lonely planet

D0561826

France

Nicola Williams

Oliver Berry, Steve Fallon, Catherine Le Nevez,
Daniel Robinson, Miles Roddis

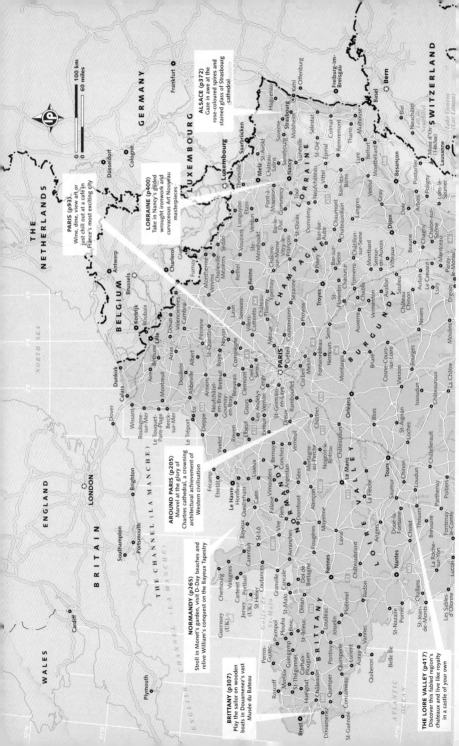

PARIS (p93)
Wine, dine, view art or just chill out at a café in France's most exciting city

LORRAINE (p400)
Take in Nancy's gilded wrought ironwork and curvaceous Art Nouveau masterpieces

ALSACE (p372)
Gaze in awe at the rose-coloured spires and stained glass of Strasbourg cathedral

AROUND PARIS (p205)
Marvel at the glory of Chartres cathedral, a crowning architectural achievement of Western civilisation

NORMANDY (p265)
Stroll in Monet's garden, visit D-Day beaches and relive William's conquest on the Bayeux Tapestry

BRITTANY (p307)
Play the sailor on wooden boats in Douarnenez's vast Musée du Bateau

THE LOIRE VALLEY (p417)
Discover this fabled region's chateaux and live like royalty in a castle of your own

100 km
60 miles

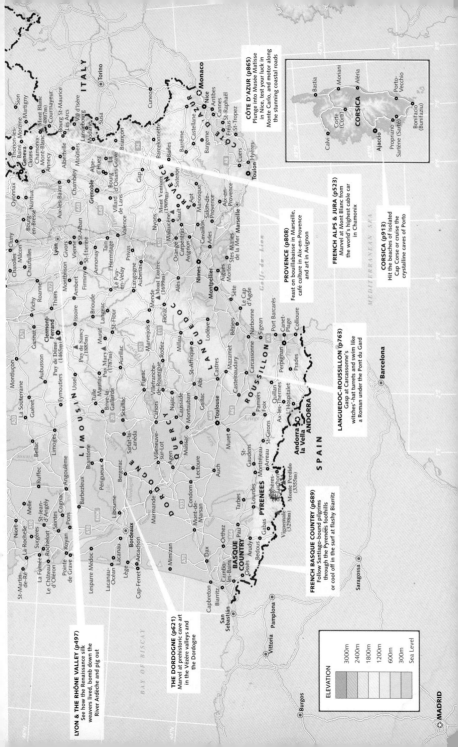

CÔTE D'AZUR (p865)
Plunge into Musée Matisse in Nice, test your luck in Monte Carlo, and motor along the stunning coastal roads

FRENCH ALPS & JURA (p523)
Marvel at Mont Blanc from the world's highest cable car in Chamonix

CORSICA (p913)
Hit the beaches of isolated Cap Corse or cruise the crystalline caves of Porto

PROVENCE (p808)
Feast on bouillabaisse in Marseille, café culture in Aix-en-Provence and art in Avignon

LANGUEDOC-ROUSSILLON (p763)
Gasp at Carcassonne's witches'-hat turrets and swim like a Roman under the Pont du Gard

FRENCH BASQUE COUNTRY (p689)
Follow Santiago-bound pilgrims through the Pyrenées foothills or cool off in the surf at flashy Biarritz

THE DORDOGNE (p621)
Marvel at prehistoric cave art in the Vézère valleys and the Dordogne

LYON & THE RHÔNE VALLEY (p497)
See how the Renaissance silk weavers lived, bomb down the River Ardèche and pig out

ELEVATION

	3000m
	2400m
	1800m
	1200m
	600m
	300m
	Sea Level

Destination France

Good, bad or ugly, everyone has *something* to say about France and the French: chic, smart, sexy, rude, racist, bureaucratic, bitchy as hell, pavements studded with dog poo, baguettes that dry out by lunchtime and a penchant for torching cars is some of the chitchat on the street. Spice up the cauldron with the odd urban riot, political scandal, presidential election and 35-hour working week – not to mention a massive box-office hit like *The Da Vinci Code* taking over Paris or superstar Angelina Jolie allegedly plumping for a chateau in Normandy to raise her kids – and the international media is all ears too.

This is, after all, that fabled land of good food and wine, of royal chateaux and perfectly restored farmhouses, of landmarks known the world over and hidden landscapes few really know. Savour art and romance in the shining capital on the River Seine. See glorious pasts blaze forth at Versailles. Travel south for Roman civilisation and the sparkling blue Med. Ski the Alps. Sense the subtle infusion of language, music and mythology in Brittany brought by 5th-century Celtic invaders. Smell ignominy on the beaches of Normandy and battlefields of Verdun and the Somme. And know that this is but the tip of that gargantuan iceberg the French call culture.

Yes, this is that timeless land whose people have a natural *joie de vivre* and savoir-faire – and have for centuries. But change is afoot. France and the French are fed up – and inspired. It's on the tip of everyone's tongues.

The Classics

Lose yourself in the formal gardens at Château de Villandry (p441), Loire Valley

Admire the vista from Paris' Eiffel Tower (p139)

Scale the steps at the Abbaye du Mont St-Michel (p305)

Plunge into the arts of the past at the Musée du Louvre (p126), Paris

DIANA MAYFIELD

CHRISTOPHER WOOD

Turn back the clock amid the architecture of Old Lyon (p503)

Cycle between vineyards in the Loire Valley (p417)

OLIVER STREWE

8

Food & Wine

Treat yourself at a patisserie (p86)

Imbibe France's regional wines (p77)

Taste mature Comté cheese in Franche-Comté (p578)

Festivals & Events

STELLA HELLANDER

Celebrate Mardi Gras in Nice (p867)

See the spectacle at the Lemon Festival (p905), Menton

DAVID TOMLINSON

TOM LEVY

Get your dancing shoes on for
Paris' Fête de la Musique (p151)

Activities

ROCCO FASANO

Pedal through the forests of Brittany (p307)

Confront the cliffs in the Gorges du Verdon (p860)

JEAN-BERNARD CARILLET

MARK WEBSTER

Dive down to gorgonians from the Îles Lavezzi (p940) in Corsica

GARETH MCCORMACK

Survey the Chamonix Valley from the
Grand Balcon Nord (p535)

Immerse yourself in the Mediterranean off the Côte
d'Azur (p865)

DAN HERRICK

Experience skiing and snowboarding heaven in the Alps (p525)

CHRISTIAN ASLUND

Arts & Architecture

Pause in Paris at the Musée Rodin (p138)

NEIL SETCHFIELD

BÉTHUNE CARMICHAEL

Absorb the artistry in the Église Notre Dame (p459) in Dijon

Wonder at the huge Grande Arche de la Défense (p208)

MARTIN MOOS

Contents

Regional Map Contents

FAR NORTHERN FRANCE p225

PARIS pp98–100

NORMANDY p266

CHAMPAGNE p355

ALSACE p372 & LORRAINE p401

AROUND PARIS p206

BRITTANY p308

THE LOIRE VALLEY p418

BURGUNDY p456

FRENCH ALPS p524 & THE JURA p573

ATLANTIC COAST p651

LIMOUSIN, THE DORDOGNE & QUERCY p610

MASSIF CENTRAL p585

LYON & THE RHÔNE VALLEY p498

FRENCH BASQUE COUNTRY p690

THE PYRENEES pp712–13

TOULOUSE AREA p739

LANGUEDOC-ROUSSILLON p764

PROVENCE p809

CÔTE D'AZUR p866 & MONACO p908

CORSICA p915

The Authors

NICOLA WILLIAMS
Coordinating Author; Introductory Chapters; Lyon & the Rhône Valley; French Alps & the Jura; Directory

Living on the southern (French) shore of Lake Geneva in a house with lake and Jura view, Nicola is well and truly spoilt...so much so she only dines in places that cook up the real McCoy lake fish (most comes from Eastern Europe), and if the sky is not blue she refuses to ski. A journalist by training, she worked in the Baltic region as a newspaper features editor and later city-guide series editor for several years before trading in Lithuanian *cepelinai* for Lyonnaise *andouillette* in 1997. Nicola has worked on dozens of Lonely Planet titles, including *The Loire* and *Provence & the Côte d'Azur*.

My Favourite Trip

With every trip I stash away a couple of business cards – special addresses to let friends in on...or use myself when a work-free weekend beckons (rare). La Fruitière in Val d'Isère (lunch on the slopes; p556), Marseille's Hôtel Le Corbusier (guided tour essential, stunning rooftop; p819) and Péron (hip seaside eating; p821) are in there, as is the Collège Hotel (wow design; p509), Le Petit Léon (quintessential bistro lunch; p510) and Bistro Fait Sa Broc' (oh so Croix-Rousse; p514) in Lyon. From my travels this time, I added the Clubhouse in Chamonix (future dirty weekend *sans* kids; p537); the Jura's Amondans (p577) and Ferme Auberge du Rondeau (activity weekend *avec* kids; go in summer next time; p577); and Château des Allues in St-Pierre d'Albigny (parents would love it; p553).

[Map of France showing: The Jura, Chamonix, Lyon, Val d'Isère, St-Pierre d'Albigny, Marseille]

OLIVER BERRY
Normandy; Limousin, the Dordogne & Quercy

Oliver graduated from University College London with a degree in English and now works as a writer and photographer in Cornwall and London. His first trip to France was at the age of two, and subsequent travels have carried him from the streets of Paris to the Alpine mountains and from the wine-fields of southern France to the chestnut forests of Corsica. For this book he got lost on the winding backroads of the Dordogne, descended into the depths of the earth around the Vézère Valley and braved the perils of the *boulevards périphériques* around Rouen. He has won several awards for his writing, including *The Guardian* Young Travel Writer of the Year.

LONELY PLANET AUTHORS

Why is our travel information the best in the world? It's simple: our authors are independent, dedicated travellers. They don't research using just the Internet or phone, and they don't take freebies in exchange for positive coverage. They travel widely, to all the popular spots and off the beaten track. They personally visit thousands of hotels, restaurants, cafés, bars, galleries, palaces, museums and more – and they take pride in getting all the details right, and telling it how it is. For more, see the authors section on www.lonelyplanet.com.

STEVE FALLON Food & Drink; Paris; Around Paris

Steve was surrounded by things French from a very young age when his neighbour's (and best friend's) mother in Boston thought it would be a 'bunny day' (or was that a *bonne idée*?) to rock them in the same cradle. Convinced that Parisians were seriously devoid of humour after he and said best friend dropped water-filled condoms on the heads of passers-by from a 5e arrondissement hotel balcony at age 16, he nevertheless went back to the 'City of Light' five years later to complete a degree in French at the Sorbonne. Based in East London, Steve will be just one Underground stop away from Paris when Eurostar trains begin departing from Stratford.

CATHERINE LE NEVEZ Brittany; Atlantic Coast; Provence; Côte d'Azur & Monaco; Corsica; Transport

Catherine's wanderlust kicked in when she lived and road-tripped throughout France aged four, and she's been hitting the road at every opportunity since, including a two-year odyssey of her native Oz. While freelance writing and editing, she completed her Doctorate in Writing, and her Masters in Professional Writing, plus editing and publishing postgrad qualifications. Previous Lonely Planet assignments in France include online accommodation reviews for the Bordeaux region and Provence, as well as Marseille and Nice – for which she's also written Lonely Planet Digital City Guides.

DANIEL ROBINSON Far Northern France; Champagne; Alsace & Lorraine; The Loire; Burgundy

Over the past 15 years, Daniel's articles and guidebooks have covered every region of France, but he has a particular fondness for those bits of the Hexagone in which Celtic, Romance and Germanic cultures have mingled for over two millennia. Seeking out enchanting corners of rust-belt France is a long-time hobby, and he takes particular interest in the creativity and panache of dynamic northern cities such as Lille, Nancy and Strasbourg.

Daniel grew up in the United States and Israel, and holds degrees from Princeton University and Tel Aviv University. He is based in Tel Aviv.

MILES RODDIS Massif Central; French Basque Country; The Pyrenees; Toulouse Area; Languedoc-Roussillon

Miles' involvement with France began when he threw up the night's red wine in a Paris café. Undeterred by the monumental hangover, he studied in French at university, where he spent an idyllic year in Neuville-sur-Saône, a place quite rightly overlooked by the best guidebooks, including the one in your hand.

Living over the Pyrenees in Valencia, Spain, he and his wife Ingrid visit France, for work or fun, at least once a year.

He has written or contributed to over 25 Lonely Planet titles including *France, Brittany, Normandy* and, perhaps most satisfyingly, *Walking in France.*

CONTRIBUTING AUTHOR

Annabel Hart wrote the Entertainment, Drinking and Transport sections of the Paris chapter. Annabel arrived in Paris planning to learn French for a few months and ended up spending the better part of six years there. Most of this was spent doing freelance writing and studying international politics and sustainable development. She has contributed to Lonely Planet's Web content as well as various guidebooks including *France*, *Paris* and *Bretagne*.

Getting Started

Be it a spontaneous city-break on the cheap or a carefully planned adventure of a lifetime, travel in France requires as little or as much money, planning and time as you do (or don't) have.

WHEN TO GO

See Climate Charts (p953) for more information

French pleasures can be indulged in any time, although many Francophiles swear spring is best. In the hot south sun-worshippers bake from June to early September (summer) while winter-sports enthusiasts soar down snow-covered mountains mid-December to late March (winter). Festivals (p956) and gastronomic temptations (p73) around which to plan a trip abound year-round.

School holidays – Christmas and New Year, mid-February to mid-March, Easter, July and August – see millions of French families descend on the coasts, mountains and other touristy areas. Traffic-clogged roads, sky-high accommodation prices and sardine-packed beaches and ski slopes are downside factors of these high-season periods. Many shops take their *congé annuel* (annual closure) in August; Sundays and public holidays (p958) are dead everywhere.

The French climate is temperate, although it gets nippy in mountainous areas and in Alsace and Lorraine. The northwest suffers from high humidity, rain and biting westerly winds, while the Mediterranean south enjoys hot summers and mild winters.

HOW MUCH?

See also LP Index, inside front cover.

Two-course midrange lunch/dinner *menu* €15/25

Munch-on-the-move stuffed baguette €3.50-5

Half-/full-day bicycle hire €10/15

Cinema ticket in the provinces/Paris €7/9

Public transport ticket €1.40

COSTS & MONEY

Accommodation is the biggest expense: count on a bill of minimum €50 a night for a double room in a midrange hotel and over €120 for a top-end hotel. Backpackers staying in hostels and living on bread and cheese can survive on €50 a day; those opting for midrange hotels, restaurants and museums will spend upwards of €90. For cent-saving discount cards, see p955.

TRAVEL LITERATURE

France inspires reams of writing. See p58 for a listing of fun-filled 'frog v Rosbif' books, p32 for books on French history and p47 for titles with a cultural focus.

A Piano in the Pyrenees (Tony Hawks) He's gone round Ireland with a fridge, played the Moldovans at tennis and now it's off to the Pyrenees with a piano for the wackiest of English travel writers.

French Revolutions (Tim Moore) Great title, great read: 'Suburban slouch' Moore cycles around France in a quest to pedal to the bottom of the Tour de France (p53).

DON'T LEAVE HOME WITHOUT...

- valid travel insurance (p958).
- ID card or passport and visa if required (p965).
- driving licence, car documents and car insurance (p977).
- sunglasses, hat, mosquito repellent and a few clothes pegs for the hot south.
- a brolly for wet 'n' soggy Brittany, neighbouring northern climes and Paris.
- an adventurous appetite, a pleasure-seeking palate and a thirst for good wine (p73).

TOP TENS
ADVENTURES

Craving excitement? Wanna feel the earth move? Dabble in daredevil France.

- Scale Europe's highest sand dune (p686)
- Sail subterranean waters (p648)
- Drive a Porsche on an ice piste (p569) or fly down the legendary Vallée Blanche off-piste (p534)
- Learn how to survive in the mountains; attend an avalanche-awareness clinic (p525)
- Embark on a surf safari (p687)
- Trek Corsica's hot tough spine with the mythical GR20 (p916)
- Splash out on some white-water sports in the Dordogne (p621), Gorges du Verdon (p861) or Parc National des Pyrénées (p724)
- Go volcanic (p591)
- Paraglide the thermals above Puy de Dôme (p591) or hang-glide off Ménez-Hom (p331)
- Live dangerously: kite-surf, *ski joër* or sledge in a Snake Gliss (p529)

CULINARY EXPERIENCES

France is your oyster as far as tickling the tastebuds with extraordinary new experiences goes. For other gastronomic-adventure ideas see p73.

- Pick and nibble our way through Paris' Marché Bastille, the capital's best open-air market (p169)
- Scoff porky-pig cuisine in a Lyonnais *bouchon* (p510)
- Sleep, eat and breathe escargots (snails) at a fabulous snail-farm *chambre d'hôte* (p579)
- Fill up on Burgundy reds at Beaune's École des Vins de Bourgogne (p467)
- Feast on *wädele braisé au pinot noir* (ham knuckles in wine), *choucroute au canard* (duck sauerkraut) and other Alsatian specialities in a cosy old *winstub* (p382)
- Dip into an authentic fondue on a Jurassien farm (p572)
- Tour Strasbourg's breweries (p381)
- Sink oysters fresh from an oyster farm in Cancale (p317)
- While away several hours in Marseille over bouillabaisse at Chez Madie Les Galinettes (p820)
- Savour a snail stuffed with foie gras in truffle- and foie gras–rich Périgord (p626)

SHOPPING SPREES

Be it street markets, chic boutiques or a farm, shopping *en France* covers the whole gambit of styles and wallets. Our favourites:

- Triangle d'Or, Paris – French couture's walk of fame (p185)
- Marché aux Puces de St-Ouen, Paris – Europe's largest flea market (p186)
- Cité Europe, Calais – alcohol shopping in bulk (p240)
- Cancale – year-round oyster market (p317)
- Le Puy-en-Velay – handmade lace (p603)
- La Maison de la Truffe, Uzès – snuffle a truffle (p771)
- Sarlat-La-Canéda – Saturday morning truffle 'n foie gras market (p629)
- Limoges – porcelain and enamel shops (p611)
- Les Halles, Lyon – for foodies seeking the very best (p513)
- Places des Lices, St-Tropez – quintessential Provençal market (p896)

Birdsong (Sebastian Faulks) The horror of trench warfare during WWI sits at the powerful heart of this novel, essential reading for anyone visiting the Battle of the Somme memorials.

The Price of Water in Finistère (Bodil Malmsten) The story of what happened when middle-aged Swedish novelist Bodil Malmsten traded in Stockholm for the heart of Breton culture portrays daily life in Brittany beautifully.

The Ripening Sun and **La Belle Saison** (Patricia Atkinson) The Atkinsons moved to Bergerac to pursue the Brit-dream of renovating an old property, only for Mr A to return home, leaving Mrs A to man the Bordeaux fort. Clos d'Yvigne wine is now award-winning.

Down and Out in Paris and London (George Orwell) Famous account of the time Orwell spent living with tramps in Paris and London in the late 1920s.

Tender is the Night and **Bits of Paradise** (F Scott Fitzgerald) Vivid accounts of life during the decadent 1920s Jazz Age on the Côte d'Azur.

A Motor-flight Through France (Edith Wharton) Classic travelogue of three pioneering automobile trips embarked on by the Whartons around *belle époque* France from 1906 to 1907.

INTERNET RESOURCES

French Government Tourist Office (www.francetourism.com) Official tourist site.

Lonely Planet (www.lonelyplanet.com)

Maison de la France (www.franceguide.com) Main tourist office website.

Météo France (www.meteo.fr in French) For details of nationwide weather conditions.

Motorist Information (www.bison-fute.equipement.gouv.fr in French) Road conditions, closures and school holiday schedule.

SNCF (www.sncf.com) France's national railways website.

Itineraries
CLASSIC ROUTES

A WHIRLWIND ROMANCE
One Week / Paris to Provence

France's soulful **capital** (p93) seduces: the **Eiffel Tower** (p139) is the peak of romance. If your inner vampire longs to be free, pop the question Gothic-style in **Hôtel St-Merry** (p155). The area around Pont St-Louis (p134) personifies romance. Nip north to chink glasses on **Champagne's wine route** (p360), or west to the **Loire Valley** (p417) with its chateaux: see love blossoming at **Villandry** (p441); a drama of passion and betrayal unfold at **Chenonceau** (p438); or meet your lover on **Chambord's** (p429) double-helix staircase. Don't miss Brittany's haunting **Île d'Ouessant** (p329). Oysters, for which **Cancale** (p317) is famed, are an aphrodisiac. Tempting to lonely hearts and lovers is **Belle Île** (p344) with its caves and beaches steeped in legend. Shouting yes from a huge **sand dune** (p686) or in the **surf** (p687) on the Atlantic Coast is not a bad idea. Or cuddling atop **Mont Aigoual** (p789) or paragliding above **Puy de Dôme** (p591). **Provence** (p808) and the **Côte d'Azur** (p865) is love at first sight. Tying the knot aboard a **St-Tropez** (p894) yacht or in a lavender field near **Mont Ventoux** (p863) is old hat. Try in a **Matisse chapel** (p873) or **Van Gogh landscape** (p834); between **kite-surfs** (p899); or on promenade des Anglais in **Nice** (p867).

Paris to Provence – 2000km-odd in all – in a whirlwind week is a love affair with old-fashioned romance. But it's not all red roses and fairy-tale castles. Thrills abound for those with a passion for the unconventional.

TIMELESS CLASSICS
Two Weeks / Paris to Nice

There's no better place to kick off a whistle-stop tour of classic French sights than Paris, where the **Eiffel Tower** (p139), **Arc de Triomphe** (p141), **Notre Dame** (p132) and **Louvre** (p126) warrant a postcard home. Stroll the banks of the Seine and gardens of **Versailles** (p211), then flee the capital for Renaissance royalty at **Châteaux de Chambord** (p429) and **Chenonceau** (p438). Or skip the Loire and spend a couple of days in Normandy, not missing Rouen's **Cathédrale Notre Dame** (p268), the **Bayeux Tapestry** (p292), **Mont St-Michel** (p304) and the **D-Day landing beaches** (p295).

Venture south through the **Bordeaux wine region** (p670). Surfers can ride waves in **Biarritz** (p696), and the faithful/faithfully curious might enjoy world-famous **Lourdes** (p717). Otherwise, it's straight to **Carcassonne** (p781) and its city walls; Roman **Nîmes** (p765) with a trip to the **Pont du Gard** (p770); and the papal city of **Avignon** (p842) with its **nursery-rhyme bridge** (p843). Finish on the Côte d'Azur, not missing Grace Kelly's **Monaco** (p906), a flutter in **Monte Carlo Casino** (p911), a portside aperitif in **St-Tropez** (p894), a strut in **Cannes** (p884) and a stroll in **Nice** (p867).

From Paris to Nice, with a few short detours along the way, is a breathtaking 2000km that can be done in a jam-packed fortnight, but definitely merits as much time as you can give it.

PORT TO PORT   Two Weeks / Calais to Marseille

Step off the boat in **Calais** (p236) and there's 40km of stunning cliffs, sand dunes and windy beaches – not to mention great views of those white cliffs of Dover across the Channel – on the spectacular **Côte d'Opale** (p243). Speed southwest, taking in a fish lunch in **Dieppe** (p272), a cathedral-stop in **Rouen** (p267) or a picturesque cliffside picnic in **Étretat** (p277) on your way to your overnight stop: the pretty Normandy seaside resort of **Honfleur** (p282), **Deauville** (p285) or **Trouville** (p285).

Devote day two to the **D-Day landing beaches** (p295) and abbey-clad **Mont St-Michel** (p304). In Brittany, flop in an old-fashioned beach tent in **Dinard** (p314) then follow fairy-tale forest trails around **Huelgoat** (p326) to art-rich **Camaret-sur-Mer** (p332).

A long drive south along the Atlantic Coast rewards with chic **La Rochelle** (p662) and its lavish seafood and oyster feasts, from where it is simply a matter of wining your way through the **Médoc** (p680) to bustling **Bordeaux** (p670). Next morning, continue south through **Toulouse** (p739) and **Carcassonne** (p781) to the Med. The **Camargue** (p838) – a wonderful wetland of flamingos, horses and incredible bird life – is a unique patch of coast to explore before hitting gritty **Marseille** (p810), immediately east.

The Atlantic to the Mediterranean in two weeks – 2500km in all – is no mean feat, but one that rewards with stunning vistas, superb coastal motoring and sensational seafood. For those with more time to play with, activities abound in, on and out of the sea – and there's always Corsica for the truly coast crazy.

TOUR DE FRANCE
One Month / Strasbourg to Paris

Get set for your race around the country in Strasbourg: stroll canal-clad **Petite France** (p375), marvel at its **cathedral** (p378) and dine in a **winstub** (p382). Moving on to greener climes, pick up the **Route du Vin d'Alsace** (p386) and tipple your way around the **Vosges** (p397) foothills. But keep a clear head for that splendid Art Nouveau architecture in **Nancy** (p400), where you should spend at least one night to enjoy romantic **place Stanislas** (p403) illuminated. From Lorraine it is guns a-ho to champagne cellars around **Épernay** (p361), then north to the sobering **Battle of the Somme memorials** (p252) in far northern France.

Devour Normandy and Brittany's best sights in week two: base yourself in **Bayeux** (p291) to see the **tapestry** (p292), **D-Day landing beaches** and **WWII memorials** (p295). **Mont St-Michel** (p304) is an astounding pit stop en route to France's Celtic **land of legends** (p307); **St-Malo** (p309) and **Dinard** (p314) make charming overnight stops. Meander around megaliths in **Carnac** (p341), then zoom south for more prehistory in the **Vézère Valley** (p630).

The pace hots up in the third week: from the **Dordogne** (p621), wiggle through the **Upper Languedoc** (p787) – through the spectacular **Gorges du Tarn** (p791) – to **Avignon** (p842). Take a break with local café culture then slog like a Tour de France cyclist up **Mont Ventoux** (p854). Explore Provence's **hilltop villages** then speed north to the majestic city of **Lyon** (p498), from where an **Alpine mountain adventure** (p523) is doable.

The last leg takes in wine-rich Burgundy: **Beaune** (p468), **Dijon** (p458) and **Vézelay** (p484) are the obvious desirable places to stop en route to **Paris** (p93).

Tour de France cyclists take three weeks to bike 3000km around the country. This 3000km tour of France can be done in one month, but warrants much more time than that. As with the world's greatest cycling race, it labours through the Pyrenees and Alps, and finishes on Paris' Champs-Élysées.

ROADS LESS TRAVELLED

GREEN FOR GO   Two Weeks / Chamonix to Cauterets

Kick-start your Alpine adventure in **Chamonix** (p530) at the foot of Europe's highest peak: ride a cable car to the **Aiguille du Midi** (p531) and **Le Brévent** (p533) or a train to the **Mer de Glace** (p533). Skiing the legendary **Vallée Blanche** (p534) and **paragliding** (p529) are daredevil choices. For the truly Alpine-dedicated there are the **Vanoise** (p549) and **Écrins** (p566) national parks to explore.

Hopping across Lake Geneva by boat, the unexplored **Jura** (p572) looms large. This gentle land of cross-country skiing, dog-mushing and cheese dining in **Métabief Mont d'Or** (p580) – not to mention Le Corbusier's **Ronchamp** (p580) chapel – is an oasis of peace.

Or head southwest for week two, breaking the journey in the **Parc Naturel Régional de Chartreuse** (p553) of potent pea-green liqueur fame or in the cave-riddled **Parc Naturel Régional du Vercors** (p566). Passing through the wild **Cévennes** (p789), walking a stage of Robert Louis Stevenson's **donkey trek** (p791) is doable before hitting the Pyrenees.

In the **Parc National des Pyrénées** (p722), revitalise weary bones with spa waters in **Bagnères de Luchon** (p734) then hit the **Vallée d'Ossau** (p727) and **Vallée d'Aspe** (p724) for a heady cocktail of mountain biking, walking and vulture spotting. Use **Cauterets** (p729) – from where you can ski in season – as your base.

This highly energetic 1500km tour from the French Alps to the Pyrenees will leave you breathless, especially if you take a few days out to indulge in an adrenaline rush of outdoor activity up, down or on the mountain slopes.

VENTURE OUT OF THE ORDINARY

One Month / Parisian Sewer to Burgundian Building Site

Forget the Eiffel Tower, St-Tropez and the lavender fields of Provence. This tour ventures out of the ordinary into France's quirkiest sights and sounds – and smells in the case of the **Paris sewer** (p140) where it starts. Gawp at more skulls than you can imagine in the capital's **catacombes** (p137), then venture north to the spot near **Compiègne** (p260) where WWI officially ended. Top off your day with a subterranean dose of V2 rocket technology in a **bunker** (p241) near St-Omer.

A few drops of Christ's blood in **Fécamp** (p275) on the Normandy coast inspired monks to concoct Bénédictine liqueur: visit the **Palais Bénédictine** (p276) and get a free shot – then tell yourself you're not drunk as you tour the 'laboratory of emotions' in Honfleur's wacky **Les Maisons Satie** (p283).

Steering south along the Atlantic Coast, cartwheel down Europe's highest sand dune near **Arcachon** (p686). Afterwards, head east to Quercy and set sail on an underground river in **Gouffre de Padirac** (p648); then nip to Toulouse to tour **Space City** (p744) and see **Airbus planes** (p744) being built.

Learning how silk weavers toiled in the 19th century and walking the tunnels they trod puts **Lyon** (p504) in a different light. Returning north, see brickies in costume at the **Chantier Médiéval de Guédelon** (p478) in La Puisaye build a castle using 13th-century tools.

It might well follow a predictable route – enabling it to be mixed-and-matched with other itineraries in this chapter – but that's about it. Covering 2400km in all, one month scarcely does quirky France justice. Take longer if you can.

TAILORED TRIPS

QUICK GETAWAY

Budget airlines (p968) make short breaks easy. For urban souls, sophisticated cities like **Paris** (p93) and **Lyon** (p498) win hands down. Big but not everyone's cup of tea is rough-cut **Marseille** (p810), a heady mix of sea breeze and city grit. Elsewhere along the Med, **Nice** (p867) beckons hardcore punters after sun, sand and sex; **Toulon** (p899) is a slick flit to **St-Tropez** (p894); **Nîmes** (p765) – the stepping-stone alongside student-driven **Montpellier** (p773) to a **Camargue safari** (p838) – combines Roman relics in town with the **Pont du Gard** (p770) out of town; while the **Pyrenees** (p710) tumble into the sea near Spanish-styled **Perpignan** (p798). **Toulouse** (p739), itself a two- or four-day itinerary, is the other Pyrenees launch pad. Fairy-tale castle-clad **Carcassonne** (p781) or the **Loire chateaux** (p431) around **Tours** (p432) vie with the capital for hottest romantic getaway.

In the Alps, **Chamonix's Clubhouse** (p537) – the ultimate in stylish dirty weekends – is a two-hour drive from **Chambéry** (p549) and **Grenoble** (p558), three from **Lyon** (p498) and **St-Étienne** (p519), and an hour from Geneva (Switzerland). All these cities are first-class stops for **skiing** (p534).

For an old-fashioned seaside paddle, **Biarritz** (p696), **Dinard** (p314) or **Brest** (p327) are best. **La Rochelle** (p662) is a bridge away from **Île de Ré** (p668); **Poitiers** (p659) neighbours **Green Venice** (p661); **Limoges** (p611) is the place to stockpile crockery; while **Nantes** (p652) and **Bordeaux** (p670) are innovative French cities that surprise and enthral.

ARTISTS' PALETTE

Provence (p808) and the **Côte d'Azur** (p865) are an art paradise: Matisse lapped up the Mediterranean sunlight and vivacity in **Nice** (p873), designing an exceptional chapel in **Vence** (p883). Picasso set up studio in **Antibes** (p881); Signac and Seurat found inspiration in **St-Tropez** (p894); while Cézanne spent his career in **Aix-en-Provence** (p824). Westward, Van Gogh painted some of his most famous canvases in **Arles** (p831) and **St-Rémy de Provence** (p835).

The Fauvist-favoured port of **Collioure** (p805) on the Côte Vermeille in Roussillon is an essential stop on any art lover's itinerary; as is Henri de Toulouse-Lautrec's hometown of **Albi** (p749), near Toulouse. Moulin Rouge cancan girls and prostitutes the bohemian artist painted in Paris hang in the town's **Musée Toulouse-Lautrec** (p751).

A day trip to Monet's garden-clad home and studio in **Giverny** (p280) is irresistible for anyone painting an artist's palette from Paris – where, incidentally, Monet's famous painting of **Rouen cathedral** (p268) hangs in the **Musée d'Orsay** (p138). Renoir hung out with his impressionist buddies in and around **Le Havre** (p278) on the serene Normandy coast, and is buried in **Essoyes** (p370) in Champagne.

AFTER DARK

France at night: illuminated capital highlights include the **Eiffel Tower** (p139), the **Sacré Cœur** (p145) seen from place du Parvis du Sacré Cœur, the banks of the **Seine** (p150) seen from a boat and the **Champs Élysées** (p141), best seen from place de l'Étoile.

In Normandy **Mont St-Michel** (p304) is beautifully lit and **Caen nightlife** (p290) rocks. Harbour-side dining in **Honfleur** (p284) is another after-dark great. Enchanting is a candle-lit stroll around the Dordogne's **Jardins de Marqueyssac** (p632) or watching **Najac's** (p646) fairy-tale castle turn gold at sunset.

Lyon (p498) is spectacular during its **Fête des Lumières** (p508) when light shows run riot on its historic squares, churches and public buildings. In summer, images are projected onto **Poitiers'** Église Notre Dame la Grande (p660), **Rouen** (p270) cathedral and some **Loire chateaux** (p431).

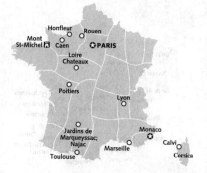

Southbound, **Toulouse** (p739) is a self-proclaimed 'City of Light'. In magical-by-night **Monaco** (p906) take in the Hong Kong–style skyline and rub shoulders with the glitterati at **Monte Carlo Casino** (p911). Or dance the night away on sand at a Cap Croisette club in **Marseille** (p822) or in an impossibly hip 1930s piano bar in **Calvi** (p927).

TREASURE-TROVE

France flaunts 30 World Heritage Sites (http://whc.unesco.org), including the banks of the Seine in **Paris** and royal palaces at **Versailles** (p211), **Fontainebleau** (p214) and **Chambord** (p429). The cathedral in **Chartres** (p220) makes a fine foray from the capital, as does the Unesco-hallmarked chunk of the **Loire Valley** (p417) between Sully-sur-Loire and Chalonnes.

Burgundy boasts a medieval Cistercian abbey in **Fontenay** (p474) and Romanesque basilica in **Vézelay** (p485), the fortified village from where pilgrims head to Santiago de Compostela in Spain. Their paths are World Heritage.

Northern jewels include Strasbourg's **Grande Île** (p375); a trio of public squares in **Nancy** (p400) and buildings in **Reims** (p355); **Amiens** (p256) cathedral; and an ode to post-WWII architecture at **Le Havre** (p278). Sea-splashed **Mont St-Michel** (p304) and its bay are priceless.

Southbound, drink Bordeaux reds from listed vineyards in **St-Émilion** (p680) and rub shoulders with prehistory in the **Vézère Valley** (p630). History oozes out of fortified **Carcassonne** (p781); Roman **Pont du Gard** (p770), **Arles** (p831) and **Orange** (p851); papal **Avignon** (p843) and silk-weaving **Lyon** (p498). Sailing a slow boat along the **Canal du Midi** (p780) is a fine way to whittle away time; as is hiking around **Corsica's** capes (p916).

Snapshot

Which direction France is helter-skeltering in is as clear as mud, although French bloggers (p49) have plenty to say on the matter. In fact, everyone seems to, world press included. This is one of the vanguards of European integration after all, albeit one which sent the fantastic notion tumbling out the window with its fierce rejection of the European constitution in May 2005. Debate has raged ever since.

'Bad bad' is the hot bet at the bookies: Paris lost its bid to host the Olympics in 2012 (to, shock horror, London). Worse, France lost to Italy in the 2006 World Cup, the infamous head-butt by the best French footballer of all time (p52) being a moment few French will forget. And in late 2005, street riots, car torching and tear-gas clashes between youths and police ripped across the country, forcing state-of-emergency curfews as authorities tried to claw back control (p53). Repeated stabs at pension reform have been met by strikes. And no one drinks French wine anymore (p73).

Then there is that infamous government U-turn: rewind to March 2006. In a determined move to outmanoeuvre high unemployment – 9.6% nationally and a shocking 20% among 18- to 25-year-olds – Prime Minister Dominique de Villepin introduced a new youth-employment law giving employers the right to sack under 26s – just like that – during the first two years of their contract. Far from being applauded (the law removed the risk for employers in hiring young inexperienced recruits, the PM argued, thus encouraging job creation for youths), the law was slammed by students who hit the streets by the thousands and stayed there for several weeks. Police stormed the Sorbonne (p134), the situation got so bad. Squeezed into a corner with street violence increasing by the day, a battered and desperately weak Chirac government backed down. Power to the people (p44)!

Determining which way France should go is almost incidental in the face of who will end up in the Élysée Palace after the 2007 elections. Discredited French president *Le Grand Jacques* is in his 70s, has two terms under his presidential belt and is far too old, haggard and old-hat say critics, for whom *sortie* (exit) is the only possible direction Chirac can take.

Then there is Sarko (as the French press call him), of the same centre-right ilk as Chirac (both belong to the UMP – Union pour un Mouvement Populaire – party) but a bitter enemy. A man of the masses, interior minister and ruling party chairman Nicolas Sarkozy (1955–) is dynamic, high-profile, highly ambitious. Ruthless in his determination to run as centre-right candidate in the presidential elections, the charismatic politician speaks a lot about crime crackdown and helping the country's substantial immigrant population (p53); Sarkozy himself is the son of a Hungarian immigrant. But punters might not forgive him for his hardliner comments during the 2005 riots or for his role – albeit that of innocent victim – in the Clearstream scandal. Falsely implicated in accepting bribes as economic minister in 1991, Sarkozy vowed to uncover whoever had framed him in 2006 after courts ruled the anonymous bribery allegations to be bogus. Chief suspect in the political smear campaign: floundering prime minister and Chirac favourite in the presidential run, Dominique de Villepin (1953–).

Standing tall, dignified and well above all this dirty political dogfighting, is socialist and squeaky-clean, glam Ségolène 'Ségo' Royal (1953–). Favourite in the presidential sweepstake, Royal can be relied on to lead France in a groundbreaking new direction where no man has dared set foot before. She would be, after all, France's first female president.

FAST FACTS

Population: 62.7 million

Area: 551,000 sq km

GDP: €1689 billion

GDP per capita: €27,000

GDP growth: 1.4%

Inflation: 1.9%

Unemployment: 9.6%

Highest point: Mt Blanc (4807m)

Internet domain: fr

Annual alcohol consumption (per person over 15 years): wine 78.9L, beer 41L, cider 6.9L, spirits 9.1L

History

PREHISTORIC PEOPLE

Neanderthals were the first people to live in France. Out and about during the Middle Palaeolithic period (about 90,000–40,000 BC), these early *Homo sapiens* hunted animals, made crude flake-stone tools and lived in caves. In the late 19th century Neanderthal skeletons were found in caves at Le Bugue in the Vézère Valley (see p630) in Dordogne.

Cro-Magnons, a taller *Homo sapiens* variety who notched up 1.7m on the height chart, followed 35,000 years ago. These people had larger brains than their ancestors, long and narrow skulls, and short, wide faces. Their hands were nimble, and with the aid of improved tools they hunted reindeer, bison, horses and mammoths to eat. They played music, danced and had fairly complex social patterns. You can view archaeological treasures from this period in Strasbourg (p379).

Cro-Magnons were also artists. A tour of Grotte de Lascaux II (p634) – a replica of the Lascaux cave where one of the world's best examples of Cro-Magnon drawings were found in 1940 – demonstrates how initial simplistic drawings and engravings of animals gradually became more detailed and realistic. Dubbed 'Périgord's Sistine Chapel', the Lascaux cave is one of 25 known decorated caves in Dordogne's Vézère Valley, the prehistory of which is covered in Les Eyzies de Tayac's Musée National de Préhistoire (p630).

The Neolithic period (about 7500 to 4000 years ago), alias the New Stone Age, produced France's incredible collection of menhirs and dolmens: the Morbihan Coast in Brittany (p339) is an ode to megalithic monuments. During this era, warmer weather caused great changes in flora and fauna, and ushered in farming and stock rearing. Cereals, peas, beans and lentils were grown, and villages were settled. Decorated pottery, woven fabrics and polished stone tools became commonplace household items.

There have been dozens of books published about it, but it's Mario Ruspoli's *Cave of Lascaux* that is the bible on France's most famous cave and its fabulous interior design.

GAULS & ROMANS

The Celtic Gauls moved into the region between 1500 and 500 BC, establishing trading links by about 600 BC with the Greeks, whose colonies included Massilia (Marseille) on the Mediterranean coast. About 300 years later the Celtic Parisii tribe built a few wattle and daub huts on what is now Paris' Île de la Cité (p132).

It was from Wissant (see p244) in far northern France that Julius Caesar launched his invasion of Britain in 55 BC. Centuries of conflict between the Gauls and Romans ended in 52 BC when Caesar's legions crushed a revolt led by Gallic chief Vercingétorix (see the boxed text, p587) in Gergovia, near present-day Clermont-Ferrand. See Vercingétorix on Clermont-Ferrand's place de la Jaude (p587) and Caesar in action on the façade of the Roman triumphal arch (p851) in Orange.

The subsequent period gave rise to magnificent baths, temples, aqueducts like the Pont du Gard (p770) and other splendid public buildings: stand like a plebeian or sit like a Roman patrician in awe-inspiring

TIMELINE

c90,000–30,000 BC	1500–500 BC
Around 30,000 BC, Cro-Magnons start decorating the caves in the Vézère Valley (Dordogne) with a riot of bestial scenes	The Celtic Parisii tribe set up camp on the Île de la Cité in Paris

theatres and amphitheatres at Autun (p489), Lyon (p503), Vienne (p520), Arles (p831) and Orange (p851). Lyon also has an excellent Gallo-Roman civilisation museum (p503). In the Dordogne, Périgueux's 1st-century Roman amphitheatre (p622) was dismantled in the 3rd century and its stones used to build the city walls. The town's stunningly contemporary Vesunna Musée Gallo-Romain (p624) is a feast to behold.

France remained under Roman rule until the 5th century, when the Franks (hence the name 'France') and the Alemanii overran the country from the east. These peoples adopted important elements of Gallo-Roman civilisation (including Christianity) and their eventual assimilation resulted in a fusion of Germanic culture with that of the Celts and the Romans.

Read all about it - the Pont du Gard, that is - at www.pontdugard.fr.

DYNASTY

The Frankish Merovingian and Carolingian dynasties ruled from the 5th to the 10th centuries, with the Carolingians wielding power from Laon (p263) in northern France. The Frankish tradition, by which the king was succeeded by all of his sons, led to power struggles and the eventual disintegration of the kingdom into a collection of small feudal states. In Poitiers (p659) in 732 Charles Martel defeated the Moors, thus preventing France from falling under Muslim rule as Spain had done.

Martel's grandson, Charlemagne (742–814), extended the boundaries of the kingdom and was crowned Holy Roman Emperor (Emperor of the West) in 800. But during the 9th century, Scandinavian Vikings (also called Norsemen, thus Normans) raided France's western coast, settling in the lower Seine Valley and forming the duchy of Normandy a century later.

With the crowning of Hugh Capet as king in 987, the Capetian dynasty was born. The king's then-modest domain – a parcel of land around Paris and Orléans – was hardly indicative of a dynasty that would rule one of Europe's most powerful countries for the next 800 years.

The tale of how William the Conqueror and his Norman forces occupied England in 1066 (making Normandy and, later, Plantagenet-ruled England formidable rivals of the kingdom of France) is told on the Bayeux Tapestry, showcased inside Bayeux's Musée de la Tapisserie de Bayeux (p293). In 1152 Eleanor of Aquitaine wed Henry of Anjou (see ornate polychrome effigies of the royal couple in Abbaye Royale de Fontevraud, p449), bringing a further third of France under the control of the English crown. The subsequent rivalry between France and England for control of Aquitaine and the vast English territories in France lasted three centuries.

Many studies have been woven around the Bayeux Tapestry and the tales it tells. Carola Hicks' The Bayeux Tapestry: The Life of a Masterpiece is the most recent.

In Clermont-Ferrand in 1095 Pope Urban II preached the First Crusade, prompting France to play a leading role in the Crusades and giving rise to some splendid cathedrals – Reims (p357), Strasbourg (p378), Metz (p407) and Chartres (p221) among them – between the 12th and 14th centuries. In 1309 French-born Pope Clement V moved the papal headquarters from Rome to Avignon (p842), with Avignon's third pope Benoît XII (1334–42) starting work on the resplendent Palais des Papes (p843). The Holy See remained in the Provençal city until 1377.

55–52 BC	c AD 455–70
Julius Caesar launches his invasion of Britain from the Côte d'Opale in northern France; the Gauls defeat the Romans at Gergovia	The Franks invade and kick out the Romans; Alsace is overrun by the Alemanii

THE HUNDRED YEARS' WAR

Incessant struggles between the Capetians and England's King Edward III (a Plantagenet) over the powerful French throne degenerated into the Hundred Years' War (1337–1453). The French suffered particularly nasty defeats at Crécy and Agincourt (home to a great multimedia battle museum; see the boxed text, p242). Abbey-studded Mont St-Michel (p304) was the only place in northern and western France not to fall into English hands.

Five years later, the dukes of Burgundy (allied with the English) occupied Paris and in 1422 John Plantagenet, duke of Bedford, was made regent of France for England's King Henry VI, then an infant. Less than a decade later he was crowned king of France at Paris' Notre Dame (p132).

Luckily for the French, a 17-year-old virginal warrior called Jeanne d'Arc (Joan of Arc) came along; her tale is told at Orléans' Maison de Jeanne d'Arc (p421). At Château de Chinon (p445) in 1429, she persuaded French legitimist Charles VII that she had a divine mission from God to expel the English from France and bring about Charles' coronation in Reims. Convicted of witchcraft and heresy by a tribunal of French ecclesiastics following her capture by the Burgundians and subsequent sale to the English in 1430, Joan was burned at the stake in Rouen in 1431: one tower of the castle (p270) where the teenager was imprisoned and the square (p268) where she was burned as a witch remain.

Charles VII returned to Paris in 1437, but it wasn't until 1453 that the English were driven from French territory (with the exception of Calais). At Château de Langeais (p442) in 1491, Charles VIII wed Anne de Bretagne, marking the unification of independent Brittany with France.

RENAISSANCE TO REFORMATION

With the arrival of Italian Renaissance culture during the reign of François I (r 1515–47), the focus shifted to the Loire Valley. Italian artists decorated royal castles in Amboise (p439), Blois (p427), Chambord (p429) and Chaumont (p430), with Leonardo da Vinci making Le Clos Lucé (p439) in Amboise his home from 1516 until his death. Artist and architect disciples of Michelangelo and Raphael were influential, as were writers such as Rabelais, Marot and Ronsard. Renaissance ideas of scientific and geographic scholarship and discovery assumed a new importance, as did the value of secular over religious life.

The Reformation swept through Europe in the 1530s, the ideas of Jean (John) Calvin (1509–64) – a Frenchman born in Noyon (Picardie) but exiled to Geneva – strengthening it in France. Following the Edict of Jan (1562), which afforded the Protestants certain rights, the Wars of Religion (1562–98) broke out between the Huguenots (French Protestants who received help from the English), the Catholic League (led by the House of Guise) and the Catholic monarchy. In 1588 the Catholic League forced Henri III (r 1574–89) to flee the royal court at the Louvre (see p126) and the next year the monarch was assassinated.

Henri IV (r 1589–1610) kicked off the Bourbon dynasty, issuing the controversial Edict of Nantes (1598) to guarantee the Huguenots many civil and political rights, notably freedom of conscience. Ultra-Catholic

Seven films have immortalised 15th-century virginal warrior Joan of Arc on the silver screen. Standouts include Carl Dreyer's controversial *The Passion of Joan of Arc* (1928), Victor Flemming's *Joan of Arc* (1948) starring Ingrid Bergman, and *Jeanne d'Arc* (1999) by Luc Besson, all available on DVD.

La Reine Margot (Queen Margot) by Alexander Dumas (1802–70) is a compelling tale of murder and intrigue in the Renaissance royal French court. The lead character is based on the queen of King Henri IV.

Five centuries of Merovingian and Carolingian rule ends with the crowning of Hugh Capet as king; the Capetian dynasty is born

Duke of Normandy William the Conqueror and his Norman forces occupy England

Paris refused to allow the new Protestant king entry to the city, and a siege of the capital continued for almost five years. Only when Henri IV embraced Catholicism at the cathedral in St-Denis (p209) did the capital submit to him.

Throughout most of his undistinguished reign, Fontainebleau-born Louis XIII (r 1610–43) remained firmly under the thumb of his ruthless chief minister, Cardinal Richelieu, best known for his untiring efforts to establish an all-powerful monarchy in France and French supremacy in Europe.

THE SUN KING

At the tender age of five, *le Roi Soleil* (the Sun King) ascended the throne as Louis XIV (r 1643–1715). Bolstered by claims of divine right, he involved France in a rash of wars that gained it territory but terrified its neighbours and nearly bankrupted the treasury. At home, he quashed the ambitious, feuding aristocracy and created the first centralised French state. In Versailles, 23km southwest of Paris, Louis XIV built an extravagant palace (p211) and made his courtiers compete with each other for royal favour, reducing them to ineffectual sycophants. In 1685 he revoked the Edict of Nantes.

Grandson Louis XV (r 1715–74) was an oafish buffoon whose regent, the duke of Orléans, shifted the royal court back to Paris. As the 18th century progressed, the *ancien régime* (old order) became increasingly at odds with the needs of the country. Enlightened anti-establishment and anticlerical ideas expressed by Voltaire, Rousseau and Montesquieu further threatened the royal regime.

The Seven Years' War (1756–63), fought by France and Austria against Britain and Prussia, was one of a series of ruinous wars pursued by Louis XV, leading to the loss of France's flourishing colonies in Canada, the West Indies and India to the British. The war cost a fortune and, even more ruinous for the monarchy, it helped to disseminate in France the radical democratic ideas that had been thrust onto the world stage by the American Revolution.

REVOLUTION TO REPUBLIC

Social and economic crises marked the 18th century. With the aim of warding off popular discontent, Louis XVI called a meeting of the États Généraux (Estates General) in 1789, made up of representatives of the nobility (First Estate), clergy (Second Estate) and the remaining 90% of the population (Third Estate). When the Third Estate's call for a system of proportional voting failed, it proclaimed itself a National Assembly and demanded a constitution. On the streets, a Parisian mob took the matter into its own hands by raiding the Invalides (p138) for weapons and storming the prison at Bastille (now a very busy roundabout; p132). Said to be something of a clueless idiot, Louis XVI is reckoned to have written 'rien' (nothing happened) in his diary that day.

France was declared a constitutional monarchy and reforms enacted. But as the new government armed itself against the threat posed by Austria, Prussia and the many exiled French nobles, patriotism and nationalism mixed with revolutionary fervour. Before long, the moderate

A critic in the British *Independent* praised the 816-page epic *That Sweet Enemy: The British and the French from the Sun King to the Present* by Robert Tombs and Isabelle Tombs as 'the *War and Peace* of Franco-British relations'. It's true.

It's as juicy as it sounds: stroll with Anne Somerset around the Sun King's court in *The Affair of the Poisons: Murder, Infanticide and Satanism at the Court of Louis XIV*. It kicks off with a marquise about to be beheaded for poisoning her father and brothers.

Mozart said he'd marry her. Her son claimed she'd sexually abused him. Read all about the dramatic and unfortunate life of Marie-Antoinette in Antonia Fraser's biography of the French queen, *Marie Antoinette*.

? WITH HIS HEAD

In a bid to make public executions more humane (hanging and quartering – roping the victim's limbs to four oxen which then ran in four different directions – was the favoured method of the day for commoners), French physician Joseph Ignace Guillotin (1738–1814) came up with the guillotine.

Several tests on dead bodies down the line, highwayman Nicolas Jacques Pelletie was the first in France to have his head sliced off by the 2m-odd long falling blade on 25 April 1792 on place de Grève on Paris' Right Bank. His head rolled into a strategically placed wicker basket. During the Reign of Terror, at least 17,000 met their death by guillotine.

By the time the last person in France (murderer Hamida Djandoubi in Marseille) to be guillotined had been given the chop in 1977 (behind closed doors – the last public execution was in 1939), the lethal contraption had been sufficiently refined to slice off a head in 2/100 of a second. France abolished capital punishment in 1981.

republican Girondins lost power to the radical Jacobins led by Robespierre, Danton and Marat, and in September 1792 France's First Republic was declared. Louis XVI was publicly guillotined in January 1793 on Paris' place de la Concorde (p142) and the head of his queen, the vilified Marie-Antoinette, rolled several months later.

The terrifying Reign of Terror between September 1793 and July 1794 saw religious freedoms revoked, churches closed, cathedrals turned into 'Temples of Reason' and thousands incarcerated in dungeons in Paris' Conciergerie (p133) before being beheaded.

Afterwards, a five-man delegation of moderate republicans led by Paul Barras set itself up as a Directoire (Directory) to rule the Republic – until a dashing young Corsican general named Napoleon Bonaparte (1769–1821) came along.

NAPOLEON BONAPARTE

Napoleon Bonaparte's skills and military tactics quickly turned him into an independent political force and in 1799 he overthrew the Directory and assumed power as consul of the First Empire. A referendum in 1802 declared him consul for life, his birthday became a national holiday and in 1804 he was crowned emperor of the French by Pope Pius VII at Paris' Notre Dame (p132). Two years on he commissioned the world's largest triumphal arch (p141) to be built.

The French invented the first digital calculator, the hot-air balloon, Braille and margarine, not to mention Grand Prix racing and the first public interactive computer network. Find out what else at http://inventors .about.com/od/french inventors.

To consolidate and legitimise his authority, Napoleon waged several wars in which France gained control of most of Europe. In 1812 his troops captured Moscow, only to be killed off by the brutal Russian winter. Two years later, Allied armies entered Paris, exiled Napoleon to Elba and restored the House of Bourbon to the French throne at the Congress of Vienna (1814–15).

But in 1815 Napoleon escaped from the Mediterranean island-kingdom, landed at Golfe Juan in southern France and marched north, triumphantly entering Paris on 20 May. His glorious 'Hundred Days' back in power ended with the Battle of Waterloo and his return to exile (to the South Atlantic island of St Helena, where he died in 1821). In 1840 his remains were moved to Paris' Église du Dôme (p139).

1515

With the reign of François I the royal court moves to the Loire Valley, where a rash of regal chateaux and hunting lodges are built

1598

Henry IV gives French Protestants freedom of conscience with the Edict of Nantes

SECOND REPUBLIC TO SECOND EMPIRE

A struggle between extreme monarchists seeking a return to the *ancien régime*, people who saw the changes wrought by the Revolution as irreversible, and the radicals of the poor working-class neighbourhoods of Paris dominated the reign of Louis XVIII (r 1815–24). Charles X (r 1824–30) responded to the conflict with ineptitude and was overthrown in the so-called July Revolution of 1830. Those who were killed in the accompanying Paris street battles are buried in vaults under the Colonne de Juillet in the centre of place de la Bastille (p132).

Louis-Philippe (r 1830–48), a constitutional monarch of bourgeois sympathies, was subsequently chosen as ruler by parliament, only to be ousted by the 1848 Revolution. The Second Republic was established and elections brought in Napoleon's almost useless nephew, Louis Napoleon Bonaparte, as president. But in 1851 Louis Napoleon led a coup d'état and proclaimed himself Emperor Napoleon III of the Second Empire (1852–70).

France enjoyed significant economic growth at this time. Paris was transformed under urban planner Baron Haussmann (1809–91), who created the 12 huge boulevards radiating from the Arc de Triomphe (p141). Napoleon III threw glittering parties at the royal palace (p261) in Compiègne, and breathed in fashionable sea air at Biarritz (p696) and Deauville (p285).

Like his uncle, Napoleon III embroiled France in various catastrophic conflicts, including the Crimean War (1853–56) and the humiliating Franco-Prussian War (1870–71), which ended with Prussia taking the emperor prisoner. Upon hearing the news, defiant and very hungry Parisian masses took to the streets demanding a republic. The Wall of the Federalists in Paris' Cimetière du Père Lachaise (p143) serves as a deathly reminder of the subsequent bloodshed.

A BEAUTIFUL AGE

There was nothing beautiful about the start of the Third Republic. Born as a provisional government of national defence in September 1870, it was quickly besieged by the Prussians who laid siege to Paris and demanded

---

REPUBLICAN CALENDAR

During the Revolution, the Convention adopted a calendar from which all 'superstitious' associations (such as saints' days) were removed. Year 1 began on 22 September 1792, the day the Republic was proclaimed. The 12 months – renamed Vendémiaire, Brumaire, Frimaire, Nivôse, Pluviôse, Ventôse, Germinal, Floréal, Prairial, Messidor, Thermidor and Fructidor – were divided into three 10-day weeks called *décades*.

The poetic names of the months were seasonally inspired: the autumn months, for instance, were Vendémiaire (derived from *vendange*, grape harvest or vintage), Brumaire (from *brume*, mist or fog) and Frimaire (from *frimas*, frost). The last day of each *décade* was a rest day, and the five or six remaining days of the year were used to celebrate Virtue, Genius, Labour, Opinion and Rewards. These festivals were initially called *sans-culottides* in honour of the *sans-culottes*, the extreme revolutionaries who wore pantaloons rather than the short breeches favoured by the upper classes.

While the Republican calendar worked well in theory, it caused no end of confusion and on 1 January 1806 Napoleon switched back to the Gregorian calendar.

1643–1715	1789–94
The Sun King (Louis XIV) assumes the French throne and shifts the royal court from Paris to a fabulous palace 23km west in Versailles	Revolutionaries storm the Bastille, leading to the public beheading of Louis XVI and Marie-Antoinette and the Reign of Terror

⌐ THE CHURCH–STATE PENAL SYSTEM

Guillotine: 15 Years among the Living Dead by René Belbenoît paints a vivid picture of the hideous island where infamous Jewish army officer Captain Alfred Dreyfus – court-martialled and sentenced to life imprisonment in 1894 for betraying military secrets to Germany – ended up. A notorious penal colony in French Guiana, South America, some 56,000 French prisoners slumbered in misery here between 1864 and 1946. Dreyfus' eventual vindication greatly discredited both the army and Catholic Church, resulting in the legal separation of Church and State in 1905.

National Assembly elections be held. Unfortunately, the first move made by the resultant monarchist-controlled assembly was to ratify the Treaty of Frankfurt (1871), the harsh terms of which – a five-billion-franc war indemnity and surrender of the provinces of Alsace and Lorraine – prompted immediate revolt. During the Semaine Sanglante (Bloody Week), several thousand rebel Communards (supporters of the hardcore insurgent Paris Commune) were killed and a further 20,000 or so executed.

Despite this bloody start, the Third Republic ushered in the glittering *belle époque* (beautiful age), with Art Nouveau architecture, a whole field of artistic 'isms' from impressionism onwards, and advances in science and engineering, including the construction of the first metro line in Paris. World Exhibitions were held in the capital in 1889 (showcased by the Eiffel Tower, p139) and again in 1901 in the purpose-built Petit Palais (p141). Bohemian Paris, with its nightclubs and artistic cafés, was conceived around this time.

Colonial rivalry between France and Britain in Africa ended in 1904 with the Entente Cordiale (literally 'Cordial Understanding'), marking the start of a cooperation that has continued, more or less, to this day.

THE GREAT WAR

Propaganda posters, rats in the trenches, battleground tours, maps, diaries and dozens of feature articles make www.firstworldwar.com stand out.

A trip to the Somme (p252) or Verdun (p414) battlefields goes some way to revealing the unimaginable human cost of WWI. Of the eight million French men called to arms, 1.3 million were killed and almost one million crippled. Much of the war took place in northeastern France, with trench warfare using thousands of soldiers as cannon fodder to gain a few metres of territory.

Central to France's entry into war against Austria-Hungary and Germany had been its desire to regain Alsace and Lorraine, lost to Germany in 1871. The Great War officially ended in November 1918 with Germany and the Allies signing an armistice in a clearing (p262) near Compiègne. But the details were not finalised until 1919 when the so-called 'big four' – French Prime Minister Georges Clemenceau, British Prime Minister Lloyd George, Italian Premier Vittorio Orlando and US President Woodrow Wilson – gathered in the Palace of Versailles (p211) to sign the Treaty of Versailles. Its harsh terms included the return of Alsace-Lorraine to France and a reparations bill of US$33 billion for Germany.

WWI: Trenches on the Web provides dozens of hot links to other Great War-related websites; find it at www.worldwar1.com.

WWI caused industrial production to drop by 40% and threw France into financial crisis. Yet somehow Paris still sparkled as the centre of the avant-garde in the 1920s and 1930s, with artists pushing into the

1799–1815	1858
The rise and fall of dashing Corsican soldier Napoleon Bonaparte	A 14-year-old peasant girl in Lourdes sees the Virgin Mary in a series of 18 visions; the town becomes a world pilgrimage site

new fields of cubism and surrealism, Le Corbusier (p63) rewriting the architectural textbook, foreign writers such as Ernest Hemingway and F Scott Fitzgerald being attracted by the liberal atmosphere of Paris, and nightlife establishing a cutting-edge reputation for everything from jazz to striptease. In 1922 the luxurious *Train Bleu* (Blue Train) made its first run from Calais, via Paris, to the Côte d'Azur.

WWII

The naming of Adolf Hitler as Germany's chancellor in 1933 signalled the end of a decade of compromise between France and Germany. Initially the French tried to appease Hitler, but two days after Germany invaded Poland in 1939, France joined Britain in declaring war on Germany.

By June 1940 France had capitulated. The British expeditionary force sent to help the French barely managed to avoid capture by retreating to Dunkirk and crossing the English Channel in small boats. The Maginot Line (see the boxed text, p373) had proved useless, with German armoured divisions outflanking it by going through Belgium.

Germany divided France into a zone under direct German occupation (in the north and along the western coast) and a puppet state led by ageing WWI hero General Pétain in the spa town of Vichy; the demarcation line between the two ran through Château de Chenonceau (p438) in the Loire Valley. Life in the Nazi-occupied north is examined at La Coupole (p241), a WWII museum inside a subterranean Nazi-built rocket-launch site.

The Vichy regime was viciously anti-Semitic, and local police proved very helpful to the Nazis in rounding up French Jews and others for deportation to Auschwitz and other death camps. Museums in Grenoble (p559) and Lyon (p506), among others, examine these deportations. The only Nazi concentration camp on French soil was Natzweiler-Struthof (see the boxed text, p388); it can be visited.

An 80km-long stretch of beach (see the boxed text, p298) and Bayeux's Musée Mémorial 1944 Bataille de Normandie (p294) tell the tale of the D-Day landings on 6 June 1944 when 100,000-plus Allied troops stormed the coastline to liberate most of Normandy and Brittany. Paris was liberated on 25 August by a force spearheaded by Free French units, sent in ahead of the Americans, so the French would have the honour of liberating their own capital.

The US general's war room in Reims (see the boxed text, p358), where Nazi Germany officially capitulated in May 1945, is open to the public.

Richard Davenport-Hin- evokes the ritzy glitz, glamour and intrigue of 1920s Paris in *A Night at the Majestic*, the true tale of the night modernist greats Proust, Joyce, Picasso, Diaghilev and Stravinsky met for dinner at the capital's legendary Hôtel Majestic.

So Churchill, Roosevelt and de Gaulle couldn't stand each other? So claims Simon Berthon's gripping *Allies at War: The Bitter Rivalry among Churchill, Roosevelt and De Gaulle*. Britain's Channel 4 televised his subsequent book, *Warlords: In the Heart of Conflict 1939–45*.

SUITE FRANÇAISE

The story behind the 2006 literary stunner, *Suite Française*, is as incredible as the novel itself. A twin set of novellas, it evokes the horror of Nazi-occupied Paris from June 1940 until July 1941 through the eyes of Ukrainian-born author Irène Némirovsky, who was arrested as a 'stateless person of Jewish descent' and carted off to Auschwitz where she died in the gas chamber in August 1942. Months later her husband suffered the same fate, leaving their oldest daughter with a bunch of leather-bound notebooks which remained unread until the 1990s – when this amazing novel (first published in French in 2004) was discovered.

1870	1914–18
The Third Republic ushers in the *belle époque*	Eight million French men are called to arms during WWI; of these, 1.3 million are killed and almost one million crippled

~NCH RESISTANCE

...te the myth of 'la France résistante' (the French Resistance), the underground movement ...er actually included more than 5% of the population. The other 95% either collaborated or ...id nothing. Resistance members engaged in railway sabotage, collected intelligence for the Allies, helped Allied airmen who had been shot down and published anti-German leaflets, among other activities. The impact of their pursuits might have been modest but the Resistance served as an enormous boost to French morale – not to mention fresh fodder for numerous literary and cinematic endeavours.

Part historical study, part social analysis, *La Vie en Bleu: France and the French since 1900* by Rod Kedward provides excellent insights into the mechanism of the French state and its people. Particularly fascinating is the issue of identity from the 1960s to 2000s.

Enthralling, exciting and hard to put down sums up Marcus Binney's *The Women who Live for Danger*. Women who worked under cover in occupied France during WWII is its savvy focus.

POSTWAR DEVASTATION

France was ruined. Over one-third of industrial production fed the German war machine during WWII, the occupiers requisitioning practically everything that wasn't (and was) nailed down: ferrous and nonferrous metals, statues, iron grills, zinc bar tops, coal, leather, textiles and chemicals. Agriculture, strangled by the lack of raw materials, fell by 25%.

In their retreat, the Germans burned bridges (2600 destroyed) and the Allied bombardments tore up railroad tracks (40,000km). The roadways hadn't been maintained since 1939, ports were damaged, and nearly half a million buildings and 60,000 factories were destroyed. The French had to pay for the needs of the occupying soldiers to the tune of 400 million francs a day, prompting an inflation riptide.

France's humiliation at the hands of the Germans was not lost on its restive colonies. As the war economy tightened its grip, the native-born people, poorer to begin with, noticed that they were bearing the brunt of the pain. In North Africa, the Algerians coalesced around a movement for greater autonomy that blossomed into a full-scale independence movement by the end of the war. The Japanese moved into strategically important Indochina in 1940. The Vietnamese resistance movement that developed quickly took on an anti-French, nationalistic tone, setting the stage for Vietnam's eventual independence.

THE FOURTH REPUBLIC & POST-WAR PROSPERITY

After the liberation, General Charles de Gaulle (1890–1970) – France's undersecretary of war who had fled Paris for London in 1940 after France capitulated – faced the tricky task of setting up a viable government. Elections on 21 October 1945 created a national assembly composed largely of pro-resistant communists. De Gaulle was appointed head of the government, but quickly sensed that the tide was turning against his idea of a strong presidency and in January 1946 he resigned.

The magnitude of France's post-war economic devastation required a strong central government with broad powers to rebuild its industrial and commercial base. Soon after the liberation, most banks, insurance companies, car manufacturers and energy-producing companies passed into the hands of the government. Other businesses remained in private hands, the objective being to combine the efficiency of state planning with the dynamism of private initiative. But progress was slow. By 1947 rationing remained and France was forced to turn to the USA for loans as part of the Marshall Plan to rebuild Europe.

1939	1944
Nazi Germany occupies France and establishes the Vichy regime	Normandy and Brittany are the first areas to be liberated by Allied troops following the June 1944 D-Day landings

One of the aims of the Marshall Plan was to financially and politically stabilise post-war Europe, thus thwarting the expansion of Soviet power. As the Iron Curtain fell over Eastern Europe, the pro-Stalinist bent of the Communist Party put it in a politically untenable position. Seeking at once to exercise power within the government and at the same time oppose its measures as insufficiently Marxist, the communists found themselves on the losing end of disputes involving the colonies, workers' demands and American aid. In 1947 they were booted out of government.

While the Communist Party fulminated against the 'imperialism' of American power, de Gaulle founded a new party, the Rassemblement du Peuple Français (RPF), which argued for the containment of Soviet power. In 1949 France signed the Atlantic Pact uniting North America and Western Europe in a mutual defence alliance (NATO). The fear of communism and a resurgent Germany prompted the first steps towards European integration with the birth of the Council of Europe in 1949, the European Coal and Steel Community in 1951 and military accords in 1954.

The economy gathered steam in the 1950s. The French government invested in hydroelectric and nuclear power plants, oil and gas exploration, petrochemical refineries, steel production, naval construction, auto factories, and building construction to accommodate a baby boom and consumer goods.

WAR IN THE COLONIES

The 1950s spelled the end of French colonialism. When Japan surrendered to the Allies in 1945, nationalist Ho Chi Minh launched a push for an autonomous Vietnam that became a drive for independence. Under the brilliant General Giap, the Vietnamese perfected a form of guerrilla warfare that proved highly effective against the French army. After their defeat at Dien Bien Phu in 1954, the French withdrew from Indochina.

The struggle for Algerian independence was nastier. Technically a French *département* (see p959), Algeria was in effect ruled by a million or so French settlers who wished at all costs to protect their privileges. Heads stuck firmly in the Saharan sands (especially in the south where the oil was), the colonial community and their supporters in the army and the right wing refused all Algerian demands for political and economic equality.

The Algerian War of Independence (1954–62) was brutal. Nationalist rebel attacks were met with summary executions, inquisitions, torture and massacres that only made Algerians more determined to gain their independence. The government responded with half-hearted reform and reorganisation programmes that failed to address the fact that most people didn't want to be part of France.

International pressure on France to pull out of Algeria came from the UN, the USSR and the USA, while *pieds noirs* (literally 'black feet', as Algerian-born French people are known in France), elements of the military and extreme right-wingers became increasingly enraged at what they saw as defeatism in dealing with the problem. A plot to overthrow the French government and replace it with a military-style regime was narrowly avoided when de Gaulle agreed to assume the presidency in 1958.

Women in France did not gain the right to vote until 1945. Find out how female politicians in France fought to have their voices heard in *Women & Politics in France: 1958–2000* by Gill Allwood and Kursheed Wadia.

Todd Shepard eloquently discusses the issues in his book *The Invention of Decolonization: The Algerian War and the Remaking of France.*

1949	1954–62
France signs the Atlantic Pact uniting North America and Western Europe in a mutual defence alliance (NATO)	The Algerian War of Independence marks the end of French colonialism

THE BIRTH OF THE BIKINI

Almost called *atome* (French for atom), rather than bikini after its pinprick size, the scanty little two-piece bathing suit was the 1946 creation of Cannes fashion designer Jacques Heim and automotive engineer Louis Réard.

Top-and-bottom swimsuits had existed for centuries, but it was the French duo which plumped for the name, bikini – after Bikini, an atoll in the Marshall Islands chosen by the USA in 1946 as the testing ground for atomic bombs.

Once wrapped around the curvaceous buttocks of 1950s sex-bomb Brigitte Bardot on St-Tropez' Plage de Pampelonne, there was no looking back. The bikini was born.

THE FIFTH REPUBLIC & YESTERDAY'S MAN

While it could claim to have successfully reconstructed the economy and created political stability, the Fourth Republic was hampered by a weak presidential branch and the debilitating situation in Algeria. De Gaulle remedied the first problem by drafting a new constitution (the Fifth Republic), which gave considerable powers to the president at the expense of the National Assembly.

Algeria was a greater problem. De Gaulle's initial attempts at reform – according the Algerians political equality and recognising their right in principle to self-determination – only infuriated right-wingers without quenching the Algerian thirst for independence. Following a failed coup attempt by military officers in 1961, the Organisation de l'Armée Secrète (OAS; a group of French settlers and sympathisers opposed to Algerian independence) resorted to terrorism. It tried to assassinate de Gaulle several times and in 1961 violence broke out on the streets of Paris. Police violently attacked Algerian demonstrators, murdering more than 100 people. In 1962 de Gaulle negotiated an end to war in Algeria with the lakeside signing of the Accord d'Évian (Evian Accord) in Évian-les-Bains.

By the late 1960s de Gaulle was appearing more and more like yesterday's man. Loss of the colonies, a surge in immigration (p53) and the rise in unemployment had weakened his government. De Gaulle's government by decree was starting to gall the anti-authoritarian baby-boomer generation, now at university and agitating for social change. Students reading Herbert Marcuse and Wilhelm Reich found much to admire in Fidel Castro, Che Guevara and the black struggle for civil rights in America, and vociferously denounced the American war in Vietnam.

Student protests of 1968 climaxed with a brutal overreaction by police to a protest meeting at Paris' most renowned university (p134). Overnight, public opinion turned in favour of the students, while the students themselves occupied the Sorbonne and erected barricades in the Latin Quarter. Within days, a general strike by 10 million workers countrywide paralysed France.

But such comradeship between worker and student did not last long. While the former wanted a greater share of the consumer market, the latter wanted to destroy it. After much hesitancy, de Gaulle took advantage of this division by appealing to people's fear of anarchy. Just as the

In *War and the Ivory Tower: Algeria and Vietnam* David L Schalk examines how the French handled Algeria, drawing analogies with the US in Vietnam and calling for intellectuals to stand up and make their voices heard in times of national crisis.

Tune into L'Imagination au Pouvoir (Power to the Imagination), Sous les Pavés, la Plage (Under the Cobblestones, the Beach) – a reference to Parisians' favoured material for building barricades and what they could expect to find beneath – and other slogans drummed up by protesting students in Daniel Singer's *Prelude to Revolution: France in May 1968*.

GAULLISH FACTS

- Charles de Gaulle was a record breaker: he is included in the *Guinness Book of Records* as surviving more assassination attempts – 32 to be precise – than anyone else in the world.
- The present constitution, known as the Fifth Republic and the 11th since 1789, was instituted by good old de Gaulle in 1958.
- 'Of course you can jump up and down on your chair like a little goat, bleating "Europe!, Europe!, Europe!" but all that leads nowhere and means nothing' said a provocative de Gaulle in 1965. Find out what else he said and did at www.charles-de-gaulle.org.

country seemed on the brink of revolution and an overthrow of the Fifth Republic, stability returned. The government immediately decentralised the higher education system and followed through in the 1970s with a wave of other reforms (lowering the voting age to 18, instituting an abortion law and so on). De Gaulle meanwhile resigned from office in 1969 after losing an important referendum on regionalisation and suffered a fatal heart attack the following year.

France has maintained an independent arsenal of nuclear weapons since 1960. It withdrew from NATO's joint military command in 1966.

POMPIDOU TO LE PEN

Georges Pompidou (1911–74), prime minister under de Gaulle, stepped onto the presidential podium in 1969. Despite embarking on an ambitious modernisation programme, investing in aerospace, telecommunications and nuclear power, he failed to stave off inflation and social unrest following the global oil crisis of 1973.

In 1974 Valéry Giscard d'Estaing (b 1926) inherited a deteriorating economic climate and sharp divisions between the left and right. Hampered by a lack of media nous and an arrogant demeanour, d'Estaing proved unpopular. His friendship with emperor and accused child-eater Jean Bédel Bokassa of the Central African Republic did little to win him friends and in 1981 he was ousted by longtime head of the Parti Socialiste (PS; Socialist Party), François Mitterrand (1916–96). As the only surviving French president to remain in politics, the French media have nicknamed d'Estaing *l'Ex* (the Ex).

Despite France's first socialist president instantly alienating the business community (the Paris stock market index fell by 30% on news of his victory) by setting out to nationalise 36 privately owned banks, industrial groups and other parts of the economy, Mitterrand did give France a sparkle. The Minitel – a potent symbol of France's advanced technological savvy – was launched in 1980 and a clutch of *grands projets* (p63) were embarked upon in the French capital. The death penalty was abolished, homosexuality was legalised, a 39-hour work week was instituted, annual holiday time was upped from four to five weeks and the right to retire at 60 was guaranteed.

Yet by 1986 the economy was weakening and in parliamentary elections that year the right-wing opposition, led by Jacques Chirac (Paris mayor since 1977), won a majority in the National Assembly. For the

Delve into the information portal of the French civil service to find hundreds of links to government websites, covering everything from defence, national security and environment to youth and employment, industry and trade, at www.service-public.fr.

Stay in tune with the moves and motions of France's National Assembly at www.assemblee-nat.fr.

1994	1995
The 50km-long Channel Tunnel linking mainland France with Britain opens after seven years of hard graft by 10,000 workers	After twice serving as prime minister, Jacques Chirac becomes president of France

Since the end of WWII France has been one of the five permanent members of the UN Security Council. Follow its movements at www .un.org/docs/sc.

Peep into the presidential palace and have a good old nosey around at www.elysee.fr.

Express yourself: sink your teeth into a meaty discussion on government policy and what France's politicians are saying at government portal www .premier-ministre.gouv.fr.

next two years Mitterrand worked with a prime minister and cabinet from the opposition, an unprecedented arrangement known as *cohabitation*. The extreme-right Front National (FN; National Front) meanwhile quietly gained ground by loudly blaming France's economic woes on immigration.

Presidential elections in 1995 ushered Chirac (an ailing Mitterrand did not run) into the Élysée Palace, the former mayor winning immediate popular acclaim for his direct words and actions in matters relating to the EU and the war raging in Bosnia. Whiz-kid foreign minister Alain Juppé was appointed prime minister and several women were placed in top cabinet positions. However, Chirac's attempts to reform France's colossal public sector in order to meet the criteria of European Monetary Union (EMU) were met with the largest protests since 1968, and his decision to resume nuclear testing on the Polynesian island of Moruroa and a nearby atoll was the focus of worldwide outrage (France didn't sign the worldwide test-ban treaty until 1998).

Always the maverick, Chirac called early parliamentary elections in 1997 – only for his party, the Rassemblement pour la République (RPR; Rally for the Republic), to lose out to a coalition of socialists, communists and greens. Another period of *cohabitation* ensued, this time with Chirac on the other side.

Presidential elections in 2002 were a shocker. Not only did the first round of voting see left-wing PS leader Lionel Jospin eliminated, it also saw the FN's racist demagogue Jean-Marie Le Pen (b 1928) – legendary for his dismissal of the Holocaust as a 'mere detail of history' in the 1980s and his 'inequality of races' jargon in the late 1990s – scoop 17% of the national vote. In the fortnight preceding the subsequent run-off ballot, demonstrators took to the streets with cries of 'Vote for the crook, not the fascist' ('crook' referring to the various party financing scandals floating around Chirac). On the big day itself, left-wing voters – without a candidate of their own – hedged their bets with 'lesser-of-two-evils' Chirac to give him 82% of votes. Chirac's landslide victory was echoed in parliamentary elections a month later when the president-backed coalition UMP (Union pour un Mouvement Populaire) won 354 of the 577 parliamentary seats, ending years of *cohabitation* and leaving Le Pen's FN seatless. Subsequent claims of nepotism in response to Le Pen trying to automatically pass the party leadership to his look-alike daughter, Marine, only weakened the party further.

POWER TO THE PEOPLE

France's outright opposition to the US-led war in Iraq in 2003 stirred up anti-French sentiment among Americans: many restaurants in the US changed 'French fries' to 'freedom fries' on their menus, to avoid having to mention the unspeakable, while US defence secretary Donald Rumsfeld publicly dismissed France (along with Germany) as 'old Europe'.

Old Europe indeed – in need of a shake-up: in November 2002 widespread strikes brought France to a standstill as public-sector workers hit out at the government's ambitious privatisation plans aimed at raising cash to reduce an increasingly too-high budget deficit. A few months

1999	2002
A fire in the Alpine Mont Blanc tunnel kills 41 people	The French franc, first minted in 1360, is dumped as France adopts the euro as its official currency

later, in a bid to appease a discontented electorate, parliament granted greater power to local government (p959) on economic and cultural affairs, transport and further education. The constitutional reform also gave the green light to local referenda – to better hear what the people on the street were saying (though the first referendum subsequently held – in Corsica – threw up a 'No' vote, putting Paris back at square one; for details see p914).

Spring 2003 ushered in yet more national strikes, this time over the government's proposed pension reform, which was pushed through parliament in July. 'We are not going to be intimidated by protestors' was the tough response of centre-right Prime Minister Jean-Pierre Raffarin, in office since May 2002. An extreme heatwave that summer, sending temperatures in the capital soaring above 40° and claiming 11,000 predominantly elderly lives, did little to cool rising temperatures.

More cracks appeared in France's assured countenance and silky-smooth veneer during 2004. Regional elections in March saw Chirac's centre-right UMP party sent to the slaughterhouse by the socialists; European elections two months later were equally disastrous. Strikes against various pension, labour and welfare reforms proposed by the government continued and in May 2005 the voice of protest was injected with a new lease of life thanks to French voters' shock rejection of the proposed EU constitution in a referendum. It was no coincidence that the constitution was something Chirac had fervently backed: the overriding message behind the humiliating 'No' vote was loud and clear – We are fed up with you. Do something!

What Chirac did was to sack his hugely unpopular punchbag of a prime minister, Raffarin, take his own foot off the reform pedal and knuckle down to some serious people-sweetening amid calls in some circles that he should resign. In the face of a five-year high in unemployment (10.2%) and an increasingly sluggish economy (GDP grew by just 1.4% in 2005 compared to 2.1% in 2004), the newly appointed prime minister – the silver-haired and -tongued career diplomat Dominique de Villepin (b 1953) who was best known as foreign minister during the Iraq invasion – assumed the gargantuan task of turning around disgruntled public opinion.

The last quarter of 2005 was the final helter-skelter downhill. The catalyst was the death of two teenagers of North African origin in October who, apparently running from police, were electrocuted while hiding in an electricity substation in a northeast Paris suburb. Rioting immediately broke out in the poor, predominantly immigrant neighbourhood and spread like wild fire. Within days, the violence was countrywide as rioters burnt cars, hurled petrol bombs, smashed windows,

Netpolitique is France's No 1 web spot for sinking your teeth into real French politics; keep up to date with what's happening and have a good laugh with its e-satire links at www .Netpolitique.net (in French).

Track France in the news, learn about its history and catch up on stacks more background info with www.discover france.net.

FRANCE ON EDGE

France is on the brink of a precipice, argues Jonathan Fenby in his insightful and provocative *France on the Brink: A Great Civilization Faces a New Century*, in which he takes a wry look at the gargantuan social and political challenges facing contemporary France. Fenby fans will equally enjoy *On the Brink: The Trouble with France*.

2003	2004
A heatwave across Europe brings sizzling temperatures of 40°C to Paris in August, killing an estimated 11,000 (mainly elderly) people	The National Assembly says yes to a controversial bill banning overtly religious symbols such as the Islamic headscarf in state schools

CHIRAC'S TAKE ON IT

A stiff-upper-lipped Chirac described the electorate's shock rejection (55%) of the EU constitution as '... a plea to be heard, a plea for action, a plea for results. Strong, diverse and sometimes contradictory expectations were expressed and came together in a feeling of dissatisfaction and insecurity in the face of today's world.'

Get the gory low-down on the 2007 presidential race – intrigue, drama, blogs, campaign speeches, political profiles et al – at www.presidentielle-2007.net (in French).

looted shops and vented months of pent-up anger. Two weeks later the government introduced emergency measures restricting people's movements and imposing curfews in 30 French towns and cities as part of its tough zero-tolerance policy on the urban chaos. Nine thousand burnt cars and buildings later, as peace returned, Chirac assured France there would be no more urban violence and steps would be made to create equal opportunities for immigrants and better opportunities for its youth. Little did he realise how loaded with irony this pledge would prove (p31).

2005

Paris loses to London in a bid to host the 2012 Olympics. In November riots force the government to declare a state of emergency

2007

The race is on for a new president, elections set for 22 April being slated as the most significant in France since WWII

The Culture

THE NATIONAL PSYCHE

There is nothing more maddening than the shop assistant who unabashedly chats to her mate while you wait, or the post-office clerk who greets you with complete disregard. Dumb insolence some say.

France is a country whose people have attracted more stubborn myths and stereotypes than any other in Europe. Arrogant, rude, bolshie, unbelievably bureaucratic (which, incidentally, is true: try getting a *carte grise*, car-ownership papers), sexist, chauvinistic, super chic and stylish are among the dozens of tags – true or otherwise – donned on the garlic-eating, beret-wearing, *sacre bleu*–swearing French over the centuries. The French, by the way, don't wear berets or use old chestnuts such as *'sacre bleu'* anymore. (Sit in a café some afternoon and you'll soon hear the gentle expressions of surprise favoured by Parisians these days as they slip on dog droppings. *'Merde'* (shit) is quite popular.)

Most people are extremely proud to be French and staunchly nationalistic to boot, a result of the country's republican stance that places nationality – rather than religion, for example – at the top of the self-identity list. This has created an overwhelmingly self-confident nation, both culturally and intellectually – a French superiority complex that manifests itself in a pompous refusal to speak any language other than French, according to many Anglophones: fair comment given the example set by none other than the French president himself at an EU summit in 2006 (p48).

Contrary to popular belief, many French speak English or another foreign language very well, travel and are perfectly happy to use their language skills should the need arise. Of course, if monolingual English-speakers don't even attempt *'bonjour'*, then there is no way proud French linguists will let on they speak fluent English with a great sexy accent! French men, by the way, deem an English gal's heavily accented French as downright sexy as many women deem a Frenchman speaking English.

Sixty Million Frenchmen Can't be Wrong: What Makes the French so French ask Jean-Benoit Nadeau and Julie Barlow in their witty, well-written and at times downright comical musings on one of Europe's most contradictory nationalities.

FRENCH KISSING

Kissing is an integral part of French life. (The expression 'French kissing', as in tongues, doesn't exist in French, incidentally.) That said, put a Parisian in Provence and there's no saying they will know when to stop.

Countrywide, people who know each other reasonably well, really well, a tad or barely at all greet each other with a glancing peck on each cheek. Southern France aside (where everyone kisses everyone), two men rarely kiss (unless they are related or artists) but always shake hands. Boys and girls start kissing as soon as they're out of nappies, or so it seems.

Kissing French-style is not completely straightforward, 'how many' and 'which side first' potentially being problematic. In Paris it is definitely two: unless parties are related, *very* close friends or haven't seen each other in an age, anything more is deemed affected. That said, in certain trendy 20-something circles friends swap three or four cheek-skimming kisses, as do many young teenagers at school *parce qu'ils ont que ça à faire…*

Travel south and the *bisous* (kisses) multiply, three or four being the norm in Provence. The bits of France neighbouring Switzerland around Lake Geneva tend to be three-kiss country (in keeping with Swiss habits); and in the Loire Valley it is four. Corsicans, bizarrely, stick to two but kiss left cheek first – which can lead to locked lips given that everyone else in France starts with the right cheek.

DON'T SPEAK ENGLISH!

Inexcusable and inadmissible was how staunch French traditionalist and patriot President Chirac deemed the behaviour of his fellow countryman, EU business lobby head Monsieur Ernest-Antoine Seillière, who had the audacity to address a meeting of the EU summit in 2006 in English. So 'deeply shocked' was Chirac that he walked out, trailed by his French-delegation flock.

'Don't speak English!' was the headline of *Le Monde* the next day, while the French blogosphere seethed with debate on linguistic patriotism: 'Open your eyes, Mr President, you are on another planet', 'it is a long time since French was the language of the international arena' taunted modern French bloggers, many of whom blog in English as well as their mother tongue.

French was the main language of the EU until 1995 when Sweden and Finland came into the EU fold.

On the subject of sex, not all French men ooze romance or light Gitanes all day. Nor are they as civilised about adultery as French cinema would have you believe. Adultery, illegal in France until 1975, was actually grounds for automatic divorce until as late as mid-2004.

Suckers for tradition, the French are slow to embrace new ideas and technologies: it took the country an age to embrace the internet, clinging on to their own Minitel system for dear life. Yet the French are also incredibly innovative (see p50) – a dichotomy reflected in practically every facet of French life: they drink and smoke more than anyone else, yet live longer. They eat like kings, but are not fat…

LIFESTYLE

Culture shock for Brits is the thrust of Helena Frith-Powell's latest book, *More More France Please*, in which the British author resident in Languedoc interviews fellow Brits who call France home.

Be a fly on the wall in the 5th-floor bourgeois apartment of Monsieur et Madame Tout le Monde and you'll see them dunking croissants in bowls of *café au lait* for breakfast, buying a baguette every day from the bakery (Monsieur nibbles the top off on his way home) and recycling little bar a few glass bottles. They go to the flicks once a month, work not an hour more than 35 hours a week and have a 20-year-old daughter who is so BCBG, darling (BCBG – bon chic, bon genre – a Sloane ranger in non-Parisian speak).

Madame buys a clutch of hot-gossip weekly mags, Monsieur enjoys *boules* and August is the *only* month a summer holiday can possibly be considered (along with the rest of France). Dodging dog pooh on pavements is a sport practised from birth and everything goes on the *carte bleue* (debit card) when shopping: this *is* the society after all that microchipped credit cards long before anyone else even dreamt of scrapping the swipe-and-sign system. The couple have a landlord: with a longstanding tradition of renting rather than buying, home ownership is low (57% of households own their own home; the rest rent).

Discover just how French women gorge themselves on the country's fabulous cakes, fill up on fresh-from-the-*boulangerie* bread and scarcely work out – or do they? *French Women don't Get Fat: The Secret of Eating for Pleasure* by Mireille Guiliano spills the beans.

Jospin's slashing of the standard French working week from 39 to 35 hours in 2000 (applicable to employers of more than 20 from 2002) created jobs, boosted domestic tourism and redefined peak hours as pleasure-thirsty workers headed out to the country on Thursday night (instead of Friday) and returned to urban life on Monday evening. Given the choice, most French workers would plump for less income and more leisure time, but a sizable chunk of the population still toils 39 hours or more a week. (Since 2003 employers can enforce a 39-hour work week for a negotiable extra cost.)

The family plays a vital role. Nonetheless, couples are marrying later (men at the age of 30.9, women at 28.8) and waiting longer to have children. More children are born out of wedlock (48.3% in 2005 compared to 38.6% in 1995 and 11.4% in 1980) and divorce is on the rise (42.5% of marriages now end in divorce compared to 30.4% in 1985).

Abortion is legal during the first 12 weeks of pregnancy, girls under 16 not needing parental consent provided they are accompanied by an adult of their choice: 30 abortions take place in France for every 100 live births.

Civil unions between two members of the same (or different) sex have been legal since the end of 1999 – and have dramatically increased year on year (by around 25% a year). But civil partnerships fall short of legal marriages say gay lobbyists, who want homosexual couples to be granted the same fiscal advantages and adoptive rights in marriage as heterosexuals. A petition calling for the legal recognition of same-sex marriages in early 2004 was topped off in June that year by the civil

THE FRENCH BLOGOSPHERE

There is no better means of tuning in to the underbelly of what French people are really thinking – right NOW – than through the French blogosphere. Growing like wildfire every second of every minute, it is the voice of the moment.

The best-known blogger in France is Paris-based Loïc Le Meur – a 33-year-old 'serial entrepreneur' who is extraordinarily influential (150,000 unique visitors read him a month), in no small part because he blogs simultaneously in French and English on separate sites; English-driven www.loiclemeur.com runs a link to French Loïc. 'Traditional media send messages; blogs start discussions' is his strapline and indeed, the discussion is rife on his blog, embracing everything from current affairs in France to his favourite jogging routes in the capital. In the office Loïc heads up the European, Middle Eastern and African arms of blog-host world leader, Six Apart. Considerately, Loïc lists his favourite French blogs in English at www.eu.socialtext.net/loicwiki /index.cgi?french_blogosphere.

The other big-name blogger is Cyrille De Lasteyrie, aka the nutty Vinvin. Jam-packed with humour and wit, his blog reviews restaurants, films etc (in French) and ranks them out of 20, hence its name, Vingt sur Vingt (http://cdelasteyrie.typepad.com). But in 2006 he switched to podcasting, wooing surfers with hilarious downloadable video clips in English aimed specifically at an American market. 'Are the French arrogant or is there a scientific explanation', 'Is French cheese good for health' and 'what about the French army' are but some of the meaningful/less questions Bonjour America (www.bonjour-america.com) poses so stylishly.

Frivolous they might seem to some, but French bloggers have serious clout. In the days preceding France's historic vote on the EU constitution (p45), the powerful 'No' blog of humble French law professor Étienne Chouard (http://etienne.chouard.free.fr in French) lured an online crowd of 25,000 a day – and contributed enormously to France's eventual rejection of the constitution say political analysts (there was no equivalent 'Yes' blog). The so-called 'workers' revolt' in Paris and elsewhere against the government's proposed new employment law in April 2006 was likewise charted in English by French bloggers who continue to cover events at www.libcom.org/blog.

Other hot blogs by the French in English:

- French Word a Day (http://french-word-a-day.typepad.com). Just that; fun language learning.

- ¡No Pasarán! (http://no-pasaran.blogspot.com). What expats and the mainstream media (French and American alike) fail to tell you about France.

- Ric's Metropole Paris (www.metropoleparis.com). Paris for students, lovers, tourists et al.

- Emmanuelle Richard (www.emmanuelle.net). Wacky musings by a French journalist in Los Angeles with 'France & Frogs' section and comprehensive links to 'frogblogs' and blogs by 'frogs in the US' and 'Americans in France'.

- Petrol Head (www.petrol-head.com). French-language blog about everything: art, babies, finance, wine, culture, health, the garden, gadgets, technology.

MADAME AVERAGE IN FIGURES

Married at 28
First child at 29
Total number of kids: 1.9
Monthly salary (gross): 12% less than Monsieur
Will live until 83

MONSIEUR AVERAGE IN FIGURES

Married at 30
Working week: 35 hours, 52 minutes
Annual holiday: five weeks, plus five public holidays
Monthly salary (gross): €2440
Will live until 76

wedding of two gay men in Bègles town hall in Bordeaux. The ground-breaking ceremony, conducted by local mayor and former Green party presidential candidate Noël Mamère, was the first in France – and just months later was declared null and void by a Bordeaux court. Gay lobbyists continue to push for equal rights, but their prospects don't look good: a parliamentary report published on the rights of the family and child in early 2006 strongly recommended France not legalise marriage and adoption for same-sex couples.

The gay scene thrives in big cities such as Paris, Marseille, Lyon and Grenoble; see p957.

ECONOMY

Tax cuts, public sector reform and combating crime were among the big things promised by Chirac upon assuming office in 2002. Some years later, hindered by a flurry of national strikes and demonstrations (p44), economic and employment reform has not panned out as the French president hoped. Unemployment, double that of Britain and a definite hot potato in light of the government's proposed youth employment law (p31), hovers around 9.6%. Inflation clocked in at 1.9% in 2005.

Despite ritual denunciations of globalisation by politicians and pundits, the French economy is heavily dependent on the global market-

DOS & DON'TS

- Say 'Bonjour, monsieur/madame' when you walk into a shop or café and 'Merci, monsieur...au revoir' when leaving. Use 'Monsieur' for any male person who isn't a child; 'Madame' for those you'd call 'Mrs' in English; and 'mademoiselle' for unmarried women (see p56).

- Touching, fondling or picking up fruit, vegetables, flowers or a piece of clothing in shops attracts immediate killer stares from shop assistants. Ask if you want to look at something.

- Take a gift – flowers (not chrysanthemums, which are only brought to cemeteries) or wine for more informal gatherings – when invited to someone's home.

- Going 'Dutch' (splitting the bill) in restaurants is an uncivilised custom for many French. The person who invites generally pays, although close friends often share the cost.

- Never discuss money, particularly income, over dinner.

- Knock what your French textbook at school taught you on the head. These days 's'il vous plaît' – never 'garçon' (meaning 'boy') – is the only way to summon a waiter in restaurants.

place. It is the fourth-largest export economy, including the products of foreign businesses implanted in France which account for a third of the export market. In mid-2006, in what analysts interpreted as a brave bid to fend off US global dominance, Chirac pledged €2 billion to fund a clutch of ground-breaking technological *grands projets:* the creation of a €450 million Franco-German search engine called Quaero (Latin for 'I search') destined to rival Google and Yahoo; a biorefinery to produce chemicals from cereals; energy-storage technology allowing electric trains to recharge automatically at stations; the invention of a hybrid electric-diesel car; mobile-phone TV; and an energy-efficient heating and lighting system regulated by wall sensors.

France is the largest agricultural producer and exporter in the EU, thanks to generous subsidies awarded to the high-voting, sympathy-inducing agricultural sector. Its production of wheat, barley, maize (corn) and cheese is particularly significant. The country is to a great extent self-sufficient in food except for tropical products such as bananas and coffee.

POPULATION

France is not that densely populated – 107 people inhabit every square kilometre (compared to 235 in Germany, 240 in the UK and 116 in the EU), although a whopping 20% of the national population is packed into the greater metropolitan area of Paris.

The last 10 years have seen rural and suburban areas steadily gaining residents; and Paris and the northeast (except Alsace) losing inhabitants to southern France, an increasingly buoyant part of the country where populations are predicted to rise by 30% over the next 30 years.

In keeping with European trends, France's overall population is ageing: on 1 January 2006 16.2% of the population were 65 or older and by 2050 one in three will be 60 or older (compared to one in five in 2000). This demographic phenomenon will be less marked in urban areas such as Paris, Lyon and the Rhône Alpes and on the Mediterranean coast where increasing work opportunities ensure a younger, more active population.

By 2050 the population of mainland France is expected to notch up 64 million – five million more than in 2000.

See p53 for a snapshot of France's foreign population.

SPORT

Most French wouldn't be seen dead walking down the street in trainers and tracksuit bottoms. Contrary to appearances though, they do love sport. Shaved-leg cyclists toil up Mont Ventoux in good weather; anyone who can flits off for the weekend to ski; and football fans fill stadiums during home matches.

France has achieved a strikingly high level in international judo, four-time world champion David Douillet being the star. Les 24 Heures du Mans and the F1 Grand Prix in Monte Carlo are the world's raciest dates in motor sports.

With the exception of mogul champion, *le boss des bosses* Edgar Gospiron, skiing bizarrely has produced very few stars since the 1968 alpine sweep of Jean-Claude Killy. Alpine downhill skier Antoine Deneriaz (1976–) scooped gold – just one of three France won – at the 2006 Olympics in Turin, while Chamonix snowboarder Karine Ruby (1978–), gold medallist in 1998 and holder of more World Cup titles than any other boarder, finished a disappointing 16th. On ice, Marina Anissina and Gwendal Peizerat scooped ice-dancing gold at Salt Lake City in 2002, and Brian Joubert finished second in the 2004 world figure-skating championships.

Find out everything you need to know about buying or selling a home in France, setting up a business, marriage and inheritance under French law with Notaires de France (French Notaries) at www.notaires.fr (click on the minuscule Union Jack for English).

French women have the highest life expectancy in the whole of the EU (along with Spanish women). Find out more from the National Institute of Demographic Studies at www.ined.fr.

Join 225,000 spectators live to watch Les 24 Heures du Mans at www .lemans.org and race around Monte Carlo's F1 Grand Prix with the big boys at www.acm.mc.

Losing out to London in its bid to host the 2012 Summer Olympics was a major loss of face for Paris. The French capital last hosted the gargantuan event in 1924.

Football

France's greatest sporting moment came at the 1998 World Cup, which the country hosted and won. But the game has produced few stars since, leaving the French line-up for the 2006 World Cup looking uncannily similar to that of eight years previous: 'Ageing players from France's golden generation' said critics who predicted at best a quarter-final finish for the national team, captained as in 1998 by Marseille-born midfielder ace Zinedine Zidane who pledged to retire immediately after the cup.

As it happened the 2006 World Cup ended up a tournament followers of French football are unlikely to forget. Against all the odds the team reached the final (against Italy) – only for Zidane to be sent off in the 110th minute for head-butting one of the Italian players in the chest. 'Shame on you!' said critics, who lamented such a shameful end to such a brilliant football career. But for the French nation, Zidane could be forgiven. 'Merci les Bleues' became the catch phrase of the moment while the song *Coup de Baile (Headbutt)*, written as something of a joke (the lyrics read 'Zidane hit him. The cup... we missed it'), soared overnight to the top of the French pop charts.

At club level, Marseille was the first French side to win the European Champions League (in 1991), thanks in no small part to Paris-born football legend Eric Cantona, who transferred to Leeds a year later and subsequently turned the fortunes of Manchester United around. In 1994 Paris-St-Germain won the European Cup Winners' Cup. Since the 1995 Bosman decision allowing European clubs to field as many European players as they wish, French football greats have been lured to richer clubs in Italy, Britain, Spain and Germany (including Zidane, who transferred from Juventus to Real Madrid in 2001 for US$64.45 million, making him the most expensive player in football history). Other hotshots out of France include Arsenal's French manager Arsène Wenger (who was awarded an OBE in 2003 for his contribution to British football) and hotshot striker Thierry Henry.

France's home matches (friendlies and qualifiers for major championships) kick off at St-Denis' magnificent 80,000-capacity Stade de France (p183), built for the 1998 World Cup. Other noteworthy stadiums (there are 250-odd in all in France) include Lyon's Stade de Gerland (p516), home to national champions (since 1993) Olympique Lyonnais. Previous champion sides include St-Étienne (1967–70) and Marseille (1989–1992).

Rugby

Rugby league has a strong following in the south and southwest of France, favourite teams being Toulouse, Montauban and St-Godens. Rugby union is more popular still, as the enduring success of the powerful Paris-St-Germain club testifies.

FRENCH BALLS

France's most traditional ball games are *pétanque* and the similar, though more formal, *boules,* which has a 70-page rule book. Both are played by village men in work clothes on a gravel or sandy pitch known as a *bouldrome,* scratched out wherever a bit of flat and shady ground can be found. World championships are held for both sports. In the Basque Country, the racquet game of pelota (p695) is the thing to do.

The indisputable contributions French footballers have made to British football is the subject of *French Revolution: 10 Years of English Football since Cantona* by Alex Hayes, Daniel Ortelli and Xavier Rivoire.

Read all about French rugby and the scores on the board at www .francerugby.fr (in French).

TOUR TRIVIA

- French journalist and cyclist Henri Desgrange came up with the Tour de France in 1903 as a means of promoting his sports newspaper *L'Auto* (*L'Équipe* today).
- With the exception of two world war–induced intervals, the Tour de France has never missed a year.
- The 1998 race was the 'tour of shame': fewer than 100 riders crossed the finish line after several teams were disqualified for doping.
- 2004 wasn't much better: even before the race began, the French team had withdrawn and the Spanish were banned on doping grounds.
- *Le blaireau* (the badger), alias Brittany-born biking legend Bernard Hinault (1954–), won the Tour de France five times before retiring in 1986.
- American sports icon Lance Armstrong (1971–) is the indisputable Tour de France king. He overcame cancer, then won the race seven consecutive times between 1999 and 2005, after which he retired.

France's home games in the Tournoi des Six Nations (Six Nations Tournament) are held in March and April. The finals of the Championnat de France de Rugby take place in late May and early June.

Cycling

The legendary Tour de France – the world's most prestigious bicycle race – brings together 189 of the world's top male cyclists (21 teams of nine) and 15 million spectators in July each year for a spectacular 3000-plus kilometre cycle around the country. The three-week route changes, but always labours through the Alps and Pyrenees and finishes on the Champs-Élysées in Paris. The publicity caravan preceding the cyclists showers roadside spectators with coffee samples, logo-emblazoned balloons, pens and other free junk-advertising gifts – and is almost more fun to watch than the cyclists themselves, who speed through in 10 seconds flat.

France is the world's top track cycling nation and has a formidable reputation in mountain biking: Christian Taillefer holds the world speed record on a mountain bike, 212.39km/h, which he hit by flying down a snow-covered ski slope.

Check annual tour dates and routes for the legendary Tour de France at www.letour.fr.

Tennis

The French Open, held in Paris' Roland Garros Stadium in late May and early June, is the second of the year's four Grand Slam tournaments. Marseille-born Sébastien Grosjean (1978–), a quarterfinalist in the 2006 Australian Open, is ranked No 23 in the world and has been the highest-ranking French player on the men's circuit for the last few years. On the women's circuit, Amélie Mauresmo – world No 1 for five weeks in 2004 and again in 2006 – is the only real French star. In April, the world's best warm up on clay at the Monte Carlo Masters in Monaco.

Follow the matches and the aces in Monte Carlo at http://montecarlo .masters-series.com and during the French Open at http://www.roland garros.com.

MULTICULTURALISM

France might be multicultural (immigrants make up 7.4% of the population) but its republican code, while inclusive and nondiscriminatory, does little to accommodate a multicultural society. This dichotomy exploded in a riot of demonstrations in 2004 when the Islamic headscarf (along with Jewish skullcaps, crucifixes and other religious symbols) was banned in French schools. The law, intended to place all school

In 1998 Fernanda Eberstadt upped and left New York with husband and two kids in tow for southwest France (around Perpignan) where she penetrated the local community of Roma. Read her story in *Little Money Street: In Search of Gypsies in the South of France.*

children on an equal footing in the classroom, was slammed by Muslims as intolerant and yet more proof that the French State is not prepared to integrate Muslims into French society. French Muslims were only given a national voice with the election of the French Muslim Council (FCMC), an umbrella organisation of 18 representatives from Muslim associations and mosques in France, in 2003.

Some 90% of the French Muslim community – Europe's largest – are noncitizens. Most are illegal immigrants living in depressing poverty-stricken *bidonvilles* (tinpot towns) around Paris, Lyon and other metropolitan centres. Many are unemployed (unemployment in France is currently 14% among foreigners compared to 9.2% among people of French origin) and face little prospect of getting any job, let alone a decent one: racial discrimination is widespread in the workplace. How many black waiters do you see in central Paris cafés and restaurants?

Years of pent-up anger, resentment and frustration exploded in a riot of lootings, car burnings and street violence in Paris in late 2005. The catalyst was the hideous death of two teenage boys of North African origin in the Paris suburb of Clichy-sous-Bois on 27 October. The boys were electrocuted to death after hiding in an electrical substation, allegedly while on the run from the police. But within days, the riots and arson had spread beyond Paris to Dijon, Lyon and other cities, as youths of all origins, French included, joined forces to express their burning discontent. On 9 November, after a particularly nasty night – 1173 burnt cars, 330 arrests and 12 injured police officers – the government declared a state of emergency, allowing local authorities in 30 towns to impose curfews. By 13 November the urban violence had receded and the EU had conjured up €50 million to help France clean up the mess on the streets, while Chirac was promising to smarten up his act.

Multicultural France has always drawn immigrants: 4.3 million from other parts of Europe arrived between 1850 and WWI and another three million came between the world wars. During the post-WWII economic boom years, several million unskilled workers followed from North Africa and French-speaking sub-Saharan Africa. Large-scale immigration peaked in the early 1960s when, as the French colonial empire collapsed, French settlers returned to metropolitan France from Algeria, other parts of Africa and Indochina.

Fadela Amara and Sylvia Zappi's portrayal of women in French Muslim society in *Breaking the Silence: French Women's Voices from the Ghetto* (translated by Helen Harden Chenut) makes for uncomfortable but vital reading.

Of France's 4.3 million foreign residents, 13% are Algerian, 13% Portuguese, 12% Moroccan and 9% Italian. Only one-third has French citizenship, not conferred at birth but subject to various administrative requirements.

MEDIA

Public licence fees subsidise public broadcaster France Télévisions, which controls 40% of the market with its three TV channels – France 2, 3 and 5 (Arte after 7pm). Yet in the face of increasingly stiff competition from private broadcasters such as TF1 and M6, its future looks bleak. That said, TF1 and France Télévisions are partners in CII, an international CNN-style station (broadcast in English, French and Arabic) that will broadcast 24-hour international news and is backed by €70 million in public funding. It will go on air in December 2006 to a predominantly Anglophone target audience.

Find out about the public broadcaster behind France 2, 3 and 5 (Arte) with www.francetele visions.fr (in French) and its biggest private competitor at www.tf1.fr (in French).

As in Britain, there is a strong distinction between broadcasting and print media. The press, like TV and radio broadcasters, are independent and free of censorship. Unlike Britain, there is no tabloid or gutter press.

On the airwaves, two out of five songs played on French radio must have French lyrics; one in five must be a newcomer.

RELIGION

Secular France maintains a rigid distinction between the Church and State. Some 55% of French identify themselves as Catholic, although no more than 10% attend church regularly. Another one million people are Protestant.

Coexisting uneasily with this nominally Christian majority is France's five million–strong Muslim community. Most Muslims adhere to a moderate Islam, although the deportation (and subsequent return) in 2004 from Lyon of an Algerian imam in favour of stoning unfaithful wives – one of 27 radical Muslim prayer leaders to be deported since 2001 – renewed fears that Islamic fundamentalists are gaining ground. It also prompted calls from more moderate Muslims for the State to help train imams in a French-style Islam and build more mosques. Most of the 1500 or so imams in France are self-taught or have been educated in more radical climes. Almost 90% are employees of Algeria, Saudi Arabia or another Islamic country and work in mosques funded by these countries.

More than half of France's 600,000-strong Jewish population (Europe's largest) live in and around Paris. Marseille and Strasbourg (p380) likewise have notable Jewish communities. French Jews, the first in Europe to achieve emancipation, have been represented by the Paris-based umbrella organisation the Consistoire since 1808.

The number and extremity of anti-Semitic and racist crimes is rising (by 43% in 2004/05), as the gruesome murder of Jewish telephone salesman Ilan Halimi, tortured for three weeks by a multiracial gang in a Paris suburb in early 2006, disturbingly highlighted. Subsequent street rallies by tens of thousands of protesters simply resulted in a trio of anti-Semitic attacks within 24 hours in Sarcelles, a predominantly Jewish neighbourhood in Paris where the country's largest Jewish community of 20,000 – mainly second-generation North African Jews – lives.

WOMEN IN FRANCE

Women were given the right to vote in 1945 by de Gaulle's short-lived postwar government, but until 1964 a woman needed her husband's permission to open a bank account or get a passport. Younger French women especially are quite outspoken and emancipated, but self-confidence has yet to translate into equality in the workplace, where women are often kept out of senior and management positions. The problem of sexual harassment (harcélement sexuel) in the workplace is finally beginning to be addressed with a new law imposing financial penalties on the offender. A great achievement in the last decade has been Parité, the law requiring political parties to fill 50% of their slates in all elections with female candidates.

Traditionally known for their natural chic, style and class, contemporary French women are bolder, more confident and sassier than ever. Take the Rykiel women: in the 1970s legendary Parisian knitwear designer Sonia Rykiel designed the skin-tight, boob-hugging sweater worn with no bra beneath. In 2006 daughter Nathalie came up with the ultimate stylish sex boutique. The shop – wedged between big-name labels in the chic Parisian quarter of St-Germain des Prés – screams design and is aimed squarely at women who know what they want.

To top it off, it might be a woman who is elected French president in 2007 (see p31).

The community of French Jews speak out at www.col.fr (in French).

Decidedly more upbeat and optimistic than most books on Jewish France, Thomas Nolden looks at the literature Jewish writers in France have produced from the 1960s to the present day in *In Lieu of Memory: Contemporary Jewish Writing in France.*

Simone de Beauvoir is essential reading: *She Came to Stay* is a compelling tale of a threesome; *The Woman Destroyed* portrays female vulnerability in three novellas; and *The Mandarins* is a bumper, 800-page epic romance.

A MADAME FROM BIRTH

'About time too' a feminist anywhere else on the planet would argue. Indeed it is only now that French women have decided no more 'Mademoiselle', meaning 'Miss', 'not married', 'virgin', 'sexually available' and so on, say Paris-based feminist group Les Chiennes de Garde (meaning 'guard dogs', or rather, 'guard bitches'). The group has launched a petition for the term 'Mademoiselle' to be eradicated from the administrative and political arena. It also wants the standard 'maiden name' box struck off official forms and documents.

'Mademoiselle' originates from the medieval word 'damoiselle', meaning a young upper-class girl (male equivalents were 'damoisel'). Later merged with 'ma' to denote an unmarried woman, the term was tantamount to 'sad old spinster who can't find a husband' in the 17th and 18th centuries. In the 19th-century, novelist Adolphe Belot borrowed the term to depict a frigid wife in *Mademoiselle Giraud, ma Femme*.

So the fight is on to become a Madame from birth. Already a Madame, I for one, not to mention practically all my 30-something-with-kids girlfriends, are delighted if someone dares call me 'Mademoiselle'. Despite the kids in tow, dirty washing and first wrinkle, it means I still look young.

ARTS
Literature
COURTLY LOVE TO SYMBOLISM

Lyric poems of courtly love composed by troubadours dominated medieval French literature, while the *roman* (literally 'the romance') drew on old Celtic tales such as King Arthur, the search for the Holy Grail and so on. With the *Roman de la Rose*, a 22,000-line poem by Guillaume de Lorris and Jean de Meung, the allegorical figures of Pleasure and Riches, Shame and Fear popped on the scene.

La Pléaide, Rabelais and Montaigne made French Renaissance literature great: La Pléaide was a group of lyrical poets active in the 1550s and 1560s, of whom the best known is Pierre de Ronsard (1524–85), author of four books of odes. The highly exuberant narrative of Loire Valley–born François Rabelais (1494–1553) blends coarse humour with encyclopaedic erudition in a vast panorama of subjects that includes every kind of person, occupation and jargon existing in mid-16th-century France. Michel de Montaigne (1533–92) wrote essays on everything from cannibals, war horses and drunkenness to the uncanny resemblance of children to their fathers.

'Le grand siècle' ushered in the great French classical writers with their lofty odes to tragedy. François de Malherbe (1555–1628) brought a new rigour to the treatment of rhythm in poetry; and Marie de La Fayette (1634–93) penned the first major French novel, *La Princesse de Clèves* (1678).

The philosophical work of Voltaire (1694–1778) dominated the 18th century. A century on, the city of Besançon gave birth to Victor Hugo – the key figure of French Romanticism. The breadth of interest and technical innovations exhibited in Hugo's poems and novels – *Les Misérables* and *Notre Dame de Paris* (The Hunchback of Notre Dame) among them – was phenomenal: after his death his coffin was laid beneath the Arc de Triomphe for an all-night vigil.

In 1857 literary landmarks *Madame Bovary* by Gustave Flaubert (1821–80) and Charles Baudelaire's (1821–67) collection of poems, *Les Fleurs du Mal* (The Flowers of Evil), were published. Émile Zola (1840–1902) meanwhile strove to convert novel-writing from an art to a science in his powerful series, *Les Rougon-Macquart*.

Contemporary France features a bit too much for comfort in the recently published *Rising from the Muck: The New Anti-Semitism in Europe* by Pierre-André Taguieff and Patrick Camiller.

It's 'Verbal Viagra' according to the *Sunday Times*. The fabulous loves, lusts and longings of French women are the focus of *Two Lipsticks & A Lover* by Helena Frith-Powell, an eye-opening account of sex, lingerie and other French femininities.

The expression of mind states rather than the detailing of day-to-day minutiae was the aim of symbolists Paul Verlaine (1844–96) and Stéphane Mallarmé (1842–98). Verlaine's poems – alongside those of Arthur Rimbaud (1854–91), with whom Verlaine shared a tempestuous homosexual relationship – were French literature's first modern poems.

MODERN LITERATURE

The world's longest novel – a seven-volume 9,609,000-character giant by Marcel Proust (1871–1922) – dominated the early 20th century. À la Recherche du Temps Perdu (Remembrance of Things Past) explores in evocative detail the true meaning of past experience recovered from the unconscious by 'involuntary memory'.

Surrealism proved a vital force until WWII, André Breton (1896–1966) capturing its spirit – a fascination with dreams, divination and all manifestations of 'the marvellous' – in his autobiographical narratives. In Paris the bohemian Colette (1873–1954) captivated and shocked with her titillating novels detailing the amorous exploits of heroines such as schoolgirl Claudine.

After WWII, existentialism developed around the lively debates of Jean-Paul Sartre (1905–80), Simone de Beauvoir (1908–86) and Albert Camus (1913–60) in Paris' Left-Bank cafés of St-Germain des Prés. In L'Étranger (The Outsider), which scooped the Nobel Prize for Literature in 1957, Camus stresses the importance of the writer's political engagement.

The 1950s' nouveau roman saw experimental young writers seek new ways of organising narratives, Nathalie Sarraute slashing identifiable characters and plot in Les Fruits d'Or (The Golden Fruits). Histoire d'O (Story of O), an erotic sadomasochistic novel written by Dominique Aury under a pseudonym in 1954 sold more copies outside France than any other contemporary French novel. In the 1960s it was Philippe Sollers' experimental novels that raised eyebrows.

> Keep up to the minute with contemporary French literature and what's being translated into English with the French Publishing Agency, online at www .frenchpubagency.com.

TOP TEN LITERARY SIGHTS

- The chateau on the French–Swiss border in the Jura where Voltaire lived from 1759 (p583).
- Colette's Paris: of her many Parisian addresses, the apartment where she died in the Palais Royal (p128) is the most illustrious. Elsewhere, there's a small museum (p478) in the Burgundian village where she was born and Hôtel de Paris (p910) in Monaco.
- The Left-Bank cafés of St-Germain des Prés, Paris (p163).
- The graves of Sartre and Beauvoir in the Cimetière du Montparnasse (p137).
- Musée du Jules Verne in Nantes (p653), home town of the author of Around the World in 80 Days.
- Île du Grand Bé (p310), burial place of St-Malo–born 18th-century writer Chateaubriand.
- Musée Jean Cocteau and Salle de Marriages (p905) in Menton, odes to one of France's most multitalented poets, dramatists, artists and film directors – Jean Cocteau.
- Museon Arlaten (p834), founded in Arles in 1896 by Nobel Prize–winning poet and dedicated Provençal preservationist Frédéric Mistral.
- Île Ste-Marguerite (p885), the speck of an island off Cannes where the Man in the Iron Mask – immortalised in Alexandre Dumas' novel Le Vicomte de Bragelonne (The Viscount of Bragelonne) – was incarcerated in the 17th century.
- Toulouse's four-day, literary star–studded Marathon des Mots (Marathon of Words) in June (p745).

TOP FIVE FROGS V ROSBIFS

Age-old rivalry between English (rosbifs) and the French (frogs) sells like hotcakes. Our favourites:

- *That Sweet Enemy: the French and the British from the Sun King to the Present* (Robert & Isabelle Tombs). Cross-Channel rivalry in a historical context, light-hearted nonetheless.

- *Au Secours, les Anglais Nous Envahissent!* (José-Alain Fralon). Help, the English Are Invading Us! They're everywhere. Slowly but surely the English are invading us...

- *Cross Channel* (Julian Barnes). Classic short stories zooming in on everything both sides of the Channel, from sex, art and love to literature, the Channel tunnel and the *Eurostar*.

- *More France Please! We're British!* (Helen Frith-Powell). Seen through the perspective of Brits who chose to live in France for good.

- *A Year in the Merde & Merde Actually* (Stephen Clarke). Dog poo everywhere, unnecessary bureaucracy, transport; Clarke spouts on about it all. You'll love it or hate it.

Treat the vast labour-intensive series of novels, known under the general title La Comédie Humaine, by Tours-born Honoré de Balzac as an extremely comprehensive social history of France.

Contemporary authors include Françoise Sagan, Pascal Quignard, Jean Auel, Anna Gavalda, Emmanuel Carrère, Stéphane Bourguignon and Martin Page whose novel, *Comment Je Suis Devenu Stupide* (How I Became Stupid) explores a 25-year-old Sorbonne student's methodical attempt to become stupid. Also popular are Frédéric Dard (alias San Antonio), Léo Malet and Daniel Pennac, widely read for his witty crime fiction such as *Au Bonheur des Ogres* (The Scapegoat) and *La Fée Carabine* (The Fairy Gunmother).

Cinema

Watching French classics in the Lyonnaise factory (p506) where the cinematographic pioneers, the Lumière brothers, shot the world's first motion picture in March 1895, is a must.

French film flourished in the 1920s. Abel Gance (1889–1981) was king of the decade with his antiwar blockbuster *J'Accuse* (I Accuse; 1918) – all the more impressive for its location filming on actual WWI battlefields. The switch to sound ushered in René Clair (1898–1981) and his world of fantasy and satirical surrealism.

WWI inspired the 1930s classic *La Grande Illusion* (The Great Illusion; 1937), a devastating portrayal of the folly of war based on the trench warfare experience of director Jean Renoir (1894–1979). Indeed, portraits of ordinary people and their lives dominated film until the 1950s when realism was eschewed by surrealist Jean Cocteau (1889–1963) in two masterpieces: *La Belle et la Bête* (Beauty and the Beast; 1945) and *Orphée* (Orpheus; 1950) are unravelled in Menton's Musée Jean Cocteau (p905) on the Côte d'Azur.

Sapped of talent and money after WWII, France's film industry found new energy by the 1950s. And so the *nouvelle vague* (new wave) burst forth. With small budgets and no extravagant sets or big-name stars, filmmakers produced uniquely personal films using real-life subject matter: Claude Chabrol (1930–) explored poverty and alcoholism in rural France in *Le Beau Serge* (Bitter Reunion; 1958); Alain Resnais (1922–) portrayed the problems of time and memory in *Hiroshima, Mon Amour* (1959); and François Truffaut (1932–84) dealt with love.

By the 1970s the new wave had lost its experimental edge, handing over the limelight to lesser known directors such as Eric Rohmer (1920–), who made beautiful but uneventful films in which the characters endlessly analyse their feelings. Two 1960s movies ensured France's invincibility as the land of romance: Claude Lelouch's *Un Homme et une Femme* (A Man and a Woman; 1966), a love story set in Deauville (p285), and Jacques Demy's *Les Parapluies de Cherbourg* (The Umbrellas of Cherbourg; 1964), a wise and bittersweet love story likewise filmed in Normandy.

Big-name stars, slick production values and a strong sense of nostalgia were the dominant motifs in the 1980s, as generous state subsidies saw film-makers switch to costume dramas and comedies in the face of growing competition from the USA. Claude Berri's portrait of prewar Provence in *Jean de Florette* (1986), Jean-Paul Rappeneau's *Cyrano de Bergerac* (1990) and *Bon Voyage* (2003), set in 1940s Paris, and *Astérix et Obélix: Mission Cléopâtre* (2001) – all starring France's best known (and biggest-nosed) actor, Gérard Depardieu – found huge audiences in France and abroad.

French film has enjoyed a massive renaissance since 2001 thanks to films such as *Le Fabuleux Destin de Amélie Poulain* (Amélie; 2001), a simple and uncontroversial feel-good story of a Parisian do-gooder directed by Jean-Pierre Jeunet of *Delicatessen* (1991) fame; Jacques Perrin's animal film *Le Peuple Migrateur* (Winged Migration; 2001), about bird migration; the big-name (Omar Sharif and Isabelle Adjani) *Monsieur Ibrahim et les Fleurs du Coran* (Mr Ibrahim and the Flowers of Coran; 2003) about an Arab grocer living on rue Bleue; and the giggle-guaranteed, Marseille comedy *Taxi 3* (2003).

The big hit of 2004 was *Les Choristes* (The Chorus; 2004), a sentimental tale of a new teacher arriving at a school for troublesome boys in 1949

View France through cinematic eyes with *France on Film*, edited by Lucy Mazdon. If *nouvelle vague*'s your thing, Jean Douchet's *French New Wave* (translated by Robert Bononno) is compulsive reading.

A HISTORY OF FRENCH CINEMA IN 10 FILMS

Grab a bottle of Burgundy, glue yourself to the screen and take a whirlwind tour through French cinematic history (all available on video or DVD) with:

- *La Règle du Jeu* (The Rules of the Game; 1939). Shunned by the public and censored, Jean Renoir's story of a 1930s bourgeois hunting party in the Loire Valley's soggy Sologne is a dark satirical masterpiece.

- *Les Enfants du Paradis* (Children of Paradise; 1945). Made during the Nazi occupation of France, Marcel Carné celebrates the vitality and theatricality of a Paris without Nazis.

- *Et Dieu Créa la Femme* (And God Created Woman; 1956). Roger Vadim's tale of the amorality of modern youth set in St-Tropez made a star out of Brigitte Bardot.

- *Les Quatre Cents Coups* (The 400 Blows; 1959). Partly based on the rebellious adolescence of the best loved of new-wave directors François Truffaut.

- *Les Vacances de M Hulôt* (Mr Hulôt's Holiday; 1953). and *Mon Oncle* (My Uncle; 1958) Two films starring the charming, bumbling figure of Monsieur Hulot and his struggles to adapt to the modern age by non-new-wave 1950s director Jacques Tati.

- *Diva* (1981) and *37°2 le Matin* (Betty Blue; 1986). Two visually compelling films by Jean-Jacques Beineix. *Diva* stars French icon Richard Bohringer.

- *Shoah* (1985). Claude Lanzmann's 9½-hour-long black-and-white documentary of interviews with Holocaust survivors worldwide is disturbing. It took 11 years to make.

- *Indochine* (Indochina; 1993). An epic love story set in 1930s French Indochina with Catherine Deneuve – timeless beauty – as a French plantation owner.

- *Subway* (1985), *Le Grand Bleu* (The Big Blue; 1988), *Nikita* (1990) and *Jeanne d'Arc* (Joan of Arc; 1999). Take your pick from these box-office hits directed by Luc Besson.

- *Code Inconnu* (Code Unknown; 2001). Intellectual art-house film starring Oscar-winning French actress Juliette Binoche as an actress in Paris.

> **OSS 117**
>
> OSS 117 is not a cinematic invention. The French secret agent was created by novelist Jean Bruce (1921–63) in 1949 – four years before Ian Fleming's 007. Making his debut in *Tu Parles d'une Ingénue* (You Speak of an Ingenue), Hubert Bonisseur de la Bath, colonel in the Office of Strategic Service (OSS), starred in 87 novels (selling 24 million copies) before his creator died in a car accident in 1963.
>
> But the silky-smooth, dark haired action man with a penchant for beautiful women, fancy gadgets and dicing with death was not dead. Three years after Bruce's death, wife Josette took over, penning another incredible 143 adventures between 1966 and 1985. Josette died in 1996.
>
> *OSS 117 est Mort* (OSS 117 is Dead) was the first book written by the couple's children, François and Martine Bruce, who picked up the family tradition in 1987 and churned out 24 more adventures. By the time *OSS 117 Prend le Large* (OSS 117 Takes Off) – the last to be published – hit the streets in 1992 the best-selling French series had been translated into 17 languages and sold 75 million copies. Previous OSS 117s on screen include Ivan Desny in Jean Sacha's 1957 film adaptation of Jean Bruce's 1953 novel *OSS 117 n'est Pas Mort* (OSS 117 is Not Dead): he's clearly not.

and starring the incredible voice of angelic actor Jean-Baptiste Maunier (1990–). A year on, *Asterix & the Vikings* (2005) by Danish director Stefan Fjeldmark wooed French cinema-goers with Europe's most expensive feature-length cartoon – its budget was €22 million – proving once and for all that France's cartoon industry, which currently produces about 15 films a year, means business.

The Palme d'Or, awarded each year at Cannes, is the world's most coveted film prize; find out winners past and present at www.festival-cannes.fr.

Charismatic comic actor Jean Dujardin (1972–) has been the hottest thing since sliced bread in France after starring in *Brice de Nice* (2005), a piss-take of cult surfing movie *Point Break* in which surfing dude and poseur Brice waits for *sa vague* (his wave) to come in waveless Nice on the French Riviera. The film features great shots of the town. In 2006 Dujardin played the sexist, racist, macho, uncultured and cringingly outdated 1950s Bond…James Bond, or rather Bonisseur de la Bath…Hubert Bonisseur de la Bath, in *OSS 117: Le Caire, Nid d'Espions* (OSS 117: Cairo Nest of Spies; 2006). The Bond parody (above) was an instant hit.

The runaway hit of the decade was indisputably American film director Ron Howard's *The Da Vinci Code* (2006). Not only did the film bring international acclaim to Audrey Tautou, the waifish French actress of *Amélie* fame who costarred with Tom Hanks in *The Da Vinci Code*. It also brought American tourists back in their droves to Paris; for the inside scoop see p136.

Find out what all the hype was about with Brice and OSS 117 at www.bricedenice.com (in French) and www.oss117.org (in French).

The French film industry honours its film-makers and actors with the Césars, named after the Marseille-born artist who created the prestigious statue awarded to winners.

Music

There's more to it than accordions and Édith Piaf.

French baroque music influenced European musical output in the 17th and 18th centuries, while French musical luminaries – Charles Gounod (1818–93), César Franck (1822–90) and *Carmen*-creator Georges Bizet (1838–75) among them – were a dime a dozen in the 19th century. Modern orchestration was founded by Hector Berlioz (1803–69), the greatest figure in the French romantic movement. He demanded gargantuan forces: his ideal orchestra included 240 stringed instruments, 30 grand pianos and 30 harps.

Claude Debussy (1862–1918) revolutionised classical music with his *Prélude à l'Après-Midi d'un Faune* (Prelude to the Afternoon of a Fawn), creating a light, almost Asian musical impressionism; while impressionist comrade Maurice Ravel (1875–1937) peppered his work, including *Boléro*, with sensuousness and tonal colour. Contemporary composer Olivier Messiaen (1908–92) combined modern, almost mystical music with natural sounds such as birdsong. His student, Pierre Boulez (1925–), works with computer-generated sound.

Jazz hit 1920s Paris in the banana-clad form of Josephine Baker, a cabaret dancer from the USA (the 15th-century chateau in the Dordogne where the African-American lived after the war can be visited; p636). Post-WWII ushered in a much-appreciated bunch of musicians – Sidney Bechet, Kenny Clarke, Bud Powell and Dexter Gordon among them. In 1934 a chance meeting between Parisian jazz guitarist Stéphane Grappelli and three-fingered Roma guitarist Django Reinhardt in a Montparnasse nightclub led to the formation of the Hot Club of France quintet. Claude Luter and his Dixieland Band was the hot sound of the 1950s.

The *chanson française*, a tradition dating from the troubadours of the Middle Ages, was eclipsed by the music halls and burlesque of the early 20th century, but was revived in the 1930s by Piaf and Charles Trenet. In the 1950s the Left Bank cabarets nurtured *chansonniers* (cabaret singers) such as Léo Ferré, Georges Brassens, Claude Nougaro, Jacques Brel and Serge Gainsbourg.

French pop music has evolved massively since the 1960s *yéyé* (imitative rock) days of Johnny Halliday. Particularly strong is world music, from Algerian raï and other North African music (artists include Cheb Khaled, Natacha Atlas, Jamel, Cheb Mami and Racid Taha) to Senegalese *mbalax* (Youssou N'Dour), West Indian *zouk* (Kassav, Zouk Machine). One musician who uses these elements to stunning effect is Manu Chao (www.manuchao.net), the Paris-born son of Spanish parents whose albums are international bestsellers.

Another hot musical export is Parisian electro-dance duo Daft Punk, whose debut album *Homework* (1997) fused disco, house, funk and techno. *Discovery* (2001) adopts a more eclectic approach. Electronica duo Air, around since the mid-1990s, remains sensational with its third

Let the hauntingly beautiful soundtrack of *Les Choristes* transport you to another world with the music on CD or film on DVD.

Surf Rohff at www.roh2f.com (in French) and Booba at http://booba92i.artistes.universalmusic.fr.

CRUDE ART

They sparked riots in Paris, said 200 French MPs who went so far as to submit a complaint to the justice ministry in November 2005 demanding seven rap groups be prosecuted for provocative lyrics.

'Is rap responsible for the crisis in the suburbs? My answer is no', retorted French Prime Minister Dominique de Villepin, who made his distaste for finger-pointing crystal clear.

'Hip-hop is a crude art, so we use crude words. It is not a call to violence', was what French rapper Monsieur R had to say on the matter. He's a fine one to talk: the rap singer of Congolese origin is currently in court for outrageously non-PC lyrics on his aptly entitled album, *Politikment incorrect* (2005). Think *'je pisse sur Napoleon et sur le général de Gaulle'* (I piss on Napoleon and General de Gaulle) or *'La France est une garce, n'oublie pas de la baiser jusqu'à l'épuiser, comme une salope il faut la traiter, mec'* (France is a bad gal', don't forget to fuck her into exhaustion, treat her like a slut, boy!').

Not all French rap is as extreme as Monsieur R's. A few fucks yes, but most rap astutely portrays immigrant life in the suburbs. Big-name rappers in France are, without exception, French 20-somethings of Arabic or African origin whose prime preoccupation is the frustrations and fury of fed-up immigrants. Take Disiz La Peste: hot-shot rapper, 27, Senegalese father, French mother, website http://disizlapeste.artistes.universalmusic.fr, title of third album *Histoires Extra-Ordinaires d'un Jeune de Banlieue* (The Extraordinary Stories of a Youth in the Suburbs; 2005).

album *Talkie Walkie* (2004). French rap was spearheaded in the 1990s by Senegal-born, Paris-reared rapper MC Solaar and Suprême NTM (NTM being an abbreviation for a French expression far too offensive to print), which split in 2000.

Keep abreast of French rap at http://rap.fr (in French).

Immigrant life in the French *banlieue* (outskirts) finds expression in the rap and hip-hop lyrics of countless French artists (see p61), among them Marseille's hugely successful IAM; Brittany's Manau trio that fuses hip-hop with traditional Celtic sounds; female rapper Diam's; and the Paris-based Triptik trio from Nantes. Hard-core rappers include Parisian heavyweights Booba of Senegalese origin and Rohff (whose fourth album, *Au delà de mes Limites,* released in 2005, sold 30,000 copies in the first week); and five-piece rap band KDD from Toulouse.

Architecture
PREHISTORIC TO ART NOUVEAU

From the prehistoric megaliths around Carnac (p341) to Vauban's 33 star-shaped citadels (below) built to defend France's 17th-century frontiers, French architecture has always been of *grand-projet* proportions.

Southern France is the place to find its Gallo-Roman legacy: the Pont du Gard (p770), amphitheatres in Nîmes (p765) and Arles (p832), the theatre at Orange (p851) and Nîmes' Maison Carrée (p766).

Several centuries later, architects adopted architectural elements from Gallo-Roman buildings to create *roman* (Romanesque) masterpieces such as Toulouse's Basilica St-Sernin (p740), Poitier's Église Notre Dame la Grande (p660) and Caen's two famous Romanesque abbeys (p289).

Northern France's extraordinary wealth in the 12th century lured the finest architects, engineers and artisans, who created impressive Gothic structures with ribbed vaults carved with great precision, pointed arches, slender verticals, chapels along the nave and chancel, refined decoration and stained-glass windows. Avignon's pontifical palace (p843) is Gothic architecture on a gargantuan scale. With the introduction of flying buttresses around 1230, Gothic masterpieces such as the seminal cathedral at Chartres (p221) and its successors at Reims (p357), Amiens (p256) and Strasbourg (p378) appeared.

By the 15th century architects had shelved size for ornamentation, conceiving the beautifully lacy Flamboyant Gothic. For an example of such decorative overkill, look at the spire of Strasbourg cathedral. To trace the shift from late Gothic to Renaissance, travel along the Loire Valley: Château de Chambord (p429) illustrates the mix of classical components and decorative motifs typical of early Renaissance architecture. In the mid-16th century, François I had Italian architects design Fontainebleau (p215).

VAUBAN'S CITADELS

From the mid-17th century to the mid-19th century the design of defensive fortifications around the world was dominated by the work of one man: Sébastien le Prestre de Vauban (1633–1707).

Born to a relatively poor family of the petty nobility, Vauban worked as a military engineer during almost the entire reign of Louis XIV, revolutionising both the design of fortresses and siege techniques. To defend France's frontiers, he built 33 immense citadels, many of them star-shaped and surrounded by moats, and he rebuilt or refined more than 100 more. Vauban's most famous citadel is situated at Lille, but his work can also be seen at Antibes, Belfort, Belle Île, Bensançon, Concarneau, Perpignan, St-Jean Pied de Port, St-Malo and Verdun.

In 1635 early-baroque architect François Mansart (1598–1666) designed the classical wing of Château de Blois (p427), while his younger rival, Louis Le Vau (1612–70), started work on Louis XIV's palace at Versailles (p211).

A quest for order, reason and serenity through the adoption of the forms and conventions of Graeco-Roman antiquity defined neoclassical architecture from 1740 until well into the 19th century. Nancy's place Stanislas (p403) is France's loveliest neoclassical square.

Under Napoleon, many of Paris's best-known sights – the Arc de Triomphe, La Madeleine, the Arc du Carrousel at the Louvre and the Assemblée Nationale building – were designed.

Art Nouveau (1850–1910) combined iron, brick, glass and ceramics in ways never before seen. See for yourself in Paris with Hector Guimard's noodlelike metro entrances, the fine Art Nouveau interiors in the Musée d'Orsay (p138) and the glass roof over the Grand Palais (p141).

http://france.archiseek .com is a fabulous online resource on French architecture, both century-old and spanking-new.

CONTEMPORARY

Chapelle de Notre-Dame du Haut in the Jura (p580) and Couvent Ste-Marie de la Tourette near Lyon (p519) are architectural icons of the 20th century. Designed in the 1950s by France's most celebrated architect, Le Corbusier (1887–1965), the structures rewrote the architectural stylebook with their sweeping lines and functionalised forms adapted to fit the human form.

French political leaders have long sought to immortalise themselves through the erection of huge public edifices, otherwise called *grands projects*. Georges Pompidou commissioned Paris' Centre Pompidou (p129) in 1977; Giscard d'Estaing transformed a derelict train station into the Musée d'Orsay (p138); while François Mitterrand commissioned the capital's best-known contemporary architectural landmarks, including IM Pei's glass pyramid at the Louvre (p126), the Opéra-Bastille (p132), the Grande Arche (p208) in the skyscraper district of La Défense, and the national library (p144). In June 2006 Jean Nouvel's fabulous new architectural icon, the Musée du Quai Branly (p138), opened in the capital.

In the provinces, notable buildings include Strasbourg's European Parliament (p379), Dutch architect Rem Koolhaas' Euralille and Jean Nouvel's glass-and-steel Vesunna Musée Gallo-Romain in Perigueux (p624), a 1920s Art-Deco swimming pool–turned–art museum in Lille (p229) and the fantastic Louvre II (p252) in unknown Lens, 37km south. Also noteworthy are an 11th-century abbey-turned–monumental sculpture gallery in Angers (p451) and a 120m-tall metallic tower planned for 2008 in Le Havre's rejuvenated 19th-century docks (p278). Then, of course, there's one of the world's tallest bridges (p794), by Sir Norman Foster no less.

For an alternative guide to contemporary architecture, look no further than the bilingual www.archi-guide.com .

Painting

France's oldest prehistoric cave paintings (drawn 31,000 years ago) adorn the Grotte Chauvet-Pont d'Arc (Ardèche, Rhône Valley) and the underwater Grotte Cosquer (near Marseille); neither can be visited.

According to Voltaire, who clearly rated the classical mythological and biblical scenes bathed in golden light that the baroque painter created, French painting proper began with Nicolas Poussin (1594–1665). Forward-wind a couple of centuries and modern still life pops onto the scene with Jean-Baptiste Chardin (1699–1779), the first to see still life as an essay in composition rather than a show of skill in reproduction. A century later, neoclassical artist Jacques Louis David (1748–1825) wooed the public with his vast portraits; several are in the Louvre.

While Romantics such as Eugène Delacroix (buried in Paris' Cimetière du Père Lachaise; p143) revamped the subject picture, the Barbizon School effected a parallel transformation of landscape painting. Barbizons included landscape artist Camille Corot (1796–1875) and Jean-François Millet (1814–75). The son of a peasant farmer from Normandy, Millet took many of his subjects from peasant life and reproductions of his *L'Angélus* (The Angelus; 1857) – the best-known French painting after the *Mona Lisa* – are strung above mantelpieces all over rural France. The original hangs in Paris' Musée d'Orsay (p138).

The latter is also the place to see the Realists, among them Édouard Manet (1832–83), who zoomed in on Parisian middle-class life and Gustave Courbet (1819–77), who depicted the drudgery of manual labour and difficult lives of the working class.

It's USA-based but it's informative, comprehensive and the height of usefulness. Keep up-to-date with what's hot in French culture at www.french culture.org.

It was in a flower-filled garden in a Normandy village (p280) that Claude Monet (1840–1926) expounded impressionism, a term of derision taken from the title of his experimental painting *Impression: Soleil Levant* (Impression: Sunrise; 1874). In summer, view some of his work projected on the façade of Rouen cathedral (p270). A trip to the Musée d'Orsay unveils a rash of other members of the school – Boudin, Sisley, Pissarro, Renoir, Degas and so on.

An arthritis-crippled Renoir painted out his last impressionist days in a villa (p884) on the Côte d'Azur. With a warmth and astonishing intensity of light hard to equal, the French Riviera inspired dozens of artists post-Renoir: Paul Cézanne (1839–1906) is particularly celebrated for his postimpressionist still lifes and landscapes done in Aix-en-Provence where he was born and worked (visit his studio; p827); Paul Gauguin (1848–1903) worked in Arles; while Dutch artist Vincent van Gogh (1853–90) painted Arles and St-Rémy de Provence. In St-Tropez pointillism took off: Georges Seurat (1859–91) was the first to apply paint in small dots or uniform brush strokes of unmixed colour, producing fine mosaics of warm and cool tones, but it was his pupil Paul Signac (1863–1935) who is best known for his pointillist works; see them in St-Tropez's Musée de l'Annonciade (p894).

Twentieth-century French painting is characterised by a bewildering diversity of styles, including Fauvism, named after the slur of a critic who compared the exhibitors at the 1906 autumn salon in Paris with *fauves* (wild animals) because of their radical use of intensely bright colours, and cubism. Henri Matisse (1869–1954) was the man behind the former (a Fauvist trail around Collioure takes you past scenes he captured on canvas in Roussillon; p806) and Spanish prodigy Pablo Picasso (1881–1973) the latter. Both chose southern France to set up studio, Matisse living in Nice (visit the Musée Matisse; p873) and Picasso opting for a 12th-century chateau (now the Musée Picasso) in Antibes. Cubism, as developed by Picasso and Georges Braque (1882–1963), deconstructed the subject into a system of intersecting planes and presented various aspects of it simultaneously.

No piece of French art better captures Dada's rebellious spirit than Marcel Duchamp's *Mona Lisa*, complete with moustache and goatee. In 1922 German Dadaist Max Ernst moved to Paris and worked on surrealism, a Dada offshoot that drew on the theories of Freud to reunite the conscious and unconscious realms and permeate daily life with fantasies and dreams.

With the close of WWII, Paris' role as artistic world capital ended, leaving critics wondering ever since where all the artists have gone. The focus shifted back to southern France in the 1960s with new realists such as Arman (1928–) and Yves Klein (1928–62), both from Nice and well represented in contemporary art museums in Paris, Lyon, St-Étienne, Nice, Lille and Strasbourg.

In 1960 Klein famously produced *Anthropométrie de l'Époque Bleue,* a series of blue imprints made by naked women (covered from head to toe in blue paint) rolling around on a white canvas – in front of an orchestra of violins and an audience in evening dress. A decade on the supports-surfaces movement deconstructed the concept of a painting, transforming one of its structural components (such as the frame or canvas) into a work of art instead.

Artists in the 1990s threw in the towel as far as the grandeur of early French art was concerned, looking to the minutiae of everyday urban life to express social and political angst and turning to mediums other than paint to let rip. Conceptual artist Daniel Buren (1938–) reduced his painting to a signature series of vertical 8.7cm-wide stripes that he applies to every surface imaginable – white marble columns in the courtyard of Paris's Palais Royal (p128) included. The painter (who in 1967, as part of the radical *groupe BMPT,* signed a manifesto declaring he was not a painter) was the *enfant terrible* of French art in the 1980s. Partner-in-crime Michel Parmentier (1938–2000) insisted on monochrome painting for a while – blue in 1966, grey in 1967 and red in 1968.

Current trends are best expressed by Paris' Palais de Tokyo (p140), a contemporary art space that opens noon to midnight or thereabouts; encourages art visitors to feel, touch, talk and interact; and bends over backwards to turn every expectation of painting and art on its head.

For anyone who reads French, www.avoir-alire .com (in French) is an essential tool for keeping a cultural eye on the latest literature, music, comic strips and films to be released.

Environment

THE LAND

Hexagon-shaped France, the largest country in Europe after Russia and Ukraine, is hugged by water or mountains along every side except its northeastern boundary – a relatively flat frontier abutting Germany, Luxembourg and Belgium.

The country's 3200km-long coastline embraces white chalk cliffs (Normandy), treacherous promontories (Brittany), fine-sand (Atlantic Coast) and pebble (Mediterranean Coast) beaches. Five major river systems crisscross the country: the Garonne (which includes the Tarn, Lot and Dordogne) empties into the Atlantic; the Rhône links Lake Geneva and the Alps with the Mediterranean; Paris is licked by the Seine, which snakes through the city en route from Burgundy to the English Channel; while tributaries of the North Sea–bound Rhine drain much of the area north and east of the capital. Then there's France's longest river, the chateau-studded Loire, which meanders from the Massif Central to the Atlantic.

Mountains run riot. Europe's highest peak, Mont Blanc (4807m), spectacularly tops the French Alps that stagger along France's eastern border. North of Lake Geneva the gentle limestone Jura Range runs along the Swiss frontier to reach heights of around 1700m, while the rugged Pyrenees lace France's entire 450km-long border with Spain and peak at 3404m.

Stunning as they are, the Alps, Jura and Pyrenees are mere babies compared to France's ancient massifs, formed 225 to 345 million years ago. The Massif Central covers one-sixth (91,000 sq km) of the country and is renowned for its chain of extinct volcanoes: Puy de Dôme (1465m) last erupted in 5760 BC, the volcanic history and geology of which is explained in the Vulcania centre near Clermont-Ferrand (p591). Other golden oldies, worn down by time, include the forested upland of the Vosges in northeast France; the Ardennes on Champagne's northern edge; and Brittany and Normandy's backbone, the Massif Armoricain.

WILDLIFE

France is blessed with a rich variety of flora and fauna, although few habitats have escaped human impact: urbanisation, pollution, intensive agriculture, wetland draining, hunting, the encroachment of industry and tourism infrastructure menace dozens of species.

The Shaping of French Environmental Policy by Joseph Skarka is a 224-page heavyweight analysis of precisely what its title suggests.

Some spectacular and quite miraculous footage of the natural world close-up is screened during the annual International Nature & Environment Film Festival, held each year in Grenoble. Follow the festival link to read all about it at www.frapna .org (in French).

RESPONSIBLE TRAVEL

Follow the local code of ethics and common decency in nature reserves and national parks:

- Pack up your litter and carry it out with you.
- Minimise waste by taking minimal packaging and no more food than you need.
- Don't use detergents or toothpaste, even if they are biodegradable, in or near watercourses.
- Stick to designated paths in protected areas, particularly in sensitive biospheres and alpine areas and on coastal dunes where flora and fauna may be seriously damaged if you stray.
- When camping in the wild (check first with the landowners or a park ranger to see if it's allowed), bury human waste in cat holes at least 15cm deep and at least 100m from any watercourse.
- Obey the 'no dogs, tents and motorised vehicles' rule in national parks.

TOP FIVE NATURAL CURIOSITIES

Several up hill and down dales later, here's what tickled us most in France's 42 regional parks:

- Dwarf mutant beech trees that have grown in all their stunted glory around Reims and Champagne since the 6th century and are protected today by the Parc Naturel Régional de la Montagne de Reims (p361) in Champagne.

- Europe's highest sand dune (which also happens to move and swallow trees), the Dune de Pilat near Arcachon on the Atlantic Coast (p686).

- Europe's largest extinct volcano (by area), Monts du Cantal, the balding slopes of which can be hiked up in summer and skied down in winter (p591).

- The lunar landscape of underground sink-hills, caves and streams beneath the *causses* (limestone plateaus) of Languedoc's Parc Naturel Régional des Grands Causses (p793).

- Prehistoric bird footprints and marine-reptile fossil skeletons in the Réserve Naturelle Géologique near Digne-les-Bains (p862).

Animals

France has more mammals to see (around 110) than any other country in Europe. Couple this with its 363 bird species, 30 types of amphibian, 36 varieties of reptile and 72 kinds of fish, and wildlife watchers are in paradise. Of France's 39,000 identified insect species, 10,000 creep 'n crawl in the Parc National du Mercantour (p70) in the Alps.

High-altitude plains in the Alps and Pyrenees shelter the marmot (it hibernates October to April) with its shrill and distinctive whistle; the nimble *chamois* (mountain antelope) with its dark-striped head; and the *bouquetin* (Alpine ibex) that can be seen in large numbers in the Parc National de la Vanoise (see p68 & p557). Mouflon, introduced in the 1950s, clamber over stony sunlit scree slopes in the mountains; and the red and roe deer and wild boar are common in lower-altitude forested areas. Winter welcomes the Alpine hare with its white coat, while 19 of Europe's 29 bat species hang out in the dark in the alpine national parks.

The wolf, which disappeared from France in the 1930s, returned to the Parc National du Mercantour in 1992 – much to the horror of the mouflon (on which it preys) and local sheep farmers. Dogs, corrals and sound machines to frighten the estimated 55 wolves believed to freely roam in the Mercantour and other alpine areas today are effective

> Follow the movement of France's precious wolf, bear and lynx populations with FERUS, France's conservation group for the wellbeing of these protected predators, online at www.ours -loup-lynx.info (in French).

WHERE TO WATCH WILDLIFE

The national parks and their smaller siblings encourage green-eyed visitors to hook up with a nature guide to watch wildlife; details are in the regional chapters. Otherwise, the following observation posts are worth a gander:

- Bison in Languedoc at the Réserve de Bisons d'Europe near Mende (p788).

- Vultures in the Pyrenees at La Falaise aux Vautours in the Vallée d'Ossau (p728) and in Languedoc at the Belvédère des Vautours in the Parc Naturel Régional des Grands Causses (p794).

- Storks in Alsace at the Centre de Réintroduction des Cigognes in Hunawihr (p391) and the Enclos Cigognes in Munster (p398); on the Atlantic Coast at the Parc Ornithologique in Le Teich (p688) and at the Parc des Oiseaux outside Villars-les-Dombes near Lyon (p518).

- Wolves in Languedoc at the wolf reserve in the Parc du Gévaudan near Mende (p788).

A SHAGGY GOAT STORY

The nippy *bouquetin des Alpes* (Alpine ibex), with its terrifyingly large, curly-wurly horns (we're talking 1m long and a good 5kg in weight) and penchant for sickeningly high crags and ledges, is the animal most synonymous with the French Alps. In the 16th century, higher altitudes were loaded with the handsome beast, the males spraying themselves with urine and sporting a strong body odour. Three centuries on, however, its extravagant and unusual horns had become a must-have item in any self-respecting gentleman's trophy cabinet, and within a few years the Alpine ibex had been hunted to the brink of extinction.

In 1963 the Parc National de la Vanoise (p557) was created in the Alps to stop hunters in the Vanoise massif shooting the few Alpine ibex that remained. The creation of similar nature reserves and the pursuit of rigorous conservation campaigns to protect the animal has seen populations surely and steadily recover – to the point where the Alpine ibex thrives today. Not that you're likely to encounter one: the canny old ibex has realised some mammals are best avoided.

alternatives to more murderous means of getting rid of the unwanted predator. A four-year action plan adopted by the government in 2004 pledges to create a favourable environment for wolf conservation while protecting the animals on which wolves traditionally prey.

The brown bear disappeared from the Alps in the mid-1930s. The 300-odd bears living in the Pyrenees at that time have dwindled to one orphaned cub following the controversial shooting of its mother – the last female bear of Pyrenean stock – by a hunter in 2004. However another 12 to 18 bears of Slovenian origin also call the Pyrenees home; see p727.

A rare but wonderful treat is the sighting of a golden eagle: 40 pairs nest in the Parc National du Mercantour, 20 pairs nest in the Vanoise, 30-odd in the Écrins and a good handful in the Pyrenees. Other birds of prey include the peregrine falcon, kestrel, buzzard and bearded vulture, with its bone-breaking habits. The latter – Europe's largest bird of prey, with an awe-inspiring wingspan of 2.8m – was extinct in the Alps from the 19th century until the 1980s when it was reintroduced. More recently, the small pale-coloured Egyptian vulture (worshipped by the Egyptians, hence its name) has been seen in springtime.

Even the eagle-eyed will have difficulty spotting the ptarmigan, a chickenlike species that moults three times a year to ensure a foolproof camouflage for every season (brown in summer, white in winter). It lives on rocky slopes and in alpine meadows above 2000m. The nutcracker, with its loud and buoyant singsong and larch-forest habitat, the black grouse, rock partridge, eagle owl and three-toed woodpecker are among the other 120-odd species to keep bird-watchers on their toes in mountainous realms.

Elsewhere on the French watch-the-birdie front, there are 400 pairs of storks to see in Alsace (p391); 10% of the world's flamingo population to see in the Camargue (p838); giant black cormorants – some with a wingspan of 170cm – on an island off the north coast of Brittany (p318); and unique seagull and fishing eagle populations in the Réserve Naturelle de Scandola on Corsica (p928). The osprey – a once-widespread migratory bird that winters in Africa and returns to France in February or March – only inhabits Corsica and the Loire Valley today.

Plants

About 14 million hectares of forest – beech, oak and pine in the main – cover 20% of France, while 4200 different species of plant and flower are

Spotted a bearded vulture? Lucky you! Note down when, where, any distinguishing marks and behaviour patterns of the bird and send it to the Beared Vulture Reintroduction into the Alps project at www.wild.unizh.ch/bg.

Find out what to spot where and when with the Ligue de Protection des Oiseaux (LPO; League for the Protection of Birds) at www.lpo.fr (in French).

known to grow countrywide (2250 alone grow in the Parc National des Cévennes). In forests near Reims in the Champagne region, beech trees grow in a bizarrely stunted, malformed shape (see p361).

The Alpine and Pyrenean regions nurture fir, spruce and beech forests on north-facing slopes between 800m and 1500m. Larch trees, mountain and arolla pines, rhododendrons and junipers stud shrubby subalpine zones between 1500m and 2000m; and a brilliant riot of spring- and summertime wildflowers carpet grassy meadows above the tree line in the alpine zone (up to 3000m).

Alpine blooms include the single golden-yellow flower of arnica, which is still used in herbal and homeopathic bruise-relieving remedies; the flame-coloured fire lily that flowers from December until May; and the hardy Alpine columbine with its beautiful, delicate blue petals. The protected 'queen of the Alps' (aka the Alpine eryngo) bears an uncanny resemblance to a purple thistle but is, in fact, a member of the parsley family (to which the carrot also belongs); you will find it on grassy ledges.

The rare twinflower only grows in the Parc National de la Vanoise (p557). Of France's 150 orchids, the black vanilla orchid is one to look out for – its small red-brown flowers exude a sweet vanilla fragrance. At Les Fermes de Marie in Megève (p541) dozens of alpine plants and seeds – gentian, St John's wort, melissa, pulsatilla, pimpernel, cyclamen, hazel seeds and so on – go into beauty products.

Corsica and the Massif des Maures, west of St-Tropez on the Côte d'Azur, are closely related botanically: both have chestnut and cork oak trees (the bark of which gets stuffed in bottles) and are thickly carpeted with *maquis* – a heavily scented scrubland where dozens of orchids, herbs (the secret behind Provençal cooking) and heathers find shelter. Particularly enchanting are the rock rose (a shrub bearing white flowers with yellow centres or pinkish-mauve flowers); the white-flowering myrtle that blossoms in June and is treasured for its blue-black berries (used to make some excellent liqueurs); and the blue-violet flowering Corsican mint with its heady summertime aroma.

NATIONAL PARKS

The proportion of land protected in France is surprisingly low, relative to the size of the country: six small national parks *(parcs nationaux)* fully protect just 0.8% of the country. Another 7% is protected to a substantially lesser degree by 42 *parcs naturels régionaux* (regional nature parks) and a further 0.4% by 136 smaller *réserves naturelles* (nature reserves), some of which are under the eagle eye of the Conservatoire du Littoral (p71).

While the central zones of national parks are uninhabited and fully protected by legislation (dogs, vehicles and hunting are banned and camping is restricted), the ecosystems they protect spill into populated peripheral zones in which tourism and other (often environmentally unfriendly) economic activities run riot.

Most regional nature parks and reserves were established not only to improve (or at least maintain) local ecosystems, but to encourage economic development and tourism in areas suffering from diminishing populations and increasing economic problems (such as the Massif Central and Corsica).

Select pockets of nature – the Pyrenees, Mont St-Michel and its bay, part of the Loire Valley and a clutch of capes on Corsica – are Unesco World Heritage Sites (see p30).

Trip through France's forests with the Office National des Forêts (National Forestry Commission) at www.onf.fr (in French).

Conservatoire du Littoral: Saving the French Coast by Dominique Legrain is a fabulous introduction to France's extraordinarily diverse and nature-rich coastline, and provides a fascinating insight to the work done by the Conservatorie du Littoral. The latter's online boutique sells it.

Tune in to France's 42 regional nature parks with the Fèdèration des Parcs Naturels Règionaux de France (Federation of French Regional Natural Parks) at www.parcs-naturels-regionaux.tm.fr (in French).

NATIONAL PARKS

Park	Features	Activities	Best Time to Visit	Page
Parc National des Cévennes	wild peat bogs, causses, granite peaks, ravines and ridges bordering the Massif Central and Languedoc (910 sq km); red deer, beavers, vultures, wolves, bison	walking, donkey trekking, mountain-biking, horse-riding, cross-country skiing, caving, canoeing, botany (2250 plant species)	spring & winter	p789
Parc National des Écrins	glaciers, glacial lakes and mountain tops soaring up to 4102m in the French Alps (1770 sq km); marmots, lynx, ibex, chamois, bearded vultures	walking, climbing, hang-gliding	spring & summer	p566
Parc National du Mercantour	Provence at its most majestic with 3000m-plus peaks and dead-end valleys along the Italian border; marmots, mouflons, chamois, ibex, wolves, golden and short-toed eagles, bearded vultures	alpine skiing, white-water sports, mountain-biking, walking, donkey trekking	spring, summer & winter	p871
Parc National de Port Cros	Island marine park off the Côte d'Azur forming France's smallest national park and Europe's first marine park (700 hectares and 1288 hectares of water); puffins, shearwaters, migratory birds	snorkelling, bird-watching, swimming, gentle strolling	summer & autumn (for bird-watching)	p899
Parc National des Pyrénées	100km of mountains along the Spanish border (457 sq km); marmots, lizards, brown bears, golden eagles, vultures, buzzards	alpine & cross-country skiing, walking, mountaineering, rock-climbing, white-water rafting, canoeing, kayaking, mountain-biking	spring, summer & winter	p722
Parc National de la Vanoise	postglacial mountain landscape of Alpine peaks, beech-fir forests and 80 sq km of glaciers forming France's first national park (530 sq km): chamois, ibex, marmots, golden eagles	alpine & cross-country skiing, walking, mountaineering, mountain-biking	spring, summer & winter	p557

ENVIRONMENTAL ISSUES

Summer forest fires are an annual hazard. Great tracts of land sizzle each year, often because of careless day-trippers but occasionally, as is sometimes the case in the Maures and Estérel ranges on the Côte d'Azur, because they are intentionally set alight by people wanting to get licences to build on the damaged lands. Since the mid-1970s, between 67 sq km and 883 sq km of land a year has been reduced to a burnt black stubble by an average of 540 fires – although the number of fires is falling according to the Office National des Forêts, the national forestry commission responsible for public forests in France. As the globe warms, avalanches have become the winter menace for mountainous areas; see p525 for details.

Wetlands, incredibly productive ecosystems that are essential for the survival of a number of bird species, reptiles, fish and amphibians, are shrinking. More than two million hectares – 3% of French territory – are considered important wetlands, but only 4% of this land is protected. The vulnerability of these areas was highlighted in 2003 when lumps of

Pick up the daily air pollution and quality forecast for France at www.prevair.org.

HIGH-FACTOR PROTECTION BY THE SEA

Some 10% of the coastline of mainland France and Corsica is managed by the **Conservatoire du Littoral** (Coastal Protection Agency; ☎ 05 46 84 72 50; www.conservatoire-du-littoral.fr; Corderie Royale, BP 10137, 17306 Rochefort Cedex), a coastal protection association that acquires threatened natural areas by the sea to restore, rejuvenate and protect.

Rare orchid-studded sand dunes east of Dunkirk (p243), a Corsican desert (p924), the Baie de Somme with its ornithological park (p249) and several wet and watery pockets of the horse-studded Camargue (p838) rank among the *conservatoire*'s rich pageant of *espaces naturels protégés* (protected natural areas).

Books, guides and maps on the 400 natural sites, 880km of coastline and 860 sq km of land managed by the Conservatoire du Littoral are sold through its online boutique.

oil landed on beaches in southwestern France following the sinking of the *Prestige* oil tanker off Spain's northwestern coast in late 2002. The slick wrecked beaches, crippled local fishing and seafood industries and killed hundreds of birds and marine life – to the horror of French environmentalists who were still seething with anger over the 1999 *Erika* oil tanker disaster that fouled more than 400km of shoreline in Brittany and cost €695 million to clean up.

Men with dogs and guns pose an equal threat to French animal life, brown bears included (p68). While the number of hunters has fallen by 20% in the last decade, there are still way more hunters in France (almost 1.5 million) than in other Western European countries (around 1 million in Spain and Italy, 625,000 in Britain). Despite the Brussels Directive being introduced in 1979 to protect wild birds, their eggs, nests and habitats in the EU, the French government didn't bother to make its provisions part of French law, meaning birds that can safely fly over other countries can still be shot as they cross France. A good handful of those not shot – at least 1000 birds of prey a year – are instead electrocuted to death by high-voltage power lines.

Many animal habitats have been destroyed by huge recreational lakes, created by the state-owned electricity company, Electricité de France, which dams rivers to produce electricity. Since the 1980s, however, almost 80% of the country's electricity (78% in 2005) has been produced by 59 nuclear reactors. (The French nuclear power-station programme is the most ambitious in the world.) Most are on main rivers or near the coast, and their environmental cost is high. Radioactive emissions spewed out by the four nuclear plants on the banks of the River Loire alone represent more than 25% of rare gas emissions in France.

As energy demands increase, President Chirac has expressed France's continuing commitment to nuclear power – in stark contrast to

Environmentalists in Languedoc (p794) were none too happy to have one of the world's tallest bridges – a vital link in the A75 motorway to boot – slicing across one of their quiet green valleys. Track the drama and decide for yourself at www.viaducdemillau.com (in French).

WORLD POWER REVOLUTION

France has a pivotal role to play in the international quest to develop fusion power: Cadarache, 40km northeast of Aix-en-Provence in southeast France, has been chosen as the hot spot where a thermonuclear experimental reactor will be built. Assuming it succeeds, the ambitious US$5 billion engineering project between the EU, the USA, China and Japan will revolutionise the production of power globally.

Unlike conventional nuclear power plants, fusion reactors produce energy through the fusion of light atom nuclei and produce dramatically less radioactive waste. The cleaner, new-generation reactor in Cadarache will start churning out energy in 2014.

A DEGRADING PROCESS

Make sure that whatever you bring to the mountains leaves with you. Decomposition, always slow, is even more protracted in the high mountains. Typical times:

- paper handkerchief: three months
- plastic bag: 450 years
- apple core: up to six months
- aluminium can: up to 500 years
- cigarette butt: three to five years
- plastic bottle: up to 1000 years
- wad of chewing gum: five years
- glass bottle: up to 4000 years
- lighter: 100 years

Learn how spent nuclear fuel is reprocessed at France's La Hague Reprocessing plant, 25km west of Cherbourg on the Cotentin Peninsula in Normandy, and pumped into the Channel, at www.cogemalahague .com.

non-nuclear policies pursued in most other European countries – and to a more sophisticated fourth-generation nuclear pressurised water reactor (not due online until 2040). The fact that the 40-year shelf life of one-third of the country's reactors will have expired by 2025 is no deterrent: plans are already panning out for a new reactor (to be constructed 2007 to 2012) at the Flamanville power plant, much to the consternation of environmentalists in France and Guernsey. They fear that it will make the water separating them even dirtier than it is already. Waste water from the reactor will be pumped directly into the Channel, while nuclear waste from France and elsewhere is already treated at a nearby plant on the Cotentin Peninsula in Normandy and pumped into the Channel.

Conservation Organisations

A growing network of environmental organisations in France monitor trouble spots:

- **Action Nature** (☎ 06 08 18 54 55; www.action-nature.info in French; 32 rue Ste-Hélène, 69002 Lyon) Follow what's happening in nature from a political perspective with Action Nature; campaigns against controversial laws etc.
- **Association Nationale de Protection des Eaux de Rivières** (TOS; ☎ 01 43 75 84 84; www.anpertos.org; 67 rue de Seine, 94140 Alfortville) Clean up French rivers with the National Association for the Protection of Rivers & Water Resources.
- **Conservatoire d'Espaces Naturels** (☎ 02 38 24 55 00; www.enf.asso.fr in French; 6 rue Jeanne d'Arc, 45000 Orléans) Safeguards 790 sq km split across 1800 sites.

Environmental facts, figures and statistics are packed with punch by the Institut Français de l'Environnement (French Institute of the Environment) at www .ifen.fr.

- **Fondation Ligue Française des Droits de l'Animal** (LFDA; www.league-animal-rights.org; 39 rue Claude Bernard, 75005 Paris) Say 'no' to force feeding and foie gras is one of the animal-friendly calls made by the French League for Animal Rights.
- **France Nature Environnement** (☎ 02 38 62 44 48; www.fne.asso.fr in French; 6 rue Dupanloup, 45000 Orléans) Umbrella organisation for 3000-odd nature-protection and environmental groups countrywide.
- **Greenpeace** (☎ 01 44 64 02 17; www.greenpeace.org; 22 rue des Rasselins, 75020 Paris) Zoom in on France's environmental hot spots.
- **Les Amis de la Nature** (☎ 01 46 27 53 56; www.amisnature-colombes.org in French; 197 rue Championnet, 75018 Paris) Ditch the car; cycle or walk instead. For other tips on reducing your impact on the environment, contact Nature's Friends.
- **Ligue pour la Préservation de la Faune Sauvage** (Ligue ROC; ☎ 01 43 36 04 72; www.roc .asso.fr; 26 rue Pascal, 75005 Paris) The League for the Protection of Wild Animals also fights for the rights of nonhunters (98% of the population).

Food & Drink

No other cuisine (with the arguable exception of Chinese) comes close to that of the French for freshness of ingredients, natural flavours and refined (and very often complex) cooking methods. It is the West's most important and influential style of cooking.

The very word 'cuisine', of course, is French in origin – the English 'cooking style' just cannot handle all the nuances, while 'French' conjures up a sophisticated, cultured people who know their arts, including gastronomy. While there is only some truth to that notion (not every French man, woman and child is a walking *Larousse Gastronomique*, the seminal encyclopaedia of French gastronomy), eating well is still of prime importance to most people here, and they continue to spend an inordinate amount of time thinking about, talking about and consuming food.

But don't suppose for a moment that this obsession with things culinary means that dining out in France has to be a ceremonious occasion or one full of pitfalls for the uninitiated. Approach food and wine here with even half the enthusiasm the French themselves do, and you will be warmly received, encouraged and very well fed.

> In the Middle Ages soups were closer to what we would call porridge today and the word *soupe* referred to a piece of bread (or sop) boiled in with the *bouillon* (broth or stock).

STAPLES & SPECIALITIES
Staples

French cuisine has long stood apart for its great use of a variety of foods – beef, lamb, pork, poultry, fish and shellfish, cereals, vegetables and legumes – but its staple 'trinity' is bread, cheese and *charcuterie* (cured, smoked or processed meat products).

BREAD

Nothing is more French than *pain* (bread). More than 80% of all French people eat it at every meal, and it comes in an infinite variety.

All bakeries have baguettes (and the similar, but fatter, *flûtes*), which are long and thin and weigh 250g, and wider loaves of what is simply called *pain*. A *pain*, which weighs 400g, is softer on the inside and has a less crispy crust than a baguette. Both types are at their best if eaten within four hours of baking. You can store them for longer in a plastic bag, but the crust becomes soft and chewy; if you leave them out, they'll soon be hard – which is the way many French people like them at breakfast the next day. If you're not very hungry, ask for a half-loaf: a demi baguette or a demi *pain*. A *ficelle* is a much thinner, crustier 200g version of a baguette – not unlike a very thick breadstick, really.

Most bakeries also carry heavier, more expensive breads made with all sorts of grains and cereals; you will also find loaves studded with nuts, raisins or herbs. These keep much longer than baguettes and standard white-flour breads.

> President Charles de Gaulle, commenting on the near impossibility of uniting the French on a single issue after WWII, famously grumbled: 'You cannot easily bring together a country that has 265 kinds of cheese'. And did you know that the number has now almost doubled to 500?

CHEESE

France has nearly 500 varieties of *fromage* (cheese) produced at farms, dairies, mountain huts, monasteries and factories. They're made from cow's, goat's or ewe's milk, which can be raw, pasteurised or *petit-lait* ('little milk'; the whey left over after the milk fats and solids have been curdled with rennet) but there are just five basic types (see the boxed text, p74).

ON BOARD WITH CHEESE

The choice on offer at a *fromagerie* (cheese shop) can be overwhelming, but *fromagers* (cheese merchants) always allow you to sample what's on offer before you buy, and are usually very generous with their advice. The following list divides French cheeses into five main groups and recommends several types to try.

- **Fromage de chèvre** 'Goat's milk cheese' is usually creamy and both sweet and a little salty when fresh, but hardens and gets much saltier as it matures and dries out. Among the best are: Ste-Maure de Touraine, a creamy, mild cheese from the Loire region; Crottin de Chavignol, a classic though saltier variety from Burgundy; Cabécou de Rocamadour from Midi-Pyrénées, often served warm with salad or marinated in oil and rosemary; and St-Marcellin, a soft white cheese from Lyon.

- **Fromage à pâté persillée** 'Marbled' or 'blue cheese' is so called because the veins often resemble *persille* (parsley). Roquefort is a ewe's-milk veined cheese that is to many the king of French cheese. Fourme d'Ambert is a very mild cow's-milk cheese from Rhône-Alpes. Bleu du Haut Jura (also called Bleu de Gex) is a mild blue-veined mountain cheese.

- **Fromage à pâté molle** 'Soft cheese' is moulded or rind-washed. Camembert, a classic moulded cheese from Normandy that for many is synonymous with French cheese, and the refined Brie de Meaux are both made from raw cow's milk. Munster from Alsace and the strong Époisses de Bourgogne are rind-washed, fine-textured cheeses.

- **Fromage à pâté demi-dure** 'Semi-hard cheese' denotes uncooked, pressed cheese. Among the finest are Tomme de Savoie, made from either raw or pasteurised cow's milk; Cantal, a cow's-milk cheese from Auvergne that tastes something like Cheddar; St-Nectaire, a strong-smelling pressed cheese that has a complex taste; and Ossau-Iraty, a ewe's-milk cheese made in the Basque Country.

- **Fromage à pâté dure** 'Hard cheese' in France is always cooked and pressed. Among the most popular are: Beaufort, a grainy cow's-milk cheese with a slightly fruity taste from Rhône-Alpes; Comté, a cheese made with raw cow's-milk in Franche-Comté; Emmental, a cow's-milk cheese made all over France; and Mimolette, an Edam-like bright-orange cheese from Lille that can be aged for as long as 36 months.

CHARCUTERIE

Traditionally *charcuterie* is made only from pork, though a number of other meats (beef, veal, chicken or goose) are used in making sausages, salamis, blood puddings and other cured and salted meats. Pâtés, terrines and *rillettes* are also considered *charcuterie*.

The difference between a pâté and a terrine is academic: a pâté is removed from its container and sliced before it is served while a terrine is sliced from the container itself. *Rillettes*, on the other hand, is potted meat or even fish that is not ground or chopped but shredded with two forks, seasoned, mixed with fat and spread cold over bread or toast.

While every region in France produces standard *charcuterie* favourites as well as its own specialities, Alsace, Lyon and the Auvergne produce the best sausages, and Périgord and the north of France some of the most acclaimed pâtés and terrines. Some very popular types of *charcuterie* are: *andouillette* (soft raw sausage made from the pig's small intestines that is grilled and eaten with onions and potatoes); *boudin noir* (blood sausage or pudding made with pig's blood, onions and spices, and usually eaten hot with stewed apples and potatoes); *jambon* (ham, either smoked or salt-cured); *saucisse* (usually a small fresh sausage that is boiled or grilled before eating); *saucisson* (usually a large salami eaten cold); and *saucisson sec* (air-dried salami).

Regional Specialities

Climatic and geographical factors have been particularly important to the amazing variety of France's regional cuisine: the hot south tends to favour olive oil, garlic and tomatoes, while the cooler northern regions prefer cream and butter. Coastal areas specialise in mussels, oysters and saltwater fish, while those near lakes and rivers make full use of freshwater fish.

Diverse though it is, French cuisine is typified by certain regions, most notably Normandy, Burgundy, Périgord, Lyon and, to a lesser extent, the Loire region, Alsace and Provence. Still others – Brittany, the Auvergne, Languedoc, the Basque Country and Corsica – have made incalculable contributions to what can generically be called French food.

NORMANDY

Cream, apples and seafood are the three essentials of Norman cuisine. Specialities include *moules à la crème normande* (mussels in cream sauce with a dash of cider) and *canard á la rouennaise* ('Rouen-style duck'; duck stuffed with its liver and served with a red wine sauce), preferably interrupted by a *trou normand* (literally 'Norman hole'; a glass of Calvados) to allow room for more courses.

> In Normandy, Calvados is sometimes drunk in the middle of a meal as a *trou norman*, a 'Norman hole', to allow room for more courses.

BURGUNDY

The 'trinity' of the Burgundy kitchen is beef, red wine and mustard. *Bœuf bourguignon* (beef marinated and cooked in young red wine with mushrooms, onions, carrots and bacon) combines the first two; Dijon, the Burgundian capital, has been synonymous with mustard for centuries.

PÉRIGORD

This southwest region is famous for its truffles and poultry, especially the ducks and geese whose fattened livers are turned into *pâté de foie gras* (duck or goose liver pâté), which is sometimes flavoured with cognac and truffles. *Confit de canard* and *confit d'oie* are duck or goose joints cooked very slowly in their own fat. The preserved fowl is then left to stand for some months before being eaten.

> Sea salt, especially that from the marshes of the Guérande peninsula in southeastern Brittany, is prized for its stronger and more pleasant taste than mined salt, which can be somewhat metallic.

LYON

Many people consider France's third-largest city to be its *temple de gastronomie* (gastronomic temple). Typical *charcuteries* are *saucisson de Lyon*, which features in Lyon's trademark dish, *saucisson aux pommes* (sausage with potatoes). Another speciality is the *quenelle*, a poached dumpling made of freshwater fish (usually pike) and served with a *sauce Nantua*, made with cream and a paste from freshwater crayfish.

OMELETTE DE LA MÈRE POULARD

Mont St-Michel's celebrated omelette, the world's first, is at its fluffiest finest when cooked over a wood-burning stove.

10 eggs	100g butter
15mL thick cream	salt and pepper

Separate the egg whites and yolks into two bowls. Beat the whites until they rise in peaks, then beat the yolks thoroughly. Place a pat of butter on a hot pan. When it begins to bubble, add the egg yolks and pepper and salt to taste. When the eggs begin to set, mix in the thick cream and beaten egg whites. Shake the pan continuously over the fire. Fold the omelette and serve on a warm plate. Serves 4.

LOIRE REGION

The cuisine of the Loire, refined in the kitchens of the region's chateaux from the 16th century onwards, ultimately became the cuisine of France as a whole; *rillettes, coq au vin* (chicken cooked in wine), *beurre blanc* sauce and *tarte Tatin* (a caramelised upside-down apple pie) are all specialities from this area. The Loire region is also known for its *pruneaux de Tours*, prunes dried from luscious Damson plums and used in poultry, pork or veal dishes.

The Food of France by Waverley Root is the seminal work on la cuisine française in English, with much focus on historical development, by a longtime American correspondent based in France.

ALSACE

A classic dish of this meaty, Teutonic-leaning cuisine is *choucroute alsacienne* (or *choucroute garnie*), sauerkraut flavoured with juniper berries and served hot with sausages, bacon, pork and/or ham knuckle. You should drink chilled Riesling or Alsatian Pinot Noir – not beer – with *choucroute* and follow it with a *tarte alsacienne*, a scrumptious custard tart made with local fruits like *mirabelles* (sweet yellow plums) or *quetsches* (a variety of purple plum).

PROVENCE

The Roman legacy of olives, wheat and wine remain the triumvirate of *la cuisine provençale*, and many dishes are prepared with olive oil and generous amounts of garlic. Provence's most famous contribution to French cuisine is *bouillabaisse*, a chowder made with at least three kinds of fresh fish, cooked for about 10 minutes in a broth containing onions, tomatoes, saffron and various herbs, and eaten as a main course with toasted bread and *rouille*, a spicy mayonnaise of olive oil, garlic and chilli peppers.

BRITTANY

Brittany may be a paradise for lovers of seafood, but the *crêpe* and the *galette* are the royalty of Breton cuisine. A *crêpe* is made from wheat flour and is almost always sweet; the flour used in a *galette* is made from buckwheat, a traditional staple of the region, and the fillings are always savoury. A *galette complète*, for example, comes with ham, egg and cheese.

CRÊPES SUCRE-BEURRE

This is the classic recipe for making traditional Breton butter and sugar *crêpes*.

250g wheat flour	4 eggs
175g sugar	3 sachets of vanilla sugar
750mL fresh full cream milk	pinch of salt
oil	250g lightly salted butter for cooking

Put the flour into a large bowl, make a well in the centre and break an egg into it. Stir in well with a wooden spoon, gradually drawing in the flour. Add the three remaining eggs one at a time. Add the sugar, vanilla sugar and salt and thin the mixture gradually with the milk, pouring it slowly into the centre of the batter. Cover the bowl with a cloth and leave the batter to rest for at least an hour.

To cook the *crêpes*, melt a knob of butter in a frying pan and tip in a small ladle of batter. Tip the pan in all directions to ensure that the batter completely covers the bottom, to produce the desired thinness of the *crêpe*. Cook the *crêpe* for one minute until the edges begin to colour. Take hold of the *crêpe* between thumb and index finger and with one swift movement lift and turn it over to finish the cooking. Continue until the batter is finished. Makes 24.

AUVERGNE

This *rude* (that is, 'rugged' or 'harsh') region of the Massif Central specialises in *charcuterie*, and its celebrated *salaisons* (salt-cured meats) are sold and consumed throughout France. Specialities include *lentilles vertes du Puy aux saucisses fumées* (smoked pork sausages with green Puy lentils) and *clafoutis*, a custard and cherry tart baked upside down like a *tarte Tatin*.

LANGUEDOC

No dish is more evocative of Languedoc than *cassoulet*, a casserole with beans and meat. There are at least three major varieties but a favourite is that from Toulouse, which adds *saucisse de Toulouse*, a fat, mild-tasting pork sausage. France's most famous (and expensive) cheese is made at Roquefort, south of Millau.

BASQUE COUNTRY

Among the essential ingredients of Basque cooking are the deep-red chillies that add the extra bite to many of the region's dishes, including its signature *jambon de Bayonne*, the locally prepared Bayonne ham. Basques love cakes and pastries but the most popular of all is *gâteau basque*, a relatively simple layer cake filled with cream or cherry jam.

CORSICA

The hills and mountains of the island of Corsica have always been ideal for raising stock and the dense Corsican underbrush called the *maquis* is made up of shrubs mixed with wild herbs. These raw materials come together to create such trademark Corsican dishes as *stufatu*, a fragrant mutton stew; *premonata*, beef braised with juniper berries; and *lonzo aux haricots blancs*, a Corsican sausage cooked with white beans, white wine and herbs.

DRINKS
Alcoholic Drinks

Although alcohol consumption has dropped by 30% in less than two decades, France still ranks 5th in the world in the boozing stakes behind Luxembourg, Portugal, Ireland and Germany.

WINE & CHAMPAGNE

Grapes and the art of wine-making were introduced to Gaul by the Romans. In the Middle Ages, important vineyards developed around monasteries as the monks needed wine to celebrate Mass. Large-scale wine production later moved closer to ports (eg Bordeaux), from where it could be exported.

In mid-19th century, phylloxera aphids were accidentally brought to Europe from the USA. These pests ate through the roots of France's grapevines, destroying some 10,000 sq km of vineyards. Wine production appeared to be doomed until root stocks resistant to phylloxera were brought from California and original cuttings grafted onto them.

Wine-making is a complicated chemical process, but ultimately the taste and quality of the wine depend on four key factors: the type(s) or blend of grape, the climate, the soil and the art of the *vigneron* (winemaker).

Some viticulturists have honed their skills and techniques to such a degree that their wine is known as a *grand cru* (literally 'great growth'). If this wine has been produced in a year of optimum climatic conditions

Le Grand Atlas des Cuisines de Nos Terroirs from Éditions Atlas is a beautifully illustrated atlas of regional cooking in France with emphasis on *cuisine campagnarde* (country cooking).

The mouldy blue-green veins running through Roquefort cheese are, in fact, the seeds of microscopic mushrooms, picked in the caves at Roquefort then cultivated on leavened bread.

France's foremost food and drink blog is C'est moi qui l'ai fait! (I made it myself!; http://scally .typepad.com) authored by Pascale 'Scally' Weeks.

it becomes a *millésime* (vintage) wine. *Grands crus* are aged first in small oak barrels and then in bottles, sometimes for 20 years or more, before they develop their full taste and aroma.

There are dozens of wine-producing regions throughout France, but the seven principal regions are Alsace, Bordeaux, Burgundy, Champagne, Languedoc, the Loire region and the Rhône. With the exception of Alsatian wines, in France wines are named after the location of the vineyard rather than the grape varietal.

> Each year, some 3% of the volume of the casks fermenting in Cognac – the so-called *part des anges* (angels' share) – evaporates through the pores in the wood.

Alsace

Alsace produces almost exclusively white wines – mostly varieties produced nowhere else in France – that are known for their clean, fresh taste and compatibility with the often heavy local cuisine. The vineyards closest to Strasbourg produce light red wines from Pinot Noir that are similar to rosé. This wine is best served chilled.

Alsace's four most important varietal wines are Riesling, known for its subtlety; the more pungent and highly regarded Gewürztraminer; the robust Pinot Gris, which is high in alcohol; and Muscat d'Alsace, which is not as sweet as that made with Muscat grapes grown further south.

Bordeaux

Britons have had a taste for the full-bodied wines of Bordeaux, known as clarets in the UK, since the mid-12th century when King Henry II, who controlled the region through marriage, tried to gain the favour of the locals by granting them tax-free trade status with England. Thus began a roaring business in wine exporting that continues to this day.

The reds of Bordeaux, which produces more fine wine than any other region in the world, are often described as well balanced, a quality achieved by blending several grape varieties. The grapes predominantly used are Merlot, Cabernet Sauvignon and Cabernet Franc. Bordeaux's foremost wine-growing areas are Médoc, Pomerol, St-Émilion and Graves. The nectar-like sweet whites of the Sauternes area are the world's finest dessert wines.

Burgundy

Burgundy developed its reputation for viticulture during the reign of Charlemagne, when monks first began to make wine here. Its red wines are produced with Pinot Noir grapes; the best vintages need 10 to 20 years to age. White wine is made from the Chardonnay grape. The five main wine-growing areas are Chablis, Côte d'Or, Côte Chalonnais, Mâcon and Beaujolais, which alone produces 13 different types of light Gamay-based red wine.

Champagne

Champagne, the region of flatlands (the name means *campania* or 'land of plains'), northeast of Paris, has been the centre for what is arguably France's best-known wine since the 17th century when the innovative monk Dom Pierre Pérignon perfected a technique for making sparkling wine.

Champagne is made from the red Pinot Noir, the black Pinot Meunier or the white Chardonnay grape. Each vine is vigorously pruned and trained to produce a small quantity of high-quality grapes. Indeed, to maintain exclusivity (and price), the amount of champagne that can be produced each year is limited to between 160 and 220 million bottles. Most of it is consumed in France and the UK, followed by the USA, Germany, Japan and China.

Making champagne – carried out by innumerable *maisons* (houses) – is a long, complex process. There are two fermentation processes, the first in casks and the second after the wine has been bottled and had sugar and yeast added. The bottles are aged in cellars for between two and five years (sometimes longer), depending on the *cuvée* (vintage).

If the final product is labelled *brut,* it is extra dry, with only 1.5% sugar content. *Extra-sec* means very dry (but not as dry as *brut*), *sec* is dry and *demi-sec* slightly sweet. The sweetest champagne is labelled *doux.*

Some of the most famous champagne houses are Dom Pérignon, Möet et Chandon, Veuve Cliquot, Mercier, Mumm, Krug, Laurent-Perrier, Piper-Heidsieck and Taittinger.

Part of the reason the 17th-century monk Dom Pierre Pérignon's technique for making sparkling wine was more successful than earlier efforts was because he put his product in strong, English-made bottles and capped them with corks brought from Spain.

Languedoc

This is the country's most productive wine-growing region, with up to 40% of France's wine – mainly cheap red *vin de table* (table wine) – produced here. About 300,000 hectares of the region is 'under vine', which represents just under a third of France's total.

In addition to the well-known Fitou label, the area's other quality wines are Coteaux du Languedoc, Faugères, Corbières and Minervois. The region also produces about 70% of France's *vin de pays,* 'country wine' from a particular named village or region, most of which is labelled Vin de Pays d'Oc.

Loire Region

The Loire's 75,000 hectares of vineyards rank it as the third-largest area in France for the production of quality wines. Although sunny, the climate

---

A TOAST IS IN ORDER

Under a 2005 agreement between the EU and USA, 'champagne' marked 'made in USA' may soon be a thing of the past. The US government agreed to limit the use of 17 prestigious European wine terms – including 'champagne', 'burgundy', 'chablis' and 'claret' – that are now considered 'semi-generic'. In exchange, the EU will end restrictions – seen by the US as a sneaky form of protectionism – on the import of American wines made with scandalously nontraditional practices such as nanofiltration and the addition of wood chips to fermentation vats in order to impart an oak-barrel flavour.

is moist and not all grape varieties thrive here. The most common grapes are the Muscadet, Cabernet Franc and Chenin Blanc varieties. Wines tend to be light and delicate. The most celebrated areas are Pouilly-Fumé, Vouvray, Sancerre, Bourgueil, Chinon and Saumur.

Rhône Region
The Rhône region is divided into northern and southern areas. The different soil, climate, topography and grapes used means there are dramatic differences in the wines produced by each.

On steep hills by the river, the northern vineyards produce red wines from the ruby-red Syrah grape; the aromatic Viognier grape is the most popular for white wines. The south is better known for quantity rather than quality. The Grenache grape, which ages well when blended, is used in the reds, while the whites use the Ugni Blanc grape.

APÉRITIFS & DIGESTIFS

The average French person consumes 10.9L of pure alcohol a year, compared to 8.2L in the UK and 6.3L in the USA.

Meals in France are often preceded by an appetite-stirring *apéritif* such as *kir* (white wine sweetened with cassis or blackcurrant syrup), *kir royale* (champagne with cassis) or *pineau* (cognac and grape juice). Pastis, a 90-proof, anise-flavoured alcoholic drink that turns cloudy when water is added, is especially popular at cafés in the warmer months.

After-dinner drinks are often ordered with coffee. France's most famous brandies are Cognac and Armagnac, both of which are made from grapes in the regions of those names. *Eaux de vie*, literally 'waters of life', can be made with grape skins and the pulp left over after being pressed for wine (Marc de Champagne, Marc de Bourgogne), apples (Calvados) and pears (Poire William), as well as such fruits as plums *(eau de vie de prune)* and even raspberries *(eau de vie de framboise)*.

BEER & CIDER
The *bière à la pression* (draught beer) served by the *demi* (about 33cL) in bars and cafés across the land is usually one of the national brands such as Kronenbourg, 33 or Pelforth and totally forgettable. Alsace, with its close cultural ties to Germany, produces some excellent local beers (eg Bière de Scharrach, Schutzenberger Jubilator and Fischer, a hoppy brew from Scilligheim). Northern France, close to Belgium and the Netherlands, has its own great beers as well, including St-Sylvestre 3 Monts, Terken Brune and the barley-based Grain d'Orge.

Cidre (apple cider) is made in many parts of France, including Savoy, Picardy and the Basque Country, but its real home is Normandy and Brittany.

Nonalcoholic Drinks
The most popular nonalcoholic beverages consumed in France are mineral water and coffee.

The English word vinegar comes from the French *vin aigre* for 'sour wine'.

WATER & MINERAL WATER
All tap water in France is safe to drink, so there is no need to buy bottled water. People in cities don't agree, however; less than 1% of the water used by a typical Parisian household each day, for example, is actually drunk. Tap water that is not drinkable (eg at most public fountains and on trains) will usually have a sign reading '*eau non potable*'.

At a restaurant, if you prefer tap water rather than pricey bottled water, make sure you ask for *de l'eau* (some water), *une carafe d'eau* (a jug of water) or *de l'eau du robinet* (tap water). Otherwise you'll most likely get bottled *eau de source* (spring water) or *eau minérale* (mineral water), which comes *plate* (flat or still) like Évian, Vittel and Volvic, or *gazeuse* (fizzy or sparkling) like Badoit and Perrier.

COFFEE
The most ubiquitous form of coffee is espresso, made by a machine that forces steam through ground coffee beans. A small espresso, served without milk, is called *un café noir, un express* or simply *un café*. You can also ask for a *grand* (large) version.

Café crème is espresso with steamed milk or cream. *Café au lait* is lots of hot milk with a little coffee served in a large cup or, sometimes, a bowl. A small *café crème* is a *petit crème*. A *noisette* (literally 'hazelnut') is an espresso with just a dash of milk. Decaffeinated coffee is *café décaféiné*.

CELEBRATIONS
A tradition that remains very much alive in France is *le jour des rois* (day of the kings), which falls on 6 January and marks the feast of the Épiphanie (Epiphany), when the Three Wise Men paid homage to the Infant Jesus. Placed on the table is a *galette des rois* (kings' cake), which is a puff pastry with frangipane cream, a little dried *fève* (broad) bean (or plastic or silver figurine) hidden inside and topped with a gold paper crown, that goes on sale in patisseries (cake shops) throughout Paris after the new year. The youngest person in the room goes under the table and calls out which member of the party should get each slice. The person who gets the bean is named king or queen, dons the crown and chooses their consort. This tradition is popular both at home among families and at offices and dinner parties.

At Chandeleur (Candlemas, marking the Feast of the Purification of the Virgin Mary) on 2 February, family and friends gather in their kitchens to make *crêpes de la Chandeleur* (sweet pancakes).

Pâques (Easter) is marked as elsewhere with *œufs au chocolat* (chocolate eggs) – here filled with candy fish and chickens – and there is always an egg hunt for the kids. The traditional meal at Easter lunch is *agneau* (lamb) or *jambon de Pâques,* which – like hot cross buns in Britain – seems to be available throughout the year nowadays.

After the *dinde aux marrons* (turkey stuffed with chestnuts) eaten at lunch at Noël (Christmas), a *bûche de Noël* (a 'Yule log' of chocolate and cream or ice cream) is served.

WHERE TO EAT & DRINK
There's a vast number of eateries in France. Most have defined roles, though some definitions are becoming a bit blurred.

Auberge
An *auberge* (inn), which may also appear as an *auberge de campagne* or *auberge du terroir* (country inn), is usually attached to a rural inn or small hotel and serves traditional country fare. A *ferme-auberge* (literally 'farm inn') is usually a working farm that serves diners traditional regional dishes made from ingredients produced there. The food is usually served *table d'hôte* (literally 'host's table'), meaning in set courses with little or no choice.

Bar
A *bar* or *bar américain* (cocktail bar) is an establishment dedicated to elbow-bending and rarely serves food. A *bar à vins* is a 'wine bar', which often serves full meals at lunch and dinner. A *bar à huîtres* is an 'oyster bar'.

The French cure the dreaded *crise de foie*, a bilious attack, bad indigestion or just another way of saying a hangover, by flushing out the system with mineral water.

Bistro

A *bistro* (also spelled *bistrot*) is not clearly defined in France nowadays. It can be simply a pub or bar with snacks and light meals or a fully fledged restaurant.

France has long been a nation of dyed-in-the-wool carnivores and until modern times the word *viande* (meat) simply meant 'food'.

Brasserie

Unlike the vast majority of restaurants in France, brasseries – which can look very much like cafés – serve full meals, drinks and coffee from morning till late at night. The dishes served almost always include *choucroute* and sausages because the brasserie, which actually means 'brewery' in French, originated in Alsace.

Buffet

A *buffet* (or *buvette*) is a kiosk usually found at train stations and airports and selling drinks, filled baguettes and snacks.

Café

The main focus of a café is, of course, *café* (coffee) and only basic food is available at most. Common options include a baguette filled with Camembert or pâté and *cornichons* (gherkins), a *croque-monsieur* (grilled ham and toasted cheese sandwich) or a *croque-madame* (a toasted cheese sandwich topped with a fried egg).

Cafétéria

Many cities in France have *cafétérias* (cafeteria restaurants), including Flunch, that offer a decent selection of dishes you can see before ordering – a factor that can make life easier if you're travelling with kids.

Crêperie

Crêperies (sometimes known as *galetteries*) specialise in sweet *crêpes* and savoury *galettes*.

Relais Routier

A *relais routier* is a transport café or truck stop, usually found on the outskirts of towns and along major roads, which caters to truck drivers and can provide a quick, hearty break from cross-country driving.

Restaurant

The restaurant, the French word for 'restorative', comes in many guises and price ranges. Generally restaurants specialise in a particular variety of food (eg regional, traditional, North African). There are lots of restaurants where you can get an excellent French meal for under €30 – Michelin's *Guide Rouge* is filled with them – and they usually offer what the French call *bon rapport qualitéa-prix* (good value for money). Chain restaurants (eg Hippopotamus and Léon de Bruxelles) are a definite step up from fast-food places and usually offer good-value (though uninspired) standard *menus*.

Almost all restaurants close for at least one and a half days (ie a full day and either one lunch or one dinner period) each week, and this schedule will be posted on the front door. Chain restaurants are usually open throughout the day, seven days a week.

Restaurants almost always have a *carte* (menu) posted outside so you can decide before going in whether the selection and prices are to your liking. Most offer at least one fixed-price, multicourse meal known as a *menu*, *menu à prix fixe* or *menu du jour* (daily menu). A *menu* (not to be confused with a *carte*) almost always costs much less than ordering à la carte.

When you order a *menu,* you usually get to choose an entree, such as salad, pâté or soup; a main dish (several meat, poultry or fish dishes, including the *plat du jour,* or 'daily special', are generally on offer); and one or more final courses (usually cheese or dessert). In some places, you may also be able to order a *formule,* which usually has fewer choices but allows you to pick two of three courses – a starter and a main course, say, or a main course and a dessert.

Boissons (drinks), including wine, cost extra unless the *menu* says *boisson comprise* (drink included), in which case you may get a beer or a glass of mineral water. If the *menu* has *vin compris* (wine included), you'll probably be served a 25cL *pichet* (jug) of wine. The waiter will always ask if you would like coffee to end the meal, but this will almost always cost extra.

> The restaurant as we know it today was born in Paris in 1765 when a certain Monsieur A Boulanger opened a small business in rue Bailleul in the 1er, selling soups, broths and other *restaurants* ('restoratives').

Restaurant Libre-Service

A *restaurant libre-service* is a self-service restaurant that's similar to a *cafétéria.*

Restaurant Rapide

A *restaurant rapide* is a fast-food restaurant, be it imported (eg Pizza Hut, McDonald's, KFC) or home-grown such as Quick.

Restaurant Universitaire

All French universities have several *restaurants universitaires* (refectories or canteens) subsidised by the Ministry of Education and operated by the Centre Régional des Œuvres Universitaires et Scolaires (better known as 'Crous'). They serve cheap meals and are usually open to nonstudents.

Salon de Thé

A *salon de thé* (tearoom) is a trendy and somewhat pricey establishment that usually offers quiches, salads, cakes, tarts, pies and pastries in addition to black and herbal teas.

VEGETARIANS & VEGANS

Vegetarians and vegans make up a small minority in a country where *viande* (meat) once also meant 'food', and they are not particularly well catered for; specialist vegetarian restaurants are few and far between, even in Paris. In fact, the vegetarian establishments that do exist in France often look more like laid-back, 'alternative lifestyle' cafés than restaurants. On the bright side, more and more restaurants are offering vegetarian choices on their set *menus,* and *produits biologiques* (organic products) are all the rage nowadays, even among carnivores.

> Strict vegetarians should note that most French cheeses are made with rennet, an enzyme derived from the stomach of a calf or young goat, and that some red wines (especially Bordeaux) are clarified with the albumin of egg whites.

DINING WITH CHILDREN

Few restaurants in France have highchairs, children's menus or even children's portions. This may explain the popularity of American-style fast-food restaurants, *cafétérias* and French chain restaurants, which cater to parents with kids in tow. Baby food is readily available in grocery shops and supermarkets throughout France.

HABITS & CUSTOMS
When the French Eat

French people do not eat in the clatter-clutter style of the Chinese or with the exuberance of, say, the Italians. A meal is an artistic and sensual delight to most people here, something to be savoured and enjoyed with a certain amount of style and *savoir-vivre.*

DOS & DON'T

■ If invited to someone's home or a party, always bring a gift, but not wine unless it's a bottle of chilled champagne. The wine your host has chosen will be an expression of his or her tastes and hospitality. Flowers are always a good idea, but chrysanthemums are only taken to cemeteries and carnations are said to bring bad luck.

■ Many French people feel that 'going Dutch' (ie splitting the bill) at restaurants is an uncivilised custom. In general, the person who did the inviting pays for dinner, though close friends and colleagues will sometimes share the cost.

■ When buying fruit and vegetables anywhere, except at supermarkets, do not touch the produce unless invited to do so. Show the shopkeeper what you want and he or she will choose the vegetables or fruit for you.

■ In a restaurant, do not summon the waiter by shouting *'garçon'*, which means 'boy'. Saying *'s'il vous plaît'* (please) is the way it's done nowadays.

■ When you're being served cheese (eg as the final course for dinner), remember two cardinal rules: never cut off the tip of the pie-shaped soft cheeses (eg Brie, Camembert) and cut cheeses whose middle is the best part (eg blue cheese) in such a way as to take your fair share of the crust.

BREAKFAST

What the French call *petit déjeuner* is not every Anglo-Saxon's cup of tea. Masters of the kitchen throughout the rest of the day, French chefs don't seem up to it in the morning. Perhaps the idea is not to fill up – *petit déjeuner* means 'little lunch' and the real *déjeuner* (lunch) is just around the corner!

In the Continental style, people traditionally start the day with a bread roll or a bit of baguette left over from the night before, eaten with butter and jam and followed by a *café au lait*, a small black coffee or even a hot chocolate. Some people eat cereal, toast, fruit and even yogurt in the morning – something they never did before.

Contrary to what many foreigners think, the French do not eat croissants every day but usually reserve these for a treat at the weekend when they may also choose *brioches, pains au chocolat* or other *viennoiserie* (baked goods).

LUNCH & DINNER

Many French people still consider *déjeuner* (lunch) to be the main meal of the day. But as the pace of life is as hectic here as elsewhere in the industrialised world, the two-hour midday meal has become increasingly rare, at least on weekdays. Dinners, however, are still turned into elaborate affairs whenever time and finances permit. A fully fledged, traditional French meal at home is an awesome event, often comprising six distinct *plats* (courses). *Plats* are always served with wine – red, white or rosé (or a combination of two or all three), depending on what you're eating. A meal in a restaurant almost never consists of more than three or four courses: the *entrée* (starter or first course), the *plat principal* (main course), *dessert* and perhaps *fromage* (cheese).

Where the French Shop

Most French people buy a good part of their food from a series of small neighbourhood shops, each with its own speciality (though people are relying more and more on supermarkets). At first, having to go to four shops and stand in four queues to fill the fridge (or assemble a picnic) may seem a waste of time, but the ritual is an important part of French people's daily lives.

It's perfectly acceptable to purchase only meal-size amounts: a few *tranches* (slices) of meat to make a sandwich, perhaps, or a *petit bout* (small hunk) of sausage. You can also request just enough *pour une/deux personne(s)* (for one/two person/s).

BOUCHERIE

A *boucherie* is a general butcher's shop selling fresh beef, lamb, pork, chicken etc, but for specialised poultry you have to go to a *marchand de volaille* (also called a *volailler*), where *poulet fermier* (free-range chicken) and *poulet de grain* (corn-fed chicken) are also sold.

BOULANGERIE

Fresh bread is baked and sold at France's 36,000 *boulangeries,* which supply three-quarters of the country's bread. Along with bread, bakeries usually sell croissants, *brioches, pains au chocolat* etc – baked goods that are lumped together under the term *viennoiserie.*

CHARCUTERIE

A *charcuterie* is a delicatessen offering sliced meats, pâtés, terrines, *rillettes* etc, though they sometimes sell things like seafood salads and even casseroles, such as *traiteurs* (see p86) do.

CONFISERIE

Sweets, including chocolate made with the finest ingredients, can be found at *confiseries*, which are sometimes combined with *boulangeries* and patisseries. A *chocolaterie* is a shop selling only chocolate and most make their own bonbons on the premises.

ÉPICERIE

Literally 'spice shop', this is a small grocery store with a little bit of everything, including fruit and vegetables; it's also known as an *alimentation générale.* Some *épiceries* are open on days when other food shops are closed, and many family-run operations close late at night.

FROMAGERIE

If you buy your cheese in a supermarket, you're likely to end up with unripe and relatively tasteless products unless you know how to select each variety. The owner of a *fromagerie*, also known as a *crémerie*, on the other hand will tell you which cheese is *fait* (ripe) to the exact degree that you request and will almost always let you taste before you decide what to buy.

MARCHAND DE LÉGUMES ET DE FRUITS

Fruits and vegetables are usually sold by a *marchand de légumes et de fruits* (greengrocer); *épiceries* (see above) usually only have a limited selection. *Biologique* (or *bio*) means grown organic (ie grown without chemicals).

MARCHAND DE VIN

Wine is sold by a *marchand de vin* (or *caviste*), such as the shops of the Nicolas chain. Wine shops in close proximity to the vineyards of Burgundy, Bordeaux, the Loire region and other wine-growing areas are often called *vinothèques* and offer tastings.

MARCHÉ

In most towns and cities, many of the aforementioned products are available one or more days a week at a *marché en plein air* (open-air market), also known as a *marché découvert*, and up to six days a week at a *marché couvert* (covered marketplace). Markets are cheaper than shops and the produce is usually fresher and of better quality.

French homemakers have never been averse to letting the experts take care of the more complicated dishes and have used the services of *traiteurs* and *pâtissiers* for centuries.

PATISSERIE

Mouth-watering pastries are available at patisseries. Some of the most common pastries include *tarte aux fruits* (fruit tarts), *pain aux raisins* (a flat, spiral pastry made with custard and sultanas) and *religieuses* (*éclairs*, or pastries filled with cream that – vaguely – resemble a nun's habit).

POISSONNERIE

Fresh fish and seafood are available from a *poissonnerie* (fishmonger). Fish is so popular in France that cities and towns inland often have as big a selection of fresh fish and crustaceans as those closer to the coast.

SUPERMARCHÉ

Both town and city centres usually have at least one department store with a large *supermarché* (supermarket) section in the basement or on the 1st floor. Most larger supermarkets have *charcuterie* and cheese counters, and many also have in-house *boulangeries*.

TRAITEUR

A *traiteur* (caterer) sells ready-to-eat dishes to take home: casseroles, salads of all shades and hues and many more elaborate dishes. *Traiteurs* are a picnicker's delight and a godsend to people who want something better than takeaway but can't be bothered to cook.

COOKING COURSES

What better place to discover the secrets of *la cuisine française* than in front of a stove? Cooking courses are available at different levels and lengths of time and the cost of tuition varies widely. In Paris one of the most popular – and affordable – for beginners is the **Cours de Cuisine Françoise Meunier** (Map pp104-5; ☎ 01 40 26 14 00; www.fmeunier.com; 2nd fl, 7 rue Paul Lelong, 2e; Ⓜ Bourse), which offers three-hour courses (adult/12-14 years €100/60) at 10.30am from Wednesday to Friday and at the same time on Saturday once a month (see the website for exact dates). 'Carnets' of five/20 courses cost €440/1700.

Other major cooking schools in Paris:

École Le Cordon Bleu (Map pp108-9; 01 53 68 22 50; www.cordonbleu.edu; 8 rue Léon Delhomme, 15e; Ⓜ Vaugirard or Convention) Dating back to 1895, the 'Blue Ribbon School' has a host of professional degree courses as well as one-day 'gourmet sessions' (€142) on subjects such as petits fours and terrines and a four-day course (€889) on French regional cuisine.

École Ritz Escoffier (Map pp102-3; ☎ 01 43 16 30 50; www.ritzparis.com; 38 rue Cambon, 1er; Ⓜ Concorde) This prestigious cooking school is in the back of what is arguably Paris' finest hotel. A four-hour Saturday themed workshop (truffles, sea scallops, asparagus, Easter lamb etc) costs €125; a three-day introductory course in summer is €530.

There are a number of regional cooking schools around France:

Domaine de la Tortinière (☎ 02 47 34 35 00; www.tortiniere.com; route de Ballan Miré, Les Gués de Veigné, 37250 Montbazon) Courses in traditional methods of Touraine cooking can be arranged at this lovely country hotel in the Loire.

École de Cuisine du Soleil (☎ 04 93 75 78 24; www.moulin-mougins.com; Notre Dame de Vie, 06250 Mougins) Mediterranean cuisine taught by chef Alain Llorca, not far from Cannes.
La Manoir d L'Aufragère (☎ 02 32 56 91 92; www.laufragere.com; L'Aufragère, La Croisée, 27500 Fourmetot) *Telegraph*-recommended cooking courses held in an 18th-century Norman manor house.
Mas de Cornud (☎ 04 90 92 39 32; www.mascornud.com; petite route des Baux, 13210 St-Rémy de Provence) Home cooking in the heart of Provence.

EAT & DRINK YOUR WORDS

For pronunciation guidelines see p987.

Useful Phrases

I'm hungry/thirsty.
J'ai faim/soif.   zhay fum/swaf
A table for two, please.
Une table pour deux, s'il vous plaît.   ewn ta·bler poor der seel voo play
Do you have a menu in English?
Est-ce que vous avez la carte en anglais? es·ker voo za·vay la kart on ong·lay
What's the speciality of this region?
Quelle est la spécialité de la région?   kel ay la spay·sya·lee·tay de la ray·zhon
What is today's special?
Quel est le plat du jour?   kel ay ler pla doo zhoor
I'd like the set menu, please.
Je prends le menu, s'il vous plaît.   zher pron ler mer·new seel·voo·play
I'd like some...
Je voudrais du/de la...   zher voo·dray doo/de la...
May I have another...please?
Puis-je avoir encore un/une...   pwee zher a·vwa ong·kor un/oon...
s'il vous plaît?   seel voo play
I'm a vegetarian.
Je suis végétarien/végétarienne. (m/f)   zher swee vay·zhay·ta·ryun/vay·zhay·ta·ryen
I don't eat (meat).
Je ne mange pas de viande.   zher ne monzh pa de vyond
Is service included?
Le service est compris?   ler sair·vees ay kom·pree
The bill, please.
L'addition, s'il vous plaît.   la·dee·syon seel voo play

Menu Decoder

STARTERS (APPETISERS)
assiette anglaise	a·syet ong·glayz	plate of cold mixed meats and sausages
assiette de crudités	a·syet der krew dee·tay	plate of raw vegetables with dressings
soufflé	soof·lay	a light, fluffy dish of egg yolks, stiffly beaten egg whites, flour and cheese and other ingredients

SOUP
bouillabaisse	bwee·ya·bes	Mediterranean-style fish soup, originally from Marseille, made with several kinds of fish, including *rascasse* (spiny scorpion fish); often eaten as a main course
bouillon	boo·yon	broth or stock
bourride	boo·reed	fish stew; often eaten as a main course
potage	po·tazh	thick soup made with puréed vegetables
soupe au pistou	soop o pee·stoo	vegetable soup made with a basil and garlic paste
soupe de poisson	soop der pwa·son	fish soup
soupe du jour	soop dew zhoor	soup of the day

MEAT & POULTRY

aiguillette	ay·gwee·yet	thin slice of duck fillet
andouille or andouillette	on·doo·yer/on·doo·yet	sausage made from pork or veal tripe
bifteck	bif·tek	steak
bleu	bler	nearly raw
saignant	sen·yon	very rare (literally: 'bleeding')
à point	a pwun	medium rare but still pink
bien cuit	byun kwee	literally: 'well cooked', but usually like medium rare
blanquette de veau	blong·ket der vo	veal stew with white sauce
bœuf bourguignon	berf boor·geen·yon	beef and vegetable stew cooked in red wine
bœuf haché	berf ha·shay	minced beef
boudin noir	boo·dun nwar	blood sausage (black pudding)
brochette	bro·shet	kebab
canard	ka·nar	duck
caneton	ka·ne·ton	duckling
cassoulet	ka·soo·lay	Languedoc stew made with goose, duck, pork or lamb fillets and haricot beans
charcuterie	shar·kew·tree	cooked or prepared meats (usually pork)
chevreuil	sher·vrer·yer	venison
choucroute	shoo·kroot	sauerkraut with sausage and other prepared meats
civet	see·vay	game stew
confit de canard (d'oie)	kon·fee der ka·nar (dwa)	duck (goose) preserved and cooked in its own fat
coq au vin	kok o vun	chicken cooked in wine
côte	kot	chop of pork, lamb or mutton
côtelette	kot·let	cutlet
cuisses de grenouille	kwees der grer·noo·yer	frogs' legs
entrecôte	on·trer·kot	rib steak
escargot	es·kar·go	snail
faisan	fer·zon	pheasant
faux-filet	fo fee·lay	sirloin steak
filet	fee·lay	tenderloin
foie	fwa	liver
foie gras de canard	fwa gra der ka·nar	duck liver pâté
fricassée	free·ka·say	stew with meat that has first been fried
gibier	zheeb·yay	game
gigot d'agneau	zhee·go da·nyo	leg of lamb
grillade	gree·yad	grilled meats
jambon	zhom·bon	ham
langue	long	tongue
lapin	la·pun	rabbit
lard	lar	bacon
lardons	lar·don	pieces of chopped bacon
lièvre	lye·vrer	hare
mouton	moo·ton	mutton
oie	wa	goose
pieds de cochon/porc	pyay der ko·shon/por	pigs' trotters
pintade	pun·tad	guinea fowl
quenelles	ker·nell	dumplings made of a finely sieved mixture of cooked fish or (rarely) meat
rognons	ron·yon	kidneys
sanglier	song·glee·yay	wild boar
saucisson	so·see·son	large sausage

saucisson fumé	so·see·son few·may	smoked sausage
steak	stek	steak
steak tartare	stek tar·tar	raw ground meat mixed with onion, raw egg yolk and herbs
tournedos	toor·ner·do	thick slices of fillet
volaille	vo·lai	poultry

FISH & SEAFOOD

anchois	on·shwa	anchovy
anguille	ong·gee·yer	eel
brochet	bro·shay	pike
cabillaud	ka·bee·yo	cod
calmar	kal·mar	squid
chaudrée	sho·dray	fish stew
coquille St-Jacques	ko·kee·yer sun·zhak	scallop
crabe	krab	crab
crevette grise	krer·vet greez	shrimp
crevette rose	krer·vet roz	prawn
écrevisse	ay·krer·vees	freshwater crayfish
fruits de mer	frwee der mair	seafood
hareng	a·rung	herring
homard	o·mar	lobster
huître	wee·trer	oyster
langouste	long·goost	crayfish
langoustine	long·goo steen	very small saltwater 'lobster' (Dublin Bay prawn)
maquereau	ma·kro	mackerel
merlan	mair·lan	whiting
morue	mo·rew	cod
moules	mool	mussels
palourde	pa·loord	clam
rouget	roo·zhay	mullet
sardine	sar·deen	sardine
saumon	so·mon	salmon
thon	ton	tuna
truite	trweet	trout

COOKING METHODS, SAUCES & CONDIMENTS

à la vapeur	a la va·per	steamed
aïoli	ay·o·lee	garlic mayonnaise
au feu de bois	o fer der bwa	cooked over a wood-burning stove
au four	o foor	baked
béchamel	bay·sha·mel	basic white sauce
en croûte	on kroot	in pastry
farci	far·see	stuffed
fumé	few·may	smoked
gratiné	gra·tee·nay	browned on top with cheese
grillé	gree·yay	grilled
huile d'olive	weel do·leev	olive oil
moutarde	moo·tard	mustard
pané	pa·nay	coated in breadcrumbs
pistou	pee·stoo	pesto (pounded mix of basil, hard cheese, olive oil and garlic)
provençal(e)	pro·von·sal	tomato, garlic, herb and olive oil dressing or sauce

rôti	ro·tee	roasted
sauté	so·tay	sautéed (shallow fried)
tartare	tar·tar	mayonnaise with herbs
vinaigrette	vee·nay·gret	salad dressing made with oil, vinegar, mustard and garlic

DESSERTS & SWEETS

crêpes suzettes	krep sew·zet	orange-flavoured pancakes flambéed in liqueur
dragées	dra·gay	sugared almonds
éclair	ay·klair	pastry filled with cream
flan	flon	egg-custard dessert
frangipane	fron·zhee·pun	pastry filled with cream and flavoured with almonds
gâteau	ga·to	cake
gaufre	go·frer	waffle
glace	glas	ice cream
île flottante	eel flo·tont	literally: 'floating island'; beaten egg white lightly cooked, floating on a creamy sauce
macaron	ma·ka ron	macaroon (sweet biscuit of ground almonds, sugar and egg whites)
sablé	sa·blay	shortbread biscuit
tarte (aux pommes)	tart (o pom)	apple tart or pie
yaourt	ya·oort	yogurt

SNACKS

croque-madame	krok·ma·dam	croque-monsieur with a fried egg
croque-monsieur	krok·mers·yer	grilled ham and cheese sandwich
frites	freet	chips (French fries)
quiche	keesh	quiche

Food Glossary

BASICS

breakfast	per·tee day·zher·nay	petit déjeuner
lunch	day·zher·nay	déjeuner
dinner	dee·nay	dîner
food	noo·ree·tewr	nourriture
menu	kart	carte
set menu	mer·new/for mewl	menu/formule
starter/appetiser	on·tray	entrée
main course	pla prun·see·pal	plat principal
wine list	kart day vun	carte des vins
waiter/waitress	sair·ver/sair·verz	serveur/serveuse
delicatessen	tray ter	traiteur
grocery store	ay·pee·sree	épicerie
market	mar·shay	marché
fork	foor·shet	fourchette
knife	koo·to	couteau
spoon	kwee·yair	cuillère
bottle	boo·tay	bouteille
glass	vair	verre
plate/dish	pla/a·syet	plat/assiette
hot/cold	sho/frwa	chaud/froid
with/without	a·vek/son	avec/sans

MEAT & FISH

beef	berf	*boeuf*
chicken	poo·lay	*poulet*
fish	pwa·son	*poisson*
lamb	a·nyo	*agneau*
meat	vyond	*viande*
pork	por	*porc*
turkey	dund	*dinde*
veal	vo	*veau*

FRUIT & VEGETABLES

apple	pom	*pomme*
apricot	ab·ree·ko	*abricot*
artichoke	ar·tee·sho	*artichaut*
asparagus	a·spairzh	*asperge*
banana	ba·nan	*banane*
beans	a·ree·ko	*haricots*
beetroot	be·trav	*betterave*
bilberry (blueberry)	meer·tee·yer	*myrtille*
blackcurrant	ka·sees	*cassis*
cabbage	shoo	*chou*
carrot	ka·rot	*carotte*
celery	sel·ree	*céleri*
cepe	sep	*cèpe*
(boletus mushroom)		
cherry	ser·reez	*ceris*
cucumber	kong·kom·brer	*concombre*
French (string) beans	a·ree·ko vair	*haricots verts*
gherkin (pickle)	kor·nee·shon	*cornichon*
grape	ray·zun	*raisin*
grapefruit	pom·pler·moos	*pamplemousse*
leek	pwa·ro	*poireau*
lemon	see·tron	*citron*
lentils	lon·tee·yer	*lentilles*
lettuce	lay·tew	*laitue*
mushroom	shom·pee·nyon	*champignon*
onion	on·yon	*oignon*
peach	pesh	*pêche*
peas	per·tee pwa	*petit pois*
pepper (red/green)	pwa·vron (roozh/vair)	*poivron (rouge/vert)*
pineapple	a·na·nas	*ananas*
plum	prewn	*prune*
potato	pom der tair	*pomme de terre*
prune	prew·no	*pruneau*
pumpkin	see·troo·yer	*citrouille*
raspberry	from·bwaz	*framboise*
rice	ree	*riz*
shallot	eh sha lot	*échalote*
spinach	eh·pee·nar	*épinards*
strawberry	frez	*fraise*
sweet corn	ma·ees	*maïs*
tomato	to·mat	*tomate*
turnip	na·vay	*navet*
vegetable	lay·gewm	*légume*

OTHER

bread	pun	*pain*
butter	ber	*beurre*
cheese	fro·mazh	*fromage*
cream	krem	*crème*
egg	erf	*œuf*
honey	myel	*miel*
jam	kon·fee·tewr	*confiture*
oil	weel	*huile*
pepper	pwa·vrer	*poivre*
salt	sel	*sel*
sugar	sew·krer	*sucre*
vinegar	vee·nay·grer	*vinaigre*

DRINKS

beer	bee·yair	*bière*
coffee	ka·fay	*café*
with milk	o lay	*au lait*
with sugar	a·vek sew·kray	*avec sucre*
juice (apple)	zhew (der pom)	*jus (de pomme)*
juice (orange)	zhew (do·ronzh)	*jus (d'orange)*
milk	lay	*lait*
mineral water	o mee·nay·ral	*eau minérale*
tea	tay	*thé*
water	o	*eau*
wine (red)	vun (roozh)	*vin (rouge)*
wine (white)	vun (blong)	*vin (blanc)*

Paris

Paris has almost exhausted the superlatives that can be reasonably applied to a city. Notre Dame, the Eiffel Tower and the Champs-Élysées have been described innumerable times. What writers rarely capture is the magic of strolling along the broad avenues that lead from impressive public buildings and exceptional museums to parks, gardens and esplanades.

First-time visitors often arrive with expectations: intellectuals pontificating at cafés, romance along the Seine, rude people. To be sure, if you look for them, you'll find those things. But another approach is to set aside these preconceptions and explore the city's avenues and back streets as if the tip of the Eiffel Tower wasn't about to pop into view at any moment.

Paris is enchanting in every season, at any time of day. And, like a good meal, it excites, it satisfies, the memory lingers. In *A Moveable Feast*, the American author Ernest Hemingway wrote: 'If you are lucky enough to have lived in Paris as a young man, then wherever you go for the rest of your life it stays with you, for Paris is a moveable feast.'

Those of us who were able to take Mr Hemingway's advice in our salad days could not agree more. We're still dining out on the memories and so will you.

HIGHLIGHTS

- Enjoy the collections and the spectacular rooftop views at the **Centre Pompidou** (p129), the world's most successful art and culture centre

- Cruise the **Champs-Élysées** (p141), Paris' broadest and most famous avenue, at ground level or view it from atop the **Arc de Triomphe** (p141)

- Play spot the departed at the **Cimetière du Père Lachaise** (p143), the world's most visited necropolis

- Go to the top of the **Eiffel Tower** (p139), the landmark that's more Parisian than Paris itself

- Visit the **Louvre** (p126), the world's richest art depository, to view old favourites such as the *Mona Lisa* and *Venus de Milo* or perhaps break your own Da Vinci Code

- Do a walking tour of **Montmartre** (p147), the Paris of song, story and myth

- Make a pilgrimage to **Notre Dame** (p132), as celebrated for the sacred (rose windows, medieval statuary) as it is for the profane (gargoyles, tourist hordes)

- Enjoy the views of the timeless **Seine** (p150) from the banks or on an evening cruise

- POPULATION: 2.144 MILLION
- AREA: 105 SQ KM

HISTORY

In the 3rd century BC a tribe of Celtic Gauls known as the Parisii settled on what is now the Île de la Cité. Centuries of conflict between the Gauls and Romans ended in 52 BC, when Julius Caesar's legions crushed a Celtic revolt led by Vercingétorix. Christianity was introduced in the 2nd century AD, but Roman rule ended in the 5th century with the arrival of the Germanic Franks. In 508 Frankish king Clovis I united Gaul as a kingdom and made Paris his seat.

In the 9th century France was beset by Scandinavian Vikings (also known as Norsemen and later Normans), who raided the western coastal areas; within three centuries they started pushing towards Paris, which had risen rapidly in importance. Construction began on the cathedral of Notre Dame in the 12th century, the Louvre began life as a riverside fortress around 1200, the beautiful Ste-Chapelle was consecrated in 1248 and the Sorbonne opened its doors in 1253.

The incursions heralded the Hundred Years' War between Norman England and Paris' Capetian dynasty, eventually bringing the French defeat at Agincourt in 1415 and English control of the capital in 1420. In 1429 the 17-year-old Jeanne d'Arc (Joan of Arc) rallied the French troops to defeat the English at Orléans. With the exception of Calais, the English were finally expelled from France in 1453.

The Renaissance helped Paris get back on its feet at the end of the 15th century, and many of the city's most famous buildings and monuments were erected at this time. But in less than a century Paris was again in turmoil, as clashes between Huguenot (Protestant) and Catholic groups increased. The worst such incident was the so-called St Bartholomew's Day massacre in 1572 in which 3000 Huguenots who had gathered in Paris to celebrate the wedding of Henri of Navarre (later King Henri IV) died.

Louis XIV, also known as the Sun King, ascended the throne in 1643 at the age of five and ruled until 1715, virtually emptying the national coffers with his ambitious building and battling. His greatest legacy is the palace at Versailles, 21km southwest of Paris. The excesses of Louis XVI and his queen, Marie-Antoinette, in part led to an uprising of Parisians on 14 July 1789 and the storming of the Bastille prison – kick-starting the French Revolution.

At first the Revolution was in the hands of moderates but within four years the so-called Reign of Terror, during which even the original patriots were guillotined, was in full swing. The unstable postrevolutionary government was consolidated in 1799 under a young Corsican general named Napoleon Bonaparte, who declared himself First Consul. In 1804 he had the Pope crown him Emperor of the French and then went forward and conquered most of Europe. Napoleon's ambitions eventually brought about his defeat, first in Russia in 1812 and later at Waterloo in Belgium in 1815. He was exiled and died in 1821.

France struggled under a string of mostly inept rulers until a coup d'état in 1851 brought Emperor Napoleon III to power. He oversaw the construction of a more modern Paris, with wide boulevards, sculpted parks and – not insignificantly – a modern sewer system. Like his pugnacious uncle, however, Napoleon had a taste for blood, which led to his costly and unsuccessful war with Prussia in 1870. When the masses in Paris heard of their emperor's capture by the enemy, they took to the streets, demanding that a republic be declared. Despite its bloody beginnings, the Third Republic ushered in the glittering and very creative period known as the *belle époque* (beautiful era), celebrated for its graceful Art Nouveau architecture and advances in the arts and sciences.

By the 1930s Paris had become a centre for the artistic avant-garde and had established its reputation among freethinking intellectuals. This was all cut short by the Nazi occupation of 1940; Paris would remain under direct German rule until 25 August 1944. After the war Paris regained its position as a creative centre and nurtured a revitalised liberalism that reached a climax in the student-led uprisings of 1968. The Sorbonne was occupied, barricades were set up in the Latin Quarter and some nine million people nationwide were inspired to join in a general strike that paralysed the country.

During the 1980s President François Mitterrand initiated several costly *grands projets*, a series of building projects that garnered widespread approval even when the results were popular failures. In the

1990s, the baton passed to right-wing President Jacques Chirac, who won a second five-year term in 2002. Nationwide support of the government reached its nadir in late 2005 and early 2006 when Paris was convulsed by demonstrations, protests and widespread rioting. In May 2001 Bertrand Delanoë, a Socialist with support from the Green Party, became Paris' – and a European capital's – first openly gay mayor. He was expected to be returned to the same post in the May 2007 elections.

ORIENTATION

Central Paris is relatively small: approximately 9.5km (north to south) by 11km (east to west). Within the 'oval' of central Paris, which Parisians call *intra-muros* (Latin for 'within the walls'), the Rive Droite (Right Bank) is north of the Seine, while the Rive Gauche (Left Bank) is south of it since the river flows from east to west.

Paris is quite an easy city to negotiate, but this chapter offers you three ways to find the addresses listed: by district, map reference and metro station.

Arrondissements

Paris is divided into 20 arrondissements (districts), which spiral out clockwise from the centre like a conch shell. City addresses always include the number of the arrondissement, because streets with the same name exist in different districts.

In this chapter, arrondissement numbers are given after a street address using the usual French notation: 1er for *premier* (1st), 2e for *deuxième* (2nd), 3e for *troisième* (3rd) and so on. On some signs or commercial maps, you will see variations such as 2ème, 3ème etc.

Maps

The most useful map of Paris is the 1:10,000-scale *Paris Plan* published by Michelin. It comes in booklet form (€5) or as a fold-out sheet (€3.75). The Lonely Planet *Paris City Map* is available from bookshops in the UK and France, as well as other countries.

For a more user-friendly street atlas than the venerable old *Paris par Arrondissement* (€23.50), choose L'Indispensable's *Paris Pratique par Arrondissement* (€4.90), which

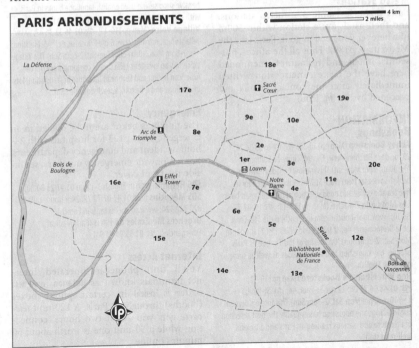

PARIS ARRONDISSEMENTS

PARIS

FINDING YOURSELF IN PARIS

In Paris, when a building is put up in a location where they've run out of consecutive street numbers, a new address is formed by fusing the number of an adjacent building with the notation *bis* (twice), *ter* (thrice) or even *quater* (four times). Therefore, the street numbers 17bis and 89ter are the equivalent of 17a and 89b in English.

The street doors (*portes cochères*) of most apartment buildings in Paris can be opened only if someone has given you the entry code (*digicode*), which is usually alphanumeric (eg 26A10) and changed periodically; the days of the concierges, who would vet every caller before allowing them in, are well and truly over. In some buildings the entry-code device is deactivated during the day but to get in (or out) you still have to push a button (usually marked *porte*) to release the electric catch.

The doors of many apartments are unmarked: the occupants' names are nowhere in sight and there isn't even an apartment number. To know which door to knock on, you'll usually be given cryptic instructions, such as *cinquième étage, premier à gauche* (5th floor, first on the left) or *troisième étage, droite droite* (3rd floor, turn right twice).

is a slim, pocket-sized atlas. The same publisher's larger *Le Petit Parisien* (€6.50) has three maps for each arrondissement, showing streets, metro lines and bus routes.

The best place to find a full selection of maps is the Espace IGN (p959 and Map pp102–3).

Metro Stations

Paris possesses some 372 metro stations, and there is always a station within 500m of wherever you need to go in Paris (see the Metro map, p189). Thus all the offices, museums, hotels and restaurants mentioned here have the nearest metro stop written immediately after the contact details and preceded by the Ⓜ icon.

INFORMATION
Bookshops

Abbey Bookshop (Map pp110–11; ☎ 01 46 33 16 24; 29 rue de la Parcheminerie, 5e; Ⓜ Cluny-La Sorbonne; ⊗ 10am-7pm Mon-Sat) This mellow Canadian-owned bookshop not far from place St-Michel is celebrated for its free tea and coffee and good selection of new and used books.

Les Mots à la Bouche (Map pp110–11; ☎ 01 42 78 88 30; www.motsbouche.com in French; 6 rue Ste-Croix de la Bretonnerie, 4e; Ⓜ Hôtel de Ville; ⊗ 11am-11pm Mon-Sat, 2-8pm Sun) 'On the Tip of the Tongue' is Paris' premier gay bookshop and stocks guides as well as some novels in English.

Red Wheelbarrow Bookstore (Map pp110–11; ☎ 01 48 04 75 08; 22 rue St-Paul, 4e; Ⓜ St-Paul; ⊗ 10am-7pm Mon-Sat, 2-6pm Sun) This foreign-owned English-language bookshop has arguably the best selection of literature and 'serious reading' in Paris and a helpful, well-read staff.

Shakespeare & Company (Map pp110–11; ☎ 01 43 26 96 50; 37 rue de la Bûcherie, 5e; Ⓜ St-Michel; ⊗ noon-midnight) Paris' most famous English-language bookshop has a varied collection of new and used books in English, including cheap used paperback novels.

Tea & Tattered Pages (Map pp108–9; ☎ 01 40 65 94 35; 24 rue Mayet, 6e; Ⓜ Duroc; ⊗ 11am-7pm Mon-Sat, noon-6pm Sun) T&TP is by far the best and most comprehensive shop selling used English-language books in Paris, with some 15,000 volumes squeezed into two floors.

Village Voice (Map pp110–11; ☎ 01 46 33 36 47; www.villagevoicebookshop.com; 6 rue Princesse, 6e; Ⓜ Mabillon; ⊗ 2-8pm Mon, 10am-8pm Tue-Sat, 2-6pm Sun) The Village Voice has an excellent selection of contemporary North American fiction and European literature in translation, lots of readings and a helpful, knowledgeable staff.

Emergency

The numbers below are to be dialled in an emergency. See p123 for hospitals with 24-hour accident and emergency departments. For nationwide emergency numbers, see inside the front cover.

SOS Helpline (☎ in English 3-11pm 01 47 23 80 80)
SOS Médecins (☎ 01 47 07 77 77, 24hr house calls 0 820 332 424; www.sosmedecins.fr in French)
Urgences Médicales de Paris (Paris Medical Emergencies; ☎ 01 53 94 94 94)

Internet Access

You'll find phonecard-operated internet terminals known as **Netanoo** (www.netanoo.com in French) in certain phone boxes (booths) throughout Paris. A 120-unit *télécarte* gets you about two hours' connection while a 50-unit one is worth about 50 minutes online.

Note that in this chapter only, the 🖳 icon is used for businesses offering wi-fi access but no actual computers, as well as for businesses offering a terminal with internet access.

The best and most central commercial internet cafés in Paris include the following:

Cyber Cube (Map pp108-9; ☎ 01 56 80 08 08; www .cybercube.fr; 9 rue d'Odessa, 14e; Ⓜ Montparnasse Bienvenüe; per 1 min €0.15, per 5/10hr €30/40; 🕑 10am-10pm) One of three branches; expensive but convenient to the Gare Montparnasse.

Toonet – The Cyber Space (Map pp114-15; ☎ 01 58 30 97 37; 74 rue de Charonne, 11e; Ⓜ Charonne or Ledru Rollin; per 1/5/15/30hr €5/16/30/45; 🕑 10.30am-9pm Mon-Sat)

Web 46 (Map pp110-11; ☎ 01 40 27 02 89; 46 rue du Roi de Sicile, 4e; Ⓜ St-Paul; per 15/30/60min €2.50/4/7, 5hr €29; 🕑 10am-midnight Mon-Fri, 10am-9pm Sat, noon-midnight Sun) This is a very pleasant, well-run café in the heart of the Marais.

XS Arena Les Halles (Map pp110-11; ☎ 01 40 13 02 60; 31 blvd de Sébastopol, 1er; Ⓜ Les Halles; 🕑 24hr) This XS Arena branch is just down from the Forum des Halles.

XS Arena Luxembourg (Map pp118-19; ☎ 01 43 44 55 55; 17 rue Soufflot, 5e; Ⓜ Luxembourg; per 1/2/3/4/5hr €3/6/8/10/11; 🕑 24hr) This minichain of internet cafés is bright, buzzy and open round the clock.

Internet Resources

Lonely Planet's website (www.lonelyplanet .com) is a good start for many useful links. Other English-language websites include the following:

Mairie de Paris (www.paris.fr) Statistics and city information direct from the town hall.

Metropole Paris (www.metropoleparis.com) Excellent online magazine in English.

Paris Pages (www.paris.org) Good links to museums and cultural events.

Paris Tourist Office (www.parisinfo.com) Super site with more links than you'll ever need.

Laundry

There's a *laverie libre-service* (self-service laundrette) around just about every corner in Paris; your hotel or hostel can point you to one in the neighbourhood. Machines usually cost €3.20 to €4 for a small load (3.5kg to 7kg) and €5.80 to €7 for a larger (10kg to 16kg) one. Drying costs €1 for 10 minutes.

LOUVRE & LES HALLES

Laverie Libre Service (Map pp110-11; 7 rue Jean-Jacques Rousseau, 1er; Ⓜ Louvre-Rivoli; 🕑 7.30am-10pm) Near the Centre International de Séjour BVJ Paris-Louvre hostel.

MARAIS & BASTILLE

Laverie Libre Service (Map pp110-11; 35 rue Ste-Croix de la Bretonnerie, 4e; Ⓜ Hôtel de Ville; 🕑 7am-10pm)

Laverie Miele Libre Service (Map pp114-15; 2 rue de Lappe, 11e; Ⓜ Bastille; 🕑 7am-10pm)

LATIN QUARTER & JARDIN DES PLANTES

Le Bateau Lavoir (Map pp118-19; 1 rue Thouin, 5e; Ⓜ Cardinal Lemoine; 🕑 7am-10pm) Near place de la Contrescarpe.

Laverie Libre Service (Map pp118-19; 63 rue Monge, 5e; Ⓜ Place Monge; 🕑 6.30am-10pm) Just south of the Arènes de Lutèce.

ST-GERMAIN, ODÉON & LUXEMBOURG

Julice Laverie (Map pp110-11; 56 rue de Seine, 6e; Ⓜ Mabillon; 🕑 7am-11pm)

GARE DU NORD, GARE DE L'EST & RÉPUBLIQUE

Laverie Libre Service (Map pp104-5; 14 rue de la Corderie, 3e; Ⓜ République or Temple; 🕑 8am-9pm)

Laverie SBS (Map pp104-5; 6 rue des Petites Écuries, 10e; Ⓜ Château d'Eau; 🕑 7am-10pm)

MÉNILMONTANT & BELLEVILLE

C'Clean Laverie (Map pp104-5; 18 rue Jean-Pierre Timbaud,11e; Ⓜ Oberkampf; 🕑 8am-10pm)

MONTMARTRE & PIGALLE

Salon Lavoir Sidec (Map p122; 28 rue des Trois Frères, 18e; Ⓜ Abbesses; 🕑 7am-8.50pm)

Media

There are no local English-language newspapers in Paris although freebies such as the **Paris Times** (www.theparistimes.com) and **Paris Where** (www.wheremagazine.com) proliferate and are available at English-language bookshops, pubs and so on. *FUSAC* (short for *France USA Contacts*), a freebie issued every fortnight, consists of hundreds of ads placed by both companies and individuals. It can be found at the same places as well as at the **American Church in Paris** (Map pp108-9; ☎ 01 40 62 05 00; www.acparis.org; 65 quai d'Orsay, 7e; Ⓜ Pont de l'Alma or Invalides; 🕑 reception 9am-noon & 1-10.30pm Mon-Sat, 9am-2pm & 3-7pm Sun), which functions as a community centre for English speakers and is an excellent source of information on au pair work, short-term accommodation etc.

Paris Live Radio (963kHz AM; www.parislive.fm), the city's only all-English station, can be heard via the internet, cable, satellite and DAB

(Continued on page 123)

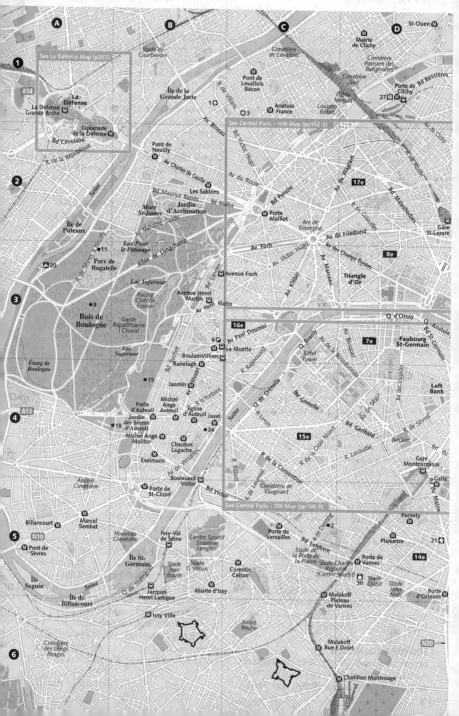

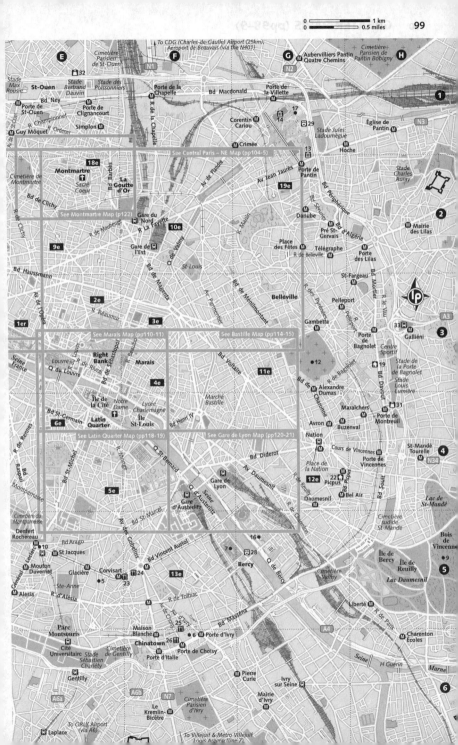

0 — 1 km
0 — 0.5 miles

INFORMATION
American Express...................(see 10)
Art Nouveau Toilets.................... 1 G5
Belgian Embassy..........................2 C4
Canadian Embassy......................3 E5
France Lodge...............................4 D2
German Consulate.....................5 A4
German Embassy.........................6 E5
Irish Embassy & Trade Office........7 C4
Japanese Embassy.......................8 D3
New Zealand Embassy & Trade
    Office..................................9 B5
Paris Convention & Visitors
    Bureau.................................. 10 H4
Paris Convention & Visitors Bureau
    (Main Branch)...................... 11 H6
Pharmacie des Champs............. 12 D4
Ski France............................... 13 G4
Spanish Embassy....................... 14 D5
UK Consulate........................... 15 G5
UK Embassy & Trade Office........16 F5
US Consulate........................... 17 G5
US Embassy & Trade Office........ 18 G5

SIGHTS & ACTIVITIES
Arc de Triomphe...................... 19 C4
Bateaux Mouches....................20 E6
Bibliothèque-Musée de l'Opéra..(see 36)
Colonne Vendôme.................... 21 H5
Église de la Madeleine.............. 22 G5
Flame of Liberty Memorial........ 23 D6
Galerie National du Jeu de
    Paume.............................(see 27)
Galeries Nationales du Grand
    Palais..............................(see 25)
Galeries du Panthéon
    Bouddhique........................24 G4
Grand Palais.............................25 F6
Jardin des Tuileries.................. 26 G6

Jeu de Paume.......................... 27 G6
L'Open Tour............................. 28 H4
Musée de l'Orangerie..............(see 30)
Musée des Beaux-Arts de la Ville de
    Paris................................(see 37)
Musée Guimet des Arts
    Asiatiques.......................... 29 C6
Orangerie............................... 30 G6
Palais de Chaillot.....................31 B6
Palais de l'Élysée......................32 F5
Palais de la Découverte.............33 E5
Palais de Tokyo........................ 34 C6
Palais des Congrès de Paris........35 B3
Palais Garnier.......................... 36 H4
Petit Palais.............................. 37 F6
Place de l'Alma........................ 38 D6
Place de la Concorde Obelisk..... 39 G6
Place de l'Opéra....................... 40 H5
Place Vendôme........................ 41 H5

SLEEPING
Hôtel Costes............................42 H5
Hôtel Eldorado.........................43 G2
Hôtel Langlois..........................44 H3
Hôtel Le A...............................45 E4
Hôtel Ritz Paris........................46 H5
New Orient Hôtel......................47 F3
Style Hôtel...............................48 G2

EATING
Bistrot du Sommelier.................49 F4
Champs-Élysée Bistro Romain.... 50 D4
Franprix..................................51 G5
Graindorge.............................52 C3
L'Ardoise.................................53 G5
Le Roi du Pot au Feu................54 G4
Lina's.....................................55 G5
Monoprix Champs-Élysées........56 E5
Monoprix Opéra.......................57 H5

DRINKING
Harry's New York Bar...............58 H5

ENTERTAINMENT
Boutique PSG...........................59 E5
Crazy Horse............................. 60 D6
Fnac Champs-Élysées................ 61 D5
Kiosque Théâtre....................... 62 G5
Le Lido de Paris........................ 63 D4
Palais Garnier
    Box Office..........................(see 36)
Salle Pleyel.............................. 64 D3
Virgin Megastore......................65 E5

SHOPPING
Boutique Maille........................66 G5
Colette................................... 67 H6
Espace IGN..............................68 E5
Fromagerie Alléosse.................69 C3
Galeries Lafayette.................... 70 H4
Galeries Lafayette.................... 71 H4
Hédiard...................................72 G5
Le Printemps de l'Homme..........73 H4
Le Printemps de la Beauté et
    Maison..............................74 H4
Le Printemps de la Mode...........75 H4
Les Caves Augé........................76 F4
Réciproque..............................77 A6
Réciproque..............................78 A6

TRANSPORT
ADA Car Rental........................ 79 G3
Air France Buses.......................80 C4
Batobus Stop...........................81 E6
Buses from Beauvais Airport.......82 B3
Parking Pershing (Buses to Beauvais
    Airport).............................83 B3
Rent A Car Système.................. 84 H6
Roissybus.................................85 H4

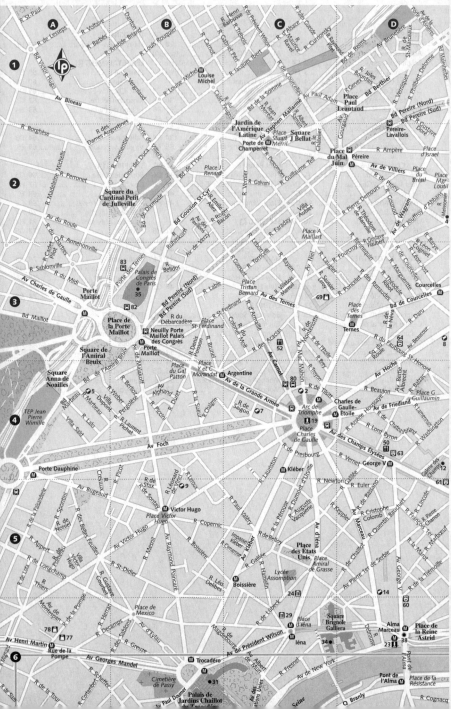

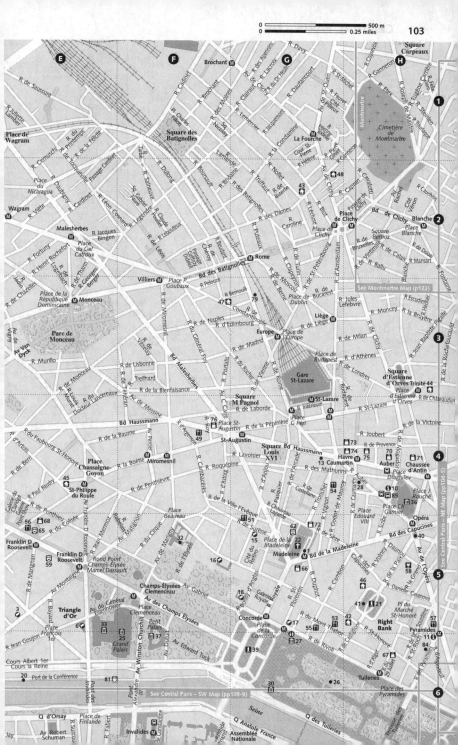

0 — 500 m
0 — 0.25 miles

E **F** **G** **H**

Square Carpeaux

Brochant

R de Saussure

Place de Wagram

Square des Batignolles

Cimetière de Montmartre

La Fourche

Place du Nicaragua

Wagram

Maleshesbes

Place du Gal Catroux

Villiers

Bd des Batignolles

Rome

Place de Clichy

Bd de Clichy Blanche

Place Blanche

Square Berlioz

Place de la République Dominicaine

Monceau

Parc de Monceau

See Montmartre Map (p122)

Europe

Place de l'Europe

Liège

Gare St-Lazare

Square d'Estienne d'Orves Trinité

Place d'Estienne d'Orves

Av Van Dyck

Square M Pagnol

St-Lazare

Bd Haussmann

St-Augustin

Square Louis XVI

Bd Haussmann

Havre Caumartin

Chaussée d'Antin

Place Chassaigne-Goyon

St-Philippe du Roule

Place Draghilev

Place J Rouché

Opéra

Franklin D Roosevelt

Place Beauvau

Madeleine

Bd des Capucines

Triangle d'Or

Champs-Élysées Clemenceau

Rond Point Champs-Élysée Marcel Dassault

Galeries Royale

Bd de la Madeleine

Place Edouard VIII

Right Bank

Pyramides

Concorde

Place de la Concorde

Tuileries

Place des Pyramides

Grand Palais

Petit Palais

Port de la Conférence

See Central Paris – SW Map (pp108-9)

Seine

Q d'Orsay

Place de Finlande

Invalides

Assemblée Nationale

See Central Paris – NE Map (pp104-5)

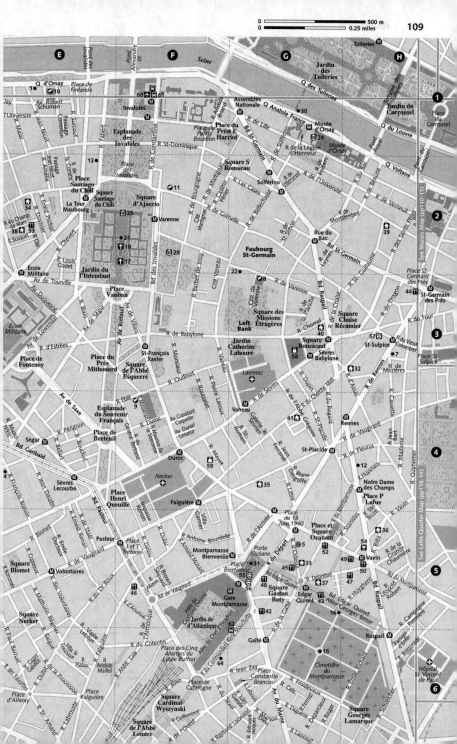

0 — 500 m
0 — 0.25 miles

E | **F** | *Seine* | **G** | **H**

Pont des Invalides | Pont Alexandre III | Jardin des Tuileries | Tuileries

Q d'Orsay | Place de Finlande | Jardin du Carrousel | Place du Carrousel

Av. Robert Schuman | Assemblée Nationale | Q Anatole France | Jardin du Carrousel

Invalides | Q des Tuileries | Q du Louvre

l'Université | Place du Palais Bourbon | Place du Prés E Harriot | Musée d'Orsay | Q Royal | Q Voltaire

Esplanade des Invalides | R de Lille | R St-Germain | Musée d'Orsay | R de Bellune

Place des Invalides | R St-Dominique | Square S Rousseau | R de la Légion d'Honneur

Place Santiago du Chili | Square Santiago du Chili | Square d'Ajaccio | Solférino | Rue du Bac

La Tour Maubourg | Varenne | Faubourg St-Germain | Place St-Germain des Prés | St-Germain des Prés

Jardin du l'Intendant | Bd des Invalides | R de Varenne | Bd St-Germain | R du Four

Place Vauban | Square des Missions Étrangères | Left Bank | Square Chaise Récamier | Place St-Sulpice

École Militaire | Av de Tourville | Jardin Catherine Labouré | Square Boucicaut | Sèvres Babylone | St-Sulpice

Place de Fontenoy | Place du Prés Mithouard | St-François Xavier | Square de l'Abbé Esquerré | Laennec | Vaneau | Rennes

Esplanade du Souvenir Français | Place de Breteuil | Duroc | St-Placide

Séminaire | Necker | Place Henri Queuille | Falguière | Notre Dame des Champs | Place P Lafue

Sèvres Lecourbe | Pasteur | Volontaires | Place J of L Tréfouel | Montparnasse Bienvenüe | Place du 18 Juin 1940 | Place et Square Ozanam | Vavin

Square Blomet | Square Necker | Porte Océane | Place Bienvenüe | Gare Montparnasse | Square Gaston Baty | Edgar Quinet

Square Necker | Jardin d'Atlantique | Gaîté | Cimetière du Montparnasse | Raspail

Place des Cinq Martyrs du Lycée Buffon | Place Constantin Brancusi | Square Georges Lamarque

Place Falguière | Square Cardinal Wyszynski | Hôpital St-Vincent de Paul

Place d'Alleray | Square de l'Abbé Lemire

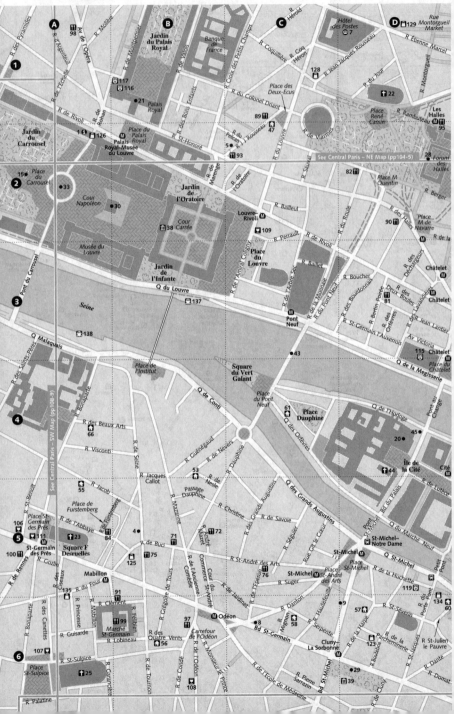

Jardin du Palais Royal

Banque de France

Hôtel des Postes

Rue Montorgueil Market

Jardin du Carrousel

Place du Carrousel

Cour Napoléon

Palais Royal

Place du Palais Royal-Musée du Louvre

Jardin de l'Oratoire

Place des Deux-Ecus

Place René Cassin

Les Halles

Place M Quentin

Place M de Navarre

Cour Carrée

Musée du Louvre

Jardin de l'Infante

Place du Louvre

Châtelet

See Central Paris – NE Map (pp104–5)

Forum des Halles

Q du Louvre

Pont Neuf

Seine

Place de l'Institut

Square du Vert Galant

Place du Pont Neuf

Place Dauphine

Place du Châtelet

Q Malaquais

See Central Paris – SW Map (pp108–9)

R des Beaux Arts

R Visconti

Île de la Cité

Cité

R Jacob

Place de Furstemberg

R Jacques Callot

Passage Dauphine

R de Nesle

R Christine

Place St-Germain des Prés

Square F Desruelles

Mabillon

St-Michel–Notre Dame

St-Michel

St-André des Arts

Place St-André des Arts

St-Michel

Q St-Michel

R Clément

Marché St-Germain

Odéon

Carrefour de l'Odéon

Bd St-Germain

Cluny–La Sorbonne

Place St-Sulpice

R Palatine

0 _____ 200 m
0 _____ 0.1 miles

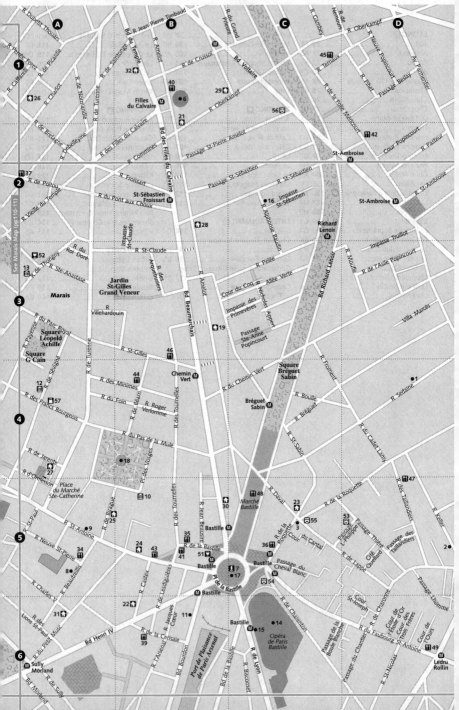

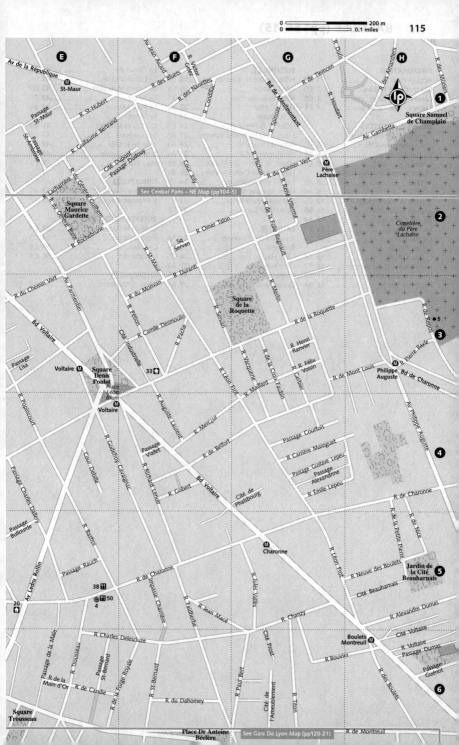

0   200 m
0   0.1 miles

E **F** **G** **H**

Av de la République

St-Maur

Passage
St-Maur

Passage
St-Ambroise

R. St-Hubert

R. Guillaume Bertrand

R. du Général Guilhem

Cité Dupont
Passage Dudouy

R. Victor
Gelez

Av Jean Aicard

R. des Bluets

R. des Nanettes

R. Godillot

Cour Joly

Bd de Ménilmontant

R. Spinoza

R. Pichon

R. du Chemin Vert

R. de Tlemcen

R. Duris

R. Houdart

R. des Amandiers

R. des Mûriers

Square Samuel
de Champlain

Av. Gambetta

Père
Lachaise

1

See Central Paris – NE Map (pp104–5)

Square Maurice
Gardette

R. Lacharrière

R. du Général Blaise

R. Rochebrune

R. St-Maur

Sq
Servan

R. Omer Talon

R. René Villermé

R. de la Folie Regnault

Cimetière
du Père
Lachaise

2

R. du Chemin Vert

Av Parmentier

R. du Morvan

R. Durant

R. Merlin

Square
de la
Roquette

R. Servan

R. de la Roquette

R. de Repos

3

Bd Voltaire

Passage
Lisa

Voltaire

Square
Denis
Poulot

Place
Léon
Blum

Voltaire

Cité Industrielle

R. Camille-Desmoulin

R. Pétion

R. Pache

33

R. Léon Frot

R. Vacquerie

R. de la Croix Faubin

R. Henri
Ranvier

R. R. Félix
Voisin

Crebec

R. de Mont Louis

R. Pierre Bayle

Philippe
Auguste

Bd de Charonne

Passage
Lisa

R. Popincourt

R. Godefroy Cavaignac

R. Auguste Laurent

R. Mercœur

R. de Belfort

Passage
Viallet

R. Richard Lenoir

R. Gobert

Bd Voltaire

Cité de
Phalsbourg

Passage Courtois

R. Carrière Mainguet

Passage Gustave Lepeu

Passage
Alexandrine

R. Émile Lepeu

Av Philippe Auguste

R. de Charonne

4

Passage Charles Dallery

Passage
Bullourde

Cour Delille

R. Bastrol

Av Ledru Rollin

Square
Rauch

Passage Rauch

R. de Charonne

Passage Chanvin

Charonne

R. Léon Frot

R. de la Petite Pierre

R. de Nice

R. Neuve des Boulets

Cité-Beauharnais

Jardin de
la Cité
Beauharnais

5

20

38

50
4

R. Charles Delescluze

R. Faidherbe

R. Jean Macé

R. Chanzy

R. Léon Frot

Boulets
Montreuil

Alexandre Dumas

Cité Voltaire

R. Voltaire
Passage Dumas

Passage
Guenot

6

Passage de la Main

R. Trousseau

Passage
St-Bernard

R. de la Forge Royale

R. de Candie

R. St-Bernard

R. du Dahomey

R. Paul Bert

Cité de
l'Ameublement

R. Titon

R. Bouvier

R. des Boulets

Square
Trousseau

R. de la
Main d'Or

Place Dr Antoine
Béclère

See Gare De Lyon Map (pp120–21)

R. de Montreuil

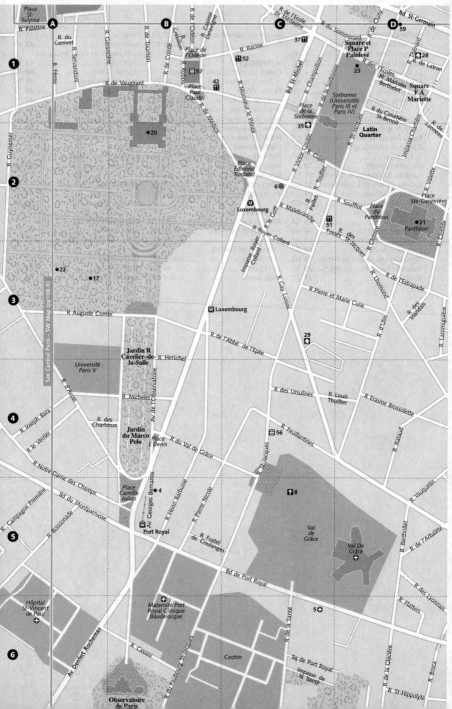

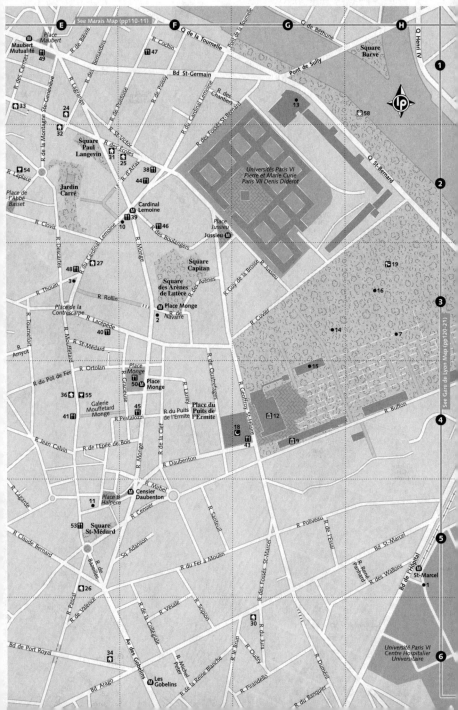

0 — 200 m
0 — 0.1 miles

See Marais Map (pp110-11)

E   F   Q de la Tournelle   G   Q de Béthune   H

Place
Maubert
M Maubert
Mutualité
49

R des Carmes
R de Bièvre
R des Bernardins
R Cochin
47

Square
Barye

Q Henri IV

Pont de Sully

Bd St-Germain

R de Poissy
R de Pontoise
R du Cardinal Lemoine
R des Chantiers
R des Fossés St-Bernard

13

58

33

24
32

R Lagrange
R St-Victor
R des Écoles
R d'Arras
Square
Paul
Langevin
31
25

38
44

Universités Paris VI
Pierre et Marie Curie
Paris VII Denis Diderot

Q St-Bernard

54

R Laplace

Jardin
Carré

Cardinal
Lemoine
39
10
46

R des Boulangers

Place
Jussieu
Jussieu M

Place de
l'Abbé
Basset

R Clovis

R Descartes

R du Cardinal Lemoine

R Monge

48
27
3

Square
Capitan

Square
des Arènes
de Lutèce

R des Arènes

R Guy de la Brosse R Jussieu

19

16

R Thouin

Place de la
Contrescarpe

R Lacépède
40

R Rollin

Place Monge
2
R de
Navarre

R Cuvier

14

7

R Amyot
R Tournefort
R Mouffetard

R St-Médard

R Ortolan

R du Pot de Fer

Place
Monge
50
Place
Monge

R de Quatrefages

R Lanneau

R Geoffroy St-Hilaire

15

36
55
41

Galerie
Mouffetard
Monge
45

R Pestalozzi

R du Puits
de l'Ermite
Place du
Puits de
l'Ermite

R Buffon

12

R Jean Calvin
R de l'Épée de Bois

R Monge

R de la Clef

R Daubenton

18
43

9

R Lagarde

11

Place B
Halpern

R Mirbel
Censier
Daubenton

R Santeuil

53
Square
St-Médard

R Censier

R Poliveau

R Claude Bernard

Sq Adanson

R de
Bazeilles

R du Fer à Moulin

R des Fossés St-Marcel

Bd St-Marcel

R René
Panhard
R des Wallons
Bd de l'Hôpital
M St-Marcel
1

26

R Pascal
R de Valence

R Vésale
R de la Collégiale
R Scipion

30

R du Jura

R Dunois

34

Bd de Port Royal

Av des Gobelins

R Michel Peter
R de la Reine Blanche

R Brun
R Oudry

R Pirandello

Bd Arago

Les
Gobelins

R du Banquier

Université Paris VI
Centre Hospitalier
Universitaire

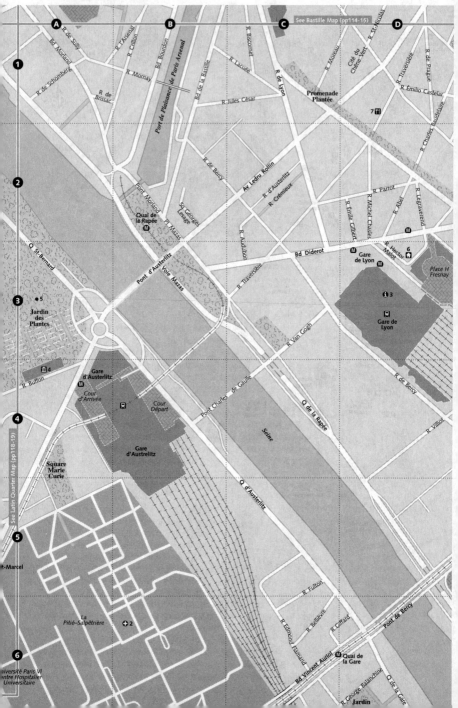

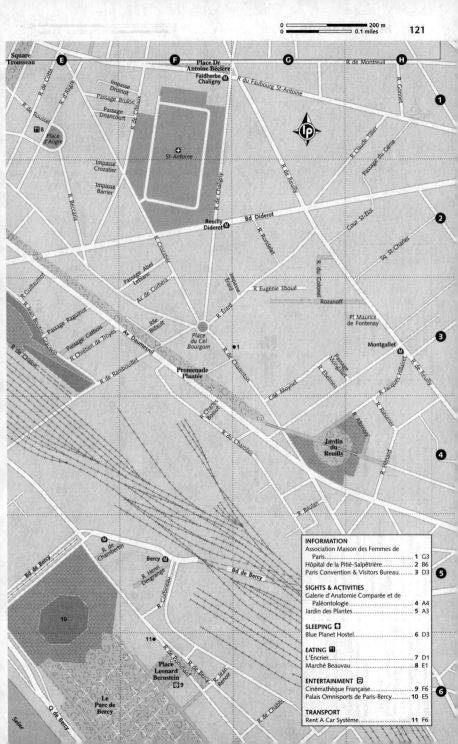

0 — 200 m
0 — 0.1 miles

INFORMATION

Association Maison des Femmes de
Paris... **1** G3
Hôpital de la Pitié-Salpêtrière................ **2** B6
Paris Convention & Visitors Bureau....... **3** D3

SIGHTS & ACTIVITIES

Galerie d'Anatomie Comparée et de
Paléontologie....................................... **4** A4
Jardin des Plantes................................. **5** A3

SLEEPING

Blue Planet Hostel................................. **6** D3

EATING

L'Encrier... **7** D1
Marché Beauvau.................................... **8** E1

ENTERTAINMENT

Cinémathèque Française......................... **9** F6
Palais Omnisports de Paris-Bercy.......... **10** E5

TRANSPORT

Rent A Car Système............................... **11** F6

0 _____ 400 m
0 _____ 0.2 miles

INFORMATION
Lariboisière................................	1 F4
Paris Convention & Visitors Bureau	2 D4
Salon Lavoir Sider...................	3 C3
Syndicate d'Initiative de Montmartre	4 C3

SIGHTS & ACTIVITIES
Basilique du Sacré Cœur.............	5 D3
Bateau Lavoir (Former Artists' Studio)	6 C3
Cimetière de Montmartre............	7 A3
Close de Montmartre..................	8 C2
Crypt & Dome Entrance..............	9 D3
Église St-Pierre de Montmartre.....	10 D3
Entrance to Montmartre Cemetery	11 A3
Moulin de la Galette...................	12 B2
Moulin Radet............................	13 C2
Musée de l'Érotisme..................	14 B4
Musée de Montmartre................	15 C2
Place du Tertre.........................	16 C3

SLEEPING 🛏
Hôtel Bonséjour Montmartre.......	17 B3
Hôtel des Arts..........................	18 B3
Hôtel du Moulin........................	19 B3
Hôtel Regyn's Montmartre.........	20 C3
Hôtel Utrillo.............................	21 B3
Le Village Hostel......................	22 D4
Terrass Hotel...........................	23 B3

EATING 🍴
Chez Toinette..........................	24 C3
Ed l'Épicier.............................	25 D4
La Maison Rose........................	26 C2
La Mascotte.............................	27 B3
La Table d'Anvers....................	28 D4
8 Huit.....................................	29 B3

DRINKING 🍷
La Fourmi................................	30 C4
Le Progrès...............................	31 C4

ENTERTAINMENT 🎭
Au Lapin Agile.........................	32 C2
L'Élysée-Montmartre.................	33 D4
La Cigale.................................	34 C4
Moulin Rouge...........................	35 A3
Virgin Megastore......................	36 E3

TRANSPORT
Funicular to Sacré Cœur............	37 D3

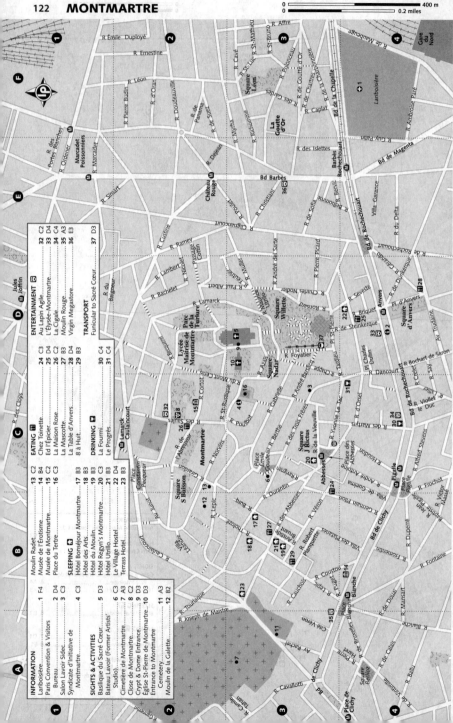

(Continued from page 97)

digital radio throughout the day and has news, music, community information etc.

Medical Services

DENTAL SURGERIES
For emergency dental care contact either of the following:

Hôpital de la Pitié-Salpêtrière (Map pp120-1; ☎ 01 42 16 00 00; rue Bruant, 13e; Ⓜ Chevaleret) This is the only dental hospital with extended hours – from 6.30pm to 8.30am. After 5.30pm use the emergency entrance (Map pp118–19) at 83 blvd de l'Hôpital, 13e, Ⓜ St-Marcel.

SOS Dentaire (Map pp118-19; ☎ 01 43 36 36 00, 01 43 37 51 00; 87 blvd de Port Royal, 14e; Ⓜ Port Royal) This is a private dental office that also offers services when most dentists are off duty (8pm to 11pm weekdays, 9.45am to 11pm at the weekend).

HOSPITALS
There are some 50 *assistance publique* (public health service) hospitals in Paris. Major hospitals in the city that have 24-hour accident and emergency departments include the following:

American Hospital in Paris (Map pp98-9; ☎ 01 46 41 25 25; www.american-hospital.org; 63 blvd Victor Hugo, 92200 Neuilly-sur-Seine; Ⓜ Pont de Levallois Bécon) Offers emergency 24-hour medical and dental care.

Hertford British Hospital (Map pp98-9; ☎ 01 46 39 22 22; www.british-hospital.org; 3 rue Barbès, 92300 Levallois-Perret; Ⓜ Anatole France) This is a less expensive English-speaking option than the American Hospital.

Hôtel Dieu (Map pp110-11; ☎ 01 42 34 82 34; 1 place du Parvis Notre Dame, 4e; Ⓜ Cité) One of the city's main government-run public hospitals; after 8pm use the emergency entrance (rue de la Cité, 4e).

PHARMACIES
Some pharmacies with extended hours:

Pharmacie Bader (Map pp110-11; ☎ 01 43 26 92 66; 12 blvd St-Michel, 5e; Ⓜ St-Michel; ⏰ 9am-9pm)

Pharmacie des Champs (Map pp102–3; ☎ 01 45 62 02 41; Galerie des Champs, 84 av des Champs-Élysées, 8e; Ⓜ George V; ⏰ 24hr)

Pharmacie des Halles (Map pp110-11; ☎ 01 42 72 03 23; 10 blvd de Sébastopol, 4e; Ⓜ Châtelet; ⏰ 9am-midnight Mon-Sat, 9am-10pm Sun)

Money

Post offices that have a Banque Postale can offer the best exchange rates, and they accept banknotes in various currencies as well as travellers cheques issued by Amex or Visa. *Bureaux de change* are usually faster and easier, are open longer hours and give better rates than most banks. For general advice on exchanging money, see p961.

Post

Each arrondissement (p95) in Paris has its own five-digit postcode, formed by prefixing the arrondissement number with '750' or '7500' (eg 75001 for the 1er arrondissement, 75019 for the 19e). The only exception is the 16e, which has two postcodes: 75016 and 75116.

The **Main Post Office** (Map pp110-11; ☎ 01 40 28 76 00; 52 rue du Louvre, 1er; Ⓜ Sentier or Les Halles; ⏰ 24hr), five blocks north of the eastern end of the Louvre, is open round the clock for basic services such as sending letters and picking up poste restante (or 'general delivery') mail (window Nos 5 to 7; €0.53 per letter). Other services, including currency exchange, are available only during regular opening hours. Be prepared for long queues after 7pm. Poste restante mail not specifically addressed to a particular branch post office in Paris will be delivered here. There is a one-hour closure from 6.20am to 7.20am Monday to Saturday and from 6am to 7am on Sunday.

Toilets

The public toilets in Paris are signposted *toilettes* or *WC*. The tan-coloured, self-cleaning cylindrical toilets you see on Paris' pavements are open 24 hours and used to cost €0.40 but for the most part are now free.

Café owners do not appreciate use of their facilities if you are not a paying customer. If you are desperate, try ducking into a fast-food place, a major department store, Forum des Halles (Map pp110-11) or even a big hotel. There are public toilets (€0.40 or free) underground in front of Notre Dame Cathedral (Map pp110–11), near the Arc de Triomphe (Map pp102–3), east down the steps at Basilisque du Sacré Cœur (Map p122), at the northwestern entrance to the Jardins des Tuileries (Map pp102–3) and also in a few metro stations. Check out the wonderful Art Nouveau public toilets below place de la Madeleine, 8e (Map pp102–3). They were built in 1905.

In older cafés and bars, the amenities may consist of a *toilette à la turque* (Turkish-style toilet), which is what the French call a squat toilet.

PARIS IN...

Two Days

If you've got only a couple of days in Paris (bad decision, that) you should definitely join a **morning tour** (p150) and then concentrate on the most Parisian of sights and attractions: **Notre Dame** (p132), the **Louvre** (p126), the **Eiffel Tower** (p139) and the **Arc de Triomphe** (p141). In the late afternoon have a coffee or a pastis on the **av des Champs-Élysées** (p141) and then make your way to **Montmartre** (p144) for dinner. The following day take in such sights as the **Musée d'Orsay** (p138), **Ste-Chapelle** (p133), **Conciergerie** (p133), **Musée National du Moyen Âge** (p134) and/or the **Musée Rodin** (p138). Have brunch on the **place des Vosges** (p130) and enjoy a night of mirth and gaiety in the **Marais** (p130).

Four Days

With another couple of days to look around the city, you should consider **a cruise** (p150) along the Seine or the Canal St-Martin and visit some place further afield – the **Cimetière du Père Lachaise** (p143), say, or **the Parc de la Villette** (p145). On one of the two nights take in a concert, opera or ballet at the **Palais Garnier** (p143) or **Opéra Bastille** (p132) or a play at the **Comédie Française** (p182), and go on a bar and club crawl along **rue Oberkampf** (p173) in Ménilmontant. The **Bastille area** (p130) is another option for a night out.

A Week

If you have one week in the French capital, you can see a good many of the major sights listed in this chapter, visit places around Paris such as **La Défense** (p206) and **St-Denis** (p208), and leave Paris proper for a day or two for excursions: **Vaux-le-Vicomte** (p217) can be easily combined with **Fontainebleau** (p214), **Senlis** (p220) with **Chantilly** (p218) and, if you travel hard and fast, **Chartres** (p220) with **Versailles** (p211).

Tourist Information

The main branch of the **Office de Tourisme et de Congrès de Paris** (Paris Convention & Visitors Bureau; Map pp102-3; ☎ 0 892 683 000; www.parisinfo.com; 25-27 rue des Pyramides, 1er; Ⓜ Pyramides; ⊗ 9am-7.30pm Jun-Oct, 10am-7pm Mon-Sat & 11am-7pm Sun Nov-May) is about 500m northwest of the Louvre. It closes on 1 May only.

The bureau also has five centres (telephone numbers and website the same as the main office), plus an independent office in Montmartre. For Paris' surrounds, contact **Espace du Tourisme d'Île de France** (Map pp110-11; ☎ 08 26 16 66 66, from abroad 33-1 44 50 19 98; www .pidf.com; Galerie du Carrousel du Louvre, 99 rue de Rivoli, 1er; Ⓜ Palais Royal-Musée du Louvre; ⊗ 10am-6pm).

Anvers (Map p122; opp 72 blvd de Rochechouart, 18e; Ⓜ Anvers; ⊗ 10am-6pm, closed Christmas Day, New Year's Day & May Day)

Eiffel Tower (Map pp108-9; btwn Pilier Nord & Pilier Est, Parc du Champ de Mars, 7e; Ⓜ Champ de Mars-Tour Eiffel; ⊗ 11am-6.40pm 25 Mar-Oct) In a kiosk beneath the Eiffel Tower.

Gare de Lyon (Map pp120-1; Hall d'Arrivée, 20 blvd Diderot, 12e; Ⓜ Gare de Lyon; ⊗ 8am-6pm Mon-Sat, closed Sun & 1 May) In the mainline trains arrivals hall.

Gare du Nord (Map pp104-5; 18 rue de Dunkerque, 10e; Ⓜ Gare du Nord; ⊗ 8am-6pm, closed Christmas Day, New Year's Day & 1 May) Located beneath the glass roof of the Île de France departures and arrivals area at the eastern end of the train station.

Opéra-Grands Magasins (Map pp102-3; 11 rue Scribe, 9e; Ⓜ Auber or Opéra; ⊗ 9am-6.30pm Mon-Sat, closed Sun, Christmas Day, New Year's Day & 1 May) In the same building as the American Express office.

Syndicat d'Initiative de Montmartre (Map p122; 21 place du Tertre, 18e; Ⓜ Abbesses; ⊗ 10am-7pm) This locally run tourist office and shop is in Montmartre's most picturesque square and open year-round.

Travel Agencies

You'll find travel agencies everywhere in Paris, but the following are among the largest and offer the best service and (usually) best deals:

Forum Voyages (www.forum-voyages.fr in French); Opéra branch (Map pp104-5; ☎ 01 42 61 20 20; 11 av de l'Opéra, 1er; Ⓜ Pyramides); St-Germain branch (Map pp108-9; ☎ 01 45 44 38 61; 1 rue Cassette, 6e; Ⓜ St-Sulpice) Forum Voyages has five outlets in Paris that are usually open 9.30am to 7pm Monday to Saturday.

PARIS

Nouvelles Frontières (☎ 0 825 000 747; www
.nouvelles-frontieres.fr in French; ☼ 9am-8pm Mon-Sat,
10am-8pm Sun); Odéon branch (Map pp110-11; ☎ 01
43 25 71 35; 116 blvd St-Germain, 6e; Ⓜ Odéon); Opéra
branch (Map pp104-5; ☎ 01 42 61 02 62; 13 av de l'Opéra,
1er; Ⓜ Pyramides) There are 19 outlets around the city
which are usually open 9am to 7pm Monday to Saturday.
OTU Voyages (☎ 01 55 82 32 32; www.otu.fr in French);
Luxembourg branch (Map pp118-19; ☎ 01 44 41 38 50;
39 av Georges Bernanos, 5e; Ⓜ Port Royal; ☼ 9am-
6.30pm Mon-Fri, 10am-noon & 1.15-5pm Sat) There is also
a branch opposite the Centre Pompidou (p152).
Voyageurs du Monde (Map pp104-5; ☎ 01 49 26
07 14, 0 892 235 656; www.vdm.com in French; 55 rue
Ste-Anne, 2e; Ⓜ Pyramides or Quatre-Septembre;
☼ 9.30am-7pm Mon-Sat) 'World Travellers' is an
enormous agency with more than a dozen departments on
three floors dealing with different destinations.

DANGERS & ANNOYANCES
Crime
In general Paris is a safe city and random
street assaults are rare. The so-called Ville
Lumière (City of Light) is generally well lit,
and there's no reason not to use the metro
before it stops running at some time between
12.30am and just past 1am. As you'll notice,
women *do* travel alone on the metro late at
night in most areas, though not all who do
so report feeling 100% comfortable.

Metro stations that are probably best
avoided late at night include: Châtelet-Les
Halles and its seemingly endless corridors;
Château Rouge in Montmartre; Gare du
Nord; Strasbourg St-Denis; Réaumur Sébastopol; and Montparnasse Bienvenüe.
Bornes d'alarme (alarm boxes) are located
in the centre of each metro/RER platform
and in some station corridors.

Nonviolent crime such as pickpocketing
and thefts from handbags and packs is a
problem wherever there are crowds, especially crowds of tourists. Places to be particularly careful include Montmartre (especially
around Sacré Cœur); Pigalle; the areas
around Forum des Halles and Centre Pompidou; the Latin Quarter (especially the
rectangle bounded by rue St-Jacques, blvd
St-Germain, blvd St-Michel and quai St-
Michel); below the Eiffel Tower; and on the
metro during rush hour.

Lost Property
All objects found anywhere across Paris –
except those picked up on the trains or in

train stations – are eventually brought in to
the city's **Bureau des Objets Trouvés** (Lost Property
Office; Map pp98-9; ☎ 0 821 002 525; 36 rue des Morillons,
15e; Ⓜ Convention; ☼ 8.30am-5pm Mon, Wed & Fri,
8.30am-8pm Tue & Thu), which is run by the Préfecture de Police. Since telephone inquiries
are impossible, the only way to find out if
a lost item has been located is to go there
and fill in the forms.

Items lost on the **metro** (☎ 0 892 987 714;
☼ 7am-9pm Mon-Fri, 9am-5.15pm Sat & Sun) are held
by station agents for three days before being
sent to the Bureau des Objets Trouvés.

Anything found on trains or in train
stations is taken to the lost-property office
(usually attached to the left-luggage office)
of the relevant station. Telephone inquiries
(in French) are possible:
Gare d'Austerlitz (☎ 01 53 60 71 98)
Gare de l'Est (☎ 01 40 18 88 73)
Gare de Lyon (☎ 01 53 33 67 22)
Gare du Nord (☎ 01 55 31 58 40)
Gare Montparnasse (☎ 01 40 48 14 24)
Gare St-Lazare (☎ 01 53 42 05 57)

Litter
In theory Parisians can be fined more than
€183 for littering but we've never heard of
anyone having to pay up. Don't be non-
plussed if you see locals drop paper wrap-
pings or other detritus along the side of
the pavement, however; the gutters in every
quarter of Paris are washed and swept out
daily and Parisians are encouraged to use
them where litter bins are not available.

A much greater annoyance are all those
dog droppings on the pavements. The Paris
municipality spends more than €11 million
each year to keep them relatively free of dog
dirt, but it seems that repeated campaigns –
including threats of heavy fines and free
plastic bags distributed in parks and along
the quays – to get people to clean up after
their pooches, which now number 200,000
plus and produce 16 tonnes of dog dirt a
year, have had only limited success, with
just 60% of dog owners saying they do so.

SIGHTS
Paris' major sights are distributed more or
less equally on the Right and Left Banks of
the Seine. We start in the heart of the Right
Bank in the area around the Louvre and
Les Halles, which largely takes in the 1er
and follows, more or less, the order of the

arrondissements (p95), ending in the Parc de la Villette in the 19e.

Louvre & Les Halles

The area around the Louvre in the 1er contains some of the most important sights for visitors in Paris. To the northeast, the mostly pedestrian zone between the Centre Pompidou and the Forum des Halles, with rue Étienne Marcel to the north and rue de Rivoli to the south, is filled with people by day and by night, just as it was for the 850-odd years when part of it served as Paris' main marketplace known as Les Halles.

MUSÉE DU LOUVRE

The vast Palais du Louvre was constructed as a fortress by Philippe-Auguste in the early 13th century and rebuilt in the mid-16th century for use as a royal residence. In 1793 the Revolutionary Convention turned it into the **Musée du Louvre** (Louvre Museum; Map pp110-11; ☎ 01 40 20 53 17; www.louvre.fr; Ⓜ Palais Royal-Musée du Louvre; admission to permanent collections/ permanent collections & temporary exhibits €8.50/13, after 6pm Wed & Fri €6/11, permanent collections free for under 18yr & after 6pm Fri for under 26yr, admission free 1st Sun of the month; ☉ 9am-6pm Mon, Thu, Sat & Sun, 9am-9.45pm Wed & Fri), the nation's first national museum.

The paintings, sculptures and artefacts on display in the Louvre Museum have been assembled by French governments over the past five centuries. Among them are works of art and artisanship from all over Europe and important collections of Assyrian, Etruscan, Greek, Coptic and Islamic art and antiquities. Traditionally the Louvre's *raison d'être* is to present Western art from the Middle Ages to about the year 1848 (at which point the Musée d'Orsay takes over) as well as the works of ancient civilisations that formed the starting point for Western art. However, in recent years it has acquired or begun to exhibit other important collections as well.

When the museum opened in the late 18th century it contained 2500 paintings and *objets d'art*; today some 35,000 are on display. The 'Grand Louvre' project inaugurated by the late President Mitterrand in 1989 doubled the museum's exhibition space, and new and renovated galleries have opened in recent years devoted to *objets d'art* such as Sèvres porcelain and the crown jewels of Louis XV (Rm 66, 1st floor, Apollo Gallery, Sully Wing), as well as ancient art collected from Africa, Asia, Australasia and the Americas (Rms 1-8, ground floor, Denon Wing), which is in the process of being moved to the new Musée du Quai Branly (p138).

The Louvre may be the most actively avoided museum in the world. Daunted by the richness and sheer size of the place (the side facing the Seine is some 700m long and it is said that it would take nine months just to glance at every piece of art here), both local people and visitors often find the prospect of an afternoon at a smaller museum far more inviting. Eventually, most people do their duty and come, but many leave overwhelmed, unfulfilled, exhausted and frustrated at having got lost on their way to da Vinci's *La Joconde*, better known as *Mona Lisa* (Rm 6, 1st floor, Salle de la Joconde, Denon Wing; opposite). Since it takes several serious visits to get anything more than a brief glimpse of the works on offer, your best bet – after checking out a few you really want to see – is to choose a particular period or section of the Louvre and pretend that the rest is in another museum somewhere across town.

The most famous works from antiquity include the *Seated Scribe* (Rm 22, 1st floor, Sully Wing), the *Code of Hammurabi* (Rm 3, ground floor, Richelieu Wing) and that armless duo, the *Venus de Milo* (Rm 12, ground floor, Sully Wing) and the *Winged Victory of Samothrace* (opp Rm 1, 1st floor, Denon Wing). From the Renaissance, don't miss Michelangelo's *The Dying Slave* (ground floor, Michelangelo Gallery, Denon Wing) and works by Raphael, Botticelli and Titian (1st floor, Denon Wing). French masterpieces of the 19th century include Ingres' *The Turkish Bath* (Rm 60, 2nd floor, Sully Wing), Géricault's *The Raft of the Medusa* (Rm 77, 1st floor, Denon Wing) and works by Corot, Delacroix and Fragonard (2nd floor, Denon Wing).

The main entrance and ticket windows in the Cour Napoléon are covered by the 21m-high **Grande Pyramide**, a glass pyramid designed by the Chinese-born American architect IM Pei. You can avoid the queues outside the pyramid or at the Porte des Lions entrance by entering the complex via the Carrousel du Louvre

---

MONA LISA: COLD, LONELY & LOVELY

  Are you warm, are you real, Mona Lisa
  Or just a cold and lonely, lovely work of art?

Jay Livingston & Ray Evans, 1950

So much has been written, most recently (and popularly) by Dan Brown in his bestselling *The Da Vinci Code* about the painting the French call *La Joconde* and the Italians *La Gioconda* yet so little has been known of the lady behind that enigmatic smile. For centuries admirers speculated on everything from the possibility that the subject was mourning the death of a loved one to that she might have been in love – or in bed – with her portraitist.

  Mona (actually *monna* in Italian) is a contraction of *madonna* while Gioconda is the feminine form of the surname Giocondo. With the emergence of several clues in recent years, it is almost certain that the subject was Lisa Gherardini (1479–1539?), the then-24-year-old wife of Florentine merchant Francesco del Giocondo, and that the portrait was painted sometime between 1503 and 1507. At the same time, tests performed in 2005 with 'emotion recognition' computer software suggest that the smile of 'Madam Lisa' is at least 83% happy. And one other point remains unequivocally certain despite occasional suggestions to the contrary: Lisa was not the lover of Leonardo, who preferred his Vitruvian Man to his Mona.

---

shopping centre entrance (Map pp110–11), at 99 rue de Rivoli, or by following the 'Musée du Louvre' exit from the Palais Royal-Musée du Louvre metro station. Those in the know buy their tickets in advance from the ticket machines in the Carrousel du Louvre, online or by ringing ☎ 0 892 683 622 or ☎ 0 825 346 346, or from the *billeteries* (ticket offices) of FNAC (rhymes with 'snack'; p178) for an extra €1.50, and walk straight in without queuing. Tickets are valid for the whole day, so you can come and go as you please.

The Musée du Louvre is divided into four sections: the Sully, Denon and Richelieu Wings and the Hall Napoléon. **Sully** creates the four sides of the Cour Carrée (literally 'square courtyard') at the eastern end of the complex. **Denon** stretches along the Seine to the south; **Richelieu** is the northern wing along rue de Rivoli.

The split-level public area under the glass pyramid is known as the **Hall Napoléon** (🕐 9am-10pm Wed-Mon). The hall has an exhibit on the history of the Louvre; a bookshop; a restaurant; a café; auditoriums for concerts, lectures and films; and **CyberLouvre** (🕐 10am-4.45 Wed-Mon), an internet research centre that allows access to some 20,000 works of art. The centrepiece of the **Carrousel du Louvre** (Map pp110-11; ☎ 01 40 20 67 30; 99 rue de Rivoli; 🕐 8.30am-11pm), the shopping centre that runs underground from the pyramid to the **Arc de Triomphe du Carrousel** (Map pp110–11) in the Jardin du Carrousel, is an **inverted glass pyramid** *(pyramide inversée),* also created by Pei.

Free maps in English of the Louvre complex, called *Louvre Plan/Information,* are available at the information desk in the centre of the Hall Napoléon. Excellent publications to guide you if you are doing the Louvre on your own are *Destination Louvre: A Guided Tour* (€7.50), *Visit the Louvre: a Guide to the Masterpieces* (€8) and the hefty, 475-page *Guide to the Louvre* (€17). All are available from the museum bookshop.

English-language guided tours (☎ 01 40 20 52 63) lasting 1½ hours depart from the area under the Grande Pyramide, marked 'Acceuil des Groupes' (Groups Welcome), at 11am, 2pm and 3.45pm Monday to Saturday. Tickets cost €5 in addition to the cost of admission. Groups are limited to 30 people, so it's a good idea to sign up at least 30 minutes before departure time. Self-paced audio guide tours in six languages with 1½ hours of commentary can be rented for €5 under the pyramid at the entrance to each wing.

JARDIN DES TUILERIES
The formal, 28-hectare **Jardin des Tuileries** (Tuileries Garden; Map pp102-3; ☎ 01 40 20 90 43; Ⓜ Tuileries or Concorde; 🕐 7am-9pm late Mar-late Sep, 7am-7.30pm late Sep-late Mar), which begins just west of the Jardin du Carrousel, was laid out in its present form – more or less – in the mid-17th century by André Le Nôtre, who also created the gardens at

Vaux-le-Vicomte (p217) and Versailles (p211). The Tuileries soon became the most fashionable spot in Paris for parading about in one's finery; today it is a favourite of joggers. It forms part of the Banks of the Seine World Heritage site listed in 1991.

The **Voie Triomphale** (Triumphal Way), also called the Axe Historique (Historic Axis), the western continuation of the Tuileries' east–west axis, follows the av des Champs-Élysées to the Arc de Triomphe and, ultimately, to the Grande Arche in the skyscraper district of **La Défense** (p206).

Jeu de Paume & Orangerie

The **Galerie Nationale du Jeu de Paume** (Jeu de Paume National Gallery; Map pp102-3; ☎ 01 47 03 12 52; www.jeudepaume.org; 1 place de la Concorde, 1er; Ⓜ Concorde; adult/senior, student & 13-18yr €6/3, under 13 free; ☉ noon-9.30pm Tue, noon-7pm Wed-Fri, 10am-7pm Sat & Sun) is housed in an erstwhile *jeu de paume* (real, or royal, tennis) court built in 1861 during the reign of Napoleon III in the northwestern corner of the Jardin des Tuileries. Once the home of a good part of France's national collection of impressionist art, now housed across the Seine in the Musée d'Orsay (p138), the two-storey Jeu de Paume stages innovative exhibitions of contemporary art. A new branch of the gallery, the Jeu de Paume-Site Sully in the **Hôtel de Sully** (p131) in the Marais concentrates on top-notch photography. A joint ticket for an adult/senior, student & 13–18 year old to both galleries costs €8/4.

The **Musée de l'Orangerie** (Orangery Museum; Map pp102-3; ☎ 01 42 97 49 21; www.musee-orangerie .fr; Jardin des Tuileries, 1er; Ⓜ Concorde; adult/senior & student €6.50/4.50; ☉ 12.30-7pm Wed, Thu & Sat-Mon, 12.30-10pm Fri) in the southwestern corner of the Jardin des Tuileries is, with the Jeu de Paume, all that remains of the once palatial Palais des Tuileries, which was razed during the Paris Commune in 1871. It reopened in 2006 after six years of extensive renovations and it exhibits important impressionist works, including a series of Monet's exquisite *Decorations des Nymphéas* (Water Lilies) in two huge oval rooms purpose-built on the artist's instructions.

PLACE VENDÔME

The octagonal **place Vendôme** (Map pp102-3; Ⓜ Tuileries or Opéra) and the arcaded and colonnaded buildings around it were constructed

---

MUSEUMS: AN OPEN & SHUT CASE

The vast majority of museums in Paris close on Monday although more than a dozen (including the Louvre, Centre Pompidou, Musée Picasso and Musée National du Moyen Âge) are closed on Tuesday instead. It's important to remember that *all* museums and monuments in Paris shut their doors or gates between 30 minutes and an hour before their actual closing times, which are the ones listed in this chapter. Therefore if we say a museum or monument closes at 6pm, don't count on getting in much later than 5.30pm or even 5pm.

---

between 1687 and 1721. In March 1796 Napoleon married Josephine, Viscountess Beauharnais, in the building at No 3. Today, the buildings surrounding the square house the posh **Hôtel Ritz Paris** (p153) and some of the city's most fashionable boutiques. The 43.5m-tall **Colonne Vendôme** (Vendôme Column), which stands in the centre of the square, consists of a stone core wrapped in a 160m-long bronze spiral made from 1250 Austrian and Russian cannons captured by Napoleon at the Battle of Austerlitz in 1805. The statue on top depicts Napoleon as a Roman emperor.

PALAIS ROYAL

The **Palais Royal** (Royal Palace; Map pp104-5; place du Palais Royal, 1er; Ⓜ Palais Royal-Musée du Louvre), which briefly housed a young Louis XIV in the 1640s, lies to the north of place du Palais Royal and the Louvre. Construction was begun in the 17th century by Cardinal Richelieu, though most of the present neoclassical complex dates from the latter part of the 18th century. It now contains the governmental **Conseil d'État** (State Council) and is closed to the public.

The colonnaded building that is opposite place André Malraux is the **Comédie Française** (p182), which was founded in 1680 and is the world's oldest national theatre.

Just north of the palace is the **Jardin du Palais Royal** (Map pp104-5; ☉ 7.30am-10.15pm Apr & May, 7am-11pm Jun-Aug, 7am-9.30pm Sep, 7.30am-8.30pm Oct-Mar), a lovely park surrounded by 19th-century shopping arcades, including **Galerie de Valois** on the eastern side and **Galerie de Montpensier** to the west. Don't miss the zany crown-like Palais Royal-Musée du Louvre **metro entrance** on the place du Palais Royal.

CENTRE POMPIDOU

The **Centre National d'Art et de Culture Georges Pompidou** (Georges Pompidou National Centre of Art & Culture; Map pp110-11; ☎ 01 44 78 12 33; www.centrepompidou.fr; place Georges Pompidou, 4e; Ⓜ Rambuteau) is the most successful art and culture centre in the world. An extensive €85-million renovation completed at the start of the new millennium gave the centre a new look, expanded its exhibition space and created a new cinema and audiovisual centre, dance and theatre venues and a posh restaurant, making it even more popular.

The Centre Pompidou, also known as the Centre Beaubourg, has amazed and delighted visitors since it was inaugurated in 1977, not just for its outstanding collection of modern art, but also for its radical architectural statement; it was among the first buildings to have its 'insides' turned outside. But it all began to look somewhat *démodé* by the late 1990s, hence the refit.

The **Forum du Centre Pompidou** (admission free; ⊗ 11am-10pm Wed-Mon), the open space at ground level, has temporary exhibits and information desks. The 4th and 5th floors of the centre exhibit about a third of the 50,000-plus works of the **Musée National d'Art Moderne** (MNAM, National Museum of Modern Art; Map pp110-11; adult/senior & 18-25yr €10/8, under 18 free & 1st Sun of month free; ⊗ 11am-9pm Wed-Mon), France's national collection of art dating from 1905 onwards and including the work of the Surrealists and Cubists, as well as pop art and contemporary works. The huge (and free)

Bibliothèque Publique d'Information (BPI; ☎ 01 44 78 12 33; www.bpi.fr in French; ⊗ noon-10pm Mon & Wed-Fri, 11am-10pm Sat & Sun), which is entered from rue du Renard, takes up part of the first as well as the entire second and third floors of the centre while the sixth floor has two galleries for **temporary exhibitions**, the admission to which is usually now included in the entrance fee.

The **Atelier Brancusi** (Map pp110-11; place Georges Pompidou; ⊗ 2-6pm Wed-Mon), west of the main building, contains some 140 examples of the work of Romanian-born sculptor Constantin Brancusi (1876–1957) as well as drawings, paintings and glass photographic plates. An MNAM ticket includes entry.

FORUM DES HALLES

Les Halles, the city's main wholesale food market, occupied the area just south of the Église St-Eustache from the early 12th century until 1969, when it was moved to the southern suburb of Rungis. In its place, the unspeakable **Forum des Halles** (Map pp110-11; ☎ 01 44 76 96 56; 1 rue Pierre Lescaut, 1er; Ⓜ Les Halles or Châtelet Les Halles), a huge underground shopping centre, was constructed in the glass-and-chrome style of the early 1970s.

Atop the Forum des Halles is a popular **park** (actually a rooftop garden). During the warmer months, street musicians, fire-eaters and other performers display their talents throughout the area, especially at **place du Jean du Bellay**, whose centre is adorned by a multitiered Renaissance fountain, the **Fontaine des Innocents**, erected in 1549. It is named after the Cimetière des Innocents, a cemetery on this site from which two million skeletons were disinterred and transferred to the Catacombes (p137) in the 14e after the Revolution.

ÉGLISE ST-EUSTACHE

The majestic **Église St-Eustache** (Map pp110-11; ☎ 01 42 36 31 05; www.st-eustache.org in French; 2 impasse St-Eustache, 1er; Ⓜ Les Halles; ⊗ 9am-7.30pm), one of the most beautiful churches in Paris and consecrated to an early Roman martyr who is the patron saint of hunters, is just north of the gardens above the Forum des Halles. Constructed between 1532 and 1640, St-Eustache is primarily Gothic, though a neoclassical façade was added on the western side in the mid-18th century. Inside, there are some exceptional Flamboyant

PARIS

Gothic arches holding up the ceiling of the chancel, although most of the interior ornamentation is Renaissance and classical. The gargantuan organ above the west entrance, with 101 stops and 8000 pipes, is used for concerts (long a tradition here) and during High Mass on Sunday (11am and 6pm). There's a 'free' audioguide available, though a donation of €3 is suggested.

TOUR ST-JACQUES

The 52m-high Flamboyant Gothic **Tour St-Jacques** (St James' Tower; Map pp110-11; place du Châtelet, 4e; Ⓜ Châtelet) is all that remains of the Église St-Jacques la Boucherie, built by the powerful butchers' guild in 1523 and demolished by the Directory in 1797. The tower is topped by a weather station and is not open to the public.

Marais & Bastille

The Marais, the area of the Right Bank north of Île St-Louis in the 3e and 4e, was exactly what its name implies – 'marsh' or 'swamp' – until the 13th century, when it was put to agricultural use. In the early 17th century, Henri IV built the place Royale (today's place des Vosges), turning the area into Paris' most fashionable residential district and attracting wealthy aristocrats who then erected their own luxurious *hôtels particuliers* (private mansions) and less expensive *pavillons* (smaller residences). Today many of them house museums and government institutions.

When the aristocracy moved from Paris to Versailles and Faubourg St-Germain during the late 17th and 18th centuries, the Marais and its townhouses passed into the hands of ordinary Parisians. The 110-hectare area was given a major face-lift in the late 1960s and early '70s. Marais has become a much desired address in recent years; while it also remains home to a long-established Jewish neighbourhood called the Pletzel, it is the centre of Paris' gay life.

Today, Marais is one of the few neighbourhoods of Paris that still have most of its pre-Revolution architecture. Examples include the oldest house in Paris, the **13th-century house** at 3 rue Volta in the 3e, parts of which date back to 1292; the **15th-century house** at 51 rue de Montmorency in the 3e (back to 1407) and the **16th-**

century **half-timbered houses** at 11 and 13 rue François Miron in the 4e.

After years as a run-down immigrant neighbourhood notorious for its high crime rate, the contiguous Bastille district (11e and 12e) has undergone a fair degree of gentrification, largely due to the opening of the Opéra Bastille back in 1989. Though the area is not the hip nightlife centre it was through most of the 1990s, it still has quite a bit to offer after dark, with numerous pubs, bars and clubs lining rue de Lappe and rue de la Roquette.

HÔTEL DE VILLE

After having been gutted during the Paris Commune of 1871, Paris' **Hôtel de Ville** (City Hall; Map pp110-11; ☎ 0 820 00 75 75, 01 42 76 50 49; www .paris.fr; place de l'Hôtel de Ville, 4e; Ⓜ Hôtel de Ville) was rebuilt in the neo-Renaissance style (1874–82). The ornate façade is decorated with 108 statues of noteworthy Parisians. There's a **Salon d'Accueil** (Reception Hall; 29 rue de Rivoli, 4e; ⏲ 10am-7pm Mon-Sat), which dispenses copious amounts of information and brochures and is used for temporary exhibitions, usually with a Paris theme.

The Hôtel de Ville faces the majestic **place de l'Hôtel de Ville**, used from the Middle Ages to the 19th century to stage many of Paris' celebrations, rebellions, book burnings and public executions. Known as place de Grève (Strand Square) until 1830, it was, in centuries past, a favourite gathering place of the unemployed, which is why a strike is called *une grève* in French to this day.

PLACE DES VOSGES

Place des Vosges (Map pp114-15; Ⓜ St-Paul or Bastille), inaugurated in 1612 as place Royale, is an ensemble of three dozen symmetrical houses with ground-floor arcades, steep slate roofs and large dormer windows arranged around a large square. Only the earliest houses were built of brick; to save time and money, the rest were given timber frames and faced with plaster, which was then painted to resemble brick.

The author Victor Hugo lived at the square's Hôtel de Rohan-Guéménée from 1832 to 1848, moving here a year after the publication of *Notre Dame de Paris* (The Hunchback of Notre Dame). The **Maison de Victor Hugo** (Victor Hugo House; Map pp114-15; ☎ 01 42 72 10 16; permanent collections admission free, temporary exhibitions adult/senior & student/14-25yr €7.50/5/3.50, under 14 free; ☼ 10am-6pm Tue-Sun) is now a municipal museum devoted to the life and times of the celebrated novelist and poet, with an impressive collection of his own drawings and portraits.

HÔTEL DE SULLY

The aristocratic mansion called **Hôtel de Sully** (Map pp110-11; 62 rue St-Antoine, 4e; Ⓜ St-Paul) dating from the early 17th century today houses the headquarters of the **Centre des Monuments Nationaux** (Monum; ☎ 01 44 61 20 00; www.monum .fr; ☼ 9am-12.45pm & 2-6pm Mon-Thu, 9am-12.45pm & 2-5pm Fri), the body responsible for many of France's historical monuments (with lots of brochures and information available), as well as the **Jeu de Paume-Site Sully** (☎ 01 47 03 12 52; www.jeudepaume.org; adult/senior, student & 13-18yr €5/2.50; ☼ noon-7pm Tue-Fri, 10am-7pm Sat & Sun), a branch of the more famous Galerie Nationale de Jeu de Paume (p128), with excellent rotating photographic exhibits. Visiting both galleries for an adult/senior, student and 13–18 year old costs €8/4. The Hôtel de Sully's two Renaissance-style courtyards alone are worth the trip here.

MUSÉE CARNAVALET

This museum, also called the **Musée de l'Histoire de Paris** (Paris History Museum; Map pp114-15; ☎ 01 44 59 58 58; www.paris.fr/musees/musee_carnav alet in French; 23 rue de Sévigné, 3e; Ⓜ St-Paul or Chemin Vert; permanent collections admission free, temporary exhibits adult/senior & student/14-25yr €7/5.50/3.50, under 14 free; ☼ 10am-6pm Tue-Sun), is in two *hôtels particuliers*. It charts the history of Paris from the Gallo-Roman period to the 20th century. Some of the nation's most important documents, paintings and objects from the French Revolution are here (Rooms 101 to 113), as is Fouquet's magnificent Art Nouveau jewellery shop from the rue Royale (Room 142) and Marcel Proust's cork-lined bedroom from his apartment on blvd Haussmann (Room 147), in which he wrote most of the 7350-page *À la Recherche du Temps Perdu*.

MUSÉE PICASSO

The **Picasso Museum** (Map pp114-15; ☎ 01 42 71 25 21; www.musee-picasso.fr; 5 rue de Thorigny, 3e; Ⓜ St-Paul or Chemin Vert; adult/18-25yr €6.70/5.20 Wed-Sat & Mon, admission for all €5.20 Sun, under 18 & 1st Sun of the month free; ☼ 9.30am-6pm Wed-Mon Apr-Sep, 9.30am-

5.30pm Wed-Mon [...] Hôtel Salé, is [...] museums and [...] the *grand m[...]* ceramic worl[...] You can also [...] sonal art coll[...] by Braque, C[...] Degas and Rousseau.

MUSÉE D'ART ET D'HISTOIRE DU JUDAÏSME

The **Musée d'Art et d'Histoire du Judaïsme** (Art & History of Judaism Museum; Map pp110-11; ☎ 01 53 01 86 60; www.mahj.org; 71 rue du Temple, 3e; Ⓜ Rambuteau; adult/student & 18-26yr €6.80/4.50, under 18yr free; ☼ 11am-6pm Mon-Fri, 10am-6pm Sun) is housed in the sumptuous, 17th-century Hôtel de St-Aignan. It was formed by combining the crafts, paintings and ritual objects from Eastern Europe and North Africa of the Musée d'Art Juif (Jewish Art Museum) in Montmartre with medieval Jewish artefacts from the Musée National du Moyen Âge (p134). Highlights include documents relating to the Dreyfus Affair (1894–1900) and works by Paris-based Jewish artists Chagall, Modigliani and Soutine.

MAISON EUROPÉENNE DE LA PHOTOGRAPHIE

The **Maison Européenne de la Photographie** (European House of Photography; Map pp110-11; ☎ 01 44 78 75 00; www.mep-fr.org in French; 5-7 rue de Fourcy, 4e; Ⓜ St-Paul or Pont Marie; adult/senior & 9-25yr €6/3, under 9 free & 5-8pm Wed free; ☼ 11am-8pm Wed-Sun), housed in the overwrought Hôtel Hénault de Cantorbe dating from the early 18th century, has cutting-edge temporary exhibits (usually retrospectives on single photographers) and a huge permanent collection on the history of photography, with particular reference to France. There are frequent showings of short films and documentaries on weekend afternoons.

MÉMORIAL DE LA SHOAH

Established in 1956, the Memorial to the Unknown Jewish Martyr has metamorphosed into the **Mémorial de la Shoah** (Memorial of the Holocaust; Map pp110-11; ☎ 01 42 77 44 72; www.memorialdelashoah.org; 17 rue Geoffroy l'Asnier, 4e; Ⓜ St-Paul; admission free; ☼ 10am-6pm Sun-Wed & Sat, 10am-10pm Thu) after a lengthy renovation. The permanent collection and temporary exhibits relate to the Holocaust and occupation of parts of France ... uring WWII; the film clips of ... orary footage and interviews are ... ending and the displays instructive ... easy to follow. The actual memorial to ... e victims of the 'Shoah', a Hebrew word meaning 'catastrophe' and synonymous in France with the Holocaust, stands at the entrance and there is a wall inscribed with the names of 76,000 men, women and children deported from France to Nazi extermination camps.

MUSÉE DES ARTS ET MÉTIERS

The **Musée des Arts et Métiers** (Arts & Crafts Museum; Map pp104-5; ☎ 01 53 01 82 00; 60 rue de Réaumur, 3e; **M** Arts et Métiers; adult/student & 18-26yr €6.50/4.50, under 18 free; ☒ 10am-6pm Tue & Wed, Fri-Sun, 10am-9.30pm Thu) is a must for anyone with a scientific (or mechanical) bent. Housed in the 18th-century priory of St-Martin des Champs, some 80,000 instruments, machines and working models from the 18th to 20th centuries are displayed across three floors. Taking pride of place is Foucault's original pendulum, which he introduced to the world in 1855.

PLACE DE LA BASTILLE

The Bastille, built during the 14th century as a fortified royal residence, is the most famous monument in Paris that no longer exists; the notorious prison – the quintessential symbol of monarchical despotism – was demolished by a Revolutionary mob on 14 July 1789 and all seven prisoners were freed. **Place de la Bastille** (Map pp114-15; **M** Bastille) in the 11e and 12e, where the prison once stood, is now a very busy traffic roundabout.

In the centre of the square is the 52m-high **Colonne de Juillet** (July Column), whose shaft of greenish bronze is topped by a gilded and winged figure of Liberty. It was erected in 1833 as a memorial to those killed in the street battles that accompanied the July Revolution of 1830; they are buried in vaults under the column. It was later consecrated as a memorial to the victims of the February Revolution of 1848.

OPÉRA BASTILLE

Paris' giant 'second' **opera house** (Map pp114-15; ☎ 0 892 899 090; www.opera-de-paris.fr in French; 2-6 place de la Bastille, 12e; **M** Bastille), designed by the Canadian architect Carlos Ott, was inaugurated

on 14 July 1989, the 200th anniversary of the storming of the Bastille. There are **guided tours** (☎ 01 40 01 19 70; adult/senior & student/under 19yr €11/9/6; 1½hr), which usually depart at 1.15pm Monday to Saturday. Tickets go on sale 15 minutes before departure at the **box office** (130 rue de Lyon, 12e; ☒ 10.30am-6.30pm Mon-Sat).

Île de la Cité

The site of the first settlement in Paris around the 3rd century BC and later the Roman town of Lutèce (Lutetia), the Île de la Cité remained the centre of royal and ecclesiastical power even after the city spread to both banks of the Seine during the Middle Ages. The buildings on the middle part of the island were demolished and rebuilt during Baron Haussmann's great urban renewal scheme of the late 19th century.

NOTRE DAME CATHEDRAL

The **Cathédrale de Notre Dame de Paris** (Cathedral of Our Lady of Paris; Map pp110-11; ☎ 01 42 34 56 10; place du Parvis Notre Dame, 4e; **M** Cité; audioguide €5; ☒ 8am-6.45pm Mon-Fri, 8am-7.45pm Sat & Sun) is the true heart of Paris; in fact, distances from Paris to all parts of metropolitan France are measured from **place du Parvis Notre Dame**, the square in front of Notre Dame. A bronze star, set in the pavement across from the main entrance, marks the exact location of **point zéro des routes de France** (point zero of French roads).

Notre Dame, the most visited site in Paris with 10 million people crossing its threshold a year, is not just a masterpiece of French Gothic architecture but has also been the focus of Catholic Paris for seven centuries. In recent years its western façade has had a thorough cleaning, which makes it even more attractive and inspiring (though be aware that many of the saints carved in stone in the main portals are modern-day copies).

Constructed on a site occupied by earlier churches – and, a millennium before that, a Gallo-Roman temple – it was begun in 1163 and largely completed by the mid-14th century. Architect Eugène Emmanuel Viollet-le-Duc carried out extensive renovations in the 19th century. The interior is 130m long, 48m wide and 35m high and can accommodate more than 6000 worshippers.

Notre Dame is known for its sublime balance, although if you look closely you'll see many minor asymmetrical elements introduced to avoid monotony, in accordance with standard Gothic practice. These include the slightly different shapes of each of the three main portals, whose statues were once brightly coloured to make them more effective as a *Biblia pauperum* – a 'Bible of the poor' to help the illiterate understand the Old Testament stories, the Passion of the Christ and the lives of the saints. One of the best views of Notre Dame is from **Square Jean XXIII**, the lovely little park behind the cathedral, where you can see the mass of ornate **flying buttresses** that encircle the chancel and support its walls and roof.

Inside, exceptional features include three spectacular **rose windows**, the most renowned of which is the 10m-wide one over the western façade above the 7800-pipe organ, and the window on the northern side of the transept, which has remained virtually unchanged since the 13th century. The central choir, with its carved wooden stalls and statues representing the Passion of the Christ, is also noteworthy. There are free guided tours of the cathedral in English at noon on Wednesday and Thursday and at 2.30pm on Saturday.

The **trésor** (treasury; adult/student/3-12yr €3/2/1; 9.30am-6pm Mon-Sat, 1.30-5.30pm Sun) in the southeastern transept contains artwork, relics, liturgical objects, and church plate – some of them of questionable origin. Among these is the Ste-Couronne, the 'Holy Crown', which is purportedly the wreath of thorns placed on Jesus' head before he was crucified, which was brought here in the mid-13th century. It is exhibited at 3pm on each first Friday of the month, every Friday during Lent and from 10am to 5pm on Good Friday (the Friday before Easter).

The entrance to the **tours de Notre Dame** (Notre Dame towers; ☎ 01 53 10 07 00; www.monum.fr; rue du Cloître Notre Dame; adult/student & 18-25yr €7.50/4.80, under 18yr & 1st Sun Oct-Mar free; 9.30am-7.30pm daily Apr-Jun & Sep, 9am-7.30pm Mon-Fri, 9am-11pm Sat & Sun Jul & Aug, 10am-5.30pm daily Oct-Mar), which can be climbed, is from the **North Tower**, to the right and around the corner as you walk out of the cathedral's main doorway. The 387 spiralling steps bring you to the top of the west façade, where you'll find yourself face-to-face with many of the cathedral's most frightening gargoyles, the 13-tonne bell Emmanuel (all the cathedral's bells are named) in the **South Tower** and a spectacular view of Paris.

STE-CHAPELLE
The **Ste-Chapelle** (Holy Chapel; Map pp110-11; ☎ 01 53 40 60 97; www.monum.fr; 4 blvd du Palais, 1er; Ⓜ Cité; adult/18-25yr €6.50/4.50, under 18yr & 1st Sun Oct-Mar free; 9.30am-6pm Mar-Oct, 9am-5pm Nov-Feb), the most exquisite of Paris' Gothic monuments, is tucked away within the walls of the **Palais de Justice** (Law Courts). The 'walls' of the **upper chapel** are sheer curtains of richly coloured and finely detailed **stained glass**, which bathe the chapel in an extraordinary light. Built in just under three years (compared with nearly 200 years for Notre Dame), Ste-Chapelle was consecrated in 1248. The chapel was conceived by Louis IX to house his personal collection of holy relics (now kept in the treasury of Notre Dame).

A joint ticket for both the Conciergerie (below) and for Ste-Chapelle costs adult/18 to 25 years €9.50/7.

CONCIERGERIE
The **Conciergerie** (Map pp110-11; ☎ 01 53 40 60 97; www.monum.fr; 2 blvd du Palais, 1er; Ⓜ Cité; adult/18-25yr €6.50/4.50, under 18yr & 1st Sun Oct-Mar free; 9.30am-6pm Mar-Oct, 9am-5pm Nov-Feb), built in the 14th century for the concierge of the Palais de la Cité, was the main prison during the Reign of Terror (p94) and was used to incarcerate alleged enemies of the Revolution before they were brought before the Revolutionary Tribunal in the Palais de Justice next door. Among the 2700 prisoners held in the *cachots* (dungeons) here before being sent in tumbrels to the guillotine were Queen Marie-Antoinette and, as the Revolution began to turn on its own, the Revolutionary radicals Danton and Robespierre.

The Gothic14th century **Salle des Gens d'Armes** (Cavalrymen's Hall) is a fine example of the Rayonnant Gothic style. It is the largest surviving medieval hall in Europe. The **Tour de l'Horloge** (clock tower; cnr blvd du Palais & quai de l'Horloge), built in 1353, has held a public clock aloft since 1370.

PONT NEUF
The sparkling-white stone of Paris' oldest bridge, **Pont Neuf** (Map pp110-11; Ⓜ Pont Neuf) – literally 'New Bridge' – has linked the western end of the Île de la Cité with both banks of the Seine since 1607, when King Henri IV inaugurated it by crossing the bridge on a white stallion. The seven arches, best

seen from the river, are decorated with humorous and grotesque figures of barbers, dentists, pickpockets, loiterers etc.

Île St-Louis

The smaller of the Seine's two islands, Île St-Louis is just downstream from the Île de la Cité. In the early 17th century, when it was actually two uninhabited islets (Île Notre Dame and Île aux Vaches), a building contractor and two financiers worked out a deal with Louis XIII to create one island out of the two and build two stone bridges to the mainland. In exchange they would receive the right to subdivide and sell the newly created real estate. This they did with great success, and by 1664 the entire island was covered with fine new and airy houses facing the quays and the river rather than the inner courtyards as was common then.

Today, the island's 17th-century, greystone houses and the shops that line the streets and quays impart a village-like, provincial calm. The central thoroughfare, **rue St-Louis en l'Île**, is home to a number of upmarket art galleries, boutiques and the French baroque **Église St-Louis en l'Île** (Map pp110-11; ☎ 01 46 34 11 60; 19bis rue St-Louis en l'Île, 4e; Ⓜ Pont Marie; ☒ 9am-noon & 3-7pm Tue-Sun), built between 1664 and 1726. We think the area around **Pont St-Louis**, the bridge linking the island with the Île de la Cité, and **Pont Louis Philippe**, the bridge to the Marais, is one of the most romantic spots in all of Paris.

Latin Quarter & Jardin des Plantes

Known as the Quartier Latin because all communication between students and professors here officially took place in Latin until the Revolution, this area of the 5e has been the centre of Parisian higher education since the Middle Ages. It still has a large population of students and academics affiliated with the Sorbonne (now part of the University of Paris system), the Collège de France, the École Normale Supérieure and other institutions of higher learning. To the southeast, the Jardin des Plantes, with its tropical greenhouses and Musée National d'Histoire Naturelle, offers a bucolic alternative to cobbles and chalkboards.

MUSÉE NATIONAL DU MOYEN ÂGE

Sometimes called the Musée de Cluny, the **Musée National du Moyen Âge** (National Museum of the Middle Ages; Map pp110-11; ☎ 01 53 73 78 16, 01 53 73 78 00; www.musee-moyenage.fr; Thermes & Hôtel de Cluny, 6 place Paul Painlevé, 5e; Ⓜ Cluny-La Sorbonne or St-Michel; adult/senior, student & 18-25yr €6.50/4.50, under 18yr & 1st Sun of month free; ☒ 9.15am-5.45pm Wed-Mon) is housed in two structures: the **frigidarium** (cooling room) and other remains of Gallo-Roman baths dating from around AD 200, and the late-15th-century **Hôtel de Cluny**, considered the finest example of medieval civil architecture in Paris.

The spectacular displays at the museum include statuary, illuminated manuscripts, armaments, furnishings, and objects made of gold, ivory and enamel. But nothing compares with *La Dame à la Licorne* (The Lady with the Unicorn), a sublime series of late-15th-century tapestries from the southern Netherlands now hung in circular Room 13 on the 1st floor. The **Forêt de la Licorne**, a medieval-style garden, is north of the museum.

SORBONNE

Paris' most renowned university, the **Sorbonne** (Map pp118-19; 12 rue de la Sorbonne, 5e; Ⓜ Luxembourg or Cluny-La Sorbonne) was founded in 1253 by Robert de Sorbon, confessor to Louis IX, as a college for 16 impoverished theology students. Today, the Sorbonne's main complex (bounded by rue de la Sorbonne, rue des Écoles, rue St-Jacques and rue Cujas) and other buildings in the vicinity house most of the 13 autonomous universities that were created when the University of Paris was reorganised after violent student protests in 1968.

PANTHÉON

The domed landmark now known simply as the **Panthéon** (Map pp114-15; ☎ 01 44 32 18 00; www.monum.fr; place du Panthéon, 5e; Ⓜ Luxembourg; adult/18-25yr €7.50/4.80, under 18yr & 1st Sun Oct-Mar free; ☒ 10am-6.30pm Apr-Sep, 10am-6.15pm Oct-Mar) was commissioned around 1750 as an abbey church dedicated to Ste Geneviève, but because of financial and structural problems it wasn't completed until 1789 – not a good year for churches to open in France. Two years later, the Constituent Assembly converted it into a secular mausoleum for the *grands hommes de l'époque de la liberté française* (great men of the era of French liberty).

The Panthéon is a superb example of 18th-century neoclassicism but its ornate marble interior is gloomy in the extreme. The 80-odd permanent residents of the crypt include Voltaire, Jean-Jacques Rousseau, Victor Hugo, Émile Zola, Jean Moulin and Nobel Prize winner Marie Curie, whose remains were moved here in 1995 – the first woman to be honoured with that privilege.

JARDIN DES PLANTES

Paris' 24-hectare **Jardin des Plantes** (Botanical Gardens; Map pp118-19 & Map pp120-1; ☎ 01 40 79 56 01, 01 40 79 36 00; 57 rue Cuvier, 5e; Ⓜ Gare d'Austerlitz, Censier Daubenton or Jussieu; ☾ 7.30am-5.30 to 7.30pm according to the season) was founded in 1626 as a medicinal herb garden for Louis XIII. Here you'll find the Eden-like **Jardin d'Hiver** (Winter Garden), which is also called the **Serres Tropicales** (Tropical Greenhouses) and currently under renovation; the **Jardin Alpin** (Alpine Garden; admission free Mon-Fri, €1.50 Sat & Sun; ☾ 8am-5pm Mon-Fri, 1.30-6pm Sat, 1.30-6.30pm Sun Apr-Sep), with 2000 mountain plants; and the gardens of the **École de Botanique** (admission free; ☾ 8am-5pm Mon-Fri), which is where students of the School of Botany 'practise'.

The **Ménagerie du Jardin des Plantes** (Botanical Garden Zoo; ☎ 01 40 79 37 94; 57 rue Cuvier & 3 quai St-Bernard, 5e; Ⓜ Jussieu or Gare d'Austerlitz; adult/senior, student & 4-15yr €7/5; ☾ 9am-6pm Mon-Sat, 9am-6.30pm Sun Apr-Sep, 9am-5pm Mon-Sat, 9am-5.30pm Sun Oct-Mar), a medium-sized (5.5-hectare, 1000 animals) zoo in the northern section of the garden, was founded in 1794. During the Prussian siege of Paris in 1870, most of the animals were eaten by starving Parisians.

Musée National d'Histoire Naturelle

The **Musée National d'Histoire Naturelle** (National Museum of Natural History; ☎ 01 40 79 30 00; www.mnhn .fr in French; 57 rue Cuvier, 5e; Ⓜ Censier Daubenton or Gare d'Austerlitz), created by a decree of the Revolutionary Convention in 1793, was the site of important scientific research during the 19th century. It is housed in several different buildings (all on Map pp118–19) along the southern edge of the Jardin des Plantes.

The **Grande Galerie de l'Évolution** (Great Gallery of Evolution; Map pp118-19; 36 rue Geoffroy St-Hilaire, 5e; adult/4-13yr €8/6; ☾ 10am-6pm Wed-Mon) has some imaginative exhibits on evolution and mankind's effect on the global ecosystem, spread over four floors and 6000 sq metres of space. The **Salle des Espèces Menacées et des Espèces Disparues** on level 2 displays extremely

rare specimens of endangered and extinct species while the **Salle de Découverte** (Room of Discovery) on level 1 houses interactive exhibits for kids.

The **Galerie de Minéralogie, de Géologie** (36 rue Geoffroy St-Hilaire; adult/4-13yr €6/4; ☾ 10am-5pm Mon-Fri, 10am-6pm Sat & Sun Apr-Oct, 10am-5pm Wed-Mon Nov-Mar), which covers mineralogy and geology, has an amazing exhibit of giant natural crystals and a basement display of jewellery and other objects made from minerals. The **Galerie d'Anatomie Comparée et de Paléontologie** (2 rue Buffon; adult/4-13yr €6/4; ☾ 10am-5pm Mon-Fri, 10am-6pm Sat & Sun Apr-Oct, 10am-5pm Wed-Mon Nov-Mar) has displays on comparative anatomy and palaeontology (the study of fossils).

INSTITUT DU MONDE ARABE

The **Institut du Monde Arabe** (Institute of the Arab World; Map pp118-19; ☎ 01 40 51 38 38; www.imarabe .org in French; 1 place Mohammed V, 5e; Ⓜ Cardinal Lemoine or Jussieu), set up by France and 20 Arab countries to promote cultural contacts between the Arab world and the West, is housed in a highly praised building (1987) that successfully mixes modern and traditional Arab and Western elements.

The **museum** (adult/senior, student & 18-25yr €5/4, under 18 free; ☾ 10am-6pm Tue-Fri, 10am-7pm Sat & Sun), spread over three floors and entered via the 7th floor, displays 9th- to 19th-century art and artisanship from all over the Arab world, as well as instruments from astronomy and other fields of scientific endeavour in which Arab technology once led the world. Temporary exhibitions (enter from quai Saint Bernard) charge a separate fee (usually between €7 and €9 for adults and €5 and €7 for the reduced tariff). Audioguides are €5. A ticket valid for the permanent collection and temporary exhibitions costs €13/11.

MOSQUÉE DE PARIS

The central **Mosquée de Paris** (Paris Mosque; Map pp118-19; ☎ 01 45 35 97 33; www.mosquee-de-paris.org; 2bis place du Puits de l'Ermite, 5e; Ⓜ Censier Daubenton or Place Monge; adult/senior & 7-25yr €3/2; ☾ 9am-noon & 2-6pm Sat-Thu), with its striking 26m-high minaret, was built in 1926 in the ornate Moorish style. Visitors must be modestly dressed and remove their shoes at the entrance to the prayer hall. The complex includes a North African–style **salon de thé** (tearoom) and **restaurant** (p169) and a **hammam**

(☎ 01 43 31 18 14, 01 43 31 38 20; admission €15; ⊙ men 2-9pm Tue & 10am-9pm Sun, women 10am-9pm Mon, Wed, Thu & Sat, 2-9pm Fri), a traditional Turkish-style bathhouse where a massage costs €10 for 10 minutes.

St-Germain, Odéon & Luxembourg

Centuries ago the Église St-Germain des Prés and its affiliated abbey owned most of today's 6e and 7e. The neighbourhood around the church began to develop in the late 17th century, and these days it is celebrated for its heterogeneity. Cafés such as Les Deux Magots and Café de Flore (p176) were favourite hang-outs of postwar, Left Bank intellectuals and the places where existentialism was born.

ÉGLISE ST-GERMAIN DES PRÉS

Romanesque Église St-Germain des Prés (Church of St Germanus of the Fields; Map pp110-11; ☎ 01 55 42 81 33; 3 place St-Germain des Prés, 6e; Ⓜ St-Germain des Prés; ⊙ 8am-7pm Mon-Sat, 9am-8pm Sun), which is the oldest church in Paris, was built in the 11th century on the site of a 6th-century abbey and was the dominant church in Paris until the advent of Notre Dame. It has since been altered many times, but Chapelle de St-Symphorien, to the right as you enter, was part of the original abbey and is the final resting place of St Germanus (AD 496–576), the first bishop of Paris. Columns in the chancel were taken from the Merovingian abbey. The bell tower over the western entrance has changed little since 990, although the spire dates only from the 19th century.

ÉGLISE ST-SULPICE

The Italianate Église St-Sulpice (Church of St Sulpicius; Map pp110-11; ☎ 01 46 33 21 78; place St-Sulpice, 6e; Ⓜ St-Sulpice; ⊙ 8.30am-7.15pm Mon-Sat, 8.30am-7.45pm Sun), lined with small side chapels inside, was built between 1646 and 1780. The façade, designed by a Florentine architect, has two rows of superimposed columns and is topped by two towers. The neoclassical décor of the vast interior is influenced by the Counter-Reformation.

The frescoes in the Chapelle des Sts-Anges (Chapel of the Holy Angels), first to the right as you enter, depict Jacob wrestling with the angel (to the left) and Michael the Archangel doing battle with Satan (to the right) and were painted by Eugène Delacroix between 1855 and 1861.

VENI, VIDI, DA VINCI

With apologies to J Caesar, we came, we saw, we Da Vinci'd – and not exactly willingly. The shooting of the film of Dan Brown's runaway bestseller was wrapping up in Paris as we researched our part of this book and la code – and we're not talking about the one to the porte cochère (p96) downstairs – was on everyone's lèvres (lips). But certainly not ours. We'll be honest – we didn't like The Da Vinci Code and what's more we don't like the idea that fiction should play any role as guidebook – especially when the author gets his compass points as mixed up as Mr Brown does. Versailles (p211) is 'northwest of Paris' while rue Haxo (where the Depository Bank of Zurich and the cryptex is located) is to the west near the Bois de Boulogne – where we get a little tour of the unusual sexual activity that takes place (we're told) there after dark (p141). Rue Haxo is actually on the opposite side of Paris near the Cimetière du Père Lachaise where, with the exception of Jim Morrison's grave (p144), there is probably little action in the wee hours. And those are just the author's directions... No, we say leave guidebooks to the experts – horses for courses and all that – so that's why if you are really keen on seeing the sites named in the book, you should take a tour like the one offered by Paris Walks (p150). No-one knows their way round like these guys do and why shouldn't they? One of the co-founders, Peter Caine, has written The Definitive Guide to the Da Vinci Code (Bartillat; €12). What we want to know is how come no-one ever mentions the fact that Leonardo gave up the ghost in France (at Amboise in the Loire region on 2 May 1519 to be precise; p438)? Is that in the sequel or have we just told Mr Brown something valuable? Can we, like the tourism industry in Paris, ca$h in? No one here is complaining about the book. It's brought the free-spending Yanks back – 1.4 million a year, in fact – after that 'significant dip' in trans-Atlantic arrivals in the wake of the 11 September attacks and the silly fracas between the USA and France over the war in Iraq. Like Mr Brown, Parisians in tourism are laughing – all the way to the bank (wherever it might be).

Until recently, Église St-Sulpice was 'just another church' visited by handfuls of dedicated architecture buffs or fans of Delacroix. Then Dan Brown used it as the setting for a crucial discovery (and murder) in his *The Da Vinci Code* (opposite) and the rest is, well, history. Use your elbows to enter.

JARDIN DU LUXEMBOURG
When the weather is fine Parisians of all ages flock to the formal terraces and chestnut groves of the 23-hectare **Jardin du Luxembourg** (Luxembourg Garden; Map pp118-19; Ⓜ Luxembourg; ☯ 7.30am to 8.15am-5pm to 10pm according to the season) to read, relax and sunbathe. There are a number of activities for children here, and in the southern part of the garden you'll find urban **orchards** as well as the honey-producing **Rucher du Luxembourg** (Luxembourg Apiary).

Jardin du Luxembourg (Luxembourg Palace; rue de Vaugirard, 6e), at the northern end of the garden, was built for Marie de Médicis, Henri IV's consort; it has housed the **Sénat** (Senate), the upper house of the French parliament, since 1958. There are **guided tours** (reservations ☎ 01 44 54 19 30; adult/under 25 €8/6) of the interior usually at 10.30am on the first Sunday of each month, but you must book by the preceding Tuesday.

The **Musée du Luxembourg** (Luxembourg Museum; ☎ 01 42 34 25 95; www.museeduluxembourg.fr in French; 19 rue de Vaugirard, 6e; Ⓜ Luxembourg or St-Sulpice; ☯ 11am-10pm Mon, Fri & Sat, 11am-7pm Tue-Thu, 9am-7pm Sun), which opened at the end of the 19th century in the orangery of the Palais du Luxembourg as an exhibition space for living artists, hosts prestigious temporary art exhibitions. Admission can cost up to €10 (students & 10 to 25 year olds €8), but it depends on the exhibit. An audioguide is €4.50.

Montparnasse
After WWI, writers, poets and artists of the avant-garde abandoned Montmartre on the Right Bank and crossed the Seine, shifting the centre of artistic ferment to the area around blvd du Montparnasse. Chagall, Modigliani, Léger, Soutine, Miró, Kandinsky, Picasso, Stravinsky, Hemingway, Ezra Pound and Cocteau, as well as such political exiles as Lenin and Trotsky, all used to hang out in the cafés and brasseries for which the quarter became famous. Montparnasse remained a creative centre until the mid-

1930s. Today, especially since the const. tion of the Gare Montparnasse comple. there is little to remind visitors of the area's bohemian past except the now very touristed restaurants and cafés.

TOUR MONTPARNASSE
A steel-and-smoked-glass eyesore built in 1974, the 210m-high **Tour Montparnasse** (Montparnasse Tower; Map pp108-9; ☎ 01 45 38 52 56; www.tourmontparnasse56.com; rue de l'Arrivée, 15e; Ⓜ Montparnasse Bienvenüe; adult/student & 16-20yr/7-15yr €8.50/6.50/4, under 7 free; ☯ 9.30am-11.30pm Apr-Sep, 9.30am-10.30pm Sun-Thu, 9.30am-11pm Fri & Sat Oct-Mar) affords spectacular views over the city – a view, we might add, that does not take in this ghastly oversized lipstick tube. A lift takes you up to the 56th-floor enclosed **observatory**, recently redesigned with an exhibition centre, a film about Paris, interactive terminals and a bar. You can finish your visit with a hike up the stairs to the **open-air terrace** on the 59th floor.

CIMETIÈRE DU MONTPARNASSE
The **Cimetière du Montparnasse** (Montparnasse Cemetery; Map pp108-9; blvd Edgar Quinet & rue Froidevaux, 14e; Ⓜ Edgar Quinet or Raspail; ☯ 8am-6pm Mon-Fri, 8.30am-6pm Sat, 9am-6pm Sun mid-Mar-early Nov; 8am-5.30pm Mon-Fri, 8.30am-5.30pm Sat, 9am-5.30pm Sun early Nov-mid-Mar) received its first 'lodger' in 1824. It contains the tombs of such illustrious personages as the poet Charles Baudelaire, writer Guy de Maupassant, playwright Samuel Beckett, sculptor Constantin Brancusi, painter Chaim Soutine, photographer Man Ray, industrialist André Citroën, Captain Alfred Dreyfus of the infamous Dreyfus affair, actress Jean Seberg, philosopher Jean-Paul Sartre, writer Simone de Beauvoir and the crooner Serge Gainsbourg. Maps showing the location of the tombs are available free from the **conservation office** (☎ 01 44 10 86 50; 3 blvd Edgar Quinet, 14e).

CATACOMBES
In 1785 it was decided to solve the hygiene and aesthetic problems posed by Paris' overflowing cemeteries by exhuming the bones and storing them in the tunnels of three disused quarries. One ossuary created in 1810 is now known as the **Catacombes** (☎ 01 43 22 47 63; Map pp98-9; www.catacombes.paris .fr in French; 1 av Colonel Henri Roi-Tanguy, 14e; Ⓜ Denfert Rochereau; adult/senior & student/14-25yr €5/3.30/2.50,

...5pm Tue-Sun), which can be ...cending 20m (130 steps) ...visitors follow 1.7km of ...ridors in which the bones ...lions of former Parisians are neatly stacked along the walls. During WWII these tunnels were used as a headquarters by the Resistance; so-called *cataphiles* looking for cheap thrills are often caught roaming the tunnels at night (there's a fine of €60).

The route through the Catacombes begins at a small, dark green *belle époque*–style building in the centre of a grassy area of av Colonel Henri Roi-Tanguy, the new name of place Denfert Rochereau. The exit is at the top of 83 steps on rue Remy Dumoncel (**M** Mouton Duvernet), 700m southwest of place Denfert Rochereau, where a guard will check your bag for 'borrowed' bones.

Faubourg St-Germain & Invalides

Paris' most fashionable neighbourhood during the 18th century was Faubourg St-Germain in the 7e, the area between the Musée d'Orsay and, a kilometre to the south, rue de Babylon. Some of the most interesting mansions, many of which now serve as embassies, cultural centres and government ministries, are along three streets running east to west: rue de Lille, rue de Grenelle and rue de Varenne. The **Hôtel Matignon** (Map pp108-9; 57 rue de Varenne, 7e) has been the official residence of the French prime minister since the start of the Fifth Republic in 1958. Here you'll also find the Hôtel des Invalides containing, among other things, the earthy remains of Napoleon Bonaparte. The architecturally impressive Musée du Quai Branly, which opened in 2006, is the feather in the cap of the 7e arrondissement.

MUSÉE D'ORSAY

The **Musée d'Orsay** (Orsay Museum; Map pp108-9; ☎ 01 40 49 48 14; www.musee-orsay.fr; 62 rue de Lille, 7e; **M** Musée d'Orsay or Solférino; adult/senior & 18-25yr €7.50/5.50, under 18 & 1st Sun of the month free; ☽ 9.30am-6pm Tue, Wed, Fri-Sun, 9.30am-9.45pm Thu) is housed in a former train station (1900) facing the Seine from quai Anatole France. It displays France's national collection of paintings, sculptures, *objets d'art* and other works produced between the 1840s and 1914, including the fruits of the impressionist, postimpressionist and Art Nouveau move-

ments. The **Musée National d'Art Moderne** (p129) at the Centre Pompidou then picks up the baton.

Many visitors to the museum go straight to the upper level (lit by a skylight) to see the famous **impressionist paintings** by Monet, Pissarro, Renoir, Sisley, Degas and Manet and the **postimpressionist works** by Cézanne, Van Gogh, Seurat and Matisse, but there's also lots to see on the ground floor, including some early works by Manet, Monet, Renoir and Pissarro. The middle level has some superb **Art Nouveau rooms**.

English-language tours (☎ information 01 40 49 48 48; admission fee plus €6.50/4.70), lasting 1½ hours, include the 'Masterpieces of the Musée d'Orsay' tour, departing at 11.30am Tuesday to Saturday, and an in-depth tour focusing on the impressionists at 2.30pm on Tuesday and 4pm on Thursday at least once a month. The 1½-hour **audioguide tour** (€5.50), available in six languages, points out around 80 major works. Be aware that tickets are valid all day so you can leave and re-enter the museum as you please. The reduced entrance fee of €5.50 applies to everyone after 4.15pm (8pm on Thursday) and all day on Sunday.

MUSÉE RODIN

The **Musée Rodin** (Rodin Museum; Map pp108-9; ☎ 01 44 18 61 10; www.musee-rodin.fr; 77 rue de Varenne, 7e; **M** Varenne; adult/senior & 18-25yr €7/5, under 18 free & 1st Sun of the month free, garden only €1; ☽ 9.30am-5.45pm Tue-Sun Apr-Sep, 9.30am-4.45pm Tue-Sun Oct-Mar), one of our favourite cultural attractions in Paris, is both a sublime museum and one of the most relaxing spots in the city, with a lovely **garden**, full of sculptures and shade trees, in which to rest. Rooms on two floors of this 18th-century residence display extraordinarily vital bronze and marble sculptures by Rodin, including casts of some of his most celebrated works: *The Hand of God, The Burghers of Calais, Cathedral,* that perennial crowd-pleaser *The Thinker* and the incomparable *The Kiss.* There are also some 15 works by Camille Claudel (1864–1943), sister of the writer Paul Claudel and Rodin's mistress.

MUSÉE DU QUAI BRANLY

The long-awaited **Musée du Quai Branly** (☎ 01 56 61 70 00; www.quaibranly.fr; 37 quai Branly, 7e; **M** Pont de l'Alma; adult/senior & 18-25yr €10/7.50, under 18 & 1st Sun of the month free; ☽ 10am-6.30pm Tue, Wed & Fri-Sun, 10am-9.30pm Thu), housed in architect

Jean Nouvel's impressive new structure of glass, wood and turf pp108–9on the Seine, opened to great fanfare – and controversy (it is President Jacques Chirac's most important *grand projet* to date) – in June 2006. The museum combines the collection of the erstwhile Musée National des Arts d'Afrique et d'Océanie in the Bois de Vincennes and some items from the Musée de l'Homme (p140) in the Palais de Chaillot. Thus you'll find art and sculpture from the south Pacific, north and western and central Africa, the Americas and Asia – from Siberia to central Asia. The idea is to raise the level of appreciation of so-called primitive and non-Western art in the minds of the general public and in sum it works. The delightful experimental garden was designed by Gilles Clément.

HÔTEL DES INVALIDES

The **Hôtel des Invalides** (Map pp108-9; M Varenne or La Tour Maubourg) was built in the 1670s by Louis XIV to provide housing for some 4000 *invalides* (disabled war veterans). On 14 July 1789 a mob forced its way into the building and, after some fierce fighting, seized 28,000 rifles before heading on to the prison at Bastille and the start of the French Revolution.

North of the Hôtel des Invalides' main courtyard, the so-called **Cour d'Honneur**, is the **Musée de l'Armée** (Army Museum; Map pp108-9; ☎ 01 44 42 38 78; www.invalides.org; 129 rue de Grenelle, 7e; adult/senior, student & 18-25yr €7.50/5.50, under 18 free; ☑ 10am-6pm Apr-Sep, 10am-5pm Oct-Mar, closed 1st Mon of the month), which holds the nation's largest collection on the history of the French military. To the south are the **Église St-Louis des Invalides**, once used by soldiers, and the **Église du Dôme**, with its sparkling dome (1677–1735) visible throughout the city, which received the remains of Napoleon in 1840. The very extravagant **Tombeau de Napoléon 1er** (Napoleon I's Tomb; ☑ 10am-6pm Apr-Sep, 10am-5pm Oct-Mar, closed 1st Mon of month), in the centre of the church, consists of six coffins that fit into one another rather like a Russian *matryoshka* doll.

Eiffel Tower Area & 16e Arrondissement

The very symbol of Paris, the Eiffel Tower, is surrounded by open areas on both banks of the Seine, which take in both the 7e and 16e, the most chichi (and snobby) part of the capital. It's not everyone's *tasse de thé* (cup of tea) but there are several outstanding museums and sights in this part of the Right Bank.

EIFFEL TOWER

The **Tour Eiffel** (Map pp108-9; ☎ 01 44 11 23 23; www.tour-eiffel.fr; M Champ de Mars-Tour Eiffel or Bir Hakeim; ☑ lifts 9.30am-11pm Sep-mid-Jun, 9am-midnight mid-Jun–Aug, stairs 9.30am-6.30pm Sep-mid-Jun, 9am-midnight mid-Jun–Aug) faced massive opposition from Paris' artistic and literary elite when it was built for the 1889 Exposition Universelle (World Fair), marking the centenary of the Revolution. The 'metal asparagus', as some Parisians snidely called it, was almost torn down in 1909 but was spared because it proved an ideal platform for the transmitting antennas needed for the new science of radiotelegraphy. It welcomed two million visitors the first year it opened and just under three times that number – 5.8 million, in fact – make their way to the top each year today.

The Eiffel Tower, named after its designer, Gustave Eiffel, is 324m high, including the TV antenna at the tip. This figure can vary by as much as 15cm, however, as the tower's 10,000 tonnes of iron, held together by 2.5 million rivets, expand in warm weather and contract when it's cold.

Three levels are open to the public. The lifts (in the west and north pillars), which follow a curved trajectory, cost €4.20 to the 1st platform (57m above the ground), €7.70 to the 2nd (115m) and €11 to the 3rd (276m). Children aged three to 11 pay €2.30, €4.20 or €6, respectively; there are no senior, youth or student discounts though children under three years go free. You can avoid the lift queues by taking the stairs (over/under 25 years €3.80/3) in the south pillar to the 1st and 2nd platforms.

CHAMP DE MARS

Running southeast from the Eiffel Tower, the grassy **Champ de Mars** (Field of Mars; Map pp108-9; M Champ de Mars-Tour Eiffel or École Militaire) is named after the Roman god of war. It was originally a parade ground for the cadets of the 18th-century **École Militaire** (Military Academy), the vast, French-classical building (1772) at the southeastern end of the park, which counted Napoleon among its graduates.

PALAIS DE CHAILLOT & JARDINS DU TROCADÉRO

The two curved and colonnaded wings of the **Palais de Chaillot** (Chaillot Palace; Map pp108-9; Ⓜ Trocadéro), built for the 1937 World Exhibition held here, and the terrace in between them afford an exceptional panorama of the Jardins du Trocadéro, the Seine and the Eiffel Tower.

The palace's western wing contains two interesting museums. The **Musée de l'Homme** (Museum of Mankind; Map pp108-9; ☎ 01 44 05 72 72; www.mnhn.fr in French; 17 place du Trocadéro, 16e; adult/senior & student/4-16yr €7/5/3; ☉ 9.45am-5.15pm Mon, Wed-Fri, 10am-6.30pm Sat & Sun) focuses on human development, ethnology, population and population growth. The **Musée de la Marine** (Maritime Museum; Map pp108-9; ☎ 01 53 65 69 69; www.musee-marine.fr; 17 place du Trocadéro; adult/student & 18-25yr €6.50/4.50, under 18 free; ☉ 10am-6pm Wed-Mon) examines France's naval adventures from the 17th century until today.

Spreading out below the Palais de Chaillot are the **Jardins du Trocadéro** (Trocadero Gardens; Map pp108-9; Ⓜ Trocadéro), whose fountains and statue garden are grandly illuminated at night. They are named after a Spanish stronghold near Cádiz that was captured by the French in 1823.

MUSÉE GUIMET DES ARTS ASIATIQUES

The **Musée Guimet des Arts Asiatiques** (Guimet Museum of Asian Art; Map pp102-3; ☎ 01 56 52 53 00; www.museeguimet.fr; 6 place d'Iéna; Ⓜ Iéna; permanent collections adult/18-25yr & everyone on Sun €7/5, under 18 & 1st Sun of the month free; ☉ 10am-6pm Wed-Mon) is France's foremost repository for Asian art and has sculptures, paintings, objets d'art and religious articles from Afghanistan, India, Nepal, Pakistan, Tibet, Cambodia, China, Japan and Korea. Part of the original collection – Buddhist paintings and sculptures brought to Paris in 1876 by collector Émile Guimet – is housed in the annexe called the **Galeries du Panthéon Bouddhique du Japon et de la Chine** (Buddhist Pantheon Galleries of Japan & China; ☎ 01 47 23 61 65; 19 av d'Iéna; Ⓜ Iéna; admission free; ☉ 9.45am-5.45pm Wed-Mon) in the sumptuous Hôtel Heidelbach a short distance to the north. Don't miss the wonderful **Japanese garden** (☉ 1-5pm Wed-Mon) here.

PALAIS DE TOKYO

The **Tokyo Palace** (Map pp102-3; ☎ 01 47 23 38 86; www.palaisdetokyo.com; 13 av du Président Wilson, 16e;

adult/senior & 18-26yr €6/4.50, under 18 free, 1st Sun of the month €1; ☉ noon-midnight Tue-Sun), like the Musée d'Art Moderne de la Ville de Paris, next door in yet another 1937 World Exhibition building, opened in 2002 as a 'Site de Création Contemporaine' (Site for Contemporary Arts). Translation: it has no permanent collection and plans no exhibitions of a single artist or theme but showcases ephemeral artwork, installations and performances. It's an event-driven rather than a static museum and well worth a visit.

FLAME OF LIBERTY MEMORIAL

Southeast of the Musée Guimet and over the border to the 8e is **place de l'Alma** (Map pp102-3; Ⓜ Alma-Marceau). This is the spot where on 31 August 1997 in the underpass running parallel to the Seine, Diana, Princess of Wales, was killed in an automobile accident along with her companion, Dodi Fayed, and their chauffeur, Henri Paul. The bronze **Flame of Liberty** is a replica of the one topping the torch of the Statue of Liberty and was placed here by Paris-based US firms in 1987 on the centenary of the International Herald Tribune newspaper as a symbol of friendship between France and the USA. It became something of a memorial to Diana and was decorated with flowers, photographs, graffiti and personal notes for almost five years. In 2002 it was renovated and cleaned and, this being an age of short (or no) memories, there are now very few reminders of the tragedy that happened so close by.

MUSÉE DES ÉGOUTS DE PARIS

The **Musée des Égouts de Paris** (Paris Sewers Museum; Map pp108-9; ☎ 01 53 68 27 81; place de la Résistance, 7e; Ⓜ Pont de l'Alma; adult/student & 5-16yr €4/3.20, under 5 free; ☉ 11am-5pm Sat-Wed May-Sep, 11am-4pm Sat-Wed Oct-Dec & Feb-Apr) is a working museum whose entrance – a rectangular maintenance hole topped with a kiosk – is across the street from 93 quai d'Orsay, 7e. Raw sewage flows beneath your feet as you walk through 480m of odoriferous tunnels, passing artefacts illustrating the development of Paris' waste-water disposal system. It'll take your breath away, it will.

Bois de Boulogne

The 845-hectare **Bois de Boulogne** (Boulogne Wood; Map pp98-9; blvd Maillot, 16e; Ⓜ Porte Maillot) on the western edge of Paris just beyond the 16e owes its informal layout to Baron Haussmann, who was inspired by Hyde Park in London. Be warned that the Bois de Boulogne becomes a distinctly adult playground after dark, especially along the Allée de Longchamp, where male, female and tranny prostitutes cruise for clients.

The wood's enclosed **Parc de Bagatelle** (info ☎ 3975, 0 820 007 575; ⊗ 8am-8pm Mon-Fri, 9am-8pm Sat & Sun May-Aug, 8am-7pm Mon-Fri, 9am-7pm Sat & Sun Sep-Apr) in the northwestern corner, is renowned for its beautiful gardens surrounding the 1775-built **Château de Bagatelle** (☎ 01 40 67 97 00; route de Sèvres à Neuilly, 16e; adult/student & 7-18yr €3/1.50, under 7 free; ⊗ 9am-6pm Apr-Sep, 9am-5pm Oct-Mar).

Located at the southeastern end of the Bois de Boulogne is the **Jardin des Serres d'Auteuil** (☎ 01 40 71 75 23; av de la Porte d'Auteuil, 16e; Ⓜ Porte d'Auteuil; adult/6-18yr €1.50/1, under 6 free; ⊗ 10am-6pm Apr-Sep, 10am-5pm Oct-Mar), a garden with impressive conservatories that opened in 1898.

The 20-hectare **Jardin d'Acclimatation** (☎ 01 40 67 90 82; av du Mahatma Gandhi; Ⓜ Les Sablons; adult/4-18yr €2.70/1.35, under 4 free; ⊗ 10am-7pm Jun-Sep, 10am-6pm Oct-May), a kids-oriented amusement park whose name is another term for 'zoo' in French, includes the high-tech **Exploradôme** (☎ 01 53 64 90 40; www.exploradome .com in French; adult/4-18yr €5/3.50, under 4yr free), a tented structure devoted to science and the media.

The southern part of the wood takes in two horse-racing tracks, the **Hippodrome de Longchamp** for flat races and the **Hippodrome d'Auteuil** (p184) for steeplechases as well as the **Stade Roland Garros** (p184), home of the French Open tennis tournament.

Rowing boats (☎ 01 42 88 04 69; per hr €9; ⊗ noon-6pm Mon-Fri, 10am-7pm Sat & Sun mid-Apr–mid-Oct) can be hired at **Lac Inférieur** (Ⓜ av Henri Martin), the largest of the wood's lakes and ponds. **Paris Cycles** (☎ 01 47 47 76 50; per 30min/1hr/day €3.50/5/10; ⊗ 10am-sunset mid-Apr–mid-Oct, 10am-sunset Wed, Sat & Sun mid-Oct–mid-Apr) hires out bicycles at two locations in the Bois de Boulogne: on **av du Mahatma Gandhi** (Ⓜ Les Sablons), across from the Porte Sablons entrance to the Jardin d'Acclimatation amusement park, and near the **Pavillon Royal** (Ⓜ av Foch) at the northern end of Lac Inférieur.

Étoile & Champs-Élysées

A dozen avenues radiate out from place de l'Étoile – officially place Charles de Gaulle –

and first among them is the av des Champs-Élysées. This broad boulevard, whose name refers to the 'Elysian Fields' where happy souls dwelt after death, according to Greek mythology, links place de la Concorde with the Arc de Triomphe. Symbolising the style and *joie de vivre* of Paris since the mid-19th century, the avenue is scuzzy in parts but remains a popular tourist destination.

Some 400m north of av des Champs-Élysées is rue du Faubourg St-Honoré (8e), the western extension of rue St-Honoré. It is home to some of Paris' most renowned couture houses, jewellers, antique shops and the 18th-century **Palais de l'Élysée** (Map pp102-3; cnr rue du Faubourg St-Honoré & av de Marigny, 8e; Ⓜ Champs-Élysées Clemenceau), the official residence of the French president.

ARC DE TRIOMPHE

The **Arc de Triomphe** (Triumphal Arch; Map pp102-3; ☎ 01 55 37 73 77; www.monum.fr; Ⓜ Charles de Gaulle-Étoile; viewing platform adult/18-25yr €8/6, under 18 & 1st Sun of the month Oct-Mar free; ⊗ 10am-11pm Apr-Sep, 10am-10.30pm Oct-Mar) is 2.2km northwest of place de la Concorde in the middle of place Charles de Gaulle (or place de l'Étoile), the world's largest traffic roundabout. It was commissioned in 1806 by Napoleon to commemorate his imperial victories but remained unfinished when he started losing battles and then entire wars. It was not completed until 1836. Since 1920, the body of an **Unknown Soldier** from WWI, taken from Verdun in Lorraine, has lain beneath the arch; his fate and that of countless others is commemorated by a **memorial flame** that is rekindled each evening around 6.30pm.

From the **viewing platform** on top of the arch (up 284 steps and well worth the climb) you can see the dozen broad avenues – many of them named after Napoleonic victories and illustrious generals (including ultra-exclusive av Foch, which is Paris' widest boulevard) – radiating towards every part of the city. Tickets are sold in the underground passageway beneath place de l'Étoile that surfaces on the even-numbered side of av des Champs-Élysées. It is the only sane way to get to the base of the arch and is not linked to nearby metro tunnels.

GRAND & PETIT PALAIS

Erected for the 1900 World Exposition, the **Grand Palais** (Great Palace; Map pp102-3; ☎ 01

44 13 17 17; reservations ☎ 0 892 684 694; www.rmn.fr /galeriesnationalesdugrandpalais; 3 av du Général Eisenhower, 8e; Ⓜ Champs-Élysées Clemenceau; with/without booking adult €11/9.30; student & 13-25yr €10/8, under 13 free; ⏰ 10am-8pm Thu-Mon, 10am-10pm Wed) now houses the **Galeries Nationales du Grand Palais** beneath its huge Art Nouveau glass roof. Special exhibitions, among the biggest the city stages, last three or four months here.

The **Petit Palais** (Little Palace; Map pp102-3; ☎ 01 53 43 40 00; www.petitpalais.paris.fr in French; av Winston Churchill, 8e; Ⓜ Champs-Élysées Clemenceau; permanent collection admission free, temporary exhibits entrance fee varies; ⏰ 10am-6pm Wed-Sun, 10am-8pm Tue), which was also built for the 1900 fair, is home to the **Musée des Beaux-Arts de la Ville de Paris**, the Paris municipality's Museum of Fine Arts, which contains medieval and Renaissance *objets d'art*, tapestries, drawings and 19th-century French painting and sculpture. It reopened in late 2005 after a protracted, four-year renovation and looks superb.

PALAIS DE LA DÉCOUVERTE

The **Palais de la Découverte** (Palace of Discovery; Map pp102-3; ☎ 01 56 43 20 21; www.palais-decouverte.fr in French; av Franklin D Roosevelt, 8e; Ⓜ Champs-Élysées Clemenceau; adult/senior, student & 5-18yr €6.50/4, under 5 free; ⏰ 9.30am-6pm Tue-Sat, 10am-7pm Sun), inaugurated during the 1937 Exposition Universelle and thus the world's first interactive museum, is a fascinating place to take kids, with hands-on exhibits on astronomy, biology, medicine, chemistry, mathematics, computer science, physics and earth sciences. The **planetarium** (admission €3.50) usually has four shows a day in French at 11.30am, and 2pm, 3.15pm and 4.30pm; ring or consult the website for current schedules.

Concorde & Madeleine

The cobblestone expanses of 18th-century place de la Concorde are sandwiched between the Jardin des Tuileries and the parks at the eastern end of av des Champs-Élysées. Delightful place de la Madeleine is to the north. Both are in the 8e arrondissement.

PLACE DE LA CONCORDE

Place de la Concorde (Map pp102-3; Ⓜ Concorde) was laid out between 1755 and 1775. The 3300-year-old pink granite **obelisk** with the gilded top in the middle of the square once stood in the Temple of Ramses at Thebes (today's Luxor) and was given to France

in 1831 by Muhammad Ali, viceroy and pasha of Egypt. The **female statues** adorning the four corners of the square represent France's eight largest cities.

In 1793 Louis XVI's head was lopped off by a guillotine set up in the northwest corner of the square, near the statue representing Brest. During the next two years, a guillotine built near the entrance to the Jardin des Tuileries was used to behead 1343 more people, including Marie-Antoinette and, six months later, the Revolutionary leaders Danton and Robespierre. The square was given its present name after the Reign of Terror (p94), in the hope that it would be a place of peace and harmony.

ÉGLISE DE LA MADELEINE

The neoclassical **Église de la Madeleine** (Church of St Mary Magdalene; Map pp102-3; ☎ 01 44 51 69 00; www.eglise-lamadeleine.com in French; rue Royale, 8e; Ⓜ Madeleine; ⏰ 10am-7pm) is 350m northeast of place de la Concorde. Built in the style of a Greek temple, what is simply called La Madeleine was consecrated in the year 1845 after almost a century of design changes and construction delays. It is surrounded by 52 Corinthian columns, and the marble and gilt interior is topped by three sky-lit cupolas. You can hear the massive organ being played at Mass at 9.30am and 11am on Sunday.

Opéra & Grands Boulevards

Place de l'Opéra (Map pp102–3) is the site of Paris' world-famous (and original) opera house. It abuts the Grands Boulevards, the eight contiguous 'Great Boulevards' – Madeleine, Capucines, Montmartre, Poissonnière, Italiens, Bonne Nouvelle, St-Denis and St-Martin – that stretch from elegant place de la Madeleine in the 8e eastwards to the more plebeian place de la République in the 3e, a distance of just under 3km.

The Grands Boulevards were laid out in the 17th century on the site of obsolete city walls and served as a centre of café and theatre life in the 18th and 19th centuries, reaching the height of fashion during the *belle époque*. North of the western end of the Grands Boulevards is blvd Haussmann (8e and 9e), the heart of the commercial and banking district and known for some of Paris' most famous department stores, including **Galeries Lafayette** and **Le Printemps** (p185).

PALAIS GARNIER

The **Palais Garnier** (Garnier Palace; Map pp102-3; ☎ 0 892 899 090; place de l'Opéra, 9e; Ⓜ Opéra), one of the most impressive monuments erected in Paris during the 19th century, stages operas, ballets and classical-music concerts. In summer it can be visited on English-language **guided tours** (☎ 01 41 10 08 10; http://visites.opera deparis.fr; adult/senior/10-26yr €11/9/6; Ⓜ 11.30am & 2.30pm Jul & Aug, 11.30am Sat & Sun Sep-Jun).

Palais Garnier houses the **Bibliothèque-Musée de l'Opéra** (Map pp102-3; ☎ 01 47 42 07 02; www .bnf.fr; adult/senior, student & 10-26yr €7/4, under 10 free; ☯ 10am-5pm Sep-Jun, 10am-6pm Jul & Aug), which contains a lot of documentation (it also functions as an important research library) and some memorabilia. More interestingly, admission to the museum includes a self-paced visit to the opera house itself as long as there's not a daytime rehearsal or performance on.

COVERED ARCADES

There are several **passages couverts** (covered shopping arcades) off blvd Montmartre (9e) and walking through them is like stepping back into the sepia-toned Paris of the early 19th century. The **passage des Panoramas** (Map pp104-5; 11 blvd Montmartre, 2e; Ⓜ Grands Boulevards), which was opened in 1800 and received Paris' first gas lighting in 1817, was expanded in 1834 with the addition of four other interconnecting passages: Feydeau, Montmartre, St-Marc and Variétés. The arcades are open till about midnight daily.

On the northern side of blvd Montmartre, between Nos 10 and 12, is **passage Jouffroy** (Ⓜ Grands Boulevards), which leads across rue de la Grange Batelière to **passage Verdeau**. Both contain shops selling antiques, old postcards, used and antiquarian books, gifts, pet toys, imports from Asia and the like. These arcades are open until 10pm.

MUSÉE GRÉVIN

Inside passage Jouffroy, the **Musée Grévin** (Grévin Museum; Map pp104-5; ☎ 01 47 70 85 05; www .grevin.com; 10 blvd Montmartre, 9e; Ⓜ Grands Boulevards; adult/student/senior/6-14yr €17/15.50/14.50/10; ☯ 10am-6.30pm Mon-Fri, 10am-7pm Sat & Sun) boasts some 250 wax figures that look more like caricatures than characters, but where else do you get to see Marilyn Monroe and Charles de Gaulle face to face or the real death masks of French Revolutiona. ers? The admission charge is positivei, rageous and just keeps a-growin'.

Ménilmontant & Belleville

A solidly working-class *quartier* with little to recommend it until just a few years ago, Ménilmontant in the 11e now boasts a surfeit of restaurants, bars and clubs. On the other hand, Belleville (20e), home to large numbers of immigrants, especially Muslims and Jews from North Africa and Vietnamese and ethnic Chinese from Indochina, remains for the most part unpretentious and working-class. **Parc de Belleville** (Map pp104-5; Ⓜ Couronnes), which opened in 1992 a few blocks east of blvd de Belleville, occupies a hill almost 200m above sea level amid 4.5 hectares of greenery and offers superb views of the city. Paris' most famous necropolis lies just to the south of the park.

CIMETIÈRE DU PÈRE LACHAISE

The world's most visited graveyard, **Cimetière du Père Lachaise** (Père Lachaise Cemetery; Map pp98-9; ☎ 01 55 25 82 10; Ⓜ Philippe Auguste, Gambetta or Père Lachaise; ☯ 8am-6pm Mon-Fri, 8.30am-6pm Sat, 9am-6pm Sun mid-Mar–early Nov, 8am-5.30pm Mon-Fri, 8.30am-5.30pm Sat, 9am-5.30pm Sun early Nov–mid-Mar) opened its one-way doors in 1804. Its 69,000 ornate, even ostentatious, tombs form a verdant, open-air sculpture garden.

Among the 800,000 people buried here are the composer Chopin, the playwright Molière, the poet Apollinaire; the writers Balzac, Proust, Gertrude Stein and Colette; the actors Simone Signoret, Sarah Bernhardt and Yves Montand; the painters Pissarro, Seurat, Modigliani and Delacroix, the chanteuse Édith Piaf; the dancer Isadora Duncan; and even those immortal 12th-century lovers, Abélard and Héloïse whose remains were disinterred and reburied here together in 1817 beneath a neogothic tombstone.

Particularly frequented graves are those of **Oscar Wilde**, interred in Division 89 in 1900, and 1960s rock star **Jim Morrison**, who died in an apartment at 17–19 rue Beautreillis, 4e in the Marais in 1971 and is buried in Division 6 (see p144).

Père Lachaise has five entrances, two of which are on blvd de Ménilmontant. Maps

d as fresh as the air, Oscar Wilde (1854–1900) is apparently as flamboyant
hotel deathbed when he proclaimed, 'My wallpaper and I are fighting
one of us has got to go.' It seems that the Père Lachaise grave of the Irish
d humorist, who was sentenced to two years in prison in 1895 for gross indecency
ming from his homosexual relationship with Lord Alfred 'Bosie' Douglas (1870–1945), is attracting gay admirers, who plaster the ornate tomb with indelible lipstick kisses.

But Wilde's tomb is not the only grave concern at Père Lachaise these days. A security guard
had to be posted near the grave of rock singer Jim Morrison (1943–71) after fans began taking
drugs and having sex on his tomb. The cemetery's conservation office has even issued a leaflet
outlining the rules of conduct when visiting the grave. Meanwhile, over in Division 92, a protest
by a woman has seen the removal of a metal fence placed around the grave of one Victor Noir,
pseudonym of the journalist Yvan Salman (1848–70), who was shot and killed by Pierre Bonaparte,
great-nephew of Napoleon I, at the age of just 22. The protest had nothing to do with anything
as 'highbrow' as freedom of the press. According to legend, a woman who strokes the amply
filled crotch of Monsieur Noir's prostrate bronze effigy will quickly become pregnant. Apparently
some would-be mothers were rubbing a bit too enthusiastically, and the larger-than-life-size
package was being worn away.

indicating the location of noteworthy graves
are available free from the **conservation office**
(Map pp114-15; 16 rue du Repos, 20e) on the western
side of the cemetery.

13e Arrondissement & Chinatown

The 13e begins a few blocks south of the
Jardin des Plantes in the 5e and has undergone a true renaissance with the advent
of the Bibliothèque Nationale de France,
the high-speed Météor metro line (No 14)
and the ZAC Paris Rive Gauche project, the
massive redevelopment of the old industrial
quarter along the Seine. The stylishness of
the neighbouring 5e extends to the av des
Gobelins, while further south, between av
d'Italie and av de Choisy, the succession of
Asian restaurants, stalls and shops in the
capital's version of Chinatown gives passers-
by the illusion of having imperceptibly
changed continents.

BIBLIOTHÈQUE NATIONALE DE FRANCE-
SITE FRANÇOIS MITTERRAND

Rising up from the banks of the Seine are
the four glass towers of the controversial, €2
billion **Bibliothèque Nationale de France** (National
Library of France; Map pp98-9; ☎ 01 53 79 53 79, 01 53 79
40 41; www.bnf.fr; 11 quai François Mauriac, 13e; Ⓜ Bibliothèque; temporary exhibitions admission adult/student 18-
26yr from €5/3.50, under 18 free; ☾ 10am-7pm Tue-Sat,
1-7pm Sun), which was conceived by the late
president François Mitterrand as a 'wonder
of the modern world' and opened in 1988.

No expense was spared to carry out a plan
that many said defied logic. While many of
the books and historical documents were
shelved in the sun-drenched, 23-storey
towers – shaped like half-open books –
readers sat in artificially lit basement halls
built around a 'forest courtyard' of 140 50-
year-old pines, trucked in from the countryside. The towers have since been fitted with a
complex (and expensive) shutter system, but
the basement is prone to flooding from the
Seine. The national library contains around
12 million tomes stored on some 420km of
shelves and can accommodate 2000 readers
and 2000 researchers. Temporary exhibitions revolve around 'the word', focusing on
everything from storytelling to bookbind-
ing. Using the study library costs €3.30/35
per day/year while the research library costs
€7/53 for three days/year.

Montmartre & Pigalle

During the late 19th and early 20th centuries
the bohemian lifestyle of Montmartre in the
18e attracted a number of important writers
and artists, including Picasso, who lived at the
studio called **Bateau Lavoir** (Map p122; 11bis Émile
Goudeau; Ⓜ Abbesses) from 1908 to 1912 during his so-called Blue Period. Although the
activity shifted to Montparnasse after WWI,
Montmartre retains an upbeat ambience that
all the tourists in the world couldn't spoil.

Only a few blocks southwest of the tranquil, residential streets of Montmartre is

lively, neon-lit Pigalle (9e and 18e), one of Paris' two main sex districts (the other, which is *much* more low-rent, is along rue St-Denis and its side streets north of Forum des Halles in the 1er). But Pigalle is more than just a sleazy red-light district; there are plenty of trendy nightspots, including clubs and cabarets, here as well.

The easiest way to reach Montmartre is via the RATP's sleek funicular (p717).

Montmartrobus, a bus run by the RATP, makes a circuitous route from place Pigalle through Montmartre to the 18e Mairie on place Jules Joffrin. Detailed maps are posted at bus stops.

BASILIQUE DU SACRÉ CŒUR

The **Basilique du Sacré Cœur** (Basilica of the Sacred Heart; Map p122; ☎ 01 53 41 89 00; www.sacre-coeur -montmartre.com; place du Parvis du Sacré Cœur, 18e; Ⓜ Anvers; ☯ 6am-11pm), perched at the very top of the Butte de Montmartre (Montmartre Hill), was built from contributions pledged by Parisian Catholics as an act of contrition after the humiliating Franco-Prussian War of 1870–71. Construction began in 1873, but the basilica was not consecrated until 1919.

Some 234 spiralling steps lead you to the basilica's **dome** (admission €5; ☯ 9am-7pm Apr-Sep, 9am-6pm Oct-Mar), which affords one of Paris' most spectacular panoramas; they say you can see for 30km on a clear day.

PLACE DU TERTRE

Half a block west of the **Église St-Pierre de Montmartre** (Map p122), which once formed part of a 12th-century Benedictine abbey, is **place du Tertre** (Map p122; Ⓜ Abbesses), once the main square of the village of Montmartre. These days it's filled with cafés, restaurants, tourists and rather obstinate portrait artists and caricaturists who will gladly do your likeness. Whether it looks even remotely like you is another matter.

CIMETIÈRE DE MONTMARTRE

Established in 1798, **Cimetière de Montmartre** (Montmartre Cemetery; Map p122; ☎ 01 53 42 36 30; Ⓜ Place de Clichy; ☯ 8am-6pm Mon-Fri, 8.30am-6pm Sat, 9am-6pm Sun mid-Mar–early Nov, 8am-5.30pm Mon-Fri, 8.30am-5.30pm Sat, 9am-5.30pm Sun early Nov–mid-Mar) is the most famous cemetery in Paris after Père Lachaise. It contains the graves of writers Émile Zola, Alexandre Dumas and Stendhal, composer Jacques Offenbach, artist Edgar

Degas, film director François Truffaut and dancer Vaslav Nijinsky – among others. The entrance closest to Butte de Montmartre is at the end of av Rachel, just off blvd de Clichy or down the stairs from 10 rue Caulaincourt. Maps showing the location of the tombs are available free from the **conservation office** (☎ 01 53 42 36 30; 20 av Rachel, 18e).

MUSÉE DE MONTMARTRE

The **Musée de Montmartre** (Montmartre Museum; Map p122; ☎ 01 49 25 89 39; www.museedemontmar tre.com; 12-14 rue Cortot, 18e; Ⓜ Lamarck Caulaincourt; adult/senior, student & 10-25yr €5.50/3.50, under 10 free; ☯ 10am-6pm Tue-Sun) displays paintings, lithographs and documents mostly relating to the area's rebellious and bohemian/ artistic past in a 17th-century manor house, the oldest structure in the quarter. It also stages exhibitions of artists still living in the *quartier*. There's an excellent bookshop here that also sells small bottles of the wine produced from grapes grown in the Clos du Montmartre (p149).

MUSÉE DE L'ÉROTISME

The **Musée de l'Érotisme** (Museum of Erotic Art; Map p122; ☎ 01 42 58 28 73; 72 blvd de Clichy, 18e; Ⓜ Blanche; adult/student €8/6; ☯ 10am-2am) tries to put some 2000 titillating statues and stimulating sexual aids and fetishist items from days gone by on a loftier plane, with erotic art – both antique and modern – from four continents spread over seven floors. But most of the punters know why they are here.

La Villette

The Buttes Chaumont, the Canal de l'Ourcq and especially the Parc de la Villette, with its wonderful museums and other attractions, create the winning trifecta of the 19th arrondissement.

PARC DE LA VILLETTE

The whimsical, 35-hectare **Parc de la Villette** (La Villette Park; Map pp98-9; ☎ 01 04 03 75 75; www.vil lette.com; Ⓜ Porte de la Villette or Porte de Pantin) in the city's far northeastern corner, which opened in 1993, stretches from the **Cité des Sciences et de l'Industrie** (Ⓜ Porte de la Vil lette) south to the **Cité de la Musique** (Ⓜ Porte de Pantin). Split into two sections by the Canal de l'Ourcq, the park is enlivened by shaded walkways, imaginative street furniture, a series of themed gardens for kids and fanciful, bright-red pavilions known as *folies*. It is the largest open green space in central Paris and has been called 'the prototype of the urban park of the 21st century'.

CITÉ DES SCIENCES ET DE L'INDUSTRIE

The huge **Cité des Sciences et de l'Industrie** (City of Science & Industry; Map pp98-9; ☎ 01 40 05 80 00, ☎ reservations 0 892 697 072; www.cite-sciences.fr; 30 av Corentin Cariou, 19e; Ⓜ Porte de la Villette; ⏲ 10am-6pm Tue-Sat, 10am-7pm Sun), at the northern end of Parc de la Villette, has all sorts of high-tech exhibits. Free attractions include the following:

Aquarium (level -2; ⏲ 10am-6pm Tue-Sat, 10am- 7pm Sun)
Carrefour Numérique (level -1; ⏲ noon-7.30pm Tue, noon-6.45pm Wed-Sun) Internet centre.
Cité des Métiers (level -1; ⏲ 10am-6pm Tue-Fri, noon-6pm Sat) Information about trades, professions and employment.
Médiathèque (levels 0 & -1; ⏲ noon-7.45pm Tue, noon-6.45pm Wed-Sun) With multimedia exhibits dealing with childhood, the history of science and health.

A free and useful map/brochure in English called *The Keys to the Cité* is available from the information counter at the main entrance to the complex.

The huge – and somewhat confusingly laid-out – **Explora** (adult/7-25yr €7.50/5.50, under 7 free) exhibitions are on levels 1 and 2 and cover everything from space exploration and automobile technology to biology and sound. Tickets are valid for a full day and allow you to enter and exit up to four times.

The **Planétarium** (level 1; admission €3, 3-7yr free, under 3 not admitted; ⏲ 11am-5pm Tue-Sun) has six shows a day on the hour (except at 1pm) on a screen measuring 1000 sq metres.

The highlight of the Cité des Sciences et de l'Industrie is the brilliant **Cité des Enfants** (Children's Village; level 0), whose colourful and imaginative hands-on demonstrations of basic scientific principles are divided into three sections: one for three- to five-year-olds, and two for five- to 12-year-olds. In the first, kids can explore, among other things, the conduct of water (waterproof lab ponchos provided). The second allows children to build toy houses with industrial robots and stage news broadcasts in a TV studio. A third section has special exhibitions on everything from electricity to light.

Visits to Cité des Enfants lasting 1½ hours begin four times a day: at 9.45am, 11.30am, 1.30pm and 3.15pm on Tuesday, Thursday and Friday and at 10.30am, 12.30pm, 2.30pm and 4.30pm on Wednesday, Saturday and Sunday. Each child (€5) must be accompanied by an adult (maximum two adults per family). During school holidays, book two or three days in advance by phone or via the internet.

CITÉ DE LA MUSIQUE

The **Cité de la Musique** (Music Village; Map pp98-9; ☎ 01 44 84 44 84; www.cite-musique.fr; 221 av Jean Jaurès, 19e; Ⓜ Porte de Pantin; ⏲ noon-6pm Tue-Sat, 10am-6pm Sun), on the southern edge of Parc de la Villette, is a striking triangular-shaped concert hall whose brief is to bring non-elitist music from around the world to Paris' multi-ethnic masses. In the same complex, the **Musée de la Musique** (Music Museum; ☎ 01 44 84 44 84; adult/senior, student & 18-25yr €7/3.40, under 18 free; ⏲ noon-6pm Tue-Sat, 10am-6pm Sun) displays some 900 rare musical instruments out of a collection of 4500 warehoused, and you can hear many of them being played through the earphones included in the admission cost. The museum's **Médiathèque** (☎ 01 44 84 89 45; ⏲ noon-6pm Tue-Sat, 1-8pm Sun) can answer your music questions via the internet; it has terminals with about 500 music-related sites.

Bois de Vincennes

The **Bois de Vincennes** (Vincennes Wood; Map pp98-9; blvd Poniatowski, 12e; Ⓜ Porte de Charenton or Porte Dorée) encompasses some 995 hectares in the southeastern corner of Paris. Most of it, however, is just outside the blvd Périphérique.

Located at the wood's northern edge, the **Château de Vincennes** (Map pp98-9; Vincennes Palace; ☎ 01 48 08 31 20; www.monum.fr; av de Paris, 12e; Ⓜ Château de Vincennes; ⏲ 10am-noon & 1.15-6pm May-Aug, 10am-noon & 1.15-5pm Sep-Apr) is a bona fide royal chateau with massive fortifications and a moat. Louis XIV spent his honeymoon at the mid-17th-century Pavillon du Roi, the westernmost of the two royal pavilions flanking the Cour Royale (Royal Courtyard). The 52m-high dungeon, closed to visitors at present, was completed in 1369 and used as a prison during the 17th and 18th centuries. You can walk round the grounds for free, but the only way to see the Gothic Chapelle Royale (Royal Chapel), built between the 14th and 16th centuries, is to take a guided tour (in French; information booklet in English). Long-tour (1½ hours) tickets are €6.50 for seniors and students, €4.50 for ages 18 to 25, under 18 free; short tours (45 minutes) €5 and €3.50. There are an average of three short and five long tours daily from April to September but only one long tour a day at 4.30pm the rest of the year; ring ahead for exact times. There are guided tours in English at 11am and 3pm daily in July and August.

The wood's main attraction, the **Parc Floral de Paris** (Paris Floral Park; ☎ info 3975, 0 820 007 575; www.parcfloraldeparis.com in French; esplanade du Château de Vincennes, 12e; Ⓜ Château de Vincennes; adult/7-18yr €1/0.50 or €3/1.50 when event is on; ☽ 9.30am-5pm to 8pm seasonally), is south of the Château de Vincennes, and amusements for kids aged six to 14 include the **Bibliothèque-Ludothèque Nature** (Nature Library & Puppetry; ☎ 01 43 28 47 63; ☽ 1.30-5.30pm Tue-Sat, to 6.30pm Sun Apr-Sep, to 5.30pm Tue-Sun Oct-Mar) and a lovely **Jardin des Papillons** (Butterfly Garden), with 40 species of butterfly.

The well-managed, 15-hectare **Parc Zoologique de Paris** (Paris Zoological Park; ☎ 01 44 75 20 10; www.mnhn.fr in French; 53 av de St-Maurice, 12e; Ⓜ Porte Dorée; admission €5, under 4 free; ☽ 9am-6pm Mon-Sat, 9am-6.30pm Sun Apr-Sep, 9am-5pm Mon-Sat, 9am-5.30pm Sun Oct-Mar), just east of Lac Daumesnil and also known as the Zoo du Bois de Vincennes, was established in 1934. It has some 600 animals.

ACTIVITIES

The best single source of information on sports in Paris is the Salon d'Accueil (Reception Hall) of the **Hôtel de Ville** (Map pp110-11; ☎ info3975, 0 820 007 575; www.sport.paris.fr; 29 rue de Rivoli, 4e; Ⓜ Hôtel de Ville; ☽ 10am-7pm Mon-Sat).

Cycling

Paris now counts some 315km of bicycle lanes running throughout the city as well as a dedicated lane paralleling a large portion of the blvd Périphérique encircling the capital. On Sundays and holidays from mid-March to mid-December, large sections of road are reserved for pedestrians, cyclists and skaters under a scheme called 'Paris Respire' (Paris Breathes).

Maison Roue Libre (☎ 0 810 441 534; www.roue libre.fr; ☽ 9am-7pm Feb-Nov, 10am-6pm Dec & Jan; Bastille branch Map pp114-15; 37 blvd Bourdon, 4e; Ⓜ Bastille; main branch Map pp110-11; Forum des Halles, 1 passage Mondétour, 1er; Ⓜ Les Halles), sponsored by RATP, the city's public transport system, is the best place to rent a bicycle in Paris.

Bicycles cost €4/9/14/20 per hour/h. day/10-hour day/24-hour day and inclu insurance, helmet and baby seat.

Other outfits that rent out bicycles:
Bike 'n' Roller (Map pp108-9; ☎ 01 45 50 38 27; 38 rue Fabert, 7e; Ⓜ Invalides; per 3hr/day €12/17; ☽ 10am-8pm Mon-Sat, 10am-6.30pm Sun)
Fat Tire Bike Tours (Map pp108-9; ☎ 01 56 58 10 54; www.fattirebiketoursparis.com; 24 rue Edgar Faure, 15e; Ⓜ La Motte-Piquet Grenelle; ☽ office 9am-7pm)
Gepetto et Vélos rue du Cardinal Lemoine (Map pp118-19; ☎ 01 43 54 19 95; www.gepetto-et-velos.com in French; 59 rue du Cardinal Lemoine, 5e; Ⓜ Cardinal Lemoine; per ½ day/day/weekend/week €7.50/14/23/50; ☽ 9am-7.30pm Tue-Sat, 9.30am-7pm Sun); Latin Quarter (Map pp118-19; ☎ 01 43 37 16 17; 46 rue Daubenton, 5e; Ⓜ Censier Daubenton; ☽ 9am-1pm & 2-7.30pm Tue-Sat).
Paris à Vélo, C'est Sympa! (Map pp114-15; ☎ 01 48 87 60 01; www.parisvelosympa.com in French; 22 rue Alphonse Baudin, 11e; Ⓜ Richard Lenoir; per ½ day/day/weekend/week €10/13/24/60; ☽ 9.30am-1pm & 2-5.30pm Mon & Wed-Fri, 9.30am-1pm & 2-6pm Sat & Sun)

Swimming

Paris has 35 swimming pools that are open to the public; check with the **Mairie de Paris** (☎ info3975, 0 820 007 575; www.paris.fr) for the one that is nearest you. Most are short-length pools and finding a free lane for lengths can be nigh on impossible. Opening times vary widely. On Wednesday afternoon and Saturday, kids off from school take the plunge. The entry cost for municipal pools in Paris is €2.60/1.50 for adults/under-21s. A carnet of 10 tickets costs €21.50/12.50.

WALKING TOUR

Montmartre, from the French words for hill (*mont*) and martyr, has been a place of legend ever since St Denis was executed here in circa AD 250 and began his headless journey on foot to the village north of Paris that still bears his name (p208). In recent times the Montmartre of myth has been resurrected by music, books and especially films like *Le Fabuleux Destin d'Amélie Poulain* (just *Amelie* in English; 2002), which presented the district in various shades of rose, and *Moulin Rouge* (2001), which also made it pretty but gave it a bit more edge.

For centuries Montmartre was a simple country village filled with the mills (*moulins*) that supplied Paris with its flour. When it was incorporated into the capital in 1860, its picturesque charm and

d painters and writers –
e Communard uprising
gan here. The late 19th
turies were Montmar-
eyday, when Toulouse-Lautrec drew
his favourite cancan dancers and Picasso,
Braque and others introduced Cubism to
the world.

After WWI such creative activity shifted
to Montparnasse, but Montmartre retained
an upbeat ambience. The real attractions
here, apart from the great views from the
Butte de Montmartre (Montmartre Hill),
are the area's little parks and steep, winding
cobblestone streets, many of whose houses
seem about to be engulfed by creeping vines
and ivy.

WALK FACTS

Start Ⓜ Blanche
Finish Ⓜ Abbesses
Distance 2.5km
Duration Two hours
Fuel Stop La Maison Rose

In English-speaking countries, Montmartre's mystique of unconventionality has
been magnified by the supposed notoriety
of places like the Moulin Rouge, a nightclub
on the edge of the Pigalle district that was
founded in 1889 and is known for its scant-
ily clad – ooooh la la! – chorus girls. The
garish nightlife that Toulouse-Lautrec loved
to portray has spread along blvd de Clichy,
and Pigalle has become decidedly sleazy,
though it's pretty tame stuff overall.

Begin the walk at the Blanche metro station. Diagonally opposite to the left is the
legendary **Moulin Rouge (1**; p183) beneath
its trademark red windmill while appropriately located to the right is the **Musée
de l'Érotisme (2**; p145), an institution that
portrays itself as educational rather than
titillating. Walk up rue Lepic and halfway up on the left you'll find the **Café des
Deux Moulins (3**; ☎ 01 42 54 90 50; 15 rue Lepic,
18e; ⏰ 7am-2am Mon-Fri, 7.30am-2am Sat, 9am-2am
Sun), where our heroine Amélie worked in
the eponymous film. Follow the curve to
the west (left); Théo Van Gogh owned the
house at No 54 (4) and his brother, the artist

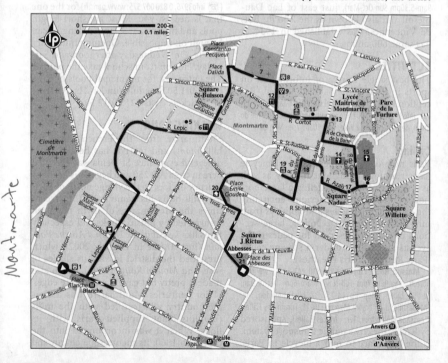

Vincent, stayed with him on the 3rd floor for two years from 1886.

Further along rue Lepic are Montmartre's famous twinned windmills. The better known **Moulin de la Galette (5)** was a popular open-air dance hall in the late 19th century and was immortalized by Pierre-Auguste Renoir in his 1876 tableau *Le Bal du Moulin de La Galette*. About 100m to the east, at the corner of rue Girardon is the **Moulin Radet (6)**. Confusingly, it's now a restaurant called Le Moulin de la Galette.

Turn left (north) into rue Girardon, cross through leafy square St-Buisson (Holy Bush) and past the charmingly named allée des Brouillards (Fog Path) and descend the stairs from place Dalida into rue St-Vincent; on the other side of the wall is **Cimetière St-Vincent (7)**, final resting place of the great and the good, including Maurice Utrillo (1883–1955), known as 'the painter of Montmartre'. Just over rue des Saules is the celebrated cabaret **Au Lapin Agile (8**; p180), whose name seems to suggest a 'nimble rabbit' but actually comes from Le Lapin à Gill, a mural of a rabbit jumping out of a cooking pot by caricaturist André Gill, which can still be seen on the western exterior wall.

Turn right (south) onto rue des Saules. Just opposite the cabaret is the **Close du Montmartre (9)**, a small vineyard dating from 1933 whose 2000 vines produce an average 850 bottles of wine each October, which is then auctioned off for charity in the 18e. You can buy sample bottles of the hooch at the **Musée de Montmartre (10**; p145), which is on rue Cortot at Nos 12–14, the first street on the left after the vineyard. The museum is housed in Montmartre's oldest building, a manor house built in the 17th century, and onetime home to painters Renoir, Utrillo and Raoul Dufy. The **house of Eric Satie (11)**, where the celebrated composer lived from 1892 to 1898 is at No 6. A great place for a bite to eat is **La Maison Rose (12**; p175), the quintessential Montmartre bistro and subject of an eponymous lithograph by Utrillo.

Turn right (south) onto rue du Mont Cenis – the attractive **water tower (13)** just opposite dates from the early 20th century – and then left onto rue de Chevalier de la Barre, which will lead you past the back of **Église St-Pierre de Montmartre (14**; p145), which was built on the site of a Roman temple to Mercury and did time as a Temple of Reason under the Revolution and as a clothing factory during the Commune. The entrance to the **Basilique du Sacré Cœur (15**; p145), and the stunning vista over Paris from **place du Parvis du Sacré Cœur (16)** are just a few steps to the south.

From the basilica follow rue Azaïs west past the upper station of the **funicular (17**; p717) and then rue Norvins north into **place du Tertre (18**; p145), arguably the most touristy place in all of Paris but buzzy and still fun. Just off the southwestern side of the square is rue Poulbot leading to the **Dalí Espace Montmartre (19**; ☎ 01 42 64 40 10; www.daliparis.com in French; 11 rue Poulbot, 18e; Ⓜ Abbesses; adult/senior/student & 8-16yr €8/7/5, under 8 free; ☑ 10am-6pm), surprisingly the only 'art' museum on the Butte. From place du Calvaire take the steps – actually called the Calvaire – into rue Gabrielle, turning right (west) to reach place Émile Goudeau. At No 11b is the so-called **Bateau Lavoir (20)**, where Kees Van Dongen, Max Jacob, Amedeo Modigliani and Pablo Picasso once lived in an old piano factory later used as a laundry. It was dubbed the 'Laundry Boat' because of the way it swayed in a strong breeze. Picasso painted his seminal *Les Demoiselles d'Avignon* (1907) here. Originally at No 13, the real Bateau Lavoir burned down in 1970 and was rebuilt in 1978.

Take the steps down from place Émile Goudeau and follow rue des Abbesses south into place des Abbesses, where you can't miss the **metro station (21)** entrance designed by Hector Guimard.

PARIS FOR CHILDREN

Paris abounds in places that will delight children, and there is always a special child's entry rate to attractions (though ages of eligibility may vary). Family visits to many areas of the city can be designed around a rest stop (or picnic) at the city's many parks. For details about Disneyland Resort Paris, see p210.

If you read French, the daily newspaper *Libération* produces a supplement every other month entitled **Paris Mômes** (Paris Kids; www.parismomes.fr in French), with listings and other information aimed at kids to age 12. *L'Officiel des Spectacles* (p177), the weekly entertainment magazine that appears on newsstands every Wednesday, lists *gardes d'enfants* (babysitters) available in Paris.

TOURS

Bicycle

Fat Tire Bike Tours (Map pp108–9; ☎ 01 56 58 10 54; www.fattirebiketoursparis.com; 24 rue Edgar Faure, 15e; Ⓜ La Motte Picquet Grenelle; office ⓧ 9am-7pm) offers four-hour English-language tours of the city (adult/student €24/22) starting at 11am from March to November, with an additional tour at 3pm from mid-May to July. Night bicycle tours (adult/student €28/26) depart at 7pm on Sunday, Tuesday and Thursday in March and November and at the same time daily from April to October. Tours depart from av Gustave Eiffel, 7e (Map pp108–9), just opposite the Eiffel Tower's South Pillar at the start of the Champ de Mars. Costs include bicycle hire and, if necessary, rain gear. Three-speeds are available from the company's office to rent for €2/15/25/50/65 per hour/day/weekend/week/month.

Boat

Based on the Right Bank just east of the Pont de l'Alma, **Bateaux Mouches** (Map pp102–3; ☎ 01 42 25 96 10; www.bateauxmouches.com in French; Port de la Conférence, 8e; Ⓜ Alma Marceau; adult/senior & 4-12yr €8/4, under 4 free; ⓧ every 15-30min mid-Mar–mid-Nov), the most famous river-boat company in Paris, runs 1000-seat tour boats, the biggest on the Seine. Cruises (70 minutes) run at 11am, 2.30pm, 4pm, 6pm and 9pm from mid-March to mid-November, with additional winter cruises available, depending on demand. Recorded commentary is in a half-dozen languages.

If you prefer to see Paris from one of its canals, **Paris Canal Croisières** (Map pp108–9; ☎ 01 42 40 96 97; www.pariscanal.com; Bassin de la Villette, 19-21 quai de la Loire, 19e; Ⓜ Jaurès or Musée d'Orsay; adult/senior & 12-25yr/4-11yr €16/13/9, under 4 free) has daily 2½-hour cruises departing from quai Anatole France, 7e, just northwest of the Musée d'Orsay (Map pp108–9), for Bassin de la Villette, 19e (Map pp104–5) via the charming Canal St-Martin and Canal de l'Ourcq. Departures are 9.30am from quai Anatole France and at 2.30pm from Bassin de la Villette.

Bus

Balabus (☎ in French 0 892 687 714, in English 0 892 684 114; www.ratp.fr; €1.40 or metro ticket or bus ticket; ⓧ departures 12.30-8pm Sun Apr-Sep) run by RATP follows a 50-minute route from Gare de Lyon (Map pp120–1) to La Défense (Map p206) that passes by many of central Paris' most famous sights. Buses depart about every 20 minutes.

L'Open Tour (Map pp102–3; ☎ 01 42 66 56 56; www.paris-opentour.com; 13 rue Auber, 9e; Ⓜ Havre Caumartin or Opéra; 1 day adult/4-11yr €25/12, 2 consecutive days €28/12) runs daily open-deck buses along four circuits (central Paris, 2¼ hours; Montmartre–Grands Boulevards, 1¼ hours; Bastille–Bercy, one hour; and Montparnasse–St-Germain, one hour). You can jump on and off at more than 50 stops. Schedules vary but buses depart roughly every 10 to 15 minutes from 9.20am to 8pm April to October and every 25 to 30 minutes from 9.30am to 6pm November to March.

Walking

Paris Walks (☎ 01 48 09 21 40; www.paris-walks.com; adult/student under 21/under 15yr €10/8/5) has English-language tours of several different districts, including Montmartre at 10.30am on Sunday and Wednesday (leaving from Ⓜ Abbesses; Map p122) and the Marais at 10.30am on Tuesday and at 2.30pm on Sunday (departing from Ⓜ St-Paul, north of Île St-Louis; Map pp110–11). There are other tours focusing on people and themes, such as Hemingway, medieval Paris, fashion, the French Revolution and, of course, the *Da Vinci Code* (which costs €12).

FESTIVALS & EVENTS

Innumerable festivals and cultural and sporting events take place in Paris throughout the year; weekly details appear in *Pariscope* and *L'Officiel des Spectacles* as well as the more colourful entertainment magazine *Zurban* (p178). You can also find them listed under 'What's On' on the tourist office's website (www.parisinfo.com).

The following abbreviated list gives you a taste of what to expect throughout the year. To ensure that your trip does not coincide with a public holiday, when most everything will be shut, see p958.

January & February

La Grande Parade de Paris (www.parisparade.com) The city's New Year's Day parade originated in Montmartre but takes place in different venues (eg along the Grands Boulevards, under the Eiffel Tower, in Chantilly) from year to year. Check the website for details.

Paris, Capitale de la Création (www.pariscapitalede lacreation.com) Prêt-à-Porter, the twice yearly ready-to-wear fashion salon in January/February and again in September, joins forces with 16 other trade shows dealing with all aspects of fashion and interior design. Held jointly at Paris des Expositions at Porte de Versailles, 15e (Ⓜ Porte de Versailles), southwest of the centre, and Parc des Expositions, Paris-Nord Villepinte, to the north of the capital.

Chinese New Year (www.paris.fr) Dragon parades and other festivities are held in late January or early February in Paris' two Chinatowns: the smaller but more authentic one in the 3e, taking in rue du Temple, rue au Maire and rue de Turbigo (Ⓜ Temple or Arts et Métiers), and the flashier one in the 13e area in the triangle formed by porte de Choisy, porte d'Ivry and blvd Masséna (Ⓜ Porte de Choisy, Port d'Ivry or Tolbiac).

Salon International de l'Agriculture (www.salon -agriculture.com) A 10-day international agricultural fair with lots to eat and drink, including dishes and wine from all over France. Held at the Parc des Expositions at Porte de Versailles in the 15e (Ⓜ Porte de Versailles) from late February to early March.

March & April
Printemps du Cinéma (www.printempsducinema.com) Cinemas across the capital welcome spring by offering film-goers a unique entry fee of €3.50 over three days (usually Sunday, Monday and Tuesday) sometime around 21 March.

Banlieues Bleues (www.banlieuesbleues.org) 'Suburban Blues' jazz and blues festival (with world, soul, funk and R&B thrown in for good measure) is held in March and April in the suburbs of Paris, including St-Denis (p208), and attracts big-name talent.

Marathon International de Paris (www.parismara thon.com) The Paris International Marathon in early April starts on the ave des Champs-Élysées, 8e, and finishes on av Foch, 16e. The Semi-Marathon de Paris is a half-marathon held in early March; see the marathon website for details.

Foire du Trône (www.foiredutrone.com in French) Huge funfair with 350 attractions is held on the pelouse de Reuilly of the Bois de Vincennes (Ⓜ Porte Dorée) for eight weeks during April and May.

May & June
Internationaux de France de Tennis (www.french open.org) The glitzy French Open tennis tournament takes place from late May to early June at Stade Roland Garros (Ⓜ Porte d'Auteuil) at the southern edge of the Bois de Boulogne in the 16e.

Fête de la Musique (www.fetedelamusique.culture .fr) A national music festival welcoming in summer on 21 June that satisfies a wide range of tastes with jazz, reggae, classical etc and features staged and impromptu live performances all over the city.

Gay Pride March (www.gaypride.fr in French) A colourful, Saturday afternoon parade held in late June through the Marais to Bastille celebrates Gay Pride Day, with various bars and clubs sponsoring floats, and participants in some eye-catching costumes.

Paris Jazz Festival (www.parcfloraldeparis.com) Free jazz concerts every Saturday and Sunday afternoon in June and July in Parc Floral de Paris (Ⓜ Château de Vincennes).

July & August
Bastille Day Paris is *the* place to be on 14 July, France's national day. Late on the night of the 13th, *bals des sapeurs-pompiers* (dances sponsored by Paris' fire brigades, who are considered sex symbols in France) are held at fire stations around the city. At 10am on the 14th, there's a military and fire-brigade parade along av des Champs-Élysées, 8e, accompanied by a fly-past of fighter aircraft and helicopters. In the evening a huge display of *feux d'artifice* (fireworks) is held at around 11pm on the Champ de Mars, 7e.

Tour de France (www.letour.fr) The last stage of the world's most prestigious cycling event has ended since 1975 with a race up av des Champs-Élysées on the 3rd or 4th Sunday of July.

Paris Plage (www.paris.fr) 'Paris Beach', one of the most unique and successful city recreational events in the world (and now duplicated in cities across Europe from Berlin to Budapest), sees 3km of embankment from the quai Henri IV (Ⓜ Sully Morland) in the 4e to the quai des Tuileries (Ⓜ Tuileries) below the Louvre in the 1er transformed from mid-July to mid-August into three sand and pebble beaches, with sun beds, umbrellas, atomisers and plastic palm trees. There's even a 38m paddling pool for kids.

September & October
Jazz à la Villette (www.villette.com) Super 10-day jazz festival with sessions in Parc de la Villette, at the Cité de la Musique and in surrounding bars in early September.

Festival d'Automne (www.festival-automne.com) 'Autumn Festival' of arts – including painting, music, dance and theatre – held in venues throughout the city from mid-September to December.

Nuit Blanche (www.paris.fr) 'White Night' is when Paris becomes 'the city that doesn't sleep', with museums across town joining bars and clubs and staying open till the very wee hours.

November & December
Jumping International de Paris (www.salon-cheval .com) The annual International Showjumping Competition in early December forms part of the Salon du Cheval at the Parc des Expositions at Porte de Versailles in the 15e (Ⓜ Porte de Versailles) with some of the best showjumpers in the world testing their limits.

Christmas Eve Mass Celebrated at midnight on Christmas Eve at many Paris churches, including Notre Dame, but get there by 11pm to find a place.

New Year's Eve Blvd St-Michel (5e), place de la Bastille (11e), the Eiffel Tower (7e) and especially av des Champs-Élysées (8e) are the places to be to welcome in the new year.

SLEEPING

Paris has a very wide choice of accommodation options that caters for all budgets. When calculating accommodation costs in Paris, assume you'll spend from €20 per person per night in a hostel and at least €35 for a wash-basin-equipped double in a budget hotel (count on anything up to €65 if you want your own shower). Bear in mind that you may be charged up to €5 to use communal showers in budget hotels. If you can't go without your daily ablutions, it is often a false economy staying at such places.

Midrange hotels in Paris offer some of the best value for money of any European capital. Hotels at this level always have en suite bathrooms; all rooms listed in this section have showers or baths unless noted otherwise. These hotels charge between €65 and €150 for a double and are generally excellent value, especially at the higher end.

Top-end places run the full gamut from tasteful and discreet boutique hotels to palaces with more than 100 rooms. Prices start at a minimum of €150 a night for two people and can reach the GNP of a medium-sized Latin American republic.

Breakfast – usually a simple continental affair of bread, croissants, butter, jam and coffee or tea, though American-style breakfast buffets are becoming more popular – is served at most hotels with two or more stars and costs from about €6 or €8.

Breakfast is usually included in the price of a bed or room at hostels.

Like most cities and towns elsewhere in France, Paris levies a *taxe de séjour* (tourist tax) of between €0.20 (camp sites, unclassified hotels) and €1.20 (four-star hotels) per person per night on all forms of accommodation.

Accommodation Services

The Paris tourist office, notably the Gare du Nord branch (p124), can find you a place to stay for the night of the day you stop by and will make the booking for free. The only catch is that you have to use a credit card. Be warned: the queues can be very long in the high season.

Some travel agencies (p124) can book you reasonably priced accommodation. The student travel agency **OTU Voyages** (Map pp110-11; ☎ 01 40 29 12 22, 01 55 82 32 32; www.otu.fr in French; 119 rue St-Martin, 4e; Ⓜ Rambuteau; ⊙ 9.30am-6.30pm Mon-Fri, 10am-6pm Sat), directly across the *parvis* (square) from Centre Pompidou, can *always* find you accommodation, even in summer. You pay for the accommodation plus a finder's/service fee of €15, and the staff give you a voucher to take to the hotel. Prices for singles are around €35; doubles start at about €40. Be prepared for long queues in high season.

An agency that can arrange bed-and-breakfast accommodation in Paris and gets good reviews from readers is **Alcôve & Agapes** (☎ 01 44 85 06 05; fax 01 44 85 06 14; www.bed-and-breakfast-in-paris.com). Expect to pay anything between €60 and €195 for a double.

Louvre & Les Halles

The very central area encompassing the Musée du Louvre and the Forum des Halles,

---

CAMPING IN PARIS

Camping du Bois de Boulogne (Map pp98-9; ☎ 01 45 24 30 00; www.campingparis.fr; 2 allée du Bord de l'Eau, 16e; sites off/mid-/peak season €11/14.90/16.50, with vehicle, tent & 2 people €20/24.50/27.50, with electricity €23/27.50/30.50, first-time booking fee €13; ⊙ 6am-2am) The Bois de Boulogne camping ground, the only one within the Paris city limits, measures 7 hectares and lies along the Seine at the far western edge of the Bois de Boulogne, opposite Île de Puteaux. With upwards of 435 camping pitches and two dozen bungalows, it gets very crowded in the summer, but there's usually space for a small tent. Fully equipped caravans accommodating four to five people are also available for rent; rates – €53.50 to €95.50 – depend on the type and the season.

Porte Maillot metro station (Map pp102–3), 4.5km to the northeast through the wood, is linked to the site by RATP bus No 244, which runs from 6am to 8.30pm, and from April to October also by a privately operated **shuttle bus** (€1.60; ⊙ 8.30am-1pm & 6pm-midnight).

effectively the 1er and a small slice of the 2e, is more disposed to welcoming top-end travellers, but there are some decent budget places, including the main branch of a popular hostel. Both airports are linked to nearby metro station Châtelet-Les Halles by the RER (Réseau Express Régional), a network of suburban lines (designated A to E and then numbered) that pass through the city centre.

BUDGET

Centre International de Séjour BVJ Paris-Louvre (Map pp110–11; ☎ 01 53 00 90 90; www.bvjhotel.com; 20 rue Jean-Jacques Rousseau, 1er; Ⓜ Louvre-Rivoli; dm €25, d per person €28; ✗ 🖳) This modern 200-bed hostel run by the Bureau des Voyages de la Jeunesse (Youth Travel Bureau) has bunks in a single-sex room for two to eight people. Guests should be aged under 35. Rooms are accessible from 2.30pm on the day you arrive and all day after that. There are no kitchen facilities and showers are in the hallway. There is usually space in the morning, even in the summer, so stop by as early as you can. Internet access is available for €1 for 10 minutes.

Hôtel Tiquetonne (Map pp110–11; ☎ 01 42 36 94 58; fax 01 42 36 02 94; 6 rue Tiquetonne, 2e; Ⓜ Étienne Marcel; s €30-40, d €50) This is a decent option if you're looking for good-value digs smack in the middle of party town. This vintage 47-room cheapie on a cobbled pedestrian street may not be inspirational, but it's clean and comfortable and some rooms are quite large.

TOP END

Hôtel Ritz Paris (Map pp102–3; ☎ 01 43 16 35 29; www.ritzparis.com; 15 place Vendôme, 1er; Ⓜ Opéra; s & d €680-770, ste from €900; ✗ 🔁 🖳) So famous it has lent its name to the English lexicon, the incomparable, unmistakable Ritz has 162 sparkling rooms and suites. Its L'Espadon restaurant has two Michelin stars and the Hemingway Bar is where the American author imbibed once he'd made a name for himself (and could afford it).

Marais & Bastille

There are quite a few top-end hotels in the heart of the lively Marais as well as in the vicinity of the elegant place des Vosges, and the choice of lower-priced one- and two-star hotels is excellent. Two-star comfort is less expensive closer to the Bastille in the

neighbouring 11e, however. Despite massive gentrification in recent years, there are some fine hostels and some less expensive hotels in the Marais as well. East of Bastille, the relatively untourised 11e is generally made up of unpretentious, working-class areas and is a good way to see the 'real' Paris up close.

BUDGET

Maison Internationale de la Jeunesse et des Étudiants (☎ 01 42 74 23 45; www.mije.com; dm €27, s/tw/tr per person €42/32/28; ✗ 🖳) The MIJE runs three hostels in attractively renovated 17th- and 18th-century *hôtels particuliers* (private mansions) in the heart of the Marais, and it's difficult to think of a better budget deal in Paris. Costs are the same for all three; there are single-sex, shower-equipped dorms with four to eight beds as well as singles, twins and triples. Rooms are closed from noon to 3pm, and the curfew is 1am to 7am. The maximum stay is seven nights. Individuals can make reservations at any of the three MIJE hostels listed below (all Map pp110–11) by calling the central switchboard or emailing; they'll hold you a bed till noon. During the summer and other busy periods, there may not be space after about mid-morning. There's an annual membership fee of €2.50.

MIJE Le Fauconnier (11 rue du Fauconnier, 4e; Ⓜ St-Paul or Pont Marie) This 122-bed hostel is two blocks south of MIJE Le Fourcy.

MIJE Le Fourcy (6 rue de Fourcy, 4e; Ⓜ St-Paul) The largest of the three branches with 185 beds. There's a cheap eatery here called Le Restaurant with a three-course *menu* including a drink for €10.50 and a two-course *formule* plus drink for €8.50.

MIJE Maubuisson (12 rue des Barres, 4e; Ⓜ Hôtel de Ville or Pont Marie) The pick of the three in our opinion, this 103-bed place is half a block south of the *mairie* (town hall) of the 4e.

Hôtel Baudin (Map pp114–15; ☎ 01 47 00 18 91; hotel baudin@wanadoo.fr; 113 av Ledru Rollin, 11e; Ⓜ Ledru Rollin; s €29-52, d €35-62, tr €40-76) This once-grand, old-fashioned hostelry has 17 brightly coloured rooms and fairly weathered public areas, with reception on the 1st floor. The rooms at the lower end of the price scale have wash basins only (hall showers are free) while more expensive ones have shower or bath and toilet.

Hôtel Rivoli (Map pp110–11; ☎ 01 42 72 08 41; 44 rue de Rivoli or 2 rue des Mauvais Garçons, 4e;

(M) Hôtel de Ville; s €30-50, d €40-50, tr €66) Long an LP favourite, the Rivoli is forever cheery but not as dirt cheap as it once was, with 20 basic, somewhat noisy rooms. The cheaper rooms have washbasins only but showers are free. The front door is locked from 2am to 7am.

Hôtel de la Herse d'Or (Map pp114-15; ☎ 01 48 87 84 09; www.hotel-herse-dor.com; 20 rue St-Antoine, 4e; (M) Bastille; s/d €40-68; (💻)) This friendly place just west of place de la Bastille has 35 servicable rooms off a long stone corridor. It's very basic and very cheap; the lower-priced rooms have washbasins only. You can check your emails at an internet station in the lobby (€1 for 15 minutes). And, just in case you wondered, *herse* in French is not 'hearse' but 'portcullis'. So let's just call it the 'Golden Gate Hotel'.

MIDRANGE

Hôtel Daval (Map pp114-15; ☎ 01 47 00 51 23; www .hoteldaval.com; 21 rue Daval, 11e; s/d/tr/q €67/71/84/98; (M) Bastille; (💻)) This 21-room property is a clean and central option if you're looking for budget accommodation just off place de la Bastille. Rooms and baths are a bit on the small side; rooms in the back (eg No 13) are quieter.

Hôtel Lyon Mulhouse (Map pp114-15; ☎ 01 47 00 91 50; www.1-hotel-paris.com; 8 blvd Beaumarchais, 11e; (M) Bastille; s €65-90, d €78-110, tr €110-130; (💻)) A former post house from where carriages would set out for Lyon and Mulhouse in Alsace, this place has 40 quiet and comfortable rooms. Place de la Bastille and the delightful market on blvd Richard Lenoir (p169) are just around the corner.

Hôtel Jeanne d'Arc (Map pp114-15; ☎ 01 48 87 62 11; www.hoteljeannedarc.com; 3 rue de Jarente, 4e; (M) St-Paul; s €58-96, d €82-96, tr €115, q €145; (♿)) This cosy, 36-room hotel near lovely place du Marché Ste-Catherine is a great little base for your peregrinations among the museums, bars and restaurants of the Marais and almost has a country feel to it. But everyone knows about it so book early.

Hôtel du Septième Art (Map pp110-11; ☎ 01 44 54 85 00; hotel7art@wanadoo.fr; 20 rue St-Paul, 4e; (M) St-Paul; s & d €85-135, tw €90-135; (💻)) This heavily themed hotel on the south side of rue St-Antoine is a fun place for film buffs (*le septième art*, or 'the seventh art', is what the French call cinema), with a black-and-white-movie theme throughout, right down

to the tiled floors and bathrooms. The 23 guestrooms spread over five floors (no lift) are sizable and quite different one from the other. A single with just washbasin is €59.

Hôtel Central Marais (Map pp110-11; ☎ 01 48 87 56 08; www.hotelcentralmarais.com; 2 rue Ste-Croix de la Bretonnerie, 4e; (🌙) Hôtel de Ville; s & d €87, tr €107; (💻 💻)) This small hotel in the centre of gay land, Paris, caters essentially for gay men, though lesbians are also welcome. It's in a lovely 17th-century building and its seven rooms are spread over as many floors; there is no lift. Also there is only one bathroom for every two rooms, though the room on the 5th floor has an adjoining bathroom and toilet.

Hôtel de Nice (Map pp110-11; ☎ 01 42 78 55 29; www .hoteldenice.com; 42bis rue de Rivoli, 4e; (M) Hôtel de Ville; s €65-75, d €95-105, tr €130) This is an especially warm, family-run place with 23 comfortable rooms, some of which have balconies high above busy rue de Rivoli. Every square inch of wall space is used to display old prints, and public areas and guestrooms are full of Second Empire-style furniture and Indian carpets.

Hôtel Castex (Map pp114-15; ☎ 01 42 72 31 52; www .castexhotel.com; 5 rue Castex, 4e; (M) Bastille; s €85-115, d & tw €95-140, ste €160-220; (💻 💻)) Equidistant from Bastille and the Marais, the 30-room Castex retains some of its 17th-century elements, including a vaulted stone cellar used as a breakfast room, terracotta tiles on the floor and Toile de Jouy wallpaper. Try to get one of the independent rooms (Nos 1 & 2) off the lovely patio.

Grand Hôtel Malher (Map pp110-11; ☎ 01 42 72 60 92; www.grandhotelmalher.com; 5 rue Malher, 4e; (M) St-Paul; s €95-120, d €115-140, ste €170-185; (♿)) This welcoming establishment run by the same family for three generations has a small but pretty courtyard at the back. The 31 guestrooms are of a decent size, and the bathrooms modern and relatively capacious.

Hôtel Bastille de Launay (Map pp114-15; 01 47 00 88 11; www.albotel.com; 42 rue Amelot, 11e; (M) Chemin Vert; s €73, d €102-129; (💻)) This 36-room hotel offers good value for money due to its central location just up from place de la Bastille. Rooms are smallish and much of a muchness, with classic lower midrange furnishings and carpets. Double room No 41 and twin No 43 face rue Amelot and the steps up to blvd Beaumarchais.

Hôtel de la Place des Vosges (Map pp114-15; ☎ 01 42 72 60 46; www.hotelplacedesvosges.com; 12 rue

de Birague, 4e; Ⓜ Bastille; s & d €107-140, ste €207; 🖳)
This superbly situated 17-room hotel is an oasis of tranquillity due south of sublime place des Vosges. The public areas are quite impressive and the rooms have recently had a facelift. There's a tiny lift from the 1st to 4th floors but stairs only from the ground floor and to the 5th floor.

Hôtel St-Louis Marais (Map pp114-15; ☎ 01 48 87 87 04; www.saintlouismarais.com; 1 rue Charles V, 4e; Ⓜ Sully Morland; s €99, d & tw €115-140, tr €150, ste €160m; 🖳) This especially charming hotel in a converted 17th-century convent is more Bastille than Marais but still within easy walking distance of the latter. Wooden beams, terracotta tiles and heavy brocade drapes tend to darken the 19 rooms but certainly add to the atmosphere. Be aware that there are four floors here but no lift.

Hôtel de la Bretonnerie (Map pp110-11; ☎ 01 48 87 77 63; www.bretonnerie.com; 22 rue Ste-Croix de la Bretonnerie, 4e; Ⓜ Hôtel de Ville; s & d €116-149, t & q €174, ste €180-205; 🖳) This is a very charming upper midrange place in the heart of the Marais nightlife area dating from the 17th century. The décor of each of the 22 guestrooms and seven suites is unique, and some rooms have four-poster and canopy beds. Three 'duplex' suites on two levels are huge and can easily accommodate three or four people.

New Hôtel Candide (Map pp114-15; ☎ 01 43 79 02 33; www.new-hotel.com; 3 rue Pétion, 11e; Ⓜ Voltaire; s/d €95/120; ⊠ 🖳) This 48-room hotel within easy striking distance of both Bastille and the Marais offers relatively good value and is very convenient to the Marché Bastille (p169) on blvd Richard Lenoir. It's on a quiet street and we've always been impressed by the friendly, helpful service.

Hôtel Caron de Beaumarchais (Map pp110-11; ☎ 01 42 72 34 12; www.carondebeaumarchais.com; 12 rue Vieille du Temple, 4e; Ⓜ St-Paul; s & d €125-162; ⊠ 🆒 🖳) Decorated like an 18th-century private house contemporary with Beaumarchais – who wrote *Le Mariage de Figaro* (The Marriage of Figaro) at No 47 of the same street, this themed hotel has to be seen to be believed. The museum-like lobby, with its prized 18th-century pianoforte, gilded mirrors, and candelabras, sets the tone of the place. Downsides: the 19 guestrooms are on the smallish side and the welcome is not very warm.

TOP END

ourpick Hôtel St-Merry (Map pp110-11; ☎ 01 42 78 14 15; www.hotelmarais.com; 78 rue de la Verrerie, 4e; Ⓜ Châtelet; d & tw €160-230, tr €205-275, ste €335-407) The interior of this small hostelry, with beamed ceilings, remade church pews and confessionals, and wrought-iron candelabra, is a goth's wet dream and just the place for the Dracula in you who yearns to breathe free. Arguably our favourite medieval number in the Marais, the 11 rooms and one suite of this hotel are in the one-time presbytery of the attached Église St-Merry. So very close are both structures that two flying buttresses straddle the double bed of room No 9; the possibilities for in-house gymnastics are endless. Some rooms are on the smallish side – although No 11 is larger than most, No 20 is a suite with eye-popping furnishings and No 12 has a bed board formed of ancient church furnishings and a large table. On the downside: there is no lift connecting the postage-stamp lobby with the four upper floors, no mod cons to speak of (including TVs) and no air conditioning in a hotel that gets quite warm in summer.

Hôtel Les Jardins du Marais (Map pp114-15; ☎ 01 40 21 22 23; www.homeplazza.com; 74 rue Amelot, 11e; Ⓜ Chemin Vert; s & d €350-455, ste from €600; ⊠ 🆒 🖳 🆓) You'd never know you were in Paris after walking through the door of this 268-room hotel housed in nine separate buildings designed by Gustave Eiffel and surrounding an enormous courtyard of cobblestones and gardens. Rooms are Art Deco, with furnishings in maple and mahogany, and the outlets are always bursting at the seams.

Île de la Cité & Île St-Louis

Believe it or not, the only hotel on the Île de la Cité is a budget one. However, Île St-Louis, the smaller of the two islands in the Seine, is by far the more romantic and has a string of excellent top-end hotels. It's an easy walk from the Marais and the Latin Quarter.

BUDGET

Hôtel Henri IV (Map pp110-11; ☎ 01 43 54 44 53; 25 place Dauphine, 1er; Ⓜ Pont Neuf or Cité; s €27-34, d €35-72, tr €47) This decrepit place, with 20 tattered and worn rooms, is popular for its location, location and – above all else – location on the very tip of the Île de la Cité. It would be impossible to find something this romantic at such a price elsewhere; just don't stay in bed too long. Singles and triples have washbasin only; doubles are equipped with shower or bath. Book well in advance.

TOP END

Hôtel St-Louis (Map pp110-11; ☎ 01 46 34 04 80; www .hotel-saint-louis.com; 75 rue St-Louis en l'Île, 4e; Ⓜ Pont Marie; d/tw €140/155, ste €220; ✖ 🖳 ⑤) One of several hotels lining posh rue St-Louis en l'Île, this place has 19 appealing but unspectacular rooms, though the public areas are lovely. The breakfast room in the basement dates from the early 17th century.

Hôtel de Lutèce (Map pp110-11; ☎ 01 43 26 23 52; www.hotel-ile-saintlouis.com; 65 rue St-Louis en l'Île, 4e; Ⓜ Pont Marie; s/d/tr €130/164/186; ✖ 🖳) An exquisite hotel and more country than city, the Lutèce has an enviable spot on delightful Île St-Louis and 23 comfortable and tastefully decorated rooms. The lobby, with its ancient fireplace aglow in the cooler months, wood panelling and antique furnishings, sets the tone of the whole place.

Latin Quarter & Jardin des Plantes

The northern section of the 5e close to the Seine has been popular with students and young people since the Middle Ages though there is precious little budget accommodation left in the area.

There are dozens of attractive two- and three-star hotels in the Latin Quarter, including a cluster near the Sorbonne and another group along the lively rue des Écoles. Midrange hotels in the area are very popular with visiting academics so rooms are hardest to find when conferences and seminars are scheduled (usually from March to July and in October). In general this part of the city offers better value among topend hotels than the neighbouring 6e does. The Luxembourg and Port Royal RER stations are linked to both airports by RER and Orlyval.

BUDGET

Young & Happy Hostel (Map pp118-19; ☎ 01 47 07 47 07; www.youngandhappy.fr; 80 rue Mouffetard, 5e; Ⓜ Place Monge; dm €21-23, d per person €24-26; ✖ 🖳) Although slightly tatty, this is a friendly spot in the centre of the Latin Quarter. It's popular with a slightly older crowd nowadays. The rooms are closed from 11am to 4pm, but the reception remains open; the 2am curfew is enforced. Beds are in very small rooms for two to eight people with washbasins. In summer the best way to get a bed is to stop by at about 8am. Internet access costs €2 for 30 minutes.

Centre International de Séjour BVJ Paris-Quartier Latin (Map pp114-15; ☎ 01 43 29 34 80; www .bvjhotel.com; 44 rue des Bernardins, 5e; Ⓜ Maubert Mutualité; dm €26, s/d per person €35/28; ✖ 🖳) This 100-bed hostel on the Left Bank is a branch of the Centre International BVJ Paris-Louvre (p153) and has the same rules. All of the rooms here have showers and telephones.

Port Royal Hôtel (Map pp118-19; ☎ 01 43 31 70 06; www.portroyal.fr; 8 blvd de Port Royal, 5e; Ⓜ Les Gobelins; s €41-89, d €52.50-89; ⑤) It's hard to imagine that this 46-room hotel, owned and managed by the same family for three generations, still only bears one star. The spotless and very quiet rooms overlook a small glassed-in courtyard (eg No 15) or the street (No 14) but we especially like room No 11 with its colourful bed frame and pretty bathroom.

Hôtel Gay-Lussac (Map pp118-19; ☎ 01 43 54 23 96; hotel.gay-lussac@club-internet.fr; 29 rue Gay Lussac, 5e; Ⓜ Luxembourg; s & d with washbasin €49, s €55-59, d €64-68.50, tr/q €90/95) The Gay-Lussac is a 35-room threadbare hotel with a certain amount of character in the southern part of the Latin Quarter. Though the single rooms are small, the others are large and have high ceilings. Rates include breakfast.

MIDRANGE

Hôtel du Collège de France (Map pp118-19; ☎ 01 43 26 78 36; www.hotel-collegedefrance.com; 7 rue Thénard, 5e; Ⓜ Maubert Mutualité; s €70-85, d €78-115, tw €80-97; 🖳) Close by its prestigious educational namesake, the 'College of France' is a 29-room hotel with fairly ordinary guestrooms; go for the ones overlooking the quiet street, especially those with two windows. The lobby, with its roaring fire, stained glass and statue of Joan of Arc, is welcoming.

Hôtel de l'Espérance (Map pp118-19; ☎ 01 47 07 10 99; www.hoteldelesperance.fr; 15 rue Pascal, 5e; Ⓜ Censier Daubenton; s €71-79, d €79-87, tw €87, tr €102; 🖳 ⑤) The 'Hotel of Hope', just a couple of minutes' walk south of lively rue Mouffetard, is a quiet and immaculately kept 38-room place with faux antique furnishings and a warm welcome. Some of the larger rooms have two double beds.

Hôtel Esmeralda (Map pp110-11; ☎ 01 43 54 19 20; fax 01 40 51 00 68; 4 rue St-Julien le Pauvre, 5e; Ⓜ St-Michel; s €35-85, d €80-95, tr/q €110/120) Tucked away in a quiet street with full views of Notre Dame, the Esmeralda has been everyone's secret 'find' for years now so book well in advance. At these prices and location the 19 guestrooms – the cheapest singles have washbasin only – are no great shakes so expect little beyond the picture postcard through the window.

Familia Hôtel (Map pp118-19; ☎ 01 43 54 55 27; www .hotel-paris-familia.com; 11 rue des Écoles, 5e; Ⓜ Cardinal Lemoine; s €72-93, d €83-125, tr €129-149, q €147-171; 🖳) This very welcoming and well-situated family-run hotel has attractive sepia murals of Paris' landmarks in its 30 rooms. Eight rooms have little balconies, from which you can catch a glimpse Notre Dame. By far the choicest rooms are Nos 61, 62 and 65 (the last has a four-poster bed). We love the flower-bedecked window and the complimentary buffet breakfast.

Hôtel St-Jacques (Map pp118-19; ☎ 01 44 07 45 45; www.hotel-saintjacques.com; 35 rue des Écoles, 5e; Ⓜ Maubert Mutualité; s €52-80, d €90-118, tr €145; ✖ 🖳 ♿) This very stylish 38-room hotel has balconies that overlook the Panthéon. Audrey Hepburn and Cary Grant, who filmed some scenes of *Charade* here in the 1960s, would commend the mod cons that now complement the original 19th-century details (trompe l'œil ceilings, iron staircase etc).

Hôtel Minerve (Map pp118-19; ☎ 01 43 26 26 04; www.hotel-paris-minerve.com; 13 rue des Écoles, 5e; Ⓜ Cardinal Lemoine; s €84-132, d €98-132, tr €150-152; ✖ 🖳) This 54-room hotel in two buildings is owned by the same family who runs the Familia Hôtel (above). It has a reception area kitted out in Oriental carpets and antique books, and we like the frescoes of French monuments and reproduction 18th-century wallpaper in some of the rooms. Some 10 rooms have small balconies, eight have views of Notre Dame and two have tiny courtyards that are swooningly romantic.

Hôtel des Grandes Écoles (Map pp118-19; ☎ 01 43 26 79 23; www.hotel-grandes-ecoles.com; 75 rue du Cardinal Lemoine, 5e; Ⓜ Cardinal Lemoine or Place Monge; s & d €105-130, tr €125-150; ✖ ♿) This wonderful and welcoming hotel, just north of place de la Contrescarpe, has one of the loveliest situations in the Latin Quarter, tucked away in a courtyard off a medieval street with its own garden. Choose a room in one of three

buildings but our favourites are those in the garden annexe, especially the five that are on the ground floor and have direct access to the garden (Nos 29 to 33).

Hôtel du Levant (Map pp110-11; ☎ 01 46 34 11 00; www.hoteldulevant.com; 18 rue de la Harpe, 5e; Ⓜ Cluny-La Sorbonne or St-Michel; s €95-115, d €111-135, tw €150, tr €165-206, ste €285-303) It's hard to imagine anything more central than this recently renovated 46-room hotel in the heart of the Latin Quarter. The lobby, done up in yellows and reds, is warm and welcoming. The rooms are of a decent size, furnishings two steps beyond pure functional and the bathrooms completely new.

TOP END

Select Hôtel (Map pp118-19; ☎ 01 46 34 14 80; www.select hotel.fr; 1 place de la Sorbonne, 5e; Ⓜ Cluny-La Sorbonne; d €139-175, tw €155-175, tr €179-189, ste €212; ✖ 🖳) What was once a popular student hotel in the thick of the Sorbonne area, the Select has metamorphosed into an Art Deco mini-palace, with an atrium and cactus-strewn winter garden, an 18th-century vaulted breakfast room and 67 stylish guestrooms. The 1920s-style cocktail bar with an attached 'library' is a delight.

Hôtel Résidence Henri IV (Map pp118-19; ☎ 01 44 41 31 81; www.residencehenri4.com; 50 rue des Bernardins, 5e; Ⓜ Maubert Mutualité; s & d €175-185, 1-/2 person apt €220-230, 3-person apt €250-260, 4-person apt €300-310; 🖳) This exquisite late 19th-century hotel at the end of a quiet cul-de-sac near the Sorbonne has eight rooms and five two-room apartments – all with kitchenettes. They are of a generous size and look out onto the street and leafy square while the bathrooms face a courtyard.

Hôtel La Demeure (Map pp118-19; ☎ 01 43 37 81 25; www.hotel-paris-lademeure.com; 51 blvd St-Marcel, 13e; Ⓜ Gobelins; s/d €155/190, ste €245; ✖ ✖ 🖳) This self-proclaimed *'hôtel de caractère'*, owned and operated by a charming father-son team, is just a bit away from the action at the bottom of the 5e. But the refined elegance of its 43 rooms, the almost 'clubby' public areas and the wraparound balconies of the corner rooms make it worth going that extra distance. Unusually for Paris, the entire hotel is nonsmoking.

St-Germain, Odéon & Luxembourg

The well-heeled St-Germain des Prés is a delightful area to stay but has very little in the way of budget offerings. On the other hand there are some excellent midrange hotels here.

MIDRANGE

Hôtel de Nesle (Map pp110-11; ☎ 01 43 54 62 41; www .hoteldenesleparis.com; 7 rue de Nesle, 6e; Ⓜ Odéon or Mabillon; s €55-75, d €75-100) The Nesle is a relaxed, colourfully decorated hotel with 20 rooms, half of which are painted with murals taken from (mostly French) literature. What is by far its greatest asset, though, is the huge back garden accessible from the 1st floor in the back, with pathways, trellis and even a small pond.

Hôtel Sèvres Azur (Map pp108-9; ☎ 01 45 48 84 07; www.hotelsevresazur.com; 22 rue de l'Abbé Grégoire, 6e; Ⓜ St-Placide; s €85-95, d €90-115, tr €135; ▯ ⚬) Well-situated on a quiet street between Montparnasse and St-Germain, this 31-room hotel offers some of the best value for money on the left bank. Rooms are of a decent size; yellows and oranges predominate and the ones facing the courtyard are as bright as those looking on to the street.

Hôtel du Globe (Map pp110-11; ☎ 01 43 26 35 50; www.hotel-du-globe.fr; 15 rue des Quatre Vents, 6e; Ⓜ Odéon; s €95-120, d €105-130, ste €160; ▯) The Globe is an eclectic caravanserai with 14 small but completely renovated rooms just south of the blvd St-Germain. Some of the rooms are verging on the minuscule, and there is no lift (but four floors to ascend via a very narrow staircase). Still, we're suckers for armour and there are at least two full sets here.

Hôtel du Lys (Map pp110-11; ☎ 01 43 26 97 57; www .hoteldulys.com; 23 rue Serpente, 6e; Ⓜ Odéon; s/d/tr €95/115/130) This 22-room hotel situated in what was a *hôtel particulier* in the 17th century has been owned and operated by the same family for six decades. We love the beamed ceiling and the *chinoiserie* wallpaper in the lobby; rooms to go for include the blue-toned No 13 with its striped ceiling and two windows or the darker (but more atmospheric) No 13 in terracotta and with rustic old furniture.

Hôtel de Danemark (Map pp108-9; ☎ 01 43 26 93 78; www.hoteldanemark.com; 21 rue Vavin, 6e; Ⓜ Vavin; s €115-132, d €132-152; ⚬ ⚬ ▯) This positively scrumptious boutique hotel southwest of the Jardin du Luxembourg has tastefully furnished rooms and eclectic contemporary décor contrasting with ancient stone walls.

The 15 guestrooms, well soundproofed and of a generous size (minimum 20 sq metres) for a boutique hotel in central Paris, contain original artwork – though not all of it is museum-quality.

TOP END

Hôtel des Marronniers (Map pp110-11; ☎ 01 43 25 30 60; www.hotel-marronniers.com; 21 rue Jacob, 6e; Ⓜ St-Germain des Prés; s €110-168, d & tw €153-173, tr €208, q €248; ⚬ ▯) At the end of a small courtyard 50m from the main street, the 'Chestnut Trees' has 37 cosy rooms and a delightful conservatory giving onto a back garden. It's a real oasis in the heart of St-Germain. Rooms on the two uppermost floors (5th and 6th) have pretty views over the courtyard and roofs of central Paris.

L'Hôtel (Map pp110-11; ☎ 01 44 41 99 00; www.l-hotel .com; 13 rue des Beaux Arts, 6e; Ⓜ St-Germain des Prés; s & d €255-640, ste €540-740; ⚬ ▯ ⚬) With 20 rooms and tucked away in a quiet quay-side street, the place with the most minimal of names is the stuff of romantic Paris legends. Rock and film star groupies alike fight to sleep in room No 16 where Oscar Wilde died a century ago or in the mirrored Art Deco room (No 36) of legendary dancer Mistinguett with its huge mirrored bed. The public areas include a fantastic bar and restaurant under a glass canopy and, in the ancient cellar, a very modern swimming pool.

Montparnasse

Just east of Gare Montparnasse, there are a number of budget and low-end midrange places on rue Vandamme and rue de la Gaîté – though the latter street is rife with sex shops and peep shows. Gare Montparnasse is served by Air France buses from both airports. Place Denfert Rochereau is also linked to both airports by Orlybus, Orlyval and RER.

BUDGET

Hôtel de Blois (Map pp98-9; ☎ 01 45 40 99 48; www .hoteldeblois.com; 5 rue des Plantes, 14e; Ⓜ Mouton Duvernet; s €45-56, d €49-62, tw €58-66, tr €55-72; ⚬ ▯) This 25-room establishment just off the av du Maine underwent major renovations recently and is now a very pleasant, very affordable place just south of Gare Montparnasse. Rooms, smallish but fully equipped, now have shower or bath but some share use of the toilet in the hallway.

Celtic Hôtel (Map pp108-9; ☎ 01 43 20 93 53; hotel celtic@wanadoo.fr; 15 rue d'Odessa, 14e; Ⓜ Edgar Quinet; s €43-56, d €57-63, tr €75) An old-fashioned, 29-room place that has undergone a few changes in recent years – there's now a small lift and a new reception area. The cheaper singles are pretty bare and even the doubles and triples with private bathrooms are not exactly *tout confort* (in possession of all the mod-cons), but the Gare Montparnasse is only 200m away.

MIDRANGE

Hôtel Delambre (Map pp108-9; ☎ 01 43 20 66 31; www .hoteldelambre.com; 35 rue Delambre, 14e; Ⓜ Montparnasse; s €75-115, d €85-115, ste €150-160; ❄ 🖳) This attractive 30-room hotel just east of the Gare Montparnasse takes wrought-iron as a theme and uses it both in functional pieces (bed board, lamps) and decorative items throughout. Room No 7 has its own little terrace while Nos 1 and 2 give on to a small private courtyard.

Hôtel Aviatic (Map pp108-9; ☎ 01 53 63 25 50; www .aviatic.fr; 105 rue de Vaugirard, 6e; Ⓜ Montparnasse Bienvenüe; s & d €139-210; ❄ 🖳) This 43-room hotel with charming, almost Laura Ashley-style décor and a delightful Art Deco entrance has been in the business since 1856 so it must be doing something right. The tiny 'winter garden' is a breath of fresh air (literally). Some rooms face the street and some the quieter (and no less light) courtyard.

Faubourg St-Denis & Invalides

The 7e is a lovely arrondissement in which to stay, but apart from the northeastern section – the area east of Invalides and opposite the Louvre – it's fairly quiet here.

MIDRANGE

Hôtel Lindbergh (Map pp108-9; ☎ 01 45 48 35 53; www .hotellindbergh.com; 5 rue Chomel, 7e; Ⓜ Sèvres Babylone; s & d €98-160, tr €156-180, q €166-190; 🖳) We still haven't figured out why but this 26-room *hôtel de charme* (charming hotel) is totally kitted out in Charles Lindbergh photos and memorabilia but it works. We also like the room number plates on the doors with little Paris landmarks, the ample-sized bathrooms and the very friendly staff.

Hôtel Lenox St-Germain (Map pp108-9; ☎ 01 42 96 10 95; www.lenoxsaintgermain.com; 9 rue de l'Université, 7e; Ⓜ Rue du Bac; s €120-152, d €125-165, tw €152-165, ste €260-275; ❄ 🖳) This midrange

hotel in the posh 7e has 34 simple, uncluttered and comfortable rooms upstairs and a late-opening 1930s-style bar called the Lenox Club downstairs that attracts a chic clientele. The Art Deco décor is a treat and the fine leather armchairs in the lobby more than comfortable.

Eiffel Tower & 16th Arrondissement

Surprisingly these very chic neighbourhoods offer some decent choices in the way of midrange hotels.

MIDRANGE

Hôtel du Champ-de-Mars (Map pp108-9; ☎ 01 45 51 52 30; www.hotelduchampdemars.com; 7 rue du Champ de Mars, 7e; Ⓜ École Militaire; s/d/tw/tr €78/84/88/105; ❄ 🖳) This charming 25-room hotel in the shadow of the Eiffel Tower is on everyone's wish list so book a good month or two in advance. The attractive shopfront entrance leads into a colourful lobby done up in yellows and greens. Rooms on the lower floors can be downright cupboard-like, though; go up higher and you might earn a glimpse of Mademoiselle Eiffel herself.

Grand Hôtel Lévèque (Map pp108-9; ☎ 01 47 05 49 15; www.hotel-leveque.com; 29 rue Cler, 7e; Ⓜ École Militaire; s €57, d €87-110, tr €125; ❄) This 50-room hotel is recommended less for its charms than for its value for money and excellent location overlooking rue Cler and its market (p169). Choose any room ending in Nos 1 to 3 (eg room No 11 with its little balcony) – these have two windows overlooking the market.

Étoile & Champs-Élysées

This area boasts some of Paris's finest hotels – including a couple of real trendsetters.

TOP END

Hôtel Le A (Map pp102-3; ☎ 01 42 56 99 99; www.paris -hotel-a.com; 4 rue d'Artois, 8e; Ⓜ St-Philippe du Roule; s & d €329-399, ste €450-590; ❄ ❄ 🖳) One of our favourite new discoveries, the 'A' (think 'list') is an über-stylish minimalist hotel that doesn't have any of the attitude that generally goes with the concept. White, black and grey predominate and help 'frame' the fabulous contemporary art. The airy spaces – the breakfast area and bar are in a glassed-in courtyard – fireplace, and real books (as opposed to decorative items) in the lobby for guests' use are as welcome as the nonsmoking floor but rooms are somewhat petite.

Hôtel Costes (Map pp102-3; ☎ 01 42 44 50 00; www .hotelcostes.com; 239 rue St-Honoré, 1er; Ⓜ Concorde; s & d €350-800, ste from €1200; ☒ 🎇 🖳 🕩 ⓺) Jean-Louis Costes' eponymous hotel offers a 'luxurious and immoderate home away from home' to the style Mafia. Outfitted in camp Second Empire cast-offs with a Byzantine twist, the 82 rooms are petite but stylish. A delightful restaurant takes pride of place in the central Italian-style courtyard in the warmer months and the basement pool, with underwater music and Art Deco–ish lounge chairs, is a stunner.

Clichy & Gare St-Lazare

These areas offer some excellent midrange hotels. The better deals are away from Gare St-Lazare but there are several places along rue d'Amsterdam beside the station worth checking out. There's also an unusual place to stay in the budget category.

BUDGET

Style Hôtel (Map pp102-3; ☎ 01 45 22 37 59; fax 01 45 22 81 03; 8 rue Ganneron, 18e; Ⓜ La Fourche; s & d €35-50, tr/q €57/67) This 36-room hotel just north of place de Clichy and west of Cimetière de Montmartre is a titch rough around the edges (rough wooden floors, old runner carpets in the hallways) but is loaded with character and the welcome is always charming. There's a lovely double courtyard, but no lift. The cheapest singles and doubles are equipped with washbasin only.

Hôtel Eldorado (Map pp102-3; ☎ 01 45 22 35 21; www.eldoradohotel.fr; 18 rue des Dames, 17e; Ⓜ Place de Clichy; s €25-50, d & tw €45-70, tr €50-80) This bohemian place is one of Paris' grooviest finds: a welcoming, somewhat well-run place with 40 colourfully decorated rooms in a main building on a quiet street and in an annexe with a private garden at the back. Is this really Paris? Be aware that the cheaper-category rooms have washbasin only.

MIDRANGE

New Orient Hôtel (Map pp102-3; ☎ 01 45 22 21 64; www.hotel-paris-orient.com; 16 rue de Constantinople, 8e; s €82-105, d €99-105, tw €105-130, tr & q €140; Ⓜ Europe; ☒ 🎇 🖳) This 30-room nonsmoking hotel, situated in a neighbourhood of the 8e north of Gare St-Lazare that seems to have only shops that sell musical instruments

and/or sheet music, has a lot of personality, especially in the common areas. Some rooms (eg twin room No 7 and double No 8) have little balconies.

Hôtel Favart (Map pp104-5; ☎ 01 42 97 59 83; www .hotel-paris-favart.com; 5 rue Marivaux, 2e; Ⓜ Richelieu Drouot; s €89-110, d €110-135, tr €130-160, q €155-176; ☒ 🎇 ⓺) With 37 rooms facing the Opéra Comique, the Favart is a stylish Art Nouveau hotel that feels like it never let go of the *belle époque*. If you're interested in shopping at the big department stores on blvd Haussmann, this is an excellent choice.

Opéra & Grands Boulevards

The avenues around blvd Montmartre are a popular nightlife area and a lively district in which to stay.

MIDRANGE

Hôtel Vivienne (Map pp104-5; ☎ 01 42 33 13 26; paris@hotel-vivienne.com; 40 rue Vivienne, 2e; Ⓜ Grands Boulevards; s €54-104, d €69-104, tw €90-104; ☒ 🎇 🖳) This stylish 45-room hotel is amazingly good value for Paris. While the rooms are not huge, they have all the mod cons, some boast little balconies and the public areas are bright and cheery. The Vivienne is a very wise choice if you want to be close to the Palais Royal or the Vivienne and Colbert covered passages (p143).

Hôtel Chopin (Map pp104-5; ☎ 01 47 70 58 10; fax 01 42 47 00 70; 46 passage Jouffroy, entrance at 10 blvd Montmartre, 9e; Ⓜ Grands Boulevards; s €58-73, d €75-86, tr €100) Dating back to 1846, the 36-room Chopin is down one of Paris' most delightful 19th-century *passages couverts* (covered shopping arcades; p143). It may be a little faded around the edges, but it's still enormously evocative of the *belle époque* and the welcome is always warm. The cheapest singles have washbasin only.

Hôtel des Arts (Map pp104-5; ☎ 01 42 46 73 30; hdag@free.fr; 7 Cité Bergère, 9e; Ⓜ Grands Boulevards; s/d/tr €74/82/98; ⓺) This quirky place with pink geraniums bedecking each exterior window is in a quiet little alley off rue du Faubourg Montmartre. It has 25 rooms recently redone in shades of plum and burgundy and there seems to be a bird theme (ancient prints, caged squawker in the lobby) throughout. There are seven other hotels on this tranquil street alone.

Hôtel Peletier-Haussmann-Opéra (Map pp104-5; ☎ 01 42 46 79 53; www.peletieropera.com; 15 rue Le

Peletier, 9e; (M) Richelieu Drouot; s €72-80, d €82-90, tr €86-95; (🖳)) This is a pleasant, 26-room hotel just off blvd Haussmann and close to the big department stores. There are attractive packages available at weekends, depending on the season. Internet access here costs €2 for 15 minutes.

Hôtel Langlois (Map pp102-3; ☎ 01 48 74 78 24; www .hotel-langlois.com; 63 rue St-Lazare, 9e; (M) Trinité; s €89-104, d & tw €104-120, ste €160) Built in 1870, this 27-room hotel has retained its charming *belle époque* look and feel despite a massive makeover in 1997. The hotel's rooms and suites are unusually large for a small-ish hotel in Paris and it is very convenient to the department stores on blvd Haussmann.

Gare du Nord, Gare de l'Est & République

The areas east and northeast of the Gare du Nord and Gare de l'Est have always had a more than ample selection of hotels and now you'll also find a hostel within striking distance. At the same time, there are quite a few two- and three-star places around the train stations in the 10e that are convenient if you are catching an early-morning train to London or want to crash immediately upon arrival. Place de la République is convenient for the nightlife areas of Ménilmontant.

Gare du Nord is linked to Charles de Gaulle airport by RER and RATP bus No 350 and to Orly airport by Orlyval. Bus No 350 to/from Charles de Gaulle airport also stops right in front of the Gare de l'Est.

BUDGET

Auberge de Jeunesse Jules Ferry (Map pp104-5; ☎ 01 43 57 55 60; www.fuaj.fr; 8 blvd Jules Ferry, 11e; (M) République or Goncourt; dm €20, d per person €20; (✗) (✗) (🖳)) This official hostel, three blocks east of place de la République, is somewhat institutional and the rooms (with 99 beds) could use a refit, but the atmosphere is fairly relaxed. Beds are in two- to six-person rooms, which are locked between 10.30am and 2pm for housekeeping; there is no curfew. You'll have pay an extra €2.90 per night if you don't have an HI card or equivalent.

Auberge de Jeunesse Le D'Artagnan (Map pp98-9; ☎ 01 40 32 34 57; www.fuaj.fr; 80 rue Vitruve, 20e; (M) Porte de Bagnolet; dm €21.50) The only other official hostel in central Paris. It's far from the centre of the action but just one metro stop from the Gare Routière Internationale de Paris-Galliéni (International Bus Termi-

nal). It has rooms with two to eight beds, big lockers, laundry facilities, a bar, cinema, and the same rules and regulations as the Jules Ferry hostel. With 435 beds on seven floors, it is the largest hostel in France.

Peace & Love Hostel (Map pp104-5; ☎ 01 46 07 65 11; www.paris-hostels.com; 245 rue La Fayette, 10e; (M) Jaurès or Louis Blanc; dm €17-21, d per person €21-26; (🖳)) This modern-day hippy hang-out is a groovy though chronically crowded hostel with beds in 20 smallish, shower-equipped rooms for two to four people. There's a great kitchen and eating area, but most of the action seems to revolve around the ground floor bar (open till 2am) that boasts more than 30 types of beer, including the cheapest blondes (that's lagers) in Paris. Internet access costs from €2 for 15 minutes.

Hôtel de Nevers (Map pp104-5; ☎ 01 47 00 56 18; www.hoteldenevers.com; 53 rue de Malte, 11e; (M) Oberkampf; s & d €35-53, tr €66-78; (🖳) (♿)) This excellent-value family-run budget hotel is around the corner from place de la République, and within easy walking distance of the nightlife of Ménilmontant. Hyperallergenics may think twice about staying here, though; there are at least two cats on hand to greet you. The 32 guestrooms are sparingly furnished but nothing is threadbare and everything is proper and *propre* (clean).

Sibour Hôtel (Map pp104-5; ☎ 01 46 07 20 74; sibour .hotel@wanadoo.fr; 4 rue Sibour, 10e; (M) Gare de l'Est; s €40-55, d €40-65, tr/q €75/85) This friendly place has 45 well-kept rooms, including some old-fashioned ones – the cheapest singles and doubles – with washbasins only. Hall showers cost €3. Some of the rooms look down on pretty Église de St-Laurent.

Hôtel La Vieille France (Map pp104-5; ☎ 01 45 26 42 37; la.vieille.france@wanadoo.fr; 151 rue La Fayette, 10e; (M) Gare du Nord; s €42, d €60-65, tr €90; (🖳)) The 'Old France' is an upbeat, 34-room place with relatively spacious and pleasant rooms though with the Gare du Nord so close it's bound to be somewhat noisy. Singles are basic, with washbasins only, but hall showers are free.

MIDRANGE

Nord-Est Hôtel (Map pp104-5; ☎ 01 47 70 07 18; hotel.nord.est@wanadoo.fr; 12 rue des Petits Hôtels, 10e; (M) Poissonnière; s/d/tr/q €63/73/97/123; (🖳)) This unusual 30-room hotel, charmingly located on the 'Street of Little Hotels', is set away from the street and fronted by a small terrace. It is convenient to both the Gare du Nord and the Gare de l'Est. Internet access costs an outrageous €8/12 for 30/60 minutes.

Grand Hôtel de Paris (Map pp104-5; ☎ 01 46 07 40 56; grand.hotel.de.paris@gofornet.com; 72 blvd de Strasbourg, 10e; Ⓜ Gare de l'Est; s/d/tr/q €77/83/102/119) The Grand Hôtel de Paris is a well-run establishment just south of the Gare de l'Est on blvd de Strasbourg. It has 49 sound-proofed rooms and a tiny lift and is a pleasant place to stay if you're in the area.

Hôtel Libertel Croix de Malte (Map pp114-15; ☎ 01 48 05 09 36; H2752@accor-hotels.com; 5 rue de Malte, 11e; Ⓜ Oberkampf; s/d €97/107; ☒ ▣) With its glassed-in courtyard sporting a giant jungle mural, this cheery hotel will have you thinking you're in the tropics not Paris. The 28 rooms are in two little buildings, only one of which has a lift.

TOP END
Murano Urban Resort (Map pp114-15; ☎ 01 42 71 20 00; www.muranoresort.com; 13 blvd du Temple, 3e; Ⓜ Filles du Calvaire; s €350, d €400-650, ste €750-950; ☒ ☒ ▣) This 52-room hotel's subtitle suggests that you should come, kick off your shoes and sink your toes in the hotel's figurative sand. And with public areas like a spa with heated pool and hammam, a courtyard restaurant under glass, a cool jazz and DJ bar and guestrooms that allow you to change their colour scheme, that's easily accomplished.

Ménilmontant & Belleville
The Ménilmontant nightlife district is an excellent area in which to spend the evening, but the selection of accommodation in all price categories is surprisingly limited.

MIDRANGE
Hôtel Beaumarchais (Map pp114-15; ☎ 01 53 36 86; www.hotelbeaumarchais.com; 3 rue Oberkampf, 11e; Ⓜ Filles du Calvaire; s €75, d €90-110, tr €170, ste €150; ☒ ▣) This brighter-than-bright 31-room boutique hotel, with its emphasis on sunbursts and bold primary colours, is just this side of kitsch. But it makes for a different Paris experience and fits in with its surroundings very well indeed. *La crème de la crème* is room No 1, which leads into the hotel's charming leafy terraced courtyard.

Hôtel du Vieux Saule (Map pp114-15; ☎ 01 42 72 01 14; www.hotelvieuxsaule.com; 6 rue Picardie, 3e; Ⓜ Filles du Calvaire; s €91, d €106-136, tr €151; ☒ ☒)

The flower-bedecked 'Old Willow Tree' is a 31-room hostelry in the northern Marais and something of a find because of its slightly unusual location. The hotel has a small sauna, there is a tranquil little 'garden' on full display behind glass off the lobby and the 'superior' rooms on the 3rd and 4th floors have been renovated.

Gare de Lyon, Nation & Bercy
The neighbourhood around the Gare de Lyon has a few budget hotels as well as a popular independent hostel.

BUDGET
Blue Planet Hostel (Map pp120-1; ☎ 01 43 42 06 18; www.hostelblueplanet.com; 5 rue Hector Malot, 12e; Ⓜ Gare de Lyon; dm €21; ☒ ▣) This 43-room hostel is very close to Gare de Lyon – convenient if you're heading south or west at the crack of dawn. Dorm beds are in rooms for two to four people and the hostel closes between 11am and 3pm. There's no curfew. Internet access costs €3 for 30 minutes.

Hôtel Le Cosy (Map pp98-9; ☎ 01 43 43 10 02; www.hotel-cosy.com; 50 av de St-Mandé, 12e; Ⓜ Picpus; s €35-85, d €48-85; ☒ ▣) This family-run budget hotel immediately southeast of place de la Nation positively oozes charm. The 28 rooms, though basic – the cheapest singles and doubles have washbasins only – are all different, decorated in original artwork and with hardwood floors. If feeling flush, choose one of four 'VIP' rooms in the courtyard annexe.

Montmartre & Pigalle
Montmartre, encompassing the 18e and the northern part of the 9e, is one of the most charming neighbourhoods in Paris. There is a bunch of top-end hotels in the area and the attractive midrange places on rue Aristide Bruant are generally less full in July and August than in spring and autumn.

The flat area around the base of the Butte Montmartre has some surprisingly good budget deals. The lively, ethnically mixed area east of Sacré Cœur can be a bit rough; some say it's prudent to avoid Château Rouge metro station at night. Both the 9e and the 18e have fine and recommended hostels.

BUDGET
Woodstock Hostel (Map pp104-5; ☎ 01 48 78 87 76; www.woodstock.fr; 48 rue Rodier, 9e; Ⓜ Anvers; dm €18-21,

d per person €21-24; ☒ ◻) Woodstock is just down the hill from raucous Pigalle in a quiet, residential quarter. Dorm beds are in rooms for four to six people, and each room has sink only; showers and toilets are off the corridor. Rooms are shut from 11am to 3pm, and the (enforced) curfew is at 2am. The spanking new eat-in kitchen down the steps from the patio has everything. Internet access is available for €2 for 30 minutes.

Le Village Hostel (Map p122; ☎ 01 42 64 22 02; www.villagehostel.fr; 20 rue d'Orsel, 18e; Ⓜ Anvers; dm €20-23, per person d €23-27 & tr €21.50-25; ☒ ◻) The 'Village' is a fine 25-room hostel with beamed ceilings and views of Sacré Cœur. Dorm beds are in rooms for four to six people and all rooms have showers and toilets. Kitchen facilities are available, and there's a popular bar too. Rooms are closed between 11am and 4pm and curfew is 2am. Internet access is available for €2.50 for 30 minutes.

Hôtel Bonséjour Montmartre (Map p122; ☎ 01 42 54 22 53; www.hotel-bonsejour-montmartre.fr; 11 rue Burq, 18e; Ⓜ Abbesses; s €25, d €32-48, tr €59) The 'Good Stay' at the top of a quiet street in Montmartre is a perennial budget favourite. It's a simple place to stay – no lift, and linoleum or parquet floors – but welcoming, comfortable, very clean and getting a much needed face-lift. Some rooms (eg Nos 14, 23, 33, 43 and 53) have little balconies attached and at least one room (No 55) offers a fleeting glimpse of Sacré Cœur. Hall showers cost €2.

MIDRANGE

Hôtel du Moulin (Map p122; ☎ 01 42 64 33 33; www .hotelmoulin.com; 3 rue Aristide Bruant, 18e; Ⓜ Abbesses or Blanche; s €55-63, d €59-67, tw €67-70; ◻) There are 27 good-sized rooms with toilet and bath or shower in both a main building and a garden annexe at this quiet little hotel. The Korean family who own the place are very kind. Check out their fun website. Internet access costs €1.60 for 30 minutes.

Hôtel Utrillo (Map p122; ☎ 01 42 58 13 44; www .hotel-paris-utrillo.com; 7 rue Aristide Bruant, 18e; Ⓜ Abbesses or Blanche; s €64, d & tw €76-82, tr €96; ☒ ◻ ⓐ) This friendly 30-room hotel, named for the 'painter of Montmartre', Maurice Utrillo, is smartly done up and can boast a few extras such as a little leafy courtyard in back and a small sauna.

Hôtel des Arts (Map p122; ☎ 01 46 06 30 52; www .arts-hotel-paris.com; 5 rue Tholozé, 18e; Ⓜ Abbesses

or Blanche; s €68, d & tw €82, tr €97; ◻) The 'Arts Hotel' is a friendly and attractive 50-room place convenient to both place Pigalle and Montmartre. Towering over it is the old-style windmills Moulin de la Galette. The resident canine is very friendly.

Hôtel Regyn's Montmartre (Map p122; ☎ 01 42 54 45 21; www.regynsmontmartre.com; 18 place des Abbesses, 18e; Ⓜ Abbesses; s €72-92, d & tw €84-104, tr €104-124; ☒ ◻) This 22-room hotel should be one of your first choices if you want to stay in old Montmartre and not break the bank. It's just opposite the Abbesses metro station, and some of the rooms have views out over Paris.

TOP END

Hôtel Résidence les Trois Poussins (Map pp104-5; ☎ 01 53 32 81 81; www.les3poussins.com; 15 rue Clauzel, 9e; Ⓜ St-Georges; s/d & tw €130/150, 1-/2-person studio €185, 3-/4-person studio €220; ☒ ◻ ⓐ) The 'Hotel of the Three Chicks' is a lovely property due south of place Pigalle with 40 rooms, half of which are small studios with their own cooking facilities. The back patio is a delightful place in the warmer months for breakfast or a drink.

Terrass Hotel (Map p122; ☎ 01 46 06 72 85; www .terrass-hotel.com; 12 rue Joseph de Maistre, 18e; Ⓜ Blanche; s €208-280, d €248-320, ste €36-360; ☒ ☒ ◻) This very sedate and stylish hotel at the southeastern corner of Montparnasse Cemetery has 100 spacious and well-designed rooms and suites. For the ultimate Parisian experience, choose junior suite No 703 for stunning views of the Eiffel Tower and Panthéon from the Jacuzzi or No 802, which boasts its own private terrace. Internet access costs from €4 for 15 minutes.

EATING

When it comes to food, Paris has everything – and nothing. As the culinary centre of the most aggressively gastronomic country in the whole world, the city has more 'generic French', regional and foreign-cuisine restaurants than any other place in France. But *la cuisine parisienne* (Parisian cuisine) is a poor relation of that extended family known as *la cuisine des provinces* (provincial cuisine). That's because those greedy country cousins have consumed most of what was once on Paris' own plate, claiming it as their own. Today very few French dishes except maybe *vol-au-vent* (light pastry shell filled

PARIS

with chicken or fish in a creamy sauce), *potage St-Germain* (thick green pea soup), onion soup and the humble pig's trotters are associated with the capital.

That said, like the Indian curry and Turkish kebabs of London, over the years foreign food has become as Parisian as that onion soup and those pig's trotters; the *nems* and *pâtés impérials* (spring or egg rolls) and *pho* (soup noodles with beef) of Vietnam, the couscous and *tajines* of North Africa, the *boudin antillais* (West Indian blood pudding) from the Caribbean and the *yassa* (meat or fish grilled in onion and lemon sauce) of Senegal are all eaten with relish throughout the capital. Indian and Japanese food are also very popular non-French cuisines in Paris. In fact, foreign food is what Paris does better than any other city in the country.

One of Paris' largest concentrations of foreign restaurants is squeezed into a labyrinth of narrow streets in the 5e arrondissement across the Seine from Notre Dame. The Greek, North African and Middle Eastern restaurants between rue St-Jacques, blvd St-Germain and blvd St-Michel, including rue de la Huchette, attract mainly foreign tourists, often under the mistaken impression that this little maze is the whole of the famous Latin Quarter. But you'd be far better off looking elsewhere for ethnic food: blvd de Belleville in the 20e for Middle Eastern; nearby rue de Belleville in the 19e for Asian (especially Thai and Vietnamese); and Chinatown in the 13e for Chinese, especially ave de Choisy, ave d'Ivry and rue Baudricourt.

Louvre & Les Halles

The area between Forum des Halles (1er) and the Centre Pompidou (4e) is filled with scores of trendy restaurants, but few of them are particularly good and they mostly cater to tourists, both foreign and French. Streets lined with places to eat include rue des Lombards, the narrow streets north and east of Forum des Halles and pedestrians-only rue Montorgueil, a market street and probably your best bet for something quick.

FRENCH

L'Épi d'Or (Map pp110-11; ☎ 01 42 36 38 12; 25 rue Jean-Jacques Rousseau, 1er; Ⓜ Louvre-Rivoli; starters €6-

15, mains €16-22, 2-/3-course menus €18/22; Ⓨ lunch & dinner Mon-Fri, Sat dinner till 10pm) This oh-so-Parisian bistro serves well-prepared, classic dishes – such as *gigot d'agneau* (leg of lamb) cooked for seven hours – to a surprisingly well-heeled crowd.

Le Petit Mâchon (Map pp110-11; ☎ 01 42 60 08 06; 158 rue St-Honoré, 1er; Ⓜ Palais Royal-Musée du Louvre; starters €7-12.50, mains €14-22, lunch menu €16.50; Ⓨ lunch & dinner Tue-Sun) An upbeat bistro with Lyon-inspired specialities; it's convenient to the Louvre. Try the *saucisson de Lyon* (Lyon sausage) studded with pistachios.

Le Vaudeville (Map pp104-5; ☎ 01 40 20 04 62; 29 rue Vivienne, 2e; Ⓜ Bourse; starters €6.50-14.50, mains €17-33, menus €19.90 & €29.90; Ⓨ lunch & dinner to 1am) This stunning brasserie just opposite the stock exchange is to Art Deco what the Bouillon Racine (p168) is to Art Nouveau. Come for the fabulous décor; the food might be something of a second thought (though you can be guaranteed a certain standard).

AMERICAN

Joe Allen (Map pp110-11; ☎ 01 42 36 70 13; 30 rue Pierre Lescot, 1er; Ⓜ Étienne Marcel; starters €7-9.80, mains €12.90-16.50, menus €12.90 lunch, €18 & €22.50; Ⓨ noon-1am) An institution in Paris for some 35 years, Joe Allen is a little bit of New York in Paris. There's an excellent brunch (€17 to €19.50) from noon to 4pm at the weekend. Ribs (€16.50) are a speciality.

ASIAN

Tana (Map pp110-11; ☎ 01 42 33 53 64; 36 rue Tiquetonne, 2e; Ⓜ Étienne Marcel; starters €7-12.50, mains €9-20; Ⓨ dinner to 11.30pm) In a street where each restaurant is more original than the next, Tana takes the tart, with sexy Thai 'waitresses' greeting and serving. The mixed hors d'oeuvre for two and the *homok pla* (steamed fish served in a banana leaf; €10) are both excellent choices.

Kunitoraya (Map pp104-5; ☎ 01 47 03 33 65; 39 rue Ste-Anne, 1er; Ⓜ Pyramides; soup & noodle dishes €8.50-16, lunch menu €12.50; Ⓨ 11.30am-10pm) With seating on two floors, this simple place has a wide and excellent range of Japanese noodle dishes and set lunches and dinners.

VEGETARIAN

La Victoire Suprême du Cœur (Map pp110-11; ☎ 01 40 41 93 95; 41 rue des Bourdonnais, 1er; Ⓜ Châtelet; starters & salads €4.70-10.70, mains €9.70-12.50, menus €12.50 lunch, €15.30 & €19.30; Ⓨ lunch & dinner to 10pm

Mon-Sat) This Indian-inspired vegan restaurant serves decent meatless dishes though you should avoid the mock-meat dishes like the seitan 'steak'. For drinks try the mango lassi or spiced tea. No smoking, no alcohol, no guilt.

QUICK EATS

L'Arbre à Cannelle (Map pp104-5; ☎ 01 45 08 55 87; 57 passage des Panoramas, 2e; Ⓜ Grands Boulevards; dishes €6.50-12; Ⓨ 11.30am-6.30pm Mon-Sat) The 'Cinnamon Tree' is a lovely tearoom in a covered passage with original 19th-century décor, *tartes salées* (savoury pies; €6.50 to €7), excellent salads (€6.50 to €9.50) and great *plats du jour* (€10).

SELF-CATERING

There are a number of supermarkets around Forum des Halles including a **Franprix Les Halles** (Map pp110-11; 35 rue Berger, 1er; Ⓜ Châtelet; Ⓨ 8.30am-7.50pm Mon-Sat). Other supermarkets include the following:

Ed l'Épicier Marais (Map pp110-11; 80 rue de Rivoli, 4e; Ⓜ Hôtel de Ville)

Franprix Châtelet (Map pp110-11; 16 rue Bertin Poirée, 1er; Ⓜ Châtelet; Ⓨ 8.30am-8pm Mon-Sat)

Marais & Bastille

The Marais, filled with small restaurants of every imaginable type, is one of Paris' premier neighbourhoods for eating out. In the direction of place de la République there's a decent selection of different national cuisines. If you're looking for authentic Chinese food but can't be bothered going all the way to Chinatown in the 13e or Belleville in the 20e, check out any of the small noodle shops and restaurants along rue Au Maire, 3e (Map pp110–11; Ⓜ Arts et Métiers), which is southeast of the Musée des Arts et Métiers. The kosher and kosher-style restaurants along rue des Rosiers, 4e (Map pp110–11; Ⓜ St-Paul), the so-called Pletzel, serve specialities from North Africa, Central Europe and Israel. Many are closed on Friday evening, Saturday and Jewish holidays. Takeaway falafel and *shwarma* (kebabs) are available at several places along the street.

Bastille is another area chock-a-block with restaurants, some of which have added a star or two to their epaulets in recent years. Narrow rue de Lappe and rue de la Roquette, 11e (Map pp114–15), just east of place de la Bastille, may not be as hip as they were a dozen years ago, but they remain popular streets for nightlife and attract a young, alternative crowd.

FRENCH

L'Encrier (Map pp120-1; ☎ 01 44 68 08 16; 55 rue Traversière, 12e; Ⓜ Ledru Rollin or Gare de Lyon; starters €5-10, mains €9-16.50, mains €13; Ⓨ lunch Mon-Fri, dinner Mon-Sat) You can always expect a relaxed atmosphere at the popular 'Inkwell'. A variety of set menus at lunch and dinner, an open kitchen, exposed beams and a large picture window make this a winner.

Le Trumilou (Map pp110-11; ☎ 01 42 77 63 98; 84 quai de l'Hôtel de Ville, 4e; Ⓜ Hôtel de Ville; starters €4-12, mains €13-21; menus €17.50 & €19) This no-frills bistro is a Parisian institution in situ for over a century. If you're looking for an authentic menu from the early 20th century and prices (well, almost) to match, you won't do better than this. The *confit de canard* is excellent.

Chez Nénesse (Map pp114-15; ☎ 01 42 78 46 49; 17 rue Saintonge, 3e; Ⓜ Filles du Calvaire; starters €4.50-14, mains €12-16; Ⓨ lunch & dinner to 10.30pm Mon-Fri) The atmosphere at Chez Nénesse, an oasis of simplicity and good taste, is 'old Parisian café' and the dishes are prepared with fresh, high-quality ingredients.

Les Galopins (Map pp114-15; ☎ 01 47 00 45 35; 24 rue des Taillandiers, 11e; Ⓜ Bastille or Voltaire; starters €6.10-10.50, mains €12.50-19, lunch menus €11.50 & €14.50; Ⓨ lunch Mon-Fri, dinner to 11pm Mon-Thu, to 11.30pm Fri & Sat) This cute little neighbourhood bistro called the 'Urchins' serves dishes in the best tradition of French cuisine: *poêlée de pétoncles* (pan-fried queen scallops), *magret de canard* (fillet of duck breast) and *compotée d'agneau aux aubergines* (lamb and eggplant ragout).

Robert et Louise (Map pp110-11; 01 42 78 55 89; 64 rue Vieille du Temple, 3e; Ⓜ St-Sébastien Froissart; starters €5-12, mains €13-18, lunch menu €12; Ⓨ lunch & dinner to 10pm Tue-Sat) This 'country inn', complete with its red gingham curtains, offers delightful, simple and inexpensive French food, including *côte de bœuf* (side of beef, €39), which is cooked on an open fire and prepared by a husband-and-wife team.

Aux Vins des Pyrénées (Map pp114-15; ☎ 01 42 72 64 94; 25 rue Beautreillis, 4e; Ⓜ Saint Paul or Bastille; starters €7.50-13, mains €13-18.50, lunch menu €12.50; Ⓨ lunch Sun-Fri, dinner daily to 11.30pm) 'At the Wines of the Pyrenees' is a good place to

---

FAST-FOOD & CHAIN RESTAURANTS

American fast-food chains have busy branches all over Paris as does the local hamburger chain **Quick** (www.quick.fr in French). In addition, a number of local chain restaurants have outlets around Paris with standard menus. They are definitely a cut above fast-food outlets and can be good value in areas such as along the av des Champs-Élysées, where restaurants tend to be bad value.

The ever popular bistro-restaurant chain **Bistro Romain** (www.bistroromain.fr in French; starters €4.90-9.70, pasta €12.80-15.90, mains €14.20-19, menus €13.90-22.70; 🕒 usually 11.30am-1am) with some 15 branches in Paris proper, is surprisingly upmarket for its price category. The **Champs-Élysées Bistro Romain** (Map pp102-3; ☎ 01 43 59 93 31; 122 av des Champs-Élysées, 8e; Ⓜ George V) one of a pair along the city's most famous thoroughfare, is a stone's throw from the Arc de Triomphe.

Buffalo Grill (www.buffalo-grill.fr; starters €3.90-9.50, mains €9.20-20.50, menus from €9; 🕒 usually 11am-11pm Sun-Thu, 11am-midnight Fri & Sat) counts eight branches in Paris, including the **Gare du Nord Buffalo Grill** (Map pp104-5; ☎ 01 40 16 47 81; 9 blvd de Denain, 10e; Ⓜ Gare du Nord). The emphasis here is on grills and steak – everything from Canadian buffalo burgers (€9.80) to 350g T-bone steaks (€17).

The ever-expanding **Hippopotamus** (www.hippopotamus.fr in French; starters €4.50-9.90, mains €10.90-19.50, menus €9.90-24.50; 🕒 usually 11.45am-12.30am Sun-Thu, 11.45am-1am Fri & Sat) chain, which now has 20 branches in Paris proper, specialises in solid, steak-based meals. Three of the outlets stay open to 5am daily, including the **Opéra Hippopotamus** (Map pp102-3; ☎ 01 47 42 75 70; 1 blvd des Capucines, 2e; Ⓜ Opéra).

Léon de Bruxelles (www.leon-de-bruxelles.com in French; starters €4.30-6.80, mains €10.50-15, menus €10.50-16.90; 🕒 usually 11.45am-11pm) focuses on one thing: *moules* (mussels). Meal-size bowls of the meaty bivalves, served with chips and bread, start at under €10. There are a dozen Léons in Paris, including **Les Halles Léon de Bruxelles** (Map pp110-11; ☎ 01 42 36 18 50; 120 rue Rambuteau, 1er; Ⓜ Châtelet-Les Halles).

---

enjoy a no-nonsense French meal with a lot of wine. The fish, meat and game dishes are all equally good, but worth a special mention is the foie gras and the top-notch *pavé de rumsteak* (thick rump steak).

L'Ambassade d'Auvergne (Map pp110-11; ☎ 01 42 72 31 22; 22 rue du Grenier St-Lazare, 3e; Ⓜ Rambuteau; starters €7-16, mains €14-21, menu €27; 🕒 lunch & dinner to 10.30pm) The 100-year-old 'Auvergne Embassy', is the place to go if you're really hungry; the sausages and hams of this region are among the best in France, as are the lentils from Puy and the sublime *clafoutis*, a custard and cherry tart baked upside down like a *tarte Tatin* (caramelised apple pie).

Le Petit Marché (Map pp114-15; ☎ 01 42 72 06 67; 9 rue Béarn, 3e; Ⓜ Chemin Vert; starters €7-16, mains €14-19, lunch menu €13.80; 🕒 lunch & dinner to midnight) This great little bistro just up from the place des Vosges attracts a mixed crowd with its hearty cooking and friendly service. Try any of the salad starters and the duck breast with ginger.

Bofinger (Map pp114-15; ☎ 01 42 72 87 82; 5-7 rue de la Bastille, 4e; Ⓜ Bastille; starters €6-18.50, mains €16.50-37.50, 2-/3-course menus €22.90/29.90; 🕒 lunch

& dinner to 1am Mon-Fri, noon-1am Sat & Sun) Founded in 1864, Bofinger is reputedly the oldest brasserie in Paris and specialities include Alsatian-inspired dishes such as *choucroute* (sauerkraut with assorted meats; €17.50 to €19), and seafood dishes.

Le Dôme Bastille (Map pp114-15; ☎ 01 48 04 88 44; 2 rue de la Bastille, 4e; Ⓜ Bastille; starters €8.70-12, mains €19.70-23) This lovely restaurant, little sister to the more established Le Dôme (p171) in Montparnasse, specialises in superbly prepared fish and seafood dishes with a blackboard that changes daily.

NORTH AFRICAN & MIDDLE EASTERN

Chez Omar (Map pp110-11; ☎ 01 42 72 36 26; 47 rue de Bretagne, 3e; Ⓜ Arts et Métiers; couscous & tajines €12-24, grills €15-22; 🕒 lunch Mon-Sat, dinner to 11.30pm daily) The quality of the couscous at Chez Omar is top notch, judging from the crowds. But apart from the food, don't expect anything else to be North African here; it's located in a century-old corner café.

404 (Map pp110-11; ☎ 01 42 74 57 81; 69 rue des Gravilliers, 3e; Ⓜ Arts et Métiers; starters €7-9, couscous & tajines €14-24, lunch menu €17, brunch €21; 🕒 lunch Mon-Fri, dinner to midnight daily, brunch to 4pm Sat &

Sun) As comfortable a Maghreb (North African) caravanserai as you'll find in Paris, the 404 not only has excellent couscous and *tajines* but superb grills (€12 to €22). You'll just love the *One Thousand and One Nights* décor, but the tables are set too close to one another.

VEGETARIAN

Grand Apétit (Map pp114-15; ☎ 01 40 27 04 95; 9 rue de la Cerisaie, 4e; Ⓜ Bastille or Sully Morland; soups €3-4, dishes €5.20-10.50; Ⓨ lunch Mon-Fri, dinner to 9pm Mon-Wed) 'The Big Appetite', a simple place near Bastille, offers light fare such as miso soup and cereals, as well as strength-building *bols garnis* (rice and vegetable bowls) and *assiettes* (platters) for big eaters only.

Piccolo Teatro (Map pp110-11; ☎ 01 42 72 17 79; 6 rue des Écouffes, 4e; Ⓜ St-Paul; €3.80-7.50, mains €8.90-11.70, lunch menus €8.90-14.70, dinner menus €15.10 & €21.50; Ⓨ lunch & dinner till 11.30pm) This is an intimate place with exposed stone walls, a beamed ceiling and cosy little tables. Try the *assiette végétarienne* (vegetarian plate; €12.10) or any of the gratin dishes, which combine vegetables, cream and cheese.

OTHER CUISINES

Paris Hanoi (Map pp114-15; ☎ 01 47 00 47 59; 74 rue de Charonne, 11e; Ⓜ Charonne; starters €3.10-7.50, mains €6.60-10; Ⓨ lunch Mon-Sat, dinner to 10.30pm daily) This upbeat, very yellow (as in the walls) restaurant is an excellent place to come for *pho* (soup noodles, usually with beef) and shrimp noodles. Judging from the clientele, the local Vietnamese community thinks so too.

Chez Heang (Map pp114-15; ☎ 01 48 07 80 98; 5 rue de la Roquette, 11e; Ⓜ Bastille; barbecue €8.50-17.50, lunch menu €9, dinner menus €11-23; Ⓨ lunch & dinner to midnight) Also known as 'Barbecue de Seoul', this is where you cook your food on a grill in the middle of your table. The *fondue maison*, a kind of spicy hotpot in which you dip and cook your food, costs €21 per person (minimum two).

Le Petit Dakar (Map pp110-11; ☎ 01 44 59 34 74; 6 rue Elzévir, 3e; Ⓜ St-Paul; starters €7, mains €13-15, lunch menu €15; Ⓨ lunch & dinner to 11pm Mon-Sat) Some people think this is the most authentic Senegalese restaurant in Paris, and with both a popular African club and the CSAO Boutique (p186) on the same street, it does feel like a bit of West Africa has fallen onto a quiet Marais street.

Les Caves St-Gilles (Map pp114-15; ☎ 01 48 87 22 62; 4 rue St-Gilles, 3e; Ⓜ Chemin Vert; tapas €5.30-17, mains €14.50-18; Ⓨ lunch & dinner till 11.30pm) This Spanish wine bar a short distance northeast of place des Vosges is the most authentic place on the Right Bank for tapas, paella (at the weekend only; €19) and sangria (€28 for 1.4L). We like (and eat) the bowls of complimentary olives on the bar and the tables.

L'Enoteca (Map pp110-11; ☎ 01 42 78 91 44; 25 rue Charles V, 4e; Ⓜ Sully Morland or Pont Marie; starters €8-14, mains €18-21; Ⓨ lunch & dinner to 11.30pm) This trattoria in the historic Village St-Paul quarter serves *haute cuisine à l'italienne*, and there's an excellent list of Italian wines by the glass (€3 to €7). Pasta dishes (€10 to €18) are good as is the generous *tavola antipasti* (antipasto buffet table) at lunch.

QUICK EATS

L'As de Felafel (Map pp110-11; ☎ 01 48 87 63 60; 34 rue des Rosiers, 4e; Ⓜ St-Paul; dishes €4-7.50; Ⓨ noon-midnight Sun-Thu, noon-5pm Fri) This has always been our favourite place for deep-fried balls of chickpeas and herbs (€3.50 to €4). It's always packed, particularly at weekday lunch, so avoid those times if possible.

Crêperie Bretonne (Map pp114-15; ☎ 01 43 55 62 29; 67 rue de Charonne, 12e; Ⓜ Charonne; starters €3.50-7, crêpes & galettes €2.30-7.20; Ⓨ lunch Mon-Fri, dinner to 11.30pm Mon-Sat) Head here if you fancy savoury buckwheat *galettes* (pancakes) – try the ham, cheese and egg *complète* – or a sweet *crêpe* and wash it down with dry cidre de Rance (€5.90 for 50cL). The Breton paraphernalia and B/W photos on display will keep you occupied.

SELF-CATERING

In the Marais, there are a number of food shops and Asian delicatessens on the odd-numbered side of rue St-Antoine, 4e (Map pp114-15) as well as several supermarkets. There's also a branch of the famous delicatessen **Le Nôtre** (Map pp114-15; ☎ 01 53 01 91 91; Ⓜ Bastille; 10 rue St-Antoine, 4e; Ⓨ 9.30am-10pm Mon-Fri, 9am-10pm Sat & Sun) nearby.

Closer to Bastille, there are lots of food shops along rue de la Roquette (Map pp114-15; Ⓜ Voltaire or Bastille) up towards place Léon Blum.

Supermarkets include the following:

Franprix Marais branch (Map pp110-11; 135 rue St-Antoine, 4e; Ⓜ St-Paul; Ⓨ 9am-8.30pm Mon-Sat);

Franprix Hôtel de Ville branch (Map pp110-11; 87 rue de la Verrerie, 4e; Ⓜ Hôtel de Ville; ☪ 9am-9pm Mon-Sat)

Monoprix Marais branch (Map pp110-11; 71 rue St-Antoine, 4e; Ⓜ St-Paul; ☪ 9am-9pm Mon-Sat); Monoprix Bastille branch (Map pp114-15; 97 rue du Faubourg St-Antoine, 11e; Ⓜ Ledru Rollin; ☪ 9am-10pm Mon-Sat).

Île St-Louis

Famed in Paris for its ice cream as much as for anything else, the Île St-Louis is generally a pricey place to eat and you'll find that its restaurants are few and far between. It's best suited to those looking for a light snack.

FRENCH

Les Fous de L'Île (Map pp110-11; ☎ 0143257667; 33 rue des Deux Ponts, 4e; Ⓜ Pont Marie; starters €6.50-9, mains €12-15, menus €15 lunch & dinner €19; ☪ lunch Tue-Sat, dinner to 10pm Thu-Sat) This friendly, down-to-earth tearoom and restaurant serves rather innovative café-style dishes and moonlights as an exhibition space.

Brasserie de l'Île St-Louis (Map pp110-11; ☎ 01 43 54 02 59; 55 quai de Bourbon, 4e; Ⓜ Pont Marie; ☪ 6pm-1am Thu, noon-1am Fri-Tue) Established in 1870, this brasserie enjoys a spectacular location on the Seine and serves standard brasserie favourites such as *choucroute garnie* (Alsatian dish of sauerkraut with sausage and other prepared meats), *jarret* (veal shank; €16.80) and *onglet de boeuf* (prime rib of beef; €16.80).

QUICK EATS

Berthillon (Map pp110-11; ☎ 01 43 54 31 61; 31 rue St-Louis en l'Île, 4e; Ⓜ Pont Marie; 1/2/3/4 scoops €2/3.50/4.50/5.50; ☪ 10am-8pm Wed-Sun) Berthillon is to ice cream what Château Lafite Rothschild is to wine. While the fruit flavours (eg cassis) produced by this celebrated *glacier* (ice-cream maker) are justifiably renowned, the chocolate, coffee, *marrons glacés* (candied chestnuts), *Agenaise* (Armagnac and prunes), *noisette* (hazelnut) and *nougat au miel* (honey nougat) are much richer. Choose from among 70 flavours.

SELF-CATERING

Along rue St-Louis en l'Île there are fromageries and groceries (usually closed on Sunday afternoon and all day Monday). There are more food shops on rue des Deux Ponts.

Latin Quarter & Jardin Des Plantes

Rue Mouffetard, 5e (Map pp118-19; Ⓜ Place Monge or Censier Daubenton), and its side streets are simply filled with places to eat. It's especially popular with students because of the number of stands and small shops selling baguettes, Italian *panini* and *crêpes*.

FRENCH

Perraudin (Map pp118-19; ☎ 01 46 33 15 75; 157 rue St-Jacques, 5e; Ⓜ Luxembourg; starters €8-19, mains €15-29, lunch menu €18, dinner menu €28; ☪ lunch & dinner to 11.30pm Mon-Fri) Perraudin is a traditional French restaurant that hasn't changed much since 1910 when it first opened its doors. If you fancy classics such as *bœuf bourguignon* (beef marinated and cooked in young red wine with mushrooms, onions, carrots and bacon; €15), *gigot d'agneau* (leg of lamb; €16) or *confit de canard* (duck joints cooked very slowly in their own fat, then left to stand for some months before being eaten; €16), try this reasonably priced and atmospheric (if somewhat shabby) place.

Bouillon Racine (Map pp118-19; ☎ 01 44 32 15 60; 3 rue Racine, 6e; Ⓜ Cluny-La Sorbonne; starters €7.50-14.50, mains €14.50-28, menus €15.50 lunch & €27 dinner) This 'soup kitchen' built in 1906 to feed city workers is an Art Nouveau palace but the classic French dishes like *caille confite* (preserved quail) and *cochon de lait* (milk-fed pork) don't hold a candle to the surrounds.

Le Petit Pontoise (Map pp118-19; ☎ 01 43 29 25 20; 9 rue de Pontoise, 5e; Ⓜ Maubert Mutualité; starters €8-13.50, mains €15-25; ☪ lunch & dinner to 10.30pm) This charming bistro offers a blackboard menu of seasonal delights. Regular dishes to look out for are the homemade foie gras with figs (€12) and *poulet fermier avec pommes purée* (roasted farm chicken with mashed potato; €13).

Chez Allard (Map pp110-11; ☎ 01 43 26 48 23; 41 rue St-André des Arts; Ⓜ St-Michel; starters €7.70-19.50, mains €19-35, 2-/3-course menus €24/32; ☪ lunch & dinner to 11.30pm Mon-Sat) One of our favourite new places on the Left Bank is this positively charming bistro where the staff couldn't be kinder and more professional – even during its enormously busy lunch time – and the food is superb. Try the excellent (and massive) *canard aux olives vertes* (duck with green olives).

NORTH AFRICAN & MIDDLE EASTERN

La Voie Lactée (Map pp118-19; ☎ 01 46 34 02 35; 34 rue du Cardinal Lemoine, 5e; Ⓜ Cardinal Lemoine; starters €5.50-7, mains €9.50-12.50, menus €11.50 & €14 lunch, €16.50-19 dinner; ⓦ lunch & dinner to 11pm Mon-Sat) The 'Milky Way' is a Turkish place with traditional and modern Anatolian cuisine, including a generous buffet of Turkish meze and salads. For mains, go for the grills, especially the various types of meatballs on offer. There's a good three-course vegetarian menu available for €16.50.

La Mosquée de Paris (Map pp118-19; ☎ 01 43 31 38 20; 39 rue Geoffroy St-Hilaire, 5e; Ⓜ Censier Daubenton or Place Monge; starters & snacks €4-12, mains €11-25; ⓦ lunch & dinner to 10.30pm) The central Mosque of Paris (p135) has an authentic restaurant serving couscous (€11 to €25) and *tajines* (€12 to €16). There's also a North African–style tearoom (open from 9 am to midnight) where you can enjoy peppermint tea (€2) and *pâtisseries orientales* (oriental pastries; €2).

VEGETARIAN

Les Cinq Saveurs d'Ananda (Map pp118-19; ☎ 01 43 29 58 54; 72 rue du Cardinal Lemoine, 5e; Ⓜ Cardinal Lemoine; soups & starters €5.20-9, mains €9.20-14.90; ⓦ lunch & dinner to 10.30pm Tue-Sun) Set back from place de la Contrescarpe, this bright semi-vegetarian restaurant is extremely popular

---

IN THE MARKET

Paris counts some five dozen *marchés découverts* (open-air markets) that pop up in public squares around the city two or three times a week and there are another 19 *marchés couverts* (covered markets) that keep more regular hours: 8am to 1pm and 3.30pm or 4pm to 7pm or 7.30pm from Tuesday to Saturday and till lunchtime on Sunday. Completing the picture are numerous independent *rues commerçantes*, pedestrian streets where the shops set up outdoor stalls. To find out when there's a market near your hotel or hostel, ask the staff or anyone who lives in the neighbourhood.

The following are favourite Paris markets rated according to the variety of their produce, their ethnicity and the neighbourhood. They are *la crème de la crème*.

Marché Bastille (Map pp114-15; blvd Richard Lenoir, 11e; Ⓜ Bastille or Richard Lenoir; ⓦ 7am-2pm Tue, 7am-2.30pm Sun) Stretching as far north as Richard Lenoir metro station, this is arguably the best open-air market in Paris with a lot more different national cuisines than ever before.

Marché Beauvau (Map pp120-1; place d'Aligre, 12e; Ⓜ Ledru Rollin; ⓦ 8.30am-1pm & 4-7.30pm Tue-Sat, 8.30am-1.30pm Sun) This covered market remains a colourful Arab and North African enclave just a stone's throw from the Bastille.

Marché Belleville (Map pp104-5; blvd de Belleville btwn rue Jean-Pierre Timbaud & rue du Faubourg du Temple, 11e & 20e; Ⓜ Belleville or Couronne; ⓦ 7am-1.30pm Tue & Fri) This market offers a fascinating (and easy) entry into the large, vibrant communities of the *quartiers de l'est* (eastern neighbourhoods), home to African, Middle Eastern and Asian immigrants as well as artists and students.

Marché Grenelle (Map pp108-9; blvd de Grenelle btwn rue de Lourmel & rue du Commerce, 15e; Ⓜ La Motte-Picquet Grenelle; ⓦ 7am-2.30pm Wed, 7am-3pm Sun) Arranged below an elevated railway and surrounded by stately Haussmann boulevards and Art Nouveau apartment blocks, the Grenelle market attracts a well-heeled clientele.

Marché St-Quentin (Map pp104-5; 85 blvd de Magenta, 10e; Ⓜ Gare de l'Est; ⓦ 8am-1pm & 4-7.30pm Tue-Sat, 8.30am-1pm Sun) This iron-and-glass covered market built in 1866 is a maze of corridors lined mostly with gourmet food stalls.

Rue Cler (Map pp108-9; rue Cler, 7e; Ⓜ École Militaire; ⓦ 7am or 8am-7pm or 7.30pm Tue-Sat, 8am-noon Sun) This commercial street market in the 7e is a breath of fresh air in a sometimes stuffy *quartier* and can almost feel like a party at the weekend when the whole neighbourhood turns out en masse to squeeze and pinch, pay and cart away.

Rue Montorgueil (Map pp104-5; rue Montorgueil btwn rue de Turbigo & rue Réaumur, 2e; Ⓜ Les Halles or Sentier; ⓦ 8am-7.30pm Tue-Sat, 8am-noon Sun) This is the closest market to Paris' 700-year-old wholesale market, Les Halles, which was moved from this area to the southern suburb of Rungis in 1969.

Rue Mouffetard (Map pp118-19; rue Mouffetard around rue de l'Arbalète; Ⓜ Censier Daubenton; ⓦ 8am-7.30pm Tue-Sat, 8am-noon Sun) Rue Mouffetard is the city's most photogenic market street – the place where Parisians send tourists (travellers go to Marché Bastille).

among health-food lovers. All ingredients are fresh and guaranteed 100% organic. Vegetarians should note that fish is served here.

Le Petit Légume (Map pp118-19; ☎ 01 40 46 06 85; 36 rue des Boulangers, 5e; Ⓜ Cardinal Lemoine; dishes €6.50-13, menus €9-15; Ⓥ lunch & dinner to 10pm Mon-Sat) The 'Little Vegetable', a tiny place on a narrow street, is a great choice for house-made vegetarian and organic fare. The ample salads are particularly good and they have organic wine.

QUICK EATS

Le Foyer du Vietnam (Map pp118-19; ☎ 01 45 35 32 54; 80 rue Monge, 5e; Ⓜ Place Monge; starters €3.10-6, mains €6-8.50, menus €8.20 & €12.20; Ⓥ lunch & dinner to 10pm Mon-Sat) The little 'Vietnam Club' is a favourite meeting spot among the capital's Vietnamese community and serves simple one-dish meals in medium and large portions. Try the 'Saigon' or 'Hanoi' soup (noodles, soya beans and pork flavoured with lemon grass, coriander and chives).

Breakfast in America (Map pp118-19; ☎ 01 43 54 50 28; 17 rue des Écoles, 5e; Ⓜ Cardinal Lemoine; meals €6.95-9.50; Ⓥ 8.30am-11pm) This almost authentic American-style diner, complete with red banquettes and Formica surfaces, serves all-day breakfast with free coffee refills, and there are generous burgers, chicken wings and fish and chips.

SELF-CATERING

Place Maubert, 5e (Map pp110–11), becomes the lively food market Marché Maubert on Tuesday, Thursday and Saturday mornings. There are also some great provisions shops here, including a cheese shop called **Crémerie des Carmes** (Map pp110-11; ☎ 01 43 54 50 93; 47ter blvd St-Germain, 5e; Ⓜ Maubert Mutualité; Ⓥ 7.30am-7.30pm Mon-Sat, 7.30am-1pm Sun).

There's a particularly lively food market set out along rue Mouffetard (p169). On place Monge there's a much smaller market, **Marché Monge** (Map pp114-15; place Monge, 5e; Ⓜ Place Monge; Ⓥ 7am-2pm Wed & Fri, 7am-2.30pm Sun).

Supermarkets located in the area include the following:

Champion (Map pp118-19; 34 rue Monge, 5e; Ⓜ Place Monge; Ⓥ 8.30am-9pm Mon-Sat)

Ed l'Épicier (Map pp118-19; 37 rue Lacépède, 5e; Ⓜ Place Monge; Ⓥ 9am-1pm & 3-7.30pm Mon-Fri, 9am-7.30pm Sat)

Franprix (Map pp118-19; 82 rue Mouffetard, 5e; Ⓜ Censier Daubenton or Place Monge; Ⓥ 8.30am-8.50pm Mon-Sat)

St-Germain, Odéon & Luxembourg

Rue St-André des Arts (Map pp110–11; Ⓜ St-Michel or Odéon) is lined with restaurants, including a few situated down the covered cour du Commerce Saint André. You'll find that there are lots of eateries between Église St-Sulpice and Église St-Germain des Prés as well, especially along rue des Canettes, rue Princesse and rue Guisarde. Carrefour de l'Odéon (Map pp110–11, Ⓜ Odéon) has a cluster of lively bars, cafés and restaurants. Place St-Germain des Prés itself is home to celebrated cafés such as Les Deux Magots and Café de Flore (p176) as well as the equally celebrated Brasserie Lipp.

FRENCH

Polidor (Map pp110-11; ☎ 01 43 26 95 34; 41 rue Monsieur le Prince, 6e; Ⓜ Odéon; starters €4-15, mains €10-19, menus €12 lunch, €20 & €30; Ⓥ lunch & dinner till 12.30am Mon-Sat, to 11pm Sun) Eating meal at this quintessentially Parisian *crémerie-restaurant* is like taking a quick trip back to Victor Hugo's Paris – the restaurant and its décor date from 1845 – but everyone knows about it and it's pretty touristy. Specialities include *bœuf bourguignon* (€11), *blanquette de veau* (veal in white sauce; €13) and the most famous *tarte Tatin* (€6) in Paris.

Brasserie Lipp (Map pp108-9; ☎ 01 45 48 53 91; 151 blvd St-Germain, 6e; Ⓜ St-Germain des Prés; starters €8.20-13.10, mains €15.60-20; Ⓥ noon-1am) The Lipp is a wood-panelled café-brasserie (1880) where politicians rub shoulders with intellectuals, editors and media moguls, and waiters in black waistcoats, bowties and long white aprons serve such brasserie favourites as *choucroute garnie* and *jarret de porc aux lentilles* (pork knuckle with lentils).

Les Éditeurs (Map pp110-11; ☎ 01 43 26 67 76; 4 Carrefour de l'Odéon, 6e; Ⓜ Odéon; starters €9-16.50, mains €17.50-25; Ⓥ 8am-2am) This place – part café, restaurant, library, bar and *salon de thé* – is intended for writers – there are a load of books on display and great big windows through which you can watch the St-Germain des Prés goings-on. The generous Sunday brunch is an absolute snip at €24.50.

OTHER CUISINES

Indonesia (Map pp118-19; ☎ 01 43 25 70 22; 12 rue de Vaugirard, 6e; Ⓜ Luxembourg; lunch & dinner menus €17-23; Ⓨ lunch Mon-Fri, dinner to 10.30pm daily) One of only a couple of Indonesian restaurants in town, this unimaginatively named eatery has all the old favourites – from an elaborate, nine-dish *rijstafel* (rice with side dishes) to *lumpia* (a type of spring roll; €5.50), *rendang* (beef cooked in peanut and chilli sauce; €8.95) and *gado-gado* (vegetable salad with peanut sauce; €6).

Le Golfe de Naples (Map pp110-11; ☎ 01 43 26 98 11; 5 rue de Montfaucon, 6e; Ⓜ Mabillon; starters €8-16, pizza & pasta dishes €10-16.50, mains €13-15; Ⓨ lunch & dinner to 11pm Tue-Sun) The 'Gulf of Naples' has some of the best pizza and fresh, shop-made pasta in Paris – though more elaborate main courses are something of a disappointment. Don't forget to try the *assiette napolitaine*, a plate of grilled fresh vegetables (€13.50).

Azabu (Map pp110-11; 01 46 33 72 05; 3 rue André Mazet, 6e; Ⓜ Odéon; starters €8.50-13.50, mains €19-26, menus lunch €18 & dinner €33; Ⓨ lunch Tue-Sat, dinner to 10.30pm Tue-Sun) For relatively cheap and somewhat cheerful Japanese food in the heart of St-Germain, head for this place. It was mostly filled with *gaijin* (non-Japanese) the last time we visited but the noodles and the *teppanyaki* looked authentic enough.

QUICK EATS

Amorino (Map pp110-11; ☎ 01 43 26 57 46; 4 rue Buci, 6e; Ⓜ St-Germain des Prés; 1/2/3 scoops €3/4/5; Ⓨ noon-midnight) We're told that Berthillon (p168) has some serious competition and that Amorino's home-made ice cream (yogurt, forest fruits, caramel, kiwi, strawberry etc) is, in fact, better. Expect long queues in season.

Guen Maï (Map pp110-11; ☎ 01 43 26 03 24; 6 rue Cardinal & 2bis rue de l'Abbaye, 6e; Ⓜ St-Germain des Prés or Mabillon; soups €4.50, mains €7-11; Ⓨ lunch Mon-Sat) Guen Maï is a health-food shop with a kitchen serving up macrobiotic and organic *plats du jour* and soups. It's a cosy, friendly place and, as the name suggests, the dishes are Asian-inspired.

SELF-CATERING

With the Jardin du Luxembourg nearby, this is the perfect area for putting together a picnic lunch. There is a large cluster of food shops on rue de Seine and rue de Buci, 6e (Map pp110–11, Ⓜ Mabillon). The renovated and covered **Marché St-Germain** (Map pp110-11; 4-8 rue Lobineau, 6e; Ⓜ Mabillon; Ⓨ 8.30am-1pm & 4-7.30pm Tue-Sat, 8.30am-1pm Sun), just north of the eastern end of Église St-Sulpice, has a huge array of produce and prepared food. Nearby supermarkets include the following: **Champion** (Map pp110-11; 79 rue de Seine, 6e; Ⓜ Mabillon; Ⓨ 1-9pm Mon, 8.40am-9pm Tue-Sat, 9am-1pm Sun) **Monoprix** (Map pp110-11; 52 rue de Rennes, 6e; Ⓜ St-Germain des Prés; Ⓨ 9am-10pm Mon-Sat)

Montparnasse

Since the 1920s the area around blvd du Montparnasse has been one of the city's premier avenues for enjoying that most Parisian of pastimes: sitting in a café and checking out the scenery on two legs. Many younger Parisians, however, now consider the area somewhat *démodé* and touristy, which it is to a certain extent, and avoid it.

Montparnasse offers all types of eateries, especially traditional *crêperies*, because Gare Montparnasse is where Bretons arriving in Paris to look for work would disembark (and apparently venture no further). There are three at 18 & 20 rue d'Odessa (Map pp108–9) alone and at least half a dozen more round the corner on rue du Montparnasse.

FRENCH

La Coupole (Map pp108-9; ☎ 01 43 20 14 20; 102 blvd du Montparnasse, 14e; Ⓜ Vavin; starters €6.50-19, mains €12.50-32, menus lunch €15, €24 & €32 dinner; Ⓨ 8am-1am Sun-Thu, to 1.30AM Fri & Sat) This 450-seat brasserie, which opened in 1927, has mural-covered columns painted by such artists as Brancusi and Chagall. Its dark-wood panelling and indirect lighting have hardly changed since the days of Sartre, Soutine, Man Ray and the dancer Josephine Baker. You can book for lunch, but you'll have to queue for dinner (and then there's always breakfast starting at €8).

Dix Vins (Map pp108-9; ☎ 01 43 20 91 77; 57 rue Falguière, 15e; Ⓜ Pasteur; lunch menu €20, dinner menu €24; Ⓨ lunch & dinner to 11pm Mon-Fri) This tiny little restaurant, which offers a set menu only, is so popular you will probably have to wait at the bar even if you've booked. Be sure to sample one of the carefully chosen wines that the owner will decant into a carafe. Excellent value, good service and stylish décor.

Le Dôme (Map pp108-9; ☎ 01 43 35 25 81, 01 43 35 23 95; 108 blvd du Montparnasse, 14e; Ⓜ Vavin; starters €12.50-25, mains €29-56; Ⓨ lunch & dinner to 12.30am)

An Art Deco extravaganza dating from the 1930s, Le Dôme is a monumental place for a meal, with the emphasis on the freshest of oysters, shellfish and fish dishes such as *sole meunière* (sole sautéed in butter and garnished with lemon and parsley).

QUICK EATS

Mustang Café (Map pp108-9 ☎ 01 43 35 36 12; 84 blvd du Montparnasse, 14e; Ⓜ Montparnasse Bienvenüe; starters €6-13.50, mains €8.20-15.45; ☯ 9am-5am Mon-Sat, 11am-5pm Sun) A café that almost never sleeps, the Mustang has passable Tex-Mex combination platters and nachos, fajitas, burgers, and salads (€6.60 to €8.90).

SELF-CATERING

Opposite the Tour Montparnasse there's the outdoor **Boulevard Edgar Quinet Food Market** (Map pp108-9; blvd Edgar Quinet; ☯ 7am-2pm Wed & Sat). Supermarkets convenient to the area include the following:

Atac (Map pp108-9; 55 av du Maine, 14e; Ⓜ Gaîté; ☯ 9am-10pm Mon-Sat)

Franprix Delambre (Map pp108-9; 11 rue Delambre; Ⓜ Vavin; ☯ 8.30am-7.50pm Mon-Sat)

Inno (Map pp108-9; 29-31 rue du Départ, 14e; Ⓜ Montparnasse Bienvenüe; ☯ 9am-9.50pm Mon-Fri, 9am-8.50pm Sat)

Étoile & Champs-Élysées

With few exceptions, eateries lining the touristy 'Avenue of the Elysian Fields' offer little value for money. Restaurants in the surrounding areas can be excellent, however.

FRENCH

Graindorge (Map pp102-3; ☎ 01 47 64 33 47; 15 rue de l'Arc de Triomphe, 17e; Ⓜ Charles de Gaulle-Étoile; starters €11-16, mains €22-25, lunch menu €28, dinner menu €32; ☯ lunch Mon-Fri, dinner to 11pm Mon-Sat) The name of this stylish restaurant, with its soft lighting and Art Deco touches, means 'barleycorn' and alludes to the great breweries of Flanders. The chef's signature dish is *potjevleesch* (€11), four different kinds of meat cooked slowly together and served in aspic.

L'Ardoise (Map pp102-3; ☎ 01 42 96 28 18; 28 rue du Mont Thabor, 1er; Ⓜ Concorde or Tuileries; menu €31; ☯ lunch & dinner to 11pm Tue-Sun) This is a little bistro with no menu as such (*ardoise* means 'blackboard', which is all there is) and the food – rabbit stuffed with plums and beef fillet with morels – is superb. It's touristy, though.

QUICK EATS

Lina's (Map pp102-3; ☎ 01 40 15 94 95; 4 rue Cambon, 1er; Ⓜ Concorde; soups & salads €4.50-6.10, sandwiches €3.50-6.90; ☯ 9.30am-4.30pm Mon-Fri, 10am-5.30pm Sat) This branch of a popular Paris chain has upmarket sandwiches, salads and soups.

There's also an **Opéra branch** (Map pp110-11; ☎ 01 47 03 30 29; 7 av de l'Opéra, 1er; Ⓜ Pyramides).

SELF-CATERING

Place de la Madeleine (metro Madeleine) is the luxury food centre of one of the world's food capitals. Supermarkets include the following:

Monoprix (Map pp102-3; 62 av des Champs-Élysées, 8e; Ⓜ Franklin D Roosevelt; ☯ 9am-midnight Mon-Sat)

Franprix (Map pp102-3; 12 rue de Surène, 8e; Ⓜ Madeleine)

Opéra & Grands Boulevards

The neon-lit blvd Montmartre (Ⓜ Grands Boulevards or Richelieu Drouot) and nearby sections of rue du Faubourg Montmartre (neither of which are anywhere near the neighbourhood of Montmartre) form one of the Right Bank's most animated café and dining districts. A short distance to the north there's a large selection of kosher Jewish and North African restaurants on rue Richer, rue Cadet and rue Geoffroy Marie, 9e, south of metro Cadet.

FRENCH

Chartier (Map pp104-5; ☎ 01 47 70 86 29; 7 rue du Faubourg Montmartre, 9e; Ⓜ Grands Boulevards; starters €2-11.50, mains €6.30-11.60, menu with wine €20; ☯ lunch & dinner to 10pm) Chartier is a real gem that is justifiably famous for its 330-seat *belle époque* dining room, virtually unaltered since 1896, and its excellent-value menu. Reservations are not accepted and lone diners will have to share a table.

Le Roi du Pot au Feu (Map pp102-3; ☎ 01 47 42 37 10; 34 rue Vignon, 9e; Ⓜ Havre Caumartin; starters €5-7, mains €16-17, 2-/3-course menus €23/28; ☯ noon-10.30pm Mon-Sat) The typical Parisian bistro atmosphere adds immensely to the charm of the 'King of Hotpots', but what you really want to come here for is a genuine *pot au feu*, a stockpot of beef, aromatic root vegetables and herbs stewed together, with the stock served as an entree and the meat and vegetables as the main course. No bookings.

Julien (Map pp104-5; ☎ 01 47 70 12 06; 16 rue du Faubourg St-Denis, 10e; Ⓜ Strasbourg St-Denis; starters

€5.90-15.50, mains €14-33, menus with wine €24.50 & €34.50; ☺ lunch & dinner to 1am) In the less-than-salubrious neighbourhood of St-Denis, Julien offers brasserie food that you wouldn't cross town for, but – *sacré bleu*! – the décor and the atmosphere: it's an Art Nouveau extravaganza perpetually in motion and a real step back in time.

Bistrot du Sommelier (Map pp102-3; ☎ 01 42 65 24 85; 97 blvd Haussmann, 8e; Ⓜ St-Augustin; starters €14-19, mains €22-27, 2-/3-course menus €32/39 & €42/54 with wine; ☺ lunch & dinner to 10.30pm Mon-Fri) The whole point of this attractive eatery is to match wine with food and the best way to do it is to order one of the testing menus (€60 to €100, including the wine).

SELF-CATERING
Both av de l'Opéra and rue de Richelieu have several supermarkets, including a large one in the basement of **Monoprix** (Map pp102-3; 21 av de l'Opéra, 2e; Ⓜ Pyramides; ☺ 9am-10pm Mon-Fri, 9am-9pm Sat).

Gare du Nord, Gare de l'Est & République
These areas offer all types of food but most notably Indian and Pakistani, which can be elusive elsewhere in Paris. There's a cluster of traditional brasseries and bistros around the Gare du Nord.

FRENCH
Le Chansonnier (Map pp104-5; ☎ 01 42 09 40 58; 14 rue Eugène Varlin, 10e; Ⓜ Château Landon or Pierre Dupont; starters €5.50-12, mains €15-18, menus €10.50 lunch, €22 & €23.50 dinner; ☺ lunch Mon-Fri, dinner to 11pm Mon-Sat) It may not be the best restaurant in Paris, but if ever there was the perfect example of a *restaurant du quartier* (neighbourhood restaurant), the 'Singer' is it. The food is authentic, very good and very substantial; the €23.50 *formule bistro* (set menu) includes *terrine maison à valonté* (all you can eat of four types of terrine).

La Marine (Map pp104-5; ☎ 01 42 39 69 81; 55bis quai de Valmy, 10e; Ⓜ République; starters €7.50-12, mains €14.10-18.80, lunch menu €12; ☺ lunch & dinner to 11.30pm Mon-Sat) This large and airy bistro overlooking the Canal St-Martin is a favourite, especially in the warmer months, and serves such delicacies as *millefeuille de rouget à la vinaigrette* (mullet in layered pastry with vinaigrette) and *brick de poisson à la crème océane* (fish fritter with seafood sauce).

QUICK EATS
Passage Brady (Map pp104-5; 46 rue du Faubourg St-Denis & 33 blvd de Strasbourg, 10e; Ⓜ Château d'Eau) This derelict covered arcade, which could easily be in Calcutta, has dozens of incredibly cheap Indian, Pakistani and Bangladeshi cafés offering excellent value lunches (meat curry, rice and a tiny salad €5 to €7; chicken or lamb biryani €8 to €12; *thalis* €12); there are dinner menus from €9 to €22. Among the best are the following:
Passage de Pondicherry (☎ 01 53 32 63 10; 84 passage Brady)
Pooja (☎ 01 48 24 00 83; 91 passage Brady)
Roi du Kashmir (☎ 01 48 00 08 85; 76 passage Brady)

SELF-CATERING
Rue du Faubourg St-Denis, 10e (Map pp104–5, Ⓜ Strasbourg St-Denis or Château d'Eau), which links blvd St-Denis and blvd de Magenta, is one of the cheapest places in Paris to buy food, especially fruit and vegetables (shop Nos 23, 27–29 and 41–43). The street has a distinctively Middle Eastern air, and quite a few of the groceries offer Turkish, North African and subcontinental specialities. Many of the food shops, including the fromagerie at No 54, are open Tuesday to Saturday and until noon on Sunday.

There are three Franprix supermarkets convenient to this area:
Franprix Faubourg St-Denis (Map pp104–5; 7-9 rue des Petites Écuries, 10e; Ⓜ Strasbourg St-Denis or Château d'Eau; ☺ 9am-7.50pm Mon-Sat)
Franprix Magenta (Map pp104-5; 57 blvd de Magenta, 10e; Ⓜ Gare de l'Est)
Franprix Bretagne (Map pp110-11; 49 rue de Bretagne, 3e; Ⓜ Arts et Métiers; ☺ 9am-8.30pm Tue-Sat, 9am-1.20pm Sun)

Ménilmontant & Belleville
In the northern section of the 11e and into the 19e and 20e arrondissements, rue Oberkampf and its extension, rue de Ménilmontant (Map pp104–5), are popular with diners and denizens of the night though rue Jean-Pierre Timbaud, running parallel to the north, is stealing some of their glory these days. Rue de Belleville and the streets running off it are dotted with Chinese, Southeast Asian and a few Middle Eastern places; blvd de Belleville has some kosher couscous restaurants, most of which are closed on Saturday.

PARIS

FRENCH

Le Clown Bar (Map pp114-15; ☎ 01 43 55 87 35; 114 rue Amelot, 11e; Ⓜ Filles du Calvaire; starters/mains €7.50/15, menus lunch €13.50, dinner €25; ☯ lunch & dinner to midnight Mon-Sat) A wonderful wine bar-cum-bistro next to the Cirque d'Hiver, the Clown Bar is like a museum with its painted ceilings, mosaics on the wall, lovely zinc bar and circus memorabilia that touches on one of our favourite themes: the evil clown. The food is simple and unpretentious traditional French.

Le Grand Méricourt (Map pp114-15; ☎ 01 43 38 94 04; 22 rue de la Folie Méricourt, 11e; Ⓜ St-Ambroise; starters €11-17, mains €16-19, menus lunch €14, dinner €17 & €27; ☯ lunch Mon-Fri, dinner to 10.30pm Tue-Sat) The speciality here is *'la cuisine créative'* (basically traditional French that is light on oils and fat and heavy on seasonal produce) in a very English, almost fussy (floral wallpaper, wooden floors, starched white tablecloths and napkins) place just a stone's throw from trendy rue Oberkampf.

our pick **Le Villaret** (Map pp114-15; ☎ 01 43 57 89 76; 13 rue Ternaux, 11e; Ⓜ Parmentier; starters €8.50-20, mains €17-35, 2-/3-course lunch menus €21/26; ☯ lunch Mon-Fri, dinner to 11.30pm Mon-Thu, to 1am Fri & Sat) An excellent neighbourhood bistro serving very rich food, Le Villaret has diners coming from across Paris to sample the house specialities. The *velouté de cèpes à la mousse de foie gras* (cep mushroom soup with foie gras mousse), the *solette au beurre citronné* (baby sole with lemon-flavoured butter) and the *gigot d'agneau de Lozère rôti et son gratin de topinambours* (roast lamb with Jerusalem artichoke gratin) are all recommended but only the chef knows what will be available as he changes the menu daily. Tasting menus can range from €45 to €80 (the latter when truffles are in season). We just can't keep away from this place.

ASIAN

Reuan Thai (Map pp104-5; ☎ 01 43 55 15 82; 36 rue de l'Orillon, 11e; Ⓜ Belleville; starters €4.50-13, mains €7.50-15, lunch buffet €8; ☯ lunch & dinner to 11.30pm) This fragrant place offers some of the most authentic Thai food in Paris and has all your favourite Thai dishes, including soups. About a half-dozen of the choices are vegetarian.

New Nioullaville (Map pp104-5; ☎ 01 40 21 96 18; 32 rue de l'Orillon, 11e; Ⓜ Belleville or Goncourt; starters €4.90-7.50, mains €7.50-16, menus €7-14; ☯ lunch & dinner to 1am) This cavernous, 400-seat place resembles the Hong Kong Stock Exchange on a busy day. The food is a bit of a mishmash – *dim sum* sits next to beef satay, as do scallops with black bean alongside Singapore noodles. Order carefully and you should be able to approach authenticity.

Ossek Garden (Map pp104-5; ☎ 01 48 07 16 35; 14 rue Rampon, 11e; Ⓜ Oberkampf; starters €6-14.80, barbecue €15.90-17.90, menus €9.50-29.90) Things Korean – especially films – seem to be taking the world by storm these days and this place not far from place de la République has excellent barbecues as well as *bibimbab* (€12 to €17.90), rice served in a sizzling pot topped with thinly sliced beef (or other meat) and cooked and preserved vegetables, which is then bound by a raw egg and flavoured with chilli-laced soy bean paste.

SELF-CATERING

Supermarkets in the area include **Franprix Jules Ferry** (Map pp104-5; 28 blvd Jules Ferry, 11e; Ⓜ République or Goncourt; ☯ 8am-8pm Mon-Sat) and a **Franprix Oberkampf branch** (Map pp104-5; 23 rue Jean-Pierre Timbaud, 11e; Ⓜ Oberkampf).

13e Arrondissement & Chinatown

Dozens of Asian restaurants – not just Chinese ones – line the main streets of Paris' Chinatown (Map pp98-9), including av de Choisy, av d'Ivry and rue Baudricourt. Another wonderful district for an evening out is the Butte aux Cailles area (Map pp98-9), just southwest of place d'Italie. It's chock-a-block with interesting addresses.

FRENCH

Chez Gladines (Map pp98-9; ☎ 01 45 80 70 10; 30 rue des Cinq Diamants, 13e; Ⓜ Corvisart; starters €4.50-9, mains €7.30-11, lunch menu €10; ☯ lunch & dinner to midnight Sun-Tue, to 1am Wed-Sat) This lively Basque bistro in the heart of the Buttes aux Cailles quarter serves enormous 'meal-in-a-bowl' salads (€5 to €9), as well as traditional Basque specialities, such as *pipérade* (omelette with tomatoes and peppers) and *poulet basque* (chicken cooked with tomatoes, onions, peppers and white wine).

L'Avant-Goût (Map pp98-9; ☎ 01 53 80 24 00; 26 rue Bobillot, 13e; Ⓜ Place d'Italie; starters/mains €9.50/16, menus lunch €14 & dinner €31; ☯ lunch & dinner to 11pm Tue-Fri) This prototype of the Parisian 'neo-bistro' (classical yet modern) in the Butte aux Cailles serves some of the most inventive modern cuisine around. It can get noisy at times and there are occasional lapses in the service, but the food is well worth it.

ASIAN

La Chine Masséna (Map pp98-9; ☎ 01 45 83 98 88; 18 av de Choisy, 13e; Ⓜ Porte de Choisy; soups & starters €4.10-11, mains €6.10-13.50) This enormous restaurant, which specialises in Cantonese and Chiu Chow cuisine, is our current favourite place in Chinatown. The dim sum here is especially good and wait staff still go around with trolleys calling out their wares.

La Fleuve de Chine (Map pp98-9; ☎ 01 45 82 06 88; 15 av de Choisy, 13e; Ⓜ Porte de Choisy; starters €3.50-9, mains €7-15; Ⓨ lunch & dinner to 11pm Fri-Wed) The 'River of China', which can also be reached through the Tour Bergame housing estate at 130 blvd Masséna, has some of the most authentic Cantonese and Hakka food to be found in Paris and, as is typical, both the surroundings and service – but definitely not the food – are forgettable. Go for the superb dishes cooked in clay pots.

Montmartre & Pigalle

The 18th arrondissement, where you will find Montmartre and the northern half of place Pigalle, thrives on crowds and little else. When you've got Sacré Cœur, place du Tertre and its portrait artists and Paris literally at your feet, who needs decent restaurants? But that's not to say everything is a write-off in this well-trodden tourist area. You just have to pick and choose a bit more carefully.

FRENCH

La Maison Rose (Map p122; ☎ 01 42 57 66 75; 2 rue de l'Abreuvoir, 18e; Ⓜ Lamarck Caulaincourt; starters €7.80-13, mains €14.50-16.50, menu €16.50; Ⓨ lunch & dinner to 11pm daily Mar-Oct, lunch Thu-Mon, dinner to 9pm Mon, Thu-Sat Nov-Feb) If you are looking for the quintessential intimate Montmartre bistro in a house that Utrillo painted, head for the tiny 'Pink House' just north of place du Tertre.

Chez Toinette (Map p122; ☎ 01 42 54 44 36; 20 rue Germain Pilon, 18e; Ⓜ Abbesses; starters €5-8, mains €14-20; Ⓨ dinner to 11pm Tue-Sat) The atmosphere of this convivial restaurant, which has somehow managed to keep alive the tradition of old Montmartre in one of the capital's most touristy neighbourhoods, is rivalled only by its fine cuisine. Game lovers in particular won't be disappointed.

La Mascotte (Map p122; ☎ 01 46 06 28 15; 52 rue des Abbesses, 18e; Ⓜ Abbesses; starters €6.50-12, mains €17-23, menus lunch €17.50 & dinner €29; Ⓨ lunch & dinner to 11.30pm Tue-Sat) The 'Mascot' is a small, unassuming spot much frequented by regulars who can't get enough of its seafood and regional cuisine. *Plats du jour* are between €14 and €16.

La Table d'Anvers (Map p122; ☎ 01 48 78 35 21; 2 place d'Anvers, 9e; Ⓜ Anvers; starters/mains €12/18, 2-/3-course lunch menus €15/23 & dinner menus €26/33; Ⓨ lunch Tue-Fri, dinner to 11pm Mon-Sat) Just far enough off the Montmartre tourist track to keep the hordes away, this local favourite overlooking a stylish square offers some great Mediterranean/Provençal dishes and some very decent fixed-price menus.

SELF-CATERING

Towards place Pigalle there are lots of grocery stores, many of them open until late at night; try the side streets leading off blvd de Clichy (eg rue Lepic). Heading south from blvd de Clichy, rue des Martyrs, 9e (Map pp104–5), is lined with food shops almost all the way to metro Notre Dame de Lorette. Supermarkets in the area include the following:

8 à Huit (Map p122; 24 rue Lepic, 18e; Ⓜ Abbesses; Ⓨ 8.30am-9pm Mon-Sat)

Ed l'Épicier (Map p122; 31 rue d'Orsel, 18e; Ⓜ Anvers)

DRINKING

Traditionally drinking in Paris revolved around a café, where a *demi* looked more like an eyewash than 330mL of beer. But all that has changed and the number of drinking establishments has mushroomed in recent years, especially in the Marais and along the Grands Boulevards. Happy hour – sometimes extending to as late as 9pm – has brought the price of a pint of beer, a glass of wine or a cocktail down to pricey, rather than extortionate, levels. Bear in mind that drinking in Paris essentially means paying the rent for the space you are occupying. So it costs more sitting at tables than it does to stand, more on a fancy square than a back street, more in the 8e than in the 18e. Just think of it as a short-term investment that varies according to the décor and the property price per square metre in that neighbourhood.

Louvre & Les Halles

Le Fumoir (Map pp110-11; ☎ 01 42 92 00 24; 6 rue de l'Amiral Coligny, 1er; Ⓜ Louvre-Rivoli; Ⓨ 11am-2am) The 'Smoking Room' is a huge, very stylish colonial-style bar-café just opposite the Louvre. It's a fine place to sip top-notch gin from quality glassware while nibbling on olives; during happy hour (6pm–8pm) cocktails are all around half price at €6.

Marais & Bastille

Andy Wahloo (Map pp110–11; ☎ 01 42 71 20 38; 69 rue des Gravilliers, 3e; Ⓜ Arts et Métiers; ☻ noon-2am) Casablanca meets candy-store in this trendy, multicoloured and very lively cocktail lounge hidden away just north of the Pompidou Centre, whose name means (more or less) 'I Have Nothing' in Arabic. During happy hour (5pm to 8pm) a cocktail/ beer is €5/3 – after that it doubles.

Au Petit Fer à Cheval (Map pp110–11; ☎ 01 42 72 47 47; 30 rue Vieille du Temple, 4e; Ⓜ Hôtel de Ville or St-Paul; ☻ 9am-2am) The original horseshoe-shaped zinc counter leaves little room for much else, but nobody seems to mind as at this tiny and very genial bar overflowing with friendly regulars enjoying a drink or a sandwich (simple meals are served from noon).

Café des Phares (Map pp114–15; ☎ 01 42 72 04 70; 7 place de la Bastille, 4e; Ⓜ Bastille; ☻ 7am-3am Sun-Thu, 7am-4am Fri & Sat) Should you wake in the night wondering 'What does speaking mean?' or 'How does one go from ethics to morality?' then head for the 'Beacons Café', the city's original philocafé (philosophers' café), established by the late philosopher and Sorbonne professor Marc Sautet (1947–98). Debates on diverse topics take place at 11am Sunday.

L'Apparement Café (Map pp110–11; ☎ 01 48 87 12 22; 18 rue des Coutures St-Gervais, 3e; Ⓜ St-Sébastien Froissart; ☻ noon-2am Mon-Fri, 4pm-2am Sat, 12.30pm-midnight Sun) Tucked not so 'Apparently' behind the Musée Picasso at a merciful distance from the Marais shopping hordes, this tasteful haven looks and feels like a private living room.

Le Pick Clops (Map pp110–11; ☎ 01 40 29 02 18; 16 rue Vieille du Temple, 4e; Ⓜ Hôtel de Ville or St-Paul; ☻ 7.30am-2am) This retro café-bar – all shades of yellow and lit by neon – has Formica tables, ancient bar stools and plenty of mirrors. Attracting a friendly flow of locals and passers by, it's a great place for morning or afternoon coffee, or that last drink.

Lizard Lounge (Map pp110–11; ☎ 01 42 72 81 34; 18 rue Bourg du Tibourg, 4e; Ⓜ St-Paul; ☻ noon-2am) This is a quality outpost of Anglo-Saxon attitude in the heart of the Marais, with pretty young expatriates with tight jeans and clutch purses filing downstairs to the cellar, which is complete with DJ and little corners in which to schmooze.

Stolly's Stone Bar (Map pp110–11; ☎ 01 42 76 06 76; 16 rue de la Cloche Percée, 4e; Ⓜ St-Paul; ☻ 4.30pm-2am) is just around the corner and run by the same team as the Lizard Lounge.

Latin Quarter & Jardin des Plantes

Le Piano Vache (Map pp118–19; ☎ 01 46 33 75 03; 8 rue Laplace, 5e; Ⓜ Maubert Mutualité; ☻ noon-2am Mon-Fri, 9pm-2am Sat & Sun) Just down the hill from the Panthéon, the 'Mean Piano' is covered in old posters and couches and drenched in 1970s and '80s rock ambience. Effortlessly underground and a huge favourite with students, it has bands and DJs playing mainly rock, plus some Gothic, reggae and pop.

Le Vieux Chêne (Map pp118–19; ☎ 01 43 37 71 51; 69 rue Mouffetard, 5e; Ⓜ Place Monge; ☻ 4pm-2am Sun-Thu, 4pm-5am Fri & Sat) The 'Old Oak', long a Mouffetard institution, is believed to be the oldest bar in Paris. Today it is popular with students and often has jazz on weekends. Happy hour is from opening to 9pm, with half pints for €2.50 (usually €3.50).

St-Germain, Odéon & Luxembourg

Café de Flore (Map pp110–11; ☎ 01 45 48 55 26; 172 blvd St-Germain, 6e; Ⓜ St-Germain des Prés; ☻ 7.30am-1.30am) The Flore is an Art Deco café where the red, upholstered benches, the mirrors and the marble walls haven't changed since the days when Sartre, de Beauvoir, Camus and Picasso bent their elbows here. The terrace is a much sought-after place to sip beer (€7.50 for 400mL), the house Pouilly Fumé (€7.50 a glass or €29 a bottle) or coffee (€4).

Café de la Mairie (Map pp110–11; ☎ 01 43 26 67 82; 8 place St-Sulpice, 6e; Ⓜ St-Sulpice; ☻ 7am-2am Mon-Sat) Plain but with an excellent terrace giving onto place St-Sulpice, this bustling yet laid-back café attracts students, writers and film people with its tattered Left Bank ambience.

Le 10 (Map pp110–11; ☎ 01 43 26 66 83; 10 rue de l'Odéon, 6e; Ⓜ Odéon; ☻ 5.30pm-2am) This is a popular cellar pub with smoke-darkened posters on the walls, an eclectic jukebox with everything from jazz and the Doors to French chansons – and sangria, the house speciality by the jug (€3.30 per person). Happy hour is from 6pm to 9pm daily.

Les Deux Magots (Map pp110-11; ☎ 01 45 48 55 25; 170 blvd St-Germain, 6e; Ⓜ St-Germain des Prés; ☿ 7am-1am) This erstwhile literary haunt, whose name derives not from a couple of disgusting white worms but from the two *magots* (grotesque figurines) of Chinese dignitaries at the entrance, dates from 1914 although it is best known as the favoured hang-out of Sartre, Hemingway, Picasso and André Breton. Everyone has to sit on the terrace here at least once and have a coffee or the famous hot chocolate served in porcelain jugs (€6).

Montparnasse
The most popular places to while away the hours over a drink or coffee in Montparnasse are large café-restaurants like La Coupole (p171) and Le Dôme (p171) on blvd du Montparnasse.

Cubana Café (Map pp108-9; ☎ 01 40 46 80 81; 47 rue Vavin, 6e; Ⓜ Vavin; ☿ 11am-3am Sun-Wed, 11am-5am Thu-Sat) The 'Cuban Café' is the perfect place to have cocktails and tapas (€2 to €8) before carrying on to the clubs of Montparnasse. The *salon fumoir* (smoking lounge) indulges cigar lovers with comfy old leather armchairs and oil paintings of daily life in Cuba.

Opéra & Grands Boulevards
Café Noir (Map pp104-5; ☎ 01 40 39 07 36; 65 rue Montmartre, 2e; Ⓜ Sentier; ☿ 8am-2am Mon-Fri, 3pm-2am Sat) An excellent, dependable bar on the edge of the Sentier garment district, the 'Black Café' is one of those watering holes you decide to make your regular. It's always packed, with a mix of both French and Anglo imbibers attracted by the friendly and very hip ambience.

Harry's New York Bar (Map pp102-3; ☎ 01 42 61 71 14; 5 rue Daunou, 2e; Ⓜ Opéra; ☿ 10.30am-4am) One of the most popular American-style bars in the interwar years, Harry's manages to evoke a golden past without feeling like a museum piece. Lean upon the bar where F. Scott Fitzgerald and Ernest Hemingway once drank and gossiped and have the expert, white-smocked gentlemen prepare you a killer martini or the house creation: the Bloody Mary. The Cuban mahogany interior dates from the mid-19th century and was brought over from a Manhattan bar in 1911. There's a basement piano bar with light jazz open in the evening.

Gare du Nord, Gare de l'Est & République
Chez Wolf Motown Bar (Map pp104-5; ☎ 01 46 07 09 79; 81-83 blvd de Strasbourg, 10e; Ⓜ Gare de l'Est; ☿ 24hr except 6am-7pm Sat) This is the place to come in the lonely wee hours when you've got a thirst and a few bob but, alas, no friends. The ambience is warm and festive, and both the staff and patrons friendly.

Le Relais du Nord (Map pp104-5; ☎ 01 48 78 03 51; 22 rue de Dunkerque, 10e; Ⓜ Gare du Nord; ☿ 6am-9pm) This gem of an Art Nouveau café is a short distance to the west of the Gare du Nord and an excellent, down-to-earth choice if you're in the mood to celebrate your departure or arrival with a drink or a light meal.

Ménilmontant & Belleville
L'Autre Café (Map pp104-5; ☎ 01 40 21 03 07; 62 rue Jean-Pierre Timbaud, 11e; Ⓜ Parmentier; ☿ 8am-1.30am Mon-Fri, 11.30am-1.30am Sat & Sun) A young mixed crowd of locals, artists and partygoers remains faithful to the 'Other Café', a quality café with long bar, spacious seating areas, relaxed environment and reasonable prices. A springboard for young artists, the Autre Café organises exhibition openings and film screenings.

Montmartre & Pigalle
La Fourmi (Map p122; ☎ 01 42 64 70 35; 74 rue des Martyrs, 18e; Ⓜ Pigalle; ☿ 8am-2am Mon-Thu, 10am-4am Fri-Sun) A perennial Pigalle favourite, the 'Ant' marches all day and night and is hip but not overwhelming with a lively yet unpretentious atmosphere. The music is mostly rock – quality well-known tunes that get you going while leaving space for conversation

Au Progrès (Map p122; ☎ 01 42 51 33 33; 7 rue des Trois Frères, 18e; Ⓜ Abbesses; ☿ 5pm-2am) A real live *café du quartier* (neighbourhood café) perched in the heart of Abbesses, the 'Progress' attracts a relaxed mix of local artists, shop staff, writers and hangers-on that is very telling of the local population.

ENTERTAINMENT
Listings
It's virtually impossible to sample the richness of Paris' entertainment scene without first studying *Pariscope* (€0.40) or *Officiel des Spectacles* (€0.35), both of which come out on Wednesday and are available at newsstands everywhere in the city. The

weekly magazine **Zurban** (www.zurban.com in French; €1), which also appears on Wednesday, offers a fresher look at entertainment in the capital. **Les Inrockuptibles** (www.lesinrocks .com in French; €2.90) is a national culture and entertainment weekly but, predictably, the lion's share of the information concerns Paris. Their website lists events and concerts.

For up-to-date information on clubs and the music scene, you might also pick up a copy of *LYLO* (an acronym for *Les Yeux, Les Oreilles*, literally 'Eyes and Ears'), a free booklet with excellent listings of rock concerts and other live music. It is available at many cafés, bars and clubs across town.

Other excellent sources for finding out what's on include Radio FG on 98.2MHz FM (www.radiofg.com in French) and Radio Nova on 101.5MHz FM (www.novaplanet .com in French). In addition to the above resources, for information on the club scene you can also check out www.france -techno.fr (in French) or www.parissi.com (in French).

Booking Agencies

You can buy your tickets for cultural events at numerous ticket outlets, including FNAC and Virgin Megastore branches, for a small commission. Both accept reservations, ticketing by phone and the internet and most credit cards. Tickets generally cannot be returned or exchanged unless a performance is cancelled.

FNAC (☎ 0 892 683 622; www.fnac.com in French) has nine outlets in Paris with *billeteries* (ticket offices) including the following:
FNAC Champs-Élysées (Map pp102-3; ☎ 01 53 53 64 64; 74 av des Champs-Élysées, 8e; Ⓜ Franklin D Roosevelt; Ⓨ 10am-midnight Mon-Sat, noon-midnight Sun)
FNAC Forum des Halles (Map pp110-11; ☎ 01 40 41 40 00; Forum des Halles shopping centre, Level 3, 1-7 rue Pierre Lescot, 1er; Ⓜ Châtelet-Les Halles; Ⓨ 10am-7.30pm Mon-Sat)
FNAC Musique Bastille (Map pp114-15; ☎ 01 43 42 04 04; 4 place de la Bastille, 12e; Ⓜ Bastille; Ⓨ 10am-8pm Mon-Sat)

Virgin (www.virginmegastore.fr in French) has a half-dozen 'megastores' in the capital; central locations:
Virgin Megastore Barbès (Map p122; ☎ 01 56 55 53 70; 15 blvd Barbès, 18e; Ⓜ Barbès Rochechouart; Ⓨ 10am-9pm Mon-Sat)

Virgin Megastore Carrousel du Louvre (Map pp110-11; ☎ 01 44 50 03 10; 99 rue de Rivoli, 1er; Ⓜ Palais Royal-Musée du Louvre; Ⓨ 10am-8pm Mon & Tue, 10am-9pm Wed-Sun)
Virgin Megastore Champs-Élysées (Map pp102-3; ☎ 01 49 53 50 00; 52-60 av des Champs-Élysées, 8e; Ⓜ Franklin D Roosevelt; Ⓨ 10am-midnight Mon-Sat, noon-midnight Sun)

DISCOUNT TICKETS

On the day of any play or musical performance, **Kiosque Théâtre** (Map pp102-3; opp 15 place de la Madeleine, 8e; Ⓜ Madeleine; Ⓨ 12.30-7.45pm Tue-Sat, 12.30-3.45pm Sun) sells tickets at half price plus commission of about €2.50. Seats are almost always the most expensive ones in the stalls or 1st balcony. There's also a **Kiosque Théâtre** (Map pp108-9; parvis Montparnasse, 15e; Ⓜ Montparnasse Bienvenüe) in Montparnasse between Gare Montparnasse and Tour Montparnasse, open the same hours. There are no telephone bookings. The French-language websites www.billetreduc.com and www .ticketac.com have online discounts.

Live Music
ROCK, POP & INDIE

There's rock, pop and indie at bars, cafés and clubs around Paris, and a number of venues regularly host acts by international performers. It's often easier to see big-name Anglophone acts in Paris than in their home countries. The most popular stadiums or other big venues for international acts are the **Palais Omnisports de Paris-Bercy** (Map pp120-1; ☎ 0 825 030 031, 01 46 91 57 57; www.bercy.fr in French; 8 blvd de Bercy, 12e; Ⓜ Bercy) in Bercy; the **Stade de France** (Map p209; ☎ 0 892 700 900, 01 55 93 00 00; www.stadedefrance.fr; rue Francis de Pressensé, ZAC du Cornillon Nord, 93216 St-Denis La Plaine; Ⓜ St-Denis-Porte de Paris) in St-Denis; and **Le Zénith** (Map pp98-9; ☎ 01 55 80 09 38; www.le-zenith.com in French; 211 av Jean Jaurès, 19e; Ⓜ Porte de Pantin) at the Cité de la Musique in the Parc de la Villette, 19e.

Café de la Danse (Map pp114-15; ☎ 01 47 00 57 59; www.cafédeladanse.com in French; 5 Passage Louis-Philippe, 11e; Ⓜ Bastille; admission €8-30; box office Ⓨ noon-6pm Mon-Fri) Just a few metres down a small passage from 23 rue de Lappe, the 'Dance Café' is a large auditorium with 300 to 500 seats. An excellent venue for modern dance, it also plays host to rock and world music concerts, musical theatre and poetry readings.

La Cigale (Map p122; ☎ 01 49 25 89 99; 120 blvd de Rochechouart, 18e; Ⓜ Anvers or Pigalle; admission

€22-45; box office ☺ noon-7pm Mon-Fri) The 'Cicada' is an enormous old music hall seating up to 2000 people and hosting international rock and jazz concerts from international and local acts. Dating back to 1887, the hall was redecorated a hundred years later by Philippe Starck.

La Java (Map pp104-5; ☎ 01 42 02 20 52; 105 rue du Faubourg du Temple, 10e; Ⓜ Goncourt; admission €8-16; ☺ 11pm-5am Thu-Sat, 2-7pm Sun) The dance hall (1922) where Édith Piaf got her first break now reverberates to the sound of live salsa and other Latino music. From 9am until midnight there are concerts, including world music. Afterwards, the Latino DJs usually bring in a festive dancing crowd.

L'Élysée-Montmartre (Map p122; ☎ 01 44 92 45 36, 01 55 07 16 00; www.elyseemontmartre.com; 72 blvd de Rochechouart, 18e; Ⓜ Anvers; admission €10-35) A huge old music hall with a great sound system, this is one of the better venues in Paris for one-off rock and indie concerts. It also hosts club events and big-name DJs at the weekend.

Le Bataclan (Map pp114-15; ☎ 01 43 14 00 30; 50 blvd Voltaire, 11e; Ⓜ Oberkampf or St-Ambroise; admission €15-50; box office ☺ 3-7pm Mon-Sat) Built in 1864 and Maurice Chevalier's debut venue in 1910, this small concert hall draws some French and international acts. It also masquerades as a theatre and dance hall. Le Bataclan usually opens from 8pm for concerts.

CLASSICAL

Paris plays host to dozens of orchestral, organ and chamber-music concerts each week. In addition to theatres and concert halls listed here, Paris' churches, especially Notre Dame Cathedral (p132), Ste-Chapelle (p133) and **Église Royale du Val-de-Grâce** (Map pp118-19; ☎ 01 42 01 47 67; 277bis rue St-Jacques, 5e; Ⓜ Port Royal) sometimes hold concerts. In general the concerts don't keep to any fixed schedule, but are advertised on posters around town. Admission fees vary but usually range from €20/10 for adults/students and children.

Châtelet-Théâtre Musical de Paris (Map pp110-11; ☎ 01 40 28 28 40; www.chatelet-theatre.com in French; 2 rue Édouard Colonne, 1er; Ⓜ Châtelet; concert tickets €9-60; box office ☺ 11am-7pm) This central venue hosts concerts (including ones by the Orchestre de Paris from October to June) as well as operas, ballets and theatre performances. Tickets go on sale 14 days before the performance date; subject to availability, anyone aged under 26 or over 65 can get reduced-price tickets from 15 minutes before curtain time. There are no performances in July and August.

Salle Pleyel (Map pp102-3; ☎ 01 42 56 13 13; www .sallepleyel.fr; 252 rue du Faubourg St-Honoré, 8e; Ⓜ Ternes) Dating from the 1920s, this highly regarded hall hosts many of Paris' finest classical music concerts and recitals. It closed in July 2002 for a massive renovation and reopened in September 2006 with prestigious French and foreign orchestras on the programme.

JAZZ & BLUES

After WWII Paris was Europe's most important jazz centre and it is again very much à la mode; the city's better clubs attract top international stars.

Cafe Universel (Map pp118-19; ☎ 01 43 25 74 20; 267 rue St-Jacques, 5e; Ⓜ Port Royal; ☺ 9.30pm-2am Mon-Sat) The 'Universal Café' hosts a brilliant array of live concerts, with everything from bebop and Latin sounds to vocal jazz sessions. Entry is free and there's a lot of freedom given to young producers and artists.

Le Baiser Salé (Map pp110-11; ☎ 01 42 33 37 71; 58 rue des Lombards, 1er; Ⓜ Châtelet; admission free-€22) The 'Salty Kiss' is one of several jazz clubs on the same street. The *salle de jazz* (jazz hall) on the 1st floor has concerts of pop, rock and *chansons* at 7pm and Afro-jazz and jazz fusion at 10pm. The cover charge depends on the act; it's free during the *soirée bœuf* (jam session) on Monday night.

Le Caveau de la Huchette (Map pp110-11; ☎ 01 43 26 65 05; 5 rue de la Huchette, 5e; Ⓜ St-Michel; adult Sun-Thu €11, Fri & Sat €13, student €10; ☺ 9pm-2.30am Sun-Thu, 9pm-4am Fri & Sat) Housed in a medieval *caveau* (cellar) that was used as a courtroom and torture chamber during the Revolution, this club is where virtually all the jazz greats have played since the end of WWII. It's touristy but the atmosphere can often be more electric than at the more serious jazz clubs. Sessions start at 9.30pm.

New Morning (Map pp104-5; ☎ 01 45 23 51 41; www .newmorning.com in French; 7-9 rue des Petites Écuries, 10e; Ⓜ Château d'Eau; admission €15-21; ☺ 8pm-2am) This informal auditorium hosts jazz concerts as well as blues, rock, funk, salsa, Afro-Cuban and Brazilian music three to seven nights a week at 9pm, with the second set ending at about 1am. Tickets are available at the box office (open 4.30pm to 7.30pm) and at the door.

FRENCH CHANSONS

When French music comes to mind, most people hear accordions and *chansonniers* (cabaret singers) such as Édith Piaf, Jacques Brel, Georges Brassens and Léo Ferré. But although you may stumble upon buskers performing *chansons françaises* or playing *musette* (accordion music) in the market, it can sometimes be difficult to catch traditional French music in a more formal setting in Paris. We list a handful of venues where you're sure to hear it – both the traditional and the modern forms.

Au Lapin Agile (Map p122; ☎ 01 46 06 85 87; www .au-lapin-agile.com; 22 rue des Saules, 18e; Ⓜ Lamarck Caulaincourt; adult €24, students except Sat €17; ☯ 9pm-2am Tue-Sun) This rustic cabaret venue in Montmartre was favoured by artists and intellectuals in the early 20th century and *chansons* are still performed here and poetry read six nights a week starting at 9.30pm. Admission includes one drink.

Le Limonaire (Map pp104-5; ☎ 01 45 23 33 33; 18 cité Bergère, 9e; Ⓜ Grands Boulevards; admission free; ☯ 6pm-midnight Tue-Sun) This little wine bar is one of the best places to listen to traditional French bistro music, but come here only if you're serious about the genre; the crowd is almost reverential. Singers (who change regularly) perform at 10pm Tuesday to Saturday and at 7pm on Sunday.

Chez Adel (Map pp104-5; ☎ 01 42 08 24 61; 10 rue de la Grange aux Belles, 10e; Ⓜ Jacques Bonsergent; admission free; ☯ lunch & dinner to 2am Tue-Fri, noon-2am Sat & Sun) Chez Adel is a truly Parisian concept: Syrian hosts with guest *chansonniers* (as well as folk and world music artists) performing most nights to a mixed and enthusiastic crowd. A main meal costs €10.

Clubs

Paris does not have a mainstream club scene like that found in most other world-class cities; the music, theme and crowd at most clubs changes regularly according to the whims of the moment. The Latin scene is still huge, with salsa dancing and Latino music nights taking place in many clubs. There's a decent R&B and hip-hop following, although these styles are far less represented here than they are in, say, London. Electronic music is high quality in Paris' clubs, with some excellent local house and techno. Recently the predominance of dark minimal sounds seems to be giving way to more funk and groove. This scene remains somewhat underground and very mobile – the best DJs and their followings tend to have short stints in a certain venue before moving on.

To keep in the loop, see Listings (p177) and pick up flyers in shops; www.audio families.com has information and downloads on top Parisian DJs. Some of the bars listed in the Drinking section have DJ nights and dancing.

Admission to clubs generally costs €10 to €15 and includes a drink; often men cannot get in unaccompanied (by women that is). Drink prices vary greatly but they're upwards of €6 for a beer and €8 for a mixed drink or cocktail.

La Favela Chic (Map pp104-5; ☎ 01 40 21 38 14; www .favelachic.com in French; 18 rue du Faubourg du Temple, 10e; Ⓜ République; admission €10; ☯ 7.30pm-2am Tue-Fri, 9.30pm-4am Sat) The ambience is more *favela* (shantytown) than chic in this restaurant-bar-cum-dancehall, where Brazilians and French alike get down to the frenetic mix of samba, *baile* funk and classic Brazilian pop.

Le Balajo (Map pp114-15; ☎ 01 47 00 07 87; 9 rue de Lappe, 11e; Ⓜ Bastille; admission €10-17; ☯ 9pm-2am Tue-Thu, 11pm-5am Fri & Sat, 3-7.30pm Sun) A mainstay of Parisian nightlife since 1936, this ancient ballroom is a bit lower shelf these days but still hosts a number of popular theme nights. Tuesday to Thursday is salsa and Latino music, on Friday and Saturday DJs play rock, disco, R&B and house and from 3pm to 7.30pm on Sunday, DJs play old-fashioned *musette* (accordion music).

Le Batofar (Map pp98-9; ☎ 01 56 29 10 33; www .batofar.net in French; opposite 11 quai François Mauriac, 13e; Ⓜ Quai de la Gare or Bibliothèque; admission free-€15; ☯ 9pm-midnight Mon & Tue, 9 or 10pm-4 to 6am Wed-Sun) What looks like an unassuming tug boat moored near the imposing Bibliothèque Nationale de France is a rollicking dancing spot that attracts some top international talent. Batofar is known for its edgy, experimental music policy and live performances, mostly electro-oriented but also incorporating other sounds such as hip hop, new wave, rock, punk and jazz.

Le Cithéa (Map pp104-5; ☎ 01 40 21 70 95; 114 rue Oberkampf, 11e; Ⓜ Parmentier or Ménilmontant; admission free-€4; ☯ 5pm-5.30am Tue-Thu, 10pm-6.30am Fri & Sat) This popular and ever-hopping concert venue picks up the post-drinking crowd from rue Oberkampf. It has a pub-meets-concert hall feel to it, with quality bands playing rock, soul, jazz and funk. Concerts usually run from 10.30pm, with DJs from 1am.

Le Nouveau Casino (Map pp104-5; ☎ 01 43 57 57 40; www.nouveaucasino.net in French; 109 rue Oberkampf, 11e; Ⓜ Parmentier; admission free-€18; Ⓥ 9 to 11pm-2am to 6am) The 'New Casino' has an eclectic program – electro, pop, deep house, rock – with both live music concerts and top DJs. Try to get there before everyone pours out of the surrounding bars at 2am.

Rex Club (Map pp104-5; ☎ 01 42 36 10 96; 5 blvd Poissonnière, 2e; Ⓜ Bonne Nouvelle; admission €8-13; Ⓥ 11.30pm-6am Wed-Sat) The Rex reigns supreme in the house and techno scene and welcomes big name local and international DJs; getting in is more a question of queuing up than looking right.

Triptyque (Map pp104-5; ☎ 01 40 28 05 55; www .letriptyque.com; 142 rue Montmartre, 2e; Ⓜ Grands Boulevards; admission €3-10; Ⓥ 9pm-2am Sun-Wed, 9pm-5am Thu-Sat) A vast club set up in three underground rooms decorated with video projections, the Triptyque fills something of a gap in inner-city clubbing. Musically it spans electro, hip-hop and funk, as well as jazz and live acts.

Gay & Lesbian Venues

The Marais, especially those areas around the intersection of rue Ste-Croix de la Bretonnerie and rue des Archives and eastwards to rue Vieille du Temple, has been Paris' main centre of gay and lesbian nightlife for two decades. There are a few other addresses scattered elsewhere on the Right Bank.

Bliss Kfé (Map pp110-11; ☎ 01 42 78 49 36; 30 rue du Roi de Sicile, 4e; Ⓜ St-Paul; Ⓥ 5.30pm-2am) This lesbian café and lounge bar at the corner of rue des Écouffes has a stylish vibe and a somewhat mixed crowd. Guys are welcome, and there's a smoky club downstairs on Friday and Saturday nights.

Le Dépôt (Map pp110-11; ☎ 01 44 54 96 96; 10 rue aux Ours, 3e; Ⓜ Rambuteau or Étienne Marcel; admission €6-12; Ⓥ 2pm-8am) With a cop shop just next door you'd think this strictly men-only bar on the 'Street of the Bears' would be a titch more subdued. Fat chance. It's a major men's pick-up joint with theme nights, DJs and notorious backrooms.

Le Pulp (Map pp104-5; ☎ 01 40 26 01 93; www.pulp -paris.com; 25 blvd Poissonnière, 2e; Ⓜ Grands Boulevards; admission from €9; Ⓥ midnight-6am Thu-Sun) A hip yet down-to-earth place with a hot little dance floor and a lounge area with couches, the Pulp is Paris' pre-eminent women's-only club. Boys are allowed in when accompanied by girls on the mixed Thursday nights, which have been known for attracting the electronic in-crowd and some of Paris' best house and electro DJs.

Le Troisième Lieu (Map pp110-11; ☎ 01 48 04 85 64; 62 rue Quincampoix, 4e; Ⓜ Rambuteau; Ⓥ 6pm-2am) This friendly bar has rapidly become the new happening place for a chic young lesbian crowd (boys are welcome). There's a large, colourful bar at street level; downstairs makes room for dancing to DJs, rock/alternative music concerts and live singers.

Open Café (Map pp110-11; ☎ 01 42 72 26 18; 17 rue des Archives, 4e; Ⓜ Hôtel de Ville; Ⓥ 11am-2am Sun-Thu, 11am-4am Fri-Sat) The huge, overflowing terrace is the place for gay men to see and be seen, especially in the warmer months (though even in winter there's a lot of outdoor posing here). It's always packed, but more social than cruisy.

Red Light (Map pp108-9; ☎ 01 42 79 94 94; 34 rue du Départ, 14e; Ⓜ Montparnasse Bienvenüe; admission €20; Ⓥ 11pm-6am Thu-Sun) Previously (and perhaps more fittingly) named L'Enfer (Hell) this seedy underground (literally) venue beneath Tour Montparnasse refuses to give up the ghost. Huge and laser-lit, it's a popular choice for student drink-fest evenings during the week, while weekends see a young, exuberant gay crowd pack out its podiums.

Cinemas

Pariscope and *L'Officiel des Spectacles* (p177) list Paris' cinematic offerings alphabetically by their French title followed by the English (or other foreign) one.

Going to the cinema in Paris is not cheap: expect to pay up to €9 for a first-run film. Students and those aged under 18 or over 60 usually get discounts of about 25% except on Friday nights, all day Saturday and until Sunday evening. On Wednesday (and sometimes Monday) most cinemas give discounts of 20% to 30% to everyone.

Cinémathèque Française (Map pp120-1; ☎ 01 71 19 33 33; www.cinemathequefrancaise.com in French; 51 rue Bercy, 12e; Ⓜ Bercy; adult/student & child €8/6.50) This national cultural institution is a veritable temple to the 'seventh art' and also sponsors

ÉDITH PIAF: URCHIN SPARROW

Like her US contemporary Judy Garland, Édith Piaf was not just a singer but a tragic and stoic figure whom the French nation took to its heart and has quite simply never let go of.

She was born Édith Giovanna Gassion to a street acrobat and a singer in the working-class district of Belleville in 1915. Piaf's early childhood was spent with her maternal grandmother, an alcoholic who neglected her, and later with her father's parents in Normandy, who ran a local brothel. At age nine she toured with her father but left home at 15 to sing alone in the streets of Paris. Her first employer, Louis Leplée, called her *la môme piaf* (the urchin sparrow) and introduced her to the cabarets of the capital.

When Leplée was murdered in 1935, Piaf faced the streets again. But along came Raymond Asso, an ex-French Legionnaire who would become her Pygmalion, forcing her to break with her pimp and hustler friends, putting her in her signature black dress and inspiring her first big hit, *Mon Légionnaire* (My Legionnaire) in 1937. When he succeeded in getting her a contract at what is now La Java (p179), one of the most famous Parisian music halls of the time, her career skyrocketed.

This frail woman, who sang about street life, drugs, unrequited love, violence, death and whores, seemed to embody all the miseries of the world yet sang in a husky, powerful voice with no self-pity. Her tumultuous love life earned her the reputation as *une dévoreuse d'hommes* (a man-eater), but she launched the careers of several, including Yves Montand and Charles Aznavour. Another of her many lovers was world middleweight boxing champion Marcel Cerdan; he was killed in a plane crash while flying over to join her on her US tour in 1949. True to form, Piaf insisted that the show go on after learning of his death and fainted on stage in the middle of *L'Hymne à l'Amour* (Hymn to Love), a song inspired by Cerdan.

After suffering injuries in a car accident in 1951, Piaf began drinking heavily and became addicted to morphine. Her health declined quickly but she continued to sing around the world, including New York's Carnegie Hall in 1956, and recorded some of her biggest hits (*Je Ne Regrette Rien, Milord* etc). In 1962, frail and once again penniless, Piaf married a 20-year-old hairdresser called Théophanis Lamboukas (aka Théo Sarapo), recorded the duet *À Quoi Ça Sert l'Amour?* (What Use Is Love?) with him and left Paris for the South of France, where she died the following year. Some two million people attended her funeral in Paris, and the grave of the beloved and much missed Urchin Sparrow at Père Lachaise Cemetery is still visited and decorated by thousands of her loyal fans each year.

cultural events, workshops and exhibitions. It always leaves its foreign offerings – often rarely screened classics – in their original versions. The association is a not-for-profit collective and largely funded by the state.

Theatre

Almost all of Paris' theatre productions, including those written in other languages, are performed in French. There are a few English-speaking troupes around, though; look for ads on metro poster boards and in English-language periodicals such as *FUSAC* (p946), *Paris Voice* and *Paris Times*, which are free at English-language bookshops, pubs, and so on.

For booking agencies for theatre tickets see p178.

Comédie Française (www.comedie-francaise.fr; tickets €5-32) Comédie Française Studio Théâtre (Map pp110-11; ☎ 01 44 58 98 58; Galerie du Carrousel du Louvre, 99 rue de Rivoli, 1er; Ⓜ Palais Royal-Musée du Louvre; box office ⊙ 1-5pm Wed-Mon); Salle Richelieu (Map pp110-11; ☎ 0 825 101 680; place Colette, 1er; Ⓜ Palais Royal-Musée du Louvre; box office ⊙ 11am-6pm Tue-Sat, 1-6pm Sun & Mon); Théâtre du Vieux Colombier (Map pp108-9; ☎ 01 44 39 87 00; 21 rue du Vieux Colombier, 6e; Ⓜ St-Sulpice; box office ⊙ 11am-6pm Tue-Sat, 1-6pm Sun & Mon) Founded in 1680 during the reign of Louis XIV, the 'French Comedy' theatre bases its repertoire around works of the classic French playwrights such as Molière, Racine and Corneille, though in recent years contemporary and even non-French works have been staged. There are three venues: the main Salle Richelieu on place Colette just west of the Palais Royal; the Comédie Française Studio Théâtre; and the Théâtre du Vieux Colombier. Tickets for regular seats cost €10 to €35; tickets for the 95 places near the ceiling (€7) go on sale one hour before curtain time (usually 8.30pm), which is when those under 27 can purchase any of the better seats remaining for €7.50 to €10. The discount tickets are available from the window round the corner from the main entrance and facing place André Malraux.

Odéon-Théâtre de l'Europe (Map pp118-19; ☎ 01 44 85 40 40; www.theatre-odeon.fr; place de l'Odéon, 6e; Ⓜ Odéon) This huge, ornate theatre built in the early 1780s has recently undergone extensive renovations. It often puts on foreign plays in their original languages (subtitled in French) and hosts theatre troupes from abroad.

Ateliers Berthier (Map pp98-9; ☎ 01 44 85 40 40; 8 blvd Berthier, 17e; Ⓜ Porte de Clichy; tickets €13-26; box office Ⓨ 11am-6.30pm Mon-Sat) Stages plays. People over 60 get a discount on pricier tickets, while students and those under 30 can get good reserved seats for as little as €7.50.

Opera

Opéra National de Paris (ONP; ☎ 0 892 899 090; www.opera-de-paris.fr in French) Splits its performance schedule between the Palais Garnier, its original home built in 1875, and the modern Opéra Bastille, which opened in 1989. Both opera houses also stage ballets and classical-music concerts performed by the ONP's affiliated orchestra and ballet companies. The season runs from September to July.

Opéra Bastille (Map pp114-15; 2-6 place de la Bastille, 12e; Ⓜ Bastille) Tickets are available from the box office (Map pp114-15; 130 rue de Lyon, 10.30am-6.30pm Monday to Saturday) some 14 days before the date of the performance, but the only way to ensure a seat is by post (120 rue de Lyon, 75576 Paris CEDEX 12) some two months in advance. Operas cost €6 to €114. Ballets cost €13 to €70; seats with limited or no visibility available at the box office only are €6 to €9. Chamber-music concerts, which are also held here throughout the season, cost €6 to €16. If there are unsold tickets, people aged under 26 or over 65 and students can get excellent seats for €20 only 15 minutes before the curtain goes up.

Palais Garnier (Map pp102-3; place de l'Opéra, 9e; Ⓜ Opéra; box office Ⓨ 11am-6.30pm Mon-Sat) Ticket prices and conditions (including last-minute discounts) at the city's original opera house are almost exactly the same as those at the Opéra Bastille.

Cabaret

Paris' risqué cabaret revues – those dazzling, pseudo-bohemian productions where the women wear two beads and a feather (or was it two feathers and a bead?) – are another one of those things that everyone sees in Paris except the Parisians themselves. But they continue to draw in the crowds as they did in the days of Toulouse-Lautrec and Aristide Bruant and can be a lot of fun. Times and prices vary with the seasons, but shows usually begin at 7.30pm or 9pm, and tickets per person cost from €40 to €100 for the performance, or from €100 to €400 when you have dinner, which usually includes champagne.

Crazy Horse (Map pp102-3; ☎ 01 47 23 32 32; www.lecrazyhorseparis.com; 12 av George V, 8e; Ⓜ Alma Marceau) This popular cabaret, whose dressing (or, rather, undressing) rooms were featured in Woody Allen's film *What's New Pussycat?* (1965), has been promoting what it calls *l'art du nu* (the art of nudity) for more than half a century.

Le Lido de Paris (Map pp102-3; ☎ 01 40 76 56 10; www.lido.fr; 116bis av des Champs-Élysées, 8e; Ⓜ George V) Founded at the close of WWII, the Lido gets top marks for its ambitious sets and the lavish costumes of its 70 artistes.

Moulin Rouge (Map p122; ☎ 01 53 09 82 82; www.moulinrouge.fr; 82 blvd de Clichy, 18e; Ⓜ Blanche) This legendary cabaret founded in 1889, whose dancers appeared in Toulouse-Lautrec's celebrated posters, sits under its trademark red windmill (actually a 1925 copy of the 19th-century original).

Sport

Parisians are mad about watching sport. For details of upcoming sporting events, consult the sports daily **L'Équipe** (www.lequipe.fr in French; €0.80) or **Figaroscope** (www.figaroscope.fr in French), an entertainment and activities supplement published with *Le Figaro* daily newspaper each Wednesday.

Most big international sporting events are held at the magnificent **Stade de France** (Map p207; ☎ 0 892 700 900; www.stadefrance.com; rue Francis de Pressensé, ZAC du Cornillon Nord, 93216 St-Denis La Plaine) at St-Denis (p208).

FOOTBALL

France's home matches (friendlies and qualifiers for major championships) are held at the **Stade de France** (tickets €12-70).

The city's only top-division football team, the red-and-blue-striped **Paris-St-Germain** (☎ 01 47 43 71 71; www.psg.fr in French) plays its home games at the 45,500-seat **Parc des Princes** (Map pp98-9; ☎ 0 825 075 078; 24 rue du Commandant Guilbaud, 16e; Ⓜ Porte de St-Cloud; tickets €12-80; box office ⊙ 9am-9pm Mon-Sat), near Stade Roland Garros. Tickets are also available at the more central **Boutique PSG** (Map pp102-3; ☎ 01 56 69 22 22; 27 av des Champs Elysées, 8e; Ⓜ Franklin D Roosevelt; ⊙ 10am-7.45pm Mon-Thu, 10am-9.45pm Fri & Sat, noon-7.45pm Sun) as well as from FNAC and Virgin Megastore outlets (p178) in central Paris.

TENNIS
In late May/early June the tennis world focuses on the clay surface of the 16,500-seat **Stade Roland Garros** (Map pp98-9; ☎ 01 47 43 48 00, 01 47 43 52 52; www.rolandgarros.com in French; 2 av Gordon Bennett, 16e; Ⓜ Porte d'Auteuil) in the Bois de Boulogne for Les Internationaux de France de Tennis (The French Open), the second of the Grand Slams. Tickets are expensive and hard to come by; they go on sale in mid-November and bookings must usually be made by March. One week prior to the competition (on the first day of the qualifiers) remaining tickets are sold from the **stadium box office** (☎ 0 825 167 516; 9.30am-5.30pm Mon-Fri) at the stadium entrance.

The top indoor tournament is the Open de Tennis de la Ville de Paris (Paris Tennis Open), which usually takes place sometime in late October or early November at the **Palais Omnisports de Paris-Bercy** (Map pp120-1; ☎ 01 40 02 60 60; www.bercy.fr in French; 8 blvd de Bercy, 12e; Ⓜ Bercy). Tickets are available from the **box office** (☎ 0 892 390 490, from abroad 33-1 46 91 57 57, 11am-6pm Mon-Sat).

CYCLING
Since 1974 the final stage of the **Tour de France** (www.letour.fr), the world's most prestigious cycling event, has ended on the av des Champs-Élysées. The final day varies from year to year but is usually the 3rd or 4th Sunday in July, with the race finishing sometime in the afternoon. If you want to see this exciting event, find a spot at the barricades before noon.

Track cycling events, a sport at which France excels, are usually held in the *vélo-drome* of the Palais Omnisports de Paris-Bercy.

HORSE RACING
One of the cheapest ways to spend a relaxing afternoon in the company of Parisians

of all ages and backgrounds is to go to the races. The most accessible of the Paris area's seven racecourses is **Hippodrome d'Auteuil** (Map pp98-9; ☎ 01 40 71 47 47; www.france-galop.com in French; Champ de Courses d'Auteuil, Bois de Boulogne, 16e; Ⓜ Porte d'Auteuil), in the southeastern corner of the Bois de Boulogne. It hosts steeplechases from February to late June/early July and early September to early December.

Races are held about six times a month (check the hippodrome's website for the exact days), with half a dozen or so heats scheduled from 2pm to 5.30pm. There's no charge to stand on the *pelouse* (lawn) in the middle of the track but a seat in the *tribune* (stands) costs around €3/1.50 for adults/students and seniors on weekdays and €4/2 on Sunday; those under age 18 get in free. Race schedules are published in almost all national newspapers. If you read French, pick up a copy of *Paris Turf* (€1.15), the horse-racing daily.

SHOPPING
Paris is a wonderful place to shop, whether you're someone who can afford an original Cartier diamond bracelet or you're an impoverished *lèche-vitrine* (literal meaning: 'window-licker') who just enjoys what you see from the outside looking in. From the ultrachic couture houses of av Montaigne and the cubby-hole boutiques of the Marais to the vast underground shopping centre at Les Halles and the flea-market bargains at St-Ouen, Paris is a city that knows how to make it, how to display it and how to charge for it.

Opening Hours
Opening times in Paris are notoriously anarchic, with each store setting its own hours. Most shops will be open at least from 10am to about 7pm Monday to Saturday, but they may open earlier, close later, close for lunch (usually 1pm to 2pm or 2.30pm) or for a full or half-day on Monday or Tuesday. In general, only shops in tourist areas (eg the Champs-Élysées, Marais and Montmartre) stay open on Sunday. Many larger shops and department stores also have a *nocturne* – one late shopping night (usually to 10pm on Thursday) a week. During sales (*soldes*) – from mid-January and from the second week in July – and around Christmas larger stores stay open later at night and all weekend.

Clothing & Fashion

HAUTE COUTURE & DESIGNER WEAR

Most of the major French couturiers and ready-to-wear designers have their own boutiques in the capital, but it's also possible to see labelled, ready-to-wear collections at major department stores such as Le Printemps, Galeries Lafayette and Le Bon Marché. The Right Bank, especially the so-called **Triangle d'Or** (Map pp102-3; **M** Franklin D Roosevelt or Alma Marceau, 1er & 8e), **rue du Faubourg St-Honoré** (Map pp102-3; **M** Madeleine or Concorde, 8e) and its eastern extension, **rue St-Honoré** (**M** Tuileries), **place des Victoires** (Map pp104-5; **M** Bourse or Sentier, 1er & 2e) and the Marais' **rue des Rosiers** (Map pp110-11; **M** St-Paul, 4e), is traditionally the epicentre of Parisian fashion though **St-Germain** (Map pp110-11; **M** St-Sulpice or St-Germain des Prés) on the Left Bank also boasts its fair share of boutiques.

FASHION EMPORIA

There are fashion shops offering creations and accessories from a variety of cutting-edge designers.

Abou d'Abi Bazar (Map pp114-15; ☎ 01 42 77 96 98; 10 rue des Francs Bourgeois, 3e; **M** St-Paul; ☺ 2-7pm Sun & Mon, 10.30am-7.15pm Tue-Sat) This fashionable boutique with the odd name is a treasure-trove of smart and affordable ready-to-wear pieces from young designers including Paul & Joe, Isabel Marant and Vanessa Bruno.

Colette (Map pp102-3; ☎ 01 55 35 33 90; www.colette .fr; 213 rue St-Honoré, 1er; **M** Tuileries; ☺ 10.30am-7.30pm Mon-Sat) If you want to know what's hot, this Japanese-inspired concept store is the place to take the temperature. Along with the exquisite selection of clothing, check out limited-edition sneakers, Prada handbags, designer hairpins and cutting-edge clocks.

Kiliwatch (Map pp110-11; ☎ 01 42 21 17 37; 64 rue Tiquetonne, 2e; **M** Étienne Marcel; ☺ 11am-7pm Tue-Sat) This barn of a shop is always packed with hip guys and gals sorting through rack after rack of new and used street wear and designs. There's a startling vintage range including hats and boots, plus the latest sneakers.

Réciproque (Map pp102-3; ☎ 01 47 04 30 28, 01 47 04 82 24; 88 & 95 rue de la Pompe, 16e; **M** Rue de la Pompe; ☺ 11am-7pm Tue-Fri, 10.30am-7pm Sat) The biggest *dépôt-vente* (resale stores that sell used or barely used clothes and accessories from one-quarter to one-half off the original price) has rack after rack of Chanel suits as well as bits and pieces from Christian Lacroix, Hermès and John Galliano in two shops. It's an excellent place to pick up bags and shoes. There are half a dozen other such shops on the same street.

Department Stores

Paris boasts a number of *grands magasins* (department stores).

Galeries Lafayette (Map pp102-3; ☎ 01 42 82 34 56; www.galerieslafayette.com; 40 blvd Haussmann, 9e; **M** Auber or Chaussée d'Antin; ☺ 9.30am-7.30pm Mon-Wed, Fri & Sat, 9.30am-9pm Thu) A vast *grand magasin* in two adjacent buildings, Galeries Lafayette features a wide selection of fashion and accessories and the world's largest lingerie department. A fashion show (☎ 01 42 82 30 25 to book a seat) takes place at 3pm on Friday.

Le Bon Marché (Map pp108-9; ☎ 01 44 39 80 00; www .bonmarche.fr; 24 rue de Sèvres, 7e; **M** Sèvres Babylone; ☺ 9.30am-7pm Mon-Wed & Fri, 10am-9pm Thu, 9.30am-8pm Sat) Opened by Gustave Eiffel as Paris' first department store in 1852, the 'Good Market' (which also means 'bargain') is less frenetic than its rivals across the Seine, but no less chic. Men's as well as women's fashions are sold.

Le Printemps (Map pp102-3; ☎ 01 42 82 50 00; www .printemps.com; 64 blvd Haussmann, 9e; **M** Havre Caumartin; ☺ 9.35am-7pm Mon-Wed, Fri & Sat, 9.35am-10pm Thu) The 'Spring' (as in the season) is actually three separate stores – one for women's fashion (De la Mode), one for men (De l'Homme) and one for beauty and household goods (De la Beauté et Maison) – offering a staggering display of perfume, cosmetics and accessories, as well as established and up-and-coming designer wear. There's a fashion show under the 7th-floor cupola at 10am on Tuesday.

Flea Markets

Paris' *marchés aux puces* (flea markets) can be great fun if you're in the mood to browse for unexpected diamonds in the rough through all the *brocante* (second-hand goods) and bric-à-brac on display. Some new items are also available, and a bit of bargaining is expected. Closing times depend on the season.

Marché aux Puces de la Porte de Vanves (Map pp98-9; av Georges Lafenestre & av Marc Sangnier, 14e; **M** Porte de Vanves; ☺ 7am-6 or 7pm Sat & Sun) The Porte de Vanves flea market is the smallest and, some say, friendliest of the big three. Av Georges Lafenestre looks like a giant car-boot sale, with lots of 'curios' that aren't quite old (or curious) enough to qualify as antiques. Av Marc Sangnier is lined with stalls offering new clothes, shoes, handbags and household items for sale.

Marché aux Puces de Montreuil (Map pp98-9; av du Professeur André Lemière, 20e; Ⓜ Porte de Montreuil; 7.30am or 8am-6pm or 7pm Sat-Mon) Established in the 19th century, this flea market is renowned for its quality second-hand clothing and designer seconds. The 500 stalls also sell engravings, jewellery, linen, crockery, old furniture and appliances.

Marché aux Puces de St-Ouen (Map pp98-9; www.les-puces.com; rue des Rosiers, av Michelet, rue Voltaire, rue Paul Bert & rue Jean-Henri Fabre, 18e; Ⓜ Porte de Clignancourt; 9am or 10am-7pm Sat-Mon) This vast flea market founded in the late 19th century and said to be Europe's largest has some 2500 stalls grouped into 10 *marchés* (market areas), each with its own speciality (eg Marché Serpette and Marché Biron for antiques, Marché Malik for second-hand clothing). For more information about the market and its stalls check www.vernaison.com.

Food & Wine

The food and wine shops of Paris are legendary and well worth seeking out. Many places will vacuum pack or shrink wrap certain food items to guard against spoilage.

Boutique Maille (Map pp102-3; ☎ 01 40 15 06 00; 6 place de la Madeleine, 8e; Ⓜ Madeleine; 10am-7pm Mon-Sat) This shop specialises in mustards, of which it stocks and/or can make up for you some two dozen different varieties.

Cacao et Chocolat (Map pp110-11; ☎ 01 46 33 77 63; 29 rue du Buci, 6e; Ⓜ Mabillon; 10.30am-7.30pm Mon-Sat, 11am-1.30pm & 2.30-7pm Sun) You have not tasted chocolate (around which there is a veritable religion in France) till you've tasted this stuff. 'Cocoa and Chocolate' is an exotic and contemporary take on chocolate, showcasing the cocoa bean in all its guises, both solid and liquid. The added citrus flavours, spices and even chilli are guaranteed to tease you back for more. We're going to say it: it's the best chocolate in the world.

Fromagerie Alléosse (Map pp102-3; ☎ 01 46 22 50 45; 13 rue Poncelet, 17e; Ⓜ Ternes; 9am-1pm & 4-7pm Tue-Sat, 9am-1pm Sun) This is without a doubt the best cheese shop in Paris – well worth a trip across town – and cheeses are as they should be: grouped and displayed in five main categories (p74).

Hédiard (Map pp102-3: ☎ 01 43 12 88 88; www.hediard.fr; 21 place de la Madeleine, 8e; Ⓜ Madeleine; 8.30am-8.30pm Mon-Sat) This famous luxury food shop established in 1854 consists of two adjacent sections selling prepared dishes, teas, coffees, jams, wines, pastries, fruits, vegetables and so on as well as a popular tearoom.

La Petite Scierie (Map pp110-11; ☎ 01 55 42 14 88; 60 rue St-Louis en l'Île, 4e; Ⓜ Pont Marie; 11am-8pm) This little hole-in-the-wall sells every edible produced by and made from ducks, with the emphasis on foie gras (€30 for 180g). The products come direct from the farm.

Les Caves Augé (Map pp102-3; ☎ 01 45 22 16 97; 116 blvd Haussmann, 8e; Ⓜ St-Augustin; 1-7.30pm Mon, 9am-7.30pm Tue-Sat) The 'Augé Cellars' should be the *marchand de vin* (wine shop) for you if you're following the advice of a certain Marcel Proust. It's now under the stewardship of a passionate and knowledgeable *sommelier*.

Gifts & Souvenirs

Paris has a huge number of speciality shops offering gift items.

Anna Joliet (Map pp104-5; ☎ 01 42 96 55 13; passage du Perron, 9 rue de Beaujolais, 1er; Ⓜ Pyramides; 10am-7pm Mon-Sat) This wonderful (and minuscule) shop at the Jardin du Palais Royal specialises in music boxes, both old and new. Just open the door and see if you aren't tempted in.

Boutique Paris-Musées (Map pp110-11; ☎ 01 42 74 13 92; 29bis rue des Francs Bourgeois, 4e; Ⓜ Chemin Vert or St-Paul; 2-7pm Mon, 11am-1pm & 2-7pm Tue-Sun) This lovely boutique stocks museum reproductions, especially of art and sculpture on exhibit at museums run by the City of Paris, such as the Musée Carnavalet and the Musée d'Art Moderne de la Ville de Paris.

CSAO Boutique (Map pp110-11; ☎ 01 44 54 55 88; 1-3 rue Elzévir, 3e; Ⓜ St-Paul or Chemin Vert; 11am-7pm Tue-Fri, 11am-7.30pm Sat, 2-7pm Sun) This wonderful gallery and shop distributes the work of African artists and craftspeople. Many of the colourful fabrics and weavings are exquisite and the handmade recycled items – small watering cans from old tuna tins, handbags and caps from soft-drink cans, lamp shades from tomato paste tins – are both amusing and heartbreaking.

E Dehillerin (Map pp110-11; ☎ 01 42 36 53 13; 18-20 rue Coquillière, 1er; Ⓜ Les Halles; 9am-12.30pm & 2-6pm Mon, 9am-6pm Tue-Sat) Spread over two floors and dating back to 1820, E Dehillerin carries an incredible selection of professional-quality *matériel de cuisine* (kitchenware).

You're sure to find something even the most well-equipped kitchen is lacking.

Mélodies Graphiques (Map pp110-11; ☎ 01 42 74 57 68; 10 rue du Pont Louis-Philippe, 4e; Ⓜ Pont Marie; ⊙ 2-7pm Mon, 11am-7pm Tue-Sat) 'Graphic Melodies' carries all sorts of items made from exquisite Florentine *papier à cuve* (paper hand-decorated with marbled designs). There are other fine stationery shops along the same street.

GETTING THERE & AWAY

For information on the transport options between the city and Paris' airports, see p188. For information on international air links to Paris, see p968.

Air
AÉROPORT D'ORLY

Orly (ORY; ☎ 01 49 75 15 15, flight info 0 892 681 515; www.adp.fr), the older and smaller of Paris' two major international airports, is 18km south of the city. Air France and some other international carriers (eg Iberia and TAP Air Portugal) use Orly-Ouest (the west terminal). The Orlyval automatic metro links both terminals and connects with RER B (see p201).

AÉROPORT PARIS-BEAUVAIS

The international airport at **Beauvais** (BVA; ☎ 03 44 11 46 86, flight info 0 892 682 066; www.aeroportbeauvais.com), 80km north of Paris, is used by discount airline Ryanair for its European flights, including those between Paris and Dublin, Shannon and Glasgow.

AÉROPORT ROISSY CHARLES DE GAULLE

Roissy Charles de Gaulle (CDG; ☎ 01 48 62 22 80, 0 892 681 515; www.adp.fr), 30km northeast of Paris in the suburb of Roissy, consists of three terminal complexes, appropriately named Aérogare 1, 2 and 3. Aérogares 1 and 2 are used by international and domestic carriers. Aérogare 3 is used mainly by charter companies.

AIRLINE OFFICES

Contacts for airline offices in Paris can be found in the *Yellow Pages* under 'Transports Aériens':

Aer Lingus (☎ 01 70 20 00 72; www.aerlingus.com)
Air Canada (☎ 0 825 880 881; www.aircanada.com)
Air France (☎ 0 820 820 820, 0 892 681 048; www.airfrance.com)
Air New Zealand (☎ 01 40 53 82 83; www.airnz.com)
British Airways (☎ 0 825 825 400; www.britishairways.com)

British Midland (☎ 01 41 91 87 04; www.flybmi.com)
Continental Airlines (☎ 01 42 99 09 01, 01 71 23 03 35; www.continental.com)
Delta Air Lines (☎ 0 800 354 080; www.delta.com)
easyJet (☎ 0 825 082 508; www.easyjet.com)
KLM (☎ 0 890 710 710; www.klm.com)
Lufthansa Airlines ☎ 0 826 103 334; www.lufthansa.com)
Northwest Airlines (☎ 0 890 710 710; www.klm.com)
Qantas Airways (☎ 0 820 820 500; www.qantas.com)
Ryanair (☎ 0 892 682 073; www.ryanair.com)
Scandinavian Airlines (☎ 0 820 325 335; www.scandinavian.net)
Singapore Airlines (☎ 0 821 230 380; www.singaporeair.com)
Thai Airways International (☎ 01 44 20 70 80; www.thaiair.com)
United Airlines (☎ 0 810 727 272; www.ual.com)
US Airways (☎ 0 810 632 222; www.usairways.com)
Virgin Atlantic (☎ 0 800 528 528; www.virgin-atlantic.com)

Bus
DOMESTIC

Because French transport is biased in favour of the excellent state-owned rail system, Société Nationale des Chemins de Fer Français (SNCF), the country has extremely limited inter-regional bus services and no internal intercity bus services to or from Paris.

INTERNATIONAL

Eurolines (p971) links Paris with destinations in all parts of Western and Central Europe, Scandinavia and Morocco. The central **Eurolines office** (Map pp118-19; ☎ 01 43 54 11 99; www.eurolines.fr; 55 rue St-Jacques, 5e; Ⓜ Cluny-La Sorbonne; ⊙ 9.30am-6.30pm Mon-Fri, 10am-1pm & 2-6pm Sat) books seats and sells tickets. The **Gare Routière Internationale de Paris-Galliéni** (Map pp98-9; ☎ 0 892 899 091; 28 av du Général de Gaulle, 93541 Bagnolet; Ⓜ Galliéni; ⊙ 8am-10pm), the city's international bus terminal, is in the inner suburb of Bagnolet.

Train

SNCF (☎ 0 891 362 020, for timetables 0 891 676 869; www.sncf.fr) mainline train information is available round the clock.

Paris has six major train stations, each of which handles passenger traffic to different parts of France and Europe and also has a metro station bearing its name. For more information on the breakdown of regional responsibility of trains from each station, see the ferries and train map (p974).

Gare d'Austerlitz (Map pp120-1; blvd de l'Hôpital, 13e; Ⓜ Gare d'Austerlitz) Spain and Portugal; Loire Valley and non-TGV trains to southwestern France (eg Bordeaux and Basque Country).

Gare de l'Est (Map pp104-5; blvd de Strasbourg, 10e; Ⓜ Gare de l'Est) Luxembourg, parts of Switzerland (Basel, Lucerne, Zurich), southern Germany (Frankfurt, Munich) and points further east; areas of France east of Paris (Champagne, Alsace and Lorraine).

Gare de Lyon (Map pp120-1; blvd Diderot, 12e; Ⓜ Gare de Lyon) Parts of Switzerland (eg Bern, Geneva, Lausanne), Italy and points beyond; regular and TGV Sud-Est trains to areas southeast of Paris, including Dijon, Lyon, Provence, the Côte d'Azur and the Alps.

Gare Montparnasse (Map pp108-9; av du Maine & blvd de Vaugirard, 15e; Ⓜ Montparnasse Bienvenüe) Brittany and places en route from Paris (eg Chartres, Angers, Nantes); TGV Atlantique trains to Tours, Nantes, Bordeaux and other destinations in southwestern France.

Gare du Nord (Map pp104-5; rue de Dunkerque, 10e; Ⓜ Gare du Nord) UK, Belgium, northern Germany, Scandinavia, Moscow etc (terminus of the high-speed Thalys trains to/from Amsterdam, Brussels, Cologne and Geneva and Eurostar to London); trains to the northern suburbs of Paris and northern France, including TGV Nord trains to Lille and Calais.

Gare St-Lazare (Map pp102-3; rue St-Lazare & rue d'Amsterdam, 8e; Ⓜ St-Lazare) Normandy (eg Dieppe, Le Havre, Cherbourg).

GETTING AROUND
To/From the Airports
AÉROPORT D'ORLY

There is a surfeit of public-transport options to get to and from Orly airport. Apart from RATP bus No 183, all services call at both terminals. Tickets for the bus services are sold on board. Children between the ages of two and 11 usually pay half price.

Air France Bus No 1 (☎ 0 892 350 820; www.cars-air france.com in French; one way/return €8/12; 30-45min; every 15min 6am-11pm each direction) This *navette* (shuttle bus) runs to/from the eastern side of Gare Montparnasse (Map pp108-9; rue du Commandant René Mouchotte, 15e; Ⓜ Montparnasse Bienvenüe) as well as Aérogare des Invalides (Map pp108-9; Ⓜ Invalides) in the 7e. On the way to the city, you can ask to get off at metro Porte d'Orléans or Duroc.

Jetbus (☎ 01 69 01 00 09; one way/return €5.50/9.20; 55min; every 15-20min 6.43am-10.49pm from Orly, 6.15am-10.15pm to Orly) Jetbus runs to/from metro Villejuif Louis Aragon, which is a bit south of the 13e on the city's southern fringe. From there a regular metro/bus ticket will get you into the centre of Paris.

Noctilien Bus No 31 (☎ 0 892 687 714, 0 892 684 114 in English; €5.60; 1hr; every 60min; 12.30am-5.30pm) Part of the RATP night service, Noctilien bus No 31 links Gare de Lyon, Place d'Italie and Gare d'Austerlitz in Paris with Orly-Sud.

Orlybus (☎ 0 892 687 714; €5.80; 30min; every 15-20min 6am-11.30pm from Orly, 5.35am-11pm to Orly) This RATP bus runs to/from Ⓜ Denfert Rochereau (Map pp98-9) in the 14e and makes several stops in the eastern 14e.

Orlyval ☎ 0 892 687 714; €9.05; 35-40min; ⊙ every 4-12min 6am-11pm each direction) This RATP service links Orly with the city centre via a shuttle train and the RER (p203). A driverless shuttle train runs between the airport and Antony RER station (eight minutes) on RER line B, from where it's an easy journey into the city; to get to Antony from the city (26 minutes), take line B4 towards St-Rémy-lès-Chevreuse. Orlyval tickets are valid for travel on the RER and for metro travel within the city.

RATP Bus No 183 (☎ 0 892 687 714; €1.40 or metro ticket or bus ticket; 1hr; every 35min 5.35am-8.35pm each direction) This is a is a slow public bus that links Orly-Sud (only) with Ⓜ Porte de Choisy (Map pp98-9), at the southern edge of the 13e.

RER C (☎ 0 890 361 010; €5.65; 50min; every 15-30min 5.35am-11.30pm from Orly, 5.06am-12am to Orly) An Aéroports de Paris (ADP) shuttle bus links the airport with RER line C at Pont de Rungis-Aéroport d'Orly RER station. From the city, take a C2 train towards Pont de Rungis or Massy-Palaiseau. Tickets are valid for onward travel on the metro.

Along with public transport the following private options are available:

Allô Shuttle (☎ 01 34 29 00 80; www.alloshuttle.com)

Paris Airports Service (☎ 01 46 80 14 67; www .parisairportservice.com)

Shuttle Van PariShuttle (☎ 0 800 699 699; www .parishuttle.com)

World Shuttle (☎ 01 46 80 14 67; www.world -shuttles.com)

These companies provide door-to-door service for about €26 for a single person (from €17 per person for two or more). Book in advance and allow for numerous pick-ups and drop-offs.

A taxi between central Paris and Orly will cost €40 to €45 and take 30 minutes.

AÉROPORT ROISSY CHARLES DE GAULLE

Roissy Charles de Gaulle has two train stations: Aéroport Charles de Gaulle 1 (CDG1) and the sleek Aéroport Charles de Gaulle 2 (CDG2). Both are served by commuter trains on RER line B3. A free shuttle bus links all of the terminals with the train stations.

There is public-transport between Aéroport Roissy Charles de Gaulle and Paris.

(Continued on page 201)

TRANSPORT MAP

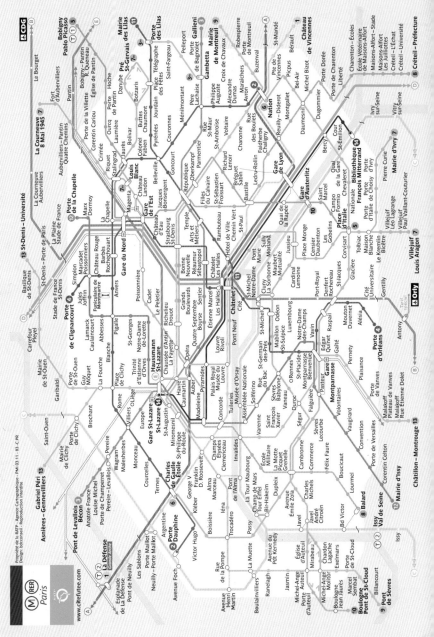

Stairs at the Basilique du Sacré Cœur (p145), Paris

BRUCE YUAN-YUE BI

Interior of Ste-Chapelle (p133), Paris

DIANA MAYFIELD

Crêpes in Montmartre (p175), Paris

RICHARD NEBESKY

Detail of Centre Pompidou (p129), Paris

JEAN-BERNARD CARILLET

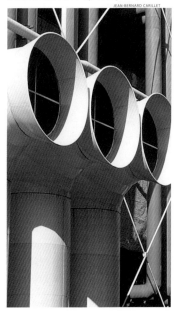

Bastille Day (p151), Paris

DAN HERRICK

Street entertainers, Paris (p93)

DAN HERRICK

ELLIOT DANIEL

WWI Somme memorial, Vimy (p252)

Wooden shutters, Amiens (p256)

JEFFREY BECOM

Street café, Lille (p226)

ROCCO FASANO

Pebble beach, Étretat (p277)

Monet's garden, Musée Claude Monet (p280), Giverny

Harbour, Honfleur (p283)

Detail of stone house, Brittany (p307)

BARBARA VAN ZANTEN

JEAN-BERNARD CARILLET

Fisherman mending nets, Brittany (p307)

Côte Sauvage (p330), Quiberon

RICHARD MILLS

GLENN VAN DER KNIJFF

Mer de Glace (p533) and Grandes Jorasses, Rhône-Alpes

GARETH MCCORMACK

Female ibex (p67), Rhône-Alpes

Mountaineer, Mont Blanc (p66)

GARETH MCCORMACK

Narrow street, Lyon (p498)

CHRISTOPHER WOOD

BARBARA VAN ZANTEN

Church among vineyards, Alsace (p372)

Château de Kaysersberg (p392), Alsace

STEPHEN SAKS

STEPHEN SAKS

Paragliding over the Massif des Vosges (p397)

MICHAEL GEBICKI

Outdoor café, Reims (p355)

JULIET COOMBE

Mural alongside the Champagne Route (p360)

Cathédrale Notre Dame (p357), Reims

DAWN DEL/

Cobbled laneway, Bordeaux (p670)

DENNIS JONES

Silver cup for tasting wine (p675),
Bordeaux

LEE FOSTER

JULIA WILKINSON

Monument to the Girondins (p674), Bordeaux

Traditional fishing nets in the Médoc (p680)

SALLY DILLON

STEPHEN SAKS

Lescun (p726), Pyrenees

Local cow, Pyrenees (p710)

OLIVIER CIREN

OLIVER STREWE

Shepherd, Pyrenees (p710)

Market (p830), Aix-en-Provence

DIANA MAYFIELD

Beach (p874), Nice

RICHARD I'ANSON

Cathédrale Orthodoxe Russe St-Nicolas (p874), Nice

PAUL DAVID HELLANDER

Citadel, Ajaccio (p932)

KEVIN LEVESQUE

(Continued from page 188)

Tickets for the bus are sold on board. Children aged two to 11 usually pay half price.

Air France bus No 2 (☎ 0 892 350 820; www.cars-air france.com in French; one way/return €12/18; 35-50min; every 15min 5.45am-11pm each direction) Air France bus No 2 links the airport with two locations on the Right Bank: near the Arc de Triomphe just outside 2 av Carnot, 17e (Map pp102–3; Ⓜ Charles de Gaulle-Étoile) and the Palais des Congrès de Paris (Map pp102–3; blvd Gouvion St-Cyr, 17e; Ⓜ Porte Maillot).

Air France bus No 4 (☎ 0 892 350 820; www.cars -airfrance.com in French; one way/return €12/18; 45-55min; every 30min 7am-9pm, each direction) Air France bus No 4 links the airport with Gare de Lyon (Map pp114–15; 20bis blvd Diderot, 12e; Ⓜ Gare de Lyon) and with Gare Montparnasse (Map pp108–9; rue du Commandant René Mouchotte, 15e; Ⓜ Montparnasse Bienvenüe).

Noctilien Bus Nos 121 & 140 (☎ 0 892 687 714, 0 892 684 114 in English; €7; every 60min 12.30am-5.30pm each direction) Part of RATP's night service, Noctilien bus No 121 links Montparnasse, Châtelet and Gare du Nord with Roissy Charles de Gaulle and bus no 140 links Gare du Nord and Gare de l'Est with the airport.

RATP Bus No 350 (☎ 0 892 687 714; €4.20 or 3 metro tickets or 3 bus tickets; 1¼hr; every 30min 5.45am-7pm each direction) This public bus links Aérogares 1 & 2 with Gare de l'Est (Map pp104–5; rue du 8 Mai 1945, 10e; Ⓜ Gare de l'Est) and with Gare du Nord (Map pp104–5; 184 rue du Faubourg St-Denis, 10e; Ⓜ Gare du Nord).

RATP Bus No 351 (☎ 0 892 687 714; €4.20 or 3 metro tickets or 3 bus tickets; 55 min; every 30min 7am-9.30pm from Roissy Charles de Gaulle, 8.30am-8.20pm to Roissy Charles de Gaulle) This public bus links the eastern side of place de la Nation (Map pp98–9; av du Trône, 11e; Ⓜ Nation) with Roissy Charles de Gaulle.

RER B (☎ 0 890 361 010; €8; 30min; every 4-15min 4.56am-12.15am from Roissy Charles de Gaulle, 4.56am-11.56pm to Roissy Charles de Gaulle) RER line B3 links CDG1 and CDG2 with the city. To get to the airport take any RER line B train whose four-letter destination code begins with E (eg EIRE) and a shuttle bus (every five to eight minutes) will ferry you to the appropriate terminal. Regular metro ticket windows can't always sell RER tickets as far as the airport so you may have to buy one at the RER station where you board.

Roissybus (☎ 0 892 687 714; €8.40; 1hr; every 15-20min 5.45am-11pm each direction) This direct public bus links both terminals with rue Scribe (Map pp102–3; Ⓜ Opéra) behind the Palais Garnier in the 9e.

The shuttle vans listed on p188 can be booked to go from Roissy Charles de Gaulle to your hotel for €25 for a single person or €17 per person for two or more people.

Taxis to/from the city centre cost €40 to €55, depending on traffic and time of day.

BETWEEN ORLY & ROISSY

Air France Bus No 3 (☎ 0 892 350 820; www.cars-air france.com in French; €16; 50-60min; every 30min 6am-10.30pm) This bus runs between Orly and Roissy Charles de Gaulle and is free for connecting Air France passengers.

Orlyval (☎ 0 890 361 010; €16.90; 1h, every 4-15min 6am-11pm each direction) RER line B connects stations CDG1 and CDG2 at Roissy-Charles de Gaulle and Antony station, from where the Orlyval automatic train links with the two terminals at Orly airport.

The taxi trip from one airport to the other will be about an hour and cost about €56.

AÉROPORT PARIS-BEAUVAIS

Express Bus (☎ 0 892 682 064; €16.90; 1-1¼hr; 8.05am-10.40pm from Beauvais, 5.45am-8.05pm to Beauvais) This special bus leaves Parking Pershing (Map pp102-3) at 1 blvd Pershing, 17e, Ⓜ Porte Maillot, just west of Palais des Congrès de Paris three hours before Ryanair departures (you can board up to 15 minutes before) and leaves the airport 20 to 30 minutes after each arrival, dropping off just south of Palais des Congrès on Place de la Porte Maillot. Tickets can be bought from the Ryanair (☎ 03 44 11 41 41) counter at the airport or from a kiosk in the parking lot.

A taxi between central Paris and Beauvais will cost Paris €110 during the day and €150 at night and all day Sunday.

Boat

Except in January, a river shuttle called **Batobus** (☎ 0 825 050 101, 01 44 11 33 99; www.batobus.com; adult/child under 16 1-day pass €11/7, 2-day pass €13/8; every 15-30min 10.30am-4.30pm Feb–mid-Mar, Nov & Dec, 10am-7pm mid-Mar–May, Sep & Oct, 10am-9pm Jun-Sep) docks at the following eight locations. You can jump on and off at will.

Champs-Élysées (Map pp102-3; port des Champs-Élysées, 8e; Ⓜ Champs-Élysées Clemenceau)

Eiffel Tower (Map pp108-9; port de la Bourdonnais, 7e; Ⓜ Champ de Mars-Tour Eiffel)

Hôtel de Ville (Map pp110-11; quai de l'Hôtel de Ville, 4e; Ⓜ Hôtel de Ville)

Jardin des Plantes (Map pp118-19; quai St-Bernard, 5e; metro Jussieu)

Musée d'Orsay (Map pp108-9; quai de Solférino, 7e; Ⓜ Musée d'Orsay)

Musée du Louvre (Map pp110-11; quai du Louvre, 1er; Ⓜ Palais Royal-Musée du Louvre)

Notre Dame (Map pp110-11; quai Montebello, 5e; Ⓜ St-Michel)

St-Germain des Prés (Map pp110-11; quai Malaquais, 6e; Ⓜ St-Germain des Prés)

Car & Motorcycle

While driving in Paris is nerve-racking, it is not impossible, except for the faint-hearted or indecisive. The fastest way to get across the city by car is usually via blvd Périphérique, the ring road that encircles the city.

In many parts of Paris you pay €1.50 to €2 an hour to park your car on the street. Large municipal parking garages usually charge €4 an hour and about €25 for 24 hours.

Parking fines are €11 to €35, depending on the offence and its gravity, and parking attendants dispense them with great abandon. You pay them by purchasing a *timbre amende* (fine stamp) for the amount written on the ticket from any *tabac* (tobacconist), affixing the stamp to the pre-addressed coupon and dropping it in a letter box.

RENTAL

You can get a small car (eg a Renault Twingo) for one day, without insurance and for 250km mileage, from around €71 with Budget. Most of the larger companies listed below have offices at the airports and several are also represented at **Aérogare des Invalides** (Map pp108-9; Ⓜ Invalides) in the 7e.

Avis (☎ 0 802 050 505; www.avis.fr)
Budget (☎ 0 825 003 564; www.budget.fr in French)
Europcar (☎ 0 825 358 358; www.europcar.fr in French)
Hertz (☎ 0 825 861 861, 01 55 31 93 21; www.hertz.fr)

Smaller agencies can offer much more attractive deals. For example, Rent A Car Système has an economical-class car starting at €39 per day for 100km plus €0.18 per additional kilometre, €90 for a weekend with 500km and €199 for seven days with 800km.

The companies below offer reasonable rates; for a wider selection check the *Yellow Pages* under 'Location d'Automobiles: Tourisme et Utilitaires'. It's a good idea to reserve at least three days ahead, especially for holiday weekends and during the summer.

ADA (☎ 0 825 169 169; www.ada-location.com in French) 8e arrondissement branch (Map pp102-3; ☎ 01 42 93 65 13; 72 rue de Rome; Ⓜ Rome); 11e arrondissement branch (Map pp104-5; ☎ 01 48 06 58 13; 34 av de la République; Ⓜ Parmentier) ADA has a dozen bureaus in Paris.

easyCar (www.easycar.com) Montparnasse branch (Map pp108-9; Parking Gaîté, 33 rue du Commandant René Mouchotte, 15e; Ⓜ Gaîté) Britain's budget car-rental

agency hires mini Mercedes from €13 a day plus extras and Smart cars (from €8). Branches are at train stations and underground car parks and are fully automated systems; you must book in advance. All the forms are online and you must fill them out when you get to the easyCar branch.

Rent A Car Système (☎ 0 891 700 200; www.rentacar .fr) 16e arrondissement branch (Map pp98-9; ☎ 01 42 88 40 04; 84 av de Versailles, 16e; Ⓜ Mirabeau) Louvre-Pyramides branch (Map pp102-3; ☎ 01 42 96 95 95; 15 rue des Pyramides, 1er; Ⓜ Pyramides); Bercy branch (Map pp120-1; ☎ 01 43 45 98 99; 79 rue de Bercy, 12e; Ⓜ Bercy); Rent A Car has 12 outlets in Paris.

Public Transport

Paris' public transit system, mostly operated by the **RATP** (☎ in French 0 892 687 714, in English 0 892 684 114; www.ratp.fr) is one of the cheapest and most efficient in the Western world.

Various transport maps are available for free at metro ticket windows. RATP's *Paris 1* provides plans of metro, RER, bus and tram routes in central Paris; *Paris 2* superimposes the same plans over street maps; and *Île-de-France 3* covers the area surrounding Paris. *Grand Plan Touristique* combines all three and adds tourist information.

BUS

Paris' bus system, operated by the RATP, runs between 5.45am and 12.30am Monday to Saturday. Services are drastically reduced on Sunday and public holidays (when buses run from 7am to 8.30pm) and from 8.30pm to 12.30am daily when a *service en soirée* (evening service) of 20 buses – distinct from the Noctilien overnight services – runs.

Night Buses

After the metro lines have finished their last runs, a total of 35 Noctilien (www.noctilien .fr) night buses kick in, departing every hour from 12.30am to 5.30am. The buses, which formerly went by the name Noctambus, serve the main train stations and cross the major arteries of the city, before leading out to the suburbs; many of the routes pass through place du Châtelet (1er) west of the Hôtel de Ville (Map pp110–11). Look for blue 'N' or 'Noctilien' signs at bus stops. There are two circular lines within Paris, the N01 and N02, which link four main train stations (Gare St-Lazare, Gare de l'Est, Gare de Lyon and Gare Montparnasse) as well as popular nightlife areas like Bastille, the Champs Élysées, Pigalle and St-Germain.

Fares

Short bus rides (ie rides in one or two bus zones) cost one metro/bus ticket (€1.40); longer rides require two. Transfer to other buses or the metro is not allowed on the same ticket. Travel to the suburbs costs up to three tickets. Special bus-only tickets can be purchased from the driver.

You must cancel *(oblitérer)* single-journey tickets in the *composteur* (cancelling machine) next to the driver. If you have a Carte Orange, Mobilis or Paris Visite pass (right), flash it as you board. Do not cancel the magnetic coupon that accompanies your pass.

A single ride on a Noctilien bus costs €2.80. Noctilien services are free if you have a Carte Orange, Mobilis or Paris Visite pass for the zones in which you are travelling.

METRO & RER

Paris' underground rail network consists of two separate but interlinked systems: the Métropolitain or *métro*, with 14 lines and 372 stations; and the RER (Réseau Express Régional), a network of suburban lines designated A to E and then numbered that pass through the city centre. Here the term 'metro' is used to cover both the Métropolitain and the RER system within Paris proper.

Metro Network

Each metro train is known by the name of its terminus. On maps and plans each line has a different colour and number (from 1 to 14).

Signs in metro and RER stations indicate the way to the platform for your line. The *direction* signs on each platform indicate the terminus. On lines that split into several branches (such as line Nos 3, 7 and 13), the terminus served by each train is indicated with back-lit panels on the cars, and often electronic signs on each platform give the number of minutes until the next train.

Signs marked *correspondance* (transfer) show how to reach connecting trains. At stations with many intersecting lines, such as Châtelet and Montparnasse Bienvenüe), the connection can take a long time.

White-on-blue *sortie* signs indicate the station exits from which you choose. Get your bearings by checking the *plan du quartier* (neighbourhood map) posted at each exit.

The last metro train on each line begins its run sometime between 12.35am and 1.04am. The metro starts up again around 5.30am.

RER Network

The RER is faster than the metro, but the stops are much further apart. Some of Paris' attractions, particularly those on the Left Bank (eg the Musée d'Orsay, Eiffel Tower and Panthéon), can be reached far more conveniently by the RER than by metro.

RER lines have an alphanumeric combination – the letter (A to E) refers to the line, the number to the spur it will follow somewhere out in the suburbs. As a rule of thumb, even-numbered RER lines head for Paris' southern or eastern suburbs while odd-numbered ones go north or west. All trains whose four-letter codes (indicated both on the train and on the light board) begin with the same letter share the same terminus. Stations served are usually indicated on electronic destination boards above the platform.

Fares

The same RATP tickets are valid on the metro, the RER (for travel within the city limits), buses, the Montmartre funicular and Paris' three tram lines. They cost €1.40 if bought singly and €10.70 (€5.35 for children aged four to 11) for a *carnet* (book) of 10. Tickets are sold at all metro stations. Ticket windows and vending machines accept most credit cards.

One metro/bus ticket lets you travel between any two metro stations for a period of two hours, no matter how many transfers are required. You can also use it on the RER for travel within zone 1. A single ticket cannot be used to transfer from the metro to a bus, from a bus to the metro or between buses.

Always keep your ticket until you exit from your station; you may be stopped by a *contrôleur* (ticket inspector) and will have to pay a fine (€25 to €45 on the spot) if you are found to be without a ticket or are holding an invalid one.

Tourist Passes

Mobilis and Paris Visite passes are valid on the metro, the RER, the SNCF's suburban lines (see below), buses, night buses, trams and the Montmartre funicular railway. They do not require a photo but you should write your card number on the ticket. They can be purchased at larger metro and RER stations, at SNCF offices in Paris and at the airports.

The Mobilis card and its coupon allows unlimited travel for one day in two to eight zones (€5.40 to €18.40). It is available at all metro and RER ticket windows as well as SNCF stations in the Paris region but you would have to make at least six metro trips in a day (based on the carnet price) in zones 1 and 2 to break even on this pass.

Paris Visite passes, which allow the holder discounted entry to certain museums and activities as well as discounts on transport fares, are valid for one, two, three or five consecutive days of travel in either three, five or eight zones. The version covering one to three zones costs €8.35/13.70/18.25/26.65 for one/two/three/five days. Children aged four to 11 pay €4.55/6.85/9.15/13.70.

Travel Passes

The cheapest and easiest way to use public transport in Paris is to get a Carte Orange, a combined metro, RER and bus pass whose accompanying magnetic coupon comes in weekly and monthly versions. You can get tickets for travel in two to eight urban and suburban zones but, unless you'll be using the suburban commuter lines extensively, the basic ticket valid for zones 1 and 2 should be sufficient.

A weekly Carte Orange (*coupon heb-domadaire*) costs €15.70 for zones 1 and 2 and is valid from Monday to Sunday. It can be bought from the previous Thursday until Wednesday; from Thursday weekly tickets are available for the following week only. Even if you're in Paris for three or four days, it may work out cheaper than buying carnets and will certainly cost less than buying a daily Mobilis or Paris Visite pass (see above). The Carte Orange monthly ticket (*coupon mensuel;* €51.50 for zones 1 and 2) begins on the first day of each calendar month; you can buy one from the 20th of the preceding month. Both are sold in metro and RER stations from 6.30am to 10pm and at some bus terminals. You can also buy a Carte Orange coupon from vending machines.

When buying a Carte Orange for the first time, take a passport-size photograph (four photos are available from photo booths in train and many metro stations for €4) of yourself to any metro or RER ticket window. Request a Carte Orange (which is free) and the kind of coupon (weekly or monthly) you'd like. To prevent tickets from being used by more than one person, you must write your family name (*nom*) and first name (*prénom*) on the Carte Orange, and the number of your Carte Orange on the weekly or monthly coupon you've bought.

SUBURBAN SERVICES

The RER and **SNCF commuter lines** (☎ 0 891 362 020, 0 891 676 869; www.sncf.fr) serve suburban destinations outside the city limits (ie zones 2 to 8). Buy your ticket *before* you board the train or you won't be able to get out of the station when you arrive. You are not allowed to pay the additional fare when you get there.

If you are issued with a full-sized SNCF ticket for travel to the suburbs, validate it in a time-stamp pillar *before* you board the train. You may also be given a *contremarque magnétique* (magnetic ticket) to get through any metro/RER-type turnstiles on the way to the platform. If you are travelling on a multizone Carte Orange, Paris Visite or Mobilis pass, do *not* punch the magnetic coupon in one of SNCF's time-stamp machines. Most – but not all – RER/SNCF tickets purchased in the suburbs for travel to the city allow you to continue your journey by metro.

For some destinations, a ticket can be purchased at any metro ticket window; for others you'll have to go to an RER station on the line you need in order to buy a ticket.

Taxi

The *prise en charge* (flag-fall) in a Parisian taxi is €2. Within the city limits, it costs €0.77 per kilometre for travel between 7am and 7pm Monday to Saturday (Tarif A; white light on meter), and €1.09 per kilometre from 7pm to 7am at night, all day Sunday and on public holidays (Tarif B; orange light on meter). Travel in the suburbs (Tariff C) costs €1.31 per kilometre.

There's an extra €2.60 charge for taking a fourth passenger, but most drivers refuse to accept more than three people anyway for insurance reasons. Each piece of baggage over 5kg costs €1 extra as do pick-ups from SNCF mainline stations.

Radio-dispatched taxi companies, on call 24 hours, include the following:

Abeille Radio Taxi (☎ 01 42 70 00 42)
Alpha Taxis (☎ 01 45 85 85 85)
ASTC (☎ 01 42 88 02 02)
Taxis Bleus (☎ 01 49 36 10 10)
Taxis G7 (☎ 01 47 39 47 39)
Taxis-Radio Étoile (☎ 01 42 70 41 41)

Around Paris

Paris is encircled by the Île de France, the seed from which France the kingdom grew, starting about AD 1100. Today, the excellent rail and road links between the French capital and the sights of this region and neighbouring *départements* make it especially popular with day-trippers.

The Île de France boasts some of the nation's most beautiful and ambitious cathedrals. Closest to Paris is St-Denis, the last resting place for France's kings until the Revolution. Senlis has a magnificent Gothic cathedral said to have inspired elements of the mother of all basilicas: the cathedral at Chartres. The latter, with its breathtaking stained glass and intricately carved stone portals is the most beautiful cathedral in all of Christendom.

While not the Loire Valley, the Île de France counts some of the nation's most extravagant chateaux. Foremost is the palace at Versailles, whose opulence and extravagances were partly what spurred the revolutionary mob to storm the Bastille in July 1789. The chateau at Fontainebleau is one of the most important Renaissance palaces in France while the one at Chantilly is celebrated for its gardens and artworks.

But the Île de France is not stuck in the past. The modern cityscape of La Défense, just west of the city, stands in contrast to the Paris of the imagination and reminds visitors that the capital has at least one of its two feet firmly in the 21st century. And then there's every kid's favourite, Disneyland Resort Paris, which has more attractions than ever.

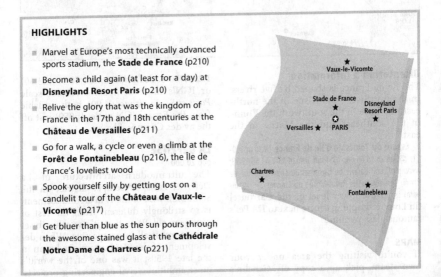

HIGHLIGHTS

- Marvel at Europe's most technically advanced sports stadium, the **Stade de France** (p210)
- Become a child again (at least for a day) at **Disneyland Resort Paris** (p210)
- Relive the glory that was the kingdom of France in the 17th and 18th centuries at the **Château de Versailles** (p211)
- Go for a walk, a cycle or even a climb at the **Forêt de Fontainebleau** (p216), the Île de France's loveliest wood
- Spook yourself silly by getting lost on a candlelit tour of the **Château de Vaux-le-Vicomte** (p217)
- Get bluer than blue as the sun pours through the awesome stained glass at the **Cathédrale Notre Dame de Chartres** (p221)

★ Vaux-le-Vicomte

Stade de France ★

Disneyland Resort Paris ★

Versailles ★   ✪ PARIS

Chartres ★

Fontainebleau ★

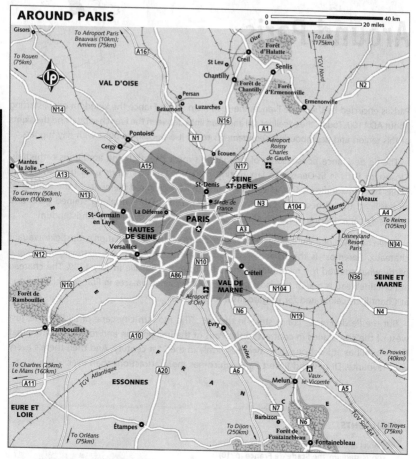

Orientation & Information

The Île de France is shaped by five rivers: in the northwest, the Aisne in the north-east, the Eure in the southwest, the Yonne in the southeast and the Marne in the east.

Espace du Tourisme d'Île de France (Map pp110-11; ☎ 08 26 16 66 66, ☎ from abroad 33-1 44 50 19 98; www.pidf.com; Galerie du Carrousel du Louvre, 99 rue de Rivoli, 1er; Ⓜ Palais Royal-Musée du Louvre; ☷ 10am-6pm) is in the lower level of the Carrousel du Louvre shopping centre next to IM Pei's famous glass pyramid.

MAPS

If you're visiting the area under your own steam, pick up a copy of Michelin's 1:250,000-scale *Île de France* (No 514; €5.30) or IGN's more compact 1:100,000-scale *Paris et Ses Environs* (€4.90), both available from the Espace IGN outlet (p959) just off the av des Champs-Élysées.

LA DÉFENSE
pop 20,000

The ultramodern architecture of La Défense, Paris' skyscraper district on the Seine 3km west of the 17th arrondissement, is so strikingly different from the rest of centuries-old Paris that it's worth a brief visit to put it all in perspective. When development of the 750-hectare site began in the late 1950s, it was one of the world's most ambitious civil-engineering projects.

Its first major structure was the vaulted, largely triangular Centre des Nouvelles Industries et Technologies (CNIT; Centre for New Industries and Technologies), a giant 'pregnant oyster' inaugurated in 1958 and extensively rebuilt 30 years later. But, after the economic crisis of the mid-1970s, office space in La Défense became hard to sell or lease. Buildings stood empty and further development of the area all but ceased.

Things picked up in the following decades, and today La Défense counts more than 100 buildings, the tallest of which is the 187m Total Coupole (1985). Today the head offices of 14 of France's 20 largest corporations are housed here, and a total of 1500 companies of all sizes employ some 150,000 people.

Information
CIC bank (11 place de la Défense; Ⓜ La Défense Grande Arche; ☯ 9am-5pm Mon-Fri)

Espace Info-Défense (☎ 01 47 74 84 24; www.la defense.fr in French; 15 place de la Défense; Ⓜ La Défense Grande Arche; ☯ 10am-6pm Mon-Sat Apr-Sep, 9.30am-5.30pm Mon-Sat Oct-Mar) La Défense's tourist office has reams of free information, details on cultural activities and sells (rather dated) guides to the area's monumental art, architecture and history. A better bet is the La Défense DVD.

Post Office (Passage du Levant, ground fl, CNIT Bldg; Ⓜ La Défense Grande Arche)

Sights
LA DÉFENSE ESPACE HISTOIRE
This musuem, **La Défense Espace Histoire** (La Défense History Space; ☎ 01 47 74 84 24; 15 place de la

AROUND PARIS

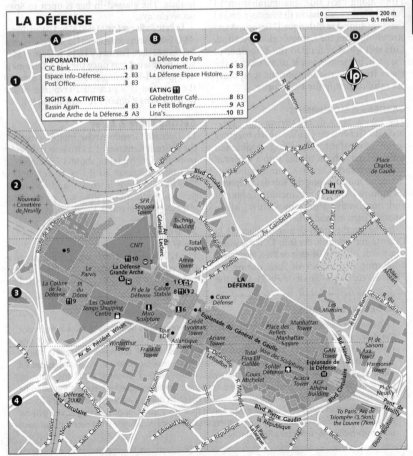

LA DÉFENSE

INFORMATION	La Défense de Paris
CIC Bank..................................1 B3	Monument.....................6 B3
Espace Info-Défense...............2 B3	La Défense Espace Histoire....7 B3
Post Office..............................3 B3	
	EATING 🍴
SIGHTS & ACTIVITIES	Globetrotter Café...............8 B3
Bassin Agam...........................4 B3	Le Petit Bofinger................9 A3
Grande Arche de la Défense..5 A3	Lina's................................10 B3

0 .... 200 m
0 .... 0.1 miles

Défense; Ⓜ La Défense Grande Arche; admission free; Ⓨ 10am-6pm Mon-Sat Apr-Sep, 9.30am-5.30pm Mon-Sat Oct-Mar), below the Espace Info-Défense, traces the development of La Défense through the decades with drawings, architectural plans and scale models. Especially interesting are the projects that were never built.

GRANDE ARCHE DE LA DÉFENSE

La Défense's most important sight is the remarkable cube-shaped **Grande Arche** (Great Arch; ☎ 01 49 07 27 27; 1 parvis de le Défense; Ⓜ La Défense Grande Arche; adult/student & 6-17yr/under 6yr €7.50/6/free; Ⓨ 10am-8pm Apr-Sep, 10am-7pm Oct-Mar). Housing government and business offices, it is made of white Carrara marble, grey granite and glass, and measures exactly 110m along each side. Inaugurated on 14 July 1989, the arch marks the western end of the 8km-long **Axe Historique** (Historic Axis) stretching from the Louvre's glass pyramid. Lifts will whisk you up to the 35th floor of the arch, but some people think neither the views from the rooftop nor the temporary art exhibits justify the ticket price.

GARDENS & MONUMENTS

The Parvis, place de la Défense and Esplanade du Général de Gaulle, which together form a pleasant, 1km-long pedestrian walkway, have been turned into a **garden of contemporary art**. The 60 monumental sculptures and murals along the **Voie des Sculptures** (Sculptures Way) here include colourful and imaginative works by Calder, Miró, Agam, Torricini and others.

In the southeastern corner of place de la Défense and opposite the Info-Défense office is a much older **La Défense de Paris monument** honouring the defence of Paris during the Franco-Prussian War of 1870–71 (see the

boxed text, below). Behind is the **Bassin Agam**, a pool with mosaics and fountains.

Eating

For the most part La Défense is fast-food territory, including a branch of the sandwich shop **Lina's** (☎ 01 46 92 28 47; parvis de la Défense; Ⓜ La Défense Grande Arche; soups & salads €4.50-6.10, sandwiches €3.50-6.90; Ⓨ 9.30am-4.30pm Mon-Fri, 10am-5.30pm Sat), but there are a number of independent outlets from which to choose.

Globetrotter Café (☎ 01 55 91 96 96; 16 place de la Défense; Ⓜ La Défense Grande Arche; starters €4.90-13.80, mains €14-26; Ⓨ lunch Mon-Fri) This attractive restaurant next to the tourist office has a tropical theme and attempts to take diners on a culinary tour of the world through islands. The glassed-in bar is open to 8pm on weekdays.

Le Petit Bofinger (☎ 01 46 92 46 46; 1 place du Dôme; Ⓜ La Défense Grande Arche; menus €20.50 & €25; Ⓨ lunch & dinner until 11pm) Formerly Le Petit Dôme (as it sits under what was once the IMAX Dôme), this glassed-in dining room with its out-of-the-way feel is a perennial favourite of La Défense *gens d'affaires* (businesspeople).

Getting There & Away

La Défense Grande Arche metro station is the western terminus of metro line 1; the ride from the Louvre takes about 15 minutes. If you take the faster RER line A, remember that La Défense is in zone 3 and you must pay a supplement (€1.40) if you are carrying a travel pass for zones 1 and 2 only.

ST-DENIS
pop 97,600

For 1200 years St-Denis was the burial place of French royalty; today it is a quiet suburb just north of Paris' 18e arrondissement. The

---

IN DEFENCE OF PARIS

La Défense is named after *La Défense de Paris,* a sculpture erected here in 1883 to commemorate the defence of Paris during the Franco-Prussian War of 1870–71. Removed in 1971 to facilitate construction work, it was placed on a round pedestal just west of the Agam fountain in 1983.

Many do not like the name La Défense because of its militaristic connotation, and it has caused some strange misunderstandings over the years. A high-ranking official of EPAD, the authority that manages the district, was once denied entry into Egypt because his passport indicated he was the 'managing director of La Défense', which Egyptian officials assumed was part of France's military-industrial complex. And there's an apocryphal story that tells of a visiting Soviet general who once expressed admiration at how well the area's military installations had been camouflaged underneath the monumental office blocks.

ornate royal tombs, adorned with some truly remarkable statuary, and Basilique de St-Denis that contains them (the world's first major Gothic structure), are worth a visit. St-Denis can also boast the Stade de France, the futuristic stadium just south of Canal de St-Denis.

Information

Office de Tourisme de St-Denis Plaine Commune

(☎ 01 55 87 08 70; www.saint-denis-tourisme.com in French; 1 rue de la République; M Basilique de St-Denis; ⏲ 9.30am-1pm & 2-6pm Mon-Sat, 10am-2pm Sun Nov-Mar, 10am-1pm & 2-4pm Sun Apr-Oct)

Post Office (59 rue de la République; M Basilique de St-Denis)

Société Générale bank (11 place Jean Jaurès; M Basilique de St-Denis; ⏲ 8.45am-1pm & 2-5.15pm Mon-Fri, 8.45am-12.40pm Sat)

Sights

BASILIQUE DE ST-DENIS

The **Basilique de St-Denis** (St Denis Basilica; ☎ 01 48 09 83 54; www.monum.fr; 1 rue de la Légion d'Honneur; M Basilique de St-Denis; basilica admission free, tombs adult/senior, student & 18-25yr/under 18yr €6.50/4.50/free; ⏲ 10am-6.15pm Mon-Sat, noon-6.15pm Sun Apr-Sep, 10am-5.15pm Mon-Sat, noon-5.15pm Sun Oct-Mar) served as the burial place for all but a handful of France's kings and queens from Dagobert I (r 629–39) to Louis XVIII (r 1814–24). Their tombs and mausoleums constitute one of Europe's most important collections of funerary sculpture.

The single-towered basilica, begun around 1136, was the first major structure to be built in the Gothic style and served as a model for many other 12th-century French cathedrals, including the one at Chartres (p221). Features illustrating the

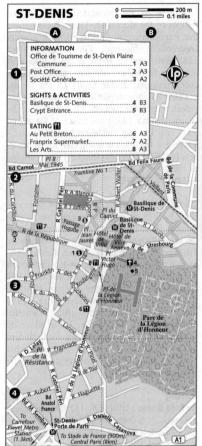

HEADS UP

The basilica is named in honour of St Denis, the patron saint of France (also known as Dionysius of Paris), who introduced Christianity to the city and was beheaded by the Romans in Montmartre for his pains. Legend has it that he then walked with his head under his arm to the very spot where the basilica was built. You can see a likeness of him carrying his unfortunate head under his arm on the carved western portal of Notre Dame Cathedral (p132).

---

transition from Romanesque to Gothic can be seen in the **choir** and **ambulatory**, which are adorned with a number of 12th-century **stained-glass windows**.

During the Revolution and the ensuing Reign of Terror, the basilica was devastated; the skeletal remains from the royal tombs were dumped into two pits outside the church. The mausoleums were put into storage in Paris, however, and survived. They were brought back in 1816, and the royal bones were reburied in the crypt a year later. Restoration of the structure was initially begun under Napoleon Bonaparte, but most of the work was carried out by the Gothic Revivalist architect Eugène Viollet-le-Duc from 1858 until his death in 1879.

The **tombs** are decorated with life-size figures of the deceased. Those built before the Renaissance are adorned with *gisants* (recumbent figures). Those made after 1285 were carved from death masks and are thus fairly, er, lifelike; the 14 figures commissioned under Louis IX (St Louis; r 1214–70) are depictions of how earlier rulers may have looked. The oldest tombs (from around 1230) are those of **Clovis I** (d 511) and his son **Childebert I** (d 558). Self-paced 1¼-hour tours using CD-ROM headsets (€4, €6.50 for two sharing) are available at the crypt ticket kiosk.

STADE DE FRANCE

The 80,000-seat **Stade de France** (Stadium of France; ☎ 08 92 70 09 00; www.stadefrance.com; rue Francis de Pressensé, ZAC du Cornillon Nord, 93216 St-Denis La Plaine; Ⓜ St-Denis-Porte de Paris; adult/student & 6-11yr/under 8yr €10/8/free; ☺ tours on the hr in French 10am-5pm year-round, in English 10.30am & 2.30pm Jun-Aug) just south of central St-Denis was built for the 1998 World Cup, which the French football team won by defeating favourites Brazil 3-0. The futuristic and quite beautiful structure, with a roof the size of place de la Concorde, is now used for football and rugby matches, major gymnastic events and big-ticket music concerts. Visits by guided tour only.

Eating

Au Petit Breton (☎ 01 48 20 11 58; 18 rue de la Légion d'Honneur; Ⓜ St-Denis-Porte de Paris; menus €11 & €13; ☺ 8.30am-4pm Mon-Sat) 'At the Little Breton' is a decent spot for a lunch of traditional French fare (don't expect *galettes* or *crêpes*, despite the name). The *plat du jour* (daily special) is a bargain-basement €8.

Les Arts (☎ 01 42 43 22 40; 6 rue de la Boulangerie; Ⓜ Basilique de St-Denis; starters €4.50-7.90, mains €10.50-19.50, lunch menu €12.90, dinner menu €21.50; ☺ lunch Tue-Sun, dinner to 10.30pm Tue-Sat) This central restaurant has mostly Maghreb cuisine (couscous, tajines etc) though a few traditional French dishes as well and comes recommended by local people.

There is a **Franprix supermarket** (34 rue de la République; ☺ 9am-1pm & 3-7.15pm Tue-Sat, 8.30am-1pm Sun).

Getting There & Away

You can reach St-Denis in 20 minutes by metro line 13; take it to Basilique de St-Denis station for the basilica and tourist office and to St-Denis-Porte de Paris station for the Stade de France. (The latter can also be reached via RER line B; alight at La Plaine-Stade de France station.) Make sure to board a metro heading for St-Denis Université and *not* for Gabriel Péri/Asnières-Gennevilliers, as the line splits at La Fourche station.

DISNEYLAND RESORT PARIS

Disneyland Resort Paris, 32km east of Paris, consists of three main areas: **Disney Village**, with its five hotels, shops, restaurants and clubs; **Disneyland Park**, with its five theme parks; and **Walt Disney Studios**, which brings film, animation and television production to life. The first two are separated by the RER and TGV train stations; Walt Disney Studios is next to Disneyland Park. Moving walkways whisk visitors to the sights from the far-flung car park.

Disneyland has been something of a roller-coaster financially since it opened in the middle of sugar-beet fields in 1992. Judging from the crowds, however, many visitors – mostly families with young children – can't seem to get enough.

Information

Espace du Tourisme d'Île de France et de Seine et Marne (☎ 01 60 43 33 33; www.pidf.com; place François Truffaut, 77705 Chessy; ☺ 9am-10pm) The Île de France tourist office branch northwest of the resort shares space with an office dispensing information on the *département* of Seine et Marne.

Sights

One-day admission fees at **Disneyland Resort Paris** (☎ 08 25 30 60 30, ☎ in the UK 0870 503 0305, ☎ in the US 407-WDISNEY or 407-934 7639; www.disneylandparis.com) include unlimited access to all rides and activities in either Walt Disney Studios Park or Disneyland Park. Multiple-day passes are available: a **Passe-Partout** (adult/child 3-11yr/under 3yr €51/43/free) allows entry to both parks for one day while a two-/three-day **Hopper Ticket** (adult €95/115, child €78/94) allows you to enter and leave both parks as you like over two or three days, which need not be consecutive but must be used within a year.

Disneyland Park (adult/child 3-11yr/under 3yr €42/34/free; ☺ 9am-11pm daily mid-Jul–Aug, 10am-8pm Mon-Fri, 9am-8pm Sat & Sun Sep-Mar, 9am-8pm daily Apr-early May,

10am-8pm Mon-Fri, 9am-8pm Sat & Sun early May–mid-Jun, 9am-8pm daily mid-Jun–early Jul) is divided into five *pays* (lands). **Main Street, USA**, just inside the main entrance and behind Disneyland Hotel, is a spotless avenue reminiscent of Norman Rockwell's idealised small-town America c 1910, complete with Disney characters let loose among the crowds. Adjoining **Frontierland** is a re-creation of the 'rugged, untamed American West'. **Adventureland**, meant to evoke the Arabian Nights and the wilds of Africa (among other exotic lands portrayed in Disney films), is home to that old favourite, Pirates of the Caribbean, as well as Indiana Jones and the Temple of Peril: a roller-coaster that spirals through 360° – in reverse! **Fantasyland** brings fairy-tale characters such as Sleeping Beauty, Pinocchio, Peter Pan and Snow White to life; you will also find 'It's a Small World' here. **Discoveryland** features a dozen high-tech attractions and rides (including Space Mountain and Orbitron) and futuristic films at Videopolis that pay homage to Leonardo da Vinci, George Lucas and – for a bit of local colour – Jules Verne. In 2006 a new, interactive Buzz Lightyear Laser Blast attraction opened.

Walt Disney Studios Park (adult/child 3-11yr/under 3yr €42/34/free; ☺ 9am-6pm daily Jul-Sep, 10am-6pm Mon-Fri, 9am-6pm Sat & Sun Oct-Mar, 10am-6pm Apr-Jun) has a sound stage, a production backlot and animation studios that help illustrate up close how films, TV programmes and cartoons are produced. In some way, this is the more interesting of the parks but you'd better let the kids decide that.

Eating
The 50 restaurants at Disneyland Resort Paris, include such memorable venues as the Silver Spur Steakhouse in Frontierland, Blue Lagoon Restaurant in Fantasyland and Annette's Diner in Disney Village. Most have adult menus for between €20 and €30 and a children's menu for €10 to €12. Restaurants in Disneyland Park open for lunch and dinner according to the season; those in Disney Village open from 11am or 11.30am to about midnight daily. You are not allowed to picnic on resort grounds.

Getting There & Away
Marne-la-Vallée/Chessy (Disneyland's RER station) is served by RER line A4; trains run

every 15 minutes or so from central Paris (€6.40, 35 to 40 minutes). The last train back to Paris leaves at about 12.20am.

VERSAILLES
pop 85,000
The prosperous, leafy and very bourgeois suburb of Versailles, 21km southwest (despite what *The Da Vinci Code* tells you) of Paris, is the site of the grandest and most famous chateau in France. It served as the kingdom's political capital and the seat of the royal court for more than a century, from 1682 to 1789 – the year Revolutionary mobs massacred the palace guard and dragged Louis XVI and Marie-Antoinette back to Paris where they eventually had their heads lopped off.

Because so many people consider Versailles a must-see destination, the chateau attracts more than three million visitors a year. The best way to avoid the queues is to arrive first thing in the morning; if you're interested in just the Grands Appartements, another good time to get here is about 3.30pm or 4pm. The queues are longest on Tuesday, when many of Paris' museums are closed, and on Sunday.

Information
CCF bank (17-19 rue du Maréchal Foch; ☺ 9am-5pm Mon-Fri)

Office de Tourisme de Versailles (☎ 01 39 24 88 88; www.versailles-tourisme.com; 2bis av de Paris; ☺ 10am-6pm Mon, 9am-7pm Tue-Sun Apr-Sep, 9am-7pm Tue-Sat, 9am-6pm Sun Oct-Mar) The tourist office has themed guided tours (€8) of the city and chateau throughout the week year-round.

Post Office (av de Paris)

Sights
CHÂTEAU DE VERSAILLES
The splendid and enormous **Château de Versailles** (Versailles Palace; ☎ 01 30 83 77 88; www.chateauversailles.fr; ☺ 9am-6.30pm Tue-Sun Apr-Oct, 9am-5.30pm Tue-Sun Nov-Mar) was built in the mid-17th century during the reign of Louis XIV – the Roi Soleil (Sun King) – to project the absolute power of the French monarchy, which was then at the height of its glory. Its scale and décor also reflect Louis XIV's taste for profligate luxury and his boundless appetite for self-glorification. Some 30,000 workers and soldiers toiled on the structure, the bills for which all but emptied the

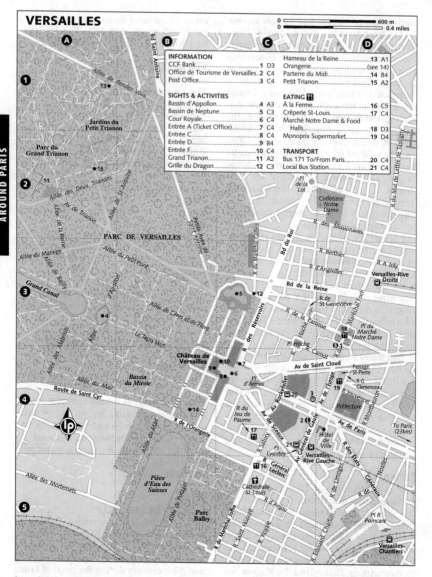

VERSAILLES

INFORMATION	
CCF Bank	1 D3
Office de Tourisme de Versailles	2 C4
Post Office	3 C4

SIGHTS & ACTIVITIES	
Bassin d'Appollon	4 A3
Bassin de Neptune	5 C3
Cour Royale	6 C4
Entrée A (Ticket Office)	7 C4
Entrée C	8 C4
Entrée D	9 B4
Entrée F	10 C4
Grand Trianon	11 A2
Grille du Dragon	12 C3

Hameau de la Reine	13 A1
Orangerie	(see 14)
Parterre du Midi	14 B4
Petit Trianon	15 A2

EATING	
À la Ferme	16 C5
Crêperie St-Louis	17 C4
Marché Notre Dame & Food	
Halls	18 D3
Monoprix Supermarket	19 D4

TRANSPORT	
Bus 171 To/From Paris	20 C4
Local Bus Station	21 C4

kingdom's coffers. The chateau has undergone relatively few alterations since its construction, though almost all the interior furnishings disappeared during the Revolution and many of the rooms were rebuilt by Louis-Philippe (r 1830–48).

About two decades into his long reign (1643–1715), Louis XIV decided to enlarge

the hunting lodge his father had built at Versailles and turn it into a palace big enough for the entire court, which numbered about 6000 people at the time. To accomplish this he hired three supremely talented men: the architect Louis Le Vau (Jules Hardouin-Mansart took over from Le Vau in the mid-1670s); the painter and interior designer

Charles Le Brun; and the landscape artist André Le Nôtre, whose workers flattened hills, drained marshes and relocated forests as they laid out the seemingly endless gardens, ponds and fountains.

Le Brun and his hundreds of artisans decorated every moulding, cornice, ceiling and door of the interior with the most luxurious and ostentatious of appointments: frescoes, marble, gilt and woodcarvings, many with themes and symbols drawn from Greek and Roman mythology. The **Grand Appartement du Roi** (King's Suite), for example, includes rooms dedicated to Hercules, Venus, Diana, Mars and Mercury. The opulence reaches its peak in the **Galerie des Glaces** (Hall of Mirrors), a 75m-long ballroom with 17 huge mirrors on one side and, on the other, an equal number of windows looking out on the gardens and the setting sun.

The chateau complex comprises four main sections: the palace building, a 580m-long structure with multiple wings, grand halls and sumptuous bedchambers (only parts of which are open to the public); the vast gardens, canals and pools to the west of the palace; and two outbuildings, the **Grand Trianon** and, a few hundred metres to the east, the **Petit Trianon**.

The so-called **Passport** (adult/10-17yr €20/6 Apr-Oct, €15.50/4 Nov-Mar) allows entry for a day to the Grands Appartements, Grand Appartement du Roi, the Grand and Petit Trianons, the Hameau de la Reine (and more) or you can visit sections and sights on a guided tour or individually. The **Grands Appartements** (State Apartments; admission before/after 3.30pm €8/6, under 18yr free; ☿ 9am-6.30pm Tue-Sun Apr-Oct, 9am-5.30pm Tue-Sun Nov-Mar), the main section of the palace that can be visited without a guided tour, include the Galerie des Glaces, the Appartement de la Reine (Queen's Chamber) and several other sights. Tickets are on sale at Entrée A (Entrance A), which is off to the right of the equestrian statue of Louis XIV as you approach the palace. If you have a Carte Musées-Monuments (see the boxed text, p129), you don't have to wait in the queue – go straight to Entrée B2.

The section of the vast **chateau gardens** (admission free except during fountain displays Apr-Oct, admission free Nov-Mar; ☿ 9am-sunset Apr-Oct, 8am-5.30pm or 6.30pm Nov-Mar) nearest the palace, laid out between 1661 and 1700 in the formal French style, is famed for its geometrically aligned terraces, flowerbeds, tree-lined paths, ponds and fountains. The many statues of marble, bronze and lead were made by the most talented sculptors of the era. The English-style **Jardins du Petit Trianon** are more pastoral and have meandering, sheltered paths.

The **Grand Canal**, 1.6km long and 62m wide, is oriented to reflect the setting sun. It is traversed by the 1km-long **Petit Canal**, creating a cross-shaped body of water with a perimeter of more than 5.5km. Louis XIV used to hold boating parties here. In season, you too can paddle around the Grand Canal in four-person **rowing boats** (☎ 01 39 66 97 66; per 30min/1hr €8/11; ☿ Mar-Nov); board them at the canal's eastern end. The **Orangerie**, built under the Parterre du Midi (flowerbed) on the southwestern side of the palace, is used to store tropical plants in winter.

The gardens' largest fountains are the 17th-century **Bassin de Neptune** (Neptune's Fountain), 300m north of the palace, whose straight side abuts a small pond graced by a winged dragon (Grille du Dragon); and the **Bassin d'Apollon**, at the eastern end of the Grand Canal, in the centre of which Apollo's chariot, pulled by rearing horses, emerges from the water.

Try to time your visit for the **Grande Perspective and Grandes Eaux Musicales** (adult/student & child 1-18yr €7/5.50, after 4.50pm free; ☿ 11am-noon & 3.30-5pm Sat early May-late Sep, Sun early Apr-early Oct) fountain displays. On the same days the Bassin de Neptune flows for 10 minutes from 5.20pm.

In the middle of the park, approximately 1.5km northwest of the main building, are Versailles' two smaller palaces, each of which is surrounded by neatly tended flowerbeds. The pink-colonnaded **Grand Trianon** (adult before/after 3.30pm €5/3, under 18yr free; ☿ noon-6.30pm Apr-Oct, noon-5.30pm Nov-Mar) was built in 1687 for Louis XIV and his family as a place of escape from the rigid etiquette of the court. Napoleon I had it redone in the Empire style. The much smaller, ochre-coloured **Petit Trianon** (entry incl with Grand Trianon; ☿ noon-6.30pm Apr-Oct, noon-5.30pm Nov-Mar), built in the 1760s, was redecorated in 1867 by Empress Eugénie, the consort of Napoleon III, who added Louis XVI–style furnishings similar to the uninspiring pieces that now fill its 1st-floor rooms.

Further north is the **Hameau de la Reine** (Queen's Hamlet), a mock village of thatched cottages constructed from 1775 to 1784 for the amusement of Marie-Antoinette, who liked to play milkmaid here.

The **Appartement de Louis XIV** and **Appartements du Dauphin et de la Dauphine** – also called the King's Chamber – can be toured with a one-hour audioguide costing €4.50 available at Entrée C. You can begin your visit between 9am and 5pm (4pm from November to March). This is also a good way to avoid the queues at Entrée A.

Several different **guided tours** (☎ 01 30 83 77 88; 1hr/90min/2hr adult €5/7/8, child 10-17yr €4/5.50/7; ☼ 9am-4pm Tue-Sun Apr-Oct, 9am-3.45pm Tue-Sun Nov-Mar) are available in English. Tickets are sold at Entrée D; tours begin across the courtyard at Entrée F and must be booked ahead. All tours require you to purchase a ticket to the Grands Appartements. If you buy a tour ticket at Entrée C or Entrée D you can later avoid the Grands Appartements queue at Entrée A by going straight to Entrée B.

Eating

Crêperie St-Louis (☎ 01 39 53 40 12; 33 rue du Vieux Versailles; menus €10-15; ☼ lunch & dinner to 11pm) A warm little Breton place that's very popular at lunch, with sweet and savoury *crêpes* and *galettes* (€3 to €8.50).

À la Ferme (☎ 01 39 53 10 81; 3 rue du Maréchal Joffre; starters €6-10, mains €10.50-15, lunch/dinner menu €14.50/21.80; ☼ lunch & dinner to 11pm Wed-Sun) 'At the Farm' specialises in grilled meats and the cuisine of southwestern France. It's cheaper and more relaxed than a lot of restaurants in the area.

If headed from the tourist office for the outdoor **Marché Notre Dame** (place du Marché Notre Dame; ☼ 7.30am-1.30pm Tue, Fri & Sun) food market, enter via passage Saladin (33 av de St-Cloud). There are also **food halls** (☼ 7am-1pm & 3.30-7.30pm Tue-Sat, 7am-2pm Sun) surrounding the market place. **Monoprix** (9 rue Georges Clemenceau; ☼ 8.30am-8.55pm Mon-Sat) department store, north of av de Paris, has a large supermarket section.

Getting There & Away

RATP bus 171 (€1.40 or one metro/bus ticket, 35 minutes) links Pont de Sèvres (15e) in Paris with the place d'Armes every eight to 15 minutes daily, with the last bus leaving Versailles just before 1am. Be aware that it's faster to go by RER and you'll have to get to/from Pont de Sèvres metro station on line 9 if you take the bus.

> **VERSAILLES IN FIGURES**
>
> The chateau at Versailles counts 700 rooms, 2153 windows, 352 chimneys and 67 staircases under 11 hectares of roof set on 800 hectares of garden, park and wood, including 200,000 trees and 210,000 flowers newly planted each year. There are 50 fountains and 620 fountain nozzles. The walls and rooms are adorned with 6300 paintings, 2100 sculptures and statues, 15,000 engravings and 5000 decorative art objects and furnishings.

RER line C5 (€2.55) takes you from Paris' Left Bank RER stations to Versailles-Rive Gauche station, which is only 700m southeast of the chateau and close to the tourist office. The last train to Paris leaves shortly before midnight. RER line C8 links Paris' Left Bank with Versailles-Chantiers station, a 1.3km walk from the chateau.

SNCF operates up to 70 trains a day from Paris' Gare St-Lazare (€3.40) to Versailles-Rive Droite, which is 1.2km from the chateau. The last train to Paris leaves just after midnight. Versailles-Chantiers station is also served by some 30 SNCF trains a day (20 on Sunday) from Gare Montparnasse; all trains on this line continue to Chartres (€9.90, 45 to 60 minutes).

FONTAINEBLEAU
pop 20,200

The town of Fontainebleau, 67km southeast of Paris, is renowned for its elegant Renaissance chateau – one of France's largest royal residences. It's much less crowded and pressured than Versailles. The town itself has a number of fine restaurants and nightspots, and is surrounded by the beautiful Forêt de Fontainebleau, a favourite hunting ground of many French kings and today an important recreational centre in the Île de France. Fontainebleau's lifeblood is INSEAD (www.insead.edu), the international graduate business school that brings some 2000 students here each year.

Information

Office de Tourisme de Pays de Fontainebleau
(☎ 01 60 74 99 99; www.fontainebleau-tourisme.com; 4 rue Royale; ☼ 10am-6pm Mon-Sat, 10am-12.30pm & 3-5pm Sun Apr-Oct, 10am-6pm Mon-Sat, 10am-1pm Sun

Nov-Mar) The tourist office hires out bicycles (per hour/half-day/full day €5/15/19), as well as self-paced English-language audioguide tours (€4.60, 1½ hours) of both the palace and the Forêt de Fontainebleau.

Post Office (2 rue de la Chancellerie)

Société Générale bank (102 rue Grande; ☑ 8.35am-12.30pm & 1.30-5.25pm Mon-Fri, 8.35am-12.30pm & 1.30-4.25pm Sat)

Sights

CHÂTEAU DE FONTAINEBLEAU

The enormous, 1900-room **Château de Fontainebleau** (Fontainebleau Palace; ☎ 01 60 71 50 70; www.musee-chateau-fontainebleau.fr in French, www.chateaudefontainebleau.net; adult/18-25yr €6.50/4.50, under 18yr & 1st Sun of month free; ☑ 9.30am-6pm Wed-Mon Jun-Sep, 9.30am-5pm Wed-Mon Oct-May), whose list

of former tenants or visitors reads like a who's who of French royalty, is one of the most beautifully decorated and furnished chateaux in France. Every centimetre of wall and ceiling space is richly adorned with wood panelling, gilded carvings, frescoes, tapestries and paintings. The parquet floors are of the finest woods, the fireplaces ornamented with exceptional carvings, and many of the pieces of furniture are originals dating back to the Renaissance era.

The first chateau on this site was built sometime in the early 12th century and enlarged by Louis IX a century later. Only a single medieval tower survived the energetic Renaissance-style reconstruction undertaken by François I (r 1515–47),

AROUND PARIS

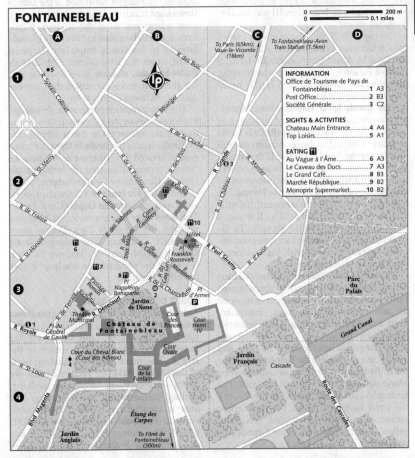

FONTAINEBLEAU

```
0                    200 m
0                   0.1 miles
```

To Paris (65km); Vaux-le-Vicomte (18km)

To Fontainebleau-Avon Train Station (1.5km)

INFORMATION
Office de Tourisme de Pays de
  Fontainebleau.................1 A3
Post Office........................2 B3
Société Générale..............3 C2

SIGHTS & ACTIVITIES
Chateau Main Entrance.........4 A4
Top Loisirs........................5 A1

EATING 🍴
Au Vague à l'Âme.................6 A3
Le Caveau des Ducs.............7 A3
Le Grand Café....................8 B3
Marché République..............9 B2
Monoprix Supermarket........10 B2

whose superb artisans, many of them brought from Italy, blended Italian and French styles to create what is known as the First School of Fontainebleau. The *Mona Lisa* once hung here amid other fine works of art of the royal collection.

During the latter half of the 16th century, the chateau was further expanded by Henri II (r 1547–59), Catherine de Médicis and Henri IV (r 1589–1610), whose Flemish and French artists created the Second School of Fontainebleau. Even Louis XIV got in on the act: it was he who hired Le Nôtre to redesign the gardens.

Fontainebleau, which was not damaged during the Revolution (though its furniture was stolen or destroyed), was beloved by Napoleon, who had a fair bit of restoration work carried out. Napoleon III was another frequent visitor.

During WWII the chateau was turned into a German headquarters. After it was liberated by Allied forces under US General George Patton in 1944, part of the complex served as the Allied and then NATO headquarters from 1945 to 1965.

The **Grands Appartements** (State Apartments) include a number of outstanding rooms. The spectacular **Chapelle de la Trinité** (Trinity Chapel), whose ornamentation dates from the first half of the 17th century, is where Louis XV married Marie Leczinska in 1725 and where the future Napoleon III was christened in 1810. **Galerie François 1er**, a jewellery box of Renaissance architecture, was decorated from 1533–40 by Il Rosso, a Florentine follower of Michelangelo. In the wood panelling, François I's monogram appears repeatedly along with his emblem, a dragon-like salamander.

The **Salle de Bal**, a 30m-long ballroom dating from the mid-16th century that was also used for receptions and banquets, is renowned for its mythological frescoes, marquetry floor and coffered ceiling. Large windows afford views of the Cour Ovale and the gardens. The gilded bed found in the 17th- and 18th-century **Chambre de l'Impératrice** (Empress' Bedroom) was never actually used by Marie-Antoinette, for whom it was built. The gilding in the **Salle du Trône** (Throne Room), the royal bedroom before the Napoleonic period, is in three shades: gold, green and yellow. Audioguide tours of the Grands Appartements in English cost €3.

The **Petits Appartements** (Small Apartments) were the private rooms of the emperor and empress, and the **Musée Napoléon 1er** (Napoleon I Museum) contains personal effects – such as ornamental swords, hats, uniforms and coats, – and knick-knacks that belonged to Napoleon and his relatives. Neither has fixed opening hours and a one-hour guided tour is an additional €3/2 for adults/18- to 25-year-olds (under 18s free).

As successive monarchs added their own wings to the chateau, five irregularly shaped courtyards were created. The oldest and most interesting is the **Cour Ovale** (Oval Courtyard), no longer oval but U-shaped due to Henri IV's construction work. It incorporates the keep, the sole remnant of the medieval chateau. The largest courtyard is the **Cour du Cheval Blanc** (Courtyard of the White Horse), from where you enter the chateau. Napoleon, about to be exiled to Elba in 1814, bade farewell to his Garde Imperiale (Imperial guard) from the magnificent 17th-century **double-horseshoe staircase** here. For that reason the courtyard is also called the Cour des Adieux (Farewell Courtyard).

The **chateau gardens** (admission free; ☺ 9am-7pm May-Sep, 9am-6pm Mar, Apr & Oct, 9am-5pm Nov-Feb) are quite extraordinary. On the northern side of the chateau is the **Jardin de Diane**, a formal garden created by Catherine de Médicis. Le Nôtre's formal, 17th-century **Jardin Français** (French Garden), or Grand Parterre, is east of the **Cour de la Fontaine** (Fountain Courtyard) and the **Étang des Carpes** (Carp Pond). The **Grand Canal** was excavated in 1609 and predates the canals at Versailles by more than half a century. The informal **Jardin Anglais** (English Garden), laid out in 1812, is west of the pond (closes one hour before the other gardens).

FORÊT DE FONTAINEBLEAU

This 20,000-hectare **Forêt de Fontainebleau** (Fontainebleau Forest), which begins 500m south of the chateau and surrounds the town, is one of the prettiest woods in the region. The many trails – including parts of the **GR1** and **GR11** (for further details, see p950) – are excellent for jogging, walking, cycling, horse riding and climbing. The area is covered by IGN's 1:25,000-scale *Forêt de Fontainebleau* map (No 2417OT; €9.80). The tourist office sells the *Guide des Sentiers de Promenades dans le Massif*

Forestier de Fontainebleau (€12), whose maps and text (in French) cover almost 20 walks in the forest, as well as the comprehensive La Forêt de Fontainebleau (€12.50), published by the Office National des Forêts, with almost three dozen walks.

Rock-climbing enthusiasts have long come to the forest's sandstone ridges, rich in cliffs and overhangs, to hone their skills before setting off for the Alps. The area presents a whole range of difficulties so anyone from beginners to expert climbers will find their feet. There are different grades marked by colours, starting with white ones, which are suitable for children, and going up to death-defying black boulders. The website http://bleau.info has stacks of information in English on climbing in Fontainebleau. If you want to give it a go, contact **Top Loisirs** (☎ 01 60 74 08 50; www.toploisirs .fr in French; 16 rue Sylvain Collinet) about equipment hire and instruction. The tourist office also sells the comprehensive Fontainebleau Climbs (€25) in English.

Eating

Le Grand Café (☎ 01 64 22 20 32; 33 place Napoléon Bonaparte; mains €9-15; ☉ 7am-1am) This modern café is spacious and airy, with a long, welcoming bar and a warm atmosphere. It's a good place for coffee, simple meals and crêpes; on weekends food is served all day long.

Au Vague à l'Âme (☎ 01 60 72 10 32; 39 rue de France; galettes & crêpes €2.50-9.50, lunch menus €11.50-16, dinner menu €25; ☉ lunch Tue-Sun, dinner to 1am Tue-Sat) This friendly café-restaurant is the place to come for Breton specialities including galettes and crêpes as well as fresh oysters and an oyster terrine to die for.

Le Caveau des Ducs (☎ 01 64 22 05 05; 24 rue Ferrare; salads €13-19, mains €15-23, lunch menus €19-21, dinner menus €24-41; ☉ lunch & dinner to 11pm) With its exposed beams, red tapestries and intimate stone cellars, not to mention the warm fire in winter, this makes an atmospheric little spot for a meal. The cellar dates from the 17th century, and there's a small terrace open during the warmer months.

Marché République (rue des Pins; ☉ 8am-1pm Tue, Fri & Sun) Fontainebleau's covered food market is just north of the central pedestrian area.

Monoprix (58 rue Grande; ☉ 8.45am-7.45pm Mon-Sat, 9am-1pm Sun) This department store has a supermarket section on the 1st floor.

Getting There & Around

Up to 30 daily commuter trains link Paris' Gare de Lyon hourly with Fontainebleau-Avon station (€7.50, 40 to 60 minutes); the last train returning to Paris leaves Fontainebleau a bit after 9.45pm weekdays, just after 10pm on Saturday and sometime after 10.30pm on Sunday. SNCF has a package (adult/10 to 17 years/four to nine years €20.80/16/7.70) that includes return transport from Paris, bus transfers and admission to the chateau.

Local buses (€1.30) link the train station with central Fontainebleau, 2km to the southwest, every 10 minutes from about 6am until about 9.30pm (11.30pm on Sunday).

VAUX-LE-VICOMTE

Privately owned **Château de Vaux-le-Vicomte** (Vaux-le-Vicomte Palace; ☎ 01 64 14 41 90; www.vaux -le-vicomte.com; adult/senior, student & 6-16yr €12.50/9.80, candlelight visit €15/13, exhibit, garden & museum only €7; ☉ 10am-1pm & 2-6pm Mon-Fri, 10am-6pm Sat & Sun late Mar–mid-Nov, candlelight visit 8pm Fri Jul & Aug, Sat May–mid-Oct) and its magnificent **formal gardens** (☉ 10am-6pm late Mar–mid-Nov), 20km north of Fontainebleau and 61km southeast of Paris, were designed and built by Le Brun, Le Vau and Le Nôtre between 1656 and 1661 as a precursor to their more ambitious work at Versailles. On the second and the last Saturday of every month from late March to late October, there are elaborate **jeux d'eau** (fountain displays) in the gardens from 3pm to 6pm.

Unfortunately the beauty of Vaux-le-Vicomte turned out to be the undoing of its owner, Nicolas Fouquet, Louis XIV's minister of finance. It seems that Louis, seething with jealousy that he had been upstaged at the chateau's official opening, had Fouquet thrown into prison, where the unfortunate ministre died in 1680. Today visitors can view the interior of the chateau, and wander through the gardens and the **Musée des Équipages** (Carriage Museum; ☉ 10am-1pm & 2-6pm Mon-Fri, 10am-6pm Sat & Sun late Mar–mid-Nov).

Getting There & Away

Unfortunately, Vaux-le-Vicomte is not an easy place to get to by public transport. The chateau is 6km northeast of Melun, is served by RER line D2 from Paris (€7, 45 minutes). A shuttle bus (€3.50 each way) links Melun station with the chateau at the weekend and on holidays; at other times you'll have to take a **taxi** (☎ 01 64 52 51 50; day/night €15/19). If you are travelling by car, take the N6 from Paris and the A5a (in the direction of Melun) and exit at Voisenon. From Fontainebleau, follow the N6 and the N36.

CHANTILLY

pop 11,000

The elegant town of Chantilly, 48km north of Paris, has a heavily restored but imposing chateau, surrounded by parkland and lakes. What's more, there's more than ample opportunity for walking, cycling and horse riding in the neighbouring Forêt de Chantilly.

Information

Office de Tourisme de Chantilly (☎ 03 44 67 37 37; www.chantilly-tourisme.com; 60 av du Maréchal Joffre; ⊗ 9.30am-12.30pm & 1.30-5.30pm Mon-Sat, 10am-1.30pm Sun May-Sep, 9.30am-12.30pm & 1.30-5.30pm Mon-Sat Oct-Apr)

Post Office (26 av du Maréchal Joffre)

Société Générale bank (1 av du Maréchal Joffre; ⊗ 8.30am-12.15pm & 1.45-5.30pm Mon-Thu, 8.30am-12.15pm & 1.45-6.30pm Fri, 9.30am-3.25pm Sat)

Sights

CHÂTEAU DE CHANTILLY

The **Château de Chantilly** (Chantilly Palace; ☎ 03 44 62 62 62; www.chateaudechantilly.com; adult/12-17yr/4-11yr €8/7/3.50; ⊗ 10.30am-6pm Mon & Wed-Fri, 10.30am-6pm Sat & Sun Apr-Oct, 10.30am-12.45pm & 2-5pm Mon & Wed-Fri, 10.30am-5pm Sat & Sun Nov-Mar), left in a shambles after the Revolution, is of interest mainly because of its gardens and a number of superb paintings. It consists of two attached buildings, which are entered through the same vestibule. The **Petit Château** was built around 1560 for Anne de Montmorency (1492–1567), who served six French kings as *connétable* (high constable), diplomat and warrior and died fighting Protestants in the Counter-Reformation. The attached Renaissance-style **Grand Château** was rebuilt 100 years after the Revolution by the Duke of Aumale, son of King Louis-Philippe. It served as a French military headquarters during WWI.

The Grand Château, to the right as you enter the vestibule, contains the **Musée Condé**. Its unremarkable 19th-century rooms are adorned with furnishings, paintings and

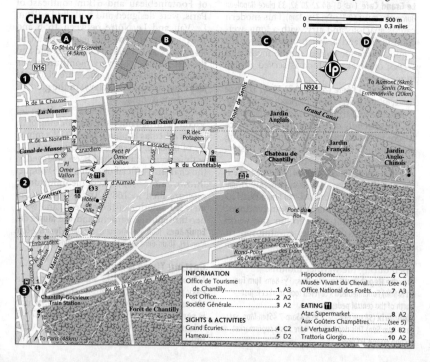

CHANTILLY

To St-Leu d'Esserent (4.5km)
N16
R de la Chaussée
La Nonette
R de la Nonette
Canal de Manse
Q de la Canardière
R de Gouvieux
R Saint Laurent
Pl Omer Vallon
Petit Pl Omer Vallon
R de Paris
R de Creil
R des Cascades
R des Potagers
Canal Saint Jean
Av de Condé
R du Connétable
Av du Connétable
R d'Aumale
Hôtel de Ville
Bd de la Libération
Route de Senlis
N924
Jardin Anglais
Grand Canal
Chateau de Chantilly
Jardin Français
Jardin Anglo-Chinois
Pont du Roi
To Aumont (6km); Senlis (7km); Ermenonville (20km)
R de l'Embarcadère
Av du Maréchal Joffre
R d'Orgemont
R de Bréauté
Chantilly-Gouvieux Train Station
Av de la Plaine des Aigles
Rond-Point de Diane
Carrefour des Lions
Forêt de Chantilly
To Paris (48km)

0 | 500 m
0 | 0.3 miles

A | B | C | D

sculptures haphazardly arranged according to the whims of the duke, who donated the chateau to the Institut de France at the end of the 19th century on the condition that the exhibits not be reorganised and that they remain open to the public. The most remarkable works are hidden away in a small room called the **Sanctuaire**, including paintings by Raphael, Filippino Lippi and Jean Fouquet.

The Petit Château contains the **Appartements des Princes** (Princes' Suites), which are straight ahead from the entrance. The highlight here is the **Cabinet des Livres**, a repository of 700 manuscripts and more than 30,000 volumes, including a Gutenberg Bible and a facsimile of the *Très Riches Heures du Duc de Berry*, an illuminated manuscript dating from the 15th century that illustrates the calendar year for both the peasantry and the nobility. The **chapel**, to the left as you walk into the vestibule, has woodwork and stained-glass windows dating from the mid-16th century and was assembled by the duke in 1882.

The chateau's excellent gardens were once among the most spectacular in France. The formal **Jardin Français**, with flowerbeds, lakes and **Grand Canal** laid out by Le Nôtre in the mid-17th century, is northeast of the main building. To the west, the 'wilder' **Jardin Anglais** was begun in 1817. East of the Jardin Français is the rustic **Jardin Anglo-Chinois**, created in the 1770s. Its foliage and silted-up waterways surround the **Hameau**, a mock village dating from 1774 whose mill and half-timbered buildings inspired the Hameau de la Reine at Versailles. Crème Chantilly – cream beaten with icing and vanilla sugar and dolloped on everything sweet that doesn't move in France – was born here (see the boxed text, p220).

A normal ticket allows entry to the chateau, Musée Condé and park, though you can visit just the **park** and **gardens** (adult/student/4-11yr €4/3.50/2.50; ☽ 10am-6pm Mar-Oct, 10am-12.45pm & 2-6pm Nov-Feb) separately. Combination tickets include the chateau, museum, park and boat or mini-train ride through the park (adult/12 to 17 years/four to 11 years €12/10.50/6.50) and the chateau, museum, park, boat and mini-train ride (adult/12 to 17 years/four to 11 years €16/13/10).

The **Grandes Écuries** (Grand Stables) of the chateau, built between 1719 and 1740 to house 240 horses and more than 400 hunting hounds, stand apart from the chateau to the west and close to Chantilly's famous **Hippodrome** (racecourse), inaugurated in 1834. They house the **Musée Vivant du Cheval** (Living Horse Museum; ☎ 03 44 57 13 13; www.musee-vivant-du-cheval.fr; adult/12-17yr/4-11yr €8.50/7.50/6.50; ☽ 10.30am-6.30pm daily Apr-Oct, 2-6pm Mon & Wed-Fri, 10.30am-7pm Sat & Sun Nov-Mar), whose 30 equines live in luxurious **wooden stalls** built by Louis-Henri de Bourbon, the seventh Prince de Condé. Displays include everything from riding equipment to rocking horses and portraits, drawings and sculptures of famous nags from the past.

The 30-minute **Présentation Équestre Pédagogique** (Introduction to Dressage; ☽ 11.30am, 3.30pm & 5.15pm Wed-Mon Apr-Oct, 3.30pm Mon & Wed-Fri, 11.30am, 3.30pm & 5.15pm Sat & Sun Nov-Mar) is included in the entry price.

FORÊT DE CHANTILLY

South of the chateau is the 6300-hectare **Forêt de Chantilly** (Chantilly Forest), once a royal hunting estate and now crisscrossed by a variety of walking and riding trails. Long-distance trails here include the **GR11**, which links the chateau with the town of **Senlis** (p220) and its wonderful cathedral; the **GR1**, which goes from **Luzarches** (famed for its cathedral, parts of which date from the 12th century) to **Ermenonville**; and the **GR12**, which goes northeast from four lakes known as the **Étangs de Commelles** to the **Forêt d'Halatte**.

The area is covered by IGN's 1:25,000-scale *Forêts de Chantilly, d'Halatte and d'Ermenonville* map (No 2412OT; €9.80). The 1:100,000-scale *Carte de Découverte des Milieux Naturels et du Patrimoine Bâti* (€6.50), available at the tourist office, indicates sites of interest (eg churches, chateaux, museums and ruins). The **Office National des Forêts** (☎ 03 44 57 03 88; www.onf.fr in French; 1 av de Sylvie; ☽ 8.30am-noon & 2-5pm Mon-Fri), just southeast of the tourist office, publishes a good walking guide for families called *Promenons-Nous dans les Forêts de Picardie: Chantilly, Halatte & Ermenonville* (€7.50).

Eating

Trattoria Giorgio (☎ 03 44 57 00 48; av du Maréchal Joffre; starters €7-12, pasta €8-12, mains €11.50-19, lunch menu €9.90; ☽ lunch & dinner to 11.30pm Tue-Sun) Spacious and popular with locals, this very central Italian restaurant is just the ticket for a pizza or more ambitious meal en route to the train station.

our pick Le Vertugadin (☎ 03 44 57 03 19; 44 rue du Connétable; starters €8-15, mains €17-40, lunch/dinner menu €15/26; ☺ lunch daily, dinner to 11pm Mon-Sat) This very friendly and highly recommended restaurant has excellent menus featuring *la cuisine traditionnelle*. In winter the little salon bar is a delight with its cosy fireplace. The walled-in garden beckons in the warmer months.

Aux Goûters Champêtres (☎ 03 44 57 46 21; Château de Chantilly; menus €17.50-37; ☺ 11am-7pm Apr-Nov) This fine restaurant in the windmill of the park's Hameau has local specialities on the menu and is a wonderful place for lunch, particularly during the summer. Expect to pay around €20 if ordering à la carte.

The large **Atac** (5 petit place Omer Vallon; ☺ 8.30am-7.30pm Mon-Sat) supermarket is midway between the train station and the chateau.

Getting There & Away
The chateau is just over 2km east of the train station (next to the bus station); the most direct route from there is to walk along av de la Plaine des Aigles through a section of the Forêt de Chantilly. You will get a better sense of the town, however, by following av du Maréchal Joffre and rue de Paris, so you can connect with rue du Connétable, Chantilly's principal thoroughfare.

Paris' Gare du Nord links with Chantilly-Gouvieux train station (€7.50, 30 to 45 minutes) by a mixture of RER and SNCF commuter trains (almost 40 a day, 20 on Sunday). The last train back to Paris departs daily just before midnight.

SENLIS
pop 17,200
Senlis, just 10km northeast of Chantilly, is an attractive medieval town of winding cobblestone streets, Gallo-Roman ramparts and towers. It was a royal seat from the time of Clovis to Henri IV and contains four small but fine **museums**, devoted to subjects as diverse as art, archaeology, hunting and the French cavalry in North Africa.

The Gothic **Cathédrale de Notre Dame** (place du Parvis Notre Dame; ☺ 8am-6pm) was built between 1150 and 1191. The cathedral is unusually bright, but the stained glass, though original, is unexceptional. The magnificent carved-stone **Grand Portal** (1170), on the western side facing place du Parvis Notre Dame, has statues and a central relief relating to the life of the Virgin Mary. It is believed to have been the inspiration for the portal at the cathedral in Chartres.

The **Office de Tourisme de Senlis** (☎ 03 44 53 06 40; www.tourisme.fr/office-de-tourisme/senlis.htm; place du Parvis Notre Dame; ☺ 10am-12.30pm & 2-6.15pm Mon-Sat, 10.30am-1pm & 2-6.15pm Sun Mar-Oct, 10am-12.30pm & 2-5pm Mon-Sat, 10.30am-12.30pm & 2-5pm Sun Nov-Feb) is just opposite (and west of) the cathedral.

Getting There & Away
Buses (€3.20, 25 minutes) link Senlis with Chantilly's bus station, just next to its train station, about every half-hour on weekdays and hourly on Saturday, with about a half-dozen departures on Sunday. The last bus returns to Chantilly at 8pm on weekdays (just after 7pm at the weekend).

CHARTRES
pop 44,200
The magnificent 13th-century cathedral of Chartres, crowned by two very different spires – one Gothic, the other Romanesque –

CHÂTEAU DE WHIPPED CREAM

Like every self-respecting 18th-century French chateau, the palace at Chantilly had its own *hameau* (hamlet) complete with *laitier* (dairy), where the lady of the household and her guests could play at being milkmaids, as Marie-Antoinette did at Versailles. But the cows at the Chantilly dairy took their job rather more seriously than their fellow bovines at other faux *crémeries*, and the *crème chantilly* (sweetened whipped cream) served at the hamlet's teas became the talk (and envy) of aristocratic Europe. The future Habsburg emperor Joseph II actually visited this '*temple de marbre*' (marble temple), as he called it, clandestinely to try out the white stuff in 1777. Chantilly (or more properly *crème Chantilly*) is whipped unpasteurised cream with a twist. It's beaten with icing and vanilla sugars to the consistency of a mousse and dolloped on berries.

HOLY VEIL

The most venerated object in the Chartres cathedral's possession is the Ste-Voile, the 'Holy Veil' said to have been worn by the Virgin Mary when she gave birth to Jesus. It originally formed part of the imperial treasury of Constantinople but was offered to Charlemagne by the Empress Irene when the Holy Roman Emperor proposed marriage to her in AD 802. It has been in Chartres since 876 when Charles the Bald presented it to the town. The cathedral was built because the veil survived the 1194 fire. It is contained in a cathedral-shaped reliquary and displayed in a small side chapel off the eastern aisle. It doesn't look like much – a yellowish bolt of silk draped over a support – but as the focus of veneration for millions of the faithful for two millennia it is priceless. We only wonder how they keep it clean.

---

rises from rich farmland 88km southwest of Paris and dominates the medieval town around its base. The cathedral's varied collection of relics, particularly the Ste-Voile (see the boxed text, below), attracted many pilgrims during the Middle Ages, who contributed to the building and extensions of the cathedral. With its astonishing blue stained glass and other treasures, the cathedral at Chartres is a must-see for any visitor.

Information

BNP Paribas bank (7-9 place des Épars; ☽ 8.30am-noon & 1.30-5.35pm Tue, 8.50am-noon & 1.45-5.35pm Wed-Fri, 8.30am-noon & 1.30-4.45pm Sat)

Office de Tourisme de Chartres (☎ 02 37 18 26 26; www.chartres-tourisme.com; place de la Cathédrale; ☽ 9am-7pm Mon-Sat, 9.30am-5.30pm Sun Apr-Sep, 10am-6pm Mon-Sat, 10am-1pm & 2.30-4.30pm Sun Oct-Mar) The tourist office, across the square from the cathedral's main entrance, rents self-paced English-language audioguide tours (for one/two people €5.50/8.50; 1½ hours) of the medieval city.

Post Office (place des Épars)

Sights

CATHÉDRALE NOTRE DAME DE CHARTRES

The 130m-long **Cathédrale Notre Dame de Chartres** (Cathedral of Our Lady of Chartres; ☎ 02 37 21 22 07; www.cathedrale-chartres.com in French; place de la Cathédrale; ☽ 8.30am-6.45pm), one of the crowning architectural achievements of Western civilisation, was built in the Gothic style during the first quarter of the 13th century to replace a Romanesque cathedral that had been devastated – along with much of the town – by fire on the night of 10 June 1194. Because of effective fund-raising and donated labour, construction took only 30 years, resulting in a high degree of architectural unity.

Excellent 1½-hour English-language **guided tours** (adult/senior & student €10/5; ☽ noon & 2.45pm Mon-Sat Apr-early Nov) are conducted by Chartres expert **Malcolm Miller** (☎ 02 37 28 15 58; millerchartres@aol.com). English-language audioguide tours (25 minutes/45 minutes/70 minutes €3.20/4.20/6.20) with three different themes can be hired from the cathedral bookshop.

The cathedral's west, north and south entrances have superbly ornamented triple **portals**, but the west entrance, known as the **Portail Royal**, is the only one that predates the 1194 fire. Carved from 1145 to 1155, its superb statues, whose features are elongated in the Romanesque style, represent the glory of Christ in the centre, and the Nativity and Ascension to the right and left. The structure's other main Romanesque feature is the 103m-high **Clocher Vieux** (Old Bell Tower; also called the Tour Sud, or 'South Tower'), which was begun in the 1140s. It is the tallest Romanesque steeple still standing anywhere.

A visit to the 112m-high **Clocher Neuf** (New Bell Tower; adult/18-25yr €6.50/4.50, under 18yr & 1st Sun of certain months free; ☽ 9.30am-noon & 2-5.30pm Mon-Sat, 2-5.30pm Sun May-Aug, 9.30am-noon & 2-4.30pm Mon-Sat, 2-4.30pm Sun Sep-Apr), which is also known as the Tour Nord (North Tower), is well worth the ticket price and the climb up the long spiral stairway. Access is just behind the cathedral bookshop. A 70m-high platform on the lacy Flamboyant Gothic spire, built from 1507 to 1513 by Jehan de Beauce after an earlier wooden spire burnt down, affords superb views of the three-tiered flying buttresses and the 19th-century copper roof, turned green by verdigris.

The cathedral's 172 extraordinary **stained-glass windows**, almost all of which date back to the 13th century, form one of the most important ensembles of medieval stained glass in the world. The three most exquisite windows dating from the mid-12th century

AROUND PARIS

CHARTRES

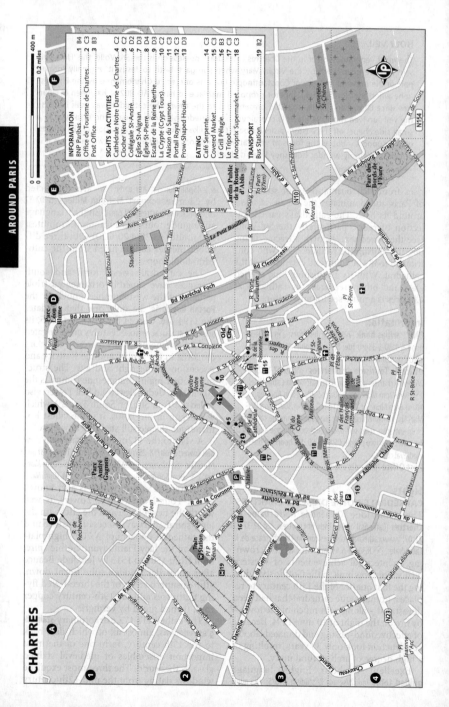

INFORMATION	
BNP Paribas................................1	B4
Office de Tourisme de Chartres.....2	C3
Post Office..................................3	B3

SIGHTS & ACTIVITIES	
Cathédrale Notre Dame de Chartres...4	C2
Clocher Neuf...............................5	C2
Collégiale St-André.....................6	D2
Église St-Aignan........................7	D3
Église St-Pierre..........................8	D4
Escalier de la Reine Berthe..........9	D3
La Crypte (Crypt Tours)..............10	C2
Maison du Saumon....................11	C3
Portail Royal.............................12	C3
Prow-Shaped House...................13	D3

EATING	
Café Serpente...........................14	C3
Covered Market.........................15	C3
Le Grill Pélagie.........................16	B3
Le Tripot..................................17	C3
Monoprix Supermarket...............18	C3

TRANSPORT	
Bus Station...............................19	B2

are in the wall above the west entrance and below the rose window. Survivors of the fire of 1194 (they were made some four decades before), the windows are renowned for the depth and intensity of their blue tones, which have become known as 'Chartres blue'.

The cathedral's 110m **crypt** (adult/senior, student & 7-18yr €2.70/2.10; ☺ 11am Mon-Sat, 2.15pm, 3.30pm, 4.30pm & 5.15pm daily late Jun-late Sep, 11am Mon-Sat, 2.15pm, 3.30pm & 4.30pm daily Apr-late Jun & late Sep-Oct, 11am Mon-Sat & 4.15pm daily Nov-Mar), a tombless Romanesque structure built in 1024, is the largest in France. Tours in French (with a written English translation) lasting 30 minutes start at **La Crypte** (☎ 02 37 21 56 33; 18 Cloître Notre Dame), the cathedral-run shop selling souvenirs, from April to October. At other times they begin at the shop below the North Tower in the cathedral.

OLD CITY
Chartres' meticulously preserved old city is northeast and east of the cathedral along the narrow western channel of the River Eure, which is spanned by a number of footbridges. From rue Cardinal Pie, the stairway called **Tertre St-Nicolas** and **rue Chantault** – the latter lined with medieval houses – lead down to the empty shell of the 12th-century **Collégiale St-André**, a Romanesque collegiate church closed in 1791 and severely damaged in the early 19th century and again in 1944.

Rue de la Tannerie and its extension **rue de la Foulerie** along the river's east bank are lined with flower gardens, mill races and the restored remnants of riverside trades: wash houses, tanneries and the like. **Rue aux Juifs** (Street of the Jews) on the west bank has been extensively renovated. Half a block down the hill there's a riverside promenade and up the hill **rue des Écuyers** has many structures dating from around the 16th century, including a half-timbered, **prow-shaped house** at No 26, with its upper section supported by beams. At No 35 is **Escalier de la Reine Berthe** (Queen Bertha's Staircase), a tower-like covered stairwell clinging to a half-timbered house that dates back to the early 16th century.

Rue du Bourg and **rue de la Poissonnerie** also have some old half-timbered houses; on the latter, look for the magnificent **Maison du Saumon** (Salmon House), also known as the Maison de la Truie qui File, at No 10-12 with its carved consoles of the Angel Gabriel and Mary, Michael the Archangel

slaying the dragon and, of course, the eponymous salmon. It is now a restaurant.

From **place St-Pierre**, you get a good view of the flying buttresses holding up the 12th- and 13th-century **Église St-Pierre** (place St-Pierre; ☺ 9am-noon & 2-6pm). Part of a Benedictine monastery in the 7th century, it was outside the city walls and vulnerable to attack; the fortress-like, pre-Romanesque **bell tower** attached to it was used as a refuge by monks and dates from around 1000. The fine, brightly coloured **clerestory windows** in the nave, choir and apse date from the early 14th century.

Église St-Aignan (place St-Aignan; ☺ 9am-noon & 2-6pm), first built in the early 16th century, is interesting for its wooden barrel-vault roof (1625), arcaded nave and painted interior of faded blue and gold floral motifs (c 1870). The stained glass and the Renaissance **Chapelle de St-Michel** date from the 16th century.

Eating
Café Serpente (☎ 02 37 21 68 81; 2 Cloître Notre Dame; salads & omelettes €5.20-11.50, dishes €13.50-15; ☺ 10am-11pm) This atmospheric brasserie and *salon de thé* (tearoom) is conveniently located opposite the cathedral.

Le Grill Pélagie (☎ 02 37 36 07 49; 1 av Jehan de Beauce; starters €3.70-7.90, mains €9.90-14.80; ☺ lunch & dinner to 10.30pm Mon-Fri, dinner to 11pm Sat) This is a popular place specialising in grills and Tex-Mex dishes such as guacamole and quesadillas (€6.50) and fajitas.

Le Tripot (☎ 02 37 36 60 11; 11 place Jean Moulin; mains €13.50-24, lunch menu €15, dinner menus €23-38; ☺ lunch Tue-Sun, dinner to 10pm Mon-Sat) This wonderful little place just down from the cathedral is one of the best bistros in Chartres.

There are a lot of food shops surrounding the **covered market** (place Billard; ☺ 7am-1pm Sat), just off rue des Changes south of the cathedral. The market itself dates from the early 20th century. The **Monoprix** (21 rue Noël Ballay & 10 rue du Bois Merrain; ☺ 9am-7.30pm Mon-Sat) department store with two entrances has a supermarket on the ground floor.

Getting There & Away
Thirty SNCF trains a day (20 on Sunday) link Paris' Gare Montparnasse (€12.40, 70 minutes) with Chartres, all of which pass through Versailles-Chantiers (€10.10, one hour). The last train to Paris leaves Chartres just after 9pm weekdays, just before 9pm on Saturday and sometime after 10pm on Sunday.

Far Northern France

France's northernmost bits have *much* more to engage the visitor than many people realise. True, a tan is easier to come by along the Mediterranean, but when it comes to culture, cuisine, shopping and dramatic views of land and sea – not to mention good old-fashioned friendliness – the far north can compete with the best France has to offer.

Lille is an ideal place to sample Flemish architecture, cuisine and beer – dark, amber and blonde. More regional flavour is on offer in Arras, whose Flemish-style squares are unique in France. Amiens, not far from a number of moving WWI memorials, boasts a magnificent Gothic cathedral.

The most picturesque of the trans-Channel ports is Boulogne-sur-Mer. Dunkirk (Dunkerque), on the other hand, is so uncomely that you actually feel sorry for the locals, though in this chapter we'll point out a few unique attractions. Although Calais has several worthwhile museums, most people see it only through the window of an accelerating vehicle, train carriage or boat.

The spectacular Côte d'Opale stretches southward from Calais along the English Channel (La Manche). Inland, you'll find WWII sites and St-Omer, known for its basilica. Further south, the Somme estuary affords watery pleasures to humans and birds alike.

Just outside Greater Paris, Compiègne serves up the glories of Napoleon III's Second Empire; Beauvais is known for its huge, unfinished cathedral; and Laon offers panoramic views from its hilltop old town.

FAR NORTHERN FRANCE (side margin)

HIGHLIGHTS

- Ramble along the spectacular, windswept **Côte d'Opale** (p243), facing the white cliffs of Dover
- Visit Lille's superb **museums** (p227) and partake of its **restaurants** (p232) and **nightlife** (p233 and p234)
- Admire Amiens' breathtaking **Gothic cathedral** (p256) both inside and out
- Explore the Flemish-style centre of **Arras** (p249)
- Ponder the sacrifices and horror of WWI at the evocative **Battle of the Somme memorials** (p252)

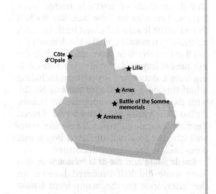

Côte d'Opale ★
★ Lille
★ Arras
★ Battle of the Somme memorials
★ Amiens

- POPULATION: 5.9 MILLION
- AREA: 31,813 SQ KM

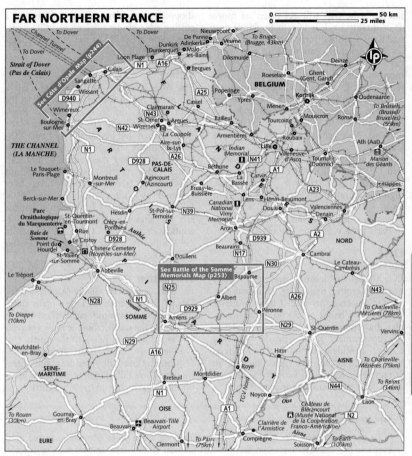

FAR NORTHERN FRANCE

History

In the Middle Ages, the Nord *département* (the administrative division of the sliver of France along the Belgian border; www.cdt nord.fr), together with much of Belgium and part of the Netherlands, belonged to 3a feudal principality known as Flanders (Flandre in French, Vlaanderen in Flemish) that has absolutely nothing to do with Homer Simpson's annoying next-door neighbour and everything to do with John McCrae's famous WWI poem *In Flanders Fields*. Today, many people in the area still speak Flemish – essentially Dutch with some variances in pronunciation and vocabulary – and are very proud of their *flamand* culture and cuisine.

The area south of the Somme estuary and Albert, towards Paris, forms the *région* of Picardy (Picardie; www.cr-picardie.fr), historically centred on the Somme *département* (www.somme-tourisme.com). The area northeast of Amiens saw some of the bloodiest and muddiest fighting of WWI. The popular British WWI love song, 'Roses of Picardy' (www.firstworldwar.com/audio /rosesofpicardy.htm), was penned here in 1916 by Frederick E Weatherley.

Getting There & Away

Far northern France is a hop, skip and a jump from England. On the **Eurostar** (www .eurostar.com) – pricey unless you snag a promotional fare – Lille is just 1¾ hours from

London (the trip will get faster as more TGV-quality track is laid in England) and one hour from Ashford. Eurotunnel (www .eurotunnel.com) can get you and your car from Folkestone to Calais in a mere 35 minutes. For those with sturdy sea legs, car ferries link Dover with Calais, Boulogne-sur-Mer and Dunkirk (see p975). From Beauvais-Tillé airport (p260), Ryanair has flights to Dublin, Shannon and Glasgow and Air Wales can sometimes get you to Cardiff.

On the Continent, superfast Eurostars and TGVs link Lille with Brussels (40 minutes) and TGVs (*train à grande vitesse*; high-speed train) make travel from Lille to Paris' Gare du Nord (one hour) a breeze. Compiègne and Beauvais are close enough to Paris to be visited on day trips.

LILLE

pop 1 million

Lille (Rijsel in Flemish) may be France's most underrated major city. In recent decades this once-grimy industrial metropolis, its economy based on declining technologies, has transformed itself – with generous government help – into a glittering and self-confident cultural and commercial hub. Highlights for the visitor include an attractive old town with a strong Flemish accent, three renowned art museums, stylish shopping, some fine dining options and a cutting-edge, student-driven nightlife scene. The Lillois are justly proud of their reputation for friendliness.

History

Lille owes its name – once spelled L'Isle – to the fact that it was founded, back in the 11th century, on an island in the River Deûle. In 1667 the city was captured by French forces led personally by Louis XIV, who promptly set about fortifying his prize (see p230). Long the centre of France's textile industry, the miserable conditions in which its 'labouring classes' lived were exposed by Victor Hugo in the 1850s. Lille's textile industry has declined but the city has shown renewed vigour and self-confidence since the TGV came to town in 1993, followed a year later by the Eurostar from London.

Orientation

Place du Général de Gaulle (also called the Grand' Place) separates Lille's main shopping precinct (around pedestrianised rue Neuve), to the south, from the narrow streets of Vieux Lille (Old Lille), to the north.

Lille's two main train stations, old-fashioned Gare Lille-Flandres and ultra-modern Gare Lille-Europe, are 400m apart on the eastern edge of the city centre.

THE GIANTS

In far northern France, *géants* (giants) – wickerwork body masks up to 8.5m tall animated by someone (or several someones) inside – emerge for local carnivals and on feast days to dance and add to the general merriment. Each has a name and a personality, usually based on the Bible, legends or local history. Giants are born, grow up, marry and have children (though never really die), creating, over the years, complicated family relationships. They serve as important symbols of town, neighbourhood and village identity. For snapshots check out http://utan.lille .free.fr/geants_1.htm.

Medieval in origin and also found in places as far afield as Catalonia (www.gegants.org in Catalan), the Austrian Tyrol, Mexico, Brazil and India, giants have been a tradition in northern France since the 16th century. More than 300 of the creatures, also known as *reuze* (in Flemish) and *gayants* (in Picard), now 'live' in French towns, including Arras, Boulogne, Calais, Cassel, Douai, Dunkirk and Lille. Local associations cater to their every need, while transnational groups such as the International Circle of Friends of the Giants (www.ciag.org) promote the creatures worldwide. In 2005 France and Belgium's giants were recognised by Unesco as 'masterpieces of the oral and intangible heritage of humanity'.

Giants make appearances year-round but your best chance to see them is at pre-Lenten carnivals, during Easter and at summer festivals. Dates and places – as well as the latest marriages and births – appear in the annual French-language brochure *Le Calendrier des Géants* (www .geants-carnaval.org in French), available at tourist offices.

Information

BOOKSHOPS

Le Furet du Nord (☎ 03 20 78 43 43; 15 place du Général de Gaulle; Ⓜ Rihour; ⏱ 9.30am-7.30pm Mon-Sat) One of the largest bookshops in Europe. The 4th floor has plenty of English books.

INTERNET ACCESS

Both the branch post office and main post office have Cyberpostes.

4 Players (☎ 03 20 07 43 18; 9 rue Maertens; Ⓜ République Beaux Arts; per 10min/hr prepaid €0.50/3; ⏱ 11am-10.30pm Mon-Fri, 10am-11.30pm Sat, 2-10pm Sun) Yes, it's pronounced 'fore-players'.

Net Arena (☎ 03 28 38 09 20; 10 rue des Bouchers; per hr €5; ⏱ 10am-10pm Mon-Sat, 2-8pm Sun) As chaotic as a teenage computer geek's bedroom. The bathroom has to be seen to be believed.

Net-K (☎ 03 20 55 13 42; 13 rue de la Clef; Ⓜ Rihour; per 10/60min €0.50/3; ⏱ 10am-11pm Tue-Sat, 2-7pm Sun)

LAUNDRY

Zombified by too much art and culture? Many experts recommend staring at washing machines going round and round.

Laundrette 4 rue Ovigneur (Ⓜ République Beaux Arts; ⏱ 7am-8pm); 13 rue de la Collégiale (⏱ 7am-9pm)

MEDICAL SERVICES

Hôpital Roger Salengro (☎ 03 20 44 61 40/41; rue du Professeur Émile Laine; Ⓜ CHR B Calmette; ⏱ 24hr) The *accueil urgences* (emergency room/casualty ward) of Lille's vast, 15-hospital Cité Hospitalière is 4km southwest of the city centre.

SOS Médecins (☎ 03 20 29 91 91; 3 av Louise Michel; Ⓜ Porte de Douai; house calls day €30, weekend €42.50-50, night €66-75, at clinic day €20, weekend €39.06/46.50, night €62.50-71.50) Doctors 24 hours a day.

MONEY

There are commercial banks with ATMs along rue Nationale. The tourist office will usually agree to exchange small sums but the rate is poor. There's a **Travelex exchange bureau** (⏱ 8am-7pm Mon-Fri, 10am-6pm Sat, Sun & holidays) in the Gare Lille-Flandres next to counter No 14.

POST

Branch Post Office (1 blvd Carnot; Ⓜ Rihour) In the Chambre de Commerce building. Changes money and has a Cyberposte.

Main Post Office (8 place de la République; Ⓜ République Beaux Arts) Changes money and has a Cyberposte.

TOURIST INFORMATION

Tourist Office (☎ from abroad 03 59 57 94 00, in France 08 91 56 20 04; www.lilletourism.com; place Rihour; Ⓜ Rihour; ⏱ 9.30am-6.30pm Mon-Sat, 10am-noon & 2-5pm Sun & holidays) Occupies what's left of the Flamboyant Gothic–style Palais Rihour, built in the mid-1400s for Philip the Good, duke of Burgundy; a war memorial forms the structure's eastern side. A brochure (€2) outlines four walking tours. City maps cost €0.30.

Sights

CITY CENTRE ARCHITECTURE

Vieux Lille (Old Lille), which begins just north of place du Général de Gaulle, is justly proud of its restored 17th- and 18th-century houses. The old brick residences along **rue de la Monnaie** (named after a mint built here in 1685) now house chic boutiques and the Musée de l'Hospice Comtesse (p229).

The Flemish-Renaissance **Vieille Bourse** (Old Stock Exchange; place du Général de Gaulle; Ⓜ Rihour) of 1652, ornately decorated with caryatids and cornucopia, actually consists of 24 separate houses. The courtyard in the middle hosts a **book market** (⏱ 2-7pm Tue-Sun).

On the southern side of place du Général de Gaulle, the 1932 Art Deco home of **La Voix du Nord** (Ⓜ Rihour), the leading regional daily, has a gilded sculpture of the Three Graces on top. The goddess-topped **column** (1845) in the square's fountain commemorates the city's successful resistance to the Austrian siege of 1792.

Nearby place du Théâtre is dominated by the Louis XVI-style **Opéra** (Ⓜ Rihour) and the neo-Flemish **Chambre de Commerce** (Ⓜ Rihour), topped by a 76m-high spire with a gilded clock. Both were built in the early 20th century.

PALAIS DES BEAUX-ARTS

Lille's world-renowned **Fine Arts Museum** (☎ 03 20 06 78 00; place de la République; Ⓜ République Beaux Arts; adult/12-25yr/under 12yr €4.60/3/free; ⏱ 2-6pm Mon, 10am-6pm Wed-Sun), built from 1885 to 1892, has a truly first-rate collection of 15th- to 20th-century paintings, including works by Rubens, Van Dyck and Manet. On the ground floor, there's exquisite porcelain and faïence, much of it of local provenance, while in the basement you'll find classical archaeology, medieval statuary and intricate 18th-century models of the fortified cities of northern France and Belgium. Tickets are valid for the whole day.

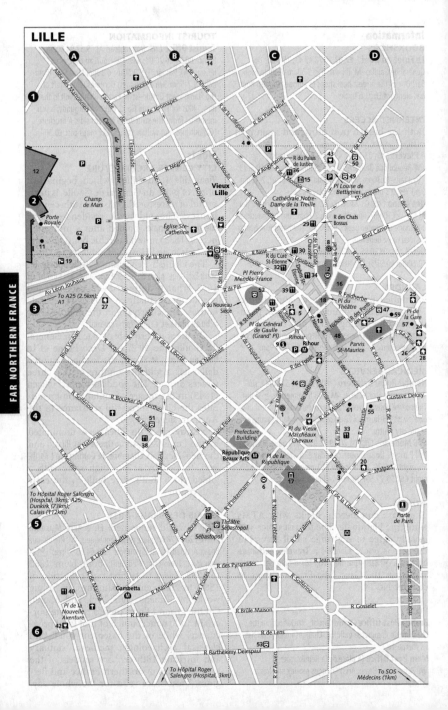

LILLE

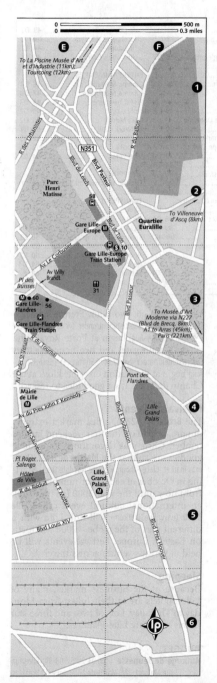

Information sheets are available in each hall. An audioguide is planned for the recently reorganised paintings section.

MUSÉE D'ART MODERNE

The highly regarded **Museum of Modern Art** (☎ 03 20 19 68 68; www.mamlm.fr; 1 allée du Musée, Villeneuve-d'Ascq), in a sculpture park 9km east of Gare Lille-Europe (the route is circuitous so if you're driving get a good map), displays colourful, playful and just plain weird works by artists such as Braque, Calder, Léger, Miró, Modigliani and Picasso. It will be closed until sometime in 2008 while a huge new wing, to house a collection of Art Brut, is built. To get there, take metro line No 1 to Pont de Bois and then bus No 41 to Parc Urbain-Musée.

LA PISCINE MUSÉE D'ART ET D'INDUSTRIE

If Paris can turn a disused train station into a world-class museum, why not take an Art Deco municipal swimming pool (built 1927–32) – an architectural masterpiece inspired by a combination of civic pride and hygienic high-mindedness – and transform it into a temple of the arts? This innovative **museum** (☎ 03 20 69 23 60; 23 rue de l'Espérance, Roubaix; Ⓜ Gare Jean Lebas; adult €3; ☯ 11am-6pm Tue-Thu, 11am-8pm Fri, 1-6pm Sat & Sun), 12km northeast of Gare Lille-Europe, showcases fine arts, applied arts and sculpture in a delightfully watery environment.

MUSÉE DE L'HOSPICE COMTESSE

Housed in an attractive 15th- and 17th-century poorhouse, the **Hospice Comtesse Museum** (☎ 03 28 36 84 00; 32 rue de la Monnaie; ☯ closed Mon morning & Tue) features ceramics, faïence wall tiles and 17th- and 18th-century paintings, furniture and religious art. The **Salle des Malades** (Hospital Hall) is decorated with Lille tapestries. The museum was undergoing renovations as we went to press.

LILLE MÉTROPOLE ALL INCLUSIVE

Available in one-/two-/three-day versions (€15/30/45), this pass gets you into almost all the museums in greater Lille and affords unlimited use of public transport. The three-day version includes 11 sites in the Nord-Pas-de-Calais region and the use of regional TER trains. Available at most Lille-area tourist offices.

FAR NORTHERN FRANCE

MAISON NATALE DE CHARLES DE GAULLE

The upper-middle-class house in which Charles André Marie Joseph de Gaulle – WWII Resistance leader, architect of the Fifth Republic and ferocious defender of French interests – was born in 1890 has been turned into a **museum** (☎ 03 28 38 12 05; 9 rue Princesse; adult/ under 26yr incl English audioguide €5/3; ⌚ 10am-noon & 2-5.30pm Wed-Sun) that presents the French leader in the context of his times, with an emphasis on his connection to France's far north. Displays include De Gaulle's dainty baptismal robe and some evocative newsreels. To get here by bus, take line 9 to the Bateliers stop.

CITADELLE

The greatest military architect of the 17th century, Sébastien le Prestre de Vauban (see p62), designed this massive **fortress**, shaped like a star, after the capture of Lille by France in 1667. Built using some 60 million bricks, it still functions as a military base but around the 2.2km-long outer ramparts you'll find central Lille's largest park. On the southeastern side there's a **children's amusement park** and a small **zoo** (admission free). To get to the Citadelle by bus, take the Citadine line.

Tours

The tourist office runs English-language **tours of Vieux Lille** (adult/student/under 4yr €7.50/6.50/ free; ⌚ 2.30pm Sat); two-hour, French-language **Citadelle tours** (adult/student/under 4yr €7.50/6.50/free; ⌚ 3pm Sun May-Aug) begin at Porte Royale, the citadel's main gate; and two-hour **bike tours** (adult/student/under 4yr €7.50/6.50/free; ⌚ 5pm Fri Jul-Aug) begin at the Station Oxygène kiosk at the Champ de Mars. It's a good idea to reserve.

Festivals & Events

The **Braderie** (p232), a flea market extraordinaire, is held on the first weekend in September. Christmas decorations and edible goodies are sold at the **Marché de Noël** (Christmas market; place Rihour; ⌚ late Nov-late Dec). Starting in October of each even-numbered year from now until the year 3000 (so they say), an international cultural event called **Lille 3000** (www.lille3000.com) will link Lille with a different part of the globe – 2008 will focus on Eastern Europe. Festival events will be held at various venues across the city.

Sleeping

Because of the business market, many of Lille's hotels are at their fullest from Monday to Thursday. Lots of two- and three-star hotels face Gare Lille-Flandres.

BUDGET

Auberge de Jeunesse (☎ 03 20 57 08 94; lille@fuaj .org; 12 rue Malpart; Ⓜ Mairie de Lille; dm with breakfast

€15.90; ☒ closed 24 Dec-late Jan) This Spartan former maternity hospital, locked from 10am to 3pm, now houses 165 beds (three to seven beds per room). Toilets and showers are down the hall.

Hôtel Le Globe (☎ 03 20 57 29 58; 1 blvd Vauban; d €38, with shower €34) The large rooms have French windows that look out on the Citadelle and (in most cases) chimneys that add a dollop of old-fashioned charm. The pillows are among the lumpiest in Europe but the prefab showers have hi-flo shower heads and the radiators don't skimp on the hot water, either. There's cheap parking across the street at the Champ de Mars. The hotel is served by bus 14B and the Citadine bus line.

Hôtel Faidherbe (☎ 03 20 06 27 93; hotelfaidherbe@wanadoo.fr; 42 place de la Gare; Ⓜ Gare Lille-Flandres; d from €46, with washbasin €32) The 39 one-star rooms are compact, cheerful and very simply furnished. The perfect choice for linoleum fans.

The Hôtel de France (see Midrange) has singles/doubles with washbasin for €35/40.

MIDRANGE

Hôtel de France (☎ 03 20 57 14 78; hotel.de.france.lille@wanadoo.fr; 10 rue de Béthune; Ⓜ Gare Rihour; s/d from €45/50) You can't get much more central than this two-star place, whose 33 rooms are awkwardly laid out but functional. Some of the top-floor rooms have great views but there's no lift. To get there by car, take blvd de la Liberté, rue Jean Sans Peur and then rue des Fossés.

Hôtel Flandre-Angleterre (☎ 03 20 06 04 12; www .hotel-flandre-angleterre.fr; 13 place de la Gare; Ⓜ Gare Lille-Flandres; s/d from €58/76, 10% less Fri-Sun & during school holidays) England certainly isn't bland and neither is Flanders, but this hotel's 44 two-star rooms, though comfortable, clean and quiet, are, shall we say, somewhat lacking in character – but hey, there's plenty of that outside. The best rooms have views of the Gare Lille-Flandres train station.

Hôtel Brueghel (☎ 03 20 06 06 69; www.hotel -brueghel.com; 5 parvis St-Maurice; Ⓜ Gare Lille-Flandres; s/d €74/80) The 65 two-star rooms here are a mix of modern and antique, though they don't have nearly as much Flemish charm as the lobby. The tiny wood-and-wrought-iron lift dates from the 1920s.

Other two-star options near Gare Lille-Flandres:

DOES THE FUTURE OF GUIDEBOOK WRITING HAVE FIVE GYROSCOPES? *Daniel Robinson*

The **Segway** (www.segway.com) sounds like a guidebook author's dream, the ultimate way to hop from museum to hotel to restaurant quickly and effortlessly. Thanks to Lille's Station Oxygène (p235), I was able to field test this thesis – €20 for four hours, including a riding lesson during which I learned the most basic Segway rule: think 'forward' and – voila! – you're off! I also learned how to turn on a dime, stop in a flash and stand motionless – look, Ma, no hands! – while taking notes on a clipboard.

True, cobblestones are not the Segway's preferred riding surface, nor can it be denied that some particularly high kerbs stopped the gadget cold, causing it to rock back and forth violently like a skittish pony. Overall, though, the gyroscopic gizmo worked superbly and the added height – so this is how basketball stars feel! – provided excellent views of the cityscape.

Cruising around the city's footpaths made me feel like a famous Hollywood actor: heads turned, couples whispered to each other and even well-brought-up children stared unabashedly and sometimes even pointed, their mouths agape. I thought to myself: is the king naked (no, I've got my trousers on and yes, my fly *is* zipped all the way up) or is this gadget just really, really cool?!

And the deference, ah, the deference! Well-dressed pedestrians willingly stepped into the gutter to give me the right-of-way, as – I thought to myself – is only proper. Are they doing so out of respect or are they terrified I'll run them down? Who cares! Rarely since the demise of the last tsar has anyone felt himself so indisputably the master of his domain.

One question kept nagging me, though: is working this way really faster than walking? My conclusion was that, most probably, it was not, and I remembered that someone had once called the Segway 'a solution of undeniable genius to a nonexistent problem'. Worse still, after dinner I had the disconcerting feeling that on that day – unlike normal research days – I had burned rather fewer calories than I had eaten…

BRADERIE DE LILLE

On the first weekend in September, Lille's entire city centre – 200km of footpaths! – is transformed into the Braderie de Lille, billed as the world's largest flea market. The extravaganza – with stands selling antiques, local delicacies, handicrafts and more – dates from the Middle Ages, when Lillois servants were permitted to hawk their employers' old garments for some extra cash.

The city's biggest annual event, the Braderie runs from 3pm on Saturday to midnight on Sunday, when street sweepers emerge to tackle the mounds of mussel shells and old *frites* (French fries) left behind by the merrymakers. Before the festivities, you can make room for all those extra calories by joining in the half-marathon held at 9am on Saturday. A free map of the market, *Braderie de Lille – Le Plan*, is available from Lille's tourist office.

Hôtel Le Floréal (☎ 03 20 06 36 21; hotel-le-floreal@ wanadoo.fr; 21 rue Ste-Anne; Ⓜ Gare Lille-Flandres; s/d €51/63; ⚙) A friendly 12-room place with linoleum floors.

Hôtel Moulin d'Or (☎ 03 20 06 12 67; www.hotel moulindor.com; 15 rue du Molinel; Ⓜ Gare Lille-Flandres; s/d Mon-Thu €55/70, Fri-Sun €50/55) Pastels hit you like a strong perfume the minute you walk into this place, whose 13 quiet rooms have first-rate carpets.

TOP END

Grand Hôtel Bellevue (☎ 03 20 57 45 64; www.grand hotelbellevue.com; 5 rue Jean Roisin; Ⓜ Rihour; d from €125) This three-star Best Western–affiliated establishment was grandly built in the early 20th century. A charmingly creaky *belle époque* lift trundles guests to the 60 spacious rooms, which have high ceilings and antique-style French furnishings.

Eating

Vieux Lille has an excellent and varied selection of restaurants, many of them serving Flemish specialities such as *carbonnade* (braised beef stewed with beer and brown sugar). Places to look for eateries include rue Royale, rue de la Barre, rue de la Monnaie and, a bit to the northeast, rue de Gand. West of the main post office, there are cheap eats on lively, studenty rue d'Inkermann, rue Solférino and rue Masséna.

La Source (☎ 03 20 57 53 07; 13 rue du Plat; Ⓜ République Beaux Arts; 2-course menus €8-13; ⚓ meals served noon-2pm Mon-Sat, 7-9pm Fri) An organic food shop founded way back in 1979 and – thanks to its light and airy restaurant – now a Lille institution. Serves vegetarian, fowl and fish *plats du jour* that are not just for the granola set. Both the décor and the diners exude health, well-being and cheer.

La Voûte (☎ 03 20 42 12 16; 4 rue des Débris St-Étienne; Ⓜ Rihour; Mon-Fri lunch menus €10.50, other menus €14.50-18.50; ⚓ closed Sun & Mon) The specialities of Flanders, including *carbonnade* (€12.80) and *lapin à la flamande* (rabbit in a white wine and prune sauce; €12.80), are served in this combination bistro, restaurant and *estaminet* (tavern).

L'Envie (☎ 03 20 15 29 39; 34 rue des Bouchers; plat du jour €8.50, menu €18.50; ⚓ closed Sun) You'll eat well, somewhere out near the cutting edge of French culinary inventiveness, at this informal but very cool establishment. The wine list, which features a white from Burgundy and a red from Alsace, reflects the chef's adventurous spirit.

Le Palais (☎ 03 20 74 53 47; 4 rue du Palais de Justice; mains €11-15; ⚓ closed Sun & dinner Mon) Serves solid cuisine of French and Flemish inspiration at eminently fair prices. Regional specialities include *carbonnade* (€11) and *potjevlesch* (a gelled pâté made with pork, rabbit, fowl and veal). Creatively lit with octopus-like light fixtures – but the brick walls never let you forget you're in Vieux Lille.

Le Barbue d'Anvers (☎ 03 20 55 11 68; 1bis rue St-Étienne; Ⓜ Rihour; menu €29; ⚓ Tue-Sat) This well-regarded regional restaurant occupies an 18th-century building at the end of a cobblestone courtyard, its three levels decorated with antique Dutch and Flemish furnishings. It's named after a race of Belgian chickens so naturally specialities include *waterzoï de volaille* (poultry and vegetables baked in a cream sauce).

our pick À l'Huîtrière (☎ 03 20 55 43 41; www .huitriere.fr; 3 rue des Chats Bossus; lunch menu €44, menu dégustation €110; ⚓ noon-2pm & 7-9.30pm, closed dinner Sun & about 21 Jul-22 Aug) Considered a good place to invite a gal before proposing. In 1928, the grandfather of the present owners turned to the nascent Art Deco movement – first exhibited (and named) in Paris just three years earlier – to find suitably elegant decoration for his fish shop, situated on 'Street of the Hunchback Cats'. The oak-panelled restaurant has held one or two Michelin stars continuously since 1930. The sea-themed mosaics and stained glass are worth a look-in even if you're not in the mood to dine on seafood fresh out of the water – accompanied, of course, by a wine or two from the 40,000-bottle cellar. Booking ahead is recommended for dinner on Friday, Saturday and holidays.

SELF-CATERING
Boulangerie Notre Dame de la Treille (26 rue Basse; Ⓜ Rihour; ⓨ 7.30am-7.30pm Mon-Sat, 10am-6pm Sun) The old-time *flûtes* and *pain à l'ancien* at this *boulangerie* are especially scrumptious.

Meert (☎ 03 20 57 07 44; 27 rue Esquermoise; Ⓜ Rihour; ⓨ 9.30am-7pm Tue-Sat, 9.30am-1pm & 3-7pm Sun) *Gaufres* (waffles; €2 each), made with Madagascar vanilla and baked in a hinged griddle over an open wood fire, are the speciality of Meert, a luxury pastry and sweets shop and tearoom that has served kings, viceroys and generals since 1761. The chocolate shop's coffered ceiling, painted wood panels, wrought-iron balcony and mosaic floor date from 1839. Luxury chocolates start at €0.085 per gram.

Other food shopping options:
Carrefour hypermarket (Euralille shopping centre; Ⓜ Gare Lille-Europe; ⓨ 9am-10pm Mon-Sat) Unbelievably huge.
Fromagerie Philippe Olivier (☎ 03 20 74 96 99; 3 rue du Curé St-Étienne; Ⓜ Rihour; ⓨ 10am-12.30pm & 3-7.30pm Mon-Thu, 9am-12.30pm & 3-7.30pm Fri, 9am-1pm & 2.15-7.30pm Sat)
Match supermarket (97 rue Solférino; ⓨ 9am-9pm Mon-Sat) Inside an old covered market.

About 1.2km southwest of the centre in Wazemmes, a *populaire* (working-class) neighbourhood that's slowly being gentrified, you'll find Lille's most beloved **Wazemmes food market** (place de la Nouvelle Aventure; Ⓜ Gambetta; ⓨ 8am-2pm Tue-Thu, 8am-8pm Fri & Sat, 8am-3pm Sun & holidays). Right outside, the city's largest **outdoor market** (ⓨ 7am-1.30pm or 2pm Tue, Thu & Sun) is at its liveliest on Sunday. There's another outdoor market, **Marché Sébastopol** (place Sébastopol; Ⓜ République Beaux Arts; ⓨ 7am-2pm Wed & Sat), a bit nearer the centre.

Drinking
Lille has two main nightlife zones: Vieux Lille (eg rue Royale, rue de la Barre and rue de Gand), where bars tend to be small and oriented towards a fairly chic clientele; and, 750m southwest of the tourist office, rue Masséna and rue Solférino, where inexpensive high-decibel bars draw mainly students.

Chocolaterie Vandyck (☎ 03 28 82 07 72; 4 rue des Bouchers; ⓨ 2-7pm Tue & Wed, 10am-7pm Thu-Sat, 3-7.30pm Sun) Hot chocolate (€4.50 to €7.50) and chocolate pralines, all 100% natural and all made right on the premises, are the highlights at this delightful *salon de dégustation de chocolat* (tearoom specialising in classic chocolates).

L'Illustration Café (☎ 03 20 12 00 90; 18 rue Royale; ⓨ 2pm-2am Sun-Thu, to 3am Fri & Sat) This mellow but smoky bar, adorned with Art Nouveau woodwork and works by local painters, attracts artists and intellectuals in the mood to read, exchange weighty ideas – or just shoot the breeze. Very French in the best sense of the word.

Café Citoyen (Citizen Café; ☎ 03 20 13 15 73; 7 place du Vieux Marché aux Chevaux; Ⓜ République Beaux Arts; lunchtime plat du jour €8.30; ⓨ noon-midnight Mon-Fri, 2-7pm Sat; ⊠ ▣) Progressive-minded volunteers turned a failing bar into a friendly, informal café forum in which social and environmental questions can be discussed. Internet access is free if you order an organic beer or a cup of fair-trade coffee from the friendly fellow wearing little, round, Lenin-style glasses. A sign in the window welcomes English-speakers. Founded, presciently, in September 2005, a month before France's suburbs exploded.

Le Balatum (☎ 03 20 57 41 81; 13 rue de la Barre; ⓨ 4pm-3am) This funky, dimly lit place, decorated with artwork that changes monthly, is ideal for a tête-à-tête. There's live music at 7.30pm on Sunday and a DJ from 10.30pm on Thursday, Friday and Saturday nights. Gay friendly.

Café Le Relax (☎ 03 20 54 67 34; 48 place de la Nouvelle Aventure; Ⓜ Gambetta; ⓨ 10.30am-midnight or later Tue-Sun) A genuine, unadulterated *café de quartier* (neighbourhood café) where locals come for an espresso or a cold Pelforth blonde and to run into friends. A great place to get a feel for this ethnically mixed, working class part of town after checking out the nearby Wazemmes market. French accordion music and chansons are performed live each Sunday from 7pm to midnight; a DJ spins reggae disks on Wednesday night.

Café Oz (☎ 03 20 55 15 15; 33 place Louise de Bettignies; ⏰ 5pm-3am Sun-Fri, 3pm-3am Sat, happy hour 6-9pm Mon-Sat) Footy on the wide screen, Australiana on the walls, Fosters on tap (€2.80) – what more could you ask for? This little piece of the Outback is packed when DJs do their thing from 10.30pm to 2.30am on Thursday, Friday and Saturday nights. The nearest bus stop is Palais de Justice, served by lines 3, 6 and 9.

Entertainment

Lille's free French-language entertainment guide, *Sortir*, comes out each Wednesday and is available at the tourist office, cinemas and event venues.

Tickets for Lille's rich cultural offerings can be bought at the **FNAC billetterie** (ticket desk; ☎ 03 20 15 58 15; Ⓜ Rihour; ⏰ 10am-7.30pm Mon-Sat), just off rue St-Nicolas inside the FNAC store. Events are posted by category on the walls.

CINEMAS

Nondubbed films are the speciality of two cinemas (☎ 08 36 68 00 73), the **Majestic** (56 rue de Béthune; Ⓜ Rihour), which has six projection spaces, and the **Metropole** (26 rue des Ponts des Comines; Ⓜ Gare Lille-Flandres), an art cinema.

GAY & LESBIAN

Vice Versa (☎ 03 20 54 93 46; 3 rue de la Barre; ⏰ 1pm-2am Mon-Thu, 1pm-2.30am or 3am Fri & Sat, 4pm-12.30am Sun) The rainbow flag flies proudly at this bar, which is as gay as it is popular (and it's very popular). Well-heeled and sophisticated, it takes eclectic décor – created by the staff and changed four times a year – in bold new directions.

Miss Marple (☎ 03 20 39 85 92; www.lemissmarple .com, 18 rue de Gand; ⏰ 4pm-midnight Tue-Thu, 4pm-1am Fri, 4pm-2am Sat, 4-10pm Sun) A friendly and unpretentious lesbian bar that welcomes gays and heteros. The upstairs lounge features upholstered cubes and low wooden tables. There's a DJ on Friday and Saturday nights.

LIVE MUSIC

The **Orchestre National de Lille** (☎ 03 20 12 82 40) plays in the circular **Nouveau Siècle concert hall** (place Pierre Mendès-France; Ⓜ Rihour; concert tickets adult €18-30, under 26yr €10).

NIGHTCLUBS

Although you no longer have to cross the Belgian frontier (eg to Gand) to dance past 4am, some locals still do because, they say, the techno is edgier, the prices lower, substances more available and the closing time even later (1pm!).

Network Café (☎ 03 20 40 04 91; 15 rue Faisan; Ⓜ République Beaux Arts; admission free; ⏰ 10.30pm-5.30am or later Tue-Sun nights) All the world may not be a stage but this discotheque, Lille's hottest late-late venue, certainly is. For dancing, you can choose between the main room, presided over by two 5m-high statues from faraway lands, and the baroque Venetian room, all crystal chandeliers and velvet settees. Hugely popular with students and the 20-to-35 crowd. Rock sets the tone on Thursday, salsa dominates on Sunday. The door policy is pretty strict.

Tchouka Club (☎ 03 20 14 37 50; www.tchoukaclub .com in French; 80 rue Barthélemy Delespaul; ⏰ 11pm-8am Fri, Sat & holiday eves) This late-late, gay and lesbian dance venue has Lille's clubbering classes chattering. The nearest bus stop is Jeanne d'Arc, on lines 13 and 14B.

La Scala (☎ 03 20 42 10 60; 32 place Louise de Bettignies; admission free; ⏰ 11pm-8am Mon-Sat) A classic cellar discothèque, with pulsating music and gyrating bodies under ancient brick arches. There are frequent student nights (Wednesday and Thursday) and theme nights (Thursday, Friday and Saturday). Things get going at about 1.30am.

Shopping

Lille's snazziest clothing and housewares boutiques are in the old city in the area bounded by rue de la Monnaie, rue Esquermoise, rue de la Grande Chausée and rue and rue d'Angleterre. The tiny pedestrian streets northwest of Cathédrale Notre-Dame de la Treille, including rue Peterinck, reward the inquisitive *flâneur* (aimless stroller).

For more practical purchases, locals often head either to the pedestrian zone south of place du Général de Gaulle (eg rue Neuve) or to the **Euralille shopping mall** (Corbusier & av Willy Brandt; Ⓜ Gare Lille Flandres or Gare Lille Europe).

Getting There & Away

BUS

Eurolines (☎ 03 20 78 18 88; 23 parvis St-Maurice; Ⓜ Gare Lille-Flandres; ⏰ 9.30am-6pm Mon-Fri, 1-6pm Sat, longer hours Jul-Aug) serves cities such as

Brussels (€14, 1½ to two hours), Amsterdam (€41, six hours) and London (€34, six hours). Buses depart from blvd de Leeds, to the left as you arrive at Gare Lille-Europe from av Le Corbusier (look for the anonymous white 'Autocar' sign behind the taxi rank).

CAR

Driving into Lille is incredibly confusing, even with a good map. To get to the city centre, the best thing to do is to suspend your sense of direction and blindly follow the 'Centre Ville' signs.

Parking at the Champ de Mars (the huge car park just east of the Citadelle) costs €3 a day (free entry and exit from 8pm to 6am), including return travel (for up to five people) to the city centre on the Citadine bus line. Parking is free along some of the streets southwest of rue Solférino and up around the Maison Natale de Charles de Gaulle.

Car hire for less than the biggies charge is available from the following companies:

ADA (☎ 03 20 57 02 25; 2 rue Gustave Delory; Ⓜ Mairie de Lille)

DLM (☎ 03 20 06 18 80; 32 place de la Gare; Ⓜ Gare Lille-Flandres; Ⓨ 8am-noon & 2-6pm Mon-Sat)

Rent-A-Car Système (☎ 03 20 40 20 20; 113 rue du Molinel; Ⓜ Rihour or République Beaux Arts)

TRAIN

Lille has been linked with Paris by rail since 1846. Its two train stations are one stop apart on metro line No 2.

Gare Lille-Flandres is used by almost all regional services and most TGVs to Paris' Gare du Nord (€35.40, at peak hours €48.40, 64 minutes, 23 daily Monday to Friday, 15 daily Saturday and Sunday).

Gare Lille-Europe – an ultramodern structure topped by what looks like a 20-storey ski boot – handles pretty much everything else, including Eurostar trains (www .eurostar.com; p973) to London (1¾ hours), TGVs/Eurostars to Brussels (Monday to Friday/weekend €24/15.50, 40 minutes, 11 to 13 daily) and TGVs to Nice (€110.30 or €130.40, 7¼ hours, two direct daily).

For details on getting to/from Amiens, Arras, Boulogne, Calais, Dunkirk and St-Omer, see those sections.

Getting Around

The city centre is being progressively pedestrianised.

BICYCLE & SEGWAY

Always wanted to try one of those nifty Segway gadgets (see the boxed text, p231)? Now's your chance! Station Oxygène, run by Transpole (below), rents out Segways for €4/15/20 (€3.50/12/18 if you have a bus ticket stamped within the hour) per 30 minutes/half-day/day, not including a mandatory first-time riding lesson (€4) that will get you an official French Segway license (we're not kidding). Riders must weigh over 40kg and be at least 12 or 13. City bikes with electric power boost are also available (€1.50/7.10 for 30 minutes/half-day). Station Oxygène's glass pavilion at the **Champ de Mars** (Ⓨ 8.30am-7pm Mon-Fri, 10am-7pm Sat winter, 8am-8pm Mon-Sat, 10am-7pm Sun summer) is easy to spot – just look for a shiny glass structure that resembles a hovering flying saucer. There's a second outlet, **Relais Oxygène** (place des Buisses; Ⓨ 11am-6.30pm Mon, 8.30am-6.30pm Tue-Fri, 2-7pm Sat, closed Jul & Aug) in the Gare Lille Flandres.

Not-for-profit **Ch'ti Vélo** (☎ 03 28 53 07 49; 10 av Willy Brandt; Ⓨ 7.30am-7.30pm Mon-Fri, 9am-7.30pm Sat, Sun & holidays), on the northern side of Gare Lille-Flandres, rents city bikes for €5 per day and can supply you with a bike path map. **DLM** (☎ 03 20 06 18 80; 32 place de la Gare; Ⓜ Gare Lille-Flandres; Ⓨ 8am-noon & 2-6pm Mon-Sat) rents city bikes per half-/whole day for €7/9 (€5/7 for students), including a helmet.

BUS, TRAM & METRO

Lille's two speedy metro lines, two tramways and many urban and suburban bus lines – several of which cross into Belgium – are run by **Transpole** (☎ 08 20 42 40 40; www .transpole.fr in French), which has an **information window** (Ⓨ closed Sun) in the Gare Lille-Flandres metro station. In the city centre, metros run until about midnight. Useful metro stops include those at the train stations, Rihour (next to the tourist office), République Beaux Arts (near the Palais des Beaux-Arts), Gambetta (near the Wazemmes market) and Gare Jean Lebas (near La Piscine). Clair de Lune night buses (lines A through G) operate from 9.30pm to 12.30am. In this chapter, places with a metro stop within 500m have the name of the stop noted next to the street address.

Tickets (single/10 €1.20/10.20) are sold on buses but must be purchased (and validated in the orange posts) *before* boarding a metro or tram. A Pass' Journée (all-day pass) costs €3.50 and needs to be time-punched just once.

TAXI
Cabs can be ordered 24 hours a day from **Taxi Gare Lille** (☎ 03 20 06 64 00) and **Taxi Rihour** (☎ 03 20 55 20 56).

CALAIS
pop 77,000

As Churchill might have put it, 'never in the field of human tourism have so many travellers passed through a place and so few stopped to visit.' Indeed, there are few compelling reasons for the 24 million people who travel by way of Calais each year to stop and explore – pity the local tourist office, whose job it is to snag a few of the Britons racing to warmer climes!

That said, the town – a mere 34km from the English town of Dover (Douvres in French) – has three speciality museums, some decent restaurants and, of course, Rodin's *The Burghers of Calais* (below). In addition Calais, once famed for its lace, makes a convenient base for exploring French Flanders and the Channel coast by train, bus or car.

Orientation
Gare Calais-Ville (the train station) is 650m south of the main square, place d'Armes, and 700m north of Calais' relatively un-touristed commercial district, which is around blvd Léon Gambetta and place du Théâtre. The town centre is ringed by canals and ship docks.

On foot, the car ferry terminal is 1.5km northeast of place d'Armes. The Channel Tunnel's vehicle loading area is about 6km southwest of the town centre.

Information
INTERNET
The Post Office has a Cyberposte.

Le Tom Souville (☎ 03 21 35 26 57; 46 rue Royale; per hr €3; ☼ 10am-11pm Mon-Thu, 10am-2am Fri & Sat) Internet access in the back of an unpretentious café. Opening hours can be unpredictable.

LAUNDRY
Be prepared for British border formalities – cross the Channel with clean undies.

Laundrette place d'Armes (☼ 7am-9pm); 36 rue de Thermes (☼ 7am-7pm)

MONEY
Currency exchange is possible aboard car ferries (at a terrible rate) but *not* at the ferry terminal, which lacks even an ATM. In town, banks (open Tuesday to Friday and Saturday morning) are clustered along rue Royale but those that still deal with foreign currency take a sizable commission. Another option is the **Exchange Bureau** (☎ 03 21 97 72 66; 5 rue Royale; ☼ 9.45am-12.30pm & 2-6pm Mon-Fri).

POST
Post Office (place de Rheims) Has a Cyberposte terminal.

TOURIST INFORMATION
Tourist Office (☎ 03 21 96 62 40; www.calais-cotedopale .com; 12 blvd Georges Clemenceau; ☼ 10am-1pm & 2-6.30pm Mon-Sat year-round, 10am-1pm Sun Jul & Aug)

THE BURGHERS OF CALAIS

Rodin sculpted *Les Bourgeois de Calais* in 1895 to honour six local citizens who, in 1347, after eight months of holding off the besieging English forces, surrendered themselves and the keys to the starving city to Edward III. Their hope: that by sacrificing themselves they might save the town and its people. Moved by the entreaties of his consort, Philippa, Edward eventually spared both the Calaisiens and their six brave leaders.

Is it worth a trip to Calais' Flemish Renaissance–style **Hôtel de Ville** (1911–25) just to see Rodin's masterpiece? Actually, you don't even have to come to France to see the work. Other casts of the six emaciated but proud figures, with varying degrees of copper-green patina (many were made posthumously), can be seen in London (next to the Houses of Parliament), the USA (New York, Washington, Philadelphia, Omaha, Stanford University) and even Japan (Shizuoka Prefecture). So moved by the work that you want one at home? You can buy a 66cm-high copy from www.bronzedirect.com – a bargain at US$2500 (plus shipping)!

CALAIS

0 ———— 400 m
0 ———— 0.2 miles

INFORMATION
Exchange Bureau.................................1 B4
Laundrette..2 C3
Laundrette..3 C4
Le Tom Souville.................................4 B4
Post Office...5 C4
Tourist Office.....................................6 B5

SIGHTS & ACTIVITIES
Burghers of Calais Statue.................7 C6
Calais Beach......................................8 A2
Children's Playground.......................9 B6
Colonne Louis XVIII.......................10 B3
Hôtel de Ville..................................11 C5

Lighthouse.......................................12 C3
Musée de la Dentelle et de la Mode....13 D6
Musée de la Guerre.........................14 B6
Musée des Beaux-Arts et de la
  Dentelle...15 C4
Tour de Guet...................................16 B4

SLEEPING
Auberge de Jeunesse......................17 A3
Bonsaï Hôtel....................................18 C5
Camping Municipal.........................19 A2
Hôtel La Sole Meunière...................20 B3
Hôtel Richelieu................................21 B4
Hôtel Victoria..................................22 C3

EATING
Au Cadre Vert..................................23 B4
Aux Mouettes..................................24 B4
Food Market....................................25 B4
Histoire Ancienne............................26 B4
La Maison du Fromage et des Vin......(see 23)
La Pléiade.......................................27 B4

Match Supermarket.........................28 C4
Tonnerre de Brest............................29 B4

ENTERTAINMENT
Cinéma Alhambra............................30 C6
Club 555..31 B4

SHOPPING
Les Quatre Boulevards.....................32 C6
Royal Dentelle..................................33 C6

TRANSPORT
ADA..34 C3
BCD Buses to Dunkirk......................35 B5
Car Ferry Terminal...........................36 D2
France Cars.......................................37 C3
Inglard Buses to Côte d'Opale &
  BCD to Bologne.............................38 C5
P&O Ferries Office & Bus Stop........39 B4
SeaFrance Office..............................40 B4
SeaFrance Shuttle Buses..................41 B4
Shuttle Buses to Ferries...................42 B5

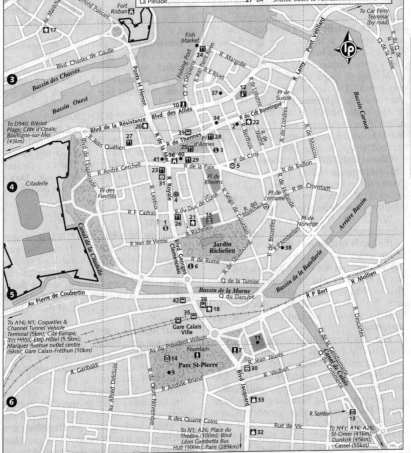

FAR NORTHERN FRANCE

Sights & Activities

The 13th-century **Tour de Guet** (watchtower; place d'Armes), square at the base but octagonal on top, is a rare remnant of pre-20th-century Calais – the rest of the town was virtually demolished during WWII.

The **Musée des Beaux-Arts et de la Dentelle** (Museum of Fine Arts & Lace; ☎ 03 21 46 48 40; 25 rue Richelieu; adult/student €3/1.50, admission free Wed; ☻ 10am-noon & 2-5.30pm Mon & Wed-Fri, 10am-noon & 2-6.30pm Sat, 2-6.30pm Sun) focuses on just two things: modern sculptures, including pieces by Rodin; and the history of lace-making both before and after the first lace machines were smuggled over from England – with French government encouragement – in 1816. Sometime during the winter of 2007–08, a brand new museum dedicated to Calais' glorious lace-making legacy, the **Musée de la Dentelle et de la Mode** (rue Sambor), is set to open in a 19th-century lace factory whose façade has been transformed to look like a giant Jacquard punched card.

Willing to burn calories for a superb panorama? Try climbing the 271 stairs to the top of the **lighthouse** (☎ 03 21 34 33 34; blvd des Alliés; adult/5-15yr €4/2; ☻ 10am-noon & 2-5.30pm or 6.30pm Sat, Sun & holidays year-round, 2-5.30pm or 6.30pm Mon-Fri Jun-Sep, 2-5.30pm or 6.30pm Wed Oct-May & during school holidays), built in 1848.

Colonne Louis XVIII (Louis XVIII Column; blvd des Alliés) commemorates the French king's return from exile in England after the fall of Napoleon (1814). A close inspection will reveal a Hollywood-style imprint of the royal foot.

World War II artefacts (weapons, uniforms, proclamations) fill the display cases of the **Musée de la Guerre** (☎ 03 21 34 21 57; adult/student/family of 5 incl audioguide €6/5/14; ☻ 10am-6pm May-Sep, 11am-5pm Wed-Mon Feb-Apr, noon-5pm Wed-Mon Oct & Nov), housed in a concrete bunker that used to be a German naval headquarters. It sits incongruously in **Parc St-Pierre**, next to a *boules* ground and a **children's playground**.

You can watch huge car ferries sailing majestically towards Dover from Calais' sandy cabin-lined **beach**, which begins 1km northwest of place d'Armes and is linked to town by a **bike path**. The sand continues westward along 8km-long, dune-lined **Blériot Plage**, named after pioneer aviator Louis Blériot, who began the first ever trans-Channel flight from here in 1909. Both beaches are served by buses 3 and 9.

Sleeping

Lots of two-star hotels can be found located along, and also just to the east of, rue Royale.

BUDGET

Camping Municipal (☎ 03 21 97 89 79; av Raymond Poincaré; per adult/site €3.35/2.27; ☻ mid-Apr–Oct) Occupies a grassy but soulless site overlooking the Channel and the ferry port, inside a section of Fort Risban. Served by buses 3 and 9.

Auberge de Jeunesse (☎ 03 21 34 70 20; www .auberge-jeunesse-calais.com; av Maréchal de Lattre de Tassigny; s €21, dm in a double r €16.20; ☻ 24hr) Modern, well-equipped and just 200m from the beach, this 87-bed hostel is a good source of information on local events. Kitchen facilities are available. Served by buses 3 and 9.

Bonsaï Hôtel (☎ 03 21 96 10 10; www.bonsai -hotel.fr; 2 quai du Danube; d/tr €31/35) A 98-room prefabricated construction with a billiard table situated next to the little bar. In triple rooms, the third bed is a bunk above the double bed.

Hôtel Victoria (☎ 03 21 34 38 32; www.hotel-victoria -calais.activehotels.com; 8 rue du Commandant Bonningue; d €39, with washbasin €28) A hotel so ordinary that it could be described as 'extraordinarily ordinary'. The 14 two-star rooms are clean but pretty basic. Don't expect an effusive welcome but overall it's good value.

MIDRANGE

Hôtel La Sole Meunière (☎ 03 21 96 86 66; 53 rue de la Mer; s/d/q €47/54/80) A family-run two-star place named after the ground-floor restaurant, which – you guessed it – specialises in butter-sautéed sole. Some of the 19 fresh, pastel rooms have electric toilets that grind every time you flush. The best rooms have views of the port.

Hôtel Richelieu (☎ 03 21 34 61 60; www.hotel richelieu-calais.com in French; 17 rue Richelieu; d/2-room q €55/110) At this quiet two-star place, the 15 cheery rooms, each one unique, are outfitted with antique furniture redeemed by the owner from local markets.

In Coquelles next to the Cité Europe shopping mall (and near the Channel Tunnel vehicle loading area) are **Etap Hôtel** (☎ 0 892 683 059; place de Cantorbéry; s/tr €36/42) and **Hôtel Ibis** (☎ 03 21 46 37 00; place de Cantorbéry; d Mon-Fri/

weekend €57/67). Both charge a bit more in July and August.

Eating

Calais is a good place for a first or last meal on the Continent. Rue Royal and place d'Armes are lined with eateries.

Tonnerre de Brest (☎ 03 21 96 95 35; 16 place d'Armes; Mon-Fri lunch menus €10-17.80; ☯ closed Mon except Jul & Aug) At this informal, rustic eatery, run by two sisters, you can wash down with *cidre* (cider) 19 kinds of savoury *galettes*, 30 sorts of sweet *crêpes* or a large salad (€9.80).

Histoire Ancienne (☎ 03 21 34 11 20; 20 rue Royale; 2-/3-/5-course menus €11/17.50/22; ☯ closed Sun & dinner Mon) Specialising in meat and fish dishes grilled over an open wood fire, this 1930s Paris-style bistro also has treats such as *escargots à l'ail* (snails with garlic) and *pied et oreille de cochon grillés* (grilled pig's trotter and ear). The toilets take full advantage of the latest self-cleaning technology.

Aux Mouettes (☎ 03 21 34 67 59; 10 rue Jean Pierre Avron; menus €16-32; ☯ closed Mon & dinner Sun) Fisherfolk sell their daily catch across the street at the quay – easy to see how this unassuming place manages to serve only the very freshest fish and seafood.

La Pléiade (☎ 03 21 34 03 70; 32 rue Jean Quéhen; menus €22-55; ☯ closed Sun & Mon) Some loyal customers come over from England just to dine here on *bar* (sea bass), *turbot*, *sole* and other superfresh fish dishes, prepared differently for each season.

Au Cadre Vert (☎ 03 21 34 69 44; 3 rue André Gerschell; ☯ closed Sun, lunch Sat & lunch Wed) A family-run French restaurant known for its generous portions and reasonable prices. Specialities include *magret de canard* (duck breast fillet) in raspberry sauce and *côte de bœuf sauce peurotte* (beef ribs in mushroom sauce).

SELF-CATERING

Picnic supplies are available at boulangeries along rue Royale and at the following places:

Food market (place d'Armes; ☯ about 7am-1pm Wed & Sat)

La Maison du Fromage et des Vins (☎ 03 21 34 44 72; 1 rue André Gerschell; ☯ 3-7.30pm Mon, 8.30am-12.30pm & 3-7.30pm Wed-Fri, 8am-1pm & 2.30-7.30pm Sat, 10am-1pm Sun) Sells delectable cheeses and fine wines.

Match supermarket (place d'Armes; ☯ 9am-7.30pm Mon-Sat year-round, 9am-noon Sun Jun-Aug)

Entertainment

Club 555 (☎ 03 21 34 74 60; 63 rue Royale; admission incl one drink €10; ☯ 11pm-5am Tue-Sun) The '70s meet techno at this discotheque, which has space for 700 revellers (mainly locals in their twenties), a polychromatic bar, plenty of banquettes for hanging out and an isolated corner for nonsmokers. The music is mixed; there's a theme party every Friday.

Cinéma Alhambra (☎ 03 21 17 73 33; 2 rue Jean Jaurès) Screens nondubbed films in its four halls.

Getting There & Around

For details on options for crossing the Channel, see p975 and p971.

BOAT

Every day, 32 to 40 car ferries from Dover dock at Calais' busy car ferry terminal, about 1.5km northeast of place d'Armes. Company bureaus:

P&O Ferries Calais town centre (41 place d'Armes); car ferry terminal (☎ 03 21 46 10 10; ☯ 6am-10pm)

SeaFrance Calais town centre (☎ 03 21 19 42 42; 2 place d'Armes); car ferry terminal (☎ 03 21 46 80 05; ☯ 5.45am-10.45pm)

Shuttle buses (€1.50 or £1, hourly from about 10am to 7pm or 7.30pm), marked 'Terminal Car Ferry/Centre Ville', link Gare Calais-Ville and place d'Armes (the stop is in front of Café de la Tour) with the car ferry terminal. Departure times are posted.

Hoverspeed, the company that pioneered the use of hovercraft – the pride of British maritime engineering in the 1960s – ceased operations in late 2005.

BUS

Inglard (☎ 03 21 96 49 54; office in the car ferry terminal) links Calais' train station, via the coastal D940, with the beautiful Côte d'Opale and Boulogne (€5.10, 1¼ hours, three daily except Sunday and holidays), where stops are at Nausicaä and 75 blvd Daunou in Boulogne.

Cariane Littoral (☎ 03 21 34 74 40; office 10 rue d'Amsterdam) operates BCD express services from Calais' train station to Boulogne (€6.90, 40 minutes, four daily Monday to Friday, two on Saturday), where bus stops are at the train station and place Dalton,

SHOP TILL YOU DROP IN CALAIS

Calais' shops and hypermarkets supply day-tripping *rosbifs* (Britons) with everything except, perhaps, roast beef. Items eagerly sought 'on the Continent' include delicious edibles (terrines, cheeses, gourmet prepared dishes) and drinkables (fine wine, cheap plonk, beer and champagne) that are hard to find – or much more expensive – in the land of the pound sterling.

The enormous steel-and-glass shopping centre **Cité Europe** (☎ 03 21 46 47 48; www.cite-europe .com; blvd du Kent; ◷ 10am-8pm Mon-Thu, 10am-9pm Fri, 9am-8pm Sat) is in Coquelles, next to the vehicle-loading area for the Channel Tunnel. Its 130 shops include a vast **Carrefour hypermarket** (◷ 9am-10pm Mon-Sat) and wine shops where buying alcohol in bulk to carry home in the boot is made easy.

Right nearby is the **Marques Avenue outlet centre** (☎ 03 21 17 07 70; www.marquesavenue.com; blvd du Parc, Coquelles; ◷ 10am-8pm Mon-Sat), whose 57 shops boast discount clothing and accessories by 80 designers.

In-town shopping options include **Les Quatre Boulevards** (blvd Jacquard), a new shopping mall with about two dozen shops right in the middle of Calais' commercial district. Genuine *dentelle de Calais* (Calais lace) – we're talking placemats and tablecloths – is available at **Royal Dentelle** (☎ 03 21 96 68 40; www.royal-dentelle.com; 106 blvd Jacquard; ◷ closed Mon morning & Sun year-round, closed Mon afternoon Jan-Mar).

To get to Cité Europe by car, take the A16 to exit Nos 12 or 14; for Marques Avenue, use exit No 12. Calais bus 5 goes to Cité Europe.

and Dunkirk (€7.40, 45 minutes, 12 daily Monday to Friday, three on Saturday).

CAR & MOTORCYCLE

To reach the Channel Tunnel's vehicle loading area at Coquelles, follow the road signs on the A16 to the Tunnel Sous La Manche (Tunnel under the Channel) at exit No 13.

Avis, Budget, Europcar, Hertz and National-Citer have bureaus at the car ferry terminal but they're not always staffed. Cheaper walk-in rates may be available from the following outfits:

ADA (☎ 03 21 36 50 12; 15 rue de Thermes)
France Cars (☎ 03 21 96 08 00; 47 blvd des Alliés)

TAXI

To order a cab, call **Taxis Radio Calais** (TRC; ☎ 03 21 97 13 14).

TRAIN

Calais has two train stations: Gare Calais-Ville in the city centre; and Gare Calais-Fréthun, a TGV station 10km southwest of town near the Channel Tunnel entrance. They are linked by the free Navette TER.

Gare Calais-Ville is linked to Amiens (€21, 2½ hours, four or five daily), Arras (€18, two hours, 12 daily Monday to Friday, five daily Saturday and Sunday), Boulogne (€6.90, 28 to 48 minutes, 17 daily Monday to Saturday, nine on Sunday), Dunkirk

(€7.40, 50 minutes, six daily Monday to Friday, three or four daily Saturday and Sunday) and Lille-Flandres (€14.70, 1¼ hours, 19 daily Monday to Friday, 10 on Saturday and Sunday).

Calais-Fréthun is served by TGVs to Paris' Gare du Nord (€37.20 or €50.60, 1½ hours, six daily Monday to Saturday, three on Sunday) as well as the Eurostar to London.

ST-OMER

pop 15,700

St-Omer is said to be the first truly French town you come to after landing at Calais – its river, the Aa, is certainly the first one you'll come across in any alphabetised list of the world's waterways. The town is justly renowned for its richly furnished 13th- to 15th-century **basilica** (entrance via the south transept arm; ◷ 8am-5pm or later), downgraded from cathedral status in 1801. The only major Gothic church in the region, it's a real gem; much of the woodwork, including the main altar and breathtaking baroque organ, dates from the 1700s. In the ambulatory, the rough-hewn tomb of the 8th-century Irish monk St-Erkembode has on top a row of toddlers' shoes, placed there by the parents of children with walking difficulties in the hope of saintly intercession.

The **tourist office** (☎ 03 21 98 08 51; www.tourisme -saint-omer.com; 4 rue du Lion d'Or; ◷ 9am-6pm Mon-Sat,

10am-1pm Sun & holidays Easter-Sep, 9am-12.30pm & 2-6pm Mon-Sat except holidays Oct-Easter) is one block north of place Foch, the typically northern-French square in front of the neoclassical **Hôtel de Ville** (1830).

The **Musée Sandelin** (☎ 03 21 38 00 94; http://m3 .dnsalias.com/sandelin in French; 14 rue Carnot; adult/15-25yr €4.50/3; ☼ 10am-noon & 2-6pm Wed-Sun, to 8pm Thu), with displays that include ceramics, *objets d'art* and paintings, is housed in a harmonious townhouse built in 1776. A number of rooms are furnished in a style that suited the refined lifestyle of the Enlightenment elite. To get there from place Foch, walk a block south and then a long block east.

North and northeast of town, the 36-sq-km **Marais Audomarois** (Audomarois Marsh), its market gardens crisscrossed by *watergangs* (canals), is home to all sorts of wildlife, including 250 kinds of bird, 19 species of dragonfly and 11 types of bat. The area can be explored on foot or by boat, including flat-bottomed *bacôves*. In Clairmarais, 5km northeast of St-Omer, **Isnor** (☎ 03 21 39 15 15; www.isnor.fr in French; 3 rue du Marais; canoe for 4hr €25; ☼ Sat, Sun & holidays Apr-Sep, daily Jul & Aug) rents canoes and runs boat excursions. The tourist office can supply a brochure with walking options.

About 5km east of St-Omer in Arques, the tableware conglomerate **Arc International** (☎ 03 21 12 74 74; www.arc-international.com; Zone Industrielle; adult/student €5.50/3.50), which markets the six million items it manufactures each day under brands such as Arcoroc, Luminarc and Mikasa, runs guided tours (often in English) of its factory – glowing globules of glass! – at 9.30am, 11am, 2pm and 3.30pm from Monday to Saturday.

Le Vivier (☎ 03 21 95 76 00; www.au-vivier-sainto mer.com; 22 rue Louis Martel; d €55), a block south of the Hôtel de Ville in St-Omer, has seven comfortable but ordinary two-star rooms and a fine fish and seafood **restaurant** (menus €17-35; ☼ closed dinner Sun).

There are quite a few good-value restaurants (lunch *menus* from €9) around the perimeter of place Foch and adjacent place P Bonhomme, and along rue Louis Martel. **Le Cygne** (☎ 03 21 98 20 52; www.restaurantlecygne.fr; 8 rue Caventou; menus €13-45; ☼ closed dinner Sun & Mon), two blocks east of the basilica, is an elegant French eatery that uses only the freshest seasonal ingredients. There's a lively **food market** (place Foch; ☼ Sat morning).

St-Omer's train station, 1.5km northeast of the Hôtel de Ville, has frequent services to Calais (€6.70, 30 minutes, 25 daily Monday to Friday, eight to 10 daily Saturday and Sunday) and Lille-Flandres (€10, 50 minutes, 17 daily Monday to Friday, five to seven on Saturday and Sunday).

LA COUPOLE

A top-secret subterranean V2 launch site just five minutes' flying time from London – almost (but not quite) put into operation in 1944 – now houses **La Coupole** (☎ 03 21 12 27 27; www.lacoupole.com; adult/5-16yr incl audioguide €9/6; ☼ 9am-6pm, to 7pm Jul & Aug, closed 2 weeks from Christmas), an innovative museum that uses lots of moving images to present Nazi Germany's secret programmes to build V1 and V2 rockets (which could fly at 650km/h and an astounding 5780km/h respectively); life in northern France during the Nazi occupation; and the postwar conquest of space with the help of V2 rocket technology – and seconded V2 engineers.

La Coupole is 5km south of St-Omer (the circuitous route is signposted but confusing) just outside the town of Wizernes, near the intersection of the D928 and the D210. From the A26, take exit No 3 or 4.

CASSEL
pop 2300

The fortified, very Flemish village of Cassel, 57km southeast of Calais atop French Flanders' highest hill (176m), affords panoramic views of the verdant Flanders plain. A **bagpipe festival** is held here each year on the weekend nearest 21 June. Cassel is enormously proud of Reuze Papa and Reuze Maman, its resident giants (p226).

The main square, fringed by austere brick buildings with steep slate roofs, is where you'll find the **Tourist Office** (☎ 03 28 40 52 55; www.cassel-horizons.com; 20 Grand' Place; ☼ 8.30am-noon & 1.30-5.30pm Mon-Fri, 8.30am-noon Sat year-round, 8.30am-noon & 2-5.30pm Sat, 2.30-6.30pm Sun May-Sep) and **Cassel Horizons** (adult €2.80; ☼ same hours;), an interactive museum which presents Cassel's history in an easily digestible form.

Eight or 10 generations ago, wheat flour was milled and linseed oil pressed just as it is today at the wooden **moulin** (windmill; adult/child €2.80/2.40; ☼ 2-6pm Mon-Sat, 9am-12.30pm & 2-6pm Sun Apr-Jun & Sep, 9am-12.30pm & 2-6pm Mon-Sat Jul & Aug, 2-6pm Sat & school holidays, 9am-12.30pm

FAR NORTHERN FRANCE

CASSEL AT WAR

Cassel served as Maréchal Ferdinand Foch's headquarters at the beginning of WWI. In 1940, it was the site of intensive rearguard resistance by British troops defending Dunkirk during the evacuation.

& 2-6pm Sun Oct–mid-Dec & mid-Jan–Mar, last tour begins 1hr before closing), perched on the highest point in town to catch the wind. The 30-minute, hands-on tour is noisy but interesting. The arms were upgraded in 2006. During the 19th century the skyline of French Flanders was dotted with 2000 such windmills.

Le Foch (☎ 03 28 42 47 73; www.hotel-foch.net in French; 41 Grand' Place; d €72; ✗) has six spacious rooms with antique-style beds, some with views of the square. The elegant, 20-seat **restaurant** (menus €13.50-23; ✒ closed Tue) specialises in traditional French cuisine made with fresh local ingredients.

Taverne Flamande (☎ 03 28 42 42 59; 34 Grand' Place; menus €12-23.50; ✒ closed Wed & dinner Tue) serves tasty Flemish dishes in a classic dining room that dates from 1933.

Cassel's train station, once linked to the town centre (3km up the hill) by a tram, is on the secondary line linking Dunkirk (€5.30, 27 minutes, five to eight daily) with Arras (€11.80, 1¼ hours, five to eight daily).

DUNKIRK

pop 191,000

Dunkirk (Dunkerque), made famous and flattened almost simultaneously (in 1940), was rebuilt during one of the most unin-

spired periods in Western architecture. Charming it may not be, but the port city has two worthwhile museums, a mellow beach and several colourful pre-Lent carnivals.

Under Louis XIV, Dunkirk – whose name means 'church of the dunes' in Flemish – served as a base for French privateers, including the daring Jean Bart (1650–1702), whose hugely successful attacks on English and Dutch merchant ships have ensured his infamy in British history and, locally, his status as a national hero: the city centre's main square, suitably adorned with a dashing **statue** (1845), bears his name, as does a high school.

Inside the base of a 58m-high **belfry** (adult €2.80), erected around 1440, is Dunkirk's **Tourist Office** (☎ 03 28 66 79 21; www.lesdunesdeflandre.fr; rue de l'Amiral Ronarc'h; ✒ 9am-12.30pm & 1.30-6.30pm Mon-Sat, 10am-noon & 2-4pm Sun & holidays, no midday closure Jul & Aug). Staff can supply you with an **MP3 tour** (€3.50) of the city's WWI and WWII sites and have details on **boat tours** (adult/7-12yr €7.50/5.50; ✒ afternoon Tue-Sat Jul & Aug, also often possible Apr-May, Sep & perhaps Oct) of the port.

Sights & Activities

The **Musée Portuaire** (Harbour Museum; ☎ 03 28 63 33 39; www.museeportuaire.com; 9 quai de la Citadelle; adult/student €4/3; ✒ 10am-12.45pm & 1.30-6pm Wed-Mon, no midday closure Jul & Aug), housed in a one-time tobacco warehouse, will delight ship-model-lovers of all ages. Forty-five-minute guided **tours** (€6/5, incl the museum €8/6.50) take visitors aboard several historic water craft, including the *Duchesse Anne*, a three-masted training ship built for the German

---

THE BATTLE OF AGINCOURT

Agincourt (Azincourt; population 275) entered the history books on 25 October 1415 when English archers and men-at-arms – led by King Henry V – inflicted an overwhelming defeat on superior French forces in one of the bloodiest engagements of the Hundred Years' War. Against minimal losses of their own, the axe- and sword-wielding English killed 6000 of their opponents, whose cavalry and foot soldiers were weighed down by heavy armour made all the more cumbersome by soggy terrain.

The **Centre Historique Médiéval Azincourt** (☎ 03 21 47 27 53; www.azincourt-medieval.com; adult/5-16yr €6.50/5; ✒ 9am-7pm Jul & Aug, 10am-5pm or 6pm Sep-Jun, closed Tue Nov-Mar) uses the latest audio-visual technology (English available) and copies of 15th-century armaments to bring alive both the battle and its context – fun for kids who are curious about knights in shining armour.

The **Champ de Bataille** (battlefield), 2.5km southeast of the museum, along the D71 (at the intersection of the D107-E2 and the D104), is marked by a granite column and a viewpoint indicator showing the battle's progression.

THE EVACUATION OF DUNKIRK

In May and June 1940, Dunkirk earned a place in the history books when the British Expeditionary Force and French and Belgian units in far northern France found themselves almost completely surrounded by Hitler's armies. In an effort to salvage what it could, Churchill's government ordered British units to make their way to Dunkirk, where naval vessels and hundreds of fishing boats and pleasure craft – many manned by civilian volunteers – braved intense German artillery and air attacks to ferry 340,000 men to the safety of England. Conducted in the difficult first year of WWII, this unplanned and chaotic evacuation – dubbed Operation Dynamo – failed to save any of the units' heavy equipment but was, nevertheless, seen as a key demonstration of Britain's resourcefulness and determination.

merchant marine in 1901 and acquired by France as WWII reparations.

The **Musée d'Art Contemporain** (☎ 03 28 29 56 00; av des Bains; 1st/2nd adult €4.50/3; ⏰ 2-5.30pm Tue, Wed & Fri, 2-8.30pm Thu, 10am-12.30pm & 2-5.30pm Sat & Sun, to 6.30pm Tue, Wed & Fri-Sun May-Sep), a few hundred metres from the western end of Malo-les-Bains' beach, features oftenwhimsical, 'evolving' expositions of contemporary art in its eight halls, each of which has some sort of theme. Outside is a sculpture garden.

The somewhat faded, turn-of-the-20th-century seaside resort of **Malo-les-Bains** is 2km northeast of Dunkirk's city centre. Its wide, promenade-lined beach, **Plage des Alliés**, is named in honour of the Allied troops evacuated to England from here in 1940 (above). Just off the coast, vessels sunk during the evacuation can be visited on scuba dives, and some can even be seen at low tide.

The **British Memorial** (rte de Furnes), honouring more than 4500 British and Commonwealth MIAs (soldiers Missing in Action) from 1940, is 1.5km southeast of the tourist office. A military museum dedicated to the evacuation, the **Memorial du Souvenir** (☎ 03 28 26 27 81; www.dynamo-dunkerque.com; rue des Chantiers de France; admission €3.50; ⏰ 10am-noon & 2-5pm Apr-Sep), is next to the Musée d'Art Contemporain.

Stretching east from Malo-les-Bains to the Belgian border, the *dunes flamandes* (Flemish dunes) represent a unique ecosystem harbouring hundreds of plant species, including rare orchids. The area – including the **Dewulf & Marchand dunes** – is linked to Dunkirk by local bus 2B (3B on Sunday and holidays), which continues on to Adinkerke in Belgium (€1.30, an extra €0.80 to cross the border). Tides permitting, you can walk or cycle along the wet sand or the GR from Malo-les-Bains to Bray-Dunes and Westhoek.

Festivals & Events

Dunkirk's **carnival**, held at the beginning of Lent, originated as a final fling for the town's cod fishermen before they set out for months on the waters off Iceland. The biggest celebration is the *bande* (parade) held on the Sunday right before Mardi Gras, when men traditionally dress up as women, costumed citizens of all genders march around town behind fife-and-drum bands and general merriment reigns. At the climax of the festivities, the mayor and other dignitaries stand on the Hôtel de Ville balcony and pelt the assembled locals with dried salted herrings.

Eating

Dunkirk is not known for its gastronomy, to put it mildly.

Entre Ciel et Mer (☎ 03 28 59 39 00; 16 rue de Flandre, Malo-les-Bains; menus €14.50-23; ⏰ closed dinner Sun & Mon) This place, between the beach and place Turenne, is a good choice for fish and seafood.

Getting There & Away

For details on links to Calais, see p239. Almost all the trains to Lille stop at Lille-Flandres (€12.20, 35 to 70 minutes, 15 to 30 daily).

Vehicle ferries run by **Norfolk Line** (☎ in the UK 0870-870 1020, in France 03 28 28 95 50; www .norfolkline.com) link Dunkirk's Car Ferry port, about 20km west of the town centre near Loon Plage, with Dover.

CÔTE D'OPALE

The 40km of cliffs, sand dunes and beaches between Calais and Boulogne, known as the Opal Coast because of the ever-changing interplay of greys and blues in the sea and sky, are a dramatic and beautiful introduction to France. The coastal peaks (frequently buffeted by gale-force winds), wide beaches and rolling farmland are dotted with the remains of Nazi Germany's Atlantic Wall, a chain of fortifications and gun emplacements built to prevent the Allied invasion that in the end took place in Normandy. The seashore has been attracting British beach-lovers since the Victorian era.

Part of the **Parc Naturel Régional des Caps et Marais d'Opale** (Opal Coast Headlands & Marshes Regional Park; www.parc-opale.fr), the Côte d'Opale area is crisscrossed by hiking paths, including the GR Littoral trail that hugs the coast. Some routes are also suitable for mountain biking and horse riding. Each village along the Côte d'Opale has at least one camp site.

By car, the D940 offers some spectacular vistas. Inglard buses (p239) link all the sights and villages mentioned below with Calais and Boulogne.

Sights

The Channel Tunnel slips under the Strait of Dover 8km west of Calais at the village of **Sangatte**, known for its wide beach. Southwest of there, the coastal dunes give way to cliffs that culminate in windswept, 134m-high **Cap Blanc-Nez**, which affords breathtaking views of the Bay of Wissant, the port of Calais, the Flemish countryside (pockmarked by Allied bomb craters) and the cliffs of Kent. The whole site is being restored and upgraded. The grey **obelisk**, a short walk up the hill from the new parking area, honours the WWI Dover Patrol.

The tidy and very French seaside resort of **Wissant** (tourist office ☎ 03 21 82 48 00), a good base for walks in the rolling countryside, boasts a vast fine-sand beach – in 55 BC Julius Caesar launched his invasion of Britain from here. **Hôtel Le Vivier** (☎ 03 21 35 93 61; www.levivier.com; place de l'Église; d with breakfast €60-82, with washbasin €44), across the street from the church and next to the mill pond, has 39 nicely appointed rooms and a homy, nautically themed **restaurant** (menus €15-35.50; ☙ closed Tue & Wed) specialising in fresh local fish and seafood.

Topped by a lighthouse and a radar station serving the 600 ships that pass by each day, the 45m-high cliffs of **Cap Gris-Nez** are only 28km from the white cliffs of the English coast. The name – in French, 'Grey Nose' – is a corruption of the archaic Eng-

lish 'craig ness', meaning 'rocky promontory'. The area is a stopping-off point for millions of migrating birds.

Oodles of WWII hardware, including a gargantuan rail-borne German artillery piece with an 86km range, are on display at the **Musée du Mur de l'Atlantique** (☎ 03 21 32 97 33; www.batterietodt.com; adult/8-14yr €5.50/2.50

FAR NORTHERN FRANCE

9am-7pm Jun-Sep, 9am-noon & 2-6pm Oct, Nov & Feb-May), which occupies a Brobdingnagian German pillbox with the word *'musée'* inscribed on the side. It is 500m off the D940 just southwest of Audinghen.

The village of **Ambleteuse**, on the northern side of the mouth of the River Slack, is blessed with a lovely beach once defended from attack by 17th-century **Fort d'Ambleteuse**, designed by Vauban. Just south of town is a protected area of grass-covered dunes known as **Dunes de la Slack**.

The neatly organised **Musée 39-45** (☎ 03 21 87 33 01; www.musee3945.com; adult/7-14yr €6/4.30; ⊙ 9.30am-6pm Apr–mid-Oct, Sat & Sun only rest of year, closed Jan, Feb & perhaps Dec), at the northern edge of Ambleteuse, features realistic tableaux of military and civilian life and a 25-minute film. The dashing but impractical French officers' dress uniforms of 1931 hint at why France fared so badly on the battlefield in 1940. The soundtrack comes from a CD entitled *The Songs that Won the War* (€12.50).

BOULOGNE-SUR-MER

pop 45,000

Boulogne, by far the most interesting of France's Channel ports, makes a pretty good first stop in France, especially if combined with a swing through the Côte d'Opale. Most of the city is an uninspiring mass of postwar reconstruction, but the attractive Ville Haute (Upper City), perched high above the rest of town, is girded by a 13th-century wall. Another draw: Nausicaä, one of Europe's premier aquariums.

Orientation

Central Boulogne consists of the hilltop Ville Haute and, on the flats below, the Basse Ville (Lower City). The main train station, Gare Boulogne-Ville, is 1.2km southeast of the centre.

Information

There are laundrettes at 235 rue Nationale and 62 rue de Lille (both open 7am to 8pm). Several commercial banks can be found on or near rue Victor Hugo.

Main Post Office (place Frédéric Sauvage; ⊙ 8am-6.30pm Mon-Fri, 8am-12.30pm Sat) Changes money and has a Cyberposte.

Tourist Office (☎ 03 21 10 88 10; www.tourisme-boulognesurmer.com; forum Jean Noël; ⊙ 9am-7pm

Mon-Sat, 10.15am-1.15pm & 3-6pm Sun & holidays Jul & Aug, 9am-12.15pm & 1.30-6.30pm Mon-Sat, 10.15am-1.15pm Sun & holidays Sep-Jun)

Tourist Office Kiosk (outside Nausicaä; ☎ 03 21 33 92 51; ⊙ Sat, Sun & holidays Easter-Sep, daily July & Aug)

Sights

You can walk all the way around the **Ville Haute** – an island of centuries-old buildings and cobblestone streets – atop of the rectangular, tree-shaded **ramparts**, making up a distance of just under 1.5km. Among the impressive buildings around place Godefroy de Bouillon are the neoclassical **Hôtel Desandrouin**, built in the 1780s and later employed by Napoleon, and the brick **Hôtel de Ville** (1735), with its square medieval belfry.

Basilique Notre Dame (rue de Lille; ⊙ 10-11.45am & 2-5pm, to 6pm May-Sep), with a towering, Italianate dome visible from all over town, was built from 1827 to 1866 with little input from trained architects. The partly Romanesque **crypt** and **treasury** (admission €2; ⊙ 2-5pm Tue-Sun) are eminently skippable.

The cultures of the world unite at the **Château-Musée** (☎ 03 21 10 02 20; adult/student €2/free; ⊙ 10am-12.30pm & 2-5pm Mon & Wed-Sat, 10am-12.30pm & 2.30-5.30pm Sun), one of the few places on earth where you can admire Egyptian antiquities (including a mummy) next to 19th-century Inuit masks and compare Andean ceramics with Grecian urns, with an *in situ*, 4th-century Roman wall thrown in for good measure – all inside a 13th-century fortified castle.

And now for something even more unexpected: the house where José de San Martín, the exiled hero of Argentine, Chilean and Peruvian independence, died in 1850 has been turned into the **Musée Libertador San Martín** (☎ 03 21 31 54 65; 113 Grande Rue; admission free; ⊙ 10am-noon & 2-6pm Tue-Sat), owned by the Argentine government. Ring the bell for a free English tour of this piece of South America, complete with memorabilia related to San Martín's life and lots of gaudy military uniforms.

The most interesting thing to do in the mostly postwar **Ville Basse** is to stroll along the **fishing port** (quai Gambetta), where you'll find fish vendors – and hungry seagulls diving and squawking overhead. The **shopping precinct** is centred on rue Victor Hugo and rue Adolphe Thiers.

FAR NORTHERN FRANCE

BOULOGNE-SUR-MER

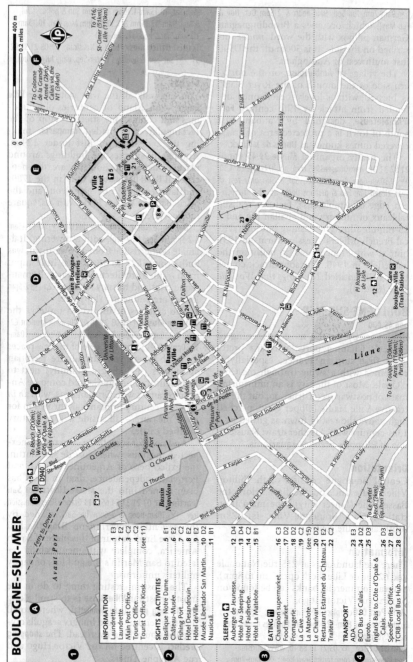

INFORMATION	
Laundrette..........................	1 E3
Laundrette..........................	2 E2
Main Post Office...................	3 C2
Tourist Office......................	4 C2
Tourist Office Kiosk..............	(see 11)

SIGHTS & ACTIVITIES	
Basilique Notre Dame............	5 E1
Château-Musée.....................	6 E2
Fishing Port.........................	7 B2
Hôtel Desandrouin................	8 E2
Hôtel deVille........................	9 E2
Musée Libertador San Martin..	10 D2
Nausicaá.............................	11 B1

SLEEPING	
Auberge de Jeunesse............	12 D4
Hôtel Au Sleeping.................	13 D4
Hôtel Faidherbe...................	14 C3
Hôtel La Matelote................	15 B1

EATING	
Champion supermarket.........	16 C3
Food market........................	17 D2
Fromagerie..........................	18 E2
La Cave...............................	19 E2
La Matelote.........................	(see 15)
Le Chativari........................	20 D2
Restaurant Estaminet du Château	21 E2
Traiteur...............................	22 C2

TRANSPORT	
ADA....................................	23 E3
BCD Bus to Calais.................	24 D2
Eurotó.................................	25 D3
Inglard Bus to Côte d'Opale & Calais	26 D3
SpeedFerries Office...............	27 B1
TCRB Local Bus Hub..............	28 C2

NAUSICAÄ

This outstanding, completely bilingual **marine aquarium** (☎ 03 21 30 98 98; www.nausicaa.fr; blvd Ste-Beuve; adult/3-12yr Apr-Sep €13/9.30, Oct-Mar €11.50/8.30, student €10.50, audioguide €3; ⊙ 9.30am-7.30pm Jul & Aug, 9.30am-6.30pm Sep-Jun, closed 3 weeks in mid-Jan), whose focus is the sustainable use of marine resources, comes with lots of kid-friendly activities (fish petting, a California sea-lion tank, feeding sessions). Educational in the best sense of the word, you can see up-close everything from see-through jellyfish and sharks to speckled caimans (in the **Submerged Forest**) and arawanas, fish that can hop out of the water to pluck birds from overhanging branches. The interactive **Environment-Friendly House** – with a bicycle parked out front, of course – looks at things we can do in our daily lives to safeguard the planet. From 2006 to 2009, an 'expedition' entitled **Cap au Sud** will take visitors on a journey of exploration to the seas around Africa. If the prices look like they'll do to your pocket what drag nets do to the oceans, remember that going to the cinema to see *Finding Nemo* and *A Fish Called Wanda* would cost about the same.

At the cafés you can dine on herring, mackerel and haddock – kind of like a zoo that sells lionburgers, some might say, but don't forget that Boulogne is Europe's most important fish-processing centre.

BEACHES

Boulogne's beach begins just north of Nausicaä, across the mouth of the Liane from the vaguely menacing steelworks (now closed and being demolished and de-contaminated) and a whirring wind farm. There are other fine beaches 4km north of town at **Wimereux** (bus 1 and 2, two to four times per hour), a partly *belle époque*–style resort founded by Napoleon in 1806; 2.5km southwest at **Le Portel** (bus 23); and 5km south at **Equihen Plage** (bus 11).

Sleeping

Auberge de Jeunesse (☎ 03 21 99 15 30; boulogne-sur-mer@fuaj.org; place Rouget de Lisle; dm with breakfast & sheets €15.85; ⊙ closed Jan, reception closed noon-5pm Sat & Sun Sep-Mar or Apr; ▢) This modern outfit has spacious rooms with shower, toilet and two to five beds – fairly luxurious as far as hostels go. Kitchen facilities are available.

Hôtel Au Sleeping (☎ 03 21 80 62 79; http://perso .wanadoo.fr/hotelsleeping; 18 blvd Daunou; s/d €30/34; ⊙ reception closed after 1pm Sun except Jul & Aug) The furnishings may be simple but the welcome is warm and the 12 two-star rooms are clean, bright and soundproofed.

Hôtel Faidherbe (☎ 03 21 31 60 93; www.hotelfaid herbe.fr; 12 rue Faidherbe; d €53-58, Jul–mid-Sep €58-64) A superfriendly two-star hotel where every guest elicits some sort of response from the house mascot, a mynah bird named Victor – his repertoire includes laughing, coughing and squawking *bonjour, au revoir* and bye-bye. The 34 rooms are smallish but modern and practical.

Hôtel La Matelote (☎ 03 21 30 33 33; www.la-mate lote.com; 70 blvd Ste-Beuve; d Sun-Thu €95-140, Fri & Sat €110-160; ⊠ ⅏) Boulogne's only four-star hotel. The 29 spacious rooms, decorated in rich shades of red and gold, have classic wood furnishings.

Eating

Thanks to its ready supply, Boulogne is an excellent place for fresh fish. In the Ville Haute, rue de Lille is lined with intimate eateries. In the Ville Basse, the area around place Dalton and rue du Doyen has a good choice of eateries.

Le Charivari (☎ 03 21 30 01 02; www.lecharivari .fr; 3-7 rue du Doyen; lunch menus €10, other menus €14.50) A Savoyard restaurant featuring hearty Alpine treats such as *potence* (grilled beef flambéed at your table; €14), *pierre chaude* (beef or poultry you cook – as you can guess from the name – on a hot rock; €14) as well as fondue and *raclette* (melted cheese and potatoes). A great hit with the locals, who seem to crave anything reminiscent of Alpine crags.

Restaurant Estaminet du Château (☎ 03 21 91 49 66; 2 rue du Château; menus €16-34; ⊠) Meat dishes are an option but this place – a veteran French restaurant with an informal rustic feel – is especially strong on fish and seafood.

La Cave (☎ 03 21 32 71 60; 24 rue du Port d'Étain; menu €22; ⊙ closed Mon, lunch Sat & dinner Sun) This restaurant–piano bar, on a desolate side street, serves excellent French cuisine, including *escargots* (six/12 for €7/14). There's live music in the cellar on Saturday night.

La Matelote (☎ 03 21 30 17 97; 80 blvd Ste-Beuve; menus €25-72; ⊙ closed dinner Sun & lunch Thu) A classy establishment with white tablecloths, fine porcelain and one Michelin star. Serves French-style *cuisine de saveurs* (cuisine that mixes savours and flavours) with an emphasis on fish.

SELF-CATERING
Food shops are sprinkled around rue de la Lampe and rue Adolphe Thiers and, in the Ville Haute, along rue de Lille. Places to pick up picnic supplies:

Champion supermarket (53 blvd Daunou; ☉ 8.30am-8pm)

Food market (place Dalton; ☉ morning Wed & Sat) Held the day before if Wednesday or Saturday is a holiday.

Fromagerie (☎ 03 21 87 58 53; 23 Grande Rue; ☉ closed morning Mon & Sun)

Traiteur (☎ 03 21 31 53 57; 1 Grande Rue; ☉ closed Sun afternoon & Mon) Ready-to-eat delicacies.

Getting There & Around
BOAT
SpeedFerries (☎ UK 0870 22 00 570, France 03 21 10 50 00; www.speedferries.com) offers an ultramodern catamaran between Boulogne and Dover (50 minutes, three to five daily). Foot passengers cannot be accommodated.

BUS
For details on bus service to the beautiful Côte d'Opale and Calais, see p239.

Most local bus lines, run by **TCRB** (☎ 03 21 83 51 51), stop at place de France.

CAR
Discount rental agencies:
ADA (☎ 03 21 80 80 82; 211 rue Nationale)
Euroto (☎ 03 21 30 32 23; 96 rue Nationale)

TAXI
To order a cab, ring ☎ 03 21 91 25 00.

TRAIN
Gare Boulogne-Ville has services to Amiens (€16.60, 1½ hours, eight to 10 daily), Calais-Ville (€6.90, 28 to 48 minutes, 17 daily Monday to Saturday, nine on Sunday), Étaples-Le Touquet (€4.90, 20 minutes, nine to 21 daily), Gare Lille-Flandres or Gare Lille-Europe (€17.60, one to 2¼ hours, nine to 14 daily) and Paris' Gare du Nord (€29, 2½ hours, five to seven daily).

LE TOUQUET
pop 5300
The beach resort of **Le Touquet** (Paris Plage), 30km south of Boulogne, was hugely fashionable during the interwar period, when the English upper crust found it positively smashing (in 1940 a politically oblivious PG Wodehouse was arrested here by the Germans). These days it remains no less posh and no less British. Good spots for a high-profile stroll include the leafy area around **place de l'Hermitage**, where you'll find the fabled Hôtel Westminster, the casino and the **Tourist office** (☎ 03 21 06 72 00; www .letouquet.com; Palais de l'Europe, place de l'Hermitage; ☉ 9am-6pm Oct-Mar, to 7pm Apr-Sep).

If you're hunting for somewhere decent to stay, you can't beat the **Hôtel Red Fox** (☎ 03 21 05 27 58; www.hotelredfox.com; 60 rue de Metz; d in winter from €53, in summer €88; ☒ ☐), a two-star hotel just off rue St-Jean, Le Touquet's sparkling main commercial thoroughfare. The 53 functional rooms go a bit overboard with the primary colours.

There are food shops along rue de Metz, between rue St-Jean and the semicircular **covered market** (☉ approx 9am-1pm Thu & Sat).

MONTREUIL-SUR-MER
pop 2400
The first thing you should know about Montreuil – so you don't have your hopes cruelly dashed upon arrival – is that the town is 15km from the sea, the 'sur-mer' a mere vestige of the time before the River Canche silted up. The second thing you should know – if you like literary trivia – is that Victor Hugo once had lunch here, the result being a mild case of indigestion and the great man's decision to set the first scenes of Les Misérables in Montreuil.

Montreuil's most interesting bits are in the fortified **Ville Haute** (Upper Town), where you'll find the star-shaped, 16th-century **Citadelle** (☉ closed Tue & Dec-Feb); **St-Saulve abbey church** (☉ 9am-noon & 2-6pm), whose 12th-century façade is topped by an 18th-century tower; quite a few attractive 18th-century **townhouses** (eg around place Darnétal and along rue de la Chaîne); and some **picturesque streets** (eg rue du Clape-en-Bas, rue du Clape-en-Haut and cavée St-Firmin). The 3km **ramparts walk** affords panoramic views of the countryside 40m below, but a lack of railings makes it inadvisable for children. Details on activities in and around Montreuil are available from the **Tourist Office** (☎ 03 21 06 04 27; www.tourisme-montreuillois.com; 21 rue Carnot; ☉ 10am-12.30pm & 2-5pm or 6pm Mon-Sat, no midday closure & open Sun Jul & Aug).

The brand new, 40-bed **auberge de jeunesse** (☎ 03 21 06 10 83; www.fuaj.org; dm €10.10; ☺ check-in 2-6pm except Tue, closed Dec-Feb) is inside the Citadelle. The three-star, 16-room **Coq Hôtel** (☎ 03 21 81 05 61; www.coqhotel.fr; 2 place de la Poissonnerie; d €95-115) occupies a 19th-century building in the heart of the Ville Haute.

The train station, in the Ville Basse, is linked to Boulogne (€6.50, 30 minutes, three or four a day).

BAIE DE SOMME

The **Somme Estuary** (www.baiedesomme.org in French), at 5km wide the largest in northern France, affords delightfully watery views as the cycle of the tides hides and reveals vast expanses of sand. **Le Crotoy** is a modest beach resort on the northern bank that makes a good base for exploring the area. From there, across the estuary you can see **Pointe du Hourdel**, famed for its colony of sand bank-lounging seals; lots of duck-hunting huts; and **St-Valéry-sur-Somme**, which can be reached on foot (with a bit of knee-deep slogging) at low tide, though only with a guide (the area is notorious for its strong currents and galloping tides) – for details, contact **Promenade en Baie** (☎ 03 22 27 47 36; www.promenade-en-baie .com in French; 5 chemin des Digues).

Le Crotoy's **Tourist Office** (☎ 03 22 27 05 25; www.tourisme-crotoy.com in French; 1 rue Carnot; ☺ 9.30am-noon & 2-6pm Mon & Wed-Sat, 10am-12.30pm & 2.30-6pm Sun & holidays, longer hours Jul & Aug) can supply you with a *horaire des marées* (tide schedule).

Les Tourelles (☎ 03 22 27 16 33; www.lestourelles .com; 2-4 rue Pierre Guerlain; s/d €49/70, with washbasin €44/60; ☐ ⚐), a sprawling old two-star hotel overlooking the beach, has an austere, Victorian feel – this is the sort of place where guests take bracing seaside walks every morning before breakfast. One room has 14 bunk beds for kids aged four to 14 (€22, including breakfast), creating a summer camp atmosphere. The attached **restaurant** (menus €21-31) serves French cuisine with Channel coast touches.

The 2-sq-km **Parc Ornithologique du Marquenterre** (Marquenterre Bird Reserve; ☎ 03 22 25 68 99; www.parcdumarquenterre.com; adult/6-16yr €9.90/7.90, binoculars €4; ☺ 10am-5pm or 5.30pm Oct-Mar, to 7.30pm Apr-Sep, last entry 2hr before closing) in St-Quentin-en-Tourmont, a circuitous 10km northwest of Le Crotoy, is a migratory stopover for more than 200 species of birds on their way from the UK, Iceland, Scandinavia and Siberia to warmer climes in West Africa. While here, our feathered friends – including 15 year-round storks – find most of their food in the sandy estuary at low tide. The green-triangle walking circuit takes at least two hours; the blue-triangle circuit takes at least three hours.

ARRAS

pop 40,500

Arras (the final 's' is pronounced), former capital of Artois, is worth seeing mainly for its harmonious ensemble of Flemish-style arcaded buildings. The city is a good base for visits to the Battle of the Somme memorials.

Orientation

The centre of Arras is the historic Grand' Place and the almost-adjoining place des Héros (the Petite Place), where you'll find the Hôtel de Ville. The train station is 600m to the southeast. The pedestrianised area southeast of place des Héros, including rue Ronville, is the main commercial precinct.

Information

Banks can be found along rue Gambetta and its continuation, rue Ernestale.

Cybega (☎ 03 21 07 94 13; 17 rue St-Aubert; ½/1hr €2/3; ☺ 10am-8pm Mon-Sat) Manga-themed internet access.

Laundrette (17 place d'Ipswich; ☺ 7am-8pm) Duds meet suds in a gripping contest of wills.

Post Office (rue Gambetta) Has a Cyberposte and changes money.

Tourist Office (☎ 03 21 51 26 95; www.ot-arras.fr; place des Héros; ☺ 9am or 10am-noon & 2-6pm or 6.30pm Mon-Sat, no midday closure May-Sep, 10am-12.30pm or 1pm & 2.30-6.30pm Sun & holidays) Inside the Hôtel de Ville.

Sights & Activities

Arras' two market squares, **place des Héros** and the **Grand' Place**, are surrounded by 17th- and 18th-century Flemish-baroque houses that are especially handsome at night. These vary in all sorts of decorative details but their 345 sandstone columns form a common arcade unique in France. The Tourist Office offers a **self-guided tour** (adult/student €5.50/3.05) of the city centre.

The Flemish-Gothic **Hôtel de Ville** (place des Héros) dates from the 16th century but was

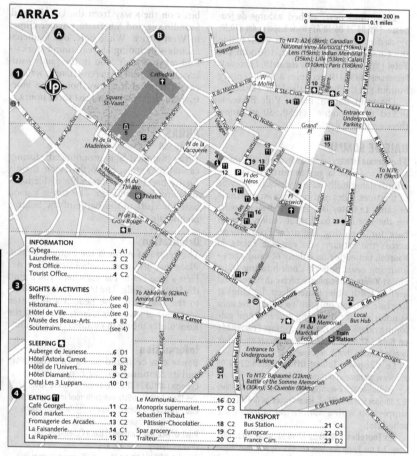

ARRAS

INFORMATION
Cybega	1 A1
Laundrette	2 C2
Post Office	3 C3
Tourist Office	4 C2

SIGHTS & ACTIVITIES
Belfry	(see 4)
Historama	(see 4)
Hôtel de Ville	(see 4)
Musée des Beaux-Arts	5 B2
Souterrains	(see 4)

SLEEPING
Auberge de Jeunesse	6 D1
Hôtel Astoria Carnot	7 C3
Hôtel de l'Univers	8 B2
Hôtel Diamant	9 C2
Ostal Les 3 Luppars	10 D1

EATING
Café Georget	11 C2
Food market	12 C2
Fromagerie des Arcades	13 C2
La Faisanderie	14 C1
La Rapière	15 D2
Le Mamounia	16 D2
Monoprix supermarket	17 C3
Sebastien Thibaut Pâtissier-Chocolatier	18 C2
Spar grocery	19 C2
Traiteur	20 C2

TRANSPORT
Bus Station	21 C4
Europcar	22 D3
France Cars	23 D2

completely rebuilt after WWI. Three giants (see p226) – Colas, Jacqueline and their son Dédé – make their home in the lobby.

The basement of the Hôtel de Ville is a veritable hub of activity. If you're in the mood for a panoramic view, this is the place to hop on the lift to the top of the 75m **belfry** (adult/student €2.30/1.60; ☉ same as tourist office). The **Historama** (€2.50/1.70) presents the city's history in a 20-minute slide show (in English). But for a truly unique perspective on Arras, head into the slimy **souterrains** (tunnels). Also known as *boves* (cellars), they run under place des Héros and were turned into British command posts, hospitals and barracks during WWI. Each spring, in a brilliant juxtaposition of underground

gloom and horticultural exuberance, plants and flowers turn the tunnels into the life-affirming **Jardin des Boves** (☉ mid-Apr–mid-Jun). **Tours** (€4.50/2.50) of the *souterrains* lasting 45 minutes (in English upon request) *generally* begin at 10am, 11am, 2.30pm, 3.30pm and 4.30pm from Monday to Friday, and every 30 minutes or so on Saturday and Sunday. All three attractions can be visited with the **combined ticket** (forfait; €7/4.20); **Le City Pass** (€10/6.20) which also gets you into the Musée des Beaux-Arts.

Highlights at the **Musée des Beaux-Arts** (Fine Arts Museum; ☎ 03 21 71 26 43; 22 rue Paul Doumer; adult/student & over 65yr €4/2; ☉ 9.30am-noon & 2-5.30pm Wed-Mon), housed in a neoclassical former Benedictine abbey, include the original copper lion from the Hôtel de Ville belfry, medieval sculpture (including a 15th-century skeletal figure whose stomach is being devoured by worms) and 17th-century religious paintings.

Sleeping

Auberge de Jeunesse (☎ 03 21 22 70 02; arras@fuaj.org; 59 Grand' Place; dm incl breakfast €14.40; ☺ reception 8am-noon & 5-9pm, hostel closed Dec & Jan) Modern and superbly situated in the town centre, this hostel has cheerful rooms for two to 10; almost all of the 54 beds are bunks. Full kitchen facilities are available.

Ostel Les 3 Luppars (☎ 03 21 60 02 03; www.ostel-les-3luppars.com in French; 47 Grand' Place; s/d/q from €44/60/75) Homy and centred on a courtyard, this 'ho(s)tel' occupies the Grand' Place's only non-Flemish-style building (it's Gothic and dates from 1370). The 42 rooms, some with fine views of the square, are comfortable, if a tad small. The sauna costs €5 per person.

Hôtel Astoria Carnot (☎ 03 21 71 08 14; www.hotelcarnot.com; 10 place du Maréchal Foch; s/d/q €50/56/75) Above a sleek brasserie, this two-star, Logis-de-France hotel has 29 spiffy, well-lit rooms with all-tile bathrooms.

Hôtel Diamant (☎ 03 21 71 23 23; www.arras-hotel-diamant.com; 5 place des Héros; s/d from €58/66; ☐) The 12 two-star rooms are newish but smallish. Internet access and coffee, both free, are available in the lobby.

Hôtel de l'Univers (☎ 03 21 71 34 01; www.hotel-univers-arras.com; 3-5 place de la Croix Rouge; d €92-132; ♿) Ensconced in a 16th-century former Jesuit monastery, this three-star, Best Western affiliated hostelry, arrayed in a U around a quiet classical courtyard, is an island of calm – though it's just 50m from No 29 on bustling rue Ernestale. Classic draperies and bedspreads give each of the 38 rooms a touch of French class. Civilised comfort at a reasonable price.

Eating

Lots of eateries are hidden away under the arches of the Grand' Place.

Café Georget (☎ 03 21 71 13 07; 42 place des Héros; plat du jour €8; ☺ noon-2pm Mon-Sat) In her unpretentious café, Madame Delforge has been serving hearty French dishes to people who work in the neighbourhood since 1985.

Sebastian Thibaut Pâtissier-Chocolatier (☎ 03 21 71 53 20; 50 place des Héros; ☺ 8am-7.30pm Tue-Sun)

Bright cases of scrumptious pastries greet you at this *salon de thé* (tearoom), a good place for a light lunch – a salad, perhaps, or a quiche. Has a terrace in summer.

La Rapière (☎ 03 21 55 09 92; 44 Grand' Place; menus €14.50-31.50; ☺ closed dinner Sun Oct-Mar) Regional cuisine, including *flan de maroilles* (flan made with a local cows' milk cheese), is elegantly served in a contemporary ambience.

Le Mamounia (☎ 03 21 07 99 99; 9 rue des Balances; mains €12-20; ☺ closed lunch Sat, dinner Sun & Mon) The elegant décor mixes the Maghreb with Provence but the couscous and *tajines* (stews) are 100% Moroccan.

La Faisanderie (☎ 03 21 48 20 76; 45 Grand' Place; menus €23-62; ☺ closed Sun & Mon) An especially elegant French restaurant under vaulted brick ceilings. The *menu* changes with the seasons so that only fresh ingredients can be used. Specialities include sole and wild turbot.

SELF-CATERING

Food market (place des Héros; ☺ morning Sat & Wed) The place to go for the best fresh produce.

Other sources for picnic supplies:

Fromagerie des Arcades (37 place des Héros; ☺ 9.30am-12.30pm & 2.30-7.15pm Tue-Sat)

Monoprix supermarket (30 rue Gambetta; ☺ 8.30am-8pm Mon-Sat)

Spar grocery (9 rue de la Taillerie; ☺ 8am-1pm & 3.30-8pm Tue-Sat, 9am-1pm Sun)

Traiteur Roger Portugal (☎ 03 21 23 44 72; 13 rue des Balances; ☺ 9am-1pm & 3-7pm Tue-Fri, 10am-1pm Sat, Sun & holidays) Delicious ready-to-eat delicacies.

Getting There & Away

BUS

For details on getting to the Canadian National Vimy Memorial, see p252.

CAR

Car rental options:

Europcar (☎ 03 21 07 29 54; 5 rue de Douai)

France Cars (☎ 03 21 50 22 22; 31 blvd Faidherbe)

TAXI

Alliance Arras Taxis-GT (☎ 03 21 23 69 69; ☺ 24 hr) can take you to Somme battlefield sites.

TRAIN

Arras is on the main line linking Lille-Flandres (€9, 40 to 70 minutes, 13 to 25 daily) with Paris' Gare du Nord (€26.90 or €38.90 by TGV, 50 minutes, seven to 13 daily).

MCDONALD'S HAS BRANCHES SO WHY SHOULDN'T THE LOUVRE?

A local branch of the Louvre is coming to a depressed former coal-mining town near you – at least if you live in France's far north. That's right, come 2009, when the Louvre II is set to open in Lens, you'll no longer have to go to Paris to visit the world's most-visited museum.

We may as well be blunt: Lens, 18km northeast of Arras and 37km south of Lille, is known for absolutely nothing, at least as far as tourism is concerned. But thanks to a high-minded effort to 'democratise' the Louvre by bringing its riches to the people – 'La culture est un acteur de la justice sociale' (culture is an agent for social justice), the French prime minister intoned – the town's 37,000 residents are hoping that what the Guggenheim Museum did for Bilbao the Louvre II will do for them. Incidentally, the decision to situate the ultraprestigious project in Lens was apparently helped along by a municipal advert that juxtaposed IM Pei's Louvre pyramid with one of Lens' very own pyramid-like slag heaps!

The new museum, which will occupy the site of long-closed Pit No 9, is being designed by the Japanese architectural firm Sanaa, led by Kazuyo Sejima (said to be the first woman to design a major public monument in France) and Ryue Nishizawa. About two-thirds of the 5500 sq metres of exhibition space will be given over to 600 to 800 major works rotated to Lens from the Louvre (Original Recipe) for two or three years at a time.

Other destinations include Amiens (€10.10, 50 minutes, six to 13 daily) and Calais-Ville (€18, two hours, 12 daily Monday to Friday, five daily Saturday and Sunday).

BATTLE OF THE SOMME MEMORIALS

The First Battle of the Somme, a WWI Allied offensive waged in the villages and woodlands northeast of Amiens, was designed to relieve pressure on the beleaguered French troops at Verdun. On 1 July 1916, British, Commonwealth and French troops 'went over the top' in a massive assault along a 34km front. But German positions proved virtually unbreachable, and on the first day of the battle an astounding 21,392 British troops were killed and another 35,492 were wounded. Most casualties were infantrymen mown down by German machine guns.

By the time the offensive was called off in mid-November, 1.2 million lives had been lost on both sides. The British had advanced 12km, the French 8km. (Today, 'Ligne de Front' signs mark where the front line stood on a specific date.) The Battle of the Somme has become a metaphor for the meaningless slaughter of war and its killing fields have since become a site of pilgrimage (see www.somme-battlefields.co.uk).

GETTING THERE & AWAY

Visiting the Somme memorials is easiest by car but quite a few sites can be reached by train or bus from Amiens and/or Arras;

details on public transport options appear after each listing. Cycling is also an option.

TOURS

Experienced companies offering minibus tours:

Salient Tours (☎ 06 86 05 61 30; www.salienttours.com; half-day per person €22 or €29) Tours begin at the Albert train station at 10am and 3pm daily except Monday from Easter to late October.

Somme-Normandy Tours (☎ 06 87 43 10 49, in Normandy 02 31 22 26 09; www.somme-normandy -tours.com; morning/afternoon/full day per person from €30/22/52) Tours begin in Arras at 10am and 3pm from March to late November, the rest of the year by appointment. Private tours tailored for various nationalities are also on offer.

North of Arras

The area towards Lille from Arras has a couple of noteworthy memorials and numerous military cemeteries.

CANADIAN NATIONAL VIMY MEMORIAL & PARK

Whereas the French, right after the war, attempted to erase all signs of battle and return the Somme region to agriculture and normalcy, the Canadians decided that the most evocative way to remember their fallen was to preserve whole sections of the crater-pocked battlefields. As a result, the best place to get some sense of the unimaginable hell known as the Western Front is at the chilling, eerie moonscape of **Vimy**

Ridge. Visitors can also see **tunnels** (admission free; ☾ with a guide May-Nov) and reconstructed **trenches** (☾ year-round)

Of the 66,655 Canadians who died in WWI, 3589 lost their lives in April 1917 taking this ridge, a German defensive line, its highest point of which was later chosen as the site of Canada's **WWI memorial** (1925–36), set to re-open in April 2007 (the 90th anniversary of the battle) after extensive renovations. The allegorical figures, carved from huge blocks of limestone, include a cloaked, downcast female figure representing a young Canada mourning her fallen. The base is inscribed with the names of 11,285 Canadians who 'died in France but have no known graves'. The 1-sq-km park also includes two **Canadian cemeteries** and, at the vehicle entrance to the main memorial, a **monument to the Moroccan Division** (in French and Arabic).

The new **Historical Interpretive Centre** (☎ 03 21 50 68 68; www.vac-acc.gc.ca; admission free; ☾ 10am-6pm May-Oct, 9am-5pm Nov-Apr), in a modest, rust-coloured building at the entrance to the trenches, is staffed by Canadian students,

who also serve as tour guides. The **Canadian Virtual War Memorial** (www.virtualmemorial.gc.ca) has details on more than 116,000 Canadian war dead.

To get to the Canadian memorials from Arras, take bus No 91 (€1, 20 minutes, six daily Monday to Saturday) towards Lens and ask the bus driver to stop a bit before the Thelus-Vert Tilleul turnoff, 3.2km from the memorial.

Trains link Arras with the town of Vimy (€2.60, 12 minutes, six daily Monday to Friday, three on Saturday), 6km east of the memorial.

A taxi from Arras costs €20 each way; the return-trip price is also €20 but then you have to pay an additional €20 for each hour the driver spends waiting. Prices are 30% higher on Sunday.

INDIAN MEMORIAL

The fascinating and seldom-visited **Mémorial Indien**, vaguely Moghul in architecture, records the names of Commonwealth soldiers from the Indian subcontinent who 'have no known grave'. The units (31st

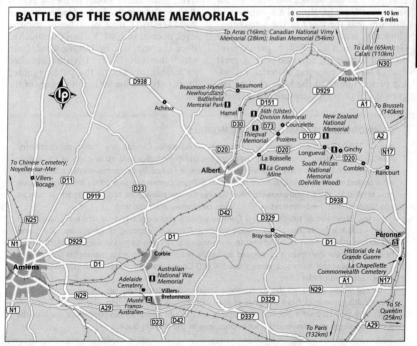

BATTLE OF THE SOMME MEMORIALS

0 — 10 km
0 — 6 miles

Punjabis, 11th Rajputs, 2nd King Edward's Own Gurkha Rifles) and the ranks of the fallen – sepoy, havildar, *naik* (chief), *sowar* (mounted soldier), labourer, follower – engraved on the walls evoke the pride, pomp and exploitation on which the British Empire was built.

To get there from La Bassée, take the northbound D947 to its intersection with the D171.

South of Arras

Some of the bloodiest fighting of WWI took place around the town of Albert. The farmland north and east of the town is dotted with scores of Commonwealth cemeteries.

PÉRONNE

Perhaps the best place to start a visit to the Somme battlefields is in the river port of Péronne (population 8400), at the well-designed and informative **Historial de la Grande Guerre** (☎ 03 22 83 14 18; www.historial.org; Château de Péronne; adult/children 6-18yr/senior incl audioguide €7.50/3.80/6, student, teacher & ex-serviceman €3.80; ☷ 10am-6pm Apr-Oct, 10am-6pm Tue-Sun Nov–mid-Dec & mid-Jan–Mar). This innovative museum tells the story of the war chronologically, with equal space given to the German, French and British perspectives on what happened, how and why. A great deal of visually engaging material, including period films and the bone-chilling engravings of Otto Dix, capture the aesthetic

sensibilities, enthusiasm, naive patriotism and unimaginable violence of the time. The proud uniforms of various units and armies are shown laid out on the ground, as if on freshly – though bloodlessly – dead soldiers. Not much glory here.

On the N17 at the southern edge of town, **La Chapellette Commonwealth Cemetery** has separate British and Indian sections.

Bus 38 links Péronne with Albert (€4, 50 minutes, three or four a day Monday to Saturday); bus 47 goes to both Villers-Bretonneux (€4, 1¼ hours, one or two daily Monday to Saturday) and Amiens' bus station (€4, 1¾ hours).

THIEPVAL MEMORIAL

Dedicated to 'the Missing of the Somme', this **memorial** – the region's most visited place of pilgrimage – was built in the early 1930s on the site of a German stronghold that was stormed on 1 July 1916 with unimaginable casualties. The columns of the arches are inscribed with the names of 73,367 British and South African soldiers whose remains were never found. The discreet, glass-walled **visitors centre** (☎ 03 22 74 60 47; ☷ 10am-6pm May-Oct, 9am-5pm Nov-Apr, closed around New Year), most of it below ground level, opened in 2004. Virtually untouched since the war, nearby **Thiepval Wood**, from which the 36th (Ulster) Division launched its assault, opened to the public (guided tours only) on the 90th anniversary of the battle.

COMMONWEALTH CEMETERIES & MEMORIALS

Almost 750,000 soldiers, airmen and sailors from Australia, Canada, the Indian subcontinent, Ireland, New Zealand, South Africa, Great Britain, the West Indies and other parts of the British Empire died on the Western Front, two-thirds of them in France. By Commonwealth tradition, they were buried where they fell, in more than 1000 military cemeteries and 2000 civilian cemeteries now tended by the **Commonwealth War Graves Commission** (www.cwgc.org). French, American and German war dead were reburied in large cemeteries after the war.

Today, hundreds of neatly tended Commonwealth plots – marked by white-on-dark-green signs – dot the landscape along a wide swathe of territory running roughly from Albert and Cambrai north via Arras and Béthune to Armentières and Ypres (Ieper) in Belgium. Many of the headstones bear inscriptions composed by family members. Twenty-six memorials (20 of them in France) bear the names of more than 300,000 Commonwealth soldiers whose bodies were never recovered or identified.

Except where noted, all the monuments listed in this chapter are always open. Many Commonwealth cemeteries have a bronze plaque with historical information. The bronze Cemetery Register boxes contain a booklet with details on the site and brief biographies of each of the identified dead; you can record your impressions in the Visitors Book.

AUSTRALIAN NATIONAL WAR MEMORIAL
During WWI, 313,000 Australians (out of a total population of 4.5 million) volunteered for military service; 46,000 met their deaths on the Western Front (14,000 others perished elsewhere). The **Australian National War Memorial**, a 32m tower engraved with the names of 10,982 soldiers who went missing in action, stands on a hill where Australian and British troops repulsed a German assault on 24 April 1918. It was dedicated in 1938; two years later its stone walls were scarred by the guns of Hitler's invading armies.

The nearest town is **Villers-Bretonneux**, an ugly bourg that still hasn't completely recovered from the war. For Aussies, though, it's a heart-warming place that bills itself as *l'Australie en Picardie*, and Anzac Day is religiously commemorated. In 1993, the unidentified remains of an Australian soldier were transferred from Adelaide Cemetery, on the N29 at the western edge of town, to the Tomb of the Unknown Soldier in Canberra.

The town's **Musée Franco-Australien** (☎ 03 22 96 80 79; www.villers-bretonneux.com/Australian.htm; École Victoria, 9 rue Victoria; adult/student €4/2.50; ☼ 10am-12.30pm & 2-6pm Wed-Sat, 2-6pm Tue, 2-6pm 1st & 3rd Sun of month) has intimate, evocative displays of WWI Australiana, including letters, photographs of life on the Western Front, and a small Anzac (Australian and New Zealand Army Corps) library. The front steps are a favoured trysting spot for local teens.

The Villers-Bretonneux train station, on the tertiary line linking Amiens (€3.10, 12 minutes, four to seven daily) with Laon (€12.70, 1¾ hours, four or five daily), is 700m south of the museum (along rue de Melbourne) and a walkable 3km south of the Australian National War Memorial. Bus No 47 links Villers-Bretonneux with Amiens (€3, 25 minutes, two daily Monday to Saturday) and Péronne (€4, 1¼ hours, one or two daily Monday to Saturday).

A **taxi** (☎ 03 22 48 49 49) to the memorial from Villers-Bretonneux costs €12 return, plus €3 for every 10 minutes spent waiting at the site.

BEAUMONT-HAMEL NEWFOUNDLAND BATTLEFIELD MEMORIAL PARK
Like Vimy (p252), the evocative **Mémorial Terre-Neuvien** preserves part of the Western Front in the state it was in at fighting's end. The zigzag trench system, which still fills with mud in winter, is clearly visible, as are countless shell craters and the remains of barbed-wire barriers.

On 1 July 1916, the volunteer Royal Newfoundland Regiment stormed entrenched German positions and was nearly wiped out; a plaque notes blandly that 'strategic and tactical miscalculations led to a great slaughter'. You can survey the whole battlefield from the **caribou statue**, surrounded by plants native to Newfoundland. Canadian students based at the **visitors centre** (☎ 03 22 76 70 87; ☼ 10am-6pm May–mid-Nov, to 5pm mid-Nov–Apr, closed late Dec–early Jan), designed to look like a typical Newfoundland fisher's house, give free guided tours year-round.

36TH (ULSTER) DIVISION MEMORIAL
Built on a German frontline position assaulted by the overwhelmingly Protestant 36th (Ulster) Division on 1 July 1916, the **Tour d'Ulster** (Ulster Tower), also known as the Mémorial Irlandais, is an exact replica of Helen's Tower at Clanboye, County Down, where the unit did its training. Dedicated in 1921, it has long been a Unionist pilgrimage site. A black obelisk known as the **Orange Memorial to Fallen Brethren** stands in an enclosure behind the tower. In a sign that historic wounds are finally healing, in 2006 the Irish Republic issued a €0.75 postage stamp, showing the 36th Division in action, to commemorate the 90th anniversary of the Battle of the Somme.

SOUTH AFRICAN & NEW ZEALAND NATIONAL MEMORIALS
The **South African National Memorial** (Mémorial Sud-Africain) stands in the middle of shell-pocked **Delville Wood**, which was almost captured by a South African brigade in the third week of July in 1916. The avenues through the trees are named after streets in London and Edinburgh. The star-shaped **museum** (☎ 03 22 85 02 17; admission free; ☼ 10am-5.45pm Apr–mid-Oct, to 3.45pm in winter, closed Mon, holidays & mid-Nov–early Feb) was dedicated amid much apartheid-related controversy in 1986.

The **New Zealand National Memorial** is 1.5km due north of Longueval.

LA GRANDE MINE
Just outside the hamlet of La Boisselle, this enormous **crater** looks like the site of a meteor impact. Some 100m across and 30m

deep and officially known as the **Lochnagar Crater Memorial**, it was created on the morning of the first day of the First Battle of the Somme by about 25 tonnes of ammonal laid by British sappers in order to create a breach in the German lines – and is a testament to the boundless ingenuity human beings can muster when determined to kill their fellow creatures.

ALBERT

The most noteworthy landmark in this rather unfetching town (population 10,000), virtually flattened during WWI, is neo-Byzantine-style **Basilique Notre-Dame de Brebières**, topped by a dazzlingly gilded statue of the Virgin Mary, famously left dangling by a German shell.

Right next to the basilica, the underground **Musée Somme 1916** (Somme Trench Museum; ☎ 03 22 75 16 17; www.musee-somme-1916.org; rue Anicet Godin; adult/6-18yr €4/2.50; ☼ 9am-noon & 2-6pm Feb–mid-Dec, no midday closure Jun-Sep) does a good job of evoking the grim, grimy lives of Tommies, *poilus* ('hairy ones', ie French WWI soldiers) and civilians at the front line.

The **Tourist Office** (☎ 03 22 75 16 42; www.tourisme-albert.net; 9 rue Léon Gambetta; ☼ 9am-noon or 12.30pm & 1.30pm or 2-6.30pm Mon-Sat, 10am-12.30pm Sun & holidays Apr-Sep, to 5pm Mon-Sat Oct-Mar) is 50m towards the train station from the basilica. Year-round, it arranges tours of the WWI memorials (phone ahead for reservations) and rents out bicycles (per half-/whole day €8/12).

Trains (eight to 19 daily) link Albert's train station – the monoplane hanging in the waiting hall is a Potez 36 from 1933 – with Amiens (€5.80, 25 minutes).

CHINESE CEMETERY

Towards the end of WWI, tens of thousands of Chinese labourers were recruited by the British government to perform noncombat jobs in Europe, including the gruesome task of recovering and burying Allied war dead. **Noyelles-sur-Mer**, 65km northwest of Amiens, served as the French base for the Chinese Labour Corps, and it was there (actually, in the neighbouring hamlet of Nolette) that the **Chinese Cemetery**, maintained by the Commonwealth War Graves Commission, bears silent testimony to 849 men from a far-off land who never made it home. To get there, follow the signs along the D111 and the C6 to the 'Cimetière Chinois'.

AMIENS

pop 135,000

The presence of one of France's most awe-inspiring Gothic cathedrals is reason enough to head to Amiens, the comfy if reserved former capital of Picardy, whose 25,000 students give the place a young, lively feel. The clean-lined city centre, rebuilt after the war, has aged remarkably well. Amiens is an excellent base for visits to the Battle of the Somme memorials.

The world's first face transplant operation was performed at Amiens' university hospital in November 2005.

Orientation

The commercial district is centred on place Gambetta, two blocks west of the cathedral. The train station is about 1km southeast of place Gambetta.

Information

Banks can be found around place René Goblet and along pedestrianised rue des Trois Cailloux.

Laundrette 10 rue André (☼ 8am-6pm); 13 rue des Majots (☼ 8am-10pm Mon-Sat)

Main Post Office (7 rue des Vergeaux) Has currency exchange and a Cyberposte.

Neurogame Cybercafé (16 rue des Chaudronniers; ☎ 03 22 72 68 79; per hr €3.50; ☼ 10am-midnight Mon-Sat, 2-8pm Sun) Internet access.

Tourist Office (☎ 03 22 71 60 50; www.amiens.com /tourisme; 6bis rue Dusevel; ☼ 9.30am-6pm or 7pm Mon-Sat, 10am-noon & 2-5pm Sun) Can supply details on visiting the Somme war monuments, including minibus tours.

Sights & Activities
CATHÉDRALE NOTRE DAME

This magnificent **Gothic cathedral** (place Notre Dame; ☼ 8.30am-6.30pm Apr-Sep, to 5.30pm Oct-Mar), the largest in France (it's 145m long) and a Unesco World Heritage site, was begun in 1220 to house the head of St John the Baptist, now enclosed in gold in the northern outer wall of the ambulatory (on view in spring and summer). Connoisseurs rave about the soaring Gothic arches (42.3m high over the transept), unity of style and immense interior but for locals, the 17th-century statue known as the **Ange Pleureur** (Crying Angel), in the ambulatory right behind the very baroque, 18th-century high altar, remains a favourite.

The black-and-white, octagonal, 234m-long **labyrinth** on the floor of the nave is easy to miss as the soaring vaults draw the eye upward. Plaques in the south transept arm honour Australian, British, Canadian, New Zealand and US troops who died in WWI.

Weather permitting, it's possible to climb the **north tower** (adult/under 18yr €3/free;

2.30-5.30pm Sat & Sun Apr-Jun & Sep, daily Jul & Aug, with a guide at 3.45pm Wed-Mon Oct-Mar). Audioguides (€4) are available inside the cathedral from mid-June to mid-September and at the tourist office the rest of the year.

A free 45-minute **light show** bathes the cathedral façade in vivid medieval colours nightly from mid-June to mid-September

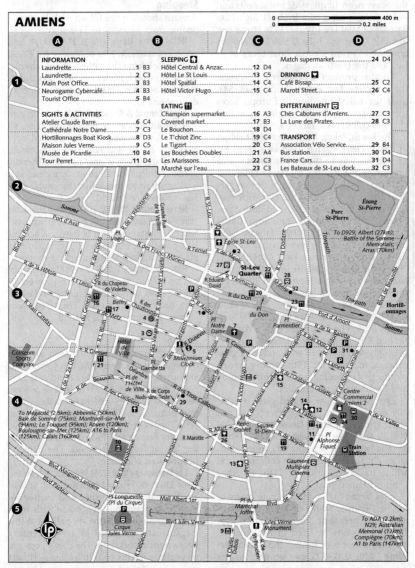

AMIENS

0 ————— 400 m
0 ————— 0.2 miles

INFORMATION
Laundrette...........................1 B3
Laundrette...........................2 C3
Main Post Office.................3 B3
Neurogame Cybercafé........4 B3
Tourist Office......................5 B4

SIGHTS & ACTIVITIES
Atelier Claude Barre............6 C4
Cathédrale Notre Dame.......7 C3
Hortillonnages Boat Kiosk...8 D3
Maison Jules Verne..............9 C5
Musée de Picardie.............10 B4
Tour Perret........................11 D4

SLEEPING
Hôtel Central & Anzac........12 D4
Hôtel Le St Louis................13 C5
Hôtel Spatial.....................14 C4
Hôtel Victor Hugo..............15 C4

EATING
Champion supermarket.......16 A3
Covered market..................17 B3
Le Bouchon.......................18 D4
Le T'chiot Zinc...................19 C4
Le Tigzirt..........................20 C3
Les Bouchées Doubles........21 A4
Les Marissons....................22 D4
Marché sur l'eau................23 C3

Match supermarket............24 D4

DRINKING
Café Bissap.......................25 C2
Marott Street.....................26 C4

ENTERTAINMENT
Chés Cabotans d'Amiens....27 C3
La Lune des Pirates............28 C3

TRANSPORT
Association Vélo Service......29 B4
Bus station.......................30 D4
France Cars.......................31 D4
Les Bateaux de St-Leu dock.32 C3

and December to 1 January; the photons start flying at 7pm in winter and sometime between 9.45pm (September) and 10.45pm (June) in summer.

OTHER SIGHTS & ACTIVITIES

Postwar renovations have left parts of the medieval **St-Leu Quarter** too cute by half, but the many neon-lit quayside restaurants and pubs make it especially lively at night. **Les Bateaux de Saint Leu** (☎ 03 22 09 06 11; quai Bélu; adult/child 11-16yr/child 3-10yr €5.50/4/3; ☼ 9am-7pm approx Apr-Oct) runs electric boat tours of St Leu and the Hortillonnages.

Another product of postwar exuberance, the concrete **Tour Perret** (built 1948–54), once the tallest building in Europe, faces the train station. In 2005 a glass cube that changes colours was tacked on top.

The lawns, lakes, waterways and bridges of **Parc St-Pierre** stretch eastwards from St-Leu all the way to the **Hortillonnages** – also known as the Jardins Flottants (Floating Gardens) – a 3.3-sq-km area of market gardens that have supplied the city with vegetables and flowers since the Middle Ages. From April to October, one-hour **cruises** (adult/11-16yr/4-10yr €5.30/4.40/2.60) of the peaceful canals – in 12-person gondola-like boats – depart from a riverside **kiosk** (☎ 03 22 92 12 18; 54 blvd de Beauvillé) daily from 1.45pm until sometime between 4.30pm and 6.30pm; get there before 4pm to buy tickets.

The **Musée de Picardie** (☎ 03 22 97 14 00; 48 rue de la République; adult/6-18yr €4.50/2.50; ☼ 10am-12.30pm & 2-6pm Tue-Sun), housed in a dashing Second Empire structure (1855–67), is surprisingly well endowed with archaeological exhibits, medieval art, 18th-century French paintings (including royal commissions) and Revolution-era ceramics.

Ever wonder how stained glass is actually designed and put together? You can see first-hand at **Atelier Claude Barre** (☎ 03 22 91 81 18; 40 rue Victor Hugo; adult/student €4/2; ☼ tour 3pm Mon-Sat), whose artisans fill commissions from churches and private collectors and which has a collection of 11th- to 20th-century stained glass.

Jules Verne (1828–1905) wrote many of his best-known works of brain-tingling – and eerily prescient – science fiction during the 18 years he lived in Amiens. His turreted home now houses the **Maison Jules Verne** (☎ 03 22 45 45 75; www.jules-verne.net; 2 rue Charles Dubois; adult/student €5/3.50; ☼ 10am-12.30pm & 2-6.30pm Mon-Wed & Fri, 2-6.30pm Tue, 11am-6.30pm Sat & Sun mid-Apr–mid-Oct, to 6pm & also closed Tue afternoon mid-Oct–mid-Apr), whose furnished rooms have been left just as they were back when going round the world in 80 days sounded utterly fantastic.

Sleeping

Amiens' hotels often fill up with business-people from Monday to Thursday.

Hôtel Victor Hugo (☎ 03 22 91 57 91; hotel victorhugo@wanadoo.fr; 2 rue de l'Oratoire; d/tr €30/56) Just a block from the cathedral, this charming family-run hostelry has two stars and 10 stylish modern rooms that retain touches of days gone by.

Hôtel Central & Anzac (☎ 03 22 91 34 08; www .hotelcentraletanzac.com; 17 rue Alexandre Fatton; s/d from €40/44, with washbasin €35/39) Founded decades ago by an Australian ex-serviceman, this two-star place is now run by a friendly French family. The 25 rooms are clean and well maintained though on the small side. Hall showers cost €2.50.

Hôtel Spatial (☎ 03 22 91 53 23; www.hotelspatial .com; 15 rue Alexandre Fatton; s/d from €42/48, with washbasin €32/38) Staying here is hardly a scintillating aesthetic experience but this two-star place is practical, welcoming and spotless.

Hôtel Le St Louis (☎ 03 22 91 76 03; www.le-saint louis.com in French; 24 rue des Otages; d/q from €49/77) All the mod cons with more than a dash of 19th-century French class. The 16 two-star rooms are spacious and tasteful.

Eating

The area around place du Don and the quays across the river in St-Leu (quai Bélu) are bursting with restaurants and cafés.

Le T'chiot Zinc (☎ 03 22 91 43 79; 18 rue de Noyon; menus €11.40-27.70; ☼ closed Sun & lunch Mon) Inviting, bistro-style décor reminiscent of the *belle époque* provides a fine backdrop for the tasty French and Picard cuisine, including lots of fish and seafood. The name is pronounced cho-zang.

Les Marissons (☎ 03 22 92 96 66; pont de la Dodane; menus €18.50-49; ☼ closed lunch Wed, lunch Sat, Sun) Traditional French dishes and *cuisine du marché* (market cuisine), made with fresh local ingredients, are the specialities at this elegant eatery, housed in a 14th-century boatwright's workshop. The chef's personal favourite – it's his own invention – is *lotte* *rôtie aux abricots* (monkfish roasted with apricots, €25).

Le Bouchon (☎ 03 22 92 14 32; 10 rue Alexandre Fatton; Mon-Fri lunch menus, €13, other menus €22-42; ✶ closed dinner Sun) A classy restaurant decorated with original artwork, changed several times a year, that serves traditional French cuisine. The mouth-watering dessert list includes all the French classics.

Le Tigzirt (☎ 03 22 91 42 55; 60 rue Vanmarcke, on weekends via 7 place du Don; dishes €10-21; ✶ closed Mon, dinner Sun & lunch Sat) The Algerian Berber-style couscous and *tajines* are steamed, boiled, grilled and baked to perfection.

Les Bouchées Doubles (☎ 03 22 91 00 85; 11bis rue Gresset; mains €12-25) A contemporary brasserie known for its succulent beef dishes.

SELF-CATERING

Marché sur l'eau (floating market; place Parmentier; ✶ until 12.30pm Sat, to 1pm in summer) Fruit and vegetables grown in the Hortillonnages are sold at this once-floating market, now held on dry land.

Other places to stock up for a picnic:
Champion supermarket (22bis rue du Général Leclerc; ✶ 8.30am-8pm Mon-Sat)
Covered market (rue de Metz; ✶ 9am-1pm & 3-7pm Tue-Thu, 9am-7pm Fri & Sat, 8.30am-12.30pm Sun)
Match supermarket (Centre Commercial Amiens 2; ✶ 9am-8pm Mon-Sat)

Drinking

Marotte Street (☎ 03 22 91 14 93; 1 rue Marotte; ✶ 11am-1am) Designed by Gustave Eiffel's architectural firm in 1892, this one-time insurance office is now a chic bar where the trendy sip champagne, suspended – on clear glass tiles – over the wine cellar.

Café Bissap (☎ 03 22 92 36 41; 50 rue St-Leu; ✶ 4pm or 6pm-1am, to 3am Thu-Sat) A very laid-back, ethnically mixed crowd, including lots of students, sips rum cocktails and West African beers amid décor from the Senegalese proprietor's native land.

Entertainment

La Lunes des Pirates (☎ 03 22 97 88 01; www.lalune .net; 17 quai Bélu) A cutting-edge venue, which has two or three live concerts a week.

Chés Cabotans d'Amiens (☎ 0)3 22 22 30 90; www .ches-cabotans-damiens.com; 31 rue Edouard-David) A theatre whose stars are all traditional Picard marionettes. Great fun even if you don't speak Picard or French.

Getting There & Away

For details on visiting the Battle of the Somme memorials by public transport, see the listing for each memorial site.

BUS

The **bus station** (☎ 03 22 92 27 03; ✶ office 6am-7pm Mon-Fri, 7am-6.45pm Sat), in the basement of the Centre Commercial Amiens 2, is accessible from rue de la Vallée.

CAR

To rent a vehicle:
ADA (☎ 03 22 46 49 49; 387 chaussée Jules Ferry) Situated 2.4km southeast of the train station and served by bus No 1.
France Cars (☎ 03 22 72 52 52; 75 blvd d'Alsace-Lorraine)

TRAIN

Rail destinations include Arras (€10.10, 50 minutes, six to 13 daily), Boulogne (€16.60, 1½ hours, eight to 10 daily), Calais-Ville (€21, 2½ hours, four or five daily), Lille-Flandres (€17.10, 1½ hours, six to 12 daily) and Paris' Gare du Nord (€17.50, one to 1½ hours, 14 to 19 daily). SNCF buses go to the Haute Picardie TGV station (45 minutes), 42km east of the city.

Getting Around

There's free parking one or two blocks north of the Victor Hugo, Spatial and Central & Anzac Hotels, along rue Lameth, rue Cardon, rue Jean XXIII and rue de la Barette.

Association Vélo Service (Buscyclette; ☎ 03 22 72 55 13; 3 rue des Corps Nuds-sans-Teste; per hr/day/weekend €1/5.50/8, tandems per hr/day €2/8; ✶ 9am-12.30pm & 1.30-7pm) is a nonprofit group that rents bikes. Helmets are free.

BEAUVAIS

pop 55,000

Famed for the titanic hubris of its cathedral, doomed to remain forever unfinished, Beauvais became an important tapestry-making centre during the reign of Louis XIV and is often mentioned in the same breath as Gobelins and Aubusson. Today, it has an excellent tapestry museum and a fascinating state-run tapestry workshop.

About 80% of the city was destroyed during WWII, mainly by Allied bombing. Unfortunately the postwar town is far from enchanting.

Information

Tourist Office (☎ 03 44 15 30 30; www.beauvais
.fr in French; 1 rue Beauregard; ⏰ 9.30am or 10am-6pm or
6.30pm Mon-Sat year-round, 10am-5pm Sun mid-Apr–mid-
Oct, 10am-1.30pm Sun rest of year except Nov-Feb) About
200m southeast of the cathedral.

Sights

The history of hapless **Cathédrale St-Pierre**
(admission free, audioguide adult/16-25yr €3/2; ⏰ 9am-
12.15pm & 2-6.15pm May-Oct, 9am-12.15pm & 2-5.30pm
Nov-Apr, no midday closure Jul & Aug) has been one
of insatiable ambition and colossal failure.
When Beauvais' Carolingian cathedral
(parts of which, known as the **Basse œuvre**,
can still be seen) was partly destroyed by fire
in 1225, the bishop and local nobles decided
that its replacement should surpass anything ever built. Unfortunately, their richly
adorned creation also surpassed the limits
of technology, and in 1284 the 48m-high
vaults – the highest ever built – collapsed.
There was further damage in 1573 when
the 153m spire, the tallest of its era, came
a-tumblin' down. One of the **astronomical
clocks** (adult/17-25yr/6-16yr €4/2.50/1) dates from
the 14th century; the other, set to solar time
and thus 52 minutes behind CET (Central
European Time), does its thing at 10.40am,
11.40am, 2.40pm, 3.40pm and 4.40pm, with
additional demonstrations at 12.40pm and
5.40pm in July and August

Just west of the cathedral, head through
the two round bastions – a relic of the early
1300s – to the excellent **Musée Départemental
de l'Oise** (☎ 03 44 11 11 30; 1 rue du Musée; adult,
18-25yr & senior/under 18y €2/€1/free; ⏰ 10am-noon &
2-6pm Wed-Mon, no midday closure Jul & Aug). Highlights in this former bishops' palace include
the *Dieu Guerrier Gaulois*, a slender and
aristocratic Celtic warrior made of ham-
mered sheet brass in the 1st century AD;
the newly acquired funerary monument of
Charles de Fresnoy, looking more pious
than he could possibly have been in life; and
a sinuous Art Nouveau dining room.

Tapestries made in the workshops of
Beauvais and Gobelins are presented in
themed temporary exhibitions at France's
national tapestry museum, **Galerie Nationale
de la Tapisserie** (☎ 03 44 15 39 10; rue St-Pierre; admission at press time free; ⏰ 9.30am-12.30pm & 2-6pm
Tue-Sun Apr-Sep, 9.30am-noon & 2-5pm Tue-Sun Oct-Mar,
closed btwn exhibitions), right next to the cathedral's choir.

You can see strikingly modern tapestries
actually being made, using techniques perfected over centuries, at the state-owned
Manufacture Nationale de la Tapisserie (☎ 03 44
14 41 90; 24 rue Henri Brispot; tours adult/7-17yr €3.20/1;
⏰ tours begin approximately 2pm & 3pm Tue-Thu), 1km
south of the cathedral (across the train
tracks). All the projects underway here
have been commissioned by the French
government to add panache to embassies
and other official buildings.

Sleeping & Eating

Hôtel Victor (☎ 03 44 45 07 51; fax 03 44 45 71 25; 15
place Jeanne Hachette; d €43) Central and soundproofed, this bar-hotel has 10 fairly spacious, modern rooms, some with French
windows looking out onto the square.

Le Palais Bleu (☎ 03 44 45 06 52; 75 rue St-Pierre;
mains €13-19; ⏰ Mon-Sat) Across the street from
the cathedral entrance, this well-lit, rustic
eatery has its daily offerings, including
French-style meat and fish dishes, posted
on a chalkboard.

Picnic supplies can be picked up at
the **Marché Plus supermarket** (4 rue Pierre Jacoby;
⏰ 7am-9pm Mon-Sat, 9am-1pm Sun), three short
blocks east of the cathedral.

Getting There & Away

Beauvais-Tillé Airport (☎ 0 892 682 066; www.aero
portbeauvais.com), a few kilometres northeast
of the centre, is thriving thanks to cheap
airlines such as Ryanair, whose destinations include Dublin, Glasgow and Shannon. Local bus 12 (€0.90, six daily except
Sunday and holidays) links the airport with
the train station and the town centre.

The **train station**, 1.2km southeast of the
cathedral, has direct services to Paris' Gare
du Nord (€11.20, 1¼ hours, 11 to 15 daily).

COMPIÈGNE

pop 41,000

Compiègne reached its glittering zenith
under Napoleon III (ruled 1852–70), whose
legacy is alive and well in the chateau and
adjacent park. The town, 80km northeast
of Paris, makes an easy day trip from the
capital.

On 23 May 1430, Joan of Arc (Jeanne
d'Arc) – honoured by two statues in the
city centre – was captured at Compiègne by
the Burgundians, who later sold her to their
allies, the English.

Information

Tourist Office (☎ 03 44 40 01 00; compiegne.tourisme
.infos@wanadoo.fr; place de l'Hôtel de Ville; ⏰ 9.15am-
12.15pm & 1.45-6.15pm Mon-Sat Apr-Sep, to 5.15pm &
closed morning Mon Oct-Mar, 10am-12.15pm & 2.15-5pm
Sun & holidays Easter-Oct) In a building attached
to the ornate, 15th-century Gothic Hôtel de
Ville, facing a statue of Joan of Arc.

Sights

CHÂTEAU DE COMPIÈGNE

Napoleon III's dazzling hunting parties
drew aristocrats and wannabes from all
around Europe to his 1337-room **royal palace** (☎ 03 44 38 47 00; www.musee-chateau-compiegne
.fr in French; place du Général de Gaulle; adult/18-25yr/under
18yr €5/3.50/free, adult Sun 3.50; ⏰ tours 10am-5.15pm
Wed-Mon), built around eight courtyards. The
sumptuous **Grands Appartements** (Imperial
Apartments), including the empress's bedroom and a ballroom lit by 15 chandeliers,
can be seen on a one-hour tour (room-by-
room English text available; departures every
15 or 20 minutes). On alternating weeks,
visitors can see either the **Musée du Second Empire**, which illustrates the life of Napoleon III
and his family, or the **Musée de l'Impératrice**,
which stars Eugénie and includes mementos of her dashing, exiled son, 'killed by the
Zulus, in Zululand, Africa' in 1879 while
serving – with Queen Victoria's express
permission – in the British army.

Vehicles that predate the internal combus-
tion engine and early motorcars – including
the Jamais Contente, a torpedo-shaped
motorcar from 1899 – are featured at the
Musée de la Voiture (Vehicle Museum; adult/under 18yr
€2.60/free, incl the Grands Appartements adult/18-25yr/
under 18yr €5.50/4/free). Tours (one hour) are
in French.

To the east of the chateau, the 20-hectare,
English-style **Petit Parc** (admission free) links
up with the **Grand Parc** and the **Forêt de
Compiègne**, which surrounds Compiègne
on the east and south and is crisscrossed
by rectilinear paths. The area is a favourite
venue for hiking and cycling (maps available at the tourist office) as well as horse
riding. Napoléon I had the 4.5km **Allée des
Beaux-Monts** laid out so that Empress Marie-
Louise wouldn't miss Schönbrunn palace in
Vienna quite so much.

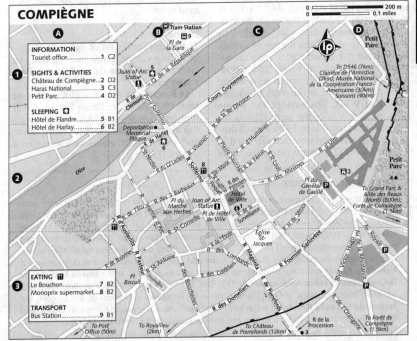

COMPIÈGNE

INFORMATION	
Tourist office..............1	C2

SIGHTS & ACTIVITIES	
Château de Compiègne..2	D2
Haras National..............3	C3
Petit Parc..............4	D2

SLEEPING	
Hôtel de Flandre..............5	B1
Hôtel de Harlay..............6	B2

EATING	
Le Bouchon..............7	B2
Monoprix supermarket..8	B2

TRANSPORT	
Bus Station..............9	B1

0 .... 200 m
0 .... 0.1 miles

FAR NORTHERN FRANCE

HARAS NATIONAL

It may be possible to get a look at the magnificent thoroughbreds, trotters, saddle horses, ponies and draught horses that live at the **National Stud Farm** (☎ 03 44 38 54 50; 6 rue de la Procession; admission free), in the chateau's former stables, which is run by the Ministry of Agriculture.

CLAIRIÈRE DE L'ARMISTICE

The armistice that came into force on 'the 11th hour of the 11th day of the 11th month' – the year of the armistice was 1918 – and finally put an end to WWI was signed 7km northeast of Compiègne (towards Soissons) inside the railway carriage of the Allied supreme commander, Maréchal Ferdinand Foch.

On 22 June 1940, in the same railway car, the French – with Hitler looking on smugly – were forced to sign the armistice that recognised the German conquest of France. Taken for exhibition to Berlin, the carriage was destroyed in April 1945 on the Führer's personal orders lest it be used for a third surrender – his own.

In the middle of a thick forest, the **Armistice Clearing** (☎ 03 44 85 14 18; adult/7-13yr €3/1.50; 🕑 9am-12.15pm & 2-6pm Wed-Mon Apr–mid-Oct, 10am-noon & 2-5pm Wed-Mon mid-Oct–Mar), staffed by volunteers (mainly French army veterans), commemorates these events with monuments and a museum whose 700 stereoscopic (3D) photos give you an eerie feeling of being right there in the mud, muck and misery of WWI. The wooden rail wagon now on display is of the same type as the original; the furnishings, hidden away during WWII, were the ones actually used in 1918. Since 1927, only visiting heads of state and government, along with a few very lucky ministers or ambassadors, have been allowed to go inside the wagon. By tradition, the president of France pays an official visit to the site every year ending in eight (1998, 2008 etc).

Festivals & Events

One of the world's most gruelling one-day cycling races, the misleadingly named **Paris-Roubaix** (www.letour.com/indexus.html), starts in front of the chateau on a Sunday right around Easter. The competition is famous for its bone-jarring sections over *pavé* (cobblestone) roads.

Sleeping

Hôtel de Flandre (☎ 03 44 83 24 40; www.hotelde flandre.com; 16 quai de la République; s/d €46/56, with washbasin €28/33) This straightforward two-star hotel offers visitors more convenience than charm. Some of the 37 rooms have river views.

Hôtel de Harlay (☎ 03 44 23 01 50; hoteldeharlay@ wanadoo.fr; 3 rue de Harlay; d €66.50) A three-star hotel whose 20 tasteful rooms have two-tone walls, rich carpeting and the latest mod cons.

Eating

The streets southwest of Église St-Jacques, including rue Magenta and narrow, ancient rue des Lombards, are home to lots of restaurants.

Le Bouchon (☎ 03 44 20 02 03; 4 rue d'Austerlitz; menus €10.50-25; 🕑 closed dinner Sun) In a half-timbered house with out-of-kilter walls, this bistro and wine bar has a sunny terrace and hearty French mains such as *magret de canard* (€12).

WHEN BENNY MET LOUIE

In these days of Franco-American disaccord, it's something of a relief to glance back at times gone by when relations between France and the USA were warmer, if not always free of rivalry. From the American Revolution (when French generals led American patriots, and Benjamin Franklin lobbied Louis XVI) through WWI (when American volunteers carried out humanitarian work long before the doughboys arrived) and WWII (when the Parisians didn't exactly liberate themselves, whatever de Gaulle might have proclaimed), the USA and France have had a prickly but ardent love affair. All this and more is presented through art and artefacts at the **Musée National de la Coopération Franco-Américaine** (☎ 03 23 39 60 16; 🕑 Wed-Mon, closed for renovations until at least Sep 2007), 30km northeast of Compiègne in the early 17th-century Château de Blérancourt. The **Jardins du Nouveau Monde** (admission free; 🕑 8am-7pm) showcase 'exotic' flowers (in bloom from May to September or October), shrubs and trees (eg sequoia) native to the Americas.

Self-catering supplies are sold at the **Monoprix supermarket** (37 rue Solférino; 🕐 8.30am-8pm Mon-Sat, to 8.30pm Fri).

Getting There & Around

Trains link Compiègne to Amiens (€11, 1½ hours, five to eight daily) and Paris' Gare du Nord (€11.90, 40 to 80 minutes, 15 to 26 daily).

Local TIC buses are free except on Sunday and holidays, when service is in any case very limited. Lines 1 and 2 link the train station with the chateau.

There's nonmetered parking in front of the chateau (place du Général de Gaulle) and southeast of there along av Royale and av de la Résistance.

LAON

pop 26,200

Laon (the name has one syllable and rhymes with *enfant*) served as the capital of the Carolingian empire until it was brought to an end in 987 by Hugh Capet, who preferred Paris. The walled, hilltop Ville Haute, an architectural gem, commands fantastic views of the surrounding plains and also boasts a fine Gothic cathedral. About 100m below sits the Ville Basse, completely rebuilt after being flattened in WWII.

Information

Tourist office (☎ 03 23 20 28 62; www.tourisme-paysde laon.com in French; place de la Cathédrale; 🕐 10am-7pm Mon-Sat, 11am-1pm & 2-6pm Sun & holidays Jun-Sep, 10am-12.30pm & 2-6pm Mon-Sat, 1-6pm Sun & holidays Oct-May) Housed in a 12th-century hospital decorated with 14th-century frescoes, in the Ville Haute next to the cathedral, the Tourist Office has excellent English brochures. A 1:600-scale model shows Laon as was in 1854.

Sights & Activities

A model for a number of its more famous Gothic sisters – Chartres, Reims and Dijon among them – **Cathédrale Notre Dame** (tourist office audioguide €3; 🕐 9am-6.30pm or 7pm, to 8.30pm in summer) was built (1150–1230) in the transitional Gothic style on Romanesque foundations. The 110m-long interior has a gilded wrought-iron choir screen and is remarkably well lit; some of the stained glass dates from the 12th century. A memorial

plaque for Commonwealth WWI dead hangs inside the west façade. It's possible to climb to the top of the cathedral's **south tower** (🕐 2pm, 4pm & 6pm Jul & Aug, 3pm Sat & Sun Easter-Jun & Sep–mid-Dec).

Underneath the cathedral (and indeed most of the old town) are three levels of **creuttes** (cellars and quarries); those underneath the Citadelle can be visited on a French-language **tour** (€3; 🕐 same days as cathedral tower). Tickets are available at the tourist office.

The Ville Haute's narrow streets, alleyways and courtyards are rich in historic buildings, making Laon a particularly rewarding place for keen-eyed wandering. The octagonal 12th-century **Chapelle des Templiers** is in the garden of the archaeologically orientated **Musée de Laon** (☎ 03 23 20 19 87; 32 rue Georges Ermant; adult/student €3.40/2.50; 🕐 11am-6pm Tue-Sun Jun-Sep, 2-6pm Tue-Sun Oct-May).

The 7km-long **ramparts**, with their three fortified gates, are lovely for a stroll; paths known as *grimpettes* take you down the steep forested slopes. For panoramic views, head to the 13th-century **Porte d'Ardon**; circular **Batterie Morlot**, a one-time optical telegraph station; and **rue du Rempart St-Rémi**.

Laon-born Jesuit missionary **Jacques Marquette** (1637–75), a pioneer explorer of the Mississippi River and the first European to live in what became Chicago, is commemorated by a haut-relief statue at square Marquette, at the bottom of rue Franklin Roosevelt (below the Ville Haute Poma station).

Sleeping & Eating

Hôtel du Commerce (☎ 03 23 79 57 16; hotel.com merce.laon@wanadoo.fr; 11 place de la Gare; d from €39, with washbasin €29) elcoming two-star hotel has 24 modestly furnished rooms that offer good value.

Hôtel Les Chevaliers (☎ 03 23 27 17 50; hotel chevaliers@aol.com; 3-5 rue Sérurier; d incl breakfast €60, s with washbasin €35) Parts of this two-star 14-room hostelry, right around the corner from the Haute Ville's Hôtel de Ville, date from the Middle Ages. Rooms are simple, with a touch of rusticity.

Les Chenizelles (☎ 03 23 23 02 34; 1 rue du Bourg; menus €13.90-29.90; 🕐 closed dinner Sun & Mon) This restaurant in the Ville Haute, across the square from the Hôtel de Ville, is an old favourite for a beer or a bite. Offerings include a variety of traditional French dishes.

Rue Chatelaine, which links the cathedral with place du Général Leclerc, is home to several food shops selling nutritional basics such as chocolate (at No 27).

Getting There & Around

There are direct rail services to Amiens (€14.70, 1½ to two hours, five daily), Paris' Gare du Nord (€18.50, 1¾ hours, 14 daily Monday to Friday, eight on Saturday and Sunday) and Reims (€8.10, 45 minutes, eight daily Monday to Friday, six on Saturday, two on Sunday).

The Ville Haute is a steep 20-minute walk away from the train station – the stairs begin at the upper end of av Carnot. A more fun way to travel is the automated, elevated **Poma funicular railway** (return €1; ☒ every 4min 7am-8pm Mon-Sat except holidays year-round, 2.30-7pm Sun Jul & Aug), which links the train station with the Ville Haute in 3½ minutes flat.

Normandy

Three things sum up Normandy – Camembert, cider and cows. Spread along the Channel coastline between Brittany and the far reaches of northeast France, Normandy is where the green, pleasant French countryside smacks hard into the rolling waves of La Manche (the Channel). It's a place of churned butter and soft runny cheese, where broad fields and dry-stone farmhouses perch on the edge of chalk-white cliffs, and the salty tang of the sea is in the air.

Ever since the armies of William the Conqueror set sail from its shores in 1066, Normandy has had a pivotal role in European history. It was the frontier for Anglo-French hostilities for much of the Hundred Years' War, and later became the crucible of impressionist art, but during the D-Day landings in 1944 Normandy sealed its place in the history books. History has certainly left its mark on the landscape, which is dotted with sturdy castles and stunning cathedrals, as well as the glorious abbey of Mont St-Michel, although many of the towns were shattered during the Battle of Normandy.

These days Normandy is an enticing blend of old and new. Fishing boats jostle with designer yachts in the harbour of Honfleur; contemporary restaurants and chic boutiques sit alongside half-timbered houses and Gothic churches in Rouen; and the reconstructed centre of Caen is a short drive away from the cobblestones of Bayeux. Whether it's browsing the Normandy fish market, mixing with the high-rollers at Deauville and Trouville, or strolling the D-Day beaches north of Bayeux, this is one part of France that will stay with you long after you leave for home.

HIGHLIGHTS

- Admire the art and architecture of the historic city of **Rouen** (p267)
- Be bowled over by the world's biggest comic strip, the **Bayeux Tapestry** (p292)
- Discover your inner impressionist at Monet's flower-filled **garden** (p280) at Giverny
- Ponder the fallen at the moving war cemeteries of **Colleville-sur-Mer** (p297), **Bayeux** (p294) and **La Cambe** (p297)
- Savour some seafood at the harbourside restaurants of **Trouville** (p286) and **Honfleur** (p284)
- Relive a century of war and peace at Caen's high-tech **Mémorial museum** (p287)
- Watch the sun sink into the sands around the abbey of **Mont St-Michel** (p304)

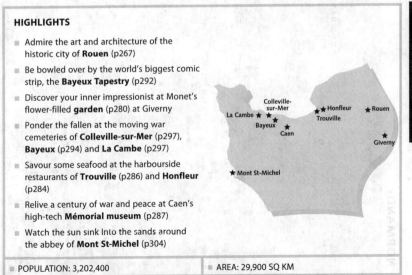

- POPULATION: 3,202,400
- AREA: 29,900 SQ KM

NORMANDY

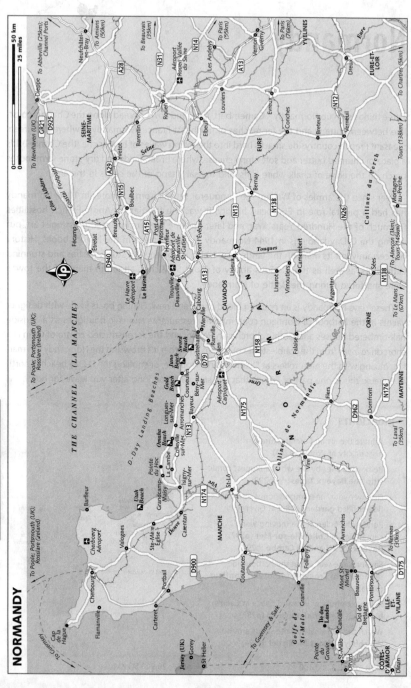

History

The Vikings invaded present-day Normandy in the 9th century. Many of the Scandinavian raiders established settlements in the area and adopted Christianity. In 911 French king Charles the Simple and Viking chief Hrölfr agreed that the area around Rouen should be handed over to these Norsemen – or Normans, as they came to be known.

In 1066 the duke of Normandy crossed the English Channel with 6000 soldiers. His forces crushed the English in the Battle of Hastings, and the duke – henceforth known as William the Conqueror – was crowned king of England (p293). The Channel Islands (Îles Anglo-Normandes), just off the Norman coast, came under English rule in the same year and remain so to this day. During the 11th and 12th centuries many churches were built in Normandy in the Romanesque style.

Throughout the Hundred Years' War (1337–1453) the duchy seesawed between French and English rule. England dominated Normandy for some 30 years until France gained permanent control in 1450. In the 16th century, Normandy, a Protestant stronghold, was the scene of much fighting between Catholics and Huguenots.

On 6 June 1944 – better known as D-Day – some 45,000 Allied troops landed on beaches near Bayeux, heralding the beginning of the Battle of Normandy (p298), the decisive campaign that led to the liberation of Nazi-occupied Europe. Freedom came at a terrible price, however – over 425,000 Allied and German casualties, and more than 15,000 civilian deaths. Eventually, the German resistance was broken and Paris was liberated on 25 August.

Getting There & Around

Ferries to and from England and Ireland dock at Cherbourg, Ouistreham, Le Havre and Dieppe. The Channel Islands are most accessible from the Breton port of St-Malo, but in the warm season from Cherbourg, Carteret, Granville and Portbail as well. For more information on ferries, see p973.

Normandy is easily accessible by train from Paris. All major towns in Normandy are well connected by rail, but the buses between smaller towns and villages are infrequent. To explore Normandy's rural areas you'll really be best on either two or four wheels.

SEINE-MARITIME

The Seine-Maritime *département* stretches from the old fishing harbour of Dieppe along the chalk-white cliffs of the Côte d'Albatre (Alabaster Coast) to Le Havre, the fifth-busiest port in France. It's a region whose history is firmly bound up with the sea, dotted with delightful country restaurants and quiet villages, and tailor-made for coastal exploring and clifftop walks. When you fancy a break from the bracing sea air, head inland to the lively, lovely metropolis of Rouen, a favourite haunt of Monet and Simone de Beauvoir and still one of the most intriguing cities in the northeastern corner of France.

ROUEN

pop 108,750

With its elegant spires, beautifully restored medieval quarter and soaring Gothic cathedral – undoubtedly one of the most stunning in northern France – the ancient city of Rouen is one of Normandy's highlights. Founded on the Roman city of Rotomagus, Rouen has had a turbulent history – the city was devastated several times during the Middle Ages by fire and plague, and was later occupied by the English during the Hundred Years' War. The young French heroine Joan of Arc (Jeanne d'Arc) was tried for heresy and burned at the stake in the central square in 1431. More recently, devastating bombing raids during WWII laid waste to much of the city, especially in the streets south of the cathedral, but in the last 60 years the city has been lavishly restored, and the medieval quarter is filled with half-timbered houses and punch-drunk, polished-up buildings. Rouen is an ideal base for exploring northern Normandy and Monet's home in Giverny.

Orientation

The main train station (Gare Rouen-Rive Droite) is at the northern end of rue Jeanne d'Arc, the main thoroughfare running south to the Seine. The old city is centred on rue du Gros Horloge between the place du Vieux Marché and the cathedral.

Information

BOOKSHOPS

ABC Bookshop (☎ 02 35 71 08 67; 11 rue des Faulx)

NORMANDY

INTERNET ACCESS

Cybernet (☎ 02 35 07 73 02; 47 place du Vieux Marché; per hr €4; ☿ 10am-10pm)

PlaceNet (☎ 02 32 76 02 22; 37 rue de la République; per 15min €1; ☿ 10am-midnight)

INTERNET RESOURCES

www.normandy-tourism.org Official site providing a whistle-stop overview of Normandy's main sights.

LAUNDRY

Laundrette (56 rue Cauchoise; ☿ 7am-8pm or 9pm)

Laundrette (55 rue d'Amiens; ☿ 7am-8pm or 9pm)

MONEY

Banks with ATMs line rue Jeanne d'Arc between Théâtre des Arts and place Maréchal Foch.

American Express (☎ 02 35 89 48 60; 25 place de la Cathédrale; ☿ 9am-1pm & 2-6pm Mon-Sat) In the tourist office.

Bureau de Change (7-9 rue des Bonnetiers; ☿ 7am-10pm) Decent exchange rates.

POST

Post Office (45 rue Jeanne d'Arc) Has a Cyberposte terminal.

TOURIST INFORMATION

Tourist Office (☎ 02 32 08 32 40; www.rouentourisme .com; 25 place de la Cathédrale; ☿ 9am-7pm Mon-Sat, 9.30am-12.30pm & 2-6pm Sun May-Sep, 9am-6pm Mon-Sat, 10am-1pm Sun Oct-Apr) Staff make hotel reservations in the area for €1.50.

Sights

OLD CITY

Rouen suffered heavy damage during WWII but has been painstakingly rebuilt. The main street, rue du Gros Horloge, runs from the cathedral to **place du Vieux Marché**, where 19-year-old Joan of Arc was executed for heresy in 1431. The futuristic **Église Jeanne d'Arc** (☿ 10am-12.15pm & 2-6pm Mon-Sat), with its fish-scale exterior and stark cast-iron cross, marks the site where Joan was burned at the stake. The church is also notable for its marvellous 16th-century stained-glass windows.

Rue du Gros Horloge is spanned by an early-16th-century gatehouse and the **Gros Horloge**, a large one-handed medieval clock.

The ornate **Palais de Justice** (Law Courts; on Place Maréchal le Foch), little more than a shell at the end of WWII, has been restored to its early-16th-century Gothic glory, though the 19th-century western façade still shows extensive damage.

The courtyard of the Palais de Justice is worth a look for its spires, gargoyles and statuary. The two-storey building overlooking the courtyard is the **Monument Juif** (Jewish Monument), the oldest such monument in France and the only reminder of Rouen's ancient Jewish community, expelled by Philippe le Bel in 1306. At the time of writing, it was closed to the public.

CATHÉDRALE NOTRE DAME

Rouen's **Cathédrale Notre Dame** (☿ 8am-6pm) is perhaps best known as the subject of a series of canvases by Claude Monet, who was fascinated by the subtle changes of light and colour on the cathedral's towering French-Gothic façade. Built between 1201 and 1514, it suffered severe damage during WWII, but the decades-long restoration process is nearly complete, and Monet would now hardly recognise its sparkling white façade. The Romanesque **crypt** was part of a cathedral completed in 1062 and destroyed by fire in 1200. The Flamboyant Gothic **Tour de Beurre** (Butter Tower) was paid for by members of the congregation who made a donation to the cathedral in return for being allowed to eat butter during the fast of Lent. The tower was supposedly built on the proceeds of their donations (although there is some argument about this – some local historians say the name simply refers to the colour of the stone). There are several guided visits to the crypt, ambulatory and **Chapel of the Virgin** on weekends, and daily in July and August.

MUSEUMS

In a desanctified 16th-century church, the fascinating **Musée Le Secq des Tournelles** (☎ 02 35 71 28 40; 2 rue Jacques Villon; adult/concession €2.30/1.55; ☿ 10am-1pm & 2-6pm Wed-Mon) is devoted to the blacksmith's craft. It displays some 12,000 locks, keys and other wrought-iron utensils made between the 3rd and 19th centuries.

The **Musée des Beaux-Arts** (Fine Arts Museum; ☎ 02 35 71 28 40; 26bis rue Jean Lecanuet; adult/student €3/2; ☿ 10am-6pm Wed-Mon) features a captivating collection of 15th- to 20th-century paintings, including canvases by Caravaggio, Rubens, Modigliani and (of course) a painting of Rouen Cathedral by Claude Monet.

ROUEN

0 ____ 400 m
0 ____ 0.2 miles

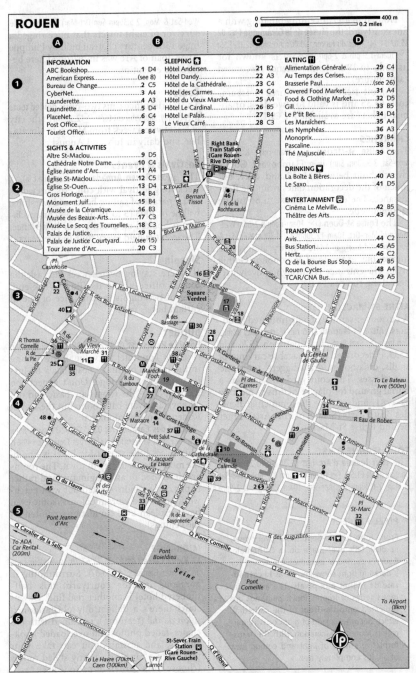

INFORMATION
ABC Bookshop.....................1 D4
American Express................(see 8)
Bureau de Change...............2 C5
CyberNet...........................3 A4
Launderette........................4 A3
Laundrette.........................5 D4
PlaceNet............................6 C4
Post Office.........................7 B3
Tourist Office......................8 B4

SIGHTS & ACTIVITIES
Aître St-Maclou....................9 D5
Cathédrale Notre Dame.........10 C4
Église Jeanne d'Arc.............11 A4
Église St-Maclou................12 C5
Église St-Ouen...................13 D4
Gros Horloge.....................14 B4
Monument Juif...................15 B4
Musée de la Céramique........16 C3
Musée des Beaux-Arts.........17 C3
Musée Le Secq des Tournelles.18 C3
Palais de Justice.................19 B4
Palais de Justice Courtyard....(see 15)
Tour Jeanne d'Arc...............20 C3

SLEEPING
Hôtel Andersen...................21 B2
Hôtel Dandy......................22 A3
Hôtel de la Cathédrale.........23 C4
Hôtel des Carmes...............24 C4
Hôtel du Vieux Marché.........25 A4
Hôtel Le Cardinal...............26 B5
Hôtel Le Palais..................27 B4
Le Vieux Carré..................28 C3

EATING
Alimentation Générale...........29 C4
Au Temps des Cerises..........30 B3
Brasserie Paul...................(see 26)
Covered Food Market..........31 A4
Food & Clothing Market.......32 D5
Gill...............................33 B5
Le P'tit Bec.....................34 D4
Les Maraîchers..................35 A4
Les Nymphéas...................36 A3
Monoprix.........................37 B4
Pascaline.........................38 B4
Thé Majuscule...................39 C5

DRINKING
La Boîte à Bières................40 A3
Le Saxo..........................41 D5

ENTERTAINMENT
Cinéma Le Melville.............42 B5
Théâtre des Arts...............43 A5

TRANSPORT
Avis..............................44 C2
Bus Station......................45 A5
Hertz............................46 C2
Q de la Bourse Bus Stop......47 B4
Rouen Cycles....................48 A4
TCAR/CNA Bus..................49 A5

NORMANDY

Housed in a 17th-century building with a fine courtyard, the **Musée de la Céramique** (☎ 02 35 07 31 74; 1 rue du Faucon; adult/concession €2.30/1.55; ☒ 10am-1.30pm & 2-6pm Wed-Sat) is known for its 16th- to 19th-century faïence (decorated earthenware).

A joint ticket for the three museums costs €5.35 and is valid for two days, or annual tickets are available for €9.15.

CHURCHES

The **Église St-Maclou** (☒ 10am-noon & 2-6pm Mon-Sat, 3-5.30pm Sun) is a Flamboyant Gothic church built between 1437 and 1521, but much of the decoration dates from the Renaissance. The entrance is next to 56 rue de la République.

The **Église St-Ouen** (☒ 10am-noon & 2-6pm Wed-Mon mid-Mar–Oct, 10am-12.30pm & 2-4.30pm Wed, Sat & Sun Nov–mid-Mar), a 14th-century abbey, is a marvellous example of Rayonnant Gothic style. The entrance is through a lovely garden along rue des Faulx.

AÎTRE ST-MACLOU

A curious ensemble of half-timbered buildings, **Aître St-Maclou** (186 rue Martainville; admission free; ☒ 8am-8pm), built between 1526 and 1533, is decorated with macabre carvings of skulls, crossbones, gravediggers' tools and hourglasses. The courtyard was used as a burial ground for plague victims as recently as 1781, and is now the municipal École des Beaux-Arts (School of Fine Arts). Enter behind Église St-Maclou.

TOUR JEANNE D'ARC

The **Tour Jeanne d'Arc** (☎ 02 35 98 16 21; rue du Donjon; adult €1.50; ☒ 10am-12.30pm & 2-6pm Wed-Sat & Mon, 2-6.30pm Sun Apr-Sep, 10am-12.30pm & 2-5pm

---

PIXEL PERFECT

From June to mid-September every year, as dusk falls over place de la Cathédrale, Rouen's cathedral becomes the venue for a dazzling light show known as **la cathédrale de Monet aux pixels**. The artist's famous series of impressionist paintings are projected onto the front of the cathedral, which becomes a kind of giant canvas, mirroring Monet's fascination with the transformative effects of light and colour. Best of all, it's completely free.

Wed-Sat & Mon, 2-5.30pm Sun Oct-Mar) is the sole survivor of eight towers that once ringed a huge 13th-century chateau built by Philippe Auge. Joan of Arc was imprisoned here before her execution.

Tours

The tourist office runs two-hour **guided tours** (French only; adult/student €6/4; ☒ 2.30pm) of the city at least twice a week from March to November, and daily in July and August.

Festivals & Events

The next **Rouen Armada** (www.armada.c.la), a week-long festival with concerts, fireworks and a parade of sailing boats and warships, will be in 2008 (5 to 14 July). Accommodation is booked up about a year in advance. The event is held every four to five years.

Sleeping

If you're staying over a weekend, ask the tourist office about its 'Bon Week-end' offer of two nights for the price of one in certain hotels (p948).

BUDGET

Hôtel Le Palais (☎ 02 35 71 41 40; 12 rue du Tambour; r from €30) Top hotel for value in town, bang in the middle of things near Palais de Justice and Gros Horloge. Don't expect too many spoils – the rooms are basic and not all have a private bathroom, but the rest of Rouen is on your doorstep.

Hôtel des Carmes (☎ 02 35 71 92 31; www.hotel descarmes.fr.st in French; 33 place des Carmes; r €45-61) This sweet little street-side hotel is one of the nicest places to stay in town. The rooms are decorated in an imaginative and rather haphazard fashion, decked out with patchwork quilts and vibrant colours (some even have cerulean-blue cloudscapes painted on the ceilings).

MIDRANGE

Le Vieux Carré (☎ 02 35 71 67 70; www.vieux-carre .fr; 34 rue Ganterie; d €55-57) Surrounding a gorgeous interior courtyard, this half-timbered hotel is another real find. Downstairs there's a delightfully old-fashioned *salon de thé* (tearoom), crammed with old chairs, faded photos and overloaded bookshelves, and upstairs you can take your pick from a range of smartly styled rooms (choose from garden or patio views).

Hôtel le Cardinal (☎ 02 35 70 24 42; www.cardinal -hotel.fr; 1 place de la Cathédrale; s €47-59, d €58-72) What this thoroughly modern hotel lacks in chara cter, it more than makes up for in location – the Cardinal sits in a fantastic spot right opposite the cathedral, and the top-floor rooms have lovely private balconies over-looking the square.

Hôtel Andersen (☎ 02 35 71 88 51; www.hotel andersen.com; 4 rue Pouchet; s €50, d €60-65) Not as central, but very handy for the station, this quietly elegant, family-run hotel is housed in a 19th-century mansion and offers an unmistakably old-world atmosphere – classical music greets you as you walk through the door, and the bedrooms ooze Laura Ashley style.

Hôtel de la Cathédrale (☎ 02 35 71 57 95; www .hotel-de-la-cathedrale.fr; 12 rue St-Romain; s €52-72, d €62-89) Another character-packed hotel down a cobbled backstreet, complete with an original 17th-century timber-panelled façade and a plant-filled inner courtyard. The rooms are pricey for what you get – some are quite poky and there's a worrying prevalence of pastel-shaded wallpaper – but the atmosphere is hard to beat.

TOP END

Hôtel Dandy (☎ 02 35 07 32 00; www.hotel-dandy -rouen.federal-hotel.com; 93 rue Cauchoise; s/d/tw €76/86/99) This hotel isn't called the Dandy for nothing – it's the perfect place to find your inner *flâneur*, decorated in Old Nor-man style with plenty of antique furniture, brass-framed mirrors and plush furnish-ings. The prices are steep, but the emphasis here is on luxury rather than low cost.

Hôtel Du Vieux Marché (☎ 02 35 71 00 88; www .hotelduvieuxmarche.com; 33 rue du Vieux Palais; s €92-98, d €102-108) In stark contrast to most of Rouen's other older-style hotels, this is very much one for the modernists – a sleek, chic boutique hotel crammed with leather furni-ture, rich mahogany and the odd touch of Zen sophistication.

Eating

BUDGET

Thé Majuscule (☎ 02 35 71 15 66; 8 place de la Calende; tartes €6.95; ⏲ noon-6.30pm Mon-Sat) Downstairs it's a typically chaotic French second-hand bookshop; upstairs it's a homely tearoom with a fine line in home-made tarts, cakes and exotic teas.

Le P'tit Bec (☎ 02 35 07 63 33; 182 rue Eau de Robec; lunch menus €11.50-14; ⏲ lunch Mon-Sat, dinner Fri & Sat) Always busy with a loyal local crowd, this down-to-earth restaurant is all about good, reliable food – the menu is stuffed with pasta, salads, *œufs cocottes* (eggs baked in cream and served in small china ram-ekins) and plenty of vegetarian options.

MIDRANGE

Brasserie Paul (☎ 02 35 71 86 07; 1 place de la Cathéd-rale; mains €10-25; ⏲ breakfast, lunch & dinner) The classic Rouennaise brasserie, favoured by artists and philosophers for over a century and still going strong. All the decorative trappings are here – starchy service, plush red seats and spinning overhead fans (not to mention the self-playing pianola) – and the menu is crammed with regional dishes, including Simone de Beauvoir's favourite smoked duck salad.

Au Temps des Cerises (☎ 02 35 89 98 00; 4-6 rue des Basnage; lunch menus €10.50, dinner menus from €15; ⏲ lunch & dinner, closed Sun, Mon & lunch Sat) There's no better place to check out Normandy's fa-mous cheeses than this ever-popular restau-rant (look out for the fox and raven murals outside). Choose your cheesy poison – the menu is packed with *tartiflette*, fondue and endless varieties of *croûtes* – and tuck in.

Pascaline (☎ 02 35 89 67 44; 5 rue de la Poterne; menus €12.95 & €15.90; ⏲ lunch & dinner) One of the top spots in town for a great-value *formule midi* (lunch *menu*, a set menu), this bus-tling bistro serves up traditional cuisine in typically French surroundings – net cur-tains, wooden tables and chuffing coffee machines abound. There's live music sev-eral nights a week.

Les Maraîchers (☎ 02 35 71 57 73; 37 place du Vieux Marché; menus from €18; ⏲ lunch & dinner) While the food here is great, it's clearly outdone by the magnificent décor. All gleaming mirrors, polished wood, pewter and tiles, the res-taurant has been classified a *café historique d'Europe*.

TOP END

Les Nymphéas (☎ 02 35 89 26 69; 7 rue de la Pie; menus €27-64; ⏲ lunch & dinner Tue-Sat) This is a more traditional establishment than Gill (p272), but the food is just as impressive – local ingredients (especially cider and Calvados) give a Norman twist to rich dishes such as foie gras and roast pigeon.

NORMANDY

Gill (☎ 02 35 71 16 14; 8 quai de la Bourse; weekday menus €38, weekend menus €58-80; ☺ lunch & dinner Tue-Sat) Rouen has no shortage of upmarket restaurants, but Gill is the only place to be for gourmands in the know. Expect classic French cuisine of the highest order (whole fresh lobster, tournedos or scallops with truffles) served in an effortlessly chic dining room.

SELF-CATERING

Rue Rollon has several good fruit stalls, cake shops and bakeries. The **covered food market** (place du Vieux Marché; ☺ 6am-1.30pm Tue-Sun) offers dairy products, fish and fresh produce. There's also a lively daily **food and clothing market** (place St-Marc).

There's an **Alimentation Générale** (78 rue de la République) and a **Monoprix** (65 rue du Gros Horloge) supermarket.

Drinking

La Boîte à Bières (☎ 02 35 07 76 47; 35 rue Cauchoise; ☺ 4pm-2am Tue-Sat) This lively half-timbered corner-bar is a good place to down a few local ales, in the company of live bands and a fanatically loyal student following.

Le Bateau Ivre (☎ 02 35 70 09 05; 17 rue des Sapins; ☺ 10pm-4am Tue-Sat) A longstanding live venue that's still one of the town's top hangouts, with a varied programme of gigs and a regular talent night open to hopeful young *chanteurs* (singers)– perfect for budding Édith Piafs and Jacques Brels.

Le Saxo (☎ 02 35 98 24 92; 11 place St-Marc; ☺ 9am-2am) This place swings to the rhythm of jazz and blues – it's a must on the nightcrawler's itinerary, especially on weekends when there are often live concerts.

Entertainment

Cinéma Le Melville (☎ 02 32 76 73 21; 12 rue St-Étienne des Tonneliers) Occasionally runs nondubbed English language films.

Théâtre des Arts (☎ 02 35 71 41 36; place des Arts; tickets from €20) Rouen's premier music venue and home to the Opéra de Normandie, the theatre also runs concerts and ballets.

Getting There & Away

The **Aéroport Rouen Vallée du Seine** (☎ 02 35 79 41 00) is 8km southeast of town at Boos. There are weekday direct flights to Lyon that connect with other cities in France as well as to international destinations.

CNA (☎ 08 25 07 60 27; 9 rue Jeanne d'Arc) runs bus services throughout Seine-Maritime, including Dieppe (€11, two hours, three daily), and towns along the coast west of Dieppe, including Fécamp (€15.10, 3¼ hours, one daily) and Le Havre (€13.80, three hours, five daily). Buses to Dieppe and Le Havre are slower and pricier than the train. Buses leave from quai du Havre and quai de la Bourse.

From Gare Rouen-Rive Droite, an Art Nouveau edifice built from 1912 to 1928, there's a frequent express train to/from Paris' Gare St-Lazare (€18.50, 70 minutes, six to eight daily). Local destinations include Caen (€20.70, two hours, 12 daily), Dieppe (€9, 45 minutes, 12 to 15 daily) and Le Havre (€12.40, one hour, 12 to 15 daily). Gare Rouen-Rive Gauche has regional services.

Getting Around

There is no public transport into town from the airport; a taxi costs about €25.

Rouen's local bus network and its flagship metro line are operated by **TCAR** (Espace Métrobus; ☎ 02 35 52 52 00; 9 rue Jeanne d'Arc). The metro runs from 5am (6am Sunday) to 11.30pm and is useful for getting from the train station to the centre of town. A ticket valid for an hour costs €1.30 a day pass is €3.70 and a 10-ticket carnet costs €10.80.

For taxis, **Radio Taxi** (☎ 02 35 88 50 50) operates 24 hour a day.

Rouen Cycles (☎ 02 35 71 34 30; 45 rue St-Éloi) rents out mountain bikes for €12 per day.

For car rental, try **ADA** (☎ 02 35 72 25 88; 34 av Jean Rondeaux). **Avis** (☎ 02 35 88 60 94) and **Hertz** (☎ 02 35 70 70 71) are both near the Gare Rouen-Rive Droite train station.

DIEPPE

pop 35,700

Sandwiched between limestone cliffs, Dieppe is one of the busiest ports on the Normandy coast. It's a salty, shabby but authentic old harbour, the kind of place where leather-skinned Dieppoise fishermen rub shoulders with British day-trippers and summertime tourists licking oversized ice creams. It's a fantastic spot to try some Norman seafood – the harbour is chockfull of restaurants serving local specialities such as *marmite Dieppoise* (seafood stew) and *moules marinières* (mussels).

Privateers based in Dieppe pillaged Southampton in 1338 and blockaded Lisbon two centuries later. The first European settlers in Canada included many Dieppois. The town was one of France's most important ports during the 16th century, when ships regularly sailed from Dieppe to West Africa and Brazil.

Orientation

The town centre is largely surrounded by water. Blvd de Verdun runs along the lawns bordering the beach. Most of Grande Rue and rue de la Barre has been turned into a pedestrianised area. Quai Duquesne and its continuation quai Henri IV follow the western and northern sides of the port area. Ferries dock at the terminal on the north-eastern side of the port, just under 2km on foot from the tourist office.

Information

INTERNET ACCESS
Art au Bar (☎ 02 35 40 48 35; 19 rue de Sygogne; per 15min/hr €1/4; ☽ 10am-7.30pm Mon-Thu, 10am-10.30pm Fri & Sat)

LAUNDRY
Laundrette (44 rue de l'Épée; ☽ 7am-9pm)

MONEY
Banque Populaire (15 place Nationale) One of several banks on place Nationale.
Crédit Maritime Mutuel (3 rue Guillaume Terrien; ☽ 8.30am-noon & 1.30-5.15pm Mon-Fri) One of the few banks open Monday.

POST
Post Office (2 blvd Maréchal Joffre) Has a Cyberposte.

TOURIST INFORMATION
Tourist Office (☎ 02 32 14 40 60; www.dieppetourisme.com; Pont Jehan Ango; ☽ 9am-7pm Mon-Sat, 10am-1pm & 3-6pm Sun Jul & Aug, 9am-1pm & 2-7pm Mon-Sat May, Jun & Sep, 9am-noon & 2-6pm Mon-Sat Oct-Apr) On the west side of the port. Hotel reservations in the area cost €3.50.

Sights

High above the city on the western cliff is the 15th-century **Château Musée** (☎ 02 35 84 19 76; adult/student €3/1.50; ☽ 10am-noon & 2-6pm Jun-Sep, 10am-noon & 2-5pm Wed-Mon Oct-May), Dieppe's most impressive landmark. The museum is devoted to Dieppe's maritime and artistic history, which often involved the dubious practice of separating African elephants

from their tusks and shipping the ivory back to Dieppe. The craft of ivory carving reached extraordinary heights in Dieppe during the 17th century and the results are on display.

The **Cité de la Mer** (☎ 02 35 06 93 20; 37 rue de l'Asile Thomas; adult/under 16yr €5/3; ☽ 10am-12.30pm & 2-6.30pm Jun-Aug, 10am-noon & 2-6pm Sep-May) is devoted to Dieppe's nautical heritage, with exhibits on fishing techniques, shipbuilding and various seaside habitats. The visit ends with five large aquariums filled with live specimens of sea creatures more usually found on French plates: octopus, lobsters, turbot and cod.

Dieppe's seafront and gravelly beach aren't terribly attractive, and are often battered by strong winds (useful for the local fishermen, but not very conducive to sunbathing). The vast **lawns** between blvd de Verdun and the beach were laid out in the 1860s by that seashore-loving imperial duo, Napoleon III and his wife, Eugénie. **Église St-Jacques**, a Norman Gothic church at place St-Jacques, has been reconstructed several times since the early 13th century.

The Canadian Military Cemetery is 4km towards Rouen. Take av des Canadiens (the continuation of av Gambetta) south and follow the signs.

The **GR21 hiking trail** follows the Côte d'Albâtre southwest from Dieppe all the way to Le Havre. Maps and topoguides for hikes and easy walks in the surrounding area are available from the tourist office.

Sleeping

Camping La Source (☎ 02 35 84 27 04; adult/site €4/6; ☽ mid-Mar–mid-Oct) This camp site is 3km southwest of Dieppe in a lovely creekside location, just off the D925 (well signposted). Take bus 4 to the Petit-Appeville train station (10 minutes), walk beneath the railway bridge and up the marked gravel drive.

Auberge de Jeunesse (☎ 02 35 84 85 73; 48 rue Louis Fromager; dm incl breakfast €11.40; ☽ mid-May–mid-Sep) About 4km southwest of the train station, this hostel provides a kitchen and laundry. From the train station, walk straight up blvd Bérigny to the Chambre de Commerce from where you take bus 2 Val Druel to the Château Michel stop.

Au Grand Duquesne (☎ 02 32 14 61 10; http://au granddunquesne.free.fr; 15 place St-Jacques; d €40-61)

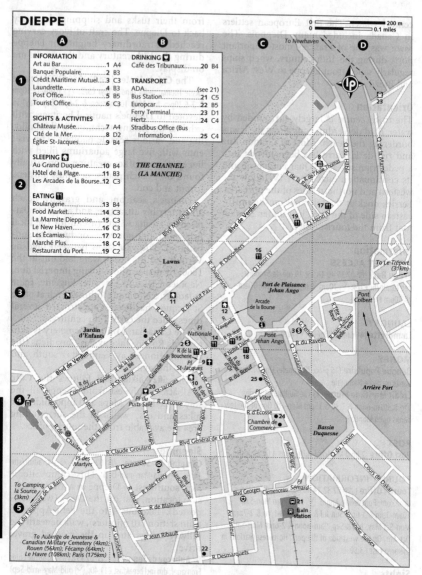

DIEPPE

0 —————— 200 m
0 —————— 0.1 miles

INFORMATION
Art au Bar....................1 A4
Banque Populaire...........2 B3
Crédit Maritime Mutuel....3 C3
Laundrette....................4 B3
Post Office....................5 B5
Tourist Office................6 C3

SIGHTS & ACTIVITIES
Château Musée..............7 A4
Cité de la Mer...............8 D2
Église St-Jacques...........9 B4

SLEEPING
Au Grand Duquesne........10 B4
Hôtel de la Plage...........11 B3
Les Arcades de la Bourse..12 C3

EATING
Boulangerie..................13 B4
Food Market................14 C3
La Marmite Dieppoise.....15 C3
Le New Haven...............16 C3
Les Écamias.................17 D2
Marché Plus................18 C4
Restaurant du Port........19 C2

DRINKING
Café des Tribunaux.........20 B4

TRANSPORT
ADA...........................(see 21)
Bus Station..................21 C5
Europcar....................22 B5
Ferry Terminal..............23 D1
Hertz.........................24 C4
Stradibus Office (Bus
  Information)...............25 C4

THE CHANNEL
(LA MANCHE)

To Newhaven

To Le Tréport
(31km)

To Camping
la Source
(3km)

To Auberge de Jeunesse &
Canadian Military Cemetery (4km);
Rouen (56km); Fécamp (64km);
Le Havre (108km); Paris (175km)

No harbour views, but this centrally located hotel is the best compromise between comfort and price in Dieppe. None of the blue-themed bedrooms are anything special, but the downstairs restaurant is good for simple seafood (*menus* €11.60 to €26.60).

Les Arcades de la Bourse (☎ 02 35 84 14 12; www .lesarcades.fr; 1-3 arcade de la Bourse; d €45-75) Perched above a colonnaded arcade right opposite the port, this is really just a restaurant with some upstairs accommodation. The plain bedrooms range from spartan to just about adequate – a bathroom and a TV is about all you'll get. Still, the port views are lovely.

Hôtel de la Plage (☎ 02 35 84 18 28; 20 blvd de Verdun; r €50-75; ☐) The best of a clutch of faded places along the seafront, although this lemon-yellow hotel certainly won't win any beauty contests. The rooms have all the mod cons – TVs, minibars and hairdryers – but the sea-view rooms come at a premium.

Eating & Drinking

Les Écamias (☎ 02 35 84 67 67; 129 quai Henri IV; menus €13.50 & €20; ☯ lunch & dinner, closed Mon, dinner Sun & Tue) This tiny, sparsely decorated restaurant only offerss a limited menu, but all the dishes are traditionally cooked and provides fantastic value. Mussels, skate and monkfish are just some of the fishy treats on offer.

Le New Haven (☎ 02 35 84 89 72; 53 quai Henri IV; menus €15.50-26.50; ☯ lunch & dinner, closed Tue & Wed in low season) The harbour front is lined with gaudy restaurants, but this is the best of the bunch. As always in Deppe, the menu is dominated by fish – the blackboard of specials changes daily depending on what's been landed on the quay.

La Marmite Dieppoise (☎ 02 35 84 24 26; 8 rue St-Jean; menus €26-39; ☯ lunch & dinner, closed Mon & dinner Sun) There's really only one thing to eat in Dieppe, and that's some fresh *fruits de mer* (seafood). This rustic little restaurant in the old city is an ideal place to sink some local seafood – especially if you go for the house speciality fish stew.

Restaurant du Port (☎ 02 35 84 36 64; 99 quai Henri IV; menus €89 & €150; ☯ lunch & dinner Fri-Wed) Currently one of the hot tips with Normandy's foodies, this eye-wateringly expensive restaurant represents seafood at its most indulgent – roast turbot, buttered sole and super-rich fish soup (the chef's secret recipe) are served up in the nautically themed dining room, and cooked to Michelin-standard perfection.

Café des Tribunaux (☎ 02 32 14 44 65; place du Puits Salé) This sprawling 18th century building was a preferred hang-out for impressionist painters in the late 19th century, and it's still an impressive spot, especially if you bag an outside table on the place du Puits Salé.

SELF-CATERING

There's a **food market** (☯ 6am-1pm Tue & Thu, 7am-5pm Sat) between place St-Jacques and place Nationale and a wonderful **boulangerie** (15 quai Henri IV; ☯ Tue-Sun; 14 rue de la Boucherie; ☯ Thu-Tue). The **Marché Plus** (22 quai Duquesne) supermarket is open long hours.

Getting There & Away

The bus station is in the same cavernous building as the train station. CNA runs services to Fécamp (€11.80, 2¼ hours, at least two daily) and Rouen (€11.10, two hours, three daily). No buses run on Saturday or Sunday afternoons.

The main ferry operator is **Transmanche Ferries** (☎ in France 08 00 65 01 00, in Britain 0800 917 1201; www.transmanche.com), which runs daily services from Dieppe to Newhaven. For further ferry information, see p973.

From Dieppe's **train station** (☎ 02 35 06 69 33) there are three trains daily to Paris St-Lazare (€24.40, 2¾ hours) and Le Havre (€13.90, two to 2½ hours), both via Rouen (€9.50, 50 minutes, 12 to 14 daily).

Getting Around

Stradibus (☎ 02 32 14 03 03; 56 quai Duquesne) operates 13 local lines that run until 6pm or 8pm. All buses stop at either the train station or the nearby Chambre de Commerce, on quai Duquesne. A single ticket costs €1.05, a 10-ticket carnet €7. Buses shuttle foot passengers between the ferry terminal and the tourist office (€2). A **taxi** (☎ 02 35 84 20 05) from the ferry pier to the city centre costs about €8.

Rental-car companies:
ADA (☎ 02 35 84 32 28; train station)
Europcar (☎ 02 35 04 97 10; 33 rue Thiers)
Hertz (☎ 02 32 14 01 70; 5 rue d'Écosse)

CÔTE D'ALBÂTRE

Stretching 100km southwest from Dieppe to Étretat, the bone-white cliffs of the Côte d'Albâtre (Alabaster Coast) are strikingly reminiscent of the limestone cliffs of Dover, just across the Channel. The coastline is dotted with small villages and hamlets, and several fine beaches, but the only towns of any note are Fécamp and Étretat.

Without a car, the Côte d'Albâtre is rather inaccessible. However, walkers can follow the coastal GR21 footpath from Dieppe to Le Havre. If you are driving, take the coastal road, which starts at the D75 west of Dieppe, and not the inland D925.

Fécamp

pop 21,500

Fécamp was a fishing village until the 6th century, when a few drops of Christ's blood miraculously found their way here and

NORMANDY

attracted hordes of pilgrims. Benedictine monks soon established a monastery, and the 'medicinal elixir' they concocted in the early 16th century helped keep Fécamp on the map. The recipe, lost during the Revolution, was rediscovered in the 19th century and the after-dinner liqueur was produced commercially. Today, Bénédictine is one of the most widely marketed *digestifs* in the world.

INFORMATION

Tourist Office (☎ 02 35 28 51 01; www.fecamptourisme .com in French; 113 rue Alexandre Le Grand; ☯ 9am-6pm Mon-Fri & 10am-6.30pm Sat Apr-Sep, 9am-6pm Mon-Fri, 9.30am-12.30pm & 2-6pm Sat Oct-Mar) There's a second outpost at the beach which opens from May to August.

SIGHTS

The ornate **Palais Bénédictine** (☎ 02 35 10 26 10; www.benedictine.fr; 110 rue Alexandre Le Grand; adult/12-18yr/under 12yr €5.80/2/free; ☯ 10am-7pm Jul-Sep, 10am-1pm & 2-6.30pm Apr-Jun, Sep–mid-Oct, 10.30am-12.45pm & 2-6pm Feb-Mar & mid-Oct–Dec, closed Jan) was inspired by the 15th-century Hôtel de Cluny in Paris, and now contains just about everything you need to know about Fécamp's trademark liqueur – except the exact recipe. Tours start in the art museum, which houses the private

---

CAMEMBERT COUNTRY

For a region that's so chock-full of cows, it's hardly surprising that Normandy is so famous for its cheese. Some of the most enduring names in the fickle world of French *fromage* cheese have their spiritual home in Normandy, including **Pont L'Evêque, Livarot** and most famous of all, **Camembert**. It's thought that monks first began experimenting with cheese-making in the Pays d'Auge sometime in the 11th century, but the present-day varieties didn't emerge until around the 17th-century. The invention of Camembert is generally credited to Marie Herel, who was supposedly given the secret of soft cheese–making by an abbot from Brie on the run from Revolutionary mobs in 1790. Whatever the truth of the legend, the cheese was a huge success at the local market in Vimoutiers, and production of Camembert quickly grew from a cottage industry into an international operation – it even received the royal seal of approval from Napoleon III at the World Fair in 1855.

These days Camembert is seriously big business. Since 1983 the Camembert name has been protected by an official AOC (Apellation d'Origine Contrôlée) designation (just like vintage French wine). Between 10,000 and 15,000 tonnes of Camembert are produced in Normandy every year, and it remains one of the country's most popular cheeses – two-thirds of French cheese buyers still consider it an essential element of any self-respecting cheeseboard.

Camembert is traditionally made from unpasteurised cow's milk, and requires two special moulds – *Penicillium candida* and *Penicillium camemberti* – to mature, a process that usually takes around three weeks from start to finish. The distinctive round wooden boxes in which Camembert is wrapped have been around since 1890; they were designed by a local engineer by the name of Monsieur Ridel to protect the soft cheese during long-distance travel.

If you're interested in seeing how the cheese is made, you can take a guided tour of the **Président Farm** (☎ 02 33 36 06 60; www.fermepresident.com; adult/child €5/3; ☯ June-Aug, by reservation Mar-May & Sep-Oct), an 18th-century farm in the centre of Camembert owned and restored by the Président brand (one of the region's main Camembert producers). The guided tour explores the way in which Camembert was traditionally made, and you can also view a collection of vintage farm tools, vats, and presses, as well as a gallery of over 500 labels from all the main Camembert brands. Naturally, there's also plenty of opportunity to try some of the village's famous cheese, and a well-stocked shop where you can pick up some Camembert-themed souvenirs.

And in case you're new to the secret science of Camembert, here are a couple of tips from those in the know. Most French people squeeze their cheese before buying it to test its ripeness – the texture should be soft, but not squelchy. A good Camembert should have a good coating of white rind with a few reddish spots, and the taste should be strong and quite fruity. Keep the Camembert in the fridge until you're ready to serve it, and then remove it around two hours before eating and let it rest at room temperature. Serve on crusty French bread with a glass of Norman cider.

NORMANDY

collection of founder Alexandre Le Grand, and continues through a hall where hundreds of bottles of bootlegged Bénédictine are proudly displayed. In the fragrant Plant & Spice Room you can smell a handful of the ingredients used to make the potent drink. The admission price even includes a free shot of Bénédictine.

Built from 1175 to 1220 under the instigation of Richard the Lion-Heart, the **Abbatiale de la Ste-Trinité** (☎ 02 35 28 84 39; place des Ducs Richard; ☺ 9am-6pm) was the most important pilgrimage site in Normandy until the construction of Mont St-Michel, thanks to the drops of holy blood that miraculously floated to Fécamp in the trunk of a fig tree. Among the many treasures inside is the late-15th-century *Dormition de la Vierge*.

Across from the abbey are the remains of the **fortified chateau** built by the earliest dukes of Normandy in the 10th and 11th centuries.

SLEEPING & EATING

Camping de Renéville (☎ 02 35 28 20 97; www .campingdereneville.com; Côte de Renéville; site €9.60-11.60) Dramatically situated on the western cliffs overlooking the beach, this is a prime position for camping.

Hôtel Normandy (☎ 02 35 29 55 11; www.normandy -fecamp.com; 4 av Gambetta; s €42-49, d €50-60) One of Fécamp's oldest hotels, in a smart *fin de siècle* (end of the 19th century) building not far from the port. Most of the original fixtures have been swept away during a recent overhaul, and the rooms are now a little on the bland side (prefab furniture, white walls and baize-green carpets dominate throughout) – but some are surprisingly spacious for the price.

La Ferme de la Chapelle (☎ 02 35 10 12 12; www .fermedelachapelle.com; Côte de la Vierge; d €75; ☒) This fine establishment is perched on the clifftops a little way from the centre of Fécamp, inside a partly converted chapel and 16th-century priory. The spick-and-span, modern rooms all overlook the grassy central courtyard, so there's no sea view. There are also five self-contained apartments complete with kitchenette.

Chez Nounoute (☎ 02 35 29 38 08; 3 place Nicolas-Selle; menus lunch €11, dinner €15-25) The perfect place to try quintessentially Norman seafood cooked in the time-honoured way. Forget your fancy sauces and fussy garnishes – this is the kind of establishment that serves up smoked herring and steamed mussels as they were meant to be eaten.

GETTING THERE & AWAY
Fécamp is accessible by bus from Dieppe, Le Havre and Rouen, and by train from Le Havre. The **train station** (☎ 02 35 28 24 82) is conveniently located. **Autocars Gris** (☎ 02 35 22 34 00) has six to eight buses daily to Le Havre (€7.50, 1½ hours) via Étretat and five on Sunday.

Étretat
pop 1650
The small village of Étretat, 20km southwest of Fécamp, is known for its twin cliffs: the **Falaise d'Amont** and the **Falaise d'Aval**, positioned on either side of the town's pebbly beach. The Falaise d'Aval is renowned for its towering arch – compared by French writer Maupassant to an elephant dipping its trunk in the sea – and the nearby Aiguille, a 70m-high spire of chalk-white rock rising from the surface of the waves. Further along the cliff is a second impressive arch, known as La Manneporte, reached by a steep path up the cliff from the western end of Étretat's beach. On the opposite headland is the Falaise d'Amont, where a memorial marks the spot where two aviators were last seen before their attempt to cross the Atlantic in 1927.

Outside opening hours the **tourist office** (☎ 02 35 27 05 21; www.etretat.net; place Maurice Guillard; ☺ 10am-7pm mid-Jun–mid-Sep, 10am-noon & 2-6pm mid-Mar–mid-Jun & mid-Sep–mid-Nov, 10am-noon & 2-6pm Fri & Sat mid-Nov–mid-Mar) posts accommodation lists for the area on the door. It also has a map of the cliff trails, and rents out bicycles.

There are a few touristy hotels in Étretat itself, but grand, clifftop **Dormy House** (☎ 02 35 27 07 88; www.dormy-house.com; rte de Havre; r €50-164, ste €130-190) is a more memorable choice thanks to its fantastic position above the beach, not to mention its sunny-coloured sea-view rooms. The room rates have an unfortunate habit of skyrocketing in summer, so try to time your visit for the off-season.

The only way to reach Étretat is on the bus line that runs from Fécamp to Le Havre, stopping at Yport. See p279.

NORMANDY

LE HAVRE

pop 193,250

Wandering around the streets of the seaside city of Le Havre, you could be forgiven for thinking you'd stumbled into a forgotten outpost of the Eastern bloc. All but obliterated by WWII bombing raids, the city was totally rebuilt by Belgian architect Auguste Perret after the war, and what emerged from the ashes of old Le Havre is something of a love letter to concrete: endless rows of breeze-block buildings and ruler-straight boulevards stretch off from the central square, which is dominated by Perret's centrepiece, the 100m-high 'Stalinist Baroque' cathedral, and looks like something straight from the pages of *1984*.

While it's probably not a place you'll want to emigrate to, Le Havre is still worth a visit as one of the great examples of postwar planning. It's a strange and oddly fascinating city – listed by Unesco as a World Heritage Site – and the sophisticated André Malraux fine-arts museum is among the best in Normandy.

Orientation

The main square is the enormous place de l'Hôtel de Ville. Av Foch runs westwards to the sea and the Port de Plaisance recreational area. Blvd de Strasbourg goes eastwards to the train and bus stations. Rue de Paris cuts south past Espace Oscar Niemeyer.

Rue de Paris ends at the quai de Southampton and the Bassin de la Manche, from where ferries to Britain set sail out of the Terminal de la Citadelle, southeast of the central square. Within easy walking distance of the terminal is the Quartier St-François, Le Havre's 'old city'.

Information

INTERNET ACCESS

Microminute (☎ 02 35 22 10 15; 7 rue Casimir Periér; per hr €3.60; ⏰ 2-7pm Mon, 10am-7pm Tue-Sat)

LAUNDRY

Laundrette (5 rue Georges Braque)

MONEY

Banks line blvd de Strasbourg.

Exchange Bureau (41 Chaussée Kennedy) Opposite the old Irish Ferries terminal.

Société Générale (2 place Léon Meyer)

POST

Post Office (62 rue Jules Siegfried) Has a Cyberposte.

TOURIST INFORMATION

Tourist Office (☎ 02 32 74 04 04; www.lehavretour isme.com in French; 186 blvd Clemenceau; ⏰ 9am-7pm Mon-Sat, 10am-12.30pm & 2.30-6pm Sun Jun-Sep, 9am-6.30pm Mon-Fri, 9am-12.30pm & 2-6.30pm Sat, 10am-1pm Sun Oct-May) On the waterfront about 650m southwest of the city hall.

Sights

The main highlight of Le Havre is the hypermodern **Musée des Beaux-Arts André-Malraux** (☎ 02 35 19 62 62; 2 blvd Clemenceau; adult/student €3.80/2.20; ⏰ 11am-6pm Mon-Wed, 11am-7pm Sat & Sun), a modernist jumble of glass and steel near the harbour entrance, which houses a fabulous collection of impressionist works by Monet, Sisley, Renoir and Le Havre native Eugène Boudin. Another section is devoted to Fauvist Raoul Dufy, also born in Le Havre.

Look out for the **Volcano**, a curving whitewashed structure at the southern end of the Bassin du Commerce that has rather unflatteringly been compared to a truncated cooling tower or, even worse, a toilet bowl. It was designed by Brazilian architect Oscar Niemeyer, after whom the surrounding square is named.

Le Havre's avant-garde ambitions look set to continue into the 21st century thanks to a massive new €31 million project to redevelop the run-down docklands area into a cutting-edge centre for shopping, culture and the arts. Architect Jean Nouvel recently beat off competition from several other famous architects (including Daniel Libeskind, designer of the new Freedom Tower in New York) to oversee the project and design its centrepiece, a 120m metallic **tower** that will house a maritime centre, an aquatic complex and a huge exhibition space. Construction began in 2006 and is set to be completed by mid-2008.

Sleeping

Chances are you won't choose to turn a day trip to Le Havre into an overnight stay, unless you happen to be catching an early-morning ferry.

Hôtel Celtic (☎ 02 35 42 39 77; www.hotel-celtic .com in French; 106 rue Voltaire; r €35-54) Overlooking the Bassin du Commerce, the Celtic might have all the exterior appeal of a city-centre car park, but inside the rooms have been refurbished in ultrafunctional style. The more expensive have views over the square, and all are equipped with private bathrooms and satellite TV.

Le Petit Vatel (☎ 02 35 41 72 07; www.multimania .com/lepetitvatel; 86 rue Louis Brindeau; s/d €40/49) This budget option dispenses with all the frills and fripperies in favour of simple décor and cheap rates. The furniture looks like it's come out of a mail-order catalogue, but it's about the best value you'll find around town.

Hôtel Vent d'Ouest (☎ 02 35 42 50 69; www.vent douest.fr; 4 rue de Caligny; r €88-135) By far and away the town's best hotel, the West Wind is decorated in shipshape maritime fashion, with plenty of nautical memorabilia dotted around the downstairs bar and a range of stylish cream-themed rooms upstairs.

Eating & Drinking

La Marine Marchande (☎ 02 35 25 11 77; 27 blvd Amiral Mouchez; lunch menus €10; ☽ lunch Mon-Sat) A great place to fill yourself up at knock-down prices before catching that afternoon ferry. The buffet table is packed with a selection of regional hors d'oeuvres, plus a main course, cheese, dessert and wine, all for just €10.

Le Bistrot des Halles (☎ 02 35 22 50 52; 7 place des Halles; menus €13.50 & €29; ☽ Mon-Sat) This is something of a rarity in ultramodern Le Havre – a bistro serving traditional food in a traditional atmosphere, with no concrete, steel or glass in sight. Expect brasserie standards (mainly steaks and seafood) and a cosy, classically French atmosphere.

L'Odyssée (☎ 02 35 21 32 42; 41 rue du Général Faidherbe; menus €21-34; ☽ lunch & dinner, closed Mon, lunch Sat & dinner Sun) One of the top restaurants in town for fish and seafood, much loved by food critics and local gourmands. The menu changes according to the daily catch, but the generous *assiettes de mer* (seafood platter) is always a popular choice.

L'Agora (☎ 02 32 74 09 70; espace Oscar Niemeyer) Not only do you get to see the inside of Le Havre's most striking building, but this funky bar is the city's best venue for live gigs.

Getting There & Away

AIR

The **airport** (☎ 02 35 54 65 00; www.havre.aeroport.fr), 6km north of town in Octeville-sur-Mer, has daily flights to Lyon, Brighton and Jersey.

BOAT

LD Lines (☎ in France 08 25 30 43 04, in UK 0870 428 4335; www.ldlines.co.uk; Terminal de la Citadelle) is the main ferry operator, offering an afternoon service from Le Havre to Portsmouth, and an overnight crossing that goes in the opposite direction. It is based in the Terminal de la Citadelle on av Lucien Corbeaux, which is 1km south of the train station.

BUS

Caen-based **Bus Verts du Calvados** (☎ 08 10 21 42 14) runs frequent services from the bus station (behind the train station) to Honfleur (€6.16, 30 minutes), Deauville-Trouville (€8.80, 1¾ hours) and Caen (€17.60, 2½ hours). There are also four daily **express buses** (two on Sundays) to Caen (€19.40, 1½ hours) via Honfleur.

CNA (☎ 08 25 07 60 27) runs daily buses to Rouen (€13, 2½ hours).

Autocars Gris (☎ 02 35 22 34 00) has 10 buses daily to Le Havre (€7.50, 1½ hours) via Étretat (one hour) and five on Sunday.

TRAIN

Le Havre's **train station** (cours de la République) is east of the city centre. Chief destinations are Rouen (€12.40, one hour, 12 to 15 daily) and Paris' Gare St-Lazare (€26.70, 2¼ hours, at least 15 daily). A secondary line goes north to Fécamp (€7.20, 1¼ hours, 10 to 12), sometimes with a change at Bréauté-Beuzeville.

Getting Around

There's no public transport to town from the airport. A taxi will cost about €15 – call ☎ 02 35 25 81 81 or ☎ 02 35 25 81 00.

Bus Océane (☎ 02 35 22 35 00; place de l'Hôtel de Ville) runs 14 lines in Le Havre. Single tickets cost €1.50; a one-day ticket costs €3.30.

EURE

Lovely day trips can be made from Rouen, particularly in the landlocked Eure *département*. The beautiful gardens of Claude Monet are at Giverny. From the 12th-century Château Gaillard in Les Andelys a breathtaking panorama takes in the bend of river banks that rise to forested hills and white bluffs.

NORMANDY

LES ANDELYS

pop 8500

Some 39km southeast of Rouen lies Les Andelys, a small town at the confluence of the mighty Seine and the tiny Gambon. The main reason for coming to the town is to visit the ruins of Château Gaillard, a 12th-century stronghold of Richard the Lion-Heart.

Orientation & Information

The town is split into two parts: Grand Andely, whose main square is place Poussin, and to the west the older Petit Andely, which lies on the banks of the mighty Seine.

The tiny **tourist office** (☎ 02 32 54 41 93; 24 rue Philippe-Auge; ☽ 9.30am-noon & 2-6pm Mon-Sat, to 5.30pm Sun Jun-Sep, 2-5.30pm Mon-Fri Oct-May) is in Petit Andely at the foot of the cliffs, which form the base of the chateau.

Sights

Built from 1196 to 1197, **Château Gaillard** (☎ 02 32 54 04 16; admission €3; ☽ 10am-1pm & 2-6pm Wed-Mon) secured the western border of English territory along the Seine until Henry IV ordered its destruction in 1603. More impressive than the ruins is the fantastic view over the Seine, whose white cliffs are best seen from the platform north of the castle. The chateau is a 20-minute climb via a path that begins about 100m north of the tourist office. By car, take the turn-off opposite Église Notre Dame in Grand Andely and follow the signs.

Sleeping & Eating

Camping Château Gaillard (☎ 02 32 54 18 20; www .chateau-gaillard80.com; rte de la Mare; sites per 2 people €18; ☽ Feb-Dec) A good choice for camping, 800m southeast of the chateau and 200m from the Seine.

Hôtel Normandie (☎ 02 32 54 10 52; www.hotel normandie-andelys.com; 1 rue Grande; d €56-62) An old Norman establishment where the slightly cramped bedrooms don't quite match up to the flowery terrace and pretty vine-covered façade. Still, it makes a very pleasant retreat, and it's pretty reasonable for the price.

ourpick Hôtel & Restaurant de la Chaine d'Or (☎ 02 32 54 00 31; www.hotel-lachainedor.com; 27 rue Grande; r €72-122; ▢) Huddled in the shadow of the chateau beside the banks of the river Seine, this dazzling little rurl hideaway in Petit Andely is perfect for exploring nearby

Giverny. It's one of those country hotels where every nook and cranny is packed with character – a marble figurine here, an antique dresser there – and the décor throughout is rustically stylish without being twee in any way. Watching dusk fall over the river is an absolutely essential experience at the Chaine d'Or, as is the buffet breakfast on the blossom-covered terrace beside the hotel. To top things off, the in-house restaurant (menus €28 to €86) is one of the best for miles around – roast partridge, and cider sorbet, are just some of the delights in store.

Getting There & Away

There's no train station in Les Andelys. **CNA** (☎ 08 25 07 60 27) buses link Grand Andely (place Poussin) and Rouen at least twice daily (€8.10, 1¼ hours).

GIVERNY

pop 550

This tiny countryside village, 15km further south from Les Andelys, is Mecca for Monet fans and devotees of the impressionist school. Monet lived here from 1883 until his death in 1926, in a rambling house surrounded by flower-filled gardens that now houses the Musée Claude Monet. First opened to the public in 1980, the museum and gardens are immensely popular, and the impressionist collection at the nearby Musée d'Art Américain is also worth a visit.

Sights

Musée Claude Monet (☎ 02 32 51 28 21; adult/student/under 12yr €5.50/4/3, gardens only €4; ☽ 9.30am-6pm Tue-Sun Apr-Oct) was Monet's home and studio. The hectare of land that Monet owned has become two distinct areas cut by the Chemin du Roy, a train line that later became the D5 road.

The northern part is the **Clos Normand**, where Monet's pastel-pink house and Water Lily studio stand. His studio is now the entrance hall, adorned with reproductions of his works and ringing with cash register bells from busy souvenir stands. Outside are the symmetrically laid-out gardens.

From the Clos Normand's far corner, a tunnel leads under the D5 to the **Jardin d'Eau** (Water Garden). Monet bought the surrounding land in 1895 and set about creating his trademark lily pond, as well as the famous Japanese bridge (which has since been rebuilt). Draped with purple wisteria, the bridge blends into the asymmetrical foreground and background, creating the intimate atmosphere for which the 'painter of light' was renowned.

Seasons have an enormous effect on the gardens at Giverny. From early to late spring, daffodils, tulips, rhododendrons, wisteria and irises appear, followed by poppies and lilies. By June, nasturtiums, roses and sweet peas are in flower. Around September, there are dahlias, sunflowers and hollyhocks.

The **Musée d'Art Américain** (☎ 02 32 51 94 65; www.maag.org; 99 rue Claude Monet; adult/student/child €5.50/4/3; ⏱ 10am-6pm Tue-Sun Apr-Oct) contains works of American impressionist painters who flocked to France in the late 19th and early 20th centuries. It's inside a garish

building 100m down the road from Musée Claude Monet.

Getting There & Away

Giverny is 76km northwest of Paris and 66km southeast of Rouen. The nearest town is Vernon, nearly 7km to the west on the Paris–Rouen train line.

From Paris' Gare St-Lazare (€11.40, 50 minutes) two early trains run to Vernon. For the return trip there's about one direct train an hour from 3pm till 8pm. From Rouen (€9.20, 40 minutes) four or five trains leave before noon; to get back, there's about one train every hour between 5pm and 10pm.

Once in Vernon it's still a hike to Giverny. **Shuttle buses** (☎ 02 35 71 32 99) meet most trains and cost €2 each way. You can rent a bike from the **Café de Chemin de Fer** (☎ 02 32 21 16 01) for €12 a day.

CLAUDE MONET

'Everyone discusses my art and pretends to understand, as if it were necessary to understand, when it is simply necessary to love.'

Claude Monet

The undisputed leader of the impressionists, Claude Monet, was born in Paris in 1840 and grew up in Le Havre, where he found an early affinity with the outdoors. Monet disliked school and spent much of his time sketching his professors in the margins of his exercise books. By 15 his skills as a caricaturist were known throughout Le Havre, but Eugène Boudin, his first mentor, convinced him to turn his attention away from portraiture towards the study of colour, light and landscape.

In 1860 military service interrupted Monet's studies at the Académie Suisse in Paris and took him to Algiers, where the intense light and colours further fuelled his imagination. The young painter became fascinated with capturing a specific moment in time, the immediate impression of the scene before him, rather than the precise detail.

From 1867 Monet's distinctive style began to emerge, focusing on the effects of light and colour and using the quick, undisguised broken brushstrokes that would characterise the impressionist period. His contemporaries were Pissarro, Renoir, Sisley, Cézanne and Dégas. The young painters left the studio to work outdoors, experimenting with the shades and hues of nature, arguing and sharing ideas. Their work was far from welcomed by critics; one of them condemned it as 'impressionism', in reference to Monet's *Impression: Sunrise* (1874). Much to the critic's chagrin, the name stuck.

From the late 1870s Monet concentrated on painting in series, seeking to re-create a landscape by showing its transformation under different conditions of light and atmosphere. *Haystacks* (1890–91) and *Rouen Cathedral* (1891–95) are some of the best-known works of this period. In 1883 he moved to Giverny, planting his property with a variety of flowers around an artificial pond (opposite), in order to paint the subtle effects of sunlight on natural forms. Here he painted the *Nymphéas* (Water Lilies) series. The huge dimensions of some of these works, together with the fact that the pond's surface takes up the entire canvas, meant the abandonment of composition in the traditional sense and the virtual disintegration of form. Despite his failing eyesight, Monet completed the series just before his death in 1926.

For more info on Monet and his work, visit www.giverny.org.

CALVADOS

The *département* of Calvados stretches from Honfleur in the east to Isigny-sur-Mer in the west. It's famed for its rich pastures and farm products: butter, cheese, cider and the distinctive apple-flavoured brandy from which the area gets its name. The D-Day beaches extend along almost the entire coast of Calvados. The Calvados tourism site (www.calvados-tourisme .com) is a comprehensive guide to hotels, sights and restaurants around the Calvados region.

HONFLEUR

pop 8350

Long a favourite subject with Normandy's painters, but now more popular with the Parisian jetset, the charming harbour of Honfleur is arguably Normandy's most attractive seaside town. The heart of Honfleur is the old port, the Vieux Bassin, which was once used by explorers setting sail for the New World and is still crammed with fishing boats and pleasure vessels. Silt from the Seine has clogged up the seafront along blvd Charles V, and the grand wooden houses that once overlooked the beach have now been stranded several hundred metres inland; but the jumble of brightly coloured buildings and busy restaurants clustered around the old port comes as a breath of fresh air after the aggressively modern lines of Le Havre.

History

Honfleur's seafaring tradition dates back over a millennium. After the Norman invasion of England in 1066, goods bound for the conquered territory were shipped across the Channel from Honfleur.

In 1608 Samuel de Champlain left from Honfleur on his way to founding Quebec City, and in 1681 Cavelier de la Salle set out from the harbour to explore the New World. He reached the mouth of the Mississippi and named the area Louisiana in honour of King Louis XIV, ruler of France at the time. During the 17th and 18th centuries Honfleur achieved a degree of prosperity through trade with the West Indies, the Azores and the colonies on the western coast of Africa.

Orientation

Just to the east of the Vieux Bassin is the centre of the old city, known as the Enclos because it was once enclosed by fortifications. To the north is the Avant Port (outer harbour) where the fishing fleet is based. Quai Ste-Catherine fronts the Vieux Bassin on the west, and rue de la République runs southwards from it. The Plateau de Grâce, with Chapelle Notre Dame de Grâce on top, is west of town.

Information

Lavomatic (4 rue Notre Dame; ☾ 8am-9pm) Laundry.
Léviathan (☎ 02 31 87 92 95; 11 blvd Charles V; per 30min €1.50; ☾ 2.30pm-1am Mon-Sat) Internet access.
Post Office (rue de la République) Southwest of the centre, just past place Albert Sorel. It has a Cyberposte terminal.
Tourist Office (☎ 02 31 89 23 30; www.ot-honfleur .fr; quai Lepaulmier; ☾ 10am-7pm Mon-Sat, 10am-5pm Sun mid-Jul–Aug, 10am-12.30pm & 2-6.30pm Mon-Sat, 10am-5pm Sun Apr–mid-Jul & Sep, 10am-12.30pm & 2-6pm Mon-Sat, 10am-5pm Sun Oct-Mar)

Sights

ÉGLISE STE-CATHERINE

The wooden **Église Ste-Catherine** (place Ste-Catherine; ☾ 10am-noon & 2-6pm, except during services), whose stone predecessor was destroyed during the Hundred Years' War, was built by the people of Honfleur during the late 15th and early 16th centuries. Wood was used as the main building material in an effort to save stone for strengthening the fortifications of the Enclos. Supposedly a temporary structure, the church has now been standing in the square for over 500 years. It's particularly notable for its double-vaulted roof and its twin naves, which resemble a couple of overturned ships' hulls.

PONT DE NORMANDIE

Opened in 1995, this futuristic bridge stretches in a soaring 2km arch over the Seine from Le Havre to Honfleur. It's a typically French affair, more artwork than architecture, with two huge V-shaped columns – somewhat reminiscent of giant tuning forks – connected by the graceful curve of the bridge itself. Driving across it is quite a thrill, and the views across the Seine are magnificent, but the price tag is a touch steep at €5 each way.

Across the square is the church's free-standing bell tower, **Clocher Ste-Catherine** (☎ 02 31 89 54 00; adult/student incl admission to Musée Eugène Boudin €4.40/2.70, Jun-Nov €5.10/3.60; ☺ 10am-noon & 2-6pm Wed-Mon mid-Mar–Sep, 2.30-5pm Mon-Fri, 10am-noon & 2.30-5pm Sat & Sun Oct–mid-Mar), supposedly built away from the church in order to avoid lightning strikes and damage from the clock's clanging bells.

MUSÉE EUGÈNE BOUDIN

Named in honour of the early impressionist painter born here in 1824, **Musée Eugène Boudin** (☎ 02 31 89 54 00; rue de l'Homme de Bois; adult/student incl admission to Clocher Ste-Catherine €4.40/2.70, Jun-Nov €5.10/3.60; ☺ 10am-noon & 2-6pm Wed-Mon mid-Mar–Sep; 2.30-5pm Mon-Fri, 10am-noon & 2.30-5pm Sat & Sun Oct–mid-Mar) has a collection of impressionist paintings from Normandy, including works by Dubourg, Dufy and Monet. One room is devoted to the works of Eugène Boudin, whom Baudelaire called the 'king of skies' for his luscious skyscapes.

LES MAISONS SATIE

The quirky **Les Maisons Satie** (☎ 02 31 89 11 11; 67 blvd Charles V; adult/student €5.10/3.60; ☺ 10am-7pm Wed-Mon Jun-Sep, 11am-6pm Wed-Mon Oct-May) captures the spirit of composer Erik Satie (1866–1925), who lived and worked in Honfleur and was born in the half-timbered house that now contains the museum. 'Esoteric' Satie was known for his surrealistic wit as much as for his starkly beautiful piano compositions. Visitors wander through the museum with a headset playing Satie's music and excerpts from his writings (in French or English). Each room is a surreal surprise – winged pears and self-pedalling carousels are just the start.

HARBOURS

The quays around the Vieux Bassin, especially **quai Ste-Catherine**, are lined with tall, taper-thin houses dating from the 16th to 18th centuries. The **Lieutenance**, once the residence of the town's royal governor, is at the mouth of the old harbour.

The **Avant Port**, on the other side of the Lieutenance, is home to Honfleur's 50 or so fishing vessels. Further north, dykes line both sides of the entrance to the port.

Either harbour makes a pleasant route for a walk to the seashore. Honfleur is a good launching pad for boat tours of the region.

MUSÉE DE LA MARINE

The **Musée de la Marine** (☎ 02 31 89 14 12; quai Saint-Etienne; adult/student €3/1.80, incl admission to Musée d'Ethnographie et d'Art Populaire Normand €4.20/2.60; ☺ 10am-noon & 2-6pm Tue-Sun Apr-Sep;,2-6pm Mon-Fri, 10am-noon & 2-6pm Sat & Sun Oct–mid-Nov & mid-Feb–Mar, closed mid-Nov–mid-Feb) is inside the deconsecrated 13th- and 14th-century Église St-Étienne, and contains several nautically themed displays of model ships, carpenters' tools and engravings.

MUSÉE D'ETHNOGRAPHIE ET D'ART POPULAIRE NORMAND

Next to the Musée de la Marine on rue de la Prison (an alley off quai St-Étienne), the **Musée d'Ethnographie et d'Art Populaire Normand** (☎ 02 31 89 14 12; adult/student €3/1.80, incl admission to Musée de la Marine €4.20/2.60; ☺ 10am-noon & 2-6pm Tue-Sun Apr-Sep, 2-6pm Mon-Fri, 10am-noon & 2-6pm Sat & Sun Oct–mid-Nov & mid-Feb–Mar, closed mid-Nov–mid-Feb) occupies a couple of period houses and a former prison. Its nine rooms recreate the world of Honfleur in the 16th to 19th centuries using a mix of costumes, furniture and other artefacts.

GRENIERS À SEL

The two huge **Greniers à Sel** (salt stores; ☎ 02 31 89 02 30; rue de la Ville), along from the tourist office, were built in the late 17th century to store the salt needed by the fishing fleet to cure its catch of herring and cod. During July and August the stores host art exhibitions and concerts.

CHAPELLE NOTRE DAME DE GRÂCE

Built between 1600 and 1613, the **Chapelle Notre Dame de Grâce** is at the top of the Plateau de Grâce, a wooded, 100m-high hill about 2km west of the Vieux Bassin. There's a great view of the town and port.

Tours

The tourist office runs guided tours of Honfleur throughout the year, including an atmospheric night-time tour. Contact the office to see what's currently available. Some tours are conducted by an English-speaking guide.

Fifty-minute **boat tours** (☎ 02 31 89 41 80; adult/child €7/5; ☺ Mar–mid-Oct) of the port are offered by Vedettes Cap Christien, Alphée and Evasion. Vedette la Jolie France goes to the Pont de Normandie (adult/child €8/5).

NORMANDY

Boarding is from the quai des Passagers or the quai de la Quarantaine.

Sleeping

Rooms don't come cheap at any time of year in Honfleur, but the hotels are all top-notch.

BUDGET

Camping La Briquerie (☎ 02 31 89 28 32; www.camp inglabriquerie.com; person/site €5/6; 🐾 🖳) A couple of kilometres south of Honfleur, this is a typically well-equipped camp site, with an on-site restaurant and laundry, and a large supermarket just down the road.

MIDRANGE

Hôtel Belvédère (☎ 02 31 89 08 13; www.hotel-bel vedere-honfleur.com; 36 rue Emile Renouf; d weekdays/ weekends €64/125) This is the closest thing to a budget hotel in Honfleur, especially if you pitch up midweek. The cosy rooms and lovely terrace-garden make this a useful option, but style-seekers should probably look elsewhere.

Hôtel du Dauphin (☎ 02 31 89 15 53; www.hotel -du-dauphin.com; 10 place Pierre-Berthelot; r €66-110; ⊗ 🖳) Behind a 17th-century cream-and-chocolate timbered façade this welcoming hotel is decorated in a more rustic fashion than many of the establishments around Honfleur. Flowery bedspreads and pastel shades dominate, and the more expensive rooms even have spa baths.

Hôtel des Loges (☎ 02 31 89 38 26; www.hotel desloges.com; 18 rue Brûlée; d €100-125; 🖳) This deliciously understated and thoroughly up-to-date hotel occupies a slate-fronted building just outside the old centre. With its muted furnishings, soft lighting and Art Deco motifs, this is a little piece of Parisian chic dropped onto the Calvados coastline.

TOP END

Hôtel L'Écrin (☎ 02 31 14 43 45; www.honfleur .com/default-ecrin.htm; 19 rue Eugène Boudin; d €90-180; 🖳) Ever fancied yourself as a member of the bourgeoisie? Then head for this lavish Norman manor house, which re-creates the splendour and opulence of a bygone age. The lobby and dining rooms are stuffed with porcelain, oil paintings and antique furniture, although most of the bedrooms themselves aren't quite as posh.

Les Maisons de Léa (☎ 02 31 89 28 61; www .lesmaisonsdelea.com; place Ste-Catherine; d €99-155, ste €235, cottage €295) Not only does this gorgeous ivy-covered hotel occupy the finest position in town, right opposite the church, but it also boasts some of its most fabulous rooms. The hotel is separated into several separate *maisons* (houses), each with its own unique style and character – choose from country cosiness, Shaker-style simplicity or maritime tranquillity.

our pick **La Maison de Lucie** (☎ 02 31 14 40 40; www.lamaisondelucie.com; 44 rue des Capucins; d €125-285) If you're looking for out-and-out luxury in Honfleur, then this marvellous little hideaway is the place to escape to. The former home of the novelist Lucie Delarue Mardrus, on a quiet backstreet leading away from the old port, the hotel combines period charm with top-notch contemporary style. The bathrooms are decked out with Moroccan tiles and rolltop baths, while the five bedrooms are panelled in oak and boast fantastic views across the harbour and the Pont de Normandie. Outside, the secluded, shady terrace makes a glorious place for a summer breakfast or a night-time apéritif, and for the truly decadent, there's a super chic spa in the old brick-vaulted cellar. Trust us – this is one place you simply won't want to leave.

Eating

Quai Ste-Catherine is lined with brasseries and terraced restaurants, mostly chock-a-block on summer weekends with sharply dressed Parisians.

La Cidrerie (☎ 02 31 89 59 85; 26 place Hamelin; menus €9; 🕑 lunch & dinner, closed Tue-Wed Oct-Jun) Budget restaurants are hard to come by in Honfleur, so this tidy little *crêperie* is a useful find – especially if you fancy washing your meal down with a few mugs of *cidre Normand.*

La Tortue (☎ 02 31 89 04 93; 36 rue de l'Homme de Bois; menus €16-30; 🕑 lunch & dinner, closed Tue & dinner Mon) Set back from the heavily touristed harbour area, this traditionally styled eatery offers fantastic value, with several multicourse *menus* and even a few vegetarian options.

L'Absinthe (☎ 02 31 89 39 00; 10 quai de la Quarantaine; menus €30, €49 & €60; 🕑 lunch & dinner) The slate-fronted 18th-century mansion may be ravishing, but it's the food that takes centre stage at this renowned restaurant near the seafront. The cuisine is sumptuous and sophisticated, even on its cheapest *menu*, but you'll need to reserve in advance.

L'Ascot (☎ 02 31 98 87 91; 76 quai Ste-Catherine; menus €22.50-28; ☺ lunch & dinner, closed Wed & Thu in low season) The perfect place for fresh French seafood on a summer evening, with tightly packed tables on the outside terrace and an intimate candle-lit ambience inside.

SELF-CATERING

The **market** (place Ste-Catherine; ☺ 9am-1pm Sat) has an excellent selection of local products and an organic food market. There's a Champion supermarket just west of rue de la République, near place Albert Sorel.

Drinking

Café L'Albatros (☎ 02 31 89 25 30; 32 quai Ste-Catherine; ☺ 8am-2am) Sailors, students, philosophers and layabouts are all at home at this café-bar, from breakfast through beer and sandwiches and on to nightcaps. It closes earlier in winter.

Le Perroquet Vert (☎ 02 31 89 14 19; 52 quai Ste-Catherine; ☺ 8am-2am) The 'green parrot' has an excellent selection of beer and a good terrace for people-watching. It also closes earlier in winter.

Getting There & Around

The **bus station** (☎ 02 31 89 28 41) is southeast of the Vieux Bassin on rue des Vases.
Bus Verts (☎ 08 10 21 42 14) No 20 runs via Deauville-Trouville (€3.52, 30 minutes) to Caen (€11.44, €12.60 by express bus, 1½ hours) several times daily. The same line goes northwards to Le Havre (€6.16, 30 minutes, five per day) via the Pont de Normandie.

TROUVILLE & DEAUVILLE

The twin towns of Trouville (population 5600) and Deauville (population 4300), 5km southwest of Honfleur, are a stone's throw from each other across the River Touques, but couldn't be more different in character. Chic Deauville has been a playground of the wealthy ever since it was founded by Napoleon III's cousin, the duke of Morny, in 1861. Packed with designer boutiques and deluxe hotels, and home to a casino, racetrack and a high-profile American film festival, Deauville is rather like the Monaco of the Normandy coast – exclusive, expensive and essentially skin-deep.

Unlike its flashy sister across the river, Trouville is still very much a working fishing port, and in many ways makes a much more attractive place to visit. The town was frequented by painters and writers during the 19th century, including Mozin and Flaubert, and many French celebrities have chosen to set up holiday homes here, lured by the town's sandy beaches and laid-back seaside ambience.

Orientation

Trouville is strung out along the eastern bank of the Touques, with Deauville on the western bank. The towns are linked by the Pont des Belges, just east of the train and bus station. Beaches line the coast to the north of both towns on either side of the port.

Information

INTERNET ACCESS

Gestimedia (☎ 02 31 14 04 61; 6 rue Thiers, Deauville; per hr €6; ☺ 9am-1pm & 2-6pm Mon-Fri)

MONEY

Crédit du Nord (84 rue Eugène Colas, Deauville)
Société Générale (9 place Morny, Trouville)

POST

Deauville Post Office (rue Robert Fossorier) Has a Cyberposte and exchanges currency.
Trouville Post Office (16 rue Amiral de Maigret)

TOURIST INFORMATION

Deauville Tourist Office (☎ 02 31 14 40 00; www .deauville.org; place de la Mairie; ☺ 9am-7pm Jul–mid-Sep, 9am-6.30pm May & Jun, 9am-12.30pm & 2-6.30pm Mon-Sat, 10am-1pm & 2-5pm Sun mid-Sep–Apr) Pick up a copy of the free glossy magazine *Deauville Passions* for an overview of annual events.
Trouville Tourist Office (☎ 02 31 14 60 70; www.trouvillesurmer.org; 32 blvd Fernand Moureaux; ☺ 9.30am-7pm Mon-Sat, 10am-4pm Sun Jul & Aug, 9.30am-noon & 2-6.30pm Mon-Sat Apr-Jun, Sep & Oct, 9.30am-noon & 1.30-6pm Mon-Sat Nov-Mar)

Sights & Activities

In Deauville, the rich and beautiful strut their stuff along the beachside **promenade des Planches**, a 500m-long boardwalk lined with private swimming huts, before losing a wad at the **Casino de Deauville** 200m to the southwest. If you still have some cash to spare, you could do exactly the same in Trouville – the casino's not quite as posh, and the beach is a little less snazzy, but the effect on your bank balance is likely to be depressingly familiar.

Musée de Trouville (☎ 02 31 88 16 26; 64 rue du Général Leclerc; adult/student €2/1.50; ⊗ 2-6.30pm Wed-Mon Apr-Sep), in the magnificent Villa Montebello, is 1km to the northeast of the Trouville tourist office. The villa has a panoramic view over the beach, and the museum recounts the history of Trouville and features work from Charles Mozin and Eugène Boudin. There are temporary exhibitions by local artists.

On Trouville's beachside promenade you'll see several illustrious **19th-century villas**. The beach is also home to the **Natur'Aquarium de Trouville** (☎ 02 31 88 46 04; adult/6-14yr/3-5yr €7/5/4; ⊗ 10am-noon & 2-6.30pm Easter-Jun, Sep & Oct, 10am-7pm Jul & Aug, 2-6pm Nov-Easter), an excellent aquarium-cum-zoo packed with multicoloured fish, fearsome reptiles and weird insects.

Festivals & Events

Deauville's **American Film Festival** (www.festival-deauville.com) is an altogether more welcoming affair than its better-known cousin at Cannes. Tickets for most screenings are on sale to the public, and you're bound to catch glimpses of a few Hollywood stars when the festival's in full swing in the first week of September. There's also an **Asian Film Festival** (www.deauvilleasian.com) at the beginning of March.

Deauville is renowned for its equestrian tradition. The **horse-racing** season, which runs from early July to mid-October, is held at two local racetracks: Hippodrome La Touques for gallop races and jumping events, and Hippodrome Clairfontaine with galloping, trotting and steeplechase.

Trouville's **Festival Folklorique** fills the streets with colourfully clad musicians and dancers in the third week of June.

Sleeping

Unless you're planning on flying in on your private jet, you'll be better off avoiding the overpriced hotels in Deauville; Trouville generally offers much better value.

Le Chant des Oiseaux (☎ 02 31 88 06 42; 11 rte d'Honfleur; sites €9-11; ⊗ Apr-Oct) About 1km east of Trouville, this camp site has a sweeping view of the coast.

La Maison Normande (☎ 02 31 88 12 25; www.maisonnormande.com in French; 4 place de Lattre de Tassigny, Trouville; r €36-65) A Norman house in quintessential Norman style, with crisscrossing beams, flowery furnishings and traditional touches. You'll feel like you're visiting your new Norman grandma.

Le Trouville (☎ 02 31 98 45 48; www.hotelletrouville.com; 1-5 rue Thiers, Trouville; s €36-37, d €46-54) This modest hotel may be small and simple but the rates are great, especially considering its proximity to the beach. The checked bedcovers and dinky bathrooms add a hint of much-needed character.

Le Fer à Cheval (☎ 02 31 98 30 20; www.hotelferacheval.com in French; 11 rue Victor Hugo, Trouville; s €48-74, d €69) This vaguely horsey hotel is inside a beautiful turn-of-the-20th-century building just off the main drag in Trouville. The rooms are simple but very comfortable, especially if you can get one of the upstairs ones with its own small balcony. Weekend rates are pricier than weekdays.

Eating

Les Vapeurs (☎ 02 31 88 15 24; 160-162 blvd Fernand-Moureaux, Trouville; menus €13-21; ⊗ lunch & dinner) A long-standing brasserie, founded in 1927 and frequented in its heyday by many famous names. These days it's still serving up the same reliable dishes – especially copious bowls of steaming-hot mussels – to an ever-changing crowd, although service can suffer when it gets a little too busy.

Brasserie Le Central (☎ 02 31 88 13 68; 158 blvd Fernand Moureaux, Trouville; menus from €17; ⊗ lunch & dinner) Right next door to Les Vapeurs, this buzzy brasserie adds a touch of Parisian class to the Trouville seafront. The menu offers few surprises – seafood and mussels are the mainstays – but the atmosphere is fantastic on a summer evening.

La Petite Auberge (☎ 02 31 88 11 07; 7 rue Carnot, Trouville; menus €28-46; ⊗ lunch & dinner, closed Tue & Wed) For something recognisably Norman in cuisine and character, this is perfect. The dining room is decorated with crockery and copper pans, and the food's just as rustic – think *sole en croûte* (sole in pastry) and *foie gras aux pommes* (foie gras with apple).

SELF-CATERING

There's a large **Monoprix** (blvd Fernand Moureaux; ⊗ closed Sun) and a **food market** (place du Maréchal Foch; ⊗ Wed & Sat mornings).

Drinking & Entertainment

Zoo Bar (☎ 02 31 81 02 61; 53 rue Désiré-le-Hoc, Deauville; ⌚ 6pm-2am, closed Tues) This is the place to be seen in style-savvy Deauville, a sleek and sophisticated urban-style hang-out, tailor-made for cocktails and checking out the beautiful people.

La Maison (☎ 02 31 81 43 10; 66 rue des Bains, Trouville; ⌚ 7pm-2am) A rather different vibe is on display at this relaxed wine bar, where the emphasis is on good wine and friendly chatter rather than measuring up to the style police. There are regular concerts and art exhibitions.

Casino de Deauville (☎ 02 31 14 31 14; av Lucien Barrière, Deauville; ⌚ 11am-2am Mon-Fri, 10am-4am Sat, 10am-3am Sun) You couldn't really come to this playground of the rich and famous without taking a few turns on the roulette wheel – just be careful with those champagne cocktails, or you could be in for an expensive night. Dress is formal, but men can borrow a jacket and tie from reception.

Getting There & Around

Aéroport de Deauville-St-Gatien (☎ 02 31 65 65 65) is 10km northeast of Deauville-Trouville. There is no public transport into town.

Bus Verts (☎ 08 10 21 42 14) has very frequent services to Caen (€8.80, 1¼ hours), Honfleur (€3.52, 30 minutes) and Le Havre (via Honfleur; €8.80, one hour).

Train services from Deauville-Trouville require changes at Lisieux (€5.30, 20 minutes, 10 to 12 daily). Trains go to Caen (€11.20, one to 1½ hours depending on connections, 10 to 12 daily) and Rouen (€18.90, one to 2½ hours depending on connection, eight daily).

CAEN

pop 117,000

The historic city of Caen, capital of Basse Normandie, has played a crucial role in Normandy's history since it was founded in the 11th century by William the Conqueror. Some six centuries after the city was sacked and torched by invading English armies in 1346, Caen's old town was levelled once more during the shattering bombardments of the Normandy campaign. The city was bombed and set ablaze on D-Day, and by the time it was liberated by Canadian troops on 9 July 1944, over 80% of the city had been razed to rubble. Practically all that remains of old Caen are the ramparts around the chateau and the city's twin abbeys; the rest has been rebuilt in a typically utilitarian post-war style, using plenty of concrete and pale stone.

Today, Caen is a busy university city and commercial centre, with a clutch of excellent museums, including the groundbreaking Caen Mémorial. It's a useful base for exploring the D-Day beaches and nearby Bayeux.

Orientation

Caen's modern heart is made up of a few pedestrianised shopping streets and some busy boulevards. The largest, av du 6 Juin, links the centre, which is based around the southern end of the chateau, with the canal and train station to the southeast. What's left of the old city is centred on rue du Vaugueux, a short distance east of the chateau.

Information

BOOKSHOPS

Hemisphères (☎ 02 31 86 67 26; 15 rue des Croisières) Guidebooks in English, including Lonely Planet titles.

INTERNET ACCESS

L'Espace Micro (☎ 02 31 53 68 68; 1 rue Basse; per hr €3.80; ⌚ 10am-11pm Mon-Sat, 10am-1pm & 3-9pm Sun)

LAUNDRY

Laundrette (☎ 02 31 53 05 35; 44 rue St-Jean)

MONEY

Crédit Agricole (1 blvd Maréchal Leclerc) There's an exchange bureau here.

POST

Post Office (place Gambetta) Has a Cyberposte.

TOURIST INFORMATION

Tourist Office (☎ 02 31 27 14 14; www.caen.fr/tourisme; place St-Pierre; ⌚ 9am-7pm Mon-Sat, 10am-1pm & 2-5pm Sun Jul & Aug, 9.30am-1pm & 2-6pm Mon-Sat, 10am-1pm Sun Oct-Mar & Apr-Jun)

Sights

MÉMORIAL – UN MUSÉE POUR LA PAIX

Located in a vast multilevel edifice on Esplanade Dwight Eisenhower, 3km northwest of the city centre, Caen's high-tech museum, **Mémorial – Un Musée pour la Paix** (Memorial – A Museum for Peace; ☎ 02 31 06 06 44;

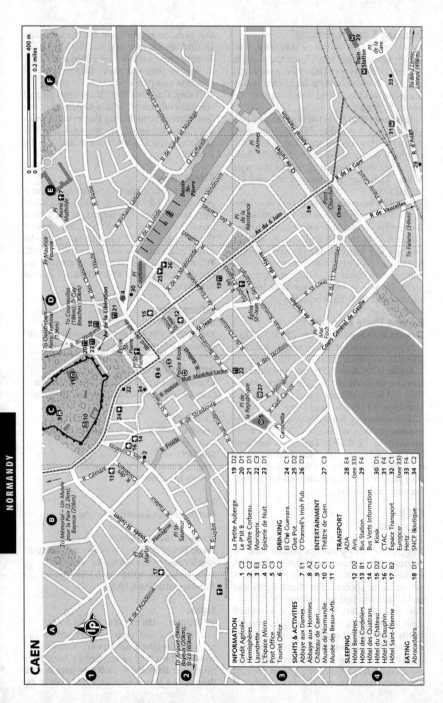

CAEN

NORMANDY

INFORMATION		
Crédit Agricole	1	C2
Hemisphères	2	C2
Laundrette	3	E3
L'Espace Micro	4	D1
Post Office	5	C3
Tourist Office	6	C2

SIGHTS & ACTIVITIES		
Abbaye aux Dames	7	E1
Abbaye aux Hommes	8	A2
Château de Caen	9	C1
Musée de Normandie	10	C1
Musée des Beaux-Arts	11	C1

SLEEPING		
Hôtel Bernières	12	D2
Hôtel des Cordeliers	13	B1
Hôtel des Quatrans	14	C1
Hôtel du Château	15	D2
Hôtel Le Dauphin	16	C1
Hôtel Saint-Etienne	17	B2

EATING		
Abracadabra	18	D1

La Petite Auberge	19	D2
Le P'tit B	20	D1
Maître Corbeau	21	D1
Monoprix	22	C3
Épicerie de Nuit	23	D1

DRINKING		
El Che Guevara	24	C1
Glue Pot	25	D2
O'Donnell's Irish Pub	26	D2

ENTERTAINMENT		
Théâtre de Caen	27	C3

TRANSPORT		
ADA	28	E4
Avis	(see 33)	
Bus Station	29	F4
Bus Verts Information		
Kiosk	30	D1
CTAC	31	F4
Espace Transport	32	C1
Europcar	(see 33)	
Hertz	33	F4
SNCF Boutique	34	C2

www.memorial-caen.fr in French; adult/student & 10-18yr/ WWII veterans €17.50/16/free; ⊙ 9am-7pm Feb-Sep, 9am-6pm Oct-Dec, closed Jan), provides an outstanding and vivid account of the Battle of Normandy and the challenges to world peace from WWII to today.

The visit begins with a whistle-stop overview of Europe's descent into total war, tracing events from the end of WWI and the Treaty of Versailles, through the rise of fascism in Europe and the French occupation, right up to the Battle of Normandy. Unsurprisingly for one of France's flagship museums, it's a hugely impressive affair, using sound, lighting, film, animation and audio testimony, as well as a range of artefacts and exhibits, to graphically evoke the realities of war and the trials of occupation and liberation.

A second section of the museum focuses on the Cold War and the prospects for world peace. There's also an underground gallery dedicated to winners of the Nobel Peace Prize, located in bunkers used by the Germans during the battle for Caen in 1944. All signs are in French, English and German. Your ticket remains valid for 24 hours, so you can split your visit over two days if you wish.

To get to the museum, take bus 2 from place Courtonne in the town centre. By car, follow signs marked 'Mémorial'.

CHÂTEAU DE CAEN

Looming above the centre of the city from a domed hilltop, and surrounded by a dry moat, the **Château de Caen** (www.chateau.caen .fr; ⊙ 6am-10pm May-Sep, 6am-7.30pm Oct-Apr) was founded by William the Conqueror in 1060 and extended by his son Henry I. It has been used over the centuries by royals, revolutionaries, townsfolk and the military.

Take a walk around the **ramparts** and visit the 12th-century **Chapelle de St-Georges** and the **Échiquier** (Exchequer), which dates from about AD 1100 and is one of the oldest civic buildings in Normandy. Of special interest is the **Jardin des Simples**, a garden of medicinal and aromatic herbs cultivated during the Middle Ages – some of which are poisonous. A book (written in French) on the garden is on sale inside the **Musée de Normandie** (☎ 02 31 30 47 50; www.musee-de -normandie.caen.fr; permanent collection admission free, temporary exhibitions adult/student €3/2; ⊙ 9.30am-6pm

Wed-Mon Oct-May, daily Jun-Sep), which contains historical artefacts illustrating traditional life in Normandy.

The **Musée des Beaux-Arts** (☎ 02 31 30 47 70; adult/concession €5/3, Wed free; ⊙ 9.30am-6pm Wed-Mon) is based in a modern building near the chateau, and provides a brief tour through the history of art from the 15th to 20th centuries. The collection includes works by Rubens, Van Dyck, Géricault, Delacroix and Rembrandt, among many others.

ABBEYS

Caen's two Romanesque abbeys were built by William the Conqueror and his wife, Matilda of Flanders, after the distant cousins had been absolved by the Roman Catholic church for marrying. The **Abbaye aux Hommes** (☎ 02 31 30 42 81; adult/student €2/1, Sun free, guided visit €4; ⊙ 8.50am-noon & 2-7.30pm, guided visits 9.30am, 11am, 2.30pm & 4pm), with its multiturreted Église St-Étienne, is at the end of rue Écuyère and was William's final resting place. The tomb was destroyed in turn by a 16th-century Calvinist mob and by 18th-century revolutionaries – a solitary thighbone is all that's left of Will's mortal remains. The convent buildings are today home to the town hall.

The **Abbaye aux Dames** (☎ 02 31 06 98 98; admission free; ⊙ guided tours 2.30pm & 4pm), at the eastern end of rue des Chanoines, incorporates the Église de la Trinité. Access to the abbey, which houses regional government offices, is by guided tour only. Look for Matilda's tomb behind the main altar.

Sleeping

None of the city's hotels are going to win any beauty contests – like much of the rest of Caen, you'll find the accent is very much on function rather than form.

Hôtel Saint-Étienne (☎ 02 31 86 35 82; www.hotel -saint-etienne.com; 2 rue de l'Académie; s €26-36, d €28-39) Just about the last thing you'll expect to find in Caen – a classic budget hotel in a charming period building, packed with oldfashioned features such as wooden wardrobes, creaky beds and cast-iron fireplaces. It's a bit rough around the edges, but in concrete Caen that's all part of the appeal.

Hôtel Bernières (☎ 02 31 86 01 26; www.hotel bernieres.com; 50 rue de Bernières; s/d €35/45) On the traffic-thronged rue de Bernières, this multistorey place initially looks unpromising,

NORMANDY

but once inside you'll find the bedrooms are more reminiscent of a British B&B than a chain hotel. The décor's a bit mix-and-match, and the rooms are on the cramped side, but you could do a lot worse.

Hôtel des Cordeliers (☎ 02 31 86 37 15; fax 02 31 39 56 51; 4 rue des Cordeliers; d from €45) One of the rare Caen hotels in an 18th-century building, this hotel has more character than most. The rooms are attractive with white walls and plain pine furniture, and open directly onto a relaxing interior garden.

Hôtel du Château (☎ 02 31 86 15 37; www.hotel -chateau-caen.com; 5 av du 6 Juin; s/d €45/55) Bang in the centre of town, right beside the tram-lines, this functional and friendly hotel makes the perfect city base. The rooms are simple but quite generous in size, and are all painted in bold primary shades. Front windows are double-glazed and there's an elevator.

Hôtel des Quatrans (☎ 02 31 86 25 57; www.hotel -des-quatrans.com; 17 rue Gémare; s/d €53/62) It might look like a set of concrete boxes piled up on top of each other from outside, but inside this typically modern hotel you'll find a surprising range of comfy, unfussy rooms, handy for exploring the city centre.

Hôtel Le Dauphin (☎ 02 31 86 22 26; www.le-dau phin-normandie.com; 29 rue Gémare; r €70-150; ✗) Just down the street, this Best Western outpost is partly housed in a former priory, though you'll be hard-pressed to find any histori-cal detail – the occasional spot of exposed stonework or a solitary woodbeam is about as good as it gets. Nevertheless, the rooms are about the swishest you'll find in central Caen.

Eating

The area around rue du Vaugueux, one of Caen's few surviving old quarters, is the best place to explore for eating out.

Abracadabra (☎ 02 31 43 71 38; 4 rue du Vaugueux; pizzas €7.50-13.50; ✓ lunch & dinner Mon-Sat) Ever heard of a Pizza Triton, Pizza Popeye or Pizza Yassa? No? Then head for this fan-tastic place a little further down the street from Le P'tit B, which serves up more va-rieties of wood-fired pizza than you ever thought possible.

La Petite Auberge (☎ 02 31 86 43 30; 17 rue des Équipes d'Urgence; menus €12-20.50; ✓ lunch & dinner Tue-Sat) A slice of the country comes to downtown Caen at this quaint little restaurant, serving

up hearty mains such as Breton sardines, *pommes de terre gratinées* (sliced oven-cooked potatoes), and the local speciality, *tripes à la Caen* (tripe cooked with carrots, onions, leeks, celery, Calvados and herbs).

Maître Corbeau (☎ 02 31 93 93 00; 8 rue Buquet; salads €9-10, fondue €12-15; ✓ lunch & dinner Tue-Fri, dinner only Mon & Sat) This is Caen's undisputed cheese specialist, serving up massive plates of *tartiflette* (oven-baked potato and Re-blochon cheese and Savoyard fondues in an Alpine-inspired atmosphere (includ-ing the all-important plastic cow in the window).

Le P'tit B (☎ 02 31 73 32 71; 15 rue du Vaugueux; mains €18-21, menus €30; ✓ lunch & dinner) Cur-rently the venue of choice with Caen's bright young things, this funky little eat-ery is all about giving traditional flavours a contemporary twist – the Provençal tuna steak or the three-fish stew are a treat for the tastebuds, and the dinky outside terrace gets lively at weekends.

SELF-CATERING

There's a **Monoprix** (45 blvd Maréchal Leclerc; ✓ 8.30am-8.30pm Mon-Sat) supermarket. Late-night purchases can be made at **Épicerie de Nuit** (23 rue Porte au Berger; ✓ 8pm-2am Tue-Sun).

For food markets check out place St-Sauveur on Friday, blvd Leroy (behind the train station) on Saturday and place Cour-tonne on Sunday.

Drinking & Entertainment

El Ché Guevara (☎ 02 31 85 10 75; 53 rue de Geôle; ✓ 6pm-1am Tue-Sat) Don't ask us how the Cuba-Caen connection started, but you'll find this is just one of many Havana-themed nightspots round town. So dig out those Cuban heels (what do mean you didn't pack them?), order a margarita and break out those bossa nova moves, baby.

O'Donnell's Irish Pub (☎ 02 31 85 51 50; 20 quai Vendeuvre; ✓ 4.30pm-2.30am) Once you've had enough of the Cuban tip, head over for a pint of the black stuff and a whiskey chaser at this authentically Irish bar, complete with upside-down barrel-tables on the out-side terrace.

Glue Pot (☎ 02 31 86 29 15; 18 quai Vendeuvre; ✓ 4pm-4am, to 2am Sun) Round off the evening with some live music at this hot-and-sweaty sinkhole next door to O'Donnell's, the best venue for Caen's new bands.

Théâtre de Caen (☎ 02 31 30 48 00; 135 blvd Maréchal Leclerc) Offers a season of opera, dance, jazz and classical concerts that runs from October to May.

Getting There & Away

AIR

Caen's **airport** (☎ 02 31 71 20 10) is 5km west of town in Carpiquet. There are regular flights to several French cities via Lyon; the only regular UK destination is Manchester. A taxi from the airport to the town centre costs around €15 (call ☎ 02 31 52 17 89).

BOAT

Brittany Ferries (☎ 02 31 36 36 36; www.brittanyferries .com) sails from Ouistreham, 14km northeast of Caen, to Portsmouth in England. For more information, see p976.

BUS

Bus Verts (☎ 08 10 21 42 14; information kiosk place Courtonne) serves the entire Calvados *département*, including Bayeux (€6.16, one hour, three daily Monday to Friday) and Courselles-sur-Mer (€4.40, 30 minutes, hourly, five on Sunday) as well as Deauville-Trouville (€8.80, 1¼ hours, hourly), Honfleur (€11.44 via Deauville, or €12.60 by express bus, at least hourly) and the ferry port at Ouistreham (€3.80, 25 minutes, six daily, one on Sunday). It also runs daily buses to Le Havre (regular bus €17.60, 2½ hours; express bus €19.40, 1½ hours, seven daily, four on Sunday).

See p300 for details on getting to the D-Day beaches.

Most buses stop at the bus station and place Courtonne. When leaving or arriving at Caen by bus, your ticket will be valid for public transport to/from the bus station.

CAR

Rental places include **Hertz** (☎ 02 31 84 64 50; 34 place de la Gare), **Europcar** (☎ 02 31 84 61 61; 36 place de la Gare), **Avis** (☎ 02 31 84 73 80; 44 place de la Gare) and **ADA** (☎ 02 31 34 88 89; 26 rue d'Auge).

TRAIN

Caen is on the Paris–Cherbourg line. There are regular connections to Paris' Gare St-Lazare (€27.70, 2½ hours, 10 direct daily), as well as Bayeux (€5.30, 20 minutes, 18 to 20 daily), Cherbourg (€17.60, 3¼ hours, 12 daily), Pontorson (€21.70, 2½ hours, nine or

10 daily) and Rouen (€20.70, two hours, six to 10 daily). Visit the **SNCF Boutique** (8 rue St-Pierre) for train information and reservations.

Getting Around

CTAC (☎ 02 31 15 55 55; www.twisto.fr) runs several of the city's buses, and both tram lines run from the train station via the city centre and place St-Pierre, outside the tourist office. Tickets cost €1.20 for single fares, or €2.90 for a 24-hour ticket.

For **taxis** call ☎ 02 31 26 62 00 or ☎ 02 31 52 17 89.

BAYEUX

pop 15,400

There's one reason why several million visitors descend on Bayeux every year – a 70m-long piece of painstakingly embroidered cloth known to the French as *La Tapisserie de la Reine Mathilde* (Tapestry of Queen Matilda), and to the rest of the world, rather more prosaically, as the Bayeux Tapestry. But there's more to the town than its impressive needlework – Bayeux was the first town to be liberated after D-Day, and is one of the few in Calvados to have survived WWII practically unscathed. Its winding streets are crammed with higgledy-piggledy period buildings, including a fine Gothic cathedral and lots of wooden-framed Norman houses, and the city is a perfect launch pad for exploring the invasion beaches just to the north.

Orientation

The Cathédrale Notre Dame, the major landmark in the centre of Bayeux and visible throughout the town, is 1km northwest of the train station. The River Aure, with several attractive little mills along its banks, flows northwards on the eastern side of the centre.

Information

Caisse d'Épargne (59 rue St-Malo)
Laundrette (13 rue du Maréchal Foch)
Post Office (14 rue Larcher) Has Cyberposte, and changes money.
Société Générale (26 rue St-Malo)
Tourist Office (☎ 02 31 51 28 28; www.bayeux-tour ism.com; pont St-Jean; ☺ 9am-7pm Mon-Sat, 9am-1pm & 2-6pm Sun July & Aug, 9.30am-12.30pm & 2-6pm Apr-Jun & Sep-Oct, 9.30am-12.30pm & 2-5.30pm Jan Mar & Nov-Dec) Changes money when the banks are closed, and books accommodation (€2 fee).

NORMANDY

Sights

BAYEUX TAPESTRY

Undoubtedly the world's most celebrated embroidery, the **Bayeux Tapestry** recounts the story of the Norman conquest of England in 58 remarkable scenes, briefly captioned in Latin, and all told from an unashamedly Norman perspective. Scholars believe that the 70m-long tapestry was commissioned by Bishop Odo of Bayeux, William's half-brother, to commemorate the opening of Bayeux cathedral in 1077. The main narrative fills up the centre of the canvas, while religious allegories and depictions of daily life in 11th-century France unfold in the borders. The tapestry is not only remarkable

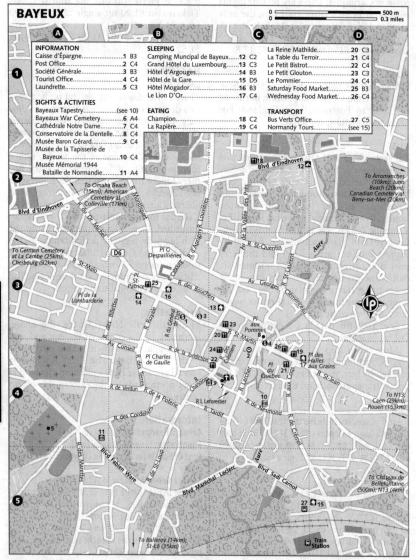

BAYEUX

0 — 500 m
0 — 0.3 miles

To Arromanches (10km); Juno Beach (20km); Canadian Cemetery at Beny-sur-Mer (20km)

To Omaha Beach (15km); American Cemetery at Colleville (17km)

Blvd d'Eindhoven

Blvd d'Eindhoven

To German Cemetery at La Cambe (25km); Cherbourg (92km)

R St-Malo

D6

Pl G-Despaillienes

R du Dr Michel

R Montinquet

R d'Aprigny

R Louviers

Av de la Vallée des Prés

Av R St-Quentin

St-Laurent

Aure

Pl St-Patrice

Pl de la Lombarderie

R des Billettes

R Royale

R du Général

des Dais

R des Bouchers

Av Georges Clemenceau

Pl aux Pommes

R St-Martin

Pl aux Grains

R des Terres

Av Conseil

R de la Juridiction

R Chartier

R Larcher

Pl des Halles

Pl Charles de Gaulle

R aux Coqs

R St-Jean

To N13; Caen (29km); Rouen (153km)

R Chanoine

Pl du Quebec

R de Verdun

R de la Poterie

R L Leforestier

R Tardif

R de Nesmond

R des Maretes

R des Cordeliers

Blvd Fabien Ware

R de St-Loup

Aure

Blvd Sadi Carnot

Blvd Maréchal Leclerc

To Château de Bellefontaine (500m); N13 (4km)

To Balleroy (14km); St-Lô (35km)

Train Station

for its astonishing size, but also its vivid pictorial detail – the final showdown at the Battle of Hastings is depicted in truly graphic fashion, complete with severed limbs, decapitated heads and a battlefield steeped in soldiers' blood. Halley's Comet, which blazed across the sky in 1066, even makes an appearance.

The tapestry is housed in the **Musée de la Tapisserie de Bayeux** (☎ 02 31 51 25 50; rue de Nesmond; adult/student incl admission to Musée Baron Gérard €7.60/3; ☒ 9am-6.30pm mid-Mar–Apr, Sep & Oct, 9.30am-12.30pm & 2-6pm Nov–mid-Mar, 9am-7pm May-Aug). Upstairs there's a short historical film and a full-sized reconstruction of the tapestry, but you'll be better off skipping both and heading downstairs to see the real thing. An audioguide is included in the admission price.

CATHÉDRALE NOTRE DAME
Most of Bayeux's spectacular Norman-Gothic **Cathédrale Notre Dame** (place de la Liberté; ☒ 8.30am-6pm Oct-Jun, 8.30am-7pm Jul-Sep) dates from the 13th century, though the crypt, the arches of the nave and the lower portions of the entrance towers are 11th-century Romanesque. The central tower was added in the 15th century; the copper dome dates from the 1860s.

WILLIAM CONQUERS ENGLAND

The son of Robert I of Normandy and his concubine Arlette, William 'the Conqueror' (born 1027, and sometimes affectionately known as 'William the Bastard') became Duke of Normandy at the tender age of five. Having survived several assassination attempts by rivals (and by members of his own family) William assumed full control of the province at age 15, and set about regaining his lost territory and feudal rights, quashing several rebellions along the way.

William had twice been promised the throne of England: once by the king himself, Edward the Confessor (William's relative), and once by the most powerful Saxon lord in England, Harold Godwinson of Wessex, who had the misfortune of being shipwrecked on the Norman coast.

In January 1066 Edward died without an heir. Harold was immediately crowned king, with the support of the great nobles of England (and very likely the majority of the Saxon people).

One of several pretenders to the throne, William was preparing to send an invasion fleet across the Channel when a rival army (consisting of an alliance between Harold's estranged brother Tostig and Harold Hardrada of Norway) landed in the north of England. In a September battle at Stamford Bridge, near York, Harold defeated and killed both Hardrada and Tostig.

Meanwhile, William had crossed the Channel unopposed with an army of about 6000 men, including a large cavalry force. They landed at Pevensey before marching to Hastings on 13 October, where Harold faced William with about 7000 men from a strong defensive position. The battle began the next day.

Although William's archers scored many hits, the Saxon army's ferocious defence ended a charge by the Norman cavalry and drove them back in disarray. William faced the real possibility of losing the battle. Summoning the knowledge and tactical ability he had gained in numerous campaigns against rivals in Normandy, he used the cavalry's rout to draw the Saxon infantry out from their defensive positions, whereupon the Norman infantry turned and caused heavy casualties on the undisciplined Saxon troops. The battle started to turn against Harold, who was slain (by an arrow through the eye, according to the Bayeux Tapestry) late in the afternoon. The embattled Saxons fought on until sunset and then fled. William immediately marched to London, ruthlessly quelled the opposition, and was crowned king of England on Christmas Day.

William thus became the ruler of two kingdoms, bringing England's feudal system of government under the control of Norman nobles. Ongoing unrest among the Saxon peasantry soured William's opinion of the country and he spent the rest of his life after 1072 in Normandy, only going to England when compelled to do so. William left most of the governance of the country to the bishops.

In Normandy William continued to expand his influence through military campaigns, strategic marriages and the ruthless elimination of all opposition. In 1087 he was injured during an attack on Mantes. He died at Rouen a few weeks later and was buried in Caen (p289).

CONSERVATOIRE DE LA DENTELLE

The fascinating **Conservatoire de la Dentelle** (Lace Conservatory; ☎ 02 31 92 73 80; 6 rue du Bienvenu; admission free; ☉ 10am-12.30pm & 2-6pm Mon-Sat) is dedicated to the preservation of traditional Norman lace-making. You can watch some of France's most celebrated lace-makers, who create intricate designs using dozens of bobbins and hundreds of pins.

MUSÉE BARON GÉRARD

The **Musée Baron Gérard** (☎ 02 31 92 14 21; 6 rue Lambert Leforestier; adult/student €2.60/1.50; ☉ 10am-12.30pm & 2-6pm) specialises in local porcelain, lace and 15th- to 19th-century paintings (Italian, Flemish and impressionist). Admission is free with a ticket to the tapestry museum.

MUSÉE MÉMORIAL 1944 BATAILLE DE NORMANDIE

Bayeux's **Musée Mémorial 1944 Bataille de Normandie** (☎ 02 31 92 93 41; blvd Fabien Ware; adult/student €6/3; ☉ 9.30am-6.30pm May–mid-Sep, 10am-12.30pm & 2-6pm mid-Sep–Apr), housing one of Normandy's main collections of D-Day memorabilia, has recently undergone refurbishment.

BAYEUX WAR CEMETERY

This peaceful cemetery, on blvd Fabien Ware a few hundred metres west of the war museum, is the largest of the 18 Commonwealth military cemeteries in Normandy. It contains 4868 graves of soldiers from the UK and 10 other countries (including Germany, in contrast with the American cemetery at Colleville-sur-Mer). Many of the soldiers buried here were never identified, and the headstones are marked 'A Soldier Known Unto God'. The bodies of 1807 other soldiers were never found, and are commemorated on the memorial across the main road. See the boxed text on p297 for details on Normandy's other war cemeteries.

Festivals & Events

On the first weekend in July, **Fêtes Médiévales de Bayeux** holds parades and medieval song and dance for the anniversary of the Battle of Formigny, which put an end to the Hundred Years' War.

Sleeping

BUDGET

Camping Municipal de Bayeux (☎ 02 31 92 08 43; blvd d'Eindhoven; adult/site €3.10/3.83; ☉ mid-Mar–

mid-Nov) This camp site is about 2km north of the town centre. Bus 3 stops three times daily at nearby Les Cerisiers.

Hôtel de la Gare (☎ 02 31 92 10 70; www.normandy -tours-hotel.com; 26 place de la Gare; s/d €19/38) A few bargain-basement rooms are available above this small brasserie opposite the station. They're old and rather tired, but offer a reasonable compromise between cost and comfort. Normandy Tours (p300) is based here.

Hôtel Mogador (☎ 02 31 92 24 58; hotel.mogador@ wanadoo.fr; 20 rue Alain Chartier; d €46-51) A reliable if slightly run-down hotel on the main market square. Floral curtains and the odd exposed beam conjure up some character, and there's a small garden courtyard that makes a lovely spot for a morning croissant.

MIDRANGE & TOP END

The tourist office has a list of *chambres d'hôtes* (B&Bs) in the Bayeux area. The average cost is around €35 to €40 for two people, with breakfast.

Le Lion d'Or (☎ 02 31 92 06 90; www.liondor-ba yeux.fr; 71 rue St-Jean; r €70-140) Another fine old hotel, tucked into the corner of a cobbled courtyard inside the town's 18th-century posthouse. The rooms vary in standard and comfort – the spacious doubles on the upstairs floors have the nicest views, but the attic rooms, sandwiched between the rafters, arguably have more character.

Hôtel d'Argouges (☎ 02 31 92 88 86; dargouges@aol .com; 21 rue St-Patrice; d €80-100) The former mansion of the d'Argouges family, this stately 18th-century residence is now a graceful hotel. Set back behind wrought-iron gates, the main house overlooks an enclosed carriage-yard and offers a range of enchanting rooms, the more expensive of which are packed with old furniture and period features. Downstairs the elegantly decorated breakfast room overlooks a private garden at the rear of the hotel.

ourpick Château de Bellefontaine (☎ 02 31 22 00 10; www.hotel-bellefontaine.com; 49 rue de Bellefontaine; s €60-90, d €90-135, ste €120-180; ✗) Surrounded by 5 acres of groomed parkland just outside Bayeux, and nestled beside the waters of a bubbling brook, this majestic 18th-century castle is top of the heap in terms of luxury. The décor is an intelligent mix of tradition and modernity, and the rural location just couldn't be bettered. Even the cheaper rooms have a tangible touch of class, but if you can afford them the beautifully appointed park-view suites are the ones to choose. Royally recommended.

Grand Hôtel du Luxembourg (☎ 02 31 92 00 04; hotel.luxembourg@wanadoo.fr; 25 rue des Bouchers; r €100-125; ✗) This venerable Bayeux landmark, with its grand façade and pale shutters, has been snapped up by the Best Western chain and reworked in typically nondescript style, though the original shell of the building is still largely untouched and the rooms have all the mod cons you could wish for.

Eating

La Reine Mathilde (☎ 02 31 92 00 59; 47 rue St-Martin; cakes €3-6; ☻ breakfast & lunch Mon-Sat, afternoon Sun) If you're looking for something sweet and sticky, this sumptuous patisserie and *salon de thé* serves the kind of wickedly indulgent cakes that would send Marie-Antoinette into overdrive.

Le Petit Bistrot (☎ 02 31 51 85 40; 2 rue du Bienvenu; mains €14-22; ☻ lunch & dinner, closed Sun & Mon Sep-Jun) The top place in town for down-to-earth regional cooking, served in a tiny dining room decked out with sunny colours, plain wooden tables and terracotta floor tiles.

La Table du Terroir (☎ 02 31 92 05 53; 42 rue St-Jean; lunch menus €11, dinner menus €16-28; ☻ lunch & dinner, closed Sun & Mon) The crimson chairs and tablecloths at this country-style restaurant are entirely fitting, as this is definitely one for the carnivores – rump steak, pork fillet and *tripes à la Caen* are just some of the meaty treats on offer.

La Rapière (☎ 02 31 21 05 45; 53 rue St-Jean; lunch menus €15, dinner menus €25 & €31; ☻ lunch & dinner, closed Wed & Thu low season) The fencing cavalier logo may be a little cheesy, but there's nothing contrived about the hearty home cooking – the *timbale de pêcheur* (fisherman's stew) is served up piping hot in its cast-iron pan, and the house speciality is a home-made sorbet spiced with a dash of Calvados.

Le Pommier (☎ 02 31 21 52 10; 40 rue des Cuisiniers; lunch/dinner menus €21.50/28.50; ☻ lunch & dinner, closed Tue & Wed in low season) For something a little bit more upmarket, this smart restaurant dishes up Norman specialities such as roast duck in apple sauce, and steamed rabbit, as well as a varied selection of classic French dishes.

SELF-CATERING
There are takeaway and sandwich shops along rue St-Martin and rue St-Jean, including **Le Petit Glouton** (☎ 02 31 92 86 43; 42 rue St-Martin). There's also a **Champion** (blvd d'Eindhoven) supermarket.

Rue St-Jean has an open-air food market on Wednesday morning, as does place St-Patrice on Saturday morning.

Entertainment
Bayeux is not known for its hot nightlife, but there are frequent concerts and theatrical events staged in venues around town. Check the free booklet *Sorties Plurielle*, available from the tourist office, for listings.

Getting There & Away
Bus Verts (☎ 08 10 21 42 14), opposite the train station, offers four or five daily buses to Caen (€6.16, one hour) leaving from the train station and place St-Patrice. Other local destinations tend to be arranged to cater for school children coming into Bayeux in the morning and going home in the afternoon.

Bus Verts also runs regular buses to the D-Day beaches (see p300).

Train services from Bayeux include Paris' Gare St-Lazare (€30.40, two to 2¼ hours, five direct daily). There are very regular trains to Caen (€5.30, 20 minutes) and Cherbourg (€14, one hour).

D-DAY BEACHES
The D-Day landings, code-named 'Operation Overlord', were the largest military operation in history. On the morning of 6 June 1944, swarms of landing craft – part of an armada of over 6000 boats – hit the beaches, and tens of thousands of soldiers from the USA, UK, Canada and elsewhere began pouring onto French soil.

The majority of the 135,000 Allied troops stormed ashore along 80km of beaches north of Bayeux code-named (from west to east) Utah, Omaha, Gold, Juno and Sword. The landings on D-Day – called Jour J in French – were followed by the Battle of Normandy, which ultimately led to the liberation of Europe from Nazi occupation. In the 76 days of fighting, the Allies suffered 210,000 casualties, including 37,000 troops killed. German casualties are believed to be around 200,000, and another 200,000 German soldiers were taken prisoner.

Caen's memorial museum (p287) provides a comprehensive overview of the events of D-Day, and many of the villages near the landing beaches have small museums packed with memorabilia relating to the invasion. Once on the coast, you can follow several sign posted circuits around the battle sites (follow signs for *D-Day-Le Choc* in the American sectors and *Overlord-L'Assaut* in the British and Canadian sectors). A free booklet called *The D-Day Landings and the Battle of Normandy*, available from tourist offices, contains details on the major routes. A useful guide to the main landing beaches is www.6juin1944.com, including maps and an hour-by-hour breakdown of the day.

Information

Maps of the D-Day beaches are available at *tabacs* (tobacconists), newsagents and bookshops in Bayeux and elsewhere. The area is also sometimes called the Côte de Nacre (Mother-of-Pearl Coast).

Arromanches

To make it possible to unload the vast quantities of cargo demanded by the invasion forces without having to capture one of the heavily defended Channel ports, the Allies installed prefabricated marinas off two of the landing beaches, code-named **Mulberry Harbours**.

These consisted of 146 massive cement blocks towed from England and sunk to form a semicircular breakwater in which floating bridge spans were moored. In the three months after D-Day, the Mulberries facilitated the unloading of some 2.5 million men, four million tonnes of equipment and 500,000 vehicles.

The harbour established at **Omaha** was completely destroyed by a ferocious gale just two weeks after D-Day, but the second, Port Winston (named after Winston Churchill), can still be see near **Arromanches**, 10km northeast of Bayeux. At low tide you can walk out to many of the caissons from the beach. The best view of Port Winston and nearby **Gold Beach** is from the hill east of town, marked with a statue of the Virgin Mary.

The **Musée du Débarquement** (☎ 02 31 22 34 31; www.normandy1944.com; place de 6 Juin; adult/child €6/4; ⏱ 9am-7pm May-Aug, 9am-6pm Sep, 9.30am-12.30pm & 1.30-5.30pm Mar, Apr & Oct, 10am-12.30pm & 1.30-5pm

Feb, Nov & Dec) in the centre of Arromanches explains the logistics and importance of Port Winston, and makes a good first stop before visiting the beaches themselves.

Dune-lined **Juno Beach**, 12km east of Arromanches, was stormed by Canadian troops on D-Day. A Cross of Lorraine marks the spot where General Charles de Gaulle came ashore shortly after the landings. Six days later, on 12 June, Winston Churchill landed here to inspect the results of the invasion, shortly followed on the 16th June by King George VI.

Longues-sur-Mer

The massive casemates and 152mm German guns near Longues-sur-Mer, 6km west of Arromanches, were designed to hit targets some 20km away, including both Gold Beach (to the east) and Omaha Beach (to the west). Half a century later, the mammoth artillery pieces are still sitting there in their colossal concrete emplacements – the only surviving large-calibre weapons in Normandy.

Parts of the classic D-Day film, *The Longest Day* (1962), were filmed both here and at Pointe du Hoc. On clear days, Bayeux's cathedral, 8km away, is visible to the south.

Omaha Beach

The most brutal fighting on D-Day took place on the 7km stretch of coastline around Vierville-sur-Mer, St-Laurent-sur-Mer and Colleville-sur-Mer, 15km northwest of Bayeux, otherwise known as Omaha Beach (or 'Bloody Omaha' to veterans). Sixty years on, little evidence of the carnage unleashed here on the 6 June 1944 remains, save for a concrete boat used to carry tanks ashore and, 1km further west, the concrete bunkers of the key German WN62 strongpoint.

These days Omaha is an altogether more peaceful place, a glorious stretch of fine golden sand lined with summer homes and popular with holiday-makers. Near the car park in St-Laurent, a memorial marks the site of the first US military cemetery on French soil. There's also a newly constructed sculpture on the beach called *Les Braves*, by the French sculptor Anilore Banon, commissioned to commemorate the 60th anniversary of the landings in 2004.

Nearby is the small **Musée Mémorial d'Omaha Beach** (☎ 02 31 21 97 44; www.musee -memorial-omaha.com; ⏱ 10am-12.30pm & 2.30-6pm mid-Feb–mid-Mar, 9.30am-6.30pm mid-Mar–mid-May, 9.30am-7pm mid-May–Sep, 9.30am-6pm Oct–mid-Nov) with uniforms, equipment and other military memorabilia relating to the Omaha landings, including a Sherman tank.

Utah Beach

The soldiers of the 4th and 8th Infantry Divisions who landed at Utah fared better than their comrades at Omaha. The weather and strong winds that caused such havoc on Omaha played into the Allies' favour on Utah – most of the landing craft landed some 2km from their intended debarkation points, in a relatively lightly protected sector of the beach. By noon the beach had been cleared and soldiers of the 4th Infantry had linked with paratroopers from the 101st Airborne; by nightfall, some 20,000 men and 1700 vehicles had arrived on French soil via Utah Beach.

Today the site is marked by memorials to the various divisions who landed here on 6 June, as well as the **Musée du Débarquement de Utah Beach** (☎ 02 33 71 53 35; www.utah -beach.com; adult/6-16yr €5/2; ☉ 9.30am-7pm Jun-Sep, 10am-6pm Apr, May & Oct. 10am-5.30pm Feb, Mar & Sep, 10am-12.30pm & 2-5.30pm Sat, Sun & holidays mid-Nov–Dec) inside the former German command post.

Pointe du Hoc Ranger Memorial

At 7.10am on 6 June 1944, 225 US Army Rangers commanded by Lt Col James Earl Rudder scaled the 30m cliffs at Pointe du Hoc, where the Germans had a battery of huge artillery guns perfectly placed to rain shells onto the beaches of Utah and Omaha. Unbeknown to Rudder and his team, the guns had already been transferred inland, and they spent the next two days repelling fierce German counterattacks. By the time they were finally relieved on 8 June, 81 of

---

FIELDS OF THE FALLEN

A visit to one of the military cemeteries scattered across Normandy is a powerful reminder of the true cost of D-Day. Strolling around one of the cemeteries, it's impossible not to be moved by the sheer scale of the devastation and to marvel at the courage of the men who gave their lives in the name of a liberated Europe.

Fittingly positioned on the bluff above the sands of Omaha Beach, the huge **American Military Cemetery** (☎ 02 31 51 62 00; ☉ 9am-6pm mid-Apr–Sep, 9am-5pm Oct–mid-Apr) at Colleville-sur-Mer, 17km northwest of Bayeux, is the largest American cemetery in Europe. Made famous by the opening scenes of Steven Spielberg's *Saving Private Ryan,* the cemetery contains the graves of 9387 American soldiers and a memorial to 1557 others whose remains were never found. Plain white crosses, interspersed with Stars of David, stretch off in seemingly endless rows, surrounded by a huge, immaculately tended expanse of lawn. The cemetery is overlooked by a large colonnaded memorial, centred on a statue dedicated to the spirit of American youth. Nearby is a reflective pond and a small chapel. Look out for the three graves decorated with gold lettering, signifying the award of a Congressional Medal Of Honour – one belongs to Brigadier General Theodore Roosevelt Jr, son of the former US President, who insisted on landing in the first wave on Utah Beach.

By tradition, soldiers from the Commonwealth killed in the war were buried near where they fell. Consequently, the 18 **Commonwealth Military Cemeteries** in Normandy follow the line of advance of British and Canadian troops. The largest is in **Bayeux** (p294), but there are many others, including the **Canadian Military Cemetery** at Bény-sur-Mer, a few kilometres south of Juno Beach and 18km east of Bayeux. In contrast to the simple inscriptions on the headstones in the American cemetery at Colleville, many graves in the Commonwealth cemeteries bear highly personal epitaphs, specially written by the families of the fallen.

The sombre **German Military Cemetery** near La Cambe, 25km west of Bayeux, contains over 21,000 German soldiers killed during the Normandy campaign, buried two or three to a grave. Here there are no flags and no noble inscriptions – each grave bears a simple plaque, inlaid almost imperceptibly into the ground. In the centre of the cemetery stands a dark Maltese cross, flanked by two hesitant figures, symbolising the parents of the soldiers whose bodies now lie buried in neat rows around the cemetery. Hundreds of other German dead were buried in the Commonwealth cemeteries, including the one in Bayeux.

NORMANDY

THE BATTLE OF NORMANDY

In early 1944 an Allied invasion of Continental Europe seemed inevitable. Hitler's disastrous campaign on the Russian front and the Luftwaffe's continuing inability to control the skies over Europe had left Germany vulnerable. Both sides knew the invasion was coming – the only question was where, and when.

Several sites were considered for the invasion. After a long period of deliberation, it was decided that the beaches along the Normandy coast would serve as the spearhead into Europe.

Code-named 'Operation Overlord', the invasion entailed an assault by three paratroop divisions and five seaborne divisions, along with 13,000 aeroplanes and 6000 vessels. The initial invasion force involved some 45,000 troops; 15 further divisions were to follow once successful beachheads had been established.

The Straits of Dover seemed the most likely invasion spot to the Germans, who set about heavily reinforcing the area around Calais and the other Channel ports. Allied intelligence went to extraordinary lengths to encourage the German belief that the invasion would be north of Normandy: double agents, leaked documents and fake radio traffic all suggested the invasion would centre on the Pas de Calais, reinforced by phoney airfields and even an entirely fictitious American army group, supposedly stationed in the southeast of England.

Because of the tides and unpredictable weather patterns, Allied planners had only a few days available each month in which to launch the invasion. On 5 June, the date chosen, the worst storm in 20 years set in, delaying the operation. The weather had only marginally improved the next day, but General Dwight D Eisenhower, Allied commander-in-chief, gave the go-ahead: 6 June would be D-Day.

In the hours leading up to D-Day, teams of the French resistance set about disrupting German communications. Just after midnight on 6 June, the first troops were on the ground. British commandos and glider units captured key bridges and destroyed German gun emplacements. The American 82nd and 101st Airborne regiments landed west of the invasion site. Although the paratroops' tactical victories were few, they caused confusion in German ranks and, because of their relatively small numbers, the German high command was convinced that the real invasion had not yet begun.

Sword, Juno & Gold Beaches

These beaches, stretching for about 35km from Ouistreham to Arromanches, were attacked by the British 2nd Army, which included the Canadian forces and smaller groups of Commonwealth, Free French and Polish forces.

At Sword Beach, initial German resistance was quickly overcome and the beach was secured within hours. Infantry pushed inland from Ouistreham to link up with paratroops around Ranville, but they suffered heavy casualties as their supporting armour fell behind, trapped in a massive traffic jam on the narrow coastal roads. Nevertheless, they were within 5km of Caen by 4pm, but a heavy German counterattack forced them to dig in. In spite of the Allies' successes, Caen was not taken on the first day as planned.

At Juno Beach, Canadian battalions landed quickly but had to clear the Germans trench by trench before moving inland Mines took a heavy toll on the infantry, but by noon they were south and east of Creuilly.

At Gold Beach, the attack by the British forces was at first chaotic, as unexpectedly high waters obscured German underwater obstacles. By 9am, though, Allied armoured divisions were on the beach and several brigades pushed inland. By afternoon they'd joined up with the Juno forces and were only 3km from Bayeux.

Omaha & Utah Beaches

The struggle on Omaha Beach (Vierville, St-Laurent and Colleville) was by far the bloodiest of the day. From the outset the Allies' best-laid plans were thrown into chaos. The beach was heavily defended by three battalions of heavily armed, highly trained Germans supported by mines, underwater obstacles and an extensive trench system. Strong winds blew many of the landing craft far from their carefully planned landing sectors. Many troops, heavily overloaded with equipment, disembarked in deep water and simply drowned; others were cut to pieces by machine-gun and mortar fire from the cliffs. Only two of the 29 Sherman tanks expected to support the troops made it to shore, equipment was scattered all over the beach, and it proved almost impossible to advance up the beach as planned.

By noon the situation was so serious that General Bradley, in charge of the Omaha Beach forces, considered abandoning the attack; but eventually, metre by metre, the GIs began to gain a precarious toehold on the beach. Assisted by naval bombardment, the US troops blew through a key German strongpoint and at last began to move off the beach; but of 2500 American casualties sustained there on D-Day, over 1000 men were killed, mostly within the first hour of the landings.

In contrast to Omaha, US forces at Utah Beach faced relatively light resistance. By noon, the beach had been cleared with the loss of only 12 men. Pockets of troops held large tracts of territory to the west of the landing site, and the town of Ste-Mère-Église was captured.

The Beginning of the End

Four days later, the Allies held a coastal strip about 100km long and 10km deep. British Field Marshal Montgomery's plan successfully drew the German armour towards Caen, where fierce fighting continued for more than a month and reduced the city to rubble. The US army stationed further west pushed northwards through the fields and *bocage* (hedgerows) of the Cotentin Peninsula.

The prized port of Cherbourg fell to the Allies on 27 June after a series of fierce battles. However, its valuable facilities were sabotaged by the retreating Germans, so it remained out of service until autumn. To overcome such logistical problems, the Allies had devised the remarkable 'Mulberry Harbours' (p296), huge temporary ports that were set up off the Norman coast.

By the end of July, US army units had smashed through to the border of Brittany. By mid-August, two German armies had been surrounded and destroyed near Argentan and Falaise (the so-called 'Falaise Pocket'), and on 20 August, US forces crossed the Seine at several points about 40km north and south of Paris. Lead by General Charles de Gaulle, France's leader-in-exile and commander of the Free French Forces, the first French troops arrived on the streets of Paris on 25 August, and by that afternoon the city – and symbolically the rest of France – had at last been liberated.

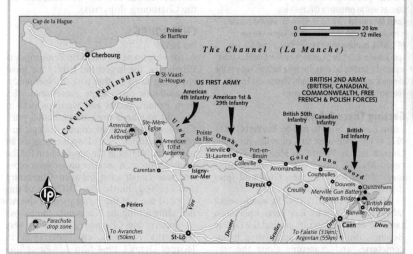

NORMANDY

the rangers had been killed and 58 more had been wounded.

Today the site, which France turned over to the US government in 1979, looks much as it did half a century ago. The ground is pockmarked with vast bomb craters, and the German command post and several of the concrete gun emplacements are still standing, scarred by bullet holes and blackened by flame-trowers.

As you face the sea, Utah Beach, which runs roughly perpendicular to the cliffs, is 14km to the left. Pointe du Hoc, which is 12km west of the American Military Cemetery, is always open. The **command post** (9am-6pm mid-Apr–Sep, 9am-5pm Oct–mid-Apr) is open the same hours as the cemetery.

Tours

An organised bus tour is an excellent way to see the D-Day beaches.

D-Day Tours (☎ 02 31 51 70 52; www.d-daybeaches .com; BP 48525, 14400 Bayeux) Offers morning tours to the American or Canadian sectors (adult/student/under 10 years €40/35/20), and afternoon tours to either the American or British sectors (adult/student/under 10 years €45/40/25). You can combine the individual tours into a full-day excursion (adult/student/under 10 years €75/65/40). Entry to one of the small D-Day museums is included.

Normandy Tours (☎ 02 31 92 10 70; www.normandy -tours-hotel.com; 26 place de la Gare; adult/student €39/34) Based at the Hotel de la Gare (p294) in Bayeux, this local operator offers twice-daily tours of the main sites, as well as personally tailored trips.

Caen Mémorial (☎ 02 31 06 06 45; www.memorial -caen.fr; afternoon tour adult/under 18yr & veteran €67.50/54, morning tour €54; 9am & 1pm Apr-Sep, 1pm Jan-Mar & Oct-Dec) Conducts excellent minibus tours around the landing beaches. The price includes entry to the museum, and guides speak French, German and English. You can book online or by telephone.

Getting There & Away

From Bayeux bus 70, run by **Bus Verts** (☎ 08 10 21 42 14), goes west to Colleville-sur-Mer, Omaha Beach, Pointe du Hoc and Grand-camp-Maisy. Bus 74 (75 during summer) serves Arromanches, Gold and Juno Beaches, and Courseulles.

D-Day Lines (☎ 08 10 21 42 14; www.busverts.fr /dday60; tour €14), run by Bus Verts, operates a range of summer circuits around the D-Day Beaches, stopping at the main sites, major cemeteries and museums along the way

(discounts are offered on museum entry). D-Day Lines departure points:

Caen (9.20am Jun-mid–Sep, return 6.05pm) To Juno Beach, Arromanches, Longues-sur-Mer, Omaha and Point du Hoc. Leaves from Caen bus station.

Bayeux (9.35am Mon, Wed & Sat mid-Jun–Sep, return 5.31pm) To Arromanches, Longues-sur-Mer, Omaha, Point du Hoc and La Cambe. Leaves from Bayeux train station.

Bayeux (9.35am Mon, Wed & Fri Jun-Sep, return 5.31pm) To La Cambe, St-Mère-Église, Azeville Battery and Utah Beach. Leaves from Bayeux train station.

Deauville (9.20am Wed, Fri & Sat Jun-Sep, return 6.05pm) To Sword Beach, Merville Battery, the Pegasus Memorial and Ouistreham. Leaves from Deauville train station.

MANCHE

The Manche *département* includes the entire Cotentin Peninsula from Utah Beach to the magnificent Mont St-Michel. The peninsula's northwest corner is especially captivating, with unspoiled stretches of rocky coastline sheltering tranquil bays and villages. Due west lie the Channel Islands of Jersey and Guernsey. The fertile inland areas, crisscrossed with hedgerows, produce an abundance of cattle, dairy products and apples.

Sadly, over the past two decades, the Manche region has become known as Europe's nuclear dump due to its uranium waste treatment plant (Cap de la Hague), its sprawling power plant (Flamanville) and its nuclear submarines' construction (at the Cherbourg shipyards).

CHERBOURG

pop 26,750

At the very tip of the Cotentin Peninsula sits Cherbourg, the largest but hardly the most appealing town in this part of Normandy. Transatlantic cargo ships, passenger ferries from Britain, yachts and warships pass in and out of Cherbourg's monumental port. Cherbourg took on enormous strategic importance during the D-Day landings as an indispensable link in the supply chain for the invasion forces. A massive underwater pipeline was constructed between Cherbourg and England shortly after D-Day, and this supplied most of the petrol used by the Allied army during the Normandy campaign.

Modern-day Cherbourg is a long way from the romantic city portrayed in Jacques Demy's 1964 film *Les Parapluies de Cherbourg* (The Umbrellas of Cherbourg), but it's a useful base if you're in transit to a cross-Channel ferry.

Orientation

The Bassin du Commerce, a wide central waterway, separates the 'living' half of Cherbourg to the west from the deserted streets to the east. The attractive Avant Port (Outer Harbour) lies to the north.

Information

Crédit Lyonnais (16 rue Maréchal Foch) ATM.
Forum Espace Culture (☎ 02 33 78 19 30; place Centrale; per 10/30min €1.50/2.35; ☷ 2-7pm Mon, 10am-7pm Tue-Sat) The internet café is on the upper floor of this cultural centre.
Laundrette (62 rue au Blé)
Post Office (1 rue de l'Ancien Quai) It has a Cyberposte and exchanges currency.
Tourist Office (☎ 02 33 93 52 02; www.ot-cherbourg -cotentin.fr in French; 2 quai Alexandre III; ☷ 9am-6.30pm Mon-Sat, 10am-12.30pm Sun Jul & Aug, 9am-12.30pm & 2-6.30pm Mon-Sat Sep-Jun)
Tourist Office Annexe (☎ 02 33 44 39 92; ferry terminal) Open for ferry arrivals.

Sights & Activities

Cherbourg is a little short on cultural highlights. **Musée Thomas Henry** (☎ 02 33 23 02 23; 4 rue Vastel; admission free; ☷ 10am-noon & 2-6pm Tue-Sat, 2-6pm Sun & Mon May-Sep, 2-6pm Wed-Sun Oct-Apr) has 200 works by French and European artists, including Van Dyck, Fra Angelico and Jean-François Millet.

Cité de la Mer (☎ 02 33 20 26 26; www.citede lamer.com; Gare Maritime Transatlantique; adult/child €14/10; ☷ 9.30am-7pm Jun–mid-Sep, 10am-6pm mid-Sep-May) is housed inside Cherbourg's former transatlantic ferry terminal, and contains half a million litres of water (making it the largest aquarium in Europe) as well as a decommissioned nuclear submarine.

Unsurprisingly, given its proximity to the Channel, Cherbourg is a big sailing centre. At the entrance to the Port de Plaisance Chantereyne, **Station-Voile Cherbourg-Hague** (☎ 02 33 78 19 29; www.cherbourg-hague-nautisme.com in French) runs half-day beginners, sailing courses (€95) and a range of other activities such as kayaking, rowing and paragliding.

Sleeping

Auberge de Jeunesse (☎ 02 33 78 15 15; cherbourg@ fuaj.org; 55 rue de l'Abbaye; dm €16) This comfort-able, ultramodern hostel is less than 10 years old and makes a great budget base, with meals available on site and a large kitchen for self-caterers. Staff can help organise sailing activities. Take bus 3 or 5 to the Hôtel de Ville stop.

La Régence (☎ 02 33 43 05 16; www.laregence .com; 42 quai de Caligny; r €55-61) Cherbourg's top hotel is a surprisingly sophisticated affair. The bedrooms have been thoroughly refurbished with a touch of Art Deco style, including scarlet bedcovers, brass light fittings and the odd cast-iron antique, but they vary in quality – get one of the top rooms overlooking the harbour, if you can.

Hôtel Moderna (☎ 02 33 43 05 30; www.moderna -hotel.com; 28 rue de la Marine; s €34-40, d €38-49; ☒) Another useful base, along a quietish side-street near the port. The concrete exterior isn't up to much, but the interior rooms are fine, decorated throughout in those stalwart shades of cream and magnolia and hooked up with satellite TV.

Hôtel Napoléon (☎ 02 33 93 32 32; www.hotel -napoleon.fr; 14 place de la République; s €23-39, d €33-43) One of the few 19th-century buildings to have survived around the heavily bombed harbour area, the Napoléon offers 14 decent if dull bedrooms, some of which have a limited view across the port.

Eating & Entertainment

Rue Tour Carrée, rue de la Paix and around place Centrale offer a wide choice in both cuisine and price.

Café de Paris (☎ 02 33 43 12 36; 40 quai de Caligny; menus €21-34.50; ☷ lunch & dinner, closed Mon & dinner Sun Oct-May) Founded in 1803 by an expat American, this has been Cherbourg's classic café for over two centuries. Sadly the original fixtures have long since been replaced (most recently by a garish puce-and-magenta colour scheme), but the food's still great – crab salad, Normandy scallops and, of course, oysters are always on the daily changing menu.

La Régence (☎ 02 33 43 05 16; www.laregence.com; 42 quai de Caligny; mains €12-18) The décor at the Régence hotel (above) is much more the ticket, with a convincing Art Deco vibe and fine French dining to match – home-made fish soup and lobster are the order of the day.

Au Diapason (☎ 02 33 01 21 43; 21 rue de la Paix) One of many nightspots along the grungy rue de la Paix, the Diapason has a little bit

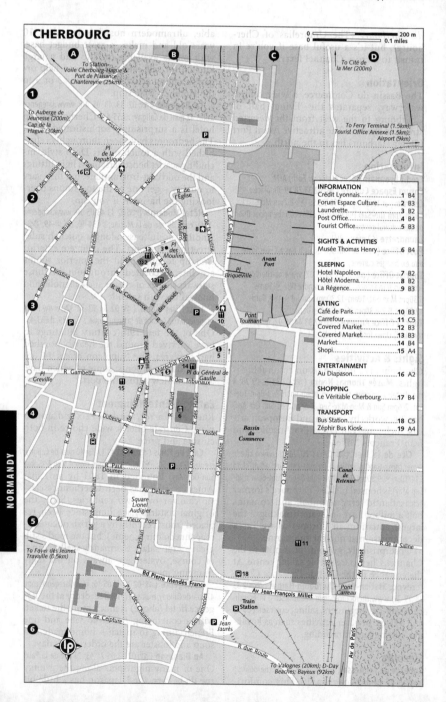

CHERBOURG

0 — 200 m
0 — 0.1 miles

INFORMATION
Crédit Lyonnais.....................**1**	B4
Forum Espace Culture...........**2**	B3
Laundrette............................**3**	B2
Post Office............................**4**	B4
Tourist Office........................**5**	B3

SIGHTS & ACTIVITIES
Musée Thomas Henry............**6**	B4

SLEEPING
Hotel Napoléon....................**7**	B2
Hôtel Moderna.....................**8**	B2
La Régence...........................**9**	B3

EATING
Café de Paris.......................**10**	B3
Carrefour............................**11**	C5
Covered Market...................**12**	B3
Covered Market...................**13**	B3
Market................................**14**	B4
Shopi..................................**15**	A4

ENTERTAINMENT
Au Diapason........................**16**	A2

SHOPPING
Le Véritable Cherbourg.........**17**	B4

TRANSPORT
Bus Station..........................**18**	C5
Zéphir Bus Kiosk..................**19**	A4

NORMANDY

of everything – live gigs, art exhibitions and a great selection of beers on tap.

SELF-CATERING
Cherbourg's market days are Tuesday and Thursday until 5pm at place de Gaulle and the covered place Centrale. The latter also operates on Saturday morning. There's a **Carrefour** (Centre Continent, quai de l'Entrepôt) supermarket and the **Shopi** (57 rue Gambetta) grocery store.

Shopping
The umbrellas of Cherbourg are beautifully made and the best place to buy them is at **Le Véritable Cherbourg** (☎ 02 33 93 66 60; 30 rue des Portes), which has a stunning selection starting at €85.

Getting There & Away
AIR
Cherbourg's airport is 9km east of town at Maupertus-sur-Mer.

BOAT
The three companies with services to either England or Ireland have bureaus in the *gare maritime* (ferry terminal). Their desks are open two hours before departure and for 30 minutes after arrivals.

Brittany Ferries (☎ 02 33 88 44 44) operates services to Poole and Portsmouth in England, while **Condor Ferries** (☎ 08 25 13 51 35, 02 99 20 03 00) sails to Portsmouth and the Channel Islands in summer. **Irish Ferries** (☎ 02 33 23 44 44) sails to Rosslare, Ireland. For further details and schedules, see p973.

BUS
The main regional bus line (which stops at the station on av Jean-François Millet) is **STN** (☎ 02 33 44 32 22). It has a couple of daily buses to Valognes (€3.90, 30 minutes, six daily) and Barfleur (€4.30, 40 minutes, two daily).

TRAIN
Services from the **train station** (☎ 02 33 57 50 50; ⏱ 6am-10pm) include direct trains to Paris' Gare St-Lazare (€39.30, 3½ hours, four to six daily) and a few more via Caen (€17.60, 1½ hours). There are also around 10 daily trains to Bayeux (€14, one hour).

Getting Around
There's no public transport from the airport into town. A taxi will cost about €20.

City buses are run by **Zéphir** (☎ 08 10 81 00 50; 40 blvd Robert Schuman). Buses leave from either outside the kiosk or place Jean Jaurès, in front of the train station. Single tickets cost €1 and a carnet of 10 is €8.70. There's a shuttle-bus service linking the ferry terminal, the town centre and the train station.

For taxis call ☎ 02 33 53 36 38. The trip between the train station and ferry terminal costs about €8.

COUTANCES
pop 9700
The medieval hilltop town of Coutances, 77km south of Cherbourg, has two major sights: a remarkable cathedral and a stunning landscape garden. Together they justify a day trip from Bayeux, or a pleasant stopover on the road to Mont St-Michel further south.

Orientation & Information
The town centre is compact and confined by blvd Alsace-Lorraine in the northwest and blvd Jeanne Paynel to the east. At the centre of town is the cathedral and town hall. The train and bus stations are about 1km southeast of the town centre.

Post Office (10 rue St-Dominique) Exchanges money and has a Cyberposte terminal.

Société Générale (8 rue Daniel) A bank opposite the tourist office.

Tourist Office (☎ 02 33 19 08 10; tourismecoutances@wanadoo.fr; place Georges Leclerc; ⏱ 10am-12.30pm & 2-5.30pm Mon, 10am-12.30pm & 2-6pm Tue, Wed & Fri, 10am-6pm Thu, 10am-12.30pm & 2-5pm Sat)

Sights & Activities
The lofty 13th-century Gothic **Cathédrale de Coutances** (admission free; ⏱ 9am-7pm) is one of France's finest, prompting Victor Hugo to call it the prettiest he'd seen after the one at Chartres. Its airy Norman-Romanesque design is enhanced by the use of light-hued limestone. There are several frescoes worth a look, including a 13th-century fresco of St George slaying the beast. There are **tours** (adult/student €5/3; ⏱ 3.30pm Mon-Fri summer) in English, which also afford sweeping views from the galleries in the lantern tower.

Opposite place Leclerc lies the splendid **Jardin des Plantes** (⏱ 9am-8pm mid-Sep–Oct & Apr-Jun, 9am-11.30pm Jul–mid-Sep, 9am-6pm Oct-Mar), a grand 19th-century landscape garden that blends symmetrical French lines with Italianate terraces, English-style copses, a maze and fountains.

Both the cathedral and gardens light up with a *son-et-lumière* (sound-and-light) show on summer nights.

Sleeping & Eating

Hôtel La Pocatière (☎ 02 33 45 13 77; www.hotel apocatiere.com; 25 blvd Alsace Lorraine; r €22-63) This welcoming hotel is the pick of the places to stay in Coutances, with a choice of rooms ranging widely in price and quality, from bare-bones budget to midrange comfort, complete with smoke-green drapes, magnolia walls and attractive little cream-coloured bathrooms.

Hôtel des Trois Piliers (☎ 02 33 45 01 31; 11 rue des Halles; r €25) Perched above a jazzy bar and usually packed with a young, boisterous crowd, this is a useful budget backup – although the hotel is often booked out by students during holiday periods. Bring your earplugs on weekend nights.

The market is held on Thursday morning. Look for the delicious local Coutances cheese with its creamy centre.

Getting There & Away

SNCF runs buses to Granville (€6.90, 30 minutes, three daily). In July and August there are buses to the beaches (20 minutes, up to five daily). Regular train services include Cherbourg (via Lison, €16.30, two hours, six to eight daily) and Caen (€14.10, 1½ hours, six direct daily), where you can hop onto trains to Paris' Gare du Nord.

MONT ST-MICHEL

pop 42

The slender towers and sky-scraping turrets of the abbey of Mont St-Michel are one of the classic images of northern France. Rising from flat white sands, the abbey sits atop a small island encircled by stout ramparts and battlements, connected to the mainland by an old causeway. Legend has it that the abbey was founded in the 8th century, when Aubert, the bishop of Avranches, was visited by the Archangel Michael in a dream; to this day the abbey is still crowned by a gilded copper statue of Michael slaying a dragon, symbolising the triumph of good over evil.

The bay around Mont St-Michel is famed for its extraordinary tides. Depending on the season and the gravitational pull of the moon, the difference between low and high tides can reach 15m, although the Mont is only completely surrounded by the sea during seasonal equinoxes. Regardless of the time of year, the waters sweep in at an astonishing rate; at low tide the Mont can be surrounded by bare sand for miles around, but at high tide, barely six hours later, the whole bay is often entirely submerged by the sea.

There are a few expensive hotels around the base of the Mont itself, but most people choose to stay at Beauvoir, right opposite the Mont, or Pontorson, about 5 miles inland from the bay. Unsurprisingly, for one of France's top tourist attractions, the Mont is always packed with coach tours and bellowing kids at the start of the day – you'll enjoy a much quieter visit if you turn up in late afternoon.

History

According to Celtic mythology, Mont St-Michel was one of the sea tombs to which the souls of the dead were sent. Following his vision of St Michael, Bishop Aubert of Avranches built a devotional chapel at the summit of the island in 708. In 966, Richard I, duke of Normandy, gave Mont St-Michel to the Benedictines, who turned it into a centre of learning and, in the 11th century, into something of an ecclesiastical fortress, with a military garrison at the disposal of the abbot and the king.

In the 15th century, during the Hundred Years' War, the English blockaded and besieged Mont St-Michel three times. The fortified abbey withstood these assaults; it was the only place in western and northern France not to fall into English hands. After the Revolution, Mont St-Michel was turned into a prison. In 1966 the abbey was symbolically returned to the Benedictines as part of the celebrations marking its millennium. Mont St-Michel and the bay became a Unesco World Heritage site in 1979.

Orientation

There is only one opening in the ramparts, Porte de l'Avancée, immediately to the left as you walk down the causeway. The Mont's single street – Grande Rue – is lined with restaurants, a few hotels and plenty of tacky souvenir shops. There are several large car parks (€4 per day) close to the Mont – staff will show you where to park your car when the high tide is due.

Pontorson (population 4200), the nearest town to Mont St-Michel, is 9km south and is the base for most travellers. Route D976 from Mont St-Michel runs right into Pontorson's main thoroughfare, rue du Couësnon.

Information
INTERNET ACCESS
Tourist Office (per 30min €4.50) You can get online at the Pontorson tourist office.

MONEY
CIN (98 rue du Couësnon, Pontorson; ☯ Tue-Sat) Better exchange rates than at the Mont.
Société Générale ATM just inside the Porte de l'Avancée.

POST
Mont St-Michel Post Office (Grande Rue)
Pontorson Post Office (place de l'Hôtel de Ville)

TOURIST INFORMATION
Mont St-Michel Tourist Office (☎ 02 33 60 14 30; www.ot-montsaintmichel.com; ☯ 9am-7pm Jul & Aug, 9am-noon & 2-5.30pm Sep-Jun) Up the stairs to the left inside Porte de l'Avancée. A *horaire des marées* (tide table) is posted outside, and a detailed map of the Mont is available for €3.50.
Pontorson Tourist Office (☎ 02 33 60 20 65; mont .st.michel.pontorson@wanadoo.fr; place de l'Église; ☯ 9am-noon & 2-7pm Mon-Fri, 10am-noon & 3-6pm Sat, 10am-noon Sun Apr-Sep; 9am-noon & 2-6pm Mon-Fri, 10am-noon & 3-6pm Sat Oct-Mar) Has heaps of information about walking tours and local events.

Sights
ABBAYE DU MONT ST-MICHEL
The Mont's major attraction is the stunning **abbey** (☎ 02 33 89 80 00; adult/18-25yr/under 18yr incl 1hr guided tour €8/5/free; ☯ 9am-7pm May-Sep, 9.30am-6pm Oct-Apr), which sits at the very top of the island at the top of the Grande Rue and a steep stairway. From Monday to Saturday between mid-May and September there are illuminated night-time visits with music from 9pm to midnight.

Most rooms can be visited without a guide, but it's worth taking the tour included in the ticket price. One-hour tours in English depart three to eight times daily (the last leaves about an hour before closing). Audioguides (€4) are also available if you miss the tour.

The **Église Abbatiale** (Abbey Church) was built at the rocky tip of the mountain cone. The transept rests on solid rock while the nave, choir and transept arms are supported by the rooms below. The church is famous for its mix of architectural styles: the nave and south transept (11th and 12th centuries) are Norman Romanesque, while the choir (late 15th century) is Flamboyant Gothic. Mass is at 12.15pm from Tuesday to Sunday.

The buildings on the northern side of the Mont are known as **La Merveille** ('the marvel'). The famous **cloître** (cloister) is surrounded by a double row of delicately carved arches resting on granite pillars. The early-13th-century **réfectoire** (dining hall) is illuminated by a wall of recessed windows – remarkable, given that the sheer drop precluded the use of flying buttresses – which diffuses the light beautifully. The Gothic **Salle des Hôtes** (Guest Hall), dating from 1213, has two giant fireplaces. Look out for the **promenoire** (ambulatory), with one of the oldest ribbed vaulted ceilings in Europe, and the **Chapelle de Notre Dame sous Terre** (Underground Chapel of Our Lady), one of the earliest rooms built in the abbey and rediscovered in 1903.

The masonry used to build the abbey was brought to the Mont by boat and pulled up the hillside using ropes. What looks like a treadmill for gargantuan gerbils was in fact powered in the 19th century by half a dozen prisoners who, by turning the wheel, hoisted the supply sledge up the side of the abbey.

ÉGLISE NOTRE DAME DE PONTORSON
Though no match for its dramatic sister to the north, the 12th-century Church of Our Lady in Pontorson is a good example of the Norman Romanesque style of architecture. To the left of the altar is a 15th-century relief of Christ's Passion, which was mutilated during the Religious Wars and again during the Revolution.

GRANDE RUE
None of the so-called **museums** (adult/child per museum €4/2) along Grande Rue are up to much, although a couple might intrigue the kids. The **Archéoscope** is a smart 20 minute multimedia history of the Mont with lights, video and even a few spurts of dry ice, while the **Musée de la Mer et de l'Écologie** explains Mont St-Michel's complex tidal patterns. Don't even think about wasting money on the others.

NORMANDY

Tours

When the tide is out, you can walk all the way around Mont St-Michel, a distance of about 1km. Straying too far from the Mont could be risky: you might get stuck in wet sand – from which Norman soldiers are depicted being rescued in one scene of the Bayeux Tapestry (p292). Several operators provide **guided walks** (tour €6.50) across the bay in summer – contact the tourist office.

Sleeping

There are eight hotels within the walls of Mont St-Michel and several more motel-style places at the end of the causeway. All tend to be booked out in summer, often by large coach parties – you'll be better off beating a retreat to the mainland. The following are in Pontorson.

Camping Haliotis (☎ 02 33 68 11 59; www.camping -haliotis-mont-saint-michel.com; Pontorson; adult/site €4.50/4; ☻ Apr-Nov; ☒) Just off blvd Général Patton, this complex has a heated pool, bike hire, tennis courts and an on site bar.

Centre Duguesclin (☎ /fax 02 33 60 18 65; aj@ville -pontorson.fr; blvd du Général Patton, Pontorson; r per person €11-14; ☻ year-round) 1km west of the train station, this modern, newly renovated hostel offers four- to six-bed rooms and kitchen facilities. The hostel closes from 10am to 6pm, but there's no curfew. It is in an old three-storey stone building opposite No 26.

Hôtel de Bretagne (☎ 02 33 60 10 55; www.lebre tagnepontorson.com; 59 rue du Couësnon, Pontorson; s €35-48, d €39-64) This timber-fronted hotel looks a touch shabby from the outside, but the flowery bedspreads and frilly curtains add a touch of brightness to the bedrooms themselves. The quasi-formal downstairs restaurant (lunch menus €11, dinner menus €15 to €38) offers generous portions of local specialities such as oysters with Camembert and scallops cooked in cider.

Hôtel Montgomery (☎ 02 33 60 00 09; www .hotel-montgomery.com; 13 rue du Couësnon, Pontorson; s €47-55, d €57-160, ste €115-250) This 16th-century mansion boasts a vine-covered Renaissance façade and a selection of quirky rooms along its creaky wood-panelled corridors. The most expensive have huge four-poster beds and hefty Renaissance furniture, although most rooms are more modestly furnished. The restaurant (dinner menus €16 to €25) is one of the best in Pontorson for French cuisine, but preference is given to guests.

Eating

MONT ST-MICHEL

The main street of the Mont is jammed with touristy restaurants, and though the views are lovely, the quality can be mediocre, especially on busy days.

Crêperie La Siréne (☎ 02 33 60 08 60; galettes €6-10, menus €14) Not a bad budget option, offering the standard selection of *crêpes* and *galettes* (savoury *crêpes*) for reasonable prices.

La Mère Poulard (☎ 02 33 89 68 68; Grande Rue; lunch menus €29-39, dinner menus €45-65; ☻ 11am-10pm) Established in 1888, this tourist institution churns out its famous *omelettes à la Mère Poulard* (soufflé omelettes cooked in a wood-fired oven) and charges astronomical prices for them. Autographed photos of visiting film stars and politicians adorn the walls.

PONTORSON

The main rue du Couësnon has a few snack bars and *crêperies*, but the best restaurants all belong to the town's hotels.

In addition to the other hotels in Pontorson, the **Hôtel La Tour Brette** (☎ 02 33 60 10 69; latourbrette@wanadoo.fr; 8 rue du Couësnon) and **Hôtel La Cave** (☎ 02 33 60 11 35; www.hotel-la-cave.com; 37 rue Libération) both have good restaurants with traditional French *menus* for €12 to €28. If you get stuck, they also both offer basic rooms.

SELF-CATERING

The nearest supermarket is across from Hôtel Mercure on the causeway, 2km from the Mont. In Pontorson, there's the **8 à Huit** (5 rue du Couësnon).

Getting There & Around

Courriers Bretons (☎ 02 33 60 11 43) buses run between Pontorson and Mont St-Michel (€1.80, 15 minutes, seven to 10 daily) and also to and from St-Malo (€8, one hour, four daily).

Local train services from Pontorson include Caen (€21.70, 2¼ hours, two daily) and Cherbourg (via Lison, €23.30, 2½ to three hours, two daily).

You can rent bicycles from **Camping Haliotis** (☎ 02 33 68 11 59; Pontorson) and **VMPS** (☎ 02 33 60 28 76, 06 86 90 95 01). VMPS, off blvd Général Patton, delivers to your hotel or camp site. For a **taxi**, call ☎ 02 33 60 33 23.

Brittany

France's westernmost promontory might be called Finistère, meaning 'land's end', but its Breton name, Penn ar Bed, translates as the 'head of the world', highlighting how Bretons have long viewed the peninsula, and, by extension, the rest of this independent region.

Historically cut off from the rest of the mainland by dense, impenetrable forest, in an era when sea travel was all, Brittany (Bretagne in French) still stands with its back to the rest of the country, looking oceanward.

The sea crashing against the granite coast and scattered islands provides numerous nautical pursuits as well as prized mussels, sea bass, oysters and lobster – ideally accompanied by cider, Breton beer, and Muscadet wine from its former capital, Nantes (Naoned in Breton), covered in the Atlantic Coast chapter (p652). Within its deep, mysterious interior, Brittany's magical forests and wending rivers and canals are ideal for hiking, cycling, or punting lazily by boat.

Brittany harbours its Celtic customs, celebrations and costumes, as well as its Breton language, which is not only reviving but forging beyond its former frontiers. Dancing needle-and-thread style, interlinked by little fingers, to music played with *biniou* (something like a bagpipe) and *bombarde* (a double-reeded oboe) at *festoù-noz* (night festivals) is a fantastic way to experience Breton culture – which is as interwoven with French culture today as the intricate lace of women's traditional headdresses and the grey churches' filigreed stone steeples.

HIGHLIGHTS

- Pop into local galleries or pick up a paintbrush at the artists' enclave, **Camaret-sur-Mer** (p332)
- Sip artisan and beers brewed on the premises as well as fine wines at Vitré's funky bar, **Bressan** (p353)
- Go on a quest for the perfect oyster in **Cancale** (p318)
- Follow wildflower-lined walking trails on pretty **Île de Bréhat** (p321)
- Shade yourself in style in a striped bathing tent at **Dinard** (p316)
- Hike enchanting forest trails fanning out from **Huelgoat** (p327)
- Play the sailor on the Musée du Bateau's wooden boats at **Douarnenez** (p333)

(map labels: Île de Bréhat, Dinard, Cancale, Camaret-sur-Mer, Huelgoat, Ménez-Hom, Douarnenez, Vitré)

- POPULATION: 2,905,000
- AREA: 27,210 SQ KM

BRITTANY

BRITTANY (BRETAGNE)

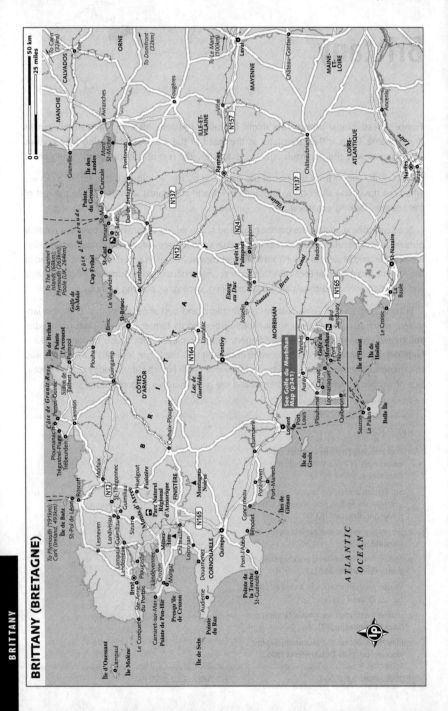

History

Brittany's earliest known Neolithic tribes left a legacy of menhirs and dolmens. Celts arrived in the 6th century BC, naming their new homeland 'Armor' (the land beside the sea). Conquered by Julius Caesar in 56 BC, the Romans withdrew in the 5th century AD, and Celts driven from what is now Britain and Ireland by the Anglo-Saxon invasions settled in Brittany, bringing Christianity.

In the 9th century, Brittany's national hero Nominoë revolted against French rule. But, sandwiched between two more-powerful kingdoms, the duchy of Brittany was contested by France and England until, after a series of strategic royal weddings, the region became part of France in 1532.

Brittany has retained a separate regional identity. Now there's a drive for cultural and linguistic renewal (see p325) – and a consciousness of Brittany's place within a wider Celtic culture embracing Ireland, Wales, Scotland, Cornwall and Galicia in Spain, with all of which ties have been established.

Getting There & Around

Ferries link St-Malo with the Channel Islands and the English ports of Portsmouth, Poole and Weymouth. From Roscoff there are ferries to Plymouth (UK) and Cork (Ireland).

Brittany's major towns and cities have rail connections but routes leave the interior poorly served. The bus network is extensive, if often infrequent.

Definitely consider renting a car or motorbike or bringing your own, especially if you're keen on exploring out-of-the-way destinations. Cycling is extremely popular, and bike-rental places are never hard to find. If touring the region by canal boat, contact the **Service de la Navigation** (☎ in Rennes 02 99 59 20 60, in Lorient 02 97 64 85 20) for information on boats, moorings and locks .

NORTH COAST

Enveloped by *belle époque* beach resorts and fishing villages, and capped by curled headlands, Brittany's central north coast spans the *départements* of Ille-et-Vilaine and Côtes d'Armor. Green shallows give rise to the name Côte d'Émeraude (Emerald Coast) to the east; west, boulders blush along the Côte de Granit Rose (Pink Granite Coast).

ST-MALO

pop 53,000

The mast-filled port of St-Malo has a cinematically changing landscape. With one of the world's highest tidal ranges, brewing storms under blackened skies see waves lash over the top of the ramparts ringing its walled city. Hours later, the blue sky merges with the deep marine-blue sea, exposing beaches as wide and flat at the clear skies above and creating land bridges to its granite outcrop islands.

Construction of the walled city's fortifications began in the 12th century. The town became a key port during the 17th and 18th centuries as a base for both merchant ships and government-sanctioned privateers (pirates, basically) against the constant threat of the English. These days English arrivals are tourists, for whom St-Malo, a short ferry hop from the Channel Islands, is a summer haven.

Orientation

The St-Malo conurbation consists of the harbour towns of St-Malo and St-Servan plus the modern suburbs of Paramé and Rothéneuf to the east. The old walled city of St-Malo is known as Intra-Muros ('within the walls') or Ville Close. From the train station, it's a 15-minute walk westwards along av Louis Martin.

Information

Cyberm@lo (☎ 02 99 56 07 78; 68 chaussée du Sillon; per 15 min/hr €1.50/4; ۞ 10am-1am Mon-Sat, 11am-11pm Sun mid-Jun–mid-Sep, 11am-9pm Tue-Thu, 11am-11pm Fri & Sat, 3-8pm Sun mid-Sep–mid-Jun) Internet access in the old town is limited or nonexistent; you'll find this place heading east along the seafront.

Laundrette (rue de la Herse; ۞ 7.30am-9pm)

Post Office (1 blvd de la République)

Tourist Office (☎ 08 25 13 52 00, 02 99 56 64 43; www.saint-malo-tourisme.com; esplanade St-Vincent; ۞ 9am-7.30pm Mon-Sat, 10am-6pm Sun Jul & Aug, 9am-12.30pm & 1.30-6pm or 6.30pm Mon-Sat Sep-Jun, 10am-12.30pm & 2.30-6pm Sun Easter-Jun & Sep)

Sights & Activities

WALLED CITY

St-Malo's first inhabitants originally lived in St-Servan but later moved to this former island, which became linked to the mainland by the sandy isthmus of Le Sillon in the 13th century.

ST-MALO IN...

Two Days

St-Malo is by no means Brittany's biggest city, but it's a great place to base yourself for a few days.
    Start by wandering the cobbled streets of the **walled city** (p309), and learn about the local history at the **Musée du Château** (below). Pick up beach picnic supplies at the **Halle au Blé covered market** (p313), pick a spot to spread out a blanket, and splash in Plage de Bon Secours' **tidal pool** (p312). Strolling along the **ramparts** (below) is at its best as the sun's setting, before dining on freshly caught seafood, followed by a drink at enchanting **L'Alchimiste** (p313) bar.
    The next day amble across the beach (at low tide only!) to **Île du Grand Bé** (below), burial place of St-Malo-born 18th-century writer Chateaubriand, then head out to St-Malo's awesome **Grand Aquarium** (p312). Sample one of St-Malo's *crêperies* (p313), then one of more than 300 beers, as well as live music, at **L'Aviso** (p313).

Four Days

Depending on the season you can catch a ferry, ride a bike, or even take a leisurely walk across to **Dinard** (p314), the quintessential beach resort immortalised by Picasso. Or make your way to the oyster port of **Cancale** (p317). Or marvel at medieval **Dinan** (p318). And Brittany's buzzing capital, **Rennes** (p349), is just a couple of hours south.

For the best views of the walled city, stroll along the top of the **ramparts**, constructed at the end of the 17th century under military architect Vauban, and measuring 1.8km. There's free access at several places, including all the main city gates.

Though you'd never guess it from the cobblestone streets and reconstructed monuments in 17th- and 18th-century style, during August 1944, the battle to drive German forces out of St-Malo destroyed around 80% of the old city. Damage to the town's centrepiece, **Cathédrale St-Vincent** (place Jean de Châtillon; ☺ 9.30am-6pm except during Mass), constructed between the 12th and 18th centuries, was severe. A mosaic **plaque** on the floor of the nave marks the spot where Jacques Cartier received the blessing of the bishop of St-Malo before his 'voyage of discovery' to Canada in 1535. Cartier's tomb – all that remains on it post-1944 is his head – is in a chapel on the north side of the choir.

The ramparts' northern stretch looks out across the remains of the former prison, **Fort National** (adult/child €4/2; ☺ Jun-Sep), accessible only at low tide. Within **Château de St-Malo**, built by the dukes of Brittany in the 15th and 16th centuries, is the **Musée du Château** (☎ 02 99 40 71 57; adult/child €5/2.50; ☺ 10am-noon & 2-6pm daily Apr-Sep, Tue-Sun Oct-Mar). The museum's most interesting exhibits – the history of cod fishing on the Grand Banks and photos of St-Malo after WWII – are in the Tour Générale.

You can visit the 18th-century mansion and historic monument **La Maison de Corsaire** (☎ 02 99 56 09 40; www.demeure-de-corsaire.com in French; 5 rue d'Asfeld; adult/child €5.50/4; ☺ 10am-noon & 2-6pm daily summer, Tue-Sun winter), once owned by corsair (privateer) François Auguste Magon. Guided tours are in French; descriptions are available in English.

ÎLE DU GRAND BÉ

At low tide, cross the beach to walk out via the Porte des Bés to the rocky islet of **Île du Grand Bé**, where the great St-Malo-born 18th-century writer Chateaubriand is buried. Once the tide rushes in, the causeway remains impassable for about six hours – check tide times with the tourist office. Depths can be deceptive; if you get caught out, stay on the islet until the tide subsides.

About 100m beyond the Île du Grand Bé is the Vauban-built 17th-century **Fort du Petit Bé** (☎ 06 08 27 51 20), also accessible at low tide.

ST-SERVAN

The pretty fishing port of St-Servan sits southwest of the walled city. Constructed in the mid-18th century, **Fort de la Cité** was used as a German base during WWII. One of the bunkers now houses **Mémorial 39-45** (☎ 02 99 82 41 74; adult/child €5/2.50; guided visits 2pm, 3.15pm & 4.30pm Tue-Sun Apr-Jun & Sep-Mar, 6 times daily Jul & Aug), which depicts St-Malo's violent WWII history and liberation and includes

ST-MALO & ST-SERVAN

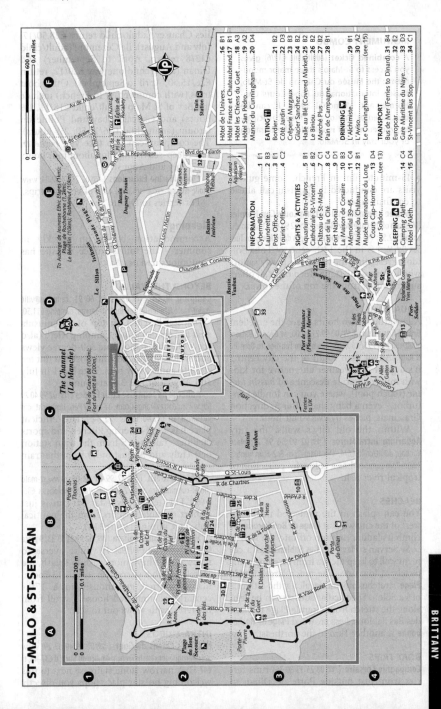

INFORMATION		
Cybermôlo	1	E1
Laundrette	2	B3
Post Office	3	E1
Tourist Office	4	C2

SIGHTS & ACTIVITIES		
Aquarium Intra-Muros	5	B1
Cathédrale St-Vincent	6	B2
Château de St-Malo	7	C1
Fort de la Cité	8	D4
Fort National	9	D1
La Maison de Corsaire	10	B3
Mémorial 39-45	11	C4
Musée du Château	12	C1
Musée International du Long		
Cours Cap-Hornier	13	D4
Tour Solidor	(see 13)	

SLEEPING		
Camping Aleth	14	C4
Hôtel d'Aleth	15	D4

Hôtel de l'Univers	16	B1
Hôtel France et Chateaubriand	17	B1
Hôtel les Chiens du Guet	18	A3
Hôtel San Pedro	19	A2
Manoir du Cunningham	20	D4

EATING		
Bordier	21	B2
Côté Jardin	22	D3
Crêperie Margaux	23	B3
Glacier Sanchez	24	B2
Halle au Blé (Covered Market)	25	B1
Le Biniou	26	B2
Marché Plus	27	B2
Pain de Campagne	28	B1

DRINKING		
L'Alchimiste	29	B1
L'Aviso	30	A2
Le Cunningham	(see 15)	

TRANSPORT		
Bus de Mer (Ferries to Dinard)	31	B4
Europcar	32	E2
Gare Maritime du Naye	33	D3
St-Vincent Bus Stop	34	C1

BRITTANY

MONUMENT COMBO

A **combined ticket** (adult/child €12/6) gives you access to St-Malo's three major monuments: the Musée du Château de St-Malo, Musée International du Long Cours Cap-Hornier and Mémorial 39-45. It can be purchased at any of the three participating museums and is valid for the duration of your stay in St-Malo.

---

a 45-minute film in French. Some guided visits are conducted in English; call ahead to confirm times.

Musée International du Long Cours Cap-Hornier (Museum of the Cape Horn Route; ☎ 02 99 40 71 58; adult/child €5/2.50; ⏰ 10am-noon & 2-6pm daily Apr-Sep, Tue-Sun Oct-Mar) is in the 14th-century Tour Solidor. Presenting the life of the hardy sailors who followed the Cape Horn route, it offers superb views from the top of the tower.

AQUARIUMS

Allow around two hours to see the excellent **Grand Aquarium** (☎ 02 99 21 19 00; av Général Patton; adult/child €13.75/9.90; ☎ 10am-6pm Feb-Dec, to 8pm Jul & Aug). About 4km south of the city centre, it's a great wet-weather alternative for kids with minisubmarine descent and *bassin tactile* (touch pool), where you can fondle rays, turbot – even a baby shark. Bus 5, direction Grassinais, passes by every half-hour.

Within the old city's walls, the tiny **Aquarium Intra-Muros** (☎ 02 99 56 94 77; place Vauban; adult/child €6/4; ⏰ 10am-1pm & 2-6pm winter, 10am-8pm summer) has a colourful collection of tropical river fish.

BEACHES

You can splash in the protected tidal pool west of the city walls at **Plage de Bon Secours** or climb its ladder to jump off into the sea.

St-Servan's **Plage des Bas Sablons** has a cement wall to keep the sea from receding completely at low tide. The much larger **Grande Plage** stretches northeast along the isthmus of Le Sillon. Spectacular sunsets can be seen along the stretch from Grande Plage to Plage des Bas Sablons. Less crowded **Plage de Rochebonne** is another 1km to the northeast.

BOAT TRIPS

Compagnie Corsaire (☎ 08 25 13 80 35) runs ferries from just outside Porte de Dinan to

Îles Chausey (adult/child return €28.50/17, July and August), Île Cézembre (adult/child €13/8 return, April to September) and Dinan (adult/child one way €20/12, return €26/15.50, April to September). Other boat trips (with commentary in French) include the Bay of St Malo (adult/child €18/11, 1½ hours) and Cancale's bay and Pointe du Grouin (adult/child €26/15.50, 2½ hours). The company can also take you *pêche en mer* (deep-sea fishing) for about four hours (€37, July and August).

Étoile Marine Excursions (☎ 02 23 18 02 04; www.etoile-marine-excursions.com) also offers boat trips.

For ferries to Dinard see p314.

Sleeping

Accommodation books up quickly in summer – the tourist office website has continuous updates.

BEYOND THE WALLS

Camping Aleth (☎ 02 99 81 60 91; camping@ville-saint-malo.fr; allée Gaston Buy, St-Servan; camping €11.50; ⏰ May-Sep) Perched on top of a peninsula next to Fort de la Cité, Camping Aleth (also spelt Alet) has panoramic 360-degree views and is close to beaches and close but not *too* close to some lively bars. Take bus 1 in July and August or bus 3 year-round.

Auberge de Jeunesse Éthic Étapes (☎ 02 99 40 29 80; www.centrevarangot.com; 37 av du Père Umbricht; dm incl breakfast €12.40-16.20; ✕ 🖳) This efficient place has a self-catering kitchen and sports facilities. Take bus 5 from the train station or 1 (July and August only) from the train station and tourist office.

Hôtel d'Aleth (☎ 02 99 81 48 08; www.st-malo-hotel-cunningham.com; 2 rue des Hauts Sablons; s €36, d €60) This terrific two-star bargain is just a short stumble upstairs from the nautical pub, Le Cunningham (p314).

Manoir du Cunningham (☎ 02 99 21 33 33; 9 place Mgr Duchesne; s/d €90/190) If you're averse to noise and/or have more cash to splash, the Hôtel d'Aleth owners operate this 13-room, mahogany-rich guesthouse, in a 17th-century half-timbered house a stroll from the ferry, with views out to sea.

INTRA-MUROS

Hôtel les Chiens du Guet (☎ 02 99 40 87 29; www.leschiensduguet.com in French; 4 place du Guet; d €37-48, tr €47-53) A narrow stone staircase next to this welcoming no-star place pops you directly up on top of the ramparts; adjacent Porte St-Pierre opens directly to the beach. The 12 simple, sunlit rooms are homey if somewhat snug. There's a convivial on site restaurant; *menus* (set menus) are €9.50 to €25.

Hôtel San Pedro (☎ 02 99 40 88 57; www.san pedro-hotel.com; 1 rue Ste-Anne; s €43-49, d €53-65; ⊗ Feb-Nov; ✗) Tucked at the back of the old city, the San Pedro has cool, crisp neutral-toned décor with subtle splashes of colour, friendly service and superb sea views, as well as welcome and all-too-rare wi-fi access. Breakfast is a €6 feast.

Hôtel France et Chateaubriand (☎ 02 99 56 66 52; www.hotel-fr-chateaubriand.com; place Chateaubriand; s €41-79, d €48-95) Opposite the chateau entrance, this grand place houses 80 rooms that combine a rarefied traditional French atmosphere with a relaxed seaside ambience. More-expensive rooms on the upper levels of this five-storey building rise over the tops of the ramparts with unfolding sea views. Good wheelchair access.

Hôtel de l'Univers (☎ 02 99 40 89 52; www.hotel -univers-saintmalo.com in French; place Chateaubriand; s €46-75.50, d €61-86) Right by the most frequently used gateway to the old city (Porte St-Vincent), and handy for the tourist office, this cream-coloured two-star place with 63 rooms is perfectly poised for all of St-Malo's attractions – not the least of which is its own all-wood, in-house maritime bar.

Eating

Restaurants, *crêperies* and pizzerias are plentiful between Porte St-Vincent, the cathedral and the Grande Porte.

Pain de Campagne (☎ 02 99 20 11 26; 7 rue Ste-Barbe; sandwiches €3.80-5.60, meals €5-9; ⊗ lunch Thu-Tue, dinner Thu-Sat, Mon & Tue Sep-Jun, noon-2am daily Jul & Aug) Sandwich shops are in no short supply in St-Malo, but many of them are sub-par and expensive. The cheerful little Pain de Campagne is where locals come for creative sandwich combinations on a variety of breads, and at least a couple of hot meals per day.

Le Biniou (☎ 02 99 56 47 57; 3 place de la Croix du Fief; crêpes €1.70-7.20, menus €8-10.20; ⊗ 10am-1am summer, closed Wed or Thu winter) With cute little illustrations of *biniou* (bagpipes), this *crêperie/salon de thé* (tearoom) has a couple of terrace tables, and a great upstairs mezzanine with velour settees where you can choose from well over 100 different artisan *galettes* (savoury *crêpes*) and *crêpes*

(including the house speciality of caramelised apples flambéed in Calvados), or the *menu* of mussels.

Crêperie Margaux (☎ 02 99 20 26 02; 3 place du Marché aux Légumes; crêpes €7.50-12, menus €12; ⊗ closed Tue & Wed) Watch the owner of this wonderful little *crêperie* on violet-filled Marché aux Légumes handmaking traditional *crêpes* (her motto: 'if you're in a hurry, don't come here'). The aromas wafting through the timber-lined dining room, and the scads of happy diners, prove it's well worth the wait.

Côté Jardin (☎ 02 99 81 63 11; 36 rue Dauphine, St-Servan; menus €18-24; ⊗ lunch Tue-Sun, dinner Tue & Thu-Sun) The charming, friendly Côté Jardin presents regional and traditional French cuisine, with a scenic terrace overlooking the marina and St-Malo's walled city. Doodlers can happily draw on the table with coloured pencils provided.

Le Bénétin (☎ 02 99 56 97 64; chemin des Rochers Sculptés, Rothéneuf; menus €25-60; ⊗ lunch & dinner Thu-Tue) Situated close to the 'sculpture rocks' (human and animal faces carved into rock by a priest) northeast of the walled city, this well-known place is a must for seafood – and for views of the sea from where it's caught.

SELF-CATERING

Cheeses and butters handmade by Jean-Yves **Bordier** (9 rue de l'Orme; ⊗ Tue-Sat) are shipped to famous restaurants all over the world. Just down the street is the covered market, **Halle au Blé** (rue de la Herse; ⊗ 8am-noon Tue & Fri).

Glacier Sanchez (☎ 02 99 56 67 17; 9 rue de la Vieille Boucherie; ⊗ Apr-Sep) serves up great ice cream (€4 for three scoops).

Pick up beach picnic supplies inside the walls at **Marché Plus** (cnr rue St-Vincent & rue St-Barbe; ⊗ 7am-9pm Mon-Sat, 7am-noon Sun).

Drinking

L'Alchimiste (☎ 02 23 18 10 06; 7 rue St-Thomas; ⊗ 5pm-1am Tue-Sun Oct-Apr, 5am-2am daily May-Sep) Ben Harper–type music creates a mellow backdrop at this magical place filled with old books and a toy flying fox. Take a seat at the bar draped with a red, tasselled theatre curtain, on the carved timber mezzanine (including a pulpit), or in the wood-heated basement.

L'Aviso (☎ 02 99 40 99 08; 12 rue Point du Jour; ⊗ 5pm-2am) Regular live music features at this cosy place, which has more than 300 beers on offer (and over 10 – including Breton beer – on tap). If you can't decide, ask the friendly owner/connoisseur.

Le Cunningham (2 rue des Hauts Sablons; ☉ 6pm-2am Mon-Fri, 4pm-3am Sat & Sun) Sail away at this fabulous curved wood bar with a wall of timber-framed windows looking out over water. Year-round live entertainment includes jazz, soul and Brazilian beats.

Entertainment

In summer, classical music concerts are held in Cathédrale St-Vincent and elsewhere in the city, and the pubs, bars and cafés have lots of live music – check the tourist office website's 'what's on' section.

Getting There & Away

AIR

See p317 for flight details.

BOAT

Brittany Ferries (☎ reservations in France 08 25 82 88 28, in UK 0870 556 1600; www.brittany-ferries.com) sails between St-Malo and Portsmouth, and **Condor Ferries** (☎ France 08 25 13 51 35, UK 0870 243 5140; www .condorferries.co.uk) runs to/from Poole and Weymouth via Jersey or Guernsey. Car ferries leave from the Gare Maritime du Naye.

From April to September, **Compagnie Corsaire** (☎ 08 25 13 80 35) and **Étoile Marine Excursions** (☎ 02 23 18 02 04; www.etoile-marine-excursions .com) run a **Bus de Mer** (Sea Bus; adult/child return €6/4; ☉ hourly) shuttle service (10 minutes) between St-Malo and Dinard.

BUS

All intercity buses stop by the train station.

Courriers Bretons (☎ 02 99 19 70 80) has services to Cancale (€2, 30 minutes), Fougères (€3, 1¾ hours, one to three daily), Pontorson (€2.50, one hour) and Mont St-Michel (€4.30, 1½ hours, three to four daily). It also offers all-day tours to Mont St-Michel – check for seasonal prices and schedules.

TIV (☎ 02 99 82 26 26) has buses to Dinard (€1.50, 30 minutes, hourly) and Rennes (€3, one to 1½ hours, three to six daily).

Tibus (☎ 08 10 22 22 22) goes to Dinan (€2, 50 minutes, three to eight daily).

CAR & MOTORCYCLE

Avis (☎ 02 99 40 18 54) has a desk at the train station and Gare Maritime du Naye. **ADA** (☎ 02 99 56 06 15) has a booth in TGV, while

Europcar (☎ 02 99 56 75 17; 16 blvd des Talards) is about 300m north towards the walled city.

TRAIN

TGV trains run between St-Malo and Rennes (€11.60, one hour, frequent), Dinan (€7.90, one hour, requiring a change), and a direct service to Paris' Gare Montparnasse (€58, three hours, three daily).

Getting Around

St-Malo city buses (single journey €1.20, 10-trip carnet €8.30, 24-hour pass €3.30) operate until about 8pm with some lines extending until around midnight in summer. Between esplanade St-Vincent and the train station, take buses 1 (July to August only), 3, 4, 6, 21 or 22.

Call ☎ 02 99 81 30 30 for a **taxi**.

DINARD

pop 10,300

Visiting Dinard 'in season' is a little bit like stepping into one of the canvases Picasso painted here in the 1920s. *Belle époque* mansions built into the cliffs preside over the beach dotted with blue-and-white striped bathing tents and the beachside carnival. Out of season, when holiday-makers have packed up their buckets and spades, the town is decidedly dormant, but wintry walks along the coastal paths are still spectacular.

Orientation

Dinard's focal point is the gently curved beach Plage de l'Écluse (also called Grande Plage), flanked by Pointe du Moulinet and Pointe de la Malouine. To get to the beach from the Embarcadère (where boats from St-Malo dock), climb the stairs and walk 200m northwest along rue Georges Clemenceau.

Information

Cyberspot (☎ 02 99 46 28 30; 6 rue Winston Churchill; per hr €6; ☉ 11am-midnight Wed-Mon winter, daily summer)

Lavomatic de la Poste (10 rue des Saules; ☉ 8am-7pm Jun-Sep, Mon-Sat Oct-May) Laundrette.

Post Office (place Rochaid)

Tourist Office (☎ 02 99 46 94 12; www.ot-dinard.com in French; place Féart; ☉ 9.30am-7.30pm Jul & Aug, 9.30am-12.15pm & 2-6pm Mon-Sat Sep-Jun) Staff book accommodation for free.

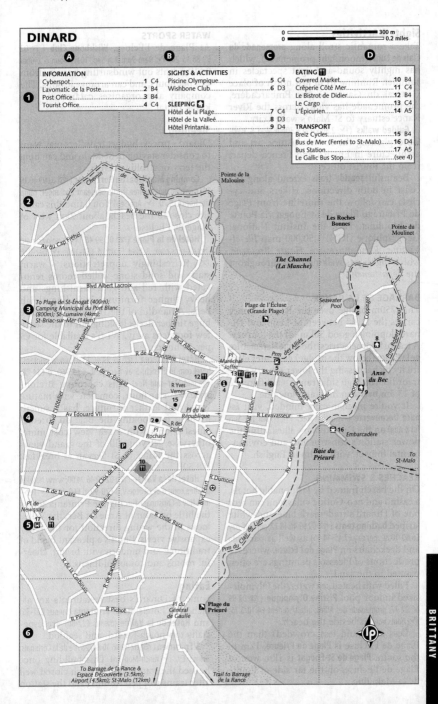

DINARD

0 _____ 300 m
0 _____ 0.2 miles

INFORMATION
Cyberspot.................................1 C4
Lavomatic de la Poste..............2 B4
Post Office...............................3 B4
Tourist Office...........................4 C4

SIGHTS & ACTIVITIES
Piscine Olympique....................5 C4
Wishbone Club.........................6 D3

SLEEPING
Hôtel de la Plage......................7 C4
Hôtel de la Vallée....................8 D3
Hôtel Printania........................9 D4

EATING
Covered Market.......................10 B4
Crêperie Côté Mer....................11 C4
Le Bistrot de Didier..................12 B4
Le Cargo.................................13 C4
L'Épicurien.............................14 A5

TRANSPORT
Breiz Cycles............................15 B4
Bus de Mer (Ferries to St-Malo)...16 D4
Bus Station............................17 A5
Le Gallic Bus Stop................(see 4)

Pointe de la Malouine

Chemin de Ronde

Av Paul Thoret

Av du Cap Fréhel

Les Roches Bonnes

Pointe du Moulinet

Blvd Albert Lacroix

The Channel
(La Manche)

To Plage de St-Énogat (400m);
Camping Municipal du Port Blanc
(800m); St-Lumaire (4km);
St-Briac-sur-Mer (14km);

R des Marettes

R de la Malouine

Blvd Albert 1er

Plage de l'Écluse
(Grande Plage)

Seawater Pool

R Coppinger

R de la Pionnière

R de St-Énogat

Pl Maréchal Joffre

Prm des Alliés

Blvd Wilson

Anse du Bec

Prm du Robert Surcouf

Blvd l'Hôtelier

Av Édouard VII

R Yves Verney

R Georges Clemenceau

R Faber

Av Georges V

Pl de la République

R Levavasseur

R des Saules

Pl Rochaid

R du Maréchal Leclerc

R l'Carine

Embarcadère

To St-Malo

Baie du Prieuré

R Clos de la Fontaine

R de la Gare

R de Verdun

Pl de Newquay

R Émile Bara

Blvd l'Éart

R Dumont

Prm du Clair de Lune

R de la Corbinais

R de Badine

R Pichot

R Pichot

Pl du Général de Gaulle

Plage du Prieuré

To Barrage de la Rance &
Espace Découverte (3.5km);
Airport (4.5km); St-Malo (12km)

Trail to Barrage
de la Rance

BRITTANY

Sights & Activities

Take a romantic stroll along **promenade du Clair de Lune** (moonlight promenade), which has nightly sound-and-light spectacles in summer. Running from just north of place Général du Gaulle to the Embarcadère, the promenade has views across the River Rance estuary to St-Malo's walled city.

Guided walks (2.30pm & 4.30pm Mon & Wed-Sat) explaining the town's history, art and architecture in English and French depart from the tourist office.

Beautiful **seaside trails** extend along the coast in both directions. Hikers and cyclists can follow the shoreline from Plage du Prieuré to Plage de St-Énogat via Pointe du Moulinet. Pack the Institut National Géographique (IGN) 1:50,000 map *Ille-et-Vilaine: Randonnées en Haute Bretagne*, which highlights walking trails throughout the *département*.

BARRAGE DE LA RANCE

This 750m bridge over the Rance estuary carries the D168 between St-Malo and Dinard, lopping a good 30km off the journey. A feat of hydroelectrics, the **Usine Marémotrice de la Rance** (below the bridge) generates electricity by harnessing the lower estuary's extraordinarily high tidal range – a difference of 13.5m between high and low tide.

If you're mechanically minded, visit **Espace Découverte** (admission free; 1-7pm Tue-Sun Jul & Aug) on the Dinard bank, illustrating the power station's construction and environmental impact, with a film in English.

BEACHES & SWIMMING

On the beach framed by fashionable hotels, a casino and neo-Gothic villas, you can rent one of Dinard's trademark blue-and-white striped **bathing tents** (02 99 46 18 12; per half-day €6.80-10.80, per day €7.45-14.15) as well as parasols and deckchairs on **Plage de l'Écluse**, where reproductions of Picasso's paintings are often planted in the sand.

Filled with heated sea water, the Olympic-sized indoor pool **Piscine Olympique** (02 99 46 22 77; promenade des Alliés; adult/student €4.10/3.25; hours vary) is beside the beach.

Less chic (and less crowded) than the Plage de l'Écluse is **Plage du Prieuré**, 1km to the south. **Plage de St-Énogat** is 1km west of Plage de l'Écluse, on the far side of Pointe de la Malouine.

WATER SPORTS

At Plage de l'Écluse, **Wishbone Club** (02 99 88 15 20; 9am-9pm Jun-Sep, 10am-noon & 2-6pm Oct-May) rents out windsurfing boards (from €15 per hour), and can arrange lessons. The company also organises catamarans and kayak rental.

Sleeping

Dinard's pricey: budget travellers may want to consider staying in St-Malo and catching the ferry or strolling across.

Camping Municipal du Port Blanc (02 99 46 10 74; camping.dinard@free.fr; rue Sergeant Boulanger; camp site from €18.70; Apr-Sep) You'll find this camp site close to the beach, about 2km west of Plage de l'Écluse.

Hôtel de la Plage (02 99 46 14 87; www.dinard-hotels-plus.com; 3 blvd Féart; d €51-100; Dec-Oct;) Refreshingly unpretentious – warm staff, and solid stone-walled rooms renovated with red-and-gold furnishings and heavy timber furniture, including sleigh beds. A handful of the 18 rooms here have huge timber decks looking out to the sea, a few footsteps away. Wi-fi's available for €5 per 24 hours.

Hôtel Printania (02 99 46 13 07; www.printania hotel.com in French; 5 av George V; s €55-60, d €54-88; mid-Mar–mid-Nov) This charming Breton-style two-star hotel, complete with mature wood and leather furniture, has a superb location overlooking the Baie du Prieuré. Guest rooms with a sea view cost more; otherwise get your fill of the grand views across the water to St-Servan at breakfast (€8.50).

Hôtel de la Vallée (02 99 46 94 00; www.hotelde lavallee.com; 6 av George V; s €70-90, d €60-105; Feb–mid-Nov & Christmas) Facing the Printania across the little harbour of Anse du Bec, the Valléc looks in the wrong direction for the really expansive views. But it's a pleasant blend of traditional and modern with bright, cheerful rooms and colourful linens.

Eating

Some of Dinard's best restaurants are attached to hotels: **Hôtel Printania** (menus €22-35) and **Hôtel de la Vallée** (menus €22-60) are especially top-notch for fish and seafood.

L'Épicurien (02 99 46 10 84; 28 rue de la Corbinais; menus €9, lunch Mon-Fri) This building once housed the station hotel, which closed well after trains stopped running and the station was demolished. Its enduring restaurant, L'Épicurien, is a fair hike from the beach but has remained a firm favourite for tasty Breton fare at good prices.

Le Bistrot de Didier (☎ 02 99 46 95 74; 6 rue Yves Verney; menus €10-20; ⊗ lunch & dinner Jul & Aug, closed Tue & Wed Sep-Jun) Young, talented chef Didier Méril has gained a reputation that extends way beyond Brittany. His culinary prowess now extends to this new, perpetually buzzing bistro serving out-of-this-world oysters, mussels and lobster. Angle for a seat on the terrace in summer.

Crêperie Côté Mer (☎ 02 99 16 80 30; 29 blvd Wilson; menus from €11.30; ⊗ lunch & dinner Jul & Aug, closed Mon Sep-Jun) A crisp little *crêperie* with pine tables on a pretty pedestrianised street, the Côté Mer serves grilled meat, salads, oysters and *moules-frites* (mussels and chips) as well as (naturally) *crêpes, galettes* and ice cream year-round.

Le Cargo (☎ 02 99 46 70 52; 3 blvd Féart; mains €15-20; ⊗ lunch & dinner) This cavernous red-brick place with classic red-and-white-checked tablecloths is a great place for steaming hot pizzas (€7.20 to €9.70) as well as rib-sticking mains like fondue with potatoes and ham.

SELF-CATERING

Dinard has a large **covered market** (place Rochaid; ⊗ 7am-1.30pm Tue, Thu & Sat).

Getting There & Away

AIR

Ryanair (☎ 02 99 16 00 66; www.ryanair.com) has daily flights to and from London Stansted. There's no public transport from the airport to town; a daytime/evening taxi from Dinard to the airport costs around €11/20.

BOAT

From April to September, **Compagnie Corsaire** (☎ 08 25 13 80 35) and **Étoile Marine Excursions** (☎ 02 23 18 02 04; www.etoile-marine-excursions.com) run the **Bus de Mer** (Sea Bus; adult/child return €6/4; ⊗ hourly) shuttle service (10 minutes) between St-Malo and Dinard.

BUS

Illenoo (www.illenoo.fr in French) buses connect Dinard and the train station in St-Malo (€2.50, 30 minutes, hourly). Le Gallic bus stop, outside the tourist office, is the most convenient. Several buses travel to Rennes (€3.50, two hours).

Getting Around

To get around you can hire bicycles (from €8 per day) and motor scooters (from €38 per day) from **Breiz Cycles** (☎ 02 99 46 27 25; 8 Rue St-Énogat).

For a taxi, telephone ☎ 02 99 46 88 80 or ☎ 02 99 88 15 15.

CANCALE

pop 5200

With brightly coloured restaurants strung along the seafront, the little fishing port of Cancale, 14km east of St-Malo, is famed for its offshore *parcs à huîtres* (oyster beds), yielding around 4000 tonnes of prize molluscs each year. A small museum dedicated to oyster farming and shellfish, the **Ferme Marine** (Marine Farm; ☎ 02 99 89 69 99; corniche de l'Aurore; adult/child €6.10/3.10; ⊗ mid-Feb–Oct) runs guided tours in English at 2pm from mid-June to mid-September.

The **tourist office** (☎ 02 99 89 63 72; www.ville -cancale.fr; ⊗ 9am-12.30pm & 2-6pm Mon-Sat Sep-Jun, to 7pm Jul & Aug) is at the top of rue du Port; opening hours may vary. There's a seasonal tourist office **annexe** (quai Gambetta; ⊗ 3-7pm Jul & Aug) in the wooden house where the fish auction takes place.

Sleeping

Camping Municipal Le Grouin (☎ 02 99 89 63 79; marie@ville-cancale.fr; Pointe du Grouin; camp site €11.85; ⊗ Mar-Oct) Overlooking a fine sand beach 6km north of Cancale near Pointe du Grouin, it has 200 well-spaced sites.

Auberge de Jeunesse (☎ 02 99 89 62 62; cancale@fuaj.org; Port Pican; dm incl breakfast €14.90; ⊗ Feb–mid-Dec) Right by the seaside, Cancale's HI-affiliated youth hostel at Port Pican is 3km northeast of the town – take the bus (July and August only) to the Cancale Église or Port Pican stop and walk 500m towards the seafront.

Hôtel La Mère Champlain (☎ 02 99 89 60 04; www.lamerechamplain.com; 1 quai Thomas; d €45-65) The 15 sweetly renovated rooms at this quay-front hotel have a relaxed port ambience and pretty-as-a-picture port views. The nautical-style restaurant (*menus €14.50 to €37.50*), complete with crisp linen, heavy cutlery and smart waiters with black bow ties, specialises in flambéed fish.

Le Continental (☎ 02 99 89 60 16; www.hotel -cancale.com in French; 4 quai Thomas; d €88-138; ⊗ late Mar–mid-Nov) In a pretty stone building above

BRIT

its red awning-shaded restaurant (*menus* €23 to €56), this *hôtel de charme* with good wheelchair access has beautiful timber-rich rooms – rooms overlooking the sea are at a premium but the views, especially on the higher floors, are worth it.

Les Maisons de Bricourt (www.maisons-de-bricourt .com) Chef Olivier Roellinger (below) rents out several seasonally opening hotel rooms (double from €160) and cottages (double from €240) under the umbrella Les Maisons de Bricourt.

Eating

From the cheap and familial to the formal and refined, Cancale has over 35 specialist seafood restaurants.

If you're on a quest for the perfect oyster, strolling along the port where the catches unload, and eyeing the oysters splayed on beds of ice outside the establishments, is the best way to whet your appetite. For us, the pearl is **L'Huitière** (☎ 02 99 89 75 05; 5 quai Gambetta; mains €7-12; ☼ 10am-10pm Easter-Sep, 10am-7pm Oct-Easter), a low-key little blue-and-yellow-painted joint on the waterfront with a chilly dining room but a warm welcome and absolutely delicious oysters, plus magnificent bowls of *moules* cooked with *créme fraîche*, and *frites* crisped to perfection.

Other standouts include **Ty Breiz** (☎ 02 99 89 60 26; 13 quai Gambetta; menus €15.50-29.50; ☼ lunch & dinner Jul & Aug, lunch Thu-Tue, dinner Thu-Mon Sep–mid-Nov & mid-Feb–Jun). Front and centre on the port, the rustic 'Breton house' framed by exposed wooden beams is also renowned for its grilled lobster and langoustine. And perennial favourite, **Le Surcouf** (☎ 02 99 89 61 75; 7 quai Gambetta; menus €18-60; ☼ lunch & dinner Jul & Aug, lunch & dinner Fri-Tue Sep–mid-Nov, lunch & dinner Fri-Tue mid-Dec–early Jan, lunch & dinner Fri-Tue early Feb-Jun) creatively combines succulent seafood with rich, regional produce and flavours.

Up the hill from the port, one of the region's (and indeed France's) most acclaimed chefs, Olivier Roellinger, has his exceptional restaurant, **O Roellinger** (☎ 02 99 89 64 76; 1 rue Duguesclin; menus €97-165; ☼ closed mid-Dec–mid-Mar). Olivier was born in this 1760-built former East India Company house, where he has been creating extraordinary cuisine for the past two-and-a-half decades. Signature dishes include the 'route of the south seas' – a knock-out combination of oysters, *iraches* (local baby squid caught only 'while the lilacs

are in bloom'), and poached Easter cabbage laced with spiced curry. Opening hours vary, so phone and book ahead.

Clustered by the Pointe des Crolles lighthouse, stalls at the **marché aux huîtres** (oyster market; ☼ 9am-6pm) sell oysters from €3.50 per dozen for small *huîtres creuses* to as much as €20 for saucer-sized *plates de Cancale*.

Getting There & Around

Buses stop behind the church on place Lucidas and at Port de la Houle, next to the pungent fish market. **Courriers Bretons** (☎ 02 99 19 70 80) and **TIV** (☎ 02 99 82 26 26) have year-round services to and from St-Malo (€2, 30 minutes). In summer, at least three daily Courriers Bretons buses continue to Port Pican and Port Mer, near Pointe du Grouin.

It's a stunning 32-km walk along the coast from Cancale to St-Malo.

Bikes can be hired at **Les 2 Roues de Cancale** (☎ 02 99 89 80 16; 7 rue de L'Industrie; per hr/day €3.50/13).

POINTE DU GROUIN

At the northern tip of the wild coast between Cancale and St-Malo, this **nature reserve** juts out on a windblown headland. Just east offshore, **Île des Landes** is home to a colony of giant black cormorants whose wingspans can reach 170cm.

Via the GR34 coastal hiking trail, Pointe du Grouin is a stunning 7km hike from Cancale and 18km from St-Malo. By the D201 road, it's 4km from Cancale. Cancale tourist office's free map covers the local coastline.

DINAN

pop 11,000

High above the rushing River Rance, Dinan's old town (webbed with narrow cobblestone streets and squares lined with crooked half-timbered houses) is straight out of the Middle Ages – something that's not lost on the deluge of summer tourists. No less than 100,000 visitors turn up to join Dinannais townsfolk dressed in medieval garb for the two-day Fête des Remparts, held every year in late July (the next is in 2008).

Orientation

Situated 22km south of Dinard, Dinan's most interesting sights – except the picturesque riverside port – are tucked within the tight confines of the old city.

Information
Post Office (7 place Duclos)
Tourist Office (☎ 02 96 87 69 76; www.dinan-tour
isme.com; 9 rue du Château; ☉ 9am-7pm Mon-Sat, 10am-
12.30pm & 2.30-6pm Sun mid-Jun–mid-Sep, 9am-12.30pm
& 2-6pm Mon-Sat mid-Sep–mid-Jun)
Zonzon (☎ 02 96 87 95 86; 9 rue des Rouairiesaux; per hr
€4; ☉ 10am-10pm Mon-Thu, 10am-1am Fri & Sat, 3-10pm
Sun) Internet access, west of the walled city.

Sights
The half-timbered houses overhanging place
des Cordeliers and place des Merciers mark
the heart of the old town. A few paces south,
climb up to the little balcony of the **Tour de
l'Horloge** (☎ 02 96 87 02 26; rue de l'Horloge; adult/under
18yr €2.75/1.75; ☉ 10am-6.30pm Jun-Sep, 2-6.30pm mid-

Apr–May), a 15th-century clock tower whose
chimes ding every quarter-hour.

Basilique St-Sauveur (place St-Sauveur; ☉ 9am-
6pm), with a soaring Gothic chancel, has in
the north transept a 14th-century grave slab
reputed to contain the heart of Bertrand du
Guesclin, a 14th-century knight noted for
his hatred of the English and his fierce battles to expel them from France. (Ironically,
Dinan today has one of the largest English
expat communities in Brittany.)

Just east of the church, beyond the tiny
Jardin Anglais (English Garden), a former
cemetery and nowadays a pleasant little
park, is the 13th-century **Tour Ste-Cathérine**,
with great views down over the viaduct and
port.

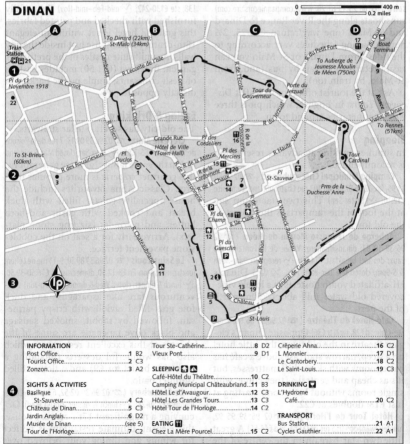

Rue du Jerzual and its continuation, the steep (and slippery-when-wet) stone **rue du Petit Fort**, both lined with art galleries, antiques shops and restaurants, lead down to the **Vieux Pont** (Old Bridge). From here the little **port** extends northwards while the 19th-century **Viaduc de Dinan** soars high above to the south.

Atmospherically housed in the keep of the ruined 14th-century castle, Dinan's **museum** (☎ 02 96 39 45 20; rue du Château; adult/child €4.20/1.65; ☼ 10am-6.30pm Jun-Sep, 2-5.30pm Oct-Dec & Feb-May) showcases the town's textile industry, with a fine collection of *coiffes* (traditional Breton lace headdresses).

Activities

Between May and September, **Compagnie Corsaire** (☎ 08 25 13 81 20; www.compagniecorsaire.com) runs boats along the River Rance to Dinard and St-Malo (one way/return €18/25, 2½ hours). Sailing schedules vary according to the tides. From Dinard or St-Malo you can easily return to Dinan by bus (and, from St-Malo, by train too).

Ask at the tourist office for its leaflet *Discovery Tours*, in English, which plots three **walking** itineraries around town.

Sleeping

In summer, making an advance reservation is recommended.

Camping Municipal Châteaubriand (☎ 02 96 39 11 96; fax 02 96 87 08 40; 103 rue Chateaubriand; camp site €12.10; ☼ Easter-Sep) This two-star camp site at the foot of the ramparts is the closest to the old town.

Auberge de Jeunesse Moulin de Méen (☎ 02 96 39 10 83; dinan@fuaj.org; Vallée de la Fontaine des Eaux; dm incl breakfast €14.90; ☼ reception 9am-noon & 5-9pm, closed late Dec-early Feb; ☒ ▣) Dinan's HI-affiliated youth hostel is in a lovely vine-covered old water mill about 750m north of the port.

Café-Hôtel du Théâtre (☎ 02 96 39 06 91; 2 rue Ste-Claire; d €28, tw & tr €36) Opposite Dinan's elegant theatre in the old town, this little hotel up a steep, narrow staircase above a café has basic rooms with skewwhiff mattresses, but it's as cheap and central as they come, with single rooms without bathrooms starting at just €16; doubles at €22.

Hôtel Tour de l'Horloge (☎ 02 96 39 96 92; hiliotel@wanadoo.fr; 5 rue de la Chaux; d €44-55) A great little two-star bargain in the centre of the old town, the 12-room Horloge occupies a charming 18th-century house on a cobbled, car-free lane. Head to the top floor, where rooms have exposed wooden beams and a lofty view of the hotel's namesake clock tower.

Hôtel Les Grandes Tours (☎ 02 96 85 16 20; www.hotel-dinan-grandes-tours.com; 6 rue du Château; d €45-48; ☼ Feb–mid-Dec) In its former life as the Hôtel des Messageries, this hotel is fabled as the place Victor Hugo stayed with his very good friend Juliette Drouet in 1836. Blue-shaded rooms (especially those on the sloped-ceiling top floor) are snug but conducive to snuggling up, and there's private lock-up parking on site.

Hôtel Le d'Avaugour (☎ 02 96 39 07 49; www.avaugourhotel.com; 1 place du Champ; d incl breakfast €63-138, ste €130-242; ☼ mid-Feb–mid-Nov) Beautifully furnished with checked and printed fabrics, this graceful hotel is set within an elegant 18th-century town house just inside the city walls. A sunlit suite nestles in the pretty rear garden. Breakfast (€11.50) includes baskets of fresh croissants; ample public parking is directly opposite.

Eating & Drinking

The old city has several stellar stalwarts.

Crêperie Ahna (☎ 02 96 39 09 13; 7 rue de la Poissonnerie; galettes €6-7.85; ☼ Mon-Sat, closed Mar & mid-end Nov) In the same family for three generations, this gourmet *crêperie* is more popular than ever. Classic Ahna favourites include the house speciality *galette* filled with duck breast and cooked with garlic-and-herb butter; and *pierrades* (sizzling stone platters). Arrive early for a seat on the cobblestone pavement terrace.

Le Saint-Louis (☎ 02 96 39 89 50; 9-11 rue de Léhon; lunch menus Mon-Fri €8-12.50, dinner menus €16.50-39.50; ☼ lunch & dinner, closed Wed & dinner Tue Sep Jun) Adventurous fare like asparagus- and duck foie gras–filled ravioli with crispy parmesan, followed by rabbit, smoked sausage and black olive tapenade are some of the choices at this excellent restaurant, which also has wonderful desserts (including a patisserie buffet for €9) and a flower-filled summer patio.

Le Cantorbery (☎ 02 96 39 02 52; 6 rue Ste-Claire; menus €12.50-24; ☼ lunch & dinner, closed Wed) Occupying a magnificent 17th-century house, this elegant, intimate restaurant is perfect for wining and dining your beloved over a romantic lunch or dinner. Its traditional menu – based on beef, grilled fish, and seafood including coquilles St-Jacques (scallops) from St-Brieuc – changes tempo in accordance with the seasons.

Chez La Mère Pourcel (☎ 02 96 39 03 80; 3 place des Merciers; menus €28-62.50, mains €18-33; ☯ lunch & dinner Tue-Sat & lunch Sun) New owners recently took over this Dinan institution, but fear not, it still turns out staples like its regional salt-marsh lamb, and the beamed dining room hasn't changed (much) since it was built in the 15th century.

L'Hydrome Café (☎ 02 96 39 25 98; cnr 20 rue de la Chaux & 13 rue de la Cordonnerie; ☯ noon-1am Tue-Sat) Between two old town streets, with entrances at either end, this lively local bar has good Breton and Belgian beers on tap at decent prices.

Port-side picnickers can pick up warm, fresh baked goods or even whole cakes, laid out on farmhouse-style wooden tables, from the *boulanger/pâtissier/chocolatier* **L Monnier** (☎ 02 96 85 03 12; rue du Petit Fort; ☯ 7.30am-1pm & 2.30-7.30pm Thu-Tue).

Getting There & Around

Buses leave from place Duclos and the bus station. **Illenoo** (☎ 02 99 26 16 00) runs five daily services to Dinard (€1.50, 25 minutes) and Rennes (€3, 1½ hours).

There are trains to St-Malo (€7.90, one hour, five daily) and Rennes (€12.20, one hour), both with a change.

Cycles Gauthier (☎ 02 96 85 07 60; 15 rue Déroyer; ☯ 9am-noon & 2-7pm Tue-Sat) rents out bikes for €17 per day.

For taxi services call ☎ 02 96 85 49 48 or ☎ 02 96 39 74 16.

PAIMPOL

pop 7900

Picturesque Paimpol (Pempoull in Breton) is a quintessential little patch of Brittany. With a charming cobblestone old town ringed by half-timbered buildings and a working fishing harbour, it's rich in history. It was the one-time home port of the Icelandic fishery, when the town's fishermen would set sail to the seas around Iceland for seven months and more at a stretch. And it's rich in legends – the fishermen lost at sea are recalled in folk tales and *chants de marins* (sea shanties). The town's **Festival de Chant de Marin** (www.paimpol-2007.com), with

traditional Breton dancing, takes place on the quays every two years.

South of the two harbours, Paimpol's town centre clusters around the market square of place du Martray. The bus and train stations are 100m south of this square.

The **tourist office** (☎ 02 96 20 83 16; www.paimpol -goelo.com; ☯ 9.30am-7.30pm Mon-Sat & 10am-1.30pm Sun Jul & Aug, 9.30am-12.30pm & 1.30-6.30pm Mon-Sat Sep-Jun) is on place de la République, and sells local rambling guides (€3).

Sights & Activities

MUSEUMS

The splendid **Musée de la Mer** (☎ 02 96 22 02 19; rue Labenne; adult/child €4.30/2.10; ☯ 10.30am-12.30pm & 2.30-6.30pm mid-Jun–Aug, 2.30-6pm mid-Apr–mid-Jun & early Sep), charting the region's maritime history, is set in a former cod-drying factory.

For land-bound history, visit the **Musée du Costume Breton** (☎ 02 96 22 02 19; rue Raymond Pellier; adult/child €2.55/1.35; ☯ 10.30am-12.30pm & 2.30-6pm Jul & Aug), containing historic traditional clothing items.

A combined ticket for both museums costs €5.50/2.50 per adult/child.

STEAM TRAIN

Between May and September, chuff along the riverbank on the 1922 steam train **La Vapeur du Trieux** (☎ 08 92 39 14 27; adult/child return €21/10.50). The train departs from Paimpol's station, travelling along the river to the artists' town of Pontrieux. Reserve ahead.

ABBAYE DE BEAUPORT

If you have wheels (or you're up for a glorious 1½-hour walk along the seashore from the town harbour), head 3.5km east to the romantic maritime **Abbaye de Beauport** (☎ 02 96 55 18 58; www.abbaye-beauport.com in French; adult/ child €5/3; ☯ 10am-7pm mid-Jun–mid-Sep, 10am-noon & 2-5pm mid-Sep–mid-Jun). En route, stop at the Pointe de Guilben for beautiful bay views. The tourist office has a free map.

ÎLE DE BRÉHAT

Paimpol is the closest port to **Île de Bréhat** (Enez Vriad in Breton), a tiny, car-free island 8km offshore to the north. With a population of 350, it stretches just 5km from north to south. The most idyllic time to visit is in spring when Mediterranean wildflowers bloom in its gentle micro climate. In the citadel on the southwestern edge you can visit the **glass-making factory** (☎ 02 96 20 09 09; www.verreriesdebrehat.com; admission €1; ⏰ hours vary). It's possible to rent bikes, but the best way to protect the fragile environment is to walk. There is a seasonal municipal camp site; contact Paimpol's tourist office for information.

Vedettes de Bréhat (☎ 02 96 55 79 50; www.vedettesdebrehat.com) operates ferries (adult/child return €8/6.50, 15 minutes, at least eight sailings daily) to Île de Bréhat from Pointe L'Arcouest, 6km north of Paimpol. Tickets are also available at Paimpol's tourist office. Bikes cost an extra €15 return to transport, which is only possible on certain in- and out-bound journeys. It's cheaper to rent a bike on the island; shops line the right-hand side of the road when you get off the boat.

Sleeping & Eating

Camping Municipal de Cruckin (☎ 02 96 20 78 47; rue de Cruckin; camping €12.40; ⏰ Easter-Sep) Near the Abbaye de Beauport, this eco-camp site, which runs an environmentally conscious programme of energy, water and waste management, is on the beautiful Baie de Kérity, 3.5km southeast of town off the road to Plouha.

L'Artimon (☎ 08 71 11 73 71, 06 24 17 73 12) The HI-affiliated hostel is no longer, but backpackers have the informal option of staying at L'Artimon, 8km southeast of town, with a pick-up service in Paimpol if required – call directly or check with Paimpol's tourist office for more info.

Hôtel Le Terre-Neuvas (☎ 02 96 55 14 14; fax 02 96 20 47 66; 16 quai Duguay Trouin; d from €31; ⏰ mid-Jan–mid-Dec) Perched right beside the harbour and a few steps from the historic town centre as well as the seafront, the two-star Terre-Neuvas has comfortable rooms, some with views out to sea.

K" Loys (☎ 02 96 20 40 01; www.k-loys.com; 21 quai Morand; d €65-95) Each of the 15 rooms at the cosy three-star 'Chez Louise', a former shipowner's mansion with good wheelchair access, is individually decorated with striped walls and paisley-pattern prints. There are lovely \private lounges with richly upholstered booths to relax over a drink.

our pick Crêperie-Restaurant Morel (☎ 02 96 20 86 34; 11 place du Martray; galettes €4.20-7, mains from €7.80; ⏰ lunch & dinner) To take the pulse of Paimpol, head no further than this cornerstone of the community. Over two timber-balustraded

levels *packed* with Paimpolaises, who wait outside for the doors to open, the buzzing Morel, on Paimpol's pretty main square, serves up great food. Head here for gargantuan salads such as tuna and hardboiled eggs tossed in rice, and perfectly buttered Breton *crêpes*, as well as *crêpes* with lush savoury and sweet fillings including a delectable chocolate-laced chestnut cream. In summer, more laden tables spill onto a pavement terrace. Arrive early – and hungry!

L'Islandais (☎ 02 96 20 93 00; 19 quai Morand; menus €17-26; ⏰ lunch & dinner) This restaurant, adjacent to K" Loys, has great brunches, and seafood platters (€36) large enough to share between two.

L'Écluse (☎ 02 96 55 03 38; quai Armand Dayot-Paimpol; menus €24; ⏰ lunch Mon-Fri, lunch & dinner Sat & Sun Sep-Jun, lunch & dinner daily Jul & Aug) Watch L'Écluse's chefs grill your fish on the big indoor barbecue at this new bistro with sleek wood interiors and an outdoor deck with timber tables.

Paimpol's Tuesday morning market spreads over place Gambetta and place du Martray. On weekends, vendors sell freshly shucked oysters at quai Duguay Trouin.

Getting There & Around

Cycles du Vieux Clocher (☎ 02 96 20 83 58; place Verdun; ⏰ 9am-noon & 2-7pm Tue-Sat Sep-Jun, Mon-Sat Jul & Aug) rents out bikes (€11 per day). It's west of the tourist office near the Vieux Clocher (Old Bell Tower).

Tibus (☎ 08 10 22 22 22) runs buses to and from St-Brieuc (€2, 1½ hours). In summer most continue to Pointe L'Arcouest.

There are several trains or SNCF buses daily between Paimpol and Guingamp (€6.10, 45 minutes), where you can pick up connections to Brest, St-Brieuc and Rennes.

CÔTE DE GRANIT ROSE

Sculpted over the millennia by wind and waves, the otter-inhabited coastline across this stretch of Brittany glows with dazzling pink granite cliffs, giving rise to the name Côte de Granit Rose (Pink Granite Coast). The area's main town, the resort of **Perros-Guirec** (population 7900), sits on a rocky peninsula at the coast's eastern end, with a new marina to its southeast, and the old fishing port of Ploumanac'h about 3km northwest.

Activities

Blissful-if-busy beaches include **Plage de Trestraou**, to the north about 1km from Perros' centre; and the smaller **Plage de Trestrignel** and **Plage du Château**, on either side of Pointe du Château.

Scale massive pink granite boulders and outcrops along the 5km walking path, **sentier des douaniers** (custom officer's trail) from Plage de Trestraou to Ploumanac'h.

Scattered offshore are the **Sept-Îles** (Seven Islands), home to more than 20,000 marine birds including puffins, razorbills and fulmars (related to the albatross). Seasonal boat trips are available with **Vendettes de Perros-Guirec** (☎ 02 96 91 10 00; www .armor-decouverte.fr; adult/child 1¼ hr from €14/9) departing from Gare Maritime Trestraou, at the western end of the Plage de Trestraou. Reservations can be made through Perros' **tourist office** (☎ 02 96 23 21 15; www.perros-guirec .com; 21 place de l'Hôtel de Ville; ⊙ 9am-7.30pm Mon-Sat, 10am-12.30pm & 4-7pm Sun Jul & Aug, 9am-12.30pm & 2-6.30pm Mon-Sat Jun-Sep), in the main town centre, about 1km uphill to the marina's north.

Sleeping & Eating

Perros-Guirec has a smorgasbord of options for families and glamorous beachgoers.

Camping de Trestraou (☎ 02 96 23 08 11; www .trestrou-camping.com; 89 av du Casino; camp site €22; ⊙ May–mid-Sep) Pricey but ideally positioned, this three-star camp site is only a few minutes' walk from Plage de Trestraou.

Le Levant (☎ 02 96 23 20 15; le-levant@wanadoo .fr; 91 rue Ernest Renan; d €55-61) Across from the yacht-filled marina, this two-star hotel has 19 airy rooms served by a lift to save you from the stairs, but its best asset is its cruise ship like gastronomic restaurant which does magnificent meat and (of course) seafood dishes, accompanied by a superb wine list. Patience is a virtue: it's not fast food, but it's worth the wait. Good deals are available for half-pension (€58.50 to €61.50) or full pension (€78.50 to €81.50). Menus range from €15 to €55. It is closed for lunch Friday and Saturday and dinner Sunday from September to June.

Au Bon Accueil (☎ 02 96 23 25 77; www.au-bon -accueil.com; 11 rue de Landerval; d €55-64.50) Fresh from a sophisticated makeover, this 21-room hotel has lovely, understated rooms in neutral tones, and a hardwood-floored restaurant (menus from €20 to €39; closed Monday

and dinner Sunday from September to June) with a canopied, sun-shaded terrace, where locals swear they have rediscovered what *bien manger* (eating well) means – high praise!

Local fishermen sell their catch directly at the **Marché des Pêcheurs** (place du Marché; ⊙ 8am-noon Fri). For a bio beach picnic, try **Biocoop** (67 rue Anatole le Braz), a cooperative that sells only organic produce; or **Distribio** (☎ 02 96 23 35 00; 137 rue du Maréchal Joffre).

Getting There & Around

Tibus (☎ 08 10 22 22 22) bus 15 (€2, 30 minutes, five to eight daily) links Perros-Guirec with Lannion's train station, calling at Ploumanac'h, Trégastel and Trébeurden. From Lannion, there are connections eastwards to Guingamp and St-Brieuc; and westwards via Morlaix to Roscoff.

TS Loisirs (☎ 02 96 91 66 61; 61 blvd des Traouïéo) rents out bikes from €10 per day.

FINISTÈRE

France's westernmost *département*, Finistère, has a wild, wind-whipped coastline scattered with lighthouses and beacons lashed by waves. Finistère's southern prow, Cornouaille, takes its name from early Celts who sailed from Cornwall and other parts of Britain to settle here, and today it's a harbour of Breton language, customs and culture.

ROSCOFF

pop 3700

Arriving across the Channel into Roscoff (Rosko in Breton) provides a captivating first glimpse of Brittany. Granite houses dating from the 16th century wreathe this pretty port, which is surrounded by emerald-green fields producing cauliflower, onions, tomatoes, new potatoes and artichokes. Roscoff farmers in distinctive horizontally striped tops, known as 'Johnnies', loaded up boats with plaited strings of locally grown small pink onions, crossed the Channel to the UK, then peddled – and pedalled – with their onions from their bikes' handlebars. Today, Johnnies have a near mythical status in the area, with about 20 still continuing the traditional trade.

Roscoff's waters conceal beds of algae (*goémon*), harvested for foodstuffs as well as *thalassothérapie* health and beauty treatments.

Orientation

Roscoff ranges around a north-facing bay, with its fishing port and pleasure harbour on the western side. Quai d'Auxerre leads northwest – becoming quai Charles de Gaulle, then rue Amiral Réveillère – to the main place Lacaze-Duthiers.

The car ferry terminal is at Port de Bloscon, 2km east of the town centre.

Information

Ferry Laverie (23 rue Jules Ferry; ☻ 7.30am-9pm)
The ferry terminal has 24-hour banknote exchange and ATM.

Post Office (19 rue Gambetta)

Tourist Office (☎ 02 98 61 12 13; www.roscoff-tourisme .com; 46 rue Gambetta; ☻ 9am-12.30pm & 1.30-7pm Mon-Sat, 10am-12.30pm Sun Jul & Aug, 9am-noon & 2-6pm Mon-Sat Sep-Jun) In an old stone building just north of place de la République.

Sights & Activities

With its Renaissance belfry rising above the flat landscape, the 16th-century Flamboyant Gothic **Église Notre Dame de Kroaz-Batz** (place Lacaze-Duthiers) is one of Brittany's most impressive churches.

Wander through 3000 species of exotic plants, many from the southern hemisphere, at **Le Jardin Exotique de Roscoff** (☎ 02 98 61 29 19; www.jardinexotiqueroscoff.com; adult/child €5/2; ☻ 10am-7pm Jun-Sep, 10.30am-12.30pm & 2-6pm Apr, May & Oct, 2-5pm Nov & Mar).

Photographs trace Roscoff's roaming onion farmers from the early 19th century at the **Maison des Johnnies** (☎ 02 98 61 25 48; 48 rue Brizeux; adult/child €4/2; ☻ 12.30-3pm & 5-7.45pm Mon-Fri, 12.30-3pm & 5-7.15pm Sat, 9.30am-noon & 3-7.15pm Sun).

You can learn about local seaweed harvesting at the **Centre de Découverte des Algues** (☎ 02 98 69 77 05; 5 rue Victor Hugo; admission free, lectures per adult/child €5/3.50; ☻ 9am-noon & 2-7pm Mon-Sat), which also organises guided walks, and gives regular lectures (often in English and German). Then immerse yourself in the stuff at **Thalasso Roscoff** (☎ 08 25 00 20 99; www.thalasso.com in French; rue Victor Hugo; ☻ closed Dec), which offers health-inducing activities including a heated sea-water pool, hammam and Jacuzzi (€10 for all three).

ÎLE DE BATZ

Bordering what is basically a 4-sq-km garden of vegetables fertilised by seaweed, the beaches on the **Île de Batz** (pronounced 'ba'; Enez Vaz in Breton) are a peaceful place to bask. The mild island climate tends the luxuriant **Jardins Georges Delaselle** (☎ 02 98 61 75 65; adult/child €4/2; ☻ 1-6pm daily Jul & Aug, 2-6pm Wed-Mon Apr-Jun & Sep-Oct), founded in the 19th century, with over 1500 plants from all five continents.

Ferries (adult/child €7/3.50 return, bike €7 return, 20 minutes each way) between Roscoff and Île de Batz run every 30 minutes between 8am and 8pm from late June to mid-September; there are about eight sailings daily during the rest of the year.

On the island, **Le Saout** (☎ 02 98 61 77 65) and **Roulez Jeunesse** (☎ 02 98 61 76 91) rent bicycles for around €9 per day.

Sleeping & Eating

Roscoff's hotels are home to some first-rate restaurants.

Camping de Perharidy (☎ 02 98 69 70 86; www .camping-aux4saisons.fr in French; Le Ruguel; camp sites €16.50; ☻ Easter-Sep) Close to a sandy beach in the grounds of a lovely 19th-century mansion, this camp site is approximately 3km southwest of Roscoff.

Hôtel Les Arcades (☎ 02 98 69 70 45; www.hotel -les-arcades-roscoff.com in French; 15 rue Amiral Réveillère; d €39-63; ☻ Easter-early Nov; ▯) Perched right above the rocks on the waterfront in the town's heart, this cosy two-star hotel, run by the same family for nearly a century, has 24 light-filled, light-coloured rooms and a glass-paned restaurant (mains around €15) serving up seafood and spectacular views.

Hôtel Les Chardons Bleus (☎ 02 98 69 72 03; www.chardonsbleus.fr.st in French; 4 rue Amiral Réveillère; d €55-70; ☻ mid-Mar–Jan) Set back just 100m from the port, in the town centre, the 'Thistles', a Logis de France, has just 10 calm, comfortable rooms, and an old fashioned, formal restaurant (menus €10 to €40) specialising in – you guessed it – seafood, with elegant fare.

Le Surcouf (☎ 02 98 69 71 89; 14 rue Amiral Réveillère; formules from €15, menus from €22; ☻ lunch & dinner) Spy your desired lobster in the live tank at this relaxed brasserie/restaurant in a central spot in town. Le Surcouf is a reliable year-round opener, making it popular with locals, but specific opening hours/days may vary slightly.

Brasserie Restaurant Les Alizés (☎ 02 98 69 75 90; quai d'Auxerre; menus €11-30; ☻ lunch & dinner Jun–mid-Sep, closed 1 day per wk mid-Sep–May)

BRETON LANGUAGE REDUX

Should you happen past some of fast food giant McDonalds' Brittany outlets, you'll receive a *trugarez* (thank you) for using the rubbish bins, and be wished *kenavo* (goodbye) in the car park.

Presumably, this bilingual French and Breton (Breizh) signage isn't included for now-elderly, first-language (non-French speaking) Bretons. And it's not for bilingual French/Breton speakers, since, of course, they already speak and read French. It's a symbolic way of localising the multinational in the region.

It's not just burger chains. Right throughout Brittany you'll see bilingual Breton street and transport signs, and many other occurrences of the language popping up.

But – what is Breton these days?

A Celtic language related to Cornish and Welsh, and more distantly, to Irish and Scottish Gaelic. Following on from the French Revolution, the government banned the teaching of Breton in schools, punishing children who spoke their mother tongue. As happened with other marginalised Celtic cultures, speakers of all ages were stigmatised. For the next century-and-a-half it remained a language spoken in the sanctum of private homes. Education, post-WWII economics, mass media, and, most of all, fluid transportation between Brittany and the rest of the country also saw French rapidly gain ground. Between 1950 and 1990 there was an 80% reduction in Breton usage.

The seeds of Breton's revival were planted in the 1960s, particularly after France's May 1968 protests, driven by the younger generation rebelling against their oppressed cultural heritage. Bringing about the rebirth of the language, no longer passed on generationally, wasn't straightforward. More often spoken than written (and both spoken and written with regional differences), settling on a standardised Breton for teaching in schools is still complex.

There's also a distinct difference between the Breton of first-generation speakers and 'neoBreton', particularly as the new incarnation often replaces French words long intermingled with Breton with completely Breton ones. Case in point: *Aotrou* and *Itron* are now used for the French *Monsieur* and *Madame*. Traditionally, though, they denote someone of exceedingly high rank (*Itron* is the respectful term of address for the Virgin Mary) – creating another generational language gap. (Imagine some stranger you encounter in the street saying 'hello, most Holy, Devout, Exalted One', or the like. Bizarre.) Some older Breton speakers also find it hard to shake the ostracisation inflicted on them for their language, and aren't comfortable conversing in it openly.

Breton now also extends beyond its historic boundaries. Originally, Basse Bretagne (Lower Brittany, in the west) spoke variants of the Breton language, while Haute Bretagne (Upper Brittany, in the east, including areas such as St-Malo), spoke Gallo, a language similar to French. But today you'll find Breton signage in Rennes' metro stations and in many other parts of the east, emblematizing Brittany's culture across the entire region.

When today's students integrate their school-taught Breton into society, Breton will evolve yet again, as France's mosaic of cultures also continues to evolve. For now as the language regenerates, so does the sense of Breton identity. Bolstered, ironically, by usage like McDonalds'. (And just in case you were wondering, the term in Brittany for a Big Mac is, yep, a Big Mac.)

With breathtaking sea views and nautical air, this 1st-floor restaurant (with a lift for wheelchair access) opened in 2005 and has quickly carved out a reputation for (yet more) seafood, cooked creatively with farm-fresh regional produce.

Getting There & Away

Brittany Ferries (☎ reservations 08 25 82 88 28; www .brittany-ferries.com) links Roscoff to Plymouth in England (five to nine hours, one to three daily year-round) and Cork in Ireland (14 hours, once weekly June to September).

Boats leave from Port de Bloscon, about 2km east of the town centre.

The combined bus and train station is on rue Ropartz Morvan.

Cars Bihan (☎ 02 98 83 45 80) operates buses from Roscoff to Brest (€2, 1½ to two hours; up to four daily), departing from the ferry terminal (Port de Bloscon) and passing by the town centre.

There are regular trains and SNCF buses to Morlaix (€8.60, 45 minutes), where you can make connections to Brest, Quimper and St-Brieuc.

BRITTANY

MORLAIX

pop 17,000

At the bottom of a deep valley sluicing through northeastern Finistère, Morlaix is an appealing and easily accessed city that's also a good gateway to the coast and the *enclos paroissiaux* (enclosed parishes), the rich sculptures surrounding many of the parish churches fanning out to the south.

Towering above the town, the arched 58m-high railway viaduct was built in 1863. Below, a few steps southwest, is the **tourist office** (☎ 02 98 62 14 94; officetourisme.morlaix@wanadoo .fr; place des Otages; ☺ 10am-2.30pm & 2-7pm Mon-Sat, 10am-12.30pm Sun Jul & Aug, 9am-12.30pm & 2-6pm Tue-Sat Sep-Jun) From the train station, take rue de Léon south, then turn left and descend the stairs of rue Courte.

Café de l'Aurore (☎ 02 98 88 03 05; 17 rue Traverse; ☺ Mon-Sat) has a free internet terminal for bar customers, and regular live music. Or log on at **Cyberarena** (☎ 02 38 88 15 83; 16 rue Basse; per hr €4.50, ☺ 11am-1am Mon-Sat, 1pm-1am Sun).

Sights & Activities

The late-15th-century Flamboyant Gothic **Église St-Melaine** (☺ 9am-noon & 2-6pm) bears a star-studded barrel-vault roof and polychrome wooden statues, including St Peter and the eponymous St Melaine.

Morlaix's newly integrated museum **Le Musée de Morlaix** (☎ 02 98 88 68 88; place des Jacobins; ☺ 10am-12.30pm & 2-6.30pm daily Jul & Aug, 10am-noon & 2-6pm Mon & Wed-Fri, 2-6pm Sat Easter-May & Sep, 10am-noon & 2-5pm Mon & Wed-Fri, 2-5pm Sat Nov-Easter), covering the area's history, archaeology and art, also incorporates the nearby, beautifully preserved half-timbered house, **La Maison à Pondalez** (☎ 02 98 62 14 94; 9 Grand' Rue; ☺ 10.30am-12.30pm & 3-6pm Tue-Sat Jul & Aug, 10.30am-12.30pm & 2-6pm Wed-Sat Sep-Jun). Tickets per adult/child cost €4.10/2.20 for both the museum and house.

Loop on a boat trip through the islands of the Baie de Morlaix and a picturesque train trip between Roscoff and Morlaix with **Le Léon à Fer et à Flots** (☎ 02 98 62 07 52; www.aferaflots.org in French; adult/child €22/11; ☺ Apr-Sep, time depending on tides).

Sleeping & Eating

The tourist office can help reserve accommodation. Rue Ange de Guernisac has several enticing restaurants.

our pick **Ty Pierre** (☎ 02 98 63 25 75, 06 80 01 37 75; 1bis place de Viarmes; s/d/tr with shared bathroom €30/46/61) At the heart-and-hearth of Morlaix's old town, Pierre-Yves Jacquet has used the timber floors, soaring ceilings and picture windows as a backdrop for his fascinating artworks and artefacts. These come from around Asia and the world and decorate his *chambre d'hôte*'s 10 guest rooms. No, at this price there's no lift (count on climbing three or four floors). And rooms don't have their own bathrooms (they're just along the wide corridors). But breakfast at a long, informal dining table with baskets of brioches and croissants is included. Bonus: the B&B's just across from the cosy Breton bar, La Chope (closed Monday), with French football on the tele and cider on tap.

Hôtel de l'Europe (☎ 02 98 62 11 99; www .hotel-europe-com.fr; 1 rue d'Aiguillon; s €58, d €63-100) Regal, refined, yet still relaxed, the Hôtel de l'Europe occupies an elegant 19th-century building. Moulded ceilings, carved panelling and sculpted woodwork fill the sweeping public areas; the romantic guest rooms have rich apricot and rose tones and mod cons.

Grand Café de la Terrasse (☎ 02 98 88 20 25; 31 place des Otages; mains €10-15.50; ☺ 7am-midnight Mon-Sat) Found right in the centre of town, Morlaix's showpiece is this stunning 1872-established brasserie with an original central spiral staircase. Sip a tea, coffee or something stronger, or sup on classical French brasserie fare.

Getting There & Away

Morlaix has frequent train services including to Brest (€9, 45 minutes), Roscoff (€5, 30 minutes) and Paris (Gare Montparnasse; €61, four hours).

HUELGOAT

pop 1709

Visitors to Brittany often stick to the coast, but the deep, mysterious interior, steeped in Breton mythology and legend, reveals a completely different side to the region. One of the most enchanting inland villages is Huelgoat (An Uhelgoat in Breton), 30km south of Morlaix. The village borders the unspoiled forest, Forêt d'Huelgoat, with curious rock formations, caves, menhirs and abandoned silver and lead mines. To the east and northeast are the Forêt de St-Ambroise and the Forêt de Fréau.

Orientation & Information

Forêt de Fréau hugs a small Y-shaped lake. Its **tourist office** (☎ /fax 02 98 99 72 32; ◷ 10am-12.30pm & 2-5.30pm Mon-Sat Jul & Aug, 10am-noon & 2.30-4.30pm Mon-Fri Sep-Jun) is in the Moulin du Chaos, an old mill beside the bridge at the eastern end of the lake.

Activities

The forest's **walking tracks** are a haven of calm in the spring and the autumn, but they get quite busy in summer, and muddy in the wet winter months. An undemanding walking trail (45 minutes round trip) leads walkers downstream from the bridge, on the opposite bank to the tourist office. From here, the trickling River Argent disappears into a picturesque, wooded valley that is punctuated by giant, moss-covered granite boulders.

Longer hikes (1½ to two hours) lead along the Promenade du Canal to some old silver mines and to the unremarkable Grotte d'Artus (Arthur's Cave).

Sleeping & Eating

Ask the tourist office about nearby cottages available for short-term rental.

Camping Municipal du Lac (☎ 02 98 99 78 80; rue Général de Gaulle; per person/site from €3/3.50; ◷ mid-Jun–mid-Sep) This 80-place camp site on the lakeside – as its name suggests – is 1km west of the town centre.

Hôtel-Restaurant du Lac (☎ 02 98 99 71 14; fax 02 98 99 70 91; 9 rue Général de Gaulle; d €49-71; ◷ closed Jan) Huelgoat's only hotel, a lime-green Logis de France with forest-green trimmings, sits right on the lake in the centre of town. Its welcome isn't the friendliest around, but the 15 rooms come with TVs, telephones and soundproofing, and it has a good on site restaurant (mains €7.50 from to €14.50) serving steak, lamb, pizza and salad, and warming Irish coffees.

Crêperie des Myrtilles (☎ 02 98 99 72 66; 26 place Aristide-Briand; crêpes €1.90-6.20, menus €9.20-14.50; ◷ lunch & dinner Jan-Oct, closed Mon except Jul & Aug) Inside this slate-floored, low wooden-ceilinged place located on the town's main square you can tuck into the signature *crêpe aux myrtilles* (*crêpes* with locally picked blueberries), or an egg- and cheese-concocted *crêpe forestière*. In case you're here in summer, there's a lovely outdoor terrace.

Getting There & Away

EFFIA (☎ 02 98 93 06 98) runs at least two services daily to Morlaix (€2, one hour) to the north. Buses stop in front of the church in place Aristide-Briand.

BREST
pop 149,600

Visiting the cobblestone, half-timbered cities of Quimper or Vannes gives you some idea of what Brest was like before it (as one of France's most important naval and commercial ports) was all but obliterated by Allied air attacks during WWII. Rebuilt quickly after the war to provide housing for its residents, many of whom lived in temporary accommodation for an entire generation, today much of Brest's mid-20th-century architecture is maturing as the city settles into its new skin.

Still a major port and military base, you'll see French sailors' blue uniforms with gold epaulettes throughout the town – as well as plenty of students from Brest's university.

Brest's built-up city centre provides a dramatic contrast to the seaswept Île d'Ouessant (p329), accessible by boat or plane from Brest.

Orientation

Brest sprawls along the northern shore of the deep natural harbour known as the Rade de Brest. Its 13th-century castle (one of the few buildings to survive the bombing), the naval base (Arsenal Maritime) and Port de Commerce are on the waterfront. From the castle, rue de Siam runs northeast to place de la Liberté, the city's main square, then it intersects with av Georges Clemenceau, the main northwest to southeast traffic artery.

Information

Point Bleu (7 rue de Siam; ◷ 7am-8.30pm) Laundry.
Net@rena (☎ 02 98 33 61 11; 30 rue Yves Collet; per hr €3.50; ◷ noon-midnight Mon-Sat, 2-8pm Sun) Internet access.
Post Office (place Général Leclerc)
Tourist Office (☎ 02 98 44 24 96; www.brest-metropole -tourisme.fr; place de la Liberté; ◷ 9.30am-7pm Mon-Sat & 10am-noon Sun Jul & Aug, 9.30am-6pm Mon-Sat Sep-Jun)

Sights & Activities

With 50 tanks in three thematic pavilions – polar, tropical and temperate – the gleaming modern aquarium **Océanopolis** (☎ 02 98 34 40 40; www.oceanopolis.com; port de Plaisance; adult/child €15.40/10.80; 9am-6pm daily Apr-Aug, 10am-5pm Tue-Sat, 10am-6pm Sun Sep-Mar) is great for spending (not uncommon) rainy days. Tip: buying your ticket from the tourist office for the same price allows you to skip the queues and head straight in to view its kelp forests, seals, crabs, anemones, penguins, sharks and more. It's about 3km east of the city centre; take bus 15 from place de la Liberté.

Learn about Brest's maritime military history at the **Musée de la Marine** (Naval Museum; ☎ 02 98 22 12 39; adult/child €4.60/free; 10am-6.30pm Apr–mid-Sep, 10am-noon & 2-6pm Wed-Mon mid-Sep–Mar). The museum is housed within the fortified, 13th-century **Château de Brest**, built to defend the harbour on the River Penfeld. Following the 1532 union of Brittany and France, both the castle and its harbour became a royal fortress. From its ramparts there are striking views of the harbour and naval base.

A sobering reminder of how Brest was on the eve of WWII can be seen at the 14th-century tower, **Tour Tanguy** (☎ 02 98 00 88 60; place Pierre Péron; admission free; 10am-noon & 2-7pm daily Jun-Sep, 2-5pm Wed-Thu & 2-6pm Sat & Sun Oct-May). Other exhibits on the town's history include the documented visit of three Siamese ambassadors in 1686 who presented gifts to the court of Louis XIV; rue de Siam was renamed in their honour.

Cruises operate around the harbour and the naval base between April and September. **La Société Maritime Azenor** (☎ 02 98 41 46 23; adult/child €15/10) offers 1½-hour trips two or three times daily from both the Port de Commerce (which is near the castle) and the Port de Plaisance (which is opposite Océanopolis).

Festivals & Events

Les Jeudis du Port (Harbour Thursdays; admission free; 7.30pm-midnight Thu mid-Jul–late Aug) Try to plan to be in Brest on a Thursday night during summer when Les Jeudis du Port fill the port with live rock, reggae and world music, as well as street performances and children's events.

Brest 2008 Over 2000 traditional sailing craft and three-quarters of a million visitors dock in Brest for its nautical spectacle held every four years in mid-July; the next is titled Brest 2008. The tourist office has a list of local families offering to host visitors in their homes.

Sleeping

Auberge de Jeunesse Éthic Étapes (☎ 02 98 41 90 41; www.ethic-etapes.fr; rue de Kerbriant; dm incl breakfast €14;) Near Océanopolis and a stone's throw from the artificial beach at Moulin Blanc, this bright, modern 118-bed hostel has bike storage and good wheelchair access. Take bus 15 from the train station to the terminus (Port de Plaisance).

Camping du Goulet (☎ 02 98 45 86 84; www.campingdugoulet.com in French; Ste-Anne du Portzic; camp site €14.50) This huge, hilly three-star camp site is in Ste-Anne du Portzic, 6km southwest of Brest and 400m from the sea. Take bus 28 from rue Georges Clemenceau (near the tourist office) to the Le Cosquer bus stop.

Hôtel Bellevue (☎ 02 98 80 51 78; www.hotelbellevue.fr in French; 53 rue Victor Hugo; d €45-52) With shades of blue and yellow throughout the 26 rooms and the welcoming bar area (open 2pm to 11pm), this cheerful, clean two-star hotel has the convenience of on site parking and a lift as well as Brest's shopping streets, train station and port a short stroll away.

Hôtel Continental (☎ 02 98 80 50 40; continental-brest@hotel-sofibra.com; rue Émile Zola; s €101-133, d 120-160;) With sleek, streamlined rooms and crisp white bathrooms finished off with tiled friezes, the classy three-star Continental has a much more lavish, Art Deco–styled interior than its plain exterior lets on. All 73 soundproofed rooms are equipped with mod cons including satellite TV.

Eating

Le Bistro de Gaëtan (☎ 02 98 43 44 10; 7 place Maurice Gillet; menus €14.90-29; lunch & dinner Tue-Sat) Opposite the Église St-Martin, the house speciality of this bistro is a twist on the traditional Breton dish *kig ha farz* – a hearty farmers' family meal based around the Breton cake, *far*, cooked in a linen bag within a boiling bacon and vegetable stew. Gaëtan does a delicious version with seafood instead of traditional *kig* (meat).

Amour de Pomme de Terre (☎ 02 98 43 48 51; 23 rue Halles St-Louis; menus €15-25; lunch & dinner, closed Sun & lunch Sat) Convivial and sweetly simple, 'Potato Love' serves up all manner of potato-oriented dishes such as gratins, along with fresh fruit and vegetable salads from the covered market opposite, and a dip into a basket of rich dried sausages, from which you hack off a hunk.

Ma Petite Folie (☎ 02 98 42 44 42; Port de Plaisance; menus €20-40; ☯ lunch & dinner Mon-Sat) Aboard an old green-and-white-painted lobster-fishing boat strung with buoys and forever beached at Moulin Blanc, this character-filled restaurant has exceptional crab, prawns and fresh fish in butter sauce, ideally finished off with pear tart for dessert and washed down with crisp white wine.

Fleur de Sel (☎ 02 98 44 38 65; 15bis rue de Lyon; mains €20-45; ☯ lunch & dinner, closed Sun, lunch Sat & Mon) Its style is minimalist Art Deco but the atmosphere is warm and welcoming at this creative place, run by the same owners as Amour de Pomme de Terre, but serving up a wider variety of creative French cuisine such as veal kidneys sizzled in truffle vinegar.

Les Halles St-Louis (☯ 9am-1pm) Head to Brest's covered market for self-catering supplies.

Getting There & Away

AIR
Check with Brest's **airport** (www.brest.aeroport .fr) for up-to-date flight services. At the time of writing, Ryanair had a daily flight to and from London (Luton), and Flybe had regular flights to Birmingham, Exeter, Southampton and Edinburgh, but routes and schedules are liable to change.

BOAT
Ferries to Île d'Ouessant (see p330) leave from the Port de Commerce.

BUS
Brest's **bus station** (☎ 02 98 44 46 73) is beside the train station. Routes include Le Conquet (€4.45, 45 minutes, six daily) and Roscoff (€9.70, 1½ to two hours, four daily).

CAR & MOTORCYCLE
Hire companies include **ADA** (☎ 02 98 44 44 88; 9 av Georges Clemenceau) and **Europcar** (☎ 02 98 44 66 88; rue Voltaire).

TRAIN
There are frequent trains or SNCF buses to Quimper (€14, 1¼ hours) and Morlaix (€9, 45 minutes), which has connections to Roscoff. There are also around 15 TGV trains daily to Rennes (€28.50, two hours) and Paris (Gare Montparnasse; €63.20, 4½ hours).

Getting Around
The tourist office has updated schedules for buses to and from the airport; a taxi for the 10km trip costs around €15.

The local bus network **Bibus** (☎ 02 98 80 30 30) sells tickets good for two hours for €1.10, carnets of 10 for €8.45 and day passes for €3. There's an information kiosk on place de la Liberté.

By the time you're reading this, the tourist office will have a bike rental service.

To order a taxi call ☎ 02 98 80 18 01 or 02 98 80 68 06.

ÎLE D'OUESSANT
pop 950
Reminiscent of Ireland's wild, windswept Aran Islands, Île d'Ouessant (Enez Eusa in Breton, meaning 'Island of Terror'; Ushant in English) has a desolate, haunting beauty.

Although frequented by summer visitors by the ferryload, free-roaming little black sheep and traditional houses give Île d'Ouessant an ends-of-the-earth feel, best experienced by hiking its 45km craggy coastal path.

Orientation & Information
Ferries land at Port du Stiff on the east coast. The island's only village is Lampaul, 4km west on the sheltered Baie de Lampaul. A handful of hotels, restaurants and shops are sprinkled along the west coast.

Île d'Ouessant's **tourist office** (☎ 02 98 48 85 83; www.ot-ouessant.fr in French; place de l'Église; ☯ 10am-noon & 1.30-5pm Mon-Sat, 10am-noon Sun) is in Lampaul. It sells an English-language version of its brochure *Circuits de Randonnée Pédestre* (€2.50) with stylised maps and descriptions of four coastal walks varying between 10km and 16km.

Sights & Activities
MUSEUMS
The black-and-white-striped **Phare de Créac'h** is the world's most powerful lighthouse. Beaming two white flashes every 10 seconds, visible for over 50km, it serves as a beacon for over 50,000 ships entering the Channel each year. Beneath is the island's main museum, the **Musée des Phares et des Balises** (Lighthouse & Beacon Museum; ☎ 02 98 48 80 70; adult/child €4.10/2.60; ☯ 10.30am-6.30pm Apr-Sep, 1.30-5pm Oct-Mar), which tells the story of these

vital navigation aids; more interesting is the section on shipwrecks and underwater archaeology.

Two typical local houses make up the small **Écomusée d'Ouessant** (☎ 02 98 48 86 37; Maison du Niou; adult/child €3.30/2.10; ☷ 10.30am-6.30pm Apr-Sep, 1.30-5pm Oct-Mar). One re-creates a traditional homestead, furnished like a ship's cabin, with furniture fashioned from driftwood and painted in bright colours to mask its imperfections; the other explores the island's history and customs.

A combined ticket giving entry to both museums costs €6.50/4.10 (adult/child).

BEACHES

Plage de Corz, 600m south of Lampaul, is the island's best beach. Other good spots to stretch out are **Plage du Prat**, **Plage de Yuzin** and **Plage Ar Lan**. All are easily accessible by bike from Lampaul or Port du Stiff.

Sleeping & Eating

Camping Municipal (☎ 02 98 48 84 65; fax 02 98 48 83 99; Stang Ar Glan, Lampaul; per person & site €2.80; ☷ Apr-Sep) About 500m east of Lampaul, it looks more like a football field than a camp site.

Auberge de Jeunesse (☎ 02 98 48 84 53; fax 02 98 48 87 42; La Croix-Rouge, Lampaul; dm incl breakfast €15; ☷ closed last 3 weeks Jan) This friendly hostel, on the hill above Lampaul, has two- to six-person rooms. It's popular with school and walking groups; reservations are essential.

Hôtel Roc'h Ar Mor (☎ 02 98 48 80 19; www.rocharmor.com in French; Lampaul; d €55-87; ☷ mid-Feb-Dec) It's worth paying a tad extra for a panoramic sea view and balcony from this appealing 15-room hotel with sunlit blue-

and-white rooms and good wheelchair access. In a superb location next to the Baie de Lampaul, there's also a good restaurant (mains from €7), with a terrace overlooking the ocean.

Crêperie Ti A Dreuz (☎ 02 98 48 83 01; Lampaul; galettes from €3; ☷ Easter–mid-Sep) You could be forgiven for thinking you'd been at sea too long, or knocked back too much Breton cider, but 'the slanting house' is so-named for its wonky walls. This quaint island *crêperie* serves delicious *galettes*: try the *ouessantine*, with creamy potato, cheese and sausage.

Ty Korn (☎ 02 98 48 87 33; Lampaul; lunch menus €14-15, dinner €27) The ground floor of this hyperfriendly place is a bar, serving midday snacks in summer; upstairs there's an agreeable restaurant.

If you forgot the sandwich filling, you'll find minimarkets in Lampaul.

Getting There & Away

AIR

Finist'air (☎ 02 98 84 64 87; www.finistair.fr) flies from Brest's small airport to Ouessant in a mere 15 minutes. There are two flights daily (one way adult/child €63/36).

BOAT

Ferries depart from Brest and the tiny town (and Brittany's most westerly point) of Le Conquet (Konk Leon in Breton). Buses operated by **Les Cars St-Mathieu** (☎ 02 98 89 12 02) link Brest with Le Conquet (€2, 45 minutes, six daily).

In high summer it's a good idea to reserve at least one day in advance and to check in 30 minutes before departure. Ferry fares quoted are all return.

BRITTANY'S TOP FIVE COASTAL DRIVES

If you're driving, cycling or motorbiking around Brittany, there's no end of detours you can take along some truly stunning stretches of coastline. Our favourites (heading anticlockwise):

Sillon de Talbert West of Paimpol on Brittany's north coast, you may see the local seaweed harvesters tossing strands of kelp into their carts.

Crozon Peninsula Trace a figure of eight around the peninsula's northern spur from Crozon to Camaret-sur-Mer; then shoot 3km south to Pointe de Pen-Hir.

Pays Bigouden Home of the up to 30cm tall lace headdress *coiffe bigoudène*, Finistère's southwestern corner has patchwork fields of green threaded with interconnecting coast roads. Spot hard-core surfers riding 'the lift' – a death-defying break off Pointe de la Torche.

Côte Sauvage On the western edge of the peninsula en route to Quiberon, the aptly named 'wild coast' swoops between barren headlands and sheer cliffs.

Golfe du Morbihan Swing southwest from Vannes to Port Navalo for fantastic views over the gulf and its islands.

Penn Ar Bed (☎ 02 98 80 80 80; www.pennarbed.fr) sails from the Port de Commerce in Brest (adult/child €30.70/18.50, 2½ hours) and from Le Conquet (€26.60/16.10, 1½ hours). Boats run between each port and the island two to five times daily from May to September and once daily between October and April. In season, Penn Ar Bed also operates from Camaret (p332) on the Crozon Peninsula (€27.50/16.60, two hours, once daily mid-April to mid-September).

Finist'mer (☎ 02 98 89 16 61; www.finist-mer.fr in French) runs faster boats to the island up to six times daily from Le Conquet (adult/child €26/15.40, 40 minutes, mid-April to September) and from Camaret (adult/child €27/16, one hour, daily mid-July to mid-August, Wednesday only Easter to mid-July).

Getting Around

BICYCLE

Several bike-hire operators have kiosks at the Port du Stiff ferry terminal and compounds just up the hill. They also have outlets in Lampaul. The going rate for town/mountain bikes is €10/14. You can save by booking and prepaying for a mountain bike (€10) at the Brest tourist office.

Cycling on the coastal footpath is forbidden – the fragile turf is strictly reserved for walkers.

MINIBUS

Several islanders, including **Dominique Etienne** (☎ 06 07 90 07 43), run minibus services. They meet the ferry at Port du Stiff and will shuttle you to Lampaul or your accommodation for a flat fare of €2 (to guarantee a seat in July and August, book ahead at the island tourist office, or at the tourist office in Brestto). For the return journey, the pick-up point is the car park beside Lampaul's church.

Minibus owners also offer two-hour guided tours (€12 per person) of the island, in French.

PRESQU'ÎLE DE CROZON

Between two bays in the centre of Finistère, the cliff-crowned Crozon Peninsula is part of the Parc Naturel Régional d'Armorique, and one of the most scenic spots in Brittany, crisscrossed by 145km of signed walking trails.

Ménez-Hom

To feel Brittany's wind beneath your wings, the **Club Celtic de Vol Libre** (☎ 02 98 81 50 27; www .vol-libre-menez-hom.com in French; hang-gliding & para-gliding from €70) offers three-hour hang-gliding and paragliding sessions off the rounded, 330m-high, heather- and grass-clad hump of Ménez-Hom. Situated at the peninsula's eastern end, a surfaced road leads to the top of the summit, which has sublime views over the Baie de Douarnenez.

Landévennec

To the north of Ménez-Hom, the River Aulne flows into the Rade de Brest beside the pretty little village of Landévennec, famous for its ruined Benedictine **Abbaye St-Guenolé**. The abbey **museum** (☎ 02 98 27 35 90; adult/child €4/2.50; ☼ 10am-7pm daily Jul–mid-Sep, 2-6pm Sun-Fri May-Jun & late Sep) records the history of the settlement, founded by St Guenolé in AD 485 and the oldest Christian site in Brittany. Nearby, a new abbey is home to a contemporary community of monks, who run a little shop selling home-made fruit jellies.

Crozon & Morgat

pop 7881

The area's largest town, Crozon, is the engine room for the peninsula. On the water 2km south, its adjoining resort, Morgat, was built in the 1930s by the Peugeot brothers (of motor vehicle fame) as a playground.

Every Tuesday during July and August free concerts take place on place d'Ys, and each year in mid-August the area hosts the **Festival du Bout du Monde** (Festival of the End of the World; www.festivalduboutdumonde.com in French), featuring world music.

INFORMATION

Housed in the former railway station, the **Crozon tourist office** (☎ 02 98 27 07 92; www.crozon .com in French; blvd Pralognan; ☼ 9.15am-12.30pm & 2-7pm Mon-Sat, 10am-noon Sun Jul & Aug, 9.15am-noon & 2-5.30pm or 6pm Mon-Sat Sep-Jun) is on the main road to Camaret.

The seasonal **Morgat tourist office** (☎ 02 98 27 29 49; ☼ 10am-1pm & 3-7.30pm Jul & Aug) overlooks the promenade at the corner of blvd de la Plage.

ACTIVITIES

Beyond the marina at the southern end of Morgat's fine sandy **beach**, the coastal path

BRITTANY

offers an excellent 8km hike along the sea cliffs to **Cap de la Chèvre**.

Morgat-based companies **Vedettes Rosmeur** (☎ 02 98 27 10 71) and **Vedettes Sirènes** (☎ 02 98 26 20 10) operate 45-minute boat trips to the colourful **sea caves** along the coast. Tours (adult/child €9/6) depart from Morgat harbour several times daily from April to September.

SLEEPING & EATING

Camping Les Pieds Dans l'Eau (☎ 02 98 27 62 43; St-Fiacre; per person/tent/car €4/4/2.30; ☒ mid-Jun–mid-Sep) 'Camping feet in the water' (almost literally, at high tide) is one of 15 camp sites along the peninsula.

Mana Mana Backpacker (☎ 02 98 26 20 97; www .mana-mana.net; rte de Penfrat, Le Pouldu; dm €12-15; ☒ closed mid-Jan–Mar) In the best free-spirited travellers' tradition, this independent hostel has just 30 beds, a self-catering kitchen, a cosy lounge/party room, good wheelchair access and a garden. Close to the surf, you can rent boards and bikes for €5 each per day. From the bus stop, head north along the beach and turn left on rue de Trelez for 900m.

Hôtel de la Baie (☎ 02 98 27 07 51; hotel.dela baie@presquile-crozon.com; 46 blvd de la Plage, Morgat; d €55) One of the *very* few hotels to remain open year-round, this simple, friendly, family-run place on Morgat's promenade has views over the ocean and is one of the best deals around – even better if you take a room with shower only (from €33). Parking's free; breakfast costs €6.

The seafront and place d'Ys are good spots to trawl for seafood restaurants.

Saveurs et Marées (☎ 02 98 26 23 18; 52 blvd Plage, Morgat; menus €15-30; ☒ lunch & dinner, closed Feb) Impossible to miss, this bright yellow house presiding over the sea has a breezy dining room and a sunny terrace, and serves up consistently good locally caught seafood, making it a favourite with locals.

Camaret-sur-Mer
pop 2600

At the western extremity of the Crozon Peninsula, Camaret is a classic little fishing village – or at least, it was until early last century, as France's then-biggest crayfish port. Abandoned fishing boat carcasses now decay in its harbour, but it remains an enchanting place that lures artists, with

over a dozen galleries dotted around town, particularly along rue de la Marne and around place St-Thomas, one block north of the waterfront.

Camaret's **tourist office** (☎ 02 98 27 93 60; www .camaret-sur-mer.com in French; 15 quai Kléber; ☒ 9am-7pm Mon-Sat & 10am-1pm Sun Jul & Aug, 10am-noon & 2-5pm Mon-Sat Sep-Jun) is on the waterfront.

The **Chapelle Notre-Dame-de-Rocamadour**, its timber roof like an inverted ship's hull, is dedicated to the sailors of Camaret, who have adorned it with votive offerings of oars, life buoys and model ships.

Pointe de Pen-Hir, 3km south of Camaret, is a spectacular headland bounded by steep, sheer sea cliffs, with two WWII memorials.

SLEEPING & EATING

Hôtel Vauban (☎ 02 98 27 91 36; fax 02 98 27 96 34; 4 quai du Styvel; d with toilet from €30, d with bathroom from €35; ☒ Feb-Nov) Its airy rooms are contemporary, but the Vauban's old-fashioned hospitality extends to its large rear garden with a barbecue to grill your own fish, and a piano to play. Its bar is a favourite with Camaret's old-timers, too. The cheapest rooms have a sink and toilet only, with showers down the hallway.

Crêperie Rocamadour (☎ 02 98 27 93 17; quai Kléber; menus €10-14, mains €10-12; ☒ lunch & dinner Wed-Sun Sep-Jun, daily Jul & Aug) Close to the tourist office, this wonderful place with beamed ceilings turns out excellent, carefully prepared *galettes* as well as mains like citrus-infused salmon. Finish off with a flaming flambéed *crêpe* or one smothered in melted chocolate.

There are supermarkets on quai du Styvel and rue de Loc'h.

Getting There & Around

Vedettes Azénor (☎ 02 98 41 46 23; www.azenor.com in French) runs seasonal ferries between Brest's Port de Commerce and the Presqu'île de Crozon.

Penn Ar Bed and Finist'mer provide a summer-only ferry service between Camaret and Île d'Ouessant (see p331).

Five buses daily run from Quimper to Crozon (€2, 1¼ hours), continuing to Camaret (€2), and up to four from Camaret and Crozon to Brest (€2, 1¼ hours, daily). Buses also run between Morgat, Crozon and Camaret several times daily (€2, 10 minutes).

To rent a bike, contact **Presqu'îles Loisirs** (☎ 02 98 27 00 09; 13 rue de la Gare, Crozon), opposite Crozon's tourist office, **Point Bleu** (☎ 02 98 27 09 04; quai Kador, Morgat) or, in summer, the open-air stall in front of Morgat's tourist office. The going rate is about €10 per day.

QUIMPER

pop 64,000

Small enough to feel like a village with its slanted half-timbered houses and cobblestone streets, and large enough to buzz as the troubadour of Breton culture and arts, Quimper (pronounced kam-pair) is Finistère's thriving capital. Derived from the Breton word *kemper*, meaning 'confluence', Quimper sits at the juncture of the small Rivers Odet and Steïr, crisscrossed by footbridges with cascading flowers.

Orientation

The magnolia-shaded, mainly pedestrianised old city clusters around the cathedral on the north bank of the Odet, overlooked by Mont Frugy on the south bank. Most of old Quimper's half-timbered houses are concentrated in the tight triangle formed by place Médard, rue Kéréon, rue des Gentilhommes and its continuation, rue du Sallé, to place au Beurre.

Information

Eixxos (☎ 02 98 64 40 56; 12 blvd Dupleix; per hr €3.50; ☼ 11am-10pm Mon-Thu, 11am-1am Fri & Sat, 2-10pm Sun) Internet access.
Laverie de la Gare (4 av de la Gare; ☼ 8am-8pm) Laundry.
Main Post Office (blvd Amiral de Kerguélen)
Stargames Café (☎ 02 98 95 71 97; 17 rue des Gentilshommes; per min €0.07; ☼ 1-11pm Tue-Thu, 1pm-midnight Fri & Sat) Log on at this chilled hookah bar.
Tourist Office (☎ 02 98 53 04 05; www.quimper-tourisme.com in French; place de la Résistance; ☼ 9am-7pm

Mon-Sat, 10am-12.45pm & 3-5.45pm Sun Jul & Aug, 9.30am-12.30pm & 1.30-6pm or 6.30pm Mon-Sat Sep-Jun, 10am-12.45pm Sun Jun & 1-15 Sep) Arranges weekly guided city tours in English, in July and August.

Sights & Activities

CATHÉDRALE ST-CORENTIN

Quimper's **cathedral** (☼ 9.30am-noon & 1.30-6.30pm Mon-Sat, 1.30-6.30pm Sun May-Oct, 9am-noon & 1.30-6.30pm Mon-Sat, 1.30-6.30pm Sun Nov-Apr) has a distinctive kink built into its soaring light-filled interior – said by some to symbolise Christ's head inclined on one shoulder as he was dying on the cross. Begun in 1239, the cathedral wasn't completed until the 1850s, with the seamless addition of its dramatic twin spires. Between them, high on the west façade, is an equestrian statue of King Gradlon, the city's mythical 5th-century founder.

MUSEUMS

Recessed behind a magnificent stone courtyard beside the cathedral, the **Musée Départemental Breton** (☎ 02 98 95 21 60; 1 rue du Roi Gradlon; adult/child €3.80/2.50; ☼ 9am-6pm daily Jun-Sep, 9am-noon & 2-5pm Tue-Sat, 2-5pm Sun Oct-May) is housed in the former bishop's palace. Superb exhibits showcase the area's history, furniture, costumes, crafts and archaeology of the area. Adjoining the museum is the **Jardin de l'Évêché** (Bishop's Palace Garden; admission free; ☼ 9am-5pm or 6pm).

Quimper's local crafts include exquisite faïence pottery, displayed at both the Musée Départemental Breton, and the **Musée de la Faïence** (☎ 02 98 90 12 72; 14 rue Jean-Baptiste Bousquet; adult/child €4/2.30; ☼ 10am-6pm Mon-Sat mid-Apr–mid-Oct), which is situated in a one-time ceramics factory and contains over 2000 pieces of china.

The ground-floor halls are home to some fairly morbid 16th- to 20th-century

---

WORTH A TRIP

Explore Brittany's maritime heritage in depth at Douarnenez' **Port-Musée** and **Musée du Bateau** (☎ 02 98 92 65 20; quai du Port Rhu; combined ticket adult/child €6.20/3.80; ☼ 10am-7pm mid-Jun–mid-Sep, 10am-12.30pm & 2-6pm Tue-Sun Apr–mid-Jun & mid-Sep–Oct). Moored at the open-air Port-Musée, traditional vessels range from a Breton *langoustier* (cray-fishing boat) to a Norwegian masted sailing ship. Within the vast Musée du Bateau, occupying a former sardine cannery (Douarnenez' locals are affectionately nicknamed *penn sardin* – sardine head), are smaller traditional boats such as an Inuit kayak and a Welsh coracle as well as local craft.

Buses run between Douarnenez and Quimper (€2, 35 minutes, six to 10 daily).

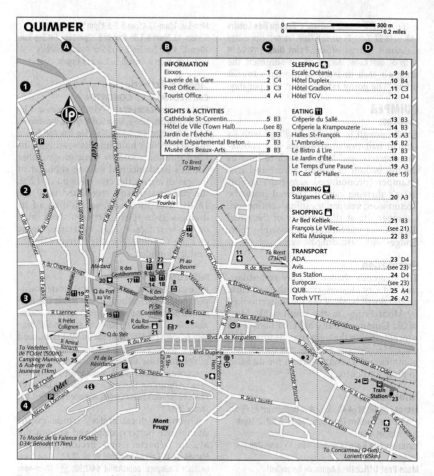

QUIMPER

INFORMATION	
Eixxos..	1 C4
Laverie de la Gare...........................	2 C4
Post Office.....................................	3 C3
Tourist Office.................................	4 A4

SIGHTS & ACTIVITIES	
Cathédrale St-Corentin....................	5 B3
Hôtel de Ville (Town Hall)...............	(see 8)
Jardin de l'Évêché...........................	6 B3
Musée Départemental Breton..........	7 B3
Musée des Beaux-Arts.....................	8 B3

SLEEPING	
Escale Océania...............................	9 B4
Hôtel Dupleix.................................	10 B4
Hôtel Gradlon.................................	11 C3
Hôtel TGV......................................	12 D4

EATING	
Crêperie du Sallé............................	13 B3
Crêperie la Krampouzerie	14 B3
Halles St-François...........................	15 A3
L'Ambroisie....................................	16 B2
Le Bistro á Lire...............................	17 B3
Le Jardin d'Été...............................	18 B3
Le Temps d'une Pause	19 A3
Ti Cass' de'Halles	(see 15)

DRINKING	
Stargames Café..............................	20 A3

SHOPPING	
Ar Bed Keltiek................................	21 B3
François Le Villec...........................	(see 21)
Keltia Musique................................	22 B3

TRANSPORT	
ADA..	23 D4
Avis...	(see 23)
Bus Station....................................	24 D4
Europcar..	(see 23)
QUB..	25 A4
Torch VTT......................................	26 A2

European paintings, but things lighten up on the upper levels of the **Musée des Beaux-Arts** (☎ 02 98 95 45 20; 40 place St-Corentin; adult/child €4/2.50; ☯ 10am-7pm daily Jul & Aug, 10am-noon & 2-6pm Wed-Mon Apr-Jun, Sep-Oct, 10am-noon & 2-6pm Wed-Sat & Mon, 2-6pm Sun Nov-Mar). A salon dedicated to Quimper-born poet Max Jacob includes sketches by Picasso.

WALKING
Following the switchback path just east of the tourist office up the 72m-high **Mont Frugy** rewards you with captivating city views.

Tours
From May to September, **Vedettes de l'Odet** (☎ 08 25 80 08 01, 02 98 57 00 58) runs boat trips

(adult/child €21.50/13, 1¼ hours) from Quimper along the serene Odet estuary to Bénodet, departing from quai Neuf.

Festivals & Events
The **Festival de Cornouaille** (www.festival-corn ouaille.com in French), a celebration of traditional Celtic music, costumes and culture, takes place between the third and fourth Sundays of July. After the traditional festival, classical music concerts are held at different venues around town.

Sleeping
Quimper unfortunately has a chronic shortage of inexpensive accommodation, and none in the old city.

BRITTANY

Camping Municipal (☎ /fax 02 98 55 61 09; av des Oiseaux; camp sites from €8.50; Apr-Sep) This wooded park is 1km west of the old city (3km from the train station). From quai de l'Odet follow rue Pont l'Abbé northwestwards and continue straight ahead where it veers left. Alternatively, take bus 1 from the train station to the Chaptal stop.

Auberge de Jeunesse (☎ 02 98 64 97 97; quim per@fuaj.org; 6 av des Oiseaux; dm incl breakfast €14.40, sheets €2.80; Apr-Sep) Beside Camping Municipal, Quimper's seasonal youth hostel has self-catering facilities.

Hôtel TGV (☎ 02 98 90 54 00; www.hoteltgv.com; 4 rue de Concarneau; d €36-46) The best bet among several hotels around the train station, 800m from the old city, the TGV has 22 small but bright en suite rooms. Light sleepers beware: the adjacent bar can be noisy at night – aim for one of the top-floor rooms.

Escale Océania (☎ 02 98 53 37 37; www.oceania hotels.com; 6 rue Théodore Le Hars; d €63-98) Formerly the Hôtel Mascotte (a rebranding that hadn't caught up with its own website at the time of writing), this two-star place has the basics covered, with 63 sizable, doubleglazed rooms in inoffensive brown-and-beige tones, good wheelchair access and an on site restaurant with menus from €15 to €25. Public parking is adjacent.

Hôtel Dupleix (☎ 02 98 90 53 35; www.hotel-du pleix.com in French; 34 blvd Dupleix; d €69-96) Part of a business complex overlooking the River Odet, this efficient, modern hotel with good wheelchair access is fronted by a concrete forecourt of fountains. Some rooms have a balcony and view of the cathedral, and it's a handy option if you're driving, with a private lock-up garage on site.

Hôtel Gradlon (☎ 02 98 95 04 39; www.hotel-grad lon.com; 30 rue de Brest; d €69-155; closed 20 Dec-20 Jan) Quimper's most charming hotel is this former 19th-century coach house, which is well set up for wheelchairs. Recently renovated with floral and checked fabrics, its 22 rooms include three elegant junior suites set around a rose garden courtyard, and there's a cosy bar with a toasty open fire, as well as wi-fi.

Eating

As a bastion of Breton culture, Quimper has some exceptional *crêperies*.

Le Temps d'une Pause (☎ 02 98 95 31 09; 10 rue St-Mathieu; dishes €2.70-7.90; 8am-7.30pm Mon-Sat, 8am-

1pm Sun) Tuck into a fresh *tartine* with goat's cheese and leek (slice of bread with topping), followed by a mini *Paris-Brest* (ring-shaped choux pastry)or a rich chocolate éclair on the two-storey premises, or pick up takeaway items for a movable feast.

Crêperie du Sallé (☎ 02 98 95 95 80; 6 rue du Sallé; galettes €3-8.60; lunch & dinner Tue-Sat) For a quarter of a century, locals have crowded into this *crêperie* on a pretty half-timbered square, hung with lace curtains, wooden dressers and painted plates lining the walls. Breton specialities include *saucisse fumée* (smoked sausage) and the house speciality, *forestière* made with mushrooms, smoked lard (fatty bacon) and cheese.

Crêperie la Krampouzerie (☎ 02 98 95 13 08; 9 rue du Sallé; galettes €3.50-7, mains from €7; lunch & dinner, closed Sun & Mon) In an atmospheric space with blue-and-white tiled wooden tables, husband and wife chefs Fanch and Laurence Savina create *crêpes* and *galettes* using organic flours and regional ingredients like *algues d'Ouessant* (seaweed from the Île d'Ouessant), Roscoff onions, and their own home-made ginger caramel.

Le Bistro á Lire (☎ 02 98 95 30 86; 18 rue des Boucheries; mains €7.40, snacks around €4.40; lunch Tue-Sat, salon de thé 9am-7pm Tue-Sat, plus Mon afternoon Jul & Aug) Hungry bookworms can take a seat among the shelves at this restaurant/bookshop/*salon de thé*. The lunch menu is a small but select offering of dishes like lasagne; or pop in for a hot drink and a slice of the *gâteau du jour* (cake of the day) for €5.

Le Jardin d'Été (☎ 02 98 95 33 00; 15 rue du Sallé; lunch menus €14, dinner menus €23-27.50; lunch & dinner Tue-Sat) Occupying a glassed-in terrace strung across with lanterns and graced by window boxes (but what's with the sprayed-on fake snow?), 'the summer garden' is a great choice for gourmands, with specialities including a duck mousse, and coquilles St-Jacques in *beurre blanc* (white sauce).

L'Ambroisie (☎ 02 98 95 00 02; www.ambroisie -quimper.com; 49 rue Elie Fréron; menus €22-60; lunch & dinner Tue-Sat, lunch Sat, closed mid-Jun–mid-Jul) Quimper's most celebrated gastronomic restaurant is sumptuously decorated with contemporary art and elegant china on snow-white tablecloths. Regional produce provided by chef Gilbert Guyon's friends are used in the creation of house specials like quail in cider sauce with peas, and a crispy almond cake with strawberries. Cooking classes are available on Tuesday afternoons by request.

SELF-CATERING
The covered market **Halles St-François** in the old town has a slew of salad and sandwich options. One of the best, with a clutch of outdoor terrace tables, is **Ti Cass' de'Halles** (☎ 09 98 95 87 56; 3 Halles St-François; dishes €3-4; ☼ 10am-3pm Mon-Thu, 10am-7pm Fri & Sat), which also has a *traiteur* (caterer) service.

Drinking
Rue du Frout near the cathedral has a couple of small pubs that attract a Breton-speaking clientele.

Fire up a hookah in the cushion-strewn Asian ambience of **Stargames Café** (☎ 02 98 95 71 97; 17 rue des Gentilhommes; ☼ 1-11pm Tue-Thu, 1pm-midnight Fri & Sat).

Entertainment
From mid-June to mid-September, traditional Breton music and dance takes place every Thursday evening at 9pm in the Jardin de l'Évêché (admission €4).

Check posters and leaflets pasted up around town or ask the tourist office for times and venues of a local **fest-noz** (night festival). On average there's one in or near Quimper every couple of weeks.

Shopping
Several shops located in the old town sell Quimper's traditional faïence pottery, including **Ar Bed Keltiek** (Celtic World; ☎ 02 98 95 42 82; 2 rue du Roi Gradlon) and **François Le Villec** (☎ 02 98 95 31 54, 4 rue du Roi Gradlon). Breton and Celtic music and art are available at **Keltia Musique** (☎ 02 98 95 45 82; 1 place au Beurre), which carries an excellent range of CDs and books.

Getting There & Away
BUS
CAT/Connex Tourisme (☎ 02 98 90 68 40) bus destinations include Brest (€6, 1¼ hours) and Douarnenez (€2, 35 minutes, six to 10 daily).

Caoudal (☎ 02 98 56 96 72) runs buses to Concarneau (€2, 45 minutes, seven to 10 daily); three daily continue to Quimperlé (€2, 1½ hours).

CAR
ADA (☎ 02 98 52 25 25), **Europcar** (☎ 02 98 65 10 05) and **Avis** (☎ 02 98 90 31 34) all have offices right outside the train station.

TRAIN
There are frequent trains to Brest (€14, 1¼ hours, up to 10 daily), Lorient (€10, 40 minutes, six to eight daily), Vannes (€16.30, 1½ hours, seven daily), Rennes (€30.10, 2½ hours, five daily) and Paris (Gare Montparnasse; €68.20, 4¾ hours, eight daily).

Getting Around
Torch VTT (☎ 02 98 53 84 41; 58 rue de la Providence; ☼ Tue-Sat) rents out mountain bikes for €18 per day. The friendly owner is a fount of information about local cycle routes.

QUB (☎ 02 98 95 26 27; 2 quai de l'Odet) has an information office opposite the tourist office; a single/day ticket costs €1/3.

For a taxi, call ☎ 02 98 90 21 21.

CONCARNEAU
pop 20,000
The sheltered harbour of Concarneau (Konk-Kerne in Breton), 24km southeast of Quimper, is known far and wide for its trawler port, which brings in close to 200,000 tonnes of *thon* (tuna) from the Indian Ocean and off the African coast (the adjacent Atlantic's too cold!). Jutting out into the port, the old town, Ville Close, is circled by medieval walls.

Orientation
Concarneau concentrates around the western side of the harbour at the mouth of the River Moros. Ville Close and its fortifications separate the Port de Plaisance, to the south, from the busy fisheries area of the Port de Pêche. Quai d'Aiguillon, becoming quai Penéroff, runs from north to south beside the harbour.

Information
Espace Informatique (☎ 02 98 60 76 37; 23 rue des Écoles; per 15min €1.20; ☼ 9am-noon & 2-7pm Mon-Fri, 9am-noon & 2-5pm Sat) Internet access.
Laundrette (21 av Alain Le Lay; ☼ 7am-8pm)
Post Office (14 quai Carnot)
Tourist Office (☎ 02 98 97 01 44; www.tourismeconcarneau.fr; quai d'Aiguillon; ☼ 9am-7pm Jul & Aug, 9am-12.30pm & 1.45-6.30pm Mon-Sat, 10am-1pm Sun Apr-Jun & 1-15 Sep, 9am-noon & 2-6pm Mon-Sat mid-Sep-March)

Sights & Activities

MUSEUMS

The **walled town**, fortified in the 14th century and modified by Vauban two centuries later, is on a small island linked to place Jean Jaurès by a footbridge. Between 15 June and 15 September the walled town can also be accessed through the **Maison du Patrimoine** (☎ 02 98 60 76 06; admission €0.80), which has exhibits on the town's history – ask for a brochure in English. Within the walls, rue Vauban and place St-Guénolé are enchanting for their old stone houses converted into shops, restaurants and galleries. Return to the mainland via the **fortifications** on the southern side of the island for magical views over the town, port and bay.

To find out about Concarneau's seafaring traditions, offshore fishing trawlers, model ships and fishing exhibits feature at the **Musée de la Pêche** (Fisheries Museum; ☎ 02 98 97 10 20; 3 rue Vauban; adult/child €6/4; ☿ 9.30am-8pm Jul & Aug, 10am-noon & 2-6pm Sep-Jun, closed 3 weeks in Jan).

Founded in 1859, the **Marinarium** (☎ 02 98 50 81 64; place de la Croix; adult/child €5/3; ☿ 10am-7pm Jul & Aug, 10am-noon & 2-6pm Apr-Jun & Sep, 2-6pm Oct-Dec, Feb-Mar) is the world's oldest institute of marine biology. Alongside its 10 aquariums are exhibits on oceanography and marine flora and fauna.

One of Concarneau's last functioning canneries, **Maison Courtin** (Conserverie Courtin; ☎ 02 98 97 01 80; 3 quai du Moros; admission free), conducts tours including a film of the cannery in peak production, and free sampling. Contact the cannery or the tourist office for tour times.

BEACHES

Plage des Sables Blancs is on Baie de la Forêt, 1.5km northwest of the town centre; take bus 2, northbound, from the tourist office. For Plage du Cabellou, 5km south of town, take bus 2, southbound.

WALKING

The tourist office sells a walking guide, *Balades au Pays des Portes de Cornouaille* (€2.50; in French), describing 17 walks around Concarneau.

SEA ANGLING

To reel in some fish of your own, the **Santa Maria** (☎ 02 98 50 69 01; adult/child incl equipment hire €35/20; ☿ sailing 8am & 1.30pm or 2pm Mon-Fri) sets

---

NAME GAME

Breton toponymy (the study of place names) gives an insight into words you'll often see on road signs and maps (sometimes with local spelling variations). And you will see them often – over 40,000 Breton place names alone incorporate the word 'ker', combined with a family name, place name or a description.

- aven, avon – river
- bihan – little
- braz – big
- conk – shelter
- ker – town, village, home
- loc (6th century), lan (8th and 9th century) – religious settlement
- men, mein – stone(s)
- menez – mount
- mor – sea
- nevet – forest
- nevez – new
- plou – parish (usually followed directly by a saint's name)
- trev, tre, treo – parish division
- ti, ty – house

out on four-hour sea-angling trips daily in July and August from quai d'Aiguillon near the tourist office. All-day deep-sea fishing expeditions (8am to 6pm) cost €80.

Tours

In July and August **Vedettes Glenn** (☎ 02 98 97 10 31; 17 av du Dr Nicolas) does four-hour river trips (adult/child €26/13.50, sailing 2.15pm Tuesday to Friday and Sunday) from Concarneau along the gorgeously scenic estuary of the River Odet. Boat trips also operate to the Îles de Glénan – a cluster of nine little islands about 20km south of Concarneau – starting from €26/14.

Vedettes de l'Odet (☎ 08 25 80 08 01; www.vedettes -odet.com in French) also runs boat trips to both

destinations – check with the tourist office or the company directly for seasonal sailing schedules and departure points.

Sleeping

Camping Moulin d'Aurore (☎ 02 98 50 53 08; www .moulinaurore.com in French; 49 rue de Trégunc; per person/car/site €5/1.50/5; Apr-Sep) Facilities at this camp site 600m southeast of the harbour and a mere 50m from the sea include a bar/ TV room and a laundry. Take buses 1 or 2 to Le Rouz stop from the tourist office or the ferry from Ville Close, then walk southeast along rue Mauduit Duplessis.

Auberge de Jeunesse Éthic Étapes (☎ 02 98 97 03 47; www.ajconcarneau.com; quai de la Croix; dm incl breakfast €13.60) Fall asleep listening to the

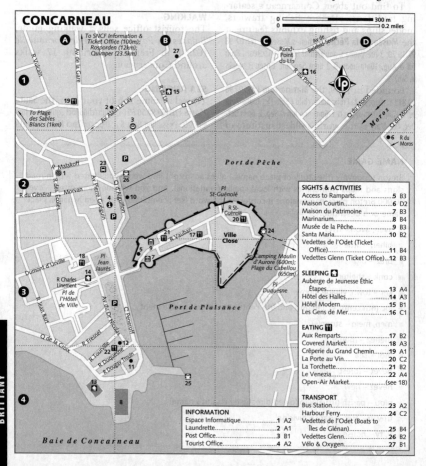

CONCARNEAU

0 ————— 300 m
0 ————— 0.2 miles

SIGHTS & ACTIVITIES	
Access to Ramparts	5 B3
Maison Courtin	6 D2
Maison du Patrimoine	7 B3
Marinarium	8 B4
Musée de la Pêche	9 B3
Santa Maria	10 B2
Vedettes de l'Odet (Ticket Office)	11 B4
Vedettes Glenn (Ticket Office)	12 B3

SLEEPING	
Auberge de Jeunesse Éthic Étapes	13 A4
Hôtel des Halles	14 A3
Hôtel Modern	15 B1
Les Gens de Mer	16 C1

EATING	
Aux Remparts	17 B2
Covered Market	18 A3
Crêperie du Grand Chemin	19 A1
La Porte au Vin	20 C2
La Torchette	21 B2
Le Venezia	22 A4
Open-Air Market	(see 18)

TRANSPORT	
Bus Station	23 A2
Harbour Ferry	24 C2
Vedettes de l'Odet (Boats to Îles de Glénan)	25 B4
Vedettes Glenn	26 B2
Vélo & Oxygen	27 B1

INFORMATION	
Espace Informatique	1 A2
Laundrette	2 A1
Post Office	3 B1
Tourist Office	4 A2

BRITTANY

waves at this welcoming waterfront hostel next to the Marinarium. Extras include a wraparound barbecue terrace, self-catering kitchen and pastries for breakfast.

Hôtel des Halles (☎ 02 98 97 11 41; www.hoteldes halles.com; place de l'Hôtel de Ville; s €42-43, d €49-71) A quiet, older-style hotel with 22 rooms renovated with marine themes and soft feather-filled quilts, the two-star Halles is only a few minutes' stroll from Ville Close. Breakfast (€8) includes home-made marmalade, and bread straight from the oven.

Also recommended:

Les Gens de Mer (☎ 02 98 97 04 01; www.lesgensdemer .fr; 9 rue du Port; d €42) A few minutes' stroll to the walled city (with views over it from some rooms).

Hôtel Modern (☎ 02 98 97 03 36; fax 02 98 97 89 06; 5 rue du Lin; d €55-60) A cosy, 1950s, put-your-feet-up kind of place with 12 rooms.

Eating

Cafés, pizzerias and *crêperies* line the waterfront, and there are more inside the walls of Ville Close.

Le Venezia (☎ 02 98 60 43 43; 4 rue Duquesne; menus €6.60-14.50; ☽ lunch & dinner, closed dinner Tue, Wed & lunch Sun) This cosy, Italian-inspired restaurant just off the main waterfront drag brims with diners, and no wonder – its pastas, fish and salads are all *bellissimo*. There are two tiny steps out the front, but otherwise excellent wheelchair access includes an internal ramp.

Crêperie du Grand Chemin (☎ 02 98 97 36 57; 17 av de la Gare; menus €8-13; ☽ lunch & dinner, closed Mon except Jul & Aug) This cheerful, cobalt-blue-painted place is great for authentic Breton *crêpes*, with seafood *crêpes* a speciality, but even the most basic *crêpe au beurre* (buttered *crêpe*) will melt in your mouth.

Aux Remparts (☎ 02 98 50 65 66; 31 rue Théophile Louarn; menus from €12, dishes from €3.70; ☽ Easter-Oct) Enjoy a very Breton lunch-time *menu* of fish soup, *moules et frites* and Breton prune cake, *far*. Aux Remparts also has an inventive range of savoury *crêpes* with fillings such as mushrooms in cream sauce.

La Porte au Vin (☎ 02 98 97 38 11; 9 place St-Guénolé; menus €11-25; ☽ lunch & dinner Apr-Nov) Highly recommended, this place in the centre of the walled city is a lovely spot in fine weather, with a pretty patio terrace shaded by a red awning. It has very good traditional cooking, specialising in (what else?) fish, seafood and *crêpes*.

SELF-CATERING

There's a **covered market** (☽ 9am-noon Tue-Sun) on place Jean Jaurès and a busy open-air market in the same square on Monday and Friday.

Enticing *biscuiteries* within Ville Close include **La Torchette** (☎ 02 98 60 46 87; 9 rue Vauban; ☽ 10.30am-6.30pm, to 11pm in Jul & Aug), with chocolate sculptures and Breton biscuits by the bucketful.

Getting There & Away

Caoudal (☎ 02 98 56 96 72) runs up to 8 buses daily between Quimper and Quimperlé, calling by Concarneau (€2 to or from Quimper).

Vélo & Oxygen (☎ 02 98 97 09 77; 65 av Alain Le Lay; ☽ Tue-Sat) rents out bikes for €10 per day.

A stubby **passenger ferry** (fare €0.80; ☽ 8am-11pm daily Jul-Aug, 8am-6.30pm or 8.30pm Mon-Sat, 9am-12.30pm & 2-6.30pm Sun Sep-Jun) links Ville Close with place Duquesne on the eastern side of the harbour.

Call ☎ 02 98 97 10 93 or ☎ 02 98 50 70 50 for a taxi.

MORBIHAN COAST

Spanning Brittany's southern coast, Morbihan is best known for its proliferation of megaliths, which are strewn throughout most of the *département*. In the crook of the coastline, the Golfe du Morbihan (Morbihan Gulf) is a haven of islands, oyster beds and birdlife.

LORIENT

pop 61,844

Like Brest, the port city of Lorient (An Oriant in Breton) was largely wiped out during WWII. Rapidly reconstructed in the following decades, today it sprawls along the western side of the Rade de Lorient, a natural harbour at the mouth of the River Scorff. Lorient's name is an abbreviation of Port de l'Orient, dating from the 17th century, when Compagnie des Indes (the French East India Company) ships docked here. It doesn't have a concentrated dining/entertainment hub, but the boat-filled port has its charms.

Orientation

The centre of town is near the canal-like Port de Plaisance, about 1km south of the train and bus stations. From these terminals, you can reach it by walking down cours de Chazelles and its continuation, rue Maréchal Foch, or by taking bus D, direction Carnel.

Information

There are two laundrettes on blvd Cosmao Dumanoir beside the bus station.

No Work Tech (☎ 02 97 84 72 09; 5 place de la Libération; per hr €4; ☽ 2pm-1am Mon, 10am-1am Tue-Sat, 3-11pm Sun) Internet access.

Post Office (9 quai des Indes)

Tourist Office (☎ 02 97 21 07 84; www.lorient -tourisme.fr in French; quai de Rohan; ☽ 9.30am-1pm & 2-7pm Mon-Sat, 10am-1pm Sun early Jul-Aug, 10am-noon & 2-6pm Mon-Fri, 10am-noon & 2-5pm Sat early Apr-early Jul & early-late Sep, 10am-noon & 2-5pm Mon-Fri, 10am-1pm Sat late Sep-early Apr)

Sights

Permanently moored at the Port de Plaisance, the research vessel **Thalassa** (☎ 02 97 35 13 00; quai de Rohan; adult/child €6.60/5.10; ☽ 9am-7pm Jul & Aug, 9am-12.30pm & 2-6pm Tue-Fri, 2-6pm Sat-Mon Sep-Jun) is now an oceanography museum with wheelchair access and hands-on exhibits.

In **Port Louis**, 5km south of Lorient, the magnificent 16th-century **citadel** (adult/child €5.50/free; ☽ 10am-6.30pm Wed-Mon Apr–mid-Sep, 2-6pm Wed-Mon mid-Sep–mid-Dec, Feb-Mar) has two museums. **Musée de la Compagnie des Indes** (☎ 02 97 82 19 13) traces the history of the French East India Company and its lucrative trade with India, China, Africa and the New World from 1660 to the end of the 18th century through its fascinating display of documents, maps and artefacts. Safety at sea and underwater archaeology are addressed at the **Musée National de la Marine** (☎ 02 97 82 56 72), with a treasure trove from the world's oceans.

To reach Port Louis and the museum, take the **Batobus** (☎ 02 97 21 28 29; one way €1.20) ferry, which runs between Lorient and Port Louis, leaving every half-hour between 6.45am and 8pm. It departs Lorient's Port de Pêche from Monday to Saturday and the Embarcadère de la Rade on Sunday.

Île de Groix, 8km long by 3km wide and about 14km offshore, was once a major tuna fishing port. With its excellent beaches and a 25km coastal footpath, it makes a great day trip (for ferries, see opposite).

Festivals & Events

Celtic communities from Ireland, Scotland, Wales, Cornwall, Isle of Man and Galicia in northwest Spain congregate with Bretons at the **Festival Interceltique** (☎ 02 97 21 24 29; www .festival-interceltique.com) over 10 days in early August.

Sleeping

Auberge de Jeunesse (☎ 02 97 37 11 65; lorient@fuaj .org; 41 rue Victor Schoelcher; dm €11.50) On the banks of the River Ter, 4km from town, Lorient's HI-affiliated hostel has a lively bar and Ping Pong tables. Skip the metallic-tasting coffee at breakfast (€3.60), though. From the bus stop on cours de Chazelles, outside the bus station, take bus B2.

Rex Hôtel (☎ 02 97 64 25 60; www.rex-hotel-lorient .com; 28 cours de Chazelles; d from €43) Rooms positively gleam at this tautly run ship – which it is almost, literally: the reception desk has the shape of a boat's prow, polished woodwork lines the public areas, each of the 23 rooms has a shining bathroom, and a tape of waves breaking and seagulls mewing plays in the small lounge. Free parking is situated opposite.

Hôtel Victor Hugo (☎ 02 97 21 16 24; www.hotel victorhugo-lorient.com in French; 36 rue Lazare Carnot; d €50-70) A handy 200m from the Gare Maritime's ferries to Île de Groix, this brightly lit, soundproofed hotel has 28 warm, welcoming rooms with cheerful striped fabrics, satellite TVs and telephones, and free wi-fi in many rooms. If you don't mind taking a shower outside the room, rates drop as low as €30. On site parking's available.

Eating

Tavarn Ar Roue Morvan (☎ 02 97 21 61 57; 1 place Polig-Montjarret; mains from €6; ☽ lunch & dinner Mon-Sat) Attracting an artistic, cultural crowd, and *the* place to hang out during the Festival Interceltique (at which time, like most places in Lorient, it's open daily), this traditional Breton tavern turns out hearty Breton cuisine, and often has live music throughout the year. A *traiteur* service is also available.

Fleur de Blé Noir (☎ 02 97 64 51 54; 3 place Polig-Montjarret; menus from €8; ☽ lunch & dinner Tue-Sat) Vegetarians have plenty of options at this classic *crêperie*, which also serves up brimming salads and regional dishes. There's a sunny outdoor terrace when the weather's fine; if you're heading off for a picnic, you can order your meal to take away.

Le Jardin Gourmand (☎ 02 97 64 17 24; 46 rue Jules-Simon; lunch menus €21-36, dinner menus €18-48; Tue-Sat) The minimalist décor and serene garden setting at this highly regarded restaurant, a couple of blocks north of the train station, contrasts with the rich, regional cuisine inspired by what's best in the market each morning.

SELF-CATERING

Stock up at the covered market **Halles de Merville** (7.30am-1pm Tue-Sun).

Getting There & Away
BOAT

The **Société Morbihannaise de Navigation** (SMN; ☎ 08 20 05 60 00; www.smn-navigation.fr in French) operates car ferries between the Gare Maritime and Île de Groix (adult/child return €24.62/12.68, 45 minutes, seven to eight daily). From mid-July to the end of August, SMN runs a passenger-only ferry to Sauzon on Belle Île (adult/child return €28.52/14.30 one hour, once daily).

BUS

The **bus station** (☎ 02 97 21 28 29) is linked to the train station by a footbridge. Destinations include Josselin (€11.80).

TRAIN

There are several trains a day from Lorient to Quimper (€10, 40 minutes), Vannes

(€8.20, 40 minutes) and Rennes (€22.30), plus TGVs to Paris (Gare Montparnasse; from €63.70, 3¾ hours).

Getting Around

City buses (☎ 02 97 21 28 29; single/day ticket €1.20/3.50) run until around 8pm.

For a taxi, call ☎ 02 97 21 29 29.

CARNAC
pop 4600

Stand aside, Stonehenge – Carnac (Garnag in Breton) has the world's greatest concentration of megalithic sites. Predating Stonehenge by around 100 years, there are over 3000 of these upright stones, most around thigh-high, erected between 5000 BC and 3500 BC.

About 32km west of Vannes, Carnac has two parts: the old stone village, Carnac-Ville, and, 1.5km south, bordered by the 2km-long sandy beach, Carnac-Plage, a seaside resort. Carnac's megaliths (p343) stretch 13km north from Carnac-Ville and east as far as the village of Locmariaquer.

Information

Main Tourist Office (☎ 02 97 52 13 52; www.ot-carnac .fr; 74 av des Druides, Carnac-Plage; 9am-7pm Mon-Sat & 3-7pm Sun Jul & Aug, 9am-noon or 12.30pm & 2-6pm Mon-Sat Sep-Jun) Hours can vary.

Post Office (av de la Poste, Carnac-Ville)

Tourist Office Annexe (☎ 02 97 52 13 52; place de l'Église, Carnac-Ville; 9.30am-12.30pm & 2-6pm Apr-Sep & school holidays)

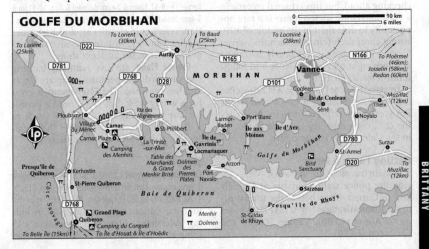

GOLFE DU MORBIHAN

Sleeping & Eating

Camping des Menhirs (☎ 02 97 52 94 67; www.les menhirs.com; 7 allée St-Michel, Carnac-Plage; camp site €29; ☺ May-late Sep; ☻) Carnac and its surrounds have over 15 camp sites including this luxury complex 300m north of the beach, complete with pool, sauna (€4) and cocktail bar.

Auberge Le Ratelier (☎ 02 97 52 05 04; www.le -ratelier.com; 4 Chemin du Douet, Carnac-Ville; d €43-55; ☺ Feb-Dec) This former farmhouse, now an eight-room hotel with low ceilings and eaturing traditional timber furnishings – is in a quiet street one block southwest of place de l'Église. Rooms with showers only start from €38. Feast on gourmet fare at its whitewashed, wood-beamed restaurant with menus from €17 to €40. Open for lunch and dinner May to September, closed Wednesday October to December and from February to April, specialising in seafood and particularly lobster.

Hôtel Le Bateau Ivre (☎ 02 97 52 19 55; fax 02 97 52 84 94; 71 blvd de la Plage, Carnac-Plage; s €64-114, d €83-160; ☻) Set in landscaped gardens with a small heated swimming pool, the Bateau Ivre is one of Carnac's more up-market hotels. All rooms have a balcony and overlook the beach, lined with jaunty yellow-and-white bathing tents in summer. Prices skyrocket in peak season. Lock-up parking is an extra €9; wheelchair access is good.

Crêperie au Pressoir (☎ 02 97 52 01 86; village du Ménec; galettes €3-7.50; ☺ lunch & dinner Easter-Aug) Opening hours fluctuate so we recommend checking ahead, but this artisanal *crêperie* in a traditional long Breton house is a rare opportunity to dine right in the middle of a 70-strong chromlech (circle of menhirs). From Carnac-Ville, take rue St-Cornély northwest and turn right on rue du Ménec and follow it north for about 1km.

Crêperie St-George (☎ 02 97 52 18 34; 8 allée du Parc, Carnac-Plage; menus from €9; ☺ lunch & dinner Apr-Sep) For great-value *crêpes* close to the beach, try the chic, contemporary Crêperie St-George in the Galeries St-George centre.

Getting There & Away

The main bus stops are in Carnac-Ville outside the police station on rue St-Cornély and in Carnac-Plage beside the tourist office. **Cariane Atlantique** (☎ 02 97 47 29 64) buses go to Auray (€3.80), Vannes (€6.30) and Quiberon (€3.80).

The nearest year-round **train** station is in Auray, 12km to the northeast. SNCF has an office in the Carnac-Plage tourist office.

Hire bikes for around €9/17 per half-day/ full day from **Lorcy** (☎ 02 97 52 09 73; 6 rue de Courdiec, Carnac-Ville) and **Le Randonneur** (☎ 02 97 52 02 55; 20 av des Druides, Carnac-Plage).

For a taxi, call ☎ 02 97 52 75 75.

QUIBERON
pop 5000

Quiberon (Kiberen in Breton) sits at the southern tip of a sliver-thin, 14km-long peninsula flanked on the western side by the rocky, windswept Côte Sauvage ('wild coast'). The town fans out around the port where ferries depart for Belle Île, and is wildly popular in summer.

Orientation & Information

The D768 leads along the peninsula and into Quiberon, ending at the seasonally operating train station. From here rue de Verdun winds down to the sheltered bay of Port-Maria, pincered by the town's main beach, La Grande Plage, to its east and the ferry harbour to the west.

The **tourist office** (☎ 08 25 13 56 00; www .quiberon.com; 14 rue de Verdun; ☺ 9am-1.30pm & 2-7pm Mon-Fri, to 5pm Sat, 10am-1pm & 2-5pm Sun Jul & Aug, 9am-12.30pm & 2-6pm Mon-Sat Sep-Jun) is between the train station and La Grande Plage.

Sights & Activities

Conserverie La Belle-Iloise (☎ 02 97 50 08 77; rue de Kerné; ☺ 9-11.30am & 2-6pm daily Jul & Aug, 10-11am & 3-4pm Mon-Fri Sep-Jun), north of the train station, offers guided visits around its former sardine cannery, with inexpensive sardines available from the adjacent shop.

Grande Plage attracts families; bathing spots towards the peninsula's tip are larger and less crowded. The **Côte Sauvage** is great for a windy walk, but you'll need a permit for any nautically based activity (such as a diving certificate) to swim in the rough seas, or risk a fine (and your safety).

Sleeping

Camping du Conguel (☎ 02 97 50 19 11; www.camping duconguel.com; blvd de la Teignouse; camp sites €12.20-41.80, electricity €3.55; ☺ Apr-Oct; ☻) This splashy four-star option, with an aqua park including waterslides, is one of the peninsula's 15 camp sites. Just 2km east of the town centre, it's beside Plage du Conguel, with cabins also available. Rates soar in July and August.

Auberge de Jeunesse – Les Filets Bleus (☎ 02 97 50 15 54; 45 rue du Roch Priol; dm €9.70; ☷ Apr-Sep) Quiberon's HI-affiliated hostel is in a quiet part of town 800m east of the train station and 500m from the beach. There's limited camping in the grounds.

Hôtel L'Océan (☎ 02 97 50 07 58; hotel-de-locean .com in French; 7 quai de l'Océan; d €37-60; ☷ Easter-Sep) Overlooking the harbour, you can't miss this huge white house with multicoloured shutters. Inside are 37 rooms. The cheapest include showers only; rooms at the other end of the price scale get you a fabulous harbour view.

MORBIHAN'S MIGHTY MEGALITHS

Two perplexing questions arise from the Morbihan region's Neolithic menhirs, dolmens, cromlechs, tumuli and cairns.

Just *how* did the original constructors hew, then haul, these blocks (the heaviest weighs 300 tonnes), millennia before the wheel and the mechanical engine reached Brittany?

And why? Theories and hypotheses abound. A phallic fertility cult? Sunworship? Representation of a long-forgotten divinity? For the moment, the vague yet common consensus is that they served some kind of sacred, religious purpose – the same spiritual impulsion behind so many monuments built by humankind.

The best way to appreciate the stones' sheer numbers is to walk or bike between the Le Ménec and Kerlescan groups, with menhirs almost continuously in view. Between June and September seven buses a day run between the two sites and both Carnac-Ville and Carnac-Plage.

Because of severe erosion the sites are fenced off to allow the vegetation to regenerate. However, between 10am and 5pm from October to May you can wander freely through parts (check site billboards or ask at the Maison des Mégalithes for updates). You can see them on a one- to 1½-hour **guided visit** (€4), regularly in French, usually twice in English on even-numbered afternoons and twice in German on odd-numbered afternoons, in July and August. Sign up for guided visits at the **Maison des Mégalithes** (☎ 02 97 52 89 99; rte des Alignements; admission free; ☷ 9am-8pm Jul & Aug, to 5.15pm Sep-Apr, to 7pm May-Jun), which also has a rolling video, topographic models and views of the menhirs from its rooftop terrace.

Opposite the Maison des Mégalithes, the largest menhir field – with no less than 1099 stones – is the **Alignements du Ménec**, 1km north of Carnac-Ville; the eastern section is accessible in winter. From here, the D196 heads northeast for about 1.5km to the equally impressive **Alignements de Kermario**. Climb the stone observation tower midway along the site to see the alignment from above. Another 500m further on are the **Alignements de Kerlescan**, a smaller grouping also accessible in winter.

Tumulus St-Michel, at the end of rue du Tumulus and 400m northeast of the Carnac-Ville tourist office, dates back to at least 5000 BC, with sweeping views.

Between Kermario and Kerlescan and 500m to the south of the D196, deposit your fee in an honour box at **Tumulus de Kercado** (admission €1; ☷ year-round). Dating from 3800 BC and the burial site of a Neolithic chieftain, during the French Revolution it was used as a hiding place for Breton royalists. From the parking area 300m further along the D196, a 15-minute walk brings you to the **Géant du Manio**, the highest menhir in the complex, and the **Quadrilatère**, a group of mini-menhirs, close-set in a rectangle.

Near Locmariaquer, 13km southeast of Carnac-Ville, the major monuments are the **Table des Marchands**, a 30m-long dolmen, and the **Grand Menhir Brisé** (adult/student/child €5/3.50/ free; ☷ 9am-8pm Jul & Aug, 9am-7pm May-Jun, 9.30am-12.30pm & 2-5.15pm Sep-Apr), the region's largest menhir, which once stood 20m high but now lies broken on its side. Both are off the D781, just before the village.

Just south of Locmariaquer by the sea is the **Dolmen des Pierres Plates**, a 24m-long chamber with still-visible engravings.

For some background, the **Musée de Préhistoire** (☎ 02 97 52 22 04; 10 place de la Chapelle, Carnac-Ville; adult/child €5/2.50; ☷ 10am-12.30pm & 1.30-6pm or 7pm Thu-Tue & Wed morning Oct-May) chronicles life in and around Carnac from the Palaeolithic and Neolithic eras to the Middle Ages.

BRITTANY

Hôtel Le Roc'h Priol (☎ 02 97 50 04 86; www.hotel rochpriol.fr; 1-5 rue des Sirènes; d €48.80-89; ☻ mid-Feb–mid-Nov) In a quiet corner of town, 800m east of the centre, the 45 rooms at the Roc'h Priol aren't out of the ordinary (think floral bedspreads and '80s-style furniture), but they're bright and spacious, and there's a salon/bar with leather lounges to sink into. Private on-site parking's available.

Eating & Drinking

La Closerie de St-Clément (☎ 02 97 50 40 00; 36 rue de St-Clément; galettes €4-8.20; ☻ lunch & dinner daily Jul & Aug, closed Wed & dinner Sun Sep-Jun) Taken over by new owners but still turning out classic *crêpes*, this rustic place with gnarled timber beams and chunky wooden furniture has a peaceful, tree-shaded garden terrace to keep diners cool in summer, and a cosy fireplace to warm your cockles in winter.

L'Embarcadère (☎ 02 97 50 17 84; 2 quai de l'Océan; menus from €13.50, mains €9.50-17.50; ☻ 7am-9pm Mon-Sat, 10am-9pm Sun) Of the *crêperies* along the quayfront, try L'Embarcadère, which also serves whopping bowls of *moules et frites* (the cheapest in town), and mixes a great kir.

Bar de la Marine (☎ 02 97 50 09 81; 20 quai de l'Océan; menus €15; ☻ 6am-8pm Mon-Sat winter, 6am-10pm Mon-Sat summer) Looking out on the quay, Bar de la Marine's dining room has an enticing selection on its blackboard *menu*, but be prepared for a long wait before ordering and a longer wait still for your meal to arrive. While you are waiting, perch at the elongated timber bar for a coffee or apéritif.

La Criée (☎ 02 97 30 53 09; 11 quai de l'Océan; mains €15-18; ☻ lunch & dinner Tue-Sun Feb-Dec) Within the former fish auction house (hence the name), and an easy walk from the ferry terminal, this splendid seaside restaurant keeps with its traditions by laying out its exceptional seafood on a table for you to take your pick.

Getting There & Away

BOAT

For ferries between Quiberon and Belle-Île, see opposite.

BUS

Quiberon is connected by **Cariane Atlantique** (☎ 02 97 47 29 64) buses with Carnac (€3.80), Auray (€6.30) and Vannes (€9.10, 1¾ hours). Buses stop at the train station and place Hoche near the tourist office and beach.

CAR & MOTORCYCLE

High-summer traffic is hellish – consider leaving your vehicle at the 1200-place Sémaphore car park (€4 for up to four hours, €12 for 24 hours), 1.5km north of the beach, and walking or taking the free shuttle bus into town.

TRAIN

In July and August only, a shuttle train called the 'Tire-Bouchon' (corkscrew) runs several times a day between Auray and Quiberon (€3, 40 minutes). From September to June a SNCF bus service links Quiberon and Auray train stations (€6.30, 50 minutes) at least seven times a day.

Getting Around

Cycles Loisirs (☎ 02 97 50 31 73; 3 rue Victor Golvan), 200m north of the tourist office, charges €8/14 a day to rent a touring/mountain bike. **Cyclomar** (☎ 02 97 50 26 00; 47 place Hoche), around 200m south of the tourist office, rents out bikes and scooters (touring/mountain bikes €9.50/11 per day, scooter including helmet €38 per day plus insurance of €6.80). It also runs an operation from the train station during July and August.

To order a **taxi** ring ☎ 02 97 50 11 11.

BELLE ÎLE

pop 5200

Accessed by ferries from Quiberon, the population of Belle-Île-en-Mer swells tenfold in summer thanks to its namesake beauty. But, as Brittany's largest island (at 20km by 9km), there's room to escape the crowds.

Information

Turn left as you leave the ferry in Le Palais to reach the main **tourist office** (☎ 02 97 31 81 93; www.belle-ile.com; quai Bonnelle; ☻ 8.45am-7.30pm Mon-Sat & 8.45am-1pm Sun Jul & Aug, 9am-12.30pm & 2-6pm Mon-Sat, 10am-12.30pm Sun Sep-Jun).

There's a summer-only **information kiosk** (☎ 02 97 31 69 49; ☻ Easter-Sep) on the quay in Sauzon.

Sights & Activities

The dramatic citadel, strengthened by Vauban in 1682, dominates the little Le Palais port. The citadel houses the **Musée Historique** (☎ 02 97 31 84 17; adult/child €6.10/3.05; ☻ 9.30am-6pm May-Oct, 9.30am-noon & 2-5pm Nov-Apr), as well as a lavish hotel with doubles for €115-450.

Belle Île's fretted southwestern coast has spectacular rock formations and caves including **Grotte de l'Apothicairerie** (Cave of the Apothecary's Shop), where waves roll in from two sides.

Plage de Donnant has awesome surf, though swimming here is dangerous. Sheltered **Port Kérel**, to the southwest, is better for children, as is the 2km-long **Plage des Grands Sables**, the biggest and busiest strand, spanning the calm waters of the island's eastern side.

The tourist office sells walking and cycling guides. The ultimate hike is a circuit of the 95km **coastal footpath** that follows the island's coastline.

Sleeping & Eating

About 10 camp sites are pitched around Belle Île; most open from April or May to September or October.

Auberge de Jeunesse Haute Boulogne (☎ 02 97 31 81 33; www.fuaj.org; Le Palais; dm €11.50; ⏰ closed Oct & Christmas) This modern 96-bed HI-affiliated hostel with a self-catering kitchen is to the north of the citadel.

Hôtel Vauban (☎ 02 97 31 45 42; www.hotelvauban.com in French; 1 rue des Remparts, Le Palais; d €62-74; ⏰ mid-Feb–Oct) Not to be confused with the swank citadel hotel, this comfy place is perched high on the coastal path, with views of the ferry landing below from many of its 16 spacious rooms. The hotel rents out mountain bikes for €13 per day, and there's good wheelchair access and a guest-only restaurant serving seafood from April to September.

Crêperies and pizzerias are scattered across the island; many of the higher-end hotels have good restaurants.

Le Goéland (☎ 02 97 31 81 26; 3 quai Vauban, Le Palais; mains around €15; ⏰ Thu-Mon Mar–mid-Nov) The Goéland (seagull) in Le Palais is reliably top-notch, whether you choose the lively bar-brasserie on the ground floor or the more formal restaurant upstairs. The menu concentrates on seafood, as well as tender lamb, fattened on the island, and salads.

Getting There & Away

FROM QUIBERON

The shortest crossing to Belle Île is from Quiberon. **SMN** (☎ 08 20 05 60 00; www.smn-navigation.fr in French) operates car/passenger ferries (45 minutes, year-round) and fast passenger ferries (20 minutes, July and August) to Le Palais, and fast passenger ferries to Sauzon (April to mid-September). An adult/child return passenger fare is €24.62/14.86; transporting a small car costs a hefty €116.28 return, plus passenger fares. There are five crossings a day (up to 13 in July and August).

FROM VANNES

Navix (☎ 02 97 46 60 29; www.navix.fr with English sections) operates ferries (oneway adult/child €19/13) between May and mid-September.

FROM LORIENT

From mid-July to the end of August, SMN runs a fast passenger-only ferry (adult/child oneway from €15.60/11.20, one hour, once daily) from Lorient to Sauzon.

Getting Around

Lots of places in Le Palais rent out bicycles/motor scooters for around €12/35 a day.

Seasonal buses run by **Taol Mor** (☎ 02 97 31 32 32) crisscross the island; single tickets cost €2.60/1.70 per adult/child.

Car rental rates on the island start at about €65 for 24 hours.

VANNES

pop 58,000

Vannes (Gwened in Breton) has a quirky, humorous creative bent. Artworks, sculptures and plays-on-words are scattered throughout this half-timbered, cobbled medieval city.

The city's integral role in Brittany's history stretches back to pre-Roman times, when it was the capital of the Veneti, a Gaulish tribe of sailors who fortified the town. Conquered by Julius Caesar in the 1st century BC, it became the centre of Breton unity in the 9th century under Breton hero Nominoë, and in 1532 the union of the duchy of Brittany with France was proclaimed here. These days it's a spirited hub for students attending the city's Université de Bretagne-Sud.

Orientation

Vannes' vibrant little marina sits at the end of a canal-like waterway about 1.5km from the gulf's entrance. Roughly 3.5km south of town, Île de Conleau, also known as Presqu'île de Conleau (Conleau Peninsula) is linked to the mainland by a causeway.

Information

Cyber Athalie (☎ 02 97 47 59 02; 4 rue Porte Poterne; per hr €3.50; 9.30am-12.30pm & 2-8pm Mon-Sat) Internet access.

Laverie Automatique (5 av Victor Hugo; 7am-9pm) For washing those clothes.

Post Office (2 place de la République)

Tourist Office (☎ 02 97 47 24 34; www.tourisme-vannes.com in French; 1 rue Thiers; 9am-7pm daily Jul & Aug, 9.30am-12.30pm & 2-6pm Mon-Sat Sep-Jun) Occupies a lovely 17th-century half-timbered house.

Sights

Surrounding Vannes' walled **old town** is a flower-filled moat. Inside, you can weave through the web of narrow alleys ranged around the 13th-century Gothic **Cathédrale St-Pierre**. Tucked away behind rue des Vierges, stairs lead to the accessible section of the **ramparts**. From here, you can see the black-roofed **Vieux Lavoirs** (Old Laundry Houses), though you'll get a better view from the **Tour du Connétable** or **Porte Poterne** to the south.

Since the 14th century, the building now housing the **Musée de la Cohue** (☎ 02 97 01 63 00; 9-15 place St-Pierre; adult/child €4/2.50; 10am-6pm Jul-Sep, 1.30-6pm Oct-Jun) has variously been a produce market, law court and the seat of the Breton parliament. Today it's a museum of fine arts, displaying mostly 19th-century paintings, sculptures and engravings.

In the summer months you can survey Roman and Greek artefacts and study up on megaliths at the **Musée d'Histoire et d'Archéologie** (☎ 02 97 01 63 00; 2 rue Noë; adult/child €3.50/2.50; 10am-6pm mid-Jun–Sep), in the 15th-century Château Gaillard.

Tours

Compagnie des Îles (☎ 08 25 13 41 00) Offers seasonal gulf cruises.

Navix (☎ 02 97 46 60 29; www.navix.fr with English sections) From April to September, Navix runs a range of cruises on the Golfe du Morbihan, departing from the Gare Maritime, 2km south of the tourist office. Adult fares range from €14/27 per two hours/half-day. Its 'Grand Tour du Golfe' (adult/child €22/14, 3¼ hours) includes optional visits to the two largest of its 40 inhabited islands, Île aux Moines and Île d'Arz (supplementary €5/4).

Festivals & Events

Festival de Jazz A four-day festival in early August.

Fêtes d'Arvor This is a three-day celebration of Breton culture in mid-August that includes parades, concerts and numerous *festoú-noz* (night festivals).

Les Musicales du Golfe Classical music concerts take place from mid-July to early August.

Sleeping

Relais du Golfe (☎ 02 97 47 14 74; fax 02 97 42 52 48; 10 place du Général de Gaulle; d €55, d/tw with shared bathroom €33/42) Its name suggests something more flash than these rooms (wedged above a café/bar) actually are. The cheapest have neither a shower nor toilet, but it's the most central budget option, and staff are welcoming.

Hôtel Le Bretagne (☎ 02 97 47 20 21; hotel.lebretagne@free.fr; 34-36 rue du Mené; d €40-42) Just outside the old city walls yet still conveniently central, Le Bretagne has a dozen decent, comfortable double rooms above its poky staircase. Budget travellers have long cottoned onto to it, so booking ahead's a good idea any time of year.

Hôtel Le Richemont (☎ 02 97 47 17 24; www.hotel-richemont-vannes.com; 26 place de la Gare; s/d €47.50/52, breakfast €6.50) If the heavy wood beams and arched stone work of the mock-medieval breakfast room aren't your cup of tea, you can pay an extra euro (€7.50) and have a laden tray brought to your very comfortable, soundproofed and much more contemporary room. Private parking's available.

Hôtel Villa Kerasy (☎ 02 97 68 36 83; www.villakerasy.com; 20 av Favrel-et-Lincy; d €118-165; closed mid-Nov–Dec) Each of this personal hotel's 12 elegant rooms is themed on historic ports of the East India trading route. In summer enjoy the tranquil garden, designed by a Japanese landscape artist. In winter relax in the cosy tearoom, where you can sip Earl Grey from fine Limoges china by the log fire.

Eating & Drinking

Vannes has a vast array of cuisine – from Afghani to Vietnamese – as well as Breton specialities. Rue des Halles has a number of tempting eateries; classical brasseries arc around the port.

Délice Café (☎ 02 97 54 23 31; 7 place des Lices; dishes €4.70-8.50; 8am-8pm Mon-Sat) Fronted by a timber decked terrace (warmed by heat lamps in winter), and flowing to a contemporary dining room of gilded mirrors and red velveteen banquettes, this smart place in the centre of the old town has outstanding salads (try the namesake house version with rice, corn, tuna and tomato), as well as hot dishes like *croques-monsieur* (grilled ham and cheese sandwiches) and mussels.

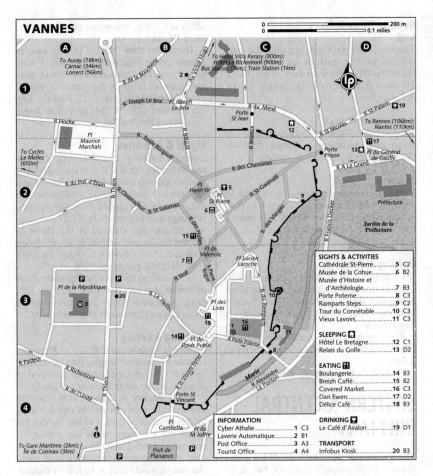

VANNES

SIGHTS & ACTIVITIES
Cathédrale St-Pierre............5 C2
Musée de la Cohue.............6 B2
Musée d'Histoire et
  d'Archéologie...................7 B3
Porte Poterne.....................8 C3
Ramparts Steps...................9 C2
Tour du Connétable............10 C3
Vieux Lavoirs....................11 C3

SLEEPING
Hôtel Le Bretagne..............12 C1
Relais du Golfe 13 D2

EATING
Boulangerie......................14 B3
Breizh Caffé......................15 B2
Covered Market.................16 C3
Dan Ewen........................17 D2
Délice Café.......................18 B3

DRINKING
Le Café d'Avalon 19 D1

TRANSPORT
Infobus Kiosk....................20 B3

INFORMATION
Cyber Athalie....................1 C3
Laverie Automatique...........2 B1
Post Office........................3 A3
Tourist Office....................4 A4

Dan Ewen (☎ 02 97 42 44 34; 3 place du Général de Gaulle; lunch menus €7.50, dinner menus €8.50-15; ☺ lunch & dinner Mon-Sat) A near-life-size statue of a sweet, smiling, wrinkled Breton lady bearing a tray greets you at the entrance of this stone and dark-wood *crêperie*. Tasty *crêpe* flavours offered by Dan Ewen include frangipani, and there's a lavish range of flambéed options topped with chantilly cream.

Breizh Caffé (☎ 02 97 54 37 41; 13 rue des Halles; lunch/dinner menus €12.90/18; ☺ lunch & dinner summer, hrs vary winter) In the heart of the old town, the 'Breton café' is renowned for Breton fare that extends well beyond *crêpes*, such as chicken with cider vinegar and honey, and cod cooked to an age-old recipe. In sum-

mer, dining's prime on the outdoor terrace; check ahead for off-season hours.

Le Café d'Avalon (☎ 02 97 47 85 44; 20 rue St-Patern; ☺ 6pm-2am Mon-Sat) A low-lit local bar with Breton and Belgian beers on tap and free nibbles.

SELF-CATERING

On Wednesday and Saturday mornings, a produce market takes over place du Poids Public and the surrounding area. Vannes' **covered market** (Les Halles; ☺ 8.30am-1.30pm) is adjacent.

Three-tiered displays of cakes, tarts and Breton pastries spin at the place du Poids Public's **boulangerie** (☎ 02 97 47 33 55; 11 place du Poids Public; ☺ 7am-8pm Mon-Sat).

BRITTANY

Getting There & Away

BUS

The small bus station is opposite the train station. Services include **Cariane Atlantique** (☎ 0297 47 29 64), which runs to Carnac (€6.30, 1¼ hours) and on to Quiberon (€9.10, ¾ hours).

CAR & MOTORCYCLE

Europcar (☎ 02 97 42 43 43) and **ADA** (☎ 02 97 42 59 10) are in the train station. **Budget** (☎ 02 97 54 25 22) is opposite, in the bus station.

TRAIN

There are frequent trains westwards to Auray (€3.40, 11 minutes), Lorient (€8.20, 40 minutes) and Quimper (€16.30, 1½ hours). Eastbound trains serve Rennes (€17.10, 1½ hours) and Nantes (€18, 1½ hours).

Getting Around

TPV (☎ 02 97 01 22 23; tickets €1.20) runs eight city bus lines till 8.15pm. Its Infobus kiosk is on place de la République. Buses 3 and 4 link the train station with place de la République.

You can hire bikes from **Cycles Le Mellec** (☎ 02 97 63 00 24; 51ter rue Jean Gougaud) for €12 a day.

To order a **taxi**, ring ☎ 02 97 54 34 34.

EASTERN & CENTRAL BRITTANY

The one-time frontier between Brittany and France, fertile eastern Brittany has at its epicentre the region's lively capital, Rennes. Central Brittany conceals the enchanting Forêt de Paimpont, sprinkled with villages.

JOSSELIN

pop 2400

In the shadow of a 14th-century castle that was the seat of the counts of Rohan for centuries, the storybook village of Josselin lies on the banks of the River Oust 43km northeast of Vannes. Today, visitors in their thousands continue to fall under its spell.

Orientation & Information

A beautiful square of 16th-century half-timbered houses, place Notre Dame, is the little village's heart. The castle and tourist

office are south, below rue des Trente, the main through street.

The **tourist office** (☎ 02 97 22 36 43; www.pays dejosselin-tourisme.com; place de la Congrégation; ⏰ 10am-6pm daily Jul & Aug, 10am-noon & 2-6pm Mon-Fri, 10am-noon Sat Sep-Jun) is beside the castle entrance.

In the village centre you'll find the **English Bookshop** (☎ 02 97 75 62 55; 4 rue des Vierges; ⏰ 10.30am-4.30pm Wed-Sat).

Sights & Activities

Guarded by three round towers, the **Château de Josselin** (☎ 02 97 22 36 45; adult/child €7/4.70; ⏰ 10am-6pm daily mid-Jul–Aug, 2-6pm Jun–mid-Jul & Sep, 2-6pm Sat & Sun Apr-May & Oct, closed Nov-Mar) can only be visited by guided tour; one English-language tour departs daily in July and August. Within the chateau is the **Musée de Poupées** (Doll Museum; adult/child €6.20/4.40; ⏰ same as chateau). A combination ticket for both costs €11.50/8 per adult/child.

Older still, parts of the **Basilique Notre Dame du Roncier** (place Notre Dame) date from the 12th century; superb 15th- and 16th-century stained glass illuminates the south aisle.

Sleeping & Eating

Camping du Bas de la Lande (☎ 02 97 22 22 20; camping basdelalande@wanadoo.fr; Guégon; camp site €8.70-11; ⏰ Apr-Oct) This peaceful spot is 2km west of Josselin, on the south bank of the Oust.

Hôtel-Restaurant du Château (☎ 02 97 22 20 11; www.hotel-chateau.com in French; 1 rue Général de Gaulle; d €59-64; ⏰ closed 3 wks Feb, 1 wk Nov, 1 wk Dec) It's worth the few extra euros for a magnificent view of the chateau looming above this cosy hotel. Cheaper rooms without in-room showers or toilets start at €33. Its restaurant menus range from €15 to €50 and regional speciailties include a moist caramel cake.

Restaurant Café France (☎ 02 97 70 61 93; 6 place Notre Dame; menus €8.90-13.90; ⏰ lunch & dinner Apr-Sep) does good omelettes, while just down the hill, **Crêperie-Grill Sarrazine** (☎ 02 97 22 37 80; 51 rue Glatinier; menus from €9.50, galettes & salads from €6; ⏰ lunch & dinner) packs in the locals.

Getting There & Away

CTM (☎ 02 97 01 22 01) bus destinations include Rennes (€11.80, 1½ hours).

FORÊT DE PAIMPONT

The Paimpont Forest (also known as Brocéliande) is about 40km southwest of Rennes, and is legendary as the place where

King Arthur received the Excalibur sword (forget that these stories are thought to have been brought to Brittany by Celtic settlers and hence probably took place offshore – it's a magical setting all the same).

The best base for exploring the forest is the lakeside village of **Paimpont**. Its **tourist office** (☎ 02 99 07 84 23; ☽ 10am-noon & 2-6pm daily Jun-Sep, Tue-Sun Oct-May) is beside the 12th-century **Église Abbatiale** (Abbey Church). A free walking/cycling map covering 50km of trails is available, or you can buy the more detailed walking guide *Brocéliande à Pied* (in French; €14), featuring 30 forest paths. In July and August the tourist office leads **guided tours** (half/full day €10/12) of the forest.

Sleeping & Eating

Camping Municipal de Paimpont (☎ 02 99 07 89 16; rue du Chevalier Lancelot du Lac; per person/tent/car €2.65/2.35/1.10; ☽ May-Sep) This small camp site has a peaceful setting by the lake.

Auberge de Jeunesse (☎ 02 97 22 76 75; www.fuaj .org; dm €9.70; ☽ Jun–mid-Sep) This 20-bed hostel occupies a lovely old stone farmhouse at Choucan-en-Brocéliande, 5km north of Paimpont.

Hôtel Le Relais de Brocéliande (☎ 02 99 07 84 94; www.le-relais-de-broceliande.fr; 5 rue du Forges, Paimpont; d €50-70) Rustic rooms at this 24-room hotel come with canopy-draped beds, TVs and telephones. On-site, there's an excellent restaurant with menus from €17to €36 specialising in local river-caught fish.

Crêperie au Temps des Moines (☎ 02 99 07 89 63; 16 av Chevalier Ponthus; crêpes €1.50-5; ☽ lunch & dinner Wed-Mon Sep-Jun, daily Jul & Aug) For a cheaper bite, try this *crêperie* in a granite house overlooking the lake.

Getting There & Around

TIV (☎ 02 99 30 87 80) runs buses to/from Rennes (€3, one hour).

You can rent mountain bikes (per half-/full day €8/12) from **Bar Le Brécilien** (☎ 02 99 07 81 13; rue Général de Gaulle), beside Paimpont's tourist office.

RENNES

pop 203,500

Brittany's capital is a hive of activity thanks to its buzzing university student population. A crossroads since Roman times, the city sits at the junction of highways linking northwestern France's major cities. Its con-temporary and medieval quarters are woven with waterways best explored by renting a boat. At night, Rennes has no end of lively places to pop in for a pint.

Orientation

The city centre is divided by La Vilaine, a river channelled into a cement-lined canal that disappears underground just before the central square, place de la République. The northern area includes the cobbled, pedes-trianised old city, while the south is garishly modern. The metro runs north through the city from the main train station.

Information

Comédie des Langues (☎ 02 99 36 72 95; 25 rue St-Malo; ☽ 9am-7pm Mon-Sat) Stocks English-language books.

E Mega (☎ 02 99 78 31 90; 15 quai Lamennais; per hr €2; ☽ 10am-midnight Mon-Sat, 2pm-11pm Sun) Central internet café.

Laundrette (23 rue de Penhoët; ☽ 7am- 8pm)

NeuroGame (☎ 02 99 65 53 85; www.neurogame.com; 2 rue Dinan; per 20min €1; ☽ 10am-1am Mon-Thu, 10am-3am Fri, noon-3am Sat, 2-10pm Sun) Internet access.

Post Office (place de la République)

Tourist Office (☎ 02 99 67 11 11; www.tourisme -rennes.com; 11 rue St-Yves; ☽ 1-6pm Mon, 9am-7pm Tue-Sat, 11am-1pm & 2-6pm Sun Jul & Aug, 1-6pm Mon, 9am-6pm Tue-Sat, 11am-1pm & 2-6pm Sun Sep-Jun) Staff can book accommodation for a fee of €1.

Sights & Activities

OLD CITY

Much of Rennes was gutted by the great fire of 1720, started by a drunken carpenter who accidentally set alight a pile of shavings. Half-timbered houses that survived line the old city's cobbled streets such as **rue St-Michel** and **rue St-Georges**. The latter bisects the place de la Mairie and the site of the 17th-century **Palais du Parlement de Bretagne**, the former seat of the rebellious Breton parliament and, more recently, the Palais de Justice. In 1994 this building too was destroyed by fire, started by demon-strating fishermen. Now restored, it houses the Court of Appeal. In July and August, guided tours in English (€6.10; book at the tourist office) take you through the ostenta-tiously gilded rooms.

Crowning the old city is the 17th-century **Cathédrale St-Pierre** (☽ 9.30am-noon & 3-6pm) with a stunning neoclassical interior.

RENNES

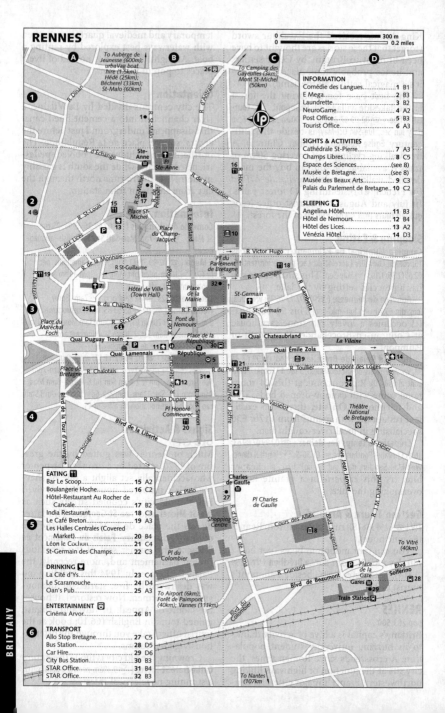

INFORMATION
Comédie des Langues	1 B1
E Mega	2 B3
Laundrette	3 B2
NeuroGame	4 A2
Post Office	5 B3
Tourist Office	6 A3

SIGHTS & ACTIVITIES
Cathédrale St-Pierre	7 A3
Champs Libres	8 C5
Espace des Sciences	(see 8)
Musée de Bretagne	(see 8)
Musée des Beaux Arts	9 C3
Palais du Parlement de Bretagne	10 C2

SLEEPING
Angelina Hôtel	11 B3
Hôtel de Nemours	12 B4
Hôtel des Lices	13 A2
Vénézia Hôtel	14 D3

EATING
Bar Le Scoop	15 A2
Boulangerie Hoche	16 C2
Hôtel-Restaurant Au Rocher de Cancale	17 B2
India Restaurant	18 C3
Le Café Breton	19 A3
Les Halles Centrales (Covered Market)	20 B4
Léon le Cochon	21 C4
St-Germain des Champs	22 C3

DRINKING
La Cité d'Ys	23 C4
Le Scaramouche	24 D4
Oan's Pub	25 A3

ENTERTAINMENT
Cinéma Arvor	26 B1

TRANSPORT
Allo Stop Bretagne	27 C5
Bus Station	28 D5
Car Hire	29 D6
City Bus Station	30 B3
STAR Office	31 B4
STAR Office	32 B3

MUSEUMS

Rooms devoted to the Pont-Aven school are the highlight of the **Musée des Beaux-Arts** (☎ 02 99 28 55 85; 20 quai Émile Zola; adult/child €4.20/2.15; ⏰ 10am-noon & 2-6pm Tue-Sun), which also has a 'curiosity gallery' of antiques and illustrations amassed in the 18th century.

Rennes' futuristic cultural centre, **Champs Libres** (☎ 02 23 40 66 00; 10 cours des Alliés) incorporates the **Musée de Bretagne** (☎ 02 23 40 66 70; www.musee-bretagne.fr), with displays on Breton history and culture. Under the same roof is **Espace des Sciences** (☎ 02 23 40 66 40; www.espace-sciences.org), an interactive science museum, along with a planetarium, a temporary exhibition space and a library. A combined ticket for all sections costs €10/7 per adult/child.

Tours

urbaVag (☎ 02 99 33 16 88; rue Canal St-Martin; per hr €25-30) Cruise Rennes' waterways on a whisper-quiet electric boat rented from urbaVag. Boats take up to seven passengers and the price drops significantly with each extra hour of rental.

Allovisit (☎ 3223 then dial 84748, then enter code 032000; per min €0.34) A nifty way to see seven city sites with commentary in English and French is with mobile phone–based Allovisit.

Festivals & Events

Tombées de la Nuit Rennes' old city comes alive with music, theatre and medieval costumes during this festival in the first week of July.

Yaouank (☎ 02 99 30 06 87) A huge *festoú-noz* (night festival), held on the third Saturday in November.

Sleeping

Camping des Gayeulles (☎ 02 99 36 91 22; fax 02 23 20 06 34; rue Professeur Audin; per person/tent/car €3.20/5.50/7) Rennes' only camp site is in Parc des Bois, about 4.5km northeast of the train station. Take bus 3 from place de la République to the Gayeulles stop.

Auberge de Jeunesse (☎ 02 99 33 22 33; rennes@fuaj.org; 10-12 Canal St-Martin; dm incl breakfast €16.25, sheets €2.80; ⏰ 7am-1am) Rennes' well-equipped youth hostel has a self-catering kitchen and a canal-side setting two kilometres north from the centre Take bus 18 from place de la Mairie.

Vénézia Hôtel (☎ 02 99 30 36 56; hotel.venezia@wanadoo.fr; 27 rue Dupont des Loges; s €28-38, d €38-48) Named for the Venice-like canals surrounding this small 'island' in the city centre,

half of this charming hotel's 16 rooms have pretty views over the canal side garden. The cheapest of these comfortable, rose-toned rooms have a toilet, but use (free) hall showers. The kind owner can recommend any number of *crêperies* nearby.

Angelina Hôtel (☎ 02 99 79 29 66; angelina-hotel@voila.fr; 1 quai Lamennais; d €43-58) It doesn't get more central than this cavernous hotel right next to République, with the old city and shopping district on the doorstep. Reception's on the 3rd floor of this creaking old building (there's a lift), but the wicker-furnished rooms are surprisingly well kept, and come with bright modern bathrooms, as well as free wi-fi.

Hôtel des Lices (☎ 02 99 79 14 81; www.hotel-des-lices.com in French; 7 place des Lices; s €55-58, d & tw €58.50-64; ✖) The Saturday morning market snakes right past the front door of this modern six-storey hotel that has good wheelchair access. You can peer down to watch the action from the steel balconies or through the floor-to-ceiling glass doors. Inside, rooms are small but sleek with pared-down contemporary furnishings and textured walls. Breakfast (€7.80) is served in a sunlit ground-floor salon with limed floorboards, white tables and fresh flowers.

Hôtel de Nemours (☎ 02 99 78 26 26; www.hotelnemours.com in French; 5 rue de Nemours; s from €52, d €60-65, tr €75; ✖ ✖) Lined with historic black-and-white photographs of Rennes, boutique Hôtel de Nemours is an understatement in elegance, with cream, chocolate, and caramel-coloured furnishings, high thread-count white linens, flat-screen TVs, and free wi-fi. Slide into a corduroy-upholstered banquette for a breakfast buffet feast (€7.50).

Eating

Rue St-Georges and rue St-Malo are lined with *crêperies* and international eateries.

Bar Le Scoop (☎ 02 99 79 10 39; 1 place Haut des Lices; dishes €8-10; ⏰ 7am-1am Mon-Sat, 10am-1am Sun) A chilled spot to relax over a coffee, or something stronger, Bar Le Scoop is also a good bet for a light brasserie-style bite (salads, sandwiches and so forth) between hitting Rennes' sights.

India Restaurant (☎ 02 99 87 09 01; 41 rue St-Georges; mains €8.50-15; ⏰ lunch & dinner) Hankering for a change from *crêpes*? This elegant eatery over two rich red-and-gold levels serves up impeccably presented, high-quality Indian cuisine with an extensive choice of vegetarian dishes.

Léon le Cochon (☎ 02 99 79 37 54; 1 rue Maréchal Joffre; menus €11.50-37; ☉ lunch & dinner, closed Sun Jul & Aug) Basking in the plaudits of almost every French gastronomic guidebook, but still fun and informal, 'Leo the Pig' specialises not just in pork but porcine products in all their many and varied manifestations.

Le Café Breton (☎ 02 99 30 74 95; 14 rue Nantaise; menus €13-30; ☉ lunch & dinner Mon-Sat) Diminutive rue Nantaise has a handful of top restaurants including this local fave for its tarts, salads and gratins. Definitely book ahead.

St-Germain des Champs (☎ 02 99 79 25 52; 12 rue du Vau St-Germain; menus around €15; ☉ lunch Tue-Sat, dinner Fri & Sat) Opposite the St-Germain church, large windows fill this vegetarian restaurant with sunlight. If you're craving a vitamin fix, this place is a bit pricey but you get what you pay for with fresh-as-it-gets organic produce (though unfortunately the juices aren't freshly-squeezed).

Hôtel-Restaurant Au Rocher de Cancale (☎ 02 99 79 20 83; 10 rue St-Michel; menus €14-25; ☉ lunch & dinner Mon-Fri) In the heart of the action, this delightful restaurant serves mainly fish. Settle into its *plateau du rocher* (€20), a seafood platter that includes oysters, winkles, whelks and *amandes de mer*, a kind of giant clam. Upstairs are four cosy guest rooms (doubles €37.30 to €46.30).

SELF-CATERING

You can pick up fresh produce at Rennes covered markets, **Les Halles Centrales** (place Honoré Commeurec; ☉ 7am-7pm Mon-Sat, 9.30am-12.30pm Sun).

Exquisite pastries and breads are enticingly displayed at **Boulangerie Hoche** (☎ 02 99 63 61 01; 17 rue Hoche, ☉ 7am-7.30pm Mon-Sat).

Drinking

Rue St-Michel – nicknamed rue de la Soif (street of thirst) for its bars, pubs and cafés – is the best-known drinking strip, but it can get rowdy (and sometimes aggressive) late at night.

Oan's Pub (☎ 02 99 31 07 51; 1 rue Georges Oottin; ☉ 2pm-1am Mon-Sat) Stone walls give this cosy place a cavelike feel. Regular jam sessions, where locals turn up with myriad instruments, add a Celtic note.

La Cité d'Ys (☎ 02 99 78 24 84; 31 rue Vasselot; ☉ noon-1am Mon-Sat) If you want to practise your Breton with Breton-speaking students and bar staff (lubricated by Breton beer), this wooden mezzanine pub is prime. *Yec'hed mat* (Cheers)!

Le Scaramouche (☎ 02 99 31 55 53; 3bis rue Duhamel; ☉ 8am-1am Mon-Sat) This huge space with art and film projected onto the walls attracts lots of local actors, artists and philosophic types.

Entertainment

Nondubbed films are screened at **Cinéma Arvor** (☎ 02 99 38 72 40; 29 rue d'Antrain). *Ciné Spectacles* is the free weekly guide.

Getting There & Away

BUS

Among Rennes' many bus services, **Illenoo** (www.illenoo.fr in French) runs five times daily to Dinard (€3.50, two hours) via Dinan (€3, 1½ hours). **TIV** (☎ 02 99 26 11 26) serves Paimpont (€3, one hour).

CAR & MOTORCYCLE

ADA (☎ 02 99 67 43 79), **Europcar** (☎ 02 23 44 02 72), **National Citer** (☎ 02 23 44 02 78) and **Hertz** (☎ 02 23 42 17 01) all have offices at the train station.

HITCHING

Allo Stop Bretagne (☎ 02 99 35 04 40; www.allostoprennes.com in French; 20 rue d'Isly; ☉ 9.30am-12.30pm & 2-6pm Mon-Fri, 9am-1pm & 1.30-3pm Sat), in the Trois Soleils shopping centre, matches up hitchers with drivers for a fee of €6.10.

TRAIN

Destinations with frequent services include St-Malo (€11.60, one hour), Dinan (€12.20, one hour including a change), Vannes (€17.10, 1½ hours), Nantes (€19.80, 1¼ hours), Brest (€30.20, two hours), Quimper (€30.10, 2½ hours) and Paris' Gare Montparnasse (€50.20, 2¼ hours).

Getting Around

Rennes has an efficient local bus network and (incredibly, for a city its size) its own single-line metro, both run by **STAR** (☎ 0811 555 535; www.star.fr in French). Bus and metro tickets (single journey €1, 10-trip carnet €9.70, 24-hour pass €3) are interchangeable.

The metro line runs northwest to southeast. Main stations include Gares (stations),

République (place de la République) in the centre, and Ste-Anne (old town).

Ring ☎ 02 99 30 79 79 for a taxi.

VITRÉ

pop 17,000

Rivalling Dinan as one of Brittany's best-preserved medieval towns – with far fewer tourists and a more laissez-faire village air – Vitré's narrow cobbled streets and half-timbered houses cluster beneath its colossal castle crowned by witches'-hat turrets.

Orientation & Information

Vitré's compact old town sits immediately north of the train station, between the castle and place de la République.

The **tourist office** (☎ 02 99 75 04 46; www.ot-vitre .fr; place Général de Gaulle; ☉ 10am-12.30pm & 2-7pm Mon-Sat, 10am-12.30pm & 3-6pm Sun Jul & Aug, 2.30-6pm Mon, 9.30am-12.30pm & 2.30-6pm Tue-Sat Sep-Jun) is right outside the train station.

Sights & Activities

You can visit Vitré's **museums** over any number of days for a single entry fee of €4/2.50 per adult/child. The highlight is the **Musée du Château** at the southern corner of the majestic **medieval castle** (☎ 02 99 75 04 54; place du Château; ☉ 10am-6pm Jul-Sep, 10am-noon & 2-5.30pm Apr-Jun, 10am-noon & 2-5.30pm Wed-Fri, 2-5.30pm Sat-Mon Oct-Mar). Rising on a rocky outcrop overlooking the River Vilaine, it was built in 1060, and expanded in the 14th and 15th centuries. A twin-turreted gateway leads you from the cobbled square of place du Château into the triangular inner courtyard.

Sleeping

Hôtel du Château (☎ 02 99 74 58 59; fax 02 99 75 35 47; 5 rue Rallon; s/d €39/45; ☎ closed last week Aug) Wake up to the aroma of freshly baked bread and,

on upper floors, fantastic vistas of the castle, at this familial hotel with good wheelchair access at the base of the ramparts. The friendly owners are a fount of local information. A brimming €6 breakfast, private garage and bike storage make this one of Brittany's gems.

Hôtel Le Petit Billot (☎ 02 99 75 02 10; www .petit-billot.com; 5bis place Général Leclerc; s/d €41.50/48) Just 100m east of the train station and five minutes' stroll from the castle, the two-star Petit Billot has 21 individually decorated rooms with striped wallpaper, bright modern bathrooms and plenty of space to stretch out. Private parking is available.

Eating & Drinking

Quaint *crêperies* and gastronomic restaurants are tucked throughout the old town.

La Gavotte (☎ 02 99 74 47 74; 7 rue des Augustins; menus €9.50-12; ☉ lunch & dinner Tue-Sun Jul & Aug, Wed-Sun Sep-Jun) Of the many top-notch, decently priced *crêperies* in town, the best is this rose-painted, wood-carved place close to the castle, where chef Marie-Christine concocts delicious fillings using organic local produce.

Bressan (☎ 02 99 75 23 64; 3 rue de la Trémouille; ☉ 3pm-3am Mon-Sat) Don't pass up a pint at this funky, low-key microbrewery with gleaming copper boilers and four artisanal beers on tap. In summer try the *blanche*, brewed with citrus zest; in winter, go for the robust *noire* (stout).

Several convivial bars offer internet access, including **Le Billy's Bar** (☎ 02 99 74 60 36; 44 rue Poterie, per 15min €1; ☉ 9.30am-10pm Mon-Sat), run by the charismatic Billy and massed with motorcycle paraphernalia.

Getting There & Away

Frequent trains travel between Vitré and Rennes (€6.40, 35 minutes).

Champagne

Known in Roman times as Campania (Land of Plains), Champagne is a largely agricultural region celebrated around the world for the sparkling wines that have been produced here since the days of Dom Pérignon. According to French law, only bubbly from the region – grown in designated areas, then aged and bottled according to the strictest standards – can be labelled as champagne. Nothing will drive the locals into fits of righteous indignation faster – or will elicit more searing expressions of contempt mixed with pity – than a mention of that absurd liquid marketed as 'California champagne'!

The production of the prestigious wine takes place mainly in two *départements*: Marne, whose metropolis is the 'Coronation City' of Reims; and the less prestigious (though increasingly respected) Aube, whose *préfecture* is the ancient and picturesque city of Troyes, home to several exceptional museums and whole streets lined with half-timbered houses.

The town of Épernay, a bit south of Reims, is the de facto capital of champagne (the drink) and is the best place to head for *dégustation* (tasting). The Champagne Route wends its way through the region's diverse vineyards, taking visitors from one picturesque – and prosperous – wine-growing village to the next. A number of name-brand *maisons* (champagne houses) have achieved international renown, but much of the region's liquid gold is made by almost 5000 small-scale *vignerons* (wine producers), many of whose family-run facilities welcome visitors.

HIGHLIGHTS

- Inhale the heady odours of maturing champagne on a cellar tour in **Épernay** (p362) or **Reims** (p358)

- Explore the rolling vineyards along Champagne's scenic **Champagne Route** (p360 and p369)

- Stroll among half-timbered houses and duck into Gothic churches in Troyes' **old city** (p364)

- Admire medieval and modern art and ancient hand tools in Troyes' fine **museums** (p366)

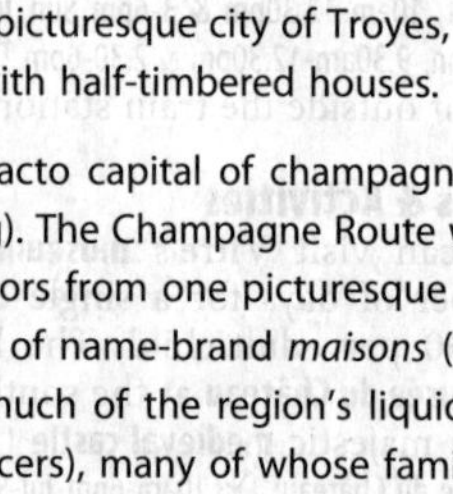

Reims
★
★ Champagne Route
★ Épernay

★ Troyes
★ Champagne Route

- POPULATION: 1,300,000
- AREA: 25,606 SQ KM

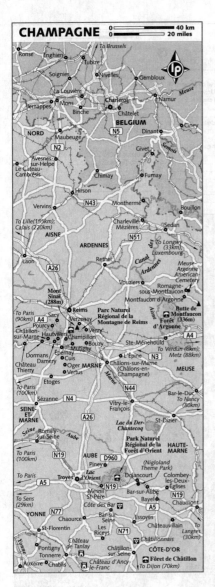

cial fairs at which merchants from around Europe bought and sold products from as far afield as the Mediterranean.

The region's name has been associated with bubbly since the late 17th century, when a Benedictine monk named Dom Pierre Pérignon perfected the process of using a second fermentation to make ho-hum still wine sparkle.

Getting There & Around

Champagne (www.tourisme-champagne -ardenne.com), just north of Burgundy, makes a refreshing stop-over if you're driving from far northern France or Paris eastward to Lorraine or Alsace. Épernay can be visited as an all-day excursion from Paris; once the TGV Est Européen line begins running in June 2007, Reims will also be day-tripable from the capital.

France's rail lines radiate out from Paris like the spokes of a wheel and, as it so happens, Reims, Épernay and Troyes are each on a different spoke (more or less). Although there are pretty good Reims–Épernay rail connections, the best way to get from Reims to Troyes is by bus.

REIMS

pop 215,000

Over the course of a millennium (816 to 1825), 34 sovereigns – among them 25 kings – began their reigns as Christian rulers in Reims' famed cathedral. Meticulously reconstructed after WWI and WWII, the city – whose name is pronounced something like 'rance' and is often anglicised as Rheims – is neat and orderly, with wide avenues and well-tended parks. Together with Épernay, it is the most important centre of champagne production.

Orientation

In the commercial centre (northwest of the cathedral), the main streets are rue Carnot, rue de Vesle, rue Condorcet and, for shopping, rue de Talleyrand. The train station is about 1km northwest of the cathedral, across square Colbert from place Drouet d'Erlon, the city's major nightlife centre. Virtually every street in the city centre is one way.

Information

Commercial banks can be found on rue Carnot and at the southern end of place

History

Champagne's most famous convert to Christianity was the Merovingian warrior-king Clovis I, who founded the Frankish kingdom in the late 5th century and began the tradition of holding royal coronations in Reims. In the Middle Ages, the region – especially Troyes – grew rich from commer-

CHAMPAGNE

REIMS

0 — 400 m
0 — 0.2 miles

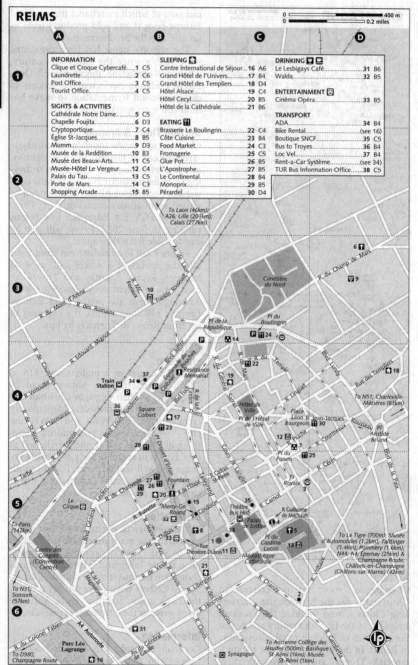

INFORMATION
Clique et Croque Cybercafé....1 C5
Laundrette...........................2 C6
Post Office..........................3 C5
Tourist Office......................4 C5

SIGHTS & ACTIVITIES
Cathédrale Notre Dame........5 C5
Chapelle Foujita....................6 D3
Cryptoportique......................7 C4
Église St-Jacques..................8 B5
Mumm..................................9 D3
Musée de la Reddition.........10 B3
Musée des Beaux-Arts.........11 C5
Musée-Hôtel Le Vergeur......12 C4
Palais du Tau......................13 C5
Porte de Mars.....................14 C3
Shopping Arcade.................15 B5

SLEEPING
Centre International de Séjour...16 A6
Grand Hôtel de l'Univers......17 B4
Grand Hôtel des Templiers....18 D4
Hôtel Alsace.......................19 C4
Hôtel Cecyl.........................20 B5
Hôtel de la Cathédrale.........21 B6

EATING
Brasserie Le Boulingrin........22 C4
Côte Cuisine.......................23 B4
Food Market........................24 C3
Fromagerie.........................25 C5
Glue Pot.............................26 B5
L'Apostrophe.......................27 B5
Le Continental.....................28 B4
Monoprix............................29 B5
Pérardel.............................30 D4

DRINKING
Le Lesbigays Café................31 B6
Waïda................................32 B5

ENTERTAINMENT
Cinéma Opéra.....................33 B5

TRANSPORT
ADA...................................34 B4
Bike Rental........................(see 16)
Boutique SNCF....................35 C5
Bus to Troyes.....................36 B4
Loc Vel..............................37 B4
Rent-a-Car Système...........(see 34)
TUR Bus Information Office...38 C5

To Laon (46km);
A26; Lille (203km);
Calais (277km)

Cimetière
du Nord

R du Champ de Mars

Pl du
Boulingrin

Pl de la
République

Resistance
Memorial

Train
Station

Square
Colbert

Hôtel de
Ville
Pl de l'Hôtel
de Ville

Place
Léon R Jean-Jacques
Bourgeois

Pl
Aristide
Briand

Pl du
Forum

Pl
Royale

To N51; Charleville-
Mézières (83km)

Le
Cirque

Merry-Go
Round

Fountain

Théâtre
Bus Hub
Palais
de Justice

R Guillaume
de Machault

To Paris
(142km)

To N31;
Soissons
(57km)

Rue
Théodore Dubois
Pl du
Cardinal
Luçon
Médiathèque
Cathédrale

To Le Tigre (700m); Musée
d'Automobiles (1.2km); Taittinger
(1.4km); Pommery (1.6km);
N44; A4; Epernay (25km) &
Champagne Route;
Châlons-en-Champagne
(Châlons-sur-Marne) (42km)

Centre des
Congrès
(Convention
Centre)

Parc Léo
Lagrange

To D980;
Champagne Route

To Ancienne Collège des
Jésuites (500m); Basilique
St-Rémi (1km); Musée
St-Rémi (1km)

Synagogue

Drouet d'Erlon. The tourist office changes money on Sunday and holidays.

Clique et Croque Cybercafé (27 rue de Vesle; per min/hr €0.07/4.20; ⏰ 10am-12.30am Mon-Sat, 2-9pm Sun) Internet access in the courtyard of a shopping arcade.

Laundrette (59 rue Chanzy; ⏰ 7am-9.30pm)

Post Office (2 rue Cérès) Through the arches on the eastern side of place Royale. Has currency exchange and a Cyberposte.

Tourist Office (☎ 03 26 77 45 00; www.reims-tourisme .com; 2 rue Guillaume de Machault; ⏰ 9am-7pm Mon-Sat, 10am-6pm Sun & holidays mid-Apr–mid-Oct, 9am-6pm Mon-Sat, 11am-4pm Sun & holidays mid-Oct–mid-Apr) Le Pass Citadine (€12) gets you a champagne house tour, an all-day bus ticket, entry to all four municipal museums and a box of *biscuits roses* (pink biscuits), traditionally nibbled with champagne.

Sights

CHURCHES & MUSEUMS

Imagine the pomp, the extravagance, the over-the-top costumes and the egos writ large of a French royal coronation… For centuries, the focal point of such affairs was **Cathédrale Notre Dame** (⏰ 7.30am-7.30pm, closed morning Mass Sun), a Gothic edifice begun in 1211 – on a site occupied by churches since the 5th century – and mostly completed a century later. The most famous event in the cathedral's history was the coronation of Charles VII, with Joan of Arc at his side, on 17 July 1429.

Very badly damaged (like the whole city) by artillery and fire during WWI, the edifice was restored with funds donated largely by John D Rockefeller; reconsecration took place in 1938, just in time for the next war. Today, the 138m-long cathedral is more interesting for its dramatic history than for its heavily restored architectural features. The finest stained-glass windows are the western façade's 12-petalled **great rose window**, its smaller downstairs neighbour, and the rose window in the north transept arm, above the Flamboyant Gothic organ case (15th and 18th centuries). Nearby is a 15th-century **astronomical clock**. There's a window by Chagall in the axial chapel (behind the high altar) and, two chapels to the left, a statue of – you guessed it! – Joan of Arc.

Persons strong-of-thigh might want to climb to the **cathedral roof** (adult/12-25yr €6.50/4.50, incl Palais du Tau €8.50/6; ⏰ Tue-Sat & afternoon Sun early May-early Sep, Sat & afternoon Sun mid-Mar–early May & early Sep-Oct) on a one-hour tour – the Palais du Tau has details.

MUSEUM PASS

All four museums run by the municipality – St-Rémi, Reddition, Beaux-Arts and the Ancienne Collège des Jésuites (closed until 2008), as well as the 1966 **Chapelle Foujita** (33 rue du Champ de Mars; ⏰ 2-6pm Thu-Tue May-Oct), are covered by the **Pass Découverte** (adult/student €3/free; valid 1 month). Visit one and you might as well visit them all!

Next door, the **Palais du Tau** (2 place du Cardinal Lucon; ☎ 03 26 47 81 79; adult/18-25yr/under 18yr €6.50/4.50/free; ⏰ 9.30am-6.30pm Tue-Sun early May-early Sep, 9.30am-12.30pm & 2-5.30pm Tue-Sun early Sep-early May), a former archbishop's residence constructed in 1690, was where French princes stayed right before their coronations – and where they played host to a sumptuous banquet right afterwards. Now a museum, it displays truly exceptional statues, ritual objects and tapestries from the cathedral, some in the impressive Salle du Tau.

The rich collections of the **Musée des Beaux-Arts** (☎ 03 26 47 28 44; 8 rue Chanzy; ⏰ 10am-noon & 2-6pm Wed-Sun), housed in an 18th-century building in which Russian troops were billeted during the Napoleonic wars (1814), include one of only four versions of Jacques-Louis David's world-famous *Death of Marat* (yes, the bloody one in the bathtub), 27 works by Camille Corot (only the Louvre has more), lots of Barbizon School landscapes, Art Nouveau creations by Émile Gallé and two works each by Monet, Gauguin and Pissarro.

Way back in the AD 400s, Bishop Remigius baptised Clovis and 3000 Frankish warriors; 121m-long **Basilique St-Rémi** (place St-Rémi) is named in his honour. Once a Benedictine abbey church and now a Unesco World Heritage site (along with the cathedral and the Palais du Tau), its Romanesque nave and transept – worn but stunning – date mainly from the mid-11th century. The choir (constructed between 1162 and 1190) is in the early Gothic style, with a large triforium gallery and, way up top, tiny clerestory windows. The 12th-century-style chandelier has 96 candles, one for each year of the life of St-Rémi, whose tomb (in the choir) is marked by a mausoleum from the mid-1600s. The basilica is about 1.5km

CHAMPAGNE

WWII IN EUROPE ENDED IN REIMS

Nazi Germany surrendered unconditionally at 2.41am on 7 May 1945 in US General Dwight D Eisenhower's war room in Reims, now a museum known as the **Musée de la Reddition** (Surrender Museum; ☎ 03 26 47 84 19; 12 rue Franklin Roosevelt; ☉ 10am-noon & 2-6pm Wed-Mon). The original Allied battle maps are still affixed to the walls of the one-time technical college, now known as Lycée Franklin Roosevelt. There's a film in French, German and English.

At Stalin's insistence, another surrender document was signed two days later in Soviet-occupied Berlin.

---

south-southeast of the tourist office; by bus take the Citadine 1 or 2 to St-Rémi.

Next door, **Musée St-Rémi** (☎ 03 26 85 23 36; 53 rue Simon; ☉ 2-6.30pm Mon-Fri, 2-7pm Sat & Sun), in a 17th- and 18th-century abbey, features local Gallo-Roman archaeology, tapestries and 16th- to 19th-century military history.

At **Musée-Hôtel Le Vergeur** (☎ 03 26 47 20 75; 36 place du Forum; adult/student/10-18yr €4/3/1; ☉ tours 2-4.50pm Tue-Sun), in a 13th- to 16th-century townhouse, highlights include a series of furnished period rooms and engravings by Albrecht Dürer.

About 1.5km southeast of the cathedral, the **Musée d'Automobiles** (☎ 03 26 82 83 84; 84 av Georges Clemenceau; adult/student/6-10yr/family of 4 €6/4/2.50/15; ☉ 10am-noon & 2-6pm Wed-Mon, to 5pm Nov-Mar, closed Christmas–mid-Jan) displays about 200 motor vehicles, most of them French and from the 1920s to the '70s. By bus, take line D to the Boussinesq stop.

OTHER SIGHTS

Pedestrianised **place Drouet d'Erlon** has almost as much neon as Las Vegas. Southeast of the **fountain** – crowned by a gilded statue of Winged Victory – is a covered **shopping arcade**. At rue Condorcet, the 12th- to 14th-century **Église St-Jacques** has some pretty awful postwar stained glass.

The handsome, mid-18th-century **place Royale**, surrounded by neoclassical arcades, reflects the magnificence of Louis XV's France (that's him up on the pedestal).

Roman relics from the 3rd century include the **Porte de Mars** (place de la République), a triumphal arch, and the **Cryptoportique** (place

du Forum; admission free; ☉ 2-5pm Tue-Sun mid-Jun–mid-Sep), a gallery that was apparently used for grain storage.

Tours

CHAMPAGNE CELLARS

The musty *caves* (cellars) and dusty bottles of eight Reims champagne houses can be visited on guided tours. The following places all have fancy websites, cellar temperatures of 8°C to 10°C and frequent English-language tours that end, *naturellement*, with a tasting session. For details on how champagne is made see p79.

Taittinger (☎ 03 26 85 84 33; www.taittinger.com; 9 place St-Niçaise; tours adult/under 12yr €7/free; tours 9.30am-11.50am & 2pm-4.20pm, closed Sat & Sun mid-Nov–mid-Mar) The headquarters of the Taittinger, 1.5km southeast of the cathedral, is an excellent place to come for a clear, straightforward presentation on how champagne is actually made – no clap-trap about 'the champagne mystique' here! On the one-hour tours visitors are shown everything from *remuage* (bottle turning) to *dégorgement* (sediment removal at -25°C) to the corking machines. Parts of the cellars occupy 4th-century Roman stone quarries; other bits were made by 13th-century Benedictine monks. For €270 you can purchase a 6L Mathusalem, though for a really big bash you'll surely want a Nabuchodonosor (15L) – and a Bible to figure out why oversized champagne bottles have such bizarre names!

Mumm (☎ 03 26 49 59 70; www.mumm.com; 34 rue du Champ de Mars; tours adult/under 16yr €7.50/free; tours 9am-11am & 2pm-5pm Mar-Oct) Mumm (pronounced 'moom') was founded in 1827 and is now the world's third-largest producer (eight million bottles a year), offering edifying, one-hour cellar tours. Phone ahead for weekday tours from November to February. A tasting session with oenological commentary is available for €13/18 for two/three champagnes.

Pommery (☎ 03 26 61 62 55; www.pommery.fr; 5 place du Général Gouraud; tours adult/student & 12-17yr/under 12yr €8/6/free; tours 10am-5.30pm Mon-Fri & to 6.15pm Sat & Sun summer, to 4pm winter) Pommery occupies an Elizabethan-style hilltop campus (built 1868–78) 1.8km southeast of the cathedral. The year-round cellar tours take you 30m underground to Gallo-Roman quarries and 25

THE EXPLOSIVE SIDE OF FIZZY WINE

The pressure inside a champagne bottle can reach six atmospheres at the end of the second fermentation. As a result, about one in 10,000 bottles explodes. Ask to see an unlucky one on a cellar tour!

---

million bottles of bubbly. Phoning ahead for reservations is recommended. The complex often hosts contemporary art exhibitions.

CATHEDRAL

The tourist office rents **audioguides** (1/2 people €7/9) and runs English-language **guided tours** (adult/student & over 60yr €5.50/3.50; 2.30pm Jul & Aug) of the cathedral.

Sleeping

BUDGET

Centre International de Séjour (CIS; ☎ 03 26 40 52 60; www.cis-reims.com; chaussée Bocquaine; bed in s/d/tr €31.80/17.80/14.20, with shared bathroom €19.80/13.10/11.90; 24hr;) The 85 brightly painted rooms are institutional and utterly devoid of charm – but look on the bright side: whingeing about luke-warm showers is a great way to break the ice with your fellow travellers. To get there take bus B, K, M or N to the Comédie stop or bus H to the Pont de Gaulle stop.

Hôtel Alsace (☎ 03 26 47 44 08; fax 03 26 47 44 52; 6 rue du Général Sarrail; s/d/tr €32/35/39, with shower only €28/32/36) Run by the friendly son of a Yorkshireman who married a French-woman during the war, this 24-room place has functional pastel rooms. The parquet floors are fake – but who cares? In winter reception is closed on Sunday afternoon.

MIDRANGE

You'll find a number of two- and three-star hotels at place Drouet d'Erlon and along adjacent rue Buirette.

Hôtel Cecyl (☎ 03 26 47 57 47; christophe.prince3@wanadoo.fr; 24 rue Buirette; d from €49) Run by two brothers, this two-star place has 27 functional rooms with sound-proofing and space-efficient bathrooms. Overall, decent value.

Hôtel de la Cathédrale (☎ 03 26 47 28 46; hoteldelacathedrale@wanadoo.fr; 20 rue Libergier; d/q from €60/80) Charm, graciousness and some very shiny brass greet guests at this family-run, two-star place, whose 17 tasteful rooms are smallish but pleasingly chintzy. Has four floors but no lift.

Grand Hôtel de l'Univers (☎ 03 26 88 68 08; www.hotel-univers-reims.com in French; 41 blvd Foch; d from €78, Nov-early Mar from €67) This venerable three-star place has 42 large rooms, tastefully appointed, with high ceilings and bathrooms big enough to do jumping jacks in.

TOP END

Grand Hôtel des Templiers (☎ 03 26 88 55 08; http://perso.wanadoo.fr/hotel.templiers; 22 rue des Templiers; d €160-250;) Built in the 1800s as the home of a rich champagne merchant, this luxurious four-star hostelry with good wheelchair access retains the original ceilings, stained glass and furnishings. The staircase imparts a certain neogothic gloominess but the 18 rooms come with luscious fabrics and modern marble bathrooms. Some of the beds even have canopies.

Eating

Place Drouet d'Erlon is lined with pizzerias, brasseries, cafés, pubs and sandwich places.

Glue Pot (☎ 03 26 47 36 46; 49 place Drouet d'Erlon; 10am-3am, meals noon-2.30pm & 7-11pm, to 1.30am Fri & Sat) Only the French genius for eclecticism could have created this Irish pub, which doubles as a Tex-Mex restaurant (*fajitas* are €16) that serves burgers (the Big Boy has an egg on top) and pizzas (€8.30 to €10.90) to patrons seated on bright red banquettes under fake Tiffany lamps. The menu is in English with French translations. Believe it or not, the food is pretty good!

Brasserie Le Boulingrin (☎ 03 26 40 96 22; 48 rue de Mars; menus €17.50-24; Mon-Sat) Offers a mini-trip back in time with original 1920s décor, including an old-time zinc bar. The culinary focus is on meat and fish. The name is derived from the English 'bowling green', as in lawn bowling. Several other buildings on the same block are just as architecturally interesting.

ourpick L'Apostrophe (☎ 03 26 79 19 89; 59 place Drouet d'Erlon; 2-course weekday menus €14, salads €11.50-14.50, mains €12.90-21.50; meals served noon-2.30pm & 7-10.45pm) This stylish café-brasserie dispenses generous portions of intellectual pretension – and some mean *piscines* (enormous cocktails for several people) – along with its French and international cuisine. A perennial favourite thanks to its chic atmosphere, summertime terrace and good value. Open as a café straight through from 9am to 1am.

Côte Cuisine (☎ 03 26 83 93 68; 43 blvd Foch; weekday lunch menus €13.50-16.90, dinner menus €30; lunch & dinner Mon-Sat) A spacious, modern place with well-regarded traditional French cuisine.

Le Continental (☎ 03 26 47 01 47; 95 place Drouet d'Erlon; menus, some incl wine €21.90-55; lunch & dinner, open all afternoon for drinks) Built in the early 20th century, this classy, marble-floored place serves up panoramic views and classic French dishes such as *magret de canard* (duck breast fillet); seafood is the speciality from September to May. A great spot for a midafternoon glass of champagne (€7 to €8).

SELF-CATERING
Pérardel (3 place Léon Bourgeois; 🕑 9am-12.30pm & 2-7.30pm Mon-Fri, 9am-7.30pm Sat), in the cellar at the end of the courtyard, is where locals buy good-value wines. The **food market** (place du Boulingrin; 🕑 until 1pm Sat), under the tent, may someday move back into the adjacent Art Deco covered market, closed since telephone numbers had six digits. Along the south side of place du Forum you'll find several food shops, including a **fromagerie** (12 place du Forum; 🕑 closed Sun & Mon). There's also a **Monoprix supermarket** (21 rue de Chativesle).

Drinking & Entertainment
Brasseries and cafés line brightly lit place Drouet d'Erlon, the focal point of Reims' nightlife; some places stay open till 3am. *Les Rendez-Vous*, a free guide published each Wednesday and available at the tourist office, lists concerts and other cultural events. **Cinéma Opéra** (☎ 03 26 47 13 54; 3 rue Théodore Dubois) screens nondubbed films.

Waïda (☎ 03 26 47 44 49; 5 place Drouet d'Erlon; 🕑 7.30am-7.30pm Tue-Sat, 7.30am-1pm & 3.30-7pm Sun) An old-fashioned *salon de thé* with mirrors, mosaics and marble unchanged since Brigitte Bardot made La Vérité in 1960.

Le Tigre (☎ 03 26 82 64 00; 2bis av Georges Clemenceau; 🕑 5pm-4am Tue-Thu, 5pm-5am Fri & Sat, weekends only in Aug) Sprawling and laid-back, this bar-disco, about 1km east of the cathedral, has more wall textures than it does beers on tap (six). There's live music (€3 to €6) from 9pm on Friday and Saturday (but not in July and August). At 11pm from Thursday to Saturday Le Tigre becomes a disco (€3 to €6).

Le Lesbigays Café (☎ 03 26 83 02 77; 89 rue Libergier; 🕑 4pm-12.30am, to 1.30am Fri & Sat) An informal bar that doesn't beat around the bush about its identity. Within sight of the cathedral.

Getting There & Away
BUS
The best way to get to Troyes (€20.45, 1¾ to 2¼ hours, three or four daily on weekdays,

two on Saturday, one on Sunday except during university breaks, none on holidays) is to take a bus operated by **TransChampagne** (STDM; ☎ 03 26 65 17 07; www.stdmarne.fr in French). The stop is next to the train station; hours are posted.

CAR
Rental companies with offices facing the train station car park:
ADA (☎ 03 26 50 08 40)
Loc Vel (☎ 03 26 40 43 38)
Rent-a-Car Système (☎ 03 26 77 87 77)

TRAIN
Direct services link Reims with Épernay (€5.50, 24 to 46 minutes, 23 daily weekdays, 14 daily weekends), Laon (€8.10, 45 minutes, eight daily Monday to Friday, six on Saturday, two on Sunday) and Paris' Gare de l'Est (€21.60, 1¾ hours, 10 to 15 daily).

In the city centre, information and tickets are available at the **Boutique SNCF** (1 cours JB Langlet; 🕑 9.30am-7pm Mon-Fri, to 6pm Sat).

The trip from Reims' newly renovated train station to Paris will take just 45 minutes once the long-awaited TGV Est Européen line starts running in June 2007.

Getting Around
The **Centre International de Séjour** (p359) rents city bikes to the public for €10/15 per half/whole day.

Two circular **bus** lines, the clockwise Citadine 1 and the anticlockwise Citadine 2 (single ticket €0.90, all-day *ticket journée* €2.50), operated by **TUR** (☎ 03 26 88 25 38; office at 6 rue Chanzy; 🕑 closed Sun & holidays), serve most of the sights mentioned in this section. Most TUR lines begin their last runs at about 8.50pm; the five night lines operate until 12.15am.

There is free **car** parking north and northwest of the train tracks. A tram line is supposed to start running in 2010 so expect traffic snafus during construction.

For a **taxi**, call ☎ 03 26 47 05 05.

AROUND REIMS
The **Champagne Route** (Route Touristique du Champagne) weaves its way among neatly tended vines covering the slopes between small villages, some with notable churches or speciality museums, some quite ordinary. All along the route, beautiful panoramas abound and small-scale *producteurs* (champagne producers) welcome travel-

FLIGHT OF THE HUMBLED KING

Louis XVI's attempt to escape from Paris in 1791 ended at **Ste-Ménehould** (pronounced Saint Menoo), 79km east of Reims, when the soon-to-be-beheaded monarch and Marie-Antoinette were recognised by the postmaster thanks to the king's portrait printed on a banknote.

lers in search of bubbly; many are closed around the *vendange* (grape harvest), ie September and into October. Tourist offices can supply you with an excellent colour-coded booklet, *The Discovery Guide*. In this region you should phone wine growers before stopping by.

The signposted tertiary roads that make up the Champagne Route meander through the Marne's three most important wine-growing areas:

- **Montagne de Reims** (70km; mainly Pinot Noir vines) – between Reims and Épernay, through villages such as **Sacy** (the church has an elegant spire), **Verzenay** (identifiable from afar by the lighthouse), **Bouzy** (famed for its nonsparkling reds) and **Mutigny** (has a 2km *sentier de vignoble* – vineyard walking path).
- **Côte des Blancs** (100km; Chardonnay vines) – south of Épernay towards Sézanne, through **Cuis** (Romanesque church), **Oger** (flowers galore), **Vertus** (fountains and a medieval church) and **Etoges** (church and 17th-century chateau).
- **Vallée de la Marne** (90km; mainly Pinot Meunier vines) – west of Épernay towards Dormans, through **Champillon** (panoramic views), **Hautvillers** (see below), **Damery** (medieval church), **Châtillon-sur-Marne** (huge statue of Pope Urban II, initiator of the First Crusade) and **Dormans** (chateau and park).

Hautvillers

It was in this tidy and conspicuously prosperous village (population 860), 7km north of Épernay, that, three centuries ago, Dom Pérignon created champagne as we know it. His tomb is next to the altar of the **Église Abbatiale** (abbey church), which has lots of 17th-century woodwork; the abbey itself was burnt down by the English during the Hundred Years' War. Great vineyard views await a few hundred metres north of the centre along route de Fismes (D386); and south along route de Cumières (a road leading to the D1). Hautvillers is twinned with Eguisheim in Alsace, which may help explain why three **storks** live in a cage 800m towards Épernay along the D386. (See the boxed text on p391.)

Details on the village and region are available at the **tourist office** (☎ 03 26 57 06 35; www.tourisme-hautvillers.com in French; place de la République; ☼ 9.30am-1pm & 1.30-6pm Mon-Sat, 10am-5pm Sun Apr–mid-Oct, 10am-5pm Mon-Sat mid-Oct–Mar).

Parc Natural Régional de la Montagne de Reims

The Montagne de Reims section of the Champagne Route skirts the Parc Natural Régional de la Montagne de Reims, endowed with extensive forests and a botanical curiosity, the mutant beech trees known as **faux de Verzy** (for photos see http://verzy .verzenay.free.fr in French). To get to the *faux* from the village of Verzy, follow the signs up the D34; the first trees can be seen about 1km from 'Les Faux' car park.

Across the D34, a short trail leads through the forest to a *point de vue* (panoramic viewpoint) atop 288m-high **Mont Sinaï**. Visitors are asked to refrain from worshipping golden calves, roasting marshmallows over the burning bush and doing impious impressions of Charlton Heston.

ÉPERNAY

pop 25,800

Well-to-do Épernay, home to many of the world's most famous champagne houses, is the best place in Champagne for touring cellars and sampling fizzy wine. The town also makes a good base for exploring the Champagne Route. By rail, Épernay, which is 25km south of Reims, can be visited as a day trip from Reims – or even Paris.

Beneath the streets in some 100km of subterranean cellars, 200 million bottles of champagne, just waiting to be popped open for some sparkling celebration, are being aged. In 1950, one such cellar – owned by the irrepressible Mercier – hosted a car rally without the loss of a single bottle!

Orientation

Mansion-lined av de Champagne, where many of Épernay's champagne houses are based, stretches east from the town's commercial heart (centred around place des Arcades), whose liveliest streets are rue Général Leclerc and rue St-Thibault. South of place de la République are car parks.

Information

Cyberm@nia (11 place des Arcades; per hr prepaid €3; ✆ 11am-midnight Mon-Sat, 2-8pm Sun) Internet access.

Post Office (place Hugues Plomb) Has currency exchange and a Cyberposte.

Tourist Office (☎ 03 26 53 33 00; www.ot-epernay .fr in French; 7 av de Champagne; ✆ 9.30am-12.30pm & 1.30-7pm Mon-Sat, 11am-4pm Sun & holidays mid-Apr–mid-Oct, 9.30am-12.30pm & 1.30-5.30pm Mon-Sat mid-Oct–mid-Apr) Has details on cellar visits, car touring, and walking and cycling options.

Tours

CHAMPAGNE HOUSES

Épernay's champagne houses cannot be accused of cowering behind excessive modesty or aristocratic understatement. When it comes to PR for brand-name bubbly, dignified razzle-dazzle is the name of the game. Many of the *maisons* on or near av de Champagne offer interesting, informative tours, followed by tasting and a visit to the factory-outlet bubbly shop. For details on the champagne production process, see p79).

Moët & Chandon (☎ 03 26 51 20 20; www.moet.com; adult/12-17yr €8/4.70; 18 av de Champagne; ✆ tours 9.30-11.15am & 2-4.15pm, closed Sat & Sun mid-Nov–Mar) This prestigious *maison* offers frequent one-hour

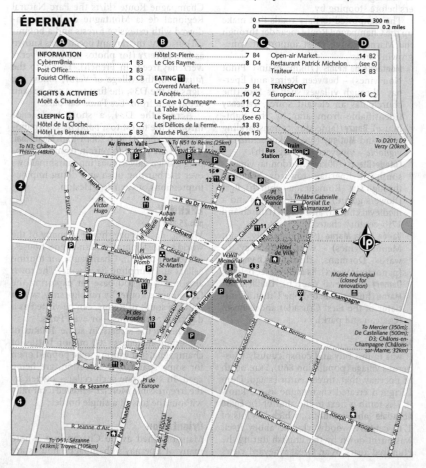

ÉPERNAY

0 ——————— 300 m
0 ——————— 0.2 miles

INFORMATION		
Cyberm@nia	1	B3
Post Office	2	B3
Tourist Office	3	C3

SIGHTS & ACTIVITIES		
Moët & Chandon	4	C3

SLEEPING 🏠		
Hôtel de la Cloche	5	C2
Hôtel Les Berceaux	6	B3

Hôtel St-Pierre	7	B4
Le Clos Rayme	8	D4

EATING 🍴		
Covered Market	9	B4
L'Ancêtre	10	A2
La Cave à Champagne	11	C2
La Table Kobus	12	C2
Le Sept	(see 6)	
Les Délices de la Ferme	13	B3
Marché Plus	(see 15)	

Open-air Market	14	B2
Restaurant Patrick Michelon	(see 6)	
Traiteur	15	B3

TRANSPORT		
Europcar	16	C2

To N3; Château Thierry (48km)

Av Ernest Vallé

R des Tanneurs

To N51 to Reims (25km)

Blvd de la Motte

Rempart Perrier

To N3; D9 Verzy (20km)

Av Jean Jaurès

R Pasteur

Pl Victor Hugo

R du Dr Verron

Auban Moët

R Flodoard

Bus Station

Train Station

Pl Mendes France

Théâtre Gabrielle Dorziat (Le Salmanazar)

R de Reims

R Léger Bertin

R de la Fauvette

Pl Carnot

R du Paulmier

Pl Hugues Plomb

R Général Leclerc

Portail St-Martin

WWII Memorial

Pl de la République

R Jean Moët

R Gambetta

Hôtel de Ville

R Pipin

Musée Municipal (closed for renovation)

Av de Champagne

Blvd du Cubry

R Professeur Langevin

Pl des Arcades

R des Berceaux

R Cussotte

R Eugène Mercier

R de Bernon

To Mercier (350m); De Castellane (500m); D3; Châlons-en-Champagne (Châlons-sur-Marne, 32km)

R Gallice

R St-Thibault

Pl de l'Europe

R de Sézanne

R J Thevenin

R Jean Chandon Moët

R Locard

R Maurice Cerveaux

R Joseph de Venoge

R Croix de Bussy

R Jeanne d'Arc

Av Paul Chandon

R de l'Hôpital Auban Moët

To D51; Sézanne (43km); Troyes (105km)

Unlike cognac, 95% of which is consumed outside France, 60% of the more than 300 million bottles of champagne produced each year are popped open, sipped and savoured in France itself. That doesn't leave much for the rest of us, especially considered how many bottles are wasted christening ships!

Large *maisons* with global brand recognition, many of them owned by international luxury-goods conglomerates, send a high percentage of their production to other countries (Moët & Chandon exports 80% of its bubbly), in part because profit margins are higher, but the many small *producteurs* continue to serve an almost exclusively domestic clientele.

tours that are among the region's most impressive. If you sell your car you might be able to buy a Methusalem of super-premium Dom Pérignon *millésime* (vintage champagne) of 1995, a bargain at €6000.

De Castellane (☎ 03 26 51 19 11; www.castellane .com in French; 64 av de Champagne; adult/10-17yr €7/5; ☺ tours 10.30-11.15am & 2.30-5.15pm mid-Mar–Dec, Sat & Sun Jan–mid-Mar, closed 3 weeks in Jan) The 45-minute tours take in the *maison's* informative bubbly museum, dedicated to elucidating the *méthode champenoise* and its diverse businesses. The reward for climbing the 237 steps up the 60m tower: a panoramic view.

Mercier (☎ 03 26 51 22 22; www.champagnemercier .com; 68-70 av de Champagne; adult/12-17yr €6.50/3; ☺ tours 9.30-11.30am & 2-4.30pm mid-Feb–mid-Dec, closed Tue & Wed mid-Feb–early-Mar & mid-Nov–mid-Dec) The most popular brand in France (and No 2 in overall production) has thrived on unabashed self-promotion since it was founded in 1847 by Eugène Mercier, a trailblazer in the field of eye-catching publicity stunts and the virtual creator of the cellar tour. Everything here is flashy, including the 160,000L barrel that took two decades to build (for the Universal Exposition of 1889) and the lift that transports you 30m underground. Alas, there's a glitch in the glitz – the laser-guided train can get confused by forward-facing camera flashes and has been known to veer into the bottles that line its route!

VINEYARDS
Champagne Domi Moreau (☎ 06 30 35 51 07, after 6.30pm 03 26 59 45 85; www.champagne-domimoreau .com; adult €20; departures 9.30am & 2.30pm except Wed, no tours 2nd half of Aug, Christmas period & Feb school holidays) Runs three-hour minibus tours (in French and

English) to nearby vineyards. Pick-up is across the street from the tourist office. Call ahead for reservations.

Sleeping
Épernay's hotels are especially full on weekends from Easter to September and on weekdays in May, June and September.

Hôtel St-Pierre (☎ 03 26 54 40 80; hotel.saint pierre@wanadoo.fr; 1 rue Jeanne d'Arc; d €36, with washbasin €24) In an early-20th-century mansion that has hardly changed in half a century, this one-star place has 15 simple rooms that retain the charm and atmosphere of yesteryear.

Hôtel de la Cloche (☎ 03 26 55 15 15; hotel-de-la-cloche.c.prin@wanadoo.fr; 5 place Mendès-France; d from €40) Has two stars and 19 cheerful rooms with bright, compact bathrooms, some with park views.

Hôtel Les Berceaux (☎ 03 26 55 28 84; www.lesber ceaux.com; 13 rue des Berceaux; d €77-86) This three-star institution, founded in 1889, has 27 comfortable rooms, each different and all with a modern *champenois* ambience.

Le Clos Raymi (☎ 03 26 51 00 58; www.closraymi -hotel.com; 3 rue Joseph de Venoge; d from €130) Staying at this delightful three-star place is like being a personal guest of Monsieur Chandon of champagne fame, whose luxurious home this was over a century ago. The seven romantic rooms have giant beds, 3.7m-high ceilings, ornate mouldings and parquet floors. In winter there's often a fire in the cosy modernist living room.

Eating
Rue Gambetta is home to four pizzerias.

La Cave à Champagne (☎ 03 26 55 50 70; 16 rue Gambetta; menus €15-36; ☺ Thu-Tue) Well-regarded by locals for its Champenoise cuisine, including *potée à la champenoise* (poultry and pork oven-baked with cabbage).

L'Ancêtre (☎ 03 26 55 57 56; 20 rue de la Fauvette; menus €15.50-25; ☺ closed Tue & lunch Wed) A rustic eatery with a grapey stained-glass door, traditional French cuisine and just six tables.

Le Sept (Hôtel Les Berceaux, 13 rue des Berceaux; menus €16-22) A bistro with traditional French fare.

La Table Kobus (☎ 03 26 51 53 53; 3 rue du Docteur Rousseau; menus €18-41; ☺ closed dinner Sun, Mon & Thu) French cuisine in versions traditional and creative, all served amid fin-de-siècle décor.

Restaurant Patrick Michelon (Hôtel Les Berceaux, 13 rue des Berceaux; menus €30-64; ☺ Wed-Sun)

A sparklingly elegant *gastronomique* restaurant whose specialities include truffles (in season) and exquisite blackcurrant sorbet.

SELF-CATERING
Covered market (Halle St-Thibault; rue Gallice; ☉ 8am-noon Wed & Sat)
Open-air market (place Auban Moët; ☉ Sun morning)
Traiteur (9 place Hugues Plomb; ☉ 8am-12.45pm & 3-7.30pm, closed Sun & Wed) Sells scrumptious prepared dishes.
Les Délices de la Ferme (19 rue St-Thibault; ☉ 9am-12.15pm & 3.15-7pm Tue-Sat) Has wonderful cheeses.
Marché Plus (13 place Hugues Plomb; ☉ 7am-9pm Mon-Sat, 9am-1pm Sun) A grocery shop.

Getting There & Around
From the **train station** (place Mendès-France) there are direct services to Nancy (€25.10, two hours, five or six daily), Reims (€5.50, 24 to 46 minutes, 23 daily weekdays, 14 daily weekends) and Paris' Gare de l'Est (€18.60, 1¼ hours, 8 to 13 daily).

Cars can be hired from **Europcar** (☎ 03 26 54 90 61; 20 rempart Perrier).

Parking in the lots south of place de la République is free for the first hour and costs €1/1.50 for the 2nd/subsequent hours.

TROYES
pop 129,000
Troyes – like Reims, one of the historic capitals of Champagne – has a lively old city that's graced with one of France's finest ensembles of Gothic churches and medieval and Renaissance half-timbered houses. It is one of the best places in France to get a sense of what Europe looked like back when William Shakespeare was alive. Several unique and very worthwhile museums provide further reasons to spend some time here.

Troyes does not have any champagne cellars. However, you can shop till you drop in its scores of outlet stores specialising in brand-name clothing and accessories, a legacy of the city's long-time role as France's knitwear capital.

Orientation
Although the Aube was almost strong-armed out of the champagne trade (p369), Troyes' medieval city centre – bounded by blvd Gambetta, blvd Victor Hugo, blvd du 14 Juillet and the Seine – is, cruelly, shaped

---

> ### TROYES AND YOU
> Chances are Troyes has already played a role in your life:
>
> ■ If you've ever enjoyed a story about Lancelot or King Arthur's search for the Holy Grail you owe a debt to the 12th-century poet Chrétien (Chrestien) de Troyes.
>
> ■ Every time you've purchased gold bullion you've done so using the troy ounce, a unit of measure derived from exchange standards established in Troyes in the 12th and 13th centuries.
>
> ■ Whenever you've put on a Lacoste shirt (www.lacoste.com), Petit Bateau kids clothing (www.petit-bateau.com) or sexy Dim undergarments (www .dim.fr in French) you've paid homage to a brand name created right here in France's knitwear capital.

---

like a champagne cork *(bouchon)*. The main commercial street is rue Émile Zola.

Information
The tourist office annexe changes money when the banks are closed but the rate is poor.
Cybercafé Viardin Net & Games (8 rue Viardin; per hr €2.50; ☉ 1pm-midnight Mon-Sat, 2-8pm Sun)
Laundrette (9 rue Georges Clemenceau; ☉ 7.30am-8pm)
Post Office (38 rue Louis Ulbach) Exchanges currency and has a Cyberposte.
Tourist Office (www.tourisme-troyes.com) Train Station (☎ 03 25 82 62 70; 16 blvd Carnot; ☉ 9am-12.30pm & 2-6.30pm Mon-Sat year-round except holidays, 10am-1pm Sun & holidays Nov-Mar); City Centre (☎ 03 25 73 36 88; rue Mignard; ☉ 10am-7pm daily Jul–mid-Sep, 9am-12.30pm & 2-6.30pm Mon-Sat, 10am-noon & 2-5pm Sun & holidays Apr-Jun & mid-Sep-Oct, closed Nov-Mar) Faces the west façade of Église St-Jean.

Sights
OLD CITY
Half-timbered houses line the streets of Troyes' old city, rebuilt after a devastating fire in 1524 – lanes worth exploring include **rue Paillot de Montabert**, **rue Champeaux** and **rue de Vauluisant**.

Off rue Champeaux (between No 30 and 32), a stroll along tiny **ruelle des Chats** (Alley of the Cats), as dark and narrow as it was

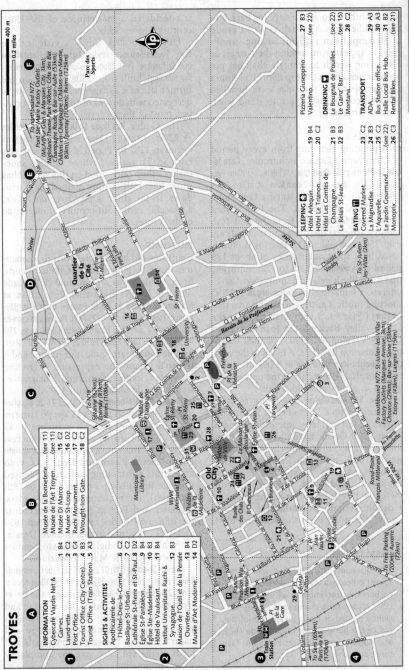

TROYES

INFORMATION
Cybercafé Viardin Net & Games..............1 B4
Laund'ette.................................2 C2
Post Office...............................3 C4
Tourist Office (City Centre).............4 B3
Tourist Office (Train Station)...........5 A3

SIGHTS & ACTIVITIES
Apothicairerie de
  l'Hôtel-Dieu-le-Comte..................6 C2
Basilique St-Urbain......................7 C2
Cathédrale St-Pierre et St-Paul..........8 D2
Église St-Pantaléon......................9 B4
Église Ste-Madeleine....................10 B3
Hôtel de Vauluisant.....................11 B4
Institut Universitaire Rachi &
Synagogue...............................12 B3
Maison de l'Outil et de la Pensée
  Ouvrière..............................13 B4
Musée d'Art Moderne.....................14 D2

Musée de la Bonneterie...............(see 11)
Musée de l'Art Troyen................(see 11)
Musée Di Marco..........................15 C2
Musée St-Loup...........................16 D2
Rachi Monument..........................17 C2
Wrought-Iron Gate.......................18 A3

SLEEPING
Hôtel Arlequin..........................19 B4
Hôtel Le Trianon........................20 C2
Hôtel Les Comtes de
  Champagne............................21 B3
Le Relais St-Jean.......................22 B3

EATING
Covered Market..........................23 C2
La Mignardise...........................24 B3
L'Aquarelle.............................25 C2
Le Jardin Gourmand..................(see 22)
Monoprix................................26 C3

Pizzeria Giuseppino.....................27 B3
Valentino...........................(see 22)

DRINKING
Le Bougnat de Pouilles..............(see 22)
Le Gainz' Bar...........................28 C2
Montana.................................(see 15)

TRANSPORT
ADA.....................................29 A3
Bus Station office......................30 A3
Halle Local Bus Hub.....................31 B2
Rental Bikes........................(see 21)

0 0.2 miles
0 400 m

four centuries ago, is like stepping back into the Middle Ages. You half expect a group of Shakespearean ruffians, singing drunkenly, to appear from around the corner, or a sneering wench to empty a chamber pot on your head from the top floor. The stones at intervals along the sides were installed to give pedestrians a place to stand when horses clattered by.

CHURCHES

Incorporating elements from every period of Champenois Gothic architecture, **Cathédrale St-Pierre et St-Paul** (place St Pierre; 10am-7pm daily Jul & Aug, 10am-1pm & 2-6pm Mon-Sat, to 5pm Sun & holidays Sep-Jun, closed Mon Nov-Mar) is a 114m-long architectural mishmash. The Flamboyant Gothic **west façade** dates from the mid-16th century, whereas the choir and transepts are over 250 years older. The interior is illuminated by a spectacular series of about 180 **stained-glass windows** (13th to 17th centuries) that shine like jewels on a sunny day. Also of interest: a fantastical baroque **organ** (1730s) sporting musical *putti* (cherubs); and a tiny **treasury** (Jul & Aug) with enamels from the Meuse Valley. Back in 1429, Joan of Arc and Charles VII stopped off here on their way to his coronation in Reims. A block to the west, the **wrought-iron gate** (rue de la Cité) of a one-time hospital – now part of the university – glitters in glamorous gilded glory.

Église Ste-Madeleine (rue Général de Gaulle; 9.30am-12.30pm & 2-5.30pm except Sun morning), Troyes' oldest and most interesting church, has an early-Gothic nave and transept from the mid-12th century; the choir and tower weren't built until the Renaissance. The main attraction is the splendid Flamboyant Gothic **rood screen**, which dates from the early 1500s. In the nave, the statue of a deadly serious **Ste Marthe** (St Martha), around the pillar from the wooden pulpit,

is considered a masterpiece of the 15th-century Troyes School.

Other churches worth a visit include the Renaissance-style **Église St-Pantaléon** (rue de Turenne; 9.30am-12.30pm & 2-5.30pm except Sun morning), built from 1508 to 1672 on the former site of a synagogue. The interior is decorated with dozens of 16th-century statues, most of them carved locally.

The Gothic **Basilique St-Urbain** (place Vernier; 9.30am-12.30pm & 2-5.30pm except Sun morning) was begun in 1262 by Pope Urban IV, who was born in Troyes and whose father's shoemaker's shop once stood on this spot. It has some fine 13th-century stained-glass windows. In the choir is *La Vierge au Raisin*, a graceful early-15th-century stone statue of the Virgin.

MUSEUMS

Centuries-old hand tools, worn to a sensuous lustre by generations of skilled hands, bring to life a world of manual skills made obsolete by the Industrial Revolution at **Maison de l'Outil et de la Pensée Ouvrière** (Museum of Tools & Crafts; 03 25 73 28 26; www.maison-de-l-outil.com; 7 rue de la Trinité; adult/student under 25yr €6.50/free; 10am-6pm, closed 25 Dec & 1 Jan). Run by a national crafts guild, this unique and – if you'll excuse the expression – riveting museum is in the magnificent Renaissance-style Hôtel de Mauroy (mid-1500s).

Musée d'Art Moderne (03 25 76 26 80; place St-Pierre; adult/student under 25yr €5/free; 11am-6pm except Mon & holidays) owes its existence to all those alligator shirts, whose global success allowed the museum's benefactors, Lacoste entrepreneurs Pierre and Denise Lévy, to amass this outstanding collection. Housed in a one-time bishop's palace (16th to 18th centuries), the museum focuses on glass, ceramics and French painting (including lots of Fauvist works) created between 1850 and 1950. Featured artists include Derain, Dufy, Matisse, Modigliani, Picasso, Soutine and local favourite Maurice Marinot.

Musée St-Loup (03 25 76 21 68; 1 rue Chrestien de Troyes; adult/student under 25yr €4/free; 10am-noon or 1pm & 2-6pm, closed Tue & holidays), across the street from the cathedral, has a wide-ranging and sometimes surprising collection of medieval sculpture, enamel, archaeology and natural history. The stuffed mammals and birds at the entrance give the completely wrong impression!

PASS' TROYES

This discount pass (€12), on sale at the tourist office, is a really great deal. Among its benefits: free entry to all seven of the city's museums, a champagne tasting session, a guided or audioguided tour of the old city, a horse-drawn carriage ride (July and August) and discounts at various factory outlet shops.

If you come down with an old-fashioned malady – scurvy, perhaps, or unbalanced humours – the place to go is the **Apothicaire de l'Hôtel-Dieu-le-Comte** (☎ 03 25 80 98 97; quai des Comtes de Champagne; adult/student under 25yr €2/free; ⏰ 10am-noon or 1pm & 2-6pm, closed Tue & holidays year-round, Thu & Fri Oct-May), a fully outfitted, wood-panelled pharmacy from 1721. Try not to think about what the two metal gadgets that look like enormous hypodermic needles were used for. The empty ground storey of the building across the little court-yard once served as a morgue.

Hôtel de Vauluisant (☎ 03 25 73 05 85; 4 rue de Vauluisant; adult/student under 25yr €3/free; ⏰ 10am-noon or 1pm & 2-6pm, closed Tue & holidays year-round, Mon Oct-May), a haunted-looking Renaissance-style mansion-turned-museum, has two sections. **Musée de l'Art Troyen** (Museum of Troyes Art) features the evocative paintings, stained glass and statuary (stone and wood) of the Troyes School, which flourished here during the economic prosperity and artistic ferment of the 1500s. **Musée de la Bonneterie** (Hosiery & Knitwear Museum) showcases the sock-strewn story of Troyes' 19th-century knitting industry. Some of the machines on display look like enormous Swiss watches.

The dramatic, action-packed drawings of Angelo Di Marco are featured at the new **Musée Di Marco** (☎ 03 25 40 18 27; www.museedimarco.com in French; 61 rue de la Cité; adult/student €5/4; ⏰ 10am-6.30pm daily Mar-Oct, 11am-6pm Wed-Sun Nov-Feb). The highlights include spellbindingly sensationalist renderings of the attempted assassination of Charles de Gaulle and of the assassination of John F Kennedy.

Sleeping

A number of two- and three-star hotels face the train station.

Hôtel Le Trianon (☎ 03 25 73 18 52; 2 rue Pithou; d with washbasin/shower €25/34; ⏰ reception 11am-8pm Mon, 6.30am-8pm Tue-Sat, 9am-1pm Sun) At this gay-friendly place the rainbow flag flies proudly from the balcony. The eight rooms, above a jaunty yellow bar, are spacious but ordinary though most have chimneys.

our pick **Hôtel Arlequin** (☎ 03 25 83 12 70; www.hotelarlequin.com; 50 rue de Turenne; d from €39.50; ⏰ reception 8am-12.30pm & 2-10pm Mon-Sat, 8am-12.30pm & 6.30-10pm Sun & holidays) The 22 cheerful rooms at this charming and very yellow two-star hostelry come with antique furnishings, high ceilings and *commedia dell'arte* playfulness. The whole place, lovingly kept, is furnished in exceptionally good taste, from the smart custard façade to the lemony breakfast room.

Hôtel Les Comtes de Champagne (☎ 03 25 73 11 70; www.comtesdechampagne.com; 56 rue de la Monnaie; d/q from €47/63, d with washbasin €29) For centuries, the same massive wooden ceiling beams have kept this super-welcoming place from collapsing into a pile of toothpicks. A huge and very romantic double goes for €69.

Le Relais St-Jean (☎ 03 25 73 89 90; www.relais-st-jean.com; 51 rue Paillot de Montabert; d €85-130; ♿) On a narrow medieval street in the heart of the old city, this four-star hotel has 25 rooms that were the last word in ultramodern back in the 1980s – gotta love the marble and lucite! Has its own little tropical hothouse (don't be startled – the chicken is stuffed) and good wheelchair access.

RASHI

During the 11th and 12th centuries, a small Jewish community was established in Troyes under the protection of the counts of Champagne. Its most illustrious member was Rabbi Shlomo Yitzhaki (Solomon son of Isaac; 1040–1105), better known as Rashi (Rachi in French).

Rashi's commentaries on the Bible and the Talmud, which combine literal and nonliteral methods of interpretation and make extensive use of allegories and parables as well as symbolic meanings, are still vastly important to Jews and have also had an impact on Christian Bible interpretation. Rashi's habit of explaining difficult words and passages in the local French vernacular – transliterated into Hebrew characters – has made his writings an important resource for scholars of Old French. In 1475 (a mere three decades after Gutenberg), Rashi's Bible commentary became the first book to be printed in Hebrew.

In Troyes (pronounced *troy*-ess in Rashi's transliteration), the striking **Rachi monument** (next to the Théâtre de Champagne) stands very near the site of a medieval Jewish cemetery where Rashi is believed to have been buried. A local institute of Jewish studies, the **Institut Universitaire Rachi** (2 rue Brunneval) is named in his honour.

CHAMPAGNE

Eating

The people of Troyes are enormously proud of the local speciality, *andouillette de Troyes* (chitterling sausage).

Rue Champeaux (just north of Église St-Jean) is lined with restaurants. Student-oriented eateries can be found just west of the cathedral along rue de la Cité and rue Georges Clemenceau. Troyes may have more kebab joints per capita than any other city in France.

Le Jardin Gourmand (☎ 03 25 73 36 13; 31 rue Paillot de Montabert; weekday lunch menus €17, mains €17-25; ☒ closed Sun & lunch Mon) Elegant without being overly formal, this intimate restaurant uses only the freshest ingredients for its French and Champenoise dishes, including no fewer than 11 kinds of *andouillette*. The estimable wine list offers 27 vintages by the glass. There's a terrace in summer.

La Mignardise (☎ 03 25 73 15 30; 1 ruelle des Chats; menus €19-45; ☒ closed dinner Sun & Mon) An elegant restaurant whose traditional French cuisine is served under ancient wood beams, 19th-century mouldings and ultramodern halogen lamps. The menu changes every six to eight weeks. The chef is a particular fan of fish.

Valentino (☎ 03 25 73 14 14; 35 rue Paillot de Montabert; menus €22-46; ☒ lunch & dinner, closed lunch Sat, dinner Sun & Mon) This is a modern restaurant whose chef takes the fusionista approach, combining classic French ingredients and *savoir-faire* with East Asian spices and forms. On a quiet medieval courtyard.

Good-value options:

Pizzeria Giuseppino (☎ 03 25 73 92 44; 26 rue Paillot de Montabert; pastas & pizzas €6.70-9.20; ☒ Tue-Sat) Serves crispy, ultrathin pizza widely considered to be Troyes' best.

L'Aquarelle (☎ 03 25 73 87 82; 24 rue Georges Clemenceau; ☒ noon-btwn 9.30pm & 1.30am, closed dinner Sun & Mon Nov-Mar) Delicious savoury *galettes* (€4.10 to €7.10), sweet crêpes (€2 to €5.50), salads (€4 to €7.50) and local Pays de l'Othe *cidre* served by a soft-spoken fellow from Belfast.

SELF-CATERING

Covered market (place de la Halle; ☒ 8am-12.45pm & 3.30-7pm Mon-Thu, 7am-7pm Fri & Sat, 9am-12.30pm Sun)

Monoprix (71 rue Émile Zola; ☒ 8.30am-8pm Mon-Sat) The edibles at this supermarket are upstairs.

Drinking

Le Bougnat de Pouilles (☎ 03 25 73 59 85; 29 rue Paillot de Montabert; ☒ 5pm-3am Mon-Sat) A funky bar/wine bar that doubles as an art gallery. The ventilation system looks like it was inspired either by the Centre Pompidou or by an extremely limited budget – in any case the antidécor seems to put people at ease. Attacks of the munchies can be overcome with plates of cold cuts or cheese (€7.50). There's live music two or three times a month, often on Thursday from 9pm.

Le Gainz' Bar (☎ 03 25 80 60 76; 37 rue de la Cité; ☒ 10am-3am Mon-Sat) Named in honour of the legendary baladeer Serge Gainsbourg (that's him in shades on the wall), this friendly, rambling place is Troyes' most popular student hang-out. There's a student night on Thursday, a DJ on Friday (10pm-1am) and a theme night on Saturday. Sports options include darts, billiards and foosball.

Montana (☎ 03 25 70 16 52; 5 place de la République, under the FNAC store; admission free, except men Thu-Sat & women Sat €11; ☒ 11pm-4.30am) From Sunday to Wednesday it's a bar with a DJ, from Thursday to Saturday a disco featuring Latino, salsa and House – but *no* 1980s! Attracts lots of students on Thursday and has a drag queen cabaret starting at 1am on Sunday.

Shopping

Troyes is famous across France for its **magasins d'usine** (factory outlets; ☒ generally 10am-7pm, closed Sun, Marques Avenue & part of Marques City also closed to 2pm Mon), a legacy of the local knitwear industry. Brand-name sportswear, underwear, baby clothes, shoes and so on – discontinued styles, unsold stock, returns, prototypes – attract bargain-hunters by the coachload.

Most stores are situated in two main zones:

- **St-Julien-les-Villas** – About 3km south of the city centre on blvd de Dijon (the N71 to Dijon). **Marques Avenue** (☎ 03 25 82 80 80; www.marquesavenue.com; 114 blvd de Dijon) boasts 240 name brands.
- **Pont Ste-Marie** – About 3km northeast of Troyes' city centre along rue Marc Verdier, which links av Jean Jaurès (the N77 to Châlons-en-Champagne) with av Jules Guesde (the D960 to Nancy). **McArthur Glen** (☎ 03 25 70 47 10; www.mcarthurglen.fr) is a huge strip mall with 84 shops. Adjacent **Marques City** (☎ 03 25 46 37 48; www.marquescity.com) brings together 30 more stores.

Getting There & Away

The **bus station office** (☎ 03 25 71 28 42; ⊙ 8.30am-12.30pm & 2-6.30pm Mon-Fri), run by Courriers de l'Aube, is in a corner of the train station building. Schedules are posted on the up-rights next to each bus berth. For details on getting to Reims see p360.

Cars can be rented from **ADA** (☎ 03 25 73 41 68; 2 rue Voltaire).

Troyes is on the rather isolated **train** line linking Basel (Bâle; Switzerland) and Mulhouse (Alsace) with Paris' Gare de l'Est (€21.10, 1½ hours, 12 to 14 daily). A change of trains gets you to Dijon (€25.70, 2½ to four hours, three to five daily).

Getting Around

There's a large free car park a block south of blvd du 1er RAM on blvd Général Charles Delestraint (the southern part of blvd Victor Hugo). The unpaved lot 200m north-west of the train station may also be free.

The Hôtel Les Comtes de Champagne (see p367) arranges **rental bikes** for €8/€12 per half/whole day; phone ahead if possible. A 42km bike path links the Troyes suburb of St-Julien-les-Villas with Lac d'Orient and two adjacent lakes farther north.

The local **bus** company, **TCAT** (☎ 03 25 70 49 00; www.tcat.fr in French), has its main bus hub, known as Halle, next to the covered market.

To order a **taxi**, call ☎ 03 25 78 30 30 or ☎ 03 25 76 06 60.

CÔTE DES BAR

Although the Aube *département*, of which Troyes is the capital, is a major producer of champagne (it has 68 sq km of vineyards, 85% of them Pinot Noir), it gets little of the recognition accorded the Marne *département* and the big *maisons* up around Reims and Épernay. Much of the acrimony dates back to 1909, when the winemakers of the Aube were excluded from the growing area for Champagne's Appellation d'Origine Contrôlée (AOC). Two years later, they were also forbidden to sell their grapes to producers up north, provoking a revolt by local *vignerons*, months of strikes and a situation so chaotic that the army was eventually called in. It was another 16 years before the Aube growers were fully certified as producers of genuine champagne but by then the Marne had established market domination.

Today, champagne production in the southeastern corner of the Aube (about 35km southeast of Troyes) – just north of Burgundy's Châtillonnais vineyards (see p474) – is relatively modest in scale, though the reputation of the area's wines has been on an upward trajectory in recent years.

The Côte des Bar section of the **Champagne Route** (p360) passes through **Bar-sur-Aube** (☎ tourist office 03 25 27 24 25), graced by a medieval quarter and two churches, which is on the rail line linking Troyes (€8.50, 30 minutes, five to 10 a day) with Langres (€10.90, 31 to 54 minutes, five or six daily). Nearby, **Bayel** (☎ tourist office 03 25 92 42 68; www.bayel-cristal.com) has long been known for crystal-making; tours of the **Cristalleries Royales de Champagne** (Champagne Royal Glassworks) begin at 9.30am and 11am Monday to Friday except holidays.

The Champagne Route also takes you to **Colombey-les-Deux-Églises**, where Charles de

---

NIGLOLAND THEME PARK

The third most popular amusement park in France (Disneyland Resort Paris, p210, is No 1), **Nigloland** (☎ 03 25 27 94 52; www.nigloland.fr; adult/under 12yr & over 60yr/child under 1m tall €17/15.50/free; ⊙ 10am-6pm or 7pm mid-Jun–Aug, to 5.30pm or 6pm most days early Apr–mid-Jun, weekends Sep–early Nov) may be even cheesier than its competitors, but the place – whose mascot is Niglo the Hedgehog – is still a huge hit with kids, especially those age three to 12. Think you're intrepid? Prepare to be *trépidé* (thrilled) on the **Grizzli**, a sort of rotating roller coaster. Homesick Americans can drop by 1950s-style Hollywood Blvd and take a road trip (without autoroute tolls!) along Route Nationale 66, both in the Village Rock and Roll. It's not clear what a Caribbean pirate galleon (a giant swing) and a paddlewheel river steamer named the *King of Mississippi* are doing in the Village Canadien (Canadian Village) but you might want to mention this peculiar arrangement the next time you hear a snooty European making condescending noises about North Americans' ignorance of geography. The park is on the N19 40km east of Troyes in Dolancourt. If you're on the A5 take exit No 22 or 23.

Gaulle is buried. **La Boisserie** (☎ 03 25 01 52 52; adult/12-18yr/under 12yr €4/4/free, incl memorial €7/6/free; ☒ 10am-12.30pm & 2-6.15pm daily mid-Apr–mid-Oct, 10am-12.30pm & 2-5.15pm Wed-Mon mid-Oct–Nov & Feb–mid-Apr), the general's family home from 1934 to 1970, is now a museum and place of Gaullist pilgrimage. The 43.5m-high Lorraine cross (1972), symbol of the Resistance, was paid for by public subscription.

Also along the route is **Essoyes** (es-*wa*), where Renoir spent his last 25 summers and is buried. **Maison de la Vigne** (☎ 03 25 29 64 64; admission €2.50, with champagne dégustation €4; ☒ 10am-12.30pm & 2.30-6.30pm Easter-1 Nov, closed Mon morning) has exhibits on wine-growing in Champagne. **Les Riceys** (☎ tourist office 03 25 29 15 38) is a *commune* noted for its three churches, three different AOCs and exceptional rosé wines.

Langres
pop 9500

Langres, 75km southeast of Bar-sur-Aube and about the same distance north of Dijon, is both an elongated hilltop bastion, with six towers and seven fortified gates, and a cheese with an orangey-yellow crust. The town's most famous son is Denis Diderot (1713–84), the great encyclopaedist; his statue graces place Diderot, the main square in the centuries-old stone-built town centre.

The **tourist office** (☎ 03 25 87 67 67; www.tourisme-langres.com; square Olivier Lahalle; ☒ Mon-Sat year-round, Sun & holidays May-Sep) is next to one of the town gates, **Porte des Moulins** (1647).

Two blocks north of place Diderot is **Cathédrale St-Mammès**, whose classical façade (1758), with its mammoth columns, hides a late-Romanesque and early-Gothic interior. The modern **Musée d'Art et d'Histoire** (☎ 03 25 87 08 05; place du Centenaire; admission free; ☒ 10am-noon & 2-5pm or 6pm Wed-Mon), two short blocks west of the cathedral, has a collection that ranges from Gallo-Roman archaeology to 17th- and 18th-century painting and sculpture. Circumambulating the **ramparts** – on the inside or the outside – is a 3.5km affair.

The two-star, Logis de France–affiliated **Grand Hôtel de l'Europe** (☎ 03 25 87 10 88; hotel-europe.langres@wanadoo.fr; 23 rue Diderot; s/d from €50/62; ☒ closed Sun evening Nov–mid-May), in a one-time post house two blocks north of place Diderot, has 26 rooms that boast 'bourgeois comfort'. The rustic French **restaurant** (menus €15-44) specialises in game (in season) and dishes made with local cheese.

Langres' train station, on the flats about 3km west of the old town centre, has services to Dijon (€12.40, one hour, three or four daily) and Troyes (€17.40, 1¼ hours, five or six daily).

Alsace & Lorraine

Though often spoken of as if they were one, Alsace and Lorraine, neighbouring *régions* in France's northeastern corner, are linked by little more than a border through the Massif des Vosges (Vosges Mountains) and the imperialism of 19th-century Germany. In 1871, after the Franco-Prussian War, the newly created German Reich annexed Alsace and the northern part of Lorraine, making the *régions'* return to rule from Paris a rallying cry of French nationalism.

Charming and beautiful Alsace, long a meeting place of Europe's Latin and Germanic cultures, is nestled between the Vosges and the River Rhine – along which the long-disputed Franco-German border has at long last found a final resting place. Popularly known as a land of storks' nests and colourful half-timbered houses sprouting geraniums, Alsace also offers a wide variety of outdoor activities – including hiking, biking and skiing – in and around its gentle, forested mountains. Throughout France, the people of Alsace have a reputation for being hard-working, well organised and tax-paying.

Lorraine, a land of prairies and forests popularly associated with quiche and de Gaulle's double-barred cross *(croix de Lorraine)*, has little of the picturesque quaintness of Alsace. However, it is home to two particularly handsome cities, both former capitals. Nancy, one of France's most refined and attractive urban centres, is famed for its Art Nouveau architecture, while Metz, 54km to the north, is known for its Germanic architecture and the stunning stained glass of its marvellous cathedral. The town of Verdun bears silent testimony to the destruction and insanity of WWI.

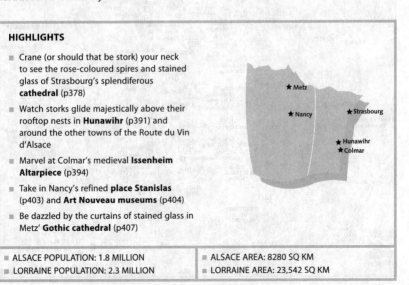

HIGHLIGHTS

- Crane (or should that be stork) your neck to see the rose-coloured spires and stained glass of Strasbourg's splendiferous **cathedral** (p378)

- Watch storks glide majestically above their rooftop nests in **Hunawihr** (p391) and around the other towns of the Route du Vin d'Alsace

- Marvel at Colmar's medieval **Issenheim Altarpiece** (p394)

- Take in Nancy's refined **place Stanislas** (p403) and **Art Nouveau museums** (p404)

- Be dazzled by the curtains of stained glass in Metz' **Gothic cathedral** (p407)

★ Metz

★ Nancy   ★ Strasbourg

★ Hunawihr
★ Colmar

- ALSACE POPULATION: 1.8 MILLION
- LORRAINE POPULATION: 2.3 MILLION

- ALSACE AREA: 8280 SQ KM
- LORRAINE AREA: 23,542 SQ KM

ALSACE

Alsace, which is 190km long and no more than 50km wide, is made up of two rival *départements* (administrative divisions): **Bas-Rhin** (Lower Rhine; www.tourisme67 .com), the area around the dynamic regional (and European) capital, Strasbourg; and **Haut-Rhin** (Upper Rhine; www.tour isme68.com), which covers the region's more southerly reaches, including the picturesque *département* capital, Colmar, and the industrial city of Mulhouse. Germany is just across the busy Rhine, whose left bank is Alsatian as far south as the Swiss city of Basel.

History

French influence in Alsace began during the Wars of Religion (1562–98) and increased during the Thirty Years' War (1618–48) when Alsatian cities, caught between opposing Catholic and Protestant factions, turned to France. Most of the region was attached to France in 1648 under the Treaty of Westphalia. Today one-fifth of Alsatians are Protestants.

By the time of the French Revolution, the Alsatians felt far more connected to France than to Germany, but the passage of time did little to dampen Germany's appetite for the region known in German as Elsass (Elsaß). The Franco-Prussian War of 1870–71, a supremely humiliating episode

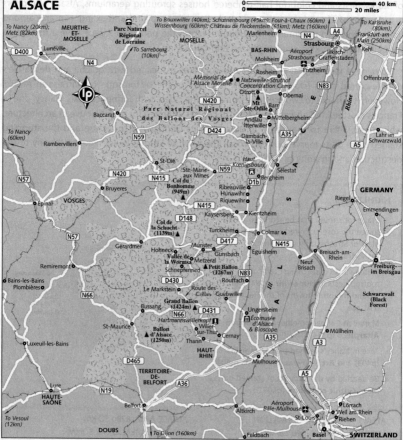

THE MAGINOT LINE

The famed **Ligne Maginot** (www.maginot.org), named after France's minister of war from 1929 to 1932, was one of the most spectacular blunders of WWII. This elaborate, mostly subterranean defence network, built between 1930 and 1940 (and, in the history of military architecture, second only to the Great Wall of China in sheer size), was the pride of prewar France. It included everything France's finest military architects thought would be needed to defend the nation in a 'modern war' of poison gas, tanks and aeroplanes: reinforced concrete bunkers, subterranean lines of supply and communication, minefields, antitank canals, floodable basins and even artillery emplacements that popped out of the ground to fire and then disappeared. The only things visible above ground were firing posts and lookout towers. The line stretched along the Franco-German frontier from the Swiss border all the way to Belgium where, for political and budgetary reasons, it stopped. The Maginot Line even had a slogan: *'Ils ne passeront pas'* (They won't get through).

'They' – the Germans – never did. Rather than attack the Maginot Line straight on, Hitler's armoured divisions simply circled around through Belgium and invaded France across its unprotected northern frontier. They then attacked the Maginot Line from the rear. With most of northern France already in German hands, some of the fortifications held out for a few weeks.

Parts of the Maginot Line are open to visitors thanks to local volunteer organisations (the French government still considers the Maginot Line an embarrassing failure and provides no funding). In Lorraine, visitors can tour more than a dozen sites, including Fort du Hackenberg (p412) and Fort de Fermont (p416). Major Maginot sites in Alsace:

Four-à-Chaux (☎ 03 88 94 48 62, Lembach tourist office ☎ 03 88 94 43 16; www.lignemaginot.fr, www.ot-lembach.com; adult/student/under 12yr €4.50/3.50/2; ☾ tours 10am, 2pm & 3pm late Mar–early Nov, also at 11am Jul–Sep & 4pm May–Sep, 10.30am & 2.30pm Sat & Sun early Nov–late Mar) Captured by the Germans after a week of fighting in June 1940, this fort is 60km north of Strasbourg and a few kilometres east of Lembach on the tiny D65. Guided tours (in French and German with English text) last 1½ to two hours and involve 1.7km of walking.

Schœnenbourg (Hunspach tourist office ☎ 03 88 80 59 39; www.lignemaginot.com; adult/6–18yr €6/4; ☾ self-guided tours 2–4pm Mon–Fri Easter–Sep, 2–4pm Sat Easter–mid-Oct, 9.30–11am & 2–4pm Sun Easter–mid-Oct) The largest visitable Maginot fortress, this concrete behemoth is about 45km north of Strasbourg. The self-guided tour follows a two-hour, 2.5km route; signs are in English.

in French history, ended with the Treaty of Frankfurt (1871), by which an embittered France was forced to cede Alsace to the Second Reich. Following Germany's defeat in WWI, the region was returned to France but it was reannexed by Nazi Germany in 1940.

After WWII, Alsace was once again returned to France. Intra-Alsatian tensions ran high, however, as those who had left came back and confronted neighbours whom they suspected of having collaborated with the Germans: 140,000 Alsatians, as annexed citizens of the Third Reich, had been conscripted into Hitler's armies. These conscripts were known as the 'Malgré-Nous' because the vast majority had gone off to war against their will; over half never returned from the Russian front and postwar Soviet prison camps. To make Alsace a symbol of hope for future Franco-German (and pan-European) coexistence and cooperation, Strasbourg was chosen as the seat of the Council of Europe (in 1949) and, later, of the European Parliament.

The impressive new **Mémorial de l'Alsace Moselle** (☎ 03 88 47 45 50; www.memorial-alsace-moselle.org in French; adult/student & over 65yr incl audio-guide €10/7; ☾ 10am–6pm or 7pm Tue–Sun, closed late Dec–late Jan), 53km southwest of Strasbourg in Schirmeck (just a few kilometres from the Natzweiler-Struthof Concentration Camp, p388), takes an unblinking but reconciliatory look at the region's traumatic modern history.

Strong Alsatian regionalism fuels support for the far-right Front National party, which received 22% of the votes in the first round of the 2004 regional elections.

Getting There & Around

Alsace is *almost* in central Europe. Situated 456km east of Paris, it's midway between Calais and Prague (about 630km from each)

THE LOCAL LINGO

Alsatian (Elsässisch; www.heimetsproch.org), the language of Alsace, is an Alemannic dialect of German not unlike the dialects spoken in nearby parts of Germany and Switzerland. It has no official written form (spelling – including on menus – is something of a free-for-all), and pronunciation varies considerably from one area to another (especially between the north and south). Despite a series of heavy-handed attempts by both the French and the Germans to impose their languages on the region, in part by restricting (or even banning) the use of Alsatian, it is – miraculously – still used in everyday life by people of all ages, in the villages as well as the cities. You're likely to hear its sing-songy cadences whenever you happen upon locals who are just being themselves – for instance, in a *bäkerlààda* (*boulangerie*; bakery).

---

and is slightly closer to Berlin (801km) than to Marseille (814km).

From Strasbourg, the A4 heads northwest towards Metz and Paris, while from Mulhouse the A36 goes southwest towards the Jura and Dijon. Heading due west from the Colmar area involves crossing the Massif des Vosges, which can be snowy in winter (winter tyres and/or chains may be required, eg to cross Col de la Schlucht).

When the long-awaited TGV Est Européen begins running in June 2007, travel time from Paris to Strasbourg will be cut almost in half, to 2¼ hours.

Special discount rail fares are available for travel within Alsace. The Pass Evasion, available on Saturday, Sunday and holidays, costs €8.10 for unlimited all-day travel within either the Bas-Rhin or Haut-Rhin *départements*, or €13 for travel anywhere in Alsace. A version valid for two or five people travelling together costs €16.20 and €26, respectively – perfect for day trips to the wine towns! You can get 25% off on all regional rail travel if you're aged 12 to 25, over 60 or travelling in a group of two to nine people.

Alsace has *lots* of bike trails. Bicycles can be brought along on almost all trains and autorails (but not SNCF buses).

STRASBOURG
pop 427,000

Prosperous, cosmopolitan Strasbourg (City of the Roads) is France's great northeastern metropolis and the intellectual and cultural capital of Alsace. Situated only a few kilometres west of the Rhine, the city is aptly named, for it is on the vital transport arteries that have linked northern Europe with the Mediterranean since Celtic times.

Strasbourg continues to serve as an important European crossroads thanks to the presence of the European Parliament, the Council of Europe, the European Court of Human Rights, the Eurocorps (www.eurocorps.org), the Franco-German TV network Arte (www.arte-tv.com in French and German) and a student population of some 48,000, 20% from outside France. Strasbourg is one of Europe's most cycle-friendly cities.

Towering above the restaurants, *winstubs* (traditional Alsatian eateries) and pubs of the lively old city – a wonderful area to explore on foot – is the cathedral, a medieval marvel in pink sandstone. Nearby you'll find one of the finest ensembles of museums anywhere in France.

Accommodation is extremely difficult to find during European Parliament sessions (see www.europarl.eu.int and click 'Activities' and then 'Parliament's Calendar' for dates).

History

Before it was attached to France in 1681, Strasbourg was effectively ruled for several centuries by a guild of citizens whose tenure accorded the city a certain democratic character. Johannes Gutenberg worked in Strasbourg from about 1434 to 1444, perfecting his printing press and the moveable metal type that made it so revolutionary. A university was founded in 1566 and several leaders of the Reformation took up residence here.

Orientation

The train station is 400m west of the Grande Île (Big Island), the core of ancient and modern Strasbourg, whose main squares are place Kléber, place Broglie (*broag*-lee), place Gutenberg and place du Château. The quaint Petite France area, on the Grande Île's southwestern corner, is subdivided by canals.

The European Parliament building and Palais de l'Europe are about 2.5km northeast of the cathedral.

Information

BOOKSHOPS

Bookworm (☎ 03 88 32 26 99; www.bookworm.fr in French; 3 rue de Pâques; ⊠ Ancienne Synagogue; ⊙ 9.30am-6.30pm Tue-Fri, 10am-6pm Sat) Carries new and used English books, including Lonely Planet guides, and is a good source of information on Strasbourg.

Géorama (☎ 03 88 75 01 95; 20-22 rue du Fossé des Tanneurs; ⊠ Homme de Fer; ⊙ 2-7pm Mon, 9.30am-7pm Tue-Sat) Has a huge selection of hiking maps and topoguides.

INTERNET ACCESS

A number of phonecard shops near the train station have internet access, eg at Nos 2 and 8 on rue du Maire Kuss.

L'Utopie (☎ 03 88 23 89 21; 21-23 rue du Fossé des Tanneurs; ⊠ Homme de Fer; per hr €3; ⊙ 7am-11.30pm Mon-Sat, 8am-10pm Sun) The computers are underground.

NeT SuR CouR (☎ 03 88 35 66 76; 18 quai des Pêcheurs; ⊠ Gallia; per hr €2; ⊙ 9.30am-9.30pm Mon-Fri, 1.30-8.30pm Sat & Sun) Hidden at the end of a narrow courtyard.

LAUNDRY

Laundrette 29 Grand' Rue (⊠ Alt Winmärik; ⊙ 7.30am-8pm); 8 rue de la Nuée Bleue (⊠ Broglie; ⊙ 7am-9pm); 15 rue des Veaux (⊙ 7am-9pm)

MEDICAL SERVICES

The Hôpital Civil (☎ 03 88 11 67 68; 1 place de l'Hôpital; ⊠ Porte de l'Hôpital) The 24-hour Accueil (reception) pavilion is inside the monumental gate 50m from Hôtel Au Cerf d'Or. A new hospital complex just west of Hôpital Civil is set to begin functioning between 2006 and 2008.

MONEY

Société Générale (☎ 03 88 23 46 50; 8 place de la Gare; ⊠ Gare Centrale; ⊙ 2-6pm Mon, 8.30am-noon & 1.45-6pm Tue-Fri)

POST

Branch Post Office (place de la Cathédrale; ⊠ Langstross Grand' Rue; ⊙ 8am-6.30pm Mon-Fri, 8am-5pm Sat) Has extended Saturday hours, currency exchange and a Cyberposte.

Main Post Office (5 av de la Marseillaise; ⊠ République) In a neogothic structure built by the Germans in 1899. Has exchange services and a Cyberposte.

TOURIST INFORMATION

Agence de Développement Touristique en Bas-Rhin (☎ 03 88 15 45 88; www.tourisme67.com; 9 rue du Dôme; ⊠ Broglie; ⊙ 9.30am-noon & 1.30-5pm Mon-Fri, to 6pm during high season) Can supply excellent English brochures on Protestant and Jewish sites, hiking, cycling, skiing and activities around Alsace for families with young children.

Main Tourist Office (☎ 03 88 52 28 28; www.ot-strasbourg.fr; 17 place de la Cathédrale; ⊠ Langstross Grand' Rue; ⊙ 9am-7pm) Next door to the ornately carved, 16th-century Maison Kammerzell. A city-centre map costs €1; bus/tram and cycling maps are free. *Strolling in Strasbourg* (€4.50) details six architectural walking tours. The Strasbourg Pass (€10.60), a coupon book valid for three consecutive days, may save you some cash.

Tourist Office Annexe (☎ 03 88 32 51 49; ⊠ Gare Centrale; ⊙ 9am-7pm Jul, Aug & Dec, 9am-12.30pm & 1.45-6pm Sep-Nov & Jan-Jun, closed Sun Jan-Mar, Oct & Nov) In front of the train station in a temporary building but is supposed to move inside the train station.

Sights

GRANDE ÎLE

With its bustling public squares, busy pedestrianised precincts and upmarket shopping streets, the Grande Île, declared a World Heritage site by Unesco, is a paradise for the aimless ambler. The narrow streets of the **old city** are especially enchanting at night, particularly right around the cathedral (eg the Nuée au Sanglier). Also worth a look is **place Gutenberg**, with its Renaissance-style **Chambre de Commerce et d'Industrie** (Chamber of Commerce) building. There are watery views from the paths along the **River Ill** and its canalised branch, the **Fossé du Faux Rempart**; the grassy quays, frequented by swans, are great venues for a picnic or a romantic stroll.

Crisscrossed by narrow lanes, canals and locks, **Petite France** is the stuff of fairy tales. The half-timbered houses, meticulously maintained and sprouting veritable thickets of geraniums, and the riverside parks attract multitudes of tourists. However, the area still manages to retain its Alsatian atmosphere and charm, especially in the early morning and late evening.

The romantic **Terrasse Panoramique** (admission free; ⊙ 9am-7.30pm) on top of **Barrage Vauban** (⊙ 7.30am-7.30pm), a dam built to prevent river-borne attacks on the city (and now used to store bits and pieces of stone statuary), affords panoramas of the River Ill.

ALSACE & LORRAINE

ALSACE & LORRAINE

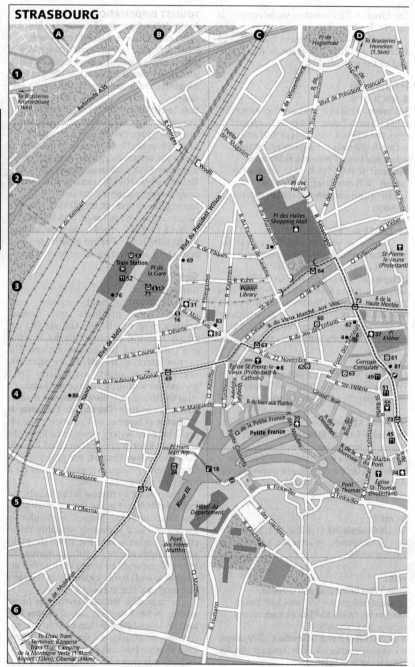

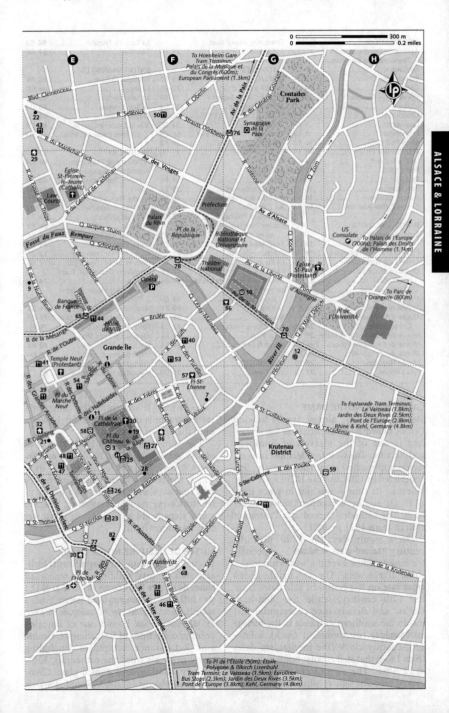

ALSACE & LORRAINE

INFORMATION		
Agence de Développement Touristique en Bas-Rhin	1	E3
Bookworm	2	C3
Branch Post Office	3	E4
Géorama	4	D3
Hôpital Civil (Hospital)	5	E6
L'Utopie	6	D3
Laundrette	7	F4
Laundrette	8	C4
Laundrette	9	E3
Main Post Office	10	G3
Main Tourist Office	11	E4
NeT SuR CouR	12	G3
Post Office	13	B3
Rest Rooms	14	C5
Rest Rooms	15	E4
Société Générale	16	B3
Tourist Office Annexe	17	B3

SIGHTS & ACTIVITIES		
Barrage Vauban & Terrasse Panoramique	18	C5
Cathedral's South Entrance	19	F4
Cathédrale Notre Dame	20	F4
Chambre de Commerce et d'Industrie	21	E4
Club Vosgien	22	E1
Musée Alsacien	23	E5
Musée Archéologique	(see 27)	
Musée d'Art Moderne et Contemporain	24	B5
Musée de l'Œuvre Notre Dame	25	F4
Musée des Arts Décoratifs	(see 27)	
Musée des Beaux-Arts	(see 27)	
Musée Historique	26	E5
Palais Rohan	27	F4

Strasbourg Fluvial Boat Excursions	28	F4

SLEEPING		
CIARUS	29	E2
Hôtel Au Cerf d'Or	30	E5
Hôtel Balladins Supérior	31	B3
Hôtel Gutenburg	32	E4
Hôtel Le Colmar	33	C3
Hôtel Patricia	34	D5
Hôtel Régent Petite France	35	C4
Hôtel Suisse	36	F4
Le Kléber Hôtel	37	D3

EATING		
Adan	38	F6
Atac supermarket	39	E4
Au Coin des Pucelles	40	F3
Au Crocodile	41	E3
Au Renard Prêchant	42	G5
Casher Price Naouri Kosher supermarket	43	E1
Food Market	44	E3
L'Assiette du Vin	45	D4
La Bourse	46	F6
La Cloche à Fromage	47	E4
La Cloche à Fromage Boutique	48	E4
Lafayette Gourmet supermarket	49	D4
Le King	50	F1
Moozé	51	D4
Petit Casino Grocery	52	B3
Tiger Wok	53	F3
Winstub Le Clou	54	E4

DRINKING		
Irish Times	55	D4

La Taverne Fraçaise	56	G3
Zanzibar	57	F4

ENTERTAINMENT		
Boutique Culture	58	E4
La Java	(see 53)	
La Salamandre	59	H4
Le Star Cinema	60	D3
Odyssée Cinema	61	D4
Star St Exupéry Cinema	62	C4
Virgin Megastore billeterie	63	D4

TRANSPORT		
Alt Winmärik Tram Stop	64	C4
Ancienne Synagogue-Les Halles Tram Stop	65	D3
Avis	(see 76)	
Broglie Tram Stop	66	E3
CTS Information Bureau	67	D3
Eurolines Office	68	F5
Europcar	69	B3
Faubourg National Tram Stop	70	B4
Gallia Tram Stop	71	G3
Gare Centrale Tram Stop	72	B3
Homme de Fer Tram Hub	73	D3
Langstross Grand' Rue Tram Stop	74	D4
Musée d'Art Moderne Tram Stop	75	B5
National-Citer	76	B3
Parc du Contades Tram Stop	77	G1
Porte de l'Hôpital Tram Stop	78	E5
République Tram Stop	79	F3
Sixt	80	A4
SNCF Boutique	81	D4
Vélocation Bicycle Rental	82	E5
Vélocation Bicycle Rental	83	C3

CATHÉDRALE NOTRE DAME

Strasbourg's lacy, almost fragile-looking Gothic **cathedral** (Langstross Grand' Rue; 7am-7pm) is one of the marvels of European architecture. The west façade, most impressive if approached from rue Mercière, was completed in 1284, but the 142m spire – the tallest of its time – was not in place until 1439; its southern companion was never built. The cathedral served as a Protestant church from 1521 to 1681.

On a sunny day, the 12th- to 14th-century **stained-glass windows** – especially the rose window over the western portal – shine like jewels. The colourful, gilded **organ case** on the northern side dates from the 14th century, while the 30m-high Gothic and Renaissance contraption just inside the southern entrance is the **horloge astronomique** (astronomical clock), a late-16th-century clock (the mechanism dates from 1842) that strikes solar noon every day at 12.30pm. There's a €1 charge to see the carved wooden figures whirl through their

paces, which is why only the cathedral's **south entrance** is open from about 11.40am until the end of the show.

The 66m-high **platform** (03 88 43 60 40; adult/student & 5-18yr €4.40/2.20; 9am or 10am-btwn 4.30pm & 7.30pm) above the façade – from which the **tower** and its Gothic openwork **spire** soar another 76m – affords a spectacular stork's-eye view of Strasbourg. The 330 spiral steps begin at the base of the tower that was never built.

MUSÉE DE L'ŒUVRE NOTRE DAME

Occupying a group of magnificent 14th- and 16th-century buildings, the renowned **Musée de l'Œuvre Notre Dame** (03 88 32 88 17; 3 place du Château; Langstross Grand' Rue; adult/student under 25yr & senior/under 18yr incl audioguide €4/2/free; 10am-6pm Tue-Sun) houses one of Europe's premier collections of Romanesque, Gothic and Renaissance sculptures (including many originals from the cathedral), 15th-century paintings and stained glass. *Christ de Wissembourg* (c 1060; Room Two) is the oldest work of stained glass in France. The celebrated figures of a blindfolded and downcast *Synagogue* (representing Judaism) and a serenely victorious *Église* (the Church), which date from approximately 1230 and once flanked the southern entrance to the cathedral (the statues there now are copies), are in Room Seven.

Hollywood gore seems pretty milquetoasty compared to what they came up with back when Hell really was hell. *Les Amants Trépassés* (the Deceased Lovers; Room 23), painted in 1470, shows a remarkably ugly couple being punished for their illicit lust: both of their entrails are being devoured by dragon-headed snakes while a toad feasts on her pudenda. If this work isn't enough to scare you into a life of chastity nothing will!

MUSÉE D'ART MODERNE ET CONTEMPORAIN

The outstanding **Musée d'Art Moderne et Contemporain** (Museum of Modern & Contemporary Art; ☎ 03 88 23 31 31; place Hans Jean Arp; 🚊 Musée d'Art Moderne; adult €5, student under 25yr & senior €2.50, under 18yr free; 🕑 11am-7pm Tue, Wed, Fri & Sat, noon-10pm Thu, 10am-6pm Sun) displays a permanent collection of 'modern' (pre-WWII) art representing all the major movements (including impressionism, symbolism, Fauvism, cubism, Dadaism and surrealism) and hosts temporary exhibits of contemporary works.

PALAIS ROHAN

The majestic **Palais Rohan** (☎ 03 88 52 50 00; 2 place du Château; 🚊 Langstross Grand' Rue; for the whole complex adult €6, student under 25yr & senior €3, under 18yr & disabled free, for each museum adult €4, student under 25yr & senior €2, under 18yr & disabled free; 🕑 10am-6pm Wed-Mon) was built between 1732 and 1742 as a residence for the city's princely bishops. In the basement, the **Musée Archéologique** (audioguide included in ticket price) takes you from the Palaeolithic period to AD 800. On the ground floor is the **Musée des Arts Décoratifs**, which has a series of lavish rooms featuring the lifestyle of the rich and powerful during the 18th century. Louis XV and Marie-Antoinette once slept here – in 1744 and 1770, respectively. On the 1st floor the **Musée des Beaux-Arts** has a rather staid collection of French, Spanish, Italian, Dutch and Flemish masters from the 14th to the 19th centuries.

MUSÉE ALSACIEN & MUSÉE HISTORIQUE

Housed in three typical houses from the 1500s and 1600s, the **Musée Alsacien** (☎ 03 88 52 50 01; 23 quai St-Nicolas; 🚊 Porte de l'Hôpital; adult €4, student under 25yr & senior €2, under 18yr & disabled free; 🕑 10am-6pm Wed-Sun Jan-Mar, Jul & Aug, noon-6pm Wed-Sat, 10am-6pm Sun & holidays Apr-Jun & Sep-Dec), affords a fascinating glimpse of Alsatian life over the centuries. Displays in the museum's two dozen rooms include kitchen equipment (stoves, ceramics, biscuit cutters), children's toys, colourful furniture and even a tiny 18th-century synagogue.

The long-closed **Musée Historique** (3 place de la Grande Boucherie; 🚊 Porte de l'Hôpital), which focuses on Strasbourg's political, economic and social history, is supposed to reopen in mid-2007.

EUROPEAN INSTITUTIONS

The home of the relatively toothless 732-member **European Parliament** (Parlement Européen; ☎ 03 88 17 20 07; www.europarl.eu.int; rue Lucien Fèbvre; 🚊 Wacken), used just 12 times a year for four-day 'part-sessions' (plenary sessions), is 2.5km northeast of the cathedral. When it's in session (dates are available from the tourist office or on the website – click 'Activities' and then 'Parliament's Calendar'), you can sit in on **debates** (🕑 5-6pm Mon, 9am-noon & 3-6pm Tue & Wed, 10am-noon & 3-5pm Thu) for up to one hour; it's first-come first-served (bring ID) and no reservations are possible. The rest of the time the building is inaccessible because of strict post-9/11 security measures.

Across the Ill, the Council of Europe's **Palais de l'Europe** (☎ 03 88 41 20 29; www.coe.int), once used by the European Parliament, can be visited on free one-hour weekday tours; ring ahead for times and reservations. During the four annual week-long sessions of

ALSACE & LORRAINE

JEWISH ALSACE

Interest in Alsace's rich Jewish heritage (www.sdv.fr/judaisme in French, http://judaisme.sdv.fr/histoire/historiq/anglais/history.htm), spanning 1000 years, has grown tremendously in recent years. Indeed, the **European Day of Jewish Culture** (www.jewisheritage.org), marked in early September in 26 countries, grew out of a local initiative in northern Alsace. Famous people of Alsatian-Jewish origin include Captain Alfred Dreyfus (of the Dreyfus Affair), the Marx Brothers (of *Duck Soup*) and Julia Louis-Dreyfus (Elaine Benes on *Seinfeld*).

Today most Alsatian Jews live in Strasbourg, whose vibrant Jewish community – proud of its unique liturgical and musical traditions – numbers about 15,000. Alsace is the only region in France in which the majority of the Jews are Ashkenazim, ie spoke various versions of Yiddish in centuries past (nationwide, some 70% of French Jews immigrated from North Africa in the mid-20th century).

Towns all over the region, including many along the Route du Vin d'Alsace, have historic **synagogues**. Museums with exhibits related to Alsatian Judaism include Strasbourg's Musée de l'Œuvre Notre Dame (p378) and Musée Alsacien (p379); Colmar's Musée Bartholdi (p394); and the **Musée Judéo-Alsacien** (☎ 03 88 70 97 17; http://judaisme.sdv.fr/today/musee in French; 62 Grand' Rue; ☺ adult/child 8-15yr €6/3; ☺ 2-5pm Tue-Fri, 2-6pm Sun & holidays, closed Sat late Apr–mid-Sep) in Bouxwiller, 40km northeast of Strasbourg. Some tourist offices (eg Strasbourg) offer walking tours of Jewish sites in French.

The Agence de Développement Touristique en Bas-Rhin (p375) publishes an excellent brochure, *Discovering Alsatian Judaism*.

---

the council's 46-country *assemblée parlementaire* (parliamentary assembly) you can sit in on debates (no reservations required). To get there by bus, take No 6, 30 or 72.

Just across Canal de la Marne, the striking **Palais des Droits de l'Homme** (☎ 03 88 41 34 95; www.echr.coe.int), home of the European Court of Human Rights, completes the city's ensemble of major European institutions. Sitting in on one of the two to five monthly court sessions, which generally begin at 9am or 9.30am Tuesday to Thursday and last about 90 minutes, is possible if there's space – check the website under 'pending cases' for dates and get there with ID a half-hour ahead (reservations are possible only for groups). The *palais* (court) is served by bus Nos 6, 30 and 72.

OTHER SIGHTS

Many of Strasbourg's most impressive (and German-built) public buildings are just northeast of the Grande Île around **place de la République** (☐ République). The neighbourhood that stretches from there eastwards to Parc de l'Orangerie is dominated by solid, stone buildings inspired by late-19th-century Prussian tastes. Most are some sort of 'neo' – romantic, Gothic or Renaissance – and you can see that some had the initials RF (République Française) hastily added

after 1918 to replace the original German insignia.

Across av de l'Europe from Palais de l'Europe, the flowerbeds, playgrounds, shaded paths and swan-dotted lake of **Parc de l'Orangerie** are hugely popular with local families, especially on sunny Sundays. In the warm months you can rent **rowboats** on Lac de l'Orangerie. To get there by bus, take No 6, 30 or 72.

Le Vaisseau (☎ 03 88 44 44 00; www.levaisseau.com; 1bis rue Philippe Dollinger; adult/3-17yr €8/7; ☺ 10am-6pm Tue-Sun, closed 3 weeks in mid-Sep), 2.5km southeast of the cathedral, is an interactive, hands-on science and technology museum aimed at kids aged three to 15. Everything is trilingual (English, French and German). From the Esplanade tram stop, the museum is one stop away on bus 7.

As a concrete (but very green) expression of Franco-German friendship, Strasbourg and its German neighbour Kehl have turned areas once used by customs posts and military installations into the 60-hectare **Jardin des Deux Rives** (Two-Shores Garden), whose play areas, promenades and parkland stretch along both banks of the Rhine just south of Pont de l'Europe. The centrepiece is a sleek (and hugely expensive) **suspension bridge**, designed by Marc Mimram (www.mimram.com in French), that's proved a big hit with pedestrians and cyclists; one of the walkways is 275m long, the other 387m long. To get to the park, take bus 2 or 21 to the Jardin des Deux Rives stop.

Tours

CITY TOURS

Boat excursions (70 minutes) with English commentary that take in Petite France and the European institutions are run by **Strasbourg Fluvial** (☎ 03 88 84 13 13, ☎ 03 88 32 75 25; behind Palais Rohan; 🚇 Porte de l'Hôpital; adult/student under 25yr €7/3.50, night tours May-Sep €7.40/3.70; ⏲ 10.30am, 1pm, 2.30pm & 4pm Dec-Feb, more frequently Mar-Nov).

The tourist office offers 1½-hour **MP3 tours** (adult/student €6/3) of the cathedral and the old city.

BREWERIES

Brasseries Kronenbourg (☎ 03 88 27 41 59; siege .visites@kronenbourg-fr.com; 68 rte d'Oberhausbergen; 🚇 Ducs d'Alsace; adult €5, student €4, 12-18yr €3, family €14; ⏲ tours 10am, 11am, 2pm, 3pm & 4pm Mon-Sat May-Sep & late Nov-Dec, 2pm, 3pm & 4pm Tue-Sat Oct & Feb-Apr, closed Jan) sells one billion litres of beer in France every year (that is enough beer to fill over 300 Olympic swimming pools!). The two-hour tours (some in English) of its brewery, 2.5km northwest of the Grande Île in the suburb of Cronenbourg, are both interesting and thirst-quenching. Call or email for reservations.

Brasseries Heineken (☎ 03 88 19 57 55; fabienne .patriat@exirys.com; 4 rue St-Charles; admission free; ⏲ tours Mon-Fri) is 2.5km north of the Grande Île in Schiltigheim, near the intersection

---

HIKING, CYCLING & SNOW-SHOEING

The Strasbourg section of the **Club Vosgien** (☎ 03 88 35 30 76; www.club-vosgien -strasbourg.net in French; 71 av des Vosges; ⏲ staffed 4-6.30pm Mon-Fri, 10am-noon Sat), a regional walking organisation founded in 1872, runs walks, cycling excursions and snow-shoe trips for its members (guests welcome) in the Vosges and other parts of Alsace; there are departures at around 8am each Sunday and sometimes on other days too. No reservations are needed for trips by private car (passengers pay €0.06 per kilometre) or train; reserve a few days ahead for bus trips (€12). Insurance costs €4.

---

of rue St-Charles and rte de Bischwiller. Tours last two hours and are sometimes in English; phone or email for reservations. Take the No 4 bus (northbound) to the Schiltigheim Mairie stop.

Festivals & Events

Strasbourg's renowned **Marché de Noël** (Christmas Market; place Broglie, place de la Cathédrale, place Kléber, Petite France & probably place de la Gare), known as Christkindelsmärik in Alsatian and a tradition since at least 1570, runs from the last Saturday in November until 5pm on 24 December (until 31 December at place de la Cathédrale).

Sleeping

It is *extremely* difficult to find last-minute accommodation from Monday to Thursday when the European Parliament is in plenary session (generally for one week each month; see www.europarl.eu.int and click 'Activities' and then 'Parliament's Calendar' for session times). Because of the Christmas Market, weekends in December are also tight so reserve ahead if at all possible.

The tourist office and its website (click 'Where to Stay') provides details about same-night room availability and, if you drop by, can help reserve a room. Hotel reservations can also be made via www .strasbourg.com.

Many hotels apply high-season rates during European Parliament sessions and in May, June, September, October and December.

BUDGET

Camping de la Montagne Verte (☎ 03 88 30 25 46; 2 rue Robert Forrer; per adult/site €3.40/4.65; ⏲ mid-Mar–Oct & late Nov-early Jan) A grassy municipal camp site a short walk from the Nid de Cigognes stop on bus line 2.

CIARUS (☎ 03 88 15 27 88; www.ciarus.com; 7 rue Finkmatt; dm in 8-/4-/2-bed room incl breakfast €20/24/26.50; 🖳) This welcoming, 101-room, Protestant-run hostel with good wheelchair access is so stylish it even counts a number of European Parliament members among its regular clients. The 700 groups it puts up (with) every year are equally international. Social events includes crêpes nights (Tuesday and Thursday). No Hostelling International (HI) card is necessary. Dorm rooms have industrial-strength furniture, toilets and showers. By bus, take No 2, 4 or 10 to the Place de Pierre stop.

Hôtel Le Colmar (☎ 03 88 32 16 89; hotel.le.colmar@ wanadoo.fr; 1 rue du Maire Kuss; ⓡ Alt Winmärik; d €42.50, with washbasin €29, hall shower €1.50) This one-star cheapie offers a unique mix of light and linoleum – stylish it ain't but it's convenient and good value. Payment is in cash only.

Hôtel Patricia (☎ 03 88 32 14 60; www.hotelpatricia .fr; 1a rue du Puits; ⓡ Langstross Grand' Rue; d from €43, with washbasin €32, hall shower €2; ⓨ reception 8am-8pm Mon-Sat, 8am-2pm Sun; ✕) The dark, rustic interior and Vosges sandstone floors – the 16th-century structure was once a convent – fit in well with the local ambience. The 22 rooms are simply furnished but immaculate and spacious; some (eg Nos 3 and 6) have great views. The best budget bet on the island.

MIDRANGE
Two- and three-star hotels, many of them chain-affiliated, line place de la Gare.

Hôtel Balladins Supérior (☎ 03 88 22 60 40; www .balladins.com; 14 rue du Maire Kuss; ⓡ Gare Centrale; d €49-70; ✕ ⓧ ⓠ) A new, 48-room place that's a cut above most chain hotels. Predictable but reliable. Rates are highly seasonal.

Le Kléber Hôtel (☎ 03 88 32 09 53; www.hotel -kleber.com; 29 place Kléber; ⓡ Homme de Fer; d €52-75; ✕) The 30 rooms (see website for photos) are named after fruits, spices, pastries and other high-calorie treats and are decorated accordingly – Meringue is all white, of course, while Noisette is light brown and, being smallish, makes you feel like you're inside a giant hazelnut. Dieters might want to avoid staying in Pavlova or Kougelopf. Very central.

Hôtel Au Cerf d'Or (☎ 03 88 36 20 05; www.cerf -dor.com in French; 6 place de l'Hôpital; ⓡ Porte de l'Hôpital; d/q from €61/86; ⓧ ⓠ) A Jacuzzi, 5m swimming pool and sauna (half-hour €8) are the cherry on the icing of this 43-room, Logis de France–affiliated hotel, which has a golden *cerf* (stag) hanging proudly out front. On the ground floor there's a traditional French restaurant and a homy sitting area with two pianos.

Hôtel Gutenberg (☎ 03 88 32 17 15; www.hotel -gutenberg.com; 31 rue des Serruriers; ⓡ Langstross Grand' Rue; d €65-98; ✕ ⓧ) One of the city's best-value two-star hotels – and it's just two blocks from the cathedral. The 42 tasteful rooms have antique touches and sparkling, all-tile bathrooms.

Hôtel Suisse (☎ 03 88 35 22 11; www.hotel-suisse .com; 2-4 rue de la Râpe; d €69-99, €10 less in Jan, Feb, Jul & Aug; ✕) A charming and very central hotel with two stars, 26 comfortable rooms and the cosy ambience of an Alpine chalet. Often full.

TOP END
Hôtel Régent Petite France (☎ 03 88 76 43 43; www .regent-hotels.com; 5 rue des Moulins; ⓡ Alt Winmärik; d from €255, ste €350-465; ⓧ ✕) Guests of this luxurious four-star hotel enjoy romantic watery views, a sauna and marble bathrooms worthy of a Roman emperor. If you're in one of the rooms over the lock your stay will be accompanied by the rush of water, which can be either calming (no need to bring along a relaxation CD) or nerve-wracking (New Yorkers might try prerecording the sound of honking cars and ambulance sirens). Wheelchair access is good. The 1970s-style breakfast room is decorated with shades of orange not seen since mood rings went out of style. Bringing along Fido or Mitzi will set you back €20.

Eating
Strasbourg is a gastronomer's dream. Just south of place Gutenberg, pedestrianised rue des Tonneliers and nearby streets are lined with midrange restaurants of all sorts. Inexpensive eateries catering to students can be found northeast of the cathedral along rue des Frères, especially towards place St-Étienne.

WINSTUBS
A *winstub* (literally 'wine room') is a traditional Alsatian restaurant renowned for its warm, homey atmosphere. Most dishes are based on pork and veal; specialities include *baeckeoffe* (meat stew), *jambonneau* (knuckle of ham), *wädele braisé au pinot noir* (ham knuckles in wine) and *jambon en croûte* (ham wrapped in a crust). Vegetarians can usually order *bibeleskas* (*fromage blanc;* soft white cheese mixed with fresh cream) and *pommes sautées* (sautéed potatoes). Few *winstubs* offer *menus* (fixed-price multicourse meals); many have non-standard opening hours.

WINSTUBS & FRENCH

L'Assiette du Vin (☎ 03 88 32 00 92; 5 rue de la Chaîne; Langstross Grand' Rue; lunch menu with wine €23, other menus €23-50; dinner daily, lunch Tue-Fri) The décor changes with the seasons (the summer flowers come from the chef's mother's garden) as does the French cuisine, inspired by what's available fresh in the marketplace. The award-winning wine list encompasses 250 vintages, 14 of which can be sampled by the glass (€4 to €7). Has an enthusiastic local following.

Au Coin des Pucelles (☎ 03 88 35 35 14; 12 rue des Pucelles; Broglie; 6.30pm-1am, closed Sun, Mon & holidays) A *winstub* with just six tables, a red-checked tablecloth on each, and solid Alsatian fare such as *choucroute au canard* (sauerkraut with six kinds of duck meat; €18). Perfect for a very late dinner.

Winstub Le Clou (☎ 03 88 32 11 67; 3 rue du Chaudron; Broglie; 11.45am-2.15pm & 5.30pm-midnight except Sun, holidays & lunch Wed) Diners sit together at long tables with paisley tablecloths, so come here for an evening in the company of fellow diners, not an intimate tête-à-tête. Specialities include *baeckeoffe* (€16.90) and *wädele braisé au pinot noir* (€14.90). A dozen Alsatian wines are available by the glass.

La Cloche à Fromage (☎ 03 88 23 13 19; 27 rue des Tonneliers; Langstross Grand' Rue; menus €24.90; closed lunch Tue) The world's largest cheese platter – with some 90 different cheeses – greets you at this haven for the lactose addicted. A plate of 15 cheeses matured and selected by a master *fromager* (cheese maker) costs €22.50; all-you-can-eat *fondue Savoyarde* (cheese fondue) will warm your insides for €22.50. Cheaper options are also on offer.

Au Renard Prêchant (☎ 03 88 35 62 87; 33 place de Zurich; mains €9.50-16.50; closed Sun & lunch Sat) A stuffed, bespectacled *renard* (fox) preaching to ducks presides over this warm, woody and very Alsatian restaurant, housed in a 16th-century chapel. *Gibier* (game) bagged by Molsheim-area hunters is an autumn and winter speciality. Take bus 30 to get here.

La Bourse (☎ 03 88 36 40 53; 1 place Maréchal de Lattre de Tassigny; Étoile; menus €21-29; 11.45am-2.30pm & 6.45-11pm, to 11.30pm Fri, Sat & Sun) While dining on excellent *flammeküche* (Alsatian pizza made with crème fraîche; €8 to €10; vegetarian available) and *bæckeoffe* (€16) at this Art Deco brasserie, you can watch vet-

eran waiters teaching trainee serveurs the art of being sullen and surly without actually causing anyone to walk out. Needless to say, there's absolutely no danger of someone coming up to your table and saying with sing-songy enthusiasm, 'Hi, my name is Jean-Jacques and I'm going to be your waiter this evening'. Sam tickles the ivories nightly from 7pm to 11pm – no, actually it's not Sam, Sam plays better than that.

our pick Au Crocodile (☎ 03 88 32 13 02; www .au-crocodile.com; 10 rue de l'Outre; Broglie; 2-/3-course lunch menus €56/78, with wine €83/110, other menus €86-128; lunch & dinner Tue-Sat) This superb restaurant, named after a stuffed toothy critter (now suspended over the foyer) brought back from Egypt by an aide-de-camp of one of Napoleon's generals, has the hushed solemnity of a true temple of French gastronomy. Elegant down to the tiniest detail, it serves up all-out *gastronomique* indulgence. Specialities include *foie de canard cuit en croûte de sel* (duck liver cooked in a crust of salt crystals; €55). Reservations are a good idea in the evening, especially on Friday and Saturday.

ASIAN

Moozé (☎ 03 88 22 68 46; 1 rue de la Demi-Lune; Langstross Grand' Rue; dishes €2.50-6; Mon-Sat) A hip and hugely popular Japanese place, given good marks by local cognoscenti, where colour-coded plates (€2.50 to €6) go round on a dual-carriageway conveyor belt. The bathrooms are integrated into a rock garden so those who come seeking physical relief will find spiritual repose as well.

Tiger Wok (☎ 03 88 36 44 87; 8 rue du Faisan; Broglie; lunch incl a drink €13.50, dinner €14, all-you-can-eat €22.90; noon-2.15pm & 7-10.30pm, to 11pm Wed & Thu, to 11.30pm Fri & Sat) Local chic-sters tired of pigs' knuckles and fois gras flock to this wokkery, where you choose your ingredients (vegies, fish, meat) and then tell your personal *wokeur* (wok guy) – muscular and short-sleeved – how to prepare them and with which sauces. The result: a quick, crunchy meal.

VEGETARIAN & KOSHER

Le King (☎ 03 88 52 17 71; 28 rue Sellénick; Parc du Contades; 2-course menu €11; closed Sat & dinner Fri) In the heart of Strasbourg's Jewish neighbourhood, this kosher place specialises in Moroccan-style grilled meats and fish.

ALSACE & LORRAINE

Adan (☎ 03 88 35 70 84; www.adan.fr in French; 6 rue Sédillot; 🚇 Porte de l'Hôpital; menu €12.50; ⏱ 11.30am-2pm Mon-Sat) An informal vegetarian-organic restaurant with tasty soups, salads, quiches and lots of legume dishes, some without milk products.

SELF-CATERING

For picnic supplies:

Atac supermarket (47 rue des Grandes Arcades; 🚇 Langstross Grand' Rue; ⏱ 8.30am-8pm Mon-Sat)

Casher Price Naouri (22 rue Finkmatt; ⏱ 8.30am-7pm or 7.30pm Sun-Thu, closes midafternoon Fri) An all-*cacher* (kosher) supermarket serving Strasbourg's large Jewish community.

Food market (place Broglie; 🚇 Broglie; ⏱ 7am-4pm, often until 6pm Wed & Fri) Moves to place Kléber during the Christmas market.

La Cloche à Fromage boutique (☎ 03 88 52 04 03; 32 rue des Tonneliers; 🚇 Langstross Grand' Rue; ⏱ 9.15am or 10am-12.15pm & 2.30-7pm Mon-Fri, 8.15am-6.30pm Sat) A first-rate *fromagerie* (cheese shop).

Lafayette Gourmet supermarket (34 rue du 22 Novembre; 🚇 Langstross Grand' Rue; ⏱ 9am-8pm Mon-Sat) On the ground floor of the department store.

Petit Casino grocery (inside the train station; ⏱ 7am-8pm, 365 days a year)

Drinking

Strasbourg has lots of pubs and bars, including a number of student-oriented places on the small streets east of the cathedral.

La Taverne Française (☎ 03 88 24 57 89; 12 av de la Marseillaise; 🚇 République or Gallia; ⏱ 8.30am-2am Mon-Thu, 8.30am-3am Fri, 2pm-3am Sat) A mellow café favoured by actors from the national theatre, musicians from the opera house and students. A mixture of the old-fashioned and the endearingly tacky creates the ideal atmosphere for stimulating conversation. Bring along some fresh salmon and by the end of the evening you'll have lox.

Irish Times (☎ 03 88 32 04 02; 19 rue St-Barbe; 🚇 Langstross Grand' Rue; ⏱ 5pm-1.30am Mon-Fri, midafternoon-1.30am Sat & Sun) A congenial and genuinely Irish pub that attracts a very international crowd. There's live music (including lots that's Irish) from about 9.30pm to 12.30am on Friday and Saturday; Thursday *may* be karaoke night; and Sunday features a trivia quiz with prizes (9pm). Major sports events – shown on the two wide screens – often push Saturday and Sunday opening back to kick-off time.

Zanzibar (☎ 03 88 36 66 18; 1 place St-Étienne; 🚇 Broglie; concerts usually €4-6; ⏱ 4pm-4am, may be closed Aug) A laid-back bar in the heart of the Grande Île's student quarter. On most nights at 9.30pm or 10pm, local groups (plus a few from abroad) play classics from the repertoires of garage trash, noisefuzz, sleaze punk, glam rock and psychobilly in the Dantesque cellar.

Entertainment

The Strasbourgeois may head to bed earlier than their urban counterparts elsewhere in France but the city's entertainment options are legion. Details on cultural events appear in the free monthly *Spectacles* (www.spectacles-publications.com in French), available at the tourist office.

Tickets are on sale at the **Virgin Megastore billeterie** (☎ 03 88 23 86 00; 30 rue du 22 Novembre; 🚇 Homme de Fer; ⏱ 9am or 9.30am-8pm Mon-Sat) and the **Boutique Culture** (☎ 03 88 23 84 65; place de la Cathédrale cnr rue Mercière; 🚇 Langstross Grand' Rue; ⏱ noon-7pm Tue-Sat).

CINEMAS

Odyssée (☎ 03 88 75 10 47/11 52; www.cinemaodyssee .com in French; 3 rue des Francs Bourgeois; 🚇 Langstross Grand' Rue) An art-house cinema pretentiously billed as an *espace cinématographique culturel européen* (European cinematographic cultural space).

Other nondubbed film venues:

Le Star (☎ 03 88 32 44 97/67 77; www.cinema-star.com in French; 🚇 Homme de Fer; 27 rue du Jeu des Enfants)

Star St-Exupéry (☎ 03 88 22 28 79/32 67 77; www .cinema-star.com in French; 18 rue du 22 Novembre; 🚇 Winmärik)

LIVE MUSIC

See Drinking for details on The Irish Times and Zanzibar, which often have live music.

La Laiterie (☎ 03 88 23 72 37; www.artefact.org in French; 11-13 rue du Hohwald; 🚇 Laiterie; ⏱ closed Jul, Aug & Christmas-early Jan) Strasbourg's most vibrant venue for live music of *every* sort puts on about 20 concerts a month. Tickets (free to €23) are available at the door (telephone bookings aren't accepted), via its website, at the Boutique Culture or, for a slight surcharge, at Virgin Megastore and FNAC ticket outlets. On Friday nights from midnight to 5am, La Laiterie turns into a laid-back, nonexclusionary disco featuring *musique électronique* (electronic; €5). It's about 1km southwest of the train station.

NIGHTCLUBS

La Salamandre (☎ 03 88 25 79 42; www.lasalamandre -strasbourg.fr in French; 3 rue Paul Janet; ⓦ Gallia; admission Fri & Sat €5, other nights €3-4; ⓨ 9pm-4am Wed-Sun Oct-Apr, 10pm-4am Wed-Sat May-Sep) Billed as a *bar-club-spectacles*, this discotheque – warmly lit, friendly and with a marble fountain in the middle – has theme nights each Friday (salsa, 1980s etc). Wednesday and Thursday events are often sponsored by student groups (open to all). Another attraction is the **bal musette** (adult/student €10/5; ⓨ 5-10pm Sun Oct-Apr), where you can dance to live French accordion music, salsa, tango and 1950s rock and roll. At the **apéritif linguistique** (admission free; ⓨ 7-10pm or later 1st Tue of each month except Jul & Aug) language fans gather at about 20 tables – one for each language – to converse and meet people from around the world.

La Java (☎ 03 88 36 34 88; www.lajava.net in French; 6 rue du Faisan; ⓦ Broglie; coat-check €2; ⓨ 7pm-4am) A lively *bar-dansant* with a stylish saloon on the ground floor and a grungy cellar – decorated like an old mine and the hold of a sailing ship – where you can boogy. Popular with the university crowd, especially on Sunday, when international students start gathering at 9pm.

Shopping

The city's fanciest shopping can be found on and around rue des Hallebards, whose super-elegant window displays are real eye candy (Baccarat is at No 44). Less exclusive shops line rue des Grandes Arcades and, to the west, the Grand' Rue.

Getting There & Away

AIR

Strasbourg's **airport** (☎ 03 88 64 67 67; www.stras bourg.aeroport.fr) is 12km southwest of the city centre (towards Molsheim) near the village of Entzheim.

BUS

Governmental strictures intended to limit private-sector competition with the state-owned SNCF mean that as of this writing, Eurolines buses must stop 2.5km south of the **Eurolines office** (☎ 03 90 22 14 60; 6d place d'Austerlitz; ⓦ Lycée Couffignal; ⓨ 10am-12.30pm & 2-6.30pm Mon-Fri, 10am-12.30pm Sat) near Stade de la

Meinau (the city's main football stadium), on rue du Maréchal Lefèbvre about 200m west of av de Colmar.

Strasbourg city bus No 21 (€1.20) links place Gutenberg with the Stadthalle in Kehl, the German town just across the Rhine.

CAR

Rental options:

Avis (☎ 03 88 32 30 44) In the train station's arrival hall.

Europcar (☎ 08 25 85 74 79; 16 place de la Gare; ⓦ Gare Centrale)

National-Citer (☎ 03 88 23 60 76) In the train station's arrival hall.

Sixt (☎ 03 88 23 72 72; 31 blvd de Nancy; ⓦ Faubourg National)

TRAIN

The train station, built in 1883 – and, as we go to press, being given a 120m-long, 23m-high glass façade and underground galleries so it can welcome the TGV in style – is linked to Metz (€20.40, 1¼ to 1¾ hours, four to eight daily), Nancy (€19.70, 1¼ hours, 10 to 17 daily) and Paris' Gare de l'Est (€50.30, four to 4¾ hours, nine to 13 daily); and, internationally, to Basel (Bâle), €18.50, 1¼ hours, 11 to 16 direct daily) and Frankfurt (€38.90, 2½ hours, eight or nine nondirect daily).

Route du Vin destinations include Colmar (€9.70, 35 to 60 minutes, 35 daily weekdays, 22 daily weekends), Dambach-la-Ville (€7.10, one hour, 12 daily on weekdays, five to six daily weekends), Obernai (€5, 26 to 45 minutes, 20 daily weekdays, five to seven daily weekends) and Sélestat (€7, 20 minutes, 24 to 42 daily).

On the Grande Île, tickets are available at the **SNCF Boutique** (5 rue des France-Bourgeois; ⓨ 10am-7pm Mon-Fri, to 5pm Sat).

Getting Around

TO/FROM THE AIRPORT

The Navette Aéroport, run by **CTS** (☎ 03 88 77 70 70; information bureau 56 rue du Jeu des Enfants; ⓨ Mon-Sat), links the Baggersee tram stop southwest of the city with the airport (€5 including tram, 15 minutes, three times an hour until at least 10.30pm).

BICYCLE

Strasbourg, a European leader in bicycle-friendly planning, has an extensive and ever-expanding *réseau cyclable* (network of cycling paths and lanes; www.strasbourg.fr /Strasbourgfr/GB/SeDeplacer/Avelo). Free maps are available at the tourist office.

The city government's *vélocation* system can supply you with a well-maintained one-speed bike (per half-/whole day €4/7, Monday to Friday €10) or a kid's bike (per day €2). A €100 deposit is required. Outlets: **City Centre** (☎ 03 88 24 05 61; 10 rue des Bouchers; 🚇 Porte de l'Hôpital; 🕑 9.30am-noon & 2-6.30pm or 7pm Apr-Oct, 10am-5pm Mon-Fri Nov-Mar)
Train Station (☎ 03 88 23 56 75; 4 rue du Maire Kuss; 🚇 Alt Winmärik; 🕑 9.30am-7pm Mon-Fri, 9.30am-noon & 2-7pm Sat, also open 9.30am-noon & 2-7pm Sun & holidays Apr-Oct)

BUS & TRAM

Four highly civilised tram lines – to which a fifth line, 13.5km of track and 22 stations are being added – form the centrepiece of Strasbourg's outstanding public transport network, run by **CTS** (☎ 03 88 77 70 70; information bureau 56 rue du Jeu des Enfants; 🕑 Mon-Sat). The main hub is at place de l'Homme de Fer. Buses – few of which pass through the Grande Île – run until about 11.30pm; trams generally operate until about 12.20am. This being earnest, hard-working Strasbourg there are no night buses.

Single bus/tram tickets, sold by bus drivers and the ticket machines at tram stops (English instructions available), cost €1.20. The Tourpass (€3.20), valid for 24 hours from the moment you time-stamp it, is sold at tourist offices and tram stop ticket machines. The weekly Hebdopass (€12) is good from Monday to Sunday.

In this chapter, tram stops less than 400m from sights, hotels, restaurants, etc are indicated next to the street address with a tram icon 🚇.

PARKING

Virtually the whole city centre is either pedestrianised or a hopeless maze of one-ways, so don't even think of getting around the Grande Île by car – or parking there for more than a couple of hours. For details on parking options check out www.parcus.com.

At Strasbourg's eight Parking-Relais (park-and-ride) car parks, all on tram lines, the €2.50 all-day fee gets the driver and each passenger a free return tram ride into the city centre. If you'd like to visit the city with-

out car hassles this is the way to do it. To get to a Park-and-Ride lot from the *autoroute* (freeway), follow the signs marked 'P+R Tram'. Locals figure that your vehicle is least likely to be burnt to a crisp by bored youths from 'the projects' if you park north of the city centre in the Rives de l'Aar P+R car park; northwest of the centre in the Rotonde P+R car park; or south of the centre at the Baggersee P+R car park. The Elsau P+R car park is said to be especially dicey.

TAXI

Round-the-clock companies:
Alsace France Taxi (☎ 03 88 22 19 19)
Taxi Treize (☎ 03 88 36 13 13)

ROUTE DU VIN D'ALSACE

Meandering for some 120km along the eastern foothills of the Vosges, the Alsace Wine Route passes through villages guarded by ruined hilltop castles, surrounded by vine-clad slopes and coloured by half-timbered houses. Combine such charms with numerous roadside *caves* (wine cellars), where you can sample Alsace's crisp white varietal wines (in particular Riesling, Pinot Blanc and Gewürztztraminer – the accent is on the 'tra'), and you have one of France's busiest tourist tracks. Local tourist offices can supply you with an English-language map-brochure, *The Alsace Wine Route* (free), and *Alsace Grand Cru Wines* (€2.30), which details Alsace's 50 most prestigious AOC (Appellation d'Origine Contrôlée; the system of French wine classification) wine-growing micro-*régions*.

The Route du Vin, at places twee and commercial, stretches from Marlenheim, about 20km west of Strasbourg, southwards to Thann, about 35km southwest of Colmar. En route are some of Alsace's most picturesque villages (and some very ordinary ones, too), many extensively rebuilt after being flattened in WWII. Ramblers can take advantage of the area's *sentiers viticoles* (sign-posted vineyard trails) and the paths leading up the eastern slopes of the Vosges to the remains of medieval bastions.

The villages mentioned below – listed from north to south – all have plenty of hotels and restaurants and some have camp sites. *Chambres d'hôtes* (B&Bs) generally cost €30 to €50 for a double – tourist offices can provide details on local options and, even when closed, often have lists of *chambres d'hôtes* posted outside.

TOURS

For minibus tours of the Route du Vin (reservations can be made at the Colmar tourist office) try the following:

LCA Top Tour (☎ 03 89 41 90 88; www.alsace-travel .com/at1en.htm; 3rd flr, 8 place de la Gare, Colmar; half-day €47.50)

Regioscope (☎ 06 88 21 27 15; www.regioscope.com; morning/afternoon tour €39/48)

GETTING THERE & AROUND

The Route du Vin is not just one road but a composite of several (the D422, D35, D1bis and so on). It is signposted but you might want to pick up a copy of Blay's colour-coded map, *Alsace Touristique* (€6). Cyclists can pick up free map-brochures at tourist offices and will find IGN maps such as *Le Haut-Rhin à Vélo* (€5.65) invaluable.

Parking can be a nightmare in the high season, especially in Ribeauvillé and Riquewihr, so your best bet is to park outside the town centre and walk. As elsewhere in France, *never* leave valuables in a parked car.

It's possible to get around much of the Route du Vin by public transport since almost all the towns and villages mentioned below are served by train from Strasbourg (p385) or by train and/or bus from Colmar (p397). Bicycles can be brought along on most trains.

Obernai

pop 10,400

The walled town of Obernai ('nai' rhymes with 'day'), 31km south of Strasbourg, is centred on the picturesque **place du Marché**, an ancient market square that's still put to use each Thursday morning. Around the square you'll find the mainly 16th-century **Hôtel de Ville** (town hall), decorated with baroque trompe l'œil; the Renaissance **Puits aux Six Seaux** (Well of the Six Buckets), just across rue du Général Gouraud (the main street); and the bell-topped **Halle aux Blés** (Corn Exchange; 1554), from whose flanks pedestrianised rue du Marché and tiny parallel ruelle du Canal de l'Ehn – just a hand's breadth wide – lead to the Vosges-sandstone **synagogue** (1876). The cool and flower-bedecked courtyards and alleyways (such as little ruelle des Juifs, next to the

tourist office) are fun to explore, as are the 1.75km-long, 13th-century **ramparts**, accessible from the lot in front of double-spired **Église St-Pierre et St-Paul** (19th century).

A number of wine growers have cellars a short walk from town (the tourist office has a map). The 1.5km **Sentier Viticole du Schenkenberg**, which wends its way through vineyards, begins at the hilltop cross north of town – to get there, follow the bright yellow signs from the cemetery behind Église St-Pierre et St-Paul.

The **tourist office** (☎ 03 88 95 64 13; www.obernai .fr; place du Beffroi; ⊙ 9.30am-12.30pm & 2-7pm daily Jul & Aug, 9am-noon & 2-6pm daily Apr-Jun & Sep & Oct, 9am-noon & 2-5pm except Sun & holidays Nov-Mar, open Sun Dec) is behind the Hôtel de Ville, across the car park from the 59m **Kapellturm** (Belfry; 1280).

La Cloche (☎ 03 88 95 52 89; www.la-cloche.com; 90 rue du Général Goraud; d €49; ⊠), a two-star Logis de France–affiliated hotel facing the Hôtel de Ville, has 20 spacious, wood-furnished rooms, some with classic views of the ancient town centre. Charming and atmospheric, the rustic ground-floor **restaurant** (menus €14-27; ⊙ closed lunch Mon, also closed dinner Sun Jan-Mar) serves delicious Alsatian cuisine.

The train station is about 300m east of the old town.

Mont Ste-Odile

Occupied by a convent founded in the 8th century (it's been destroyed and rebuilt several times since), the 763m-high summit of Mont Ste-Odile is a place of great spiritual meaning for many Alsatians, in part because it affords spectacular views of the wine country and, nearer the Rhine, the fields of white cabbage (for sauerkraut) around Krautergersheim. Vestiges of the 10km **Mur Païen** (Pagan Wall), built by the Celts around 1000 BC and fixed up by the Romans, are nearby. The summit, surrounded by conifer forests, can be reached on foot via a network of trails (see IGN trail map 3716 ET), including the GR5, that come from every direction. The **Sentier des Pèlerins** (Pilgrims' Trail) links Otrott's village church with the summit (four hours return).

Mittelbergheim

pop 620

A solid hillside village with no real centre, Mittelbergheim sits amid a sea of Sylvaner grape vines and seasonal wild tulips, its tiny streets lined with ancient houses in subdued tones of tan, mauve and terracotta. From **Parking du Zotzenberg** (on the D362 at the upper edge of the village next to the cemetery), named after the local *grand cru* (Alsace's top AOC wine designation), a paved *sentier viticole* heads across the slopes towards the two towers of the **Château du Haut Andlau** and the Vosges. A stroll along rue Principale (the main street, perpendicular to the D362) takes you past the red sandstone **Catholic Église St-Martin** (next to No 17), built in 1893, and a block down the Protestant **Église St-Étienne** (next to No 30), dating from the 12th to 17th centuries. Each of Mittelbergheim's *caves* has an old-fashioned, wrought-iron sign out front.

The two-star **Hôtel Gilg** (☎ 03 88 08 91 37; www.reperes.com/gilg; 1 route du Vin, D362; d €52-85; ☾ reception closed Tue & Wed, hotel closed Jan & 2 weeks mid-Jul), built in 1614 (the trompe l'oeil dates from 2001), has wood-panelled rooms – reached via a spiral stone staircase – that are almost as romantic as the village. Reserve well in advance for May, September and October. The rustically elegant **restaurant** (menus €27-70; ☾ closed Tue & Wed) serves classic French and Alsatian cuisine.

Private accommodation is easy to come by – you'll see *'chambres/zimmer'* signs in windows all over town. A list of about two dozen options is usually posted outside the Renaissance **Hôtel de Ville** (☎ tourist office 03 88 08 01 66; 2 rue Principale; ☾ Jul & Aug).

Dambach-la-Ville
pop 2000

Surrounded by vines, this village has plenty of *caves* but manages to avoid touristic overload. The 14th-century, pink-granite **ramparts** are pierced by four **portes** (gates), three holding aloft ancient watchtowers and bearing quintessentially Alsatian names: Ebersheim, Blienschwiller and Dieffenthal. Some of the superb half-timbered houses date from before 1500.

Neo-Romanesque **Église St-Étienne** (place de l'Église) and the **synagogue** (rue de la Paix), unused since WWII, both date from the 1860s.

NATZWEILER-STRUTHOF CONCENTRATION CAMP

A mere 50km southwest of Strasbourg stands the only concentration camp established by the Nazis on French territory (there were also a number sof French-run transit camps, such as the notorious Camp de Drancy, 22km northeast of Paris), Natzweiler-Struthof. The site was chosen by Hitler's personal architect, Albert Speer, because of the nearby deposits of valuable pink granite, in whose extraction – in the **Grande Carrière** (Large Quarry) – many inmates were worked to death. In all, some 10,000 to 12,000 of the camp's prisoners died, including many who were shot or hanged. In early September 1944, as the Allies were approaching, the 5517 surviving inmates were sent to Dachau.

The camp provided the Reichsuniversität (Reich University) in Strasbourg with inmates for use in often lethal pseudo-medical experiments involving chemical warfare agents (mustard gas, phosgene) and infectious diseases (hepatitis, typhus). In April 1943, 86 Jews – 56 men and 30 women – specially brought from Auschwitz were gassed here to supply the university's anatomical institute with skulls and bones for its anthropological and racial skeleton collection. After liberation, their bodies, preserved in alcohol, were found by Allied troops in Strasbourg. In December 2005, a memorial plaque to the 86 was unveiled at the Jewish cemetery in Cronenbourg, a suburb of Strasbourg.

Today, visitors can see the remains of the **camp** (☎ 03 88 47 44 57; adult €5, student & under 18yr €2.50; ☾ 10am-6pm May–mid-Sep, 10am-5pm Mar, Apr & mid-Sep–24 Dec), whose barracks – one housing a **museum** – are still surrounded by guard towers and two rows of barbed wire. The **four crématoire** (crematorium oven), the **salle d'autopsie** (autopsy room) and the **chambre à gaz** (gas chamber; ☾ same hr but closed 1-2pm), an ordinary-looking building 1.7km down the D130 from the camp gate, bear grim witness to the atrocities committed here. The nearby **Centre Européen du Résistant Déporté**, inaugurated in November 2005 by Jacques Chirac, pays homage to the resistance fighters from around Europe deported to Natzweiler-Struthof and other Nazi concentration camps.

To get to Natzweiler-Struthof from Obernai, take the D426, D214 and D130; follow the signs to 'Le Struthof' or 'Camp du Struthof'.

The **tourist office** (☎ 03 88 92 61 00; www.pays-de-barr.com; place du Marché; ⏰ 9am-noon & 1.30-6pm Mon-Sat, 10am-noon Sun Jul & Aug, 10am-noon & 2-5pm or 6pm Mon-Fri, 10am-noon Sat Sep-Jun), in the mid-16th-century Renaissance-style **Hôtel de Ville**, can supply you with a brochure for a walking tour of Dambach and with details on cycling trails to Itterwiller.

The renowned Frankstein *grand cru* vineyards cover the southern and southeastern slopes of four granitic hills west and southwest of Dambach. The 1½-hour **Sentier Viticole du Frankstein**, which begins 70m up the hill from the tourist office on rue du Général de Gaulle, meanders among the hallowed vines, passing by hillside **Chapelle St-Sebastien** (⏰ 9am-7pm May-Oct, also open Sat, Sun & holidays Nov-Apr though you may have to knock), known for its Romanesque tower, Gothic choir, Renaissance windows and baroque high altar.

The train station is about 1km east of the old town.

Sélestat

pop 17,200

Sélestat is the largest town between Strasbourg, 50km to the north, and Colmar, 23km to the south. Its claim to cultural fame is the 15th- and 16th-century **Bibliothèque Humaniste** (Humanist Library; ☎ 03 88 58 07 20; 1 rue de la Bibliothèque; adult/student €3.70/2.15, audioguide €1.55; ⏰ 9am-noon & 2-6pm Mon & Wed-Fri year-round, 9am-noon Sat year-round, 2-5pm Sat & Sun Jul & Aug), whose displays include a 7th-century book of Merovingian liturgy, a 10th-century treatise on Roman architecture and a copy of *Cosmographiae Introductio*, printed in 1507 in the Vosges town of St-Dié, in which the New World was referred to as 'America' for the very first time. Explanatory sheets are available in six languages.

Maison du Pain (☎ 03 88 58 45 90; www.maisondupain-d-alsace.com; rue du Sel; admission €4.60; ⏰ 10am-noon & 2-6pm Tue-Fri, 2-6pm Sat & Sun except school holidays, 10am-5pm or 6pm Tue-Sun Jul & Aug), 50m from the Bibliothèque Humaniste, showcases not S&M but rather the art of bread-making. It is run by local *boulangers* (bakers).

The 13th- to 15th-century **Église St-Georges**, one of Alsace's loveliest Gothic churches, has curtains of stained glass – some from the 1300s and 1400s – in the choir. Nearby, 12th-century Romanesque **Église St-Foy** was heavily restored in the 19th century.

Vieux Sélestat, the old town area south and southwest of the churches, is a mainly postwar commercial precinct dotted with half-timbered and trompe-l'oeil shop buildings. A huge **outdoor market**, held since 1435, takes over the streets all around Église St-Foy from 8am to noon every Tuesday. Locally-grown fruits and vegies are sold on Saturday morning at square A Ehm, on the southern edge of the old town.

The turn-off to the **cimetière israélite** (Jewish cemetery; ⏰ 8am-6pm Apr-Sep except Sat & Jewish holidays, to 4pm Oct-Mar), one of many around Alsace, is 1.8km north of Sélestat's yellow-brick water tower along the N83; look for the black-on-white sign. The key is kept by the people in the house facing the entrance – just beep the horn or knock on the door.

The **tourist office** (☎ 03 88 58 87 20; www.selestat-tourisme.com; blvd du Général Leclerc; ⏰ 9am-noon & 2-5.45pm except Sun & holidays, to 5pm Sat, open longer hr & 10.30am-3pm Sun & holidays Jul & Aug) is on the edge of the town centre two short blocks from the Bibliothèque Humaniste. It has an inexpensive car park and is well signposted.

The train station is 1km west of the Bibliothèque Humaniste.

Bergheim

pop 1830

The delightful walled town of Bergheim – overflowing with geraniums, dotted with flowerbeds and enlivened by half-timbered houses in shocking pastels – is more spacious than its neighbours. But things have not always been so cheerful: over the centuries the town has passed from one overlord to another, having been sold, ceded or captured some 20 times; and between 1582 and 1630, 35 women and one man were burnt at the stake here for witchcraft. **Maison des Sorcières** (House of the Witches; ☎ 03 89 73 85 20; rue de l'Église; adult €3; ⏰ 2-6pm Wed-Sun Jul & Aug, 2-6pm Sun Sep & Oct), run by volunteers from the local historical society, takes a hard look at the local witch hunts.

The centre, spared the ravages of WWII, is dominated by an early-Gothic **church** (14th century), significantly modified in the early 1700s. The wall-mounted **sundial** at 44 Grand' Rue has its origins in 1711. The 14th-century, Gothic **Porte Haute**, square and imposingly medieval, is the only one of the village's original three main gates still extant. Outside across the

---

NAH-NAH!

At eye-level on the exterior of Bergheim's 14th-century Porte Haute (p389), a bas-relief sandstone figure exposes his posterior and thumbs his nose at his pursuers, recalling the time, from the 14th to 17th centuries, when Bergheim granted asylum to people guilty of nonpremeditated crimes.

---

grassy park, the **Herrengarten linden tree**, planted around 1300, is hanging in there but looks like it could use a hug. A map of town stands nearby. A 2km path, marked 'Remparts XIVème Siècle', circum-navigates the town's ramparts. Bergheim's *grands crus* are Kanzlerberg and Altenberg de Bergheim.

The tiny **tourist office** (☎ 03 89 73 31 98; 🕙 Jul & Aug) is between the well-proportioned **Hôtel de Ville** (1767), which can supply you with a brochure on the town (€1), and the deconsecrated **synagogue**, built in 1863 on the site of an early-14th-century synagogue and now used for cultural activities.

Just inside the Porte Haute, **La Cour du Bailli** (☎ 03 89 73 73 46; www.cour-bailli.com; 57 Grand' Rue; 2-8-person studio Easter-Oct & Dec €68-113, rest of yr €60-102; 🕙 reception 10am-7pm; 🔊), a three-star apartment hotel built around a flowery, 16th-century courtyard, has 24 spacious, rustic studios with kitchenettes and, in the cellar, an **Alsatian restaurant** (🕙 dinner daily, lunch Fri-Sun, closed Jan–mid-Feb). There are several more **restaurants** between here and the Hôtel de Ville.

Haut Kœnigsbourg

Perched on a lushly forested promontory and offering superb vistas, the imposing red-sandstone **Château du Haut Kœnigsbourg** (☎ 03 88 82 50 60; adult/18-25yr/under 18yr €7.50/4.80/free; 🕙 9.30am-6.30pm Jun-Aug, 9.30am-5.30pm Apr, May & Sep, 9.45am-5pm Mar & Oct, 9.45am-noon & 1-5pm Nov-Feb) makes a very medieval impression despite having been reconstructed in the early 1900s – with German imperial pomposity – by Kaiser Wilhelm II (r 1888–1918).

Ribeauvillé

pop 4900

Ribeauvillé, some 19km northwest of Colmar, is arguably the most heavily touristed of all the villages on the Route du Vin. It's easy to see why: this little village, nestled in a valley and brimming with 18th-century overhanging houses and narrow alleys, is picture-perfect. The local *grands crus* are Kirchberg de Ribeauvillé, Osterberg and Geisberg.

Don't miss the 17th-century **Pfifferhüs** (Fifers' House; 14 Grand' Rue), which once housed the town's fife-playing minstrels and is now home to a friendly *winstub*; the **Hôtel de Ville** (across from 64 Grand' Rue) and its Renaissance fountain; or the nearby clock-equipped **Tour des Bouchers** (Butchers' Belltower; 13th and 16th centuries).

Just across two traffic roundabouts from the tourist office, the bright yellow **Cave de Ribeauvillé** (☎ 03 89 73 61 80; www.cave-ribeauville .com; 2 rte de Colmar; admission & tasting free; 🕙 8am-noon & 2-6pm Mon-Fri, longer hr Jul & Aug, 10am-12.30pm & 2.30-7pm Sat & Sun, slightly shorter hr Jan-Easter), France's oldest winegrowers' cooperative (founded 1895), has a small viniculture museum, exceptionally informative brochures and excellent wines made with all seven of the grape varieties grown in Alsace.

West and northwest of Ribeauvillé, the ruins of three 12th- and 13th-century hilltop castles – **St-Ulrich** (530m), **Giersberg** (530m) and **Haut Ribeaupierre** (642m) – can be reached on a hike (three hours return) beginning at place de la République (at the northern tip of the Grand' Rue).

The **tourist office** (☎ 03 89 49 08 40; www.ribeau ville-riquewihr.com; 1 Grand' Rue; 🕙 9.30am or 10am-noon & 2-6pm Mon-Sat Apr-Oct & Dec, 10am-1pm Sun & holidays May-Oct & Dec, 10am-noon & 2-5pm Mon-Fri & alternate Sat rest of yr), the area's best equipped, is at the southern end of the main street, the one-way (south-to-north) Grand' Rue.

Hunawihr

pop 510

You're absolutely guaranteed to see storks in the quiet hamlet of Hunawihr, about 1km south of Ribeauvillé, which is surrounded by a 14th-century wall and feels more solid and serious than its neighbours. On a hillside just outside the centre, the 16th-century fortified **church**, surrounded by a hexagonal wall, has been a *simultaneum* – that is, it has served both the Catholic and Protestant communities – since 1687.

About 500m east of Hunawihr, the delightful **Centre de Réintroduction des Cigognes** (Stork Reintroduction Centre; ☎ 03 89 73 28 48;

STORKS

White storks (cigognes), long a feature of Alsatian folklore, are one of the region's most beloved symbols. Believed to bring luck (as well as babies), they winter in Africa and then spend the warmer months in Europe, feeding in the marshes (their favourite delicacies include worms, insects, small rodents and even frogs) and building their nests of twigs and sticks on church steeples and rooftops.

When mid-August arrives, instinct tells young storks – at the age of just a few months – to fly south for a two- or three-year, 12,000km trek to sub-Saharan Africa (Alsatian storks are particularly fond of Mali and Mauritania), from where they return to Alsace ready to breed – if they return at all. Research has shown that something like 90% die en route because of electrocution, pesticides (eg those used to combat locusts), hunting, exhaustion and dehydration. In subsequent years, the adult storks – 1m long, with a 2m wingspan and weighing 3.5kg – make only a short trek south for the winter, returning to Alsace to breed after a few months in Africa.

In the mid-20th century, environmental changes, including the draining of the marshes along the Rhine, and high-tension lines reduced stork numbers catastrophically. By the early 1980s there were only two pairs left in the wild in all of Alsace.

Research and breeding centres were set up with the goal of establishing a permanent, year-round Alsatian stork population. The young birds spend the first three years of their lives in captivity, which causes them to lose their migratory instinct and thus avoid the rigours and dangers of migration. The programme has been a huge success, and today Alsace is home to 400 pairs.

See opposite and p398 for details on stork-breeding centres.

www.cigogne-loutre.com; adult/5-14yr €8/5; ☑ 10am-12.30pm & 2pm-btwn 5.30pm & 7pm, no midday closure weekends & Jun-Aug, closed 11 Nov-late Mar) is home base for more than 100 free-flying storks (above). Cormorants, penguins, otters and a sea lion show off their fishing prowess several times each afternoon.

At the nearby **Jardins des Papillons** (Butterfly Gardens; ☎ 03 89 73 33 33; www.jardinsdespapillons.fr; adult/5-14yr €7/4.50; ☑ 10am-btwn 5pm & 7pm Apr-1 Nov) you can stroll among exotic free-flying butterflies.

Riquewihr
pop 1200

Some Alsatians complain that this largely pedestrianised town, 5km south of Ribeauvillé, has become a tourist trap, and an un-haimisch (unfriendly) one to boot. However, it's still the most medieval stop along the Route du Vin, with 13th- and 16th-century **ramparts** and a maze of alleyways and courtyards that are great for exploring.

The **Sentier Viticole des Grands Crus** (2km; yellow signage) takes you away from the souvenir shops and out to the most prestigious local vineyards, Schœnenbourg (north of town) and Sporen (southeast of town), while a 15km trail with red trail markers takes you to five nearby villages. Both can be picked up next to Hôtel-Restaurant Le

Schœnenbourg, 100m to the right of the Hôtel de Ville as you approach the old town from the Route du Vin.

The late-13th-century **Dolder** (admission €2; ☑ daily Jul & Aug, Sat, Sun & holidays Easter-Jun & Sep-1 Nov) is a stone and half-timbered gate – topped by a bell tower – with a small local-history museum inside. From there, rue des Juifs leads down the hill to the medieval **Tour des Voleurs** (Thieves' Tower; admission incl the Dolder €3; ☑ Easter-1 Nov), a former dungeon containing some extremely efficient-looking implements of torture. The Château des Princes de Wurtemberg-Montbéliard (1540) now houses the **Musée de la Communication** (☎ 03 89 47 93 80; ☑ 10am-5.30pm Wed-Mon late March-1 Nov), whose exhibits trace the history of written and voice communications, especially in Alsace. The **Maison de Hansi** (☎ 03 89 47 97 00; 16 rue du Général de Gaulle; €2; ☑ 10am-6pm Tue-Sun Apr-Dec) presents the work of the celebrated Alsatian illustrator Jean-Jacques Waltz (1873–1951), whose idealised images of Alsace are known around the world.

The **tourist office** (☎ 03 89 49 08 40; www.ribeau ville-riquewihr.com; 2 rue de la Première Armée; ☑ 9.30am or 10am-noon & 2-6pm Mon-Sat Apr-Oct & Dec, 10am-1pm Sun & holidays May-Oct & Dec, 10am-noon & 2-5pm Mon-Fri & alternate Sat rest of yr) is smack in the centre of the old town.

Kaysersberg

pop 2700

In the middle of picture-perfect Kaysersberg, 10km northwest of Colmar, is the ornate Renaissance **Hôtel de Ville** (1605). Next door stands red-sandstone **Église Ste Croix** (🕐 9am-4pm), a 12th- to 15th-century Catholic church whose **altar** (1518) has 18 painted haut-relief panels of the Passion and the Resurrection. Out front, a Renaissance **fountain** holds aloft a statue of Emperor Constantine. Up the main street, av du Général de Gaulle (one way going west to east, ie downhill), there are lots of colourful old houses, many half-timbered, others showing baroque influences; further along is the squat, **fortified bridge** (next to No 84), built to span the River Weiss in 1514.

You can see master glass-blowers practising their magic at **Verrerie d'Art** (☎ 03 89 47 14 97; 30 rue du Général de Gaulle; 🕐 2-6pm Mon, 10am-12.30pm & 2-6pm Tue-Sat).

The house where the musicologist, medical doctor and 1952 Nobel Peace Prize winner Albert Schweitzer (1875–1965) was born is now a **museum** (☎ 03 89 47 36 55; 126 rue du Général de Gaulle; adult/child €2/1; 🕐 9am-noon & 2-6pm Apr-11 Nov, 2-6pm Fri, Sat & Sun late Nov-22 Dec) with exhibits on the good doctor's life in Alsace and Gabon.

Footpaths lead in all directions through glen and vineyard. A 10-minute walk above town, the remains of the massive, crenulated **Château de Kaysersberg** stand surrounded by vines; other destinations include Riquewihr (two hours one-way via the chateau and over the hill). The path begins through the arch to the right as you face the Hôtel de Ville.

The **tourist office** (☎ 03 89 78 22 78; www.kaysersberg.com; 37 rue du Général de Gaulle; 🕐 9.30am-noon or 12.30pm & 2-5.30pm or 6pm Mon-Sat year-round, 10am-1pm Sun mid-Jun–mid-Sep), inside the Hôtel de Ville, can supply you with a Kaysersberg walking tour brochure as well as hiking and cycling maps, and helps with *chambres d'hôtes* reservations.

Hôtel Constantin (🕐 03 89 47 19 90; www.hotel-constantin.com; 10 rue du Père Kohlmann; d €60-70), a three-star place in the heart of the old town (half a block from 38 rue du Général de Gaulle), has 20 modern rooms whose wood furnishings fit in well with the local vibe.

COLMAR

pop 65,000

The centre of the harmonious – and very conservative – town of Colmar, capital of the Haut-Rhin *département*, is a maze of cobbled pedestrian malls and centuries-old Alsatian-style buildings, many painted in tones of blue, orange, red or green. The Musée d'Unterlinden is renowned worldwide for the profoundly moving *Issenheim Altarpiece*.

Colmar is an excellent base from which to explore the Route du Vin by bike, train, bus or car. And for something a bit different, it's easy to take day trips to the German university city of Freiburg (by bus) and the Swiss city of Basel (by train), each about an hour away (see www.tourismtrirhena.com).

Orientation

Avenue de la République links the train station and the bus terminal with the Musée d'Unterlinden and the nearby tourist office, a distance of about 1km. The old city, much of it pedestrianised, is southeast of the Musée d'Unterlinden. The Petite Venise quarter runs along the River Lauch, at the southern edge of the old city.

Information

Cyber Didim (☎ 03 89 23 20 44; 9 rue du Rempart; per hr €2; 🕐 10am-11pm Mon-Sat, 2-11pm Sun) Upstairs at the doner kebab place.

Hôpital Pasteur (☎ 03 89 12 40 94; 39 av de la Liberté; 🕐 24hr) Situated 700m west of the train station and served by bus lines 1, 3, 10, A, C and S. The casualty ward is in Building 39.

Laundrette (1b rue Ruest; 🕐 7am-9pm)

Main Post Office (36 av de la République) Has exchange services.

Tourist Office (☎ 03 89 20 68 92; www.ot-colmar.fr; 4 rue d'Unterlinden; 🕐 9am-noon & 2-6pm Mon-Sat, 10am-1pm Sun & holidays, longer hr in Jul & Aug) Can help find accommodation and supply you with information on hiking, cycling and bus travel along the Route du Vin and in the Massif des Vosges.

Sights

OLD CITY

The medieval streets of the old city, including **rue des Clefs**, the **Grand' Rue** and **rue des Marchands**, are lined with dozens of restored, half-timbered houses – and lots of attractive shops – and are great for an aimless

ALSACE & LORRAINE

ALSACE & LORRAINE

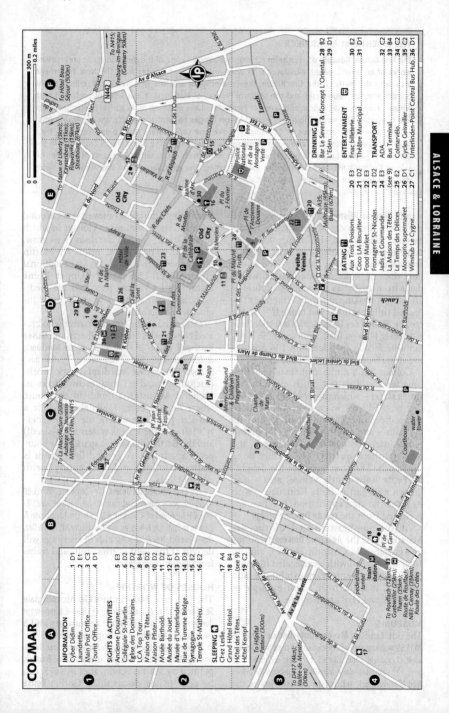

COLMAR

INFORMATION
Cyber Didim...........................1	D1
Laundrette.............................2	E1
Main Post Office.....................3	C3
Tourist Office........................4	D1

SIGHTS & ACTIVITIES
Ancienne Douane..................5	E3
Collégiale St-Martin...............6	D2
Église des Dominicains...........7	D2
LCA Top Tour........................8	B4
Maison des Têtes...................9	D2
Maison Bartholdi.................10	D2
Maison Pfister.....................11	D2
Musée du Jouet...................12	E1
Musée d'Unterlinden............13	D2
Rue de Turenne Bridge.........14	D3
Synagogue.........................15	E2
Temple St-Mathieu..............16	E2

SLEEPING ☐
Chez Leslie........................17	A4
Grand Hôtel Bristol..............18	B4
Hôtel des Têtes...............(see 9)
Hôtel Kempf......................19	C2

EATING ☐
Aux Trois Poissons...............20	E3
Coco LM Biscuiter................21	D2
Food Market.......................22	E3
Jadis et Gourmande.............23	D2
La Maison des Têtes.........(see 9)
Le Temps des Délices...........25	E2
Monoprix supermarket..........26	D1
Winstub Le Cygne...............27	C1

DRINKING ☐
Bar Le Seven & Koncept L'Oriental..28	B2
L'Eden.............................29	D1

ENTERTAINMENT ☐
Fnac billeterie....................30	E2
Théâtre Municipal..............31	D1

TRANSPORT
ADA..................................32	C2
Bus Terminal......................33	B4
Colmarvélo.........................34	C2
Cycles Geiswiller.................35	C2
Unterlinden-Point Central Bus Hub..36	D1

ALSACE & LORRAINE

THE ISSENHEIM ALTARPIECE

The late Gothic **Rétable d'Issenheim** (c1500), acclaimed as one of the most dramatic and moving works of art ever created, illustrates with unrelenting realism scenes from the New Testament, including the Nativity, the Crucifixion, the Entombment and the Resurrection. Ascribed to the painter Mathias Grünewald and the sculptor Nicolas of Haganau, it is a work of profound faith whose emotion, imagination and layers of symbolism have engaged and captivated spectators for five centuries. The work originally opened up on hinges to form three different configurations.

The gruesome *Temptation of St Anthony* shows the unfortunate saint being set upon by a mob of hideous monsters far more grotesque than anything in the bar scene of *Star Wars*. In the *Concert of Angels*, Lucifer is portrayed covered in feathers – but why? An excellent booklet on sale at Colmar's Musée d'Unterlinden (below), where the altarpiece is the star attraction, helps decipher many of the panels' mysteries.

---

stroll. **Maison Pfister** (1537), opposite 36 rue des Marchands, is remarkable for its exterior decoration, including delicately painted panels, an elaborate oriel window and a carved wooden balcony. The house next door at 9 rue des Marchands, which dates from 1419, has a wooden sculpture of an uptight-looking *marchand* (merchant) – has his tulip portfolio just tanked? – on the corner. **Maison des Têtes** (Kopfhüs in Alsatian; House of the Heads; 19 rue des Têtes), built in 1609, has a fantastic façade crowded with 106 grimacing stone faces and animal heads.

Colmar has a number of small *quartiers* (quarters) – often not much more than a single street – which preserve the ambience that reigned back when each was home to a specific guild. **Rue des Tanneurs**, with its tall houses and rooftop verandas for drying hides, intersects **quai de la Poissonnerie**, the former fishers' quarter, which runs along the Lauch. The river provides the delightful **Petite Venise** (Little Venice) area – also known as Quartier de la Krutenau – with its rather fanciful appellation. It is best appreciated from the **rue de Turenne bridge**.

At the southeastern end of rue des Marchands is the **Ancienne Douane** (Koïfhus in Alsatian; Old Customs House), built in 1480 and topped with a variegated tile roof. Now used for temporary exhibitions and concerts, it is the town's best example of late-medieval civil architecture.

MUSEUMS

The outstanding **Musée d'Unterlinden** (☎ 03 89 20 15 58; www.musee-unterlinden.com; 1 rue d'Unterlinden; adult €7, student under 30yr €5, over 65yr €6, under 12yr free; ☼ 9am-6pm daily May-Oct, 9am-noon & 2-5pm Wed-Mon Nov-Apr), whose pride and joy is the

Issenheim Altarpiece (above), is set around a Gothic-style Dominican cloister in which several dwarf-mutant hazelnut trees grow. Medieval stone statues, prints by Martin Shongauer (late 1400s) and an exceptional ensemble of 15th-century Upper Rhine Primitives let visitors peer into the medieval European mind. The entry price includes audioguides.

Dedicated to the Colmar native who created New York's Statue of Liberty, the **Musée Bartholdi** (☎ 03 89 41 90 60; 30 rue des Marchands; adult/student/under 12yr €4.30/2.70/free; ☼ 10am-noon & 2-6pm Wed-Mon Mar-Dec) displays the works (including models) and memorabilia of Frédéric Auguste Bartholdi in the house where he was born. Highlights include a full-size plaster model of the Lady Liberty's left ear (the lobe is watermelon-sized!) and the Bartholdi family's sparklingly bourgeois apartment. A ground-floor room is dedicated to 18th- and 19th-century Jewish ritual objects.

At the **Musée du Jouet** (Toy Museum; ☎ 03 89 41 93 10; www.museejouet.com; 40 rue Vauban; adult/8-17yr €4/3, groups of 4 or more €3/1.50; ☼ 10am-noon & 2-6pm, to 7pm July & Aug, no midday closure Jul, Aug & Dec, closed Tue Oct, Nov & Jan-Jun), kids of every age will delight at the sight of toys, dolls and trains from generations past.

HOUSES OF WORSHIP

The 13th- and 14th-century Gothic **Collégiale St-Martin** (place de la Cathédrale; ☼ 8am-6.30pm except during services) has a sombre ambulatory and a peculiar, Mongol-style copper spire (1572).

The celebrated triptych *La Vierge au Buisson de Roses* (The Virgin in the Rose Bush), painted by Martin Schongauer in 1473, can be seen inside desanctified Gothic **Église**

des Dominicains (place des Dominicains; adult/student €1.30/1; ☼ 10am-1pm & 3-6pm late Mar-Dec). In 1972 the work made world headlines when it was stolen, not to be recovered for 18 months. The stained glass dates to the 14th and 15th centuries.

Temple St-Matthieu (Grande' Rue; ☼ 10am-noon & 3-5pm late Apr-May & late July–mid-Oct), quintessentially Protestant in its austerity, has something of a split personality. From 1715 to 1987, a wall cut off the soaring 14th-century Gothic choir – a Catholic hospital chapel until 1937 – from the nave, long a Protestant church. This arrangement allowed the 14th-century *jubé* (rood screen) to survive the counter-Reformation. The elaborate Silbermann organ is used for concerts.

God only knows why Colmar's classical-style 1843 **synagogue** (☎ 03 89 41 38 29; 3 rue de la Cigogne) has its very own belfry (Jews have no tradition of ringing bells), but if 19th-century neo-Moorish synagogues (eg the Great Synagogue of Budapest) can have minarets, why not? Call ahead to visit the interior.

Festivals & Events
From mid-May to mid-September, **Soirées Folkloriques** (free performances of Alsatian music and dancing) are held at 8.30pm (or a bit later) on Tuesday at place de l'Ancienne Douane.

During summer, villages all over Alsace hold **Fêtes du Vin** (Wine Festivals) featuring wine and song; the tourist office has details.

LADY LIBERTY IN COLMAR
Colmar celebrated the centenary of the death of Frédéric Auguste Bartholdi (1834–1904) by inaugurating a 12m-high replica of the Statue of Liberty. Made of stratified resin supported by an Eiffelesque internal metal frame, Lady Liberty – given a convincing copper-green patina – bears her torch aloft 3km north of the old city on route de Strasbourg (the N83), in the middle of a traffic roundabout near Colmar-Houssen airfield. Around her base congregate the huddled masses, yearning to shop at the nearby American-style strip malls... By the way, the copper-skinned New York original (www.nps.gov/stli), dedicated in 1886, is four times as tall (eight times as tall including the pedestal).

Colmar's magical **Marché de Noël** (Christmas Market; www.noel-colmar.com) runs from the last Saturday in November to 31 December.

Sleeping
In December (during the Christmas market), around Easter and from mid-July to mid-August most hotels are booked up well in advance.

BUDGET
Auberge de Jeunesse Mittelhart (☎ 03 89 80 57 39; fax 03 89 80 76 16; 2 rue Pasteur; dm/d with 2 bunks incl breakfast €12.50/35; ☼ reception 7-10am & 5-11pm, to midnight during daylight-saving time, closed mid-Dec–mid-Jan) This one-time orphanage isn't cheery (it's not hard to imagine lonely children crying themselves to sleep) but the management does its best. An old-style place with 110 beds, hall showers and kitchen facilities, it's situated 1.2km northwest of the tourist office, just around the corner from 76 rte d'Ingersheim. Curfew is 11pm or midnight. By bus take No 4, 5 or 15 to the Pont Rouge stop.

Hôtel Kempf (☎ 03 89 41 21 72; http://hotel.kempf .site.voila.fr/index.html; 1 av de la République; d from €45, with washbasin €33) The phone system may date from before Sputnik and the rooms may be plain Jane, but this family-run, two-star place, with 18 rooms, is making a valiant effort to survive in a world of cheap, soulless chain hotels. The showers squirt torrents of hot water. To get there by car, follow the signs to the Rapp car park.

MIDRANGE & TOP END
Chez Leslie (☎ 03 89 79 98 99; www.chezleslie.com; 31 rue de Mulhouse; d incl breakfast €68, 4-person apt per week €400; ✗) Run by an expat from San Francisco, this superfriendly, four-room *chambre d'hôte* occupies a private home of the sort that made bourgeois Germans of a century ago pat their paunches with satisfaction. Each spacious room is unique.

Hôtel Beau Séjour (☎ 03 89 20 66 66; www.beause jour.fr; 25 rue du Ladhof; d depending on size & season €60-95; ✗) Everything about this venerable two-star hostelry, run by the Keller family for five generations, oozes charm, from the 38 rooms – some with Provençal or Louis XV décor – to the elegant restaurant. Situated about 1km northeast of the centre.

Grand Hôtel Bristol (☎ 03 89 23 59 59; www .grand-hotel-bristol.com; 7 place de la Gare; d €59-135; ✗) A marble stairway leads from the Persian-carpeted lobby of this Best Western–affiliated, three-star place with good wheelchair access, built in 1925, to grand hallways and 91 comfortable rooms. A sauna and fitness room should open in 2006.

Hôtel des Têtes (☎ 03 89 24 43 43; www.maison destetes.com; 19 rue des Têtes; d €131-269, low season €91-209; ✗ ✗) This impeccable four-star hostelry, luxurious but never flashy, occupies the magnificent Maison des Têtes (p394). Each of its 21 rooms offers rich wood panelling, an elegant sitting area, a mostly-marble bathroom and romantic views – definitely honeymoon material.

Eating

Restaurants are sprinkled around Colmar's old city, especially around place de l'Ancienne Douane (eg Grand' Rue, rue St-Jean).

ALSATIAN & FRENCH

Jadis et Gourmande (☎ 03 89 41 73 76; 8 place du Marché aux Fruits; plat du jour €8-9.50; ☾ 8am-6pm Mon-Sat) A wood-panelled *salon de thé* (tea room) that serves breakfast (€4.90 to €6.10), light lunches (eg quiche, salad; from noon to 3pm), Alsatian wines by the glass (€2.20 to €3) and luscious homemade desserts, including apple strudel with vanilla ice cream (€4.80).

Winstub Le Cygne (☎ 03 89 23 76 26; 17 rue Édouard Richard; ☾ noon-2pm & 7pm-midnight, closed Sun, lunch Sat & dinner Mon) Hidden on an untouristed side-street, this is where locals come when they want to 'eat Alsatian' – and eat well – but are tired of sauerkraut, mild though the Alsatian version may be. Authentic specialities include *fleischschnacka* (literally 'meat snails'; dough filled with chopped beef and baked with beef broth; €13) and *lawerknaepfa* (grilled heifer liver dumplings; €12.50).

Aux Trois Poissons (☎ 03 89 41 25 21; 15 quai de la Poissonnerie; menus €21-45; ☾ closed Wed & dinner Sun & Tue) Oil paintings on the walls and Persian carpets on the floor give this mainly-fish restaurant a hushed atmosphere of civilised elegance. The chef's speciality is *sandre à la choucroute* (pike-perch with sauerkraut; €18). Provençal frogs' legs will hop onto your plate for €15.

La Maison des Têtes (☎ 03 89 24 43 43; 19 rue des Têtes; menus €29-60; ☾ closed Mon, lunch Tue & dinner Sun) Behind the leaded windows of the spectacular Maison des Têtes awaits a truly grand dining room, built in 1898 and decorated with grape bunches in wood, wrought iron and stained glass. The chef's *cuisine française actuelle* (creative, contemporary French cuisine) includes *foie gras au Riesling* (foie gras and Riesling) and, in season, fish and game. Known for its superb wine list.

Le Temps des Délices (☎ 03 89 23 45 57; 23 rue d'Alspach; lunch menu €19, other menus €35-48; ☾ noon-1.30pm & 7-9pm, closed Sun & Mon; ✗) A classy Franco-Italian restaurant – the chef is half-Alsatian, half-Piedmontese – with space for just 20 diners. All ingredients are fresh, and there's a terrace in summer.

SELF-CATERING

Coco LM Biscuitier (16 rue des Boulangers; www.coco -lm.com; ☾ closed Mon morning & Sun) Bakes scrumptious Alsatian cookies *(lekerli, brünsli)*, cakes *(kougelhopf)*, sweet and salty *bretzels* and a type of startlingly spicy ginger biscuit dubbed a *'gingerli'*.

Fromagerie St-Nicolas (☎ 03 89 24 90 45; 18 rue St-Nicolas; ☾ 9am-12.30pm & 2-7pm, closed Mon morning & Sun, usually no midday closure Sat) Prepare yourself to be overcome by the heady odours of unpasteurised cheese. BYOB (bring your own baguette) and they'll make you a sandwich.

Other places to buy edibles:

Food market (around the covered market on rue des Écoles; ☾ 8am-noon, to 12.30pm Thu) Market gardeners once unloaded their produce directly from boats at the handsome sandstone 1865 *marché couvert* (covered market).

Monoprix supermarket (across the square from the Musée d'Unterlinden; ☾ 8am-8pm Mon-Sat)

Drinking

There are several pubs and cafés right around the Ancienne Douane.

L'Eden (☎ 03 89 24 40 47; 17 rue du Rempart; ☾ 10am-1.30am Mon-Sat, 3pm-1.30am Sun) A *bar australien* with the best fake Australiana in south-central Alsace ('emus next 7km') and the region's only boomerang-shaped 'roo meat sandwiches (€4). Hosts occasional didgeridoo nights.

Bar Le Seven (☎ 03 89 23 32 72; 6 rue des Trois Épis; ☾ 6pm-3am) Music videos play on huge TVs while patrons play darts or down pints at high, round tables. Becomes a disco on

Friday and Saturday from 10pm to 3am. The adjacent **Koncept L'Oriental** is a dimly lit lounge that attracts a mainly over-30 crowd and charges €10 for a *nargila* (*shisha*; water pipe).

Entertainment

Colmar's main performance venues, hosting concerts, ballet, theatre and even the occasional opera, are **La Manufacture** (☎ 03 89 24 31 78; www.atelierdurhin.com in French; 6 rte d'Ingersheim), housed in a former factory 400m northwest of the tourist office, and the **Théâtre Municipal** (☎ 03 89 20 29 02), next to the Musée d'Unterlinden.

Tickets are available at the **FNAC billeterie** (☎ 03 89 23 32 12; 1 Grand' Rue; � 2-7pm Mon, 10am-7pm Tue-Sat).

Getting There & Away

BUS

Public buses are certainly not the quickest way to explore Alsace's Route du Vin but they *are* a viable option; destinations served include Riquewihr, Hunawihr, Ribeauvillé, Kaysersberg and Eguisheim. In the Vosges you can bus it to Munster, Col de la Schlucht and Col du Bonhomme.

The bus terminal – little more than a car park – is to the right as you exit the train station. Timetables are posted and available at the tourist office or online (www.l-k.fr in French). Services are severely reduced on Sunday and holidays.

CAR

Cars can be hired from **ADA** (☎ 03 89 23 90 30; 22bis rue Stanislas).

TRAIN

Colmar has train connections to Basel (Bâle; €10.90, 44 to 70 minutes, 14 to 20 daily), Mulhouse (€6.90, 25 minutes, 21 to 26 daily), Paris' Gare de l'Est (€50.20 or €55.60, five to six hours via Strasbourg) and Strasbourg (€9.70, 35 to 60 minutes, 35 daily weekdays, 22 daily weekends).

Route du Vin destinations accessible by rail include Dambach-la-Ville (€5.10) and Obernai (€7.20), both of which require a change of trains at Sélestat (€3.90, 13 minutes, 34 daily weekdays, 21 daily weekends). About 16 daily autorails or SNCF buses (eight to 12 daily on weekends) link Colmar with the Vallée de Munster towns of

Munster (€3.30, 35 minutes) and Metzeral (€4.10, 45 minutes); the last run back begins at 7.24pm.

Getting Around

BICYCLE

Colmarvélo (☎ 03 89 41 37 90; place Rapp; per half-/whole day €3/4.50; � 8.30am-noon & 1pm or 2-8pm Jun-Sep, no midday closure Wed, 9am-noon & 2-7pm Apr, May & Oct), run by the municipality, rents city bikes (deposit €50).

Hybrid bikes for Route du Vin touring can be rented from **Cycles Geiswiller** (☎ 03 89 41 30 59; 4-6 blvd du Champ de Mars; per half-/whole day €6/11; � Tue-Sat).

BUS

Colmar's local bus lines, operated by **TRACE** (☎ 03 89 20 80 80; www.trace-colmar.fr in French), run until sometime between 6pm and 8.30pm Monday to Saturday; there's only limited service on Sunday and holidays. The main hub is Unterlinden-Point Central.

PARKING

Unmetered parking can be found a few blocks east of the train station (around the water tower) and in *part* of the car park at place de la Montagne Verte.

TAXI

For a cab call **Radios Taxis** (☎ 03 89 80 71 71) or **Taxi Gare** (☎ 03 89 41 40 19).

MASSIF DES VOSGES

The sublime **Parc Naturel Régional des Ballons des Vosges** covers about 3000 sq km in the southern part of the Vosges range. In the warm months, the gentle, rounded mountains, deep forests, glacial lakes and rolling pastureland are a walker's paradise, with an astounding 10,000km of marked trails, including GRs (*grande randonnée;* long-distance hiking trails) and their variants. Cyclists have hundreds of kilometres of idyllic trails and hang-gliding enthusiasts have plenty of places to take off. In winter three dozen inexpensive skiing areas offer modest downhill pistes and cross-country options.

For details on outings sponsored by the Strasbourg section of the Club Vosgien, see p381.

For information on bus and train connections to the Vosges area, see left and left.

Vallée de Munster

This lush river valley – its pastureland dotted with 16 villages, its upper slopes thickly forested – is one of the loveliest in the Vosges. From the town of Metzeral, hiking destinations include Schnepfenried, Hohneck, the Petit Ballon and Vallée de la Wormsa, which plays host to a section of the GR5 and has three small lakes.

MUNSTER

pop 4900

This streamside town (the name means 'monastery'), famed for its notoriously smelly eponymous cheese, is a good base for exploring the valley (the GR531 passes by here). At **place du Marché** (food market on Tuesday and Saturday mornings), it's easy to spot several storks' nests. About 10 young storks live in an enclosure 250m behind the Renaissance **Hôtel de Ville** – cross the creek and turn left.

Information

Maison du Parc (☎ 03 89 77 90 34; www.parc-ballons -vosges.fr in French; 1 cour de l'Abbaye; ☒ 10am-noon & 2-6pm Tue-Sun Jun–mid-Sep, 2-6pm Mon-Fri mid-Sep–May, 10am-noon Mon-Fri during school holidays mid-Sep–May) The regional park's tourist office has ample printed information in English, including a translation of the exhibits. To get there walk through the arch from place du Marché.

Tourist Office (☎ 03 89 77 31 80; www.la-vallee-de -munster.com; 1 rue du Couvent; ☒ 9.30am-12.30pm & 1.30-6pm or 6.30pm Mon-Sat, 10am-12.30pm Sun Jul & Aug, 9.30am-12.30pm & 2-6pm Mon-Fri, 10am-noon & 2-4pm Sat Sep-Jun) Has information, some in English, on the Munster Valley, including visits to cheese-makers. In the same building as the Maison du Parc but downstairs (or around the other side).

Sleeping & Eating

Hôtel des Vosges (☎ 03 89 77 31 41; www.hoteld esvosges.fr; 58 Grand' Rue; d €47, without shower €35; ☒ reception closes at 1pm Sun except Jul & Aug) This family-run, two-star hotel, on the main commercial street, has 15 nondescript but well-tended rooms with spacious bathrooms.

Super U supermarket (☒ 8am-7pm Mon-Sat, to 8pm Fri, to 6.30pm Sat) If you're looking to stock up on picnic supplies this supermarket is 1.7km south of the tourist office on the D417 (towards Colmar).

Nearby to the Hôtel des Vosges you'll find several **restaurants** and a delightful **salon de thé** (☎ 03 89 77 37 56; 11 Grand' Rue; ☒ closed Sun afternoon except Jul, Aug & Dec, closed Mon all year).

Route des Crêtes

The **Route of the Crests**, part of it built during WWI to supply French frontline troops, takes you to (or near) the Vosges' highest *ballons* (bald, rounded mountain peaks) as well as to several WWI sites. Mountaintop lookouts afford spectacular views of the Alsace plain, the Schwartzwald (Black Forest) across the Rhine in Germany and, on clear days, the Swiss Alps and Mont Blanc.

The route links **Col du Bonhomme** (949m), about 20km west of Kaysersberg, with Cernay, 15km west of Mulhouse, along the D148, D61, D430 and D431. To minimise disruption to the lives of local fauna, sections north and south of Col de la Schlucht are left unploughed and thus closed from about November to March, depending on the snow.

At the dramatic, windblown summit of the **Grand Ballon** (1424m), the highest point in the Vosges, a trail takes you to an aircraft-radar ball and a weather station. If the unsurpassed panorama doesn't blow you away, the howling wind just might.

our pick **Chalet Hôtel du Grand Ballon** (☎ 03 89 48 77 99; www.chalethotel-grandballon.com in French; d €55, with washbasin from €42), built all in wood in 1922 and run by the Club Vosgien, sits atop the Grand Ballon in splendid isolation –

THE CONTINENTAL DIVIDE

The Massif des Vosges serves as a *ligne de partage des eaux* (continental divide): a raindrop that falls on the range's eastern slopes will flow to the Rhine and eventually make its way to the icy waters of the North Sea, while a drop of rain that lands on the southern slopes of the Ballon d'Alsace – perhaps only a few metres from its Rhine-bound counterpart – will eventually end up in the Rhône before merging with the warm waters of the Mediterranean. The Vosges' western slopes feed the Moselle, which joins the Rhine at Koblenz.

The Danube (Donau), which meanders through Vienna and Budapest on its way to the Black Sea, rises just 100km east of the Vosges in the mountains of the Black Forest.

amid a web of hiking and cycling trails. The rooms are Spartan but with views this breathtaking you won't be spending much time inside. The Alsatian restaurant (menus €14.50 to €24) is perfect for hearty après-hike dining. By car, it's 17km up the hill from Willer-sur-Thur (the road is kept open year-round).

From **Col de la Schlucht** (1139m), home to a small ski station, trails lead in various directions; walking north along the GR5 will take you to three lakes, **Lac Vert, Lac Noir** and **Lac Blanc** (Green, Black and White Lakes). **Cimes et Sentiers** (☎ 06 74 32 12 59; www .cimesetsentiers.com in French) offers guided walking and cycling tours year-round and, in winter, snow-shoe hikes.

Ballon d'Alsace

This 1250m-high *ballon*, 20km southwest of the Grand Ballon as the crow flies (by road, take the D465 from St-Maurice), is the meeting point of four *départements* (Haut-Rhin, Territoire de Belfort, Haute-Saône and Vosges) and of three regions (Alsace, Franche-Comté and Lorraine). Between 1871 and WWI, the frontier between France and Germany passed by here, attracting French tourists eager to catch a glimpse of France's 'lost province' of Alsace from the heroic **equestrian statue of Joan of Arc** (1909) and the cast-iron **orientation table** (1888). During WWI the mountaintop was heavily fortified, but the trenches, whose shallow remains can still be seen, were never used in battle.

The Ballon d'Alsace is a good base for day walks. The GR5 passes by here, as do other trails; possible destinations include **Lac des Perches** (four hours).

MULHOUSE
pop 234,000

The multi-ethnic industrial city of Mulhouse (moo-*looze*), 43km south of Colmar, was allied with the cantons of nearby Switzerland before voting to join revolutionary France in 1798. Largely rebuilt after the ravages of WWII, it has little of the quaint Alsatian charm that you find further north – but the city's world-class industrial museums are well worth a stop.

About 700m northwest of the train station, the **tourist office** (☎ 03 89 66 93 13; place de la Réunion; www.tourism-mulhouse.com; 🕑 10am-6pm

Mon-Sat, 10am-noon & 2-6pm Sun & holidays year-round, to 7pm Jul, Aug & Dec) is in the heart of the old city in the 16th-century, trompe l'oeil–covered former **Hôtel de Ville**, now also home to the municipal **Musée Historique** (☎ 03 89 33 78 17; Historical Museum; 🕑 closed Tue).

The wonderful **Musée National de l'Automobile** (☎ 03 89 33 23 23; www.collection-schlumpf .com; 192 av de Colmar; 🚊 Musée de l'Auto; adult/student incl audioguide €10.50/8; 🕑 10am-6pm, to 5pm early Nov-Mar, opens 1pm Mon-Fri early Jan–early Feb) displays 400 rare and beautiful European motorcars produced since 1878 by more than 100 different companies, including Bugatti, whose factory was in nearby Molsheim. The collection was secretly assembled by Fritz Schlumpf, a self-made textile magnate whose passion – indeed, obsession – for fast cars only grew as his worsted-wool empire nose-dived. In 1977, after he had gone bust and fled to Switzerland, outraged former workers occupied the one-time factory housing the glittering collection, which they saw as the ultimate symbol of capitalist greed. By car, get off the A36 at the Mulhouse Centre exit.

A gricer's dream, the **Cité du Train** (French Railway Museum; ☎ 03 89 42 83 33; www.citedutrain .com; 2 rue Alfred de Glehn; adult incl audioguide €10, 7-17yr & student incl audioguide €7.50, adult with the Musée National de l'Automobile €15.50, 7-17yr & student with the Musée National de l'Automobile €11.50), reopened in 2005 after a complete renovation, displays the SNCF's wonderful collection of locomotives and carriages. To get there by car, follow the signs to the 'Musée du Chemin de Fer'.

One long block northeast of the train station, the **Musée de l'Impression sur Étoffes** (Museum of Textile Printing; ☎ 03 89 46 83 00; www .musee-impression.com; 14 rue Jean-Jacques Henner; adult/ student €6/3; 🕑 10am-noon & 2-6pm Tue-Sun) covers the history of the industry that made Mulhouse – the 'French Manchester' – incredibly wealthy. Its unique collection of more than six million printed fabric samples, assembled since 1833, is a mecca for fabric designers.

Has wallpaper always been something of a wallflower in your life? The delightful **Musée du Papier Peint** (Wallpaper Museum; ☎ 03 89 64 24 56; www.museepapierpeint.org; 28 rue Zuber, Rixheim; adult/student/under 12yr €6/4.50/free; 🕑 10am-noon & 2-6pm, closed Tue Oct-May), home to an unparalleled collection of wallpaper, and the machines used to make it since the 18th century, will change all that. Situated a couple of kilometres southeast of central Mulhouse on the D66, it's easy to get to: by car take the A36 and get off at Rixheim; by bus take line No 10 from place de l'Europe to the Commanderie stop.

Getting There & Around

France's second train line, linking Mulhouse with Thann, opened in 1839. Today, the **train station** (10 av du Général Leclerc), just south of the city centre, has direct services to Colmar (€6.90, 25 minutes, 21 to 26 daily) and Strasbourg (€14.80, one hour, 24 to 30 daily).

Most of the museums mentioned above are served by bus 17. Mulhouse's first tram line is set to begin running in mid-2006.

ÉCOMUSÉE D'ALSACE

In Ungersheim about 17km northwest of Mulhouse (off the A35 to Colmar), **Écomusée d'Alsace** (☎ 03 89 74 44 74; www.ecomusee-alsace.com in French; adult/4-16yr/student/family €9.50/6.50/8/22, in Jul & Aug €12/6.50/10.50/26, cheaper after 3pm; ☉ tickets sold & artisans at work 9.30am-7pm Jul & Aug, 10am-6pm Apr-Jun & Sep–mid-Nov, restaurant & park open until later) is a 'living museum' in which smiths, cartwrights and coopers do their thing in and among 70 centuries-old Alsatian buildings – a veritable village – brought here for preservation (and so storks can build nests on them). That industrial relic next door, now affiliated with the Écomusée, is the **Rodolphe Potassium Mine** (☉ tours Jul & Aug), shut in 1976; parts can be visited with a retired miner.

Set to open in mid-2006, the nearby **Bioscope** (www.projet-bioscope.net in French) is supposed to make it fun to learn about the relationship between human beings and the environment though *vulgarisation scientifique* – no, not scientifically turning your children into vulgarians (TV is probably taking care of that already) but rather the 'popularisation of science'.

LORRAINE

Lorraine, between Champagne and the Massif des Vosges, is fed by the Rivers Meurthe, Moselle and Meuse – hence the names of three of its four *départements* (the fourth is Vosges).

History

Lorraine (Lothringen in German) got its name – Lotharii regnum, ie Lothair's kingdom – in the 9th century when it came to be ruled by the Frankish king Lothair II, who got himself into hot water with Pope Nicholas I by seeking to have his marriage annulled in order to wed his mistress. The area became part of France in 1766 upon the death of Stanisław Leszczyński, the deposed king of Poland who ruled Lorraine as duke in the middle decades of the 18th century. In 1871 the Moselle *département* (along with Alsace) was annexed by Germany and remained part of the Second Reich until 1918, which is why much of Metz looks so stolid and serious while Nancy, which remained French, is so stylishly Gallic. The two cities are rivals to this day.

Getting There & Away

Metz is on the A4, which links Paris and Reims with Strasbourg. Both Nancy and Metz are on the A31 from Dijon to Luxembourg.

When the TGV Est Européen line opens in June 2007, rail travel from Paris to Lorraine will take just 80 minutes to Metz and 90 minutes to Nancy.

NANCY

pop 331,000

Delightful Nancy has an air of refinement found nowhere else in Lorraine. With a magnificent central square, several fine museums and sparkling shop windows, the former capital of the dukes of Lorraine seems as opulent today as it did in the 16th to 18th centuries, when much of the city centre was built.

Nancy has long thrived on a combination of innovation and sophistication. The Art Nouveau movement flourished here (as the Nancy School) thanks to the rebellious spirit of local artists, including Émile Gallé (1846–1904), who set out to prove that everyday objects could be drop-dead gorgeous. As you walk around, keep an eye out for the stained-glass windows and dreamlike, sinuous grillwork that grace the entrances to many offices, shops and private homes.

Orientation

Pedestrians-only place Stanislas connects the narrow, twisting streets of the medieval Vieille Ville (Old Town), centred on the Grande Rue, with the rigid right angles of

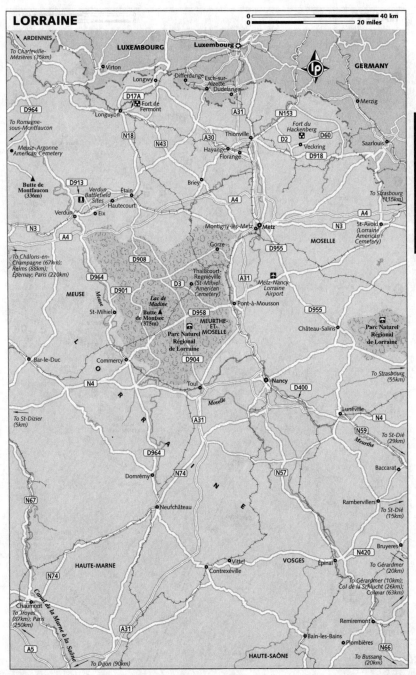

LORRAINE

0 — 40 km
0 — 20 miles

ARDENNES

To Charleville-
Mézières (35km)

LUXEMBOURG

Luxembourg

GERMANY

Virton

Longwy

Differdange

Esch-sur-
Alzette
Dudelange

Merzig

D17A
Fort de
Fermont

D964

To Romagne-
sous-Montfaucon

Longuyon

A31

N153

Fort du
Hackenberg

N18

N43

A30

Thionville

D2

D60

Veckring

Saarlouis

Meuse-Argonne
American Cemetery

Hayange
Florange

D918

Butte de
Montfaucon
(336m)

D913

Verdun
Battlefield
Sites

Étain

Briey

A4

To Strasbourg
(115km)

Hautecourt

Verdun

Eix

Montigny-lès-Metz

Metz

N3

St-Avold
(Lorraine
American
Cemetery)

A4

N3

A4

Gorze

MOSELLE

D908

D955

D964

D901

Thiaucourt-
Regniéville
(St-Mihiel
American
Cemetery)

D3

A31

Metz–Nancy-
Lorraine
Airport

To Châlons-en-
Champagne (67km);
Reims (88km);
Épernay; Paris (220km)

MEUSE

Lac de
Madine

St-Mihiel

Butte
de Montsec
(375m)

D958

Pont-à-Mousson

D955

Château-Salins

Parc Naturel
Régional
de Lorraine

Parc Naturel
Régional
de Lorraine

MEURTHE-
ET-
MOSELLE

Bar-le-Duc

Commercy

D904

To Strasbourg
(55km)

N4

Toul

Nancy

D400

To St-Dizier
(5km)

Moselle

A31

Lunéville

N4

D964

Moselle

N59

To St-Dié
(29km)

Meurthe

Domrémy

N74

N57

Baccarat

N67

Rambervillers

Neufchâteau

To St-Dié
(15km)

N420

Bruyères

HAUTE-MARNE

N74

Vittel

VOSGES

Épinal

To Gérardmer
(20km)

Contrexéville

To Gérardmer (10km);
Col de la Schlucht (26km);
Colmar (63km)

Chaumont

To Troyes
(87km); Paris
(250km)

Canal de la Marne à la Saône

Remiremont

A5

A31

Bain-les-Bains

Plombières

N66

HAUTE-SAÔNE

To Dijon (90km)

To Bussang
(20km)

ALSACE & LORRAINE

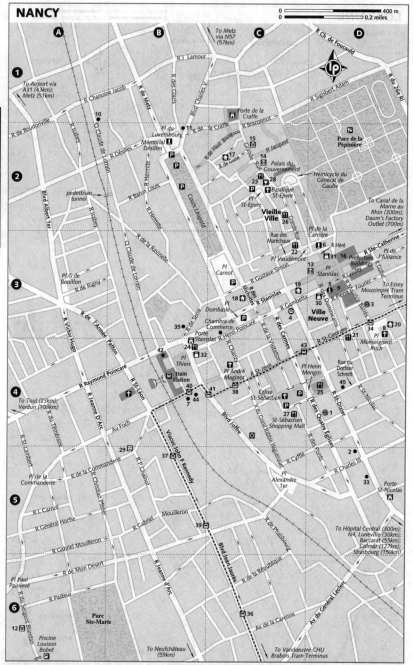

NANCY

0 — 400 m
0 — 0.2 miles

the 16th-century Ville Neuve (New Town) to the south. The train station is 800m southwest of place Stanislas.

Information

E-café Cyber Café (☎ 03 83 35 47 34; 11 rue des Quatre Églises; per min/hr €0.09/5.40; 🕙 11am-9pm Mon & Sat, 9am-9pm Tue-Fri, 2-8pm Sun) Internet access with qwerty keyboards.

Laundrette (124 rue St-Dizier; 🕙 7.45am-9.30pm)

Musée du Téléphone (☎ 03 83 86 50 00; 11 rue Maurice Barrès; per hr adult/student & senior €3/1.50; 🕙 10am-7pm Tue-Fri, 2-7pm Sat) A telecommunications museum that has saved itself from obsolescence by offering internet access.

Post Office (10 rue St-Dizier; 🕙 8am-6.30pm Mon-Fri, 8am-noon Sat) Does currency exchange.

Tourist Office (☎ 03 83 35 22 41; www.ot-nancy.fr; place Stanislas; 🕙 9am-7pm Mon-Sat, 10am-5pm Sun & holidays Apr-Oct, 9am-6pm Mon-Sat, 10am-1pm Sun & holidays Nov-Mar) Inside the Hôtel de Ville. Has free brochures outlining walking tours of the city centre and Art Nouveau architecture.

Sights

Neoclassical **place Stanislas**, whose 250th anniversary was celebrated with great fanfare in 2005, is one of the most beautiful public spaces in Europe. It is named after the enlightened, Polish-born Duke of Lorraine who commissioned it in the 18th century and whose **statue** stands in the middle. With its opulent buildings (including the **Hôtel de Ville** and the **theatre**), dazzling gilded wrought-iron gateways by Jean Lamour and rococo fountains by Guibal, the square – designed by Emmanuel Héré – has been recognised by Unesco as a World Heritage site. The ensemble – all 360-degrees of it – is reflected in a **stainless-steel half-globe** near the statue (keep an eye out around town for other such half-buried spheres).

A block to the east, 90m-square **place de l'Alliance** is graced by lime trees and a **baroque fountain** by Bruges-born Louis Cyfflé (1724–1806); it was inspired by Bernini's *Four Rivers* fountain in Rome's Piazza Navona.

Adjoining place Stanislas – on the other side of Nancy's own **Arc de Triomphe**, built in the mid-1750s to honour Louis XV – is quieter **place de la Carrière**, once a riding and jousting arena and now graced by four rows of linden trees and stately rococo gates in gilded wrought iron. A bit to the northeast is **Parc de la Pépinière**, a delightful formal garden that boasts cafés, a rose garden and a small zoo.

North of the Vieille Ville, Art Nouveau townhouses include **Maison Weissenburger** (1 blvd Charles V), built in 1904, and **Maison Huot** (92 quai Claude de Lorrain), constructed a year earlier.

The interior of the domed, 18th-century **cathédrale** (rue St-Georges) is a sombre mixture of neoclassical and baroque. The organ loft is from 1757.

Next to the Nancy Gare tram stop, a clue to the meaning of the **bizarre bronze sculpture**, a square column with a pile of – no, it can't be! – on top, is to be found on one of the nearby horizontal brass plaques.

MUSEUMS

A dazzling highlight of any visit to Nancy is the brilliant **Musée de l'École de Nancy** (School of Nancy Museum; ☎ 03 83 40 14 86; 36-38 rue du Sergent Blandan; adult/student & senior €6/4; ☾ 10.30am-6pm Wed-Sun), which brings together a heady collection of furnished rooms and curvaceous glass produced by the turn-of-the-20th-century Art Nouveau (Jugendstil) movement. It's housed in a 19th-century villa about 2km southwest of the city centre – to get there take bus 123 to the Nancy Thermal stop or buses 122, 126, 134 or 135 to the Painlevé stop.

Star attractions at the excellent **Musée des Beaux-Arts** (Fine Arts Museum; ☎ 03 83 85 30 72; 3 place Stanislas; adult/student & senior €6/4; ☾ 10am-6pm Wed-Mon) include a superb collection of Daum-made Art Nouveau glass and a rich and varied selection of paintings from the 14th to 18th centuries. Laminated information sheets are available.

The mostly 16th-century Palais Ducal, the splendid former residence of the dukes of Lorraine, now houses the **Musée Historique Lorrain** (Lorraine Historical Museum; ☎ 03 83 32 18 74; 64 & 66 Grande Rue; adult/student for both sections €4.60/3.10, for 1 section €3.10/2.30, for students on Wed free; ☾ 10am-12.30pm & 2-6pm Wed-Mon). The part dedicated to **fine arts & history** (at No 64) possesses rich collections of medieval statuary, engravings and faïence, as well as Judaica originating from before and after the Revolution; the section dedicated to **regional art & folklore** (at No 66) is housed in the 15th-century **Couvent des Cordeliers**, a former Franciscan monastery. Inside, the late-15th-century Gothic **Église des Cordeliers** and the adjacent **Chapelle Ducale** (Ducal Chapel; 1607) modelled on the Medici Chapel in Florence, served as the burial place of the dukes of Lorraine.

MUSEUM PASSES

The discount **Pass Nancy Trois Musées** (€8) gets you into the Musée de l'École de Nancy, the Musée Historique Lorrain and the Museé des Beaux-Arts and is available at each museum.

Le Pass Nancy (€13), available only at the tourist office, gets you reduced-price entry to six museums, a guided or MP3 tour of the city, a discount on bike rental, a bus/tram return trip, a cinema ticket and a *baba au rhum* (rum cake), invented by Stanislas.

Tours

The tourist office offers MP3 tours (€5) of the historic centre (1½ or two hours) and the Art Nouveau quarters (3½ hours if you check out every site).

Sleeping

Hôtel de l'Académie (☎ 03 83 35 52 31; fax 03 83 32 55 78; 7bis rue des Michottes; d €32, with shower €25) This offbeat, 29-room place has a tacky fountain that sounds like a broken urinal and cheaply furnished rooms with acoustic tile ceilings and plastic shower pods. Gallé would have been appalled but it's clean and you can't beat the price.

Hôtel des Portes d'Or (☎ 03 83 35 42 34; www.hotel-lesportesdor.com; 21 rue Stanislas; d €50-60) This welcoming and very cosy two-star hostelry, superbly situated just metres from place Stanislas, has 20 charming rooms with upholstered doors. It's often full so call ahead. By car, take rue St-Dizier, turn right onto pedestrians-only rue Stanislas and press the intercom button – the intercom opens the barrier to let authorised cars (eg those going to the hotel) into the pedestrians-only zone.

Hôtel de Guise (☎ 03 83 32 24 68; www.hotel deguise.com; 18 rue de Guise; d €59-95; ☒) A grand stone staircase leads to extra-wide hallways and 48 bright, spacious rooms. The bathrooms are as modern as the 18th-century hardwood floors are charmingly creaky. The building, in the heart of the old city, dates from 1680.

Hôtel des Prélats (☎ 03 83 30 20 20; www.hotel desprelats.com in French; 56 place Monseigneur Ruch; ☒ Cathédrale; d €92; ☒ ☒) In a grand building that's been a hotel since 1906, this two-star place with good wheelchair access, completely renovated in 2005, has 41 rooms with parquet floors, huge beds, antique furnishings and creative tile bathrooms.

Eating

No fewer than 21 reasonably priced eateries of all sorts line rue des Maréchaux, just west of the Arc de Triomphe; lunch *menus* start at €10. North of there, intimate eateries can be found all along the Grande Rue. There are lots of cheapies in the vicinity of the covered market along rue St-Dizier and rue des Quatre Églises.

Aux Délices du Palais (☎ 03 83 30 44 19; 69 Grande Rue; 1st course or dessert €4, mains €8; ☽ Mon-Fri) Billing itself as *bistronomique* (whatever that means), this informal place serves whatever the jovial chef's muse inspires him to make – everything from chicken *tajine* (North African-style stew) to beef fajitas to endive tarts. Great value so it's no surprise it's got an enthusiastic local following.

Le Gastrolâtre (☎ 03 83 35 51 94; 23 Grande Rue; lunch menu €18, other menus €30-40; ☽ Tue-Sat) A 16th- and 17th-century townhouse has been transformed into a homey, intimate eatery specialising in mouth-watering Lorraine- and Provence-inspired cuisine, including *gibier* and truffles. One of the chef's favourites is vol-au-vent filled with veal sweetbread, ham and morilles mushrooms.

Brasserie Excelsior (☎ 03 83 35 24 57; 50 rue Henri Poincaré; ☐ Nancy Gare; after-10pm menu €18.90, other menu €28.90; ☽ 8am-12.30am Mon-Sat, 8am-11pm Sun; meals served noon-3pm & 7pm-closing time) Built in 1910, this sparkling brasserie's Art Nouveau décor makes every glance at the ceiling memorable – and the food's pretty good, too. The sauerkraut options include *choucroute à trois poissons* (ie sauerkraut with salmon, haddock and burbot).

SELF-CATERING

Au Vieux Gourmet (26 rue St-Georges; ☽ 9am-8pm Mon-Fri, 9am-7.30pm Sat) This place has been a grocery since 1889. It carries luxury products (Fauchon, Hédiard) as well as staples.

Other places to pick up picnic supplies:
Aux Croustillants (10 rue des Maréchaux; ☽ 24hr except from 9.30pm Sun to 5.30am Tue) An almost-24/7 *boulangerie*.
Covered market (place Henri Mengin; ☐ Point Central; ☽ 7am-6pm Tue-Thu, 7am-6.30pm Fri & Sat)
Monoprix supermarket (rue des Ponts; ☽ 8.30am-8.30pm Mon-Sat) Deep inside the St-Sébastien shopping mall.

Drinking

There are quite a few bars along the Grande Rue.

Le Ch'timi (☎ 03 83 32 82 76; 17 place St-Epvre; ☽ 9am-2am Mon-Sat, 9am-8pm Sun) On three brick-and-stone levels, Le Ch'timi is *the* place to go for beer. Especially popular with students, this unpretentious bar has 150 brewskies, 16 of them (including Guinness) on tap.

Le Varadero (☎ 03 83 36 61 98; 27 Grande Rue; ☽ 6pm-2am Tue-Sat May-Sep, 8.30pm-2am Tue-Sat Oct-Apr) Named after a beach in Cuba, this laid-back bar has live Latino music 8.30pm to 10pm on some Saturdays and a Latino-oriented DJ 11pm to 2am on Thursday, Friday and Saturday.

Entertainment

Details on cultural events appear in the free monthly *Spectacles* (www.spectacles-publications.com in French).

CINEMA

Caméo Commanderie (☎ 03 83 28 41 00; www.cine-cameo.com in French; 16 rue de la Commanderie; ☐ Kennedy) Nondubbed films, including some Hollywood blockbusters, are screened at this cinema.

LIVE MUSIC

Blue Note Why Not Club (☎ 03 83 30 31 18; 3 rue des Michottes; admission Fri, Sat & theme nights €10; ☽ 11pm-4am Wed, Thu & Sun, 11pm-5am Fri, 11pm-6am Sat) This vaulted subterranean discotheque, at the far end of the courtyard, has jazz and blues concerts (€8 to €10) each Thursday (except during school holidays) from 9pm to 11pm or midnight; karaoke on Sunday from 11.30pm to 2am; and, from about 11pm (2am on Sunday), two dance floors, one Latino and African, the other disco.

Shopping

Nancy's main – and most sparkling – commercial thoroughfares are rue St-Dizier, rue St-Jean and rue St-Georges.

Baccarat shops (☎ 03 83 30 55 11; 2 rue des Dominicains & next door at 3 rue Gambetta; ☽ closed Mon morning & Sun) Exquisite crystal and jewellery of the sort enjoyed by royalty the world over are on display at these shops, where the simplest wine glass – impossibly delicate – costs €57.

Daum (☎ 03 83 32 21 65; 14 place Stanislas; ☽ closed Mon morning & Sun) At this flagship shop, you can watch a video showing crystal artisans at work and visit a small museum of early-20th-century pieces.

Daum's factory outlet (☎ 03 83 32 14 55; 17 rue des Cristalleries; ☒ Cristalleries; ☽ 9.30am-12.30pm & 2.30-6.30pm Mon-Sat) About 1km northeast of place Stanislas, sells discontinued Daum designs and unsigned seconds.

Bergamotes de Nancy, the local confectionery speciality, are hard candies made with bergamot, a citrus fruit – also used to flavour Earl Grey tea – that grows on the slopes of Mt Etna. The only confectioner allowed to sell *bergamottes* (with two Ts) is **Lefèvre-Lemoine** (☎ 03 83 30 13 83; Au Duché de Lorraine; 47 rue Henri Poincaré; ☒ Nancy Gare; ☽ 9.30am-7pm Mon-Sat, 9.30am-12.30pm Sun), founded in 1840 and last redecorated – with Gilded Age panache – way back in 1928. One of its old-fashioned sweets tins made a cameo appearance in the film *Amélie*.

Getting There & Away
CAR
Rental options:
ADA (☎ 03 83 36 53 09; 138 rue St-Dizier)
Europcar (☎ 03 83 37 57 24; 18 rue de Serre)
National-Citer (☎ 03 83 37 38 59; in the train station departure hall; ☒ Nancy Gare)

TRAIN
The **train station** (place Thiers; ☒ Nancy Gare) is on the line linking Paris' Gare de l'Est (€37.80, 2¾ hours to 3¼ hours, 13 to 17 daily) with Strasbourg (€19.70, 1¼ hours, 10 to 17 daily). Other destinations include Baccarat (€5, 38 to 70 minutes, seven to 14 daily) and Metz (€5, 38 to 61 minutes, 30 to 55 daily).

Tickets can be purchased at the **SNCF office** (18 place St-Epvre; ☽ 12.30-6pm Mon, 9.30am-1pm & 2-6pm Tue-Fri).

Getting Around
There's free parking along the north and east sides of Parc de la Pepinière (rue Sigisbert Adam and rue du 26e RI) and on side streets in the working-class neighbourhoods west of the train tracks.

The local public transport company, **STAN** (☎ 03 83 30 08 08; www.reseau-stan.com in French; offices at 3 rue du Docteur Schmitt & Nancy République bus hub; ☽ 7am-7.30pm Mon-Sat), has its main transfer points at Nancy République and Point Central. One/10 ticket/s cost €1.20/8.90.

STAN rents bicycles for €2 a day at the park-and-ride (*parking relais*, or P+R) car parks next to the St-Georges and Essey Mouzimpré tram stops.

A **taxi** (☎ 03 83 37 65 37) is just a telephone call away.

BACCARAT
pop 4700

The most famous *cristallerie* (crystal glassworks) of all, founded in 1764, is at Baccarat, 55km southeast of Nancy. At the **Musée du Cristal** (☎ 03 83 76 61 37; www.baccarat.fr; 2 rue des Cristalleries; adult/under 10yr €2.50/free; ☽ 9.30am-12.30pm & 2-6.30pm Apr-Oct, 10am-noon & 2-6pm Nov-Mar), on the grounds of the Baccarat factory, you can admire 1100 exquisite pieces.

Across the River Meurthe, the dark sanctuary of **Église St-Rémy** (☽ 8am-5pm), built in the mid-1950s to replace an earlier church destroyed by Allied bombing in 1944, is lit by 20,000 Baccarat crystal panels sent in brutalist-style concrete walls.

The **tourist office** (☎ 03 83 75 13 37; www.ville-baccarat.fr/accotgb.htm; ☽ 9am-noon & 1.30pm or 2-5pm or 5.30pm Mon-Sat, closed Sat Nov-Mar, open 10am-noon Sun Jul & Aug) is around the back side of the steep-roofed **Hôtel de Ville** (1924), which faces the riverside roundabout. It has hiking maps and details on group hikes run on most Thursday afternoons by the Club Vosgien.

Hôtel La Renaissance (☎ 03 83 75 11 31; www.hotel-la-renaissance.com; 31 rue des Cristalleries; d €49; ☽ reception & restaurant closed Fri & evening Sun; ☒), down the block from the museum, is a two-star Logis de France–affiliated hotel with 16 spacious if uninspired rooms and an excellent French restaurant (*menus* €17 to €37).

Baccarat's train station, a few hundred metres north of the Musée du Cristal, has trains to Nancy (€5, 38 to 70 minutes, seven to 14 daily).

METZ
pop 323,000

Present-day capital of the Lorraine *région*, Metz (pronounced 'mess') is a dignified city with stately public squares, shaded riverside parks, a large university and a lively, pedestrians-only commercial centre. Quite a few of the city's most impressive buildings date from the 48-year period when Metz was part of the German empire. The Gothic cathedral, with its stunning stained glass, is the most outstanding attraction; the city also has a truly excellent museum of antiquities and art.

Orientation

The cathedral, on a hill above the River Moselle, is a bit over 1km north of the train station. The city centre's main public squares are place d'Armes, next to the cathedral; place St-Jacques, in the heart of the pedestrianised commercial precinct; place St-Louis; and, 400m to the west of the latter, place de la République.

Information

The tourist office charges a 5.5% commission to change money.

Diacom Internet Café (per hr €3; 9am-8pm Mon-Sat, to 9pm Jun-Aug, closed noon-2pm Fri, 10am-8pm Sun) 34 rue du Pont des Morts (03 87 16 27 40); 20 rue Gambetta; (03 87 63 08 85)

Hospital (Notre Dame de Bonsecours CHR; Bldg F emergency room/casualty ward 03 87 55 34 91/2; 1 place Philippe de Vigneulles; 24hr)

Laundrettes 11 rue de la Fontaine (7am-8pm); 4 rue des Allemands (9am-8pm); 22 rue du Pont des Morts (7am-8pm); 23 rue Taison (7am-8pm)

Main Post Office (9 rue Gambetta; 8am-7pm Mon-Fri, 8.30am-12.30pm Sat) Has currency exchange and a Cyberposte.

Police (Hôtel de Police; 03 87 16 17 17; 10 rue Belle Isle; 24hr)

Tourist Office (03 87 55 53 76; http://tourisme .mairie-metz.fr; 2 place d'Armes; 9am-7pm Mon-Sat, 10am-3pm Sun, to 5pm Sun Apr-Sep) In a one-time guardroom built in the mid-1700s. Has a free walking and cycling map and an internet terminal that works with a télécarte (phonecard).

Sights

CATHÉDRALE ST-ÉTIENNE

Metz' stupendous Gothic **Cathédrale St-Étienne** (place St-Étienne; 8am-7pm May-Sep, to 6pm Oct-Apr), built between 1220 and 1522, is famed for its veritable curtains of 13th- to 20th-century stained glass, among the finest in France. The superb **Flamboyant Gothic windows** (1504), on the main wall of the north transept arm, provide a remarkable stylistic contrast with the glorious **Renaissance windows** on the main wall of the south transept arm, created a mere two decades later. There are windows by **Chagall** on the western wall of the north transept arm (yellow predominates) and in the nearby section of the ambulatory (over

the entrance to the Grande Sacristie; reds and blues set the tone), where you'll also find the **treasury** (adult/student €2/1; closed Jan). In the 15th-century **crypt** (below the altar; adult/student €2/1; closed Jan) you can see a 15th-century sculpture of the **Graoully** ('grau-lee' or 'grau-yee'), a dragon that is said to have terrified pre-Christian Metz. Try to visit on a bright day. Like the city centre's other major monuments, the cathedral is beautifully illuminated at night (until 1am).

MUSÉE LA COUR D'OR

The superb **Musée La Cour d'Or** (03 87 68 25 00; 2 rue du Haut Poirier; adult/student under 26yr/over 65yr/ under 18yr €4.60/2.30/3.30/free, 1st Sun of month free; 9am-5pm Mon & Wed-Fri, 10am-5pm Sat & Sun) has a first-rate collection of Gallo-Roman antiquities, among them a statue of the Egyptian goddess Isis unearthed right here in Metz; art from the Middle Ages, including objects from around the year 1000 and several rare painted ceilings; paintings from the 15th century onwards, among them some fine works by lesser-known local artists; and objects that trace the history of Metz' ancient Jewish community. A room-by-room brochure in English is available.

CITY CENTRE

On the eastern edge of the city centre, triangular **place St-Louis** is surrounded by medieval arcades and merchants' houses dating from the 14th to 16th centuries.

Neoclassical **place de la Comédie**, bounded by one of the channels of the Moselle, is home to the city's **Théâtre** (1738–53), the oldest theatre building in France that's still in use. During the Revolution, place de l'Égalité (as it was then known) was the site of a guillotine that lopped the heads off 63 'enemies of the people'. The neo-Romanesque **Temple Neuf** (Protestant Church), sombre and looming, was constructed under the Germans in 1903.

The formal flowerbeds of the **Esplanade** – and its statue of a gallant-looking Marshall Ney, sword dangling at his side (1859) – are flanked by imposing public buildings, including the **Arsenal Cultural Centre** (1863) and the sober, neoclassical **Palais de Justice** (late 18th century). **Église St-Pierre-aux-Nonains** (admission free; 1-6pm Tue-Sat & 2-6pm Sun mid-Jun–Sep, 1-6pm Sat & 2-6pm Sun Oct–mid-Jun) was originally built around AD 400 as part of

ALSACE & LORRAINE

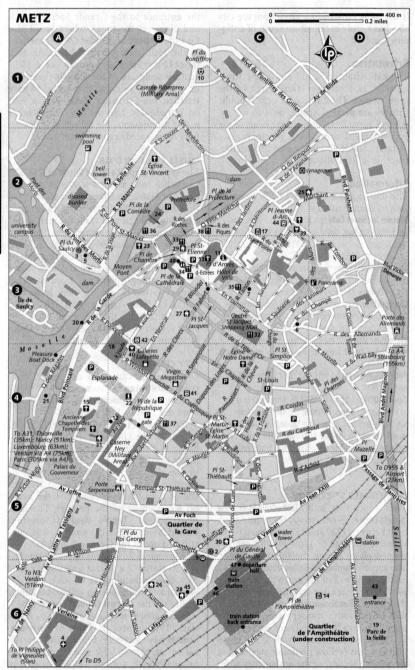

a Gallo-Roman spa complex (the wall sections with horizontal red-brick stripes are Roman originals). For a thousand years – from the 6th to the 16th centuries – the structure served as the abbey church of a women's monastery.

West and northwest of the Esplanade, on both sides of blvd Poincaré, is a lovely **riverside park** graced with statues, ponds, swans and a fountain. In the warm months, **pedal boats** and **rowboats** can be rented on quai des Régates.

QUARTIER DE LA GARE
The solid, bourgeois buildings and broad avenues of the **Train Station Quarter**, including rue Gambetta and av Foch, were constructed in the decades before WWI. Built with the intention of Germanising the city by emphasising Metz' post-1871 status as an integral part of the Second Reich, its neo-Romanesque and neo-Renaissance buildings are made of dark-hued sandstone, granite and basalt, rather than the yellow-tan Jaumont limestone characteristic of French-built, neoclassical structures.

The massive, grey-sandstone **train station**, completed in 1908, is decorated with Teutonic sculptures – some of them quite amusing – whose common theme is German imperial might; it could detrain 20,000 troops and their equipment in just 24 hours. The massive **main post office**, built in 1911 of red Vosges sandstone, is as solid and heavy as the cathedral is light and lacy.

QUARTIER DE L'AMPHITHÉÂTRE
'The wrong side of the tracks', until recently a wasteland of abandoned hangars and depots, is undergoing a transformation thanks to Metz' seemingly boundless cultural ambitions (and development budget). The Amphitheatre Quarter already boasts **Les Arènes** (Palais Omnisports), a vast steel-and-glass venue for sports events and concerts, and the green riverside lawns of **Parc de la Seille**.

But you ain't seen nothin' yet: come spring of 2008, the **Centre Pompidou-Metz** (www .centrepompidou-metz.com) – a branch of the inside-out original in Paris – is supposed to open its doors to aficionados of modern and contemporary art. The design, by Shigeru Ban (Tokyo) and Jean de Gastines (Paris), is like nothing else ever conceived by the human mind. The whole thing will be covered by an undulating, translucent 'membrane' of Teflon-coated fibreglass. It may do for Metz what the Guggenheim did for Bilbao.

Tours
The tourist office's 1½-hour *visites audioguidées* (MP3 tours; €7) of the city centre are available in six languages.

Sleeping
In general, Metz' hotels offer excellent value. Except in summer, they are at their fullest from Monday to Thursday.

BUDGET
Auberge de Jeunesse Carrefour (☎ 03 87 75 07 26; ascarrefour@wanadoo.fr; 6 rue Marchant; dm €14.90, s/d

incl breakfast €17.50/35; 24hr;) A hostel for young working people (mainly women) that also functions as a youth hostel. The rooms, accessible all day long, are Spartan; some have shower and toilet. From the train station, take bus Nos 3 or 11 to the St-Georges stop.

Hôtel Bristol (03 87 66 74 22; www.hotel-bristol-57.com in French; 7 rue Lafayette; s/d from €28/32, larger d €45) Bring your bell-bottoms – at the Bristol it's still the 1970s, the period authenticity certified by the fusty furnishings undisturbed since Elvis didn't die. The 53 rooms can charitably be termed 'compact'. If your company puts you up here, cash in your stock options and start preparing a résumé – but cash-strapped backpackers should do just fine.

MIDRANGE

Several two-star hotels face the train station.

Hôtel Métropole (03 87 66 26 22; www.hotel metropole-metz.com; 5 place du Général de Gaulle; d €48-59;) Built at the tail end of the German period (1912), this two-star place has 72 orange-yellow rooms that are so bright and cheery they're almost uplifting.

Cécil Hôtel (03 87 66 66 13; www.cecilhotel-metz .com; 14 rue Pasteur; d €58;) Built right after Metz was returned to France (1920), this two-star hotel, mercifully devoid of pastels, is popular with budget-minded business people. The 39 modern rooms, most renovated in 2006, have spacious tile bathrooms. If you stay Friday and Saturday, the buffet breakfast (€7) is free.

our pick Hôtel de la Cathédrale (03 87 75 00 02; www.hotelcathedrale-metz.fr in French; 25 place de Chambre; d €58-95, ste €105). Ensconced in a gorgeous 17th-century townhouse, this three-star place positively oozes romance! The 20 large rooms (soon to be joined by 10 more in the annexe) – some with spectacular views of the cathedral – are tastefully furnished with antiques and rugs that complement perfectly the ancient wooden beams overhead. The wrought ironwork is by Jean Lamour (1698–1771), creator of the gilded masterpieces that adorn Nancy's place Stanislas.

Grand Hôtel de Metz (03 87 36 16 33; www.grand hotelmetz.com; 3 rue des Clercs; d from €59;) At this 62-room, two-star place, you can luxuriate in a giant bathtub in a minisuite (€90) big enough for ballroom dancing (our advice to

management: lose the plastic plants), and make your own poached eggs at the buffet breakfast (€7). By car, take rue Fabert from the cathedral, push the button on the 'appel' upright and explain you're going to the hotel.

TOP END

La Citadelle (03 87 17 17 17; www.citadelle-metz .com; d €195-265; 5 av Ney;) Opened in 2005 in a one-time military supplies depot built 4½ centuries ago, Metz' only four-star hotel has good wheelchair access and 79 huge, ultramodern rooms – in stark red, white and black – with more than a hint of Japanese sleekness. There's Casablanca-style piano music in the lobby on Friday and Saturday evenings.

Eating

Place St-Jacques is taken over by cafés in the warmer months. Cheap student eats are available near the university on grungy rue du Pont des Morts.

Canada'Venture (03 87 18 99 74; www.canada -venture.com in French; lunch menu €13; 12 rue des Roches; closed Sun & lunch Mon) So you're tired of French food, eh? How about *brochettes de bison grillées* (grilled bison brochettes; €16) washed down with a Canadian beer, eh? At this themed eatery, the cuisine, like the décor – snow shoes, a wooden canoe, stuffed racoons and even a cigar store Indian straight out of 'Seinfeld' – are the Canadophilic owners' heartfelt, if cringe-inducing, homage to the Great White North.

Crêperie Le Chouchen (03 87 18 50 50; courtyard, 10 rue Taison; lunch Mon-Sat, dinner Thu-Sat) Gussied up like a Breton village, this restaurant – named after Breton honey wine – is the best place in town for sweet and savoury crêpes (€2.20 to €8.50) washed down with *cidre* (cider) or a beer from Brittany. Salads (€3.50 to €7) are also available.

La Baraka (03 87 36 33 92; 25 rue de Chambre; closed Wed & mid-Jul–mid-Aug) Serves Metz' finest Algerian Berber couscous (€10 to €14), *tajines* (€12) and *brick* (a fried pastry filled with egg, capers and either chopped meat or tuna; €4).

El Theatris (03 87 56 02 02; 2 place de la Comédie; 2-/3-/4-course menus €15.50/20.50/35; Mon-Sat) Serves traditional French cuisine with 'echoes from *ailleurs*' (elsewhere). The neoclassical décor mirrors the architecture outside.

The candles are calming and so is the music, which ranges from Glenn Miller to light opera.

ourpick **L'Étude** (☎ 03 87 36 35 32; www.l-etude .com in French; 11 av Robert Schuman; 2-/3-course lunch menus €12.70/14.50, dinner menus €20.60/25.80, during concerts €24.90/29.80; ◷ Mon-Sat) Hugely popular with local cognoscenti, this eatery is a quintessentially French mixture of the intellectual (the walls are lined with books) and the gastronomic (French, of course) – a coming together of the mind and the stomach, if you will. There's live music (jazz, chansons, Roma – the website has the schedule) from about 8pm on Friday and Saturday (except in July and August; reservations recommended).

Restaurant Thierry (☎ 03 87 74 01 23; www.res taurant-thierry.fr; 5 rue des Piques; menu €21.50, Fri night & Sat €31.50; ◷ closed Wed & Sun) Brings culinary insights from the Caribbean Basin, Louisiana and Vietnam together with French gastronomic methods and traditions to create avant-garde cuisine 'without taboos'. The bistro ambience is both chic and relaxed. Often full.

SELF-CATERING
For picnic supplies:

Atac supermarket (near place St-Jacques; ◷ 8.30am-7.30pm Mon-Sat) On the lowest level of the Centre St-Jacques shopping mall.

Covered market (place de la Cathédrale; ◷ approx 7am-6pm Tue-Sat)

Drinking
Café Jehanne d'Arc (☎ 03 87 37 39 94; place Jeanne d'Arc; ◷ 11.30am-2am Mon-Fri, 3pm-3am Sat) This bar bears its long history – the roof beams are from the 1500s, the faint frescoes two or three centuries older – with good humour and mellowness. The sound track ranges from Dizzie Gillespie to Brel to Gainsbourg. There's a refreshing terrace in the warm months.

L'Appart (☎ 03 87 18 59 26; 2 rue Haute Pierre; ◷ 8pm-2.30am Sun & Tue-Thu, 8pm-3.30am Fri & Sat) The house in which the poet Paul Verlaine – Arthur Rimbaud's lover and, almost, his assassin – was born in 1844 is now a laid-back mainly-gay bar with campy light fixtures, a retro 1950s ceiling, a bright-orange floor and centuries-old carved wood panelling that's protected by law. Drag queens do their thing at 11.30pm on Sunday.

Entertainment
Details on cultural events appear in the free monthly *Spectacles* (www.spectacles -publications.com in French) and the free monthly *Ce Mois-Ci à Metz*, available at the tourist office. The city's main concert venues are the **Arsenal cultural centre** (☎ 03 87 39 92 00; av Ney), **Les Arènes** (Quartier de L'Ampithéâtre; www .arenes-de-metz.com in French), and the recently-reopened **Salle des Trinitaires** (place Jeanne d'Arc).

Le Tiffany (☎ 03 87 75 23 32; 24 rue du Coëtlosquet; admission free except Thu/Fri & Sat €5/12; ◷ 11pm-5am Wed-Mon) The gyrating bodies at Le Tiffany would have knocked the socks off the medieval people who built the vaulted cellar it has occupied since 1972. This classic discotheque was given a sleek modern look in 2005. Friday and Saturday are theme nights.

L'Endroit (☎ 03 87 18 59 26; 20 rue aux Ours; admission €10; ◷ midnight-5.30am Fri, Sat & Sun night & holiday eve) A gay-friendly disco with industrial style interior design, including a stainless-steel dance floor, and House music on the turntable. Male strippers go the full Monty every other Sunday night.

Getting There & Away
CAR
Rental options:

Budget (☎ 03 87 66 36 31; 5 rue Lafayette)
Europcar (☎ 03 87 62 26 12; in the train station's arrival hall)
National-Citer (☎ 03 87 38 09 99; in the train station's arrival hall)

TRAIN
Metz' **train station** (pl du Général de Gaulle) spiffed up for the TGV, is on the line linking Paris' Gare de l'Est (€37.80, three hours, 10 daily) with Luxembourg (€12.40, 50 minutes, 16 to 21 daily). Direct trains also go to Nancy (€5, 38 to 61 minutes, 30 to 55 daily), Strasbourg (€20.40, 1¼ to 1¾ hours, four to eight daily) and Verdun (€6, 1¼ hours, five each weekday, one or two daily weekends).

Getting Around
BICYCLE
Three-speed city bikes can be rented from **Vélocation** (per half-/whole day €3/5), a non-profit outlet with two bureaus:

Rue d'Estrées (☎ 03 87 74 50 43; ◷ 9am-6pm)
Train station (☎ 03 87 62 61 79; in the departure hall; ◷ 9am-8pm Mon-Fri)

PARKING

Free parking can be found near the train station under the trees on av Foch; northeast of the train station at place Mazelle; and east of Auberge de Jeunesse Carrefour along blvd Paixhans.

TAXI

Radio Taxis de Metz (☎ 03 87 56 91 92) is on duty day or night.

FORT DU HACKENBERG

The largest single Maginot Line bastion (p373) in the Metz area was the 1000-man **Fort du Hackenberg** (☎ 03 82 82 30 08; adult/under 16yr €6/3.50; tours begin every 15min 2-3.30pm Sat, Sun & holidays & at 3pm Wed Apr-Oct), 30km northeast of Metz near the village of Veckring, whose 10km of galleries were designed to be self-sufficient for three months and, in battle, to fire four tonnes of shells a minute. An electric trolley takes visitors along 4km of the fortress' underground tunnels – always at 12°C – past a variety of subterranean installations (kitchen, hospital, electric plant etc). Tours last two hours.

Readers have been enthusiastic about the Fort du Hackenberg **tours** (www.maginot -line.com) led by Jean-Pascal Speck, an amateur historian and owner of the three-star **Hôtel L'Horizon** (☎ 03 82 88 53 65; www.lhorizon.fr in French; 5 rte du Crève Coeur; d €96; closed Jan & Feb) in Thionville. If he's unavailable he'll give you the name of other English-speaking guides.

VERDUN

pop 19,600

The horrific events that took place in and around Verdun between February 1916 and August 1917 – *l'enfer de Verdun* (the hell of Verdun; p415) – have turned the town's name into a byword for wartime slaughter. These days, Verdun is an economically depressed and profoundly provincial backwater – some would say it's a throwback to the more insular France of 50 years ago – though the dispatch of French troops based near Verdun to peacekeeping missions abroad has made world politics a very local and, for some, personal affair.

History

After the annexation of Lorraine's Moselle *département* and Alsace by Germany in 1871, Verdun became a frontline outpost.

Over the next four decades, it was turned into the most important – and most heavily fortified – element in France's eastern defence line.

During WWI Verdun itself was never taken by the Germans, but the evacuated town was almost totally destroyed by artillery bombardments. In the hills to the north and east of Verdun, the brutal combat – carried out with artillery, flame-throwers and poison gas – completely wiped out nine villages. During the last two years of WWI, more than 800,000 soldiers (some 400,000 French and almost as many Germans, along with thousands of the Americans who arrived in 1918) lost their lives near here.

Orientation

The main commercial street, known as rue St-Paul and rue Mazel, and the Ville Haute (Upper Town) are on the west bank of the River Meuse. The train station is 700m northwest of the cathedral.

Information

The tourist office exchanges US and British cash.

Laundrette (2 place Chevert; 6.30am-8pm, to 9pm Jun-Sep)

Main Post Office (av de la Victoire) Has currency exchange and a Cyberposte.

Tourist Office (☎ 03 29 86 14 18; www.verdun-tourisme .com; place de la Nation; 8.30am-6.30pm Mon-Sat May-Sep, 9am-noon & 2-5pm or 5.30pm Mon-Sat Oct-Apr, 9am-5pm Sun & holidays May-Sep, 10am-1pm Sun & holidays Oct-Apr)

Sights

Verdun's huge **Citadelle Souterraine** (☎ 03 29 86 62 02; tourist entrance on av du 5e RAP; adult/5-15yr €6/2.50; 9am or 10am-noon & 2pm-btwn 5pm & 7pm, no midday closure Apr-Sep, closed Jan), with its 7km of underground galleries, was designed by Vauban (p62) in the 17th century and completed in 1838. In 1916 it was turned into an impregnable command centre in which 10,000 *poilus* (French WWI soldiers) lived, many while waiting to be dispatched to the front. About 10% of the galleries have been converted into an imaginative audiovisual re-enactment of the war, making this an excellent introduction to the WWI history of Verdun. Half-hour tours in battery-powered cars are available in six languages.

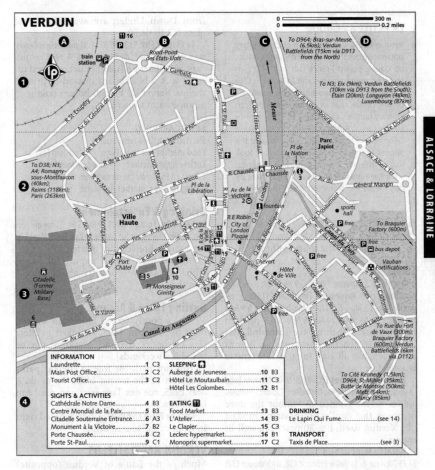

The **Centre Mondial de la Paix** (World Centre for Peace; ☎ 03 29 86 55 00; www.centremondialpaix.asso.fr in French; place Monseigneur Ginisty; adult/student €3/1.50; ⏰ 9.30am-7pm Jul & Aug, 9.30am-noon & 2-6pm Sep-Jun, closed Jan), which Verdun's mayor is rather unpeaceably trying to shut down (he wants the building), has imaginative exhibits on the horrific carnage of WWI. It is housed in Verdun's handsomely classical (and classically handsome) former bishop's palace, built in 1724.

Inside **Cathédrale Notre Dame** (place Monseigneur Ginisty; ⏰ 8am-6pm or 7pm), a gilded baroque **baldachin** and 18th-century furnishings add character to the Romanesque and Gothic structure, restored after WWI damage. Much of the stained glass is interwar.

The almost Fascist-looking **Monument à la Victoire** (Victory Monument; overlooking rue Mazel, built from 1920 to 1929, is softened somewhat by a cascading fountain.

Two of the city's gates are extant. **Porte Chaussée** (rue Chaussée) was built in the 14th century and later used as a prison. **Porte St-Paul** (rue St-Paul) was built in 1877 and rebuilt between 1919 and 1929; the Rodin bronze was given to the city by the Netherlands.

Tours

Dragées (pronounced 'dra-zhay'; sugared almonds) – not to be confused with *draguer* (dra-*gay*), which means to chat up – have long been a Verdun speciality. You can see how they're made at the **Braquier**

ALSACE & LORRAINE

LA PETITE AMERIQUE

Verdun had a significant American military presence from the end of WWII until Charles de Gaulle pulled France out of NATO's integrated military command in 1966. In **Cité Kennedy**, a neighbourhood 2km southeast of the centre that once housed American military families, the streets still bear names such as av d'Atlanta, av de Floride, av de Géorgie and impasse de Louisiane, and the almost-identical ranch-style houses look like a dull version of suburban America, circa *The Feminine Mystique*. To get there by car, follow the signs to Lycée Freyssinet.

---

factory (☎ 03 29 84 30 00; 50 rue du Fort de Vaux; €2; ☟ tours 9.30am, 10.30am & 2.30pm Mon-Thu & Fri morning), 1.5km east of the tourist office.

Sleeping

Auberge de Jeunesse (☎ 03 29 86 28 28; ajverdun@ wanadoo.fr; place Monseigneur Ginisty; dm €11.50; ☟ reception 8am-12.30pm & 5-11pm Mon-Fri, 8-10am & 5-9pm Sat & Sun, hostel closed 20 Jan-20 Feb) This modern hostel, situated behind the cathedral, has 70 bunks of generous proportions. Rooms are accessible all day long; a kitchenette is available.

Hôtel Les Colombes (☎ 03 29 86 05 46; www.hotel -a-verdun.com in French; 9 av Garibaldi; d €35-60; ☟ closed mid-Dec–mid-Jan) Named to honour the dove of peace, this family-run hostelry, modest like Verdun itself, has 30 practical, well-lit rooms.

Hôtel Le Montaulbain (☎ 03 29 86 00 47; fax 03 29 84 75 70; 4 rue de la Vieille Prison; d €38, with shower €32) The 10 rooms at this family-run, two-star place are cheerful, well-tended and fairly spacious.

Eating

Near the river, you'll find brasseries and fast-food joints along attractive, pedestrianised quai de Londres (a plaque on the wall near rue Beaurepaire explains the origin of the name).

L'Atelier (☎ 03 29 84 45 29; 33 rue des Gros Degrés; weekday lunch menus €10.50-13.50, other menus €29-45; ☟ closed dinner Sun & Mon) French cuisine meets herbs, sauces and creative ideas from around the world – at least some locals relish the thought that there's a whole world out there! About 20 wines, including some

from Down Under, are available by the glass (€2 to €4.50).

Le Clapier (☎ 03 29 86 20 14; 34 rue des Gros Degrés; menu €13; ☟ closed Sun & lunch Mon) A real *restaurant du quartier* (neighbourhood restaurant) with a blackboard instead of printed menus. Serves up French home cooking in a homey atmosphere.

SELF-CATERING
Picnic supplies options:
Food market (rue Victor Hugo; ☟ 7am-1pm Fri)
Leclerc hypermarket (☟ 9am-8pm Mon-Sat, to 8.30pm on Fri) Across the car park from the train station.
Monoprix supermarket (rue Mazel; ☟ Mon-Sat)

Drinking & Entertainment

Le Lapin Qui Fume (☎ 03 29 86 15 84; 31 rue des Gros Degrés; ☟ 11am-2am Tue-Sat, 6pm-2am Sun & Mon) Up for a micro-brewed pint in a friendly neighbourhood bar? Try Le Lapin Qui Fume, which hosts live concerts about once a month.

Getting There & Around

Verdun's poorly served little train station, built by Eiffel in 1868, is linked to Metz (€6, 1¼ hours, five each weekday, one or two daily weekends).

You can park for free in the car parks southeast of the tourist office on av du 8 Mai 1945, rue des Tanneries and rue Léon Gambetta.

Taxis de Place (☎ 03 29 86 05 22) is based right in front of the tourist office.

VERDUN BATTLEFIELDS

Much of the Battle of Verdun (opposite) was fought 5km to 8km (as the crow flies) northeast of Verdun. Today, the area – again forested – is served by the D913 and D112; by car follow the signs to the 'Champ de Bataille 14–18'. The opening hours given below may be modified in 2007. Almost all site interiors are closed in January.

The Verdun tourist office (p412) can supply visitors with practical and historical information on the local battlefields; books on offer include Alistair Horne's *The Price of Glory: Verdun 1916*, as well as several works by Lyn MacDonald. The tourist office's four-hour **minibus tours** (English text available; incl admission fees €25.50) of four battle sites begin at 2pm from May to mid-September.

VERDUN: THE STRATEGY BEHIND THE CARNAGE

The outbreak of WWI in August 1914 was followed on the Western Front by a long period of trench warfare in which neither side made any significant gains. To break the stalemate, the Germans decided to change tactics, attacking a target so vital for both military and symbolic reasons that the French would throw every man they had into its defence. These troops would then be slaughtered, 'bleeding France white' and causing the French people to lose their will to resist. The target selected for this bloody plan by the German general staff was the heavily fortified city of Verdun.

The Battle of Verdun began on the morning of 21 February 1916. After the heaviest shelling of the war to that date (something like two million shells were fired in 10 hours), German forces went on the attack and advanced with little opposition for four days, capturing, among other unprepared French positions, Fort de Douaumont. Thus began a 300-day battle fought by hundreds of thousands of cold, wet, miserable and ill-fed men, sheltering in their muddy trenches and foxholes amid a moonscape of craters.

French forces were regrouped and rallied by General Philippe Pétain (later the leader of the collaborationist Vichy government during WWII), who slowed the German advance by launching several French counterattacks. The Germans weren't pushed back beyond their positions of February 1916 until American troops and French forces launched a coordinated offensive in September 1918.

Mémorial de Verdun

The village of Fleury, wiped off the face of the earth in the course of being captured and recaptured 16 times, is now the site of the **Mémorial de Verdun** (Musée Mémorial de Fleury; ☎ 03 29 84 35 34; adult/11-16yr €7/3.50; ☺ 9am-6pm Apr-Aug, 9am-noon & 2-5pm or 5.30pm Sep-late Dec, Feb & Mar). The story of the battle is told using evocative (and in some cases gruesome) photos, documents, weapons and other objects. Downstairs is a re-creation of the battlefield as it looked on the day the guns finally fell silent. Admission includes a film, available in English.

In the grassy crater-pocked centre of **Fleury**, a few hundred metres down the road from the memorial, signs among the low ruins indicate the village's former layout.

Ossuaire de Douaumont

The sombre, 137m-long **Douaumont Ossuary** (☎ 03 29 84 54 81; www.verdun-douaumont.com), inaugurated in 1932, is one of France's most important WWI memorials. It contains the remains of about 130,000 unidentified French and German soldiers collected from the Verdun battlefields and buried together in 52 mass graves according to where they fell. A ticket to the excellent, 20-minute **audiovisual presentation** (adult/8-15yr €3.50/2.50; ☺ no screenings in Jan or mornings in Dec & Feb) on the battle and its participants lets you climb the 46m-high **bell tower**, which houses a small

museum. The ossuary appears on a French €0.53 stamp issued in March 2006.

Fort de Douaumont

About 2km northeast of the Douaumont Ossuary on the highest of the area's hills stands **Fort de Douaumont** (☎ 03 29 84 41 91; adult/8-15yr €3/1.50; ☺ 10am-6.30pm Apr-Aug, 10am-1pm & 2-5pm or 5.30pm Sep-Mar, closed Jan), the strongest of the 39 fortresses and bastions built along a 45km front to protect Verdun. Because the French high command disregarded warnings of an impending German offensive, Douaumont – whose 3km network of cold, dripping galleries was built between 1885 and 1912 – had only a skeleton crew when the Battle of Verdun began. By the fourth day it had been captured easily; four months later it was retaken by colonial troops from Morocco.

Tranchée des Baïonnettes

On 12 June 1916 two companies of the 137th Infantry Regiment of the French army were sheltering in their *tranchées* (trenches), *baïonnettes* (bayonets) fixed, waiting for a ferocious artillery bombardment to end. It never did – the incoming shells covered their positions with mud and debris, burying them alive. They weren't found until three years later, when someone spotted several hundred bayonet tips sticking out of the ground. The victims were left where they died, their bayonets still poking through the soil. The site is always open. The tree-filled valley across the D913 is known as the **Ravin de la Mort** (Ravine of Death).

Fort de Vaux

On 1 June 1916 German troops managed to enter the tunnel system of the **Fort de Vaux** (☎ 03 29 88 32 88; adult/8-15yr €3/1.50; ☼ 9am-6pm Apr-Sep, 10am-noon & 1-5pm Oct-Mar, closed Jan), attacking the French defenders from inside their own ramparts. After six days and seven nights of brutal, metre-by-metre combat along the narrow passageways (the most effective weapons were grenades, flame throwers and poison gas), the steadfast French defenders, dying of thirst (licking drops of moisture off the walls had become their only water source), were forced to surrender. The fort was recaptured by the French five months later.

The interior of Vaux, built between 1881 and 1912 and encased in 2.5m of concrete, is smaller, more reconstructed and less dreary – and thus less interesting – than Douaumont.

AMERICAN MEMORIALS

More than one million American troops participated in the Meuse-Argonne Offensive of late 1918, the last Western Front battle of WWI. The bitter fighting northwest of Verdun, in which more than 26,000 US troops were killed, convinced the Kaiser's government to cable US President Woodrow Wilson with a request for an armistice. The film *Sergeant York* (1941) starring Gary Cooper is based on events that took place here.

The largest US military cemetery in Europe, the WWI **Meuse-Argonne American Cemetery**, is at Romagne-sous-Montfaucon, 41km northwest of Verdun along the D38 and D123. Just east of Montfaucon d'Argonne (about 10km southeast of the cemetery), a 58m-high Doric column atop the 336m-high **Butte de Montfaucon** commemorates the Meuse-Argonne Offensive.

About 40km southeast of Verdun, the WWI **St-Mihiel American Cemetery** is on the outskirts of Thiaucourt-Regniéville. From there, a 15km drive to the southwest takes you to the 375m-high **Butte de Montsec**, site of a US monument with a bronze relief map surrounded by a round, neoclassical colonnade.

The WWII **Lorraine American Cemetery** is about 45km east of Metz just outside of St-Avold.

These sites are managed by the **American Battle Monuments Commission** (www.abmc.gov).

FORT DE FERMONT

One of the larger underground fortresses on the Maginot Line (p373), **Fermont** (☎ 03 82 39 35 34; www.ligne-maginot-fort-de-fermont.asso.fr; tours adult/7-12yr €6/4; ☼ tours begin 2pm or 3pm Sat, Sun & holidays Apr-Oct, Mon-Fri May-3rd weekend in Sep, to 4.30pm Jul & Aug) is approximately 56km north of Verdun. Around 30m deep, it withstood three days of heavy bombardment in 1940. During the 2½-hour tour (printed translation available), an electric trolley transports you from one subterranean army block to another.

The Loire Valley

The word 'chateau' brings to mind images of grand towers rising to the heavens, of extravagant dining rooms for hundreds of guests, of exquisite gardens and shimmering moats. It says banquets, balls and decadence, crystal chandeliers and silver candelabras. It encapsulates both the intrigue of French history and our vision of romantic France. It's a word that belongs to the Loire Valley.

From the 15th to the 18th centuries this region served as the playground of kings, princes, dukes and nobles who expended family fortunes and the wealth of the nation to turn it into a vast neighbourhood of lavish (and not-so-lavish) chateaux. The result is a rich and concentrated collection of architectural treasures – indeed, its historical importance was recognised in 2000 when Unesco named much of the area a World Heritage Site. The Renaissance architecture to be found at Azay-le-Rideau, Chambord, Chaumont and Chenonceau is truly stunning. Earlier defensive fortresses, simpler in design and far more massive, can be appreciated at Angers, Chinon and Loches. Numerous other chateaux, big and small, dot the landscape.

The untamed Loire is France's longest, most regal river. From its source in the Massif Central it follows a 1020km course to the Atlantic, cutting a wide, flat valley through stunning countryside that's ideal for cycling. Vineyards stretch along much of the Loire from Blois to Angers.

There are other attractions here too – religious architecture, curious caves and regional gastronomy, in particular – but the real stars of the Loire are the chateaux.

THE LOIRE VALLEY

HIGHLIGHTS

- Explore the huge, gracious **Château de Chambord** (p429) and its famous double-helix staircase.
- Take in the quiet grandeur of the **Château de Chenonceau** (p438) and its formal gardens.
- Stroll around **Tours** (p432) and enjoy its excellent restaurants and bustling bars.
- Look for François I's emblem, the salamander, around the eclectic **Château de Blois** (p427).
- Marvel at the control of the trainers when the hounds are fed at the **Château de Cheverny** (p431).

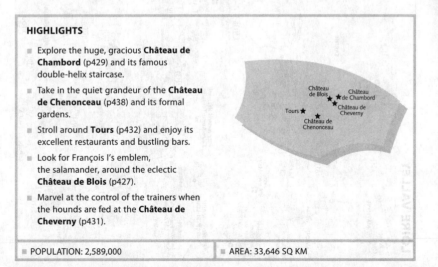

- POPULATION: 2,589,000
- AREA: 33,646 SQ KM

LOIRE VALLEY

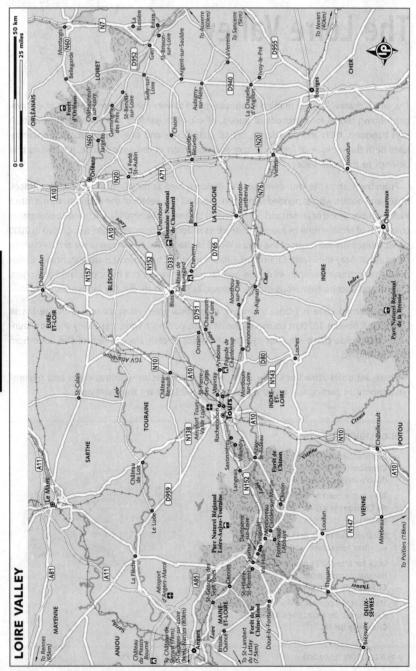

HOT-AIR BALLOONING

There's nothing quite like floating silently high above the Loire Valley and its chateaux in a hot-air balloon.

France Montgolfières (☎ 02 54 32 20 48 or 08 10 60 01 53; www.franceballoons.com; adult/6-12yr/couple €230/150/395; ☯ early Apr–late Oct or early Nov) runs 1½-hour flights that end with a toast of Loire Valley sparkling wine. Departures are from Chenonceaux or Loches and you pay only if the flight actually takes place (ie isn't cancelled because of bad weather). Flights in August and on Saturday night are the most heavily booked, but the rest of the time reserving a week or two in advance is usually enough. Of course it's also worth trying your luck to see if places have opened up at the last minute. Bookings can be made at the Tours tourist office.

Another company offering balloon flights is **Air Magic Loire Valley** (☎ 06 20 55 40 70; www .loire-et-montgolfiere.com; ☯ year-round weather permitting). Reservations can be made via the Chinon tourist office.

History

The River Loire was one of Roman Gaul's most important communications and trade arteries. Its earliest chateaux were medieval fortresses thrown up in the 9th century to fend off marauding Vikings. By the 11th century massive walls topped with battlements, fortified keeps, arrow slits and moats spanned by drawbridges were all the rage.

During the Hundred Years' War (1337–1453) the Loire marked the boundary between French and English forces and the area was ravaged by fierce fighting. After Charles VII regained his crown with the help of Joan of Arc, he began devoting his time to the pursuit of pleasure and the Loire Valley emerged as the centre of French court life. Charles took up residence in Loches with his mistress and it became fashionable among the French nobility and bourgeois elite to build extravagant chateaux with landscaped gardens as an expression of their wealth and power.

Defensive fortresses were superseded by ornate palaces for pleasure and recreation as the Renaissance – introduced to France from Italy at the tail end of the 1400s – ushered in an era of humanism and more comfortable living.

Starting in the 17th century, grand country houses built in the neoclassical style and set amid formal gardens took centre stage.

Getting There & Away

Ryanair links Tours with London-Stansted. The Angers airport has flights to Cork, Luton, Manchester and Southampton.

The Loire Valley is served by the TGV Atlantique, which whizzes down to Tours

(or nearby St-Pierre-des-Corps) from Paris' Gare Montparnasse and Charles de Gaulle Airport in just over an hour. Rapid Aqualys trains connect Paris' Gare d'Austerlitz (and sometimes Gare de Lyon) with Orléans, Blois, Amboise and Tours.

By car, the A10 links Paris with Orléans, Blois and Tours and then continues southwest to Poitiers and Bordeaux. West of Tours, the A85 to Angers still has a few segments that have yet to be upgraded to autoroute grade.

Getting Around

Having your own wheels is the easiest way to see the region, but during July and August traffic jams are common. Some of the loveliest drives are along tiny rural roads such as the tertiary D80 from Loches to Chenonceaux.

Seeing the chateaux by public transport is possible but requires a bit of planning. Trains link the major towns, but many chateaux are served only by rather infrequent buses. One option for the carless is to join an organised bus excursion from either Blois or Tours.

Cycling is a popular and invigorating means of getting around; details for hiring bicycles appear in this chapter's Getting Around sections. Tourist offices can supply you with La Loire à Vélo, an excellent map-brochure in French and English that details bike paths and cyclable back roads around Blois and between Tours and Angers. From Easter to 1 November, **Détours de Loire** (☎ 02 47 66 22 23 in Tours; www.locationdevelos .com) rents out bicycles at three shops (Tours, p437; Blois, p429; and Saumur, p448) and

THE LOIRE VALLEY

13 hotels between Orléans and Angers. You can mix and match pick-up and return sites and as a bonus you'll pay the group rate at the chateaux.

The GR3 long-distance trail links Gien and Orléans with Tours, Chinon, Saumur, Angers and Nantes.

ORLÉANAIS

The historical region of Orléanais is the Loire Valley's northern gateway. Orléans, an ancient Roman city and the region's capital, had its place in history secured by a simple French peasant girl, Joan of Arc, in 1429. Upstream, the sandbank-lined River Loire twists past ecclesiastical treasures.

ORLÉANS

pop 113,000

Many French cities claim Jeanne d'Arc (Joan of Arc), France's national heroine, as their own, but Orléans did indeed play a central role in the eventful life of La Pucelle d'Orléans (the Maid of Orléans). It was here, in May 1429, that the peasant girl from Lorraine rallied Charles VII to liberate the city from besieging English forces, a crucial turning point in the Hundred Years' War. Today, Joan remains omnipresent – as you explore the city, see how many statues, paintings and patriotic references to the virgin liberator you can spot!

For the visitor, Orléans offers an excellent fine arts museum and ample opportunities for strolling (the city is elegantly lit at night). Especially appealing are the old quarters, with their narrow cobbled streets, and the commercial precincts around rue Royale and rue de la République, where window-shopping can easily turn into the other kind of shopping.

After the devastation wrought on New Orleans – named in honour of an early 18th-century Duke of Orleans, not the city – by Hurricane Katrina in 2005, the residents of old Orléans invited about 50 displaced students to continue their studies at the local university.

Orientation

The mostly pedestrianised old city, whose main thoroughfares are east–west rue de Bourgogne and perpendicular rue Louis Rouget, stretches from the River Loire north to rue Jeanne d'Arc. North of there, around the northern end of rue Royale, is the commercial centre. The tram line running along rue de la République links place du Martroi, the city's main square, with Gare d'Orléans, the centrepiece of a postwar architectural disaster area. Gare des Aubrais-Orléans, the city's other train station, is on the tram line 2km further north.

Information

There are several banks on place du Martroi.

BSP Info (125 rue Bannier; per 15/60min €1/4; ☾ 10am-8pm Tue-Sat, 2-8pm Sun & Mon) Internet access.

Exagames (5 rue Parisie; per 30/60min €2.50/5; ☾ 2-7pm Mon, 11am-7pm Tue-Thu, 11am-10pm Fri & Sat) Internet access.

Laundrettes Rue du Poirier (26 rue du Poirier; ☾ 7am-10pm); Rue de Bourgogne (176 rue de Bourgogne; ☾ 7am-9pm)

Librairie Paes (184 rue de Bourgogne; ☾ 10am-12.30pm & 1.30-7pm Tue-Sat) A foreign-language bookshop.

Post Office (place du Général de Gaulle) Does currency exchange and has a Cyberposte.

Tourist Office (☎ 02 38 24 05 05; www.tourisme-orleans.com; 2 place de l'Étape; ☾ 10am-1pm & 2-6pm Mon-Sat, also open 10am-1pm Sun Jul & Aug)

Sights

HÔTEL GROSLOT

Built as a *hôtel particulier* (private mansion) in the mid-1500s for Jacques Groslot, a city bailiff, the Renaissance **Hôtel Groslot** (☎ 02 38 79 22 30; place de l'Étape; admission free; ☾ 10am-noon & 2-6pm Sun-Fri Oct-Jun, 9am-7pm Sun-Fri, 5-8pm Sat Jul-Sep) became Orléans' Hôtel de Ville during the Revolution. Its over-the-top, neomedieval interior – complete with multiple references to Joan – dates from the 1850s. The bedroom in which the 17-year-old King François II died in 1560 is today used as a marriage hall.

MUSÉE DES BEAUX-ARTS

Highlights at the outstanding **Fine Arts Museum** (☎ 02 38 79 21 55; 1 rue Fernand Rabier; adult/student €3/1.50, during special exhibitions €1 more; ☾ 9.30am-12.15pm & 1.30-5.45pm Tue-Sat, 2-6.30pm Sun) include a superb ensemble of 18th-century pastel portraits whose subjects almost look alive (1st floor, room 8) and Claude Dervet's *Les Quatre Éléments* (mid-

1600s) illustrating air, fire, land and (frozen) water (1st floor, room 2). Don't miss the action tableau starring a larger-than-life Joan of Arc (1887) looking a bit stoned (on being a heroine or, perhaps, on heroin) in her shining armour (on the ground floor next to the lift). There are explanation sheets in English in each room.

CATHÉDRALE STE-CROIX
Orléans' Flamboyant Gothic **cathedral** (place Ste-Croix; ⊙ 10am-noon & 2-5.30pm, till 6pm or later in summer) was built under Henri IV from 1601. Louis XIII (1610–43) had the choir and nave restored, Louis XIV (1638–1715) built the transept, and the next two Louis (1715–74) rebuilt the western façade and its towers, topped with crownlike colonnades. The spire (1858) completed the project. Stained-glass windows (1895) in the lower nave depict the life of Saint Joan of Arc, who was canonised in 1920. The best views of the cathedral are from **rue Jeanne d'Arc**, a handsome neoclassical shopping street.

MAISON DE JEANNE D'ARC
The brick and half-timber **Home of Joan of Arc** (☎ 02 38 52 99 89; 3 place du Général de Gaulle; adult/student & over 65yr €2/1; ⊙ 10am-12.30pm & 1.30-6.30pm Tue-Sun May-Oct, 1.30-6pm Tue-Sun Nov-Apr) is a Disneylandlike reconstruction of the 15th-century house where Joan of Arc stayed for 11 days in April and May 1429 (the original was destroyed by British bombing in 1940, something the locals politely avoid mentioning). Inside, eight scale models portray crucial moments in Joan's brief but eventful life.

Walking Tours
Guided tours of the city (in French with partial English commentary) run by the tourist office take place regularly in July and August and irregularly the rest of the year.

Festivals & Events
Since 1430 the Orléanais have celebrated the annual **Fêtes de Jeanne d'Arc**, which fall in early May and commemorate the liberation of the city. A week of street parties, medieval costume parades and concerts ends with a solemn morning Mass at the cathedral on 8 May.

Sleeping
Auberge de Jeunesse (☎ 02 38 53 60 06; auberge .crjs45@wanadoo.fr; 7 av de Beaumarchais; dm €8.80, breakfast €3.50; ⊙ reception 8am-7pm, may be closed Sat & Sun) Under the bleachers of the Stade Omnisports (sports stadium), this brand new, 60-bed hostel is 10km south of the city centre in the suburb of La Source. A kitchen is planned. Most rooms have four beds. Phone ahead if you're planning to arrive on a weekend. To get there take the tram to Université L'Indien.

Hôtel Le Bannier (☎ 02 38 53 25 86; 13 rue du Faubourg Bannier; d €31-37; ⊙ reception closed Sun) This zero-star hotel above a bar is a good choice for the budget crowd but be prepared – the owners run a tight ship. The 19 rooms are strictly no-frills.

Le Brin de Zinc (☎ 02 38 53 38 77; www.brindezinc .fr; 62 rue Ste-Catherine; d €36; ⊙ reception closed 3-6pm) The six simply furnished rooms above the restaurant have marble chimneys and walk-in closets. Clean, central and excellent value.

Hôtel de l'Abeille (☎ 02 38 53 54 87; www.hotelde labeille.com; 64 rue Alsace-Lorraine; s/d from €47/54) This lovingly maintained 30-room hotel, opened in 1903, is furnished with beautiful antiques and loads of Jeanne d'Arc memorabilia. The creaky floorboards can definitely be excused at such a charming place, which was named after the industrious bee so long ago that no one remembers why. The odour of honey often wafts through the lobby.

Hôtel St-Aignan (☎ 02 38 53 15 35; hotelsaintaig nan@laposte.net; 3 place Gambetta; s/d from €51/57) This high-rise two-star hotel with 27 practical rooms is 70s-style modern, comfortable

THE LOIRE VALLEY

LIVE LIKE A KING (OR AT LEAST A DUKE)

Living in a chateau may be beyond the reach of most of us, but it's possible to experience the romantic magic of aristocratic life by staying in chateaux that have been turned into *chambres d'hôtes* (B&Bs). You can't send the staff to the gallows on a whim, but in most cases you'll get a queen-sized bed and breakfast fit for a king. Two of our favourites are **Château de Brissac** (p454) and **Château de Verrières** (p448), but you can find others through www .chateaux-france.com.

THE LOIRE VALLEY

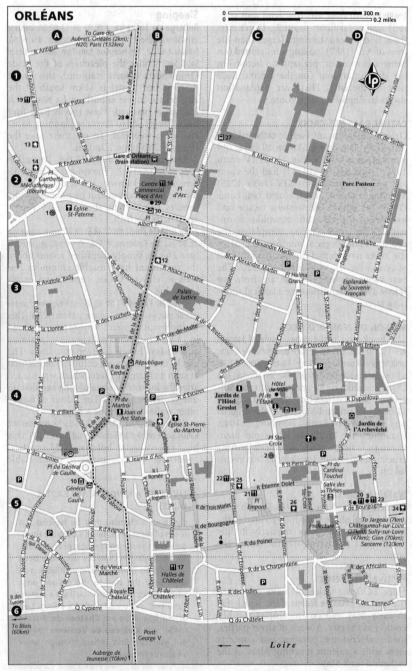

ORLÉANS

0   300 m
0   0.2 miles

and spacious. It's popular with business travellers so it's busiest Monday through Thursday.

Eating

The stretch of rue de Bourgogne from rue Parisie east to rue St-Étienne is loaded with inexpensive places to eat, including Indian (*menus* from €10), Chinese, Korean, Lebanese and North African.

Le KT Self (☎ 02 38 52 90 69; 13 rue des Pastoureaux; menu €6, plat du jour €5.40-6.90; ✆ 11.30am-2pm Mon-Fri) Serves the sort of dishes your grandmother would have made had she been French. Remarkably good value.

L'Estaminet (☎ 02 38 54 27 57; 148 rue de Bourgogne; mains €8-14; ✆ 7-11pm Tue-Sun) An atmospheric place with just seven tables where French fare has an international twist. The menu is a chalkboard; specialities include *gratin de crabe newyorkaise* (crab with parmesan; €7).

Le Dariole (☎ 02 38 77 26 67; 25 rue Étienne Dolet; menus €16.50-21; ✆ lunch Mon-Fri, dinner Fri, salon de thé 2.30-7pm Mon-Sat) In a half-timbered building in the old city. A tiny, well-regarded French restaurant with an equally tiny menu; functions as a tearoom in the afternoon.

Eugène (☎ 02 38 53 82 64; 24 rue Ste-Anne; menus €22.50-45; ✆ closed Sun & lunch Mon & Sat) A very civilised French and regional eatery whose menu changes with the seasons. Winter specialities include game from La Sologne such as *noisette de chevreuil poivrade* (venison prepared with red wine and pepper).

La Petite Marmite (☎ 02 38 54 23 83; 178 rue de Bourgogne; menus €20-34; ✆ closed Tue; ✗) Warm, cosy and often busy, this nonsmoking restaurant – in a beautiful old timber-framed house – serves up tasty French and regional fare.

SELF-CATERING
Places for picnic supplies:
Carrefour supermarket (inside the Centre Commercial Place d'Arc; ✆ 8.30am-9pm Mon-Sat) Huge and cheap.
Covered market (place du Châtelet; ✆ 7.30am-7.30pm Tue-Sat, 8am-1pm Sun) Inside the Halles de Châtelet shopping centre.
Intermarché supermarket (49 rue du Faubourg Bannier; ✆ 8.45am-7.30pm Mon-Sat, 9am-12.30pm Sun)

Drinking & Entertainment

What's-on listings fill **Orléans Poche** (www.orleanspoche.com in French), a free events magazine issued on the first Wednesday of each month. It's available at the tourist office.

In the lively old city, bars are concentrated along rue de Bourgogne and at the western end of rue du Poirier (near the covered market).

Le Petit Barcelone (☎ 02 38 53 69 26; 218 rue de Bourgogne; ✆ 3pm-1am Mon-Sat) An informal bar that's popular with students. Serves tapas and meals from April to December. Perfect for a casual tête-à-tête.

Le Metalic (☎ 02 38 53 84 29; 119 rue de Bourgogne; ✆ 7pm-3am) The bar of the moment among in-the-know locals. A mellow place with antidécor décor and a full-time DJ.

Le Pentagram (☎ 02 38 62 53 41; 41 rue Étienne Dolet; ✆ 6pm-1am Mon-Sat, till 2am mid-May–Oct) A welcoming, hetero-friendly gay and lesbian bar with some real hunks adorning the postcard-plastered walls, if not always the bar stools and banquettes.

THE LOIRE VALLEY

Getting There & Away

BUS

From the desolate **bus station** (☎ 02 38 53 94 75; www.rvl-info.com in French; 1 rue Marcel Proust; ☺ 7.30-9am, 11am-1pm & 1.30-7pm Mon-Fri, 10.30am-12.30pm Sat, shorter hours & closed Sat Jul, Aug & school holidays), Les Rapides du Val de Loire's bus 3 (six daily Monday to Saturday, one Sunday) follows the Loire east to Châteauneuf-sur-Loire (€5.80, 40 to 60 minutes), Sully-sur-Loire (€8.10, 1¼ hours) and Gien (€12.20, two hours). Some services go to Jargeau (€4.70, 50 minutes, three daily Monday to Friday).

SNCF buses go to Chartres (€11.70, 1¼ hours, four Monday to Saturday, two on Sunday).

CAR

Ecoto (☎ 02 38 77 92 92; www.ecoto.fr in French; 19 av de Paris), behind the Ibis hotel, offers competitive car-rental rates.

TRAIN

The city's two train stations, the central Gare d'Orléans (in the process of being completely rebuilt) and Gare des Aubrais-Orléans, 2km to the north, are linked by tram and frequent shuttle trains. Most westbound trains along the Loire Valley stop at both stations, whereas most trains to/from Paris' Gare d'Austerlitz (€16.40, one hour, hourly) use Gare des Aubrais-Orléans.

Orléans has frequent services to Blois (€9, 45 minutes, 14 to 28 daily) and Tours (€15.60, one to 1½ hours, 13 to 20 daily).

Getting Around

Tickets and timetables for Semtao trams (service until about 12.30am) and buses (service until 8pm or 9pm) are available at **Espace Transport** (☎ 08 00 01 20 00; www.semtao.fr in French; Gare d'Orléans tram stop; ☺ 6.45am-7.15pm Mon-Fri, 8am-6.30pm Sat); Journée and Week-end tickets (each €2.90) allow unlimited all-day or all-weekend (Saturday and Sunday) travel. One-way tickets purchased at tram stops or from bus drivers cost €1.30.

ORLÉANS TO SULLY-SUR-LOIRE

Upriver from Orléans, medieval chateaux are overshadowed by ecclesiastical treasures. North of this stretch of the Loire is the 350-sq-km Forêt d'Orléans (Orleans Forest), one of the only places in France to shelter nesting ospreys.

The riverside town of Jargeau (population 4000; www.jargeau.fr in French), 20km east of Orléans, is home to the Confrérie des Chevaliers du Goûte Andouille (Tripe Sausage Brotherhood), dedicated to *andouille* – a fat tripe sausage typical of the region that's sold at Monsieur Guibet's *charcuterie* at 14 place du Martroi.

The history of riverine trade along the Loire comes alive in Châteauneuf-sur-Loire, 7km east of Jargeau, at the **Musée de la Marine** (☎ 02 38 46 84 46; 1 place Aristide Briand; adult/child over 7yr €3.50/2; ☺ 10am-6pm Wed-Mon Apr-Oct, 2-6pm Wed-Mon Nov-Mar), housed in the stables of an 11th- to 17th-century chateau.

Châteauneuf's **tourist office** (☎ 02 38 58 44 79; 3 place Aristide Briand; ☺ 9.30am-12.30pm & 2-7pm Mon-Sat Jun-Sep, also open 9.30am-12.30pm Sun & holidays Jul & Aug, 9.30am-12.30pm & 2-6pm Oct-May, closed Mon & Tue afternoon Oct-Mar) has information on hiking options.

In Germigny-des-Prés, 6km further southeast, the historically significant **Église de Germigny-des-Prés** is a rare example of Carolingian architecture. Of special interest are the Greek cross–shaped floor plan and the 9th-century mosaic.

Travel another 12km further upstream and you come to St-Benoît-sur-Loire, whose 11th-century Romanesque **basilique** shelters the relics of St Benedict (480–547). The heavily ornamented capitals supporting the monumental porch illustrate scenes from the Book of Revelations.

In Sully-sur-Loire, 9km southeast of St-Benoît, the **Château** (☎ 02 38 36 36 86; adult/7-15yr €5/3.50; ☺ 10am-6pm Tue-Sun Apr-Sep, also open Mon Jul & Aug, 10am-noon & 2-5pm Tue-Sun Feb, Mar & Oct-Dec), with its fairy-tale moats and its thickset towers, is a quintessential medieval fortress. Built from 1395 to defend one of the Loire's few crossings, it is set to reopen after renovations in late 2007.

Sully's **tourist office** (☎ 02 38 36 23 70; ot.sully.sur .loire@wanadoo.fr; place du Général de Gaulle; ☺ 9.45am-12.15pm & 2.30-6.30pm Mon-Sat May-Sep, also open 10.30am-1pm Sun & holidays May-Aug, 10am-noon & 2-6pm except Sun, Mon afternoon & Thu morn Oct-Apr) has information on accommodation. The 24-room, two-star **Hôtel de la Poste** (☎ 02 38 36 26 22; fax 02 38 36 39 35; 11 rue Faubourg St-Germain; d €46; ✗) has comfortable rooms and a lovely courtyard restaurant (*menus* €15 to €31) with traditional French cuisine.

For public transport options see left.

LA SOLOGNE

The French associate the soggy wetland of La Sologne with one thing: hunting. A vast 500 sq km of ponds and woodland south of Orléans between the Rivers Loire and Cher, it has forests rich in deer, while eels, carp and pike fill its lakes and rivers. The area became a royal hunting playground under François I (who reigned 1515 to 1547) but years of war, disease and floods turned it into waterlogged, malaria-infested swamp. Only in the mid-19th century, after it was drained under Napoleon III, did La Sologne regain its hunting prestige.

La Sologne's 'capital' is **Romorantin-Lanthenay**, a pretty little town straddling the River Sauldre 41km southeast of Blois on the D765. The **tourist office** (☎ 02 54 76 43 89; www.tourisme-romorantin.com in French; ⏰ 10am-12.15pm & 2-6.30pm Mon, 8.45am-12.15pm & 1.30-6.30pm Tue-Fri, 8.45am-12.15pm & 1.30-6pm Sat, also open 10am-noon holidays Easter-Aug & Sun Jul & Aug) has a map of hiking circuits.

It comes as something of a surprise to find that Romorantin-Lanthenay is home to an exceptionally luxurious, four-star hostelry, the **Grand Hôtel du Lion d'Or** (☎ 02 54 94 15 15; www.hotel-liondor.fr; 69 rue Georges Clemenceau; r €125-180, ste 250-480; ⏰ closed mid-Feb–Mar & 10 days in late Nov; 🔀 🖳). Occupying a 16th-century *hôtel particulier*, its 16 rooms are huge and gorgeously furnished. The hotel's acclaimed restaurant (menus €90 to €140) holds two Michelin stars and is open for lunch except on Tuesdays.

Aside from hunting, La Sologne's other claim to fame is the *tarte Tatin*, the delicious upside-down apple tart accidentally created in 1888 by the Tatin sisters of Lamotte-Beuvron, 40km south of Orléans along the N20.

There are trains to Romorantin-Lanthenay from Tours (via Gièvres; €12.70, 1¼ to 1½ hours, six daily except Sunday morning) and Orléans (via Salbris; €12.40, at least 1½ hours, two or three daily).

BLÉSOIS

The Blésois (the area around Blois) is graced with some of the Loire's most outstanding chateaux, including the mix-and-match Château de Blois, stunning Chambord, magnificently furnished Cheverny and romantic Chaumont.

For details on public transport options see p429 and each chateau listing.

Tours

Half-day chateau excursions are run by the *départemental* bus company **TLC** (☎ 02 54 58 55 44; adult/student & child not incl admission fees €10.75/8.60; ⏰ departures at 9.10am & 1.45pm mid-May–early-Sep) from Blois to Chambord and Cheverny. Tickets are sold at the tourist office or on the bus.

Blois' Taxi Radio (p429) hires out air-conditioned eight-person minibuses for chateau visits. Options include a return trip to Chambord and Cheverny with an hour at each (€75); travel to Chaumont, Amboise and Chenonceau will set you back €128. Prices are 50% higher on Sundays and holidays.

BLOIS
pop 49,200

Blois (pronounced blwah) has a long history of aristocratic intrigue and bloody royal politics. In the Middle Ages it was the seat of the powerful counts of Blois, from whom France's Capetian kings were descended, and in the 16th century it served as a second capital of France. Several supremely dramatic events – involving some of the most important personages in French history, including Kings Louis XII, François I and Henri III – took place inside the city's outstanding attraction, the Château de Blois.

For more than 150 years the town has been home to the Poulain chocolate firm – but whereas even Willy Wonka let five lucky winners visit his factory, secretive Poulain has a strict no-tours policy.

Orientation

Blois, on the northern bank of the Loire, is a compact town – almost everything is within 10 minutes' walk of the train station. The old city is southeast and east of the chateau, which towers over place Victor Hugo. The modern commercial centre is centred on pedestrianised rue du Commerce, rue Porte Chartraine and rue Denis Papin; the latter is connected to rue du Palais by a monumental 19th-century staircase.

Information

3e Monde (39 av Dr Jean Laigret; per min/hr €0.10/6; ⏰ 9am-9pm Mon-Sat, also 2-8pm Sun Jun-Oct) Internet access.

THE LOIRE VALLEY

BLOIS

THE LOIRE VALLEY

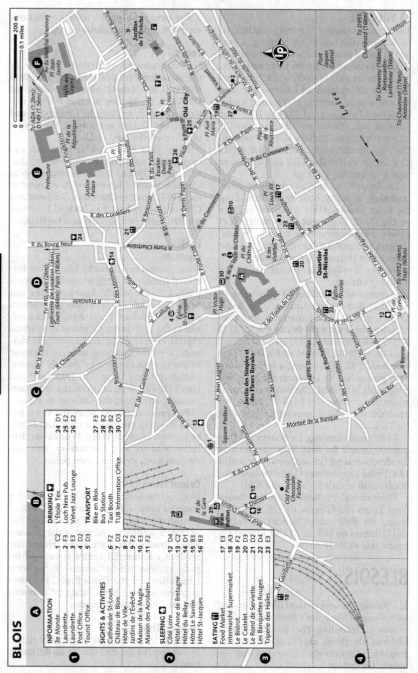

Laundrettes 1 rue Jeanne d'Arc (✇ 7am-9pm); 4 rue St-Lubin (✇ 7am-9pm)

L'Étoile Tex (☎ 02 54 78 46 93; www.letoiletex.fr.st in French; 9 rue du Bourg Neuf; per min €0.10; ✇ 7.30am-9pm Mon-Thu, 7.30am-2am Fri, 2pm-2am Sat, 2pm-9am Sun) Internet access.

Post Office (rue Gallois) Has a Cyberposte and changes money.

Tourist Office (☎ 02 54 90 41 41; www.loiredeschateaux.com; 23 place du Château; ✇ 9am-7pm Mon-Sat, 10am-7pm Sun Apr-Sep, 9am-12.30pm & 2-6pm Mon-Sat, 9.30am-12.30pm Sun Oct-Mar) Gives away a free walking tour brochure.

Sights

CHÂTEAU DE BLOIS

Blois' **chateau** (☎ 02 54 90 33 32; place du Château; adult/6-17yr/student €6.50/3/5; ✇ 9am-7pm Jul & Aug; 9am-6pm Apr-Jun, Sep & Oct; 9am-12.30pm & 2-5.30pm Nov-Mar) can serve as an excellent crash course in Loire château architecture because each of its four wings – arrayed around a central courtyard – reflect the favoured style of a different period: Gothic (13th century); Flamboyant Gothic (1498–1503), from the reign of Louis XII; early Renaissance (1515–24), from the reign of François I; and classical (1630s). Most signs are in English.

During the Middle Ages, the counts of Blois meted out justice in the huge **Salle des États Généraux** (Estates General Hall), part of the feudal castle that survived wars, rebuilding and, most dangerous of all, changes in style and taste. The dramatic trial scene in Luc Besson's box-office hit *Jeanne d'Arc* (1999) was filmed here.

A few steps away but worlds apart in terms of design, the distinctive brick-and-stone **Louis XII section**, which includes the hall where entrance tickets are sold, is ornamented with porcupines, Louis XII's heraldic symbol. The king himself is also featured in the intricate decoration on the façade, cutting a dashing figure on horseback. His royal apartments, on the first floor, house the **Musée des Beaux-Arts**, where the most grotesque (and popular) work is *Portrait de Antonietta Fille de Gonsalvos*, a portrait of a very hairy little girl (she suffered from a rare disease) by the Italian female painter Lavinia Fontana (1552–83).

Begun just 15 years later, the furnished **François I wing**, restored to its polychrome Renaissance glory in 2006, illustrates the speed at which Italian-influenced Renaissance styles gained popularity in France. The famous **spiral staircase**, a magnificent structure decorated with François I's insignia (ornate capital 'F's and dragonlike salamanders), dominates the courtyard. Inside more salamanders await, as do a number of ermines, the symbol of Claude de France, François' wife.

The last section to be built, the **Gaston d'Orléans wing**, is an impressive example of French classical architecture. Again, a richly carved monumental staircase is the most notable feature of the construction – look up and then up further to see the double vaulting.

The most infamous episode in the history of the chateau occurred during the chaotic 16th century. King Henri III summoned his great rival, the ultra-powerful duke of Guise – a leader of the Catholic League (which threatened the authority of the king, himself a Catholic) – to the **Chambre du Roi** (king's bedchamber). There, on 23 December 1588, he was set upon by royal bodyguards armed with daggers and swords. When the violence was over, the joyous king, who had been hiding behind a tapestry, stepped into the room to inspect the duke's perforated body. Henri III was himself assassinated eight months later. Paintings of personages and events associated with these bloody doings are on display in the **Salle de Guise**.

In the warm season the chateau courtyard hosts a 45-minute **son et lumière** (☎ 02 54 55 26 31; adult/child/student €6.50/3/5, incl chateau €10/8.50/5.50; ✇ mid-Apr–late Sep), held in English on Wednesday.

MAISON DE LA MAGIE

The **House of Magic** (☎ 02 54 55 26 26; www.maisondelamagie.fr in French; 1 place du Château; adult/6-17yr/student €7.50/5/6.50, incl chateau €12/5.50/8.50; ✇ 10am-12.30pm & 2-6pm Mar–late Sep & late Oct-early Nov, until 6.30pm Jul & Aug, closed Mon except Jul & Aug), facing the chateau, features a magic show, interactive exhibits and clocks invented by the Blois-born magician Jean-Eugène Robert-Houdin (1805–71), after whom the great Houdini named himself.

OLD CITY

Blois' old city, seriously damaged by German attacks in 1940, retains its steep, twisting medieval streets. **Cathédrale St-Louis** (place

St-Louis; 9am-6pm) was rebuilt in late-Gothic style following the devastating hurricane of 1678. Right behind it is the **Hôtel de Ville** – note the unusual double-aspect **sundial** across the courtyard on a corner of the Ecclesiastical Tribunal building. A few paces east, there's a great view from the **Jardins de l'Évêché** (Gardens of the Bishop's Palace).

Across the square from the cathedral, the 15th-century **Maison des Acrobates** (House of the Acrobats; 3bis rue Pierre de Blois), is so-named because its timbers are decorated with characters taken from medieval farces. It was one of the few medieval houses to survive WWII.

Walking Tours

The tourist office offers **self-guided MP3 tours** (half/whole day €6/8) of the old town.

Sleeping

Hôtel du Bellay (☎ 02 54 78 23 62; http://hoteldubel lay.free.fr; 12 rue des Minimes; d €30-35, with washbasin €25) It's easy to miss the tiny entrance to this ancient stone house – the original doorway is obviously from a time when people were much shorter. Some of the 12, one-star rooms are tiny too; though simply furnished they are eminently serviceable. Guests have access to basic kitchen facilities.

Hôtel St-Jacques (☎ 02 54 78 04 15; www.hotel saintjacquesblois.com; 7 rue Ducoux; s/d €33/43;) A cheerful, well-managed hotel near the station, recently renovated and upgraded to two stars. The 25 rooms have metal and glass furniture and offer good value.

Hôtel Le Savoie (☎ 02 54 74 32 21; www.citotel .com; 6 rue Ducoux; d €48-54) A well-kept, family-run hotel conveniently located a few steps from the train station. The 25 two-star rooms are modern and spotless.

Côté Loire (☎ 02 54 78 07 86; www.coteloire.com; 2 place de la Grève; d early Nov–Mar €48-67, Apr–early Nov €53-72) Full of wooden-beamed character, this small, higgledy-piggledy two-star hotel is a good choice if you can get one of the seven charming rooms.

Hôtel Anne de Bretagne (☎ 02 54 78 05 38; http://annedebretagne.free.fr; 31 av Dr Jean Laigret; d €52-58; closed early Jan–early Feb) A vine-covered, two-star hotel with 28 bright, comfortable rooms overlooking a leafy crescent.

Eating

Popular restaurants line rue Foulerie, which is two blocks from the Loire.

Le Castelet (☎ 02 54 74 66 09; 40 rue Saint Lubin; menus incl vegetarian €16-26.40; closed Wed & Sun;) A convivial restaurant whose motto, 'homemade cooking in tune with the seasons', translates into traditional French and Touraine cuisine prepared with market-fresh ingredients. Specialities include *escargots à l'amboisienne* (snails served with butter, garlic, parsley, ground hazelnut and rosé wine; six/12 €7.80/11.40) and that old dessert classic, *mousse au chocolat noir* (chocolate mousse; €5).

Les Banquettes Rouges (☎ 02 54 78 74 92; 16 rue des Trois Marchands; lunch menu €13.50, other menus €20.50-37.50; noon-1.45pm & 7-9.45pm Tue-Sat) Serves hearty French favourites, including *jarret d'agneau* (lamb shin) and various fish dishes, with a smile. Excellent value, especially for lunch. Child friendly.

Le Bistrot (☎ 02 54 78 47 74; 12 rue Henry Drussy; 8am-midnight Mon-Thu, 8am-2am Fri & Sat, also open Sun approx Apr-Sep, to 2am daily in summer) An informal bar-brasserie–wine bar serving family-style French dishes at all hours, including steaks with *lots* of fries (€11.50 to €13.50), salads (€8.50) and hot open-faced sandwiches (€8.50).

Le Rond de Serviette (☎ 02 54 74 48 04; 18 rue Beauvoir; menus €7.90-9.50, salads €8; closed Sun & lunch Mon, also closed dinner Mon Nov-Apr) This little pizzeria markets itself as Blois' cheapest and most humorous restaurant, declaring optimistically 'yes, we try to speak English'. The Lonely Planet sign out the front has nothing to do with us.

SELF-CATERING

To stock up for a picnic:

Food market (rue Anne de Bretagne; to 1pm Tue, Thu & Sat)

Intermarché supermarket (16 av Gambetta)

Triperie des Halles (5 rue Anne de Bretagne) For local tripe specialities.

Drinking

The best of the bars are in the old town, particularly in the small alleys and squares off rue Foulerie.

Velvet Jazz Lounge (☎ 02 54 78 36 32; www.vel vetjazz.fr; 15bis rue Haute; 6pm-2am Mon, 3pm-2am Tue-Sat;) A very cool boutique bar that's Gothic in the architectural sense of the word (the vaults are 13th-century). Creative light fixtures illuminate the orange walls while Buddha presides over the lit-from-below whiskies. Has live jazz on Thursday from 7pm to 10.30pm and a *salon de thé* (think Italian hot chocolate and Russian tea) from 3pm to 7pm Tuesday to Saturday.

Loch Ness Pub (☎ 02 54 56 08 67; cnr rue des Juifs & rue Pierre de Bois; �y 3pm-3am) A vaguely Scottish watering hole popular with the younger crowd. The two floors get busier and noisier as the night gets longer, especially on karaoke Thursdays (from 10.30pm) and on Fridays when there are live concerts (twice a month at 10pm). Footy and rugby matches are projected on giant TVs.

L'Étoile Tex (☎ 02 54 78 46 93; www.letoiletex.fr.st in French; 9 rue du Bourg Neuf; �y 7.30am-9pm Mon-Thu, 7.30am-2am Fri, 2pm-2am Sat, 2pm-9am Sun) For a youthful vibe (or internet access) head to this busy Tex-Mex bar at the top of the hill. Hosts live music every Saturday at 10pm (admission free). Modern, trendy and sophisticated it's not, but the unpretentious atmosphere is refreshing.

Getting There & Away
BUS
The *départemental* bus company, **TLC** (☎ 02 54 58 55 44) no longer has any sort of information office. Line 2 links Blois' train station and the TUB information office (see right) with Chambord (40 minutes, two to four daily Monday to Saturday); a good option is to take the 12.15pm bus from Blois and the 6.46pm bus back. TLC line 4 to Romorantin stops at Cheverny (€2.40, 30 minutes, two to four daily). The tourist office has timetables. TLC also runs chateau tours (see p425).

CAR
To rent a vehicle:
ADA (☎ 02 54 74 02 47; 108 av du Maréchal Maunoury) Situated 3km northeast of the train station; served by TUB bus 1 from the train station.
Avis (☎ 02 54 45 10 61; 58 ave de Vendôme) About 2km north of the centre.
Ligérienne de Location (☎ 02 54 78 25 45; 96-100 av de Vendôme) About 3km north of the centre; served by TUB bus 2 from the train station.

TRAIN
The train station has frequent services to towns along the Loire's right bank, including Amboise (€5.60, 19 minutes, 10 to 20 daily), Orléans (€9, 45 minutes, 14 to 28 daily) and Tours (€8.70, 40 minutes, 11

to 22 daily). There are also trains to Paris' Gare d'Austerlitz (€22.10, two hours, seven to 13 daily).

Getting Around
BICYCLE
Bike en Blois (☎ 02 54 56 07 73; 8 rue Henry Drussy; �y 9am-12.30pm & 2-6.30pm Mon-Sat, 10am-1pm & 6-7pm Sun Easter-Sep, 9.30am-12.30pm & 2-6pm Mon-Sat Oct-Christmas) is one of the 16 bike rental locations run by Détours de Loire (see p419 and, for prices, p437).

BUS
TUB operates bus services in and around Blois; tickets are available at the **TUB information office** (☎ 02 54 78 15 66; information office at 2 place Victor Hugo; �y 1.30-6pm Mon, 8am-noon & 1.30-6pm Tue-Fri, 9am-noon & 1.30-4.30pm Sat). A one-way ticket costs €1; buses run until about 8pm Monday to Saturday (Sunday service is extremely limited).

TAXI
Taxi Radio (☎ 02 54 78 07 65; place de la Gare; �y 24hr) is based in front of the train station.

CHÂTEAU DE CHAMBORD
Chateaux don't get any grander than **Chambord** (☎ 02 54 50 50 20; www.chambord.org; adult/under 18yr/18-25yr €8.50/free/6; �y 9am-6.30pm May-Sep, 9am-5.30pm Oct-Apr, to 8.30pm 14 Jul–15 Aug, ticket sales end 45 min before closing), built starting in 1519 by François I so he could hunt in the Sologne forests. You'll see his emblems – the royal monogram (a letter 'F') and salamanders of a particularly fierce disposition – adorning many parts of the complex, which has a feudal ground plan. Though forced by liquidity problems to leave his two sons unransomed in Spain and to help himself to both the wealth of his churches and his subjects' silver, François I kept 1800 workers and artisans busy here for 15 years. In the end, though, he stayed at Chambord for a total of only 42 days during his long reign (1515–47).

The chateau's most famous feature is the **double-helix staircase**, attributed by some to Leonardo da Vinci (see p439), which consists of two spiral staircases that wind around a central axis but never meet. It's easy to imagine dukes in tights chasing (Loire) Valley Girls in long skirts up one spiral while countesses in crinolines

THE LOIRE VALLEY

pursued ruddy gardeners down the other... In the nearby *donjon* (castle keep) you can see a visually engaging 15-minute film (subtitled in English) on the chateau's history and architecture.

This giant strand of DNA leads up to the Italianate **rooftop terrace**, where you're surrounded by so many towers, cupolas, domes, chimneys, mosaic slate roofs and lightning rods that it's like standing on a gargantuan chessboard. It was here that the royal court assembled to watch military exercises, tournaments and the hounds and hunters returning from a day of stalking deer.

Chambord's 1½-hour **audioguide** (€4) is available in two versions, one for adults, the other for children aged seven to 12. From about June to August, 1½-hour **guided tours** (€4) in English are held once or twice a day. Free son et lumière shows, known as **Les Clairs de Lune**, are projected onto the chateau's façade nightly from July to mid-September.

From May to September, a 45-minute **Spectacle Équestre** (dressage show; ☎ 02 54 20 31 01; www.chambord-horse-show.fr; adult/child €7.50/5) with costumed riders and some very regal horses begins daily at 11.45am. On weekends and in July and August there's a second show at 4.30pm.

Domaine National de Chambord

The chateau sits inside a 54-sq-km hunting preserve, surrounded by a 32km stone wall, reserved solely for the use of high-ranking French government personalities and their guests (Jacques Chirac has chosen not to exercise his venery prerogatives). About 10 sq km on the northwest side of the domaine is open to the public and can be explored on **walking and mountain bike trails**. From the **aires de vision** (observation towers) your chances of spotting animals such as stags, does, wild boars, wild sheep, roe deer and foxes are best early in the morning (from 6am to 8am) and before nightfall.

Bicycles, perfect for exploring the domaine, can be rented from a **kiosk** (☎ 02 54 33 37 54; half/whole day €10/13; ☼ Apr–early Nov) near Parking Lot 1, facing the Hôtel St-Michel. From early August to early September the state authorities organise two-hour **Evasion d'Été cycling excursions** (adult/under 18yr €10/6, not incl bike hire). Rowboats (per hour €11) can be rented at the *embarcadère* on the River Cosson.

The estate runs fun and informative 1½-hour **Land Rover tours** (☎ 02 54 50 50 06; adult €15; ☼ Apr–Sep) of the domaine's closed section (in French).

Getting There & Away

Chambord is 16km east of Blois, 45km southwest of Orléans and 17km northeast of Cheverny. For details on public transport options see p429. At Chambord, TLC buses use the wooden bus shelter under the giant chestnut tree on the westbound D33.

CHÂTEAU DE CHEVERNY

Built between 1625 and 1634, **Cheverny** (☎ 02 54 79 96 29; www.chateau-cheverny.fr; adult/7-14yr/ student under 25yr €6.50/3.20/4.10; ☼ 9.15am-6.45pm Jul & Aug, 9.15am-6.15pm Apr-Jun & Sep, 9.45am-btwn 5 & 5.30pm Oct-Mar) is the region's most magnificently furnished chateau. Sitting like a sparkling white ship amid a sea of beautifully manicured gardens, it presents to the world a finely proportioned classical façade. Inside visitors are treated to room after sumptuous room decked out with the finest period appointments. The most richly furnished rooms are the **Chambre du Roi** (in which no king ever slept because no king ever stayed here) and the **Grand Salon**. In the 1st-floor **dining room**, 34 painted wooden panels illustrate the story of *Don Quixote*.

Across the lawn behind the chateau is the 18th-century **Orangerie**, where Leonardo da Vinci's *Mona Lisa* was hidden during WWII.

At the gift shop you can pick up a suit of armour for €3400.

Cheverny inspired Moulinsart (Marlinspike) Hall, home of the French comicbook hero Tintin. **Les Secrets de Moulinsart** (adult/7-14yr/student under 25yr €5/3.20/4.30), which re-creates scenes from some of the character's best-known adventures, will delight Tintin fans and mystify everyone else.

Cheverny is 16km southeast of Blois and 17km southwest of Chambord. For information on the bus from Blois see p429.

CHÂTEAU DE CHAUMONT

It's a short, healthy climb up to the 15th- and early 16th-century **Château de Chaumont-sur-Loire** (☎ 02 54 51 26 26; adult/under 18yr/18-25yr €6.50/ free/4.50; ☼ 9.30am-6.30pm 8 May–mid-Sep, 10am-5pm mid-Sep–7 May, no ticket sales 12.30-1.30pm Oct-Mar), set on a bluff overlooking the Loire. Reached via

---

SOUPE DES CHIENS

As was the custom among the nobility of centuries past, Marquis Charles-Antoine de Vibraye – whose family has owned Cheverny since it was built – hunts with dogs. His 100 canines, most of them a cross between English fox hounds and French poitevins, are quite beautiful, no matter what you think of the practice of using them to kill stags. A sign at the *chenils* (kennels) asks that visitors not *exiter les chiens* (excite the dogs) – and, yes, that includes playing air-guitar while belting out 'you ain't nuthin' but a hound dog'.

The *soupe des chiens* (feeding of the dogs) is an awe-inspiring demonstration of the complete control Cheverny's two dog trainers – who know every dog by name and lineage – exercise over the pack. Some 70kg (100kg in winter) of boneless cow and chicken parts and boiled biscuits are brought from the canine kitchen by wheelbarrow into the dogs' cement enclosure and arranged in a 3m-long strip while the hounds whimper and sniff from inside the kennel. When the tiny door is opened, the dogs bundle and squeeze out as fast as they can – but they don't so much as nibble a kibble until the dog master snaps his whip. Crack! – and the raw meat is ripped to shreds and gobbled up in a flash. The *soupe des chiens* takes place at 5pm daily from April to mid-September; the rest of the year it begins at 3pm on Monday, Wednesday, Thursday and Friday.

From about September to March, the pack hunts in the privately owned Forêt de Cheverny on Tuesday and Saturday, setting out at about 9am. According to rules set down centuries ago, the horse-mounted hunters (mainly local landowners), in full hunting kit, chase only the first stag picked up by the dogs, either killing it or, as happens half the time, returning home empty handed; all other stags seen over the course of the day are spared. Fanfares played on circular brass horns help lost canines rejoin the pack. The dogs have a vested interest in all this because it is they who either eat the stag in the field or return to their kennels feeling peckish, to be fed on biscuits and offal later on.

---

a wooden drawbridge, the feudal-style castle was bought in 1875 by Princess de Broglie, heiress to the Say sugar fortune, who with her husband added many of its 'historicist' (eg neo-Renaissance) features. In the late 1800s, many were the sparkling parties held here – but by the 1930s the poor princess was bankrupt and had to sell the property to the French government. Down the cedar of Lebanon–shaded path from the main entrance are the luxurious **écuries** (stables), built by the Broglies in 1877. The chateau will be closed for several months in early 2007.

Each year, Chaumont's park – which affords spectacular river views – plays host to the **Festival International des Jardins** (☎ 02 54 20 99 22; www.chaumont-jardin.com; adult/8-12yr/concession €8.50/4/7; ☟ 9.30am-nightfall May–mid-Oct), a themed garden festival with lots of colourful flowers.

Getting There & Away

Chaumont-sur-Loire is on the Loire's south bank 17km southwest of Blois and 20km northeast of Amboise. The path leading through the park to the chateau starts at the intersection of rue Maréchal Leclerc (the D751) and rue du Village Neuf. To get to

the parking lot behind the chateau, drive up rue du Village Neuf, take the first right and follow the signs to the *stade* (stadium).

Onzain, an easily walkable 2km (across the Loire) from Chaumont, is on the Orléans–Tours rail line. Frequent trains go to Blois (€2.90, 10 minutes, 10 to 20 daily) and Tours (€6.90, 35 minutes, 11 to 22 daily).

By bicycle, the sleepy back roads on the southern bank of the river are a tranquil option. The Chaumont-sur-Loire **tourist office** (☎ 02 54 20 91 73; 24 rue du Maréchal Leclerc; ☟ 9.30am-12.30pm & 2-7pm Mon-Sat May-Sep, also open Sun & holidays Jun-Aug, 9.30am-12.30pm & 1.30-btwn 5 & 5.30pm except Sun & holidays Feb-Apr & Oct–late Dec) rents bicycles for €5/10 per half/whole day.

TOURAINE

With the exception of the medieval fortresses at Chinon and Loches, the castles of Touraine (www.monuments-touraine.fr) – Azay-le-Rideau, Chenonceau, Langeais and Villandry – date to the Renaissance. They were designed purely to inspire the soul and pamper the king, the queen, their offspring and hordes of courtiers.

Tours, the historical capital of Touraine, is a lively, convenient and reasonably priced base for exploring the central Loire Valley. The city has extensive public transport links with nearby chateaux.

Tours

Visiting chateaux by train and bus can be slow, so even veteran backpackers might want to consider taking a bus tour, a surprisingly relaxed and informal way to see the area. Expect to pay €19 to €31 for a half-day minibus trip, not including entrance fees (tour participants qualify for group discounts). Get five to eight people together and you can design your own itinerary.

Companies offering minibus tours from Tours include:

Acco-Dispo (☎ 06 82 00 64 51; www.accodispo-tours .com; morning/afternoon tours €19/31)

Alienor (☎ 02 47 61 22 23 or 06 10 85 35 39; www .locationdevelos.com; ☾ Easter–1 Nov & Christmas)

Quart de Tours (☎ 06 85 72 16 22; www.quartdetours .com; morning/afternoon tours €19/25-31)

Reservations for all three can be made at the Tours tourist office. **The Wine Tour** (☎ 02 47 61 22 23 or 06 03 10 31 11; ☾ Easter–1 Nov) offers vineyard tours that include *dégustation* (wine tasting).

If you really want to get away from peak-season crowds, take to the air for a bird's-eye view of the chateaux. The Tours tourist office (right) has details on aerial excursions by **helicopter** (☎ 02 47 30 28 29; www.jet-systems.fr; 10-/20-/50-min flights adult €60/115/235, child €48/95/190), plane, ultralight and hot-air balloon.

Getting Around

Chateaux accessible by train or SNCF bus from Tours include Chenonceau, Villandry, Azay-le-Rideau, Langeais, Amboise, Chaumont, Chinon and Loches – transport details are listed on p436 and at the end of each chateau listing.

By bicycle, worthwhile destinations from Tours include Villandry and Langeais.

TOURS

pop 298,000

Lively Tours has the cosmopolitan, bourgeois air of a miniature Paris, with wide 18th-century avenues, formal public gardens, café-lined boulevards and a thriving university with 25,000 students. Graced with imposing public buildings in the purest classical style and an atmospheric old city, it's both elegant and self-confident – and thus, in its inimitable way, quintessentially French. The French spoken in Tours is said to be the purest in France.

Orientation

Thanks to the spirit of the 18th century, Tours is efficiently laid out. Its focal point is semicircular place Jean Jaurès, where the city's major thoroughfares – rue Nationale, blvd Heurteloup, av de Grammont and blvd Béranger – meet, Champs-Élysées–style, at a flowery fountain. The train station is 300m east of place Jean Jaurès. The old city is centred on place Plumereau, which is about 400m west of rue Nationale. The northern boundary of the city is demarcated by the River Loire, which flows roughly parallel to the River Cher, 3km to the south.

Information

There are commercial banks around place Jean Jaurès.

Bureau de Change (☾ 8.45am-6pm Mon-Sat, to 6.30pm Jun-Sep; closed Jan) Inside the train station. The commission is €4.50.

Emega Cyberstation (43 rue du Grand Marché; per hour €2; ☾ noon-midnight Mon-Sat, 2-11pm Sun) Internet access.

La Boîte à Livres de l'Étranger (☎ 02 47 05 67 29; 2 rue du Commerce; ☾ Mon-Sat) Books in lots of languages, including English.

Laundrettes 22 rue Bernard Palissy (☾ 7am-8pm); 149 rue Colbert (☾ till 7.45pm); cnr rue Bretonneau & rue Mûrier (☾ 7am-8.30pm)

Le Paradis Vert (☎ 02 47 66 00 94; 9 rue Michelet; per hour €6; ☾ 10am-2am) Internet access.

Police Station (☎ 02 47 33 80 69; 70-72 rue Marceau; ☾ 24hr)

Post Office (1 blvd Béranger) Has a Cyberposte and does currency exchange.

Top Communication (129 rue Colbert; per 20min €1; ☾ 10am-10pm Mon-Sat, 3-10pm Sun) Internet access.

Tourist Office (☎ 02 47 70 37 37; www.ligeris.com; 78-82 rue Bernard Palissy; ☾ 8.30am-7pm Mon-Sat, 10am-12.30pm & 2.30-5pm Sun & holidays mid-Apr–mid-Oct; 9am-12.30pm & 1.30-6pm Mon-Sat, 10am-1pm Sun & holidays mid-Oct–mid-Apr)

Sights

MUSÉE DES BEAUX-ARTS

Occupying three floors of an impressive 17th- to 18th-century archbishop's palace, the **Musée des Beaux-Arts** (☎ 02 47 05 68 73; 18 place François Sicard; adult/under 13yr/student €4/free/2; ❧ 9am-12.45pm & 2-6pm Wed-Mon) has an excellent collection of paintings, furniture and *objets d'art* from the 14th to the 20th centuries. Highlights include a Rembrandt miniature, a Rubens portrait of the Virgin Mary (both in room 114) and a whole room of Orientalist works (on the 2nd floor). The new lift makes the museum wheelchair accessible. In the lovely formal garden the 1804 cedar of Lebanon is a whopping 7.5m around the base.

CATHÉDRALE ST-GATIEN

Various parts of Tours' Gothic-style **Cathédrale St-Gatien** (place de la Cathédrale; ❧ 9am-7pm) represent the 13th century (the choir), the 14th century (the transept), the 14th and 15th (the nave) and the 15th and 16th centuries (the west façade). The domed tops of the two 70m-high **towers** date from the Renaissance. There's a fine view of the **flying buttresses** from around the back. The interior is renowned for its marvellous 13th- to 15th-century **stained-glass windows**.

On the north side of the cathedral, **Cloître de la Psallette** (☎ 02 47 47 05 19; adult/under 18yr €2.50/free; ❧ 9.30am-12.30pm & 2-6pm Mon-Sat, 2-6pm Sun Apr-Sep, 9.30am-12.30pm & 2-5pm Wed-Sat & 2-5pm Sun Oct-Mar) is a cloister built from 1442 to 1524.

MUSÉE DU GEMMAIL

Gemmail (zheh-*mai*) – pieces of coloured glass embedded in colourless enamel and lit from behind – never quite fulfilled its mid-century promise, but the pieces on display at the **Gemmail Museum** (☎ 02 47 61 01 19; rue du Mûrier; adult/student €5.40/3.90; ❧ 2-6.30pm Tue-Sun Easter–mid-Oct) really capture the aesthetic of the 1950s and 1960s.

MUSÉE DE L'HÔTEL GOÜIN

This **archaeological museum** (☎ 02 47 66 22 32; 25 rue du Commerce; adult/student €4.50/3; ❧ 10am-1pm & 2-6pm Tue-Sun) is housed in the Hôtel Goüin, a Renaissance residence built for a wealthy merchant around 1510. Its Italianate façade is worth a peek even if an eclectic assemblage of prehistoric, Gallo-Roman, medieval, Renaissance and 18th-century artefacts seems unlikely to scintillate.

JARDIN BOTANIQUE

About 1.6km west of place Jean Jaurès, the **botanic garden** (blvd Tonnelle; admission free; ❧ 7.45am-sunset) is a great place for a stroll or a picnic. Created between 1831 and 1843 on reclaimed land on the banks of St Anne stream, the five-hectare landscaped park has a tropical greenhouse, medicinal herb garden and petting zoo. There are also emus and kangaroos bouncing around. To get there, it's a short walk or take Bus 4 along blvd Béranger.

Sleeping

Tours is blessed with lots of good-value hotels.

THE LOIRE VALLEY

JOURNEYMAN COMPANIONS

In an era of mass production, the 20,000 craftsmen – all of them male – of France's three umbrella *compagnonnages* (guilds of journeyman companions), whose roots go back to the medieval cathedrals, continue to practice their age-old skills, express solidarity with their fellow artisans and affirm the dignity of skilled manual labour. When the Statue of Liberty was restored in the mid-1980s, *compagnons* (the word derives from the Latin for 'sharing bread') sent over from France did some of the most intricate metalwork.

You can get a glimpse of the *compagnons'* world at the **Musée du Compagnonnage** (☎ 02 47 61 07 93; 8 rue Nationale; adult/under 12yr/student & over 65yr €4.80/free/2.80; ❧ 9am-noon or 12.30pm & 2 to 6pm, closed Tue except mid-Jun–mid-Sep), which displays virtuoso examples of the master craftsman's art. Pieces by locksmiths include a booby-trapped 19th-century door lock designed to shoot anyone who doesn't open it properly; carpenters are represented by the model of a quadruple staircase made by a French prisoner of war in 1943; and the *pâtissiers* (pastry chefs) weigh in with an all-sugar fairy castle in white and pink. Shoemakers, horse-shoers, iron smiths, roof slaters, stonemasons and coopers are also represented by impossibly fine scale models.

Visitors interested in disappearing crafts may also want to check out the Maison de l'Outil et de la Pensée Ouvrière in Troyes (p366).

TOURS

INFORMATION
Bureau de Change	1 E3
Emega Cyberstation	2 C2
La Boite à Livres de l'Étranger	3 D2
Laundrette	4 E2
Laundrette	5 E3
Laundrette	6 C2
Le Paradis Vert	(see 35)
Police (Commissariat Central)	7 D3
Post Office	8 D3
Top Communication	9 E1
Tourist Office	10 E3

SIGHTS & ACTIVITIES
Cathédrale St-Gatien	11 F1
Cloître de la Psallette	12 E1
Musée de l'Hôtel Goüin	13 D2
Musée des Beaux-Arts	14 F2
Musée du Compagnonnage	15 D1
Musée du Gemmail	16 C2

SLEEPING
Auberge de Jeunesse du Vieux Tours	17 C1
Hôtel de l'Univers	18 E3
Hôtel du Cygne	19 E1
Hôtel Mondial	20 D2
Hôtel Régina	21 E2
Hôtel Val de Loire	22 F3

EATING
Atac Supermarket	23 E3
Atac Supermarket	24 D3
Comme Autre Foueé	25 C2
L'Hedoniste	26 E1
La Rôtisserie Tourangelle	27 D2
Le Bœuf' Salad	28 E3
Les Halles	29 C3
Les Maris Morgans	30 C2
Vinothèque de Tours	31 E3

DRINKING
Bistro 64	32 B2
Le Baromètre	33 C2
Le Palais	34 D3
Le Paradis Vert	35 E3

ENTERTAINMENT
Cinémas Les Studios	36 F2
Fnac Billeterie	37 D2
GI Club Discothèque	38 E1
Grand Théâtre	39 E2
Le Petit Faucheux	40 C3
Les Trois Orfèvres	41 C2

TRANSPORT
Avis	42 E3
Bus Station & Touraine Fil Vert Bus Information Desk	43 E3
Détours de Loire	44 F3
Ecoto	45 F3
Europcar	(see 10)
Fil Bleu	46 D3
Vélomania	47 E1

BUDGET

Auberge de Jeunesse du Vieux Tours (☎ 02 47 37 81 58; www.ajtours.org in French; 5 rue Bretonneau; s, d or tr per person incl breakfast €16.90; ☙ reception 8am-noon & 5-10pm Oct-Mar, 8am-noon & 6-11pm Apr-Sep; ☐) A well-equipped, 146-room hostel near the old town that also functions as a dorm for foreign students. It has a friendly feel, eight kitchens and three lounges for hanging out. Toilets and showers are in the hall. Having a small fridge in your room costs €0.50 a day; bike rental is €10 a day. Rooms are open all day long.

Hôtel Régina (☎ 02 47 05 25 36; fax 02 47 66 08 72; 2 rue Pimbert; s/d €30/34, with washbasin €22/26) This popular one-star place has 20 clean, functional rooms with superb mattresses. The matronly manageress, who has the air of a mother superior, doesn't stand for any mischief. Curfew is 1am.

Hôtel Val de Loire (☎ 02 47 05 37 86; hotel.val .de.loire@club-Internet.fr; 33 blvd Heurteloup; s/d €33/42, with washbasin €22/31) This 14-room, two-star hotel, in a bourgeois home built in 1870, has heaps of charm. The ceilings get lower the higher up you go but all the rooms are lovingly cared for and have real parquet floors, antique furniture and, where needed, double glazing. The breakfast room faces the owners' cute little house, which looks like it should be made of gingerbread.

The midrange **Hôtel Mondial** has a few singles/doubles with shower for €36/42.

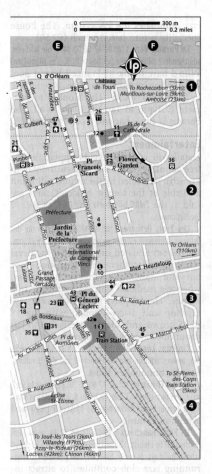

MIDRANGE

Hôtel du Cygne (☎ 02 47 66 66 41; http://perso.wana doo.fr/hotelcygne.tours; 6 rue du Cygne; d €44-74) A pretty two-star, 18-room hotel on a quiet side street. Wooden-shuttered windows, blooming window boxes, high ceilings and chandeliers add charm. The spacious 1st-floor rooms tick all the boxes. Has a private garage.

Hôtel Mondial (☎ 02 47 05 62 68; www.hotel mondialtours.com; 3 place de la Résistance; s/d from €46/50) A postwar two-star accommodation option with 19 immaculate, carpeted rooms overlooking a public square. There's a sunny room on the second floor to enjoy the buffet breakfast. Reception is upstairs.

TOP END

Hôtel de l'Univers (☎ 02 47 05 37 12; www.hotel -univers.fr; 5 blvd Heurteloup; d €193-265; ⊗ ⊠ 및) Tours' swishest town-centre hotel, with four stars, 85 rooms and good wheelchair access, occupies an imposing old building that dates from 1846. The painted figures looking down from the lobby balcony are supposed to resemble some of the hotel's more famous guests, including Winston Churchill, Thomas Edison, Edward VII, Guiseppe Garibaldi and, of course, Ernest Hemingway. If Tours were a war zone, the wood-panelled bar would be where the correspondents would hang out and swap stories over whisky. Some of the rooms have openable windows between the bath and the sleeping area, making it possible to play Peeping Tom while lying on the bed – ideal for a honeymoon!

Eating

In the old city, place Plumereau and nearby rue du Grand Marché and rue de la Rôtisserie are loaded with restaurants and cafés. Further east, cheap eats are available along rue Colbert.

ourpick Comme Autre Fouée (☎ 02 47 05 94 78; 11 rue de la Monnaie; lunch menu €10, other menus €16-19.50; ⏱ lunch Fri & Sat, dinner Tue-Sat, also open lunch Tue-Thu mid-May–mid-Sep) This place specialises in *fouée* (or *fouaces*), an age-old regional speciality – mentioned by Rabelais – that's created by baking a small, flat disc of dough in a wood-fired oven for 45 seconds. Served piping hot, these mini-pitas are filled with pork *rillettes, haricots blancs* (white beans) or fresh goat's cheese for a hearty, all-you-can-eat meal. The restaurant's name is a pun on *comme autrefois* (like the old days).

La Rôtisserie Tourangelle (☎ 02 47 05 71 21; 23 rue du Commerce; menus €16-49; ⏱ 12.15-1.30pm & 7.30-9.30pm, closed Mon, lunch Sat & dinner Sun; ⊗) A traditional French gastronomic restaurant renowned for its meat and fish dishes. Elegant and modern but not excessively formal.

Les Maris Morgans (☎ 02 47 64 95 34; 6 rue de la Rôtisserie; menus €15.90-28.90; ⏱ 7-10.30pm except Wed) Named after luminous sea-fairies who beckon passing mariners, this innovative eatery specialises in meat and fish dishes that you cook yourself on a *pierre chaude* (hot rock); and *bisquines*, an invention of the chef that brings together – on a giant cork platter – seafood in a cream, saffron, garlic and olive oil sauce, and chips. Desserts come in half-metre-tall glass cups.

L'Hedoniste (☎ 02 47 05 20 40; 16 rue Lavoisier; lunch menu €11.50, other menus €18-45; ☷ Tue-Sun; ☒) A convivial cavelike restaurant lined with bottles, whose regional and French cuisine is enhanced by a wide range of fine wines and the proprietor's extensive viticultural knowledge. Offers good value.

Le Bœuf' Salad (☎ 02 47 66 70 58; 19 rue du Grand Marché; menus €14-22; ☷ may be closed Tue & Wed) An informal eatery decked out in white and blue, with French (and a few Antillean) dishes and Tours' cheapest steak-and-fries platter (€6.90; available October to May).

SELF-CATERING

For all your picnicking needs:

Atac supermarkets 5 place du Général Leclerc (☷ 7.30am-8pm Mon-Sat); 19 place Jean Jaurès (☷ 9am-7.30pm Mon-Sat) Inside the shopping centre.

Les Halles (covered market; place Gaston Pailhou; ☷ 7am-7pm, fewer shops Mon)

Vinothèque de Tours (16 rue Michelet; ☷ 9am-12.30pm & 2-7.30pm, closed Mon morning & Sun) Carries 900 different wines.

Drinking

The old town is full of bars – a good starting point is place Plumereau, which fills to bursting in the summer, and nearby rue du Grand Marché.

Le Palais (☎ 02 47 61 48 54; 15 place Jean Jaurès; ☷ 7am-2am, closed Sun Nov-Mar) Each Monday this trendy bar-brasserie hosts a *café des langues* from 8.30pm, where you can meet linguistically motivated locals by conversing with them in English (and lots of other languages). Thursday is karaoke night (from 10.30pm). Hugely popular with students.

Le Baromètre (☎ 02 47 38 49 80; 33 rue du Grand Marché; ☷ 10am-2am) A smoky corner bar whose animated habitués often take advantage of an old guitar that's kept in the cellar (don't worry, all they do is play it, albeit with varying degrees of talent). Annie, the *patronne*, has a personality that's much larger than her establishment, kept warm in winter by a roaring fire. The background music is jazz, blues and chansons.

Bistro 64 (64 rue du Grand Marché; ☷ 11am-2am Mon-Sat) An intimate bar made smoky by both cigarettes and the candles on the tiny square tables. Hosts live music (usually jazz) from 9.30pm on Thursday; the rest of the time

jazz dominates the PA system. The house speciality is rum-based punch (€2.50).

Le Paradis Vert (☎ 02 47 66 00 94; 9 rue Michelet; adult/student billiard table per hour €10/8; ☷ 10am-2am) Who'd have thunk it? France's largest pool hall, with an incredible 36 tables, is right here in (Loire) River City. The Monday tournament (7.30pm to 1am) is open to all. The Paradis is also a bar and a pricey cybercafé.

Entertainment

Details on cultural events appear in the free monthly *Tours.infos* (www.tours.fr in French), published by the municipality and available at the tourist office. Tickets are sold at the **FNAC billeterie** (☎ 08 92 68 36 22; 72 rue Nationale).

Les Trois Orfèvres (☎ 02 47 64 02 73; 6 rue des Orfèvres; admission €2 plus an obligatory drink; ☷ 11pm-5am Wed-Sat) Situated on a narrow medieval street, this discotheque has a ground-floor bar and dancing in the vaulted cellar, whence a medieval stairway spirals up to a lounge. The DJ plays anything except rap, hip-hop and disco. Popular with the 18 to 35 crowd and hosts concerts (€3 to €9) about once a week at 8.30pm.

Cinémas Les Studio (☎ 08 92 68 37 01 for recording; www.studiocine.com in French; 2 rue des Ursulines) Screens nondubbed films.

Grand Théâtre (☎ 02 47 60 20 20; 34 rue de la Scellerie; ☷ box office 9.30am-12.30pm & 1.30-5.45pm Mon-Sat & 30 min before performances) Hosts opera and symphonic music.

Le Petit Faucheux (☎ 02 47 38 29 34; www.petit faucheux.fr in French; 12 rue Leonard de Vinci; ☷ closed school holidays & early Jul–early Oct) This long-running jazz club continues to attract international talent, local up-and-comers and an appreciative crowd. Hosts one to three concerts a week.

GI Club Discothèque (☎ 02 47 66 29 96; www.gidis cotheque.com in French; 13 rue Lavoisier; admission Fri/Sat €7/10; ☷ 11pm-5am Wed-Sun) A gay and lesbian nightclub, in a barrel-vaulted cellar, of the flashing-lights-and-nude-torsos variety. Has theme nights two Fridays a month; Sunday is dedicated to disco.

Getting There & Away

AIR

Aéroport Tours-Val de Loire (☎ 02 47 49 37 00; www .tours-aeroport.com), about 5km northeast of central Tours, is linked to London-Stansted by Ryanair.

BUS

Buses operated by **Touraine Fil Vert** (☎ 02 47 47 17 18; www.touraine-filvert.com in French) serve destinations in the Indre-et-Loire department, including Amboise (€2.10, 45 minutes, seven daily Monday to Saturday). They leave from the **bus station** (place du Général Leclerc), which has an **information desk** (☎ 02 47 05 30 49; ⊙ 7am-7pm Mon-Sat). Tickets are sold by drivers.

From Monday to Saturday in July and August, you can make an all-day chateau circuit by public bus by taking the 10am bus to Chenonceaux (€2.10, 1¼ hours), the 12.42pm bus from Chenonceaux to Amboise (€1.05, 25 minutes), and the 5.50pm bus from Amboise back to Tours (€2.10).

CAR

Car-rental companies:

Avis (☎ 02 47 20 53 27) Inside the train station.

Ecoto (☎ 02 47 66 75 00; www.ecoto.fr; 8 rue Marcel Tribut) A cheaper regional company.

Europcar (☎ 02 47 64 47 76; 76 blvd Bernard Palissy)

TRAIN

Tours is the Loire Valley's main rail hub. The **train station** is linked to St-Pierre-des-Corps, Tours' TGV train station, by frequent shuttle trains.

Trains run 13 to 20 times a day between Tours and Orléans (€15.90, one to 1½ hours). Stops en route include Montlouis-sur-Loire (€2.30, 12 minutes), Amboise (€4.50, 20 minutes) and Blois (€8.70, 35 minutes). SNCF lines go west to Saumur (€9.60, 29 to 52 minutes, 10 to 16 daily) and Angers (€14.70, one hour, eight to 14 daily); southwest to Chinon (€7.70, 45 to 70 minutes, 10 daily weekdays, four or five daily weekends); southeast to Loches (€7.50, 45 to 65 minutes by bus or train, 15 daily weekdays, five to eight daily weekends); east to Chenonceaux (€5.50, 30 minutes, four to six daily); and northeast (by bus) to Chartres (€20.30, 2½ hours, one to three direct daily).

Paris options include TGVs to/from Gare Montparnasse (€37.60 or €50.30, 1¼ hours, 13 to 15 daily) and corail services to/from Gare d'Austerlitz (€28.50, two to 2¾ hours, nine to 14 daily). TGVs go to Bordeaux (€40.40, 2½ hours) and La Rochelle (€31.30, two to three hours) and TGV/corail services serve Poitiers (€16.70/13.80, 40 to 60 minutes) and Nantes (€26.70/23.80, about two hours).

Getting Around

TO/FROM THE AIRPORT

A shuttle bus (€5), timed to coincide with Ryanair flights, links Tours' bus station with the airport.

BICYCLE

Détours de Loire (☎ 02 47 61 22 22; www.locationde velos.com; 31 blvd Heurteloup; hybrid per day/5 days/week/ additional day €13/43/56/4; ⊙ 9am-1pm & 2-7pm Mon-Sat, 9.30am-12.30pm & 6-7pm Sun & holidays Easter–early Oct, 9am-1pm & 2-6pm Mon-Sat early Oct–Easter) is part of a network of 16 Loire Valley bike rental sites (see p419). Prices include a lock, a helmet, a puncture repair kit and a pump.

Vélomania (☎ 02 47 05 10 11; 109 rue Colbert; ⊙ 10.30am-1.30pm & 3.30-7.30pm except Mon morning & Sun, no midday closure Sat, bike return at 6pm Sun) rents hybrids (per 24 hours/3 days/week €14.50/28/50.50) and tandems (per day €32).

BUS

Information on local buses is available at the **Fil Bleu information office** (☎ 02 47 66 70 70; www.filbleu.fr in French; information office 5bis rue de la Dolve; ⊙ closed Sat afternoon & Sun). Most lines stop around the periphery of place Jean Jaurès. Tickets (€1.15) are sold on the bus and are valid for one hour after being stamped. Most lines run until about 8.30pm; from 9pm to midnight, hourly Bleu de Nuit night buses take over. Park-and-ride costs €1.50 for all-day parking plus return bus travel for up to four passengers.

AROUND TOURS

Vineyards carpet the area around Vouvray (population 3100) and Montlouis-sur-Loire (population 8000), 10km east of Tours on the northern and southern banks of the Loire respectively. Frankly, neither village is particularly attractive but this stretch of the Loire offers ample opportunity to taste and buy wine. For centuries wine growers have stored their vintages in caves hewn out of the white tufaceous cliffs facing the river.

The **Vouvray tourist office** (☎ 02 47 52 68 73; 12 rue Rabelais; ⊙ 9.30am-1pm & 2-6.30pm May-Oct, 9.30am-1pm & 2-5.30pm Tue-Sat Nov-Apr), on a side street two short blocks from the intersection of the N152 and the D46, has a list of wine cellars posted in the window.

THE LOIRE VALLEY

Fil Bleu's bus No 61 links Tours' place Jean Jaurès with Vouvray (€1.15, 20 minutes). Montlouis-sur-Loire is linked to Tours' train station by Fil Vert lines C1 and C2 (10 minutes, hourly).

ourpick **Les Hautes Roches** (☎ 0247528888; www .leshautesroches.com; 86 quai de la Loire, Rochecorbon; d €135-265; ☒ closed Feb-late Mar; ☒), on the N152 about midway between Tours and Vouvray, is where you, too, can be a troglodyte (see p446) – and do so in style! Caves carved into the sheer cliff face have been transformed into a luxurious four-star hotel with spectacular panoramas of the Loire. Excavated by monks, the 12 rooms – used as a haven during the Wars of Religion and, later, to store wine and grow both silkworms and mushrooms – have walls and ceilings made of natural tufa stone that keeps them cool in summer and warm in winter. Ample wine-tasting opportunities are right nearby. The attached French restaurant (menus €48 to €90) has one Michelin star and specialises in fish and seafood.

CHÂTEAU DE CHENONCEAU

With its stylised moat, turrets and towers, the 16th-century **Château de Chenonceau** (☎ 02 47 23 90 07; www.chenonceau.com; adult/student under 27yr & 7-18yr €9/7.50; ☒ 9am-7pm mid-Mar–mid-Sep, 9am-btwn 4.30 & 6.30pm rest of year) is everything a fairy-tale castle should be, although the interior – crammed with period furniture, tourists, paintings, tapestries and tourists – is less inspiring than the elegant exterior and the delightful **formal gardens** (at their blooming best from May to September). The **park**, which covers 70 hectares on both banks of the River Cher, affords some stunning vistas of the chateau and includes a yew-tree **labyrinthe** (maze; in the grove to the left as you approach the chateau along the alley of plane trees). The MP3 audioguide (€3.50) comes in 12 languages and in an English version for children aged seven to 12.

Several remarkable women played crucial roles in the history of Chenonceau. Diane de Poitiers, mistress of King Henri II, planted the flowery formal garden to the left (east) as you approach the chateau. After Henri's death in 1559, she was forced to give up Chenonceau (and accept the Château de Chaumont instead) by Henri II's widow, the vengeful Catherine de Médi-

cis, who applied her own energies to the chateau and laid out the equally formal, if smaller, rose garden to the right (west). In the 18th century, Madame Dupin, the chateau's owner, brought Jean-Jacques Rousseau to Chenonceau as a tutor for her son. During the French Revolution, the affection with which the peasantry regarded Madame Dupin saved the chateau from the violent fate of its neighbours.

During WWI the 60m-long **Grande Gallerie** over the Cher was converted into a hospital. From 1940 to 1942 the demarcation line between German-occupied northern France and the Vichy-run south ran down the middle of the Cher. For many people fleeing the Nazis, this room served as a vital crossing point to relative safety.

Getting There & Away

The Château de Chenonceau, in the town of Chenonceaux (the village has an 'x' at the end), is 34km east of Tours, 10km southeast of Amboise and 40km southwest of Blois. By rail, it's an easy day trip from Tours (€5.50, 30 minutes, four to six daily); Chenonceaux train station, on the line to Romorantin, is right in front of the chateau.

AMBOISE
pop 11,500

The picturesque town of Amboise, nestling under its fortified chateau on the southern bank of the Loire, reached its peak during the decades around 1500, when luxury-loving Charles VIII enlarged the chateau and François I held raucous parties there. These days the town makes the most of its association with Leonardo da Vinci, who lived out his last years here under the patronage of François I. Amboise is protected from the river by a dyke whose flower-covered heights are a great place for a riverside promenade.

Amboise makes a convenient base for visiting the chateaux between Tours and Blois.

Orientation

The train station, across the river from the town centre, is about 800m north of the Château d'Amboise. Le Clos Lucé is 500m southeast of the chateau along rue Victor Hugo. The island in the middle of the Loire is called Île d'Or.

Place Michel Debré (effectively an extension of rue Victor Hugo), sometimes called place du Château, stretches west from rue de la Tour to pedestrianised rue Nationale, Amboise's main commercial street.

Information

Several banks dot rue Nationale.

Laundrette (7 allée du Sergent Turpin; ☺ 7am-8pm)

Playconnect (119 rue Nationale; per hr €3; ☺ 3-10pm Sun & Mon, 10am-10pm Tue-Sat) Internet access.

Post Office (20 Quai du Général de Gaulle)

Tourist Office (☎ 02 47 57 09 28; www.amboise-valdeloire.com; ☺ 9.30am-1pm & 2-6pm Mon-Sat, 10am-1pm & 2-6pm Sun Apr-Jun & Sep, 9am-8pm Mon-Sat & 10am-6pm Sun Jul & Aug, 10am-1pm & 2-6pm Mon-Sat & 10am-1pm sometimes Sun Oct-Mar) In a dykeside pavilion opposite 7 quai du Général de Gaulle. Stocks maps for walking (*Balades Royales*; €4) and cycling (*5 Circuits Vélos*; €2) and supplies a free English-language brochure for a walking tour of Amboise.

Sights & Activities

CHÂTEAU ROYAL D'AMBOISE

Amboise's **royal chateau** (☎ 02 47 57 00 98; place Michel Debré; adult/7-14yr/15-25yr €8/4.80/6.80; ☺ 9am-7pm Jul & Aug, 9am-btwn 6 & 6.30pm mid-Mar–Jun, Sep & Oct, 9am-noon & 2-4.45pm Nov–mid-Mar) is perched high above town on a rocky outcrop, affording panoramic views of the town and the Loire. The entrance is at the top of the ramp at place Michel Debré.

Charles VIII (r 1483–98), who was born and brought up here, enlarged the chateau in 1492 after a visit to Italy that left him deeply impressed by that country's artistic creativity and luxurious lifestyle. He died six years later after hitting his head on a low lintel while on his way to a game of *jeu de paume* (a precursor of tennis).

King François I (r 1515–47) also grew up here as did his sister, the reform-minded French Renaissance author Margaret of Angoulême (also known as Margaret of Navarre). François I lived in the chateau during the first few years of his reign, a lively period marked by balls, masquerade parties, tournaments and festivities of all sorts.

Today, just a few of the chateau's 15th- and 16th-century structures survive. These include the Flamboyant Gothic **Chapelle St-Hubert**, said to be the final resting place of Leonardo da Vinci; and the **Salle des États** (Estates Hall), where a group of Protestant conspirators were tried before being hanged from the balcony in 1560. From 1848 to 1852, Abd el-Kader, the political and spiritual leader of the Algerian resistance to French colonialism, and his family and entourage were imprisoned here, an event commemorated by a memorial.

A re-enactment of the life and times of François I is staged at 10pm or 10.30pm on Wednesday and Saturday from late June to August. Tickets are sold by **Animation Renaissance Amboise** (☎ 02 47 57 14 47; www.renaissance-amboise.com in French; adult seat/bench €16/13, child €16/7), based at the chateau's entrance.

LE CLOS LUCÉ

Leonardo da Vinci – known locally as Léonard de Vinci (van-*see*) – came to Amboise in 1516 at the invitation of François I. Until his death three years later at the age of 67, he lived and worked at **Le Clos Lucé** (☎ 02 47 57 00 73; www.vinci-closluce.com; 2 rue du Clos Lucé; adult/6-15yr/student Apr–mid-Nov €12/7/9.50, mid-Nov–Mar €9/6/7; ☺ 9am-8pm Jul & Aug, 9am-7pm Apr, Jun, Sep & Oct, 9am-6pm Nov, Dec, Feb & Mar, 9am-5pm Jan), a brick mansion that now houses scale models of his inventions. The proto-automobile, armoured tank, parachute and hydraulic turbine on display offer unique insights into the mind of one of history's true geniuses. Ticket sales end an hour before closing.

The house is set in a lovely **park** with life-sized models of some of Da Vinci's prototypes and a short video (in French). Many of the models are operational, though you're not likely to get the spiral helicopter to take off! The park is open the same hours as the chateau.

The road from the chateau up to Le Clos Lucé, rue Victor Hugo, passes by some **maisons troglodytes** (cave houses) dug into the cliffs. At No 19, stairs lead up the hill to a viewpoint indicator and a fine view of town.

MINI CHÂTEAUX VAL DE LOIRE

A sort of Bekonscot-sur-Loire, this **park** (☎ 08 25 08 25 22; www.mini-chateaux.com; adult/child €12.50/8.50; ☺ Apr–early Nov), 3km from the city centre towards Chenonceaux, features 1:20-scale models of 44 of the Loire Valley's most famous chateaux. With a bit of creative cropping and liberal use of soft focus you'll be able to convince your friends back home that you really 'did' the Loire Valley!

THE LOIRE VALLEY

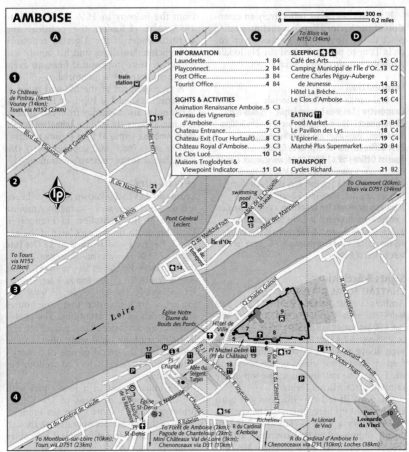

AMBOISE

INFORMATION
Laundrette..............................1 B4
Playconnect...........................2 B4
Post Office.............................3 B4
Tourist Office..........................4 B4

SIGHTS & ACTIVITIES
Animation Renaissance Amboise..5 C3
Caveau des Vignerons
d'Amboise.............................6 C4
Chateau Entrance....................7 C3
Chateau Exit (Tour Hurtault)......8 B4
Château Royal d'Amboise...........9 C3
Le Clos Lucé.........................10 D4
Maisons Troglodytes &
Viewpoint Indicator..............11 D4

SLEEPING
Café des Arts........................12 C4
Camping Municipal de l'Île d'Or..13 C2
Centre Charles Péguy-Auberge
de Jeunesse.........................14 B3
Hôtel La Brèche......................15 B1
Le Clos d'Amboise...................16 C4

EATING
Food Market..........................17 B4
Le Pavillon des Lys..................18 C4
L'Epicerie.............................19 C4
Marché Plus Supermarket..........20 B4

TRANSPORT
Cycles Richard.......................21 B2

WINE TASTING

At the **Caveau des Vignerons d'Amboise** (☎ 02 47 57 23 69; at the base of the chateau opposite 42 place Michel Debré; ☼ 10am-7pm Mar-Nov), run by enterprising Amboise-area wine growers, you can taste four white, three red and two rosé wines as well as two types of *crémant de Loire*, the region's sparkling wine. Also on offer are local goat cheeses and foie gras.

Sleeping
BUDGET

Camping Municipal de l'Île d'Or (☎ 02 47 57 23 37; Île d'Or; per adult/site €2.40/3.20; ☼ Apr–early Oct) Has transriver views of the chateau and mini-golf; the open-air municipal swimming pool is next door.

Centre Charles Péguy-Auberge de Jeunesse (☎ 02 47 30 60 90; www.mjcamboise.fr in French; dm €11, sheets €4; ☼ reception 2-8pm Mon-Fri, usually 5.30-7.30pm Sat & Sun) This is an efficiently run 72-bed youth hostel on the Île d'Or in the middle of the Loire, with rooms available for one to six people. If reception is closed when you arrive, try screeching into the intercom.

Café des Arts (☎ /fax 02 47 57 25 04; 32 rue Victor Hugo; s/d/q with washbasin €25/33/54, in Jul & Aug €25/36/73; ☼ reception 9am-9pm, later in summer, closed Tue except Jul & Aug). This funky little place, in a centuries-old house, is situated above a hip corner bar. The six simple rooms have bunk beds. The best budget deal in town.

MIDRANGE

Hôtel La Brèche (☎ 02 47 57 00 79; www.labreche -amboise.com; 26 rue Jules Ferry; d with bkfst €66; ✷ Mar-Oct) Located down the block from the train station, this 14-room place is comfortable and full of charm. The friendly owner is knowledgeable about the local area. Breakfast is served to visitors on the tree-shaded terrace.

Château de Pintray (☎ 02 47 23 22 84; www .chateau-de-pintray.com; d with breakfast €96) Six kilometres west of Amboise in Lussault-sur-Loire, this small 16th-century chateau has five traditionally furnished rooms and a delightful garden. You can taste and buy wines produced on the estate.

Le Clos d'Amboise (☎ 02 47 30 10 20; www.leclos amboise.com; 27 rue Rabelais; r high season €79-170, low season €69-140; ✷ closed late Nov–mid-Feb; ▨) This place is a gem – a grand old 17th-century ecclesiastical residence with a tranquil walled garden and a fantastic selection of individually and lavishly furnished rooms. The terrace is perfect for a pre-chateau breakfast, the outdoor pool ideal for an after-tour splash. Also has a fitness room.

Eating

The southern side of place Michel Debré is lined with eateries; more restaurants as well as food shops can be found along pedestrianised rue Nationale.

Le Pavillon des Lys (☎ 02 47 30 01 01; 9 rue d'Orange; menus €22-33; ✷ closed Tue in winter; ✗) An exceptionally elegant establishment whose gastronomic French cuisine is the perfect way to conclude a day of chateauing.

L'Épicerie (☎ 02 47 57 08 94; 46 place Michel Debré; lunch menu €10.80, other menus €19.50-37.50; ✷ Wed-Sun, also open Mon & Tue Jul-Sep, closed late Oct–mid-Dec) A quaint and friendly little restaurant with traditional French cuisine, including *tournedos de canard aux baies poivrées* (duck breast in a sauce of pink peppercorns and red Chinon wine; €16.10).

For self-caterers:

Food market (along the Loire near the tourist office; ✷ 8am-1pm Fri & Sun) An open-air market.

Marché Plus supermarket (5 quai du Général de Gaulle; 7am-9pm Mon-Sat, 10am-2pm Sun)

Getting There & Around

Amboise is 34km downstream from Blois and 23km upstream from Tours.

BICYCLE

Hire mountain bikes at **Cycles Richard** (☎ 02 47 57 01 79; 2 rue de Nazelles; per day €15; ✷ 9am-noon & 2.30-7pm Tue-Sat).

BUS

Touraine Fil Vert's line C1 links Amboise's post office with Tours' bus terminal (€2.10, 45 minutes, seven daily Monday to Saturday). In July and August, you can take this line to Chenonceaux (at 10.52am) and back (at 5.08pm) from Monday to Saturday.

TRAIN

The **train station** (blvd Gambetta), across the river from the centre of town, is served by trains from Paris' Gare d'Austerlitz (€24.20, 2¼ to three hours, 11 daily), Blois (€5.60, 20 minutes, 10 to 20 daily) and Tours (€4.50, 15 minutes, 10 to 20 daily).

CHÂTEAU DE VILLANDRY

This **chateau** (☎ 02 47 50 02 09; www.chateauvil landry.com; adult/student under 26yr chateau & gardens €8/5, gardens only €5.50/3.50; ✷ chateau 9.30am-btwn 4.30 & 6.30pm early Feb–mid-Nov & around Christmas, gardens 9am-btwn 5 & 7.30pm year-round) has some of the most magnificent formal gardens in France.

The **Jardin d'Ornement** (Ornamental Garden) comprises intricate, geometrically pruned hedges and flowerbeds loaded with romantic symbolism. Between the chateau and the village church, the nine squares of the **potager** (kitchen garden) are a cross between the vegetable plots in which medieval monks grew their food and the formal gardens so beloved of 16th-century France. All told, Villandry's gardens – in flower from April to September or October – occupy 6 hectares and include 1260 lime trees, hundreds of grape trellises and 52km of landscaped plant rows. Once inside the gardens you can stay as long as you like; the after-hours exit is next to the village church. Picnicking is forbidden. The nearby town of Villandry has several places to eat.

The chateau was completed in 1536, making it the last of the major Renaissance chateaux to be built in this area. Furnished in comfortable 18th-century style, the rooms and hallways are adorned with dark, moody Spanish paintings and large, faded tapestries; the **bibliothèque** (library) and the **bedroom** of Joachim Carvallo, the scientist who founded the gardens as we know them, were opened in 2006 to mark the centenary of his horticultural exploits. An unusual 13th-century **Moorish ceiling** is thought to have been bought here from Toledo, Spain.

From the corner **tower** (all that remains of the original medieval chateau) and the **Belvédère**, the intricate gardens can be seen in their entirety, as can the parallel Rivers Loire and Cher.

Getting There & Away

Villandry is 17km southwest of Tours, 31km northeast of Chinon and 11km northeast of Azay-le-Rideau. By road the shortest route from Tours is the D7, but cyclists will find less traffic on the D88 (which runs along the southern bank of the Loire) and the D288 (which links the D88 with Savonnières). If heading southwest from Villandry towards Langeais, the best bike route is the one-lane D16, which has no verges but very light traffic.

The nearest train station is in Savonnières, about 4km northeast of Villandry. It is linked to Tours (€2.80, 15 minutes) and Saumur (35 minutes) three times daily Monday to Saturday (once on Sunday). Daily in July and August, Touraine Fil Vert (p437) has a 2.10pm bus from Tours to Villandry (€2.10) and a 5.15pm bus back to Tours.

CHÂTEAU D'AZAY-LE-RIDEAU

Built in the 1500s on an island in the River Indre and surrounded by a quiet pool and park, **Azay-le-Rideau** (☎ 02 47 45 42 04; adult/under 18yr/18-25yr €7.50/free/4.80; ☽ 9.30am-7pm Jul & Aug, 9.30am-6pm Apr-Jun & Sep, 10am-12.15pm & 2-5.15pm Oct-Mar) is harmonious and elegant, its stylised fortifications and turrets intended both as decoration and to indicate the rank of the owners. Inside, 14 less-than-spellbinding rooms and an extraordinary staircase with ornamented loggias on each floor are open to the public. Audioguide tours (€4) last 1½ hours; in July and August there are free 45-minute tours in English.

The bloodiest incident in the chateau's history occurred in 1418. During a visit to Azay, then a fortified castle, the crown prince (later King Charles VII) was insulted by the Burgundian guard. Enraged, he had the town burned and executed some 350 soldiers and officers. The present chateau was begun exactly a century later by Gilles Berthelot, one of François I's less-than-selfless financiers who, when the prospect of being audited and hanged drew near, fled abroad.

There are several pizzeria-type eateries just paces from the chateau.

Getting There & Away

Château d'Azay-le-Rideau is 26km southwest of Tours. The D84 and D17, on either side of the Indre, are a delight to cycle along.

Azay-le-Rideau's train station, 2.5km from the chateau, is on the SNCF bus and rail line (10 daily weekdays, five or six daily weekends) linking Tours (€4.60, 26 to 26 minutes) with Chinon (€2.10, 20 minutes).

CHÂTEAU DE LANGEAIS

Built in the late 1460s to cut off the most likely invasion route from Brittany, this **chateau** (☎ 02 47 96 72 60; adult/under 10yr/10-17yr €7.20/free/4; ☽ 9.30am-7pm July & Aug, 9.30am-6.30pm Feb-Jun & Sep-mid-Nov, 10am-5pm mid-Nov-Jan) presents two faces to the world. From the town, you see a 15th-century fortified castle – nearly windowless with machicolated ramparts (ie walls from which missiles and boiling liquids could be dropped on attackers) – rising forbiddingly from the drawbridge, which is still lowered each morning and raised each evening. The sections facing the courtyard, however, are outfitted with the large windows, dormers and decorative stonework characteristic of later chateaux designed for more refined living. The **ruined donjon** out back dates from around 944 and is the oldest such structure in France.

Langeais has a truly interesting interior. The unmodernised configuration of the rooms and the **period furnishings** – the most authentic in the valley – give you a pretty good idea of what the place looked like during the 15th and 16th centuries. The walls are decorated with fine but somewhat faded Flemish and Aubusson **tapestries** that are not anywhere near as colourful as the 15th-century tiles underfoot, restored in the 1800s. In one room, **wax figures** re-enact the marriage of King Charles VIII and Duchess Anne of Brittany, held here on 6 December 1491, which brought about the final union of France and Brittany. Up top, you can get a soldier's-eye view of the town (the chicken wire is there to keep visitors in and pigeons out).

The chateau is owned by the Institut de France, whose five constituent academies include the Académie Française, fierce guardian of the French language. So while visiting it's, um, like, totally OK to speak, ya know, rully bad English – but use anything other than the purest French (that includes the subjunctive!) and a tapestry may fall off the wall and smother you!

The chateau is right next to Langeais' pedestrianised town centre, where you'll find a number of restaurants and food shops.

Getting There & Away

Langeais is 14km west of Villandry and about 24km southwest of Tours. Its train station, 400m from the chateau, is on the line linking Tours (€4.50, 15 to 25 minutes, six to nine daily) with Savonnières (near Villandry; €2.30, 10 minutes, one to three daily) and Saumur (€6.50, 25 minutes, six to nine daily).

PAGODE DE CHANTELOUP

The 44m-high, Chinese-style **Pagode de Chanteloup** (☎ 02 47 57 20 97; www.pagode-chanteloup.com in French; adult/7-15yr/student €6.90/6/4.70; ⏲ 9.30am-7.30pm Jul & Aug, 10am-7pm Jun, 10am-6.30pm May & Sep, 10am-noon & 2-6pm Mon-Fri, 10am-6pm Sat & Sun Apr, 10am-5pm Sat, Sun, bank holidays & school holidays Oct-mid-Nov) is one of the Loire Valley's more pleasing follies. Built between 1775 and 1778, it combines contemporary French architectural fashions with elements from China, a subject of great fascination at the time. From the top visitors are rewarded with an impressive view of the Loire Valley.

This eccentric pagoda is a delightful picnic venue. *Paniers de pique-nique* (hampers; €10) bursting with regional treats are sold from May to September. You can hire a boat (per hour €6) to row your sweetheart around the lake (almost dry due to drought at the time of research) and there's a fun collection of old-fashioned wooden games to play for free.

The pagoda is about 2km south of Amboise. To get there, take rue Bretonneau and follow the signs to 'La Pagode'. Some buses on Touraine Fil Vert's C1 line between Amboise and Tours (€2.10) stop at 'Pagode'.

LOCHES
pop 6300

Perched on a rocky spur and surrounded by lush countryside, medieval Loches – with its louche history, cobbled streets and imposing fortified chateau – bills itself as the 'capital of southern Touraine'.

In the Citadelle, the 11th-century keep was built by Foulques Nerra (Falcon the Black; r 987–1040), while the feudal chateau witnessed Joan of Arc persuade Charles VII to march north to be crowned (June 1429). The royal court he consequently established here was notorious for its wild banquets, thrown primarily to woo the stunningly beautiful Agnès Sorel, she of the lush blonde hair and ravishing lashes, who tragically died at the age of just 30. The town's golden age ended in 1461 with the coronation of Louis XI, who turned the keep into a prison, a function it served until 1926.

Orientation & Information

The Ville Haute (Citadelle or Cité Médiévale) is south of the Ville Basse (lower town, also known as the Vieille Ville). Rue de la République, the main commercial street, is northwest of the Ville Basse, just outside the walls.

Post Office (rue Descartes) Has a Cyberposte.

Tourist Office (☎ 02 47 91 82 82; www.loches-touraine cotesud.com; place de la Marne; ⏲ 9am-12.30pm & 1.30-7pm Mon-Sat Apr-Sep, 10am-12.30pm & 2.30-6pm Mon-Fri, 9.30am-12.30pm & 2-6pm Sat Oct-Mar) Situated between the train station and the northeastern end of rue de la République. Sells a packet of detailed walking maps, *Paysages Lochois* (€1), many of whose circuits are also suitable for mountain bikes.

Sights

From 2 rue de la République, the 15th-century **Porte Picois** takes you into the Vieille Ville. Just inside is the Renaissance-style **Hôtel de Ville** (mid-1500s), from which cobblestone rue du Château leads up the hill to the forbidding **Porte Royale** (Royal Gate), flanked by two 13th-century towers, the only opening in the 2km wall encircling the citadel. To the left, a bit up the hill, is **Maison Lansyer** (adult/child €4.60/0.90; ⏲ Jun–early Nov and part of spring), a museum dedicated to the works of landscape painter Emmanuel Lansyer (1838–93).

At the southern end of the promontory is the 36m-high, Norman-era **Donjon** (adult/

12-18yr €5/3.50; 9am-7pm Apr-Sep, 9.30am-5pm Oct-Mar), the oldest structure within the citadel (built 1010–35). The notorious **Tour Ronde** (Round Tower) and **Martelet** were constructed under Louis XI as prisons. In pre-Revolutionary times, selected inmates were kept in solitary confinement in a 2.5-tonne cage, a replica of which is on display.

At the northern end of the Citadelle is the **Logis Royal** (Royal Residence; ☎ 02 47 59 01 32; adult/12-18yr €5/3.50, including the Donjon €7/4.50; same hours), built for Charles VIII and Anne de Bretagne in the 16th century. It is now hung with faded tapestries and copies of historically important paintings (though the painted wood triptych of 1485 is an original) and decorated with pikes, lances and instruments that may help visitors better understand the precise meaning of the word 'impale'.

The 15th-century white marble tomb of Agnès Sorel, which portrays her recumbent figure flanked by two sheep and two winged angels, is in **Collégiale St-Ours**, an 11th- and 12th-century church. Recent genetic testing has confirmed that Sorel – about whom Pope Pius II (in reference to Charles VII) said, 'at the table, in bed, at meetings-of-state, she always had to be at his side' – was a natural-born blond. But was she murdered? Paleopathologists detected high mercury levels in her remains, but this may have been the result of mercury salts administered by her doctors, perhaps to combat intestinal worms or ease difficulties during childbirth.

Sleeping & Eating

Hôtel de France (☎ 02 47 59 00 32; www.hoteldefranceloches.com; 6 rue Picois & 11 rue de la République; d €53-60) At the foot of the medieval district, this two-star hotel has a piano-equipped foyer and 17 rooms with marble fireplaces and cheap antique furnishings; many look out onto the quiet courtyard. The hotel's traditional French restaurant is elegant but doesn't put on airs. It is closed for lunch on Monday and Tuesday and for dinner on Sunday and Monday (except July and August). To get to the hotel's private parking, drive to the far end of the public car park whose entrance is on rue Alfred de Vigny.

CAK'T (pronounced kek-tee, as in 'cake-tea'; ☎ 02 47 59 39 35; 6 Grande Rue; lunch €12-15; noon-7pm Tue-Fri, 3-7pm Sat & Sun Sep-Jun, 10am-7pm Jul & Aug) A

quirky little tearoom with art on the walls and tempting cakes on the trolley. Proves that Loches can be truly delish.

For picnic supplies:

Atac supermarket (5 rue Descartes; 8.30am-12.45pm & 2.45-8pm Mon-Sat, no midday closure Wed & Sat, 9.30am-12.30pm Sun)

Outdoor market (rue de la République, perpendicular rue Descartes & nearby streets; 7am-3pm Wed, 7am-1pm Sat)

Getting There & Around

Loches is 67km southwest of Blois and 41km southeast of Tours. Trains and SNCF buses link the train station, across the River Indre from the tourist office, with Tours (€7.50, 45 to 65 minutes, 15 daily weekdays, five to eight daily weekends).

Bicycles can be hired from **Peugeot Cycles** (☎ 02 47 59 02 15; 7 rue des Moulins; hybrid/mountain-bike hire per day €8/12; 9am-noon & 2-7pm Tue-Sat), which is 150m south of the tourist office.

CHINON

pop 8700

Chinon's massive 400m-long fortress looms above the town's medieval quarter, whose narrow cobblestone streets are lined with ancient houses, many made of whitish-tan tufa stone. The contrast between the triangular, black slate roofs and the tufa, some of it worn smooth by centuries of rain, gives the town its distinctive appearance. The Humanist author François Rabelais (1483–1553), whose works include *Pantagruel* and *Gargantua* (names you'll see around town), apparently grew up in Chinon.

The Forêt de Chinon (Chinon Forest), a wooded area ideal for walking and cycling, begins a couple of kilometres northeast of town and stretches along the D751 all the way to Azay-le-Rideau. Chinon's vineyards stretch north and south of town on both sides of the Vienne.

Orientation & Information

Rue Haute St-Maurice, the main street of the hillside medieval quarter, becomes rue Voltaire as you move east. The train station is 1km east of the commercial hub, place du Général de Gaulle (also called place de l'Hôtel de Ville).

Laundrette (40 rue Jeanne d'Arc; 7am-9pm)
Post Office (80 quai Jeanne d'Arc)

Stic (60 quai Jeanne d'Arc; per hour €3; 🕙 10am-noon &
2-7pm Tue-Sat) Internet access during business hours.

Tourist Office (☎ 02 47 93 17 85; www.chinon.com;
place de Hofheïm; 🕙 10am-7pm May-Sep, 10am-noon &
2-6pm except Sun & holidays Oct-Apr) Has a free walking
tour brochure and details on kayaking, and can arrange
hot-air balloon flights (see p419).

Sights

CHÂTEAU DE CHINON

Perched atop a rocky spur high above the
River Vienne, this huge, mostly ruined
medieval **chateau** (☎ 02 47 93 13 45; adult/student
€6/4.50; 🕙 9am-7pm Apr-Sep, 9.30am-5pm Oct-Mar)
consists of three sections separated by
waterless moats: the 12th-century **Fort St-
Georges**, which protected the chateau's vulnerable eastern flank and is being excavated
by archaeologists through 2008; the **Château
du Milieu** (the Middle Castle), some of whose
structures will soon get new roofs; and, at
the western tip, the 13th-century **Fort du
Coudray**.

After crossing the **dry moat** – once spanned
by a drawbridge – and entering the Château du Milieu, you pass under the 14th-

century **Tour de l'Horloge** (Clock Tower),
whose top offers a superb panorama. Four
rooms inside are dedicated to Joan of Arc,
who in 1429 picked out Charles VII from
among a crowd of courtiers in the Château
du Milieu's **Salle du Trône** (Throne Room).
Other parts of the almost undecorated **Logis
Royal** (Royal Apartments), built during the
12th, 14th and 15th centuries, are in slightly
better condition.

To get to the chateau, walk up the hill to
the western end of rue du Puits des Bancs
(this route may be closed during the excavations). By car, av François Mitterand (the
continuation of the D751 from Tours) will
take you to the rear of the chateau.

QUARRY TOUR & WINE TASTING

Underneath the ruins of the chateau are the
Caves Painctes de Chinon (☎ 02 47 93 30 44; impasse
des Caves Painctes; admission €3; 🕙 guided tours 11am,
3pm, 4.30pm & 6pm, Tue-Sun Jul–mid-Sep), former
quarries converted into wine cellars during the 15th century and hardly touched
since. Tours of the caves, which are run
by the Confrérie des Bons Entonneurs

THE LOIRE VALLEY

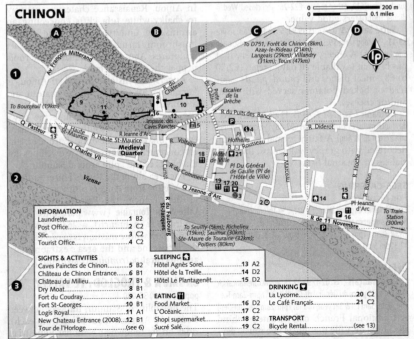

CHINON

0 —— 200 m
0 —— 0.1 miles

To D751, Forêt de Chinon (8km),
Azay-le-Rideau (21km);
Langeais (29km); Villandry
(31km); Tours (47km)

Escalier
de la
Brèche

To Bourgueil (19km)

Impasse des
Caves Painctes

R du Puits des Bancs

R Diderot

Medieval
Quarter

Pl
Hofheïm

Hôtel
de Ville

Pl Du Général
de Gaulle (Pl de
l'Hôtel de Ville)

Vienne

R Jeanne d'Arc

Pl Jeanne
d'Arc

To Train
Station
(300m)

R de 11 Novembre

To Seuilly (5km); Richelieu
(19km); Saumur (30km);
Ste-Maure de Touraine (32km);
Poitiers (80km)

INFORMATION	
Laundrette	1 B2
Post Office	2 C2
Stic	3 C2
Tourist Office	4 C2

SIGHTS & ACTIVITIES	
Caves Painctes de Chinon	5 B2
Château de Chinon Entrance	6 B1
Château du Milieu	7 B1
Dry Moat	8 B1
Fort du Coudray	9 A1
Fort St-Georges	10 B1
Logis Royal	11 B1
New Chateau Entrance (2008)	12 B1
Tour de l'Horloge	(see 6)

SLEEPING	
Hôtel Agnès Sorel	13 A2
Hôtel de la Treille	14 D2
Hôtel Le Plantagenêt	15 D2

EATING	
Food Market	16 D2
L'Océanic	17 C2
Shopi supermarket	18 B2
Sucré Salé	19 C2

DRINKING	
La Lycorne	20 C2
Le Café Français	21 C2

TRANSPORT	
Bicycle Rental	(see 13)

Rabelaisiens (www.entonneursrabelaisiens .com), a brotherhood of local wine growers, include a free glass of a local vintage.

Sleeping

Hôtel de la Treille (☎ 02 47 93 07 71; fax 02 47 93 94 10; 4 place Jeanne d'Arc; d €38-40, with washbasin €30) Simple but rustic, with a 14th-century stone staircase leading to five cosy rooms.

Hôtel Le Plantagenêt (☎ 02 47 93 36 92; www .hotel-plantagenet.com in French; 12 place Jeanne d'Arc; d €48-65; ✗ ⊠) A family-run two-star hotel whose 32 well-kept rooms, all with sparkling bathrooms, occupy three adjacent buildings, two of them from the 1800s. The cheaper rooms are smallish.

Hôtel Agnès Sorel (☎ 02 47 93 04 37; www.agnes -sorel.com; 4 quai Pasteur; d €47-75) An especially friendly riverside hotel with good wheelchair access and 10 lovingly kept rooms, some with balconies and delightful river views, others with decks, and all with spotless, all-tile bathrooms.

Eating

The restaurant of **Hôtel de la Treille** (☎ 02 47 93 07 71; fax 02 47 93 94 10; 4 place Jeanne d'Arc; weekday lunch menu €12, other menus €22-26; ⊗ closed Wed & dinner Thu) offers good value.

Sucré Salé (☎ 02 47 93 99 93; 5 rue Rabelais; mains €9-13; ⊗ food served 9.30am-11.30pm Mon-Sat, also open Sun Jul & Aug) A cheery and playful eatery that has brunch (available all day), *crêpes* (€2.50 to €8), meat dishes and *chaud' patats* (sautéed or baked potatoes served with meat and/or cheese).

L'Océanic (☎ 02 47 93 44 55; 13 rue Rabelais; weekday lunch menu €15, other menus €22-50; ⊗ closed dinner Sun except Jul & Aug) A fairly formal restaurant, decorated with grapey wall lamps, that specialises in seasonal fish.

SELF-CATERING

For picnickers:

Food market (place Jeanne d'Arc; ⊗ Thu morning)

Shopi supermarket (22 place du Général de Gaulle; ⊗ 7.30am-1pm & 2.30-7.30pm Mon-Sat, 8.30am-12.30pm Sun)

Drinking

Le Café Français (☎ 02 47 93 32 78; www.cafefrancais.fr in French; 37 place du Général de Gaulle; ⊗ 6pm-2am Tue-Thu, 6pm-3am Fri & Sat year-round, 7pm-2am Sun Jun-Sep) A traditional French café situated behind the Hôtel de Ville that hosts live music several times a month, sponsors discussions of issues of public import and shows footy and rugby on a giant TV.

La Lycorne (☎ 02 47 93 94 94; 15 rue Rabelais; ⊗ 10.30am-1am Mon-Sat, closed Mon Oct or Nov-Apr) A large, lively pub-brasserie with billiard tables and a €10.50 lunch *menu*. Adorned with an old British phone box and flags from several English-speaking islands.

Getting There & Around

Chinon is 47km southwest of Tours, 21km southwest of Azay-le-Rideau and 80km north of Poitiers.

From the train station, 300m east of place Jeanne d'Arc, trains or SNCF buses (10 daily weekdays, four or five daily weekends) go to Tours (€7.70, 45 to 70 minutes) and Azay-le-Rideau (€4.10, 20 minutes).

The Hôtel Agnès Sorel can arrange **bicycle rental** (per half-/full-day €8/14) for guests and nonguests alike. The tourist office has details on other bike rental options.

ANJOU

In Anjou, Renaissance chateaux give way to chalky-white tufa cliffs concealing an astonishing underworld of wine cellars, mushroom farms and monumental art sculptures. Above ground, black slate roofs pepper the vine-rich land.

Angers, the historic capital of Anjou, is famous for its fortified hilltop chateau and a stunning medieval tapestry. Architectural gems in Anjou's crown include the city's cathedral and, to the southeast, the Romanesque Abbaye de Fontevraud. Europe's highest concentration of troglodyte dwellings dot the banks of the Loire around Saumur.

The area along the Rivers Loire, Authion and Vienne from Angers southeast to Azay-le-Rideau form the **Parc Naturel Régional Loire-Anjou-Touraine** (www.parc-loire-anjou -touraine.fr in French), a 2530-sq-km regional park whose mission is to protect both the landscape and the area's extraordinary architectural *patrimoine* (patrimony).

SAUMUR & TROGLODYTE VALLEY

pop (Saumur) 30,000

The notability of Saumur, midway between Tours and Angers (about 65km from each), rides on its renowned National Equestrian

School, stabled on the town's western outskirts. In the town centre, uniformed personnel from the cavalry school – stationed here since 1599 – buzz around town on bicycles, creating an old-fashioned atmosphere.

During the Revolution, *habitations troglodytes* – caves carved into the chalky bluffs that dominate the river banks around Saumur – provided a refuge for the local population. Today they are used to store wine, grow mushrooms and even bake *fouaces* (Loire Valley pita bread).

You can download maps of Saumur-area hikes at www.saumur-rando.com (in French).

Orientation & Information

Saumur's main commercial streets are rue Franklin Roosevelt and its southeastern continuation, rue d'Orléans, which lead inland from pont Cessart (a trans-Loire bridge); and perpendicular rue St-Jean, which is pedestrianised.

The **Saumur Tourist Office** (☎ 02 41 40 20 60; www.saumur-tourisme.com; 🕑 9.15am-7pm Mon-Sat, 10.30am-12.30pm & 2.30-5.30pm Sun mid-May–mid-Oct; 9.15am-12.30pm & 2-6pm Mon-Sat, 10am-noon Sun mid-Oct–Apr) is in the Theatre building, facing the river.

Sights & Activities

The south bank of the Loire is dominated by the **Château de Saumur** (☎ 02 41 40 24 40; adult/under 11yr €2/1; 🕑 gardens open 10am-1pm & 2-5.30pm Wed-Mon Apr-Sep), a stunning, fairy-tale castle cornered by turreted towers. It was built under Louis XI starting in 1246 and has served as a dungeon, a fortress and a country residence. In 2001 part of the chateau's western ramparts suddenly collapsed, necessitating complicated and costly repairs

that have left the structure closed at least through mid-2007.

The **École Nationale d'Équitation** (National Equestrian School; ☎ 02 41 53 50 60; www.cadrenoir.fr; route de Marson), 3km west of the town centre in St-Hilaire-St-Florent, trains instructors and riders at competition level, prepares France's Olympic teams and is home to the elite Cadre Noir (below). The school, which sports Europe's largest indoor riding arena, can be visited on guided **tours** (adult/under 12yr morning €7/4, afternoon €5/3; 🕑 every 20 minutes 9.30-11am & 2-4pm Tue-Sat Apr–early Oct). On morning tours you get to see a Cadre Noir training session. Advance reservations are essential; tours are held in English when there are enough Anglophones.

Nearby **mushroom farms** recycle the 10 tonnes of droppings dumped daily by the school's 400 horses. The **Musée du Champignon** (☎ 02 41 50 31 55; www.musee-du-champignon .com in French; route de Gennes; adult/child/student €7/4.50/5.50; 🕑 10am-7pm Feb–mid-Nov), tucked in a cave at the western edge of St-Hilaire-St-Florent, is a living example of the area's thriving button-mushroom industry, which occupies 800km of Saumurois caves and accounts for 65% of national production.

Sleeping & Eating

Camping l'Île d'Offard (☎ 02 41 40 30 00; www.cvtloi sirs.com in French; rue de Verden; sites incl car parking €14.50-22.50; 🕑 Mar-Oct) On an island in the middle of the Loire 1.3km from the centre of town.

Centre International de Séjour Île d'Offard (☎ 02 41 40 30 00; dm incl breakfast in 8-person room €14.50, s/d with shower €22/31; 🕑 reception 24hrs, closed Nov-Feb; 🖳) A hostel built in classic early 1980s style next to the camping ground. The rooms are institutional but well-tended. Kitchen facilities are available.

CADRE NOIR

Three moves set the Cadre Noir apart from its equestrian counterparts in Vienna: the *croupade*, which requires the horse to stretch its hind legs 45° into the air while its front legs stay on the ground; the *courbette*, which sees the horse's front legs raised and tucked firmly into its body; and the demanding *cabriole*, which elevates the horse into the air in a powerful four-legged leap. These acrobatic feats, far from being crude or cruel, are considered the height of grace, elegance and classicism. They are achieved after 5½ years of training, which starts when a horse is three years old. Daily training sessions last 1½ hours; the horse is then untacked, washed down, dried and boxed for the remaining 22 hours of the day.

A black cap and jacket, gold spurs and three golden wings on the rider's whip are the distinctive trademarks of the elite Cadre Noir rider.

THE LOIRE VALLEY

ABSINTHE: NO LONGER ABSENT (IN FRENCH IT RHYMES)

During the Belle Époque, absinthe was the drink of choice among Europe's bohemians, and came to define the era and its mystique. Artists painted absinthe drinkers, often while under its influence, and poets sung its praises – even as the medical profession blamed it for causing convulsions, insanity and death. Temperance campaigners amplified its terrifying reputation, claiming that drinkers were sure to go 'straight to the madhouse or the courthouse', and some went so far as to warn that the drink would bring about racial degeneration.

Following popular agitation – led, in part, by postphylloxera vintners eager to get back their wine and cognac customers – Swiss voters banned the 'Green Fairy' in 1910; the US federal government outlawed it two years later (distillation and sales, though not possession and consumption, remain illegal to this day); and the French government proscribed the stuff during WWI out of fear that absinthe-befuddled French soldiers would be no match for their robust German enemies.

In the 1990s, a number of dedicated absintheurs decided to reverse-engineer the vivid green liqueur, chemically analysing century-old bottles that somehow survived the decades of suppression. The trick was to rediscover the secret process by which anise, fennel, wormwood (Artemisia absinthium) – notorious for containing a toxic and reputedly psychoactive substance called thujone – and other herbs are soaked in alcohol, creating a bitter macerate that is then distilled.

The result of their efforts is that absinthe is back – and Saumur has become a centre of absinthe distillation thanks to the hissing copper alembics of **Distillerie Combier** (☎ 02 41 40 23 00; www.combier.fr; 48 rue Beaurepaire; adult €3; ☯ tours 10.30am, 2.30pm, 4pm & 5.30pm Jun-Sep, also noon Jul & Aug, closed Tue Jun & Sep, 10.30am, 2.30pm & 4.30pm Wed-Sun Apr, Mar & Oct), which rents out its century-old facilities to small-scale distillers. The factory, parts of which were designed by Eiffel, can be visited on a bilingual guided tour; ask nicely and you'll probably be able to sample some genuine absinthe.

THE LOIRE VALLEY

Cristal Hôtel (☎ 02 41 51 09 54; www.cristal-hotel .fr; 10-12 place de la République; d €40-68) Facing the river next to the Hôtel de Ville, this two-star place, completely renovated in 2006, has 22 rooms and four small apartments, some with *Life of Brian*-style balconies, others with low hardwood lintels (people were shorter back in the 1700s). The more you pay the larger the room and the better the view. The ground-floor **restaurant** (lunch menus €9.50-15.30; ☯ closed dinner Sun; ☒) is brasserie-style.

Château de Verrieres (☎ 02 41 38 05 15; http: //chateau-verrieres.com; 53 rue d'Alsace, Saumur; r €100-240, dinner €38; ☒) An elegant chateau in the southwest of town set in a tree-filled 1.6-hectare English park. It was built in 1890 and inside, the furnishings and décor remain pretty much as they were then – graceful, refined and ornate.

There are a number of restaurants at place St-Pierre (near the northeastern end of rue St-Jean). An Atac supermarket is at 6 rue Franklin Roosevelt.

Getting There & Around

See p453 for details on bus options from Angers.

Agglobus (☎ 08 20 50 77 82) line 1 links Saumur with Fontevraud via Dampierre and Souzay (30 minutes, four daily Monday to Friday when school is in session). This service is available 'on demand' (ie you need to phone ahead) on Saturday and during school holidays.

Saumur is on the train line between Tours (€9.60, 29 to 52 minutes, 10 to 16 daily) and Angers (€7.10, 20 minutes, five to nine daily).

Détours de Loire (☎ 02 41 53 01 01; 2 rue David d'Angers; ☯ 9-12.30pm & 2-6.30pm Mon-Sat, 10am-1pm & 6-7pm Sun Easter–1 Nov, shorter hrs Oct) rents out bikes (see p419 and, for prices, p437).

EAST OF SAUMUR

Fruity Saumur-Champigny red wine (www .producteurs-de-saumur-champigny.fr; in French), the most hallowed Saumurois appellation, can be sampled at various cellars along the riverside D947 between **Dampierre-sur-Loire** and **Montsoreau**, whose many troglodytic houses are perched on the cliff face. The attractive village of **Candes-sur-Martin** is situated right where the Vienne and the Loire conflow.

The breathtaking Romanesque **Abbaye Royale de Fontevraud** (☎ 02 41 51 71 41; www .abbaye-fontevraud.com; adult/under 18yr/18-25yr €6.50/free/4.50, during expositions €7.90/free/5.90; ☉ 9am-6.15pm Jun-Sep, 10am-btwn 5 & 5.30pm Oct-May), 4km south of Montsoreau in the centre of Fontevraud-l'Abbaye, forms the largest monastic ensemble in France. Until it closed in 1793, it was unique in that its nuns and monks were governed by a woman: the abbess. Between 1804 and 1963 the complex served as a prison.

Inside the abbey church are the **tombs** – decorated with polychrome recumbent effigies – of some extraordinarily famous Plantagenets: Henry II, king of England from 1154 to 1189; his wife Eleanor of Aquitaine, described by the Britannica as 'perhaps the most powerful woman in 12th-century Europe'; their son Richard the Lion Heart; and Henry II's daughter-in-law, Isabelle of Angouleme. The conical kitchen, built entirely of stone to make it fireproof, looks like the tip of an Apollo space rocket. In the Middle Ages each of the gardens had its role growing edible, aromatic and medicinal plants.

Prieuré St-Lazare (☎ 02 41 51 73 16; www.hotelfp -fontevraud.com; d €60-112; ☉ closed Nov–early Apr), a converted priory in the grounds of the Abbaye de Fontevraud, has 52 two- and three-star rooms that, despite their 12th-century origins, are modern and comfortable. The attached restaurant, **Le Cloître** (buffet menu €18, other menus €37-48), is well-regarded for its gastronomic menu and wine list.

WEST OF SAUMUR

Caves riddle this stretch of the Loire, dubbed the 'Troglodyte Valley'. **St-Georges des Sept Voies**, 23km northwest of Saumur, is home to the **Hélice Terrestre de l'Orbière** (☎ 02 41 57 95 92; Espace d'Art Plastique Contemporain; adult/child €4/2; ☉ 11am-8pm May-Sep, 2-6pm Wed-Sun Oct-Apr), a startling piece of monumental art sculpted underground by local artist Jacques Warminski (1946–96). The screw-shaped subterranean gallery, duplicated in reverse above ground, can be explored on foot.

In **Gennes**, 8km east of St-Georges, there's a **Gallo-Roman amphitheatre** (☎ 02 41 51 55 04; adult/child €3/1; ☉ 10am-6.30pm Sun-Fri Jul & Aug, 3-6.30pm Sun Apr-Jun & Sep), built around AD 150, which in summer hosts lively, bloodless re-enactments of the spectacles once staged

by the Romans. From here, the scenic D69 cuts south through forests to **Doué-la-Fontaine** (population 7200), an ideal base for exploring the Troglodyte Valley. In the town **zoo** (☎ 02 41 59 18 58; www.zoodoue.fr in French; adult/3-10yr €14/8; ☉ 9 or 10am-6.30 or 7.30pm approx Feb-Nov), off route de Cholet (D960), giraffes hang out in former quarries and crocodiles bathe in pools inside clammy caves. Other troglodytic sites here include **Les Perrières** (☎ 02 41 59 71 29; 545 rue des Perrières; adult/child €4.40/2.75; ☉ 10am-12.30pm & 2-7pm May–mid-Oct), where stone composed of ancient shells was quarried in the 18th century; and the **Cave aux Sarcophages** (☎ 02 41 59 24 95; adult/child €4.20/2.70; ☉ 2-7pm early May–Sep), a Merovingian mine where sarcophagi were produced from the 6th to the 9th centuries.

See p453 for details on **Anjou Bus** (☎ 08 20 16 00 49) services from Angers to Doué-la-Fontaine. Anjou Bus line 23 links Saumur with Doué (30 minutes; two or three daily Monday to Saturday).

The abandoned troglodytic village of **Rochemenier** (☎ 02 41 59 18 15; www.troglodyte.info; adult/student €4.70/2.50; ☉ 9.30am-7pm Apr–1 Nov, 2-6pm Sat, Sun & holidays Nov, Feb & Mar) is about 6km north of Doué along the D761.

ANGERS
pop 151,000

The River Maine city of Angers, which dates to the time of the Gauls, is dominated by its mighty medieval chateau, whose interior would be eminently skippable were it not for the presence of one of the great masterpieces of medieval weaving. The city centre is pleasantly walkable and has a number of flowery public parks – perfect for a relaxing picnic lunch.

Orientation

Angers' historic quarter, on the eastern bank of the Maine, is bordered by blvd Ayrault and its continuation, blvd Carnot, on the northeast; blvd du Maréchal Foch on the southeast; and blvd du Roi René to the southwest. The commercial centre is southeast of the cathedral. Two lovely parks, Jardin de la Préfecture and Jardin du Mail, are a few hundred metres south and east of the city centre, respectively.

The train station is located 800m south of the place du Président Kennedy, the square at the northwestern end of blvd du Roi René.

THE LOIRE VALLEY

ANGERS

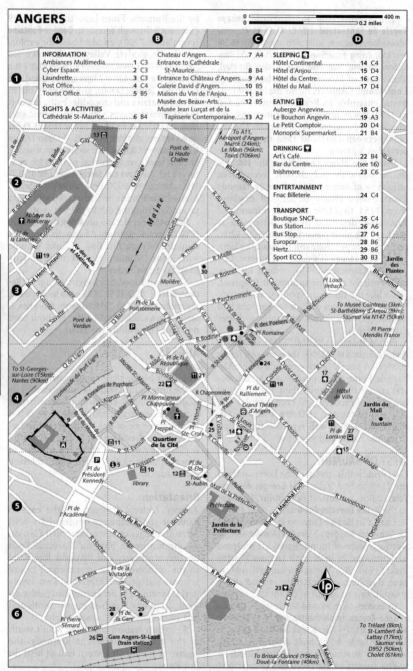

INFORMATION
Ambiances Multimedia................1 C3
Cyber Espace................................2 C3
Laundrette....................................3 C3
Post Office...................................4 C4
Tourist Office..............................5 B5

SIGHTS & ACTIVITIES
Cathédrale St-Maurice.................6 B4

Chateau d'Angers.........................7 A4
Entrance to Cathédrale
   St-Maurice................................8 B4
Entrance to Château d'Angers....9 A4
Galerie David d'Angers..............10 B5
Maison du Vin de l'Anjou..........11 B4
Musée des Beaux-Arts................12 B5
Musée Jean Lurçat et de la
   Tapisserie Contemporaine......13 A2

SLEEPING
Hôtel Continental......................14 C4
Hôtel d'Anjou............................15 D4
Hôtel du Centre.........................16 C3
Hôtel du Mail............................17 D4

EATING
Auberge Angevine.....................18 C4
Le Bouchon Angevin.................19 A3
Le Petit Comptoir.....................20 D4
Monoprix Supermarket..............21 B4

DRINKING
Art's Café..................................22 B4
Bar du Centre......................(see 16)
Inishmore.................................23 C6

ENTERTAINMENT
Fnac Billeterie..........................24 C4

TRANSPORT
Boutique SNCF.........................25 C4
Bus Station...............................26 A6
Bus Stop...................................27 D4
Europcar...................................28 B6
Hertz..29 B6
Sport ECO................................30 B3

THE LOIRE VALLEY

Information

The tourist office handles currency exchange but does not accept US$50 or US$100 bills; the commission is €4. There are commercial banks on blvd du Maréchal Foch.

Ambiances Multimedia (10 rue Bodinier; per hr €3; 9am-10pm Mon-Thu, 9am-midnight Fri & Sat, 3-8pm Sun) Internet access.

Cyber Espace (25 rue de la Roë; per hr €3; 9am-10pm Mon-Thu, 9am-midnight Fri & Sat, 2-8pm Sun & holidays) Internet access.

Laundrette (2 rue St-Laud; 7am-9pm)

Post Office (1 rue Franklin Roosevelt) Has a Cyberposte and exchanges currency.

Tourist Office (02 41 23 50 00; www.angersloire tourisme.com; 7 place du Président Kennedy; 9am-7pm Mon-Sat, 10am-6pm Sun & holidays May-Sep, 2-6pm Mon, 9am-6pm Tue-Sat, 10am-1pm Sun Oct-Apr)

Sights & Activities

CHÂTEAU D'ANGERS

Other than the view, the only good reason to pay to get into this 13th-century **fortress** (02 41 86 48 77; 2 promenade du Bout du Monde; adult/under 18yr/18-25yr €7.50/free/4.80; 9.30am-6.30pm May–early Sep, 10am-5.30pm early Sep–Apr) – whose feudal features are, in any case, best admired from outside – is to see the magnificent **Tenture de l'Apocalypse** (Apocalypse tapestry), a 101m-long series of 70 tapestries commissioned by Louis I, Duke of Anjou in 1375 to illustrate the *Revelation to John*, the last book of the New Testament. Among the scenes – all of them resolutely medieval in architecture and dress – are those featuring especially nasty goings-on: St Michel doing battle with a seven-headed dragon (panel 34); the dragon vomiting from all seven mouths as he pursues the Woman (panel 35); and the fall of Bablyon (panel 66), which looks like a medieval version of King Kong.

From June to August free guided tours begin at 10.30am and 4pm. There are plans to introduce free audioguides. *Tapestry of the Apocalypse at Angers: Front and Bank* (€33), available in the gift shop, explains all, scene by scene. Ticket sales end 45 minutes before closing.

CATHÉDRALE ST-MAURICE

Angers' austere, mostly 12th- to 13th-century **Cathédrale St-Maurice** (8.30am-7pm Apr-Nov, 8.30am-5.30pm Dec-Mar), in the centre of the historic **Quartier de la Cité**, has a striking Norman porch and nave (mid-1100s); the latter's three convex vaults, forming a perfect square, are outstanding examples of mid-12th-century Angevin (Plantagenet) vaulting. The **stained-glass windows** date from the 12th to the 16th centuries. In the 18th century a humungous organ was erected inside the western façade, facing the very baroque high altar (1758). Long home to the Apocalypse tapestry, the cathedral continues to exhibit religiously-themed tapestries.

The square in front of the cathedral is linked to the river by a monumental staircase, **Montée St-Maurice**. Behind the cathedral on place Ste-Croix is the **Maison d'Adam** (c 1500), a half-timbered house on whose ornate façade wooden sculptures run riot. The Tree of Life, on the corner, used to be flanked by Adam and Eve (another lovey-dovey couple can be seen nearby).

MUSÉE DES BEAUX-ARTS

In the **Fine Arts Museum** (02 41 05 38 00; 14 rue du Musée; adult/under 18yr/student €4/free/3, during special expositions €6/free/5; 10am-7pm Jun-Sep, noon or 1-6pm Tue-Sun Oct-May) objects illustrating the history of Angers are gorgeously displayed on the ground floor. Upstairs, the paintings – none of them consciousness-changing but many of them excellent – include some compelling Italian works from the first half of the 1800s, such as the dramatic, Dante-inspired *Paolo et Francesca* by Jean-August-Dominique Ingres, in which Francesca's elderly and deformed husband, a homicidal look on his face, discovers his wife in the arms of his younger brother Paoli (in one of the two red rooms). Audioguides are being prepared.

GALERIE DAVID D'ANGERS

Larger-than-life sculptures by the Angers-born sculptor David d'Angers (1788–1856) are displayed in **Galerie David d'Angers** (02 41 05 38 90; 33bis rue Toussaint; adult/under 18yr/student €4/free/3; 10am-7pm Jun-Sep, 10am-noon & 2-6pm Tue-Sun Oct-May), housed in a 12th-century abbey church transformed into contemporary architecture in the early 1980s. The cloister next door leads to a garden overlooked by Nikki de St-Phalle's colourful *Serpent Tree*, a children's playground (behind the library) and the Musée des Beaux-Arts.

MUSÉE JEAN LURÇAT ET DE LA TAPISSERIE CONTEMPORAINE

Ensconced in the opulent, Gothic-vaulted sick wards of a one-time hospital (1180–1865), the **Jean Lurçat Museum of Contemporary Tapestry** (☎ 02 41 24 18 45; 6 blvd Arago; adult/under 18yr €4/free; ☯ 10am-7pm approx Jun-Sep, 10am-noon & 2-6pm Tue-Sun approx Oct-May) showcases monumental 20th-century tapestries by Jean Lurçat, Thomas Gleb and others.

MUSÉE COINTREAU

At the **Cointreau Museum** (☎ 02 41 31 50 50; www .cointreau.com; blvd des Bretonnières; adult/12-17yr €5.50/2.60; tours ☯ 10.30am, 1.30pm, 2.30pm, 3.30pm & 4.30pm Jul & Aug, 10.30am & 3pm Mon-Sat plus additional tour 4.30pm Sun May, Jun, Sep & Oct, 3pm Mon-Sat plus additional tour 4.30pm Sun Nov-Apr) you won't discover the top-secret recipe for the famous orange liqueur – every bottle of which is made right here – but you will find yourself inhaling some pretty intoxicating aromas. The 1.30pm tour in July and August is in English.

The museum is off the ring road to the east of Angers. By bus, take No 7 from the train station.

WINE TASTING

The **Maison du Vin de l'Anjou** (☎ 02 41 88 81 13; www.valdeloire-wines.com in French; 5bis place du Président Kennedy; admission free; ☯ 9 or 9.30am-1pm & 3-6.30pm Tue-Sat Mar–mid-Jun, also open Sun morning Apr-Sep, closed mid-Jan–Feb), facing the chateau, is a good place to sample Anjou and Saumur wines.

Sleeping

Hôtel du Centre (☎ 02 41 87 45 07; 12 rue St-Laud; d approx €35-50) On a pretty pedestrian street, this 14-room cheapie has newly renovated rooms above a very popular bar.

Hôtel du Mail (☎ 02 41 25 05 25; www.hotel-du -mail.com; 8-10 rue des Ursules; s/d from €48/55) This almost-boutique hotel, behind the Hôtel de Ville, occupies a lovely 17th-century convent set around a quiet courtyard. The 30 rooms are large, well-furnished and charming. Excellent value.

Hôtel Continental (☎ 02 41 86 94 94; www.hotel lecontinental.com; 12-14 rue Louis de Romain; s/d €49/62; ☒ ☯) Right in the centre of town, this reliable two-star hotel with good wheelchair access has a stylised 1920s logo and 25 rooms in happy pastels.

Hôtel d'Anjou (☎ 02 41 21 12 11; www.hoteldanjou .fr; 1 blvd du Maréchal Foch; d €114-168; ☒ ☯) With an ornate lobby reminiscent of times long past, this three-star, Best Western–affiliated hotel occupies a grand mid-19th-century building. Some of the 53 refined rooms, all of them spacious and sound-proofed, have his-and-hers sinks.

Eating

Restaurants are sprinkled around the city centre, especially along the streets near place Romain, though there are also several good-value places across the river. Cheap eats can be found southeast of the centre along rue Bressigny.

Le Bouchon Angevin (☎ 02 41 24 77 97; 44 rue Beaurepaire; lunch menus €9.90-11.50, dinner menu €16.50; ☯ Tue-Sat) A French restaurant whose reasonably priced bourgeois cuisine has given it a loyal local following. It has an impressive wine list and serves about 15 wines by the glass (€2.60). Worth the walk across the river.

Le Petit Comptoir (☎ 02 41 88 81 57; 40 rue David d'Angers; lunch menus €17-19, dinner menu €28; ☯ Tue-Sun) A modern, elegant place on two levels whose traditional French cuisine is made only with fresh local ingredients. Considered by some to be Angers' best restaurant.

Auberge Angevine (☎ 02 41 20 10 40; 9 rue Cordelle; lunch menu €12, set menus Tue & Wed/Thu/Fri/Sat €17.50-26/21-27/29/38; ☯ Tue-Sat) Wenches and knaves in medieval costume serve up platters of roasted pork and goblets of red wine – and all-you-can-eat *fouaces* (Loire Valley pitas) – in this themed restaurant that doesn't take itself too seriously. The venue is a cavernous old chapel, with wooden benches and candelabras. A medieval wardrobe is available for adults and kids alike. On Thursday, Friday and Saturday nights there are jesters and live medieval music – book in advance.

SELF-CATERING

Edibles are available at the **Monoprix supermarket** (across from 59 rue Plantagenêt; ☯ 8.30am-9pm Mon-Sat).

Drinking & Entertainment

Cultural options appear in *Angers Poche*, a free weekly guide available at the tourist office. Tickets are on sale at the **FNAC billeterie** (☎ 08 92 68 36 22; 25-29 rue Lenepveu; ☯ 10am-7pm Mon-Sat).

There are a number of drinking spots near place Romaine.

Bar du Centre (☎ 02 41 87 45 07; 12 rue St-Laud; ☺ 9am-2am) A very popular bar with comfy leather sofas.

Art's Café (☎ 02 41 86 70 53; 66 rue Baudrière; ☺ 2-9pm Mon, 11am-2am Tue-Sat) A modern, arty place that attracts a pretty cool crowd.

Inishmore (☎ 02 41 88 10 09; 20 rue Chateaugontier; ☺ 5pm-2am Mon-Sat) A genuine Irish bar (the *patron* hails from Roscommon) with football and rugby on the telly and live traditional Irish music on most Fridays at 9pm or 10pm. A favoured hangout of English-speaking students.

Getting There & Away
Angers is 107km west of Tours and 90km east of Nantes.

AIR
Aéroport d'Angers-Marcé (☎ 02 41 33 50 00; www .angers.aeroport.fr), 24km northeast of the centre in Marcé (off the A11), has flights to Cork, Luton, Manchester and Southampton.

BUS
Regional services from the new bus station (next to the train station) are operated by **Anjou Bus** (☎ 08 20 16 00 49; www.cg49.fr/services /voyager/anjou-bus in French; ☺ 6.15am-7pm Mon-Sat). Bus 9 goes to Brissac-Quincé (€1.45, 30 minutes, five to seven Monday to Saturday) and Doué-la-Fontaine (€5, 55 minutes, five or six daily Monday to Saturday); buses 7, 18 and 18B will take you to St-Georges-sur-Loire (€1.45, 40 minutes, seven daily Monday to Saturday); and buses 5 (along the south bank of the Loire) and 11 (along the north bank) serve Saumur (€6.80, 1½ hours, five daily Monday to Saturday).

TRAIN
Angers' glass and steel train station, Gare Angers-St-Laud, has direct trains to Nantes (€13.50, 40 minutes, half-hourly Monday to Saturday, hourly Sunday and holidays), Saumur (€7.10, 20 minutes, five to nine daily) and Tours (€14.70/17.60 for a non-TGV/ TGV, about 1¼ hours, nine to 14 daily). TGVs link Angers with Paris' Gare Montparnasse (€57.10, 1½ hours, hourly).

Tickets can be purchased in the city centre at the **Boutique SNCF** (5 rue Chaperonnière; ☺ 1.30-7pm Mon, 9.30am-7pm Tue-Fri, to 6.30pm Sat).

Getting Around
In 2009 Angers is supposed to get its first tram line, so be prepared for traffic snafus until then.

BICYCLE
The tourist office rents bicycles from June to September. **Sport ECO** (☎ 02 41 87 07 77; 45 rue Maillé; per day/weekend/week €13/25/65; ☺ 10am-12.30 & 2-7pm Tue-Sat) hires bicycles.

BUS
Local buses are run by **Keolis Angers** (☎ 02 41 33 64 64; www.cotra.fr), whose main hub is at place Lorraine.

CAR
Car-rental companies facing the train station:
Europcar (☎ 02 41 87 87 10; place de la Gare)
Hertz (☎ 02 41 88 15 16; rue Denis Papin)

AROUND ANGERS
South of Angers, the River Maine conflows with the Loire for the final leg of its journey to the Atlantic. The river banks immediately west of this confluence remain the source of some of the valley's most notable wines, including Savennières and Coteaux du Layon.

St-Georges-sur-Loire
The **Château de Serrant** (☎ 02 41 39 13 01; www .chateau-serrant.net; adult/student €9.50/6; ☺ tours 10am, 11am & hourly 2.15-5.15pm, closed Tue except Jul & Aug, also closed mid-Nov–mid-Mar), 15km south-west of Angers (and 2km northeast of St-Georges) on the N23, is an excellent example of Renaissance architecture. The interior is unusually well furnished: the library has more than 12,000 books and in the drawing room a 17th-century ebony cabinet conceals 33 secret drawers. From Angers, Anjou Bus lines 7, 18 and 18B serve St-Georges-sur-Loire (€1.45, 40 minutes, seven daily Monday to Saturday).

Founded 800 years ago, **Prieuré de l'Epinay** (☎ 02 41 39 14 44; http://monsite.wanadoo.fr/prieure -epinay; d with breakfast €75; ☺ Easter–early Oct; 🚭), several kilometres southwest of St-Georges-sur-Loire (turn south off the N23 1.5km from St-Georges), is a delightful place to stay (and eat), especially for wine lovers. This three-suite *chambre d'hôte* is run by a wine connoisseur who takes guests on tours of nearby cellars. Bike rental is available.

Château de Brissac

A highly ornate chocolate-box folly that's been home to the dukes of Brissac since 1502, this **chateau** (☎ 02 41 91 22 21; www.chateau -brissac.fr; adult/7-14yr/student incl tour €8.50/4.50/7.50; ۞ 10am-6pm Jul & Aug, 10-11.45am & 2-5.30pm Wed-Mon Apr-Jun, Sep & Oct, 2-5.30pm during school holidays Nov-Mar), 15km south of Angers in Brissac-Quincé, is the tallest castle in the Loire at seven storeys. It stands regally amid 8 sq km of grounds studded with cedar trees.

Inside, flamboyant furnishings and extravagant ornamentation fill its 204 rooms. The theatre, lit with chandeliers, was the whimsical creation of the Vicomtesse de Trèdene, a soprano with a passion for the arts. Tours leave hourly.

Four huge, extravagantly furnished rooms serve as **chambres d'hôtes** (d incl breakfast €390, dinner €77; ⊜) that have to be seen to be believed: antique four-posters, wood panelling, hidden doors and historically significant tapestries are extras you won't find anywhere else.

Anjou Bus line 9 links Angers' bus station with the chateau (€1.45, 25 minutes, six daily).

Burgundy

With the plains of Champagne to the north and the Rhône Valley, gateway to the Midi, to the south, Burgundy (Bourgogne in French) can make a strong case for being the real heartland of France. Amid some of the country's most gorgeous countryside, two great French passions, wine and food, come together here in a particularly enticing and hearty form.

Burgundy's towns and its dashingly handsome capital, Dijon, are heirs to a glorious architectural heritage that goes back to the Renaissance, the Middle Ages and beyond, into the mists of Gallo-Roman and Celtic antiquity. Many civil and religious buildings, including Beaune's stunning Hôtel-Dieu, are topped with colourful tile roofs. Dijon, Beaune, Châtillon-sur-Seine and other towns have truly outstanding museums (www.musees-bour gogne.org in French).

Burgundy is a paradise for lovers of the great outdoors. You can hike and cycle through the highly civilised vineyards of the Côte d'Or, or in the wild reaches of the Parc Naturel Régional du Morvan (Morvan Regional Park); glide along the waterways of the Yonne in a canal boat; or float above the vineyards in a hot-air balloon.

The majority of Burgundy's most interesting historical sights are to be found in three *départements*: Côte d'Or (capital: Dijon) in the northeast; Yonne (capital: Auxerre) in the northwest, almost at the gates of Paris; and Saône-et-Loire (capital: Mâcon) in the south. Most of the lightly populated Parc Naturel Régional du Morvan is in the region's fourth *département*, Nièvre.

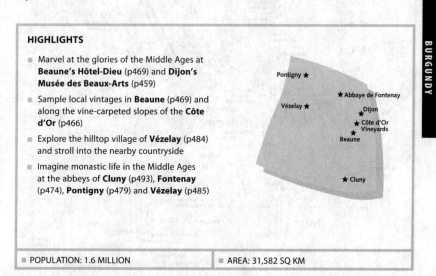

HIGHLIGHTS

- Marvel at the glories of the Middle Ages at **Beaune's Hôtel-Dieu** (p469) and **Dijon's Musée des Beaux-Arts** (p459)

- Sample local vintages in **Beaune** (p469) and along the vine-carpeted slopes of the **Côte d'Or** (p466)

- Explore the hilltop village of **Vézelay** (p484) and stroll into the nearby countryside

- Imagine monastic life in the Middle Ages at the abbeys of **Cluny** (p493), **Fontenay** (p474), **Pontigny** (p479) and **Vézelay** (p485)

Pontigny ★

★ Abbaye de Fontenay

Vézelay ★

★ Dijon

★ Côte d'Or
Vineyards

Beaune

★ Cluny

■ POPULATION: 1.6 MILLION   ■ AREA: 31,582 SQ KM

BURGUNDY

History

At its height during the 14th and 15th centuries, the duchy of Burgundy was one of the richest and most powerful states in Europe, a vast swathe of territory stretching from modern-day Burgundy to Alsace and from there northwest to Lorraine, Luxembourg, Flanders and Holland. This was a time of bitter rivalry between Burgundy and France – indeed, it was the Burgundians who sold Jeanne d'Arc (Joan of Arc) to the English – and for a while it seemed quite possible that the kingdom of France would be taken over by Burgundy. In the end, though, it worked out the other way around and in 1477 Burgundy was incorporated into France.

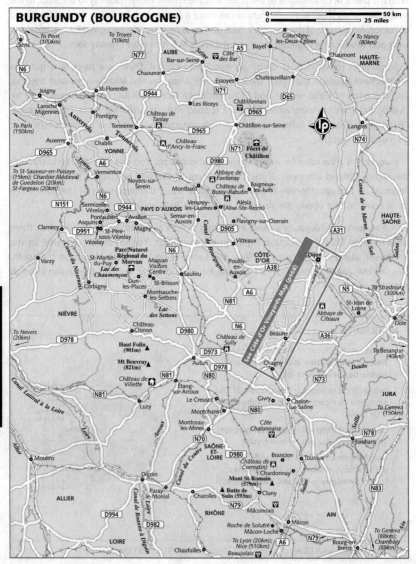

ON THE GROUND, UPON THE WATER & IN THE AIR

Tasting fine wines often involves hanging out in dimly lit cellars – but Burgundy is also a paradise for lovers of outdoor activities.

The **Comité Régional de Tourisme de Bourgogne** (Regional Tourism Board; ☎ 03 80 28 03 00; www.burgundy-tourism.com; postal address BP 20623, 21006 Dijon CEDEX) publishes an excellent brochure on Burgundy's great outdoors, available at tourist offices.

Hiking & Cycling

Burgundy has thousands of kilometres of walking and cycling trails, including sections of the GR2, GR7 and GR76. A variety of local trails take you through some of the most beautiful wine-growing areas in France, among them the world-renowned Côte d'Or (p467, p467 and p471), the vineyards of Chablis (p479) and the Mâconnais (p495). Footpaths through the countryside are especially numerous in the Parc Naturel Régional du Morvan, departing from places such as the Morvan Visitors Centre (p487) and Saulieu (p488), but you can also set out from the Abbaye de Fontenay (p474), Autun (p491), Avallon (p482), Cluny (p495), Noyers-sur-Serein (p481) and Vézelay (p485).

You can cycle on or very near the towpath of the **Canal de Bourgogne** all the way from Dijon to Tonnerre (180km). The section from Montbard to Tonnerre (65km) passes by the Château d'Ancy-le-Franc; between Montbard and Pouilly-en-Auxois (58km), spurs go to the Abbaye de Fontenay, Flavigny-sur-Ozerain, Alésia and Semur-en-Auxois.

Canal & River Boating

Few activities are as serene and relaxing as floating in a houseboat along Burgundy's 1200km of placid waterways, which include the Rivers Yonne, Saône and Seille and a network of canals such as the 242km Canal de Bourgogne. Reliable rental companies offering boats from March to November are:

- **Bateaux de Bourgogne** (☎ 03 86 72 92 10; www.bateauxdebourgogne.com in French; 1-2 quai de la République, 89000 Auxerre) A grouping of five large companies that offers 20 points of departure. Based upstairs from Auxerre's tourist office.

- **France Afloat** (Burgundy Cruisers; ☎ 03 86 81 54 55, ☎ in the UK 08700 110 538; www.franceafloat.com; 1 quai du Port, 89270 Vermenton) Based 23km southeast of Auxerre.

- **Locaboat Holidays** (☎ 03 86 91 72 72; www.locaboat.com; Port au Bois, BP 150, 89303 Joigny CEDEX) Rents out boats at many locations around France, including Joigny (27km northwest of Auxerre).

Hot-Air Ballooning

From about April to October you can take a stunning *montgolfière* (hot-air balloon) ride over Burgundy for around €220 per adult. Note that flights are contingent on good weather, though one company reports that only 7% of its scheduled flights end up being cancelled. Veteran companies include:

- **Air Adventures** (☎ 03 80 90 74 23; www.airadventures.fr) Based just outside Pouilly-en-Auxois, 50km west of Dijon.

- **Air Escargot** (☎ 03 85 87 12 30; www.air-escargot.com) Based 16km south of Beaune in Remigny. Bookings can be made through the **Beaune tourist office** (☎ 03 80 26 21 30; www.beaune -burgundy.com; 1 rue de l'Hôtel-Dieu, Beaune).

During the Middle Ages, two Burgundy-based monastic orders exerted significant influence across much of Christendom. The ascetic Cistercians were headquartered at Cîteaux (see the boxed text, p468), while their bitter rivals, the powerful and worldly Benedictines, were based at Cluny (p493).

Getting There & Around

By car or rail (including TGV Sud-Est), Burgundy makes an easy stopover on the way from the English Channel or Paris to the Alps, Lyon, Provence or the Côte d'Azur. From Dijon, *autoroutes* stretch northeast to Alsace (A36), north to Lorraine (A31), north

BURGUNDY

and then west to Champagne (A31, A5 and A26) and south to the Rhône Valley (A6). There's no quick way west to the Loire.

All the cities and towns and some of the villages mentioned in this chapter are served by trains and public buses, though patience and planning are a must as services in many areas are infrequent, especially on Sunday and during school holiday periods. For details on touring the Côte d'Or wine villages by public transport, see p472 and p465.

Tourist offices can supply brochures and maps with details on dedicated bike paths and cycling circuits.

CÔTE D'OR

The Côte d'Or *département* is named after one of the world's foremost wine-growing regions, which stretches from Dijon – bursting with cultural riches – south to the wine town of Beaune and beyond. In the far northwest, on the border with Champagne, Châtillon-sur-Seine displays spectacular Celtic treasures, while in the west you can explore the walled, hilltop town of Semur-en-Auxois.

DIJON
pop 237,000

Dijon, mustard capital of the universe, is one of France's most appealing provincial cities. Filled with elegant medieval and Renaissance buildings, the lively centre is wonderful for strolling, especially if you like to leaven your cultural enrichment with good food and shopping.

Dijon wears its long and glorious history with grace, and with a self-confidence that's never smug or off-putting because it's so obviously deserved. The city's 25,000 students get much of the credit for keeping the nightlife scene snappy, though people of all ages participate in the city's thriving cultural life.

History
Dijon served as the capital of the duchy of Burgundy from the 11th to 15th centuries, enjoying a golden age during the 14th and 15th centuries under Philippe-le-Hardi (Philip the Bold), Jean-sans-Peur (John the Fearless) and Philippe-le-Bon (Philip the Good). During their reigns, some of the finest painters, sculptors and architects from

around the Burgundian lands were brought to Dijon, turning the city into one of the great centres of European art.

Orientation
Dijon's main thoroughfare, known for much of its length as rue de la Liberté, stretches from the train station eastwards past the tourist office and the Palais des Ducs to Église St-Michel. The main shopping precinct is around rue de la Liberté and perpendicular rue du Bourg. The focal point of the old town is place François Rude. The main university campus is 2km east of the centre.

Information
EMERGENCY
Police Station (☎ 03 80 44 55 00; 2 place Suquet; ☽ 24hr) Night-time access is on rue du Petit Cîteaux.

INTERNET ACCESS
Cyberbisey (53 rue Berbisey; per hr €3; ☽ 10am-10pm Mon-Sat)
Multi-Rezo (per 15min/1hr €1/4) Inside the bus station (☽ 9am-midnight Mon-Sat, 3-10pm Sun); 74 rue Vannerie (☽ noon-9pm Mon-Sat)
Netwave (10 rue de la Liberté; per hr €4; ☽ 10am-9pm Mon-Sat, to 10pm in warm season)

LAUNDRY
Laundrettes 41 rue Auguste Comte (☽ 6am-9pm); 28 rue Berbisey (☽ 6am-8.30pm); 55 rue Berbisey (☽ 7am-8.30pm); 8 place de la Banque (☽ 7am-8.30pm)

MEDICAL SERVICES
Centre Hospitalier Universitaire (hospital; ☎ 03 80 29 30 31; 3 rue du Faubourg Raines; ☽ 24hr)
SOS Médecins (☎ 03 80 59 80 80) Has 24-hour doctors.

POST
Main Post Office (place Grangier) Has a Cyberposte and does currency exchange.

TOURIST INFORMATION
Tourist Office (☎ 08 92 70 05 58, cost per min €0.34; www.dijon-tourism.com; place Darcy; ☽ 9am-7pm May–mid-Oct, 10am-6pm mid-Oct–Apr) A new city-centre annexe is planned. The *Owl's Trail* (€2) details a self-guided city-centre walking tour whose route is marked on the pavement with bronze triangles.

Sights
MEDIEVAL & RENAISSANCE ARCHITECTURE
Once home to the region's powerful dukes, the **Palais des Ducs et des États de Bourgogne** (Pal-

ace of the Dukes & States of Burgundy) is in the heart of old Dijon. Given a neoclassical façade in the 17th and 18th centuries while serving as the seat of the States-General (parliament) of Burgundy, it overlooks **place de la Libération**, a semicircular public square designed by Jules Hardouin-Mansart (one of the architects of Versailles) in 1686.

The western wing is occupied by Dijon's **city hall**. Inside the arch across the street from 92 rue de la Liberté is **Escalier Gabriel** (1730s), a monumental marble stairway with gilded railings that's named after its architect.

The eastern wing houses the **Musée des Beaux-Arts** (right), whose entrance is next to the **Tour de Bar**, a squat 14th-century tower that once served as a prison.

The 46m-high, mid-15th-century **Tour Philippe le Bon** (Tower of Philip the Good; ☎ 03 80 74 52 71; adult/student/under 12yr €2.30/1.20/free; ☺ accompanied climbs every 45min-1hr 9am-noon & 1.45-5.30pm Easter-late Nov, 9am-11pm & 1.30-3.30pm Wed afternoon, Sat & Sun late Nov-Easter) affords fantastic views over the city. Rumour has it that on a clear day you can see all the way to Mont Blanc.

Many of Dijon's finest **hôtels particuliers** (aristocratic townhouses) are north of the Palais des Ducs on and around rues Verrerie, Vannerie and des Forges, whose names reflect the industries that once thrived along them (glassmakers, basket-weavers and metalsmiths, respectively). The early-17th-century **Maison des Cariatides** (28 rue Chaudronnerie), its façade a riot of stone caryatids, vines and horns, is particularly fine. A bit west you'll find the 13th-century **Hôtel Aubriot** (40 rue des Forges), the Renaissance-style **Maison Maillard** (38 rue des Forges) and the truly splendid **Hôtel Chambellan** (34 rue des Forges), from whose courtyard a spiral stone staircase leads up to some remarkable stone vaulting and a great view of the building's 17th-century architecture.

CHURCHES
All of Dijon's major churches are open 8am to 7pm.

A block north of the Palais des Ducs stands **Église Notre Dame**, built between 1220 and 1240. The façade's three tiers are decorated with leering gargoyles separated by two rows of pencil-thin columns; high on top is a 14th-century **Horloge à Jacquemart** (Jacquemart Clock) transported from Flanders in 1382 by Philip the Bold, who claimed it as a trophy of war. It chimes every quarter-hour. The interior has a vast transept crossing and 13th-century stained glass.

Around the north side, **rue de la Chouette** is named after the small stone *chouette* (owl) carved into the exterior corner of a chapel. Said to grant happiness and wisdom to those who stroke it, it has been worn smooth by generations of fortune-seekers. All sorts of superstitions surround the owl – some insist that walking by the dragon in the lower left corner of the adjacent window will annul your wish, while others insist that approaching the dragon will actually help make your wish come true. Loiter for a while and locals may approach with sage (and perhaps contradictory) advice.

Nearby, the 17th-century **Hôtel de Vogüé** (8 rue de la Chouette) is renowned for the ornate carvings around its exquisite Renaissance courtyard – definitely worth a peek into. Perched high atop the roof of the 15th-century **Maison Millière** (10 rue de la Chouette) are figures of an owl and a cat.

Église St-Michel (place St-Michel) began life as a Gothic church but subsequently underwent a façade-lift operation in which it was given a richly ornamented Renaissance west front considered among the most beautiful in France, perhaps because it looks like it should be in Italy. The two 17th-century towers are topped with cupolas and, higher still, glittering gold spheres.

Situated above the tomb of St Benignus (who is believed to have brought Christianity to Burgundy in the 2nd century), Dijon's Burgundian Gothic-style **Cathédrale St-Bénigne** (☺ 9am-7pm) was built around 1300 as an abbey church. Some of Burgundy's great figures are buried inside. The **crypt** (admission €1; ☺ approximately 9am-5.30pm or 6pm) is all that's left of an 11th-century Romanesque basilica.

MUSEUMS
All of Dijon's municipal museums are free except, occasionally, for special exhibitions.

Housed in the eastern wing of the Palais des Ducs, the **Musée des Beaux-Arts** (☎ 03 80 74 52 70; audioguide €3.90; ☺ 9.30am-6pm Wed-Mon May-Oct, 10am-5pm Wed-Mon Nov-Apr) is one of the most outstanding museums in France. The wood-panelled **Salle des Gardes** (Guards' Room), once warmed by a gargantuan fireplace that's as Gothic as Gothic can be, houses three impossibly intricate gilded

BURGUNDY

DIJON

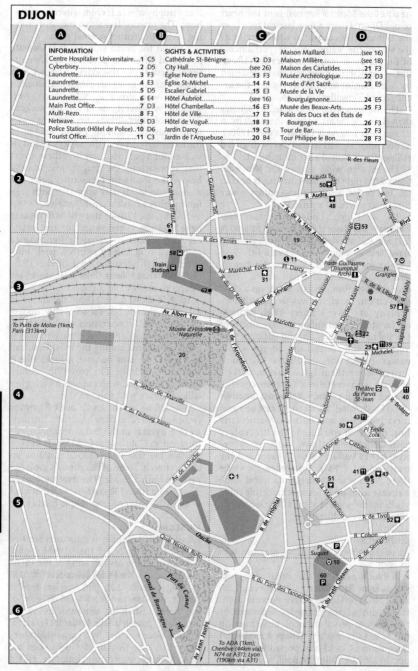

INFORMATION
Centre Hospitalier Universitaire	1	C5
Cyberbisey	2	D5
Laundrette	3	F3
Laundrette	4	E3
Laundrette	5	D5
Laundrette	6	E4
Main Post Office	7	D3
Multi-Rezo	8	F3
Netwave	9	D3
Police Station (Hôtel de Police)	10	D6
Tourist Office	11	C3

SIGHTS & ACTIVITIES
Cathédrale St-Bénigne	12	D3
City Hall	(see 26)	
Église Notre Dame	13	F3
Église St-Michel	14	F4
Escalier Gabriel	15	E3
Hôtel Aubriot	(see 16)	
Hôtel Chambellan	16	E3
Hôtel de Ville	17	E3
Hôtel de Vogüe	18	F3
Jardin Darcy	19	C3
Jardin de l'Arquebuse	20	B4

Maison Maillard	(see 16)	
Maison Millière	(see 18)	
Maison des Cariatides	21	F3
Musée Archéologique	22	D3
Musée d'Art Sacré	23	E5
Musée de la Vie Bourguignonne	24	E5
Musée des Beaux-Arts	25	F3
Palais des Ducs et des États de Bourgogne	26	F3
Tour de Bar	27	F3
Tour Philippe le Bon	28	F3

BURGUNDY

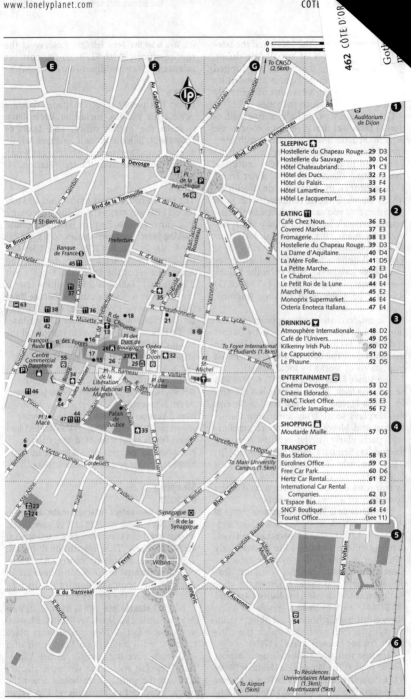

BURGUNDY

SLEEPING
Hostellerie du Chapeau Rouge..29	D3
Hostellerie du Sauvage.............30	D4
Hôtel Chateaubriand...............31	C3
Hôtel des Ducs......................32	F3
Hôtel du Palais.....................33	F4
Hôtel Lamartine....................34	E4
Hôtel Le Jacquemart...............35	F3

EATING
Café Chez Nous.....................36	E3
Covered Market....................37	E3
Fromagerie.........................38	E3
Hostellerie du Chapeau Rouge....39	D3
La Dame d'Aquitaine...............40	D4
La Mère Folle.......................41	D5
La Petite Marche...................42	E3
Le Chabrot.........................43	D4
Le Petit Roi de la Lune............44	E4
Marché Plus.........................45	E2
Monoprix Supermarket............46	E4
Osteria Enoteca Italiana...........47	E4

DRINKING
Atmosphère Internationale........48	D2
Café de l'Univers...................49	D5
Kilkenny Irish Pub..................50	D2
Le Cappuccino......................51	D5
Le Phaune.........................52	D5

ENTERTAINMENT
Cinéma Devosge...................53	D2
Cinéma Eldorado...................54	G6
FNAC Ticket Office.................55	E3
La Cercle Jamaïque.................56	F2

SHOPPING
Moutarde Maille....................57	D3

TRANSPORT
Bus Station.........................58	B3
Eurolines Office.....................59	C3
Free Car Park.......................60	D6
Hertz Car Rental...................61	B2
International Car Rental Companies.........................62	B3
L'Espace Bus........................63	B3
SNCF Boutique.....................64	E4
Tourist Office.................(see 11)	

...ic retables from the 1300s and the late-
...edieval sepulchres of two Valois dukes.
Restored in 2005, the tombs are topped
by life-size recumbent figures attended by
angelic guardians; processions of delicately
carved mourners adorn the sides.

Other highlights include: a fine collection of **primitives** that give you a good sense
of how artistic and aesthetic sensibilities
varied between Italy, Switzerland and the
Rhineland in the 13th and 14th centuries;
the painting *Galerie d'Objets d'Art* (mid-
17th century) by Cornelis de Baellieur,
which shows a room rendered with such
precision that you can actually enjoy the miniscule artwork hanging on its walls (photography made this sort of painterly *tour
de force* obsolete; hung at eye level in room
119); and quite a few nude (though never
lewd) **Rude sculptures** – they're by the Dijon-
born artist François Rude (1784–1855)
so don't be a prude or become unglued,
Dude!

The modern and contemporary art section, which has one work each by Manet
and Monet, is closed 11.30am to 1.45pm. In
the courtyard, the **ducal kitchens** (1433) host
exhibitions of works by local artists.

The **Musée Archéologique** (☎ 03 80 30 88 54; 5
rue du Docteur Maret; ☼ 9am-6pm Wed-Mon mid-May–
Sep, 9.30am-12.30pm & 1.35-6pm Wed-Sun Oct–mid-
May) displays some truly surprising Celtic,
Roman and Merovingian artefacts, including a particularly fine 1st-century bronze of
the goddess Sequana standing on a boat. Upstairs, the early-Gothic hall (12th and 13th
centuries), with its ogival arches held aloft
by two rows of columns, once served as the
dormitory of a Benedictine abbey.

The **Musée de la Vie Bourguignonne** (☎ 03 80
44 12 69; 17 rue Ste Anne; ☼ 9am-noon & 2-6pm Wed-
Mon), in a 17th-century Cistercian convent,
explores village and town life in Burgundy
in centuries past with evocative tableaux
illustrating dress, headgear, cooking, traditional crafts and the like. Down the alley
just outside the cloister, the **Musée d'Art Sacré**
(☎ 03 80 44 12 69; 15 rue Ste Anne; ☼ same hours) displays gleaming Catholic ritual objects from
the 12th to 19th centuries inside the convent's copper-domed chapel (1709).

Homage to Dijon's most famous export
can be paid at the **Musée de la Moutarde** (Musée
Amora; Mustard Museum; 48 quai Nicolas Rolin; adult/under
12yr incl tour €3/free; ☼ bilingual tours 3pm Mon-Sat May-
Oct, Wed & Sat Nov, Dec & Feb-Apr). Reserve at the
tourist office (☎ 08 92 70 05 58, cost per
minute €0.34; www.dijon-tourism.com).

PARKS
Dijon has plenty of green spaces that are
perfect for picnics, including **Jardin Darcy**,
next to the tourist office; and **Jardin de
l'Arquebuse**, Dijon's botanic gardens, whose
stream, pond and formal gardens are south
across the tracks from the train station.

Tours
The tourist office offers a two-hour **MP3 tour**
(€6, incl a PDA with images €12) of the city centre
and runs various English-language **guided
walking tours** (adult/couple/student €6/9/3; ☼ 5pm
Mon-Fri May-Oct, 3pm Mon & Thu Nov, Dec & Feb-Apr),
including *nocturnes* at 10pm in July and
August (meet at the Palais des Ducs' Cour
d'Honneur). Taking a tourist office tour is
the only way to see the famous **Puits de Moïse**
(Well of Moses; 1395–1405), a grouping of
six Old Testament figures by Claus Sluter
that's 1.2km west of the train station on the
grounds of a psychiatric hospital.

Segway tour (www.segway.com; adult/12-16yr €15/7;
daily Jul & Aug, Sat, Sun & holidays Apr-Jun, Sep & Oct,
also Fri Jun, Sep & Oct) Gadget lovers and couch potatoes
alike may react to the tourist office's 1½-hour Segway tour
like cats do to catnip!

Wine & Voyages (☎ 03 80 61 15 15; www.wineand
voyages.com; 2/3hr tours €50/60; ☼ Mar–mid-Dec) Runs
minibus tours in English of the Côte de Nuits vineyards.
Reservations can be made by phone or internet; last-
minute bookings can be made via the tourist office.

Sleeping
BUDGET
**Centre de Rencontres Internationales et de Sé-
jour de Dijon** (CRISD; ☎ 03 80 72 95 20; www.auberge
-cri-dijon.com; 1 blvd Champollion; dm/s/d with breakfast
€16.80/32.30/42.60) This institutional hostel,
2.5km northeast of the centre, was completely renovated in 2006. Most beds are in
modern, airy rooms for four or six. By bus,
take Liane 4 to the Epirey CRI stop.

Hôtel Chateaubriand (☎ 03 80 41 42 18; www
.hotelchateaubriand.fr in French; 3 av Maréchal Foch; d €38,
with washbasin €34) A 23-room, no-star place
near the train station that has the air of a
well-worn dive but, thanks to the Victorian breakfast room, has far more character than the sterile chain hotels down the
block. Alas, not as romantic as the writer

and nowhere near as self-indulgent as the legendarily thick steak named after him.

Hôtel Lamartine (☎ 03 80 30 37 47; fax 03 80 30 03 43; 12 rue Jules Mercier; s/d from €33/39; ☒ closed noon-3pm) The 14 rooms are Spartan – linoleum connoisseurs will love the floors – but the Palais des Ducs is just a few steps from the front door.

Hôtel Le Jacquemart (☎ 03 80 60 09 60; www.hotel-lejacquemart.fr; 32 rue Verrerie; d with washbasin €30)

MIDRANGE

Hôtel du Palais (☎ 03 80 67 16 26; hoteldupalais-dijon@wanadoo.fr; 23 rue du Palais; d €40-68) A great little two-star place in a 17th-century *hôtel particulier*. The 13 rooms are spacious and welcoming and the public spaces exude old-fashioned charm. Staying on the 3rd floor will get you rooftop views and help build muscle mass in your thighs.

Hostellerie du Sauvage (☎ 03 80 41 31 21; hotel dusauvage@free.fr; 64 rue Monge; d €44-54) In a 15th-century *relais de poste* (relay posthouse) set around a cobbled, vine-shaded courtyard, this great-value two-star hotel is just off lively rue Monge. The 22 rooms are spare and practical.

Hôtel Le Jacquemart (☎ 03 80 60 09 60; www.hotel-lejacquemart.fr; 32 rue Verrerie; d €47-60) Right in the heart of old Dijon, this two-star hotel has 31 tidy, comfortable rooms; the pricier ones are quite spacious and some come with marble fireplaces. The window boxes make the 17th-century building especially pretty in summer.

Hôtel des Ducs (☎ 03 80 67 31 31; www.hoteldes ducs.com; 5 rue Lamonnoye; d low season €52-74, high season €69-99; ☒ ☒) A modern, three-star hotel with 37 rooms. Comfortable and convenient if you want to stay smack-dab in the centre of things and still park nearby (€5.70).

TOP END

Hostellerie du Chapeau Rouge (☎ 03 80 50 88 88; www.chapeau-rouge.fr; 5 rue Michelet; d €135-150; ☒ ☒) A Dijon institution since 1847, this place has four stars, 30 rooms – some with Jacuzzi – that are modern but ultimately soulless and a *très correct* – some would say snooty – atmosphere.

Eating

Lots of restaurants can be found on buzzy rue Berbisey, around place Émile Zola and near the covered market (along rue Banne-lier and rue Quentin). Rue Amiral Roussin is lined with intimate eateries.

RESTAURANTS

Café Chez Nous (☎ 03 80 50 12 98; impasse Quentin; ☒ 10am-2am, closed Mon morning & Sun) A quintessentially French – and often crowded – *bar du coin* (neighbourhood bar), down a tiny alleyway from the covered market, that serves lunches generally made with organic ingredients. The *plat du jour* (meat or fish) costs €6.50 to €9 (details are on the chalkboard); salads are about €7; wine by the glass is a bargain at €1 to €2.20.

La Petite Marche (☎ 03 80 30 15 10; 27-29 rue Musette; menus €10.50-14; ☒ lunch Mon-Sat) An organic restaurant with seven types of salad and lots of vegetarian options (as well as meat and fish) – a good choice if you're tired of heavy Burgundian classics. Upstairs from the organic food shop.

La Mère Folle (☎ 03 80 50 19 76; 102 rue Berbisey; lunch menu €9.50, other menus €14.50-23; ☒ closed lunch Sat, Tue & lunch Wed) A rather camp French restaurant that bills itself as a *resto extravagant* and serves unusual variations on traditional dishes. The result: dishes like *magret de canard au miel, thym et mirabelles* (fillet of duck with honey, thyme and cherry plums; €13). Crammed with character, from the baroque wall mirrors to the pineapple-shaped table lamps.

Le Chabrot (☎ 03 80 30 69 51; 36 rue Monge; menus €12-31) A relaxed wine bar and restaurant whose Burgundian and French cooking, candle-lit tables and rustic décor make it popular with gourmets and wine-lovers alike. Among the 200 vintages on the wine list: a lone Australian white.

Osteria Enoteca Italiana (☎ 03 80 50 07 36; 32 rue Amiral Roussin; lunch/dinner menu €14/39; ☒ Tue-Sun) An intimate *ristorante* that's proud of its authentic, traditional-Italian pasta, meat and fish dishes, some made with white Italian truffles (in season), and its scrumptious home-made desserts (think *tiramisú*). The décor hints at Venice.

Le Petit Roi de la Lune (☎ 03 80 49 89 93; 28 rue Amiral Roussin; mains €15; ☒ closed Sun) 'The Little King of the Moon' serves French cuisine that – explains the chef – has been *revisitée, rearrangée et decalée* (revisited, rearranged and shifted), resulting in dishes such as the hugely popular *Camembert frit avec gelée de mûre* (Camembert wrapped in bread crumbs, fried, baked and then served with blackberry jelly).

La Dame d'Aquitaine (☎ 03 80 30 45 65; 23 place Bossuet; lunch menus €14.90-21.10, dinner menus €32.50-39; ☾ closed Sun & lunch Mon) Excellent Burgundian and southwestern French cuisine served under the bays of a 13th-century cellar. Options include *coq au vin rouge* and *magret de canard aux baies de cassis* (duck's breast with blackcurrant sauce). The Middle Ages at their most cultured.

Hostellerie du Chapeau Rouge (☎ 03 80 50 88 88; www.chapeau-rouge.fr; 5 rue Michelet; lunch menu without/with wine €38/44, 7/11 course menus €75-100) A formal restaurant with one Michelin star featuring bold, creative French gastronomy based on traditional ingredients and top-quality local produce. Specialities include red tuna and salmon.

SELF-CATERING
For picnic treats:

Covered Market (Halles du Marché; rue Quentin; ☾ 6am-1pm Tue-Sat)

Fromagerie (28 rue Musette; ☾ closed Mon morning & Sun)

Marché Plus (rue Bannelier; ☾ 7am-9pm Mon-Sat, 9am-noon Sun)

Monoprix Supermarket (11-13 rue Piron; ☾ 9am-8.45pm Mon-Sat)

Drinking
There are quite a few bars set out along rue Berbisey.

Le Cappuccino (☎ 03 80 41 06 35; 132 rue Berbisey; ☾ 5pm-2am Mon-Sat) Coffee isn't even served at this convivial and often jam-packed bar (the name is left over from an earlier Starbucksian incarnation) but wine by the glass and a varied selection of about 100 beers are, including Mandubienne, the only beer brewed in Dijon. Regularly hosts live music.

Kilkenny Irish Pub (☎ 03 80 30 02 48; 1 rue Auguste Perdrix; ☾ 6pm-3am Mon-Sat) Irish décor and a mellow air under the cellar vaults. Hosts live traditional Irish music once a month.

Café de l'Univers (☎ 03 80 30 98 29; 47 rue Berbisey; ☾ 5pm-2am) One of many convivial café-bars along rue Berbisey, this place has live music from 9pm to 1am on Friday and Saturday. In the cellar there's a small dance floor (open approximately 8pm to 2am Thursday to Sunday). For the late-late-late crowd there's an *after* from 5am to 9am on Saturday and Sunday mornings.

Atmosphère Internationale (☎ 03 80 30 52 02; 9 rue Audran; ☾ 6pm-6am) A spacious student-oriented bar and disco that's long been a favourite with international students. Has a comfy lounge area for chatting and a billiard hall.

Le Phaune (☎ 03 80 50 01 69; http://lephaune.free.fr in French; 4bis rue de Serrigny; ☾ 8pm-2am Sun-Thu, 6pm-2am Fri & Sat) A hetero-friendly gay and lesbian bar with a small dance floor and a rainbow flag in the window. Thursday is theme night.

Entertainment
For the latest on Dijon's cultural scene, pick up *Spectacles* (www.spectacles-publications.com in French), available free from the tourist office. Events tickets are sold at the **FNAC ticket office** (☎ 08 92 68 36 22; 24 rue du Bourg; ☾ 10am-7pm Mon-Sat).

A number of nightclubs are just north of place de la République. Several places listed under Drinking (left) host live music.

Le Cercle Jamaïque (☎ 03 80 73 52 19; 14 place de la République; admission free; ☾ 2pm-5am Tue-Sat) Decked out in lovably tacky baroque décor, this nightclub has live music (Cuban, flamenco, jazz, rock-and-roll) nightly from 11pm to 3.30am. Rum-based cocktails are the speciality. The downstairs disco (open 11pm to 5am Thursday to Saturday) plays everything but techno.

Nondubbed films flicker nightly at:

Cinéma Devosge (☎ 03 80 30 74 79, ☎ recorded information 03 80 49 83 83; www.cinealpes.fr in French; 6 rue Devosge)

Cinéma Eldorado (☎ 03 80 66 51 89, ☎ recorded information 03 80 66 12 34; www.cinema-eldorado.com in French; 21 rue Alfred de Musset) A three-screen art cinema.

Shopping
Moutarde Maille (☎ 03 80 30 41 02; 32 rue de la Liberté; ☾ 9am-7pm Mon-Sat) The factory outlet of the company that makes Grey Poupon. When you walk in, tangy odours assault the nostrils, as they well should in a place with 32 different kinds of mustard, including three on tap (€76 to €149.50 per kilogram).

Getting There & Away
AIR
As we go to press, no scheduled international flights use **Aéroport Dijon-Bourgogne** (☎ 03 80 67 67 67; www.dijon.aeroport.fr), 5km southeast of the city centre.

BUS

The bus station is in the train station complex. Details on bus options are available at the **Transco information counter** (☎ 03 80 42 11 00; ☼ 6am-8pm Mon-Fri, 7am-2pm & 3-6pm Sat, 10am-1pm & 4-8pm Sun). Schedules appear in the free *Guide Horaire* booklet; tickets are sold on board.

Transco bus 60 (12 to 17 daily Monday to Saturday, two Sunday) links Dijon with the northern Côte de Nuits wine villages of Marsannay-la-Côte, Couchey, Fixin and Gevrey-Chambertin (30 minutes); the Pass Tourisme (€9) lets two to five people travelling together get on and off all day long. Dijon's local Divia Ligne 15 (right) goes to Marsannay-la-Côte.

Information on bus services to/from Dijon appear under Avallon, Beaune, Châtillon-sur-Seine, Saulieu and Semur-en-Auxois.

International bus travel is handled by **Eurolines** (☎ 03 80 68 20 44; 53 rue Guillaume Tell; ☼ Mon-Fri & Sat morning).

CAR

Avis, National-Citer and Europcar have *bureaux* at the train station's eastern tip; a block north is **Hertz** (8 rue Charles Briffaut). **ADA** (☎ 03 80 51 90 90; 109 av Jean Jaurès) is 2km south of the train station (take the Liane 4 bus line to Bourroches Jaurès).

TRAIN

The **train station** (rue du Docteur Remy) is linked with Lyon-Part Dieu and/or Lyon-Perrache (€23.80, two hours, 14 to 17 daily), Nice (€72.40, supplement sometimes required, six hours, two daily), Paris' Gare de Lyon (€49 by TGV, 1¾ hours, 15 daily weekdays, eight to 10 weekends, most frequent in the early morning and evening) and Strasbourg (€40, four hours, three or four nondirect daily).

For details on going by rail to destinations within Burgundy, see the city and town listings in this chapter.

In the city centre tickets can be purchased at the **SNCF Boutique** (55 rue du Bourg; ☼ 12.30-7pm Mon, 10am-7pm Tue-Sat).

Getting Around

BICYCLE

The **tourist office** (☎ 08 92 70 05 58, cost per min €0.34; www.dijon-tourism.com; place Darcy; ☼ 9am-7pm May–mid-Oct, 10am-6pm mid-Oct–Apr) rents bikes year-round for €12/17 per half-/full day, €50 for three days. Helmets are free.

BUS

Details on Dijon's bus network, operated by Divia, are available from **L'Espace Bus** (☎ 08 00 10 20 04; www.divia.fr in French; place Grangier; ☼ 7.30am-6.45pm Mon-Fri, 8.30am-6.30pm Sat). Single tickets, sold by drivers, cost €0.90 and are valid for an hour; a Forfait Journée ticket is good all day and costs €3, available from the tourist office (p458) or L'Espace Bus.

Dijon has two kinds of bus line: 'Liane' lines, which are numbered 1 through 7 and run every 10 minutes or less from about 5.30am to 12.30am (on Sunday from 9am to midnight); and somewhat less frequent 'Ligne' lines, which are numbered 10 to 51 and run from about 5.40am to 8.30pm (from 1pm on Sunday). Bus lines are known by their number and end-of-the-line station.

The free Diviaciti minibus shuttle does a city centre circuit from 7am to 8pm Monday to Saturday. Liane 1, 3, 5 and 6 run along rue de la Liberté.

CAR & MOTORCYCLE

All city centre parking is metered. Free spots are available (clockwise from the train station): northwest of rue Devosge, northeast of blvd Thiers, southeast of blvd Carnot, south of rue du Transvaal and on the other side of the train tracks from the city centre. There's a big free car park at place Suquet, just south of the police station.

The tourist office is easy to find – signs to the 'Office de Tourisme' are everywhere.

TAXI

A cab is just a phone call away on ☎ 03 80 41 41 12 (24 hours a day).

CÔTE D'OR VINEYARDS

Burgundy's most renowned vintages come from the vine-covered Côte d'Or (Golden Hillside), the narrow, eastern slopes of a range of hills made of limestone, flint and clay that runs south from Dijon for about 60km. The northern section, the **Côte de Nuits**, stretches from Marsannay-la-Côte south to Corgoloin and produces reds known for their robust, full-bodied character. The southern section, the **Côte de Beaune**, lies between Ladoix-Serrigny and Santenay and produces great

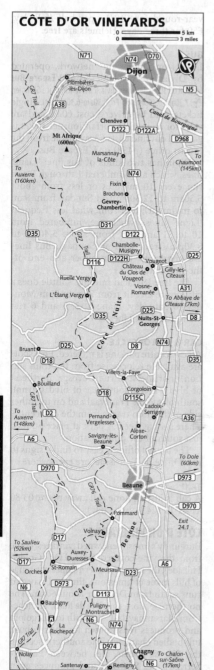

CÔTE D'OR VINEYARDS

reds and great whites. Tourist offices en route can provide brochures.

Activities

WINE TASTING

The villages of the Côte d'Or offer innumerable places to sample and purchase world-class wines – a short walk from where they were grown! Look for signs reading *dégustation* (tasting), *domaine* (wine-making estate), *château*, *cave* (wine cellar), *caveau* (a small cellar), *vente* (sales) or just plain *vins* (wines). Another key term is *gratuit* (free), though visitors are expected to be serious about making a purchase.

ROUTE DES GRANDS CRUS

Burgundy's most famous wine route, the Route des Grands Crus (www.route-des-grands-crus-de-bourgogne.com+ in French) and its variants, some almost (but not quite) as wide as two motorcars, wends its way between the region's stone-built villages, each with its ancient steeple-topped church, some with the turrets of a chateau peeping above the trees of a private park. Neatly tended vines cascade down the slopes between hamlets with impossibly beautiful names – Chambertin, Chambolle, Chassagne, Montrachet (the two Ts are silent) – that cause oenophiles to salivate at the mere sound of the syllables. The lower slopes offer luscious seas of wine fields, but don't neglect the Côte's upper slopes, where the vines give way to forests and cliffs and the views are breathtaking. Signposted in brown, the Route des Grands Crus generally follows the tertiary roads west of the N74.

If you're coming from Dijon, the Côte de Nuits begins in earnest just south of **Marsannay-la-Côte**. Most of the area's *grand cru* vineyards are between **Gevrey-Chambertin** and **Vosne-Romanée**, famed for its Romanée Conti wines, among Burgundy's most prestigious – and priciest. **Vougeot** is known for its imposing chateau. **Nuits-St-Georges** (see the boxed text, opposite) is a proper town with several hotels, restaurants and food shops.

On the Côte de Beaune, **Aloxe-Corton's** Château Corton-André, just off the hamlet's one-lane main street, is easy to spot thanks to its impossibly steep coloured-tile roof. **Pernand-Vergelesses** (see Eating, p468) is nestled in a little valley that's completely hidden from the N74.

FROM BURGUNDY TO THE MOON

In 1971, the astronauts of NASA's Apollo 15 moon mission named one of the lunar craters they found 'St George' in honour of the bottle of Nuits-St-Georges consumed on the way to the moon in Jules Verne's sci-fi epic, *From the Earth to the Moon* (1865):

'And lastly, to crown the repast, Ardan had brought out a fine bottle of Nuits, which was found "by chance" in the provision-box. The three friends drank to the union of the earth and her satellite.'

South of Beaune, **Pommard's chateau** (www .chateau-de-pommard.tm.fr), surrounded by a stone wall, is on the D973 on the northeast edge of town. **Volnay** is notable for its hillside church. A bit off the main track, **St-Romain** is a bucolic village situated right where vine-yardland meets pastureland, forests and cliffs. Hiking trails from here include the spectacular **Sentier des Roches**, a circuit that follows part of the GR7 and the D17I along the top of the **Falaises de Baubigny** (Baubigny cliffs) 300m above the Saône. This trail takes you via the hillside hamlet of **Orches** to the 15th-century **Château de La Rochepot** (☎ 03 80 21 71 37; www.larochepot.com; adult/under 15yr €6/3.50; ⊙ tours 10am-6pm Wed-Mon Jul-Aug, 10-11.30am & 2-5.30pm Wed-Mon Apr-Jun & Sep, to 4.30pm Oct), whose conical towers rise from thick woods above the ancient village of Rochepot. The tours are in French but most guides speak English and an English text is provided.

WALKING

The GR7 and it variant, the GR76, run along the Côte d'Or from a bit west of Dijon to the hills west of Beaune, from where they continue southwards. The **Beaune tourist office** (☎ 03 80 26 21 30; www.beaune-burgundy .com; 1 rue de l'Hôtel-Dieu, Beaune) sells an excellent guide, *Walks in the Beaune Countryside* (€3), which details 28 marked routes.

CYCLING

To get from Dijon to Beaune by bike, follow the quiet (but almost vergeless/ shoulderless) D122, which starts to become pretty south of Couchey, to Nuits-St-Georges. From there, take either the challenging D8 and the D115C, or the flatter D20, just east of the N74, which offers fine views of the wine slopes. The ride takes three or four hours and covers about 50km. To avoid cycling both ways (or through Dijon's ugly and heavily trafficked urban sprawl, which stretches as far south as Marsannay-la-Côte), you can take your bike along on most Dijon–Beaune trains – look for the bicycle icon on the train schedule. Bikes can also be taken along on Transco bus 60 (p465).

The new 20km **Voie des Vignes**, a bike route marked by rectangular green-on-white signs, goes from Beaune's Parc de la Bouzaise via Pommard, Volnay, Meursault, Puligny-Montrachet and Chassagne-Montrachet to Santenay, where you can pick up the northern segment of the **Voie Verte** (from Chalon-sur-Saône to St-Léger-sur-Dheune along the Canal du Centre). About 20km further south, another section of the Voie Verte (p495) links Givry with Cluny and beyond.

Sleeping

Along the Route des Grands Crus, signs reading *chambres* announce the presence of a B&B. Tourist offices have lists of accommodation options.

WANT TO KNOW MORE?

Two of the most authoritative tomes on Burgundy wines, *Burgundy* by Anthony Hanson (€44) and *Côte d'Or: A Celebration of the Great Wines of Burgundy* by Clive Coates (€76), were written by Brits, inspiring among French wine connoisseurs a mixture of awe (because of their erudition) and chagrin (because they have yet to be translated into French). A good reference guide is Sylvain Pitiot and Jean-Charles Servant's *The Wines of Burgundy* (€14.25, 11th edition). All three works are available at Beaune's Athenaeum de la Vigne et du Vin (p469).

The **École des Vins de Bourgogne** (☎ 03 80 26 35 10; www.ecoledesvins-bourgogne.com in French; 6 rue du 16e Chasseurs, Beaune) offers a variety of courses (1½/3hr €15/45) to refine your vinicultural vocabulary as well as your palate.

On the internet, useful sites include www.bourgogne-wines.com and www.frenchwines.com.

Gilly-lès-Cîteaux may be on the 'wrong' (ie eastern) side of the N74 but it's home to one of the Côte d'Or's most luxurious hotels, the four-star **Château de Gilly** (☎ 03 80 62 89 98; www.chateau-gilly.com; d €150-290, ste €390-690; ✸ ✺), which occupies the 14th- and 17th-century residence of the abbots of Cîteaux. The 48 spacious rooms are luxuriously appointed and all have lovely views.

Nearby, **La Closerie de Gilly** (☎ 03 80 62 87 74; www.closerie-gilly.com; d €70-85, per week €400; ✺) is a homey, five-room B&B inside a delightful 18th-century *maison bourgeoise*.

In Ladoix-Serrigny, 10 two-star rooms are available at **Les Terrasses de Corton** (☎ 03 80 26 42 37; www.terrasses-de-corton.com; d from €48), on the N74 near the southern edge of town.

Eating

Lots of excellent restaurants can be found in the villages of the Côte d'Or.

Les Terrasses de Corton (☎ 03 80 26 42 37; www.terrasses-de-corton.com; menus €17.50-40; ✹ noon-1.45pm & 7.30-9pm, closed Wed & lunch Thu, also closed dinner Sun Nov–mid-Jan; ✖) In Ladoix-Serrigny, on the N74 near the southern edge of town, this place looks a bit like a motel, but in fact it serves excellent-value French and Burgundian cuisine under Murano chandeliers from Venice.

La Cabotte (☎ 03 80 61 20 77; 24 Grand' Rue, Nuit-St-Georges; menus €27-42; ✹ noon-1.15pm & 7.30-8.45pm, closed Mon, lunch Tue, lunch Sat & dinner Sat) In Nuits-St-Georges, serves up 'inventive' versions of traditional Burgundian cuisine in a spare, modern setting. You won't find any artifice or posing here, just great food served by waiters in golf shirts. To get there walk half a block south from Beffroi de Nuits, the town's 17th-century chiming clock tower.

Le Chambolle (☎ 03 80 62 86 26; 28 rue Basse, Chambolle-Mussigny; 4-/6-course menus €25/38; ✹ 12.15-1.30pm or 2pm, 7.15-8.30pm, closed Wed & Thu) In Chambolle-Mussigny on the D122, a bit east of Vougeot, traditional Burgundian cuisine made with the freshest ingredients is served at this rustic restaurant (that some local connoisseurs would prefer be kept a secret).

our pick **Le Charlemagne** (☎ 03 80 21 51 45; www.lecharlemagne.fr in French; Pernand-Vergelesse; lunch menus Mon-Fri €22-28, other menus €35-75; ✹ noon-1.30pm & 7.30-9.30pm, closed Tue & Wed) Mixes French tradition with techniques and products from Japan, where the chef – whose wife is Japanese – worked for four years. The *escargots* are served with *katsuobushi* (flakes of dried bonito), and other delicious surprises involving *gari* (pickled ginger-root), *nori* (dried seaweed) and *yazu* (a tiny Japanese lemon) await. The vineyard views from the Japanese-inspired dining room are marvellous. It's on the D18 at the southern entrance to the Côte d'Or wine village of Pernand-Vergelesses.

Getting Around

See information on visiting the Côte d'Or by train and bus from Beaune on p472 or from Dijon on p464.

BEAUNE

pop 21,900

Beaune (pronounced similarly to bone), 44km south of Dijon, is the unofficial capital of the Côte d'Or. This thriving town's *raison d'être* is wine – making it, tasting it, selling it but, most of all, drinking it. Consequently Beaune is one of the best places in France for wine tasting.

ABBAYE DE CÎTEAUX

In contrast to the showy Benedictines of Cluny, the medieval Cistercian order was known for its austerity, discipline and humility – and for the productive manual labour of its monks. Named after **Cîteaux Abbey** (Cistercium in Latin; ☎ 03 80 61 32 58; www.citeaux-abbaye.com in French), where it was founded in 1098, the order enjoyed phenomenal growth in the 12th century under St Bernard (1090–1153), and some 600 Cistercian abbeys soon stretched from Scandinavia to the Near East.

Cîteaux was pretty much destroyed during the Revolution and the monks didn't return until 1898 but today it's home to a group of about 30 modern-day monks. From May to early October except Sunday morning, it's possible to visit the monastery on 1¾-hour guided tours described as 'more spiritual than architectural' (in French with printed English commentary; adult/student €7.50/4). Phone ahead for reservations.

The jewel of Beaune's old city is the magnificent Hôtel-Dieu, France's most splendiferous medieval charity hospital.

Orientation

The amoeba-shaped old city, enclosed by ramparts and a stream, is encircled by a one-way boulevard with seven names. The tourist office and the old town's commercial centre are about 1km west of the train station.

Information

Athenaeum de la Vigne et du Vin (☎ 03 80 25 08 30; www.athenaeumfr.com; 7 rue de l'Hôtel-Dieu; 🕑 10am-7pm) Stocks thousands of titles on oenology (the art and science of wine making), including quite a few in English, as well as recipe books and wine-related gifts.
Laundrette (19 rue du Faubourg St-Jean; 🕑 6am-9pm)
Post Office (7 blvd St-Jacques)
Tourist Office (☎ 03 80 26 21 30; www.beaune -burgundy.com) 1 rue de l'Hôtel-Dieu (🕑 9am or 10am-1pm & 2-7pm Jun-3rd weekend Nov, to 6pm late Mar-May, to 5pm 4th week Nov-late Mar); 6 blvd Perpreuil (🕑 same hr but midday closure noon-1pm)

Sights

Founded in 1443 and used as a hospital until 1971, the celebrated Gothic **Hôtel-Dieu des Hospices de Beaune** (☎ 03 80 24 45 00; rue de l'Hôtel-Dieu; adult/student/under 18yr €5.60/4.80/2.80; 🕑 ticket counter 9am-6.30pm Easter–mid-Nov, 9am-11.30am & 2-5.30pm mid-Nov–Easter, interior closes 1hr later), open 365 days a year, is topped by ornate turrets and pitched rooftops covered in multicoloured tiles. Interior highlights include the barrel-vaulted **Grande Salle** (look for the dragons up on the roof beams); an 18th-century **pharmacy** lined with flasks once filled with volatile oils, unguents, elixirs and powders such as *beurre d'antimoine* (antimony butter) and *poudre de cloportes* (woodlouse powder); the huge **kitchens**, with their open hearths and industrious nuns; and the brilliant **Polyptych of the Last Judgement** (see the boxed text, right).

Basilique Collégiale Notre Dame (🕑 closed noon-2pm & Sun morning), built in the Romanesque and Gothic styles from the 11th to 15th centuries, was once affiliated with the monastery of Cluny. Medieval tapestries are displayed inside from mid-April to October.

The exhibits at the **Musée du Vin de Bourgogne** (Museum of Burgundy Wines; ☎ 03 80 22 08 19;

> ## REPENT, O SINNERS, BEFORE IT'S TOO LATE!
>
> On the left side of the *Polyptych of the Last Judgement* (1443) by the Flemish painter Roger van der Weyden, on display in Beaune's Hôtel-Dieu (left), naked dead people climb out of their graves and are welcomed into Heaven (a golden cathedral) by a winged angel, while on the right the terror-stricken damned are dragged shrieking into the fiery depths of Hell, their faces frozen in horror.
>
> Judgement Day has arrived and that means it's payback time, boys and girls! The trumpets are a-blarin', the scales are a-swingin' and your fate for all Eternity lies in the balance. God is loving and beneficent but that angel – the one holding the scales – ain't gonna cut anyone any slack, so if you think that supplications, implorations and entreaties will help at this late stage – fugedaboudit! Repent, repent, O Sinners, for this is what awaits you! Rated PG13 – parental discretion advised, depicts nudity and harsh divine justice.

rue d'Enfer; admission incl Musée des Beaux-Arts €5.40; 🕑 9.30am-5pm Wed-Mon Jan-Mar, 9.30am-6pm Wed-Mon Apr-Dec) are dryer than the driest Chablis. The **Musée des Beaux-Arts** (☎ 03 80 24 98 70; 6 blvd Perpreuil; 🕑 2-6pm Apr-Oct) features Gallo-Roman carvings and assorted paintings, including works by Beaune-born Félix Ziem (1821–1911).

Beaune's thick stone **ramparts**, which shelter wine cellars and are surrounded by overgrown gardens, are ringed by a pathway that makes for a lovely afternoon stroll.

Activities
WINE TASTING

Underneath Beaune's buildings, streets and ramparts, millions of dusty bottles of wine are being aged to perfection in cool, dark, cobweb-lined cellars. At a number of places you can sample and compare fine Burgundy wines.

Marché aux Vins (☎ 03 80 25 08 20; www.marcheaux vins.com in French; 2 rue Nicolas Rolin; admission €10; 🕑 visits begin 9.30-11.30am & 2-5.30pm, no midday closure mid-Jun–Aug) Using a *tastevin* (flat silvery cup whose shiny surfaces help you admire the wine's colour) you can sample a whopping 16 wines (including three

BURGUNDY

whites) in the candle-lit former Église des Cordeliers and its cellars. Wandering among the vintages takes about an hour. The best wines are at the end – look for the *1er cru* and the *grand cru*.

Reine Pédauque (☎ 03 80 22 23 11; www.reine -pedauque.com in French; rue de Lorraine; admission €7.50; ⏰ tours 10.30am, 11.30am, 2.30pm, 3.30pm & 4.30pm, also at 5.30pm Mar-Nov, closed Mon Dec-Feb) Over the course of a 45-minute guided tour (in English upon request) of the 18th-century cellar, visitors sample at least one white, two reds and Belen, an apéritif. Given the thick cobwebs on the ceiling, you wouldn't want to be in here if gravity reversed itself.

Patriarche Père et Fils (☎ 03 80 24 53 78; www .patriarche.com; 5 rue du Collège; audioguide tour €10; ⏰ 9.30-11.30am & 2-5.30pm) The largest cellars in Beaune are rather like Paris' Catacombes except that the corridors are lined with dusty wine bottles instead of human bones. You get to sample and compare 13 wines.

Lycée Viticole (☎ 03 80 26 35 81; www.lavitibeaune .com in French; 16 av Charles Jaffelin; ⏰ 8am-noon & 2-5.30pm Mon-Thu, to 5pm Fri, 8am-noon Sat, may be closed 2 weeks mid-Aug) One of 19 French secondary schools – at least one in each wine-growing region – that train young people in every aspect of wine growing, from tending the vines to fermentation, bottling and ageing. You can visit the cellars and taste the excellent wines made by the students, something they're officially not allowed to do till they're 18 (decades ago wine used to be served with lunch in the school cafeteria!).

Cellier de la Vieille Grange (27 blvd Georges Clemenceau; ⏰ 9am-noon & 2-7pm Wed-Sat) This is where locals come to buy Burgundy wines *en vrac* (in bulk) for as little as €1.15 per litre (from €3.40 per litre for AOC). Tasting is done direct

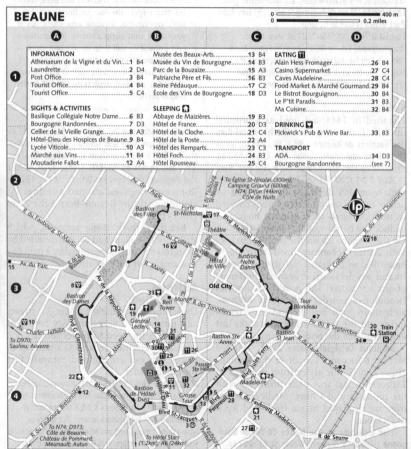

BEAUNE

0 — 400 m
0 — 0.2 miles

INFORMATION	
Athenaeum de la Vigne et du Vin....1	B4
Laundrette..2	D4
Post Office..3	B4
Tourist Office...................................4	B4
Tourist Office...................................5	C4

SIGHTS & ACTIVITIES	
Basilique Collégiale Notre Dame....6	B3
Bourgogne Randonnées....................7	D3
Cellier de la Vieille Grange.............8	A3
Hôtel-Dieu des Hospices de Beaune.9	B4
Lycée Viticole.................................10	A3
Marché aux Vins.............................11	B4
Moutaderie Fallot...........................12	A4

Musée des Beaux-Arts...................13	B4
Musée du Vin de Bourgogne.........14	B3
Parc de la Bouzaize.......................15	A3
Patriarche Père et Fils...................16	B3
Reine Pédauque.............................17	C2
École des Vins de Bourgogne........18	D3

SLEEPING 🏠	
Abbaye de Maizières.....................19	B3
Hôtel de France.............................20	D3
Hôtel de la Cloche........................21	C4
Hôtel de la Poste..........................22	A4
Hôtel des Remparts.......................23	C3
Hôtel Foch....................................24	B3
Hôtel Rousseau.............................25	C4

EATING 🍴	
Alain Hess Fromager.....................26	B4
Casino Supermarket.......................27	C4
Caves Madeleine...........................28	C4
Food Market & Marché Gourmand.29	B4
Le Bistrot Bourguignon..................30	B4
Le P'tit Paradis..............................31	B3
Ma Cuisine....................................32	B4

DRINKING 🍷	
Pickwick's Pub & Wine Bar............33	B3

TRANSPORT	
ADA...34	D3
Bourgogne Randonnées.............(see 7)	

from 114L, 228L and 600L barrels using a pipette. Bring your own jerry can or buy a *cubitainer* (5/20L for €2.75/7.60).

HIKING & CYCLING

A number of walking circuits begin at Parc de la Bouzaize, just northwest of the Lycée Viticole. See also p467 and p467.

Bourgogne Randonnées (☎ 03 80 22 06 03; www .bourgogne-randonnees.com; 7 av du 8 Septembre; ⊗ 9am-noon & 1.30-7pm Mon-Sat, 10am-noon & 2-7pm Sun Apr-Oct) Arranges tailor-made self-guided bike tours, some including lunch with a wine grower. Bike rental costs €15/80 per day/week; maps are provided.

Tours

The **tourist office** (☎ 03 80 26 21 30; www.beaune -burgundy.com; 1 rue de l'Hôtel-Dieu) runs English-language **walking tours** (per person/couple €6.90/11.10) daily at noon from July to mid-September. It also handles reservations for **minibus tours** (€34/68) of the vineyards and **hot-air balloon rides** (see the boxed text, p457).

Moutarderie Fallot (Fallot mustard factory; ☎ 03 80 26 21 30; www.fallot.com; 31 rue du Faubourg Bretonnière; 1hr tour €10; ⊗ 10am & 11.30am Mon-Sat) Come prepared for some powerful odours and tastes.

Festivals & Events

Trois Glorieuses Festival (Third Sunday in November) As part of this three-day festival, the Hospices de Beaune auctions off the wines from its endowment, 61 hectares of prime vineyards bequeathed by benefactors. Proceeds go to medical facilities and research. The event, which has been running since 1859, ends with a lavish candle-lit dinner inside the Hôtel-Dieu.

Sleeping

The tourist office has a list of accommodation options in nearby villages and can help with reservations.

BUDGET

Camping ground (☎ 03 80 22 03 91; 10 rue Auguste Dubois; per adult/tent €3.50/4.30; ⊗ mid-Mar–Oct) Four-star camping 700m north of the centre.

Hôtel Rousseau (☎ 03 80 22 13 59; 11 place Madeleine; d €52, s/d/tr/q with washbasin from €25/32/48/56, with hall shower €3) An endearingly shabby, 12-room hotel run since 1959 by a friendly woman who's been *d'un certain âge* for quite some time. Some of the old-fashioned rooms have showers or toilets. Reception occasionally shuts for a while without warning. Prices include breakfast.

Hôtel Foch (☎ 03 80 24 05 65; fax 03 80 24 75 59; 24 blvd Foch; d €33, with washbasin €25) A cheapie, run by a friendly older lady whose 10 rooms are pretty basic but clean. What you save on accommodation you can spend on wine!

MIDRANGE

Hôtel de France (☎ 03 80 24 10 34; www.hoteldefrance -beaune.com; 35 av du 8 Septembre; s/d/tr/q €46/52/65/75; 🏿) An unsurprising but comfortable two-star place with 22 decent rooms. Ideal if you're arriving by train.

Hôtel de la Cloche (☎ 03 80 24 66 33; www.hotel -cloche-beaune.com in French; 40-42 place Madeleine; d €55-70) The 32 rooms at this veteran three-star establishment mix old-fashioned character with contemporary comfort.

Abbaye de Maizières (☎ 03 80 24 74 64; www .abbayedemaizieres.com in French; 19 rue Maizières; d €77-107) A quirky three-star hotel inside a 12th-century chapel with 13 lovingly converted rooms that make use of the old brickwork and wooden beams.

Hôtel des Remparts (☎ 03 80 24 94 94; www.hotel -remparts-beaune.com; 48 rue Thiers; d low season €78-92, high season €91-105; 🏿 🏿) Set around two delightful courtyards, this three-star place – in a 17th-century townhouse – has 22 rooms with red tile floors, antique furniture and luxurious bathrooms. An excellent bet.

TOP END

Hôtel de la Poste (☎ 03 80 22 08 11; www.hoteldela postebeaune.com; 1 blvd Georges Clemenceau; d €120-200; 🏿 🏿) A four-star establishment on a site that's been home to a hostelry since 1660. Has 36 spacious and exceptionally comfortable rooms (24 more will be added by 2008) – no bling here, just understated elegance. Good wheelchair access. Very romantic.

Eating

Local restaurants are renowned for helping diners select just the right wine to go with each dish. You'll find quite a few cafés and restaurants around place Carnot, place Félix Ziem and place Madeleine.

Caves Madeleine (☎ 03 80 22 93 30; 8 rue du Faubourg Madeleine; menus €12-22; ⊗ closed Thu, Sun & lunch Fri) A convivial Burgundian restaurant, much appreciated by locals who value good value, with regional classics such as *bœuf bourguignon, cassolette d'escargots* and *jambon persillé* (jellied moulded ham). Most guests sit at long communal tables.

BURGUNDY

Le Bistrot Bourguignon (☎ 03 80 22 23 24; 8 rue Monge; menus €12.90-27; ☺ closed Sun & Mon) A bistro-style restaurant and wine bar that serves good-value cuisine billed as *régionale et originale* and 15 Burgundian wines by the glass (€2.90 to €8). Hosts live jazz at least once a month.

Ma Cuisine (☎ 03 80 22 30 22; passage Ste Hélène; menu €19; ☺ 12.15-1.30pm & 7.30-9pm Mon, Tue, Thu & Fri) An intimate place whose traditional French and Burgundian dishes, all excellent, include *pigeon de Bresse entier rôti au jus* (whole Bresse pigeon roasted in its juices; €25). The award-winning wine list includes 700 vintages listed by colour, region and ascending price (€12 to €1578).

Le P'tit Paradis (☎ 03 80 24 91 00; 25 rue Paradis; lunch menu €20, other menus €25-32; ☺ closed Sun & Mon) An intimate restaurant on a narrow medieval street – an excellent place for Burgundian specialities. Has a terrace in summer.

SELF-CATERING
The covered market at place de la Halle hosts a **food market** (☺ until 12.30pm Sat) and a much smaller **marché gourmand** (gourmet market; ☺ Wed morning).

Alain Hess Fromager (7 place Carnot; ☺ Tue-Sat) The nearest *fromagerie* to the market.

Casino Supermarket (28 rue du Faubourg Madeleine; ☺ 8.30am-7.30pm Mon-Sat) Through an archway on rue du Faubourg Madeleine.

Drinking
Pickwick's Pub & Wine Bar (☎ 03 80 22 55 92; 2 rue Notre Dame; ☺ 6pm-5am Mon-Sat) A convincingly English-style pub with leather armchairs, an open fireplace and lots of whiskies behind the counter. Serves nine fine wines by the glass. There's live music two Saturdays a month.

Getting There & Away
BUS
Bus 44, run by **Transco** (☎ 03 80 42 11 00), links Beaune with Dijon (€5.95, one hour, seven Monday to Friday, four Saturday, two Sunday and holidays), stopping at Côte d'Or wine-growing villages such as Vougeot, Nuits-St-Georges and Aloxe-Corton. Except in July and August, bus 44 (three daily weekdays, one or two daily weekends) also serves villages south of Beaune, including Pommard, Volnay, Meursault and La Rochepot.

In Beaune, buses stop along the boulevards around the old city. Timetables can be consulted at the tourist office.

CAR
You can rent a car from **ADA** (☎ 03 80 22 72 90; 26 av du 8 Septembre).

TRAIN
Beaune has frequent services to Dijon (€6.20, 20 minutes, 16 to 22 daily) via the Côte d'Or village of Nuits-St-Georges (€2.90, 10 minutes). The last train from Beaune to Dijon leaves at 11.32pm.

Other destinations include Paris' Gare de Lyon (€42.70, two direct TGVs daily), one or both of Lyon's train stations (€20.50, two hours, 11 to 17 daily) and Mâcon (€12.40, one hour, 12 to 18 daily).

Getting Around
Parking is free outside the town walls.

If your legs feel weak from walking or wine you can take a **taxi** (☎ 06 09 42 36 80, 06 09 43 12 08).

Bourgogne Randonnées (☎ 03 80 22 06 03; www.bourgogne-randonnees.com; 7 av du 8 Septembre; ☺ 9am-noon & 1.30-7pm Mon-Sat, 10am-noon & 2-7pm Sun Apr-Oct) hires bikes.

PAYS D'AUXOIS
The area northwest of Dijon along and around the Canal de Bourgogne is verdant and rural, with broad fields, wooded hills and escarpments dotted with fortified hilltop towns such as Semur-en-Auxois and Flavigny. This part of Burgundy was a Celtic stronghold; at Alésia the Romans confronted Gaulish resistance and crushed it forever.

Semur-en-Auxois
pop 4450
Surrounded by a hairpin curve in the River Armançon, this beguiling hilltop town is guarded by four massive, 13th- and 14th-century pink-granite bastions. Fear not, the 44m-high **Tour de la Orle d'Or** is not likely to collapse anytime soon – those menacing cracks have been there since 1589!

Next to two concentric medieval gates, **Porte Sauvigne** (1417) and fortified **Porte Guillier** (13th century), the **tourist office** (☎ 03 80 97 05 96; www.ville-semur-en-auxois.fr in French; 2 place Gaveau; ☺ 9am-noon & 2-6pm Tue-Sat Sep-Jun, longer hours & open Sun & Mon Jul & Aug) has a free walking tour brochure.

About 100m to the east, you can go online at **Cyber Kafé** (19 rue de la Liberté; per 30min €2; ☺ 7am-8.30pm or 9pm Mon-Sat).

The handsome buildings in the **old city**, easily explorable on foot, were built when Semur was an important religious centre boasting no less than six monasteries. Pedestrianised **rue Buffon**, through the gates from the tourist office, is lined with 17th-century houses; the **confectionary shop** (14 rue Buffon; Tue-Sun) produces **Semurettes**, delicious dark-chocolate candies invented here a century ago. The **Promenade du Rempart** affords panoramic views from atop the western part of Semur's medieval battlements.

Inside twin-towered, Gothic **Collégiale Notre Dame** (9am-noon & 2-6.30pm, until 5pm Nov-Easter), a collegiate church restored in the mid-19th century, are a stained-glass window (1927) and a plaque commemorating American soldiers who fell in WWI.

The **Musée Municipal** (03 80 97 24 25; rue Jean-Jacques Collenot; adult/student €3.25/1.65; 2-5pm Mon & Wed-Fri Oct-Mar, 2-6pm except Tue & holidays Apr-Sep) is fun because its eclectic exhibits – from fossils and stuffed fauna to archaeology, sculpture and oil paintings – are still arranged just as they were back in the 19th century.

SLEEPING & EATING

Hôtel & Restaurant Les Gourmets (03 80 97 09 41; 4 rue Varenne; d €42, with washbasin €27; menus €16-28; reception & restaurant closed Mon, Tue & Dec) In a 16th-century bourgeois house owned by the same family since 1927. The restaurant serves home-style Burgundian cooking. Upstairs, the eight rooms have plenty of old-time atmosphere.

Hôtel Cymaises (03 80 97 21 44; www.hotelcymaises.com; rue du Renaudot; d/q €60.50/88) Set around a quiet courtyard in an 18th-century *maison bourgeoise*, this two-star hotel with good wheelchair access has 18 comfortable, modern rooms, four apartments and a bright veranda for breakfast. It's just 100m from the tourist office – to get there go through the ancient gates and turn right.

Le Calibressan (03 80 97 32 40; 16 rue Févret; menus €13-34.50; closed Mon, lunch Sat & dinner Sun) A rustic eatery that mixes Burgundian tradition (the chef, whose hobby is inventing sauces, is from Bresse) with California panache (his wife is from San Diego). In fact, once inside you can't really tell if it's a French restaurant in Napa or a California-style eatery in France.

Le St Vernier (03 80 97 32 96; 13 rue Févret; menus €10.70-23) A tiny restaurant, much appreciated by locals, that serves up traditional Burgundian dishes, including some made with the strong-smelling Époisses de Bourgogne cheese (see also the boxed text, p74). Situated 150m down the hill from the church

There's a **Petit Casino grocery** (32 place Notre Dame; 8am-12.30pm & 3-7.30pm, closed Sun afternoon & Mon) near the church.

DRINKING

Pub Le Lion (03 80 97 26 68; 4 rue de l'Ancienne Comédie; 4pm-2am Wed-Mon) Just 100m from the tourist office, this popular bar has four billiard tables and a good beer selection, including Guinness on tap. There's dancing to salsa, merengue and folk music on Sunday and Latino dance lessons on Wednesday and Thursday.

GETTING THERE & AWAY

Transco (03 80 42 11 00) bus 49 goes to Dijon (€10.20, 1¼ hours, two or three daily), while bus 70 goes to Saulieu (€5.95, 25 to 50 minutes, four to six daily Monday to Friday, three Saturday and Sunday) and Montbard

---

ESCARGOTS

One of France's trademark culinary habits, the consumption of gastropod molluscs – preferably with butter, garlic, parsley and fresh bread – is inextricably linked in the public mind with Burgundy because *Helix pomatia*, though endemic in much of Europe, is best known as *escargot de Bourgogne* (the Burgundy snail). Once a regular – and unwelcome – visitor to the fine wine vines of Burgundy and a staple on Catholic plates during Lent, the humble hermaphroditic crawler has been decimated by overharvesting and the use of agricultural chemicals and is now a protected species. As a result, the vast majority of the critters impaled on French snail forks (the ones with two tongs) are now imported from Turkey, Greece and Eastern Europe.

For *lots* more information, see the article 'Start Your Own Snail Farm', issued by the **United States Department of Agriculture** (www.totse.com/en/technology/science_technology/snails.html).

(on the Paris–Dijon line; 30 to 60 minutes, seven to nine daily Monday to Friday, three to five Saturday and Sunday).

Abbaye de Fontenay

Fontenay Abbey (☎ 03 80 92 15 00; www.abbayedefontenay.com; adult/student under 26yr €8.90/4.20; ☼ 10am-noon & 2-5pm), founded in 1118 and restored to its stone-built medieval glory a century ago, offers a fascinating glimpse at the austere, serene surroundings in which Cistercian monks lived lives of contemplation, prayer and manual labour. Set in a bucolic wooded valley along a stream called the Ru de Fontenay, the abbey – a Unesco World Heritage Site – includes an exquisitely unadorned Romanesque church, a barrel-vaulted monks' dormitory, landscaped gardens and an old forge designated by ASM International (www.asminternational.org) as the 'first metallurgical factory in Europe'. Guided **tours** (☼ departures hourly 10am-noon & 2-5pm Apr-11 Nov) are in French (printed information is available in six languages).

From the parking lot, the **GR213 trail** (marked in red and white) leads to Montbard (13km); it also forms part of an 11.5km circuit that passes through Touillon and Le Petit Jailly.

The abbey is 25km north of Semur-en-Auxois. A **taxi** (☎ 03 80 92 04 79, 03 80 92 31 49) from the Montbard train station – served from Dijon (€10.60, 40 minutes) and Paris' Gare de Lyon (non-TGV/TGV train €28/43.70, two to 2½ hours) – costs €10.50 (€14 on Sunday and holidays).

Flavigny-sur-Ozerain & Alésia

Flavigny, 16km east of Semur, is a delightful hilltop village surrounded by ramparts and rolling pastureland. Neither overrestored nor touristy, it's straight out of the Middle Ages, which is why movies such as *Chocolat* have been filmed here. The local sweet, *anis de Flavigny*, consists of an anise seed wrapped in rock-hard candy.

Flavigny's only hotel, **Le Relais de Flavigny** (☎ 03 80 96 27 77; www.le-relais.fr; rue des Anciennes Halles; d with shower €35; ☼ reception closed approximately 3-6pm, hotel closed 3 weeks Jan), is above a bar-restaurant in the middle of the old city. The seven rooms are very basic.

Local farmers cook up their produce at **La Grange des Quatre Heures Soupatoires** (☎ 03 80 96 20 62; plat du jour €8-10; ☼ 12.30-5pm Tue-Fri, 12.30-

6pm Sat & Sun Jul–mid-Sep, 12.30-6pm Sun & holidays Mar-Jun & mid-Sep–Oct, also perhaps Nov), next to the church – a fantastic way to try traditional Burgundy cooking.

Die-hard fans of Roman military history might want to drop by **Alésia** (the modern-day village of Alice-Ste-Reine), a few kilometres northwest of Flavigny, where the Celtic chief Vercingétorix was defeated by Julius Caesar in 52 BC. In addition to the **archaeological excavations** (adult/7-16yr €5/3; ☼ 10am-12.30pm & 2-6pm late Mar-11 Nov, longer hr Jul & Aug) a few hundred metres from the village there's a small **museum** and a hilltop **statue of Vercingétorix**, erected by Napoleon III. The nearby indicator shows the presumed battle lines.

CHÂTILLON-SUR-SEINE

pop 6300

Châtillon's main claim to fame is the **Trésor de Vix**, a treasure-trove of Celtic, Etruscan and Greek objects from the 6th century BC found in the tomb of a Celtic princess believed to have controlled the trade in British tin and Baltic amber. The collection is displayed at the **Musée du Châtillonnais** (☎ 03 80 91 24 67; rue du Bourg; adult/child €4/2.50; ☼ 9.30am-noon & 2-5pm Wed-Mon Sep-Jun, 10am-6pm Jul & Aug) and includes the princess' half-kilogram gold torque and a 1.64m-high, bronze Greek krater (vase) that held a bladder-bursting 1100L of wine.

Châtillon's **tourist office** (☎ 03 80 91 13 19; www.pays-chatillonnais.fr in French; place Marmont; ☼ 2-5pm Mon, 9am-noon & 2-5pm Tue-Sat, also 10am-noon Sun & holidays May-Sep) is at the fountain roundabout. The town's commercial centre, rebuilt after the war, is bordered by two branches of the Seine, here hardly more than a stream.

A short walk east, **Source de la Douix** (☼ 24hr), a 600L-a-second artesian spring situated at the bottom of a 30m cliff, is ideal for a picnic. Nearby you can climb up to the round, crenellated **Tour de Gissey** (1500s), which affords a fine view; access is via the cemetery. Overlooking the village is the 10th-century **Église St-Vorles**.

Among the wines produced in the **Châtillonnais vineyards**, north and northwest of town, is Burgundy's own bubbly, *crémant de Bourgogne*. The Champagne region's **Côte des Bar vineyards** (p369) are just a few kilometres further north.

The nine-room **Hôtel de la Côte d'Or** (☎ 03 80 91 13 29; remillet.gerard@club-internet.fr; 2 rue Charles-Ronot;

d €54-69), off the main street, is a pleasant Logis de France place with shuttered windows.

Bus 50, run by **Transco** (☎ 03 80 42 11 00), goes to Dijon (€13.20, 1½ hours, two or three daily).

YONNE

The Yonne *département,* roughly midway between Dijon and Paris, has long been Burgundy's northern gateway. The area is best known for its verdant countryside, the magical hilltop village of Vézelay, the white-wine centre of Chablis and canal boat cruising from ancient river ports such as Auxerre.

AUXERRE

pop 37,800

The alluring riverside town of Auxerre (pronounced oh-*sair*) has been a river port since Roman times. Wandering through the maze of cobbled streets in the old city, you'll pass Roman remains, Gothic churches and timber-framed medieval houses – and gaze across a jumble of belfries, spires and steep tiled rooftops leading down to the boats bobbing on the River Yonne.

Auxerre makes a good base for visiting northern Burgundy, including Chablis (p478), and the city's port makes it an excellent place to rent a canal boat (see the boxed text, p457).

Auxerre boasts one of the country's top football teams.

Orientation

The old city climbs up the hillside on the left (west) bank of the River Yonne, while the train station is 700m east of the river. The commercial centre stretches from the cathedral to the post office, with shops lining rue de Paris and rue du Temple. The liveliest areas are around pedestrianised rue de l'Horloge and place Charles Surugue.

Information

The tourist office changes small amounts of money on Sunday and holidays.

Laundrette (138 rue de Paris; ☽ 6am-9pm)

Post Office (place Charles Surugue) Has a Cyberposte and changes currency.

Speed Informatique 89 (32 rue du Pont; per 10min/1hr €1/5; ☽ 10am-10pm Tue-Fri, noon-5am Sat, 2-10pm Sun & Mon) Internet access.

Tourist Office (☎ 03 86 52 06 19; www.ot-auxerre .fr in French; 1-2 quai de la République; ☽ 9am-1pm & 2-7pm Mon-Sat, 9.30am-1pm & 3-6.30pm Sun & holidays mid-Jun–mid-Sep, 9.30am-12.30pm & 2-6pm Mon-Fri, 9.30-12.30pm & 2-6.30pm Sat, 10am-1pm Sun mid-Sep–mid-Jun)

Sights

Wonderful views of the city, perched on the hillside, can be had from **Pont Paul Bert** (1857) and the arched footbridge opposite the tourist office.

ABBAYE ST-GERMAIN

The ancient **St-Germain Abbey** (☎ 03 86 18 05 50; place St-Germain; adult/student under 26yr €4.30/free; ☽ 10am-12.30pm & 2-6.30pm Wed-Mon Jun-Sep, 10am-noon & 2-6pm Wed-Mon Oct-May) began as a basilica above the tomb of St Germain, the 5th-century bishop who made Auxerre an important Christian centre. Over the centuries, as the site's importance grew, so did the abbey, and by the Middle Ages it was attracting pilgrims from all over Europe.

The **crypts**, visitable only on a tour (in French with printed information in English; hourly departures until 5pm in winter, 5.30pm in summer), contain some of Europe's finest examples of Carolingian architecture. Supported by 1000-year-old oak beams, the walls and vaulted ceiling are decorated with 9th-century frescoes; the far end houses the tomb of St Germain himself. Excavations under the nave have uncovered sarcophagi – left in situ – from as early as the 6th century.

Housed around the abbey's cloister, the **Musée d'Art et d'Histoire** displays prehistoric artefacts, Gallo-Roman sculpture and pottery discovered in and around Auxerre. The new medieval section includes a mock-up of a scriptorium (where monks copied over manuscripts); nearby rooms have medals and coinage.

The same ticket includes entry to **Musée Leblanc-Duvernoy** (☎ 03 86 52 44 63; 9bis rue d'Églény; separate admission €2.10; ☽ 2-6pm Wed-Mon), which has a pretty good collection of faïence.

CATHÉDRALE ST-ÉTIENNE

The vast Gothic **Cathédrale St-Étienne** (place St-Étienne; ☽ 7.30am-6pm Easter-Oct, 7.30am-5pm 15 Nov-Easter) and its stately 68m-high bell tower dominate Auxerre's skyline (and most of the postcards too). The building was constructed

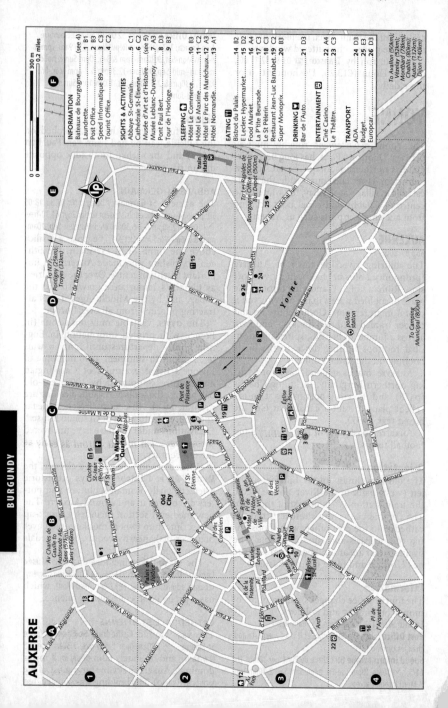

AUXERRE

0 ____ 300 m
0 ____ 0.2 miles

BURGUNDY

INFORMATION	
Bateaux de Bourgogne	(see 4)
Laundrette	1 B1
Post Office	2 B3
Speed Informatique 89	3 C3
Tourist Office	4 C2

SIGHTS & ACTIVITIES	
Abbaye St-Germain	5 C1
Cathédrale St-Étienne	6 C2
Musée d'Art et d'Histoire	(see 5)
Musée Leblanc-Duvernoy	7 A3
Pont Paul Bert	8 D3
Tour de l'Horloge	9 B3

SLEEPING	
Hôtel Le Commerce	10 B3
Hôtel Le Maxime	11 C2
Hôtel Le Parc des Maréchaux	12 A3
Hôtel Normandie	13 A1

EATING	
Bistrot du Palais	14 B2
E Leclerc Hypermarket	15 D2
Food Market	16 A4
La P'tite Beursade	17 C3
Le St Pèlerin	18 C3
Restaurant Jean-Luc Barnabet	19 C3
Super Monoprix	20 B3

DRINKING	
Bar de l'Auto	21 D3

ENTERTAINMENT	
Ciné Casino	22 A4
Le Théâtre	23 C3

TRANSPORT	
ADA	24 D3
Budget	25 E3
Europcar	26 D3

mainly between the 13th and 16th centuries, though the choir, ambulatory and some of the vivid **stained-glass windows** (eg in the axial chapel and the ambulatory) date from the 1200s. The Gothic western front was badly damaged by the hammer-happy Huguenots, who decapitated most of the statues during the Wars of Religion.

The 11th-century Romanesque **crypt** (adult/under 12yr €2.80/free; ☻ 9am-6pm except Sun morning Easter-Oct, 10am-5pm Mon-Sat Nov-Easter) is ornamented with remarkable frescoes, including a scene of **Christ à Cheval** (Christ on horseback; late 11th century) unlike any other known in Western art. Upstairs, the **treasury** (admission €1.70; ☻ same as crypt) displays illuminated manuscripts, Limoges enamels and the usual chalices. Tickets are sold in the gift shop off the choir.

From June to September a 75-minute sound-and-light show is held nightly in the cathedral. In July and August organ concerts (€5) are held every Sunday at 5pm.

TOUR DE L'HORLOGE
The spire-topped **Tour de l'Horloge** (clock tower; rue de l'Horloge) was built in 1483 as part of the city's fortifications. On the 17th-century clock faces (there's one on each side), the sun-hand indicates the time of day; the moon-hand shows what day of the lunar month it is, making a complete rotation every 29½ days. At the time of writing, the nearby fibreglass statue of **Marie Noël**, Auxerre's best known poet, had been taken away for de-graffiti treatment.

Sleeping
Camping Municipal (☎ 03 86 52 11 15; 8 route de Vaux; adult/site €2.95/2.60; ☻ Apr-Sep) A shaded, grassy place 1.5km south of the train station (and across the street from the football stadium). From place de l'Arquebuse, take bus A (two to three per hour until 7pm) to the Stades Arbre Sec stop.

Hôtel Le Commerce (☎ 03 86 52 03 16; hoteldu commerceauxerre@wanadoo.fr; 5 rue René Schaeffer; s/d/f €41/45/57) A cheap, welcoming place smack in the centre of town. The 16 deep-pastel rooms have shower pods but the old building's cheerfully creative décor has been inspired by distant sunny lands.

Hôtel Normandie (☎ 03 86 52 57 80; www.hotel normandie.fr; 41 blvd Vauban; d €58-71; ☻ closed early Feb; ✗ ☷) In a 19th-century building on

tree-lined blvd Vauban, this great-value hotel has ivy-covered frontage, friendly staff and 47 tasteful rooms that make it feel like a much more expensive country hotel. Amenities include a billiard table, a workout room and a sauna (€10 for two).

Hôtel Le Maxime (☎ 03 86 52 14 19; www.lemaxime .com; 2 quai de la Marine; s/d €70/80, mid-Nov–mid-Mar less €5, ste €125; ☷) In a wonderful spot overlooking the River Yonne, this three-star place offers spacious, impeccable rooms – some with river views, others with views of the old city – and first-class service.

Hôtel Le Parc des Maréchaux (☎ 03 86 51 43 77; www.hotel-parcmarechaux.com; 6 av Foch; d €85-115, mid-Dec–mid-Mar less €5; ☷) Housed in a one-time private mansion just outside the old city, this three-star place was totally refurbished in 2006. The 25 rooms, all named after French marshals, are decorated with exceptional taste and are ideal for a romantic getaway; the two best ones have balconies overlooking the peaceful garden.

Eating
Bistrot du Palais (☎ 03 86 51 47 02; 69 rue de Paris; mains €11; ☻ Tue-Sat) A classic French bistro with tiny tables, checked tablecloths and the essential sound of clattering saucepans. Among the specialities: Lyonnais sausages and *bœuf bourguignon*.

Le St Pèlerin (☎ 03 86 52 77 05; 56 rue St-Pèlerin; menu €25; ☻ Tue-Sat) Diners come back satiated from this rustic restaurant, where French and Burgundian dishes are prepared over a wood fire.

La P'tite Beursade (☎ 03 86 51 10 21; 55 rue Joubert; menus €17-26; ☻ closed dinner Sun, Mon & lunch Tue) An intimate place with a small selection of fish and meat dishes prepared the traditional French way. Specialities include *entrecôte poêlée à la crème de Chaource* (fried rib steak with Chaource cheese). The waitresses wear traditional Morvan dress.

Restaurant Jean-Luc Barnabet (☎ 03 86 51 68 88; 14 quai de la République; menus €32-73, children's menu €16; ☻ closed dinner Sun & lunch Tue) A true temple of gastronomy. The chef's innovative versions of traditional French dishes have earned many accolades, including a Michelin star.

SELF-CATERING
Places for picnic supplies:
E Leclerc Hypermarket (14 av Jean Jaurès; ☻ 9am-8pm Mon-Sat)

BURGUNDY

Food Market (place de l'Arquebuse; ☽ 7am-1pm Tue & Fri)
Super Monoprix Supermarket (place Charles Surugue; ☽ 8.30am-8pm Mon-Sat)

Drinking

There are a number of small bars along rue Joubert near Le Théâtre.

Bar de l'Auto (☎ 03 86 46 91 78; 4bis av Gambetta; ☽ Mon-Sat) Across the river is this very average-looking saloon with jazz jam sessions every Monday at 9.30pm and occasional concerts on Tuesday or Thursday.

Entertainment

Ciné Casino (☎ 03 86 52 36 80; 1 blvd du 11 Novembre) generally screens one or two nondubbed films. **Le Théâtre** (☎ 03 86 72 24 24; www.auxerre-le-theatre.com in French; 54 rue Joubert), the city's clean-lined, Art Deco theatre, puts on dance, drama and theatre and hosts **top jazz talent** (www.jazzclubdauxerre.com) at 9pm on several Fridays a month from mid-October to early June.

Getting There & Away
BUS

Buses operated by **Les Rapides de Bourgogne** (☎ 03 86 94 95 00) link the train station and place de l'Arquebuse with Chablis (€2, 35 minutes, two or three daily except Sunday and holidays) and Pontigny (€2, 35 minutes, two or three daily except Sunday and holidays). The tourist office can provide timetables. Some services operate only if you call the day before, prior to 5pm (☎ 08 00 30 33 09).

CAR

Car-rental companies:
ADA (☎ 03 86 46 01 02; 6bis av Gambetta)
Budget (☎ 03 80 18 00 88; 32 av Gambetta)
Europcar (☎ 03 86 46 99 08; 9 av Gambetta)

TRAIN

Trains run from **Gare Auxerre-St-Gervais** (rue Paul Doumer) to the mainline Laroche-Migennes station (€3.40, 15 minutes, six to 11 daily), where you can change for Dijon (€22.10, two hours, five to seven daily) and Paris' Gare de Lyon (€21.90, two hours, five to nine daily). Trains also go to Sermizelles-Vézelay (€6.70, 45 minutes, three to five daily) and Avallon (€8.50, one hour, three to five daily).

Getting Around

Free parking is available on quai de la Marine and quai de la République, and on the boulevards around the old city: de la Chainette, Vauban, du 11 Novembre and Vaulabelle.

Phone for a **taxi** (☎ 03 86 94 02 02, 03 86 46 95 67).

AROUND AUXERRE

Between the River Yonne and the Canal de Bourgogne lie the Auxerrois and the Tonnerrois, rural areas covered with forests, fields, pastures and vineyards. The quiet back roads (eg the D124) and many of the walking trails make for excellent cycling.

La Puisaye

The countryside west of Auxerre is known as **La Puisaye**, a sparsely populated landscape of woods, winding creeks and dark hills. The area is best known as the birthplace of Colette (1873–1954), author of *La Maison de Claudine* and *Gigi*, who was born in the tiny town of St-Sauveur-en-Puisaye, 40km southwest of Auxerre, and of particular interest because much of her work explores her rural Burgundian childhood.

Musée Colette (☎ 03 86 45 61 95; adult/student €4.50/2; ☽ 10am-6pm Wed-Mon Apr-Oct, 2-6pm Sat & Sun, public holidays & school holidays Nov-Mar), on the outskirts of St-Sauveur-en-Puisaye, houses a collection of her manuscripts, letters and belongings.

At the fantastic **Chantier Médiéval de Guédelon** (☎ 03 86 45 66 66; www.guedelon.org; adult/child €9/7; ☽ 10am-7pm Jul & Aug, 10am-5.30pm or 6pm Thu-Tue mid-Mar–Jun & Sep-early Nov), 45km southwest of Auxerre and 7km southwest of St-Sauveur-en-Puisaye, a team of builders, stonemasons and carpenters (in period costume) are constructing a medieval castle using only 13th-century tools, techniques and materials. No one seems to have any idea when the project is likely to be finished.

Chablis
pop 2600

The well-to-do but sleepy town of Chablis, 19km east of Auxerre, has made its fortune growing, ageing and marketing the dry white wines that bear its name.

Chablis is made exclusively from Chardonnay grapes and is divided into four

Appellations d'Origine Contrôlées (AOC): Petit Chablis, Chablis, Chablis Premier Cru and, most prestigious of all, Chablis Grand Cru. The seven *grands crus*, lovingly grown on just 1 sq km of land on the hillsides northeast of town, are Blanchot, Bougros, Les Clos, Grenouilles, Preuses, Valmur and Vaudésir.

ORIENTATION & INFORMATION

Chablis' main street is known as rue Auxerroise (west of the main square, place Charles de Gaulle) and rue du Maréchal de Lattre de Tassigny (east of place Charles de Gaulle). Most of Chablis' shops are closed on Monday and noon to 3pm on other days.

Tourist Office (☎ 03 86 42 80 80; www.chablis.net; 1 rue du Maréchal de Lattre de Tassigny; ✆ 10am-12.30pm & 1.30-6pm, closed Sun Dec-Mar) Just east of place Charles de Gaulle.

SIGHTS & ACTIVITIES

The 12th- and 13th-century Gothic **Église St-Martin** (✆ Jul & Aug), founded in the 9th century by monks fleeing the Norman attacks on Tours, is two short blocks northwest of place Charles de Gaulle. Southeast along rue Porte Noël are the twin bastions of **Porte Noël** (1778), which hosts art exhibitions from late May to mid-September. Nearby, the enigmatic 16th-century building known as the **synagogue** (12 rue des Juifs) is being restored. The 12th-century cellar of the **Petit Pontigny** (rue de Chichée) was once used by Pontigny's Cistercian monks to ferment wine.

Vineyard walks from Chablis include the **Sentier des Grands Crus** (8km) and the **Sentier des Clos** (13km to 24km, depending on your route). The tourist office sells a French-language topoguide (€5.50).

Cycling is a great way to tour the surrounding countryside. The tourist office helpfully hires **bikes** in the warm season.

Nearby villages worth exploring include **Courgis**, which offers great views; **Chichée** and **Chemilly**, both on the River Serein; and **Chitry-le-Fort**, famous for its fortified church.

Wine tasting can be enjoyed and wine bought at dozens of places – the tourist office has a comprehensive list. All the various Chablis *crus* can be sampled at **La Chablisienne** (☎ 03 86 42 89 98; 8 blvd Pasteur; ✆ 9am-12.30pm & 2-7pm, to 6pm Jan-Mar), a large cooperative cellar 700m south of place Charles de Gaulle

along rue Auxerroise and then av de la République.

SLEEPING & EATING

Hôtel Le Bergerand's (☎ 03 86 18 96 08; www.chablis-france.fr in French; 4 rue des Moulins; d €65-75; 🖳) A rustic hotel whose 22 attractively furnished rooms, including one with a Jacuzzi (€135), occupy a one-time coaching inn. The French-born *patronne* lived in Los Angeles for 35 years.

Hostellerie des Clos (☎ 03 86 42 10 63; www.hostellerie-des-clos.fr; rue Jules-Rathier; d €60-86, ste €125-183; ✆ closed mid-Dec–mid-Jan; 🔀) A luxurious, three-star hotel housed in the town's former hospices, with 36 lavish rooms and enclosed gardens. The attached French restaurant (menus €38 to €73) holds one Michelin star, and as you'd expect the wine list is impressive.

Le Bistrot des Grands Crus (☎ 03 86 42 19 41; 8-10 rue Jules Rathier; menu €20) A block southeast of Porte Noël, this is a sleek, modern place whose *cuisine du terroir* (cooking that's deeply connected to the land) is made with the freshest local ingredients, including Chablis.

Au Vrai Chablis (☎ 03 86 42 11 43; place Charles de Gaulle; menus €13.50-29; ✆ closed dinner Tue & Wed) At this rustic, informal place several dishes take advantage of the culinary potential of the local wines. It has a warm-season terrace, as do other restaurants nearby.

Chablis has an **outdoor food market** (place Charles de Gaulle; ✆ until 1pm Sun). Except for the **Petit Casino grocery** (rue du Maréchal Leclerc; ✆ 7.30am-12.30pm & 3-7.30pm Mon-Sat), 50m down the hill from place Charles de Gaulle, all the food shops along rue Auxerroise are closed on Sunday afternoon and Monday.

GETTING THERE & AWAY

Buses run by **Les Rapides de Bourgogne** (☎ 03 86 94 95 00) link Chablis' place Charles de Gaulle with Auxerre (€2, 35 minutes) and Tonnerre (€2, 30 minutes) two or three times a day except Sunday and holidays. Some services operate only if you call the day before, prior to 5pm (☎ 08 00 30 33 09).

Pontigny
pop 800

Rising from flat fields 25km north of Auxerre, Pontigny's **Abbatiale** (abbey church; ☎ 03 86 47 54 99; admission free; ✆ 9am or 10am-5pm in winter,

BURGUNDY

THE ENGLISH CONNECTION

Three archbishops of Canterbury played a role in the history of Pontigny's abbey: Thomas à Becket spent the first three years of his exile here (1164–66); Stephen Langton, a refugee from political turmoil in England, lived here for six years (from 1207 to 1213); and Edmund Rich, who fell ill and died at Soissy in 1240 while on his way to the Vatican, was brought here for burial.

to 7pm in summer), is one of the last surviving examples of Cistercian architecture in Burgundy. The simplicity and purity of its construction reflects the austerity of the Cistercian order. On summer days sunshine filtering through the high windows bathes the abbey in light, creating an amazing sense of peace and tranquillity.

The Gothic sanctuary, 108m long and lined with 23 chapels, was built in the mid-12th century, but the wooden choir screen, stalls and organ loft were added in the 17th and 18th centuries. Monks from the abbey were the first to perfect the production of Chablis wine.

The **tourist office** (☎ 03 86 47 47 03; pontigny@ wanadoo.fr; 22 rue Paul Desjardins; ☘ 10am-12.30pm & 2-6pm Easter-Sep or Oct, 10.30am-12.30pm & 2-4pm Tue-Sat Oct or Nov-Mar), across the road from the Abbatiale, has information on accommodation and hikes.

The only hotel in Pontigny is **Le Relais de Pontigny** (☎ 03 86 47 96 74; d €28; ☘ reception closed Sat & Sun Oct-May, hotel closed mid-Dec–early Jan), a roadside bar 400m along the N77 from the tourist office. The 10 upstairs rooms are basic but cheap, and you can find food at the attached truckers' **restaurant** (menus €13-17; ☘ closed dinner Sat & Sun, also closed lunch Sat & Sun Oct-May). Or try the nearby **Moulin de Pontigny** (☎ 03 86 47 44 98; menus €15-30; ☘ closed Mon & lunch Tue, also closed dinner Tue & Wed, plus closed dinner Thu Oct-Mar), on the N77 down by the river, which offers rural cooking in the town's old mill – frogs' legs, braised ham and *andouillette* (tripe sausage) are all on the menu.

Supplies are available at the **Alimentation Générale** (grocery; 43 rue Paul Desjardins; ☘ 7.30am-1pm & 3.30-8pm, closed Sun afternoon).

Les Rapides de Bourgogne (☎ 03 86 94 95 00) runs buses to Pontigny from Auxerre (€2, 35 minutes, two or three daily except Sun-

day and holidays). Some services operate only if you call the day before, prior to 5pm (☎ 08 00 30 33 09).

Tonnerre

pop 5900

The town of Tonnerre, on the Canal de Bourgogne, is best known for the **Hôtel-Dieu** (Vieil Hôpital; rue de l'Hôpital; adult/12-18yr €4.50/3.50; ☘ 9am-12.30pm & 2-6.30pm Mon-Sat, 10am-noon & 2-5pm Sun Apr-Oct, 9am-noon & 2-6pm except Sun & holidays Nov-Mar), a charity hospital founded in 1293 by Marguerite de Bourgogne, sister-in-law of St Louis. At the eastern end of the barrel-vaulted patients' hall, near the chapel and Marguerite's tomb, is an extraordinary 15th-century Entombment of Christ, carved from a single block of stone. The **tourist office** (☎ 03 86 55 14 48; ☘ same as Hôtel-Dieu) is at the entrance.

About 400m west at the base of the cliffs below **Église St-Pierre**, some 200L of water per second gushes from **Fosse Dionne**, a natural spring that was sacred to the Celts and whose weird blue-green tint hints at its great depth. The pool is surrounded by a mid-18th-century washing house and a semicircle of ancient houses. Legend has it that a serpent lurks at the bottom of the spring. To get there, follow the signs on rue François Mitterrand (across the street from the tourist office) past the **covered market** (1903).

Tonnerre's most delightful hostelry is **La Ferme de Fosse Dionne** (☎ 03 86 54 82 62; www .fermefossedionne.com; 11 rue de la Fosse Dionne; d with breakfast €56), a late 18th-century farm overlooking Fosse Dionne, which has six lovingly kept rooms of varying shapes and colours. Downstairs, the friendly owner runs a café and antique shop that stocks local edibles, including Tonnerre's almost unknown wines. Ask nicely and he might provide some hiking tips, or even play one of his old gramophones.

By rail, Tonnerre – 16km northeast of Chablis – is linked to Dijon (€16.10, one hour, eight to 10 daily) and, via Laroche-Migennes, to Auxerre (€9.10, 45 minutes, five to seven daily).

Les Rapides de Bourgogne (☎ 03 86 94 95 00) runs two or three buses a day, except Sunday and holidays, to Auxerre (€2, 80 minutes) and Chablis (€2, 35 minutes). Some services operate only if you call the day before, prior to 5pm (☎ 08 00 30 33 09).

A KNIGHT IN SHINING PETTICOATS

Speculation about the cross-dressing habits of the French secret agent Charles Geneviève d'Éon de Beaumont (1728–1810), born in Tonnerre, has been rife for centuries, especially in sex-obsessed England, where he spent part of his life wearing the latest women's fashion and spying for Louis XV. The locals, at least, have no doubt about the brave chevalier's suitability as a role model for today's youth – they've named the local high school after him – though a local tourist brochure refers to him as a 'chevalier(e) tonnerrois(e)'.

Château de Tanlay

The French Renaissance-style **Château de Tanlay** (☎ 03 86 75 70 61; adult/child €8/3.50; ☉ tours begin 10am, 11.30am & 2.15pm, 3.15pm, 4.15pm & 5.15pm Wed-Mon Apr–mid-Nov), an elegant product of the 17th century, is surrounded by a wide moat and elaborately carved outbuildings. Interior highlights include the **Grande Galerie**, whose walls and ceiling are completely covered with trompe l'oeil. The chateau is 10km east of Tonnerre in the village of Tanlay.

Château d'Ancy-le-Franc

The Italian Renaissance makes a cameo appearance at **Château d'Ancy-le-Franc** (☎ 03 86 75 14 63; www.chateau-ancy.com; adult/student/6-15yr €8/7/5; ☉ tours 10.30am, 11.30am, 2pm, 3pm & 4pm Tue-Sun Apr–mid-Nov, also 5pm Apr-Sep), built in the 1540s by the celebrated Italian architect Serlio. The richly painted interior is mainly the work of Italian artists brought to Fontainebleau by François I.

Overlooking huge stables, a large park and the Canal de Bourgogne, the chateau is 19km southeast of Tonnerre.

Noyers-sur-Serein

pop 880

The medieval village of Noyers (pronounced nwa-yer), 30km southeast of Auxerre, is surrounded by rolling pastureland, wooded hills and a hairpin curve in the River Serein. Stone ramparts and fortified battlements enclose much of the village, and between the two imposing stone gateways, cobbled streets lead past 15th- and 16th-century gabled houses, half-timbered buildings and a number of art galleries. Many of the streets still bear their medieval names – look out for place du Grenier-à-Sel (salt store) and place du Marché-au-Blé (flour market). Noyers lives by its own rules so don't be surprised if things are closed when they're supposed to be open and vice versa.

Lines carved into the façade of the 18th-century **mairie** (town hall), next to the library, mark the level of historic floods. Diagonally across the street is the **tourist office** (☎ 03 86 82 66 06; www.noyers-sur-serein.com; 22 place de l'Hôtel de Ville; ☉ 10am-1pm & 2-6pm Tue-Sat Oct-May, same hr daily Jun-Sep).

Musée de Noyers (☎ 03 86 82 89 09; rue de l'Église; adult/student/senior €4/2/3; ☉ 11am-6.30pm Wed-Mon Jun-Sep, 2.30-6.30pm Sat, Sun & school holidays Oct-Dec & Feb-May), near the 15th-century church, displays a colourful collection of **naive art**.

Just outside Noyers' clock-topped southern gate, Chemin des Fossés leads eastwards to the River Serein and a **streamside walk** around the village's 13th-century **fortifications**, 19 of whose original 23 towers are extant. The 9km **Balade du Château**, trailmarked in red, follows the Serein's right bank past the ruined chateau just north of Noyers.

There's a municipal **camping ground** (adult €1.40; ☉ Easter-Oct) outside the city walls, on the left as you approach the southern gates, near the post office.

Both of Noyer's **grocery shops**, situated on either side of the *mairie*, are closed 12.30pm to 3pm or 4pm and on Sunday afternoon.

Les Rapides de Bourgogne (☎ 03 86 94 95 00) runs buses to/from Avallon (€2, one hour, two or three daily except Sunday and holidays).

AVALLON

pop 8200

The once-strategic walled town of Avallon, on a picturesque hilltop overlooking the green terraced slopes of two River Cousin tributaries, was in centuries past a stop on the coach road from Paris to Lyon. At its most animated during the Saturday morning market, the city makes a good base for exploring nearby Vézelay and the rolling countryside of the Parc Naturel Régional du Morvan.

A tourist brochure cheerfully and succinctly sums up the city's history: 'Avallon was often burned, pillaged, and its inhabitants slaughtered or decimated by outbreaks of the plague. The Tourism Office wishes you a pleasant stay.'

BURGUNDY

Orientation

The old city, built on a triangular granite hilltop with ravines to the east and west, is about 1km southwest of the train station. The main commercial thoroughfares are the old city's Grande Rue Aristide Briand and, outside the walls, rue de Paris and rue de Lyon.

Information

Internet Access (per 30min €3) In the tourist office.

Post Office (9 place des Odebert)

Tourist Office (☎ 03 86 34 14 19; www.avallonnais -tourisme.com; 6 rue Bocquillot; ☺ 10am-1pm & 2.30-7pm mid-Jun–mid-Sep, 10am-12.30pm & 2-6pm Mon-Sat rest of yr, closed Mon morning Oct-Mar, open Sun morning school holidays) In a 15th-century house.

Sights

Tour de l'Horloge, a solid, 15th-century clock tower, spans Grande Rue Aristide Briand. The nearby **Musée de l'Avallonnais** (☎ 03 86 34 03 19; place de la Collégiale; admission free; ☺ 2-6pm Wed-Mon Jul-Sep & school holidays, also open Sat & Sun Oct-Jun), founded in 1862, displays religious art, fossils and expressionist sketches by Georges Rouault (1871–1958).

Eight centuries ago, the early-12th-century **Collégiale St-Lazare** (rue Bocquillot; ☺ until about 4.30pm winter, to 6pm summer) drew huge numbers of pilgrims thanks to a piece of the skull of St Lazarus, believed to provide protection from leprosy. The church once had three **portals** but one was crushed when the northern belfry came a-tumblin' down in 1633; the two remaining portals are grandly decorated in the Burgundian Romanesque style, though much of the carving has been damaged. Summertime art exhibitions are held next door in **Église St-Pierre** and across the street in the 18th-century **Grenier à Sel** (Salt Store).

South of the church is one of the city's ancient gateways, the **Petite Porte**, from where a pathway descends and gives fine views over the Vallée du Cousin. Walking around the walls, with their 15th- to 18th-century towers, ramparts and bastions, is a good way to get a sense of the town's geography.

About 100 costumes from the 18th to 20th centuries are on display at the **Musée du Costume** (☎ 03 86 34 19 95; 6 rue Belgrand; adult/ student €4/2.50; ☺ 10.30am-12.30pm & 1.30-5.30pm Easter-Oct).

Activities

An excellent route for a bucolic walk or bike ride in the **Vallée du Cousin** is the shaded, one-lane D427, which follows the gentle rapids of the River Cousin through dense forests and lush meadows. From the Hôtel du Rocher (below), you can head either west towards Pontaubert (under the viaduct; 3km) and Vézelay, or east towards Magny.

The tourist office (left) sells maps (eg IGN 2722 ET) for walking tours in and around Avallon and has limited information on the Parc Naturel Régional du Morvan.

Sleeping

Camping Municipal sous Roche (☎ /fax 03 86 34 10 39; per adult/tent/car €2/2/2; ☺ mid-Mar–mid-Oct) A delightfully woody site 2km southeast of the old city on the forested banks of the Cousin.

Hôtel du Rocher (☎ 03 86 34 19 03; rue des Îles Labaume; d with washbasin/shower €20/27, hall shower €1; ☺ reception closed Mon except holidays) The best budget deal in town, with 14 old-fashioned, wood-panelled rooms. Extremely rustic. Situated in the lovely Vallée du Cousin.

Hôtel Les Capucins (☎ 03 86 34 06 52; hotellescapucins@wanadoo.fr; 6 av Paul Doumer; d €35-60, 7-person f ste €100; 🛇) At this two-star, Logis-de-France place with good wheelchair access, all eight rooms are comfortable though some have more charm than others.

Hôtel d'Avallon Vauban (☎ 03 86 34 36 99; www .avallonvaubanhotel.com; 53 rue de Paris; s/d €51/57, studio apt €80-90) The trompe l'oeil trees make the façade look a bit like a camouflaged battleship but there really are trees – lots of them – in this two-star hotel's park-like private garden. The 26 rooms and four ski-chalet-like studio apartments are tidy and spacious though functional as far as furnishings go. Bicycle parking available.

Hôtel Le Moulin des Templiers (☎ 03 86 34 10 80; www.hotel-moulin-des-templiers.com; 10 rte de Cousin, Pontaubert; d €52-60) This beautifully converted mill is tucked away in a shady spot in the Vallée du Cousin, on the D427 about 5km southwest of Avallon. The 15 cosy bedrooms, rustic dining room and country furnishings are brimming with charm, and there's a delightful terrace next to the rushing river – an ideal place for an early evening apéritif.

Le Moulin des Ruats (☎ 03 86 34 97 00; www .moulin-des-ruats.com; Vallée du Cousin; d €73-129) This

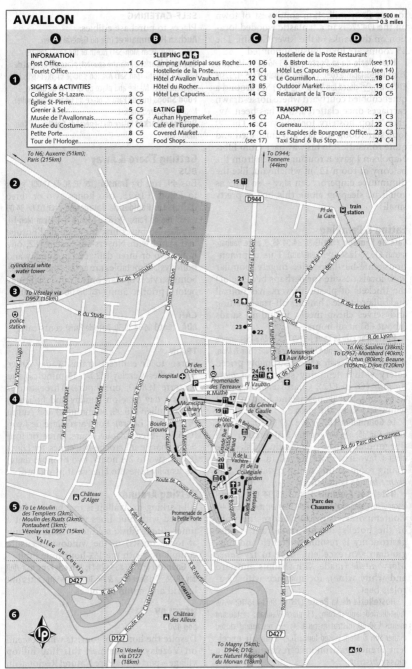

AVALLON

0 — 500 m
0 — 0.3 miles

INFORMATION
Post Office...................................1 C4
Tourist Office..............................2 C5

SIGHTS & ACTIVITIES
Collégiale St-Lazare.....................3 C5
Église St-Pierre...........................4 C5
Grenier à Sel..............................5 C5
Musée de l'Avallonnais.................6 C4
Musée du Costume.......................7 C4
Petite Porte................................8 C5
Tour de l'Horloge.........................9 C5

SLEEPING
Camping Municipal sous Roche.....10 D6
Hostellerie de la Poste.................11 C4
Hôtel d'Avallon Vauban................12 C3
Hôtel du Rocher..........................13 B5
Hôtel Les Capucins......................14 C3

EATING
Auchan Hypermarket....................15 C2
Café de l'Europe..........................16 C4
Covered Market...........................17 C4
Food Shops............................(see 17)

Hostellerie de la Poste Restaurant
& Bistrot................................(see 11)
Hôtel Les Capucins Restaurant......(see 14)
Le Gourmillon............................18 D4
Outdoor Market..........................19 C4
Restaurant de la Tour...................20 C5

TRANSPORT
ADA...21 C3
Gueneau.....................................22 C3
Les Rapides de Bourgogne Office....23 C3
Taxi Stand & Bus Stop..................24 C4

BURGUNDY

former flour mill, 4km southwest of town on the D427, is in a fantastic wooded location on the banks of the River Cousin. The 25 rooms are luxuriously appointed.

Hostellerie de la Poste (☎ 03 86 34 16 16; www .hostelleriedelaposte.com; 13 place Vauban; d €99-123, ste €145-181; ⊙ closed Jan & Feb; ✗ 🐾) Set around a quiet cobbled courtyard where horse-drawn carriages once clattered, this has been Avallon's top hostelry for 300 years. The 30 four-star rooms are lavishly furnished and quite romantic. On his way back from Elba, Napoleon I gave a rousing speech from the balcony of room 12, in which you, like the diminutive emperor, can stay – so long as you'll be sleeping alone (his bed is pretty small).

Eating & Drinking

Café de l'Europe (☎ 03 86 34 04 45; 7 place Vauban; menus €10.50-12.50; ⊙ 7am-1am) This unpretentious café-bar-brasserie, hugely popular with locals despite (or perhaps because of) the thickets of plastic flowers, has pinball and billiard tables, handles off-track betting and serves cheap meals, including salads (about €6) at all hours.

Restaurant de la Tour (☎ 03 86 34 24 84; 84 Grande Rue Aristide Briand; menu €12; ⊙ closed lunch Sun & Mon, open daily mid-Jun–early Sep) A reasonably priced eatery with a tempting selection of *plats du jour* (€8 to €12), Charolais steaks (€10 to €12.50), pizzas, pastas and four to eight wines served by the glass.

Le Gourmillon (☎ 03 86 31 62 01; 8 rue de Lyon; menus €16-35; ⊙ closed dinner Sun) French and Burgundian dishes, including fish (the chef's favourite), are served in the bright dining room of this stylish restaurant. The *crème brûlée* is delicious.

Hôtel Les Capucins (☎ 03 86 34 06 52; hotel lescapucins@wanadoo.fr; 6 av Paul Doumer; menus €17-44) Contemporary canvasses adorn the walls of the hotel's elegant restaurant, whose gastronomy is resolutely French and Burgundian. An excellent place to try *sauce Morvandelle* (made with shallots, mustard and white wine), for instance with Charolais beef.

Hostellerie de la Poste (☎ 03 86 34 16 16; www .hostelleriedelaposte.com; 13 place Vauban; restaurant menus €30-60, bistrot menu €14; ⊙ restaurant closed dinner Sun & Mon, closed lunch Tue) Has an excellent French gastronomic restaurant and a classy *bistrot*.

SELF-CATERING
Places to purchase edibles:
Auchan Hypermarket (rue du Général Leclerc; ⊙ 8.30am-9pm Mon-Sat) North of the town centre.
Covered Market (marché couvert; place du Général de Gaulle ⊙ until 1pm Sat) Avallon's huge market spills into adjacent place Mathé and place du Général de Gaulle.
Food Shops (rue de Paris & place du Général de Gaulle) Near the covered market.
Outdoor Market (place du Général de Gaulle; ⊙ Thu morning)

Getting There & Away
BUS
Bus 49, run by **Transco** (☎ 03 80 42 11 00), goes to Dijon (€16.15, two hours, two or three daily). **Les Rapides de Bourgogne** (☎ 03 86 34 00 00; 39 rue de Paris; ⊙ 8am-noon & 3-4.45pm Mon-Fri, 8am-noon Sat) buses link the Café de l'Europe taxi stand with Noyers-sur-Serein (€2, one hour, two or three daily except Sunday and holidays). Timetables are at the tourist office. Some services operate only if you call the day before, prior to 5pm (☎ 08 00 30 33 09).

CAR
ADA (☎ 03 86 34 30 30; 2 rte de Paris) rents cars.

TRAIN
Three to five direct trains a day serve Sermizelles-Vézelay (€2.80, 15 minutes) and Auxerre (€8.50, one hour). Three trains/ buses a day (one on Sunday and holidays) go to Saulieu (€6.90, 50 minutes) and Autun (€12.30, 1¾ hours). For Paris' Gare de Lyon (€26.80, three to four hours, three or four daily) change at Laroche-Migennes; for Dijon (€7.60, two to 2½ hours, two or more daily) it's usually fastest to change at Montbard.

Getting Around
All parking in Avallon is free but in places marked with blue lines you have to put a timer *disque* (disk; sold for a nominal sum at tobacconists) in the window to ensure compliance with the 1½-hour time limit.

Gueneau (☎ 03 86 34 28 11; 26 rue de Paris; half-/full day €8/16; ⊙ 8am-noon & 2-6.30pm Tue-Sat) rents out hybrid and mountain bikes.

VÉZELAY
pop 490
Despite the hordes of tourists who descend on Vézelay in summer, this tiny hilltop village – part of the Parc Naturel Régional du

Morvan (p487) and a Unesco World Heritage site – is one of France's architectural gems. Perched on a rocky spur crowned by a medieval basilica and surrounded by a patchwork of vineyards, sunflower fields and grazing sheep, Vézelay seems to have been lifted from another age.

History

Thanks to the relics of St Mary Magdalene, Vézelay's Benedictine monastery became an important pilgrimage site in the 11th and 12th centuries. It also served as a point of convergence for pilgrims heading from northern Europe to Santiago de Compostela in Spain.

The town reached the height of its influence in the 12th century, when St Bernard, leader of the Cistercian order, preached the Second Crusade here; and King Philip Augustus of France and King Richard the Lion-Heart of England met up in Vézelay before setting out on the Third Crusade.

Vézelay's vineyards, founded in Gallo-Roman times, were wiped out in the late 1800s by phylloxera and only re-established in 1973.

Information

Post Office (17 rue St-Étienne) Has an ATM.

Tourist Office (☎ 03 86 33 23 69; www.vezelaytour isme.com; 12 rue St-Étienne; ☿ 10am-1pm & 2-6pm, closed Thu Oct-May & Sun Nov-Easter) Sells postcards (€0.80) with details on four 1½- to three-hour walking circuits with yellow trail markings, each heading out of Vézelay in a different direction.

Sights & Activities

BASILIQUE STE-MADELEINE

Founded in the 880s, **Basilique Ste-Madeleine** has had a turbulent history. Rebuilt between the 11th and 13th centuries, it was trashed by the Huguenots in 1569, desecrated during the Revolution and, to top off the human ravages, repeatedly struck by lightning. By the mid-1800s it was on the point of collapse. In 1840 the architect Viollet-le-Duc undertook the daunting task of rescuing the structure. His work, which included reconstructing the western façade and its doorways, helped Vézelay – previously a ghost town – spring back to life.

On the 12th-century **tympanum**, visible from the narthex (an enclosed porch), Romanesque carvings show Jesus seated on a

throne, radiating his holy spirit to the Apostles. The **nave**, rebuilt following the great fire of 1120, has round arches and tiny windows, typical features of the Romanesque style; the transept and choir (1185) have ogival arches and larger windows, hallmarks of Gothic architecture. Under the transept is a mid-12th-century **crypt** with a reliquary containing one of Mary Magdalene's bones.

The abbey can be visited all day except during prayers (sometimes held in the cloister chapel), sung in haunting four-voice harmonies by the monks and nuns of the Fraternité Monastique de Jérusalem. Visitors are welcome to observe on Monday (6.30pm Mass), Tuesday to Friday (7am, 12.30pm and 6pm Mass), Saturday (8am, 12.30pm Mass, 6pm and 7.15pm Mass) and Sunday (8am, 11am Mass and 5.30pm). Most services (in French) are about 30 to 40 minutes long; Mass lasts 1¼ hours. Concerts of sacred music are sometimes held in the nave from May to mid-October.

Squirrels frolic in the **park** behind the basilica, which affords wonderful views of the Vallée de Cure and nearby villages, including St-Père-sous-Vézelay. A dirt road leads down (north) to the **old** and **new cemeteries**. **Promenade des Fossés** circumnavigates Vézelay's medieval ramparts. A footpath with fine views of the basilica links the north-western side of the ramparts with the village of **Asquins**, from where trails lead to the River Cure.

About half-a-dozen **art galleries**, a couple of wine cellars and some small shops selling local crafts and edibles can be found along rue St-Pierre and rue St-Étienne.

At **Maison Jules Roy** (☎ 03 86 33 35 10; admission free; ☿ 2-5pm Mon & 2-6pm Wed-Sun Apr-Sep), at the upper end of rue des Écoles, you can walk around the gardens and see the Algerian-born writer's study.

Paintings, sculptures and mobiles by Calder, Giacometti, Kandinsky, Léger, Mirò and Picasso will be featured in the new **Musée Zervos** (rue St-Étienne), set to open in 2006 in the former home of the Nobel Prize–winning pacifist writer Romain Rolland (1866–1944).

CYCLING & CANOEING

Mountain bikes are rented out (year-round; €25 per day), kayak trips arranged (€15 to €28) and other outdoor activities (eg rafting

BURGUNDY

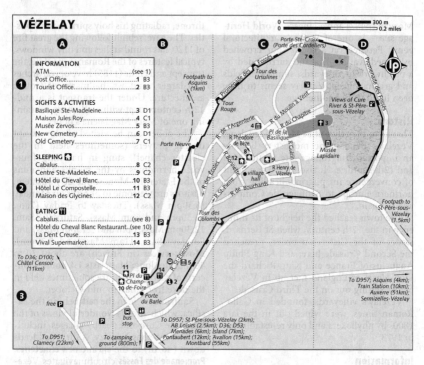

VÉZELAY

INFORMATION
ATM...(see 1)
Post Office....................................1 B3
Tourist Office...............................2 B3

SIGHTS & ACTIVITIES
Basilique Ste-Madeleine..............3 D1
Maison Jules Roy.........................4 C1
Musée Zervos..............................5 B3
New Cemetery..............................6 D1
Old Cemetery...............................7 C1

SLEEPING
Cabalus..8 C2
Centre Ste-Madeleine..................9 C2
Hôtel du Cheval Blanc................10 B3
Hôtel Le Compostelle.................11 B3
Maison des Glycines...................12 C2

EATING
Cabalus.....................................(see 8)
Hôtel du Cheval Blanc Restaurant..(see 10)
La Dent Creuse..........................13 B3
Vival Supermarket......................14 B3

and cave exploration) organised by **AB Loisirs** (☎ 03 86 33 38 38; www.abloisirs.com; rte du Camping, St-Père-sous-Vézelay; ☟ 9.30am-6.30pm Mar-Oct & most days Nov-Feb), whose base is a few kilometres southeast of Vézelay (400m southeast of the D957 along the D36). If you call ahead, bikes can be brought to where you're staying.

Sleeping

Centre Ste-Madeleine (☎ 03 86 33 22 14; fax 03 86 33 22 14; rue St-Pierre; dm €7, s/d €13.50/19; ☟ reception closed noon-1.30pm) This very basic 38-bed hostel, set around an ancient stone courtyard, is run by surprisingly with-it Franciscan nuns who are as modest as the facilities. The dormitories look a bit like a medieval charity hospital that no one endowed. Someone with a few million euros could turn this old place into a luxury hotel.

Hôtel du Cheval Blanc (☎ 03 86 33 22 12; fax 03 86 33 34 29; place du Champ-de-Foire; d €35-43; ☟ closed Dec, reception open 8.30am-3.30pm & 6-11.30pm, closed Wed & Thu) Above the restaurant are seven no-frills, good-value rooms.

Cabalus (☎ 03 86 33 20 66; www.cabalus.com in French; rue St-Pierre; d €38-54; ☟ closed Mon & Tue)

This charming B&B, housed in the abbey's former guesthouse, offers four rooms with exposed stonework, wrought-iron balconies, stone floors and huge windows.

Hôtel Le Compostelle (☎ 03 86 33 28 63; http://compostelle.vezelay.monsite.wanadoo.fr in French; 1 place du Champ-de-Foire; d €48-59, tr/q €72/82; ☟ closed early Jan-early Feb) The 18 spotless, two-star rooms, all of them recently renovated, afford romantic views of either the valley or the basilica.

Maison des Glycines (☎ 03 86 32 35 30; fax 03 86 33 21 67; rue St-Pierre; d €54-74; ☟ reception closed Thu Oct-Easter) A bourgeois townhouse built in 1763 has been turned into an extraordinary hotel that's positively overflowing with old-fashioned character. The hexagonal floor tiles, doors and wooden beams haven't changed in several generations at least. The 11 rooms are all named after famous artists – 'Paul Claudet' is the one to get. No TV or telephones.

Eating

Eateries can be found along rue St-Pierre and rue St-Étienne and around place du Champ-de-Foire.

Cabalus (☎ 03 86 33 20 66; www.cabalus.com in French; rue St-Pierre; ☺ 11am-6pm Wed-Sun) This B&B runs an excellent tearoom with an open fire in the old kitchens – perfect for a light meal.

Hôtel du Cheval Blanc (☎ 03 86 33 22 12; fax 03 86 33 34 29; place du Champ-de-Foire; menus €20-28; ☺ closed Wed & Thu except holidays) Serves French cuisine that mixes traditional recipes with *nouvelle* ideas.

La Dent Creuse (☎ 03 86 33 36 33; place du Champ-de-Foire; lunch menu €13.50, other menus €17.50-34; ☺ closed mid-Nov–mid-Mar except around Christmas; ✗) A large brasserie-restaurant that specialises in Burgundian roasts, fish and chicken dishes and boasts the town's most scenic terrace.

Vival Supermarket (☺ 8.30am-12.30pm & 3.30-7.30pm except Sun afternoon, open daily & longer hr summer) For groceries; near the bottom of rue St-Étienne.

Getting There & Away

Vézelay is 15km from Avallon (19km if you take the gorgeous D427 via Pontaubert). There's a free car park 250m from place du Champ-de-Foire (towards Clamecy).

Three to five trains a day link Sermizelles-Vézelay train station, about 10km north of Vézelay, with Avallon (€2.80, 15 minutes) and Auxerre (€6.70, 50 minutes).

In summer one SNCF bus a day links Vézelay with Avallon (€3.60, 22 minutes) and Montbard (€10.10, 70 minutes), on the Paris–Dijon line.

Taxis (☎ 03 86 32 31 88, 03 86 33 19 06) to/from Sermizelles-Vézelay cost about €16 (€21 at night and on Sunday).

AROUND VÉZELAY

Southeast of Vézelay at the base of the hill, **St-Père-sous-Vézelay** has a Flamboyant Gothic church but is best known for **L'Espérance** (☎ 03 86 33 39 10; www.marc-meneau.com; r €120-420; menus €95-220; ☺ closed Tue & lunch Wed, also closed late Jan-early Mar), a legendary French restaurant (and 26-room hotel) that holds three Michelin stars.

Three kilometres south along the D958 are the **Fontaines Salées** (☎ 03 86 33 26 62; adult/student €4/1.60; ☺ Apr-Oct), saltwater hot springs where excavations have uncovered a Celtic sanctuary (2nd century BC) and Roman baths (1st century). A few kilometres south is the village of **Pierre-Perthuis**, named after a natural stone arch; nearby, a graceful stone bridge (1770) spans the River Cure underneath a modern highway bridge.

PARC NATUREL RÉGIONAL DU MORVAN

The 2854-sq-km Parc Naturel Régional du Morvan, bounded more or less by Vézelay, Avallon, Saulieu and Autun and situated mainly in the Nièvre *département*, encompasses 700 sq km of dense woodland, 13 sq km of lakes and vast expanses of rolling farmland broken by hedgerows, stone walls and stands of beech, hornbeam and oak. The sharp-eyed can observe some of France's largest and most majestic birds of prey perched on trees as they scan for field rodents – or, perhaps, wait lazily for road kill.

The majority of the thinly populated area's 71,000 residents earn their living from farming, ranching, logging and – it's a tough job but someone has to do it – growing Christmas trees. The time when the impoverished Morvan (a Celtic name meaning 'Black Mountain') supplied wet nurses to rich Parisians passed long ago.

Activities

The Morvan offers an abundance of options to fans of outdoor activities. On dry land you can choose from rambling (the park has over 1500km of marked trails; see Morvan Visitors Centre, below), mountain biking, horse riding, rock climbing and fishing, while waterborne activities such as rafting, canoeing and kayaking are possible on several lakes and the Rivers Chalaux, Cure and Yonne.

The following outfits rent out bikes and can also arrange water sports such as canoeing and rafting:

AB Loisirs (☎ 03 86 33 38 38; www.abloisirs.com; rte du Camping, St-Père-sous-Vézelay; ☺ 9.30am-6.30pm Mar-Oct & most days Nov-Feb) Near Vézelay.

Activital (www.activital.net in French) Lac des Settons (☎ 03 86 84 51 98) Based in Montsauche-les-Settons; Lac de Chaumeçon (☎ 03 86 22 61 35) Based in St-Martin-du-Puy.

Okheanos (☎ 03 86 84 60 61; www.okheanos.com in French) Based in Dun-les-Places.

MORVAN VISITORS CENTRE

Surrounded by hills, forests and lakes, the complex known as **Espace St-Brisson** (☎ 03 86 78 79 00; www.parcdumorvan.org) is 14km west of Saulieu in St-Brisson. To get there by car, follow the signs to the 'Maison du Parc'.

BURGUNDY

All sorts of information, including hiking and cycling guides, is on offer at the **tourist office** (☎ 03 86 78 79 57; ☺ 9.30am or 10am-12.30pm & 2-5pm Mon-Sat, 10am-1pm & 3-5.30pm Sun Apr–mid-Nov, 9.30am-12.30pm & perhaps 2-7pm Mon-Fri mid-Nov–Mar). Guided walks of the park (€4 to €8), some at night (eg to observe owls), set out from March to October. Activities for children take place in July and August. Useful websites include www.morvan-tourisme.org and www.patrimoinedumorvan.org, both in French.

The **Écomusée du Morvan** (☎ 03 86 78 79 10), which explores traditional Morvan life and customs, has five sites around the park, including one at Espace St-Brisson whose theme is **hommes et paysages** (humans & landscapes; adult/student €3/1.50; ☺ 10am-1pm & 2-6pm May-Sep, to 5pm Apr & Oct–mid-Nov).

The Morvan was a major stronghold for the Resistance during WWII; the **Musée de la Résistance en Morvan** (☎ 03 86 78 79 10/06; adult/student €4/2.50, incl Écomusée €6/3.50) chronicles key events and characters.

The nearby **Verger Conservatoire** (admission free) is an orchard that preserves some 200 varieties of fruit trees that are no longer commercially grown.

Trails that pass by St-Brisson include three different 5km circuits ('Coteaux de St-Brisson', 'Autour de la Maison du Parc' and 'Autour du Vignan'), a 12km circuit to Dolmen Chevresse and a 20km circuit to the village of Gouloux.

SAULIEU

pop 2800

The town of Saulieu – approximately 40km from Avallon and Autun and once a stop on the Paris–Lyon coach road – learned centuries ago to cater to visitors with high culinary expectations. Today, despite the advent of *autoroutes*, it remains a gastronomic centre and is also a good base for exploring the Morvan park. A number of **footpaths**, including the GR Tour du Morvan, pass by here, and mountain-bike enthusiasts can choose from **bike trails** leading north to Étang de l'Argentalet, west to St-Brisson and southwest to Lac de Chambout.

The **tourist office** (☎ 03 80 64 00 21; saulieu.tourisme@cegetel.net; 24 rue d'Argentine; ☺ 9am-12.30pm & 2-7pm mid-Jun–mid-Sep, 9am-noon & 2-5pm Tue-Sat mid-Sep–mid-Jun), on the N6, can supply you with information on outdoor activities and B&Bs in the Parc Naturel Régional du Morvan.

Musée François Pompon (☎ 03 80 64 19 51; 3 rue du Docteur Roclore; adult/student €4/2.50; ☺ 10am-12.30pm & 2-5pm or 6pm Wed-Sat, 10am-12.30pm Mon, 10.30am-noon & 2.30-5pm Sun & holidays, closed Jan & Feb) displays medieval statuary and work by the local animal sculptor François Pompon (1855–1933). Next to the museum, **Basilique St-Andoche** (☺ closed Sun morning & Mon, also closed Sun afternoon Nov-Easter) is known for its 60 vividly carved capitals depicting flora, fauna and Bible stories.

Sleeping & Eating

La Vieille Auberge (☎ 03 80 64 13 74; 15 rue Grillot; d/tr €35/42; menus €12.50-32; ☺ hotel & restaurant closed Tue evening & Wed, also closed mid-Jan–early Feb & 2 weeks in Jul) This traditional inn, 200m down the hill from the Côte d'Or, serves French cuisine at a fair price. Rustic one-star rooms are available upstairs.

Auberge du Relais (☎ 03 80 64 13 16; 8 rue d'Argentine; r €45-52; menus €15-36; ☺ may be closed dinner mid-Nov–mid-Feb) A rustically elegant restaurant a block from the tourist office with reasonably priced Burgundian and French cuisine, including a local favourite, *jambon à la sédélocienne* (ham with a cream, shallot, white wine, Gruyère, tomato and mushroom sauce). There are five rooms for staying in.

La Côte d'Or (☎ 03 80 90 53 53; www.bernard-loiseau.com; 2 rue d'Argentine; lunch menu with wine €98, other menus €120-185; d from €150, ste €260-470; ☙) Run by Bernard Loiseau's widow since the great

---

MAQUIS BERNARD RÉSISTANCE CEMETERY

Seven RAF airmen – the crew of a bomber shot down near here in 1944 – and 21 *résistants* are buried in the neatly tended **Maquis Bernard Résistance Cemetery** (www.ouroux-en-morvan.com), surrounded by the dense forests in which British paratroops operated with Free French forces. The nearby **drop zone** is marked with signs.

The cemetery is about 8km southwest of Montsauche-les-Settons (along the D977) and 5.6km east of Oroux-en-Morvan (along the D12), near the tiny hamlet of Savelot. From the D977, go 2.8km along the narrow dirt road to Savelot.

chef's tragic suicide in 2003, this four-star, 32-room inn, whose dazzling restaurant holds three Michelin stars, strives for – and achieves – almost impossible standards of perfection. The garden is almost as delightful as the sophisticated country cuisine.

Atac supermarket (rue Jean Bertin; ☺ 8.45am-12.15pm & 2.45-7pm Mon-Sat, no midday closure Sat) On the D26 about 300m downhill from the Côte d'Or.

Getting There & Away

Transco (☎ 03 80 42 11 00) runs bus 48 to Dijon (€12.75, 1½ hours, once daily except Sunday and holidays). Trains and/or SNCF buses (three daily Monday to Saturday, one on Sunday and holidays) go to Autun (€7.20, 50 minutes) and Avallon (€6.90, 50 minutes).

SAÔNE-ET-LOIRE

In the southern Saône-et-Loire *département* (www.bourgogne-du-sud.com), midway between Dijon and Lyon, highlights include the Gallo-Roman ruins in Autun, Cluny's glorious Romanesque heritage, the fascinating industrial history of Le Creusot and, around Mâcon, vineyards galore. Several rivers and the Canal du Centre meander among its forests and pastureland.

AUTUN

pop 16,400

Autun, 85km kilometres southwest of Dijon, is now a quiet subprefecture, but two millennia ago – under the name of Augustodunum – it was one of the most important cities in Roman Gaul, boasting 6km of ramparts, four monumental gates, two theatres, an amphitheatre and a system of aqueducts. Beginning in AD 269 the city was repeatedly sacked by barbarian tribes and its fortunes declined, but things improved considerably in the Middle Ages, making it possible to construct an impressive cathedral.

If you have a car, Autun is an excellent base for exploring the southern parts of the Parc Naturel Régional du Morvan (p487).

Orientation

The train station is linked to Autun's common-turned-car park, the Champ de Mars, by the town's main thoroughfare, av Charles de Gaulle. The hilly area around Cathédrale St-Lazare, reached via narrow cobblestone streets, is known as the old city. The main shopping area is just south of the Champ de Mars around rue St-Saulge and rue des Cordeliers.

Information

Elge Interactive (6 Grande Rue Chauchien; per hr €4.50; ☺ 9am-noon & 2-7pm Mon-Fri, closed morning Oct-early Apr) Internet access.

Laundrettes 18 rue de l'Arquebuse (☺ 7am-9pm); 1 rue Guérin (☺ 6am-9pm)

Librairie À La Page (☎ 03 85 52 24 72; 17bis av Charles de Gaulle; ☺ closed Mon morning & Sun) Carries hiking maps and topoguides.

Post Office (8 rue Pernette)

Tourist Office (☎ 03 85 86 80 38; www.autun-tourisme.com; 2 av Charles de Gaulle; ☺ 9am-7pm May-Sep, 9am-12.30pm & 2-6pm Mon-Sat Oct-Apr) Sells a self-guided walking-tour brochure (€2) and local IGN map 2825E (€7.70); also has free pamphlets in French on the Parc Naturel Régional du Morvan.

Tourist Office Annexe (☎ 03 85 52 56 03; 5 place du Terreau; ☺ 9am-7pm May-Oct) Near the cathedral.

Sights & Activities

GALLO-ROMAN SITES

Built during the reign of Constantine, **Porte d'Arroux** was once one of Augustodunum's four gates. Constructed wholly without mortar, it supports four semicircular arches of the sort that put the 'Roman' in Romanesque: two for vehicles and two for pedestrians. **Porte St-André** is similar in general design and here, too, it's not difficult to imagine a Roman chariot clattering through, a helmeted legionnaire at the reins.

You can also let your imagination run wild at the **Théâtre Romain** (Roman Theatre), designed to hold 16,000 people – try picturing the place filled with cheering (or jeering), toga-clad spectators. From the top look southwest and you'll see the **Pierre de Couhard** (Rock of Couhard), the 27m-high remains of a Gallo-Roman pyramid that was probably a tomb.

Long associated (wrongly) with the Roman god Janus, the 24m-high **Temple de Janus** (www.temple-de-janus.net in French for a 3D visit) – in the middle of farmland 800m north of the train station – is thought to have been a site for Celtic worship. Only two of its massive walls are still standing.

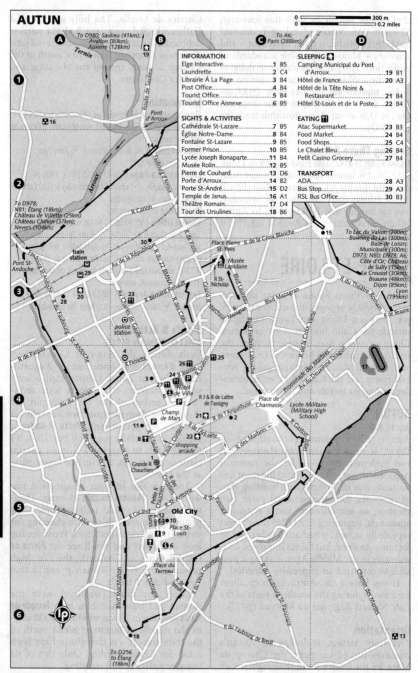

AUTUN

0 — 300 m
0 — 0.2 miles

INFORMATION
Elge Interactive.............................1 B5
Laundrette....................................2 C4
Librairie Á La Page.......................3 B4
Post Office....................................4 B4
Tourist Office...............................5 B4
Tourist Office Annexe...................6 B5

SIGHTS & ACTIVITIES
Cathédrale St-Lazare....................7 B5
Église Notre-Dame........................8 B5
Fontaine St-Lazare.......................9 B5
Former Prison.............................10 B5
Lycée Joseph Bonaparte.............11 B4
Musée Rolin................................12 B5
Pierre de Couhard.......................13 D6
Porte d'Arroux............................14 B2
Porte St-André...........................15 D2
Temple de Janus.........................16 A1
Théâtre Romain..........................17 D4
Tour des Ursulines.....................18 B6

SLEEPING
Camping Municipal du Pont
  d'Arroux..................................19 B1
Hôtel de France..........................20 A3
Hôtel de la Tête Noire &
  Restaurant...............................21 B4
Hôtel St-Louis et de la Poste.....22 B4

EATING
Atac Supermarket.......................23 B3
Food Market...............................24 B4
Food Shops.................................25 C4
Le Chalet Bleu...........................26 B4
Petit Casino Grocery..................27 B4

TRANSPORT
ADA..28 A3
Bus Stop....................................29 A3
RSL Bus Office...........................30 B3

To D980; Saulieu (41km);
Avallon (80km);
Auxerre (128km)

To A6;
Paris (288km)

Ternin

Route de Saulieu

Pont
d'Arroux

Faubourg d'Arroux

Arroux

To D978;
N81; Étang (18km);
Château de Villette (25km);
Château Chinon (37km);
Nevers (104km)

R Canon

R de Paris

Place Pierre
St-Yves

R de la Croix Blanche

Musée
Lapidaire

R St-
Nicholas

Blvd Laureau

Blvd Mazagran

To Lac du Vallon (200m);
Bowling du Lac (300m);
Base de Loisirs;
Municipale (300m);
D973; N80; D978; A6;
Côte d'Or; Château
de Sully (15km);
Le Creusot (30km);
Beaune (48km);
Dijon (85km);
Lyon (195km)

R du Théâtre Romain

R de Beaune

Pont St-
Andoche

train
station

Av de la République

R du 22 BMNA

Grand R Marchaux

Av Charles de Gaulle

Av Bernard Renault

R des Clés

Blvd Frédéric Latouche

Blvd Mazagran

R de la Croix Verte

R du Faubourg St-Andoche

police
station

R de Parpas

R Pernette

R Jeannin

Grand R Guérin

Av du Deuxième Dragon

Promenade des Marbres

Av du Morvan

Hôtel
de Ville

R J & B de Lattre
de Tassigny

Place de
Charmasse

Lycée Militaire
(Military High
School)

R Gaston Joliet

Blvd des Résistants Fusillés

Champ
de Mars

R de l'Arbalète

R de l'Arquebuse

R des Marbres

R aux Raz

R aux Cordiers

shopping
arcade

Grande R
Chauchien

Petite R
Chauchien

R des
Cordeliers

R St-
Antoine

R St-Pancrace

Faubourg Talus

R Cocand

R Dufraigne

Old City

Place St-
Louis

R du Vieux Colombier

R du Faubourg St-Pancrace

Blvd MacMahon

Place du
Terreau

R de
Breuil

Chemin des Marbres

To D256
to Étang
(18km)

R du Faubourg de Breuil

OLD CITY

Many of Autun's buildings date from the 17th and 18th centuries.

Napoleon Bonaparte and his brothers Joseph and Lucien studied in Autun as teenagers. Their old Jesuit college, now a high school known as **Lycée Joseph Bonaparte**, on the west side of the Champ de Mars, has a wrought-iron gate (1772) decorated with the municipal coat-of-arms. Next door is classical **Église Notre Dame** (1757).

Cathédrale St-Lazare (place du Terreau; ☾ 9am-noon & 1.30-7pm, no midday closure, often open later in summer) was built in the 12th century to house the sacred relics of St Lazarus. Later additions include the 15th- to 16th-century bell tower over the transept and the 19th-century towers over the entrance. Over the main doorway, the Romanesque **tympanum** showing the Last Judgement was carved in the 1130s by Gislebertus, whose name is written below Jesus' right foot. Across the bottom, the saved are on the left while the damned – including a woman whose breasts are being bitten by snakes (symbolising lust) – are on the right. The Renaissance-style fountain next to the cathedral, **Fontaine St-Lazare**, dates from the 16th century.

The **Musée Rolin** (☎ 03 85 52 09 76; 5 rue des Bancs; adult/student €3.30/1.70; ☾ 9.30am-noon & 1.30-6pm Wed-Mon Apr-Sep, 10am-noon & 2-5pm Wed-Mon Oct-Mar) has a worthwhile collection of Gallo-Roman artefacts; 12th-century Romanesque art, including the *Temptation of Eve* by Gislebertus; and 15th-century paintings such as the *Autun Virgin* by the Maître de Moulins. A new hall features 20th- and 21st-century art. There are plans to expand exhibition space by taking over the adjacent **prison** (2bis place St-Louis), a forbidding circular structure built in 1854 and used to house baddies until 1955.

WALKING & CYCLING

For a **stroll** along the city walls (part-Roman but mostly medieval), walk from av du Morvan south to the 12th-century **Tour des Ursulines** and follow the walls to the northeast. The Chemin des Manies leads out to the Pierre de Couhard, where you can pick up the **Circuit des Gorges**, three marked forest trails ranging from 4.7km to 11.5km. The map to take along is IGN 2925 O (€7.70 at the tourist office).

Bicycles can be rented at the **Base de Loisirs Municipale** (☎ 03 85 86 95 80; rte de Chalon; ☾ May-Sep), a few hundred metres east of the old city on the shore of Lac du Vallon (across the street from the McDonald's), which also hires out pedalboats and sailboats.

Sleeping

Camping Municipal du Pont d'Arroux (☎ 03 85 52 10 82; rte de Saulieu; per adult/site/car €3.10/2.80/1.50, site in Jul & Aug €5.60; ☾ Apr-Oct) At a beautiful (if cramped) spot on the River Ternin.

Hôtel de France (☎ 03 85 52 14 00; www.hotel-de-france-autun.fr; 18 av de la République; d €40, with washbasin €24; ☾ reception closed after 3pm Sun & 3 weeks in Feb) A one-star, family-run hostelry with 26 basic, clean rooms.

Hôtel de la Tête Noire (☎ 03 85 86 59 99; www.ho teltetenoire.fr; 3 rue de l'Arquebuse; d €64-74; ☾ closed 20 Dec-Jan; ✗) A two-star, Logis de France place with 31 stylish rooms, some quite large, accessible by lift. Offers solid value and has a restaurant.

Hôtel St-Louis et de la Poste (☎ 03 85 52 01 01; 6 rue de l'Arbalète; d from €65 winter, €75 summer, Napoleonic ste €1250; ✗) An enchanting three-star establishment that's justly proud of its 17th-century building, its lavish 1920s lobby, its mention in the first (1900) edition of Michelin's *Guide Rouge* – and the fact that Napoleon stayed here four times. The 44 rooms are spacious and luxurious. Under new ownership.

ourpick Château de Villette (☎ 03 86 30 09 13; www.stork-chateau.com; d €120-350, the whole shebang per week €8750) Set in a 2-sq-km private estate, this delightful chateau lets you sample the life of luxury once lived by the landed aristocracy. After waking up in a ravishingly furnished period room, you can ramble, cycle or hunt *escargots* in the nearby forests and fields before sitting down to a superb French meal made using the freshest of local products. Worthy of a honeymoon! Situated 25km southwest of Autun along the N81 (just past the hamlet of Poil).

Eating

There are a number of restaurants located along the north side of the Champ de Mars and several more up towards the cathedral, along Grande Rue Chauchien and Petite Rue Chauchien and around place du Terreau.

BURGUNDY

Le Chalet Bleu (☎ 03 85 86 27 30; 3 rue Jeannin; menus €15-45; ☒ closed Tue & dinner Mon, also closed dinner Sun mid-Nov–Mar) Serves creative French gastronomic cuisine in a light, leafy dining room. Specialities include *meurette d'oeufs pochés et escargots* (poached eggs with red wine sauce and *escargots*), *coq au vin* and thick Charolais steaks.

Stock up for a picnic at:

Atac Supermarket (av Charles de Gaulle; ☒ 8.30am-7pm Mon-Sat)

Food Market (just outside the Hôtel de Ville; ☒ until noon or 12.30pm Wed & Fri)

Food Shops There are several on rue Guerin, northeast of the Champ de Mars.

Petit Casino Grocery (6 av Charles de Gaulle; ☒ 7.30am-12.30pm & 3-8pm Tue-Sat, 8.30am-1pm & 4-7pm Sun)

Entertainment

Autun is pretty sleepy but its nightlife scene has one bright spot: **Bowling du Lac** (☎ 03 85 52 06 06; rte de Chalon; ☒ 11am-2am Sun-Thu, 11am-4am Fri & Sat, from 9am in summer), a few hundred metres east of the old city next to the McDonald's. Hugely popular with locals of all ages, it has eight bowling lanes, billiard tables, a bar and a restaurant and hosts live music twice a month.

Getting There & Away

BUS

From the bus shelters next to the train station, buses travel to Le Creusot (€5.18, 45 minutes, three daily Monday to Friday, two Saturday except school holidays) and destinations in the Parc Naturel Régional du Morvan; timetables are posted. Details are available at the **RSL bus office** (☎ 03 85 86 92 55; www.r-s-l.fr in French; 13 av de la République; ☒ 8.15am-noon & 2-6pm Mon-Thu, to 5pm Fri).

CAR

You can rent cars from **ADA** (☎ 03 85 86 37 36; 8 av de la République).

TRAIN

Autun's **train station** (av de la République) is on a slow tertiary line that requires a change of train (or bus) to get almost anywhere except Auxerre (€18.70, 2¾ hours, one or two daily except Sunday and holidays), Avallon (€12.30, 1¾ hours, three daily Monday to Saturday, one Sunday) and Saulieu (€7.20, 50 minutes, three daily Monday to Saturday, one Sunday).

CHÂTEAU DE SULLY

This Renaissance-style **chateau** (☎ 03 85 82 09 86; www.chateaudesully.com; adult/student & senior €6.20/4.50, gardens only €2.60/1.90; ☒ Apr-Nov), on the outskirts of the village of Sully (15km northeast of Autun along the D973), has a beautifully furnished interior and a lovely English-style garden. It was the birthplace of Marshall Mac Mahon, duke of Magenta and president of France from 1873 to 1879, whose ancestors fled Ireland several centuries ago and whose descendents still occupy the property. Tours begin hourly on the half-hour from 10.30am to 4.30pm (to 5.30pm July and August).

LE CREUSOT
pop 26,300

Let's be frank: Le Creusot – 30km southeast of Autun along the gorgeous N80 – is an ugly industrial town, but the story of how it got that way is fascinating (at least if you like industrial history). After all, this is where the power hammer was invented in 1841 – the towering gadget at the southern entrance to town that looks like a Jules Verne spaceship was the mightiest power hammer in the world when it was built in 1876.

Thanks to nearby coal deposits and cheap transport via the **Canal du Centre** (1793), which links the Saône with the Loire and thus the Mediterranean with the Atlantic, Le Creusot became a major steelmaking centre during the 19th century. The story of the smoke-belching Schneider steelworks is told at **Château de la Verrerie** (☎ 03 85 73 92 00; adult/11-18yr/f €6/3.80/15.25), an 18th-century glassworks turned into a private mansion by the paternalistic Schneiders, undisputed masters of their company town.

The chateau's **Musée de l'Homme et de l'Industrie** (☒ 10am-noon & 2-6pm Mon-Fri, 2-6pm Sat & Sun, longer hr summer) tells the story of the Schneider dynasty and exhibits some marvellous 1:14-scale steam locomotives. Across the courtyard, the **Académie François Bourdon** (☒ 11am-12.30pm & 3-6pm Mon-Fri, 3-6pm Sat & Sun, longer hr summer, closed Jan) has models of various flagship Schneider products, including railway locomotives, bridges, naval vessels and nuclear power plants. The 18-hectare forested **park** behind the chateau is always open.

The **tourist office** (☎ 03 85 55 02 46; www.creusot .net in French; ☒ 9am-noon & 2-6pm Mon-Fri, 2-5pm or

6pm Sat, Sun & holidays) is inside the chateau's gatehouse. To get there follow the road signs to the 'office de tourisme'.

Le Creusot's train station, a 10-minute walk northeast of the chateau, is linked to Le Creusot TGV station by the **Navette TGV** (☎ 03 85 73 01 10), costing €2.50 (20 minutes, four or five daily Monday to Saturday) and by bus to Autun (for transport details, see opposite).

CLUNY
pop 4400
The remains of Cluny's great abbey – Christendom's largest church until the construction of St Peter's Basilica in the Vatican – are fragmentary and scattered, barely discernible among the houses and green spaces of the modern-day town. But with a bit of imagination, it's possible to picture how things looked in the 12th century, when Cluny's Benedictine abbey, renowned for its wealth and power and answerable only to the Pope, held sway over 1100 priories and monasteries stretching from Poland to Portugal.

George Clooney has nothing to do with Cluny – his name is Irish.

Orientation & Information
Cluny's main street is known (from southeast to northwest) as place du Commerce, rue Filaterie, rue Lamartine and rue Mercière.

Post Office (rue de la Levée) Changes foreign currency.
Tourist Office (☎ 03 85 59 05 34; www.cluny-tour isme.com; 6 rue Mercière; ☒ 10am-6.45pm Jul & Aug, 10am-12.30pm & 2.30-6.45pm Apr-Sep, closed Sun Apr, 10am-12.30pm & 2.30-6pm Tue-Sat Oct-Mar) Has excellent English-language brochures.

Sights
Cluny's vast **Église Abbatiale** (abbey church; ☎ 03 85 59 89 99; adult/18-25yr/under 18yr €6.50/4.50/free), built between 1088 and 1130, once stretched from the rectangular **map table** in front of the **Musée d'Art et d'Archéologie** (☒ 9.30am-6.15pm May-Aug, 9.30am-noon & 1.30-4.45pm Sep-Apr) all the way to the trees near the octagonal **Clocher de l'Eau Bénite** (Tower of the Holy Water) and its neighbour, the square **Tour de l'Horloge** – a distance of 187m!

A visit to the remains of the abbey begins at the Musée d'Art et d'Archéologie, where tickets are sold and an English brochure is available. Displays include a model of the Cluny complex and some superb Romanesque carvings. It continues on the grounds of the **École Nationale Supérieure d'Arts et Métiers** (Ensam; place du 11 Août), an institute for training mechanical and industrial engineers that's centred on an 18th-century cloister. The visit includes a 12-minute computer-generated 'virtual tour' of the abbey as it looked in the Middle Ages. You can wander around the grounds at midday and for an hour after the museum closes. Free guided tours in English are held in July and August.

The best place to appreciate the abbey's scale is from the top of the **Tour des Fromages** (adult/student €1.25/0.80; ☒ 10am-6.45pm Jul & Aug, 10am-12.30pm & 2.30-6.45pm Apr-Sep, closed Sun Apr, 10am-12.30pm & 2.30-6pm Tue-Sat Oct-Mar), once used to ripen cheeses. Access to the tower's 120 steps is through the tourist office.

Cluny has two other churches: **Église St-Marcel** (rue Prud'hon; ☒ closed to public), topped by an octagonal, three-storey belfry; and 13th-century **Église Notre Dame** (☒ 9am-7pm), across from the tourist office; the entrance is around the other side on rue Notre Dame.

The **Haras National** (National Stud Farm; 2 rue Porte des Prés), founded by Napoleon in 1806, houses some of France's finest thoroughbreds, ponies and draught horses. It can be visited on a **guided tour** (☎ 06 22 94 52 69; adult/4-11yr/12-17yr €/5/2/3; 11am Fri & Sun, 2pm Tue-Fri & Sun, 3.30pm & 5pm Tue-Thu & Sun).

Sleeping
Camping Municipal St Vital (☎ 03 85 59 08 34; rue des Griottons; camping €10.20; ☒ May-Sep) A grassy camping area slightly east of town.

Hôtel du Commerce (☎ 03 85 59 03 09; www.hotel ducommerce-cluny.com in French; 8 place du Commerce; d €40, with washbasin €24.50) A family-run one-star hotel with cheerful peach-coloured hallways and 17 tidy rooms that offer clean, basic accommodation. Very central. Reception closes noon to 4.30pm.

Hôtel de l'Abbaye (☎ 03 85 59 11 14; www.abbaye -cluny.fr; 14ter av Charles de Gaulle; d €51-54; ☒ closed 3 weeks in Feb; ☒) A bit out of the centre so parking is a breeze. The 12 comfortable rooms have antique furnishings. A good option so long as you don't want to stay over Sunday or Monday nights, when this place is totally shut.

Hôtel de Bourgogne (☎ 03 85 59 00 58; www .hotel-cluny.com; place de l'Abbaye; d €78-118; ☒ closed

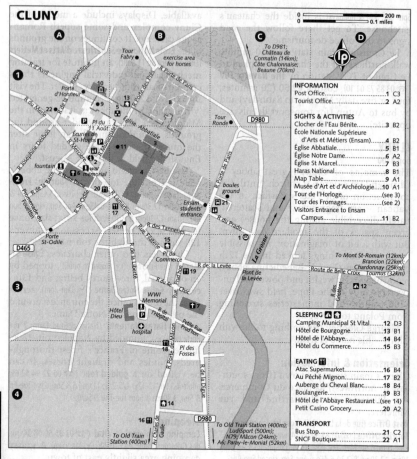

CLUNY

INFORMATION
Post Office.................................1 C3
Tourist Office............................2 A2

SIGHTS & ACTIVITIES
Clocher de l'Eau Bénite..............3 B2
École Nationale Supérieure
    d'Arts et Métiers (Ensam)......4 B2
Église Abbatiale.......................5 B1
Église Notre Dame....................6 A2
Église St Marcel.......................7 B3
Haras National.........................8 B1
Map Table................................9 A1
Musée d'Art et d'Archéologie....10 A1
Tour de l'Horloge................(see 3)
Tour des Fromages...............(see 2)
Visitors Entrance to Ensam
    Campus.............................11 B2

SLEEPING
Camping Municipal St Vital.......12 D3
Hôtel de Bourgogne.................13 B1
Hôtel de l'Abbaye....................14 B4
Hôtel du Commerce.................15 B3

EATING
Atac Supermarket....................16 B4
Au Péché Mignon.....................17 B2
Auberge du Cheval Blanc.........18 B4
Boulangerie............................19 B3
Hôtel de l'Abbaye Restaurant ..(see 14)
Petit Casino Grocery................20 A2

TRANSPORT
Bus Stop................................21 C2
SNCF Boutique.......................22 A1

Dec & Jan, also Tue & Wed Feb) This three-star hotel, Cluny's most comfortable, is right next to the remains of the abbey. Built in 1817, it has 13 charming, antique-furnished rooms and three apartments.

Eating

There are cafés and restaurants around place du Commerce and rue Lamartine.

Hôtel de l'Abbaye restaurant (☎ 03 85 59 11 14; www.abbaye-cluny.fr; 14ter av Charles de Gaulle; menus €18.50-46; ☺ noon-2pm & 7.30-9pm Tue-Sat) A quietly elegant place that serves up regional and French gastronomic cuisine. Specialities include desserts and, from October to February, venison. Has a good selection of Mâconnais and Beaujolais wines.

Auberge du Cheval Blanc (☎ 03 85 59 01 13; 1 rue Porte de Mâcon; menus €16-38; ☺ usually closed dinner Fri & Sat, also closed Dec-Feb) Reputed for its traditional Burgundian cuisine, including *coq au vin* and *bœuf bourguignon*.

Au Péché Mignon (☎ 03 85 59 11 21; www.chocolaterie-germain.fr; 25 rue Lamartine; ☺ 7am-8pm) A gourmet patisserie-*chocolaterie* (pastry and chocolate shop) with all kinds of sweet and sticky delights, including *truffes du moine* (monk's truffles; hazelnut pralines) and *perles d'or* (golden pearls; brandy-soaked cherries with marzipan and pistachio). The *salon de thé* (lunch menu €10.50) serves breakfast and light meals (eg quiche and salad).

Most of Cluny's food shops are along place du Commerce, rue Lamartine and rue Mercière; all – except one **boulangerie** (36 rue Prud'hon) – are closed on Monday. For picnic supplies:

Atac Supermarket (av Charles de Gaulle; ☺ 8.45am-7.15pm Mon-Sat, 9am-noon Sun)

Petit Casino Grocery (29 rue Lamartine; ☺ 8am-12.30pm & 3-7.30pm Tue-Sat, 8.30am-noon Sun, also open Mon Jul & Aug)

Getting There & Away

The bus stop on rue Porte de Paris is served by the SNCF coach line linking Chalon-sur-Saône's train station (€7.90, 1½ hours, four daily), Mâcon's train station (€5.70, 45 minutes, six daily) and the Mâcon-Loché TGV station (€4.10, 30 minutes, six daily). Tickets are available at the **SNCF Boutique** (9 rue de la République; ☺ 9.10am-noon & 1.55-5.40pm Tue-Fri, 8.40am-1.40pm Sat).

NORTH OF CLUNY

An old railway line and parts of a former canal towpath have been turned into the **Voie Verte** (Green Road), a 120km paved path in three segments that's perfect for walking, cycling and in-line skating. One 65km section links Cluny via vineyards and valleys with Givry (to the north) and Charnay-les-Mâcon (to the south, just west of Mâcon).

One stop on the Voie Verte is Cormatin, 14km north of Cluny, where you'll find the **Musée du Vélo** (bicycle museum; ☎ 03 85 50 16 00; http://museeduvelo.free.fr; adult/under 12yr €4.50/2.50; ☺ 10am-6.30pm Jun–mid-Sep, 2-6.30pm Apr, May & mid-Sep–11 Nov) and the Renaissance-style **Château de Cormatin** (☎ 03 85 50 16 55; adult/student under 25yr/under 17yr €8/5/4; ☺ 10am-noon & 2-5.30pm Apr-May & Oct–mid-Nov, to 6.30pm Jun-Sep, no midday closure mid-Jul–mid-Aug), renowned for its opulent 17th-century, Louis XIII-style interiors. Cormatin is linked to Cluny by six SNCF buses daily (€2.60, 25 minutes).

Tournus (www.tournugeois.fr), on the Saône 33km northeast of Cluny, is known for its 10th- to 12th-century Romanesque abbey church, **Abbatiale St-Philibert** (☺ 8.30am-6pm, to 7pm May-Sep), whose superb and extremely rare 12th-century **mosaic** of the calendar and the zodiac was discovered by chance in 2002.

The scenic roads which link Cluny with Tournus, including the D14, D15, D82 and D56, pass through lots of tiny villages, many with charming churches. The medieval village of **Brancion** (www.brancion.fr in French) sits at the base of its chateau, while **Chardonnay** is – as one would expect – surrounded by vineyards. There's a panoramic view from 579m **Mont St-Romain**.

The **Côte Chalonnaise** wine-growing area runs from St-Gengoux-le-National north to **Chagny** and is just south of the Côte de Beaune (p465).

MÂCON

pop 34,500

The town of Mâcon, 70km north of Lyon on the right (west) bank of the Saône, is a good base for exploring the **Mâconnais**, Burgundy's southernmost wine-growing area, which produces mainly dry whites.

The **tourist office** (☎ 03 85 21 07 07; www.macon-tourism.com; 1 place St-Pierre; ☺ 9.30am-7pm Mon-Sat, 10-noon Sun & holidays early May–mid-Oct, 10am-noon & 2-6pm Mon-Sat rest of year) has information on visiting the vineyards of the Mâconnais and, a tiny bit further south, the **Beaujolais** (p517). It's across the street from the 18th-century **town hall** but may move to quai Lamartine, part of which is being turned into a riverfront promenade.

Mâcon's main commercial streets are rue Carnot and rue Dombey, a block west of the river, and perpendicular rue Sigorgne. The all-wood **Maison de Bois** (☎ 03 85 38 37 70), facing 95 rue Dombey and built around 1500, is decorated with carved wooden figures, some of them very cheeky indeed.

The **Musée Lamartine** (☎ 03 85 38 96 19; 41 rue Sigorgne; adult/student €2.50/free; ☺ 10am-noon & 2-6pm Tue-Sat, 2-6pm Sun & holidays) explores the life and times of the Mâcon-born Romantic poet and left-wing politician Alphonse de Lamartine (1790–1869). His name is also associated with the charming wine villages of **Bussières**, **Pierreclos** (known for its chateau), **Milly-Lamartine**, **Berzé-la-Ville** (the Chapelle des Moines has some 12th-century frescoes) and **Berzé-le-Châtel**, in the so-called 'Val Lamartinien' (Lamartine Valley), all of them on or near the road to Cluny.

The **Musée des Ursulines** (☎ 03 85 39 90 38; adult/student €2.50/free, for 2 museums €3.40/free; ☺ 10am-noon & 2-6pm Tue-Sat, 2-6pm Sun & holidays), housed in a 17th-century Ursuline convent, features Gallo-Roman archaeology, 16th- to 20th-century paintings and 19th-century Mâconnais life.

About 10km west of town in the wine country, the **Musée de Solutré** (☎ 03 85 35 85

BURGUNDY

24; ⏰ 10am-6pm Apr-Sep, 10am-noon & 2-5pm Wed-Sun Feb, Mar, Oct & Nov) displays some impressive local prehistory finds. A 20-minute walk will get you to the top of the rocky outcrop known as the **Roche de Solutré**, from where Mont Blanc can sometimes be seen (especially at sunset).

The *fin de siècle* grandeur of the two-star **Hôtel d'Europe et d'Angleterre** (☎ 03 85 38 27 94; europangle@wanadoo.fr; 92-109 quai Jean Jaurès; d €50-70; ⏰ reception closed noon-3pm Sun & winter), facing the river two blocks north of Pont St-Laurent, has faded considerably since Queen Victoria stayed here but some of the old-time atmosphere remains, eg in the 19th-century breakfast room. Many of the

30 rooms have marble fireplaces and river views.

Au P'tit Pierre (☎ 03 85 39 48 84; 10 rue Gambetta; menus €14-31; ⏰ closed Wed & dinner Tue Sep-Jun, Sun & lunch Mon Jul & Aug), two blocks south of the tourist office, is a modern bistro whose specialities include locally grown Charolais steak (€15).

The Mâcon-Ville train station is linked to Beaune (€12.40, one hour, 12 to 18 daily), Dijon (€16.90, 1½ hours, 19 to 25 daily) and Lyon's two stations (€10.60, 35 to 60 minutes, 19 to 33 daily). SNCF buses go to Cluny (€5.70, 45 minutes, six daily). The Mâcon-Loché TGV station is 5km southwest of town.

Lyon & the Rhône Valley

Gourmets, eat your heart out: Lyon *is* the gastronomic capital of France with a lavish table of piggy-driven dishes and delicacies to savour, and a fabulous bounty of eating spaces in which to do it. Be it old-fashioned bistro with checked tablecloths and slipper-shuffling Grandma or smart, minimalist space with state-of-the-art furnishings and chic city-slicker crowd to match, this French cuisine king thrills. Throw two mighty rivers, a couple of majestic Roman amphitheatres and a generous dose of elegant Renaissance architecture into the pot and the city will have you captivated. This is, after all, the city that most travellers turn up in unexpectedly (for business or en route south from Paris) – yet instantly yearn to return to.

Plumb at the crossroads to central Europe and the Atlantic, the Rhineland and the Mediterranean, the Rhône Valley has been the envy of many a soul for centuries. Ensnaring the Rhône River on its 813km-long journey from Lake Geneva to the Mediterranean, the valley forges downstream from Lyon past Gallo-Roman ruins at Vienne (of jazz festival fame), sweet nougat-making workshops in Montélimar and an extraordinary wealth of centuries-old Côtes du Rhône vineyards from which some of France's most respected reds are born.

Design-driven St-Étienne with its no-frills airport is a handy gateway to this region. For youthful, action-seeking souls, the green 'n' wild Gorges de l'Ardèche, which bring the River Ardèche tumbling to the gates of Provence and Languedoc, promises adventure by the kayak load.

HIGHLIGHTS

- Revel in the old-fashioned village atmosphere of **Croix Rousse** (p504)
- Get lost in the incredible **traboule maze** (see the boxed text, p506) of Vieux Lyon
- Ride the funicular up **Fourvière** (p503) for a stunning city panorama – from terrace or basilica
- Pig out in a **bouchon** (bistro; see the boxed text, p510)
- Jazz it up like the Romans at the legendary **Vienne Jazz Festival** (p520)
- Revel in the romance of a bygone era: sleep in a 1920s *roulotte* (traditional caravan) or centuries-old chateau in wine-rich **Beaujolais** (p517)
- OD on action in the racy white waters of the **Gorges de l'Ardèche** (p521)

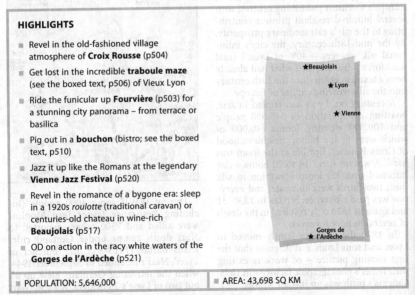

★ Beaujolais
★ Lyon
★ Vienne
Gorges de
★ l'Ardèche

- POPULATION: 5,646,000
- AREA: 43,698 SQ KM

LYON
pop 445,450

Commercial, industrial and banking powerhouse for the past 500 years, grand old Lyon (Lyons in English) is the focal point of a prosperous urban area of almost two million people, France's second-largest conurbation. Outstanding art museums, a dynamic cultural life, a busy clubbing and drinking scene, not to mention a thriving university and fantastic shopping, lend the city a distinctly sophisticated air.

Green parks, riverside paths and a historical old town sufficiently precious to be protected on Unesco's World Heritage list ensure a bounty of discoveries – on foot or bicycle – for the first-time visitor, while adventurous gourmets (particularly those with a penchant for piggie parts) can indulge their wildest gastronomic fantasies in a dining scene that is chic, sharp and savvy.

History

In 43 BC the Roman military colony of Lugdunum (Lyon) was founded. It served as the capital of the Roman territories known as the Three Gauls under Augustus, but had to wait until the 15th century for fame and fortune to strike: with the arrival of moveable type in 1473, Lyon became one of Europe's foremost publishing centres, with several hundred resident printers contributing to the city's extraordinary prosperity. By the mid-18th century, the city's influential silk weavers – 40% of Lyon's total workforce – transformed what had already been a textiles centre since the 15th century into the silk-weaving capital of Europe.

A century on, Lyon had tripled in size, boasting a population of 340,000 people and 100,000 weaving looms (40,000 of which were in the hilltop neighbourhood of Croix Rousse). But life at the loom was hard. A weaver spent 14 to 20 hours a day hunched over his loom breathing in silk dust; two-thirds were illiterate; and everyone was paid a pittance. Strikes in 1830–31 and again in 1834 only resulted in the death of several hundred weavers.

In 1870 the Lumière family moved to Lyon, and sons Louis and Auguste shot the first moving picture – of workers exiting their father's photographic factory – in 1895. Cinema's birth was an instant winner.

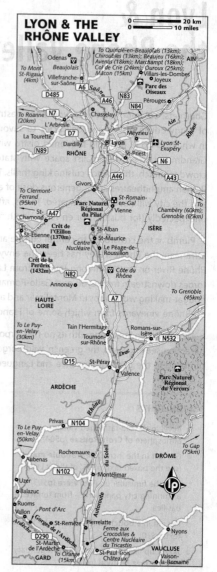

During WWII some 4000 people (including Resistance leader Jean Moulin) were killed and 7500 others deported to Nazi death camps under Gestapo chief Klaus Barbie (1913–91), the 'butcher of Lyon'. Nazi rule ended in September 1944, when the retreating Germans blew up all but two of Lyon's 28 bridges. A Lyon court sentenced Barbie to death in absentia in 1952 and again in 1954, but it was not until 1987, following his extradition from Bolivia (where he had settled after WWII), that he was tried in person in Lyon for crimes against humanity and sentenced to life imprisonment. The 72-year-old died in prison three years later.

The international police agency Interpol has been headquartered in Lyon since 1989. Urban violence (see p54 and p31) on central place Bellecour in late 2005 served as a poignant reminder that Lyon is not as picture-postcard perfect as its trim city centre suggests. Impoverished suburbs with substantial immigrant populations are as much a fact of life in Lyon as in other large French cities.

Orientation

The city centre is on the Presqu'île, a 500m- to 800m-wide peninsula bounded by the rivers Rhône and Saône. Public squares (north to south) include place de la Croix Rousse in the quarter of Croix Rousse; place Louis Pradel, just north of the opera house; place des Terreaux; place de la République, attached to pedestrianised rue de la République; vast place Bellecour; and place Carnot, just north of Gare de Perrache, one of Lyon's two mainline train stations. The other station, Gare de la Part-Dieu, is 1.5km east of the Rhône in Part-Dieu, a commercial shopping centre dominated by a pencil-shaped tower nicknamed *le crayon*.

On the Saône's western bank, Vieux Lyon (Old Lyon) is sandwiched between the river and the hilltop area of Fourvière.

Lyon comprises nine arrondissements (districts); the arrondissement number appears after each street address in this chapter.

Information

BOOKSHOPS

Decitre (Map pp500-1; ☎ 04 26 68 00 30; 6 place Bellecour, 2e; Ⓜ Bellecour; ☻ 9.30am-7pm Mon-Sat) English-language fiction, travel guides and maps.

Raconte-Moi La Terre (Map pp500-1; ☎ 04 78 92 60 22; www.raconte-moi.com; 38 rue Thomassin, 2e; Ⓜ Cordeliers; ☻ 10am-7.30pm Mon-Sat) Fab travel bookshop.

EMERGENCY

Police Station (Commissariat de Police) 47 rue de la Charité, 2e (Map pp500-1; ☎ 04 78 42 26 56; Ⓜ Perrache or Ampère); 5 place Sathonay, 1er (Map pp500-1; ☎ 04 78 28 11 87; Ⓜ Hôtel de Ville)

SOS Médecins (☎ 04 78 83 51 51) Medical emergencies.

INTERNET ACCESS

Espace Internet (Map pp500-1; ☎ 04 78 39 72 41; cnr rue Romarin & rue Terraille, 1er; Ⓜ Hôtel de Ville; per hr €2; ☻ 10am-8.30pm Mon-Sat) Cheap access in a cheap phone-calling centre.

Raconte-Moi La Terre (Map pp500-1; ☎ 04 78 92 60 22; www.raconte-moi.com; 38 rue Thomassin, 2e; Ⓜ Cordeliers; per hr €4; ☻ 10am-7.30pm Mon-Sat) Stylish surfing on one of two terminals in this 1st-floor travel bookshop café.

INTERNET RESOURCES

www.bullesdegones.com What to do with the kids (0–12 years) in/around Lyon (in French).

www.lyonclubbing.com The latest (in French) on Lyon's nightlife scene: bars, clubs, live music, celebrities, hot gossip and so on.

www.lyon.fr Official city website.

www.lyonresto.com Restaurant listings (in French) with reviews, menu prices and ratings for food, atmosphere, service, quality and quantity.

www.petitpaume.com Electronically search through the best city guide (in French) on Lyon, compiled by university students and distributed for free just one day a year in October.

www.rhonealpes-tourisme.com Regional tourist information site.

CITY SLICKER

The **Lyon City Card** (for 1/2/3 days adult €18/28/38, 4-18yr €9/14/19) covers admission to every museum in Lyon as well as the roof of Basilique Notre Dame de Fourvière and Fourvière's Tour de l'Observatoire. It also includes a guided or audioguided city tour organised by the tourist office, a river excursion (April to October) and 10% discount on Cyclotours and Le Grand Tour (for details, see p507).

To top it off, the card – sold by the tourist office and some hotels – allows you unlimited travel on buses, trams, the funicular and the metro; and 10% discount in Richart (see the boxed text, p514) and other selected shops.

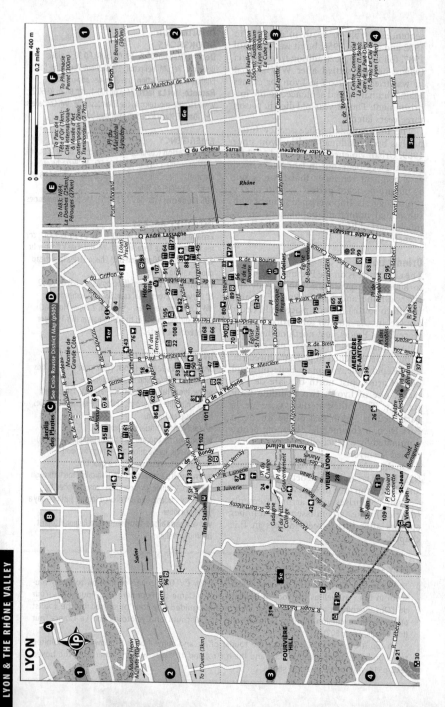

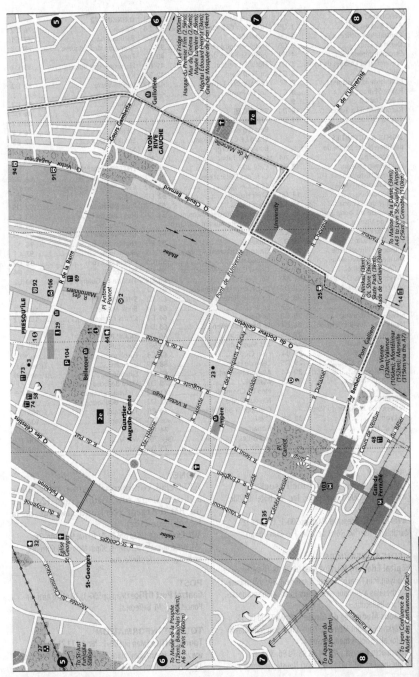

LAUNDRY

Pay €3 to wash 5kg of smelly socks at:

Lav'+ (Map pp500-1; rue Terme, 1er; M Hôtel de Ville; 🕒 6am-9pm)

Laverie de la Fresque (Map pp500-1; 1 rue de la Martinière, 1er; M Hôtel de Ville; 🕒 6am-10pm)

MEDICAL SERVICES

Hôpital Édouard Herriot (☎ 08 20 08 20 69; www .chu-lyon.fr in French; 5 place d'Arsonval, 3e; M Grange Blanche) Has a 24-hour emergency room, 4km southeast of place Bellecour.

Maisons Médicales de Garde (☎ 04 72 33 00 33; 🕒 8pm-midnight Mon-Sat, 8pm-11pm Sun & holidays) Call for after-hours medical care.

Pharmacie Perret (☎ 04 78 93 70 96; 30 rue Duquesne, 6e; M Foch; 🕒 24hr) Nonstop pharmacy.

MONEY

ATM-clad commercial banks are a dime a dozen along rue Victor Hugo (2e), rue du Bât d'Argent (1er) and also rue de la République (1er).

AOC Exchange (Map pp500-1; 20 rue Gasparin, 2e; M Bellecour; 🕒 9.30am-6.30pm Mon-Sat) Currency exchange off place Bellecour.

POST

Central Post Office (Map pp500-1; 10 place Antonin Poncet, 2e; M Bellecour)

TOURIST INFORMATION

Tourist Office (Map pp500-1; ☎ 04 72 77 69 69; www.lyon-france.com; place Bellecour, 2e; M Bellecour; 🕒 10am-5.30pm Mon-Sat)

Sights

VIEUX LYON

Old Lyon, with its cobblestone streets and **medieval & Renaissance houses** below Fourvière hill, is divided into three quarters: St-Paul at the northern end, St-Jean in the middle and St-Georges in the south. Facing the river is the grandiose **Palais de Justice** (Law Courts; Map pp500–1; quai Romain Rolland; Ⓜ Vieux Lyon).

Lovely old buildings languish on **rue du Bœuf**, **rue St-Jean** and **rue des Trois Maries**. Crane your neck upwards to see gargoyles and other cheeky stone characters carved on window ledges along **rue Juiverie**, home to Lyon's Jewish community in the Middle Ages.

Partly Romanesque **Cathédrale St-Jean** (Map pp500–1; place St-Jean, 5e; Ⓜ Vieux Lyon), seat of Lyon's 133rd bishop, was built from the late 11th to the early 16th centuries. The portals of its Flamboyant Gothic façade (completed in 1480) are decorated with 280 square stone medallions (early 14th century). The **astronomical clock** in the north transept arm chimes at noon, 2pm, 3pm and 4pm.

The **Musée Gadagne** (Map pp500–1; ☎ 04 78 42 03 61; www.museegadagne.com in French; place du Petit Collège, 5e; Ⓜ Vieux Lyon), in a 16th-century mansion once owned by two rich Florentine bankers, will house a local history and puppet museum when it reopens in 2007 after extensive renovations.

FOURVIÈRE

Over two millennia ago, the Romans built the city of Lugdunum on the slopes of Fourvière. Today, Lyon's 'hill of prayer' – topped by a basilica and the **Tour Métallique** (Map pp500–1), an Eiffel Tower–like structure built in 1893 and used as a TV transmitter – affords spectacular views of the city and its two rivers. Footpaths wind uphill but the funicular departing from place Édouard Commette is the least taxing way up; use a metro ticket or buy a return funicular ticket (€2.20).

Crowning the hill – and proffering a stunning city view from its terrace – is the **Basilique Notre Dame de Fourvière** (Map pp500–1; www.lyon-fourviere.com in French), a superb example of the exaggerated enthusiasm for embellishment that dominated French ecclesiastical architecture in the late 19th century. Free organ and other musical **concerts** (6pm 2nd & 4th Sun of the month Sep-Jun) are

fabulous for lapping up the basilica's magnificence. Otherwise, 1¼-hour **guided tours** (☎ 04 78 25 86 19; adult/under 16yr €5/3; 2.30pm & 4pm Mon-Sun Jun-Sep, 2.30pm & 4pm Wed & Sun Oct, Apr & May, 2.30pm & 3.30pm Wed & Sun Nov) take in the roof, various bits inside, and climax atop the **Tour de l'Observatoire** (Observatory Tower; adult/under 16yr €2/1; 10.30am-noon & 2-6.30pm Wed-Sun), from where an even better city panorama unfolds. The tower can be scaled without a tour too.

Artefacts found in the Rhône Valley, including the remains of a four-wheeled vehicle from around 700 BC and several sumptuous mosaics, are displayed in the **Musée de la Civilisation Gallo-Romaine** (Museum of Gallo-Roman Civilisation; Map pp500–1; ☎ 04 72 38 81 90; www.musees-gallo-romains.com in French; 17 rue Cléberg, 5e; Fourvière funicular station; adult/18-25yr/under 18yr €3.80/2.30/free, free Thu; 10am-6pm Tue-Sun). Next door the **Théâtre Romain**, built around 15 BC and enlarged in AD 120, sat an audience of 10,000. Romans held poetry readings and musical recitals in the smaller **odéon** next door.

PRESQU'ÎLE

The centrepiece of Presqu'île's beautiful **place des Terreaux** (Ⓜ Hôtel de Ville), 1er, is a 19th-century fountain made of 21 tonnes of lead and sculpted by Frédéric-Auguste Bartholdi of Statue of Liberty fame. The four horses pulling the chariot symbolise rivers galloping seawards. The **Hôtel de Ville** (Map pp500–1) fronting the square was built in 1655 but given its present ornate façade in 1702; get a bird's-eye view of its lovely interior courtyard from Les Muses (see the boxed text, p512).

Nearby, the **Musée des Beaux-Arts** (Museum of Fine Arts; Map pp500–1; ☎ 04 72 10 17 40; 20 place des Terreaux, 1er; Ⓜ Hôtel de Ville; adult/under 18yr €6/free; 10am-6pm Wed-Mon, from 10.30pm Fri) showcases France's finest collection of sculptures and paintings from every period of European art outside Paris. Its **cloister garden** is a great picnic venue.

Lyon's neoclassical **opera house** (Map pp500–1; 1 place de la Comédie, 1er; Ⓜ Hôtel de Ville) was built in 1832 and topped with its striking glass-domed roof by French architect Jean Nouvel in 1993. Boarders and bladers buzz around the fountains of riverside **place Louis Pradel**, surveyed by the **Homme de la Liberté** (Man of Freedom) on roller-skates, sculpted

---

WATCH THIS SPACE

The **Lyon Confluence** (www.lyon-confluence.fr) – the spot where the Rhône and the Saône meet south of Gare de Perrache – is the city's most exciting urban space. An industrial wasteland for decades, the riverside site is now the subject of a mammoth €780 million rejuvenation project.

Watch this space for the incredible **Musée des Confluences** (Confluence Museum), a spacey science- and society-focused museum set to open in 2008. As much stunning piece of contemporary architecture as museum, it will be housed in a futuristic steel-and-glass transparent crystal topped by a floating 'cloud'. Inside, three of the 10 vast exhibition areas will grapple with eternal questions like 'Where do we come from?', 'Where are we going?' and 'Who are we and what are we doing?'. Remaining spaces will home in on hot issues of the future – cloning, genetically modified organisms, global warming and so on.

Two auditoriums, a café, restaurants, shop and riverside garden will complete the ambitious cultural ensemble, the creation of world-famous Austria-based architect agency Coop Himmelb(l)au.

---

from scrap metal by Marseille-born César (1921–98).

West of place des Terreaux, some 25 famous Lyonnais peer out from the sevenstorey **Fresque des Lyonnais** (Map pp500-1; cnr rue de la Martinière & quai de la Pêcherie, 1er; **M** Hôtel de Ville), a mural featuring loom inventor Joseph-Marie Jacquard (1752–1834), Renaissance poet Maurice Scève (c 1499–c 1560), superstar chef Paul Bocuse (see p511) and the yellow-haired Little Prince, created by Lyon-born author Antoine de St-Exupéry (1900–44).

The **Musée de l'Imprimerie** (Printing Museum; Map pp500-1; ☎ 04 78 37 65 98; www.imprimerie.lyon .fr in French; 37 rue de la Poulaillerie, 2e; **M** Cordeliers; adult/under 18yr €3.80/free; ♥ 9.30am-noon & 2-6pm Wed-Sun) focuses on a technology established in Lyon by the 1480s.

Extraordinary Lyonnais silks, French and Asian textiles, and carpets are showcased at the **Musée des Tissus** (Textile Museum; Map pp500-1; ☎ 04 78 38 42 00; www.musee-des-tissus.com in French; 34 rue de la Charité, 2e; **M** Ampère; adult/under 18yr €5/free; ♥ 10am-5.30pm Tue-Sun). Next door, the **Musée des Arts Décoratifs** (Decorative Arts Museum; Map pp500-1; with Musée des Tissus ticket free; ♥ same as Musée des Tissus) displays 18th-century furniture, tapestries, wallpaper, ceramics and silver.

Laid out in the 17th century, **place Bellecour** (**M** Bellecour) – one of Europe's largest public squares – is pierced by an equestrian **statue of Louis XIV**. From here, pedestrianised **rue Victor Hugo** runs southwards to place Carnot and Gare de Perrache.

South of Perrache, across the Pont de la Mulatière next to the confluence of the Rhône and Saône (see the boxed text,

above), is the well thought-out **Aquarium du Grand Lyon** (☎ 04 72 66 65 66; www.aquariumlyon .fr; 6 place du Général Leclerc, La Mulatière; adult/under 12yr/under 1m €11/7/free; ♥ 11am-7pm Tue-Sun & Mon-Fri, 10am-7pm Tue-Sun school holidays), where adults can dive with dolphins and kids stroke fish. Bus 15 links it with place Bellecour.

CROIX ROUSSE

Soulful **Croix Rousse** (Map p505; **M** Croix Rousse) – a gargantuan step back in time from the Lyon Confluence – is known for its village air, bohemian inhabitants and lush outdoor food market. The hilltop neighbourhood quietly buzzes north up the steep *pentes* (slopes).

Historically, this old quarter is famed for its silk-weaving tradition, illustrated by the **Mur des Canuts** (cnr blvd des Canuts & rue Denfert-Rochereau, 4e; **M** Hénon) on the side of an apartment block. Following the introduction of the mechanical Jacquard loom in 1805, Lyonnais *canuts* (silk weavers) built workshops in this quarter with large windows to let in light and hefty wood-beamed ceilings more than 4m high to accommodate the huge new machines. Most of these workshops are today chic loft apartments.

During the bitter 1830–31 *canut* uprisings, triggered by low pay and dire working conditions, hundreds of weavers were killed. Gen up on their labour-intensive life at the **Maison des Canuts** (Map p505; ☎ 04 78 28 62 04; 10-12 rue d'Ivry, 4e; **M** Croix Rousse; adult/child €5/2.50; ♥ 10am-6.30pm Tue-Sat, guided tours 11am & 3.30pm), a museum with a shop opposite that sells silk; and the riveting **Atelier de Passementerie** (☎ 04 78 27 17 13; www.soierie-vivante.asso.fr in French; 21 rue Richan, 4e; adult/child €3/2; ♥ 30min guided tour with demonstration 2pm & 4pm Tue-Sat), an authentic

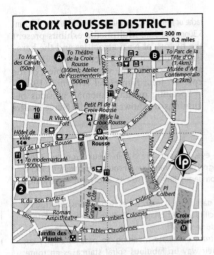

CROIX ROUSSE DISTRICT

workshop where weavers lived and worked until 1979. Its **boutique** (2-6.30pm Tue, 9am-noon & 2-6.30pm Wed-Sat) also sells contemporary Lyonnais silk.

Silk, stained glass and other visual arts are the soul of **Montée de la Grand Côte** (Map p505; Croix Rousse), a walkway lined with artists workshops that links Croix Rousse with place des Terreaux, 1er.

RIVE GAUCHE

Lyon's graceful 117-hectare **Parc de la Tête d'Or** (04 72 69 47 60; blvd des Belges, 6e; Masséna; 6am-11pm mid-Apr–mid-Oct, to 9pm mid-Oct–

mid-Apr), landscaped in the 1860s, is graced by a lake, botanic garden with greenhouses, an Alpine garden, rose garden and zoo. When it's warm you can rent boats, ride ponies, play miniature golf, take a twirl on a fairground ride or watch a puppet show. The park is served by bus 41 or 47 from metro Part-Dieu.

The park's northern realms sit snug against the brick-and-glass **Cité Internationale**, designed by Italian architect Renzo Piano to host the G7 summit in 1996. Inside, the **Musée d'Art Contemporain** (Museum of Contemporary Art; 04 72 69 17 17; www.moca-lyon.org;

A CROIX-ROUSSE SOUL

Name: Lise

Job: Journalist

In a Nutshell: Loves walking in the countryside – Monts du Lyonnais and Monts du Forez are favourites – and exotic holidays with her boyfriend.

Why Croix Rousse & since when? Five years ago, I moved here to start a new job. The plan was to stay no more than a year...

What makes you stay? The quality of life, the wonderful food, the skiing just over an hour's drive away, and the Mediterranean just a hop and skip down the motorway.

Your favourite character? The cheese-man in the market who never has anything nice to say about anyone but sells the best (and smelliest!) St-Félicien this side of the Alps.

Typical Sunday morning: Drag the boyfriend and the dog to the market, fill up the basket with fresh goodies, then settle down for oysters and white wine at one of the cafés on the plateau.

Biggest gripe? No parking space!

Hottest tip for uncovering the 'real' Croix Rousse? Head to the **Comptoir du Vin** (Map p505; 04 78 39 89 95; 2 rue Belfort, 4e; Croix Rousse; lunch & dinner Mon-Fri, lunch Sat) any day of the week for a hearty meal, and you will instantly be thrown into the deep end. But beware. It's not for the faint-hearted: a steak tartare can easily reach the half-kilo!

81 quai Charles de Gaulle, 6e; adult/under 18yr variable depending on exhibition/free; ☼ noon-7pm Wed-Sun) displays works created after 1960.

The WWII headquarters of Gestapo commander Klaus Barbie (p498) from 1942 to 1944 houses the evocative **Centre d'Histoire de la Résistance et de la Déportation** (CHRD; Map pp500-1; ☎ 04 78 72 23 11; 14 av Berthelot, 7e; Ⓜ Per-

rache or Jean Macé; adult/under 18yr €3.80/free; ☼ 9am-5.30pm Wed-Sun). Multimedia exhibits present the history of Nazi atrocities and the heroism of French Resistance fighters. The life and times of Barbie were the subject of the epic 4½-hour film *Hôtel Terminus* (1988).

Speaking of film, cinema's glorious beginnings are showcased at the **Musée Lumière**

TRABOULES

There's more to parts of Lyon than meets the eye. Beneath the city in Vieux Lyon and Croix Rousse, dark and dingy *traboules* (secret passages) wind their way through apartment blocks, under streets and into courtyards. In all, 315 passages link 230 streets and have a combined length of 50km.

Although a couple of Vieux Lyon's *traboules* date from Roman times, most were constructed by *canuts* (silk weavers) in the 19th century to facilitate the transport of silk in inclement weather. Resistance fighters found them equally handy during WWII.

Genuine *traboules* (derived from the Latin *trans ambulare* meaning 'to pass through') cut from one street to another, often wending their way up fabulous spiral staircases en route. Passages that fan out into a courtyard or lead into a cul de sac are not *traboules*, but rather *miraboules*.

Vieux Lyon's most celebrated *traboules* include those linking 27 rue St-Jean with 6 rue des Trois Maries; 54 rue St-Jean with 27 rue du Bœuf (push the intercom button to buzz open the door); 10 quai Romain Rolland with 2 place du Gouvernement; 17 quai Romain Rolland with 9 rue des Trois Maries; and 31 rue du Bœuf with 14 rue de la Bombarde.

Step into Croix Rousse's underworld at 9 place Colbert, crossing cours des Voraces – renowned for its monumental staircase that zigzags up seven floors – and emerging at 29 rue Imbert Colomès. Other well-known *traboules* in this fashionable quarter include those linking 1 place Colbert with 10 montée St-Sébastien and 9 place Colbert with 14bis montée St-Sébastien; and the plethora of passages on rue des Capucins: at Nos 3, 6, 13, 22 and 23.

The tourist office runs guided *traboule* tours (opposite) and distributes a free map of Croix-Rousse and Vieux Lyon marked up with all the *traboules* alongside interesting courtyards, building façades and staircases.

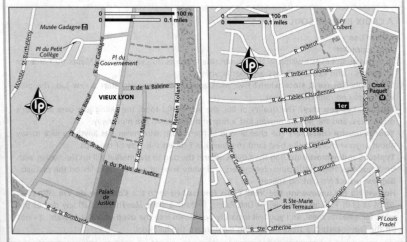

(☎ 04 78 78 18 95; www.institut-lumiere.org; 25 rue du Premier Film, 8e; Ⓜ Monplaisir-Lumière; adult/under 18yr €6/5; ☉ 11am-6.30pm Tue-Sun), a film-buff must 3km southeast of place Bellecour along cours Gambetta. The museum is inside the Art Nouveau home (1899–1902) of Antoine Lumière who, with his sons Auguste and Louis, moved to Lyon in 1870 and shot the first reels of the world's first motion picture, *La Sortie des Usines Lumières* (Exit of the Lumières Factories) in one of their factories here on 19 March 1895. Today classic films are screened in the **Hangar du Premier Film** (see also p514) – the film set for *La Sortie des Usines Lumières* – that somehow escaped demolition when the rest of the Lumière factories were bulldozed in the 1970s.

Nearby, the **Mur du Cinéma** (Cinema Wall; cnr cours Gambetta & Grand Rue de la Guillotière, 7e; Ⓜ Guillotière) – a painted wall – recaps Lyon's marvellous cinematic story in still-image form.

The **Grande Mosquée de Lyon** (☎ 04 78 76 00 23; 146 blvd Pinel, 8e; Ⓜ Laënnec; ☉ 9am-noon Sat-Thu), 5km east of Presqu'île, fuses traditional North African architecture and calligraphy with contemporary Western styles.

NORTHERN BURBS

Two museums make it worth an outing to Lyon's predominantly residential northern suburbs.

Dolls of all ages and origins grace the elegant rooms of the **Musée de la Poupée** (Doll Museum; ☎ 04 78 87 87 00; www.lacroix-laval.com in French; Parc de Lacroix-Laval, rte de St-Bel, Marcy l'Étoile; adult/under 18yr €3.80/free, Thu free; ☉ 10am-5pm Tue-Sun), inside a fairy-tale castle 12km northwest from the centre. A vast green wooded **park** (☉ 6am-10pm summer, 7am-8pm winter) hugs the 16th-century chateau and an electric train takes punters on park tours in summer. The fountain-studded paddling pool makes cooling down on hot summer days great fun.

Of a different ilk are the exhibits inside 15th-century Château de Rochetaillée: motoring enthusiasts can drool over 120 vintage cars (not to mention Hitler's Mercedes and Jean-Paul II's Renault Espace!), 50-odd motorbikes, bicycles and modes of Lyonnais public transport over the centuries at the chateau-museum **Musée de l'Automobile Henri Malartre** (Car Museum; ☎ 04 78 22 18 80; www.musee-malartre.com in French; 645 rue du Musée, Rochetaillée-sur-Saône; adult/under 18yr €5.30/free; ☉ 9am-6pm Tue-Sun

Sep-Jun, 10am-7pm Jul & Aug), 11km north of central Lyon along the Saône-side D433. Take bus 40 or 70 to the 'Rochetaillée' stop.

Activities

Rollerbladers (www.generationsroller.asso.fr in French) hook up for a mass scoot around town at 9pm on Friday on place Bellecour. Otherwise, they blade by the rivers; in Parc de la Tête d'Or (p505); and in the **skate park** (☎ 04 78 69 17 86; 24 rue Pierre de Coubertin, 7e; Ⓜ Gerland) in Parc de Gerland.

Skate shop **Le Cri du Kangourou** (Map pp500-1; ☎ 04 72 00 99 10; www.cdk.fr in French; 21 rue d'Algérie, 1er; Ⓜ Hôtel de Ville) rents blades for €5.50/7.50/12 per half-day/day/weekend.

Cycling paths run beside both rivers and more are planned. For bike hire, see p517.

Tours

The tourist office runs 1½- to two-hour thematic English-language **walking tours** (adult/8-18yr €9/5) of Vieux Lyon and Croix Rousse. Alternatively, DIY with an MP3 or a copy of *Lyon Balades: Decouvrez Lyon à pied* (Lyon Walks: Discover Lyon on foot) or *à vélo* (by bike) in hand. The tourist office stocks both.

Tiny and/or tired feet might prefer the seasonal Presqu'île tours run by **Cyclopolitain** (☎ 08 26 10 00 03; www.cyclopolitain.com in French; 1/2 people €7/10.50; tours Mar-Dec; ☉ 10.30am-7pm Mar-Sep, 10.30am-5.30pm Oct-Dec) or those aboard an open-top double-decker bus run by **Le Grand Tour** (☎ 04 78 56 32 39; lyon.legrandtour@voyages-naime.com; 1-/2-day ticket €17/20; ☉ 10am-6.30pm Apr-Oct, 10.45am-5pm Nov-Mar), which allow passengers to hop on/off as they please.

April to October, **Navig-Inter** (☎ 04 78 42 96 81; www.naviginter.fr in French) runs 1¼-hour afternoon **river excursions** (Map pp500-1; Ⓜ Bellecour or Vieux Lyon; adult/child €8/5) from the dock at 3 quai des Célestins, 2e. Advance bookings are vital for its **lunch and dinner cruises** (Map pp500-1; 23 quai Claude Bernard, 7e; Ⓜ Ampère or Guillotière; adult/child from €24/37).

Festivals & Events

Les Nuits de Fourvière (mid-June to early August; www.nuitsdefourviere.fr in French) Brings a multitude of fabulous open-air concerts to Fourvière's Théâtre Romain (Map pp500-1).

Biennale d'Art Contemporain (Contemporary Art Biennial; July to September; www.biennale-de-lyon.org) Odd-numbered years hail the Art Biennial.

Biennale de la Danse (Dance Biennial; September; www.biennale-de-lyon.org) Even-numbered years host the month-long Dance Biennial.

Fête des Lumières (Festival of Lights; December) For several days around 8 December, Lyon is lit up by the marking of the Feast of the Immaculate Conception. Sound-and-light shows are projected onto the city's most important buildings (place des Terreaux is always a key festival venue) and everyone puts candles in the windows of their homes.

Sleeping

Sleeping here is sweet: be it traditional village hotel, riverside Renaissance mansion or historic college fusing old-fashioned nostalgia with hard-hitting design (see Collège Hotel, opposite), there is something to every taste and budget. The **hotel booking office** (☎ 04 72 77 72 50; resa@lyon-france.com), run by the tourist office, has a full list of what's available.

Under the 'Bon Weekend à Lyon' scheme (see the boxed text, p948), valid year-round, some hotels offer two consecutive nights for the price of one (and a free City Card; see the boxed text, p499) to guests checking in on a Friday or Saturday. Bookings must be made at least 24 hours in advance through the hotel booking office.

BUDGET

Auberge de Jeunesse du Vieux Lyon (Map pp500-1; ☎ 04 78 15 05 50; lyon@fuaj.org; 41-45 montée du Chemin Neuf; Ⓜ Vieux Lyon, 5e; dm €15.70; Ⓨ reception 7am-1pm, 2-8pm & 9pm-1am) Rates include breakfast at this superbly located hostel above Vieux Lyon. Its 180 beds are split between rooms for two to seven people. Guests without an HI card pay an extra €2.80 a night.

Hôtel de la Poste (Map p505; ☎ 04 78 28 62 67; 1 rue Victor Fort, 4e; Ⓜ Croix Rousse; s/d/tr/q €37/35/45/66, with shower & toilet €39/44/58/70; reception Ⓨ 7am-9pm Mon-Fri, 8am-9pm Sat & Sun) Price – not prettiness – pulls in the punters at this bright but basic hotel overlooking the lovely central square in Croix Rousse. Skip the hotel breakfast (€5.50) and instead nip down to place de la Croix Rousse for coffee and a croissant on a café pavement terrace. Square-eyed punters can pay €3.50 extra a night to have a box in their room (French channels only).

Hôtel Iris (Map pp500-1; ☎ 04 78 39 93 80; hoteliris@freesurf.fr; 36 rue de l'Arbre Sec, 1er; Ⓜ Hôtel de Ville; s/d €37/39, with shower & toilet €45/47) The location of this two-star number inside a

four-centuries-old convent could not be better (the street it sits on is littered with hip places to eat and drink), so get in quick to snag one of its simple rooms overlooking a quiet courtyard.

Hôtel St-Pierre des Terreaux (Map pp500-1; ☎ 04 78 28 00 95; 8 rue Paul Chenevard, 1er; Ⓜ Hôtel de Ville; s/d/tr from €34.50/44/59; Ⓨ Sep-Jul) Given it's about the only budget choice on Lyon's main shopping street, St-Pierre is a not bad deal. Should hotel life lack colour or stress levels rise, manhandle a few balls in the juggling shop next door.

MIDRANGE

Gîtes de France (Map pp500-1; ☎ 04 72 77 17 50; www.gites-de-france-rhone.com; 1 rue Général Plessier, 2e; Ⓜ Perrache; B&B for 2 people €40-120; Ⓨ 9am-noon & 1-6pm Mon-Fri) organises B&B around Lyon.

Le Patio des Terreaux (Map pp500-1; ☎ 04 78 28 11 01; www.lepatiodesterreaux.fr in French; 9 rue Ste-Catherine, 1er; Ⓜ Hôtel de Ville; street-/patio-facing d €50/60) 'Patio' translates as an interior courtyard with a couple of flowerbeds which, small as it might be, ensures a peaceful night's sleep for guests in this kebab-joint busy neck of the city. Rooms are modern with preserved old features: thumbs up for the rickety terracotta floor tiles and the stone wall behind glass in the bathroom of room 112.

Hôtel de Paris (Map pp500-1; ☎ 04 78 28 00 95; www.hoteldeparis-lyon.com; 16 rue de la Platière, 1er; Ⓜ Hôtel de Ville; small s/d €45/50, luxury d €58-74; Ⓧ) Middle-of-the-road sums up this good-value hotel bang slap on central Lyon's shop-packed heart – in a lovely 19th-century bourgeois building no less. Pricier doubles are bigger and sport a big bath to swim in as well as shower.

Hôtel St-Vincent (Map pp500-1; ☎ 04 78 37 75 79; www.hotel-saintvincent.com in French; 9 rue Pareille, 1er; Ⓜ Hôtel de Ville; s/d/tr €45/55/65) High-beamed ceilings, giant-sized windows, a couple of old stone walls and original wooden floors make this three-floor, 32-room hotel a fine place for lapping up authentic Lyonnais atmosphere. Ask for a room on the 1st floor if your suitcase weighs a tonne; two-star hotels don't have lifts.

Hôtel des Célestins (Map pp500-1; ☎ 04 72 56 08 98; www.hotelcelestins.com; 4 rue des Archers, 2e; Ⓜ Bellecour; low season s/d/tr €58/65/90, high season €90/90/135; Ⓧ) On the same square as the elegant Théâtre des Célestins built in 1792, this comfortable hotel is surrounded by designer clothes shops, cafés and bistros. The most expensive rooms overlook the theatre; cheaper ones look out on a courtyard. Best of all, the guest-friendly hotel staff is full of recommendations on where to eat and what to see, making city navigation a breeze.

Hôtel St-Antoine (Map pp500-1; ☎ 04 78 92 91 91; www.hotel-saintantoine.fr; 1 rue du Port du Temple, 2e; Ⓜ Cordeliers; s/d €63/69; ✖ 🖵) A stylish mix of old and new – wi-fi zone and period furnishings – greets guests at this thoroughly modern hotel that occupies an 18th-century townhouse a pebble throw from the Saône. Guests staying a couple of days or more should look into its good-value 'weekend' and 'discovery' packages.

ourpick Collège Hotel (Map pp500-1; ☎ 04 72 10 05 05; www.college-hotel.com; 5 place St-Paul, 5e; Ⓜ Vieux Lyon; undergraduate/graduate/postgraduate d €105/125/140; ✖ 🖵) What style this college hotel has, although those with a dislike of white might not appreciate its cutting-edge interior design! With reception decked out in warm cosy ochre tones – think old-fashioned library lined with books, the odd antique, leather chair and lovely wood-plank floor – the dazzling *white* minimalism of the bedrooms does come as something of a shock. Flat-screen TV is a basic commodity, and breakfast (€11) can be enjoyed on the guest's own balcony or in the *salle de classe petit dejeuner* (breakfast classroom), bedecked like a classroom of a yesteryear. A rooftop panorama from a small roof-terrace garden tops off this imaginative hotel.

TOP END

Sofitel Royal Lyon (Map pp500-1; ☎ 04 78 37 57 31; H2952@accor-hotels.com; 20 place Bellecour, 2e; Ⓜ Bellecour; s/d/ste from €170/200/450; ✖ ✖ 🖵) Wedged between the Rhône and the Saône, Lyon's most prestigious visiting card has wrapped guests in cotton wool since 1895 when it opened as the Hôtel Royal. Service is four star and royal. Avoid November during trade fairs when the hotel bumps up its prices.

Cour des Loges (Map pp500-1; ☎ 04 72 77 44 44; www.courdesloges.com; 2-8 rue du Bœuf, 5e; Ⓜ Vieux Lyon; d/ste from €230/500; ✖ ✖ 🖵 ☎) Four 14th- to 17th-century houses wrapped around a *traboule* in Old Lyon make this a beautiful place to stay. A treat out of the ordinary, individually designed rooms woo guests with Philippe Stark bathroom fittings

and a bounty of antiques and carefully preserved historical features. Italianate loggias and spiral staircases add a twist to public areas.

La Tour Rose (Map pp500-1; ☎ 04 78 92 69 10; www.tour-rose.com; 22 rue du Bœuf, 5e; Ⓜ Vieux Lyon; d €250-540; ✖ ✖ 🖵) The Pink Tower – and indeed, there is a pink tower amid the Renaissance ensemble – is the top-end boutique-hotel option. A dozen rooms furnished by 11 different contemporary silk manufacturers illustrate the story of the city's vibrant silk industry. The restaurant with cobblestone floor and glass roof in a former chapel is a must-dine.

Eating

Memorable dining is a sure thing. This is the French gastronomic capital after all, with a flurry of big-name chefs behind a sparkling restaurant line-up that embraces all genres. Be it French, fusion or fast you want, Lyon has it.

Cobbled rue Mercière, rue des Marronniers and the northern side of place Antonin Poncet – all in the 2nd arrondissement (metro Cordeliers) – are chock-a-block with eating options, outside terraces overflowing in summer. Near the opera house, rue Verdi, 1er, is table-filled.

Planning lunch in a traditional Lyonnais *bouchon*? Write off the afternoon (see the boxed text, p510).

BOUCHONS

Reservations are vital at these Lyonnais classics.

Café des Fédérations (Map pp500-1; ☎ 04 78 28 26 00; www.lesfedeslyon.com in French; 8 rue Major Martin, 1er; Ⓜ Hôtel de Ville; lunch/dinner menu €19.50/23.50; ⚅ lunch & dinner Mon-Fri) B&W photos of old Lyon speckle the wood-panelled walls of this legendary *bouchon*, easily one of the city's best-known, where nothing has changed for decades. Its *caviar de la Croix Rousse* (lentils dressed in a creamy sauce) is divine.

Comptoir Restaurant des Deux Places (Map pp500-1; ☎ 04 78 28 95 10; 5 place Fernand Rey, 1er; Ⓜ Hôtel de Ville; starters/mains €10/15, menu €27; ⚅ lunch & dinner Tue-Fri) Red-and-white checked curtains, an old-world interior crammed with antiques and a menu hand-scribed in black ink contribute to the overwhelmingly traditional feel here. Annick and Jean-Marc follow a strict four-day week and the pavement terrace beneath trees on a quiet village-like square off place Sathonay is idyllic.

Chez Paul (Map pp500-1; ☎ 04 78 28 35 83; 11 rue Major Martin, 1er; Ⓜ Hôtel de Ville; menu €21.50; ☙ lunch & dinner Mon-Fri May-Jul, lunch & dinner Mon-Fri, dinner Sat Sep-Apr; ☒) Another red-and-white checked tablecloth place, Paul's Place – nothing to do with Paul – touts a piggy outside and a line-up of tightly packed tables inside. The Full Monty feast comprises salad, *gratons* (a chunkier version of pork scratchings) and *charcuterie* (cold meats), followed by one of 11 *bouchon* classics, cheese and dessert.

Chez Hugon (Map pp500-1; ☎ 04 78 28 10 94; 12 rue Pizay, 1er; Ⓜ Hôtel de Ville; menu €23; ☙ lunch & dinner Mon-Fri) Madame Hugon serves typical meaty treats on red-and-white checked tablecloths in an interior that is a total blast to the past – 1937 to be exact.

Other *bouchons* worth a trotter bite:

Le Garet (Map pp500-1; ☎ 04 78 28 16 94; 7 rue du Garet, 1er; Ⓜ Hôtel de Ville; lunch/dinner menu €17/21; ☙ lunch & dinner Mon-Fri)

Chez Georges (Map pp500-1; ☎ 04 78 28 30 46; 8 rue du Garet, 1er; Ⓜ Hôtel de Ville; menu €14; ☙ lunch & dinner Mon-Fri)

FRENCH

Le Petit Léon (Map pp500-1; ☎ 04 72 10 11 11; www .leondelyon.com; 3 rue Pléney, 1er; Ⓜ Hôtel de Ville; menu €18.50, plat du jour €11.20; ☙ lunch Tue-Sat) Tables are highly sought after at this soulful old-world bistro – the affordable arm of Michelin-starred big brother Léon de Lyon around the corner. But forget romancing here: the fascinating collections of old clocks, carafes etc are far too distracting.

Bistro Le Casse Museau (Map pp500-1; ☎ 04 72 00 20 52; 2 rue Chavanne, 1er; Ⓜ Hôtel de Ville; ☙ lunch Tue-Sat, dinner Thu-Sat) Fabulous find! Cram into this tiny but heaving wine bar, alias *bistrot sans chiqué* (bistro with no pretension) for a slurp of local Côtes du Rhone in the company of a retro tick-tock clock collection and weathered floor tiles with a thousand stories to tell.

GO LOCAL

A *bouchon* might be a 'bottle stopper' or 'traffic jam' elsewhere in France, but in Lyon it's a small, friendly, more local-than-local bistro that cooks up traditional city cuisine.

Kick-start what will definitely be a memorable gastronomic experience with a *communard*, an apéritif of red Beaujolais wine and *crème de cassis* (blackcurrant liqueur), named after the supporters of the Paris Commune killed in 1871. Blood-red in colour, the mix would be considered criminal elsewhere in France. When ordering wine, don't bother asking for a wine list. Simply order a *pot* – a thick glass bottle adorned with an elastic band to prevent wine drips – of local Brouilly, Beaujolais, Côtes du Rhône or Mâcon.

Next comes the entrée of *tablier de sapeur* (literally 'fireman's apron', but actually meaning breaded, fried stomach) or *salade de cervelas* (salad of boiled pork sausage, sometimes studded with pistachio nuts or specks of black truffle) perhaps. Hearty main dishes to sink meat-frantic gnashers into include *boudin blanc* (veal sausage), *boudin noir aux pommes* (blood sausage with apples), quenelle (a lighter-than-light flour, egg and cream dumpling), *quenelle de brochet* (pike quenelle, usually served in a creamy crayfish sauce) and *andouillette* (sausages made from pigs' intestines). If none of those appeal, wrap your lips around some *pieds de mouton/veau/couchon* (sheep/calf/piggie trotters) instead.

The cheese course usually comprises a choice of three things: a bowl of *fromage blanc* (a cross between cream cheese and natural yogurt) with or without cream; *cervelle de canut* (literally 'brains of the silk weaver'), which is *fromage blanc* mixed with chives and garlic that originated in Croix Rousse and accompanied every meal for 19th-century weavers; or a round of local St-Marcellin ripened to perfection by the legendary Mère Richard for three generations. Desserts are unadventurous and rarely that inspiring. Think *tarte aux pommes* (apple tart) or *fromage blanc* (again) with a fruit coulis dribbled on top.

Little etiquette is required to eat in *bouchons*. Seldom do you get clean cutlery for each course, so mopping your plate with a chunk of bread is fine; and, if the tablecloth is of the paper variety, that's probably where your bill will be added up.

In keeping with tradition, most *bouchons* don't accept diners after 9.30pm and are closed weekends and the entire month of August.

Plato (Map p505; ☎ 04 72 00 01 30; 1 rue Ville-neuve, 4e; Ⓜ Croix Rousse; lunch menus €15 & €19.50, dinner menu €33; Ⓧ lunch & dinner Mon-Sat) Sweep through thick pink curtains into this stylish plateau restaurant, decked out with contemporary flair and oozing theatre. Inventive dishes – creamy chestnut soup au foie gras or coriander-roasted *magret de canard* (duck) with an iced turnip and port creation – are even more delicious than their poetic names suggest.

Commanderie des Antonins (Map pp500-1; ☎ 04 78 37 19 21; www.commanderie-antonins.fr in French; 30 quai St-Antoine, 2e; Ⓜ Bellecour; starters/mains €7/13.50, menu €19.90; Ⓧ lunch & dinner Tue-Sat) This meat-lover's paradise cooks meat the old-fashioned way – slowly over a low heat in a wood-burning oven – and serves it with a flourish in a medieval banquet hall. Atmosphere is grandiose old style.

Gaston Restaurant Agricole (Map pp500-1; ☎ 04 72 41 87 86; 41 rue Mercière, 2e; Ⓜ Cordeliers; two/three-course menu €11.50/14.50; Ⓧ lunch & dinner Mon-Sat) Pack a hearty thirst and giant-sized appetite before venturing into this feisty agricultural restaurant complete with rusty old tractor parked up front and a liberal scattering of farm tools and veggie-filled wheelbarrows throughout.

Lolo Quoi (Map pp500-1; ☎ 04 72 77 60 90; 40-42 rue Mercière, 2e; Ⓜ Cordeliers; pasta €12-13.50, menus €2.50-20.50; Ⓧ lunch & dinner) Sleekly kitted out in wood and slate, Italianate Lolo Quoi is trendy, chic and commands a good wait at the bar if you roll up *sans réservation*. Pasta with innovative sauces is the speciality.

Brasserie Georges (Map pp500-1; ☎ 04 72 56 54 54; www.brasseriegeorges.com; 30 cours de Verdun, 2e; Ⓜ Perrache; mains €14.50-20, menus €21.50 & €24.50; Ⓧ 8am-11.15pm Sun-Thu, 8am-12.15am Fri & Sat) It's listed every time but it has to be: in fashion since 1836, the original 1920s Art Deco interior is breathtaking – as is the sheer size of the place. Food is a mix of onion soup, mussels, sauerkraut, seafood platters and Lyon specialities.

Le Bec (Map pp500-1; ☎ 04 78 42 15 00; www.nicolaslebec.com; 14 rue Grolée, 2e; Ⓜ Cordeliers; mains €35-40, lunch menu €45, dinner menus €85-155; Ⓧ lunch & dinner Tue-Sat Sep-Jul; Ⓧ) One of Lyon's great culinary addresses, this modern eating space showcasing gastronomic creations by Michelin-starred chef Nicolas Le Bec screams design – on the plate included. The priciest menu is an 11-course gastronomic

adventure. A magic mirror in one room allows privileged diners to peep into the kitchen.

OTHER

Oxalis (Map pp500-1; ☎ 04 72 07 95 94; www.lessar dinesfilantes.fr in French; 23 rue de l'Arbre Sec, 1er; Ⓜ Hôtel de Ville; lunch menu €15, dinner menus €28 & €35; Ⓧ lunch & dinner Mon-Fri) Thanks to an Armenian grandmother and a generous dose of far-flung travel, Lyon-born chef Sonia Ezgulian fuses Mediterranean with Asian and African to create a cuisine that stuns, surprises and spans the globe. Wanna' know how to cook an Oxalis-style dinner in 45 minutes or how to make the most of Lyon's Halle de la Martinière? Sign up for one of Sonia's cooking courses.

Fubuki (Map pp500-1; ☎ 04 78 30 41 48; 17 rue Gentil, 2e; Ⓜ Cordeliers; menus €17-42; Ⓧ lunch & dinner Mon-Sat) Tables are hot – literally – at this highly rated Japanese restaurant where traditionally dressed chefs armed with big knives chop up and cook a sizzling fiesta of grilled and raw fish right before your eyes. Book ahead to snag a hot seat.

Alyssaar (Map pp500-1; ☎ 04 78 29 57 66; 29 rue du Bât d'Argent, 1er; Ⓜ Hôtel de Ville; menus €12-23; Ⓧ dinner Tue-Sat) Aleppo is undoubtedly 'the gastronomic capital of the Middle East' as far as the Syrian-born owner of this cheap, cheerful and Syrian restaurant is concerned. *Daabill* (meatballs in spicy tomato sauce), *kharouf* (lamb in a sesame cream sauce) and *kebab karaz* (cherry beef) are all cooked here.

Yinitial G&G (Map pp500-1; ☎ 04 78 42 14 14; 14 rue Palais Grillet, 2e; Ⓜ Cordeliers; menus €19 & €26; Ⓧ lunch & dinner Tue-Sat Sep-Jul) Tastebuds are kept on the move at this ode to design – a stylish minimalist space with low-hanging table lights, an open kitchen and a world cuisine that throws a pinch of European in the wok alongside Asian.

Seiz'âmes by Garioud (Map pp500-1; ☎ 04 78 42 16 16; 16 rue Palais Grillet, 2e; Ⓜ Cordeliers; plat du jour €10, 2-/3-course menu €14/18; Ⓧ lunch & dinner Tue-Sat Sep-Jul) Next-door neighbour Seiz'âmes flouts a baby-pink Smeg fridge in its entrance and a playful littering of shocking-pink feather dusters, toasters and other design gadgets throughout its dramatic pink interior. Cuisine is a mix 'n' match world affair.

L'Ouest (☎ 04 37 64 64 64; www.bocuse.com; 1 quai du Commerce, 9e; Ⓜ Gare de Vaise; starters/mains around €13/20; Ⓧ lunch & dinner) With the

---

CITY-SCAPE GASTRO TRIO

For drinking 'n' dining with a city-scape view look no further than this trio of panoramic terraces:

■ **Les Muses de l'Opéra** (Map p500-1; ☎ 04 72 00 45 58; 1 place de la Comédie, 1er; Ⓜ Hôtel de Ville; lunch/dinner menu €15/29; ⏲ lunch & dinner Mon-Sat) Ride the lift up to the top floor of the opera house – the only spot in Lyon where you can peep into the fabulous interior courtyard of the historic Hôtel de Ville (closed to the public).

■ **Le Ciel de Lyon** (☎ 04 78 63 55 00; 129 rue Servient, 3e; Ⓜ Part-Dieu; ⏲ 11am-1am) The Lyon Sky is sky-high; find it on the 32nd floor of Lyon's legendary 'crayon' – that pencil-shaped building sticking out of the skyline – inside the Radisson hotel.

■ **Café de l'Esplanade** (Map p505; ☎ 04 78 28 54 06; Esplanade de la Grand Côte, 4e; Ⓜ Croix Rousse; ⏲ 9am-midnight or 1am Mon-Sat) The café itself is nothing more than your quintessential French local, but its outside seating upon Esplanade de la Grand Côte is enviable. Soak in the Lyon panorama then strut down the hillside along artist workshop-studded Montée de la Grand Côte to place des Terreaux.

---

emphasis at West being island (any island) cuisine, chefs trained by legendary Lyon chef Paul Bocuse cook up everything from king prawn spring rolls with fresh mint and saffron-spiced crab soup to wok-fried Asian cod and straightforward roast fish in a state-of-the-art open kitchen. Décor is minimalist, avant garde and includes a vast wood decking space outside overlooking the Saône.

CAFÉS
In summer outdoor cafés spill across place des Terreaux and much of Vieux Lyon.

In winter (December to April), café life in Croix Rousse (4e; metro Croix Rousse) revolves around oyster breakfasts eaten outdoors on crisp sunny mornings: **Café des Voyageurs** (Map p505; ☎ 04 78 28 00 17; 159 blvd de la Croix Rousse) and adjoining **Café Jutard** (Map p505; ☎ 04 78 28 22 06; 2 rue Terrasse) or **Chantecler** (Map p505; ☎ 04 78 28 13 69; 151 blvd de la Croix Rousse) and **Grand Kfé de la Soierier** (Map p505; ☎ 04 78 28 11 26; 1 place des Tapis) opposite all have buzzing pavement terraces to sink a dozen (€8.90 to €12.90).

Maison Perroudon (Map pp500-1; ☎ 04 78 37 49 19; www.perroudon.fr in French; 6 rue de la Barre, 2e; Ⓜ Bellecour; ⏲ 7am-7.30pm Tue-Sun; ✗) Smoking is no go at this cake shop where a predominantly female and couple crowd lunches on light salads. Its giant white chocolate and almond-coated *tuile* (sweet ultra-crispy sail-shaped biscuits of giant proportions; €3.50) are quite divine, darling.

Grand Café des Négociants (Map pp500-1; ☎ 04 78 42 50 05; 2 place Francisque Regaud, 2e; Ⓜ Cordeliers;

⏲ 7am-1am) Affectionately called Les Négos by the in-crowd who goes here, this refined café-cum-brasserie with mirror-lined walls and impeccable service has been a favourite meeting point with Lyonnais since 1864.

QUICK EATS
Rue Ste-Marie des Terreaux and rue Ste-Catherine, 1er (metro Hôtel de Ville) are lined with cheap-eat Chinese, Turkish and Indian joints.

Matsuri (Map pp500-1; ☎ 04 72 27 83 06; www .matsuri.fr in French; 7 rue de la Fromagerie, 1er; Ⓜ Hôtel de Ville; ⏲ lunch & dinner Mon-Sat) For a stylish quick eat look no further than this elegant sushi bar. Flop down on a bar stool and take your pick from the plates of sushi, sashimi, temaki etc that glide past on a sleek conveyer belt.

Ninkasi Opéra (Map pp500-1; ☎ 04 78 28 37 74; www.ninkasi.fr in French; 27 rue de l'Arbre Sec, 1er; Ⓜ Hôtel de Ville; ⏲ salads €6-9, burgers €5.20; ⏲ 11am-1am Mon-Thu, 11am-3am Fri & Sat, 6pm-1am Sun) If meaty burgers with all the garish trimmings or fish and chips is your cup of tea, then this microbrewery-run grub stop is for you. Film screenings, live bands, the odd magic show and so on fulfil its Sunday-evening entertainment pledge.

Best Bagels (Map pp500-1; ☎ 04 78 27 65 61; 1 place Tobie Robatel, 1er; Ⓜ Hôtel de Ville; ⏲ 11.30am-7pm Mon, 9am-7pm Tue, 9am-11pm Wed-Sat) Filled or frosted bagels, coffee to go and other American gastronomic delights designed to munch on the move are doled out at this well-thought-out bagel bar.

SELF-CATERING

Central Lyon has two fantastic **outdoor food markets** Presqu'île (Map pp500-1; quai St-Antoine, 2e; Ⓜ Bellecour or Cordeliers; Ⓣ Tue-Sun morning); Croix Rousse (Map p505; blvd de la Croix Rousse, 4e; Ⓜ Croix Rousse; Ⓣ Tue-Sun morning).

Les Halles de Lyon (102 cours Lafayette, 3e; Ⓜ Part-Dieu; Ⓣ 7am-noon & 3-7pm Tue-Thu, 7am-7pm Fri & Sat, 7am-noon Sun) and **La Halle de la Martinière** (Map pp500-1; 24 rue de la Martinière, 1er; Ⓜ Hôtel de Ville; Ⓣ 8am-7.30pm Tue-Sun) are the main indoor food markets.

Drinking

The bounty of café-terraces on place des Terreaux (1er; metro Hôtel de Ville) buzz with drinkers day and night. English-style pubs are clustered on rue Ste-Catherine (1er; metro Hôtel de Ville) and in Vieux Lyon: the **Albion** (Map pp500-1; ☎ 04 78 28 33 00; 12 rue Ste-Catherine, 1er; Ⓣ 6pm-1am) and the **Smoking Dog** (Map pp500-1; ☎ 04 78 28 38 27; www.smoking-dog.fr; 16 rue Lainerie, 5e; Ⓜ Vieux Lyon; Ⓣ 2pm-1am) are firm favourites.

Ké Pêcherie (Map pp500-1; ☎ 04 78 28 26 25; quai de la Pêcherie, 1er; Ⓜ Hôtel de Ville; Ⓣ 7am-1.30am)

Seemingly open all hours and very trendy, this Saône-side space spans the whole spectrum of drinking: daytime café drifts into lounge bar come late afternoon, followed by heaving music venue after dark.

Le Bar (Map pp500-1; ☎ 04 78 31 51 08; 10bis rue de la Bourse, 1er; Ⓜ Cordeliers; Ⓣ 11am-3am) Its name is a pallid reflection of the striking minimalist interior and imaginative cocktails shaken with panache at this cocktail bar, one of Lyon's most chic. Plastic curtains add a surreal touch.

Comptoir de la Bourse (Map pp500-1; ☎ 04 72 41 71 52; 33 rue de la Bourse, 2e; Ⓜ Cordeliers; Ⓣ 7.30am-3.30am Mon-Sat) If Le Bar is full, try the equally chic Comptoir de la Bourse opposite.

Le Voxx (Map pp500-1; ☎ 04 78 28 33 87; 1 rue d'Algérie, 1er; Ⓜ Hôtel de Ville; Ⓣ 8am-2am Mon-Sat, 10am-2am Sun) It's invariably a case of not seeing the chairs (orange and black Arne Jacobsen creations) for the people at this trendy design bar with minimalist interior and Saône-side pavement terrace snug against a set of traffic lights. Just watch those impatient motorists rev.

WANNA' MEET FOR LUNCH?

Our five faves:

- **Jim-Deli** (Map pp500-1; ☎ 04 78 38 31 67; 14 rue des Quatre Chapeaux, 2e; Ⓜ Hôtel de Ville; starters/pasta €7/13; Ⓣ lunch & dinner Mon-Sat) A newbie on the luncheon scene, this adjoining Italian duo stuns. One half serves authentic *panini* to take away; the other half *carpaccio*, pasta, salads and other delicious Italian dishes clearly emblazoned with an Italian Mama stamp of approval.

- **Le Pain Quotidien** (Map pp500-1; ☎ 04 78 38 29 84; 13-15 rue des Quatre Chapeaux, 2e; Ⓜ Hôtel de Ville; tartines €6-8, salads €12; Ⓣ 7am-10.30pm Mon-Sat, 7am-7pm Sun) Daily Bread is a city-lunch staple: come here for a fabulous choice of well-topped *tartines* (thick toast with topping), meal-sized salads and other rustic-styled lunch dishes. Its tiny street terrace buzzes.

- **Neo Le Comptoir** (Map pp500-1; ☎ 04 78 30 51 01; www.neolecomptoir.com in French; 21 rue du Bât d'Argent, 1er; Ⓜ Hôtel de Ville; salads €8-15; Ⓣ 7am-2am) Pick and mix your own salad ingredients, select a dressing and, while it's being tossed, decide which room you fancy eating in. Find this refreshingly different eating space (with lime green and pink walls) in a bourgeois townhouse.

- **Café 203** (Map pp500-1; ☎ 04 78 28 66 65; 9 rue du Garet, 1er; Ⓜ Hôtel de Ville; menu €13; Ⓣ 7am-2am) One of the busiest addresses in city-slick circles, Parisian-styled 203 is great for breakfast, lunch, dinner or a drink. Nonsmokers can step around the corner to Café 100 Tabac at 23 rue de l'Arbre Sec from 11am to 2am Monday to Saturday – same food, same genre but *cent* (*sans*; without) *tabac* (tobacco).

- **Giraudet** (Map pp500-1; ☎ 04 72 77 98 58; www.giraudet.fr in French; 2 rue Colonel Chambonnet, 2e; Ⓜ Bellecour; Ⓣ 11am-7pm Mon, 9am-7pm Tue-Sat) This small sleek quenelles (flour, egg and cream dumplings) boutique off place Bellecour has a bar where you can taste the Lyonnais speciality and unusual soups (eg watercress, curry, broad bean and cumin).

modernartcafé (☎ 04 72 87 06 82; www.modern artcafe.net; 65 blvd de la Croix Rousse, 4e; Ⓜ Croix Rousse; ☺ 11.30am-2am Mon-Fri, 3.30pm-2am Sat, 11am-2am Sun, shorter hours in winter & rain) Retro furnishings, changing art on the walls, a pocket-sized beach with deckchairs, free wi-fi zone, weekend brunch and a clutch of music- and video-driven happenings make this art bar one cool place to lounge.

Bistro Fait Sa Broc' (Map p505; ☎ 04 72 07 93 97; 1-3 rue Dumenge, 4e; Ⓜ Croix Rousse; ☺ 6pm-1am Mon-Sat) A hip lime-green and candyfloss-pink façade greets punters at this retro wine bar where no two chairs match and the furniture is constantly rearranged. Pick from floppy sofa seating or an eclectic sun umbrella-topped table. Bands occasionally play here and regional cheese, meat and other light snacks are served.

Bauhaus Bar (Map pp500-1; ☎ 04 72 00 87 22; 17 rue Sergent Blandant, 1er; Ⓜ Hôtel de Ville; ☺ 5.30pm-1am) Pocket-sized and overwhelmingly hip is the overriding feel of this chic little bar, a tad alternative, where a cool crowd hangs out between authentic Bauhaus furnishings.

Furib'Arts (Map pp500-1; ☎ 04 72 00 26 41; www .furib-arts.com in French; 12 rue Sergent Blandant, 1er; Ⓜ Hôtel de Ville; ☺ 11am-until last person leaves) A jumble of second-hand objects strewn around the place (many for sale), changing art by local artists and a cellar that hosts local up-and-coming bands make for a refreshing change at this small arts-driven bar. Bio products – micro-brewery

bottled beer, organic Coteaux du Lyonnais wine and fresh juice – served are equally refreshing.

Oblik (Map pp500-1; ☎ 04 72 30 14 97; 26 rue Hippolyte Flandrin, 1er; Ⓜ Hôtel de Ville; ☺ 10am-1am) Warm ochre and rust tones quietly frame low retro lighting at this stylish lounge bar with wi-fi, a stone stumble from the Saône. The set here is nearer 30.

La Fée Verte (Map pp500-1; ☎ 04 78 28 32 35; www .lafeeverte.fr in French; 4 rue Pizay, 1er; Ⓜ Hôtel de Ville; ☺ 9am-2am Mon-Wed, 9am-3am Thu-Fri, 10am-1am Sat & Sun) Hit the Green Fairy (as in the bar, not devilish old absinthe) for a drink in a steely setting set alive with live bands come dusk. Steel aside, furnishings are a predictable green.

Harmonie des Vins (Map pp500-1; ☎ 04 72 98 85 59; www.harmoniedesvins.com in French; 9 rue Neuve, 1er; Ⓜ Hôtel de Ville; ☺ 10am-2am Tue-Sat) Find out all about it – French wine that is – at this stylish wine bar with old stone walls and contemporary furnishings. Tasty weekday *plats/menus du jour* (€10/14.50) fill the place at lunchtime.

Entertainment

The tourist office has the most and best information about Lyon's dynamic entertainment scene. Local listings guides include weekly publication **Lyon Poche** (www .lyonpoche.com in French; €1 at newsagents); the free weekly **Le Petit Bulletin** (www.petit-bulletin.fr in French), which is available on street corners and at the tourist office; and the quarterly **Scope** (www.progrescope.com) distributed every three months with local daily newspaper **Le Progrès** (www.leprogres.fr in French; €0.80 at newsagents).

Tickets are sold at the **FNAC Billetterie** (Map pp500-1; ☎ 08 92 68 36 22; www.fnac.com/spectacles; 85 rue de la République, 2e; Ⓜ Bellecour; ☺ 10am-7pm Mon-Sat).

CINEMAS

Nondubbed films are the staple diet of **CNP-Terreaux** (Map pp500-1; ☎ 08 92 68 69 33; 40 rue du Président Édouard Herriot, 1er; Ⓜ Hôtel de Ville) and among many films screened at **Cinema Ambiance** (Map pp500-1; ☎ 08 92 68 20 15; www .cinema-ambiance.com in French; 12 rue de la République, 2e; Ⓜ Cordeliers).

Hangar du Premier Film (☎ 04 78 78 18 95; www .institut-lumiere.org; 25 rue du Premier Film, 8e; Ⓜ Monplaisir Lumière; tickets €6.50-8) shows films of all

---

TOP FIVE LYON LEGENDS

Easily the finest for …

■ Fish: **Poissonerie Vianey** (Map p505; 112 blvd de la Croix Rousse, 1er; Ⓜ Croix Rousse)

■ Meat and homemade savoury dishes: **Reinier** (Map p505; 6 rue de Pierres Plantées, 1er; Ⓜ Croix Rousse)

■ Wine: **La Vieille Réserve** (Map pp500-1; 1 place Tobie Robatel, 1er; Ⓜ Hôtel de Ville)

■ Designer chocolates: **Richart** (Map pp500-1; 1 rue du Plat, 2e; Ⓜ Bellecour)

■ Cakes and pastries: **Bernachon** (www .bernachon.com in French; 42 cours Franklin Roosevelt, 6e; Ⓜ Foch)

GAY & LESBIAN LYON

The city has its fair share of gay and lesbian haunts, freebie monthly newspaper *Hétéoculte* being a one-stop shop for finding out what's on where. Otherwise try **Forum Gai et Lesbien de Lyon** (Map pp500-1; ☎ 04 78 39 97 72; www.fgllyon.org in French; 17 rue Romarin, 1er; Ⓜ Croix Paquet) or **ARIS** (Accueil Rencontres Informations Service; ☎ 04 78 27 10 10; www.aris-lyon.org in French; 19 rue des Capucins, 1er; Ⓜ Croix Paquet). Lyon's Lesbian & Gay Pride march hits the streets in June.

Gay bars include **Le Forum** (Map pp500-1; ☎ 04 78 37 19 74; 15 rue des Quatre Chapeaux, 2e; Ⓜ Cordeliers; ☽ 5pm-1am Sun-Thu, 5pm-3am Fri & Sat), **XL Bar** (Map pp500-1; ☎ 04 78 27 83 18; 19 rue du Garet, 1er; Ⓜ Hôtel de Ville; ☽ 5pm-1am) and **La Ruche** (Map pp500-1; ☎ 04 78 37 42 26; 22 rue Gentil, 2e; Ⓜ Cordeliers; ☽ 5pm-3am). After hours, don your dancing shoes at gay nightclub **Le New York Le Medley** (Map pp500-1; ☎ 04 78 38 23 96; 19 rue Childebert, 2e; Ⓜ Cordeliers; admission free; ☽ 10pm-5am Wed, 11pm-5am Thu-Sat).

LyonGay.net is an online gay guide to Lyon.

---

genres and eras. The screen moves outside in summer (June to September).

LIVE MUSIC

Hot Club de Lyon (Map pp500-1; ☎ 04 78 39 54 74; www.hotclubjazz.com in French; 26 rue Lanterne, 1er; Ⓜ Hôtel de Ville; admission €9-12; ☽ 9pm-1am Tue-Thu, 9.30pm-1am Fri, 4-7pm & 9.30pm-1am Sat) A nonprofit musical landmark since 1948, Lyon's premier jazz club stages five weekly concerts of live jazz (big band, swing, bebop, contemporary etc); the programme is online.

Ninkasi (☎ 04 72 76 89 00; www.ninkasi.fr in French; 267 rue Marcel Mérieux, 7e; tram stop Stade de Gerland; ☽ 10am-1am Mon-Wed, 10am-3am Thu-Sat, 4-11pm Sun) This micro-brewery near the stadium lures a frenetic crowd who stream in to drink beer, listen to DJ beats and jive to bands. In summer everything (including films) spills onto the vast bamboo terrace outside.

Le Transbordeur (☎ 04 72 43 09 99; www.transbordeur.fr in French; 3 blvd de Stalingrad, Villeurbanne) Lyon's prime concert venue in an old industrial building is on the big-time European concert-tour circuit and draws international concert stars. Take bus 59 from metro Part-Dieu to the 'Echangeur Poincaré stop or bus 4 from metro Foch to the Cité Internationale stop.

NIGHTCLUBS

The nightclub scene is buoyant; track new offerings at www.lyonpeople.com and www.lyonclubbing.com.

La Chapelle (Map pp500-1; ☎ 04 78 37 23 95; www.lachapelle-lyon.fr in French; 60 montée du Coulands, 5e; Ⓜ Bellecour; admission before/after 8.30pm free/€15; ☽ 6.30pm-4am Tue-Sat, closed Tue winter) 'Open-minded' and 'a garden of Eden' are labels

the Chapel wears. Set in the chapel of a 16th-century chateau surrounded by a vast green park (in which the drinking 'n' dancing spills), the setting is unique. Décor: Art Deco and age-old. Music: house and techno.

Fish (Map pp500-1; ☎ 04 72 84 98 98; 21 quai Victor Augagneur, 3e; Ⓜ Guillotière; admission before/after 11pm with 1 drink free/€11; ☽ 8pm-5am Wed & Thu, 8pm-6am Fri & Sat) Another hot venue for Lyon's trendy set, this one is a boat moored on the Rhône's left bank. DJs spin varied sounds.

La Marquise (Map pp500-1; ☎ 04 72 61 92 92; www.marquise.net in French; 20 quai Victor Augagneur, 3e; Ⓜ Guillotière; admission free-€8; ☽ 10pm-5am Wed-Sat) Step aboard this concert club – another moored barge – for an ear-popping barrage of electronic, hip-hop, breakbeat, boogie, soul and rap. 'Good vibes generator' is its sales pitch.

Le Fridge (☎ 04 72 61 13 61; www.lefridge.com in French; 67 rue des Rancy, 3e; Ⓜ Guillotière; admission incl 1 drink €10-12; ☽ 11pm-5am Thu-Sat) Hip-hop, house, groove and techno are the order of the day at this DJ-driven club crammed with young rather than old.

Le Cube (☎ 04 78 17 29 84; 115 blvd Stalingrad, Villeurbanne; admission free; ☽ 8pm-5.30am Wed-Sat) The Cube is just that – a glass box where the Lyonnais jet set flock to eat, drink and jive the night away. House reigns at this trend temple.

In the increasingly hip quarter of Gare de Brotteaux, 6e start the evening at **ApériKlub** (☎ 04 37 24 19 46; 13-14 place Jules Ferry; Ⓜ Brotteaux; ☽ 6.30pm-3am Wed-Fri, 8.30pm-4am Sat) and end it at **First Tendency** (☎ 04 37 24 19 46; 13-14 place Jules Ferry; Ⓜ Brotteaux; admission free; ☽ 11pm-6am Thu-Sat) next door. Dress hip for both.

A trio of mainstream dancing venues sits at the top end of rue Terme, 1er (metro Hôtel de Ville) and there is a Saône-side bunch north of Vieux Lyon on quai Pierre Scize, 5e.

SPORT

When at home, national football champions **Olympique Lyonnais** (http://olweb.fr) kick off at the 44,000-seater **Stade de Gerland** (Gerland Stadium; ☎ 04 72 76 01 70; 353 av Jean Jaurès, 7e), the city stadium built in 1920 and overhauled for the 1998 World Cup. Match tickets costing €15 to €70 are sold online and at club boutiques **OL Store** (☎ 04 72 76 76 14; 60 av Tony Garnier, 7e; ☼ 10am-7pm Mon-Sat & before/after matches) opposite the stadium and **Planète OL** (Map pp500-1; ☎ 04 78 37 49 49; cnr rue de Jussieu & rue Grolée, 2e; ☒ Cordeliers; ☼ 10am-1.30pm & 2-6pm Tue-Sat) in town.

THEATRE, DANCE & CLASSICAL MUSIC

Opéra de Lyon (Map pp500-1; ☎ 08 26 30 53 25; www .opera-lyon.com in French; place de la Comédie, 1er; ☒ Hôtel de Ville; ☼ box office noon-7pm Tue-Sat & 2hr before performances) Opera, ballet and classical concerts mid-September to early July.

Maison de la Danse (☎ 04 72 78 18 00; www.maison deladanse.com in French; 8 av Jean Mermoz, 8e; tram stop Bachut-Mairie du 8e; ☼ box office 11.45am-6.45pm Mon-Fri, 2-6.45pm Sat) Stunning performances of contemporary dance, tango, flamenco etc.

Auditorium de Lyon (☎ 04 78 95 95 95; www.audi torium-lyon.com in French; 82 rue de Bonnel, 3e; ☒ Part-Dieu; ☼ box office 11am-6pm Mon-Fri, 2-6pm Sat) Home to the National Orchestra of Lyon; hosts workshops, jazz and world music concerts September to late June.

Théâtre Le Guignol de Lyon (Map pp500-1; ☎ 04 78 28 92 57; zonzons@club-internet.fr; 2 rue Louis Carrand, 5e; ☒ Vieux Lyon; tickets adult/under 15yr €9/7) Traditional puppet theatre.

Shopping

The Presqu'île (Map pp500–1) is the hot spot to shop: Mainstream shops line rue de la République and rue Victor Hugo. Upmarket boutiques and big-name design houses stud parallel rue du Président Édouard Herriot, rue de Brest and the trio of streets fanning from place des Jacobins to place Bellecour.

More big-name fashion designers are clustered amid art galleries and antique shops in Quartier Auguste Comte (Map pp500–1), an exclusive quarter south of place Bellecour around rue Auguste Comte, 2e.

Centre Commercial La Part-Dieu (☒ Part-Dieu; ☼ 9.30am-7.30pm Mon-Sat) is Lyon's vast indoor shopping centre, with a large supermarket, cafés and dozens of shops.

Market fans will love the riverside **Book Market** (Map pp500-1; quai de la Pêcherie, 1er; ☒ Hôtel de Ville; ☼ 7am-6pm Sat & Sun) and **Crafts Market** (Map pp500-1; quai de Bondy, 5e; ☒ Vieux Lyon; ☼ 9am-noon Sun).

Getting There & Away

AIR

Flights to/from dozens of European cities land at **Aéroport Lyon-St-Exupéry** (Lyon St-Exupéry airport; ☎ 08 26 80 08 26; www.lyon.aeroport.fr), 25km east of the city.

BUS

In the Perrache complex, **Eurolines** (Map pp500-1; ☎ 04 72 56 95 30), **Intercars** (Map pp500-1; ☎ 04 78 37 20 80) and Spain-oriented **Linebús** (Map pp500-1; ☎ 04 72 41 72 27) have offices on the bus-station level of the Centre d'Échange (follow the 'Lignes Internationales' signs).

CAR & MOTORCYCLE

Major car-rental companies have offices at both Gare de la Part-Dieu and Gare de Perrache.

TRAIN

Lyon has two mainline train stations: **Gare de la Part-Dieu** (☒ Part-Dieu), 1.5km east of the Rhône, which handles long-haul trains; and **Gare de Perrache** (Map pp500-1; ☒ Perrache), a stop for many long-distance as well as regional trains. Just a few local trains stop at **Gare St-Paul** (Map pp500-1; ☒ Vieux Lyon) in Vieux Lyon. Tickets are sold at all three stations and in town at the **SNCF Boutique** (Map pp500-1; 2 place Bellecour, 2e; ☒ Bellecour; ☼ 9am-6.45pm Mon-Fri, 10am-6.30pm Sat).

Destinations by direct TGV include Paris' Gare de Lyon (€58.70 to €76.30, two hours, every 30 to 60 minutes), Lille-Europe (€77.20, 3¼ hours, nine daily), Nantes (€72.20, 4½ hours, five daily), Beaune (€20.50, 2¼ hours, up to nine daily), Dijon (€23.40, 2¾ hours, at least 12 daily) and Strasbourg (€45.60, 5¼ hours, five daily).

Getting Around

TO/FROM THE AIRPORT

Satobus (☎ 04 72 68 72 17; www.satobus.com) links the airport with the centre every 20 minutes between 5am or 6am to midnight. Journey time is 35/45 minutes to Gare de la Part-Dieu/Gare de Perrache and the single/return fare (€8.40/14.90) includes one hour's travel on public transport.

By taxi, the 30-minute trip to/from the airport to the city centre costs upwards of €45 depending on the time of day.

BICYCLE
Pick up a set of red-and-silver wheels at one of 200-odd bike stations dotted around the city and drop them off at another with the city's hugely successful **vélo'v** (☎ 08 00 08 35 68; www.velov.grandlyon.com in French) bike-rental scheme. The first 30 minutes are free and the first/subsequent hours cost €1/2 with a *carte courte durée* (a short-duration card, costing €1 and valid for seven days) and €0.50/1 if you buy a *carte longue durée* (long-duration card, costing €5 and valid for one year). Buy either card with a credit card from machines installed at bike stations: central stations include in front of the town hall on blvd de la Croix Rousse, 4e (Map p505; metro Croix Rousse); beside the opera house (1er; Map pp500–1; metro Hôtel de Ville); and opposite Cathédrale St-Jean on place St-Jean (5e; Map pp500–1; metro Vieux Lyon). A city map showing every station and cycling path is posted at each station.

Motorists who park in the **car park** (☎ 04 78 42 50 09; www.vincipark.com in French; parking per 40min/24hr €1.20/23.30; ☉ 24hr) beneath place Bellecour borrow a bike for free.

Far less leg work is required with the covered, chauffeur-driven electric tricycles operated by **Cyclopolitain** (☎ 08 26 10 00 03; www .cyclopolitain.com in French; ☉ 10.30am-7pm Mar-Sep, 10.30am-5.30pm Oct-Dec). Pick up a cyclo at one of seven points around the city centre or beckon one by telephone; they cost €1 per kilometre.

PUBLIC TRANSPORT
Public transport – buses, trams, a four-line metro and two funiculars linking Vieux Lyon to Fourvière and St-Just – is run by **TCL** (☎ 08 20 42 70 00; www.tcl.fr in French; Vieux Lyon Place Éduard Commette, 5e; Ⓜ Vieux Lyon; ☉ 10am-12.30pm & 2-5pm Mon-Fri, 10am-12.30pm & 1.30-5pm Sat; Presqu'île 5 rue de la République, 1er; Ⓜ Bellecour; ☉ 7.30am-6.30pm Mon-Fri, 9am-noon & 1.30-5pm Sat). Public transport runs from around 5am to midnight.

Tickets cost €1.50/12.20 for one/10 and are available from bus and tram drivers and from machines at metro entrances. Tickets allowing unlimited travel for two hours/one day €2.10/4.30 are also available, as is a Ticket Liberté Soirée (€2.10) covering unlimited travel after 7pm. Tickets must be time-stamped on all forms of public transport.

TAXI
Taxis hover at stands in front of both train stations; on the place Bellecour end of rue de la Barre (2e); and at the northern end of rue du Président Édouard Herriot (1er). Otherwise call:

Allo Taxi (☎ 04 78 28 23 23; www.allotaxi.fr in French)

Taxis Lyonnais (☎ 04 78 26 81 81; www.taxilyonnais .com in French)

NORTH & WEST OF LYON
Cosmopolitan Lyon is ensnared by a contrasting patchwork of green hills, lakes and vineyards.

Beaujolais
Hilly Beaujolais, 50-odd kilometres northwest of Lyon is a land of streams (all tributaries of the Saône), granite peaks (the highest is 1012m Mont St-Rigaud), pastures and forests. The region is famed for its fruity red wines, especially its 10 premium *crus*, and the Beaujolais *nouveau*, drunk at the tender age of just six weeks. Vineyards stretch south from Mâcon along the right bank of the Saône for some 50km.

At the stroke of midnight on the third Thursday in November (late Wednesday night) – as soon as French law permits – the *libération* or *mise en perce* (tapping; the opening) of the first bottles of cherry-bright Beaujolais *nouveau* is celebrated with much hype and circumstance around France and the world. In **Beaujeu** (population 1904), 64km northwest of Lyon, there's free Beaujolais *nouveau* for all during the **Sarmentelles de Beaujeu** – one big street party.

For details on wine cellars where you can taste and buy wine, contact Beaujeu's **tourist office** (☎ 04 74 69 22 88; www.beaujeu.com in French; place de l'Église; ☉ 10am-noon & 2.20-6pm Wed-Sun), next to the church.

Beaujolais' other gastronomic highlights include fine oils made from pecan, almond, pine kernel, turnip and so on at the **Huilerie**

Beaujolaise (☎ 04 74 69 28 06; 29 rue des Écharmeaux) on Beaujeu's northern edge; and the sweet prize-winning honey sold at the **Miellerie du Fût d'Avenas** (☎ 04 74 69 92 03) in **Avenas** (population 106), an attractive village with a 12th-century Romanesque church and surrounded by pastures and forests.

Exploring Beaujolais by **mountain bike** is uplifting, its gentle hills being suitable for the least experienced/laziest of cyclists. Fifteen routes (230km) for two-wheelers are detailed in the Topoguide *Le Beaujolais à VTT*. **Évasion Beaujolaise** (☎ 04 74 02 06 84) in Marchampt, 10km south of Beaujeu, rents bicycles and maps showing thematic circuits for cyclists. **Walking** the area's many footpaths is equally delightful.

Chambres d'hôtes (B&Bs) are rife in this nature-rich neck of the woods and really are the best way to taste the region (not to mention snagging vineyard views from your bedroom window). **Domaine de la Grosse Pierre** (☎ 04 74 69 12 17; www.chiroubles-passot.com in French; s/d €48/55), a blue-shuttered house lovingly run by *vignerons* Alain and Véronique in Chiroubles, 12km northeast of Beaujeu, is a small wine-producing estate that provides B&B. Manicured **Domaine de Romarand** (☎ 04 74 04 34 49; s/d €48/58; dinner €22; 🕮) with vaulted wine cellar, pool and fields of vines is the restored French farmhouse Brits dream of. Find it languishing 6km southeast of Beaujeu in Quincie-en-Beaujolais.

Your own wheels or walking boots are the only ways to explore Beaujolais.

OUR PICK **Les Roulottes de la Serve** (☎ 04 74 04 76 40; www.lesroulottes.com in French; La Serve, Ouroux; d €45-48, dinner €15, heating €3-5/day; 🕮 Apr-Nov) is one of only five-odd traditional caravan-

makers in France, run by Pascal and his hippy wife, Pascaline. Something of a life-long dream for the bohemian couple, guests sleep in one of three lovingly restored *roulottes* dating from the 1920s and 1950s and can visit Pascal's workshop where he hammers away. Nostalgia for the romance of a wayward vagabond life fills every last frill and flourish of the two-room Roulotte des Amoureux (caravan of love), complete with old stove (that no longer functions). Caravans have electric heaters but modern shower, toilets, breakfast (and an optional evening meal) are provided in the main farmhouse, a two-second walk away. To find the farm, surrounded by fields and grazing horses, follow the road from Avenas to the Col de Crie for 5km and at the La Serve crossroads, head to 'Ouroux'; after 100m turn right down the track (signposted 'chambres d'hôtes en roulottes').

Pérouges & La Dombes

Film star **Pérouges** (population 850), a yellow-stone medieval village too perfectly restored, lures day-trippers like crazy in spring and summer. They flock there to stroll its cobbled alleys, admire its half-timbered stone houses, ogle at the weary old **liberty tree** planted in 1792 on place de la Halle and wolf down *galettes de Pérouges* (sweet tarts, served warm and crusted with sugar) and cider. Buses 126 and 130 link the village, on a hill 27km northeast of Lyon, with Lyon's Gare de Perrache.

Northwest is **La Dombes**, a marshy area whose hundreds of *étangs* (shallow lakes), created from malarial swamps over the past six centuries by local farmers, are used as fish ponds and then drained so crops can be grown on the fertile lake bed. The area, famed for its production of frogs' legs, attracts lots of wildlife, particularly waterfowl. Local and exotic birds, including dozens of pairs of storks, can be observed at the **Parc des Oiseaux** (☎ 04 74 98 05 54; admission depending on season €7.50-11; 🕮 10am-nightfall), a beautifully landscaped bird park and ornithological research centre just outside Villars-les-Dombes on the N83.

Lunch the local way at **La Bicyclette Bleue** (☎ 04 74 98 21 48; www.labicyclettebleue.fr in French; menus €18.50-34; 🕮 lunch & dinner Thu-Mon, lunch Tue), a family-run place 7.5km southeast of

---

GREEN BEAUJOLAIS

Tap into green Beaujolais with **Billebaudez en Beaujolais Vert** (☎ 04 74 04 77 07; www.billebaudez.com in French; La Serve, Ouroux), a group formed by a bunch of local farmers, cheese makers, artists and so on to promote the nature-rich region in which they live and work. Through the organisation tourists can, among other things, visit local farms, horse-ride, take part in a six-day botany course, participate in a fruit harvest, learn how to paint in watercolour, discover the secret of bee-keeping and so on.

AN ARCHITECTURAL PILGRIMAGE

It is definitely only for hardened fans of architecture, 'it' being a futuristic concrete priory that is far from pretty. But with the signature of modern-architecture icon Le Corbusier (for more, see p63) behind it, stark **Couvent Ste-Marie de la Tourette** (☎ 04 74 26 79 70; www.couventlatourette.com; adult/student/under 12yr €5/4/free; ☼ guided tours 10.30am & hourly 2.30-5.30pm Mon-Sat, hourly 2.30-5.30pm Sun Jul & Aug, 10.30am & hourly 2.30-4.30pm Sat, hourly 2.30-4.30pm Sun Apr, Jun, Sep & Oct, 2.30pm Sun Nov-Mar), 30km west of Lyon in La Tourette, lures a prestigious set into its lair. Inhabited by white-robed Dominican monks, the working monastery can be visited by one-hour guided tour.

From Lyon's Gare de Perrache (10 daily) and Gare St-Paul (20 daily) in Vieux Lyon, trains go to L'Arbresle (€6.40, 45 minutes), 2km north of La Tourette, from where you can call ☎ 04 74 26 90 19 for a taxi or walk (around 25 minutes). By car follow the westbound N7 or more scenic D7 from Lyon.

Villars-les-Dombes in Joyeux. As well as frying up *grenouilles fraîches en persillade* (fresh frogs' legs in butter and parsley), it rents wheels (bikes/tandems per hour €4.50/8, per half-day €12.50/20) to explore the lakeland. Cyclists can pick from 11 different mapped circuits, 12km (one hour) to 59km (four hours) long.

ST-ÉTIENNE
pop 185,000

No doubt about it: down-to-business St-Étienne, an industrial hub 62km southwest of Lyon, is dreary. But it does have a couple of redeeming features.

Enter St-Étienne's **Musée d'Art Moderne** (MAM; Modern Art Museum; ☎ 04 77 79 52 52; La Terrasse; adult/12-18yr/under 18yr €4.50/3.70/free, 1st/2nd Sun of month free/€2; ☼ 10am-6pm Wed-Mon), with its internationally renowned collection of 20th-century and contemporary paintings, sculptures and photographs. Tram 4 links the centre with La Terrasse on the northern edge of the city. The cutting-edge **Biennale Internationale Design** (www.citedudesign .com), a high-profile design fair hosted every two years in November, is the city's other big drawcard. The next design fair is in 2008.

Industrial heritage, including the local bicycle industry founded in 1886, feature at the **Musée d'Art et d'Industrie** (☎ 04 77 49 73 00; museemai@saint-etienne.fr; 2 place Louis Comte; adult/12-18yr €4.50/3.70; ☼ 10am-6pm Wed-Mon) and the **Musée de la Mine** (☎ 04 77 43 83 26; 3 blvd Franchet d'Espérey; adult/12-18yr €5.60/4.10, 1st Sun of month free; ☼ 10am-12.45pm & 2-7pm Wed-Mon), a mine active from 1910 to 1973 where you can see coal-extraction technology in situ and get a sense of what it was like to work as a collier.

Underground tours by train depart once or twice daily.

The **tourist office** (☎ 08 92 70 05 42; www.tour isme-st-etienne.com; 16 av de la Libération; ☼ 9am-7pm Mon-Sat, 9am-noon Sun Apr-Sep, 9am-6pm Mon-Sat, 9am-noon Sun Oct-Mar) is 1km southwest of the train station.

Sleeping & Eating

Hotel Brasserie d'Anjou (☎ 04 77 32 34 36; www .hotel-brasserie-anjou.com in French; 32 av Enfert Rochereau; d €44; ☼ lunch & dinner Mon-Sat) Sleek or chic it is not, but this glass-fronted brasserie with 18 rooms up top opposite the train station does make a handy halt for thirsty, hungry and/or weary travellers. A menu starring *grenouilles* (frogs' legs) and *escargots* (snails) tops off the quintessential provincial French-town experience.

Aux Deux Cageots – Aux D.K.D (☎ 04 77 32 89 85; 3 place Grenette; menus €15-20; ☼ lunch & dinner Tue-Sat) and **Absinthe Café** (☎ 04 77 25 06 89; 23 rue Léon Nautin; ☼ 8am-1.30am Tue-Fri, 10am-1.30am Sat) are two hip and trendy eating and drinking spaces. Both scream design.

Getting There & Around

Let's face it: the main reason most people come to St-Étienne is for its no-frills airport, **Aéroport International St-Étienne** (☎ 04 77 55 71 71; www.saint-etienne.aeroport.fr), 12km northwest of the city, serviced by cheap Ryanair flights to/from London Stansted. Local bus 100 links the roundabout outside the airport with place Chavanelle in town (€2.80, 30 minutes, hourly). Shuttle buses to/from Lyon (€25, 1½ hours) are coordinated with flight times.

Hourly trains link St-Étienne Châteaucreux with Lyon (€9, 50 minutes).

DOWNSTREAM ALONG THE RHÔNE

South of Lyon, vineyards meet nuclear power plants – not the most auspicious juxtaposition, but worth a stop for Lyon-based day-trippers or for those bound for the south.

Vienne

pop 29,900

This one-time Gallo-Roman city, now a disappointingly average town 30km south of Lyon, only really appeals to aficionados of the Romans or jazz fans: its two-week **jazz festival** (☎ 08 92 70 20 07; www.jazzavienne.com in French) in June is famous.

The Corinthian columns of the **Temple d'Auguste et de Livie** (place Charles de Gaulle), built about 10 BC to honour the Emperor Augustus and the lovely Livia (his wife), in the small old town are superb. Across the river in St-Romain-en-Gal, the excavated remains of the Gallo-Roman city form the **Musée Gall-Romain** (☎ 04 74 53 74 01; 2 chemin de la Plaine Gal; adult/under 18yr €3.80/free, 1st Sun of month free; ☯ 10am-6pm Tue-Sun). Savour great town views from the **Belvédère de Pipet**, a balcony with a 6m-tall statue of the Virgin Mary, immediately above Vienne's fabulous **Théâtre Romain** (☎ 04 74 85 39 23; rue du Cirque; adult/under 18yr €2.20/free, 1st Sun of month free; ☯ 9.30am-1pm & 2-6pm Apr-Aug, 9.30am-1pm & 2-6pm Tue-Sun Sep & Oct, 9.30am-12.30pm & 2-5pm Tue-Sat, 1.30-5.30pm Sun Jan-Mar, Nov & Dec). The vast Roman amphitheatre, built around AD 40-50, tumbles majestically down the hillside and is a key jazz-festival venue.

Gen up on guided walks, festivals, markets and other sights and activities around town at the **tourist office** (☎ 04 74 53 80 30; www.vienne-tourisme.com in French; 3 cours Brillier; ☯ 9am-noon & 1-6pm Mon-Sat, 10am-noon & 2-5pm Sun Sep-Jun, 9am-6pm Mon-Sat, 9am-5pm Sun Jul & Aug).

SLEEPING & EATING

Auberge de Jeunesse (☎ 04 74 53 21 97; mjcvienne.auberge@laposte.net; 11 quai Riondet; dm €8.90; ☯ reception 5-8pm Mon-Thu mid-Sep–mid-Jun, 5-9pm daily mid-Jun–mid-Sep) Vienne's 54-room riverside hostel is a two-minute strut south of the tourist office. At weekends and in winter, call ahead to make sure someone is in when you arrive.

La Tuilière (☎ 04 78 96 32 82; www.latuiliere.fr in French; chemin de la Tuilière, St-Just Chaleyssin; B&B s/d/tr €53/66/86) This *chambre d'hôte* might be 18km northeast of Vienne but it's worth the ride. Three beautiful rooms with terracotta floor tiles, stone walls and old-fashioned rustic furnishings languish in an ivy-clad 17th-century stone house, once the village tilery (hence the name). Vineyards surround it.

Hôtel de la Pyramide (☎ 04 74 53 01 96; www.lapyramide.com in French; 14 blvd Fernand-Point; s/d/ste from €180/190/250; menus €53-145; ☯ restaurant Thu-Mon; ☒ ☒ ☒) So-called because of its location overlooking La Pyramide de la Cirque (a 15.5m-tall obelisk that in Roman times pierced the centre of a hippodrome), this apricot villa with powder-blue shutters is a four-star haven of peace. French chef Patrick Henriroux works wonders in the kitchen with lobsters, foie gras, black truffles, scallops and other seasonal gourmet treats.

Run-of-the-mill eating options abound along cours Romestang and cours Brillier near the tourist office.

GETTING THERE & AWAY

Trains link Vienne with Lyon (€5.60, 20 to 32 minutes, at least hourly), Valence (€14.30, one hour, at least hourly) and Valence TGV station (€18.70, 40 minutes, at least hourly).

NUCLEAR TOURISM

Nuclear tourism enjoys a twist at the **Ferme aux Crocodiles** (☎ 04 75 04 33 73; www.lafermeaux crocodiles.com in French; adult/3-12yr €9/6.80; ☯ 9.30am-7pm Mar-Sep, 9.30am-5pm Oct-Feb), a crocodile farm, 20km south of Montélimar in Pierrelatte, where 350-odd grouchy Nile crocodiles slumber in tropical pools heated by a neighbouring nuclear power plant.

The **Centre Nucléaire du Tricastin** plant has four 915-megawatt reactors, sufficiently productive to heat 42 hectares of greenhouses and 2400 local homes. Nearby, the **Centre Nucléaire de St-Alban-St-Maurice**, 20km south of Vienne on the Rhône's left bank, has two pressurised water reactors rated at a mighty 1300 megawatts, enough to supply the needs of Lyon 10 times over.

LYON & THE RHÔNE VALLEY

AS NUTTY AS NOUGAT

There is just one sweet reason to stop in Montélimar – to chew its nutty nougat.

Produced in the otherwise ordinary town, 46km south of Valence, since the 17th century, *nougat de Montélimar* took off after WWII when holidaying motorists on their way to the French Riviera stopped off in the Rhône-side town to buy the sweeter-than-sweet treat to munch en route.

Traditional Montélimar nougat consists of at least 28% almonds, 25% lavender honey, 2% pistachio nuts, sugar, egg white and vanilla. Nougat varies in texture (more or less tender), honey taste (more or less strong) and crispness of the nuts. Some nougats are coated in chocolate and others have fruit (try the one with figs), but traditional Montélimar nougat is quite simply off-white.

A dozen nougat producers offer free tours of their factories; pick a small (rather than an industrial) confectioner such as Le Gavial or Le Chaudron d'Or. The **tourist office** (☎ 04 75 01 00 20; www.montelimar-tourisme.com; allées Provençales; ⏰ 9am-12.15pm & 2-6.30pm Mon-Sat) posts a list of producers online.

Montélimar is on the train line linking Valence-Ville (€7.20, 20 minutes, five daily) with Avignon-Centre (€11.50, 50 minutes, hourly).

Towards Valence

The **Parc Naturel Régional du Pilat** spills across 650 sq km southwest of Vienne and offers some breathtaking panoramas of the Rhône Valley from its highest peaks, Crêt de l'Œillon (1370m) and Crêt de la Perdrix (1432m). The Montgolfier brothers, inventors of the hot-air balloon in 1783, were born – and held their first public *montgolfière* demonstration – in **Annonay**, 50km northwest of Valence on the park's southeastern boundary.

The north section of the Côtes du Rhône wine-growing area, known for vintages offering particularly good value, stretches from Vienne south to Valence. Two of the area's most respected appellations, St-Joseph and Hermitage, grow around **Tain l'Hermitage** on the Rhône's left bank. Its **tourist office** (☎ 04 75 08 06 81; place de l'Église; ⏰ 9am-noon & 2-6pm Mon-Sat) has a list of wine cellars.

One or two trains an hour link Tain l'Hermitage with Valence (€3.30, 10 minutes) and Lyon (€12.30, 50 minutes).

Valence

pop 63,400

Several Rhône Valley towns claim to be the happy gateway to Provence, including Valence, complete with quaint old town and a crunchy, orange-rind-flavoured shortbread shaped like a Vatican Swiss guard to commemorate Pope Pius VI's imprisonment and death in Valence in 1799. Fancy a bite? Ask for *un suisse* in any cake shop.

Vieux Valence is crowned by the **Cathédrale St-Apollinaire**, a late-11th-century pilgrimage church (thus the ambulatory), largely destroyed in the Wars of Religion and rebuilt in the 17th century. Allegorical sculpted heads adorn **Maison des Têtes** (57 Grande Rue), a blend of Flamboyant Gothic and Renaissance from 1530. The main commercial streets are rue Émile Augier and Grande Rue. Get the full low-down from the **tourist office** (☎ 04 75 44 90 40; www.tourisme-valence.com; Parvis de la Gare; ⏰ 9.30am-12.30pm & 1.30-6pm Mon-Fri, until 5pm Sat Sep-May, 9.30am-6.30pm Mon-Fri Jun-Aug) at the train station.

Anne-Sophie Pic (b 1969), the only female chef in France with two Michelin stars, reigns over Valence gastronomy. Her culinary creations form the backbone of **Hôtel des Senteurs** (☎ 04 75 44 15 32; www.pic-valence.com; 285 av Victor Hugo; d low/high season from €200/240; menus €30-150; ⏰ Feb-Dec; ✗ ✗ ▢ ▣), a century-old inn run by her family for four generations and oozing style alongside a couple of stunning restaurants.

From the central train station, Valence-Ville, there are trains to/from Montélimar (€6.90, 23 minutes, five daily), Lyon (€13.70, 1¼ hours, 12 daily), Avignon (€15.90, 1¼ hours, four to six direct daily) and Grenoble (€12.80, 1¼ hours, nine daily). Many trains stop at Valence TGV Rhône-Alpes Sud station, 10km east.

Gorges de l'Ardèche

The serpentine River Ardèche slithers past towering cliffs of mauve, yellow and grey limestone, dotted with vegetation typical of the Midi, as it makes its way from near **Vallon Pont d'Arc** to **St-Martin de l'Ardèche**, a few kilometres west of the Rhône. Eagles nest in the cliffs and there are numerous caves to explore. One of the area's most famous features is the **Pont d'Arc**, a natural stone bridge created by the river's torrents.

About 300m above the waters (which can be canoed) of the gorge is the **Haute Corniche** (D290), which affords a magnificent series of *belvédères* (panoramic viewpoints). It turns into a huge and chaotic traffic jam in summer. On the plateaus above the gorges, typically Midi villages (eg St-Remèze) are surrounded by garrigue, lavender fields and vineyards.

From Vallon Pont d'Arc, the scenic D579 takes cyclists and motorists northwest to **Ruoms**; across the river, the D4 snakes wildly along the **Défilé de Ruoms** (a narrow tunnel of rock) and the **Gorges de la Ligne** for 8km. From Bellevue, bear north on the D104 for 2km to Uzer, then east on the D294 to **Balazuc**, one of France's prettiest villages.

From Balazuc the D579 leads northwards to **Aubenas**, from which point a multitude of scenic roads fan into the surrounding countryside. This is chestnut land, where the dark brown fruit is turned into everything from *crème de châtaigne* (a sweet purée served with ice cream, *crêpes* or cake) to *bière aux marrons* (chestnut beer). Unique to the region is *liqueur de châtaigne,* a 21% alcohol-by-volume liqueur which makes a sweet apéritif when mixed with white wine. Buy a bottle at the **Palais du Marron** (☎ 04 75 64 35 16; 10 cours de l'Esplanade) in **Privas**.

WHITE-WATER SPORTS

Bombing down the River Ardèche in a canoe or kayak is thrilling. Arrange your own half-, full- or several-day river adventure at the **Base Nautique du Pont d'Arc** (☎ 04 75 37 17 79; www.canoe-ardeche.com; rte des Gorges; ⏱ Apr-Nov) in Vallon Pont d'Arc. A typical half-day, beginner-friendly descent (8km) costs €13/8 per adult/seven to 12 years (July and August €16/10) and a one-day 24km, 28km or 32km trip is €21/13 (July and August €26/16).

French Alps & the Jura

An isolated pristine wilderness, oh no no! The most trampled bits of this region can resemble a mad old circus in high season. Yet this fabulous 44-million-year-old landscape that excited Roman generals, Romantic poets and madcap mountaineers still excites and inspires. We are talking the French Alps after all, spiritual home of winter sports and one of the most awesome mountain ranges in the world. Think of 370km of green valleys meeting soaring peaks, topped with spiky snowbound summits and climaxing in a firework-fuelled 'bang-flash-wallop' of grandeur with Mont Blanc, Europe's highest peak at a mightier-than-man 4807m.

But there's mountains more to the French Alps – split between the historic regions of Savoy (north) and Dauphiné (south) – than skiing, snowboarding and free-riding fresh powder in high-octane resorts like Chamonix, Megève and Val d'Isère. There's the fabulous après-ski scene for starters – dynamic, fast-paced and constantly on the move. Then there's that contagious Alpine rash of small, chic boutique chalets and hotels which, let's be frank, go out of their way to entice guests to do things they wouldn't dream of doing at home. Summer stays – a wildflower infusion of hiking, hang-gliding, biking, white-water sports and eagle-spotting in the Vanoise or Écrins national parks – are no short straw.

The Jura quietly beckons dreamy souls seeking a hideaway far from all this ruthlessly modern Alpine madness. In this unassuming mountain range, north of Lake Geneva, it is the earthy rhythms of traditional dairy farming, cheese-making and wine-producing that beat out life. Stay on a farm to get a true taste.

HIGHLIGHTS

- Scare the living daylights out of yourself in **Chamonix** (p531) then head for a stiff drink or three at the town's **bars** (p538)

- Jive with jazz greats at the **Grenoble Jazz Festival** (p561)

- Shop, cycle and blade in chic lakeside **Annecy** (p544)

- Experience life (not to mention a feast of a dinner) on a **Jurassien farm** (p577)

- Go Jurassien: pedal through **Arbois vineyards** (p577), explore around pretty **Baume-les-Messieurs** (p578) and sleep on a **snail farm** (p579)

- Eat your way around the Jura – **cheese** (p578) only

- Make an architect's pilgrimage to Le Corbusier's chapel in **Ronchamp** (p580)

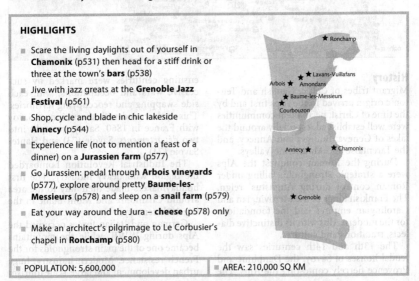

■ POPULATION: 5,600,000   ■ AREA: 210,000 SQ KM

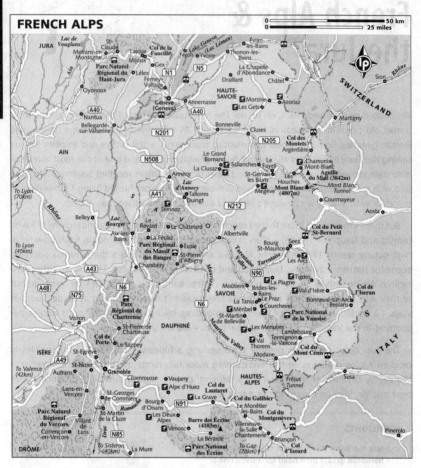

History

Migrant tribes of Celtic, Gaulish and Teutonic origin arrived in the Alps first and by the time of Christ, permanent communities were well established, especially around the lakes of Geneva, Bourget and Annecy, and the Tarentaise and Maurienne Valleys.

During the Roman conquest the Alps were a strategic stronghold, falling under Roman control during Augustus' reign. The Frankish kings of the Merovingian and Carolingian empires laid the foundations for the modern Alps with its distinctive dialects, traditions and cultures.

The 13th and 14th centuries saw the feudal houses of Savoy, the Dauphiné and Provence fiercely contesting the Alps. The ensuing centuries were marked by successive wars and occupations, with each side swapping and reoccupying territories. This cycle ended with the union of Savoy with France in 1860. Savoy was split into two *départements,* Savoie (73) and Haute-Savoie (74).

The Industrial Revolution bombarded the region with heavy industry. The first holidaymakers made their way to the area around Chamonix and Mont Blanc in the late 19th century.

German and Italian forces occupied the Alps during WWII, while the mountains became one of the main strongholds for the French resistance. Modern industry, huge urban development and large-scale tourism all contributed to the regeneration of the Alps in the post-war years.

Climate

Extreme climatic diversity and weather conditions that change alarmingly quickly are the main characteristics. Snow covers even lower-altitude stations most years from December to April. Pick up the latest weather report at the tourist office, your hotel reception or call:

Regional Weather Report (☎ 0 836 680 000)

Local Weather Report (☎ 0 836 680 2 plus two-digit *département* number)

Météoroute (road weather conditions; ☎ 0 836 682 000)

Snow & Avalanche Report (☎ 0 836 681 020)

National & Regional Parks

Wildlife is carefully protected in two national parks – Vanoise and Écrins – although even in these, there are large zones in which industry and human habitation is allowed. That said, together with four regional parks – Queyras (on the Italian border south of Briançon), the Vercors (southwest of Grenoble), Chartreuse (north of the Vercors) and Massif des Bauges (north of Chartreuse) – the Alps enjoys the greatest concentration of parks in France. The Jura is home to the Parc Naturel Régional du Haut-Jura.

Dangers & Annoyances

Avalanches (below) pose an increasing danger in snowbound areas. An accident in an isolated area can be fatal, so never ski, hike or climb alone. At high altitudes, where the sun's ultraviolet radiation is much stronger than at sea level (and is intensified by reflection off the snow), wear sunglasses and put sunscreen on exposed skin.

The air is dry in the Alps. Carry water when hiking, and drink more than you would at lower altitudes. Be aware of the possibility of hypothermia after a long climb or a sudden storm, as you'll cool off quickly while enjoying the cold, windy panorama.

Litter on the slopes is nasty and annoying. Smokers can buy a *cendrier de poche* (pocket ashtray) to hang around their neck and stick butts in from the local tourist offices.

Skiing & Snowboarding

Alpine slopes are busier than ever as bumper numbers of winter holidaymakers hit the 200-plus resorts in the French Alps to ski, snowboard and après-ski in the sun and snow. The season starts just before Christmas and ends in late April. High-season prices kick in over Christmas, New Year and during French school holidays in late February and early March; low season

---

AVALANCHE AWARENESS

The dramatic increase in avalanches in the French Alps is unnerving, and experts say this increase is the deadly result of global warming. During the winter of 2005-06, 55 people were killed in avalanches – more than double that of any other season since records began in 1971.

Ski resorts announce the daily avalanche risk through signs and coloured flags outside ticket kiosks, at the base of ski lifts and dotted around the resort and slopes. Yellow means 'low risk', black-and-yellow checks means 'heightened risk' and black is 'severe risk'. Ignoring an avalanche warning can be the death of you. Once buried beneath snow, you have no more than 15 minutes to get out.

Off-piste *(hors piste)* skiers should never leave home without an avalanche pole, ARVA transceiver, a shovel – and, most importantly, a professional local mountain guide. Staying firmly *on* piste is safer still.

Essential surfing for snow adventurers is **pistehors.com** (http://pistehors.com), an excellent English-language website devoted to French off-piste and snowboarding news. **Henry's Avalanche Talk** (☎ 04 79 06 16 58; www.henrysavalanchetalk.com), among other things, translates the daily avalanche forecast issued by Méteo France into English during the ski season and runs links to other useful avalanche-related sites. Val d'Isère-based Henry also runs mountain-safety and avalanche-awareness clinics – something more and more resorts are doing in a bid to, bluntly put, save lives. Most are free.

The French courts have adopted a zero-tolerance policy towards irresponsible skiers and boarders who trigger avalanches.

RESORT RECCE

Resort	Profile	Elevation	Alpine Runs	Cross-country Trails	Difficulty	Lifts	One-/Six-Day Lift Pass
Chamonix-Mont Blanc	High in altitude & attitude; young, trendy & full of fun	1037m	155km	45km	Intermediate, advanced, serious off-piste	47	€44/186
St-Gervais & Megève	Pricey, chic & oozing Alpine charm	810m & 1113m	445km	76km	Beginners, intermediate	111	€33/159
Les Portes du Soleil	14 connected resorts luring a tad older crowd	1000-1800m	650km	130km	All abilities	209	€37/179
Morzine-Les Gets	Busiest 'n biggest resort in Portes du Soleil	1000m	107km	18km	All abilities	56	€26.80/134.40
Avoriaz	Chic 1960s Portes du Soleil village-resort; family-driven	1800m	70km	45km	All abilities, super kid-friendly	36	€30.50/na
La Clusaz	Cheaper spot; ski for the day from Annecy	1100m	132km	70km	Beginners, intermediate	55	€27.50/143.50
Le Grand Bornand	Day trip from Annecy, hot locally	1000m	90km	62km	Beginners, intermediate	37	€25.50/122.60
Savoie Grand Révard	Day-trip from Chambéry; cheap, local & big on cross-country	1100m	50km	140km	Beginner, intermediate	14	€11.50/na
Les Trois Vallées	Hot, trendy, vast & fast ski area	2000m	600km	130km	All levels, advanced	200	€42/210
Méribel	Heavy traffic & Brit-packed bars in Les Trois Vallées	1450m	150km	24.5km	All abilities, kid-friendly	53	€35.50/170
Courchevel	Super-chic 'Three Valleys' skiing	1550m, 1650m & 1850m	150km	58km	All abilities, advanced	63	€35.50/170
Val Thorens	Europe's highest; third of the Three-Valley trio	2300m	140km	0km	All abilities	29	€34.50/166

Resort	Profile	Elevation	Alpine Runs	Cross-country Trails	Difficulty	Lifts	One-/Six-Day Lift Pass
St-Martin de Belleville	Authentic, picture-postcard Savoyard village linked to Les Trois Vallées	1450m	160km	28km	All abilities	36	€34.50/166
Val d'Isère	Unrivalled winter/summer skiing & boarding; buzzy nightlife	1850m	300km	44km	Intermediate, advanced, off-piste	97	€40/192.50
Tignes	Ruthlessly modern (ugly); summer skiing & glacial snowpark for boarders	2100m	300km	44km	Intermediate, advanced, off-piste	97	€40/192.50
Chamrousse	Weekend skiing from Grenoble	1700m	92km	44km	Beginner, intermediate	23	€26/134
Les Deux Alpes	Snowboarders' delight; summer ski & board	1660m	220km	20km	Intermediate, advanced	54	€34.70/165
Venosc	Low-altitude link to Les Deux Alpes	900m	220km	20km	Intermediate, advanced	54	€34.70/165
Alpe d'Huez	Snowboarding park; longest black run; summer skiing	1860m	245km	50km	All abilities	87	€36.20/187
Vaujany	Season's hot tip, linked to Alpe d'Huez	1250m	32.9km	0km	All abilities	20	€23/107.50
Serre Chevalier	Door-to-door skiing from 13 resorts	1200m	250km	35km	All abilities, off-piste	68	€35/173
Métabief Mont d'Or	Predominantly cross-country in the Jura	1000m	40km	250km		20	€18.40/99.30
Les Rousses	Predominantly cross-country; ideal for French & Swiss day-trippers	1100m	42km	220km		40	€19.20/100.20

is the start and end of the season and most of cold January.

Dependent on snow conditions, summer Alpine skiing on glaciers in high-altitude resorts Val d'Isère, Les Deux Alpes and Alpe d'Huez runs for anything from two weeks to two months, June to August.

Downhill skiing (ski alpin) is faster then ever, rendering helmets a sensible idea. Helmets can be rented alongside skis (Alpine, cross-country, monoski, telemark), snowboards, boots and poles at sport shops in every resort. Rental typically costs €35/150 per day/six days for Alpine equipment, €30/130 for snowboarding gear and €11/58 for cross-country; reserving in advance online invariably yields a 15% discount. Lost equipment must be paid for by you or your insurance policy; rental shops offer insurance for a small additional charge.

Downhill runs range from a few hundred metres to 20km long and are colour-coded to indicate how kid-easy or killer-hard they are: green (beginners), blue (intermediate), red (advanced) and black (very advanced). Summer glacial skiing is on short greens or blues. Snowboarders are brilliantly catered for in larger resorts with a riot of snow-parks kitted out with half-pipes, quarter-pipes, shape kickers, gaps and ramps. Long, rambling cross-country (ski de fond) trails are at their most scenic in the Jura.

France's leading ski school, the **École de Ski Français** (ESF; www.esf.net) – its instructors wear red – teaches snowboarding and skiing. It has a branch in every resort and touts competitive rates against the crop of smaller private schools it competes against; lessons typically cost €37/47 per hour for two/four people and €30 per person for a two-hour group lesson. Kids can start learning from the age of four; from the age of three, nappyless tots can lark about in the jardin de neige (snow garden).

LIFT PASSES

You must buy a lift pass (forfait) to ride the various remontées mécaniques – drag lifts or buttons (téléskis), chairlifts for two to eight people (télésièges), gondolas (télécabines), cable cars (téléphériques) and funicular railways (funiculaires).

Passes – a big chunk out of your budget – give access to one or more ski sectors and often include a day's skiing in a neighbouring resort. They can be valid for a half or full day or as many days as you want, and rarely require a passport photo. Any self-respecting lift pass is 'hands-free' – like a credit card with a built-in chip that barriers detect automatically – and can be bought and recharged online. One-way and return tickets are available on chairlifts and cable cars for walkers.

Children aged under five ski for free but still need a pass; bring along a passport as proof of age. Many places offer the same deal to veterans aged 75 or more.

Cheaper passes – usually around €6 a day – are also needed for cross-country ski trails, although passes are rarely checked.

INSURANCE

When buying your lift pass, think about insurance – a vital necessity. If you're hurt on the slopes, all the services that come to your aid – the helicopter, the guy who skis you and your stretcher down the mountain, the doctor who treats you – charge lots of money.

Most packages include insurance or you might have the **Carte Neige** (www.ffs.fr/carteneige

---

SOS

If you need help getting off the mountain, the Gendarmerie de Montagne is the emergency service to SOS. Comprising 15 Pelotons de Gendarmerie de Haute-Montagne (PGHM) and five Pelotons de Gendarmerie de Montagne (PGM) countrywide, these highly skilled mountain-rescue specialists are based in key towns and stations in the French Alps:

Annecy (☎ 04 50 09 47 47; 33 av Plaine)
Bourg St-Maurice (☎ 04 79 07 04 25; 945 av Maréchal Leclerc)
Briançon (☎ 04 92 22 22 22; 37 rue Pasteur)
Chamonix (☎ 04 50 53 16 89; 69 rue de la Mollard)

When an emergency strikes, if you don't know which number to call, don't waste time looking for it. Local tourist offices have a list of emergency numbers or simply call ☎ 17.

THE DAREDEVIL'S CHOICE

Go jump on a pair of skis, grab a horse and whoosh, away you go … at around 60km/h once you've got the knack of **ski joëring** – the art of being pulled along the flat on skis by a horse. Try it in the Parc Naturel Régional du Massif des Bauges (p553).

Kite-surfing is the dangerous daredevil choice. It can be done on snow (December to March) or grass (April to September) in the Parc Naturel Régional du Vercors (p566) and on water near Annecy (p549). High-flyers will likewise get a kick out of **paragliding** (landing on winter snow or summer grass) and **skydiving**, both practised in practically every Alpine ski station.

In Val d'Isère (p555), anyone with a smattering of daredevil in them can fly down the slope on a **babyboard** steered by weight transfer or dabble in **snakegliss sledging** – bombing downhill in a hybrid tramway-bobsleigh.

Heliskiing, illegal in France since the 1980s on environmental grounds, is still organised in resorts like Chamonix (p534), and Courchevel (p554), where heliskiers are simply taken across the border into Italy instead.

---

in French), an annual policy that covers mountain-rescue costs and medical treatment. It costs €40 to €60 per year (€20 to €30 for cross-country skiers), depending on the level of cover you choose and where you buy it. Resorts sell it (usually through the ESF, opposite) and it's sold online.

If you are not insured, buy **Carré Neige** (www.carreneige.com) with your lift pass. Every resort offers the daily insurance scheme – effectively a daily version of *Carte Neige* – that covers mountain rescue, transport and medical costs and costs €2.50 a day.

Getting There & Away

On a clear day the view through the plane window is the best introduction to the Alps you could dream of: chances are you're landing at **Lyon-St-Exupéry airport** (p516; www .lyon.aeroport.fr), 25km east of Lyon; or **Geneva Airport** (Aéroport International de Genève; www.gva.ch) in neighbouring Switzerland.

From both international airports there are buses to numerous ski resorts with Geneva's **Aeroski-Bus** (☎ 022-798 20 00; www.alpski -bus.com) and Lyon's **Satobus-Alpes** (from abroad ☎ 04 79 68 32 96, within France ☎ 0 820 320 368; www .satobus-alpes.com); fares and frequencies are listed in this chapter under Getting There & Away in resort sections.

Traffic on steeply climbing, winding mountain roads leading to resorts can be hellish, especially on Friday and Saturday. After heavy snowfalls, you may need snow chains. Winter long, winter tyres (automatically provided with most hire cars picked up at Lyon and Geneva airports) are a good idea. The Fréjus and Mont Blanc road tunnels connect the French Alps with Italy, as do several mountain passes. Road signs indicate if passes are blocked.

For Eurostar snow trains speeding from London to/from Moûtiers and Bourg St-Maurice, see p973. Within France, train services to the Alps are excellent.

SAVOY

The setting couldn't be grander. Hugged by Switzerland and Italy, Savoy (Savoie; pronounced sav-*wa*) rises from the southern shores of Europe's largest Alpine lake to the foot of Europe's biggest mountain. A sweet sprinkling of spa towns on Lake Geneva's shores and chic ski resorts around Mont Blanc top off this region's indisputable 'wow!' effect.

To the southwest, long U-shaped valleys resemble ancient glaciers that created lakes such as Lake Annecy – a chic hang-out these days – and France's largest natural lake, Lac Bourget. Next door in the historical capital of Chambéry a magnificent chateau recalls the heritage of the dukes who ruled Savoy and much of northern Italy from here until the mid-19th century.

The harsh reality of rural life, unchanged for centuries, strikes in the region's most remote realms like the Chartreuse massif, where monks quietly make pea-green liqueur, and the wild Parc National de la Vanoise, where France's largest colony of Alpine ibex roams. Despite centuries of French cultural influence, people here tenaciously cling to their Savoyard roots and

FRENCH ALPS & THE JURA

TOP 10 SURFS

The Alps (www.thealps.com) Useful resort guide with great photo galleries.

ANENA (www.anena.org in French) Get to the bottom of what makes an avalanche with the in-depth studies of the National French Association for the Study of Snow & Avalanches.

Carré Neige (www.carreneige.com) Insure yourself on the mountain.

Fédération Française de Ski (www.ffs.fr in French) Delve into the world of French skiing with the French Ski Federation; includes a *Carte Neige* lowdown.

French Alps Travel & Tourism (www.frenchalps.worldweb.com) Book hotels and tours, bone up on the sights, and mountains more with this nuts-and-bolts site.

Natives (www.natives.co.uk) Well-written website aimed at seasonal resort workers; insightful bar and club reviews (not always up-to-date) and busy discussion board.

pistehors.com (http://pistehors.com) Essential surfing for anyone heading off-piste.

Planet Subzero (www.planetsubzero.com) Book seasonal and long-term accommodation online.

Ski France International (www.ski-ride-france.com) Official website for skiing in France; excellent snow reports and resort profiles.

SkiFrance (www.skifrance.fr) Official website for the main Alpine ski resorts.

---

land, a handful still speaking an age-old dialect not dissimilar to Provençal.

CHAMONIX

pop 10,000 / elevation 1037m

Grungy and gritty, rough-cut Chamonix is where the serious Alpine action kicks in – with bags of natural panache! This is France's legendary mountaineering centre where world-class skiers, boarders and climbers push themselves to extremes on Europe's most challenging, adrenaline-pumping pistes and rock faces. This is the stuff of James Bond movies: yes, that spectacular stunt-riddled ski chase by 007 in *The World Is Not Enough* (1999) was filmed in Chamonix.

Chamonix is ensnared by scenery so mind-blowingly spectacular it's practically Himalayan (think deeply crevassed glaciers pointing towards a valley from the icy crown of mighty Mont Blanc). Summer playground since the 18th century and winter one since 1903, it was here that the first Winter Olympics happened in 1924. Since 1965 the world's highest rock-covered tunnel (2840m; p540) has provided a road link between Chamonix and Courmayeur in Italy.

But there's no obligation to overdo it: a once-in-a-lifetime-experience of a cable car, a little red mountain train leading to an ice cave carved in a glacier, and a tramway nearby means this incredible overdose of natural magnificence can also be revelled in without barely lifting a finger.

Orientation

Chamonix town runs along the banks of the River Arve for about 2km, wedged in a valley between the Mont Blanc massif (east) and the Aiguilles Rouges massif (west) with 2525m-high Le Brévent as its peak.

Sports and souvenir shops, restaurants, cafés and bars line the main street, pedestrianised rue du Docteur Paccard and its continuation, rue Joseph Vallot. Cross the river to reach the bus and train stations and the happening Chamonix Sud quarter where hip bars and clubs cluster around the foot of the Aiguille du Midi cable car (opposite).

Chamonix's most exceptional downhill skiing is in Les Grands Montets (1235m to 3300m), a ski area accessible from Argentière, 9km north of Chamonix; shuttlebuses (p540) link the two.

Information

BOOKSHOPS

Librairie VO (☎ 04 50 53 24 41; 20 av Ravanel-le-Rouge) English-language novels and books, many with a mountaineering theme.

Photo Alpine Tairraz (☎ 04 50 53 14 23; 162 av Michel Croz) Skiing and walking guides, maps, mountaineering books and local guidebooks.

EMERGENCY

Centralised First-Aid Post (☎ 04 50 54 04 73) Call this number if there's an accident on the slopes.

PGHM (Peloton de Gendarmerie de Haute Montagne; ☎ 04 50 53 16 89; 69 rue de la Mollard) Mountain rescue service for the entire Mont Blanc area.

Police Station (☎ 04 50 53 00 55; 111 rue de la Mollard)

INTERNET ACCESS

Surf for free on your own laptop in the wi-fi–savvy tourist office (right).

Le Bureau (☎ 04 50 90 68 37; 7–13 quai du Vieux Moulins; 10min/1hr €1/4.50; 10am-10pm Mon-Fri, noon-9pm Sat & Sun) Riverside office with internet access.

INTERNET RESOURCES

http://agenda.chamonix.com Cultural happenings.
www.chamonix.com Tourist office website.
www.chamonix.net Independent companion site; advice on accommodation, entertainment and nightlife.
www.compagniedumontblanc.com Buy ski passes online, download piste maps, ski area opening and closing times for the day.

LAUNDRY

Laverie Automatique (174 av de l'Aiguille du Midi; 7/16kg wash €5.50/10; 9am-8pm)

MEDICAL SERVICES

The tourist office (right) has a list of doctors, dentists, pharmacists, physiotherapists etc.

Central Hospital (Centre Hospitalier; ☎ 04 50 53 84 00; 509 rte des Pélerins) In Les Favrands, 2km south of Chamonix centre.

Duty Dentist (☎ 04 50 66 17 19)
Duty Doctor (☎ 15)

MONEY

There are several seasonal exchange places between the tourist and post offices.

Banque de Savoie (☎ 04 50 53 30 25; 1 place Balmat; 9am-1pm & 3-7pm May, Jun & early Sep–Nov, 8am-8pm Jul–early Sep & Dec-Apr) Exchange bureau with competitive rates.

Banque Laydernier (☎ 04 50 53 26 39; 2 place Balmat)

POST

Post Office (89 place Balmat)

TOURIST INFORMATION

Tourist Office (☎ 04 50 53 00 24; www.chamonix.com; 85 place du Triangle de l'Amitié; 8.30am-12.30pm & 2-7pm mid-Dec–Mar & mid-Jun & Sep, 9am-12.30pm & 2-6.30pm Mon-Sat Apr–mid-Jun, 8.30am-12.30pm & 1.30-7pm early Jul, 8.30am-7.30pm mid-Jul–mid-Aug, 8.30am-7pm mid–end Aug, 9am-12.30pm & 2-6.30pm Mon-Sat Oct–mid-Dec) Accommodation and activity information, sells ski passes, free wi-fi zone.

Sights

AIGUILLE DU MIDI

A jagged pinnacle of rock rising above glaciers, snowfields and rocky crags, 8km from the domed summit of Mont Blanc, the **Aiguille du Midi** (3777m) is one of Chamonix's most famous landmarks. If you can handle the height, the unique panoramic views from the summit are breathtaking and unforgettable.

Year round the **Téléphérique du l'Aiguille du Midi** (Aiguille du Midi cable car; ☎ 04 50 53 30 80, advance reservations 24hr ☎ 0 892 680 067; 100 place de l'Aiguille du Midi; adult/12-15yr/4-11yr/family return €36/30.60/25.20/108, adult/12-15yr/4-11yr return to mid-station Plan de l'Aiguille €16/13.60/11.20; 6.10am-6pm Jul & mid-Aug, 7.10am or 8.10am-5.30pm mid-Aug-late Sep & mid-May–Jun, 8.30am-4pm mid-Dec–Jan, 8.10am-4pm Feb & Mar, 8.10am-4.30pm Apr, 8.30am-5pm May) links Chamonix with the Aiguille du Midi; its halfway point, Plan de l'Aiguille (2317m) is an excellent place to start hikes or paraglide in summer. Be prepared for long queues, especially in summer when you need to obtain a boarding card (marked with the

---

TOP OF THE WORLD

Not spooked by the scariest ride at the funfair? Then try Chamonix's top-of-the-world stab at scaring the living daylights out of punters – the Aiguille du Midi cable car, best known as Europe's highest (and scariest) cable car.

The idea of a floor-to-peak cable car was born in 1909, but the technical challenges proved enormous and engineers initially had to settle for a lower-altitude version, completed in 1924. After WWII the original dream was revived and the spectacular cable car swung into action in 1955.

Climbing from the valley floor to a terrace beneath the Aiguille at 3777m in just 20 minutes is an amazing feat of engineering. From far below, the Aiguille looks like a single peak; in fact, it has twin spires connected by a gravity-defying footbridge. There is a café-restaurant (p538) where you can savour the afternoon tea of a lifetime, a souvenir shop (surprise surprise) and Europe's highest letterbox to send a postcard to Grandma back home.

The final few metres to the 3842m-high summit are by elevator. From the viewing platform at the top, there are frighteningly dramatic 360° views of the surrounding mountains, with the odd climber clinging to a ridge or skier setting off on the daunting Vallée Blanche descent (p534).

FRENCH ALPS & THE JURA

CHAMONIX

0 ————— 300 m
0 ————— 0.2 miles

INFORMATION
Banque de Savoie.........................**1** B5
Banque Laydernier......................**2** B5
Club Alpin Français.....................**3** C5
Laverie Automatique...................**4** B6
Le Bureau..................................**5** B4
Librairie VO...............................**6** A6
PGHM (Pelotons de Gendarmerie
  Haute Montagne).....................**7** A4
Photo Alpine Tairraz...................**8** C5
Police Station.............................**9** B5
Post Office................................**10** B5
Tourist Office............................**11** B4

SIGHTS & ACTIVITIES
Association International des
  Guides du Mont Blanc..............**12** B4
Centre Sportif Richard Bozon......**13** C3
Cham' Aventure.....................(see 17)
Compagnie des Guides.............(see 17)
École de Ski Français...............(see 17)
Espace Tairraz............................**14** B4
Ice-Skating Rink.........................**15** C3
Les Ailes du Mont Blanc.............**16** D3
Maison de la Montagne..............**17** B4
Museé Alpin..............................**18** C4
Musée des Cristaux..................(see 14)
Office de Haute Montagne.........(see 17)
Summits....................................**19** B4
Télécabine du Brévent................**20** A4
Téléphérique de l'Aiguille du Midi..**21** B6
Télésiège des Planards................**22** D4

SLEEPING
Gîte Le Vagabond.......................**23** A6
Grand Hôtel Les Alpes **24** B5
Hameau Albert 1er......................**25** C4
Hôtel de l'Arve...........................**26** B4
Hôtel El Paso.............................**27** B4
Hôtel Faucigny..........................**28** B4

Hôtel Gustavia..........................**29** C5
Hôtel Richemond.......................**30** B5
Hôtel Vallée Blanche..................**31** B5
The Clubhouse..........................**32** C3

EATING
Annapurna................................**33** A6
La Calèche................................**34** B5
Le Bistrot..................................**35** B6
Le Panier des Quatre Saisons......**36** B5
Le Refuge Payot.........................**37** B4
Le Sanjon.................................**38** B6
Munchie....................................**39** B4
No Escape.................................**40** C5
Poco Loco.................................**41** B5
Super U....................................**42** B4

DRINKING
Bar du Moulins.....................(see 44)
Bar Le Vagabond...................(see 23)
Bar'd Up..................................**43** B4
Chambre Neuf.......................(see 29)
Cybar.......................................**44** B4

Dick's Tea Bar......................(see 44)
Elevation 1904..........................**45** C5
Goophy....................................**46** C5
La Terrasse...............................**47** B5
Le Tof......................................**48** B6
L'Expédition.............................**49** B4
MBC..**50** D4
O'Byrne's.............................(see 31)
Poco Loco............................(see 41)

ENTERTAINMENT
3 Cinémas................................**51** B5
BPM...**52** B5
Cantina Club.........................(see 27)
Le Garage.................................**53** B6

TRANSPORT
Chamonix Autoloc-Hertz............**54** B4
Chamonix Bus Station.................**55** C5
Europcar..............................(see 55)
Le Grand Bi Cycles.....................**56** C4
Taxi Stand................................**57** C5
Trajectoire................................**58** A6

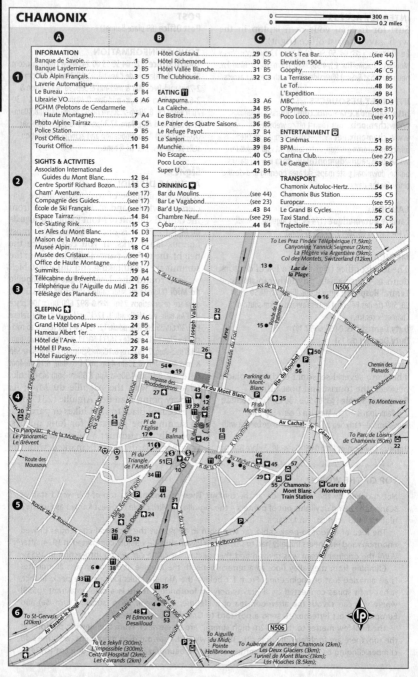

number of your departing *and* returning cable-car cabins) from the ticket desks in addition to a ticket. Making advance reservations on the 24-hour phone number incurs a €2 booking fee. The ascent is not recommended for children aged under two. Even in summer the temperature rarely rises above minus 10°C at the top – so bring warm clothes!

From the Aiguille du Midi, between mid-May and mid-September the unrepentant can continue for a further 30 minutes (5km) of mind-blowing scenery – think suspended glaciers and spurs, séracs, snow plains and shimmering ice-fields – in the smaller bubbles of the Télécabine Panoramic Mont Blanc (Panoramic Mont Blanc Cable Car) to **Pointe Helbronner** (3466m) on the French–Italian border. From Pointe Helbronner another **cable car** (☎ 04 50 53 30 80; adult/12-15yr/4-11yr/family return from Chamonix €54/45.90/37.80; ☼ 8.50am-4pm mid-May–Jun & Sep, 7.45am or 8.15am-4.30pm Jul & Aug) descends to the Italian ski resort of Courmayeur.

LE BRÉVENT
The highest peak on the western side of the valley, **Le Brévent** (2525m) has fabulous views of the Mont Blanc massif and a multitude of hiking trails, ledges to paraglide from and a summit restaurant (p538).

Reach it with the **Télécabine du Brévent** (☎ 04 50 53 13 18; 29 rte Henriette d'Angeville; Chamonix–Brévent adult/12-15yr/4-11yr/family return €15/17/14/60, Chamonix–Planpraz adult/12-15yr/ 4-11yr return €12/10.20/8.40; ☼ 8am-5.45pm Jun-Aug, 8.45am-4.45pm mid-Dec–Apr), from the end of rue de la Mollard to mid-station **Planpraz** (2000m), then continuing on another cable car to the top.

MER DE GLACE
The **Mer de Glace** (Sea of Ice), the second-largest glacier in the Alps, is 14km long, 1800m wide and up to 400m deep. During a visit to Chamonix in 1741, Englishman William Windham was the first foreigner to set eyes on the glacier, which he described as 'a sort of agitated sea that seemed suddenly to have become frozen' (hence the name). The glacier moves 45m a year at the edges, and up to 90m a year in the centre, and has become a popular tourist attraction thanks to the rack-and-pinion railway line built between 1897 and 1908.

Since 1946, the **Grotte de la Mer de Glace** (☼ late May-late Sep) – an ice cave – has been carved every spring. Work begins in February and takes three months. The interior temperature is between -2°C and -5°C. Look down the slope for last year's cave to see how far the glacier has moved. Be prepared to climb 150 steps to access the cave.

A quaint red mountain train links **Gare du Montenvers** (☎ 04 50 53 12 54; 35 place de la Mer de Glace; adult/12-15yr/4-11yr return €16/13.60/11.20; ☼ 10am-4.30pm mid-Dec–Apr, 8.30am-5.30pm May-Jun & Sep, 8am-6.30pm Jul & Aug) in Chamonix with Montenvers (1913m), from where a cable car transports tourists in summer down to the glacier and cave. The journey takes 20 minutes and a **combined ticket** valid for the train, cable car and cave costs €22.50/19.10/15.80 per adult/12-15yr/4-11yr. Before catching the train back to Chamonix, nip into the **Grand Hôtel de Montenvers** (1880; p538) for a gander at its nine-room local history museum and a drink on its dramatically placed terrace.

The Mer de Glace can be reached on foot via the Grand Balcon Nord trail from Plan de l'Aiguille. The two-hour uphill trail from Chamonix starts near the summer luge track. Traversing the glacier and its crevasses requires proper equipment and an experienced guide.

MUSEUMS
Pay for one Chamonix museum and visit the other for free.

The town's illustrious Alpine history (the cliffhanging tale of local crystal hunter Jacques Balmat and doctor Michel Gabriel Paccard summiting Mont Blanc for the first time in 1786, the creation of the winter season etc) zooms into focus at the **Musée Alpin** (Alpine Museum; ☎ 04 50 53 25 93; 89 av Michel Croz; adult/12-18yr €5/1.50; ☼ 2-7pm plus 10am-noon school holidays). Find it inside 19th-century Chamonix Palace, one of three palace hotels built in Chamonix for the 1924 Olympics.

Rocks, minerals and geology are examined in the **Musée des Cristaux** (Crystal Museum; ☎ 04 50 55 53 93; Esplanade St-Michel; adult/12-18yr €5/1.50; ☼ 2-7pm, closed 1 week in Jun & Nov), in the Espace Tairraz.

Activities
WINTER ACTIVITIES
Make the **Maison de la Montagne** (190 place de l'Église), across the square from the tourist

office, your first port of call for finding out everything about the Mont Blanc area.

Inside is the highly regarded **Compagnie des Guides** (below); the **École de Ski Français** (ESF; Chamonix ☎ 04 50 53 22 57; www.esf-chamonix.com; Argentière ☎ 04 50 54 00 12; www.esf-argentiere.com; 329 rue Charlet Straton); and the **Office de Haute Montagne** (OHM; ☎ 04 50 53 22 08; www.ohm-chamonix .com in French), which has information on trails, hiking conditions and *refuges*.

Skiing & Snowboarding

Of Chamonix's nine main skiing and snowboarding areas, the best for beginners are Le Tour, Les Planards and Les Chosalets. Le Brévent, La Flégère (connected by *téléphérique*) and Les Grands Montets, accessible from Argentière 9km north of Chamonix, offer accomplished skiers the greatest challenges. For boarders, there is a snowpark with half-pipe, kicker ramps and other thrill-filled obstacles in Les Grands Montets and a natural half-pipe in Le Tour.

The region has several marked but ungroomed trails suitable for skiers looking for off-piste thrills. The famous 20km **Vallée Blanche descent** – a lifelong dream for most serious skiers – is one of the world's most celebrated runs. The route leads from the Aiguille du Midi over the Mer de Glace and through the forests back to Chamonix, covering a drop in altitude of up to 2800m. It must *only* be tackled with a guide; the route crosses the crevasse-riddled glacier and passes through avalanche-prone areas. It takes four to five hours and a guide costs €250 for up to four people (€16 per per-

son for additional four people) through the Compagnie des Guides, ESF or Chamonix Guide (left).

Lift Passes

The tourist office, some hotels and kiosks next to ski lifts sell hands-free ski passes for the Chamonix area. The **Cham' Ski pass** (1/2/6 days €44/82/186) gives access to all Chamonix Valley lifts (including the Aiguille du Midi cable car and the Montenvers train and cable car) and free bus transport. Cheaper passes covering single ski areas are available, as is the more expensive **Ski-Pass Mont Blanc** which covers Megève–St-Gervais (p541) too. View all options and buy online at www.compagniedumontblanc.com.

Ski Touring & Heliskiing

Ski de randonnée (ski touring) is big in Chamonix, the range of tours being seemingly endless. The king of ski tours is the classic six-day **Haute Route** (from €1000 per person including guide) from Chamonix to Zermatt in Switzerland, opened by guides in 1927. Skiers need to be experienced in off-piste skiing and extremely fit. Other classics include the **Oberland** to Switzerland (six days, from €900), which traverses steep mountain descents and glacial areas including the famous Konkordiaplatz, and the **Tour des Jorasses** from Argentière to the Géant glacier through the rocky spires of the Grandes Jorasses range (five days, starting from €750).

Heliskiing (€240 to €400 per person) is reserved strictly for top-level skiers, as pro-

---

ADVENTURE KNOW-HOW

These guides have it. So go, create your own adventure:

Association International des Guides du Mont Blanc (☎ 04 50 53 27 05; www.guides-du-montblanc .com; 98 rue des Moulins) Chamonix-based international guides; extreme skiing, mountaineering, glacier trekking, ice and rock climbing, and paragliding.

Aventure en Tête (☎ 04 50 54 05 11; www.aventureentete.com; 620 rte du Plagnolet, Argentière) Ski touring and ski-alpinism expeditions, heliskiing/boarding, free ride and off-piste security courses; mountaineering and climbing in summer.

Chamonix Experience (☎ 04 50 54 09 36; www.chamex.com; 141 rue Charlet Straton, Argentière) Courses in off-piste skiing, avalanche awareness, heliskiing, ice climbing and ski touring; in summer, rock and alpine climbing.

Chamonix Guide (☎ 04 50 55 66 47, 06 03 60 21 03; www.chamonixguide.com in French; 840 rte des Chavants, Les Houches) Mountain guides in Les Houches covering most winter and summer Alpine sports.

Compagnie des Guides (☎ 04 50 53 00 88; www.chamonix-guides.com; 190 place de l'Église) *Crème de la crème* of mountain guides, founded in the 1820s and the oldest organisation of its kind in the world. Guides for skiing, mountaineering, snowshoeing, ice climbing, hiking, mountain biking and every other Alpine pastime.

ficient off as on killer-black pistes: contact the Compagnie des Guides (opposite), ESF (p528) or **Chamonix Mont-Blanc Hélicoptères** (CMBH; ☎ 04 50 54 13 82; www.cmbh.net in French).

SUMMER ACTIVITIES
Walking
From late spring until October, 310km of spectacular walking trails open up to hikers. The most rewarding are the high-altitude trails reached by cable car; lifts shut down in the late afternoon but in June and July it is light enough to walk until at least 9pm.

From the top of Les Praz-Index cable car (€15) or La Flégère (€10), the line's midway point, easy 1¼ to two-hour trails lead to **Lac Blanc** (literally 'White Lake'), a turquoise-coloured lake ensnared by mountains at 2352m. Star-lovers can overnight in the **Refuge du Lac Blanc** (☎ 04 50 53 49 15; dm with half-board €46; ☼ Jun-Sep), a wooden chalet with romantic Mont Blanc views.

The **Grand Balcon Sud** trail along the western side of the valley stays at around 2000m and also affords great MB views. Reach it on foot from behind Le Brévent's *télécabine* station. For less uphill walking, take the Planpraz or La Flégère lifts.

Several routes start from Plan de l'Aiguille, including the **Grand Balcon Nord**, which takes you to the Mer de Glace, from where you can walk or take the Montenvers train down to Chamonix.

For the less ambitious, **Parc de Merlet** (☎ 04 50 53 47 89; adult/4-12yr €4.50/3; ☼ 10am-6pm May, Jun & Sep, 9.30am-7.30pm Jul & Aug) in Les Houches offers a unique opportunity to see marmots, chamois and other typical Alpine animals close-up. Some marked footpaths through the animal park are wheel-/pushchair friendly.

White-Water Sports
Cham' Aventure (☎ 04 50 53 55 70; www.cham-aventure.com; 190 place de l'Église), with an office inside the Maison de la Montagne, organises canyoning (half-day €60 per person), rafting (€33/125 for two hours/day) and hydrospeed (€41 for two hours) on Chamonix's River Arve and the Dora Baltea in neighbouring Italy (an hour's drive).

Chamonix Guide (opposite) arranges canyoning, as does **Canyoning Yannick Seigneur** (☎ 06 77 88 24 50; www.canyoning-chamonix.com; 44 chemin de l'Ordon), a smaller set-up that offers some excellent expeditions.

Summer Luge
The highlight of the **Parc de Loisirs de Chamonix** (☎ 04 50 53 08 97; www.planards.com in French; ☼ 1.30-6pm Sat & Sun May & Oct, 1.30-6pm Jun & Sep, 10am-7.30pm Jul & Aug) is the **summer luge track** (luge d'été; 1/6 descents €5/25, one/1½ hours €12.50/15) which winds through trees at an electrifying speed near the chairlift in Les Planards. Kids under six ride for free with an adult. Other activities for kidding around include trampolines, electric cars and boats, a forest-adventure obstacle course and funfair rides.

Cycling
Lower-altitude trails like the Petit Balcon Sud (250m) from Argentière to Servoz are perfect for biking; for bike rental see p540. Most outdoor-activity specialists (opposite) arrange guided mountain-biking expeditions.

Paragliding
The sky above Chamonix is often dotted with paragliders wheeling down from the snowy heights. Starter flights from Planpraz (elevation 2000m) cost €90 (€220 from the Aiguille du Midi). Paragliding schools include **Summits** (☎ 04 50 53 50 14, 06 84 01 26 00; www.summits.fr; 27 allée du Savoy); **Les Ailes du Mont Blanc** (☎ 04 50 53 92 76, 06 20 46 55 57; www.lesailes dumontblanc.com; 24 av de la Plage) and **Baptême Biplace** (☎ 04 50 55 92 47, 06 80 42 59 55).

Ice-Skating, Swimming et al
An **ice-skating rink** (☎ 04 50 53 12 36; adult/child €4.20/3.40, skate rental €3.10; ☼ 2-5pm or 6pm Tue & Thu-Sun, 2-5pm & 9-11pm Wed) is inside the **Centre Sportif Richard Bozon** (☎ 04 50 53 20 70; http://sports.chamonix.com in French; 214 av de la Plage; ☼ 12.30-8pm Mon-Fri, 2-8pm Sat & Sun), a sports complex with indoor and outdoor **swimming pools** (adult/child €4.20/3.40), **sauna and hammam** (€10.40 including pool); **climbing wall** (€3.80); **squash** (€8) and **tennis courts** (per hr €13.20).

Festivals & Events
The two-day **Fête des Guides** in mid-August sees Chamonix's illustrious Compagnies des Guides welcome new members and honour lost ones with a dramatic *son-et-lumière* (sound and light) show, fireworks, concerts and mountaineering displays.

Sleeping
In July, August and during the ski season, hotels get heavily booked. The tourist-office

---

CHAMONIX CLIFFHANGERS

Cliffhanging is an understatement for many of the 15 *refuges* (mountain huts) that the **Club Alpin Français** (CAF; ☎ 04 50 53 16 03; www.clubalpin-chamonix.com; 136 av Michel Croz; ☼ 3.30-7pm Mon, Thu & Fri, 9am-noon Sat Jun-Jun, 9.30am-noon Jul & Aug) runs in the Mont Blanc massif, poised perilously on the mountain edge or teetering precariously over a stomach-churning drop. 'You can risk your life overnighting in the hut without acclimatisation', 'Beware rock fall from the Aiguille du Midi!' or 'Constant rockfall in the corridor; wear helmet and cross quickly' are some of the cheerier turns of phrase used to describe the mountain huts where hikers seek refuge after a hard day's walking and/or climbing. Ice axes, crampons and ropes are vital for accessing some of the most remote huts placed at altitudes above 3000m.

Most *refuges* are manned by a warden from around mid-June to mid-September and must be reserved in advance by telephone (obligatory). Snow permitting, many are open – albeit without a warden – for several more months of the year. Expect to pay anything from €8 to €15 for a dorm bed (with or without a warden) plus around €6/15 for breakfast/dinner prepared by the hut-keeper.

---

based **Centrale de Réservation** (Central Booking Office; ☎ 04 50 53 23 33; www.chamonix.com; ☼ 24hr) accepts reservations by telephone, email or online. In high season many hotels, hostels and *refuges* only offer half-board.

For a complete list of accommodation options, pick up a copy of *Les Carnets de l'Hébergement* from the tourist office.

BUDGET

Chamonix sports 13 camp sites, open May or June to September or October. In summer the **Grand Hôtel de Montenvers** (p538) has atmospheric backpacker-basic rooms dramatically perched at the foot of a glacier.

Les Deux Glaciers (☎ 04 50 53 15 84; glaciers@clubInternet.fr; 80 rte des Tissières; 2-adults tent pitch €12.70; ☼ mid-Dec–mid-Nov) The only camp site to stay open almost all year (it has five heated chalets with bathroom to rent), the Two Glaciers is a three-star ground in Les Bossons, 3km south of Chamonix. Ride the train to Les Bossons or the Chamonix bus to the Tremplin-le-Mont stop.

Gîte Le Vagabond (☎ 04 50 53 15 43; www .gitevagabond.com; 365 av Ravanel-le-Rouge; dm €14.40, with breakfast/half-board €19.40/31.40, d with breakfast €62; reception ☼ 8-10am & 4.30-10pm; ☐ ☒) '*Bed et bar et cuisine*' is the house motto of this legendary hang-out where cool dudes freeride by day and eat, drink and party by night. Find Chamonix's hippest hostelry in a 150-year-old stagecoach inn. Beds are in four- or six-person dorms and comfy doubles have their own bathroom.

Auberge de Jeunesse Chamonix (☎ 04 50 53 14 52; chamonix@fuaj.org; 127 montée Jacques Balmat; dm mid-Apr–Oct €16.70, Dec–mid-Apr €22; reception ☼ 8am-noon, 5-7.30pm & 8.30-10pm; ☼ Dec-Oct) Three- to six-night stays are the trend in winter, although one-nighters are possible if there's a bed free when you turn up (no advance reservations for single nights from December to mid-April) at this large well-run hostel, 2km south of Chamonix in Les Pélerins. Take the Chamonix-Les Houches bus line and get off in Les Pélérins d'en Haut (in front of the hostel). Non–HI-cardholders must buy a €3.50 nightly stamp. There's no kitchen but a decent snack bar.

Hôtel El Paso (☎ 04 50 53 64 20; www.cantina.fr; 37 impasse des Rhododendrons; dm/s/d/tr/q €15/35/45/55/70, with shower & toilet €45/55/65/80) The accommodation leg of nightclub Cantina Club (p540), El Paso looks like a cheap hotel in a Mexican border-town. But young boarders revel in the rowdy atmosphere and Tex-Mex *menu* – all at a price that's hard to beat.

MIDRANGE

What you get for your money varies wildly.

Hôtel Faucigny (☎ 04 50 53 01 17; www.hotelfau cigny-chamonix.com; 118 place de l'Église; d/tr/q low season €66/86/96, high season €73/86/104, d with shower low/high season €38/42; ☼ mid-May–mid-Nov & mid-Dec–mid-Apr) There is something special about this old house that in soul is '*chambre d'hôte*' rather than 'two-star hotel'. Jacqueline and Guy Écochard traded in high-flying jobs in the city for a hotel in the mountains five years ago and are naturals! Look for the peppermint-green shutters behind the church.

Hôtel Gustavia (☎ 04 50 53 00 31; www.hotel-gusta via.com; 272 av Michel Croz; s/d/tr/q from €46/74/102/180)

'Une belle addresse' (a beautiful address) since 1890, this charming manor-house hotel with bottle-green wooden shutters and wrought-iron balconies oozes soul. Its wintertime clientele is young and fun, due in part to Chambre Neuf (Room 9; p539) – the stylish après-ski bar it runs next door.

Hôtel Vallée Blanche (☎ 04 50 53 04 50; www .vallee-blanche.com; 36 rue du Lyret; s/d/tr/q low season €58/68/84/96, high season €112/124/130) A candy pink exterior, green neon lights and a British red telephone box makes White Valley Hotel – a former 18th-century water mill – hard to miss. Inside, cosy rooms tout flower-painted wooden furniture and a young, snow- and drink-loving clientele who split their time between the ground-floor pub, O'Byrne's (p539), and the slopes.

Hôtel de l'Arve (☎ 04 50 53 02 31; www.hotelarve -chamonix.com; 60 impasse des Anémones; d low/mid/ high season from €58/74/83; ☒ mid-Dec–mid-Oct) The Arve is one of the last great family-run hotels left in Chamonix. Opened by cartwright Karl Knecht in the 1890s, the sweet chalet-hotel has gone through four generations to land in the hands of granddaughter Isabelle today. The best rooms look down the valley to Mont Blanc.

our pick **Hôtel Richemond** (☎ 04 50 53 08 85; www .richemond.fr; 228 rue du Docteur Paccard; s/d/tr/q low season €56/87/108/123, high season €64/102/130/145) The same family has run this ginger-shuttered hotel with wrought-iron balconies facing Mont Blanc since 1914. That's when the great great-grandparents of Madame Sarraz-Bournet (who runs it today with her father and brother) opened up for business one month before WWI shut the place down again. WWII saw the hotel taken over by the Gestapo (who painted a huge red cross on the roof of the building to avoid it getting bombed). English prisoners were kept on the 5th floor and Americans followed. Two-star rooms today reflect this colourful past. Most tout flower-power wallpaper, carpets of various lurid colours and other kitsch 1960s furnishings which just about get away with a hip 'retro' tag. Ski lockers in the basement command a €10 deposit and parking out the back is free (drive in from allée Recteur Payot).

TOP END
Hameau Albert 1er (☎ 04 50 53 05 64; www .hameaualbert.fr; 38 rte du Bouchet; d low/mid/high season from €115/130/150; ☐ ☒) Five generations

of Carriers have run this exquisite hotel – a hamlet of traditional Savoyard farms and wooden chalets bizarrely placed in the centre of town. Interiors are rustic and the futuristic swimming pool is a dream.

Grand Hôtel Les Alpes (☎ 04 50 55 37 80; www .grandhoteldesalpes.com; 89 rue du Docteur Paccard; d low/ high season from €150/300; ☒ mid-Dec–mid-Apr, mid-Jun–Sep; ☒ ☒ ☐) Dating from 1840, this grand old dame goes down in the chronicles of Chamonix history as one of the resort's first and finest. Pricier rooms face Mont Blanc while the *pièce de résistance* – a stunning lux-clad suite with dual Mont Blanc and Brévent view – resides up high like Sleeping Beauty in the post-WWI *ancienne tour* (old tower).

The Clubhouse (☎ 04 50 90 96 56; www.clubhouse .fr; 74 promenade des Sonnailles; d 3-nights full-board from €850; ☐ ☒ ; ☒ Dec-Sep) Provocatively decadent, the Clubhouse lures a moneyed set into its luxurious lair – Chamonix's only remaining Art Deco mansion dating from 1927. Seven quirky rooms scream design and Tuesday's lobster and steak snow BBQ is not to be missed. Members only (membership €150 valid until December 2007) and stays are restricted to three, four or six nights. All rates are full-board.

Eating

For a casual meal or something quick, try an après-ski hot spot (p538).

Le Panier des Quatre Saisons (☎ 04 50 53 98 77; 24 Galerie Blanc Neige; mains €15; ☒ dinner Thu, lunch

---

SKIER OF THE IMPOSSIBLE

L'Impossible (☎ 04 50 53 20 36; 9 chemin du Cry; lunch menu €20, dinner menus €24.50-29.50; ☒ lunch & dinner daily Dec-Apr, Jul & Aug) Impossibly irresistible, the Impossible is a barn dating back to 1754 near the Aiguille du Midi cable car that has been transformed into a rustic but modern eating space – lots of wood, wicker, warm lighting, gilded gold frames and glass chandeliers. Quail stuffed with foie gras, garlic butter–oozing snails or pineapple carpaccio with ginger and mango sorbet are quintessential French dishes cooked with a twist at this ode to Sylvain Saudan (b 1936), extreme-skiing pioneer and self-proclaimed 'skier of the impossible'.

A LOFTY LUNCH

Feast on fine fodder and even finer mountain views at these high-altitude favourites:

Grand Hôtel du Montenvers (☎ 04 50 53 87 70; 35 place de la Mer de Glace; menus €8-10, half-board per person dm/d €36.40/51.40, dm/d with half-board €36/51; ☿ mid-Jun–early Sep) Ride the red mountain train up to Montenvers and dine in Alpine splendour at the foot of the Alps' second-largest glacier. The place dates back to 1880.

Le 3842 (☎ 04 50 55 82 23; Aiguille du Midi; restaurant ☿ mid-Jun–mid-Sep, snack bar ☿ year-round) Simple summit dining, drinking or snacking at the top of the Aiguille du Midi in what claims to be Europe's highest café. It certainly feels like it.

La Crémerie du Glacier (☎ 04 50 54 07 52; 766 chemin de la Glacière; menus €10-23) In 1926 Georges Ravanel started selling drinks to hikers from a little wooden hut at the foot of the Argentière's glacier. In the 1950s his son added home-made tarts and croûtes aux fromages (chunky slices of toasted bread topped with melted cheese) to the repertoire, and by the 1980s when the next son took charge of the business La Crémerie – at a heady height of 1300m in Argentière – was known far and wide for its cheesy croûtes (€5 to €9.50), fondue and other Savoyard staples. It still is today. Ski to it with the red Pierre à Ric piste in Les Grands Montets.

Le Panoramic (☎ 04 50 53 44 11; Le Brévent; menus from €15; ☿ mid-Dec–Apr & Jun-Sep) Lunch on local cheese, cured meat and an incredible view of Mont Blanc in the company of a vin chaud (hot mulled wine) at this terrace restaurant next to Le Brévent cable-car station (2500m).

& dinner Fri-Tue Dec-May & mid-Jun–Oct) A firm favourite, the Basket of Four Seasons cooks up a veritable feast of season-driven, quintessentially French dishes. Reservations recommended.

Annapurna (☎ 04 50 55 81 39; 62 av Ravanel-le-Rouge; mains €15) Named after the 8000m-plus Himalayan mountain first summited by French Alpine climbers in 1950, Indian Annapurna does not disappoint. Cuisine is authentic, delicious and hot. All the regulars are here – biryani, tandoori etc – as well as more unusual dishes like curried lobster tail (€38).

Le Sanjon (☎ 04 50 53 56 44; 5 av Ravanel-le-Rouge; menus €16.90-24, fondue from €12.30) Colourfully painted portraits of fair maidens and lasses in Savoy fields around 1830 decorate the dark wood exterior of this picturesque chalet where the fare is cheesy, very cheesy.

La Calèche (☎ 04 50 55 94 68; 18 rue du Docteur Paccard; menus €21.50-26.50, raclette/fondue per person €22/14) One of many restaurants around place Balmat aimed squarely at undiscerning holidaymakers (a folk group sings every Tuesday evening), La Calèche appeals nonetheless. Décor is rustic, with several forests worth of wood on the walls and cheese by the dairy load. Traditional Alpine dishes like fondue and raclette are musts.

Le Bistrot (☎ 04 50 53 57 64; www.lebistrotchamonix .com; 151 av de l'Aiguille du Midi; lunch menu €15, evening menus €25-50; ☿ 9am-11pm) Mickie, as the Bistro's young champion chef is known, cooks up fine French food which – alongside a stunning wine cellar – will bowl over the most discerning of food and wine lovers.

Munchie (☎ 04 50 53 45 41; 87 rue des Moulins; mains €17-25; ☿ dinner Mon-Sun) Think fusion at this trendy hang-out with great pan-Asian food. Mains include blackened salmon sashimi, sushi, Thai blue crab soup and a couple of imaginative vegetarian dishes.

No Escape (☎ 04 50 93 80 65; www.noescape.fr; 27 rue de la Tour; mains €25; ☿ 3pm-2am) Antipasti, tapas and only the gourmet best – ravioli à la truffe (black truffle), king prawns, scallops etc – make the menu at this minimalist lounge-bar a change from the norm.

SELF-CATERING

A food market fills place du Mont Blanc on Saturday morning.

Le Refuge Payot (☎ 04 50 53 18 71; www.refuge payot.com; 166 rue Joseph Vallot) Local produce: cheese, smoked and air-dried meats, sausages, wine, honey etc.

Super U (117 rue Joseph Vallot) Supermarket.

Drinking

Chamonix nightlife rocks. In the centre, quaint old riverside rue des Moulins touts a line-up of drinking holes, including a trio of firm favourites damaged by fire in February 2006. Still cleaning up at the time of research, Cybar, Bar du Moulins and Dick's Tea Bar, all at No 80, have pledged it will be business as usual for the 2006–07 winter season. **Bar'd Up** (☎ 04 50 53 91 33; 123 rue des Moulins; ☽ 4.30pm-2am) and lounge bar **L'Expedition** (☎ 04 50 53 57 68; 26 rue des Moulins; ☽ 4pm-2am) are still going strong. Elsewhere, young 'n' fun **Bar Le Vagabond**, at Gîte Le Vagabond (p536), and Irish **O'Byrne's**, at Hôtel Vallée Blanche (p537), popular with an older Murphy-slurping crowd, are worth knowing. Online, check www.lepetitcanardchx.com.

All these après-ski joints serve grub alongside grog:

MBC (☎ 04 50 53 61 59; www.mbchx.com; 350 rte du Bouchet; ☽ 4pm-2am) This trendy microbrewery run by four Canadians is fab. Be it a burger, pint or live music you're after, it is a unique drinking and dining spot. Find it just off place du Mont Blanc, on the road to Les Praz and Argentière.

Le Jekyll (☎ 04 50 55 99 70; www.thejekyll.com; 78 rte des Pélerins; ☽ 4pm-2am Mon-Fri, 11am-2am Sat & Sun) Fill up on BBQ ribs, Irish lamb and Guinness stew washed down with a pint of Murphy's at Chamonix's Irish pub – or descend to the cellar for a shot with Hyde. Happy hour is 8pm to 10pm, DJs and live bands play 'til late and Sunday breakfast/roast (€10/14) is a hit.

Goophy (☎ 04 50 55 53 42; 239 av Michel Croz; ☽ 4.30pm-2am) Goophy by name, goophy by nature at this large pub-style space with wooden floor, high ceilings and a bounty of merrymaking punters near the train station. Those who never quite make it back to their chalet can enjoy surprisingly tasty food – spare ribs with BBQ sauce, blackened chicken filet, a cheese and bacon Goophy burger and so on – from 7pm to 11pm.

Elevation 1904 (☎ 04 50 53 00 52; 259 av Michel Croz; ☽ 7-2am) Another merry bet by the train station, this is a small smoky joint with indestructible stone floor, wood panelling

and an Anglophone staff rushed off its feet day and night serving breakfast, burgers and well-stuffed *panini*.

Chambre Neuf (☎ 04 50 55 89 81; 272 av Michel Croz; ☽ 7am-2am) Drink two cocktails for the price of one between 8pm and 10pm at Room 9. Live bands play some nights, otherwise it's hip hanging at candle-lit bar seating. Food is limited but creative (crayfish soup, veggie chang mai etc).

La Terrasse (☎ 04 50 53 09 95; www.laterrassechamonix.com; 43 place Balmat; ☽ 4pm-1am) The street terrace buzzes at this two-floor bar and dance venue, with live music, shooters and bar snacks such as chicken wings, nachos, onion rings etc to munch.

Poco Loco (☎ 04 50 53 43 03; 47 rue du Docteur Paccard; ☽ 11am-2am) Chip-eating punters love this grungy café-bar – a takeaway counter downstairs and five-odd tables topped by a ceiling of corrugated iron. Well-stuffed toasted sandwiches (large round baps in fact) are served in a brown paper bag.

Le Tof (☎ 04 50 53 45 28; 58 place Edmond Desailloud) Chamonix's gay scene struts its stuff in Chamonix's only wholly gay bar and disco. Sip aperitifs, munch tapas and dance to house, new wave and retro in a trendy lounge atmosphere.

Le Office (☎ 04 50 54 15 46; www.officebar.net; 274 rue Charlet Stratton, Argentière; ☽ 3pm-late) In Argentière, Le Office, with its resident DJs, Sunday roasts, pool tables and live sport, is the hot place to hang.

See also below.

Entertainment
NIGHTCLUBS
Le Garage (☎ 04 50 53 64 49; 200 av de l'Aiguille du Midi; ☽ midnight-4am) Club-'n'-dance-wise, there's this cheesy disco down an alleyway off av Michel Croz.

CULINARY HIGHS

Chalk and cheese, yes, but these two Megève favourites are definite culinary highs:

L'Igloo (☎ 04 50 93 05 84; www.ligloo.com; 3120 rte du Crêt; mains €5-15; ☽ lunch & dinner mid-Jun–mid-Sep & mid-Dec–mid-Apr) Feast on a fiesta of incredible Mont Blanc mountain views at this high-altitude eating joint plump on the top of Mont d'Arbois (1833m). Ski here or ride the Télécabine du Mont d'Arbois. In summer the Igloo has an open-air swimming pool.

La Ferme de Mon Père (☎ 04 50 21 01 01; www.marc-veyrat.com; 367 rte du Crêt; mains from €70; ☽ lunch & dinner mid-Dec–mid-Apr) Dining here is sky-high – think €295 for the cheapest set menu – but the astonishingly creative and decadent dishes created by top chef Marc Veyrat at this strictly winter hide-out take taste buds to truly new heights.

Cantina Club (☎ 04 50 53 83 80; www.cantina.fr; 37 impasse des Rhododendrons; ☼ 7pm-2am) Deep house, afrobeat, drum & bass, breakbeat and hip hop are the varied DJ sounds pumped out at this happening bar-cum-club that cooks up Tex-Mex food from 7pm. Live bands make it Chamonix's prime concert venue.

BPM (☎ 06 70 63 64 88; 269 rue du Docteur Paccard; ☼ 11pm-4am) The most recent nightclub to open its doors in dance-mad Chamonix, BPM is glam and glitzy. It is at the end of the passage next to Rip Curl.

CINEMA
Films are shown in English at **3 Cinémas** (☎ 04 50 55 89 98; cour du Bartavel; adult/student €7/5.80). Check out the programme at www .chamonix.com.

Getting There & Away
BUS
From **Chamonix bus station** (☎ 04 50 53 07 02; www.altibus.com; ☼ 6.45-10.30am & 1.25-4.45pm Mon-Fri, 6.45-11am Sat & Sun), located at the train station, there are buses travelling to/from Geneva airport and bus station (www.sat montblanc.com; one way/return €34/55, 1½ to 2¼ hours, three daily) and Courmayeur (one way/return €10/18, three daily).

CAR
Approaching Chamonix from Italy, you arrive via the 11.6km-long **Tunnel de Mont Blanc** (Mont Blanc Tunnel; www.atmb.net; car one way/ return €31.20/38.90), which enters town in the southern suburb of Les Pélerins. From France, the A40 motorway – the **Autoroute Blanche** – hooks up with the Chamonix-bound N205, dual carriageway for the last leg.

Parking in town can be tricky although **Parking du Mont-Blanc** (place du Mont Blanc; 1st hour free then per hour/week €1/32) is a reliable car park. Other car parks are scattered along rte du Bouchet, around rue des Allobroges and in Chamonix Sud. Another option: park outside town and connect by bus or train; contact **Chamonix Parc-Auto** (☎ 04 50 53 65 71).

Car rental companies:
Chamonix Autoloc-Hertz (☎ 04 50 53 73 68; 11 av du Savoy)
Europcar (☎ 04 50 53 63 40; 36 place de la Gare)

TRAIN
From Chamonix-Mont Blanc **train station** (☎ 04 50 53 12 98; place de la Gare) the **Mont Blanc Express** narrow-gauge train trundles between St-Gervais-le Fayet, 23km west of Chamonix, to Martigny, 42km northeast of Chamonix in Switzerland, stopping en route in Les Houches, Chamonix and Argentière. There are nine to 12 return trips a day and a one-way/return Chamonix–St-Gervais fare is €9 (40 minutes).

From St-Gervais-le Fayet, there are trains to most major French cities; see opposite.

Getting Around
BICYCLE
June to September, **Le Grand Bi Cycles** (☎ 04 50 53 14 16; 240 av du Bois du Bouchet; ☼ 9am-7pm Jul & Aug, 9am-7pm Tue-Sat Jun & Sep) and **Trajectoire** (☎ 04 50 53 18 95; 91 av Ravanel-le-Rouge) rent bikes for €10 to €15 a day.

BUS
Local bus transport is handled by **Chamonix Bus** (☎ 04 50 53 05 55; chamonixbus@transdev.fr; 591 promenade Marie-Paradis; ☼ 7am-7pm winter, 8am-noon & 2-7pm Jun-Aug).

Mid-December to the end of April numerous lines to the ski lifts and central car parks depart every 10 minutes or so between 7am and 7pm (town centre shuttles 8.30am to 6.30pm). Buses are free for ski-pass holders (otherwise one-way ticket €1.50) with the exception of the Chamo-Nuit night buses linking Chamonix with Argentière and Les Houches (last departures from Chamonix 11.30pm or midnight; €2).

TAXI
There's a **taxi stand** (☎ 04 50 53 13 94) outside the train station. Minibuses for two to eight people are available from **Chamonix Transfer** (☎ 06 07 67 88 85, 06 62 05 57 38; www.chamonix-trans fer.com in French).

MEGÈVE & ST-GERVAIS
It looks like Christmas all winter in sweet **Megève** (pop 4700, elevation 1113m), a chic ski village developed in the 1920s for a French baroness following her disillusionment with Switzerland's crowded St-Moritz. It's straight out of a fairy tale, with horse-drawn sleds and exquisitely arranged boutique windows filling its medieval-

style streets and chapels tracing the Stations of the Cross in baroque, rococo and Tuscan-style woodcarvings on its eastern outskirts.

Sitting snug below Mont Blanc, 36km southwest of Chamonix, Megève's neighbour is **St-Gervais** (pop 5400, elevation 810m), another picture-postcard winter and summer resort linked to Chamonix by the legendary *Mont Blanc Express*.

Information

Megève Tourist Office (☎ 04 50 21 27 28; www.me geve.com; 70 rue de Monseigneur Conseil; ☒ 9am-7pm mid-Dec–mid-Apr, Jul & Aug, 9am-12.30pm & 2-6.30pm Mon-Sat Sep–mid-Dec & mid-Apr–Jun)
St-Gervais Tourist Office (☎ 04 50 47 76 08; www .st-gervais.com; 115 av Mont Paccard; ☒ 9am-noon & 2.30-7.30pm mid-Dec–mid-Apr, Jul & Aug, 9am-noon & 2-6pm Sep–mid-Dec & mid-Apr–Jun)

Activities

Skiing is the winter biggie, Megève downhill being split into three separate areas: Mont d'Arbois-Princesse (linked to St-Gervais), Jaillet-Combloux and Rochebrune-Côte 2000. Ski passes for the 445km of piste served by 111 lifts are sold online at **SAEM** (www.skiamegeve.com in French); a one-/six-day pass covering the entire area costs €33/159 but cheaper passes valid for one area are available.

Megève's **ESF** (☎ 04 50 21 00 97; www.megeve -ski.com) and **Compagnie des Guides et Accompagnateurs** (☎ 04 50 21 55 11; www.guidesmegeve.com) are inside the **Maison de la Montagne** (176 rue de la Poste). The latter organises off-piste skiing, heliskiing, ice climbing, rock climbing and paragliding.

Summer hiking trails in the Bettex, Mont d'Arbois and Mont Joly areas are accessible from both villages. Mountain biking is also popular; some of the best terrain is found along marked trails between Val d'Arly, Mont Blanc and Beaufortain. **Accro'bike** (☎ 04 50 47 76 77; 78 impasse Bédière) in St-Gervais runs guided biking expeditions (from €30).

For staggering mountain views with no legwork, hop aboard France's highest train. The **Tramway du Mont Blanc** (☎ 04 50 47 51 83; rue de la Gare; adult/12-15yr/4-11yr/family return €17/14.50/11.90/51; ☒ mid-Dec–mid-Apr, Jul & Aug) has laboured up to Bellevue (1800m) from St-Gervais-le Fayet in winter and further up

to the Nid d'Aigle (Eagle's Nest) at 2380m in summer since 1913.

Sleeping & Eating

Both tourist offices run an **accommodation service** (Megève ☎ 04 50 21 29 52; reservation@megeve .com; St-Gervais ☎ 04 50 93 53 63).

Alp Hôtel (☎ 04 50 21 07 58; www.alp-hotel.fr; 434 rte de Rochebrune; d €53-85) This two-star chalet with 20 rustic rooms near the Rochebrune cable car is the cheapest you'll get in pricey Megève. Count another €7.25 for a wholesome *petit déjeuner* (breakfast) each morning.

Au Coeur de Megève (☎ 04 50 21 25 30; www .hotel-megeve.com; 44 rue Charles Feige; d mid-/high winter season from €139/155, Jul & Aug from €92) Bang-slap in pedestrian Megève, this three-generation family affair doesn't disappoint. Delightful rooms with flower-bedecked balconies peep out on the traditional bustle of the central square, place du Village.

Les Fermes de Marie (☎ 04 50 93 03 10; www .fermesdemarie.com; chemin de Riante Colline; d low/mid-/ high season from €140/174/318, ☒ mid-Dec–mid-Apr, Jul & Aug; ☐ ☒) One of the most renowned Alpine spa-resorts, this gorgeous nine-chalet hamlet oozes opulence. Hotel rooms are of the pillows-piled-up variety and a trio of restaurants – formal dining room, *rôtisserie* specialising in roast meats, and fondue-driven bistro – pleases the most demanding of palates.

Getting There & Away

From **Megève bus station** (☎ 04 50 21 25 18), on the right as you enter town via the N212, there are four daily buses to/from Chamonix (€9, 55 minutes) and seven daily to/from St-Gervais-le Fayet and Sallanches train stations; all buses stop in St-Gervais en route. In winter, airport shuttles run five times daily to/from Geneva airport (one way/return €38/65, 1½ hours) from both villages.

The closest train station to Megève is in Sallanches, 12km north; for train information in Megève go to the **SNCF office** (☎ 04 50 21 23 42) inside the bus station.

St-Gervais is the main train station for Chamonix and is linked to the latter by the legendary **Mont Blanc Express** (opposite). Services to/from St-Gervais include several day and one night train to/from Paris Austerlitz (€81.30 to €88.30, six to seven hours; overnight train €87.80, 9½ hours), Lyon (€33.50, four hours), Annecy (€18.20, 1½hours), Geneva (€16.80, 2½ hours via La Roche-sur-Foron), and Grenoble (€29, five hours via Aix-les-Bains).

LES PORTES DU SOLEIL

Poetically dubbed 'the Gates of the Sun' (elevation 1000–2466m; www.portesduso leil.com), this gargantuan ski area – the world's largest – is formed from a chain of villages strung along the French–Swiss border. Some 650km of downhill slopes and cross-country trails crisscross it, served by 209 ski lifts covered by a single ski pass, or a cheaper more-restricted pass valid for one pocket. In spring and summer mountain-bike enthusiasts revel in 380km of invigorating biking trails, including the 100km-long circular Portes du Soleil tour.

Morzine (pop 3000, elevation 1000m) – the best-known of the 14 interconnected ski resorts – retains a smidgen of traditional Alpine village atmosphere. It's frantically busy in winter but summer sees the pace slow as enchanting visits to Alpine cheese dairies and traditional slate workshops kick in. For local know-how on summer activities – hiking, biking, climbing, canyoning and paragliding – contact the **Bureau des Guides** (☎ 04 50 75 96 65; www.bureaudesguides.net), which can advise on mountain-bike hire and Morzine's heart-stopping 3300m-long **bike descent** (free; ☼ Jun-Sep) from the top of the Pleney cable car (one/10 ascents €4.10/35). Accommodation can be booked through **Morzine Réservation** (☎ 04 50 79 11 57; www.resa-morzine.com) inside the **tourist office** (☎ 04 50 74 72 72; www.morzine-avoriaz.com; place de la Crusaz).

ourpick The Farmhouse (☎ 04 50 79 08 26; www.thefarmhouse.co.uk; Morzine; d with breakfast from €100-240, dinner €40) is well known to everyone in Morzine, not least for its vibrant candle-lit *raclette* evenings thrown around a huge shared table and its superb location in a 1771 farmhouse – Morzine's oldest and loveliest building, run with unfailing flair and fun for the past 11-odd years by the charming Dorrien Ricardo. Otherwise known as 'le vieux château' (the old castle) or Mas de la Coutettaz, the Farmhouse is your quintessential wood-beamed manor house. Five rooms (including the ro-

mantic Blue Room with canopy bed and Victorian-style bathroom overlooking Morzine's main square, and the Cell which was indeed, once upon a time, Morzine's only prison cell) are in the main house and a trio of cottages (including the old *mazot*, or miniature mountain chalet, where the family bible and deeds of the house would have been stored) sit in the lovely grounds. Dining – open to non-guests too and strictly around one huge long table – is a lavish affair and very much an experience in itself.

Chic but small **Avoriaz** (elevation 1800m), purpose-built a few kilometres up the valley atop a rock, appeals for its no-cars policy. Horse-drawn sleighs piled high with luggage romantically ferry new arrivals – wealthy families in the main – to/ from the snowy village centre where wacky 1960s mimetic architecture gets away with an 'avant-garde' tag. The place is so hip in fact that French chef Christophe Leroy has moved here, creating an Alpine equivalent of his St-Tropez restaurant with La Table du Marché inside **Hôtel des Dromonts** (☎ 04 94 97 91 91; www.christophe-leroy.com in French; place des Dromonts; d with half-board from €230). Outside, the funky three-star spa hotel looks like something from the Smurfs.

With just three other hotels, accommodation in Avoriaz is limited to self-catering studios and apartments, which can be booked through the **tourist office** (☎ 04 50 74 02 11; www.avoriaz.com; place Centrale). Motorists unload in bays next to the office but must park in car parks (per day/week €12.50/76) a short walk away.

Arriving by road via Cluses you hit **Les Gets** (pop 1300, elevation 1172m) – way less pretentious than Morzine and Avoriaz and a good deal for those looking to surf the same slopes but save a bob. Its **tourist office** (☎ 04 50 75 80 80; www.lesgets.com; place de la Mairie) and **accommodation service** (☎ 04 50 75 80 51; reservations@lesgets.com) in the same building can point you in the right direction. For ski-pass information see www.sagets.fr.

Should scrimping not be your cup of tea, check into spa-clad **Ferme de Montagne** (☎ 04 50 75 36 79; www.fermedemontagne.com; full board €1500-2800 per person a week; ☼ Jun-Sep & Nov-Apr), a five-star Savoyard farmhouse labelled one of Europe's top boutique ski hotels by glossy-mag critics.

Getting There & Away

Free shuttle buses serve the lifts of Télécabine Super Morzine, Télécabine du Pléney and Téléphérique Avoriaz.

During the ski season, Morzine (one way/return €32.50/54), Avoriaz (one way/return €36/61.50) and Les Gets (one way/return €29.50/50) are linked by bus to Geneva airport, 50km-odd west. From Morzine there are regular **SAT buses** (☎ 04 50 79 15 69) to Les Gets and Avoriaz. There are also buses from Morzine to its closest train stations: Thonon-les-Bains (34km north) and Cluses (31km south).

THONON-LES-BAINS

pop 30,000 / elevation 430m

Just across the water from the Swiss city of Lausanne on the French side of Lake Geneva (Lac Léman), Thonon-les-Bains – a fashionable spa town during the *Belle Époque* – sits on a bluff above the lake. Winter is deathly dull, but its summer lake cruises and lakeside strolls appeal.

A 230m-long **funicular railway** (☎ 04 50 71 21 54; one way/return €1/1.80; ☼ 8am-9pm Sep-Jun, 8am-11pm Jul & Aug) links the upper town and **tourist office** (☎ 04 50 71 55 55; www.thononlesbains .com; place du Marché; ☼ 9am-12.30pm & 1.30-6.30pm Mon-Fri, 10am-12.30pm & 1.30-6.30pm Sat Sep-Jun, 9am-7pm Mon-Fri, 10am-7pm Sat Jul & Aug) with the marina. Buy boat tickets (www.cgn.ch) at the lakeside **tourist office chalet** (☎ 04 50 26 19 94; ☼ 10am-12.30pm & 2-6.30pm Jul & Aug) here.

Château de Ripaille (☎ 04 50 26 64 44; www .ripaille.fr in French; 1hr guided tour €6; 1-5 tours Feb-Nov; forest ☼ 10am-7pm Tue-Sun May-Sep, 10am-4.30pm Tue-Sun Oct-Apr), 1km east along quai de Ripaille, is a turreted castle rebuilt in the 19th century on the site of its 15th-century ancestor. It has vineyards, a garden for summer dining (mid-June to mid-September) and forested grounds to explore.

Sleeping-wise, garden-clad **Hôtel à l'Ombre des Marronniers** (☎ 04 50 71 26 18; www.hotellesmar ronniers.com in French; 17 place de Crète; d from €50) is an in-town option, but out-of-town **La Ferme du Château** (☎ 04 50 26 46 68; www.lafermeduchateau .com; Hameau de Maugny; d €60-80; ✗ ▣), 10km inland in Draillant, is way more charming. Sophie and Didier run the *chambre d'hôte* in a renovated 18th-century stone Savoyard

---

TAKING THE WATERS

Trot 9km east from Thonon along Europe's largest Alpine lake and you hit **Évian-les-Bains** (pop 7500), the spa town from which that world-famous mineral water originates. Dubbed the 'Pearl of Lake Geneva', lakeside Évian was a favourite country retreat of the dukes of Savoy, was razed during the Wars of Religion and reinvented as a luxury spa resort in the 18th century when wallowing in tubs of mineral water was all the rage. Wallowing in a tub of Évian can still be done, although it is the bottled mineral water that accounts for the biggest chunk of the town's economy. The water takes 15 years to trickle down through the Chablais mountains, gathering minerals en route, before emerging at a constant temperature of 11.4°C (52.8°F). It was 'discovered' in 1790 and has been bottled since 1826.

In Évian's heyday, punters taking the waters would ride a funicular railway from whichever grand hotel they were staying in to the **thermal pump room** (19 rue Nationale) – a fantastic Art Nouveau structure today housing the information centre of mineral water company Eaux Minérales Évian (www.evian.fr) – and on to the famous thermal baths, housed in the stunning Palais Lumière from 1902 until 1984. The train now chauffeurs tourists along the same route. Of the many springs built around town, the **Cachet Spring** (av des Sources), dating back to 1902, is the most guzzled.

Tours (☎ 04 50 26 93 23, 04 50 26 80 29; visits-usine-evian@danone.com; admission free, transport €1.70; ☼ mid-Jun–Sep) of the Évian bottling plant, on an industrial estate 5km out of town, can be arranged through the factory. The **tourist office** (☎ 04 50 75 04 26; www.eviantourism.com; place d'Allinges) can also help.

Decidedly more glamorous and designed (like the mineral water) to suit all tastes are **Les Thermes Evian** (☎ 04 50 75 02 30; www.lesthermesevian.com; place de la Libération; ☼ Mon-Sat) – the town's state-of-the art thermal spa where visitors to Évian, as in the old days, take the waters in a mind-boggling orgy of slimming, detox, de-stress, rebirth, youth, hydro-Zen and beat-the-blues body treatments.

FRENCH ALPS & THE JURA

farm and cook up excellent evening meals (€22 with wine).

From **Thonon bus station** (11 av Jules Ferry), SAT (☎ 04 50 71 00 88) runs regular buses to/from Évian (€2, 15 minutes) and into the Chablais Mountains, including to Morzine. The **train station** (place de la Gare) is southwest of place des Arts, the main square. Trains run to/from Geneva (€6.60, one hour) via Annemase (€5.30, 25 minutes).

ANNECY

pop 50,000 / elevation 448m

Chic Haute-Savoie capital Annecy is perfect for a good old mosey. Nestled around the northwestern end of Lake Annecy against a pretty backdrop of Alpine peaks, the town is crisscrossed by ancient canals, geranium-covered bridges, medieval houses and arched alleyways perfect for meandering. A cycling path snakes along the lake's southwestern shore and pedalos, canoes and cruise-boats pepper its water in summer.

This is *the* hot spot to kick back and relax after the high-altitude and attitude-fuelled Alpine resorts – except in summer when bumper-to-bumper traffic makes it a tad taxing.

Orientation

The train and bus stations are 500m northwest of Vieil Annecy, also called the Vieille Ville (Old Town), which is huddled around the River Thiou (split into Canal du Thiou to the south and Canal du Vassé to the north). The town centre is between the post office and the purpose-built Centre Bonlieu, near the shores of Lake Annecy.

Annecy-le-Vieux, a primarily residential quarter not to be confused with Vieil Annecy, straddles the lake's north.

Information

EMERGENCY

Hospital (☎ 04 50 88 33 33; 1 av de Trésum)
Police Station (☎ 04 50 52 32 00; 15 rue des Marquisats)

INTERNET ACCESS

The post office has Cyberposte.
Internet – Red Sector Café (☎ 04 50 45 39 75; 3bis av de Chevène; per 15min/hr €1/4; 10am-7pm Fri-Wed)

Larache Télécom (☎ 04 50 33 08 95; 3 rue de l'Industrie; per 15min/hr €1/3; 9am-10pm)

LAUNDRY

Lav'Confort Express (6 rue de la Gare; 7am-9pm)

MONEY

Crédit Lyonnais (1 rue Jean Jaurès, Centre Bonlieu)

POST

Post Office (4bis rue des Glières)

TOURIST INFORMATION

Tourist Office (☎ 04 50 45 00 33; www.lac-annecy .com; 1 rue Jean Jaurès, Centre Bonlieu; 9am-12.30pm & 1.45-6pm Mon-Sat mid-Sep–mid-May, 9am-6.30pm Mon-Sat mid-May–mid-Sep, Sun Mar-Oct)

Sights & Activities

Wandering around the Vieille Ville and lakefront are the essence of Annecy. Just east, behind the town hall, are the **Jardins de l'Europe**, linked to popular park **Champ de Mars** by the poetic iron arch of **Pont des Amours** (Lovers' Bridge).

VIEILLE VILLE

A warren of narrow streets and colonnaded passageways, the old town retains much of its 17th-century appearance. On the central island, imposing **Palais de l'Isle** (☎ 04 50 33 87 31; 3 passage de l'Île; adult/student/under 12yr €3.20/1.20/ free, free 1st Sun of month Oct-May; 10.30am-6pm Jun-Sep, 10am-noon & 2-5pm Wed-Mon Oct-May) was a prison, but now hosts local-history displays. A combined ticket covering palace and castle (below) costs €6.

CHÂTEAU D'ANNECY

In the 13th- to 16th-century castle above town, the **Musée Château** (☎ 04 50 33 87 30; adult/student/under 12yr €4.70/2/free; 10.30am-6pm Jun-Sep, 10am-noon & 2-5pm Wed-Mon Oct-May) explores traditional Savoyard art, crafts and Alpine natural history.

SUNBATHING & SWIMMING

Parks and grassy areas in which to picnic and sunbathe line the lakefront. Public beach **Plage d'Annecy-le-Vieux** (admission free; Jul & Aug) is 1km east of Champ de Mars. Closer to town, privately run **Plage Impérial** (admission €3; Jul & Aug) slumbers in the shade of the elegant pre-WWI **Impérial Palace**.

ANNECY

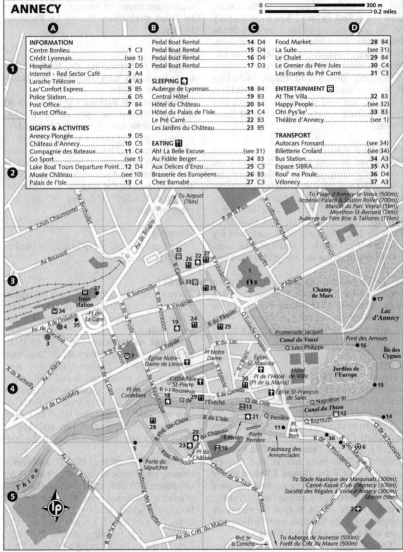

Plage des Marquisats (admission free; [Jul & Aug) is 1km south of the Vieille Ville along rue des Marquisats. Located next door is a water-sports centre, the **Stade Nautique des Marquisats** (04 50 45 39 18; 29 rue des Marquisats), which sports three outdoor swimming pools.

WALKING

A fine stroll goes from the Jardins de l'Europe along quai Bayreuth and quai de la Tournette to the Stade Nautique des Marquisats and beyond. Another excellent walk begins at Champ de Mars and meanders eastwards around the lake towards Annecy-le-Vieux.

Forêt du Crêt du Maure, south of Annecy, has many walking trails, as do the nature reserves of **Bout du Lac** (20km from Annecy on the southern tip of the lake) and **Roc de Chère** (10km from town on the eastern shore of the lake); Voyages Crolard buses (see Billetterie Crolard, p548) serve both.

Walking guides and maps, including IGN's excellent *Lac d'Annecy* (No 3431OT; 1:25,000), are sold at the tourist office and neighbouring sports shop, **Go Sport** (Centre Bonlieu).

CYCLING & BLADING

Biking and blading are big, thanks to the two-way cycling track – equally popular with rollerbladers – that starts in Annecy-le-Vieux and follows the entire western shore *(rive ouest)* of the lake for 20km through Sevrier, St-Joriaz and Duingt to Bout du Lac. The path then continues for another 10km south to Marlens. The tourist office and rental outlets (p548) have free maps.

The Friday-evening jaunts around town organised by local rollerblading club **Roll 'n Cy** (☎ 06 76 73 47 12; www.roll-n-cy.org in French; ☼ 8pm Fri Mar–mid-Dec) are fun, free and open to anyone on rollerblades. The club meets on place de la Mairie.

WATER SPORTS

Late March to late October, pedal boats and small motorboats can be hired at several points along the quays of the Canal du Thiou and Canal du Vassé.

June to September the **Stade Nautique des Marquisats** (31 rue des Marquisats) is an aquatic-activity hub: the **Canoë-Kayak Club d'Annecy** (☎ 04 50 45 03 98) rents kayaks and canoes; and the **Société des Régates à Voile d'Annecy** (SRVA; ☎ 04 50 45 48 39; 31 rue des Marquisats; sailing boat hire per 2hr €40) rents sailing boats. Nearby, **Annecy Plongée** (☎ 04 50 45 40 97; www.annecy plongee.com; 6 rue des Marquisats) rents/sells diving gear and arranges baptism dives.

On the other side of the lake, Station Roller (p548) also rents kayaks (per hour/day €5/20).

Festivals & Events

Highlights include a **Venetian carnival** in March, fireworks over the lake in August during the **Fête du Lac**, and **Le Retour des Alpages**, a street festival celebrating Savoyard traditions and folklore in October. The night-time streets of Annecy are taken over by street performers during **Les Noctibules** in July.

Tours

Mid-June to September, the tourist office organises **guided tours** (adult/under 12yr €5.50/free) of the Vieille Ville.

Compagnie des Bateaux (☎ 04 50 51 08 40; www.annecy-croisieres.com; 2 place aux Bois; 1/2hr lake cruise adult €10.90/13.30; ☼ mid-Mar–Oct) runs lake cruises departing from Canal du Thiou on quai Bayreuth. Tickets are sold 15 minutes before departure at blue wooden huts on the lakeside. April to September boats also sail across the lake to Menthon-St-Bernard (€4.30), Talloires (€5.30) and other villages.

Sleeping

In July and August cheap hotels are hard to find; book in advance.

BUDGET

There are several camp sites near the lake in Annecy-le-Vieux and a handful of *chambres d'hôtes* around the lake; the tourist office has details.

Auberge de Jeunesse (☎ 04 50 45 33 19; annecy@fuaj.org; 4 rte du Semnoz; dm €17.30; reception ☼ 8am-12.30pm & 1.30-10pm mid-Jan–Nov) Annecy's smart wood-clad hostel with plain décor, large picture windows and modern furnishings sits south of town in Forêt du Semnoz. Take bus 6 to the 'Hôtel de Police' stop and walk 1km or, in July and August only, take a Semnoz-bound bus to the hostel door.

Central Hôtel (☎ 04 50 45 05 37; www.hotelcen tralannecy.com in French; 6bis rue Royale; d/tr €33/47, d/tr with shower €38/52, d/tr/q with shower & toilet €43/57/64) Madame Parel has run this century-old hotel in a quiet, shabby courtyard since 1988. It's very much a homely affair, with Bouba the dog padding around the place. Four of the 16 rooms enjoy a table-clad balcony overhanging the canal (ask for room 8, 9, 14 or 15). Stick a pin in your country of origin on the map in the breakfast room before leaving.

Auberge du Lyonnais (☎ 04 50 51 26 10; 9 rue de la République; s/d €40/50, with shower & toilet €55/70, menu €28.50) This traditional nine-room hotel-restaurant is ideal for a quintessential taste of Vieil Annecy. Idyllically set astride the canal, the inn is old, quaint and as recommended a place to eat as sleep.

MIDRANGE & TOP END

Hôtel du Château (☎ 04 50 45 27 66; www.an necy-hotel.com; 16 rampe du Château; s/d/tr/q Oct-Apr €49/60/69/79, May-Sep €49/99/71/81) Just below one of the towers of the chateau, this hilltop hotel is hard to beat for its serene view over Annecy's lantern-lit lanes. Rooms are small, beige and have seen better days.

Les Jardins du Château (☎ 04 50 45 72 28; jardinduchateau@wanadoo.fr; 1 place du Château; d €64-95, tr/q €90/120) It's impossible to miss this big period house next door to Hôtel du Château thanks to the oversized B&B sign it sports. Location is everything for this *chambre d'hôte* – the only one of its type in Annecy to boot. Oddly, breakfast (included in the rates) is only served June to September.

Hôtel du Palais de L'Isle (☎ 04 50 45 86 87; www .hoteldupalaisdelisle.com; 13 rue Perrière; s/d from €62/76; ▨) Guests slumber in the heart of old-town action at this 18th-century house where the crisp contemporary décor is an oasis of peace after the tourist mayhem outside. The best rooms peek out onto the canal and Palais de l'Isle.

Le Pré Carré (☎ 04 50 52 14 14; www.hotel-annecy .net; 27 rue Sommeiller; s/d €125/135; ▨) Very designled, the contemporary interior of this modern four-star hotel makes a refreshing change from the older norm. Service is predictably impeccable and the sauna a dream. Internet costs €8 an hour.

Eating

The quays along both sides of Canal du Thiou in the Vieille Ville are jam-packed with touristy cafés and restaurants. Cheap places dot pedestrian rue du Pâquier.

Chez Barnabé (☎ 04 50 45 90 62; 29 rue Sommeiller; mains €3.40; ◷ 10am-7pm Mon-Sat) Cartoons on the walls set the tone of this trendy and innovative quick-eat joint where healthier-than-healthy 'fast food' – salads, hot dishes, fresh juices, cookies and so on – is religiously baked on the premises. Vegetarians and non–pork-eaters are well catered for.

Au Fidèle Berger (☎ 04 50 45 00 32; 2 rue Royale; ◷ 9.15am-7pm Tue-Fri, 9am-7.30pm Sat) This traditional tearoom and cake shop with a fantastic old-world feel is the spot for a sweet breakfast (€7.50), cakes and chocolates. Look for the old wood panelling façade.

Aux Delices d'Enzo (☎ 04 50 45 35 36; 17 rue du Pâquier; mains €10; ◷ lunch & dinner) What you see is what you get at this typically French restaurant-bar where the menu is handwritten and the Italian pasta home-made. Find it tucked under the arched colonnades of rue du Pâquier.

Ah! La Belle Excuse (☎ 04 50 51 20 05; cour du Pré Carré, 10 rue Vaugelas; mains €10-15; ◷ lunch & dinner Mon-Sat) Ah! The Beautiful Excuse is a funky, red and green wood-clad bistro with a cosy retro interior and unbeatable wooden-decking summer terrace. What's more, the ensemble sits in an attractive interior courtyard. Grilled meats, salads and *parmentiers* (mashed potato baked with different toppings) are menu mainstays.

Les Écuries du Pré Carré (☎ 04 50 45 59 14; cour du Pré Carré, 10 rue Vaugelas; menus €13.90 & €18.90; ◷ lunch & dinner) In the same charming courtyard, the Stables ooze theatre. Cuisine is imaginative, as is the décor – a mix of wood, '70s retro and glasses that don't match. Upstairs, **La Suite** – billowing white cloth, leather armchairs and

---

LAKESIDE LEGENDS

Dining à la lakeside legend requires a certain amount of nous and loads of dosh.

La Maison de Marc Veyrat (☎ 04 50 60 24 00; www.marcveyrat.fr; 13 vieille rte des Pensières; d €300-670; menus €290 & €380; ◷ late May–early Nov) Small fortune needed aside, snagging a table is tough at Marc Veyrat's lakeside 'Maison Bleue', a powder-blue house with a handful of extraordinary hotel rooms up top, 1km east of the centre. Cuisine is highly creative and flamboyant – very much 'once-tried-never-forgotten' calibre. Come winter Veyrat moves to Megève (p539).

Auberge du Père Bise (☎ 04 50 60 72 01; www.perebise.com; rte du Port, Talloires; d from €300; menus €80, €125 & €185) The other big name on Lake Annecy's chic shores, this one is substantially more affordable in the form of a fab Sunday brunch worth-every-last-cent feast. It's run by four generations of Bise since 1901; female chef Sophie Bise currently heads up the kitchen.

pink lighting – is evening only; last orders are at midnight.

Le Grenier du Père Jules (☎ 04 50 45 41 18; www .restaurant-chez-le-pere-jules.com in French; 11 rue Grenette; menus €11.50, €15.50 & €21; ⏰ lunch & dinner) Checked tablecloths, mountain-dried sausages hung up to dry and a menu heaving with diet-busting dishes like fondue, *tartiflette* (sliced potatoes oven-baked in cream and *reblochon* cheese) and other cheese-heavy Savoyard dishes create an overwhelmingly rustic atmosphere at Father Jules' busy attic.

Brasserie des Européens (☎ 04 50 51 30 70; 23 rue Sommeiller; mains €15-20; ⏰ lunch & dinner) This popular brasserie with a 1920s ambience is known for the mountains of mussels it cooks up, not to mention seasonal oysters, seafood platters (climaxing with a *plateau royale* for four at €180) and 10 types of tartare.

Le Chalet (☎ 04 50 51 82 55; www.restaurant -lechalet.com; quai de l'Evêché; menus €16, €26 & €50; ⏰ lunch & dinner Tue-Sat, lunch Sun) Well on the tourist trail it might be, but this waterside restaurant decked out to resemble a cosy old Savoyard chalet (think wood everywhere) does have a certain charm. Cuisine is cheese-fuelled.

SELF-CATERING
In the Vieille Ville, there is a **food market** (rue Faubourg Ste-Claire; ⏰ 8am-noon Sun, Tue & Fri).

Entertainment
Théâtre d'Annecy (☎ 04 50 33 44 11; www.bonlieu-an necy.com in French; Centre Bonlieu) is the main stage in Annecy for theatre.

Hip lounge bars worth a glug 'n jive include DJ bar **Oh! Pys'ke'** (☎ 04 50 51 20 05; cour du Pré Carré, 10 rue Vaugelas); and minimalist **At The Villa** (☎ 04 50 52 93 28; 48 rue Carnot), with red-neon bar. Next door, disco-bar **Happy People** (☎ 04 50 51 08 66; 48 rue Carnot; admission €12; ⏰ 6pm-5am) is Annecy's main gay venue.

Getting There & Away
AIR
From Annecy's small **airport** (☎ 04 50 27 30 06; www.annecy.aeroport.fr in French; 8 rte Côte Merle), north of the city in Meythet, Air France operates daily flights to/from Paris' Orly Ouest (€220, 1¼ hours).

BUS
From the **bus station** (Gare Routière Sud; rue de l'Industrie), adjoining the train station, the

Billetterie Crolard (☎ 04 50 45 08 12; www.voyages -crolard.com; ⏰ 7.15am-12.30pm & 1.45-7.30pm Mon-Sat, Sun in peak seasons) sells tickets for hourly buses to other lakeside destinations including Menthon (€2.10, 20 minutes) and Talloires (€2.90, 30 minutes), and for local ski resorts La Clusaz (€10, 50 minutes) and Le Grand Bornand (€10, 60 minutes). The January-to-March day-trips it runs to La Clusaz/Le Grand Bornand (€25/27 including lift pass) are particularly good value. It also runs up to five buses daily to/from Lyon-St-Exupéry airport (one way/return €30/45).

Next door, **Autocars Frossard** (☎ 04 50 45 73 90; ⏰ 7.45-11am & 2-7.15pm Mon-Fri, 7.45am-1pm Sat) sells tickets for Geneva (€10.30, 1¾ hours, up to 12 daily), Thonon (€14.90, 1¾ hours, twice daily) and Évian (€17.40, 2¼ hours, twice daily); and a bus four times weekly to/from Nice (€66.50, 9¼ hours) via Chambéry (€9.20, one hour) and Grenoble (€16.60, two hours).

TRAIN
From the **train station** (place de la Gare), there are frequent trains to/from Aix-les-Bains (€6.50, 30 minutes), Chambéry (€8.20, 50 minutes), St-Gervais (€18.40, 3¼ hours), Lyon (€20.50, 2¼ hours) and Paris'Gare de Lyon (€109, 3¾ hours).

Getting Around
BICYCLES & ROLLERBLADES
Bikes can be hired from **Vélonecy** (☎ 04 50 51 38 90; place de la Gare; ⏰ 9.30am-noon & 1.30-6.30pm Mon-Sat Apr-Sep, 9am-noon & 1-6pm Thu-Sat Oct-Mar), situated at the train station, for €6/10 per half-/full day.

Roul' ma Poule (☎ 04 50 27 86 83; www.roul mapoule.com in French; 4 rue des Marquisats; ⏰ 9am-noon & 1.30-7.30pm Mar-Jun & Sep, 9am-7.30pm Jul & Aug) rents rollerblades (€8/12 per half-/full day), bikes (€7/11), tandems (€16/25) and trailers (€4/6).

Near the Impérial at the start of the lakeside cycling path (p546), **Station Roller** (☎ 04 50 66 04 99; www.roller-golf-annecy.com in French; 2 av du Petit Port; ⏰ 9am-10pm) is another bike and blade outlet.

BUS
Get info on local buses at **Espace SIBRA** (☎ 04 50 10 04 04; www.sibra.fr; 21 rue de la Gare; ⏰ 7.30am-7pm Mon-Fri, 9am-noon & 2-5pm Sat) opposite the

---

WHERE TO CATCH THE SURF

You'll catch them early in the morning on the lake before anyone else has woken up, or any time on frisky winter days when no-one else is daft enough to dip their toes in ... kite-surfers, that is. Those wanting to follow in their wake – on water or snow – should contact the Sévrier-based **Kitesurfers Centre** (☎ 04 50 52 46 21; www .snowkiteschool.fr in French; 610 rte de Piron, Sévrier; 1/3hr initiation €30/80), which runs snow-kiting classes and five-day courses (€340) in Semnoz.

---

bus station. Buses run between 6am to 8pm and a single ticket/day pass/carnet of 10 costs €1/2.60/8.80.

TAXI
Taxis (☎ 04 50 45 05 67) hover outside the bus and train stations; otherwise call **Taxi Plus** (☎ 04 50 68 93 33).

AROUND ANNECY
When the sun shines, the villages of **Sévrier**, 5km south on Lake Annecy's western shore, and **Menthon-St-Bernard**, 7km south on the lake's eastern shore, make good day trips (p546). South of Menthon, **Talloires** is the most exclusive lakeside spot.

In winter, ski-keen Annéciens make a beeline for the cross-country resort of **Semnoz** (elevation 1700m), 18km south; or downhill stations **La Clusaz** (elevation 1100m; www.laclusaz.com), 32km east, and **Le Grand Bornand** (elevation 1000m; www.legrand bornand.com), 34km northeast.

CHAMBÉRY
pop 56,000 / elevation 270m
Chambéry, plopped in a valley between Annecy and Grenoble, has long served as one of the principal gateways between France and Italy. Occupying the entrance to the valleys that lead to the main Alpine passes, the town was Savoy's capital from the 13th century until 1563 when the dukes of Savoy shifted their capital to Turin in Italy.

The highlight of the disarmingly shabby old city, crammed with courtyards and cobbled streets, is the castle which once served as the seat of power for the House of Savoy,

founded by Humbert I (the Whitehanded) in the mid-11th century.

Busy dual carriageways along a narrow canal separate Chambéry's compact old section from the unfortunate new-town northern sprawl. But look beyond the latter and a couple of beautiful green parks (p553) unfold.

Information
BOOKSHOPS
Decitre (☎ 04 79 62 80 80; 75 rue Sommeiller) English-language novels, travel guides and maps.

LAUNDRY
Laverie Automatique (1 rue Doppet; €4 per 7kg wash; ☻ 7.30am-7pm).

MONEY
Crédit Agricole (place du Château)
Crédit Lyonnais (26 blvd de la Colonne)

POST
Main Post Office (sq Paul Vidal)
Post Office (11 place de l'Hôtel de Ville)

TOURIST INFORMATION
Parc National de la Vanoise Office (☎ 04 79 62 30 54; www.vanoise.com; 135 rue du Docteur Julliand; ☻ 8am-noon & 2-6pm Mon-Fri) Vanoise National Park HQ; see p557.
Tourist Office (☎ 04 79 33 42 47; www.chambery -tourisme.com; 24 blvd de la Colonne; ☻ 9am-noon & 1.30-6pm Mon-Sat Sep-Jun, 9am-6pm Mon-Sat, 9.30am-12.30pm Sun Jul & Aug) Guided old-town tours and evening 'Chambéry 3001: back to the future' jaunts on foot.

Sights
CHÂTEAU DES DUCS DE SAVOIE
Now home to the region's Conseil Général (County Council), Chambéry's forbidding 14th-century **Château des Ducs de Savoie** (place du Château; adult/student 18 €4/3, under 18 free; tours ☻ 2.30pm May-Sep, 10.30am Mon-Sat, 3.30pm & 4.30pm Jul & Aug) can only be visited by guided tours. Tours vary in length (45 minutes to 1½ hours) and depart from the **Accueil des Guides office** (☎ 04 79 85 93 73; place du Château), tucked beneath the terrace of Hôtel Montfalcon, opposite the chateau steps.

Tours take in the adjoining **Ste-Chapelle**, built in the 15th century to house the Shroud of Turin. Chambéry lost the relic to Turin in 1860 when Savoy became part of France. Visit the 70-bell **Grand Carillon** in

FRENCH ALPS & THE JURA

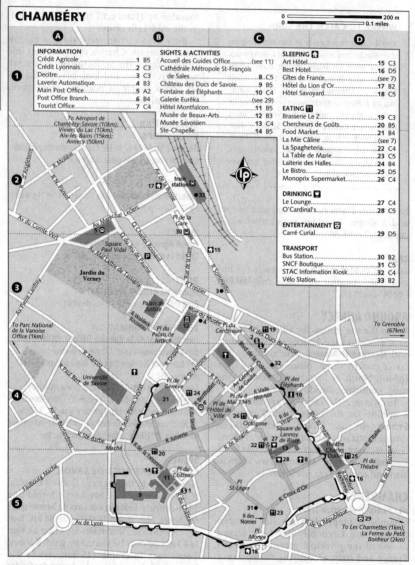

CHAMBÉRY

0 ————————— 200 m
0 ————————— 0.1 miles

INFORMATION
Crédit Agricole	1	B5
Crédit Lyonnais	2	C3
Decitre	3	C3
Laverie Automatique	4	B3
Main Post Office	5	A2
Post Office Branch	6	B4
Tourist Office	7	C4

SIGHTS & ACTIVITIES
Accueil des Guides Office	(see 11)	
Cathédrale Métropole St-François de Sales	8	C5
Château des Ducs de Savoie	9	B5
Fontaine des Éléphants	10	C4
Galerie Eurêka	(see 29)	
Hôtel Montfalcon	11	B5
Musée de Beaux-Arts	12	B3
Musée Savoisien	13	C4
Ste-Chapelle	14	B5

SLEEPING
Art Hôtel	15	C3
Best Hôtel	16	D5
Gîtes de France	(see 7)	
Hôtel du Lion d'Or	17	B2
Hôtel Savoyard	18	C5

EATING
Brasserie Le Z	19	C3
Chercheurs de Goûts	20	B5
Food Market	21	B4
La Mie Câline	(see 7)	
La Spagheteria	22	C4
La Table de Marie	23	C5
Laiterie des Halles	24	B4
Le Bistro	25	D5
Monoprix Supermarket	26	C4

DRINKING
Le Lounge	27	C4
O'Cardinal's	28	C5

ENTERTAINMENT
Carré Curial	29	D5

TRANSPORT
Bus Station	30	B2
SNCF Boutique	31	C5
STAC Information Kiosk	32	C4
Vélo Station	33	B2

Ste-Chapelle – Europe's largest bell chamber – on a guided tour or enjoy it in full concert on the first and third Saturdays of the month at 10.30am and 5.30pm.

FONTAINE DES ÉLÉPHANTS
With its four mighty carved elephants, this bizarre **Fontaine des Éléphants** (place des Éléphants)

could be the model for an Indian postage stamp. It was sculpted in 1838 in honour of Général de Boigne (1751–1830), a local who made his fortune in the East Indies. When he returned home, he bestowed some of his wealth on the town and was honoured posthumously with this monument. Among his various local projects was the construction of the arcaded street – named after him no less – that leads from the fountain to Château des Ducs de Savoie.

MUSEUMS
Admission is free on the first Sunday of the month.

South of the fountain in an old Franciscan monastery near the 15th- and 16th-century **Cathédrale Métropole St-François de Sales** (place de la Metropole; 8am-noon & 2-6.30pm), is the **Musée Savoisien** (☎ 04 79 33 44 48; sq Lannoy de Bissy; adult/student/under 18 €3/1.50/free; 10am-noon & 2-6pm Wed-Mon), home to various local archaeological finds including a gallery of 13th-century wall paintings discovered behind a false roof inside a local mansion. Traditional Savoyard mountain life zooms into perspective on the 2nd floor.

Musée des Beaux-Arts (☎ 04 79 33 75 03; place du Palais de Justice; adult/student/under 18 €3/1.50/free; 10am-noon & 2-6pm Wed-Mon) houses a rich collection of 14th- to 18th-century Italian works in addition to some fascinating temporary exhibitions.

French philosopher and writer Jean-Jacques Rousseau lived with his lover, Baronne Louise Éléonore de Warens, at **Les Charmettes** (☎ 04 79 33 39 44; 890 chemin des Charmettes; adult/student/under 18 €3/1.50/free; 10am-noon & 2-6pm Wed-Mon Apr-Sep, to 4.30pm Oct-Mar), 1km southeast of the town, from 1736 to 1742. Herbs, flowers and plants flourish in the surrounding gardens and the country house stages night-time shows in period costume (visite-spectacle costumée) in July and August; the tourist office has details.

Science and mountaineering displays are part of the hi-tech lure of **Galerie Eurêka** (☎ 04 79 60 04 25; www.ccsti-chambery.org in French; rue de la République; admission free; 2-6pm Tue-Sat Jul & Aug, 5-7pm Tue & Fri, 2-6pm Wed, 10am-noon & 2-6pm Sat Sep-Jun), an interactive mixed-media–driven gallery in the Carré Curial.

Sleeping
Gîtes de France (☎ 04 79 33 22 56; www.gites-de-france-savoie.com; 24 blvd de la Colonne) takes bookings for chambres d'hôtes (B&B) and self-catering accommodation in or around Chambéry; find it inside the tourist office on the 4th floor. The nearest hostel is in Aix-les-Bains (p553).

Hôtel du Lion d'Or (☎ 04 79 69 04 96; 13 av de la Boisse; s/d €29/49, ste €69) This two-star far-from-

wonder is bang-smack opposite the train station, making it an obvious choice for late-night arrivals. Rooms are large and inoffensively drab; station-facing ones sport wrought-iron balconies and clickety-clack ginger shutters. Breakfast costs an extra €6.50 a night and come lunchtime, the adjoining brasserie buzzes with punters wolfing down €8.50 plats du jour.

Hôtel Savoyard (☎ 04 79 33 36 55; savoyard@noos.fr; 35 place Monge; s/d from €36/46) A tasty choice on the sleeping and eating front, recommended all-rounder Hôtel Savoyard is a midrange ode to Savoy. Its welcome is as warm as one would expect of this region's mountain folk and its cuisine appropriately hearty and cheese-driven.

Art Hôtel (☎ 04 79 62 37 26; www.arthotel-chambery.com; 154 rue Sommeiller; road/station-facing d €53/46, tr €63) Flags fly from the uninspiring concrete façade of this modern five-floor hotel where the name seemingly has nothing to do with the décor (ask owner Monsieur Allanet why it's called such and he'll tell you he doesn't know). Reception, unusually, opens around the clock and breakfast/garage parking is €7/7 a night.

Best Hotel (☎ 04 79 85 76 79; www.best-hotel-chambery.com; 9 rue Denfert Rochereau; s/d/tr/q €40/58/75/88) The best rooms overlook place du Théâtre at this functional, modern hotel near the theatre and happening Carré Curial – a handy choice for entertainment fiends. And there's plenty of surrounding kebab shops and snack bars to dip into when late-night hunger bites. Breakfast is €9.

La Ferme du Petit Bonheur (☎ 04 79 85 26 17; www.chambresdhotes-chambery.net; 538 chemin Jean-Jacques; s/d/tr €70/80/100) If walking, mountain biking and an overdose of green views and fresh air is your cup of tea, then Chantal and Eric's homely pad is for you. Eric plays the piano, Chantal paints and they are fabulous B&B hosts. Find the Farm of Good Humour 2km from town, near the Rousseau museum.

Eating
Le Bistro (☎ 04 79 33 10 78; 6 rue du Théâtre; plat du jour €8.50, 2-/3-course menus €12.50/14; lunch & dinner Tue-Sat) With its typical lace curtains, handful of tightly packed tiled-topped tables and hardy terracotta tiled floor, the Bistro – as far as quintessential bistros go – does not disappoint. Fare is filling and Savoyard.

ourpick **Brasserie Le Z** (☎ 04 79 85 96 87; www
.zorelle.com in French; 12 av des Ducs de Savoie; 2-/3-course
menu €12.50/15.50; ⊙ lunch & dinner) Stuffed to the
gills with cheese? Can't stomach one more
morsel of the Savoyard staple? Then head
straight for what has to be Chambéry's
hippest, coolest, funkiest eating spot. From
outside it's unextraordinary. But step inside and be wooed by a vast airy dining
space with minimalist décor and an open
steel kitchen. Chefs wear grey, bold orange
water glasses add a dashing flash of colour
to stark, crisp tables and cuisine is predominantly light and fishy: shellfish galore,
lobster risotto, house-smoked salmon and
oysters – dozens of them.

La Spagheteria (☎ 04 79 33 27 62; 43 rue St-Réal; plat
du jour €7.90, menus €13-17; ⊙ lunch & dinner Mon-Sat)
This pizza and pasta house oozes Mediterranean atmosphere and instantly befriends less
adventurous diners or anyone sick of Savoyard cooking. In true Italian fashion, kids are
welcomed with a €6.50 spag bol menu.

La Table de Marie (☎ 04 79 85 99 76; 193 rue Croix
d'Or; menus €13-18; ⊙ lunch & dinner Mon-Sat) This
intimate, pocket-sized restaurant overflows
with eccentricity. Take the shocking-pink
table parked out front or the mishmash of
flowers and neon strung between candle-lit
tables inside. Nothing beats Marie's lunchtime steak, chips and salad (€10).

Chercheurs de Goûts (103 rue Juiverie; mains €16,
menus €28 & €45; ⊙ lunch Tue, lunch & dinner Wed-Sat)
This imaginative old-town bistro smacks
of something different. The bread is home-
baked, the cuisine a twist on regional fare
and the interior an inspired mix of predictable old (stone walls, wooden beams)
and funky new (contemporary light installations, crisp white/beige linen).

SELF-CATERING
Chambéry's Saturday morning **food market**
(place de Genève) is a gastronomic ball, as is a
stroll down pedestrian rue du Sénat – an
alley with butcher, baker and chocolate-
maker shops.

Laiterie des Halles (☎ 04 79 33 77 17; 2 place de
Genève) Pongy, yes, but this cheese shop is pure heaven
for cheese aficionados.

La Mie Câline (☎ 04 79 60 80 58; 22 blvd de la
Colonne; ⊙ 6.45am-7.30pm Mon-Sat) Well-stuffed
sandwiches (€4.50).

Monoprix (place du 8 Mai 1945; ⊙ 8.15am-7.30pm
Mon-Sat) Supermarket.

Drinking
The huge open square of place St-Léger
is the summertime heart of Chambéry's
drinking scene.

O'Cardinal's (☎ 04 79 85 53 40; 5 place de la
Métropole; ⊙ 5pm-1.30am Sun & Mon, 10-1.30am Tue-
Sat) Leather banquet seating, super-friendly
staff (service *à l'irlandais* from 7pm, ie
service at the bar only) and great pub grub
(noon to 2pm Tuesday to Saturday) make
this a fine pub. In warmer weather the cheer
spills out onto cathedral-shaded place de la
Métropole.

Le Lounge (☎ 04 79 85 53 40; 68 rue St-Réal)
Twenty cocktails, six types of champagne,
10 whiskies and a gaggle of different DJs
are trademarks of this laid-back music pub
where low seating woos a late 20s to 30-
something crowd.

Getting There & Away
AIR
Aéroport de Chambéry-Savoie (☎ 04 79 54 49
66; www.chambery-airport.com), 10km north in
Viviers du Lac, is serviced by no-frills
flights to/from Amsterdam, Brussels and a
bunch of regional British airports; see p968
for details.

BUS
From the **bus station** (☎ 04 79 69 11 88; place
de la Gare; ticket office ⊙ 6am-7pm Mon-Fri, 6.50am-
12.30pm & 2.30-5.30pm Sat) there are buses to/
from local ski resort La Féclaz (€6.40, 50
minutes, up to seven daily), Aix-les-Bains
(€2.80, 35 minutes, five daily), Annecy
(€8.20, 50 minutes, seven daily), and Grenoble (€5.10, 1½ hours, 10 daily). There's
one daily bus to/from Geneva (€17.40, two
hours) and Nice (€60.70, 8¾ hours) and
up to five a day to/from Lyon St-Exupéry
airport (€20, one hour).

TRAIN
From Chambéry **train station** (place de la Gare;
ticket office ⊙ 5.45am-8.30pm Mon-Sat, 6.45am-
9.30pm Sun) there are major rail connections
running to/from Paris' Gare de Lyon
(€106.50, three hours, 11 daily), Lyon (€18,
1½ hours, 12 daily), Annecy (€8.20, 50
minutes, 25 daily) and Grenoble (€9.50,
one hour, 10 to 13 daily). Trains also run up
the Maurienne Valley to Modane (€13.70,
1¼ hours, nine daily) and onwards into
Italy.

In town buy tickets at the **SNCF Boutique** (21 place St-Léger; ⊙ 9.20am-1pm & 2-6.45pm Mon-Fri, 9.30am-12.15pm & 2-5pm Sat).

Getting Around

TO/FROM THE AIRPORT

Buses timed to coincide with flight arrivals/departures link the airport and the bus station; a one-way fare is €1.50 and journey time is 20 minutes.

BICYCLE

Pick up wheels for €3/5/10 per hour/day/week and advice on marked trails and itineraries from **Vélo Station** (☎ 04 79 96 34 13; ⊙ 6.30am-7pm Mon-Fri, 9am-7pm Sat & Sun Apr-Oct, closed Sun Nov-Mar) at the train station.

BUS

City buses run from 6am to around 8pm Monday to Saturday and are operated by **STAC** (☎ 04 79 68 67 00). A single ticket/carnet of 10 costs €1/6.38 and are sold at tobacconists and the **STAC information kiosk** (blvd de la Colonne; ⊙ 7.15am-7.15pm Mon-Fri, 8.30am-12.15pm & 2.30-6.30pm Sat) near Fontaine des Éléphants.

Bus 7 links the train station with Fontaine des Éléphants.

AROUND CHAMBÉRY

Chambéry is sandwiched by two green-rich regional nature parks. Southwest, the **Parc Naturel Régional de Chartreuse** (www.parc-chartreuse.net in French) safeguards the gentle Chartreuse massif, dubbed the 'emerald of the Alps' by 19th-century novelist Stendhal and best known for the startling pea-green liquor – a mind-blowing 55% proof – made by monks here since 1737. The **park headquarters** (☎ 04 76 88 75 20; www.chartreuse-tourisme .com) in St-Pierre-de-Chartreuse, 40km south of Chambéry, has information on visiting the Voiron distillery where fiery Chartreuse is produced.

Northeast, outdoor enthusiasts can delve into 800 sq km of royal hiking and biking opportunities in the little-known **Parc Naturel Régional du Massif des Bauges** (www .parcdesbauges.com). Several marked trails kick off from the **Maison Faune-Flore** (☎ 04 79 52 22 56; adult/7-18yr €2/1; ⊙ 10.30am-12.30pm & 1.30-7pm Tue-Sun mid-Jun–mid-Sep) in École where you can learn how to spot some of the 600-odd chamois and plethora of mouflon inhabiting the park.

Alpine skiers seeking piste action on the cheap could do worse than **Savoie Grand Révard** (www.savoiegrandrevard.com), the nearest ski resort to Chambéry where Baujus (people from the Massif des Bauges) ski at weekends. Downhill skiing is limited to 50km of pistes but ski passes are a steal at €11.50 a day and there's always ski joëring (p529) to dabble in! Tourist offices in **Le Revard** (☎ 04 79 54 01 60), **La Féclaz** (☎ 04 79 25 80 49) and **Le Châtelard** (☎ 04 79 54 84 28; www.lesbauges.com) – the main office in the park – have more information.

Self-pamperers can seek solace in **Aix-les-Bains** (pop 25,271), a small thermal spa 11km northwest of Chambéry from where you can boat around France's largest natural lake, **Lac Bourget**. Contact **Bateaux d'Aix-les-Bains** (☎ 04 79 88 92 09; www.gwel.com) at the waterfront Grand Port or the **tourist office** (☎ 04 79 88 68 00; www.aixlesbains.com; place Maurice Mollard) next to the main thermal baths in town. A two-hour lake cruise costs €14.80 and a return trip to the 12th-century **Abbaye d'Hautecombe** on the other side of the lake is €11.70.

The highs and lows of the 1992 Winter Olympics are colourfully retold by host of 18 of the 57 sporting events, **Albertville** – a disappointingly uninspiring town 39km east of Chambéry – at its **Maison des Jeux Olympiques d'Hiver** (☎ 04 79 37 75 71; 11 rue Pargoud; adult/family €3/8; ⊙ 9am-7pm Mon-Sat, 2-7pm Sun Jul & Aug, 9am-noon & 2-6pm Mon-Sat Sep-Jun).

SLEEPING

our pick **Château des Allues** (☎ 06 75 38 61 56; www .chateaudesallues.com; Les Allues, St-Pierre d'Albigny; d/q €95-125/165, dinner adult/child €35/15) The attention to detail at this stylish, off-the-beaten-track *maison d'hôtes de charme* reminiscent of a 19th-century bourgeois family home is awesome. Hip 'n trendy owner Stéphane Vandeville bought the 17th-century Savoyard manor – then a very sorry old sight four years ago – and spent two years sanding, sawing, scrubbing and goodness knows what else to spruce up the place to its current impeccable standard. Oozing elegance, the wood panelling in the dining room was salvaged from a 17th-century pharmacy and the floor tiles are the chateau's original – as is the re-enamelled bathtub with legs in one of the five spacious, lavishly furnished rooms. Much of the produce cooked up is straight from the chateau *potager* (veggie patch), aperitifs are served on the lawn in summer and breakfast is a truly copious and magnificent affair.

LES TROIS VALLÉES

Named after its valley trio, this super-sexy ski area is vast, fast and the largest in the world – 600km of piste and 200 lifts headed up by three ritzy resorts: **Val Thorens**, Europe's highest at a heady 2300m; wealthy old **Méribel** created by Scotsman Colonel Peter Lindsay in 1938; and trendsetting **Courchevel** (a fave of Victoria Beckham) where fashion is as hot on as off the slopes. In between is a sprinkling of lesser-known villages – **Le Praz** (elevation 1300m), **St-Martin de Belleville** (elevation 1450m) and **La Tania** (elevation 1400m) – where savvy skiers can revel in awesome skiing at less painful prices.

Purpose-built **Méribel** (elevation 1450m), 42km southeast of Albertville and 88km from Annecy and Chambéry, is one of the most 'British' resorts in France. A mon-eyed international set hits **Courchevel**, 18km from Méribel, a series of purpose-built resorts that scale the mountain at altitudes of 1550m, 1650m and 1850m; prices rise the higher you get.

Information

Courchevel 1850 Tourist Office (☎ 04 79 08 00 29; www.courchevel.com; ◷ 9am-7pm) Sister offices at 1650m, 1550m and 1300m.

Méribel Tourist Office (☎ 04 79 08 60 01; www .meribel.net; Maison du Tourisme; ◷ 9am-7pm Dec-Apr, 9am-noon & 3-7pm Jun-Sep, 9am-noon & 3-6pm Mon-Fri, 9am-noon Sat May, Oct & Nov)

Val Thorens Tourist Office (☎ 04 79 00 08 08; www .valthorens.com; Maison de Val Thorens; ◷ 9am-7pm Mon-Fri, 9am-6.30pm Sat & Sun)

Activities

All three valleys appease the feistiest of outdoor-action appetites, Méribel Valley alone boasting 73 downhill ski runs (150km), 53 ski lifts, two snowboarding parks, a slalom stadium, and two Olympic downhill runs. In Courchevel there's another 150km of downhill piste to explore and a superb 2km-long floodlit toboggan run (a great adrenaline-pumping après-ski alternative); while Val Thorens, though smaller, proffers summer skiing on the Glacier de Péclet. A

Trois Vallées pass costing €42/210 for one/six days covers the entire area – 600km of piste in all – but cheaper solo valley passes are available.

Courchevel is big on alternative snow action, the key info point being **La Croisette** (place du Forum; ◷ 7am-8pm) in Courchevel 1850, where the **ESF** (☎ 04 79 08 07 72; www.esfcourchevel .com) resides in winter and the super-friendly **Maison de la Montagne** can be found year-round. The latter takes bookings for guided off-piste adventures, heliskiing, snowshoeing and ski mountaineering as well as go-karting or driving on ice, snowmobile treks and snow-rafting, and is home to the **Bureau des Guides** (☎ 04 79 01 03 66).

Rock climbing, mountain biking, hiking and paragliding are rife in all three valleys. In July and August **Chardon Loisirs** (☎ 04 79 24 08 84; www.chardonloisirs.com) organises canyoning and rafting on the Doron de Belleville and Isère Rivers from its riverside hut 1km south of Moutiers in Salins les Termes.

Sleeping & Eating

All three resorts have a **central accommodation service** (Courchevel ☎ 04 79 08 14 44; www .courchevel-reservation.com; Méribel ☎ 04 79 00 50 00; reservation@meribel.net; Val Thorens ☎ 04 79 00 01 06; www.valthorens.com/resa).

Hôtel Les Bleuets (☎ 04 79 08 24 73; rue des Tovets, Courchevel 1850; d from €56) It's far from flash and ranks among Courchevel 1850's cheapest but *tant pis!* Martine and Jean-Luc keep rooms maniacally clean and beds are comfy. When Les Bleuets is shut, neighbouring clothing and souvenir shop 'Elle & Lui' doubles as reception.

Les Peupliers (☎ 04 79 08 41 47; www.lespeupliers .com; Le Praz; d €80, half-board per person low/high season from €100/135; ◷ Jul & Aug, mid-Dec–Apr) This authentic village hotel – not to mention the stylish country-style dining in its restaurant, La Table de Mon Grand-Père – is a rare breed. Where else does carbonara come topped with raw egg in a raw onion shell?

Le Doron (☎ 04 79 08 60 02; hotel_doron@wanadoo .fr; rte de la Chaudanne, Méribel; d/tr/q low season €95/125/140, high season €115/150/170) Among the cheapest options – not cheap – is this place, above a rowdy Brit-styled pub opposite Méribel tourist office.

La Bouitte (☎ 04 79 08 96 77; www.la-bouitte.com; St-Marcel; s/d/tr from €122/190/285, 2-/3-course menu

€62/78; [Y] Jul & Aug, mid-Dec–Apr) Book ahead to snag a bed at this divine chalet-style hotel-restaurant where five exquisitely decorated rustic rooms and top-notch cuisine form a fearsome duo. The heart carved in wood on the front door sums up its spirit. Find it in the hamlet of St Marcel, 1km south of St-Martin de Belleville.

Legendary hang-outs at Courchevel 1850 for the *really* rich 'n famous include **Byblos des Neiges** (☎ 04 79 00 98 00; www.byblos.com) – St-Tropez in the Alps – and 10-chalet spa hotel, **Le Kilimandjaro** (☎ 04 79 01 46 46; www .hotelkilimandjaro.com).

Getting There & Away

The four-lane A43, built for the 1992 Olympics, links Chambéry (88km northwest) with the nearest town, Moûtiers, 18km north of Méribel. From Moûtiers follow signs for 'Vallée des Belleville' for Val Thorens, and 'Haute Tarentaise' for Méribel and Courchevel.

Shuttle buses link all three resorts with Geneva (€65.50, four hours) and Lyon St-Exupéry (€56, three to four hours) airports. From Moûtiers, the nearest train station, there are trains to/from Chambéry (€11.20, 1¼ hours).

Transavoie Moûtiers (☎ 04 79 24 21 58; www .altibus.com) operates up to 12 regional buses daily between Moûtiers and Méribel (€11.60, one hour), Courchevel (€9.80 to €11.60, 40 to 60 minutes) and Val Thorens (€14.80, 1½ hours).

VAL D'ISÈRE

pop 1750 / elevation 1850m

The party never ends in Val d'Isère, a hip-to-be-seen resort in the upper Tarentaise Valley, 31km southeast of Bourg St-Maurice. Here cosmopolitan snow junkies revel in mountains of groomed snow, off-piste thrills, trendy shops and a hopping après-ski scene. Hard to believe this high-altitude hunting ground for the dukes of Savoy was once a remote village in the upper reaches of the eastern Alps. If you're seeking traditional Alpine atmosphere, forget it.

Lac du Chevril looms up large on the approach to Val d'Isère. The mammoth lake and dam slumbers on the grave of Tignes-le-Lac, the village flooded by the 1950s electricity-generating project. Out of its ashes rose **Tignes** (elevation 2100m), a purpose-built lakeside village that – together with Val d'Isère – forms the **Espace Killy** skiing area.

As legendary as the man this fabulous skiing estate is named after (triple Olympic gold medallist Jean-Claude Killy, who grew up here) is **La Face de Bellevarde**, a black 63% Olympic ski run with a kick-off altitude of 2809m and vertical drop of 973m. In 2009 the very best will fly down it during the World Alpine Skiing Championships (www.valdisere2009.org). Between now and then anyone daring or reckless enough to do it can have a bash.

Information

Tourist Office (☎ 04 79 06 06 60; www.valdisere .com; place Jacques Mouflier; [Y] 8.30am-7.30pm Sun-Fri, 8.30am-8pm Sat Dec-Apr, Jul & Aug, 9am-noon & 2-6pm Mon-Sun May, Jun, Sep-Nov) Public internet access here costs €9 per hour.

Activities

WINTER ACTIVITIES

Espace Killy offers fabulous skiing on 300km of marked pistes between 1550m and 3450m. Ski touring is also excellent, especially in the Parc National de la Vanoise. The snowboarders' Snowspace Park in La Deille has a half-pipe, tables, gaps, quarter-pipes, and kicker ramps, while the runs around Tignes are popular with both snowboarders and skiers. In July and August you can ski on the glacier.

Ski schools teaching boarding, cross-country and off-piste skiing are a dime a dozen. The **ESF** (☎ 04 79 06 02 34; carrefour des Dolomites; www.esfvaldisere.com) is in Val Village, a hub of shops and services backing onto the slopes. Nearby, **Ski Pass** (place des Dolomites; [Y] 8.30am-7pm Mon-Fri & Sun, 8am-8pm Sat Dec-Apr) sells lift passes covering Espace Killy (one/ six days €40/192.50) and – for six-day or more passes – one day's skiing in La Plagne, Les Arcs, Les Trois Vallées or Valmorel. Unusually, beginner lifts opposite Val Village are free. Glacial summer skiing starts in late June and lasts for anything from two weeks to two months.

Heliskiing in Italy, ice diving, ice climbing, snowshoeing, snowmobiling and paragliding with skis (to land!) are other snow-driven activities. Fun-driven are the floodlit airboarding and snakegliss sledging (p529) sessions held a couple of times a week on the Savonette nursery slope opposite Val Village.

SUMMER ACTIVITIES

The valleys and trails from Val d'Isère into the nearby Parc National de la Vanoise (opposite) proffer an orgy of outdoor action. Be it walking, mountain biking, trekking with a donkey or paragliding, the Bureau des Guides or ESF can arrange it. **Safari Photo Vanoise** (☎ 04 79 06 00 03; www.valgliss.com in French) organises botanical *balades* (walks) and animal-photography safaris in the Vanoise.

Sleeping

Find out about availability and make hotel reservations (essential in high season) through the **Centre de Réservation Hôtellerie** (☎ 04 79 06 18 90; valhotel@valdisere.com). For self-catering accommodation, contact **Val Location** (☎ 04 79 06 06 60; vallocation@valdisere.com). Prices vary widely, pricey being the common factor.

Hôtel Bellevue (☎ 04 79 06 00 03; d with half-board per person €74, with bathroom & half-board per person €87-92) This central family-run hotel – Mattis is the family name – on the main street screams 1960s. Rooms are basic but excellent value for skiers who are in town to ski rather than self-pamper.

Relais du Ski & La Bailletta (☎ 04 79 06 02 06; http://lerelaisduski.valdisere.com; rte Fornet; s/d/tr/q with shared bathroom Dec-Apr €76/86/96/116, with bathroom €124/146/171/208, s/d/tr/q with shared bathroom Jul & Aug €64/70/81/88, with bathroom €77/90/99/116; ☙ Dec-Apr, Jul & Aug) A 500m stroll from the centre on the east side of town is this twin-

set of restaurant-clad hotels rolled into one. Touting 35 comfy midrange rooms (La Bailletta) and nine budget-basic (Relais du Ski) with shared bathrooms, its stand-out feature is the central fireplace in the restaurant-bar.

Eating

Many restaurants cater to a largely English clientele, making quality varied and unpredictable. Better deals can be had opting for full-board in your hotel. Well-stuffed baguettes (€3.50) to takeaway are sold at main-street **Maison Chevallot** (☙ 6.30am-8pm), and self-caterers can borrow fondue and *raclette* gadgets from the **Cooperative Laitière de Haute Tarentaise** (☎ 04 79 06 08 94; Val Village); the Beaufort and other local cheeses sold here are divine.

Salon de Thé Moris (☎ 04 79 22 68 61; pasta €10, tarts €5; ☙ 7am-9pm) Enjoy breakfast, lunch or afternoon tea for two at this stylish tearoom on the sunny side of the main street. The home-made savoury and sweet tarts are unbeatable.

Quicksilver & Billabong Coffee Shops (☎ 04 79 06 09 54; burgers & wraps €8.50-12; ☙ 9am-10pm) Two of the trendiest names in streetwear have joined forces to create this American-style diner with menu to match. Kids are well catered for here.

La Fruitière (☎ 04 79 06 07 17; mains €20; ☙ lunch Dec-Apr, Jul & Aug) At the top of the La Daille bubble at 2400m, this piste-side oasis of fine dining is legendary. Snuggle under a rug and savour traditional but creative cuisine in a hip dairy setting.

TOP FIVE PARTY HOT SPOTS

Val d'Isère is bar loaded. To tune in to the hippest spot of the moment, track down (in any bar) a copy of *The Mountain Echo*, a tongue-in-cheek resort mag put together and written for Val d'Isère's Anglophone seasonal workers. In 2006 Mullit was the live band worth turning up to see.

Dick's Tea Bar (☎ 04 79 06 14 87; www.dicksteabar.com; admission before/after 1am free/€12; ☙ 3pm-4am) The Val d'Isère outpost of the Alpine nightclub chain. Live music from 4.30pm.

Warm Up (☎ 04 79 08 27 00; rue Olympique; ☙ 11.30-2am) Large, pub-style drinking hole on the main street with stylish retro furnishings (great leather sofas) and free wi-fi. Find **Bar Rodeo** (☙ 3pm-2am), complete with pool tables and rodeo bull, in its basement.

Le Lodge (☎ 04 79 06 02 01; ☙ 11.30-2am) Combining good food with a hopping drinking scene, the Lodge sits a few doors down from Dick's on the same street.

Café Face (☙ 4pm-2am) Count on live music from 5pm, lounge from 6.30pm and a DJ mix from 10pm at this après-ski institution opposite Dick's.

Bananas (☎ 04 79 06 04 23; ☙ 11.30-2am) A bizarre mix of Tex-Mex and Indian is dished up at this party shack found at the bottom of La Face, behind the Bellevarde Express.

La Montagne (☎ 04 79 40 04 12; mains €20; ⊙ lunch & dinner) St Marcellin pizza or grilled salmon with saffron-spiced tagliatelle are conventional dishes served with a creative twist at this clean-cut eating spot with sunny street terrace near the bus station.

Le Blizzard (☎ 04 79 06 02 07; www.hotelblizzard .com; mains €25) A Val d'Isère highlight is lunch by the snow-framed outdoor pool with a quick dip in the steaming hot tub for good measure at this rustic-modern four-star hotel. Find the entrance to the poolside restaurant behind the Bellevarde Express.

Casino (⊙ 7.30am-9pm) Supermarket on the main street opposite the Boutique Autocars Martin.

Getting There & Away

Hourly buses in season link Val d'Isère with Tignes (€6.70) and Bourg St-Maurice train station (€12.10, 1¼ hours). Tickets must be reserved 48 hours in advance at the **Boutique Autocars Martin** (☎ 04 79 06 00 42; ⊙ 9am-noon & 1.15-6.45pm Mon-Fri, 6.30am-6.45pm Sat, 7.30am-noon & 1.15-6.45pm Sun) on the main street in the resort centre. The **SNCF desk** (⊙ 9am-noon & 3-6.30pm Tue-Sat) here sells train tickets.

Other seasonal bus services include three or four daily to/from Geneva airport (one way/return €52.50/89.50, four hours) and two to five daily to/from Lyon St-Exupéry airport. Again, advance reservations are obligatory.

PARC NATIONAL DE LA VANOISE

A wild mix of high mountains, steep valleys and vast glaciers, the Parc National de la Vanoise sports 530 sq km of spectacular scenery between the Tarentaise (north) and Maurienne (south) Valleys: snowcapped peaks mirrored in icy lakes is just the start! It was the country's first national park in 1963 and is very much a green haven. Five designated nature reserves and an inhabited peripheral zone embracing 28 villages border the highly protected core of the park where marmots, chamois and France's largest colony of Alpine ibex graze freely and undisturbed beneath the larch trees. Overhead, 20 pairs of golden eagle and the odd bearded vulture fly in solitary wonder.

A hiker's heaven, yes, although **walking trails** are limited and accessible for a fraction of the year – June to late September usually. The **Grand Tour de Haute Maurienne**, a hike of five days or more around the upper reaches of the valley, takes in the very best of the national park. The **GR5** and **GR55** cross it and other trails snake south to the Park National des Écrins (p566) and east into Italy's Grand Paradiso National Park.

Lanslebourg and **Bonneval-sur-Arc**, two pretty villages along the southern edge of the park, are the main accommodation bases from which to explore. The **Maison du Val Cénis** (☎ 04 79 05 23 66; www.valcenis.com; ⊙ 9am-noon & 3-7pm) in Lanslebourg and Bonneval-sur-Arc's **tourist office** (☎ 04 79 05 95 95; www.bon neval-sur-arc.com; ⊙ 9am-noon & 2-6.30pm Mon-Sat in season, to 6pm rest of year) stock practical information on the limited skiing (cross-country and downhill), walking and other activities in the park. In Termignon-la-Vanoise, 6km southwest of Lanslebourg, the tiny national park–run **Maison de la Vanoise** (☎ 04 79 20 51 67; admission free; ⊙ 9am-noon & 2-6pm Tue, Wed, Fri & Sat) portrays the park through ethnographical eyes; opening hours are variable. The park headquarters are in Chambéry (p549).

Getting There & Away

All three mountain passes linking the national park with Italy – the Col du Petit St-Bernard, Col de l'Iseran and Col du Mont Cénis – are shut in winter.

Trains serving the valley leave from Chambéry and run as far Modane, 23km southwest of Lanslebourg, from where **Transavoie** (☎ 04 79 05 01 32; www.transavoie.com) runs five daily buses to/from Termignon-la-Vanoise (€7.30, 30 minutes), Lanslebourg (€9.80, 50 minutes) and Bonneval-sur-Arc (€14.50, 1¼ hours).

DAUPHINÉ

Dauphiné, which encompasses the territories south and southwest of Savoy, stretches from the River Rhône in the west to the Italian border in the east. It includes the city of Grenoble and, a little further east, the mountainous Parc National des Écrins. The gentler terrain of the western part of Dauphiné is typified by the Parc Naturel Régional du Vercors, much loved by cross-country skiers. In the east, the town of Briançon stands guard on the Italian frontier.

First inhabited by the Celts and the Romans, Dauphiné fell in the 11th century

FRENCH ALPS & THE JURA

under the rule of Guigues I, the count of Albon, whose great-grandson Guigues IV (ruled 1133–42) was the first count to bear the name of 'dauphin'. By the end of the 13th century, the name 'dauphin' had become a title and the fiefs held by the region's ruling house, La Tour du Pin, were known collectively as Dauphiné. The rulers of Dauphiné continued to expand their territories, which gave them control of all the passes that run through the southern Alps.

In 1339 Humbert II established a university at Grenoble. A decade later, lacking money and a successor, he sold Dauphiné to the French king, Charles V, who started the tradition whereby the eldest son of the king of France (the crown prince) ruled Dauphiné and bore the title 'dauphin'. The region was annexed to France by Charles VII in 1457.

GRENOBLE

pop 156,000

Elegant Grenoble is the Alps' modern economic soul. Spectacularly sited in a broad valley surrounded by snow-capped mountains – Chartreuse (north), Vercors (southwest) and the Italian Alps (east) – the city sits plump in the centre of the Dauphiné region. It gained a reputation for social, artistic and technological innovation in the 1960s thanks to Socialist mayor Hubert Dubedout, and still lures Europe's top dogs with its nuclear and microelectronic research. Shops thrive, boulevards are broad and architecturally fine, and a gregarious student population adds a big-city buzz to the air.

Orientation

Grenoble is tricky to negotiate from behind the wheel thanks to the bewildering one-way system and disorientating tram network. The old city is centred around place Grenette and place Notre Dame, both 1km east of the train and bus stations. The main university campus is a couple of kilometres east of the old centre on the southern side of the River Isère.

Information

BOOKSHOPS

Decitre (☎ 04 76 03 36 36; 9-11 Grande Rue) Mainstream bookshop and café with English titles.

EMERGENCY

Duty Pharmacy (☎ 04 76 60 40 40)

Grenoble University Hospital (☎ 04 76 76 75 75) Two main sites: Hôpital Nord de la Tronche (av de Marquis du Grésivaudan; tram stop 'La Tronche' on tramway line B) and Hôpital Sud (av de Kimberley; bus 11 and 13).

INTERNET ACCESS

Log in at the tourist office (below) for €2 per 15 minutes or €5 an hour.

Arobase (☎ 04 76 19 08 49; 22 rue de la Poste; 15/30/60mins €1/1.50/2.50; ☼ 10am-11pm Mon-Sat, 1-9pm Sun) Slick 'n' stylish with flat-screen TV.

Neptune Internet (☎ 04 76 63 94 18; 2 rue de la Paix; 60mins €2.50; ☼ 9am-9pm Mon-Fri, 10am-8pm Sat, 1-8pm Sun) Wi-fi and laptop connection points; happy hours.

Pl@net Internet (☎ 04 76 47 44 74; 1 place Vaucanson; 15/30/60mins €1.50/2.50/3.50; ☼ 10am-11pm Mon-Sat, 1-8pm Sun)

INTERNET RESOURCES

www.grenoble.fr Official city website (in French).

LAUNDRY

Pay around €3 to wash a 5kg load at:

Au 43 Viallet (43 av Felix Viallet; ☼ 7am-8pm)

Laverie Berriat (88 cours Berriat; ☼ 7am-8pm)

POST

Post Office (rue de la République) Next to the tourist office.

TOURIST INFORMATION

Tourist Office (☎ 04 76 42 41 41; www.grenoble-isere .info; 14 rue de la République; ☼ 9am-6.30pm Mon-Sat, 10am-1pm Sun, longer hours in summer) Inside the Maison du Tourisme. Sells maps and guides, arranges city tours.

Sights

FORT DE LA BASTILLE

Looming above the old city on the northern side of the River Isère, this grand 16th-century fort is Grenoble's best known

---

CITY PASS

In town for a few days? Invest in a **Multipass'Grenoble**, sold at the tourist office for €10.50. It includes a return trip on the Grenoble Bastille cable car (opposite), a guided city tour (p561), reduced admission to several museums and discounts in a clutch of shops.

landmark. Built to control the approaches to the city, the stronghold has long been a focus of military and political action.

These days, the strategic importance of **Fort de la Bastille** (498m; www.bastille-grenoble.com) might have waned, but the city and mountain views it proffers are spectacular. Three viewpoint indicators explain the surrounding vistas (glimpse Mont Blanc on clear days) and panels map out hiking trails, some of which lead down the hillside.

To get to the fort, hop aboard the riverside **Téléphérique Grenoble Bastille** (☎ 04 76 44 33 65; quai Stéphane Jay; adult/student/under 5yr one way €3.90/3.20/free, adult/student return €5.70/4.60; ☽ 10.45am-6.30pm Tue-Sun, 11am-6.30pm Mon Nov-Feb, 9.30am-11.45pm Tue-Sat, 9.30am-7.25pm Sun, 11am-7.25pm Mon Mar-May & Oct, 9.15am-11.45pm Tue-Sat, 9.15am-7.25pm Sun, 11am-11.45pm Mon Jun & Sep, 9.15-12.15am Tue-Sun, 11-12.15am Mon Jul & Aug). The ascent in egg-shaped pods, which climb 264m from the quay over the swift waters of the River Isère, is almost more fun than the fort itself. Unsurprisingly, it gets crowded in summer – leave early to avoid the worst queues.

MUSEUMS
The city has a wealth of great museums, many free.

Musée de Grenoble
The sleek glass and steel exterior of Grenoble's boldest museum stands at the southern end of place Notre Dame. Also called Musée des Beaux-Arts, **Musée de Grenoble** (☎ 04 76 63 44 44; www.museedegrenoble.fr in French; 5 place de Lavalette; adult/student €5/2, free 1st Sun of month; ☽ 10am-6.30pm Wed-Mon) is renowned for its distinguished modern collection, including various works by famous artists Chagall, Matisse, Modigliani, Monet, Picasso, Pissaro and Gauguin, among others.

Centre National d'Art Contemporain
Housed in the city's other architectural biggie, Grenoble's National Centre of Contemporary Art is a must-see. Considered one of Europe's leading centres of contemporary art, it is dramatically placed in **Le Magasin** (☎ 04 76 21 95 84; www.magasin-cnac.org in French; 155 cours Berriat; adult/student/under 10yr €3.50/2/free; ☽ 2-7pm Tue-Sun), a vast and hugely impressive glass and steel warehouse built by employees of Gustave Eiffel. There are two exhib-

ition areas – a permanent 1000-sq-m space with a huge glass roof called 'The Rue' and a flexible space of about 900 sq m known as 'The Galleries'. Charles Saatchi would be green with envy.

Musée d'Histoire Naturelle
Alpine flora and fauna, a 'carnival of insects' and an aquarium are housed in the **Natural History Museum** (☎ 04 76 44 05 35; 1 rue Dolomieu; adult/18-25yr/under 18yr €2.20/1.10/free; ☽ 9.30am-noon & 1.30-5.30pm Mon-Fri, 2-6pm Sat & Sun), overlooking Jardin des Plantes. The grounds include a botanical garden.

Musée Dauphinois
The **Musée Dauphinois** (☎ 04 76 85 19 01; www.musee-dauphinois.fr in French; 30 rue Maurice Gignoux; admission free; ☽ 10am-7pm Wed-Mon Jun-Sep, until 6pm Oct-May) documents the cultures, crafts and traditions of Alpine life, including a fantastic exhibition devoted to the region's skiing history. The museum occupies a beautiful 17th-century convent, nestled at the foot of the hill below Fort de la Bastille. From the city centre, it is most easily reached by the Pont St-Laurent footbridge.

East of the museum, also in the historic St-Laurent quarter, is the **Musée Archéologique** (Archaeological Museum; ☎ 04 76 44 78 68; www.musee-archeologique-grenoble.com; ☽ 9am-6pm Wed-Mon), in a 12th-century church.

Musée de l'Ancien Évêché
On place Notre-Dame the imposing **Cathédrale Notre Dame** and adjoining 14th-century **Bishops' Palace** – home to Grenoble's bishops until 1908 – form the **Musée de l'Ancien Évêché** (☎ 04 76 03 15 25; www.ancien-eveche-isere.com; 2 rue Très Cloîtres; admission free; ☽ 9am-6pm Wed-Sat & Mon, 10am-7pm Sun). The palace museum traces local history and takes visitors beneath the cathedral square to a crypt safeguarding old Roman walls and a baptistry dating from the 4th to 10th centuries.

Musée de la Résistance et de la Déportation de l'Isère
This moving **Museum of Resistance & Deportation** (☎ 04 76 42 38 53; www.resistance-en-isere.com in French; 14 rue Hébert; admission free; ☽ 9am-6pm Mon & Wed-Fri, 1.30-6pm Tue, 10am-6pm Sat & Sun Sep-Jun, 10am-7pm Mon & Wed-Sun, 1.30-7pm Tue Jul & Aug) examines the deportation of Jews and other 'undesirables' from Grenoble to Nazi

GRENOBLE

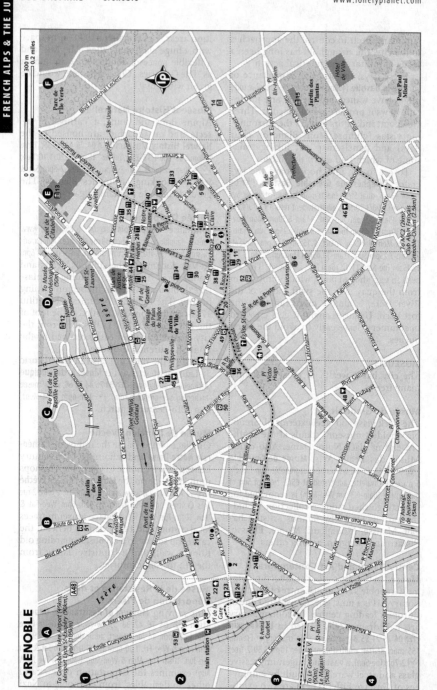

camps during WWII, and explores the role of the Vercors region in the French Resistance. Captions are in French, English and German.

Activities

The authorities on mountain activities around Grenoble – skiing, snowboarding, ski mountaineering, ice climbing, walking, mountain biking, rock climbing etc – reside in the **Maison de la Montagne** (☎ 0 825 825 588; 3 rue Raoul Blanchard; ☼ 9am-6pm Mon-Fri, 10am-1pm & 2-5pm Sat). For help in planning your mountain adventure, including information on local clubs, *gîtes* and *refuges*, make a beeline for the **Bureau Info-Montagne** (☎ 04 76 42 45 90; www.grande-traversee-alpes.com in French), which additionally runs a well-stocked library of hiking maps and guides that are free to consult. If it's a guide you're after there is the **Bureau des Guides de Grenoble et Accompagnateurs** (☎ 04 38 37 01 71; www.guide-grenoble.com in French; ☼ 9am-noon & 2-6pm Mon-Fri) or **SIPAVAG** (☎ 04 76 24 48 59; www.sipavag.fr in French; ☼ 1.45-4pm Wed & noon-4pm Fri), which organises some great thematic half- and full-day hikes as well as walks with a donkey.

The best-known (but not, depending on your interests, necessarily the best) club is **Club Alpin Français Grenoble-Oisans** (☎ 04 76 47 04 22; www.cafgo.org in French; 16 rue Marcel Peretto; ☼ 3-6pm Mon, Wed & Fri, 10am-noon & 2.30-7pm Tue, 6-8.30pm Thu) with a regional counterpart,

Club Alpin Français de l'Isère (☎ 04 76 87 03 73; 32 av Félix Viallet; www.clubalpin-grenoble.com in French; ☼ 2-6pm Tue & Wed, 2-8pm Thu & Fri). For *refuge* information and/or reservations contact the latter.

Skiers not keen to waste precious piste time queuing for a lift pass at one of Grenoble's surrounding **ski resorts** (p565) can buy passes in advance from the tourist office or the *billetterie* inside FNAC (p564). Amateur walkers will appreciate the 50 short walks and strolls suggested by public transport company TAG (p565) in its free booklet *Guide Balades* (French only).

Tours

The tourist office organises imaginative thematic **walking tours** (adult/student €7.50/5.50), including a two-hour stroll in the footsteps of Grenoble-born novelist Stendhal; a two-hour 'doors, staircases and courtyards' discovery tour and various industry-focused tours. Those who'd rather go it alone can rent an MP3 audioguide (€7 plus €80 deposit; one-hour tour with 13 stops) at the tourist office.

Festivals & Events

Jazz greats have hit Grenoble for a fiesta of concerts during the annual **Grenoble Jazz Festival** (programme information ☎ 04 76 51 00 04, festival office ☎ 04 76 51 65 32; www.jazzgrenoble.com in French; tickets free-€25, 3-/6-evening pass €42/78) in March for the last 34 years; the venue for many concerts is MC2 (p564).

Sleeping

Grenoble hotels aren't the cheapest but compared to those in nearby ski resorts, many offer good value. Special deals are available at certain hotels through the 'Bon Weekend en Ville' scheme (p948).

Parking in Grenoble is a pain. Few hotels have private garages, meaning you have to park in a public car park (€10 a night), generally a five-minute walk from your hotel. Guests at some hotels get discounted parking rates; check at your hotel reception.

BUDGET

Auberge de Jeunesse (☎ 04 76 09 33 52; grenoble@fuaj.org; 10 av du Grésivaudan; B&B €16.70; reception ☁ 7.30am-11pm) Five kilometres south of the train station in the Echirolles district. From cours Jean Jaurès, take bus 1 to the Quinzaine stop (look for the Casino supermarket).

Hôtel Alizé (☎ 04 76 43 12 91; www.hotelalize.com; 1 rue Amiral Courbet; s with washbasin €28, d with washbasin/shower €35/39, tr €47) The major drawcard of this small, simple, well-run one-star pad opposite the train station is its cheapness; book in advance to snag one of its 35 rooms.

Hôtel Acacia (☎ 04 76 87 29 90; 13 rue de Belgrade; s/d €39/43-60) As boxy and boring as it is, this dead-central hotel with pallid apricot façade and handy car park opposite could not be closer to the action. Count five floors and 20 rooms.

MIDRANGE & TOP END

Hôtel Gloria (☎ 04 76 46 12 93; hotelgloria@wanadoo.fr; 12 rue Aristide Berges; s/d €46/50) Gloria is a simple number, tucked down an appealing side street in the train station area. The hotel is clearly past her heyday, but Eric runs it with a certain dry grace. B&W snaps of old Grenoble decorate the corridor.

Hôtel Institut (☎ 04 76 46 36 44; www.institut-hotel.fr; 10 rue Barbillon; d/tr €52/70; ☒) There's good reason why the SNCF book out a certain number of rooms at this excellent-value two-star hotel with ginger-and-white façade. Refreshing air-con – sweet in steamy July and August – costs an extra €6. There's an overload of tourist information in reception.

Hôtel Suisse et Bordeaux (☎ 04 76 47 55 87; www.hotel-sb-grenoble.com; 6 place de la Gare; s/d/tr/q €44/53/65/70) The decidedly odd corridor décor of this vast century-old hotel facing the train station – bathroom tiles plastered around the door frames – is the only real element of surprise. Otherwise it's bog-standard three-star furnishings throughout. Breakfast (€7), notably, is served from 6am.

Hôtel de l'Europe (☎ 04 76 46 16 94; www.hoteleurope.fr; 22 place Grenette; s with washbasin/shower €29/39, s/d from €52/56) This classic late-17th-century Grenoblois building above place Grenette, a hotel since 1820, is among the city's oldest establishments. And its range of 45 comfortable, spacious rooms designed to suit all budgets are fantastic value to boot. A fabulously elegant staircase spirals up four floors past a bunch of caged budgies, while rooms facing the front proffer balconies offering Fort de la Bastille and mountain views.

Hôtel Angleterre (☎ 04 76 87 37 21; www.hotel-angleterre-grenoble.com; 5 place Victor Hugo; d €98-170; ☐) Hotel England – the pick of several three-star hotels in the area – has a lovely outlook over elegant, fountain-adorned and tree-shaded place Victor Hugo. Rooms are appropriately luxurious (if small) and the in-room kettle to make tea and coffee is a welcome (if unusual in France) touch. Breakfast/a day's internet access each cost €12.

Eating

Dining embraces the whole gamut of cuisines. The main food thoroughfares being around place Grenette, place Notre Dame, place St-André and rue Brocherie, but there are interesting places scattered all over the city.

As Dauphiné capital, Grenoble is *the* place to sample that quintessential French dish *gratin dauphinois* (finely sliced potatoes oven-baked in cream and a pinch of nutmeg). *Noix de Grenoble* (a sweet walnut candy) and *gâteau aux noix* (walnut cake) are local specialities for the sweeter-toothed.

RESTAURANTS

Altitude 4810 (☎ 04 76 87 40 79; 49 av Alsace Lorraine; menus €9.90 & €13.50; ☁ 8am-midnight) Cheap and cheerful is the trademark of this cheesy but popular fake chalet where specialities like *tartiflette* (€10.50), fondue (€14.50) and *raclette* (€14.50) are served up to a fairly undiscerning but hungry crowd.

Shaman Café (☎ 04 38 37 23 56; 1 place Notre Dame; menu from €11; ◷ 8am-midnight) Submerge yourself in oriental opulence at this cavernous restaurant-cum-bar with low lighting and a cuisine that flits between India, Japan, Morocco and Italy. Particularly good value is its lunchtime buffet (€10).

La Mandala (☎ 04 76 44 49 80; 4 rue Raoul Blanchard; mains €10-15; ◷ lunch & dinner Mon-Sat, lunch Sun) No more than a dozen tables fill this modern eating space with steely façade, kitchen behind glass, retro ceramic-green tiled bar and the day's market-driven specials chalked up *au tableau* (on the blackboard). Note *les afters* are obligatory!

Les Archers (☎ 04 76 46 27 76; 2 rue Docteur Bailly; mains €10-15; ◷ 11am-2am Tue-Sat, 11am-1am Sun & Mon) This busy brasserie has great outside summer seating, cosy red leather banquet seating inside and a shellfish repertoire that is hard to beat. October to March an oyster-charged seafood platter is the thing to order. Home-cooked tripe is the other standout.

Le Mal Assis (☎ 04 76 54 75 93; 9 rue Bayard; mains €15; ◷ dinner Tue-Sat) 'The Badly Seated' translates as a small but cosy, conventional, upmarket restaurant favoured by a smart, cultured crowd. Cuisine deviates little from old-school *bourgeoise*; think a choice of four traditional meats in the company of *gratin dauphinois*. Reservations recommended.

L'Amphitryon (☎ 04 76 51 38 07; 9 rue Chenoise; mains €15; ◷ dinner Mon-Sat) Push your way through what must be Grenoble's biggest steel door to enter this stark, minimalist space – a seriously funky restaurant with orange walls – to feast on great Mediterranean cuisine.

La Mère Ticket (☎ 04 76 44 45 40; 13 rue Jean-Jacques Rousseau; menus €18.50 & €24; ◷ lunch & dinner Mon-Sat) The homely cooking at this tiny, old-style French restaurant – think red-and-white checked tablecloths, lace curtains, handwritten menu and just four mains to choose from – hasn't changed for years! The *poulet aux écrevisses* (chicken with crayfish) and *gratin dauphinois* come highly recommended.

Italian's Café (☎ 04 76 17 14 72; 4 rue de Belgrade; pasta €11-19, meat mains €15-25, menus €17-37; ◷ lunch & dinner Mon-Sat) The funky furnishings – shocking-pink leather chairs, cutlery lampshades, beer on tap pulled from a sax – lure a cut above the student set to stylish IC, a restaurant-bar with a wholly Italian cuisine.

La Panse (☎ 04 76 54 09 54; 7 rue de la Paix; menus €19 & €31; ◷ lunch & dinner Mon-Sat) Herring and whisky pâté, quail with foie gras in sweet madeira sauce, brill in sorrel sauce or a simple deer stew are among the traditional dishes cooked with a contemporary twist at this relaxed dining spot. Media types particularly like it.

Le Supplice de Tantale (☎ 04 76 44 28 29; 13 rue Jean-Jacques Rousseau; menu €25; ◷ lunch & dinner Tue-Sat) No more than a handful of tables at a time can savour the exceptional seasonal fare cooked up from strictly local produce at this stylish upmarket bistro. The *suggestion du moment* (€13 to €20) invariably surprises.

our pick **La Fondue** (☎ 04 76 15 20 72; 5 rue Brocherie; salads from €5.90, fondue per person €12.50-22.50, raclette €21-23; ◷ dinner Mon, lunch & dinner Tue-Sat) The stream of hungry people who pile into this overly rustic hide-out on a Friday and Saturday night – only to be turned away or told to come back at 11pm (it doesn't accept telephone reservations at weekends) – confirms that, old-hat décor aside, this is Grenoble's fondue hot spot. Leave your waistline worries at the door and dip into one of 15 fondue types (minimum two people). Otherwise, there's regular *raclette* (a hunk of *raclette* cheese melted before your very eyes) or the decidedly more rare mouthwatering *raclette aux 3 fromages* (three-cheese *raclette*) starring blue and goat's cheese as well as *raclette*. Tricky it is but save space if you can for dessert: for a truly decadent taste of the region go hell-for-leather for *fondue des Pères Chartreux* – fruit chunks dipped in a bowl of warm melted chocolate laced with fiery pea-green Chartreuse liqueur.

CAFÉS & QUICK EATS

Pivano (☎ 04 76 50 62 13; 33 av Alsace Lorraine; mains €4; ◷ 7.15am-6pm Mon-Fri, 8am-6pm Sat) 'Gastronomic snacks' are the hallmark of this chic boutique-café where imaginative sandwiches, warm and cold, are served in a mellow peach and amber setting.

China Moon (☎ 04 76 43 14 15; 52 av Alsace Lorraine; mains €4; ◷ 9am-11pm daily) The Chinese fare at this vast self-service canteen opposite the train station is definitely not startling – but its 100-year-old setting is.

Le Tonneau de Diogène (☎ 04 76 42 38 40; 6 place Notre Dame; menu from €8, plat du jour €8.40; ☒ 11.30am-midnight) Grenoble's best known philo-café is a cramped, wonderfully atmospheric place, decked out with polished wood, leather booths, tightly packed tables and an academic crowd.

Café de la Table Ronde (☎ 04 76 44 51 41; www.cafetableronde.com in French; 7 place St-André; lunch menu €10, dinner menu €22; ☒ 7am-midnight Mon-Sat) This historic café from 1739 was a favoured haunt of Stendhal and Rousseau, its old-world atmosphere, period furnishings and moulded bar changing little since the 19th century. In summer its tables and chairs spill onto place St-André, easily the city's loveliest (and liveliest) drinking square.

SELF-CATERING

Les Halles Ste-Claire (place Ste-Claire; ☒ 7am-1pm Tue-Thu & Sun, 7am-1pm & 3-7pm Fri & Sat) Grenoble's lovely old covered market since 1874.

Monoprix (22 rue Lafayette; ☒ 8.30am-8pm Mon-Sat) Supermarket with street-level *boulangerie* (bakery; rue Raoul Blanchard entrance).

Drinking

Le 365 (☎ 04 76 51 73 18; 3 rue Bayard; ☒ 3pm-1 or 2am Tue-Sat) This Pandora's box of knick-knacks oozes an atmosphere so relaxed it really is difficult to leave whatever the time of day. Hang out around low tables on comfy leather chairs and sip a hot *chocolat Chartreuse* (which comes with whipped cream, spiced bread, chocolate and dried fruit!) or something stronger. Look for the Michelin rubber-tyre man outside.

Barberousse (☎ 04 76 57 14 53; www.barberousse.com in French; 8 rue Hache; ☒ 6pm-2am Tue-Sat) There are 70-odd types of aromatic rum (think cherry, apple, papaya etc) to try – many fermenting in giant pirate-style glass flasks behind the counter – at this superbly hip shooter bar hidden down an alley. Down a shot of cherry, apple, papaya or other fruit-flavoured liqueurs. Note that a *planteur* is fruitier than a *shooter*, and backpacks must be left in the wardrobe (€1).

Les 3 Canards (☎ 04 76 46 74 74; 2 av Félix Viallet; ☒ 5pm-2am) A studenty in-the-know set

favours this candle-lit bar with violet tables and a décor that seriously distracts. Locals call it 'Les 3C' ('the three ducks').

momento (☎ 04 76 26 21 59; 2 rue Beccaria; ☒ until 1am Sun-Wed, until 2am Thu-Sat) Steel and neon mingle with a well-dressed set at this trendy lounge bar (no capital M please) where tapas whets appetites and DJs set toes tapping from 10.30pm.

Subway (☎ 04 76 87 31 67; 22 blvd Gambetta; ☒ 8.30am-1am Mon-Wed, 8.30am-2am Thu & Fri, 2pm-2am Sat, 4pm-1am Sun) Seeking out fellow drink-happy students? Hit this rough-cut student bar where DJs mix live some nights.

Styx (☎ 04 76 44 09 99; 6 place Claveyson; ☒ 1pm-2am Mon-Sat) The air is vodka heavy at hip, chic and steely Styx where a cooler-than-cool clientele sip shots and cocktails beneath a vaulted stone ceiling. Designer bites include beef and salmon carpaccio.

Le Couche Tard (☎ 04 76 44 18 79; 1 rue du Palais; ☒ 4pm-1am) This grungy pub is another busy late-night drinking spot, but there are loads more to discover: Rue Brocherie, place St-André, tiny place de Gordes and the streets around rue Thiers are made for late-night exploring.

Entertainment

Pick up the weekly *Sortir* and *Le Petit Bulletin* (both free) at the tourist office to discover what's happening when and where.

La Nef (☎ 04 76 46 53 25; 18 blvd Édouard Rey; tickets €7.50) shows a great selection of art-house and independent films. For new releases try **Les 6 Rex** (☎ 08 92 68 00 31; 13 rue St-Jacques; tickets €7.80). Find programmes (in French) at www.cine-loisirs.com.

The most exciting all-rounder for theatre, dance, opera, jazz (p561) and other music is **MC2** (Maison de la Culture; ☎ 04 76 00 79 00; www.mc2grenoble.fr in French; 4 rue Paul Claudel; box office ☒ 12.30-7.30pm Tue-Fri, 2-7pm Sat), 2km south of the centre on tram line A (tram stop MC2).

As a thriving student city, Grenoble boasts music venues galore. **La Soupe aux Choux** (☎ 04 76 87 05 67; http://jazzalasoupe.free.fr in French; 7 rte de Lyon; admission €20; ☒ 8.30pm-1am Tue-Sat) is the tip-top address for getting down to live jazz but you can get into the groove of dozens more venues with flyers at the *billetterie* (ticket office) inside **FNAC** (☎ 04 76 85 85 85; 4 rue Félix Poulet; ☒ 10am-7pm Mon-Sat).

GAY GRENOBLE

Student-studded Grenoble enjoys a rich gay life, kicking off with a wealth of gay organisations (think everything from gay rugby to gay mountain-sports, singing and a support network for gay and lesbian parents) spearheaded by **CIGALE** (Collectif Inter-Associations Gays et Lesbiennes; www .cigalegrenoble.free.fr in French; 8 rue Sergent Bobillot). The fabulously cutting-edge **Festival Vues d'en Face** (www.vuesdenface.com), an international gay and lesbian film festival, is held each year in April followed by June's hugely gay **Semaine Gay et Lesbienne** (Gay & Lesbian Week).

    Le Georges V (☎ 04 76 84 16 20; 124 cours Berriat; admission €12; ☾ 11pm-5.30am Wed-Sun) is a happening gay nightclub and **Le Code Bar** (☎ 04 76 43 58 91; 9 rue Étienne Marcel; ☾ 6pm-1am Tue-Sun), a hip gay bar.

    Gay Grenoble is online at www.grenoble-lgbt.com (in French).

Getting There & Away

AIR

A clutch of budget airlines, including Ryanair and easyJet, fly to/from **Grenoble-Isère Airport** (☎ 04 76 65 48 48; www.grenoble-airport.com), 45km northwest of Grenoble, from London, Bristol, Stockholm, Warsaw and Rome; see p968 for details.

BUS

The **bus station** (☎ 04 76 87 90 31; rue Émile Gueymard) next to the train station is the main terminus for several bus companies, including **VFD** (☎ 0 820 833 833; www.vfd.fr in French) and **Transisère** (☎ 04 76 87 90 31; www.transisere .fr in French). Destinations include Chambéry (€5.10, 1¾ hours), Lyon St-Exupéry airport (€20, 65 minutes), Chamrousse (€4, 1¼ hours), Bourg d'Oisans (€5.10, 50 minutes), Les Deux Alpes (€5.10, 1¾ hours) and the Vercors ski stations (p566).

    Intercars (☎ 04 76 46 19 77; www.intercars.fr in French; ☾ 9am-noon & 2-6pm Mon-Fri, 9am-noon & 2-5pm Sat) handles international destinations (p972).

TRAIN

From the **train station** (rue Émile Gueymard), next to the Gare Europole tram stop, trains run to/from Paris' Gare de Lyon (from €86, three hours), Chambéry (€9.50, one hour, 10 to 13 daily) and Lyon (€17.30, 1-¾ hours, five daily). Train tickets are sold at the station and in town at the **SNCF boutique** (15 rue de la République; ☾ 9am-6.30pm Mon-Fri, 10am-6pm Sat).

Getting Around

TO/FROM THE AIRPORT

Shuttle buses run by **Transisère** (☎ 04 76 87 90 31) to/from Grenoble-Isère Airport use the bus station (one way/return €4/8, 45 minutes, four to eight daily).

BICYCLE

Métrovélo (☎ 0 820 223 838; ☾ 7am-8pm Mon-Fri, 9am-noon & 2-7pm Sat & Sun), underneath the train station, rents out bikes for €1.20/3/5 per hour/half-day/day plus €2 for a helmet and/or kid's seat.

BUS & TRAM

Grenoble's three pollution-free tram lines – called A, B and C – run through the heart of town. A bus and tram ticket costs €1.30 from ticket machines at tram/bus stops or drivers. Time-stamp tickets in the blue machines at stops before boarding. Carnets of 10/20 tickets (€10.50/19.50) can only be bought at the **TAG office** (☎ 04 76 20 66 66; ☾ 8.30am-6.30pm Mon-Fri, 9am-6pm Sat) inside the tourist office or next to the train station. Trams run from around 5am to midnight; buses stop between 6pm and 9pm.

CAR

Find the major car-rental agencies in the Europole complex underneath the train station. Otherwise, **Rent a Car Système** (☎ 04 76 86 27 60; 10 place de la Gare) is opposite.

TAXI

Call the **central reservation line** (☎ 04 76 54 42 54) to order a taxi.

AROUND GRENOBLE

Grenoble's low-altitude surrounds lure city dwellers seeking a weekend fix of snow action, and a relaxed crowd from elsewhere who travel here for the cheap winter skiing and summer walking its small ski resorts sport. The Vercors is sweet for cross-country;

and family-driven **Chamrousse** (elevation 1700m), built for the 1968 Winter Olympics 35km southeast, is hot for beginner-level downhill; its **tourist office** (☎ 04 76 89 92 65; www.chamrousse.com in French; 42 place de Belledonne) has the full lowdown. Further east again, glacial skiing in Les Deux Alpes, Alpe d'Huez and La Grave gets extreme skiers very excited.

Several daily VFD buses link Grenoble with all its surrounding resorts (details listed in respective sections), including Chamrousse (€4, 1¼ hours). For day-trippers, the Skiligne operated by VFD to 13 different ski resorts in the region are a good deal; rates (€13 to €25) include a one-day ski pass as well as return bus fare.

Parc Naturel Régional du Vercors

Immediately southwest of Grenoble, this gently rolling nature park (1750 sq km) is a slow-paced oasis of peace and calm, known for its cross-country skiing, snowshoeing, caving and hiking. During WWII it was a Resistance stronghold, nicknamed 'Fortresse de la Résistance'.

From humble **Lans-en-Vercors** (pop 1450, elevation 1020m), 25km southwest of Grenoble, buses shuttle downhill skiers 4km east to its 14-piste Montagnes de Lans ski area. **Villard de Lans** (pop 3350, elevation 1050m), 9km up the valley, is linked by ski lifts and roads to **Corrençon-en-Vercors** (pop 320, elevation 1111m). In the tiny hamlet of **Font-d'Urle** (elevation 1500m), 45km south

of Villard de Lans, **GlissKite** (☎ 06 61 43 54 23, 06 07 47 47 23; www.gliss-kite.com in French) runs kite-surfing courses on snow.

The **Maison du Parc** (☎ 04 76 94 38 26; www.pnr-vercors.fr; 255 chemin des Fusillés; ☉ 8.30am-12.30pm & 2-5pm Mon-Fri) and **tourist office** (☎ 08 11 46 00 38; www.ot-lans-en-vercors.fr; 246 av Léopold Fabre) in Lans-en-Vercors have information on outdoor activities. In Villard de Lans, half- and full-day snowshoe discovery treks organised by **Les Accompagnateurs Nature & Patrimoine** (☎ 04 76 95 08 38; www.accompagnateur-vercors.com in French) offer a fantastic opportunity to learn about the park's flora and fauna. The **tourist office** (☎ 0 811 460 015; www.villarddelans.com; place Mure Ravaud) here is also useful. Accommodation throughout the park, including on farms, is handled by **Vercors Réservations** (☎ 04 76 95 96 96; www.vercors-reservations.com).

GETTING THERE & AWAY
Up to six **VFD** (☎ 0 820 833 833; www.vfd.fr in French) buses daily link Lans-en-Vercors with Grenoble (€5.10, 45 minutes), Villard de Lans (€1.80, 15 minutes) and Corrençon-en-Vercors (€1.80, 35 minutes).

Parc National des Écrins

The spectacular Parc National des Écrins (930 sq km), France's second-largest national park, was created in 1973. Stretching between the towns of Bourg d'Oisans, Briançon and Gap, the area is enclosed by steep, narrow valleys, sculpted by the Ro-

---

INSIDE TASTE

Sleeping and eating on a farm or *chambre d'hôte* yields an immediate insider taste of the Vercors. This author's top (albeit vastly different) three:

Château de Pâquier (☎ 04 76 72 77 33; http://chateau.de.paquier.free.fr; St-Martin de la Cluze; s/d from €51/62, evening meal €21) Moulded ceilings, period furnishings and hospitality by the tractor-load set off this secluded, 16th-century feudal manor house ensnared by garden, field and mountain. St-Martin de la Cluze is 25km south of Grenoble, 4km off the N75 on the eastern fringe of the Parc Naturel Régional de Vercors.

Entre Chiens et Loups (☎ 04 76 95 36 64; fbdumoulin@free.fr; Autrans; s/d/tr €42/52/74, evening meal €18) 'Between Dogs & Wolves' cannot disappoint. Inside this cosy wooden cabin, deep in the forested heart of the Vercors at 1100m, Florence cooks up hearty mountain fare while husband Bernard, professional musher and fisherman, takes guests mushing with his 40 dogs in winter and fishing for trout in the river come summer. Find Autrans 10km north of Lans-en-Vercors.

À la Crécia (☎ 0 870 390 776; www.gite-en-vercors.com in French; Lans-en-Vercors; s/d/tr/q €49/54/69/84, evening meal €17) Goats, pigs, poultry and lambs rule the roost at this authentic 16th-century farm, renovated with zeal by Véronique and Pascal who run this charming *chambre d'hôte*. Stylish rooms are rustic but modern with wooden beams, delicate natural tones and lots of wood.

manche, Durance and Drac rivers and their erstwhile glaciers. It peaks at 4103m.

Bourg d'Oisans (pop 3000, elevation 720m), 50km southeast of Grenoble, and **Briançon** (p569), another 67km in the same direction, are good bases for exploring the park. In Bourg d'Oisans, the **Maison du Parc** (☎ 04 76 80 00 51; rue Gambetta; ⏰ 8am-noon & 1.30-7pm Jul & Aug, 8am-noon & 1.30-5.30pm Mon-Fri Sep-Jun) sells maps and guides. The town's **tourist office** (☎ 04 76 80 03 25; www.bourgdoisans.com; quai Girard; ⏰ 8.30am-noon & 2.30-6pm Mon-Sat, 8.30-11.30am Sun Dec-Apr; 9am-noon & 2-6pm Mon-Sat May, Jun & Sep-Nov, 9am-noon Mon-Sat, 10am-noon & 3-6pm Sun Jul & Aug) is equally useful. The **national park headquarters** (☎ 04 92 40 20 10; Domaine de la Charance; www.les -ecrins-parc-national.fr) are in Gap.

SIGHTS & ACTIVITIES
In Bourg d'Oisans the **Musée des Mineraux et de la Faune des Alpes** (☎ 04 76 80 27 54; place de l'Église; adult/6-18yr €4.60/2; ⏰ 2-6pm Sep-Jun, 10am-6pm Jul & Aug) paints park geology, flora and fauna, including ibex, chamois and stoats.

In summer you can mammal-spot amid spectacular scenery from the window of **Chemin de Fer de la Mure** (☎ 0 892 391 426; www .trainlamure.com; adult/student/4-16yr return €18.50/12/9; ⏰ 2-4 departures daily Apr-Oct), a little red 1920s mountain train that chugs 30km (1¾ hours) between St-Georges de Commiers and La Mure.

Age-old footpaths used by shepherds and smugglers centuries before – 740km in all – ensnare the national park, making it prime **hiking** territory. From Bourg d'Oisans a trail climbs up to Villard Notre Dame (1525m, two hours). From Venosc, a mountain village in the Vénéon Valley, 12km southeast of Bourg d'Oisans, a trail leads to Les Deux Alpes (1660m, 1½ hours).

Kayaking along the Drac's turquoise river waters, rock climbing, via ferrata, **paragliding** and **mountain biking** are other activities; park offices have details.

SLEEPING & EATING
Grenoble's Maison de la Montagne (p561) has a list of seasonal **refuges** (dm €10-15) and the tourist office in Bourg d'Oisans knows about **gîtes d'étape** (dm €13-21) open year-round.

There are camp sites galore in and around Bourg d'Oisans, open June to Sep-

tember, including **La Cascade** (☎ 04 76 80 02 42; lacascade@wanadoo.fr; rte de l'Alpe d'Huez; 2-adult tent pitch €16.30-23.30, extra adult/under 5yr €4.40-5.80/free; ⏰ mid-Dec–Sep), 1.5km from the centre; and well-equipped **Le Colporteur** (☎ 04 76 79 11 44; www.camping-colporteur.com; Le Mas de Plan; 2-adult tent pitch €21, extra adult/under 5yr €5.50/free; ⏰ mid-May–mid-Sep), with restaurant, a two-second hop from town.

Bourg has a clutch of uninspiring hotels. Rather, try **Au Fils des Saisons** (☎ 04 76 30 07 01; www.chambresdhotes-afs.com in French; Ferme du Cros, Les Côtes de Corps; d with B&B €50, dinner €17; ⏰ Feb–mid-Dec). With enormous smiles, Dany (Danielle) and Domi (Dominique) welcome guests to their five rustic rooms with beamed ceiling in an old stone farmhouse dating back to 1731. Evening dining is around a large wooden table and breakfasts are built wholly from farm produce – think home-made bread and jam, *fromage frais* and *chèvre* (goat's cheese) made with milk from the farm. Find the Ferme du Cros 2km from Corps in Les Côtes de Corps in the south of the park; follow the southbound N85 from Grenoble. Advance reservations essential.

GETTING THERE & AWAY
From Bourg d'Oisans **bus station** (☎ 04 76 80 00 90; av de la Gare), on the main road into town, there are one to four buses daily to/from Briançon (€13.20, two hours), Les Deux Alpes (€1.80, 45 minutes) and Alpe d'Huez (€1.80, 30 minutes); and up to eight daily to/from Grenoble (€5.10, 50 minutes).

Les Deux Alpes
elevation 1600m

It's Glacier du Mont de Lans – an enormous 3200m- to 3425m-high glacier – that creates the buzz in Les Deux Alpes (elevation 1600m), a busy ski resort 28km southeast of Bourg d'Oisans. The village's lowly beginnings as mountain pasture for sheep flocks are belied by the never-ending stream of traffic that clogs up the main street, av de la Muzelle.

Wacky wall frescoes of extreme skiers in the resort's feisty **Auberge de Jeunesse** (☎ 04 76 79 22 80; les-deux-alpes@fuaj.org; dm €11) drum up images of Europe's top off-piste skiers, who head for **La Grave** (www.la-grave.com), 21km east, to tackle the legendary Vallons

de la Meije descent. The stuff of legend,
the off-piste run plummets 2150m and is
strictly for the *crème de la crème* of free-
riders.

INFORMATION
Slope-side **Maison des Deux Alpes** (place des Deux
Alpes) is the key source: inside you'll find
the **tourist office** (☎ 04 76 79 22 00; www.les2alpes
.com; ☯ 8am-7pm mid-Dec–mid-Apr, Jul & Aug, 9am-noon
& 2-6pm Mon-Fri rest of year), **accommodation service**
(☎ 04 76 79 24 38; res2alp@les2alpes.com), **ESF** (☎ 04
76 79 21 21; esf.les2alpes@wanadoo.fr) and the **Bureau
des Guides** (☎ 04 76 11 36 29; guides2alpes@yahoo.fr).
Radio 2 Alpes (96.2 FM) is also handy.

SIGHTS
Metre-tall animals, Alpine flowers and
shepherds are among the monumental
ice sculptures filling the **Grotte de Glace** (Ice
Cave; admission €3.60; ☯ 9.30am-4.30pm), a cave
carved into the Glacier du Mont de Lans
at Dôme de Puy Salié (3425m). To reach it
ride the Jandri Express *télécabine* to 3200m
(change of *télécabine* at 2600m), then the
underground Funiculaire Dôme Express
to 3400m. A ticket covering cable cars and
cave costs €20.30/16.10 per adult/under
13 years.

Most people are amazed by **La Croisière
Blanche** (The White Cruise; ☎ 04 79 79 75 03; adult
€5.70; ☯ 10.15-11.45am & 1.15-3.30pm mid-Dec–mid-
Apr, 9.30-11.45am & 1-3.15pm Jul & Aug), which is an
incredible James Bond-style journey on the
glacier by caterpillar-track minibus with
guided commentary in French. Count on
it taking 50 minutes for the glacial ride,
plus one hour to get to the glacier (using

the same cable cars as for the Grotte de
Glace, left). La Croisière Blanche is not recommended for children aged under five
and advance reservations are essential.
Cruise plus cable cars plus ice cave costs
€26/21.80.

Marginally more down-to-earth are the
informative Alpine-orientated exhibitions
held seasonally in the **Maison de la Montagne**
(☎ 04 76 79 53 15; av de la Muzelle; admission free;
☯ 2-6pm Dec-May, 10am-noon & 3-7pm Jun-Aug).

ACTIVITIES
Les Deux Alpes sports 200km of marked
downhill pistes, 20km of cross-country
trails and also a snowpark (2600m) with
600m-long axe pipe, 110m-long half-pipe
and numerous jumps. The main skiing
domain at Les Deux Alpes lies below La
Meije (3983m), one of the highest peaks
in the Parc National des Écrins. A one-/
six-day pass covering the entire area costs
€34.70/165 and a one-day Les Deux Alpes–
La Grave pass – you can ski from one resort
to the other – is €45.

Skiing and snowboarding aside, snow
fiends can bomb downhill on a mountain bike at the Bike Park des Lutins, ice
skate, or nip around the rink in an ice-
glider car. Contact the **Bureau des Guides** (left)
for organised ice climbing, snowshoeing,
off-piste skiing, ski mountaineering and
ruisseling (walking along iced brooks with
crampons and ice axe). In summer guides
run rock climbing, walking, rafting and biking expeditions.

The summer skiing season on the
glacier – Europe's largest summer skiing
area against a panoramic backdrop of Mont
Blanc, Massif Central and Mont Ventoux –
runs mid-June to the end of August.
Otherwise there are three nail-biting descents and 22 marked trails for mountain-
bikers; numerous hiking trails; and plenty
of paragliding.

GETTING THERE & AWAY
VFD buses link Grenoble (€5.10, 1¾ hours,
eight daily) and Les Deux Alpes via Bourg
d'Oisans; return journeys to Grenoble must
be booked 72 hours in advance in Les Deux
Alpes at **Agence VFD** (☎ 04 76 87 90 31; 112 av
de la Muzelle). There are also services to/from
Briançon and Lyon St-Exupéry and Geneva
airports.

Alpe d'Huez

elevation 1860m

A Tour de France classic – the great *Montée de l'Alpe d'Huez* – helter-skelters cyclists and motorists around 21 hair-raising hair-pin bends to Alpe d'Huez, a purpose-built resort, 14.5km above Bourg d'Oisans in the Massif des Grandes Rousses. Here, 245km of motorway pistes range from dead-easy to deadly; at 16km La Sarenne, accessible from the Pic Blanc cable car, is the French Alps' longest black run. Experienced skiers can also ski in July, August and, unusually, for one week around late October, on glaciers ranging from 2530m to 3330m. Off the slopes, speed fiends can ice-drive … in a Porsche.

The panorama from Pic du Lac Blanc (3330m), the highest point accessible year-round by the Tronçons and Pic Blanc cable cars, is impressive – as is the ice art show-cased mid-station (2700m) at the **Grotte de Glace** (Ice Cave; adult/child €3.50/2.50, with cable cars €11.50/7.50). Summer unveils mountains threaded through with marked hiking and biking trails.

Information hub **Maison de l'Alpe** (place Paganon) sells ski passes (€36.20/day) and houses the **tourist office** (☎ 04 76 11 44 44; www.alpedhuez.com; ⌚ 8.45am-7pm), **accommodation reservation centre** (☎ 04 76 80 90 90; www.alpes-vacances.com; ⌚ 9am-1pm & 2-7pm Mon-Fri, 9am-noon & 2-6pm Sat & Sun) and **ESF** (☎ 04 76 80 31 69; www.esf-alpedhuez.com).

GETTING THERE & AWAY

VFD buses (opposite) link Alpe d'Huez and Grenoble (€5.10, 1¾ hours, eight daily) via Bourg d'Oisans. Two days a week buses shuttle skiers from Alpe d'Huez to Les Deux Alpes (return €6, 45 minutes, twice daily).

> **BEHIND THE SNOWY SCENES**
>
> Ever wondered where all that snow comes from? Wonder no more. Take a tour of Alpe d'Huez's hi-tech **Usine à Neige du Plat des Marmottes** (Plat des Marmottes Snow Factory; admission & cable cars €15; ⌚ 2pm Thu) at 2300m where artificial snow is made; the resort has 770 snow-making machines in all. ...cess Plat des Marmottes with the Mar-...tes cable car.

BRIANÇON

pop 11,300 / elevation 1320m

Jutting out from a rocky outcrop at the meeting of five valleys, hilltop Briançon stands like a sentinel between the French Alps and Italy, 20km northeast. Long a frontier post, it was fortified by military architectural great, Vauban, in the 17th century and, at 1320m high, can happily claim to be Europe's highest town (blessed by 300-odd days of sunshine a year to boot). But peep behind Briançon's lofty ramparts and sheer walls reminiscent of the great towns of northern Burgundy and there's one too many shut shop fronts and *à vendre* (for sale) signs for comfort.

Cheap skiing (with no après-ski scene or nightlife to speak of) or walking are the best reasons to bed down in Briançon. From the modern lower town, linked to the old upper town by the steep hill of av de la République, a cable car lumbers up to Le Prorel (2566m) from where a bounty of pistes in the Serre Chevalier ski area (p570) unfold. West lies the Parc National des Écrins (p566); south is the Parc Naturel Régional du Queyras.

Information

Crédit Agricole (10 Grande Rue; ⌚ 8.15am-noon & 1.30-4.45pm Mon-Fri, until 3.45pm Sat) Bank with currency exchange.

Maison du Parc (☎ 04 92 21 42 15; ecrins.brianconnais@espacesnaturels.fr; place Médecin Général Blanchard; ⌚ 9.30am-7pm Jul & Aug, 2-6pm Sep-Jun) Comprehensive information on the Parc National des Écrins (p566).

Post Offices (place du Champ de Mars; av du 159 RIA)

Tourist Office (☎ 04 92 21 08 50; www.ot-briancon.fr in French; Maison des Templiers, 1 place du Temple; ⌚ 9am-noon & 2-6pm Mon-Sat, 10am-12.30pm & 3-5pm Sun Sep-Jun, 9am-7pm Jul & Aug) In Vieille Ville.

Sights

Take a walk on the slow side around the pretty if run-down Vieille Ville (Old Town). Enter from place du Champ de Mars (north) through **Porte de Pignerol**, a daunting gateway hewn from dark stone, or up the hill from the lower town through **Porte d'Embrun**. The two gates are linked by the steep main street, Grande Rue, known as **Grande Gargouille** (Great Gargoyle) because of the drain that gushes down its

FRENCH ALPS & THE JURA

middle. The tiny **Musée de la Mesure du Temps** (☎ 04 92 21 07 93; 45 Grande Rue; adult/child €4.50/2; ☺ variable) is as interesting for the old house in which it is crammed as for its sundial collection.

Meander away from the main tourist track to uncover a couple of tiny, tumble-down chapels in the shabby back streets. The coral-pink **Collégiale Notre Dame et St Nicholas** (place du Temple) – a characteristically heavy and fortified twin-towered church – is an early 18th-century Vauban creation. The baroque paintings and gilt chapels inside are worth a closer look.

Crowning the old city is the slumbering 18th-century **Fort du Château**, affording magnificent mountain views from its bat-

tlements. If you can't face the hike up, av Vauban along the town's northern ramparts affords equally spectacular views of the snowy Écrins peaks.

Activities

Serre Chevalier (www.serre-chevalier-ski.com) – which is properly called Le Grand Serre Chevalier – links 13 villages and 250km of piste along the Serre Chevalier Valley between Briançon and Le Monêtier-les-Bains, 15km northwest. From the Briançon–Serre-Chevalier station at 1200m in Briançon's lower town, it takes just a few minutes to reach the slopes with the **Télécabine du Prorel** (Prorel Cable Car; av René Froger; return ticket/day pass for pedestrians €4.80/10;

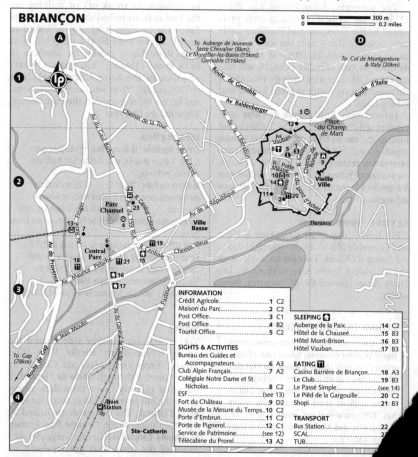

BRIANÇON

0 300 m
0 0.2 miles

To Auberge de Jeunesse
Serre Chevalier (8km);
Le Monêtier-les-Bains (15km);
Grenoble (116km)

To Col de Montgenèvre
& Italy (20km)

Route de Grenoble

Av Baldenberger

Route d'Italie

Chemin de la Tour

Av du Clair Barnol

Av de la Libération

Av du Laillard

Av
Vauban

Place
du Champ
de Mars

R. Porte
Méane

R. des
Cordes

Chemin de
la Ronde

Porte
Méane

Vieille
Ville

R. Cental Colaul

Av de la République

Parc
Channel

R. Central Colaul

Grande Rue

Pont d'Asfeld

Ville
Basse

Durance

Av de Provence

Av René Froger

R. Centrale

Chemin Vieux

Central
Parc

Av Maurice Petsché

R. Pasteur

R. du Général de Gaulle

R. Jean Moulin

To Gap
(78km)

Route de Gap

Train
Station

Ste-Catherin

8.45am-4.15pm Mon-Thu, 8.45am-5.15pm Fri-Sun mid-Dec–mid-Apr & mid-Jun–mid-Sep). A one-day Briançon/Grand Serre Chevalier ski-lift pass costs €23/35.

The **ESF** (☎ 04 92 20 30 57; www.esf-serrechevalier .com; 7 av René Froger; 8.45am-6pm Dec-Apr) runs a seasonal office inside the Prorel cablecar station and **Club Alpin Français** (CAF; ☎ 04 92 20 16 52; caf.briancon@wanadoo.fr; 6 av René Froger; 5-7pm Tue-Sat) is opposite. The latter runs many of the mountain *refuges* in this neck of the woods and organises ice climbing and ski tours.

For summer activities, including walking in the Briançon, Oisans and Vanoise regions, visit the Maison du Parc (p569) and **Bureau des Guides et Accompagnateurs** (☎ 04 92 20 15 73; bgb05@club-internet.fr; Central Parc) which organises treks, parapente, rafting, cycling, canyoning and via ferrata.

Tours

The **Service de Patrimoine** (☎ 04 92 20 29 49; patrimoine@mairie-briancon.fr; Porte de Pignerol; 2-5.30pm Mon, 9.30am-noon & 2-5.30pm Tue-Fri), tucked in one of the old-town city gates, organises guided old-town walks (€5.15, 1½ hours), some in English.

Sleeping

Contact the tourist office–run accommodation service, **Briançon Réservations** (☎ 04 92 21 01 01; resa@ot-serrechevalier.fr), for the complete lowdown. Hotel parking in the pedestrian old town is a headache; park along the ramparts and walk.

Auberge de Jeunesse Serre Chevalier (☎ 04 92 24 74 54; serre-chevalier@fuaj.org; Le Bez, Serre-Chevalier 1400; dm summer €11.50; late Dec–Apr & mid-Jun–mid-Sep) This trio of attractive Savoyard houses set at the foot of the piste collectively forms the nearest hostel, 8km northwest at Serre Chevalier-le-Bez near Villeneuve-la-Salle. Hop aboard a bus heading to Monêtier-les-Bains, get off at Villeneuve Pré Long and walk 600m. Half- or full-board on a weekly basis is obligatory during winter school holidays; otherwise you can check in for one night on a full-board basis. Weekly rates include a six-day ski pass. Winter low/mid/high season dorm accommodation with full-board is €36/40/50, weekly half-board is €281/345/410, and weekly full board is €326/398/445.

Hôtel Mont-Brison (☎ 04 92 21 14 55; 3 av du Général de Gaulle; d with sink/shower €30/38, d/tr/q with bathroom €43/60/70; Jan-Oct) Lime-green shutters and emerald-green balconies flag this shabby two-star joint overlooking a busy road. Inside, beige is king.

Auberge de la Paix (☎ 04 92 21 37 43; www.auberge-de-la-paix.com; 3 rue Porte Méane; s/d/tr €37/39/50, s/d/tr with shower €39/41/60, s/d/tr with shower & toilet €43/46/60) Three floors, no lift, creaky wooden floors, minuscule windows and plenty of 1960s flower power are the trademarks of Briançon's oldest hotel, an old-town inn dating from 1845. The attached restaurant is recommended for Savoyard specialities (menus from €19).

Hôtel de la Chaussée (☎ 04 92 21 10 37; hotel-de-la-chaussee@wanadoo.fr; 4 rue Centrale; d/tr/q €68/75/85) Five generations of Bonnaffoux have run this author top-choice – a small hotel oozing with charm on Briançon's most appealing street. Renovated rooms are rustic-modern and copper cooking pots add an inventive touch to the busy restaurant.

Hôtel Vauban (☎ 04 92 21 12 11; www.hotel-vauban.fr; 13 av du Général de Gaulle; s/d/tr/q €75/84/102/115;) A definite old-fashioned air lingers in this super-friendly, family-run, well-organised hotel in the new town, going strong since 1956. Logis de France (p948) rates it.

Eating

Every other restaurant in the touristy Vieille Ville, including Le Passé Simple at the Auberge de la Paix (above), cooks up a *menu Vauban* starring traditional 17th-century recipes: think fennel-stuffed pigeon, lamb cutlets, snail and mushroom casserole and roast hare.

Le Club (☎ 04 92 21 99 06; 3 place Centrale; mains €8; lunch & dinner Mon-Sat) Kitchen & Bar is the strapline of this hip hang-out where the young and trendy feast on burgers, fries, pasta, jumbo salads and club sandwiches. Its sunny square-facing terrace is probably Briançon's best.

Casino Barrière de Briançon (☎ 04 92 20 66 66; 7 av Maurice Petsche; lunch menu €11, mains €10.50-16.60; lunch & dinner Mon-Sun) The contemporary décor at this casino restaurant arranged around a central fireplace comes as a whiff of fresh air in – dare we say it – super-staid Briançon. The mushroom and white truffle ravioli in asparagus cream is sublime.

Le Pied de la Gargouille (☎ 04 92 20 12 95; 64 Grande Rue; menus €17.50 & €19.50; ☻ dinner Mon-Sun; ✗) The Gargoyle's Foot – an old-town homage to fondue, *raclette* and *tartiflette* – is one of the friendliest, homeliest and most simple in town. Call ahead to reserve the house speciality – *gigot d'agneau à la ficelle* (whole leg of lamb strung over an open fire).

SELF-CATERING

Shopi (av Maurice Petsche; ☎ 8.30am-12.30pm & 2.30-7.30pm Mon-Sat, 8.45am-noon Sun) Supermarket.

Getting There & Away

BUS

Tickets for buses to Grenoble (€26.20, 2¾ hours, two to five daily) via Bourg d'Oisans must be booked at least 72 hours in advance at the **SCAL** (☎ 04 92 21 12 00; 14 av du 159 RIA; ☎ 9am-noon & 2-6pm Mon-Fri) office or by calling ☎ 04 76 60 47 07. Other services from the bus station on the corner of av du 159 RIA and rue Général Colaud include a daily bus to/from Gap (€9.50, two hours), Digne (€19, 3¼ hours, no bus Sunday), Marseille (€27, 5¾ hours) and Aix-en-Provence (€25, five hours). At least 10 daily services shuttle skiers and boarders to/from Villeneuve-la-Salle (€4.50, 20 minutes, 10 daily).

CAR & MOTORCYCLE

The Col de Montgenèvre (1850m), the ancient Roman mountain pass made into a reliable road by Napoleon, is the main road link between Briançon and neighbouring Italy. It stays open year-round but does occasionally get snow-bogged; to check road conditions for the Col de Montgenèvre and the nearby Col de Lautaret (2058m; open April to November), call ☎ 04 92 24 44 44.

TRAIN

From the **train station** (av du Général de Gaulle), about 1.5km from the Vieille Ville, an overnight train to Paris' Gare d'Austerlitz departs at 8.30pm (€115.50, 10¼ hours) and a speedier daytime service goes to/from the capital via Grenoble (€99.50, 6¾ hours). Other destinations include Gap (€11.70, 1¼ hours, five daily), Grenoble (€25.80, 3½ hours, one daily) and Marseille (€34.90, 4¾ hours, one daily).

Getting Around

Local buses run by **TUB** (☎ 04 92 20 47 10; tub@wanadoo.fr; place de Suse; ☎ 9am-noon & 1.30-5.30pm Tue-Fri) connect the train station with place du Champ de Mars and the Prorel cable-car station. A single ticket/carnet of 10 costs €1.10/8.

THE JURA

From its fragrant yellow wine left to mature in oak casks for six years to its unusual hot-box cheese, Jesus sausage and generous dose of authentic farmstays, Jurassien travel really is a memorable feast. Moreover, the dark wooded hills and granite plateaus of the Jura Mountains that stretch in an arc for 360km along the Franco–Swiss border from the Rhine to the Rhône are one of the least explored pockets in France. If it is peace, tranquillity and a true taste of humble mountain life you're seeking, the Jura is an instant winner.

The Jura – from a Gaulish word meaning 'forest' – is France's premier cross-country skiing area. The range is dotted with ski stations from Pontarlier south to Bellegarde; Métabief Mont d'Or, north of the Parc Naturel Régional du Haut-Jura, is the main station, as popular for its superb hiking and nature trails as for its gentle slopes. Every year the region hosts the Transjurassienne, one of the world's toughest cross-country skiing events.

BESANÇON

pop 125,000

Old town, young heart: that's Besançon, capital of the Franche-Comté region. One of France's most liveable cities, Besançon boasts one of the country's largest foreign student populations and an innovative spirit that finds expression in an old town humming with hip bars and bistros and a blog it can call its own (http://besancon info.blogspirit.com in French). The Battant quarter, originally settled by wine-makers, is the most historic.

First settled in Gallo-Roman times, Besançon became an important stop on the early trade routes between Italy, the Alps and the Rhine. In the 18th century it was a noted clock-making centre (it remains so), and in the 19th century Victor Hugo

THE JURA

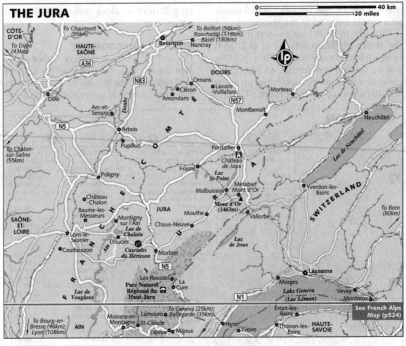

0 — 40 km
0 — 20 miles

(who penned *Les Misérables*) and the film-pioneering Lumière brothers were born on place Victor Hugo in the old town.

Orientation

The old city is encased by the curve of the River Doubs (Boucle du Doubs). The tourist office and train station sit just outside this loop. The Battant quarter straddles the northwest bank of the river around rue Battant. Grande Rue, the pedestrianised main street, slices through the old city from the bank of the river to the gates of the citadel.

Information

Blanc-Matic (14 rue de la Madeleine; 🕑 7am-8pm) Laundrette.

ID PC (28 rue de la République; per hr €3; 🕑 9.30am-noon & 2-7pm Tue-Sat) Computer shop with internet terminal.

Post Office (23 rue Proudhon; 🕑 8am-7pm Mon-Fri, 8am-noon Sat) In the old city.

Tourist Office (☎ 03 81 80 92 55; www.besancon-tourisme.com; 2 place de la 1ère Armée Française; 🕑 9.30am-7pm Mon-Sat, 10am-5pm Jun-Sep,

9.30am-6pm Mon-Sat, 10.30am-12.30pm Sun Apr, May & Oct, 9.30am-12.30pm & 1.30-5.30pm Mon-Sat, 10.30am-12.30pm Sun Nov-Mar) Sells city maps and guides; organises thematic city tours.

Sights

MUSEUMS

Built by Vauban for Louis XIV between 1688 and 1711, Besançon's **citadel** (☎ 03 81 87 83 33; www.citadelle.com; rue des Fusillés de la Résistance; adult/4-14yr €7.80/4.50; 🕑 9am-7pm Jul & Aug, 9am-6pm Apr-Jun, Sep & Oct, 10am-5pm Nov-Mar) is a steep 15-minute walk from **Porte Noire** (Black Gate; rue de la Convention), a triumphal arch left over from the city's Roman days, dating from the 2nd century AD. Inside the citadel walls there are three museums to visit: the **Musée Comtois** zooms in on local traditions, the **Musée d'Histoire Naturelle** covers natural history, and the **Musée de la Résistance et de la Déportation** examines the rise of Nazism and fascism and the French Resistance movement.

Less sobering are the insects, fish and nocturnal rodents inhabiting the **insectarium**, **aquarium**, **noctarium** and **parc zoologique** where Siberian tigers prowl. Citadel admission covers entry to all the museums.

Thought to be France's oldest museum, the **Musée des Beaux-Arts** (☎ 03 81 87 80 49; 1 place de la Révolution; adult/student €3/free; ⏱ 9.30am-noon & 2-6pm Wed-Mon) houses an impressive collection of paintings, including primitive and Renaissance works. Franche-Comté's

long history of clock-making is also displayed here.

HORLOGE ASTRONOMIQUE

Housed in the 18th-century **Cathédrale St-Jean** (rue de la Convention; adult/under 18yr €2.50/free; ⏱ 7 guided tours a day Wed-Mon Apr-Sep, Thu-Mon Oct-Mar), this incredible astronomical clock has

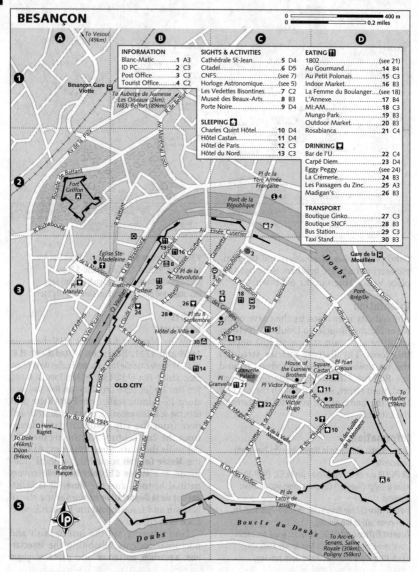

BESANÇON

0 _____ 400 m
0 _____ 0.2 miles

INFORMATION	
Blanc-Matic............1	A3
ID PC...................2	C3
Post Office..............3	C3
Tourist Office..........4	C2

SIGHTS & ACTIVITIES	
Cathédrale St-Jean............5	D4
Citadel...................6	D5
CNFS.....................7	A3
Horloge Astronomique.......(see 7)	
Les Vedettes Bisontines.......7	C2
Musée des Beaux-Arts........8	B3
Porte Noire................9	D4

SLEEPING	
Charles Quint Hôtel..........10	D4
Hôtel Castan...............11	D4
Hôtel de Paris.............12	C3
Hôtel du Nord.............13	C3

EATING	
1802.....................(see 21)	
Au Gourmand...............14	B4
Au Petit Polonais............15	C3
Indoor Market.............16	B3
La Femme du Boulanger.....(see 18)	
L'Annexe.................17	B4
MI:AM...................18	C3
Mungo Park...............19	B3
Outdoor Market............20	B3
Rosabianca...............21	C4

DRINKING	
Bar de l'U................22	C4
Carpé Diem...............23	D4
Eggy Peggy...............(see 24)	
La Crémerie..............24	B3
Les Passagers du Zinc......25	A3
Madigan's................26	B3

TRANSPORT	
Boutique Ginko.............27	C3
Boutique SNCF............28	C3
Bus Station...............29	C3
Taxi Stand................30	B3

30,000 moving parts, 57 faces, 62 dials and, among other things, tells the time in 16 places, the tides in eight different ports, and the time of sunrise and sunset. It really has to be seen to be believed.

Tours
In summer vessels dock beneath Pont de la République to take passengers on 1¼-hour river cruises along the Boucle du Doubs: **CNFS** (☎ 03 81 68 05 34; www.saut-du-doubs .org; adult/child €9.50/7.50; ⊙ Jul & Aug) and **Les Vedettes Bisontines** (☎ 03 81 68 13 25; www.saut dudoubs.fr in French; adult/child €9.50/7.50; ⊙ Apr–Oct). In summer there are usually three trips a day. Both companies sail along a 375m-long tunnel underneath the citadel.

Sleeping
Auberge de Jeunesse Les Oiseaux (☎ 03 81 40 32 00; 48 rue des Cras; dm incl breakfast €23; reception ⊙ 8am-8pm) Two kilometres east of the train station is this hostel. Rates include breakfast and bedding; subsequent nights cost €5 less. Take bus 7 from the tourist office in the direction of Orchamps and get off at Les Oiseaux.

Hôtel du Nord (☎ 03 81 81 34 56; www.hotel-du -nord-besancon.com in French; 8 rue Moncey; s/d/tr from €35/38/48) This excellent-value hotel, strung with wrought-iron balconies and flower boxes, sits on a smart street in the old quarter. Pricier rooms are huge with vast bathrooms to wallow in. Parking is off-site in an underground garage.

Hôtel de Paris (☎ 03 81 81 36 56; www.hotel-de paris.com; 33 rue des Granges; d €50-64; ☐) Originally called Hôtel de France, the Paris prides itself on being the city's oldest hotel where a clutch of celebrities stayed, including Colette and George Sand in 1932. Skip breakfast in the hotel and revel in a coffee and croissant in chandelier-grandeur in the Brasserie du Commerce next door.

Charles Quint Hôtel (☎ 03 81 82 05 49; www.hotel -charlesquint.com; 3 rue du Chapitre; d €82-125) Oldy world and oozing charm, Charles Quint is a flashback to a bygone era. Find this nine-room oasis of old-style elegance – an 18th-century townhouse – slumbering in the shade of the citadel, behind the cathedral.

Hôtel Castan (☎ 03 81 65 02 00; www.hotelcastan .fr; 6 square Archéologique Castan; d €110-70; ☐) Original monumental fireplaces, canopy beds, hunted stag heads, terracotta floors and ornate grandfather clocks add authenticity to this lovely ivy-covered 18th-century townhouse, exquisitely furnished by a retired dentist with a passion for collecting antiques. Find Besançon's loveliest boutique hotel on a peaceful old-town square.

Eating
Au Gourmand (☎ 03 81 81 40 56; 5 rue Mégevand; menus from €9; ⊙ lunch & dinner Tue-Fri, lunch Sat) Going strong for 22 years, this legendary bistro is loved by everyone – students, couples and old ladies alike. Décor is a retro-theatrical cross and *les parmentières* (a mound of mashed potato with various toppings) are the humble speciality. Best of all, it's cheap – €6.70 for the *plat du jour* and €7 for the pick of 40 salads. No credit cards.

L'Annexe (☎ 03 81 53 17 12; 11 rue du Palais de Justice; meat/vegetarian plat du jour €12.50/11.50, menu €18; ⊙ lunch & dinner Tue-Sat) At the other extreme stands the Annexe, a contemporary space with a strong design-led interior and chic crowd to match. Black and white dominates and reservations are vital. Summer dining is alfresco in an interior courtyard.

Au Petit Polonais (☎ 03 81 81 23 67; 81 rue des Granges; menus €11-14.50; ⊙ lunch & dinner Mon-Fri, lunch Sat) One of Besançon's oldest restaurants, founded in 1870 by Polish émigrés (hence the name), still pulls in the punters with its delicious cooked meats, fondues and sausages.

MI:AM (☎ 03 81 82 09 56; 8 rue Morand; mains €15; ⊙ 11.30am-midnight Tue-Sun) *Apéro et dînatoire* – aperitif and a light casual dinner – is what trendy MI:AM (as in YUM!) is best at. Waltz through the heavy velvet curtain to enter or snag a seat on the buzzing street terrace. The same set run next-door **La Femme du Boulanger** (☎ 03 81 82 86 93; 6 rue Morand; salads €10; ⊙ 8am-7pm Mon-Sat), paradise for cake and tart lovers.

Mungo Park (☎ 03 81 81 28 01; 11 rue Jean Petit; lunch menu €36, dinner menus €51-95; ⊙ lunch & dinner Tue-Sat) Named after a Scottish explorer, this is Besançon's most elegant and renowned restaurant, headed up by Parisian female chef Jocelyne Lotz-Choquart. Braised fish in peppered artichokes and Charollais beef fillet are just some of the items you might try.

FRENCH ALPS & THE JURA

Place Granvelle sports a trendy twinset of design-led eating spaces, both with large terraces overlooking the action-packed square: Italian brasserie **Rosabianca** (☎ 03 81 81 05 60; place Granvelle; ☺ lunch & dinner) and **1802** (☎ 03 81 82 21 97; place Granvelle; ☺ 8am-midnight).

Self-caterers can food shop at the **indoor market** (cnr rue Paris & rue Claude Goudimel) or **outdoor market** (place de la Révolution).

Drinking

Nightlife is concentrated in the old Battant quarter and around the river; tune into Besançon's most happening street, rue Claude Pouillet (and parallel quai Vauban), at www .nuitdespouillets.com (in French).

Madigan's (☎ 03 81 81 17 44; 19 place du 8 Septembre; ☺ 7.30-1am) If it's an Irish pint and pub grub you're after, try this easy-going spot.

La Crémerie (☎ 03 81 83 55 00; http://lacremerie1 .free.fr; 9 rue Claude Pouillet; ☺ 5pm-1am Tue-Thu, 5pm-2am Fri & Sat) Hotshot concert venue on the city's buzziest street. Bars are constantly coming and going along this ramshackle strip, but the Dairy has long been strong. Next-door neighbour **Eggy Peggy** (9 rue Claude Pouillet; menus €16 & €20; ☺ 7pm-1am) is another great one, for eating … eggs too!

Carpé Diem (☎ 03 81 83 11 18; 2 place Jean Gigoux; ☺ 9-1am Mon-Thu, 9-2am Fri & Sat, 9am-8pm Sun) Play chess, drink, smoke and hang out with a student set at this small, rough-and-ready café-bar through which a decidedly bohemian wind blows.

Les Passagers du Zinc (☎ 03 81 81 54 70; 5 rue de Vignier; ☺ 5pm-1am Tue-Fri, 5pm-2am Sat & Sun) A grungy bar and club that hosts tapas nights, live bands and music nights; it's where Besançon's hip brigade can be found by night. Step through the bonnet of an old Citröen DS to reach the cellar.

Bar de l'U (☎ 03 81 81 55 95; 5 rue Mairet; ☺ 7.30pm-1am Mon-Thu, 7.30-2am Fri, 10-2am Sat) Concert and live music venue, this hip hang-out is a mainstay on the student drinking circuit.

Getting There & Away

BUS

From the **bus station** (9 rue Proudhon), there are daily services to Ornans and Pontarlier.

TRAIN

From **Besançon Gare Viotte**, 800m uphill from the city centre, there are trains to/

from Paris' Gare de Lyon (€86, 2¾ hours, three daily), Dijon (€14.40, 50 minutes, 20 daily), Lyon (€24.10, 2¾ hours, seven daily), Belfort (€13.40, 1¼ hours, six daily), Arbois (€7.70, 45 minutes, eight to 10 daily) and Arc-et-Senans (€5.60, 35 minutes, up to 10 daily). Buy tickets at the train station or from the **Boutique SNCF** (44 Grand Rue; ☺ 9am-7pm Mon-Fri, 9am-6pm Sat) in town.

Getting Around

Borrow a bicycle, pushchair or shopping caddie on wheels to cruise around town– free with a valid bus ticket – from local bus company office, **Boutique Ginko** (☎ 0 825 002 244; www.ginkobus.com; 4 place du 8 Septembre; ☺ 10am-7pm Mon-Sat). The boutique sells bus tickets costing €1.05/3.20/8.90 for a single ticket/day ticket/carnet of 10.

Call a **taxi** (☎ 03 81 88 80 80) or pick one up next to the town hall.

AROUND BESANÇON
Saline Royal

Envisaged by its designer, Claude-Nicolas Ledoux, as the 'ideal city', the 18th-century **Saline Royale** (Royal Saltworks; ☎ 03 81 54 45 45; www.salineroyale.com in French; adult/16-25yr/6-15yr €7/4.50/2.80; ☺ 9am-7pm Jul & Aug, 9am-noon & 2-6pm Apr-Jun, Sep & Oct, 10am-noon & 2-5pm Nov-Mar) in **Arc-et-Senans** (pop 1400), 30km south-west of Besançon, is a showpiece of early Industrial Age town planning. Although his urban dream was never realised, Ledoux's semicircular saltworks is now listed as a Unesco World Heritage site. Arc-et-Senans **tourist office** (☎ 03 81 57 43 21; www.ot-arcetsenans.fr; Saline Royale; ☺ 2-5pm Mon-Wed, 10am-noon & 2-5pm Fri & Sat, closed Thu & Sun), inside the gateway of the saltworks, has more information.

Regular trains link Besançon (€5.60, 35 minutes, up to 10 daily) and Arc-et-Senans.

Route Pasteur

Practically every Jurassienne town has a street, square, garden or all three named after Louis Pasteur, the great 19th-century chemist who invented pasteurisation and developed the first rabies vaccine (he also made great leaps in the treatment of ailing silkworms). And rightly so. Although much of his working life was spent in Paris,

---

THE STUFF OF DREAMS

Get away from it all at these two more-idyllic-than-idyllic Jurassien hideouts.

Amondans (☎ 03 81 86 53 53; www.amondans.com; place du Village, Amondans; half-board s/d/tr €69/98/132; May-Oct) This funky find of a village inn – a stunning 18th-century farm 30km south of Besançon in sleepy Amondans (pop 77) – fuses retro 1930s to 1960s furnishings (picked up in second-hand shops and jumble sales) with century-old features to create a contemporary eating and sleeping space. Rooms overlook open fields and are vast and minimal with crisp white bed linen, wooden floors and designery power-showered bathrooms. Guests – groups and couples rather than families – are very much hip, happy, outdoor types who mountain bike, hike, canoe, cave or horse-ride by day and hang out after dinner in the inn's magnificent *coin salon* – an entire converted barn with the most enormous fireplace you're ever likely to see. Swiss couple George and Geneviève, who run the place (they summer in Amondans and winter in Geneva) can organise most outdoor activities, rent mountain bikes (€15/day), supply picnics (€10) and occasionally serve a barbecued dinner in the hills. Half-board only.

Ferme Auberge du Rondeau (☎ 03 81 59 25 84; Lavans-Vuillafans; half-board s/d/tr €69/98/132, menus €20-29; mid-Feb–mid-Nov; ✗) Coo over 200 goats, 50 boar and a handful of horses at this idyllic organic farm, 2km from the village of Lavans-Vuillafans along a forest track. Run by the friendly Bourdier family for three generations since 1961, this farm really is the stuff childhood dreams are made of: cosy rooms are wood-panelled and breakfast is a veritable feast of farm produce – home-made yoghurt and jam, fresh farm-baked bread and sweet cakes. And lunching or dining on summer evenings on the outdoor terrace is unforgettable – wafer-thin slices of melt-in-your-mouth air-dried *sanglier* (boar), seven different types of *chèvres* (goats cheese) and a main course of goat, kid or boar depending on the season. Advance reservations for eating, sleeping or both are essential.

Pasteur was a born-and-raised Jura lad, returning to the region for holidays until his death in 1895.

Pasteur was born in **Dole**, 20km west of Arc-et-Senans along the D472. His childhood home, **La Maison Natale de Pasteur** (☎ 03 84 72 20 61; www.musee-pasteur.com; 43 rue Pasteur; adult/under 12yr €4.50/free; 10am-6pm Mon-Sat, 2-6pm Sun Jul & Aug, 10am-noon & 2-6pm Mon-Sat, 2-6pm Sun Apr-Jun, Sep & Oct, 10am-noon & 2-6pm Sat & Sun Nov-Mar), overlooking the Canal des Tanneurs in the old town, is now an atmospheric museum housing letters, artefacts and exhibits including his university cap and gown.

In 1827 the Pasteur family settled in the rural community of **Arbois** (pop 4569), 35km east of Dole. His laboratory and workshops in Arbois are on display at **La Maison de Louis Pasteur** (☎ 03 84 66 11 72; 83 rue de Courcelles; adult/7-15yr €5.50/2.80; guided tours 9.45am, 10.45am, 11.45am & hourly 2-6pm Jun-Sep, hourly 2.15-5.15pm Apr, May & 1-15 Oct). The house is still decorated with its original 19th-century fixtures and fittings.

Despite his international reputation, Pasteur was an active member of village life, and often found himself called upon to dispense neighbourly advice on subjects ranging from sickly vines to sickly children (despite the fact that he was a chemist by profession). He also regularly took part in the **Fête de Biou**, a traditional harvest festival still held at the beginning of September every year in Arbois.

Route du Vin

No visit to Arbois, Jura wine capital, would be complete without a glass of *vin jaune*. The history of this nutty 'yellow wine', which is matured for six years in oak casks, is told in the **Musée de la Vigne et du Vin** (☎ 03 84 66 26 14; museevignevin@wanadoo .fr; adult/child €3.30/2.50; 10am-noon & 2-6pm Wed-Mon Mar-Jun, Sep & Oct, 10am-12.30pm & 2-6pm Jul & Aug, 2-6pm Wed-Mon Nov-Feb). Don't miss out on doing the **Chemin des Vignes**, a 2.5km-long walking trail that wends its way in a loop through vineyards from the museum. Cyclists might prefer the 8km-long **Circuit des Vignes**, a mountain-bike trail likewise through vineyards.

Complete the wine trip with lunch at Arbois' **la balance mets & vins** (☎ 03 84 37 45 00; 47 rue de Courcelles; menus €21 & €28; lunch & dinner Thu-Sat, lunch Sun & Tue), a fantastic rustic bistro created by six local *vignerons* (wine producers). Its rooster casserole and *créme brulée* doused in local *vin jaune* are must-tastes, as are its fixed three-course menus accompanied by five different glasses of either Jurassienne wine (€15.60) or *vin jaune* (€26.60, including one from 1976).

High above Arbois is **Pupillin** (pop 220), a cute yellow-brick village famous for its wine production. Some 10 different *caves* (wine cellars) are open to visitors, but there is no public transport to Pupillin and it's a long 2.5km walk uphill from Arbois. Mountain-bikers can follow the **Circuit de Pupillon** (13km) marked trail from Arbois.

Arbois **tourist office** (☎ 03 84 66 55 50; www.arbois.com; rue de l'Hôtel de Ville; �9.30am-noon & 2-6pm Sep-Apr, 9am-12.30pm & 2-6.30pm May-Sep) has cycling itinerary information and a list of *caves* where you can taste and buy the local vintage.

Trains link Arbois and Besançon (€7.70, 45 minutes, eight to 10 daily).

POLIGNY TO BAUME-LES-MESSIEURS

Comté is indisputable king of the Jura, small-town **Poligny** (pop 4518) serving as the capital of the industry that produces 40 million tonnes of the venerable cheese a year. Learn how 450 litres is transformed into a 40kg wheel of cheese and smell some of its 83 different aromas at the **Maison du Comté** (☎ 03 84 37 23 51; www.comte.com; av de la Résistance; adult/6-16yr €4/2.50; � 2-5pm Tue-Sun Sep-Jun, 10-11.30am & 2-6pm Tue-Sun Jul & Aug). Hardened cheese aficionados can follow the **Comté Cheese Route** (below). Poligny **tourist office** (☎ 03 84 37 24 21; tourisme.poligny@wanadoo.fr; rue Victor Hugo; �9am-noon & 2-6pm Mon-Fri, 9am-noon & 2-5.30pm Sat) stocks an abundance of cheesy info.

Heading south, wiggle along the pretty D68 to Plasne then continue south to **Château-Chalon** (pop 162; www.chateau-chalon.info in French), the pretty hilltop village of medieval yellow stone ensnared by vineyards known for the Jura's legendary *vin jaune*.

Baume-les-Messieurs (pop 200) is another extraordinarily pretty village of cob houses and red-tiled rooftops, wedged between three glacial valleys, 20km south of Poligny. Its abandoned Benedictine **Abbaye Impériale** (Imperial Abbey; ☎ 03 84 44 99 28; admission €3.50; � 10am-noon & 2-6pm mid-Jun–mid-Sep) can only be visited by guided tour. Nearby, the 30-million-year-old **Grottes de Baume** (Baume Caves) are accessible by road from the foot of the 10m-tall **Cascade de Baume** (Baume Waterfall).

Immediately east lies the Jura's **Région des Lacs** (Lakes District), the highlight being the majestic waterfalls of the **Cascades du Hérisson**.

South sits **Lons-le-Saunier** (pop 20,000; www.ville-lons-le-saunier.fr in French), a must-visit on the first weekend in February during **La Percée du Vin Jaune** (www.jura-vins.com). The wine festival celebrates the opening of the first vat of *vin jaune* after six years maturing in oak casks.

Sleeping & Eating

Sleeping and dining options are vastly different and all fantastic in this rural neck of the woods.

THE CHEESE ROUTE

Easily the best way to taste local Jura cheese is to follow **Les Routes du Comté** (www.lesroutesducomte.com), studded with traditional *fruitières* (cheese dairies) where you can see cheese being made and sample regional varieties like Comté, Morbier, Bleu de Gex and Mont d'Or. Our top three stops:

Le Hameau du Fromage (☎ 03 81 62 41 51; Cléron, 7km west of Ornans; www.hameaudufromage.com in French; adult/10-16yr €5.50/3.85; � 9am-7pm) Industrial and touristy, yes, but a great place to start your tour. Two films on cheese-making (in English), cheese museum, restaurant and shop.

Musée des Maisons Comtoises (☎ 03 81 55 29 77; www.maisons-comtoises.org in French; Nancray, 10km east of Besançon; adult/6-16yr €7.50/4; � 1.30-6pm Mon-Sat mid-Mar–Apr, 10.30am-6.30pm Mon-Fri, 1.30-6.30pm Sat, 10.30am-7pm Sun May–mid-Sep, 1.30-6pm Sat, 10.30am-6.30pm Sun mid-Sep–Oct) Reconstructed 19th-century cheese farm-turned-intriguing museum.

Les Fructeries Vagne (☎ 03 84 44 92 25; rue St-Jean, Château-Chalon; � 10am-12.30pm & 2-7pm Jul–mid-Sep, 11am-12.30pm & 2-6.30pm Wed-Sun mid-Sep–Jun) Charming village dairy in one of the Jura's prettiest villages; hourly tours 2.30pm to 5.30pm summer, at 2.30pm only in winter.

Le Comptois (☎ 03 84 25 71 21; restaurant. comtois@wanadoo.fr; Doucier; d €40-50, half-board per person €52, starters/mains €15/15) This simple village restaurant opposite the post office with eight rooms up top (four dead basic for hikers) really has no airs and graces, despite it being run by one of France's most renowned *sommeliers* (wine experts). Always behind the bar or taking curious parties around the vineyards, Christophe Menozzi happily guides wine buffs and is a mine of local gastronomic information – making Le Comptois an irresistible must for food and drink lovers. Find it 25km southeast of Baume in Doucier.

Au Douillet Gourmet (☎ 03 84 51 27 24; www.au-douillet-gourmet.com; rue du Château, Montigny sur l'Ain; s/d/tr with breakfast €32/44/57, dinner €17) Pascal and Cristelle are gregarious, warm-hearted and full of smiles, happy to show guests around their chaotic but cheerful farm. Watch the cows being milked, help bottle-feed the calves, collect the eggs from the hen hutch and later dip into one of the most delicious fondues you'll ever taste around the kitchen table with the happy duo and their four kids.

Le Grand Jardin (☎ 03 84 44 68 37; rue des Grands Jardins, Baumes-les-Messieurs; s/d/tr/q with breakfast €39/47/57/74; Feb–mid-Dec) Book well ahead in summer to snag one of three rooms at this delightful *chambre d'hôte*, enviably placed opposite the abbey in Baume-les-Messieurs. Rooms, one of which sleeps six, are quainter than picture-postcard quaint.

ourpick Escargot Comtois (☎ 03 84 24 15 29; www.escargot-comtois.com in French; 215 rue de Montorient, Courbouzon; s/d/tr with breakfast €40/48/56, dinner with/without snails €21/17;) Spending a night at this highly original *chambre d'hôte* makes a great story to tell the folks back home. This is one of France's 400 snail farms so, depending on the season, you might see (a) the 200,000 miniscule boxed snails arriving by mail in mid-May; (b) baby snails with soft white shells; (c) soap and oil being rubbed along the edge of the snail field to keep the snails in and slugs out; (d) six-month-old adults munching grass in the field; (e) 90,000 surviving snails being harvested in late September; or (f) net bags of 100-odd harvested snails in hibernation, alias 'drying out' before the 'big boil'. The snail farm is run by Muriel and David Blanchard from a beautifully

renovated, old stone *maison de village* (which the Blanchards totally gutted and rebuilt themselves), dating back to 1747. Rooms are modern and sport a computer with ADSL internet access. Evening meals are around a shared table, the optional entrée being snails stuffed with cheese or laced in garlic butter served in the company of wine made by the village maths teacher. Find Courbouzon 22km south of Baumes-les-Messieurs.

Le Relais des Abbesses (☎ 03 84 44 98 56; www.chambres-hotes-jura.com; rue de la Roche, Château-Chalon; d €61-63, dinner €22) Another beautiful B&B in the heart of another beautiful village, this one has the added attraction of a view-studded terrace on which to breakfast or dine come dusk.

Café Restaurant de l'Abbaye (☎ 03 84 44 63 44; Baumes-les-Messieurs; menu €20; lunch & dinner Mon-Sat Feb-Dec) Tucked in one of the abbey's old buildings, this old-fashioned eating and drinking venue hits the spot as far as tasty lunches go. Its *cassolette franc-comtoise* (a casserole of potatoes, onions, cheese and local sausage; €9.20), *tartiflette* (€8.20) and kirsch-fuelled *fondue jurassienne* (€11) are all tasty but a trifle filling.

BELFORT
pop 50,125

A mere hop, jump and fairy skip across the border from Germany and Switzerland, Belfort is as Alsatian as it is Jurassien. Historically part of Alsace, it only became part of the Franche-Comté region in 1921 and is best known today as the manufacturer of the speedy TGV train and host to three-day open-air rock festival **Les Eurockéennes** (www.eurockeennes.fr) in early July and international film festival **Entre Vues** (www.festival-entrevues.com) in late November.

The city centrepiece is a **Vauban citadel** (p62), host to open-air concerts in summer and the **Musée d'Art et d'Histoire** (☎ 03 84 54 25 51; 10am-6pm, Wed-Mon Apr-Sep, 10am-noon & 2-6pm Wed-Mon Oct-Apr) year-round. On duty at its foot is an 11m-tall lion sculpted in sandstone by Frédéric-Auguste Bartholdi (of Statue of Liberty fame) to commemorate Belfort's resistance to the Prussians in 1870–71. While the rest of Alsace was annexed as part of the greater German Empire, Belfort stubbornly remained part of France.

Belfort **tourist office** (☎ 03 84 55 90 90; www
.ot-belfort.fr; 2bis rue Clémenceau; ☎ 9am-noon & 2-
6pm Mon-Fri) distributes free city maps and
has plenty of information on accommodation and things to see and do around
Belfort. Car enthusiasts can visit the **Musée
de l'Aventure Peugeot** (☎ 03 81 99 42 03; Carrefour
de l'Europe; www.peugeot.com/default_histoire_musee
.htm in French; adult/10-18yr €7/3.50; ☎ 10am-6pm),
12km south in Sochaux; the modern-
ist **Église du Sacré Cœur**, 4km southeast in
Audincourt, is an architecture-buff must;
and outdoor adventures are bountiful in
the **Massif du Ballon d'Alsace** (1247m), 20km
north of Belfort in the southern Vosges
Mountains.

RONCHAMP

The only reason to rendezvous in Ronchamp, 20km west of Belfort, is to visit Le
Corbusier's striking modernist chapel on a
hill overlooking the old mining town. Built
between 1950 and 1955, the surreal **Chapelle
de Notre Dame du Haut** (Chapel of our Lady of the
Height; ☎ 03 84 20 65 13; www.chapellederonchamp
.com in French; adult/student €2/1.50; ☎ 9.30am-6.30pm
Apr-Sep, 10am-5pm Oct & Mar, 10am-4pm Nov-Feb) with
sweeping concrete roof inspired by a hermit
crab shell is one of the 20th century's architectural masterpieces. It's a pilgrimage site
for thousands of architects every year, and
for 3000-odd religious pilgrims each year
on 8 September. Sunday mass is celebrated
in summer at 11am.

A 15-minute walking trail leads uphill to
the chapel from the centre of Ronchamp
village; the **tourist office** (☎ 03 84 63 50 82; 14 place
du 14 Juillet; ☎ 9am-noon & 2-5pm Tue-Fri, 9-11.30am
Sat) can guide you.

Sleeping & Eating

Don't leave Belfort without biting into a
Belfore, a scrumptious almond-flavoured
pastry filled with raspberries and topped
with hazelnuts.

Relais d'Alsace (☎ 03 84 22 15 55; www.arahotel
.com; 5 av de la Laurencie; s/d/tr/q from €28/40/45/50)
Do not let its somewhat tinpot appear-
ance deter you. Step inside and the
incredible warmth, love and laughter of Italian-
Yugoslav Georges and Franco-Algerian
Kim astonishes. Very much their baby for
the last 20-odd years, this colourful 10-
room hotel oozes charm. Room 12 peeps
out on the citadel, works of art penned by

little guests decorate the breakfast room-
cum-reception and nothing – absolutely
nothing – is too much trouble for the love-
able G & K. This is the place where musicians and artists stay when in town.

Getting There & Away

Connections from Belfort **train station** (av
Wilson) include Paris' Gare de Lyon via Besançon (from €66.30, four hours, three
daily), Montbéliard (€3.30, 15 minutes,
20 daily), Besançon (€13.40, 1¼ hours, six
daily) and Ronchamp (€3.90, 20 minutes,
four daily).

MÉTABIEF MONT D'OR

pop 700 / elevation 1000m

Métabief Mont d'Or, 18km south of Pontarlier on the main road to Lausanne,
is the region's leading cross-country ski
resort. All year, lifts take you almost to
the top of Mont d'Or (1463m), the area's
highest peak, from where a fantastic 180°
panorama stretches over the foggy Swiss
plain to Lake Geneva (Lac Léman) and
all the way from the Matterhorn to Mont
Blanc.

Métabief is famed for its unique *vacherin Mont d'Or* cheese, produced alongside
Comté and Morbier by the Sancey-Richard
family at the **Fromagerie du Mont d'Or** (☎ 03 81
49 02 36; www.fromageriedumontdor.com in French; 9 rue
Moulin; cheese shop ☎ 9am-12.15pm & 3-7pm Mon-Sat,
9am-noon Sun) since 1953. The dairy produces
over 200 tonnes of cheese a year and can
be visited by guided tour. To see cheese
being made, arrive with the milk lorry before 10.30am.

The **tourist office** (☎ 03 81 49 16 79; www
.tourisme-metabief.com in French; 6 place Xavier Authier;
☎ 9am-noon & 2-5pm, closed Sun Sep–mid-Dec) has
information on winter skiing and summer
strolling, mountain biking, hang-gliding
etc. It also has a comprehensive list of hotels and apartments to rent in Métabief.
Or wine, dine and sleep at the family-run
Hôtel Étoile des Neiges (☎ 03 81 49 11 21; www
.hoteletoiledesneiges.fr in French; 4 rue du Village; s/d/tr/q
€54/66/80/94; half-board €65/96/132/160). Tickle your
taste buds with a hearty shot of *anis de Pontarlier* (a liquorice-flavoured aperitif), the
Jura's answer to Provençal pastis, then continue your indulgence with a feisty portion of
raclette, fondue Comtoise, *Mont d'Or chaud*
or *la saucisse Jésus de Morteau* (opposite).

Two of the 22 hotel rooms are wheelchair-friendly.

Getting There & Away: use your own wheels!

AROUND MÉTABIEF MONT D'OR

Skiers can break from the slopes at **Odyssée Blanche** (White Odyssey; ☎ 03 81 69 20 20; www.parcduchienpolaire.com in French; adult/4-11yr €6.50/4.90; ☺ 10am-7pm Sun & Tue-Fri Jul & Aug, 2-5pm Sep & Oct, 10am-5pm Feb, 10am-6pm Feb, 10am-noon & 2-6pm Tue-Sun Mar-Jun), a husky park in Chaux-Neuve where you can mush with a dog-drawn sledge or simply tour the kennels and coo over 40 huskies instead.

Château de Joux (☎ 03 81 69 47 95; www.chateaudejoux.com in French; adult/6-14yr €5.80/3; ☺ 9am-6pm Jul & Aug, 10-11.30am & 2-4.30pm Feb-Jun & Sep, four guided tours only Oct-May), 10km north of Métabief, guards the entrance from leaving Switzerland into northern and central France. It sits atop Mont Larmont (922m), overlooking a dramatic *cluse* (transverse valley). Part of *Les Misérables* (1995) was filmed here, and during the First Empire the castle was a state prison. Today it houses France's most impressive arms museum. The music and theatre festival, **Festival des Nuits de Joux**, takes place here in mid-July.

Montbenoît (pop 230), 20km further north, is the capital of the **République du Saugeais** (Saugeais Republic). The tiny folkloric republic, declared in 1947, has its own flag, national anthem, postage stamp and female president. During summer a customs officer greets tourists as they enter the town.

PARC NATUREL RÉGIONAL DU HAUT-JURA

Experience the Jura at its rawest in the Haut-Jura Regional Park, an area of 757 sq km stretching from Chapelle-des-Bois in the north almost to the western tip of Lake Geneva. Each year in February its abundant lakes, mountains and low-lying valleys host the Transjurassienne, the world's second-longest cross-country skiing race (p582). Forget exploring the region without private transport.

There's not much to **St-Claude** (pop 12,704) – the largest town in the park – bar the world's biggest wooden pipe (8.2m tall, 7.5m long and 600kg in weight) propped up next to the **tourist office** (☎ 03 84 45 34 24; 19 rue du Marché; ☺ 9am-noon & 2-6pm Mon-Sat) and an illustrious diamond-cutting industry that, with its strict rules permitting factory visits for buying customers only, is pretty much

---

HOT BOX, CHRISTMAS ICE & JESUS

It's hot, it's soft and it's packed in a box. *Vacherin Mont d'Or* is the only French cheese to be eaten with a spoon – hot (or cold for that matter). Made between 15 August and 15 March with *lait cru* (unpasteurised milk), it derives its unique nutty taste from the spruce bark in which it's wrapped.

Louis XV adored it. In the 18th century it was called fat cheese, wood cheese or box cheese. Today, *vacherin Mont d'Or* is named after the mountain village from which it originates. Connoisseurs top the soft-crusted cheese with chopped onions, garlic and white wine, wrap it in aluminium foil and bake it for 45 minutes to create a *boîte chaude* (hot box).

Only 11 factories in the Jura are licensed to produce *vacherin Mont d'Or* which, ironically, has sold like hot cakes since 1987, when 10 people in Switzerland died from listeriosis after consuming the Swiss version. Old-fashioned cheese buffs in Mont d'Or believe the bacterial tragedy, which claimed 34 lives between 1983 and 1987, happened because the Swiss copycats pasteurised their milk.

Mouthe, 15km south of Métabief Mont d'Or, is the mother of *liqueur de sapin* (fir-tree liqueur). *Glace de sapin* (fir-tree ice cream) also comes from Mont d'Or, known as the North Pole of France due to its seasonal sub-zero temperatures (record low -38°C). Sampling either is rather like ingesting a Christmas tree. Then there's Jesus. *Jésus* – a small, fat version of *saucisse de Morteau* (Morteau sausage) – is the gastronomic delight of the village of Morteau. *Jésus* is easily identified by the wooden peg on its end, attached after the sausage is smoked with pine-wood sawdust in a traditional *tuyé* (mountain hut). Morteau residents claim their sausage is bigger and better than any other French sausage. They host a sausage festival every August.

a closed shop as far as curious tourists are concerned.

Well worth the short detour is **Les Louvières** (☎ 03 84 42 09 24; www.leslouvieres.com in French; Pratz; 2-/3-/4-course menu €19/25/29; ☺ lunch & dinner Wed-Sat, lunch Sun), a farmhouse restaurant to rave about 14km north of Ste-Claude in the middle of nowhere. Contemporary creations cooked up by Philippe are strictly fusion and the whole place – solar-powered – smacks of trendiness and hip living. Front of house is Canadian Sol.

As the so-called French capital of wooden toys, **Moirans-en-Montagne**, 14km west, hosts the **Musée du Jouet** (Toy Museum; ☎ 03 84 42 38 64; www.musee-du-jouet.com/musee in French; 5 rue du Murgin; adult/6-15yr/3-5yr €5/2.50/2; ☺ 10am-noon & 2-6pm Sat Sep-Jun, 10am-6.30pm Jul & Aug) – a far from playful 'look but don't touch' (rather than interactive) museum.

Les Rousses (pop 2850, elevation 1100m), on the northeastern edge of the park, is the park's prime sports hub, winter (skiing) and summer (walking and mountain biking) alike. Dubbed *'le station aux 4 villages'* (the four-village resort), it comprises four small ski areas – predominantly cross-country with a dash of downhill thrown in for good measure: Prémanon, Lamoura, Bois d'Amont and the village Les Rousses. Find out more at the **Maison du Tourisme** (square du 19 Mars 1962; ☺ 9am-noon & 2-6pm Mon-Sat), home to the **tourist office** (☎ 03 84 60 02 55; www.lesrousses.com in French; square du 19 Mars 1962), **ESF** (☎ 03 84 60 01 61; www.esf-lesrousses.com) and **Espace Loisirs Les Rousses** (☎ 03 84 60 02 55)

where ski passes for both Les Rousses and the neighbouring ski resorts of La Dôle and St Cergue in Switzerland are sold. Lunch, dinner and/or kip the night on the Swiss border (opposite).

The Jura's most staggering view is from the **Col de la Faucille**, 20km south of Les Rousses. Savour incredible views (extra incredible at sunset) from the restaurant terrace of **La Mainaz** (☎ 04 50 41 31 10; www.la-mainaz.com; 5 rte du Col de la Faucille; d from €70; ☺ mid-Dec–mid-Oct; 🅿), a hotel-restaurant midway along the mountain pass.

As the N5 twists and turns its way down the Jura Mountains past the small ski resort of **Mijoux**, the panoramic view of Lake Geneva embraced by the French Alps and Mont Blanc beyond is equally startling. For the best vantage point, ride the **Telesiège Val Mijoux** (chairlift; ☺ 9.30am-12.30pm & 2-6pm Jul & Aug; return €6) from Mijoux to the foot of the **Télécabine du Mont Rond** and continue up to Mont Rond (elevation 1533m). Alternatively, continue 8km south along the D991 to **Lélex** and hop aboard the **Télécabine de la Catheline** (cable car; ☺ 9am-1pm & 2-15-5.30pm Sat-Mon Jul & Aug; return €6). The latter is a particular hit with mountain-bikers (half-/full day ticket €9/15.50) who take the cable car up and free-pedal down. For more details, visit the **Maison du Tourisme** (☎ 04 50 20 91 43; www.monts-jura.com; ☺ 9am-noon & 2-5.30pm Mon-Fri, 9am-noon Sat) inside Lélex's cable-car building.

Continuing a further 25km southeast you arrive at the French–Swiss border, passing through **Ferney-Voltaire** (tourist office ☎ 04 50 28

GRANDE TRAVERSÉE DU JURA

The Grande Traversée du Jura (GTJ) – the Grand Jura Crossing – is a 210km cross-country skiing track from Villers-le-Lac (north of Pontarlier) to Hauteville-Lompnes (southwest of Bellegarde) that can also be done on foot or mountain bike. The path peaks at 1500m near the town of Mouthe (south of Métabief) and follows one of the coldest valleys in France. After the first 20km the route briefly crosses into Switzerland, but mostly runs along the border on the French side. Well maintained and very popular, the track takes 10 full days of skiing to cover – a feat even for the ultrafit.

Part of the GTJ, the 76km from Lamoura to Mouthe is covered each year by 4000 skiers during the world's second-largest cross-country skiing competition, the **Transjurassienne** (www .transjurassienne.com), held in late February, and several hundred rollerbladers and rollerskiers during the **Trans' Roller** (www.transroller.transjurassienne.com in French) in September.

For complete information on the GTJ, including maps and accommodation along the route, contact **Les Grandes Traversées du Jura** (☎ 03 84 51 51 51; www.gtj.asso.fr; 15 & 17 Grande Rue, Les Planches-en-Montagne).

CROSS-BORDER

Sleep in Switzerland, breakfast in France and pay in euros or Swiss francs at **Hôtel Franco-Suisse** (☎ 03 84 60 02 20, +41 22 360 13 96; www.hotelarbez.fr.st; La Cure; s/d/tr/q €49/59/65/70, with half-board €68/110/150/180; bistro ☒ lunch & dinner Wed-Mon), a fabulously unique bistro inn with a French and a Swiss telephone number (!) that sits smack on the French–Swiss border, 2.5km from Les Rousses. Run by the Arbez family since 1920 (think fourth generation), the place dates from 1870 and is an old-fashioned mix of weathered floor tiles, Parisian bistro-style red-and-white checked tablecloths and Alpine wood panelling. Ten rooms up top are simple but comfortable, and the next-door neighbour is the Douane La Cure (La Cure customs and border crossing). In winter, the bistro gets jammed to the rafters with cross-country skiers refuelling on hearty Savoyard fodder after a hard day's skiing. Find Hôtel Franco-Suisse in the hamlet of La Cure, wedged between the Col de la Faucille (France) and Col de la Givrine (Switzerland).

09 16; www.ferney-voltaire.net), 5km north of Geneva en route. Following his banishment from Switzerland in 1759, Voltaire lived in Ferney until his return to Paris and death in 1778. Guided tours (55 minutes) of his humble home, **Château de Voltaire** (☎ 04 50 40 53 21; allée du Château; admission free; ☒ 11am-1pm & 2-6pm Tue-Sun mid-May–mid-Sep), take in the chateau, chapel and surrounding seven-hectare park. Past visitors include Auden, Blake and Flaubert, all of whom wrote about the philosopher's home in exile.

Massif Central

The Massif Central is France's spine, its vertebrae the spiky plugs and rounded grassy cones of extinct volcanoes called *puys* (pronounced 'pwee'). Down in the relatively rich volcanic soil of its plains and valleys, maize, tobacco and vines thrive. Its rumpled slopes are clad in either dense forest or pasture, offering sweet grazing for the cattle and sheep that are the source of Auvergnat cheeses, some of France's finest.

At valley level you'll also find spa towns that these days pull in both the hale and those seeking health. Vichy is for those who treasure a touch of faded elegance while St-Nectaire, home to the smooth, eponymous cheese, and Le Mont-Dore, ski resort in winter and summer-time trekking base, both still speak of *la belle époque*.

Clermont-Ferrand is the only city of consequence. It's home to the Michelin tyre giant – though you'd never guess it as you roam the narrow streets of the old quarter. It's a great base for exploring the northern *puys* – and for visiting Vulcania, a breathtaking multimedia exhibition about all things volcanic.

But the Massif Central, with its superb walking and mountain biking, is above all for those who love the great outdoors. Two large regional parks, the dramatic Parc Naturel Régional des Volcans d'Auvergne and its tamer eastern neighbour, the Parc Naturel Régional du Livradois-Forez, together make up France's largest environmentally protected area. And from the Massif Central, which is roughly coextensive with the Auvergne, trickle the myriad streams that band together to form a trio of France's mightiest rivers: the Dordogne, Allier and Loire.

HIGHLIGHTS

- Drink in views of all southeastern France from the summit of **Mont Mézenc** (p608)
- Live a little of the *belle époque* life in the spa town of **Vichy** (p592)
- Puff your way to the tiptop of spectacular **Puy Mary** (p600)
- Survive a virtual volcanic eruption at state-of-the-art **Vulcania** (p591)
- Crunch across volcanic cinders, tiny and light as Rice Krispies, in the **Parc Naturel Régional des Volcans d'Auvergne** (p591)
- Tuck into windy picnics up high, each day sampling a different **Auvergnat cheese** (p600)

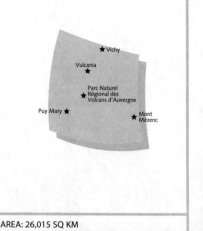

- POPULATION: 1,310,000
- AREA: 26,015 SQ KM

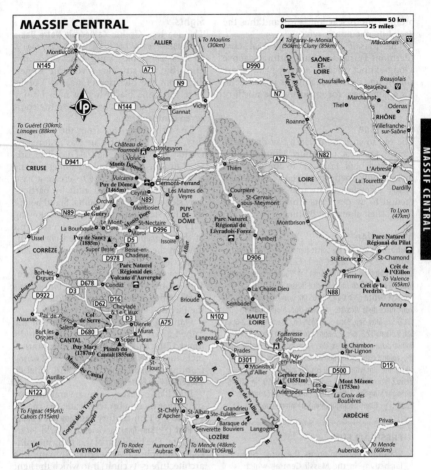

MASSIF CENTRAL

MASSIF CENTRAL

GEOGRAPHY & CLIMATE

The Massif Central's three geographical regions were formed at very different times. The northernmost range, the Monts Dômes, are mere babes, thrust up less than 100,000 years ago and still spurting intermittently a mere 5000 years ago. The central Monts Dore are in the middle of the age band and took shape between 100,000 and three million years ago. The oldest of the even more ancient Monts du Cantal near Murat go back a good nine million years. Less recognisably volcanic in shape, they were formed when a giant volcano collapsed in on itself, leaving only its fragmented rim, or caldera.

Unlike the rest of France and inconveniently for holiday-makers, the Massif Central gets the major part of its rainfall in summer, frequently as late-afternoon storms. This said, days may pass without a drop falling to dampen your vacation.

CLERMONT-FERRAND & AROUND

CLERMONT-FERRAND

pop 141,000 / elevation 400m

Bibendum, the roly-poly Michelin car man, started life in Clermont-Ferrand, centre of France's rubber industry and power base of the Michelin tyre empire. As did the first Michelin guidebook, published in 1898 to promote motor-car tourism – and thus the use of its pneumatic tyres.

The Massif Central's only real city, Clermont-Ferrand, is built, fittingly, above a long-extinct volcano. A lively place where almost one in five inhabitants is a student, it's a good base for exploring the north of the region.

Orientation

The old town is bounded by av des États-Unis to the west, rue André Moinier to the north and blvd Trudaine to the east. The increasingly pedestrianised commercial centre stretches westwards from the cathedral to av des États-Unis and place de Jaude, then along rue Blatin.

Information

Laundrette (6 place Hippolyte Renoux; 7am-8pm)
Lepton (22 av des Paulines; per hr €2.50; 10am-midnight Mon-Fri, 2pm-midnight Sat & Sun) Internet access.
Main Post Office (rue Maurice Busset)
Tourist Office (04 73 98 65 00; www.clermont-fd .com; place de la Victoire; 9am-7pm Mon-Fri, 10am-7pm Sat & Sun May-Sep, 9am-6pm Mon-Fri, 10am-1pm & 2-6pm Sat, 9.30am-12.30pm & 2-6pm Sun Oct-Apr) *Espace Art Roman* downstairs is an excellent free exhibition highlighting the region's outstanding Romanesque churches. There's a 30-minute film with optional English audio.
Visio2 Paulines (14 av des Paulines; per hr €2.50; 10am-midnight Mon-Sat, 1-8pm Sun); Carnot (11 av Carnot; per hr €2.50; 10am-midnight Mon-Sat) Internet access.

FRESH-AIR FUN

Walking rivals skiing as the most popular activity in the Massif Central, which is crisscrossed by as many as 13 GR tracks (including the spectacular GR4, which cuts through the range from north to south) and hundreds of other footpaths. Some of these trails are also suitable for mountain biking; the publisher Chamina puts out a series of excellent topoguides for the region.

Several ski resorts, particularly Le Mont-Dore, Super Besse and Super Lioran (near Murat), provide full alpine skiing facilities, and the Massif Central's undulating terrain is great for cross-country sorties.

The region's topography and thermal currents also mean it's ideal for hang-gliding and *parapente* (paragliding), for which the *puys* are used as take-off platforms.

Sights

The soaring, Gothic **Cathédrale Notre Dame** (7.30am-noon & 2-6pm Mon-Sat, 9.30am-noon & 3-7.30pm Sun) looks smog-blackened and grim. But the structure's volcanic stones, dug from the quarries of nearby Volvic, were the same blackish-grey hue the day the finishing touches were put to the choir seven centuries ago.

The twin towers are from the 19th century, when the west façade was restored by Gothic revivalist Viollet-le-Duc. The original architects took full advantage of the strong, light Volvic stone to create a vast, double-aisled nave, held aloft by particularly slender pillars and vaults. Stand before the altar steps and marvel at the glowing 14th-century rose windows at each end of the transept. Several stained-glass windows in the choir and side chapels are also medieval.

From place de la Poterne and its early-16th-century **Fontaine d'Amboise**, two blocks north of the cathedral, there's a fine view of the Puy de Dôme and nearby peaks.

Flanking the narrow streets east of the cathedral are some of Clermont-Ferrand's finest 17th- and 18th-century townhouses, including **Hôtel Reboul-Sadourny** (9 rue Savaron), fronting a small courtyard, and **Hôtel de Chazerat** (4 rue Blaise Pascal).

Rue Blaise Pascal, with several antique shops that merit a browse, leads, via rue du Port, to the 12th-century **Basilique Notre Dame du Port** (8am-7pm), a Unesco World Heritage Site. The highlight of this truly magnificent example of Auvergnat-Romanesque architecture is its choir, into which the light streams on a summer's day. Notice too the delightfully naive carving on the capitals of the four easternmost pillars.

The **Musée d'Archéologie Bargoin** (04 73 91 37 31; 45 rue Ballainvilliers; adult/child/student €4.20/ free/2.70; 10am-noon & 1-5pm Tue-Sat, 2-7pm Sun) has excellent prehistory and Gallo-Roman sections on the ground floor. Upstairs, the **Musée du Tapis et des Arts Textiles**, in addition to its unique collection of carpets and rugs from the Near and Middle East, mounts excellent temporary textile-related exhibitions (during which the permanent collection is withdrawn).

Just down the street, the **Musée d'Histoire Naturelle Henri-Lecoq** (04 73 91 93 78; 15 rue Bardoux; adult/under 18/student €4.20/free/2.70; 10am-noon &

CELTIC HERO

Vercingétorix, chief of the Celtic Arverni tribe, almost foiled Julius Caesar's conquest of Gaul. With most of Gaul overrun and Caesar slyly playing one tribe off against the other, Vercingétorix pulled together the tribes between the Loire and Garonne rivers and forged a force that could match the Roman legions in discipline.

In summer 52 BC, the Gauls' thrashing of Caesar's troops at Gergovia near Clermont-Ferrand, in the tribe's heartland, inspired a general uprising by most Gallic tribes, led by Vercingétorix.

For a couple of years the Gauls hounded the Romans with guerrilla warfare and stood up to them in several match-drawn pitched battles. But gradually Gallic resistance collapsed and Roman rule in Gaul reigned supreme.

Vercingétorix was captured and taken to Rome, where he was paraded in chains in Caesar's triumphal procession. As a final insult he was left languishing in prison for six years before being strangled.

2-5pm or 6pm Mon-Sat, 2-6pm Sun) is a natural history museum with an impressive collection of rocks, fossils, stuffed fauna and pickled things that creep. A new section presents the sad litany of animals of the region that have become extinct over the centuries.

Place de Jaude, the city's main square, has recently been pedestrianised. Fountains splash and kids play in this recovered urban space, watched over at its northern end by the equestrian **statue of Vercingétorix**, the Celtic chief who so nearly foiled Julius Caesar's conquest of Gaul (above).

The quiet, none-too-prosperous suburb of **Montferrand**, 2.5km northeast of the cathedral, beyond the vast Michelin works, is worth a visit for its many **Gothic and Renaissance houses**, especially around where rue de la Rodade meets rue des Cordeliers. Many of the houses have stone-built ground floors and overhanging, half-timbered upper storeys.

The **Musée d'Art Roger Quilliot** (☎ 04 73 16 11 30; place Louis Deteix; adult/child €4.10/free; ☽ 10am-6pm Tue-Sun) is an excellent fine arts museum within an architecturally exciting complex in Montferrand. It has a fascinating, chronologically arranged collection of sculpture, painting and art objects from the late Middle Ages to the 20th century. Take bus 16 from place de Jaude or buses 1 and 9 from the bus station.

Sleeping

Camping Le Chanset (☎ 04 73 61 30 73; camping .lechanset@wanadoo.fr; av Jean Baptiste, Ceyrat; per person/car/tent €2.95/1.85/5.50; ☽ year-round) The nearest camp site is in Ceyrat, virtually a suburb of Clermont-Ferrand. Bus 4 stops right outside.

Hôtel de la Gare (☎ 04 73 92 07 82; www.hotel -gare-clermont.com in French; 76 av Charras; s/d €39/42) One of several hotels in a quiet street near the train station, the 20 rooms of Hôtel de la Gare (four are in a rear annexe) have been recently and comprehensively renovated.

Hôtel Ravel (☎ 04 73 91 51 33; hotelravel63@ wanadoo.fr; 8 rue de Maringues; s/d €37.50/47) With its eccentric mosaic façade and pleasant old-fashioned rooms, the Ravel (which recently celebrated its first centenary) is a good bet if you like your accommodation with character – something the lady housekeeper also has, in spades! Rooms vary in their facilities; but all have full bathroom facilities, and those overlooking the street are a little larger. It's in a quiet part of town, where the only bustle comes from the St-Joseph morning market, around which you can park for free once evening falls.

Hôtel de Lyon (☎ 04 73 17 60 80; hotel.de.lyon@ wanadoo.fr; 16 place de Jaude; s €60-68, d €67-85; ☒) This 33-room hotel right on place de Jaude couldn't possibly be more central – and it has private parking (€5.50) so your car needn't be an encumbrance. Most rooms overlook the square and are double glazed, so don't be apprehensive about noise from the pub below.

Hôtel Lafayette (☎ 04 73 91 82 27; www.hotel-le -lafayette.com; 53 av de L'Union Soviétique; r €85-115; ☒ ☒ ▱) Behind Hôtel Lafayette's brash lavender-blue façade lies a very comfortable, welcoming option where staff speak good English. Its 49 double-glazed rooms, all with bathtub, are light and bright, decorated with prints of Clermont by a local artist. Tall mirrors give a sense of greater space. The beds all have firm mattresses

MASSIF CENTRAL

CLERMONT-FERRAND

INFORMATION
Laundrette.....................................1 B3
Laundrette.....................................2 D3
Main Post Office...........................3 B3
Tourist Office................................4 B2
Visio2..5 D2
Visio2..(see 2)

SIGHTS & ACTIVITIES
Basilique Notre Dame du Port...6 C1
Cathédrale Notre Dame...............7 B2
Fontaine d'Amboise.....................8 B1
Hôtel de Chazerat.......................9 C2
Hôtel Reboul-Sadourny............10 C2
Musée du Tapis et des Arts
  Textiles................................(see 11)
Musée d'Archéologie
  Bargoin....................................11 C3
Musée d'Histoire Naturelle
  Henri-Lecoq.............................12 C3
Pl de Jaude.................................13 B2
Statue of Vercingétorix.............14 B2

SLEEPING
Hôtel de la Gare........................15 E2
Hôtel de Lyon............................16 A2
Hôtel des Puys...........................17 D1
Hôtel Kyriad Prestige................18 B4
Hôtel Lafayette..........................19 F1
Hôtel Ravel.................................20 D2

EATING
Brasserie Danièle Bath.........(see 21)
Covered Market.........................21 B2
Crêperie-Grill le 1513...............22 B2
Fleur de Sel................................23 C2

L'Alambic...................................24 B1
Le Lypocan.................................25 B3
Les Godtiers de Justine.............26 C2
Ostréo Bar..................................27 C1
Relais du Pascal.....................(see 26)

DRINKING
Bar des Beaux Arts....................28 C3
Café Pascal.................................29 B2
John Barleycorn.........................30 C3
Le Tout du Cru...........................31 B3
Still...32 B3

ENTERTAINMENT
Ciné Capitole.............................33 A3
Oxxo...34 B1

TRANSPORT
Boutique SNCF..........................35 B4
Boutique SNCF..........................36 B2
Bus Station.................................37 B4
Eurolines....................................38 B4
MoovíCité...................................39 E1
T2C Information Office..............40 B4

and comfy duvets. The hotel has wi-fi and free parking.

Hôtel Kyriad Prestige (☎ 04 73 93 22 22; www.hotel
-kyriadprestigeclermont.com; 25 av de la Libération; r €99-
150; ☒ ☒ ☒) Comprehensively renovated in 2005, this is a very enticing option. A full four of the five floors are nonsmoking and all rooms are attractively furnished, their dark furniture contrasting with the light-coloured, snug duvets. All have free tea and coffee, safe and ironing board. There's also a good restaurant, Le Bistrot de Clermont. The hotel has wi-fi, and parking for €10.

Hôtel des Puys (☎ 04 73 91 92 06; www.hotel
despuys.fr; 16 place Delille; s €70-112, d €101-112;
☒ ☒ ☒) This is a safe, reliable but not too exciting landing stage. Toilets and bathrooms are separate in all rooms and the majority share a balcony overlooking busy place Delille. All have been recently and comprehensively renovated. One floor is reserved for nonsmokers, there's wi-fi, parking is €7 and a couple of rooms are wheelchair-accessible.

Eating
BUDGET
Two blocks north of place de Jaude, rue St-Dominique and nearby rue St-Adjutor sprawl with reasonably priced French and ethnic restaurants, including Tunisian, Italian, Portuguese, Cuban, Japanese and Slav.

Les Goûters de Justine (☎ 04 73 92 26 53; 11bis rue
Blaise Pascal; ☟ noon-7pm Tue-Sat) This charming tearoom – it's rather like stepping into your great aunt's parlour – is a haven of calm and mellowness in the heart of the city. It also offers a range of snacks.

Relais de Pascal (☎ 04 73 92 21 04; 15 rue Blaise
Pascal; weekday lunch menus €8.50-12; ☟ Tue-Sat)
This seething *bar–restaurant du quartier* (neighbourhood restaurant) serves Auvergnat dishes, mainly based on pork, on marble tables. Ample platters of pig-based *charcuterie* (€5.60 to €9.20) are dished up any old time and it does an excellent *menu du terroir* of regional delights (€24).

Le Lypocan (☎ 04 73 92 67 24; 16 place Hippolyte
Renoux; pizzas €8-10; ☟ dinner Tue-Fri, lunch & dinner
Sat, lunch Mon) More than 25 years in business, this informal, immensely popular pizza and pasta joint also does meaty mains with an Italian touch.

Crêperie-Grill le 1513 (☎ 04 73 92 37 46; 3 rue
des Chaussetiers; menus €13.50-23, crepes €3-5.50; open

daily) This cavernous restaurant occupies the ground floor of a sumptuous mansion built in 1513 – hence the name. For a hefty snack, go for a *galette* (savoury buckwheat *crêpe*). For the ravenous, the French fries that accompany the mains must have depleted half a potato field. Go downstairs to the lovely internal terrace for summer dining.

MIDRANGE
Brasserie Danièle Bath (☎ 04 73 31 23 22; place
St-Pierre; menu €21, mains €15-25; ☟ Tue-Sat, closed
mid-end Aug) This classy little place, where contemporary art hangs from the walls, serves top-quality dishes based on fresh local ingredients from the adjacent central market. Dining is a delight on its summer terrace.

Ostréo Bar (☎ 04 73 91 58 28; 63bis rue du Port;
☟ 7.30am-8pm Mon-Sat) This tiny hole in the wall offers oysters whenever there's an 'r' in the month.

L'Alambic (☎ 04 73 36 17 45; 6 rue Ste-Claire; menus
€23-33, mains €14-16; ☟ closed Sun & lunch Mon & Wed)
Meaning the Still (there's a handsome brass example on display and photos of artisan distilling around the walls), this is *the* place to sample Auvergnat dishes. The house speciality (so much a favourite that 15 kilos of Cantal cheese is purchased every week) is *aligot*, a stretchy confection of potato, cheese, garlic and cream.

Fleur de Sel (☎ 04 73 90 30 59; 8 rue Abbé Girard;
menus €28-48, mains around €25; ☟ Tue-Sat Sep-Jul)
Fleur de Sel specialises in fine fish and seafood, which feature in every dish except the desserts. It's small, stylishly furnished and popular, so you'll need to book.

SELF-CATERING
The city's **covered market** (☟ 6am-7pm Mon-Sat) is a jumble of blue, yellow and grey cubes splaying over place St-Pierre.

Drinking
Café Pascal (4 place de la Victoire) This favourite exchange-student hangout is usually packed to the gunnels inside and you'll be lucky to find a chair on its popular summertime terrace.

Bar des Beaux Arts (4 rue Ballainvilliers) This bar also pulls in the student crowd, crammed into its interior or sitting and sipping at the tables that take over most of the adjacent square.

John Barleycorn (9 rue du Terrail; ☻ 2pm-2am Mon-Sat May-Aug, 5pm-2am Mon-Sat Sep-Apr) This long-established Celtic pub serves liquids brewed from both barley and corn.

Le Tout du Cru (9 blvd Léon Malfreyt; dishes €8) This pleasant, intimate wine bar with its wooden counter and tables serves snacks and a variety of wines by the glass. You'll enjoy its plate of cold cuts and salad.

Still (9 blvd Léon Malfreyt) Right next door to Le Tout du Cru and altogether rowdier, this popular new addition to Clermont's drinking scene is your usual turnkey instant Irish pub. Mix cultures and down a glass of its smooth draft Lucifer Belgian beer.

Entertainment

Pocket-sized *Le P'tit Bougnat* lists the best of pubs and clubs, while *After Magazine*, out monthly, is your best bet for info about concerts and ephemeral events. You'll find them in selected pubs, clubs and hotels.

Le B-Box (☎ 04 73 28 59 74; www.bboxclub.com in French; ave Ernest Cristal, La Pardieu; ☻ 11pm-5am Thu-Sat) This vast new architecturally stunning complex is a few kilometres south of town beside the A75 (take exit 1). Split into various levels with the DJ perched up high surveying all, it claims to be Europe's largest dance area.

Oxxo (☎ 04 73 14 11 11; 14-16 rue des Deux Marchés; admission €5; ☻ 10pm-4am Wed-Sat) This rough-hewn discothèque-bar is hugely popular with the student community. Upstairs is La Rhûmeraie, where you can psych yourself up on beer cocktails and shooters. Downstairs is a sweatbox of a dance floor.

The city's main venue for concerts and spectacles is the striking, ultramodern **Zénith** (☎ 04 73 77 24 24), which can accommodate up to 8500 spectators. Part of the Grande Halle d'Auvergne complex, it too is southeast of the city centre.

There are nondubbed films at the five-screen **Ciné Capitole** (☎ 0 892 687 333; 32 place de Jaude).

Getting There & Away

AIR

Clermont-Ferrand Auvergne airport (☎ 04 73 62 71 00), a major Air France hub for domestic and European flights, is 7km east of the city centre. An **airport bus** (☎ 04 73 84 72 57; adult one-way €4) runs four to seven times daily, stopping at the bus and train stations.

BUS

The **bus station** (☎ 04 73 93 13 61; place Gambetta) has an efficient information office.

Bus 73 runs to Riom (€4, 25 to 45 minutes, nine daily) and bus 1 serves Thiers (€8, 1¼ hours, eight daily). For Vichy, you're better to travel by train.

Linebus (☎ 04 73 34 81 16; ☻ 10am-7pm Mon-Sat), with a kiosk at the bus station, runs to many cities in Spain. For other European destinations, consult **Eurolines** (☎ 04 73 29 70 05; 82 blvd François Mitterand).

CAR & MOTORCYCLE

Car-rental agencies:

Avis town (☎ 04 73 91 72 94); airport (☎ 04 73 91 18 08)
Europcar town (☎ 04 73 92 70 26); airport (☎ 04 73 91 18 07)
Hertz town (☎ 0 825 845 220); airport (☎ 04 73 62 71 93)

TRAIN

Clermont-Ferrand is the Massif Central's most important rail junction. It has two **boutiques SNCF** (ticketing offices; ☎ 0 892 353 535; 43 rue du 11 Novembre & 80 blvd François Mitterand).

Major destinations include Paris' Gare de Lyon (€43.10, 3½ hours, six to nine daily) and Lyon (€24.30 via St-Étienne, three hours, more than 10 daily). The route through the Gorges de l'Allier to Nîmes (€34, 4¾ hours, two or three daily) via Langeac (€14.10) and Monistrol d'Allier (€17.10), known as Le Cévenol, is one of the most scenic in France.

Short-haul trains run to/from Le Mont-Dore (€11.20, 1¼ hours, four or five daily), Le Puy-en-Velay (€19.30, 2¼ hours, four daily), Murat (€16.30, 1½ hours, four to seven daily), Riom (€2.80, 10 minutes, frequent), Vichy (€8.50, 40 minutes, frequent) and Thiers (€7.40, 45 minutes, eight to 10 daily).

Getting Around

MooviCité (☎ 0 810 630 063; av de l'Union Soviétique; ☻ 7.30am-7pm Mon-Sat), a splendid public-sector initiative, rents bikes for a bargain €3/6 per half-/full day. You need a refundable deposit of €150.

The **T2C information office** (☎ 04 73 28 00 00; 24 blvd Charles de Gaulle) provides information on local T2C buses.

Call **Allo Taxi Radio** (☎ 04 73 19 53 53) or **Taxi 63** (☎ 04 73 31 53 15) for taxis.

> **VIRTUAL VOLCANOES**
>
> **Vulcania** (☎ 0 820 827 828; www.vulcania.com; adult/child €19.50/12; ☺ 9am-6pm or 7pm Apr-Aug, 9am-6pm or 7pm Wed-Sun late Mar & Sep) is 15km to the west of Clermont-Ferrand on the D941B. A hugely spectacular multimedia visitors centre in an architecturally innovative site, it illustrates the workings of volcanoes and their role in the development of our planet.

AROUND CLERMONT-FERRAND
Puy de Dôme

Covered in outdoor adventurers in summer and snow in winter, the balding Puy de Dôme (1465m) gives a panoramic view of Clermont-Ferrand and scores of volcanoes. The Celts then the Romans worshipped their gods from the summit. Nowadays, dominated by a TV transmission tower resembling a giant rectal thermometer, it's a popular launching platform for *parapente* (paragliding) and hang-gliding enthusiasts.

You can reach the summit either by the 'mule track' – a steepish hour's climb starting at the Col de Ceyssat, 4km off the D941A – or by the 4km **toll road** (per vehicle €4.50; ☺ 8am-dusk Mar-Nov, weekends only Dec). This road is closed to private cars from 10am to 6pm daily in July and August and between 12.30pm and 6pm on weekends in May, June and September – at those times you can take a shuttle bus (per adult/child €3.50/1.40 return).

Riom
pop 19,300

Riom, 15km north of Clermont-Ferrand on the train line to Vichy, makes for a convenient day or half-day trip from either town. The streets of the austere old quarter, in the Middle Ages the capital of the Auvergne region, are lined with mansions built of dark Volvic stone.

The main arteries of the old city are the north–south rue du Commerce, plus its northern extension, rue de l'Horloge, and the east–west rue de l'Hôtel de Ville.

The **tourist office** (☎ 04 73 38 59 45; www.tourisme-riomlimagne.fr; 16 rue du Commerce; ☺ 9.30am-1pm & 2-6.30pm Mon-Sat, 10am-1pm Sun Jul & Aug; 9.30am-noon & 2-5.30pm Tue, Wed, Fri & Sat, 2-5.30pm Mon & Thu Sep-Jun), 100m south of rue de l'Hôtel de Ville, carries *Laissez-vous Conter*

Riom, a free English-language walking-tour brochure.

The 15th-century **Église Notre Dame du Marthuret** (rue du Commerce; ☺ 9am-6pm), about 200m from the tourist office, has a fine pair of 14th-century statues of the Virgin: the *Vierge à l'Oiseau* (Virgin with Bird; the figure over the entrance is a copy – the original is inside, in the first chapel to the right) and the squat *Vierge Noire* (Black Virgin), in the next chapel eastwards.

Transitional **Église St-Amable** (rue St-Amable; ☺ 9am-5pm Oct-May, 9am-7pm Jun-Sep) has a Romanesque nave and a Gothic choir that ranks as one of Auvergne's finest.

The excellent **Musée Régional d'Auvergne** (☎ 04 73 38 17 31; 10bis rue Delille; admission €4.20; ☺ 10am-noon & 2.30-6pm Tue-Sun mid-May–Oct) has displays documenting rural life in Auvergne. The **Musée Francisque Mandet** (☎ 04 73 38 18 53; 14 rue de l'Hôtel de Ville; admission €4.20; ☺ 10am-noon & 2.30-6pm Tue-Sun Jun-Sep, 10am-noon & 2-5.30pm Tue-Sun Oct-May) has a collection of classical antiquities, medieval sculptures and 17th- to 19th-century paintings. A combined ticket giving entry to both costs €5.70.

Volvic
pop 4400

About 7km southwest of Riom, the town of Volvic is famous for its spring water and its quarries, which provided the lightweight but strong volcanic stone used in so many local buildings, including Clermont-Ferrand's cathedral.

Even if you don't go inside, it is well worth the walk up to the ruins of the nearby **Château de Tournoël** (☎ 04 73 33 53 06; adult/child €5/3; ☺ 10am-6pm Jul & Aug, 2-6pm Wed-Mon Apr-Jun & Sep) to enjoy the splendid panoramic view from its base.

PARC NATUREL RÉGIONAL DES VOLCANS D'AUVERGNE

The 3950-sq-km, 120km-long **Parc Naturel Régional des Volcans d'Auvergne** (☎ information office 04 73 65 64 00; www.parc-volcans-auvergne.com in French) makes for great walking.

The Monts Dômes, in the north, are a chain of some 80 'recent' cinder cones, the

MASSIF CENTRAL

best known being the Puy de Dôme (p591). The Monts Dore culminate in the Puy de Sancy (1885m), the Massif Central's highest point and a popular alpine ski station in winter. At its foot lies the spa town of Le Mont-Dore, an ideal base from which to explore the area.

The wilder, rugged Monts du Cantal, all that remains of a super-volcano worn down over the millennia, dominate the south of the park. The highest point is the Plomb du Cantal (1855m), a desolate peak often shrouded in heavy, swirling clouds, even in summer.

For more information on the geography of the area, see p585.

VICHY

pop 26,900

The spa resort of Vichy can be a bleak place in winter. The pollarded trees are bare and most hotels are shuttered as ageing residents walk ridiculously small dogs, muffled in their canine coats. In spring the town wakens, shakes itself and once more flirts its *belle époque* charm.

Vichy became enormously fashionable after visits by Napoleon III in the 1860s. These days, however, the average age of *curistes* (patients taking the waters) must equal that of any old folks' home. Most come seeking relief from rheumatism, arthritis and digestive ailments under France's generous social security system.

During WWII, Vichy, with its plentiful hotel rooms and phone lines, was the capital of Marshal Philippe Pétain's collaborationist 'Vichy French' government.

Orientation

The heart of Vichy is its triangular Parc des Sources, 800m west of the train station. Rue Georges Clemenceau, the main shopping thoroughfare, crosses the partly pedestrianised city centre.

Information

Échap (☎ 04 70 32 28 57; 12 rue Source de l'Hôpital; per hr €4; ☼ noon-midnight Tue-Sat, 2pm-midnight Sun) Internet access, coffee and snacks and live jazz if you're lucky.

Le Grenier (☎ 04 70 32 10 04; 23 rue E Gilbert; per hr €2; ☼ 10.30am-9.30pm Mon-Fri, 11am-9.30pm Sat & Sun) Internet access with changing art exhibitions and delightful salads and sandwiches. Free wi-fi.

Main Post Office (place Charles de Gaulle)

Tourist Office (☎ 04 70 98 71 94; www.vichytourisme .com; 19 rue du Parc; ☼ 9am-7pm Mon-Sat, 9.30am-12.30pm & 3-7pm Sun Jul & Aug, 9am-12.30pm & 1.30-7pm Mon-Sat, 9.30am-12.30pm & 3-7pm Sun Apr-Jun & Sep, 9am-noon & 1.30-6pm Mon-Fri, 9am-noon & 2-6pm Sat, 2.30-5.30pm Sun Oct-Mar) Makes hotel and spa reservations without charge.

Sights & Activities

To savour the full richness of Vichy's Second Empire and *belle époque* heritage, pick up *Vichy Pas à Pas*, available in English, from the tourist office. It outlines a couple of **walking routes** and lists five themed **walking tours** (each €6, Jun-Sep). *Quartier Thermal Vichy: Exercices de Styles*, in French but very visual, explores the spa area in more depth.

The bench-lined walkways of **Parc des Sources**, created in 1812, are enclosed by a covered promenade. At the park's northern end is the glass-enclosed **Hall des Sources** (☼ 6.15am-6pm, 7pm or 8.30pm according to season), whose taps deliver five types of mineral water, three of them warm (up to 43.3°C). You can sit on the metal chairs for free, but taking a drink costs €1.65 from April to October. A graduated, urine-sample-style cup is included in the price – the taste of the hotter brews suits the cup's design.

Across the northern end of the park stretches the Indo-Moorish–style **Centre Thermal des Dômes**, adorned with tiled domes and towers and nowadays a shopping arcade.

The brass taps of **Source de l'Hôpital** (admission free; ☼ 8am-8.30pm Apr-Dec), first used in Gallo-Roman times, dispense unlimited quantities of the warmish, odoriferous and rather acrid mineral waters of the Hôpital and Célestins springs.

In the decorated oval pavilion of **Source des Célestins** (blvd du Président Kennedy; ☼ 8am-8.30pm Apr-Sep, 8am-6pm Oct-Mar) you can drink your fill of the famous slightly saline, slightly bubbly mineral water, of which more than 60 million bottles are sold annually. The taps are shut in winter to prevent the pipes freezing, but you can still fill your bottles at the Hall des Sources, to which the fizzy fluid is piped.

Art-Deco **Église St-Blaise** (rue de l'Allier), built in the 1930s, has rich, glowing stained-glass windows and splendid neo-Byzantine mosaics in its barrel-vaulted roof (to illuminate

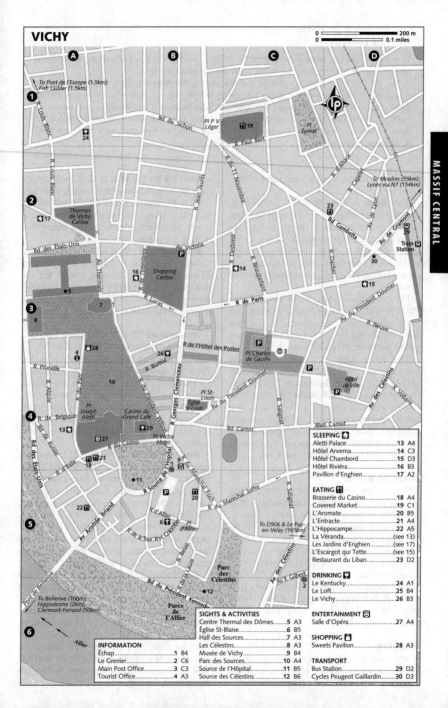

VICHY

MASSIF CENTRAL

MASSIF CENTRAL

LADY OF LETTERS

That *grande dame* of letter writing, Mme de Sévigné, visiting Vichy in 1676, wrote to her friend and confidante Mme de Grignon in her usual breezy epistolary style:

'So, my dearest, I took the plunge and the waters this morning. Lord, how foul they are! About six in the morning you go to the spring, where just everyone who matters is already there. You all sip and sup and pull the ugliest of faces because – just imagine – the waters are boiling hot and have the quite vilest of sulphury tastes. You stroll up and down, come and go, listen to Mass, go walkabout, throw up, confide discreetly just how you threw up – and that's it, all the way to midday...'

---

them, press the button to your right as you enter by the west door).

Tiny **Musée de Vichy** (☎ 04 70 32 12 97; 15 rue du Maréchal Foch; admission free; ◷ 2-6pm Tue-Fri, 2-5pm Sat) occupies three small rooms in an Art-Deco theatre. Surprisingly slight for a city with such a history, it displays paintings, sculpture, a couple of cases of archaeological finds and a few telegrams from Marshal Pétain.

For a little flutter, visit Vichy's **Hippodrome** (☎ 04 70 32 47 00), one of France's finest and most prestigious racecourses, just across the river on the Bellerive bank. The horses gallop between May and September.

The River Allier is one of the few in France where salmon still swim. Northwest of the centre, beside the Pont de l'Europe on the right bank, is a **fish ladder** (◷ 2-6pm Fri-Tue Apr-Aug) where, according to the season, you can see migratory salmon, sea trout, eels and lampreys, in addition to local species. Call up www.fondation-saumon.org (in French) and you can track them in real time.

THERMAL BATHS

The most luxurious of Vichy's three active spas is the ultramodern **Les Célestins** (☎ 04 70 30 82 82; 111 blvd des États-Unis) with its beauty, fitness and slimming programmes. Walk-in treatments include a *douche de Vichy* (a four-hand massage as you're sprayed with hot spring water; €45), *hydromassage* (a 20-minute massage with water jets; €30) and the *jet tonifiant* (a high-powered water jet – the sort that disperses riots; €30). They'll even rip the hairs from your legs, should you so wish (€28).

Sleeping

Vichy's many hotels offer some of the country's best deals. Those included here are open year-round unless otherwise noted.

Hôtel Riviéra (☎ 04 70 98 22 32; www.hotelrivier avichy.com in French; 5 rue de l'Intendance; r €28, with bathroom €34-40) One-star, friendly Hôtel Riviéra with its 20 large, recently renovated rooms is one of several places on this street that offer great value.

Hôtel Chambord (☎ 04 70 30 16 30; le.chambord@ wanadoo.fr; 82-84 rue de Paris; s €38-45, d €42-57) This 25-room Logis de France, handy for the station, has been run by the same family for three generations. Welcoming and relaxed, it runs a creditable restaurant, L'Escargot qui Tette.

Hôtel Arverna (☎ 04 70 31 31 19; www.hotels-vichy .com in French; 12 rue Desbrest; s €42-46, d €50-60; ⊠ 🅿) Tautly run by an engaging couple who fled Paris for quieter quarters, the Arverna is an excellent choice. All rooms are double glazed and most overlook the small internal patio, where vines creep up the walls. For more space at marginal extra cost, ask for one of their four large, attractive rooms with a small salon.

Pavillon d'Enghien (☎ 04 70 98 33 30; www.pavil londenghien.com; 32 rue Callou; r €46-78; closed 20 Dec-Jan; 🅿) The rooms here are trim and attractive, each individually furnished without a square centimetre of plastic in sight, except for the minibar. Nearly all have a bathtub and most overlook the internal garden and small pool. The hotel offers wi-fi for those with laptops. Next door is its outstanding restaurant, Les Jardins d'Enghien.

Aletti Palace (☎ 04 70 30 20 20; www.aletti.fr; 3 place Joseph Aletti; s €104-146, d €119-161; ⊠ 🅿 🖳 🅿) Here's *the* place to stay to get a feel for what a visit during the *belle époque* must have been like for the affluent. Nothing could be more of the era and more French – except that, as signs of more modern times, it's now part of a multinational chain and offers wi-fi connections. It too runs a stylish restaurant, La Véranda.

Eating

Les Jardins d'Enghien (☎ 04 70 98 33 30; www.pavillondenghien.com; 32 rue Callou; ☻ Tue-Sun) at Pavillon d'Enghien, **L'Escargot qui Tette** (The Suckling Snail; ☎ 04 70 30 16 30; le.chambord@wanadoo.fr; 82-84 rue de Paris; menus €19-40; ☻ Tue-Sat & lunch Sun) at Hôtel Chambord and **La Véranda** (☎ 04 70 30 20 20; www.aletti.fr; 3 place Joseph Aletti) at Aletti Palace are three excellent hotel restaurants open to all-comers.

Restaurant du Liban (☎ 04 70 31 14 79; 51 blvd Gambetta; mezze €3.50-6.50; closed lunch Mon) This unpretentious place serves tasty Lebanese food, offering more than 40 different kinds of *mezze*. For a variety of taste sensations, go for the *mini mezze* (€24 for two people), a selection of 10 of the best.

L'Entracte (☎ 04 70 59 85 68; 10 rue du Casino; ☻ Tue-Sat) This tiny wine bar, clad in attractive antique wood panelling, is a great place for a toasted sandwich (€8.50) or a platter of Auvergnat cheese (€6), sluiced down with one of their fine wines, all available by the glass.

Brasserie du Casino (☎ 04 70 98 23 06; 4 rue du Casino; mains €16-22, lunch menu €15, fish menu €25; ☻ Thu-Mon Mar–mid-Oct & mid-Nov–mid-Feb) This is a wonderful pre-WWII brasserie, its walls plastered with signed photos of the once-famous artistes who dropped in from the Opéra, just across the road.

our pick **L'Aromate** (☎ 04 70 32 13 22; 9 rue Besse; menus €15-36, mains €18-20; ☻ mid-Aug–mid-Jul, closed Wed, dinner Tue & dinner Sun) With its pillars topped by ornate capitals holding up the high ceiling – which, it must be said, bears a crack or two – its softly piped classical music and tall, gilded mirrors, L'Aromate speaks of a lost elegance. But the food is imaginative, stylishly presented and strictly contemporary. It's a fairly formal place; reservations are all but essential and even if you strike it lucky with a lunchtime walk-in, you won't be all that well regarded. And don't expect lightning service; good food, as the menu points out, takes time. So set aside a good two hours. You won't regret it and, as a souvenir of a special meal, you can take away a pot of exotic homemade jam.

L'Hippocampe (☎ 04 70 97 68 37; 3 blvd de Russie; menus €21-48; ☻ Tue-Sun) Oysters, lobsters, sole and scallops – even humble sardines, here smoked over oak; the menu leans heavily towards the freshest of fish and seafood, retaining all its juices and attractively pre-sented, even though L'Hippocampe's far from the nearest salt water. The place is normally packed and staff are rushed off their feet so bring along a little patience. The lunch *menu* (€15) is excellent value.

SELF-CATERING

The cavernous covered market, built in the mid-1930s in a heavy, unadorned Stalinist style, is on place PV Léger.

Drinking

There's little after dark in Vichy to make young blood tingle.

Le Kentucky (14 blvd du Sichon; ☻ 5pm-2am Mon-Sat) pulls in a young crowd and has a decent range of draught beers. **Le Vichy** (15 rue Burnol) with its glowing sky-blue bar and multiple televisions playing MTV is equally popular.

Le Loft (☎ 04 70 97 16 46; 7 rue du Casino; admission €8; ☻ from 11pm Thu-Sun), below the Casino du Grand Café, is a discotheque that makes the walls of the genteel spa shudder.

Entertainment

Pick up *Vichy Mensuel*, a free monthly what's-on guide, at the tourist office or around town.

Vichy was once known as the 'French Bayreuth'. Operas, operettas, dance performances and concerts are still staged regularly in the ornate 1902 **Salle d'Opéra** (☎ 04 70 30 50 50; rue du Casino) within the Palais des Congrès (formerly Vichy's Grand Casino).

Shopping

You can sample and buy the octagonal mint, aniseed and lemon lozenges known as *pastilles de Vichy*, pride of the city since 1825, at the **sweets pavilion** (☻ Apr-Oct) of the Parc des Sources and at sweets shops around town. Why are they so popular? See the boxed text on p731.

Getting There & Around

Major train destinations include Paris' Gare de Lyon (€38.80, three hours, six daily), Clermont-Ferrand (€8.50, 40 minutes, frequent), Riom (€6.70, 25 minutes, frequent) and Lyon (€21.80, 2½ hours, six daily).

Year round, **Cycles Peugeot Gaillardin** (☎ 04 70 31 52 86; 48 blvd Gambetta; ☻ Mon morning & Tue-Sat) hires out both town and mountain bikes (half-/full-day €5/8) with a refundable deposit of €80.

MASSIF CENTRAL

ORCIVAL
pop 250 / elevation 860m

The delightful, slate-roofed village of Orcival lies midway between the Puy de Dôme and Le Mont-Dore. Situated beside the gurgling River Sioulet, it's a perfect base for day hikes and, despite the coachloads of quick-fix tourists, a lovely spot to spend a few soothing days.

Hanging over the entrance of the superb 12th-century Auvergnat-Romanesque **basilica** are balls and chains left in gratitude by released prisoners. Perched on a pillar behind the altar is a squat 12th-century statue of the Virgin, fashioned from gilded silver over wood.

Turreted 15th-century **Château de Cordès** (☎ 04 73 65 81 34; adult/child/student €4/2.30/3; ☼ 10am-noon & 2-6pm Easter-Oct) is about 2.5km to the north. It's well worth the short detour to enjoy the rich 18th-century furnishings and the formal gardens, laid out by Le Nôtre, designer of the gardens of Versailles and of London's Greenwich and St James's parks.

Orcival's **tourist office** (☎ 04 73 65 89 77; www .terresdomes-sancy.com in French; ☼ 10am-noon & 2-6pm Mon-Sat, 10am-noon Sun Jun-Sep & school holidays) is opposite the church.

Sleeping & Eating

Les Bourelles (☎ 04 73 65 82 28; d €27-30; ☼ Easter-Sep) Set back from the road, Les Bourelles has a lovely, flowery terrace and seven simple rooms giving beautiful views.

Hôtel Notre Dame (☎ & fax 04 73 65 82 02; d €33-38, q €46; ☼ Feb-Dec) This hotel belongs to the same friendly couple who run Les Bourelles and is excellent value. All seven rooms have views of the basilica and have been recently renovated. Ask for No 26, which has its own large terrace. The hostel runs a decent restaurant (menus €11.50 to €22).

COL DE GUÉRY

The D27 from Orcival to the Col de Guéry (1268m), 8.5km to its south, passes through spectacular scenery.

In summer, the **Maison des Fleurs d'Auvergne** (☎ 04 73 65 20 09; http://maisondesfleurs.free.fr; ☼ 10am-7pm mid-Jun–mid-Sep, 10am-7pm Sat & Sun May–mid-Jun), beside the pass, presents the area's flora. Although in French, the display is highly visual and the *jardin écologique* (ecological garden) grows many of the plants and trees you'll see on walks in the area. From the first snowfall, the centre becomes the **Foyer Ski de Fond Orcival Guéry** (www.leguery .fr in French; ☼ 9am-5pm), a cross-country skiing centre with a children's play area and pony-drawn sleigh rides (€2.50). From here radiate 35km of groomed pistes. Hire of cross-country gear costs €9.20 per day and snowshoes are €5.50.

Auberge du Lac de Guéry (☎ 04 73 65 02 76; www .auberge-lac-guery.fr in French; d €54; ☼ mid-Jan–mid-Oct) The rooms are comfortable if relatively plain but the site, beside the southern shore of Lac de Guéry, is unbeatable. You'll eat well in its restaurant (menus €16.50 to €30). The fish, selected from the nearby fish farm, couldn't come fresher. In late winter, you can pull out your own; the hotel sells permits for this, the only lake in France where there's ice fishing.

LE MONT-DORE
pop 1700 / elevation 1050m

This trim little spa town, 44km southwest of Clermont-Ferrand, is ideal for exploring the Puy de Sancy area on foot, by bicycle or

---

TOP TRAILS

The rounded summits of the Massif Central and the gentle valleys in-between are cobwebbed by a network of signed trails, varying in length from a few kilometres to long-distance treks that can take a couple of weeks.

Week-end Dans le Massif Central, published in French by Chamina, describes 24 one- or two-day walks, while *Week-end en Auvergne* presents eight two- and three-dayers.

The **Traverse of the High Auvergne** is a magnificent 290km linear route that winds southwards from Volvic (p591) across the Massif Central's most spectacular summits, mainly following the GR4. It's described in detail in Alan Castle's excellent *Walks in Volcano Country*.

Less rugged but not as spectacular, the **Robert Louis Stevenson Trail**, designated the GR70, also heads southwards into the Cévennes, starting from Monastier-sur-Gazelle, near Le Puy-en-Velay. See the boxed text on p790.

by car. It stretches along a narrow, wooded valley beside the Dordogne, not far from the river's source. Built from locally quarried dark stone, the town bustles with skiers in winter, then hikers and *curistes*, attracted by the hot springs and spa, in summer.

Information

Laundrette (place de la République; ☺ 9am-7pm)
Post Office (place Charles de Gaulle)
Tourist Office (☎ 04 73 65 20 21; www.sancy.com; av de la Libération; ☺ 9am-noon & 2-6pm Mon-Sat, 9am-noon Sun, also 2-5pm Sun school holidays)

Sights & Activities

The waters (37°C to 40°C) of the huge **Thermes** (spa complex; ☎ 04 73 65 05 10; 1 place du Panthéon; ☺ May–mid-Oct) soothe respiratory ailments and rheumatism. The spa also offers fitness programmes for the hale and hearty (from €95, minimum three days), or you can test the waters with its one-day introductory programme (€43). There are 30-minute **guided tours** (adult/child €3.20/2.20; ☺ hourly 2-5pm Mon-Sat May-Sep, 3pm Mon-Fri Jan-Apr & Oct), of the sumptuous 19th-century neo-Byzantine interior, which retains vestiges from Gallo-Roman times.

The **Funiculaire du Capucin** (av René Cassin; single/return €3.30/4.20; ☺ May–mid-Oct) runs to Les Capucins, a 1270m-high wooded plateau above town. France's oldest funicular railway, built in 1898, it creeps up at precisely one metre per second. From the upper station, multiple signed walking possibilities open up, including linking with the GR30, which wends its way southwards towards the Puy de Sancy, continuing to the Pic du Capucin (1450m; about 45 minutes one way) or dropping steeply back to town.

A cable-car lift, the **Téléphérique du Sancy** (single/return €5.40/6.80), about 3.5km south of town, swings to the summit of the Puy de Sancy (also known as the Pic de Sancy). Here you can take in the stunning panorama of the northern puys and the southern Monts du Cantal before starting a hike or, in winter, slip-sliding down the slopes.

A session at the town's **ice-skating rink** (☎ 04 73 65 06 55; av Georges Lagaye; ☺ Dec-Aug), where there's also a bowling alley, costs €6.35, including skate hire.

Mont-Dore Aventures (☎ 04 73 65 00 00; www .montdoreaventures.com; le Salon du Capucin; adult/under 12/12-15yr €19/11/14; ☺ 10am-7.30pm Jul & Aug, 1-7pm Sat & Sun Apr-Jun & Sep-Nov) is great for playing Tarzan for an hour or two, as you clamber and swing your way around the circuits up in the trees. It's 150m from the Funiculaire du Capucin's upper station. Alternatively, take the winding 4km road via the D465.

SKIING

The northern side of the spectacular Puy de Sancy has 42km of runs. Another 43km splay over the hill down to **Super Besse**, on the mountain's southeastern slopes. There's a good cross-country network around the Puy de Sancy ski fields, with nearly 40km of trails.

A lift ticket, good for both Le Mont-Dore and Super Besse, costs €22/57.20 (under 12s €15.40/41.20) for one/three days.

WALKING

Lonely Planet's *Walking in France* describes two of the best treks around the area's forests, lakes and peaks. Routes are superbly indicated; a signpost at every major junction bristles with arrows showing distance or time to the next landmark. Buy Chamina's 1:30,000-scale map *Massif du Sancy* (€5.35). This sterling Auvergnat company also produces a walking guide with the same title (€6.70), describing 30 hikes in the area.

CYCLING

You can't avoid the ups and downs (even though the Funiculaire du Capucin does allow bikes on board) but this is still great cycling terrain. The tourist office has a free mountain-bike trail map, *Circuit VTT: Le Mont-Dore Sancy*.

Sleeping

Camping Les Crouzets (☎ 04 73 65 21 60; camping .crouzets@wanadoo.fr; per person/site €2.90/2.55; ☺ mid-Dec–mid-Oct) It's municipal and conveniently opposite the train station.

Camping L'Esquiladou (☎ 04 73 65 23 74; camping .esquiladou@wanadoo.fr; route des Cascades; per person/site €3/2.65; ☺ May–mid-Oct) About 1.5km north of town and signposted from the train station, L'Esquiladou, also municipal, is altogether more tranquil and roomy.

Auberge de Jeunesse (☎ 04 73 65 03 53; le-mont -dore@fuaj.org; route du Sancy; B&B €14.90; ☺ Dec–mid-Nov; ▣) This HI-affiliated youth hostel, Le Grand Volcan (The Big Volcano), sits in

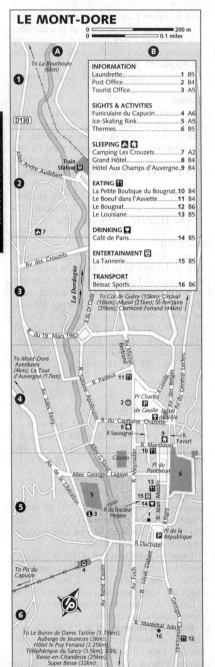

LE MONT-DORE

0 _____ 200 m
0 _____ 0.1 miles

INFORMATION	
Laundrette.....................................1	B5
Post Office...................................2	B4
Tourist Office..............................3	A5

SIGHTS & ACTIVITIES	
Funiculaire du Capucin...............4	A6
Ice-Skating Rink...........................5	A5
Thermes.......................................6	B5

SLEEPING	
Camping Les Crouzets.................7	A2
Grand Hôtel.................................8	B4
Hôtel Aux Champs d'Auvergne.9	B4

EATING	
La Petite Boutique du Bougnat.10	B4
Le Bœuf dans l'Assiette...............11	B4
Le Bougnat..................................12	B6
Le Louisiane................................13	B5

DRINKING	
Café de Paris................................14	B5

ENTERTAINMENT	
La Tannerie.................................15	B5

TRANSPORT	
Bessac Sports..............................16	B6

the shadow of Puy de Sancy about 3.5km south of town. Rooms accommodate from two to six hostellers. Book ahead during the ski season and in summer.

Hôtel Aux Champs d'Auvergne (☎ 04 73 65 00 37; www.auxchampsdauvergne.com in French; 18 rue Favart; s/d €19/26, with bathroom €31/38, half-board per person €31.50-41; ◉ late Dec–mid-Oct) This friendly, laid-back place has 23 cosy rooms divided between the main building and a couple of annexes. Go for half-board; dinner is a splendid five-course affair and there's a choice of homemade jams at breakfast to smear on your warm croissant.

our pick **Grand Hôtel** (☎ 04 73 65 02 64; www .hotel-mont-dore.com; 2 rue Meynadier; d €40-57, tr €53-60; ◉ mid-Dec–mid-Mar & mid-Apr–mid-Nov) In 2004, Murielle and Patrick Perrot took over a classic old hotel, constructed in 1850. While still majestic from the outside, it was desperately run down (even the local Red Cross refused half of the furniture they tried to give away) and very far from grand within. They've turned it around with great flair and style yet prices remain moderate and excellent value. In the cosy lounge with its soft leather chairs – in red, a theme that's picked up throughout the hotel's décor – there's a flat-screen TV and piles of tourist information for guests. Rooms are furnished with taste and those on the 3rd floor have balconies. Our favourite is No 33 with its huge angled bathtub. Behind the building there's a large garden, ideal for a little sun-worshipping. Parking is free.

Hôtel le Puy Ferrand (☎ 04 73 65 18 99; www .hotel-puy-ferrand.com; d €62-72, studio flats €72-82; ◉ late Dec–Oct; 🏊) This midrange hotel, built chalet-style from local stone, is an easy stomp, even in ski boots, from the Puy de Sancy cable car. It has an excellent restaurant, sauna and year-round covered pool. The considerably larger studio flats have self-catering facilities. Half-board is obligatory in February. Wi-fi available.

Eating

Le Bœuf dans l'Assiette (Beef on the Plate; ☎ 04 73 65 01 23; 9 av Michel Bertrand; mains €8-12, menus €12-16.80; ◉ Tue-Sun) As its name suggests, this place is for serious carnivores as photographs of cows gaze down on you from the walls like film stars' portraits.

Le Louisiane (☎ 04 73 65 03 14; 2 rue Jean Moulin; menus €13-25; ◉ closed Wed mid-Oct–Apr) Spacious and airy, Le Louisiane is an odd yet pleasing marriage with its décor, which owes much to the deep south of the USA, grafted onto the vast dining room of what was once the largest luxury hotel in the region. The cuisine too is hybrid: plenty of local dishes and a good choice of seafood.

Le Buron de Dame Tartine (☎ 04 73 65 28 40; route du Sancy; menus €17-22) A *buron* is, traditionally, a mountain shepherd's simple summer hut. This place is altogether more comfortable and modern (indeed, perhaps a tad *too* new for some). But the food's fine and it's an easy walk from the base of the ski slopes.

Le Bougnat (☎ 04 73 65 28 19; 23 av Georges Clemenceau; menus €17-23; ☾ early Dec–Oct) With its low-beamed wooden interior hung with appealing farmhouse clutter and an attractive, flowery terrace, this splendid place offers rich Auvergnat dishes confected from local produce.

SELF-CATERING
La Petite Boutique du Bougnat (1 rue Montlosier) positively bursts with the best local cured and canned meats, hams, sausages and more than 30 varieties of Auvergnat wine. Right opposite, its *fromagerie* is just as pungent and enticing.

Drinking & Entertainment
Café de Paris (8 rue Jean Moulin) is a convivial, crowded old-time café where clients, mainly from the town, play cards, flirt and chat until the cows come home.

La Tannerie (☎ 04 73 65 25 86; rue du Docteur Perpère; drinks from €5) is the town's sole disco theque.

Getting There & Around
From the sleepy train station, change at Clermont-Ferrand (€11.20, 1¼ hours, up to five daily) for Paris' Gare de Lyon (€49, 5½ hours).

In winter, a free skiers shuttle bus *(navette)* plies regularly between Le Mont-Dore and the Sancy cable car. From mid-May to September, the service operates four times daily (single/return €2.15/3.25), continuing to La Bourboule (single/return €4/5.90).

Bessac Sports (☎ 04 73 65 02 25; 3 rue Maréchal Juin) hires out mountain bikes from €12/18 per half-/full day and can also put you wise about the most attractive routes.

AROUND LE MONT-DORE
Only 7km downriver westwards, La Bourboule, Le Mont-Dore's slightly larger sister spa, has some lovely *belle époque* buildings. The **tourist office** (☎ 04 73 65 57 71; www.sancy.com; place de la République; ☾ 9am-9pm Mon-Sat, 10am-noon & 2-6pm Sun Jul & Aug; 9am-noon & 1.30-6pm Mon-Sat, 10am-noon & 2-4/5pm Sun Sep-Jun) is in the Hôtel de Ville. The train trip to/from Le Mont-Dore (€1.40, seven daily) takes just eight minutes.

About 10km east of Le Mont-Dore, the 12th-century **Château de Murol** (☎ 04 73 88 67 11; adult/child €4/3; ☾ Apr-Oct, Sat & Sun Nov-Mar) sits squat atop a knoll overlooking the village of the same name. From April to October, there's a lively **pageant** (adult/child €7.50/5), where actors in period costume recreate medieval castle life.

Lac Chambon
This pleasant little resort, beside the natural lake of the same name, is 1.5km west of Murol.

Hôtel Restaurant Beau Site (☎ 04 73 88 61 29; www.beau-site.com in French; d €43-48; menus €17-28; ☾ Feb-Oct) is one of a string of hotels that fringe the lake. At its northern end, it's just that little bit higher and offers the best views. It also runs a highly recommended restaurant.

Also at the northern end is **Sancy Loisirs** (☎ 04 73 88 67 07), which rents canoes, dinghies and windsurfers.

Besse-en-Chandesse
Picturesque Besse-en-Chandesse is 25km southeast of Le Mont-Dore. There's a small **tourist office** (☎ 04 73 79 52 84; www.sancy.com; place du Docteur Pipet; ☾ 9am-noon & 2-6pm Dec-Sep, 9am-noon & 2-6pm Mon-Sat Oct-Nov).

With cobbled streets and houses of solid rectangular basalt blocks, it's known for its cheese production (in fact processing much more St-Nectaire cheese than the town of St-Nectaire itself). Several of the 15th- to 18th-century houses along rue de la Boucherie were built of basalt quarried right beside each home – and the quarry became the cheese cellar.

The 15th-century Maison de la Reine Margot is home to a small **ski museum** (☎ 04 73 79 57 30; admission €2.50; ☾ 9am-noon & 2-7pm school holidays). Pierre-André, who's collected more than 300 pairs of vintage skis and other mountain gear, will himself guide you around in his charmingly eccentric English.

The mostly Romanesque **Église St-André** has a 12th-century nave with finely carved capitals.

The ski station of **Super Besse** (see p597), established in the 1960s as a purpose-built resort, is 7km to the west. About 4km towards Super Besse is **Lac Pavin**. A near-circular lake and Auvergne's deepest, it sits in the hollow of an extinct volcano. A gentle walk around its wooded perimeter takes about 45 minutes.

St-Nectaire

This tiny town is famed for its 50 natural springs and eponymous soft and flavoursome cheese. Straggling for more than 2km from St-Nectaire-le-Haut (the upper) to St-Nectaire-le-Bas (the lower), it's a lively place with a whiff of faded charm from its days as a spa town.

The efficient **tourist office** (☎ 04 73 88 50 86; www.ville-saint-nectaire.fr; ☼ 9am-12.15pm & 2-6.45pm Jul & Aug, 9-11.45am & 2-4.45pm Mon-Sat Sep-Jun) is in St-Nectaire-le-Bas. It has seven sheets in English that outline circular walks around the town.

At the top of the town, highlights of the delightful Romanesque **church** (☼ 9am-7pm Apr-Oct, 10am-12.30pm & 2-6pm Nov-Mar) are its 103 carved polychrome capitals and a fine 12th-century statue of the Virgin.

The Romans were the first to steep themselves in the waters, both hot and cold, of the **Grottes du Cornadore** (☎ 04 73 88 57 97; adult/child €4.50/3; ☼ mid-Feb–Oct). Perfect natural baths, these caves today make an impressive underground spectacle.

At the **Site Troglodyte de Jonas** (☎ 04 73 88 57 98; adult/child €4.40/3; ☼ Easter-Sep), 6km south of town, are more than 60 interconnecting troglodyte caves hewn into the cliff, several retaining traces of medieval frescoes.

Maison du St-Nectaire (☎ 04 73 88 57 96; adult/child €3.40/2.70; ☼ mid-Feb–Oct) is a small exhibition that takes you through the cheese-making process. Also included is a guided tasting and introductory film.

PUY MARY

Majestic Puy Mary (1787m) is an easy 30-minute ascent from **Pas de Peyrol**, a 1582m pass on the D680 that's blocked by snow-drifts between late October and May.

North of Puy Mary is **Col de Serre** (1364m), a notch 3km northeast of the Pas de Peyrol. From here the D62 drops tortuously to the green River Cheylade valley, passing through rich pasture and deciduous forests.

Alternatively, take the D680 from Col de Serre to follow the Santoire Valley eastwards to the tidy little village of **Dienne**, and continue to the town of Murat.

MURAT

pop 2300 / elevation 930m

The dark grey stone houses of Murat huddle and tumble at the foot of a basalt crag topped by a giant white statue of the Virgin Mary.

Information

The **tourist office** (☎ 04 71 20 09 47; www.ville-de-murat.com in French; 2 rue du Faubourg Notre-Dame; ☼ 9am-noon & 2-6pm daily Jul & Aug, Mon-Sat Sep-Jun) is beside the Hôtel de Ville.

Sights & Activities

Murat makes a good base for exploring the Monts du Cantal, including **Puy Mary** and the 1855m **Plomb du Cantal**. Walks bagging each peak, starting from the ski station of

---

AUVERGNAT CHEESES

From as early as the 1st century AD, the lush grasses of Auvergne's volcanic soils have fed the cows that gave the milk that farmers ferment into the region's excellent cheeses. The region has no fewer than five cheeses classified as Appellation d'Origine Contrôlée (AOC; the highest category of French cheese, with an officially controlled declaration of origin): Cantal, white and full flavoured; Salers, similar to Cantal and from the same area, but made only from the milk of cows that graze on high summer pastures; St-Nectaire, rich-scented, flat and round like a discus; Fourme d'Ambert, a mild, smooth blue cheese; and Bleu d'Auvergne, also blue and stronger, with a creamier texture than its much-touted cousin, Rocquefort.

Take your pick; each in its distinct way makes a delightful sandwich filling.

Super Lioran, are described in Lonely Planet's *Walking in France*.

With the English version of the tourist office's audioguide or its free pamphlet, *The Picturesque Visit in the Old Murat* (sic; the text flows better than the title), you can happily spend a pleasant hour or so browsing Murat's steep, narrow streets. A steepish ascent (45 minutes round trip from the tourist office) takes you up to **Rocher de Bonne Vie** with its statue of the Virgin. Follow the red-and-white GR flashes northwestwards out of town, then signs for the Rocher, to enjoy a magnificent view of the town and the higher peaks to the west.

Maison de la Faune (☎ 04 71 20 00 52; just above place de l'Hôtel de Ville; adult/child €4/2.50; ☯ core hours 10am-noon & 3-5pm Mon-Sat, 2-6pm Sun) occupies an elegant 16th-century house. On the ground and 1st floors are more than 10,000 mounted insects, starring some truly dazzling tropical butterflies. Upper levels display local stuffed and mounted wildlife in a natural, well documented – in French – setting. This said, there's a chilling irony – the frequent green spots on individual labels denote endangered species; lift your eyes and there's the hapless creature, staring back at you in death.

Sleeping & Eating

Camping Municipal Stalapos (☎ 04 71 20 01 83; rue du Stade; per person/site €2/1.60; ☯ May-Sep) Beside the River Alagnon, this attractive camp site is 750m south of the train station. In high summer they organise nights of Auvergnat food and folklore.

Hôtel Les Messageries (☎ 04 71 20 04 04; www .hotel-les-messageries.com in French; 18 av Docteur Mallet; s/d/tr/q €35/45/60/70; ☯ closed 1-10 Jan; 🖳) Overlooking the train station, this Logis de France, with notices, warnings and admonishments plastered everywhere, is more characterful than its bland exterior suggests. The restaurant (*menus* €11 to €31) is strong on Auvergnat dishes and there's a sauna, pool and mini-gym, should you still have energy to expend after a day's hiking.

Auberge de Maître Paul (☎ 04 71 20 14 66; www .auberge-paul.fr; 14 place du Planol; s/d/tr/q €35/46/60/70; ☯ closed last week Jun, 1st week Nov; ✗) This jolly, family-friendly *gîte* with attitude has winding corridors and spruce, charmingly decorated rooms. If you're a couple, you really should go for half-board at a terrific value

€70. Popular with walkers in summer and skiers when the snow's on the heights, its restaurant serves pizzas the size of flying saucers (€6.90 eat in or take away) and does an excellent *menu* (€16).

Hostellerie Les Breuils (☎ 04 71 20 01 25; www .hostellerie-les-breuils.com; 34 av du Docteur Mallet; r €62-77; ☯ Feb, mid-May-Oct; 🖳) Converted from a private 19th-century mansion and still in the hands of the original family, Les Breuils' more modern features include a sauna and heated pool. Ivy-clad and welcoming with a lovely garden, its pricier rooms are particularly large, while those on the 1st floor still have the original family furniture.

For fine picnic fare, stock up at **Caldera** (3 rue Justin Vigier), no more than 100m from the tourist office, which has a magnificent selection of local cheese, cold cuts, honey, jam and liqueur.

Getting There & Around

Trains running between Clermont-Ferrand (€16.30, 1½ hours) and Aurillac (€7.60, 45 minutes) call by Murat four to seven times daily. Two continue beyond Aurillac to Toulouse (€30.70, 4½ hours).

The countryside around makes for splendid if fairly taxing cycling. Both **Loisirs et Deux Roues** (☎ 04 71 20 06 54; rue Bon Secours) and **Ô Ptit Montagnard** (☎ 04 71 20 28 40; rue Faubourg Notre Dame) rent reliable machines.

PARC NATUREL RÉGIONAL LIVRADOIS-FOREZ

One of France's largest protected areas, this nature park slopes away gently to the west to the plains of Limagne while the Monts du Forez, dropping abruptly to the upper Loire Valley, form a natural eastern limit.

The **park information office** (☎ 04 73 95 57 57; www.parc-livradois-forez.org in French; ☯ 9am-12.30pm & 1.30-7pm Mon-Fri, 3-7pm Sat & Sun May-Sep; 9am-12.30pm & 1.30-5.30pm Mon-Fri Oct-Apr) is just off the D906 in St-Gervais-sous-Meymont. Its excellent brochure, *La Route des Métiers* (The Cottage Industry Trail), describes and pinpoints on the map 40 small museums and cottage industries. All open to the public, they produce items as diverse as lace,

MASSIF CENTRAL

honey, medicinal plants and perfumes. The park's *Guide de la Randonnée et des Loisirs de Plein Air* gives a host of suggestions for treks and mountain-bike routes, cross-referring to the relevant topoguides. Both are in French and free.

Getting Around

The **Train de la Découverte** (Discovery Train; ☎ 04 73 82 43 88) is a superb way to see the heart of the park. In July and August, it runs between Courpière (15km south of Thiers) via Ambert (adult/child €13/9) to La Chaise-Dieu (adult/child €18/13). Check the variable timetable with the park office, or Ambert and La Chaise Dieu tourist offices.

THIERS

pop 14,000 / elevation 420m

Down below, beside the Gorges de la Durolle, you could convince yourself that Thiers is a town seriously on the skids. The thundering river that once drove the mills that ground the knives roars on, but the abandoned factories along its banks are a sad testament to an outmoded way of production.

Nevertheless, Thiers remains Steel City with more than 60 workshops and factories producing some 70% of the knives and cutlery sold in France. To understand its unique industrial history, you need to visit the Musée de la Coutellerie and the Vallée des Rouets.

The friendly **tourist office** (☎ 04 73 80 65 65; www.tourisme-thiers.fr in French; 1 place du Pirou; ☷ 9am-1pm & 1.30-7pm Mon-Sat, 10am-noon & 2-6pm Sun mid-Jun–mid-Sep, 9.30am-noon & 2-6pm Mon-Sat mid-Sep–mid-Jun) is in the Château du Pirou.

The **Musée de la Coutellerie** (Cutlery Museum; ☎ 04 73 80 58 86; 23 & 58 rue de la Coutellerie; adult/child €4.90/2.40; ☷ 10am-12.30pm & 1.30-6.30pm Jul & Aug, 10am-noon & 2-6pm Tue-Sun Sep-Dec & Feb-Jun) presents cottage-industry cutlery manufacturing. No 23 gives the historical perspective and includes an eight-minute film (with optional English version) while No 58 has demonstrations by skilled craftspeople and an impressive collection of knives, present and past. Ask for the accompanying guide sheet in English.

The **Vallée des Rouets** (Valley of the Waterwheels; ☷ noon-7pm Jul & Aug, noon-6pm Tue-Sun Jun & Sep), about 4km upstream from Thiers, is an open-air museum to the self-employed knife grinders who spent their working days stretched along a wooden plank above their grindstone. You can follow either an easy 1km signed walking trail or the scarcely more arduous 2.5km trail. In July and August a shuttle bus runs hourly from Thiers. Driving, take the N89 towards Lyon. A combined ticket (adult/child €6.20/2.60) covers the shuttle bus and admission to both the museum and Vallée des Rouets.

Near the tourist office is the **Maison de l'Homme de Bois** (21 rue de la Coutellerie), named after the bizarre figure in skins carved in wood on the left of the façade. It's one of several fine wood and half-timbered 15th-century mansions in the old quarter.

AMBERT

pop 7700

In the 16th century, Ambert, 30km north of La Chaise-Dieu, had more than 300 small water-powered mills. The little town fed the printing presses of Lyon and was France's most important paper producer until the industrial revolution. Today it's renowned for the fine Fourme d'Ambert cheese and is a centre for the surrounding agricultural area.

The **tourist office** (☎ 04 73 82 61 90; www.tourisme.fr/office-de-tourisme/ambert.htm in French; 4 place de l'Hôtel de Ville; ☷ 9.30am-12.30pm & 1.30-6pm Mon-Sat, 10am-noon Sun Jul & Aug; 2-5pm or 6pm Mon, 10am-12.30pm & 2-5pm or 6pm Tue-Sat Sep-Jun) is opposite the Hôtel de Ville.

Maison de la Fourme d'Ambert (☎ 04 73 82 49 23; 29 rue des Chazeaux; adult/child €4.60/3.70; ☷ 9am-7pm Jul & Aug; 9am-noon & 2-7pm Sep, 9am-noon & 2-7pm & Thu-Sat Oct-Dec, Feb & Mar, 9am-noon & 2-7pm Tue-Sat Apr-Jun) explains via a short video in French the production process of rich, mellow blue Fourme d'Ambert cheese. It has a display of traditional cheese-making implements – and also graciously displays Auvergne's other fine cheeses.

Musée Agrivap (☎ 04 73 82 60 42; rue de l'Industrie; adult/child €5/3.30; ☷ 10am-12.30pm & 2-6.30pm Jul & Aug; 2-6pm Easter-Jun & Sep–mid-Oct) is a collection of vintage agricultural machinery and traction engines.

Moulin Richard de Bas (☎ 04 73 82 03 11; adult/child €5.50/3.60; ☷ 9am-8pm Jul & Aug, 9am-noon & 2-6pm Sep-Jun) occupies a 14th-century mill and produces handmade paper using traditional techniques. It's 4km out of town on the D57 towards Valeyre.

Ambert's round **Hôtel de Ville** was originally the town's grain store. Notice the grotesque gargoyles sprouting like warts all along the exterior southern wall of Gothic **Église St-Jean**. There are some lovely half-timbered, mainly **15th-century houses** along rue du Château, rue de la République and place Minimes.

LA CHAISE DIEU

Early in the 14th century, an 11-year-old novice monk, Pierre Roger de Beaufort, joined the **Église Abbatiale de St-Robert** (adult/child/student €3/1/2; 🕑 9am-noon & 2-7pm Jun-Sep, 10am-noon & 2-5pm Mon-Sat, 2-5pm Sun Oct-May). Later, as Pope Clement VI, he bequeathed funds for a fundamental reconstruction of this abbey church, originally built in 1044 – and for the placing of his tomb at its heart.

Although sacked by Huguenots in 1562, ravaged by fire in 1695 and despoiled by revolutionary mobs in the late 18th century, it's still deeply impressive.

At the west end is an elaborately carved 18th-century wooden organ gallery. Plumb in the centre of the choir sits the black-and-white marble tomb of the good pope, surrounded by 144 14th-century choir stalls carved in pale oak. Lift your eyes to take in the magnificent 16th-century Flemish tapestries above them.

By the northern aisle is an unfinished 15th-century **fresco** of the Dance of Death, where sinuous skeletons mock human figures representing the various classes of society.

Outside, the **Salle de l'Écho** has led to all sorts of speculation. Whisper, facing the wall, in one corner and someone listening in the opposite corner will hear you perfectly. Was it, as some maintain, for hearing the confession of lepers? Or of indiscreet fellow monks? Or is it no more than an unanticipated architectural and acoustic fluke?

The abbey and village of La Chaise Dieu are internationally renowned for their annual **festival of sacred music**, held during the second half of August.

LE PUY-EN-VELAY

pop 22,000 / elevation 630m
Lentils and lace, Le Puy-en-Velay's main claim to contemporary fame, make odd bedfellows. Lace, alas, has fallen on hard times and all but the oldest lengths will have been imported. But oh, the lentils! They bear an Appellation d'Origine Contrôlée (AOC) label, just like a fine wine, thanks to the area's uniquely rich volcanic soil.

In medieval times, the cathedral of Le Puy was one of four French departure points for pilgrim routes to Santiago de Compostella in Spain. Known as the Via Podiensis, it's today called, more prosaically, the GR65, a 1600km long-distance walking trail.

Capital of the Haute-Loire *département*, Le Puy-en-Velay is immediately recognisable by the trio of striking volcanic plugs that thrust up from the valley floor.

Orientation

North of the main square, place du Breuil, lies the pedestrianised old quarter, its narrow streets leading uphill to the cathedral. Le Puy's commercial centre is around the Hôtel de Ville and between blvd Maréchal Fayolle and rue Chaussade.

Information

Cyb'Aire (17 rue Général Lafayette; per hr €3.50; 🕑 11am-11pm Mon-Sat, 3-7pm Sun Jul & Aug, 11am-9pm Mon-Sat, 3-7pm Sun Sep-Jun) Internet access.
Laundrette (24 rue Portail d'Avignon; 🕑 8am-7.30pm)
Main Post Office (8 av de la Dentelle)
Tourist Office (☎ 04 71 09 38 41; www.ot-lepuyenvelay.fr; 2 place du Clauzel; 🕑 8.30am-7.30pm Jul & Aug, 8.30am-noon & 1.30-6.15pm Mon-Sat Sep-Jun) Has a walking tour leaflet in English, *Historical Visits*, describing three walks around town.

Sights & Activities

Medieval, Gothic and Renaissance houses of dark volcanic stone border rue Chaussade, rue du Collège, rue Porte Aiguière and rue Pannessac around the Hôtel de Ville.

God beams down from each of Le Puy's three lava pinnacles: the largest, around whose skirts the old city fans, has the cathedral; the highest bears a giant statue of the Virgin; and on the steepest, a few hundred metres further north, perches a 10th-century gravity-defying chapel.

Cathédrale Notre Dame is a heavily restored Romanesque cathedral. The most impressive way to enter it is up the steep stairs and through the massive arches at the top of cobbled rue des Tables. Byzantine and Moorish elements include the six domes over the nave and the ornately patterned stonework. A 17th-century **Black Virgin** takes pride of place on the high altar.

MASSIF CENTRAL

LE PUY-EN-VELAY

0 ————————— 300 m
0 ————————— 0.2 miles

INFORMATION
Cyb'Aire...................................1 C4
Laundrette...............................2 C5
Main Post Office......................3 C5
Tourist Office...........................4 B4

SIGHTS & ACTIVITIES
Atelier-Conservatoire National de la
 Dentelle...............................5 A3
Cathédrale Notre Dame............6 B4
Centre d'Enseignement de la Dentelle
 au Fuseau............................7 B4
Chapelle St-Michel d'Aiguilhe.....8 B2

Children's Zoo...........................9 B6
Cloister...................................10 B4
Jardin Henri Vinay...................11 B6
Musée Crozatier.......................12 B6
Rocher Corneille Entrance........13 B3

SLEEPING
Auberge de Jeunesse..............14 C4
Camping Le Puy-en-Velay........15 A2
Dyke Hôtel.............................16 C5
Hôtel Bristol...........................17 C6
Hôtel du Parc.........................18 A5
Hôtel Le Régina......................19 A5

Hôtel St-Jacques.....................20 C4
Le Bilboquet..........................21 D4

EATING
Chez Chantal.........................22 B5
Fromagerie Coulaud...............23 A4
Lapierre.................................24 A5
Le Croco................................25 B5
Le Poivrier.............................26 A4
Restaurant Francóis Gagnaire......(see 18)

DRINKING
Café l'Aviation........................27 B5
La Distillerie...........................28 B5
Le Bistrot...............................29 B5
Yam's Bar...............................(see 27)

ENTERTAINMENT
Le Clandestin.........................30 D4

SHOPPING
Boutique de la Lentille Verte du
 Puy.....................................31 B4
Les Portraits du Velay.............32 B4

TRANSPORT
Bus Information Office.............33 D4
Bus Stop................................34 B5

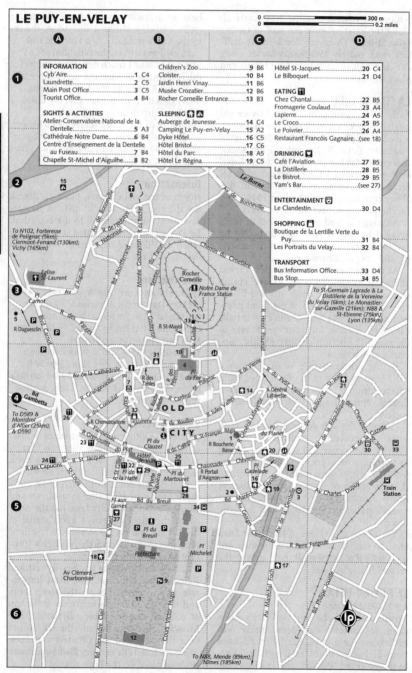

To N102, Forteresse
de Polignac (5km);
Clermont-Ferrand (130km);
Vichy (165km)

Le Borne

Av. de Bonneville

Église
St-Laurent

Rocher
Corneille

Notre Dame
de France Statue

To St-Germain Laprade & La
Distillerie de la Verveine
du Velay (6km); Le Monastier-
sur-Gazeille (21km); N88 &
St-Étienne (75km);
Lyon (135km)

Pl
Carnot

R Duguesclin

R St-Mayol

Av. de la Cathédrale

R des
Tables

Pl
du For

R Cardinal de Polignac

Bd
Gambetta

To D589 &
Monistrol
d'Allier (25km);
& D590

OLD

CITY

R Boucherie
Basse

Pl
du Planet

Train
Station

R des Capucins

Pl de
la Halle

Pl du
Martouret

Pl du
Clauzel

Pl du
Plat

Hôtel
de Ville

R Chaussade

Pl
Cadelade

Av Charles Dupuy

Pl aux
Laines

Bd du Breuil

Pl du
Breuil

Pl
Michelet

Préfecture

Av Clément
Charbonnier

To N88, Mende (89km);
Nîmes (185km)

The 12th-century **cloister** (adult/under 18/18-25 yr/€5/free/3.50; 9am-6.30pm Jul & Aug, 9am-noon & 2-6.30pm mid-May–Jun & Sep, to 5pm Oct–mid-May) with its multicoloured building blocks would look perfectly at home in Moorish Spain.

Massive **Rocher Corneille** (adult/child €3/1.50; 9am-6pm or 7pm mid-Mar–Sep; 10am-5pm Oct–mid-Nov & Feb–mid-Mar) is just north of the cathedral and accessible via rue du Cloître. It was crowned in 1860 by a jarringly red, 16m-high statue of Notre Dame de France, made from melted-down cannons captured in the Crimean War. She looks for all the world like something in raspberry from the top of a wedding cake, but the view from her feet is superb.

Octagonal **Chapelle St-Michel d'Aiguilhe** (adult/child €2.75/1.25; 9.30am-6.30pm May-Sep, 9.30am-noon & 2-5.30pm mid-Mar–Apr & Oct–mid-Nov, 2-5pm Feb–mid-Mar) perches at the summit of an 85m-high volcanic plug. Haul yourself up the 276 steps to enjoy traces of its 12th-century murals, recently revealed, and a magnificent view to reward you for all the huffing and puffing. On the way down, take in the informative DVD with English subtitles. From town, it's an easy walk – as far as the base, that is! – or take bus 6 to the foot of the pinnacle.

You can admire antique and modern lace and take lace-making classes (€15 per hour) at the **Centre d'Enseignement de la Dentelle au Fuseau** (04 71 02 01 68; www .ladentelledupuy.com; 38-40 rue Raphaël; adult/child €3/free; 9am-noon & 1.30-5.30pm Mon-Fri, 9.30am-4.30pm Sat Jul–mid-Sep, 10am-noon & 2-5pm Mon-Fri mid-Sep–Jun), a nonprofit educational centre that seeks to preserve what was once an important local industry (in 1900 the Haute-Loire *département* had 5000 lace workshops).

From state-owned **Atelier-Conservatoire National de la Dentelle** (04 71 09 74 41; 2 rue Dug-

uesclin), the French government orders some of the prestigious gifts it gives to visiting heads of state. It was closed for renovations when we last visited.

Jardin Henri Vinay, in the heart of town, is a pleasant park with a swan lake and tiny **children's zoo**. At its southern end is **Musée Crozatier** (04 71 06 62 40; adult/child €3.20/free; 10am-noon & 2-6pm Wed-Mon Feb-Nov). Exhibits include some impressive Romanesque capitals, local folk costumes and lace, a sad collection of stuffed birds and animals and some ingenious late-19th-century mechanical devices, among them the first patented sewing machine.

La Distillerie de la Verveine du Velay (04 71 03 04 11; 45min tour adult/child/student €5.80/2/4.20; 10am-noon & 1.30-6.30pm Jul & Aug, 10am-noon & 1.30-6.30pm Tue-Sat Mar-Jun & Sep-Dec) is famous for its bright green firewater, first brewed in 1859. The distillery is 6km east of town in St-Germain Laprade; take the N88 then the C150.

Festivals & Events

The **Fêtes Renaissance du Roi de l'Oiseau** are four days of street fun in mid-September. The tradition dates to 1524 when the title of King *(Roi)* was first accorded to the archer who brought down a straw bird, the *oiseau*. Among other concessions, the winner was exempt from all local taxes for the following year. Today's prize, alas, is markedly less generous, but there's still heaps of fun for all.

Interfolk, Le Puy's annual week-long folk festival, in the second half of July, is nearly 40 years old but remains as fresh as ever.

Sleeping

Camping Le Puy-en-Velay (04 71 09 55 09; chemin de Bouthezard; sites €12; Easter-Sep) Le Puy's camp site enjoys an attractive site beside the River Borne. Bus 6 delivers you outside.

Auberge de Jeunesse (04 71 05 52 40; auberge@ maire-le-puy-en-velay.fr; 9 rue Jules Vallès; per person €7; daily Easter-Nov, Mon-Fri Nov-Easter) This HI-affiliated youth hostel, which occupies part of Centre Pierre Cardinal, has a members kitchen. Accommodation is in dorms or rooms for four.

Dyke Hôtel (04 71 09 05 30; dykehotel@wanadoo .fr; 37 blvd Maréchal Fayolle; s €35, d €40-48) This

MASSIF CENTRAL

DISCOUNT ADMISSION

Between February and mid-November you can visit Le Puy's four major sights – the cathedral cloister, Rocher Corneille, Chapelle St-Michel d'Aiguilhe and Musée Crozatier – with an open-dated discount combination ticket (€8), available at the tourist office and at each location.

particularly welcoming place has 15 attractive, modern rooms painted in buttercup yellow, some with balconies. That name may be something of a *faux ami* – or *fausse amie*; *dyke* (pronounced 'deek') here means a volcanic spire. Parking is available for €5.

Le Bilboquet (☎ 04 71 09 74 24; fax 04 71 02 70 51; 52 rue du Faubourg St-Jean; s €42, d €48-53; ☒) Australian readers are assured of a special welcome at this friendly 10-room Logis de France; just ask the *patronne* about her brother in Brisbane. Rooms facing the interior all have a decent-sized balcony. Ideal for families and close friends, the largest rooms (€60 to €67) have aircon, an independent mezzanine with its own bathroom and can accommodate up to four. Parking is €4 a night. Le Bilboquet also runs a great little restaurant.

Hôtel Bristol (☎ 04 71 09 13 38; www.hotelbristol -lepuy.com; 7-9 av Maréchal Foch; s €41, d €48-54; ☺ closed 1-15 Jan & 2 weeks in Mar) This Logis de France, its 40 rooms trim and recently refurbished, is a good two-star option with its garden, attractively retro restaurant and small, cosy bar. Parking costs €3.80.

Hôtel St-Jacques (☎ 04 71 07 20 40; www.hotel -saint-jacques.com; 7 place Cadelade; s/d/tr €43/55/65; ☺ Feb-Dec; ☒) Intimate and well maintained, Hôtel St-Jacques has 12 tidy rooms, one with disabled access. Occupying four floors, most overlook a pedestrian square, where you can take breakfast on the hotel's summer terrace. Parking is €5.

Hôtel du Parc (☎ 04 71 02 40 40; www.hotel-du -parc-le-puy.com; 4 av Clément Charbonnier; r €54-70; ☒) This family-run hotel has 21 comfortable, simply furnished rooms. Choose one, for no extra cost, that overlooks the green space of Jardin Henri Vilay. Parking is available for €6.

Hôtel Le Régina (☎ 04 71 09 14 71; www.hotel restregina.com; 34 blvd Maréchal Fayolle; s €49 d €59-66; ☒ ☒) Nearly all the Régina's 25 comfortable, well-furnished rooms have bathtub and separate toilet. At the corner of the building and all soft angles, its junior suites (€89) can accommodate up to four. There's wi-fi, and parking for €6.50. You'll eat very well at its restaurant (*menus* €21 to €37.50).

Eating

Chez Chantal (☎ 04 71 09 09 16; 8 place de la Halle; menu €11; ☺ lunch only) Popular with down-town workers, this unpretentious restaurant offers unbeatable value for the few euros you drop.

Le Croco (☎ 04 71 02 40 13; 5 rue Chaussade; menus €8-18; ☺ Tue-Sat) While not eschewing red meat, Le Croco (The Crocodile) tuck into your cheek the pair of croc jelly babies/jellybeans that come with your bill) is particularly strong on bushy salads and equally enormous, mainly vegetarian *plats composés* (mixed platters).

Lapierre (☎ 04 71 09 08 44; 6 rue des Capucins; menus €18-28, mains around €15; ☺ Mon-Sat) Estelle Lapierre, the chef, is a rarity on two counts: a woman in the male world of French cuisine, and one who undertook her apprenticeship in the UK, including time at London's Grosvenor Hotel. The restaurant is comfortably traditional with floral wallpaper, lacey lampshades and fresh plants. The food too is traditional, tasty and very reliable. Savour her *soufflé glacé à la verveine*, a featherlight soufflé with a hint of the local liqueur (verveine and a raspberry sauce trickled over it.

Le Poivrier (☎ 04 71 02 41 30; 69 rue Pannessac; menus €20-29; ☺ Wed-Sat, lunch Mon & Tue) Don't be put off by the tacky, pull-you-in exterior. Within, Le Poivrier, which was thoroughly made over in 2006, is all smoky mirrors, blacks, greys and soft terracotta colours. It's particularly strong on meat dishes and all desserts are homemade. You may find the service lackadaisical.

The splendid **restaurant François Gagnaire** (☎ 04 71 02 40 40; www.hotel-du-parc-le-puy.com; 4 av Clément Charbonnier; menus €23 to – oh yes! – €115), bearing one Michelin star, is attached to Hôtel du Parc – it's where the husband weaves his culinary magic.

SELF-CATERING

Just west of the Hôtel de Ville, there's a good Saturday morning food market sprawling over place du Plot, place de la Halle and rue St-Jacques. **Fromagerie Coulaud** (24 rue Grenouillit; ☺ Tue-Sat) is one of France's disastrously declining number of specialist cheese shops. It merits your patronage.

Drinking & Entertainment

Café l'Aviation (place aux Laines) and its neighbour **Yam's Bar** pack in a youthful crowd. **Le Bistrot** (7 place de la Halle) is a great watering hole if you've a taste and thirst for good beer. **La Distillerie**, in a small square just north of place du Breuil, is a large drinking space equipped with a huge, nonfunctioning still. It does snacks and grills and has free wi-fi.

Le Clandestin (☎ 04 71 05 77 53; www.leclandestin .fr in French; 25 rue des Chevaliers St-Jean; ☾ Thu-Sat) is Le Puy-en-Velay's only discotheque.

Shopping
Several shops sell handmade lace. Pieces marked *dentelle du Puy* were made in Le Puy-en-Velay many years ago (there's no longer any commercial lace production here); lace marked *fait main* (handmade) has probably been imported from China.

Les Portraits du Velay (☎ 04 71 06 00 94; www .dentelledupuy.com in French; 10 rue Raphaël), a lace shop, has lace-making demonstrations between Easter and August.

Le Puy's other Big L is the humble lentil. But not just any old pulse. To be sure of the real AOC thing – and to learn more than you ever thought you wanted to know about lentils – visit **Boutique de la Lentille Verte du Puy** (☎ 04 71 02 60 44; 23 rue des Tables; ☾ Jul & Aug).

Getting There & Away
The bus station and **bus information office** (☎ 04 71 09 25 60) are just north of the train station. Three buses run to/from Mende (€16.50, 1¾ hours) on weekdays, and two travel to/from St-Étienne (€9.90, two hours), which has good onward bus and rail connections.

Le Puy-en-Velay's sleepy **train station** (av Charles Dupuy) has limited rail services. Destinations include Lyon (€19.30, 2½ hours, three daily), Clermont-Ferrand (€19.30, 2¼ hours, four daily) and St-Étienne (€12.40, 1½ hours, six daily), where you can connect with the TGV network.

Getting Around
All five lines of the local TUDIP bus network (single ticket/10-trip carnet €1.05/7.20) stop at place Michelet.

For a taxi call ☎ 04 71 05 42 43.

AROUND LE PUY-EN-VELAY
Fortresse de Polignac
Perched atop yet another volcanic plug, about 5km northwest of Le Puy's centre, are the crumbling remains of this 11th-century **fortress** (☎ 04 71 04 06 04; adult/child

€5/3; ☾ May-Sep, Tue-Sun Apr & Oct–mid-Nov). Once home to the powerful Polignac family, who virtually ruled Velay from the 11th to the 14th centuries, its 32m-high **donjon** (keep) remains nearly intact, if much restored over the years.

Gorges de l'Allier
About 30km west of Le Puy, the salmon-filled River Allier – paralleled by the scenic Langeac–Langogne stretch of the Clermont-Ferrand–Nîmes rail line – weaves between rocky, scrub-covered hills and steep cliffs. Above the river's right (east) bank, the narrow D301 gives fine views as it passes through wild countryside and remote, mud-puddle hamlets. Several villages in the area have Romanesque churches. The one in **Prades** – where you can laze on the village's small sand beach – has an expressive 15th-century polychrome wood entombment of Christ and a rich baroque altarpiece.

Tonic Rafting (☎ 04 71 57 23 90; www.raft-canyon .fr in French; ☾ Apr-Sep)), in scenic Monistrol d'Allier, does river descents to Prades by raft and inflatable canoe (€40) between April and September and also organises canyon descents and rock climbing.

Hôtel des Gorges (☎ 04 71 57 24 50; fax 04 71 57 25 36; d/tr €42/48; ☾ Apr-Sep) does a special deal for pilgrims and hikers: €20 for dinner and a bunk bed in a double room – it'll want to see your backpack to confirm that you're more than a motorist on the scrounge, though. The hotel does a plentiful *menu* for all comers at €15.50.

In tidy Langeac, at the northern extremity of the Allier's most interesting stretch, drop into the **Collégiale St-Gal**, a 15th-century Gothic church and, beside it, **Le Jaquemard**, a small museum of local traditions.

Langeac's **tourist office** (☎ 04 71 77 05 41; www.langeac.com in French; ☾ 9am-noon & 2-7pm Mon-Sat, 9am-1pm Sun May-Sep, 9am-noon & 2-5.30pm Tue-Sat Oct-Apr) is on place Aristide Briand.

Le Chambon-sur-Lignon
'L'espace ouvert, l'esprit aussi' (open space, open mind) is the motto of this quiet, neat village, 45km east of Le Puy-en-Velay, which played a courageous role in WWII.

Across the street from the Protestant **temple** is a bronze **plaque** which was erected in

MASSIF CENTRAL

QUIET HEROISM IN LE CHAMBON-SUR-LIGNON

The village of Le Chambon-sur-Lignon is in the Montagne Protestante, a remote highland area with a long-standing Protestant majority. Its tradition of sheltering the persecuted began in the 17th century, when Huguenots fled here. Throughout WWII, Chambon and nearby hamlets 'hid, protected and saved' around 3000 refugees, including hundreds of Jewish children, hunted by French police and the Gestapo. A crucial role in this resistance to the Nazis was played by the local religious leadership, led by Pastor André Trocmé.

Today Chambon continues its venerable tradition of welcoming the disadvantaged by taking in orphans and children from troubled families, both in institutions (such as the Collège-Lycée International Cévenol) and in local homes.

Chambon's honour by Jews who sheltered here as children. Every July and August there's an exhibition on the town's WWII history. Ask at the **tourist office** (☎ 0471597156; www.ot-lechambonsurlignon.fr; rue des Quatre Saisons; ☻ 9am-noon & 2-6.30pm Mon-Sat, 10am-noon Sun Jun-Sep, 9am-noon & 3-6pm Mon-Sat Oct-May) for details.

Mont Mézenc

South of Le Chambon-sur-Lignon, the D500 and D262 take you to the scenic D410, from which the D400 winds its way up to the col of La Croix des Boutières (1508m). Here you can link up with the GR7 and GR73 trails for the half-hour hike to the summit of Mont Mézenc (1753m; pronounced meh-*zang*).

On a clear day, you can see the entire southeastern quarter of France, from Mont Blanc, 200km to the northeast, right around to Mont Ventoux, 140km southeastwards.

Limousin, the Dordogne & Quercy

The neighbouring regions of the Limousin, Dordogne and Quercy are in many ways the rural heartland of France. This is the land of the black truffle and the fattened goose, a province of jewel-green fields, dark oak forests and silvery rivers, where honey-stoned medieval towns sit side by side with hilltop villages and towering chateaux. Rich food, red wine and rustic architecture meet here and wooden-hulled *gabarres* still ply the waterways.

Limousin is the most rural of the three areas, a deeply traditional landscape devoted mostly to agriculture, where plump cows, ducks and geese far outnumber humans. Life in Limousin moves at a languid pace, especially in countryside villages, but it's also home to the thriving university town of Limoges, famous for its fine porcelain and delicate enamelware.

Slightly to the south, the Dordogne is best-known for its astonishingly rich ancient heritage. Its highest concentration of prehistoric sites in Europe includes the stunning cave paintings of Lascaux and the stone-age caves around the Vézère Valley. Throughout the Hundred Years War the Dordogne was the frontline between the French and English, and the area is littered with castles and fortified *bastide* towns, as well as beautifully preserved medieval cities.

Quercy is hotter, drier and distinctly more Mediterranean than its neighbours to the north, home to most of the region's vineyards, especially around the riverside city of Cahors. Cut through by the winding course of the Lot River, Quercy is the perfect place for some back-country walking or a leisurely canoe ride, but there are fascinating historical sites to explore, including the fairy-tale *fortresse royale* of Najac and the holy city of Rocamadour.

HIGHLIGHTS

- Wander the lantern-lit lanes of the medieval town of **Sarlat-la-Canéda** (p626)
- Marvel at some prehistoric graffiti at **Lascaux** (p634) and **Font de Gaume** (p632)
- Get your paddle going on a canoe ride down the **Dordogne** and **Vézère Rivers** (p611)
- Drink in the views from the gravity-defying village of **St-Cirq Lapopie** (p643)
- Admire the beautifully preserved *bastides* of **Domme** (p635) and **Monpazier** (p637)
- Be king for a day at the fabulous chateaux of **Beynac** (p636) and **Castelnaud** (p636)

Lascaux ★
Font de Gaume ★ ★ Sarlat-la-Canéda
Dordogne & ★ ★ ★
Vézère Rivers ★ Domme
Monpazier ★
Château ★ St-Cirq Lapopie
de Beynac &
Château de
Castelnaud

■ POPULATION: 1,134,959   ■ AREA: 25,654 SQ KM

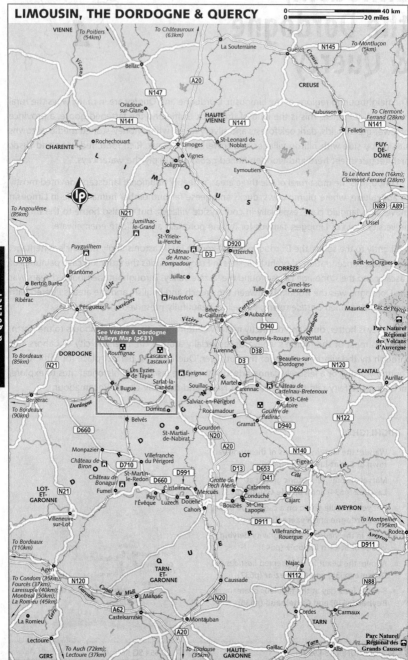

LIMOUSIN, THE DORDOGNE & QUERCY

0 — 40 km
0 — 20 miles

Activities

BOATING
One of the most relaxing ways to see the cliffs and villages along the 64km navigable stretch of the River Lot between St-Cirq Lapopie and Luzech (Cahors is about midway) is to rent a houseboat. There are plans to open up more of the River Lot to navigation, making it possible to travel downstream to Fumel and upstream to Cajarc.

For detailed information, contact the Centrale de Réservation Loisirs Accueil (p641), **Les Bateaux Safaraid** (☎ 05 65 30 22 84; fax 05 65 35 98 89) in Bouziès, **Baboumarine** (☎ 05 65 30 08 99; fax 05 65 23 92 59) in Cahors, **Crown Blue Line** (☎ 05 65 20 08 79; fax 05 65 30 97 96) in Douelle, or **Locaboat Plaisance** (☎ 03 86 91 72 72; fax 03 86 62 42 41) in Luzech.

KAYAKING & CANOEING
Kayaking and canoeing are excellent ways to explore the Rivers Dordogne and Lot, and there are plenty of places where you can hire gear or organise trips. Operators are obliged to provide you with lifejackets (*gilets*) and an introduction to basic safety procedures.

Trips generally follow a course downriver, passing through Carsac, Vitrac, Domme, La Roque Gageac, Vezac, Beynac and Les Milandes. There's also a popular route from St-Léon-sur-Vézère via Le Moustier, Tursac and La Madeleine to Les Eyzies. Trips usually last from two to four hours, and prices vary from around €12 to €25. You'll generally be dropped at your starting point by minibus and then paddle your own way back to base.

Dordogne
Canoë Dordogne (☎ 05 53 29 58 50; contact@canoe -dordogne.fr; La Roque Gageac)
Canoës-Loisirs (☎ 05 53 28 23 43; www.perigord -insolite.net; Vitrac)
Randonnée Dordogne (☎ 05 53 28 22 01; randodordogne@wanadoo.fr; Domme)

Vézère
Canoës Vallée Vézère (☎ 05 53 05 10 11; www.canoes valleevezere.com; Les Eyzies)
Location Canoës-Kayaks (☎ 05 53 06 92 64; www .canoe-loisirsevasion-vezere-dordogne.com; Les Eyzies)

WALKING & CYCLING
In addition to the GR36 and the GR65, both of which pass through Cahors, Quercy has numerous marked trails for day walks. Other Grande Randonnée trails that cross the Lot *département* include the GR6, GR46 and GR652. An excellent range of topo-guides and route guides for walkers and cyclists are available from tourist offices.

Getting There & Around
The major transport hub is Limoges (p616) which has regular flights to many French and UK cities. Bergerac (p638) also has flights to the UK. The A20 motorway heads north from Limoges to Paris and continues south through the region to Toulouse.

As always in rural France, the best way to explore the region is by car (although in the height of summer when the holiday traffic's at its worst, you might think otherwise). The bus network is patchy and operated by a number of companies – generally you'll be better off catching the train. A useful rail link meanders down to Toulouse from Limoges via Brive, Souillac and Cahors, and Limoges and Périgueux are both on the main route to the southwest from Paris. Train services are often supplemented by SNCF buses.

LIMOUSIN

The rich green fields and hills of Limousin have long been overshadowed by the Dordogne and Lot Valleys nearby, and while it's true that tourist sights are few and far between, that doesn't mean that the region is without its charms. With its quiet lanes, flower-filled villages and country markets, it's the perfect place to escape the summertime crowds further south, tailor-made for walkers and cyclists, and a destination *par excellence* for fans of homely, hearty French cuisine.

Limousin is made up of three *départements*: Haute-Vienne, in the west, whose *préfecture* is the city of Limoges; the rural Creuse, in the northeast; and, in the southeast, the Corrèze, home to many of the region's most beautiful sights.

LIMOGES
pop 200,000
The city of Limoges is renowned for its production of enamelware and fine porcelain, and if you're looking to pick up some French crockery, then this is certainly the

place to do it; but these days Limoges is better known as a buzzy university town, home to around 17,000 students and plenty of bars, clubs and drinking holes. Nevertheless, if you're a fine-china fan, there are several museums dedicated to the city's most famous export, and you can even visit a working porcelain factory – just remember to leave the pet bull at home.

Orientation

The train station is 500m northeast of place Jourdan. The Cité Quarter and its cathedral are southeast of place Jourdan and east of the partly pedestrianised commercial centre, the chateau-less Château Quarter.

Information

INTERNET ACCESS

Point Cyber (☎ 05 55 79 03 28; 7 av Charles de Gaulle; 9.30am-midnight Mon-Sat, 2pm-midnight Sun)
TendanceWeb (☎ 05 55 10 93 61; 5 blvd Victor Hugo; 8am-4am Mon-Fri, 9am-6am Sat, 2pm-4am Sun)

LAUNDRY

Laundrette (28 rue Delescluze; to 9pm)
Laundrette (9 rue Monte à Regret; to 9pm)

MONEY

There are several banks on place Jourdan and place Wilson and the post office changes cash.
Banque de France (8 blvd Carnot)

POST

Main Post Office (29 av de la Libération) Offers currency exchange services, a Cyberposte and an ATM.
Post Office (6 blvd de Fleurus) Has a Cyberposte and ATM.

TOURIST INFORMATION

Maison du Tourisme (☎ 05 55 79 04 04; 4 place Denis Dussoubs; 8.30am-noon & 1.30-6.30pm Mon-Sat) Provides information on the Haute-Vienne, including B&B reservations and organised cycling and hiking trips.
Tourist Office (☎ 05 55 34 46 87; www.tourisme-limoges .com; 12 blvd de Fleurus; 9am-7pm Mon-Sat & 10am-6pm Sun Jun-Sep, 9.30am-6pm Mon-Sat Jan-Apr & Nov-Dec) Offers a range of guided walks and themed visits around the town – contact them to see what's on offer.

Sights

PORCELAIN & ENAMEL

One of the main draws to the porcelain capital of France is obviously the chance to check out its famous enamelware. The

Musée National Adrien Dubouché (☎ 05 55 33 08 50; 8bis place Winston Churchill; adult/18-25yr/under 18yr €4/2.60/free; 10am-12.30pm & 2-5.45pm Wed-Mon, no lunch break Jul & Aug) has one of France's two outstanding ceramics collections (the other is in Sèvres, southwest of Paris). An English-language brochure is available at the entrance.

The **Bernardaud porcelain factory** (☎ 05 55 10 55 91; 27 av Albert Thomas), 1km northwest of the Musée National Adrien Dubouché, can be visited daily June to September; **tours** (adult/under 12yr €4/free) are from 9.15am to 11am and 1pm to 4.30pm. The rest of the year tours take place Monday to Friday (and sometimes on Saturday), but you have to phone ahead.

In Limoges *émail* (eh-*my*) has nothing to do with the internet, it means 'enamel', which has been produced here since the 12th century. The Musée Municipal de l'Évêché (p614) has a fine collection of *émaux* (plural of *émail*). Contemporary works can be admired at **Galerie du Canal** (☎ 05 55 33 14 11; 15 rue du Canal; 10am-noon & 2-7pm Tue-Sat, Mon-Sat Jul, Aug & Dec), a cooperative gallery run by six master enamellists.

Many traditional porcelain and enamel galleries can be found south of the tourist office along blvd Louis Blanc.

CHÂTEAU QUARTER

All that remains of the great pilgrimage abbey of St-Martial, founded in AD 848, is an outline on place de la République. The **Crypt of St-Martial** (mid-Jun–mid-Sep), from the 9th century, contains the tomb of Limoges' first bishop, who converted the population to Christianity.

Église St-Pierre du Queyroix (place St-Pierre) half a block southeast of place de la République, has an impressive 13th-century **tower**. Across place St-Pierre is the **Pavillon du Verdurier**, an octagonal, porcelain-faced structure that dates from 1900.

Église St-Michel des Lions (rue Adrien Dubouché), named for the two granite lions on either side of the tower door, has a huge copper ball perched atop its 65m-high spire. Built between the 14th and 16th centuries, it contains St-Martial's **relics** (including his head) and a number of beautiful 15th-century stained-glass windows.

Just off place St-Aurélien, the pedestrianised **rue de la Boucherie** – so named because

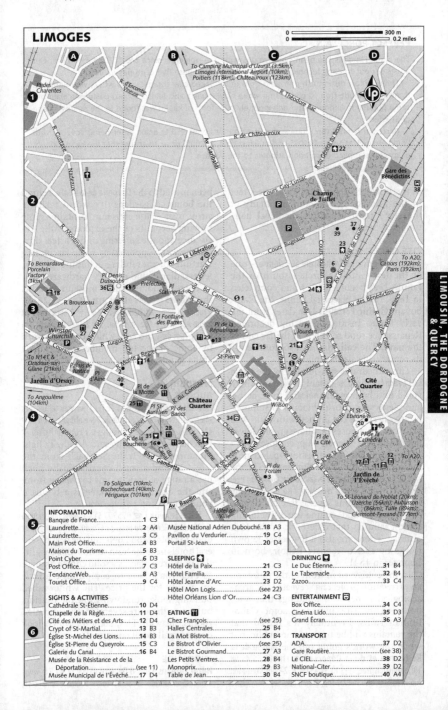

LIMOGES

0 _____ 300 m
0 _____ 0.2 miles

LIMOUSIN, THE DORDOGNE & QUERCY

INFORMATION
Banque de France	1 C3
Laundrette	2 A4
Laundrette	3 C5
Main Post Office	4 B3
Maison du Tourisme	5 B3
Point Cyber	6 D3
Post Office	7 C3
TendanceWeb	8 A3
Tourist Office	9 C4

SIGHTS & ACTIVITIES
Cathédrale St-Étienne	10 D4
Chapelle de la Règle	11 D4
Cité des Métiers et des Arts	12 D4
Crypt of St-Martial	13 B3
Église St-Michel des Lions	14 B3
Église St-Pierre du Queyroix	15 C3
Galerie du Canal	16 B4
Musée de la Résistance et de la Déportation	(see 11)
Musée Municipal de l'Évêché	17 D4

Musée National Adrien Dubouché	18 A3
Pavillon du Verdurier	19 C4
Portail St-Jean	20 D4

SLEEPING
Hôtel de la Paix	21 C3
Hôtel Familia	22 D2
Hôtel Jeanne d'Arc	23 D2
Hôtel Mon Logis	(see 22)
Hôtel Orléans Lion d'Or	24 C3

EATING
Chez François	(see 25)
Halles Centrales	25 B4
La Mot Bistrot	26 B4
Le Bistrot d'Olivier	(see 25)
Le Bistrot Gourmand	27 A3
Les Petits Ventres	28 B4
Monoprix	29 B3
Table de Jean	30 B4

DRINKING
Le Duc Étienne	31 B4
Le Tabernacle	32 B4
Zazoo	33 C4

ENTERTAINMENT
Box Office	34 C4
Cinéma Lido	35 D3
Grand Écran	36 A3

TRANSPORT
ADA	37 D2
Gare Routière	(see 38)
Le CIEL	38 D2
National-Citer	39 D2
SNCF boutique	40 A4

PERFECT PORCELAIN

The name Limoges has been synonymous with fine porcelain since the 1770s, when European artists set out to copy techniques perfected by the Chinese five centuries earlier.

Three factors distinguish porcelain from other baked-clay ceramics: it is white, very hard and translucent. Made from kaolin (a fine white clay), quartz and feldspar, hard-paste porcelain became popular in Limoges after an extremely pure form of kaolin was found in the nearby village of St-Yrieix.

Porcelain is fired three times: the first time at about 950°C; again, after being covered with liquid enamel, at about 1450°C; and one last time, at 900°C or so, to ensure that the hand-painted or machine-applied decoration adheres to the surface.

of the butcher's shops that lined the street in the Middle Ages – contains many of the city's most attractive medieval half-timbered houses.

CITÉ QUARTER

The dark granite **Cathédrale St-Étienne** – one of the few Gothic churches south of the Loire – was begun in 1273 and completed in 1888. Facing place St-Étienne, the Flamboyant Gothic **Portail St-Jean** dates from the early 1500s. Inside, the richly decorated Renaissance rood screen is at the far end of the nave. The cathedral is also notable for its remarkably slender pillars.

The cathedral is surrounded by the **Jardin de l'Évêché**, Limoges' botanical garden, where you'll find both medicinal and toxic herbs, and plenty of colourful blooms in summer. Nearby **rue Haute Cité** is lined with 16th- and 17th-century houses that have granite lower floors and half-timbered upper storeys.

Housed in the former bishop's palace near the cathedral, the **Musée Municipal de l'Évêché** (☎ 05 55 45 98 10; place de la Cathédrale; admission free; ☒ 10-11.45am & 2-6pm Wed-Mon, also Tue Jul-Sep, to 5pm Oct-May) contains several fine collections of porcelain and enamelware, including some examples that date back to the 12th century. There are also a few lesser-known works by Pierre-Auguste Renoir, born in Limoges in 1841.

In the courtyard in front of the museum, an excavation project has revealed the archaeological remains of buildings that once occupied the site, including some Gallo-Roman ruins. Eventually it's hoped that the remains will be open to the public, but while the work's going on, the **Musée de la Résistance et de la Déportation** (☎ 05 55 45 98 10; admission free; ☒ 10-11.45am & 2-6pm Wed-Mon Jun–mid-Sep, also Tue Jul-Sep, 2-5pm mid-Sep–May) has

been moved to the **Chapelle de la Règle**, behind the botanical gardens. It's worth taking a stroll over – the museum contains some moving accounts of the exploits of the Resistance and the suffering of deportees during the war, supported by some fascinating wartime memorabilia, including photos, letters, diaries and military hardware.

There's another small museum nearby, the **Cité des Métiers et des Arts** (☎ 05 55 32 57 84; 5 rue de la Règle; adult/child €5/2.50; ☒ 2-6pm Wed, Sat & Sun Apr-May, 2-6pm daily Jun, Sep & Oct, 10.30am-1pm & 2.30-7pm daily Jul & Aug), which contains work by some of the top members of France's crafts guilds.

Sleeping

BUDGET

Hôtel Mon Logis (☎ 05 55 77 41 43; www.hotel-limoges-monlogis.com in French; 16 rue du Général du Bessol; d €31-42) This is a classic budget French hotel – welcoming, easy-going and decidedly light on unnecessary frills. Set back from the street around a small courtyard, the hotel has a range of basic rooms to choose from, and the easy onsite parking is a bonus if you're travelling *par voiture*.

Hôtel Familia (☎ 05 55 77 51 40; www.hotelfamilia.fr; 18 rue du Général du Bessol; s €36-40, d €40-46) Next door to Hôtel Mon Logis and the best of several hotels near the train station, this cosy little family-run place is a solid choice, though as ever you'll have to compromise a little on quality for the price. The whitewashed building looks rundown from the outside, but inside there are several nicely appointed rooms, all with TVs, some of which look over a small floral courtyard.

MIDRANGE

Hôtel Orléans Lion d'Or (☎ 05 55 77 49 71; www.orleansliondor.com; 9 & 11 cours Jourdan; s €32-49, d €39-51) Part of the Citôtel chain, this old station hotel has been sensibly modernised with an emphasis on functionality rather than character. None of the rooms are particularly exciting, but they're comfy and clean enough – even if some of the floral colour schemes are a little challenging on the eye – and it's dead handy for the station.

Hôtel de la Paix (☎ 05 55 34 36 00; fax 05 55 32 37 06; 25 place Jourdan; s/d from €38/64) Tucked into the corner of place Jourdan, this rambling old hotel makes a great bolthole for exploring the rest of central Limoges. The reception and breakfast area downstairs are cluttered with antique gramophones, phonographs and all kinds of musical memorabilia (forming the owner's Mechanical Music Museum), while upstairs you'll find a selection of plain, serviceable rooms, most looking out across the square.

Hôtel Jeanne d'Arc (☎ 05 55 77 67 77; www.hotel jeannedarc-limoges.fr; 17 av du Général de Gaulle; s €57-73, d €67.50-84.50) For something more upmarket, head for this grand hotel on the main road towards the station, a former coaching inn that's been overhauled with sensitivity and impeccable good taste. The downstairs lobby and dining room are furnished with drapes, pale shades and plenty of polished wood, and the theme continues into the upstairs bedrooms – the best have antique writing desks, freestanding dressers and wooden-framed beds.

Eating

The best places for eating out are around the Halles Centrales and place de la Motte.

Le Bistrot d'Olivier (☎ 05 55 33 73 85; Halles Centrales; menus €10 & €15; ☉ lunch Mon-Sat) After a spot of lunch on the cheap? Then do as the locals do and head straight for this great little French diner inside the main market hall. Squeeze yourself onto one of the wooden benches and tuck into a hearty, three-course set for €10 or €15. There's a limited choice, and if you don't like the look of the set menu, head over to the almost identical Chez François opposite to see what's on offer there.

Le Bistrot Gourmand (☎ 05 55 10 29 29; 5-7 place Winston Churchill; mains €7.90-16.50; ☉ noon-3pm & 7-11.30pm Mon-Sat) This reliable bistro has a good-value menu centring on gourmet salads, *gratins* and casseroles, and a choice of dining areas – take your pick from the traditionally themed *salle à manger* (dining room) or the bright conservatory overlooking place Winston Churchill.

La Mot Bistrot (☎ 05 55 34 47 19; 22 place de la Motte; mains €8-15; ☉ lunch & dinner, closed Sun) One of many cafés and brasseries dotted around place de la Motte, this little brasserie is usually packed at lunchtime with local shop workers, and it's an excellent place to soak up the market atmosphere. The menu is stuffed with brasserie standards – mainly salads, steaks and casseroles.

Table de Jean (☎ 05 55 32 77 91; 5 rue de la Boucherie; mains €13-22; ☉ dinner Mon-Sat) Just along the street from Les Petits Ventres, this is a cosy little restaurant that's all about hearty, down-to-earth country cooking – dishes such as braised beef and *brandade de morue* (cod brandade) are house specialities, and there's always a blackboard of daily specials.

Les Petits Ventres (☎ 05 55 34 22 90; 20 rue de la Boucherie; menus €20.50, €26.50, €28 & €32; ☉ dinner) Looking at the meat-heavy menu of the 'Small Stomachs', you might well wonder whether the restaurant's name refers more to the customers or to what's being served up on their plates. If you're going to try regional delicacies such as *tripes de la rue* (tripe cooked to a regional recipe), *andouillettes* (sausage made of chitterlings) or *tête de veau* (boiled calf's head) then this is the place to do it – but it's definitely one for the carnivores.

SELF-CATERING

The **Halles Centrales** (covered market; place de la Motte; ☉ to 1pm) is the best place for supplies, with plenty of fresh seafood, vegetables and meat – but if you only need the basics, there's a **Monoprix** (42 rue Jean Jaurès; ☉ 8.30am-8.30pm Mon-Sat) supermarket.

Drinking

Like any city with a healthy student population, Limoges is riddled with drinking holes. Most of the nightlife centres on the rundown streets around rue Charles Michels.

Le Duc Étienne (place St-Aurélien; ☉ 2pm-2am Mon-Sat, 6pm-2am Sun) One of the longest standing nightspots in the city, next door to the Église St-Aurilien in the medieval quarter. The atmosphere is classically French – think wooden stools, lively chatter and plenty of Gauloises smoke – and the drinks range from *eaux de vie* right through to Irish pints.

Le Tabernacle (☎ 05 55 34 69 80; 19 rue de la Loi; ⏱ 11pm-5am Wed-Sat) One of the city's hot spots for new bands and live music, this grungy place is half rock venue, half backstreet pub. There are regular gigs, cheap drinks and it's open very late, so it gets jammed on weekends.

Zazoo (☎ 05 55 32 13 93; 6 rue Charles Michels; ⏱ 6pm-1am Mon-Sat) The owner of this quirky bar has a real thing about the colour purple – just check out the royal-purple cushions, mauve walls and lilac furniture. There are even a few plum-coloured cocktails to try if you're in the mood.

Entertainment

Tickets for cultural events are available from **box office** (☎ 05 55 33 28 16; 15 rue Jean Jaurès; ⏱ Tue-Sat).

Limoges has a couple of good cinemas – the multiplex **Grand Écran** (☎ 0 892 682 015; 9-11 place Denis Dussoubs), which mainly screens new releases, and the more arty **Cinéma Lido** (☎ 05 36 68 20 15; 3 av du Général de Gaulle).

Getting There & Away

AIR

Just off the A20, **Limoges International Airport** (☎ 05 55 43 30 30; www.aeroportlimoges .com in French) is 10km west of Limoges. It is served by domestic flights to destinations including Paris, Nice and Lyon, and international Ryanair flights to UK cities including Liverpool, Nottingham and London Stansted. There's no shuttle bus into town; a taxi takes 15 minutes and will cost around €20.

BUS

The *gare routière* is across the tracks from the train station, where you'll find an information kiosk for the main local bus operator **Le CIEL** (Centre Intermodal d'Échanges de Limoges; ☎ 05 55 45 10 10). The local bus network operates on a zone system, where the tariffs are based on how many zones you cross. Destinations include Oradour-sur-Glane (€3), Solignac (€3) and Rochechouart (€5).

Other local destinations can be reached via SNCF bus, including Tulle (€16.60, 1½ hours, two daily) and St-Léonard de Noblat (€4.10, 30 minutes, five daily).

CAR

Hire cars from **ADA** (☎ 05 55 79 61 12; 27 av du Général de Gaulle) or **National-Citer** (☎ 05 55 77 10 10; 3 cours Bugeaud).

TRAIN

The stunning Art Deco **Gare des Bénédictins** (☎ 0 836 353 535) is one of the most striking train stations in France. Completed in 1929, the station is graced by a vast copper dome, and the exterior is covered in lavish frescoes inspired by the region's rural heritage. The elegant copper-topped clocktower has been thoroughly restored since a fire in 1997.

Main destinations include Paris' Gare d'Austerlitz (€41.50, three hours, 10 daily), Périgueux (€13.70, one hour, 11 daily) and Cahors (€25.90, 2¼ hours, four direct daily), as well as local destinations including Aubusson (€12.90, 1¾ hours, three daily, one on Sunday) and Brive-la-Gaillarde (€16.10, 1 hour, at least fifteen daily).

Tickets are also available from the **SNCF boutique** (4 rue Othon Péconnet; ⏱ 9am-7pm Mon-Sat).

AROUND LIMOGES
Solignac

pop 1350

The pretty medieval village of Solignac, 10km south of Limoges on the River Briance, owes its elaborate 11th-century **church** to its position on the pilgrimage route to Santiago de Compostela (in Spain; p639). The church is known for its unusually wide domed roof, which measures almost 14m across. The stalls in the nave, made for the Benedictines in the late 1400s, are decorated with carved human heads, bizarre animals and a monk mooning the world, and the capitals of the columns – intended to further the moral education of the faithful – are decorated with human figures being devoured by dragons. There's a 15th-century fresco of St Christophe on the right-hand wall of the choir.

Solignac's **tourist office** (☎ 05 55 00 42 31; tourisme-solignac@wanadoo.fr; ⏱ 10am-1pm & 2.30-6.30pm Tue-Sat, 10am-1pm & 3-6pm Sun May-Sep, 9am-noon & 2-6pm Tue-Fri, 9am-noon Sat Oct-Apr) is in the car park across the street from the church.

Welcoming **Hôtel Le St-Eloi** (☎ 05 55 00 44 52; lesaint.eloi@wanadoo.fr; 66 av St-Eloi; r from €43), 150m from the church's western front, has 15 recently refurbished Provençal-style rooms

---

SILENCE BEARS WITNESS

Oradour-sur-Glane, 21km northwest of Limoges, was an unexceptional Limousin town until the afternoon of 10 June 1944, when German lorries bearing an SS detachment rumbled into town.

The town's population was ordered to assemble at the market square. The men were divided into groups and forced into *granges* (barns), where they were machine-gunned before the structures were set alight. Several hundred women and children were herded into the church, inside which a bomb was detonated; those who tried to escape through the windows were shot before the building was set on fire, along with the rest of the town. Of the people rounded up that day – among them refugees from Paris and a couple of Jewish families living under assumed names – only one woman and five men survived; 642 people, including 205 children, were killed.

Since these events, the entire **village** (admission free; 9am-5pm, to 7pm mid-May–mid-Sep) has been left untouched, complete with tram tracks, prewar electricity lines, the blackened shells of buildings and the rusting hulks of 1930s automobiles – an evocative and moving memorial to a once-peaceful village caught up in the brutal tide of war.

Entry is via the **Centre de la Mémoire** (adult €6, 7-18yr, students & war veterans €4) which describes the village before the massacre and shows survivors' testimonies and executioners' confessions. After the war, a larger Oradour was built a few hundred metres west of the ruins.

Several buses daily link Le CIEL in Limoges with Oradour-sur-Glane (€3, 30 minutes). By car, take the D9 and follow the road signs to the *village martyr* (martyred village).

---

inside an enchanting lemon-stone building topped with original chimneys and decorated with timber beams. There's an attached **restaurant** (menus €16-42; lunch & dinner, closed Sun evening, Mon, Tue & Sat lunch).

Three or four buses daily (except Sunday) link Le CIEL in Limoges with Solignac (€3, 25 minutes) and the neighbouring hamlet of Le Vigen (€3, 35 minutes). The Solignac-Le Vigen train station is linked to Limoges (€2.50, 10 minutes) and Uzerche (€9.20, 40 minutes) by two or three trains daily.

Uzerche
pop 3500

Set on a promontory high above the River Vézère, the picturesque town of Uzerche is known for its 15th- and 16th-century **Maisons à Tourelles**, which look like miniature castles thanks to their turrets. The best examples can be seen around **Porte Bécharie**, a 14th-century town gate near place Marie Colein. The main street into the old city leads uphill from place Marie Colein to the **Église St-Pierre**, a barrel-vaulted, Romanesque abbey church, with a typically Limousine belfry and an 11th-century crypt.

The **tourist office** (05 55 73 15 71; www.pays-uzerche.com; place de la Libération; 10am-7pm Mon-Fri, 10am-12.30pm & 2.30-6.30pm Sat & Sun Jul & Aug, 10am-noon & 2-6pm daily Jun & Sep, 10am-noon Mon-Fri Oct-May, 10am-noon & 2-5pm Mon-Sat during school holidays) is near the church.

Run by the same family for three generations, **Hôtel Ambroise** (05 55 73 28 60; fax 05 55 98 45 73; 34 av de Paris; d €30-60; closed Nov, reception closed Sun evening & Mon Sep-Jun) is a great little hideaway in Uzerche, with snug, old-fashioned rooms (some with river-views) and a pleasant **restaurant** (menus €13-31) overlooking the hotel gardens.

Rambling old **Hôtel Jean Teyssier** (05 55 73 10 05; http://hotelteyssier.free.fr in French; rue du Pont-Turgot; d €47-63), situated on the edge of the village, is just about the best place to stay. The décor in most of the bedrooms is a bit mix-and-match (stripey bedcovers meet floral curtains) but the rooms are cosy enough, and downstairs there's a lovely country **restaurant** (menus €18-33), complete with curved saloon bar and leather-topped stools.

Uzerche is linked to Limoges, 56km to the north, by train (€9.20, 40 minutes, six to 10 daily). The train station is 2km north of the old city along the N20.

BRIVE-LA-GAILLARDE
pop 51,590

Brive-la-Gaillarde (Brive) is one of the region's main administrative and commercial centres. There's not a great deal to see round town, and although you probably won't want to spend too much time here, Brive is useful as an overnight stop on the way south to the Dordogne.

THE CARPET CAPITAL OF FRANCE

For over 500 years, the town of **Aubusson**, 90km southeast of Limoges, has been famous for its exquisite **carpets** and **tapestries**. From the mid-16th century onwards, the tapestry-work of weavers from Aubusson and the Creuse valley was highly prized by royalty, aristocrats and rich merchants across Europe. Characterised by their vivid colours, fine detail and exquisite craftsmanship, the tapestries were often inspired by literature, nature and contemporary society, as well as religious iconography, landscapes and rural scenes. Sadly, such shamelessly decorative items met with the disapproval of the defiantly pragmatic Revolutionaries, and many tapestries and workshops were destroyed during the French Revolution. The looms slowly went back to work throughout the 19th century, but the industry had to wait until after the Second World War for its real renaissance, when the work of inventive new designers such as Jean Lurçat and Sylvaine Dubuisson reinvented the traditional Aubusson tapestry for the modern world.

Today, there are some 30 tapestry workshops in Aubusson and nearby Felletin (10km to the south). You can see recent work at the **Exposition Tapisseries d'Aubusson-Felletin** (admission €3; ☢ 9am-12.30pm & 2-6pm Jun-Sep, 9am-6pm Jul & Aug), held inside the town hall on the Grande Rue in Aubusson.

For a historical overview, head to the **Musée Départemental de la Tapisserie** (☎ 05 55 83 08 30; adult/child €4/2.50; ☢ 9.30am-noon & 2-6pm Wed-Mon, 9.30am-6pm Jul & Aug), which houses changing exhibits of antique and modern tapestries.

If you'd like to visit a tapestry workshop, contact Aubusson's **tourist office** (☎ 05 55 66 32 12; ☢ 10am-7pm Mon-Sat, 10am-noon & 2.30-5.30pm Sun Jul & Aug, 9.30am-12.30pm & 2-6pm Jun & Sep), which organises visits to many local tapestry *ateliers*.

The **tourist office** (☎ 05 55 24 08 80; www.brive -tourisme.com in French; place du 14 Juillet; ☢ 9am-7pm Mon-Sat, 10am-1pm Sun Jul & Aug, 9am-noon & 2-6pm Mon-Sat Sep-Jun) is beside the bus station. Its usual home in a 19th-century water tower is currently undergoing refurbishment, so the office is temporarily located in a building directly opposite.

As always, there are plenty of basic hotels clustered around the station, but miniscule **Hôtel Andrea** (☎ 05 67 73 29 93; fax 05 67 73 29 99; 39 av Jean-Jaurés; d €43-49) is probably the best budget option, with nine dinky bedrooms (only a couple of which are en suite).

Centrally located **Hôtel du Chapon Fin** (☎ 05 55 74 23 40; www.chaponfin-brive.com; 1 place de Lattre-de-Tassigny; s/d from €48/58; 🖳) is a useful base if you've got to stick around in Brive for a night or two. Housed in a graceful white-shuttered building on one of the city's main market squares, the hotel has a selection of recently modernised rooms, some of which overlook the grassy garden at the rear.

Brive is one of the region's major rail and bus junctions – see the relevant town and city listings for details. The **bus station** (☎ 05 55 17 91 19; place du 14 Juillet; ☢ 8.15am-noon & 2-6.15pm Mon-Sat) is next to the tourist office. Local and intercity buses generally don't run on Sunday or holidays.

The train station is linked to the tourist office and bus station, 1.3km to the southwest, by the hourly bus No 5, which runs until a little before 7pm.

NORTHEAST OF BRIVE
Aubazine
pop 800

The idyllic village of Aubazine sits on a hilltop surrounded by forests, sloping pastures and verdant valleys. The small **tourist office** (☎ 05 55 25 79 93; place de l'Église) is in the village hall on the main square. Opening hours vary according to season.

The 12th-century Romanesque **church** contains an extremely rare oak armoire liturgique (liturgical chest) from the late 1100s, as well as the elaborately carved, 13th-century tomb of Étienne d'Obazine, founder of the Cistercian abbey to which the church once belonged. About 300m north, along route de Tulle, the small, Greek Catholic monastery has a modern, Byzantine-style chapel.

One of the area's footpaths heads up the hill to the **Puy de Paulliac** (or Pauliat; 520m), which has a *cromlech* (dolmen) at the top and affords fine views. For part of the way it follows the abbey's one-time aqueduct, the **Canal des Moines**.

Hôtel Le Saint Étienne (☎ 05 55 25 71 01; hotel .saint-etienne@netcourrier.com; place du Bourg; r from €43; Mar-Nov), a two-star inn, is housed in a 14th-century chateau in the centre of the village. Its 41 rooms are simply designed but comfortable. The adjoining **restaurant** (menus €15-19.50; lunch & dinner, closed Mon & dinner Sun) serves traditional French cuisine in a sunny courtyard.

Gimel-les-Cascades

pop 670

This tiny hamlet, 37km northeast of Brive-la-Gaillarde, is one of the prettiest villages in the Corrèze, and it makes a perfect rural retreat for exploring the surrounding countryside – except in high summer, when its flower-filled streets prove an irresistible draw for legions of day-trippers and coach-parties.

A few hundred metres down the hill from the late-15th-century **Église St-Pardoux** are the village's best-known landmarks: the **Cascades**, three waterfalls that drop 143m into a gorge aptly named the Inferno. They're situated inside a privately owned **park** (☎ 05 55 21 26 49; adult/6-14yr €4/3; 10am-6pm Mar-Oct).

Other sights around Gimel-les-Cascades include the **Pont de Péage**, a medieval toll bridge rebuilt in the 1700s; the ruins of the **Château de Roche Haute**; the remains of the Romanesque **Église St-Étienne de Braguse**; and the **Étang de Ruffaud**, a glassy lake that offers a refreshing dip and a shady picnic spot. Walking options include the trails along the **Gorges de la Vallée de la Montane**; details are available at the **tourist office** (☎ 05 55 21 44 32; www.gimellescascades.fr; 10am-6pm Jul & Aug), 50m up the hill from the church.

The nine simple, newly renovated rooms of quaint **Hostellerie de la Vallée** (☎ 05 55 21 40 60; hostellerie_de_la_vallee@hotmail.com; d €49.50-52.50; Mar-Dec) are small, but the view of the nearby cascades from the bedroom windows more than make up for the lack of space. The attached **restaurant** (menus €19.50-30; lunch & dinner Thu-Tue), overlooking the gorge, offers delicious home-cooked food using local produce.

SOUTHEAST OF BRIVE

This part of Limousin is near Carennac (p648), Rocamadour (p647), Château de Castelnau-Bretenoux (p648) and the Gouffre de Padirac (p648).

Turenne

pop 770

The pretty hilltop village of Turenne, 11km west of Collonges-la-Rouge on the D8, is dominated by the stern **chateau** (☎ 05 55 85 90 66; www.chateau-turenne.com; adult/under 12yr €3.50/ free; 10am-7pm Jul & Aug, 10am-noon & 2-6pm Apr-Jun, Sep & Oct, 2-5pm Sun Nov-Mar), constructed as a stronghold for the local viscount and balanced on a sheer limestone outcrop with superb panoramas over the surrounding countryside. The massive 17th-century **Collégiale** (Collegiate Church) is in the style of the Counter-Reformation. Turenne is on the GR46 footpath.

The **tourist office** (☎ 05 55 85 94 38; 9am-12.30pm & 3-6.30pm Jul & Aug, 10am-12.30pm & 3-6pm Apr-Jun & Sep) is a few metres from place du Foirail on the D8.

Elegant **La Maison des Chanoines** (☎ 05 55 85 93 43; www.maison-des-chanoines.com; d €65-90; Apr-Oct) is surrounded by slate-roofed houses in the centre of the village, and offers six smart, surprisingly contemporary rooms, all slightly different in style and décor, and each named after a different notable from Turenne's historical past. The country views are the real draw, and the well-respected restaurant is worth a visit even if you're not staying overnight – house specialties include foie gras in truffle sauce and home-made walnut bread.

Turenne Gare, 3km southeast of the village, is served by a daily train from Brive (€2.90, 15 minutes). From Monday to Saturday there are buses from Brive (€2.80, 25 minutes, one or two daily).

Collonges-la-Rouge

pop 50

Red by name, red by nature, the village of Collonges-la-Rouge is one of the classic postcard villages of the Corrèze region, with its skyline of conical turrets, grey-slate tiles and rickety rooftops, and the jumble of rust-coloured houses at the village's heart. Surrounded by rolling farmland, this tiny hamlet is a fine place to just sit and soak up the rural atmosphere, and it's well worth at least an overnight stay.

The part Romanesque **church**, constructed from the 11th to the 15th centuries on the foundations of an 8th-century Benedictine priory, was an important resting place on the pilgrimage to Santiago de Compostela

---

A LOAD OF HOT AIR

Fancy seeing from a different viewpoint? Hot-air ballooning has to be one of the most spectacular ways to explore the region, and there are several operators who will happily give you a bird's-eye view. Half-day trips cost around €190/100 per adult/child under 12 – but do be aware that you'll have to get up early, and the weather can play havoc with your carefully laid plans. Needless to say, you'll also need a head for heights...

Mistral Montgolfière (☎ 05 53 59 56 75; www.mistralmontgolfiere.com; Calviac-en-Périgord) and **Montgolfières du Périgord** (☎ 05 53 28 18 58; www.perigordballoons.com; La Roque Gageac) both specialise in balloon-trips around the Périgord region, while **Corrèze Montgolfière** (☎ 06 83 43 36 01; www.montgolfiere.fr; Juillac) is the best for the Limousin area.

(p639). In the late 16th century local Protestants held prayers in the southern nave and their Catholic neighbours prayed in the northern nave. Nearby, the ancient wood and slate roof of the old **covered market**, held up by stone columns, shelters an ancient baker's oven.

The **tourist office** (☎ 05 55 25 47 57; ☷ 10am-7pm Jul & Aug, 10am-12.30pm & 2-6pm Apr-Jun & Sep, 10am-noon & 2-5pm Mon-Sat Oct-Mar) is next to the town hall on the village's 'main' road, off the D38.

In the centre of the village, welcoming family hotel **Relais de St-Jacques de Compostelle** (☎ 05 55 25 41 02; relais_st_jacques@yahoo.fr; d €41-64; ☷ mid-Mar–mid-Nov) is located in a beautifully refurbished 15th-century building a stone's throw from the church. The rustic rooms have been sympathetically updated while still retaining plenty of period touches, and the **restaurant** is all about fresh local produce and classic Corrèze cooking.

For a real home away from home, **Jeanne Maison d'Hôtes** (☎ 05 55 25 42 31; www.jeannemaisondhotes.com; r with breakfast €80) is a wonderful *chambre d'hôte* (B&B) that is tough to beat. Located on the edge of the village, the majestic house is split over several floors, with five character-filled bedrooms, complete with original fireplaces, wooden rafters, antique furnishings and tiny windows. Home-cooked meals are available for €32 extra per day.

Collonges is linked by bus with Brive, 18km to the northwest along the D38 (€3.30, 30 minutes, six on weekdays and one on Saturday).

Beaulieu-sur-Dordogne
pop 1300

Poised in a restful curl of the river on the banks of the upper Dordogne, the medieval town of Beaulieu thoroughly deserves its name (literally 'beautiful place'). With a brace of excellent hotels, an attractive rural location and one of the best-preserved medieval quarters in the region, Beaulieu makes an excellent base for exploring the Corrèze.

INFORMATION
Tourist Office (☎ 05 55 91 09 94; www.beaulieu-sur-dordogne.fr in French; place Marbot; ☷ 9.30am-1pm & 2.30-7pm daily Jul & Aug, 9.30am-12.30pm & 2.30-6pm Mon-Sat, 9.30am-12.30pm Sun Apr-Jun & Sep, 10am-12.30pm &2.30-5pm Oct-Mar)

SIGHTS
Beaulieu is known for the majestic **Abbatiale St-Pierre**, a 12th-century Romanesque abbey church that was once a stop on the Santiago de Compostela pilgrimage (p639). The southern portal's amazing **tympanum** (c 1130), based upon prophecies from the books of Daniel and the Apocalypse, illustrates the Last Judgement in vivid detail, including monsters devouring the condemned and the dead rising from their graves. The **treasury**, with its 12th-century gilded Virgin and 13th-century enamel reliquary, is on view inside.

Surrounding the abbatiale is Beaulieu's picturesque **medieval quarter**, littered with timber-framed houses and medieval mansions, many dating from the 14th and 15th centuries. Nearby is the **Faubourg de la Chapelle**, a neighbourhood of 17th- and 18th-century houses on the banks of the Dordogne, which leads to the Romanesque **Chapelle des Pénitents**. The river can be crossed on foot at the dam. The GR480, a spur of the GR46, passes by here.

SLEEPING & EATING
Camping des Îles (☎ 05 55 91 02 65; per person €8.60-12.50; ☷ Apr-Oct) On the other side of the old

city from the tourist office, this shady campsite is on an island sandwiched between two branches of the Dordogne. Its three-star facilities include tennis, children's play area and fishing.

Auberge de Jeunesse (☎ 05 55 91 13 82; www.fuaj .org/aj/beaulieu; place du Monturu; dm €12; ❤ Mar-Nov) Housed in a partly 14th-century building (complete with miniature windows, timber-beamed gallery and even a small turret), this has to be one of the most intriguing youth hostels in France. Inside the rooms are more modern than you might expect, even if they are on the small side.

Hôtel Le Turenne (☎ 05 55 91 10 16; hotelleturenne@ wanadoo.fr; blvd de Turenne; s €50, d €50-56, tr €61) A cleverly converted hotel on the outskirts of the medieval quarter, located inside a former Benedictine Abbey. The bedrooms are crammed with character – some boast huge overhead beams and creaky furniture, while others contain their own grand stone fireplaces. The **restaurant** is equally good, serving regional cooking in a lovely dining room full of period fixtures and fittings. The monks certainly never had it this good.

Auberge Les Charmilles (☎ 05 55 91 29 29; www .auberge-charmilles.com; 20 blvd Rodolphe de Turenne; d/tr €55/65) This homey hotel, in a beautifully converted *maison bourgeoise* on the banks of the river, is a cross between an upmarket hotel and a supremely stylish B&B. All the rooms are named after different types of strawberry and are decorated in suitably summery shades – the ones at the back have tall windows overlooking the garden and the river beyond. The downstairs restaurant (menus €17 to €43) offers excellent-value menus full of delicious country dishes such as perch on a bed of lentils or a salad of *confits de canard*.

On Wednesday and Saturday mornings, an open-air market is held next to the village church. At least one of the grocery stores on place Marbot – the Suprette and the Casino – is open daily (closed Sunday afternoon except in July and August); midday closure for both lasts from 12.30pm to 2.30pm or 3pm.

GETTING THERE & AWAY
Beaulieu is situated 70km east of Sarlat-la-Canéda and 47km northeast of the Gouffre de Padirac (p648).

From Monday to Saturday, there are buses linking Beaulieu with Brive (€6.50, one hour, one to three daily). Schedules are posted at the bus shelter on place du Champ de Mars and outside the tourist office.

THE DORDOGNE

The Dordogne *département* is for many people the picture-perfect image of the French countryside, a gentle landscape of patchwork fields, hilltop towns, turreted mansions and jade-green woods. Named after the most important of the region's seven rivers, the Dordogne is better-known to the French as Périgord, spiritual home to two of the country's enduring culinary passions – foie gras and the black truffle. The Dordogne is famous for its stunning cave paintings, as well as for its many fortified chateaux and *bastide* towns (p637) – reminders of the bloody battles waged here during the Middle Ages and the Hundred Years' War.

Périgord has been divided into four colour-coded areas: in the centre, the area around the capital, Périgueux, is known as Périgord Blanc (white) after its pale limestone hills. The fields and forests to the north and northwest are known as Périgord Vert (green), while the wine-growing area of Périgord Pourpre (purple) lies to the southwest, around Bergerac. Périgord Noir (black) encompasses the Vézère Valley and the upper Dordogne Valley, as well as the beautiful medieval town of Sarlat-la-Canéda.

With such a rich variety of attractions, it's hardly surprising that the Dordogne is crammed to bursting-point in the summer months, especially with holidaying Brits and French families during the *grandes vacances*. In winter the region goes into hibernation, and many hotels, restaurants and tourist sites close.

PÉRIGUEUX
pop 33,294
Périgueux, prefecture of the Dordogne *département,* is a busy provincial city filled with modern boutiques, restaurants, bars and chain stores, but turn the clock back a couple of millennia and you would have discovered the thriving Roman town of

Vesunna, one of the most important settlements in Roman Gaul. Remnants of the city's Roman past survive in the rather run-down area known as La Cité, and you'll find traces of the city's more recent history around the heavily restored medieval and Renaissance quarter.

Périgueux is at its liveliest during the Wednesday and Saturday **truffle and foie gras markets** (p625), and the city is home to one of the country's best museums of prehistory, but most visitors tend to move on pretty quickly, lured away by the attractions of the Vézère Valley 45km to the southeast.

Orientation

The medieval and Renaissance old city, known as Puy St-Front, is on the hillside between the River Isle (to the east) and blvd Michel Montaigne and place Bugeaud (to the west). On the other side of place Bugeaud is the old city's historic rival, the largely residential Cité, centred around the ruins of a Roman amphitheatre. The train station is about 1km northwest of the old city.

Information

EMERGENCY

Hôtel de Police (police station; ☎ 05 53 06 44 44; place du Président Roosevelt; ⊗ 24hr) Across from 20 rue du 4 Septembre.

LAUNDRY

Laundrette (place Hoche; ⊗ 8am-8pm)
Laundrette (18 rue des Mobiles de Coulmiers; ⊗ to 9pm)
Laundrette (61 rue Gambetta; ⊗ to 9pm, to 8pm Sat)

MONEY

There are several banks on place Bugeaud.
Banque de France (1 place du Président Roosevelt)

POST

Post Office (1 rue du 4 Septembre) Offers money exchange and a Cyberposte.

TOURIST INFORMATION

Espace Tourisme Périgord (☎ 05 53 35 50 24; 25 rue du Président Wilson; ⊗ 8.30am-5.30pm Mon-Fri) Provides information on the Dordogne *département*.
Tourist Information Kiosk (place André Maurois; ⊗ 9am-8pm Jun-Sep)
Tourist Office (☎ 05 53 53 10 63; www.tourisme-peri gueux.fr in French; 26 place Francheville; ⊗ 9am-6pm Mon-Sat, 10am-1pm & 2-6pm mid-Jun–mid-Sep, 9am-1pm & 2-6pm Mon-Sat mid-Sep–mid-Jun)

Sights

PUY ST-FRONT

The **Musée du Périgord** (☎ 05 53 06 40 70; 22 cours Tourny; adult/student/under 18yr €4/2/free, free admission noon-2pm Mon-Fri mid-Sep–mid-Jun; ⊗ 10am-5pm Mon & Wed-Fri, 1-6pm Sat & Sun) is renowned for its collection of prehistoric tools and implements, as well as several fine Roman mosaics and some unique examples of prehistoric scrimshaw.

Crowned by five bump-studded domes, the curious **Cathédrale St-Front** (place de la Clautre; admission free; ⊗ 8am-12.30pm & 2.30-7.30pm) looks more like something you might stumble across in ancient Istanbul than modern-day France. Heavily restored by Abadie (the creator of Paris' Sacré Cœur) during the late 19th century, the result is dramatic but feels rather overdone. The carillon sounds the same hour chime as Big Ben. The best views of the cathedral (and the town) are from **Pont des Barris**.

The ancient cobblestone streets north of the cathedral are lined with centuries-old limestone houses, best seen along **rue du Plantier**, **rue de la Sagesse** and **rue de la Miséricorde**. The area's main thoroughfare, **rue Limogeanne**, has graceful Renaissance buildings at Nos 3 and 12, and the opulent **Maison du Pâtisser** is found at the end of rue Éguillerie at place St-Louis.

Most impressive of all is the **Hôtel d'Abzac de Ladouze** (16 rue Aubergerie), a fortified merchant's house built sometime in the 15th century. The tourist office supplies a useful street map detailing most of the main sights.

The **Musée Militaire** (☎ 05 53 53 47 36; 32 rue des Farges; admission €3.50; ⊗ 1-6pm Mon-Sat Apr-Sep, 2-6pm Mon-Sat Oct-Dec, 2-6pm Wed & Sat Jan-Mar, closed holidays) founded right after WWI, has a varied collection of swords, firearms, uniforms and insignia from the Napoleonic wars and the two world wars.

Of the 28 towers that once formed Puy St-Front's medieval fortifications, only the 15th-century **Tour Mataguerre**, a stout, round bastion next to the main tourist office, is still standing.

LA CITÉ

A few solitary arches are all that remain of Périgueux' 1st-century **Roman amphitheatre** – the rest of the massive structure, designed to hold 30,000 spectators, was disassembled

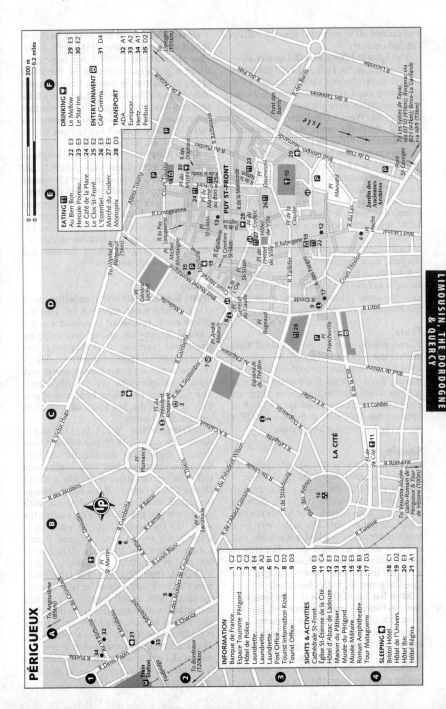

PÉRIGUEUX

0	300 m
0	0.2 miles

EATING 🍴
Au Bien Bon..............	22 E3
Hercule Poireau.........	23 E3
Le Café de la Place.....	24 E2
Le Clos St-Front........	25 E2
L'Essentiel.............	26 E3
Marché du Coderc.......	27 E3
Monoprix...............	28 D3

DRINKING 🍷
Le Mellow.............	29 E3
Le Star Inn............	30 E2

ENTERTAINMENT 🎭
CAP Cinéma...........	31 D4

TRANSPORT
ADA...................	32 A1
Europcar..............	33 A2
Hertz.................	34 A1
Peribus...............	35 D2

INFORMATION
Banque de France.......	1 C2
Espace Tourisme Périgord.	2 C3
Hôtel de Police.........	3 C3
Laundrette.............	4 E4
Laundrette.............	5 A2
Laundrette.............	6 B1
Post Office............	7 C2
Tourist Information Kiosk.	8 D2
Tourist Office.........	9 D3

SIGHTS & ACTIVITIES
Cathédrale St-Front.....	10 E3
Église St-Étienne de la Cité.	11 C4
Hôtel d'Abzac de Ladouze.	12 E3
Maison du Pâtisser......	13 E2
Musée du Périgord......	14 E2
Musée Militaire.........	15 E3
Roman Amphitheatre.....	16 B3
Tour Mataguerre........	17 D3

SLEEPING 🛏
Bristol Hôtel...........	18 C1
Hôtel de l'Univers......	19 D2
Hôtel Ibis.............	20 E3
Hôtel Regina...........	21 A1

LIMOUSIN, THE DORDOGNE & QUERCY

and carried off to construct the city walls in the 3rd century.

The **Église St-Étienne de la Cité** (place de la Cité), constructed in the 11th and 12th centuries, served as Périgueux's cathedral until 1669. Only two cupolas and two bays survived the devastation wrought by the Huguenots during the Wars of Religion (1562–98). Two blocks to the south, the **Vesunna Musée Gallo-Romain de Périgueux** (☎ 05 53 53 00 92; www .semitour.com; rue Claude Bernard; adult/child €5.50/3.50; ☒ 10am-7pm Jul & Aug, 10am-12.30pm & 2-5.30pm Sep-Jun) is a new museum built to showcase the ruins of a grand 1st-century Roman villa uncovered in 1959. The excavations have revealed a treasure-trove of Roman arte-facts, jewellery and some incredible wall murals.

In the grounds stands the **Tour de Vésone**, shaped like a gargantuan anklet, the only remaining section of a Gallo-Roman temple thought to have been dedicated to the god-dess Vesunna, protector of the town (and the Roman name for Périgueux).

Tours

There are French-language **guided tours** (adult/12-18yr & student €5/3.80) of the city on Monday to Saturday throughout the year, leaving from outside the tourist office at 2.30pm. From June to September, there are extra tours at 10.30am and 4pm, as well as 3pm on Sundays. Ask at the tourist office about the less regular **bicycle tours**.

Sleeping

Hôtel Régina (☎ 05 53 08 40 44; comfort.perigueux@ wanadoo.fr; 14 rue Denis Papin; d €42-53) The best of several places in the hotel ghetto around the station, the Régina might be showing its age from the outside, but inside it's had a half-decent facelift. The bedrooms are a touch institutional – a bed, a wardrobe and a TV is about all you'll get – but they're functional enough, and downstairs there's a bright dining room where you can tuck into the generous buffet breakfast.

Hôtel Ibis (☎ 05 53 53 64 58; ho636@accor.hotels .com; 8 blvd Georges Saumande; d from €45-61) Not the most characterful choice, but as always with chain hotels, the real attraction is that you know exactly what you're going to get in advance. The rooms are completely unre-markable, but the hotel's in a convenient position not far from the city centre.

Hôtel de l'Univers (☎ 05 53 53 34 79; fax 05 53 06 70 76; 18 cours Michel Montaigne; s/d €47/58; ☒ Feb-Dec) This pleasant old-school hotel is perched above a popular restaurant in the heart of town. The top bedrooms have pleasant bathrooms and high ceilings, and are a little removed from the hustle of the restaurant downstairs – but the standard of rooms is variable, so if you don't like the one you've been given, ask to see another.

Bristol Hôtel (☎ 05 53 08 75 90; www.bristolfrance .com; 37-39 rue Antoine Gadaud; s €54-62, d €59-71; ☐) If you don't mind splashing out a few more euros, you won't regret opting for this thor-oughly modern hotel in a quiet quarter near the city centre. It looks a bit like a Lego ex-periment gone wrong from the outside, but once you get past the box-based exterior you'll find a range of nicely finished and surprisingly traditional rooms.

Eating

Au Bien Bon (☎ 05 53 09 69 91; 15 rue des Places; mains €11-13; ☒ lunch Mon-Fri, dinner Fri & Sat) This ex-cellent rustic restaurant is nestled along a cobbled alleyway just off the main shopping street, and makes an ideal spot for trying some traditional Périgord country cooking – try the *confit de canard* or *omelette aux cèpes* (omelette with cèpe mushrooms). The tables are packed in tight and it gets busy at lunchtime, but that's all part of its considerable charm.

Le Café de la Place (☎ 05 53 08 21 11; 7 place du Marché au Bois; mains €11-15; ☒ lunch & dinner) Over-looking lively place du Marché au Bois, this is the quintessential French streetside café. The interior décor looks like it hasn't changed in decades – think brass fittings, burnished wood and tobacco tones, with old photos and faded posters decorating the walls. It's the perfect place to while away a few hours over a *petit café*, and there's a simple menu of brasserie standards if you're after something more substantial.

Le Clos St-Front (☎ 05 53 46 78 58; 12 rue St-Front; mains €15-25; ☒ lunch & dinner Tue-Sat) Another upmarket and much-respected gourmet restaurant, with a reputation for imagina-tive menus and an emphasis on seasonal ingredients sourced from local producers. The interior dining room is elegant and un-derstated, but the lovely enclosed courtyard is *the* place to be in summer – so you'd be wise to reserve ahead.

Hercule Poireau (☎ 05 53 08 90 76; 2 rue de la Nation; mains €18-31; ☺ lunch & dinner Mon-Fri) Long considered one of the city's *grandes tables*, the Hercule Poireau is a more refined option, with gingham-topped tables artfully arranged around a vaulted dining room, and a menu that's stuffed to the gunnels with rich, classic French cuisine.

L'Essentiel (☎ 05 53 35 15 15; 8 rue de la Clarté; menus €20-42; ☺ lunch & dinner, closed Sun & Mon) A new and popular restaurant in the shadow of the cathedral, whose *raison d'être* seems to be giving regional classics an original spin. Fresh seafood and seasonal meats form the core of the menu, and you're guaranteed to find foie gras and truffles on the blackboard in season.

SELF-CATERING

Périgueux is renowned for its lively markets, especially the food market on place de la Clautre, which happens on Wednesday and Saturday mornings year-round. At other times, the **Marché du Coderc** (covered market; ☺ to about 1.30pm) is great for fresh local produce, and you'll find lots of *charcuteries* and *fromageries* along the cobbled streets of rue de la Sagesse and rue Limogeannes. There's also a **Monoprix** (☺ 8.30am-8pm Mon-Sat) between place Bugeaud and place Francheville.

On Wednesday and Saturday mornings from mid-November to mid-March, black truffles, wild mushrooms, foie gras, *confits* (duck or goose conserve), cheeses and other local delicacies are sold at the **Marché de Gras** (place St-Louis) in Puy St-Front.

Drinking

The liveliest areas after dark, especially in summer, are place St-Louis, place du Coderc and the surrounding streets.

Le Mellow (☎ 05 53 08 53 97; 4-6 rue de la Sagesse; ☺ 5pm-2am Tue-Sat) This is as close as Périgueux gets to urban chic, a *bar d'ambience* decked out with contemporary art, neutral tones and self-consciously stylish furniture. It's more of a wine bar than a beer den, so make sure you're wearing your glad rags.

Le Star Inn (☎ 05 53 08 56 83; 17 rue des Drapeaux; ☺ 7pm-1am Mon-Sat) For a decidedly less continental atmosphere, head for this Anglo-themed pub run by an expat English couple, popular with local students and homesick Brits alike. There's even darts, a weekly pub quiz and Guinness on tap.

Entertainment

The ten-screen **CAP Cinéma** (☎ 0 892 680 121; place Francheville) screens mainly new release films, some in v.o. (*version originale*).

Getting There & Away

BUS

The main local operator is **Peribus** (☎ 05 53 53 30 37; place Michel Montaigne; ☺ 9.45am-12.30pm & 1.30-5.45pm Mon-Fri). The tourist office and the train station information office can supply you with timetables – single fares around town cost €1.25.

For buses further afield, you'll need to head to the train station or the tourist office for information – there are lots of companies and routes, but no central point of contact.

Except on Sunday and holidays, the bus service's destinations include Bergerac (€6.80, 70 minutes, three daily), Ribérac (€5.15, one hour, four daily, one on Saturday) and Sarlat-la-Canéda (€8.35, 1½ hours, two daily, fewer in July and August) via the Vézère Valley town of Montignac (€5.85, 55 minutes).

CAR

All the main rental agencies are around the station, including **Europcar** (☎ 05 53 08 15 72; 7 rue Denis Papin), **ADA** (☎ 05 53 05 40 28; 4 rue Henri Barbusse) and **Hertz** (☎ 05 53 54 61 80; angle rue Puebla et Barbusse 1).

TRAIN

The **train station** (rue Denis Papin) is served by buses 1, 4 and 5. Destinations with direct services include Bordeaux (€17.30, 1½ hours, nine daily), Brive-la-Gaillarde (€10.80, one hour, three daily), Les Eyzies (€6.60, 30 minutes, two to four daily) and Limoges (€13.70, one hour, seven to nine daily).

Train services to Paris' Gare d'Austerlitz (€54.80, three to five hours, five to nine daily) are via Limoges. To get to Sarlat-la-Canéda (€12.60, two daily) you have to change at Le Buisson.

Getting Around

Allo Taxi (☎ 05 53 09 09 09) is available 24 hours a day.

LIMOUSIN, THE DORDOGNE & QUERCY

BERTRIC BURÉE

This tiny village (population 399), 35km northwest of Périgueux on the D708, draws thousands of gourmands and onlookers for the annual **snail festival** (☎ 05 53 91 94 96), held on the first Monday in May. It's estimated that up to 18,000 snails are devoured during the course of the festival, ranging from the traditional *escargots* in garlic butter sauce to the haute-cuisine version – snail stuffed with foie gras.

SARLAT-LA-CANÉDA
pop 10,000

Nestled at the bottom of a sheltered valley enclosed by hills, Sarlat-la-Canéda is one of the most attractive medieval towns in France. It's certainly one of the best-restored – a maze of cobbled alleyways, unexpected culs-de-sacs and snaking lanes, hemmed in on every side by the town's distinctive honey-bricked buildings and elegant mansions. One of the great pleasures of a visit to Sarlat is simply wandering around the old town, soaking up the atmosphere and admiring the architecture, but there are plenty of intriguing little shops and galleries to explore, as well as some excellent regional restaurants. The only drawback to such a good-looking place is its inevitable popularity – Sarlat is one of the most visited spots in the Dordogne, and the summertime rush in July and August tends to take the shine off things.

Sarlat makes an excellent base for exploring the prehistoric sites of the Vézère Valley and the Périgord Noir, although you'll need your own wheels, as the bus and train links from town leave a lot to be desired.

Orientation

The heart-shaped Cité Médiévale (Medieval Town) is bisected by the rue de la République (La Traverse), which joins up with the main roads north and south from town. The train station is around 2km from the Cité Médiévale, which is centred around place de la Liberté, rue de la Liberté and place du Peyrou.

Information

There are several banks along rue de la République, all with ATMs.

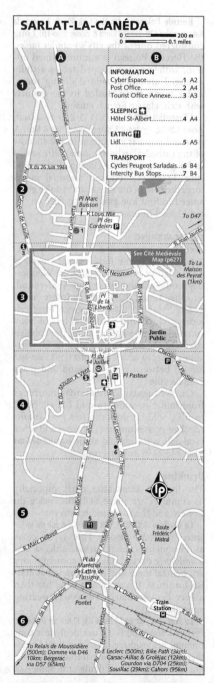

SARLAT-LA-CANÉDA

INFORMATION	
Cyber Éspace...............1 A2	
Post Office....................2 A4	
Tourist Office Annexe......3 A3	
SLEEPING 🛏	
Hôtel St-Albert.............4 A4	
EATING 🍴	
Lidl...............................5 A5	
TRANSPORT	
Cycles Peugeot Sarladais...6 B4	
Intercity Bus Stops..........7 B4	

See Cité Médiévale Map (p627)

Cyber Éspace (☎ 05 53 31 22 37; av Gambetta; ⏰ 4.30-8pm Tue & Thu, 9am-noon & 1.30-8pm Wed, 1-8pm Fri, 9am-1pm & 2-8pm Sat)

Post Office (Map p626; place du 14 Juillet) Currency exchange and a Cyberposte.

Tourist Office (Map p627; ☎ 05 53 31 45 45; www .ot-sarlat-perigord.fr; rue Tourny; ⏰ 9am-7pm Mon-Sat, 10am-noon Sun Apr-Oct, 9am-noon & 2-7pm Mon-Sat Nov-Mar) Staff can supply several booklets and maps detailing walks around the medieval centre. In summer there is a €2 charge for making hotel and B&B bookings.

Tourist Office Annexe (Map p626; ☎ 05 53 59 18 87; av du Général de Gaulle; ⏰ 9am-noon & 2-6pm Mon-Sat Jul & Aug).

Sights & Activities

Once part of Sarlat's Cluniac abbey, **Cathédrale St-Sacerdos** (Map p627) is a real hotchpotch of styles. The wide, airy nave and its chapels date from the 17th century; the cruciform chevet (at the far end from the entrance) is from the 14th century; and the western entrance and much of the belfry above it are 12th-century Romanesque. The organ dates from 1752.

Behind the town's cathedral is **Jardin des Enfeus** (Map p627), Sarlat's first cemetery,

and the 12th-century **Lanterne des Morts** (Lantern of the Dead; Map p627), a short tower that looks like the top of a missile. It may have been built to commemorate St Bernard, who visited Sarlat in 1147 and whose relics were given to the abbey.

Across the square from the cathedral is the lavish façade of the Renaissance **Maison de la Boétie** (Map p627), the birthplace of the writer Étienne de la Boétie (1530–63), who was a close friend of the great French essayist Michel de Montaigne (1533–92).

The alleyways of the quiet, largely residential area west of rue de la République, many of them lined with centuries-old stone houses, are also worth exploring. **Rue Jean-Jacques Rousseau** makes a good starting point.

A **bicycle path** *(piste cyclable)* begins 3km southeast of Sarlat (near the intersection of the D704 and the D704A), and takes you along an old railway grade to Carsac-Aillac (12km from Sarlat) and across the river to Groléjac. It will eventually reach Souillac (about 30km from Sarlat).

LIMOUSIN, THE DORDOGNE & QUERCY

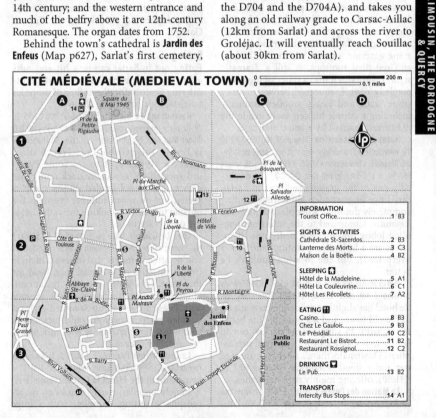

CITÉ MÉDIÉVALE (MEDIEVAL TOWN)

200 m
0.1 miles

INFORMATION	
Tourist Office	1 B3

SIGHTS & ACTIVITIES	
Cathédrale St-Sacerdos	2 B3
Lanterne des Morts	3 C3
Maison de la Boétie	4 B2

SLEEPING	
Hôtel de la Madeleine	5 A1
Hôtel La Couleuvrine	6 C1
Hôtel Les Récollets	7 A2

EATING	
Casino	8 B3
Chez Le Gaulois	9 B3
Le Présidial	10 C2
Restaurant Le Bistrot	11 B2
Restaurant Rossignol	12 C2

DRINKING	
Le Pub	13 B2

TRANSPORT	
Intercity Bus Stops	14 A1

Sleeping

Sarlat is one of the most popular tourist spots in the Dordogne, and on holiday weekends and in July and August every hotel is booked up way in advance. Budget rooms are thin on the ground at any time of year – shoestring travellers might be better off asking at the tourist office for a list of the area's many *chambres d'hôtes*.

Hôtel Les Récollets (Map p627; ☎ 05 53 31 36 00; www.hotel-recollets-sarlat.com; 4 rue Jean-Jacques Rousseau; d from €43-63) Lost in the tangle of narrow alleys of the Medieval Town, this delightful hotel is one of the best deals in Sarlat. The peculiar old building has bags of period appeal (expect quirky layouts and the odd spot of exposed brickwork) and all the bedrooms have a slightly different colour and character – the only headache is the lack of any parking nearby.

Hôtel La Couleuvrine (Map p627; ☎ 05 53 59 27 80; www.la-couleuvrine.com; 1 place de la Bouquerie; d from €45-60) This lovely hotel once formed the corner tower of the old medieval wall surrounding Sarlat, and the grand lemon-stone exterior, topped with tall chimneys and red-tiled rooftops, is still a dramatic sight. Inside you'll find a range of higgledy-piggledy rooms, squeezed between sturdy stone walls and heavy wooden beams – including a couple hidden away inside the old turret, reached by a spiral staircase.

Hôtel de la Madeleine (Map p627; ☎ 05 53 59 10 41; www.hoteldelamadeleine-sarlat.com; 1 place de la Petite Rigaudie; s low season €57-66, d €64-78, s high season €67-86, d €76-99; 🗘 Feb-Dec; 🗶 🐾) Undoubtedly one of the grandest edifices in Sarlat, this imposing wooden-shuttered building completely dominates the place de la Petite Rigaudie. Compared to the smart antique-filled lobby, the modern bedrooms themselves are a little disappointing (and rather overpriced), but the location couldn't be better.

Hôtel St-Albert (Map p626; ☎ 05 53 31 55 55; www .sarlathotel.com; place Pasteur; r €45-58) This cosy little hotel lies slightly outside the busy streets of the old town, and it's probably the better for it, with 25 snug rooms decked out in sunny tones and a calm, convivial atmosphere. Downstairs there's a baroque-themed bar and a good restaurant (*menus* €17 to €31.50), offering mainly regional dishes.

La Maison des Peyrat (☎ 05 53 59 00 32; www.mai sondespeyrat.com; le Lac de la Plane; r €47-95) This beautifully renovated 17th-century house, formerly a nun's hospital and later an aristocratic hunting lodge, is set on a hill about 1.5km from the town centre. The eleven generously sized rooms are impeccably tasteful but still manage to maintain a sense of country-tinged charisma; the best have views over the lovingly tended gardens and the countryside beyond.

Le Relais de Moussidière (☎ 05 53 28 28 74; www .hotel-moussidiere.com; Moussidière Basse; r €112-162; 🗪 🖳) If you're looking to stay in Sarlat with style, then this fabulous country hotel is the place for you. A couple of miles from town on the road towards Domme, this former charterhouse has been renovated in lavish fashion, with boldly decorated bedrooms, private landscaped grounds and several relaxing lounges filled with bric-a-brac, burnished-wood furniture and stone fireplaces. To get to the hotel, head south from the old town onto the av de la Dordogne, and turn left at the Citroën Garage.

Eating

Eating out in Sarlat can be a hit-and-miss affair; the town is packed with restaurants catering mainly for the influx of summer tourists, so it pays to be choosy.

Restaurant Le Bistrot (Map p627; ☎ 05 53 28 28 40; place du Peyrou; menus €17.50 & €22; 🗘 lunch & dinner Mon-Sat) Next door to the Maison de la Boétie, this reliable little French diner makes a perfect spot to try some Périgord specialities, especially duck and goose dishes. The pastel-shaded dining room is pretty, but on warm summer evenings the outside terrace overlooking the cathedral is the only place to be.

Chez Le Gaulois (Map p627; ☎ 05 53 59 50 64; 3 rue Tourny; mains €9-13; 🗘 lunch & dinner Tue-Sat) If you're after a menu that doesn't include twelve varieties of foie gras, then head for this excellent Alpine-inspired restaurant. Huge selections of smoked meats, sausage and cheese are served up Savoyard-style on wooden platters, or you could tuck into a traditional *tartiflette* made with mountains of *réblochon* cheese.

La Couleuvrine (Map p627; 1 place de la Bouquerie; menus €18-32; 🗘 lunch & dinner mid-Feb–mid-Jan) The restaurant at the Hôtel la Couleuvrine (left) is hugely popular, partly thanks to its atmospheric setting, complete with a huge

THE BLACK DIAMONDS OF THE DORDOGNE

Championed by chefs, guzzled by gourmands and pursued by people and pigs alike, the *diamant noir* – more commonly known as the **black truffle** – is one of the great culinary experiences of French cuisine, and the Périgord and Lot Regions are at the heart of the country's truffle trade. The Lot area alone produces over ten tonnes of truffles every year, and it's become seriously big business – this curious little fungus is quite literally worth its weight in gold, and prices can reach truly astronomical heights during a vintage year.

The black truffle is notoriously fussy about where it grows, preferring specific types of soil, nutrients and shade, and it's proved enormously difficult to farm on any serious scale, which explains its inflated price tag. The art of truffle-hunting is a closely guarded secret; it's a matter of luck, judgement and hard-earned experience, and serious truffle hunters often employ specially trained dogs (and sometimes even pigs) to help them in the search. The height of truffle season is between December and March, when you'll often find special truffle markets are held across the region. Preserved truffles are available year-round.

As for the best way to eat them – well, those in the know say that the best way to savour the taste of truffles is in a plain omelette, perched on a slice of foie gras, or simply on a piece of fresh crusty bread. Whether the truffle deserves its culinary reputation is something only your tastebuds can tell you...

medieval fireplace, glowing chandeliers and a smattering of French antiques, but mainly for its regionally themed menus and wholesome cooking.

Restaurant Rossignol (Map p627; ☎ 05 53 31 02 30; 15 rue Fénelon; menus €20-60; ☻ lunch & dinner Fri-Wed) At first sight this small restaurant might look a little bit starchy, with its crisp white tablecloths and plain wooden chairs, but in fact the atmosphere is closer to a homely *ferme auberge* (farm stay) than a gourmet restaurant. Local fish, meat and foie gras dominate the menu, and you'll be in for a treat if you're here during truffle season.

ourpick Le Présidial (☎ 05 53 28 92 47; 6 rue Landry; menus from €29; ☻ lunch Tue-Sat, dinner Mon-Sat) There are some top-notch restaurants around Sarlat's medieval quarter, but if you're looking for the finest that the region's got to offer, then make a beeline for Le Présidial. Hidden away behind sturdy gates, this grand restaurant is arranged around a glorious flower-filled courtyard and a delightful terrace, where you're positively encouraged to dine during the warmer months. The food, unsurprisingly, is stunning, providing a whistle-stop tour of the signature dishes of the Périgord – *magret de canard* (duck breast), *carre d'agneau* (lamb), *pommes sarlaidaises* (potatoes fried in goose fat) and of course the ubiquitous foie gras. There's also a comprehensive selection of homemade desserts and local cheeses. Our

own tip? Try the profiteroles – they're belt-bustingly good.

SELF-CATERING

The **Saturday market** (place de la Liberté & rue de la République) bustles into action from around 8.30am, with food and fresh produce in the morning, and other goods such as clothes and souvenirs in the afternoon. Depending on the season, Périgord delicacies on offer include truffles, foie gras, mushrooms and goose-based products. A smaller **fruit and vegetable market** (☻ 8.30am-1pm) is held on Wednesday morning on place de la Liberté. Plenty of shops around town sell foie gras and other pricey regional specialities, but you'll usually get better prices from the market stalls.

There are a couple of supermarkets on the edge of town, including **E.Leclerc** (☎ 05 53 31 35 35; route de Souillac; ☻ Mon-Sat 9am-8pm) and **Lidl** (Map p626; av Aristide Briand; ☻ 9am-12.30pm & 2.30-7.30pm Mon-Fri, 9am-7pm Sat). The **Casino** (Map p627; 32 rue de la République; ☻ 8am-12.15pm & 2.30-7.15pm Tue-Sat, 8.30am-12.15pm Sun) supermarket in town keeps longer hours in July and August.

Drinking

Le Pub (☎ 05 53 59 57 98; 1 passage de Gérard du Barry; ☻ from 7pm) Housed in a typically impressive medieval building, this is one of Sarlat's most popular drinking spots, especially in summer, when the enclosed courtyard springs into life with alfresco drinkers.

Getting There & Away

Bus services from Sarlat are practically nonexistent – about the only destination is Périgueux (€7.10, 1½ hours, two to four daily) via Montignac. There's no bus station – departures are from the train station, place Pasteur or place de la Petite Rigaudie, depending on where you're going.

Sarlat's **train station** (Map p626; ☎ 05 53 59 00 21) is 1.3km south of the old city at the southern end of av de la Gare.

Destinations include Périgueux (via Le Buisson; €12.60, 1¾ hours, two daily), Les Eyzies (change at Le Buisson; €7.90, 50 minutes to 2½ hours depending on connections, two daily) and Bordeaux (€21.20, 2½ hours, five to seven direct daily), on the same line as Bergerac.

The SNCF bus to Souillac (€5.10, 40 minutes, two daily) passes through Carsac-Aillac (on the scenic D703) and links up with trains on the Paris (Gare d'Austerlitz)–Limoges–Toulouse line.

Getting Around

The Sarlat area has nine bike-rental outlets including **Cycles Peugeot Sarladais** (Map p626; ☎ 05 53 28 51 87; 36 av Thiers).

Free parking is available around the perimeter of the Medieval Town along blvd Nessmann, blvd Voltaire and blvd Henri Arlet. Cars are banned from the Medieval Town from June to September, and rue de la République is pedestrianised in July and August.

PREHISTORIC SITES & THE VÉZÈRE VALLEY

The Vézère Valley is famed for its spectacular Stone-Age cave paintings, especially the celebrated Lascaux Caves near Montignac. The landscape around the Vézère Valley certainly feels ancient, flanked by sharply eroded limestone cliffs stained black with time, topped by ancient woods and copses, and bisected by the meandering course of the Vézère River.

Most of the prehistoric sites are situated between Le Bugue (near the confluence of the Vézère and Dordogne) and Montignac, 25km to the northeast. The most convenient bases you will find for exploring the area are Les Eyzies (right), Montignac (p634) and Sarlat-la-Canéda (p626), all well-stocked with hotels and

camp sites. Bear in mind that most of the valley's sites are closed in winter; the best time to visit is in spring or autumn, when the sites are open but the crowds are not overwhelming.

Getting Around

Public transport in the area is limited, especially if you're travelling by bus. Generally you'll find you'll have to take a train between the major towns, and then find some way of getting to the caves themselves – cycling is sometimes an option, and hire bikes are often available from camp sites, tourist offices or rental outlets. But as always in rural France, having your own car is the most convenient option.

However you choose to travel around, you'll find the Vézère Valley is well signposted; arrows at every crossroads direct you to all the main sights.

Les Eyzies de Tayac
pop 850

There's not much to the modest town of Les Eyzies, strung out along one street a stone's throw away from the banks of the Vézère. The town has devoted itself to catering for the thousands of visitors who pass through the valley every year in search of their prehistoric ancestors, and the main street is jampacked with souvenir shops, postcard-sellers and touristy restaurants. Still, it's a convenient base, with several good hotels and camp sites, and the town's fantastic museum of prehistory is worth a visit on its own.

INFORMATION

Librairie de la Préhistoire (☯ 8.30am-12.30pm & 3-7pm Mar-Nov, 8.30am-7pm Jun-Aug, 8.30am-noon Dec-Feb) Sells IGN maps and topoguides.

Tourist Office (☎ 05 53 06 97 05; www.leseyzies.com; ☯ 9am-7pm Mon-Sat, 10am-noon & 2-6pm Sun Jul & Aug, 9am-noon & 2-6pm Mon-Sat, 10am-noon & 2-5pm Sun Sep-Jun, closed Sun Oct-Apr) On Les Eyzies' main street, the D47.

SIGHTS

The main reason to stop in Les Eyzies is the **Musée National de Préhistoire** (National Museum of Prehistory; ☎ 05 53 06 45 45; adult/18-25yr/under 18yr €5/3.50/free, adult Sun €3; ☯ 9.30am-6.30pm Jul & Aug; 9.30am-6pm Wed-Mon Jun & Sep, 9.30am-noon & 2-5.30pm Wed-Mon Oct-May), tucked in beneath the cliffs near the tourist office, and now housed in a startling new sandstone building opened in 2004. It contains the most comprehensive collection of prehistoric finds in France, over 18,000 in total, including Stone-Age tools and implements, a collection of seashell buttons found in a Stone-Age burial chamber, and a famous bas-relief carving of a bison turning its head to lick its flank.

About 250m north of Musée National de Préhistoire is the **Abri Pataud** (☎ 05 53 06 92 46; www.semitour.com; adult/6-12yr €5.50/3.50; ⌚ 10am-7pm Jul-Sep, 10am-12.30pm & 2-6pm Mon-Sat Sep-Jun), a Cro-Magnon shelter *(abri)* inhabited over a period of 15,000 years starting some 37,000 years ago; bones and other artefacts discovered during the excavations are on display.

The ibex carved into the ceiling dates from about 19,000 BC. The admission price includes a one-hour guided tour in French (and some English if you're lucky).

SLEEPING & EATING

Camping is a good way to cut costs in the Vézère, though in the height of summer you might find half of France seems to have had the same idea. Contact the tourist office for full listings.

Camping Le Vézère Périgord (☎ 05 53 06 96 31; www.levezereperigord.com; route de Montignac, Tursac; per person €8-13; ⌘) Excellent camp site in the middle of a forest 6km north of Les Eyzies (on the D706), with plenty of facilities (including a pizzeria, bakery and

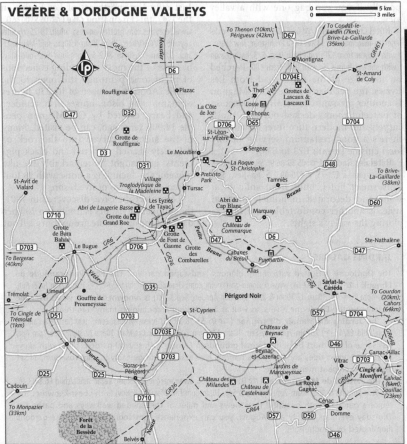

VÉZÈRE & DORDOGNE VALLEYS

tennis courts) as well as mountain-bike and kayak hire.

Camping La Rivière (☎ 05 53 06 97 14; www.lari viereleseyzies.com; per person €8.20-12.50; ⚌ ▣) More a small village than a camp site, in a tree-shaded spot around a former post-house. There's a restaurant, bar and onsite grocery, and it's only a five-minute walk from town (west across the river).

Hostellerie du Passeur (☎ 05 53 06 97 13; www .hostellerie-du-passeur.com; place de la Mairie; d €65-100; ☾ Feb-Oct) Right in the centre of Les Eyzies, in a lovely position overlooking the Vézère, this delightful ivy-clad hotel is by far the most comfortable place to stay in town. There are three categories of accommodation – it's worth paying the premium for the Grand Confort or Élégance rooms, especially if you can bag one with a valley view.

Hôtel Cro-Magnon (☎ 05 53 06 97 06; www.hostel lerie-cro-magnon.com; 54 ave de la Préhistoire; low season r with shower from €70, with bath from €73, high season r with shower from €75, with bath from €80) Perched on the edge of the main road from Les Eyzies, the peculiarly named Cro-Magnon is another pleasant choice, with a selection of peaceful rooms decked out with plush carpets and modern furniture. Downstairs there's a good restaurant serving mainly local cuisine (*menus* €23 to €33).

Hôtel des Roches (☎ 05 53 06 96 59; www.roches -les-eyzies.com; s €71-75, d €76-89; ☾ Apr-Nov; ⚌) This smart hotel, built from solid local stone and decorated in homely pastoral style, is another comfortable base for exploring the valley's sights.

GETTING THERE & AWAY

There are no buses to Les Eyzies. The **train station** (☎ 05 53 06 97 22; ☾ 7am-6pm Mon-Fri, noon-6pm weekends) is 700m north of the tourist office, just off the main D47 road.

Destinations include Bordeaux (change at Le Buisson or Périgueux; €21.10, three hours, three to five daily), Sarlat-la-Canéda (change at Le Buisson; €7.90, 50 minutes to 2½ hours depending on connections, two daily) and Périgueux (€6.60, 30 minutes, two to four daily).

GETTING AROUND

Bicycles can be rented at the tourist office for €8 per half-day or €12 per day.

Grotte de Font de Gaume

Just over 1km northeast of Les Eyzies on the D47, this fascinating **cave** (☎ 05 53 06 86 00; www.leseyzies.com/grottes-ornees; adult/18-25yr/under 18yr €6.10/4.10/free; ☾ 9.30am-5.30pm mid-May–mid-Sep, 9.30am-12.30pm & 2-5.30pm mid-Sep–mid-May) has one of the most astounding collections of prehistoric paintings still open to the public. About two dozen of its 230 figures of mammoths, bison, horses, fish, reindeer and bears, created by Cro-Magnon people 14,000 years ago, can be visited. Many of the animals, carved into the rock or delicately shaded with red and black pigments, are caught in remarkably life-like movement – including a horse with its foot raised and a fresco of five bison.

To protect the cave, discovered in 1901, the number of visitors is limited to 200 per day, and the 45-minute group tours sell out

---

JARDINS GALORE

The Dordogne is dotted with many glorious landscaped gardens. The **Parc Panoramique de Limeuil** (☎ 05 53 57 52 64; www.perigord-patrimoine.com; Limeuil; adult/child €5/4; ☾ 10am-7pm Jul & Aug, 2.30-6pm Mon-Sat, 10am-12.30pm & 2.30-6pm Sun Apr-Jun, Sep & Oct) is renowned for its views over the Vézère and the Dordogne Rivers, as well as an arboretum containing many rare trees.

The **Jardins du Manoir d'Eyrignac** (☎ 05 53 28 99 71; www.eyrignac.com; near Sarlat-la-Canéda; adult/child €8/4; ☾ 9.30am-7pm May-Sep, 10am-12.30pm & 2pm-dusk Oct-Mar, 10am-12.30pm & 2-7pm Apr) has some of the most beautiful formal grounds in France, with several gardens filled with alley-ways of trimmed trees and hedges, a tranquil lake and an unforgettably fragant rosarium, all set around an elegant manor house.

The **Jardins de Marqueyssac** (☎ 05 53 31 36 36; www.marqueyssac.com; Vézac; adult/child €6.80/3.40; ☾ 9am-8pm Jul & Aug, 10am-7pm Apr-Jun & Sep, 10am-6pm Feb, Mar, Oct & Nov) is the best-known of the region's gardens, with beautiful river views and miles of tree-shaded walkways and paths. On Thursday evenings in July and August, you can experience a memorable visit to the gardens illuminated by candle-light.

lightning-fast – you'll need to book at least a few days in advance during high season, and a week or two ahead from July to September. Reservations can be made via telephone or online.

Grotte des Combarelles

The long, narrow Combarelles Cave, 3km northeast of Les Eyzies and 1.6km east of the Grotte de Font de Gaume, averages barely 80cm in width (so claustrophobes should probably steer clear). Discovered in 1901, the cave is renowned for its 600 engravings of reindeer, bison, horses and human figures, often superimposed on top of each other, dating from around 12,000 to 14,000 years ago.

To reserve a place in a six-person group (tours last 45 to 60 minutes), call the Grotte de Font de Gaume – opening hours, admission costs and contact numbers are the same for both sites.

Abri du Cap Blanc

Discovered in 1909, this privately owned **shelter** (☎ 05 53 59 21 74; adult/7-15yr €5.90/3.50; ☽ 9.30am-7pm Jul & Aug, 10am-noon & 2-6pm Apr-Jun & Sep-Nov) is unusual in that it only contains carved sculptures, rather than the combinations of engravings and cave paintings you'll see elsewhere. Figures of horses, reindeer and bison, created some 14,000 years ago, are cut into the interior rock of this natural shelter, formed by an overhanging outcrop and peacefully situated on a wooded hillside. The *abri* is 8km east of Les Eyzies along the D48.

Grotte du Grand Roc

The **Grand Roc Cave** (☎ 05 53 06 92 70; www.grandroc.com; adult/under 12yr €7/3.50; ☽ 9.30am-7pm Jul & Aug, 10am-6pm Feb-Jun & Sep-Dec), known for its masses of iridescent stalactites and stalagmites, is a few kilometres northwest of Les Eyzies along the D47. Nearby is the prehistoric site of **Abris de Laugerie Basse** (adult/child €6/3; ☽ same as Grand Roc). Joint tickets to both sites cost €9/4.50 for adults/children.

Grotte de Rouffignac

About 15km north of Les Eyzies, the huge **cavern** (☎ 05 53 05 41 71; www.grottederouffignac.fr; adult/child €6.10/3.80; ☽ tours in French 9am-11.30am & 2-6pm Jul & Aug, from 10am Sep-Nov & Apr-Jun) at Rouffignac is one of the largest in the area,

with over 10km of galleries, including 250 engravings and paintings of bison, mammoths, ibex and even a few rhinoceros.

Village Troglodytique de la Madeleine

This cave-dwelling **village** (☎ 05 53 06 92 49; adult/family/5-12yr €5/16/3; ☽ 9.30am-7pm Jul & Aug, 10am-6pm Sep-Jun, to 5pm Dec & Jan), 8km north of Les Eyzies along the D706, lies in a lush forest overlooking a hairpin curve in the River Vézère. The site has two levels: 10,000 to 14,000 years ago, prehistoric people lived on the bank of the river, and 500 to 700 years ago, medieval French people built a fortified village – now in ruins – halfway up the cliff face. Their chapel, dedicated to Ste Madeleine, gave its name to the Magdelenian era. Many of the artefacts discovered here are at the prehistory museum (p630) in Les Eyzies.

Guided tours (in French; 50 minutes) begin every half-hour or so; a free English-language brochure is available.

La Roque St-Christophe

This 900m-long series of terraces and **caves** (☎ 05 53 50 70 45; www.roque-st-christophe.com; adult/student/12-16yr/5-11yr €6/5/4/3; ☽ 10am-7pm Jul & Aug, 10am-6.30pm Apr-Jun & Sep, 10am-6pm Mar & Oct, 11am-5pm Jan-Feb & Nov-Dec) sits on a sheer cliff face 80m above the Vézère. Thanks to its commanding position high above the valley, the cave complex makes a unique and practically unassailable stronghold, and it's been employed as a natural fortress for almost 50 millennia – initially by Mousterian (Neanderthal) people some 50,000 years ago, and then by successive generations of human settlers up until the 16th century. The sweeping views are stunning, though the caverns themselves are largely empty and some of the plastic reconstructions are a little lame.

La Roque St-Christophe is on the D706, 9km northeast of Les Eyzies.

Le Thot

The museum and animal park at **Le Thot – Espace Cro-Magnon** (☎ 05 53 50 70 44; www.semitour.com; adult/6-12yr €5/3, joint ticket with Lascaux €10/7; ☽ 9am-7pm Jul & Aug, 10am-noon & 2-5.30pm Tue-Sun Sep-Jun, closed Jan) is intended as an introduction to the world of prehistoric people. There are fibreglass models of many of the animals that feature in prehistoric art (and

---

TOP FIVE PREHISTORIC SITES

Grotte de Font de Gaume (p632) Near Les-Eyzies-de-Tazac.

Grottes de Lascaux (right) Near Montignac.

Grotte de Pech Merle (p642) Near Figeac.

Musée National de Préhistoire (p630) In Les-Eyzies-de-Tazac.

Abri du Cap Blanc (p633) Near Les-Eyzies-de-Tazac.

---

a few live beasties that are roughly equivalent), as well as informative exhibits on the creation of Lascaux II. You'll even get the chance to try your own hand at a spot of cave painting.

Montignac
pop 3101

Spread out over the banks of the River Vézère, the previously peaceful town of Montignac, 25km northeast of Les Eyzies, achieved sudden fame after the discovery of the nearby Grotte de Lascaux. The attractive old city and commercial centre is on the river's right bank, but of more use for touristic logistics is the left-bank area around place Tourny. The Lascaux Caves themselves are a couple of miles along a well-signposted back road.

INFORMATION

There are three banks right around the tourist office.

Post Office (place Tourny) Offers currency exchange.

Tourist Office (☎ 05 53 51 82 60; www.bienvenue-montignac.com in French; place Bertrand de Born; ☿ 9am-7pm Jul–mid-Sep, 9am-noon & 2-6pm Mon-Sat Apr-Jun & mid-Sep–Oct, 10am-noon & 2-5pm Mon-Sat Nov-Mar) Around 200m west of place Tourny, next to the 14th-century Église St-Georges le Prieuré.

SLEEPING & EATING

Hôtel de la Grotte (☎ 05 53 51 80 48; hoteldelagrotte@wanadoo.fr; place Tourny; d €49-57) You won't find better value in Montignac than this sweet little hotel, which – with its red-and-white striped awnings and chichi furnishings – seems to have dropped out of a timehole to the 1930s. The rooms themselves are a little pokey (especially the attic ones, jammed in around the roofbeams), but they're reasonably priced and quite comfortable. The pretty **restaurant**, bedecked with chandeliers and rose-pink

tablecloths, is worth a look for its regional menus (€19.50 to €32.50).

Le Relais du Soleil d'Or (☎ 05 53 51 80 22; www.le-soleil-dor.com in French; 16 rue du 4 Septembre; d €81-110; ☿ closed mid-Jan–mid-Feb; ⊠) For something substantially more upmarket, this old posthouse-turned-hotel should fit the bill. The antique-filled lounge and waxed-wood furniture are a little misleading, as the bedrooms themselves tend more towards modern comfort and minibars rather than period elegance – still, they're well kitted-out, and handy for the fine-dining **restaurant** downstairs (menus €24 to €53).

La Roseraie (☎ 05 53 50 53 92; www.laroseraie-hotel.com; 11 pl des Armes; s €81-96, d €92-152, f €172-182; ⊠) This splendid hotel, housed in one of the town's grandest mansions overlooking the peaceful place des Armes, is the top choice in town. The traditionally furnished rooms, full of plumped-up cushions, floral wallpaper and polished furniture, might not be to everyone's taste – but it's hard not to fall in love with the beautiful rose garden and the tranquil breakfast terrace, especially on a clear-blue summer's day.

Bar des Arcades (☎ 05 53 51 95 73; 37 rue du 4 Septembre; mains from €8; ☿ 8am-8pm in winter, to 2am in summer) A cosy, traditional café, popular with locals, serving good snacks and regional specialities such as cassoulet de canard (duck casserole; €8.50).

Le Tourny (☎ 05 53 51 59 95; place Tourny; mains €7-15) A lively brasserie-cum-bar in the centre of town, good for coffee and a light lunch, and for late-night music and DJs at the weekend. It's usually open till around 2am, and sometimes till later on summer nights.

Casino (place Tourny; ☿ Tue-Sat & Sun morning, closed 12.30-3pm) A supermarket next to the post office.

ENTERTAINMENT

Nondubbed films are screened at **Cinéma Vox** (☎ 05 53 51 87 24), across the car park from the tourist office.

GETTING THERE & AWAY

For information on buses to and from Montignac, see p625 and p630. There's a bus stop (hours posted) at place Tourny.

Grottes de Lascaux & Lascaux II

Of the many spectacular prehistoric sites in the Vézère Region, none can match the scale and complexity of the **Lascaux Cave**, high on a tree-shaded hilltop 2km southeast of Montignac. Discovered in 1940 by four teenage boys who were supposedly out searching for their dog, the cave's main chamber and adjoining galleries are adorned with some of the most extraordinary prehistoric paintings ever found. The walls are covered with an astonishing menagerie of animals and figures, etched onto the rock using natural pigments of red, black, yellow and brown; there are wild oxen, deer, horses, reindeer and mammoths, as well as many human figures and an amazing depiction of a 5.5m bull, the largest cave drawing ever found. Carbon dating has shown the drawings are between 15,000 and 17,000 years old, but the exact reason for their existence is still shrouded in mystery.

The cave was opened to visitors in 1948, and public interest was unsurprisingly massive; but within a few years it quickly became apparent that human breath and body heat was causing irreparable damage to the fragile paintings, and they were closed just fifteen years later in 1963.

In response to continuing public demand, a precise replica of the most famous section of the original cave was meticulously re-created a few hundred metres away – a massive undertaking that required the skills of some twenty artists and took over eleven years. **Lascaux II** (☎ 05 53 51 95 03; www.semitour .com; adult/6-12yr €8/5, joint ticket with Le Thot €10/7; ☽ 9am-8pm Jul & Aug, 9.30am-6.30pm Sep & Apr-Jun, 10am-12.30pm & 2-6pm Oct–mid-Nov, mid-Nov–Mar 10am-12.30pm & 2-5.30pm) was opened in 1983, and although the idea sounds rather contrived, the reproductions are surprisingly evocative and well worth a visit.

Lascaux II can handle up to 2000 visitors daily (in guided groups of 40). The last tours (which last 40 minutes) begin about an hour before the morning and afternoon closing times. From April to October, tickets are sold only in Montignac (next to the tourist office). Reservations are not necessary except when you plan to visit in a group.

DORDOGNE PÉRIGOURDINE

The term Dordogne Périgourdine is used to describe the part of Périgord that stretches along the River Dordogne.

Domme
pop 1030

Set on a steep promontory high above the Dordogne, the walled village of Domme is one of the few *bastides* to have retained most of its 13th-century ramparts, including three fortified gates. Approached via a tortuous switchback road that winds its way up the hillside from the valley below, it's easy to see what made the town such an attractive site for Philippe III of France, who founded the town in 1281 as a stronghold against the English. The town's imposing clifftop position is best appreciated from the **esplanade du Belvédère** and the adjacent **promenade de la Barre**, which both offer panoramic views across the valley.

Across from the **tourist office** (☎ 05 53 31 71 00; place de la Halle; ☽ 10am-7pm Jul & Aug, 10am-noon & 2-6pm Feb-Jun & Sep–mid-Nov, 2-5pm Mon-Fri mid-Nov–Dec, closed Jan) is the 19th-century reconstruction of a 16th-century *halle* (covered market). This houses the entrance to the **grottes** (adult/student/child €6.50/5.50/3.50; ☽ 10am-7pm Jul & Aug, 10am-noon & 2-6pm Sep-Jun, closed Jan), a series of stalactite-filled galleries below the village; a lift whisks you back up at the end of the 30-minute tour. Tickets are available from the tourist office.

On the far side of the square from the tourist office, the **Musée d'Arts et Traditions Populaires** (adult/student/child €3/2.50/2; ☽ Apr-Sep) has nine rooms of artefacts, including clothing, toys and tools, mainly from the 19th century.

From March to September or mid-October (unless the river is too high), canoe and kayak trips can be arranged through **Randonnée Dordogne** (☎ 05 53 28 22 01; randodordogne@wanadoo.fr), a highly professional, English-speaking outfit based in Cénac. Two-hour trips cost €12 to €14, and five-hour trips €19 to €22.

SLEEPING
Les Quatre Vents (☎ 05 53 31 57 57; fax 05 53 31 57 59; d €40-48; ☒) A kilometre or so from Domme itself, this lovely stone-fronted complex is a good place to escape the summer rush. The hotel offers twenty pleasantly furnished, spacious rooms, as well as a small holiday apartment, all overlooking private grounds, landscaped terraces and a swimming pool.

Le Nouvel Hôtel (☎ 05 53 28 38 67; www.domme -nouvel-hotel.com; 1 Grand Rue; d €42-62) This small but perfectly formed hotel is in a lovely position on the corner of the town's main square. The décor throughout is farmhouse-chic, with plenty of rough stonework and wood-beamed character, and the homely restaurant is all about down-to-earth regional dishes and hearty portions.

our pick L'Esplanade (☎ 05 53 28 31 41; rue du Pont-Carral; www.esplanade-perigord.com; d low season €72-128, high season €84-148) This bewitching hotel has one of the most spectacular positions in the whole Dordogne, perched right on the edge of the village ramparts beside the esplanade du Belvédère. The bedrooms are stylish, understated and beautifully furnished – the best have grand wooden four-poster beds, armchairs and writing desks, and of course the obligatory balcony above the valley offering truly jaw-dropping views. Downstairs there's a fantastic gourmet restaurant (*menus* €80 to €135), serving superindulgent dishes ranging from roast pigeon to lobster with truffle vinaigrette, best savoured on the tree-shaded terrace at the front of the house. This is very much an old-world French establishment, closer to a country house than a hotel; it's certainly on the expensive side, but then again, who ever said good things in life come cheap?

Château de Castelnaud

The 12th- to 16th-century **Château de Castelnaud** (☎ 05 53 31 30 00; www.castelnaud.com; adult/10-17yr €7.20/3.60; ◷ 9am-8pm Jul & Aug, 10am-7pm Apr-Jun & Sep, 10am-6pm Feb, Mar, Oct & Nov, 2-5pm Dec & Jan), 11km west of Domme along the D50 and D57, has everything you'd expect from a clifftop castle: walls up to 2m thick (as you can see from the loopholes, some designed for crossbows, others for small cannons), a superb panorama of the Dordogne, and fine views of the fortified chateaux (including arch rival Château de Beynac) on the nearby hilltops. The interior rooms contain a **museum of medieval warfare**, whose displays range from daggers and spiked halberds to huge catapults. An English-language guidebook can be borrowed from the ticket counter.

La Roque Gageac

This hamlet of tan stone houses is built halfway up the cliff above a *cingle* (hairpin curve) in the River Dordogne. When the tiny **tourist office** (☎ 05 53 29 17 01; ◷ 9am-12.30pm & 2-6pm Easter-Oct) in the car park is closed, brochures can be picked up at the post office.

The **Fort Troglodyte** (☎ 05 53 31 61 94; adult/child €4/2; ◷ 10am-7pm Mon-Fri Apr–mid-Nov, Mon-Sat Jul & Aug) consists of a number of medieval military positions built into the cliff. There's some tropical foliage in the small, free **Jardin Exotique** (Exotic Garden), next to the tiny **church**.

The main reason for a visit to La Roque is a spot of outdoor activity – several canoeing companies have bases in town, including **Canoë Dordogne** (☎ 05 53 29 58 50; contact@canoe -dordogne.fr) next to the car park. Down below, the quay also serves as a launch point for short **river cruises** aboard a traditional *gabarre* (see boxed text, p643).

Château de Beynac

This dramatic **fortress** (☎ 05 53 29 50 40; adult/5-11yr €7/3; ◷ 10am-6pm Mar-Sep, 10am-dusk Oct-Feb) occupies a sheer clifftop, dominating a strategic bend in the Dordogne. A steep trail links it to the centre of the village of **Beynac-et-Cazenac**, 150m below on the river bank (and the D703).

Loyal to the king of France, the fort, built from the 12th to 14th centuries (and later modified), was long a rival of Castelnaud, just across the river, which owed its allegiance to the king of England. The interior is architecturally interesting – you get a good idea of the layout of a medieval fortress – but is only partly furnished. From mid-March to mid-November, one-hour guided tours (in French) take place every half-hour.

In a stunning position with the chateau high above and the river just below, is the stylish **Hôtel-Restaurant du Château** (☎ 05 53 29 19 20; www.hotelduchateau-dordogne.com; s €40-60, d €40-65; ◷ Feb-Dec) with a range of swishly refurbished rooms decorated with style and just a touch of minimalist chic. Four rooms have castle views. The **restaurant** (menus €17.50-22) specialises in traditional Périgord cuisine.

Château des Milandes

The claim to fame of the late-15th-century **Château des Milandes** (☎ 05 53 59 31 21; www.mil andes.com; adult/4-15yr €7.80/5.50; ◷ 9.30am-7.30pm Jul & Aug, 10am-6.30pm May, Jun, Sep & Oct) is its postwar role as the home of the African-American dancer and music-hall star Josephine Baker (1906–75), who helped bring

---

PAYS DES BASTIDES

The countryside of the southern Dordogne and the Lot Valley is littered with fortified towns known as **bastides**. Though many were conceived as strategic strongholds from the outset, the purpose of the earliest *bastides* was generally economic rather than military – rich local landlords saw them as a way of opening up new farmland and trading routes, swelling their own pockets in the process. But as Anglo-French hostilities intensified during the late 13th century, *bastides* were increasingly constructed as defensive strongpoints along the hotly contested frontier between the English- and French-controlled areas. Over the next 150 years, more than 300 *bastide* towns and villages were established, largely thanks to the efforts of the opposing kings of France and England, Alphonse de Poitiers and Edward I. Though all the *bastide* towns are slightly different in size and layout, they generally share some common characteristics – a regular street pattern, numbered building lots, fortified walls and an arcaded market square, often with a church tucked into one corner.

The best-preserved *bastides* include Monpazier (below), Domme (p635), Najac (p646) and Villefranche de Rouergue (p645), but there are many others to explore, including Monflanquin, Villeneuve-Sur-Lot and Gourdon.

---

black-American culture to Paris in the 1920s with her *Revue Nègre* and created a sensation by appearing on stage wearing nothing but a skirt of bananas.

Baker was awarded the Croix de Guerre and the Legion of Honour for her work with the French Resistance during WWII, and was later active in the US civil rights movement. She established her Rainbow Tribe here in 1949, adopting 12 children from around the world as 'an experiment in brotherhood'.

The last bilingual guided tour (lasting about 60 minutes) begins about an hour before closing time. The fierce-looking birds of prey in the courtyard are the stars of **falconry displays** several times a day (afternoons only in April, September and October).

MONPAZIER
pop 560

Founded by a representative of the king of England in 1284, Monpazier is perhaps the best preserved of all the *bastide* towns in southwestern France. Poised on a hilltop some 45km from both Sarlat-la-Canéda and Bergerac, it's a fascinating and reassuringly ramshackle kind of place, mercifully spared from overzealous restoration, and in stark contrast to towns such as Najac and Rocamadour, there's not a tourist shop in sight.

Passing through one of the town's three gateways, you'll find that Monpazier's grid of streets all lead to the arcaded market square, **place des Cornières** (place Centrale), surrounded by a motley collection of stone houses that reflect centuries of building and rebuilding. In one corner is an old *lavoir*, once used for washing clothes. Thursday is market day, as it has been since the Middle Ages.

The **tourist office** (☎ 05 53 22 68 59; www.pays-des -bastides.com in French; place des Cornières; ⏰ 10am-7pm Jul & Aug, 10am-12.30pm & 2-6.30pm Mon-Sat & 3-6pm Sun Apr-Jun & Sep, to 6pm rest of year), in the southeastern corner of the square, has an informative historical brochure in English.

Square, auberge-style **Hôtel de Londres** (☎ 05 53 22 60 64; fax 05 53 22 61 98; Foirail Nord; d €40-50) stands on its own just outside the town's main gates, and offers 10 plain shuttered rooms above a down-to-earth **restaurant** (menus from €15).

The **Casino** (place des Cornières; ⏰ 8am-12.30pm & 2.30-7pm Tue-Sat & Sun morning, also Mon in Jul & Aug) supermarket is on the northern side of the square.

BERGERAC
pop 27,000

Bergerac, the capital of the Périgord Pourpre wine-growing area, is surrounded by 125 sq km of vineyards, which ensures it's a hive of activity during harvest time, and a relatively sleepy backwater most of the rest of the year. A Protestant stronghold in the 16th century, it sustained heavy damage during the Wars of Religion, but the old city and harbour have retained some of their old-time ambience and are worth a stroll.

LIMOUSIN, THE DORDOGNE & QUERCY

Bergerac is a convenient stopover on the way from Périgueux (47km to the northeast) to Bordeaux (93km to the west).

The dramatist and satirist Savinien Cyrano de Bergerac (1619–55) may have put the town on the map, but his connection with his namesake is extremely tenuous: it is believed that during his entire life he stayed here a few nights at most.

The **tourist office** (☎ 05 53 57 03 11; www.ber gerac-tourisme.com; 97 rue Neuve d'Argenson; ❤ 9.30am-7.30pm Mon-Sat, 10.30am-1pm & 2-7pm Sun Jul & Aug, 9.30am-1pm & 2-7pm Mon-Sat Sep-Jun) supplies useful brochures in English, including information on cycling and wine-tasting in the region.

Sights

Bergerac has long been at the centre of two great French vices – wine and tobacco – and the town's museums are both dedicated to its ongoing love-affair with the pernicious weed and the fruits of the vine.

The **Musée du Tabac** (☎ 05 53 63 04 13; 10 rue de l'Ancien Port; adult/child €3/1.50; ❤ 10am-noon & 2-6pm Tue-Fri year-round, 2-6pm Sat & Sun Mar-Nov & Mon Jul & Aug), housed in the elegant, early-17th-century Maison Peyrarède, explores the history of tobacco through various exhibits, including some impressively ornate pipes.

The **Musée du Vin et de la Batellerie** (☎ 05 53 57 80 92; place de la Mirpe; adult/child €1/0.60; ❤ 10am-noon & 2-5.30pm Tue-Fri, 10am-noon Sat) showcases local wine-making and the historic role of the river as a vital trade route.

Maison des Vins (☎ 05 53 63 57 55; admission free; ❤ 10am-12.30pm & 2-6pm Mon-Sat May-Sep, Tue-Sat Oct-Apr), inside a 16th-century cloister along the river, offers free wine-tasting and sells local vintages.

Sleeping & Eating

Le Moderne (☎ 05 53 57 19 62; 19 av du 108e RI; d from €38) One of a few small hotels near the station, this two-star option has 11 rooms above a fairly quiet **brasserie-bar**. Nothing to write home about, but the rooms are clean, simple and quite comfy.

Hôtel de Bordeaux (☎ 05 53 57 12 83; www.hotel -bordeaux-bergerac.com; 38 place Gambetta; d €50-76; ☒) This pleasantly refurbished hotel is one of the best bases in Bergerac, with a selection of practical if rather characterless rooms – the hotel's guestbook includes such illustrious names as Georges Simenon, Antony Eden and François Mitterand.

Le Poivre et Sel (☎ 05 53 27 02 30; 11 rue de l'Ancien-Pont; menus €15-38; ❤ lunch & dinner, closed Sun evening, Mon & Tue in winter) This reliable restaurant opposite the Musée du Tabac specialises in hearty fish, seafood and meat dishes, served in a small dining room or a lovely outside terrace.

L'Enfance de Lard (☎ 05 53 57 52 88; place Pélissière; menus from €26; ❤ dinner Wed-Mon) One of the town's most respected restaurants, serving huge portions of traditionally themed southwest cuisine, from grilled fish to slabs of perfectly cooked steak accompanied by *pommes sarladaises*.

Getting There & Away

Bergerac is on the tertiary train line that links Bordeaux and St-Émilion with Sarlat. The airport, 4km southeast of town, is served by flights from Paris (Air France) and the UK (Ryanair).

QUERCY

Southeast of the Dordogne *département* lies the warm, unmistakably southern region of Quercy, many of whose residents still speak Occitan (Provençal). The dry limestone plateau in the northeast is covered with oak trees and riddled with canyons carved by the serpentine River Lot. The main city of Cahors is surrounded by some of the region's finest vineyards.

CAHORS

pop 21,432

There is something unmistakably Mediterranean about the laidback town of Cahors, the former capital of the Quercy region – a reminder that the sunbaked regions of Toulouse and Languedoc lie just to the south. Practically encircled by a hairpin loop in the River Lot and ringed by hills, the city has been inhabited since Roman times, but its most celebrated landmark is the three-towered medieval Pont Valentré, which spans the river on the west side of the city. There's also an intriguing medieval quarter to explore. The vineyards around Cahors produce much of the region's best wine – long known in this part of France for its special relationship with *le diamant noir* (black truffle).

Orientation

The main commercial thoroughfare, north–south blvd Léon Gambetta, is named in honour of Cahors-born Léon Gambetta (1838–82), one of the founders of the Third Republic and briefly premier of France (1881–82). It divides Vieux Cahors (Old Cahors) to the east from the new quarters to the west. At its northern end is place Général de Gaulle, essentially a giant car park; about 500m to the south is place François Mitterrand, home of the tourist office. An even-numbered street address is often blocks away from a similar odd-numbered one.

Information

INTERNET ACCESS

INIT (☎ 05 65 22 00 81; 100 rue Jean Vidal; ✆ 8.30am-noon & 1.30-6pm Mon-Fri)**Les Docks** (430 allées des Soupirs; per hr €3; ✆ 2-6pm & 8-10pm Tue & Thu, 2-6pm Wed, Fri & Sat)

LAUNDRY

Laundrette (place de la Libération; ✆ 7am-9pm)
Laundrette (208 rue Georges Clémenceau; ✆ 7am-9pm)

MEDICAL SERVICES

Centre Hospitalier Jean Rougier (☎ 05 65 20 50 50) The ramp to the 24-hour Urgences (casualty ward) is across from 428 rue Président Wilson.

MONEY

There are several high-street banks along blvd Léon Gambetta, open either Tuesday to Saturday or Monday to Friday.

POST

Post Office (257 rue Président Wilson)

TOURIST INFORMATION

Tourist Office (☎ 05 65 53 20 65; cahors@wanadoo .fr; place François Mitterrand; ✆ 9am-6.30pm Mon-Sat, 10am-1pm Sun Jul & Aug, 9am-12.30pm & 1.30-6pm Mon-Sat Sep-Jun) Typically efficient, with several excellent brochures and walking tours available in English.
Comité Départemental du Tourisme (☎ 05 65 35 07 09; www.tourisme-lot.com; 1st fl, 107 quai Eugène Cavaignac; ✆ 8am-12.30pm & 1.30-6pm Mon-Thu, to 5.30pm Fri) Provides information on the Lot *département*.

Sights & Activities

Cahors is ringed on three sides by the **quays**, once the bustling centre of the city's river-going traffic, but these days more often frequented by cyclists, rollerbladers and people out for an afternoon stroll. First port of call is the **Pont Valentré**, one of France's finest medieval bridges, consisting of six arches and three tall towers, two of which have projecting parapets designed to allow defenders to drop missiles on attackers below. The main body of the bridge was built in the 14th century and the towers were added later. The bridge was always intended to serve as part of the town's defences, not to carry traffic, and it's still open only to pedestrians.

Two millennia ago, the **Fontaine des Chartreux** was used in the worship of Divona, the namesake of Gallo-Roman Cahors. Many coins, minted between 27 BC and AD 54 and thrown into the water as offerings, were discovered by archaeologists a few years back. The flooded cavern under the pool has been explored by divers to a depth of 137m.

The old medieval quarter is east of blvd Léon Gambetta, which cuts through the

LIMOUSIN, THE DORDOGNE & QUERCY

SANTIAGO DE COMPOSTELA

In the early 9th century a hermit, Pelayo, inspired by a holy vision, stumbled across the 800-year-old tomb of the apostle James, brother of John the Evangelist, near the small town of Santiago de Compostela in northern Spain. A shrine was quickly established above the tomb, and by the 12th century, this once-sleepy town had become as important a site of pilgrimage as Jerusalem and Rome.

There are four traditional pilgrimage routes through France, the most popular of which passes through Figeac (p644) and Cahors (opposite) – the nearest thing to a medieval motorway. You can pick up the trail in many places, but if you've got time to spare (and legs of iron), it's possible to follow a single route all the way from Paris – a blister-inducing trek of over 2000km. Early pilgrims were inspired to undertake the arduous journey in the hope of securing a few less years in purgatory, but for modern-day pilgrims the reward is more tangible – walkers or horse-riders who complete the final 100km to Santiago (cyclists the final 200km) qualify for a unique Compostela Certificate, issued on arrival at the cathedral.

www.lonelyplanet.com

CAHORS

LIMOUSIN, THE DORDOGNE & QUERCY

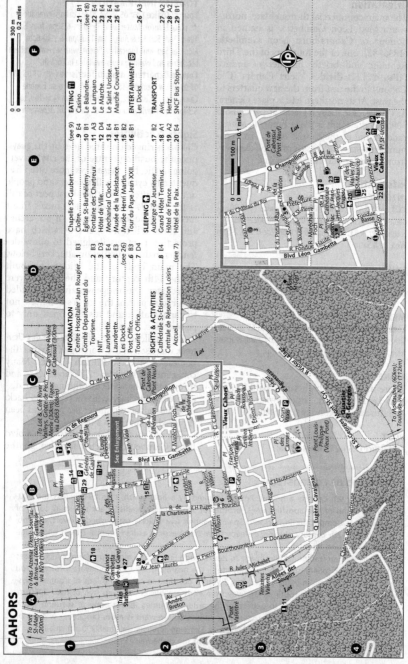

INFORMATION	
Centre Hospitalier Jean Rougier..1 B3	
Comité Départemental du	
Tourisme.................................2 B3	
INIT..3 D3	
Laundrette.................................4 E4	
Laundrette.................................5 E3	
Les Docks...............................(see 26)	
Post Office................................6 B3	
Tourist Office............................7 D4	

SIGHTS & ACTIVITIES	
Cathédrale St-Étienne..................8 E4	
Centrale de Réservation Loisirs	
Accueil..................................(see 7)	
Chapelle St-Gaubert..................(see 9)	
Cloître......................................9 E4	
Église St-Barthélémy................10 B1	
Fontaine des Chartreux.............11 A3	
Hôtel de Ville..........................12 D4	
Mechanical Clock....................13 E4	
Musée de la Résistance.............14 B1	
Musée Henri Martin..................15 B2	
Tour du Pape Jean XXII..............16 B1	

SLEEPING	
Auberge de Jeunesse................17 B2	
Grand Hôtel Terminus...............18 A1	
Hôtel de France.......................19 A2	
Hôtel de la Paix......................20 E4	

EATING	
Casino....................................21 B1	
Le Balandre.........................(see 18)	
Le Lamparo............................22 E4	
Le Marché..............................23 E4	
Le Saint Urcisse......................24 E4	
Marché Couvert.......................25 E4	

ENTERTAINMENT	
Les Docks...............................26 A3	

TRANSPORT	
Avis..27 A2	
Hertz......................................28 A2	
SNCF Bus Stops.......................29 B1	

centre of the modern city. In the Middle Ages Cahors was a prosperous commercial and financial centre, and reminders of the city's wealth are clearly visible along the narrow streets and alleyways of **Vieux Cahors**, densely packed with elegant houses and *hôtels particuliers* (private mansions). At place St-Urcisse, there's a fascinating **mechanical clock** (1997) that drops metal balls through a series of improbable contraptions.

The cavernous nave of the Romanesque-style **Cathédrale St-Étienne** (admission free), which was consecrated in 1119, is crowned with two 18m-wide cupolas (the largest in France). The chapels along the nave (repainted in the 19th century) are Gothic, as are the choir and the massive western façade. The wall paintings between the organ and the interior of the western façade are early 14th century.

Accessible from the cathedral's choir, the badly damaged **cloître** (cloister; ☉ Jun-Sep), is in the Flamboyant Gothic style of the early 16th century. Off the cloister, **Chapelle St-Gausbert** (admission €3) houses a small collection of liturgical objects. The frescoes of the final judgement date from around 1500.

The **Musée Henri Martin** (Musée Municipal; ☎ 05 65 30 15 13; 792 rue Émile Zola; adult/under 18yr/under 6yr €3/1.50/free; ☉ 11am-6pm Mon-Sat, 2-6pm Sun, closed Tue) has a collection of works by the Cahors-born pointillist painter Henri Martin (1893–1972).

The **Tour du Pape Jean XXII** (1-3 blvd Léon Gambetta), a square, crenellated tower – the tallest structure in town at 34m – was built in the 14th century as part of the home of Jacques Duèse, later Pope John XXII from 1316 to 1334. The second of the Avignon popes, he established a university in Cahors in 1331. The interior is closed to the public. Across the street is the 14th-century **Église St-Barthélémy**, with its massive brick and stone belfry.

The small **Musée de la Résistance** (☎ 05 65 22 14 25; place Général de Gaulle; admission free; ☉ 2-6pm), on the northern side of the square, presents illustrated exhibits on the Resistance, the concentration camps and the liberation of France.

Tours

The **Centrale de Réservation Loisirs Accueil** (☎ 05 65 53 20 90; loisirs.accueil.lot@wanadoo.fr; place François Mitterrand; ☉ 8am-noon & 1.30-6.30pm Mon-Fri, also Sat

Jun-Sep), in the same building as the tourist office, arranges canoe, bicycle and horse-riding excursions and various guided walks around town. They can also organise accommodation in the area's many *chambres d'hôtes* and *gîtes ruraux*.

Festivals & Events

Around Bastille Day (14 July), the week-long **Festival de Blues** brings big-name jazz stars to town.

Sleeping

Camping Rivière de Cabessut (☎ 05 65 30 06 30; www .cabessut.com; site/person €8/3; ☉ Apr-Sep; ☒) This three-star camp site is situated on the left bank of the River Lot about 1km north of Pont de Cabessut (east of Vieux Cahors).

Auberge de Jeunesse (☎ 05 65 35 64 71; fjt46@ wanadoo.fr; 20 rue Frédéric Suisse; dm €9.50; ☉ check-in 24hr; ☐) The 40-bed youth hostel's staff are helpful and efficient and there's a cheap canteen. There are a limited number of private rooms, so accommodation is usually in dorms of four to 10 beds; telephone reservations advisable.

Hôtel de France (☎ 05 65 35 16 76; www.hotelde france-cahors.fr in French; 252 av Jean Jaurès; s €43-81, d €47-91; ☒ ☒) A more modern option on the main ring road near the train station and the Pont Valentré. As you'd expect from a mainstream chain hotel, the rooms are generously sized and kitted out with minibars and international TV channels.

Hôtel de la Paix (☎ 05 65 35 03 40; www.hotelde lapaix-cahors.com; 30 pl St-Maurice; s €48, d €54-70, ste €75) Probably the best option near the old town, inside a tall, pale-pink building. The rooms are a little hit-and-miss – the suites are unsurprisingly better equipped than the budget singles, but most of the doubles are roomy and freshly decorated. Downstairs there's a *salon du thé*, the Blue Angel, tailor-made for a sticky treat or two.

Grand Hôtel Terminus (☎ 05 65 53 32 00; www .balandre.com; 5 av Charles de Freycinet; d €60-160; ☒) Not your run-of-the-mill station hotel, this exceptional place is luxurious and full of character. Built around 1920, the hotel has recently been refurbished to a high standard with period detail including ornamental radiators, stained-glass windows and roll-top baths. The rooms are beautifully furnished and the huge beds are perfect for holiday lie-ins.

Eating

Le Lamparo (☎ 05 65 35 25 93; 76, rue Georges Clémenceau; menus €11.40-26; ☒ lunch & dinner) This popular and great-value bistro caters for all moods, from pizza, pasta and gourmet salads to regional fish and meat dishes, all served in an unstuffy dining room with overhead beams and warm Mediterranean tones.

Le Saint Urcisse (☎ 05 65 35 06 06; place St-Urcisse; mains €18-30; ☒ lunch & dinner Tue-Sat) With a delightful walled garden and birds chattering away outside, this place is hard to beat for summer lunch. There's a good choice of traditional French cuisine, including some mouthwatering desserts – just don't plan too much for the afternoon…

Le Marché (☎ 05 65 35 27 27; place Jean Jacques Chapon; menus €21/28; ☒ lunch & dinner Tue-Sat) Fusion cuisine hits Cahors at this funky new restaurant, where you'll find Asian-tinged dishes such as blackened salmon and soy-soaked steak sit alongside more traditional fare. The décor's stark and minimalist, the food's generous, and the outside terrace is one of the best in town.

Le Balandre (☎ 05 65 53 32 00; www.balandre.com; 5 av Charles de Freycinet; menus €38-85; ☒ lunch & dinner) It might be pricey, but you won't regret spending a single cent at this regionally renowned restaurant on the ground floor of the Grand Hôtel Terminus. The smart antique-filled dining room simply smacks of class the minute you walk through the doors, and the impeccably prepared food doesn't disappoint – the varied menus include treats such as a duo of *foie gras de canard* (duck foie gras) and *mignon de veau* (fillet of veal) in truffle sauce.

SELF-CATERING

Marché Couvert (place des Halles; ☒ 7.30am-12.30pm & 3-7pm Tue-Sat, 9am-noon Sun & most holidays) The city's main covered market is usually just referred to as Les Halles. There's an open-air market on Wednesday and Saturday mornings around the covered market and on place Jean-Jacques Chapou. Nearby, food shops can be found around place des Halles and along rue de la Préfecture.

There's a **Casino** (☒ closed Wed) supermarket on place Général de Gaulle.

Entertainment

Les Docks (☎ 05 65 22 36 38; 430 allées des Soupirs) This one-time warehouse is now a municipal cultural centre, with a concert hall, small-scale theatre, practice rooms (€1 per hour per musician), a free skate park and an internet café (p639).

Getting There & Away

BUS

The bus services linking Cahors with destinations around the Lot *département*, designed primarily to transport school children, are a mess. To check your limited options, ask at the tourist office.

There are three or four daily SNCF bus services from Cahors' train station and place Charles de Gaulle to Bouziès (€4.60, 30 minutes), Tour de Faure (St-Cirq Lapopie, €5.10, 40 minutes) and Figeac (€10.70, 1½ hours).

CAR

Choose from **Avis** (☎ 05 65 30 13 10; place de la Gare) or **Hertz** (☎ 05 65 35 34 69; 385 rue Anatole France) opposite the train station.

Free parking is available all along the river and in the westernmost sections of the car parks along allées Fénelon (behind the tourist office) and also at place Charles de Gaulle.

TRAIN

Cahors' **train station** (place Jouinot Gambetta, aka place de la Gare) is on the main SNCF line (four to eight daily) linking Paris' Gare d'Austerlitz (€60.90, five hours). Trains stop at Limoges (€24.10, 2¼ hours), Souillac (€9.60, 45 minutes), Brive-la-Gaillarde (€13.90, one hour) and Toulouse (€15.60, 1¼ hours). To get to Sarlat-la-Canéda, take a train to Souillac and an SNCF bus from there (€13, three hours, two daily).

EAST OF CAHORS

The narrow, winding and wonderfully scenic D662 (signposted 'Vallée du Lot') tracks the banks of the River Lot eastwards from Cahors towards Figeac, passing through the peaceful towns of Bouziès and Conduché and the gravity-defying hillside village of St-Cirq Lapopie.

Grotte de Pech Merle

The spectacular, 1200m-long **Pech Merle Cave** (☎ 05 65 31 27 05; www.pechmerle.com; adult/5-18yr mid-Jun–mid-Sep €7.50/4.50, mid-Sep–mid-Jun €6/3.80; ☒ 9.30-noon & 1.30-5pm Apr-Nov) is only 30km

MESSING ABOUT ON THE RIVER

One of the most atmospheric ways to explore the region's scenery is aboard a **gabarre**, a flat-bottomed, wooden boat used to transport freight up and down the riverways of the Périgord and Lot Valley. *Gabarres* were once a common sight in this part of France, but they had practically died out by the early 20th century, eclipsed by the rise of the railway and the all-conquering automobile; but these days they've been reinvented as river-going pleasure-vessels, and you can hop aboard for a tranquil cruise in several places, including the small village of La Roque Gageac.

Gabarres de Bergerac (☎ 05 53 24 58 80; perigord.gabarres@worldonline.fr; Bergerac)
Gabarres de Beynac (☎ 05 53 28 51 15; www.gabarre-beynac.com; St-Martial de Nabirat)
Gabarres Caminade (☎ 05 53 29 40 95; vecchio@tiscali.fr; La Roque Gageac)
Gabarres Norbert (☎ 05 53 29 40 44; www.norbert.fr; La Roque Gageac)

northeast of Cahors, perched on the hills high above the riverside town of Les Cabrerets. The cave would be dazzling enough simply for its stalactites and stalagmites, but it also contains a stunning array of cave paintings, arguably even more impressive than those at Les Eyzies or Font de Gaumes. There are dozens of paintings of mammoths, bears, horses and bison drawn by Cro-Magnon people some 16,000 to 20,000 years ago, but the most memorable part of the cave is saved till last – a beautifully preserved human footprint, clearly imprinted into the muddy clay floor.

From April to October guided tours (in French, with an English translation available) take place every 45 minutes or so – the time of your tour will be given to you when you buy your ticket. During busy months (especially July and August), get there early or reserve ahead, as only 700 people daily are allowed to visit.

St-Cirq Lapopie
pop 50

St-Cirq Lapopie, 25km east of Cahors and 44km southwest of Figeac, is balanced precariously on the side of a sheer cliff high above the River Lot. With its narrow

AN AWFULLY BIG ADVENTURE

Le Bureau des Sports Nature (☎ 05 65 24 21 01; http://perso.wanadoo.fr/bureau-sports-nature; ⏰ Mon-Fri year-round, Sat & Sun Jul & Aug) in the village of Conduché offers rock climbing and caving, guided hikes, canoe trips and mountain biking, weather permitting. Prices vary depending on the activity; guided canoe trips start at €20 for half a day.

cobbled alleyways, tumbledown medieval houses and glorious views, it's a beautiful place to while away an afternoon – unfortunately, it's also on the itineraries of all the local coach tours, which tends to spoil the sense of peace and tranquillity during the summer months.

The best views are from the ruins of the 13th-century **chateau** at the summit of the village.

Nearby is an early-16th-century **Gothic church** and below, along the narrow streets of the village itself, there are lots of lovingly restored stone and half-timbered houses, topped with steep, red-tiled roofs. Many of the houses have been occupied by local artists, producing pottery, craftwork, jewellery and souvenirs for the summertime tourists. The **Musée Rignault** (admission €2; ⏰ 10am-12.30pm & 2.30-6pm Apr-Oct, to 7pm Jul & Aug) has a delightful garden and an eclectic collection of French furniture and African and Chinese art.

The **tourist office** (☎ 05 65 31 29 06; saint-cirq .lapopie@wanadoo.fr; ⏰ 10am-1pm & 2-7.30pm Jun-Sep, to 6pm Apr, May & Oct, to 5pm Sun, closed Mon Nov-Mar) is in the village hall.

The riverside **Camping de la Plage** (☎ 05 65 30 29 51; site for 2 people €19-21; ⏰ Apr-Nov) is on the left bank of the Lot at the bridge linking the D662 (Tour de Faure) with the road up to St-Cirq Lapopie.

The fine pale-stone **Hôtel de La Pelissaria** (☎ 05 65 31 25 14; http://perso.wanadoo.fr/hoteldelapelis saria; r €71-130; ⏰ Apr-Oct; ⓟ), just down the hill from the tourist office, dates back to the 16th century, and offers several quaintly decorated rooms, most of which are in the main house, although a few are dotted around the courtyard in converted outbuildings. Needless to say, if you want one of the lovely valley-view rooms, you'll need to book well ahead.

LIMOUSIN, THE DORDOGNE & QUERCY

There are several pleasant restaurants in town, but the nicest is **Lou Bolat** (☎ 05 65 30 29 04; mains €9-15; ☽ lunch & dinner Feb-Nov), a trusty little brasserie with a panoramic terrace at the top of the village that specialises in local *galettes* (savoury *crêpe*), cassoulets (casserole) and home-made ice-creams.

St-Cirq Lapopie is 2km across the river and up the hill from Tour de Faure (on the D662), from where SNCF buses travel to Cahors (€5.10, 40 minutes, three or four daily) and Figeac (€7.40, one hour, four or five daily). If you want to get up to the village itself, there's no option but to face the long walk uphill.

Figeac

pop 9500

The riverside town of Figeac, on the River Célé 70km northeast of Cahors, is something of a rarity in this part of France, an old medieval city that has refused to smarten itself up simply to cater for camera-toting tourists. It makes a refreshing change from the meticulously restored buildings of the area's better-known towns, and in many ways feels much more authentic. Most of the houses in the old city date from the 12th to 18th centuries, and many have open-air wooden galleries on their top floors that were once used for drying out leather. Founded in the 9th century by Benedictine monks, Figeac became a prosperous medieval market town, an important stopping place for pilgrims travelling to Santiago de Compostela (p639) and, later, a Protestant stronghold.

ORIENTATION & INFORMATION

The main commercial thoroughfare is the north–south blvd Docteur G Juskiewenski, which runs perpendicular to the Célé and its right-bank quays. Pedestrianised rue Gambetta, four short blocks east, is also perpendicular to the river. The train station, about 600m to the southeast, is across the river from the centre of town, at the end of av Georges Clémenceau.

The **tourist office** (☎ 05 65 34 06 25; http://figeac .quercy-tourisme.com; place Vival; ☽ 10am-7.30pm Jul & Aug, 10am-12.30pm & 2.30-6pm Mon-Sat & 10am-12.30pm Sun May, Jun & Sep, 10am-noon & 2.30-6pm Mon-Sat Oct-Apr) is one block north of the river and two blocks east of blvd Docteur G Juskiewenski.

The **post office** (8 av Fernand Pezet), a block west of blvd Docteur G Juskiewenski, offers currency exchange. There are a couple of banks along the same street.

The **Allo Laverie laundrette** (☽ 6am-10pm) is next to the tourist office.

SIGHTS

The tourist office is in a handsome arcaded building dating from the 13th century. Upstairs is the **Musée du Vieux Figeac** (adult/child €2/1; ☽ 10am-7.30pm Jul & Aug, 10am-12.30pm & 2.30-6pm Mon-Sat & 10am-12.30pm Sun May, Jun & Sep, 10am-noon & 2.30-6pm Mon-Sat Oct-Apr), with a collection of antique clocks, coins, minerals and a propeller blade made by a local aerospace firm.

Figeac's most illustrious son is the brilliant linguist and founder of the science of Egyptology, Jean-François Champollion (1790–1832), who managed to decipher the written language of the pharaohs by studying the Rosetta Stone. Discovered by Napoleon's forces in 1799 during their abortive invasion of Egypt, the stone was captured by the English in 1801 and taken to the British Museum, where it remains; an enlarged copy fills the ancient courtyard next to Champollion's childhood home, now the **Musée Champollion** (☎ 05 65 50 31 08; rue des Frères Champollion), which, at the time of research, is closed to the public while it undergoes a massive facelift.

North of the Musée Champollion and place Champollion, **rue de Colomb**, favoured by the local aristocracy in the 18th century, is lined with centuries-old mansions in sandstone, half-timbers and brick. Near the river on rue du Chapitre, the musty **Église St-Sauveur**, a Benedictine abbey church built from the 12th to 14th centuries, features stained glass installed during the last half of the 19th century.

SLEEPING

Hôtel des Bains (☎ 05 65 34 10 89; 1 rue Griffoul; d €43-64) This dinky family-run hotel is just along the river from the Pont d'Or (just look out for the bright blue neon sign). Once a public bathhouse, it's now a charming low-key hotel with a range of refurbished rooms, the best of which have river views. There's also a pleasant outside terrace, perfect for breakfast on a warm summer morning.

Hostellerie de l'Europe (☎ 05 65 34 10 16; 51 allée Victor Hugo; www.hostelleriedeleurope.com; r €45-65;

⊠) Set back from the river on one of the main roads out of town, this large hotel is housed in a typically French building, complete with solid-stone exterior and russet-coloured shutters on every window. The bedrooms themselves aren't quite as exciting, with plain interior colours and furnishings to match.

Grand Hôtel le Pont d'Or (☎ 05 65 50 95 00; hotel .pont.or@free.fr; 2 av Jean Jaurès; d €60-76; ⊠ ⊠ ⊠) Overlooking the River Célé, this 13th-century building has been renovated in typical Best Western style, so you won't find much period detail, but you will be able to burn off that lavish three-course meal in the sauna and fitness room. The riverside rooms are larger (and more expensive), but most have riverside balconies.

EATING

Hôtel-Café Champollion (☎ 05 65 34 04 37; fax 05 65 34 61 69; 3 place Champollion; mains from €8; ☻ lunch & dinner) In the centre of Figeac, this funky, contemporary café-bar is currently the town's hottest ticket, decorated with bold primary colours and a mix of old and new furnishings. It's always buzzy and busy, especially for the varied lunchtime menu.

La Table de Marinette (☎ 05 65 50 06 07; 51 allée Victor Hugo; menus €12-20; ☻ lunch & dinner) A much-loved and endearingly old-fashioned restaurant, run in the traditional way with the emphasis very much on lovingly prepared food and face-to-face service. The menus are chock-a-block with local dishes, and the three-course €12 *menu* served only during the week is fabulous value.

Cuisine du Marché (☎ 05 65 50 18 55; 15 rue Clermont; menus €29-40; ☻ lunch & dinner Mon-Sat) Unashamedly upmarket, but if you're looking for a slap-up supper in Figeac, then this is the place to find it. The tastefully elegant dining room is full of gleaming wood, potted plants and razor-edged tablecloths, and the menu is stuffed to bursting with rich Quercy cuisine.

There's a **Centre L Gambetta (Leclerc) supermarket** (32 rue Gambetta; ☻ 8.30am-12.30pm & 2pm-7.30pm Mon-Sat), and place Carnot hosts a food market on Saturday morning.

GETTING THERE & AWAY

Three SNCF buses daily travel to Cahors (€10.70, 1¾ hours) via Bouziès and Tour de Faure (St-Cirq Lapopie). Stops are at Figeac's train station and on av Maréchal Joffre (which runs along the river) behind Lycée Champollion.

The **train station** (☎ 05 65 04 94 79) has useful links in a couple of directions. One line links the town with Najac (€8.10, 50 minutes) and Villefranche de Rouergue (€6, 40 minutes) on the way south to Toulouse. A second line travels north via Rocamadour-Padirac (€7, 40 minutes), Brive-la-Gaillarde (€12.40, 80 minutes) and Limoges (€22.90, 2½ hours). There are usually four or five trains daily to each destination.

Villefranche de Rouergue
pop 12,300

At first sight, it's difficult to recognise Villefranche, 61km east of Cahors as a *bastide* town, since the old city has almost disappeared behind the main roads and contemporary buildings of the modern-day town. But a short stroll soon leads to the arcaded central square, **place Notre Dame** – such a typical feature of the *bastides* – and the soaring square pillars of the 15th-century **Collégiale Notre Dame**, along with its never-completed bell tower in one corner. Inside, the 15th-century choir stalls are ornamented with a menagerie of comical and decidedly cheeky figures.

A few blocks to the southwest along streets lined with stone and half-timbered houses, the **Musée Urbain Cabrol** (☎ 05 65 45 44 37; rue de la Fontaine; ☻ Mon-Sat Jun–mid-Sep, Mon-Fri mid-Sep–May) has an eclectic but fascinating collection of religious art, local folk art and 19th-century medical equipment. The **fountain** at the front, decorated with stone carvings from 1336, gushes from a natural spring.

The large Thursday-morning market on place Notre Dame is a real draw for tourists and locals alike, where everything from Chinese herbal medicine to organic produce and handmade kites is sold.

The **tourist office** (☎ 05 65 45 13 18; www.ville franche.com in French; promenade du Guiraudet; ☻ 9am-noon & 2-6pm Mon-Sat May-Oct, 10am-noon Sun Jul & Aug, 9am-noon & 2-6pm Mon-Fri Nov-Apr) is next to the town hall.

Three-star **Le Relais de Farrou** (☎ 05 65 45 18 11; www.relaisdefarrou.com; route de Figeac; s from €45-65.50, d from €51-82, ste €91.50-108; ⊠), housed in a totally modernised *relais de poste* (postal station), 4km from town, has all the comforts and mod-cons you could ask for, including tennis courts, minigolf, secluded gardens and even a heli-pad (just in case you brought your personal chopper).

Logis de France's **L'Univers** (☎ 05 65 45 15 63; 2 place de la République; d €55-58) is in a convenient spot beside the river, opposite one of the road bridges into the old city. The décor could do with some serious sprucing-up – some of the interior furnishings look like they've come as a job-lot from a seventies jumble sale – but if you manage to get one of the river-view rooms, you probably won't even notice.

Near the tourist office, **Le Globe** (☎ 05 65 45 23 19; 1 place de la République; menus €9-23) is another classically French brasserie that's always packed with locals sipping a *petit café* (espresso), but it's just as good for a cheap two-course lunch or a more substantial sit-down dinner.

L'Assiette Gourmande (☎ 05 65 45 25 95; place Andrée Lescur; menus €13-30; ☻ lunch & dinner, closed all Sun, Tue & Wed dinner), just off place Notre Dame, is a snazzy restaurant with an outside terrace, offering reliable regional and French cuisine.

Villefranche's train station (across the river from the tourist office) has regular trains to Figeac (€6, 40 minutes). Buses to Najac (€4.20, 45 mins, one daily), Figeac (€5.70, 40 minutes, three daily) and Cahors (€9.20, 80 minutes, two daily), all leave from the train station.

Najac
pop 250
Of all the *bastide* towns, Najac is unquestionably one of the most beautiful. Clustered on the hilltop above a hairpin curve in the River Aveyron, the town is best known for its soaring medieval castle, the **Fortresse Royal** (☎ 05 65 29 71 65; admission €3.75; ☻ 10am-1pm & 3-7pm Jul & Aug, 10am-12.30pm & 3-6.30pm Jun, 10am-12.30pm & 3-5.30pm Apr, May & Sep), which with its slender turrets, sturdy ramparts and fluttering flags looks like it could have fallen straight from the pages of a fairy tale. Thanks to its sturdy defenses and practically impregnable hilltop position, the chateau was a key strongpoint throughout the Middle Ages, and it's well worth visiting for a look at its beautifully preserved medieval architecture and the superb views from the central keep.

The medieval parts of the town itself are spread out along one central street that runs 1.2km from the crest of the hill to the sloping **place du Faubourg**, a beguiling central square surrounded by a hotch-potch of timber-framed houses, some dating from the 13th century. Slightly to the west of the castle is the massive Gothic **Église St-Jean l'Évangéliste**, which the locals were forced to construct by the Inquisition in 1258 as punishment for their Catharist tendencies.

The **tourist office** (☎ 05 65 29 72 05; otsi.najac@ wanadoo.fr; place du Faubourg; ☻ 9am-12.30pm & 2-6.30pm Mon-Sat, longer in Jul & Aug) is on the southern side of the square.

Surrounded by peaceful gardens on the edge of the River Aveyron, quiet family-run **Le Belle Rive** (☎ 05 65 29 73 90; hotel.bellerive .najac@wanadoo.fr; Le Roc du Pont; d €52-56; ☒) is 1.5km from the village, past the train station. It's a relaxing and welcoming place to base yourself in Najac, with up-to-date, unfussy rooms and an excellent inhouse restaurant.

Huddled into the corner of the square opposite the tourist office, **Oustal del Barry** (☎ 05 65 29 74 32; www.oustaldelbarry.com; place du Faubourg; d €70-90; ☻ late Mar–mid-Nov) is by far the most comfortable place to stay in Najac, a rustic and well-worn old *auberge* with plenty of pleasant rooms, including some which overlook the surrounding valley. It's perhaps better known for the downstairs **restaurant** (menus €23-49; ☻ closed lunch Mon & Tue Oct-Jun), renowned for its regionally inspired cuisine.

Most people end up sitting down for dinner at the Oustal del Barry, but simple little **La Salamandre** (☎ 05 65 29 74 09; rue du Barriou; menus €15-20; ☻ lunch & dinner, closed dinner Wed Dec & Jan) is worth a look for its local dishes and a wonderful panoramic terrace overlooking the castle.

The most scenic way to get to Villefranche de Rouergue, 23km to the north, is via the twisting, one-lane D638, which intersects the D339 about 5km northeast of Najac. There are also regular trains from Figeac (€8.10, 50 minutes, four or five daily).

WEST OF CAHORS
Downstream from Cahors, the lower River Lot twists its way through the rich **vineyards** of the Cahors Appellation d'Origine Contrôlée (AOC) region, passing the dams at **Luzech**, whose medieval section sits at the

CASTLE COUNTRY

The Dordogne and Quercy aren't in quite the same league as the Loire Valley, but there are still plenty of chateaux to explore. Here's a whistle-stop guide to some of the region's lesser-known castles and mansions.

Biron (Map p610; ☎ 05 53 63 13 39; adult/student & child €5.50/3.50; ☒ Feb-Dec) This much-filmed chateau, 8km south of Monpazier, is a glorious mish-mash of styles, having been fiddled about with by successive generations of heirs for the last eight centuries, until the castle was sold off in the early 1900s to pay for the extravagant lifestyle of a particularly irresponsible son.

Jumilhac-le-Grand (Map p610; ☎ 05 53 52 42 97; adult/child €6/4; ☒ Jun-Sep, weekends & holidays May, Oct–mid-Nov) This spiky-turreted, slate-topped chateau, 50km northeast of Périgueux, is renowned for its formal gardens and lavishly decorated rooms. Guides dressed in period costume conduct night-time tours in summer.

Hautefort (Map p610; ☎ 05 53 50 51 23; adult/child €8/4; ☒ late Mar-Oct, afternoon Sun Nov–mid-Mar, closed mid-Dec–mid-Jan) An imposing neoclassical chateau 40km east of Périgueux, set around a central square and surrounded by formal gardens and flower terraces.

Losse (Map p631; ☎ 05 53 50 80 08; www.chateaudelosse.com; adult/student/child €7/5/3; ☒ Easter-Oct) Château de Losse, 5km southwest of Montignac, is worth visiting for its well-preserved 15th-century architecture, including the original moat and crenellated battlements, and its grandly furnished rooms, filled with antique tapestries and furniture.

Puymartin (Map p631; ☎ 05 53 59 29 97; adult/child €6.50/3; ☒ Apr-Nov) A partly furnished chateau 8km northwest of Sarlat, best known for its lavishly decorated interior and the mysterious tale of the Dame Blanche, whose restless spirit is said to haunt the chateau corridors.

base of a donjon, and **Castelfranc**, with a dramatic suspension bridge. Sights in this region are few and far between – this is working land first and foremost, and the landscape becomes increasingly industrial the further west you travel from Puy l'Évêque. Along the river's right bank, the D9 affords superb views of the vines and the river's many hairpin curves.

Puy l'Évêque
pop 2200

The riverside town of Puy l'Évêque, on a rocky hillside above the right bank of the Lot, was once one of the most important ports in the valley, but these days the river traffic's long-gone, and the once-grand merchants' houses are looking a little worse for wear. Still, the oldest part of town is well worth a stroll, with many fine stone mansions and tumbledown medieval buildings, best appreciated from the road bridge that spans the Lot River just outside town.

The Puy l'Évêque **tourist office** (☎ 05 65 21 37 63; www.puyleveque.fr; ☒ 9.30am-1pm & 2.30-6.30pm Mon-Fri, 9.30am-1pm & 2.30-5.30pm Sat, 10am-12.30pm Sun Jul & Aug, 9am-noon & 2-6pm Mon, 9am-noon & 2-5pm Tue-Fri, 9.30am-12.30pm Sat Sep-Jun) is at the base of a square, 13th-century donjon.

Five to seven SNCF buses each day link Cahors with Puy l'Évêque (€5.70, 45 minutes).

Château de Bonaguil

This imposing feudal **fortress** (☎ 05 53 71 90 33; www.bonaguil.org; Fumel; adult/7-16yr €6/3.50; ☒ 10am-6pm Jun-Aug, 10.30am-1pm & 2.30-5pm Sep, 11am-1pm & 2.30-5pm Oct, 11am-1pm & 2.30-5.30pm Feb & Mar, 11am-1pm & 2.30-5.30pm Apr & May, 2.30-4.30pm Sun & holidays Nov-Jan) is a fine example of late-15th-century military architecture, featuring the artful integration of cliffs, outcrops, towers, bastions, loopholes, machicolations and crenellations. It's situated about 15km west of Puy l'Évêque (and on the GR36 footpath). Optional guided tours (1½ hours), in English three times daily in July and August, generally take place on the hour, with the last one about an hour before closing time.

About 5km to the southeast is the attractive village of **St-Martin-le-Redon**, in a quiet little valley along the River Thèze (and just off the D673).

NORTHERN QUERCY

The northern edge of Quercy is not far from Collonges-la-Rouge (p619), Beaulieu-sur-Dordogne (p620) and Turenne (p619).

Rocamadour
pop 630

The hillside silhouette of Rocamadour, clinging to the cliffs above the River Alzou

59km north of Cahors and 51km east of Sarlat, is one of the classic sights of northern Quercy. For hundreds of years the town has been a centre for Christian pilgrims from across France and Europe, thanks to the supposedly miraculous powers of the Black Madonna housed in the **Chapelle Notre Dame** in the heart of the Cité (old city). From the 12th to 14th centuries, the town became an important stop on the main pilgrimage route to Santiago de Compostela (p639), but these days, the penitents have mostly been replaced by coach tourists plodding their way around the city's over-restored Gothic chapels, and in summer the crowds can be pretty unbearable.

The Cité's only street is connected to the chapels and the plateau above, known as **L'Hospitalet**, by the **Grand Escalier** (Great Staircase). The pious once climbed this on their knees, and there's a path whose switchbacks are marked with graphic Stations of the Cross. At the top of the stairs is the 14th-century **chateau** (charging €2.50 for a view from the ramparts).

There's not a great deal to see in L'Hospitalet itself, a straggling and unattractive hilltop suburb that's almost entirely devoted to tourism. The **Grotte des Merveilles** (☎ 05 65 33 67 92; Apr–mid-Nov) contains some stalactites and prehistoric cave paintings – it's next door to the **tourist office** (☎ 05 65 33 22 00) in L'Hospitalet. There's a second **tourist office** (☎ 05 65 33 62 59) on the main street in La Cité.

You'd be better off giving the overpriced hotels and restaurants around Rocamadour a wide berth – prices for even the dingiest room skyrocket in summer, and most hotels are booked out well in advance by coach parties.

Gouffre de Padirac

The spectacular **Padirac Cave** (☎ 05 65 33 64 56; www.gouffre-de-padirac.com; adult/6-9yr €8.50/5.40; 9am-6pm Jul, 8.30am-6.30pm Aug, 9am-noon & 2-6pm Apr-Jun & Sep-early Oct), 15km northeast of Rocamadour and 10km southeast of Carennac, offers the closest thing – at least in *this* world – to a cruise to Hades across the River Styx. Discovered in 1889, the cave's navigable river, 103m below ground level, is reached through a 75m-deep, 33m-wide chasm.

Boat pilots ferry visitors along a 500m stretch of the subterranean waterway, guid-

ing them along a series of stairways to otherworldly pools and vast, floodlit caverns.

The whole cave operation is unashamedly mass-market, but it retains an innocence and style reminiscent of the 1930s, when the first lifts were installed. The temperature inside the cave is a constant 13°C. The 1¼-hour visits take place from April to early October.

Château de Castelnau-Bretenoux

Towering above the valleys of the Dordogne, Cère and Bave Rivers, 9km east of Carennac, this feudal **fortress** (☎ 05 65 10 98 00; adult/18-25yr/under 18yr €6.10/4.10/free; 9.30am-7pm Jul & Aug, 9.30am-12.30pm & 2-6.30pm May & Jun, 10am-12.30pm & 2-5.30pm Wed-Mon Sep-Apr) is one of the most impressive castles in France. Set around a roughly triangular courtyard, the chateau's stout towers are linked by a series of high defensive walls and bulwarks. Most of the complex dates from the 12th to the 15th centuries, and has been sympathetically restored after the castle fell into disrepair during the 19th and early 20th centuries.

Ticket sales stop 45 minutes before the morning and afternoon closing times. The seven eclectically furnished rooms must be visited with a guide (English information sheet available).

Carennac

pop 370

Teetering above the fast-running river on the left bank of the Dordogne, this delightful medieval village is a gorgeous place for an overnight stop. The village is crisscrossed by a maze of alleyways and winding lanes, lined by solid dry-stone houses built from amber-coloured brick, some dating from the 10th century (and most occupied only in summer).

An arched stone gate near the river leads to the 16th-century **Château du Doyen**, which houses a heritage centre, **L'Espace Patrimoine** (☎ 05 65 33 81 36; patrimoine-vallee-dordogne@wanadoo .fr; admission free; 10am-noon & 2-6pm Tue-Fri Apr-Jun, Tue-Sun Jul-Sep), showcasing the art and history of the region. Above is the square **Tour de Télémaque**, named after the hero of Fénelon's *Les Aventures de Télémaque*, written here in 1699.

Next to the chateau is the **priory** and the Romanesque **Église St-Pierre**, distinguished by its remarkable tympanum depicting Jesus in majesty, carved in the Languedoc Romanesque style in the mid-12th century. Just off the **cloître** (cloister; adult/child €2.50/0.80), heavily damaged in the Revolution, is a remarkable, late-15th-century **Mise au Tombeau** (Statue of the Entombment), once brightly painted. Its opening hours are the same as the **tourist office** (☎ 05 65 10 97 01; ot.intercom .carennac@wanadoo.fr; ☼ 10am-7pm mid-Jun–Sep; 10am-noon & 2-6pm Mon-Sat, 2-6pm Sun Oct–mid-Jun) next door.

The only place to buy food is the small **grocery** (☼ closed 12.30-3pm & afternoon Sun & Mon) next to the post office.

Fine creeper-covered **L'Auberge de Vieux Quercy** (☎ 05 65 10 96 59; www.vieuxquercy.com; d low season €45-60, high season €60-90; ☒ ☐) is housed inside a 19th-century inn on the edge of the village and makes for a luxurious night's sleep. The bedrooms are chic and contemporary; some overlook the pool, while others have views over the hotel's private gardens. The **restaurant** (menus €20-36) is excellent, too, with plenty of rich Quercy cuisine on offer.

Right on the banks of this river, **Hôtel Fenelon** (☎ 05 65 10 96 46; www.hotel-fenelon.com; s €48-52, d €50-62; ☒) is another picturesque country hotel with shades of an Alsatian summer home, thanks to its red-tiled roof, floral décor and geranium-filled hanging baskets. The **restaurant** has views overlooking the tree-covered Île Calypso.

Atlantic Coast

Hemmed in by Brittany above and the Basque country below, the area in this chapter cuts a swath through three regions: Pays de la Loire around Nantes; Poitou-Charentes from Poitiers to the coast; and Aquitaine, south of the Gironde Estuary. Within these are numerous smaller *départements* (administrative divisions), stitched with rows of vineyards.

At the upper extent, the animated city of Nantes is infused with maritime and Breton heritage and imaginative cultural spaces. In the centre, riches include the ancient university city of Poitiers, with its resplendent Romanesque churches; the charming town of Cognac, tantamount with its celebrated double-distilled spirit; and the ancient, arcaded port of La Rochelle.

Approaching the area's lower edge, the elegant city of Bordeaux is blessed with 18th-century architecture and borders the country's largest wine-growing area, encompassing the Médoc's magnificent chateaux, and the medieval hilltop hamlet, St-Émilion. Westwards, the tranquil Bay of Arcachon is home to a dazzling variety of birdlife and weathered wooden oyster shacks.

Interwoven with the area's historical fabric are shimmering modern additions like the cinematic theme park Futuroscope, and smooth-as-silk bicycle paths crisscrossing the Île de Ré.

Fringing this patchwork are countless kilometres of fine-sand beaches soaked in more sunshine than anywhere in France (apart from the Mediterranean). Less moneyed than the Med, all along this stretch of the Atlantic Coast you'll find relaxed, reasonably priced beach havens including the Côte d'Argent (Silver Coast), with world-class surf breaks backed by rolling sand dunes blanketed by pine forests – just one of this region's affordable treasures.

HIGHLIGHTS

- Ascend the 15th-century belfry at **Cathédrale St-André** (p674) for a bird's-eye view of Bordeaux
- Board Cap Ferret's **P'tit Train** (p687), running from the bay to the beach
- Tour the centuries-old **towers** (p662) guarding La Rochelle
- Sip **wine** (see the boxed text, p675), **Cognac** (see the boxed text, p669), or a combination of both, Poitiers' speciality, **pineau** (p661)
- Be enchanted by the dreams of **Jules Verne** (p653) in Nantes

- ★ Nantes
- Poitiers ★
- ★ La Rochelle
- ★ Cognac
- The Médoc ★
- Cap Ferret ★
- ★ Bordeaux

■ POPULATION: 4,529,642	■ AREA: 51,597 SQ KM

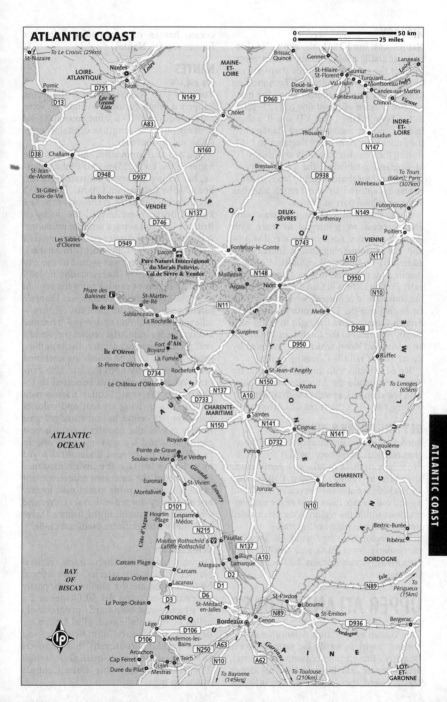

ATLANTIC COAST

HISTORY

Nantes was, until 1941, the capital of Brittany, and still retains strong Breton roots. Most of the other areas in this chapter were historically part of Aquitaine. The Aquitaine came under English control when the marriage of Eleanor of Aquitaine (c 1122–1204) to the French king Louis VII was dissolved in 1152 and she married Henry Plantagenet, the future King Henry II of England. In 1361, during the Hundred Years' War, Edward III of England established the principality of Aquitaine. Less than a century later, in 1453, it was recaptured by the French and has since remained part of France.

Along the Atlantic Coast, the area's ports and harbours were integral to trade with France's colonies, notably in salt and wine – and slaves, something that is increasingly addressed in historical exhibits. Voyagers inspired by the coast included many of the early French settlers in Canada, among them the founders of Montreal, who set sail from La Rochelle in the 17th century. The loss of French Canada (and the right to trade with North America) to the English in 1763 dealt an economic blow, which was softened by the arrival of rail the following century.

Rapid rail links with the rest of the country have today made the Atlantic coast popular with sea-changers, as well as with students attending the area's many major universities.

GETTING THERE & AWAY

Bordeaux is the main transport hub for the region, reached in three hours by TGV from Paris. From here, trains can take you pretty much anywhere in France. Nantes, Poitiers and La Rochelle are also well served by TGV, and a good rail service links most of the main attractions within the region. A car gives added freedom for the wine-tasting trail.

The region also has good air services, particularly from Paris and the UK with airports at Nantes, Poitiers, La Rochelle and Bordeaux.

UPPER ATLANTIC COAST

This swatch of the Loire-Atlantique *département* might as easily be termed 'lower Brittany'. Breton in every sense – cultural, architectural and historical – this upper tract, where the Loire empties into the ocean, has as its centrepiece Brittany's former capital, Nantes.

NANTES

pop 280,600

You can take Nantes out of Brittany (as happened when regional boundaries were redrawn during WWII), but you can't take Brittany out of its longtime capital, Nantes ('Naoned' in Breton).

Spirited and innovative, this city on the banks of the Loire, 55km east of the Atlantic, has a long history of reinventing itself. Founded by Celts around 70 BC, in AD 937 Alain Barbe-Torte, the grandson of the last king of Brittany, established the duchy of Brittany here following a series of invasions. A landmark royal charter guaranteeing civil rights to France's Huguenots (Protestants), the Edict of Nantes, was signed in the city by Henri IV in 1598. Its revocation in 1685 led to a Huguenot exodus from the region.

By the 18th century Nantes was France's foremost port, and in the 19th century – following the abolition of slavery – it became a cutting-edge industrial centre; the world's first public transport service, the omnibus, began here in 1826. Shipbuilding anchored the city's economy until the late 20th century. When the shipyards relocated to St-Nazaire to the west, Nantes transformed itself into a thriving student and cultural hub. The city centre has now nudged past Bordeaux's as the country's sixth-largest metropolis, and it's growing, with one in two Nantais today aged under 40. Buoyed by its Breton heritage, the city's renaissance extends from the extensive redevelopment of the former shipyards to its iconic former biscuit factory–turned–cultural centre, and a brand new museum in the former Dukes of Brittany's magnificent medieval castle.

Orientation

On the Loire's northern bank, central Nantes' two main arteries, both served by tram lines, are the north–south, partly pedestrianised cours des 50 Otages and a broad east–west boulevard (progressively called blvd de Stalingrad, alleé Commandant Charcot, cours John Kennedy, and cours Franklin Roosevelt) that connects the train station with quai de la Fosse. They intersect near the Gare Centrale bus/tram hub.

The old city is to the east, between cours des 50 Otages and the Château des Ducs de Bretagne.

Information

EMERGENCY

Hôtel de Police (☎ 02 40 37 21 21; 6 place Waldeck Rousseau) Police Nationale's 24-hour station is 1km northeast of the Monument des 50 Otages. Go to tram stop Motte Rouge.

INTERNET ACCESS

Cyber City (☎ 02 40 89 57 92; 14 rue de Strasbourg; per hr €3; ☺ 10am-1am Mon-Sat, 11am-midnight Sun)

MEDICAL SERVICES

CHR de Nantes hospital (☎ 02 40 08 38 95; quai Moncousu) Has a *service d'urgence* (emergency room).

MONEY

Commercial banks line rue La Fayette.

POST

Main Post Office (place de Bretagne)

TOURIST INFORMATION

Tourist Office (☎ 02 72 64 04 79; www.nantes-tour isme.com; cours Olivier de Clisson; ☺ 10am-6pm, from 10.30am Thu, closed Sun)
Tourist Office Annexe (2 place St-Pierre; ☺ 10am-1pm & 2-6pm, from 10.30am Thu, closed Mon)

Sights

The Nantes **city pass** (Pass Nantes; 24/48/72hr €10/16/22), available from the tourist office, includes unlimited bus and tram transport as well as entry to museums and monuments, and extras like a free hot chocolate at the Art Nouveau brasserie, La Cigale (p657).

MUSEUMS

By the time you're reading this, the grand **Château des Ducs de Bretagne** (Castle of the Dukes of Brittany; ☎ 02 51 17 49 00; museum/exhibitions each adult/child €5/3 or both €8/4.80, admission to grounds free; ☺ 9am-7pm mid-May–mid-Sep, 10am-6pm Wed-Mon mid-Sep–mid-May) will have reopened after 15 years of renovations to house a multifaceted, multimedia-rich new museum (with good wheelchair access) covering the city's history.

Duchess of Brittany, Anne de Bretagne (1477–1514), was born in the chateau; her heart (encased in ivory and gold) is dis-

played at the **Musée Dobrée** (☎ 02 40 71 03 50; 18 rue Voltaire; adult/student & child €3/1.50; ☺ 1.30-5.30pm Tue-Fri, 2.30-5.30pm Sat & Sun). Exhibits also include classical antiquities, Renaissance furniture, and medieval and French Revolution artefacts.

Showcasing one of the finest collections of French paintings outside Paris in sumptuous gallery spaces linked by grand stone staircases, Nantes' exceptional **Musée des Beaux-Arts** (Fine Arts Museum; ☎ 02 51 17 45 00; 10 rue Georges Clemenceau; adult/child €3.10/1.60; ☺ 10am-6pm Wed-Mon, to 8pm Thu) displays works by artists including Georges de La Tour, Chagall, Monet, Picasso and Kandinsky.

Overlooking the river 2km southwest of the tourist office, the **Musée Jules Verne** (☎ 02 40 69 72 52; www.julesverne.nantes.fr in French; 3 rue de l'Hermitage; adult/student & child €3/1.50; ☺ 10am-noon & 2-6pm Mon & Wed-Sat, 2-6pm Sun) is a magical place with first-edition books, hand-edited manuscripts, cardboard theatre cut-outs, good wheelchair access and some delightful child-friendly interactive displays to introduce or reintroduce you to the work of Jules Verne, who was born in Nantes in 1828. Verne's books, like *Around the World in 80 Days*, are so well known that it's still worthwhile visiting even if you're not *au fait* with the French-language interpretative signs. A few metres east of the museum in a little park are a pair of life-size **statues**, dedicated to the writer in 2005, showing his creation Captain Nemo looking out to sea, and behind him, Verne as a small boy with big dreams.

If you're squeamish about reptiles, skip the vivarium packed with live pythons, crocodiles and iguanas at the **Musée d'Histoire Naturelle** (☎ 02 40 99 26 20; 12 rue Voltaire; adult/child €3.10/1.60; ☺ 10am-6pm Wed-Mon). Prehistory and ethnography collections also figure largely here, including a gigantic skeleton of a rorqual that takes up an entire room.

OTHER ATTRACTIONS

Île Feydeau (the quarter south of the Gare Centrale) ceased to be an island after WWII when the channels of the Loire that once surrounded it were filled in following the riverbeds drying up. Today, you can still see where ships docked at the doors of the area's 18th-century mansions – some of which are adorned with stone carvings of the heads of African slaves.

NANTES

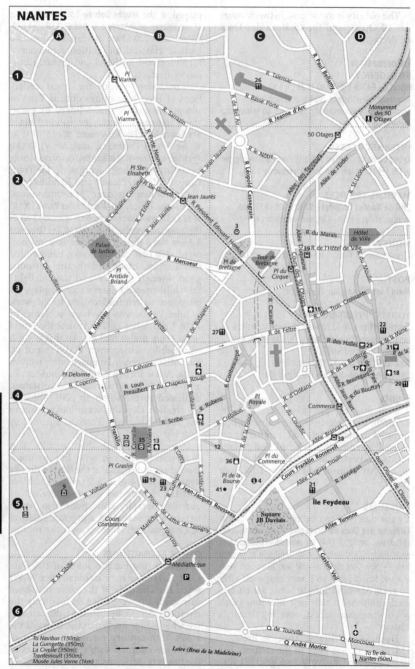

ATLANTIC COAST

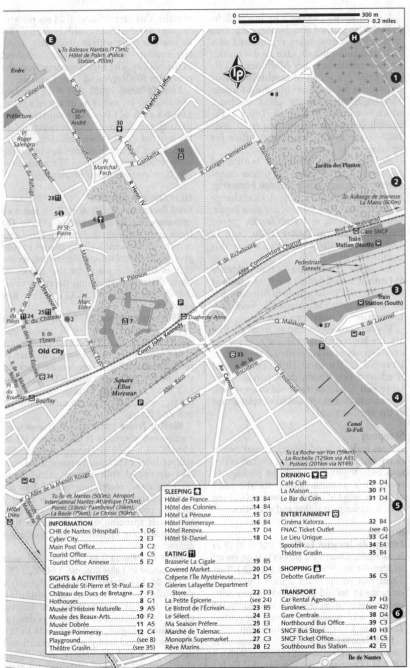

ATLANTIC COAST

INFORMATION
CHR de Nantes (Hospital)............1 D6
Cyber City.....................................2 E3
Main Post Office...........................3 C2
Tourist Office...............................4 C5
Tourist Office Annexe..................5 E2

SIGHTS & ACTIVITIES
Cathédrale St-Pierre et St-Paul....6 E2
Château des Ducs de Bretagne....7 F3
Hothouses...................................8 G1
Musée d'Histoire Naturelle...........9 A5
Musée des Beaux-Arts................10 F2
Musée Dobrée............................11 A5
Passage Pommeraye...................12 C4
Playground............................(see 8)
Théâtre Graslin.....................(see 35)

SLEEPING
Hôtel de France..........................13 B4
Hôtel des Colonies......................14 B4
Hôtel La Pérouse........................15 D3
Hôtel Pommeraye.......................16 B4
Hôtel Renova..............................17 D4
Hôtel St-Daniel...........................18 D4

EATING
Brasserie La Cigale......................19 B5
Covered Market..........................20 D4
Crêperie l'Île Mystérieuse...........21 D5
Galeries Lafayette Department
  Store....................................22 D3
La Petite Épicerie...................(see 24)
Le Bistrot de l'Écrivain...............23 B5
Le Sélect....................................24 E3
Ma Seaison Préfere.....................25 E3
Marché de Talensac....................26 C1
Monoprix Supermarket...............27 C3
Rêve Marins...............................28 E2

DRINKING
Café Cult...................................29 D4
La Maison..................................30 F1
Le Bar du Coin...........................31 D4

ENTERTAINMENT
Cinéma Katorza.........................32 B4
FNAC Ticket Outlet................(see 4)
Le Lieu Unique..........................33 G4
Spoutnik....................................34 B4
Théâtre Graslin..........................35 B4

SHOPPING
Debotte Gautier.........................36 C5

TRANSPORT
Car Rental Agencies...................37 H3
Eurolines..............................(see 42)
Gare Centrale............................38 D4
Northbound Bus Office...............39 C3
SNCF Bus Stops.........................40 H3
SNCF Ticket Office.....................41 C5
Southbound Bus Station.............42 E5

Still an island (accessed by bridges), **Île de Nantes** languished after Nantes' shipyards closed, but is now being regenerated as a civic and cultural hub. One of the quirkiest new residents is Les Machines de l'Île de Nantes – a group of machinists/artists responsible for creations like the 40-tonne, 12m-high, 30-passenger giant elephant, which is a fixture at festivals. Tours of the workshop are planned starting from mid-2007 – check with the tourist office for updates.

Pedestal statues symbolise traditional Nantais industries inside the ornate three-tiered shopping arcade **Passage Pommeray**, built in 1843 to link the then-stock exchange with the post office. Nearby are **place Royale**, laid out in 1790, and **place Graslin**, graced by the neoclassical **Théâtre Graslin**, built in 1788 and beautifully renovated earlier this decade (see p658).

Inside the Flamboyant Gothic **Cathédrale St-Pierre et St-Paul** (place St-Pierre), the **tomb of François II** (r 1458–88), duke of Brittany, and his second wife, Marguerite de Foix, is a masterpiece of Renaissance art.

If you need some respite from all that art, the **Jardin des Plantes** is one of the most exquisite botanical gardens in France. Founded in the early 19th century, and filled with flowerbeds, duck ponds, fountains and towering redwoods (sequoias), there are **hothouses** and a **children's playground** at the northern end.

Sleeping

Nantes makes a good weekend break, when hotel rates often drop. The tourist office also puts together a weekend package of two nights' accommodation for the price of one in selected hotels at weekends, along with discounts on sights and activities.

BUDGET

Auberge de Jeunesse La Manu (☎ 02 40 29 29 20; nanteslamanu@fuaj.org; 2 place de la Manu; dm incl breakfast €14.90; ☯ early Jan-late Dec; 🖳) Just 600m east of the train station's northern entrance in an old converted factory with good wheelchair access, this well-equipped hostel is a 15-minute walk from the centre. Take tram 1 to the Manufacture stop.

Hôtel Renova (☎ 02 40 47 57 03; www.hotel-renova .com in French; 11 rue Beauregard; s €34-43, d €38-48, tr & q €55; ✗) Over six steep mosaic-tiled flights of stairs, this narrow hotel of 24 rooms with original polished floorboards is a simple little one-star place with an absolutely super-star location – it's in a pedestrianised street in the old city, just a few footsteps from the cours des 50 Otages and Gare Centrale.

Hôtel St-Daniel (☎ 02 40 47 41 25; www.hotel -saintdaniel.com in French; 4 rue du Bouffay; s €32-40, d €45, tr & q €50; ✗) Peacefully situated overlooking the St-Croix church courtyard in the heart of the old town, this clean, cheery place has a variety of room sizes including some whoppers, as well as (French) cable TV, hairdryers and double-glazing.

MIDRANGE & TOP END

Hôtel Pommeraye (☎ 02 40 48 78 79; www.hotel -pommeraye.com; 2 rue Boileau; s €45-64, d €53-84; 🖳) Sleek and chic with shimmering short-pile carpet and textured walls in shades of pale grey, gold, chocolate and violet blue, rooms at this boutique place on the corner of Nantes' smartest shopping street are sized like clothes (M, L, XL, XXL), with prices to match.

Hôtel des Colonies (☎ 02 40 48 79 76; www .hoteldescolonies.fr in French; 5 rue du Chapeau Rouge; s €56-64, d €63-71; ✗ 🖳) Local art exhibitions rotate monthly in the lobby of this cherry-red place featuring snazzy rooms fitted out with purple, green and orange feature walls and boxy resin light fittings. Book ahead for free wi-fi, which only beams to the 1st and 2nd floors.

Hôtel de France (☎ 02 40 73 57 91; www.hotels -exclusive.com/hotels/france; 24 rue Crébillon; s €83-88, d & tw €87-92, tr €107-118) Through an ornately sculpted stone entrance passage, this Louis XVI–decorated 18th-century grand dame offering good wheelchair access has recently changed owners – and with any luck the rooms' faded grandeur won't see too much sprucing up to the point that they lose their charming, old-fashioned character.

Hôtel La Pérouse (☎ 02 40 89 75 00; www .hotel-laperouse.fr; 3 allée Duquesne; s €81-95, d €91-133; ✗ ✗ 🖳) Styled to reflect the city's shipbuilding traditions, this stunning pad in the city centre is Nantes' hottest choice for travellers into all things design. A wooden gangway entrance leads to the stone-and-wood lobby with international newspapers and 46 rooms with zigzag chairs, canvas sail-like curtains, and glass bathroom basins and wardrobes. Breakfast (€11.15) includes 17 flavours of jam and freshly squeezed OJ.

Eating

Nantes' most cosmopolitan dining is in the medieval Bouffay quarter, a couple of blocks west of the chateau around rue de la Juiverie, rue des Petites Écuries and rue de la Bâclerie. Breton *crêperies* are plentiful throughout town. West of cours des 50 Otages, rue Jean-Jacques Rousseau and rue Santeuil are lined with eateries.

Ma Seaison Préfere (☎ 02 40 47 13 12; 10 rue de Château; dishes €6-7; ☽ 10am-8pm Mon-Sat) Though not exclusively vegetarian, this little lemon- and lime-coloured hole in the wall is a great place for homemade vegetable tarts and lasagnes. At lunchtime, its nine tables fill quickly.

Brasserie La Cigale (☎ 02 51 84 94 94; 4 place Graslin; breakfast €9.50, brunch €20, mains €7.30-13.80; ☽ 7.30am-12.30am) No visit to Nantes is complete without a café and cake or all-out feast at the Art Nouveau showpiece, La Cigale – several salons of original 1890s gilded tilework and frescoed ceilings, attended by white-aproned waiters. The name comes from the cautionary fable of the *cigale* (cicada) and the ant, in which the cicada is too busy enjoying himself to plan for the winter ahead. But this lavish brasserie embraces the cicada wholeheartedly – just allow plenty of time to savour the experience.

Crêperie l'Île Mystérieuse (☎ 02 40 47 42 83; 13 rue Kervégan; menus €8-14; ☽ lunch & dinner Tue-Sat) Jules Verne's legacy lives on at this lovely little place in the town centre serving *crêpes* with local cheeses and cured hams amid décor such as a hot-air balloon, old-fashioned maps and books lining uneven stone walls glittering with coins.

Rêve Marins (☎ 02 40 47 00 96; 2 rue du Roi Albert; mains €7.50-12; ☽ lunch & dinner Tue-Sat) Accompanied by an outstanding list of local wines, this much-lauded place combines classic *crêpes* and buckwheat *galettes* with very un-classic (but delicious) fillings like chicken curry, or kangaroo and Muscadet grapes.

Le Bistrot de l'Écrivain (☎ 02 51 84 15 15; 15 rue Jean-Jacques Rousseau; menus €17; ☽ lunch & dinner Mon-Sat) Splashed in shades of red, with checked-clothed tables and wine bottles lining the walls, Le Bistrot de l'Écrivain serves authentic Nantaise cuisine like *sandre* (pikeperch) in *beurre blanc* (white sauce), as well as fine foie gras.

Le Sélect (☎ 02 40 89 04 49; 14 rue du Château; mains €9-13; ☽ 2-7pm Mon, 10.30am-midnight Tue-Sat) A spiral wooden staircase leads to an upper mezzanine level at this arty café/restaurant/ *salon de thé* (tearoom), with mellow jazz playing in the background. The huge sandwich board is chalked with daily specials including reliable favourites like salads, steak and fries.

La Petite Épicerie (☎ 02 40 48 65 91; 14 rue du Château; mains from €7.20; ☽ 10am-7.30pm Tue-Sat) One half of this petite shopfront is stocked high with homemade jams and preserves and glass jars of sugared hearts; the other half has a clutch of wooden tables. If you're easing into the day, it's a great place for a late breakfast; at lunch it serves fabulous fresh fish.

For a romantic night out and about, glide along the River Erdre with an ever-changing view of chateaux as you dine aboard **Bateaux Nantais** (☎ 02 40 14 51 14; www.bateaux-nantais.fr; quai de la Motte Rouge; lunch €50-80, dinner €57-80; ☽ by reservation), accompanied by ambient music, local Muscadet wines, and chef-prepared regional specialities. There are regular departures in summer; in winter boats operate only when there are sufficient numbers.

ACROSS THE RIVER

For the cost of a tram ticket, the little **Navibus** (☎ 08 10 44 44 44) shuttles across the river from the Gare Maritime tram stop to the villagelike quarter of **Trentemoult**. Lined with fishermen's cottages and ships captains' houses, this artsy community has an island feel, despite being on the Loire's southern banks. Overlooking the river, **La Civelle** (☎ 02 40 75 46 60; 21 quai Marcel Broissard; mains €13-15; ☽ 11am-midnight Mon-Fri) is a buzzing designer place of burnished chrome, funky light fittings, and art exhibits, serving contemporary market fare like spiced smoked salmon. On weekends especially, drop by **La Guingette** (☎ 02 40 75 88 96; 20 quai Marcel Broissard; mains €8.50-11.50; ☽ lunch & dinner), when locals congregate for board-game tournaments, French tapas, and a drink at the boat-shaped timber bar.

SELF-CATERING

Sardines are sold at street stalls throughout town between March and November.

Marché de Talensac (rue Talensac; 🕑 7.30am-1pm Tue-Sun) Stock up on picnic supplies at this huge marketplace.

Monoprix supermarket (2 rue du Calvaire; 🕑 9am-9pm Mon-Sat)

Galeries Lafayette department store (rue de la Marne) This massive store has a basement food section open 9am to 7.30pm Monday to Saturday.

Drinking

Nantes has no shortage of lively spots for a drink.

La Maison (☎ 02 40 37 04 12; 4 rue Lebrun; 🕑 3pm-2am) You have to see to believe this trip of a place, decorated room by room like a home furnished in *bad* 1970s taste, playing (what else?) house music – but not so loud that you can't chat with the local students who make it their home away from home.

Café Cult (☎ 02 40 47 18 49; www.lecult.com in French; place du Change; mains €11.50-14.50; 🕑 2pm-2am Mon & Sat, noon-2am Tue-Fri) Squeezed inside a dark, smoky half-timbered house in the centre of town, and hung with local art, this bohemian place draws a student crowd.

Le Bar du Coin (☎ 02 40 47 55 05; 21 rue de la Juiverie; 🕑 11am-2am Apr-Oct, closed Sun Nov-Mar) This 'corner bar' in the heart of the medieval Bouffay quarter is where most Nantais nights out get started.

Entertainment

Le Mois Nantais, available at the tourist office and tobacconists, has day-by-day details of cultural events. Good what's-on websites include www.leboost.com (in French). Tickets for most events are available across the hall from the tourist office at the **FNAC billeterie** (ticket outlet; ☎ 02 51 72 47 23; 🕑 10am-8pm Mon-Sat).

Le Lieu Unique (☎ 02 40 12 14 34; www.lelieu unique.com in French; 2 rue de la Biscuiterie) Within the one-time Lu biscuit factory (crowned by a replica of its original tower), this former artists' squat is the venue for dance and theatre performances, eclectic and electronic music, philosophical sessions and contemporary art. Also incorporated in these industrial chic premises is an always-busy restaurant (menus €8.50-15, open lunch Monday to Friday and dinner Tuesday to Saturday from July to August, plus lunch Monday to Saturday and dinner Tuesday to Saturday September to June) and a polished concrete bar.

Beautifully refurbished, **Théâtre Graslin** (☎ 02 40 69 77 18; place Graslin) is the home of the Nantes Opera.

In a small turquoise-coloured space with a quirky collection of stainless steel and brass clocks (none of which show the same time), **Spoutnik** (☎ 02 40 47 65 37; 6 allée du port Maillard; 🕑 5pm-2am Mon-Sat) has regular live independent rock as well as 40 different flavours of vodka and good tap beer.

The six-screen **Cinéma Katorza** (☎ 02 51 84 90 60; 3 rue Corneille) shows nondubbed films.

Shopping

Debotte Gautier (☎ 02 40 48 18 16; 9 rue de la Fosse; 🕑 9am-7.15pm Tue-Sat) When Jules Verne was a young boy he too was awed by this beautiful chocolate shop decorated with chandeliers, marble floors and a circular velvet banquette where Nantais have waited while their orders were filled since 1823. Handmade specialities include *mascarons* (finely ground chocolates encased in a dark chocolate shell) and a rainbow of hard-boiled sweets.

Getting There & Away

AIR

Aéroport International Nantes-Atlantique (☎ 02 40 84 80 00; www.nantes.aeroport.fr) is 12km southeast of town.

BUS

The southbound **bus station** (☎ 08 25 08 71 56), across from 13 allée de la Maison Rouge, is used by CTA buses serving areas of the Loire-Atlantique *département* south of the Loire River.

The northbound **bus office** (☎ 08 25 08 71 56; 1 allée Duquesne, cours des 50 Otages), run by Cariane Atlantique, handles buses to destinations north of the Loire.

Eurolines (☎ 02 51 72 02 03; allée de la Maison Rouge; 🕑 9.30am-12.30pm & 1.30-6pm Mon-Fri, 9.30am-12.30pm & 1.30-6pm Sat) has an office in town.

CAR

Budget, Europcar and Hertz are right outside the train station's southern entrance.

TRAIN

The **train station** (☎ 36 35; 27 blvd de Stalingrad) is well connected to most of the country.

Destinations include Paris' Gare Montparnasse (€49.10 to €61.40, 2¼ hours, 15 to 20 daily), Bordeaux (€37, four hours, three or four daily) and La Rochelle (€21, 1¾ hours, three or four daily).

Tickets and information are also available at the **SNCF ticket office** (La Bourse, 12 place de la Bourse; ⏰ 10am-7pm Mon, 9am-7pm Tue-Sat) in the city centre.

Getting Around
TO/FROM THE AIRPORT
The public bus TAN-Air links the airport with the Gare Centrale bus/tram hub and the train station's southern entrance (€6, 20 minutes) from about 5.30am until 9pm. For information call **Allotan** (☎ 08 10 44 44 44).

BUS & TRAM
The **TAN network** (☎ 08 01 44 44 44; www.tan.fr in French) includes three modern tram lines that intersect at the Gare Centrale (Commerce), the main bus/tram transfer point. Buses run from 7.15am to 9pm. Night services continue until 12.30am. At press time, planning was under way for a 'Busway' that will be the first of its kind in France – check with the tourist office or TAN for updates.

Bus/tram tickets can be individually purchased (€1.20) from bus (but not tram) drivers and at tram stop ticket machines. They're valid for one hour after being time-stamped. A *ticket journalier*, good for 24 hours, costs €3.30; time-stamp it only the first time you use it.

CAR & MOTORCYCLE
For a full list of free and pay parking areas in Nantes – including access maps – click on www.nantesmetropole.fr/67868597/0/fiche_pagelibre (in French) .

TAXI
To order a taxi, call ☎ 02 40 69 22 22.

AROUND NANTES
Venture across the river from Nantes city centre (see the boxed text, p657), or further afield to the classic seaside town of **Le Croisic** (population 4300). Centred on a pretty, half-timbered fishing harbour, where shrimp, lobster, crab, scallop and sea bass are unloaded, adjacent to the old town, Le Croisic has retained an authentic air. The **tourist office** (☎ 02 40 23 00 70; www.ot-lecroisic.com; place du 18 Juin

1940; ⏰ 9am-1pm & 2-7pm Mon-Sat, 10am-1pm & 3-5pm Sun May-Sep, 9am-12.30pm & 2-6.30pm Tue-Sat Oct-Apr) is in a little cottage to the right as you exit the train station, just east of the harbour.

From Nantes, an all-day *MétrOcéane* (www.metroceane.fr in French) train ticket to Le Croisic costs €14.60 and includes public transport throughout Nantes. En route to Le Croisic, the same ticket allows you to stop at **St-Nazaire** (population 68,600), where cruise ships – including the recent *Queen Mary II* – are built and where Airbus has a factory that can be toured. The train also stops at the glamorous *belle époque* resort of **La Baule** (population 16,400), purportedly boasting Europe's largest beach.

TGVs also run directly from Paris' Gare Montparnasse to Le Croisic (€57.70, 3¼ hours).

CENTRAL ATLANTIC COAST

The Poitou-Charentes region, midway along the Atlantic Coast, scoops a potpourri of attractions – from the history-rich capital, Poitiers, to the portside panache of La Rochelle, the languid beaches of Île de Ré, and the eponymous home of Cognac.

POITIERS
pop 87,000
Inland from the coast, the cobblestone city of Poitiers is packed with history. Founded by the Pictones, a Gaulish tribe, it is the former capital of Poitou, the region governed by the Counts of Poitiers in the Middle Ages. A pivotal turning point came in AD 732, when somewhere near Poitiers (the exact site is not known) the cavalry of Charles Martel defeated the Muslim forces of Abd ar-Rahman, governor of Córdoba, thus ending Muslim attempts to conquer France. The Romans built up the city, and there are numerous reminders still evident, such as extensive ruins uncovered when the large Cordeliers shopping centre was built in the town centre about a decade ago. The city's remarkable Romanesque churches are in part a legacy of Eleanor of Aquitaine's financial support.

Poitiers has one of the oldest universities in the country, first established in 1432 and today a linchpin of this lively city.

Orientation

The train station is about 600m downhill (west) from the old city, which begins just north of Poitiers' main square, place du Maréchal Leclerc, and stretches northeast to Église Notre Dame la Grande. Rue Carnot heads south from place du Maréchal Leclerc.

Information

Banks can be found around place du Maréchal Leclerc.

Post Office (21 rue des Écossais) Has a Cyberposte and changes money.

Tourist Office (☎ 05 49 41 21 24; www.ot-poitiers .fr; 45 place Charles de Gaulle; ☯ 10am-11pm Mon-Sat, 10am-6pm & 7-11pm Sun 21 Jun–Aug, 10am-10pm Mon-Sat, 10am-6pm & 7-10pm Sun 1-17 Sep, 10am-6pm Mon-Sat 18 Sep-20 Jun) Near Église Notre Dame.

Virtual 86 (☎ 05 49 53 63 42; 13 rue Magenta; per 15min/1hr €0.50/2; ☯ 10am-2am)

Sights

Strolling Poitiers' history-trodden streets is the best way to get a feel for the city's past. Along the pavements, red, yellow and blue lines correspond with three **self-guided walking tours** of the city detailed on a free city map handed out by the tourist office.

Every evening from 21 June to 17 September, spectacular colours are cinematically projected onto the west façade of the Romanesque **Église Notre Dame la Grande** (place Charles de Gaulle; ☯ 8.30am-7pm Mon-Sat, 2-7pm Sun). The earliest parts of the church date from the 11th century; three of the five choir chapels were added in the 15th century, with the six chapels along the northern wall of the nave added in the 16th century. The only original frescoes are the faint 12th- or 13th-century works that adorn the U-shaped dome above the choir.

Within today's Palais de Justice (law courts), at the northeastern end of rue Gambetta, the vast, partly 13th-century great hall, **Salle des Pas-Perdus** (☯ 8.45am-6pm Mon-Fri), flanked by three huge fireplaces, is a not-so-subtle reminder of the building's history as the former palace of the counts of Poitou and the dukes of Aquitaine.

About 500m east of Église Notre Dame la Grande, the Gothic-style **Cathédrale St-Pierre** (rue de la Cathédrale; ☯ 8am-6pm) was built between 1162 and 1271; the west façade and the towers date from the 14th and 15th centuries. At the far end of the choir, the 13th-century stained-glass window illustrating the Crucifixion and the Ascension is one of the oldest in France.

Constructed in the 4th and 6th centuries on Roman foundations, **Baptistère St-Jean** (rue Jean Jaurès; adult/child €1/0.50; ☯ 10.30am-12.30pm & 3-6pm Wed-Mon Apr-Oct, 2.30-4.30pm Wed-Mon Nov-Mar), 100m south of the cathedral, was redecorated in the 10th century and used as a parish church. The octagonal hole under the frescoes was used for total-immersion baptisms, practised until the 7th century.

Poitou's history from prehistoric times to the 19th century is detailed at the **Musée Ste-Croix** (☎ 05 49 41 07 53; www.musees-poitiers.org in French; 3 rue Jean Jaurès; adult/child €3.70/free; ☯ 1.15-6pm Mon, 10am-noon & 1.15-6pm Tue-Fri, 10am-noon & 2-6pm Sat & Sun Jun-Sep, to 5pm Mon-Fri & afternoons Sat & Sun Oct-May). Admission here is also good for the **Musée Rupert de Chièvre** (☎ 05 49 41 07 53; 9 rue Victor Hugo; ☯ same hr as Musée Ste-Croix), which displays 19th-century furniture, paintings and art.

Sleeping

Poitiers has a handful of atmospheric, well-located hotels.

Hôtel Central (☎ 05 49 01 79 79; www.centralho tel86.com in French; 35 place du Maréchal Leclerc; d €34-51) Facing directly onto place du Maréchal at the southern edge of this charming pedestrian district of half-timbered houses, this two-star place is a terrific little bargain. It has snug but sunlit rooms with showers or bathtubs, and a lift to save you and your suitcases from scaling its three storeys. Breakfast's €6.50.

Hôtel de l'Europe (☎ 05 49 88 12 00; www.hotel -europe-poitiers.com; 39 rue Carnot; d €49.50-79) Behind a dramatically recessed entrance, the main building of this elegant, very un-two-star-like hotel with good wheelchair access dates from 1710, with a sweeping staircase, oversized rooms and refined furnishings. The annexe has modern rooms for the same price.

Hôtel du Plat d'Étain (☎ 05 49 41 04 80; hoteld uplatdetain@wanadoo.fr; 7-9 rue du Plat d'Étain; d €28-62) Its location in a hidden little pedestrian backstreet half a block north of place du Maréchal Leclerc (through the arch next to the theatre) might appear peaceful, but it's next to a lively, late-opening bar, which is either a good or bad thing depending on your predilection for partying. Things are a bit quieter in the 3rd-floor attic rooms, which have sweeping views across the town.

Le Grand Hôtel (☎ 05 49 60 90 60; www.grandho telpoitiers.fr; 28 rue Carnot; s €65.50-68, d €80.50-83; 🖳) Poitiers' premier hotel lives up to its name. Faux Art Deco furnishings and fittings fill the public areas with character, and rooms are spacious and well equipped. Service comes with all the trimmings including a porter and a private, lock-up garage.

Eating & Drinking
Prime dining spots tend to be south of place du Maréchal Leclerc.

our pick La Serrurerie (☎ 05 49 41 05 14; 28 rue des Grandes Écoles; mains €11-16, weekend brunch €14.50; 🖳 8am-2am) In a fantastic space of mosaic tiles and steel balustrades showcasing local art and sculpture (plus an entire wall displaying cute retro toys), this vibrant bistro/bar is Poitiers' communal lounge/dining room. Its social scene peaks during the weekend brunches, where you have the option of a vegetarian-friendly version or the full post-hangover bacon-and-eggs works. A chalked blackboard menu lists specialities like *tournedos* (thich slices) of salmon, sensational pastas, and a *crème brûlée* you'll be dreaming about until your next visit.

Aux 40 Gourmands (☎ 05 49 37 01 37; 40 rue Carnot; mains €10.40-12.50, menus €14 & €16.50; 🖳 lunch & dinner Tue-Sat) Spread over a succession of skylit rooms painted in bright oranges and reds, this relaxed place has friendly staff and awesome *moules et frites* (mussels and fries); try them cooked with *crème fraîche* and *Pineau des Charentes* – a sweet white wine with a Cognac base that you can also order by the glass.

The covered market **Marché Notre Dame** (🖳 7am-1pm Tue-Sat) is right next to Église Notre Dame la Grande; the area out front hosts an open-air market from 7am to 1pm on Saturdays. About 200m to the south, the **Monoprix supermarket** (🖳 9am-7.30pm Mon-Sat) is across from 29 rue du Marché Notre Dame (behind the Palais de Justice).

You'll find the best bars and pubs one block north of place du Maréchal Leclerc along rue du Chaudron d'Or; and around place Notre Dame.

Getting There & Away
The **train station** (☎ 08 36 35 35 35; blvd du Grand Cerf) has direct links to Bordeaux (€30.30,

1¾ hours), La Rochelle (€19.30, one hour and 20 minutes), Nantes (€24.40, 3¼ hours) and many other cities. TGV tickets from Paris' Gare Montparnasse (1½ hours, 12 daily) cost from €46.40.

AROUND POITIERS
Futuroscope
Piercing the countryside with gleaming domes, pods and towers, **Futuroscope** (☎ 05 49 49 30 80; www.futuroscope.com; Jaunay-Clan; adult 1/2 days €31/59, child under 16yr €24/44; 🖳 10am-10pm, closed Jan-early Feb) is a futuristic theme park with 22 whizz-bang attractions and lakeside laser and firework shows. Schedules change annually, as do many of the attractions. Most are motion seat setups that require a minimum height of 120cm, so it's not really ideal for littlies.

Highlights include **Digitalworld**, an action-packed 3-D trip, and a **Zoo Safari**, starring a giant robotic giraffe. At **Cosmos** you can board a spaceship for a journey through the solar system and beyond.

Films last four to 40 minutes and showcase the park's cinematic technological wizardry, so don't come expecting convincing acting or intelligent plots. Free infrared headsets provide soundtracks in English, German and Spanish.

Allow at least five hours to see the major attractions; two days to see everything.

Futuroscope is 10km north of Poitiers in Jaunay-Clan (take exit No 28 off the A10). TGV trains link the park's TGV station with cities including Paris (from €46.40, 1½ hours) and Bordeaux (€31.20, 1¾ hours).

Local **STP buses** (☎ 05 49 44 66 88) 9, 16 and 17 (€1.20, 30 minutes) link Futuroscope (Parc de Loisirs stop) with Poitiers' train station (the stop in front of Avis car rental); there are one to two buses an hour from 6.15am until 7.30pm or 9pm.

Marais Poitevin
The bird-filled wetlands of the Marais Poitevin (Poitevin marsh) fall within the protected Parc Naturel Interrégional du Marais Poitevin. A maze of green waterways, this Venise Verte (Green Venice) covers 80,000 hectares of wet and drained marsh, interspersed with villages and woods.

Canoeing and **boating** are ideal for exploring the area (except in hot weather when the marshes dry up). To rent a boat or bicycle, or to organise *gîte* (guesthouse) and *chambre d'hôte* (B&B) accommodation, contact **Venise Verte Loisirs** (☎ 05 49 35 43 34; www.veniseverteloisirs .fr in French; 10 chemin du Charret, Arçais). Poitiers' **tourist office** (☎ 05 49 41 21 24; www.ot-poitiers.fr; 45 place Charles de Gaulle) also has information.

LA ROCHELLE

pop 80,000

Known as La Ville Blanche ('the white city'), La Rochelle's luminous limestone façades are topped by 14th- and 15th-century towers glowing white in the bright coastal sunlight.

The arcaded walkways; half-timbered houses protected from the salt air by slate tiles; and ghoulish protruding gargoyles are rich reminders of La Rochelle's seafaring past. One of France's foremost seaports from the 14th to 17th centuries, early French settlers in Canada, including the founders of Montreal, set sail from here in the 17th century. La Rochelle's cobblestone streets are fashioned in part by ships' ballast brought back across the Atlantic.

La Rochelle might be called the white city, but it's also commendably green, with innovative public transport and open spaces. It's kid-friendly too, with lots of activities for little visitors.

Southwest of the old city, the late 20th-century district of Les Minimes was built on reclaimed land, and now has one of the largest marinas in the country. Unlike the Med with its motor cruisers, the 3500 moorings here are mostly used by yachts that fill the harbour with billowing spinnakers.

Orientation

La Rochelle is centred on its vibrant Vieux Port (old port). The old city unfolds to its north. To the southeast, the train station is linked to the Vieux Port by the 500m-long av du Général de Gaulle, with the tourist office tucked about halfway between in a quarter of brightly painted wooden buildings known as Le Gabut. Place du Marché and place de Verdun are at the northern edge of the old city. Les Minimes is 3km southwest of the city centre.

Information

BOOKSHOPS

Planète Bleue (☎ 05 46 34 23 23; 54 rue St-Nicolas; ☽ 10am-noon & 2-7pm Mon-Sat)

EMERGENCY

Hospital (☎ 05 46 45 50 50; fur du Dr Schweitzer) Has an emergency room.
Police Station (Hôtel de Police; ☎ 05 46 51 36 36; 2 place de Verdun; ☽ 24hr)

INTERNET ACCESS

Akromicro (☎ 05 46 34 07 94; rue de l'Aimable Nanette; per hr €2; ☽ 10am-midnight) Right behind the tourist office.

MONEY

There are a number of banks on rue du Palais in the old city.

POST

Post Office (6 rue de l'Hôtel de Ville) Exchange services and a Cyberposte.

TOURIST INFORMATION

Tourist Office (☎ 05 46 41 14 68; larochelle-tourisme .com or www.ville-larochelle.fr; Le Gabut; ☽ 9am-8pm Mon-Sat, 11am-5.30pm Sun Jul & Aug, 9am-7pm Mon-Sat, 11am-5pm Sun Jun & Sep, 10am-12.30pm & 1.30-6pm Mon-Sat, 10am-1pm Sun Oct-May) Sells the *Pass Rochelais*, offering various discounts for public transport, sights and activities.

Sights & Activities

TOWERS

The three defensive **towers** (☎ 05 46 34 11 81; admission per tower adult/18-25 yr/child €4.60/3.10/free; ☽ 10am-7pm Jul & Aug, 10am-12.30pm & 2-6.30pm 15 May-Jun & 1-15 Sep, 10am-12.30pm & 2-5.30pm Tue-Sun Oct-May) can be visited individually, or on a combined ticket (€10/6.50/free).

To protect the harbour at night in times of war, an enormous chain was raised between the two 14th-century stone towers at the harbour entrance, giving rise to the name of **Tour de la Chaîne** ('chain tower'). There are some informative exhibits on the history of the local Protestant community, and superb views from the top.

Across the harbour it's also possible to climb the 36m-high, pentagonal **Tour St-Nicolas**.

So named because of its role as the harbour's lighthouse (lit by an enormous candle), and one of the oldest of its kind in the world, the conical 15th-century **Tour de la Lanterne** is also referred to as Tour des Quatre Sergents in memory of four local sergeants held here (for plotting to overthrow the newly reinstated monarchy) before their

LA ROCHELLE

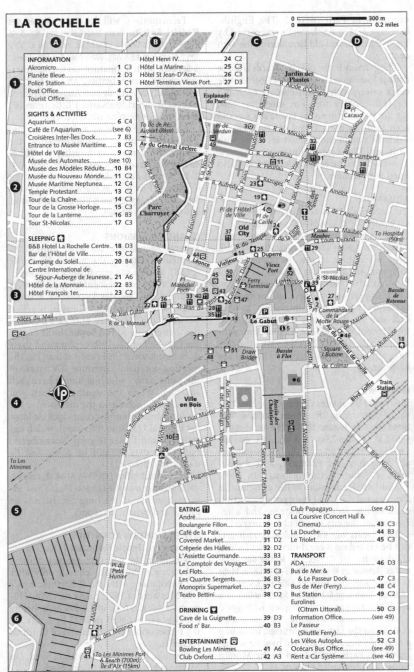

0 | 300 m
0 | 0.2 miles

INFORMATION
Akromicro............................. 1 C3
Planète Bleue........................ 2 D3
Police Station........................ 3 C1
Post Office............................ 4 C2
Tourist Office........................ 5 C3

SIGHTS & ACTIVITIES
Aquarium.............................. 6 C4
Café de l'Aquarium................(see 6)
Croisières Inter-Îles Dock....... 7 B3
Entrance to Musée Maritime.... 8 C5
Hôtel de Ville....................... 9 C2
Musée des Automates...........(see 10)
Musée des Modèles Réduits..... 10 B4
Musée du Nouveau Monde..... 11 C2
Musée Maritime Neptunea..... 12 C4
Temple Protestant.................. 13 C2
Tour de la Chaîne.................. 14 C3
Tour de la Grosse Horloge...... 15 C3
Tour de la Lanterne............... 16 B3
Tour St-Nicolas..................... 17 C3

SLEEPING
B&B Hôtel La Rochelle Centre.. 18 D3
Bar de l'Hôtel de Ville............ 19 C2
Camping du Soleil.................. 20 B4
Centre International de
  Séjour-Auberge de Jeunesse.. 21 A6
Hôtel de la Monnaie............... 22 B3
Hôtel François 1er.................. 23 C2

Hôtel Henri IV....................... 24 C2
Hôtel La Marine.................... 25 C3
Hôtel St Jean-D'Acre............. 26 C3
Hôtel Terminus Vieux Port...... 27 D3

EATING
André.................................. 28 C3
Boulangerie Fillon................. 29 D3
Café de la Paix..................... 30 C2
Covered Market..................... 31 D2
Crêperie des Halles................ 32 D2
L'Assiette Gourmande............ 33 B3
Le Comptoir des Voyages....... 34 B3
Les Flots.............................. 35 C3
Les Quartre Sergents.............. 36 B3
Monoprix Supermarket........... 37 C3
Teatro Bettini....................... 38 D2

DRINKING
Cave de la Guignette.............. 39 D3
Food n' Bar........................... 40 B3

ENTERTAINMENT
Bowling Les Minimes.............. 41 A6
Club Oxford.......................... 42 A3

Club Papagayo.....................(see 42)
La Coursive (Concert Hall &
  Cinema)............................ 43 C3
La Douche............................ 44 B3
Le Triolet............................. 45 C3

TRANSPORT
ADA..................................... 46 D3
Bus de Mer &
  & Le Passeur Dock.............. 47 C3
Bus de Mer (Ferry)................ 48 C2
Bus Station........................... 49 C2
Eurolines
  (Citram Littoral)................. 50 C3
Information Office.................(see 49)
Le Passeur
  (Shuttle Ferry)....................51 C4
Les Vélos Autoplus................ 52 C3
Océcars Bus Office...............(see 49)
Rent a Car Système...............(see 46)

ATLANTIC COAST

execution in Paris in 1822. The English-language graffiti on the walls was carved by English privateers held here during the 18th century.

The gateway to the old city, **Tour de la Grosse Horloge** (quai Duperré) is a steadfast Gothic-style clock tower, with a 14th-century base and an 18th-century top. For safety reasons, it's not possible to enter. The tower's grand arch leads to the arcaded **rue du Palais**, La Rochelle's main shopping street, lined with 17th- and 18th-century shipowners' homes. Two blocks to the east, **rue des Merciers** is also lined with arcades.

AQUARIUM

La Rochelle's 21st-century, state-of-the-art **aquarium** (☎ 05 46 34 00 00; adult/student & child €12.50/9.50, with audioguide €16/13; ☼ 9am-11pm Jul & Aug, to 8pm Apr-Jun & Sep, 10am-8pm Oct-Mar) with good wheelchair access is a fantastic way to spend an afternoon. As well as lots of local Atlantic fish and sea creatures, you can also peer at some spectacular tropical fish and sea flora, and ominous 2.7m-long bull sharks. While you're here, head up to the rooftop Café de l'Aquarium with mains from €10 to €20. Open late, the cafe has panoramic views over the city and the harbour.

MUSEUMS

Moored at Bassin des Chalutiers are the two ships comprising the **Musée Maritime Neptunea** (Maritime Museum; ☎ 05 46 28 03 00; adult/child €7.60/5.30; ☼ 10am-7.30pm Jul & Aug, until 6.30pm Apr-Jun & Sep, 2-6.30pm Oct-Mar): the meteorological research vessel *France 1*, and *Angoumois*, a *chalutier* (fishing boat). In 2008, a land-based extension of the museum on the adjacent dock will incorporate a section dedicated to Jacques Cousteau, and a re-creation of the city's ancient fish market.

Two treats for kids (and kids-at-heart) can be visited on a combined ticket (adult/child under 10 €11/6.50). **Musée des Automates** (Automation Museum; ☎ 05 46 41 68 08; 14 rue La Désirée; adult/child 3-10yr €7.50/5; ☼ 9.30am-7pm Jul & Aug, 10am-noon & 2-6pm Jan-Jun & Sep-Dec) is a small theme-park style display with good wheelchair access showing 300 automated dolls from the last two centuries, including a near-life-size re-creation of bygone Montmartre in Paris, right down to the Moulin Rouge and funicular railway.

Trainspotters will love the **Musée des Modèles Réduits** (Scale Model Museum; ☎ 05 46 41 64 51; rue La Désirée; adult/child under 10yr €7.50/5; ☼ 9.30am-7pm Jul & Aug, 10am-noon & 2-6pm Jan-Jun & Sep-Dec), with miniature cars, computer-automated naval battles, and a tootling model railway. In July and August, children under 10 can ride aboard a little train (€2 train only or €1 plus entrance fee).

La Rochelle's role as a departure point for North America is interpreted at the 18th-century mansion housing the **Musée du Nouveau Monde** (New World Museum; ☎ 05 46 41 46 50; 10 rue Fleuriau; adult/child under 18yr €3.50/free; ☼ 10am-12.30pm & 2-6pm Mon & Wed-Sat, 2.30-6pm Sun Apr-Sep, 9.30am-12.30pm & 1.30-5pm Mon & Wed-Fri, 2.30-6pm Sat & Sun Oct-Mar).

ISLAND EXCURSIONS

Several islands are scattered around La Rochelle, including the nearby Île de Ré (p668), as well as a trio further offshore.

The car-free, crescent-shaped **Île d'Aix** (pronounced 'eel dex'), 16km due south of La Rochelle, has some blissful beaches. Between the Île d'Aix and **Île d'Oléron** is the fortress-island **Fort Boyard**, built during the first half of the 19th century and these days best known (in France at least) as the location for the 'adventure' TV show of the same name, which is filmed here each summer. When the weather's clear, you can see La Rochelle in the distance.

Companies offering cruises include **Inter-Îles** (☎ 08 25 13 55 00; cours des Dames), which has sailings from Easter to early November to Fort Boyard (€18) and Île d'Aix and Île d'Oléron (each €23).

The **tourist office** (☎ 05 46 41 14 68; larochelle-tourisme.com or www.ville-larochelle.fr) also has information about reaching the islands by public and private transport.

OTHER SIGHTS & ACTIVITIES

The austere **Temple Protestant** (2 rue St-Michel) was built in the late 17th century, though it became a Protestant church only after the Revolution. After the St Bartholomew's Day Massacre of 1572, many surviving Huguenots took refuge in La Rochelle before the city was besieged in 1627 by Louis XIII's forces under the command of Cardinal Richelieu.

If you're looking for a patch of sand, Les Minimes has a small artificial **beach**.

Tours

Flanked by a 15th-century Flamboyant Gothic wall and stunning 17th-century Renaissance-style courtyard, the **Hôtel de Ville** (Town Hall; ☎ 05 46 41 14 68; place de l'Hôtel de Ville) has guided tours in French (€3.50/1.50 for adult/child) at 3pm on weekends and school holidays; at 3pm daily in June and September; and, 3pm and 4pm daily in July and August.

In summer, **city tours** (☎ 05 46 41 14 68) are run in French, including a **horse-drawn carriage tour** (adult/child €9/6) and **night tours** (adult/child €10/7) led by characters in costume operate; reservations are essential.

Festivals & Events

Festival International du Film (☎ 01 48 06 16 66, 05 46 51 54 00) Silent classics as well as new films in original languages are screened during the 10-day film festival in early July.

Francofolies (☎ 05 46 28 28 28; www.francofolies.fr in French) A cutting-edge, contemporary music and performing arts festival held over six days in mid-July.

Jazz Festival (☎ 05 46 27 11 19) October sees jazz fans jive to La Rochelle's jazz festival, which is themed each year according to an artist or genre.

Sleeping

BUDGET

During the warmer months, dozens of camp sites open up (and fill up just as quickly) around La Rochelle and Île de Ré. The tourist office has a list of camping grounds outside the town. The closest to the city is **Camping du Soleil** (☎ 05 46 44 42 53; av Michel Crepeau; adult/tent €8.50/8.50; ⊙ late Jun-late Sep). Take bus 10.

Centre International de Séjour-Auberge de Jeunesse (☎ 05 46 44 43 11; www.fuaj-aj-larochelle.fr.st in French; av des Minimes; dm incl breakfast €14-16, tw incl breakfast €34; ⊙ closed Christmas period) This popular hostel is 2km southwest of the train station in Les Minimes. A membership card is compulsory for stays of more than one night.

B&B Hotel La Rochelle Centre (☎ 08 92 78 80 48; www.hotelbb.com; 140 blvd Joffre; s & d €36-47, tr & q €51-63) Not *a* B&B, but part of the ubiquitous B&B chain popping up all over France and Germany. Sure, it's formulaic, but the extra-spacious tiled rooms have funky touches like moulded lime-green chairs, as well as phones and TVs; there's a lift; and best of all, it's just 150m from the train

station, and an easy five-minute stroll to the Vieux Port.

Bar de l'Hôtel de Ville (☎ 05 46 41 30 25; 5 rue St-Yon; d from €47, with shared bathroom €35) This bustling place attached to the Bar de l'Hôtel de Ville has just nine rooms. Don't expect luxury – rooms are super-simple, but they offer great value for money given the price and proximity to the Vieux Port and old town.

MIDRANGE

Hôtel Terminus Vieux Port (☎ 05 46 50 69 69; www.tourisme-francais.com/hotel/terminus; 7 rue de la Fabrique; d €46-68) Bedecked with navy blue awnings, this welcoming hotel with good wheelchair access has 32 comfortable, freshly renovated rooms, each whimsically named after one of the islands offshore from La Rochelle. The pick are the bright, sun-filled rooms at the front. There's also a cheery in-house bar.

Hôtel La Marine (☎ 05 46 50 51 63; www.hotel-marine.com in French; 30 quai Duperré; d €55-95; ⊠) For captivating views of La Rochelle's iconic towers, try for rooms 1, 6, 9 or 13 in this exquisite boutique hotel, occupying a superb position in the northwest corner of the Vieux Port. Each of the 13 rooms is individually decorated with cool neutral-toned décor and smart designer furniture.

Hôtel Henri IV (☎ 05 46 41 25 79; henriIV@wanadoo.fr; 31 rue des Gentilshommes; d €58-80, with shared bathroom €44) Housed in a classified late-16th-century building, even the cheapies among the Hôtel Henri IV's 24 rooms have satellite TVs. It's smack-bang in the middle of the pedestrianised old city, a block back from the Vieux Port, but if you're arriving with wheels, you'll find public parking 500m away.

Hôtel François 1er (☎ 05 46 41 28 46; www.hotelfrancois1er.fr; 15 rue Bazoges; d €60-106) A number of 15th- and 16th-century French kings have stayed in this building that's set back behind a cobbled courtyard. The 40 rooms are atmospheric, if a bit heavy-handed with the heritage décor, and have good wheelchair access. King-size rooms cost proportionately more. On-site private parking makes it a handy option if you're driving.

Hôtel St Jean-D'Acre (☎ 05 46 41 73 33; www.hotel-la-rochelle.com; 4 place de la Chaîne; d €85-135; ⊠ ▦) A good bet for business travellers, this light-filled hotel is in an epicentral location with lush views of the port and La Rochelle's definitive towers. All 60 airy, whitewashed rooms are soothingly decorated and equipped with in-room kettles, and there's free wi-fi in the lobby and good access for wheelchairs as well as a power buffet breakfast (€10).

Hôtel de la Monnaie (☎ 05 46 50 65 65; www .hotel-monnaie.com; 3 rue de la Monnaie; d €98-112; 🖳) The rooms at the three-star Hôtel de la Monnaie are more up-to-the-minute than the vine-draped 17th-century floodlit façade and statue-studded courtyard suggest, and come with all mod cons and good wheelchair access. From the hotel it's a mere one block to the Tour de la Lanterne and Vieux Port.

Eating

Most restaurants offer a kids' menu for around €8.

The port has a plethora of restaurants and cafés, especially on the northern side. In summer, the quays in front of the Vieux Port are closed to traffic from 8pm to midnight Monday to Saturday and 2pm to midnight on Sunday, giving it the ambience of a giant street party (and saving you from dining amid the traffic fumes).

Away from the tourist crowds, locals' favoured dining areas are rue St-Jean du Pérot and the streets surrounding place du Marché.

Teatro Bettini (☎ 05 46 41 07 03; 3 rue Thiers; mains from €9.50; 🕑 lunch & dinner Tue-Sat) Combining a strong Italian influence with an even stronger Rochelais spirit (the owner's likeness appears in the Michelangelo paintings adorning the walls), fare at this decades-old, much-loved restaurant includes a hearty lasagne and seafood.

Café de la Paix (☎ 05 46 41 39 79; 54 rue Chaudrier; mains €11-20; 🕑 7am-10pm Mon-Sat) A visual feast as much as a dining one, this *belle époque* brasserie-bar serves up traditional cuisine including beef, duck, foie gras and fish, as well as bountiful breakfasts and afternoon teas amid the splendour of soaring, lavishly painted ceilings and gold-edged arched mirrors.

Le Comptoir des Voyages (☎ 05 46 50 62 60; www.coutanceau.com; 22 rue St-Jean du Perot; menu €26; 🕑 lunch & dinner) This chic place done out with rattan chairs, palms and red walls takes you on a stylish world tour of international flavours, infusing regional produce cooked according to traditional

techniques under the direction of chef Grégory Coutanceau, and accompanied by a global wine list.

Les Flots (☎ 05 46 41 32 51; 1 rue de la Chaîne; menus €24 & €79; 🕑 lunch & dinner) You'll feel like you're floating in the water at this place by the Tour de la Chaîne, with fabulous port views and sunshine streaming in through timber-framed windows. Another string in Grégory Coutanceau's bow (he also has several other restaurants, and a catering sideline), this place is especially renowned for its stylishly presented seafood.

André (☎ 05 46 41 28 24; www.bar-andre.com; 8 place de la Chaîne; mains €15-30; 🕑 noon-4pm & 7pm-midnight) A legend in its own time, this place first opened in the 1950s as a small seafood café; as its popularity grew, André began buying adjacent shops. There's now a maze of interconnecting rooms, each with its own individual ambience (like a port-holed cabin) but all with the same menu of fish caught the night before. Many people swear it's the best seafood restaurant in France. And they may just be right.

Also recommended:

Crêperie des Halles (☎ 05 46 27 93 97; 1 rue des Cloutiers; dishes €5-8; 🕑 lunch & dinner Mon-Sat) Cosy, convivial *crêperie* tucked behind the covered market serving sweet *crêpes* and savoury *galettes* at equally convivial prices.

L'Assiette Gourmande (☎ 05 46 52 07 98; 39 rue St-Jean du Pérot; menus €19-38; 🕑 dinner Mon-Sat) Sleek new hot spot serving traditional cuisine.

Les Quartre Sergents (☎ 05 46 41 35 80; 49 rue St-Jean du Pérot; menus €15.20-37; 🕑 lunch & dinner) White tableclothed elegance and gastronomic French fare.

SELF-CATERING

The lively, 19th-century **covered market** (place du Marché; 🕑 7am-1pm) seethes with stallholders selling fresh fruit and vegetables, fish splayed on beds of ice, and just-killed meat.

In the old city you can pick up staples at **Monoprix supermarket** (30-36 rue du Palais; 🕑 8.30am-8pm Mon-Sat) and freshly baked breads and pastries at **Boulangerie Fillon** (18 quai Louis Durand; 🕑 6am-9pm Mon & Thu-Sat, 6am-8pm Tue, 6am-1pm Sun).

Drinking

Cave de la Guignette (☎ 05 46 41 05 75; 8 rue St-Nicolas; 🕑 4-8pm Mon, 10am-1pm & 4-8pm Tue & Wed, 10am-1pm & 3-8pm Thu-Sat) Keep your cool on a hot summer's afternoon with a glass of *Guignette* (white wine with tiny bubbles, flavoured with natural fresh fruit) at this young, busy, vivacious place.

Food n' Bar (☎ 05 46 52 26 69; 35 rue St-Jean du Pérot; menu €29; ☺ lunch & dinner) Hipsters head to this ultracontemporary new restaurant/lounge bar of streamlined metal, and ultralow UV-style lights in subtly changing shades of pink, blue, red and green, to quaff on cocktails, champagne and nouvelle cuisine (no, you can't see it under those lights, but hey, it tastes great).

Entertainment

The dual discos **Club Oxford & Club Papagayo** (☎ 05 46 41 51 81 for both; complexe de la Pergola; admission with 1 drink €10; ☺ 11pm-5am Wed-Mon, plus Tue Jul-Sep) are on the waterfront about 500m west of Tour de la Lanterne. Oxford spins techno and house; Papagayo goes for '70s and '80s, with karaoke on Sundays. Further east, **La Douche** (☎ 05 46 41 24 79; 14 rue Léonce; admission €10, free Thu & Sun; ☺ 11pm-5am Thu-Sun) draws a trendy gay and straight crowd.

Le Triolet (☎ 05 46 41 03 58; 8 rue des Carmes; ☺ 11pm-3am) has been *le* cool club for an older crowd since 1970.

For a change of pace from the café scene, have a spin at **Bowling Les Minimes** (☎ 05 46 45 40 40; rue Trinquette; bowling €4-6.30; ☺ 10am-2am Sun-Fri, to 3am Sat), in an alley next to the youth hostel.

The two auditoriums at **La Coursive** (☎ 05 46 51 54 00; 4 rue St-Jean du Pérot; tickets €21-28.50; ☺ late Aug–mid-Jul) host regular concerts and nondubbed art films.

Getting There & Away

AIR

La Rochelle Airport (☎ 05 46 42 30 26; www.larochelle.aeroport.fr in French), north of the city centre off the N237, has flights to destinations throughout France as well as London Stansted (with Ryanair) and Southampton and Birmingham (with Flybe) in the UK.

BUS

From the **bus station** (place de Verdun), **Océcars** (☎ 05 46 00 95 15) runs services to regional destinations. See p669 for details on bus services to Île de Ré.

Eurolines ticketing is handled by **Citram Littoral** (☎ 05 46 50 53 57; 30 cours des Dames; ☺ closed Sat afternoon, Mon morning & Sun).

CAR

Inexpensive car rental companies close to the train station include **ADA** (☎ 05 46 41 02 17; 19 av du Général de Gaulle) and **Rent A Car Système** (☎ 05 46 27 27 27; 27 av du Général de Gaulle).

TRAIN

The **train station** (☎ 08 36 35 35 35) is linked by TGV to Paris' Gare Montparnasse (€57.60, three hours, five or six direct daily). Other destinations served by regular direct trains include Nantes (€22.30, two hours), Poitiers (€19.30, 1½ hours) and Bordeaux (€23.80, two hours).

Getting Around

TO/FROM THE AIRPORT

Bus 7 runs from the airport to the town centre (€1.20); schedules are available at www.rtcr.fr in French. A taxi costs about €7 to €10.

BICYCLE

The city's distinctive yellow bikes can be rented at **Les Vélos Autoplus** (☎ 05 46 34 02 22; ☺ 9am-7pm Jul & Aug, 9am-12.30pm & 1.30-7pm May, Jun & Sep, 9.15am-12.15pm & 1.50-6pm Mon-Sat Oct-Apr). The first two hours are free; after that bikes cost €1 per hour. Child seats, but not bike helmets, are available. From May to September, bikes can also be picked up at the Vieux Port (across the street from 11 quai Valin).

BOAT

Le Passeur (tickets €0.60; ☺ 7.45am-8pm, to 10pm Apr & May, to midnight Jul & Aug) is a three-minute ferry service linking Tour de la Chaîne with the Avant Port. It runs when there are passengers – press the red button on the board at the top of the gangplank.

The ferry **Bus de Mer** (tickets €1.50, €1.70 Jul & Aug) links Tour de la Chaîne with Les Minimes (20 minutes). It runs daily April to September; at weekends and holidays only from October to March. Boats from the Vieux Port depart every hour on the hour (except at 1pm) from 10am to 7pm (every half-hour and until 11.30pm in July and August).

BUS

The innovative local transport system, **RTCR** (☎ 05 46 34 02 22), has a main bus hub and **information office** (place de Verdun; ☺ 7.30am-6.30pm

ATLANTIC COAST

Mon-Fri, 8am-6.30pm Sat). Most lines run until sometime between 7.15pm and 8pm. Tickets cost €1.20.

Bus 1 runs from place de Verdun to the train station, returning via the Vieux Port. Bus 10 links place de Verdun with the youth hostel and Les Minimes.

CAR & MOTORCYCLE

There is free parking on the side streets north of the concrete transport hub, place de Verdun; at esplanade des Parcs, which is a few hundred metres northwest of place de Verdun; and around Neptunea. There's an underground garage at place de Verdun.

TAXI

Call ☎ 05 46 41 55 55 or 05 46 34 02 22 for a taxi.

ÎLE DE RÉ

pop 16,000

Spanning 30km from its most easterly and westerly points, and just 5km at its widest section, Île de Ré is scattered with 10 villages of traditional green-shuttered, whitewashed buildings with red Spanish-tile roofs. Even with the advent of the bridge linking it to La Rochelle, Île de Ré retains an isolated islet feel. Its name is thought to originate from the Egyptian sun god, Ra, as, due to a combination of the offshore gulf stream and the westerly winds, the island gets more hours of sunshine than anywhere except the Mediterranean. The gentle rays and fine sand beaches make the island ideal for frolicking in summer (when hotels and camp sites fill *completely*).

Sights & Activities

On the northern coast about 12km from the toll bridge, the island's main town is the quaint fishing port, **St-Martin-de-Ré** (population 2500). Surrounded by 17th-century fortifications, you can stroll along most of the ramparts, but the **citadel** (1681), which has been a prison for over two centuries, is closed to the law-abiding public. St-Martin's **tourist office** (☎ 05 46 09 20 06; www.iledere .com; av Victor Bouthillier; ⏰ 10am-6pm Mon-Sat, 10am-noon Sun May-Sep, 10am-noon & 2-6pm Mon-Sat Oct-Apr) is about 100m on your right, across the port, from the Rébus stop.

The island's best **beaches** are along the southern edge, including unofficial

naturist beaches at Rivedoux Plage and La Couarde-sur-Mer; and around the western tip (northeast and southeast of Phare-des-Baleines). Many beaches are bordered by dunes that have been fenced off to protect the vegetation.

Crisscrossed by an extensive network of well-maintained bicycle paths, the pancake-flat island is ideal for **cycling**. A biking map is available at tourist offices. In summer practically every hamlet has somewhere to hire bikes. At Sablanceaux, from mid-June to mid-September, bikes can be hired at **Cycland's kiosk** (☎ 05 46 09 97 54) in one of the little buildings to the left as you come off the bridge. It's best to call one to two days in advance. The rest of the year, call **Cycland's office** (☎ 05 46 09 65 27) in La Flotte and it will deliver a bike to the bridge in about 15 minutes. Bicycles/mountain bikes/tandems cost €7/11.50/18 per day.

Sleeping & Eating

Île de Ré is an easy day trip from La Rochelle; however, if you want to spend longer on the island, each village has a tourist information office with lists of local accommodation options, including camp sites. Pitching your tent anywhere but designated camping areas is forbidden. St-Martin's **Camping Municipal** (☎ 05 46 09 21 96; camp sites €15; ⏰ mid-Feb–mid-Nov) has grassy, shaded sites.

Hôtel la Jetée (☎ 05 46 09 36 36; www.hotel-la jetee.com; 23 quai Georges Clemenceau; d €60-180 Oct-Jun, €78-99 Jul-Sep) Also in St-Martin, this pretty, portside hotel is a highly recommended three-star place of 30 modern rooms, wrapping around a peaceful, flowering courtyard; split-level mezzanine rooms offer extra space for families.

The town's bustling **Bistrot du Marin** (☎ 05 46 68 74 66; 10 quai Nicolas Baudin; mains €10-15) is a quaint, friendly bar-*bistrot* dishing up 'grandma's cooking'. Elegant seafood restaurants overlook the harbour's flotilla of boats.

Pick up beach picnic supplies at the **covered market** (rue Jean Jaurès; ⏰ 8.30am-1pm Tue-Sun) in St-Martin on the southern side of the port, or from a cluster of nearby food shops. You'll also find minimarts and restaurants dotted around the island's villages, although it's cheaper to buy food in La Rochelle.

Getting There & Away

The one-way automobile toll (paid on your way to the island) is €9 (a whopping €16.50 from mid-June to mid-September).

Year-round, excruciatingly slow buses run by **Rébus** (☎ 05 46 09 20 15) link La Rochelle (the train station car park, Tour de la Grosse Horloge and place de Verdun) with all the major towns on the island; the one-hour trip to St-Martin costs €5. The company also covers intra-island routes.

COGNAC

pop 20,000

On the banks of the River Charente amid vine-covered countryside, Cognac is known worldwide for the double-distilled spirit that bears its name, and on which the local economy thrives. Most visitors head here to visit the famous Cognac houses, but the town makes a picturesque stop even if you're not a fan of the local firewater.

Orientation

The train station is 1.5km south of the town centre, on av du Maréchal Leclerc. Heading about 1.5km north of the centre brings you to the River Charente; nearby are many major Cognac houses, which can be reached on foot. The central, café-ringed roundabout place François 1er, 200m northeast of the tourist office (follow rue du 14 Juillet), is linked to the river by blvd Denfert Rochereau.

Information

There are banks in the town centre, but nowhere to exchange foreign currency.

THE HOME OF COGNAC

According to local lore, divine intervention plays a role in the production of Cognac. Made of grape *eaux de vie* (brandies) of various vintages, Cognac is aged in oak barrels and blended by an experienced *maître de chai* (cellar master). Each year some 2% of the casks' volume – *la part des anges* (the angels' share) – evaporates through the pores in the wood, nourishing the tiny black mushrooms that thrive on the walls of Cognac warehouses.

The best-known **Cognac houses** are open to the public, and also run tours of their cellars and production facilities, ending with a tasting session. If you plan to visit more than one, ask for the free *Cognac Passeport* at the first house, for discounts on subsequent visits to Cognac houses around town. Opening times may be reduced in winter; in summer, in particular, foreign-language tours are often available. Year-round it's a good idea to reserve in advance.

■ **Camus** (☎ 05 45 32 28 28; www.camus.fr; 29 rue Marguerite de Navarre; adult €6-8, child free; ⏱ 2-6pm Mon, 10.30am-12.30pm & 2-6pm Tue-Sat) Located 250m northeast of the Jardin Public.

■ **Hennessey** (☎ 05 45 35 72 68; 8 rue Richonne; tours €7; ⏱ 10am-6pm Jun-Sep, 10am-5pm Mar-May & Oct-Dec, closed Jan & Feb) Situated 100m uphill from quai des Flamands. Tours include a film (in English) and a boat trip across the Charente to visit the cellars.

■ **Martell** (☎ 05 45 36 33 33; www.martell.com; place Édouard Martell; adult/child €5.50/3; ⏱ 10am-5pm Mon-Fri, noon-5pm Sat & Sun) Found 250m northwest of the tourist office; last entry is one hour prior to closing.

■ **Otard** (☎ 05 45 36 88 86; www.otard.com; 127 blvd Denfert Rochereau; adult/child €6/3; ⏱ tours 11am, 2pm, 3pm, 4pm, 5pm & 6pm Jul & Aug, 11am, 2pm, 3.30pm & 5pm Apr-Jun, Sep & Oct, 11am, 2pm & 4pm Mon-Fri Nov-Dec, tours sometimes possible by appointment Jan-Mar) Housed in the 1494 birthplace of King François I, the Château de Cognac, 650m north of place François 1er.

■ **Rémy Martin** (☎ 05 45 35 76 66; www.remy.com) Two locations: the **estate** (adult/child €12/6; ⏱ by appointment May-Sep), 4km southwest of town towards Pons; and, in town, the **house** (adult €20; ⏱ by appointment Mon-Fri year-round, plus Sun May-Sep), for intimate tastings in groups of eight.

The tourist office has a list of smaller Cognac houses near town; most close between October and mid-March.

To stock up, **Cognathèque** (☎ 05 45 82 43 31; 10 place Jean Monnet; ⏱ 9am-7pm), 100m from the tourist office, sells over 250 different Cognacs costing up to €1500 a bottle.

Cyber Espace (☎ 05 45 36 55 36; 68 blvd Denfert Rochereau; per 30min €0.75; ☯ 2-6pm Mon-Fri & 10am-noon Wed) Internet access.

Tourist Office (☎ 05 45 82 10 71; www.tourism -cognac.com; 16 rue du 14 Juillet; ☯ 9am-7pm Mon-Sat, 10am-4pm Sun Jul & Aug, 9.30am-5.30pm Mon-Sat May, Jun & Sep, 10am-5pm Mon-Sat Oct-Apr) Dispenses maps and a comprehensive English-language brochure covering the town's sights.

Sights & Activities

Half-timbered 15th- to 17th-century houses line the narrow streets of the **Vieille Ville** (old city), which sits snugly between the partly Romanesque **Église St-Léger** (rue Aristide Briand) and the river.

At the southern corner of the leafy **Jardin Public** (public park) is the **Musée de Cognac** (☎ 05 45 32 07 25; 48 blvd Denfert Rochereau; adult/student €5.50/2.25; ☯ 10am-6pm Apr-Oct, 2-5.30pm Wed-Mon Nov-Mar), showcasing the town's history. Admission here also covers **Le Musée des Arts du Cognac** (☎ 05 45 32 07 25; 48 blvd Denfert Rochereau; adult/student €5.50/2.25; ☯ 10am-6pm Apr-Oct, 2-5.30pm Tue-Sun Nov-Mar), taking you step by step through the production of Cognac and including exhibits on the vineyards, distilling process and barrel making (and a wonderful collection of bottles).

See the boxed text, p669, for information on tours and tastings.

Sleeping & Eating

Hôtel Le Cheval Blanc (☎ 05 45 82 09 55; www .hotel-chevalblanc.fr; 6 place Bayard; s/d €43/48; 🛋) Miniature bottles of Cognac in the vending machine satiate midnight cravings at this two-star place (with good wheelchair access) 100m west of the tourist office in the town centre, a block south of the old town. Although the rooms here aren't vast, they're immaculate, well-equipped and have wi-fi.

Hôtel Héritage (☎ 05 45 82 01 26; www.hherit age.com; 25 rue d'Angoulême; d €60) Renovated in striking shades of lime green, fuchsia and cherry red, this 17th-century mansion in the heart of town proves period elegance and contemporary style don't have to be mutually exclusive. Adjacent to the beautifully restored *belle époque* bar (open 8am to 9pm Tuesday to Saturday), the hotel's restaurant, La Belle Époque (open lunch and dinner Tuesday to Saturday) specialises in reintroducing long-lost regional classics (menus from €17).

La Boune Goule (☎ 05 45 82 06 37; 42 allée de la Corderie; menus €11.50 & €23; ☯ lunch & dinner summer, lunch & dinner Tue-Sat winter) In a central spot just across the square from the Martell complex, this cosy local favourite dishes up local Charentaise cuisine at reasonable prices.

La Ribaudière (☎ 05 45 81 30 54; www.laribaudiere .com in French; menus €35 & €70; ☯ lunch Tue-Sun, dinner Tue-Sat) For a real gourmet treat, head 10km out of town through the vineyards to Bourg-Charente, in the direction of Angoulême. Set among orchards overlooking the river, chef Thierry Verrat grows his own vegetables to accompany his exquisite Michelin-starred creations such as almond-encrusted filet of sole with a *mousseline* made from St-Jacques scallops. A taxi (☎ 05 45 82 14 31) from town costs about €15 one way.

You'll find an **Ecofrais supermarket** (32 place Bayard; ☯ 9am-12.30pm & 3-7.30pm Mon-Fri, 8am-noon Sun) opposite the post office. About 300m to the north of place François 1er, the **covered market** (57 blvd Denfert Rochereau; ☯ until 1pm) is just across from the Musée de Cognac.

Getting There & Away

Cognac's train station has regular daily trains to/from La Rochelle (€13.70, 1¼ hours).

LOWER ATLANTIC COAST

At the lower edge of the Atlantic Coast, the expansive Aquitaine region extends to the Dordogne in the east, and the Basque Country in the south. The gateway to the region's wealth of attractions, set amid glorious vine-ribboned countryside, is its capital, Bordeaux.

BORDEAUX

pop 229,500

The city long known as La Belle Au Bois Dormant (Sleeping Beauty) is well and truly awake after years of slumber. The turn of the millennium was a major turning point for Bordeaux, when the former mayor, controversial ex-Prime Minister Alain Juppé, roused this graceful city, pedestrianising its boulevards, restoring its neoclassical architecture, and implementing a high-tech public transport system. These days, bolstered by its high-spirited university student population, La Belle Bordeaux never seems to sleep at all.

History

Rome colonised the Aquitaine region in 56 BC, naming the area 100km east of the Atlantic at the lowest bridging point on the River Garonne, Burdigala. From 1154 to 1453, after Eleanor of Aquitaine married would-be King Henry II of England, the city prospered under the English. Their fondness for the region's red wine (known across the Channel as claret) provided the impetus for Bordeaux's international reputation for quality wines. Centuries on, this reputation continues to flourish.

Orientation

The city centre lies between flower-filled place Gambetta and the wide River Garonne, which flows both ways depending on the tides. From place Gambetta, place de Tourny is 500m northeast, from where the tourist office is 200m to the southeast.

Bordeaux's train station, Gare St-Jean, is about 3km southeast of the city centre. Cours de la Marne stretches from the train station to place de la Victoire, which is linked to place de la Comédie by the elongated pedestrianised shopping street, rue Ste-Catherine.

Information

BOOKSHOPS

Bradley's Bookshop (☎ 05 56 52 10 57; 8 cours d'Albret; ⏰ 9.30am-7pm Tue-Sat, 2-7pm Mon)
Librarie Mollat (☎ 05 56 56 40 40; 15 rue Vital Carles; ⏰ 9.15am-7pm Mon-Sat) A succession of rooms, including one dedicated to travel guides (with Lonely Planet titles in English) and maps.

INTERNET ACCESS

Cyberstation (☎ 05 56 01 15 15; 23 cours Pasteur; per hr €3; ⏰ 9.30am-2am Mon-Sat, 2pm-2am Sun)
NetZone (☎ 05 57 59 01 25; 209 rue Ste-Catherine; per hr €3; ⏰ 9.30am-midnight Mon-Sat, noon-midnight Sun)

LAUNDRY

Laundrettes 31 rue du Palais Gallien (⏰ 7am-9pm); 32 rue des Augustins (⏰ 7.30am-9pm); 5 rue de Fondaudège (⏰ 7am-10pm)

MEDICAL SERVICES & EMERGENCY

Hôpital St-André (☎ 05 56 79 56 79; 1 rue Jean Burguet) Has a 24-hour casualty ward.
Police Station (☎ 05 56 99 77 77; 29 rue Castéja; ⏰ 24hr)

MONEY

Banks offering currency exchange can be found near the tourist office on cours de l'Intendance, rue de l'Esprit des Lois and cours du Chapeau Rouge.

BORDEAUX IN...

Two Days

Bordeaux is virtually synonymous with its famous *vin* (wine), but there's much more to this revitalised riverside city than just the local drop. Start with a stroll along the polished **rue Ste-Catherine** (p679), lined with chic boutiques – except Sundays, when the shops shut; in which case fossicking through place St-Michel's **antique markets** (p679) before lunching on locally harvested **oysters** (p678) is better yet. Imbibe culture at the city's magnificent **museums** (p674), then knock back the knock-out nectar at place de la Victoire's lively **cafés** (p678), and groove to French tunes at funky **Café Pop** (p678).

Since no visit to Bordeaux is complete without venturing into the vineyards, on the second day, pay homage to **St-Émilion** (p680), the golden-hued medieval village with its spider's web of cobblestone laneways and legendary, full-bodied reds.

Four Days

On the third day, spin with your own wheels (or take a tour – see the boxed text, p675) among the chateaux in the nearby **Médoc** (p680) wine-growing region.

On the fourth day, less than an hour brings you to the boat-filled **Bassin d'Arcachon** (Bay of Arcachon; p683), and its namesake seaside holiday township. From here, a peaceful ferry trip transports you to rustic **Cap Ferret** (p686), with its red-and-white lighthouse rising above a canopy of pine trees, and crashing surf.

BORDEAUX

0 _____ 200 m
0 _____ 0.1 miles

ATLANTIC COAST

INFORMATION		
American Express	**1**	B3
Bordeaux Monumental	**2**	C3
Bradley's Bookshop	**3**	A4
Cyberstation	**4**	B5
Hôpital St-André	**5**	B5
Laundrette	**6**	C5
Laundrette	**7**	B2
Laundrette	**8**	A3
Librarie Mollat	**9**	B3
Main Post Office	**10**	A4
Main Tourist Office	**11**	C3
Maison du Tourisme de la Gironde	**12**	B3
NetZone	**13**	C5
Police Station	**14**	A3
Post Office	**15**	C4
Post Office (extended hours)	**16**	A3
SIGHTS & ACTIVITIES		
CAPC Musée d'Art Contemporain	**17**	C1
Cathédrale St-André	**18**	B4
École du Vin	(see 22)	
Esplanade des Quinconces	**19**	C2
Galerie des Beaux-Arts	**20**	A4
Girondins Fountain Monument	**21**	B2
Maison du Vin de Bordeaux	**22**	B2
Musée d'Aquitaine	**23**	B5
Musée d'Histoire Naturelle	**24**	B1
Musée des Arts Décoratifs	**25**	B4
Musée des Beaux-Arts	**26**	A4

Palais Gallien	**27**	A1
Tour Pey-Berland	**28**	B4
SLEEPING 🏠		
Hôtel de France	**29**	B3
Hôtel Majestic	**30**	C2
Hôtel Boulan	**31**	A4
Hôtel de la Presse	**32**	C3
Hôtel de la Tour Intendance	**33**	B3
Hôtel des 4 Soeurs	**34**	C3
Hôtel Studio	**35**	B2
Hôtel Touring	**36**	B2
La Maison Bordeaux	**37**	A2
La Maison du Lierre	**38**	A2
Petit Hôtel Labottiere	**39**	A1
Une Chambre en Ville	**40**	A4
EATING 🍴		
Baillardran	(see 44)	
Baud et Millet	**41**	B2
Brasserie Le Noailles	**42**	B3
Cassolette Café	**43**	C6
Champion Supermarket	**44**	B3
Fromagerie	**45**	B3
Fruit & Vegie Stalls	**46**	D6
L'Entrecôte	**47**	C3
Le Café du Musée	(see 17)	
Le Fournil des Capucins	**48**	D6
Marché des Capucins	**49**	D6
Moshi Moshi	(see 17)	
Restaurant Jean Ramet	**50**	C3

DRINKING 🍷 🍺		
Absolut Lounge	**51**	C3
Bodega Bodega	**52**	C3
Café Brun	**53**	C3
Café Pop	**54**	C6
Chez Auguste	**55**	C6
ENTERTAINMENT 🎭		
Bar de l'Hôtel de Ville	**56**	B4
Box Office	(see 65)	
Centre Jean Vigo	**57**	B3
Cinéma Utopia	**58**	C4
Connemara Bar	**59**	A4
Galerie Bordelaise	(see 65)	
Grand Théâtre	**60**	C3
Théâtre Femina	**61**	B3
Virgin Megastore Billeterie	**62**	A3
SHOPPING 🛍		
Antique Market	**63**	D5
Bordeaux Magnum	**64**	B2
Galerie Bordelaise	**65**	C3
L'Intendant	**66**	B3
TRANSPORT		
Citram Aquitaine Information Kiosk	**67**	C2
Jet'Bus (Airport Bus)	**68**	A3
Le 63	**69**	C4
TBC Bus Information Office	**70**	A3

American Express (☎ 05 56 00 63 36; 11 cours de l'Intendance; ⏰ 9am-noon & 1.30-5.30pm Mon-Fri Apr-Sep, to 5pm Mon-Fri Oct-Mar, plus 9.30am-12.30pm Sat Jun-Sep)

POST
Main Post Office (37 rue du Château d'Eau) Currency exchange and Cyberposte.

Post Office 43 place Gambetta (⏰ 10am-7pm Mon & Thu, 9am-7pm Tue, Wed & Fri, 9am-5pm Sat) Has extended hours; place St-Projet Adjacent to rue Ste-Catherine.

TOURIST INFORMATION
Bordeaux Monumental (☎ 05 56 48 04 24; 28 rue des Argentiers; ⏰ 10am-1pm & 2-6pm Mon-Sat, 2-6pm Sun) Specialist tourist office dedicated to the city's history. Offers free multimedia presentations, and presents temporary exhibitions for €7/6.50/5 per adult/student/child.

Main Tourist Office (☎ 05 56 00 66 00; www .bordeaux-tourisme.com; 12 cours du 30 Juillet; ⏰ 9am-7.30pm Mon-Sat, 9.30am-6.30pm Sun Jul & Aug, 9am-7pm Mon-Sat, 9.30am-6.30pm Sun May, Jun, Sep & Oct, 9am-6.30pm Mon-Sat, 9.45am-4.30pm Sun Nov-Apr) Runs an excellent range of city and regional tours – see p676 and the boxed text, p675; and sells the comprehensive *Plan Guide du Patrimoine* (€1) which suggests four walking itineraries covering the city's architectural heritage. Its *Passport Gourmand* (€53) offers reductions on restaurants as well as on a range of activities and museums.

Maison du Tourisme de la Gironde (☎ 05 56 52 61 40; www.tourisme-gironde.cg33.fr in French; 21 cours de l'Intendance; ⏰ 9am-6pm Mon-Fri, to 7pm Apr-Oct, 10am-1pm & 2-6.30pm Sat) Information on the Gironde *département*.

Train Station Tourist Office (⏰ 9am-noon & 1-6pm Mon-Sat, 10am-noon & 1-3pm Sun May-Oct, 9.30am-12.30pm & 2-6pm Mon-Fri Nov-Apr) Limited information.

Dangers & Annoyances
Bordeaux is a safe city, but the train station and its surrounding streets can be dicey, especially at night. Keep your luggage in sight at all times, and keep your passport, cash and credit cards on your person, not in bags or backpacks. Place de la Victoire can become aggressive late at night.

Sights & Activities
On the first Sunday of every month, Bordeaux's city centre is closed to cars, and attractions often have extended hours. Added events on the day include a **contemporary art bus** (tickets €5; commentary in French), which visits galleries showcasing emerging artists. Reserve through the **tourist office** (☎ 05 56 00 66 00; www.bordeaux-tourisme.com; 12 cours du 30 Juillet).

ATLANTIC COAST

CATHÉDRALE ST-ANDRÉ

Lording it over the city is **Cathédrale St-André** (☎ 05 56 81 26 25; admission free; ☼ 7.30am-6pm Tue-Fri, 9am-7pm Sat, 9am-6pm Sun, 2-6pm Mon). A Unesco World Heritage site, the cathedral's oldest section dates from 1096; most of what you see today was built in the 13th and 14th centuries. Exceptional masonry carvings can be seen in the north portal. Even more imposing than the cathedral itself is the 50m gargoyled, Gothic belfry, **Tour Pey-Berland** (adult/student/child €5/3.50/free; ☼ 10am-noon & 2-6pm). Erected between 1440 and 1466, its spire was added in the 19th century, and in 1863 it was topped off with the statue of Notre Dame of Aquitaine (Our Lady of Aquitaine). Scaling the tower's 232 steep, narrow steps rewards you with an unfolding panorama of the city.

MUSEUMS

Bordeaux's museums have free entry for permanent collections; temporary exhibits cost €5 for adults, €2.50 for children.

Gallo-Roman statues and relics dating back 25,000 years are among the highlights at the impressive **Musée d'Aquitaine** (Museum of Aquitaine; ☎ 05 56 01 51 00; 20 cours Pasteur; ☼ 11am-6pm Tue-Sun). Ask to borrow an English-language catalogue.

Built in 1824 as a warehouse for French colonial produce like coffee, cocoa, peanuts and vanilla, the cavernous Entrepôts Lainé creates a dramatic backdrop for more than 900 post-1960s works at the **CAPC Musée d'Art Contemporain** (Museum of Contemporary Art; ☎ 05 56 00 81 50; Entrepôt 7, rue Ferrére; ☼ 11am-6pm Tue, Thu-Sun, to 8pm Wed, closed Mon).

Occidental art buffs can trace its evolution from the Renaissance to the mid-20th century at Bordeaux's exceptional **Musée des Beaux-Arts** (Museum of Fine Arts; ☎ 05 56 10 20 56; 20 cours d'Albret; ☼ 11am-6pm Wed-Mon). Occupying two wings of the 1770s-built Hôtel de Ville, either side of the elegant public park, **Jardin de la Mairie**, the museum established in 1801 houses a superb collection of paintings, particularly 17th-century Flemish, Dutch and Italian works. Temporary exhibitions are regularly hosted at its nearby annexe, **Galerie des Beaux-Arts** (place du Colonel Raynal).

Exquisite faïence pottery, porcelain, gold, iron and glasswork and furniture are displayed at the **Musée des Arts Décoratifs** (Museum of Decorative Arts; ☎ 05 56 00 72 50; 39 rue Bouffard; ☼ museum 2-6pm Wed-Mon, temporary exhibits from 11am Mon-Fri); for your own decorative treasures, you can browse rue Bouffard's antique and homewares shops.

The **Musée d'Histoire Naturelle** (Natural History Museum; ☎ 05 56 48 29 86; ☼ 11am-6pm Mon & Wed-Fri, 2-6pm Sat & Sun) is really only worthwhile if you're a natural-history nut.

CROISEUR COLBERT

The 180m-long French navy missile cruiser, **Croiseur Colbert** (☎ 05 56 44 96 11; adult/student/child €7.80/6/5.50; ☼ 11am-6pm Wed, Sat & Sun Nov, Dec, Feb & Mar, 11am-6pm daily Apr-Oct, closed Jan), was in service from 1957 to 1991, and gives you a rather expensive glimpse of life aboard a battleship. It's proven so expensive for the city to maintain that it may be departing its dock at the quai des Chartrons – check ahead.

PALAIS GALLIEN

The only remains of Burdigala today are the crumbling ruins of the 3rd-century amphitheatre, **Palais Gallien** (rue du Dr Albert Barraud; adult/child €2.50/free; ☼ 2-7pm Jun-Sep), just northwest of the city centre.

PARKS

Leafy oases of green abound in Bordeaux.

Landscaping is artistic as well as informative at the **Jardin Public** (cours de Verdun). Established in 1755 and laid out in the English style a century later, the grounds incorporate the meticulously catalogued **Jardin Botanique** (☎ 05 56 52 18 77; admission free; ☼ 8.30am-6pm), founded in 1629 and at this site since 1855. If you're a tango fan but never learnt the moves (and you happen to be in town on the first Sunday of the month), the Jardin Public is the venue for free **tango lessons** (☎ 05 56 44 06 34).

At the vast square **esplanade des Quinconces**, laid out in 1820, you'll see the fountain **monument to the Girondins**, a group of moderate, bourgeois National Assembly deputies during the French Revolution, 22 of whom were executed in 1793 after being convicted of counter-revolutionary activities.

The 4km-long **riverfront esplanade** is gradually being redeveloped as part of the town's face-lift, with the addition of playgrounds and bicycle paths.

Pretty **place Gambetta**, a central open area ringed by shaded benches and bursting with

ON THE WINE TRAIL

Thirsty? The 1000-sq-km wine-growing area around the city of Bordeaux is, along with Burgundy, France's most important producer of top-quality wines.

The Bordeaux region is divided into 57 appellations (production areas whose soil and micro climate impart distinctive characteristics on the wine produced there) that are grouped into seven *familles* and also then subdivided into a hierarchy of designations (eg *premier grand cru classé*, the most prestigious) that often vary from appellation to appellation. The majority of the Bordeaux region's reds, rosés, sweet and dry whites and sparkling wines have earned the right to include the abbreviation AOC (Appellation d'Origine Contrôlée) on their labels, indicating that the contents have been grown, fermented and aged according to strict regulations that govern such viticultural matters as the number of vines permitted per hectare and acceptable pruning methods.

Bordeaux has over 5000 chateaux (also known as *domaines, crus* or *clos*), referring not to pala-tial residences but rather to the properties where grapes are raised, picked, fermented and then matured as wine. The smaller chateaux sometimes accept walk-in visitors, but at many places, especially the better-known ones, you have to make advance reservations. Many chateaux are closed during the *vendange* (grape harvest) in October.

Whet your palate with the tourist office's inexpensive and informal **introduction to wine and cheese courses** (cost €22) every Thursday at 4.30pm year-round at the restaurant Baud et Millet (p678), where you sip several different wines, and sup on cheese straight from the cellar. Classes are limited to 25 people; definitely reserve ahead.

Serious students of the grape and its many and wonderful uses can enrol at the **École du Vin** (Wine School; ☎ 05 56 00 22 66; ecole.vins-bordeaux.fr; 3 cours du 30 Juillet). Within the Maison du Vin de Bordeaux (Bordeaux House of Wine), across the street from the tourist office, introduc-tory two-hour courses are held in English on Monday and Thursday from 10am to noon, and Wednesday and Friday from 3pm to 5pm between May and October (€20). More comprehensive are the all-day classes held from 9am to 5pm on selected Saturdays in July and August (€150), which offer some tastings and also your lunch into the bargain. To really develop your nose (and your dinner party skills), sign up for one of three progressively more complex, intensive three- to four-day courses (from €375/230 per adult/student). The courses provide an entertaining overview of the techniques and vocabulary of tasting and wine making, and include chateaux visits to test your new skills.

Chateaux visits are also included in many tours run by Bordeaux's tourist office. The program changes annually, with most tours operating between May and October. Day trips generally start at €50 per adult for those closest to town, and around €75 for areas such as the **Médoc** (p680) or **St-Émilion** (p680). Tours include wine tastings and lunch. Some tours also incorporate a tour of the city's Chartrons' wine merchants' district.

For DIY wine trailing, the **Maison du Vin de Bordeaux** (☎ 8.30am-4.30pm Mon-Fri) can supply you with a free, colour-coded map of production areas, details on chateau visits, and the addresses of local *maisons du vin* (tourist offices that mainly deal with winery visits).

To stock your own cellar, speciality shops in Bordeaux's city centre include **Bordeaux Magnum** (☎ 05 56 48 00 06; 3 rue Gobineau; ☿ 10am-7.30pm Mon-Sat) and the stunning **l'Intendant** (☎ 05 56 48 01 29; 2 allées de Tourny; ☿ 10am-7.30pm Mon-Sat), with a central spiral staircase climbing four floors, surrounded by cylindrical shelves holding 15,000 bottles of regional wine.

And to immerse yourself, literally, in the local liquid, at the **Spa de Vinothérapie Caudalie** (☎ 05 57 83 83 83; www.sources-caudalie.com; chemin de Smith Haut Lafitte, Martillac) you can take a red-wine bath, enjoy a Merlot wrap or order a Cabernet body scrub. Apart from the sheer novelty factor, the vine and grape extracts are said to promote blood-strengthening and anti-ageing. The spa is 20 minutes south of Bordeaux next to Chateau Smith Haut Lafitte. It's best reached by your own wheels; exit the A62 at junction 1.

But even if the wine trail only leads you as far as the supermarket, it's possible to pick up exceptional wines off the shelves from just a couple of euros – the same wines that command a small fortune at some very flash restaurants around the world.

yellow and orange blooms in spring, also has its share of history – during the Reign of Terror that followed the Revolution, a guillotine placed here severed the heads of 300 alleged counter-revolutionaries.

Tours

Guided tours, including a two-hour bilingual **city walking tour** (adult/senior or student €7/6.50) departs from the tourist office at 10am daily, with an extra tour at 3pm from mid-July to mid-August. Tours can accommodate wheelchairs.

See the boxed text, p675, for details of tours further afield.

Sleeping

Budget and midrange options are plentiful and competitive, but true top-end accommodation is scarce in the city itself – consider the nearby countryside areas such as St-Émilion (p682).

The *Découverte* package is a neat little offering from the tourist office that bundles up one or two nights at your choice of participating hotels (predominantly, but not only, chains) along with free public transportation, free city parking, and a free drink in one of the selected restaurants, as well as a little souvenir in your room (plus, with two-night stays, a bottle of wine). Prices start at €72 for a one-night package for two people in a one-star hotel, going up to €354 for two nights for two people in a four-star establishment.

BUDGET

Auberge de Jeunesse (☎ 05 56 33 00 70; www.centres-animation.asso.fr in French; 22 cours Barbey; dm incl sheets & breakfast €19.90; ☒ ☐) Bordeaux's only hostel is housed in a schmick lino-and-glass building with a self-catering kitchen and good wheelchair access, mostly four-share en suite dorms, and foosball (table soccer), to boot. From the train station, follow cours de la Marne northwest for about 300m and turn left opposite the park; the hostel's about 250m up on your left.

Hôtel Studio & annexes (☎ 05 56 48 00 14; www.hotel-bordeaux.com; 26 rue Huguerie; s/d/tw/tr €18/27/32/45; ☐) The Hôtel Studio and its annexes have 42 rooms spread across four establishments. Incredibly, the en suite single rooms cost less than a dorm bed at Bordeaux's hostel (though breakfast here's an

extra €4). Sure, none of the buildings have lifts, and the blue-and-white rooms are pretty plain. But they're comfortable, and some have small balconies and/or TVs.

Hôtel Touring (☎ 05 56 81 56 73; le-touring@ wanadoo.fr; 16 rue Huguerie; s €25-42, d €30-50, tr €57) The Touring is a leading budget contender, run with pride by a warm-hearted local family. Its 12 impeccable rooms are furnished with original 1940s and '50s furniture, like flip-up school-style desks and club chairs. Most rooms have fridges, TVs and telephones; the cheapest have showers but share toilet facilities.

Also recommended:

Hôtel Boulan (☎ 05 56 52 23 62; fax 05 56 44 91 65; 28 rue Boulan; s €20-28, d €25-32) Situated on a secluded little side street, but still handy for a slew of Bordeaux's sights.

Hôtel de France (☎ 05 56 48 24 11; fax 05 56 48 78 30; 7 rue Franklin; s/d €47/49) Sweet two-star place in the heart of the city.

MIDRANGE

Hôtel de la Presse (☎ 05 56 48 53 88; www.hotelde lapresse.com; 6-8 rue Porte-Dijeaux; d €49-109; ☒) Just off the pedestrianised rue Ste-Catherine, this three-star hotel has elegant touches like silk and dried flowers, and guest baskets of fruit and nuts in the rooms. Service is polished and professional.

Hotel California II (☎ 05 56 91 17 25; hotel california@wanadoo.fr; 22 rue Charles Domercq; s/d/tr €48/54/65) Directly opposite the train station, this is your best bet to stop for the night if you're arriving late or leaving early. Windows are all double-glazed, and rose-motif rooms and natural light lend a countrified ambience to the rooms, which have kettles for a late-night cuppa, and BBC.

Hôtel de la Tour Intendance (☎ 05 56 44 56 56; www.hotel-tour-intendance.com; 14-16 rue de la Vieille Tour; d €58-129; ☒) Wake up to soaring exposed sandstone walls, stone-laid floors and wood-beamed ceilings at this stylised boutique hotel tucked into a quiet corner of the city. All 26 light-filled rooms have neutral-toned natural fabrics and fibres, interleaved with lime-washed timber panelling and geometric embossed vinyl walls, with pebbled bathrooms screened by milky opaque glass. Private parking costs €10.

Hotel Majestic (☎ 05 56 52 60 44; www.hotel-ma jestic.com; 2 rue de Condè; d €65-110;) This 18th-century Bordelaise private mansion is home to 49 spacious rooms in a bouquet of colours opening from wide buttercup-yellow hallways. Just 10 parking spaces are available (€10 – reserve ahead!), and there's free wi-fi in most rooms.

La Maison du Lierre (☎ 05 56 51 92 71; www .maisondulierre.com; 57 rue Huguerie; d €69-85) The delightfully restored 'house of ivy' has a welcoming *chambre d'hôte* feel. A beautiful Bordelaise stone staircase (no lift, unfortunately) leads to 12 sunlit rooms with polished floorboards, buttery yellow walls, rose-printed fabrics and sparkling white bathrooms. Rear rooms are a tad smaller, but overlook the vine-draped garden – a perfect spot for sipping freshly squeezed orange juice at breakfast (€6.50).

Hôtel des 4 Soeurs (☎ 05 57 81 19 20; 4soeurs .free.fr; 6 cours du 30 Juillet; s €65, d €75-90; ☒ ☒ ☐) A romantic relic from the reign of Louis-Philippe, Hôtel des 4 Soeurs' 34 sophisticated rooms recall the private home it once was, with stencilled wood-panelling, soft, snow-white damask drapes, and old-fashioned chrome bathroom fittings. Try for one of the front rooms overlooking place de la Comédie, such as balconied room 22, where Richard Wagner stayed in 1850.

Une Chambre en Ville (☎ 05 56 81 34 53; www .bandb-bx.com; 35 rue Bouffard; d €79, junior ste €89) Within the walls of a former gallery and adjoining Bordelaise town house, each of these five *chambres en ville* (rooms in the city) is an individual work of art, created by owners/hosts Rémi Labory and Rudolfus van de Pol. Burnished chrome kettles let you brew up your own tea and coffee. Une Chambre en Ville is gay-friendly (and all-welcoming).

TOP END

`our pick` **Petit Hôtel Labottiere** (☎ 05 56 48 44 10; www.chateauxcountry.com; 14 rue Francis Martin; d €180, extra bed €20; ☒) Staying in one of just two guest rooms in this splendid freestanding private 18th-century mansion is like sleeping in a museum (because essentially, you are sleeping in a museum). Saved from demolition in 1960, the heritage-listed restored mansion now houses innumerable antiques. You'll breakfast/brunch in a grand, triple-chandeliered gallery space or hedged central courtyard, and overnight in one of just two salubrious guest rooms with free fully stocked minibars. Secure parking

costs €8. Even if you're not staying here, you can tour the property by appointment for €8; guests receive a free private tour.

La Maison Bordeaux (☎ 05 56 44 00 45; www .lamaisonbordeaux.com; 113 rue du Docteur Albert Barraud; s €113-163, d €133-183) You'd expect to find a sumptuous 18th-century chateau with a stately conifer-flanked courtyard and stable house in the countryside, but this stunning *maison d'hôte* is right in the middle of the city. Public areas include a library with curved pistachio-coloured banquettes and shelves of books and CDs. Breakfast's included.

Eating

All that wine needs fine cuisine to accompany it, and Bordeaux has some excellent restaurants. Place du Parlement and rue du Pas St-Georges have a plethora. There are also scads of inexpensive cafés and restaurants around place de la Victoire.

Sandwich joints become pricier but offer better quality around the top end of rue Ste-Catherine; you'll also find good ones scattered along rue du Palais Gallien.

The tourist office's *Passport Gourmand* (€53) offers reductions on restaurants as well as on a range of activities and museums.

Cassolette Café (☎ 05 56 92 94 96; www.cassolet tecafe.com in French; 20 place de la Victoire; lunch menu €9.90, dinner menu €11.90; ☾ noon-midnight) Fun, friendly and fantastic value, this lively place at the southwestern edge of place de la Victoire serves up cassoulets (casserole dishes) cooked on a terracotta plate, created from ingredients you tick off on a checklist.

L'Entrecôte (☎ 05 56 81 76 10; 4 cours du 30 Juillet; menus €14-29; ☾ lunch & dinner) Opened in 1966, this popular, unpretentious place doesn't take reservations. However, Bordeaux locals queue for hours for its succulent thin-sliced meat (heated underneath by tea-light candles) and unlimited homemade *frites*.

Brasserie Le Noailles (☎ 05 56 81 94 45; 12 allées de Tourny; mains €12-30; ☾ lunch & dinner) Fronted by a winter garden opening to a dark timber-panelled interior with red velour booths, this classical French brasserie is an elegant affair, with delicious fare including Le Noaille's signature king prawn salad. *Plats du jour* (daily specials) are available at dinner as well as lunch.

Moshi Moshi (☎ 05 56 79 22 91; 8 place Fernand Lafargue; mains from €15; ☾ 8pm-2am Tue-Sat) Japan

ATLANTIC COAST

meets France head-on at this superchic minimalist place. The open kitchen lets you watch its celebrated chefs roll out sushi with unusual twists like foie gras and *magret de canard* (duck breast meat).

Baud et Millet (☎ 05 56 79 05 77; 19 rue Huguerie; menus €15-30; ☸ 9.30am-midnight Mon-Sat) Over 250 different cheeses are offered at this cosy vegetarian-friendly place, with almost as many international wines lining the walls. If too much French cheese is barely enough, try the all-you-can-eat *raclette* (cheese buffet).

Le Café du Musée (brunch €18, menus €18-25; ☸ 11am-6pm Tue-Sun) On the rooftop of the stunning CAPC Musée d'Art Contemporain, Le Café du Musée is renowned for its artistic, international cuisine such as satays and stir-fries, and especially its sumptuous Sunday brunch.

Restaurant Jean Ramet (☎ 05 56 44 12 51; 7 place Jean Jaurès; menus from €30; ☸ lunch & dinner Tue-Sat) Go the whole gastronomic hog at this fabulously formal establishment of white tablecloths and sparkling silverware, serving classy French and Bordelaise cuisine and the finest of wines.

SELF-CATERING
Near the covered market, **Marché des Capucins** (☸ 6am-1pm Tue-Sun), are super-cheap **fruit and vegie stalls** (rue Élie Gintrec; ☸ 8.30am-12.45pm Mon-Sat).

Champion supermarket (place des Grands Hommes; ☸ 8.30am-7.30pm Mon-Sat) is in the basement of the circular Marché des Grands Hommes shopping centre. Nearby, you'll find Jean D'Alos' fine **fromagerie** (4 rue Montesquieu; ☸ closed Mon morning & Sun).

Le Fournil des Capucins (62-64 cours de la Marne), near place de la Victoire, is a bakery that never closes.

For a taste of Bordeaux (that for once doesn't involve wine!), head to **Baillardran** (☎ 05 56 79 05 89; Galerie des Grands Hommes) to watch them make *canelès*, a local cake distinguished by its moist, vanilla-infused interior encased in a hard exterior shaped like a rippled jelly mould.

On Sunday mornings, pick up fresh **oysters** (per half-dozen around €3.50) at quai des Chartrons' open-air market.

Drinking
Bodega Bodega (☎ 05 56 01 24 24; 4 rue des Piliers de Tutelle; ☸ noon-3.15pm & 7pm-2am Mon-Sat,

7pm-2am Sun) The biggest and best Spanish bar in town has two floors of tapas, tunes and trendy types. Mind your head on the giant hams hanging up above the bar when you order a drink.

Café Brun (☎ 05 56 52 20 49; 45 rue St-Rémi; ☸ 10am-2am) This bar-bistro with a warm atmosphere and cool jazz is great for an evening apéritif.

Absolut Lounge (☎ 05 56 48 80 00; 14 rue de la Devise; mains around €33; ☸ 6pm-2am Mon-Sat) Chill to electro-jazz amid turquoise décor and red lamps.

Student hang-outs ring place de la Victoire. Our favourite is **Chez Auguste** (☎ 05 56 91 77 32; 3 place de La Victoire; ☸ 7am-2am). For a postmodern vibe and cool French tunes, pop into nearby **Café Pop** (Café Populaire; ☎ 05 56 94 39 06; 1 rue Kleber; ☸ 8pm-2am Tue-Sat).

Entertainment
Bordeaux buzzes by night. Details of events appear in the free publications *Bordeaux Plus* and *Clubs & Concerts* (www.clubset concerts.com in French), available at the tourist office.

Concert and event tickets can be purchased from the **Virgin Megastore billeterie** (☎ 05 56 56 05 56; 17 place Gambetta; ☸ 9.30am-8pm Mon-Thu, 9.30am-10pm Fri & Sat, noon-7pm Sun) or the **Box Office** (☎ 05 56 48 26 26; Galerie Bordelaise; ☸ 10am-7pm Mon-Fri, 10am-6pm Sat).

NIGHTCLUBS & LIVE MUSIC
Trendy pedestrianised streets like rue St-Rémi are good bets to get the evening started. For zoning reasons, many of the city's late-night dance venues are a few blocks northeast of Gare St-Jean along the river, on quai de la Paludate, such as the dark, smoky jazz club **Le Port de la Lune** (☎ 05 56 49 15 55; portdelalune@wanadoo.fr; 58 quai de la Paludate; ☸ 7pm-2am). Clubs also cluster along the river north of the city centre. Bouncers can be selective but there's normally no cover charge.

Catch regular live bands as well as football on the big screen at the lively **Connemara Bar** (☎ 05 56 52 82 57; 18 cours d'Albret; ☸ noon-2am), which also has free wi-fi, darts, pool and good pub grub.

A mainly gay crowd kicks up its heels at **Bar de l'Hôtel de Ville** (☎ 05 56 44 05 08; 4 rue de l'Hôtel de Ville; ☸ 6pm-2am), which often has shows on Sundays.

THEATRE & CLASSICAL MUSIC

The 18th-century **Grand Théâtre** (☎ 05 56 00 85 95; place de la Comédie; ☺ ticket office 11am-6pm Tue-Sat Oct-Jul) stages operas, ballets and concerts of orchestral and chamber music. For the operettas, plays, dance performances and variety shows held at **Théâtre Femina** (10 rue de Grassi), there is a ticket office in the nearby **Galerie Bordelaise** (☎ 05 56 48 26 26; ☺ 10am-7pm Tue-Sat, 2-7pm Mon).

CINEMAS

Nondubbed art-house films are screened at **Centre Jean Vigo** (☎ 05 56 44 35 17; 6 rue Franklin; tickets adult/student €4.60/3.80), and **Cinéma Utopia** (☎ 05 56 52 00 03; 3 place Camille Jullian; matinees €3.50, evening sessions from €5.50).

Shopping

Europe's longest pedestrian shopping street, rue Ste-Catherine, is paved with raised, polished Bordelaise stone, becoming increasingly upmarket as it stretches 1.2km north from place de la Victoire to place de la Comédie.

Galerie Bordelaise (rue de la Porte Dijeaux & rue Ste-Catherine) is a 19th-century shopping arcade. Luxury label boutiques concentrate within 'le triangle', formed by the allées de Tourny, cours Georges Clemenceau and cours de l'Intendance. An **antique market** (place St-Michel) fills the square on Sunday mornings.

See the boxed text, p675, for wine shops.

Getting There & Away

AIR

Bordeaux airport (☎ 05 56 34 50 50; www.bordeaux .aeroport.fr) is in Mérignac, 10km west of the city centre, with domestic and some international services. A taxi from the airport into town costs about €20.

BUS

Citram Aquitaine runs most buses to destinations in the Gironde and has an **information kiosk** (☎ 05 56 43 68 43; ☺ 1-8pm Mon-Fri, 9am-1.30pm & 5-8pm Sat) at esplanade des Quinconces.

Eurolines (☎ 05 56 92 50 42; 32 rue Charles Domercq; ☺ 7am-7.30pm Mon-Fri, 9am-7pm Sat) faces the train station.

CAR

Rental companies have offices in the train station building, to the far left as you exit.

TRAIN

Bordeaux is one of France's major rail transit points. The station, Gare St-Jean, is about 3km from the city centre at the southern terminus of cours de la Marne.

Destinations include Paris' Gare Montparnasse (€63.70, three hours, at least 16 daily), Bayonne (€25.70, 1¾ hours), Nantes (€39.60, four hours), Poitiers (€30.30, 1¾ hours), La Rochelle (€23.80, two hours) and Toulouse (€31.60, 2¼ hours).

Getting Around

TO/FROM THE AIRPORT

The train station and place Gambetta are connected to the airport (single/return €6.50/11) by **Jet'Bus** (☎ 05 56 34 50 50) from 5.30am until 9.30pm (last departure from the airport 10.45pm). The trip takes approximately 45 minutes.

BICYCLE

Le 63 (☎ 05 56 51 39 41, 06 74 82 27 62; 63 cours d'Alsace et Lorraine; ☺ by appointment 24hr) rents out bicycles (€14 for eight hours).

BUS

Urban buses are run by **TBC** (☎ 05 57 57 88 88; www.infotbc.com in French). The company has *Espace Bus* information/ticket offices at the train station and place Gambetta (4 rue Georges Bonnac).

Line No 1 runs along the waterfront from the train station north to Le Croiseur Colbert and beyond. Single tickets (€1.30), sold on board, aren't valid for transfers.

On weekends, night buses run on line S11, between place de la Victoire and the nightclub zone on quai de la Paludate.

CAR

Traffic can be horrendous during peak hour(s). Parking in the city centre is hard to find and pricey. Try looking for free spaces in the side streets north of the Musée d'Art Contemporain and west of the Jardin Public.

TAXI

To order a taxi call ☎ 05 56 99 28 41.

TRAM

The city's whizz-bang tramway has three lines. Line C links the train station with esplanade des Quinconces via the riverside, a continuation north along the riverfront was in the works at press time.

Trams run every 10 minutes between 5am and 1am. Purchase a ticket (€1.30) from the machine at your tram stop and stamp it on board.

THE MÉDOC

Northwest of Bordeaux, along the western shore of the Gironde Estuary – formed by the confluence of the Rivers Garonne and Dordogne – lie some of Bordeaux's most celebrated vineyards. To the west, fine-sand beaches, bordered by dunes and *étangs* (lagoons), stretch for some 200km from Pointe de Grave south along the Côte d'Argent (Silver Coast) to the Bassin d'Arcachon and beyond, with some great surf – see the boxed text, p687. The coastal dunes are enveloped by a vast pine forest planted in the 19th century to stabilise the drifting sands and to prevent them from encroaching on areas further inland.

Orientation & Information

On the banks of the muddy Gironde, the port town of **Pauillac** (population 1300) is at the heart of the wine country, surrounded by the distinguished Haut-Médoc, Margaux and St-Julien appellations. The Pauillac wine appellation encompasses 18 *crus classés* including the world-renowned Mouton Rothschild, Latour and Lafite Rothschild.

Pauillac's tourist office houses the **Maison du Tourisme et du Vin** (☎ 05 56 59 03 08; www.pauillac-medoc.com; La Verrerie; ⌚ 9.30am-7pm Jul–mid-Sep, 9.30am-12.30pm & 2-6.30pm Jun & mid-Sep–Nov, 9.30am-12.30pm & 2-6pm Mon-Sat, 10.30am-12.30pm & 3-6pm Sun Dec-May), which has information on chateaux and how to visit them.

Sleeping & Eating

From Bordeaux, the Médoc makes an easy and enjoyable day trip. To stay and/or dine under the vines, the tourist offices in Bordeaux and in the Médoc have information on the many *chambres d'hôtes* in the area.

Le Pavillon de Margaux (☎ 05 57 88 77 54; www.pavillondemargaux.com; 3 rue Georges Mandel, Margaux; d €60-110) In an old schoolhouse, this welcoming, family-run place has 14 rooms styled according to famous local chateaux. The family has four vineyards in the vicinity; you can taste the fruits of their labour at the on-site restaurant (mains €15 to €20; closed Tuesday mid-November to March), which serves a small but stellar selection of dishes such as honey-glazed, truffle-stuffed lamb under a canopy of fairy lights.

Getting There & Away

The Médoc's northern tip, Pointe de Grave, is linked to Royan by **car ferries** (☎ 05 46 38 35 15; per person/bicycle/motorcycle/car one way €3/1.50/9.40/20.80) that operate six times daily in winter and every 45 minutes in summer. The service runs around 6.30pm to 8.30pm (7.15pm and 9.30pm from Royan, 25 minutes one-way), depending on the season.

Another **car ferry** (☎ 05 57 42 04 49; per person/bicycle/car/motorcycle one way €3/1.50/12.40/9.50) links Lamarque (between Pauillac and Margaux on the D2) with Blaye, running five to 10 times daily (every 1½ hours June to September). The service starts around 7.30am and ends between 6.30pm and 8pm (until 9pm Saturday and Sunday June to September).

Citram Aquitaine buses (☎ 05 56 43 68 43) link Bordeaux with Margaux (€6.20, 50 minutes), Pauillac (€9.40, 1½ hours) and Lesparre Médoc (€12.50, 1½ hours). In Lesparre, buses depart for Soulac-sur-Mer (€7.30, two hours) and Point de Grave (€8.30, 2¼ hours).

To reach the Médoc by car from Bordeaux, take *sortie* (exit) 7 to get off the Bordeaux Rocade (ring road).

Trains run from Bordeaux's Gare St-Jean station to Margaux (€6.50, 50 minutes) several times a day.

ST-ÉMILION

pop 2500

Glowing with halolike golden hues as the sun sets over the valley, the medieval village of St-Émilion perches above vineyards renowned for producing full-bodied, deeply coloured red wines. Named after Émilion, a miracle-working Benedictine monk who lived in a cave here between 750 and 767, it soon became a stop on pilgrimage routes, and the village and its vineyards are now Unesco-listed. Today, although it's definitely a stop on the tourist route, too, it's well worth venturing 40km east from Bordeaux to experience St-Émilion's magic.

Orientation & Information

Unfortunately the village's steep, uneven streets make it difficult for travellers with disabilities to get around.

The pharmacy and banks are along rue Guadet.

Post Office (rue Guadet) Can exchange currency.

Tourist Kiosk (place de l'Église Monolithe) During the summer the tourist office opens a kiosk. Opening times vary (usually 10am to noon and 2pm to 6pm Monday to Friday and some weekends).

Tourist Office (☎ 05 57 55 28 28; www.saint-emilion -tourisme.com; place des Créneaux; ⏰ 9.30am-7pm mid-Jun–mid-Sep, 9.30am-12.30pm & 1.45-6pm mid-Sep–mid-Jun) Has brochures in English and details on visiting almost 100 nearby chateaux.

Sights

The only (but highly worthwhile) way to visit the town's most interesting historical sites (many of them concealed beneath the village streets in a labyrinth of cata-combs) is with one of the tourist office's 45-minute **guided tours** (adult/student/child incl site entry €6/3.80/3). Highlights are the hermit saint's famous cave, **Grotte de l'Ermitage**, and the 11th-century church **Église Monolithe**, carved out of limestone from the 9th to the 12th centuries. Tours in French de-part regularly throughout the day – call ahead to check English tour times (usually 2pm).

For captivating views of the hilltop ham-let, collect the key from the tourist office to climb the **clocher** (bell tower; ☎ 05 57 55 28 28; admission €1; ⏰ 9.30am-7pm mid-Jun–mid-Sep, 9.30am-12.30pm & 1.45-6pm mid-Sep–mid-Jun) above

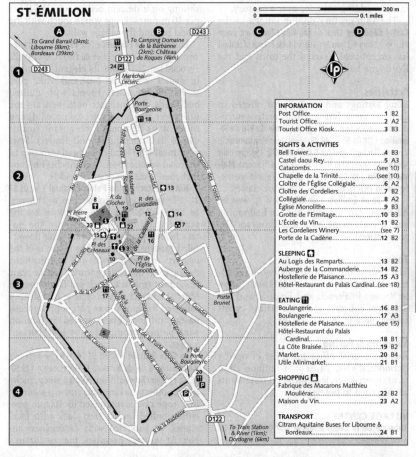

ST-ÉMILION

0 —————— 200 m
0 —————— 0.1 miles

To Grand Barrail (3km);
Libourne (8km);
Bordeaux (39km)

To Camping Domaine
de la Barbanne
(2km); Château
de Roques (4km)

Pl Maréchal
Leclerc

Porte
Bourgeoise

INFORMATION
Post Office.....................................1 B2
Tourist Office................................2 A2
Tourist Office Kiosk......................3 B3

SIGHTS & ACTIVITIES
Bell Tower.....................................4 B3
Castel daou Rey............................5 A3
Catacombs.............................(see 10)
Chapelle de la Trinité...............(see 10)
Cloître de l'Église Collégiale........6 B2
Cloître des Cordeliers...................7 B2
Collégiale.....................................8 A2
Église Monolithe..........................9 B3
Grotte de l'Ermitage...................10 B3
L'École du Vin.............................11 B2
Les Cordeliers Winery..............(see 7)
Porte de la Cadène.....................12 B2

SLEEPING 🏠
Au Logis des Remparts................13 B2
Auberge de la Commanderie.......14 B2
Hostellerie de Plaisance..............15 A3
Hôtel-Restaurant du Palais Cardinal..(see 18)

EATING 🍴
Boulangerie.................................16 B3
Boulangerie.................................17 A3
Hostellerie de Plaisance...........(see 15)
Hôtel-Restaurant du Palais
  Cardinal..................................18 B1
La Côte Braisée............................19 B2
Market..20 B4
Utile Minimarket.........................21 B1

SHOPPING 🛍️
Fabrique des Macarons Matthieu
  Mouliérac.................................22 B2
Maison du Vin............................23 A2

TRANSPORT
Citram Aquitaine Buses for Libourne &
  Bordeaux.................................24 B1

Porte
Brunet

To Train Station
& River (1km);
Dordogne (6km)

the church; the entrance is on place des Créneaux.

A domed Romanesque 12th-century nave dominates the former **Collégiale** (Collegiate Church), which also boasts an almost-square vaulted choir built between the 14th and 16th centuries. Free concerts are held here every Thursday at 6pm during summer. **Cloître de l'Église Collégiale**, the church's tranquil 14th-century cloister, is accessible through the tourist office building.

Surviving sections of the town's medieval walls and gates include **Porte de la Cadène** (Gate of the Chain), off rue Guadet.

Within the ruined monastery **Cloître des Cordeliers** (rue des Cordeliers; admission free; ☾ year-round), the winery **Les Cordeliers** (☎ 05 57 24 76 99; guided cellar tours €4; ☾ tour hrs vary daily) has made sparkling wine for over a century.

The 13th-century donjon known as the **Castel daou Rey** (Tour du Roi, King's Tower; admission €1; ☾ 9.30am-8.30pm Jun-Sep, variable hrs out of season) has exceptional views of the town and the Dordogne Valley.

Activities

Blind tastings and games (also offered in English) are a fun and informative introduction to wine tasting at **L'École du Vin de St-Émilion** (☎ 05 57 74 44 29; www.vignobleschateaux.fr; 4 rue du Clocher; Vignobles & Châteaux €20; ☾ 3pm daily Apr-Oct, by reservation Nov-Mar). The adjacent **Maison du Vin** (☎ 05 57 55 50 55; €17; ☾ mid-Jul–mid-Sep) also offers bilingual, 1½-hour classes.

See Saint Émilion (☎ 05 57 74 46 78; www.see-travel.com) can arrange hot-air ballooning and private wine education courses (by reservation).

Tours

The tourist office organises two-hour afternoon **chateau visits** (adult/child €9.60/6; ☾ Mon-Sat May-Sep) in French and English, and has details of concerts and wine-tasting events taking place in local chateaux.

Sleeping & Eating

Ask the tourist office for a list of nearby *chambres d'hôtes*. Most of St-Émilion's best (and surprisingly, least touristy) restaurants are attached to hotels.

VILLAGE CENTRE

Auberge de la Commanderie (☎ 05 57 24 70 19; www.aubergedelacommanderie.com; rue des Cordeliers;

d €60-100, q duplex apt €120; ☾ mid-Feb–mid-Jan) Inside this hotel's 13th-century walls, rooms have been dramatically modernised. The medieval and contemporary eras are now married by massive murals depicting a techni-colourised pop art version of an old black-and-white postcard of the village. Perks include a private lock-up car park, wi-fi and an online computer (both €5 per hour), and fun, friendly staff.

Au Logis des Remparts (☎ 05 57 24 70 43; logis-des-remparts@saint-emilion.org; 18 rue Guadet; d €70-150; ☾ mid-Jan–mid-Dec; ☒ ☙) This boutique hotel has elegantly renovated rooms and suites, but its highlight is the swimming pool set in lush gardens overlooking the vineyards. Stretching right up to the ceiling, timber bed-heads have recessed halogen downlights shining on iridescent bedspreads. Wi-fi (€5 per 30 minutes) keeps you in touch with the world beyond the village walls.

Hostellerie de Plaisance (☎ 05 57 55 07 55; www.hostellerie-plaisance.com; place du Clocher; d €150-435; ☾ closed Jan; ☒) From its elegant salon/bar in shades of eggshell blue and white gold to its 14 whimsical rooms with quilted bed-heads, this intimate hotel beneath the bell tower also has a spice-coloured dining room at its destination restaurant (mains €40 to €44; open lunch and dinner). Start your meal with local caviar and move on to charcoal-smoked beef; or go for chef Philippe Etchebest's 'discovery menu' (€80).

Hôtel-Restaurant du Palais Cardinal (☎ 05 57 24 72 39; www.palais-cardinal.com; place du 11 Novembre 1918; s €60-203, d €70-266; ☙) Run by the same family for five generations, the hotel's heated pool is set in rambling flower-filled gardens and framed by sections of the original medieval town wall fortifications dating from the 13th century. Gastronomic restaurant (menu €36, closed December to March) fare includes Cognac-glazed shrimp followed by duck's liver pâté topping fresh pasta, and for dessert spiced St-Émilion wine plums accompanied by blackcurrant sorbet.

La Côte Braisée (☎ 05 57 24 79 65; www.la-cote-braisee.com; 3 rue du Tertre de la Tente; menus €13.50-25.50; ☾ lunch & dinner) Slanted on a steep, rocky little cobblestone lane, this rustic restaurant in a stone cave is renowned for its foie gras, either stuffed inside roast duck with local grapes, or pan-fried with caramelised apples. At separate premises, the restaurant's proprietors rent out five charming guest rooms (doubles €75).

AROUND ST-ÉMILION
Camping Domaine de la Barbanne (☎ 05 57 24 75 80; www.camping-saint-emilion.com; rte de Montagne; camping €15.50-27.90, cabins €50-61; ﾁ Apr-Sep; ⏴) This family-friendly, three-star place is about 2km north of St-Émilion on the D122. There's a five-night minimum for camping in July and August. Cabins, sleeping up to five people, are spacious and well equipped.

Château de Roques (☎ 05 57 74 55 69; www.chateau-de-roques.com; d €43-100) If you've dreamed of staying in a romantic countryside chateau but your budget – or lack of – was a rude awakening, you'll adore this affordable 16th-century place with good wheelchair access in the vineyards of Puisseguin, 5km outside St-Émilion. Its restaurant (menus €18 to €32, open lunch and dinner, closed late December to early February) serves foie gras with Cognac and jelly made from locally produced Sauternes white wine. The best road is the D122 (head north from St-Émilion) – the chateau is just near the junction of the D21, just before you get into the town of Puisseguin.

Grand Barrail (☎ 05 57 55 37 00; www.grand-barrail.com; rte de Libourne/D243; ⏴ ⏴ ⏴) Grand doesn't even begin to describe this immense 1850-built chateau 3km from the village, with its decadent on-site spa, stone-flagged, heated swimming pool, free state-of-the-art fitness room, good wheelchair access and, if you happen to be arriving by helicopter, its own helipad on the front lawns. Undoubtedly the best seat in the on-site restaurant (mains from around €20) is the corner table surrounded by 19th-century stained glass.

SELF-CATERING
Boulangeries (bakeries) on rue Guadet and rue de la Grande Fontaine open to around 6pm. A market fills place de la Porte Bouqueyre every Sunday.

Utile Grocery (ﾁ 8am-7pm Mon-Sat, 8am-1pm Sun Jun–mid-Sep, 8am-12.30pm & 2-7pm Mon-Fri, 8am-1pm Sun mid-Sep–May) On the D122, 150m north of town.

Shopping
St-Émilion's quaint streets and squares are lined with about 50 wine shops – one for every eight of the old city's residents.

Maison du Vin (☎ 05 57 55 50 55; place Pierre Meyrat; ﾁ 9.30am-12.30pm & 2-6pm Sep-Jul, 9.30am-7pm Aug) Owned by the 250 chateaux whose wines it sells, this place has exhibitions and publications on local wines.

Ursuline nuns brought the recipe for *macarons* (macaroons – almond biscuits with a soft, fluffy interior) to St-Émilion in the 17th century. Bakeries including **Fabrique des Macarons Matthieu Mouliérac** (Tertre de la Tente; ﾁ closed mornings Jan-Mar) charge €5 per two dozen.

Getting There & Away
Citram Aquitaine (☎ 05 56 43 68 43) buses to/from Bordeaux's Halte Routière run at least once daily (except on Sunday and holidays from October to April) to Libourne (€5.70, 45 minutes); from there you take a **Marchesseau** (☎ 05 57 40 60 79) bus to St-Émilion (€2, 10 minutes). A direct service from Bordeaux may operate during July and August – phone to check.

Trains run three times daily (two on Sunday and holidays) from Bordeaux (€6.80, 40 minutes); the train station is 1km south (downhill) from the village.

By car from Bordeaux, follow the signs for Libourne and take the D243.

Year-round, the tourist office rents out bicycles for €9.50/14 per half-day/day.

Call for a **taxi** (☎ 05 57 25 17 59; www.taxi-St-Emilion.com).

ARCACHON
pop 11,800
A longtime oyster harvesting area on the southern side of the tranquil, triangular Bassin d'Arcachon (Arcachon Bay), this seaside town lured bourgeois Bordelaise at the end of the 19th century. Its four little quarters are romantically named for each of the seasons, with villas that evoke the town's golden past amid a scattering of 1950s architecture.

Arcachon seethes with sun-seekers in summer, but you'll find practically deserted beaches a short bike ride away.

Orientation
Arcachon's main commercial streets run parallel to the beach: blvd de la Plage, cours Lamarque de Plaisance and cours Héricart de Thury. Perpendicular to the beach, busy streets include av Gambetta and rue du Maréchal de Lattre de Tassigny.

Information

Crédit Agricole (252 blvd de la Plage) Only bank with currency exchange.

Le Bistrot du Boulevard (☎ 05 56 83 45 67; 230 blvd de la Plage; per hr €7.50; ⏰ 11am-11pm)

Post Office (place Président Roosevelt) Cyberposte.

Tourist Office (☎ 05 57 52 97 97; www.arcachon.com; place Président Roosevelt; ⏰ 9am-7pm Jul & Aug, 9am-6.30pm Mon-Fri, 9am-5pm Sat, 10am-noon & 1-5pm Sun Apr–Jun & Sep, 9am-6pm Mon-Fri, 9am-5pm Sat Oct-Mar)

Sights

In the **Ville d'Été** (Summer Quarter), Arcachon's sandy beach, **Plage d'Arcachon**, is flanked by two piers. Lively **Jetée Thiers** is at the western end. In front of the eastern pier, **Jetée D'Eyrac**, stands the town's turreted **Casino de la Plage** – built by Adalbert Deganne in 1953 as an exact replica of Château de Boursault in the Marne. Inside, it's a less-grand blinking and bell-ringing riot of poker (slot) machines and gaming tables.

The **Aquarium et Musée** (☎ 05 56 83 33 32; 2 rue du Professeur Jolyet; adult/student/under 10yr €4.40/3/2.80; ⏰ 9.45am-12.15pm & 1.45-7pm Jun-Aug, to 6.30pm Mar-May & Sep-Nov, closed Dec-Feb), in a wooden shack opposite the casino, has a small collection of fish.

On the tree-covered hillside south of the Ville d'Été, the century-old **Ville d'Hiver** (Winter Quarter) has over 300 villas, many decorated with delicate wood tracery, ranging in style from neogothic through to colonial. It's an easy stroll or a short ride up the Art Deco–style **public lift** (tickets €0.15; ⏰ 9am-12.45pm & 2.30-7pm) in Parc Mauresque.

A lovely **pedestrian promenade** lined with trees and playgrounds runs west and then south from the Plage d'Arcachon to **Plage Péreire**, **Plage des Abatilles** and the **Dune du Pilat** (p686).

Activities

Cycle paths link Arcachon with the Dune du Pilat and Biscarosse (30km to the south), and around the Bassin d'Arcachon to Cap Ferret. From here, a cyclable path parallels the beaches north to Pointe de Grave.

The exposed ocean beaches to the south of town generally offer good conditions for surfing. **Ocean Roots** (☎ 06 62 26 04 11; oceanrclub@hotmail.com; 27 av St-Francois Xavier) offers

ARCACHON

INFORMATION
Crédit Agricole...................................1 C1
Le Bistrot du Boulevard.....................2 C1
Main Post Office................................3 C2
Tourist Office....................................4 C2

SIGHTS & ACTIVITIES
Aquarium et Musée............................5 D1
Casino...6 C1
Public Lift...7 B2
UBA Boats to Cap Ferret &
    Cruises..8 D1
UBA Boats to Cap Ferret &
    Cruises..9 C1

SLEEPING
Hôtel La Paix...................................10 C2
Hôtel le Dauphin.............................11 D2
Hôtel Point France...........................12 C1

EATING
Aux Mille Saveurs...........................13 D2
Casino Supermarket.........................14 C2
E Leclerc Supermarket......................15 C1
Food Market....................................16 C2
La Paix.......................................(see 10)
Monoprix Supermarket.....................17 B2
St-Christaud....................................18 A1

TRANSPORT
Autobus d'Arcachon Office...............19 C2
Dingo Vélos.....................................20 C1
Locabeach.......................................21 B1

lessons and rents out equipment. For more surf spots, see the boxed text, p687.

Centre Nautique d'Arcachon (☎ 05 56 22 36 83; quai Goslar; ⓨ Apr-Sep), 1.5km east of the Jetée d'Eyrac at the Port de Plaisance (Pleasure Boat Port), rents out sea kayaks and windsurfing and diving equipment, and offers courses.

Tours

Les Bateliers Arcachonnais (UBA; ☎ 05 57 72 28 28; www.bateliers-arcachon.asso.fr in French) runs daily, year-round cruises around the **Île aux Oiseaux** (adult/child €13.50/9.50), the uninhabited 'bird island' in the middle of the bay. It's a haven for tern, curlew and redshank, so take your binoculars. In summer there are regular all-day excursions to the **Banc d'Arguin**, the sand bank off the Dune du Pilat (€16/11).

Sleeping

La Forêt (☎ 05 56 22 73 28; www.campinglaforet.fr; rte de Biscarosse; camp sites €12.25-26.50; ⓨ Apr–mid-Oct; 🛋) A well-run, three-star camp site, 'the forest' has shady pine trees and spotless amenities.

Hôtel La Paix (☎ 05 56 83 05 65; fax 05 56 83 05 65; 8 av de Lamartine; s/d €33.30/36.10, with shared bathroom €25.80/28.90, half-board d €54-62; ⓨ May-Sep) Many of these 23 simple, sweet rooms 200m from the beach have scrubbed timber floors, and some open onto a sunny rear courtyard. Upstairs are three breezy, beach-housey self-contained apartments (€152.40 to €487 per week) available from Easter to early November. Rates include breakfast; from June to September, half-board is obligatory.

Hôtel le Dauphin (☎ 05 56 83 02 89; www.dauphin-arcachon.com; 7 av de Gounod; tw €52-79, d €57-88, tr €64-95, q €71-107; 🛋 🛋) You won't be able to miss this late-19th-century gingerbread place with patterned red-and-cream brickwork graced by twin semicircular staircases, magnolias and palms. Several eras have left their legacy, with a '50s marble foyer, '70s backlit frosted glass and cork-panelled walls, plus '80s pine furniture. Parking is free.

Hôtel Point France (☎ 05 56 83 46 74; www.hotel-point-france.com; 1 rue Grenier; s €82-140, d €85-181; 🛋) All 34 rooms at this strobe-lit retro-chic place near the beach have balconies. Rooms facing the sea have knock-out views (some have side views), and postcolonial Indian styling; rooms facing the town side have Jetsons-style moulded plastic chairs, geometric prints and funky pistachio-tiled bathrooms.

Eating

The beachfront promenade between Jetée Thiers and Jetée d'Eyrac is lined with restaurants and places offering pizza and *crêpes*. Locals tend to avoid this slightly tacky strip, but it has an animated atmosphere, and competition keeps prices reasonable.

Be sure to try the bay's oysters served raw, and accompanied by the local small, flat sausages, *crepinettes*.

La Paix (☎ 05 56 83 05 65; fax 05 56 83 05 65; 8 av de Lamartine; menus around €10-21.50; ⓨ early Jun–mid-Sep) Hôtel La Paix's rambling guesthouse is fronted by a theatrical glass-paned summerhouse restaurant wound with vines and filled with silk, paper and real flowers that harks back to its heyday when the owner's grandfather was one of the original team of chefs cooking here. All the traditional French fare's good, particularly the gourmet seafood *menu* (set meals).

St-Christaud (☎ 05 56 83 38 53; 8 allée de la Chapelle; menus from €12.50; ⓨ lunch & dinner summer, by reservation winter; ✗) Opening to a sun-baked concrete courtyard a hop, skip and a jump from the beachfront and La Chapelle jetty, this authentic family-run place serves just one hearty *plat* (dish) a day in the low season (but can cater to vegetarians with advance notice). Out back there's a maze of austere but appealing guest rooms (doubles €50).

La Calypso (☎ 05 56 83 65 08; 84 blvd de la Plage; menu €20; ⓨ closed Wed & Thu Sep-Jun) With beamed ceilings, red tablecloths and a cosy open fireplace flickering in the chillier months, this good-natured restaurant is an amiable place to tuck into specialities like sole stuffed with crab; honey-glazed duck; and a delicious *bouillabaisse arcachonnaise* (fish soup) made from local sea critters.

Aux Mille Saveurs (☎ 05 56 83 40 28; 25 blvd du Général Leclerc; menus €15-31; ⓨ closed dinner Tue, Wed low season) In a light-filled space of flowing white tablecloths, this genteel restaurant is renowned for its traditional French fare artistically presented on fine china. Specialities include rabbit with thyme and coriander as well as seafood, or leave it to the experts and go for the 'chef's suggestion'.

SELF-CATERING

Find fresh beach picnic supplies at the **food market** (ⓨ 8am-1pm) adjacent to the train station.

Nearby there's a **Casino supermarket** (57 blvd du Général Leclerc; 9am-12.30pm & 3-7pm Mon-Sat, 9am-noon Sun). Other supermarkets include **E Leclerc** (224 blvd de la Plage; 9am-7.30pm Mon-Sat, 9.30am-12.30pm Sun) and **Monoprix** (46 cours Lamarque de Plaisance; 8.30am-12.30pm & 2-7.30pm Mon-Sat).

Getting There & Away

Frequent trains between Bordeaux and Arcachon (€9, 50 minutes) coordinate with TGVs from Paris' Gare Montparnasse.

Getting Around

Free Ého buses A, B and C loop around town. Buses can be hailed anywhere along the route; the tourist office has maps.

Locabeach (05 56 83 39 64; www.locabeach .com in French; 326 blvd de la Plage; 9am-12.30pm & 2.30-7pm) rents out scooters and motorcycles starting at €15/39 per hour/day, and bicycles per half-day/day from €7/10.

Dingo Vélos (05 56 83 44 09; www.dingovelos .com; rue Grenier; 9.30am-6.30pm Apr-Sep, until midnight Jul & Aug) rents out five-speeds/mountain bikes from €10/13 per day, plus tandems and bikes for multiple riders.

To order a cab, call 05 56 83 88 88.

AROUND ARCACHON
Dune du Pilat

Situated 8km south of Arcachon, this colossal sand dune (sometimes referred to as the Dune de Pyla because of its location in the resort town of Pyla-sur-Mer) stretches from the mouth of the Bassin d'Arcachon southwards for almost 3km. Already the largest in Europe, studies have shown it to be spreading eastwards at about 4.5m a year – it has swallowed trees, a road junction and even an entire hotel, and at this rate the camp site at the base of the dune's steep eastern side appears to have a limited lifespan.

The view from the top – approximately 114m above sea level – is magnificent. To the west you can see the sandy shoals at the mouth of the Bassin d'Arcachon, including the **Banc d'Arguin bird reserve** and **Cap Ferret**. Dense dark-green pine forests stretch from the base of the dune eastwards almost as far as the eye can see.

Take care swimming in this area: powerful currents swirl out to sea from the deceptively tranquil *baïnes* (baylets) that jut into the beach.

SLEEPING & EATING

In addition to a swag of seasonal camp sites, there are a couple of stand-out accommodation options.

Hôtel Yatt (05 57 72 03 72; www.yatt-hotel.com in French; 253 blvd Côte d'Argent, Moulleau village; d €40-85, q €60-115; closed mid-Nov–Mar, minimum 5 nights Aug;) Built in 1950 and renovated with a designer's eye, this hip hotel in the café-clad Moulleau fishing village, 400m north of Pyla-sur-Mer, has good wheelchair access and a *très* cool coastal ambience. Footsteps from the jetty and beach, rooms have backlit floor-to-ceiling woodcut panels, floating blond-timber floors, funky yellow bath towels, and free wi-fi.

Côte du Sud (05 56 83 25 00; www.cote-du-sud .fr; 4 av du Figuier; d €59-120; closed Dec-early Feb) Splashed in bright, bold colours and south-of-France sunshine, this chic little beachside boutique hotel has eight exotic rooms. Inspired by a spectrum of continents, details include rattan ceilings, stainless steel basins, sea shells and cacti. Choose your crustacean from the live tank at the raked-ceilinged restaurant (mains €15 to €39).

GETTING THERE & AWAY

Cycling is the most popular way to reach the dune from Arcachon (see left).

The local bus company, **Autobus d'Arcachon** (05 57 72 45 00; 47 blvd du Général Leclerc), has daily buses from Arcachon's train station to the Pyla Plage (Haïtza), 1km north of the dune (€2.70).

From mid-June to mid-September, buses continue south to the dune's car park at the northern end.

Cap Ferret
pop 6392 (peninsula)

Crowned by its red-and-white lighthouse, the tiny village of Cap Ferret is hidden among a canopy of dark-green pine trees at the southernmost tip of the Cap Ferret peninsula, spanning a mere 2km between the bay and the crashing Atlantic surf.

INFORMATION

Tourist Office (05 56 60 63 26; www.lege-capferret .com in French; 12 av de l'Océan; 10am-6.30pm Mon-Sat, 10am-1pm & 3-6pm Sun Jul & Aug, 10am-1pm & 3-6pm Mon-Sat Jun & Sep) Opens seasonally. The rest of the year, an outlying office can be reached on the same telephone number and website.

SIGHTS & ACTIVITIES

From approximately early April until late August, a tiny choo-choo, the **P'tit Train** (☎ 05 56 60 60 20; return journey €5), rattles on narrow tracks between the bay and the beach.

Federation Française de Surf member **Surf Center** (☎ 05 56 60 61 05; 22 allées des Goe'lands; ☾ approx Jun-Sep) rents out boards and offers lessons for all levels, starting from around €20 an hour. See the boxed text, below, for more about surfing the Atlantic Coast.

SLEEPING & EATING

Auberge de Jeunesse (☎ 05 56 60 64 62; 87 av de Bordeaux; dm incl breakfast €13.10; ☾ Jul & Aug) The ultrabasic youth hostel, 500m from the beach, lets campers pitch a tent in the grounds.

Hôtel L'Océane (☎ 05 56 60 68 13; www.hotel-oceane.com in French; 62 av de l'Océane; d €39-117, q €75-158) Two of Hôtel L'Océane's coir-carpeted, marine-coloured rooms open to private breezy decks (others open on to a communal timber-decked patio), with mechanically operated toilets reminiscent of being on board a ship.

There's a clutch of cafés and pizzerias footsteps from the hotel, or try a seafood platter at the laid-back on-site **Restaurant l'Hippocampe** (mains around €15; ☾ lunch & dinner Apr-Oct).

Hôtel du Cap (☎ 05 56 60 60 60; fax 05 56 60 63 59; 58 av de l'Océane; d €41-95, tr €64-103, q €84-135) Framed by pretty sky-blue timber fretwork and even prettier on the inside, this boutique place has sky-blue rooms (some opening to balconies) with a trendy beach-house vibe. Strewn with brightly coloured cotton-covered cushions, the long wooden bench in the restaurant (mains €15 to €25; lunch and dinner summer, closed dinner Friday and Sunday winter and January) makes a perfect perch to dine on fresh local seafood.

Hôtel des Pins (☎ 05 56 60 60 11; fax 05 56 60 67 41; 23 rue des Fauvettes; d €52-72, ste €110-142; ☾ closed mid-Nov–mid-Mar) This 1920-built guesthouse has lovely creaking old corridors leading to 16 romantic rooms. Some are basic, with bathrooms screened only by curtains, but are charmingly furnished. All rooms have telephones, but no TVs (there's a guest lounge with a communal TV and billiard table). The *Great Gatsby*-style glass-paned **restaurant** (mains €22-29; ☾ lunch & dinner Jul & Aug, closed Mon Sep–mid-Nov & mid-Mar–Jun), with an original geometric mosaic tiled floor, opens to a vine-draped alfresco deck where you can dine on freshly caught fish.

La Maison du Bassin (☎ 05 56 60 60 63; www.lamaisondubassin.com; 5 rue des Pionniers; s €90-195, d €110-215, apt €300) Four dreamy rooms the size of suites are in a separate annexe of this quixotic hideaway; the cosy rooms in the main house have details like a muslin-canopied sleigh bed, or a curtained bathtub in the centre of the room. Its chocolate-toned, contemporary restaurant, Le Bistrot du Bassin, serving dinner daily except Tuesday and lunch on weekends, with mains for €23-50, has a wi-fi'd bar area.

TOP SURF SPOTS ON THE ATLANTIC COAST

France's Atlantic Coast has some of Europe's best surf. Autumn is prime time for riding the waves, with warm(ish) water temperatures, consistent(ish) conditions and few(er) crowds. The biggest swells tend to roll in around Biarritz (p696), but the waves along this stretch of coast are mighty *malade* (sick)!

■ Hit the beaches south of Arcachon around the **Dune du Pilat** (opposite).

■ Take a lesson in the mellow waves at **Soulac-sur-Mer**. Reservations can be made through Soulac's **tourist office** (☎ 05 56 09 86 61; www.soulac.com; 68 rue de la Plage).

■ Watch the pros contest August's ASP (Association of Surfing Professionals; www.aspeurope.com) event at **Lacanau-Océan**.

■ Paddle out from the tip of pine-forested **Cap Ferret peninsula** (opposite).

■ Other hot spots (but don't let on we told you!) are **Le Porge-Océan**, **Montalivet** and **Hourtin-Plage**.

And for the best wave *away* from the coast, longboarders can attempt the **mascaret** (bore; mascaretgironde.free.fr), a tidal wave travelling inland from the Gironde Estuary. The best place to pick it up is St-Pardon (you'll need boots to get in).

GETTING THERE & AWAY

Les Bateliers Arcachonnais (UBA; ☎ 05 57 72 28 28; www.bateliers-arcachon.asso.fr in French) runs ferries from Jetée Thiers to Cap Ferret (adult/child return €10/6), across the mouth of the Bassin d'Arcachon. From April to October, boats run four to 20 times daily, depending on the season; the rest of the year there are two sailings on Monday, Wednesday and Friday and four on Saturday and Sunday.

Cap Ferret is a scenic drive around Bassin d'Arcachon or you can drive here directly from Bordeaux (71.8km) – take the D106 to the tip.

Gujan Mestras

pop 15,367

Picturesque oyster ports are dotted around the town of Gujan Mestras, which sprawls along 9km of coastline.

You'll find the **tourist office** (☎ 05 56 66 12 65; www.ville-gujanmestras.fr in French; 19 av de Lattre de Tassigny; ⏰ 8.30am-12.30pm & 2-6.30pm Mon-Sat, 9.30am-12.30pm Sun mid-Jun–Aug, 8.30am-12.30pm & 2-6.30pm Mon-Sat early Sep–mid-Sep, 8.30am-noon & 1.30-5.30pm Mon-Sat mid-Sep–mid-Jun, plus 9.30am-12.30pm Sun Apr) at the western edge of town in La Hume.

Flat-bottom oyster boats moored to weathered wooden shacks line the largest

port, **Port de Larros**, about 4km to the east. The small **Maison de l'Huître** (☎ 05 56 66 23 71; adult/child €2.80/2; ⏰ 10am-12.30pm & 2.30-6pm Mon-Sat) has a display on oyster farming, including a short film in English. The area's finest Banc d'Arguin oysters are sold direct from the growers 100m away at the little shop **Cap Noroit** (☎/fax 05 56 66 04 15; 112 allée du Haurat). A dozen medium oysters costs around €3, served at seafood restaurants with water-side terraces.

The Gujan Mestras train station is on the train line linking Bordeaux with Arcachon.

Le Teich Parc Ornithologique

Just 29% of the shallow 155-sq-km Bassin d'Arcachon is under water at low tide, attracting 260 species of migratory and nonmigratory birds each year. Committed to their preservation is the idyllic **Parc Ornithologique** (Bird Reserve; ☎ 05 56 22 80 93; www.parc-ornithologique-du-teich.com in French; adult/child €6.80/4.80; ⏰ 10am-8pm Jul & Aug, to 7pm mid-Apr–Jun & early Sep–mid-Sep, to 6pm mid-Sep–mid-Apr) situated in Le Teich, 15km east of Arcachon. Le Teich's train station, 1.2km south of the park, is linked with Bordeaux and Arcachon.

French Basque Country

The Basque Country ('Euskal Herria' in the Basque language) – the area around the western foothills of the Pyrenees as it slopes down to the Bay of Biscay – has been home to the Basque people for many centuries. The area straddles modern-day France and Spain (with roughly 20% on the French side) but it's still a land apart, stubbornly independent and profoundly different from either of the nation-states that have adopted it.

The French side (called 'Iparralde' in Basque or 'Le Pays Basque' in French), less populous and industrialised than the Spanish Basque region, is perhaps best known for its glitzy beach resort, Biarritz. But this medium-rise town, with bronzed surfers hooning around on mopeds and swarms of peak-season sun-seekers, is the least Basque of the area's towns.

More authentic is the cultural and administrative capital, Bayonne. Traditional Basque music, sports and festivals are a big part of the summer's entertainment and it's not just for the benefit of tourists. Bayonne, with its good transport links, restaurants and sleeping options, also makes an excellent base for exploring the region.

To the southwest is St-Jean de Luz, a relaxed family beach resort. There's also a bustling fishing port there, so bring along an appetite and tuck into some tasty Basque seafood specialities.

You'll find the Iparralde of old away from the coast, up in the hills, with little one-street villages to discover and green valleys to explore. St-Jean Pied de Port offers a likely base for such excursions, as an age-old pit stop for pilgrims heading over the border to Santiago de Compostela.

HIGHLIGHTS

- Indulge yourself with the delicious chocolates of **Bayonne** (p695)
- Surf the world-class waves at **Anglet beach** (p696)
- Catch a frantic game of high-speed **pelote basque** (p695)
- Creep up the mountainside railway on **Le Petit Train de la Rhune** (p706)
- Follow the centuries-old footsteps of pilgrims near **St-Jean Pied de Port** (p706)

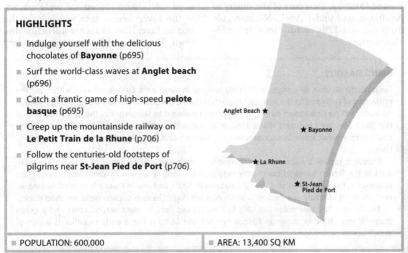

Anglet Beach ★

★ Bayonne

★ La Rhune

★ St-Jean Pied de Port

- POPULATION: 600,000
- AREA: 13,400 SQ KM

FRENCH BASQUE COUNTRY

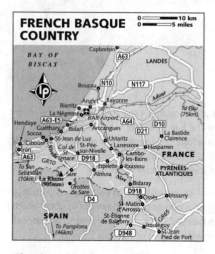

History

The origins and early history of the Basque people are a mystery. Roman sources mention a tribe called the Vascones living in the area and it's attested that the Basques took over what is now southwestern France in the 6th century. Converting to Christianity in the 10th century, they are still known for their strong devotion to Catholicism.

After resisting invasions, the Basques on both sides of the Pyrenees emerged from the turbulent Middle Ages with a fair degree of local autonomy, which they retained in France until the Revolution. The French Basque Country, then part of the duchy of Aquitaine, was under Anglo-Norman rule from the mid-12th century until the mid-15th century.

Basque nationalism flourished before and during the Spanish Civil War (1936–39). Until the death of Franco, the Spanish dictator, in 1975, many Basque nationalists and anti-Franco guerrillas from the other side of the Pyrenees sheltered in France. More recently, Spanish Euskadi ta Azkatasuna (ETA) terrorists would often seek sanctuary in France too but, with the organisation's declared renunciation of violence in March 2006, this may be a thing of the past.

Getting There & Away

All roads and train lines lead to Bayonne, which is easily accessible from the rest of France.

For rail travel to Spain, switch trains at the frontier since the Spanish track gauge is narrower. Take an SNCF train to Hendaye, where you can pick up the EuskoTren, familiarly known as 'El Topo' (The Mole), a shuttle train that runs regularly via Irún to San Sebastián.

Year-round, the Spanish company Sema runs twice-daily buses between Bayonne and San Sebastián via St-Jean de Luz, while ATCRB operates a summer-only service.

The airport (p695) serving Bayonne and Biarritz has domestic flights as well as services to the UK and Ireland.

BAYONNE
pop 41,800

Bayonne ('Baiona' in Basque) means 'the good river'. And indeed the wide estuary of the River Adour, into which leaks the smaller River Nive, in a sense still defines the town. The pair establish a watery boundary

---

BEING BASQUE

Euskara, the Basque language, is the only tongue in southwest Europe to have withstood the onslaught of Latin and its derivatives. Linguists reckon it's probably unrelated to any other tongue on earth and no-one knows its origins. Theories relating it to languages of the Caucasus, east of the Black Sea, are nowadays discredited, and similarities with the long-dead Iberian language could simply result from contact between the Iberians and Basques rather than from a common source.

Basque is spoken by about a million people in Spain and France, nearly all of whom are bilingual. In the French Basque Country, the language is widely spoken in Bayonne, but is even more common in the hilly hinterland. Two TV stations in Spain and one in France broadcast in Basque, and you'll occasionally see 'Hemen Euskara emaiten dugu' (Basque spoken here) on shop doors.

The Basque flag resembles the UK's but with a red field, a white vertical cross and a green diagonal one. Another common Basque symbol, the lauburu, like a curly swastika, is a sign of good luck or protection.

for Petit Bayonne with its narrow streets, attractive riverside buildings clad in red and green shutters, student bars and shoals of waterside restaurants. Here, Euskara is spoken almost as much as French.

Bayonne, cultural and economic capital of the French Basque country, forms, together with sprawling Anglet (that final 't' is pronounced) and Biarritz, 8km to the west, an urban area often called BAB (population around 100,000).

In addition to its yummy chocolates, Bayonne is famous for its marzipan and prime smoked ham. Incidental fact, if you're prepared to believe tradition: the *baïonnette* (bayonet) was developed here in the early 17th century.

History

Bayonne prospered from the 13th to 15th centuries under the dubious protection of the Anglo-Norman kings who ruled Aquitaine. A century later, Jews, expelled en masse from Spain, injected fresh commercial vitality and must be forever thanked for establishing chocolate making as a local trade. The town's 18th-century commercial prosperity was fuelled in no small measure by Basque pirate ships, which landed cargoes much more valuable and sweeter scented than the tonnes of cod caught off the coast of Newfoundland by the substantial Basque fishing fleet.

Orientation

The Rivers Adour and Nive split Bayonne into three: St-Esprit, the area north of the Adour; Grand Bayonne, the oldest part of the city, on the western bank of the Nive; and the very Basque Petit Bayonne quarter to its east.

Information

BOOKSHOPS

Elkar (☎ 05 59 59 35 14; place de l'Arsenal) A wealth of texts on Basque history and culture; walking in the Basque Country; maps and CDs of Basque music.

INTERNET ACCESS

Taxiphone (1 place Ste-Ursule; per hr €2; ☺ 11am-10pm) A welcoming new place that also does cheap international phone calls.

LAUNDRY

Hallwash (6 rue d'Espagne; ☺ 8am-8pm)

POST

Post Office (11 rue Jules Labat)
Post Office (21 blvd Alsace-Lorraine)

TOURIST INFORMATION

Tourist Office (☎ 05 59 46 01 46; www.bayonne-tourisme.com; place des Basques; ☺ 9am-7pm Mon-Sat, 10am-1pm Sun Jul & Aug, 9am-6.30pm Mon-Fri, 10am-6pm Sat Sep-Jun) Useful free brochures include *Fêtes*, listing French Basque Country cultural and sporting events, and the free booklet *Guide des Loisirs en Béarn & Pays Basque*, a detailed summary of almost everything to do and see in Aquitaine. From mid-July to mid-September, the office organises guided tours of the city (€5) in French at 10.30am except Sunday.

Sights & Activities

RAMPARTS

Thanks to Vauban's 17th-century fortifications (see the boxed text, p62), now grass-covered and dotted with trees, a slim, green belt surrounds the city centre. You can walk the stretches of the old ramparts that rise above blvd Rempart Lachepaillet and rue Tour de Sault.

CATHÉDRALE STE-MARIE

The twin towers of Bayonne's Gothic **cathedral** (☺ 8am-noon & 3-7pm Mon-Sat) soar above the city. Construction began in the 13th century, when Bayonne was ruled by the Anglo-Normans, and was completed well after France assumed control in 1451. The nave's vaulted ceiling reflects these political changes: up there are both the English coat of arms (three lions) and that most French of emblems, the fleur-de-lys. Above the north aisle are three lovely stained-glass windows, mainly Renaissance with 19th-century neogothic additions. The entrance to the stately 13th-century **cloister** (☺ 9am-12.30pm & 2-6pm Jun-Sep, to 5pm Oct-May) is on place Louis Pasteur.

MUSÉE BASQUE ET DE L'HISTOIRE DE BAYONNE

This **museum** (☎ 05 59 46 61 90; www.musee-basque.com in French; 37 quai des Corsaires; adult/student/under 18yr €5.50/3/free; ☺ 10am-6.30pm Tue-Sun May-Oct, 10am-12.30pm & 2-6pm Tue-Sun Nov-Apr) is a must if you want to get under the skin of the unique Basque people. There's a reconstructed farm and interior of a typical *etxe* (home), and plenty on Basque fisherfolk, pastoralists and popular traditions. You'll

FRENCH BASQUE COUNTRY

BAYONNE

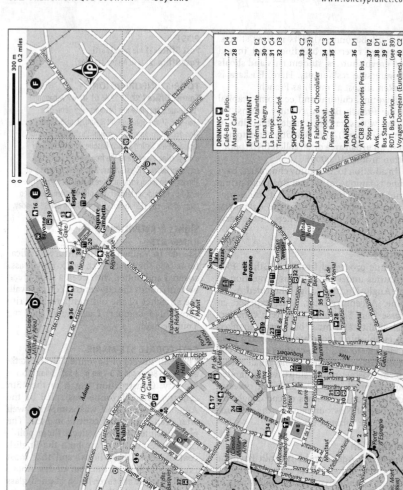

INFORMATION	
Elkar................................	1 D4
Hallwash...........................	2 C4
Post Office.......................	3 E2
Post Office.......................	4 D1
Taxiphone.........................	5 D1
Tourist Office....................	6 C2

SIGHTS & ACTIVITIES	
Cathédrale Ste-Marie............	7 C3
Cloister...........................	8 C3
Musée Basque et de l'Histoire	
de Bayonne.......................	9 D3
Musée Bonnat...................	10 D3
Riverboat (Le Bayonne)........	11 E3

SLEEPING	
Adour Hôtel.......................	12 D1
Hôtel Côte Basque.............	13 E1
Hôtel des Arceaux.............	14 D1
Hôtel Loustau....................	15 D1
Hôtel Paris-Madrid.............	16 E1
Le Grand Hôtel..................	17 C2

EATING	
Auberge du Cheval Blanc.....	18 D3
Bar-Restaurant du Marché.....	19 C4
Bistrot Ste-Cluque.............	20 D1
Bodega Ibaia.....................	21 C4
Covered Market..................	22 C4
La Grange........................	23 C3
Le Chistera.......................	24 C3
Restaurant Agadir..............	25 E1
Restaurant François Miura....	26 D3

DRINKING	
Café-Bar Le Patio..............	27 D4
Massaï Café......................	28 D4

ENTERTAINMENT	
Cinéma L'Atalante..............	29 E2
La Luna Negra..................	30 C4
La Pompe.........................	31 C4
Trinquet St-André..............	32 D3

SHOPPING	
Cazenave.........................	33 C2
Daranatz.........................	(see 33)
La Fabrique du Chocolater....	34 C3
Puyodebat........................	35 D4
Pierre Ibaïalde..................	

TRANSPORT	
ADA................................	36 D1
ATCRB & Transportes Pesa Bus	
Stop...............................	37 B2
Avis...............................	38 D1
Bus Station......................	39 E1
RDTL Bus Service...............	(see 39)
Voyages Domejean (Eurolines)...	40 C2

also learn lots about Bayonne, French Basque Country's prime fishing port and maritime window on the wider world.

MUSÉE BONNAT

More art gallery than museum **Musée Bonnat** (☎ 05 59 59 08 52; 5 rue Jacques Lafitte; adult/student/child €5.50/3/free; ☼ 10am-6.30pm Wed-Mon May-Oct, 10am-12.30pm & 2-6pm Wed-Mon Nov-Apr), contains a multitude of treasures, including canvases by El Greco, Goya, Ingres and Degas, and a roomful of works by Rubens.

A **combined ticket** (adult/student €9/4.50) admits you to both the Musée Basque and Musée Bonnat.

RIVER TRIPS

The riverboat **Le Bayonne** (☎ 06 80 74 21 51; ☼ 10am-noon & 2.45-7pm mid-Jun–mid-Sep) runs two-hour cruises on the River Adour – if a minimum of 15 passengers show up.

Festivals & Events

Fêtes de Bayonne The town's premier fiesta is the five-day Fêtes de Bayonne, beginning on the first Wednesday in August. They do a 'running of the bulls', as in Pamplona, Spain, only here it's more benign; they use cows not bulls and most of the time participants are chasing the frisky heifers rather than vice versa. The festival also includes Basque music, bullfights, fireworks, a parade of floats, and rugby.

Ham Fair During Easter week, the town hosts a Ham Fair, honouring *jambon de bayonne*, the acclaimed local ham.

Journées du Chocolat May brings the Journées du Chocolat (below).

La Ruée au Jazz Four days of stompin' in mid-July, attracting jazz lovers from all over France.

CHOCOLATE WEEKEND

In 1870, Bayonne boasted 130 *chocolatiers* (specialist makers of chocolate), more than in all of Switzerland. Eleven are still in business (for a trio of the best, see p695). During the **Journées du Chocolat**, celebrated on a variable weekend in May, rivalry is keen as the master chocolatiers set up the tools of their craft in front of their shops so that all can watch them weave their sticky magic.

Each year features another country with a tradition of making miracles from the humble cocoa bean. In 2006, the honoured guest was Ecuador.

And yes, there are free samples...

Sleeping

It's tough to find a bed from mid-July to mid-August and near impossible during the Fêtes de Bayonne.

Auberge de Jeunesse (☎ 05 59 58 70 00; www .hibiarritz.org); 19 rte des Vignes, Anglet; dm incl breakfast €16.50, camping per person incl breakfast €10.40; ☼ Apr-Oct) Complete with a Scottish pub, this hostel is lively and popular. Reservations are essential in summer. The hostel also has a small camp site.

Hôtel Paris-Madrid (☎ 05 59 55 13 98; sorbois@ wanadoo.fr; place de la Gare; s/d €18/24, r with shower only €27, d/tr with bathroom €32/47) You can tumble off the train straight into this highly recommended, hyperfriendly place. The owners speak English, and rooms, surrounding a peaceful inner patio, are excellent value. Bright murals and the large papier-mâché giraffe and crocodile add colour and flair. Parking free.

Hôtel Côte Basque (☎ 05 59 55 10 21; fax 05 59 55 39 85; 2 rue Maubec; s/d/tr from €35/47/57) Here's another place, also near the station, that's had a massive face-lift. Ask for one of the recently renovated rooms (the majority), which are pleasant and comfortable, if unexceptional.

Adour Hôtel (☎ 05 59 55 11 31; www.adourhotel .net; 13 place Ste-Ursule; d/tr from €55/70) Just north of the River Adour and conveniently near the station, this friendly family establishment has bright, airy rooms, comprehensively renovated in 2005. Each one is decorated according to a Basque theme – bullfighting, rugby, chocolate, cuisine and more.

Hôtel des Arceaux (☎ 05 59 59 15 53; www.hotel -arceaux.com in French; 26 rue Port Neuf; r €60) In two years, the young family who took over this hotel has turned it around. Each of the 17 rooms is now spick and span and individually decorated with style. Nos 3 and 8, with large windows overlooking the bustling pedestrian street below, can sleep up to four (€7 supplement per person).

Hôtel Loustau (☎ 05 59 55 08 08; www.hotel-loustau .com; 1 place de la République; s/d/tr/q from €77/84/89/94; ✖ ✖) This tall, attractive 18th-century building on the St-Esprit side of the town has comfortable rooms. On the southern side of the building, the full-length windows open out onto views of the River Adour. It also runs a good restaurant. Wi-fi available.

Le Grand Hôtel (☎ 05 59 59 62 00, www.bw-legrand hotel.com; 21 rue Thiers; s €62-128, d €68-140; ✖ ✖)

This tastefully refurbished hotel, part of the Best Western chain, offers spacious cream-toned rooms. The old building was once a convent though you'd never guess from the slick, modern interior. It has a good restaurant and a particularly cosy bar. Wi-fi available. Parking €12.50.

Eating

You have a great choice of medium-priced restaurants around the covered market and all along quai Amiral Jauréguiberry. Over the River Nive, quai Galuperie and quai des Corsaires offer other tempting choices.

Bar-Restaurant du Marché (☎ 05 59 59 22 66; 39 rue des Basques; ☺ lunch Mon-Sat) You can fill yourself to bursting point for under €15 at this unpretentious place with its ample, homely cooking, all but a stone's throw from the market and run for 30 years by the same welcoming, Basque-speaking family.

Bodega Ibaia (☎ 05 59 59 86 66; 45 quai Amiral Jau-réguiberry; mains €8-12; ☺ lunch & dinner Tue-Sat, dinner Mon) This atmospheric Basque restaurant/tapas bar with wooden benches, sawdust on the floor and traditional Spanish tiling is more informal than most of the terrace restaurants on this popular stretch.

Bistrot Ste-Cluque (☎ 05 59 55 82 43; 9 rue Hugues; menus €10-16, mains 9.50-15; ☺ lunch & dinner) There's only one menu here – a large blackboard that's propped up before you. Noisy (the music's a decibel or two too loud), smoky and with waiters bustling about everywhere, it's a wonderful, no-pretensions place.

Le Chistera (☎ 05 59 59 25 93; 42 rue Port Neuf; menus €15, mains €10-14; ☺ lunch & dinner Thu-Sun, lunch Tue & lunch Wed) This very Basque place deservedly features in many a French gastronomic guide. It's aptly named (the chistera is the basket that pelota players strap to their wrists) and decorated with motifs from the sport, the owner having spent 14 years in the US as a professional player.

Restaurant Agadir (☎ 05 59 55 66 56; 3 rue Ste-Catherine; menus €16; ☺ lunch & dinner, closed lunch Mon) This enthusiastically decorated restaurant in St-Esprit, shimmering with red and gold, serves up southern Moroccan-style couscous dishes (€9 to €13).

La Grange (☎ 05 59 46 17 84; 26 quai Galuperie; mains €14-22; ☺ lunch & dinner Mon-Sat) With a shady outside terrace, this popular place overlooks the River Nive. Basque music plays sotto voce in the cosy interior, hung

with hanks of dried peppers and garlic. Traditional French flavours include plenty of seafood options and the desserts are to die for.

Restaurant François Miura (☎ 05 59 59 49 89; 24 rue Marengo; menus €19-30; ☺ lunch & dinner, closed dinner Sun & Wed) This ultrastylish place has a strictly postmodern décor. It's one of the places to be seen in Petit Bayonne, where the food, such as tender pigeon stuffed with foie gras, is just as fashionable as the clientele.

Auberge du Cheval Blanc (☎ 05 59 59 01 33; 68 rue Bourgneuf; menus €28-75; ☺ lunch & dinner Tue-Fri, dinner Sat & lunch Sun) Renowned as one of the town's most exclusive restaurants, this refined eatery with its pastel tones and original artwork fully deserves its Michelin star for its mouthwatering creative French cuisine. A must with the business set at lunchtime.

SELF-CATERING

The **covered market** (quai Commandant Roquebert) occupies an imposing riverside building. There are a number of tempting food shops and delicatessens along rue Port Neuf and rue d'Espagne.

Drinking

The greatest concentration of pubs and bars is in the Petit Bayonne area, especially along rue Pannecau, rue des Cordeliers and quai Galuperie. Two lively night-time spots are **Café-Bar Le Patio** (38 rue Pannecau) and **Massaï Café** (14 rue des Cordeliers).

Entertainment

Two free publications with news of upcoming cultural events are À l'Affiche and the trimestrial Les Saisons de la Culture, both carried by the tourist office.

Every Thursday in July and August, there's traditional **Basque music** (admission free; ☺ 9.30pm) in place Charles de Gaulle.

Between October and June **Trinquet St-André** (☎ 05 59 59 18 69; rue du Jeu de Paume; tickets around €9) stages main nue matches (opposite) every Thursday at 4.30pm.

In summer, bullfights are held from time to time at **Les Arènes** (☎ 05 59 25 65 30; 19 av Maréchal Foch), 1km west of the city centre. The tourist office has details of upcoming corridas and also sells tickets.

Cinéma l'Atalante (☎ 05 59 55 76 63; www.cinema-atalante.org in French; 7 rue Denis Etcheverry) screens art-house nondubbed films.

PELOTA

Pelota (*pelote basque* in French) is the generic name for a group of games native to the Basque Country, all played using a hard ball with a rubber core (the *pelote*), which is struck with bare hands *(mains nues)*, a wooden paddle *(pala or paleta)*, or a scooplike racquet made of wicker, leather or wood and strapped to the wrist *(chistera)*.

Cesta punta, also known as jai alai, the world's fastest ball game and the most popular variety of pelota, became faster and faster after the introduction of rubber made it possible to produce balls with more bounce. The game is played with a *chistera*, with which players catch and hurl the ball. Matches take place in a jai alai *(cancha)*, a three-walled court, usually a precise 53m long.

The walls and floor are made of materials that can withstand the repeated impact of the ball, which can reach speeds of up to 300km/h. A cancha and its tiers of balconies for spectators constitute a fronton. Other types of pelota (such as *joko-garbi, main nue, pala, paleta, pasaka, rebot* and *xare*) are played in outdoor, one-wall courts, also known as frontons, and in enclosed structures called *trinquets*.

La Luna Negra (☎ 05 59 25 78 05; rue des Augustins; ⏱ 7pm-2am Wed-Sat) is a creative cabaret and alternative theatre venue that puts on live jazz, salsa and tango evenings and concerts of world music.

La Pompe (☎ 05 59 25 48 12; 7 rue des Augustins; admission €8; ⏱ midnight-5am Fri & Sat Sep-Jul), a tiny sweatbox of a place where the music comes in all styles, is the only discotheque in central Bayonne.

Shopping

Bayonne is famous throughout France for its ham. For the lowest prices, visit the covered market (opposite). For the best produce, visit a specialist shop such as **Pierre Ibaïalde** (☎ 05 59 25 65 30; 41 rue des Cordeliers) where you can taste before you buy.

The town's other claim to gastronomic fame is its chocolate. Two traditional *chocolateries* are **Daranatz** (☎ 05 59 59 03 05; 15 rue Port Neuf) and **Cazenave** (☎ 05 59 59 03 16; 19 rue Port Neuf), where you'll find pralines (the size of apples) to challenge even the most devout chocoholics. You can also see chocolates being made at **La Fabrique du Chocolatier Puyodebat** (☎ 05 59 59 20 86; 9 rue des Gouverneurs).

Getting There & Away

AIR

Biarritz-Anglet-Bayonne airport (☎ 05 59 43 83 83; www.biarritz.aeroport.fr in French) is 5km southwest of central Bayonne and 3km southeast of the centre of Biarritz. Ryanair flies daily to/from London Stansted and three times weekly to/from Dublin. Air France has several daily flights to/from Paris (Orly and Roissy) and Lyon.

Bus 6 links both Bayonne and Biarritz with the airport (buses depart roughly hourly). A taxi from the town centre costs around €15.

BUS

From place des Basques, **ATCRB buses** (☎ 05 59 26 06 99) follow the coast to the Spanish border. There are nine services daily to St-Jean de Luz (€3, 40 minutes) with connections for Hendaye (€3, one hour). Summer beach traffic can double journey times. **Transportes Pesa** (☎ in Spain 902 10 12 10) buses leave twice a day for Bilbao in Spain, calling by Irún and San Sebastián.

From the train station, **RDTL** (☎ 05 59 55 17 59; www.rdtl.fr in French) runs services northwards into Les Landes. For beaches north of Bayonne, such as Mimizan Plage and Moliets Plage, get off at Vieux Boucau (1¼ hours, six or seven daily).

Eurolines is represented by **Voyages Domejean** (☎ 05 59 59 19 33; 3 place Charles de Gaulle). Buses stop in the square, opposite this travel agent's office.

CAR & MOTORCYCLE

Among several rental agencies near the train station are **ADA** (☎ 05 59 50 37 10; 10bis quai de Lesseps) and **Avis** (☎ 05 59 55 06 56; 1 rue Ste-Ursule).

TRAIN

TGVs run between Bayonne and Paris' Gare Montparnasse (€75.60, five hours, eight daily).

There are five trains daily to St-Jean Pied de Port (€7.90, one hour) and fairly frequent services to/from Biarritz (€2.20, 10 minutes), St-Jean de Luz (€4.10, 25 minutes), plus the Franco-Spanish border towns of Hendaye (€6.20, 40 minutes) and Irún (€6.50, 45 minutes).

There are also train services to Bordeaux (€24.90, 2¼ hours, at least 10 daily), Pau (€14.30, 1¼ hours, nine daily) and Toulouse (€35.50, 3¾ hours, five daily).

Getting Around

BICYCLE
Near the train station, Adour Hôtel (p693) rents out bikes for €9/12.50/30 per half-/full/three days.

BUS
STAB buses link Bayonne, Biarritz and Anglet. A single ticket costs €1.20 while carnets of five/10 are €4.75/9.50. STAB's **information office** (☎ 05 59 52 59 52; www.bus-stab.com in French) was besieged by builders when we last visited and no-one yet knew its new home. Buses 1 and 2 run between Bayonne and Biarritz about 50 times daily, stopping at the Hôtels de Ville and stations of both towns. No 1, which runs every 15 minutes until 8.30pm, is the fastest and most frequent.

A free bright-orange *navette* (shuttle bus) describes a wriggling route around the heart of town.

For information on buses to and from the airport, see p690.

CAR & MOTORCYCLE
There's free parking along the southern end of av des Allées Paulmy, within easy walking distance of the tourist office.

TAXI
Call **Taxi Bayonne** (☎ 05 59 59 48 48) or **Taxi Gare** (☎ 05 59 55 13 15).

BIARRITZ
pop 30,700
The stylish coastal town of Biarritz, 8km west of Bayonne, took off as a resort in the mid-19th century when Napoleon III and his Spanish-born wife, Eugénie, visited regularly. For years the darling of wealthy French families, Biarritz was dumped in the second half of the 20th century by many who preferred the fleshpots of the Mediterranean and cheaper holidays in coastal Spain. Nowadays, everyone from the *jeu-*

nesse dorée (golden youth) of Paris to beach bums in camper vans are flocking back to this lovely seaside resort, renowned for its beaches and some of Europe's best surfing.

The town is expensive. If you're travelling on a budget, consider staying in Bayonne and travelling through, as many French holidaymakers do. Many surfers camp or stay at one of the two excellent youth hostels in Biarritz and Anglet.

Orientation
Place Clemenceau, the heart of town, is just south of the main beach (Grande Plage). Pointe St-Martin, topped with a lighthouse, rounds off Plage Miramar, the northern continuation of the Grande Plage, which is bounded on its southern side by Pointe Atalaye.

Both the train station and airport are about 3km southeast of the centre.

Information
Form@tic (☎ 05 59 22 12 79; 15 av de la Marne; per hr €4; ⊙ 10am-8pm daily Jul-Sep, 10am-7pm Mon-Sat Oct-Jun, closed Sat afternoon Nov-May) Internet access.
Laundrette (11 av de la Marne; ⊙ 7am-9pm)
Post Office (rue de la Poste)
Tourist Office (☎ 05 59 22 37 00; www.biarritz.fr; square d'Ixelles; ⊙ 8am-8pm daily Jul & Aug, 9am-6pm Mon-Sat, 10am-5pm Sun Sep-Jun) Publishes *Biarritz Scope et Shops*, a free monthly what's-on guide. There's a tourist office annexe at the train station in July and August.

Sights & Activities

BEACHES
Biarritz' fashionable beaches are end-to-end bodies on hot summer days. In the high season, the **Grande Plage** and also **Plage Miramar** to its north are lined with striped bathing tents. North of Pointe St-Martin, the superb surfing beaches of **Anglet** stretch northwards for more than 4km. Take eastbound bus 9 from place Clemenceau.

Beyond long, exposed **Plage de la Côte des Basques**, some 500m south of Port Vieux, are **Plage de Marbella** and **Plage de la Milady**. Take westbound bus 9.

MUSÉE DE LA MER
Biarritz' **Musée de la Mer** (Sea Museum; ☎ 05 59 22 33 34; www.museedelamer.com; Esplanade du Rocher de la Vierge; adult/child €7.50/4.60; ⊙ 9.30am-12.30pm & 2-6pm, closed Mon Nov-Mar) overlooks Rocher de la Vierge. The ground-floor aquarium has 24

BIARRITZ

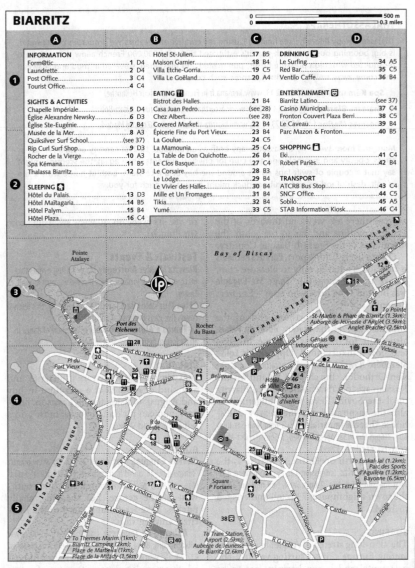

INFORMATION
Form@tic...1 D4
Laundrette.......................................2 D4
Post Office.......................................3 C4
Tourist Office..................................4 C4

SIGHTS & ACTIVITIES
Chapelle Impériale..........................5 D4
Église Alexandre Newsky................6 D3
Église Ste-Eugénie.........................7 B4
Musée de la Mer.............................8 A3
Quiksilver Surf School...............(see 37)
Rip Curl Surf Shop..........................9 D3
Rocher de la Vierge......................10 A3
Spa Kémana..................................11 B5
Thalassa Biarritz...........................12 D3

SLEEPING
Hôtel du Palais.............................13 D4
Hôtel Maïtagaria...........................14 B5
Hôtel Palym..................................15 B4
Hôtel Plaza...................................16 C4

Hôtel St-Julien..............................17 B5
Maison Garnier.............................18 B4
Villa Etche-Gorria.........................19 C5
Villa Le Goëland...........................20 A4

EATING
Bistrot des Halles..........................21 B4
Casa Juan Pedro.....................(see 28)
Chez Albert.............................(see 28)
Covered Market............................22 B4
Épicerie Fine du Port Vieux............23 B4
La Goulue.....................................24 C5
La Mamounia................................25 C4
La Table de Don Quichotte............26 B4
Le Clos Basque..............................27 C4
Le Corsaire....................................28 B3
Le Lodge.......................................29 B4
Le Vivier des Halles.......................30 B4
Mille et Un Fromages....................31 B4
Tikia...32 B4
Yumé..33 C5

DRINKING
Le Surfing.....................................34 A5
Red Bar..35 C5
Ventilo Caffe................................36 B4

ENTERTAINMENT
Biarritz Latino.........................(see 37)
Casino Municipal..........................37 C4
Fronton Couvert Plaza Berri..........38 C5
Le Caveau.....................................39 B4
Parc Mazon & Fronton..................40 B5

SHOPPING
Eki...41 C4
Robert Pariès...............................42 B4

TRANSPORT
ATCRB Bus Stop............................43 C4
SNCF Office..................................44 C4
Sobilo..45 A5
STAB Information Kiosk..................46 C4

tanks seething with underwater life from the Bay of Biscay (Golfe de Gascogne). On the 1st floor are exhibits on commercial fishing and whaling, recalling Biarritz' whaling past. On the 3rd floor, it's seal feeding time at 10.30am and 5pm. In a nearby pool sleek baby sharks grin back at you, while the top floor has a rather mournful display of stuffed birds.

Tickets are €1 cheaper if you buy them at the tourist office.

OTHER ATTRACTIONS

Stroll over the footbridge at the end of Pointe Atalaye to **Rocher de la Vierge** (Rock of the Virgin), named after the white statue of the Virgin and child. From this impressive

---

THALASSOTHERAPY

Thalassotherapy (literally, 'sea healing'), using the curative and restorative properties of sea water, is big, booming business. Each year it's estimated that over 200,000 French allow themselves to be squirted with high pressure hoses, pummelled and massaged, smeared in mud and seaweed and come away smiling. Biarritz has three such centres.

■ **Spa Kémana** (☎ 05 59 22 12 13; www.kemana.fr in French; 3 carrefour Hélianthe)

■ **Thalassa Biarritz** (☎ 05 59 41 30 01; www.accorthalassa.com; 11 rue Louison-Bobet)

■ **Thermes Marins** (☎ 05 59 23 01 22; www.biarritz-thalasso.com; 80 rue de Madrid)

More and more swear by thalassotherapy both as an antidote to 21st-century problems such as stress, obesity and insomnia and as a cure for physical ailments. Then again, the sceptical might say that a couple of swift laps swum around the bay or a nice warm bath at home with a kilo of salt, dash of iodine and a rubber duck might do just as much for you.

---

outcrop there are views northwards of the Landes coastline and, far to the south, the mountains of the Spanish Basque Country.

Once a lively fishing port, **Port des Pêcheurs** is nowadays a haven only to pleasure craft. Above it, the neogothic **Église Ste-Eugénie** was built in 1864 for – who else? – Empress Eugénie.

Dominating the northern end of the Grande Plage is the stately **Hôtel du Palais**, also built for Empress Eugénie in 1854 and now a luxury hotel. Opposite is **Église Alexandre Newsky** (8 av de l'Impératrice), a Russian Orthodox church built by and for the Russian aristocrats who frequented Biarritz until the Soviet Revolution. Eugénie was also the inspiration for the nearby doll's-house **Chapelle Impériale** (☻ 3-6pm Mon-Sat Jul & Aug, 3-6pm Thu & Sat Apr-Jun & Sep, 3-5pm Thu Oct-Mar), constructed in 1864.

To the north on Pointe St-Martin is the **Phare de Biarritz** (admission €2; ☻ 10am-noon & 3-7pm Tue-Sun Jul & Aug, 2-6pm Sat & Sun mid-Apr–Jun), the town's lighthouse, 73m tall and erected in 1834.

SURFING
The 4km-long stretch of Anglet beach ranks among Europe's finest surfing venues. The best rental and lesson bargains are to be had at the Bayonne/Anglet (p693) and Biarritz Auberges de Jeunesse. Alternatively, for gear and lessons, try **Rip Curl Surf Shop** (☎ 05 59 24 38 40; 2 av de la Reine Victoria) or the **Quiksilver Surf School** (☎ 05 59 22 03 12; www.biarritz-boardrid ers.com in French) under the Casino Municipal.

For details of surf conditions ring the French-language **Swell Line** (☎ 08 92 68 40 64)

or see its webcam at www.swell-line.com (in French).

Festivals & Events
Biarritz Maider Arosteguy Major surfing events take place year-round, including this three-day event around Easter.

Fêtes Musicales de Biarritz More sedately, this festival covers five days of classical music in April.

Le Temps d'Aimer A two-week celebration of dance in all its forms, held in mid-September.

Sleeping
Inexpensive hotels are rare in Biarritz, and any kind of room is at a premium in July and August. Outside the high season, however, you can pick and choose; most prices fall by a good 25%.

BUDGET
Biarritz Camping (☎ 05 59 23 00 12; www.biarritz -camping.fr; 28 rue d'Harcet; pitch €15-21.50; ☻ mid-May–mid-Oct; ⬛) This camp site, 2km south-west of the centre, has spacious, shady pitches. Take westbound bus 9 to the Biarritz Camping stop.

Auberge de Jeunesse (☎ 05 59 41 76 00; www .hibiarritz.org; 8 rue Chiquito de Cambo; dm incl breakfast €17.20; ☻ year-round) Like Anglet's youth hostel, this popular place, with rooms for two to four hostellers, offers outdoor activities such as surfing, sailing and guided walks. From the train station, follow the railway westwards for 800m.

MIDRANGE & TOP END
Hôtel Palym (☎ 05 59 24 16 56; www.le-palmarium .com; 7 rue du Port Vieux; d with bathroom €50-55,

d/tr without bathroom €42/52; mid-Jan–mid-Nov) This welcoming 20-room, family-run place occupies a brightly painted town house on a street packed with hotels. Bedrooms, on the floors above the family's bustling restaurant, are colourful though the bathrooms are a squeeze.

Villa Etche-Gorria (05 59 24 00 74; www.hotel -etche-gorria.com; 21 av du Maréchal Foch; r €50-90, without bathroom €45; mid-Dec–3rd week Nov) This pretty Basque villa, set back from the main road, is run by Pierre, the amiable, English-speaking owner. First-floor rooms are huge and high-ceilinged. Two have large balconies overlooking the public garden. The three small, cheaper attic rooms on the 2nd floor are particularly good value.

Hôtel St-Julien (05 59 24 20 39; www.saint-julien -biarritz.com in French; 20 av Carnot; s €60-80, d €66-99) The friendly new owners have taken a new broom to this attractive late-19th-century villa, to which you're immediately drawn by its bright façade and shutters. Inside, there's the original parquet flooring and lots of pleasing woodwork. Third-floor rooms have views of both mountains and sea. Parking is free.

Hôtel Maïtagaria (05 59 24 26 65; www.hotel -maitagaria.com; 34 av Carnot; d €56-64, tr €74-80) Spotless, modern rooms and swish bathrooms make this friendly place good value – especially its large, two-roomed family suite (€80). Not least of its charms is its rear summer terrace and ornamental pool.

Maison Garnier (05 59 01 60 70; www.hotel-bi arritz.com in French; 29 rue Gambetta; r €95-130) The seven rooms of this elegant mansion are delightfully decorated and furnished. All are large (the two with twin beds particularly so) while those up at attic level (especially No 5) have a special charm of their own.

Hôtel Plaza (05 59 24 74 00; www.groupe-segeric .com; 20 av Édouard VII; s/d from €105/125;) The Plaza is a three-star Art Deco delight overlooking Grande Plage. Refurbished to great effect, the original 1930s glass-fronted lift and plenty of decorative detail throughout give the feel of a glamorous hotel in its heyday. Spacious rooms, many with beach views, have Art Deco dressing tables, plum-coloured armchairs and marble-effect bathrooms. Wi-fi available.

Villa Le Goëland (05 59 24 25 76; www.vil lagoeland.com; 12 plateau de l'Atalaye; r €130-250;) This stunning family home with its chateau-like spires, perches high on a plateau above Pointe Atalaye. Rooms, tastefully furnished with antiques, family photos and mementos, have panoramic views of town, the sea and across to Spain. There are only three rooms (opt for *chambre Goëland* with its huge private terrace) so advance booking is essential. Wi-fi available.

Eating

Le Corsaire (05 59 24 63 72; Port des Pêcheurs; mains €11-15; lunch & dinner Tue-Sat) The service may be excruciatingly slow at peak times, but you can savour the delightful harbourside setting from the terrace. It's all about seafood here at the water's edge, with dishes including dorado *à l'espagnole* and grilled cod with chorizo. It's one of three popular fish restaurants, with neighbours **Casa Juan Pedro** (05 59 24 00 86) and **Chez Albert** (05 59 24 43 84; mains €17-25) offering similar fares.

Tikia (05 59 24 46 09; 1 place Ste Eugénie; menus €12.80-20; lunch & dinner) 'Tikia' is the Basque word for small. The restaurant's indeed modestly sized, though the same can't be said of the giant *brochettes* (skewers) of duck, steak or seafood. For lighter appetites there's a good selection of salads and local wines, all topped off with friendly service.

Le Lodge (05 59 24 73 78; 1 rue du Port Vieux; mains €13-17; lunch & dinner Tue-Sat) Disregard the indifferent African art and naff zebra- and leopard-skin tablecloths. Concentrate instead upon the pleasures of Le Lodge's traditional cuisine and you'll enjoy a fine dining experience.

La Mamounia (05 59 24 76 08; 4 rue Jean Bart; lunch & dinner) The extravagant North African décor, the centrepiece a ridiculously huge Moroccan teapot, makes this a suitable place to tuck into delicious tagine (€16) and couscous (€13 to €19.50).

Le Clos Basque (05 59 24 24 96; 12 rue Louis Barthou; menus €24, mains €12; lunch & dinner Tue-Sat) With its tiles and exposed stonework this tiny place could have strayed in from Spain. The cuisine, however, is emphatically Basque, traditional with a contemporary twist or two. In summer, reserve a place on its popular terrace.

La Goulue (05 59 24 90 90; 3 rue Étienne Ardoin; menus €24, mains €14; lunch & dinner Tue-Fri, dinner Sat & Sun) This brasserie with its reproduction *belle époque* décor, mirrors and ancient gramophones offers traditional French cooking with a nod or two towards the Basque country and Les Landes, to the north.

Bistrot des Halles (☎ 05 59 24 21 22; 1 rue du Centre; mains €14-17; Ⓨ lunch & dinner) One of a cluster of decent restaurants along rue du Centre that take their produce fresh from the nearby covered market, this bustling place serves three-course meals from the blackboard menu for about €25, including wine.

Le Vivier des Halles (☎ 05 59 24 58 57; 8 rue du Centre; menus €25; Ⓨ lunch & dinner daily Jul-Sep, Tue-Sun Oct-Jun) The fish could almost flap their way up the road from the nearby covered market to this place, where the seafood is very reasonably priced and the hot fish soup a special delight.

Yumé (☎ 05 59 22 01 02; 6 rue Jean Bart; menus €34-47; Ⓨ lunch & dinner Mon-Fri, lunch Sat) This stylish, gastronomic Japanese restaurant offers authentic, well-presented sushi, sashimi and tempura dishes.

SELF-CATERING
Just downhill from Biarritz' **covered market**, **La Table de Don Quichotte** (12 av Victor Hugo) sells all sorts of Spanish hams, sausages, pickles and wines, while you'll find a tempting array of cheeses, wines and pâtés at nearby **Mille et Un Fromages** (8 av Victor Hugo). Down at sea level, **Épicerie Fine du Port Vieux** (41bis rue Mazagran) is another excellent delicatessen.

Drinking
There are several good bars along rue du Port Vieux and the streets radiating from it. It's also well worth snooping around place Clemenceau and the central food market area.

Le Surfing (☎ 05 59 24 78 72; 9 blvd Prince des Galles; Ⓨ daily) After a hard day's surfing, drop in here to discuss waves and wipe-outs. The bar is full of surfing memorabilia and there's an outside terrace with decent views.

Red Bar (9 ave Maréchal Foch; Ⓨ Tue-Sun) The huge frame of owner Philippe Bernat-Salles, a *rugbyman* who played for France and Biarritz Olympique (their colours red and white – hence the name), leans over the bar of this temple to the oval ball.

Ventilo Caffe (rue du Port Vieux; Ⓨ Wed-Sun, daily in summer) Playing great music, this café, which has recently had a makeover, continues to attract a young crowd and gets packed to the gills on summer nights.

Entertainment
In high summer there are free Friday-evening **classical music concerts** in front of Église Ste-Eugénie and at other venues.

If you fancy frittering away your travel money, step into the white slab of Biarritz' **Casino Municipal** (1 av Édouard VII). Constructed in 1928, its over 200 fruit machines whir and chink until the wee hours.

Two discos near the town centre are **Le Caveau** (☎ 05 59 24 16 17; 4 rue Gambetta; Ⓨ 11pm-5am) and **Biarritz Latino** (☎ 05 59 22 77 59; Ⓨ 11pm-5am Tue-Sat), within the Casino Municipal.

At the **Fronton Couvert Plaza Berri** (☎ 05 59 22 15 72; 42 av du Maréchal Foch) there's pelota (p695) at 7.15pm every Tuesday and Friday in July and August. Other tournaments are held year-round. From July to mid-September, the open-air fronton at **Parc Mazon** has regular *chistera* matches at 9pm on Monday. Admission to each is around €8.

Between mid-June and mid-September, **Euskal-Jaï** (☎ 05 59 23 91 09; av Henri Haget) in the Parc des Sports d'Aguiléra complex, 2km east of central Biarritz, has regular professional *cesta punta* matches (admission €10 to €20) at 9pm. Bus 1 stops nearby.

Shopping
For Basque music, crafts and guidebooks, visit **Eki** (☎ 05 59 24 79 64; 21 av de Verdun). For scrumptious chocolates and Basque sweets, call by **Robert Pariès** (1 place Bellevue).

Getting There & Away
AIR
Ryanair flies to Biarritz-Anglet-Bayonne airport daily from London (Stansted) and four times weekly from Dublin. Take STAB bus No 6 or, on Sunday, line C to/from Biarritz' Hôtel de Ville. Each runs once or twice hourly, from 7am until about 7pm.

BUS
Stopping on Av Jean Petit, nine daily **ATCRB buses** (☎ 05 59 26 06 99) follow the coast southwestwards to St-Jean de Luz (€3, 30 minutes) and Hendaye (€3, one hour). For other destinations, it's better to go from Bayonne – not least in order to ensure a seat in the high season.

TRAIN
Biarritz–La Négresse train station is about 3km from the town centre. Buses 2 and 9

connect the two. **SNCF** (13 av du Maréchal Foch; ☒ Mon-Fri) has a town-centre office. Times, fares and destinations are much the same as Bayonne's (p695).

Getting Around

BICYCLE

Sobilo (☎ 06 80 71 72 88; 24 rue Peyroloubilh) rents out mountain bikes (€12 per day), scooters (from €31) and even in-line skates (€12).

BUS

Most services stop beside the Hôtel de Ville, from where route Nos 1 and 2 (€1.20, about 50 daily) go to Bayonne's Hôtel de Ville and station. **STAB** (☎ 05 59 24 26 53) has an information kiosk beside Square d'Ixelles.

For information on buses to Biarritz-Anglet-Bayonne airport, see opposite.

TAXI

Call **Taxis Biarritz** (☎ 05 59 23 05 50).

ST-JEAN DE LUZ & CIBOURE

pop 13,600

St-Jean de Luz, 24km southwest of Bayonne, sits at the mouth of the River Nivelle. Hugging one side of a sheltered bay, it's just plain lovely. There's a long stretch of sand and it's also an active fishing port, pulling in large catches of sardines, tuna and anchovies.

Ciboure is the town's quiet alter ego. Several timber-framed whitewashed Basque houses, with shutters in green or ox-blood red, survive just south of rue Agorette.

Orientation

St-Jean de Luz and its long beach are on the eastern side of Baie de St-Jean de Luz, with smaller Ciboure on the western curve of the bay. A tiny but active fishing harbour nestles at the mouth of the River Nivelle, dividing the two towns. The axis of St-Jean de Luz is pedestrianised rue Gambetta with bustling place Louis XIV at its southwestern end.

Information

Internet World (☎ 05 59 26 86 92; 7 rue Tourasse; per hr €6; ☒ 9am-9pm daily Jun-Aug, 10am-6pm Mon-Sat Sep-May) Internet access.

Laverie du Port (place Maréchal Foch; ☒ 7am-9pm) Laundrette.

Post Office St-Jean de Luz (cnr blvd Victor Hugo & rue Sallagoïty); Ciboure (quai Maurice Ravel)

Tourist Office (☎ 05 59 26 03 16; www.saint-jean-de-luz.com; place Maréchal Foch; ☒ 9am-7.30pm Mon-Sat, 10am-1pm & 3-7pm Sun Jul & Aug, 9am-12.30pm & 2.30-6.30pm Mon-Sat, 10am-1pm Sun Sep-Jun)

Sights & Activities

A stroll to the promontory of **Pointe Ste-Barbe**, at the northern end of the Baie de St-Jean de Luz and about 1km beyond the town beach, gives you a great panorama of the town. Go to the end of blvd Thiers and keep walking.

The heart of **Socoa** is about 2.5km west of Ciboure along the continuation of quai Maurice Ravel. Its prominent **fort** was built in 1627 and later improved by Vauban. You can walk out to the **Digue de Socoa** breakwater or climb to the **lighthouse** via rue du Phare, then out along rue du Sémaphore for fabulous coastal views.

BEACHES

St-Jean de Luz' family-friendly sandy beach sprouts bathing tents (€6.25 per day) from June to September. Ciboure has its own modest beach.

Plage de Socoa, 2km west of Socoa on the corniche (the D912), is served by ATCRB buses (p705) en route to Hendaye and in the high season by boats (p705).

CHURCHES

The plain façade of France's largest and finest Basque church, **Église St-Jean Baptiste** (rue Gambetta; ☒ 8.30am-noon & 2-7pm), conceals a splendid interior with a magnificent Baroque altarpiece. Before it, Louis XIV and Maria Teresa (Marie Thérèse), daughter of King Philip IV of Spain, were married in 1660. After rings were exchanged, the couple walked down the aisle and out of the south door, which was then sealed to commemorate peace between the two nations after 24 years of hostilities. You can still see its outline, opposite No 20 rue Gambetta.

Until as recently as the Second Vatican Council (1962–65), many Basque churches had separate areas for men and women. The men occupied the tiers of grand oak galleries and sang as a chorus, while the women's seating was on the ground floor.

In Ciboure, the 17th-century **Église St-Vincent** (rue Pocalette) has an octagonal bell tower topped by an unusual three-tiered

ST-JEAN DE LUZ

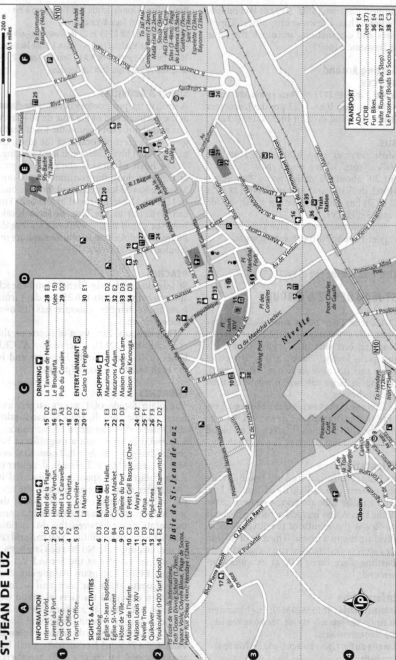

INFORMATION
Internet World....................	1 D3
Laverie du Port..................	2 D3
Post Office........................	3 C4
Post Office........................	4 F2
Tourist Office...................	5 D3

SIGHTS & ACTIVITIES
Billabong.........................	6 D3
Église St-Jean Baptiste.......	7 D2
Église St-Vincent..............	8 B4
Hôtel de Ville...................	9 D3
Maison de l'Infante...........	10 C3
Maison Louis XIV..............	11 D3
Nivelle Trois....................	12 D3
Quiksilver.......................	13 E2
Youkoulélé (H2O Surf School).....	14 E2

SLEEPING
Hôtel de la Plage.............	15 D2
Hôtel de Verdun..............	16 E3
Hôtel La Caravelle............	17 A3
Hôtel Ohartzia.................	18 D2
La Devinière....................	19 E2
La Marisa........................	20 D3

EATING
Buvette des Halles............	21 E3
Covered Market...............	22 E3
Grillerie du Port...............	23 D3
Le Petit Grill Basque (Chez Maya).....	24 D2
Olatua............................	25 F1
Pilpil-Enea......................	26 F3
Restaurant Ramuntcho.......	27 D2

DRINKING
La Taverne de Nesle..........	28 E3
Le Brouillarta..................	(see 15)
Pub du Corsaire...............	29 D2

ENTERTAINMENT
Casino La Pergola.............	30 E1

SHOPPING
Macarons Adam................	31 D2
Macarons Adam................	32 E2
Maison Charles Larre.........	33 D3
Maison du Kanouga..........	34 D3

TRANSPORT
ADA................................	35 E4
ATCRB............................	(see 37)
Fun Bikes.......................	36 E4
Halte Routière (Bus Stop)...	37 E3
Le Passeur (Boats to Socoa)...	38 C3

wooden roof. Inside, the lavish use of wood and tiered galleries are typically Basque.

ÉCOMUSÉE BASQUE

Beside the N10, this multimedia **museum** (☎ 05 59 51 06 06; adult/student/child €5.50/5/2.30; ☼ 10am-6.30pm daily Jul & Aug, 10-11.15am & 2.45-4.45pm Mon-Sat Apr-Jun, Sep & Oct), 2km north of St-Jean de Luz, will tell you all you want to know about Basque life and traditions – and probably a good deal more. Once you've embarked on the 1½-hour guided tour, there's no escape.

PLACE LOUIS XIV

Beside this pleasant pedestrianised square sits **Maison Louis XIV** (☎ 05 59 26 01 56; ☼ 10.30am-noon & 2.30-5.30pm Jun & Sep, 10.30am-12.30pm & 2.30-6.30pm Jul & Aug), built in 1643 by a wealthy shipowner and furnished in period style. Here, Louis XIV lived out his last days of bachelorhood before marrying Maria Teresa. Half-hour guided tours (with English text) cost €4.80/3 per adult/child.

Alongside, and rather dwarfed by its more imposing neighbour, is St-Jean de Luz' **Hôtel de Ville**, built in 1657.

In the days before her marriage, Maria Teresa stayed in another shipowner's mansion, the brick-and-stone Maison Joanoenia, off place Louis XIV and nowadays called **Maison de l'Infante** (☎ 05 59 26 36 82; quai de l'Infante; adult/child €2.50/free; ☼ 11am-12.30pm & 2.30-6.30pm Tue-Sat, 2.30-6.30pm Mon mid-Jun–mid-Oct).

SURFING

For some prime surfing, head 5.5km northeast of St-Jean de Luz to **Plage de Lafitenia**; ATCRB's Biarritz and Bayonne buses pass within 1km (Martienia or Bubonnet stop).

Surf schools based in the **Youkoulélé** (H2O surf school; ☎ 05 59 26 81 95; 72 rue Gambetta), **Quiksilver** (☎ 06 86 94 95 27; 64 rue Gambetta) and **Billabong** (☎ 05 59 26 07 93; 16 rue Gambetta) surf shops will transport you to the waves. Typical prices for a two-hour daily lesson are €40/115/160 per one/three/ five days.

OTHER ACTIVITIES

École de Voile International (☎ 05 59 47 06 32) and **Espace Voile** (☎ 05 59 47 21 21) in Socoa offer windsurfing lessons and yachting courses. The former also rents out dinghies and motor-boats and the latter, sea kayaks.

Diving schools in Socoa:

Tech Ocean (☎ 05 59 47 96 75; 45 av Commandant Passicot)

Odysée Bleue (☎ 06 63 54 13 63; hangar 4, chemin des Blocs)

Pottorua Sokoa (☎ 05 59 47 1 7; 53 av Commandant Passicot)

From May to mid-September, the **Nivelle Trois** (☎ 05 59 47 06 24) leaves quai du Maréchal Leclerc for morning deep-sea fishing trips and afternoon cruises.

Festivals & Events

Fêtes de la St-Jean This is celebrated with bonfires, music and dancing on the weekend nearest 24 June, the longest day.

La Nuit de la Sardine The Night of the Sardine sounds like a horror movie. In fact, it's a night of music, folklore and dancing held twice each summer on a Saturday in early July and the Saturday nearest 15 August.

La Fête du Thon The Tuna Festival, on another July weekend, fills the streets with brass bands, Basque music and dancing while stalls sell sizzling tuna steaks.

Danses des 7 Provinces Basques Folk dancers from all across the Spanish and French Basque Country meet in early summer.

Régates de Traînières A weekend of whaleboat races on the first weekend in July.

Sleeping

Reserve well in advance if you plan to visit between July and mid-September. There are very few budget hotels, although off-season prices for midrange hotels can drop significantly.

Between St-Jean de Luz and Guéthary, 7km northeast up the coast, are no fewer than 16 camp sites. ATCRB's Biarritz and Bayonne buses stop within 1km of them all.

Hôtel de Verdun (☎ 05 59 26 02 55; 13 av de Verdun; r €32-40, without bathroom €28) Opposite the train station in St-Jean de Luz, this simple place is a popular staging post for Chemin de St-Jacques pilgrims. Rooms are relatively spacious, if plain. Half-board (€44 per person) is obligatory from July to September.

Hôtel La Caravelle (☎ 05 59 47 18 05; www .hotellacaravelle.com; blvd Pierre Benoît; r €60-140) In Ciboure, this nautical themed place was originally two fishermen's cottages. Recently upgraded (notably by the creation of an airy new breakfast room), it has 19 modern rooms, seven of which have great views over the bay. Parking €10.

FRENCH BASQUE COUNTRY

Hôtel Ohartzia (☎ 05 59 26 00 06; www.hotel-ohartzia.com in French; 28 rue Garat; r low-season €60-77, high season €72-85) This delightful, flower-bedecked Basque house is just a few steps from the beach. Immaculate rooms are well furnished and equipped and the welcome's friendly. The highlight is its large rear garden courtyard, an oasis of calm. Wi-fi available.

La Marisa (☎ 05 59 26 95 46; www.la-marisa.com; 16 rue Sopite; r €75-145; ✗) Each of the 16 rooms at this charming, family-run hotel is individually decorated and furnished with antiques. The bright breakfast room with its cheerful Brazilian-theme murals gives onto a delightful, secluded patio. Parking €9.

Hôtel de la Plage (☎ 05 59 51 03 44; www.hoteldelaplage.com; 33 rue Garat; r low season €86-118, high season €106-138; ☺ Easter–mid-Nov & school holidays; ☻) This attractive white-painted, red-shuttered building overlooks the beach. Sixteen of the 22 rooms, all with gleaming tiled bathrooms, have sea views. Most have small balconies, enough to fit a table and two chairs. It runs a good bar/restaurant (opposite) and staff speak excellent English. Wi-fi available. Valet parking €10.

ourpick La Devinière (☎ 05 59 26 05 51; www.hotel-la-deviniere.com; 5 rue Loquin; r €110-150) Here's a true home from home (indeed, the owners used to live here). One difference is that you won't find a TV in the place. Instead, browse their collection of antiquarian books (room 11 has its own mini-library). Another is that at home you probably don't have some 20 kinds of tea to choose from (they also run the tea house just down the road). Beyond the living room, with its piano and comfy armchairs, there's a delightful small patio equipped with lounges.

Eating

There are a number of tempting restaurants along rue de la République, and more, interspersed with cafés, around place Louis XIV.

ourpick Buvette des Halles (☎ 05 59 26 73 59; blvd Victor Hugo; dishes from €6; ☺ 6am-2pm Tue-Sat Oct-May, 6am-2pm & dinner daily Jun-Sep) This minuscule restaurant, tucked into a corner of the covered market, has been run by the same family for well over a century. Between June and September, outside beneath the plane trees on the small square, it offers the finest local produce – goats' cheese, Bayonne ham, grilled sardines, fish soup, mussels and much more – prepared simply, with care and at very reasonable prices. For the rest of the year, it serves the tastiest of sandwiches to market visitors and traders and all who care to drop by.

Grillerie du Port (☎ 05 59 51 18 29; quai du Maréchal Leclerc; ☺ mid-Jun–mid-Sep) In this old shack by the port join the crowds gorging themselves on fresh sardines, salads and slabs of tuna steak fresh off the boat. It's informal, economical and enormously popular.

Restaurant Ramuntcho (☎ 05 59 26 03 89; 24 rue Garat; menus €18-30; ☺ closed Mon low season) This lively place, whose jovial owner hails from Normandy, successfully blends the cuisine of north and southwest France. Duck and fish dishes feature prominently. It's also the headquarters of the local veteran car club (president, your host); you can scarcely see the walls for the photos and posters of vintage vehicles and motorbikes.

Le Petit Grill Basque (Chez Maya) (☎ 05 59 26 80 76; 2 rue St-Jacques; menus €20-27; ☺ lunch & dinner Fri-Tue & dinner Thu) This authentically Basque restaurant, run by the same family for over half a century, offers plenty of regional specialities including a tasty *ttoro* (fish soup). It's Madame who pulls the strings in this place, activating an ingenious system of cloth sheets that act as giant fans when things get too hot.

Olatua (☎ 05 59 51 05 22; 30 blvd Thiers; lunch menus €18, dinner €28; ☺ lunch & dinner) Olatua's interior is bright and cheerful, enlivened by plenty of plants. The two young owners of this brasserie-type place stick to basic dishes with a strong regional slant, all made with the freshest of ingredients.

Pilpil-Enea (☎ 05 59 51 20 80; 3 rue Sallagoïty; mains €10-14, menus €30; ☺ lunch & dinner Thu-Mon) This popular restaurant – small, simple and unostentatious – is set apart from the tourist throng. It fills its few wooden tables by the sheer quality of its cooking and its relaxed ambience.

SELF-CATERING

There's a food market every Tuesday and Friday morning inside the covered market.

Drinking & Entertainment

La Taverne de Nesle (☎ 05 59 26 60 93; 5 av Labrouche; ☺ 5pm-2am Wed-Mon Oct-Jun, daily Jul-Sep) This cheery neighbourhood pub has a DJ every Friday year-round, twice a week in July and August.

Pub du Corsaire (☎ 05 59 26 10 74; 16 rue de la République; ⏰ 5pm-2am) This place has nearly 100 different beers, including 10 on draft, and whiskies galore, and mixes some mean cocktails.

Le Brouillarta (☎ 05 59 51 29 51; 33 rue Garat) Locals drop into this, the bar and restaurant of Hôtel de la Plage (opposite), to enjoy an early-evening apéritif, then move on or linger to enjoy its tapas or, if the mood takes them, dinner.

Mata Hari (☎ 05 59 26 04 28; 48 av André Ithurralde) Although swarming with people in the high season, St-Jean de Luz has only three discos, all outside town. Mata Hari, 2km east of the train station and open year-round, is far and away the most popular.

Casino La Pergola (☎ 05 59 51 58 58; rue Dalbarade; ⏰ slot machines 11am-3am daily, gaming 9pm-3am Tue-Sun) Bang on the beach.

SPORT
In July and August there's *cesta punta* at the **Jaï Alaï Compos Berri** (☎ 05 59 51 65 30; rte de Bayonne, N10), 1km northeast of the train station. Matches start at 9pm every Tuesday and Friday, and half-time is spiced up with music or dancing. Tickets are available at the tourist office and cost €8 to €18, depending on the crowd-pulling capacity of the players.

Shopping
Agonise over the rich choice of high-calorie Basque pastries and sweets at **Maison du Kanouga** (9 rue Gambetta) – *kanouga* are chewy chocolate cubes, invented by the owner's grandfather – with more varieties of marzipan that you've imagined in your sweetest dreams. Equally tempting are the two branches of **Macarons Adam** (49 rue Gambetta & 6 rue de la République).

St-Jean de Luz is also a good place to purchase Basque linen – for example, at **Maison Charles Larre** (4 rue de la République).

Getting There & Away
BUS
Buses run by **ATCRB** (☎ 05 59 26 06 99) pass the Halte Routière bus stop near the train station on their way northeast to Biarritz (€3, 30 minutes, nine daily) and Bayonne (€3, 40 minutes, nine daily). Southwestwards, there are around 10 services daily to Hendaye (€1, 35 minutes).

Also passing the Halte Routière, Spanish company **Transportes Pesa** (☎ in Spain 902 10 12 10) has twice-daily buses to San Sebastián (€4, one hour), to which ATCRB also runs twice daily.

From April to October **Le Basque Bondissant** (The Leaping Basque; ☎ 05 59 26 25 87) runs buses to La Rhune (below; including Le Petit Train adult/child €11/7) and the Grottes de Sare (p706; including admission €10/7). Buses leave from the Halte Routière.

TRAIN
There are frequent trains to Bayonne (€4.10, 25 minutes) via Biarritz (€2.60, 15 minutes) and to Hendaye (€2.60, 15 minutes), with connections to San Sebastián.

Getting Around
BICYCLE
Based at the train station, **Fun Bikes** (☎ 06 27 26 83 01) rents out cycles (€7 per half-day) and scooters (from €21 per half-day).

BOAT
Between June and September, the good ship **Le Passeur** (☎ 06 81 20 84 98) plies between quai de l'Infante and Socoa (€2 one way) every half-hour.

BUS
Between June and September, the Navette Intercommunale, run by ATCRB, provides a local daily bus service and a skeleton service during the rest of the year. Take Line A for Erromardie and the camp sites north of town, Line D for Socoa via Ciboure.

CAR
Car-rental company **ADA** (☎ 05 59 26 26 22) has an office at the train station.

TAXI
Call ☎ 05 59 26 10 11.

AROUND ST-JEAN DE LUZ
La Rhune
La Rhune ('Larrun' in Basque), a 905m-high, antenna-topped mountain, lies 10km south of St-Jean de Luz. Half in France and half in Spain, it's something of a Basque symbol. Views are spectacular from its peak, best approached from **Col de St-Ignace**, 3km northwest of Sare on the D4 (the St-Jean de Luz road). From here, you can take

a fairly strenuous walk or hop onto **Le Petit Train de la Rhune** (☎ 05 59 54 20 26; www.rhune.com; single/return adult €11/13, child €6/7). This charming little wooden train takes 35 minutes to haul itself up the 4km from col to summit. It runs from Easter to October with departures roughly every half-hour, depending on the crowds. Be prepared for a wait of up to an hour in high summer.

Grottes de Sare

Along the D306, 6km south of the village of Sare, are the **Grottes de Sare** (☎ 05 59 54 21 88; www.grottesdesare.com; adult/child €6.50/3.50; 🕑 10am-7pm Jul & Aug, 10am-6pm Apr-Jun & Sep, 10am-5pm Oct & school holidays, 2-5pm Feb, Mar, Nov & Dec) A 45-minute multilingual tour takes you through a gaping entrance via narrow passages to a huge central cavern, first inhabited at least 20,000 years ago.

Ainhoa

'Un des plus jolis villages de la France', says the sign as you enter this, indeed, very pretty village. Only this being the Basque country, someone has painted out 'la France'…

Ainhoa's long main street is flanked by imposing 17th-century houses, half-timbered and brightly painted. Look for the rectangular stones set above many of the doors, engraved with the date of construction and the name of the family to whom the house belonged. The fortified church has the Basque trademarks of internal gallery and a particularly embellished altarpiece.

Espelette

Whether you like your food sweet or spicy, Espelette will appeal. The village is famous for its dark red peppers, an essential ingredient of so much Basque cuisine. So prized is *le piment d'Espelette* that it's been accorded *Appellation d'Origine Contrôlée* (AOC) status, much like a fine wine. Arrive in the autumn and you can scarcely see the walls of the houses, masked by rows of peppers, threaded with string and hung up to dry. The last weekend in October marks Espelette's **Fête du Piment**, with processions, a formal blessing of the peppers and the ennoblement of a *chevalier du piment* (a knight of the pimento).

Although some like it hot, others may prefer sweeter pleasures. **Chocolats Anton** (☎ 05 59 93 80 58; place du Marché) is a specialist chocolate-maker that offers free tastings of its scrumptious confections.

The **tourist office** (☎ 05 59 93 95 02; www.espe lette.fr in French), within a small stone chateau, shares its premises with the Hôtel de Ville. On the castle's 2nd floor is a photographic exhibition about – what else? – peppers around the world.

It's strictly regional cuisine at renowned **Hôtel Restaurant Euzkadi** (☎ 05 59 93 91 88; r €42-52, menus €16-32; 🍽️), beamed, cavernous and enlivened by cheerful artwork all around the walls. Begin with the *elzecaria*, a tureen of thick mixed vegetable soup followed by *axoa*, tender minced veal simmered with onions and fresh peppers. Rooms are comfortable and a true bargain, the only downside being the growling toilet flush.

ST-JEAN PIED DE PORT

pop 1700

For centuries, the walled Pyrenean town of St-Jean Pied de Port, 53km southeast of Bayonne, was the last stop in France for pilgrims, converging from all over Europe. Refreshed, they headed south over the Spanish border, a mere 8km away, and on to Santiago de Compostela in western Spain. Nowadays too, it's a popular departure point for hikers and bikers attempting the pilgrim trail.

It makes for a pleasant day trip from Bayonne. Half the reason for coming here is the scenic journey south of Cambo-les-Bains, as both railway and road (the D918) pass through rocky hills, forests and lush meadows dotted with white farmhouses whose signs announce *ardi* (the Basque word for 'cheese') for sale.

The town can be hideously crowded in summer. Consider staying the night and exploring before breakfast or visit in the low season. Even better, to leave it all behind, rent a bike or pull on your boots and head for the surrounding hills.

Information

Bar Paris (☎ 05 59 37 01 47; 33 av Renaud; per hr €3; 🕑 7.15am-12.30pm & 3-8.30pm) Internet access; a few steps from the station.

Tourist Office (☎ 05 59 37 03 57; www.terre-basque .com; place Charles de Gaulle; 🕑 9am-7pm Mon-Sat, 10am-4pm Sun Jul & Aug, 9am-noon & 2-6pm Mon-Sat Sep-Jun)

Sights & Activities

OLD TOWN

The **Église Notre Dame du Bout du Pont**, with foundations as old as the town itself, was thoroughly rebuilt in the 17th century. Beyond **Porte de Notre Dame** is the photogenic **Vieux Pont** (Old Bridge) from where there's a fine view of whitewashed houses with balconies leaning out above the water. Fishing is forbidden where the River Nive passes through town, and the fat, gulping trout seem to know it. A pleasant 500m riverbank stroll upstream leads to the steeply arched **Pont Romain** (meaning Roman Bridge, but in fact dating from the 17th century).

Rue de la Citadelle is edged by substantial, pink-granite 16th- to 18th-century houses.

Look for the construction date on door lintels (the oldest we found was 1510). A common motif is the scallop shell, symbol of St Jacques (St James or Santiago) and of the Santiago de Compostela pilgrims, and perhaps an early example of come-hither advertising by the boarding-house keepers of the time. Pilgrims would enter the town through the **Porte de St-Jacques** on the northern side of town, then, refreshed and probably a little poorer, head for Spain through the **Porte d'Espagne**, south of the river.

LA CITADELLE

From the top of rue de la Citadelle, a rough cobblestone path ascends to the massive citadel itself, from where there's a

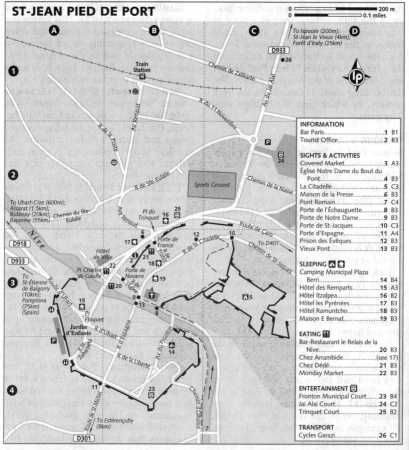

ST-JEAN PIED DE PORT

FRENCH BASQUE COUNTRY

splendid panorama of town and the surrounding hills. Constructed in 1628, the fort was rebuilt around 1680 by military engineers of the Vauban school. Nowadays it serves as a secondary school and is closed to the public.

If you've a head for heights, descend by the steps signed *escalier poterne* (rear stairway). Steep and slippery after rain, they plunge beside the moss-covered ramparts to **Porte de l'Échauguette** (Watchtower Gate).

PRISON DES ÉVÊQUES

The so-called **Prison des Évêques** (Bishops' Prison; 41 rue de la Citadelle; admission €3; ⏰ 10.30am-9pm daily Jul & Aug, 11am-12.30pm & 2.30-6.30pm Wed-Mon Easter-Jun & Sep-Oct), a claustrophobic vaulted cellar, gets its history muddled. It indeed served as the town jail from 1795, as a military lockup in the 19th century, then as a place of internment during WWII for those caught trying to flee to nominally neutral Spain. And the lower section indeed dates from the 13th century when St Jean Pied de Port was a bishopric of the Avignon papacy. But the building above it dates from the 16th century, by which time the bishops were long gone.

WALKING & CYCLING

St-Jean Pied de Port is a fine place from which to walk or cycle into the Pyrenean foothills, where the loudest sounds you'll hear are cowbells and the wind. Both the GR10 (the trans-Pyrenean long-distance trail running from Atlantic to Mediterranean) and the GR65 (the Chemin de St-Jacques pilgrim route) pass through town. **Maison de la Presse** (place Charles de Gaulle) carries a good selection of walking maps.

Pick up a copy of *55 Balades et Randonnées en Pays Basque* (€8) from the tourist office. Written in French but with explicit maps, it gives enough ideas for walking or mountain-bike excursions to keep you active and happy for a good two weeks.

To cycle the easy way while enjoying the best of the views of the Nive Valley, load your bicycle onto the train in Bayonne – they're carried free – and roll back down the valley from St-Jean Pied de Port. If you find the ride all the way back to the coast daunting, rejoin the train at Pont-Noblia, for example, or Cambo-les-Bains. For local bike hire, see opposite.

Tours

In July and August, the tourist office organises tours of the old town and visits to the citadel in French.

Festivals & Events

In high summer there's a weekly handicraft and food fair, held most Thursdays, in the covered market.

Sleeping & Eating

The tourist office has details of *gîtes* and *chambres d'hôtes* in the area, primarily, but not exclusively, for walkers and pilgrims.

Camping Municipal Plaza Berri (☎ 05 59 37 11 19; av du Fronton; per adult/tent/car €2.50/2/2; ⏰ Apr-Oct) Beside the river, this smallish camp site has ample shade.

Hôtel Itzalpea (☎ 05 59 37 03 66; itzalpea@wanadoo .fr; 5 place du Trinquet; d/tr €40/55) This family-run hotel, above a pleasant tearoom, has seven decent, very reasonably priced rooms. No 4 (€49), one of two in the original 19th-century building, has two large beds and a gorgeous view over the mountains.

Hôtel des Remparts (☎ 05 59 37 13 79; www.tou radour.com/hotel-remparts.htm; 16 place Floquet; r €44-54; ⏰ Feb-Sep) With a well-stocked bar/café beneath, this hotel has functional, good-sized rooms and sturdy wooden furniture. An excellent budget option, it's popular with walkers and pilgrims swapping tips and comparing blisters.

ourpick Maison E Bernat (☎ 05 59 37 23 10; www .ebernat.com; 20 rue de la Citadelle; d Jul & Aug €57-67, Easter-Jun & Sep–mid-Oct €47-57) There are only four bedrooms in this delightful 17th-century building with its thick stone walls. But they're airy, well furnished and meticulously kept. The welcome's a warm one and your fellow guests will probably be hikers or Chemin de St-Jacques pilgrims spending their last night in France. No need to step outside once you've pulled your boots off because they run a great little restaurant open for lunch and dinner daily July and August, lunch Tuesday to Sunday Easter to June and September to mid-October.

Hôtel Ramuntcho (☎ 05 59 37 03 91; hotel .ramuntcho@wanadoo.fr; 1 rue de France; d €49-74; ⏰ closed Wed low season) Within the old walls, this rustic place offers smallish but well-maintained rooms with sparkling, freshly renovated bathrooms. Some rooms have balconies that directly overlook the red-brown ramparts and beyond to the mountains. It runs a good restaurant (menus from €11.50 to €17.50) offering modestly priced family-style regional cuisine.

Hôtel les Pyrénées (☎ 05 59 37 01 01; www.hotel -les-pyrenees.com; 19 place Charles de Gaulle; r €92-155; ⓨ mid-Jan–mid-Nov; ☒ ☒ ☐ ☒) This one-time coaching inn has large, well-furnished rooms. Those on the top (third) floor were comprehensively renovated in 2005. Balconies reveal stunning views of the surrounding mountains. Chez Arrambide (menus from €40 to €85, mains €28 to €45), its much- acclaimed restaurant, is reason alone to come to St-Jean. Wi-fi available. Parking €10.

Chez Dédé (☎ 05 59 37 16 40; 3 rue de France; menus €9-18; ⓨ lunch & dinner Sun-Thu, lunch Fri, daily high season) Nestled in the ramparts of the old town up a little alley, this busy place is hot on Basque peppers. Try the *piquillos farcis à la morue* (sweet peppers stuffed with cod in a rich tomato sauce).

Bar-Restaurant le Relais de la Nive (☎ 05 59 37 04 22; place du Marché; menus €18.50 & €25; ⓨ lunch & dinner Fri-Sun Mar-Nov) Occupying a prize spot right beside the river, it has views of the Vieux Pont, perfectly reflected by day and floodlit at night.

SELF-CATERING

Farmers bring in their fresh produce for the town's **Monday market** (place Charles de Gaulle).

Entertainment

In high summer, there are performances of Basque music and dancing in the jai alai court at 9.30pm on Thursdays.

At 5pm every Monday, coinciding with market day, there's a bare-handed pelota tournament at the **trinquet court** (place du Trinquet).

In summer, variants of pelota (admission €7 to €10) are played according to the day

of the week at the *trinquet,* fronton *municipal* and jai alai courts. Check schedules at the tourist office.

Getting There & Away

Train is the best option since the irregular bus service to/from Bayonne makes a huge detour. The rail journey (€7.90, one hour, five daily) from Bayonne up the Nive Valley to St-Jean, the end of the line, is just beautiful.

For a day trip, take the 8.55am from Bayonne. The last train back leaves St-Jean Pied de Port at (let's be specific!) 4.51pm (do check these times, which can vary according to season).

Getting Around

Cycles Garazi (☎ 05 59 37 21 79; 32 av du Jaï Alaï) has mountain bikes and scooters for hire year-round.

Parking is a real pain in summer. The car parks beside the covered market and by the jai alai pelota court, both free, are the largest.

To order a taxi, call ☎ 05 59 37 05 00 or ☎ 05 59 37 13 37.

AROUND ST-JEAN PIED DE PORT

The village of **St-Étienne de Baïgorry** along with its outlying hamlets straggle across the Vallée de Baïgorry. Tranquillity itself after busy St-Jean Pied de Port and stretched thinly along a branch of the Nive, the village has, like so many Basque settlements, two focal points: the church and the fronton court.

Irouléguy (white, rosé and red) is the French Basque Country's only AOC wine – and most of it comes from the Vallée de Baïgorry. Just north of town, the **wine-growers' cooperative** (☎ 05 59 37 41 33) organises vineyard visits (€3) in July and August. It's open year-round for sales and tasting.

The Pyrenees

The Pyrenees (Pyrénées) stretch for 430km, forming a natural boundary between France and Spain. Had you sufficient time and energy, you could follow the GR10 walking trail that bucks and twists from Hendaye beside the Bay of Biscay on France's Atlantic Coast all the way to Banyuls beside the Mediterranean Sea – but you'll probably have to select from its three distinct zones.

The Pyrénées-Atlantiques rise steadily from the Atlantic through mist and cloud.

The Hautes Pyrénées, the focus of this chapter, are wilder and higher. Their rugged peaks and ridges, deep valleys and high cols are protected territory, falling within the narrow strip of the Parc National des Pyrénées that shadows the frontier for about 100km. Here, you can disappear into the mountains for days and spot only other walkers, marmots, izards (cousin to the chamois) – and, if you're *very* lucky, one of the Pyrenees' few brown bears.

Stunning valleys, such as the Vallée d'Aspe and the Vallée d'Ossau, cut laterally into the central Pyrenees, their lower reaches rich pasture, their narrow, southern necks steeper and more enclosed. Here, high, shimmering lakes and tarns are fed by swift mountain streams. Towns, such as the winter ski resorts and summer walking bases of Cauterets and Bagnères de Luchon, are appropriately small, deferring to the sheer grandeur of the mountains.

To the north sits Lourdes, one of Christianity's most important pilgrim towns.

Eastwards, in the Pyrénées Orientales, the climate becomes warmer and drier, and the vegetation pricklier, squatter and more abundant as the mountains taper down into Roussillon, then finally dip into the Mediterranean.

HIGHLIGHTS

- Catch a first glimpse of **snow-capped mountains** (p712) from Pau's stylish blvd des Pyrénées
- Mingle with the faithful at **Lourdes** (p719), one of the world's most important pilgrimage sites
- Trek in **Parc National des Pyrénées** (p722), one of Western Europe's wildest areas
- Trundle in the open-topped **Petit Train d'Artouste** (p729) at a constant 2000m
- Gasp at the magnificent wraparound sweep of the **Cirque de Gavarnie** (p734)

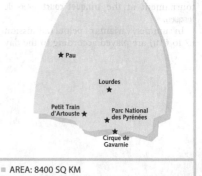

- POPULATION: 3,050,000
- AREA: 8400 SQ KM

GEOGRAPHY & CLIMATE

The lush beech forests of the lower, western hills give way to the higher, more rugged mountains, valleys and lakes of the central Pyrenees, where the real action lies. The Pyrénées Orientales, warmer and drier, taper away towards the Mediterranean.

Snow can tumble even in summer on higher ground and is the norm on the tops between October and May. Summer's weather can be temperamental with warm, caressing sunshine giving way to afternoon downpours in the twinkling of an eye.

THE TOWNS

PAU

pop 80,600

Pau (rhymes with 'so') is famed for its mild climate, flower-filled public parks and magnificent views of the Pyrenees. In the 19th century it was a favourite wintering spot for wealthy English and Americans. In recent years the city has owed its prosperity to a high-tech industrial base and the huge natural gas field, plus spin-off chemical plants, at nearby Lacq. Nowadays it's also at the cutting edge of communications technology and has attracted such giants as Microsoft, Intel, IBM and Toshiba.

Elegant, stylish (the shopping's great, especially for gourmets) Pau also has a fun-loving undertow, as befits a long-standing university city, and makes a good base for forays into the Pyrenees.

Orientation

The town centre sits on a small hill with the River Pau (Gave de Pau) at its base. Along its crest stretches blvd des Pyrénées, a wide promenade offering Cinemascope views of the mountains. The town's east–west axis is the thoroughfare of cours Bosquet, rue Maréchal Foch and rue Maréchal Joffre. When we last visited, the main square, place Clemenceau, had disappeared. In time, the giant hole in the ground will become an underground car park, masked by a landscaped, pedestrian piazza above.

Information

C Cyber Café (☎ 05 59 82 89 40; 20 rue Lamothe; per hr €4.50; ⊗ 10am-2am Mon-Fri, 2pm-2am Sat & Sun) Internet access.

Laundrette (66 rue Émile Garet; ⊗ 7am-8pm)

Librairie des Pyrénées (☎ 05 59 27 78 75; 14 rue St-Louis) Carries an excellent selection of walking maps and guidebooks in French.

Main Post Office (21 cours Bosquet)

Tourist Office (☎ 05 59 27 27 08; www.pau-pyrenees .fr; place Royale; ⊗ 9am-6pm Mon-Sat, 9.30am-noon & 2-6pm Sun, closed Sun afternoon Sep-Jun) Carries the free booklet *Guide des Loisirs en Béarn & Pays Basque*, a detailed summary of almost everything to do and see in Aquitaine.

Sights

CHATEAU

Originally the residence of the monarchs of Navarre, Pau's **chateau** (☎ 05 59 82 38 02; www .musee-cha teau-pau.fr in French; adult/18-25yr/under 18yr €5/3.50/free; ⊗ 9.30am-12.15pm & 1.30-5.45pm mid-Jun–mid-Sep, 9.30-11.45am & 2-5pm mid-Sep–mid-Jun) was transformed into a Renaissance chateau, bedecked with gardens, by Marguerite d'Angoulême in the 16th century. Marguerite's grandson, the future Henri IV, was born here – cradled, so the story goes, in an upturned tortoise shell.

Neglected in the 18th century and used as barracks after the Revolution, the chateau was in a sorry state by 1838, when King Louis-Philippe ordered a complete interior renovation. The whole, especially the façade, has again been recently and painstakingly re-restored.

The chateau holds one of Europe's richest collections of 16th- to 18th-century Gobelins tapestries and some fine Sèvres porcelain. These items apart, most of the ornamentation and furniture, including an oak dining table that can seat 100, dates from Louis-Philippe's intervention. In the

---

THE CHAMELEON OF PAU

Frédéric Bourdin, aged 31, is quite an impostor. In 2005 he spent a month at Pau's Jean Monnet secondary school, masquerading as a 15-year-old Spanish orphan. 'He seemed a bit older than his mates, maybe by a year or two', said the headmaster, presumably a wearer of pebble glasses. For Bourdin, this was a minor coup compared with an earlier impersonation; despite his thick French accent and the wrong colour eyes, he'd managed to convince a Texan couple he was their 14-year-old son who'd gone missing three years earlier.

room where Henry IV was born is what's claimed to be that tortoise-shell cradle.

Within the brick-and-stone **Tour de la Monnaie** below the main chateau, a free, modern lift hauls you from place de la Monnaie up to the ramparts.

Admission includes an obligatory guided tour in rapid-fire French. Tag along, armed with a guide sheet in English, offered at the reception desk.

PYRENEES PANORAMA

From majestic blvd des Pyrénées there's a breathtaking panorama of the Pyrenean summits on clear days, prevalent in autumn and winter. The **orientation table** opposite Australia Bar details the names of the peaks.

VIEILLE VILLE

Of Pau's old centre, only an area of around 300m in diameter abutting the chateau remains, yet it is rich in restored medieval and Renaissance buildings.

MUSÉE BERNADOTTE

The **Musée Bernadotte** (☎ 05 59 27 48 42; 8 rue Tran; adult/child €3/free; ☗ 10am-noon & 2-6pm Tue-Sun) has exhibits illustrating the improbable yet true story of how a French general, Jean-Baptiste Bernadotte, born in this very building, became king of Sweden and Norway (see the boxed text, p715). You'll spot the building from a distance by the blue and yellow Swedish flag fluttering outside.

PYRENEES (PYRÉNÉES)

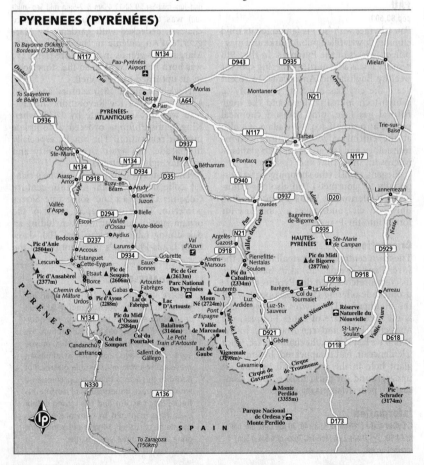

MUSÉE DES BEAUX-ARTS

Pau's **Musée des Beaux-Arts** (Fine Arts Museum; ☎ 05 59 27 33 02; adult/child €3/free; ☷ 10am-noon & 2-6pm Wed-Mon) is rich in 15th- to 20th-century European paintings, including works by Rubens, El Greco and Degas. The entrance is on rue Mathieu Lalanne.

Walking Tour

For do-it-yourself walking tours of the town, the tourist office has a pair of free booklets in English: *History & Heritage* and *Parks & Gardens*.

Festivals & Events

If cars, venerable and distinguished or mean and growling, captivate you, plan to spend the week before Whitsuntide in Pau. On the first weekend there's a parade of vintage vehicles, followed by the **Grand Prix Historique**. On the second weekend a Formula 3 Grand Prix motor race howls and whines through the city's streets.

Other festivals include the following:

L'Été à Pau (Summer in Pau) A time for free music concerts, often of high quality, at venues throughout the town – notably the amphitheatre in Parc Beaumont.

Carnival Week (late February) The prelude to Lent normally brings winter gaiety to the town.

Festival de Dance (March) A month-long celebration of contemporary dance.

Concours Complet International (October) Brings together some of the world's best horse riders in a gruelling competition embracing dressage, cross-country and jumping.

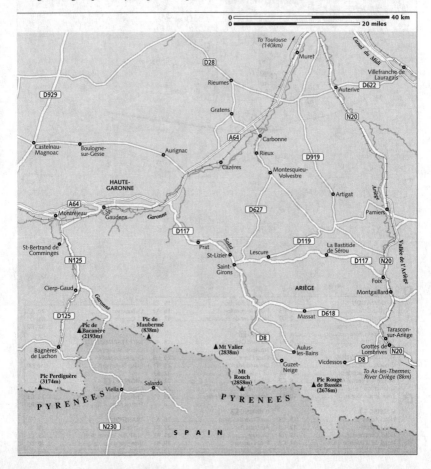

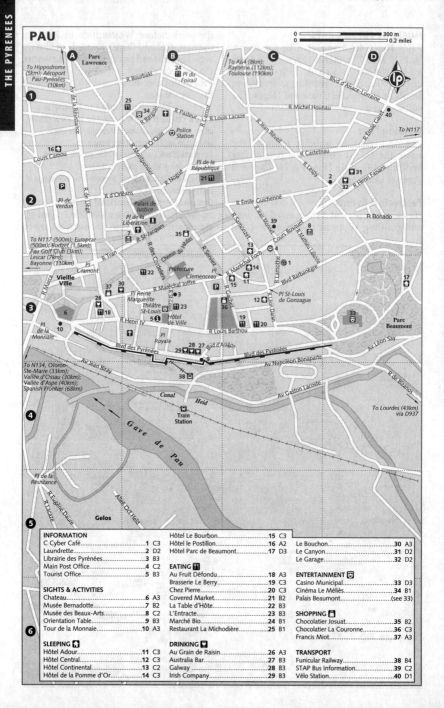

PAU

Sleeping

Hôtel de la Pomme d'Or (☎ 05 59 11 23 23; fax 05 59 11 23 24; 11 rue Maréchal Foch; s/d from €31/35, with shared bathroom from €20/23, with shower from €24/28) On the 1st floor of a former coaching inn, this is a more than decent economical choice. Ask for a room facing away from the busy street. Go into the recessed courtyard and you'll find the entrance on the left.

Hôtel Adour (☎ 05 59 27 47 41; www.hotel-adour-pau.com; 10 rue Valérie Meunier; r from €45, with shower €32; ✗) Even though the street isn't particularly noisy, rooms overlooking this central hotel are *triple* glazed. The other client-sensitive touch is its nonsmoking rooms – a welcome feature absent from many hotels with greater pretensions. Secure overnight parking at €4 is a bargain.

Hôtel le Postillon (☎ 05 59 72 83 00; www.hotel-le-postillon.fr in French; 10 cours Camou; s €42, d €45-65) Take your pick: a room giving onto the charming, flower-bedecked inner courtyard of this former coaching inn, or one of the three top-floor rooms offering views of vast place de Verdun (where there's free parking) and the Pyrenees beyond. Each room is individually decorated in soft pastel tones and two are equipped for disabled people.

Hôtel Central (☎ 05 59 27 72 75; www.hotelcentralpau.com in French; 15 rue Léon Daran; s €39-49, d €49-56; ✗ 🖳) We scarcely recognised the place on our most recent visit. The new owners are renovating it with vigour and style. Ask for one of the excellent-value rooms they've already upgraded. Each is individually and charmingly decorated (can they sustain such individuality for all 28 rooms, we wonder?). Has wi-fi; parking costs €7.

Hôtel Le Bourbon (☎ 05 59 27 53 12; www.hotel-le-bourbon.com; 12 place Clemenceau; s/d/tr €50/60/69; ✗) Reception is on the 1st floor of Le Bourbon, which offers cosy, practical rooms in a central location. Most overlook Pau's pedestrianised central square – as does the breakfast room. Top-floor rooms have air-con.

Hôtel Continental (☎ 05 59 27 69 31; www.hotel-continental-pau.com in French; 2 rue Maréchal Foch; s €59-90, d €69-115; ✗) The less expensive rooms, in particular, at this long-established Pau landmark are excellent value. The grandeur is far from faded; savour the abundance of glass in the restaurant, the eclectic antique furniture and the rich mosaics in the main hallway. Parking is free.

Hôtel Parc de Beaumont (☎ 05 59 11 84 00; www.hotel-parc-beaumont.com; 1 av Edouard VII; r €175-240; ✗ ✗ 🖳 🛒) This new confection of steel, wood and glass is hugely stylish with original works of art in public areas. Most rooms have ample balconies overlooking the park. Shower cubicles and bathtubs are separate and rooms are large. So are the 2m by 2m beds – why, they can even hitch on an extension when visiting basketball teams are staying! There's an attractive indoor pool, sauna, hammam (Turkish bath) and Jacuzzi, all free to guests. Has wi-fi; parking costs €12.

Eating

L'Entracte (☎ 05 59 27 68 31; 2bis rue St-Louis; dishes €7.50-10; ☽ lunch Mon-Sat, dinner Thu-Sat) For something light, L'Entracte (The Interval – it's right opposite Pau's main theatre) is a winner. Tablecloths and furnishings are as bright and cheerful as the young owners, who speak excellent English. It serves up a wide selection of crunchy salads and toasted sandwiches, and in summer tables spill onto the pavement.

Au Fruit Défondu (☎ 05 59 27 26 05; 3 rue Sully; ☽ dinner only) This intimate place offers participatory dinners, with seven different kinds of fondue (€12 to €15), as well as grill-it-yourself duck or beef *pierrades*, sizzled over a hot stone (€12 to €15).

Brasserie Le Berry (☎ 05 59 27 42 95; 4 rue Gachet; mains €12-16; ☽ from 6pm) Top-value Le Berry,

70 years in the same family and preserving its original 1950s brasserie ambience, serves Béarnaise specialities. Save a cranny for something from its tempting range of desserts. They don't take reservations so arrive early, especially at lunchtime.

Restaurant La Michodière (☎ 05 59 27 53 85; 34 rue Pasteur; menus €14-25, mains €11-22; ☺ Mon-Sat, closed Aug; ☒) This gem of a place, a little apart from the main action, is well worth seeking out. Run by two brothers, the cuisine is imaginative and matched by the attractive décor. It's on two levels; choose a table on the ground floor and you can watch the chef sibling working his magic. Head upstairs and you're in air-conditioned coolness.

Sunken rue Hédas, like a little country lane sneaking through the heart of town, has several restaurants worth visiting.

La Table d'Hôte (☎ 05 59 27 56 06; 1 rue Hédas; menus €22-28, mains €12.50-16.50; ☺ closed lunch Mon Jul & Aug, Sun & Mon Sep-Jun) This 17th-century tannery is all beams, mellow exposed brickwork and rough plaster. Service is cheerful and dishes are creative and delightfully presented. We enjoyed the *cochon noir Gascon*, a thick, juicy hunk of locally reared pork stuffed with frilly mushrooms and soaked in its juices.

Chez Pierre (☎ 05 59 27 76 86; 16 rue Louis Barthou; menu €34; ☺ closed Sun, lunch Sat & lunch Mon) Chez Pierre, its walls hung with Kashmiri fabrics, is highly reputed and much garlanded. Salivate over the lobster and crayfish or tuck into the *sole braiseée au Jurançon et aux morilles et foie gras* (sole simmered in local Jurançon wine with wild mushrooms).

SELF-CATERING
Stock up on picnic goodies at the big **covered market** (place de la République). Marché Bio, much smaller and selling exclusively organic food, takes over the gaunt concrete hulk of a building on place du Foirail every Wednesday and Saturday morning. For other tempting food choices, see Shopping, right.

Drinking
'Le Triangle', bounded by rue Henri Faisans, rue Émile Garet and rue Castetnau, is the centre of student nightlife. Good bets are **Le Garage** (☎ 05 59 83 75 17; 49 rue Émile Garet) – look for the giant stucco mechanic sitting on the roof – and **Le Canyon** (☎ 05 59 83 92 37; 35 rue Émile Garet; ☺ 7pm-2am Wed-Sat), which sometimes has live music.

A short string of bars, new and newish, extends along blvd des Pyrénées and around the corner into blvd d'Aragon. The orientation of Galway and Irish Company speaks for itself (is there any city left in Europe that doesn't serve Guinness?) though Australia Bar has no manifest link with Oz.

You'll find a couple of congenial wine bars near the chateau. **Au Grain de Raisin** (11 rue Sully) has a tempting range and also runs several draught beers. Round the corner, **Le Bouchon** (46 rue Maréchal Joffre) specialises in wine and Corsican goodies and does delightful sandwiches and salads.

Entertainment
For theatre, music, dance and upcoming exhibitions, get hold of *La Culture à Pau*, published every three months and available free from the tourist office.

The excellent **Cinéma Le Méliès** (☎ 05 59 27 60 52; 6 rue Bargoin), Pau's only cinema, shows exclusively nondubbed films.

Casino Municipal (☎ 05 59 27 06 92; ☺ 10am-3am Mon-Fri, 10am-4am Sat & Sun) occupies a sumptuous building, the Palais Beaumont, within Parc Beaumont.

The renowned **Hippodrome du Pont Long** (☎ 05 59 13 07 07; 462 blvd du Cami-Salié), 5km north of the town centre, has steeplechases from December to April. Rugby fans will want to take in a home game (check the website) of **Section Paloise** (www.section-paloise.com/accueil.php in French), one of France's leading club sides.

Shopping
Pau is renowned for its chocolate. Two of the best *chocolatiers* are **La Couronne** (place Clemenceau) and **Josuat** (23 rue Serviez).

Francis Miot (48 rue Maréchal Joffre) Still on things sweet, this several times champion jam maker of all France also makes wonderful sweets/candies and handmade chocolates (how about a box of *couilles du Pape* – the Pope's testicles – for a loved one back home?).

Getting There & Away
AIR
The **Aéroport Pau-Pyrénées** (☎ 05 59 33 33 00; www.pau.aeroport.fr) is about 10km northwest of town. Ryanair flies daily to/from London (Stansted), and Transavia flies direct to/from Amsterdam. Air France has four to six flights daily to Paris (Orly) and three to Paris (Roissy).

BUS
Citram Pyrénées (☎ 05 59 27 22 22) buses roll up the Vallée d'Ossau to Laruns (€4, one hour, two to four daily).

TRAIN
Up to 10 daily trains or SNCF buses link Pau and Oloron-Ste-Marie (€5.90, 40 minutes) via Buzy-en-Béarn (€3.60, 25 minutes). There are three onward SNCF bus connections from Buzy into the Vallée d'Ossau and three to four from Oloron-Ste-Marie into the Vallée d'Aspe. Most of the latter continue to the Spanish railhead of Canfranc, from where trains run to Zaragoza (Saragossa). There are frequent trains to Lourdes (€6.50, 30 minutes).

Around 10 direct trains run to Bayonne (€14.30, 1¼ hours) and Toulouse (€25.70, 2¾ hours). There are five daily TGVs to Paris' Gare Montparnasse (€79, 5½ hours).

Getting Around
TO/FROM THE AIRPORT
A daily bus (€5) runs from the train station to the airport, serving the London Ryanair flight. A taxi costs around €25.

BICYCLE
Vélo Station (☎ 05 59 02 27 54; 9 blvd Alsace Lorraine) rents out town bikes (per day/week €5/25) and electric bikes (€10/50).

CAR & MOTORCYCLE
There's extensive free parking on place de Verdun. Rental agencies at the airport include **Europcar** (☎ 05 59 33 24 31) and **Budget** (☎ 05 59 33 77 45).

FUNICULAR RAILWAY
The train station is linked to blvd des Pyrénées by a free funicular railway, a wonderful creaky little contraption. But unless you're heavily laden or a railway nut, it's scarcely worth the wait; the walk itself, even uphill, takes much the same time.

PUBLIC TRANSPORT
The local bus company, **STAP** (☎ 05 59 14 15 16; www.bus-stap.com in French), has a sales and information office on rue Jean Monnet. Single tickets/daily passes/eight-ride *carnets* (books of tickets) cost €1/2.50/5.50.

TAXI
For a taxi, call ☎ 05 59 02 22 22.

LOURDES
pop 15,700 / elevation 400m
Lourdes, 43km southeast of Pau, was just a sleepy market town until 1858, when Bernadette Soubirous (1844–79), a near-illiterate, 14-year-old peasant girl, saw the Virgin Mary in a series of 18 visions that came to her in a grotto. After long deliberation, the Vatican confirmed them as bona fide apparitions and the little country girl, having lived out her short life as a nun, was declared Ste Bernadette in 1933.

Nowadays Lourdes is one of the world's most important pilgrimage sites, descended upon annually by some five million visitors from all over the world. Well over half are pilgrims, including many invalids seeking cures. Nowadays, 58% of pilgrims come from beyond France's frontiers – and two-thirds are over 45 years old.

Accompanying the fervent piety of the pilgrims is an astounding display of tacky commercial exuberance – shake-up snow domes, packets of sugared almonds saying 'I prayed for you at the Grotte of Lourdes' and plastic bottles in the shape of the Virgin (just add holy water at the shrine) are but a sample. Even the best bookshop in town had a notice 'Special Price To Clear: Quality Crucifixes €5.50'. Yes, it's easy to mock, but it's also worth remembering that some people spend their life savings to come here.

Orientation
Lourdes' two main east–west streets are rue de la Grotte and blvd de la Grotte, both leading to the Sanctuaires Notre Dame de Lourdes. The principal north–south thoroughfare, called av du Général Baron Maransin where it passes above blvd de la Grotte, connects the train station with place Peyramale, where you'll find the tourist office.

The huge religious complex that has grown up around the original cave where Bernadette's visions took place is west of the River Pau.

Information
BOOKSHOPS
Book Shop (☎ 05 62 42 27 94; www.lourdes-bookshop .com; 13 rue du Bourg) Mainly stocks titles relating to Lourdes plus a few novels, travel titles and walking maps.

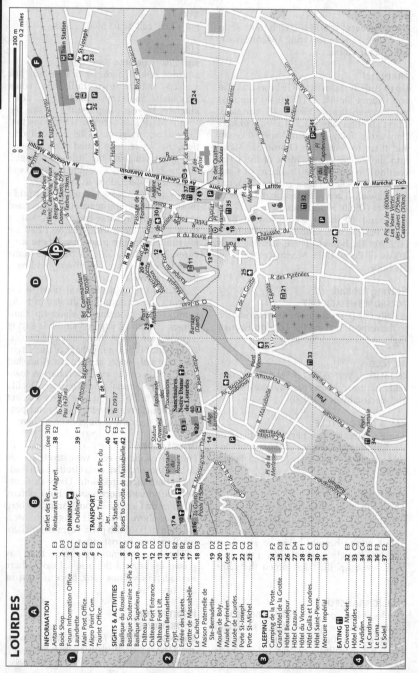

INTERNET ACCESS

Antares (5 rue de la Grotte; per hr €3; 🕑 9am-noon & 2-7pm Mon-Sat) Fairly creaky machines.
Micro Point Com (8 place du Champ Commun; per hr €4; 🕑 2-7pm Mon, 9.30am-noon & 2-7pm Tue-Sat)

LAUNDRY

Laundrette (10 av du Général Baron Maransin; 🕿 8am-7pm)

POST

Main Post Office (1 rue de Langelle)

TOURIST INFORMATION

Forum Information office (🕿 05 62 42 78 78; www.lourdes-france.com; Esplanade des Processions; 🕑 8.30am-6.30pm Apr-Oct, 9am-noon & 2-6pm Nov-Mar) For information on the Sanctuaires Notre Dame de Lourdes.
Tourist Office (🕿 05 62 42 77 40; www.lourdes-info tourisme.com; place Peyramale; 🕑 9am-7pm Mon-Sat, 10am-6pm Sun Jul & Aug, 9am-6.30pm Mon-Sat, 10am-12.30pm Sun Apr-Jun & Sep, 9am-noon & 2-6pm Mon-Sat Jan-Mar & Oct-Dec)

Sights

SANCTUAIRES NOTRE DAME DE LOURDES

The development of the Sanctuaries of Our Lady of Lourdes began within a decade of the miraculous events of 1858. The most revered site is known variously as the **Grotte de Massabielle** (Massabielle Cave or Grotto), the Grotte Miraculeuse (Miraculous Cave) and the Grotte des Apparitions (Cave of the Apparitions). Open 24 hours, its walls are worn smooth by the touch of millions of hands over the years. Hundreds of candles, donated by pilgrims, flicker, the fatter ones bearing the names of the groups that donated them. Here too are 19 baths in which 400,000 pilgrims seeking cures immerse themselves each year. Medically certifiable miraculous cures are becoming rarer; about one every decade. The most recent one, the 67th overall, confirmed in 2005, was that of an Italian, Anna Santaniello, crippled by and cured of chronic rheumatism.

The main 19th-century section of the sanctuaries has three parts. On the western side of Esplanade du Rosaire, between the two ramps, is the neo-Byzantine **Basilique du Rosaire** (Basilica of the Rosary). One level up is the **crypt**, reserved for silent worship. Above is the spire-topped, neogothic **Basilique Supérieure** (Upper Basilica).

From Palm Sunday to at least mid-October, there are solemn **torchlight processions** nightly at 9pm from the Massabielle Grotto, while at 5pm there's the **Procession Eucharistique** (Blessed Sacrament Procession), where pilgrims bearing banners process along the Esplanade des Processions.

When it's wet, the latter ceremony is held inside the vast, bunkerlike **Basilique Souterraine St-Pie X** (Underground Basilica of St Pius X), with a capacity for 20,000 worshippers. Built in 1959 in the fallout-shelter style then all the rage, it's redeemed to some extent by vibrantly warm backlit works of *gemmail* (superimposed pieces of coloured glass embedded in enamel).

All four places of worship open 6am to 10pm in summer and 7am to 7pm in winter. You can enter the grounds around the clock via the **Entrée des Lacets** (rue Monseigneur Theas). The **Porte St-Michel** and **Porte St-Joseph** entrances are open 5am to midnight year-round.

CHEMIN DE LA CROIX

Also called Chemin du Calvaire (Way of Calvary), the 1.5km **Chemin de la Croix** (Way of the Cross), leading up the forested hillside from near the Basilique Supérieure, is punctuated by the 14 Stations of the Cross. Especially devout pilgrims mount to the first station on their knees.

OTHER BERNADETTE SITES

You can also visit other places that figured prominently in the life of Ste Bernadette.

PASSPORTS & PASSES

If you're intent upon doing Lourdes thoroughly, pick up a *Sejour Futé* pass (adult/child €29.50/15), giving free access to Lourdes' seven most popular sites, transport from one to another on the little train that circumnavigates the town and a trip up the spectacular Pic du Jer funicular railway, plus an audioguide to the Grotte de Massabielle.

Alternatively, pick up the free *Lourdes Pass*, pay the normal tariff for five of the seven attractions (Musée de Lourdes, Château Fort/Musée Pyrénéen, Musée de la Nativité, Musée Grévin, Funiculaire du Pic du Jer, Musée du Petit Lourdes, Le Petit Train) and get the last two free.

THE PYRENEES

On rue Bernadette Soubirous are the **Moulin de Boly** (Boly Mill; No 12; admission free), Bernadette's birthplace, and the **Maison Paternelle de Ste-Bernadette** (No 2; admission €1), the house that the town of Lourdes bought for the Soubirous family after Bernadette saw the apparitions. **Le Cachot** (15 rue des Petits Fossés; admission free), a former prison, is where Bernadette lived during the period when she saw the apparitions.

MUSÉE DE LOURDES

The **Musée de Lourdes** (☎ 05 62 94 28 00; adult/child €5.50/2.70; ⓨ 9am-noon & 1.30-6.30pm Apr-Oct), in the Parking de l'Égalité, portrays the life of Ste Bernadette as well as the general history of Lourdes.

CINÉMA BERNADETTE

If you've a yen to learn yet more about Ste Bernadette or simply want to rest your feet, **Cinéma Bernadette** (☎ 05 62 42 79 19; 6 av Monseigneur Schoepfer; adult/under 18yr €6/4.50) shows the same two-hour feature film entitled (you've guessed it) *Bernadette* with optional English dialogue at 2pm, 4.30pm and 6.30pm daily from Easter to October.

CHÂTEAU FORT

There are great bird's-eye views of town from the **Château Fort** (Fortified Castle; adult/child €5/2.50; ⓨ 9am-noon & 1.30-6.30pm Easter-Sep, 9am-noon & 2-6pm Oct-Easter), up on its rocky pinnacle. Within is the **Musée Pyrénéen**, with displays on folk art and tradition.

Take the free lift (elevator) from rue Baron Duprat or walk up the ramp at the northern end of rue du Bourg.

PIC DU JER

There's a truly splendid panoramic view of Lourdes and the central Pyrenees from the summit of Pic du Jer (948m). It's but a six-minute ride from valley level by the **funicular railway** (☎ 05 62 94 00 41; blvd d'Espagne; adult/child one way €6.50/5, return €8.50/6.50; ⓨ 10am-6pm Mar-Nov).

More strenuously and much more satisfyingly, follow the signed trail to the summit from the lower station (allow 2½ to three hours for the return journey) or simply ride up and walk down. The ticket booth has a free stylised map.

Take Bus 2 from place Monseigneur Laurence.

Activities

To get away from Bernadette Soubirous for a day, hire a cycle (see p722) and head for the mountains along all or part of **Les Voies Vertes des Gaves** (Mountain Streams Green Routes). This follows the old, long-abandoned Lourdes–Cauterets train line up the lovely Vallée des Gaves all the way to Cauterets, where you can catch a bus back to Lourdes.

Festivals & Events

Lourdes' renowned **Festival International de Musique Sacrée** is a week of sacred music held around Easter.

Sleeping

Since Lourdes has well over 200 hotels, you shouldn't need our help to find a bed. Even so, you may have to scout around during Easter, Whitsuntide, Ascension Day, May and from August to the first week of October. By contrast, the town is so quiet in winter, when most hotels shut down, that it would need a miracle to bring it to life. Given the nature of their clientele, a high proportion have facilities for the disabled.

BUDGET

Camping de la Poste (☎ 05 62 94 40 35; 26 rue de Langelle; per person/pitch €2.80/4, d/tr/q €26/35/44; ⓨ Easter-mid-Oct) Right in the heart of town, it's tiny and friendly – and consequently often full. It also rents out eight excellent-value rooms with bathroom.

Among the nearest of the dozen or so camp sites ringing town are **Camping Vieux Berger** (☎ 05 62 94 60 57; ⓨ mid-Jun–mid-Oct) and **Camping Domec** (☎ /fax 05 62 94 08 79; ⓨ Easter-Oct). Both are on route de Julos, just off blvd de Centenaire, the eastern ring road.

Hôtel Cazaux (☎ 05 62 94 22 65; hotelcazaux@yahoo .fr; 2 chemin des Rochers; s/d €30/35; ⓨ Easter-mid-Oct) This small 20-room hotel is a converted house. It's friendly, a true bargain and sparkling clean from the immaculate white and salmon-pink exterior with its boxes of fresh flowers to the deepest bedroom corner.

Hôtel Saint-Pierre (☎ 05 62 42 30 31; fax 05 62 94 80 32; 4-6 passage de la Fontaine; s/d/tr/q €25/30/35/40; ⓨ Easter-Oct) Rooms at this spruce hotel are smallish but quite satisfactory. There's a bar for guests, a patio, and a restaurant, Reflet des Îles (opposite), serving exotic fare.

Hôtel du Viscos (☎ 05 62 94 08 06; fax 05 62 94 26 74; 6 av St-Joseph; d €35, with shared bathroom €30;

Feb–mid-Dec) This friendly, family-run place has a bustling bar (strictly for guests), offers great value, has free parking and couldn't be handier for the station.

MIDRANGE

Hôtel Beauséjour (☎ 05 62 94 38 18; www.hotel -beausejour.com; 16 av de la Gare; s/d/tr from €60/72/82; ☒ ▣) The Beauséjour, with its scrubbed white and oxblood façade, offers free parking, and a full third of its 45 rooms are non-smoking. It runs a good restaurant (menu €15). Rooms at the rear have impressive views of town and the Pyrenees beyond.

Grand Hôtel de la Grotte (☎ 05 62 94 58 87; www .hotel-grotte.com; 66 rue de la Grotte; s/d/tr from €64/72/88; Apr-Oct; ☒) Established in 1872, this charming *fin de siècle* place has belonged to the same family for four generations. With a gorgeous garden, bar and a couple of prestige restaurants, it's an excellent choice for those who like comfort, maturity and old-world courtesy.

Hôtel Gallia et Londres (☎ 05 62 94 35 44; www .hotelgallialondres.com; 26 av Bernadette Soubirous; s €73-78, d €86-96; Apr-Oct; ☒ ▣) The spacious bedrooms (add €7 for views of the sanctuary) are individually and attractively decorated à la Louis XVI. You'll gasp at the chandeliers and wooden panelling of the dining room with its side alcoves for intimate eating. Equally seductive is the lovely little garden, a rarity in this town of stone and concrete.

Mercure Impérial (☎ 05 62 94 06 30; www.mer cure.com; 3 av du Paradis; r €89-109; Feb–mid-Dec; ☒ ☒ ▣) Overlooking the river and Pont Vieux (do sip an apéritif on its roof terrace and savour the panorama), this hotel, fundamentally renovated in 2005, is strictly 21st century. Yet constructed in the 1930s, it pleasingly preserves the ambience of that era. The lounge opens out onto a rear garden, and the restaurant (mains €11 to €15) is splendid. It has wi-fi; parking costs €11 to €13.

Eating

Your options aren't great in this town of pack-'em-in, fill-'em-up hotels with accompanying restaurants. Most offer half- or full board; some even require guests to stay on those terms, especially in the high season.

our pick **Restaurant le Magret** (☎ 05 62 94 20 55; 10 rue des Quatre Frères Soulas; menus €26 & €33, mains €17-23; Tue-Sun Feb-Dec) This restaurant, its agreeably rustic décor embellished with early

photos of Lourdes, offers an innovative menu with a pronounced regional flavour. The friendly, courteous *maître* – a dead ringer for a portly Lenin – talks you through the dishes you've ordered and offers informed rugby chat too, if you've the inclination. It's prudent to make a reservation.

Le Cardinal (☎ 05 62 42 05 87; 11 place Peyramale; salads €5-5.50; Mon-Sat) Le Cardinal is an unpretentious bar/brasserie where the staff of the tourist office lunch – and they should know what's best. Tuck into steak, pork or chicken with chips and salad for only €6.

Le Luma (☎ 05 62 94 27 25; 23 av du Général Leclerc; Mon-Fri) This great little neighbourhood place with barely half a dozen tables is well worth the short walk from the tourist eating emporiums. The three-course set menu at a bargain €10 includes buffet hors d'oeuvres.

Le Soleil (☎ 05 62 94 53 22; 8 rue des Quatre Frères Soulas; Tue-Sun) This North African restaurant – a bold Muslim presence in such a fervently Catholic town – specialises in couscous (€12 to €14).

L'Ardiden (☎ 05 62 94 30 55; 48 av Peyramale; lunch menu €11, dinner menus €12.50-16, mains €8-14; Wed-Sun) It's well worth the short walk upstream to L'Ardiden, pleasantly situated beside Pont Peyramale and the river and strong on pizza and pasta.

Reflet des Îles (☎ 05 62 42 30 31; fax 05 62 94 80 32; 4-6 passage de la Fontaine; Easter-Oct) The restaurant of Hôtel Saint-Pierre serves spicy dishes (around €15) from the Indian Ocean island of La Réunion, as well as less exotic French cuisine.

Hôtel Arcades (☎ 05 62 94 20 59; 13 av du Paradis; menus €15-19.50, mains €10.50-13) The restaurant of Hôtel Arcades, open daily year-round, could save you from starvation. Entry is directly from the street, the service is swift and smiling and the food more than acceptable.

SELF-CATERING

Covered Market (place du Champ Commun) Occupies most of the square.

Drinking

There's not much to rave about after dark; Lourdes has only one Madonna and she's far from being a Material Girl.

Le Dubliner's (☎ 05 62 42 16 38; 7 av Alexandre Marqui) However, poke your nose into Le Dubliner's. It's a rarity in France – you stand a chance of actually meeting an Irish drinker in an Irish pub; every year over 30,000 Hibernians make the pilgrimage to Lourdes.

Getting There & Away

BUS

The small **bus station** (place Capdevieille) has services northwards to Pau (€7.40, 1¼ hours, four to six daily) and is a stop for buses running between Tarbes and Argelès-Gazost (at least eight daily), to the south and gateway to the Pyrenean communities of Cauterets, Luz-St-Sauveur and Gavarnie. SNCF buses to Cauterets (€6.40, one hour, at least five daily) leave from the train station.

TRAIN

Many pilgrims arrive by rail and Lourdes is well connected by train to French cities including Bayonne (€18.90, 1¾ hours, up to four daily), Pau (€6.50, 30 minutes, 10-plus daily) and Toulouse (€22.20, 1¾ hours, six daily). There are four daily TGVs to Paris' Gare Montparnasse (€91.80, six hours).

Getting Around

BICYCLE

Opposite Leclerc supermarket, **Cycles Arbes** (☎ 05 62 94 05 51; 10 av François Abadie) hires out both mountain and town bikes.

BUS

Citybus (☎ 08 00 10 02 39) No 1 links the train station with place Monseigneur Laurence and the Sanctuaries.

CAR & MOTORCYCLE

Lourdes is one big, fuming traffic jam in summer. If you have a vehicle, leave it near the train or bus stations, where there's free parking, and walk.

TAXI

For a taxi, call ☎ 05 62 94 31 30.

AROUND LOURDES

The **Grottes de Bétharram** (☎ 05 62 41 80 04; www .grottes-de-betharram.com; adult/child €10/6; ☺ visits 9am-6pm Jul & Aug, 9am, noon, 1.30pm & 5.30pm Apr-Jun, Sep & Oct, 2.30pm & 4.30pm Mon-Fri Feb-Mar), 14km west of Lourdes along the D937, are among France's most spectacular limestone caves. Guided visits, by mini-train and barge, last 1½ hours.

To see fauna that you would be extremely lucky to stumble across in the Parc National

---

> **HONOURING THE BERET**
>
> The archetypal Frenchman in beret, a Gauloise dangling from his lip and a baguette under his arm, is nowadays consigned to caricature. But only France could have a museum dedicated exclusively to his headgear. 'Unique in the World,' says the publicity and it's not a statistic we'd choose to challenge.
>
> The little town of Nay, 24km west of Lourdes along the D937, is home to the **Musée du Béret** (Beret Museum; ☎ 05 59 61 91 70; place St-Roch; admission €4; ☺ 10am-noon & 2-6pm Tue-Sun Apr-Oct, 2-6pm Tue-Sat Nov-Mar).

des Pyrénées, visit **Parc Animalier des Pyrénées** (☎ 05 62 97 91 07; www.parc-animalier-pyrenees.com in French; adult/child €9/6; ☺ 9am-7pm Jun-Aug, 9am-noon & 2-6pm Apr-May & Sep, 1-6pm Oct), at the northern side of the village **Argelès-Gazost**. Animals in this small park include marmots, wolves, lynx, otters and a couple of brown bears.

PARC NATIONAL DES PYRÉNÉES

The Parc National des Pyrénées (Pyrenees National Park) extends for about 100km along the Franco-Spanish border, from the Vallée d'Aspe in the west to the Vallée d'Aure in the east. Its boundaries are marked by a red izard head on a rectangular white background, painted on rocks and trees. Never broad, its width varies from 1.5km to 15km. Within are 230 lakes and Vignemale (3298m), the French Pyrenees' highest summit. It interlinks and collaborates closely with Spain's 156-sq-km Parque Nacional de Ordesa y Monte Perdido, to its south.

The park's many streams are fed by springs and some 2000mm of annual precipitation, much of which falls as snow. The French slopes are much wetter and greener than the dun-coloured Spanish flanks.

The park is exceptionally rich in both fauna and plant life (over 150 species of flora are endemic). Keep glancing up: its wilder reaches rank among the best places in Europe to see large birds of prey such as golden eagles, griffon and bearded vultures, booted eagles, buzzards and falcons.

The animal population includes 42 of France's 110 species of mammal. Look out for marmots – or rather, listen out for their distinctive whistle. Having become extinct in the Pyrenees, they were reintroduced from the Alps, where they thrive. Another success story is that of the izard, a close relative of the chamois, all but blasted out of existence half a century ago. Nowadays, thanks to careful control, the park has about 5000 izards while numbers on both sides of the Pyrenees exceed 20,000. By contrast, brown bears, once numerous, are now extremely scarce despite the introduction of cousins from Slovenia (see the boxed text, p727).

Each year the park receives over two million visitors, 80% of whom increase the pressure upon three beleaguered sites: Cirque de Gavarnie, Pont d'Espagne above Cauterets and the Réserve Naturelle de Néouvielle in the eastern sector.

MAPS & BOOKS
Each of the six park valleys (Vallée d'Aure, Vallée de Luz, Vallée de Cauterets, Val d'Azun, Vallée d'Ossau and Vallée d'Aspe) has a national park folder or booklet in French, *Randonnées dans le Parc National des Pyrénées*, describing 10 to 15 walks. Worthwhile for the route maps alone, they're on sale at local parks and tourist offices.

The park is covered by IGN's 1:25,000 Top 25 maps 1547OT *Ossau*, 1647OT *Vignemale*, 1748OT *Gavarnie* and 1748ET *Néouvielle*.

The Pyrenees chapter in Lonely Planet's *Walking in France* describes in detail a variety of day walks and longer treks in the Vallée d'Aspe and around both Cauterets and Bagnères de Luchon.

Fleurs des Pyrénées Faciles à Reconnaître by Philippe Mayoux, published by Rando Éditions, is a handy, well-illustrated pocket guide in French.

Information
There are national park offices with visitor centres at (from west to east) Etsaut, Laruns, Arrens-Marsous, Cauterets, Luz-St-Sauveur, Gavarnie and St-Lary-Soulan. All except the Cauterets and Gavarnie ones close during the cold half of the year.

For information about the park, call up www.parc-pyrenees.com.

Activities
WALKING
The park is crisscrossed by 350km of way-marked trails (including the Mediterranean to Atlantic GR10), some of which link up with trails in Spain.

It has about 20 *refuges* (mountain huts), most run by the Club Alpin Français (CAF). Most are staffed only from July to September but retain a small wing year-round.

SKIING
The Pyrenees receive less snow than the much higher Alps and the snows that fall

---

TOP FIVE FRENCH PYRENEES SKI RESORTS

Let's be frank: the best Pyrenees skiing lies across the watershed, in Spain's Baqueira-Beret and Andorra's Gran Valira. But the more modest resorts on the French side can make for a satisfying family break and offer reasonable downhill skiing and snowboarding for beginners and intermediates.

- **Cauterets** This long-established spa town (p729) has recently installed a fast new cabin lift. Snows linger late; you can still whiz downhill here when other resorts have closed down.

- **Superbagnères** A cabin lift hurtles up from the spa town of Bagnères de Luchon (p734) for satisfying skiing above the tree line at 1800m.

- **Barèges-La Mongie** This combined resort, on either side of Col du Tourmalet and at the foot of the Pic du Midi de Bigorre (p733), has 69 runs and offers the French Pyrenees' most extensive skiing area.

- **Ax Trois Domaines** Above Ax-les-Thermes (p736) are 75km of gentle runs, tracing their way through pine forest and, higher up, the open spaces of Campels.

- **La Pierre St-Martin** Wow, it can be windy at this small custom-built resort that gazes up to Pic d'Aniet. But here it's wilder and you're more in tune with the mountains.

are generally wetter and heavier. In addition to downhill skiing, the potential for cross-country skiing, ski touring and, increasingly, snowshoeing, is also good.

The French side has over 20 downhill ski stations, most of them quite modest, and more than 10 cross-country areas.

For the best cross-country skiing, head for **Val d'Azun** (tourist office in Arrens-Marsous ☎ 05 62 97 49 49), about 30km southwest of Lourdes, where you can plough along 110km of trails between 1350m and 1600m.

WHITE-WATER SPORTS

Rivers racing from the Pyrenean heights offer some of France's finest white water, which, since spring snowmelt is supp lemented by modest year-round rain, have a fairly steady annual flow. Organisations offering rafting and canoeing within or downstream from the national park include **A Boste Sport Loisir** (☎ 05 59 38 57 58; www.aboste .com in French; rue Léon Bérard, 64390 Sauveterre de Béarn) and **Centre Nautique de Soeix** (☎ 05 59 39 61 00; fax 05 59 39 65 16; quartier Soeix, 64400 Oloron-Ste-Marie).

THE VALLEYS

VALLÉE D'ASPE

The River Aspe (Gave d'Aspe) flows for some 50km from the Col du Somport, which marks the frontier with Spain, down to Oloron-Ste-Marie. Fewer than 3000 people live in the valley's 13 villages. Its upper reaches are still among the remotest corners of the French Pyrenees and one of the final refuges of their more timid wildlife.

But such seclusion may soon be lost as juggernauts plough through the Tunnel de Somport, the Pyrenees' newest, 8km-long road tunnel. Despite concessions such as ring roads around the luckier villages of the lower valley, its impact upon the fragile higher reaches of the valley can only be negative. So far, locals admit, the impact hasn't been as great as they feared. But final judgement must wait until remaining stretches of the original road have been upgraded, making the route even more tempting for truckers.

The Vallée d'Aspe has been a transfrontier passage ever since Julius Caesar's Roman legionnaires marched through. A railway line, completed in 1928 and a minor masterpiece of engineering, forged its way

up the valley and tunnelled through to meet the Spanish railhead at Canfranc. Services stopped when a bridge collapsed in 1970, and the railway, still visible for most of its length, rusts away.

MAPS

The 1:50,000-scale *Béarn: Pyrénées Carte No 3*, published by Rando Éditions, is a practical general trekking map of the area. A more detailed option is IGN's 1:25,000-scale Top 25 map No 1547OT, *Ossau*.

The national park's *Randonnées dans le Parc National des Pyrénées: Aspe* is a pack of information sheets on 11 walks, varying from 1½ hours to eight hours, in and around the valley.

Information

The valley's **tourist office** (☎ 05 59 34 57 57; www.aspecanfranc.com in French & Spanish; place Sar-raillé; ◔ 9am-12.30pm & 2-5.30pm or 6.30pm Mon-Sat) is in the main square of Bedous. It carries a reasonable selection of walking maps.

The **Maison du Parc National des Pyrénées** (Park Information Centre; ☎ 05 59 34 88 30; ◔ 10.30am-12.30pm & 2-6.30pm May-Oct) occupies the old train station in Etsaut and houses a good display (in French) about the fauna of the Pyrenees.

Getting There & Away

SNCF (☎ 08 92 35 35 35) buses and trains connect Pau and Oloron-Ste-Marie up to 10

VALLEY HOPPING

To cut the kilometres and avoid leaving the Pyrenean valleys altogether, opt for one of the pretty roads that roll over their lower flanks.

The narrow, steeply winding D294 between Escot and Bielle makes for a dramatic 21km drive over the Col de Marie-Blanque (1035m) between the Aspe and Ossau valleys. The road linking Asasp-Arros and Arudy is a gentler alternative, primarily through forest.

Once the snows melt, the drive along the D918 between Laruns (Vallée d' Ossau) and Argelès-Gazost (Vallée des Gaves) is a true summer spectacular. The D35 between Louvie-Juzon and Nay is an easier year-round alternative, flanked by plenty of farms selling cheese.

times daily. From Oloron there are three to four onward bus connections into the valley via Bedous to Etsaut, the majority continuing to Somport and the Spanish railhead of Canfranc.

Bedous

Bedous, the valley's biggest village – with, despite this superlative, under 600 inhabitants – is 25km south of Oloron-Ste-Marie, where the valley is still wide.

Moulin d'Orcun (☎ 05 59 34 51 70; adult/child €4/3; ☺ visits 11am, 3pm & 6pm Jul, Aug & school holidays), 500m out of Bedous on the Aydius road, is a working 18th-century watermill.

ACTIVITIES

The tourist office in Bedous, and other outlets in the valley, sell the excellent locally produced guide *45 Randonnées en Béarn: la Vallée d'Aspe* (€9). It can also put you in touch with organisers of a whole host of outdoor activities: mountain biking, canyon clambering, rafting, climbing, skiing, snowshoeing and winter mountaineering trips.

SLEEPING & EATING

Camping Municipal de Carole (☎ 05 59 34 59 19; per person/tent/car €2.50/2/2; ☺ Mar–mid-Nov) Small and quiet (it's a good 300m west of the N134), it's well signposted from the main highway.

Le Mandragot (☎ 05 59 34 59 33; place Sarraillé; beds €10) This welcoming *gîte d'étape* (walkers' guesthouse) is a frequent staging post for walkers undertaking the Chemin de St Jacques. There's a cosy common room, accommodation is in rooms for two to eight and it has self-catering facilities.

Chez Michel (☎ 05 59 34 52 47; abr.michel@free .fr; rue Gambetta; r with breakfast €45, menus €10-20) On the main street, Chez Michel has a sauna, free for overnighters, and also runs a neat little restaurant (closed Saturday lunch July and August, as well as lunch Friday and Saturday and dinner Sunday September to June). Go for the *menu saveur du pays* ('flavours of the region'; €15.50) of *garbure* (a scrumptious local pork-based gruel, thick with vegetables and pulses), trout with *cèpe* mushrooms, and bilberry pie.

Restaurant des Cols (☎ 05 59 34 70 25; d €29; ☺ closed dinner Sun & dinner Mon except school holidays, also 1-15 Oct) nearby merits a 50km detour for its sumptuous *menus* (€10 to €21.50) and wonderful views. Happily it's a mere 6.5km

uphill drive east of Bedous in the hamlet of Aydius. It also has three delightful doubles with self-catering facilities. The only downsides: the stuffed wildlife in the restaurant and those rabbit skin (or could it be cat?) bar-stool cushions…

Accous

This little village, 2.5km south of Bedous and 800m east of the highway, sits at the yawning mouth of the Vallée Berthe with a splendid backdrop of 2000m-plus peaks. North of here, the Vallée d'Aspe is broad and fertile. To the south, it closes in dramatically.

The **Fermiers Basco-Béarnais cheese centre** (☎ 05 59 34 76 06; ☺ 8.30am-noon & 2-6pm Mon-Fri, 10am-noon & 2.30-6pm Sat, Sun & school holidays), a farmers' cooperative and thriving *fromagerie* (cheese shop), is beside the N134. It has free sampling and offers a 20-minute audiovisual presentation in French, plus the opportunity to buy the best of local ewe, goat and cow's-milk cheeses.

ACTIVITIES

Tiny Accous boasts two *parapente* (paragliding) schools. **Ascendance** (☎ 05 59 34 52 07; www.ascendance.fr in French) offers accompanied 15-minute introductory flights (€65) and five-day induction courses (€366). **Air Attitude** (☎ 05 59 34 50 06; www.air-attitude.com in French) offers a wider range of courses and flights and has similar prices.

Between Easter and November, a horse ride with guide at **Auberge Cavalière** (☎ 05 59 34 72 30; www.auberge-cavaliere.com) costs €45/70 per half-/full day. Alternatively, for an investment of €580, you can enjoy half-board and half a day's riding for an entire week. The hotel also arranges horse treks of four to seven days and, for walkers, supplies detailed maps outlining circular day walks from the hotel.

SLEEPING & EATING

Camping Despourrins (☎ 05 59 34 71 16; per person/ site €2.65/2.60; ☺ Mar-Oct) This tiny camp site is just off the N134, tucked behind the Fermiers Basco-Béarnais cheese centre.

Auberge Cavalière (☎ 05 59 34 72 30; www.au berge-cavaliere.com; d €38.50, menus €20-25.50; ☺ year-round) About 3km south of Accous and just off the main road, this well-established place has a strong equine flavour. Dining – and you dine well – in the low-beamed restaurant with sheep and goat pelts around the walls is rather like eating in a particularly cosy barn.

Lescun

The bridge at L'Estanguet that collapsed in 1970 and finished off the valley's train traffic is about 4km south of Bedous. Nearby, a steeply hairpinned, 5.5km detour climbs southwest to the mountain village of Lescun (900m), whose slate roofs once sheltered a leper colony.

It's worth a touch of vertigo on the ascent for the breathtaking, photogenic view westwards of the Cirque de Lescun, an amphitheatre of jagged limestone mountains, backed by the 2504m Pic d'Anie.

WALKING

Several great walks start from Lescun. For a day walk with spectacular views back over the Vallée de Lescun and the distinctive Pic du Midi d'Ossau, follow the GR10 northwest via the Refuge de Labérouat and along the base of Les Orgues de Camplong (Camplong Organ Pipes) up to the Cabane du Cap de la Baigt, a *fromagerie* (open only in summer), where you can buy fresh cheese directly from the shepherd.

Lonely Planet's *Walking in France* describes other tempting walks from Lescun and also from Etsaut (right), higher up the Vallée d'Aspe.

SLEEPING & EATING

Gîte & Camping du Lauzart (☎ 05 59 34 51 77; campinglauzart@wanadoo.fr; per person/tent/car €2.50/ 3.80/1.20; ☻ May–mid-Sep) Spacious, friendly and beautifully situated, this pleasant camp site is 1.5km southwest of the village. A dorm bed in the *gîte* costs €10.

Maison de la Montagne (☎ 05 59 34 79 14; lescun.dom@clubinternet.fr; per person €12, half-board €27) This cosy, rustic *gîte*, where rooms sleep four or five, has been adapted from an old barn. The owner, a qualified guide, leads mountain walks.

Hôtel du Pic d'Anie (☎ 05 59 34 71 54; www.vallee -aspe.com/hebergement/pic-anie in French; r €43; ☻ mid-Jun–mid-Sep) In the village itself, this summertime-only hotel has 10 simple, well-maintained rooms. It does particularly hearty meals (*menus* €15 including a vegetarian option, and €23). A couple of doors

away is its year-round *gîte* (dorm bed €13 to €15) with self-catering facilities.

our pick Au Château d'Arance (☎ 05 59 34 75 50; www.auchateaudarance.com in French; r €58-63) From the hamlet of Cette-Eygun, climb eastwards up a narrow, winding lane for 2.25km to reach this delightfully renovated 13th-century castle. For a castle, it's decidedly intimate with only eight rooms, one of which has facilities for the disabled. Its restaurant (menus €16 and €26) is equally stylish, and the sweeping view of the valley below from the terrace makes a sundowner taste all the sweeter.

Etsaut & Borce

The twin villages of Etsaut and Borce are set back on either side of the N134, 11km south of Bedous. Both are popular bases for higher-elevation walks. The **Maison du Parc National des Pyrénées** (Park Information Centre; ☎ 05 59 34 88 30; ☻ 10.30am-12.30pm & 2-6.30pm May-Oct) is in the old train station in Etsaut. To get more background, visit www.haute-aspe.net (in French).

Up the hill, Borce is one of the trimmest little hamlets in all the Pyrenees, restored and documented with care – just see how the telephone booth and public toilets blend harmoniously with the village's mellow stone domestic architecture! – yet still a living community, just the right side of twee.

One route for medieval pilgrims heading for Santiago de Compostela (nowadays the GR653 long-distance trail) was via the Vallée d'Aspe, through Borce and over the Col du Somport. **Hospitalet de St-Jacques de Compostelle** (☎ 05 59 34 88 99; admission free; ☻ 10am-6.30pm) in Borce is a tiny museum, housed in a former pilgrims' lodging and 15th-century chapel. Pop a euro in the slot for 10 minutes of haunting plainsong.

Espace Animalier (☎ 05 59 34 89 33; adult/child €7.50/4.60; ☻ 9.30am-7pm Jun-Sep, 1.30-6pm Apr, May, Oct & Nov) is a large open area above the village where three brown bears together with izards, roe deer, marmots and mouflons live in semicaptivity – though higher authority, under pressure from local herders, did veto plans to introduce a small pack of wolves.

WALKING

For a challenging half-day walk, pick up the GR10 in Borce or Etsaut and follow it south

THE BROWN BEAR HANGS ON

At the time of the last edition of this guide, only two mature Pyrenean brown bears still roamed the mountains, as far as experts were aware: Papillon, a venerable old male, and Cannelle, the only surviving female. Papillon (Butterfly) died of old age but the fate of Cannelle (Cinnamon) has the makings of true tragedy. On 1 November 2004 in the Vallée d'Aspe, a boar hunter shot the one animal that might, with a great deal of luck, have ensured the genetic survival of the Pyrenean bear. 'In self-defence', he claimed, maintaining that, trying to protect her cub, she charged him. France was in uproar. Many believed that the excuse had all the truthfulness of the classic 'Shot while trying to escape'. Even President Chirac weighed in, regretting 'a great loss for French and European biodiversity'.

So the Pyrenean brown bear is emphatically dead. But between 12 and 18 brown bears still hang on precariously. Three bears, Pyros, Mellba and Ziva, imported from Slovenia in 1996 and released amid great controversy, have successfully bred. Then, in April 2006 – and adjudged newsworthy enough to feature on that evening's main TV bulletins – four females and one male bear, also from Slovenia, were released into the mountains.

Great for the survival of this magnificent mammal, once so widespread throughout Europe but now confined to its most remote fastnesses. But spare a thought too for the shepherds, the principle source of opposition. A 0.1% loss rate (86 animals out of an estimated 100,000 that roam the high summer pastures were killed by bears in 2005) may seem an acceptable statistic overall but not if it's your sheep that have been savaged. And truly effective provision requires nightly vigils or the construction of kilometres of fencing to protect flocks.

to Fort du Portalet, a 19th-century fortress used as a prison in WWII by the Germans and Vichy government. Here, head east to negotiate the Chemin de la Mâture, a vertiginous path, originally hacked into the vertical cliff face to allow bullock trains to transport timber for ships' masts from the upper slopes.

Prefer hands-in-pockets walking? Rand'en Âne, run by the friendly folk at **La Garbure** (☎ 05 59 34 88 98; www.garbure.net in French), can line you up with a donkey (per hour/half-/full day €11/23/35) to take the strain.

SLEEPING & EATING

La Garbure (☎ 05 59 34 88 98; www.garbure.net in French; per person €11, half-board €23.50) This popular *gîte d'étape*, down the alleyway beside Etsaut's parish church, has donkeys to rent and can arrange a host of other outdoor activities. The owners have a mountain of information about local walks, and there's a kitchen for self-caterers and even free wi-fi, should you have packed your laptop in your rucksack. Rooms accommodate between two and eight people.

The same family also runs **La Maison de l'Ours** (same rates & hrs as La Garbure) in the village square. In July and August you can sit on its terrace and savour its lip-smacking home-made ice cream.

VALLÉE D'OSSAU

The River Ossau makes a 60km journey from the watershed at Col du Pourtalet (1794m) to its confluence with the Aspe at Oloron-Ste-Marie. The Vallée d'Ossau, through which the river cuts a swath, is one of contrasts. The lower, northern reaches as far as Laruns are broad, green and pastoral. Then, as it cuts more deeply, more steeply into the Pyrenees, it becomes narrow, confined, wooded and looming before broadening out again near the hamlet of Gabas.

MAPS & BOOKS

The most practical general walking map of the area is the 1:50,000-scale *Béarn: Pyrénées Carte No 3*, published by Rando Éditions. For more detail, consult three IGN 1:25,000-scale Top 25 maps – Nos 1547OT *Ossau*, 1647OT *Vignemale* and 1546ET *Laruns*.

The tourist office produces *Randonnées en Vallée d'Ossau* (€7), describing 30 signed walks between 5km and 16km, plus five mountain-bike routes. The national park visitor centre stocks *Randonnées dans le Parc National des Pyrénées: Vallée d'Ossau* (€6.40), describing 14 more challenging walks in the area, supported by 1:50,000-scale maps.

THE PYRENEES

Information

La Maison de la Vallée d'Ossau (☎ 05 59 05 31 41; ossau.tourisme@wanadoo.fr; place de La Mairie, Laruns; ☼ 9am-noon & 2-6pm Mon-Sat, 9am-noon Sun & school holidays, closed Mon, Wed, Thu & afternoon Sun rest of year) The valley's tourist office, on Laruns' main square.

National Park Visitor Centre (☎ 05 59 05 41 59; pnpossau@espaces-naturels.fr; ☼ 9am-noon & 2-5.30pm Jun-Sep, Tue-Sat Oct-May) Beside the tourist office.

Activities

La Maison de la Vallée d'Ossau (☎ 05 59 05 31 41; ossau.tourisme@wanadoo.fr; place de La Mairie, Laruns), where staff speak good English, can reserve a whole host of summer activities such as caving, climbing, kayaking and rafting; and winter fun too, including snowshoe treks and guided cross-country ski outings.

Getting There & Around

Citram Pyrénées (☎ 05 59 27 22 22) runs buses from Pau to Laruns (€4, one hour, two to four daily).

SNCF trains from Pau stop at Buzy-en-Béarn from where there are three onward bus connections daily as far as Laruns (40 minutes).

During school holidays, **Transports Canonge** (☎ 05 59 05 30 31) runs a morning and an evening bus between Laruns and Artouste-Fabrèges (€2 return, 40 minutes, daily). The summer service continues as far as Col du Pourtalet.

For scenic routes between the Ossau and Aspe valleys, see the boxed text, p724.

Falaise aux Vautours

The gliding flight of the griffon vulture (*Gyps folvus*) is once more a familiar sight over the Pyrenees. It feeds exclusively on carrion, fulfilling the role of alpine dustman.

The 82-hectare protected area of the Falaise aux Vautours was originally a haven for 10 griffon vulture pairs nesting in the limestone cliffs above the villages. Now, there are more than 120 couples, plus various other raptors – notably a couple of Egyptian vultures who come back every springtime; the miniature cameras beam images from the heart of their nest.

La Falaise aux Vautours (Cliff of the Vultures; ☎ 05 59 82 65 49; www.falaise-aux-vautours.com in French; adult/child €7/5; ☼ 10.30am-12.30pm & 2-6.30pm Jun-Aug, 2.30-5.30pm or 6.30pm May, Jun, Sep & other school

holidays) in Aste-Béon shows live, big-screen, round-the-clock images from nests on the cliffs 500m higher up. If the moment's right, you can peek in on nesting, hatching and feeding in real time. There's also a good display about vultures, with captions in English.

Laruns

pop 1500 / elevation 536m

Laruns, 6km south of Aste-Béon and 37km from Pau, is the valley's principal village.

SLEEPING & EATING

Camp sites sprawl nearby. At most, however, you're hemmed in by caravans and mobile homes.

Camping du Valentin (☎ 05 59 05 39 33; pelphi@infonie.fr; per person/pitch €3.35/7.05; ☼ May-Oct) By contrast, this highly recommended camp site, 2.4km south of the village beside the D918, has separate zones for mobile homes, caravans and family tents. Overlooking all, and enjoying the best of the impressive views northwards, is a grassy area for lightweight campers.

Refuge-Auberge L'Embaradère (☎ 05 59 05 41 88; lembaradere.@wanadoo.fr; 13 av de la Gare; dm €10, half-board €26, menu €12, mains €9-16; ☼ closed 1-21 May) A long-standing walkers' favourite that's had a couple of new owners in quick succession – always a warning sign. It's still a reasonable budget option, despite the loss of internet access and self-catering facilities.

Hôtel de France (☎ 05 59 05 33 71; www.vallee-ossau.com/hotel/france in French; av de la Gare; r €48, with shared bathroom €31) Although no longer young (and all the more characterful for that), this place is spotless and spruce. It serves real jam for breakfast, unlike the usual sealed-plastic goo. The friendly family owners readily dispense information about hiking opportunities.

L'Arrégalet (☎ 05 59 05 35 47; 37 rue du Bourguet; menus €14-27, mains €9-13; ☼ Tue-Sun lunch) Offering excellent value, L'Arrégalet, about 200m northeast of Lescun's main square, smokes its own trout, bakes all its bread and marinates its own duck foie gras in Armagnac. Every one of its tempting desserts is home-made, too.

Eaux-Bonnes

If you've a penchant for faded glam, allow yourself the briefest of detours to this sad spa that got left behind. Frequented by no less than the Empress Eugénie herself in its 19th-century heyday, it's now all but a ghost resort. The once magnificent Hôtel des Princes stares unseeing, all shutters closed, across the oval square at Hôtel du Parc, once its keenest rival, and now closed over 40 years. More recently, some slick, quick-buck cartel took over the casino – and promptly dropped the place when it failed to squeeze out the profit it had banked on. The **tourist office** (☎ 05 59 05 33 08), God bless it, squats lonely in what was once the town's bandstand.

The small ski resort of Gourette is a mere 10-minute drive away, higher up the valley. Even higher, the col beyond is a favourite torture point of the Tour de France.

Gabas

Tiny Gabas, with less than 50 souls, is now mainly a trekking base, 13km south of Laruns. Its equally small-scale 12th-century **chapel** is the only vestige of what was once a monastery, the very last Chemin de St-Jacques pilgrim hostel before the Spanish frontier. Pick up a hunk of tangy *fromage d'Ossau*, made here in the high mountains from ewe's milk and matured in this very hamlet.

The CAF **refuge** (☎ 05 59 05 33 14; per person €8.20, half-board €28; 🕑 Jun-Sep & school holidays, Sat & Sun only other times, closed Nov-Dec), 500m south of Gabas, offers cheery accommodation in rooms for four to 12 and a culinary reputation that extends way beyond the valley; Marie-France's homemade desserts are to die for.

Hôtel-Restaurant le Biscaü (☎ 05 59 05 31 37; fax 05 59 05 43 23; s/d €27.50/40, with shower €17/32.50; menus €10-15; 🕑 mid-Dec–Oct) Le Biscaü is the most comfortable option in Gabas, offering hearty cuisine (do save room for the cheese course; the owner himself matures cheeses brought in by the local shepherds).

From the CAF *refuge*, a 3.5km forest track brings you to Lac de Bious-Artigues (1420m) and a superb view southeast to Pic du Midi d'Ossau and southwest to Pic d'Ayous.

Le Petit Train d'Artouste

Winter skiers and summer holidaymakers converge upon charmless, lakeside Artouste-Fabrèges (1250m), 6km by road east of Gabas, to squeeze into the cable car which soars up the flanks of the 2032m Pic de la Sagette. Between June and September, an open-topped **train** (☎ reservations 05 59 05 36 99; www.trainartouste.com in French; adult/child €20/16; 🕑 half-hourly 9am-5pm Jul & Aug, hourly 10am-3pm Jun & Sep), built for dam workers in the 1920s, runs for 10km at 2000m from the upper cable car station to Lac d'Artouste (1991m). Views are heart-stopping and the 'little train' tucks away over 100,000 passengers in its four months of operation. Allow a good four hours. For walkers, the one-way/return **cable-car** (🕑 9.30am-6pm) fare is €4.20/6.20.

There's a seasonal **tourist office** (☎ 05 59 05 34 00; 🕑 Jun-Sep & other school holidays) beside the cable car.

CAUTERETS

pop 1300 / elevation 930m

The thermal spa and ski resort of Cauterets, less than 30km south of Lourdes, nestles in a tight valley, crowded in by steep slopes rising to 2800m. In summer it's a superb base for exploring the forests, meadows, lakes and streams of the Parc National des Pyrénées. In winter Cauterets is blessed with an abundance of snow; it's usually the first of France's Pyrenean ski stations to open and the last to close.

Information

INTERNET ACCESS
Pizzeria Giovanni (☎ 05 62 92 57 80; 5 rue de la Raillère; per hr for nondiners €3)

LAUNDRY
Laundrette (19 rue Richelieu; 🕑 8am-8pm)

TOURIST INFORMATION
Maison de la Presse (8 place Maréchal Foch) For walking maps and international newspapers.
Maison du Parc National des Pyrénées (☎ 05 62 92 52 56; place de la Gare; 🕑 9.30am-noon & 3-7pm Jun–mid-Sep, 9.30am-noon & 3-6pm Mon-Fri mid-Sep–Apr) Sells walking maps, has an impressive free exhibition on Pyrenean flora and fauna and shows park-related films. Organises guided walks (per half-/full day €9.15/15.25 in July and August).
Pont d'Espagne Information Office (☎ 05 62 92 52 19; 🕑 Dec-Sep)
Tourist Office (☎ 05 62 92 50 50; www.cauterets.com in French; place Maréchal Foch; 🕑 9am-12.30pm & 2-7pm Mon-Sat, 9am-noon & 3-6pm Sun school holidays, otherwise 9am-noon & 2-6pm Mon-Sat, 9am-noon Sun)

THE PYRENEES

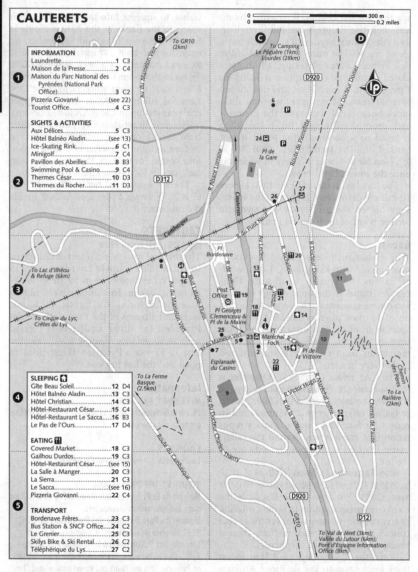

CAUTERETS

0   300 m
0   0.2 miles

INFORMATION
Laundrette...........................1 C3
Maison de la Presse................2 C4
Maison du Parc National des
  Pyrénées (National Park
  Office)..............................3 C2
Pizzeria Giovanni..............(see 22)
Tourist Office.......................4 C3

SIGHTS & ACTIVITIES
Aux Délices..........................5 C3
Hôtel Balnéo Aladin............(see 13)
Ice-Skating Rink...................6 C1
Minigolf.............................7 C4
Pavillon des Abeilles..............8 B3
Swimming Pool & Casino.........9 C4
Thermes César.....................10 D3
Thermes du Rocher...............11 D3

SLEEPING
Gîte Beau Soleil....................12 D4
Hôtel Balnéo Aladin..............13 C3
Hôtel Christian.....................14 C3
Hôtel-Restaurant César..........15 C4
Hôtel-Restaurant Le Sacca......16 B3
Le Pas de l'Ours...................17 D4

EATING
Covered Market....................18 C3
Gailhou Durdos....................19 C3
Hôtel-Restaurant César........(see 15)
La Salle à Manger.................20 C3
La Sierra...........................21 C3
Le Sacca.........................(see 16)
Pizzeria Giovanni.................22 C4

TRANSPORT
Bordenave Frères..................23 C3
Bus Station & SNCF Office....24 C2
Le Grenier..........................25 C3
Skilys Bike & Ski Rental........26 C2
Téléphérique du Lys.............27 C2

Sights & Activities
WALKING

Cauterets makes a particularly good base for day walks because so many start right from town or from Pont d'Espagne at the end of the spectacular D920 road, 8km south, 600m higher and accessible in season by shuttle bus (p733). For a week or more of stimulating walking in the area, consult Lonely Planet's *Walking in France*.

The area west of Cauterets is covered by IGN's 1:25,000-scale Top 25 map No 1647OT *Vignemale;* land east of town features on No 1748OT *Gavarnie.* Rando Éditions' *Bigorre Carte No 4* covers the region at 1:50,000.

The national park produces *Randonnées dans le Parc National des Pyrénées: Vallée de Cauterets* (€6.40), a loose-leaf pack describing, in French and with a detailed map, 15 walks. The tourist office carries *Sentiers du Lavaudon* (€5), describing seven easy walks in the area.

A painless way to gain height from Cauterets is to take the Télécabine du Lys cable car (p733).

For a pleasant day walk from Cauterets (allow around six hours), follow the Vallée de Lutour southwards as far as Lac d'Estom, where the lakeside *refuge* offers refreshments.

From the giant car park at **Pont d'Espagne**, Chemin des Cascades passes by a series of spectacular waterfalls as it drops northwards towards Cauterets.

Heading south from Pont d'Espagne, you've a choice of two valleys, each different in character. Following the Gave de Gaube upstream through a pine wood brings you to the popular **Lac de Gaube** and, nearby, Hôtellerie de Gaube, which does drinks, snacks and midday *menus*. Three hours, not counting breaks, is generous for this out-and-back walk.

A longer trek up the gentler, more open **Vallée de Marcadau** leads to **Refuge Wallon** (☎ 05 62 92 64 28; ☺ Feb–mid-Apr & Jun-Sep) at 1866m. Allow about five hours for the roundtrip.

SKIING

Cauterets is linked to the 21-run **Cirque du Lys** by the shining new Télécabine du Lys cabins, which can shoot up 2000 skiers per hour – nearly three times the throughput of the creaky lift it has replaced. The 36km of runs, ranging from 2415m to 1850m, are best for beginner and intermediate **downhill skiers**. Lift passes cost €25.50/133 per day/week.

Pont d'Espagne (1450m) is primarily a **cross-country skiing** area. From it, 37km of maintained trails, paralleled in their lower reaches by a 6km circuit for walkers and snowshoers, lead up the Vallée du Marcadau. A one-day/week trail pass costs €7.20/33.

Several shops in Cauterets hire out ski equipment. Typical prices per day are downhill €12 to €20, snowboards €19 to €25 and cross-country gear €8 to €10.

SNOWSHOE TREKS

Several mountain guides organise day and half-day treks into spectacular scenery. Typical prices are around €21 to €26 for a three-hour outing and €29 to €32 for a full day including transport and hire of snowshoes and poles. Ask at the tourist office or ring the **Bureau des Guides** (☎ 06 12 94 81 88).

THERMAL SPAS

Cauterets' hot springs, blooping from the earth at 36°C to 53°C, have attracted *curistes* (those seeking a cure) since the 19th century. **Thermes César** (☎ 05 62 92 14 20; www .thermesdecauterets.com in French; rue Docteur Domer; ☺ Feb-Nov) offers a variety of water-based, tone-up activities (around €10) for weary walkers, skiers and those who just want to indulge. Particularly sensuous is the *pelothérapie* option (€18.50), where you get plastered in mud. **Thermes du Rocher**, the other large thermal establishment, is primarily for water-based cures.

Year-round, **Hôtel Balnéo Aladin** (☎ 05 62 92 60 00; www.hotelbalneoaladin.com in French; 11 av Général Leclerc) does the same, though its water is artificially heated, not deep from the earth.

OTHER ACTIVITIES

About 200m southwest of the tourist office are Esplanade du Casino and Esplanade des Oeufs (Egg Esplanade, so named, in an age before public-relations officers and spin doctors held sway, for the stench the sulphurous waters gave off). Here you'll find cafés, an indoor swimming pool, minigolf

---

A LITTLE SWEETENER

Halitosis is never fun. Back in the 19th century, once the *curistes* (those seeking a cure) of Cauterets had swallowed their daily dose of sulphurous spa water, they – and their nearest and dearest – complained of dog's breath.

An enterprising villager, seeing a chance, set about making a boiled sweet that would mask the odour. Shaped like a humbug and made in a rainbow of colours, *berlingots*, a speciality of Cauterets, are on sale in town. **Aux Délices** (place de la Mairie) is one of a quartet of small producers. They'll always give you a sample and if you call by between 4.30pm and 5.30pm you can usually see a batch being made.

and the town's large casino. It would be an even more lovely little open space for promenading if they'd banish the parked cars.

Pavillon des Abeilles (☎ 05 62 92 50 66; 23bis av du Mamelon Vert; admission free; ☽ 10.30am-12.30pm & 2.30-7pm Mon-Sat school holidays, otherwise 3-7pm Wed-Sat) is all about bees, with a glass-sided hive, video and honey of every possible flavour.

Cauterets also has an **ice-skating rink** (place de la Gare; adult/child €8/5.50).

Sleeping
BUDGET

Camping Le Péguère (☎ 05 62 92 52 91; www.les -campings.com/peguere; per pitch €10.65; ☽ May-Sep) This grassy, shady camp site, 1.5km north of town on the D920, has some choice pitches right beside the Gave de Cauterets.

Cauterets has two particularly attractive *gîtes*.

Gîte Beau Soleil (☎ 05 62 92 53 52; gite.beau .soleil@wanadoo.fr; 25 rue Maréchal Joffre; per person €18, half-board €34; ☽ closed Nov-first snows) The Beau Soleil has the comfort of a hotel as well as the friendly informality of a *refuge*. Beds are in spick-and-span doubles or quads with bathrooms, and there's a kitchen for self-caterers, a green rear garden and a large lounge.

Le Pas de l'Ours (☎ 05 62 92 58 07; www.lepas delours.com in French; 21 rue de la Raillère; per person €17, half-board €33, d/tr/q €47/60/75, with half-board per person €37.50-48; ☽ mid-May–Sep & Dec–mid-Apr) 'The Bear's Footstep' is both hotel and *gîte*. Prices for the dorms (two to six people) include use of the kitchen, and all guests can use the sauna (€8 to €15).

MIDRANGE

Hôtel-Restaurant César (☎ 05 62 92 52 57; www .cesarhotel.com in French; 3 rue César; r €42-52; ☽ closed May & Oct) This cosy option, run by an engaging husband and wife, has attractive rooms and represents excellent value. Opt for the recently renovated 3rd-floor rooms. The hotel also runs an impressive restaurant.

Hôtel-Restaurant Le Sacca (☎ 05 62 92 50 02; hotel.le.sacca@wanadoo.fr; 11 blvd Latapie-Flurin; r €41-70; ☽ closed 10 Oct-20 Dec) Le Sacca has recently taken over its neighbour, nearly doubling its capacity and creating a spacious ground-floor guest area. It's another excellent mid-range choice, run by the same husband and wife team for three decades. It too has a great restaurant and many rooms have separate bathroom and toilet.

Hôtel Christian (☎ 05 62 92 50 04; www.hotel -christian.fr in French; 10 rue Richelieu; s/d/tr/q incl break-fast €49/68/86/103; ☽ Dec-Sep) Rooms are large and comfortable at this friendly hotel, in the hands of the same Cauterets family for three generations. There's a charming rear garden, and wi-fi.

Hôtel Balnéo Aladin (☎ 05 62 92 60 00; www .hotelbalneoaladin.com in French; 11 av Général Leclerc; d incl breakfast €100-130, half-board per person €61-106; ☽ Christmas–mid-May & Jun-Sep) The Aladin also doubles as a private spa (p731). Strikingly modern – brash even – in a resort where venerable hotels are closing or converting into apartments, it offers every luxury. A stay of four nights is normally expected, although this is negotiable outside peak periods. Half-board is obligatory during the ski season. Rates include access to the fitness centre and sauna.

Eating

La Sierra (☎ 05 62 42 68 97; 8 rue Verdun; lunch menu €10.50, dinner menus €13.50-19; ☽ Thu-Tue) This intimate little place, tucked away down a side street, will warm you through and through. It offers as much *garbure* as your tummy will take, plus 25cl of wine and coffee for €12.

La Salle à Manger (☎ 05 62 92 06 57; 22 rue Richelieu; lunch menu €14, mains €14-20; ☽ Dec-Apr only, closed lunch Mon) Although in the mountains, you're guaranteed the freshest of fish at this welcoming recent addition to Cauteret's eating choices. The well-travelled owner (see the souvenirs of her globetrotting all around the walls) regularly drops down to her home town, coastal St-Jean de Luz, to pick up a box, fresh from the ocean. Meat mains are equally impressive.

Pizzeria Giovanni (☎ 05 62 92 57 80; 5 rue de la Raillère; menu €15; ☽ lunch & dinner daily school holidays, otherwise dinner only, closed Wed & mid-May–mid-Jun & Nov–mid-Dec) Pizzas (around €9, to eat in or take away) are superior, a generous steak costs €13 and the home-cooked desserts (€4 to €4.60) are a dream. A nice touch: diners can check out their emails for free.

Le Sacca (☎ 05 62 92 50 02; hotel.le.sacca@wanadoo .fr; 11 blvd Latapie-Flurin; menus €16.50-42) Here is by common consent the finest place to eat in Cauterets, with a range of *menus* to suit most pockets. Whether you're down from the mountains or fresh from Lourdes and the plains, make a pilgrimage to savour its subtle cuisine.

Hôtel-Restaurant César (☎ 05 62 92 52 57; www
.cesarhotel.com in French; 3 rue César; menus €22-32;
🕑 closed lunch in winter, also dinner Wed except school
holidays) With its crisp white tablecloths and
napkins, the César offers elegant dining. The
food is excellent and there's a good range of
regional wines at reasonable prices.

La Ferme Basque (☎ 05 62 92 54 32; rte de Cam-
basque) About 4km by road west of town,
this place has a superb plunging view of
Cauterets from its terrace and makes a great
spot for a daylight drink. You can eat great
farm-produced fare though the service can
be excruciatingly slow.

SELF-CATERING
Stalls are few but Cauterets' **covered market**
(av Leclerc) is a gastronome's delight. Inside,
a couple of stalls do tasty takeaway dishes
while another sells wonderful mountain
cheeses. Just follow your nose…

Gailhou Durdos (rue de Belfort), opposite the
post office, has a rich selection of local
wines and specialities.

Getting There & Away
The last train steamed out of Cauterets'
magnificent, all-wood station in 1947. Like
something left over from a cowboy film set,
it now serves as the **bus station** (☎ 05 62 92
53 70).

SNCF buses run between Cauterets and
Lourdes train station (€6.40, one hour, at
least five daily).

Getting Around
BICYCLE
Skilys (☎ 05 62 92 58 30; rte de Pierrefitte) and its
affiliate, **Le Grenier** (4 av du Mamelon Vert) rent out
winter ski equipment and mountain bikes
(per half-/full day from €16/25) in summer.

BUS
Navette d'Espagne is a shuttle service (single/
return €4/6) between the bus station and
Pont d'Espagne during the ski season (twice
daily) and in summer (six times daily).

CABLE CAR
The fast new Télécabine du Lys operates
mid-June to mid-September and from December to the end of the ski season. It rises
over 900m to the Cirque du Lys, where you
can catch the Grand Barbat chairlift up to
Crêtes du Lys (2400m). A return trip costs
€7.50/5 per adult/child to Cirque du Lys or
€9.50/6.50 to Crêtes du Lys.

TAXI
Ring **Bordenave Frères** (☎ 05 62 92 53 68; place Clemenceau), which also calls itself Allo Taxis. A
taxi between Cauterets and Pont d'Espagne
costs €16.

VALLÉE DES GAVES & AROUND
Vallée des Gaves (Valley of the Mountain
Streams), gentle and pastoral, extends south
from Lourdes to Pierrefitte-Nestalas. Here,
the valley forks, narrows, twists and becomes more rugged. The eastern tine pokes
into the Pyrenees via Gavarnie while the
western prong leads up to Cauterets.

Pic du Midi de Bigorre
Lament it or love it, the Pic du Midi (2877m),
once the preserve of astronomers and scien-
tists, is now accessible to all by **cable car** (☎ 08
25 00 28 77; adult/student/child €23/18/12; 🕑 daily

NO PASARÁN!
'No pasarán', say the banners and posters around Lourdes and the Vallée des Gaves: 'They shall
not pass', echoing the famous Republican slogan of the Spanish Civil War. The long environmental campaign to save the Vallée d'Aspe (p724) was lost and the tunnel de Somport now allows
easy truck access to this fragile valley. The battlefield has now moved two valleys westwards, to
Vallée des Gaves, as residents and environmentalists resist plans for the Traversée Centrale des
Pyrénées (TCP), or Central Pyrenees Crossing.

The TCP is being actively pursued by the governments of the Midi-Pyrenees region and of
Aragón, over the Spanish frontier, despite the opposition of every mayor and local council in
the valley. What's proposed is a 42km tunnel between Biescas in Spain and Pierrefitte-Nestalas.
Should it go ahead, more than 250 trains daily will use this twin-track rail freight link, burrowed
under Vignemale, France's highest Pyrenean peak, then continuing down the valley to loop
around Lourdes.

THE PYRENEES

Mar-Jan, Wed-Fri Feb). Leaving from the ski resort of La Mongie (1800m), it gives access to one of the Pyrenees' most soul-stirring panoramas, albeit at heart-stopping prices.

Gavarnie
pop 165 / elevation 1360m

In winter, Gavarnie, 52km south of Lourdes at the end of the D921, offers limited downhill and decent cross-country skiing plus snowshoe treks. In summer it's a popular take-off point for walkers. And take off they do, as quickly as their feet will carry them: by 10am the village and its tawdry souvenir stalls are overrun by tourists.

Consult the IGN Top 25 map No 1748OT *Gavarnie* or the National Park pack *Randonnées dans le Parc National des Pyrénées: Vallée de Luz* (€6.40) for the rich menu of routes.

The most frequented trail, accessible to all (in winter too; pull on your skis or snowshoes), leads to the **Cirque de Gavarnie**, a breathtaking rock amphitheatre, 1500m high, fringed by ice-capped peaks. The round-trip walk to its base takes around two hours. Between Easter and October you can clip-clop along on a horse or donkey (€22 round trip). In mid-July, Gavarnie hosts an **arts festival** in the dramatic setting of the Cirque.

The **tourist office** (☎ 05 62 92 49 10; www.gavarnie.com; ☼ 8.30am-12.30pm & 2-6.30pm daily school holidays, otherwise 9am-noon & 2-6.30pm Mon-Sat) is at the northern entrance to the village.

The **national park office** (☎ 05 62 92 42 48; ☼ 9.30am-noon & 1.30-5.30pm Tue-Sat school holidays, Mon-Fri rest of year) is 200m beyond.

Camping Le Pain de Sucre (☎ 05 62 92 47 55; www.camping-gavarnie.com; per person/site €3.60/3.80; ☼ mid-Dec–mid-Apr & Jun-Sep) enjoys a lovely riverside spot a little north of town.

Hôtel Le Marboré (☎ 05 62 92 40 40; www.lemarbore.com; s/d/tr €49/63.50/77, half-board per person €58; ☼ mid-Dec–mid-Nov; ✗) stands out among Gavarnie's few overnight options as much for its acclaimed restaurant as for the comfort of its rooms. In a characterful, thoroughly modernised 19th-century building, it's family-run and friendly (kick back in Le Swan, its pub) and has a fitness centre. Half-board is compulsory in the ski season and high summer.

During school holidays only, two buses run daily between Gavarnie and Luz-St-Sauveur, from where there are connections to Lourdes.

Cirque de Troumouse

From Gèdre, 6.5km north of Gavarnie, a toll road (€4 per vehicle) winds southeast up a desolate valley into the Pyrenees to the base of the Cirque de Troumouse, wilder, infinitely less trodden and almost as stunning as the Cirque de Gavarnie. Snows permitting, the road is open between May and October.

UPPER GARONNE VALLEY
St-Bertrand de Comminges

On an isolated hillock, St-Bertrand and its **Cathédrale Ste-Marie** (adult/child incl audioguide in English €4/1.50; ☼ 9am-7pm Mon-Sat, 2-7pm Sun May-Sep, 10am-noon & 2-5pm Mon-Sat, 2-5pm Sun Oct-Apr) loom protectively over the Vallée de Garonne and the much-pillaged remains of the Gallo-Roman town of Lugdunum Convenarum, where you can wander at will for free.

The splendid Renaissance oak choir stalls sit below the soaring Gothic east end of the cathedral. Carved in 1535 by local artisans, they blend the serene and spiritual with an earthy realism.

Bagnères de Luchon
pop 3000 / elevation 630m

Bagnères de Luchon (or simply Luchon) is a trim little town of gracious 19th-century buildings, expanded to accommodate the *curistes* who came to take the waters at its splendid spa.

Tourist Office (☎ 05 61 79 21 21; www.luchon.com; 18 allées d'Étigny; ☼ 8.30am-7pm Mon-Sat, 8.30am-12.30pm & 2.30-6pm Sun Jul, Aug & Dec-Mar, 8.30am-12.30pm & 1.30-7pm Sep-Nov & Apr-Jun)

SIGHTS & ACTIVITIES

Once only for the ailing, the **Thermes** (Health Spa; ☎ 05 61 79 22 97; ☼ Apr–mid-Oct), at the southern end of allées d'Étigny, now also offer relaxation and fitness sessions for weary skiers and walkers, mainstay of the town's tourism-based economy. It's €13 to loll in the scented steam of the 160m-long underground *vaporarium*, then dunk yourself in the caressing 32°C waters of its pool. Follow this with a flutter in the elegant surroundings of the casino and you'll have had a good night out.

The stylish allées d'Étigny, flanked by cafés and restaurants, link place Joffre with the Thermes. Just to the west of this boulevard is the base of the **cabin lift** (single/return €5.30/8.10) that hauls you up to **Superbagnères**, at 1860m the starting point for winter skiing and summer walking. It operates daily in the ski season and during July and August (weekends only during most other months).

Cycling

Although you'll huff and puff, the area is rich in opportunities for mountain biking. The tourist office has copies of the free *Guide des Circuits VTT,* prepared by the local mountain-bike club, and also a miniguide to four runs starting from the top of the cabin lift. To rent a bike, see right.

Walking

An amazing 250km of marked trails, ranging from gentle valley-bottom strolls to more demanding high-mountain treks, thread their way from Luchon and Superbagnères. Lonely Planet's *Walking in France* describes five days of walks in the area and the tourist office carries a useful free pamphlet, *Sentiers Balisés du Pays de Luchon.* Pick up IGN 1:25,000 map No 1848OT *Bagnères de Luchon,* pull on your boots and head for the hills.

Other Activities

For the full range of outdoor possibilities, ask the tourist office for a copy of its free *La Montagne Active* brochure. The skies above Superbagnères are magnificent for **parapenting**. Contact **École Soaring** (☎ 05 61 79 29 23; www.soaring.fr in French; 31 rue Sylvie). More down-to-earth, **Pyrénées Aventure** (☎ 05 61 79 20 59; www.pyreneesaventure.com in French; 9 rue Docteur Germès) arranges canyon clambering and guided walks.

SLEEPING & EATING

Camping Beauregard (☎ 05 61 79 30 74; camp.beauregard@wanadoo.fr; 37 av de Vénasque; per person/pitch €4/5; ♥ Apr–mid-Oct) This is the larger and more welcoming of Luchon's two camp sites. A mere 300m from Les Thermes, it's popular with *curistes.*

Hôtel des Sports (☎ 05 61 79 97 80; www.hotel-des-sports.net; 12 av Maréchal Foch; d €42-52, tr €58; ✗)

This hotel is that rare institution in France – an entirely nonsmoking hotel, where the friendly owner, himself a hiker, happily dispenses local walking information and advice. Within the lifespan of this book, he'll probably have retired and be indulging in some major travelling of his own.

Hôtel des Deux Nations (☎ 05 61 79 01 71; www .hotel-des2nations.com; 5 rue Victor Hugo; r €45-55, with shared bathroom €25-35) Nearly into its second century, this hotel has been run by the same family for five generations. Rooms are comfortable and good value but its major attraction is the restaurant (*menus* €14 to €33, closed Sunday dinner and Monday November to January), which serves hearty local cuisine in gargantuan quantities. Try the locally reared lamb chops, brought flaming to your table and deftly doused with a lettuce leaf.

The Allées d'Étigny are packed with bars and restaurants, some fine delicatessens and the usual pizza 'n' pasta joints.

L'Arbesquens (☎ 05 61 79 33 69; 47 allées d'Étigny; menus €14.35-22.50) Its speciality is fondue (€14, minimum two people) in 17 varieties. Help it down with a jug of fine Jurançon white wine.

Caprices d'Étigny (☎ 05 61 94 31 05; 30bis allées d'Étigny; menus €15-22.50; ♥ closed dinner Thu) Just across the road and staffed by a young, friendly crew, it does great grilled meats on its open fire.

Self-caterers should pass by Luchon's daily **market** (rue Docteur Germès), established in 1897 and offering fine fresh fare ever since.

GETTING THERE & AROUND

SNCF trains and buses run between Luchon and Montréjeau (€6, 50 minutes, seven daily), which has frequent connections to Toulouse (€18.40) and Pau (€19.50).

There's free parking around the Casino and cabin lift station.

For bicycle hire, contact **Liberty Cycles Demiguel** (☎ 05 61 79 12 87; 82 av Maréchal Foch) – look for the Statue of Liberty holding aloft a bike wheel – or **Cycles Sanson** (☎ 05 61 79 88 56; place du Comminges), barely a turn of the pedals away.

VALLÉE DE L'ARIÈGE

The Vallée de l'Ariège offers some great pre-Pyrenean walking, caving and canoeing. Ask at any tourist office for the *Carte*

Touristiques: Guide Pratique, which lists in French a host of local entrepreneurs.

Foix

pop 9700

Foix, county seat of the Ariège *département*, merits a small detour from the N20 to visit its castle, 11th-century church and streets lined with medieval, half-timbered houses.

The town sits in the crook of the confluence of the Rivers Ariège and Arget. Its oldest, most attractive quarter is on the west bank of the Ariège.

INFORMATION

Tourist Office (☎ 05 61 65 12 12; www.ot-foix.fr in French; ⊙ 9am-7pm Mon-Sat, 9.30am-12.30pm & 2-6pm Sun Jul & Aug, 9am-noon & 2-6pm Mon-Sat Sep-Jun) Near the covered market on cours Gabriel Fauré, the wide main thoroughfare.

SIGHTS

The imposing **Château des Comtes de Foix** (☎ 05 34 09 83 83; www.sesta.fr in French; adult/child €4.20/3; ⊙ 9.45am-6.30pm Jul & Aug, 9.45am-noon & 2-6pm Jun & Sep, 10.30am-noon & 2-5.30pm Wed-Sun & daily in school holidays Oct-Dec & Feb-May, Sat & Sun only Jan), with its three crenellated, gravity-defying towers, stands guard over the town. Constructed in the 10th century as a stronghold for the counts of Foix, it served as a prison from the 16th century onwards; look for the graffiti scratched into the stones by some hapless inmate. Today it houses a small **archaeological museum**.

ACTIVITIES

Go canyon clambering, canoeing, mountain biking or hiking with **Pyrénévasion** (☎ 05 61 65 01 10; www.pyrenevasion.com). The tourist office sells *Le Pays de Foix à Pied* (€7.80), an excellent guide to short and more challenging walks in the area.

SLEEPING & EATING

Camping du Lac (☎ 05 61 65 11 58; www.campingdulac.com in French; per 2 people & car €13-19; ⊙ year-round; ⛲) Beside the RN20 2.5km north of Foix, this attractive camp site has both pool and restaurant.

Hôtel Lons (☎ 05 34 09 28 00; www.hotel-lons-foix.com; 6 place Dutilh; d €42-71) Once a coaching inn, it's now a three-star Logis de France with attractive, good-value rooms, nine of which

overlook the river. The hotel's restaurant (closed lunch Saturday September to mid-July) offers similar river views through its picture windows.

Le Sainte Marthe (☎ 05 61 02 87 87; place Lazéma; menus €22-37; ⊙ daily Jul & Aug, Thu-Mon Sep-Jun) Under new management, all the indications are that this gourmet restaurant will continue to serve fine fare. Specialising in Ariègeois cuisine, its signature dish is cassoulet (€16), a hearty platter of beans and duck that's almost a meal in itself. Staff can rustle up a vegetarian menu on request.

GETTING THERE & AWAY

Regular trains (€11.80, 1¼ hours, 10-plus daily) connect Toulouse and Foix.

Around Foix

Beneath **Labouiche**, 6km northwest of Foix on the D1, flows Europe's longest navigable underground river ('Venice of the Ariège' proclaims the publicity, with more than a whiff of hyperbole). You can take a spectacular 1500m, 75-minute **boat trip** (☎ 05 61 65 04 11; adult/child €8/6; ⊙ 9.30am-5.15pm Jul & Aug, 10-11.15am & 2-5.15pm Apr-Jun & Sep, 10-11.15am & 2-4.30pm Sat & Sun Oct–mid-Nov) along part of its length.

Les Forges de Pyre'ne (☎ 05 34 09 30 60; adult/child €7.50/3.50; ⊙ 10am-7pm Jul & Aug, 1.30-6pm Apr–mid-Nov, plus 10am-noon Jun & Sep), in Montgaillard, 4.5km south of Foix, is a living museum of Ariège folk tradition with its own blacksmith, baker, cobbler and basket weaver. Spread over 5 hectares, it illustrates a host of lost or dying trades such as glass blowing, tanning, thatching and nail making.

Ax-les-Thermes

pop 1500 / elevation 720m

Ax-les-Thermes flourishes as a small base for skiing in winter and, with over 60 hot-water springs, as a spa town. Like Foix, it lies at the confluence of two rivers: the Ariège and – here's scope for confusion – the Oriège. The **tourist office** (☎ 05 61 64 60 60; www.vallees-ax.com in French; ⊙ 9am-noon & 2-6pm) is on av Delcassé. It sells two walking guides (each €5) – *D'un Village à L'Autre: 23 Balades au De'part de 15 Villages* and *Lacs et Torrents: 20 Randonneés.*

The heart of town is place du Breilh. On one side of the square is the faded elegance of the casino. On the other is the **Bassin de Ladres**, a shallow pool originally built to soothe the wounds of Knights Templar injured in the Crusades and the ulcers of the town's leper colony. Pull off your socks, follow the example of the knights and steep your feet in its waters.

There are a couple of interesting narrow streets with overhanging buildings between place du Breilh and place Roussel. The **Thermes du Teich** (☎ 05 61 65 86 60; ☼ Apr–mid-Nov), beside the River Oriège, have a pool, sauna, hammam and aquagym (€12.80 per session), open to all comers.

La Petite Fringale (☎ 06 87 74 03 21; 6 rue Rigal; mains around €15, menus €15-30) This popular, friendly place, down a pedestrianised alley near the Bassin de Ladres, has a small summertime terrace. It does four kinds of fondues (€14 to €17), lots of tempting cheese-based dishes, and meaty mains.

Most trains serving Foix (see opposite) continue as far as Ax.

Around Ax-les-Thermes

At **Lombrives** (☎ 05 61 05 98 40; ☼ May-Sep & school holidays), 22km north of Ax on the N20 near the village of Ussat-les-Bains, is Europe's largest underground cave. There are several different routes, ranging from 1½ hours underground (€6.60/3.70) to (cave owners are given to exaggeration hereabouts) a five-hour 'journey to the centre of the earth' (€33, prior reservation).

Toulouse Area

Toulouse, not quite the Pyrenees, is no longer part of Languedoc-Roussillon, having been hived off when regional boundaries were redrawn almost half a century ago. The area, once Languedoc's traditional centre, may be in geographical limbo but, rich in historical sights, it remains a fascinating one to explore.

Toulouse itself, the only city of any size hereabouts, is one of France's liveliest and fastest-growing. Bolstered by its booming hi-tech industries (notably aerospace; this is the epicentre of the huge Europe-wide EADS aircraft manufacturing consortium), the city is increasingly confident. In its vibrant centre, enlivened by students, you'll sense more than a whiff of Spain.

South of Toulouse lie the Pyrenees, while within easy reach are five towns with historical connections: Albi, 75km to the northeast, all red brick and birthplace of Toulouse-Lautrec; Montauban, 53km north, a Huguenot stronghold in the 16th century; Moissac with its magnificent Abbaye St-Pierre, once a stop for Chemin de St-Jacques pilgrims en route to Spain and Santiago de Compostela; Condom, 110km to the northwest, with its 18th-century *hôtels particuliers;* and Auch, 77km west, a trade and communications crossroads ever since Roman times.

West of Toulouse city, the region of Gascony (Gascogne) rolls all the way to the Atlantic. Famous for its lush countryside, fine wines, foie gras and Armagnac liqueur, slow-paced Gascony is ideal for experiencing some of France's finest examples of medieval and Renaissance architecture. Allow yourself a whole day, for example, to explore the cluster of sleepy *bastides,* fortified medieval villages northwest of Toulouse.

HIGHLIGHTS

■ Trace the development of an artistic master at the **Musée Toulouse-Lautrec** (p751), in Albi

■ Invade the **bastide villages** (p760) around Condom for a day

■ Carouse until late, enjoying Toulouse's busy **bar scene** (p747)

■ Expand your mind and universe at **Cité de l'Espace** (p744)

■ Take a trip from Castres along the River Agoût in a replica **river barge** (p753)

★ Condom   ★ Albi

Toulouse ★   ★ Castres

■ POPULATION: 2,560,000   ■ AREA: 45,350 SQ KM

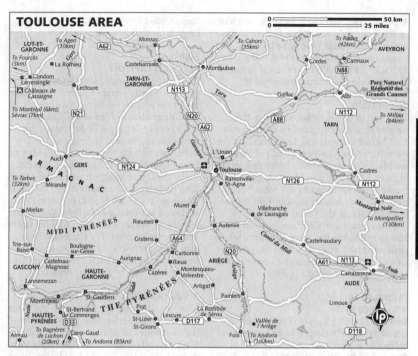

TOULOUSE

pop 389,500

Be warned, even the grannies will want to fight you in Toulouse according to the lyrics of *Oh! Toulouse,* a bittersweet tribute to the city by the late French crooner Claude Nougaro, born and bred here.

Nougaro may have had a hard time growing up on the streets of *la ville rose* (the pink city – so named because of the profusion of rose-red brick buildings), but these days you're more likely to find a good time in Toulouse than you are to bump into pugilistic pensioners.

This lively, friendly city, pink by day, is bright at night. 'Toulouse, Ville de Lumière' (City of Light) is the city's latest tourist slogan, and the illuminated main sights indeed fight back the night.

Anywhere that's home to 130,000 students can't really fail to be a buzzing, busy place with a terrific café and bar scene, lots of clubbing alternatives and dozens of good, affordable places to eat.

Signs of a rich and tumultuous history crowd around you in the narrow medieval streets and inside the many churches and cathedrals of the city, capital of the Midi-Pyrénées region and France's fourth-largest city.

History

Toulouse, known to the Romans as Tolosa, was the Visigoth capital from AD 419–507. In the 12th and 13th centuries the counts of Toulouse supported the Cathars (see p804). Three centuries later, during the Wars of Religion, the city prudently sided with the Catholic League. Toulouse merchants grew rich in the 16th and 17th centuries from the woad (blue dye) trade, which collapsed when the Portuguese began importing indigo from India. The Toulouse parliament ruled Languedoc from 1420 until the 1789 Revolution.

During WWI, Toulouse became a centre for the manufacture of arms and aircraft. In the 1920s, Antoine de St-Exupéry, author of *Le Petit Prince (The Little Prince),* and other daring pilots pioneered mail flights to northwestern Africa and South America, often staying in the city between sorties.

After WWII, Toulouse became the nucleus of the country's aerospace industry. Passenger planes built here have included the Caravelle and Concorde as well as the latest 555-seat Airbus A380, and local factories also produce the Ariane space rocket.

Orientation

The heart of Toulouse is bounded to the east by blvd de Strasbourg and its continuation, blvd Lazare Carnot, and, to the west, by the River Garonne. Its two principal squares are place du Capitole and, 200m east, place Wilson. From the latter, the wide allées Jean Jaurès leads northeast to the main bus station and Gare Matabiau, the train station, both just across the Canal du Midi.

From place du Capitole, rue du Taur runs north to the Basilique St-Sernin, while pedestrianised rue St-Rome and rue des Changes lead south from the square to the transport hub of place Esquirol.

Information

BOOKSHOPS

Bookshop (Map p743; ☎ 05 61 22 99 92; 17 rue Lakanal) Has an excellent range of English-language books and operates an information board.

Ombres Blanches (Map p743; ☎ 05 34 45 53 33; 48-50 rue Gambetta) Friendly, specialising in maps and travel guides, including Lonely Planet titles.

INTERNET ACCESS

Alerte Rouge (Map p743; 21 place St-Sernin; per hr €3; ☼ 10am-11pm Mon-Sat) Free wi-fi connection if you buy a drink. Free webcam use.

Cyber King (Map p743; 31 rue Gambetta; per hr €4; ☼ 11am-11pm Mon-Sat, 2-9pm Sun)

LAUNDRY

Befitting a city with so many students, Toulouse is well endowed with laundrettes. Two central ones are:

Hallwash (Map p743; 7 rue Mirepoix; ☼ 7.30am-9.30pm)

Lavarie Atoraya (Map p741; 29 rue Pargaminières; ☼ 7.30am-9.30pm)

POST

Post Office (Map p743; 9 rue la Fayette)

TOURIST INFORMATION

Tourist Office (Map p743; ☎ 05 61 11 02 22; www.toulouse-tourisme.com; square Charles de Gaulle; ☼ 9am-7pm Mon-Sat, 10am-1pm & 2-6.15pm Sun Jun-Sep; 9am-6pm Mon-Fri, 9am-12.30pm & 2-6pm Sat, 10am-12.30pm & 2-5pm Sun Oct-May) In the base of the Donjon du Capitole, a 16th-century tower.

Sights

PLACE DU CAPITOLE

Bustling pedestrianised **place du Capitole** (Map p743) is the city's main square. On the ceiling of the arcades on its western side are 29 vivid illustrations of the city's history, from the *Venus of Lespugue* (a prehistoric representation of woman) through to the city's status as a hub for the aeronautics industry, by contemporary artist Raymond Moretti.

On the square's eastern side is the 128m-long façade of the **Capitole** (☼ 10am-7pm), Toulouse's city hall, built in the early 1750s. Within is the **Théâtre du Capitole** (☎ 05 61 63 13 13), one of France's most prestigious opera and operetta venues. The Capitole's interior also includes the over-the-top (can't you just tell by the name), late 19th-century **Salle des Illustres** (Hall of the Illustrious).

VIEUX QUARTIER

The small, mainly 18th-century **Vieux Quartier** (Old Quarter; Map p743) is a web of narrow lanes and squares south of place du Capitole and place Wilson. Place de la Daurade is the city's 'beach' beside the River Garonne, peaceful by day and romantic by night, overlooking floodlit Pont Neuf.

BASILIQUE ST-SERNIN

The **Basilique St-Sernin** (Map p743; ☎ 05 61 21 80 45; place St-Sernin; ☼ 8.30am-6.15pm Mon-Sat, 8.30am-7.30pm Sun Jul-Sep; 8.30-11.45am & 2-5.45pm Mon-Sat, 8.30am-12.30pm & 2-7.30pm Sun Oct-Jun) was once an important stop on the Chemin de St-Jacques pilgrimage route. Simply vast (it's 115m long) it ranks as France's largest and most complete Romanesque structure. The basilica is topped by a magnificent eight-sided 13th-century tower and spire, added in the 15th century.

Directly above the double-level crypt is the 18th-century tomb of St-Sernin beneath a sumptuous canopy. In the north transept is a well-preserved 12th-century fresco of Christ's Resurrection. Visiting hours for the ambulatory chapels and **crypt** (admission €2) are shorter than those for the basilica.

MUSÉE DES AUGUSTINS

The **Musée des Augustins** (Map p743; ☎ 05 61 22 21 82; 21 rue de Metz; €3/free; ☼ 10am-6pm) houses

TOULOUSE AREA

TOULOUSE

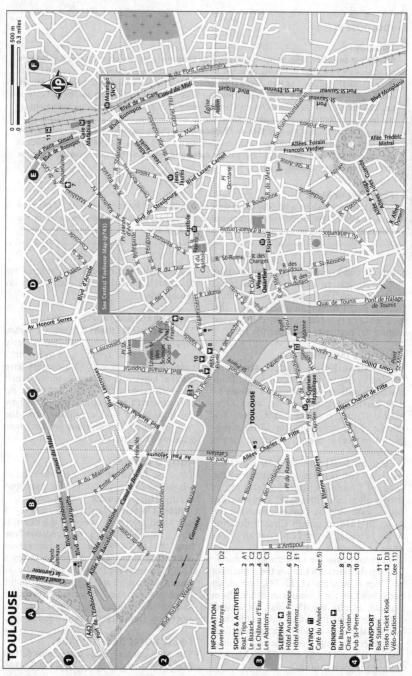

INFORMATION	
Laverie Atoraya........................	1 D2

SIGHTS & ACTIVITIES	
Boat Trips.................................	2 A1
Le Bazacle..............................	3 C2
Le Château d'Eau....................	4 C3
Les Abattoirs..........................	5 C3

SLEEPING	
Hôtel Anatole France...............	6 D2
Hôtel Mermoz.........................	7 E1

EATING	
Café du Musée........................	(see 5)

DRINKING	
Bar Basque..............................	8 C2
Chez Tonton...........................	9 C2
Pub St-Pierre...........................	10 C2

TRANSPORT	
Bus Station..............................	11 E1
Tisséo Ticket Kiosk..................	12 D3
Vélo-Station............................	(see 11)

See Central Toulouse Map (p743)

0 500 m
0 0.3 miles

TOULOUSE IN...

Two Days

Breakfast at one of the cafés on handsome **place du Capitole** (p740), before exploring the **Capitole** building (city hall), and the many churches in the **Vieux Quartier** (p740). Lunch at the cheap, tasty restaurants above **Les Halles Victor Hugo** (p747), then it's a toss-up between the **Musée des Augustins** (p740) or a walk to the river and beyond to the modern art spaces and café at **Les Abattoirs** (p744). Browse on hearty Gascon fodder back in the Vieux Quartier before hitting the many excellent bars (p747) and clubs (p748) in town.

Next day head out of town to **Cité de l'Espace** (p744) in the morning and the **Airbus factory** (p744) in the afternoon or, if this is too much hi-tech stuff for one day, window-shop back in the Vieux Quartier or relax back in the various **cafés and salons de thé** (p748; tearooms) in the city centre's shady squares.

Four Days or More

Take a boat or a bike for a lazy day along the **Canal du Midi** (p745) and then head out to towns such as **Albi** (p749) for the striking cathedral and excellent Toulouse-Lautrec museum or the **Condom area** (p760) for fine dining and pretty *bastide* villages.

---

a superb collection ranging from Roman stone artefacts to paintings by Rubens, Delacroix and Toulouse-Lautrec. It's in a former Augustinian monastery, and the gardens of its two 14th-century cloisters are among the prettiest in southern France.

ÉGLISE DES JACOBINS

This extraordinary Gothic structure, flooded by day in multicoloured light from the huge stained-glass windows, seems to defy gravity. A single row of seven 22m-high columns, running smack down the middle of the nave, look for all the world like palm trees as they spread their fanned vaulting.

Église des Jacobins (Map p743; Parvis des Jacobins; ☽ 9am-7pm) is the mother church of the order of Dominican friars (or Jacobins, as they're often called in France). Construction began soon after St Dominic founded the order in 1215 to preach Church doctrine to the heretical Cathars and took all of 170 years to complete.

Interred below the modern, grey-marble altar on the northern side are the remains of St Thomas Aquinas (1225–74), himself an early head of the Dominican order. From outside, admire the 45m-high, octagonal, 13th-century belfry. Admission to the tranquil cloister costs €1.50. Miraculously, little permanent damage was done as a result of the church serving as an artillery barracks during the 19th century.

The 14th-century refectory, entered via the church, nowadays hosts temporary art exhibitions.

CATHÉDRALE ST-ÉTIENNE

The **Cathédrale St-Étienne** (Cathedral of St Stephen; Map p743; place St-Étienne; ☽ 7.30am-7pm), severely modified over the centuries, is in a hotchpotch of styles. The vast, 12th-century nave is out of kilter with the equally monumental late-13th-century choir, designed to realign the cathedral along a different axis (see how the improvised Gothic vaulting links the two sections). The glorious western rose window dates from 1230.

HÔTEL D'ASSÉZAT

Toulouse boasts about 50 handsome *hôtels particuliers* – grand, private mansions mostly dating from the 16th century.

Hôtel d'Assézat (Map p743), built by a rich woad merchant, is one of the finest. It now houses a museum, the **Fondation Bemberg** (☎ 05 61 12 06 89; www.fondation-bemberg.fr; rue de Metz; adult/student €4.60/2.75; ☽ 10am-12.30pm & 1.30-6pm Tue-Sun, to 9pm Thu), with a collection of paintings, bronzes and *objets d'art* from the Renaissance to the 20th century assembled and donated to the city by Georges Bemberg, a cosmopolitan Argentinean collector.

ÉGLISE NOTRE DAME DU TAUR

The 14th-century **Église Notre Dame du Taur** (Map p743; 12 rue du Taur; ☽ 2-7pm Mon-Sat, 9am-

CENTRAL TOULOUSE

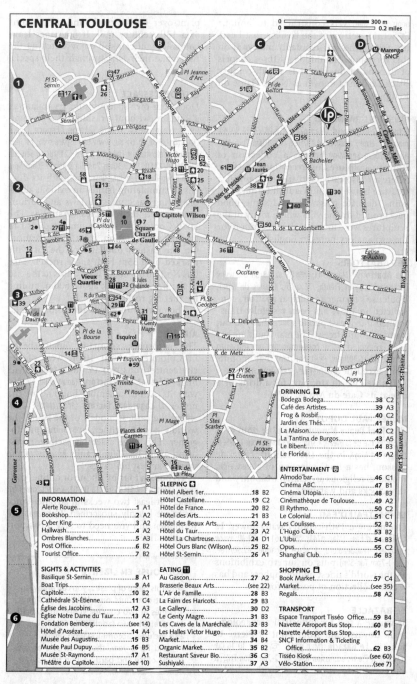

TOULOUSE AREA

INFORMATION
Alerte Rouge...............................	**1** A1
Bookshop....................................	**2** A2
Cyber King.................................	**3** A2
Hallwash....................................	**4** A2
Ombres Blanches.......................	**5** A3
Post Office.................................	**6** B2
Tourist Office............................	**7** B2

SIGHTS & ACTIVITIES
Basilique St-Sernin......................	**8** A1
Boat Trips...................................	**9** A4
Capitole......................................	**10** B2
Cathédrale St-Étienne.................	**11** C4
Église des Jacobins.....................	**12** A3
Église Notre Dame du Taur.........	**13** A2
Fondation Bemberg................(see 14)
Hôtel d'Assézat..........................	**14** A4
Musée des Augustins...................	**15** B3
Musée Paul Dupuy......................	**16** B5
Musée St-Raymond.....................	**17** A1
Théâtre du Capitole...............(see 10)

SLEEPING
Hôtel Albert 1er.........................	**18** B2
Hôtel Castellane.........................	**19** C2
Hôtel de France..........................	**20** B2
Hôtel des Arts............................	**21** B3
Hôtel des Beaux Arts..................	**22** A4
Hôtel du Taur.............................	**23** A2
Hôtel La Chartreuse....................	**24** D1
Hôtel Ours Blanc (Wilson)..........	**25** B2
Hôtel St-Sernin..........................	**26** A1

EATING
Au Gascon..................................	**27** A2
Brasserie Beaux Arts.............(see 22)
L'Air de Famille..........................	**28** B3
La Faim des Haricots...................	**29** B3
Le Gallery...................................	**30** D2
Le Genty Magre..........................	**31** B3
Les Caves de la Maréchale..........	**32** B3
Les Halles Victor Hugo...............	**33** B2
Market.......................................	**34** B4
Organic Market...........................	**35** A2
Restaurant Saveur Bio.................	**36** C3
Sushiyaki....................................	**37** A3

DRINKING
Bodega Bodega..........................	**38** C2
Café des Artistes.........................	**39** A3
Frog & Rosbif.............................	**40** C2
Jardin des Thés...........................	**41** B3
La Maison...................................	**42** C2
La Tantina de Burgos.................	**43** A5
Le Bibent...................................	**44** B3
Le Florida....................................	**45** A2

ENTERTAINMENT
Almodo'bar................................	**46** C1
Cinéma ABC...............................	**47** B1
Cinéma Utopia............................	**48** B3
Cinémathèque de Toulouse.........	**49** A2
El Rythmo..................................	**50** C2
Le Colonial.................................	**51** C1
Les Coulisses..............................	**52** B2
L'Hugo Club...............................	**53** B2
L'Ubu...	**54** B3
Opus..	**55** C2
Shanghai Club............................	**56** B3

SHOPPING
Book Market...............................	**57** C4
Market..................................(see 35)
Regals..	**58** A2

TRANSPORT
Espace Transport Tisséo Office...	**59** B4
Navette Aéroport Bus Stop.........	**60** B1
Navette Aéroport Bus Stop.........	**61** C2
SNCF Information & Ticketing Office	**62** B3
Tisséo Kiosk..........................(see 60)
Vélo-Station..........................(see 7)

noon Sat & Sun) was constructed to honour St-Sernin, patron of the basilica that bears his name, who was reputedly martyred on this very spot. The middle of three chapels at the end of the nave has a 16th-century Black Madonna known as Notre Dame du Rempart.

MUSÉE ST-RAYMOND

Musée St-Raymond (Map p743; ☎ 05 61 22 31 44; place St-Sernin; adult/child €3/free; ☼ 10am-7pm Jun-Aug, to 6pm Sep-May) houses a collection of Roman sculptures of exceptional quality. There are also early Christian sarcophagi, a treasure house of gold Gaulish torques and coins, delicate glassware and some good background on the villa where many of the sculptures were found. Ask at reception for the explanatory notes in English.

LES ABATTOIRS

Les Abattoirs (Map p741; ☎ 05 62 48 58 00; www .lesabattoirs.org in French; 76 allées Charles de Fitte), Toulouse's former municipal abattoir, con-structed in 1831, has been tastefully trans-formed into a vast public space that you can wander around freely. The main building has been recycled as a **contemporary art museum** (adult/child €6.10/free; ☼ 11am-7pm) that mounts some excellent temporary exhibitions.

It's well worth stopping for a drink or a bite at its Café du Musée (p746).

MUSÉE PAUL DUPUY

The **Paul Dupuy Museum** (Map p743; ☎ 05 61 14 65 50; 13 rue de la Pléau; €3/free; ☼ 10am-6pm Jun-Sep, to 5pm Oct-May), in the 18th-century Hôtel de Besson, has a fine collection of glasswork, medieval religious art, china, weaponry and rare clocks and watches.

LE CHÂTEAU D'EAU

Occupying a 19th-century water tower, **Le Château d'Eau** (Map p741; ☎ 05 61 77 09 40; www .galeriechateaudeau.org; 1 place Laganne; €2.50/free; ☼ 1-7pm Tue-Sun) puts on superb exhibitions by the world's finest photographers and has a great collection of posters for sale.

LE BAZACLE

If you've a feel for industrial archaeology, walk downstream from Pont St-Pierre to take in **Le Bazacle** (Map p741; ☎ 05 62 30 16 00; 11 quai St-Pierre; admission free; ☼ 2-7pm Mon-Fri), a monument to water power with a hydro plant over 100 years old and the remains of a 13th-century mill. If machines leave you cold, you can still enjoy watching the fish make their way through their special bypass.

CITÉ DE L'ESPACE

Dock your own space shuttle, try to launch a satellite without crashing it and jump as if weightless inside **Cité de l'Espace** (Space City; ☎ 05 62 71 64 80; www.cite-espace.com; av Jean Gonord; adult/student/child Jul & Aug €21/18/14, Sep-Jun €19/15.50/12.50; ☼ 9.30am-7pm Jul & Aug; 9.30am-5pm or 6pm Sep-Dec & Feb-Jun, closed Jan), with its doz-ens of stimulating hands-on exhibits dem-onstrating basic physical laws and various space-based technologies. 'Astralia: The Sixth Continent', with a simulated visit to the Mir space station, is its latest creation. On the eastern outskirts of the city, it's marked by a 55m-high space rocket. Take bus No 15 from allées Jean Jaurès to the end of the line, then walk about 600m, aiming for that big rocket.

The tourist office sells admission tickets.

AIRBUS

The aerospace company **Airbus** (based in Colomiers, about 10km west of the city centre) runs two 1½-hour **tours**: of its huge **Clément Ader factory** (adult/child €9.50/8) with its Airbus assembly line and the newer **JJ Lagardère factory** (adult/child €14/11), where the earliest models of the A380, the world's largest airliner, are being put to-gether. This huge assembly facility, meas-uring 490m by 250m, ranks as one of the world's largest buildings.

To book a tour by phone or online, con-tact **Taxiway** (☎ 05 61 18 06 01; www.taxiway.fr), ideally at least two weeks in advance since visits are heavily subscribed. Cameras are forbidden and you need to take a passport or other ID.

TOULOUSE EN LIBERTÉ

With this piece of plastic, you can enjoy sig-nificant discounts on admission to sights. It comes in two colours: violet (adult/child €10/5) and brown (adult/child €13/7), which also includes accommodation offers.

Valid for a year, they're on sale at the tourist office and participating hotels.

Activities

The city's canalside paths are peaceful places to walk, run or cycle. Port de l'Embouchure (Map p741) is where the Canal du Midi (1681; linking Toulouse with the Mediterranean), meets the Canal Latéral à la Garonne (1856; flowing to the Atlantic) and the Canal de Brienne (1776).

Tours

Taxis Touristiques (1/2 hr for up to 4 people €45/60) are ideal for an overview of the city. They'll call by your hotel, plug in a multilingual CD and drive you around the major sights. Ring **Capitole Taxi** (☎ 05 34 25 02 50) or **Taxi Radio Toulousain** (☎ 05 61 42 38 38) to reserve.

Boats run short trips on the canals, including Canal du Midi, and River Garonne, leaving from Quai de la Daurade (Map p743) or Ponts Jumeaux (Map p741). Try **Toulouse Croisières** (☎ 05 61 25 72 57; www.toulouse-croisieres.com in French) or **Baladines** (☎ 06 07 43 48 28; www.bateaux-toulousains.com).

Festivals & Events

Toulouse has a lively cultural scene with several festivals that extend over three weeks or more. Major annual events include:

Festival de la Violette (weekend in early February) Celebrates Toulouse's favourite flower.

Le Marathon des Mots (four days in June) 'Word Marathon' celebrates language and literature in all their many manifestations. Guests in 2006 included Umberto Eco, Michel Tournier and Hanif Kureishi.

Toulouse d'Été (July, August) Jazz, classical, accordion and other music all around town.

Piano aux Jacobins (September) Classical piano recitals in the Église des Jacobins.

Jazz sur Son 31 (October) An international jazz festival.

Sleeping

Since many Toulouse hotels cater for business people, there can be great discounts at weekends and during the July and August holiday period. Strangely for such a major city, Toulouse has no youth hostel.

BUDGET

Camping de Rupé (☎ 05 61 70 07 35; 21 chemin du Pont de Rupé; camp site €13.50; ☺ for caravans year-round, tents Jul & Aug) Often packed, this camp site is 6km northwest of the train station. From place Jeanne d'Arc take bus No 59.

Hôtel Anatole France (Map p741; ☎ 05 61 23 19 96; fax 05 61 21 47 66; 46 place Anatole France; r €30-36,

with shared bathroom €25) This is a quiet (there's double glazing throughout) and intimate (there are only 18 rooms) option. Rooms are bright and the décor is minimalist. There's free public parking right in front.

Hôtel des Arts (Map p743; ☎ 05 61 23 36 21; fax 05 61 12 22 37; 1bis rue Cantegril; s/d €30.50-33.50, with shared bathroom €28/32) Price is the trump card for this modest place. Rooms are small but well maintained. Those with shower can get steamy since only a plastic curtain separates the cubicle from the room itself. Toilets are in the corridor.

Hôtel La Chartreuse (Map p743; ☎ 05 61 62 93 39; la.chartreuse@wanadoo.fr; 4bis blvd Bonrepos; r €33) You can tumble out of the station and straight into this family-run hotel, a decent budget bet among some fairly scruffy offerings hereabouts. Rooms, all with bathroom, are on the small side but represent great value.

MIDRANGE

Hôtel de France (Map p743; ☎ 05 61 21 88 24; www.hotel-france-toulouse.com; 5 rue d'Austerlitz; r €51-75; ✷) The 64 rooms at this hotel, just around the corner from Les Halles Victor Hugo, are spotless. They're agreeably furnished in bright fabrics and the larger ones can accommodate three.

Hôtel St-Sernin (Map p743; ☎ 05 61 21 73 08; fax 05 61 22 49 61; 2 rue St-Bernard; s/d/tr from €50/55/70) This peaceful, well-located place has private parking (€10) for only three cars, so do reserve a slot when you book. Ask for a room overlooking the Basilique. The fun-size baths are only for munchkins or very supple contortionists.

Hôtel du Taur (Map p743; ☎ 05 61 21 17 54; www.hotel-du-taur.com; 2 rue du Taur; s/d/tr from €49/55/72) Rooms bear the naff-paintings-and-textured-wallpaper look but it's a comfortable, welcoming place overlooking a quiet interior courtyard. Its killer attraction is location: roll out of bed and you'll find yourself on place du Capitole.

Hôtel Ours Blanc (Wilson) (Map p743; ☎ 05 61 21 62 40; www.hotel-oursblanc.com; 2 rue Victor Hugo; s €51, d €61-73; ✷) The most central of Toulouse's trio of Ours Blanc (Polar Bear; no, nobody could tell us why) hotels, it has smart, modern rooms, to which a tiny vintage lift creaks you upwards. Risk it to the uppermost floor, where rooms have great pigeon's eye views over the rooftops.

MY BAD HER DAY *Miles Roddis*

It's not all honey and kisses, writing for Lonely Planet. I rolled up at the reception desk of a top-end hotel to be greeted with 'You have a reservation, M'sieur?' 'Well no, actually, I'm here on behalf...'. 'Why not?'

I patiently explained my mission. 'Not sure if my boss would like that'. 'But, Madame, you've been in our guide for the last two years.' 'It's what exactly, Le Leunly?' And so on in the same vein as I teased out grudgingly given information like working splinters from my thumb.

Barely ten minutes later, I'm checking out with the pleasant young barman a place that has clearly changed both name and atmosphere since we last passed by. Up bustles the manageress. 'Bonsoir, Madame, I was explaining to your colleague....' 'He's not my colleague, he's an employee.' 'They're the same in my vocabulary, Madame.' 'Ah, not in mine.' I made my excuses, striking out the bar with a flourish as I left.

Crossing a nearby bridge over the Garonne, I read on the pavement a graffito in English, 'f**k out'. Not quite how I would have put it but oh yes, how I endorsed the sentiment...

Hôtel Castellane (Map p743; ☎ 05 61 62 18 82; www.castellanehotel.com in French; 17 rue Castellane; r €66-82; 🅿 💻) Rooms are comfortable, simple and trim at this well-established hotel just off place Wilson. They're ranged for the most part around an airy, quiet central patio and some have small balconies. Parking €10.

Hôtel Albert 1er (Map p743; ☎ 05 61 21 17 91; www.hotel-albert1.com; 8 rue Rivals; s €49-72, d €70-87; 🅿 🅿 💻) Two amiable young brothers represent the third generation to run this pleasant, well-maintained family hotel. They've prepared their own shopping and restaurant guide in English for visitors. Rooms, all with safe and minibar, have robust wooden furniture, and breakfast (€10) is ample with home-made bread, fresh fruit salad and fresh orange juice.

ourpick Hôtel Mermoz (Map p741; ☎ 05 61 63 04 04; www.hotel-mermoz.com; 50 rue Matabiau; d/tr €115/135; 🅿) Cars whiz by on the ugly street outside. But as soon as you walk into this pretty little Art Deco nook with its peaceful garden and bright, welcoming rooms, you leave the city behind. The theme of its décor recalls aviation's pioneering days from Vol de Nuit (Night Flight), its smart little bar, to the posters and prints that bedeck the walls. Weekend rates (s/d €75/85 including breakfast) are a particularly good deal. Wi-fi; parking €9.

TOP END

Hôtel des Beaux Arts (Map p743; ☎ 05 34 45 42 42; www.hoteldesbeauxarts.com; 1 place du Pont Neuf; r €119-168, suite €210; 🅿) This is surely the most romantic spot in town, where all rooms offer

great views over river and bridge by day or night. They're soothingly decorated and there's a smart, modern brasserie downstairs (opposite). Reception, however, could do with a crash course at charm school. Wi-fi.

Eating

Plenty of places around town offer excellent-value lunch *menus* for under €15. Both blvd de Strasbourg and the perimeter of place du Capitole are lined with restaurants and cafés. The terrace cafés of place St-Georges are especially lively in summer.

ourpick Les Halles Victor Hugo (Map p743; menus €11-19; 🕑 lunch Tue-Sun) Many of Toulouse's best-value places are the small, spartan, lunchtime-only restaurants above the appetite-sharpening food stalls of Toulouse's busy covered market. Fast, packed and no-nonsense, catering for market vendors and shoppers alike, they serve up generous, delicious *menus* of hearty fare.

Café du Musée (Map p741; ☎ 05 61 59 33 56; 76 allées Charles de Fitte; plat du jour €8, daily special €12; 🕑 11am-7pm Tue-Sun) This bright and light space in one of the outbuildings of Les Abattoirs (p744) is very good value for both lunch and an afternoon coffee, cake or ice cream.

La Faim des Haricots (Map p743; ☎ 05 61 22 49 25; 3 rue du Puits Vert; menus €9-12; 🕑 lunch Mon-Sat, dinner Thu-Sat; 🅅) This simple place offers pick-n-mix all-vegetarian, all-you-can-eat *menus* from its salad and dessert bars and dispenses home-made soups in winter.

Le Gallery (Map p743; ☎ 05 61 99 30 81; 8 rue Maury; mains around €12, lunch menus €8.50-12.50; 🕑 lunch Mon-Fri, dinner Wed-Sat) The enterprising young owner of Le Gallery (regularly changing exhibitions line the walls) has run his own restaurant in London. The lunch *menu* (pick from the blackboard), relying on fresh produce, changes daily, most wines are selected from small-scale independent producers and desserts are all homemade.

Au Gascon (Map p743; ☎ 05 61 21 67 16; 9 rue des Jacobins; menus €11-18; ☺ lunch & dinner Mon-Sat) Here's terrific value for hearty, filling and artery-thickening Gascon cuisine – duck, foie gras and dauntingly large, oily and utterly delicious servings of *cassoulet au confit* (a haricot bean stew with confit of duck).

Sushiyaki (Map p743; ☎ 05 61 12 00 60; 9 rue Ste-Ursule; menus €11-20; ☺ lunch & dinner Mon-Sat) Head for this small, intimate, reasonably priced sushi and *teppanyaki* place when you can't face any more duck or *cassoulet*.

Restaurant Saveur Bio (Map p743; ☎ 05 61 12 15 15; 22 rue Maurice Fonvieille; menus €15.50 & €20.30; ☺ lunch & dinner Mon-Sat; ⓥ) This earnest place is given to proselytising about all things organic. It serves tasty, imaginative vegetarian food, including a lunchtime mixed plate (€8.80) and a great-value evening buffet (€8.80).

Les Caves de la Maréchale (Map p743; ☎ 05 61 23 89 88; 3 rue Jules Chalande; menus €15-28, mains €18-21; ☺ lunch & dinner Tue-Fri, dinner Mon, lunch Sat) Dine under the eyeless gaze of classical statues in the magnificently vaulted brick cellar of a pre-Revolution convent. The excellent lunchtime three-course *menu* (€15) is an absolute steal. The *menu* at €28 has a wide choice of inventive dishes.

Brasserie Beaux Arts (Map p743; ☎ 05 61 21 12 12; 1 quai Daurade; menus €20-32; ☺ lunch & dinner) This smart, modern brasserie with a retro 1930s feel serves fresh seafood and classic French dishes with style and bustling efficiency.

L'Air de Famille (Map p743; ☎ 05 61 29 85 89; 1bis rue Jules Chalande; 3-course lunch €16, dinner €25-30; ☺ lunch Mon-Fri, dinner Thu & Fri) This intimate restaurant (30 places at a squeeze plus a small summertime terrace) has a talented young owner-chef, an inventive lunch menu that changes daily, a short dinner menu with a weekly turnover and only the freshest of local produce on your plate.

Le Genty Magre (Map p743; ☎ 05 61 21 38 60; 1 rue Genty Magre; menus €20-42, mains €12-20; ☺ lunch & dinner Wed-Sat & lunch Tue; closed mid-Jul–mid-Aug) Here's another exciting newcomer to Toulouse's already rich gastronomic scene. Go

for one of its creative *menus* or select à la carte from the giant slate. Invest an extra €15 for a champagne apéritif and glass of white and red, specially selected to accompany your meal.

SELF-CATERING

For fresh produce, visit **Les Halles Victor Hugo** (Map p743; place Victor Hugo), the large covered food market, or the **market** (Map p743; place des Carmes) to its south. Both open until 1pm, Tuesday to Sunday. Another small **market** (Map p743; place du Capitole) spreads across the square selling organically grown food on Tuesday and Saturday mornings.

Drinking
PUBS & BARS

Almost every square in the Vieux Quartier has at least one café, busy day and night. Other busy after-dark areas include rue Castellane and rue Gabriel Péri and, near the river, around place St-Pierre.

Bodega Bodega (Map p743; 1 rue Gabriel Péri) Once the headquarters of the local tax authority but now altogether more fun and less straitlaced (it's a particular haunt of rugby fans, local and visiting), this huge, heaving place has live music and lively crowds, especially at weekends.

La Tantina de Burgos (Map p743; 27 av de la Garonnette; ☺ Tue-Sat) This popular bodega has a strong Spanish flavour – bullfighting posters, over 40 varieties of tapas and a buzzing atmosphere most nights. Here too there's live music at weekends.

Frog & Rosbif (Map p743; 14 rue de l'Industrie) Very British. This lively expat pub has a dartboard and its own microbrewery churning out very palatable real ales and stouts. Tuesday night is student night with beer at €4 per pint.

La Maison (Map p743; 9 rue Gabriel Péri) Very French. This cosy place has a log fire in winter where you can smoke while arguing animatedly, or at least watch the youngish local crowd doing so over a glass of excellent wine.

Rue des Blanchers has several 'alternative' joints. Those clustered around place St-Pierre beside the Garonne pull in a predominantly young crowd. **Chez Tonton** (Map p741; place St-Pierre) and Spanish-flavoured **Bar Basque** (Map p741; place St-Pierre) are sports bars. **Café des Artistes** (Map p743; 13 place de la Daurade) is primarily an art-student hang-out while **Pub St-Pierre** (Map p741; 10 place St-Pierre), with 1½L jugs of beer at €11.50 and a litre of Margharita for €15, is for those with major thirsts.

CAFÉS & TEAHOUSES

Jardin des Thés (Map p743; ☎ 05 61 23 46 67; 16 place St Georges) This civilised teahouse serves a good range of darjeelings and green teas along with rich, filling desserts inside and (if you're lucky enough to find a free seat) on the pleasant square.

Two of the best places to linger in place du Capitole (Map p743) over a coffee or something stronger are **Le Florida** (No 12) and **Le Bibent** (No 5), with its ornate plastered, chandeliered and mirrored interior.

Entertainment

For what's on where, grab yourself a copy of *Toulouse Hebdo*, *Le Flash* (both weekly) or *Intramuros* (free from major hotels and cinemas).

NIGHTCLUBS

Toulouse has dance venues aplenty. There are a fair few fully fledged nightclubs, and several bars in town also double up as clubs on certain nights.

Opus (Map p743; 24 rue Bachelier; ✆ midnight-5am Mon-Wed, 2-6am Thu-Sat) has a huge blackboard on which to pen your thoughts, and dancing all night (rock upstairs, funk and disco down below). **L'Hugo Club** (Map p743; 18 place Victor Hugo) is a slightly smarter dance bar attracting an older crowd. **L'Ubu** (Map p743; 16 rue St-Rome; ✆ Mon-Sat), a hot spot nearer the centre, has a choosy door policy, so dress smartly.

Out of town, the intrepid may like to risk **Le Clap** (146 chemin des Étroits); take exit 24 off the A64.

GAY VENUES

Toulouse is a very gay city – it's not called *la ville rose* just for those pink bricks. Popular **Shanghai Club** (Map p743; 12 rue de la Pomme; ✆ midnight-dawn) is a long-established gay club and disco. Downstairs is men only, while the first floor has a mixed clientele. **Le Colonial** (Map p743; 8 place de Belfort; ✆ noon-1am) is an exclusively male sauna. Nearby, **Almodo'bar** (Map p743; 27 rue Stalingrad) is a bright, sassy gay bar. Sunday is disco night from

10pm. **Les Coulisses** (Map p743; 5 blvd de Strasbourg; ✆ Mon-Sat) is a mixed, gay-friendly place with live music where the dominant colour is black. **El Rythmo** (Map p743; 6 rue de la Colombette) is a friendly bar that's strictly for the girls.

CINEMAS

The three-screen **Cinéma Utopia** (Map p743; ☎ 05 61 23 66 20; 24 rue Montardy) and **Cinéma ABC** (Map p743; ☎ 05 61 29 81 00; 13 rue St-Bernard) both show nondubbed foreign films. Arthouse **Cinémathèque de Toulouse** (Map p743; ☎ 05 62 30 30 10; www.lacinemathequedetoulouse.com in French; 69 rue du Taur) also mostly has nondubbed screenings and great classics series (a complete retrospective of John Huston when we last sat in the stalls).

Shopping

Toulouse's main shopping district, flanked by department stores and expensive boutiques, embraces rue du Taur, rue Alsace-Lorraine, rue de la Pomme, rue des Arts and nearby streets. Place St-Georges is also ringed by fashionable shops.

Regals (Map p743; 25 rue du Taur) sells edible specialities such as chocolates, cakes, liqueurs and sweets containing or made of violets or violet flavourings (a local speciality). Place du Capitole hosts a huge **market** (including books; Map p743) each Wednesday, and there's a **flea market** (Map p743) each Saturday and Sunday on place St-Sernin. There's an antiquarian **book market** (Map p743) on place St-Étienne every Saturday.

Getting There & Away

AIR

Aéroport Toulouse-Blagnac (☎ 08 25 38 00 00; www.toulouse.aeroport.fr) is 8km northwest of the city centre. Air France and easyJet between them have well over 30 flights daily to and from Paris (Orly and Charles de Gaulle). There are also regular flights to and from many other cities in France and Europe. EasyJet and BA each fly from Gatwick at least twice daily. Flybe serves Birmingham and Bristol while BMIbaby flies to and from Manchester.

BUS

Toulouse's modern **bus station** (Map p741; ☎ 05 61 61 67 67; blvd Pierre Sémard; ✆ information office 8am-7pm) is just north of the train station. Regional destinations include:

destination	one-way fare (€)	duration (hr)	daily frequency
Albi	12.40	1½	3
Andorra	28	3½	2
Auch	10.40	1¼	2
Castres	10	1½	6
Millau	25.40	4	1
Montauban	7.20	1¼	4

CAR
Several car-rental agencies have desks at both airport and train station

ADA (☎ train station 05 34 30 48 60, airport 05 61 30 00 33)

Europcar (☎ train station 08 25 00 43 46, airport 08 25 82 55 14)

Budget (☎ train station 05 61 63 18 18, airport 05 61 71 85 80)

TRAIN
The **train station** (Gare Matabiau; ☎ 08 92 35 35 35; blvd Pierre Sémard) is about 1km northeast of the city centre. Local destinations served by frequent direct trains include:

destination	one-way fare (€)	duration (hr)
Albi	10.90	1¼
Auch	12.40	1½
Bayonne	35.50	3¾
Bordeaux	31.10	2-3
Carcassonne	12.70	1
Castres	12.20	1¼
Foix	11.80	1¼
Lourdes	22.20	1¾
Montauban	8	½
Pau	25.70	2¾

The fare from Toulouse to Paris is €71 by Corail (6½ hours, to Gare d'Austerlitz) and €95 by TGV (5½ hours, to Gare Montparnasse via Bordeaux).

There's an **SNCF information and ticketing office** at 5 rue Peyras.

Getting Around
TO/FROM THE AIRPORT
The **Navette Aéroport bus** (☎ 05 34 60 64 00; www.navettevia-toulouse.com) links town and airport every 20 minutes from 5am and costs €3.90/5.90 single/return. The last run to the airport is at 8.20pm. Pick it up at the bus station, outside Jean Jaurès metro station or

place Jeanne d'Arc. From the airport, the last bus leaves at 12.15am.

An airport **taxi** costs about €20.

BICYCLE
Vélo-Station (☎ 05 34 30 03 00; www.movimento .coop in French; per half/full day €1/2) is an extraordinarily reasonable cycle hire scheme with bases located at the bus station (Map p741) and in front of the tourist office (Map p743). It requires a €260 deposit (cash, credit card or a cheque on a French bank).

BUS & METRO
The local bus network and 18-station metro line are run by **Tisséo** (☎ 05 61 41 70 70; www .tisseo.fr in French). A single/return ticket for either service costs €1.30/2.40 and a 10-ticket *carnet* is €10.70.

Most bus lines run daily until at least 8pm. The seven 'night' bus lines all start at the train station and run from 10pm to just after midnight.

The metro is fully automated – no driver, no conductor, just lots of short, swift trains speeding under the city. A second line is due to be completed in 2007.

Pick up a route map at the **Espace Transport Tisseo office** (Map p743; 7 place Esquirol) or at the tourist office.

CAR
Parking is tight in the city centre. There are huge car parks under place du Capitole, beneath allées Jean Jaurès and just off place Wilson. Simply show your metro or bus ticket to enjoy free parking at the two terminuses of the metro line and at the Argoulets station.

TAXI
Call **Capitole Taxi** (☎ 05 34 25 02 50) or **Taxi Radio Toulousain** (☎ 05 61 42 38 38).

ALBI
pop 49,100

The massive, fortress-like Gothic cathedral dwarfing the rest of town is an unmissable reminder of Albi's violent religious past. The town was at the heart of the so-called Albigensian heresy of the 12th and 13th centuries and the bloody crusade that crushed it (see The Cathars, p804). Almost all of central Albi, including the cathedral, is built from bricks of reddish clay, dug from the River Tarn that meanders through the town.

Two things make a trip here well worthwhile: that extraordinary cathedral and the excellent museum dedicated to artist Henri de Toulouse-Lautrec, who hailed from Albi; it has the most extensive collection of his work anywhere.

Orientation

Cathédrale Ste-Cécile rears above the old quarter. From it, a web of narrow, semi-pedestrianised streets stretches southeast to place du Vigan, Albi's commercial hub. The train station is about 1km southwest of the city centre.

Information

Lavomatique (10 rue Émile Grand; ☉ daily) For spinning your smalls.

Ludi.com (64 rue Séré de Rivières; per hr €4; ☉ 11am-midnight Mon-Sat) Internet access.

Post Office (place du Vigan)

Tourist Office (☎ 05 63 49 48 80; www.albi-tourisme .fr; place Ste-Cécile; ☉ 9am-7pm Mon-Sat, 10am-12.30pm & 2.30-6.30pm Sun Jul & Aug; 9am-12.30pm & 2-6pm Mon-Sat, 10am-12.30pm & 2.30-5pm Sun Oct-Jun) Has a free pamphlet in English, *To Discover*, describing four signposted walks around the old quarter.

Sights

CATHÉDRALE STE-CÉCILE

As much fortress as church, the mighty **Cathédrale Ste-Cécile** (place Ste-Cécile; ☉ 9am-6.30pm

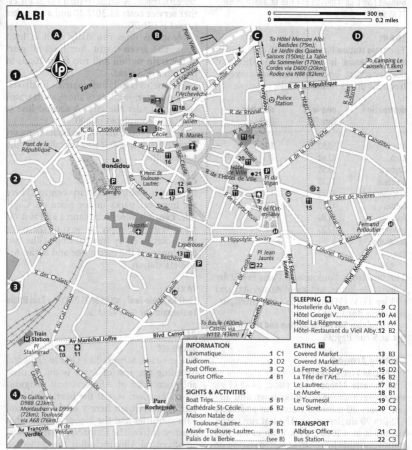

ALBI

		0	300 m
		0	0.2 miles

To Hôtel Mercure Albi Bastides (75m); Le Jardin des Quatre Saisons (150m); La Table du Sommelier (170m); Cordes via D600 (20km); Rodez via N88 (82km)

To Camping Le Caussels (1.8km)

To Gaillac via D988 (22km); Montauban via D999 (72km); Toulouse via A68 (76km)

To Basile (400m); Castres via N112 (43km)

ALBI PASS

This card, sold at the tourist office for €5.50, gives free admission to the Musée Toulouse-Lautrec and cathedral choir and offers a variety of other reductions and concessions around town.

Jun-Sep; 9am-noon & 2-6.30pm Oct-May) was begun in 1282, not long after the Cathar movement was crushed. Built to impress and subdue, it took over a hundred years to complete. Attractive isn't the word – what strikes you most is its sheer mass rising over town like some Tolkienesque dark lord's tower rather than a place of Christian worship.

When you step inside, however, the contrast with that brutal exterior is total. No surface was left untouched by the Italian artists who, in the early 16th-century, painted their way, chapel by chapel, the length of its vast nave.

An intricately carved, lacy rood screen, many of its statues smashed in the Revolution, spans the sanctuary. The stained-glass windows in the apse and choir date from the 14th to 16th centuries.

On no account miss the **grand chœur** (great choir; admission €1) with its frescoes, chapels and 30 biblical polychrome figures, finely carved in stone.

At the western end, behind today's main altar, is *Le Jugement Dernier* (The Last Judgement; 1490), a particularly vivid Doomsday horror-show of the damned being boiled in oil, beheaded or tortured by demons and monsters.

MUSÉE TOULOUSE-LAUTREC

Beside the tourist office, the **Musée Toulouse-Lautrec** (☎ 05 63 49 48 70; place Ste-Cécile; adult/student/child €5/2.50/free, audioguide €3; ☺ 9am-6pm Jul & Aug; 9am-noon & 2-6pm Jun & Sep; 10am-noon & 2-5pm or 6pm Oct-May, closed Tue Oct-Mar) occupies the **Palais de la Berbie**, the vast, fortress-like 13th- to 15th-century archbishop's palace.

The museum boasts over 500 examples of the artist's work, giving both an excellent idea of his development as an artist and the way individual works evolved – everything from simple pencil sketches and rough pastel drafts to the final works such as his celebrated Parisian brothel scenes, with the *Salon de la rue des Moulins* taking pride of place. On the top floor are works by Degas, Matisse and Rodin. The attractive ornamental palace courtyard and **gardens** (☺ 8am-7pm) are also well worth a wander.

A short walk away, a plaque on the wall of the privately owned **Maison Natale de Toulouse-Lautrec** (14 rue Henri de Toulouse-Lautrec) marks the house where the artist was born.

Tours

From mid-June to mid-September you can take half-hour **boat trips** (€5/3) from just north of the Palais de la Berbie on a *gabarre*,

---

PAINTER, LITHOGRAPHER, POSTER DESIGNER &...COOK?

Henri de Toulouse-Lautrec (1864–1901), Albi's most famous son, was famously short. As a teenager he broke both legs in separate accidents, stunting his growth and leaving him unable to walk without his trademark canes.

He spent his early twenties studying painting in Paris where he mixed with other artists including Van Gogh. In 1890, at the height of the *belle époque,* he abandoned impressionism and took to observing and sketching Paris' colourful nightlife. His favourite subjects included cabaret singer Aristide Bruant, cancan dancers from the Moulin Rouge and prostitutes from the rue des Moulins, sketched to capture movement and expression in a few simple lines.

With sure, fast strokes he would sketch on whatever was to hand – a scrap of paper or a tablecloth, tracing paper or buff-coloured cardboard. He also became a skilled and sought-after lithographer and poster designer until drinking and general overindulgence in the heady nightlife scene led to his premature death in 1901.

If you want to taste, rather than see, a Toulouse-Lautrec creation, you may find some of Albi's restaurants offering versions of the recipes devised by the keen amateur chef Lautrec (for more information, ask at the tourist office). *The Art of Cooking* (alas, out of print) is a collection of his amusing, whimsical recipes, which include advice on how to cook a squirrel or stew a 'marmot you caught that very same morning sunning himself on a rock'.

a flat-bottomed sailing barge of the kind that used to haul goods down the Garonne to Bordeaux.

Festivals & Events

Voix-lá In May, Voix-lá (get it?) celebrates vocal music in all its richness.

Pause Guitare Early July's Pause Guitare, held in the sumptuous space of place Ste-Cécile, brings together the best of French singing and accompaniment (Georges Moustaki and Graeme Allwright were there in 2006).

Carnaval More frivolously, Albi celebrates Carnaval at the beginning of Lent (February or March) with particular gusto and confetti galore.

Sleeping

Camping Le Caussels (☎ /fax 05 63 60 37 06; camp site €11.50; ☼ Apr–mid-Oct) This fairly basic camp site is just off route de Millau, 2km north-east of place du Vigan. Take bus No 5 from place du Vigan to the terminus.

Hôtel La Régence (☎ 05 63 54 01 42; www.hotel laregence.com in French; 27 av Maréchal Joffre; r €30-42) Next door to Hôtel George V and with prices more than coincidentally tagged in parallel, this child-friendly hotel with its 13 rooms is just as warm in its welcome. Staff speak good English and there's a small rear garden. Parking €5.

Hôtel George V (☎ 05 63 54 24 16; www.hotel georgev.com; 29 av Maréchal Joffre; d €33-44) Friendly, welcoming and family-run, this nine-room hotel offers excellent value. Rooms are spacious, it's handy for bus and train stations and there's a small breakfast terrace. Unlike many a more grasping upmarket establishment, it offers wi-fi for free.

Hôtel-Restaurant du Vieil Alby (☎ 05 63 54 14 69; levieilalby@wanadoo.fr; 25 rue Henri de Toulouse-Lautrec; r €47-68; ☼ closed 2nd half Jan & late Jun-early Jul; ☒) This tiny hotel is set above an excellent restaurant (right) and represents great value. There's a small internal courtyard, each of its spacious nine rooms is nonsmoking. Private parking, difficult hereabouts, costs €7.

Hostellerie du Vigan (☎ 05 63 43 31 31; www .hotel-vigan.com in French; 16 place du Vigan; d/tr from €50/65; ☒) At the heart of town, overlooking pedestrianised place du Vigan, this hotel of the same name has 40 spacious, modern, if unexceptional rooms and a popular **brasserie** (menus €16-23; ☼ lunch & dinner Mon-Sat) below.

Hotel Mercure Albi Bastides (☎ 05 63 47 66 66; www.mercure.com; 41 rue Porta; s/d €76/85, with river views €85/95; ☒ ☒) Occupying a handsome 18th-century brick building (originally a mill and latterly a pasta factory), this hotel enjoys a prime riverside spot. Its 58 rooms are handsomely furnished and there's a great restaurant terrace from which to gaze back across to town. Parking free. Wi-fi.

Eating

Le Tournesol (☎ 05 63 38 38 14; 11 rue de l'Ort-en-Salvy; daily special €8.50; ☼ lunch Tue-Sat & dinner Fri; ⓥ) This highly popular vegetarian restaurant – why, even the beers and wines are organic – is airy and full of light. The aircon blows in summer or you can eat outside on the terrace. Mixed salad platters start at €8.50.

La Table du Sommelier (☎ 05 63 46 20 10; 20 rue Porta; menus €12.50-35; ☼ lunch & dinner Tue-Sat) This place marries the best of wines (the owner's a qualified sommelier) with fine food, whether a one-dish snack or a full meal. Or abnegate all responsibility, place yourself in the chef's hands and enjoy the *menu vin passion* (€35), his selected delights of the day, each accompanied by an equally carefully chosen wine.

La Tête de l'Art (☎ 05 63 38 44 75; 7 rue de la Piale; menus €14-29; ☼ lunch & dinner daily May-Jul & Sep; Thu-Mon Aug & Oct-Apr) Dishes for the adventurous such as jugged hare, tripe and boned pig's trotter mix with more traditional local stuff. It does excellent desserts (sink your spoon into the pistachio and chocolate tart) and gourmet takeaways.

Le Musée (☎ 05 63 47 17 17; 15bis place de L'Archevêché; menus €14.50-25, mains €6.50-14.50; ☼ lunch & dinner) Beneath the brick vaulting of what was once the bishop's stables, this attractive brasserie, its dominant colours deep red and black, offers traditional fare with a strong emphasis on meat dishes. Pizzas too (€9.50 to €11).

Hôtel-Restaurant du Vieil Alby (☎ 05 63 38 28 23; 25 rue Henri de Toulouse-Lautrec; menus €18-45, lunch menus €12; ☼ lunch & dinner Mon-Fri, dinner Sat, lunch Sun) The very best in local fare is served with local Gaillac wine. Foie gras with caramelised apples and filet mignon with a cep sauce are just a couple of tempting mains. There are also vegetarian options.

Le Lautrec (☎ 05 63 54 86 55; 13-15 rue Henri de Toulouse-Lautrec; ☼ lunch & dinner Tue-Sat, lunch Sun) Dine on the shady summer terrace or in what were once the stables of the Lautrec family. It's one of those restaurants where the plates come in all shapes but round. Portions are smallish but delightfully crafted. Choosing's easy: you simply select from one course (€16) to four (€32) from their enticing *promenade gourmande*.

Le Jardin des Quatre Saisons (☎ 05 63 60 77 76; 19 blvd de Strasbourg; menus €20-33; ⊗ lunch & dinner Tue-Sat, dinner Sun) Here too you've got a choice of eating environments: the light, bright main dining room giving onto the street, or the intimate rear room with its cosy fireplace. Strong on tempting desserts, it also has a particularly tempting wine list.

Lou Sicret (☎ 05 63 38 26 40; 1 rue Timbal; mains €12-15, menus €20-30; ⊗ lunch & dinner Tue-Sat, dinner Sun & Mon) Tucked away down an alley at the north-west corner of place du Vigan, this friendly, very Occitan, arty restaurant serves delight-ful regional cuisine in a secluded courtyard.

SELF-CATERING

Buy fresh fare at the temporary (until at least 2007) **covered market** (place Lapérouse; ⊗ morn-ing-early afternoon Tue-Sun) while a car park is completed beneath the old, architecturally striking market on place St-Julien.

Pick up the very best in cheese from **La Ferme St-Salvy** (53 rue Séré de Rivières), one of France's dwindling number of *fromageries* (specialist cheese shops).

Getting There & Away

The **bus station** (☎ 05 63 54 58 61), little more than a parking area, is on the southwest corner of place Jean Jaurès. Ask at the tour-ist office for timetable information since there's nothing but a sign here. Services include Castres (€5.40, 50 minutes, up to 10 daily). For other destinations, the train's your better option.

Bus No 1 links the **train station** (place Stalin-grad) with the bus station and place du Vigan. There are trains to/from Rodez (€11.80, 1½ hours, seven daily), Millau (€19, 2¾ hours, two daily) and Toulouse (€10.90, 1¼ hours, 10+ daily). For Montauban (€10.70), change in Toulouse.

Getting Around

You can rent town bikes from **Basile** (☎ 05 63 38 43 09; 18 av Maréchal Foch; per day/week €15/73).

Leave your vehicle in the large car park at Le Bondidou near the cathedral or in the underground one beneath place du Vigan.

Local bus services are run by **Albibus** (☎ 05 63 38 43 43), Monday to Saturday. It has an information office at 14 rue de l'Hôtel de Ville.

For a **taxi**, call ☎ 05 63 54 85 03.

CASTRES
pop 45,400

Castres was founded by the Romans as a settlement, or *castrum*. At its heart is newly pedestrianised place Jean Jaurès, named in honour of Castres' most famous son and founding father of French socialism.

The **tourist office** (☎ 05 63 62 63 62; www .tourisme-castres.fr in French; 3 rue Milhau Ducommun; ⊗ 9.30am-12.30pm & 1-6pm Mon-Sat, 10.30am-noon & 2-4pm Sun Jul & Aug, 9.30am-12.30pm & 2-6pm Mon-Sat, 2.30-4.30pm Sun Sep-Jun) is on the eastern bank of the River Agoût, near Pont Vieux. Just downstream, the attractive multistorey **houses**, whose cellars open onto the river, were once the homes and workshops of tanners, weavers and dyers, creators of the city's wealth.

The **Musée Goya** (☎ 05 63 71 59 30; Hôtel de Ville, rue de l'Hôtel de Ville; adult/child €2.30/free; ⊗ 10am-6pm daily Jul & Aug; 9am-noon & 2-5pm or 6pm Tue-Sun Sep-Jun) has an important collection of Span-ish art, including several paintings and en-gravings by Goya himself and canvases by Murillo, Ribera, Picasso and many others. Its lovely formal gardens were designed by Le Nôtre, architect of Versailles' parkland.

Parc de Gourjade (av de Roquecourbe, D89) is a vast municipal park north of the town cen-tre with camp sites, golf course, about 15km of jogging trails, riding centre, **L'Archipel** (☎ 05 63 62 54 00) water park and an ice-skating rink. You can take bus No 6 or 7 from the Arcades stop on place Jean Jaurès, but it's more fun to hop aboard **Le Miredames** (☎ 05 63 62 41 76; adult/child €4/1.60 return), a replica river barge that runs to and from the park from the quay in front of the tourist office two to five times daily from mid-May to October.

MONTAUBAN
pop 54,400

Montauban, on the right bank of the River Tarn, was founded in 1144 by Count Al-phonse Jourdain of Toulouse who, legend has it, was so charmed by its trailing willow trees (*alba* in Occitan) that he named the place Mont Alba.

Montauban, southern France's second-oldest *bastide*, was badly battered during the Albigensian crusade. It later became a Huguenot stronghold, only to again suffer persecution when the Edict of Nantes (1598), which had brought royal concessions to the Huguenots, was repealed by Louis XIV a century later.

Montauban's many classical townhouses date from the prosperous decades following the Catholic reconquest.

Orientation

Place Nationale, surrounded by attractive arcaded 17th-century brick buildings and a grid of semipedestrianised streets, sits at the heart of the old city. Place Franklin Roosevelt, overlooked by the cathedral, lies to its south.

The train station is about 1km from place Nationale, across the River Tarn at the western end of av Mayenne.

Information

3D Gamma (103 Faubourg Lacapelle; per hr €4; ☺ 11am-midnight Mon-Fri, 2pm-midnight Sat) Internet access.

Laundrette (26 rue de l'Hôtel de Ville; ☺ 7am-7.30pm)

Tourist Office (☎ 05 63 63 60 60; www.montauban-tourisme.com; place Prax-Paris; ☺ 9.30am-6.30pm Mon-Sat, 9.30am-12.30pm Sun Jul & Aug, 9.30am-12.30pm & 2-6.30pm Sep-Jun) Its free pamphlet in English, *On the Paths to Heritage*, describes an exhaustive walking tour around the old town.

Sights

Jean Auguste Dominique Ingres, the sensual neoclassical painter and accomplished violinist, was a native of Montauban. Many of his works, plus canvases by Tintoretto, Van Dyck, Courbet and others, are in the **Musée Ingres** (☎ 05 63 22 12 91; 13 rue de l'Hôtel de Ville; adult/student & under 18yr €4.50/free; ☺ 10am-6pm daily Jul & Aug; 10am-noon & 2-6pm Tue-Sat Sep-Jun, 10am-noon & 2-6pm Sun Easter-Jun & Sep–mid-Oct), a former bishop's palace. Reception has explanatory notes in English. Your entry ticket also admits you to the nearby museums of Histoire Naturelle (natural history), Terroir (local costumes and traditions) and Résistance et Déportation (with mementos of WWII).

The 18th-century **Cathédrale Notre Dame de l'Assomption** (place Roosevelt; ☺ 10am-noon & 2-6pm Mon-Sat) with its clean, classical lines contains one of Ingres' masterpieces, *Le Vœu de Louis XIII*, depicting the king pledging France to the Virgin. The fine 13th-century **Église St-Jacques**, also in mellow pink brick, still bears cannonball marks from Louis XIII's 1621 siege of the town.

Festivals & Events

Alors Chante (May) A festival of traditional French song.

Jazz à Montauban (July) A giant week-long jam.

Légende des Quatre-Cent Coups (400 Blows, end of August) This weekend street festival commemorates the moment when, says local lore, a fortune-teller told Louis XIII, besieging Montauban, to blast off 400 cannons simultaneously against the town, which still failed to fall.

Sleeping

Hôtel d'Orsay (☎ 05 63 66 06 66; www.hotel-restaurant-orsay.com in French; 29 av Roger Salengro; r €44-64; ⌨) A stone's throw from the station, this hotel has comfortable enough if rather dated rooms within a solid building of mellow red brick. In summer, you can lounge on its lovely floral terrace and the upmarket restaurant (opposite) merits a visit any day of the year.

Hôtel du Commerce (☎ 05 63 66 31 32; 9 place Franklin Roosevelt; d €49-75) Central and overlooking the cathedral, this traditional building has 27 well-maintained, comfortably furnished rooms. It does a very generous buffet breakfast (€7) and some fine knick-knacks and furniture decorate public areas. Parking €6.

Eating

Couvert des Drapiers (☎ 05 63 92 91 03; 27 place Nationale; daily special €8, salads €10-14; ☺ lunch & dinner, closed dinner Mon Nov-Easter) Across the square from Brasserie des Arts and more attractive internally (large gleaming mirrors give a greater sense of space), it serves fine fare, including eight varieties of salad, frondy, colourful and piled high on your plate.

Brasserie des Arts (☎ 05 63 20 20 90; 4 place Nationale; menus €12-16, mains €13.50-18; ☺ lunch & dinner, closed dinner Sun Nov-Easter) One of several *brasseries* with summer terraces on arcaded place Nationale, it offers a good range of fish dishes, mussels prepared five different ways and plenty of pizzas.

Bistrot du Faubourg (☎ 05 63 63 49 89; 111 Faubourg Lacapelle; menus €12-26.50; ☺ Mon-Fri) It's all intimate tables for two at this cosy bistro. Montauban's best value for money is perhaps found here, as its 'house full' notice regularly attests.

La Cuisine d'Alain (☎ 05 63 66 06 66; Hôtel d'Orsay, 29 av Roger Salengro; menus €23-58; ☺ lunch & dinner Wed-Sun, lunch Mon) Especially strong on seafood including oysters, scallops and fish such as *rouget*, Alain's place offers free wine and coffee with lunch and wheels in a dessert trolley that will tempt all but the most dedicated weight watcher.

Restaurant Au Fil de l'Eau (☎ 05 63 66 11 85; 14 quai du Dr Lafforgue; menus €25-53; ☺ lunch & dinner Tue-Sat & lunch Sun) Beside the River Tarn, tempting *menus* and a window full of merited recommendations from Gallic gastronomic guides beckon you in. Typical *menu* examples include frog soufflé and pork with confit onions and mustard.

Morning **farmers markets** are on Saturday (place Prax-Paris) and Wednesday (place Lalaque), as well as a smaller, daily one (place Nationale).

Getting There & Around

The **train** is your best option. There are frequent services to Toulouse (€8, 30 minutes, frequent) and Bordeaux (€24.70, two hours, frequent) via Agen (€12.10, 45 minutes) and Moissac (€5.10, 20 minutes, five daily). For Albi, change in Toulouse.

The combined **train and bus stations** are connected with the town centre by bus Nos 3 and 5.

There's free parking under Pont Vieux. **Parking Occitan** is opposite the tourist office, on place Prax-Paris, beneath which a large underground carpark was being gouged when we last visited.

For a taxi, call **Radio Taxis** (☎ 05 63 66 99 99).

MOISSAC

pop 12,700

Moissac, an easy day trip from Montauban or Toulouse, was once a stop for Santiago de Compostela pilgrims. **Abbaye St-Pierre** (☺ 9am-7pm Jul & Aug; 9am-noon & 2-6pm Apr-Jun & Sep; 10am-noon & 2-5pm Mon-Fri, 2-5pm Sat & Sun Oct-Mar), resplendent with France's finest Romanesque sculpture, became a model for more modest ecclesiastical buildings throughout southern France.

Above the **south portal**, completed around 1130, is a superb tympanum depicting St John's vision of the Apocalypse, with Christ in majesty flanked by the apostles, angels and 24 awestruck elders.

In the **cloister** 116 delicate marble columns support wedge-shaped, deeply carved capitals, each a little masterpiece of foliage, earthy figures or biblical scenes. The Revolution's toll is sickening – nearly every face is smashed.

You enter the cloister through the **tourist office** (☎ 05 63 04 01 85; www.moissac.fr; place Durand de Bredon; ☺ as Abbaye St-Pierre). It shows a free 10-minute video (English version available) and sells a detailed guidebook, also in English. Admission to the cloister also includes a museum of folk art and furnishings, and a library containing replicas of the monastery's beautiful illuminated manuscripts.

Hôtel Le Moulin de Moissac (☎ 05 63 32 88 88; www.lemoulindemoissac.com in French; esplanade du Moulin; r €55-70) Overlooking the River Tarn and once a giant grain mill, it has a long history. In the 18th century it exported flour to the young USA; during WWI, a fire destroyed all but the shell; in WWII it sheltered Jewish children and clandestine Resistance activity. Nowadays, it's a fine hotel with unparalleled views of the river from the rooms and from the **restaurant** (menus €27-33; ☺ lunch & dinner Mon-Fri, dinner Sat) with its large picture windows.

Five trains daily run to and from Montauban (€5.10, 20 minutes), the majority also serving Toulouse (€7.90). You can park for free in place des Récollets (the market square) and just above (north of) the tourist office.

AUCH

pop 23,500

Auch (rhymes with Gosh!) has been an important trade crossroads ever since the Romans conquered a Celtic tribe called the Auscii and established Augusta Auscorum on the flats east of the River Gers. The town's heyday was in the Middle Ages when the counts of Armagnac and their archbishops together ran the city and built its cathedral. Its second flowering was in the late 18th century, as new roads were pushed southwards to Toulouse and into the Pyrenees. A slide into rural obscurity followed the Revolution in 1789.

Orientation

Hilltop Auch, with place de la Libération, place de la République and the cathedral at its heart, has most of the sights, restaurants, shops and hotels. Pedestrianised rue Dessoles is the principal shopping street.

The old town, tumbling away to the south, is a web of lanes, steps and little courtyards. Across the River Gers is the 'new' Auch and adjacent train and bus stations.

Information

Keynet (4 rue d'Étigny; per hr €3.50; ☉ 10am-10pm Wed-Fri, 10am-1am Fri & Sat, 2-8pm Sun) Internet access.

Post Office (rue Gambetta)

Tourist Office (☎ 05 62 05 22 89; www.auch-tourisme .com; 1 rue Dessoles; ☉ 9.30am-6.30pm Mon-Sat, 10am-12.15pm & 3-6pm Sun mid-Jul–mid-Aug, 9.15am-noon & 2-6pm Mon-Sat mid-Aug–mid-Jul, 10am-12.15pm Sun May–mid-Jul & mid-Aug-Sep) In Maison Fedel, a handsomely restored 15th-century building. Its town map shows a couple of signposted walking tours. Ask for the English version of the exhaustively detailed accompanying leaflet.

Sights

CATHÉDRALE STE-MARIE

This magnificent building, a Unesco World Heritage Site, moved Napoleon II to exclaim 'A cathedral like this should be put in a museum!' Constructed over two centuries, **Cathédrale Ste-Marie** (☉ 9.30am-noon & 2-5pm) ranges in style from pure Gothic to Italian Renaissance. To appreciate the contrast, take a look at the doorway in the external north wall; the lower part is lacy Gothic while the upper, unadorned arch is purest Florentine.

The heavy western façade impresses by its sheer bulk – and looks imposingly grand illuminated at night – but the real splendour lies within: 18 vivid 16th-century

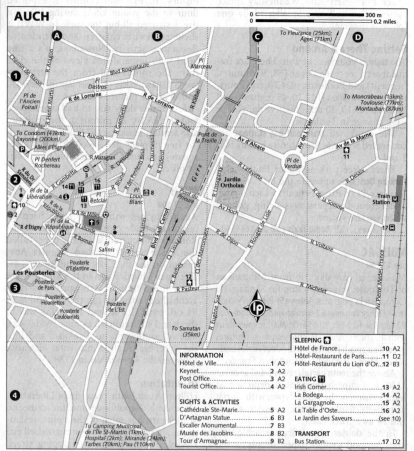

INFORMATION	
Hôtel de Ville	1 A2
Keynet	2 A2
Post Office	3 A2
Tourist Office	4 A2

SIGHTS & ACTIVITIES	
Cathédrale Ste-Marie	5 A2
D'Artagnan Statue	6 B3
Escalier Monumental	7 B3
Musée des Jacobins	8 B2
Tour d'Armagnac	9 B2

SLEEPING 🏠	
Hôtel de France	10 A2
Hôtel-Restaurant de Paris	11 D2
Hôtel-Restaurant du Lion d'Or	12 B3

EATING 🍴	
Irish Corner	13 A2
La Bodega	14 A2
La Gargagnole	15 A2
La Table d'Oste	16 A2
Le Jardin des Saveurs	(see 10)

TRANSPORT	
Bus Station	17 D2

Renaissance stained-glass windows and the astonishing **choir** (admission incl guide sheet in English €1.50), featuring over 1500 individual carvings of biblical scenes and mythological creatures in the 113 oak choir stalls.

For a multisensory experience, enjoy a free **recital** (🕑 6pm Sun Jul & Aug) on the cathedral's grand booming organ.

Behind the cathedral, the 14th-century, 40m-high **Tour d'Armagnac** (closed to the public) served Auch's archbishops as their archive, then briefly became a lock-up during the Revolution and later times of trouble.

MUSÉE DES JACOBINS
The **Musée des Jacobins** (☎ 05 62 05 74 79; 4 place Louis Blanc; adult/child €3/1.50; 🕑 10am-noon & 2-6pm daily May-Sep, to 5pm Tue-Sun Oct-Apr), also called the Musée d'Auch, was established in 1793. Its original collection came from property seized during the Revolution, when this elegant 14th-century Dominican monastery briefly served as a stable, then as a weapons workshop. Show your entry ticket to the cathedral's choir and admission costs only €1.50.

Highlights of this eclectic collection include frescoes from an early Gallo-Roman villa, copious pre-Columbian artefacts from the Americas and a rich collection of 19th-century Gascon costumes and everyday items.

MAISON GASCOGNE
In its time a vast grain market, this imposing space with its elaborate wooden ceiling is nowadays the venue for temporary exhibitions. In July and August it becomes a showcase for the best of Gascon produce – handicrafts, food and, of course, Armagnac.

ESCALIER MONUMENTAL
Auch's 234-step Monumental Stairway drops to the river from place Salinis. Near the bottom postures a statue of d'Artagnan, the fictional swashbuckling Gascon hero immortalised by Alexandre Dumas in *Les Trois Mousquetaires* (The Three Musketeers). Nearby, a series of narrow, stepped alleyways, collectively called Les Pousterles, also plunge to the plain.

Sleeping
Camping Municipal de l'Île St-Martin (☎ 05 62 05 00 22; person/tent/car €2.30/1.15/0.30; 🕑 mid-Apr–mid-Oct) This fairly spartan place is 1.5km south of town. Take bus No 5 from place de la Libération to the Mouzon stop.

Accommodation options with a roof over your head are decidedly limited unless you're happy in a chain hotel.

Hôtel-Restaurant de Paris (☎ 05 62 63 26 22; fax 05 62 60 04 27; 38 av de la Marne; s/d from €38/41, with shared bathroom from €25/28; 🕑 Dec-Oct) This agreeably old-fashioned hotel has been in the hands of the same family for over 70 years. With few concessions to the passing years, it offers nevertheless cosily furnished rooms, has a well-stocked bar and runs a good restaurant that serves copious quantities. Parking €3.50.

Hôtel-Restaurant du Lion d'Or (☎ 05 62 63 66 00; e.liondor@wanadoo.fr; 7 rue Pasteur; s/d from €35/45; ✗) There's been an inn on this spot since at least 1706. Today's hotel is a rambling old place in the same genre as Hotel-Restaurant de Paris. You won't find it listed by the tourist office, with whom the fiercely independent owner maintains a running battle.

Hôtel de France (☎ 05 62 61 71 71; www.hotelde france-auch.com; 1 place de la Libération; s/d from €66/81, half-board from €99/148; ✗) This is the only independent medium-range hotel in the old town – indeed in all of Auch – and it's a very comfortable option indeed. What it terms its *chambres privilège* (s/d from €95/118) are on the grand scale, in both size and décor. For fine dining, go no further than Le Jardin des Saveurs (p758), its splendid restaurant.

Eating & Drinking
La Gargagnole (☎ 05 62 05 09 64; 10 rue Dessoles; plat du jour €7, salads €6.50-7.50, mains around €10; 🕑 lunch Mon-Sat) This bustling, popular place offers fine fare at lunchtime and operates as a friendly, popular bar with a strictly contemporary feel throughout the day.

La Bodega (☎ 05 62 05 69 17; 7 rue Dessoles; daily special €7, mains €10-17; 🕑 lunch & dinner Mon-Sat, dinner Sun) At lunchtime you can enjoy full meals of Spanish and Basque origin. In the evening, go à la carte or simply pick at a tapa or two and enjoy the Latino ambience.

Irish Corner (1 place Betclar; menu €16.50) French-run with not an Irish accent in earshot, this is a convivial and lively place and the Guinness is as good as anywhere. Like La Gargagnole, it also lays on food – pizzas, pasta and a *menu* – and has a pleasant, shady terrace.

La Table d'Oste (☎ 05 62 05 55 62; 7 rue Lamartine; menus €16-23; ⏰ lunch Tue-Sat, dinner Mon-Fri mid-Jun–Oct; lunch & dinner Tue-Sat Nov–mid-Jun) New owners have taken over this longstanding local favourite. Time will tell if they keep the clientele. What's sure is that it still offers a cosy dining experience and the ample grill of beef, pork and duck will fill you to bursting.

Le Jardin des Saveurs (☎ 05 62 61 71 71; 2 place de la Libération; menus from €27; ⏰ lunch & dinner Mon-Sat, lunch Sun) Elegant dining indeed in a glorious Second Empire salon. Chef Roland Garreau is an acknowledged specialist in Gascon food but it needn't bust your budget: enticing *menus* begin at €27, rising to the gastronomic revelations of his *menu gourmand du chef* at €52.

Shopping

On Wednesday, there's a farmers market flanking Jardin Ortholan in the new town and a smaller Saturday one on place de la Cathédrale.

Getting There & Around

Bus connections include Condom (€6.10, 50 minutes, three daily) and Agen (€10.60, 1½ hours, five to seven daily). The **bus station** (☎ 05 62 05 76 37) is beside the **train station** (☎ 05 62 05 76 37). Eight to 12 trains or SNCF buses link Auch with Toulouse (€12.40, 1½ hours). There's extensive free parking along the length of allées d'Étigny.

CONDOM

pop 7500

Poor Condom, whose name has made it the butt of so many nudge-snigger, English-language jokes (the French don't even use the word, preferring *préservatif* or, more familiarly, *capote anglaise,* meaning 'English hood' – touché!).

Condom is actually a self-confident town beside the River Baïse, and is well worth a visit for its decorative cathedral, some fine restaurants and a clutch of sober neoclassical mansions.

Information

La Lavandière (5 rue Jules Ferry; ⏰ 8am-8pm) Laundrette.

Tourist Office (☎ 05 62 28 00 80; www.tourisme-tenareze.com; place Bossuet; ⏰ 9am-7pm Mon-Sat, 10.30am-12.30pm Sun Jul & Aug; 9am-noon & 2-5.30pm Mon-Sat Sep-Jun) Within the 13th-century Tour Auger d'Andiran. Has free descriptive leaflets (in French only but useful for the maps) of three signed walks around town, each with multilingual descriptive panels.

Sights

Condom's 16th-century **Cathédrale St-Pierre** (place St-Pierre), with its lofty nave and elaborately carved chancel, is a rich example of southern Flamboyant Gothic architecture. Its most richly sculpted entrance – much defaced during the Revolution – gives onto the square. Abutting the cathedral on its northern side is the delicately arched 16th-century cloister, now occupied in part by the Hôtel de Ville.

Musée de l'Armagnac (☎ 05 62 28 47 17; 2 rue Jules Ferry; adult/child €2.20/1.80; ⏰ 10am-noon & 3-6pm Wed-Mon Apr-Oct; 2-5pm Wed-Sun Nov, Dec, Feb & Mar, closed Jan) portrays the traditional production of Armagnac, Gascony's fiery rival to Cognac, distilled to the north in the Bordeaux vineyards.

For a taste of the real stuff, head to **Ryst-Dupeyron** (☎ 05 62 28 08 08; 36 rue Jean Jaurès; ⏰ 10am-noon & 2-6.30pm Mon-Fri year-round, 3.30-6.30pm Sat & Sun Jul & Aug), one of several Armagnac producers offering free sampling. It occupies the 18th-century Hôtel de Cugnac.

Among the town's most elegant 18th-century *hôtels particuliers* (private mansions) are **Hôtel de Marie Dorlan de Polignac**, (rue Jules Ferry), **Hôtel de Gensac** (rue de Roquepine),

---

VULGAR VILLAGES

The more puerile English-speaking visitors to France have long been amused by place names such as Condom (not to mention the likes of Pissy or Stains), but the French are in on the act now too. In an attempt to really put themselves on the map, in 2003 a group of French villages with names that mean silly or rude things in French staged their first summit meeting of 'Villages of lyric or burlesque names' in a tiny village outside Toulouse called Mingocebos (or 'eat onions' in the old Occitan tongue). Members include Saligos ('filthy pig'), Beaufou ('beautiful mad'), and Cocumont ('cuckold hill'), although Trecon ('very stupid') and Montcuq ('my arse') have yet to join.

Hôtel du Bouzet de Roquepine (rue Jean Jaurès) – the future Hôtel de Ville, currently being restored – and **Hôtel de Cadignan** (allées de Gaulle). None is open to the public.

Tours

During July and August, **Gascogne Navigation** (☎ 05 62 28 46 46; www.gascogne-navigation.com; quai Bouquerie) runs 1½-hour **cruises** (adult/child €7.20/5.50) from its quayside base, La Capitainerie. It also hires small motor boats (hour/day €25/92) and bigger ones by the week.

Festivals & Events

Bandas à Condom (www.festival-de-bandas.com in French, second weekend in May) Marching and brass bands from all over Europe for 48 hours of nonstop oompah.

Les Nuits Musicales (July and August) Listen to operetta in the cloister.

Sleeping

Camping Municipal de L'Argenté (☎ 05 62 28 17 32; campingmunicipal@condom.org; Chemin de L'Argenté; person/tent €3.10/3.30; ☼ Apr-Sep) This well equipped camp site is beside the River Baïse,

2.3km southwest of town along the D931. There's a sports centre with pool nearby.

Hôtel-Restaurant Le Relais de la Ténarèze (☎ 05 62 28 02 54; fax 05 62 28 46 96; 22 av d'Aquitaine; d/tr/q from €38/48/64) This welcoming place gives priority to cyclists and Chemin de St-Jacques pilgrims. For hearty home cooking, invest in half-board (€41) and enjoy the evening *menu du terroir* in its restaurant (p760) and home-made jams with breakfast. Reservations are all but essential between April and October.

Hôtel Continental (☎ 05 62 68 37 00; www.lecontinental.net; 20 av Maréchal Foch; r from €40; ☒ ☒ ☐) This welcoming, recently upgraded hotel overlooks the river. It runs an impressive restaurant, Les Jardins de la Baïse, and has a pleasant rear garden. There's ample parking space on the quayside if the slots in front of the hotel are full. Wi-fi.

Le Logis des Cordeliers (☎ 05 62 28 03 68; www.logisdescordeliers.com; rue de la Paix; d €49-64; ☼ Feb-Dec; ☒ ☒ ☒) Set in a modern building, it's family-run, family-friendly, peaceful and well set back from the nearest road. Most rooms have small balconies through which

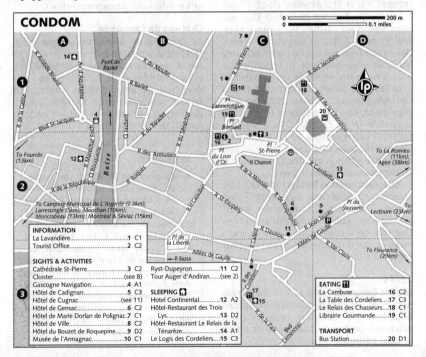

CONDOM

0 ——— 200 m
0 ——— 0.1 miles

To Fourcès (13km)

To Camping Municipal de L'Argenté (2.3km); Larressingle (5km); Mouchan (10km); Moncrabeau (13km); Montréal & Séviac (15km)

To La Romieu (11km); Agen (38km)

To Lectoure (23km)

To Fleurance (29km)

INFORMATION	
La Lavandière.....................1 C1	
Tourist Office.....................2 C2	

SIGHTS & ACTIVITIES	
Cathédrale St-Pierre.....................3 C2	
Cloister.....................(see 8)	
Gascogne Navigation.....................4 A1	
Hôtel de Cadignan.....................5 C3	
Hôtel de Cugnac.....................(see 11)	
Hôtel de Gensac.....................6 C2	
Hôtel de Marie Dorlan de Polignac.7 C1	
Hôtel de Ville.....................8 C2	
Hôtel du Bouzet de Roquepine.....9 D2	
Musée de l'Armagnac.....................10 C1	

Ryst-Dupeyron.....................11 C2	
Tour Auger d'Andiran.....................(see 2)	

SLEEPING ☐	
Hotel Continental.....................12 A2	
Hôtel-Restaurant des Trois Lys.....................13 D2	
Hôtel-Restaurant Le Relais de la Ténarèze.....................14 A1	
Le Logis des Cordeliers.....15 C3	

EATING ☐	
La Cambuse.....................16 C2	
La Table des Cordeliers.....................17 C3	
Le Relais des Chasseurs.....18 C1	
Librairie Gourmande.......19 C1	

TRANSPORT	
Bus Station.....................20 D1	

climbing flowers wind. The majority overlook the garden and pool. Parking €6.50.

Hôtel-Restaurant des Trois Lys (☎ 05 62 28 33 33; www.lestroislys.com; 38 rue Gambetta; r €90-150; 🔲 🈶) Each of the ten large rooms within this 18th-century mansion is individually and tastefully furnished, often with artefacts of the era. The pool, a cosy bar and its superb restaurant (below) make it an ideal self-contained retreat.

Eating

La Cambuse (☎ 05 62 68 48 95; place Bossuet; salads €6.50-12, sandwiches €2.50-3.50, daily special €8; 🕑 lunch Mon-Sat, dinner Fri & Sat) This quick-fix place beside the tourist office offers a whole variety of snacky and more substantial fare. Good for eating in or takeaway, it spills onto place Bossuet in summertime.

Le Relais des Chasseurs (☎ 05 62 28 20 14; 3 blvd de la Libération; menus €10-28; 🕑 lunch & dinner Tue-Sat & lunch Mon) This unpretentious place is a popular midday venue for local workers. Its weekday lunch *menu* at €11 including wine is particularly good value.

Hotel-Restaurant Le Relais de la Ténarèze (☎ 05 62 28 02 54; 22 av d'Aquitaine; €13-22; 🕑 lunch & dinner Apr-Sep, lunch Mon-Sat Oct-Mar) This no-nonsense place dishes up lipsmacking, hearty meals. Often as not out of season, there's no menu and you take what Madame has simmering in the pot. In season, go for her *menu du terroir*, strong on local dishes.

La Table des Cordeliers (☎ 05 62 68 43 82; 1 rue Cordeliers; menus €20-50, mains €20-25; 🕑 lunch & dinner Tue-Sat, lunch Sun) Adjacent to, but run separately from, Le Logis des Cordeliers (p759) it offers sumptuous dining indeed, beneath the sweeping arches of a former chapel. Furnishings are strictly modern yet sit harmoniously in such a setting.

Hôtel-Restaurant des Trois Lys (☎ 05 62 28 33 33; 38 rue Gambetta; menus €20-32, mains €21-35; 🕑 lunch & dinner) The finest Gascon cuisine is rustled up here, with such delights as cod terrine with ceps, crab ravioli in bisque and a *menu autour de Gascogne* (around Gascony menu) at €32.

CAFÉS

Librairie Gourmande (☎ 05 62 28 17 35; 3 place Bossuet; 🕑 Tue-Sun) Within this recently opened bookshop is a charming little tea room where you can browse and relax over a plate of local pastries.

Getting There & Around

Condom, its nearest train station in Auch, is ill served by public transport. There are three daily buses to Auch (€6.10, 50 minutes), including one that goes on to Toulouse (€14.90, 2½ hours), and an early-bird run to Bordeaux (€18.75, 2¾ hours Monday to Saturday). Frequent buses run daily to Agen (€8, 45 minutes).

There's free parking in the raised area between allées de Gaulle and rue Jean Jaurès.

AROUND CONDOM

This swath of the ancient province of Gascon was, in its time, wild frontier country, caught between the French, entrenched in Toulouse, and the English with their power base in Bordeaux. The better endowed of the hapless villages caught in the crossfire fortified themselves against all comers, creating what are known as *bastides*.

You can drive from one to another in a long morning. But better to take them at a more gentle pace; these mild undulating lands are ideal for cycling.

The area's claim to contemporary fame is as a producer of Armagnac (below).

Château de Cassaigne

At 13th-century **Château de Cassaigne** (☎ 05 62 28 04 02; www.chateaudecassaigne.com; 🕑 10am-7pm daily Jul & Aug, 9am-noon & 2-6pm Tue-Sun Sep-Jul), the old country house of the bishops of Condom, you can enjoy a video, a visit, then sample Armagnac from its 18th-century distillery. It's 6.5km southwest of Condom, just off the D931 to Eauze.

ARMAGNAC

As any good Gascon will tell you, Armagnac slips down just as smoothly as the more heavily produced and marketed Cognac to the north. Produced from white grapes that ripen in the sandy soils hereabouts and aged in barrels of local black oak, it was originally taken for medicinal reasons. You too may care to try a little pick-me-up. A couple of major distillers have their headquarters in Condom (p758). Travelling among the vineyards, you'll also come across many a siren-call notice, inviting you in for a taste and the chance to buy direct from a small-scale farmer-distiller.

Fourcès

Fourcès (pronounce that 's'), 13km north-west of Condom via the D114, is a pictur-esque *bastide* on the River Auzoue. Uniquely circular (but not so incongruous really since the houses once surrounded a small castle, demolished by royal order in the 15th cen-tury), it was founded by the English invad-ers. Nowadays, its shady expanse is ringed by well-restored medieval houses. In one corner is the tiny, dusty **Musée des Vieux Mé-tiers** (Museum of Ancient Crafts).

The village bursts into colour during the last weekend of April as thousands pour in for its **Marché aux Fleurs**, more a flower festival than market.

The tiny seasonal **tourist office** (☎ 05 62 29 50 96; www.fources.fr; ☉ Jun-Sep) is in the square (or, more accurately, circle).

Larressingle

Larressingle, 5km west of Condom on the D15, must be France's cutest fortified village. It's certainly the most besieged, bravely withstanding armies of tourists and Com-postela pilgrims.

This textbook bastion bears witness to the troubled times of medieval Gascony. Within the largely intact original walls are the remains of a **castle-keep**, once the principal residence of the bishops of Con-dom, and the sturdy Romanesque **Église St-Sigismond**.

There's a seasonal **tourist office** (☎ 05 62 68 22 49; 10am-noon & 3-7pm Tue-Sat May, Jun & Sep; Tue-Sun Jul & Aug). It organises **guided visits** (☉ 11am & 4.30pm Mon-Sat).

Within the walls, **La Halte aux Pèlerins** (☎ 05 62 28 11 58; adult/child €3/2.50; ☉ 10.30am-noon & 2-6.30pm Jun-Sep, 2-6pm school holidays, Sat & Sun Oct-May) is a fun waxwork museum of medieval village life with optional English commentary. Outside the fortifications, **Cité des Machines du Moyen Âge** (☎ 05 62 68 33 90; admission adult/child €5/3; ☉ May-Oct) is a display of medieval war machines, drawn up as if about to assault the city.

Montréal & Séviac

Montréal, established in 1255, was one of Gascony's first *bastides*. Its chunky Gothic church squats beside place Hôtel de Ville, the arcaded main square.

At Séviac, 1.5km southwest of Montréal, are the excavated remains of a 4th-century

Gallo-Roman villa (admission €4; ☉ 10am-7pm Jul & Aug, 10am-noon & 2-6pm Mar-Jun & Sep-Nov). Dis-covered by the local parish priest in 1868, the site is still being excavated. What ar-chaeologists have revealed are the remains of a luxurious villa, including baths and outbuildings, on the agricultural estate of a 4th-century Roman aristocrat. Large areas of the villa's spectacular mosaic floors (over 450 mosaics have been uncovered) have survived.

Admission includes entry to the **museum**, within Montréal's **tourist office** (☎ 05 62 29 42 85; place Hôtel de Ville; ☉ 9.30am-12.30pm & 2-6pm Tue-Sat), where artefacts from Séviac are displayed. Ask for its explanatory sheet in English.

La Romieu

La Romieu, 11km northeast of Condom and once an important stopover on the Santiago de Compostela route, takes its name from the Occitan *roumieu*, meaning pilgrim. It's dominated by the magnificent 14th-century collegiate **Église St-Pierre** (admission €4.50). Just opposite the entrance is the **tourist office** (☎ 05 62 28 86 33; ☉ 10am-6.30pm or 7pm May-Sep, 10am-noon & 2-6pm Oct-Apr, closed Sun morning year-round), whose staff will let you into the fine Gothic cloister that gives onto the church. Left of the altar is the **sacristy** where original medieval frescoes include arcane biblical characters, black angels and esoteric sym-bols. Climb the 136 steps of the double-helix stairway to the top of the octagonal tower for a good view over the countryside.

About 500m west of the village is the **Ar-boretum Coursiana** (☎ 05 62 68 22 80; admission €6; ☉ 9am-8pm Easter-Oct), an initiative of a local agricultural engineer, where over 650 trees and rare plants flourish.

Lectoure

Lectoure's main claim to fame, its renowned juicy melons aside, is the superb **Musée Archéologique** (☎ 05 62 68 70 22; place Général de Gaulle; adult/child €4/free; ☉ 10am-noon & 2-6pm daily Mar-Sep; 10am-noon & 2-6pm Wed-Mon Oct-Feb) in the former Episcopal palace, today the Hôtel de Ville. The museum displays finds from local Gallo-Roman sites (including 20 bull- or ram-head pagan altars, used for sacri-fice), Roman jewellery and mosaics.

Rearing up over the archaeological museum is the bulk of the 15th-century

TOULOUSE AREA

Cathédrale St-Gervais et St-Protais with its curious, ornate tower.

Bleu de Lectoure (☎ 05 62 68 78 30; www.bleu-de-lectoure.com; ⏳ 10am-12.30pm & 2-6.30pm Mon-Sat, 2-6.30pm Sun; closed Mon Jan & Feb) occupies a former tannery, near the old railway station on the road to Condom. A dedicated Franco-American couple have revived the extraction of blue dye from the fermented leaves of the woad plant. You can visit the workshop and buy a whole host of products dyed in woad – though the owner's blue Jaguar with its woad-based paint is strictly not for sale.

The **tourist office** (☎ 05 62 68 76 98; www.lectoure.fr in French; ⏳ 9am-12.30pm & 2.30-7pm Jul & Aug; 9am-noon & 2-6pm Mon-Sat, 2-5pm Sun Sep-Jun) is next door.

Slip 50m down the alley opposite the cathedral for **Le Bastard** (☎ 05 62 68 82 44; rue Lagrange; menus €28 & €48; ⏳ closed Mon, dinner Sun & lunch Tue) and the finest in Gascon cuisine. Dine inside this highly regarded restaurant or on its ample terrace overlooking the valley.

Languedoc-Roussillon

Languedoc-Roussillon is a three-eyed hybrid, cobbled together in the 1980s by the merging of two historic regions. Bas-Languedoc (Lower Languedoc), land of bullfighting, rugby and robust red wines, looks towards the more-sedate Provence. On the plain are the major towns: Montpellier, the vibrant capital, sun-baked Nîmes with its fine Roman amphitheatre – and fairy-tale Carcassonne, with its witches'-hat turrets. On the coast, good beaches abound, old Agde lies somnolent beside the River Hérault and Sète, a thriving port, adds commercial vigour.

Deeper inland, Haut-Languedoc (Upper Languedoc) is quite distinct from the sunny lowlands. A continuation of the Massif Central, this sparsely populated mountainous terrain shares trekking, mountain pasture, forests and hearty cuisine with Auvergne, to its north. The small towns of Mende, Florac, Alès and Millau are like oases within the greater wilderness. The Parc National des Cévennes has long been the refuge of exiles and crisscrossed by marked trails. Trekking country too are the bare limestone plateaus of the Grands Causses, sliced through by deep canyons such as the Gorges du Tarn, perfect for a day's canoeing.

Roussillon, abutting the Pyrenees, glances over the frontier to Catalonia, in Spain, with which it shares a common language and culture. Alongside the rocky coastline are attractive resorts such as Collioure, which drew the likes of Matisse and Picasso, while the gentle Têt and Tech Valleys stretch away inland. To their south, the Pic de Canigou, highest summit in the eastern Pyrenees and symbol of Catalan identity, pokes its nose to the clouds while, further east, the foothills are capped by stark, lonely Cathar fortresses.

LANGUEDOC-ROUSSILLON

HIGHLIGHTS

- Gasp at your first glimpse of La Cité's witches'-hat turrets above **Carcassonne** (p783)
- Spot vultures looping and swooping high above **Gorges de la Jonte** (p794)
- Swim under the bridge for an original perspective of the **Pont du Gard** (p770)
- Drift lazily down the **Gorges du Tarn** (p792) in a canoe
- Walk a stage or two of Robert Louis Stevenson's **donkey trek** (p790) in Parc National des Cévennes
- Enjoy spectacular Pyrenean scenery from the trundling **Train Jaune** (Yellow Train; p804), near Villefranche de Conflent
- Take a slow boat along the **Canal du Midi** (p780) from Agde

■ POPULATION: 2,300,000	■ AREA: 27,375 SQ KM

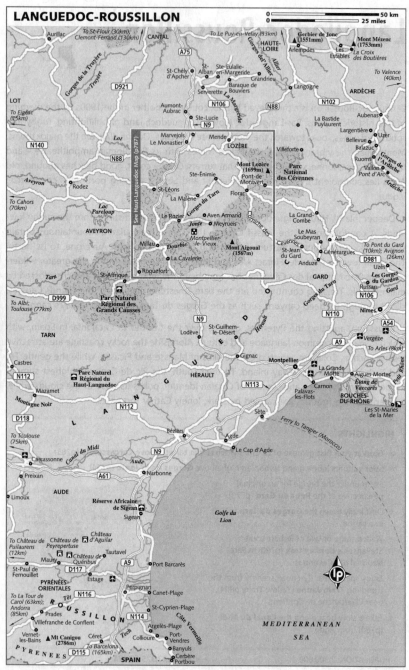

LANGUEDOC-ROUSSILLON

0 — 50 km
0 — 25 miles

BAS-LANGUEDOC

Languedoc takes its name from *langue d'oc*, a language closely related to Catalan. It's quite distinct from *langue d'oïl*, the forerunner of modern French, spoken to the north (the words *oc* and *oïl* meant 'yes'). The plains of Bas-Languedoc boast all Languedoc's towns of consequence, its beaches, rich Roman heritage and France's largest wine-producing area.

History

Phoenicians, Greeks, Romans, Visigoths and Moors all passed through Languedoc before it came under Frankish control in the 8th century. The Franks were generally happy to leave affairs in the hands of local rulers and around the 12th century Occitania (today's Languedoc) reached its zenith. At the time, Occitan was the language of the troubadours and the cultured speech of southern France. However, the Albigensian Crusade, launched in 1208 to suppress the 'heresy' of Catharism, led to Languedoc's annexation by the French kingdom. The treaty of Villers-Cotterêts (1539), which made *langue d'oïl* the realm's official language, downgraded Occitan. Continuing to be spoken in the south, it enjoyed a literary revival in the 19th century, spearheaded by the poet Frédéric Mistral, and is nowadays more often called Provençal.

NÎMES

pop 137,700

Plough your way through the bleak, traffic-clogged outskirts of Nîmes to reach its true heart, still beating there where the Romans established their town more than two millennia ago. Here, you'll find some of France's best-preserved classical buildings, together with some stunning modern constructions as the city continues its centuries-old rivalry with Montpellier, just down the autoroute.

The city's other less obvious claim to fame is sartorial. During the 1849 Californian gold rush, one Levi Strauss was making trousers for miners. Looking for a tough, hardwearing fabric, he began importing the traditionally blue *serge de Nîmes*, nowadays known as denim.

Orientation

Almost everything, including traffic, revolves around Les Arènes, the roman amphitheatre. North of here, the fan-shaped, largely pedestrianised old city is bounded by blvd Victor Hugo, blvd Amiral Courbet and blvd Gambetta. The main squares are place de la Maison Carrée, place du Marché and place aux Herbes.

Information

Laundrette (14 rue Nationale; ☻ 7am-9pm)
Main Post Office (blvd de Bruxelles)
Net@Games (place de la Maison Carrée; per hr €3; ☻ 10am-midnight) Internet access.
PC Gamer (2 rue Nationale; per hr €2.50; ☻ 9.30am-12.30am Mon-Sat, noon-12.30am Sun) Internet access.
Tourist Office (☎ 04 66 58 38 00; www.ot-nimes.fr; 6 rue Auguste; ☻ 8am-8pm Mon-Sat, 10am-6pm Sun Jul & Aug, 8.30am-7pm Mon-Sat, 10am-5pm or 6pm Sep-Jun)

Sights

LES ARÈNES

The **Roman Amphitheatre** (adult/under 16/under 11 including audioguide €7.70/5.60/free; ☻ 9am-7pm Jun-Aug, 9am-5.30pm Mar-May & Oct-Sep, 9.30am-4.30pm Nov-Feb), built around AD 100 to seat 24,000 spectators, is wonderfully preserved, even retaining its upper storey, unlike its counterpart in Arles. The interior of this magnificent arena has a system of exits and passages (called, engagingly, *vomitories*), designed so that patricians attending animal and gladiator combats never had to rub shoulders with the plebs up top. A couple of multimedia presentations on bullfighting and gladiatorial combat were in preparation when we last visited.

Les Arènes lives on as a frequent sporting and cultural venue – an excellent thing in itself though the scaffolding and temporary barriers do detract from its appeal as a

---

THE CROCODILE OF NÎMES

Around town and on tourist literature, you'll see the city's shield: a crocodile chained to a palm tree. It recalls the city's foundation, when retiring Roman legionaries who had sweated with Caesar during his River Nile campaign, were granted land to cultivate hereabouts.

NÎMES DISCOUNT PASSES

Tariffs for Nîmes' three major monuments, recently privatised, have increased hugely. Limit the damage by purchasing a **combination ticket** (adult/child €9/7) – also hiked way in excess of inflation – which admits you to Les Arènes, La Maison Carrée and Tour Magne.

---

historical site. Buy your ticket at the reception point, tucked into its northern walls.

MAISON CARRÉE

The **Maison Carrée** (Square House; place de la Maison Carrée; adult/11-16yr/under 11yr €4.50/3.60/free; ☻9am-7pm Jun-Aug, 9am-5.30pm Mar-May & Oct-Sep, 9.30am-4.30pm Nov-Feb) is a remarkably preserved rectangular Roman temple, constructed around AD 5 to honour Emperor Augustus' two adopted sons. It's survived the centuries as a medieval meeting hall, private residence, stable, church and, after the Revolution, archive.

The striking glass and steel building across the square, completed in 1993, is the **Carré d'Art** (Square of Art), which houses the municipal library and Musée d'Art Contemporain (right). The work of British architect Sir Norman Foster, it harmonises well with the Maison Carrée and is everything modern architecture should be: innovative, complementary and beautiful – a wonderful, airy building to just float around.

JARDINS DE LA FONTAINE

Nîmes' other major Roman monuments enrich the elegant Fountain Gardens. The **Source de la Fontaine** was the site of a spring, temple and baths in Roman times. The **Temple de Diane** – 'it is strictly forbidden to escalade this monument,' says the sign in quaint near-English – is in the lower northwest corner.

A 10- to 15-minute uphill walk to the top of the gardens brings you to the crumbling shell of the 30m high **Tour Magne** (adult/11-16yr/under 11yr €2.70/2.30/free; ☻9am-7pm Jun-Aug, 9am-5.30pm Mar-May & Oct-Sep, 9.30am-4.30pm Nov-Feb), raised around 15 BC and the largest of a chain of towers that once punctuated the city's 7km-long Roman ramparts. From here, there's a magnificent view of Nîmes and the surrounding countryside.

MUSEUMS

Each of Nîmes' **museums** (☻10am-6pm Tue-Sun) follows a common timetable. Most are in sore need of a new broom.

Musée du Vieux Nîmes (place aux Herbes; admission free), in the 17th-century Episcopal palace, is a small museum that, in addition to the usual period costumes and furniture, has a whole room showcasing denim, with smiling pin-ups of Elvis, James Dean and Marilyn Monroe.

Musée d'Archéologie (Archaeological Museum; 13 blvd Amiral Courbet; admission free) brings together some interesting Roman and pre-Roman tombs, mosaics, inscriptions and artefacts unearthed around Nîmes. It also houses a hotchpotch of artefacts from Africa, piled high and tagged with yellowing captions such as 'Abyssinia' and 'Dahomey'. In the same building, **Musée d'Histoire Naturelle** (Natural History Museum) has a musty collection of stuffed animals gazing bleakly out. Only the custodians, protected from importunate visitors inside their own glass case, have life.

Musée des Beaux-Arts (Fine Arts Museum; rue de la Cité Foulc; adult/11-16yr/under 11yr €4.90/3.60/free) has a wonderfully preserved Roman mosaic (look down upon it from the 1st floor). This apart, it houses a fairly pedestrian collection of Flemish, Italian and French works.

The refreshing **Musée d'Art Contemporain** (Contemporary Art Museum; place de la Maison Carrée; adult/11-16yr/under 11yr €4.90/3.60/free) in the Carré d'Art makes a welcome contrast. Housing permanent and rotating exhibitions of modern art, it merits a visit, if only to prowl the innards of the striking building.

Tours

The tourist office runs two-hour French-language city tours (€5.50) at 10am on Tuesday, Thursday and Saturday in summer, and 2.30pm on Saturday the rest of the year.

Taxi TRAN (☎ 04 66 29 40 11) offers a one-hour tour of the city (around €25 for up to six people) with a cassette commentary in English. Inquire at the tourist office.

Festivals & Events

In July and August there's an abundance of dance, theatre, rock, pop and jazz events. The tourist office produces *Festivités à Nîmes*, a free annual calendar of events.

FÉRIAS & BULLFIGHTS

Nîmes becomes more Spanish than French during its *férias* (bullfighting festivals). Each *féria* – the five-day **Féria de Pentecôte** (Whitsuntide Festival) in June, and the three-day **Féria des Vendanges** coinciding with the grape harvest on the third weekend in September – is marked by daily *corridas* (bullfights). The **Bureau de Locations des Arènes** (☎ 04 66 02 80 90; 2 rue de la Violette) sells tickets.

JEUDIS DE NÎMES

Every Thursday between 6pm and 10.30pm in July and August, artists, artisans and vendors of local food specialities take over the main squares of central Nîmes.

Sleeping

During Nîmes' *férias*, many hotels raise their prices significantly and accommodation is hard to find.

BUDGET

Camping Domaine de la Bastide (☎ 04 66 62 05 82; www.camping-nimes.com; site €12.80; ☺ year-round) is 4km south of town on the D13. Take bus D and get off at La Bastide, the terminus.

Auberge de Jeunesse (☎ 04 66 68 03 20; www .hinimes.com; 257 chemin de l'Auberge de Jeunesse, la Cigale; dm €11.65, d/q €27.30/46.60) This sterling, well equipped youth hostel has everything from dorms to cute houses for two to six in its extensive grounds, 3.5km northwest of the train station. It offers a children's playground,

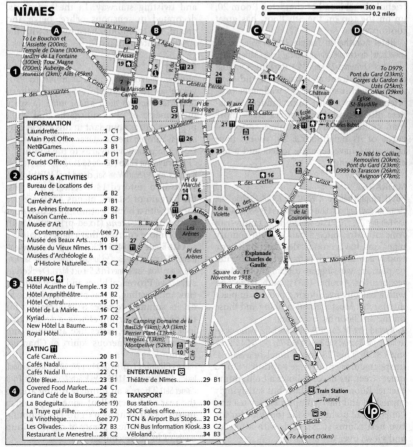

NÎMES

INFORMATION	
Laundrette.......................1	C1
Main Post Office..............2	C3
Net@Games.....................3	B1
PC Gamer........................4	D1
Tourist Office..................5	B1

SIGHTS & ACTIVITIES	
Bureau de Locations des Arènes.........................6	B2
Carrée d'Art....................7	B1
Les Arènes Entrance........8	B2
Maison Carrée.................9	B1
Musée d'Art Contemporain...........(see 7)	
Musée des Beaux Arts.....10	B4
Musée du Vieux Nîmes....11	C2
Musées d'Archéologie & d'Histoire Naturelle......12	C2

SLEEPING	
Hôtel Acanthe du Temple..13	D2
Hôtel Amphithéâtre.........14	B2
Hôtel Central..................15	D1
Hôtel de La Mairie..........16	C2
Kyriad...........................17	D2
New Hôtel La Baume........18	C1
Royal Hôtel....................19	B1

EATING	
Café Carré.....................20	B1
Cafés Nadal...................21	C2
Cafés Nadal II................22	C2
Côte Bleue.....................23	B1
Covered Food Market......24	C1
Grand Café de la Bourse..25	B2
La Bodeguita.............(see 19)	
La Truye qui Fume..........26	B2
La Vinothèque...........(see 27)	
Les Olivades..................27	C2
Restaurant Le Menestrel..28	C2

ENTERTAINMENT	
Théâtre de Nîmes............29	B1

TRANSPORT	
Bus station....................30	D4
SNCF sales office...........31	C2
TCN & Airport Bus Stops..32	D4
TCN Bus Information Kiosk.33	C2
Véloland.......................34	B3

LANGUEDOC-ROUSSILLON

self-catering facilities and bike hire (per day €14) and there's limited camping (per person €5.85). Take bus No I, direction Alès or Villeverte, and get off at the Stade stop.

Hôtel de La Mairie (☎ 04 66 67 65 91; hotelnimes@ aol.com; 11 rue des Greffes; r €43-52, with shower €34, with shared bathroom €26) Several rooms in this friendly family-run two-star 13-room hotel have separate bathroom and toilet. Ceilings are high and rooms cool, even in high summer. To watch the world go by in the quiet street below, ask for room three with its tiny balcony.

Hôtel Central (☎ 04 66 67 27 75; www.hotel-cen tral.org; 2 place du Château; d/tr/q €45/55/65, r with shared bathroom €35) Parking €8. With its creaky floorboards and bunches of wild flowers painted on each bedroom door, this friendly hotel is full of character. Room 20, up on the top on the 5th floor, has great rooftop views.

Hôtel Acanthe du Temple (☎ 04 66 67 54 61; www.hotel-du-temple.com in French; 1 rue Charles Babut; ☾ closed Christmas-23 Jan; ☒) Parking €9. Just opposite the Central, it has spick-and-span rooms, even if some of the wallpaper (different in every room) might induce biliousness. Room and garage prices are – more than coincidentally – within a couple of euros of its neighbour's. All rooms have fans, some have separate toilets and a few are nonsmoking.

MIDRANGE

Hôtel Amphithéâtre (☎ 04 66 67 28 51; hotel-am phitheatre@wanadoo.fr; Blvd des Arènes; s €34-39, d €44-61; ☾ Feb-Dec; ☒ ☒) The welcoming, family-run Amphithéâtre, once a pair of 18th-century mansions, has 15 rooms decorated in warm, woody colours. Each is named after a writer or painter; we suggest dipping into Montesquieu or Arrabal (€61), both large and with a balcony overlooking pedestrian place du Marché. Most are nonsmoking and those on the 3rd floor have air-con.

Kyriad (☎ 04 66 76 16 20; www.hotel-kyriad-nimes .com; 10 rue Roussy; s €58-66, d €63-75; ☒ ☒) Parking €8.50. This 28-room hotel is a safe if unspectacular midrange option. On a quiet street, its décor follows a bullfighting theme. Rooms are smallish but satisfyingly furnished and have complimentary tea and coffee. Head up high to the top floor for the two best rooms (€75), each with a terrace and views over the city.

Royal Hôtel (☎ 04 66 58 28 27; rhotel@wanadoo.fr; 3 blvd Alphonse Daudet; s €45-65, d €60-85) New owners have preserved the raffishly bohemian atmosphere of this hotel, popular with visiting artistes. The huge dove cage still sits beside reception and the local intelligentsia continue to discourse over coffee in its very Spanish café. Rooms, all with ceiling fan and nearly all with bathtubs, are furnished with flair. Some overlook pedestrian place d'Assas; fine for the view though the noise might be intrusive on summer nights.

New Hôtel La Baume (☎ 04 66 76 28 42; www.new -hotel.com; 21 rue Nationale; s/d €95/120; ☒ ☒ 💻) Wi-fi. In an unfashionable part of town and in fact far from new, this 34-room hotel occupies an attractive 17th-century town mansion with a glorious interior courtyard and twisting stairway. In the bedrooms, decorated in sensuous ochre, beige and cream, the traditional harmonises with the strictly contemporary.

Eating

Nîmes' gastronomy owes as much to Provence as to Languedoc. Spicy southern delights, such as aïoli and *rouille* (a spicy mayonnaise of olive oil, garlic and chilli peppers), are as abundant in this city as cassoulet. Sample the Costières de Nîmes wines from the pebbly vineyards to the south.

La Truye qui Filhe (☎ 04 66 21 76 33; 9 rue Fresque; menu €9.20; ☾ lunch Mon-Sat, closed Aug) Within the vaults of a restored 14th-century inn, this, the bargain of Nîmes, blends a self-service format with a homely atmosphere and does a superb-value *menu* (fixed-price meal with two or more courses) that changes daily.

Côte Bleue (☎ 04 66 67 36 12; rue du Grand Couvent; menu €17, mains €9-13; ☾ lunch & dinner Mon-Sat Jun-Sep, lunch Mon-Sat, dinner Fri & Sat Oct-May) Decked in attractive Provençal blues and deep yellows, tiny and bustling, it's as attractive inside as on its summer terrace. Save a cranny for the *gâteau de marrons et noix*, a dessert that looks like sludge, tastes like ambrosia and comes with a generous squirt of Chantilly cream.

Les Olivades (☎ 04 66 21 71 78; 18 rue Jean Reboul; lunch/dinner menu €11/26; ☾ lunch & dinner Tue-Fri & dinner Sat) There's an intimate dining area to the rear of this excellent wine shop, which merits a visit in its own right. The tempting dinner *menu* offers plenty of choice within each of its three courses.

Restaurant Le Menestrel (☎ 04 66 67 54 45; 6 rue École Vieille; menus €24-30, mains €15-18; ☾ dinner Thu-Mon, lunch only with prior reservation Thu-Mon; Ⓥ) The husband and wife team who have taken over the Menestrel offer a range of gastronomic delights. Meat and fish are of the freshest and all desserts are homemade. Peek at the guest book with its multilingual tributes to the quality of the cuisine and observe yourself in the giant overhead mirror as you tuck in. There's always a choice for vegetarians and menus are in both English and French.

Le Bouchon et L'Assiette (☎ 04 66 62 02 93; 5bis rue Sauve; menus €25-44, mains €16-18; ☾ lunch & dinner Thu-Mon, closed 3 weeks Aug) Refined cuisine indeed. Dishes are attractively presented and described sotto voce as they're slipped before you. For dessert, go for the *blanc manger*, a smooth, creamy confection of white chocolate beneath a bed of stewed berries and worlds away from the synthetic blancmange of childhood parties. Service can be slow so come with a thick book or a scintillating companion.

CAFÉS
Place aux Herbes is one communal outside café in summer. Equally bustling, beneath the huge palm tree that flops its fronds over the centre, is place du Marché.

Grand Café de la Bourse (blvd des Arènes) Great for breakfast or a quick coffee. Sit on the terrace or inside this vast, flamboyant café bang opposite Les Arènes. It was closed when we visited, but it should again be serving, in the proprietor or his successor's hands, soon.

Other cafés:

Café Carré (1 place de la Maison Carrée) Overlooking Maison Carré. Lounge on one of the terrace's wicker chairs or sit inside, with fresh flowers on the table and lots of gleaming aluminium.

La Bodeguita (☾ 6pm-late Mon-Sat) A popular meeting place for the local intelligentsia. Inside Royal Hôtel.

SELF-CATERING
There are colourful Thursday markets in the old city in July and August. The large and particularly rich covered food market is on rue Général Perrier.

La Vinothèque (18 rue Jean Reboul) Knowledgeable staff at La Vinothèque can guide you through their unbeatable choice of local wines.

Quaint **Cafés Nadal**, overlooking place aux Herbes, specialises in local herbs, oils and spices, while its branch on rue St-Castor sells the finest coffees and chocolate.

Entertainment
Pick up *À Nîmes*, a free fortnightly entertainment listing, available at the tourist office and major hotels. Les Arènes is a major venue for theatre performances and concerts.

Théâtre de Nîmes (☎ 04 66 36 02 04; place de la Calade) This theatre has drama, music and opera performances throughout the year.

Getting There & Away
AIR
Nîmes' **airport** (☎ 04 66 70 49 49), 10km southeast of the city on the A54 is served only by Ryanair, which flies to/from London (Stansted and Luton), Liverpool and Nottingham East Midlands in the UK.

BUS
The **bus station** (☎ 04 66 29 52 00; rue Ste-Félicité) connects with the train station. International operators **Eurolines** (☎ 04 66 29 49 02) and **Line Bus** (☎ 04 66 29 50 62) both have kiosks there.

Regional destinations include Pont du Gard (€6.20, 30 minutes, five daily), Uzès (€6.20, 45 minutes, at least five daily) and Alès (€7.60, 1¼ hours, five daily).

CAR & MOTORCYCLE
Europcar has kiosks at both the airport (☎ 04 66 70 49 22) and train station (☎ 04 66 29 07 94).

TRAIN
There's an **SNCF sales office** (11 rue de l'Aspic).

At least eight TGVs daily run to/from Paris' Gare de Lyon (€72.70 to €88.80, three hours). There are frequent services to/from Alès (€7.90, 40 minutes), Arles (€6.90, 30 minutes), Avignon (€7.70, 30 minutes), Marseille (€17.20, 1¼ hours), Sète (€11.10, one hour) and Montpellier (€7.90, 30 minutes). Up to five SNCF buses or trains go to Aigues Mortes in the Camargue (€6.50, 1¼ hours).

Getting Around
TO/FROM THE AIRPORT
A TCN airport bus (€4.50, 30 minutes) meets and greets Ryanair flights, leaving

from the train station. To confirm times, ring ☎ 04 66 29 52 00.

BICYCLE
Véloland (☎ 04 66 01 80; 4 rue de la République; ☻ Tue-Sat & Mon 9am-noon) rents mountain bikes (per half/full day €9/15).

PUBLIC TRANSPORT
Local buses are run by **TCN** (☎ 08 20 22 30 30), which has an information kiosk in the northeast corner of esplanade Charles de Gaulle, the main centre for buses. A single ticket/five-ticket *carnet* (booklet) costs €1/4.

TAXI
Ring ☎ 04 66 29 40 11.

AROUND NÎMES
Perrier Plant
Ever wondered how they get the bubbles into a bottle of Perrier water? Or why it's that stubby shape? Take the one-hour tour in French of **Perrier's bottling plant** (☎ 04 66 87 61 01; adult/child €6/3; ☻ tours 9.15am-5pm daily Jul & Aug, 9.30am-4pm Mon-Fri Sep-Dec & Feb & May). It's in Vergèze, on the RN113, 13km southwest of Nîmes. We trust their tongue is firmly in their cheek when they advertise '*dégustation gratuité*' (free tasting)! Ring to reserve; recommended in high summer and required for the rest of the year.

Pont du Gard
The Pont du Gard (Gard Bridge), a Unesco World Heritage site, is an exceptionally well-preserved, three-tiered Roman aqueduct, once part of a 50km-long system of canals built about 19 BC to bring water from near Uzès to Nîmes. The scale is huge: the 35 arches of its 275m-long upper tier, running 50m above the River Gard, contain a watercourse designed to carry 20,000 cubic metres of water per day. Its largest construction blocks weigh more than five tonnes.

From car parks on either bank of the River Gard, you can walk along the road bridge, built in 1743 and running parallel with the aqueduct's lower tier. The best view of the aqueduct is from upstream, beside the river, where you can swim on hot days.

You won't be alone; the complex receives well over a million visitors each year, averaging a horrendous 15,000 or so daily in high summer.

There's a **museum** (admission €6) – with captions in English – featuring the bridge, aqueduct and the role of water in Roman society, a 25-minute large-screen **film** (€3), with an English version, and **Ludo** (€4.50), a children's activity play area.

You can walk, for free, **Mémoires de Garrigue**, a 1.4km trail with interpretive signs that winds through this typical Mediterranean bush and scrubland – though you'll need the explanatory booklet in English (€4) to get the most out of it.

A combination ticket (adult/child €10/8) gives access to all three activities with a free walking trail guidebook thrown in. A family ticket (€20) gives the same concession to two adults and up to four children.

A spectacular free **light show** (nightly Jul & Aug, Fri & Sat Jun & Sep) beams out into the summer night sky. From mid-June to mid-September, if there are enough takers, it's

---

BUBBLE, BUBBLE...
Perrier water is H_2O, injected carbon dioxide, minute traces of mineral that you probably get in your diet anyway, and that's it. But thanks to one of the world's slickest marketing operations, it sells more than 400 million bottles every year in France alone.

Its bottling and bottle manufacturing plant occupies the equivalent of 150 football pitches. Here's automated industry on the grand scale. A green hillock of pulverised glass (crushed from those empty bottles that you gently ease into the recycling container) is fed into furnaces that transform the molten goo back into little green bottles. On the vast floor of the bottling plant, ranks of bottles clank and shuffle along feeder lines like soldiers in formation. Once they're filled and boxed, driverless fork lift trucks carry them in a slow-moving ballet across the shop floor to where metal claws shake out giant sheets of plastic, billowing like spinnakers and envelop them in bales. Amazingly, the whole operation is controlled and monitored by no more than eight workers.

possible to walk the bridge's topmost tier (€6) with a guide.

If, like many, you simply want to enjoy the bridge, head on down. You can walk about for free around the clock, though the car parks close between 1am and 6am.

GETTING THERE & AWAY

The Pont du Gard is 21km northeast of Nîmes, 26km west of Avignon and 12km southeast of Uzès. Buses to/from each town normally stop 1km north of the bridge beside the Auberge Blanche. In summer, some make a diversion to the Pont du Gard car park. There are five buses daily from Nîmes and three from Avignon.

The extensive car parks on each bank of the river cost a whopping €5 (reimbursed if you sign on for the combination or family ticket).

River Gard

The wild, unpredictable River Gard descends from the Cévennes mountains. Torrential rains can raise the water level by as much as 5m in a flash. During long dry spells, by contrast, it sometimes almost disappears.

The river has sliced itself a meandering 22km gorge (Les Gorges du Gardon) through the hills from **Russan** to the village of **Collias**, about 6km upstream from the Pont du Gard. The GR6 trail runs beside it most of the way.

In Collias, 4km west of the D981, **Kayak Vert** (☎ 04 66 22 80 76; www.canoefrance.com/gardon) and **Canoë Le Tourbillon** (☎ 04 66 22 85 54; www .canoe-le-tourbillon.com), both based near the village bridge, rent out kayaks and canoes.

You can paddle 7km down to the Pont du Gard (€18 per person, two hours), or arrange to be dropped upstream at Russan, from where there's a great descent back through Gorges du Gardon (€30, full day), usually possible only between March and mid-June, when the river is high enough.

Uzès

pop 8400

Uzès is a laid-back little hill town 25km northeast of Nîmes. With its faithfully restored Renaissance façades, impressive Duché (Ducal Palace), ancient towers and narrow, semipedestrianised streets flanked by art galleries, craft and antique shops, it's a charming place for a brief wander.

The **tourist office** (☎ 04 66 22 68 88; www.uzes -tourisme.com; ☽ 9am-6pm Mon-Fri, 10am-1pm & 2-5pm Sat & Sun Jun-Sep, 9am-12.30pm & 2-6pm Mon-Fri, 10am-1pm Sat Oct-May) is on place Albert I, beside the ring road and just outside the old quarter.

SIGHTS & ACTIVITIES

The tourist office carries a useful free pamphlet in English, *Tour of the Historic Town*. Whether you follow this guided walk or not, let your steps take you through **Place aux Herbes**, Uzès' shady, arcaded central square, with its odd angles.

The **Duché** (☎ 04 66 22 18 96; ☽ 10am-1pm & 2-6.30pm Jul–mid-Sep, 10am-noon & 2-6pm mid-Sep–Jun) is a fortified chateau that has been the Dukes of Uzès' for more than 1000 years. Altered almost continuously from the 11th to 18th century, it has fine period furniture, tapestries and paintings. You can take the French-language one-hour **guided tour** (adult/child €12/9) or wander at will around the **keep** (€7).

Close by, just off rue Port Royal, is the beautifully landscaped **Jardin Médiéval** (Medieval Garden; admission €3; ☽ 10.30am-12.30pm & 2-6pm daily Jul & Aug, 2-6pm Mon-Fri, 10.30am-12.30pm & 2-6pm Sat & Sun Apr-Jun & Sep, 2-5pm daily Oct).

Musée du Bonbon (☎ 04 66 22 74 39; Pont des Charrettes; adult/child €4.50/2.50; ☽ 10am-7pm daily Jul-Sep, 10am-1pm & 2-6pm Tue-Sun Oct-Dec & Feb-Jun) is the place for a little indulgence. As a plaque at the entrance declares, 'This museum is dedicated to all who have devoted their lives to a slightly guilty passion – greed'. Signs at this shrine to sticky sweets are multilingual and you come away with a copious goody bag.

FESTIVALS & EVENTS

Uzès positively reeks on 24 June, the date of the **Foire à l'Ail** (Garlic Fair), while the third Sunday in January sees a full-blown **Truffle Fair**. The town is also renowned for its **Nuits Musicales d'Uzès**, an international festival of baroque music held in the second half of July.

SHOPPING

At the splendid **Maison de la Truffe** (27 place aux Herbes), it's truffles with everything – adding aroma to chocolate, steeped in oil, bagged with rice and much more.

GETTING THERE & AWAY

The bus station – grandly named and in fact merely a bus stop – is on av de la Libération, beside Banque Populaire. Buses running between Avignon (€8.40, one hour) and Alès (€7, 50 minutes) call by three to four times daily. There are also at least five daily services to/from Nîmes (€6.20, 45 minutes).

ALÈS & AROUND

pop 41,100

Alès, 45km from Nîmes, 70km from Montpellier and snuggled against the River Gard, is the Gard *département*'s second-largest town. Coal was mined here from the 13th century, when monks first dug into the surrounding hills, until the last pit closed in 1986.

The pedestrianised heart of town, having long ago shed its sooty past, is pleasant, if unexciting. Gateway to the Cévennes and bright with flowers in summer, Alès is also a convenient base for visiting a quartet of unique exhibitions close by.

The **tourist office** (☎ 04 66 52 32 15; tourisme@ville-ales.net; place Hôtel de Ville; ☒ 9am-7pm Mon-Sat, 9am-noon Sun Jul & Aug, 9am-noon & 1.30-5.30pm Mon-Sat Sep-Jun) occupies a modern building set into the shell of a baroque chapel.

Sights & Activities

From April to October the little **Train à Vapeur des Cévennes** (Cévennes steam train; ☎ 04 66 60 59 00; adult/child one-way €8.50/6, return €11/7; ☒ daily Apr–mid-Sep, Tue-Sun mid-Sep–Oct) takes 40 minutes to chug the 13km between St-Jean du Gard and Anduze via the Bambouseraie, making four return trips each day.

MINE TÉMOIN

Mine Témoin (☎ 04 66 30 45 15; chemin de la Cité Ste-Marie; adult/child €6.70/4; ☒ 10am-6pm Jul & Aug, 9am-5pm Jun, 9am-11am & 2.30-4pm Apr, May & Sep–mid-Nov) in Alès is no museum. Don a safety helmet and take the cage down an actual mine. Preceded by a 20-minute video (in French), the one-hour **guided tour** (option in English, July to mid-August, if you ring to reserve; at other times, ask for the free pamphlet in English) leads you along 700m of underground galleries.

BAMBOUSERAIE DE PRAFRANCE

This huge, mature **bamboo grove** (☎ 04 66 61 70 47; adult/child €7.50/3.50; ☒ 9.30am-dusk Mar–mid-Nov), which celebrated its 150th birthday in 2006, was founded by a spice merchant who returned from the tropics. Here in Générargues, 12km southwest of Alès, 150 bamboo species sprout amid aquatic gardens, an Asian village and a green feng shui space. A fun way to get there is on the Cévennes steam train (left), which travels between St-Jean du Gard and Anduze.

MUSÉE DU DÉSERT

Musée du Désert (☎ 04 66 85 02 72; adult/child €4.50/3; ☒ 9.30am-7pm Jul & Aug, 9.30am-noon & 2-6pm Mar-Jun & Sep-Nov) portrays the way of life of the Camisards (see below), their persecution and clandestine resistance. It's in the charming hamlet of Le Mas Soubeyran, 5km north of the Bambouseraie.

LA CARACOLE

Here's one to make the kids squirm. **La Caracole** (☎ 04 66 25 65 70; www.lacaracole.fr; St-Florent sur Auzonnet; adult/child €5.30/3.50; ☒ visits 10.30am, 3pm, 4.30pm & 6pm daily Jul & Aug, 3pm & 4.30pm Wed &

THE CAMISARD REVOLT

Early in the 18th century, a guerrilla war raged through the Cévennes as Protestants took on Louis XIV's army. The revocation of the Edict of Nantes in 1685 removed rights that the Protestant Huguenots had enjoyed since 1598. Many emigrated, while others fled deep into the wild Cévennes, from where a local leader named Roland, only 22 at the time, led the resistance against the French army sent to crush them.

Poorly equipped but knowing every bush and hill of the countryside, the outlaws resisted for two years. They fought in their shirts – *camiso* in langue d'oc; thus their popular name, Camisards. Once the royal army gained the upper hand, the local population was either massacred or forced to flee. Roland was killed and most villages were methodically destroyed.

Each year, on the first Sunday of September, thousands of French Protestants meet at Roland's birthplace in Le Mas Soubeyran, a sleepy hamlet near the village of Mialet, just off the Corniche des Cévennes. It's now the Musée du Désert (above), which details the persecution of Protestants in the Cévennes between 1685 and the 1787 Edict of Tolerance, which marked the reintroduction of religious freedom.

Sun, Apr-Jun & Sep), with a cast of over 250,000, presents 'the astonishing, exciting world of the snail'. In fact, it's a snail farm with big ideas. There are sections on – oh yes – the snail in religion, the snail in art and the snail through the centuries. After the one-hour tour (in English and French), there's free sampling and the chance to buy a tin of two of former farm members embalmed in a variety of tempting sauces. It's 12km from Alés. Take the D904 northwards, direction Aubenas, then turn left onto the D59.

Sleeping & Eating

Camping la Croix Clémentine (☎ 04 66 86 52 69; www.clementine.fr in French; 2 people with car according to season €10.60-23; ☺ Apr–mid-Sep) This four-star camp site is in Cendras, 5km northwest of Alès. Sites, within or on the fringes of an oak wood, are shady.

Hôtel Durand (☎ 04 66 86 28 94; fax 04 66 30 52 68; 3 blvd Anatole France; s/d/tr €32/35/43; ☒) New owners have comprehensively renovated this modest choice, down a side street 100m east of Hôtel Le Riche. Its 17 rooms are all freshly painted and furnished and the three overlooking the small rear garden have air-con.

Hôtel Le Riche (☎ 04 66 86 00 33; www.leriche.fr in French; 42 place Pierre Sémard; s/d/tr €43/52/60; ☺ Sep-Jul; ☒ ☒) Parking €4. Opposite the train station, this hotel is highly recommended, as much for its fine **restaurant** (menus €18-48) as for its 19 pleasant, modern rooms.

Getting There & Away

BUS

From the **bus station** (place Pierre Sémard), south of the train station, one bus heads into the Cévennes to Florac (€12.50, 1¼ hours), daily except Sunday, and two to four serve Uzès (€7, 50 minutes), continuing to Avignon (€14.20, 1¾ hours). Five daily link Alès and Nîmes (€7.60, 1¼ hours).

TRAIN

There are up to 10 trains daily to/from Montpellier (€14, 1½ hours), some requiring a change in Nîmes (€7.90, 40 minutes). Three trains daily run between Alès and Mende (€16, 2¼ hours).

MONTPELLIER

pop 229,100

The 17th-century philosopher John Locke may have had one glass of Minervois wine too many when he wrote: 'I find it much better to go twise (sic) to Montpellier than once to the other world'. Paradise it ain't, but Montpellier, where students make up nearly a quarter of the population, is innovative, fast-growing, self-confident and a worthy rival to Toulouse for the title of southern France's most vital city. Every time we visit, there's some exciting new development afoot, designed to improve the quality of life of its inhabitants. These days, €425 million are being invested in a second metro line that will cut across this most pedestrian-friendly of cities, where more than 12,000 parking spaces around the centre encourage motorists to leave their cars behind.

History

Montpellier, one of the few cities in southern France without a Roman heritage, started lateish. Founded by the Counts of Toulouse, it's first mentioned in a written document in 985. By medieval times, it had become a prosperous city with trading links all over the Mediterranean. Its scholastic tradition is a long one: Europe's first medical school was founded here in the 12th century. The population swelled dramatically in the 1960s when many French settlers left independent Algeria and settled here.

Orientation

Montpellier's mostly pedestrianised historic centre, girdled by wide boulevards, has place de la Comédie at its heart.

Northeast of this square sits esplanade Charles de Gaulle, a pleasant, tree-lined promenade. To the east is Le Polygone, a vast shopping complex, and Antigone, a mammoth neoclassical housing project designed by the Spanish architect Ricardo Bofill.

Westwards, between rue de la Loge and Grand Rue Jean Moulin, sprawls the city's oldest quarter, a web of narrow alleys and fine *hôtels particuliers* (private mansions).

Information

BOOKSHOPS

Book in Bar (☎ 04 67 66 22 90; www.bookinbar.com in French; 8 rue du Bras de Fer) Large stock of new and second-hand books in English. Runs conversation exchanges and cultural events. Browse the British press for free.

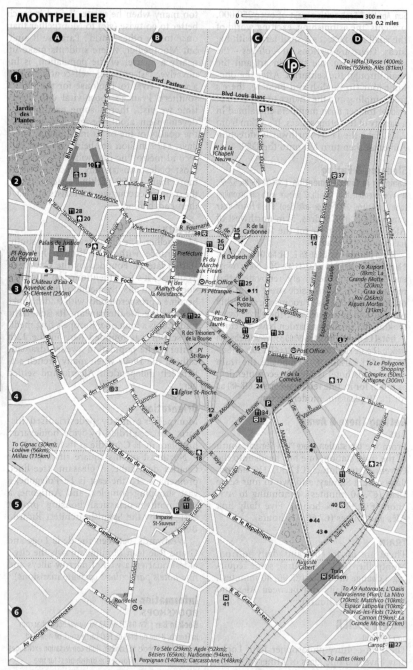

MONTPELLIER

0   300 m
0   0.2 miles

Bookshop (☎ 04 67 66 09 08; 4 rue de l'Université) Carries a good selection of novels and travel guides in English.

Les Cinq Continents (☎ 04 67 66 46 70; 20 rue Jacques Cœur) Specialist travel bookshop with an excellent stock of maps and travel literature including Lonely Planet guides.

INTERNET ACCESS
Dimension 4 Cybercafé (☎ 04 67 60 57 57; 11 rue des Balances; per hr €3; ☺ 10am-midnight)
Point Internet (☎ 04 67 54 57 60; 54 rue de l'Aiguillerie; per hr €1.60; ☺ 9.30am-midnight Mon-Sat, 10.30am-midnight Sun)

LAUNDRY
Lavasud (19 rue de l'Université; ☺ 7am-9pm)

POST
Main Post Office (13 place Rondelet)

TOURIST INFORMATION
Main Tourist Office (☎ 04 67 60 60 60; www.ot-mon tpellier.fr; ☺ 9am-6.30pm Mon-Fri, 10am-6pm Sat, 10am-1pm & 2-5pm Sun) At southern end of esplanade Charles de Gaulle.

Sights
HÔTELS PARTICULIERS
In the span of the 17th and 18th centuries, Montpellier's wealthier merchants built grand private mansions with large inner courtyards. Fine examples are **Hôtel de Varennes** (2 place Pétrarque), a harmonious blend of Romanesque and Gothic, and **Hôtel St-Côme** (Grand Rue Jean Moulin), the city's first anatomy theatre for medical students and nowadays its Chamber of Commerce. The 17th-century **Hôtel des Trésoriers de France** (7 rue

Jacques Cœur) today houses the Musée Languedocien (below). Within the old quarter are several other mansions, each marked by a descriptive plaque in French.

MUSEUMS
Musée Fabre (☎ 04 67 14 83 00; 39 blvd Bonne Nouvelle) is the city's cultural showpiece. Founded in 1825, it has one of France's richest collections of French, Italian, Flemish and Dutch works from the 16th century onwards. Undergoing radical renovation, it's expected to reopen in 2007.

Musée Languedocien (☎ 04 67 52 93 03; 7 rue Jacques Cœur; adult/student €6/5; ☺ 3-6pm Mon-Sat Jul & Aug, 2.30-5.30pm Mon-Sat Sep-Jun) displays the area's rich archaeological finds as well as *objets d'art* from the 16th to 19th centuries.

Musée du Vieux Montpellier (☎ 04 67 66 02 94; 2 place Pétrarque; admission free; ☺ 9.30am-noon & 1.30-5pm Tue-Sat), a storehouse of the city's memorabilia from the Middle Ages to the Revolution, is upstairs in the Hôtel de Varennes.

Musée Atger (☎ 04 67 66 27 77; 2 rue de l'École de Médecine; admission free; ☺ 1.30-5.45pm Mon, Wed & Fri Sep-Jul), housed within the medical faculty, displays a striking collection of French, Italian and Flemish drawings.

AROUND PLACE ROYALE DU PEYROU
At the eastern end of this wide, tree-lined esplanade is the **Arc de Triomphe** (1692); at its western limit, the **Château d'Eau**. Leading from this hexagonal water tower is the 18th-century **Aqueduc de St-Clément**, under which there's an organic food and second-hand books market on Saturday and

---

MONTPELLIER CITY PASS

The **City Pass** (per day/2 days/3 days €12/18/22, children half price) gives admission to a number of sites, unlimited bus and metro travel and a place on a guided walking tour (below). Sold at the tourist office, it also entitles you to reduced admission at several other sites and spectacles.

---

pétanque (a game not unlike lawn bowls played with heavy metal balls on a sandy pitch; also called *boules*) most afternoons. To the north, off blvd Henri IV, is the **Jardin des Plantes** (1593), France's oldest botanic garden. Opposite is **Cathédrale St-Pierre**, with its disproportionately tall 15th-century porch.

Tours

The tourist office offers two-hour **walking tours** (€6.50; ☉ in English 3.30pm Sat Oct-Jun, more frequently in summer, in French 10am & 5pm daily Jul & Aug, 5pm daily Sep, 3pm Wed, Sat & Sun Oct-Jun) of the old town. Ring to reserve.

Festivals & Events

Montpellier hosts **Le Printemps des Comédiens** (☎ 04 67 63 66 67; www.printempsdescomediens.com in French), a popular theatre festival, in June and **Montpellier Danse** (☎ 08 00 60 07 40; www.montpellierdanse.com in French), a two-week international dance festival in June/July. The **Festival de Radio France et Montpellier** (☎ 04 67 02 02 01; www.festivalradiofrancemontpellier.com in French) in the second half of July brings in top-notch classical music and jazz. Most events are free.

Sleeping

The closest camp sites are around the suburb of Lattes, some 4km south of the city centre.

L'Oasis Palavasienne (☎ 04 67 15 11 61; www.oasis-palavasienne.com; rte de Palavas; site according to season €16-28; ☉ mid-May–Aug; ☒) This shady camp site, 4.5km from town, has a large pool. Take bus No 17 from the bus station.

Auberge de Jeunesse (☎ 04 67 60 32 22; montpellier@fuaj.org; 2 impasse de la Petite Corraterie; B&B €14.40; ☉ mid-Jan–mid-Dec) Montpellier's HI-affiliated youth hostel is just off rue des Écoles Laïques. Rooms sleep two to six and there's a small, shaded garden. Take the tram to the Louis Blanc stop.

Hôtel des Étuves (☎ 04 67 60 78 19; www.hoteldesetuves.fr; 24 rue des Étuves; s €23-42, d €37-42) This welcoming, 13-room family hotel creeps around a spiral staircase like a vine. Room two, one of six overlooking the quiet pedestrian street, has a bath while the rest are equipped with showers.

Hôtel le Mistral (☎ 04 67 58 45 25; www.hotel-le-mistral.com in French; 25 rue Boussairolles; s €39-42, d €41-48.50) Parking €8. Behind its 19th-century façade, this spruce, friendly 20-room place offers great value and is handy for both the station and heart of town. Some rooms have small, wrought-iron balconies.

Hôtel de la Comédie (☎ 04 67 58 43 64; hotel delacomedie@cegetel.net; 1bis rue Baudin; s €42-47, d €52-69; ☒) This welcoming, family-run place, just off place de la Comédie, is a favourite with visiting musicians and theatre troupes. All 20 rooms have air-con and heating and are double glazed.

Hôtel Ulysse (☎ 04 67 02 02 30; www.hotel-ulysse.com; 338 av St-Maur; s €46-55, d €58-68) Parking €5. The Ulysse, in a quiet neighbourhood no more than a 10-minute walk from place de la Comédie, has a small garden and attractive breakfast salon. Each of its 23 rooms, all with bathtubs, is decorated individually and pleasingly furnished in wood and wrought iron.

Hôtel du Palais (☎ 04 67 60 47 38; www.hoteldupalais-montpellier.fr; 3 rue du Palais des Guilhem; s €54, d €59-71; ☒) All 26 rooms of this delightful hotel overlooking a quiet square are decorated by a local artist and tastefully and individually furnished.

our pick Hôtel Le Guilhem (☎ 04 67 52 90 90; www.hotel-le-guilhem.com; 18 rue Jean-Jacques Rousseau; s €72-79, d €83-136; ☒ ☒ ☐) Occupying a couple of interconnecting 16th-century buildings, Hôtel Le Guilhem's 35 guest rooms are exquisitely and individually furnished. Nearly all have views of the cathedral and overlook the tranquil garden of nearby Restaurant Le Petit Jardin. Room 100 (€136) has its own little terrace and garden. All rooms have bathtubs and some have sepa-

---

SLEEPING & DRIVING

Most hotels have a special arrangement with municipal car parks that allows guests to leave their cars overnight for €6. Ask for the relevant form at reception.

---

rate toilets. It's wise to reserve at any time of year since Le Guilhem has its faithful clientele who return again and again.

Eating

You'll find plenty of cheap and cheerful eateries on rue de l'Université, rue des Écoles Laïques and the streets interlinking them.

Chez Fels (3 Grand Rue Jean Moulin; ☻ 8am-7.30pm Mon-Sat) Just off place de la Comédie, this hole-in-the-wall sandwich shop does the crunchiest of baby baguettes, stuffed with salad and Alsatian goodies.

Tripti Kulai (☎ 04 67 66 30 51; 20 rue Jacques Cœur; salads €9.50, menus €11.50-16; ☻ noon-9.30pm Mon-Sat; Ⓥ) Barrel-vaulted and cosy, this popular vegetarian place stands out for the inventiveness of many of its dishes. You could drink a tea a day for more than a month and still not exhaust their selection.

Welcomedia (☎ 04 67 02 82 65; place de la Comédie; daily special €12; ☻ 8am-1am Mon-Sat) This exciting new bar and bistro could figure just as well within the Drinking section. In the southwest corner of the Opéra-Comédie theatre, it's smart, stylish, does great regional wines by the glass and has a terrace that lords it over the square.

Roule Ma Poule (☎ 04 67 60 36 15; 20 place Candolle; menus €15-19) Like most places in the area, it pulls in a mainly student crowd with its decent, uncomplicated fare. Happy-go-lucky and with rapid service, it has a large terrace that spills over the square and does a filling midday *formule rapide* (similar to a *menu* but allows choice of whichever two of three courses you want; €12.50 including coffee).

Restaurant Cerdan (☎ 04 67 60 86 96; 8 rue Collot; menus €13.50-34; ☻ lunch & dinner Tue-Fri, dinner Sat, dinner Mon) This much garlanded family restaurant carries a good list of local wines and offers five different *menus*, each rich in local fare with a leavening of dishes from Normandy, Mme Cerdan's home region.

Le Ban des Gourmands (☎ 04 67 65 00 85; 5 place Carnot; menu €30, mains €16-20; ☻ lunch & dinner year-round, Tue-Fri & dinner Sat Sep-Jul) South of the train station and a favourite of locals in the know, this appealing restaurant, run by a young family team, serves delicious local cuisine.

Caves Jean Jaurès (☎ 04 67 60 27 33; 3 rue Collot; menu €18, mains €12-15; ☻ lunch & dinner Tue-Sat, Sun dinner & Mon dinner) Scan this attractive restaurant's range of tasty dishes on the

chalkboard that the waiter props against a nearby table. A glass of wine? Select from the bottles of the day on the bar counter. Rather more? Pick from the shelves; every bottle has its price marked and the range is superlative.

Restaurant Verdi (☎ 04 67 58 68 55; 10 rue Aristide Olivier; menus €18-26, mains €18-20; ☻ Mon-Sat) This restaurant does delicious Italian fare, especially fish dishes, in an Italian ambience (walls are plastered with posters relating to the eponymous Verdi). It has an outstanding wine list. Two doors away, **Pizzeria Aïda** (menu €14.50) serves pasta, pizzas and salads from the same kitchen and in a more informal setting.

La Diligence (☎ 04 67 66 12 21; 2 place Pétrarque; lunch menu €15, dinner menus €20-59; ☻ lunch & dinner Tue-Fri, dinner Sat & dinner Mon) Dine beneath attractive vaults and arches and savour the creative cuisine, impressive wine cellar and elegant rear patio overlooked by a gallery of the Hôtel de Varennes.

Le Petit Jardin (☎ 04 67 60 78 78; 20 rue Jean-Jacques Rousseau; mains €22-45, mains €21-28; ☻ Tue-Sun Feb-Dec) 'The Little Garden' is just that: a restaurant offering imaginative cuisine, its big bay windows overlooking a shady, fairytale greenness at the rear, where you could be 100km from Montpellier's bustle. The lunch *menu* (€14) is excellent value.

ourpick Tamarillos (☎ 04 67 60 06 00; 2 place Marché aux Fleurs; menus €50-80; ☻ Tue-Sat & dinner Mon) 'A cuisine of fruit and flowers' is Tamarillos' motto, and indeed all dishes, sweet or savoury, have fruit as an ingredient or main element. Dine on the terrace or inside, where the décor's part of the experience. It's bright with fresh flowers, palm fronds nudge your elbow and apples bob in giant vases. Pace yourself; chef Philippe Chapon is *'double champion de France de dessert'* and taught a young Gordon Ramsay his pastrycooking. The lunchtime *formule de midi* (€18 to €29) makes this gourmet place accessible to travellers on more modest budgets.

SELF-CATERING

There's a farmers market every Sunday morning on av Samuel de Champlain in the Antigone complex.

The city's other food markets:

Castellane Market (rue de la Loge) The biggest market.

Laissac Market (rue Anatole France)

Drinking

All summer long, place de la Comédie is alive with cafés where you can drink, grab a quick bite and watch street entertainers strut their stuff. Smaller, more intimate squares include place Jean Jaurès and place St-Ravy.

L'Heure Bleue (1 rue de la Carbonnerie; ✆ Tue-Sun) At this tea salon, you can sip Earl Grey to a background of classical music. It also does light lunches (around €12) with plenty of choice for vegetarians.

With more than 60,000 student residents, Montpellier has a multitude of places to drink and dance. You'll find dense concentrations around rue En-Gondeau, off Grand Rue Jean Moulin, around place Jean Jaurès and around the intersection of rue de l'Université and rue Candolle.

Entertainment

To find out what's on where, pick up the free weekly *Sortir à Montpellier*, available around town and at the tourist office.

Tickets for Montpellier's numerous theatres are sold at the box office of the **Opéra-Comédie** (☎ 04 67 60 05 45; place de la Comédie). **Le Corum** (☎ 04 67 61 67 61; Esplanade Charles de Gaulle) is the city's prime concert venue.

Rockstore (☎ 04 67 06 80 00; 20 rue de Verdun) In the heart of town, you'll recognise this longstanding discothèque by the rear of a classic American '70s car protruding above the entrance.

There's a critical mass of discos outside town in Espace Latipolia, about 10km from Montpellier on rte de Palavas heading towards the coast:

La Nitro (☎ 04 67 22 45 82) Thumps out techno and house.

Matchico (☎ 04 67 64 19 20) Retro music.

L'Amigo, a night bus (€2.40), does a circuit of Espace Latipolia and other dance venues on the periphery of town, leaving Le Corum at midnight, 12.45am and 1.30am, returning at 2.30am, 3.30am and (yawn!) 5am, Thursday to Saturday.

To tune into the active men-on-men scene (many reckon Montpellier is France's most gay-friendly city), call by the following places:

Café de la Mer (☎ 04 67 60 79 65; 5 place du Marché aux Fleurs) Just around the corner, where the friendly staff will arm you with a map of gay venues.

Le Heaven (1 rue Delpech) An exclusive men's bar that gets busy from 8pm.

Le Village (☎ 04 67 60 29 05; 3 rue Fournarié) A shop specialising in queer gear.

Getting There & Away

AIR

Montpellier's **airport** (☎ 04 67 20 85 00; www .montpellier.aeroport.fr) is 8km southeast of town. Air France flies at least four times daily to both Paris (Orly) and Paris (Roissy). Ryanair operates daily to/from London (Stansted).

BUS

The **bus station** (☎ 04 67 92 01 43; rue du Grand St-Jean) is an easy walk from the train station. **Hérault Transport** (☎ 08 25 34 01 34) runs hourly buses to La Grande Motte (No 106; €1.40, 35 minutes) via Carnon from Odysseum at the end of the tram line. Some services continue to Aigues Mortes (€6.30, 1½ hours, five daily) and, in July and August, Stes-Maries de la Mer in the Camargue (€9.80, two hours).

Eurolines (☎ 04 67 58 57 59; 8 rue de Verdun) has buses to Barcelona (€31, five hours) and most European destinations. **Linebus** (☎ 04 67 58 95 00) mainly operates services to destinations in Spain.

TRAIN

Major destinations from Montpellier's two-storey train station include Paris' Gare de Lyon by TGV (€74.20 to €83, 3½ hours, 10 daily), Carcassonne (€20.20, 1½ hours, six daily), Millau (€23.10, 1½ hours, two daily) and Perpignan (€20.50, two hours, frequent).

More than 20 trains daily go northwards to Nîmes (€7.90, 30 minutes) and southwards to Narbonne (€13.40, one hour) via Sète (€4.80), Agde (€7.90) and Béziers (€10.40).

Getting Around

TO/FROM THE AIRPORT

A **shuttle bus** (☎ 08 25 34 01 34) runs between the airport and bus station (€4.80, 15 minutes, nine to 11 daily; until works on the new metro line are completed, it terminates at metro stop Léon Blum).

BICYCLE

Montpellier encourages cycling and has over 100km of bicycle track. **TaM Vélo** (☎ 04 67 22 87 22; 27 rue Maguelone; ✆ 9am-7pm Mon-Sat,

LANGUEDOC-ROUSSILLON

9am-12.30pm & 2-7pm Sun), an admirable urban initiative, rents town bikes and electric bikes per hour/half-day/full day for €1.50/3/6. You'll need to leave a deposit (cheque, credit card or cash) of €150/300 per bike/electric bike.

PUBLIC TRANSPORT
Take a ride, even just for fun, on Montpellier's hi-tech, high-speed, leave-your-car-at-home tram. Like city buses, it's run by **TaM** (☎ 04 67 22 87 87; www.tam-way.com in French; 6 rue Jules Ferry) and runs until midnight. Regular buses run until about 8.30pm daily.

Single-journey tickets, valid for bus or tram, cost €1.30. A one-day pass/10-ticket *carnet* costs €3.10/10.50. Pick them up from newsagents or any tram station.

TAXI
Ring **Taxi Bleu** (☎ 04 67 03 20 00) or **Taxi 2000** (☎ 04 67 04 00 60).

AROUND MONTPELLIER
The closest beaches are at **Palavas-les-Flots**, 12km south of the city and Montpellier-on-Sea in summer. Take TaM bus No 131 from the Port Marianne tram stop. Heading north on the coastal road towards Carnon, you stand a good chance of seeing flamingos hoovering the shallows of the lagoons on either side of the coastal D21.

Carnon itself comes out fairly low in the charm stakes despite its huge marina. Better to continue hugging the coast along the D59 (Le Petit Travers), bordered by several kilometres of white sand beach, uncrowded and without a kiosk or café in sight.

Further northwards, about 20km southeast of Montpellier, is **La Grande Motte**. Purpose-built on the grand scale back in the 1960s to plug the tourist drain southwards into Spain, its architecture, considered revolutionary at the time, now comes over as fairly heavy and leaden, contrasting with the more organic growth of adjacent **Grau du Roi**, deeper rooted and a still-active fishing port.

Aigues Mortes, on the western edge of the Camargue, is another 11km eastwards.

SÈTE
pop 40,200
Twenty-six kilometres to the southwest of Montpellier, Sète is France's largest Mediterranean fishing port and biggest commercial entrepôt after Marseille. Established by Louis XIV in the 17th century, it prospered as the harbours of Aigues Mortes and Narbonne, to north and south, were cut off from the sea by silt deposits.

Huddled east of Mont St-Clair, from where there's a great panorama, Sète has lots in its favour: waterways and canals, beaches, outdoor cafés and shoals of fish and seafood restaurants.

The **tourist office** (☎ 04 67 74 71 71; www.ot-sete.fr; 60 Grand' Rue Mario Roustan; ⏰ 9.30am-7.30pm daily Jul & Aug, 9.30am-6pm Mon-Fri, 9.30am-5.30pm Sat & Sun Apr-Jun, 9.30am-6pm Mon-Fri, 9.30am-12.30pm & 2-5.30pm Sat & Sun Sep-Mar) rents multilingual **audioguides** (for 1/2 routes €7/12) covering six walks in and around town.

Sète was the birthplace of the symbolist poet Paul Valéry (1871–1945), whose remains lie in the **Cimetière Marin**, inspiration for and title of his most famous poem. Overlooking this cemetery is **Musée Paul Valéry** (☎ 04 67 46 20 98; rue François Desnoyer; adult/child €3/1.50; ⏰ 10am-noon & 2-6pm daily Jul & Aug, Wed-Mon Sep-Jun), which hosts temporary exhibitions and has one room devoted to the poet.

The town was also the childhood home of singer and infinitely more accessible poet Georges Brassens (1921–81), whose mellow voice still speaks on the audioguide at multimedia **Espace Georges Brassens** (☎ 04 67 53 32 77; 67 blvd Camille Blanc; adult/child €5/2; ⏰ 10am-noon & 2-6pm Tue-Sun). Ask for the English synopsis.

In July and August, **Sète Croisières** (☎ 04 67 46 00 46; www.sete-croisieres.com in French; quai Général Durand) does a variety of boat trips, including a one-hour **harbour tour** (adult/child €10/5), leaving from Pont de la Savonnerie.

Over a long weekend in mid-July, Sète celebrates **La Fête de la St-Pierre**, or Fête des Pêcheurs (Fisherfolks Festival). The **Fête de la St-Louis** fills six frantic days around 25 August with *joutes nautiques*, where participants in competing boats try to knock each other into the water.

Sleeping & Eating
Auberge de Jeunesse (☎ 04 67 53 46 68; fax 04 67 51 34 01; rue Général Revest; dm €15.25; ⏰ mid-Jan–mid-Dec) Scarcely a kilometre northwest of the tourist office, it enjoys a lovely wooded site with great views over town and harbour.

Most hotel options are beside La Corniche, running alongside the beaches west of the port.

Hôtel la Conga (☎ 04 67 53 02 57; www.conga .fr: plage de la Corniche; r €32-49 Oct-Jun, €45-61 Jul-Sep; ⊠) Parking free. This pleasant 19-room hotel is beside the corniche, overlooking the beach, 2.25km west of the port area. You'll need to reserve at its popular restaurant **La Table de Jean** (menus €12-25), justifiably famous for its fish dishes and worth a visit in its own right.

Les Demoiselles Dupuy (☎ 04 67 74 03 46; 4 quai Maximin Licciardi; mains €10-18; ♥ Thu-Tue) This tiny, vital place, crowded and rough and ready, serves up deliciously fresh seafood at economical prices in unpretentious surroundings. The oysters, shucked before you, come straight from Les Demoiselles Dupuy's own offshore beds.

Au Bord du Canal (☎ 04 67 51 98 39; 9 quai Maximin Licciardi; menu €28; ♥ Tue-Sun) One among an infinity of canalside choices, it prepares the freshest of fish and does a splendid midday grill (€15) of whatever with fins that takes the chef's fancy that day.

Getting There & Away

Both **Comanav** (☎ 04 67 46 68 00) and **Comarit** (☎ 04 67 80 75 40) have offices at the port and run ferries to Morocco from quai d'Alger about every four days.

AGDE
pop 20,300

Originally a Phoenician, then a Greek settlement at the mouth of the River Hérault, Agde (from *agathos*, Greek for 'good') is a small fishing port with an attractive inland old quarter. Both **Bateaux du Soleil** (☎ 04 67 94 08 79) and **Bateau Millésime** (☎ 04 67 01 71 93) do short boat trips along the Canal du Midi, which joins the River Hérault just upstream from the old quarter. The tourist office sells tickets.

The **tourist office** (☎ 04 67 94 29 68; www .agde-herault.com in French; ♥ 9am-7pm daily Jul & Aug, 9am-noon & 2-6pm Mon-Sat Sep-Jun) is at 1 place Molière.

The dark grey basalt of older buildings, such as the fortresslike, mainly 12th-century **Cathédrale St-Étienne**, motivated Marco Polo to describe the town as the 'black pearl of the Mediterranean'.

Twenty-room **Hôtel le Donjon** (☎ 04 67 94 12 32; www.hotelledonjon.com; place Jean Jaurès; r €42-81; ⊠), in its time a convent, then coaching inn (today's garage was once its stable), is

full of character and particularly well maintained (the owner's an expert handyman). Rooms are large and attractively decorated in typical Midi blues and yellows. Parking is free.

A battery of restaurants with terraces splay along the quayside.

ourpick Lou Pescadou (☎ 04 67 21 17 10; 18 rue Chassefière; menu €15) has been serving the same magnificent value take-it-or-leave-it five-course *menu* (€15) ever since 1965. First, the do-it-yourself soup: smear a slice of toast with a clove of garlic, sprinkle on grated cheese and dunk it in the rich, fishy broth. Next, a steaming plate, piled high, of mussels. There follows a big bowl of *pâté de campagne* (country-style pâté), left on the table with no-one looking or caring how much you dollop onto your plate. Then it's a giant grilled fish or slab of steak staring up at you from the plate. For dessert, there are orange pancakes. Come back tomorrow, next week, next year and repeat the experience; Lou Pescadou is one of life's few constants.

Buses (€2) ply the 6km route at least hourly to the modern tourist resort of **Le Cap d'Agde**, famed for its long beaches and large nudist colony – a little township in itself with more than 20,000 bare bodies in high season.

BÉZIERS
pop 71,400

Béziers, first settled by the Phoenicians, became an important military post in Roman times. It was almost completely destroyed in 1209 during the Albigensian Crusade, when some 20,000 'heretics', many seeking refuge in the cathedral, were slaughtered. In happier times, the local tax collector Paul Riquet (1604–80) moved heaven and earth to build the Unesco World Heritage-listed **Canal du Midi**, a 240km-long marvel of engineering with its aqueducts and more than 100 locks, enabling cargo vessels to sail from the Atlantic to the Mediterranean without having to circumnavigate Spain. There's a fine statue to Béziers' most famous son on allées Jean-Jaurès, a wide, leafy esplanade at the heart of the town.

The **tourist office** (☎ 04 67 76 84 00; www.beziers -tourisme.fr; 29 av St-Saens; ♥ 9am-7pm Mon-Sat, 10am-1pm & 3-6pm Sun Jul & Aug, 9am-noon & 2-6pm Mon-Sat Sep-Jun) is in the Palais des Congrès.

Fortified **Cathédrale St-Nazaire** (☼ 9am-noon & 2.30-5.30pm), surrounded by narrow alleys, is typical of the area, with massive towers, an imposing façade and a huge 14th-century rose window.

Musée du Biterrois (☎ 04 67 36 81 61; place St Jacques; adult/child €2.45/1.70; ☼ 10am-6pm Tue-Sun Jul & Aug, 9am-noon & 2-5pm or 6pm Tue-Sun Sep-Jun) is a well displayed and illuminated museum of the town's history, its largest sections devoted to Roman artefacts and wine-making.

Popular annual events include the week-long **Festa d'Oc**, a celebration of Mediterranean music and dance, in late July, and the **féria** around 15 August.

NARBONNE
pop 48,000

Once a coastal port but now a whole 13km inland because of silting-up, Narbonne in its time was capital of Gallia Narbonensis and one of the principal Roman cities in Gaul.

The **tourist office** (☎ 04 68 65 15 60; place Roger Salengro; ☼ 8am-7pm Mon-Sat, 9.30am-12.30pm Sun Jun–mid-Sep, 8.30am-noon & 2-6pm Mon-Sat mid-Sep–May) is just northwest of the massive cathedral.

The splendid **Cathédrale St-Just** (entry on rue Armand Gauthier; ☼ 10am-7pm Jul-Sep, 9am-noon & 2-6pm Oct-Jun) is, in fact, no more than its towers and a soaring choir (at 41m, one of France's highest), construction having stopped in the early 14th century. The Notre Dame de Bethlehem ambulatory chapel has a haunting alabaster Virgin and Child and fine, much knocked about polychrome stone carving. The **treasury** (admission €2.20) has a beautiful Flemish tapestry of the Creation while grotesque gargoyles peer down upon the 16th-century **cloister**.

Adjoining the cathedral to the south and facing place de l'Hôtel de Ville, the fortified **Palais des Archevêques** (Archbishops' Palace) includes the **Donjon Gilles Aycelin** (admission €2.20; ☼ 10am-6pm Jul-Sep, 9am-noon & 2-6pm Oct-Jun), a large, square 13th-century keep.

The **Hôtel de Ville**, its mock-Renaissance 19th-century façade designed by Viollet-le-Duc, is home to Narbonne's **Musée d'Art** and **Musée Archéologique**, the latter with an impressive collection of Roman mosaics and paintings on stucco. Nearby is the **Horreum**, an underground gallery of Gallo-Roman shops. A combined ticket (adult/child €5.20/3.70) gives access to all three sites.

Take in too Narbonne's imposing Art Nouveau **covered market**, a colourful place to stock up on food and itself an architectural jewel.

Just off the A9, 15km south of Narbonne, is the **Réserve Africaine de Sigean** (☎ 04 68 48 20 20; www.reserveafricainesigean.fr; adult/child €22/18; ☼ 9am-4.30pm or 6.30pm according to season), where lions, tigers and other 'safari' animals live in semiliberty. If you arrive by bike or on foot, there's free – in a manner of speaking – transport around the reserve. Allow at least half a day. From the A9, take exit 39.

CARCASSONNE
pop 46,200

From afar, Carcassonne looks like some fairy-tale medieval city. Bathed in late-afternoon sunshine and highlighted by dark clouds, La Cité, as the old walled city is known, is truly breathtaking. But once you're inside, La Cité loses its magic and mystery. Luring an estimated 3.5 million visitors annually, it can be a tourist hell in high summer. This said, you'll have to be fairly stone-hearted not to be moved.

But Carcassonne is more than La Cité. The Ville Basse (Lower Town), altogether more tranquil and established in the 13th century, is a more modest stepsister to camp Cinderella up the hill and also merits a browse.

History
The hill on which La Cité stands has been fortified across the centuries – by Gauls, Romans, Visigoths, Moors and Franks. In the 13th century, the walls protected one of the major Cathar strongholds (see p803). Once Roussillon was annexed to France in 1659, Carcassonne, no longer a frontier town, sank into slow decline. By the 19th century La Cité was simply crumbling away. It was rescued by the elaborate intervention of Viollet-le-Duc, who also set his controversial stamp upon, for example, the cathedrals of Notre Dame in Paris and Vézelay in the Massif Central.

Orientation
The River Aude separates the Ville Basse from the Cité, up on a hill 500m to the southeast. Pedestrianised rue Georges Clemenceau leads from the train station and Canal du Midi southwards through the heart of the lower town.

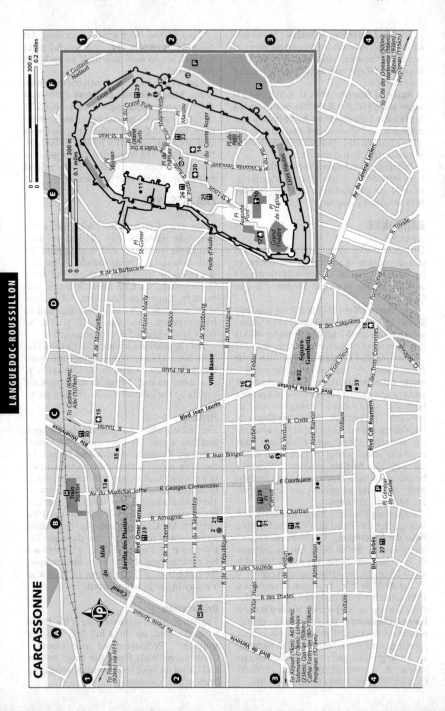

CARCASSONNE

LANGUEDOC-ROUSSILLON

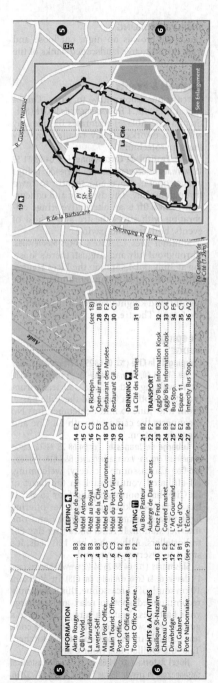

Information

INTERNET ACCESS

Alerte Rouge (73 rue de Verdun, Ville Basse; per hr €3; ⏲ 10am-11pm Mon-Sat) Buy a drink and you can wi-fi for free for an hour. And here's a rare internet café that actually does great coffee.

C@ll World (32 rue de la République, Ville Basse; per hr €3.50; ⏲ 9am-10pm Mon-Sat, 2-10pm Sun Jun-Sep; 9am-12.30pm & 2-8pm Mon-Sat, 2-10pm Sun Oct-May)

LAUNDRY

La Lavandière (31 rue Aimé Ramon, Ville Basse; ⏲ 8am-7pm Mon-Sat)

Laverie-Self (63 rue Aimé Ramon, Ville Basse; ⏲ 7am-9pm)

POST

Main Post Office (40 rue Jean Bringer, Ville Basse)

Post Office (rue Porte d'Aude, La Cité)

TOURIST INFORMATION

Main Tourist Office (☎ 04 68 10 24 30; www.carcas sonne-tourisme.com; 28 rue de Verdun, Ville Basse; ⏲ 9am-7pm daily Jul & Aug, 9am-6pm Mon-Sat, 9am-noon Sun Sep-Jun)

Tourist Office Annexe La Cité (Porte Narbonnaise; ⏲ year-round); Ville Basse (av du Maréchal Joffre; ⏲ mid-Apr–Oct) The Ville Basse kiosk just south of the train station.

Sights & Activities

LA CITÉ

La Cité, dramatically illuminated at night and enclosed by two rampart walls punctuated by 52 stone towers, is one of Europe's largest city fortifications. But only the lower sections of the walls are original; the rest, including the anachronistic witches'-hat roofs (the originals were altogether flatter and weren't covered with slate), were stuck on by Viollet-le-Duc in the 19th century.

From square Gambetta, it's an attractive walk to La Cité across Pont Vieux, along rue de la Barbacane, then up and in through Porte d'Aude. Catching a bus to the main entrance is also an option (p786).

If you pass over the **drawbridge** and enter via the main entrance, you're faced with a massive bastion, the **Porte Narbonnaise** and, just inside, the tourist office annexe. Rue Cros Mayrevieille, suffocating in kitschy souvenir shops, leads up to place du Château, heart of La Cité.

Through another archway and across a second dry moat is the 12th-century

Château Comtal (adult/student/under 18 €6.50/4.50/free; ◷ 9.30am-6.30pm Apr-Sep, 9.30am-5pm Oct-Mar). The entrance fee lets you look around the castle itself and also join a 30- to 40-minute guided tour of both castle and ramparts. For the latter, you may have to wait some time until a critical mass of visitors assembles.

South of place du Château is **Basilique St-Nazaire**. Highlights are the graceful Gothic transept arms with a pair of superb 13th- and 14th-century rose windows at each end.

There's a rash of hole-in-the-wall private museums and initiatives, each eager to separate you from your money, including Memories of the Middle Ages, a Schooldays Museum, the Haunted House – and a particularly repellent exhibition of replica medieval torture instruments. All are very resistible.

LA CITÉ DES OISEAUX
This **bird park** (☎ 04 68 47 88 99; adult/child €8.50/5; ◷ 10.30am-noon & 2.30-6.30pm Jul & Aug, 2-6pm Mar-Jun, Sep & Oct), 800m south of the Cité walls, has more than 300 different species. Raptors, swans and parrots swooping over the audience provide in-flight entertainment and there's also a small pack of wolves.

BOAT RIDES
The **Lou Gabaret** (☎ 04 68 71 61 26; adults €7.50-10, child €6.50-7.50; ◷ sailings 4 times daily Jul & Aug, 2.30pm Tue-Sun Apr-Jun, Sep & Oct) chugs along the Canal du Midi, departing from the bridge just south of the train station. Prices vary according to the length of the trip.

FANGS FOR THE MEMORY

'The furtive silhouettes of the wolves slink across the plain. Of a sudden their prey dashes across the ground, as though flushed out by these predators. The wolves leap forward in merciless pursuit. In a cloud of dust, right before the audience, they leap upon it.'

So went the publicity for the Cité des Oiseaux's innovation of 2005, adding in much smaller letters 'NB the prey is artificial, pulled by a mechanical device.' All the same, it was scarcely wholesome family fun. You can still see the wolves in their park but as a result of public pressure they no longer take star billing in the show.

SIMPLY STROLLING
Leave the crowds up high, cut loose and walk the attractive landscaped banks of the River Aude.

Festivals & Events
Carcassonne knows how to party. On 14 July at 10.30pm, **L'Embrasement de la Cité** (Setting La Cité Ablaze) celebrates Bastille Day with a fireworks display rivalled only by Paris' pyrotechnics.

The **Festival de Carcassonne** (☎ 04 68 11 59 15; www.festivaldecarcassonne.com in French) brings music, opera, dance and theatre to town throughout July. The dynamic and concurrent **Festival Off** is an alternative fringe celebration with street theatre and a host of events, both free and paying.

Summer sees La Cité's **Fêtes Médiévales**. Throughout July and August, there's jousting at 3pm and 4.45pm in the Lices Hautes, between the inner and outer ramparts while in the first three weeks of August there's a nightly (and knightly) pageant at 9.30pm in the Grand Théatre.

Sleeping
BUDGET
Camping de la Cité (☎ 04 68 25 11 77; www.campeole.fr; site €16-21.40, for walkers €9-11; ◷ mid-Mar–mid-Oct) A walking and cycling trail leads from the site to both La Cité and the Ville Basse. From mid-June to mid-September, bus No 8 connects the camp site with La Cité and the train station.

Auberge de Jeunesse (☎ 04 68 25 23 16; carcassonne@fuaj.org; rue Vicomte Trencavel; B&B €16; ◷ Feb–mid-Dec) Carcassonne's cheery, welcoming, HI-affiliated youth hostel, in the heart of La Cité, has rooms sleeping four to six. It has a members kitchen, snack bar offering light meals, great outside terrace and one internet station. It rents bikes (per day €8) to hostellers. Although it has 120 beds, it's smart to reserve year-round.

Sidsmums (☎ 04 68 26 94 49; www.sidsmums.com; 11 chemin de la Croix d'Achille; dm €18) In Preixan, 10km south of Carcassonne, this is a warmly recommended spot to relax and recharge your batteries. You can hire a bike, take a guided walk with George the dog and cook for yourself in the self-contained kitchen. Take the Quillan bus (four daily).

Hôtel Astoria (☎ 04 68 25 31 38; www.astoriacarcassonne.com in French; 18 rue Tourtel; d/tr/q €45/52/66, r with shared bathroom €28; ☺ Mar-Jan) Parking free. Rooms are fresh and pleasant, each with tiles or parquet, at this hotel and its equally agreeable annexe. Bathrooms are a bit pokey but all in all it's a welcoming place that offers very good value.

MIDRANGE

Hôtel au Royal (☎ 04 68 25 19 12; 22 blvd Jean Jaurès; s €43 d €50; ☺ mid-Jan–mid-Dec) Parking €7. This attractive midrange option serves a copious, varied breakfast. Its 24 rooms are comfortable, well appointed and equipped with ceiling fans, while those facing the busy street all have double glazing.

Hôtel du Pont Vieux (☎ 04 68 25 24 99; www .hoteldupontvieux.com in French; 32 rue Trivalle; d mid-Aug–mid-Jul €48-60, mid-Jul–mid-Aug €77-82; ✖ ✖) Bedrooms, most with a bathtub, have attractively rough-hewn walls. On the 3rd floor, rooms 18 and 19 have unsurpassed views of the Cité and there's a small terrace, accessible to all guests. The buffet breakfast (€7) is truly gargantuan and there's a large garden.

Hôtel des Trois Couronnes (☎ 04 68 25 36 10; www.hotel-destroiscouronnes.com; rue des Trois Couronnes; s €57-73 d €73-89; ✖ ✖) Wi-fi. Parking €5 to €8. Set back from the River Aude, this attractive modern hotel has uninterrupted views of La Cité from east-facing rooms (€16 extra) and from the summertime terrace restaurant. On the 4th floor (where there's also a heated indoor pool) there's a nice restaurant (see Le Richepin, right).

TOP END

La Cité has a couple of splendid top-of-the-market choices.

Hôtel Le Donjon (☎ 04 68 11 23 00; www.hotel -donjon.fr; 2 rue du Comte Roger; d €100-155 tr €120-175; ✖ ✖ ▯) Parking €10. Wi-fi. Low-beamed, thick-walled, venerable and cosy, 15th-century Le Donjon was originally an orphanage. Rooms overlook either its shady garden or the ramparts. Its two annexes, Les Remparts and Maison du Comte Roger, are equally comfortable but shorter on period charm.

Hôtel de la Cité (☎ 04 68 71 98 71; www.hotelde lacite.orient-express.com; place Auguste Pont; d €250-500; ☺ closed Feb & Dec; ✖ ✖) Parking €15. Neogothic Hôtel de la Cité has rooms fit for royalty (literally so: 'A favourite hideaway for Europe's crowned heads, film stars,

writers and intellectuals,' proclaims its glossy brochure), should you fancy a retreat in such august company.

Eating

Even if it's a boiling summer's day, don't leave town without trying cassoulet, a piping-hot dish blending white beans, juicy pork cubes, even bigger cylinders of meaty sausage and, in the most popular local variant, a hunk of duck.

VILLE BASSE

Au Bon Pasteur (☎ 04 68 25 49 63; 29 rue Armagnac; menus €15-28; ☺ closed Sun & Mon Jul & Aug, Sun & Wed Sep-Jun) At this welcoming, intimate family restaurant, the simple wooden tables and chairs belie the sophistication of the cooking. You can warm yourself in winter with the yummy cassoulet or *choucroute* (sauerkraut), 100% authentic since the chef hails from the Vosges. Year-round, its *menu classique* (classic menu; €15) and *formules de midi* (lunch specials; €10 to €11.50) both represent excellent value.

Restaurant Gil (☎ 04 68 47 85 23; 32 rte Minervoise; menus €18-28, mains €9-18; ☺ Tue-Sat) Go downstairs, below street level, to enjoy quality, Catalan-influenced cuisine. A particular strength is its fresh seafood and fish dishes (€10 to €15), mostly served grilled and unsmothered by superfluous sauces or adornment.

Le Richepin (☎ 04 68 25 36 10; www.hotel-destr oiscouronnes.com; rue des Trois Couronnes; menus €21-28.50) This restaurant, on the 4th floor of Hôtel des Trois Couronnes serves fine food year-round.

Chez Fred (☎ 04 68 72 02 23; 31 blvd Omer Sarraut; menus €21-31; ☺ lunch & dinner daily mid-Jun–mid-Oct, lunch & dinner Mon-Fri & Sat dinner mid-Oct–mid-Jun) With a large window pierced in one of the walls of the oxblood-red interior, you can peek at what Fred's chefs are confecting; it's sure to be something creative. The scrummy desserts are as pretty as they're tasty and the weekday *menu bistrot* (lunch €15, dinner €18) is superb value.

L'Écurie (☎ 04 68 72 04 04; 43 blvd Barbès; menus €22-29; ☺ closed Wed & dinner Sun) Enjoy fine fare either within this attractively renovated 18th-century stable, all polished woodwork, brass and leather, or in the large, shaded garden. Pick from its long and choice selection of local wines.

LANGUEDOC-ROUSSILLON

LA CITÉ

Place Marcou is hemmed in on three sides by eateries and throughout La Cité every second building seems to be a café or restaurant. For those we recommend, it's wise to reserve, particularly for lunch.

Restaurant des Musées (☎ 06 17 05 24 90; 17 rue du Grand Puits; menus €8.50-18; ☒ Mon-Sat lunch & dinner; Ⓥ) This simple unpretentious place has three rear terraces with views of the ramparts. It bakes its own organic bread and offers excellent-value meals, including a few vegetarian *menus* (€9.50). It doesn't serve alcohol but you can bring in a bottle from the wine shop next door and there's no corkage charge. It doesn't take credit cards.

Auberge de Dame Carcas (☎ 04 68 71 23 23; 3 place du Château; menus €14-24.50; ☒ Thu-Tue Feb-Dec) This casual restaurant specialises in pork products (model piggies, large and small, displayed around the restaurant give you a clue) and carries a fine selection of well-priced local wines. Downstairs is cosy and agreeably rustic and you can see the chefs at work, the larger upstairs room offers more light and there's a summer terrace too.

L'Écu d'Or (☎ 04 68 25 49 03; 7-9 rue Porte d'Aude; menus €20-30) Here's a spot for stylish dining. It serves, among many other delightful dishes, five varieties of cassoulet and a delicious range of creative desserts.

SELF-CATERING

L'Art Gourmand (13 rue St-Louis) Chocolate fiends should descend upon this place, which sells a huge range of goodies. The ice cream is pretty great too – all 33 varieties of it.

Markets:

Covered market (rue du Verdun; ☒ Mon-Sat)

Open-air market (place Carnot; ☒ Tue, Thu & Sat)

Drinking

Cafés overlooking place Carnot in the Ville Basse spill onto the square in summer.

La Cité des Arômes (14 place Carnot) In the northwestern corner of place Carnot this cafe wafts out scents of rich arabica and carries a huge selection of coffees.

In La Cité, place Marcou is one big outside café.

Getting There & Away

AIR

Ryanair is the only airline to fly in and out of Carcassonne's **airport** (☎ 04 68 71 96

46), 5.5km from town. It has daily flights to/from London (Stansted) and Brussels (Charleroi) and flies to Dublin, Liverpool and UK East Midlands at least three times weekly.

BUS

We can only reiterate the advice of the tourist office: take the train. Eurolines and such intercity buses as there are stop on blvd de Varsovie, 500m southwest of the train station.

TRAIN

Carcassonne is on the main line linking Toulouse (€12.70, 50 minutes, frequent) with Narbonne (€9, 30 to 45 minutes), Béziers (€12, 50 minutes) and Montpellier (€20.20, 1½ hours, six daily). For Perpignan (€16.50), change in Narbonne.

Getting Around

TO/FROM THE AIRPORT

Agglo'Bus's Navette Aéroport runs to/from the airport (€5, 25 minutes), leaving the train station two hours before each Ryanair departure. By car, take the Carcassonne Ouest A61 motorway exit.

BICYCLE

Espace 11 (☎ 04 68 25 28 18; 3 rte Minervoise; ☒ Tue-Sat) rents mountain bikes (per day/three days/week €13/35/61).

CAR & MOTORCYCLE

Several operators including **Europcar** (☎ 04 68 72 23 69), **Ada** (☎ 04 68 11 71 92) and **Hertz** (☎ 04 68 71 00 55) have booths at the airport.

Cars are forbidden in La Cité during the day. Leave your vehicle in the huge car park (cars/camper vans €3.50/5) just east of the main entrance.

PUBLIC TRANSPORT

Agglo'Bus, the city bus company, has an **information kiosk** (☎ 04 68 47 82 22). It was in and may return to square Gambetta, currently being excavated for a megaparkark. For the moment, it's about 150m south, beside a large concrete dome.

Buses run until about 7pm, Monday to Saturday. A single ticket/10-ticket *carnet* costs €1/7.

Bus No 2 runs about every 40 minutes from the Ville Basse to La Cité's main entrance. From mid-June to mid-September, a **navette** (shuttle service; 9.30am-7.30pm Mon-Sat) plies between La Cité, downtown and the train station (€1.50, every 15 minutes).

TAXI
Ring 04 68 71 50 50.

HAUT-LANGUEDOC

Haut-Languedoc is a world away from the towns, vineyards and beaches of the broad coastal plain. More sparsely populated, it's a land of deeply incised gorges, high windswept plateaus and dense forest, ideal for those who love the open air.

MENDE
pop 13,100

Mende, a quiet little place straddling the River Lot, is the capital of Lozère, France's least populous *département*. Its oval-shaped centre is ringed by a one-way road that acts as something of a *cordon sanitaire*, leaving the old quarter almost traffic-free.

Information
Salle Antirouille (place du Foirail; per hr €1.50; 3-8pm Tue-Fri, 9am-noon & 2-5pm Sat) Internet access.
Tourist Office (04 66 94 00 23; www.ot-mende.fr; place Charles de Gaulle; 9am-12.30pm & 2-7pm Mon-Sat, 9am-noon & 2-5pm Sun Jul & Aug, 9am-12.30pm & 2-6pm Mon-Fri, 9am-noon Sat Sep-Jun)

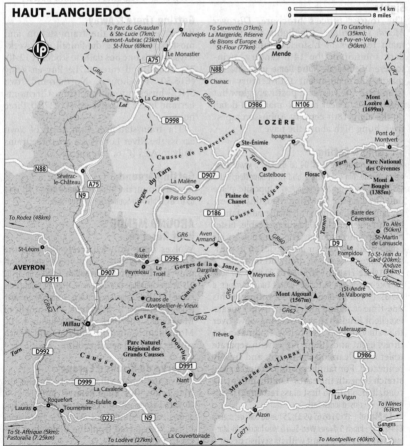

HAUT-LANGUEDOC

0 —— 14 km
0 —— 8 miles

To Parc du Gévaudan & Ste-Lucie (7km); Aumont-Aubrac (23km); St-Flour (69km)
To Serverette (31km); Marvejols La Margeride, Réserve de Bisons d'Europe & St-Flour (77km)
To Grandrieu (35km); Le Puy-en-Velay (90km)

Le Monastier
A75
N88
Mende

Chanac

La Canourgue
Lot
D986 **N106**
LOZÈRE
Mont Lozère (1699m)

D998
Causse de Sauveterre
Ste-Énimie
Ispagnac
Pont de Montvert

N88
Sévérac-le-Château
A75
N9
Gorges du Tarn
La Malène
D907
Castelbouc
Florac
Tarn
Parc National des Cévennes
Mont Bougès (1385m)

Pas de Soucy
Plaine de Chanet
D186
Causse Méjean
Barre des Cévennes

To Rodez (48km)
GR6
Aven Armand
GR60
Tarnon
D9
Le Pompidou
To Alès (50km); St-Martin de Lansuscle
To St-Jean du Gard (20km); Anduze (34km)

St-Léons
Le Rozier
D996
Gorges de la Jonte
Dargilan
Meyrueis
Jonte
Corniche des Cévennes

AVEYRON
D907
Peyreleau Le Truel
Causse Noir
GR6
St-André de Valborgne

D911
Chaos de Montpellier-le-Vieux
Mont Aigoual (1567m)
GR62

Millau
Gorges de la Dourbie
GR62
Trèves
Vallerauge

Parc Naturel Régional des Grands Causses
Montagne du Lingas
D986

D992
Tarn
Causse du Larzac
D991
Nant
GR7

D999
La Cavalerie
Le Vigan
To Nîmes (63km)

Lauras
Roquefort Tournemire
Ste-Eulalie
D23 **N9**
Alzon
GR71
Ganges

To St-Affrique (5km); Pastoralia (7.25km)
To Lodève (27km)
La Couvertoirade
To Montpellier (40km)

LANGUEDOC-ROUSSILLON

SOME DINGDONG!

In 1512, the largest church bell ever cast until then, all 25 tonnes of it, was hauled to the top of the newly completed steeple of Mende's cathedral. 'Non Pareille', it was called, The Unrivalled One. It swung and clanged for only 67 years. On Christmas Eve 1579, while the faithful were attending mass, the Huguenots captured Mende, slaughtered most of the congregation, hacked loose the bell, then melted it down to make cannons. They spared nothing but the clanger, which itself weighs in at a hefty 470 kilograms. It's displayed just to the left of the west end entrance.

Sights

The tourist office's brochure, *Discover Mende's Heritage*, highlights the town's main features of historical interest. The dark interior of the 14th-century, twin-towered **Cathédrale Notre Dame** (place Urbain V) makes the magnificent 17th-century rose window at the west end positively glow but you'll have to peer hard to make out detail on the eight 18th-century Aubusson tapestries, hung high above the nave.

Sleeping & Eating

Hôtel le Commerce (☎ 04 66 65 13 73; www.lecommerce-mende.com in French; 2 blvd Henri Bourrillon; s/d/tr €33/42/48; ☽ closed 2 weeks in Apr) Opposite place du Foirail on the busy ring road, this agreeably labyrinthine hotel, run by the same family for three generations, has impeccable, tastefully furnished rooms. The owner is an ale fanatic and its popular bar carries an impressive range of beers, on draft and in bottle.

Hôtel de France (☎ 04 66 65 00 04; www.hoteldefrance-mende.com in French; 9 blvd Lucien Arnault; d €49-85; ☽ mid-Jan–Dec; ☐) Most rooms at this one-time coaching inn (whose owner speaks excellent English) have sweeping views over the valley and gardens below. Rooms one to three, eight and 10 are large, with separate toilet and gleaming bathroom, and freshly renovated. For families, a duplex and a suite stretch beneath the eaves. On the inner ring road, it also runs a first class **restaurant** (menus €23-26; ☽ closed lunch Sat).

Le Mazel (☎ 04 66 65 05 33; 25 rue du Collège; menus €14-27; ☽ lunch & dinner Wed-Sun & Mon lunch mid-Mar–mid-Nov) This restaurant with its stylish décor – don't be deterred by the bleakly modern surroundings – offers mainly local cuisine, imaginatively prepared. A recognised gourmet venue, it offers exceptional value.

Restaurant Les Voûtes (☎ 04 66 49 00 05; 13 rue d'Aigues-Passes; menus €18-24, mains around €15; ☽ daily May-Aug, Tue-Sun Sep-Apr, closed 15-30 Sep) This restaurant has a splendid setting, deep in the vaults of an ex-convent. Run by three brothers, it offers salads big enough to fill a fruit bowl (€7 to €8.50), pizzas (€6.50 to €8.50) and grills (€10 to €13.50), all to eat in or takeaway. It does a great all-on-one-plate lunchtime special (€11.50).

La Fromagerie (28 rue Soubeyran) Overlooked by the buttresses of the cathedral's east end, this cheese shop has an impressive range of cheeses and regional meats and pâtés.

Getting There & Away

Buses leave from the train station and most pass by place du Foirail. On weekdays, there's one bus daily to Rodez (€12.40, 3½ hours) and three to Le Puy-en-Velay (€16.50, 1¾ hours). Northbound, two SNCF buses run daily to/from Clermont-Ferrand in the Massif Central (€27.20, three hours).

The train station is 1km north of town across the River Lot. There are three trains daily to Alès (€16, 2¼ hours).

Getting Around

Rent a mountain bike at **Espace Bike** (☎ 04 66 65 01 81; 1 blvd du Soubeyran; ☽ Tue-Sat).

AROUND MENDE
Wolf Reserve

Wolves once prowled freely through the Lozère forests but today you'll see them only in the **Parc du Gévaudan** (☎ 04 66 32 09 22; www.loupsdugevaudan.com in French; adult/child €6.50/3.50; ☽ 10am-7pm Jun-Aug, 10am-5pm or 6pm Feb-May & Sep-Dec) in Ste-Lucie, 7km north of Marvejols. The park sustains around 100 Mongolian, Canadian, Siberian and Polish wolves living in semifreedom.

Réserve de Bisons d'Europe

Above the small village of Ste-Eulalie-en-Margeride, this **Bison Reserve** (☎ 04 66 31 40 40; www.bisoneurope.com in French; ☽ 10am-4pm, 5pm or 6pm) was established with 25 European bison, transferred from the Bialowieza forest in Poland.

Within their 200-hectare reserve, the bison roam freely. Visitors, by contrast, must follow a 50-minute guided tour, either by horse-drawn carriage (adult/child €11/6) or, in winter, by sledge (€14/8). From mid-June to September, you can follow a 1km walking path (€5.50/4).

PARC NATIONAL DES CÉVENNES

Drier, hotter and in general leafier than the Auvergne to its north, the Cévennes have more in common with Mediterranean lands. Dotted with isolated hamlets, the park harbours a huge diversity of fauna and flora (an astounding 2250 plant species have been logged). Animals such as red deer, beavers and vultures, long gone from the park, have been successfully reintroduced. The park covers four main areas: Mont Lozère, much of the Causse Méjean, the Vallées Cévenoles (Cévennes Valleys) and Mont Aigoual.

The park possesses four **ecomuseums**: the Écomusées du Mont Lozère, de la Cévenne, de L'Aigoual and du Causse, each of which has several different sites. For more details, ask at the excellent Maison du Parc National des Cévennes (p790).

History

The 910-sq-km park was created more than 35 years ago to bring ecological stability to an area that, because of religious and later economic upheavals, has long had a destabilising human presence. Population influxes, which saw the destruction of forests for logging and pasture, were followed by mass desertions as people gave up the fight against the inhospitable climate and terrain. Emigration led to the abandonment of hamlets and farms, many of which have been snapped up by wealthy Parisians and foreigners.

Maps

The best overall map of the park is the IGN's *Parc National des Cévennes* (€6.20) at 1:100,000.

Mont Lozère

This 1699m-high lump of granite in the north of the park is shrouded in cloud and ice in winter and covered with heather and blueberries, peat bogs and flowing streams in summer. **Écomusée du Mont Lozère** (☎ 04 66 45 80 73; ◷ 10.30am-12.30pm & 2.30-6.30pm Easter-Sep) has a permanent exhibition at Pont de Montvert, 20km northeast of Florac.

Vallées Cévenoles

First planted back in the Middle Ages, *châtaigniers* (sweet-chestnut trees) carpet the Vallées Cévenoles, the park's central *région* of plunging ravines and jagged ridges, along one of which runs the breathtaking Corniche des Cévennes.

Mont Aigoual

Mont Aigoual (1567m) and the neighbouring Montagne du Lingas region are renowned for their searing winds and heavy snowfall. The area is dense with beech trees, thanks to a successful reforestation programme that counteracts years of uncontrolled logging. The observatory atop the breezy summit has an **exhibition** (admission

CHESTNUT: THE ALL-PURPOSE TREE

In the Cévennes, the chestnut tree (known as *l'arbre à pain*, or bread tree) was the staple food of many Auvergnat families. The nuts were eaten raw, roasted and dried, or ground into flour. Blended with milk or wine, chestnuts were the essence of *bajanat*, a nourishing soup. Part of the harvest would feed the pigs while the leaves of pruned twigs and branches provided fodder for sheep and goats.

Harvested at ground level with small forks – of chestnut wood, of course – the prickly husks (called *hèrissons*, or hedgehogs) were removed by being trampled upon in spiky boots. Nowadays, they're the favourite food of the Cévennes' wild boars and still feature in a number of local sauces and desserts.

Nothing was wasted. Sections of hollowed-out trunk would serve as beehives, smaller branches would be woven into baskets while larger ones were whittled into stakes for fencing or used to build trellises. The wood, hard and resistant to parasites was used for rafters, rakes and household furniture – everything from, quite literally, the cradle to the coffin.

TRAVELS WITH A DONKEY

The Cévennes were even wilder and more untamed back in October 1878, when Scottish writer Robert Louis Stevenson crossed them with only a donkey, Modestine, for company.

'I was looked upon with contempt, like a man who should project a journey to the moon, but yet with a respectful interest, like one setting forth for the inclement Pole,' Stevenson wrote in his *Travels with a Donkey in the Cévennes*.

Accompanied by the wayward Modestine, bought for 65 francs and a glass of brandy, Stevenson took a respectable 12 days to travel the 232km on foot (Modestine carried his gear) from Le Monastier-sur-Gazelle, southeast of Le Puy-en-Velay, to St-Jean du Gard, west of Alès. Afterwards, he sold his ass – and wept.

The Stevenson trail, first retraced and marked with the cross of St Andrew by a Scottish woman in 1978, is nowadays designated the GR70.

Whether you're swaying on a donkey or simply walking, you'll find *The Robert Louis Stevenson Trail* by Alan Castle an excellent, practical, well-informed companion. Consult too www.chemin-stevenson.org and pick up the free pamphlet *Sur Le Chemin de Robert Louis Stevenson* (On The RLS Trail), stocked by tourist offices, which has a comprehensive list of accommodation en route.

---

free; ☼ May-Sep), portraying the mountain through the seasons and the play of wind and water upon it.

Activities

In winter there's **cross-country skiing** (more than 100km of marked trails) on Mont Aigoual and Mont Lozère, and **donkey treks** are popular in the park in warmer months. There are 600km of donkey- and horse-riding trails and 200km marked out for mountain-bike enthusiasts.

An equally well-developed network of trails makes the park a **walking** paradise year-round. It's crisscrossed by a dozen GR *(grande randonnée)* trails and there are over 20 shorter signposted walks lasting between two and seven hours.

Florac's Maison du Parc (right) has more than 11 excellent wallets (€5 each) describing circular walks from various starting points within the park. Ask about the **Festival Nature**, a summertime mix of outdoor activities, lectures and field trips.

Getting There & Away

By car, the most spectacular route is the Corniche des Cévennes, a ridge road that winds along the mountain crests of the Cévennes for 56km from St-Jean du Gard to Florac.

FLORAC

pop 2100

Florac, 79km northwest of Alès and 38km southeast of Mende, makes a great base for exploring the Parc National des Cévennes

and the upper reaches of the Gorges du Tarn. Lively in summer and moribund for most of the rest of the year, it's draped along the west bank of River Tarnon, one of the tributaries of the Tarn, with the sheer cliffs of the Causse Méjean looming 1000m overhead.

Information

Laundrette (11 rue du Pêcher; ☼ 8.30am-7.30pm)

Tourist Office (☎ 04 66 45 01 14; www.mesce vennes.com; av Jean Monestier; ☼ 9am-12.30pm & 1.30-7pm daily Jul & Aug, 9am-noon & 2-6pm Mon-Sat Sep-Jun)

Activities

The tourist office has details of a whole summer's worth of outdoor activities. For information on the park's rich walking potential, contact **Maison du Parc National des Cévennes** (☎ 04 66 49 53 01; www.cevennes-parcnational .fr; ☼ 9am-6.30pm Jul & Aug, 9.30am-12.30pm & 1.30-5.30pm daily Easter-Jun, 9.30am-12.30pm & 1.30-5.30pm Mon-Fri Sep-Easter). It occupies the handsome restored 17th-century Château de Florac, stocks an English version of the guidebook *Parc National des Cévennes* (€15) and has a splendidly informative **interactive exhibition** (adult/child €3.50/2.50), *Passagers du Paysage*, with captions and a recorded commentary in English (delivered, alas, by a couple of glum, monotone native speakers) and a 15-minute slide show.

See too Activities, left. Lonely Planet's *Walking in France* describes three varied day walks, each accessible from Florac.

DONKEY TREKS

Why not follow the lead of Robert Louis Stevenson and hire a pack animal? Several companies are in the donkey business. They include **Gentiâne** (☎ 04 66 41 04 16; anegenti@free.fr) in Castagnols and **Tramontane** (☎ 04 66 45 92 44; chantal.tramontane@nomade.fr) in St-Martin de Lansuscle. Typical prices are €40 to €45 per day and €200 to €245 per week and both outfits can reserve accommodation along the route. Though each is outside Florac, they'll transport the dumb creatures to town or a place of your choosing for a fee (around €0.75 per kilometre).

OTHER ACTIVITIES

Cévennes Évasion (☎ 04 66 45 18 31; www.cevennes-evasion.com in French; 5 place Boyer) rents mountain bikes for €13/19 per half-/full day and furnishes riders with handy colour route maps. In summer Cévennes Évasion will take you for free up to the Causse Méjean, from where you can whiz effortlessly back down (minimum five persons). It also arranges caving, rock-climbing and canyon-clambering expeditions (trust these guys; they hung the fireworks up high for the spectacular opening and closing ceremony pyrotechnics at the Athens Olympics and Turin Winter Olympics). It also runs guided and independent walking holidays, where your accommodation is prebooked and your luggage transported onwards daily.

Sleeping

Florac has a pair of municipal riverside camp sites, each 1.5km from town.

Camping Le Pont du Tarn (☎ 04 66 45 18 26; pontdutarne@aol.com; per person/tent/car €2.95/2.95/1.40; Apr–mid-Oct; 🏊) To the north, off the N106.

Camping La Tière (☎ 04 66 45 04 02; mairie@ville-florac.fr; per person/tent/car €2.50/2.40/1.60; Jul & Aug) Smaller and south of town, is right beside the river and may well be less crowded than Camping Le Pont du Tarn.

La Carline (☎ 04 66 45 24 54; lagrave.alain@wanadoo.fr; 18 rue du Pêcher; per person €12; Apr–Oct) This welcoming trekkers' favourite with doubles and quads occupies an 18th-century house and has self-catering facilities.

Grand Hôtel du Parc (☎ 04 66 45 03 05; www.grandhotelduparc.fr; 47 av Jean Monestier; r €44-62, with shared bathroom €32; mid-Mar–Nov; 🏊) This venerable building has spacious rooms and sits in its own extensive grounds with a pool, terrace and delightful gardens shaded by mature cedars. It also runs a creditable restaurant (see below).

Hôtel Les Gorges du Tarn (☎ 04 66 45 00 63, gorges-du-tarn.adonis@wanadoo.fr; 48 rue du Pêcher; r €52, with shower €36; Easter-Oct) Beside a quiet street, rooms in the main building have greater character while those in the annexe are more spacious, if less sparkling. It has a good restaurant (below).

Eating

L'Esplanade, a shady, pedestrianised path, becomes one long dining area in summer. Then, you can eat well and economically at one of the restaurant terraces.

La Source du Pêcher (☎ 04 66 45 03 01; 1 rue de Remuret; menus €28-50; Apr-Oct) With a wonderful open-air terrace, perched above the little River Pêcher, it's very good and oh, they know and show it (just look at the ostentatious display of medallions and shields from gastronomic bodies known and obscure that fringe the door) and it still observes the outmoded practice of handing Madame a menu with nothing so vulgar as prices indicated. This said, you'll eat very well indeed, if you can stomach a little ritual humiliation. They don't take reservations, so arrive early.

Maison du Pays Cévenol (3 rue du Pêcher) This gastronomic treasure-trove sells local specialities – liqueurs, jams, Pélardon cheese and chestnuts in all their guises.

Impressive hotel restaurants:

Grand Hôtel du Parc restaurant (☎ 04 66 45 03 05; www.grandhotelduparc.fr; 47 av Jean Monestier; menus €18-36)

L'Adonis (☎ 04 66 45 00 63; 48 rue du Pêcher; menus €17-37) At Hôtel Les Gorges du Tarn.

Getting There & Away

It's a pain without your own vehicle. One **Transports Reilhes** (☎ 04 66 45 00 18) minibus runs to/from Alès (€12.50, 1¼ hours), Monday to Saturday, calling by the old railway station.

GORGES DU TARN

From the village of Ispagnac, 9km northwest of Florac, the spectacular Gorges du Tarn wind southwestwards for about 50km, ending just north of Millau. En route are two villages: medieval Ste-Énimie (a good base for canoeing and walking along the gorges) and, 13km downstream, La Malène, smaller but equally attractive.

The gorge, 400m to 600m deep, marks the boundary between the Causse Méjean to its south and the Causse de Sauveterre to the north. From these plateaus, the gorge looks like a white, limestone abyss, its green waters dotted here and there with bright canoes and kayaks. In summer the riverside road (the D907bis) is often jammed with cars, buses and caravans: every summer's day, more than 3000 vehicles grind through Ste-Énimie.

Activities
CANOEING
Riding the River Tarn is at its best in high summer when the river is usually low and the descent a lazy trip over mostly calm water. You can get as far as the impassable Pas de Soucy, a barrier of boulders about 9km downriver from La Malène, downstream from which are further canoeing possibilities.

The Ste-Énimie tourist office carries information on the veritable flotilla of companies offering canoe and kayak descents. These include the following:

ADN La Cazelle (☎ 04 66 48 46 05; www.lacazelle.com in French) In Ste-Énimie.

Au Moulin de la Malène (☎ 04 66 48 51 14; www .canoeblanc.com) In La Malène.

Canoë Paradan (☎ 04 66 48 56 90; www.canoe paradan.com) In Ste-Énimie.

Locanoë (☎ 04 66 48 55 57; www.canoe-gorges-du -tarn.com in French) In Castelbouc.

Typical trips and tariffs for canoe and kayak descents include: Ste-Énimie to La Malène (€16 to €18, 3½ hours, 13km) and Ste-Énimie to Pas de Soucy (€22 to €23, 6½ hours, 23km).

If you'd rather someone else did the hard work, spend a lazy, effortless hour with **Les Bateliers de la Malène** (☎ 04 66 48 51 10; ☼ Apr-Oct), who, for €18.50 per person, will punt you down an 8km stretch of the gorge, leaving from La Malène, then drive you back.

WALKING & CYCLING
The Sentier de la Vallée du Tarn trail, blazed in yellow and green, runs for around 250km, from Pont de Montvert on Mont Lozère, down the Gorges and all the way to Albi, near Toulouse. The GR60 follows an old drovers' route, winding down from the Causse de Sauveterre to Ste-Énimie, crossing the bridge and continuing southwards up to the Causse Méjean in the direction of Mont Aigoual.

Less strenuously, there are well over a dozen circular, signposted day and half-day walks in the stretch between Ispagnac and La Malène.

ADN La Cazelle (☎ 04 66 48 46 05; www.lacazelle .com in French) In Ste-Énimie, rents out mountain bikes (per half-/full day €20/30).

The Ste-Énimie tourist office (below) sells the useful *Vallée et Gorges du Tarn – Balades à Pied et à VTT* (€15), which details walking and cycling routes in the area.

Sleeping & Eating
Camping Les Gorges du Tarn (☎ 04 66 48 59 38; fax 04 66 48 59 37; 2 people tent & car €7.50; ☼ Easter-Oct) About 800m upstream from Ste-Énimie, this is the cheapest of the several riverside camp sites. It also hires out canoes and kayaks.

Château de la Caze (☎ 04 66 48 51 01; www.cha teaudelacaze.com; d €108-162; ☼ Easter–mid-Nov) This fairy-tale 15th-century castle, overlooking the River Tarn between Ste-Énimie and La Malène, is a fabulous top-end option. Rooms are the last word in luxury and it boasts a renowned gourmet restaurant. Accommodation in the annexe is less romantic but easier on the pocket and guests have access to all the hotel's facilities.

Ste-Énimie
pop 500
Ste-Énimie, 27km from Florac and 56km from Millau, tumbles like an avalanche of grey-brown stone, blending into the steep, once-terraced slope behind it. Long isolated, it's now a popular destination for day-visitors from Millau, Mende and Florac and one of the starting points for descending the Tarn by canoe or kayak (see left).

Ste-Énimie's **tourist office** (☎ 04 66 48 53 44; www.gorgesdutarn.net in French; ☼ 9am-1pm & 2-7pm Mon-Sat, 9.30am-12.30pm Sun Jul & Aug, 9.30am-12.30pm & 2-5.30pm Mon-Fri Oct-Easter, 9.30am-12.30pm & 2-5.30pm Mon-Sat Easter-Jun & Sep) is 100m north of the bridge. It stocks maps and walking guides, including IGN Top 25 map No 2640OT *Gorges du Tarn*. There's also a small seasonal **annexe** in La Malène.

Highlights are the Romanesque **Église de Ste-Énimie** and, just behind it, the tiny **Écomusée Le Vieux Logis** (adult/child €2/1; ☉ Easter-Sep), its one vaulted room crammed with antique local furniture, lamps, tableware and costumes.

PARC NATUREL RÉGIONAL DES GRANDS CAUSSES

The Grands Causses, the Massif Central's most southerly expression, are mainly harsh limestone plateau. Scorched in summer and windswept in winter, the stony surface holds little moisture as water filters through the limestone to form an underground world ideal for cavers.

The Rivers Tarn, Jonte and Dourbie have sliced deep gorges through the 5000-sq-km plateau, creating four *causses* ('plateaus' in the local patois): Sauveterre, Méjean, Noir and Larzac, each different in its delicate geological forms. One resembles a dark lunar surface, another's like a Scottish moor covered with the thinnest layer of grass, while the next is gentler and more fertile. But all are eerie and empty except for the occasional shepherd and his flock – and all offer magnificent walking and mountain biking.

Millau, at the heart of the park, is a good base for venturing into this wild area. The southern part of the park, home to France's 'king of cheeses', is known as Le Pays du Roquefort (Land of Roquefort). The Gorges de la Jonte, where birds of prey wheel and swoop, skim the park's eastern boundary, rivalling in beauty the neighbouring, more famous Gorges du Tarn.

Information

Parc Naturel Régional des Grands Causses office
(☎ 05 65 61 35 50; info@parc-grands-causses.fr; 71 blvd de l'Ayrolle, Millau; ☉ 9am-noon or 12.30pm & 2-5pm or 6pm Mon-Fri)

Causse de Sauveterre

The northernmost of the *causses* is a gentle, hilly plateau dotted with a few compact and isolated farms resembling fortified villages. Every possible patch of fertile earth is cultivated, creating irregular, intricately patterned wheat fields.

Causse Méjean

Causse Méjean, the highest, is also the most barren and isolated. It's a land of poor pas-

ture enriched by occasional fertile depressions, where streams gurgle down into the limestone through sinkholes, funnels and fissures.

This combination of water and limestone has created some spectacular underground scenery. The cavern of **Aven Armand** (☎ 04 66 45 61 31; www.aven-armand.com; adult/child €8.30/5.70; ☉ 9.30am-6pm Jul & Aug, 9.30am or 10am-noon & 1.30-5pm or 6pm Mar-Jun & Sep-Nov), on the plateau's southwestern side, lies about 75m below the surface. Stretching some 200m, it bristles with a subterranean forest of stalagmites and stalactites. A **combination ticket** (adult/child €11.50/7.80) also includes admission to the Chaos de Montpellier-le-Vieux.

Nearby is the equally spectacular, even larger cavern of **Dargilan** (☎ 04 66 45 60 20; www.grotte-dargilan.com; adult/child €8.30/5.70; ☉ 10am-6.30pm Jul & Aug, 10am-noon & 2-4.30pm or 5.30pm Easter-Jun, Sep & Oct). The highlight of the one-hour tour is the sudden, final exit onto a ledge with a dizzying view of the Gorges de la Jonte way below.

Causse Noir

Rising immediately east of Millau, the 'Black Causse' is bounded by gorges. It's best known for the **Chaos de Montpellier-le-Vieux** (☎ 05 65 60 66 30; adult/child €5.20/3.75; ☉ 9.30am-6pm or 7pm Apr–mid-Nov), an area of jagged rocks 18km northeast of Millau overlooking the Gorges de la Dourbie. Water erosion has created more than 120 hectares of tortured limestone formations with fanciful names such as the Sphinx and the Elephant. Three trails, lasting one to three hours, cover the site, as does a tourist train (adult/child €3.40/2.40).

If you're here outside official opening times, there's nothing to stop you wandering around freely.

Causse du Larzac

The Causse du Larzac (800m to 1000m) is the largest of the four *causses*. An endless sweep of distant horizons and rocky steppes broken by medieval villages, it's known as the 'French Desert'.

You'll stumble across old, fortified villages such as **Ste-Eulalie** (not to be confused with Ste-Eulalie-en-Margeride, which is further north near Réserve de Bisons d'Europe), long the capital of the Larzac *région,* and **La Couvertoirade**, both built by the Knights Templar, a religious military order that distinguished itself during the Crusades.

Gorges de la Jonte

The dramatic Gorges de la Jonte slice east–west from Meyrueis to Le Rozier, below the western slopes of the Aigoual massif. West of Le Truel on the D996 is **Belvédère des Vautours** (Vulture Viewing Point; ☎ 05 65 62 69 69; www.vautours-lozere.com; adult/child €6.50/3; ☼ 10am-5pm or 6pm Apr-Oct), above which the birds nest high in the cliffs. Reintroduced after having all but disappeared locally, the vultures now freely wheel and plane in the Causses skies.

The viewing point has an impressive multimedia exhibition, including live video transmission from the nesting sites of what must be the world's most heavily researched vultures. It also organises half-day **birding walks** (adult/student/child €7/6/3.50; reservation essential) to the surrounding gorges.

MILLAU

pop 22,000

Millau (pronounced mee-yo) squeezes between the Causse Noir and Causse du Larzac at the confluence of the Rivers Tarn and Dourbie. Though falling just over the border into the Midi-Pyrénées *département* of Aveyron, it's tied to Languedoc historically and culturally. Millau is famous within France for glove-making. The main centre for the Parc Naturel Régional des Grands Causses, it comes to life at holiday time as a take-off point for hiking and other outdoor activities – particularly hang-gliding and parapente, exploiting the up-lifting thermals.

Information

Laundrette (14 av Gambetta; ☼ 7am-9pm)
Main Post Office (12 av Alfred Merle)
Metr@net (1 rue J-F Alméras; per hr €3; ☼ 9am-noon & 2-7pm Mon-Sat) Internet access.
Posanis (5 rue Droite; per hr €3; ☼ 10am-10pm Mon-Sat Jul & Aug, 10am-12.30pm & 1.30-8pm Mon-Sat Sep-Jun) Internet access.
Tourist Office (☎ 05 65 60 02 42; www.ot-millau.fr; 1 place du Beffroi; ☼ 9am-7pm daily Jul & Aug, 9am-12.30pm & 2-6.30pm Mon-Fri, 9am-6.30pm Sat, 9.30am-4pm Sun Sep-Jun)

Sights

The 42m-tall **beffroi** (belfry; rue Droite; adult/child €2.50/free; ☼ 10am-noon & 2.30-6pm Jul & Aug, 2.30-6pm mid-end Jun & Sep) has a square base dating from the 12th century and tapers into a 17th-century octagonal tower, from where there's a great view.

Musée de Millau (☎ 05 65 59 01 08; place Maréchal Foch; adult/student/under 18yr €5/3.50/free; ☼ 10am-6pm daily Jul & Aug, 10am-noon & 2-6pm daily May, Jun & Sep, 10am-noon & 2-6pm Mon-Sat Oct-Apr) has a rich collection of fossils, including mammoth molars and a dinosaur skeleton from the Causse du Larzac. In the basement is a huge array of plates and vases from **La Graufesenque**, in its time the largest pottery workshop in the western Roman Empire. The 1st-floor leather and glove section illustrates Millau's tanneries and their products through the ages.

A **combined ticket** (€6) includes admission to La Graufesenque archaeological site, at the confluence of the Rivers Tarn and Dourbie.

Activities

HANG-GLIDING & PARAPENTE

Outfits running introductory courses (around €300 for five days) and tandem

---

VIADUC DE MILLAU

This toll bridge, slung across the wide Tarn Valley to link the Causse du Larzac and Causse Rouge, takes the breath away. Designed by the British architect Sir Norman Foster, it carried a massive 4.43 million vehicles in 2005, its first year of operation. It's a true work of industrial art and an amazing feat of engineering. Only seven pylons, hollow and seemingly slim as needles, support 2.5km of four-lane motorway. Rising to 343m above the valley bottom, it ranks among the tallest road bridges in the world.

More than three years in construction and costing more than €400 million, it gobbled up 127,000 cu metres of concrete, 19,000 tonnes of reinforcing steel and 5000 tonnes of cables and stays. Yet despite these heavyweight superlatives, it still looks like a gossamer thread. Far from detracting from the charms of the hitherto unspoilt countryside around the town of Millau, this vital link in the A75 motorway is a true 21st-century icon.

LANGUEDOC-ROUSSILLON

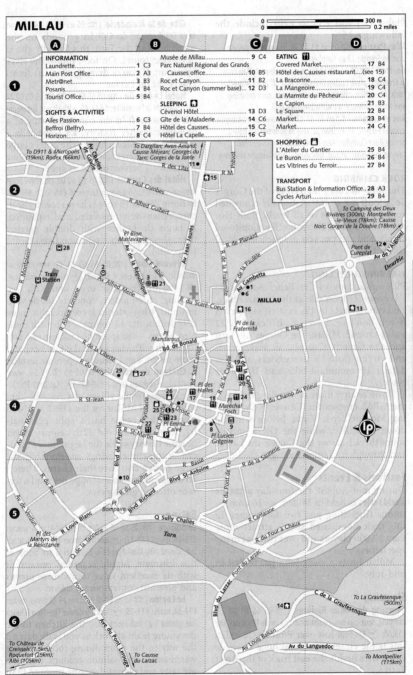

MILLAU

0 ____ 300 m
0 ____ 0.2 miles

A **B** **C** **D**

INFORMATION
Laundrette................................ 1 C3
Main Post Office....................... 2 A3
Metr@net................................ 3 B3
Posanis.................................... 4 B4
Tourist Office........................... 5 B4

SIGHTS & ACTIVITIES
Ailes Passion............................ 6 C3
Beffroi (Belfry)......................... 7 B4
Horizon................................... 8 C4

Musée de Millau....................... 9 C4
Parc Naturel Régional des Grands
  Causses office...................... 10 C4
Roc et Canyon......................... 11 B5
Roc et Canyon (summer base)... 12 D3

SLEEPING
Cévenol Hôtel.......................... 13 D3
Gîte de la Maladerie................. 14 C6
Hôtel des Causses..................... 15 C2
Hôtel La Capelle....................... 16 C3

EATING
Covered Market........................ 17 B4
Hôtel des Causses restaurant....(see 15)
La Braconne............................. 18 C4
La Mangeoire........................... 19 C4
La Marmite du Pêcheur............. 20 C4
Le Capion................................ 21 B3
Le Square................................ 22 B4
Market.................................... 23 B4
Market.................................... 24 C4

SHOPPING
L'Atelier du Gantier.................. 25 B4
Le Buron................................. 26 B4
Les Vitrines du Terroir.............. 27 B4

TRANSPORT
Bus Station & Information Office.. 28 A3
Cycles Arturi........................... 29 B4

LANGUEDOC-ROUSSILLON

flights (around €35 to €70) include the following:

Ailes Passion (☎ 05 65 61 20 96; www.ailes-passion .com in French; 12 av Gambetta)

Horizon (☎ 05 65 59 78 60; www.horizon-millau.com in French; 6 place Lucien Grégoire) Just off place Maréchal Foch. Also offers caving, canyon descents, rock climbing and Naturaventure, a multiadventure trail.

Roc et Canyon (☎ 05 65 61 17 77; www.roc-et-canyon .com in French; 55 av Jean Jaurès) In summer it's based beside Pont Cureplat. Also offers caving, rock climbing, canyon descents, rafting, canoeing – and bungee jumping.

ROCK CLIMBING
The 50m- to 200m-high cliffs of the Gorges de la Jonte are an internationally renowned venue for climbers of all levels. Both Horizon and Roc et Canyon offer monitored climbs and can put you in touch with local climbers.

WALKING & CYCLING
Pick up a copy of *Les Belles Balades de l'Aveyron* (€8), on sale at the tourist office. You can navigate by the explicit maps even if you don't read French. It describes 22 walks around Millau, the Gorges du Tarn and the Grands Causses, all waymarked and varying from 1½ to six hours, and also details 10 mountain-bike and 10 tourer routes.

If you're after more demanding trekking, the GR62 crosses the Causse Noir, passing Montpellier-le-Vieux before winding down to Millau, while the GR71 and its spurs thread across the Causse du Larzac and through its Templar villages.

Festivals & Events
During mid-August, the four-day **pétanque world series** is held in Millau. Its 16 competitions (including just two for women in this male-dominated sport) attract more than 10,000 players and over twice as many spectators.

Millau hosts a week-long **jazz festival** in mid-July.

Sleeping
Camping des Deux Rivières (☎ 05 65 60 00 27; camping.deux-rivieres@wanadoo.fr; 61 av de l'Aigoual; site €13.80; ☸ Apr-Sep) Just over Pont de Cureplat, this is the closest of several huge riverside camp sites beside the east bank of the River Tarn.

Gîte de la Maladerie (☎ 05 65 60 41 84; chemin de la Graufesenque; dm €10) In grounds on the south bank of the Tarn, this friendly gîte is open year-round. On foot, follow the river upstream. If you're driving, turn left (east) after Pont du Larzac.

Hôtel La Capelle (☎ 05 65 60 14 72; fax 05 65 60 22 69; 7 place de la Fraternité; d €42-45, with shared bathroom €28; ☸ year-round) In the converted wing of a one-time leather factory, La Capelle is a quite lovely budget choice. The hotel's large terrace with views towards the Causse Noir makes for a perfect breakfast spot.

Hôtel des Causses (☎ 05 65 60 03 19; www.hotel -des-causses.com; 56 av Jean Jaurès; d €46-55, tr €60-70) Parking €6. All 19 rooms have recently been comprehensively renovated and repainted. A Logis de France with double glazing throughout, it also has a good restaurant (opposite).

Cévenol Hôtel (☎ 05 65 60 74 44; www.cevenol -hotel.fr; 115 rue Rajol; d €58-62; ☸ mid-Mar–mid-Nov; ☒) On the fringe of town and with free parking, this modern concrete block with its uninspiring exterior is considerably more cosy within. Its 42 rooms – two with disabled access – are spacious (ask for one facing south with views over the Causses) and there's a pool and pleasant open-air terrace.

Château de Creissels (☎ 05 65 60 16 59; www .chateau-de-creissels.com; r €59-89; ☸ Mar-Dec) Parking is free. In the village of Creissels, 2km southwest of Millau on the D992 and well signed, this castle has a split personality. Rooms in the old 12th-century tower breathe history while the larger, more modern 20th-century wings overlooking the large garden also have their charm. There's an excellent restaurant (opposite) and a terrace offering great views.

Eating
Le Square (☎ 05 65 61 26 00; 10 rue St-Martin; menus €16-26, mains €13-17; ☸ lunch & dinner Thu-Mon & lunch Tue, closed mid-Mar–Apr) It's essential to book at this intimate, highly regarded restaurant with its excellent value four-course *menus* and pleasant contemporary décor.

Le Capion (☎ 05 65 60 00 91; 3 rue J-F Alméras; menus €17-38, mains €13-18; ☸ lunch & dinner Thu-Mon & lunch Tue, closed 1-21 Jul) Peer into the kitchen to see the young team at work as you walk past on the way to the main dining room with its warm ochre and salmon colours. Portions are tasty and plentiful – none more so than the rich cheese platter (where, of course, Roquefort stars) and trolley of tempting homemade desserts.

La Mangeoire (☎ 05 65 60 13 16; 8 blvd de la Capelle; menus €16-45; ☑ lunch & dinner Tue-Sun; closed dinner Sun Nov-Apr) Millau's oldest restaurant, in the vaults beneath the former city walls, serves delightful mainly regional dishes. Its pride is the open wood-fire barbecue. In winter, spits pierce wild game such as hare and partridge. Year-round, meat and fish (€12 to €16) are sizzled to perfection.

La Marmite du Pêcheur (☎ 05 65 61 20 44; 14-16 blvd de la Capelle; menus €16-45, mains €14-22; ☑ Wed-Mon) A few doors from La Mangeoire and run by an engaging young couple, it's also attractively vaulted and has hearty regional *menus* within much the same price range. Within the *menu del país* (regional menu; €24) are some especially enticing regional specialities.

La Braconne (☎ 05 65 60 30 93; 7 place du Maréchal Foch; menus €17-37; ☑ lunch & dinner Tue-Sat & dinner Sun) Choose the cosy interior with its thick, 13th-century stone walls and vaulted roof or dine on the terrace overlooking Millau's main square. The Braconne has excellent regional *menus* and keeps a good selection of local Faugères wines.

Two good hotel restaurants:

Hôtel des Causses restaurant (☎ 05 65 60 03 19; www.hotel-des-causses.com; 56 av Jean Jaurès; menus €16-26) Has a pair of enticing regional *menus* and several hearty dishes from the Lyon area, the chef/owner's home town.

Château de Creissels restaurant (☎ 05 65 60 16 59; www.chateau-de-creissels.com; menus €23-50)

SELF-CATERING

There are markets on Wednesday and Friday morning in place du Maréchal Foch, place Emma Calvé and the covered market at place des Halles.

Shopping

L'Atelier du Gantier (21 rue Droite) A wonderful little shop that sells gloves and only gloves of the softest leather. Hit the right moment and you can see staff sewing away at a pair of vintage Singer machines.

Les Vitrines du Terroir (17 blvd de l'Ayrolle) and **Le Buron** (18 rue Droite) are delightfully rich and pungent *fromageries* (cheese shops) selling local specialities including Roquefort and Perail du Larzac cheeses.

Getting There & Away

The **bus station** and its **information office** (☎ 05 65 59 89 33) are beside the train station. Buses travel to Toulouse (€25.40, four hours, one daily), Montpellier (€16, 2¼ hours, eight daily), and Rodez (€11, 1½ hours, eight daily).

Train connections from Millau include Béziers (€16.10, 1¾ hours, two daily), plus Montpellier (€23.10, 1½ hours, two daily) and Rodez (€10.80, 1½ hours, six daily).

Getting Around

Cycles Arturi (☎ 05 65 60 28 23; 2 rue du Barry; ☑ Mon-Sat Jul & Aug, Tue-Sat Sep-Jun) rents city bikes for €9/12 per half-/full day and mountain bikes for €11/15.

AROUND MILLAU
Roquefort

In the heart of Parc Naturel Régional des Grands Causses and 25km southwest of Millau, the village of Roquefort-sur-Soulzon (population 680) turns ewe's milk into France's most famous blue cheese. Its steep, narrow streets lead to the cool natural caves, where seven producers ripen 22,000 tonnes of Roquefort cheese every year.

La Société (☎ 05 65 59 93 30; www.roquefort-soci ete.com) has one-hour **guided tours** (adult/under 16yr €3/free; ☑ 9.30am-6.30pm Jul & Aug, 9.30am-noon & 1.30-5pm Sep-Jun) that include a fairly feeble sound-and-light show and sampling of the

THE KING OF CHEESES

The mouldy blue-green veins that run through Roquefort are, in fact, the spores of microscopic mushrooms, cultivated on leavened bread.

As the cheeses are ripened in natural caves, enlarged and gouged from the mountainside, draughts of air called *fleurines* flow through, encouraging the blue *Penicillium roqueforti* to eat its way through the white cheese curds.

Roquefort is one of France's priciest and most noble cheeses. In 1407 Charles VI granted exclusive Roquefort cheese-making rights to the villagers, while in the 17th century the Sovereign Court of the Parliament of Toulouse imposed severe penalties against fraudulent cheese makers trading under the Roquefort name.

three varieties the company makes. Established in 1842, it's the largest Roquefort producer, churning out 70% of the world's supply, over 30% of which is exported.

Tours of the equally pungent caves of **Le Papillon** (☎ 05 65 58 50 08; www.roquefort-papillon .com in French; rue de la Fontaine; ☯ 9am-6.30pm Jul & Aug, 9.30am-12.30pm & 1.30-4.30pm or 5.30pm Sep-Jun) are free and include a 15-minute film.

Between mid-June and mid-September, you can also visit farms in the catchment area, from which some 130 million litres of ewe's milk are collected annually. For details, contact the **tourist office** (☎ 05 65 58 56 00; www.roquefort.com; ☯ 9am-7pm daily Jul & Aug, 9am-6pm Mon-Sat Apr-Jun, Sep & Oct; 10am-5pm Mon-Fri Nov-Mar) at the western entry to the village.

Micropolis

'La Cité des Insectes' (Insect City), **Micropolis** (☎ 05 65 58 50 50; www.micropolis.biz; adult/child with audioguide €10/7.40; ☯ 10am-6pm daily Jul & Aug, 10am-5pm Tue-Sun Jun & Sep; 11am-4pm Tue-Fri, 10am-5pm Sat & Sun Mar, May & Oct) is outside the village of St-Léons, off the D911 19km northwest of Millau.

Ever felt small? This mind-boggling hi-tech experience happens in a building where grass grows 6m high. The swarms of facts about insect life, all compellingly presented, seem equally tall but all are true. Captions are in French and English. Allow a good 1½ hours, perhaps rounding off with a meal at its pleasant, reasonably priced restaurant.

Pastoralia

Pastoralia (☎ 05 65 98 10 23; adult/child €4.50/3; ☯ 10am-6pm Jul & Aug, 10am-noon & 2-6pm daily May-Jun, 10am-noon & 2-6pm Mon-Fri Apr & Sep), 2.25km west of St-Affrique, tells the story of the 700,000 ewes who graze the high plateaus, producing around 170 million litres of milk annually, over half of which is turned into Roquefort and other regional cheeses. There are interactive panels with English translation, a 10-minute film and in summer you can feed the sheep.

ROUSSILLON

Roussillon, sometimes known as French Catalonia, sits on Spain's doorstep at the eastern end of the Pyrenees. It's the land of the Tramontane, a violent wind that howls down from the mountains, chilling to the bone in winter and in summer strong enough to overturn a caravan. The main city is Perpignan, capital of the Pyrénées-Orientales *département*.

Long part of Catalonia (which nowadays officially designates only the autonomous region over the border in northeast Spain), Roussillon retains many symbols of Catalan identity. The *sardane* folk dance is still performed and the Catalan language, closely related to Provençal, is fairly widely spoken.

History

People have lived here since prehistoric times, and one of Europe's oldest skulls was found in a cave near Tautavel (p803).

Roussillon's relatively modern history was for a long time closely bound with events over the Pyrenees in present-day Spain. In 1172 it came under the control of the realm of Catalonia-Aragon. After flourishing in its own right as the capital of the kingdom of Mallorca for most of the next two centuries, it again fell under alien Aragonese rule for much of the late Middle Ages.

In 1640 the Catalans on both sides of the Pyrenees revolted against the Castilian kings in distant Madrid, who had engulfed Aragon. Perpignan endured a two-year siege, only relieved with the support of the French to the north. Peace came in 1659 with the Treaty of the Pyrenees, defining the border between Spain and France once and for all and ceding Roussillon (until then the northern section of Catalonia) to the French, much to the indignation of the locals.

PERPIGNAN

pop 107,200

As much Catalan as French, Perpignan (Perpinyà in Catalan) is far from being a 'villainous ugly town' – the verdict of traveller Henry Swinburne in 1775. Its population is a mixed one. Iberian blood flows in the veins of the descendants of the thousands of refugees who fled over the mountains at the end of the Spanish Civil War. Many others, Arab and displaced French settlers alike, have their recent origins in Algeria.

At the foothills of the Pyrenees and with the Côte Vermeille to its southeast, Perpignan is a good base for day trips along the coast or to the mountains and Cathar castles of the interior. It's commendably well

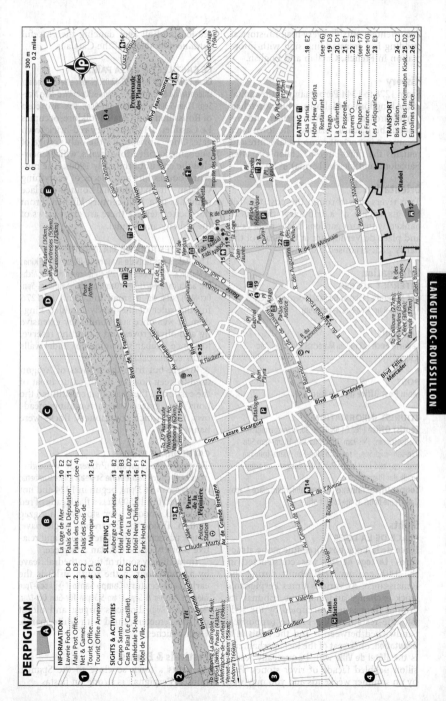

PERPIGNAN

INFORMATION
Lavenie Foch...................	1 D4
Main Post Office.............	2 D3
Net & Games..................	3 C2
Tourist Office.................	4 F1
Tourist Office Annexe......	5 D3

SIGHTS & ACTIVITIES
Campo Santo..................	6 E2
Casa Pairal (Le Castillet)...	7 D2
Cathédrale St-Jean..........	8 E2
Hôtel de Ville.................	9 E2
La Loge de Mer..............	10 E2
Palais de la Députation.....	11 E2
Palais des Congrès...........	(see 4)
Palais des Rois de	
Majorque.....................	12 E4

SLEEPING 🛏
Auberge de Jeunesse.......	13 B2
Hôtel Avenir...................	14 B3
Hôtel de La Loge............	15 D2
Hôtel New Christina.........	16 F1
Park Hotel.....................	17 F2

EATING 🍴
Casa Sansa.....................	18 E2
Hôtel New Cristina	
Restaurant...................	(see 16)
L'Arago........................	19 D3
La Galinette...................	20 D1
La Passerelle..................	21 E1
Laurens'O......................	22 E3
Le Chapon Fin...............	(see 17)
Le France.....................	23 E2
Les Antiquaires...............	(see 10)

TRANSPORT
Bus Station....................	24 C2
CTPM Bus Information Kiosk.	25 D2
Eurolines office...............	26 A3

LANGUEDOC-ROUSSILLON

documented; outside every major historical building is a freestanding sign with information in French, Catalan and English.

History

From 1278 to 1344 Perpignan was the capital of the kingdom of Mallorca, which stretched northwards as far as Montpellier and included the Balearic Islands. The town later became an important commercial centre and remains the third-largest Catalan city after Barcelona and Lleida (Lérida) in Spain.

Orientation

Two rivers flow through the city: the Têt and its trickle of a tributary, the Basse, banked with trim gardens. Place de la Loge and place de Verdun are at the heart of the partly pedestrianised old town.

Information

INTERNET ACCESS
Net & Games (45bis av Général Leclerc; per hr €3; ☻ noon-1am Mon-Sat, 1-8pm Sun)

LAUNDRY
Laverie Foch (23 rue du Maréchal Foch; ☻ 7am-8.30pm)

POST
Main Post Office (quai de Barcelone)

TOURIST INFORMATION
Tourist Office (☎ 04 68 66 30 30; www.perpignan tourisme.com; ☻ 9am-7pm Mon-Sat, 10am-4pm Sun mid-Jun–mid-Sep, 9am-6pm Mon-Sat, 10am-1pm Sun mid-Sep–mid-Jun) In the Palais des Congrès, off promenade des Platanes.
Tourist Office Annexe (Espace Palmarium, place Arago) Open same hours as the tourist office.

Sights

PLACE DE LA LOGE
Place de la Loge has three fine stone structures. **La Loge de Mer** was constructed in the 14th century and rebuilt during the Renaissance. At various times Perpignan's stock exchange and maritime tribunal, its ground floor is now occupied by the stylish café-restaurant Le France (opposite). Sandwiched between it and the **Palais de la Députation**, once seat of the local parliament, is the **Hôtel de Ville** with its typically Roussillon pebbled façade of river stones. Pass by on summer weekends and you may well

see locals of all ages dancing the graceful *sardane*, folk dance of the Catalans.

LE CASTILLET & CASA PAÏRAL
Casa Païral (☎ 04 68 35 42 05; place de Verdun; adult/student/child €4/2/free; ☻ 10am-6.30pm Wed-Mon May-Sep, 11am-5.30pm Wed-Mon Oct-Apr), the museum of Roussillon and Catalan folklore, occupies Le Castillet, a 14th-century red-brick town gate. Once a prison, it's the only vestige of Vauban's fortified town walls, which encircled the city until the early 1900s. The museum houses bits and pieces of everything Catalan – from traditional bonnets and lace mantillas to a 17th-century kitchen. From the rooftop terrace there are great views of the old city and citadel.

PALAIS DES ROIS DE MAJORQUE
The **Palais des Rois de Majorque** (Palace of the Kings of Mallorca; ☎ 04 68 34 48 29; entrance on rue des Archers; adult/child €4/2; ☻ 10am-6pm Jun-Sep, 9am-5pm Oct-May) sits on a small hill. Built in 1276 for the ruler of the newly founded kingdom, it was once surrounded by extensive fig and olive groves and a hunting reserve, lost once Vauban's formidable citadel walls enclosed the palace.

Bizarre but true: the princes of Aragon used to keep lions in the dried-up moat of the castle and the goats that constituted the lions' diet grazed the surrounding meadows, from which commoners' flocks were banned.

CATHÉDRALE ST-JEAN
Topped by a typically Provençal wrought-iron bell cage, **Cathédrale St-Jean** (place Gambetta; ☻ 9am-noon & 3-6.30pm), begun in 1324 and not completed until 1509, has a flat façade of red brick and smooth river stones in a zigzag pattern. Inside the cavernous single nave, notice particularly the fine carving and relative sobriety of the Catalan altarpiece.

Immediately south of the cathedral (leave by a small door in the south aisle) is the early-14th-century **Campo Santo** (☻ noon-7pm Tue-Sun Apr-Jun & Sep, 11am-5.30pm Tue-Sun Oct-Mar, closed Jul & Aug), France's largest and oldest cloister-cemetery, lined with white-marble Gothic niches.

Festivals & Events

As befits a town so close to the Spanish border, Perpignan is strong on fiestas.

For the Good Friday **Procession de la Sanch**, penitents wearing the *caperutxa* (traditional hooded red or black robes) parade silently through the old city.

A 'sacred' flame is brought down from Mont Canigou during the week-long **Fête de la Sant Joan**, marking midsummer, while in September half the town pulls on tights and wimples for the **Marché Médiéval** (Medieval Market).

Shutterbugs will be in their element in the first half of September, when, for a full two weeks, the town hosts **Visa Pour l'Image**, the world's major festival of photojournalism, open to the general public.

Perpignan holds a **jazz festival** throughout October and, on the third weekend in October, a **wine festival**, when a barrel of the year's new wine is ceremonially borne to Cathédrale St-Jean to be blessed.

Sleeping

Camping La Garrigole (☎ 04 68 54 66 10; 2 rue Maurice Lévy; 2 adults, tent & car €13; ⊗ year-round) This small camp site is 1.5km west of the train station. Take bus No 2 and get off at the Garrigole stop.

Auberge de Jeunesse (☎ 04 68 34 63 32; perpignan@fuaj.org; allée Marc Pierre; dm €12; ⊗ Mar–mid-Nov) Perpignan's HI-affiliated youth hostel is just north of Parc de la Pépinière. There's a members kitchen.

Hôtel Avenir (☎ 04 68 34 20 30; www.avenirhotel.com; 11 rue de l'Avenir; r €33.60, with shower from €28, s/d with shared bathroom from €17/23.30) Parking €4.50. Among the budget hotels along and around av Général de Gaulle, the Avenir is a particularly friendly, highly recommended place. Several rooms have a small terrace and each is uniquely and charmingly decorated by the proprietor. Savour too the delightful 1st-floor terrace, open to all.

Hôtel de La Loge (☎ 04 68 34 41 02; www.hoteldelaloge.fr; 1 rue des Fabriques Nabot; s €37, d €42-64; 🅿) Disregard the gruff owner and the threadbare stair carpet; the bedrooms themselves are rather more pleasant though their furniture varies from attractive and antique to flea market. Of the more expensive rooms, which have air-con and separate toilets, Nos 106 and 206 (each €57) overlook place de la Loge.

Park Hotel (☎ 04 68 35 14 14; www.parkhotel-fr.com; 18 blvd Jean Bourrat; s/d from €60/70; 🅿 🅿 🖥) Wi-fi. Parking €10. How to generalise when each of this pleasant hotel's soundproofed rooms is individually and engagingly furnished and decorated? What's sure is that their *supérieure* rooms (€85/100), with separate bathroom, shower cubicle and toilet, are indeed a cut above the already attractive rest. The largest of them (ending in 04 and 05) overlook the park. It also runs a superb Michelin one-star restaurant (see Le Chapon Fin, p802).

Hôtel New Christina (☎ 04 68 35 12 21; www.hotel-newchristina.com; 51 cours Lassus; s/d €64/69; 🅿 🅿) Parking €9. At the excellent, family-run New Christina, rooms are attractively decorated in blue and beige and bathrooms, all with bathtubs, are separate from toilets. Those at the front overlook a public park. The open-air pool, up on the roof (together with Perpignan's only Jacuzzi), has an even better view. There's also a good restaurant (p802).

Eating

L'Arago (☎ 04 68 51 81 96; 1 place Arago; mains €13-20.50; ⊗ daily) L'Arago is much in demand so you may have to hang around a while for a free table. It bakes mean pizzas (€8.50 to €10) and has a strong and varied à la carte selection. Choose from the good range of Roussillon and Côtes Catalanes wines.

Casa Sansa (☎ 04 68 34 21 84; entrances 2 rue Fabrique Nadal & rue Fabrique Couverte; menus €19-29, mains €15-21; ⊗ daily) This is another highly popular spot – or rather two adjacent places. Choose the older, more southerly one, its walls scarcely visible for posters and the photos of the famous and less than famous who have enjoyed its fine Catalan cuisine. It too has a great selection of wines, most also available by the glass.

Le France (☎ 04 68 51 61 71; place de la Loge; mains €15-24; ⊗ noon-10pm daily) Popular and stylish, Le France manages to blend harmoniously the modern – right down to the all-glass hand basins in the toilets – within a historical setting. Portions are smallish but attractively presented and the wine list is almost as vast as the palatial setting of what was once Perpignan's stock exchange. The lunchtime *formule rapide* at €12 is great value.

Laurens'O (☎ 04 68 34 66 66; 5 place des Poilus; mains €16-19; ⊗ Tue-Sat) This cheerful modern locale with its striped tablecloths and orange and black décor offers innovative Mediterranean cooking. Its distinctly Italian flavour is garnished with a creative French twist, a whiff of North Africa and a little Thai touch here and there.

Les Antiquaires (☎ 04 68 34 06 58; place Desprès; menus €22-40, mains €16-21; ☯ lunch & dinner Tue-Sat & lunch Sun) The day we dined here, there wasn't a soul under 40 – much the same age as the splendid line of vintage bottles displayed above the fireplace. The cuisine is traditional, reliable and as mature and bourgeois as the clientele. Portions, from the giant 50g pack of butter discreetly placed before you to the three huge dollops of chocolate mousse for dessert, are generous.

La Passerelle (☎ 04 68 51 30 65; 1 cours Palmarole; menu €30, mains €19-22; ☯ dinner Mon-Sat) Its attractive marine décor hints at the riches within the kitchen. La Passerelle is *the* restaurant in Perpignan for Mediterranean fish, guaranteed fresh and without a hint of freezer or fish farm.

La Galinette (☎ 04 68 35 00 90; 23 rue Jean Payra; lunch menu €15, mains around €25; ☯ Tue-Sat) In an elegant, contemporary setting with bright murals and flowers on every table, La Galinette offers refined cuisine and has an ample selection of regional wines. For a frisson of the unexpected, go for the *'menu surprise'* fish menu (€42) and let the chef select the best that the sea can offer that day.

Recommended hotel restaurants:

Le Chapon Fin (☎ 04 68 35 14 14; www.parkhotel-fr .com; 18 blvd Jean Bourrat; mains €38-45, menus €59-69, lunch menu €25; ☯ closed 1-21 Jan, 15-31 Aug) At Park Hotel.

Hôtel New Christina restaurant (☎ 04 68 35 12 21; www.hotel-newchristina.com; 51 cours Lassus; menu €19)

Entertainment

The tourist office publishes *L'Agenda*, a comprehensive free monthly guide to exhibitions and cultural events. *So Aware*, published monthly, is the best of several competing free, what's-on tap-ins to the club scene and nightlife.

Getting There & Away

AIR

Perpignan's **airport** (☎ 04 68 52 60 70) is 5km northwest of the town centre. Air France flies three to four times daily to/from Paris (Orly). Ryanair runs a daily flight to/from London Stansted, Flybe serves Birmingham and Southampton and BMI Baby flies to/from Manchester.

The Navette Aéroport bus runs from the train station via place Catalogne and the bus station.

BUS

From the **bus station** (☎ 04 68 35 29 02; av Général Leclerc), **Courriers Catalans** (☎ 04 68 55 68 00) services coastal resorts, running two to five buses daily (€6.90) to/from Collioure and Port-Vendres, most continuing to Banyuls (1¼ hours).

Five buses daily travel along the Têt Valley to Vernet-les-Bains (€10, 1½ hours) via Prades (€8.40) and Villefranche (€10). Up to seven daily buses run up the Tech Valley to Céret (€6.10, 50 minutes).

For long-distance buses, the **Eurolines office** (☎ 04 68 34 11 46; 10 av Général de Gaulle) is just east of the train station.

CAR

Rental companies include **Avis** (airport ☎ 04 68 34 26 71) and **Budget** (airport ☎ 04 68 56 95 95).

TRAIN

Perpignan's small train station – centre of the universe according to Salvador Dalí (below) – is served by bus Nos 1 and 2.

Trains cross the Pyrenees to Barcelona (€32 direct, €16.50 changing at Cerbère/Portbou, up to three hours, at least three daily). There are frequent services to Montpellier (€20.50, two hours) via Narbonne (€9.50, 45 minutes) and Béziers (€12.50). Nine TGVs daily run to Paris,

---

DALÍ'S TRAIN OF THOUGHT

You may choose to dissent from Salvador Dalí's no doubt chemically induced claim that Perpignan's train station is the centre of the universe. According to local lore (reinforced by a plaque in front of the building), the Catalan surrealist painter (1904–89) was visiting the capital of French Catalonia in 1965 when he experienced an epiphany. 'Suddenly before me, everything appeared with the clarity of lightning,' he wrote. 'I found myself in the centre of the universe.' Dalí went on to describe this decidedly nondescript place as *'la source d'illuminations'* and *'la cathédrale d'intuitions'* – no doubt putting a smile on the faces of local tourism authorities and most Perpignanais.

Gare de Lyon (€83 to €96, five hours). For Carcassonne (€16.50), change in Narbonne.

Closer to home is Cerbère/Portbou on the Spanish border (€6.90, 40 minutes, around 15 daily) via Collioure (€4.80), Port-Vendres (€5.30) and Banyuls (€6).

The nearest you can get to Andorra by train is La Tour de Carol (€21.60, four hours, four daily, most changing in Ville-franche (€6.60, 45 minutes) and Villefranche (€7.40, one hour, five daily). From La Tour de Carol, a connecting bus takes you on to Andorra.

Getting Around

The local bus company, CTPM, has an **information kiosk** (☎ 04 68 61 01 13; 27 blvd Clemenceau). A ticket costs €1.10, a one-day pass is €4.10 and a 10-ticket *carnet*, €7.80. Bright yellow and red, *Le P'tit Bus* is a free hop-on, hop-off minibus that plies a circular route around the town centre.

For a taxi, call **Accueil Perpignan Taxis** (☎ 04 68 35 15 15).

AROUND PERPIGNAN
Coastal Beaches

The nearest beach – all 5km of it – is at **Canet-Plage**, backed by a sprawl of hotels and apartment blocks. There's a small **tourist office** (☎ 04 68 86 72 00; www.ot-canet.fr; ☼ 9am-7pm daily Jul & Aug, 9am-noon & 2-6pm Mon-Sat, 9.30am-12.30pm & 2-5pm Sun Sep-Jun).

Rent a bicycle (first day €15, then €5 per day) from **Sun Bike 66** (☎ 04 68 73 88 65) and cruise the promenade or ride around the Étang de Canet, a small inland lake and nature reserve.

South of Argelès-Plage, wide sandy beaches give way to rocky coastline as the Pyrenees tumble to the sea, their steep flanks terraced with vineyards.

Céret

It's mainly the **Musée d'Art Moderne** (☎ 04 68 87 27 76; www.musee-ceret.com; 8 blvd Maréchal Joffre; adult/student/child €5.50/3.50/free; ☼ 10am-6pm or 7pm daily May-Sep, 10am-6pm or 7pm Wed-Mon Oct-Apr) that draws visitors to this town of scarcely 8000 souls, settled snugly in the Pyrenean foothills just off the Tech Valley. Superbly endowed for such a small community, its collection owes much to an earlier genera-tion of visitors and residents, who included Picasso, Braque, Chagall, Matisse, Miró, Dalí, Juan Gris and Manolo, all of whom donated works (53 from Picasso alone).

Firmly Catalan, Céret is also splendidly disproportionate in the number and vigour of its festivals. Famous for its juicy cherries (the first pickings of the season are packed off to the French president), it kicks off with the **Fête de la Cerise** (Cherry Festival) in late May. Summer sees the **féria** with bullfights and roistering and **La Fête de la Sardane**, cel-ebrating the *sardane*, folk dance par excel-lence of the Catalans – and, it goes without saying, yet more bullfights. More sedately, **Les Méennes** is a festival of primarily classical music. Contact the **tourist office** (☎ 04 68 87 00 53; www.ot-ceret.fr; 1 av Clemenceau) for details.

Tautavel

The Arago Cave, on the slopes above the village of Tautavel, 30km northwest of Perpignan along the D117, has yielded a human skull, estimated to be 450,000 years old, along with a host of other prehistoric items. The **Musée de Préhistoire** (Prehistory Mu-seum; ☎ 04 68 29 07 76; www.tautavel.com; av Jean Jau-rès; adult/child with audioguide €7/3.50; ☼ 10am-7pm Jul & Aug, 10am-12.30pm & 2-5pm or 6.30pm Sep-Jun) has a full-size reproduction of the cave, complete with holograms, dioramas, TVs dispensing knowledge from every corner and lots of fossilised bones and stone tools. There's also a secondary exhibition, **Musée des Premiers Habitants d'Europe** (ask for the English-language sheet 'The First Inhabit-ants of Europe'), 300m away on rue Anatole France. Allow a good 1½ hours to take in both elements.

Cathar Fortresses

When the Albigensian Crusade forced the Cathars into the arid mountains that once marked the frontier between France and Aragon, they sought refuge in these inac-cessible fortresses that had long protected the border. In a long but fulfilling 195km day of driving between Carcassonne and Perpignan – or vice versa – you can take in the four major sites of **Puilaurens** (☎ 04 68 20 65 26; adult/child €3.50/1.50; ☼ 9am-8pm Jul & Aug, 10am-6pm Apr-Jun & Sep, 10am-5pm Oct), which later functioned as a prison; **Peyrepertuse** (☎ 04 68 45 40 55; adult/child €5/3, audioguide €4; ☼ 9am-8.30pm Jun-Aug, 10am-5pm, 6pm or 7pm Sep-May), the largest with a drop of several hundred metres on

THE CATHARS

The term *le Pays Cathar* (Cathar Land) recalls the cruel Albigensian Crusade – the hounding and extermination of a religious sect called the Cathars.

The Cathars were the fundamentalists of their day: people of extreme beliefs, warily regarded by the mainstream yet convinced that they alone knew the one true way to salvation. Cathars (from the Greek word *katharos* meaning 'pure') believed that God's kingdom was locked in battle with Satan's evil world and that humans were base at heart. But, they reckoned, a pure life followed by several reincarnations could free the spirit from its satanical body. Reacting against worldly Rome and preaching in *langue d'oc*, the local tongue, the sect gained many followers. Their most extreme followers, the ascetic *parfaits* ('perfects'), who followed strict vegetarian diets and abstained from sex, weren't your ideal fun travelling companions.

In 1208 Pope Innocent III preached a crusade against the Cathars. The Albigensian Crusade had a political as much as spiritual dimension; here was the chance for northern rulers to expand their territory into Languedoc.

After long sieges, the major Cathar centres at Béziers, Carcassonne, Minerve and the dramatically sited fortresses of Montségur, Quéribus and Peyrepertuse were taken and hundreds of 'perfects' were burned as heretics. In Béziers as many as 20,000 of the faithful were slaughtered. Montségur witnessed another cruel massacre in 1244, when 200 Cathars, refusing to renounce their faith, were burned alive in a mass funerary pyre. In 1321 the burning of the last 'perfect', Guillaume Bélibaste, marked the end of Catharism in Languedoc.

all sides; **Quéribus** (☎ 04 68 45 03 69; adult/child €5/2, audioguide €4; ☉ 9am-8pm Jul & Aug, 9.30am-7pm Apr-Jun & Sep, 10am-5pm or 5.30pm Oct-Mar), which marked the Cathars' last stand in 1255; and **Aguilar** (☎ 04 68 45 51 00; adult/child €2.30/1; ☉ 10am-12.30pm & 3.30-7pm Jun-Sep), the smallest and sadly in need of care and attention. See too the boxed text, above). Each clings to the clifftop, offers a dramatic wraparound panorama and requires a short, stiff climb from its car park. This is wild country, hot as hell in summer, so be sure to pack extra water.

A combined ticket (€14) allows entry to Peyrepertuse, Quéribus and the Musée de Préhistoire in Tautavel (p803), which can be visited in the same day if you've the stamina. Those deeply into Catharism might want to invest €4 in a *Carte Inter-Sites*, which gives reductions to 17 sites, major and minor.

TÊT VALLEY

Fruit orchards carpet the lower reaches of the Têt Valley. Beyond the strategic fortress town of Villefranche de Conflent, the scenery becomes wilder, more open and undulating as the valley climbs towards Spanish Catalonia and Andorra.

Le Train Jaune

Carrying nearly half a million passengers during the three peak months of high sum-

mer, **Le Train Jaune** (Yellow Train) runs from Villefranche to La Tour de Carol (return €34) through spectacular Pyrenean scenery. There are five trains daily in July and August, four in June and September and two between October and May. You can't reserve and it's wise to arrive an hour before departure time in high summer.

Prades
pop 6300

Prades, at the heart of the Têt Valley, is internationally famed for its annual classical music festival. It's an attractive town with houses of river stone and brick, liberally adorned with pink marble from nearby quarries.

The **tourist office** (☎ 04 68 05 41 02; www.prades -tourisme.com; 4 rue des Marchands; ☉ 9am-noon & 2-6pm Mon-Sat, 10am-noon Sun Jul & Aug, 9am-noon & 2-6pm Mon-Fri Sep-Jun, 9am-noon Sat Jun & Sep) is just off the main square, place de la République.

The belltower of **Église St-Pierre** (☉ 8.30am-noon & 2.30-6pm Mon-Sat, 8.30am-noon Sun) is all that remains of the original 12th-century Romanesque church. The wonderfully expressive, ill-lit 17th-century *Entombment of Christ* at the western end is by the Catalan sculptor Josep Sunyer, who also carved the exuberant main altarpiece, a *chef-d'oeuvre* of Catalan baroque and reputedly the largest in France.

Hiking & Walking Around Prades details in English 20 easy-to-moderate walks lasting from 2½ to four hours. *Six Grandes Randonnées en Conflent* in French describes six more challenging day walks, including the classic ascent of Mont Canigou (2786m). The tourist office sells both guides at €3 each.

VTT en Conflent details 10 mountain-bike routes varying from easy to seriously tough. **Cycles Flament** (☎ 04 68 96 07 62; 8 rue Arago) rents out mountain bikes.

The **Musée Pablo Casals** (☎ 04 68 96 28 55; 33 rue de L'Hospice; admission free; ☷ 9am-1pm & 2-5pm Tue-Fri, 9am-1pm Sat Jul & Aug, 10am-noon & 3-7pm Tue, Wed & Sat, 3-7pm Fri Sep-Jun) commemorates the world-renowned Spanish cellist, who settled in Prades after fleeing Franco's Spain. Look out among the mementoes for the photo of a youthful Yehudi Menuhin staggering under a giant grape-harvesting basket. The **Festival Pablo Casals** (☎ 04 68 96 33 07; www.prades-festival-casals.com in French), held over two weeks in late July/early August, brings top-flight classical musicians to this small town.

There's a robust farmers market on place de la République every Tuesday and Saturday.

Villefranche de Conflent

Villefranche, sitting at the strategic confluence of the valley of the Rivers Têt and Cady (hence the 'de Conflent' of its name), is encircled by thick fortifications, built by Vauban in the 17th century to strengthen and augment the original 11th-century defences, which have survived intact.

Villefranche has a small **tourist office** (☎ 04 68 96 22 96; otsi-villefranchedeconflent@wanadoo.fr; 2 rue St-Jean; ☷ 9am-noon & 2-6pm daily Jul & Aug, 9am-noon & 2-5pm Tue-Sun Jun & Sep, 10am-noon & 2-5pm Sat-Wed Oct-May). Access to the spectacular **ramparts** (adult/student/child €4/3/free, audioguide €3; ☷ 10am-7pm Jun-Sep, variable Oct-May) is next door.

Vernet-les-Bains

pop 1600

Busy in summer and almost a ghost town for the rest of the year, this small spa was much frequented by the British aristocracy in the late 19th century (there's still a small Anglican church). Nowadays, it's an alternative to Prades for hiking and particularly for attacking **Mont Canigou**, the Pyrenees'

> **MAKING ENDS MEET**
>
> In an early example of multitasking, the menfolk of Vernet would work the long-closed iron ore mines for some eight months of the year, tend their crops during summer and autumn and, during the hours left to them, pick up extra pin money as croupiers in the town's casino.

easternmost major peak. Three tracks wind up from Vernet. To bag the summit the easy way, bounce up in a 4WD (about €25 per person return) with **Garage Villacèque** (☎ 04 68 05 51 14; rue du Conflent) or **Taxi de la Gare** (☎ 04 68 05 62 68; 17 blvd des Pyrénées) as far as Les Cortalets (2175m), from where the summit is a three-hour return trip.

Vernet's **tourist office** (☎ 04 68 05 55 35; www.ot-vernet-les-bains.fr; ☷ 9am-noon & 2-6pm Mon-Fri, 9am-noon & 3-5pm Sat, 10am-noon Sun) is on place de la République, the main square. Upstairs, there's a well-mounted free exhibition recounting Vernet's past.

CÔTE VERMEILLE

The Côte Vermeille (Vermilion Coast) runs south from Collioure to Cerbère on the Spanish border, where the Pyrenees foothills reach the sea. Against a backdrop of vineyards and pinched between Mediterranean and mountains, it's riddled with small, rocky bays and little ports.

If you're driving from Perpignan, leave the N114 at exit 13 and follow the lovely coastal corniche all the way to Banyuls.

Collioure

pop 2900

Collioure, where boats (look out for the *llaguts,* traditional lateen-rigged fishing vessels) bob against a backdrop of houses washed in soft pastel colours, is the smallest and significantly the most picturesque of the Côte Vermeille resorts. Once Perpignan's port, it found fame in the early 20th century when it inspired the Fauvist art of Henri Matisse and André Derain (see The Fauvistes & Collioure, p806). Later both Picasso and Braque came here to paint.

Collioure is almost overwhelmed in summer by visitors, drawn by its artistic reputation (there are more than 30 galleries), its wine and the chance to buy at source the

THE FAUVISTES & COLLIOURE

'No sky in all France is more blue than that of Collioure. I only have to close the shutters of my room and there before me are all the colours of the Mediterranean.' So effused Henri Matisse (1869–1954), father of Fauvism. *Les Fauves* (The Wild Animals) worked with pure colour, filling their canvases with firm lines and stripes, rectangles and splashes of bright colour.

The **Chemin du Fauvisme** (Fauvism Trail) is a walking route around Collioure that takes you by 20 reproductions of works that Matisse and his younger colleague André Derain painted while living here. The tourist office carries a French-language guide booklet (€5.50).

famed Collioure anchovies (see Something Fishy in Collioure, below).

The **tourist office** (☎ 04 68 82 15 47; www.collioure.com; ⊗ 9am-8pm Mon-Sat, 10am-6pm Sun Jul & Aug, 9am-noon & 2-7pm Mon-Sat Jun & Sep, 9am-noon & 2-6pm Tue-Sat Oct-May) is on place 18 Juin.

Across the creek is the **Château Royal** (☎ 04 68 82 06 43; adult/child €4/2; ⊗ 10am-5.15pm Jun-Sep, 9am-4.15pm Oct-May). Originally a Templar settlement built upon Roman foundations, the castle enjoyed its greatest splendour as the summer residence of the kings of Mallorca. Vauban added its towering defensive walls in the 17th century.

The medieval church tower of **Notre Dame des Anges** at the northern end of the harbour once doubled as a lighthouse (the pink dome that gives it the air of a giant penis was added in 1810). Inside is a superb altarpiece, crafted by the Catalan master Josep Sunyer.

The **Musée d'Art Moderne** (☎ 04 68 82 10 19; Villa Pams, rte de Port-Vendres; adult/child €2/1.50; ⊗ 10am-noon & 2-6pm or 7pm, closed Tue Oct-May) has a good collection of 20th century and contemporary canvases.

To sample and pick up some of the best local Collioure wine, visit the **Cellier des Dominicains** (⊗ 8am-noon & 1.30-8pm Mon-Fri, 9.30am-noon & 3-6pm Sat year-round, 10am-noon & 3-7.30pm Sun Jun-Sep). It overlooks the beach from rue de la Démocratie. In summer, **La Maison de la Vigne et du Vin** (☎ 04 68 82 49 00; ⊗ daily Jul & Aug, weekends May, Jun & Sep), another grouping of local wine producers, sets itself up on place 18 Juin.

Collioure's Good Friday evening procession of hooded penitents is about the most elaborate this side of the Pyrenees. Altogether more joyous are **Fêtes de la St-Vincent** (14–18 August), celebrations in honour of the town's patron saint, their highlight a spectacular fireworks display on the 16th.

From mid-June to mid-September, leave your car in Parking Cap Dourats and take the shuttle bus that runs to the village every 10 minutes. Year-round, there's a large car park behind the castle.

Port-Vendres

pop 6000

Three kilometres south of Collioure, Port-Vendres, Roussillon's only natural harbour

SOMETHING FISHY IN COLLIOURE

The anchovies of Collioure in their many guises (canned, bottled, fresh, pickled, salted or marinated in oil) are something special.

Their flesh is so delicate that they can't be processed mechanically. So, even today, women still skilfully process the anchovies by hand. These *anchoieuses* first rub the fish with salt to maintain their sheen. After degutting, they arrange them, layer by layer like bicycle spokes, and sprinkle on lots more salt, in plastic barrels. The barrels are then topped by a heavy stone so that the anchovies *font le sang* (literally 'bleed', losing a lot of their liquid). After three months, each fillet is rinsed, dried on absorbent paper, then marinated in oil. Then, after another brief saline bath, they're packed into cans or jars.

No Catalan kitchen cupboard is complete without a jar or two of this tiny fish, an ingredient of so much local cuisine.

Only two salting plants remain, down from a one-time peak of 30, and each is still a family business. At the showroom of **Anchois Desclaux** (3 rte Nationale), you can sample, buy, see a 15-minute video in French and (between April and October) watch the deft way the *anchoieuses* work. Just up the road at **Anchois Roque** (17 rte d'Argelès), you can watch, sample and buy year-round.

and deep-water port, has been exploited ever since Greek mariners roamed the rocky coastline. Until the independence of France's North African territories in the 1960s, it was an important port linking them with the mainland. It's still an important fishing harbour with everything from small coastal chuggers to giant deep-sea vessels bristling with radar. There's also a large leisure marina.

The **tourist office** (☎ 04 68 82 07 54; 1 quai François Joly; www.port-vendres.com in French; ☼ 9am-7pm daily Jul & Aug, 9am-noon & 2-6pm Mon-Sat Sep-Jun) is located in the port's northwestern corner.

Banyuls
pop 4600

Banyuls, 7km south of Port-Vendres, has a pebbly beach, overlooked by the **tourist office** (☎ 04 68 88 31 58; www.banyuls-sur-mer.com; av de la République; ☼ 9am-8pm daily Jul & Aug, 9am-noon & 2-6pm Mon-Sat Sep-Jun). The town, where the Pyrenees dip their feet in the Mediterranean, is the starting point for the GR10,

a long-distance trail that snakes along the chain all the way to Hendaye, beside the Atlantic.

At the promenade's southern limit is the **Aquarium du Laboratoire Arago** (☎ 04 68 88 73 39; adult/child €4.40/2.20; ☼ 9am-1pm & 2-9pm Jul & Aug, 9am-noon & 2-6.30pm Sep-Jun). Much more than yet another commercial enterprise with smiling dolphins, this aquarium, which displays local Mediterranean marine life (and a collection of more than 250 stuffed sea and mountain birds) also functions as the oceanographic research station of Paris' Université Pierre et Marie Curie.

More strenuously aquatic but well worth the effort is snorkelling for free around a 500m **underwater trail** (☼ noon-6pm Jul & Aug). Situated just off Plage de Peyrefite, which is midway between Banyuls and Cerbère and within a protected marine area, it has five underwater information points. You can hire fins and masks (€5 to €7). If you have your own gear, you can swim the trail at any time.

Provence

The palette of Provence – orange blossoms, ochre-rich earth, fields of poppies and sunflowers, plane-shaded squares, cobalt skies deepening to midnight-blue, pink flamingos, snowy peaks, and perfusive deep-purple lavender – has been vividly rendered by painters such as Van Gogh, Gauguin and Cézanne.

Provence's picturesque hues, brought out by its brilliant light, are fragranced with wild herbs, alpine moss and salt blown through the Camargue's bulrush-filled marshes. They're steeped in the sounds of passionate crowds cheering matadors in Arles' Roman arena, metal *boules* clunking on dirt *pétanque* pitches often accompanied by players muttering in Provence's traditional language, and pastis glasses clinking on outdoor café terraces. They're flavoured with market stalls' lavender honeys, oven-warm breads, candied fruits, crisp rosé wines, and earthy black truffles. And they're textured with centuries-old cobblestones, Avignon's palaces, Les Baux's craggy limestone spurs, Aix-en-Provence's lavish fountains, and the surging River Rhône.

The region spans the Rhône from just north of Orange to the Mediterranean and from the Rhône delta east along France's southern coast to Marseille; and stretches east across the top of the Côte d'Azur through rugged Alpine terrain to the Italian border. As well as transcending the tangible senses, Provence's history-soaked streets, bucolic farms, the prehistoric Gorges du Verdon, and age-old legends and lore have a way of stirring a mystical sixth sense, too.

HIGHLIGHTS

- Soak up seething, sultry **Marseille** (p810)

- Trail **Van Gogh** (p834) around Arles to spots where he set up his easel to paint some of his best-known canvases

- Ride the **Camargue's white horses** (p840) along windswept beaches, or take a 4WD **wetlands safari** (p840)

- Admire the impressive collection housed in Avignon's private **Musée Angladon** (p844)

- Hike, bike, or drive with the windows down to **Digne-les-Bains** (p862) through hillsides carpeted with serried, scented lavender

- Sip a *café* on the table-lined terrace of Aix-en-Provence's legendary 1792 **Les Deux Garçons** (p829)

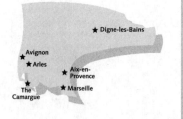

- POPULATION: 4,632,600   - AREA: 25,851 SQ KM

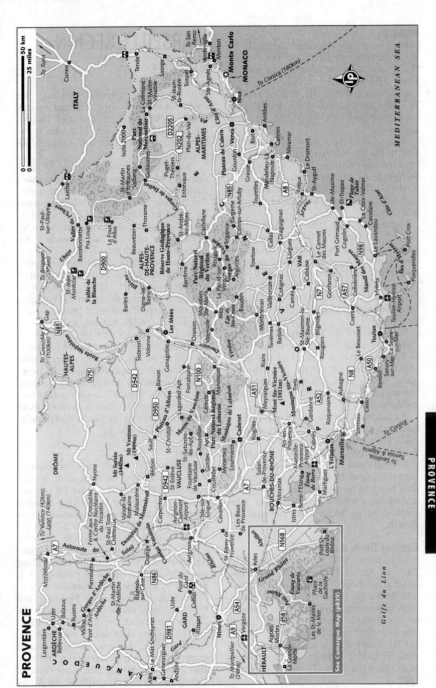

PROVENCE

History

Settled over the centuries variously by the Ligurians, the Celts and the Greeks, the area between the Alps, the sea and the River Rhône flourished following Julius Caesar's conquest in the mid-1st century BC. The Romans called the area *Provincia Romana*, which evolved into the name Provence.

After the collapse of the Roman Empire in the late 5th century, Provence was invaded several times, by the Visigoths, Burgundians and the Ostrogoths. The Arabs – who held the Iberian Peninsula and parts of France – were defeated in the 8th century.

During the 14th century, the Catholic Church – under a series of French-born popes – moved its headquarters from feud-riven Rome to Avignon, thus beginning the most resplendent period in the city's – and region's – history. Provence became part of France in 1481, but Avignon and Carpentras remained under papal control until the Revolution.

From around the 12th to the 14th centuries, Provençal was the literary language of France, northern Spain and also as far afield as Italy, and was the principal language of the medieval troubadours who romanticised courtly love in poems and melodies.

A movement for the revival of Provençal literature, culture and identity began in the mid-19th century, spearheaded by the poet Frédéric Mistral (1830–1914), recipient of the Nobel Prize for literature in 1904 (the region's furious 100km/h winds are named after him). In recent years the language has undergone a further revival, and in some areas signs are written in Provençal and French.

Getting There & Away

Thanks to the TGV, you can travel from Paris to Aix-en-Provence (three hours), Arles (four hours), Avignon (2¾ hours), and Marseille (three hours). On Saturdays in summer, there's a direct Eurostar service from London to Avignon (p849). Marseille-Provence International Airport (p823) is served by a smorgasbord of carriers, including Ryanair. Ferries sail from Marseille to Sardinia, Tunisia and Corsica (p823).

MARSEILLE REGION

MARSEILLE

pop 807,071

With its terracotta-roofed buildings the colour of cracked wheat, ripened apricot and blanched almond scattered around the mistral-whipped sea, Marseille is infused with a perceptible and irrepressible energy.

This gritty, grimy and gloriously real city – France's oldest, and largest after Paris – isn't gentrified like its Provençal counterparts. But its rough-and-tumble edginess, wailing sirens and litter-swirled streets, and its coastal corniches, chicaning around rocky inlets, coves and sun-baked beaches, are chock-a-block with treasures.

Pulsing to a sultry southern European tempo, Marseille also beats to the drum of neighbouring North Africa. Its fusion of cultures is best experienced at its thronging street markets of Provençal produce stalls, Moroccan *souk*-like bazaars, and fresh-off-the-boat catches splayed along the Vieux Port's docks at its centuries-old fish market, selling the base ingredients for the local speciality fish stew, *bouillabaisse*. Its name literally translates to its cooking method: when it boils *(bouillir)*, lower the heat to a simmer *(baisser)* – which is maybe a good recipe for handling the heady, heated melting pot that is Marseille.

History

Around 600 BC Greek mariners founded Massilia, a trading post, at what is now Marseille's Vieux Port. In the 1st century BC, the city lost out by backing Pompey the Great rather than Julius Caesar, whose forces captured Massilia in 49 BC and directed Roman trade elsewhere. Massilia stayed a free port, remaining the last Western centre of Greek learning before falling into ruin until its revival in the early 10th century by the counts of Provence.

Marseille became part of France in the 1480s, but retained its rebellious streak. Its citizens embraced the Revolution, sending 500 volunteers to defend Paris in 1792. Heading north, they sang a rousing march recently composed in Strasbourg and ever after dubbed *La Marseillaise* – now France's national anthem. Trade with North Africa escalated after France occupied Algeria in 1830, and after the 1869 opening of the Suez Canal. During WWII Marseille was bombed by the Germans and Italians in 1940, and by the Allies in 1943–44.

The English spelling, Marseilles (pronounced the same), is passing out of use.

Marseille is one of Europe's largest and most important ports, and is burgeoning with myriad expansion projects including a redevelopment of its docklands. Just three hours from Paris by TGV, it's arguably France's city most on the rise.

Orientation

The city's main thoroughfare, the wide boulevard La Canebière (from the Provençal word *canebe*, meaning 'hemp', after Marseille's rope industry manufacturing ships' rigging), stretches eastwards from the Vieux Port (Old Port). The Gare St-Charles train station is north of La Canebière at the northern end of blvd d'Athènes. Just a few blocks south of La Canebière, near the Notre Dame du Mont-Cours Julien metro station, is cours Julien, a bohemian, graffitied concourse with a water garden and palm trees, with hip cafés, restaurants and theatres and a Berlin vibe. To the north of the Vieux Port is Le Panier, Marseille's oldest quarter. The city's commercial heart is around rue Paradis, which becomes more fashionable as you head south. The new ferry terminal is west of place de la Joliette.

Greater Marseille is divided into 16 arrondissements; addresses in this book indicate the arrondissement (1er, 2e etc).

Information
BOOKSHOPS
FNAC (Map p815; ☎ 04 91 39 94 00; Centre Bourse shopping centre; Ⓜ Vieux Port) On the top floor of the centre off cours Belsunce (1er).

Librairie de la Bourse (Map p815; ☎ 04 91 33 63 06; 8 rue Paradis, 1er; Ⓜ Vieux Port) The best range of maps, travel books and Lonely Planet guides in Provence.

EMERGENCY
Préfecture de Police (Map p815; ☎ 04 91 39 80 00; place de la Préfecture, 1er; Ⓜ Estrangin Préfecture; ☾ 24hr)

INTERNET ACCESS
Info Cafe (Map p815; ☎ 04 91 33 74 98; 1 quai du Rive Neuve, 1er; Ⓜ Vieux Port; per 30 min/hr €2/3.60; ☾ 9am-10pm Mon-Sat, 2.30-7.30pm Sun)

INTERNET RESOURCES
Discover South of France (www.discoversouthoffrance .com). Comprehensive information on the region, including eco-travel.
Visit Provence (www.visitprovence.com)

LAUNDRY
Laverie des Allées (Map p815; 15 allées Léon Gambetta, 1er; Ⓜ Réformés Canebière; ☾ 8am-8pm)
Laverie Self-Service (Map p815; 5 rue Breteuil, 1er; Ⓜ Vieux Port; ☾ 6.30am-8pm)

MEDICAL SERVICES
Hôpital de la Timone (☎ 04 91 38 60 00; 264 rue St-Pierre, 5e; Ⓜ La Timone) East of the city centre.

MONEY
There are a number of banks and exchange bureaus on La Canebière near the Vieux Port.
Canebière Change (Map p815; 39 La Canebière, 1er; Ⓜ Vieux Port).

POST
Main Post Office (Map p815; 1 place de l'Hôtel des Postes, 1er; Ⓜ Colbert) Offers currency exchange.

TOURIST INFORMATION
Tourist Office (Map p815; ☎ 04 91 13 89 00; www .marseille-tourisme.com; 4 La Canebière, 1er; Ⓜ Vieux Port; ☾ 9am-7pm Mon-Sat, 10am-5pm Sun, to 7.30pm mid-Jun–mid-Sep)
Tourist Office Annexe (Map p815; ☎ 04 91 50 59 18; Gare St-Charles train station; Ⓜ Gare St-Charles; ☾ 10am-1pm & 2-6pm Mon-Sat)

Dangers & Annoyances
Forget everything you have heard about Marseille being a hotbed of crime: it's no more dangerous than other French cities. In fact, its integration of cultures meant Marseille wasn't marred by France's 2005 riots.

As with any big city, keep your wits about you, and your valuables hidden from view. *Never* leave anything of value in a parked car, even in the boot. At night, take extra care in the Belsunce area, southwest of the train station bounded by La Canebière, cours Belsunce and rue d'Aix, rue Bernard du Bois and blvd d'Athènes.

Sights & Activities
MUSEUMS
Unless otherwise noted, museums listed here are open 10am to 5pm Tuesday to

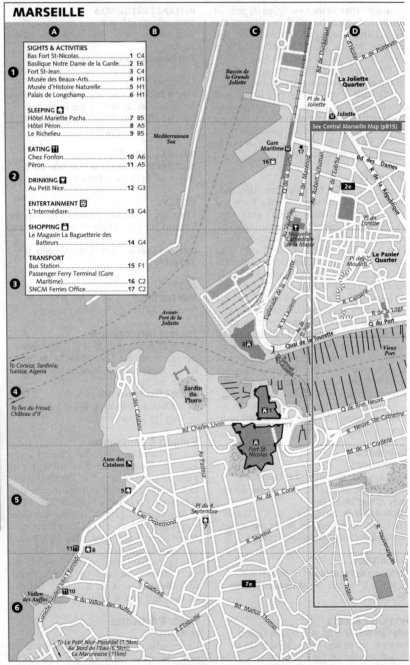

MARSEILLE

SIGHTS & ACTIVITIES
Bas Fort St-Nicolas.........................1 C4
Basilique Notre Dame de la Garde......2 E6
Fort St-Jean...................................3 C4
Musée des Beaux-Arts.....................4 H1
Musée d'Histoire Naturelle...............5 H1
Palais de Longchamp.......................6 H1

SLEEPING
Hôtel Mariette Pacha.......................7 B5
Hôtel Pèron..................................8 A5
Le Richelieu.................................9 B5

EATING
Chez Fonfon................................10 A6
Pèron.......................................11 A5

DRINKING
Au Petit Nice...............................12 G3

ENTERTAINMENT
L'Intermédiare.............................13 G4

SHOPPING
Le Magasin La Baguetterie des
    Batteurs.................................14 G4

TRANSPORT
Bus Station.................................15 F1
Passenger Ferry Terminal (Gare
    Maritime)...............................16 C2
SNCM Ferries Office.......................17 C2

PROVENCE

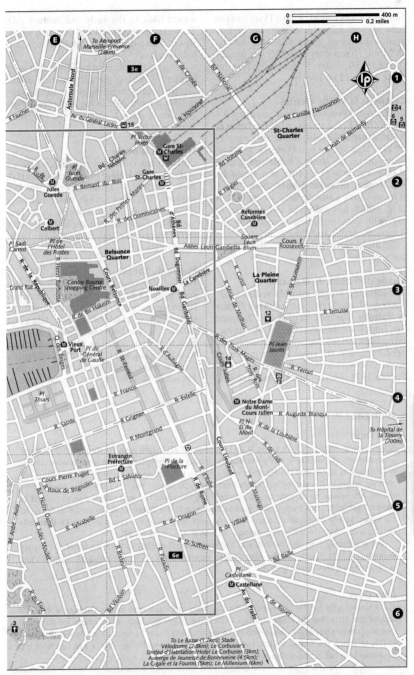

Sunday October to May, and 11am to 6pm June to September. Admission to permanent exhibitions costs €2/1 for adults/children. Temporary exhibitions usually cost €3/1.50. Entry is generally free for those under 12 or over 60.

Centre de la Vieille Charité

Built around Provence's most imposing baroque church, the courtyard of the **Centre de la Vieille Charité** (Old Charity Cultural Centre; Map p815; ☎ 04 91 14 58 80; 2 rue de la Charité, 2e; Ⓜ Joliette) incorporates the **Musée d'Archéologie** (Museum of Archeology; ☎ 04 91 14 58 80) and **Musée des Arts Africains, Océaniens & Amérindiens** (Museum of African, Oceanic & American Indian Art; ☎ 04 91 14 58 38), which has a diverse and often striking collection, including masks from the Americas, Africa and the Pacific.

An all-inclusive ticket for adults/students costs €5/2.50.

Musée d'Histoire de Marseille

A fascinating insight into Marseille's composited cultural heritage, the **Musée d'Histoire de Marseille** (Map p815; ☎ 04 91 90 42 22; ground floor, Centre Bourse shopping centre, 1er; Ⓜ Vieux Port; ☿ noon-7pm Mon-Sat) has some extraordinary exhibits such as the remains of a merchant vessel discovered by chance in the Vieux Port in 1974, which plied the surrounding waters back in the early 3rd century AD. To preserve the soaked and decaying wood, it was freeze-dried right where it now sits behind glass.

Fragments of Roman buildings that were unearthed during the construction of the Centre Bourse shopping centre can be seen outside the museum in the **Jardin des Vestiges** (Garden of Ruins), which fronts rue Henri Barbusse (1er).

Musée de la Mode

Contemplate contemporary fashion trends at the **Musée de la Mode** (Fashion Museum; Map p815; ☎ 04 91 56 59 57; 11 La Canebière, 1er; Ⓜ Vieux Port; adult/child €3/1). This stylish space has over 2000 garments and accessories in its permanent collection, and regularly features retro temporary exhibitions like 1920s beachwear.

Musée du Santon

One of Provence's most enduring – and endearing – Christmas traditions is *santons* (from *santoùn* in Provençal, meaning 'little saint'). These plaster-moulded, kiln-fired nativity figures between 2.5cm and 15cm high were first created by Marseillais artisan Jean-Louis Lagnel (1764–1822). *Santonniers* (santon makers) still use his method today. There are 55 *santons* from the tambourine

---

MARSEILLE IN...

Two Days

Savour home-made jam from **Le Goût de l'Enfance** (p822) before weaving through the pedestrianised streets of the historic **Le Panier quarter** (p822). Stopping by the **fashion museum** (above) is a fitting way to get into the Marseille mode. Follow the African drums, swaying accordions and clinking masts to the yacht-filled **Vieux Port** (p817) to sample the city's signature *bouillabaisse* (p820). Afterwards, stroll, cycle or rollerblade along the corniches, and take the open-topped **Le Grand Tour** (p817) bus back, jumping off at **Basilique Notre Dame de la Garde** (p816) for celestial views, before dining alfresco around lively place Thiars. Catch a jazz session at **La Caravelle** (p822), and – if you're still going strong – kick on at the clubs (p822).

Get a leisurely start the next day at **Le Pain Quotidien** (p821), then meander the myriad **museums** (p811). Check out the **cours Julien quarter** (p811) before feasting on couscous and up-and-coming **live music** (p822).

Four Days

Put a slower spin on the city with a boat trip from the Vieux Port to the **Château d'If** (p816) and/or the little **Îles du Frioul** (p816). Mooch the many **markets** (p823), then for the most peaceful perspective of the city, climb up to the sculpted stone benches at the **Jardin du Pharo** (p817) to watch the sunset sizzling over the water. On the fourth day, plan a summer boat trip or winter hike out to the **Calanques** (p817).

CENTRAL MARSEILLE

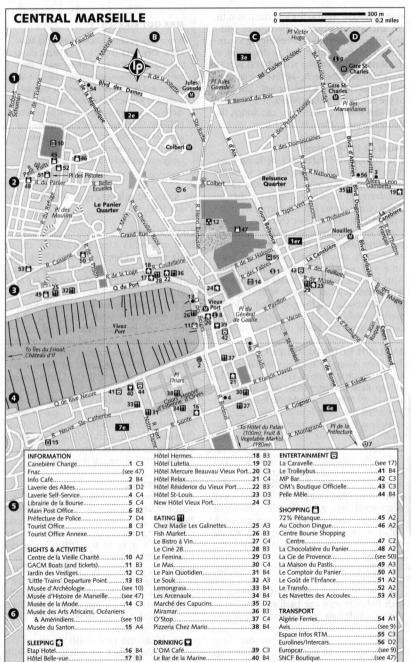

INFORMATION	
Canebière Change	1 C3
Fnac	(see 47)
Info Café	2 B4
Laverie des Allées	3 D2
Laverie Self-Service	4 C4
Librairie de la Bourse	5 C4
Main Post Office	6 B2
Préfecture de Police	7 D4
Tourist Office	8 C3
Tourist Office Annexe	9 D1

SIGHTS & ACTIVITIES	
Centre de la Vieille Charité	10 A2
GACM Boats (and tickets)	11 B3
Jardin des Vestiges	12 C2
'Little Trains' Departure Point	13 B3
Musée d'Archéologie	(see 10)
Musée d'Histoire de Marseille	(see 47)
Musée de la Mode	14 C3
Musée des Arts Africains, Océaniens & Amérindiens	(see 10)
Musée du Santon	15 A4

SLEEPING	
Etap Hotel	16 B4
Hôtel Belle-vue	17 B3
Hôtel Hermes	18 B3
Hôtel Lutetia	19 D2
Hôtel Mercure Beauvau Vieux Port	20 C3
Hôtel Relax	21 C4
Hôtel Résidence du Vieux Port	22 B3
Hôtel St-Louis	23 C3
New Hôtel Vieux Port	24 C3

EATING	
Chez Madie Les Galinettes	25 A3
Fish Market	26 B3
Le Bistro à Vin	27 C4
Le Ciné 28	28 B3
Le Femina	29 D3
Le Mas	30 C4
Le Pain Quotidien	31 B4
Le Souk	32 A3
Lemongrass	33 B4
Les Arcenaulx	34 B4
Marché des Capucins	35 D2
Miramar	36 B3
O'Stop	37 C4
Pizzeria Chez Mario	38 B4

DRINKING	
L'OM Café	39 C3
Le Bar de la Marine	40 B4

ENTERTAINMENT	
La Caravelle	(see 17)
Le Trolleybus	41 B4
MP Bar	42 C3
OM's Boutique Officielle	43 C3
Pelle Mêle	44 B4

SHOPPING	
72% Pétanque	45 A2
Au Cochon Dingue	46 A2
Centre Bourse Shopping Centre	47 C2
La Chocolatière du Panier	48 A2
La Cie de Provence	(see 50)
La Maison du Pastis	49 A3
Le Comptoir du Panier	50 A3
Le Goût de l'Enfance	51 A2
Le Transfo	52 A2
Les Navettes des Accoules	53 A3

TRANSPORT	
Algérie Ferries	54 A1
Avis	(see 9)
Espace Infos RTM	55 C3
Eurolines/Intercars	56 D2
Europcar	(see 9)
SNCF Boutique	(see 47)

PROVENCE

man to the chestnut seller and the tinsmith. An enchanting private collection of 18th- and 19th-century *santons* belonging to *santonnier* Marcel Carbonnel is displayed at the **Musée du Santon** (Map p815; ☎ 04 91 54 26 58; 47 rue Neuve Ste-Catherine, 7e; Ⓜ Vieux Port; admission free; ◷ 10am-noon & 2-6.30pm Tue-Sun). Entrance to the adjoining **ateliers** (workshops; ◷ 8am-1pm & 2-5.40pm Mon-Thu), where you can watch the figures being crafted, is also free.

Palais de Longchamp

The colonnaded **Palais de Longchamp** (Longchamp Palace; Map pp812-13; blvd Philippon, 4e; Ⓜ Cinq Avenues Longchamp), constructed in the 1860s, was designed in part to disguise a *château d'eau* (water tower) at the terminus of an aqueduct from the River Durance. Its two wings house Marseille's oldest museum, the **Musée des Beaux-Arts** (☎ 04 91 14 59 30), undergoing extensive renovations at press time and slated to reopen during 2008. Also housed here, the **Musée d'Histoire Naturelle** (Museum of Natural History; ☎ 04 91 62 30 78) is for serious fans of the genre, but its lovely gardens with a children's playground and carousel are a good spot to placate littlies.

BASILIQUE NOTRE DAME DE LA GARDE

Be blown away by the celestial views and knockout 19th-century architecture at the hilltop **Basilique Notre Dame de la Garde** (Map pp812-13; ☎ 04 91 13 40 80; admission free; ◷ basilica & crypt 7am-7pm, longer hours in summer), the resplendent Romano-Byzantine basilica 1km south of the Vieux Port that dominates Marseille's skyline.

The domed basilica was built between 1853 and 1864 and is ornamented with coloured marble, intricate mosaics superbly restored in 2006 and murals. Its bell tower is crowned by a 9.7m-tall gilded statue of the Virgin Mary on a 12m-high pedestal. Bullet marks and vivid shrapnel scars on the cathedral's northern façade mark the fierce fighting that took place here during Marseille's Battle of Liberation (15-25 August 1944).

Bus 60 links the Vieux Port (from cours Jean Ballard) with the basilica. Otherwise, there's a **little train** (€5; ◷ contact the tourist office for seasonal schedules), which departs from the port for the 20-minute trip up the steep hill, giving you 20 minutes to look around before taking it back down. By foot, count

---

MAX OUT MARSEILLE

To max out your time in Marseille, the **Marseille City Pass** (1-/2-day pass €18/25), gives you access to the city's museums, guided tours of the town, unlimited travel on all metro and bus services as well as the little train, and a boat trip to either Île d'If or Îles du Frioul, as well as various discounts like Le Grand Tour tourist bus. The pass quickly pays for itself for adults; it's not necessary for children under 12, as many attractions are greatly reduced or free.

---

on about 30 minutes each way from the Vieux Port.

CHÂTEAU D'IF

Immortalised in Alexandre Dumas' classic 1840s novel *Le Comte de Monte Cristo* (The Count of Monte Cristo), the 16th-century fortress-turned-prison **Château d'If** (☎ 04 91 59 02 30; adult/student €5/3.50; ◷ 9.30am-6.30pm Jun-Aug, 9.30am-5.30pm Sep-Dec, 9am-5.30pm Jan-May) sits on a 30-sq-km island 3.5km west of the Vieux Port. Political prisoners of all persuasions were incarcerated here, along with hundreds of Protestants (many of whom perished in the dungeons), the Revolutionary hero Mirabeau and the Communards of 1871.

Boats run by **GACM** (Map p815; ☎ 04 91 55 50 09; www.answeb.net/gacm in French; 1 quai des Belges, 1er) to the Château d'If leave from outside the GACM office in the Vieux Port. There are boats at 9am, 10.30am, noon, 2pm and 3.30pm (€10 return, 20 minutes).

ÎLES DU FRIOUL

A few hundred metres west of the Château d'If are the islands of **Ratonneau** and **Pomègues**. The tiny islands (each about 2.5km long; totalling 200 hectares) were linked by a dyke in the 1820s. From the 17th to 19th century they were used as a place of quarantine for people suspected of carrying plague or cholera. Marseille's population was ravaged in 1720 when the plague, carried by a merchant vessel from Syria, killed around 50,000 of the city's 90,000 inhabitants.

Sea birds and rare plants thrive on the islands today, which are still sprinkled with the ruins of the old quarantine hospital,

Hôpital Caroline, and Fort Ratonneau (used by German troops during WWII).

Boats to the Château d'If also serve the Îles du Frioul (€10 return; €15 to stop at Château d'If too). There are also departures at 6.45am, 5pm and 6.30pm for the Îles du Frioul alone.

VIEUX PORT AREA

Ships have docked for more than 26 centuries at Marseille's colourful Vieux Port. Although the main commercial docks were transferred to the Joliette area on the coast north of here in the 1840s, it still overflows with fishing craft, yachts and local ferries.

Guarding the harbour are **Bas Fort St-Nicolas** (Map pp812–13) on the southern side and, across the water, **Fort St-Jean** (Map pp812–13), founded in the 13th century by the Knights Hospitaller of St John of Jerusalem.

In 1943 the neighbourhood on the northern side of the quai du Port, the historic Le Panier quarter (Map p815; see p822), was dynamited and much of it rebuilt afterwards. Today its winding, narrow streets are a jumble of authentic artisan shops and washing lines strung outside terraced houses that evoke the area's past.

On the Vieux Port's southern side, late-night restaurants and cafés pack the **place Thiars** and **cours Honoré d'Estienne d'Orves** pedestrian zone (Map p815).

Northeast of La Canebière and cours Belsunce, the run-down **Belsunce** (Map p815) area is slowly being rehabilitated.

For chic, street-smart shopping, stroll the fashionable **6th arrondissement**, especially pedestrianised **Rue St-Ferréol**.

Heading west of the Vieux Port brings you to the serene **Jardin du Pharo** (Map pp812–13) gardens overlooking the sea; continuing southwest leads you around to the beaches.

LE CORBUSIER'S UNITÉ D'HABITATION

Visionary International Style architect Le Corbusier redefined urban living in 1952 with the completion of his vertical 337-apartment 'garden city', **Unité d'Habitation** (☎ 04 91 16 78 00; www.hotellecorbusier.com; 280 blvd Michelet, 8e; ☯ by appointment), also known as Cité Radieuse (Radiant City), elevated on tapering pylons like a titanic dry-docked ship. Along its darkened hallways, primary-coloured downlights create a glowing tunnel leading to a mini-supermarket, architectural bookshop and panoramic rooftop 'desert garden' with an avocado-tiled, ankle-deep pool producing rippling sunlit patterns, and a cylindrical tower (camouflaging the building's utilities), which tops off the steamship effect. Even if you're not staying at the **hotel** (p819), you can arrange to visit this *tour de force*, including its private apartments, or dine at its **restaurant** (mains €8-12), with its shimmering views of the Mediterranean – and of the proliferation of high-rises that Le Corbusier inspired. Catch bus 83 or 21 to Le Corbusier stop.

Tours

Le Grand Tour (☎ 04 91 91 05 82; adult/student/child €16/13/8; ☯ 10am-at least 4pm) is handy for getting around as well as seeing the city. This hop-on-hop-off, open-topped double-decker bus travels between the main sights and museums, taking in the Vieux Port, the corniche and Notre Dame de la Garde, accompanied by a five-language audio guide. Buy tickets from the tourist office or on the bus. The best place to join the tour is at the Vieux Port.

The tourist office offers various **guided tours**, including an English-language walking tour of the city once a week at 2pm on either Monday or Saturday.

THE CALANQUES

Get away from it all just a few miles east of busy, built-up Marseille along the **Calanques** (☯ closed 15 Jun–15 Sep): small inlets along the rocky, indented coast, sometimes with a small patch of beach on which to soak up the sun. Even when the inland area's closed due to the threat of forest fires, you can still rent a boat from Marseille's Vieux Port to pull up at the beaches and coves. A trip to the pretty nearby fishing village of Cassis makes an ideal day out and is a good place to grab lunch and sample the subtle local white wine. **Cassis' tourist office** (☎ 04 42 01 71 17; quai des Moulins; ☯ 9am-12.30pm & 2-6pm Tue-Sat) supplies a free list and map of all the *caves* (cellars) you can visit for tastings.

For a DIY walking tour, the free city map handed out by the tourist office outlines three **walking circuits**. Of these, one, around the historic Le Panier quarter, corresponds with a red line painted along the route, though once in a while it dead-ends (and at one point runs straight into a concrete-bound tree).

From the Vieux Port, the **little train** (p816) also tootles around Le Panier's hilly streets.

In summer **GACM** (☎ 04 91 55 50 09; www.an sweb.net/gacm in French; 1 quai des Belges, 1er) runs boat trips (with French commentary only) from the Vieux Port to Cassis and back (€20). Trips pass by the coves and clear turquoise waters of the Calanques (p817).

Sleeping

Because Marseille's not geared around tourists (like, say, Nice), there's a shortage of rooms during summer – book ahead.

BUDGET
Hostels

Frustratingly, France's second-biggest city has no central hostel. Remember that regular buses stop running around 9pm – check with these outlying hostels for late-night transportation alternatives.

Auberge de Jeunesse de Bonneveine (☎ 04 91 17 63 30; fax 04 91 73 97 23; impasse du Docteur Bonfils, 8e; dm €14.60-15.60, d €33.70-35.70 incl sheets & breakfast; 🕙 Feb-Dec; ✗ 🖳) A fair hike from the centre, this HI with good wheelchair access makes up for it with its proximity to the beach, and outdoor terrace and bar. Take bus 44 from the Rond Point du Prado metro stop and get off at the Place Bonnefons stop, then turn right, take your first left (Av Joseph Vidal), then your first left again; it's on your left, through the car park.

La Cigale et la Fourmi (☎ 04 91 40 05 12; 19 rue Théophile Boudier, Mazargues, 9e; dm/d €15/30) Also heading toward the Calanques, the tiny, independent 'Cicada and Ant' has miniature staircases, loft-style rooms and freebies including wi-fi and bikes. There are self-catering facilities, but no breakfast. From the Rond Point du Prado metro stop, take bus 21 to the Obelisque stop or bus 22 to the Robespierre stop.

Hotels

Le Richelieu (Map pp812-13; ☎ 0491310192; www.leriche lieu-marseille.com; 52 corniche Président John F Kennedy,

7e; d €34-53) With a breezy, beach-house vibe, and marine-motif rooms, most opening to balconies, this artists' haven is built onto the rocks next to the plage des Catalans. Bathrooms are mostly tiny and tucked behind shower curtains. Jutting over the water, the sun-drenched terrace is idyllic for feasting on fresh pastries at breakfast (€7).

Hôtel St-Louis (Map p815; ☎ 04 91 54 02 74; www .hotel-st-louis.com; 2 rue des Récollettes, 1er; Ⓜ Noailles; d €45-47, tw €52, tr €63) This charmingly simple pied-à-terre is in the heart of Marseille's chic shopping district. Behind blue-painted doors, rooms have towering ceilings, French-washed walls and hexagonal-tiled terracotta floors, extending to double sets of French doors opening to Juliet balconies in many of the 22 rooms.

Etap Hotel (Map p815; ☎ 08 92 68 05 82; fax 04 91 54 95 67; 46 rue Sainte, 1er; Ⓜ Vieux Port; s €46, d & tr €48-50; ✗ 🐾) Try for one of the large, wood-beamed rooms in the old building (a former sea galley captain's house) of this hotel, four short blocks back from the port. Onsite covered parking costs €7.10. English-speaking staff are friendly and accommodating, through the 'do not disturb' signs don't always register with staff servicing your room (hey, but at least it's kept spotlessly clean).

MIDRANGE

Hôtel Relax (Map p815; ☎ 0491331587; 4 rue Corneille, 1er; Ⓜ Vieux Port; s €35, d €50-55; 🐾) In a dress-circle location overlooking Marseille's Art Deco Opera House, this 20-room hotel is framed by sunflower-yellow canvas awnings above geranium-filled window boxes. Some rooms are pint-sized but they're all button-cute with Provençal fabrics, TVs, telephones and an in-room fridge to stash your pre-opera champagne.

Hôtel Mariette Pacha (Map pp812-13; ☎ 04 91 52 30 77; mpacha@hotelselection.com; 5 place du 4 Septembre; s €47-52, d €57-68) Close to the city and just 200m from the sea, colourful rooms here are creatively configured to be adapted for a range of accommodation, including family rooms that offer independence for kids (and privacy for parents).

Hôtel Lutètia (Map p815; ☎ 04 91 50 81 78; www .hotelmarseille.com; 38 allées Léon Gambetta, 1er; Ⓜ Réformès-Canabière s/d/tr from €55/60/69) Awaken to the cacophony of church bells ringing on

Sunday mornings from Les Rèformès, the distinctive twin-steepled church just up the street from the sweet, petite Hôtel Lutètia. There's free wi-fi.

Hôtel Hermès (Map p815; ☎ 04 96 11 63 63; www .hotelmarseille.com; 2 rue de la Bonneterie, 2e; Ⓜ Vieux Port; s €47, d €69-78, nuptial ste €89; ✗ 🕸) On the Vieux Port, with prime proximity to Le Panier quarter and La Canebière, Hôtel Hermès' cute, cosy rooms are a steal. The communal rooftop terrace with tables and chairs is perfect for a sunset picnic; above it, up a metal stairway-to-heaven, the rooftop nuptial suite feels like you're on top of the world.

our pick Hôtel Péron (Map pp812-13; ☎ 04 91 31 01 41; www.hotel-peron.com; 119 corniche Président John F Kennedy, 7e; d €69.50-72.50, tw €78-97; 🖵) Wow. This authentic and utterly unassuming 1920s period piece has been in the same family for four generations. Its faded exterior conceals museum-like rooms with preserved original Art Deco turquoise-and-black ceramic bathrooms (some only partly partitioned), and parquet floors inlaid with Provençal olive-picking scenes. Many rooms are set at an angle to accentuate the sea views, and all have balconies. Breakfast (€8) isn't a meal so much as an event, when the family plays traditional Marseille music.

Hôtel Saint-Ferréol (Map p815; ☎ 04 91 33 12 21; www.hotel-stferreol.com; 19 rue Pisançon, 1er; Ⓜ Vieux Port; s €72-82, d €77-92; 🖵) On the corner of the city's most beautiful lamp-lit pedestrian shopping street, this hotel now has renovations that match its fashionable surrounds. There's free wi-fi; breakfast (€8.50) includes fresh-squeezed orange juice. It's opposite the Galeries Lafayette department store – look for the world globe on the hotel's sign.

Hôtel Le Corbusier (☎ 04 91 16 78 00; www.hotel lecorbusier.com; 280 blvd Michelet, 8e; cabin without bathroom €50, d €80-90; ✗ 🕸) Staying at the restored 20-room hotel within this iconic concrete monolith gives architectural aficionados the opportunity to absorb Le Corbusier's legacy. A few extra euros get you a sublime sea view and some rooms have balconies with distinctive bold colour panels. Catch bus 83 or 21 to Le Corbusier stop.

Hôtel du Palais (Map p815; 04 91 37 78 86; www .hotelmarseille.com; 26 rue Breteuil, 6e; Ⓜ Estrangin-Préfecture; d €80-100; ✗ 🕸 🖵) For a stylish

sleep, head a few blocks further south of the Vieux Port than you otherwise might, in order to reach this chic little place. Its 22 intimate rooms are done out in designer shades, with chrome minibar fridges with glass doors, free wi-fi, a sleek red lobby and cachet to spare.

Hôtel Belle-vue (Map p815; ☎ 04 96 17 05 40; fax 04 96 17 05 41; 34 quai du Port, 2e; Ⓜ Vieux Port; s €68-115, d €68-122, tr €137; 🕸) Inside this classical cream building cased in duck-egg–blue shutters on the Vieux Port are Hôtel Belle-vue's artistic rooms, and the very funky jazz bar La Caravelle (see p822). Wrapping around a wrought-iron staircase, claret-coloured walls create a dramatic backdrop for up-and-coming painters who exhibit their work in the de facto gallery of the hotel's public spaces.

Hôtel Résidence du Vieux Port (Map p815; ☎ 04 91 91 91 22; www.hotelmarseille.com; 18 quai du Port, 2e; Ⓜ Vieux Port; d €91-135, apt €164; 🕸 🖵) Blending modern and traditional furnishings like classical lemon, lime, blue, pink and white candy-striped curtains and bedspreads, most rooms give onto the port, with a small loggia to lap up the breathtaking basilica views. The two-room apartments are great for families.

TOP END

Le Petit Nice-Passédat (☎ 04 91 59 25 92; www.petit nicepassedat.com; Anse de Maldormé, 7e; d €150-470; 🕸 🖵 🛁) Nestled into the rocks above a petite cove and rock-ledge beach, this is an intimate little hideaway of just 16 individually and exquisitely appointed rooms overlooking the orchid mosaic-tiled saltwater pool. It's also home to Gerald Passédat's virtuoso, two-Michelin-starred restaurant (mains €53-85).

New Hôtel Vieux Port (Map p815; ☎ 04 91 99 23 23; www.new-hotel.com; 3bis rue Reine Elisabeth, 1er; Ⓜ Vieux Port; s €135-165, d €155-185; ✗ 🕸) Incorporating state-of-the-art technology, this sophisticated, central hotel has rooms reflecting exotic locales such as Mexico, India, Morocco, Japan and Africa.

Hôtel Mercure Beauvau Vieux Port (Map p815; ☎ 04 91 54 91 00; www.mercure.com; 4, rue Beauvau, 1er; s €132-190, d €144-205; ✗ 🕸 🖵) First opened in 1816, and receiving luminaries like Chopin and George Sand, Marseille's most historic hotel was recently gutted and refitted, while its antique Louis-Philippe and Napoleon III

PROVENCE

furniture was also restored. Above down-quilted beds, suspended embroideries give rooms a regal feel. Wheelchair access is good. Sleep under the stars in six mezzanine rooms beneath retractable shuttered skylights.

Eating

African, Middle Eastern and Mediterranean cuisines, along with Provençal specialities, are the mainstays of Marseille's restaurants. Fish, *huîtres* (oysters), *moules* (mussels) and mounds of other shellfish are predominant and plentiful.

RESTAURANTS

The quai de Rive Neuve (1er) teems with touristy restaurants touting *bouillabaisse*; those along quai du Port (2e) are better but pricier. Behind quai de Rive Neuve, the pedestrian streets around place Thiars brim with umbrella-filled dining terraces in the warmer months.

For fare as diverse as Marseille itself, cours Julien and its surrounding streets are jammed with French, Indian, Antillean, Pakistani, Thai, Armenian, Lebanese, Tunisian and Italian restaurants.

Le Femina (Map p815; ☎ 04 91 54 03 56; 1 rue Musée, 1er; **M** Noailles; menus €8-18; ☺ closed Sun & Mon) Heading east from the Vieux Port towards cours Julien, Le Femina is a great – and affordable – traditional Algerian place for couscous cooked to perfection.

ourpick Chez Madie Les Galinettes (Map p815; ☎ 04 91 90 40 87; 138 quai du Port, 2e; mains €10-28, bouillabaisse €35; ☺ lunch & dinner Mon-Sat, closed Sat lunch in summer) Decked out with colourful original pop art and mural panels, this *très* Marseille portside place is great for *bouillabaisse* (you'll need to order before Mme Roux's expedition to the fish markets around 3pm, so the day before if you're

headed here for lunch). The house speciality fish, *Les Galinettes*, is full of flavours, and there are some creative starters such as marinated capsicums with anchovy tapenade, as well as delectable seasonal desserts such as winter's chestnut ice cream.

Le Bistro à Vin (Map p815; ☎ 04 91 54 02 20; 17 rue Sainte, 6e; **M** Vieux Port; dishes €12; ☺ closed Sat lunch & Sun) As its name implies, the wine offerings at this beamed-ceiling rustic bistro are outstanding. The accompanying fare – including tapenade, and a mouthwatering selection of artisanal cheeses – is exceptional value.

Au Bord de l'Eau (☎ 04 91 72 68 04; 15 rue des Arapèdes, port de la Madrague Montredon, 8e; menus €25-30; ☺ closed Tue, lunch Sun, Dec & Jan, open daily Jul & Aug) Promise you won't tell *too* many people about this little harbourside haven literally 'at the water's edge' of the Calanques. Chances are you can thank the fishing boats moored below the sundrenched terrace for catching the fish on your plate just hours before. Catch bus 83 along the coast to Av du Prado (by the statue of David), then take bus 19 further south along the coast.

Miramar (Map p815; ☎ 04 91 90 10 40; 12 quai du Port, 2e; **M** Vieux Port; mains €25-50; ☺ lunch & dinner Tue-Sat) Dine on Marseille's celebrated dish in style, beneath glowing burgundy wall-mounted lamps in the dining rooms, or on a burgundy velveteen settee at the white-clothed tables elegantly arranged on the quai-side terrace. This is the place locals herald as having the best *bouillabaisse* anywhere in the city centre.

Lemongrass (Map p815; ☎ 04 91 33 97 65; 8 rue Fort Notre Dame, 1e; **M** Vieux Port; menus €30; ☺ closed Sun) Spice up your day or night at this refreshing fusion place. Lemongrass serves lush menus of Asian/French fare such as peeled lobster in curry with Granny Smith apples, and coconut rice pudding in banana leaf.

CULINARY CASTOFFS

What began as a humble means of fishermen feeding their families (by salvaging scraps after they'd sold the best of their catch) is, centuries on, Marseille's most sought-after meal. No trip here is complete without tasting *bouillabaisse*: seafood stew made with at least five or six types of Mediterranean fish plus crab or shrimp, along with onions, white wine and tomatoes, flavoured with fennel and saffron and served with *rouille* (garlic mayonnaise) and croutons. Variations throughout Provence (scorned by purists) include potatoes, lobster, langoustines or mussels. Expect to pay about €35 to €50 per person (it's worth it), and note that the better places require you to order up to 48 hours ahead, and may require a minimum of two diners.

PROVENCE

Le Souk (Map p815; ☎ 04 91 91 29 29; 98 quai du Port, 2e; **M** Vieux Port; menus €20-30; ☺ lunch Tue-Sun, dinner Tue-Sat Sep-Jun, lunch Sat & Sun, dinner Sun, Jul & Aug) Taste the authentic *tajine* (a heaping slow-cooked meat and vegetable stew elegantly delivered in a conical-covered earthenware dish) amid Moroccan orange-and-red mosaic walls, iron furniture and tiny tealight candles.

Le Mas (Map p815; ☎ 04 91 33 25 90; 4 rue Lulli; **M** Estrangin Préfecture; menu €25; ☺ 11am-4am, ☺ closed Sun Oct-Apr) Le Mas' walls are lined with photographs of stars, showbiz types, celebs and other insomniac artists who dine at this little late-night place. It serves fab French fare with excellent wine included in *menu* prices.

Les Arcenaulx (Map p815; ☎ 04 91 54 85 38; 27 cours Honoré d'Estienne d'Orves, 1er; **M** Vieux Port; menus €30-50; ☺ Mon-Sat) Wrapped around cours des Arcenaulx on the Vieux Port's left bank, this cavernous complex contains an antiquarian and contemporary bookshop with a specialist interest in gastronomy, as well as a restaurant and *salon de thé* (tearoom) serving ice creams named after literary classics.

Chez Fonfon (Map pp812-13; ☎ 04 91 52 14 38; 140 rue du Vallon des Auffes, 7e; mains around €40; ☺ closed Mon lunch & Sun) Overlooking the enchanting little harbour Vallon des Auffes, near the corniche, Chez Fonfon is famed for its *bouillabaisse*. Choose from a lush list of local rosés and crisp Cassis white wines to accompany it. Book ahead.

Péron (Map pp812-13; ☎ 04 91 52 15 22; 56 corniche Kennedy, 7e; menus €60; ☺ lunch & dinner) If you're going to throw budgetary caution to the wind, do it at this designer, truffle-coloured place, opposite Hôtel Pèron (p819) but no longer owned by the same family. The food – especially the lobster risotto – is phenomenal and the views of the Med mesmerising.

CAFÉS
Cafés crowd quai de Rive Neuve and cours Honoré d'Estienne d'Orves (6e), a large, long, open square two blocks south of the quay. Another cluster overlooks place de la Préfecture, at the southern end of rue St-Ferréol (1er).

Le Ciné 28 (Map p815; ☎ 04 91 91 52 72; 28 quai du Port, 2e; **M** Vieux Port; juice €4, dishes €4-6.50; ☺ 9am-6pm winter, 9am-8pm summer) Get a vitamin fix with a fresh-squeezed fruit-juice cocktail or salad at this bright, breezy place overlooking the port.

O'Stop (Map p815; ☎ 04 91 33 85 34; 15 rue St-Saëns, 1er; **M** Vieux Port; menu €10; ☺ 24hr) With a tiny daytime terrace and just four two-person tables plus bar stools at night, O'Stop does fantastic sandwiches and simple regional specialities round-the-clock.

Locals tuck into eggs for breakfast at **Le Pain Quotidien** (Map p815; ☎ 04 91 33 55 00; 18 place aux Huiles, 1er; **M** Vieux Port; breakfast €5-8); and fast, fresh Italian fare at **Pizzeria Chez Mario** (Map p815; ☎ 04 91 54 48 54; 8 rue Euthymènes, 1er; **M** Vieux Port; mains €8.50-15).

SELF-CATERING
Stock up on fruit and vegetables at **Marché des Capucins** (Map p815; place des Capucins, 1er; **M** Noailles; ☺ Mon-Sat), one block north of La Canebière; and at the **fruit and vegetable market** (Map p815; cours Pierre Puget, 6e; **M** Estrangin Préfecture; ☺ Mon-Sat).

See p823 for more market listings.

There are a couple of supermarkets in the monstrous concrete bunker that is the Centre Bourse shopping centre (Map p815).

Drinking
Options for a coffee or something stronger abound on and around the Vieux Port. Students and artists congregate at the alternative cafés and bars of cours Julien and its surrounding streets.

Le Bar de la Marine (Map p815; ☎ 04 91 54 95 42; 15 quai de Rive Neuve, 7e; **M** Vieux Port; ☺ 7am-1am) Marcel Pagnol filmed the card party scenes in *Marius* at this Marseille institution that draws folks from every walk of life.

L'OM Café (Map p815; ☎ 04 91 33 80 33; 3 quai des Belges, 1er; **M** Vieux Port; menus €14-25; ☺ 7am-1am) Decked out in football team Olympique de Marseille's pale blue-and-white, with footballs suspended from the ceiling and press clippings and posters plastering the walls, this place (and especially the terrace) becomes a giant party when it screens each and every game.

Au Petit Nice (Map pp812-13; ☎ 04 91 48 43 04; 28 place Jean Jaurès, 6e; **M** Notre Dame du Mont-Cours Julien; ☺ 6am-2am) This cosy Brit boozer-type place is a local favourite.

Entertainment
Cultural events are covered in Wednesday's *L'Hebdo* (in French; €1) available around town. The website www.marseillebynight .com (in French) also has listings.

PROVENCE

Tickets for most events are sold at *billet-teries* (ticket counters) including **FNAC** (p811) as well as the tourist office.

Match tickets to see the city's cherished football team, Olympique de Marseille (OM), play at their home ground **Stade Vélodrome** (3 blvd Michelet, 8e; M rond-point du Prado) are sold in town at **OM's Boutique Officielle** (Map p815; ☎ 04 91 33 52 28; 44 La Canebière, 1er; M Noailles; 10am-7pm Mon-Sat) and **L'OM Café** (p821).

LIVE MUSIC

La Caravelle (Map p815; ☎ 04 96 17 05 40; 34 quai du Port, 2e; M Vieux Port; 7am-2am) Catch legendary jazz sessions or just catch the vibe at Hôtel Belle-vue's (p819) first-floor bar lined with timber walls, black and red vinyl upholstered chairs, bold murals and a sky blue ceiling. On balmy nights the balcony is a prized portside perch.

Pelle Mêle (Map p815; ☎ 04 91 54 85 26; 8 place aux Huiles, 1er; M Vieux Port; 7pm-1am Mon-Sat) Jive to more good jazz at this lively bistro near the port. Bands start around 10pm.

L'Intermédiaire (Map pp812-13; ☎ 04 91 47 01 25; 63 place Jean Jaurès, 6e; M Notre Dame du Mont-Cours Julien; 7pm-2am Mon-Sat) Groovers gather at this artsy, intimate place for live music like blues and breaking new bands (from 10.30pm most nights).

NIGHTCLUBS

La Maronnaise (☎ 04 91 73 98 58, 04 91 72 42 65; rte de la Maronnaise, 8e; admission €10; 9am-4am Wed-Sat early May–early Sep) Arrive early to slide into a sun lounge or earlier still for a patch of sand to bask on the tiny beach, before dancing under the stars till dawn at this hipsters' hang-out at Les Goudes on Cap Croisette. You can also dine on the seaside terrace (lunch €15, dinner €30). Take bus 19.

Other happenin' haunts:

Le Bazar (Map pp812-13; ☎ 04 91 79 08 88; 90 blvd Rabatau, 8e; admission €15; midnight-6am Thu-Sun) Vast Moroccan-style space with bungalows and palms.

Le Millenium (☎ 08 92 88 80 13; rte de Cassis, 9e; 11pm-6am Thu-Sun) Five kinds of music across five gyrating floors, and a record-producer/rock star–type crowd aged 20 to 50. About 6km from the city. Free entry.

Le Trolleybus (Map p815; ☎ 04 91 54 30 45; 24 quai Rive Neuve, 7e; M Vieux Port; 11pm-dawn Wed-Sat) Shake your booty to techno, funk, indie and more inside this tunnel-like harbourside club. Wicked sound system.

GAY & LESBIAN

The website www.petitfute-gay.com (in French) has good coverage of Marseille's gay scene. **MP Bar** (Map p815; ☎ 04 91 33 64 79; 10 rue Beauvau, 1e; M Vieux Port) is a perennial hotspot, attracting a mostly young, gay, male crowd.

MARSEILLE'S BASKET

North of the Vieux Port, Marseille's old city, Le Panier quarter (2e) translates as 'the basket', and was the site of the Greek agora (marketplace). In its history-woven streets you can get your fill of its past, as well as fill your shopping basket with artisan products handmade in Marseille.

Sniff Marseille's scented soaps at **La Cie de Provence** (Map p815; ☎ 04 91 56 20 94; 1 rue Caisserie; M Vieux Port), and pick up bathroom accoutrements like colourful towels at the neighbouring **La Comptoir du Panier** (Map p815; ☎ 04 91 56 20 94; 1 rue Caisserie; M Vieux Port). Olive-wood carvings, olive soaps and olive oils fill **72% Pétanque** (Map p815; ☎ 04 91 91 14 57; 10 rue du Petit Puits; M Vieux Port). Nearby are a clutch of ceramic ateliers with shops attached to their workshops, including **Le Transfo** (Map p815; ☎ 04 91 56 21 93; 3 rue du Petit Puits; M Vieux Port). Squeal over the cute **Au Cochon Dingue** (the Mad Pig; Map p815; ☎ 06 71 39 96 16; 6 place de Lorette; M Vieux Port), selling handmade pig ornaments.

And to fill your picnic basket? Try **La Chocolatière du Panier** (Map p815; ☎ 04 91 91 67 66; 4 place des 13 Cantons), with weird-and-wonderful flavours of handmade chocolates such as onion and lavender; and **Les Navettes des Accoules** (Map p815; ☎ 04 91 90 99 42; 68 rue Caisserie) for traditional canoe-shaped biscuits made from orange-flavoured flour. At **Le Goût de l'Enfance** (Map p815; ☎ 04 91 54 11 25; 6 place des Pistoles; mains €8-9; 9am-6pm Tue-Sat) you can buy Le Panier legend Madame Brigitte Garelli's home-made jam. Wash it down with the local firewater at **La Maison du Pastis** (Map p815; ☎ 04 91 90 86 77; 108 quai du Port), where you can sample more than 60 varieties of pastis (a liquorice-flavoured apéritif) or splash out on absinthe.

To empty your picnic basket, cross the port and head up to **Jardin du Pharo** (p817).

Shopping

You'll find artisan specialities in the streets spiralling out from the Vieux Port, especially in **Le Panier** (see opposite).

Music shops are massed around cours Julien, including **Le Magasin La Baguetterie des Batteurs** (Map pp812-13; ☎ 04 91 36 55 55; 42 cours Julien; Ⓜ Notre Dame du Mont-Cours Julien; ✿ closed Sun & Mon), a specialist drum shop jam-packed with *djembes* (goblet-shaped West African hand drums), kits, sticks and more.

MARKETS

Mooch among Marseille's Moroccan *souk*-style bazaars. The small but enthralling **fish market** (Map p815; quai des Belges; Ⓜ Vieux Port; ✿ 8am-1pm) is a daily fixture at the Vieux Port docks. **Cours Julien** hosts a Wednesday-morning fruit and vegetable market. Stalls laden with everything from second-hand clothing to pots and pans fill nearby **place Jean Jaurès** (✿ 8am-1pm Sat; Ⓜ Notre Dame du Mont-Cours Julien).

Marseille's biggest market, the daily **Prado Market** (Map pp812-13; Ⓜ Castellane or Perier; ✿ mornings) stretches from the Castellane metro station along av du Prado to the Perier metro station, with a staggering array of clothes, fruit, vegetables and speciality items; and a flower market on Friday morning.

Getting There & Away

AIR

Aéroport Marseille-Provence (☎ 04 42 14 14 14; www.mrsairport.com), also known as Aéroport Marseille-Marignane, is 28km northwest of town in Marignane.

BOAT

Marseille's **passenger ferry terminal** (Map pp812-13; ☎ 04 91 56 38 63; fax 04 91 56 38 70; Ⓜ Place de la Joliette) is 250m south of place de la Joliette (1er).

The **Société Nationale Maritime Corse-Méditerranée** (SNCM; Map pp812-13; ☎ 08 36 67 95 00; www.sncm.fr; 61 blvd des Dames, 2e; Ⓜ Place de la Joliette; ✿ 8am-6pm Mon-Fri, 8.30am-noon & 2-5.30pm Sat) links Marseille with Corsica (see p914), Sardinia and Tunisia. It also serves the ports of Algiers, Annaba, Bejaia, Oran and Skikda in Algeria, although services are prone to disruption/cancellation because of the political troubles there.

For more information on ferry services to/from North Africa (p975) and Sardinia (p974) see the Transport chapter.

There is an office for **Algérie Ferries** (Map p815; ☎ 04 91 90 64 70; 29 blvd des Dames, 2e; Ⓜ Jules Guesde; ✿ 9-11.45am & 1-4.45pm Mon-Fri).

BUS

The **bus station** (Map pp812-13; ☎ 04 91 08 16 40; 3 place Victor Hugo, 3e; Ⓜ Gare St-Charles) is 150m to the right as you exit the train station. Tickets are sold at company ticket counters (closed most of the time) or on the bus.

Buses travel to Aix-en-Provence (€4.40, 35 minutes via the *autoroute* or one hour via the N8, every five to 10 minutes), Avignon (€17.20, two hours, one daily), Cannes (€23.50, two hours, four daily), Carpentras (€12, two hours, infrequent), Nice (€25, 2¾ hours, up to three daily), Nice airport, Orange and other destinations.

Services to some destinations including Cassis use the stop on **place Castellane** (Map pp812-13; ☎ 04 91 79 81 82; 6e; Ⓜ Castellane), south of the centre. Bus drivers sell tickets.

Eurolines (☎ 08 92 89 90 91; www.eurolines.com) has buses to Spain, Switzerland, Germany, Italy, Morocco, the UK and beyond; see p971. Its counter is inside the bus station. **Intercars** (☎ 04 91 50 08 66; www.intercars.fr in French), with an office next to Eurolines in the bus station, also serves numerous countries (p972). There's also a joint **office** (Map p815; ☎ 04 91 50 57 55; 3 allées Léon Gambetta, 1er; Ⓜ Rèformès-Canabière) for these two firms nearer the Vieux Port.

CAR

Rental agencies offering decent rates include **Avis** (Map p815; ☎ 04 91 64 71 00) and **Europcar** (Map p815; ☎ 04 91 99 40 90), both at the train station.

TRAIN

Marseille's passenger train station, **Gare St-Charles** (Map p815) is served by both metro lines. There's an **information and ticket reservation office** (✿ 9am-8pm Mon-Sat; ticket purchases 4am-1am); plus a **left-luggage office** (rates from €3.50; ✿ 7.30am-10pm) next to platform A.

In town, tickets can be bought at the SNCF Boutique inside the Centre Bourse shopping centre (Map p815), near place de la Préfecture.

From Marseille there are trains to pretty much anywhere in France and beyond.

PROVENCE

Sample destinations and starting fares include Paris' Gare de Lyon (€75.20, three hours, 17 daily), Nice (€26.40, 2½ hours, 21 daily), Avignon (€16.40, 30 minutes, 27 daily) and Lyon (€43.10, 3¼ hours, 16 daily).

Getting Around

TO/FROM THE AIRPORT

Navette (Marseille ☎ 04 91 50 59 34; airport ☎ 04 42 14 31 27) shuttle buses link Marseille-Provence airport (€8.50, one hour) with Marseille's train station. Buses heading to the airport leave from outside the station's main entrance every 20 minutes between 5.30am and 9.50pm, and buses to the train station depart the airport between 6.10am and 10.50pm.

BUS & METRO

Marseille has two metro lines (Métro 1 and Métro 2) and an extensive bus network.

The metro and most buses run from 5am only until 9pm. From 9.25pm to 12.30am, metro routes are covered every 15 minutes by buses M1 and M2; stops are marked with the fluorescent green signs reading *métro en bus* (metro by bus). Most night buses begin their runs in front of the **Espace Infos RTM** (Map p815; ☎ 04 91 91 92 10; 6 rue des Fabres, 1er; Ⓜ Vieux Port; Ⓨ 8.30am-6pm Mon-Fri, 9am-12.30pm & 2-5.30pm Sat), where you can obtain information and tickets for public transport.

Bus/metro tickets (€1.70) can be used on any combination of metros and buses for one hour after they've been time-stamped. A pass for one/three days costs €4.50/10.

TAXI

There's a taxi stand to the right as you exit the train station through the main entrance. **Marseille Taxi** (☎ 04 91 02 20 20) and **Taxis France** (☎ 04 91 49 91 00) run taxis 24 hours a day. Flagfall is €1.50, or €3 if you order one by phone.

TRAM

At the time of research, Marseille's new tramway was in the works, though hampered by delays; check www.metro-tram way-marseille.com (in French) for updates.

AIX-EN-PROVENCE

pop 137,067

A pocket of Left Bank Parisian chic deep in Provence, it's hard to believe Aix-en-Provence is just 25km from chaotic, exotic Marseille. Aix (pronounced like the letter X)

is all class: its plane tree–shaded boulevards and public squares are lined with 17th- and 18th-century mansions, and punctuated by gurgling, moss-covered fountains. The city's grandest avenue, cours Mirabeau, is guarded by haughty stone lions – and by fashionable Aixois sipping espresso on wicker chairs on elegant café terraces.

Like Paris' Left Bank, Aix is a prestigious student hub (and like Paris' Left Bank, it's expensive, too). First established in 1409, the Université de Provence Aix-Marseille has a 30,000-strong campus, including many intensive French-language foreign students.

Aix marks the spot where, under the proconsul Sextius Calvinus, Roman forces enslaved the inhabitants of the Ligurian Celtic stronghold of Entremont, 3km to the north. In 123 BC the military camp was named Aquae Sextiae (Waters of Sextius) for the thermal springs, which still flow today. In the 12th century the counts of Provence proclaimed Aix their capital, which it remained until the Revolution, when it was supplanted by Marseille. The city became a centre of culture under arts patron King René (1409–80); two of Aix's most famous sons are painter Paul Cézanne and novelist Émile Zola. But for all its polish, it's still a laid-back Provençal town at heart.

Forty kilometres northeast of age-old Aix is Cadarache, a revolutionary new thermonuclear experimental reactor - see p71.

Orientation

Cours Mirabeau extends eastwards to place Forbin from place du Général de Gaulle, a roundabout with a huge fountain commonly just referred to as La Rotonde. The city's mostly pedestrianised old town, Vieil Aix, is north of cours Mirabeau. Radiating from La Rotonde, av des Belges leads southwest to the bus station; while av Victor Hugo brings you southeast to the train station – the tourist office is on the southern edge of La Rotonde between the two. The TGV station is 8km from the city centre, linked by shuttle buses.

South of cours Mirabeau is the Mazarin Quartier, with a street grid laid out in the 17th century. The entire city centre is ringed by a series of maddening one-way boulevards.

AIX-EN-PROVENCE

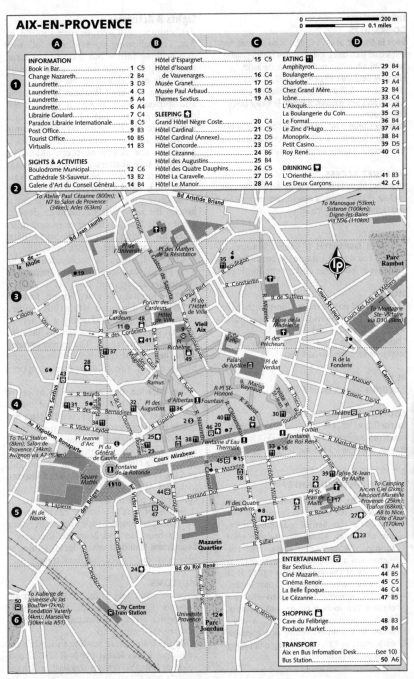

INFORMATION
Book in Bar	1	C5
Change Nazareth	2	B4
Laundrette	3	D3
Laundrette	4	C3
Laundrette	5	A4
Laundrette	6	A4
Librairie Goulard	7	C4
Paradox Librairie Internationale	8	C5
Post Office	9	B3
Tourist Office	10	B5
Virtualis	11	B3

SIGHTS & ACTIVITIES
Boulodrome Municipal	12	C6
Cathédrale St-Sauveur	13	B2
Galerie d'Art du Conseil Général	14	B4

Hôtel d'Espargnet	15	C5
Hôtel d'Isoard de Vauvenarges	16	C4
Musée Granet	17	D5
Musée Paul Arbaud	18	C5
Thermes Sextius	19	A3

SLEEPING
Grand Hôtel Nègre Coste	20	C4
Hôtel Cardinal	21	C5
Hôtel Cardinal (Annexe)	22	D5
Hôtel Concorde	23	D5
Hôtel Cèzanne	24	B6
Hôtel des Augustins	25	B4
Hôtel des Quatre Dauphins	26	C5
Hôtel La Caravelle	27	D5
Hôtel Le Manoir	28	A4

EATING
Amphityron	29	B4
Boulangerie	30	C4
Charlotte	31	A4
Chez Grand Mère	32	B4
Icône	33	C4
L'Aixquis	34	A4
La Boulangerie du Coin	35	C3
Le Formal	36	B4
Le Zinc d'Hugo	37	A4
Monoprix	38	C4
Petit Casino	39	D5
Roy René	40	C4

DRINKING
L'Orienthé	41	B3
Les Deux Garçons	42	C4

ENTERTAINMENT
Bar Sextius	43	A4
Ciné Mazarin	44	B5
Cinéma Renoir	45	C5
La Belle Époque	46	C4
Le Cézanne	47	B5

SHOPPING
Cave du Felibrige	48	B3
Produce Market	49	B4

TRANSPORT
Aix en Bus Infomation Desk	(see 10)	
Bus Station	50	A6

PROVENCE

Information

BOOKSHOPS

Book in Bar (☎ 04 42 26 60 07; 1bis rue Cabassol) Buys/sells second-hand books, and stocks new English-language books. With a bohemian reading café out the back.

Librairie Goulard (☎ 04 42 27 66 47; 37 cours Mirabeau; ⊙ 10.30am-7.30pm Mon, 9am-7.30pm Tue-Sat) Aix's best selection of English-language Lonely Planet guides.

Paradox Librairie Internationale (☎ 04 42 26 47 99; 15 rue du 4 Septembre) Dublin-style bookshop paradoxically selling foreign-language books and groceries.

INTERNET ACCESS

Virtualis (☎ 04 42 26 02 30; 40 rue des Cordeliers; per hr €3.80; ⊙ 9am-midnight Mon-Fri, noon-midnight Sat & Sun) Central and state-of-the-art.

LAUNDRY

Loads of **laundrettes** (⊙ 7am or 8am-8pm) include 3 rue de la Fontaine, 34 cours Sextius, 3 rue de la Fonderie and 60 rue Boulegon.

MONEY

Commercial banks mass along cours Mirabeau and cours Sextius, which runs north–south to the west of La Rotonde.

Change Nazareth (7 rue Nazareth; ⊙ 9am-7pm Mon-Sat year-round, 9-5pm Sun Jul & Aug)

POST

Post Office (place de l'Hôtel de Ville)

TOURIST INFORMATION

Tourist Office (☎ 04 42 16 11 61; www.aixenprovence tourism.com; 2 place du Général de Gaulle; ⊙ 8.30am-7pm Mon-Sat, 10am-1pm & 2-6pm Sun) Longer hours in summer.

OLD FASHIONED PAMPERING

When in Aix, do as the Romans did when they were here in the 1st century BC and bliss out at the thermal spas. Built on the site of Roman Aquae Sextiae's thermal springs, the excavated remains of the Roman spa are displayed beneath glass in the lobby of **Thermes Sextius** (☎ 04 42 23 81 82; www.thermes-sextius.com; 55 cours Sextius). Decadent remedies for weary travellers include a 'Zen spray massage' and a host of other hydrotherapy treatments. A day's access to the fitness centre or a massage each starts at €37, with all-day pampering packages available.

Sights & Activities

Art, culture, and architecture abound in Aix. The following sights can be followed as a walking tour – but taking your time, and taking detours at whim, is the ultimate way to discover this strollable city.

The graceful **cours Mirabeau** is the literal and spiritual heart of Aix. It was laid out during the latter half of the 1600s and named after the Revolutionary hero Comte de Mirabeau. Cafés spill out onto the footpaths on the sunny northern side. The southern side shelters a string of elegant Renaissance *hôtels particuliers* (private mansions); **Hôtel d'Espargnet** (1647) at No 38 is among the most impressive (today it houses the university's economics department). The Marquis of Entrecasteaux murdered his wife in their family home, **Hôtel d'Isoard de Vauvenarges** (1710), at No 10.

Cours Mirabeau is bookended to the west by the cast-iron fountain **fontaine de la Rotonde**, dating from 1860. At its eastern end, the fountain by place Forbin, **fontaine du Roi René**, is decorated with a 19th-century statue of King René clasping a bunch of Muscat grapes, which he's said to have introduced to the region. The mossy **fontaine d'Eau Thermale**, at the intersection of cours Mirabeau and rue du 4 Septembre, spouts 34°C water.

Rue Mazarine, one block south of cours Mirabeau, also has some splendid buildings. Two blocks further south, **place des Quatre Dauphins'** fountain dates from 1667. More fine architectural examples are found at the eastern continuation of cours Mirabeau, **rue de l'Opéra** (at Nos 18, 24 and 26); and the pretty, fountain-clad **place d'Albertas**, just west of place St-Honoré, where musicians often play on midsummer nights.

South of Aix's historic centre is the peaceful **parc Jourdan**, dominated by Aix's largest fountain and home to the town's **Boulodrome Municipal** where locals gather to play *pétanque* under the plane trees.

MUSEUMS

Save on entry fees with the **Visa for Aix-en-Provence** (€2), available from the tourist office, which gives you discounts at many city and regional museums.

By the time you're reading this, Aix's exceptional **Musée Granet** (☎ 04 42 52 88 32; place St-Jean de Malte; ⊙ 11am-6pm Wed-Mon) will have reopened after nearly three years of massive works, tripling it in size. Housed in a 17th-century priory of the Knights of Malta, its collections include 16th- to 20th-century Italian, Flemish and French paintings, including the museum's pride and joy, eight of Cézanne's works.

Musée Paul Arbaud (☎ 04 42 38 38 95; 2a rue du 4 Septembre; adult/student €3/1.50; ☒ 2-5pm Mon-Sat) connects you to Aix's literary heritage with displays of books and manuscripts, as well as exhibiting Provençal faïence – tin-glazed earthenware.

Galérie d'Art du Conseil Général (☎ 04 42 93 03 67; 21bis cours Mirabeau; admission free; ☒ 10.15am-12.45pm & 1.30-6.30pm Mon-Sat) showcases photography and contemporary art.

CATHÉDRALE ST-SAUVEUR
A potpourri of architectural styles, the **Cathédrale St-Sauveur** (rue Laroque; ☒ 8am-noon & 2-6pm) was built between 1285 and 1350. A Romanesque 12th-century nave is incorporated in its southern aisle, the chapels were added in the 14th and 15th centuries, and there's a 5th-century sarcophagus (stone coffin) in the apse. More recent additions include the 18th-century gilt baroque organ. The acoustics make the Gregorian chants (usually sung at 4.30pm Sunday) an unforgettable experience.

Mass is held here at 8am (Saturday at 6.30pm, and Sunday at 9am, 10.30am and 7pm).

CÉZANNE SIGHTS
His star may have reached its giddiest heights after his death, but the life of local lad Paul Cézanne (1839–1906) is treasured in Aix. To see where he ate, drank, studied and painted, you can follow the **Circuit de Cézanne** (Cézanne Trail), marked by footpath-embedded bronze plaques inscribed with the letter C. Corresponding with the plaques is an informative English-language guide, *Cézanne's Footsteps*, available free from the tourist office, where the circuit begins.

Though none of his works hang here, Cézanne's last **studio** (Atelier Paul Cézanne; ☎ 04 42 21 06 53; www.atelier-cezanne.com; 9 av Paul Cézanne; adult/student €5.50/2; ☒ 10am-noon & 2-5pm Oct-Mar, to 6pm Apr-Jun & Sep, 10am-6pm Jul & Aug) is a must for anyone interested in his works. It's painstakingly preserved as it was at the time of his death, strewn with his tools and still life

models; you get the impression he's just popped out to the shops and will be back any moment. The atelier's 1.5km north of the tourist office on a hilltop; take bus 1 to the Cézanne stop.

Both the atelier and the tourist office have information about trailing Cézanne further afield in the surrounding countryside where he painted his landscapes.

Tours
Between April and October, the tourist office runs a packed schedule of guided bus tours throughout the region in English and in French. Literary buffs can take a guided Émile Zola literary walk, or follow the free, self-guided *Literary Walk* brochure. Ask for the free *Guide Map* at the tourist office for details of all tours or check its website (www.aixenprovencetourism.com). Prices start from around €28.

Festivals & Events
Aix's sumptuous cultural calendar is capped off by the month-long **Festival International d'Art Lyrique d'Aix-en-Provence** (International Festival of Lyrical Art; www.festival-aix.com) in July, bringing classical music, opera and ballet to city venues such as the Théâtre de l'Archevêché, outside the Cathédrale St-Sauveur, while buskers keep cours Mirabeau's festive spirits high.

Comic books, animation and cartoon art feature during the **Rencontres du 9ème Art** (www.bd-aix.com in French) festival in March. Other highlights are the two-day **Festival du Tambourin** (Tambourine Festival) in mid-April and the **Fête Mistralienne**, marking the birthday of Provençal troubadour Frédéric Mistral on 13 September.

Sleeping
The city centre fills up fast in summer and during busy conference and law exam times. The tourist office has lists of *chambres d'hôtes* (B&Bs) and *gîtes ruraux* (country cottages) in and around Aix as well as longer-term accommodation including farmhouses. Hotel bookings are coordinated through the email address resaix@aixenprovencetourism.com.

BUDGET
Camping Arc-en-Ciel (☎ 04 42 26 14 28; rte de Nice; camping €17.10; ☒ Apr-Sep) There are tranquil

wooded hills out the back of this four-star place, but a busy motorway in front. It's 2km southeast of town, at Pont des Trois Sautets. Take bus 3 to Les Trois Sautets stop.

Auberge de Jeunesse du Jas de Bouffan (☎ 04 42 20 15 99; fax 04 42 59 36 12; 3 av Marcel Pagnol; dm incl breakfast & sheets €15.70; reception 🕑 7am-1pm & 5pm-midnight, closed 20 Dec–9 Feb) Flash and cyclist-friendly, with a bar and tennis courts, this HI hostel is 2km west of the centre. Take bus 4 from La Rotonde to the Vasarely stop.

Hôtel Concorde (☎ 04 42 26 03 95; fax 04 42 27 38 90; 68 blvd du Roi René; d €43-69; ✗) Definitely ask for a room with views over the hills at this 50-room place with good wheelchair access just on the southeastern edge of the city centre. Some have small balconies, and higher-priced rooms come with air-con and minibars; try and avoid the dark ground-floor rooms out the back. Handy onsite parking is available for €7.50.

MIDRANGE

Hôtel La Caravelle (☎ 04 42 21 53 05; www.lacara velle-hotel.com; 20 blvd du Roi René; s €40, d €43-70; ✗) Central and serviceable, the 30 rooms here range from air-conditioned doubles overlooking a pretty (and sadly, neighbouring) garden to singles with toilets situated just outside the rooms. The hotel is on the southeastern ring; if you're driving you can pull up to drop off your luggage right out front. Wi-fi's free and wheelchair access is good.

Hôtel Le Manoir (☎ 04 42 26 27 20; www.hotel manoir.com; 8 rue d'Entrecasteux; d €57-85, tr €78-85; 🕑 closed Jan) In a 14th-century cloister re-constructed in the 16th century, Le Manoir has 40 antique-furnished rooms in a secluded but super-central wedge of the old town. There's a lovely leafy garden and private parking.

Hôtel des Quatre Dauphins (☎ 04 42 38 16 39; fax 04 42 38 60 19; 54 rue Roux Alpheran; s €55, d €65-85; ✗) Close to cours Mirabeau, this hotel's skylit central staircase gives on to 13 coir-carpeted rooms with freshly laundered Wedgewood-blue and pale-pink quilts and curtains. Four quaint attic rooms have sloped beamed ceilings (maybe not ideal if you're pushing 6ft tall). Wi-fi's available for €5 per day.

Hôtel Cardinal (☎ 04 42 38 32 30; fax 04 42 26 39 05; 24 rue Cardinale; s/d €58/68, self-catering ste €80) Beneath stratospheric ceilings, Hôtel Cardinal's 29 romantic rooms are beautifully furnished with antiques, tasselled curtains, and newly tiled bathrooms. Try for Room 8, with double sets of French doors opening to a narrow, street-facing balcony. Small self-catering suites are annexed a few doors up.

Grand Hôtel Nègre Coste (☎ 04 42 27 74 22; www .hotelnegrecoste.com; 33 cours Mirabeau; d €70-140; ✗) The only hotel right on cours Mirabeau isn't as grand as when Louis XIV stayed here in 1660, with musty corridors and blasé service, but rooms are cheered up with Provençal colours, and it doesn't get more central than this. Garage parking is €10.

TOP END

Hôtel des Augustins (☎ 04 42 27 28 59; www.hotel -augustins.com; 3 rue de la Masse; standard/superior d €97-240; ✗) A heartbeat from the hub of Aixois life, this former 15th-century convent has volumes of history: Martin Luther stayed here after his excommunication from Rome. Decorated with hand-painted furniture, the largest, most luxurious abodes have Jacuzzis; and two have private terraces beneath the filigreed bell tower. The stained-glass foyer has free wi-fi.

Hôtel Cézanne (☎ 04 42 91 11 11; www.hotelaix .com; 40 av Victor Hugo; d €140-155; ✗ 🖳) In an elegant white building with royal-purple canvas awnings and interiors, this fash-ionable hotel has personalised touches like monogrammed towels, free stamped postcards and free (non-alcoholic) stocked in-room fridges. Downstairs, the open bar is lit by designer lamps, and strewn with purple glass pebbles plus bowls of sea-sonal nuts and fruits such as cherries and clementines – like Cézanne himself would have painted.

Eating

Aix excels for Provençal cuisine. You'll also find a concentration of Vietnamese and Chinese restaurants, particularly around Rue de la Verrerie and rue Félibre Gaut.

Charlotte (☎ 04 42 26 77 56; 32 rue des Bernardines; 2-/3-course menu €13/16; 🕑 lunch & dinner Tue-Sat) Townspeople congregate like a big ex-tended family at this bustling place, which turns out delicious, simple home cooking, including incredible crème brûlée, from the open kitchen. In summer, feasting takes place outdoors in the garden, and there's a comfy lounge room to unwind pre- or post-repast.

Chez Grand Mère (☎ 04 42 53 33 47; 1 rue des Bernardines; mains €12.50-21.50; ☾ closed Sun dinner & Mon) In the old town, this friendly place characterised by colourful murals is a fine choice for frogs' legs and the like. The multicourse menus are great value. If you missed out on *bouillabaisse* in Marseille, this is your chance to make up for it (minimum of two; order two days before).

Le Zinc d'Hugo (☎ 04 42 27 69 69; 22 rue Lieutaud; mains €14-18; ☾ lunch & dinner Tue-Sat) This rustic bistro of stone walls, wooden tables packed with convivial locals, and a blackboard menu chalking up daily specials like a terrine of foie gras with *confit* of vegetables, also has a lush, 80-strong wine list.

Icône (☎ 04 42 27 59 82; 3 rue Frédéric Mistral; 2-/3-course menu €17/25; ☾ lunch & dinner Mon-Sat) The designer Italian/Mediterranean fare matches the designer box-like teal armchairs and dark timber lining at this glam place just off cours Mirabeau. There's a stainless steel bar and DJ spinning electro lounge beats.

L'Aixquis (☎ 04 42 27 76 16; 22 rue Victor Leydet; mains €18-25; ☾ lunch & dinner Tue-Sat) You'll be tempted to whip out your camera to photograph elaborately presented *plats* like truffle-infused *St-Jacques* (scallops) at this small peach-coloured restaurant, which has a way of giving even the most humble vegetables panache. The *carte* (no *menus*) changes seasonally, but the magical *minute chocolat noir* (a tray of petite desserts) is a year-round fixture.

Amphitryon (☎ 04 42 26 54 10; 2-4 rue Paul-Doumer; mains €23; ☾ lunch & dinner Tue-Sat; ✗) Run by Patrice Lesné, who masterfully oversees the sleek dining rooms of studded red banquettes and outdoor 15th-century cloister terrace, and co-owner and passionate chef Bruno Ungaro, who visits the markets each morning. The attached *Comptoir de l'Amphi* (mains €12-14) is an affordable alternative, and there's a piano where guests knock out a tune after a cognac or two.

Le Formal (☎ 04 42 27 08 31; 32 rue Espariat; mains starting from €14; ☾ lunch & dinner Tue-Fri, dinner Sat; ✗) Actually named after its chef, Jean-Luc Le Formal, who's making a splash in France's foodie circles, this first-class establishment has impeccably mannered service both at its whitewashed stone lounge/reception area at street level, and in its vaulted cellar dining rooms.

SELF-CATERING
Fresh, often still-warm loaves cram the shelves of **La Boulangerie du Coin** (4 rue Boulegon; ☾ Tue-Sun). It's also one of the few *boulangeries* to bake on Sunday, along with the **boulangerie** (5 rue Tournefort; ☾ 24hr) that never closes.

Aix is blessed with bountiful markets – see p830.

Pick up groceries at **Monoprix** (cours Mirabeau; ☾ 8.30am-9pm Mon-Sat) and at **Petit Casino** (rue d'Italie; ☾ 9am-7pm Mon-Sat).

Drinking
Pavement cafés offer a plethora of people-watching and posing ops. Open-air cafés also saturate the city's squares, especially place des Cardeurs, forum des Cardeurs, place de Verdun and place de l'Hôtel de Ville.

Les Deux Garçons (☎ 04 42 26 00 51; 53 cours Mirabeau) The best choice – since 1792 and still resplendent – is the legendary Les Deux Garçons, where Cézanne and Zola used to hang out. In its gilded olive-painted salon and on its outdoor terrace you're attended by waiters wearing dinner suits and long white aprons, whisking between tables with trays held aloft. Above the café there's a jazz club/piano bar.

L'Orienthé (5 rue de Félibre Gaut; ☾ 1pm-1am) A languorous place for lounge music, *shishas* (Turkish water pipes), and a Zen atmosphere, as well as over 50 different flavours of tea.

Entertainment
Flip though a copy of the monthly *In Aix* (free from the tourist office) to find out what's on where.

The locally-based dance company, **Le Ballet Preljocaj** (www.preljocaj.org) presents cutting-edge works when not on tour.

CINEMA
Aix's arty-intellectual student population ensures great cinema offerings, from Oscar contenders to cult flicks, very often in English. Programmes for the following cinemas can be found at www.lescinemasaixois.com (in French):

Ciné Mazarin (☎ 08 92 68 72 70; 6 rue Laroque; adult/student €7.50/6.50)

Cinéma Renoir (☎ 08 92 68 72 70; 24 cours Mirabeau; adult/student €7.50/6.50)

PROVENCE

Le Cézanne (☎ 08 92 68 72 70; 1 rue Marcel Guillaume; ticket adult/student €8.50/6.70)

BARS & CLUBS

Like all good student cities, the scene here is fun but fickle. The areas on and around rue de la Verrerie and place Richelme are prime for nightlife. Listings on the website www.marseillebynight.com (in French) also cover Aix.

La Belle Époque (☎ 04 42 27 65 66; 29 cours Mirabeau; ☺ hours vary) Many a 'beautiful time' has been had at this place, which sees DJs spinning Latino, house and funk every evening.

Bar Sextius (☎ 04 42 26 07 21; 13 cours Sextius; ☺ 7am-2am Mon-Sat) With live music and DJs spinning house, reggae and ragga, depending on the night, Bar Sextius is a local gathering spot – ask the in-the-know crowd here about Aix's latest in-spots.

Shopping

Aix's chicest shops are clustered along pedestrian rue Marius Reinaud, which winds behind the Palais de Justice on place de Verdun. Elegant boutiques also grace cours Mirabeau.

Local wine vendors include **Cave du Felibrige** (18 rue des Cordeliers), which has a splendid array – some *very* expensive.

There are around 20 *calisson* makers in town (see below), as well as plenty of enticing patisseries.

MARKETS

Trestle tables set up each morning for the **produce market** on place Richelme, displaying olives, goat's cheese, garlic, lavender, honey, peaches, melons and other sunkissed products. Another **food market** (place des Prêcheurs) takes place on Tuesday, Thursday and Saturday morning.

Rainbows of flowers fill place des Prêcheurs during the Sunday-morning **flower market**; and place de l'Hôtel de Ville (Tuesday, Thursday and Saturday mornings). Quirky vintage items can also be found at the **flea market** (Tuesday, Thursday and Saturday mornings) on place de Verdun.

Getting There & Away

AIR

Aéroport Marseille-Provence (☎ 04 42 14 14 14; www.mrsairport.com), also known as Aéroport Marseille-Marignane, is 25km from Aix-en-Provence and is served by regular shuttle buses.

BUS

Aix's **bus station** (information office ☎ 08 91 02 40 25; av de l'Europe) is a 10-minute walk southwest from La Rotonde. Numerous companies' services include buses to Marseille (€4.40, 35 minutes, every 10 minutes, every 20 minutes on Sunday), Arles (€10, 1¾ hours, five daily), Avignon (€13.90, one hour, six daily) and Toulon (€10, one hour, six daily Monday to Saturday).

CAR

Circumnavigating the one-way, three-lane orbital system circling the old town is nightmarish in heavy traffic. Street parking spaces are like hen's teeth, but secure, pricier covered parking is plentiful.

TRAIN

Aix's tiny **city centre train station** (☺ 5am-9.15pm Mon-Fri, 6am-9.15pm Sat & Sun, information office ☺ 9am-7pm) is at the southern end of av Victor Hugo. There are frequent services to Briançon (€31.20, 3½ hours), Gap (€23.80, two hours) and Marseille (€6.20, 35 minutes, at least 18 daily), from where there are connections to just about everywhere.

Aix's **TGV station** is 8km from the city centre, accessible by shuttle bus.

Getting Around

TO/FROM THE AIRPORT & TGV STATION

Aix's bus station is linked to both the TGV station (€3.90) and the airport (€7.90) from

---

SWEET TREAT

Aix's sweetest treat since King René's wedding banquet in 1473 is the marzipan-like local speciality, *calisson*, a small, diamond-shaped, chewy delicacy made with ground almonds and fruit syrup, wrapped in a communion-wafer base and glazed with white icing sugar. Traditional *calissonniers* still make the sweets, including **Roy René** (☎ 04 42 26 67 86; www.calisson.com; 10 rue Clémenceau), which also runs guided tours at its out-of-town **factory-museum** (€1; ☺ 10am Tue & Thu). Eight or nine plainly wrapped *calissons* (100g) cost around €3 to €4.

PROVENCE

around 5am to 11.30pm by the half-hourly **Navette** (☎ 04 42 93 59 13) shuttle-bus services.

BUS
The city's 14 bus and three minibus lines are operated by **Aix en Bus** (☎ 04 42 26 37 28; 🕑 8.30am-7pm Mon-Sat). The information desk is inside the tourist office.

La Rotonde is the main bus hub. Most services run until 8pm. A single/carnet of 10 tickets costs €1.10/7.70; a day pass costs €3.50. Minibus 1 links the bus station with La Rotonde and cours Mirabeau. Minibus 2, starting at the train station, follows much the same route.

TAXI
You can find taxis outside the bus station. To order one, call **Taxi Radio Aixois** (☎ 04 42 27 71 11) or **Taxi Mirabeau** (☎ 04 42 21 61 61).

ARLES & THE CAMARGUE

ARLES
pop 51,000
If Arles' winding streets, stone squares and colourful houses baking in the sun seem familiar, it's probably because they feature in Vincent Van Gogh's prolific outpouring of art.

Long before Van Gogh captured on canvas this spot on the Grand Rhône River, just south of where the Petit Rhône diverges, the Romans had already been turned on to its charms. (Even before that, Arles was a Celtic settlement in the Bronze Age, before becoming a Greek colony known to the Romans as Arelate.)

In 49 BC, Arles' prosperity and political standing rose meteorically when it backed a winner in Julius Caesar (who would never meet defeat in his entire career). After Caesar seized and plundered Marseille, which had supported his rival Pompey the Great, Arles eclipsed Marseille as the region's major port. Within a century and a half, it boasted a 12,000-seat theatre and a 20,000-seat amphitheatre to entertain its citizens with gruesome gladiatorial spectacles and chariot races. Still impressively intact, the two structures now stage events including *corrida* (bullfighting), which sends the town into fever-pitched excitement when the season starts with fanfare each spring.

Orientation
Arles is shoehorned between the Grand Rhône River to the northwest, blvd Émile Combes to the east and, to the south, blvd des Lices and blvd Georges Clemenceau. The city centre is shaped like a foot, with the train station, place de la Libération and place Lamartine (where Van Gogh once lived) at the top, les Arènes at the anklebone and the tourist office under the arch. And (fittingly enough) its compact size means it's easily walkable.

Information
BOOKSHOPS
Librairie Van Gogh (☎ 04 90 49 39 39; 1 place Félix Rey; 🕑 10am-12.30pm & 2-6.30pm Tue-Sat) Wrapped around the courtyard of the Espace Van Gogh cultural centre, with an extensive range of art and history books in French and English, and regional travel guides.

INTERNET ACCESS
Point Web (☎ 04 90 18 91 54; 10 rue du 4 Septembre; per 10min €1; 🕑 9am-7pm Mon-Sat)

LAUNDRY
Laundrette (6 rue de la Cavalerie; 🕑 7am-7pm)

MONEY
There are several banks along rue de la République.

POST
Post Office (5 blvd des Lices)

TOURIST INFORMATION
Tourist Office main office (☎ 04 90 18 41 20; www .tourisme.ville-arles.fr; esplanade Charles de Gaulle; 🕑 9am-6.45pm Apr-Sep, 9am-4.45pm Mon-Sat, 10am-1pm Sun Oct-Mar); train station (☎ 04 90 49 36 90; 🕑 9am-1pm & 2-5pm Tue-Sat Apr-Sep; hours may vary) The main office is adjacent to the busy blvd des Lices. Both offices sell a discounted combination ticket to all of Arles' sights for adult/student €13.50/12.

Sights & Activities
Unless otherwise noted, the last entry to all sights listed in this section is 30 minutes prior to closing.

ROMAN MONUMENTS
If you're keen to dig into Arles' Roman past, a combination ticket costing €9/7 for adults/children gives you access to the four following sites.

Les Arènes

Arles' remarkable Roman amphitheatre, **Les Arènes** (☎ 04 90 96 03 70; adult/student €5.50/4; ⏰ 9am-6.30pm May-Sep, 9am-5.30pm Mar, Apr & Oct, 10am-4.30pm Nov-Feb), was built around the late 1st or early 2nd century. With a slightly smaller capacity but marginally larger dimensions than its counterpart in Nîmes, it was the venue for chariot races, and gladiatorial displays where slaves and criminals met their demise before jubilant crowds.

During the Arab invasions of early medieval times, Les Arènes became a fortress. Three of the four defensive towers still stand (one of which is accessible), and parts of Les Arènes are undergoing restoration,

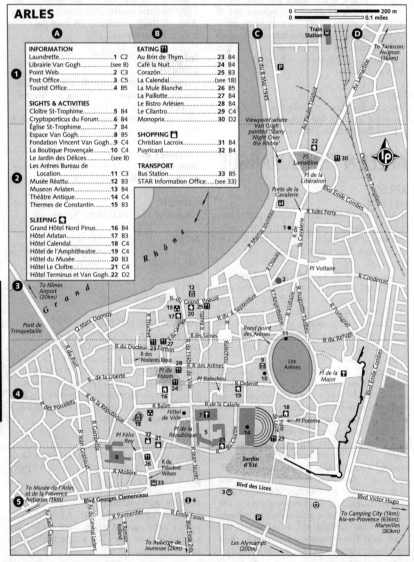

ARLES

0 — 200 m
0 — 0.1 miles

INFORMATION
Laundrette...............................1 C2
Librairie Van Gogh................(see 8)
Point Web...............................2 C3
Post Office..............................3 C5
Tourist Office..........................4 B5

SIGHTS & ACTIVITIES
Cloître St-Trophime...............5 B4
Cryptoporticus du Forum......6 B4
Église St-Trophime.................7 B4
Espace Van Gogh....................8 B4
Fondation Vincent Van Gogh.9 C4
La Boutique Provençale.......10 C4
Le Jardin des Délices.........(see 8)
Les Arènes Bureau de
    Location............................11 C3
Musée Réattu........................12 B3
Museon Arlaten.....................13 B4
Théâtre Antique....................14 C4
Thermes de Constantin........15 B3

SLEEPING
Grand Hôtel Nord Pinus.......16 B4
Hôtel Arlatan........................17 B3
Hôtel Calendal......................18 C4
Hôtel de l'Amphithéatre.......19 C4
Hôtel du Musée....................20 B3
Hôtel Le Cloître....................21 C4
Hôtel Terminus et Van Gogh.22 D2

EATING
Au Brin de Thym...................23 B4
Café la Nuit..........................24 B4
Corazón................................25 B3
La Calendal......................(see 18)
La Mule Blanche...................26 B5
La Paillotte...........................27 B4
Le Bistro Arlésien.................28 B4
Le Cilantro...........................29 C4
Monoprix..............................30 D2

SHOPPING
Christian Lacroix...................31 B4
Puyricard..............................32 B4

TRANSPORT
Bus Station...........................33 B5
STAR Information Office.....(see 33)

PROVENCE

A CLOSE SHAVE

Hemingway might have scoffed – *mise-à-mort* bullfighting *(corrida)* isn't a classic contest between matador and bull, hence in Spain, Latin America and parts of southern France, it's not considered a sport. But Hemingway would no doubt have appreciated the high drama of this tragedy in three acts.

In a *corrida*, a bull bred to be aggressive is killed in a colourful and bloody spectacle involving picadors, bandilleros, matadors and horses. When performed correctly (which is rarely the case) the matador and bull execute a kind of dance, each demonstrating heroism under pressure. Theatrics aside, killing the bull is crucial because, after having been in a *corrida*, it's said to be too dangerous to revisit the ring with a matador. After the event, the bull is carved up and sold for meat (giving it a different taste than ordinary steers' since bulls bred for fighting graze free-range on grass).

Animal lovers fear not: not all types of bullfight end with deceased beasts. The local Camargue variation, *course Camarguaise*, sees amateur *razeteurs* (from the word 'shave'), wearing tight white shirts and trousers, get as close as they dare to the bulls to try and remove rosettes and ribbons tied to the bull's horns, using hooks held between their fingers.

Arles' bullfighting season begins around Easter with a festival known as the Feria (or Féria) Pascale and charges through until the September rice harvest festival.

---

creating community debate about whether the structure should remain in its original condition. But the amphitheatre is far from a forgotten ruin – today it fills to its 12,000 capacity during Arles' bullfighting season (see above).

Les Arènes crowns a hilltop in the city centre, reached by a web of narrow streets. The *bureau de location* (ticket office) is on the northern side of the amphitheatre on Rond Point des Arènes.

Thermes de Constantin

Admission to the amphitheatre is also good for the **Thermes de Constantin** (rue du Grand Prieuré; adult/student €3/2.20; ☉ 9am-noon & 2-6.30pm May-Sep, 9am-noon & 2-5.30pm Mar, Apr & Oct, 10am-noon & 2-5pm Feb & Nov), partly preserved Roman baths near the river, built for Emperor Constantin's private use in the 4th century.

Théâtre Antique

Now a summer outdoor cinema and concert venue, the **Théâtre Antique** (Roman Theatre; ☎ 04 90 96 93 30; enter via the Jardin d'Été on blvd des Lices; adult/student €3/2.20; ☉ 9am-6.30pm May-Sep, 9am-noon & 2-6pm Mar, Apr & Oct, 10am-noon & 2-5pm Nov-Feb) dates from the end of the 1st century BC. For hundreds of years it was used as a convenient source of construction materials, chipping away at the 102m diameter structure (the remaining column on the right-hand side near the entrance indicates the height of the original arcade).

Les Alyscamps

Van Gogh and Gauguin both painted this large **necropolis** (adult/student €3.50/2.60; ☉ 9am-7pm May-Sep, 9am-noon & 2-6pm Mar & Apr, 9am-noon Oct, 10am-noon & 2-5pm Nov-Feb). Situated 1km southeast of Les Arènes, it was founded by the Romans and taken over by Christians in the 4th century, becoming a coveted resting place because of the apparent presence of miracle-working Christian martyrs among its dead.

Other Roman Sites

Under your feet as you stand on the place du Forum are the underground storerooms *Cryptoporticus du Forum*, carved out in the 1st century BC; and closed at press time for repairs – check with the tourist office for reopening dates.

ÉGLISE ST-TROPHIME

Arles was an archbishopric from the 4th century until 1790, and this Romanesque-style **church** was once a cathedral. Built in the late 11th and 12th centuries on the site of several earlier churches, it's named after St Trophime, a late-2nd- or early-3rd-century bishop of Arles. If you look on the far right of the left-hand side of the intricately sculpted façade of biblical scenes on the western portal (more spectacular than the interior), St Trophime is depicted holding a spiral staff in his right hand. Inside the austere church, the most fascinating feature

PROVENCE

is the 'treasury', containing pieces of bone of Arles' bishops who were later canonised. Many of the broken statues inside were decapitated during the French Revolution.

Across the courtyard, **Cloître St-Trophime** (St-Trophime Cloister; ☎ 04 90 49 36 36; adult/student €3.50/2.60; ☻ 9am-6.30pm May-Sep, 9am-6pm Mar, Apr & Oct, 10am-5pm Nov-Feb) is flanked by highly detailed stone and marble columns. Its two Romanesque galleries date from the 1100s, while the two Gothic galleries were added in the 14th century.

MUSEUMS

Within a striking, state-of-the-art cobalt-blue building, the **Musée de l'Arles et de la Provence Antique** (☎ 04 90 18 88 88/89; adult/student/ under 18 €5.50/4/free; ☻ 9am-7pm Apr-Oct, 10am-5pm Nov-Mar) has amassed a rich collection of pagan and Christian art. Among its stand-out exhibits are Roman statues and artefacts and 4th-century Christian sarcophagi. The museum is 1.5km southwest of the tourist office at av de la 1ère Division Française Libre on the Presqu'île du Cirque Romain.

Museon Arlaten (☎ 04 90 93 58 11; 29 rue de la République; adult/student €4/3; ☻ 9.30am-12.30pm & 2-6pm Tue-Sun Apr & May, 9.30am-1pm & 2-6.30pm Tue-Sun Jun, 9.30am-1pm & 2-6.30pm daily Jul & Aug, 9.30am-12.30pm & 2-6pm daily Sep, 9.30am-12.30pm & 2-5pm Tue-Sun Oct-Mar) was founded by Nobel Prize–winning poet and dedicated Provençal preservationist Frédéric Mistral. It occupies a 16th-century townhouse, with displays of traditional Provençal furniture, crafts, costumes, ceramics, wigs, and a model of the mythical people-eating amphibious monster, the *Tarasque*. The last entry is one hour prior to closing.

Housed in a former 15th-century priory, this splendid **Musée Réattu** (☎ 04 90 96 37 68; 10 rue du Grand Prieuré; adult/student €4/3; ☻ 10am-noon & 2-5pm Mar, Apr & Oct; 10am-noon & 2-6.30pm May-Sep, 1-5pm Nov-Feb) has two Picasso paintings, and 57 of his sketches from the early 1970s, as well as works by 18th- and 19th-century Provençal artists, but it's best known for its cutting-edge photographic displays. Temporary exhibitions incur an additional admission fee depending on the exhibits.

VAN GOGH SIGHTS

Although Van Gogh painted around 200 canvases in Arles, not a single one remains here today (the only Van Gogh canvas in Provence is in Avignon's Musée Angladon – see p844). There's a certain poetic justice, considering that following his altercation with housemate Paul Gauguin in place Victor Hugo (in which he threatened him with a cut-throat razor before using it to slice off part of his own left ear), a petition was raised by fearful neighbours, and he was committed for one month on the mayor's orders.

But Arles has admirably made up for it. Fitting tributes to his art include **Fondation Vincent Van Gogh** (☎ 04 90 49 94 04; 24bis Rond Point des Arènes; adult/student €7/5; ☻ 10am-6pm Apr-Jun, 10am-7pm Jul-Sep, 11am-5pm Tue-Sun Oct-Mar), where important modern-day artists, including David Hockney, Francis Bacon and Fernando Botero, pay homage to the artist's distinctive style.

Temporary art exhibitions regularly take place at **Espace Van Gogh** (☎ 04 90 49 39 39; place Félix Rey), housed in the former hospital where Van Gogh had his ear stitched, and was later locked up.

The best way to get a sense of Van Gogh's time in Arles is the excellent **Van Gogh Trail**, a walking circuit of the city marked by foot-path-embedded plaques. Accompanied by a brochure (in English) handed out by the tourist office, the trail takes in spots where Van Gogh set up his easel to paint canvases such as *The Yellow House* (1888) on place Lamartine, where he lived, but which was wiped out during WWII, and *The Amphitheatre* (1888). At each stop along the circuit, a lectern-style signboard with a reproduction of the painting has interpretative information (also in English). If you stand by the river at twilight as the sky deepens to midnight blue with the yellow moon rising in a sea of fiery stars, where he painted *Starry Night Over the Rhône* (1888), Van Gogh's presence seems strangely palpable.

See also the boxed text on opposite.

Tours

In addition to the Van Gogh Trail (left), several other self-guided walking tours are marked along Arles' footpaths, in conjunction with an explanatory brochure.

From mid-June to mid-September the tourist office runs several thematic city tours for around €5 for two hours, usually with a couple of tours a week in English.

Jeep tours of the Camargue are organised by several companies, costing around €30/15 per adult/child for a half-day trip. The tourist office has information and seasonal schedules; reservations can also be made at **La Boutique Provençale** (☎ 04 90 49 84 31; 8 Rond Point des Arènes). For further operators in the Camargue, see p840.

Festivals & Events

Arles heralds the beginning of the bullfighting season with the festive **Feria Pascale** around Easter. May sees Camargue cowboys parade through the streets of town, the crowning of the Queen of Arles and Camargue games in the amphitheatre during the **Fête des Gardians**. Dance, theatre, music and poetry readings feature during the two-week **Fêtes d'Arles** (☎ 04 90 96 47 00) from around the end of June. Other events include the **Festival Ame Gitane** in mid-August, which celebrates *Gitane* ('Gypsy' or Romany) culture, and the 10-day-long **Fête des Prémices du Riz**, held in September, which

---

VINCENT

Vincent Van Gogh may have been poor – he sold only one painting in his lifetime – but he wasn't old. It's easy to forget from his self-portraits, in which he appears much older (partly the effects of his poverty), that he was only 37 when he died. But his short life, especially his ephemeral time in Provence, would leave an indelible legacy.

Born in 1853, the Dutch painter arrived in Arles in 1888 after living in Paris with his younger brother Theo, an art dealer, who financially supported him from his modest income. In Paris he became acquainted with seminal artists Edgar Degas, Camille Pissarro, Henri de Toulouse-Lautrec and Paul Gauguin. Revelling in Arles' intense light and bright colours, Van Gogh painted sunflowers, irises and other vivid subjects with a burning fervour, unfazed by howling mistrals, during which he knelt on his canvases and painted horizontally or lashed his easel to iron stakes driven deep into the ground. He sent paintings to Theo in Paris to try and sell, and dreamed of founding an artists' colony here, but only Gauguin followed up his invitation. Their differing artistic approaches – Gauguin believed in painting from imagination, Van Gogh painting what he saw – and their artistic temperaments, fuelled by absinthe, came to a head with the argument that led to Van Gogh lopping his ear, and his subsequent committal. Gauguin left Provence immediately (at times Gauguin too suffered from mental illness and also attempted suicide).

During Van Gogh's hospitalisation in Arles, he produced, among other works, a portrait of his doctor, Dr Rey, which he presented as a gift. The doctor didn't throw it away, exactly; using it to plug a hole in his chicken coop. It's now in Moscow's Pushkin Museum.

In May 1889 Van Gogh voluntarily entered an asylum in St-Rémy de Provence, 25km northeast of Arles over the Alpilles, where he painted another 150-odd canvases during his one year, one week, and one day's infirment, including masterpieces like *Starry Night* (not to be confused with *Starry Night Over the Rhône*, painted in Arles). While here, Theo sent him a positive critique of his work that had appeared in the *Mercure de France* newspaper in January 1890, and the following month, his 1888 Arles-painted work *The Red Vines* was bought by Anne Boch, sister of his friend Eugene Boch, for 400 francs (around €50 today). It also now hangs in the Pushkin Museum. You can visit a reconstruction of Van Gogh's room at St-Rémy's Monastère St-Paul de Mausole, and the St-Rémy de Provence tourist office (www.saintremy-de-provence.com) also runs Van Gogh tours.

On 16 May 1890 Van Gogh moved to Auvers-sur-Oise, just outside Paris, to be closer to Theo, but on 27 July that year he shot himself, possibly to avoid further financial burden on his brother, whose wife had just had a baby son, named Vincent. Theo was also supporting their ailing mother. Van Gogh died two days later with Theo at his side. Theo subsequently had a breakdown and was also committed, prior to succumbing to physical illness. He died, aged 33, just six months after Van Gogh.

It would be less than a decade before Van Gogh's talent would start to achieve wide recognition, with major museums acquiring his works. By the early 1950s he'd become a household name. His tormented life is documented in countless books, films, and Don McLean's poignant song, 'Vincent'.

---

marks the start of the rice harvest. The tourist office has detailed information.

In early July, **Les Rencontres Internation-ales de la Photographie** (International Photography Festival; www.rencontres-arles .com) attracts photographers from around the world; with works displayed until September.

Sleeping

Except during festivals, bullfights and July and August, Arles has plenty of reasonably priced accommodation (most of which shuts during January, if not the entire low season – check ahead). There are lots of **gîtes ruraux** (for reservations ☎ 04 90 59 49 40) in the surrounding countryside, especially the Camargue. Ask the tourist office for a list.

BUDGET

Camping City (☎ 04 90 93 08 86; www.camping-city .com; 67 rte de Crau; camping €17; ✆ Apr-Sep) This well-situated (if not very French-sounding) camp site is the closest to town, 1km south-east on the road to Marseille. Take bus 2 to the Hermite stop.

Auberge de Jeunesse (☎ 04 90 96 18 25; arles@fuaj .org; 20 av Maréchal Foch; dm incl breakfast & sheets €14.55; ✆ 5 Feb–20 Dec) This sunlit, 100-bed place, made up of eight-bed dorms, is 2km south of the centre. There's a microwave but no self-catering kitchen. Take bus 3 or 8 from blvd Georges Clemenceau (bus 8 from place Lamartine) to the Fournier stop.

Hôtel Terminus et Van Gogh (☎ /fax 04 90 96 12 32; 5 place Lamartine; d €36.60-42) On the same little square where Van Gogh lived and handy for the station and shops, this welcoming one-star hotel comes highly recommended, and has a dozen cosy rooms with private bathrooms, telephones and TVs.

MIDRANGE

Hôtel Le Cloître (☎ 04 90 96 29 50; www.hotelcloitre .com; 16 rue du Cloître; d €42-65; ✆ 15 Mar–31 Oct) This pistachio-shuttered hotel is atmospherically housed in a 12th-century former cloister cleric residence. Its terrazzo lobby leads to 30 rooms with private glazed-tiled bath-rooms – especially coveted are Rooms 1 and 2, with traces of 12th-century paint that were revealed during renovations and left exposed; and Rooms 18 and 20, look-ing into the stone and marble St-Trophime cloister.

Hôtel de l'Amphitheatre (☎ 04 90 96 10 30; www .hotelamphitheatre.fr; 5-7 rue Diderot; s €41-45, d €45-83; ✇ 🖳) Deep crimson décor dresses the steadfast, solid bones of this 1600s–built structure with contemporary flair. Right near the hotel's namesake Roman amphi-theatre, guests can have breakfast (€6.50) beneath the shadowed hands of the salon's slide-projected clock, or in a high-walled, red-painted courtyard. Wheelchair access is good.

Hôtel du Musée (☎ 04 90 93 88 88; www.hoteldu musee.com.fr; 11 rue du Grand Prieuré; d €48-78; ✆ closed mid-Jan–mid-Feb; ✇) An appealing period hotel in a fine 12th- to 13th-century building, this impeccably maintained option has 28 sunny, beautifully furnished rooms, a tiled lobby and tranquil terrace garden. Rooms with showers only are significantly cheaper than those with bathtubs.

Hôtel Calendal (☎ 04 90 96 11 89; www.lecalen dal.com; 5 rue Porte de Laure; d €64-104; ✆ closed Jan; ✇ ✇ 🖳) Next to the amphitheatre and overlooking the Théâtre Antique, this pic-ture of a place with good wheelchair ac-cess, rendered in sand and ochre with sky-blue shutters, is best known for its wonderful *salon de thé* (see opposite). Its 38 rooms have beamed ceilings and bright Provençal fabrics, and are well equipped. There's a peaceful garden terrace at the back. Garage parking costs €10.

Hôtel Arlatan (☎ 04 90 93 56 66; www.hotel-arla tan.fr; 26 rue du Sauvage; d €85-153; ✆ closed mid-Jan–mid-Feb; ✇ 🖳) Swim in the heated pool set in flowering gardens at this three-star hotel near the river, sections of which were once part of the palace of Emperor Con-stantin. Gorgeous stone-and-wood rooms are individually decorated in flowing, sub-tle floral fabrics, with views over Arles' old town rooftops. Wheelchair access is good; garaged parking (including help carrying your bags) is €11 to €14.

TOP END

Grand Hôtel Nord Pinus (☎ 04 90 93 44 44; www .nord-pinus.com; place du Forum; r €145-190; ✇) On the café-clad place du Forum, and incor-porating the only remaining chunk of the original Roman Forum wall in its façade, this 1927–established hotel with good wheelchair access is an intimate 26-room affair offering American breakfasts (€20) as well as classic continental fare (€14). Even if you're not staying here, stop by the bar and check out the fab photo exhibits.

Eating

Arles' restaurant terraces give even the most upmarket eating establishments a relaxed café atmosphere.

RESTAURANTS

La Paillotte (☎ 04 90 96 33 15; 28 rue du Docteur Fanton; mains €11-15; ☺ lunch Fri-Tue, dinner Thu-Tue) In keeping with its stone walls, red tablecloths and terracotta tiles, this very Provençal place has a whole range of different *menus*, some hearty and others more gourmet, but you won't go wrong with the Chef Specialities *menu* (€20), sure to be fresh and fabulous.

La Calendal (☎ 04 90 96 11 89; 22 place Pomme; mains €11.50-13, buffet €14; ☺ lunch daily, dinner Oct-Mar) This quaint-as-can-be *salon de thé–*restaurant is popular with locals as well as guests at its equally quaint hotel (opposite), for its buffet brimming with garden-crisp veges in its cool, stone-walled dining room or in the leafy courtyard garden.

La Mule Blanche (☎ 04 90 93 98 54; 9 rue du Président Wilson; mains €12.20-20; ☺ lunch Tue-Sun, dinner Wed-Sun summer, lunch Tue-Sat, dinner Wed-Sat winter) Jazz is often performed at the piano in the White Mule's domed interior, but the hottest tables are on the pavement terrace, which is the prettiest in town and gets packed in fine weather.

Au Brin de Thym (☎ 04 90 49 95 96; 22 rue du Docteur Fanton; menus €14-22; ☺ lunch Thu-Mon, dinner Wed-Mon) Market-fresh produce is made to look like a work of art at this pretty place fronted by a lavender and white awning and damask-clothed tables. The Provençal *menu* (€17) is a great way to sample the creative dishes laced in local olive oil, and there's a strong wine list.

Corazón (☎ 04 90 96 32 53; 1bis rue Réattu; mains €16.50-24.50; ☺ lunch & dinner Tue-Sat) This funky, contemporary space in a recessed arcade combines a contemporary art gallery with long pink- and red-accented dining areas highlighted by quirky-chic lighting and furnishings. Modern Mediterranean fare includes warm goat's cheese drizzled with lavender honey.

Le Cilantro (☎ 04 90 18 25 05; 29 rue Porte de Laure; mains €18-23; ☺ lunch Tue-Fri & Sun, dinner Tue-Sat) Arles' newest, most buzzing tables are a

result of the homecoming of Arlésian chef Jêrome Laurant, cooking accomplished dishes like saddle of lamb in almond oil with mash and braised carrots. Great lunchtime specials include a starter and main or main and dessert for €19, or all three for €23.

CAFÉS

The Roman place du Forum, shaded by outstretched plane trees, turns into a giant dining table at lunch and dinner during summer. It's also where you'll find **Café la Nuit** (place du Forum), thought to be the café captured on canvas by Van Gogh in his *Café Terrace at Night* (1888). Painted in bright yellow tones, to recreate the effect used by Van Gogh to indicate bright night-time lights, it's invariably packed with tourists dining in front of its famous façade. A few doors down, **Le Bistrot Arlésien** (place du Forum) is the locals' pick of places on the square, with decently priced Provençal fare.

Blvd Georges Clemenceau and blvd des Lices are also lined with plane trees and brasserie terraces, though depending on the time of day, you may find yourself dining à la traffic fumes.

SELF-CATERING

Amble the Saturday morning **market** (blvd Georges Clemenceau & blvd des Lices) stretching the length of the main boulevard, selling strong cheese, Camargue salt, olive oil and bull sausages. On Wednesday, market stalls set up along blvd Émile Combes.

Pick up groceries at **Monoprix** (place Lamartine; ☺ 8.30am-7.25pm Mon-Sat).

Shopping

Next door to the first-ever boutique of home-grown fashion designer **Christian Lacroix** (52 rue de la République) is **Puyricard** (54 rue de la République), purveying exquisite Provençal chocolates.

Getting There & Away

AIR

Nîmes airport (p769) is 20km northwest of the city on the A54. There is no public transport between the airport and Arles.

BUS

The **bus station** (☎ 08 10 00 08 16; 24 blvd Georges Clemenceau; ☺ 7.30am-4pm Mon-Sat) is served by companies including **Telleschi** (☎ 04 42 28 40 22),

PROVENCE

which runs services to/from Aix-en-Provence (€9.80, 1¾ hours).

Buses also link Arles with various parts of the Camargue, including Les Stes-Maries de la Mer (€4.90, one hour).

Long-haul, international bus company **Eurolines** (☎ 04 90 96 94 78; www.eurolines.com) stops here, though there's no ticket office.

TRAIN

Some major rail destinations from Arles' **train station** (information office 9am-12.30pm & 2-6.30pm Mon-Sat) include Nîmes (€6.90, 30 minutes), Montpellier (€12.90, one hour), Marseille (€12.20, 45 minutes) and Avignon (€6, 20 minutes).

Getting Around

BUS

Local buses are operated by **STAR** (☎ 09 10 00 08 16; information office 24 blvd Georges Clemenceau; 8am-12.30pm & 1.30-6pm Mon-Fri). STAR's office, situated west of the tourist office, is the main bus hub, although most buses also stop at place Lamartine, a short walk south of the train station. In general, STAR buses run from 7am to 7pm (to 5pm on Sunday). A single ticket costs €0.80. In addition to its 11 bus lines, STAR runs free minibuses called Starlets that make a circle around most of the old city every 30 minutes from 7.15am to 7.40pm Monday to Saturday.

TAXI

For a taxi call ☎ 04 90 96 90 03.

THE CAMARGUE

Provence's brightly coloured landscapes become bleached out in the haunting, desolate beauty of the Camargue. Roamed by black bulls and white horses, France's 'wild west' is a wetland wilderness, interspersed with saltpans and rice fields. Pale-pink flamingos wade in the bulrush-blown marshes during spring and summer. Migratory birds from both the north and the south visit year-round, and the area is home (at least temporarily) to more than 500 species.

This 780-sq-km delta of the River Rhône was formed over the ages by sediment flowing to the Mediterranean. Enclosed by the Petit Rhône and Grand Rhône Rivers, most of the Camargue wetlands are within the 850-sq-km park, Parc Naturel Régional de Camargue, established in 1970 to preserve the area's fragile ecosystems while sustaining local agriculture. On the periphery, the Étang de Vaccarès and nearby peninsulas and islands form the Réserve Nationale de Camargue, a 135-sq-km nature reserve. Exploring by bike, jeep, boat or horseback is a buzz – literally. Be sure to pack plenty of mosquito repellent.

The Camargue's two largest towns are the seaside pilgrim's outpost, Les Stes-Maries de la Mer, and to the northwest, the walled town of Aigues Mortes.

INFORMATION

Parc Naturel Régional de Camargue Information Centre (☎ 04 90 97 86 32; www.parc-camargue.fr in French; Pont de Gau; admission free; 10am-6pm

---

PRETTY IN PINK

The pink or greater flamingo (Phoenicopterus ruber) in flight is a breathtaking sight. Equally majestic is the catwalk stance – neck high, breast out – adopted by this elegant, long-legged creature when strutting through shallow waters.

Flamingo courtship starts in January, with mating taking place from March to May. The single egg laid by the female in April or May is incubated in a mud-caked nest for one month by both parents. The young chicks shakily take to the skies when they are about three months old. By the time they reach adulthood (around five years old), their soft grey down has become a fine feather coat of brilliant white or pretty rose-pink.

This well-dressed bird lives to the grand old age of 34 (longer if kept in captivity). It stands between 1.5m and 2m tall and has an average wing span of 1.9m. When the flamingo feels threatened, its loud hiss is similar to the warning sound made by a goose. It feeds on plankton, sucking in water and draining it off with its disproportionately heavy, curved bill.

Some flamingos remain in the Rhône delta year-round. Come September, several thousand take flight to Spain, Tunisia and Senegal, where they winter in warmer climes before returning to the Camargue in February in time for early spring.

Apr-Sep, 10am-5pm Sat-Thu Oct-Mar) Watch birds through powerful binoculars from the glassed-in foyer of this interpretive centre, 4km north of Les Stes-Maries. Plenty of information on walking and bird-watching is also available.

Réserve Nationale de Camargue Office (☎ 04 90 97 00 97; La Capelière; ☻ 9am-noon & 2-5pm Mon-Sat) Along the D36B, on the eastern side of Étang de Vaccarès; with exhibits on the Camargue's ecosystems, flora and fauna. Many trails and paths fan out from here.

SIGHTS & ACTIVITIES
Musée Camarguais

Inside an 1812-built sheep shed, the **Camargue Museum** (Museon Camarguen in Provençal; ☎ 04 90 97 10 82; Mas du Pont de Rousty; adult/student €5/2.50; ☻ 10am-6pm Wed-Sat Apr-Oct, 10.15am-4.45pm Wed-Sat Nov-Mar) is a fantastic introduction to this unique area, covering its history, ecosystems, flora and fauna, with a glimpse into traditional life in the region. From here, a 3.5km nature trail leads to an observation tower with bird's-eye views. The museum is 10km southwest of Arles on the D570 to Les Stes-Maries.

Le Parc Ornithologique du Pont de Gau

Especially good if you're travelling with kids, 4km north of Les Stes-Maries on the D570 is **Le Parc Ornithologique du Pont de Gau** (☎ 04 90 97 82 62; adult/child €6.50/4; ☻ 9am-sunset Apr-Sep, 10am-sunset Oct-Mar), with hides to peek at the area's dazzling array of bird life.

Walking

Walking paths and trails wend through the Parc Naturel Régional and the Réserve Nationale, on the embankments and along the coast. Both park offices sell detailed walking maps of the area, including the 1:25,000 IGN Série Bleue maps Nos 2944E and 2944O.

Boating & Watersports

Experience the waterlogged Camargue by a boat excursion departing from Port Gardian in the centre of Les Stes-Maries with **Camargue Bateau de Promenade** (☎ 04 90 97 84 72; 5 rue des Launes) or **Quatre Maries** (☎ 04 90 97 70 10; 36 av Théodore Aubanel). Or ply the delta's shallow waters on the beat-up old paddle boat **Le Tiki III** (☎ 04 90 97 81 68), docked at the

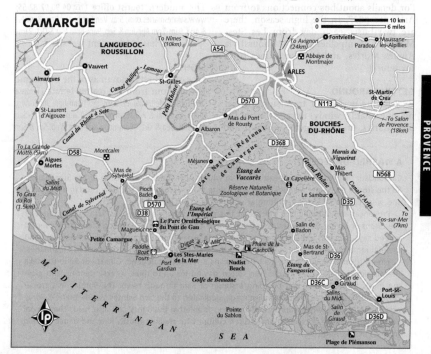

mouth of the Petit Rhône 1.5km west of Les Stes-Maries. All charge around €10/5 per adult/child for a 1½-hour trip.

If you prefer to paddle under your own steam, **Kayak Vert Camargue** (☎ 06 09 56 06 47, 04 66 73 57 17; Mas de Sylvéréal; prices vary), 14km north of Les Stes-Maries off the D38, arranges canoeing and kayaking on the Petit Rhône.

Horse-riding

Saddle up for a horse-ride *(promenade à cheval)* along the beach on the region's white horses. Farms along the D570 (Rte d'Arles) leading into Les Stes-Maries have signs advertising riding and lessons. Expect to pay around €13 to €16 per hour, or €55 to €80 per day.

TOURS

Jeep safaris costing about €15 to €30 for 1½ hours are offered by **Le Gitan** (☎ 04 66 70 09 65; 17 av de la République) on Les Stes-Maries' seafront, and L'Auberge Cavaliere (opposite).

GETTING THERE & AWAY

For details about bus connections to/from Arles see p837. In the high season, there are two buses each day from Les Stes-Maries to Montpellier (€10, 1¼ hours) via Aigues Mortes, and two for Nîmes (€10, 1¼ hours).

GETTING AROUND

Bicycles are perfect for traversing the Camargue's flat (if windy) terrain. East of Les Stes-Maries, areas along the seafront and further inland are reserved for walkers and cyclists.

For an English-language list of cycling routes go to **Le Vélo Saintois** (☎ /fax 04 90 97 74 56; 19 rue de la République, Les Stes-Maries), which hires out mountain bikes for €15/34 per day/three days. **Le Vélociste** (☎ 04 90 97 83 26; place des Remparts, Les Stes-Maries) also rents bikes, and organises cycling, horse-riding (€36) and canoeing (€28) packages.

Les Stes-Maries de la Mer

pop 2478

You could be forgiven for thinking you'd crossed into Spain in this remote little town by the seaside. With some of the most captivating light in Provence, especially in early spring and autumn, its dusty streets are lined with whitewashed buildings thatched with pitched rooves of bulrush reeds. Les-Stes-Maries comes alive during festivals, when flamenco dancers spin in its squares and flag-carrying horse-riders in traditional costumes trot into town.

INFORMATION

The modern **tourist office** (☎ 04 90 97 82 55; www.saintesmaries.com; 5 av Van Gogh; ✆ 9am-8pm Jul & Aug, 9am-7pm Apr-Jun & Sep, 9am-6pm Mar & Oct, 9am-5pm Nov-Feb) has an excellent website.

SIGHTS

One of the best panoramas of the Camargue is rolled out from the **rooftop terrace** (Terrasse de l'Église; adult/child €2/1.30; ✆ 10am-8pm Jul & Aug, 10am-12.30pm & 2-6.30pm Mon-Fri, 10am-7pm Sat & Sun Mar-Jun, Sep & Oct, 10am-noon & 2-5pm Wed, Sat & Sun

---

A WASHED-UP LEGEND?

Catholicism first reached European shores in what's now the little township of Les Stes-Maries. So the stories go, Sainte Marie-Salomé and Sainte Marie-Jacobé fled the Holy Land in a tiny boat and were caught in a storm, drifting at sea until washing ashore here.

Provençal and Catholic lore diverge at this point: Catholicism believes Sara (patron saint of the *Gitans* or Roma, also known as Gypsies), travelled with the two Marys on the boat; Provençal legend says Sara was already here and was the first person to recognise their holiness. In 1448 skeletal remains said to belong to Sara and the Marys were found in a crypt in Les Stes-Maries.

Finer historical points aside, it's by no means a washed-up legend. Gitans continue to make the pilgrimage here on 24 and 25 May (often staying for up to three weeks), dancing and playing music in the streets, and parading a statue of Sara through town. The Sunday in October closest to the 22nd sees a second pilgrimage, dedicated to the two Saintes Maries (Marie-Salomé and Marie-Jacobé), when *courses Camarguaises* (nonlethal bullfights) are also held. The annual Festival Ame Gitane, a celebration of Gitan culture with theatre, music, film and dance, is held in Arles in mid-August.

Nov-Feb) of the **Église des Stes-Maries** (place de l'Église). In this church, dating from the 12th to the 15th century, the relics of St Sara – the highly revered patron saint of the Roma – were found in the crypt by King René in 1448 and are enshrined in a wooden chest, stashed in the stone wall above the choir.

Les Stes-Maries spills over with colour and life during the animated Gitan pilgrimages (opposite).

Tickets for **bullfights** at Les Stes-Maries' Arènes are sold at the arena – check with the tourist office for schedules.

Les Stes-Maries is fringed by around 30km of uninterrupted fine-sand **beaches**. For an all-over tan, the area around **Phare de la Gacholle**, the lighthouse 11km east of town, is the place for bathing sans suit.

SLEEPING & EATING

Low-rise 'ranch style' hotels line the D570 heading into Les Stes-Maries. A number of old *mas* (farmhouses) also surround the town, and often let rooms. Accommodation is more limited in the winter off-season; in summer there are more options open, but they fill quickly.

Camping La Brise (☎ 04 90 97 84 67; fax 04 90 97 72 01; av Marcle Carrière; camping €13 winter, €18-20 summer; ☉ closed mid-Nov–mid-Dec; ☎) Right on the beach, this three-star camp site northeast of the town centre has a refreshing pool and a friendly, family atmosphere.

Auberge de Jeunesse (☎ 04 90 97 51 72; fax 04 90 97 54 88; Pioch Badet; dm incl breakfast, dinner & sheets €27.30; reception ☉ 7.30-10.30am & 5-11pm, to midnight Jul & Aug) Half-board is part of the package at this rural hostel 8km north of Les Stes-Maries on the D570 to Arles. Buses from Arles' bus station drop you at the door.

Hôtel Méditerranée (☎ 04 90 97 82 09; fax 04 90 97 76 31; 4 av Frédéric Mistral; r €39-52) Handily located in the centre of town (so a good bet if you don't have your own wheels), this place is one of the cheapest options and also offers a homey, familial environment with a flower-decked terrace on which to enjoy breakfast.

Mas de la Grenouillère (☎ 04 90 97 90 22; fax 04 90 97 08 58; d/tr incl breakfast from €60/80; ☎ ☎) Be sung to sleep by an open field full of frogs at 'The Frog Farm', in small but cosy rooms. The farm's stables organise horse-riding trips. It's 1.5km down a dirt track signposted 1km north of Les Stes-Maries off the D570.

L'Auberge Cavaliere (☎ 04 90 97 88 88; www.auberge cavaliere.com in French; rte d'Arles (D570); s €87-164, d €92-164; ☎ ☎ ☎) Approximately 1.5km north of Les Stes-Maries, this sophisticated yet salt-of-the-earth, family-run place with good wheelchair access has mezzanine loft-style apartments, luxurious guest quarters overlooking the wetlands, and thatched cabins. Although horses are commonly eaten in France, you won't find them at the on-site **restaurant** (menus €24-38), but you can ride them on a guided sunrise, sunset or lunchtime picnic expedition.

Le Delta (☎ 04 90 97 81 12; 1 place Mireille; menus €18-26) A local favourite, Le Delta is a great place to try Camargue specialities like *gardianne de taureau* (bull stew) and the area's thumbnail-sized clams called *tellines*.

Aigues Mortes
pop 6084

Actually over the border from Provence in the Gard *département* (department), the town of Aigues Mortes (meaning, somewhat eerily, 'dead waters') is 28km northwest of Les Stes-Maries at the western extremity of the Camargue. Aigues Mortes is set in flat marshland and encircled by walls. The town was established in the mid-13th century by Louis IX to give the French crown a Mediterranean port under its direct control, and in 1248 Louis IX's flotilla of 1500 ships massed here before setting sail to the Holy Land for the Seventh Crusade.

To minimise traffic, parking within the walls is charged at €5 per hour.

INFORMATION

Tourist Office (☎ 04 66 53 73 00; www.ot-aigues mortes.fr; place St-Louis; ☉ 9am-noon & 1-6pm Sep-Jun, 9am-8pm Jul & Aug) Inside the walled city at Porte de la Gardette.

SIGHTS & ACTIVITIES

Scaling the ramparts rewards you with a sweeping overview of the town's history, and of surrounding marshes. Head to the top of the tower, **Tour de Constance** (☎ 04 66 53 61 55; adult/under 17yrs €6.50/free; ☉ 10am-5.30pm winter, 10am-7pm summer). The 1.6km wall-top walk takes about 30 minutes.

The southern ramparts afford views of the stretching saltpans, which you can travel through aboard the **salt train** (☎ 04 66 51 17 10; www.salins.fr; adult/child €6.80/5; ☉ Mar-Oct),

PROVENCE

accompanied by commentary in English. La Baleine train stop is on the left before the bridge heading towards Salins du Midi.

SLEEPING & EATING

Within the walls, place St-Louis, at the southern foot of Grande Rue, is (in fine weather, at least) filled with open-air cafés and terrace restaurants. Grande Rue is also where self-caterers and picnickers can find bakeries, groceries and butchers selling bull sausages.

Le Victoria (☎ 04 66 51 14 20; www.victoria.ca margue.fr in French; place Anatole-France; d €49-58, tr €80-95; mains €15-21) Just opposite the Tour de Constance, this elegant place with blue-toned rooms is at least as well known for its traditional restaurant serving local classics such as *soupe de poissons* (fish soup) and the ubiquitous Camargue bull stew, *gardienne de taureau*.

L'Hermitage de St-Antoine (☎ 06 03 04 34 05; www.hermitagesa.com; 9 blvd Intérieur Nord; d €50-60; ✗ ✗) Inside the walled town, this *chambre d'hôte* has just three rooms beautifully appointed with crisp linens and canopied beds, and a lovely courtyard garden for a relaxing – and filling – breakfast in the sunshine (€7). You won't be disturbed by littlies running around – L'Hermitage de St-Antoine only caters to children aged over 12. Get a pass for free parking.

L'Oustau Camarguais (☎ 04 66 53 79 69; 2 rue Alsace-Lorraine; mains €11-22; ☽ lunch & dinner, closed Thu in low season) Accompanied by rotating art exhibitions and often live music, this wood-beamed place in the old town is a great place to try the local miniature clams, *tellines*, but the main event here is *civet de taureau aux saveurs de garrigue* (bull stew flavoured with Provence scrubland herbs).

THE VAUCLUSE

All those postcard images of Provence come to life in this, its most picturesque region. Shaped like a fan, with its elegant capital, Avignon, at its hinge, the Vaucluse (meaning 'closed valley') unfolds across undulating countryside strewn with lavender, wild herbs, vineyards, and enchanting villages and towns where locals gather at farmers' markets. Presiding over the region, Provence's highest peak, Mont Ventoux

(1909m) is a snowy spectacle in winter and a maze of hiking trails in summer.

A car is the ideal way to cover the Vaucluse, but it's possible (if not expedient) to get from town to town by local bus.

AVIGNON

pop 88,312

Hooped by 4.3km of superbly preserved stone ramparts, this graceful city is the belle of Provence's ball. Its turn as the papal seat of power has bestowed Avignon with a treasury of magnificent art and architecture, none grander than the massive medieval fortress and papal palace, the Palais des Papes.

Famed for its annual performing arts festival, these days Avignon is also an animated student city and an ideal spot from which to step out into the surrounding region. In France and beyond, Avignon is perhaps best known for its fabled bridge, the Pont St-Bénézet, aka the Pont d'Avignon.

History

Avignon first donned its ramparts and its reputation as a city of art and culture during the 14th century, when Pope Clement V and his court fled political turmoil in Rome for Avignon. From 1309 to 1377, the seven French-born popes invested huge sums of money in building and decorating the papal palace. Under the popes' rule, Jews and political dissidents took shelter here. Pope Gregory XI left Avignon in 1376, but his death two years later led to the Great Schism (1378–1417), during which rival popes – up to three at one time – resided at Rome and Avignon, denouncing and excommunicating one another. Even after the schism was settled and an impartial pope – Martin V – established himself in Rome, Avignon remained under papal rule. The city and Comtat Venaissin (now the Vaucluse *département*) were ruled by papal legates until 1791, when they were annexed to France.

Orientation

The main avenue within the walled city (*intra-muros*) runs northwards from the train station to place de l'Horloge. South of the tourist office it's called cours Jean Jaurès, north of it it's rue de la République.

The café-clad central square place de l'Horloge is located 300m south of place du Palais, which abuts the Palais des Papes. The city gate nearest the train station is Porte de la République, while the city gate next to Pont Édouard Daladier, which leads to Villeneuve-lès-Avignon, is Porte de l'Oulle. The Quartier des Teinturiers (Dyers' Quarter), centred on rue des Teinturiers, southeast of place Pie, is the hangout of Avignon's population of bohemian artists.

Information

BOOKSHOPS

The tourist office has a small boutique (open April to October) that sells maps and regional guides in French and English.

Shakespeare (☎ 04 90 27 38 50; 155 rue de la Carreterie; ⊙ 9.30am-12.30pm & 2-6.30pm Tue-Sat) Enjoy scones with your tomes at this English bookshop and *salon de thé*.

INTERNET ACCESS

There are loads of internet cafés in the streets surrounding place Pie.

Webzone (☎ 04 32 76 29 47; 3 rue St-Jean le Vieux; per 30/60 min €2/3.50; ⊙ 10am-10pm)

INTERNET RESOURCES

Provence Guide (www.provenceguide.com). Covers the Vaucluse region including B&Bs.

Visit Provence (www.visitprovence.com)

LAUNDRY

Lavmatic (27 rue du Portail Magnanen; ⊙ 7am-7.30pm)

MONEY

CIC (13 rue de la République) Also in the train station forecourt, with a currency changing machine and ATM.

POST

Main Post Office (cours Président Kennedy) Currency exchange and Cyberposte available.

TOURIST INFORMATION

Tourist Office (☎ 04 32 74 32 74; www.avignon -tourisme.com; 41 cours Jean Jaurès; ⊙ 9am-6pm Mon-Sat, 10am-5pm Sun Apr-Jun & Aug-Oct, 9am-6pm Mon-Fri, 9am-5pm Sat, 10am-noon Sun Nov-Mar, 9am-7pm Mon-Sat, 10am-5pm Sun Jul) Around 300m north of the train station.

Sights & Activities

Ticket offices for most sights close 30 minutes to one hour before overall closing times.

PONT ST-BÉNÉZET (LE PONT D'AVIGNON)

The fabled **Pont St-Bénézet** (St Bénézet's Bridge; ☎ 04 90 27 51 16; full price/pass €4/3.30; ⊙ 9am-9pm Jul, 9am-8pm Aug-Sep, 9am-7pm mid-Mar–Jun & Oct, 9.30am-5.45pm Nov–mid-Mar) was completed in 1185, a bridge linking Avignon with the settlement across the Rhône that later became Villeneuve-lès-Avignon. The 900m-long wooden structure (see the boxed text p844) was repaired and rebuilt several times before all but four of its 22 spans were washed away in the mid-1600s.

Entry is via cours Châtelet. There are some dreamy distant (but free) views from the Rocher des Doms park or Pont Édouard Daladier; or from across the river on the Île de la Barthelasse's promenade des Berges.

WALLED CITY

Wrapping around the city, Avignon's ramparts were built between 1359 and 1370. They were restored during the 19th century, minus their original moats – though even in the 14th century this defence system was hardly state-of-the-art, lacking machicolations (openings in the parapets for niceties such as pouring boiling oil on attackers, or shooting arrows at them).

Within the walls are a wealth of fine museums – the Avignon *Passion* booklet (below) lists the whole gamut.

Palais des Papes

Flanked by the sprawling courtyard cours d'Honneur, the cavernous stone halls and extensive grounds of the **Palais des Papes** (Palace of the Popes; ☎ 04 90 27 50 00; place du Palais; full price/pass €9.50/7.50; ⊙ 9am-9pm Jul, 9am-8pm Aug & Sep, 9am-7pm mid-Mar–June & Oct, 9.30am-5.45pm Nov–mid-Mar) testify to the fortune amassed

---

AVIGNON PASSION

Anyone passionate about Avignon's rich cultural heritage will want to pick up a free Avignon *Passion* pass from the tourist office. This nifty pass entitles you to 20% to 50% discounted entry on your second and subsequent visits to museums and monuments (the equivalent of student prices), as well as reduced prices on the tourist office walking tours. It's good for 15 days in all the museums of Avignon as well as Villeneuve-lès-Avignon, and covers a family of five.

UNDER THE BRIDGE *Catherine Le Nevez*

OK, so I don't quite remember dancing on Avignon's broken bridge (see p843) as a pinafored four-year-old, but family snaps show that I did. The bridge continues to capture kids' imaginations everywhere with its namesake nursery rhyme, 'Sur le Pont d'Avignon'. All together now:

Sur le pont d'Avignon
L'on y danse, l'on y danse
Sur le pont d'Avignon
L'on y danse tout en rond...

(On the bridge of Avignon
Everyone is dancing, everyone is dancing
On the bridge of Avignon
Everyone is dancing in a circle...)

And so on.

But actually, apart from rhyming better in French, because the bridge was too narrow for dancing (much less in a circle), people are believed to have danced *sous* (under) its arches, where it straddled the island Île de Barthelasse. Previously pleasure gardens hosting folk dancing, the island is another prime spot for a bridge panorama today.

The 16th-century composer Pierre Certon penned the original song, albeit to a different tune, under the title of 'Sus (sic) le Pont d'Avignon'. In the mid-19th century, Adolphe Adam featured the present-day version in the 1853 operetta *l'Auberge Pleine*, but it wasn't until it was popularised in 1876 that it was inverted.

The alleged inspiration for the now Unesco-listed bridge is an even older tale. Construction is said to have begun in 1177 when Bénézet (Benedict the Bridge Builder), a pastor from Ardèche, was told in three visions to span the Rhône at any cost.

At the entrance is a new museum (included in the entry price) where you can make your own CD of the song. And regardless of the song's or bridge's origins, chances are you'll see kids (and maybe even a Lonely Planet author) doing a jig on the bridge for posterity.

by the papacy during the 'Babylonian Captivity'. Built during the 14th century and intended as a fortified palace for the pontifical court, it's the largest Gothic palace in the world, but its undecorated rooms are all but empty, except during occasional art exhibitions.

The admission price includes a multilanguage audio guide.

Musée du Petit Palais

During the 14th and 15th centuries, **Musée du Petit Palais** (☎ 04 90 86 44 58; place du Palais; full price/pass €6/3; ☯ 10am-1pm & 2-6pm Wed-Mon Jun-Sep, 9.30am-1pm & 2-5.30pm Wed-Mon Oct-May) served as a bishops' and archbishops' palace. These days it is home to an outstanding collection of lavishly coloured 13th- to 16th-century Italian religious paintings created by artists including Botticelli, Carpaccio and Giovanni di Paolo. English-language interpretive information is available.

Musée Calvet

Impressive architecture and art intertwine at the elegant Hôtel de Villeneuve-Martignan (1741–54), where **Musée Calvet** (☎ 04 90 86 33 84; 65 rue Joseph Vernet; full price/pass €6/3; ☯ 10am-1pm & 2-6pm Wed-Mon) has among its collections 15th century wrought-iron works and paintings from the 16th to 20th centuries.

Musée Lapidaire

Museum buffs on a budget will appreciate the **Musée Lapidaire** (☎ 04 90 86 33 84; 27 rue de la République; full price/pass €2/1; ☯ 10am-1pm & 2-6pm Wed-Mon), with a random but interesting collection of Egyptian, Roman, Etruscan and early Christian pieces ranging from large sections of marble statuary and hieroglyphics to delicate vases and bronze figurines.

Musée Angladon

From the private collection of couturier Jacques Doucet (1853–1929), the charming

Musée Angladon (☎ 04 90 82 29 03; www.angladon .com; 5 rue Laboureur; full price/pass €6/4; ⏰ 1-6pm Wed-Sun Sep-Jun, Tue-Sun Jul & Aug) harbours the only Van Gogh painting in Provence, *Railway Wagons*. You can see that the 'earth' isn't paint but the bare, underlying canvas. Also housed in this gracious mansion are original works by Picasso, Cézanne, Sisley, Manet, Degas and others, with antiquities upstairs.

BOATING

Les Grands Bateaux de Provence (☎ 04 90 85 62 25; www.mireio.net in French; allées de l'Oulle) runs excursions down the Rhône to Arles, vineyard towns and the Camargue on two restaurant boats (from €44, including a meal). Less ambitious destinations include Villeneuve-lès-Avignon and Île de la Barthelasse from two to six times daily in July and August.

A free **shuttle boat** (⏰ 10am-12.30pm & 2-6.30pm Apr-Jun & Sep, 11am-9pm Jul & Aug, 2-5.30pm Wed, 10am-noon & 2-5.30pm Sat & Sun Oct-Dec) adjacent to Pont St-Bénézet connects the walled city with the Île de la Barthelasse.

Tours

Two-hour **Avignon l'Italienne tours** (adult/child €10/7) in English and French depart from the tourist office at 10am on Thursday and Saturday between April and October.

Also in English and French, Avignon at the time of the Popes (including a tour of the Palais des Papes) departs from the tourist office at 10am Tuesday and Friday from April to October, and costs €15 for adults and €7 for children.

Autocars Lieutaud (☎ 04 90 86 36 75; www.cars -lieutaud.fr), based at the bus station, runs terrific thematic half- and full-day bus tours throughout the greater region between April and October.

Festivals & Events

More than 600 *spectacles* take to the stage and streets during Avignon's world-famous **Festival d'Avignon** (www.festival-avignon.com), founded in 1946 and held every year from early July to early August. Tickets for official festival performances in the Palais des Papes' cours d'Honneur cost around €30; reservations can be made from mid-June. Information can be obtained from the **Bureau du Festival** (☎ 04 90 27 66 50; Espace St-Louis, 20 rue du Portail Boquier).

Paralleling the official festival, the fringe event, **Festival Off** (☎ 01 48 05 01 19; www.avignon -off.org), has an eclectic, che[...] of experimental performan[...] lic Adhérent (€14) gives y[...] on all Festival Off performances.

Sleeping

You'll need to book many months ahead for a room during the festival. Many places close for a few weeks mid-winter.

BUDGET

Camping Bagatelle (☎ 04 90 86 30 39; camping. bagatelle@wanadoo.fr; Île de la Barthelasse; camping €9-15; reception ⏰ 8am-9pm) You'll find this shaded camp site just north of Pont Édouard Daladier, 850m from the walled city.

Auberge Bagatelle (☎ 04 90 85 78 45; auberge .bagatelle@wanadoo.fr; Île de la Barthelasse; dm €15, s €29-33, d €35-37) Adjoining the camp site, this hostel has 180 beds in a mix of two- to eight-bed rooms, plus snazzier private digs (including family rooms) in its adjoining hotel. All rates include breakfast; sheets are €2.50. Take bus 10 from the main post office to La Barthelasse stop, then follow the river to the camp site.

YMCA-UCJG (☎ 04 90 25 46 20; www.ymca-avignon .com; 7bis chemin de la Justice; s €23-34, d €29-43, tr €34-52; reception ⏰ 8.30am-6pm, closed Dec–early Jan) If you're after your own space on a shoestring budget (the cheapest rooms share bathrooms), head to this spotless hostel with good wheelchair access just across the river in Villeneuve-lès-Avignon. Sheets are included; breakfast costs €5. Take bus 10 to the Monteau stop.

Hôtel Mignon (☎ 04 90 82 17 30; www.hotel-mig non.com; 12 rue Joseph Vernet; s €36, d €40-55; 🖧 🖵) Cute and comfy, this 16-room place within the walled city is a favourite for its boutique rooms in pretty shades, friendly, helpful staff, wi-fi, and a decent breakfast of croissants and rolls (€5).

MIDRANGE

Hôtel le Provençal (☎ 04 90 85 25 24; www.hotel leprovencal.com; 13 rue Joseph Vernet; s €41-60, d €43-60) Rooms painted the colour of sunshine are clean, cosy and welcoming at this charming, well-priced place in the northeastern corner of the walled city centre. There are only 11 rooms, so get in early.

Hôtel Boquier (☎ 04 90 82 34 43; www.hotel-bo quier.com; 6 rue du Portail Boquier; d €45-62) Handy for the train and bus stations, this 18th-century

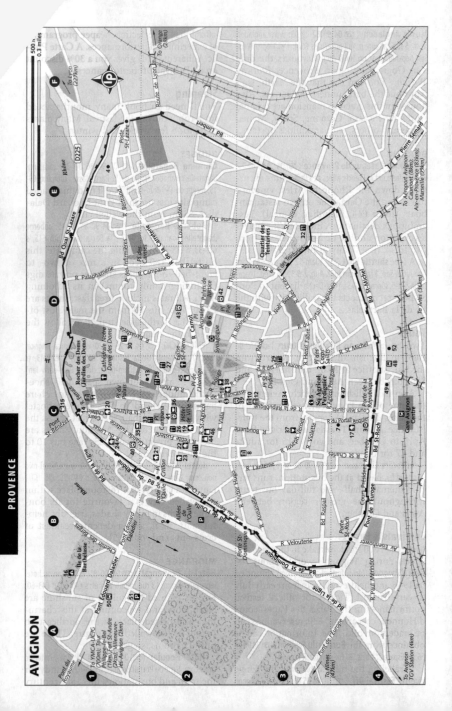

AVIGNON

PROVENCE

manor has attractive rooms with bathrooms, telephones and TVs. Some are inspired by far-off destinations like southern Africa and India. A little wrought-iron gate opens to the breakfast room 'café' (for guests only; €7) with wood-beamed ceilings.

Hôtel de Garlande (☎ 04 90 80 08 85; www.hotelgarlande.com; 20 rue Galante; d €62-110; ✗ ✗) Central for just about everything including the bus and train stations, Hôtel de Garlande is a sweet, familial little 12-room place housed in a historic *hôtel particulier* (private mansion) overlooking a narrow street.

Hôtel du Palais des Papes (☎ 04 90 86 04 13; www.hotel-avignon.com; 1 rue Gérard Philippe; d €65-75) No, it's not taking the Palais' name in vain. This might be an old-fashioned abode of 25 rooms with wrought-iron furniture, frescoed ceilings and exposed stone walls, but pricier rooms sport a view of the Palais des Papes opposite. There's also a wonderfully authentic, cave-like restaurant, **Le Lutrin** (mains €24-28).

Hôtel de l'Horloge (☎ 04 90 16 42 00; www.hotels-ocre-azur.com; place de l'Horloge; s €72-122, d €82-132; ✗) On Avignon's main square, this hotel's refined rooms are tastefully decorated in natural fabrics and fibres, with muslin curtains overlaid by stone-coloured checked linen drapes and lustrous chocolate-brown carpet. Even the sprayed concrete interiors manage to look refined and tasteful, thanks to smart two-toned colour schemes. Wheelchair access is good. Breakfast is an impressive buffet banquet (€13).

Le Limas (☎ 04 90 14 67 19; www.le-limas-avignon.com; 51 rue du Limas; d €86-135, tr €139-165 incl breakfast; ✗) Behind its discreet (easily missed) entrance in a quiet street 50m from the papal palace, this chic B&B in an 18th-century mansion is like something out of *Vogue Living*, with four white-on-white rooms with hardwood floors. Breakfast on home-made jam by the cosy fireplace or on the sundrenched terrace.

TOP END
Hôtel L'Europe (☎ 04 90 14 76 76; www.heurope.com; 12 place Crillon; d €141-449; ✗ ✗) You're in good company at this antique-laden hotel, established in 1799: guests have included illustrious leaders and dignitaries from Napoleon to King Edward VII of England, Charles Dickens, Jacqueline Kennedy-Onassis and Jacques Chirac. The 44 rooms are befittingly resplendent, subtly incorporating mod cons like English and Japanese TV channels, and free wi-fi in about half the rooms.

Eating
Place de l'Horloge is a riot of restaurants and cafés from Easter until mid-November. They're popular with tourists, but generally fun and decent value. Most *menus* start at around €16.

Numéro 75 (☎ 04 90 27 16 00; 75 rue Guillaume Puy; mains from €10; ☺ lunch & dinner Mon-Sat, daily during Festival) This place is in a lovely old house

PROVENCE

where, incidently, Pernod was concocted in 1870 by absinthe inventor Jules Pernod while he was living here. It's is now one of Avignon's in-spots for Mediterranean cuisine with succulent flavours like mango; and a fantastic €15 'chef's suggestion' *menu*.

Restaurant Brunel (☎ 04 90 27 16 00; 46 rue de la Balance; mains €10-18; ☽ lunch & dinner Tue-Sat) A local favourite for authentic Provençal food, especially at lunch, when there are super-duper deals on main courses (which always include a fish of the day) and desserts. The handful of outdoor tables is hotly contested in warm weather.

Le Caveau du Théâtre (☎ 04 90 82 60 91; 16 rue des Trois Faucons; lunch menu €10.60, dinner menu €18; ☽ closed Sat lunch & Sun) Swing over to the south of the square for mellow, moody jazz and a monthly-changing *carte* of traditional southern French fare with extra zip, such as butter-fried fish in a curry paste with sun-dried tomatoes.

Le Grand Café (☎ 04 90 27 04 96; 4 rue des escaliers Ste-Anne; mains from €13) Within the rustic Manutention cultural centre, the duck breast/mushroom tart–type fare at Le Grand Café could be described as 'almost gastronomic' (ie, delectable but affordable).

La Fourchette (☎ 04 90 85 20 93; 17 rue Racine; menus from €28; ☽ Mon-Fri) An enduring classic French restaurant west of place de l'Horloge, La Fourchette offers a tempting choice of dishes on its fixed-price *menu* (prices are the same for lunch or dinner). Along with tender *agneau* (lamb), house specialities include sardines, and for dessert, a sinful ice-cream meringue with praline.

Christian Etienne (☎ 04 90 86 16 50; 10 rue de Mons; mains €38-58; ☽ lunch & dinner Tue-Sat, daily Jul) Spanning an elevated dining room and leafy outdoor terrace in a 12th-century palace neighbouring the Palais des Papes, this is Avignon's top table. Provençal cuisine such as Avignonnaise wild boar stew is prepared by its eponymous Master Chef, who has returned home to Avignon after wowing Paris.

Le Marmiton (☎ 04 90 85 93 93; www.la-mirande .fr; 4 place de l'Amirande; lunch menu €38, dinner menu €49, table d'hôte €85; ☽ restaurant lunch & dinner Thu-Mon, table d'hôte dinner Tue-Sat) Watch the preparation of classic Provençal food then dine on the four-course feast cooked before you in the intimate kitchen of this 14th-century cardinals' palace-turned-hotel (the exclusive Hôtel de la Mirande). Or try your own hand at its masterpieces – a week-long cooking school is held each month.

SELF-CATERING

Over 40 outlets fill Les Halles' **food market** (place Pie; ☽ 7am-1pm Tue-Sun); or pick up groceries at **Shopi** (23 rue de la République; ☽ 7am-9pm Mon-Sat, 8am-noon Sun) and St-Tropez's famous cream-and-cake concoction at **La Tropézienne** (☎ 04 90 86 24 72; 22 rue St-Agricol; ☽ 8.30am-7.30pm Mon-Sat). Then make your way to Avignon's most picturesque picnic spot, **Rocher des Doms**, a bluff-top park with views spanning the Rhône, Pont St-Bénézet, Villeneuve-lès-Avignon and the Alpilles. Finish off with a *papaline d'Avignon*, a pink chocolate ball of potent Mont Ventoux herbal liqueur that packs a punch (available from speciality shops around town).

Drinking

Tapalocas (☎ 04 90 82 56 84; 15 rue Galante; dishes from €2.30; ☽ 11.45am-1am) In the pedestrian area, tuck into a seemingly endless array of traditional Spanish tapas over a sangria or two.

La Compagnie des Comptoirs (☎ 04 90 85 99 04; 83 rue Joseph Vernet; mains €25-29; ☽ doors close 1am) Sink back on raised Moroccan-style beds beneath the arches of this former convent cloister, also incorporating a snazzy restaurant wrapped around an 18th-century courtyard. Cutting-edge DJs mix it up on weekends.

L'Echappée Belle (☎ 04 90 82 52 61; 13 rue de la Balance; mains €14; ☽ noon-10pm) For flavours of cumin, saffron and ginger infusing regional produce; or for just a home-made pastry and tea, Avignon's newest restaurant/*salon de thé* is a treat. Named after the Nicolas Bouvier novel of the same name (which translates as 'The Beautiful Escape'), it's a chic yet relaxed spot amid Avignon's architectural and artistic highlights.

L'Opéra Café (☎ 04 90 86 17 43; 24 place de l'Horloge; lunch formule/plat du jour €13/9, menu €32; ☽ lunch & dinner) DJs keep the beats coming at this contemporary place with a thespian bent in the centre of action-station place de l'Horloge.

Entertainment

The free *César* weekly magazine and the tourist office's fortnightly newsletter, *Rendez-vous d'Avignon* (both in French), carry

PROVENCE

events listings. Tickets for most events are sold at **FNAC** (☎ 04 90 14 35 35; 19 rue de la République; ☻ 10am-7pm Mon-Sat); the tourist office also sells tickets for many cultural fixtures.

Opéra d'Avignon (☎ 04 90 82 23 44; place de l'Horloge; box office ☻ 11am-6pm Mon-Sat) Housed in an imposing structure built in 1847, Opéra d'Avignon stages operas, operettas, plays, symphonic concerts, chamber music concerts and ballet.

Cinéma Utopia (☎ 04 90 82 65 36; 4 rue des escaliers Ste-Anne; admission €3-5) In the cultural centre tucked behind the Palais des Papes, this cinema screens dubbed and subtitled films.

NIGHTCLUBS

Red Lion (☎ 04 90 86 40 25; 21-23 rue St Jean le Vieux) Looking like someone picked it up from central London and plonked it in Avignon, this cherry-red English pub has gigs a couple of nights a week, and theme nights a couple of times a month.

Red Zone (☎ 04 90 27 02 44; 25 rue Carnot) A studenty crowd gathers here for its regular gigs and always-buzzing bar.

L'Esclave (☎ 04 90 85 14 91; 12 rue du Limas; ☻ from 11pm Tue-Sun) Avignon's inner-city gay hotspot is tucked behind a blank backstreet façade.

Shopping

Comtesse du Barry (☎ 04 90 82 62 92; 25 rue St-Agricol) Stock up on gourmet goodies like fine wine and foie gras.

Instant du Sud (☎ 04 90 82 24 48; 1 place Nicolas Saboly) Make your own perfume in an instant or two.

Oliviers & Co (☎ 04 92 70 48 20; 19 rue St-Agricol) Fine olive oil and olive oil–based products such as soap, hand cream and biscuits.

Getting There & Away

AIR

The **Aéroport Avignon-Caumont** (☎ 04 90 81 51 51) is 8km southeast of Avignon.

BUS

The **bus station** (☎ 04 90 82 07 35; blvd St-Roch; information window ☻ 10.15am-1pm & 2-6pm Mon-Fri) is in the basement of the building down the ramp to the right as you exit the train station. Tickets are sold on the buses.

Bus services include Aix-en-Provence (€13.90, one hour), Arles (€7.10, 1½ hours), Carpentras (€4.20, 45 minutes), Marseille

(€20, 35 minutes), Nîmes (€7.60, 1¼ hours) and Orange (€5.60, 40 minutes). Most lines operate on Sunday at reduced frequency.

Long-haul bus companies **Linebus** (☎ 04 90 85 30 48) and **Eurolines** (☎ 04 90 85 27 60; www .eurolines.com) have offices at the far end of the bus platforms.

CAR

Most car-rental agencies, such as **Europcar** Ibis Bldg (42 blvd St-Roch; ☎ 04 90 85 01 40); TGV station (☎ 04 32 74 63 40), are either inside the main train station complex or nearby (and well signed).

To reduce traffic within the walls, the city has over 900 free, monitored parking spaces at **Parking de L'Ile Piot**, served by a free shuttle bus.

TRAIN

Avignon has two train stations: **Gare Avignon TGV**, 4km southwest in the suburb of Courtine, and central **Gare Avignon Centre** (42 blvd St-Roch), where local trains to/from Orange (€5, 20 minutes), Arles (€6, 20 minutes) and Nîmes (€7.70, 30 minutes) arrive/depart.

Some TGVs to/from Paris stop at Gare Avignon Centre, but TGV services such as to/from Marseille (€20.90, 30 minutes) and Nice (€47.80, 3¼ hours) only use Gare Avignon TGV.

From early July to early September, there's a direct **Eurostar** (www.eurostar.com) service on Saturdays from London (six hours) and Ashford (five hours). See p973 for more details.

Getting Around

TO/FROM THE AIRPORT

There is no public transport from the airport into town; a taxi costs about €15.

BICYCLE

Bike-hire places in town include **Provence Bike** (☎ 04 90 27 92 61; www.provence-bike.com in French; 52 blvd St-Roch), which also rents scooters and motorbikes.

BUS

Local **TCRA** (www.tcra.fr in French) bus tickets cost €1.10 each on board. Buses run from 7am to about 7.40pm (less frequently on Sunday from 8am to 6pm). The two most important bus transfer points are the Poste stop at the main post office and place Pie.

PROVENCE

Carnets of 10 tickets (€9) and free bus maps *(plan du réseau)* are available at the **Agence Commerciale TCRA** (☎ 04 32 74 18 32; av de Lattre de Tassigny; �v 8.30am-12.30pm & 1.30-6pm Mon-Fri).

Villeneuve-lès-Avignon is linked with Avignon by bus 10, which stops in front of the main post office and on the western side of the walled city near Porte de l'Oulle.

Navettes (shuttle buses) link Gare Avignon TGV with the centre (€1.10, 10 to 13 minutes, twice hourly between 6.15am and 11.30pm); buses use the bus stop in front of the post office on cours Président Kennedy Monday to Saturday, and the Cité Administrative bus stop around the corner on cours Jean Jaurès on Sunday.

TAXI

Pick up a taxi outside the train station or call ☎ 04 90 82 20 20 around the clock.

AROUND AVIGNON
Villeneuve-lès-Avignon
pop 11,791

Across the Rhône from Avignon (and in a different *département*), the 13th-century Villeneuve-lès-Avignon (sometimes written as Villeneuve-lez-Avignon, and almost always just called Villeneuve, meaning 'new city') became known as the City of Cardinals because many primates affiliated with the papal court built large residences in the town. This was despite the fact that it was situated in territory ruled by the French crown, which in turn established a garrison here to keep an eye on events in the papal-controlled city across the river.

Just 3.5km from Avignon, Villeneuve is easily reached by foot (around 30 minutes) or bus 10 from Avignon's main post office. Sights are included in the Avignon *Passion* (p843).

Chartreuse du Val de Bénédiction (☎ 04 90 15 24 24; 60 rue de la République; full price/pass €6.10/4.10; �v 9am-6.30pm May-Aug, 9.30am-5.30pm Sep-Apr) was once the largest and most important Carthusian monastery in France and still looks it today.

If you're remotely interested in religious art, check out Enguerrand Quarton's lavish and dramatic 1453 painting *The Crowning of the Virgin* at **Musée Pierre de Luxembourg** (☎ 04 90 27 49 66; rue de la République; full price/pass €3/2; �v 10am-12.30pm & 2-6.30pm, closed Mon mid-Sep–mid-Jun). Ask for the accompanying notes for an insight into its commissioning and underpinning religious dogma.

If you're up for it, take the steep spiral steps to the top of **Tour Philippe-le-Bel** (☎ 04 32 70 08 57; full price/pass €1.80/1; �v 10am-12.30pm & 2-6.30pm, closed Mon mid-Sep–mid-Jun). This 14th-century defensive tower built at what was – then – the northwestern end of Pont St-Bénézet has awesome views of Avignon's walled city.

Provençal panoramas are also speccy from the turreted, 14th-century **Fort St-André** (☎ 04 90 25 45 35; full price/pass €4.60/3.10; �v 10am-1pm & 2-6pm Apr-Sep, 10am-1pm & 2-5pm Oct-Mar).

Les Baux de Provence
pop 500

Along a twisting, turning road 25km south of Avignon towards Arles, and about 7km past the small town of St-Rémy de Provence (population 10,000), Les Baux de Provence was vividly immortalised on canvas – albeit from a distance – by Van Gogh during his infirment in St-Rémy (p835).

Clawing precariously to a 245m-high grey limestone *baou* (Provençal for rocky spur) is **Château des Baux** (☎ 04 90 54 55 56; adult/child €7.50/5; �v 9am-8.30pm Jul & Aug, 9am-6.30pm Mar-Jun & Sep-Nov, 9am-5pm Dec-Feb). Thought to date back to the 10th century, it was largely destroyed during the reign of Louis XIII in 1633. Its remains are pitched above vineyards and olive groves. Audio guides in several languages detail the history of the castle, village and region, and demonstrations of medieval warfare frequently feature in summer. Opening hours can vary.

This ancient outcrop is one of the most visited villages in France – aim for early evening after the caterpillar of tourist coaches has crawled back downhill. The **tourist office** (☎ 04 90 54 34 39; www.lesbauxde provence.com; �v 9.30am-1pm & 2-6pm Mon-Sat) can give visitors information on Les Baux's handful of accommodation options. There's metered but no free parking within 800m of the village, but you can park for free at **Cathédrale d'Images** (www.cathedrale-im ages.com; adult/child €7.30/3.50), which screens large-scale sound-and-light projections flickering against the backdrop of a former quarry cave just a few minutes' stroll north of the village.

ORANGE

pop 28,889

This friendly little city has a refreshingly down-to-earth, untouristy ambience among its plazas, fountains and cobweb of pedestrian streets; and it's generally more affordable than its Provençal neighbours, too.

The House of Orange – the princely dynasty that had ruled Orange since the 12th century – made its mark on the history of the Netherlands through a 16th-century marriage with the German House of Nassau; and later on English history through William III (William of Orange). Known as Arenja in Provençal, it had earlier been a stronghold of the Reformation, and was ceded to France in 1713 by the Treaty of Utrecht. To this day many members of the royal house of the Netherlands are known as the princes and princesses of Orange–Nassau.

Orange is home to two of France's juiciest Roman treasures: a steep, spectacular theatre and a magnificent triumphal arch.

Orientation

Orange's train station is about 1.5km east of the city centre's place de la République, along av Frédéric Mistral then rue de la République. Rue St-Martin links place de la République and nearby place Clemenceau with the tourist office, which is 250m to the west. Théâtre Antique, Orange's magnificent Roman theatre, is two blocks south of place de la République. The tiny River Meyne lies north of the centre. From the train station, bus 1 from the École Mistral school goes to the centre of town; get off at Pourtoules for the Théâtre Antique.

Information

Crédit Lyonnais (7 place de la République)
La Bugado (5 av Général Leclerc; ☯ 7am-midnight) Laundrette.
Post Office (679 blvd Édouard Daladier) The only place in Orange that changes money.
Tourist Office (☎ 04 90 34 70 88; www.otorange.fr; 5 cours Aristide Briand; ☯ 9.30am-7pm Mon-Sat, 10am-4pm Sun Apr-Sep, 10am-1pm & 2-5pm Mon-Sat Oct-Mar) Closed mid-January, but phones are manned.

Sights

THÉÂTRE ANTIQUE

For an unforgettable first ogle at Orange's **Roman theatre** (☎ 04 90 51 17 60; adult/student €7.70/5.60; ☯ 9am-7pm Jun-Aug, 9am-6pm Apr, May & Sep, 9.30am-5.30pm Mar & Oct, 9.30am-4.30pm Nov-Feb), take the steep back stairs to the top, which affords an awesome view down the raked seating to the stage. Designed to seat 10,000 spectators, it's thought to have been built during Augustus Caesar's rule (27 BC–AD 14). The 103m-wide, 37m-high stage wall (*mur de scène*) is the only such Roman structure still standing in the world in its entirety, minus a few mosaics and the roof. A brand new roof was under construction at the time of research, striking another claim as the only modern enhancement of its kind to an ancient structure. Admission includes a seven-language audio guide.

The admission price for the theatre is also good for entry to the **museum** (museum only adult/child €4.50/3.50; ☯ 9.15am-6.45pm Jun-Aug, 9.15am-6.45pm May & Sep, 9.45am-12.15pm & 1.30-5.15pm Apr, Mar & Oct, 9.45am-12.15 & 1.30-4.15pm Nov-Feb) across the road, with some unassuming treasures of its own. These include segments of the Roman survey registers (essentially the precursor to the tax department) and the friezes that formed part of the theatre's scenery.

Follow montée Philbert de Chalons or montée Lambert to the top of **Colline St-Eutrope** (St Eutrope Hill; elevation 97m) for an elevated theatre panorama, where a circular viewing table explains what's what. En route you pass the ruins of a 12th-century **chateau**, the former residence of the princes of Orange.

ARC DE TRIOMPHE

Uncannily like Paris' iconic arch, Orange's 1st-century AD **triumphal arch** stands a proud 19m high and wide, and 8m thick, at the northern end of plane tree–lined av de l'Arc de Triomphe, about 450m northwest of the town centre. On its façade, ornate sculptures commemorate the Romans' victories over the Gauls in 49 BC as a not-so-subtle reminder to travellers approaching the city.

Festivals & Events

In June and August Théâtre Antique comes alive with all-night concerts, cinema screenings and musical events during **Les Nocturnes d'Été** (the Summer Nights) series. During late July and early August, it hosts **Les Chorégies d'Orange** (www.choregies.com), a series

PROVENCE

of weekend operas, classical concerts and choral performances. Festival tickets (€20 to €200) must be reserved months beforehand. A week-long **jazz festival** swings into town in June.

Sleeping

Camping Le Jonquier (☎ 04 90 34 49 48; www.camp inglejonquier.com in French; 1321 rue Alexis Carrel; camping €22.80; ☺ mid-Mar–Sep; ⚲) Splash in the pool, or play minigolf or tennis at this place near the Arc de Triomphe. Take bus 1 from the République stop (av Frédéric Mistral, 600m from the train station) to the Arc de Triomphe. From there, walk 100m back, turn right onto rue des Phocéens and right again onto rue des Étudiants and cross the football field.

Hôtel l'Herbier d'Orange (☎ 04 90 34 09 23; www .lherbierdorange.com in French; 8 place aux Herbes; s €25-32, d €30-47, tr €45-52; reception ☺ 8am-noon & 3-5pm winter, 7am-11pm summer) A groovy choice for style-conscious, budget-conscious travellers, this retro-funky pad run by a hip young team has 20 rooms with Arctic-white walls starkly contrasted with lavender, maroon, yellow or dark chocolate-brown, and designer lighting. The cheapest rooms come with a sink only but all have TVs, telephones, and fridges (yay for being able to chill supermarket-bought Provençal wine!).

Hôtel St-Florent (☎ 04 90 34 18 53; fax 04 90 51 17 25; 4 rue du Mazeau; s €27, d €35-75) A trip of a place, the St-Florent has 17 colourful, chintzy rooms with giant murals and antique wooden beds with crushed and studded velvet, plus a breakfast room filled with a riot of fake flowers, iridescent orange tablecloths and Christmas lights. Cheapies have toilets outside the rooms.

Le Glacier (☎ 04 90 34 02 01; www.le-glacier.com; 46 cours Aristide-Briand; d €47-95; ⚲) A cosy and bright option, with cute blue and yellow rooms, and close to the Théâtre Antique. Le Glacier's staff are welcoming and kind-hearted, and also rent bikes (per half-/full day €12/16) and can recommend touring itineraries of the nearby countryside and villages.

Hôtel Arène (☎ 04 90 11 40 40; www.hotel-arene.fr; place de Langes; s €56-64, d €77-140; ⚲ ⚲ ⚲) With a whole floor dedicated to hypoallergenic, ecological rooms, the personable Arène is privately owned and run with meticulous attention to the smallest of details. Furnish-

ings across all 35 rooms, even its whimsically named 'Romantique' and 'Charme' rooms, are modern and streamlined. Downstairs there's a light, bright bar/breakfast room with wi-fi.

Eating

Orange's pedestrianised streets and squares overflow with well-priced, well-patronised restaurants and cafés.

Brasserie Le Palace (☎ 04 90 34 13 51; 7 rue de la République; mains €7; ☺ 8am-7.30pm Mon-Sat summer, shorter hrs winter) Squeeze in with the locals over a drink or casual *plat* at this clattering old-school place with red vinyl booths, aromatic coffees and a collection of old clocks.

La Table D'Angélina (☎ 04 90 30 28 36; 23 rue Victor Hugo; mains €12; ☺ lunch & dinner Tue-Sat summer, lunch Tue-Sat, dinner Fri & Sat winter) A pastel-pretty place tucked in a 16th-century vaulted dining room, the tiny La Table D'Angélina specialises in cooking up whatever's freshest at the markets in and around Orange.

L'Olivier (☎ 04 90 11 05 22; 12 rue Petite Fusterie; mains €15-19.80; ☺ closed dinner Wed, lunch Sat & all day Sun winter, closed Sun summer) Remember the name Olivier Teissendre – it's unlikely to be the last time you hear of this rising chef, who is creating a buzz at his little French-washed place. Must-tries from the blackboard are Olivier's *tartes* (including vege ones), *ravioles* (itty-bitty cheese-and-herb local specialities), and his handmade *nougat glacé* (nougat ice cream). The restaurant's wi-fi'd.

Classic fare stars at the terrace-only **Festival Café** (☎ 04 90 34 65 58; 5 place de la République; mains €8-10; ☺ lunch & dinner Apr-Oct, closed Nov-Mar), which sets up a marquee in inclement weather; and at **Le Parvis** (☎ 04 90 34 82 00; 55 cours Pourtoules; mains €17; ☺ closed Sun dinner and all day Mon), Orange's gastronomic gem.

The town's central streets are lined with stalls each Thursday for its weekly **market** (if you need to move your car before the market wraps up, park at the edges of the city). Self-caterers can also pick up supplies at **Petit Casino** (35 rue St-Martin).

Getting There & Away

BUS

There's no longer a bus station, but buses stop on blvd Edouard Daladier, southwest of the post office, and travel to destinations including Avignon (€5.60, 40 minutes) and Vaison-la-Romaine (€5.10, 45 minutes).

TRAIN

Orange's **train station** (☎ 04 90 11 88 64, 3635; av Frédéric Mistral) has services south to Avignon (€5, 20 minutes), Marseille (€19.50, 1½ hours) and beyond, and north including Lyon (€24.30, 2¼ hours).

VAISON-LA-ROMAINE

pop 5986

This quintessential Provençal village has an enchanting pedestrianised centre dappled by plane trees, and stretches across the River L'Ouvèze to the walled Cité Médiévale (Medieval City) on the hilltop.

Vaison has a rich Roman legacy, with the largest archaeological site in France. Originally a Celtic city, it was conquered by Romans in the 2nd century BC. They left a treasure-trove including the picturesque bridge that connects the Cité Médiévale – where the counts of Toulouse built their 12th-century castle – with the town's heart.

Situated at the crossroads of Provence, 23km and 47km northeast of Orange and Avignon respectively, and 10km north of Carpentras, Vaison is also a prime jumping-off point for exploring the Mont Ventoux region.

Orientation

The ever-flooding River Ouvèze bisects Vaison. The modern centre is on the river's north bank; the Cité Médiévale is on its south side.

Pedestrianised Grand-rue heads northwest from the Pont Romain, changing its name near the Roman ruins to become av du Général de Gaulle.

To get from the bus station to the tourist office, turn left as you leave the station then left again into rue Colonel Parazols, which leads past the Fouilles de Puymin excavations along rue Burrhus.

Information

Vaison's **tourist office** (☎ 04 90 36 02 11; www .vaison-la-romaine.com; place du Chanoine Sautel; ✆ 9am-noon & 2-6.45pm daily Jul & Aug, 9am-noon & 2-5.45pm Mon-Sat, 9am-noon Sun Apr-Jun & Sep–mid-Oct, 9am-noon & 2-5.45pm Mon-Sat mid-Oct–Mar) is inside the Maison du Tourisme et des Vins, just off av du Général de Gaulle.

The post office, opposite place du 11 Novembre, has an exchange service and Cyberposte.

Sights

GALLO-ROMAN RUINS

The ruined remains of Vasio Vocontiorum, the Roman city that flourished here from the 6th to 2nd centuries BC, are unearthed at two sites, covered by a single admission.

At **Puymin** (av du Général de Gaulle; adult/child €7.50/4 for both; ✆ 10am-noon & 2-5pm Oct-Dec & early Feb, 10am-noon & 2-6pm Mar, 9.30am-6pm Apr & May, 9am-noon & 6.30pm Jun-Sep, closed Jan-early Feb) you can see houses, mosaics, the still-functioning Théâtre Antique (built around AD 20 for an audience of 6000) and an **archaeological museum** (✆ 10am-noon & 2-5pm Oct-Dec & early Feb, 10am-noon & 2-6pm Mar, 10.30am-6pm Apr & May, 10.30am-6.45pm Jun-Sep, closed Jan–early Feb) with a swag of statues – including likenesses of Hadrian and his wife Sabina.

Colonnaded shops and a limestone-paved street with an underground sewer are visible at **La Villasse** (✆ 10am-noon & 2-5pm Oct-Dec & early Feb, 10am-noon & 2-6pm Mar-May, 10.30am-noon & 2.30-6pm Jun-Sep, closed Jan-early Feb), to the west of the same road.

Admission includes an audio guide and entry to the 12th-century Romanesque **cloister** (€1.50; ✆ 10am-noon & 2-5pm Oct-Dec & early Feb, 10am-noon & 2-6pm Mar, 10am-noon & 2-6pm Apr-May, 10am-12.15pm & 2-5.45pm Jun-Sep, closed Jan-early Feb) of the **Cathédrale Notre Dame de Nazareth**, a five-minute walk west across rue du Bon Ange from Fouilles de la Villasse.

From April to September, there are free guided tours in English; check the schedule at the tourist office.

CITÉ MÉDIÉVALE

Across the pretty **Pont Romain** (Roman Bridge), cobblestone alleyways carve through the stone walls up to the Cité Médiévale. The highest point is home to an imposing 12th-century **chateau** built by the counts of Toulouse, which was modernised in the 15th century only to be later abandoned. Entry to the chateau is available by guided tours (in French, €2) only – check with the tourist office for schedules.

Sleeping

The tourist office has comprehensive accommodation lists, including details on *chambres d'hôtes* and self-catering places in the surrounding region. The hotels are few and far between.

Camping du Théâtre Romain (☎ 04 90 28 78 66; www.camping-theatre.com; chemin de Brusquet; camping €18.50; ☒ 15 Mar-15 Nov; ☒) Located opposite Théâtre Antique in the northern section of the Fouilles de Puymin.

Escapade (☎ 04 90 36 00 78; www.escapade-vacances.com/vaison in French; av César Geoffray; d with half-board €38-42; ☒ closed Dec-Feb) Around 500m southeast of town along the river, this modern family resort is set over peaceful, sprawling grounds with views of Mont Ventoux. This being France, half-board (obligatory) includes wine; breakfast is €5.50.

Hôtel Le Burrhus (☎ 04 90 36 00 11; www.burrhus.com; 1 place de Montfort; d €44-69; ☒ closed 12 Nov-20 Dec & Sun in Jan & Feb) Right on Vaison's vibrant central square, this might look like a quaint old place from the outside, but inside its 38 rooms have stunning cutting-edge colours (including one vision in all-white), funky streamlined furnishings, mosaic bathrooms and designer lighting.

Hostellerie Le Beffroi (☎ 04 90 36 04 71; www.le-beffroi.com; rue de l'Évêché; d €68-130; ☒ closed late Jan-late Mar; ☒) Within the medieval city's walls, this 1554-built *hostellerie* is housed over two buildings (the 'newer' one was built in 1690). A fairy-tale hideaway, its 22 rough-hewn stone-and-wood-beam rooms are romantically furnished, and there's a glass-paned breakfast room and summer terrace tumbling onto a rambling rose-and-herb garden with kids' swings. It's been held by the same family since 1904.

Eating

Le Bateleur (☎ 04 90 36 28 04; 1 place Théodore Aubanel; lunch menu €16-19.50, dinner €28-38; ☒ lunch Tue-Fri & Sun, dinner Tue, Wed & Fri-Sun) In two cosy rooms, one of which overlooks the rushing river, this is a great, convivial place for Provençal fare. Vegan alert: lunchtime mains consist of just two choices, meat or fish.

Moulin à Huile (☎ 04 90 36 20 67; www.moulin-huile.com; quai Maréchal Foch; mains €18-35; ☒ lunch & dinner Tue-Sat, lunch Sun) Master Chef Robert Bardot refines and redefines the art of gastronomic cooking at this old, orange-painted oil mill by the river, in the shadow of the Cité Médiévale. Sample a cross-section of his creations with his €76 tasting plate.

SELF-CATERING

Wines (available at the tourist office's on-site boutique), as well as honey and honey nougat, are local specialities, but nothing compares with the area's delectable black truffles hidden underground in the surrounding hillsides. They don't come cheap (€500 to €1000 per kilogram depending on the season and rainfall), but a few shavings are enough to transform any dish.

A magnificent **market** snakes through the central streets every Tuesday from 6.30am to 1pm.

Getting There & Away

The bus station, where **Lieutard buses** Vaison (☎ 04 90 36 05 22; av des Choralies; ☒ 9am-noon & 2-7pm Mon-Fri, 9am-noon Sat); Avignon (☎ 04 90 86 36 75) has an office, is 400m east of the town centre. There are limited services from Vaison to Orange (€5.10, 45 minutes), Avignon (€7.70, 1¼ hours) and Carpentras (€4.30, 45 minutes).

MONT VENTOUX

Visible from as far away as Avignon, Mont Ventoux (1909m) presides over northern Provence. From its antenna-studded summit, accessible by road between May and October, vistas extend to the southern Alps and – on a clear day – as far as the Pyrenees.

Unique species including the snake eagle and an assortment of spiders and butterflies are found only on this isolated peak, which marks the divide between northern and southern France's flora and fauna. Ship-building in the 17th century felled much of its forests, but since the 1860s, reforested species such as cedar create an autumnal kaleidoscope of red, yellow and golden brown.

As you ascend the relentless gradients (which regularly feature in the Tour de France), temperatures can plummet by 20°C, and there's twice as much precipitation as on the plains below. Bring warm clothes and rain gear, even in summer. Snow blankets the areas above 1300m from December to April; in summer it appears snow-capped because of the *lauzes* – broken white stones covering the top.

Piercing the sky to the west of Mont Ventoux are the sharp limestone pinnacles of **Dentelles de Montmirail**. At the eastern end of Mont Ventoux massif, the village of **Sault** (population 1190) is cloaked in purple lavender in summer – see p863.

The most common starting point for forays into the region is the town of **Malaucène**, the former summer residence of the Avignon popes. It's about 10km south of Vaison-la-Romaine and 21km west of Mont Ventoux.

In winter, you can ski **Mont Serein** (1445m), about 16km east of Malaucène and 5km from Mont Ventoux's summit on the D974 – the website www.stationdumontserein.com has a webcam showing conditions. A lift ticket including insurance costs €15.10 per day.

Information

Destination Ventoux (www.destination-ventoux.com)

Malaucène Tourist Office (☎ 04 90 65 22 59; ot-malaucene@wanadoo.fr; place de la Mairie; ☒ 10am-noon & 2-4.30pm Apr-Jun, 9.30am-12.30pm & 2.30-6pm Jul & Aug, 10am-noon & 2-4.30pm Mon-Sat Sep-Mar)

Sault Tourist Office (☎ 04 90 64 01 21; www.saultenprovence.com; av de la Promenade; ☒ 10am-noon & 2-6pm Apr-Jun & Sep, 9am-1pm & 2-7pm Jul & Aug, 10am-noon & 2.30-4.30pm Tue-Sat Oct-Mar)

Walking

Running from the River Ardèche west, the GR4 crosses the Dentelles de Montmirail before scaling the northern face of Mont Ventoux, where it meets the GR9. Both trails traverse the ridge before the GR4 branches eastwards to the Gorges du Verdon (p860).

Continuing on the GR9 takes you across the Monts du Vaucluse and the Luberon Range. Lonely Planet's *Walking in France* has details of walking in the latter.

MAPS

Didier-Richard's 1:50,000 map No 27, *Massif du Ventoux*, includes Mont Ventoux, the Monts du Vaucluse and the Dentelles de Montmirail. It's available at some of the area's larger tourist offices, bookshops and newsagents. More detailed is IGN's Série Bleue 1:25,000 *Mont Ventoux* (No 3140ET).

Getting There & Around

Mont Ventoux can be reached by car from Sault via the D164 or – in summer – from Malaucène or St-Estève via the switchback D974, often snow-blocked until April. For information on bus services in the area, see p857.

ACS (☎ 04 90 65 15 42) in Malaucène rents mountain bikes.

CARPENTRAS

pop 27,249

If you can, plan to be in Carpentras on a Friday morning, when the streets spill over with more than 350 stalls laden with breads, honeys, cheeses, olives, nuts, fruits (especially the area's juicy, blood-red strawberries), brittle almond nougat, *nougalettes* (like the nougat but finely crushed), and a rainbow of *Berlingots* – Carpentras' striped, pillow-shaped hard-boiled sweets. During winter there's also a truffle market.

Carpentras' mouthwatering markets aside, this charming agricultural town equidistant from Avignon (25km) to the southwest and Orange to the northwest has a handful of architectural treats too. A Greek trading centre and later a Gallo-Roman city, Carpentras became the capital of the papal territory of the Comtat Venaissin in 1320. Pope Clement V was a frequent visitor in the 14th century, during which time Jews expelled from French crown territory took refuge in the Comtat Venaissin under papal protection. The 14th-century synagogue is the oldest in use in France; a wonderful Jewish music festival runs from late July to early August.

Orientation

A heart-shaped ring of boulevards replaced the city's fortifications in the 19th century; the largely pedestrianised old city sits inside.

If you're arriving by bus, walk northeastwards to place Aristide Briand, a major intersection at the boulevards' southernmost point, where you'll find the tourist office. From here, the pedestrian-only rue de la République, which heads due north, takes you to the 17th-century Palais de Justice and the cathedral. The town hall is a few blocks northeast of the cathedral.

Information

There are commercial banks on central place Aristide Briand and blvd Albin Durand.

Laundrette (118 rue Porte de Monteux; ☒ 7am-8pm) On the road linking place du Général de Gaulle and blvd Albin Durand.

PROVENCE

Post Office (65 rue d'Inguimbert)

Tourist Office (☎ 04 90 63 00 78; www.tourisme.fr /carpentras; place Aristide Briand; ☺ 9am-7pm Mon-Sat, 9.30am-1pm Sun Jul & Aug, 9.30am-12.30pm & 2-6pm Mon-Sat Sep-Jun) Sells regional maps and guides, and organises guided city tours (adult/child €4/2.50) from April to September. Also hands out a free English-language *Discovery Circuit* brochure, corresponding with a walking circuit of signposts marked with *Berlingots*.

Sights & Activities

SYNAGOGUE

The centre of Jewish life for centuries and still a place of worship today, Carpentras' moving **synagogue** (☎ 04 90 63 39 97; place Juiverie; admission free; ☺ 10am-noon & 3-5pm Mon-Thu, 10am-noon & 3-4pm Fri) was founded here in 1367, rebuilt between 1741 and 1743 and restored in 1929 and 1954. In the first-floor wood-panelled sanctuary you can see 18th-century liturgical objects. It's inconspicuously situated opposite the town hall; look for the stone plaque inscribed with Hebrew letters.

CATHEDRAL

Église St-Siffrein, once Carpentras' **cathedral** (☺ 10am-noon & 2-6pm Tue-Sat), was built in the Méridional (southern French) Gothic style between 1405 and 1519 and is topped by a distinctive contemporary bell tower. Sadly, due to theft, its **Trésor d'Art Sacré** (Treasury of Religious Art) holding precious 14th- to 19th-century religious relics is now salted away from the public except during the Fête de St-Siffrein (opposite).

MUSEUMS

Carpentras' museums are open 10am to noon and 2pm to 4pm Wednesday to Monday (till 6pm April to September). Admission is €2.

Musée Comtadin (243 blvd Albin Durand), which displays artefacts related to local history and folklore, and **Musée Duplessis** (243 blvd Albin Durand), with paintings from the personal collection of Monseigneur d'Inguimbert, are on the western side of the old city.

Musée Sobirats (112 rue du Collège), one block west of the cathedral, is an ornate 18th-century private residence filled with furniture, faïence and *objets d'art* in the Louis XV and Louis XVI styles.

Behind the tourist office, the former 18th-century hospital in **Hôtel Dieu** (place Aris-

tide Briand; ☺ by arrangement with tourist office) has an incredibly preserved old-fashioned **pharmacy** and a **chapel**. Guided tours in English run at 3.30pm on Wednesday between June and late September (€4).

SWIMMING

Art Deco fans can dive into the 1930-built, geometric **piscine couverte** (covered swimming pool; ☎ 04 90 60 92 03; rue du Mont de Piété; adult/3-15yrs €2/1.50; ☺ hours vary, closed end Jun–mid-Sep), which is closed, weirdly enough, in summer.

Sleeping & Eating

Hôtel La Lavande (☎ 04 90 63 13 49; 282 blvd Alfred Rogier; d €30-40) Hôtel La Lavande has nine cheerful, cheap-as-*frites*, frill-free rooms (the very cheapest have shared bathrooms), accessed by staircases running between the floors at random angles. Downstairs there's a bustling, old-fashioned **restaurant** (menus €11-15) dishing up home cooking and good deals on half-board. It's on the left just past the intersection of rue Porte de Mazan.

Hôtel du Fiacre (☎ 04 90 63 03 15; www.hotel-du -fiacre.com; 153 rue Vigne; d €62-90; ✗) The genuine warmth of the welcome at this family-owned hotel makes you feel as if you're staying with favourite relatives. Set around a central walled stone courtyard in a beautifully restored 18th-century mansion, the 18 rooms are furnished with floral quilts, canopied beds, antiques and original art. All have TVs (including BBC), telephones and private bathrooms.

Le Marijo (☎ 04 90 60 42 65; 73 rue Raspail; mains €14.50-16.50; ☺ lunch & dinner Mon-Fri, dinner Sat, lunch Sun) Behind green timber-framed windows, this local place has rich regional fare like goat's cheese marinated for 15 days in herbs and olive oil. Proof of just how sweet a tooth Carpentras has, the list of desserts, like nougat and honey ice cream, runs longer than the choice of mains.

Chez Serge (☎ 04 90 63 21 24; 90 rue Cottier; lunch menus from €14, dinner menu from €26.50; ☺ lunch Sun-Fri, dinner Mon-Sat) Paris meets Provence by way of Armenia at this bistro where Serge serves up his culinary creations like cider-braised salmon, and piping hot pizzas made with local produce. There's a good kid's menu (€6.50).

Franck Restaurant (☎ 04 90 60 75 00; 30 place de l'Horloge; lunch menus from €20, dinner menu from €26.50; ☺ lunch & dinner Thu-Mon) Flanked by a sophisticated bar area, this burgundy-coloured place with stone walls and a white tableclothed terrace is frequented by those in the know for Franck's seasonal gastronomic cooking, including a heavenly truffle menu (€92).

Shopping

Rue d'Inguimbert and most of av Jean Jaurès (and often the streets spilling off) are the site of Carpentras' fantastic **Friday morning market**. The town gets *very* quiet in the long lunch hours following.

In winter, Carpentras' 'black diamonds' are traded at the **truffle market** (place Aristide Briand; ⏰ 9-10am Fri late Nov-Mar), attended by brokers, merchants and wholesalers from all over France. Carpentras' biggest fair, held on the Fête de St-Siffrein (Feast of St Siffrein) on 27 November, marks the opening of the truffle season.

In July and August, drop by the **wine market** outside the tourist office.

A Hansel and Gretel fantasy, **Chocolats Clavel** (☎ 04 90 63 07 59; 30 Porte d'Orange; ⏰ Mon-Sat) has spectacularly sculptured sweets.

Getting There & Away

The train station is served by goods trains only, so buses operated by Cars Comtadins and Cars Arnaud provide Carpentras' only intercity public transport. The **bus station** (place Terradou) is 150m southwest of place Aristide Briand.

Schedules are available from **Cars Comtadins** (☎ 04 90 67 20 25; 192 av Clemenceau) across the square and from **Cars Arnaud** (☎ 04 90 63 01 82; 8 av Victor Hugo).

There are hourly services to Avignon (€4.20, 45 minutes) and infrequent runs to Vaison-la-Romaine (€4.30, 45 minutes) via Malaucène and Bédoin (€3.40, 40 minutes) at the southwestern foot of Mont Ventoux; and Cavaillon (€5.10, 45 minutes) and to L'Isle-sur-Sorgue (€3.70, 20 minutes), 7km west of Fontaine de Vaucluse.

FONTAINE DE VAUCLUSE

pop 611

Water, water everywhere. All of the rain that falls around Apt, as well as melting snow, gushes out here in Fontaine de Vaucluse (Vau-Cluso La Font in Provençal) at the edge of the Luberon. The world's fifth most powerful spring – and France's most powerful – Fontaine (meaning fountain) is where the River Sorgue surges surfaceward from its subterranean course. Jacques Cousteau was one of many who attempted unsuccessfully to plumb the spring's depths before an unmanned submarine touched base, 315m, in 1985. It's at its most dazzling after heavy rain, when the water is an azure, almost violet, blue.

The spring's crystal waters flow through the pretty village of Fontaine de Vaucluse about 1km downstream... as do the 1.5 million or more tourists that pour through here each year. Aim to arrive early morning before the trickle of visitors becomes a deluge.

Information

Tourist Office (☎ 04 90 20 32 22; www.oti-delasorgue .fr; chemin de la Fontaine; ⏰ 9.30am-5.30pm Tue-Sat low season, daily in high season) Southeast of central place de la Colonne on the way to the spring.

Sights

Most visitors, of course, come to see the spring, but this tiny village also has an eclectic collection of museums.

Musée d'Histoire 1939–1945 (☎ 04 90 20 24 00; adult/child €3.50/1.50; ⏰ 10am-noon & 2-6pm Sat & Sun Mar, 10am-noon & 2-6pm Wed-Mon Apr-Jun & Sep-Oct, 10am-7pm Wed-Mon Jul & Aug, 10am-noon & 2-5pm Sat & Sun Nov & Dec) showcases the resistance movement during WWII.

Moulin à Papier (⏰ 04 90 20 34 14; chemin de la Fontaine; admission free; ⏰ 9am-12.30pm & 2-5pm Mon-Sat, 10.30am-12.30pm & 2-5pm Sun Sep-Jun, 9am-7pm Jul & Aug) is a reconstructed paper mill on the river. Beautiful flower-encrusted paper, made as it was in the 16th century, is sold in the adjoining boutique and art gallery.

Musée Pétrarque (☎ 04 90 20 37 20; admission €3.50; ⏰ 10am-noon & 2-6pm Wed-Mon Apr-Sep, 10am-noon & 2-5pm Oct) is devoted to the Italian Renaissance poet Petrarch, who lived in Fontaine de Vaucluse from 1337 to 1353, expressing in heartbreaking verse his futile love for Laura, wife of Hugues de Sade.

Sleeping & Eating

Ask the tourist office for a regularly updated list of *chambres d'hôtes*.

Auberge de Jeunesse (☎ 04 90 20 31 65; fax 04 90 20 26 20; chemin de la Vignasse; dm €11; reception ⏰ 8-10am & 5.30-9pm, closed mid-Nov–Jan) In a lovely old farmhouse, south of Fontaine de Vaucluse in the direction of Lagnes, this peaceful hostel is popular with families and hikers. From the bus stop, walk 800m uphill.

Hôtel du Poète (☎ 90 20 34 05; www.hoteldupoete .com; r €70-240; ✆ closed late Dec–mid-Feb; ✆ ✆) On the right-hand side of the road as you enter the village, on the river bank, the peach-tinged Hôtel du Poéte has 23 lyrically categorised rooms like 'Melody' and 'Symphony' with creamy furnishings, a poolside terrace on which to feast on fresh fruit at breakfast (€17), and can recommend nearby dining options.

Les Sources (☎ 04 90 20 31 84; rte de Cavaillon; menus €22-35; ✆ lunch Tue-Sun, dinner nightly early Apr–mid-Nov) Regional cuisine is at its freshest at Les Sources, an almond-coloured place with sage-green shutters flanked by potted palms, along the road to Cavaillon. Other restaurants are sprinkled around the village.

Getting There & Away

Fontaine de Vaucluse is 21km southeast of Carpentras, 30km west of Apt, and 7km east of L'Isle-sur-Sorgue, a popular antiques centre. From Avignon, **Cars Arnaud** (☎ 04 90 82 07 35) has a bus (€4.60, one hour, two or three daily) with a stop at Fontaine de Vaucluse.

Fontaine is most easily reached by car, but you'll have to fork out for the privilege of parking. (Don't duck down the little lane opposite the pay parking area instead – it dead-ends with nowhere to turn around, and reversing out is tricky. Trust us, we tried.)

THE LUBERON

The Luberon's lush hills stretch from Cavaillon in the west to Manosque in the east, and from Apt southwards to the River Durance. The area is named after the main range, a compact massif culminating in a 1100m-high summit. Whether you're on the steep, oak-covered northern face or the more Mediterranean southern tract, the countryside vistas are captivating.

Hiking, biking and roadtripping are ideal for taking in the Luberon's landscapes, including its scattering of ancient igloo-like stone *bories* (opposite).

Much of the range is within the boundaries of the Parc Naturel Régional du Luberon, headquartered in the area's main centre, Apt (right). The park's 1200 sq km encompass numerous villages, deso-

late forests, unexpected gorges and abandoned farmhouses on the way to ruin – or restoration by fans of Peter Mayle. The British author's light-hearted, lavishly detailed books *A Year in Provence* and *Toujours Provence* recount his renovation of a house just outside the village of Ménerbes in the late 1980s. Their spectacular success spawned a still-booming genre of expat armchair travel tales – and spawned a spectacular number of tourists traipsing by. Peter Mayle subsequently sold up and moved abroad, but the Luberon's charm recently lured him back, this time to the village of Lourmarin – where, as it happens, Nobel Prize–winning writer Albert Camus (1913–60) is buried.

Apt

pop 11,172

Anchoring the Luberon is its capital, Apt. The agricultural town's festive spirit comes alive at its Saturday morning market brimming with its local specialities (cherries, grapes, and candied and crystallised fruits) and peaks during its wine and cheese festival, held on the Ascension (May or June), when up to 30 chateaux show off their wares.

MAPS

For hardcore exploring, the tourist office sells regional maps such as the Top 25 (3242OT) *Map of Apt and the Parc Naturel Régional du Luberon* (€11.50), or the *Cavaillon* map (3142OT), for €9.

The Maison du Parc sells an extensive range of guides and maps including hiking and cycling, such as the recommended topoguide *Le Parc Naturel Régional du Luberon à Pied* (€11.90), which details 24 walks including the GR9, GR92 and GR97 trails (in French only).

INFORMATION

Maison du Parc (☎ 04 90 04 42 00; www.parcdulu beron.fr in French; 60 place Jean Jaurès; ✆ 8.30am-noon & 1.30-7pm Mon-Sat Apr-Sep) Has information on the Parc Naturel Régional du Luberon, including details of the park's two dozen *gîtes d'étape* (hikers' accommodation).

Tourist Office (☎ 04 90 74 03 18; www.ot-apt.fr; 20 av Philippe de Girard; ✆ 9am-noon & 2-6pm Mon-Sat Oct-Apr, 9am-noon & 2-6pm Mon-Sat, 9am-12.30pm Sun May, Jun & Sep, 9am-7pm Mon-Sat, 9am-12.30pm Sun Jul & Aug) Ask for the leaflet *Apt à Découvrir*, which details, in English and French, two one-hour city tours signposted around town with colour-coded markers.

SIGHTS & ACTIVITIES

You can appreciate Apt's roots at the **Musée de l'Aventure Industrielle du Pays d'Apt** (Industrial History Museum; ☎ 04 90 74 95 30; 14 place du Postel; adult/under 12yrs €4/free; ☺ 10am-noon & 3-6.30pm Mon-Sat, 3-7pm Sun). In an old candied-fruit factory, it interprets the area's candied-fruit trade, ochre mining, and earthenware production from the 18th century.

SLEEPING & EATING

Camping Municipal Les Cèdres (☎ /fax 04 90 74 14 61; rte de Rustrel; camping €13; ☺ Mar–mid-Nov) This back-to-basics riverside camp site is just out of town.

Hôtel L'Aptois (☎ 04 90 74 02 02; www.aptois .fr.st; 289 cours Lauze de Perret; d €32-56) Above an inexpensive café, this surprisingly stylish, cyclist-friendly hotel with good wheelchair access rents bikes to guests, which can be dropped off at points along the *Luberon A Vélo* bike routes, and does repairs. The

TO É OR NOT TO É

Luberon may be spelt Lubéron by many leading cartographic publishers, but no – as any local will emphatically explain, regardless of what the rest of the country might heedlessly claim, there's no accent on the E. (In fact, to really sound like a local, it's pronounced as if there's no E at all.)

cheapest rooms have toilets only, but they're all done out with chic fuschia, purple and red taffeta and funky touches like designer lamps and slimline vases of silk flowers.

Auberge du Lubéron (☎ 04 90 74 12 50; www .auberge-luberon-peuzin.com; 8 place Faubourg du Ballet; d €58-118) This cosy inn just across the river from the historic town centre is best known as the home of Apt's finest **restaurant** (menus €29-62), the magnum opus of chef Serge Peuzin. But it also has 14 guestrooms in rich Provençal colours like (aptly enough) cherry red. Higher priced rooms have minibars, air conditioning and more room to move.

WORTH A TRIP

You'll see beehive-shaped *bories* while you're buzzing around Provence (1610 have been counted to date), but the **Village des Bories** (☎ 04 90 72 03 48; adult/child €5.50/3; ☺ 9am-5.30pm Oct-May, 9am-8pm Jun-Sep) has hordes of them.

Reminiscent of Ireland's *clochàn*, these one- or two-storey dry-walled huts constructed from slivers of limestone were first built in the area in the Bronze Age. Right up until the 18th century, they were lived in, renovated and even built from scratch. Their original purpose isn't known (shelter would seem most likely), but over time they've also been used as workshops, wine cellars and storage sheds. This 'village' contains about 20, best visited early morning or just before sunset for the interplay of light and shadows.

Getting here requires your own wheels. You'll find the village 4km southwest of **Gordes** (population 2127), just off the D2 heading for Cavaillon. Gordes' **tourist office** (☎ 04 90 72 02 75; www.gordes-village.com; place du Château; ☺ 9am-12.30pm & 2-6pm Jun-Sep, 9am-noon & 2-5pm Oct-May) has information.

To see more stunning stonework, combine it with a trip to the ochre-rich earth at **Roussillon** (population 1200), between the Vaucluse plateau and the Luberon Range. Two millennia ago the Romans used this distinctive earth to produce pottery glazes. These days the whole village – even the cemetery's gravestones – is built of the reddish stone.

From the town, take a 45-minute walk along the **Sentier des Ocres** (Ochre Trail; admission €2; ☺ 9.30am-5.30pm Mar-11 Nov). Within fairy-tale groves of chestnuts, maritime pines and scrub, the trail leads you through nature's powdery sunset-coloured paint palette of ochre formations created over centuries by erosion and winds. Don't wear white!

For more information, Roussillon's central **tourist office** (☎ 04 90 05 60 25; www.roussillon-provence .com in French; place de la Poste; ☺ 10am-noon & 2-5.30pm Mon-Sat) has details about restaurants and lodging in and around the area.

Roussillon is 9km east of Gordes in the direction of Apt (11km further east). If you don't have wheels but you do have hiking boots, the GR6 walking trail passes through here.

PROVENCE

Le Couvent (☎ 04 90 04 55 36; www.loucouvent.com in French; 36 rue Louis Rousset; d incl breakfast €75-120; ✕ 🖳) Within a 17th-century convent, this B&B is exceptional value for what you get, which is one of just five sumptuous rooms with high-speed internet, and breakfast (included) in a vaulted stone dining room. It's right in the town centre, but screened by flowering gardens. Between April and October there's a two-night minimum at weekends.

Thym, te voilà (☎ 04 90 74 28 25; 59 rue St-Martin; mains €10; ⏰ 11.30am-6pm Tue-Sat) Head to this sweet little tearoom any time, but especially on Saturday when they boil up a fresh-as-it-gets market soup.

GETTING THERE & AWAY

Buses going to Aix-en-Provence (€9.40, 1½ hours, two daily) leave from the **bus station** (☎ 04 90 74 20 21; 250 av de la Libération) east of the centre. There are services to/from Avignon (€7.90, 1¼ hours, three or four daily), Digne-les-Bains (€7.30, two hours, one or two daily), Cavaillon (via Coustellet; €4.80, 40 minutes, two or three daily) and Marseille (€10.90, 2½ hours, two daily).

NORTHEASTERN PROVENCE

Northeastern Provence crowns the top of the Côte d'Azur with snowy peaks and spectacular Alp-cradled valleys.

The Route Napoléon (www.route-napoleon.com), which Bonaparte followed in 1815 en route to Paris after escaping from Elba, passes through Castellane. The route is now the N85, one of the gateways to the Gorges du Verdon, Europe's largest canyon. The route continues north to Digne-les-Bains, a thermal spa retreat surrounded by serried lavender fields. Further north again are the winter ski slopes and summer mountain retreats of the Ubaye and Blanche Valleys.

GORGES DU VERDON

Europe's largest canyon, the plunging Gorges du Verdon (also known as the Grand Canyon du Verdon) slices a 25km swathe through Provence's limestone plateau.

The gorges begin at Rougon near the confluence of the Verdon and the Jabron Rivers, and wind westwards until the Verdon's green waters flow into Lac de Ste-Croix. A dizzying 250m to 700m deep, the gorges' floor is just 8m to 90m wide, with its overhanging rims 200m to 1500m apart.

The two main jumping-off points for exploring the gorges are the villages of Castellane (population 1349), northeast of Rougon; and the magical Moustiers Ste-Marie (population 600), which has a centuries-old gold star on a 227m-long chain strung between its cliffs.

Information

Castellane Tourist Office (☎ 04 92 83 61 14; www.castellane.org; rue Nationale; ⏰ 9am-12.30pm & 1.30-7pm Mon-Sat, 10am-12.30pm Sun Jul & Aug, 9am-noon & 2-6pm Mon-Fri, 10am-noon & 3-6pm Sat Sep-Jun)
Moustiers Ste-Marie Tourist Office (☎ 04 92 74 67 84; www.moustiers.fr; ⏰ 10am-12.30pm & 2-5.30pm Mar, 10am-12.30pm & 2-6pm Apr, 10am-12.30pm & 2-6pm May, 10-12.30pm & 2-6.30pm Jun, 9.30am-12.30pm & 2-7.30pm Jul-Sep, 10am-12.30pm & 2-5.30pm Oct, 10am-noon & 2-5pm Nov, 2-5pm Dec-Feb)

Sights & Activities

The gorges' depths are only accessible by foot or raft. Motorists and cyclists can take in staggering panoramas from two vertigo-inducing cliff-side roads.

CYCLING & DRIVING

The D952 corkscrews along the northern rim, past **Point Sublime**, which offers a fish-eye-lens view of serrated rock formations falling away to the river below. Between March and October, the best view from the northern side is from **Belvédère de l'Escalès** along rte de Crêtes (D23). Drive to the third bend and steel your nerves for the stunning drop-off into the gorge.

Also heart-palpitating, **La Corniche Sublime** (the D19 to the D71) twists along the southern rim, taking in landmarks such as the **Balcons de la Mescla** (Mescla Terraces) and **Pont de l'Artuby** (Artuby Bridge), the highest bridge in Europe.

A complete circuit of the Gorges du Verdon via Moustiers Ste-Marie involves about 140 unremitting kilometres of driving. Castellane and Moustiers tourist offices have English-language driving itineraries. The only village en route is **La Palud-sur-Verdon** (930m), 2km northeast of the northern bank of the gorges. Traffic on the single-lane roads frequently slows to snail's pace in summer; in winter, roads can be icy. Any time of year watch out for falling (and fallen) rocks.

WALKING

From Point Sublime, the GR4 descends to the bottom of the canyon. Walkers and white-water rafters can experience an overwhelming series of cliffs and narrows. The GR4 is detailed by Didier-Richard's 1:50,000 map No 19, *Haute Provence-Verdon*. It's also included in the excellent English-language book *Canyon du Verdon – The Most Beautiful Hikes* (€4.12), available at the tourist offices, which lists 28 walks in the gorges. The full route takes two days, though short descents into the canyon are possible from a number of points. Bring a torch (flashlight) and drinking water. Camping on gravel beaches is illegal, but is generally tolerated if you break camp early the next morning (and, of course, camp responsibly).

OUTDOOR SPORTS

Castellane and Moustiers tourist offices have complete lists of companies offering rafting, canyoning, horse riding, mountaineering, biking and more.

Aboard Rafting (☎/fax 04 92 83 76 11; www.aboard -rafting.com; 8 place Marcel Sauvaire, Castellane; ☻ Apr–Sep) runs white-water rafting trips (€33 to €75) as well as canyoning (€33 to €65).

Bungee jumping (*élastique*), usually on weekends only, can be arranged through Marseille-based **Latitude Challenge** (☎ 04 91 09 04 10; www.latitude-challenge.fr in French).

The newest thrill-seeking pursuit is 'floating' (€45/90 per half-/full day): like white-water rafting minus the raft, with a buoyancy bag strapped to your back. Contact **Guides Aventure** (www.guidesaventure.com).

Sleeping & Eating

Both tourist offices have lists of numerous camp sites and accommodation options, as well as restaurants and food shops.

CASTELLANE & AROUND

The nearby river is lined with seasonal camping areas. Hotels and restaurants cluster around the central square, place Marcel Sauvaire and place de l'Église.

Domaine de Chasteuil Provence (☎ 04 92 83 61 21; www.chasteuil-provence.com; camping €11-16;

☻ May–mid-Sep; ☒) Just south of Castellane, this camp site has lovely, leafy grounds, optional powered sites, and timber chalets (from €111 for two nights for four people).

Ma Petite Auberge (☎ 04 92 83 62 06; fax 04 92 83 68 49; rue de la République; d €43-67; ☻ closed early Dec–early Mar) An intimate two-star place, Ma Petite Auberge has 15 bright, airy rooms, a lime tree–shaded garden, and a highly recommended regional **restaurant** (mains from €12) that's worth popping into even if you're not bedding down here.

MOUSTIERS & AROUND

Domaine de Le Petit Lac (☎ 04 92 74 67 11; www .lepetitlac.com; rte du lac de Ste-Croix; camping €14-22.50, 4-person eco-cabins from €45; ☻ camping mid-Jun–Sep, cabins Apr–mid-Oct; ☒) In a peaceful lakeside spot, this activity-oriented camp site has brand new eco-cabins (two-night minimum) with hemp walls, solar hot water and low-output electricity.

Hôtel le Baldaquin (☎ 04 92 74 63 92; place Clerissy; d €60-99; ☻ Mar–mid-Nov) Experience heart-warming hospitality at this 17th-century, blue-shuttered place in the village centre; with seven romantic rooms hung with Renoir and Degas prints, garaged parking (€5), and a buffet breakfast (€9) to assuage the heartiest hiker's appetite.

La Ferme Rose (☎ 04 92 74 69 47; www.lafermerose .fr.fm; chemin de Quinson; d €80-145) This fabulous converted farmhouse contains wonderfully quirky collections including antique toys, a Wurlitzer jukebox with 45rpm records, a display case of coffee grinders, and old telephones, telex machines, theatre lighting and projectors. Its dozen boutique rooms are named for the colour dramatising each chic sleeping area and glazed bathroom; some are air conditioned. It's off the D952 on Moustiers' fringe.

La Bastide de Moustiers (☎ 04 92 70 47 47; www .bastide-moustiers.com; d low/high season from €155/180; menus €42-57; ☒ ☒) Some of France's finest chefs get their start at this bastion belonging to Alain Ducasse. Inside the thick stone-walled old master-potter's studio with good wheelchair access are poetic rooms in which to pamper yourself, and yes, there's a place to park the helicopter.

For local fare, try **La Treille Muscate** (☎ 04 92 74 64 31; place de l'Église; menus €25-34; ☻ closed dinner Wed and all day Thu in low season, all day Wed in high season, plus mid-Nov–Jan); or dine under the

PROVENCE

oak trees at **Côte-Jardin** (☎ 04 92 74 68 91; rue de Lérins; mains €19-27; ✆ closed dinner Tue, all day Wed, plus Nov & Dec).

Getting There & Away

Public transport to, from and around the Gorges du Verdon is limited. **Autocars Sumian** (☎ 04 42 67 60 34) runs buses from Marseille to Castellane (€19.90, 2¼ hours) via Aix-en-Provence (€16.30, 1¾ hours); and from Castellane to Moustiers (€7.30, 1 hour).

Getting Around

In July and August **Navettes Autocar** (☎ 04 92 83 40 27, 04 92 83 64 47) runs shuttle buses around the gorges daily except Sunday, linking Castellane with Point Sublime, La Palud, La Maline and Moustiers. Ask at the tourist offices for schedules; fare segments start at €3.80. Both tourist offices (p860) have bike rental information.

DIGNE-LES-BAINS

pop 17,680

At the foot of the Alps, Digne-les-Bains is named for its curative thermal springs. Situated 100km northeast of Aix-en-Provence and 152km northwest of Nice, it's most enchantingly reached by the mountain train from Nice (p864). The town has a couple of top museums and rich fossils in the surrounding shale.

Wild and cultivated lavender carpets the mountains and plains around Digne, which celebrates the annual lavender harvest with a five-day festival starting the first weekend in August.

Orientation

Digne hugs the eastern bank of the shallow River Bléone. The major roads into town converge at the Point Rond du 11 Novembre 1918 roundabout 400m northeast of the train station. The main street, blvd Gassendi, heads northeastwards from the Point Rond and passes the large place du Général de Gaulle, the main square of Digne-les-Bains.

Information

INTERNET ACCESS

Cybercafé (☎ 04 92 32 00 19; 48 rue de l'Hubac; per hr €5; ✆ 10am-noon & 2-7pm Tue-Sat) In the centre of the town.

LAUNDRY

There are laundrettes at 4 place du Marché, in the old city (open 8am to 7pm Monday to Saturday), and 99 blvd Gassendi (open 9am to 7pm).

TOURIST INFORMATION

Relais Départemental des Gîtes de France (☎ 04 92 31 30 40; www.gites-de-france.com; ✆ 9am-noon & 1-5pm Mon-Fri, 9am-noon Sat) Adjacent to the tourist office. Between 9am and 11am and 1pm to 4pm it can book *gîtes* in the area.

Tourist Office (☎ 04 92 36 62 62; www.ot-digneles bains.fr; place du Tampinet; ✆ 8.45am-noon & 2-6pm Mon-Sat, 10am-noon Sun Sep-Jun, 8.45am-12.30pm & 1.30-6.30pm Jul & Aug) Has comprehensive regional info including walking and cycling maps; reserves accommodation free of charge.

Sights & Activities

FONDATION ALEXANDRA DAVID-NÉEL

Tibetan culture is celebrated at the **Fondation Alexandra David-Néel** (☎ 04 92 31 32 38; www.alex andra-david-neel.org; 27 av Maréchal Juin; admission free), in memory of Paris-born writer and philosopher Alexandra David-Néel, who made an incognito voyage in the 1900s to Tibet before settling in Digne. Year-round, free two-hour tours (available in English) commence at 10am, 2pm and 3.30pm. Drive 1km along the Nice road or take bus 3 to the Stade Rolland stop.

MUSÉE GASSENDI

Everything from modern art by Andy Goldsworthy to still-lifes by 19th-century painter Etienne Martin, natural history, and exhibits on the 16th-century philosopher/scientist/painter Pierre Gassendi are displayed at the **Musée Gassendi** (☎ 04 92 31 45 29; place des Récollets; adult/child €4/2; ✆ 11am-7pm Apr-Sep, 1.30-5.30pm Wed-Mon Oct-Mar) in the town centre.

RÉSERVE NATURELLE GÉOLOGIQUE

Prehistoric birds' footprints, outsized ammonites and ram's horn spiral shells are some of the amazing fossil deposits in the **Réserve Naturelle Géologique**, which surrounds Digne. Getting to the 18 sites requires your own wheels; ask the tourist office for a detailed regional map.

Definitely try to visit the fascinating **Centre de Géologie** (☎ 04 92 36 70 70; www.resgeol04 .org; adult/child €4.60/2.75; ✆ 9am-noon & 2-5.30pm, to

---

THE PERFUME OF PROVENCE

If Provence has a defining colour, it's purple; and a defining fragrance is the astringent aroma of lavender *(lavande)*, which flowers between mid-July and mid-August. Farmed lavender, serried in rows throughout the region, is harvested in full bloom in hot, dry conditions. The cut *paille* (straw) is then packed tight in a steam still and distilled to extract the essential oils. Wild lavender *(lavande sauvage)* grows in the mountains; its more concentrated essences linger longer.

Lavender farms, distilleries and gardens open to visitors are listed in the English-language brochure *Les Routes de la Lavande* (Lavender Roads; free from tourist offices or online at www .routes-lavande.com). You'll see lavender fields in the Vaucluse near **Gordes**, around the **Musée de la Lavande** (Lavender Museum; ☎ 04 90 76 91 23) in Coustellet, and massed in the arid **Sault** region east of Mont Ventoux; as well as the hillsides around Digne-les-Bains. The Digne tourist office has information on tours and hiking trails.

4.30pm Fri, closed Sat & Sun Nov-Mar) at St-Benoît, 2km north of town off the road to Barles. Up a **steep** hill, trails lead to a museum containing aquarium tanks, insect displays, and fossils and plants put into evolutionary context. Take TUD bus 2 to the Champourcin stop; then take the road to the left.

THERMAL SPA

Ahhhh… Float in the thermal pool, slather yourself in mud and seaweed, or luxuriate in a lavender bath at the **Établissement Thermal** (☎ 04 92 32 32 92; www.eurothermes.com in French; ☺ Feb-early Dec), 2km east of Digne's centre. A 20-minute spa or massage starts at €45.

Sleeping & Eating

Digne's hotels often require half-board in July and August. France's first *gîte* (holiday cottage) was founded here in 1951; the Relais Départemental des Gîtes de France's headquarters (opposite) has a list of locations.

Hôtel L'Origan (☎ /fax 04 92 31 62 13; 6 rue Pied de Ville; d €25-35) Good thing the rooms at this hotel in the heart of town are so cheap (though still charmingly comfy), because it means you can spend up at its respected regional **restaurant** (menus €20-40; ☺ closed Tue).

Hôtel Central (☎ 04 92 31 31 91; www.lhotel-central.com; 26 blvd Gassendi; d €30-49) You guessed it, this corner hotel is super-central, which means the road-facing rooms can be noisy, but it's a bright, very clean place with wood-beamed rooms, colourful quilts and accommodating staff. The cheapest of the cheapies have shared facilities in the hall. Right outside are a scattering of cafés.

Hôtel du Golf (☎ 04 92 30 58 00; www.golfdigne .com in French; 57 rte du Chaffaut; d €45-68; ☺) Swing a club through fields of lavender. A well-

signed 8km from town, this resort takes the so-called 'good walk spoiled' *très* seriously, with accommodation/dining/golfing packages, multistage lessons, golf buggy and GPS rental. Rooms are modern, utilitarian arrangements; there's a relaxed **restaurant** (menus €13-25; ☺ lunch year-round, dinner Jul & Aug).

Hôtel Villa Gaïa (☎ 04 92 31 21 60; www.hotelvil lagaia.fr; 24 rte de Nice; d €85-95; ☺ Apr-Oct) Set in Italianate fountained gardens, this antique-filled 19th-century villa 2km west of town feels like the private mansion it once was, complete with a tennis court and grand **dining room** (menus €26-39).

SELF-CATERING

On Wednesday and Saturday mornings, place du Général de Gaulle overflows with fresh market produce.

The bevy of bakeries in town includes **Boulangerie Patisserie Andre Michel** (16 rue Pied de Ville).

Stock up on groceries at the **Casino Supermarket** (42 blvd Gassendi; ☺ 7.30am-12.30pm & 3.30-7.30pm).

Getting There & Away

The **bus station** (☎ 04 92 31 50 00; place du Tampinet; ☺ 9am-12.30pm & 3-6.30pm Mon-Sat) is behind the tourist office. Destinations include Nice (€23.30, 2¼ hours, Monday, Tuesday, Friday and Saturday) via Castellane (€11, 1¼ hours); Marseille (€15.10, 2½ hours) and Apt (€11, Monday to Saturday).

A shuttle bus links Digne with Aix-en-Provence's TGV station, timed to coincide with the TGV to and from Paris (€16.46, 1½ hours).

Digne's **train station** (☎ 04 92 31 00 67; av Pierre Sémard; ticket windows ☺ 8.15am-12.30pm & 1-8pm

PROVENCE

THE PINE CONE TRAIN

Chug along the picturesque, narrow-gauge railway on *le Train des Pignes* (the Pine Cone Train). Operated by **Chemins de Fer de la Provence** (Digne ☎ 04 92 31 01 58, Nice ☎ 04 97 03 80 80; www.trainprovence.com), the entire trip from Digne to Nice's Chemins de fer de Provence station (4bis rue Alfred Binet) takes about 3¼ hours (€17.65, four daily each direction). It was conceived in 1861 and fully inaugurated in 1911; there are some endearing Christmassy theories, but no-one knows the history behind the name.

Mon-Fri, 8.15am-12.30pm & 1.45-4.45pm Sat) is a 10-minute walk westwards from the tourist office. There are four services daily to Marseille (€19.60, 2¼ hours).

Gallardo (☎ 04 92 31 05 29; 8 cours des Arès; ⏲ 9am-noon & 3-7pm Tue-Sat) rents bikes (€15 per day).

THE PROVENCE ALPS

Powdery winter wonderlands crisscrossed by ski trails or glorious summer mountain retreats? Head north for a whole other slant on Provence.

Vallée de la Blanche

Like a little swatch of Switzerland, the Vallée de la Blanche (www.valleedelablanche.com in French) has over 110km of ski runs split between three resorts. The main one, well set up for families with amenities including a crèche, is the 1350m **St-Jean Montclar**. Its **tourist office** (☎ 04 92 30 92 01; www.montclar.com; ⏲ call for seasonal hours) is adjacent to the ski station. The area is the home of Montclar spring water, but you won't need to buy it while you're here – just turn on the tap.

Ski passes for St-Jean Montclar's slopes cost €16 to €18.50 per day. One of the sweetest *chambres d'hôtes* is **Les Alisiers** (☎ 04 92 35 30 88; fax 04 92 35 02 72; d incl breakfast €48-52, apt €53; ⏲ closed mid-Nov–mid-Dec), 800m past the

ski station on your left, with *pension* (half-board) options available and good wheelchair access.

St-Jean Montclar is 50km north of Dignes-les-Bains. Between late December and March, there's a bus service from Gap (€11, 45 minutes); the rest of the year it's best reached by your own wheels.

Vallée de l'Ubaye

At the edge of the wild, isolated **Parc National du Mercantour** (www.parc-mercantour.fr; p871), spanning 136,500 majestic hectares, the Vallée de l'Ubaye is ringed by a rollercoaster of rugged mountains. The area's main town, Barcelonnette (population 3300), has a fascinating Mexican heritage, resulting in some exceptional, very un-alpine architecture. Rising 8.5km southwest are the twin ski resorts of **Pra Loup 1500** (sometimes called Les Molanes) and **Pra Loup 1600** (which has more infrastructure and nightlife). Both are connected by a lift system with the ski resort of La Foux d'Allos. Pra Loup's 50 lifts are between 1600m and 2600m, with 180km of runs and a vertical drop of almost 1000m. In summer, it's a hiker's heaven.

The Pra Loup **tourist office** (☎ 04 92 84 10 04; www.praloup.com; ⏲ 9am-noon & 2-6pm Jul & Aug, 9am-noon & 2-6pm Mon-Fri May, Jun & Sep-Nov, 9am-7pm Dec-Apr) and **École de Ski Français** (ESF; ☎ 04 92 84 11 05) are in Pra Loup 1600. Ski passes cost €26.50 per day.

Studios and apartments start from around €190 per week, climbing to around €650 in peak ski season – the tourist office has lists. There's also a handful of hotels, like the sloped-ceiling, storybook chalet, **Hôtel Le Prieuré** (☎ 04 92 84 11 43; www.prieure -praloup.com in French, Pra Loup 1500; d €68-92 summer, €65-90 winter; ✕ ☻), just across the road from the ski lift, with a **restaurant** (mains €13-26.55) serving fondue.

The nearest train station to Pra Loup is Gap, from where buses (usually a couple a day) travel to Pra Loup (€7, 1¾ hours) with a change in Barcelonnette.

Côte d'Azur & Monaco

With its glistening seas and charming, tangled old town streets, foreigners have admired the Côte d'Azur (Azure Coast) for centuries. Known also as the French Riviera due to a string of influential sojourners, from Queen Victoria to F Scott Fitzgerald, this lustrous stretch of shoreline is still the destination *de rigueur* for today's jet set. But its flashiness is balanced by its Provençal heritage. Think of the Côte d'Azur as a glittering, glamorous (and yes, expensive) ring, adorning a warm, gracefully aging hand (Provence). Distinct yet intertwined, these two regions enhance each other's allure; with the Côte d'Azur home to colourful markets in ancient plane-shaded squares as well as *belle époque* villas and brazen new palaces.

The Côte d'Azur wraps around the sapphire-blue Mediterranean from Toulon to the Italian border. Its intense, radiant light quality inspired artists like Renoir, Picasso, Matisse and Chagall; numerous works are showcased in the areas where they lived and painted. Coastal towns like Nice, Cannes and St-Tropez sparkle with fashionable restaurants and nightlife, sun-kissed beaches and significant museums.

If the coastline is the Côte d'Azur's jewel, the infinitely less touristed hinterland – spanning Grasse's perfume-producing fields of flowers, the rugged red Massif de l'Estérel and forested Massif des Maures mountain ranges, rows of rosé-yielding vineyards, and a myriad of medieval hilltop villages – is its ornate setting.

And the Côte d'Azur encircles another separate gem, the miniature principality (and world's second-smallest country), Monaco.

HIGHLIGHTS

- Trace Matisse's artistic evolution at Nice's **Musée Matisse** (p873)
- Take a chef-run **cooking course** or **watercolour classes** (p898) in Hostellerie Berard
- Pit yourself against Monaco's high-rolling **Casino de Monte Carlo** (p911)
- Head to Hyères' beaches for prime **kite-surfing** (p899)
- Survey Fréjus' **Roman ruins** (p892)
- Catch a ferry to Cannes' **Îles de Lérins** (p885)

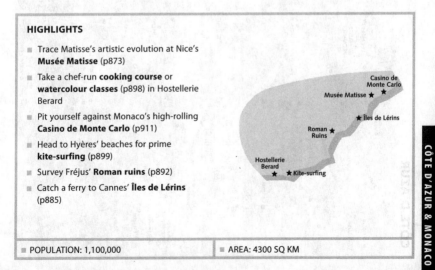

- POPULATION: 1,100,000
- AREA: 4300 SQ KM

CÔTE D'AZUR & MONACO

CÔTE D'AZUR

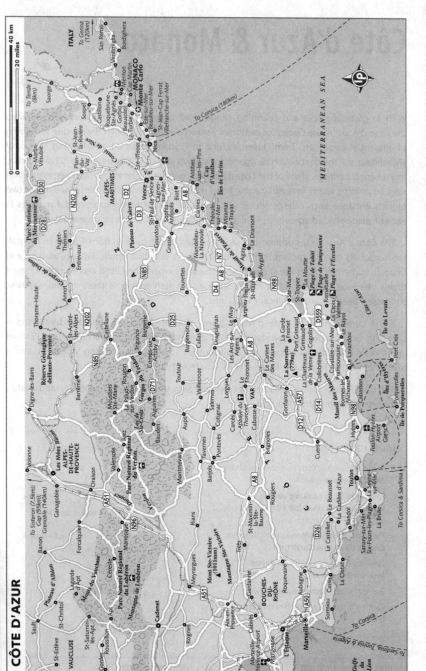

History

The eastern part of France's Mediterranean coast, including the area now known as the Côte d'Azur, was occupied by the Ligurians from the 1st millennium BC. It was colonised around 600 BC by Greeks from Asia Minor, who settled along the coast in the areas of present-day Marseille, Hyères, St-Tropez, Antibes and Nice. Called in to help Massalia against the threat of invasion by Celto-Ligurians from Entremont, the Romans triumphed in 125 BC. They created Provincia Romana – the area between the Alps, the sea and the River Rhône – which ultimately became Provence.

In 1388 Nice – along with the Haute-Provence mountain towns Barcelonette and Puget-Théniers – was incorporated into the House of Savoy, while the rest of the surrounding Provençal region became part of the French kingdom in 1482. After an agreement between Napoleon III and the House of Savoy in 1860 drove the Austrians from northern Italy, France took possession of Savoy.

Within the Provence–Alpes–Côte d'Azur *région*, the Côte d'Azur encompasses most of the *départements* of the Alpes-Maritimes and the Var. In the 19th century, wealthy French, English, American and Russian tourists flocked to the Côte d'Azur to escape cold northern winters, along with celebrated artists and writers, whose presence added to the area's cachet. Little fishing ports morphed into exclusive resorts. Paid holidays for all French workers from 1936 and improved transportation saw visitors arrive in summer, making it a holiday playground year round. But it's not all play, no work: since the late 20th century, the area inland of Antibes has been home to France's 'Silicon Valley', Sophia Antipolis, the country's largest industrial/technological hub.

Dangers & Annoyances

The Côte d'Azur isn't a dangerous area, but theft – from backpacks, pockets, bags, cars and even laundrettes – is rife. Watch your belongings, especially at train and bus stations, on overnight trains, in tourist offices, in fast-food restaurants and on the beaches (don't set your camera down next to you while you momentarily gaze at the sunset!). Keep your passport, credit cards and cash on your person, not in your bags. Always drive with the doors locked and windows up as thieves often pounce at red lights. If you're travelling by bicycle, store it off-street overnight.

Getting There & Away

The efficient SNCF train network and regular bus connections link the Côte d'Azur with Provence and the rest of France. Excellent road networks make the region easy to access by car from the rest of the country. There are international airports at Nice (the country's second busiest after Paris) and outside Toulon.

For information on ferry services from Nice and Toulon to Corsica, see p914.

Getting Around

SNCF trains shuttle back and forth along the coast between St-Raphaël and the Italian border, and north to Grasse. The coastal area between St-Raphaël and Toulon (where the train line veers inland) is served by regular buses. Boat services operate to St-Tropez in summer.

Except for the traffic-plagued high-summer season, the Côte d'Azur is easily accessible by car (and to get off the main tourist routes, you'll need one). The fastest thoroughfare is the uninspiring A8 motorway which, travelling west to east, starts near Aix-en-Provence, approaches the coast at Fréjus, skirts the Estérel range and runs more or less parallel to the coast from Cannes to the Italian border at Ventimiglia (Vintimille in French).

NICE TO TOULON

NICE

pop 345 892

It might be a cliché to say Nice has something for everyone, but the Côte d'Azur's cosmopolitan capital pretty much does.

Sure, sun seekers sip cocktails on parasoled lounges lining its polished pebbled shores, and kids splash in the azure sea, while bladers cruise the curved Baie des Anges (Bay of Angels) against a backdrop of fairy-lit palm trees flanking the promenade des Anglais.

But Nice is much more than just a place for fun in the sun. Art aficionados'

NICE

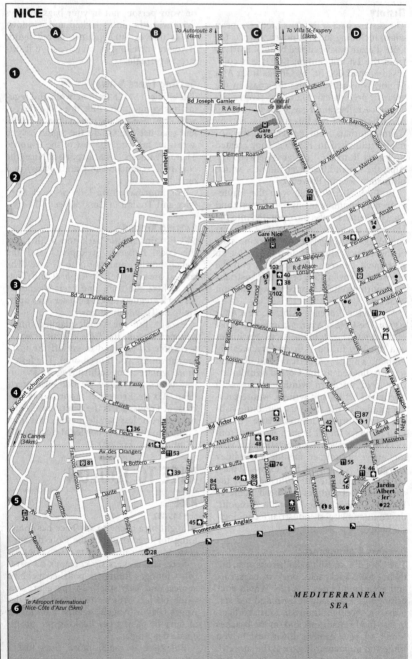

To Autoroute 8 (4km)

To Villa St-Exupery (3km)

Bd Joseph Garnier

R A Binet

Pl Général de Gaulie

Gare du Sud

R Clément Roassal

R Vernier

R Trachel

Gare Nice Ville

R de Belgique

R d'Alsace-Lorraine

Av Thiers

Av Georges Clemenceau

R de Châteauneuf

R Rossini

R Paul Déroulède

R F Passy

R Caffarelli

R Verdi

To Cannes (34km)

Av des Fleurs

Bd Victor Hugo

Av des Orangers

R du Maréchal Joffre

R Bottero

R de la Buffa

R de France

Promenade des Anglais

To Aéroport International Nice-Côte d'Azur (5km)

MEDITERRANEAN SEA

Jardin Albert Ier

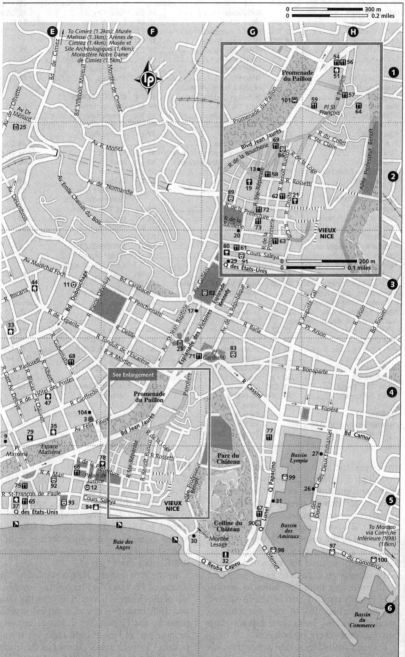

must-sees include major museums. Archaeological buffs ruminate over the ruins of the ancient Roman city of Cemenelum. Flaneurs ferret out secret passages leading to narrow pedestrian laneways in the romantic old town, lingering over the sights and scents of the colourful flower and produce markets, and trawling for antiques. Festival fans descend for animated events. Gastronomes go gaga over finely prepared food, from chic little bolt holes to family-style French cooking and Michelin-starred cuisine. Barflies flit to the perpetually-buzzing watering holes, and hipsters hop between ever-emerging hotspots.

France's fifth-largest city is naughty, it's nice…and it's everything in between.

History

Nice was founded around 350 BC by the Greek seafarers who had settled Marseille. They named the colony Nikaia, apparently to commemorate a nearby victory (*nike* in Greek). In 154 BC the Greeks were followed by the Romans, who settled further uphill around what is now Cimiez, where there are still Roman ruins (p874).

By the 10th century, Nice was ruled by the counts of Provence but turned to Amadeus VII of the House of Savoy in 1388. In the 18th and 19th centuries it was occupied several times by the French, but didn't definitively become part of France until 1860, when Napoleon III struck a deal (known as the treaty of Turin) with the House of Savoy.

CÔTE D'AZUR & MONACO

During the Victorian period the English aristocracy and European royalty enjoyed Nice's mild winter climate. Its relatively recent status as a French city, combined with its long-standing tradition of international visitors, gives Nice something of an Italian flair and an open, welcoming attitude towards travellers. Today it's the second-most visited city in France after Paris.

Orientation

Av Jean Médecin runs south from near the Gare Nice Ville (the main train station) to place Masséna. The modern city centre, the area north and west of place Masséna, includes the pedestrianised shopping streets rue de France and rue Masséna. The bus station is located three blocks east of place Masséna.

Promenade des Anglais follows the gently arced beachfront from the city centre to the airport, 6km west. Vieux Nice (old Nice) is delineated by blvd Jean Jaurès, quai des États-Unis and, east, the hill known as Colline du Château.

The wealthy residential neighbourhood of Cimiez, home to outstanding museums, is just north of the city centre.

Information

BOOKSHOPS

Cat's Whiskers (☎ /fax 04 93 80 02 66; 26 rue Lamartine; ☒ closed all Sun, Mon morning & lunchtime) New and second-hand guides and English-language novels.
Magellan Librairie de Voyages (☎ 04 93 82 31 81; 3 rue d'Italie) Stellar selection of maps and travel guides, including Lonely Planet titles in English.
Maison de la Presse (place Masséna; ☒ to 7.30pm Oct-Jun, to midnight Jul-Sep) Maps and guides, plus books and magazines in English.

EMERGENCY

Police (☎ 04 92 17 22 22, Foreign Tourist Department 04 92 17 20 63; 1 av Maréchal Foch)

INTERNET ACCESS

New internet cafés open in Nice seemingly every week (there are around 10 on rue Pertinax alone); you'll have no problems staying connected.
Cyberpoint (☎ 04 93 92 70 63; 10 av Félix Faure; per hr €4; ☒ 10am-10pm Mon-Sat, 3-9pm Sun) Organised internet café with English keyboards.

INTERNET RESOURCES

Nice Tourism (www.nicetourism.com) Comprehensive info about the capital.
Riviera Guide (www.guideriviera.com) Covers the eastern Côte d'Azur.
Var Destination (www.vardestination.com) Info on the Côte d'Azur's western Var region.
PACA (www.crt-paca.fr) Umbrella site for all of Provence and the Côte d'Azur.

LAUNDRY

Self-service laundrettes are plentiful, especially around Gare Nice Ville. Expect to pay about €3.50 for a small load of around 5kg.
Laundrette (rue de la Buffa; ☒ 7am-9pm)
Taxi Lav (22 rue Pertinax & 13 rue du Pont Vieux; ☒ 7am-9pm)

MONEY

Barclays Bank (2 rue Alphonse Karr) Has a change counter.
Le Change (☎ 04 93 88 56 80; 17 av Thiers; ☒ 7.30am-8pm) Opposite the Gare Nice Ville, to the right as you exit the terminal building. It has decent rates.

POST

Main Post Office (23 av Thiers)
Post Office (2 rue Louis Gassin) In Vieux Nice.

TOURIST INFORMATION

Airport Tourist Information Desk (☎ 0 892 707 407; ☒ 8am-9pm daily high season, closed Sun low season) In Terminal 1.
Main Tourist Office (☎ 0 892 707 407; 5 promenade des Anglais; ☒ 8am-8pm Mon-Sat, 9am-7pm Sun Jun-Sep; 9am-6pm Mon-Sat Oct-May) Right by the beach.
Parc National du Mercantour headquarters (☎ 04 93 16 78 88; www.parc-mercantour.fr; 23 rue d'Italie; ☒ hours vary) Stocks numerous guides including the free Les Guides Randoxygène series, which details 25 canyoning routes, 40 mountain-biking (VTT) trails and hiking trails in the park. See p864 for more park information.

CULTURE CARTE

The **Carte Musées Côte d'Azur** pass is good for admission to some 62 Côte d'Azur museums. Available from tourist offices and participating museums, it makes for great savings at €10/17/27 for one/three/seven days. If you're only visiting Nice, ask about the **Carte Musées Ville de Nice** (€6 for seven days, €18.30 for 15 visits), which allows entry into all of Nice's museums except the Chagall.

NICE IN...

Two Days

Kick-start the day with a *café* and croissant from **Chez Maître Pierre** (p879) before an invigorating run or rollerblade along **promenade des Anglais** (p874). Browse the fragrant flower and produce **markets** (p880) for picnic supplies to take up to the **Parc du Château** (below), or pop into **Cave de la Tour** (p878) to see what's on the menu. Amble the little alleys of **Vieux Nice** (below), then laze the afternoon away on the beach, or sail the Baie des Anges on a **catamaran** (p874). After an aperitif at **La Banane** (p878) and dinner at the lovely little **La Table Alziari** (p877), set off on a quest to find your favourite old town **bar** or **pub** (p879). The following day, trace Matisse's artistic evolution at the **Musée Matisse** (opposite), muse over the **Musée Marc Chagall** (opposite), and get a dose of pop culture at **Marmac** (below), before catching dinner and a cabaret at **Le Bar des Oiseaux** (p879).

Four Days

Traverse the twisting cliff-side **corniches** (p902) to the medieval village of **Èze** (p903), taking time out in its rocky cacti and sculpture garden. Continue east to the pint-sized principality of **Monaco** (p906) for a punt at the **Casino de Monte Carlo** (p911) and a peek at the **Palais du Prince** (Prince's Palace; p909). On the fourth day, go inland to **Grasse** (p891) to tour its **perfumeries** (p891) and, in season, its **flower-filled fields** (p891), or venture west to tackle one of the hundred-odd hiking trails crisscrossing the jagged red crags of the **Massif de l'Estérel** (p892).

Train Station Tourist Office (☎ 0 892 353 535; av Thiers; ☒ 8am-8pm Mon-Sat, 9am-7pm Sun Jun-Sep; 8am-7pm Mon-Sat, 9am-6pm Sun Oct-May) Next to the Gare Nice Ville.

Sights

VIEUX NICE

Abandon your map and lose yourself in the old town's tangle of tiny 18th-century pedestrian passages and laneways. The area between quai des États-Unis and the Musée d'Art Moderne et d'Art Contemporain conceals a trove of Aladdin's cave–like specialised shops and café-clad squares. On the seaward side, cours Saleya is the venue for one of the most vibrant, vividly-hued local markets (p880) in the south of France.

Jutting above the rooflines are the spires of some historic churches including the baroque **Cathédrale Ste-Réparate** (place Rossetti), built around 1650; the blue–grey and yellow **Église du Gésu St-Jacques le Majeur** (place du Gésu), close to rue Rossetti, whose baroque ornamentation also dates from the mid-17th century; and the mid-18th-century **Chapelle de la Miséricorde**, next to place Pierre Gautier.

Rue Benoît Bunico, which runs perpendicular to rue Rossetti, was Nice's Jewish quarter when a 1430 law subjugated Jews' habitation rights and forced them to live here, imprisoned behind gates that were locked at each end at sunset.

PARC DU CHÂTEAU

Zigzag up the scenic steps or zip up the lift for glittering city- and seascapes from this 92m hilltop park presiding over Nice at the eastern end of quai des États-Unis.

With a gushing artificial waterfall tempering hot summer days, this shaded hill and park are named after a 12th-century château, which was razed by Louis XIV in 1706 and never rebuilt. To reach it you can walk up montée Lesage or climb the steps at the eastern end of rue Rossetti, or take the **ascenseur** (lift; €0.70; ☒ 10am-5.30pm Oct-Mar, 9am-7pm Apr, May & Sep, 9am-8pm Jun-Aug) under Tour Bellanda.

MUSÉE D'ART MODERNE ET D'ART CONTEMPORAIN (MARMAC)

Designed by Yves Bayard and Henri Vidal, **Marmac** (Museum of Modern & Contemporary Art; ☎ 04 93 62 61 62; www.mamac-nice.org; av St-Jean Baptiste; adult/student €4/2.50; ☒ 10am-6pm) is worth a visit for its stunning architecture alone, but it also houses some fantastic avant-garde art from the 1960s to the present, including iconic pop art from Roy Lichtenstein, and Andy Warhol's 1965 *Campbell's Soup Can*. The marbled towers' glass walkways lead to highlights like Niki de St-Phalle's papier-mâché sculptures and a shopping trolley wrapped by Christo. An awesome panorama of Vieux Nice unfolds from the rooftop garden/gallery, which features works by Nice-born Yves Klein (1928–62).

Next door is Nice's library, **Bibliothèque Louis Nucéra** (☎ 04 97 13 48 00; 2 place Yves Klein; ✆ 1-6pm Tue-Sat Jul & Aug; 10am-7pm Tue & Wed, 2-7pm Thu & Fri, 10am-6pm Sat Sep-Jun), with cubical admin offices above its underground reading rooms.

MUSÉE NATIONAL MESSAGE BIBLIQUE MARC CHAGALL

This freshly renovated **museum** (Marc Chagall Biblical Message Museum; ☎ 04 93 53 87 20; 4 av Docteur Ménard; permanent collection adult/student €5.50/4, temporary exhibitions additional €1.20; ✆ 10am-6pm Wed-Mon Jul-Sep, 10am-5pm Oct-Jun), northeast of the train station, reopened in spring 2006. It houses the largest public collection of the Russian-born artist's seminal paintings of *Old Testament* scenes. Be sure to peek through a plate-glass window across a reflecting pond to view a mosaic of the rose window at Metz Cathedral. Take bus No 15 from place Masséna to the front of the museum or walk. Chagall (1887–1985) is buried in St-Paul de Vence (p883). Bus travel between the Chagall museum and the Matisse and Archaeology museums is free – ask at the museums' ticket desks.

MUSÉE MATISSE

Heading northeast from the Chagall museum (about 2.5km from the city centre) brings you to the **Musée Matisse** (☎ 04 93 81 08 08; www.musee-matisse-nice.org; 164 av des Arènes de Cimiez; adult/student €4/2.50; ✆ 10am-6pm Wed-Mon). Housed in a *trompe l'oeil* 17th-century Genoese mansion, the depth and range of the diverse exhibits spanning Matisse's career let you follow his artistic evolution. In addition to well-known pieces in the permanent collection, like his blue paper cut-outs *Blue Nude IV* and *Woman with Amphora,* are his works using a host of media, including cloth, paper, oils, pen and ink, and sculptures, particularly of the human form. Temporary exhibits focus on specific œuvres.

MAGICAL MATISSE TOUR

If you're mad about Matisse, you can cherry-pick a Côte d'Azur itinerary that takes in the regions where he created, drawing inspiration from what he described as the 'radiant colours and luminosity of the daylight'.

Born on New Year's Eve in 1869, Henri Matisse arrived from Paris in Nice in 1917 to recover from bronchitis, and remained here until his death in 1954 at his home and studio in the mansion-lined suburb, Cimiez.

Checking into the **Hôtel Beau Rivage** (p876), he went on to rent a flat on quai des États-Unis, then moved to what is now the **Palais de la Mediterranée** (p877), where he also exhibited. Many of the works he painted in Nice are housed in the city's **Musée Matisse** (above).

Matisse's visits to **Renoir's villa** (p884) in Cagnes-sur-Mer provided further inspiration for paintings including *Oliviers, Jardin de Renoir à Cagnes* (Olive trees, Renoir's garden in Cagnes, 1917).

During WWII, Matisse rented **Villa Le Rêve** in Vence, where he was visited by Picasso and Aragon, among others. (If your own creative streak is unleashed, you can take **painting classes** at the villa, with seven nights' accommodation, from March to November from around €650; call ☎ 04 93 58 82 68, visit www.mclean.dk, or email villalereve@wanadoo.fr for info.) While living here, Matisse's friendship with his former model-turned-Dominican Sister Jacques Marie saw him design his masterwork, the nearby **Chapelle du Rosaire** (Rosary Chapel; ☎ 04 93 58 03 26; 468 av Henri Matisse Vence; admission €2.50; ✆ 2-5.30pm Mon, Wed & Sat, 10-11.30am & 2-5.30pm Tue & Thu, closed mid-Nov–mid-Dec), completed in 1951. Midmorning is the prime time to see sunlight streaming through the vast stained-glass windows. See p884 for directions. Matisse's artistic blueprints for the chapel, including 42 drawings, 21 paper cuttings, two stained-glass windows, two ceramic pieces and a sculpture, are on display in the Musée Matisse.

Matisse is buried at the **Monastère Notre Dame de Cimiez** (Cimiez Notre Dame Monastery; ☎ 04 93 81 00 04; ✆ 8.30am-12.30pm & 2.30-6.30pm), near the Musée Matisse; signs lead to his grave.

Tourist offices throughout the Côte d'Azur have an info-packed brochure (available in English) about retracing Matisse's footsteps.

CÔTE D'AZUR & MONACO

Take buses 15, 17, 20, 22 or 25 from Gare Routière to the Arènes stop. For other Matisse highlights in the Côte d'Azur, see p873.

MUSÉE ET SITE ARCHÉOLOGIQUES

Nice's little-spoken but lingering language, Nissart, derives most of its vocab from the Roman city of Cemenelum, founded by Augustus in 14 BC. Its ruins lie behind the Musée Matisse, on the eastern side of the Parc des Arènes, and are the focus of the **Musée et Site Archéologiques** (Archaeology Museum & Site; ☎ 04 93 81 59 57; 160 av des Arènes de Cimiez; adult/student €4/2.50; ☯ 10am-noon & 2-6pm Wed-Mon Apr-Sep, 10am-1pm & 2-5pm Wed-Mon Oct-Mar), where you can visit the public baths, amphitheatre and original paved streets, and view relics like ceramics, glass, coins and tools.

From Museé Matisse, turn left out of the main park entrance on av des Arènes de Cimiez, walk 100m, then turn left again onto av Monte Croce.

CATHÉDRALE ORTHODOXE RUSSE ST-NICOLAS

Crowned by six onion domes, the multicoloured **Cathédrale Orthodoxe Russe St-Nicolas** (Russian Orthodox Cathedral of St-Nicolas; ☎ 04 93 96 88 02; av Nicolas II; ☯ 9am-noon & 2.30-6pm, closed Sun morning), was built between 1902 and 1912 in early-17th-century style, and is the largest outside Russia. It's an easy 15-minute walk from Gare Nice Ville; shorts, miniskirts and sleeveless shirts are forbidden.

MUSÉE DES BEAUX-ARTS

In a resplendent 1878 *belle époque* villa, the **Musée des Beaux-Arts** (Fine Arts Museum; ☎ 04 92 15 28 28; 33 av des Baumettes; adult/student €4/2.50; ☯ 10am-noon & 2-6pm Tue-Sun) displays works by Boudin, Dufy, Fragonard, Sisley and Rodin.

Activities

For information on the region's **walking** and **mountain-biking** trails, visit the headquarters of Parc National du Mercantour (see p871).

CITY WALKING

Established by English expats in 1822, wide, palm-lined **promenade des Anglais** (English promenade) is a timelessly elegant place for a beachfront stroll.

Continuing east along **quai des États-Unis** (named for the 1917 decision by President Wilson for the USA to enter WWI) to the end brings you to a colossal **WWI memorial** carved in the rock, commemorating the 4000 people from Nice who died during the war.

Behind the quay is the ultimate flaneur's fantasy, Vieux Nice (p872).

Other pleasant spots are **Jardin Albert 1er**, laid out in the late 19th century; **Espace Masséna**, a public square enlivened by fountains; **place Masséna**, with early-19th-century, neoclassical arcaded buildings in shades of ochre and red; **av Jean Médecin**, Nice's main commercial street; and **Cimiez**, the most exclusive quarter in Nice, just north of the city.

INLINE SKATING

Smooth and flat, with great views to boot, promenade des Anglais is a perfect place to skate. **Roller Station** (☎ 04 93 62 99 05; 49 quai des États-Unis) rents skates and kneepads for €7 a day and bikes for €15 a day. Some ID's required as a deposit.

BEACHES & WATER SPORTS

Made up of round pebbles, you'll need at least a beach mat to cushion your tush from Nice's **beaches**. Free sections of beach alternate with 15 sun lounge–lined **plages concédées** (private beaches; ☯ late Apr or early May–15 Sep), for which you have to pay by renting a chair (around €11 a day) or mattress (around €9).

On the beach, operators hire catamarans, paddleboats, sailboards and jet skis; you can also parascend, water-ski, or paraglide.

There are outdoor showers on every beach, and indoor showers and toilets opposite 50 promenade des Anglais.

Dive companies **PH+ Plongée** (☎ 04 93 26 09 03; 3 quai des Deux Emmanuel) and **Nice Diving** (☎ 04 93 89 42 44; www.nicediving.com; 14 quai des Docks) offer courses, organise diving expeditions and rent gear. An introductory dive costs around €33 with equipment.

Tours

The tourist office–run **guided walking tours** (tour €12; ☯ 9.30am Sat May-Oct) of Vieux Nice in English depart from the main office on the promenade des Anglais.

With headphone commentary in several languages, the open-topped **Le Grand Tour** (☎ 04 92 29 17 00; adult/student/child €17/14/9) buses give you a good overview of Nice. Tours (1½hr) depart from the Jardin Albert 1er on the promenade des Anglais.

Trans Côte d'Azur (☎ 04 92 00 42 30; www.trans -cote-azur.com; quai Lunel) runs cruises in summer to the Îles de Lérins (adult/child €25/17; p885), and transfers to St-Tropez (adult/child €45/27) and Monaco (adult/child €20/15).

To tour the coast in style, take a DIY daytrip in a classic convertible. **Le Road-Show** (☎ 04 92 04 01 05; www.azur-roadshow.com) offers packages for two people including car rental, lunch at a gourmet restaurant en-route and a detailed driving itinerary plus fuel and insurance for €390.

Festivals & Events

Carnaval de Nice (www.nicecarnaval.com) Festival fans descend for February's Carnaval de Nice, especially its battles of the flowers, where thousands of blooms are tossed into the crowds from passing parade floats, as well as its fantastic fireworks display.

Nice Jazz Festival (www.nicejazzfest.com) In July, Nice swings to the week-long jazz festival at the Arènes de Cimiez, amid the Roman ruins. Music starts around 7pm, with up to 15 bands throughout the park each night.

Les Nuits Musicales de Nice Moonlight classical-music concerts are held over three weeks in late July/early August – contact the tourist office for venues and performance dates.

Sleeping

Nice has a suite of places to sleep, from stellar independent backpacker hostels to international art-filled icons. Onsite parking's often limited – reserve ahead, or ask about nearby public parking, which is plentiful. Prices jump during summer and also for festivals such as February's Carnaval de Nice. Prices listed here span seasonal variations.

BUDGET
Hostels

ourpick Villa Saint-Exupéry (☎ 04 93 84 42 83; www.vsaint.com; 22 av Gravier; dm €18-22, s/d €30/52 incl breakfast; ✗ ▣ 및) In a lovely former monastery, this fabled independent hostel is fit for St-Exupéry's little prince, and absolutely worth the few kilometres' trek north from the city centre. As well as a dozen free on-line computers, wi-fi and a king-size 12-cereal breakfast, this palatial 240-bed place has terrazzo-tiled, mostly ensuite dorms and private rooms, a slate-and-steel self-

catering kitchen, wrap-around barbecue terrace, and a 24-hour common room/night-time bar within the stained-glass chapel. Upper-level rooms have magical views across Nice to the Med. Take bus No 1, direction St-Sylvestre along av Jean Médecin to the Gravier stop, then call from the phone boxes and they can usually pick you up (otherwise follow a series of steps).

Auberge de Jeunesse – Les Camèllias (☎ 04 93 62 15 54; www.fuaj.org; 3 rue Spitalieri; dm €20 incl breakfast, sheets €2.70; ✗ 및) Flash backpacking. The 4- to 8-bed dorms (136 beds all-up) have space-age metallic bunks and in-room showers, and there's a self-catering kitchen. A funky citrus-coloured bar stays open to 11pm, and there's good wheelchair access and no curfew, though there is a lock-out from 11am to 3pm.

Backpackers Chez Patrick (☎ 04 93 80 30 72; www.chezpatrick.com; 32 rue Pertinax; dm/d €21/45; ✗) Ultrahandy for the station, you'll find this friendly 24-bed independent hostel inconspicuously situated on the first floor above a restaurant (look for Chez Patrick's doorbell on the street below). Chill out in the air-conditioned, French-washed tiled common room, or in the high-ceilinged rooms, which have stacks of space, hand basins, brand new beds and double-glazed windows.

Budget hotels that also have dorm beds available:

Hôtel Belle Meunière (☎ 04 93 88 66 15; 21 av Durante; dm €17-22, d €36-55) Near the train station with posh, panelled rooms, an iron-lace balcony and (limited) free parking.

Hôtel/Hostel Meyerbeer Beach (☎ 04 93 88 95 65; www.hotel-meyerbeer-beach-nice.cote.azur.fr; 15 rue Meyerbeer; dm €15-35, d €72; 및) Kitchenette-equipped rooms near the sea with free internet, cookies and cordial.

Hôtel Paradis (☎ 04 93 87 71 23; www.paradishotel. com; 1 rue Paradis; dm €25-30, d €90; ✗) Boutique-style budget hotel and dorms 60m from the beach.

Hotels

Hôtel Wilson (☎ 04 93 85 47 79; www.hotel-wilson -nice.com; 39 rue de l'Hôtel des Postes; s/d/tr €45/50/60.50, without bathroom €27/33-50/43.50) Owner and multilingual *bon vivant* Jean-Marie Martinez lives in this rambling old apartment building, and willingly shares his convivial dining table, books and classical music with his guests. Some of the 16 rooms, like the sky-blue Matisse room, have small balconies. It's a hike up three flights, but it's worth it.

Hôtel de la Buffa (☎ 04 93 88 77 35; www .hotel-buffa.com; 56 rue de la Buffa; d €48-73; 🔀 💻) Up a spiral staircase in a character-filled building, old-fashioned corridors with ornate cornices and baskets of dried and silk flowers open to 13 bright, airy, sun-washed rooms with lofty ceilings, oval-shaped windows and angular bathrooms.

MIDRANGE

Villa la Tour (☎ 04 93 80 08 15; www.villa-la-tour.com; 4 rue de la Tour; s €45-127, d €48-135; 🔀) This intimate B&B-style hotel in Nice's old town has organza curtains framing rustic rooms with fragrant Fragonard Perfumery soaps and quirky details like bedside lamps designed like chic little paper shopping bags. Have breakfast (€7) at a long candlelit communal table, and listen to birdsong from the petite rooftop patio.

Hôtel Armenonville (☎ 04 93 96 86 00; www .hotel-armenonville.com; 20 av des Fleurs; d €49-96; 💻) Graced by grand Grecian-style columns, this dove-white, triple-decker 1905-built pavilion is secluded in gardens filled with citrus trees. A marble staircase leads to rooms in romantic hues like rose and olive.

Hôtel Acanthe (☎ 04 93 62 22 44; www.hotel -acanthe-nice.cote.azur.fr; 2 rue Chauvain; d €57-61) Facing the fountained Albert 1er gardens, this place is perfectly positioned for the beach and old town. Behind its peach-coloured curved corner facade, the pick are the four 'round' rooms, which have semi-circular balconies. Some bathrooms are tiny but bright and clean. Free wi-fi.

Hôtel Lépante (☎ 04 93 62 20 55; www.hotel lepante.com; 6 rue de Lépante; s €59-99, d €59-109; 🔀) Renovated in a palette of French-washed colours, this homey, unpretentious hotel in the city's heart is housed in a landmark 1915 *belle époque* building, with free wi-fi. Two rooms have pretty balconies just big enough for a tiny table and chairs.

Hôtel Windsor (☎ 04 93 88 59 35; www.hotelwind sornice.com; 11 rue Dalpozzo; d €80-165; 🔀 💻 🌊) Half of this boutique hotel's rooms feature Impressionist murals, and the other half are the wonderful, often whacky work of experimental contemporary artists, in a wild mix of styles. Art apart, there's also an exotic private garden with a birdcage, a zen fitness room, hammam and meditation area.

Hôtel Les Cigales (☎ 04 97 03 10 70; www.hotel -lescigales.com; 16 rue Dalpozzo; s €70-130, d €80-140, 🔀) 'The Cicadas' is a bright, chirpy boutique establishment just a couple of minutes' walk from the promenade des Anglais and the beach, with red and gold brocade rooms, good wheelchair access and a sundeck.

Villa Victoria (☎ 04 93 88 39 60; www.villa-victoria .com; 33 blvd Victor Hugo; s €75-155, d €90-170; 🔀 💻) How many inner-city hotels can boast their own botanic garden (complete with a fairy-lit gazebo overlooked by a marble breakfast room flanked by five sets of French doors)? All of the Provençal-decorated rooms here have wi-fi.

Hôtel Excelsior (☎ 04 93 88 38 69; www.excelsior nice.com; 19 av Durante; s €80-95, d €95-125; 🔀) Looking as if it belongs on a tree-lined Parisian boulevard, this handsome 1892-built hotel with good wheelchair access and wrought-iron balconies is so close to the train station. A couple of courtyard rooms incorporate kitchenettes.

Hôtel La Petite Sirène (☎ 04 97 03 03 40; www .sirene-fr.com; 8 rue Maccarani; s €72-86, d €107-117, apt €147-176; 🔀) Fresh, frescoed rooms at 'the Little Mermaid' have stylin' extras like opaque glass basins and heavy, professional chrome hairdryers, and there's good wheelchair access and a sun lounge–lined terrace (albeit with rather unfortunate fake grass).

TOP END

Hôtel Beau Rivage (☎ 04 92 47 82 82; www.nice beaurivage.com; 24 rue St-François de Paule; d €145-385; 🔀 💻) Matisse and Chekhov both stayed at the 1860-built Beau Rivage in its *belle époque* heyday, but they wouldn't recognise the place after its new millennium strip and refit. Wheelchair access is good and Nice's pebbled beaches cue urban architect/ interior designer Jean-Michel Wilmotte's cool minimalist décor, including real pebbles decoupaged beneath some bathroom floors (and yep, there's a private beach).

Hôtel Hi (☎ 04 97 07 26 26; www.hi-hotel.net; 3 av des Fleurs; s from €165, d €185-395; 🔀 💻 🌊) Imagine you're invited to stay with ultra-connected, urbanite friends in their techno-funky, futuristic pad designed in part by Philippe Starck, with a panoramic rooftop splash pool and in-room surround-sound stereos programmed by DJ Laurent Garnier. The party vibe here means, you are (for a price!).

Palais de la Mediterranée (☎ 04 92 14 77 00; www.lepalaisdelamediterranee.com; 13 promenade des Anglais; d €280-780; 🚫 🖳 🏊) This brand new, opulent edifice is spectacularly recessed behind the massive pillars of its majestic 1929 Art Deco facade; with a mosaic indoor/outdoor swimming pool, good wheelchair access and private beach.

Hôtel Negresco (☎ 04 93 16 64 00; www.hotel-negresco-nice.com; 37 promenade des Anglais; r €250-525; 🚫 🖳) Built in 1912 and now a protected historical site, the pink-domed Negresco houses priceless art and architecture (like, for instance, one of only three Hyacinthe Rigaud Louis XIV portraits – the others are in the Louvre and Versailles – and the Gustave Eiffel–designed stained-glass Salon Royale, bearing a one-tonne Baccarat crystal chandelier). Two hundred and fifty staff await, and there's a private beach.

Eating

Niçois nibbles include *socca* (a thin layer of chickpea flour and olive oil batter fried on a large griddle, served with pepper), salade niçoise, ratatouille and *farcis* (stuffed vegetables, each with a unique filling).

Generally, you'll find the most authentic and atmospheric restaurants in the back streets of Vieux Nice.

RESTAURANTS
Budget

Chez René Socca (☎ 04 93 92 05 73; 2 rue Miralhéti; dishes from €2; 🕑 9am-9pm Tue-Sun, to 10.30pm Jul & Aug, closed Nov) The cheapest fare in town and it's good. Split into two sides (order food on one and drinks on the other), this is a great, casual place for tapas-style bites like spiced fish cakes, washed down with local wine.

Lou Pilha Leva (place Centrale; dishes from €3; 🕑 11am-10pm) Seated at outdoor wooden tables under an awning, this down-to-earth place is a good bet for vegetarians. Try the *soupe au pistou* (soup of vegetables, noodles, beans, basil and garlic). Order at the counter and carry your meal to your table where you order drinks from a waiter.

Nissa Socca (☎ 04 93 80 18 35; 5 rue Ste-Réparate; menus €13, dishes from €6; 🕑 lunch & dinner, closed Sun & lunch Mon) Locals love this inexpensive *socca* joint in Nice's ambient old town, making it a prime bet for visitors to taste-test authentic Niçois cuisine.

Pasta Basta (☎ 04 93 80 03 57; 18 rue de la Préfecture; mains €6.80-9.50; 🕑 noon-2pm & 7-11pm) Nice's proximity to the border means you can count on Italian restaurants here to be *bellissimo*. This inexpensive old-town place dishes up authentic pasta and primo pizzas on stylish plates. There's a canopied front terrace, intimate main room, and upstairs dining room that attracts lively groups.

Midrange

our pick La Table Alziari (☎ 04 93 80 34 03, 4 rue François Zanin, mains €8-14, 🕑 noon-2pm & 7.30-10pm Tue-Sat) It takes some serious wending through Vieux Nice's labyrinth of twisting, turning laneways to happen upon the pretty-as-a-picture La Table Alziari, but once you do, it appears like something out of an Impressionist painting. Framed by a tiny front terrace, this traditional Provençal place opens to lime- and lemon-painted dining rooms. There's no menu, just a blackboard chalking up the day's selection of seasonal dishes, such as wonderful vege terrines, accompanied by the pick of locally-grown wines.

Le Nautique (☎ 04 93 26 77 79; 20 quai Lunel; mains €9.50-35; 🕑 lunch & dinner) Decked out in gleaming polished timber like a grand old yacht sailing its way around the Med, this vast place appears to merge with the boat-filled port directly in front. Over four separate dining rooms, the order of the day is, appropriately enough, seafood, with a selection of salads (such as octopus salad with local olive oil), pastas (tagliatelle with seafood, or perhaps spaghetti tossed with scampi and parsley), and premium *plats* like grilled giant tiger prawns. Vegetable and meat dishes feature.

L'Adresse (☎ 04 93 80 15 66; 27 rue Benoit Bunico; mains €10-21; 🕑 7pm-midnight Thu-Tue) Tucked away on an itty bitty Vieux Nice laneway but well worth looking up, L'Adresse dishes up an array of globe-trotting specialities, from tapas to fondue, in low-lit, cosy surrounds.

Texas City (☎ 04 93 16 25 75; 10 rue Dalpozzo; mains €11-24; 🕑 noon-2pm & 7-11pm, closed lunch Sun) You'll find excellent enchiladas and gourmet guacamole at this adobe-walled place adorned with authentic Americana including quirky curios like an 1844 framed certificate for the Ladies Fort Hill Total Abstinence Society (from alcohol that is; but don't let it put you off your margarita). It mainly caters to a local clientele, hence portions aren't Texan-sized.

Escalinada (☎ 04 93 62 11 71; 22 rue Pairolière; mains €12-20; ⊗ lunch & dinner) Dine on the candlelit terrace with a decent bottle of wine and good, unpretentious fare such as *daube* (stew) and (if you're game) the house speciality, *testicules de mouton panés* (battered sheep's testicles).

Zucca Magica (☎ 04 93 56 25 27; 4bis quai Papacino; lunch/dinner menus €18/22; ⊗ lunch & dinner Tue-Sat) The Italian-vegetarian 'magic pumpkin' is packed with regulars – along with a profusion of pumpkins and squash. Book ahead, and bring an appetite: lunch comprises four set dishes plus dessert (five for dinner), depending on what chef Marco Folicaldi finds at the markets.

Le Merenda (4 rue de la Terrasse; starters from €9, mains €12-20; ⊗ lunch & dinner Mon-Fri) Infamous for having no phone, no credit cards, and (obviously) no phone reservations (but beloved nonetheless), you'll need to try for a reservation in person for Le Merenda's regional comfort food such as stockfish, a local speciality soaked for days in running water to triple its size, then simmered with onions, tomatoes, garlic, black and green olives, bell peppers, olive oil and potatoes.

Les Epicureans (☎ 04 93 80 85 00; 6 place Wilson; mains €18-45.50; ⊗ lunch & dinner Mon-Fri, dinner Sat) If you don't have time to visit the glamorous, pint-sized principality of Monaco, 18km east of Nice, this wood-and-white-tableclothed place overlooking a pretty fountained square brings Monégasque cuisine to you. What's more, it's so expertly prepared that Monaco's monarch, Prince Albert, comes to dine here (look for the photo of him next to the bar). House specialities include *barbajuans* (tiny fried ravioli with gaspacho sauce) and *cocottes* (cast-iron casserole dishes). French fare includes foie gras with grape compote.

Top End

Le Comptoir (☎ 04 93 92 08 80; 20 rue St-François de Paule; menus €30; ⊗ lunch & dinner, closed Sat & lunch Sun) These trendy Art Deco digs near the seaside serve smart Italian and French fare and people-watching opportunities in equal measure.

Terres de Truffes (☎ 04 93 62 07 68; 11 rue St-François de Paul; mains €29-42; ⊗ lunch & dinner) At

this small, exquisite place, head chef Arnaud Leclercq creates seasonal sensations using Provençal truffles ranging from pastry-wrapped pigeon stuffed with foie gras and truffles to brie layered with truffles, to truffle ice cream topped with caramel of truffles.

Chantecler (☎ 04 93 16 64 00; 37 promenade des Anglais; mains €30-70; ⊗ lunch & dinner Wed-Sun Feb-Dec) Up there in the fame stakes, along with the historic hotel in which it's housed, is the Negresco's crimson-coloured, Michelin-starred restaurant, where Bruno Turbot's classical cuisine might include oscietre caviar on egg-white mousse, followed by Rossini beef on truffle brioche.

CAFÉS

Fenocchio (☎ 04 93 80 72 52; 2 place Rossetti; ice cream from €2; ⊗ 9am-midnight Feb-Oct) The best place to beat Nice's heat is this *glacier* serving ice cream and sorbet made on the premises in scores of unique flavours like lavender and thyme.

La Banane (☎ 06 03 18 61 40; 6 rue de la Poissonnerie; dishes €3.50-9; ⊗ 9am-9pm Mon, Wed & Thu, 9am-midnight Fri-Sun) This hidden little bolt hole in the old town is a chic spot for a drink or a Grand Marnier–flambéed *crêpe* or *croque banane* (grilled banana sandwich that is much more elegant than it sounds).

Cave de la Tour (☎ 04 93 80 03 31; 3 rue de la Tour; mains around €7.50; ⊗ 7am-7pm Tue-Sat, 7am-noon Sun) An utterly untouristy old-town treasure that combines a wonderful wine shop and a café/bar serving just one main dish a day, prepared from ingredients sourced at the nearby markets.

Scotch Tea House (☎ 04 93 87 75 62; 4 av de Suède; breakfast & brunch €12-15, mains €10-18.50; ⊗ 9am-8pm Mon-Sat) On a swank shopping street near the promenade des Anglais, this classic, timber-lined place has elegant homemade cake- and *tarte*-type treats.

La Rotonde (☎ 04 93 16 64 00; 37 promenade des Anglais; mains €15-43, ⊗ 7am-11.30pm) At this delightful carousel-designed bistro, dine on delicate fare at fairy floss–coloured circular booths as painted horses on golden poles mechanically glide up and down around you.

SELF-CATERING

Pack the ultimate picnic hamper from cours Saleya's **fruit & vegetable market** (p880), and pick up fresh-caught fish from the **fish market** (place St-François; ⊙ 6am-1pm Tue-Sun).

Crisp, flaky croissants and freshly cut sandwiches can be taken away from the boulangerie-patisserie **Chez Maître Pierre** (☎ 04 93 87 77 95; 41 rue Masséna; dishes €2.50-3.80; ⊙ 7am-8pm Mon-Sat), which also has pavement seating.

Supermarkets and mini-markets abound around town.

Casino (27 blvd Gambetta; ⊙ 8.30am-8pm Mon-Sat) On the western side of the city.

Monoprix av Jean Médecin (33 av Jean Médecin; ⊙ 8.30am-8.30pm Mon-Sat); place Garibaldi (place Garibaldi; ⊙ 8.30am-8pm Mon-Sat)

Drinking

Vieux Nice's little streets runneth over with local bars and cafés in which to sip a perfect *pastis* (anise-flavoured alcoholic drink). (Half the fun is stumbling across them – and, later, out of them – on your own.)

Raucous watering hole **Chez Wayne's** (☎ 04 93 13 46 99; 15 rue de la Préfecture), a magnet for carousing locals and visitors alike, has live bands every night. Next door, **Master Home** (☎ 04 93 80 33 82; 11 rue de la Préfecture) is a Scottish pub with similar pulling power. Not far away is the Danish bar and boisterously fun backpacker haunt, **Thor Pub** (☎ 04 93 62 49 90; 34 cours Saleya). All three close around midnight on weekdays and around 3am on weekends.

If you're above those sorts of shenanigans, head for the rarefied rooftop bar at the **Grand Hotel Aston** (☎ 04 92 17 53 00; 12 av Félix Faure; ⊙ 8am-11pm, closed Sun & Mon in winter), which has champagne views over Nice and the Med. Cocktail connoisseurs quaff at **Hôtel La Petite Sirène** (p876). Cocktails are half-price from 5pm to 7pm Tuesday to Sunday; there are also regional wines. And the latest hotel to herald a smart in-house bar for guests and nonguests is the **Hôtel Beau Rivage** (p876), featuring oversize pebble-shaped sofas, pebble-shaped cushions and pebble-shaped paper light fittings, along with a couple of turntables, and a cocktail house special sex-on-the-beach.

Entertainment

The tourist office has info on Nice's cultural activities, which are listed in its free publications, *Nice Rendezvous* and *Côte d'Azur en Fêtes*; or consult the weekly *Semaine*

des Spectacles (€0.80), available from newsstands on Wednesday. All are in French. Event tickets can be purchased at **FNAC** (☎ 04 92 17 77 77; 44 av Jean Médecin).

CINEMA

Catch nondubbed flicks at **Cinéma Nouveau Mercury** (recorded message in French ☎ 04 93 55 32 31; 16 place Garibaldi) and **Cinéma Rialto** (☎ 04 93 88 08 41; 4 rue de Rivoli). Art films (usually in the original version with French subtitles) are screened at **Cinemathèque de Nice** (☎ 04 92 04 06 66; 3 esplanade Kennedy; ⊙ Tue-Sun), which is at the Acropolis conference centre and concert hall.

LIVE MUSIC

Opéra de Nice (☎ 04 92 17 40 40; 4-6 rue St-François de Paule; ⊙ box office 10am-5pm Tue-Sat, closed mid-Jun–Sep) Built in 1885 and recently renovated, this *grande dame* hosts operas, ballets and orchestral concerts. Tickets cost €7 to €84.

Le Bar des Oiseaux (☎ 04 93 80 27 33; 5 rue St-Vincent; ⊙ noon-midnight Tue-Sat summer, 6pm-12.30am Tue-Sat winter) Artistic types flock to this bohemian bar (and adjoining theatre) for live jazz, blues and cabaret. There's a cover charge of about €5 when entertainment's on the bill; you can also dine here (*menus* around €20).

Jonathan's (☎ 04 93 62 57 62; 1 rue de la Loge; ⊙ 8-11.30pm) Live Irish folk-type music is played every night in summer at this laidback place.

La Havane (☎ 04 93 16 36 16; www.lahavaneice.com; 32 rue de France; mains €16.50-21; ⊙ 2pm to 2.30am) Show off your smoothest moves on the dance floor of this sultry Latin restaurant/bar with live samba and salsa from 9.30pm nightly (at which time a €1.60 surcharge on drinks kicks in), or watch on from the mezzanine.

NIGHTCLUBS

Happy Bar (☎ 04 97 07 26 26; www.hi-hotel.com; 3 av des Fleurs; ⊙ DJs Tue, Fri & Sat until late) The heart and soul of the hip Hôtel Hi hosts the gurus of the DJ world. Red Bull's illegal in France, but you can rev up with a sleek designer can of Hi's own energy drink.

Les Trois Diables (☎ 04 93 92 93 37; 2 cours Saleya; ⊙ 5pm-2.15am) The 'Three Devils' tempts a mainly local crowd with trip-hop, house and electro top-ten dance. Wednesday's karaoke features French tracks.

CÔTE D'AZUR & MONACO

L'Ôdace (☎ 04 93 82 37 66; 29 rue Alphonse Karr; ☾ until late Thu-Sat Jul & Aug, Fri & Sat Sep-Jun) The vast industrial-style party temple formerly known as Le Grand Escurial is now hipper and even more hyper after its recent relaunch.

Other party options:

Blue Boy Enterprise (☎ 04 93 44 68 24; 9 rue Spinetta; ☾ from 11pm) A timelessly trendy gay nightclub that also welcomes a straight crowd.

Le White Lab (☎ 06 88 08 26 15; 26 quai Lunel; ☾ from midnight) Party on at the port's hottest spot.

Liqwid (☎ 04 93 76 14 28; 11 rue Alexandre Mari) Loosen up here with nightly DJs.

Shopping

Cours Saleya is split between its famous **flower market** (☾ 6am-5.30pm Tue-Sat, to 1pm Sun) selling bucketfuls of blooms in the western half, and a magnificent **food market** (☾ 6am-1pm Tue-Sun) at the eastern end, with long trestle tables displaying exotic spices, hand-moulded chocolates, pastries, *fruits glacés* (glazed or candied fruits like figs, ginger, tangerine and pears) and more. On Mondays from 6am to 1pm, cours Saleya is the venue for an **antiques market**.

The best-value place for wine-tasting and buying is a traditional wine cellar; try Cave de la Tour (p878).

Designer names abound above the beautiful fashion boutiques along rue Paradis, av de Suède, rue Alphonse Karr and rue du Maréchal Joffre.

The massive **Nice Étoile shopping mall** (av Jean Médecin) spans a city block.

Getting There & Away

AIR

Nice's international airport, **Aéroport International Nice-Côte d'Azur** (☎ 0 820 423 333; www .nice.aeroport.fr), is about 6km west of the city centre. Its two terminals are connected by a free **shuttle bus** (☾ at least every 10min 6am-11pm). The airport's served by numerous carriers, including the cut-price **BMIBaby** (www.bmibaby .com) and **easyJet** (www.easyjet.com).

For the shortest and most stylish transport to Monaco, aboard a **helicopter** (☎ for calls outside Monaco 00 377 92 05 00 50; www.heliairmonaco.com). Seven-minute flights departing from Nice airport start from €75 per person, one way.

BOAT

The fastest and least expensive ferries from mainland France to Corsica depart from Nice (see p914). The **SNCM office** (☎ 0493 13 66 66; ferry terminal, quai du Commerce) issues tickets (otherwise try a travel agency in town). Italian-run **Corsica Ferries** (☎ 0 825 095 095; www .corsicaferries.com; quai Lunel) also sells tickets at the port. From av Jean Médecin take buses 1 or 2 to the Port stop.

BUS

Buses stop at the **bus station** (Gare Routière; ☎ 04 93 85 03 90; 5 blvd Jean Jaurès).

A single €1.30 fare can take you anywhere in the Alpes-Maritimes *département* (with a few exceptions such as the airport), provided you're making direct connections (within around an hour).

There are services until about 7.30pm daily to Antibes (1¼ hours), Cannes (1½ hours), Grasse (1¼ hours), Menton (1¼ hours) and Monaco (45 minutes). Buses also run to Vence (50 minutes) and St-Paul de Vence (one hour).

For long-haul travel, **Intercars** (☎ 04 93 80 08 70), at the bus station, serves various European destinations; it also sells Eurolines tickets for buses to London, Brussels and Amsterdam.

TRAIN

Nice's main train station, **Gare Nice Ville** (av Thiers) is 1.2km north of the beach.

There are fast and frequent services (up to 40 trains a day in each direction) to coastal towns including Antibes (€3.60, 25 minutes), Cannes (€5.50, 40 minutes), Menton (€4.10, 35 minutes), Monaco (€3.10, 20 minutes) and St-Raphaël (€9.60, 1¼hr).

Direct TGV trains link Nice with Paris' Gare de Lyon (€103.20, 5½ hours), with additional connecting services.

From July to September, the SNCF's **Carte Isabelle** (€11, available from train stations) lets you make unlimited trips in a single day (except TGV express trains) from Théoule-sur-Mer to Vintimiglia in Italy, and from Nice to Tende.

Lost luggage and other problems are handled by **SOS Voyageurs** (☎ 04 93 16 02 61; ☾ 9am-noon & 3-6pm Mon-Fri).

For an enchanting train trip through the mountains, two-car diesel trains operated by **Les Chemins de Fer de la Provence** (www.train provence.com; ☎ in Nice 04 97 03 80 80, in Digne-les-Bains 04 92 31 01 58) chug four times daily from Nice's **Gare du Sud** (☎ 04 93 82 10 17; 4bis rue

Alfred Binet) to Digne-les-Bains (p864; €17.65, 3¼ hours).

Getting Around

TO/FROM THE AIRPORT

Ligne d'Azur (☎ 0 810 061 007; www.lignedazur .com; ticket €4) runs two airport bus services. Route 99 shuttles approximately every half hour direct between Gare Nice Ville and both airport terminals daily from around 8am to 9pm. Route 98 departs from the Gare Routière bus station every 20 minutes (every 30 minutes on Sunday) from around 6am to around 9pm.

A taxi from the airport to the centre of Nice will cost €25 to €30, depending on the time of day and terminal.

BUS

Local buses are handled by **Ligne d'Azur** (www .lignedazur.com). Fares are €1.30/4/20 for a single fare/day pass/17 rides. All tickets can be purchased on the bus. After you time-stamp your ticket, it's valid for one hour and can be used for one transfer or return.

Buses are rerouted while the tramway's under construction, so you may find it's quicker to walk to destinations within Nice's city centre. Four night buses (N1, N2, N3 and N4) run north, east and west from place Masséna every half-hour from 9.10pm until 2am.

CAR & MOTORCYCLE

Easycar (☎ in London 44-0906 33 33 33 3; www.easycar .com) rents out subcompacts from Nice starting from €62 per day, including 100km. Cars must be reserved either on the website or through its London call centre.

Holiday Bikes (☎ 04 93 16 01 62; 34 av Auber; ☯ closed noon-2pm & Sun) rents 50cc scooters for €26 a day, and 125cc motorcycles for €51 a day; as well as bicycles from €14 a day, and small cars for €58 a day. There's a hefty security deposit.

Also try the following places.

Budget av Gustave V (☎ 04 97 03 35 03; 1bis av Gustave V); Auber branch (38 av Auber)

JML (☎ 04 93 16 07 00; fax 04 93 16 07 48; 34 av Auber)

TAXI

To avoid getting taken for a ride (as it were), make sure the driver is using the meter and applying the right rate, clearly outlined in a laminated card that they're required to display. There are taxi stands right outside the Gare Nice Ville and on av Félix Faure close to place Masséna; otherwise you can order one on ☎ 04 93 13 78 78.

TRAM

By the time you're reading this, sections of Nice's brand new tram system *should* be operational, following lengthy delays. For updates on construction, traffic rerouting and proposed tram stops, check www.tram way-nice.org.

ANTIBES-JUAN-LES-PINS

pop 75,000

On the shore of the French Riviera… stood a large, proud, rose-coloured hotel. Deferential palms cooled its flushed facade and before it stretched a short dazzling beach. Now it has become a summer resort of notable and fashionable people…In the early morning the distant image of Cannes, the pink and cream of old fortifications, the purple Alp that bounded Italy, were cast across the water and lay quavering in the ripples and rings sent up by sea-plants through the clear shallows…

F Scott Fitzgerald, Tender is the Night, 1934

Fitzgerald romanticised the 'French Riviera' in perpetuity. His fictional Hôtel des Étrangers in *Tender is the Night* was (and still is) the Hôtel du Cap Eden Roc (p882), the venue for a post-WWI salon attended by Fitzgerald, Hemingway, Picasso and others, which transformed the neighbouring towns of Antibes, Cap d'Antibes and Juan-les-Pins from a winter resort to the summer playground it remains today.

Settled around the 4th century BC by Greeks from Marseille, who named it Antipolis, Antibes was later taken over by the Romans, and then by Monaco's Grimaldi family, who ruled it from 1384 to 1608. Its position on the border of France and Savoy saw it fortified in the 17th and 18th centuries, and demolished in 1894 so the town could expand.

The contiguous towns of Antibes-Juan-les-Pins span a shimmering sweep of the Mediterranean, which unfurls like a bolt of breeze-ruffled lilac-hued silk. Antibes' flower-filled cobblestone streets branch out from a central, covered marketplace, while Cap d'Antibes' luxurious walled mansions are hidden amid dense pines. Juan-les-Pins sprawls along a 2km sandy beach.

Orientation

Across the Baie des Anges from Nice, Antibes centres on place du Général de Gaulle, linked to Juan-les-Pins by blvd du Président Wilson (1.5km) and to Cap d'Antibes by blvd Albert 1er (700m). Av Robert Soleau links Antibes' train station (300m) with place du Général de Gaulle. The bus station is just a few steps away, linked by rue de la République, which continues east to the old town.

Information

Antibes Books-Heidi's English Bookshop (☎ 04 93 34 74 11; 24 rue Aubernon; ☽ 10am-7pm) One of the best on the *Côte*, this fantastic bookshop stocking new and used English-language books also acts as a quasi Anglo info centre.

Antibes Tourist Office (☎ 04 92 90 53 00; www.antibesjuanlespins.com; 11 place de Gaulle, Antibes; ☽ 9am-7pm daily Jul & Aug; 9am-12.30pm & 1.30-6pm Mon-Fri, 9am-noon & 2-6pm Sat Sep-Jun) In the town centre.

Exchange Office (17 blvd Albert 1er, Antibes; ☽ 9am-7pm Mon-Sat, 10am-1pm Sat)

Juan-les-Pins Tourist Office (☎ 04 92 90 53 05; fax 04 92 90 55 13; 55 blvd Charles Guillaumont, Juan-les-Pins) Similar hours to the Antibes office.

Post Office (place des Martyrs de la Résistance, Antibes)

Xtreme Cyber (☎ 04 93 34 09 96; 8 blvd d'Aguillon, Antibes; per min €0.12; ☽ 9.30am-9pm)

Sights & Activities

Picasso used the 12th-century Château Grimaldi as a studio for six months in 1946, where he would paint late into the night in a kind of trance, his work lit by powerful arc-lights. It's now home to the Musée Picasso, which at the time of writing was closed for extensive renovations – check with the tourist office for updates.

The light-hearted **Musée Peynet** (☎ 04 92 90 54 30; place Nationale, Antibes; adult/concession/under 18yr €3/1.50/free; ☽ 10am-6pm Tue-Sun mid-Jun–mid-Sep, to 8pm Wed & Fri Jul & Aug; 10am-noon & 2-6pm Tue-Sun mid-Sep–mid-Jun) displays over 300 humorous pictures, cartoons, sculptures and costumes by Raymond Peynet. The Antibes-born cartoonist also designed a 'Diploma of Love'; formally presented at weddings in the town

hall, leading many couples from around the world to marry here.

Antibes' small, sandy beach, **Plage de la Gravette**, gets packed; but you'll find the best ones in Juan-les-Pins, including some free beaches on blvd Littoral and blvd Charles Guillaumont.

Festivals & Events

Next to the casino, Antibes' La Pinède park swings during mid-July's **Jazz à Juan** (also known as the Festival de Jazz d'Antibes-Juan-les-Pins). Reserve tickets via the tourist office or try at the gate an hour before show time.

Sleeping & Eating

Relais International de la Jeunesse (☎ 04 93 61 34 40; 60 blvd de la Garoupe; dm incl breakfast €15, sheets €3) Beautifully located in Cap d'Antibes, with the option of pitching a tent on site. Take bus 2A from the bus station to L'Antiquité stop.

Le Relais du Postillon (☎ 04 93 34 20 77; www.relaisdupostillon.com; 8 rue Championnet, Antibes; d €45-83; mains €15-30) Dating back to when it was the border to France, Antibes' earliest hotel is housed in a 17th-century coach house right in the old town. Its 16 rooms have tassel-tied curtains and old wooden chests; try for the Capri room which opens to a sunny private patio. There's a stone walled restaurant (dinner Monday to Saturday) specialising in seafood.

Auberge Provençal (☎ 04 93 34 13 24; fax 04 93 34 89 88; 61 place Nationale; d €80-90) Clustered around a vine-arbored terrace, this rambling place is best known for its exceptional Provençal cuisine (mains €25 to €60, lunch and dinner), but upstairs are five atmospheric guest rooms including two enormous antique-filled *grande* rooms with sleigh beds and beamed ceilings.

Hôtel Belle Rives (☎ 04 93 61 02 79; www.bellesrives.com; blvd Edouard Baudoin, Juan-les-Pins; d from €130; ☒) In the mid-1920s, F Scott and Zelda Fitzgerald rented this small villa (then the St-Louis). Since the early 1930s it's housed this mahogany-lined hotel with a private beach and pier (with boat rental available), and two top-notch restaurants (mains €21 to €48) as well as a bar named after the author, and a humidor.

Hôtel du Cap Eden Roc (☎ 04 93 61 39 01; www.edenroc-hotel.fr; blvd JF Kennedy; d from €550; ☽ closed mid-Oct–mid-Apr; 🔀 🔁) The list of celebrities who have stayed at the 1870-built star of Fitzgerald's famous novel is so long it's alphabetised. A teak cable car ferries you from the paradisaical hotel to its cabana-fringed private beach (accessible for non-guests from €40).

Other dining recommendations:

L'Oursin (☎ 04 93 34 13 46; 16 rue de la République, Antibes; mains €12-35; 🕑 lunch & dinner Tue-Sun) A seafood institution since the '60s, especially for mussels.

Oscar's (☎ 04 93 34 90 14; rue Rostan, Antibes; mains €22-24; 🕑 lunch & dinner Tue-Sat) Silver plates, soft muslin curtains, stone floors and statues; with divine gourmet cuisine.

Les Vieux Murs (The Old Walls; ☎ 04 93 34 06 73; promenade Amiral de Grasse, Antibes; mains €30-40; 🕑 lunch & dinner, closed Mon & Tue in winter) One of Antibes' top tables, aptly housed within the former fortifications' old walls on the seaside promenade.

SELF-CATERING

Marché Provençal (cours Masséna, Antibes; 🕑 morning daily Jun-Aug, Tue-Sun Sep-May) Antibes' heady Provençal marketplace is perfect for picking up picnic supplies.

Getting There & Away

Antibes is an easy day trip by train from Nice (€3.60, 30 minutes) or Cannes (€2.30, 15 minutes).

Antibes' **bus station** (🕑 04 93 34 37 60) has buses to surrounding towns such as Biot; some buses also depart from adjacent to the tourist office.

BIOT

pop 9000

From the 15th century, this little village perched on an old volcano was a vital pottery-manufacturing centre for vast oil and wine jars. Since 1956 – when ceramist Eloi Monod married a master potter's daughter Lucette Auge-Laribe and created handmade (or rather, 'mouth blown') pottery shapes from glass – the village has become known worldwide for its glass production, especially bubbled glass.

Biot's famous bubbles are produced by rolling molten glass in baking soda to create a chemical reaction, then trapping the bubbles with a second layer of glass; the latest frosted look uses acid dips. You can watch work underway at the factory **La Verrerie de Biot** (☎ 04 93 65 03 00; www.verreriebiot.com;

Chemin des Combes; admission free, 45-min guided tour in English €6; 🕑 9.30am-8pm Mon-Sat, 10am-1pm & 2.30-7.30pm Sun summer, 9.30am-6pm Mon-Sat, 10.30am-1pm & 2.30-6.30pm Sun winter) at the foot of the village, which also houses a locally-patronised **restaurant** (mains €6-10; 🕑 lunch Mon-Sat summer, reduced hr in winter), and an international glass sculpture gallery.

In the enchanting old village, ancient pottery is displayed at the local **museum** (☎ 04 93 65 54 54; 9 rue St-Sébastien; adult/under 15yr €2/free; 🕑 10am-6pm Wed-Sun Jul-Sep, 2-6pm Wed-Sun Oct-Jun). Within the 13th- and 14th-century **place des Arcades** you'll find the Brottier family's gastronomic restaurant **Galerie des Arcades** (☎ 04 93 65 01 04; 16 place des Arcades; mains €25-30; 🕑 lunch & dinner, closed Mon & dinner Sun). Dining here (or staying here – there are 14 guest rooms for €70 to €100 per double), gives you a peek at the private collection of art and glass, donated by the artists (including César, Novaro, Vasarely and Folon) as payment for food and lodging. Definitely book ahead.

Biot's **tourist office** (☎ 04 93 65 78 00; www.biot-coteazur.com in French; 46 rue St-Sébastien; 🕑 10am-7pm Mon-Fri, 2.30-7pm Sat & Sun Jul & Aug, 9am-noon & 2-6pm Mon-Fri, 2-6pm Sat & Sun Sep-Jun) has info and maps, as well as a list of *chambres d'hôtes*.

Note that Biot village is a *steep* three footpathless kilometres from the Biot Gare (train station), linked by bus No (€1, 5 minutes, hourly), which travels from Antibes (€1, 20 minutes).

ST-PAUL DE VENCE & AROUND

pop 2900

The medieval hilltop village of St-Paul de Vence and its surrounds are a veritable feast of fine art thanks to the legacy of seminal artists, including Russian painter Marc Chagall, who moved to the village in 1966 and lived here for 25 years until his death. He's buried in the village's interdenominational cemetery. St-Paul is also a favourite of 007 Roger Moore, who has a house in the area.

St-Paul de Vence's cobblestone streets and 16th-century fortifications, dramatically floodlit at night, remain virtually intact, despite it attracting 2.5 million visitors a year. A total of 64 art galleries are within the village fortifications – one for every 6.25 of the 400 intramural residents.

The nearby Fondation Maeght showcases an exceptional collection of 20th-century works, including some by Matisse, whose masterwork, the Chapelle du Rosaire (Rosary Chapel), is nearby.

Orientation & Information

Inside the fortifications, St-Paul de Vence is delineated by its main pedestrian thoroughfare, rue Grande. The best way to approach it is to turn right just by the **tourist office** (☎ 04 93 32 86 95; www.saint-pauldevence.com; 2 rue Grande; ☯ 10am-7pm Jun-Sep, 10am-6pm Oct-May), follow the ramparts around to the far end, then turn left into rue Grande against the tourist tide.

Matisse's **Chapelle du Rosaire** and his former home Villa Le Rêve (see p873) are 4.8km north of St-Paul de Vence (800m north of the attractive medieval town of **Vence**, population 18,000), on route de St-Jeannet (the D2210). From Vence's place du Grand Jardin, head east along av de la Résistance, then turn right along av Tuby. At the next junction, bear right along av de Provence, then left onto av Henri Matisse.

Sights & Activities

Browsing the gallery-lined village streets is a fine entrée for art lovers, but the main course is the **Fondation Maeght** (☎ 04 93 32 81 63; adult/student €11/9.50; ☯ 10am-7pm Jul-Sep, 10am-12.30pm & 2.30-6pm Oct-Jun). With an outdoor sculpture 'labyrinth' by the Spanish surrealist, Joan Miró, interspersed with reflecting pools and mosaics, it was designed by architect Josep Luis Sert in conjunction with its earliest artists including Chagall, who created an exterior mosaic, and inaugurated in 1964. Its extraordinary permanent collection of 40,000 works is exhibited on a rotating basis, in addition to several temporary exhibitions a year.

The Fondation Maeght is about 1km uphill from the bus stop outside the old village.

Sleeping & Eating

Malabar (☎ 04 93 32 60 14; Rempart Ouest; mains €7-16.50; ☯ 11am-6pm Thu-Tue) Locals chill to world music while tucking into huge, homemade hamburgers and *frites*.

La Colombe d'Or (The Golden Dove; ☎ 04 93 32 77 78; lunch mains €20-60, dinner mains €60-70; ☯ lunch & dinner, call to confirm winter opening hr) At the entrance to the village, fronted by a beautiful table-lined terrace, this once-humble inn is now known around the world: Chagall, Braque, Dufy and Picasso often ate here, paying for their meals with their creations, resulting in an incredible private art collection, which you can see if you dine on the top-end Provençal cuisine, or stay in one of the guest rooms (€200 to €330).

There's a seven-day **grocery store** immediately to your right after entering the village and plenty of benches for picnicking along the ramparts.

Getting There & Away

From Nice, St-Paul de Vence (one hour) and Vence (50 minutes) are served by frequent buses (€1.30).

CANNES

pop 68,000

These days Cannes is tantamount to its International Film Festival, when it twinkles with a constellation of silver-screen stars, and a meteor shower of camera flashes. Though the festival lasts less than two

---

WORTH A TRIP

The conglomerated city Cagnes-sur-Mer (population 45,000) comprises Le Haut de Cagnes, a medieval hill town; Le Cros de Cagnes, a former fishing village by the beach; and Cagnes Ville, euphemistically referred to as a 'modern town'. Amid the urban and semi-industrial sprawl are two pilgrimages for art devotees.

On the Haut de Cagnes hilltop, the 14th-century **Château Grimaldi** (☎ 04 92 02 47 30; place Grimaldi; adult/child €3/1.50, combined ticket with Musée Renoir €4.50; ☯ 10am-noon & 2-5pm Wed-Mon summer, 10am-noon & 2-5pm Wed-Mon winter, closed Nov) houses a museum showcasing contemporary Mediterranean art.

Near Cagnes Ville is Renoir's home and studio from 1907 to 1919, now the **Musée Renoir** (☎ 04 93 20 61 07; chemin des Collettes; adult/concession/under 18 €3/1.50/free; ☯ 10am-noon & 2-5pm Wed-Mon summer, 10am-noon & 2-5pm Wed-Mon winter, closed Nov), set in dappled olive groves with original décor and several of Renoir's works on display.

weeks, the city basks in its aura for the rest of the year.

Long before it started screening flicks, Cannes' offshore islands, the Îles de Lérins, were inhabited by the Ligurians, then the Romans; and the town was first mentioned by name in the 11th century. Like elsewhere along the coast, its star ascended in the 19th century when newly arrived British luminaries triggered an influx of London's high society.

Cannes' palatial hotels lining palm-shaded blvd de la Croisette, and the city's chic boutiques cater to *très* affluent travellers, and/or delegates for an ever-increasing number of festivals and congresses such as January's Shopping Festival.

Orientation

Cannes' glitter starts to appear along its main shopping street, rue d'Antibes, a couple of blocks south of the train station on rue Jean Jaurès. Several blocks further south, east of the Vieux Port, is the huge Palais des Festivals et des Congrès, home of both the film festival and the tourist office.

The resplendent waterfront promenade blvd de la Croisette begins at the Palais des Festivals and goes east along the Baie de Cannes to Pointe de la Croisette. Place Bernard Cornut Gentille, with the bus station to Nice, is on the northwestern corner of Vieux Port. The old town, Le Suquet quarter, is to the west of the Vieux Port.

Information

BOOKSHOPS

Cannes English Bookshop (☎ 04 93 99 40 08; 11 rue Bivouac Napoléon) Stocks English-language novels for beach reading.

INTERNET ACCESS

Cap Cyber (12 rue 24 Août; per 15/60min €1.30/3; ☺ 10am-9pm Mon-Sat) Close to the town centre and handy for the train station.

LAUNDRY

Laverie du Port (☎ 04 93 38 06 68; 36 rue Georges Clemenceau; 7kg load €5.50, drying per 10min €1.50; ☺ closed Sun & from noon Sat) Multilingual staff onsite.

MONEY

Scads of banks line rue d'Antibes and rue Buttura.

Crédit Lyonnais (13 rue d'Antibes)

POST

Post Office (22 rue Bivouac Napoléon; ☺ 8am-7pm Mon-Fri, 8am-noon Sat) Has an ATM.

TOURIST INFORMATION

Tourist Office (☎ 04 92 99 84 22; www.cannes.com; ☺ 9am-8pm daily Jul & Aug, 9am-7pm Mon-Sat Sep-Jun) On the ground floor of the Palais des Festivals.
Tourist Office Annexe (☎ 04 93 99 19 77; ☺ 9am-7pm Mon-Sat) Next to the train station.

Sights & Activities

Proving how long Cannes really has been on the scene, **Musée de la Castre** (☎ 04 93 38 55 26; adult/concession €3/2; Le Suquet; ☺ 10am-1pm & 3-7pm Tue-Sun Jun-Aug, 10am-1pm & 2-6pm Tue-Sun Apr, May & Sep, 10am-1pm & 2-5pm Wed-Mon Oct-Mar) is memorable not just for its ethnographic exhibits – including a collection of musical instruments from various continents – but its setting, within the remains of a medieval castle at the pinnacle of Cannes' old town.

The central, sandy **beaches** along blvd de la Croisette are sectioned off for hotel guests, where sun worshippers pay around €19 a day to stretch out in a lounge chair and another €6 for a parasol. A small strip of sand near the Palais des Festivals is free, but you'll find the best public (aka free) beaches, **Plages du Midi** and **Plages de la Bocca**, stretching westwards from the Vieux Port along blvd Jean Hibert and blvd du Midi.

Cinephiles can pick up a brochure titled *Itineraries of Shooting Locations* from the tourist office, spotlighting **film shoot locales** from James Bond instalments to 2005's cult spy thriller, *Anthony Zimmer*, starring Sophie Marceau.

ÎLES DE LÉRINS

Just 20 minutes by boat, the tranquil Îles de Lérins feel far from the madding crowd.

The closest of these two tiny islands is the 3.25km by 1km **Île Ste-Marguerite**, where the enigmatic Man in the Iron Mask was incarcerated during the late 17th century. Immortalised in Alexandre Dumas' novel *Le Vicomte de Bragelonne* (The Viscount of Bragelonne) and dozens of films, including the 1998 Hollywood version starring Leonardo DiCaprio, the identity of the masked man (or woman?) remains a mystery.

As you get off the boat, a map indicates a handful of rustic restaurants, and trails and paths through the cool eucalyptus and

CÔTE D'AZUR & MONACO

pine forest. It also directs you to the steep track to Fort Royal, built in the 17th century, and now harbouring the **Musée de la Mer** (Museum of the Sea; ☎ 04 93 38 55 26; adult/student/under 18yr €3/2/free; ☒ museum & cells 10.30am-1.15pm & 2.15-5.45pm Wed-Mon Apr–mid-Jun, to 4.45pm Jan-Mar & Oct-Dec, 10.30am-5.45pm daily mid-Jun–mid-Sep). The door to the left as you enter leads to the old state prisons, built under Louis XIV. Exhibits interpret

the fort's history; with displays on shipwrecks off the island's coast.

Smaller still, at just 1.5km long by 400m wide, **Île St-Honorat** has been a monastery since the 5th century. Its Cistercian monks welcome visitors to their community including seven small chapels around the island.

The islands' shorelines are littered with dried seaweed drifts, giving them a castaway

---

STARRING AT CANNES

For 12 days in May, Cannes becomes the centre of the cinematic universe. Over 30,000 producers, distributors, directors, publicists, stars and hangers-on descend on Cannes each year to buy, sell or promote more than 2000 films. As the premier film event of the year, it attracts some 4000 journalists from around the world, guaranteeing a global spotlight.

When the festival is in town, frenzied negotiations take place on the city's streets in dozens of languages, and tuxedos and evening gowns come out at night for lavish and highly exclusive parties. Meanwhile, the uninvited mass around the stars as they emerge from chauffeured limos to climb the red-carpeted stairs into the Palais des Festivals. (The carpet's there most of the year, making it a prime photo opp.)

At the centre of the whirlwind is the 60,000-sq-m Palais des Festivals (Festival Palace; dubbed 'the bunker' by locals) where the official selections are screened. Its stark concrete base is adorned with the hand prints and autographs of celebrities.

The original palace on blvd de la Croisette was set to accommodate the first Cannes Film Festival on 1 September 1939 as a response to Mussolini's fascist propaganda film festival in Venice. Hitler's invasion of Poland abruptly halted the festival but it restarted in 1946; shifting to its new digs in 1982, which were expanded in 1999.

Over the years the festival split into 'in competition' and 'out of competition' sections. The goal of 'in competition' films is the prestigious Palme d'Or, awarded by the jury and its president to the film that best 'serves the evolution of cinematic art'. Notable winners include Francis Ford Coppola's *Apocalypse Now* (1979), David Lynch's *Wild at Heart* (1990 – who could forget Nicolas Cage's snakeskin jacket?), and documentary maker Michael Moore's anti–Bush administration polemic *Fahrenheit 9/11* (2004). The 2006 winner was British director Ken Loach for his war drama *The Wind That Shakes the Barley*, which drew parallels between the Irish fight against British rule in 1920 and contemporary events in Iraq.

The vast majority of films are 'out of competition'. Behind the scenes, the Marché (marketplace), sees an estimated US$200 million worth of business negotiated in distribution deals; and it's this combination of hard-core commerce and Tinseltown glitz that gives the film festival its special magic. Its breadth of films and international focus means that although many of the films are obscure, art-house showings, they often define new mainstream trends – when Cannes sneezes, Hollywood catches a cold.

Tickets to the festival are governed by a complex system of passes that determine who gets entry to which film. Passes are generally restricted to film-industry high fliers, but you may get free tickets to some films, usually after their first screening. Look for the booth of the **Cannes Cinephiles** (☎ 04 93 99 04 04), outside the Palais des Festivals, which distributes film tickets daily from 9am to 5.30pm. For the film festival programme, consult the official website www.festival -cannes.org.

Also starring at Cannes is the **Cannes Lions International Advertising Festival** (www.canneslions .com). Hot on the heels of the film festival, the festival, now over 50 years old, is the advertising industry's equivalent of the Olympics, with Gold, Silver and Bronze Lions awarded for the world's most creative, persuasive advertising. Other accolades bestowed during the week-long event each June include adland's own Palme d'Or. More than 75 countries take part; presenting over 22,000 ads, at least some of which, you can be sure, will be finding their way to a medium near you.

CANNES

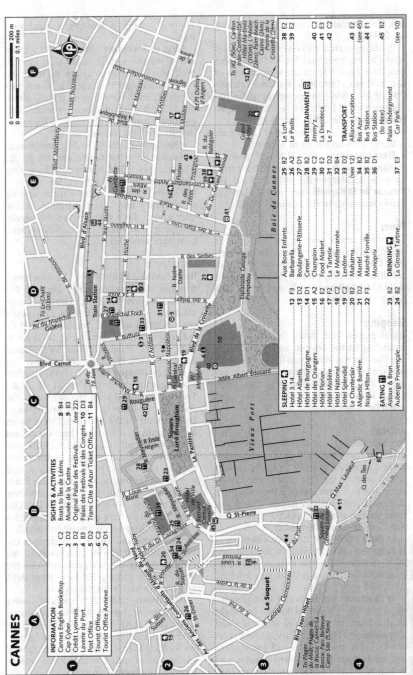

INFORMATION
Cannes English Bookshop......	**1** C2
Cap Cyber......	**2** D2
Crédit Lyonnais......	**3** D2
Laverie du Port......	**4** B3
Post Office......	**5** D2
Tourist Office......	**6** C2
Tourist Office Annexe......	**7** D1

SIGHTS & ACTIVITIES
Boats to Îles de Lérins......	**8** B4
Musée de la Castre......	**9** B3
Original Palais des Festivals......	(see 22)
Palais des Festivals et des Congrès......	**10** D3
Trans Côte d'Azur Ticket Office......	**11** B4

SLEEPING
Hotel 3.14......	**12** F3
Hôtel Atlantis......	**13** D2
Hôtel de Bourgogne......	**14** D1
Hôtel des Orangers......	**15** A2
Hôtel Molière......	**16** F2
Hôtel National......	**17** F2
Hôtel Splendid......	**18** C2
Le Chantedai......	**19** C2
Majestic Barrière......	**20** B2
Noga Hilton......	**21** D2
	22 F3

EATING
Astoux & Brun......	**23** B2
Auberge Provençale......	**24** B2
Aux Bons Enfants......	**25** B2
Barbarella......	**26** A2
Boulangerie-Pâtisserie......	**27** B2
Ceneri......	**28** D1
Champion......	**29** C2
Food Market......	**30** E2
La Tarterie......	**31** D2
Le Méditerranée......	**32** B4
LenÔtre......	**33** D2
Mahatma......	**34** B2
Mantel......	**35** B2
Marché Forville......	**36** B2
Monoprix......	**37** D1

DRINKING
La Grosse Tartine......	**37** E3

ENTERTAINMENT
Le Loft......	**38** E2
Le Pastis......	**39** E2
Jimmy'z......	**40** C2
La Discoteca......	**41** C3
Le 7......	**42** C3

TRANSPORT
Alliance Location......	**43** E2
Bus Azur......	(see 45)
Bus Station......	**44** E1
Bus Station......	**45** B2
(to Nice)......	
Palais Underground......	(see 10)
Car Park......	

CÔTE D'AZUR & MONACO

feel. To maintain it, camping and cycling are forbidden.

Boats operated by several companies leave Cannes from quai des Îles (along from quai Max Laubeuf) on the western side of the harbour. **Compagnie Maritime Cannoise** (CMC; ☎ 04 93 38 66 33) runs ferries to Île Ste-Marguerite (€11 return), while **Compagnie Estérel Chanteclair** (☎ 04 93 39 11 82) operates boats going to Île St-Honorat (€12 return); with skeleton schedules in winter.

Trans Côte d'Azur (☎ 04 92 98 71 30; www.trans-cote-azur.com; quai St-Pierre) charges €10 for trips to/from Ste-Marguerite. In St-Raphaël, **Les Bateaux de St-Raphaël** (see p893) also has daily excursions to the islands.

Tours

The most serene way to see the coast is gazing back from out at sea. In summer, **Trans Côte d'Azur** runs daytrips to St-Tropez (adult/child €32/17 return), Monaco (adult/child €34/17 return) and Île de Porquerolles (adult/child €49/24 return).

Sleeping

Hotel prices in Cannes fluctuate wildly according to the season, and soar during the film festival when you'll need to book months in advance. Many places only accept 12-day bookings during this time. Check ahead to confirm rates for the dates you'll be in town.

BUDGET

Parc Bellevue (☎ 04 93 47 28 97; www.parcbellevue.com; 67 av Maurice Chevalier, Cannes-La Bocca; powered site for 2 adults, tent & car €24; ☉ Apr-Sep) About 5.5km west of the city, this is the closest camp site to Cannes, with a near-Olympic size pool and facilities galore. The 9 bus from the bus station on place Bernard Cornut Gentille stops 400m away.

Le Chalit (☎ 04 93 99 22 11; www.le-chalit.com; 27 av du Maréchal Galliéni; dm from €20, sheets €3) Just 300m northwest of the station, this independent hostel has a self-catering kitchen, wi-fi, and (yay!) no curfew.

Le Chanteclair (☎/fax 04 93 39 68 88; 12 rue Forville; d from €37; ☉ closed mid-Oct–early Jan) Right in the heart of Le Suquet old town and just moments from the Forville Provençal market, this sweet, simple 15-room place has an enchanting courtyard garden, and is handy for the harbourside restaurants.

There's usually a two-night minimum stay.

Hôtel de Bourgogne (☎ 04 93 38 36 73; www.hotel-de-bourgogne.com; 11 rue 24 Août; d from €50) Well placed for easy access to both the train station and the centre of town, this comfy, homey hotel has spacious, clean, old-fashioned, pink-tinged rooms with mottled brown marble tiling with toilet-less, shower-less rooms from €25.

Hôtel National (☎ 04 93 39 91 92; hotelnationalcannes@wanadoo.fr; 8 rue Maréchal Joffre; d from €60; ☒ ☒) The friendly Hôtel National is in a nifty location in the centre of town. Soundproofing keeps its rooms whisper quiet, and air conditioning keeps them refreshingly cool after a hard day's shopping on the nearby shopping strip, rue d'Antibes. Rooms with courtyard views fill quickly.

MIDRANGE

Hôtel Florian (☎ 04 93 39 24 82; www.hotel-le-florian.com; 31 rue Commandant André; d from €50; ☒) It's simple, but the Hôtel Florian is sensationally located smack bang in between rue d'Antibes and the beachfront blvd de la Croisette. A lift takes you up to 20 fresh, floral rooms kitted out with TVs, phones and hairdryers. Parking's €12 per day.

Hôtel des Orangers (☎ 04 93 39 99 92; www.hotel-orangers.com; 1 rue des Orangers; d from €71; ☒ ☐ ☒) Perched at the edge of the old town, the water views from the light, bright west-facing rooms on the second and third floors are an unexpected treat. There's a decent onsite restaurant (mains €12 to €20), and in summer you can breakfast by the stone-flagged, sun-shaded pool. Be quick to nab one of just six free car spaces out the front.

Hôtel Atlantis (☎ 04 93 39 18 72; www.cannes-hotel-atlantis.com; 4 rue 24 Août; d from €80; ☒ ☐) This cheerful place offers outstanding bang for your buck. Top-notch amenities include a lift, guest spa and sauna, plus cheaper use of two different private beaches (€9). Air conditioning costs a few euros extra. To top it off, there's parking (€8 to €15 per day), and it's also handy for the station.

Hôtel Molière (☎ 04 93 38 16 16; www.hotel-moliere.com; 5 rue Molière; d from €80; ☒) This elaborately colonnaded pretty-in-pink period piece has restrained, subtle rooms. Most have balconies looking over the storybook manicured gardens lined with conifers. Rates include a classic continental breakfast.

Hôtel Splendid (☎ 04 97 06 22 22; www.splen did-hotel-cannes.com; 4 & 6 rue Félix Faure; s/d from €112/124; ❸) You'd never know this place was a chain. Looking like an elaborately sculpted, white-frosted wedding cake, this 1871 confection with iron-lace balconies is right on the old port, across the street from the Palais des Festivals. Breakfast and broadband internet are included.

TOP END
There are top end places…
Hôtel 3.14 (☎ 04 92 99 72 00; www.3-14hotel.com; 5 rue François Einesy; d from €120; ❸ ❷) Otherwise known as *trois-quatorze* (three-fourteen) or more often, Pi, this is the hottest design choice in Cannes. Each individually perfumed floor is themed after an aspect of a continent such as North America's '70s psychedelia. Lounge on the private beach (a mere 50m away) or by the rooftop swimming pool.

…and in a stratosphere of their own, there are the beachfront palaces garlanding blvd de la Croisette.
Carlton Inter-Continental (☎ 04 93 06 40 06; www .cannes.intercontinental.com; 58 blvd de la Croisette; d from €160; ❸ ❷) Understated African-colonial ambience with a colossal, columned lobby and legendary domed façade.
Majestic Barrière (☎ 04 92 98 77 00; www.lucien barriere.com; 10 blvd de la Croisette; d from €235; ❸ ❷ ❷) Miami-style Art Deco edifice with soaring statues, good wheelchair access and a double Michelin-starred restaurant.
Hôtel Martinez (☎ 04 92 98 73 00; www.hotel -martinez.com; 73 blvd de la Croisette; d from €260; ❸ ❷ ❷) The *crème de la crème*, with an onsite Givenchy spa.
Noga Hilton (☎ 04 92 99 70 00; www.cannes.hilton .com; 50 blvd de la Croisette; d from €280; ❸ ❷ ❷) On the historic site of the original Palais des Festivals, but a bit too 1992. Good wheelchair access.

Eating
Generally you'll find the least expensive restaurants on and around rue du Marché Forville. Quaint, if somewhat pricier places are tucked along the stone streets of rue St-Antoine and rue du Suquet.
Aux Bons Enfants (80 rue Meynadier; mains around €15.50; ❂ lunch & dinner, closed Sun & dinner Sat low season) A familial little place that operates like a private dining room. There's no phone, and credit cards aren't accepted, but if you're

able to get a table, you'll be rewarded with earthy regional cuisine made from ingredients from the adjacent market.
Mahatma (☎ 04 92 99 72 00; 5 rue François Einesy; mains €15-40) Within the ode to design that is Hôtel 3.14, this opulent purple restaurant under the direction of chef Mario D'Orio does majestic Indian/Mediterranean fusion cuisine using exotic spices. On sultry nights, a table on the outdoor terrace is pure magic.
Mantel (☎ 04 93 39 13 10; 22 rue St-Antoine; lunch menus €23, dinner menus €32-70; ❂ lunch & dinner, closed Wed & lunch Thu) With a charming owner who may well also be your waiter, this cosy little gem of a restaurant dishes up gastronomic bliss. Don't miss Mantel's signature *crêpe Suzette* for dessert.
Barbarella (☎ 04 92 99 17 33; 16 rue St-Dizier; mains €23-38; ❂ 7-11.30pm Tue-Sun) At the top of the old town in a *trompe l'oeil*–painted building with groovy, upbeat interiors, this gay-friendly establishment, named after the psychedelic sci-fi '60s flick, does ab-fab fusion food like roasted duck filet glazed in coffee sauce.
Auberge Provençale (☎ 04 92 99 27 17; 10 rue St-Antoine; mains €24-38; ❂ lunch & dinner) Established in 1860, Cannes' oldest restaurant nestles between exposed stone walls, and is a time-honoured tradition for long classic Provençal lunches accompanied by very fine bottles of wine. One of the few signs of the post-millennium times is the free wi-fi.
Astoux & Brun (☎ 04 93 39 21 87; 21 rue Félix Faure; menus from €28; ❂ 10am-1am) If you're a seafood connoisseur, this world-renowned place needs no introduction. Every type and size of oyster is available by the dozen, as well as sophisticated fish platters, scallops and mussels. In summer chefs prepare the shellfish out front.
Le Méditerranée (☎ 04 93 99 73 02; 2 blvd Jean Hibert; lunch menus €35-55, dinner menus €45-65; ❂ lunch & dinner). On top of the portside Sofitel hotel, adjoining the rooftop pool, it's hard to say which makes more of an impression – this contemporary French restaurant's culinary prowess or its 360-degree views across the Med to the red Massif de l'Estérel mountains.

CAFÉS
Cannes has copious numbers of coffee-houses, cafés and *salons de thé* (tearooms).

Lenôtre (☎ 04 92 92 56 00; 63 rue d'Antibes; breakfast from €8.95, lunch around €20; ☽ 9am-6pm) Cannes' classy branch of this patisserie chain is run by chefs who put an inordinate amount of effort into the plates' presentation. Like its Parisian sister, it runs cooking courses from €90 for three hours, as well as courses for children (€40 for two hours). Classes are in French, but for a fee you can book an interpreter. Programmes are at www.lenotre.fr.

La Tarterie (☎ 04 93 39 67 43; 33 rue Bivouac Napoléon; most dishes from €3-9; ☽ 8.30am-4.30pm) Fashionistas and backpackers jostle for stellar salads and specialities like *clafoutis* – a fruit tart baked in sweet batter.

SELF-CATERING

The daily **food market** (place Gambetta; ☽ morning, closed Mon in winter) is one of Cannes' main markets. **Marché Forville** (rue du Marché Forville), a fruit and vegetable market two blocks north of place Bernard Cornut Gentille, comes to life every morning except Monday (when a flea market takes its place).

Square Lord Brougham, next to the Vieux Port, is a great place for a picnic – buy filled baguettes and other lunch-time snacks from the **Boulangerie-Pâtisserie** (12 rue Maréchal Foch). Locals go to **Ceneri** (22 rue Meynadier) for its wondrous cheeses.

Large supermarkets:
Champion (6 rue Meynadier)
Monoprix (9 rue Maréchal Foch) Take the second entrance on the corner of rue Jean Jaurès and rue Buttura.

Drinking

The streets north of blvd de la Croisette between the Grand Hotel and the rue des États Unis tend to offer the best bar-and-club-hopping turf.

To mingle with the rich and famous, Cannes' four hotel palaces (p889) all have drop-dead-posh bars.

Le Pastis (☎ 04 92 98 95 40; 28 rue du Commandant André; ☽ lunch & evening) The perfect start to a night on the town. The convivial Le Pastis only recently opened, but fits so seamlessly into the Cannes scene it might have been here forever. Charismatic barman Manuel mixes show-stopping cocktails, and there's a great wine list as well as a blackboard menu.

Also recommended:
Le Loft (☎ 04 93 39 40 39; 13 rue du Dr Gérard Monod; ☽ 10.30am-2.30am Mon-Sat) A great second stop after Le Pastis with a friendly, cruisy vibe.

La Grosse Tartine (☎ 04 93 68 59 28; 9 rue Batéguier; ☽ hours vary) Fun local bistro that's not even a little bit pretentious (any place that calls itself 'the big tart' can't be).

Entertainment

Ask the tourist office for a copy of the free monthly *Le Mois à Cannes*, which lists what's on where. Nondubbed films are screened from time to time at the cinemas along rue Félix Faure and rue d'Antibes.

Come dressed up and cashed up to experience nightlife Cannes-style.

L'Atelier (www.lepalmbeach.com; place Franklin Roosevelt; ☽ 11pm-4am) Anyone who's anyone heads to this club within the Art Deco Palm Beach Casino; recently saved from the bulldozers and spectacularly restored.

Jimmy'z (☎ 04 92 98 78 00; Palais des Festivals, blvd de la Croisette; ☽ midnight-dawn daily Jun-Sep; Fri, Sat & Sun Oct-May) Part of the Palais des Festivals complex, and still popular, despite losing it's 'it' status to L'Atelier.

La Discoteca (☎ 06 11 91 69 99; 22 rue Macé; ☽ hr vary) If you want that casting director to notice you, ordering a jeroboam of champagne sees your table spot-lit as a gong goes off.

Le 7 (☎ 04 93 39 10 36; 7 rue Rouguière; ☽ hr vary) Don't sit in the front row of the drag shows at this disco-and-house gay club unless you're up for being part of the spectacle.

Getting There & Away

BUS

Regular bus services to Nice (€1.30, 1½ hours), Nice airport (€12.90, 40 minutes, hourly from 8am to 7pm) and other destinations leave from place Bernard Cornut Gentille, next to Hôtel de Ville in Cannes' centre.

TRAIN

There's an **information desk** at the train station, but no left-luggage office.

Destinations within easy reach include Nice (€5.50, 30 minutes), Grasse (€3.40, 25 minutes) and Marseille (€23.60, two hours), as well as St-Raphaël (€5.70, 30 minutes), from where you can get buses to St-Tropez and Toulon.

Getting Around

BUS

Serving Cannes and destinations up to 7km away is **Bus Azur** (☎ 0 825 825 599, 04 93 45 20 08; place Bernard Cornut Gentille). Tickets cost

€1.30. Bus 8 runs along the coast from place Bernard Cornut Gentille to the port and Palm Beach Casino on Pointe de la Croisette.

For €0.50 per day, you can flag down the **Élo Bus** anywhere you see it passing through the city; there are no set stops.

CAR & MOTORCYCLE
Car-rental agency **JKL** (☎ 04 97 06 37 77; www .jkl-forrent.com; 59 angle de la Croisette) offers cars fit for a star. There are plenty of pay car parks, including the Palais underground car park right next to the tourist office, which lends out free bicycles if you park here. The easy-to-spot entry is off blvd de la Croisette.

Alliance Location (☎ 04 93 38 62 62; 19 rue des Frères Pradignac) rents motorcycles (from €53 a day) and scooters (€38).

TAXI
Taxis (☎ 04 93 38 91 91, 04 93 49 59 20) can be ordered by phone.

GRASSE
pop 43,000
In 2005, the brand new train line opened, connecting the flourishing, centuries-old hilltop town with the coast. Surrounded by fields of lavender, jasmine, centifolia roses, mimosa, orange blossom and violets, Grasse is one of France's leading perfume producers. Its tightly coiled streets make for an absorbing stroll – the tourist office hands out maps directing you along a trail of golden plates embedded in the cobblestones, with multilanguage interpretive signs highlighting points of historical interest along the way.

Orientation & Information
While the town of Grasse and its suburbs sprawl over a wide area of hill and valley, the old city is packed into the compact area formerly ringed by ramparts. The N85, better known as **Route Napoléon** (www.route-napo leon.com), runs right through Grasse, where it becomes the town's main thoroughfare, blvd du Jeu de Ballon.

The town's helpful **tourist office** (☎ 04 93 36 66 66; www.grasse-riviera.com; 22 cours Honoré Cresp; ☺ 9am-7pm Mon-Sat, 9am-1pm & 2-6pm Sun Jul-Sep; 9am-12.30pm & 2-6pm Mon-Fri Oct-Jun) is inside the Palais de Congrès, and has information on accommodation in the town and surrounding area.

Banks abound on blvd du Jeu de Ballon. You can also change money at the **Change du Casino** (☎ 04 93 36 48 48; Palais de Congrès).

Spiralling out from place aux Aires, home to a flower-filled morning **market** from Tuesday to Sunday, are some excellent little **restaurants** – just follow your nose.

Sights & Activities
Grasse has more than 40 **perfumeries**, creating essences sold primarily to factories and by mail order, as well as for aromatically enhanced foodstuffs and soaps. Several perfumeries offer free tours, taking you stage by stage through the perfume production process, from extraction and distillation to the work of the 'noses' – perfume creators who, after 10 years' training, are able to identify more than 6000 scents with one whiff. Just 250 qualified noses exist worldwide. The perfumeries' showrooms sell fragrances for much less than traditional retailers, where you're mainly paying for the bottle.

Situated at the foot of the old town, **Fragonard** (☎ 04 93 36 44 65; 20 blvd Fragonard; ☺ 9am-6.30pm Jun-Sep, 9am-12.30pm & 2-6pm Oct-May) is the easiest perfumery to reach by foot; the tourist office can provide information about other perfumeries that can be visited further afield.

And for the ultimate field trip, if you're travelling with wheels, it's possible to visit the **flower-growing fields** to learn about the blooms' cultivation and harvest. Contact **Domaine de Manon** (☎ 04 93 60 12 76; admission €6) to see roses from mid-May to mid-June, and jasmine from July to late October.

Getting There & Away
There's a ticket office (to 5.15pm) at the **bus station** (☎ 04 93 36 37 37; place de la Buanderie). **TAM** (☎ for travel to Nice 04 93 36 49 61, for Cannes 04 93 36 08 43) has buses to Nice (€1.30, 1¼ hours) via Cannes (€1.30, 45 minutes) approximately every 30 minutes (hourly on Sunday).

About 2km south of the centre, Grasse's train station is served by free **Sillages** shuttle buses to the old town and bus station from 6.40am to 8pm, in addition to fare-paying buses (€1.30). Regular trains depart to Cannes (€3.40, 25 minutes) and Nice (€7.70, one hour).

CÔTE D'AZUR & MONACO

MASSIF DE L'ESTÉREL

Punctuated by pine, oak and eucalyptus trees, the rugged red mountain range Massif de l'Estérel contrasts dramatically with the brilliant blue sea.

Extending east from St-Raphaël to Mandelieu-La Napoule (near Cannes), a curling coastal road, the Corniche de l'Estérel (also known as the Corniche d'Or and the N98), passes through summer villages and inlets ideal for swimming including **Le Dramont**, where the 36th US Division landed on 15 August 1944; **Agay**, a sheltered bay with an excellent beach; and **Mandelieu-La Napoule**, a large pleasure-boat harbour near a fabulously restored 14th-century castle.

More than 100 hiking trails traverse the Massif de l'Estérel's interior, but for the more challenging trails you'll need a good map, such as IGN's *Série Bleue* (1:25,000) No 3544ET. Many of the walks, such as those up to Pic de l'Ours (496m) and Pic du Cap Roux (452m), are signposted. Trails are open from 9am to 7pm (hence camping's not possible); and they're often closed in summer when fire danger's high.

FRÉJUS & ST-RAPHAËL

The twin towns of Fréjus (population 50,536) and St-Raphaël (population 32,000) bear the hallmarks of the area's history over the millennia.

The site of some exceptional Roman ruins, France's 'little Pompeii', Fréjus, was settled by Massiliots (the Greeks who founded Marseille) and colonised by Julius Caesar around 49 BC as Forum Julii. Its commercial activity largely ceased after its harbour silted up in the 16th century; and its ruins are scattered in and around the lively pedestrianised town centre, with pastel-shaded Provençal buildings and leafy *piazzas*.

St-Raphaël sits on a pretty harbourfront at the foot of the Massif de l'Estérel, and is blessed with a bounty of beaches. It became a fashionable hangout in the 1920s, when F Scott Fitzgerald wrote *Tender is the Night* here. Two decades on, St-Raphaël was one of the main landing bases of US and French troops in August 1944.

Orientation

St-Raphaël is 2km southeast of Fréjus, but their suburbs have become so intertwined they essentially now form a single town.

Fréjus comprises the hillside Fréjus Ville, about 3km from the seafront, and Fréjus Plage, on the Golfe de Fréjus. Most of the Roman remains are in Fréjus Ville.

Information

MONEY

Banque National de Paris (BNP; rue Jean Jaurès, Fréjus) Just west of the Fréjus tourist office; there's an ATM.

POST

Fréjus Post Office (264 av Aristide Briand)
St-Raphaël Post Office (av Victor Hugo)

TOURIST INFORMATION

Fréjus Tourist Office (☎ 04 94 51 83 83; www.frejus .fr in French; 325 rue Jean Jaurès; ☽ 9.30am-noon & 2-6pm Mon-Sat year-round, 10am-noon & 3-6pm Sun Jul & Aug) Distributes an excellent, free map of Fréjus' archaeological treasures.
St-Raphaël Tourist Office (☎ 04 94 19 52 52; www .saint-raphael.com; rue Waldeck Rousseau; ☽ 9am-7pm daily Jul & Aug, 9am-12.30pm & 2-6.30pm Mon-Sat Sep-Jun) Across the street from the train station.
Tourist Office Kiosk (☎ 04 94 51 48 42; ☽ 9.30am-noon & 3-6pm Jul-Aug) By the beach opposite 11 blvd de la Libération in Fréjus.

Sights

The most economical entry to Fréjus' Roman sights is the seven-day **Le Fréjus Pass** (adult/child €4.60/3.10), available from the tourist office. An extended version (€6.20) includes five local sites as well as the Episcopal ensemble.

ROMAN RUINS

Fréjus' Roman-times population is calculated at 10,000, based on the capacity of its 1st- and 2nd-century **arènes** (amphitheatre; ☎ 04 94 51 34 31; rue Henri Vadon; ☽ 10am-1pm & 2.30-6.30pm Mon-Sat Apr-Oct; 10am-noon & 1.30-5.30pm Mon-Fri, 9.30am-12.30pm & 1.30-5.30pm Sat Nov-Mar). Modern-day gladiatorial spectators fill this restored venue, west of Fréjus' old city past the Porte des Gaules, for rock concerts and bullfights.

Other highlights are the **Porte d'Orée**, the remaining arcade of the thermal baths at the southeastern end of rue des Moulins; and a **Roman theatre** (rue du Théâtre Romain; ☽ as for amphitheatre) north of the old town.

LE GROUPE ÉPISCOPAL

The best time to visit this dramatic **Episcopal ensemble** (☎ 04 94 51 26 30; place Formigé, Fréjus;

adult/18-25yr/under 18yr €5/3.50/free; 9am-noon & 2-5pm Tue-Sun Oct-May, 9am-6.30pm daily Jun-Sep) is in the morning, when the sunlight illuminates the intricate 14th-century painted cornices of the cloister, which is supported by columns fashioned from the Roman amphitheatre.

In the centre of the old town on the site of a Roman temple, the ensemble includes an 11th- and 12th-century **cathedral**, and a 5th-century octagonal **baptistry** as well as the stunning 12th- and 13th-century **cloister**. Admission includes a 10-minute film in multiple languages.

Adjoining the cloister is the **Musée Archéologique** (Archaeological Museum; adult/student €3.80/2.50; 10am-1pm & 2.30-6.30pm Mon & Wed-Sat Apr-Oct; 10am-noon & 1.30-5.30pm Mon & Wed-Sat Nov-Mar), whose unearthed treasures include a marble statue of Hermes, a head of Jupiter and a stunning 3rd-century mosaic depicting a leopard.

Activities

Fréjus and St-Raphaël both have sandy **beaches** to frolic on.

St-Raphaël is a leading **dive** centre, with numerous **WWII shipwrecks** off the coast, ranging from a 42m-long US minesweeper to a landing craft destroyed by a rocket in 1944 during the Allied landings.

Aventure Sous-Marine (06 09 58 43 52; 56 rue de la Garonne, St-Raphaël) and **CIP** (04 94 52 34 99; www.cip-frejus.com; Fréjus east port) organise night and day dives and courses for beginners.

Tours

A **guided tour**, run by the Fréjus tourist office for around €5 for two hours, and conducted by English-speaking local guides, is an ideal way to see the spread-out Roman ruins, especially if you don't have your own wheels.

Les Bateaux de St-Raphaël (04 94 95 17 46; tmr-saintraphael.com; Gare Maritime, St-Raphaël) organises boat excursions from St-Raphaël to the Îles de Lérins (€16 return), and daily boats to St-Tropez (€20) and St-Tropez and Port Grimaud (€32 return); check for seasonal schedules.

Sleeping & Eating

Holiday Green (04 94 19 88 30; www.holiday-green .com; route de Bagnols, Fréjus; camping €25-35;

Apr–end Sep;) Within a pungent pine forest, the camp site is 7km from the beach but has fantastic facilities including a pool to cool off in.

Auberge de Jeunesse Fréjus-St-Raphaël (04 94 53 18 75; fax 04 94 53 25 86; chemin du Counillier, Fréjus; dm incl breakfast €15; reception 8-11am & 5.30-8.30pm; closed mid-Nov–Feb) A rambling HI-affiliated hostel amid a 7-hectare park. From St-Raphaël's train station, take bus No 7. From the Fréjus train station or place Paul Vernet (opposite the tourist office), take bus Nos 7, 10 or 13 to Les Chênes, cross the roundabout and take chemin de Counillier on your left; the hostel's 600m ahead, on your right.

Hôtel Le Flore (04 94 51 38 35; fax 04 94 55 59 89; 35 rue Grisolle, Fréjus; d from €46) In an unbeatable location for exploring Fréjus' fascinating old town, the ambient two-star Hôtel Le Flore has 11 appealing rooms with telephones. Some also have TVs, and a handful have balconies.

L'Aréna (04 94 17 09 40; www.arena-hotel .com; 145 rue du Général de Gaulle, Fréjus; s €65-90, d €85-145;) Near the Roman amphitheatre, as its name implies, this perennially delightful, highly recommended hotel with good wheelchair access has a flower-festooned terrace shaded by market umbrellas overlooking the pool, and bright, summery rooms. The restaurant (mains around €20) is a local favourite for its refined and imaginative regional food, paired with exceptional wines.

Hôtel Provençal (04 98 11 80 00; www.hotel -provencal.com; 195 rue de la Garonne, St-Raphaël; d €52-75;) Close to the cafés of St-Raphaël's port, the Provençal is a comfy, spick-and-span two-star place with friendly staff, a little lift, and a secure (if squished) garage half-a-block up the road. Hôtel Provençal's handy for some of St-Raphaël's best restaurants, such as L'Arbousier.

La Cave Blanche (04 94 51 25 40; place Calvini, Fréjus; mains €14-38; lunch & dinner, closed Mon & dinner Sun) Just opposite the cathedral, La Cave Blanche is set in a medieval cave that was once part of the town's ramparts. Foie gras is a speciality.

L'Arbousier (04 94 95 25 00; 6 av de Valescure; lunch menus €27, dinner menus €34-58; lunch & dinner, closed Mon & lunch Tue) One of St-Raphaël's best restaurants with a flower-scented garden and seasonally changing cuisine.

Getting There & Away

Bus 5, run by **Estérel Cars** (☎ in St-Raphaël 04 94 95 16 71), links Fréjus train station and place Paul Vernet with St-Raphaël.

Fréjus and St-Raphaël are on the train line from Nice to Marseille. There's a frequent service (€9.60, 45 minutes) from Nice to **St-Raphaël-Valescure train station** (☎ 0 892 353 535; ☿ information office 9.15am-1pm & 2.30-6pm), southeast of the centre.

ST-TROPEZ

pop 5754

Characterised by sunset-hued pink, orange and deep red townhouses framing its flotilla-filled port, St-Tropez is, effectively, two different towns, depending on the season. If you visit during the madness that is midsummer, when the population increases tenfold, you'll tear your hair out looking for a parking space or a seat at a quay-side café, and be hard pressed to squeeze past the tourist throngs clogging the cobblestone streets. But if you visit in spring, autumn, or even the mild winter, when the central square transforms into a fairy-lit forest complete with an ice rink, you'll instantly appreciate what lured artists, writers and film makers to this picturesque village.

Outside peak summer, you'll probably still see celebs hiding behind designer sunglasses. But you'll also see locals playing *pétanque* in the shade of age-old plane trees, spirited market stallholders selling handmade products, and have the wildflower-lined coastal walking paths pretty much to yourself.

History

St-Tropez acquired its name in AD 68 when a Roman officer named Torpes was beheaded on Nero's orders in Pisa, and packed into a boat with a dog and a rooster to devour his remains. His headless corpse washed up here intact, leading the villagers to adopt him as their patron saint.

For centuries St-Tropez remained a peaceful little fishing village, attracting painters like the pointillist Paul Signac, but few tourists. That changed dramatically in 1956 when *Et Dieu Créa la Femme* (And God Created Woman) was shot here starring Brigitte Bardot (aka BB), catapulting it into the international limelight.

Orientation

The beaches where A+-listers lounge start about 4km southeast of the town. The village itself is at the tip of a petite peninsula on the southern side of the Bay of St-Tropez, across from the Massif des Maures. The old town sits snugly between quai Jean Jaurès (the main quay of the luxury yacht–packed Vieux Port), place des Lices (an elongated square a few blocks back from the port) and a lofty 16th-century citadel overlooking the town from the northeast edge.

Information

INTERNET ACCESS

Kreatik Café (☎ 04 94 97 40 61; 19 av Gal Leclerc; ☿ 10am-9pm, closed Mon winter) State-of-the-art internet access.

LAUNDRY

Laverie du Port (quai de l'Épi; ☿ 7am-10pm) Close to the town-facing edge of the car park near the port.

MONEY

There are a couple of exchange bureaus with decent rates at the old port.
Crédit Lyonnais (21 quai Suffren) At the port.

POST

Post Office (place Celli) One block from the port.

TOURIST INFORMATION

A good information resource for the surrounding towns and beaches is the Central Tourist Office of the Bay of St-Tropez/Pays Des Maures' English-language website, www.bay-of-saint-tropez.com.
Tourist Office (☎ 04 94 97 45 21; www.ot-saint-tropez .com; quai Jean Jaurès; ☿ 9.30am-8.30pm Jul & Aug, 9.30am-12.30pm & 2-7pm Apr-Jun, Sep & Oct, 9.30am-12.30pm & 2-6pm Nov-Mar).

Sights

Threading your way through the web of history-woven old city streets is the best way to get a feel for the town's timeless traditions and culture. The tourist office organises 1½- to two-hour **guided walking tours** (tour €2.50; ☿ Wed Apr-Oct) in French; call to check departure times, and to see if an English-speaking guide is available.

Dramatically displayed in a disused chapel, the **Musée de l'Annonciade** (☎ 04 94 97 04 01; place Grammont, Vieux Port; adult/student €4.50/2.50; ☿ 10am-noon & 3-7pm Wed-Mon Jun-Sep, 10am-noon &

2-6pm Wed-Mon Oct & Dec-May) are an impressive collection of works by Matisse, Bonnard, Dufy, Derain, Rouault, and especially Signac, who set up his home and studio in St-Tropez.

For a panorama of St-Tropez' bay, the elevated 17th-century **Citadelle de St-Tropez** (☎ 04 94 97 59 43; adult/concession €4/2.50; ⏱ 10am-12.30pm & 1.30-6.30pm Apr-Sep, 10am-12.30pm & 1.30-5.30pm Oct-Mar) is a top spot. Inside its stone walls you can learn about the local maritime history; including the Allied landings in 1944.

Activities
BEACHES
The glistening sandy beach, **Plage de Tahiti**, 4km southeast, morphs into the 5km-long **Plage de Pampelonne**, which in summer incorporates a sequence of exclusive restaurant/clubs. To get here on foot, head out of town along av de la Résistance (south of place des Lices) to route de la Belle Isnarde and then route de Tahiti. Otherwise, the bus to Ramatuelle, south of St-Tropez, stops at various points along a road that runs about 1km inland from the beach. Beach mats rent for around €15 per day.

WALKING
Marked by yellow ('easy') blazes, a 35km **sentier du littoral** (coastal path) starts from St-Tropez' sandy fishing cove to the east of the 15th-century Tour du Portalet, in the old fishing quarter La Ponche, and arcs around to Cavalaire-sur-Mer along a spectacular series of rocky outcrops and hidden bays. If you're short on time or energy, you can walk as far as Ramatuelle and return by bus. The tourist office has a free, easy-to-follow map showing distances and average walking times.

Sleeping
BUDGET & MIDRANGE
St-Tropez is no shoestring destination, but to the southeast along Plage de Pampelonne there are plenty of multistar camping grounds – check with the tourist office for openings and rates. Alternatively, during summer St-Tropez makes a scenic daytrip by boat from St-Raphaël or Nice, which have hostels.

Hôtel La Méditerranée (☎ 04 94 97 00 44; www .hotelmediterranee.org; 21 blvd Louis Blanc; d low season €50-120, high season €90-170; ⚏) The kind of unpretentious, old fashioned place you hoped still existed in St-Trop. The Méditerranée has 16 charming rooms and a courtyard restaurant beneath the trees (mains €16 to €20). Opening hours for reception and the restaurant can be erratic.

Les Palmiers (☎ 04 94 97 01 61; www.les-palmiers .com; 26 blvd Vasserot; d low season €63-133, high season €75-177; ⚏) Opposite the place des Lices, screened by a garden scattered with citrus trees and shaded benches, this comfortable, unadorned place has friendly staff, good wheelchair access and free wi-fi throughout. Pet pooches are welcome.

Hôtel Sube (☎ 04 94 97 30 04; www.hotel-sube.com; 15 quai Suffren; d low season €65-150, high season €90-250; ⏱ closed early Jan-early Feb; ⚏) This nautically styled hotel has a crows nest perch above the old port. Portside rooms cost more, but they're worth it to peer down onto the decks of the floating palaces pulled up in front. A favourite with the town's movers and shakers, the first-floor bar with model boats and a chandelier in the shape of a tall ship opens to a much-coveted balcony.

TOP END
When in St-Tropez, hey? Many top-end places only open from Easter to October.

AU NATUREL

Not a fan of tan-lines? The coastline from Le Lavandou to the St-Tropez peninsula is well endowed with *naturiste* (nudist) beaches. Naturism is also legal in some other spots in the area, like the secluded beach, **Plage de l'Escalet**, on the southern side of Cap Camarat. There's a bus to Ramatuelle from St-Tropez, but you'll have to walk the 4km southeast to the beach.

Closer to St-Tropez is **La Moutte**, 4.5km east of town – take route des Salins.

The coast's laidback, let-it-all-hang-out attitude was the premise of Jean Girault's cult 1964 farce film *Le Gendarme de St-Tropez*, in which Louis de Funès starred as the policeman of the title, who attempted to crack down on local nudists.

Most isolated is the oldest and largest *naturiste* colony in the region, which occupies half of the 8km-long island **Île du Levant** (p899).

CÔTE D'AZUR & MONACO

The following stay open (more or less) year-round:

La Maison Blanche (☎ 04 94 97 52 66; www.hotel lamaisonblanche.com; place des Lices; d low season €168-290, high season €221-374; ☒ closed Feb; ☒) Behind a hedged courtyard, the nine white-on-white rooms at 'the white house' are a statement in chic minimalism. There's an outdoor champagne bar in summer; breakfast is served in a marquee. Good wheelchair access.

Pastis (☎ 04 98 12 56 50; www.pastis-st-tropez.com; 61 av du Général Leclerc; d low season €175-350, high season €275-500; ☒ ☒) The newest kid on the bay-side block, the pop art–themed Pastis has good wheelchair access and mixes things up with bleached oak floorboards, stainless steel minibars and in-room coffee plungers, and a dramatic black lagoon-like swimming pool. Parking's free.

La Mistralée (☎ 04 98 12 91 12; www.hotel-mist ralee.com; 1 av du Général Leclerc; d low season €190-370, high season €450-760; ☒ ☒) The flamboyant former home of hairdresser-to-the-stars, Alexandre (famously sans surname), the totally over-the-top 1960s-decorated rooms in this historic mansion incorporate, for example, fabric presented to Alexandre by the king of Morocco. Breakfast is served in the glass-paned winter garden or by the mosaic pool.

Eating

Quai Jean Jaurès on the old port is littered with restaurants and cafés, most with *menus* from around €20 to €30 and a strategic view of the silverware and crystal of those dining aboard their yachts. Appealing places can also be found on Port des Pêcheurs at La Ponche at the northern end of rue des Remparts, and wedged in the pedestrian alleys running south of rue Allard.

Le Petit Charron (☎ 04 94 97 73 78; 5 rue Charrons; mains €18-22; ☒ dinner Tue-Sat) Off place des Lices in a charming little lane, this traditional restaurant is true to its name, with a tiny dining room and itty bitty terrace, but it's worth trying for a table to sample its classical Provençal *menus*.

La Nouvelle Bohême (☎ 06 65 67 97 51; 3 rue Charrons; menus €23; ☒ lunch & dinner Tue-Sun) Across from Le Petit Charron, the former La Bohême has a new chef and new management, but is still hidden inside the same cosy cave of exposed stone walls, low-beamed ceilings

and candlelit tables, and is still a winner for solid regional cooking at decent prices.

La Table du Marché (☎ 04 94 97 85 20; 38 rue Georges Clemenceau; mains €26-36; ☒ lunch & dinner) Slide into wine-coloured velvet booths to dine on Christophe Leroy's rave-worthy risotto, and finish off with his lemon meringue *tarte* for dessert. Christophe also runs cooking classes on request for a minimum of eight people.

Lei Mouscardins (☎ 04 94 97 29 00; Tour du Portalet; mains €33-62; ☒ lunch & dinner Easter-Jun & Sep–mid-Oct; dinner Jul & Aug) Set in a sun-baked stone tower above the crashing waves at the start of the *sentier du littoral*, this legendary place sums up St-Tropez. Laurent Tarridec's inspired twin-Michelin-starred cuisine is accompanied by a sublime wine list. And yep, that probably *is* Bruce Willis/George Clooney/Victoria Beckham at the next table.

CAFÉS

Sénéquier (☎ 04 94 97 00 90; cnr quai Jean Jaurès & place aux Herbes; dishes €5-12.50; ☒ 8am-2am Apr-Oct, 8am-6pm Nov-Mar) This quintessential St-Trop quay-side café opened in 1887, and Sartre worked on *Les Chemins de la Liberté* (Roads to Freedom) here. Instantly recognisable for its vivid red director's chairs propagating on the pavement like a field of poppies, splurge on stellar coffee, elaborate ice creams, and nougat made on the premises (€8 for 200g).

Le Café (☎ 04 94 97 44 69; place des Lices; mains €17-33; ☒ lunch & dinner) Not to be confused with the nearby Le Café des Arts on the corner of av du Maréchal Foch, this venerable institution dishes up phenomenal Provençal specialities like *bouillabaisse de poissons blancs en crème d'aïoli* (monkfish soup with garlic mayonnaise) in portions to defeat the heartiest yachtie's appetite. It's a loose, lively place for a drink, and they'll lend you a set of *boules* to play *pétanque* out front.

SELF-CATERING

The entire village turns out for the **place des Lices market** (☒ morning Tue & Sat), brimming with colourful stalls selling jars of jams and preserves, rounds of rich cheeses, and all sorts of other delicacies. There's also a centuries-old **fish market** on place aux Herbes behind quai Jean Jaurès, open until about noon Tuesday to Sunday (daily in summer); as well as a **fruit and vegetable market** daily in summer.

A must-try is the local speciality, *tarte Tropézienne*, a sweet, orange blossom-flavoured double sponge cake filled with cream, created nearby by a Polish baker, and christened by BB. **La Tarte Tropézienne** (☎ 04 94 97 71 42; 36 rue Georges Clemenceau ☉ 6.30am-7.30pm & ☎ 04 94 97 04 69; place des Lices ☉ 6am-8pm) turns them out along with freshly filled sandwiches on home-baked bread.

There are four supermarkets in the village including **Prisunic** (9 av du Général Leclerc; ☉ 8am-8pm Mon-Sat).

Entertainment

The good news: most bars open from around 11pm to dawn. The bad? Upwards of €15 to €20 for a standard drink is the norm and door policies are formidable. Try to look as famous as possible.

St-Tropez' fab five:
Le Pigeonnier (☎ 04 94 97 84 26; 13 rue de la Ponche; ☉ daily summer, weekends winter) Petite and discreet.
Les Caves du Roy (☎ 04 94 97 16 02; Hôtel Byblos, av Foch) Celeb-heavy.
L'Esquinade (☎ 04 94 97 87 45; 2 rue du Four) Gay-friendly.
Papagayo (☎ 04 94 54 82 89; Résidence du Nouveau Port; ☉ summer & Christmas-time) Your best bet for gaining entry, and usually the most fun.
VIP Room (☎ 04 94 97 14 70; Résidence du Nouveau Port) Ultraswanky.

Shopping

Custom-moulded for your foot, cobblers like the 1927-established **Atelier Rondini** (☎ 04 94 97 19 55; 16 rue Georges Clémenceau) can make you a pair of strappy St-Tropez sandals (around €90). The style is thought to have been inspired by a set made here for the writer, Collette.

The old town streets and arcades are dripping in designer boutiques.

Getting There & Away
BOAT
Les Bateaux Verts (☎ 04 94 49 29 39; www.bateaux verts.com; Ste-Maxime) operates a shuttle-boat service from St-Tropez to Ste-Maxime (one way adult/child €6/3.20, 20 minutes) and Port Grimaud (one way adult/child €5.50/3, 15 minutes), with reduced schedules outside peak season. In summer and autumn, **Les Bateaux de St-Raphaël** (☎ 04 94 95 17 46; www.tmr-saintraphael.com; St-Raphaël) runs boats from St-Tropez to St-Raphaël (adult/child €11/7, 50 minutes).

Trans Côte d'Azur runs day trips from Nice (see p875) and Cannes (see p888) between Easter and September.

BUS
St-Tropez **bus station** (av Général de Gaulle) is on the southwestern edge of town on the main road. There's an **information office** (☎ 04 94 54 62 36; ☉ 8am-noon & 2-6pm Mon-Fri, 8am-noon Sat) at the station. **Sodetrav** (☎ 04 94 12 55 12; Hyères) has eight buses daily from St-Raphaël-Valescure train station to St-Tropez bus station, via Fréjus (€9.50, 1¼ hours). Eight daily buses from St-Tropez to Toulon (€18.20, 2½ hours) also stop at Le Lavandou and Hyères.

CAR
To avoid the worst of the high season traffic, approach from the Provençale Autoroute (the A8) and exit at Le Muy (exit 35). Take the D558 road across the Massif des Maures and via La Garde Freinet to Port Grimaud, then park here and take the shuttle boat that runs to St-Tropez from Easter to October.

Getting Around
MAS (☎/fax 04 94 97 00 60; 3-5 rue Joseph Quaranta) rents mountain bikes. There are several car-hire places lining av du Général Leclerc.

To order a taxi ring ☎ 04 94 97 05 27. To order a taxi boat call **Taxi de Mer** (☎ 06 09 53 15 47; 5 quartier Neuf).

ST-TROPEZ TO TOULON
Massif des Maures
Shrouded by a forest of pine, chestnut and cork oak trees, the Massif des Maures arcs inland between Hyères and Fréjus. Roamed by wild boars, its near-black vegetation gives rise to its name, derived from the Provençal word *mauro* (dark pine wood).

Within the forest, the village of **Collobrières** concocts wonderful chestnut purée and *marrons glacé* (candied chestnuts).

Hiking and cycling opportunities abound, especially around La Sauvette (779m), the massif's highest peak. St-Tropez' tourist office distributes an English-language map/guide called *Tours in the Gulf of St-Tropez – Pays des Maures*, detailing driving, cycling

VAR AWAY, SO CLOSE

A handful of kilometres from the Côte d'Azur's crowded shores, the hidden villages and grape-laden vineyards of the Var *département*'s hinterland are steeped in Provençal traditions. These roads-less-travelled – from the Massif des Maures west to just near Marseille; and south of the Gorges du Verdon – take you deep into the dark-green wooded countryside, and make for a romantic roadtrip.

Highlights here appear roughly northeast to southwest. (And chances are you'll find your own.)

At Les Arcs-sur-Argens, on the N7 gateway to this rich wine-producing region is the **Maison des Vins Côtes de Provence** (☎ 04 94 99 50 29; www.provencewines.com; ⏰ 10am-8pm Jul & Aug, 10am-7pm Apr-Jun, 10am-6pm Sep-Mar). Representing the appellation's 60+ wineries, which specialise in rosés, it offers free wine tastings and refreshingly unpretentious explanations in English; and can give you directions to chateaux that can be visited in the area for free.

The remote, otherworldly Cistercian monastery **Abbaye du Thoronet** (☎ 04 94 60 43 90; Le Thoronet; adult/under 25yr/child €6.50/4.50/free; ⏰ 10am-6.30pm Mon-Sat, 10am-noon & 2-6.30pm Sun Apr-Sep; 10am-1pm & 2-5pm Mon-Sat, 10am-noon & 2-5pm Sun Oct-Mar) provides free guided tours in English if you book ahead. Its early-12th-century stone library, chapter house, dormitory, cloisters and grape presses have all been preserved, as has its church. Phenomenal acoustics make the church, in effect, a musical instrument. If you're lucky, your guide may sing beautiful plainsong.

The abbey is one of some two dozen sites in the region (including the coast) where you can score savings with a **Var Pass** – you can pick one up for free at any of the participating cultural attractions for discounts at subsequent sites.

About an hour west of the abbey in the rural hamlet of Pontevès, the inexpensive little inn **Le Rouge Gorge** (☎ 04 94 77 03 97; le.rouge.gorge.free.fr; Quartier les Costes; d €51-58; mains €20-32; 🍴) has a family-friendly regional restaurant serving stockfish, and a swimming pool under the trees.

In the pastel-hued town of **St-Maximin-La-Ste-Baume** (www.la-provence-verte.net), biblical pilgrims (or those of the ubiquitous blockbuster *The Da Vinci Code*) won't want to miss the **Ste-Madeleine Basilica**, where Mary Magdalene came after Jesus' death; she later died in the township. The adjacent convent has been converted into a sumptuous guesthouse, **Hôtellerie le Couvent Royal** (☎ 04 94 86 55 66; www.hotelfp-saintmaximin.com; place Jean Salusse; d €80-140), with a celebrated **restaurant** (menus €26-35, ⏰ lunch daily, dinner Mon-Sat) overlooking the cloister.

The area is dotted with cake decoration–like hilltop villages (if you're renting a car, make it a small one for the precipitous roads). One of the sweetest is **Le Castellet** (www.coteprovencale.com), with artisan bakeries and confectioners lining its cobblestone lanes, and breathtaking views.

With its own glorious view across the valley to Le Castellet, just five kilometres from the sea, the family-run **Hostellerie Berard** (☎ 04 94 90 11 43; www.hotel-berard.com; rue Gabriel Péri; d €98-263; menus from €45; 🍴 💻 🐾), in the tiny town of La Cadière d'Azur, houses a collection of guest rooms throughout four rambling buildings. You can splash in the pool or a milk-and-rose-petal bath, dine at the gastronomic restaurant, or take chef-run **cooking courses** in a 1780 farmhouse, or **water colour workshops** with a local painter.

More information about the region is online at www.vardestination.com. Restaurants, hotels and camping options are listed at www.var-provence.com. The Toulon (p900) and Fréjus (p892) tourist offices also have free maps and can suggest itineraries.

and walking itineraries. To explore the villages west of here, see above.

Corniche des Maures

At the edge of the Massif des Maures, this 26km-long coastal road (part of the D559) snakes southwest from La Croix-Valmer to Le Lavandou. In addition to stunning views, there are some superb spots for swimming,

sunbathing, windsurfing and walking; the website www.provence-azur.com supplies information.

Just a few kilometres before you reach La Croix-Valmer on the D559 from the north, you'll see directions to its beach, Gigaro. From here, the walking path towards Cap Lardier, is one of the most magnificent, least trodden coastal paths.

Blanketing the cliff-side at Le Rayol is a patchwork of international Mediterranean gardens, **Le Domaine du Rayol** (☎ 04 98 04 44 00; www.domainedurayol.org; av des Belges; adult/child €7/3.50; 9.30am-12.30pm & 2-5.30pm Tue-Sun Feb, Mar, Oct & Nov, 9.30am-12.30pm & 2.30-6.30pm Apr-Sep). A 2km self-guided walking trail threads through exotic species: Canary Islands dragon trees, Australian bottlebrush, South African aloes, Asian bamboo and New Zealand cabbage trees. Coastal buses run by **Sodetrav** (☎ 0 825 000 650; www.sodetrav.fr in French) pass Le Rayol.

Le Lavandou
pop 5508

Its name may sound like a variation on the region's purple flowers, but as recently as the mid-20th century, Provençal was by and large the only language spoken in this 17th-century village. The Provençal name for its local lavender is the entirely unrelated *queirélé;* and the village's name is thought to be a version of the Provençal *Lou Lavandou,* meaning washhouse.

Once a traditional fishing port and now home to an 1100-boat marina, Le Lavandou retains a quaint pedestrianised old town, garrotted by beach resort developments in light of its popularity. Undeterred dolphins frequent Le Lavandou's bay, which is scalloped by a 12km-long perimeter of sandy beaches made up of 12 different colours of sand, variegating from red to a spectrum of yellows to charcoal-grey.

Le Lavandou's **tourist office** (☎ 04 94 00 40 50; www.lelavandou.com; quai Gabriel Péri; 9am-noon & 3-6pm) has local info.

Îles d'Hyères

Shimmering mica rock is responsible for this trio of island's alternate name, Îles d'Or (islands of gold). The easternmost island is the *naturiste* colony, **Île du Levant**. In the middle, the smallest island, **Port-Cros**, is also France's smallest **parc national** (national park; ☎ 04 94 12 82 30; www.portcrosparcnational.fr in French; 50 rue St Claire, Hyères), home to a marine reserve and butterfly haven (but no campers, to protect its environmental treasures). The largest, westernmost island, Porquerolles, has a handful of hotels, restaurants and a post office, and is a cherished local holiday spot.

Boats to the Îles d'Hyères leave from various towns along the coast, including Le Lavandou and Hyères; with reduced crossings in winter. **Vedettes Îles d'Or** (☎ 04 94 71 01 02; www.vedettesilesdor.fr), which has an office at the ferry terminal in Le Lavandou, operates boats to Île du Levant and Port Cros (adult/child return €22/18.20, 35 to 55 minutes). For both adults and children, there's a supplement of €13 return for visiting both islands. Return adult/child crossings to Porquerolles cost €28/22. Boats also sail from Hyères (one hour) in the high season; and from Toulon between Easter and September.

Hyères
pop 53,000

Also known as Hyères-les-Palmiers for its profusion of palms, Hyères has a fine medieval old town, but its prized asset is the Giens Peninsula to the south. A protected wetland area, its amazing birdlife includes pink flamingos, herons, terns, egrets, sandpipers, teals and cormorants. The **tourist office** (☎ 04 94 01 84 50; 3 av Ambroise Thomas; 8.30am-7.30pm daily Jul & Aug; 9am-6pm Mon-Fri, 10am-4pm Sat Sep-Jun) runs 1½-hour tours for €6.

Ferries depart for the Îles d'Hyères from the café-lined port on the northwest of the peninsula. Directly across on the northeastern side, the beaches at l'Almanarre are internationally famed for windsurfing and kite-surfing. For lessons (around €23 for windsurfing, and €70 for a maiden kite-surf) and gear rental, contact **Funboard Center** (☎ 04 94 57 95 33; www.funboardcenter.com; rte l'Almanarre) which operates year-round; several other places open in summer.

The town and peninsula also have a number of designated cycling tracks.

TOULON
pop 168,000

Times are a'changin' in Toulon. France's second-largest naval port after Brest and the base for the French navy's Mediterranean fleet, Toulon was a rough diamond compared to its glittering coastal counterparts. Then former French Government minister, and passionate local, Hubert Falco became mayor in 2002 and set about revitalising the city. The pedestrianised old town and the boat-filled port are starting to buzz with bars and restaurants. The opulent 1862 Opéra de Toulon, designed by Charles Garnier (the only other outside Paris) has been restored. And the polished place de la Liberté is fringed by newly planted palm trees.

CÔTE D'AZUR & MONACO

The western gateway of the Côte d'Azur, Toulon has excellent train connections as well as ferry services, a brand new bus station, and an international airport at neighbouring Hyères.

History

Initially a Roman colony, Toulon became part of France in 1481 – the city grew in importance after Henri IV founded an arsenal here. In the 17th century the port was enlarged by Vauban. The young Napoleon Bonaparte made a name for himself in 1793 during a siege in which the English, who had taken over Toulon, were expelled. The city was badly bombed in WWII, and languished for much of the second half of the 20th century until its current revival. It's the birthplace of France's beloved actor Raimu, the star of Marcel Pagnol's 1931 classic, *Marius*.

Orientation

Toulon wraps around the *rade*, a sheltered bay lined with quays. To the west is the naval base and to the east the ferry terminal, where boats sail for Corsica. The city is at its liveliest along quai de la Sinse and quai Stalingrad (the departure point for Îles d'Hyères ferries) and in the old city. The train station is northwest of the old city.

Separating the old city from the Hausmannian northern section is a multilane, multinamed thoroughfare (known as av du Maréchal Leclerc and blvd de Strasbourg as it runs through the centre), which teems with traffic.

Although you're unlikely to have any hassles, women travelling solo should take care in some of the old city streets at night, such as rue Chevalier Paul and the western end of rue Pierre Sémard.

Information

Many commercial banks flourish along blvd de Strasbourg.

Laverie (10 rue Zola; 7am-9pm) One of several laundrettes in the old city.

Post Office (rue Dr Jean Berthelot) Second entrance on rue Ferrero.

Société Generale (1bis av Vauban; 8.30am-noon & 1.30-4.45pm Mon-Fri) With an ATM.

Tourist Office (04 94 18 53 00; www.toulontourisme .com; 334 av de la République; 9am-6pm Mon-Sat, 10am-noon Sun high season; 9.30am-5.30pm Mon-Sat, 10am-noon Sun low season).

Sights & Activities

Housed in an imperial arsenal building, the **Musée de la Marine** (Naval Museum; 04 94 02 02 01; place Monsenergue; adult/child €5/free; 9.30am-noon & 3-7pm daily Jul & Aug, 9.30am-noon & 2-6pm Wed-Mon Sep-Jun) has some intricate scale models of old ships and historic paintings of Toulon.

The compact but high-calibre photographic museum, **Maison de la Photographie** (04 94 93 07 59; rue Nicolas Laugier, place du Globe; admission free; noon-6pm Tue-Sat mid-Jun–mid-Sep, 1-7pm Tue-Sat mid-Sep–mid-Jun), exhibits contemporary works in a two-tiered, light-filled space.

Towering over the old city to the north is **Mont Faron** (580m), offering a fantastic panorama of the port. Near the summit is the **Tour Beaumont Mémorial du Débarquement**, commemorating the Allied landings that took place along the coast here in August 1944. The steep road up to the summit is part of the Tour de Méditerranée (February) and Paris–Nice (March) professional cycling races. A **téléphérique** (cablecar; 04 94 92 68 25; adult/child return €6/4; 9am-noon & 2-5.30pm Tue-Sun) ascends the mountain from av de Vence. Take bus 40 from place de la Liberté. See p902 for combined bus, boat and cable-car tickets.

Good **beaches** for soaking up some rays are two kilometres southeast at Mourillon.

Tours

On summer afternoons, a little **tourist train** (06 20 77 44 42; adult/child €5/2.50; closed Sat) departs from the port to the beaches every 30 minutes – call or check with the tourist office for departure times.

From the port, you can take a spin around the *rade*, with a commentary (in French only) on the local events of WWII (€8.50); or take a day trip to the Îles d'Hyères (€22; p899) with **Le Batelier de la Rade** (04 94 46 24 65; quai de la Sinse). **Cie Maritime des Îles d'Hyères** (04 94 92 96 82) also runs boat tours to the islands from Easter to September departing from quai Stalingrad. The trip to Porquerolles (€22 return) takes one hour. It's another 40 minutes to Port Cros, from where it's a 20-minute hop to Île du Levant (€30 return to tour all three islands). Pack a picnic lunch.

Sleeping

Unlike the rest of the coast, Toulon isn't a typical tourist magnet – yet – but appealing places are popping up.

TOULON

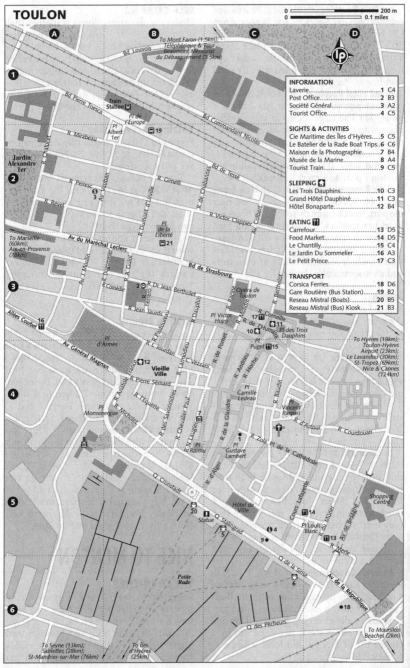

INFORMATION
Laverie................................**1**	C4
Post Office.........................**2**	B3
Société Général.................**3**	A2
Tourist Office....................**4**	C5

SIGHTS & ACTIVITIES
Cie Maritime des Îles d'Hyères....**5**	C5
Le Batelier de la Rade Boat Trips.**6**	C6
Maison de la Photographie.......**7**	B4
Musée de la Marine...............**8**	A4
Tourist Train......................**9**	C5

SLEEPING
Les Trois Dauphins..............**10**	C3
Grand Hôtel Dauphiné..........**11**	C3
Hôtel Bonaparte.................**12**	B4

EATING
Carrefour...........................**13**	D5
Food Market.......................**14**	D5
Le Chantilly.......................**15**	C4
Le Jardin Du Sommelier.........**16**	A3
Le Petit Prince....................**17**	C3

TRANSPORT
Corsica Ferries....................**18**	D6
Gare Routière (Bus Station)....**19**	B2
Reseau Mistral (Boats)..........**20**	B5
Reseau Mistral (Bus Kiosk)....**21**	B3

Les Trois Dauphins (☎ 04 94 92 65 79; www.hotel destroisdauphins.com; 9 place des Trois Dauphins; d from €30) Next to the opera house, this simple little one-star, lime-shuttered place above a ritzy boutique is a great little budget option, with 14 rooms equipped with TVs and telephones. Breakfast is €7.

Grand Hôtel Dauphiné (☎ 04 94 92 20 28; www .grandhoteldauphine.com; 10 rue Dr Jean Berthelot; d €43-57; 🌣) The large rooms at this modern place with good wheelchair access are simply but elegantly done out in contemporary soft furnishings and have extras like minibars and safes. It's in a handy location for Toulon's port and market. Breakfast's €7.

Hôtel Bonaparte (☎ 04 94 93 07 51; 17 rue Anatole France; s €45-50, d €50-55) Ideally positioned near the port, this charmingly renovated boutique hotel has spotless, spacious terracotta-tiled rooms with sponged yellow walls and rose-stencilled furniture. The laden breakfast tables include wicker baskets of croissants and an assortment of breads for €7.

Eating

Relaxed restaurants, terraces and bars ring the port; *menus* start at around €20. Place Victor Hugo and neighbouring place Puget are also lively areas.

Le Petit Prince (☎ 04 94 93 03 45; 10 rue de l'Humilité; mains from €9; 🌣 lunch & dinner, closed Sun, 2 weeks in Feb & 3 weeks in Aug) Named after Antoine de St-Exupéry's book for children, the 'Little Prince' dishes up traditional family-style cooking with three meat and two fish specialities on the menu each day. Wheelchairs – and pets – are well catered for.

Le Chantilly (☎ 04 94 92 24 37; place Puget; mains €12.50-15; 🌣 7am-8.30pm) Established in 1907, this wonderfully old fashioned brasserie/ restaurant/glacier was a favourite with actor Raimu and doesn't look like it's changed much in the intervening years. Lunch (the only meal served here, from noon to 2pm) is an institution which will see you dining alongside loyal locals; it's also an animated spot for a coffee or aperitif.

Le Jardin Du Sommelier (☎ 04 94 62 03 27; 20 allées Courbet; mains €27-39; 🌣 lunch & dinner, closed Sun & lunch Sat) This inauspicious, intimate double decker townhouse turns out adventurous, seasonally changing Provençal cuisine and knock out desserts, accompanied by a choice list of foreign and local wines and impeccable service.

SELF-CATERING

Under the plane trees along the southern half of cours Lafayette you'll find the elongated, open-air **food market** (🌣 9am-4pm Tue-Sun). Once the picnic-perfect food stalls have packed up for the day, bric-a-brac and clothes traders take over the trellises. A **Carrefour** (av de Besagne; 🌣 8.30am-8pm Mon-Sat) supermarket is two blocks behind the eastern end of the port.

Getting There & Away

Ferries to Corsica and Sardinia are run by **Corsica Ferries** (☎ 0 825 095 095; Port de Commerce). See p914 for details.

From Toulon's **bus terminal** (gare routière; ☎ 04 94 24 60 00; blvd Tessé), near the train station, bus 103 to Hyères runs east along the coast via Le Lavandou to St-Tropez (€16.60, two hours, eight daily).

There are frequent **train** connections to coastal cities including Marseille (€12, 40 minutes), St-Raphaël (€15.10, 50 minutes), Cannes (€17.10, one hour 20 minutes), Monaco (€24, 2½ hours) and Nice (€22.30, 1¾hr).

Getting Around

Local buses are run by **Reseau Mistral** (☎ 04 94 03 87 03), which has an **information kiosk** (rue Revel; 🌣 7.30am-7pm Mon-Fri, 8am-12.30pm & 1.30-6.30pm Sat) at the main local bus hub. Single/10 tickets cost €1.40/8.60. Buses generally run until around 7.30pm or 8.30pm. Sunday service is limited. Buses 7 and 13 link the train station with quai Stalingrad.

Reseau Mistral also runs boats that link quai Stalingrad with the towns on the peninsula across the harbour, including La Seyne (line 8M), St-Mandrier-sur-Mer (line 28M) and Sablettes (line 18M). The 20-minute ride costs the same as a bus ticket: €1.40 (€1.70 if you buy your ticket onboard, or €5.50 for an all-day bus, boat and cable-car ticket). Boats run from around 6am to 8pm.

NICE TO MENTON

THE CORNICHES

Some of the Côte d'Azur's most spectacular scenery stretches between Nice and Menton. A trio of corniches (coastal roads) hug the cliffs between Nice and Monaco, each higher up the hill than the last. The middle corniche ends in Monaco, the upper and lower continue to Menton. (If you're in a hurry, you can take the uninspiring A8, a bit further inland.)

Corniche Inférieure

Skimming the villa-lined waterfront, the Corniche Inférieure (also known as the Basse Corniche, the Lower Corniche or the N98) sticks pretty close to the train line, passing (west to east) through Villefranche-sur-Mer, St-Jean-Cap Ferrat, Beaulieu-sur-Mer, Èze-sur-Mer and Cap d'Ail.

VILLEFRANCHE-SUR-MER
pop 8080

This postcard-pretty little terracotta-rooved port overlooking the Cap Ferrat peninsula was a favourite with Jean Cocteau, who painted the frescoes in the 17th-century **Chapelle St-Pierre**. Steps split the steep cobblestone streets that weave through the old town, including the oldest, rue Obscure, a vaulted covered passageway built in 1295. Looking down on the township is the 16th-century citadel, which today houses the town hall along with three museums and an open air theatre.

ST-JEAN-CAP FERRAT
pop 2248

The fishing-village-turned-exclusive-seaside-haven of St-Jean-Cap Ferrat on the Cap Ferrat peninsula conceals an enclave of millionaires' villas, with illustrious residents present and past, including Somerset Maugham, whose house guests included Ian Fleming. On the narrow isthmus of St-Jean-Cap Ferrat, the extravagant **Musée de Béatrice Ephrussi de Rothschild** (☎ 04 93 01 33 09; www.villa-ephrussi.com; adult/student €9/6.60; ☉ 10am-7pm daily Jul & Aug, 10am-6pm daily mid-Feb–Jun & Sep-early Nov, early-Nov–Dec & Jan–mid-Feb 2-6pm Mon-Fri, 10am-6pm Sat & Sun) gives you an appreciation of the area's wealth. Housed in a garden-set 1912 Tuscan-style villa built for the Baroness de Rothschild, it abounds with antique furniture, paintings, tapestries and porcelain. Admission includes entry to the gardens and the collections on the rez-de-chaussée (ground floor). It costs an extra €2 to view those on the 1st floor.

BEAULIEU-SUR-MER
pop 4013, boats 800

Some of the best preserved *belle époque* architecture along the coast is in the seaside holiday town of Beaulieu-sur-Mer, including its elaborate 1904 **rotunda** with Corinthian columns capped by a cupola. Another *belle époque* beauty is the **Villa Grecque Kérylos** (☎ 04 93 76 44 09; www.villa-kerylos.com; av Gustave Eiffel; adult/student €7.80/5.50; ☉ 10am-7pm daily Jul & Aug, 10am-6pm daily mid-Feb–Jun & Sep-early Nov, early-Nov–Dec & Jan–mid-Feb 2-6pm Mon-Fri, 10am-6pm Sat & Sun), a reproduction of an Athenian villa built by archaeologist Théodore Reinach in 1902.

Moyenne Corniche

The Moyenne Corniche, the middle coastal road (the N7), clings to the hillside. It was here that Alfred Hitchcock filmed *To Catch a Thief* starring Grace Kelly, who met Prince Rainier of Monaco during that time; and it was here that she later lost her life in a car crash. It's a hair-raising road, even if you do keep your eyes on it, and not the dazzling views. From Nice, the Moyenne Corniche travels past the Col de Villefranche and Èze to Beausoleil, the French town bordering Monte Carlo.

ÈZE
pop 2742

At the pinnacle of a 427m peak is the medieval stone village of Èze. Once occupied by Ligurians and Phoenicians, today it's home to one-off galleries and artisan boutiques within its enclosed walls (there's only one doorway in or out of the village). The high point is the **Jardin Èze** (admission €5; ☉ 9am-sunset), a slanting cliff-side garden of exotic cacti interspersed with ethereal sculptures.

To explore the village's nooks and crannies after the tour buses have left, donkeys can cart your luggage uphill from the car park to the **Château Eza** (☎ 04 93 41 12 24; www .thesteingroup.com/chateau; rue de la Pise; d from €150; ✗ ✸), which also has a lofty gastronomic restaurant and terrace (lunch *menu* €37 to €47, dinner *menu* €95) with views of the Med on a plate.

On the seaside below is the village's coastal counterpart, Èze-sur-Mer (where U2's Bono and The Edge have neighbouring houses). Èze-sur-Mer and Èze village are connected by a spectacular (and steep!) walking path, where German philosopher Friedrich Nietzsche (1844–1900) mused about the theories that formed the basis of his work *Thus Spoke Zarathustra*. The rocky path takes about an hour, and in winter it's the only link without your own wheels. In summer a shuttle bus meets every train. Year round, buses 82 and 112 run direct to Èze village from Nice (€1.30; 20 minutes). There's a helpful **tourist office** (☎ 04 93 41 26 00; www.eze-riviera.com; place du Général de Gaulle) at the base of the village.

Grande Corniche

The Grande Corniche, whose panoramas are the most dramatic of all, leaves Nice as the D2564. It passes **La Turbie** (population 2609), which sits on a promontory directly above Monaco and offers stunning views of the principality. The best views are from the town's **Trophée des Alps** (☎ 04 93 41 20 84; 18 av Albert 1; adult/child €4/2.50; ☽ 10am-5pm Tue-Sun winter, longer in summer), one of only two Roman Trophy monuments in the world (the other's in Romania), built by Augustus in 6 BC. The corniche continues to **Roquebrune** (population 12,376), a hilltop village of tortuous streets, arcaded passages and stairways, leading to a 10th-century castle. The architect Le Corbusier is buried in Roquebrune's cemetery.

MENTON

pop 30,000

To the east of Monaco, the pastel-shaded, palm-lined seaside town of Menton is within walking distance of the Italian border.

Bordered by lush gardens and lemon groves, Menton has a pretty pebbled beach and a charming old town. Overall, it's a lot less touristed (and, hence, generally less expensive) than other spots on the Côte d'Azur. And it's warmer. Thanks to the surrounding hills, which trap the warm air from the Mediterranean within the town, Menton is said to have the highest temperatures on the coast; it's not unheard of for it to be snowing in Ventimiglia a few kilometres away while the sun's shining in Menton.

Menton's mild subtropical microclimate makes it ripe for cultivating lemons, which take centre stage during the town's exuberant annual Fête des Citrons (Lemon Festival).

Orientation

Promenade du Soleil runs southwest to northeast along the beach; the train line runs approximately parallel about 500m inland. Av Édouard VII links the train station with the beach. Av Boyer, home to the tourist office, is 350m to the east. From the station, turn left and walk along av de la Gare, then take the second right; the tourist office is about halfway down av Boyer. The Gare Routière (bus station) is approximately 500m north along av Boyer from the tourist office.

Av Boyer and its parallel to the west, av Verdun, are divided by the Jardins Biovès, an elongated sequence of parks where the annual Lemon Festival displays are held.

On and around the hill at the northeastern end of promenade du Soleil is the old town; the Vieux Port lies just beyond it.

Information

BOOKSHOPS

Librairie de la Presse (25 av Félix Faure) Stocks a fine range of guides, travel books and foreign-language newspapers.

INTERNET ACCESS

Café des Arts (☎ 04 93 35 78 67; 16 rue de la République; per 15min €1.15; ☽ 7.30am-11am & 2.15-10pm Mon-Sat; restaurant 7.30am-10pm Mon-Sat) Also a funky café with mains from €7 to €13.

MONEY

There are plenty of banks with exchange facilities along rue Partouneaux.
Barclays Bank (☎ 04 93 28 60 00; 39 av Félix Faure) Has an automatic exchange machine outside.
Crédit Lyonnais (av Boyer) Two doors down from the tourist office. There's a 24-hour currency machine outside.

POST

Post Office (cours George V) With a Cyberposte.

TOURIST INFORMATION

Service du Patrimoine (Heritage Office; ☎ 04 92 10 97 10; fax 04 93 28 46 85; 24 rue St-Michel; ☽ 10am-12.30pm & 1.30-6pm Tue-Sat) Runs thematic organised tours (Menton and the belle époque, artists, gardens etc) for €5 per person.
Tourist Office (☎ 04 92 41 76 76; www.menton.fr; 8 av Boyer; ☽ 9am-7pm summer; 8.30am-12.30pm & 1.30-6pm Mon-Fri, 9am-noon & 2-6pm Sat winter) In the Palais de l'Europe.

Sights & Activities

Step back in time in the peaceful **old town**, where you might hear a choir singing in the **Basilic St-Michel** (☽ 3-5.15pm). The ornate, Italian-inspired early-17th-century basilica sits above the centre of the old town, accessed by a labyrinth of little staircases from the old town's narrow lanes.

In a seafront bastion dating from 1636, the **Musée Jean Cocteau** (☎ 04 93 57 72 30; quai Napoléon III; admission €3; ☼ 10am-noon & 2-6pm Wed-Mon) displays drawings, tapestries and mosaics by the multitalented poet, dramatist, artist and film director. You can view Cocteau's frescoes in the **Salle des Mariages** (Marriage Hall; place Ardoïno; admission €1.50; ☼ 8.30am-noon & 1.30-5pm Mon-Fri) in the Hôtel de Ville.

Yes, Menton has a **beach**, along promenade du Soleil, and yes, it's free, but no, like Nice there's no sand, only pebbles. You'll find sandy private beaches directly north of the Vieux Port, and east of Port de Garavan, the main pleasure-boat harbour.

Base Nautique (☎ 04 93 35 49 70; promenade de la Mer; ☼ closed Sun) rents laser-class dinghies/catamarans/kayaks for €19/31/8 per hour. The **sailing school** also runs courses that cost €115 for five two-hour sessions.

Sleeping

Auberge de Jeunesse (☎ 04 93 35 93 14; www.fuaj .org; Plateau St-Michel; dm €15.70, sheets €2.70; ☼ reception 7am-10am & 5-10pm, closed Nov-Jan) Menton's HI hostel is a 1.5km hike uphill from the train station. Take the (infrequent) bus 6 to the camp site, situated 500m from the hostel.

Camping Saint Michel (☎ 04 93 35 81 23; route des Ciappes de Castellar; 2 adults, tent & car around €15; ☼ 1 Apr-15 Oct) This two-star ground has good kids' play areas. Get here on bus 6.

Hôtel Claridges (☎ 04 93 35 72 53; www.claridges -menton.com; 39 av de Verdun; s €37-50, d €47-67)

Handy for the bus and also for the train stations, although a brisk couple of kilometres' walk from the old town, this early-1900s hotel has 39 rooms that won't set the design world alight, but with their own bathroom (tub or shower) at this price, who cares?

Hôtel Richelieu (☎ 04 93 35 74 71; www.hotel richelieumenton.com; 26 rue Partouneaux; s €39-48, d €49-89) Some of the 2.5m ceilinged rooms here have air conditioning, and all have modernised bathrooms and floating floors. There's nearby public parking, and an owner who's kind to travellers.

Hôtel des Arcades (☎ 04 93 35 70 62; fax 04 93 35 35 97; 41 av Félix Faure; s €40-61, d €51-74) At the edge of the pedestrian district 50m from the sea, this colourfully colonnaded ochre hotel with pale blue shutters and lemon coin work has basic but character-filled rooms with TVs and phones. Rooms 110 and 111 open to a sweeping terrace. Pet pooches are free, and rates include breakfast. Wheelchair access is good.

Le Royal Westminster (☎ 04 93 28 69 69; www .vacancesbleues.com; 1501 promenade du Soleil; s €58-85, d €75-133; ☼ 🖳) It's a chain but you wouldn't know it from the 1870 building, which has just been completely renovated. It has good wheelchair access. In a great spot right on the promenade, there's discounted parking (€8 per 24 hours) close by.

Eating

You'll find cheerful, casual eating places galore along av Félix Faure and its pedestrianised continuation, rue St-Michel. Place Clemenceau and place aux Herbes in the Vieille Ville are also fruitful for inexpensive

---

FRUITY FÊTE

Since the 1930s, Menton's lemon cultivation has been embraced during its **Fête des Citrons** (Lemon Festival). Every February, lemon-adorned floats weave processions along the seafront, accompanied by marching bands; houses are decorated Hansel-and-Gretel-style with lemons on the roofs; and giant wire-framed sculptures bearing thousands of lemons fill the Jardins Biovès. The sculptures are based around an annual narrative theme, which might be anything from Asterix to Alice in Wonderland.

Five metric tonnes of the total 120 metric tonnes are used to replace fruit that rots during the course of the festival. Afterwards, the sculptures and floats are dismantled, and undamaged fruit is sold off at bargain prices out the front of the Palais de l'Europe.

Year round you can view Europe's largest variety of citrus in the gardens of the **Palais Carnolès** (☎ 04 93 35 49 71; 3 av de la Madone; admission free; ☼ 10am-noon & 2-6pm Wed-Mon). The tourist office has bucket loads of info about the town's favourite fruit.

MONACO'S NEW MONARCH

Recently Monaco mourned the loss of its beloved monarch, Prince Rainier (1923–2005), who had a fairytale marriage to Hollywood actress Grace Kelly (1929–82) in 1956, and who ruled from 1949 until his death on 6 April 2005. Their son, Albert (1958–), undertook his official advent on 12 July 2005, and was enthroned on 19 November 2005.

Monaco's new monarch is renowned for his athletic achievements (he played on the national soccer team, is a black belt in judo, and competed in several Olympics with the Monaco bobsleigh team), and his humanitarian efforts (he set up Monaco's Aid & Presence Association). But like his sisters, Princess Caroline (1957–) and Princess Stephanie (1965–), the 'world's most eligible bachelor' (at the time of writing, at least), has garnered his share of space in the tabloids, thanks to a string of high-profile relationships and his 2005 confirmation that he has a son, born in 2003 to Togolese Nicole Coste; and 2006's revelation that he has a daughter, born in 1992, to American Tamara Rotolo. Under the monarchy, however, heirs must be born in wedlock; and the constitution was modified to take Albert's bachelor status into account; making his elder sister Caroline next in line, for now.

dining options, as is quai de Monléon. The pricier restaurants with terraces fanned by cool breezes are along promenade du Soleil.

Du Centre Beaux-Arts (☎ 04 93 35 70 62; fax 04 93 35 35 97; 41 av Félix Faure; mains €9-20; �ّ closed Mon Oct-Apr) In the bygone grandeur of the Hôtel des Arcades, you can dine under the arches or in the coffered-ceiling, timber-lined dining room on Italian favourites like tagliatelle with scampi.

Abraijade (☎ 04 93 35 65 65; 66 rue Longue; mains €15-24; ☟ lunch & dinner Thu-Mon Sep-Jun, dinner Jul-Aug) Menton's hidden treasure is this very local little place along the main narrow street in the old town, cooking gastronomic Mediterranean meals served by candlelight.

Le Louvre (☎ 04 93 28 75 75; 3 rue Partouneaux; breakfast €20, mains €27-39; ☟ breakfast, lunch & dinner) The resplendent, rose-coloured 19th-century Grand Hotel des Ambassadeurs (doubles from €330) houses four floors of original art along with a marble and white-table-cloth restaurant with gourmet cuisine. There's also an annexe restaurant at the hotel's private beach, reached by a shuttle bus.

If you're planning a beach picnic, fill your basket at the old town's covered market, **Marché Municipal** (Les Halles; quai de Monléon; ☟5am-1pm Tue-Sun), or pop into the supermarket **8 à Huit** (7 rue Amiral Courbet; ☟ 9am-7.45pm Mon-Sat, 12.30-7.45pm Sun).

Getting There & Away

The **bus station** (☎ 04 93 28 43 27, information office 04 93 35 93 60) is next to 12 promenade Maréchal Leclerc, the northern continuation of av Boyer. There are buses to Monaco (€2.20 return, 30 minutes), Nice (€5.20 return, 1¼ hours), Ste-Agnès (€7.20 return, 45 minutes) and Sospel (€4.20 return, 45 minutes). There are also buses to the Nice-Côte d'Azur airport (€16.40, 1½ hours) via Monaco run by **Bus RCA** (☎ 04 93 85 64 44).

Trains going to Ventimiglia cost €2.20 and take 10 minutes. For more information on train services along the Côte d'Azur see p880.

TUM (Transports Urbains de Menton; ☎ 04 93 35 93 60) runs nine bus lines in the area. Lines 1 and 2 link the train station with the old town. Tickets cost €1.20.

MONACO (PRINCIPAUTÉ DE MONACO)

pop 32,000 / ☎ 377

After scaling Monaco's steep terraced steps, shiny escalators and gleaming marble corridors tunnelling through the rocks to a series of free public lifts running up and down the hillside (not to mention navigating the 3D road system encircling its towering high rises!), you could be forgiven for thinking you're inside a life-size MC Escher illustration of an illusionary maze.

Squeezed into 1.95 sq km, making it the world's second smallest country, after the Vatican, this pint-sized principality is a sovereign state, with its own red-and-white flag, national holiday (19 November), country telephone code and traditional Monégasque dialect. French is the official language, although many street signs, especially in the old Monaco Ville quarter, are in French and Monégasque, and children of all 107 nationalities that form Monaco's population are required to study the language at school. Neither is Monaco part of the EU, but because of its close ties with France it participates in the EU customs territory, and there are no border formalities crossing to and from France.

Monaco's manicured streets presided over by palaces and its lush fountained parks are eminently safe thanks to a prolific police presence backed up by plain-clothed patrollers and omnipresent CCTV cameras.

Monaco is most famed for its glamorous Monte Carlo casino, Formula One cars roaring through the streets during its glamorous Grand Prix, and the scintillating lives of its glamorous royal family, the Grimaldis.

History
Originally from the nearby Genoa region of Italy (hence the Monégasque language's similarity with the Genoese dialect), the Grimaldi family has ruled Monaco for most of the period since 1297, except for its occupation during the French Revolution, and loss of territories in 1848. Its independence was again recognised by France in 1860. Five years later, a monetary agreement with France and the opening of the Monte Carlo casino revived the country's fortunes. Today there are just 7800 Monégasque citizens, by either parentage or marriage, out of the total population; they live an idyllic tax-free life of cradle-to-grave security. Alas, all other residents and businesses pay tax.

Orientation
Monaco is made up of six main areas: Monaco Ville (also known as the old city and Rocher de Monaco), with its narrow, fairy-tale streets leading to the Palais du Prince (Prince's Palace) on a 60m-high outcrop of rock on the southern side of the port; the capital, Monte Carlo, which is north of the port; La Condamine, the predominantly

flat area immediately to the southwest of the port; Fontvieille, the industrial area southwest of Monaco Ville; Moneghetti, the hillside suburb west of La Condamine; and Larvotto, the beach area north of Monte Carlo, from where the French town of Beausoleil is just three streets uphill.

Information
BOOKSHOPS
Scruples (☎ 93 50 43 52; 9 rue Princesse Caroline) Well-stocked English-language bookshop.

INTERNET ACCESS
Stars 'n' Bars (☎ 93 50 95 95; www.starsnbars.com; 6 quai Antoine 1er; per 15min €2; ☑ 11am-midnight) There's a cybercorner and wi-fi inside this rockin' restaurant/bar (p911).

LAUNDRY
Laverie Laundrette (1 Escalier de la Riviera, Beausoleil; ☑ 7am-7pm) On the border between Monaco and France.

MEDICAL SERVICES
Centre Hospitalier Princesse Grace (☎ emergencies 97 98 97 69; ☎ switchboard 97 98 99 00; av Pasteur)

MONEY
Monaco-imprinted Euro coins are rarely spotted in circulation, and are quickly pocketed by collectors.

There are (of course!) numerous banks near the casino. In La Condamine, you'll find banks on blvd Albert 1er.
Change Bureau (Jardins du Casino; ☑ 9am-7.30pm)

POST
Monégasque stamps must be used to post mail within Monaco and to countries beyond; rates are the same as France. There are post office branches in each of Monaco's districts.
Post Office (1 av Henri Dunant) In Monte Carlo inside the Palais de la Scala.

TELEPHONE
Calls between Monaco and France are international calls. Dial 00 followed by Monaco's country code (377) when calling Monaco from France or elsewhere abroad. To phone France from Monaco, dial 00 and France's country code (33), even if you're only calling from the eastern side of blvd de France (in Monaco) to its western side (in France)!

CÔTE D'AZUR & MONACO

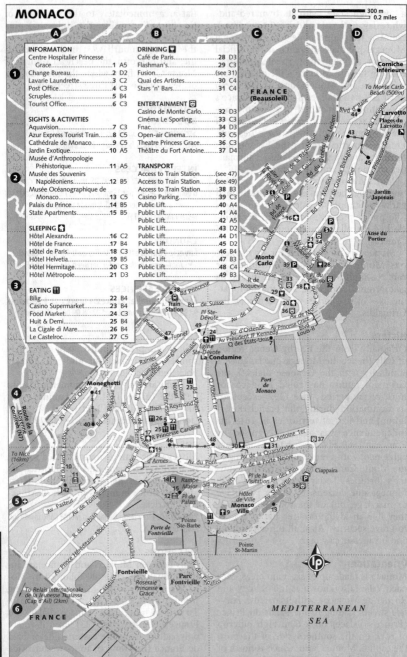

MONACO

0 _____ 300 m
0 _____ 0.2 miles

INFORMATION
Centre Hospitalier Princesse
  Grace..............................1 A5
Change Bureau.....................2 D2
Lavarie Laundrette.................3 C2
Post Office..........................4 C3
Scruples.............................5 B4
Tourist Office.......................6 C3

SIGHTS & ACTIVITIES
Aquavision..........................7 C3
Azur Express Tourist Train........8 C5
Cathédrale de Monaco.............9 C5
Jardin Exotique.....................10 A5
Musée d'Anthropologie
  Préhistorique.....................11 A5
Musée des Souvenirs
  Napoléoniens.....................12 B5
Musée Océanographique de
  Monaco............................13 C5
Palais du Prince....................14 B5
State Apartments..................15 B5

SLEEPING
Hôtel Alexandra....................16 C2
Hôtel de France....................17 B4
Hôtel de Paris......................18 C3
Hôtel Helvetia.....................19 B5
Hôtel Hermitage...................20 C3
Hôtel Métropole...................21 D3

EATING
Bilig..................................22 B4
Casino Supermarket...............23 B4
Food Market........................24 C3
Huit & Demi.........................25 B4
La Cigale di Mare..................26 C5
Le Castelroc........................27 C5

DRINKING
Café de Paris.......................28 D3
Flashman's..........................29 C3
Fusion...........................(see 31)
Quai des Artistes..................30 C4
Stars 'n' Bars......................31 C4

ENTERTAINMENT
Casino de Monte Carlo...........32 D3
Cinéma Le Sporting...............33 C3
Fnac.................................34 C3
Open-air Cinema..................35 C5
Theatre Princess Grace..........36 C3
Théâtre du Fort Antoine.........37 D4

TRANSPORT
Access to Train Station........(see 47)
Access to Train Station........(see 49)
Access to Train Station...........38 B3
Casino Parking.....................39 C3
Public Lift...........................40 A4
Public Lift...........................41 A4
Public Lift...........................42 A5
Public Lift...........................43 D2
Public Lift...........................44 D1
Public Lift...........................45 D2
Public Lift...........................46 B4
Public Lift...........................47 B3
Public Lift...........................48 C4
Public Lift...........................49 B3

FRANCE
(Beausoleil)

Corniche
Inférieure

To Monte Carlo
Beach (500m)

Larvotto
Plages du
Larvotto

Jardin
Japonais

Monte
Carlo

Anse du
Portier

Train
Station

Pl Ste-
Dévote

La Condamine

Port
de
Monaco

Moneghetti

To Nice
(16km)

Pl
d'Armes

Ciappaira

Pointe
Ste-Barbe

Hôtel
de Ville

Monaco
Ville

Pointe
St-Martin

Porte de
Fontvieille

Fontvieille

Parc
Fontvieille

Roseraie
Princesse
Grace

To Relais Internationale
de la Jeunesse Thalassa
(Cap d'Ail) (2km)

FRANCE

MEDITERRANEAN
SEA

TOURIST INFORMATION

Direction du Tourisme et des Congrès de la Principauté de Monaco (☎ 92 16 61 16; www.monaco -tourisme.com; 2a blvd des Moulins; ☺ 9am-7pm Mon-Sat, 10am-noon Sun) Across the public gardens from the casino. From mid-June to late-September additional tourist information kiosks open around the harbour and the train station.

Sights & Activities

PALAIS DU PRINCE

They're changing guard at Monaco's **Palais du Prince** (Prince's Palace; ☎ 93 25 18 31), at the southern end of rue des Remparts in Monaco Ville, every day at 11.55am. Dressed in spiffy white uniforms in summer, black in winter, the guards appear apparently resigned to the comic-opera nature of their duties. For a half-hour inside glimpse into royal life, you can tour the **state apartments** (adult/child €4/2; ☺ 9.30am-6.30pm Jun-Sep, 10am-5pm Oct, closed Nov-May) with a 10-language audio guide.

A combined ticket, which also lets you view a display of Napoleon's personal effects in the southern wing of the palace at the **Musée des Souvenirs Napoléoniens** (☺ 9.30am-6.30pm Jun-Sep, 10am-5pm Oct, closed Nov-May), costs €8 (children €4).

MUSÉE OCÉANOGRAPHIQUE DE MONACO

Rising imperially from the sheer cliff face, the 1910-built **Musée Océanographique de Monaco** (☎ 93 15 36 00; av St-Martin; adult/student €11/6; ☺ 9.30am-7pm Jul & Aug, to 6.30pm Apr-Jun & Sep) houses one of the world's best aquariums, with tropical coral, eerie sharks, and cunning chameleon fish. One vast, columned floor explores the evolution of oceanography. Even if you're not dining at the rooftop **restaurant** (mains €11-21; ☺ noon-4pm, closed Jan) or adjoining **brasserie** (mains €10-17; ☺ 10am-5pm, closed Jan), come up for a squiz at the spectacular views. It's a hilly but exhilarating walk along the exposed cliff-face from Monte Carlo (best avoided in high winds); alternatively take buses 1 or 2.

CATHÉDRALE DE MONACO

Prince Rainier and Princess Grace are buried on the western side of the cathedral choir of the 1875 Romanesque–Byzantine **Cathédrale de Monaco** (4 rue Colonel). Monaco's boys' choir, Les Petits Chanteurs de Monaco, sings Sunday Mass at 10am between September and June.

JARDIN EXOTIQUE

Flowering year-round, over a thousand species of cacti and succulents tumble down the slopes of the **Jardin Exotique** (☎ 93 15 29 80; 62 blvd du Jardin Exotique; adult/student €6.80/3.50; ☺ 9am-7pm mid-May–mid-Sep, 9am-6pm mid-Sep–mid-May); Apart from the spectacular vistas over the principality, your admission also includes entry to the **Musée d'Anthropologie Préhistorique** and, 279 steps down the hillside, a half-hour guided visit of the stalactites and stalagmites in the **Observatory Caves**. From the tourist office, take bus 2 to the Jardin Exotique terminus.

BEACHES

A few kilometres east of Monte Carlo, Monaco's nearest beaches are the free **Plages du Larvotto** and the €60-a-day **Monte Carlo Beach** including a sun lounge, security for your accoutrements while you bathe, and parking.

Tours

A saviour from all those hills is the **Azur Express tourist train** (☎ 92 05 64 38; tour €6). Starting opposite the Musée Océanographique, multilanguage, 30-minute city tours run every day from 10.30am to 6pm (11am to 5pm in winter).

Festivals & Events

Triple Brazilian world champion Nelson Piquet famously likened driving Monaco's **Formula One Grand Prix** to 'riding a bicycle around your living room'. Monaco's cachet nonetheless means it's the most coveted trophy; and the narrow lanes, tortuous road layout and hairpin bends (the MC Escher painting, remember?) means spectators can get closer to the action than most circuits. Trackside tickets (from about €50) for the May event can be purchased from the Automobile Club de Monaco (www.amc.mc), but get in early as demand is steeper than the near-vertical streets (as are ticket prices for the better locations).

Also death-defying, the **International Circus Festival of Monaco** (www.montecarlofestivals.com) held each year in late January, showcases heart-stopping acts from around the globe.

Sleeping

BUDGET

If your shoestring budget's fraying, consider basing yourself at one of Nice's hostels or budget hotels and taking the quick 20-minute train trip to Monaco.

Otherwise try the **Relais Internationale de la Jeunesse Thalassa** (☎ 04 93 78 18 58; blvd de la Mer, Cap d'Ail; dm €14; ☺ closed Nov-Mar), the closest hostel to Monaco, in a beautiful spot right by the sea on Cap d'Ail.

The neighbouring French town of Beausoleil is also a good hunting ground for lower-priced accommodation.

MIDRANGE

Hôtel Helvetia (☎ 93 30 21 71; www.monte-carlo .mc/helvetia; 1bis rue Grimaldi; s without bathroom €56-70, s with bathroom €73-83, d without bathroom €68-78, d with bathroom €78-91; ☒) Overlooking the alfresco cafés of rue Princesse Caroline, and place d'Armes, the Helvetia is handy for the port and the train station. Its simple rooms have an old-fashioned charm. Rates include breakfast; for a bit extra you can get air conditioning.

Hôtel de France (☎ 93 30 24 64; fax 92 16 13 34; 6 rue de la Turbie; s/d/tr €70/80/93) Your best bet for bargain accommodation in Monaco is this well-located little almond-coloured place within walking distance of the old city and the casino, with parking available nearby for €7.20 for 24 hours. Appealing ensuite rooms are equipped with cable TV, telephones and hair dryers; breakfast costs €9.

Hôtel Alexandra (☎ 93 50 63 13; fax 92 16 06 48; 35 blvd Princesse Charlotte; s €95-115, d €120-150, tr €160-180; ☒) This turn-of-the-twentieth-century hotel is the closest you'll find to a midrange place in Monaco. It's in a great Monte Carlo location near the train station, and its 56 rooms are spacious, comfy and modernised; with minibars and soundproofing.

TOP END

Here are some world-famous places to blow your winnings:

Hôtel Métropole (☎ 93 15 15 35; www.metropole .com; 4 av de la Madone; d low season from €355, high season €440, 'very high season' €460; ☒ 🖳 🐾) A sumptuously renovated 1889 palace in the heart of Monte Carlo, with black and white diamond-laid marble floors, a massive mosaic-tiled swimming pool and considerate staff.

Hôtel Hermitage (☎ 92 16 40 00; www.montecar loresort.com; square Beaumarchais; d low season from €355, high season €440, 'very high season' €490; ☒ 🖳 🐾) This fresco-cloistered Italianate landmark

with good wheelchair access is replete with soaring pink marble columns, elegant rooms in soothing Wedgwood blues, and a stained-glass winter garden built by Gustave Eiffel.

Hôtel de Paris (☎ 92 16 30 00; www.montecar loresort.com; place du Casino; d low season from €390, high season €480, 'very high season' €580; ☒ 🖳 🐾) The Palais du Prince pales in comparison with this 1864 domed palace a dice's throw from the casino, where the writer Colette spent her final years. Swim in the serene pool overlooking the sea, and dine on Alain Ducasse's cuisine.

Eating

Decent-priced restaurants congregate in La Condamine along place d'Armes and rue Princesse Caroline; you'll find sandwich bars along quai Albert 1er. In Monte Carlo, there are a few snack stops inside the Métropole shopping centre.

If you're living it *way* up, head to the dining rooms of the sumptuous hotels.

Bilig (☎ 97 98 20 45; 11bis rue Princesse Caroline; mains €5-10.50; ☺ to 6pm winter, to 10pm summer, closed Sun) This small, charming *crêperie* has a cute wooden outdoor deck and cosy interior and serves superior savoury and sweet *crêpes*.

La Cigale di Mare (☎ 97 77 14 64; 4 rue Baron de Ste-Suzanne; mains €9-20; ☺ noon-3pm & 7.30-11pm Mon-Fri) As unpretentious as it gets, this little pink-tablecloth, family-run place specialises in scrumptious seafood/pasta combinations like fusili with baby octopus, or gnocchi with red mullet.

Huit & Demi (☎ 93 50 97 02; cnr rue Langlé & rue Princesse Caroline; mains €12-27; ☺ noon-3pm & 7-11pm, closed Sun & lunch Sat) Dine on tasty Italian dishes surrounded by crimson curtains and crimson walls hung with black and white movie-star posters. The pavement terrace occupying the adjoining pedestrian lane is prime when the weather's warm.

Le Castelroc (☎ 93 30 36 68; place du Palais; ☺ 9am-3pm daily, dinner Tue-Sat May-Sep; mains €22-27) Right across from the Palace, the entrance is lined by T-shirt and souvenir shops but amazingly Le Castelroc is no tourist trap. Spilling out to an alfresco terrace, its twin dining rooms are the best place around to try authentic Monégasque specialities like *barbadjuan* (a beignet filled with spinach and cheese) and *pissaladière* (onion tart with tomato; France's version is sans tomato).

SELF-CATERING

Self-catering pit-stops include a **food market** (place d'Armes; ⏲ from 7am Mon-Sat) and a **Casino Supermarket** (blvd Albert 1er), both in La Condamine. Unfortunately, spreading out a picnic blanket in the manicured parks is illegal.

Drinking

Café de Paris (☎ 92 16 20 20; place du Casino; mains €17-53; ⏲ 7am-2am) Adjacent to the opulent Monte Carlo Casino, this is a fabulous spot for classy French fare, and for limo-spotting from the sprawling 300-seat terrace.

Stars 'n' Bars (☎ 93 50 95 95; 6 quai Antoine 1er; mains €14.50-22; ⏲ noon-2.30am Tue-Sun) On the south side of the port, this huge American western saloon has a stratospheric reputation as an international party spot. Chow down on humungous hamburgers and homemade apple pie (served until midnight), and swig €5.50 bottles of Bud or €160 bottles of Dom Pérignon before playing the Grand Prix arcade games and foosball.

Fusion (☎ 97 97 95 95; 6 quai Antoine 1er; mains €15-25; ⏲ 7pm-2.30am, closed Sun). The Love Boat just sailed into the 21st century via Asia at this place built like the interior of a cruise liner above Stars 'n' Bars, overlooking the port. Lots of sushi, lots of glittering views.

Quai des Artistes (☎ 97 97 97 77; 4 quai Antoine 1er; mains €18-29; ⏲ noon-1am) This posh portside restaurant/cocktail bar in a large warehouse-style space stages monthly rotating contemporary art exhibitions.

Flashman's (☎ 93 30 09 03; 7 av Princesse Alice; ⏲ 8am-5am Mon-Fri, 7am-5am Sat & Sun) An upstairs concrete and steel bar leads underground to a disco area at this Brit-run bolt hole.

Entertainment

Pack your evening wear for concerts, opera and ballet, held in the various venues. The tourist office has a schedule of local events. Tickets for most cultural events are sold at **FNAC** (☎ 93 10 81 81; Centre Commercial le Métropole, 17 av des Spélugues).

CASINOS

It doesn't get better for living out your James Bond fantasies than at Monte Carlo's monumental showpiece, the 1910-built **Casino de Monte Carlo** (☎ 92 16 20 00; www.casino-monte-carlo .com; ⏲ European & Private Rooms from noon Sat & Sun, from 2pm Mon-Fri). You have to pay even before you play: admission is €10 for the European Rooms, with poker/slot machines, French roulette and *trente et quarante;* and €20 for the Private Rooms, which offer baccarat, blackjack, craps and American roulette.

Punters can also pop into the (slightly) less glitzy gaming rooms adjoining the **Café de Paris** (see left), which have lower minimum bets.

Minimum entry age for both is 18; bring photo ID.

CINEMAS

Cinéma Le Sporting (☎ 0 836 680 072; place du Casino; tickets €9) often has movies in their original language. An **open-air cinema** (parking des Pêcheurs; €10-15) has nightly shows at 9.30pm in July and August, specialising in crowd-pleasing blockbusters.

THEATRE

The 18th-century fortress-turned-outdoor theatre, **Théâtre du Fort Antoine** (☎ 93 50 80 00; av de la Quarantaine; ⏲ plays usually 9pm Mon Jul & Aug), is a wonderful spot to while away a summer evening.

In winter, Monte Carlo's **Theatre Princess Grace** (☎ 93 25 32 27; www.tpgmonaco.com; 12 rue d'Ostende; tickets around €25-39), designed by the late Princess, stages anything from magic shows to gospel music and comedy.

Getting There & Away

BUS

Buses to France leave from various stops around the city; the tourist office has schedules and maps.

CAR

Some 25 official pay car parks are scattered around the principality. One of the most convenient is the casino parking from where you exit directly to the door of the tourist office. The first hour is free, the second costs €2.40, and every hour after that is €0.60.

If you're driving (not really necessary in this compact little country), note you can't take your car into Monaco Ville unless you have either a Monaco or a 06 (Alpes-Maritimes) licence plate.

TRAIN

Trains to and from Monaco's **train station** (av Prince Pierre) are run by the French SNCF.

CÔTE D'AZUR & MONACO

A train trip along the coast offers mesmerising views of the Mediterranean Sea and the mountains. There are frequent trains to Nice (€3.10, 25 minutes), and east to Menton (€1.70, 10 minutes), and the first town across the border in Italy, Ventimiglia (Vintimille in French; €3.10, 25 minutes).

Getting Around
BUS
Several urban bus lines traverse Monaco; No 4 links the train station with the tourist office and also with the casino. Tickets cost €1.30.

LIFTS
Some 15 public lifts (ascenseurs publics) whisk you up and down the hillsides. Most operate 24 hours, others run between 6am and midnight or 1am.

TAXI
Expect to pay around €12 for a 10-minute taxi ride. To order one, call ☎ 93 15 01 01.

Corsica

Shaped like a bunch of vine-ripened grapes, Corsica (Corse) ripples with mountain ranges covered in vivid green chestnut and pine forests, lush hillside pastures and fragrant *maquis* scrubland. Grape cultivation dates back over 3000 years, with exceptional vineyards on the island.

Corsica's coastline curls around 1000km of aquamarine and jade-green coves and glistening beaches and bays beneath cliffs. But until the early 19th century, the coast was considered worthless, susceptible to invasion. Corsicans took shelter in the mountains, and even today it's the interior that defines the culture. Typical Corsican cuisine consists of inland victuals like cured sausages, cheeses and lamb seasoned with wild herbs. Fishing traditionally took place around Cap Corse (the rugged 'stem' in the northeast). Away from the coastal resorts and bustling ports, the interior – which often stays snow-capped until July – is still where you're most likely to encounter Corsica's language, Corsu, as well as its distinctive customs and festivals.

The mountains make for exhilarating hikes, the most famous and challenging of which is the legendary GR20. (The death-defying switchback roads make for some dizzying driving, too.)

Pick your timing carefully – Corsica swells to bursting with summer visitors; all but withering in winter when many activities, accommodation and transport services slow or cease. The wildflower-filled spring and red-hued autumn months let you experience this *Île de beauté* (island of beauty) at its best.

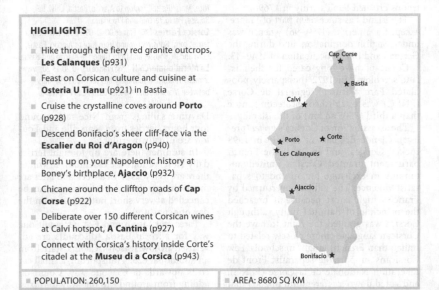

HIGHLIGHTS

- Hike through the fiery red granite outcrops, **Les Calanques** (p931)
- Feast on Corsican culture and cuisine at **Osteria U Tianu** (p921) in Bastia
- Cruise the crystalline coves around **Porto** (p928)
- Descend Bonifacio's sheer cliff-face via the **Escalier du Roi d'Aragon** (p940)
- Brush up on your Napoleonic history at Boney's birthplace, **Ajaccio** (p932)
- Chicane around the clifftop roads of **Cap Corse** (p922)
- Deliberate over 150 different Corsican wines at Calvi hotspot, **A Cantina** (p927)
- Connect with Corsica's history inside Corte's citadel at the **Museu di a Corsica** (p943)

Cap Corse • Bastia • Calvi • Porto • Corte • Les Calanques • Ajaccio • Bonifacio

■ POPULATION: 260,150 | ■ AREA: 8680 SQ KM

CORSICA

History

From the 11th to 13th centuries Corsica was ruled by the Italian city-state of Pisa, superseded in 1284 by its arch rival, Genoa. To prevent seaborne raids, mainly from North Africa, a massive defence system was constructed that included citadels and coastal watchtowers, many of which still dot the coastline.

On several occasions, Corsican discontent with foreign rule led to open revolt. In 1755, after 25 years of sporadic warfare against the Genoese, Corsicans declared their independence, led by Pasquale Paoli (1725–1807), under whose rule they established a National Assembly and adopted the most democratic constitution in Europe. They also adopted La Tête de Maure (the Moor's Head) – a profile of a black head wearing a white bandanna and a hooped earring, which first appeared in Corsica in 1297 – as a national emblem. According to legend, the bandanna originally covered the Moor's eyes, and was raised to the forehead to symbolise the island's liberation.

Corsicans made the inland mountain town of Corte their capital, outlawed blood vendettas, founded schools and established a university, but the island's independence was short-lived. In 1768 the Genoese ceded Corsica to the French king Louis XV, whose troops crushed Paoli's army in 1769.

The island has since been part of France, except for a period (1794–96) when it was under English domination, and during the German and Italian occupation of 1940–43.

Corsicans have long cared for their island's ecology. In 1972 the sparsely populated Parc Naturel Régional de Corse (PNRC) was established, protecting more than a third (3505 sq km) of the island.

The assassination of Corsica's préfet (prefect), Claude Erignac, in Ajaccio in 1998 rocked Corsica, and in 2001, the French parliament granted Corsica limited autonomy in exchange for an end to separatist violence. The bill was overturned by France's high court because it breached the principle of national unity, although Corsica was granted the right to have the Corsican language (more closely related to Italian than French) taught in schools. Few Corsicans support the separatist Front de Libération Nationale de la Corse (FLNC); and voted down a referendum in 2003 that would have seen the island gain greater autonomy. For now, Corsica remains part of France's rich mix of cultures.

Information

Visit Corsica (www.visit-corsica.com) This website features island-wide information.

Getting There & Away

AIR

Corsica's main airports are at Ajaccio, Bastia, Figari (near Bonifacio) and Calvi.

Air France (☎ 08 20 82 08 20; www.airfrance.com) has year-round flights from Paris and Lyon to all airports except Figari. Seasonal flights operate from Bordeaux, Lille, Nantes, Mulhouse and Strasbourg to Bastia or Ajaccio. Air France also flies regularly from London to Corsica's main airports.

Compagnie Corse Méditerranée (CCM; ☎ 08 20 82 08 20; www.ccm-airlines.com) flies from Bastia and Ajaccio to Marseille, Lyon and Nice year-round, and to Bordeaux, Lille, Lyon, Mulhouse, Nantes and Strasbourg in summer.

BOAT
Mainland France

Ferries between France and Corsica are operated by several lines:

Société Nationale Maritime Corse-Méditerranée (SNCM; ☎ 08 91 70 18 01; www.sncm.fr) Services from Nice, Marseille and Toulon to Ajaccio, Bastia, Calvi, Île Rousse, Porto Vecchio and Propriano.

Corsica Ferries (☎ France 08 25 09 50 95; www.corsica ferries.com) Runs year-round from Nice to Ajaccio, Bastia, Calvi and Île Rousse, and from Toulon to Ajaccio and Bastia.

La Méridionale/CMN (☎ France 08 10 20 13 20; www .cmn.fr) This SNCM subsidiary has year-round sailings between Marseille and Ajaccio, Bastia and Propriano.

Daytime sailings from Nice take around four hours; ferries from Marseille and Toulon are usually overnight.

In summer there are up to eight ferries daily (reservations are essential); in winter there are as few as eight a week and fares are much cheaper. In bad weather, boats can be cancelled at very short notice (often on the day of departure).

Fares start at around €24 per adult one way for Nice to Bastia (discounts are advertised in low season). Cabins start from an additional €25. Transporting a small car costs upwards of €53 one way. Count on adding from around €18 one way for taxes.

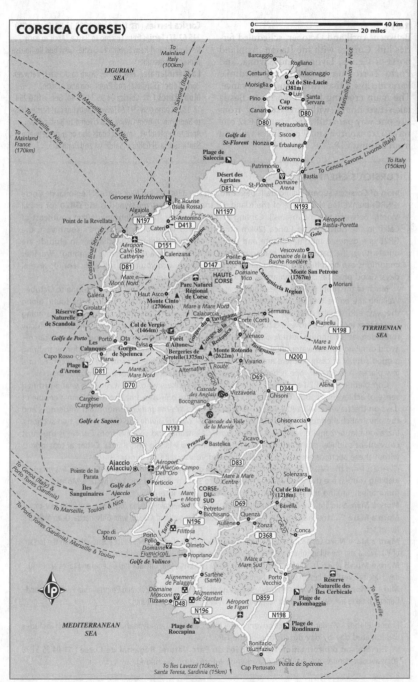

CORSICA (CORSE)

0   40 km
0   20 miles

CORSICA

Italy

Between April and October, scheduled ferries link Corsica with the Italian mainland ports of Genoa, Livorno and Savona, and Porto Torres on neighbouring Sardinia. Fares are lower than from mainland France. The main crossing from Livorno to Bastia takes two hours, with fares starting from €16 one way per adult, and around €32 one way to transport a small car. Taxes will add from around €18.

Corsica Ferries (☎ Livorno 0586 88 13 80, Savona 019 215 62 47) Ferries from Livorno to Bastia (April to early November) and from Savona to Bastia, Calvi and Île Rousse (April to September).
La Méridionale/CMN Ferries (April to October) between Porto Torres (Sardinia) and Propriano and Ajaccio.
Moby Lines (☎ Corsica 04 95 34 84 94, Genoa 010 254 15 13, Livorno 0565 93 61; www.mobylines.it) Ferries (May to September) from Genoa and Livorno to Bastia. From April to September, smaller boats also operate between Santa Teresa di Gallura (Sardinia) and Bonifacio.

CORSICA'S GREAT HIKES

Most of Corsica's superb hiking trails pass through the 3300-sq-km Parc Naturel Régional de Corse (PNRC) blanketing the centre of the island. Of them, the most renowned is the **GR20** (or Frá Li Monti, 'between the mountains'). Carving a 168km swathe from Calenzana (10km southeast of Calvi) in the northeast to Conca (20km north of Porto Vecchio) in the island's southwest, the GR20 is a genuine mountain route and shouldn't be taken lightly. The changes in altitude are unrelenting, the path is rocky and sometimes steep (be prepared for some climbing). Weather conditions can be difficult and you have to carry enough with you to be self-sufficient for several days. Good physical condition and advance training are essential.

Much of the route is above the snowline at 2000m and passable only from mid-June to October. Walking the entire trail takes at least 15 days. PNRC *refuges* (mountain huts) can be found along the way, and usually offer light meals, but reservations aren't accepted, so you'll need camping equipment including a stove and fuel – lighting fires at any point along a route in the park is strictly forbidden, as is camping outside designated areas. Drinking water along the route is also scarce – avoid drinking stream water unless absolutely necessary, and always purify it. Don't forget to bring a good supply of cash, as there are no ATMs on the GR20 and credit cards are only accepted in a few places. A length of rope is handy to lower your backpack down steep sections of the trail.

Completing the GR20 end to end gives the 10,000 walkers who take it on each year a justified sense of achievement. But for a taste, it's possible to bite off just a small section. Even a couple of days on the traverse will allow you to experience Corsica's magnificent mountain wilderness and the physical challenges of the trail. The most logical way to divide the GR20 is into two sections. Vizzavona (approximately a nine-day walk from Calenzana, and six days from Conca) is the most convenient midway point, with train and road links to Ajaccio and Bastia. Other access points within these sections are also possible, allowing you to take on shorter stages.

Apart from the GR20, Corsica's most celebrated *grandes randonnées* (long-distance, waymarked walking routes) are the three Mare a Mare ('sea to sea') trails, and the two Mare e Monti (sea and mountains), linking the west coast with Corsica's alpine interior.

Mare a Mare Sud This five-day trail connects Propriano to Porto Vecchio, passing Zonza en route. Open year-round.
Mare a Mare Centre This seven-day trail links Porticcio (25km south of Ajaccio) with Ghisonaccia. Open May to November.
Mare a Mare Nord Connects Cargèse with Moriani (40km south of Bastia), one route passing through the forest of Vizzavona and the village of Vénaco. Allow seven to 12 days. Open May to November.
Mare e Monti Nord Travels from Cargèse to Calenzana (via Évisa, Ota, Girolata and Galéria) and takes about 10 days. Open all year, but best in spring and autumn.
Mare e Monti Sud This walk runs between the bays of the resorts of Porticcio and Propriano via Porto Pollo and Olmeto. It takes five days and is open year-round, but is best in spring and autumn.

Lonely Planet's *Walking in France* covers many hikes, as does Lonely Planet's *Corsica*, which includes a dedicated day-by-day description of the GR20.

The **Maison d'Information Randonnées du Parc Naturel Régional de Corse** (☎ 04 95 51 79 10; www.parc-naturel-corse.com) has island-wide information on hiking.

Getting Around
BUS
Corsica's slow, infrequent buses are handled by several independent companies. On longer routes, which are mostly operated by **Eurocorse** (☎ Ajaccio 04 95 21 06 30, Porto Vecchio 04 95 70 13 83), there are one, two or, at most, four runs daily. Except in high summer, buses very rarely run on Sunday and holidays.

CAR & MOTORCYCLE
Driving is the most convenient way to explore Corsica, but navigating its narrow, twisting roads is not easy – see p929. A good road map (such as Michelin's yellow-jacketed 1:200,000 map No 90) is indispensable.

TRAIN
Corsica's single-track railway **Chemins de Fer de Corse** (CFC; ☎ Bastia 04 95 32 80 61; www .ter-sncf.com/trains_touristiques/corse_anglais.htm) is a great (if bone-shattering) way for visitors to explore the island. In Corsica, trains are known as *U Trinighellu* ('the trembler'), and you only have to spend five minutes on one to understand why. The tiny trains screech and judder their way through the mountains, stopping at rural stations and, when necessary, for sheep, goats and cows.

The network's two lines meet at Ponte Leccia. Between September and July, the Ajaccio–Corte–Bastia line is served by four daily trains (two on Sunday and holidays). Two daily trains (coordinated with the Ajaccio–Corte–Bastia service) link Bastia with Ponte Leccia, Île Rousse and Calvi. Services are reduced in winter and increased in August.

Fares for train travel range from €9.70 (Bastia–Corte) to €24.50 (Ajaccio–Calvi). Children under 12 travel half-price; under fours travel free. Transporting a bicycle costs €18.

For return journeys of less than 200km within 48 hours, the *billet touristique* (tourist ticket) is 25% cheaper than a regular ticket (for example a Bastia–Ajaccio return ticket costs €31), but is unavailable from July to September.

Holders of InterRail passes get 50% off normal fares. The CFC sells its own rail pass – the Carte Zoom – which costs €47 for seven days' unlimited train travel.

BASTIA AREA

BASTIA
pop 37,800
With its colourful jumble of tenement buildings built into the hillside and atmospheric old port, Bastia is in some ways like a miniature version of mainland Marseille: a thriving, lively city that's not tizzed up for tourists. Basking beneath the Mediterranean sun, the city's narrow streets are crowned by a crumbling 15th-century citadel.

Orientation
Bastia's focal point is place St-Nicolas. On the northern side, av Maréchal Sébastiani links the ferry port with the train station. Parallel to the square to the west are the main shopping thoroughfares, blvd Paoli and rue César Campinchi. The city's three older neighbourhoods are south of place St-Nicolas: Terra Vecchia (centred on place de l'Hôtel de Ville), the Vieux Port (old port) and the citadel.

Information
BOOKSHOPS
Librairie Album (☎ 04 95 31 08 59; 19 blvd Paoli; ☑ 8am-noon & 1.30-7.30pm Mon-Sat, 9am-12.30pm Sun) Big bookshop with an excellent travel section.
Librairie-Papeterie Papi (☎ 04 95 31 00 96; 5 rue César Campinchi; ☑ 7.30am-noon & 1.30-7pm Mon-Sat) Sells walking maps, topoguides and travel books.

EMERGENCY
Centre Hospitalier Général Paese Nuovo (☎ 04 95 59 11 11; Route Impériale)
Police National (☎ 04 95 54 50 22; av Paul Giacobbi) Near the northern ferry terminal.

INTERNET ACCESS
Cyber Space (☎ 04 95 30 70 83; 3 blvd Paoli; per 15min/hr €1/3.80; ☑ 9am-midnight Mon-Sat, 4pm-midnight Sun)

LAUNDRY
Le Lavoir du Port (☑ 7am-9pm) This laundrette is in the car park near the end of rue du Commandant Luce de Casabianca.

MONEY
Banks are dotted along place St-Nicolas and along rue César Campinchi and rue du Conventionnel Saliceti. Most have ATMs.

CORSICA

BASTIA (AND BEYOND) IN...

Two Days

Corsica covers less than 200km by 90km, and even a few days is enough to hit at least some of the island's highlights. The bustling port city of Bastia is a great gateway to the island, with some fine highlights of its own. Start with a stroll up to the city's **citadel** (below), with a stop in pretty **Jardin Romieu** (below), and a peek inside the amazing **Ortoire Baroque Ste-Croix** (below). While you're here, introduce your tastebuds to 'new Corsican cuisine' at **A Casarella** (p921). In the afternoon, spin along the clifftop roads of the pristine peninsula, **Cap Corse** (p922). Back in Bastia, head to **Osteria U Tianu** (p921) for a unique dining experience, then descend to the cave-like nightclub, **La Onzieme** (p921).

From Bastia, day two might carry you to the mountain-cradled former capital, **Corte** (p942). Or it might take you west to the north coast's village-like **Île Rousse** (p923), or the classy Mediterranean port, **Calvi** (p924); both are bounded by blissful beaches.

Four Days

Depending on your trajectory, day three could bring you down the wild west coast to the eucalyptus groves of **Porto** (p928). Or it might zip you to the glamorous capital, **Ajaccio** (p932), with its elegant alfresco eateries and swank shopping streets.

On day four, take a trip to 'Corsica's Gibraltar', **Bonifacio** (p938), perched on the island's southernmost promontory, and a **boat ride** (p940) through its stunning strait.

POST

Post Office (av Maréchal Sébastiani; ☒ 8am-7pm Mon-Fri, 8am-noon Sat)

TOURIST INFORMATION

Tourist Office (☎ 04 95 54 20 40; www.bastia-tourisme .com; place St-Nicolas; ☒ 8.30am-noon & 2-6pm Mon-Sat) Friendly multilingual office at the northern end of place St-Nicolas.

Sights

A half-day stroll is ideal to absorb Bastia's charms. Just back from the ferry terminal, **place St-Nicolas**, a vast seafront esplanade laid out in the 19th century, makes a good starting point. The square is lined with trees and cafés, and at the southern end a bizarre **statue** of Napoleon Bonaparte depicted as a muscle-bound Roman emperor stands guard, ringed by a phalanx of palm trees.

Between place St-Nicolas and the old port lies **Terra Vecchia**, a historic neighbourhood of old houses and tumbledown tenement blocks. Its centre is the shady **place de l'Hôtel de Ville**, now an open-air marketplace. On rue Napoléon, the baroque **Oratoire de l'Immaculée Conception** once served as the seat of the Anglo-Corsican parliament.

The Vieux Port (old port) is an enchanting jumble of boats, restaurants and ramshackle sunset-shaded buildings (magically illumi-

nated at night), dominated by the twin towers of the **Église St-Jean Baptiste**, which loom over the north side of the harbour. The best views are from **Jetée du Dragon** (Dragon Jetty) on the southern side of the harbour, where you can admire the luxury pleasure cruisers and watch the local blue-and-white fishing boats setting out to sea.

Bastia's **citadel** was built by the Genoese between the 15th and 17th centuries to protect the harbour. To reach it, climb the stairs through **Jardin Romieu**, the hillside park on the southern side of the harbour. Close by, the fiery-orange **Palais des Gouverneurs** (Governors' Palace; place du Donjon) is undergoing major renovations. Due to open in 2008, it will house Bastia's new history museum – check with the tourist office for updates.

Inside the citadel, winding streets lead to the former cathedral, **Église Ste-Marie**. Inside, depositing €0.20 in a coin box illuminates the treasured, glass-encased silver Virgin Mary for two minutes; the Italian organ is one of the finest on the island. Just behind the church on the southern side is the gilded Rococo **Ortoire Baroque Ste-Croix** (Brotherhood of Ste-Croix), which – apart from a riot of angels – contains one of the city's most precious relics, a mysterious black-oak crucifix hauled from the sea by fishermen in the 14th century. Also look for

CORSICA

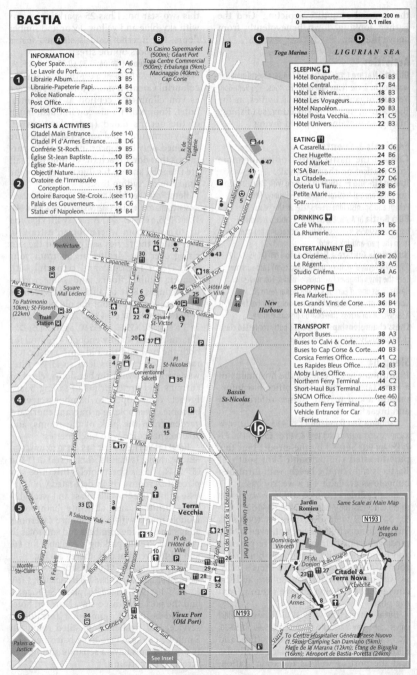

BASTIA

0 _____ 200 m
0 _____ 0.1 miles

INFORMATION
Cyber Space.....................................1 A6
Le Lavoir du Port...........................2 C2
Librairie Album...............................3 B5
Librairie-Papeterie Papi...............4 B4
Police Nationale..............................5 C2
Post Office.......................................6 B3
Tourist Office..................................7 B3

SIGHTS & ACTIVITIES
Citadel Main Entrance.............(see 14)
Citadel Pl d'Armes Entrance......8 D6
Confrérie St-Roch..........................9 B5
Église St-Jean Baptiste................10 B5
Église Ste-Marie..........................11 D6
Objectif Nature.............................12 B3
Oratoire de l'Immaculée
  Conception.................................13 B5
Ortoire Baroque Ste-Croix....(see 11)
Palais des Gouverneurs..............14 C6
Statue of Napoléon.....................15 B4

SLEEPING
Hôtel Bonaparte...........................16 B3
Hôtel Central.................................17 B4
Hôtel Le Riviera............................18 B3
Hôtel Les Voyageurs....................19 B3
Hôtel Napoléon.............................20 B3
Hôtel Posta Vecchia.....................21 C5
Hôtel Univers................................22 B3

EATING
A Casarella....................................23 C6
Chez Hugette................................24 B6
Food Market.................................25 C5
K'SA Bar..26 C5
La Citadelle...................................27 D6
Osteria U Tianu............................28 B6
Petite Marie..................................29 B6
Spar...30 B3

DRINKING
Café Wha......................................31 B6
La Rhumerie.................................32 C6

ENTERTAINMENT
La Onzieme.............................(see 26)
Le Régent.....................................33 A5
Studio Cinéma.............................34 A6

SHOPPING
Flea Market...................................35 B4
Les Grands Vins de Corse............36 B4
LN Mattei......................................37 B3

TRANSPORT
Airport Buses................................38 A3
Buses to Calvi & Corte.................39 A3
Buses to Cap Corse & Corte........40 B3
Corsica Ferries Office...................41 C2
Les Rapides Bleus Office..............42 B3
Moby Lines Office.........................43 C3
Northern Ferry Terminal..............44 C2
Short-Haul Bus Terminal.............45 B3
SNCM Office...........................(see 46)
Southern Ferry Terminal.............46 C3
Vehicle Entrance for Car
  Ferries.......................................47 C2

Toga Marina   LIGURIAN SEA

To Casino Supermarket (500m); Géant Port Toga Centre Commercial (500m); Erbalunga (9km); Macinaggio (40km); Cap Corse

R de l'Impératrice Eugénie

Av Emile Sari

R du Commandant Luce de Casablanca

R du Chanoine Leech

R Notre Dame de Lourdes

R Capanelle

Préfecture

Av Jean Zuccarelli

Square Mal Leclerc

To Patrimonio 10km); St-Florent (22km)

Train Station

R Gabriel Péri

Av Maréchal Sebastiani

Blvd Général Graziani

R César Campinchi

R du Nouveau Port

Hôtel de Ville

Av Pierre Guidicelli

Square St-Victor

New Harbour

R du Conventionnel Salicetti

Pl St-Nicolas

Bassin St-Nicolas

Blvd Paoli

Blvd Général de Gaulle

R Miot

R St-François

Blvd Hyacinthe de Montera

Blvd Auguste Gaudin

Montée Ste-Claire

R Favalelli

Terra Vecchia

Cours Henri Pierangeli

Q des Martyrs de la Libération

Tunnel Under the Old Port

Pl de l'Hôtel de Ville

R St-Jean

Q des Zéphirs

R Napoléon

R Fontaine Neuve

R des Terrasses

Blvd Paoli

R de la Marine

R Général Carbuccia

Vieux Port (Old Port)

Q du Sud

N193

Palais de Justice

See Inset

Inset map (Citadel & Terra Nova):

Same Scale as Main Map

Jardin Romieu

N193

Jetée du Dragon

Pl Dominique Vincetti

R du Dragon

Pl du Donjon

Citadel & Terra Nova

R de l'Évêché

Pl d'Armes

Vauban

To Centre Hospitalier Général Paese Nuovo (1.5km); Camping San Damiano (5km); Plage de la Marana (12km); Étang de Biguglia (16km); Aéroport de Bastia-Poretta (24km)

CORSICA

the unusual sculpture depicting 'God the Father' looking down benevolently from above the altar.

Activities

Objectif Nature (☎ /fax 04 95 32 54 34; objectif-nature@ wanadoo.fr; 3 rue Notre Dame de Lourdes; ⏳ 9am-6pm Mon-Sat) organises outdoor activities in the Bastia area, including kayaking, sea fishing, hiking, mountaineering and diving.

Festivals & Events

Contact the Bastia tourist office for more information on these festivals.

Italian Cinema Festival In keeping with Bastia's Italian roots, this annual festival is held in February. There are British and Spanish film weeks later in the year.

BD à Bastia In April, Bastia hosts France's trendiest bandes dessinées (comics) festival, attracting big names from the pen-and-ink world.

Nuits de la Guitare à Patrimonio (☎ 04 95 37 12 15; www.festival-guitare-patrimonio.com) Late summer sees the tiny village of Patrimonio, about 10km west of Bastia, host one of Europe's major guitar festivals.

Corsican music festival This vivacious October festival is a showcase for across-the-board Corsican culture.

Chess championships The island's hotly contested chess championships are held in November.

Sleeping

If you want to experience the hospitality of a local family, the tourist office has information about private homes offering bed and breakfast.

Camping San Damiano (☎ 04 95 33 68 02; www .campingsandamiano.com; tent & vehicle €5-7, person €5-7; ⏳ Apr-Oct) Served by the airport bus, this pine-forested campground 5km south of Bastia is right on the beach, with furnished bungalows available on a weekly basis.

Hôtel Le Riviera (☎ 04 95 31 07 16; www.corsehotel riviera.com; 1bis rue Adolphe Landry; s €40-50, d €50-60; ☒) Le Riviera describes its rooms as 'luxury', and while they're not, even by the most generous definition, they're pleasant and light-filled with cornflower-blue bathrooms, phones and TVs, and there's a lift, as well as a convivial atmosphere and the convenience of being a stone's throw from the port.

Hôtel Univers (☎ 04 95 31 03 38; www.hoteldel univers.com; 3 av Maréchal Sébastiani; s €45-60, d €50-70; ☒) Situated opposite the post office, a hop, skip and a jump to place St-Nicolas and the port as well as the train station, this two-star hotel has 25 sparkling rooms with sky-blue and yellow décor and timber floors. An internet café is situated just a couple of doors up the street.

Hôtel Napoléon (☎ 04 95 31 60 30; 43 blvd Paoli; s €45-60, d €50-70, tr €60-90, q €80-110) A dramatic, colourful Corsican mural lines the staircase as you climb to reception at this central hotel. Rooms aren't air conditioned, much of the décor's dated (red velour carpet, heavy furniture), and some bathrooms are screened only by concertina-style '60s partitions that don't reach the ceiling, but staff are friendly, and wi-fi's due to arrive by the time you're reading this.

Hôtel Posta Vecchia (☎ 04 95 32 32 38; www.hotel -postavecchia.com; quai des Martyrs de la Libération; d €40-47, tr €70-95, q €80-105; ☒) A teensy lift zips you up to your room where, for an extra €10, you watch the ferries sail past and the sun rising over the Mediterranean from your bed. Décor is bright and colourful with floating timber floors, and some rooms have fridges. Best of all is Posta Vecchia's position, footsteps from the old port.

Hôtel Central (☎ 04 95 31 71 12; www.centralhotel .fr; 3 rue Miot; s €55-60, d €65-90, apt €85-105; ☒) Charming and – aptly enough – central for both the new and the old ports, rustic terracotta-tiled corridors lead to airy white-washed rooms with timber floors, checked curtains and pretty prints of sailing boats. French doors open to bamboo-screened balconies overlooking a fragrant courtyard garden from the pick of the rooms, and apartments come with kitchenettes.

Hôtel Les Voyageurs (☎ 04 95 34 90 80; www.hotel -lesvoyageurs.com; 9 av Maréchal Sébastiani; s €63, d €73-83, tr €83-93; ☒) Bastia's best hotel is this three-star place of 24 rooms, chicly decorated with Matisse prints, lemon walls, glass and wrought-iron furniture and all-white bathrooms. Double rooms with bath tubs are cavernous affairs and include minibars and soft sofas to sink into. Private parking's available for €6, and wi-fi's free, but alas, there's no lift.

Hôtel Bonaparte (☎ 04 95 34 07 10; www.hotel -bonaparte-bastia.com; 45 blvd Général Graziani; s €60-80, d €85-160; ☒) Close to place St-Nicolas and the port, this three-star, 23-room hotel has old-fashioned, somewhat formidable service, and freshened-up, tiled rooms in Santa Fe colours. Five have balconies, and two vast rooms have a separate sitting area screened by curtains.

Eating

Restaurants for all budgets cluster around the old port, quai des Martyrs de la Libération and place de l'Hôtel de Ville.

A Casarella (☎ 04 95 32 02 32; rue du Dragon; mains €9-28; ☺ lunch Mon-Fri, dinner Mon-Sat) At this fab little find, artistically decorated with contemporary paintings, artefacts and striking navy tablecloths, charismatic chef Joseph 'Rocky' Rocche concocts cuisine based on classical Corsican produce but combined and presented in innovative ways. His €15 'discovery' degustation plate lets you sample his latest creations.

Petite Marie (☎ 04 95 32 47 83; 2 rue des Zéphyrs; plats du jour €11-17, mains €13-20; ☺ lunch Tue-Fri, dinner Mon-Sat) Squeezed into a cross-vaulted room just back from the port, this tucked away little place serves *plats du jour* of the freshest seafood imaginable; otherwise you can order meat dishes à la carte. Petite Marie also does exceptional paella as well as its prepared-to-perfection *poissons* (fish).

K'SA Bar (☎ 04 95 36 60 20; quai des Martyrs Libération; mains €15-30; ☺ lunch & dinner) Touting 'flavours without borders', this retro-chic place on the quay has an outdoor timber deck at street level and a subterranean stone-walled room with Arctic white modular furniture and moulded bar stools. 'Discovery plates' include the Japanese-inspired Le Zen, a Brazilian plate and one for the veges with herb-infused tofu.

our pick **Osteria U Tianu** (☎ 04 95 31 36 67; 4 rue Rigo; menus €19; ☺ 7pm-2am Mon-Sat, closed Aug) For a memorable taste of Corsica – culturally as well as culinary – climb the narrow, creaking wooden stairs in a hidden back lane behind the old port to this quarter-of-a-decade-old restaurant/local gathering spot lined with posters of Che Guevara, old yellowing bank notes and hunting rifles. Chef Albertu Filidori and his family and friends serve up five incredible courses of authentic Corsican fare including an aperitif, wine, cheese, dessert, coffee and a *digestif*. Later in the night, chances are Albertu will pick up his guitar and play for the invariably packed house.

Chez Hugette (☎ 04 95 31 37 60; rue de la Marine; mains €19-29; ☺ lunch & dinner Mon-Sat year-round, dinner Sun mid-Jun–mid-Sep) Like dining aboard a luxury yacht, this sleek, slate and timber-decked place framed by glass walls has uninterrupted views of the boats bobbing in the Vieux Port. At your elegant white-clothed table, savour exquisite seafood like oysters presented on beds of ice, followed by a 'symphony' of desserts.

La Citadelle (☎ 04 95 31 44 70; 6 rue du Dragon; menus €33, mains €21-28; ☺ closed Jan) Up in the citadel, these two interlinked French-washed rooms serve some of Bastia's most celebrated gastronomic cuisine. Blending French and Corsican traditions results in dishes like smoked duck with Corsican cheese, or tender veal with chestnuts; accompanied by an excellent wine list. Unfortunately there's no terrace, but the intimate, ancient stone dining area makes for a romantic meal.

SELF-CATERING

Pick up fresh produce at the lively morning **food market** (place de l'Hôtel de Ville; ☺ Tue-Sun). The large **Spar** (rue César Campinchi) supermarket is the most convenient place for staples. Out of town, the huge Géant Port Toga Centre Commercial houses a **Casino** supermarket.

Drinking

Inexpensive terraced cafés line place St-Nicolas. You'll find dozens more scattered on and around the Vieux Port.

La Rhumerie (☎ 06 86 37 09 32; place Galetta; ☺ 8pm-2am Mon-Sat Jun-Aug, Wed-Sat Sep-May) Past the giant pirate guarding the entrance, this bolt hole serves 23 different types of rum between its stone walls. The owners are in the process of opening another, bigger 'rumery' in Corte.

Café Wha (☎ 04 95 34 25 79; Vieux Port; ☺ 11am-2am) Decked out in tutti-frutti colours, this animated, contemporary bar/restaurant on the old port dishes up decent Tex-Mex by the plateful (mains €8 to €15) as well as frequent entertainment and is nearly always chock-a-block with Bastiais and tourists alike.

Entertainment

La Onzieme (☎ 06 22 09 47 30; 11 rue Sisco; ☺ until 5am Thu-Sat) Down a small flight of steps just off quai des Marthyrs, this bar/*discoteque* inside a dungeon-like succession of rooms spins French house.

Le Régent (☎ 04 95 31 30 31; www.leregent.fr; rue César Campinchi) A large multiscreen cinema screening the latest releases (nearly always in French).

Studio Cinéma (☎ 04 95 31 12 94; www.studio-cinema.com; rue Miséricorde) A small arts cinema near the Palais de Justice that shows both French and international films.

Shopping

Les Grands Vins de Corse (☎ 04 95 31 24 94; www.lesvinscorse.com in French; 24 rue César Campinchi) has been stocking Corsican wines for over 50 years. **LN Mattei** (15 blvd Général de Gaulle) is the place to buy the local liqueur, Cap Corse, invented by Louis Napoléon Mattei in the late 19th century. Both shops sell Corsican jams, honeys and other delicacies.

Arrive at the Sunday **flea market** (place St-Nicolas) before 9am for the best bargains.

Getting There & Around

AIR

Aéroport Bastia-Poretta (☎ 04 95 54 54 54; www.bastia.aeroport.fr) is 24km south of the city. Buses (€8, seven to nine daily, fewer on Sunday) depart from outside the Préfecture building. The tourist office has schedules, and timetables are posted at the bus stop. A taxi to the airport costs around €30.

BOAT

The southern ferry terminal is at the eastern end of av François Pietri. The vehicle entrance is 600m north.

There's an **SNCM** (☎ 04 95 54 66 81; www.sncm.com; ☺ 8-11.45am & 2-5.45pm Mon-Fri, 8am-noon Sat) office in the southern terminal. Tickets are sold two hours before departure in the Corsica Marittima section of the terminal building.

Moby Lines (☎ 04 95 34 84 94; www.mobylines.it; 4 rue du Commandant Luce de Casabianca) has a bureau in the ferry terminal, open two hours before each sailing.

The **Corsica Ferries** (☎ 04 95 32 95 95; www.corsicaferries.com; 15bis rue Chanoine Leschi; ☺ 8.30am-noon & 2-6pm Mon-Fri, 9am-noon Sat) office is across the road from the northern ferry terminal.

BUS

In the absence of a central terminus, Bastia's buses leave from several locations around town. The tourist office can provide timetables and show you where to catch your bus.

Autocars Cortenais (☎ 04 95 46 02 12) travels to Corte (€10, two hours) on Monday, Wednesday and Friday. Buses leave from outside the train station.

Eurocorse (☎ 04 95 31 73 76) travels to Ajaccio (€20, three hours) via Corte (€11, two hours) twice daily except on Sundays.

Les Beaux Voyages (☎ 04 95 65 11 35) travels to Île Rousse and Calvi (€15, two hours) daily except Sunday. Buses leave from outside the train station.

Les Rapides Bleus (☎ 04 95 31 03 79; 1 av Maréchal Sébastiani) runs buses to Porto Vecchio (€20 plus €1 per item of baggage), with connections to Bonifacio and Sartène.

TRAIN

The **train station** (☎ 04 95 32 80 61; av Maréchal Sébastiani; ☺ 6am-8.30pm Mon-Sat, 8.30am-8.30pm Sun) is beside the large roundabout on Square Mal Leclerc. Main destinations include Ajaccio (€20.70, four hours, four daily) via Corte, and Calvi (€15.70, three hours, three or four daily) via Île Rousse.

CAP CORSE

Corsica's spiny northeastern peninsula, Cap Corse, is shot through with mountains and dotted with crumbling Genoese watchtowers, sandy coves and rocky cliffs.

Buses only run along its eastern edge, as far as Macinaggio – and if you drive around the twisting clifftop roads on the western side, you'll know why. Be prepared for some adventurous driving. If you and your legs are keen, cycling is also a great way to cover the cape's 100km perimeter.

Leaving Bastia's city centre, the road at first seems little more than a wealthy seaside suburban sprawl, but soon winds through gentle bays and quiet fishing villages, starting with **Erbalunga**, 9km north, and the venue each August for the two-week **Festival d'Erbalunga** (☎ 04 95 33 20 84). Open-air concerts held on the intimate, charming central square across from the Genoese tower include jazz, rock and classical music. Further north at **Pietracorbara**, you'll find one of the coast's best beaches.

At Santa Servara, the road splits in two. The western branch climbs though the village of Luri to the hilltop tower at **Col de Ste-Lucie**, where the Roman poet-philosopher Seneca was exiled in the 1st century. The second branch continues north to **Macinaggio**, a pretty port that has the cape's only **tourist office** (☎ 04 95 35 40 34; www.ot-rogliano-macinaggio.com; Port de Plaisance de Macinaggio; ☺ 9am-noon & 3-7.30pm Mon-Sat, 9am-noon Sun Jul &

Aug, 9am-noon & 3-6pm Mon-Fri, 9am-noon Sat May, Jun & Sep, 9am-noon & 2-5pm Oct-Apr). Ask the tourist office for the free brochure *Le Cap à Pied* (in French) outlining 21 different walking trails around the peninsula.

Near the tip is Barcaggio. From here, the road swings south around the wilder western side, with villages perched high on the steep cliffs and jagged inlets cut into the coastline. Heading south takes you past the villages of **Centuri**, with its traditional Corsican houses clustered around a pretty harbour, then Pino and Canari, and on to **Nonza**, one of the cape's most captivating villages. Famous for its 11th-century chapel of St Julia (who was martyred in Nonza in the 5th century), houses tumble down the cliff in steep terraces to a vast bay presided over by a fortified tower.

The final stretch passes sweeping bays on the way to **St-Florent**, a busy harbour at the southwestern end of Cap Corse.

Sleeping & Eating

Camping La Pietra (☎ 04 95 35 27 49; www.la-pietra .com; Marine de Pietracorbara; adult €6.30-7, tent €3.30-4.50; ☺ Apr–mid-Oct) This large, family-oriented camping ground shaded by approximately 50 different types of tree has all the creature comforts including a free tennis court and good wheelchair access.

Les Tamaris (☎ 04 95 37 81 91; www.lestamaris .com; Canari; d €53-77; ☺ May-Nov) Close to the beach, this modern hotel in Canari organises activities like horse riding and local walks. Half pension is available for an additional €18 for adults, €10 for children (plus drinks); or if you'd rather whip something up yourself, self-catering apartments cost €305 to €615 per week.

Gîte i Fioretti (☎ 04 95 37 80 17; Canari; d €55-70) In an old Franciscan monastery built in 1506, this *gîte rural* (country cottage) offers an atmospheric sleep in six rooms rustically fitted out within its former cells. Adjacent to the main building, another three two-room apartments sleeping up to six people are available from €283 to €339 per week, with self-catering kitchens.

Hôtel Castel Brando (☎ 04 95 30 10 30; www.castel brando.com; Erbalunga; d €99-199; ☒ ☐ ☒) Romance reigns at this 19th-century mansion in the postcard-perfect village of Erbalunga. Rooms are furnished with creamy peach décor and elegant antiques, there's a library

to curl up in with a book, a pool to lounge by, and homemade breakfasts (€12) to feast on, and wi-fi. If you can bring yourself to leave, the sea's just 50m away.

Osteria di U Portu (☎ 04 95 35 40 49; Macinaggio; menus €21-22, mains €9-22; ☺ lunch & dinner) On Macinaggio's pretty port, this rustic restaurant with red and yellow décor and a cosy ambience serves seafood straight off the boats moored in front, and also rents out four guest rooms (double room for €50 to €70). Room reservations aren't taken in advance for July and August, so it's worth trying your luck when you arrive.

Getting There & Away

The main road around Cap Corse is the D80. **Société des Transports Interurbains Bastiais** (☎ 04 95 31 06 65) handles buses from Bastia to Cap Corse. Destinations include Erbalunga (€2, six to eight daily), Pietracorbara (€2.60) and Macinaggio (€6.40, two daily except Sunday). Buses leave from av Pierre Guidicelli, opposite the tourist office, in Bastia.

THE NORTH COAST

ÎLE ROUSSE (ISULA ROSSA)
pop 2300

With a central, tree-shaded square, quaint streets, and amenities for the coastal area including schools, Île Rousse remains a vibrant village year round compared with its seasonal neighbour, Calvi, 24km southwest.

Named for the red granite of Île de la Pietra, a rocky island (now connected to the mainland), the port was founded by Pasquale Paoli in 1758 to compete with pro-Genoese Calvi, and became an important commercial harbour. These days passenger ferries dock here from the mainland.

Orientation

From the main square, place Paoli (home to a large open-air carpark), the old city stretches 400m northwest to the train station. The ferry port is on a peninsula north of town. The **tourist office** (☎ 04 95 60 04 35; www.balagne-corsica.com; place Paoli; ☺ 9am-7pm mid-Jun–mid-Sep, 9am-12.30pm & 2-6pm May, early Jun & late Sep, 9am-noon & 2-6pm Mon-Fri Oct-Apr) is on the southern side of place Paoli.

Sights

Promenade a Marinella runs along the seafront; more beaches extend east of town. **Île de la Pietra**, the island-turned-peninsula where the ferries dock, has a **Genoese watchtower** and a **lighthouse**.

If you're seeking empty sand in the busy bucket-and-spade summer months, try nearby **Lozari** (7km east) or **Guardiola** (4km west).

Sleeping & Eating

L'Amiral (☎ 04 95 60 28 05; www.hotel-amiral.com; 163 blvd Charles Marie Savelli; d €60-90; tr €70-90; ✿ Apr-Oct; ✖) All 20 fresh, contemporary rooms at this appealing two-star hotel have balconies, and the best have sea views. You can take breakfast (€9) on the timber deck overlooking the beach and a nightcap in the nautical bar.

Splendid Hotel (☎ 04 95 60 00 24; www.le-splendid -hotel.com; s €50-70.50, d €54-95, tr €74-130.50; ✿ late Mar-Oct; ✖ ✿) Near place Paoli in the town's heart, this grand old period building has 51 somewhat dated rooms and a cocktail bar beside its paradisaical palm-shaded swimming pool. Splendid deals are available for half and full board (buffets in peak season; regional specialities other times).

Restaurant L'Île d'Or (☎ 04 95 60 12 05; place Paoli; menus €12.50-35) Salads, pasta, fresh fish and authentic Corsican specialities (including a €10 *plat du jour*) keep regulars returning to this buzzy restaurant, which has ringside seats on the terrace for the town's nightly *boules* contests.

Brasserie du Port (☎ 04 95 60 10 66; Port de Commerce; menus €14.50-16.50; ✿ 6am-midnight) You can easily kill time waiting for your ferry at this excellent portside brasserie with a panoramic terrace overlooking the town. Fish, mussels and sea urchins are all specialities, and the desserts are delectable.

A Siesta (☎ 04 95 60 28 74; blvd Charles Marie Savelli; menus from €20; ✿ lunch & dinner mid-Mar–Oct) Serving (what else?) fish, A Siesta is one of the restaurants with tables right on the sand (weather permitting).

Le Cocotier (☎ 04 95 60 45 45; rue Paoli; dishes €3.10-5.40; ✿ 8am-midnight Mon-Sat, daily Apr-Oct, closed Feb) For quick fixes like tiramasu *crêpes* and chestnut paninis, pop into this little hole in the wall, adjacent to the covered market and decorated with coconut shells.

The daily **covered market** (place Paoli; ✿ 8.30am-1.30pm) sells fish, vegetables, fruit and Corsican delicacies.

Shopping

On the first and third Friday of each month, a large market selling crafts, jewellery and clothes spills out around the covered market, and the first five days of September see Île Rousse host a giant market/festival.

Getting There & Away

On the Calvi–Bastia line, **Les Beaux Voyages** (☎ 04 95 65 11 35) depart daily except Sunday from av Paul Doumer. The **train station** (☎ 04 95 60 00 50) is between place Paoli and the ferry port.

Corse Voyages (☎ 04 95 60 11 19; place Paoli) handles ferry tickets, as does **Tramar** (☎ 04 95 60 09 56; av Joseph Calizi; ✿ 8.30am-noon & 2-5.30pm Mon-Fri, 8.30am-noon Sat).

LA BALAGNE

Known as the 'garden' or 'orchard' of Corsica for its lush landscapes, fertile soil and gentle microclimate, the Balagne's low hills unfurl from the Monte Cinto massif to the sea. The area's coastline stretches from the **Désert des Agriates**, the 5000-hectare maquis-covered desert east of Île Rousse, all the way southwest to Galéria. Between Île Rousse and Calvi, fine-sand beaches include **Algajola**, **Aregno** and **Renalta**. Many are served by Le Tramway de la Balagne rail line (p928).

Inland, the main town of **Calenzana** marks the northern terminus of the GR20 and Mare e Monti trails (p916).

The area is rich in traditional crafts, with a dedicated **Route des Artisans de Balagne** ('Balagne craft trail'). Essentially the trail follows the N197 southwest from Île Rousse to Calvi with occasional detours through mountain villages. Signposts indicate artisan workshops such as potters and stringed-instrument makers, as well as wineries. Many are open to the public for free. The Île Rousse and Calvi tourist offices hand out the free leaflet *Strada di l'Artigiani* detailing stops along the trail.

CALVI

pop 5600

More like a glamorous mainland Mediterranean resort than perhaps anywhere else in Corsica, Calvi curves around a crescent-

CORSICA'S TOP FIVE BEACHES

Rondinara (10km northeast of Bonifacio) Circular bay of crystal-clear water, with superb snorkelling and sheltered sunbathing, ringed by white sand.

Algajola (8km west of Île Rousse) Silken white-sand beach served by the Tramway de la Balagne in summer.

Palombaggia (3km southeast of Porto Vecchio) Secluded sandy cove ringed by pines and rocks.

Rocapina (12km south of Sartène, 20km north-west of Bonifacio) Wild and windswept. Look for the 'Lion of Rocapina' rock up above.

Saleccia (10km northwest of St-Florent) Pristine beach deep in the Désert des Agriates, accessible only by sea or an arduous trek on foot or quad-bike.

shaped bay, basking beneath the snowy peaks of Monte Cinto (2706m). Watching over the town, the citadel remains as a relic of the town's past as a strategic military outpost, with a huddle of 13th-century hilltop houses cosseted by 15th-century bastions.

In 1794, a British expeditionary fleet assisting Pasquale Paoli's Corsican nationalist forces besieged and bombarded the Genoese stronghold. In the course of the battle, Captain Horatio Nelson was wounded by rock splinters and lost the use of his right eye.

Orientation

The citadel – also known as the Haute Ville (upper city) – sits on a rocky promontory northeast of the Basse Ville (lower city). Blvd Wilson, the major thoroughfare through town, is uphill from the marina.

Information

Banks, including Crédit Lyonnais, can be found along blvd Wilson.

Antenne Médicale du SAMU (☎ 04 95 65 11 22; route du Stade)

Café de l'Orient (☎ 04 95 65 00 16; quai Landry; connection/per min €1/0.10; 🕙 9am-late)

Hall de la Presse (☎ 04 95 65 05 14; 13 blvd Wilson; 🕙 9am-noon & 2-6pm Mon-Sat) Sells topoguides and walking maps.

Post Office (blvd Wilson)

Tourist Office (☎ 04 95 65 16 67; www.balagne-corsica .com) main office (Port de Plaisance; 🕙 9am-noon & 3-7pm Mon-Fri, 9am-12.30pm & 2.30-6.30pm Sat & Sun Jul & Aug, 9am-noon & 2-6pm Mon-Sat Apr-Jun & Sep, 9am-noon & 2-6pm Mon-Fri Oct-Mar); Citadel (🕙 9am-noon Mon-Sat Jun-Sep) The main office is opposite the marina.

Sights & Activities
CITADEL

Glowing the colour of topaz in the late-afternoon light, Calvi's 15th-century citadel dominates the harbour skyline. Set atop a granite promontory surrounded by massive Genoese fortifications, the town's loyalty to Genoa is recalled by the motto *Civitas Calvi Semper Fidelis* (the city of Calvi, forever faithful) carved over the citadel gateway. The majority of its buildings are closed to the public.

Within the walls, the **Palais des Gouverneurs** (Governors' Palace; place d'Armes) was once the seat of power for the Genoese administration and now serves (under the name Caserne Sampiero) as a base for the French Foreign Legion. Look out for soldiers wearing the regiment's distinctive white caps around town.

Up the hill from Caserne Sampiero is the 13th-century **Église St-Jean Baptiste**, rebuilt in 1570. The women of the local elite sat in the screened boxes, with grilles sheltering them from the rabble's inquisitive gaze. Near the altar is the *Christ des Miracles,* an ebony statue that was paraded around town in 1553 shortly before the besieging Turkish forces fell back. Credited with saving Calvi from the Saracens, the statue has become a much-revered relic.

In the northern part of the citadel, a **plaque** marks the house where navigator Christopher Columbus was supposedly born during the Genoese rule – though the historical jury is out. According to supporters of the theory, when Columbus went looking for underwriting at the Spanish court, he could not very well admit to being of Calvian origin because the Calvians had massacred a Spanish garrison, thus putting an end to Spanish ambitions in Corsica, in 1521. Certainly numerous Calvians figured in his crews.

BEACHES

Sunworshippers don't have far to stroll – Calvi's stellar 4km beach begins at the marina and runs east around the Golfe de Calvi.

Tours

Croisières Colombo Line (☎ 04 95 65 32 10; www .colombo-line.com in French; marina; 🕙 Apr-Oct) offers visitors a variety of glass-bottomed boat

CORSICA

CALVI

0 .... 200 m
0 .... 0.1 miles

INFORMATION	
Antenne Médicale du SAMU	1 B3
Café de l'Orient	2 C2
Crédit Lyonnais	3 C2
Hall de la Presse	4 C1
Post Office	5 B2
Tourist Office	6 C2
Tourist Office Annexe	(see 7)

SIGHTS & ACTIVITIES	
Citadel Gate	7 C1
Croisières Colombo Line	8 C2
Église St-Jean Baptiste	9 D1
Palais des Gouverneurs	10 D1
Plaque Marking the Home of Christopher Columbus	11 D1

SLEEPING	
Bel Ombra	12 C1
Hôtel Balanea	13 C2
Hôtel Le Belvedere	14 C1
Hôtel Le Rocher	15 C2

EATING	
A Cantina	16 C2
Alimentation du Golfe	17 C2
Annie Traiteur	18 C2
Best Of	19 C2
Casino	20 B4
Covered Market	21 C2
Emile's	(see 22)
Île de Beauté	22 C2
Super-U	23 B4
U Minellu	24 C2

ENTERTAINMENT	
Chez Tao	25 D1

TRANSPORT	
Buses to Galéria & Porto	26 C1
Buses to Porto	27 B4
Corsica Ferries	(see 29)
Ferry Terminal	28 D2
Les Beaux Voyages	29 B2
SNCM Tickets	(see 31)
Taxi Rank	30 B2
Tramar	31 C2

excursions including to the Réserve Naturelle de Scandola nature reserve, starting from €44.

Festivals & Events

La Granitola An Easter procession on Good Friday.
Jazz festival Corsica's biggest jazz festival, in June.
Rencontres Polyphoniques Traditional Corsican chants – traditionally sung a cappella – can be heard at this five-day music festival in September. The stirring *paghjellas* feature three male voices – a tenor, baritone and bass – and mark the passage of life.
Le Festival du Vent (☎ 04 95 65 16 67; www.le-festival -du-vent.com) In autumn, this festival celebrates wind in all its forms, with musical instrument and theatre performances, art exhibitions, sailing and windsurfing, and paragliding and air displays.

Sleeping

Calvi's hotels aren't cheap at any time of year and most are closed in winter.

Camping Les Castors (☎ 04 95 65 13 30; www .castors.fr; route de Pietra Maggiore; adult €7.60-9.20, tent €2.90-3.95, car €2.30-3.20; ☉ May-Sep; ☒) An 800m stroll southeast of town, this three-star camping ground has an aquatic park and also rents studios and mobile homes starting from €290 per week.

Bel Ombra (☎ 04 95 65 93 50; www.residence-bel ombra.com in French; av Gérard Marche; d €38-72, q €50-93; ☉ Apr-Oct; ☒) A terrific deal, especially if you're looking to save money by self-catering, the two-star Bel Ombra has 37 studios, all kitted out with kitchenettes. Tiled rooms are spacious, and many open to balconies with views over the citadel. There's one wheelchair-equipped room, but it's on the third floor, so if the lift's not working, access can be a problem.

Hôtel Le Belvedere (☎ 04 95 65 01 25; www.resa -hotels-calvi.com; place Christophe Colomb; d €45-115, tr €70-130; 🌂) Both the standard and deluxe rooms at this pleasant two-star place have views over the sparkling blue Golfe de Calvi. Breakfast (€6.50) is served in a pretty wood-beamed room, wi-fi's available, and unlike most of the town's accommodation, it's open all year round.

Hôtel Le Rocher (☎ 04 95 65 20 04; www.hotel-le -rocher.com in French; blvd Wilson; d €70-170, f €105-200; 🌂 Apr-Sep; 🌂) Elegant and equipped with all the comforts, this three-star hotel also has mezzanine family rooms sleeping up to four people. Understated touches include crimson fabrics contrasted with soothing neutral furnishings. Breakfast, in a *trompe l'oeil*–adorned room, is a bit hefty at €12, but offers a generous buffet spread.

Hôtel Balanea (☎ 04 95 65 94 94; www.hotel -balanea.com; 6 rue Clemenceau; d €79-209, ste €199-299; 🌂 Apr-Sep; 🌂 🌂) Wedged between the port and pretty pedestrianised av Georges Clémenceau, this stylish hotel has a sleek polished timber lobby and 37 fashionable rooms with wicker chairs, glass-topped tables, and bright, beachy colours. If you're bringing Fido along, he'll cost you an extra €16.

Eating

Restaurants in Calvi are generally high quality (and generally priced accordingly). Quai Landry and rue Clemenceau are the chicest people-watching spots in summer.

A Cantina (☎ 06 25 78 10 42; quai Landry; tapas dishes €3-7, plates €10; 🌂 7pm-2am Apr-Nov, plus lunch May-Sep) Set back on the port by a terrace with tables fashioned from wooden wine barrels, this adobe-rendered cantina serves 'Corsican tapas' made from local produce, and over 150 Corsican wines (plus 30 international varieties). The kitchen stays open until 1.30am.

Île de Beauté (☎ 04 95 65 00 46; quai Landry; menus €20-50, mains €12-35; 🌂 lunch & dinner mid-Mar–Dec) Looking like it's straight out of St-Tropez with bright-red chairs on its waterfront terrace, this eminently stylish café specialises in fish and Corsican cuisine. Chef Bernard Guillot's signature dishes include St Jacques (scallops) marinated in

seaweed and olive oil, and patisseries and sorbets 'of the moment' for dessert.

U Minellu (☎ 04 95 65 05 52; Traverse à l'Église; menus from €14; 🌂 lunch & dinner closed Sun in winter) This delightful family-run restaurant opposite Église Ste-Marie serves Corsican dishes under a wooden awning lit by lanterns. The *menu Corse* includes regional specialities such as *brocciu* cannelloni, Corsican cooked pork, and chestnut and apple cake.

Emile's (☎ 04 95 65 09 60; quai Landry; menus €40-100, mains €28; 🌂 lunch & dinner Apr, dinner May-Oct) Adjacent to the Île de Beauté up a flight of steps, the elevated terrace at this gastronomic temple has divine views over the bay and exceptional cuisine created by chef Vincent Deyres, whose *menus* include 'the sea', 'the island' and an 'invitation' to try his latest innovations.

QUICK EATS & SELF-CATERING

If you're looking for a snack on the move, head for **Best Of** (1 rue Clemenceau; sandwiches €4-7; 🌂 11.30am-10pm), which creates original sandwiches, paninis and wood-fired bread topped with local specialities.

The **covered market** (marché couvert; 🌂 8am-noon Mon-Sat) is near Église Ste-Marie Majeure. In the old town, try the well-stocked **Alimentation du Golfe** (rue Clemenceau; 🌂 Apr-Oct) for staples, and the wonderful **Annie Traiteur** (rue Clemenceau; 🌂 Apr-Oct) for a mouthwatering range of Corsican products including fresh cheeses and handmade sweet biscuits.

South of the train station there's a large **Casino** (av Christophe Colomb) supermarket; and also, next door, a **Super-U** (av Christophe Colomb) supermarket.

Entertainment

Chez Tao (☎ 04 95 65 00 73; citadel; 🌂 May-Oct) A-listers dance until dawn at this impossibly hip piano bar. Founded in 1935 by Tao Kanbey de Kerekoff, an escaping member of the Russian White Cavalry, it's run in the same opulent style by his descendents today.

Getting There & Around
AIR

Southeast of town (7km) is **Aéroport Calvi-Ste-Catherine** (☎ 04 95 65 88 88; www.calvi.aeroport .fr). Air France links Calvi with Nice, Marseille, Lyon and other French cities. There is no bus service from Calvi to the airport.

Taxis (☎ 04 95 65 03 10) can be picked up from place de la Porteuse d'Eau for around €20.

BOAT
The ferry terminal is below the southern side of the citadel. From Calvi there are express NGV ferries to Nice (2½ hours, five a week).

Ferry tickets can be bought at the port two hours before departure. At other times, SNCM tickets are handled by **Tramar** (☎ 04 95 65 01 38; quai Landry; ⓨ 9am-noon & 2-5pm Mon-Fri, 9am-noon Sat). Tickets for Corsica Ferries are handled by **Les Beaux Voyages** (☎ 04 95 65 15 02; place de la Porteuse d'Eau).

BUS
Buses to Bastia (€15, 2¼ hours) are run by **Les Beaux Voyages** (☎ 04 95 65 15 02; place de la Porteuse d'Eau).

From mid-May to mid-October, **Autocars SAIB** (☎ 04 95 22 41 99) runs buses from the carpark opposite the Super-U supermarket to Galéria (1¼ hours) and Porto (three hours). Except in July and August, there are no buses on Sunday.

TRAIN
Calvi's **train station** (☎ 04 95 65 00 61; ⓨ to 7.30pm) is off av de la République. There are two departures daily to Ajaccio (€24.10), Bastia (€15.70) and the stations between.

From April to October, the single-car trains of CFC's **Tramway de la Balagne** (see p924) make 19 stops along the coast between Calvi and Île Rousse (45 minutes). The line is divided into three sectors – you need one ticket for each sector. *Carnets* of six tickets (€8) are sold at stations.

PORTO TO AJACCIO

PORTO (PORTU)
pop 250

Nestled at the bottom of a deep eucalyptus-filled gully etched by the burbling Le Porto River trickling over a bed of stones to the sea, Porto is a rustic little seasonal town. Diving here is among the island's finest. The town is an ideal departure point for hiking the Réserve Naturelle de Scandola, Les Calanques (p931), as well as exploring the nearby mountain villages of Ota and Évisa (p930).

Orientation
Porto is split into three sections: the seaside marina, the Vaita quarter (Guaïta in Corsican), 800m further uphill, and the main road from Calvi, 1.3km from the sea. There are shops, hotels and restaurants in all three districts.

Information
In the Vaita quarter, Crédit Agricole and the post office have ATMs.

Tourist Office (☎ 04 95 26 10 55; www.porto-tourisme .com in French; ⓨ 9am-7pm Mon-Sat Jun-Sep, 9am-6pm Mon-Sat Apr-May, 9am-5pm Mon-Fri Oct-Mar) The area's tourist office is built into the wall below the marina's upper car park.

Sights & Activities
From Porto's seafront, a short trail leads up the rocks to a **Genoese tower** (admission €2.50; ⓨ 11am-7pm Apr-Oct). Nearby, the marina overlooks the estuary of the Porto River. On the far side, a footbridge takes you through one of Corsica's best-known, heady-scented **eucalyptus groves** to a pebbly beach.

HIKING
Porto's tourist office publishes an excellent English-language brochure, *Hikes & Walks in the Area of Porto* (€2.50).

BOATING & BOAT TOURS
You can rent a boat from **Porto Bateaux Locations** (☎ 04 95 21 44 72; half/full day without permit €75/115) to visit the Réserve Naturelle de Scandola and Girolata independently. You'll be missing out on the educational experience of one of the excursions, but you'll have more freedom to explore and for a group it would be cheaper.

From April to October **Nave Va Promenades en Mer** (☎ 04 95 26 15 16; www.naveva.com) and **Porto Linéa** (☎ 04 95 26 11 50; jrostini@club -internet.fr) offer excursions (€34 to €44) to the Réserve Naturelle de Scandola, listed by Unesco for its unique marine environment. The boats afford incredible views of the coastline ablaze with fiery colours, and stop at Girolata, a remote fishing village only accessible by sea. There are shorter trips to Les Calanques (from €20).

DIVING
For underwater adventures, the Golfe de Porto's top diving spots include Capo

Rosso and the outskirts of the Réserve Naturelle de Scandola, where you'll glimpse multicoloured coral forests and all kinds of Mediterranean marine life.

Porto's accredited diving operators include **École de Plongée Génération Bleue** (☎ 04 95 26 24 88; www.generation-bleue.com; Porto Marina; ☻ May-Oct), **Centre de Plongée du Golfe de Porto** (☎ 04 95 26 10 29; www.plongeeporto.com in French; Porto Marina; ☻ Apr-Nov) and **Méditerranée Porto Sub** (MPS; ☎ 04 95 26 19 47; www.le-mediterranee.com in French; Porto Marina; ☻ mid-Apr–mid-Oct). All three companies run diving courses and trips into the bay, with dives starting from €26 without gear, or €42 including gear rental.

Sleeping

Camping Municipal (☎ 04 95 26 17 76; fax 04 95 26 14 12; person €5-5.50, tent €2.20-2.30, car €2.20; ☻ mid-Jun–mid-Sep) The sea is just a gentle 500m stroll from this pleasant one-star campground.

Camping Les Oliviers (☎ 04 95 26 14 49; www.campinglesoliviers.com; person €6.50-8.50, tent €2.50-6, car €2.50-3.50, chalet from €48; ☻ late Mar-early Nov; 🖭) Amid olive groves, this luxe retreat has a natural rock-lined swimming pool, a fitness centre and an onsite restaurant and pizzeria, with glorious views of the mountains. Timber chalets sleep up to seven people.

Bon Accueil (☎ /fax 04 95 26 19 50; Vaita quarter; d €35-46; 🗷) Above a convivial café/souvenir shop, this homey, welcoming place has 23 modern rooms, spartan but immaculately furnished; many with balconies. Try for a room at the front with views through the eucalypts to the river.

Le Riviera (☎ 04 95 26 10 15; hotel.riviera.porto@laposte.net; marina; d €35-51; ☻ Easter-Oct) There are just six rooms at the Riviera, which – incredibly for the price – enjoys an idyllic location on the marina at the foot of the Genoese tower. Rooms come with TVs; breakfast costs €6.50.

Le Colombo (☎ 04 95 26 10 14; www.hotellecolombo.com in French; route de Calvi; d €62-125, tr €85-159, q €102-177; ☻ Apr-Oct; 🗷) This charming little two-star place on the Calvi road has sky-blue rooms with quirky décor like lamps fashioned from tree branches, and a serene, shady garden. Breakfast is included in the room rate.

Hôtel La Calypso (☎ 04 95 26 11 54; www.hotel-la-calypso.com in French; marina; d €54-104; ☻ Apr-Oct; 🗷 🖵) In a pretty stone building decorated with awnings and window boxes, this small, smart, sophisticated hotel offers excellent value, with eight spacious rooms and a panoramic terrace where you can linger over breakfast (€8); the terrace transforms into

---

CORSICA'S CORKSCREW ROADS

The *Tour de Corse*, held over three days each April, is perhaps the most prized driving circuit in the WRC (World Rally Championship; www.wrc.com and www.rallyedefrance.com). And with good reason. Most of Corsica's roads are spectacular but narrow, with huge drops that demand nerves of steel and hair-raising hairpin curves (leading to the *Tour de Corse*'s nickname 'rally of 10,000 corners').

If you're roadtripping around Corsica, count on averaging 50km/h, and look out for livestock – as well as Corsican drivers!

One of the island's most memorable stretches of road is the only direct route between Calvi and Porto, the D81 (known as the D81B as far as Galéria). But beware: the switchback bends are wrist-breaking, the drops to the thundering waves below sheer, and rock falls common, as are meandering mountain goats. Guard rails? Ha! Despite being continually patched, the surface is ridden with unexpected cavities. Added to that, the road's narrowness makes passing vehicles coming at you a nerve-racking game of chicken.

If you chicken out (and you may have to – it's frequently closed due to roadworks and accidents; check road conditions before setting out), you can take the inland mountain route splintering off the N193 to Calacuccia, Évisa and Porto. Although, as the highest road pass in Corsica, it's not for the vertigo-prone either. It is, however, a magnificent trip through mountains, chestnut forests and canyons. Otherwise, a longer but (somewhat) less daunting alternative route is via Corte and Ajaccio.

But the tortuous tarmacs help to preserve the island's wild, rugged beauty. In the words of one life-long Calvian, 'We don't want a freeway full of cars. We want to keep Corsica just as she is.'

a guests-only bar by night. Private lock-up parking is available.

Le Subrini (☎ 04 95 26 14 94; www.hotels-porto .com; marina; d €70-110; ☯ Apr-Oct; ☒) Ideally aspected to take in a front-row view of the Genoese tower, this luxury three-star hotel on the marina has poised, polished rooms with gleaming bathrooms. Private parking is available, and there's a lift. Breakfast jumps from €8 to €10 in peak season.

Eating

Most of Porto's restaurants and portside cafés only open during spring, summer and early autumn.

Le Soleil Couchant (☎ 04 95 26 10 12; menus €15.50-22.50; ☯ Apr-Oct) In the shadow of the Genoese tower, with two tiers of open-air terraces. Standouts on Le Soleil Couchant's seafood-oriented menu include spaghetti with langoustines caught in the Golfe du Porto, and a spectacular seafood paella. Salads are fresh and filling, and there's also a good range of inland Corsican specialities.

Le Sud (☎ 04 95 26 14 11; menus from €29; ☯ Apr-Oct) Sit back and savour Mediterranean-style seafood, especially freshly caught fish, as well as Corsican cooking on a veranda overlooking the vivid rocks at this sophisticated restaurant also right near the Genoese tower.

Self-caterers can find **supermarkets** near the pharmacy on the road from Calvi, as well as a terrific **boulangerie** in the Vaita quarter, but stock up beforehand if you're heading here between November and March, as most shops open only seasonally.

Getting There & Around

Autocars SAIB (☎ 04 95 22 41 99) has one or two buses daily, linking Porto (€11) and Ota (€11.50) with Ajaccio (two hours, none on Sunday). From May to October a bus braves the road between Porto and Calvi (€16, three hours). Buses depart from the pharmacy.

Transports Mordiconi (☎ 04 95 48 00 44) connects Porto with Corte (€20, 2½ hours, one daily) via Évisa and Ota. Buses leave from the restaurant 'Le Mini-Golf' near the eucalyptus forest and beach.

From May to late September, scooters (€46 per day), cars (€58 to €98) and mountain bikes (€15) can be hired from **Porto Locations** (☎ /fax 04 95 26 10 13), across the street from the supermarkets.

For a taxi contact **Chez Félix** (☎ 04 95 26 12 92).

ÉVISA
pop 300

The fact that the magical mountain village of Évisa is more populous than portside Porto (in winter at least) says a lot about Corsican culture. Sitting above a deep valley between the Gorges de Spelunca and the Forêt d'Aïtone, this authentic township is a terrific starting point for hikes. Several trails leave near the village, including the path through the Spelunca gorge itself, which ends near the tiny village of Ota.

The Porto tourist office has information on Évisa and surrounding areas.

Sights & Activities

The **Forêt d'Aïtone** (Aïtone Forest) contains Corsica's most impressive stands of laricio pines. These arrow-straight trees reach 60m in height and once provided beams and masts for Genoese ships. The forest begins east of Évisa and stretches to the 1477m-high **Col de Vergio** (Vergio Hill). The **Cascades d'Aïtone** (Aïtone Falls) are 4km northeast of Évisa via the D84 and a short footpath.

The partly paved trail linking Ota and Évisa via the **Gorges de Spelunca** was originally a mule track that carried supplies from Porto to the highland villages. These days, it's one of Corsica's most exhilarating hikes. The trail winds along the plunging valley of the River Porto, past huge rock formations and soaring orange cliffs, some more than 1000m high. The trail passes the Genoese pont de Zaglia en route and takes about five hours return, but it's worth the effort (and the blisters).

Other good walks near Évisa include the Sentier du Châtaigner (1½ hours), which travels through chestnut groves to a waterfall and mountain lake; and the 1½-hour hike uphill through the Forêt d'Aïtone to the Bocca au Saltu (1391m) hilltop.

Sleeping & Eating

For cheap accommodation, dorm beds are available at **Gîte d'Étape Chez Marie** (☎ 04 95 26 11 37; dm €15) in Ota, 19km further down the valley towards Porto.

Hôtel L'Aïtone (☎ 04 95 26 20 04; www.hotel -aitone.com; d low season €35-110; ☯ Feb-Nov; ☻) Évisa's main hotel has rustic rooms, an unpretentious restaurant and a welcoming country atmosphere. Kids will get a kick out of the Aïtone's play areas, which include a pool and tennis court as well as a children's garden. More expensive rooms have balconies with panoramic valley views.

La Châtaigneraie (☎ 04 95 26 24 47; hotellachataig neraie@wanadoo.fr; d from €50) Ideal after a long day's hike, this traditional Corsican house offers simple, homey rooms on the western edge of the village.

Bar de la Poste (☎ 04 95 26 24 39; mains €6-12), This village bar opens daily and serves meals, cakes, chestnut ice cream and good coffee.

Getting There & Away

There's a daily bus from Monday to Saturday from Évisa to Porto (€7, 40 minutes) and Corte (€15, two hours).

PIANA

pop 500

Perched above the Golfe de Porto, the picturesque hillside town of Piana is ideally positioned for exploring Les Calanques. Good Friday is marked by La Granitola, a traditional festival during which hooded penitents parade through the village to Piana's Église Ste-Marie.

The **syndicat d'initiative** (tourist office; ☎ 04 95 27 84 42; www.sipiana.com; Pl Mairie; ☒ 8.30-5pm Mon-Fri) is next to the post office. It has lots of information on exploring Les Calanques, and distributes the free leaflet *Piana Randonnées*.

Nearby beaches include **Anse de Ficajola**, reached by a narrow 4km road from Piana, and **Plage d'Arone**, 11km southwest of town via the scenic D824. From the D824, a trail leads to the tower-topped **Capo Rosso**.

Sit in the rambling gardens out the back of **Hôtel Continental** (☎ 04 95 27 83 12; www.contin entalpiana.com; s €40-44, d €49-52, tr €59-62; ☒ Apr-Sep), an old, converted townhouse in the town centre 100m uphill from the church, listening to donkeys braying in the adjacent paddock. Inside, the 17 old-fashioned rooms are furnished with antiques, and it's just a few footsteps from place de la Coletta, the main town square.

Welcoming **Le Casanova** (☎ 04 95 27 84 20; pl Coletta; menus €14.80-16, mains €8.50-19; ☒ 8am-midnight Apr-Oct) has two locations right on place de la Coletta – a bar with an open-air terrace, and diagonally opposite, a cosy restaurant reached via a narrow spiral staircase. Both serve the same fresh fare includ-ing a slew of salads and woodfired pizza plus a classical menu.

There's no more romantic place in Corsica (or perhaps on earth) than the majestic 1912 **Hôtel des Roches Rouges** (☎ 04 95 27 81 81; www.lesrochesrouges.com in French; D81; d €75-80, tr €110, q €125; ☒ mid-Mar–mid-Nov). With a fading façade of peeling pastel paint and flowing rooms, the 'red rocks' is immediately and impossibly seductive. Without question, it's worth spending an extra €5 for a room with a view of the still, deep blue Mediterranean out of which the mountains rise like icebergs. After watching the sun set in a rainbow of colours over the rugged red Calanques, dine in the glass-paned, white-tableclothed restaurant (menus €30 to €38, mains €23 to €29), then wander out to the wide terrace to take in the constellations.

Buses between Porto and Ajaccio stop near the church and the post office.

LES CALANQUES

Flaming a fiery red in the sunlight, the giant granite cliffs and outcrops of Les Calanques de Piana (E Calanche in Corsican) are contrasted by the green foliage of pine and chestnut forests. Though dazzling from the road, you have to take to one of the clifftop walking trails to truly appreciate the views. Eight kilometres southwest of Porto on the D81 is Le Chalet des Roches Bleues, an isolated souvenir shop that makes a useful landmark. Four trails begin nearby:

Chemin des Muletiers The steep, one-hour 'Mule-Drivers' Trail' begins 400m towards Piana from the chalet;

THAT OLD CHESTNUT

Since the 16th century, Corsicans have planted *châtaigniers* (chestnut trees), dubbed *l'arbre à pain* (the bread tree) because of the vast variety of uses for chestnut flour *(farine de châtaigne)*, including pastries still baked today.

Free-range pigs raised on chestnuts have a distinctive flavour. Chestnut treats also include *falculelli* (pressed, frittered *brocciu* cheese served on a chestnut leaf), *beignets au brocciu à la farine de châtaigne* (brocciu cheese frittered in chestnut flour), and *délice à la châtaigne* (chestnut cake); washed down with *bière à la châtaigne* (chestnut beer).

CORSICA

the trailhead is 15m downhill from the sanctuary dedicated to the Virgin Mary.

Chemin du Château Fort A one-hour trail to a fortress-shaped rock with stunning views of the Golfe de Porto. It begins 700m towards Porto from the chalet; the trailhead is on the D81 right of the Tête de Chien (Dog's Head) rock.

La Châtaigneraie A three-hour circuit through chestnut groves, beginning 25m uphill from the chalet.

La Corniche A steep, forested, 40-minute walk to a fantastic view of Les Calanques. Begins on the bridge 50m towards Porto from the chalet.

Buses travelling from Ajaccio to Porto stop at the chalet.

CARGÈSE (CARGHJESE)

pop 900

The Greek-founded fishing port of Cargèse is best known for its **twin churches** – one Eastern (Orthodox), the other Western (Catholic). The interior of the 19th-century Greek church is adorned with icons brought across by the original settlers, who fled their Ottoman-controlled homeland in the 17th century.

Cargèse's main street, the D81, is called av de la République towards Ajaccio, and rue Colonel Fieschi towards Porto. The **tourist office** (☎ 04 95 26 41 31; www.cargese.net; rue du Docteur Dragacci; ☯ 9am-noon & 2-6pm Mon-Sat) is a few streets up from the Latin Church, and has information about local activities including boat excursions. Cargèse's **port** is downhill from the churches. **Genoese towers** atop Pointe d'Omigna and Pointe de Cargèse overlook **Plage de Pero**, a long beach of white sand 1km north of Cargèse.

Cosy, comfortable rooms can be found at **M'hôtel Punta e Mare** (☎ 04 95 26 44 33; www .hotel-puntaemare.com in French; chemin de Paomia; d €40-65; ☯ closed Jan), a welcoming two-star hotel set back from the main town, where you can enjoy breakfast on a tree-shaded terrace framed by climbing plants.

Hôtel Le St-Jean (☎ 04 95 26 46 68; www.lesaint jean.com; place St-Jean; d from €70; ☒), on the main road from Porto on the village square, has an elevated café-restaurant terrace and modern, villa-style rooms, most with balconies overlooking the bay.

There are a few summer-only **restaurants** on Pero beach offering pizzas, seafood and regular music.

Two daily buses from Ota (1½ hours) via Porto (one hour) to Ajaccio (one hour) stop in front of the post office.

AJACCIO (AJACCIU)

pop 52,880

If you didn't happen to know that Napoleon Bonaparte was born in Ajaccio (pronounced Ajaxio) you will within a few minutes of arriving here. With a glittering harbourfront, designer boutiques and fashionable restaurants, Corsica's cosmopolitan capital honours its famous son with street names, statues and several stellar museums.

Orientation

Ajaccio's main street, cours Napoléon, stretches from place de Gaulle northwards to the train station and beyond. The old city is south of place Foch. The port is on the eastern side of town, from where a promenade leads west along plage St-Francois.

Information
BOOKSHOPS
Album (☎ 04 95 21 81 18; 2 place Foch; ☯ 8.30am-noon & 2.30-7pm Mon-Sat, 8.30am-noon Sun Oct-May)

EMERGENCY
Centre Hospitalier Notre-Dame de la Miséricorde (☎ 04 95 29 90 90; 27 av Impératrice Eugénie; ☯ 24hr)
Police Station (☎ 04 95 11 17 17; rue Général Firoella)

INTERNET ACCESS
Absolut Game (☎ 04 95 21 56 60; av de Paris; per hr €3; ☯ 9-2am)

LAUNDRY
Lavomatique (rue Maréchal Ornano; ☯ 8am-10pm)

MONEY
Banks with ATMs are found along place de Gaulle, place Foch and cours Napoléon.

POST
Post Office (13 cours Napoléon)

TOURIST INFORMATION
Tourist Office (☎ 04 95 51 53 03; www.ajaccio-tourisme .com; 3 blvd du Roi Jérôme; ☯ 8am-7pm Mon-Sat, 9am-1pm Sun) Free internet.
Maison d'Information Randonnées du Parc Naturel Régional de Corse (☎ 04 95 51 79 10; www .parc-naturel-corse.com in French; 2 rue Sgt Casolonga; ☯ 8am-noon & 2-6pm Mon-Fri Jun-Sep, 8am-noon & 2-5pm Oct-May) Information on Parc Naturel Régional de Corse and its hiking trails.

AJACCIO (AJACCIU)

0   200 m
0   0.1 miles

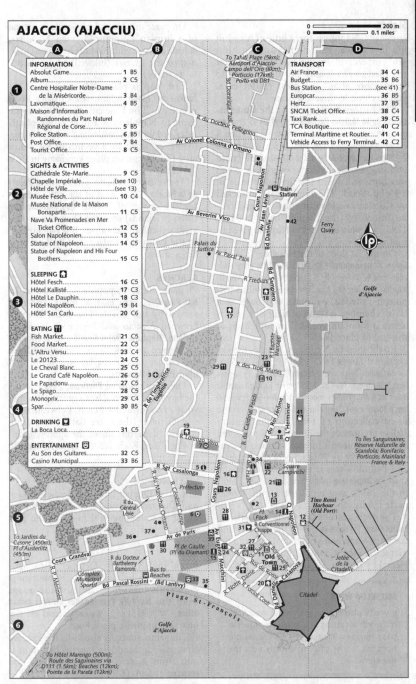

INFORMATION

Absolut Game	1 B5
Album	2 C5
Centre Hospitalier Notre-Dame de la Miséricorde	3 B4
Lavomatique	4 B5
Maison d'Information Randonnées du Parc Naturel Régional de Corse	5 B5
Police Station	6 B5
Post Office	7 B4
Tourist Office	8 C5

SIGHTS & ACTIVITIES

Cathédrale Ste-Marie	9 C5
Chapelle Impériale	(see 10)
Hôtel de Ville	(see 13)
Musée Fesch	10 C4
Musée National de la Maison Bonaparte	11 C5
Nave Va Promenades en Mer Ticket Office	12 C5
Salon Napoléonien	13 C5
Statue of Napoleon	14 C5
Statue of Napoleon and His Four Brothers	15 C5

SLEEPING

Hôtel Fesch	16 C5
Hôtel Kallisté	17 C3
Hôtel Le Dauphin	18 C3
Hôtel Napoléon	19 B4
Hôtel San Carlu	20 C6

EATING

Fish Market	21 C5
Food Market	22 C5
L'Altru Versu	23 C4
Le 20123	24 C5
Le Cheval Blanc	25 C5
Le Grand Café Napoléon	26 C5
Le Papacionu	27 C5
Le Spago	28 C5
Monoprix	29 C4
Spar	30 B5

DRINKING

La Boca Loca	31 C5

ENTERTAINMENT

Au Son des Guitares	32 C5
Casino Municipal	33 B6

TRANSPORT

Air France	34 C4
Budget	35 B6
Bus Station	(see 41)
Europcar	36 B5
Hertz	37 B5
SNCM Ticket Office	38 C4
Taxi Rank	39 C5
TCA Boutique	40 C2
Terminal Maritime et Routier	41 C4
Vehicle Access to Ferry Terminal	42 C2

CORSICA

Sights

Ironically, Napoleon spent little of his adult life in Corsica, and after crowning himself Emperor of France in 1804, he never returned to the island. But if you want to learn more about the great (little) man, you've come to the right place.

The history book opens at the **Musée National de la Maison Bonaparte** (☎ 04 95 21 43 89; rue St-Charles; adult/concession €5/3.50; 9-11.30am & 2-5.30pm Tue-Sun, 2-5.50pm Mon Apr-Sep, 10-11.30am & 2-4.15pm Tue-Sun, 2-4.15pm Mon Oct-Mar), the grand building in the old city where Napoleon was born and spent the first nine years of his childhood. The house was ransacked by Corsican nationalists in 1793, and requisitioned by the English from 1794 to 1796, but was later rebuilt by Napoleon's mother.

On the 1st floor of the Hôtel de Ville, the **Salon Napoléonien** (☎ 04 95 21 90 15; place Foch; adult/child €2.30/free; 9-11.45am & 2-5.45pm Mon-Fri mid-Jun–mid-Sep, to 4.45pm rest of year) exhibits Napoleonic medals, paintings and busts in a lavish chamber. A **statue** of Napoleon stands above a fountain guarded by four lions at the end of place Foch.

Established by Napoleon's uncle, the exceptional **Musée Fesch** (☎ 04 95 21 48 17; 50-52 rue du Cardinal Fesch; adult/student €5.35/3.80; 2-6pm Mon, 9.30am-6pm Tue-Thu, 2-9.30pm Fri, 10.30am-6pm Sat & Sun Jul & Aug; 9.30am-noon & 2-6pm Tue-Sun Apr-Jun & Sep; 9.30am-noon & 2-6pm Tue-Fri & Sun Oct-Mar) has the finest collection of 14th- to 19th-century Italian art outside the Louvre (mostly looted during Napoleon's foreign campaigns), including works by Titian, Botticelli, Raphael and Bellini. There is a separate fee for the **Chapelle Impériale** (adult/student €1.50/0.75), built in the 1850s as a sepulchre for the Bonaparte family.

The 16th-century **Cathédrale Ste-Marie** (rue Forcioli Conti; hours vary) is in the old city and contains Napoleon's baptismal font and the *Vierge au Sacré-Cœur* (Virgin of the Sacred Heart) by Eugène Delacroix (1798–1863).

MUSEUM PASS

If you're planning to see several museums, it's worth investing in a seven-day **Ajaccio pass musées** (museum pass €10), available from the tourist office or directly from the museums.

On place du Général de Gaulle is a **statue** of a Roman Emperor–dressed Napoleon astride a horse with his four brothers (nicknamed the *encrier* (inkwell) by locals due to its shape).

Last stop is place d'Austerlitz and the **Jardins du Casone**, 800m west of place Foch, where you'll find the city's grandest monument to Napoleon – a huge stone plinth, inscribed with his battles and other achievements, crowned by a replica of the statue atop the column on place Vendôme in Paris (p128).

At the black-granite promontory **Pointe de la Parata**, 12km west of the city, you can see the group of islands **Îles Sanguinaires** (Bloody Islands) so named because of their vivid red colours at sunset. Bus No 5 travels to the point from place de Gaulle several times daily.

BEACHES

Plage de Ricanto, popularly known as **Tahiti Plage**, is 5km east of town, and it is served by bus No 1. The small beaches between Ajaccio and Pointe de la Parata (**Ariane**, **Neptune**, **Palm Beach** and **Marinella**) are served by bus No 5. Buses run from the corner of rue du Dr Ramoroni and blvd Pascal Rossini.

The ritzy resort of **Porticcio**, 17km across the bay from Ajaccio, has a great – if somewhat overcrowded – beach. Between April and October, there are daily boats from Ajaccio, departing from the quayside opposite place Foch (€5/8 single/return, 30 minutes).

WALKING

The free English-language leaflet *Hiking and Discovery,* available from the tourist office, describes several hikes in the area around Ajaccio.

Tours

From mid-April to October, Îles Sanguinaires can be visited on 2½-hour boat excursions (€22) that sail most afternoons from the **Nave Va Promenades en Mer ticket office** (☎ 04 95 51 31 31; www.naveva.com) on the quayside opposite place Foch.

The same company also visits the Réserve Naturelle de Scandola (see p928). A boat sails from Ajaccio's old port at 9am and returns at 6pm (€46).

Festivals & Events

Fêtes Napoliennes, Ajaccio's annual celebration of its beloved Boney, features displays, outdoor shows, processions and exhibitions. The highlight is a huge street parade in which the participants dress up as Napoleonic soldiers. Usually the festival coincides with the fireworks display that lights up the night sky on 15 August to mark Napoleon's birthday.

Sleeping

There are no budget options in Ajaccio, short of sleeping in your car – which you might have to do if you don't reserve ahead in summer or during events such as April's WRC car rally (p929).

Hôtel Kallisté (☎ 04 95 51 34 45; www.hotel-kalliste-ajaccio.com in French; 51 cours Napoléon; s €45-56, d €52-69, tw €58-76, tr €69-89; ✗ ☒ ☒ ☐) With clean lines and 50 contemporary rooms, this stylish city hotel – complete with a glass lift, terracotta-tiled floors and exposed brickwork – is a fantastic deal. The hotel also rents cars and has laundry facilities and good wheelchair access. Parking costs €12 (€5 for bikes).

Hôtel Fesch (☎ 04 95 51 62 62; www.hotel-fesch .com; 7 rue du Cardinal Fesch; s €56-79, d €61-89; ✗ closed mid-Dec–mid-Jan; ☒) Presiding over one of Ajaccio's oldest pedestrianised streets, shops and restaurants are on your doorstep at this grand, old fashioned 77-room hotel. Depending on availability, you may have to pay a €19 to €23 supplement for an extra bed in the room – even if you're not using it. Wi-fi's available for free – ask reception for the code.

Hôtel Marengo (☎ 04 95 21 43 66; 2 rue Marengo; www.hotel-marengo.com; d €61-79, tr €75-95; ☒) A former private villa, this family-run place is a charming spot with airy rooms and elegant public areas. On the fringe of Ajaccio's pastel-shaded city centre, it's in a blind alley, so there are no sea views, but you're just a three-minute walk to the beach.

Hôtel Napoléon (☎ 04 95 51 54 00; www.hotel-napoleon-ajaccio.com; 4 rue Lorenzo Vero; s €65-89, d €75-105; ☒) Just off cours Napoléon, rooms at this smart hotel aren't large, but they're tastefully decorated in cool neutral tones, and come with crisp white-tiled bathrooms and free wi-fi. Secure parking's available for €9. If you're travelling solo and don't stipulate that you want a single bed you'll be slugged

the full double room rate (we're still smarting about that).

Also recommended:

Hôtel Le Dauphin (☎ 04 95 21 12 94; www.ledauphin hotel.com; 11 blvd Sampiero; s €52-59, d €56-69, tr €69-85; ☒) One of the cheapest options in town, this local café is opposite the ferry port with clean, modern rooms, some with balconies.

Hôtel San Carlu (☎ 04 95 21 13 84; www.hotel-san carlu.com; 8 blvd Danielle Casanova; s €76-86, d €85-99; ☒) In a prime position overlooking the citadel. The top rooms have views out to sea.

Eating

The old city's rue St-Charles and rue Conventionnel Chiappe are lined with tiny terraced restaurants. It's a great place for a night-time wander, even if you're not planning on eating.

Le Papacionu (☎ 04 95 21 27 86; 16 rue St-Charles; mains €7.50-18, pizza €9-12; ✗ dinner Mon-Sat, closed Nov-Feb) Ajaccio's best pizza is served on bright pink, purple and cobalt-blue plates at this fabulous, funky little hole in the wall. Fortunately the tables are sturdy, otherwise it's unlikely they'd bear the weight of the enormous elliptical pizzas and whopping calzones fired in the open kitchen's wood oven. Corsican wine is served by the pitcher.

L'Altru Versu (☎ 04 95 50 05 22; 16 rue J Baptiste Marcaggi; mains €15-22; ✗ lunch Tue-Sat, dinner Tue-Sun) Situated behind a tiny park (hence its name, which translates as 'the other side'), this exquisite place with stencilled walls, beams and tea lights creates classic French cooking using local produce, such as filet mignon of pork with Corsican honey. Friday and Saturday nights feature live guitar performances and Corsican chants.

Le 20123 (☎ 04 95 21 50 05; 2 rue du Roi de Rome; menus €26; ✗ dinner Tue-Sun) These days an Ajaccio institution, this trip of a Corsican bistro started life in the village of Pila Canale (postcode 20123). When the owner upped sticks, he decided to re-create his old restaurant – village square, water-pump, washing lines and all.

Le Grand Café Napoléon (☎ 04 95 21 42 54; 10 cours Napoléon; menus €28-45, mains €23-30; ✗ Mon-Sat) Inconspicuously situated behind its grand street-front café (p936) is Ajaccio's grandest dining room, replete with soaring cream arches, black-and-white terrazzo floors and red tablecloths. Dine alongside

Ajaccio's elite on elegantly presented fare including excellent fish, duck and the finest *fromages*.

Other recommendations:

Le Spago (☎ 04 95 21 15 71; rue Emmanuel Arène; mains €13-22.50; ☽ lunch & dinner Mon-Fri, dinner Sat) Hip lime-green designer restaurant serving Italian-influenced dishes.

Le Cheval Blanc (☎ 04 95 21 17 98; 18 rue Bonaparte; dishes €8-15; ☽ lunch & dinner Mon-Sat) Rough-hewn stone walls hung with horse saddles, and meat, meat and more meat on the menu.

SELF-CATERING

Ajaccio's open-air **food market** (square Campinchi; ☽ to noon, closed Mon) fills the area with Corsican atmosphere every morning. Chefs vie over the day's catch at the daily **fish market** in the building behind the food market.

Spar (cours Grandval; ☽ 8.30am-12.30pm & 3-7.30pm Mon-Sat) supermarket is close to place de Gaulle, while **Monoprix** (☽ 8.30am-7.15pm Mon-Sat; cours Napoléon) is not far away from the port.

Drinking & Entertainment

Ajaccio isn't known for its nightlife – tipples tend to take place at trendy cafés and restaurants rather than bars, clubs or pubs. Blvd du Roi Jérôme, quai Napoléon and place de Gaulle are the most popular with quaffers.

Le Grand Café Napoléon (10 cours Napoléon; ☽ 8am-midnight) Fronting its famous dining room (p935), Le Grand Café Napoléon's street-side brasserie and terrace are as glam as it gets for a coffee or an aperitif.

La Boca Loca (☎ 06 11 09 52 94; 2 rue de la Porta; tapas €3; ☽ 7.30pm-2am) Catch Latino music on Thursday, Friday and Saturday nights and great tapas and wine anytime.

Au Son des Guitares (☎ 04 95 51 15 47; 7 rue du Roi de Rome) Local guitar bands perform most evenings from around 10pm.

Casino Municipal (☎ 04 95 50 40 60; blvd Pascal Rossini; ☽ 1pm-3am) If you're not up for a flutter on roulette or blackjack, the piano bar is an elegant spot to relax.

Getting There & Away

AIR

Aéroport d'Ajaccio-Campo dell'Oro (☎ 04 95 23 56 56) is 8km east of the city centre.

Air France (☎ 08 20 82 08 20; 3 blvd du Roi Jérôme) has an office in town.

BOAT

Boats depart from the combined bus/ferry **Terminal Maritime et Routier** (quai l'Herminier). The **SNCM ticket office** (☎ 04 95 29 66 99; 3 quai l'Herminier; ☽ 8am-8pm Tue-Fri, to 6pm Mon, to 1pm Sat) is across the street. Inside the terminal, the SNCM bureau sells tickets a few hours before departure for evening ferries. Tickets for vehicles are available at the port's vehicle entrance.

BUS

Most bus companies have ticket kiosks on the right as you enter the **Terminal Maritime et Routier** (quai l'Herminier). The **information counter** (☎ 04 95 51 55 45; ☽ 7am-7pm Jul & Aug, hours vary rest of year) provides schedules.

Eurocorse (☎ 04 95 21 06 30) travels to Bastia (€18, three hours, two daily), Bonifacio (€19.50, four hours, two or three daily), Calvi (€19.85, change at Ponte Leccia, 2½ hours, one daily), Corte (€10.50, 2¾ hours, two daily) and Sartène (€11.50, two hours, two daily). Services run daily except Sundays; some routes operate reduced services out of season.

Ceccaldi/SAIB (☎ 04 95 22 41 99) travels to Porto (€11, two hours, two daily).

Autocars Ricci (☎ 04 95 51 08 19) also travels to Sartène (€10.70, two hours, two daily).

CAR

The main car-rental companies also have airport bureaus.

Budget (☎ 04 95 21 17 18; 1 blvd Lantivy)

Europcar (☎ 04 95 21 05 49; 16 cours Grandval)

Hertz (☎ 04 95 21 70 94; 8 cours Grandval)

Hôtel Kallisté (p935) rents cars and mopeds cheaply.

TRAIN

The **train station** (☎ 04 95 23 11 03; place de la Gare) is staffed until 6.30pm (to 8pm May to September). Services include Bastia (€20.70, four hours, three to four daily), Corte (€11, two hours, three to four daily) and Calvi (€24.10, five hours, two daily; change at Ponte Leccia).

Getting Around

TO/FROM THE AIRPORT

Transports Corse d'Ajaccio (TCA) bus No 8 links the airport with Ajaccio's train and bus stations (€4.50). Hourly buses run from around 8am to 7pm from the bus station, 9am to 11pm from the airport. A taxi from the airport to Ajaccio costs €25 to €35.

BUS
TCA Boutique (☎ 04 95 23 29 41; 75 cours Napoléon) distributes bus maps and timetables. A single ticket/*carnet* of 10 costs €1.20/9. Most buses operate from place Général de Gaulle and cours Napoléon.

TAXI
There's a **taxi rank** (☎ 04 95 21 00 87) on place de Gaulle.

SOUTH OF AJACCIO

SARTÈNE (SARTÈ)
pop 3500

Said to be the most Corsican of Corsica's towns, the grey-granite mountain town of Sartène has a sombre past. In 1583 Barbary pirates raided the town and carried 400 people into slavery in North Africa; raids only ended in the 18th century. Sartène was notorious for its banditry and bloody vendettas. In the early 19th century a disagreement between rival landowners deteriorated into fighting, forcing most of the population to flee.

These days, the town is best known for its increasingly famous **Procession du Catenacciu**, a colourful re-enactment of the Passion, which dates back to the Middle Ages. Each year on Good Friday, the Catenacciu ('the chained one'), an anonymous, barefoot penitent covered in a red robe and cowl (to preserve anonymity), carries a huge cross through the town while dragging a heavy chain shackled to the ankle. The penitent is chosen by the parish priest from applicants seeking to expiate a grave sin.

Orientation & Information
Sartène's main square, place de la Libération, is often referred to locally as place Porta. Cours Sœur Amélie leads south from the square, while cours Général de Gaulle heads north. The Santa Anna quarter is north of place de la Libération. The **tourist office** (☎ 04 95 77 15 40; cours Sœur Amélie; ☿ 9am-noon & 2-6pm Mon-Fri) is 1km downhill from place de la Libération. **Crédit Lyonnais** (14 cours Général de Gaulle) has an ATM.

Sights & Activities
Strolling Sartène's cool cobblestone streets is a pleasant way to spend a hot summer's afternoon. The tourist office has a multilingual brochure marking out suggested walking tours.

Near the **WWI memorial** on place de la Libération is the granite **Église Ste-Marie**. Inside hangs the 35kg cross and 17kg chain used in the Procession du Catenacciu.

An archway through the **town hall** (formerly the Governors' Palace), on the northern side of the square, leads to the web of little alleyways that make up the residential **Santa Anna quarter**.

To ride on Corsican horses amid wild countryside, **Le Domaine de Croccano** (☎ 04 95 77 11 37; christian.perrier@wanadoo.fr) offers short treks (from €16) as well as longer day and overnight trips, and pony rides for kids. You'll find the stables a well-signed 3km northeast from town from cours Bonaparte.

Sleeping & Eating
Hôtel des Roches (☎ 04 95 77 07 61; www.sartenehotel .fr in French; s €49-82, d €54-90; ☿ Apr-Oct) In a typical grey granite building, Sartène's only central hotel has snug rooms with good wheelchair access, some with French doors opening to loggias with plunging views over the valley, and more mesmerising views from its excellent restaurant (mains around €15).

Hôtel La Villa Piana (☎ 04 95 77 07 04; www.lavilla piana.com; d €50-115; ☿ Apr–mid-Oct; ☿) A landmark on the N196, 1.5km outside Sartène, this rustically styled three-star hotel has 32 rooms, some with private terraces, a tennis court and a pool perched above the valley with sublime views.

Piazza Porta (☎ 04 95 77 07 15; 1 place de la Libération; dishes €8-10; ☿ 8am-2am Jul & Aug, 8am-11pm Apr-Jun & Sep, closed Oct-Mar) With a terrace overlooking all the comings and goings of Sartène on the town's central square, this friendly, family-run bar has healthy salads and paninis, and top-notch coffee.

La Chaumière (☎ 04 95 77 07 13; 39 rue Médecin-Capitaine Louis Bénédetti; menus €15; ☿ lunch & dinner) This traditional restaurant serves Corsican food and Sartenaise specialities, including a delicious lamb-and-bean stew.

Self-caterers can stock up at the **Spar** (14 cours Général de Gaulle) or **Atac** (cours Sœur Amélie) supermarkets.

Getting There & Away

Sartène is on the **Eurocorse** (☎ 04 95 21 06 30) bus line linking Ajaccio (€11.50, two hours, two daily) with Bonifacio (€10.50, two hours, two daily). Buses stop at the **Ollandini travel agency** (☎ 04 95 77 18 41; cours Gabriel Péri), near the end of cours Sœur Amélie.

BONIFACIO (BUNIFAZIU)

pop 2700

The most vivid view of Bonifacio is from aboard a boat in the sapphire-blue Bouches de Bonifacio (Strait of Bonifacio). This stunning 12km strait channels between Corsica's southernmost tip and the Italian island of Sardinia. From the water, the tall, sun-bleached buildings of Bonifacio's citadel appear to morph seamlessly into the serrated white limestone cliffs rising up from the sea. Within the clifftop citadel is a charming maze of alleyways with a distinct medieval feel.

A sheer 70m below, on the northern side, is Bonifacio's vibrant port, which spills over with café terraces, shops and – as Corsica's most visited town – more than a few tourists in summer.

Orientation

The citadel (often referred to as Haute Ville – upper town) is the main town centre. Set on the cliff-top promontory above the harbour, it's reached by car via av Charles de Gaulle, or on foot by two steep sets of steps. Bonifacio's boat-filled port lies at the southeastern corner of Bouches de Bonifacio. The ferry terminal is further west along the port.

Information

Boniboom (☎ 04 95 73 55 45; quai Jérôme Comparetti; per 30 min/hr €3/5; ☼ 7am-midnight) Friendly café carved into the cliff with internet access.

Lavoir de la Marine (1 quai Jérôme Comparetti; €6.10; 7am-10pm) Laundrette.

Post Office (place Carrega; ☼ 8.30am-6pm Mon-Sat Jul–mid-Sep, 9am-noon & 2-5pm Mon-Fri, 9am-noon Sat mid-Sep–Jun).

Société Générale (38 rue St-Érasme; ☼ Mon-Fri) Exchanges currency and has the only ATM in town. In summer, there are exchange bureaus along the port.

Tourist Office (☎ 04 95 73 11 88; www.bonifacio.fr; 2 rue Fred Scamaroni; ☼ 9am-8pm daily Jul & Aug, 9am-7pm daily May, Jun & Sep, 9am-noon & 2-6pm Mon-Fri Oct-Apr) In Haute Ville.

Tourist Office Annexe (☼ 10am-6pm daily Jun-Sep) Next to the docks for the boats departing for the islands, at the port's eastern end.

Sights & Activities

CITADEL (HAUTE VILLE)

Towering above both the port to the north and the brilliant blue sea to the south, the citadel is linked by steps from rue St-Érasme to Porte de Gênes known as Montée Rastello and Montée St-Roch further up. At the top of Montée St-Roch, the **Porte de Gênes** is accessed by a dramatic drawbridge dating from 1598.

Just inside the Porte de Gênes you'll find the **Bastion Memorial** (admission €2.50; ☼ 9am-7pm daily mid-Apr–Sep). Newly renovated, the 13th-century bastion sets an atmospheric stage for life-size scenes depicting major events in the town's history including the discovery of the 6500-year-old skeleton of the 'lady of

---

SOUTHWESTERN CORSICA'S PREHISTORIC SITES

If you have a fascination with prehistory (and you have wheels), the areas around Sartène offer a treasure-trove of megalithic sites.

Northwest of Sartène and Propriano is **Filitosa**, Corsica's most important prehistoric site. Filitosa's megaliths and menhirs have been surveyed since their accidental discovery in 1946 by the land's owner, Charles-Antoine Césari. Set among 1000-year-old olive trees, some of these extraordinary monuments date as far back as the early Neolithic era; others date from as (relatively) recently as Roman times. The oldest findings on the site suggest a human population living in caves, and remnants of pottery, arrow heads and farming tools point to fixed settlements beginning as early as 3300 BC. A small **museum** (☎ 04 95 74 00 91; admission €5; ☼ 8am-sunset) at the site displays major finds.

Southwest of Sartène near the D48, other prehistoric sites include the figures and menhirs of the **Alignement de Stantari** and the **Alignement de Palaggiu**, and the eerie megaliths of **Cauria**. Theories abound regarding their purpose, ranging from magical armies to celestial communication centres, but as with Brittany's megalithic sites, no one really knows.

BONIFACIO

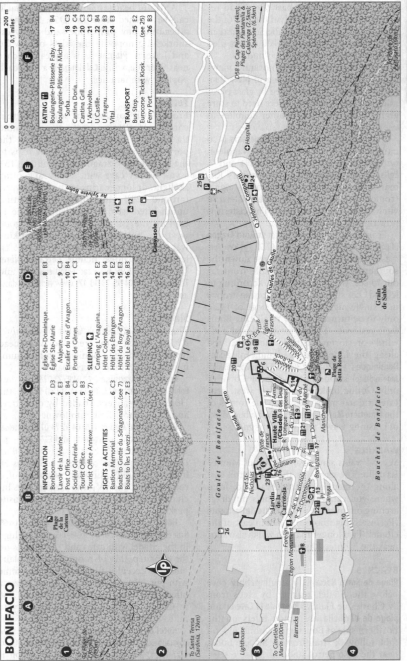

| 0 | 200 m |
| 0 | 0.1 miles |

INFORMATION
Boniboom	**1**	D3
Lavoir de la Marine	**2**	E3
Post Office	**3**	B4
Société Générale	**4**	C3
Tourist Office	**5**	B3
Tourist Office Annexe	(see 7)	

SIGHTS & ACTIVITIES
Bastion Memorial	**6**	C3
Boats to Grotte du Sdragonato	(see 7)	
Boats to îles Lavezzi	**7**	E3
Église Ste-Dominique	**8**	B3
Église Ste-Marie	**9**	C3
Majeure	**10**	B4
Escalier du Roi d'Aragon	**11**	C3
Porte de Gênes		

SLEEPING 🛏
Camping L'Araguina	**12**	E2
Hôtel Colomba	**13**	B4
Hôtel des Etrangers	**14**	E2
Hôtel du Roy d'Aragon	**15**	E3
Hôtel Le Royal	**16**	B3

EATING 🍴
Boulangerie-Pâtisserie Faby	**17**	B4
Boulangerie-Pâtisserie Michel		
Sorba	**18**	C3
Cantina Doria	**19**	C4
Cantina Grill	**20**	C3
L'Archivolto	**21**	C3
U Castille	**22**	B4
U Fragnu	**23**	B3
Vital	**24**	E3

TRANSPORT
Bus Stop	**25**	E2
Eurocorse Ticket Kiosk	(see 25)	
Ferry Port	**26**	B3

Bonifacio' its Genoese past (Bonifacio remained Genoese longer than the rest of the island) and the sinking of the *Sémillante* in 1855, in which more than 700 sailors died when it struck an off-shore island.

Along the ramparts, panoramic views unfold from **place du Marché** and **place Manichella**. The two holes covered by glass pyramids in place Manichella were used to store grain, salted meats and other supplies to use during times of siege.

The old city's **rue des Deux Empereurs** is so named because Charles V and Napoleon once slept in the houses at Nos 4 and 7. **Église Ste-Marie Majeure**, a 14th-century Romanesque church, is known for its loggia (roofed porch) and communal cistern, a vital asset in times of siege. The cistern is now used as a conference hall.

From the citadel, the **Escalier du Roi d'Aragon** (King of Aragon's stairway; admission €2.50; ☉ 9am-7pm mid-Apr–Sep) slices a diagonal line down the southern cliff-face that's visible from far out to sea. Its 187 steps were, according to legend, constructed by Aragonese troops in a single night during the siege of 1420, only to be turned back by retaliating Bonifacio residents. The stairway is closed if it's windy or stormy. Outside the walls, west along the limestone headland, **Église Ste-Dominique** (☉ 9.30am-12.30pm & 3-6pm Mon-Sat mid-Jun–mid-Sep) stands out as one of Corsica's only Gothic buildings. Further west, near three ruined mills, the elaborate tombs of the **Cimetière Marin** are set against a backdrop of crashing waves and wheeling gulls.

WALKING

Several walks start near the top of Montée Rastello. The easiest is the 2km stroll east along the maquis-covered headland, from where you can view Bonifacio's buildings arching out over the water. **Phare de Pertusato** (Pertusato Lighthouse) is 5.6km east of the citadel. Two longer marked walks also start near the Montée Rastello.

BEACHES

Plage de Sotta Rocca is a small pebbly cove below the citadel, reached by steps from av Charles de Gaulle. **Plage de la Catena** and **plage de l'Arinella** are sandy inlets on the northern side of Bouches de Bonifacio – on foot, follow the trail from av Sylvère Bohn, near the Esso petrol station.

A trio of beaches 3km east of Bonifacio can be reached from the D58. **Spérone** is a beautiful bay with white sand and great snorkelling opposite the islets of Cavallo and Lavezzi. **Piantarella** is a pleasant cove near Spérone, while **Calalonga** is a big beach popular with families.

Tours

From April to October, seven different companies offering boat cruises around the Strait of Bonifacio operate from the port. Most offer either one-hour trips to the Grotte du Sdragonato (around €15), a vast watery cave with a natural rooftop skylight, or longer trips to the Îles Lavezzi (around €29), wild, impossibly beautiful uninhabited islands. You'll have time to explore the islands, and swim in good weather, but bring food and drinking water as there are no supplies on the islands. Companies include **Rocca Croisières** (☎ 04 95 73 13 96; www.rocca-croisieres.com) and **Thalassa** (☎ 04 95 73 10 17; www.vedettesthalassa .com in French).

Sleeping

The tourist office has a list of *chambres d'hôtes* (B&Bs) in the area. Book *way* ahead if you're heading to Bonifacio in high summer, at which time prices soar.

Camping L'Araguina (☎ 04 95 73 02 96; av Sylvère Bohn; camping from €13.50; ☉ Mar-Oct) Near the Hôtel des Étrangers, shaded by olive trees and only a short walk into town.

Hôtel des Étrangers (☎ 04 95 73 01 09; hoteldes etrangers.ifrance.com; av Sylvère Bohn; d €37-74; ☉ Apr-Oct; ☒) Bonifacio's best deal is just 300m outside town. This rambling hotel has 30 light, airy, old-fashioned soundproofed rooms with cable TVs, the bargain rates include breakfast, and there's plenty of onsite parking – a rare treat in these parts.

Hôtel Le Royal (☎ 04 95 73 00 51; fax 04 95 73 04 68; 8 rue Fred Scamaroni; s €40-95, d €45-105; ☒) Set high in the citadel with cafés and restaurants on the doorstep, this 14-room place has plain, modern, decently fitted out rooms, some with port views too. Its restaurant/pizzeria offers port views and *menus* from €13.50 to €20.50, and is open from February to mid-November.

Hotel du Roy d'Aragon (☎ 04 95 73 03 99; www .royaragon.com; 13 quai Jérôme Comparetti; d €49-145, ste €127-197; ☒ ☒) Hotel du Roy d'Aragon is the pick of places to stay on the crowded quay. This sophisticated three-star place has minimalist rooms furnished in blond wood; higher-priced rooms come with port views and breezy balconies. Staff are friendly and accommodating.

Hôtel Colomba (☎ 04 95 73 73 44; www.hotel-boni facio.fr; rue Simon Varsi; d €72-165; 🈂) The boutique Colomba has 10 white-glove-test-clean rooms, elegant wrought-iron and rustically painted furniture, and luxuries like minibars and – a saving grace after scaling the citadel's steps – a lift to whisk you between floors. There's a seasonally opening, exposed stone-walled restaurant on site, or head to U Castille (below) opposite.

Eating

The citadel invariably offers better value than the pricey – if pretty – harbourside terraces.

Cantina Doria (☎ 04 95 73 50 49; 27 rue Doria; menus €12-15; 🈂 Apr-Oct) Sit alongside locals on wooden benches, surrounded by copper pots and pans, black-and-white photos and rusty signs, for classic Corsican fare like hearty soup and the local specialty, *aubergines à la Bonifacienne*, eggplant stuffed with breadcrumbs soaked in basil and olive oil and three kinds of cheese. For dessert try the *gateau à la châtaigne* (chestnut cake).

Cantina Grill (☎ 04 95 70 49 86; 3 quai Banda del Ferro; menus €12-15; 🈂 Apr-Oct) The sister establishment of Cantina Doria is the best spot to pull up a pew on the port. Unlike Doria's earthy menu and décor, the lighter, brighter Cantina Grill specialises in fresh fish and seafood both expertly grilled and reasonably priced.

L'Archivolto (☎ 04 95 73 17 58; rue de l'Archivolto; plats du jour €7-14; 🈂 dinner Mon-Sat mid-Mar–Oct) Specialities like chicken in Pietra beer and a fresh herb tart with *brocciu* cheese are long-standing favourites at this wonderfully quirky restaurant-cum-antique-shop in the citadel, serving imaginative food in a dining room filled with bric-a-brac.

U Castille (☎ 04 95 73 04 99; rue Simon Varsi; menus €16.50-19, mains €13-23, pizzas €7.50-11.50; 🈂 lunch & dinner daily Mar-Oct, Tue-Sat Nov-Feb) U Castille is the umbrella for four separate dining premises carved out of the rocks and run by the same welcoming family, but the Corsican menu, wood-fired pizzas and excellent wine list are interchangeable among all. For

a romantic meal, ask for a table with views over the clear gemstone-coloured coves of the sea.

U Fragnu (☎ 04 95 73 51 69; rue Fred Scamaroni; mains €15-26; 🈂 lunch & dinner Apr-Oct) Next door to the Hôtel Le Royal in the citadel, this refined restaurant has spectacular views over the port and harbour from on high. Seafood such as grilled red mullet is the order of the day here, but there's also a lengthy list of veal options, as well as pizzas.

SELF-CATERING

Be sure to taste Bonifacio's pastry speciality, *pain des morts* (literally, 'bread of the dead'), a nut and raisin brioche traditionally eaten for the Fête des Morts (Festival of the Dead) on the 2nd of November, but baked year round. In the citadel you can pick it up, along with other sweet treats, at **Boulangerie-Pâtisserie Faby** (4 rue St-Jean Baptiste; 🈂 8am-8pm Jul & Aug, 8am-12.30pm & 4-7pm Sep-Jun). On the port, try **Boulangerie-Pâtisserie Michel Sorba** (1-3 rue St-Érasme; 🈂 6am-8pm Jul & Aug, 8am-12.30pm & 4.30-7pm Tue-Sat, 8am-12.30pm Sun Sep-Jun).

You'll find a handful of supermarkets on the port including **Vital** (93 quai Jérôme Comparetti; 🈂 8am-12.30pm & 3.30-7.30pm Mon-Sat, 8am-12.30pm Sun).

Getting There & Away

AIR

Bonifacio's airport, **Aéroport de Figari** (☎ 04 95 71 10 10), is 21km north of town. An airport bus runs from the town centre in July and August (€7 to €8).

BOAT

In summer, ferries to Santa Teresa in Sardinia are operated by **Saremar** (☎ 04 95 73 00 96; www.saremar.it in Italian) and **Moby Lines** (☎ 04 95 73 00 29; www.mobylines.it) from Bonifacio's ferry port (50 minutes, two to seven daily). Fares start from €8 one way, plus taxes (around €6.20 one way).

BUS

Eurocorse (Porto Vecchio ☎ 04 95 70 13 83) runs two buses to Ajaccio (€19.50, four hours) via Sartène from Monday to Saturday. For Bastia, change at Porto Vecchio (€6.50, 45 minutes, two to four buses daily). Buses leave near the Eurocorse kiosk on the port, with only a few services a week outside summer.

CORTE AREA

CORTE (CORTI)

pop 5700 / elevation 400m

To truly experience Corsican culture, head to Corte (pronounced Cor-tay), its heartland. Since Pasquale Paoli created an independent nation in 1755 and made this fortified town its capital, Corte continues to be a potent symbol of Corsican independence. Paoli founded a national university here in 1765, but it was closed four years later when the short-lived Corsican republic foundered. Università di Corsica Pasquale Paoli was reopened in 1981. It has about 3000 students and is a lynchpin in the revival of the Corsican language.

Cradled by mountains, hiking in the area is some of the island's best. The town marks the midpoint on the Mare a Mare Nord trail.

Orientation

Corte's main street is cours Paoli, which is lined with shops and cafés. At its southern end is place Paoli, from where the narrow streets of the Haute Ville (upper town) continue uphill to the fortified citadel. The train station is about 500m downhill from cours Paoli.

Information

Banks with ATMs are found along cours Paoli.

Grand Café (22 cours Paoli; per 15min/hr €1/3.50; ☺ 7am-2am) Internet access while you dine.

Hôpital Civile (☎ 04 95 45 05 00; allée du 9 Septembre)

Maison de la Presse (24 cours Paoli; ☺ 8am-6pm) Sells maps and walking guides and has a good Corsican section.

Post Office (av du Baron Mariani) Has an ATM.

Tourist Office (☎ 04 95 46 26 70; www.centru-corsica .com; La Citadelle; ☺ usually 9am-noon & 2-5pm Mon-Fri, longer hours summer)

Sights

Of Corsica's six citadels, Corte's is the only one not on the coast. Jutting out above the Rivers Tavignanu and Restonica and

---

THE VINEYARDS OF CORSICA

France's fine wines aren't confined to the mainland. The rich soils, pure air and gentle rainfall of Corsica's sunkissed slopes and mountain plateaus gives rise to three distinct grape varieties. Vermentinu (also called Malvasia) is a white grape with floral aromas that also combines with red varietals to produce rosés. Niellucciu, a soft red grape, has aromas including liquorice, violets and spices. From the granite grounds around Ajaccio, the firm grape Sciaccarellu has a peppery bouquet.

Dozens of vineyards ribbon the island, many of which (including those listed here) can be visited for free and offer tastings. In all there are nine AOCs (*Appelations d'Origine Contrôlée*) across Corsica.

A smattering of the island's best:

Domaine Vico (☎ 04 95 47 61 35; rte de Calvi, Ponte Leccia; ☺ Mon-Sat) Sample reds, rosés and whites in an ancient vaulted stone cellar in the inland Ponte Leccia region.

Domaine Arena (☎ 04 95 37 08 27; Rogliano; ☺ daily) This friendly estate is situated at the intersection of the roads to Cap Corse and Patrimonio (and they speak English).

Domaine Fiumicicoli (☎ 04 95 76 14 08; Olmeto; ☺ Mon-Sat) From Sartène, head 8km along the road to Levie after the Genoese bridge to this family-run winery. Bring cash if you're planning to stock up your cellar: credit cards aren't accepted.

Domaine Mosconi (☎ 04 95 77 00 27; Sartène; ☺ Jun-Sep) Straddling prehistoric sites and surrounded by menhirs and dolmens, Domaine Mosconi's wines are equally steeped in history.

Domaine de la Ruche Roncière (☎ 04 95 58 40 80; Vescovato; ☺ daily) In the Castagniccia region of the island, you can learn (in English) about all sorts of Corsican products including these hillside-ripened, ancestral wines.

For more information, contact the Corsican winegrowers association, **Les Vignerons Uvacorse** (☎ 04 95 25 19 61).

Heed the Corsican advice, '*A chi beie sempre acqua finisce per avé granochie in corpu*' ('Drink nothing but water and you'll have frogs growing in your belly'). Just take care on the rollercoaster roads afterwards!

the cobbled alleyways of the Haute Ville, the citadel's highest point is the **château** (known as the Nid d'Aigle, or Eagle's Nest), built in 1419 by a Corsican nobleman allied with the Aragonese. It was expanded during the 18th and 19th centuries and served as a Foreign Legion base from 1962 until 1983.

The citadel's outstanding **Museu di a Corsica** (Museum of Corsica; ☎ 04 95 45 25 45; adult/student €5.30/3; ⏰ 10am-6pm summer, to 5pm Nov-Apr, closed Mon low season) has an excellent permanent exhibition of Corsican traditions, crafts, agriculture and anthropology. Temporary art and music exhibitions are held on the ground floor. Captions are in French and Corsican.

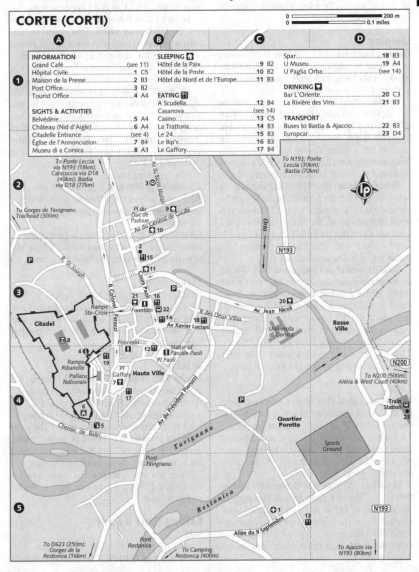

CORTE (CORTI)

0 — 200 m
0 — 0.1 miles

INFORMATION
Grand Café..................................(see 11)
Hôpital Civile..................................**1** C5
Maison de la Presse.......................**2** B3
Post Office.....................................**3** B2
Tourist Office.................................**4** A4

SIGHTS & ACTIVITIES
Belvédère......................................**5** A4
Château (Nid d'Aigle).....................**6** A4
Citadelle Entrance.......................(see 4)
Église de l'Annonciation................**7** B4
Museu di a Corsica.......................**8** A3

SLEEPING 🏠
Hôtel de la Paix.............................**9** B2
Hôtel de la Poste..........................**10** B2
Hôtel du Nord et de l'Europe.........**11** B3

EATING 🍴
A Scudella....................................**12** B4
Casanova...................................(see 14)
Casino..**13** C5
La Trattoria..................................**14** B3
Le 24...**15** B3
Le Bip's.......................................**16** B3
Le Gaffory...................................**17** B4

Spar..**18** B3
U Museu......................................**19** A4
U Paglia Orba.............................(see 14)

DRINKING 🍷
Bar L'Oriente...............................**20** C3
La Rivière des Vins......................**21** B3

TRANSPORT
Buses to Bastia & Ajaccio...........**22** B3
Europcar.....................................**23** D4

To N193; Ponte Leccia (30km); Bastia (70km)

To Ponte Leccia via N193 (18km); Calacuccia via D18 (40km); Bastia via D18 (77km)

To Gorges de Tavignanu Trailhead (300m)

Pl du Duc de Padoue

Av du Bastion Mattei

Av du Général de Gaulle

Orta

N193

R St-Joseph

R. Colonel Feracci

Cours Paoli

Rampe Ste-Croix

Fountain

R des Deux Villas

Av Jean Nicoli

Av Xavier Luciani

Citadel

Fountain

Statue of Pascale Paoli

Pl Paoli

Università di Corsica

Basse Ville

Rampe Ribanelle

Pl Gaffory **Haute Ville**

Pallazu Nationale

Av du Président Pierucci

N200

To N200 (500m); Aléria & West Coast (40km)

Chemin de Baliri

Tavignanu

Quartier Porette

Train Station

Pont Tavignanu

Sports Ground

Restonica

N193

Allée du 9 Septembre

To D623 (250m); Gorges de la Restonica (16km)

Pont Restonica

To Camping Restonica (400m)

To Ajaccio via N193 (80km)

Outside the ramparts, a path leads to the **belvédère** (viewing platform), which has views of the city and the Eagle's Nest. Close by, a precarious staircase leads down to the river.

Further down the hill is the 15th-century **Église de l'Annonciation** (place Gaffory). The walls of nearby houses are pockmarked with bullet holes, reputedly from Corsica's war of independence.

Sleeping

Camping Restonica (☎ /fax 04 95 46 11 59; faubourg de St-Antoine; per adult/car/tent €6/2.50/3; ☾ mid-Apr–mid-Oct) This basic but leafy campground is a 400m stroll south of town.

Hôtel de la Paix (☎ 04 95 46 06 72; socoget@wanadoo.fr; av du Général de Gaulle; d €35-62; ☾ Apr-Oct) With 63 spic-and-span rooms, this comfortable two-star hotel is calmly but conveniently located on a quiet square off cours Paoli. Bike storage is available and there's a decent in-house Corsican restaurant (*menu* €14).

Hôtel de la Poste (☎ 04 95 46 01 37; 2 place du Duc de Padoue; d €46-57) Situated on the same square as Hôtel de la Paix in the heart of the town, and open all year round, the Hôtel de la Poste is a typically Corsican no-frills hotel of 11 good-sized rooms with charmingly mismatched décor and good wheelchair access.

Hôtel du Nord et de l'Europe (☎ 04 95 46 00 68; www.hoteldunord-corte.com; 22 cours Paoli; d low season €64-85) Corte's oldest hotel is also its best. Freshly renovated, this sweeping family-run place has 15 rooms with soaring ceilings, double-glazed windows and timber floors; the best rooms have mountain views. There's free parking 50m away. The cosy onsite café (open to nonguests) is a treat.

Eating

La Trattoria (☎ 04 95 46 00 76; 6 cours Paoli; menus €9-14; ☾ lunch & dinner, closed Sun) A family-run restaurant held in high esteem by locals, La Trattoria trots out classic Corsican meat dishes and enormous salads. The next-door patisserie is the best in town, so the cakes are rather good, too.

Le Gaffory (☎ 04 95 46 36 97; place Gaffory; menus from €11.50; ☾ lunch & dinner Apr-Sep) Nestling in the shadow of Église de l'Annonciation and shaded by a dark green awning, this respectable restaurant is a good bet for cheap Corsican food, with most main courses averaging just €8.

U Museu (☎ 04 95 61 08 36; rampe Ribanelle; menus €13-15, mains around €20; ☾ lunch & dinner, closed mid-Nov–Mar) This celebrated Corsican restaurant serves traditional cuisine on a gazebo-covered terrace with panoramic views. Its *menus* include *civet de sanglier aux myrtes sauvages* (wild boar with myrtle), *soissons Corses* (Corsican lima beans) and *truite au peveronata* (trout in red pepper sauce).

Le Bip's (☎ 04 95 46 06 26; 14 cours Paoli; menus from €14; ☾ lunch & dinner Sun-Fri) This cellar restaurant is always packed with a boisterous crowd who come for the atmosphere and home-style food. The restaurant is down a flight of stairs beside the buzzy Brasserie Le Bip's.

Le 24 (☎ 04 95 46 02 90; 24 cours Paoli; menus €19; ☾ lunch & dinner Mon-Sat) Formerly Chez Julien, this elegant place on Corte's main street has been completely revamped and now offers 'semigastronomic' fare (read: beautifully presented, top-quality food without the matching price tag).

Also recommended:

A Scudella (☎ 04 95 46 25 31; 2 place Paoli; menus €9-18; ☾ lunch & dinner, closed Christmas period) Rustic and rich in regional produce, this snug place is on the northern side of place Paoli.

U Paglia Orba (☎ 04 95 61 07 89; 5 av Xavier Luciani; menus from €14; ☾ lunch & dinner Mon-Sat) U Paglia Orba serves classic Corsican cuisine on a flower-decked terrace.

SELF-CATERING

Practically the whole town comes to buy its cakes at Corte's top *boulangerie*, **Casanova** (6 cours Paoli). Stock up on supplies at **Spar** (7 av Xavier Luciani) or **Casino** (allée du 9 Septembre) supermarkets.

Drinking

Funky **Bar L'Oriente** (☎ 04 95 61 11 17; av Jean Nicoli; ☾ 9am-midnight) is popular with students from the university across the street.

For a glass of fine Corsican wine accompanied by *charcuterie* and cheese, try the cosy **La Rivière des Vins** (☎ 04 95 46 37 04; 5 rampe Ste-Croix; menus €12-16; ☾ closed Sun Oct-Mar) with pine tables on a red awning-shaded outdoor terrace.

Keep an eye out for the rum bar La Rhumerie (p921), set to roll out its barrel in Corte soon.

Getting There & Away

BUS

Eurocorse travels through town twice daily from Ajaccio (€10.50, 2¾ hours) towards

Bastia (€10, two hours) except Sunday. Buses stop outside Brasserie Majestic at 19 cours Paoli.

CAR
Europcar (☎ 04 95 46 06 02; place de la Gare), at the train station, offers the only car rental in town.

TRAIN
The **train station** (☎ 04 95 46 00 97; ⊗ 6.30am-8.30pm Mon-Sat, 9.45am-noon & 4.45-8.35pm Sun) is east of the city centre. Destinations include Bastia (€9.70, two hours, three to four daily) and Ajaccio (€11.00, two hours, three to four daily).

AROUND CORTE
Southwest of Corte are the grey-granite **Gorges de la Restonica**. Some of the area's best walking trails begin 16km southwest

of Corte at **Bergeries de Grotelle** (1375m), which is accessible via the D623. The **Lac de Mello** (Melu; 1711m) is a one-hour walk from the Bergeries (sheepfolds), while **Lac de Capitello** (Capitellu; 1930m) is 40 minutes further. Both lakes are iced over for much of the year.

West of Corte, there are walking trails around the **Gorge du Tavignanu**. **Lac Nino** (Ninu; 1743m) is a 9½-hour walk departing from Corte. Twenty kilometres south from there, the 15-sq-km **Forêt de Vizzavona** has 43km of forest trails. Two waterfalls, the **Cascade des Anglais**, accessible from Vizzavona, and the **Cascade du Voile de la Mariée**, near Bocognano, are both worth the walk.

If you're hiking in the area, call the **Peloton de Gendarmerie de Haute Montagne** (PGHM, mountain police; ☎ 04 95 61 13 95) for route conditions and information.

Directory

CONTENTS

ACCOMMODATION

Be it boutique bunkhouse, village hotel, fairytale castle or mountain refuge, France has accommodation to suit every taste and budget.

In general, accommodation options listed under 'budget' in this guide have doubles costing up to €50 (€65 in Paris). Listings in this book are assumed to have a private bathroom, but the bathroom may be just a basin and/or shower without a private toilet. Hall showers are free, although, very rarely these days, the odd hotel still charges €2.

Accommodation listed under 'midrange' costs €50 to €120 for a double (up to €150 in Paris) with private shower and toilet. Top-end accommodation costs anything upwards of €120 (€150 in the capital).

During periods of heavy domestic or foreign tourism (eg Easter, Christmas–New Year, the February–March school holidays, as well as July and August and most long weekends) popular destinations are packed out and accommodation prices soar. This is particularly noticeable in coastal hot spots like the Côte d'Azur and Alpine ski resorts

PRACTICALITIES

- Use the metric system for weights and measures.

- Plugs have two round pins, meaning you need an international adaptor; the electric current is 220V at 50Hz AC (you may need a transformer for 110V electrical appliances).

- Videos in France work on the PAL system; TV is Secam.

- Read the French news in *Le Monde* (www.lemonde.fr), right-wing *Le Figaro* (www.lefigaro.fr) or left-leaning *Libération* (www.liberation.fr).

- Tune in to Radio France Info (105.5 FM) or the multilanguage RFI (738AM) for round-the-clock news; BBC World Service/Europe (648AM); Nova (101.5FM) for an eclectic blend of modern beats; Paris Jazz (98.1 FM) for jazz in the capital; and Nostalgie (www.nostalgie.fr), Skyrock (www.skyrock.com) or Fun Radio (www.funradio.fr) for commercial hits (check their websites for local frequencies).

- Pick up *FUSAC* (France USA Contacts) magazine (www.fusac.fr) in Anglophone haunts in Paris for classified ads about housing, babysitting, jobs and language exchanges.

- Switch on French TV: private stations TF1 and M6; and state-owned France 2, France 3 and Arte.

where high-season rates are double those charged in low season. Rates listed in this guide are generally peak rates.

Some tourist offices make room reservations (occasionally for a fee of €5), but many will only do so if you stop by the office in person. In the Alps, tourist offices for ski resorts run a central reservation service through which the whole spectrum of accommodation – hotels, studios, apartments and chalets – can be booked.

B&Bs

Some of the best accommodation exists in the shape of *chambres d'hôtes* (B&Bs) – bed and breakfast in a private home. Many hosts cook up a scrumptious home-made evening meal too *(table d'hôte)* for an extra charge (€20–25). Tourist offices have lists of *chambres d'hôtes* in their areas – urban rarities but rife in rural areas.

Gîtes de France acts as an umbrella organisation for B&B properties. Ask about local Gîtes de France offices, brochures and guides at local tourist offices, or contact the **Fédération Nationale des Gîtes de France** (Map pp102-3; ☎ 01 49 70 75 75; www.gites-de-france.fr; 59 rue St-Lazare, 9e, Paris; Ⓜ Trinité) directly.

Bienvenue à la Ferme (☎ 01 53 57 11 44; www .bienvenue-a-la-ferme.com; 9 av George V, Paris; Ⓜ Alma-Marceau, George V) is another fantastic contact for those seeking a dreamy *chambre d'hôte* on a farm. Search for properties online or order a catalogue.

Other useful websites: **Fleurs de Soleil** (http://fleursdesoleil.fr) and **...en France** (www.bb france.com).

Camping

Thousands of France's camp sites are near rivers, lakes or the sea. Most open March or

April to October. Some hostels let travellers pitch tents in their grounds.

In this book 'camping' refers to fixed-price deals for two or three people including a tent and a car. Otherwise the price is broken down per person/tent/car. Camping-ground offices are often closed for most of the day. Getting to/from many sites without your own transport can be slow and costly.

Wild camping *(camping sauvage)* in non-designated spots is illegal. Except in Corsica, you probably won't have problems if you're at least 1500m from a camping area (or, in national parks, at least an hour's walk from the road). Camping on the beach is not a good idea in areas with high tidal variations. Always ask permission before camping on private land.

Gîtes de France (left) and Bienvenue à la Ferme (left) coordinate camping on farms and publish the joint annual guide, *Séjours à la Ferme* (€14).

Homestays

Under an arrangement known as *hôtes payants* or *hébergement chez l'habitant*, students, young people and tourists stay with French families. In general you rent a room and have access to the bathroom and kitchen (sometimes limited). Ask tourist offices for details. Language schools often arrange this style of accommodation for their students, as do the following organisations:

Accueil Familial des Jeunes Étrangers (Map pp108-9; ☎ 01 45 49 15 57; www.afje-paris.org; 23 rue du Cherche Midi, 6e, Paris; Ⓜ Sèvres Babylone) Homestays in Paris; €540 a month with breakfast.

France Lodge (Map pp102-3; ☎ 01 56 33 85 85; www .apartments-in-paris.com; 2 rue Meissonier, 17e, Paris;

ICONOGRAPHY

A note on the icons used in this book... Those hotels that bear a nonsmoking icon (✖) really do have at least a handful of rooms – in the case of some, entire floors – reserved for those who do not smoke. They are not places that make claims to 'airing out our rooms thoroughly after guests' use'. Also most hotels and hostels in Paris have some form of internet access available nowadays. We have included an internet icon (▢) only if the hotel has a terminal which guests can use; we haven't used it for places that offer wi-fi only. Use of the terminal is usually free of charge for guests; where the business (usually a hostel) charges its guests an access fee, we have generally noted this in the review text. Only hotels that possess one or two rooms fully equipped for disabled guests (bathrooms big enough for a wheelchair user to turn around in, access door on bath tubs, grip bars alongside toilets etc) get a wheelchair icon (♿).

(M) Wagram) Accommodation in private Parisian homes; B&B €23 to €70 a night.

Hostels

A dormitory bed in a hostel (auberge de jeunesse) costs €25 in Paris, and anything from €9.70 to €35 in the provinces, geographic-location dependent; breakfast/dinner is often available for €3/10. Bring your own sleeping bag or rent sheets for €2.80.

Guests need to purchase an annual Hostelling International card (€10.70/15.25 for under/over 26s) or a nightly Welcome Stamp (€1.50–2.80) to stay at hostels run by French hostelling associations **Ligue Française pour les Auberges de la Jeunesse** (LFAJ; Map pp98-9; ☎ 01 44 16 78 78; www.auberges-de-jeunesse.com; 7 rue Vergniaud, 13e, Paris; (M) Glacière) and **Fédération Unie des Auberges de Jeunesse** (FUAJ; Map pp110-11; ☎ 01 48 04 70 30; www.fuaj.org; 9 rue de Brantôme, 3e, Paris; (M) Rambuteau).

In university towns, foyers d'étudiant (student dormitories) are sometimes converted for use by travellers during summer.

Hotels

Hotels in France are rated with one to five stars, although ratings are based on objective criteria (eg the size of the entry hall), not the quality of the service, décor or cleanliness. Prices often reflect these intangibles far more than they do the number of stars.

French hotels almost never include breakfast in their advertised nightly rates. Unless specified otherwise, prices quoted in this guide don't include breakfast. Breakfast costs around €6/8/20 in a budget/midrange/top-end hotel.

A double room generally has one double bed (albeit two singles pushed together often!); a room with twin beds (deux lits séparés) is always more expensive, as is a room with a bathtub instead of a shower. Triples and quads usually have two or three beds.

Logis de France (www.logis-de-france.fr), which publishes an annual guide with maps, and **Citotel** (www.citotel.com) group together affiliated hotels that meet strict standards of service and amenities while retaining their own identity and charm. They are usually reliable and good value. **Best Western** (www.bestwestern.com) has muscled in on the upper end of midrange accommodation.

BON WEEKEND EN VILLES

In 32 cities and larger towns across France kip two nights for the price of one with Bon Weekend en Villes (Great Weekend in Towns), a countrywide city-break deal that kicks in at weekends year-round in less-visited destinations and from November to March in hotter tourist spots. Reservations must be made at least 24 hours in advance. Read all about it at www.bon-week-end-en-villes.com.

A remarkably cheap option for those travelling by car are the Accor group 'clones' in convenient but horribly uninspiring locations on town and city outskirts, usually on the main access route: with **Etap** (www.etap hotel.com) and **Formule 1** (www.hotelformule1.com) you can sleep in a soulless but functional box for €28 per double a night.

Hotels usually ask for a credit card number and occasionally written (faxed) confirmation; some require a deposit.

Refuges & Gîtes d'Étape

A refuge (mountain hut or shelter) is a bog-basic cabin established along trails in uninhabited mountainous areas and operated by national park authorities, Club Alpin Français (CAF; p950) or other private organisations. Refuges are marked on hiking and climbing maps. A bunk in the dorm costs €10 to €20 a night. Advance reservations and a weather check are essential before setting out.

Gîtes d'étape, better equipped and more comfortable than refuges (some even have showers), are situated in less remote areas, often villages. Gîtes de France (p947) publishes an annual guide, Gîtes d'Étapes et de Séjour (€10).

Rental Accommodation

Renting a furnished studio, apartment or villa can be an economical alternative for stays of a few days or more, plus it gives you the opportunity to live as a local. Cleaning, linen rental and electricity fees usually cost extra.

In rural areas, Gîtes de France (p947) handles some of the most charming gîtes ruraux (self-contained holiday cottages) up for rental grabs; drool over the best of the bunch in its annual catalogue *Gîtes de Charme* (€20). As with urban accommodation, weekly rates vary enormously depending on geographic location, size and comfort – anything from €250 to €2500 a week.

Finding an apartment for a long-term rental can be gruelling. Landlords usually require substantial proof of financial responsibility and sufficient funds in France; many ask for a *caution* (guarantee) and a hefty deposit.

Classified ads appear in **De Particulier à Particulier** (www.pap.fr) and **La Centrale des Particuliers** (www.lacentrale.fr in French), both published Thursday and sold at newsstands. **FUSAC** (p946) also has short- and long-term apartment ads.

For the best selection of apartments outside Paris it's best to be on-site. Check places like bars and *tabacs* for free local newspapers (named after the number of the *département*) with classifieds listings.

ACTIVITIES

From the peaks, rivers and canyons of the Alps to the mountains and volcanic peaks of the Massif Central – not to mention 3000km of coastline stretching from the Med to the Dover Straits – France lends itself to exhilarating outdoor adventures by the mountain load.

See the individual destinations for details and check with local and regional tourist offices and websites for information on local activities, clubs and companies.

Some hostels, for example those run by the Fédération Unie des Auberges de Jeunesse (FUAJ; opposite), offer week-long sports-driven *stages* (courses).

Adventure Sports

Be it canyoning, diving, ice-driving or kite-surfing (on snow or water!), France sets hearts soaring. In larger cities and picturesque places like the Côte d'Azur and the Alps, local companies offer all kinds of high-adrenaline pursuits; see regional chapters for details.

Adventures in *alpinisme* (mountaineering), *escalade* (rock climbing), *escalade de glace* (ice climbing) and other alpine activities with a professional guide can be arranged through the Club Alpin Français (p950).

Deltaplane (hang-gliding) and *parapente* (paragliding) are all the rage in the Pyr-

enees, Brittany, Massif Central and Languedoc-Roussillon regions; see those chapters for details and/or contact the Nice-based **Fédération Française de Vol Libre** (☎ 04 97 03 82 82; www.ffvl.fr in French), a melting pot for regional clubs specialising in *le kite-surf* (kitesurfing), a high-flying adventure sport big around Lake Annecy (p549) and the Vercors (p566).

Vol à voile (gliding) is popular in southern France where temperatures are warmer and thermals better. Causse Méjean (p793) in Languedoc is a popular spot. The **Fédération Française de Vol à Voile** (FFVV; ☎ 01 45 44 04 78; www.ffvv.org; 29 rue de Sèvres, 6e, Paris) provides details of gliding clubs countrywide. Helicopter flights are big in the Loire Valley (p417), Burgundy (p455) and the Côte d'Azur (p865).

Speleology, the scientific study of caves, was pioneered in France and there are still some great spots for cave exploration; the CAF (p950) has information.

Cycling

The French take cycling very seriously. Whole parts of the country grind to a halt during the famous annual Tour de France (p53).

A *vélo tout-terrain* (VTT, or mountain bike) is a fantastic tool for exploring the countryside. Some GR *(grandes randonnées)* and GRP *(grandes randonnées de pays)* trails (p950) are open to mountain bikers. A *piste cyclable* is a cycling path.

Some of the best areas for cycling (with varying grades of difficulty) are around Annecy (p544) and Chambéry (p549) in the Alps and throughout the Pyrenees (p710). In southwestern France (p609), the Dordogne and Quercy offer a vast network of scenic, tranquil roads for pedal-powered tourists. The Loire Valley (p417), the Lubéron in Provence (p858) and coastal regions like Brittany, Normandy and the Atlantic coast offer a wealth of easier (flatter) options.

For maps, see p959. Lonely Planet's *Cycling France* includes essential maps, advice, directions, and technical tips. For information on transporting your bicycle and bike rental, see p976. Details on places that rent out bikes and all the accessories – helmet, kid's seat, etc – appear in each city or town listing under Getting Around.

DIRECTORY

SKIING SUPERLATIVES

France can claim a fair few superlatives in the world of skiing.

- The world's largest ski area is Les Portes du Soleil (p542), northwest of Chamonix.

- France's longest vertical drop (2500m) is at Les Arcs (p555), near Bourg St-Maurice.

- Europe's highest resort is Val Thorens (2300m), west of Méribel (p554).

- Europe's largest skiable glacier, which measures almost 200 hectares, is at Les Deux Alpes (p567) in the spectacular Parc National des Écrins.

- One of France's longest off-piste trails (20km) is the legendary Vallée Blanche (p534) at Chamonix; the longest official (groomed) one – some 16km – is black-marked La Sarenne (p569) at Alpe d'Huez.

Skiing & Snowboarding

France sports more than 400 resorts in the Alps, the Jura, the Pyrenees, the Vosges, the Massif Central and the mountains of Corsica. The season lasts from mid-December to late March or April. January and February tend to have the best overall conditions, but the slopes get very crowded during the February–March school holidays.

The Alps have some of Europe's priciest and most fashionable resorts (see p525 for the full scoop on winter and summer Alpine skiing) although smaller, low-altitude stations in the Pyrenees and the Massif Central are cheaper. Cross-country skiing is possible in high-altitude resorts but best done in the valleys; the Jura (p572) has some lovely trails.

One of the cheapest ways to ski and board is with a package deal. Thanks to budget airlines flying to/from Lyon (p516), Grenoble (p565), Chambéry (p552) and Geneva (Switzerland) though, arranging Alpine breaks independently is equally viable.

Paris-based **Ski France** (Map pp102-3; ☎ 01 47 42 23 32; www.skifrance.fr; 61 blvd Haussmann, 8e, Paris; Ⓜ Opéra) has information and an annual brochure covering more than 50 ski resorts. CAF (right) can also provide information on alpine activities.

Walking

The countryside is crisscrossed by a staggering 120,000km of *sentiers balisés* (marked walking paths), which pass through every imaginable terrain in every region of the country. No permit is needed to hike.

Probably the best known trails are the *sentiers de grande randonnée*, long-distance footpaths marked by red-and-white-striped track indicators. Some – like the GR5 which goes from the Netherlands through the French Alps to Nice – are hundreds of kilometres long.

The *grandes randonnées de pays* (GRP) trails, whose markings are yellow, are designed for intense exploration of one particular area. Other types of trails include *sentiers de promenade randonnée* (PR), walking paths marked in yellow; *drailles*, paths used by cattle to get to high-altitude summer pastures; and *chemins de halage*, canal towpaths. Shorter day-hike trails are often known as *sentiers de petites randonnées* or *sentiers de pays*.

The **Fédération Française de la Randonnée Pédestre** (FFRP; French Ramblers' Association) has an **information centre** (Map pp104-5; ☎ 01 44 89 93 93; www.ffrp.asso.fr in French; 14 rue Riquet, 19e, Paris; Ⓜ Pernety) in Paris, as does the **Club Alpin Français** (CAF; Map pp104-5; ☎ 01 53 72 87 00; www.ffcam .fr in French; 24 av de Laumière, 19e, Paris; Ⓜ Laumière).

Lonely Planet's *Walking in France* is full of lively detail and essential practical information. For details on *refuges* (mountain huts) and other overnight accommodation for walkers, such as *gîtes d'étape*, see p948. For maps, see p959.

Water Sports

France has fine and dandy beaches along all its coasts – the English Channel, the Atlantic and the Mediterranean. The beautifully sandy beaches stretching along the family-oriented Atlantic Coast (eg near La Rochelle; p662) are less crowded than their rather pebbly counterparts on the Côte d'Azur. Corsica has some magnificent spots. Brittany and the north coast are also popular, albeit cooler, beach destinations. The general public is free to use any beach not marked as private.

The best surfing in France is on the Atlantic Coast around Biarritz (p687) where waves reach heights of 4m. Windsurfing is popular wherever there's water and a breeze, and renting equipment is often possible on lakes.

White-water rafting, canoeing and kayaking are practised on many French rivers, especially in the Massif Central and the Alps. The **Fédération Française de Canoë-Kayak** (FFCK; ☎ 01 45 11 08 50; www.ffck.org in French) supplies information on canoeing and kayaking clubs around the country.

For kite-surfing see p949.

BUSINESS HOURS

French business hours are regulated by the 35 hour-week work limit. Shop hours are usually 9am or 9.30am to 7pm or 8pm, often with a midday break from noon or 1pm to 2pm or 3pm. The midday break is uncommon in Paris. French law requires that most businesses close on Sunday; exceptions include grocery stores, boulangeries, cake shops, florists and businesses catering exclusively to the tourist trade. Many close one weekday too, often Monday.

Restaurants open for lunch between noon or 12.30pm and 2pm and for dinner from 7.30pm; they are often closed on one or two days of the week. Cafés open early morning until around midnight. Bars usually open early evening and close at 1am or 2am.

National museums are closed on Tuesday and local museums are closed on Monday. In summer some open daily. Local or less famous regional museums may close at lunchtime.

Banks usually open 8am or 9am to 11.30am or 1pm and then 1.30pm or 2pm to 4.30pm or 5pm, Monday to Friday or Tuesday to Saturday. Exchange services may end half an hour before closing time.

Post offices generally open from 8.30am or 9am to 5pm or 6pm on weekdays (perhaps with a midday break) and Saturday morning from 8am to noon.

Supermarkets open Monday to Saturday usually from about 9am or 9.30am to 7pm or 8pm (plus a midday break in smaller towns); some open on Sunday morning. Small food shops may shut on Monday also, so Saturday morning may be your last chance to stock up on provisions until Tuesday. Open-air markets start at about 6am and finish at 1pm or 1.30pm. Many service stations have small groceries open 24 hours a day.

CHILDREN

Country France can be a great place for travel with children and, while big cities can be more difficult, lots of activities are on offer for *les enfants*, especially in Paris.

Practicalities

France is reasonably child-friendly, although French parents don't usually take their children to a restaurant any more

---

TOP TEN KID PLEASERS

Amusements abound for the biggest and smallest of budgets and ages. Our favourite kid-pleasers include the following:

- Marvelling at Airbus planes being assembled and docking our own space shuttle, Toulouse (p744)
- Canal cruising and hot-air ballooning, Burgundy (p457)
- Jardin du Luxembourg (p137) & Cité des Sciences et de l'Industrie, Paris (p146)
- Playing dragons and princesses around fairytale castles, the Loire Valley (p438)
- Taking an action-packed 3D trip through Digital World at cinematic theme park Futuroscope (p661)
- Lavender-field cavorting, Provence (p808)
- Volcanic Vulcania, near Clermont-Ferrand (p591)
- Riding Cap Ferret's little train from bay to beach (p687)
- Mushing with Bernard and his 40 dogs in the forested Vercors (p566)
- Fish-feeling 'n' peering at aquariums in Cherbourg (p301), St-Malo (p312), Brest (p328) and Lyon (p504)

sophisticated than a corner café. Chain restaurants like Hippopotamus and Bistro Romain are casual and serve food that most kids like; many restaurants have a children's menu. Take drinks and snacks with you on sightseeing days if you want to avoid costly stops in cafés. Picnics are a great way to feed the troops and enjoy local produce.

In Paris, weekly entertainment magazine *L'Officiel des Spectacles* (p177) advertises babysitting services *(gardes d'enfants)*. Elsewhere, tourist offices often have lists of babysitters or try www.bebe-annonce.com (in French).

Car-rental firms have children's safety seats for hire at a nominal cost; book them in advance. The same goes for highchairs and cots (cribs) – standard in midrange restaurants and hotels. The choice of baby food, infant formula, soy and cow's milk, nappies (diapers) and the like is as great in French supermarkets as it is back home, but the opening hours may be different. Run out of nappies on Saturday afternoon and you could be facing a long and messy weekend. (Should disaster strike note that in France, pharmacies – of which there is always one open for at least a few hours on a Sunday – also sell all the baby paraphernalia.)

Staying in a *chambre d'hôte* (B&B; p947) which also does *table d'hôte* is fab for families; little kids can sweetly slumber upstairs while weary parents wine and dine in peace downstairs (don't forget your baby monitor!). Fancier camping grounds have pools and facilities for kids.

Sights & Activities

Include the kids in the trip planning: Lonely Planet's *Travel with Children* is a useful info source.

Paris' narrow streets and metro stairways can be a trial, but the capital has wonderful parks with amusements and activities like pony rides and puppet shows, as well as attractions like La Villette (p145) and Disneyland Resort (p210).

Beaches are great kid-pleasers (p951), the Atlantic coast being especially popular with families. The French Alps also have lots of outdoor activities year-round, like horse riding, snow-shoeing, light hiking and biking.

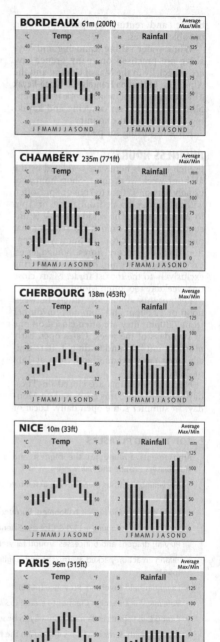

RAIN, HAIL, SNOW OR SHINE

Tune into the French weather forecast at www.meteo.fr (in French) or call one of the following:

National forecast	☎ 0 836 701 234
Regional forecasts	☎ 0 836 680 000
Département forecasts	☎ 0 836 6802 +
2-digit *département* number	
Mountain areas & snow forecasts	☎ 0 836 680 404
Marine forecast	☎ 0 836 680 808

CLIMATE

France has a temperate climate (see climate charts opposite) with mild winters, except in mountainous areas and Alsace. For climatic considerations, see p20.

COURSES

Art, food, wine, language, film – the best of France is there for the learning. The website www.edufrance.fr/en has information about higher education, and www.study abroadlinks.com can help you find specific courses and summer programmes.

Cooking

For short cooking courses and specialised sessions such as pastry making, see p86.

Language

All manner of French language courses are available in Paris and provincial towns and cities. Many also arrange accommodation. Prices and courses vary greatly and the content can often be tailored to your needs (for

a fee). Expect to pay upwards of €500 for an intensive four-week course.

The government site www.diplomatie .gouv.fr and www.europa-pages.com/france list language schools in France.

CUSTOMS

Goods brought in and out of countries within the EU incur no additional taxes, provided duty has been paid somewhere within the EU and the goods are for personal consumption. There is no longer duty-free shopping within the EU; you have to be leaving Europe.

Coming from non-EU countries, duty-free allowances (for adults) are: 200 cigarettes, 50 cigars, 1L of spirits, 2L of wine, 50ml of perfume, 250ml *eau de toilette* and other goods up to the value of €183. Anything over the limit must be declared and paid for.

DANGERS & ANNOYANCES

France is generally a safe place in which to live and travel, but crime has risen dramatically in the last few years. Property crime is a major problem but it is extremely unlikely that you will be physically assaulted while walking down the street. Always check your government's travel advisory warnings. Advice for women is on p967.

Hunters

The hunting season is September to February. If you see signs reading *'chasseurs'* or *'chasse gardée'* strung up or tacked to trees, think twice about wandering into the area.

CINQ OF THE BEST

Amboise Eurocentre (☎ 02 47 23 10 60; www.eurocentres.com; 9 Mail St-Thomas, Amboise) Small, well-organised school in the charming Loire Valley.

Alliance Française (☎ 01 42 84 90 00; www.alliancefr.org; 101 blvd Raspail, 6e, Paris; Ⓜ St-Placide) Venerable institution for the worldwide promotion of French language and civilisation offering various classes including literature, cooking or business French.

Centre de Linguistique Appliquée de Besançon (☎ 03 81 66 52 00; http://cla.univ-fcomte.fr; 6 rue Gabriel Plançon, Besançon) One of France's largest language schools, in a beautiful city, with a variety of language and culture classes.

Centre Méditerranéen d'Études Françaises (☎ 04 93 78 21 59; www.monte-carlo.mc/centremed; chemin des Oliviers, BP 38, Cap-Ail) French Riviera school dating to 1952 with open-air amphitheatre designed by Jean Cocteau overlooking the sparkling blue Med.

Université de Provence (☎ 04 42 95 32 17; www.up.univ-mrs.fr/wscefee; 29 av Robert Schumann, Aix-en-Provence) A hot choice in lovely Aix: academic language and methodology courses, as well as writing workshops and basic French classes.

As well as millions of wild animals, fifty French hunters die each year after being shot by other hunters. Hunting is traditional and commonplace in all rural areas in France, especially Les Vosges, Sologne, the southwest and the Baie de Somme.

Natural Dangers

There are powerful tides and strong undertows along the Atlantic Coast, Brittany and Normandy. Only swim in *zones de baignade surveillée* (beaches monitored by life guards). Many people drown each year, especially on the Atlantic Coast. Be aware of tide times, and if sleeping on a beach, always ensure you are above the high tidemark.

Thunderstorms in the mountains and hot southern plains can be extremely sudden and violent. So check the weather report before you set out on a long walk and be very well prepared if you're heading into the high country of the Alps or Pyrenees.

Avalanches are an enormous natural danger in the French Alps; see p525 for details.

Smoking

Laws banning smoking in public places do exist, but no-one pays much attention to them. In restaurants, diners will often smoke in nonsmoking sections – and the waiter will happily bring them an ashtray.

Strikes & Riots

France is the only European country in which public workers enjoy an unlimited right to strike and avail themselves of it with carefree abandon. Aggrieved truck drivers have been known to block motorways and farmers agitating for more government support occasionally dump tonnes of produce on major arteries.

Getting caught in one of the 'social dialogues' that characterise labour relations in France can put a serious crimp in your travel plans. It's best to leave some wriggle room in your schedule, particularly around the departure times.

Street riots such as those that struck dozens of towns and cities countrywide in November 2005 (p54) are by no means the norm.

Theft

The problems you're most likely to encounter are thefts (which can be aggressive), mainly pick-pocketing/bag snatching, especially in dense crowds and public places. A common ploy is for one person to distract you while another steals your wallet, camera or bag. Tired tourists on the train from the airport are a frequent target for thieves. Big cities – notably Paris, Marseille and Nice – have high crime levels. Particularly in Paris, museums are beset by organised gangs of seemingly innocuous children who are actually trained pickpockets.

There's no need whatsoever to travel in fear. Taking a few simple precautions will minimise travellers' chances of being ripped off.

- Photocopy your passport, credit cards, plane tickets, driver's licence, and other important documents – leave one copy at home and keep another one with you, separate from the originals.
- A hidden money belt remains the safest way to carry money and valuable documents.
- Take only what you need on busy sightseeing days: use the hotel/hostel safe.
- On trains, keep bags as close as possible: the luggage racks (if in use) at the ends of the carriage are an easy target for thieves; in sleeping compartments, lock the door carefully at night.
- Be especially vigilant at train stations, airports, fast-food outlets, cinemas, outdoor cafés and beaches and on public transport.

TRAVELLING BY CAR

Car thefts and break-ins to parked cars are a frequent problem. Gangs cruise seemingly tranquil tourist areas for unattended vehicles. Foreign or out-of-town plates and rental stickers are a dead giveaway and will be targeted. Never, ever leave anything valuable (or otherwise) inside your car. Hiding your bags in the trunk is risky; in hatchbacks it is an open invitation to theft.

Aggressive theft from cars stopped at red lights is occasionally a problem, especially in the south (specifically in and around Marseille and sometimes Nice) at intersections and motorway exits. Thieves are usually on motorcycle. Your car should have autolocking doors (and air-conditioning).

DISCOUNT CARDS
Camping Card International
The Camping Card International is a form of ID that can be used instead of a passport when checking into a camping ground and includes third-party insurance. As a result, many camping grounds offer a small discount if you sign in with one. CCIs are issued by automobile associations, camping federations and, sometimes, on the spot at camping grounds.

Seniors Cards
Senior citizens are entitled to discounts in France on things like public transport, museum admission fees and public theatres. The **SNCF** (☎ 0 892 353 535; www.sncf.com) issues the **Carte Senior** (€50; www.senior-sncf.com) to those aged more than 60 years, which gives reductions of 25% to 50% on train tickets, valid for one year.

Student, Youth & Teachers' Cards
These cards, available from student unions and travel agencies, yield fantastic discounts, but not all places will recognise them. An **International Student Identity Card** (ISIC; €12) can pay for itself through half-price admissions, discounted air and ferry tickets, and cheap meals in student cafeterias. Many places stipulate a maximum age, usually 24 or 25. For more details, check the **International Student Travel Confederation** (ISTC; www.istc.org) website.

If you're under 26 but not a student, you can apply for an **International Youth Travel Card** (IYTC or Go25, €12), also issued by ISTC, which entitles you to many of the same discounts as an ISIC. The European Youth Card (Euro<26 card) offers similar discounts across 35 European countries for nonstudents under 26; see www.euro26.org.

Teachers, professional artists, museum conservators and certain categories of students are admitted to some museums free. Bring along proof of affiliation – for example, an International Teacher Identity Card (ITIC).

EMBASSIES & CONSULATES
French Embassies & Consulates
France's diplomatic and consular representatives abroad are listed on the website www.france.diplomatie.fr. For some of the following countries, additional consulates exist.

Australia Canberra (☎ 02-6216 0100; www.ambafrance-au.org; 6 Perth Av, Yarralumla, ACT 2600); Sydney Consulate (☎ 02-9261 5779; www.consulfrance-sydney.org; Level 26, St Martin's Tower, 31 Market St, Sydney, NSW 2000)
Belgium Brussels (☎ 02-548 8700; www.ambafrance-be.org; 65 rue Ducale, Brussels 1000); Brussels Consulate (☎ 02-229 8500; www.consulfrance-bruxelles.org; 12a place de Louvain, Brussels 1000)
Canada Ottawa (☎ 613-789 1795; www.ambafrance-ca.org; 42 Sussex Drive, Ottawa, Ont K1M 2C9); Toronto Consulate (☎ 416-925 8041; www.consulfrance-toronto.org; 2 Bloor Est, Suite 2200, Toronto M4W 1A8)
Germany Berlin (☎ 030-590 039 000; www.botschaft-frankreich.de; Pariser Platz 5, Berlin 10117); Munich Consulate (☎ 089-419 4110; www.consulfrance-munich.de; Heimeranstrasse 31, 3rd floor, Munich 80339)
Ireland Dublin (☎ 01-277 5000; www.ambafrance-ie.org; 36 Ailesbury Rd, Dublin 4)
Italy Rome (☎ 06-686 011; www.ambafrance-it.org; Piazza Farnese 67, 00186 Rome)
Netherlands The Hague (☎ 070-312 5800; www.ambafrance-nl.org; Smidsplein 1, 2514 BT Den Haag); Amsterdam Consulate (☎ 020-530 6969; www.consulfrance-amsterdam.org; Vijzelgracht 2, 1017 HR Amsterdam)
New Zealand Wellington (☎ 04-384 2555; www.ambafrance-nz.org; 13th fl, Rural Bank Building, 34-42 Manners St, PO Box 11-343, Wellington)
South Africa Pretoria Embassy Apr-Jan (☎ 012-425 1600; www.ambafrance-za.org; 250 Melk St, New Muckleneuk, 0181 Pretoria); Pretoria Embassy Feb-Mar (☎ 021-422 1338; www.ambafrance-za.org; 78 Queen Victoria St, 8001 Cape Town)
Spain Madrid (☎ 91-423 8900; www.ambafrance-es.org; Calle de Salustiano Olozaga 9, 28001 Madrid); Barcelona Consulate (☎ 93-270 3000; www.consulfrance-barcelone.org; Ronda Universitat 22, 08007 Barcelona)
Switzerland Bern (☎ 031-359 2111; www.ambafrance-ch.org; Schosshaldenstrasse 46, 3006); Zürich Consulate (☎ 01-268 8585; www.consulatfrance-zurich.org; Signaustrasse 1, 8008 Zürich)
UK London Embassy (☎ 020-7073 1000; www.ambafrance-uk.org; 58 Knightsbridge, London SW1X 7JT); London Consulate (☎ 020-7073 1200; www.consulfrance-londres.org; 21 Cromwell Rd, London SW7 2EN); London Visa Section (☎ 020-7073 1250; 6A Cromwell Place, London SW7 2EW)
USA Washington (☎ 202-944 6000; www.ambafrance-us.org; 4101 Reservoir Rd NW, Washington, DC 20007); New York Consulate (☎ 212-606 3600; www.consulfrance-new york.org; 934 Fifth Av, New York, NY 10021)

Embassies & Consulates in France
All foreign embassies are in Paris. Many countries – including the UK, USA, Canada, Japan and most European countries –

also have consulates in other major cities such as Nice, Marseille and Lyon. To find an embassy or consulate not listed here, look up *'ambassades et consulats'* under Paris in the super user-friendly **Pages Jaunes** (Yellow Pages; www.pagesjaunes.fr).

Australia Paris (Map pp108-9; ☎ 01 40 59 33 00; www .austgov.fr; 4 rue Jean Rey, 15e; Ⓜ Bir Hakeim)

Belgium Paris (Map pp102-3; ☎ 01 44 09 39 39; www .diplomatie.be/paris; 9 rue de Tilsitt, 17e; Ⓜ Charles de Gaulle-Étoile)

Canada Paris (Map pp102-3; ☎ 01 44 43 29 00; www .amb-canada.fr; 35 av Montaigne, 8e; Ⓜ Franklin D Roosevelt); Nice consulate (☎ 04 93 92 93 22; 10 rue Lamartine)

Germany Paris embassy (Map pp102-3; ☎ 01 53 83 45 00; www.amb-allemagne.fr; 13-15 av Franklin D Roosevelt, 8e; Ⓜ Franklin D Roosevelt); Paris consulate (Map pp102-3; ☎ 01 53 83 46 40; 28 rue Marbeau, 16e; Ⓜ Porte Maillot)

Ireland Paris (Map pp102-3; ☎ 01 44 17 67 00; www .embassyofirelandparis.com; 12 av Foch/4 rue Rude, 16e; Ⓜ Argentine)

Italy Paris Embassy (Map pp108-9; ☎ 01 49 54 03 00; www.amb-italie.fr; 51 rue de Varenne, 7e; Ⓜ Rue du Bac); Paris Consulate (Map pp98-9; ☎ 01 44 30 47 00; 5 blvd Émile Augier, 16e; Ⓜ La Muette)

Japan Paris (Map pp102-3; ☎ 01 48 88 62 00; www.amb -japon.fr; 7 av Hoche, 8e; Ⓜ Courcelles)

Netherlands Paris (Map pp108-9; ☎ 01 40 62 33 00; www.amb-pays-bas.fr; 7 rue Eblé, 7e; Ⓜ St-François Xavier)

New Zealand Paris (Map pp102-3; ☎ 01 45 01 43 43; www.nzembassy.com; 7ter rue Léonard de Vinci, 16e; Ⓜ Victor Hugo)

South Africa Paris (Map pp108-9; ☎ 01 53 59 23 23; www.afriquesud.net; 59 quai d'Orsay, 7e; Ⓜ Invalides)

Spain Paris (Map pp102-3; ☎ 01 44 43 18 00; www.amb -espagne.fr; 22 av Marceau, 8e; Ⓜ Alma Marceau)

Switzerland Paris Embassy (Map pp108-9; ☎ 01 49 55 67 00; www.amb-suisse.fr; 142 rue de Grenelle, 7e; Ⓜ Varenne); Paris Consulate (☎ 01 45 66 00 80; 13 rue du Laos, 15e)

UK Paris (Map pp102-3; ☎ 01 44 51 31 00; www.amb -grandebretagne.fr; 35 rue du Faubourg St-Honoré, 8e; Ⓜ Concorde); Paris Visa Section (Map pp102-3; ☎ 01 44 51 31 01; 16 rue d'Anjou, 8e; Ⓜ Madeleine); Paris Consulate (Map pp102-3; ☎ 01 44 51 31 02; 18bis rue d'Anjou, 8e; Ⓜ Madeleine); Marseille Consulate (☎ 04 91 15 72 10; 24 av du Prado)

USA Paris Embassy (Map pp102-3; ☎ 01 43 12 22 22; www.amb-usa.fr; 2 av Gabriel, 8e; Ⓜ Concorde); Paris Consulate (Map pp102-3; ☎ 01 43 12 47 08; 2 rue St-Florentin, 1er; Ⓜ Concorde); Nice Consulate (Map pp868-9; ☎ 04 93 88 89 55; 7 av Gustave V); Marseille consulate (☎ 04 91 54 92 00; place Varian Fry)

FESTIVALS & EVENTS

Most French cities and towns have at least one major music, dance, theatre, cinema or art festival each year. Villages hold *foires* (fairs) and fêtes (festivals) to honour anything from a local saint to the year's garlic crop. We list these important annual events in city and town sections. During big events, towns get extremely busy and accommodation can get booked out in advance.

FEBRUARY

Carnaval de Nice (p875; www.nicecarnaval.com) Merrymaking on the Riviera during France's largest street carnival, Nice.

MARCH & APRIL

Feria Pascale (p835; www.feriaarles.com in French) In the ancient *arène* of Arles, this Feria kicks off the bullfight season with much cavorting and merriment (Easter).

MAY & JUNE

May Day Across France, the workers' day is celebrated with trade union parades and diverse protests. People give each other *muguet* (lilies of the valley) for good luck. No-one works – except waiters and *muguet* sellers (1 May).

International Film Festival (p884; www.festival -cannes.com) The stars walk the red carpet at Cannes, the epitome of see-and-be-seen cinema events in Europe (mid-May).

Fête de la Musique (www.fetedelamusique.culture.fr) Bands, orchestras, crooners, buskers and spectators take to the streets for this national celebration of music (21 June).

Pélerinage des Gitans (p840; www.gitans.fr in French) Twice a year *gitans* (Roma Gitano people) from all over Europe make their way to the Camargue for a flamboyant street fiesta of music, dancing and dipping their toes in the sea (24-25 May & 22 October).

JULY

National Day Fireworks, parades and all-round hoo-ha to commemorate the storming of the Bastille in 1789, symbol of the French Revolution (14 July).

Gay Pride (www.gaypride.fr in French) Effervescent street parades, performances and parties throughout Paris and other major cities (July).

Festival d'Aix-en-Provence (p827; www.festival-aix .com) Attracting the world's best classical music, opera, ballet and buskers, Aix-en-Provence is the place to be for the discerning visitor (July).

Festival d'Avignon (p842; www.festival-avignon.com) Actors, dancers and musicians flock to Avignon to perform in the official and fringe art festivals (late July & early August).

Fêtes de Bayonne (p693; www.fetes-de-bayonne.com in French) Bullfighting, cow-chasing and Basque music are the order of the day at Bayonne's biggest event (July).

Nice Jazz Festival (p875; www.nicejazzfest.com) See jazz cats and other pop, rock and world artists take over public spaces and the Roman ruins of Nice (July).

Paris Plage (p151; www.paris.fr) Flop on a sandy beach in the capital (mid-July–mid-August).

AUGUST & SEPTEMBER

Fêtes d'Arvor (p346; www.fetes-arvor.org in French) A passionate celebration of local Breton culture, this three-day fest in mid-August includes street parades, concerts and numerous *festoú noz* (night festivals).

Festival Interceltique de Lorient (p340; www.festival -interceltique.com in French) This massive event pulls hundreds of thousands of Celts to Lorient from all over Brittany and the UK for a massive celebration of their shared Celtic culture (August).

Festival du Cinema Américain (p286; www.festival -deauville.com) The silver screen comes to the seaside at this celebration of American cinema in Deauville (September).

Braderie de Lille (p232) Three days of madness and mussel-munching as this colossal flea market engulfs the city with antiques, handicrafts and bric-a-brac (early September).

Journées du Patrimoine Countrywide festivals which see some of France's most important public buildings unusually open to the public (21 September).

DECEMBER

Fête des Lumières (p508) France's biggest and best sound-and-light show transforms Lyon (8 December).

Christmas Markets Alsace (p381) Alsace is the place to be for a traditional-style festive season, with world-famous Christmas markets, decorations and celebrations.

FOOD

Our special food and drink chapter (p73) bursts with succulent information about French gastronomy.

In this book, we usually indicate the price of *menus* (two- or three-course set menus); ordering *à la carte* (from the menu) is generally more expensive.

Budget eating options are usually more casual places with simple meals under €10 or set *menus* for €8 to €15. Midrange restaurants have more atmosphere and offer seasonal specialities and fine local flavours, with meals/*menus* from €20/15–30 (less at lunchtime). In France, 'top-end' restaurants are superb establishments with impeccable quality and service and meals from €50 and *menus* costing anything upwards of €30.

GAY & LESBIAN TRAVELLERS

France is one of Europe's most liberal countries when it comes to homosexuality, in part because of the long French tradition of public tolerance towards people who choose not to live by conventional social codes. Paris has been a thriving gay and lesbian centre since the late 1970s. Montpellier, Lyon, Toulouse, Bordeaux and many other towns also have significant active communities. Attitudes towards homosexuality tend to become more conservative in the countryside and villages. France's lesbian scene is much less public than its gay male counterpart and is centred mainly on women's cafés and bars, which are the best places to find information.

Gay Pride marches (opposite) are held in major French cities in July.

Internet Resources

Gayscape (www.gayscape.com) Hundreds of links to gay- and lesbian-related sites.

France Queer Resources Directory (www.france.qrd .org in French) Directory for gay and lesbian travellers.

CitéGAY (http://citegay.fr in French) Lowdown on gay events.

Organisations

Most major gay and lesbian organisations are based in Paris:

Act Up-Paris (Map pp114-15; ☎ 01 48 06 13 89; www .actupparis.org in French; 45 rue Sedaine, 11e; Ⓜ Voltaire) This organisation represents France's gay community and can provide advice and information. Its free monthly newsletter *Action* is useful.

AIDES (☎ 0 820 160 120, 01 53 27 63 00; www.aides .org in French; 119 rue des Pyrénées, 20e; Ⓜ Jourdain) France-wide organisation fighting against HIV/AIDS and for the rights and wellbeing of those affected.

Association des Médecins Gais (☎ 01 48 05 81 71; www.medecins-gays.org in French; 3 rue Keller, 11e; Ⓜ Ledru Rollin) Association of Gay Doctors, based in the Centre Gai et Lesbien; deals with gay-related health issues.

DIRECTORY

Centre Gai et Lesbien (CGL; Map pp114-15; ☎ 01 43 57 21 47; www.cglparis.org in French; 3 rue Keller, 11e; Ⓜ Ledru Rollin) A welcome and support centre. Friday is women's (only) day, with meetings, debates, outings and workshops.

SIDA-info service (☎ 0 800 840 800; www.sida-info-service.org in French) HIV/AIDS information service that helps with anonymous testing and treatment; advice available in foreign languages.

Publications

Damron Women's Traveller (www.damron.com) English-language travel guide for lesbians.

Guide Gai Pied (www.gayvox.com/guide3 in French) Online travel guide.

Lesbia (www.lesbiamag.com) Women's monthly with articles and useful listings.

Spartacus International Gay Guide (www.spartacusworld.com) Annual English-language travel guide for men.

Têtu (www.tetu.com in French) A glossy men's monthly with a France-wide directory of bars, clubs and hotels. Listings for lesbians too.

HOLIDAYS

The following *jours fériés* (public holidays) are observed in France:

New Year's Day (Jour de l'An) 1 January – parties in larger cities; fireworks are subdued by international standards.

Easter Sunday & Monday (Pâques & lundi de Pâques) Late March/April.

May Day (Fête du Travail) 1 May – traditional parades.

Victoire 1945 8 May – the Allied victory in Europe that ended WWII.

Ascension Thursday (Ascension) May – celebrated on the 40th day after Easter.

Pentecost/Whit Sunday & Whit Monday (Pentecôte & lundi de Pentecôte) Mid-May to mid-June – celebrated on the seventh Sunday after Easter.

Bastille Day/National Day (Fête Nationale) 14 July – the national holiday.

Assumption Day (Assomption) 15 August.

All Saints' Day (Toussaint) 1 November.

Remembrance Day (L'onze novembre) 11 November – celebrates the WWI armistice.

Christmas (Noël) 25 December.

The following are not public holidays in France: Shrove Tuesday (Mardi Gras; the first day of Lent); Maundy (or Holy) Thursday and Good Friday just before Easter; and Boxing Day (26 December). Good Friday and Boxing Day, however, are public holidays in Alsace.

INSURANCE

See p984 for health insurance and p979 for car insurance.

Travel Insurance

A travel-insurance policy to cover theft, loss and medical problems is a good idea. Some policies specifically exclude dangerous activities, which can include scuba diving, motorcycling, even trekking.

You may prefer a policy that pays doctors or hospitals directly rather than you having to pay on the spot and claim later. If you have to claim later ensure you keep all documentation. Check that the policy covers ambulances or an emergency flight home. Paying for your airline ticket with a credit card often provides limited travel accident insurance. Ask your credit card company what it's prepared to cover.

INTERNET ACCESS

Thing are improving rapidly for wi-fi users: wireless access points have been installed in major airports, hotel chains and cafés, while many tourist offices tout wi-fi hot spots allowing laptop owners to hook up for free; the website www.laptopkfe.com (in French) lists 58 wi-fi cafés in the capital alone. Check sites like www.wifinder.com for access points countrywide.

Internet cafés are fairly abundant in towns and cities countrywide; they are listed under Information in the regional chapters. You'll pay €3 to €5 per hour. In museums, tourist offices and other public buildings, you may come across phonecard-operated Borne Internet terminals (www.netanoo .com in French); a 120-unit France Telecom *télécarte* (€15) gets you two hours online.

Roughly 1000 post offices across France are equipped with a Cyberposte, a card-

---

WHAT THE COMPUTER ICON MEANS

Throughout this guide, only accommodation providers that have an actual computer that guests can use to access the internet are flagged with a computer icon like this: 🖳 ; those that are wi-fi friendly, but have no computer, are not. Paris is the exception: places offering wi-fi only as well as places offering the use of a computer receive the 🖳 icon in Paris.

operated internet terminal for public use. Access cards cost €7.60 for the first hour and €4.60 for a one-hour recharge. Find a list of Cyberposte-equipped post offices at www.cyberposte.com (in French).

If you're using your laptop, check that it is compatible with the 220V current in France; if not you will need a converter. You'll also need a telephone plug adaptor. Having a reputable global modem will prevent access problems that can occur with PC-card modems brought from home.

If you do not go with a global Internet Service Provider (ISP; such as AOL) make sure your ISP has a dial-up number in France. Local ISPs Free (www.free.com), Tiscali (www.tiscali.fr) and Orange (www .orange.fr in French) have cheap or free short-term membership (look out for free trial membership CD-ROMs).

For useful travel websites, see p22.

LEGAL MATTERS
Drugs & Alcohol
Contrary to popular belief, French law does not distinguish between 'hard' and 'soft' drugs. The penalty for any personal use of *stupéfiants* (including cannabis, amphetamines, ecstasy, heroin etc) can be a one-year jail sentence and a €4000-odd fine, but depending on the circumstances it might be anything from a stern word to a compulsory rehab programme.

Importing, possessing, selling or buying drugs can get you up to 10 years' prison and massive fines. Police have been searching chartered coaches, cars and train passengers for drugs just because they are coming from Amsterdam.

Being drunk in public places is punishable with a €150 fine.

LEGAL AGE

- Driving: 18
- Buying alcohol: 16
- Age of majority: 18
- Age of sexual consent for everyone: 15
- Age considered minor under anti-child-pornography and child-prostitution laws: 18
- Voting: 18

Police
French police have wide powers of search and seizure, and can ask you to prove your identity at any time – whether or not there is plausible cause. Foreigners must be able to prove their legal status in France (eg passport, visa, residency permit) without delay.

If the police stop you for any reason, be polite and remain calm. Verbally (and of course physically) abusing a police officer can carry a hefty fine, and even imprisonment. You may refuse to sign a police statement, and have the right to ask for a copy.

People who are arrested are considered innocent until proven guilty, but can be held in custody until trial. The website www.service-public.fr has information on legal rights.

French police are very strict about security. Do not leave baggage unattended at airports or train stations: suspicious objects will be summarily blown up.

LOCAL GOVERNMENT
Metropolitan France (the mainland and Corsica) is made up of 22 *régions* (regions) which are subdivided into 96 *départements* (departments), which are subdivided into 324 *arrondissements*, which are in turn subdivided into *cantons*, which are subdivided into 36,400 *communes* (communes).

Invariably named after a geographic feature, *départements* tout a two-digit code (see the map, p960) which make up the first two digits of the area's postcode.

MAPS
France's two major map producers are Michelin (www.viamichelin.com) and Institut Géographique National (IGN; www .ign.fr), which also publishes themed maps about wine, museums and so on. Their websites list sales outlets, including the **Espace IGN** (Map pp102-3; ☎ 01 43 98 85 12; 107 rue la Boétie, Paris 8e; Ⓜ Franklin D Roosevelt) – definitely the capital's best bet for a full selection of maps. Countrywide, road and city maps are available at Maisons de la Presse (large newsagencies), bookshops, tourist offices and newspaper kiosks.

The book in your hand contains more than 135 city and town maps. Lonely Planet publishes a laminated *Paris City Map*.

RÉGIONS & DÉPARTEMENTS

0 —— 200 km
0 —— 120 miles

ALSACE
67 Bas-Rhin
68 Haut-Rhin

AQUITAINE
24 Dordogne
33 Gironde
40 Landes
47 Lot-et-Garonne
64 Pyrénées-Atlantiques

AUVERGNE
03 Allier
15 Cantal
43 Haute-Loire
63 Puy-de-Dôme

BASSE-NORMANDIE
14 Calvados
50 Manche
61 Orne

BRETAGNE
22 Côtes d'Armor
29 Finistère
35 Ille-et-Vilaine
56 Morbihan

BOURGOGNE
21 Côte d'Or
58 Nièvre
71 Saône-et-Loire
89 Yonne

CENTRE
18 Cher
28 Eure-et-Loir
36 Indre
37 Indre-et-Loire
41 Loir-et-Cher
45 Loiret

CHAMPAGNE-ARDENNE
08 Ardennes
10 Aube
51 Marne
52 Haute-Marne

CORSE
2A Corse-du-Sud
2B Haute-Corse

FRANCHE-COMTÉ
25 Doubs
39 Jura
70 Haute-Saône
90 Territoire de Belfort

HAUTE-NORMANDIE
27 Eure
76 Seine-Maritime

LANGUEDOC-ROUSSILLON
11 Aude
30 Gard
34 Hérault
48 Lozère
66 Pyrénées-Orientales

LIMOUSIN
19 Corrèze
23 Creuse
87 Haute-Vienne

LORRAINE
54 Meurthe-et-Moselle
55 Meuse
57 Moselle
88 Vosges

MIDI-PYRÉNÉES
09 Ariège
12 Aveyron
31 Haute-Garonne
32 Gers
46 Lot
65 Hautes-Pyrénées
81 Tarn
82 Tarn-et-Garonne

NORD-PAS-DE-CALAIS
59 Nord
62 Pas-de-Calais

PAYS DE LA LOIRE
44 Loire-Atlantique
49 Maine-et-Loire
53 Mayenne
72 Sarthe
85 Vendée

PICARDIE
02 Aisne
60 Oise
80 Somme

POITOU-CHARENTES
16 Charente
17 Charente-Maritime
79 Deux-Sèvres
86 Vienne

PROVENCE-ALPES-CÔTE D'AZUR
04 Alpes-de-Haute-Provence
05 Hautes-Alpes
06 Alpes-Maritimes
13 Bouches-du-Rhône
83 Var
84 Vaucluse

RÉGION PARISIENNE
75 Ville de Paris
77 Yvelines
78 Seine-et-Marne
91 Essonne
92 Haut-de-Seine
93 Seine-St-Denis
94 Val-de-Marne
95 Val-d'Oise

RHÔNE-ALPES
01 Ain
07 Ardèche
26 Drôme
38 Isère
42 Loire
69 Rhône
73 Savoie
74 Haute-Savoie

—·—· International Boundary
——— Région Boundary
‖‖‖ Département Boundary

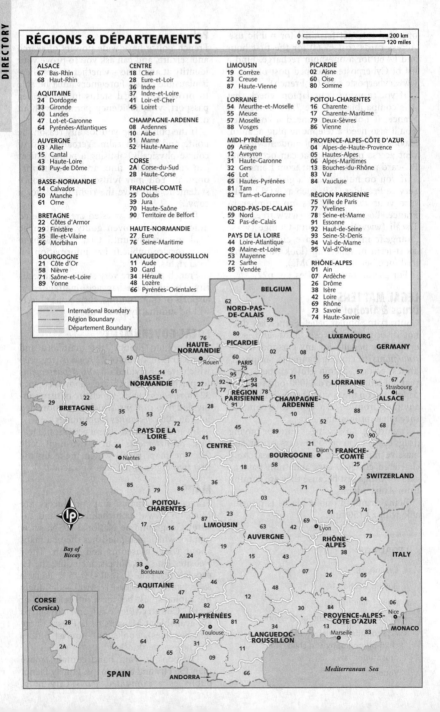

Michelin has excellent road maps of cities and towns, which are coordinated with its travel guides. Plans-Guides Blay offers orange-jacketed street maps of 125 French cities and towns.

For road maps, *Environs de Paris* (Michelin) will help you with the very confusing drive out of Paris. Michelin's *Atlas Routier France,* which covers the whole country in 1:200,000 scale (1cm = 2km), is the best for long-distance driving. *France – Routes, Autoroutes* (IGN) is also good for plotting cross-country travel.

If you're concentrating on just a few regions, it is easier and more cost effective to buy Michelin's yellow-jacketed regional fold-out maps or IGN's fold-out regional maps.

Walking & Cycling

The FFRP (p950) publishes some 120 topoguides – map-equipped booklets about major trails – in French. Local organisations also produce topoguides with details on trail conditions, flora and fauna, mountain shelters and so on; ask local bookshops and tourist offices. English translations of a handful of topoguides are available through UK publisher Robertson McCarta.

IGN has a variety of great maps and topoguides that are ideal for hiking, biking or walking. Its specialised *cyclocartes* (cycle maps) show dozens of suggested bicycle tours around France. Didier et Richard publishes a series of 1:50,000-scale trail maps, perfect for walking or for off-road cycling.

MONEY
ATMs

Automated Teller Machines (ATMs) – known as *distributeurs automatiques de billets* (DAB) or *points d'argent* in French – are the cheapest and most convenient way to get money. ATMs are situated in all major cities and towns (though are more scarce in rural areas), and usually offer an excellent exchange rate. Many are linked to the international Cirrus, Plus and Maestro networks so that you can draw on your home account. Cash advances on credit cards are also possible at ATMs, but incur charges.

Cash

You always get a better exchange rate in-country, though it's a good idea to arrive with enough local currency to take a taxi to a hotel if you have to. Carry as little cash as possible while travelling around.

Credit & Debit Cards

Credit and debit cards are convenient and relatively secure and will usually offer a better exchange rate than travellers cheques or cash exchanges.

Visa and MasterCard (Access or Eurocard) are widely accepted; AmEx cards are useful at more upmarket establishments, and allow you to get cash at AmEx offices and certain ATMs. In general, all three cards can be used in shops and supermarkets, for train travel, car rentals and motorway tolls and for cash advances. Don't assume that you can pay for a meal or a budget hotel with a credit card – inquire first.

Getting a cash advance against a credit card is usually an expensive way to go because fees (and interest) are charged. Debit card fees are usually much less.

For lost cards, these numbers operate 24 hours:

AmEx (☎ 01 47 77 72 00) AmEx offices arrange on-the-spot replacements.
Diners Club (☎ 0 810 314 159)
MasterCard, Eurocard & Access (Eurocard France; ☎ 0 800 901 387, 01 45 67 84 84)
Visa (Carte Bleue; ☎ 0 800 902 033)

Currency

The euro has been the official currency of France since 2002. One euro is divided into 100 cents or centimes, with one, two, five, 10, 20 and 50 centime coins. Notes come in denominations of five, 10, 20, 50, 100, 200 and 500 euros. Euro notes and coins issued in France are valid throughout the other 11 countries in the euro zone: Austria, Belgium, Finland, Germany, Greece, Ireland, Italy, Luxembourg, the Netherlands, Portugal and Spain.

Exchange rates are given on the inside front cover of this book and a guide to costs can be found on p20.

Moneychangers

Commercial banks usually charge a stiff €3 to €5 per foreign-currency transaction (eg BNP Paribas charges 3.3% or a minimum of about €4). Rates offered vary, so it pays to compare. Banks charge roughly €3.40 to €5.30 to cash travellers cheques (eg BNP

Paribas charges 1.5%, with a minimum charge of €4).

In Paris, exchange bureaux (bureaux de change) are faster and easier, open longer hours and give better rates than most banks. In general, post offices in Paris can offer the best exchange rates and accept banknotes in various currencies as well as American Express and Visa travellers cheques. The commission for travellers cheques is 1.5% (minimum about €4).

Familiarise yourself with rates offered by the post office and compare them with those at exchange bureaux. On small transactions, even exchange places with less-than-optimal rates may leave you with more euros in your pocket.

Travellers Cheques

The most flexible travellers cheques are those issued by AmEx (in US dollars or euros) and Visa (in euros) because they can be changed at many post offices as well as commercial banks and exchange bureaux. Note that you will not be able to pay most merchants with travellers cheques directly. AmEx offices don't charge commission on their own travellers cheques.

For lost travellers cheques call **AmEx** (☎ 0 800 908 600) and **Thomas Cook** (☎ 0 800 908 330) for replacements. For Visa and Mastercard, see p961.

PHOTOGRAPHY & VIDEO

Photo development in France is generally of excellent quality but it is expensive compared with the cost of developing photos in many other countries. Expect to pay around €0.25/0.20 per print for up to 50/100 digital prints (tirages numériques). Transferring your images onto a CD usually costs an additional €5, although some photo shops throw a CD in for free.

Colour-print film remains widely available but costly, so stock up ahead of time. For slides (diapositives), avoid Kodachrome: it's difficult to process quickly in France and may not be handled correctly. You can easily obtain video cartridges in large towns, but it's good to come with a few from home.

A good companion when on the road is Travel Photography: A Guide to Taking Better Pictures, by travel photographer Richard I'Anson.

POST

French post offices are flagged with a yellow or brown sign reading 'La Poste'. Since La Poste also has banking, finance and bill-paying functions, queues can be long, but there are automatic machines for postage.

Postal Rates

Domestic letters of up to 20g cost €0.53. For international post, there are three different zones: a letter/package under 20g/2kg costs €0.55/12.50 to Zone A (EU, Switzerland, Iceland, Norway); €0.75/14 to Zone B (the rest of Europe and Africa); and €0.90/20.50 to Zone C (North and South America, Asia & Middle East, Australasia).

Rates are automatically given for prioritaire (priority post, reasonably fast); specify if you want the cheaper tarif écopli or service d'économique (economy post, snail slow).

Worldwide express-mail delivery, called **Chronopost** (☎ 0 825 801 801; www.fr.chronopost .com), costs a fortune and is not as rapid as advertised.

All mail to France must include the five-digit postcode, which begins with the two-digit number of the département (postcodes are listed under the main city or town headings in this book). The notation 'CEDEX' after a town name simply means that mail sent to that address is collected at the post office, rather than delivered to the door.

Receiving Mail

Picking up poste-restante mail costs €0.50; you must show your passport or national ID card. Mail will be kept 15 days. Poste-restante mail not addressed to a particular branch goes to the city's main post office.

SHOPPING

France is renowned for its luxury goods, particularly haute couture, high-quality clothing accessories (eg Hermès scarves), lingerie, perfume and cosmetics. Such goods may not be any cheaper here than at home. For our favourites shopping sprees, see p21.

Sale periods (soldes) – held for three weeks in January and July – can be a gold mine for fashion finds. The fashion- and budget-conscious should also look out for the words degriffés (cut price; usually the labels have been cut out) or dépôt-vente (ex-showroom garments sold at steep mark-downs).

For local crafts and art go directly to the source. In Brittany, look for colourful Quimper *faïence* (earthenware) and in Normandy pick up unique Rouen *faïence* or intricate lace from Alençon. Other good buys include crystal and glassware from Baccarat in southern Lorraine or enamel and porcelain from Limoges in Limousin.

Even though wines originating from Bordeaux, Burgundy, Alsace and Champagne are available everywhere, you'll get a better selection in a local wine shop. Local brandies make good souvenirs since they may not be available in your home country, such as cognacs (from Cognac!) and Calvados, *pommeau* or Fécamp Bénédictine (from Normandy). Corsicans sell unusual liqueurs in local markets and Charentes is the place to pick up Pineau de Charentes.

Goodies that travel well include macaroons from St-Émilion, *calissons* from Aix-en-Provence and candied fruit from Nice. For information on local shopping options, see the individual towns and cities.

Non-EU residents can get a rebate of some of the 19.6% value-added tax (VAT) for large purchases, including when several different purchases are made in the one department store. There are forms to fill out in-store which must be shown, with the purchases, upon departure.

SOLO TRAVELLERS

Travelling solo in France is easy and rewarding. Many hotels charge the same price for single and double rooms, and if singles are available, they tend not to be significantly cheaper. It is quite common for people to eat in restaurants alone in France, particularly at lunch, when menus are also considerably cheaper – you might want to make that the main meal of the day. Women shouldn't encounter any particular problems travelling alone in France, but may come across some minor hassles.

TELEPHONE

A quarter of a century ago, France had one of the worst telephone systems in Western Europe. But thanks to massive investment, the country now has one of the most modern and sophisticated telecommunications systems in the world.

Domestic Dialling

France has five telephone dialling areas. You dial the same 10-digit number no matter where you are, but it is cheaper to call locally.

For France Telecom's directory inquiries *(services des renseignements)*, dial ☎ 118 712. Not all operators speak English.

Domestic rates are billed at about €0.20 for three minutes with a *télécarte*, but numbers starting with 08 are more expensive.

Emergency numbers (see inside the front cover) and 0 800 numbers can be dialled free from public and private telephones.

International Dialling

To call France from another country, dial your country's international access code, then dial ☎ 33 (France's country code), then omit the 0 at the beginning of the 10-digit local number.

To call someone outside France, dial the international access code (☎ 00), the country code, the area code (without the initial zero if there is one) and the local number. International Direct Dial (IDD) calls to almost anywhere in the world can be placed from public telephones.

To make a reverse-charges (collect) call *(en PCV)* or a person-to-person call *(avec préavis)*, dial ☎ 3123 or ☎ 0 800 990 011 (for the USA and Canada) and ☎ 0 800 990 061 for Australia.

For directory inquiries for numbers outside France, dial ☎ 3212. The cost is about €2.50.

Hotels, *gîtes,* hostels and pensions are free to meter their calls as they like. The surcharge is usually around €0.30 per minute but can be higher.

Phonecards offer much, much better international rates than those offered by Country Direct services (which allow you to be billed by the long-distance carrier you use at home).

Mobile Phones

France uses GSM 900/1800, which is compatible with the rest of Europe and Australia but not with the North American GSM 1900 or the totally different system in Japan (though some North Americans have GSM 1900/900 phones that do work here). If you have a GSM phone, check with your service provider about using it in France, and beware of calls being routed internationally (very expensive for a 'local' call).

The three major providers of mobile phone access are **SFR** (☎ 0 800 106 000; www.sfr.com), **Bouygues** (☎ 0 810 630 100; www.bouygtel.com) and France Telecom's **Orange** (☎ 0 800 830 800; www.orange.fr). If you already have a compatible phone, you can buy a 'prepay' phone kit which gives you a SIM card with a mobile phone number and a set number of calls. When these run out you can purchase a recharge card at most *tabacs* (tobacconists). You can also get similar 'prepay' deals that include the phone itself.

Mobile phone numbers in France always begin with 06. France has a 'caller pays' system which means that you do not pay to receive a call on your mobile phone unless it is an international call.

Public Phones & Telephone Cards

Public telephones in France are card-operated. Most have a button displaying two flags which you push for explanations in English.

Phonecards *(télécartes)* cost €8 or €15 at post offices, *tabacs* and anywhere that you see a blue sticker reading *'télécarte en vente ici'*. There are two kinds of phonecards, *cartes à puce* (cards with a magnetic chip, that are inserted chip-first into public phones) and *cartes à code* (that you can use from public or private phones by dialling the free access number and then punching in the card's scratch-off code).

Your choice of card will depend on your needs. France Telecom offers different cards suited to national and international dialling. For help in English on all France Telecom's services, see www.francetelecom.com or call ☎ 0 800 364 775.

A whole bevy of other cards are available for cheap international calls, especially in Paris, and most can be used elsewhere in Europe. Compare advertised rates, or ask which one is best for the place you're calling.

TIME

France uses the 24hr clock and is on Central European Time, which is one hour ahead of GMT/UTC. During daylight-saving time, which runs from the last Sunday in March to the last Sunday in October, France is two hours ahead of GMT/UTC.

Without taking daylight-saving time into account, when it's noon in Paris it's 3am in San Francisco, 6am in New York, 11am in London, 8pm in Tokyo, 9pm in Sydney and 11pm in Auckland. The Australian eastern coast is between eight and 10 hours ahead of France. Refer to the time-zone world map on pp1022–3 for additional data.

TOURIST INFORMATION
Local Tourist Offices

Almost every city, town, village and hamlet has an *office de tourisme* (a tourist office run by some unit of local government) or *syndicat d'initiative* (a tourist office run by an organisation of local merchants). Both are excellent resources for local maps, accommodation, restaurants and activities. Very few of their many, many brochures are on display. If you have a special interest, such as walking tours, cycling or wine sampling, ask about it. Some have limited currency-exchange services. Many tourist offices make local hotel reservations, sometimes for a small fee.

Regional tourist offices *(CRTs; comités régionaux de tourisme)* and their websites are great for regionwide information; click through to the CRT website you desire from www.fncrt.com (in French).

Details on local tourist offices appear under Information at the beginning of each city, town or area listing.

Tourist Offices Abroad

French government tourist offices (usually called Maisons de la France) provide every imaginable sort of tourist information on France. The general website www.franceguide.com lets you access the site for your home country.

Australia (☎ 02-9231 5244; info.au@franceguide.com; Level 13, 25 Bligh St, Sydney, NSW 2000)
Belgium (☎ 0902 88 025; info.be@franceguide.com; av de la Toison d'Or 21, 1050 Brussels)
Canada (☎ 514-288 2026; canada@franceguide.com; 1981 McGill College Av, Suite 490, Montreal, Que H3A 2W9)
Germany (☎ 09001 57 00 25; info.de@franceguide.com; Zeppelinallee 37, 60325 Frankfurt)
Ireland (☎ 01560 235 235; info.ie@franceguide.com; 10 Suffolk St, Dublin 2)
Italy (☎ 899 199 072; info.it@franceguide.com; Via Larga 7, 20122 Milan)
Netherlands (☎ 0900 11 22 332; info.nl@franceguide.com; Prinsengracht 670, 1017 KX Amsterdam)

Spain Madrid (☎ 807 117 181; info.es@franceguide.com;
Plaza de España 18, 28008 Madrid); Barcelona (☎ 807 117
181; Fontanella 21-23, 08010 Barcelona)
Switzerland Zurich (☎ 01-211 3085; info.
ch@franceguide.com; Rennweg 42, 8023 Zurich); Geneva
(☎ 0900 900 699; c/o SNCF-Rail Europe, 2 rue de
Lausanne 11, 1201 Geneva)
UK (☎ 09068 244 123; info.uk@franceguide.com; 178
Piccadilly, London W1V 9AL)
USA New York (☎ 514-288 1904; info.us@franceguide
.com; 444 Madison Av, 10022 New York); Los Angeles
(☎ 310-271 6665; info.losangeles@franceguide.com;
9454 Wilshire Blvd, Ste 715, Beverly Hills, CA 90212-2967)

TRAVELLERS WITH DISABILITIES

France is not well equipped for *handicapés*
(people with disabilities): kerb ramps are
few and far between; older public facilities
and budget hotels often lack lifts; cobblestone streets are a nightmare to navigate in
a wheelchair; and the Paris metro, most of it
built decades ago, is hopeless. But disabled
people who would like to visit France can
overcome these difficulties.

The French government has increased
efforts to improve conditions for disabled
people, creating the national *Tourisme et
Handicap* rating. This classification is given
to sites, restaurants and hotels that meet
strict requirements and standards: different symbols indicate whether establishments have access for people with physical,
mental, hearing and/or seeing disabilities.
Places marked *Accessible normes handicapés* subscribe to certain access standards,
but the rating is not officially verified.

With the SNCF, a traveller in a wheelchair (*fauteuil roulant*) can travel in TGV
and regular trains (make a reservation at
least a few hours before departure). Details are available in SNCF's booklet *Guide
du Voyageur à Mobilité Réduite*. You can
also contact **SNCF Accessibilité** (☎ 0 800 154 753)
which has information (French only) for
travellers with physical, sight and hearing
disabilities.

Tourism for All (☎ 0845-124 9971; outside UK
☎ 44-208 760 0027; www.tourismforall.info) is a UK-
based group that publishes an information
guide to France which can be ordered on-
line. **Access Project** (www.accessproject-phsp.org; 39
Bradley Gardens, West Ealing, London W13 8HE) publishes a dated but useful guide, *Access in
Paris*. The **Paris Tourist Office** (p124) also has
information and brochures.

If you speak French, specialised guidebooks
with comprehensive information for travellers with physical disabilities include Bernic's
Guide Rousseau and the Petit Futé *Handigu-
ide*. They're available at major bookshops.
The portal www.jaccede.com (in French) has
loads of information and reviews.

Michelin's *Guide Rouge* indicates those
hotels with lifts and facilities for disabled
people, while Gîtes de France (see p947)
can provide a list of *gîtes ruraux* and *chambres d'hôtes* with disabled access.

Specialised travel agencies abroad include US-based **Wheels Up!** (☎ 1-888 38 4335;
www.wheelsup.com) and UK-based **Access Travel**
(☎ 01942 888 844; www.access-travel.co.uk).

Organisations
Association des Paralysées de France (AFP; ☎ 01
40 78 69 00; www.apf.asso.fr in French; 17 blvd Auguste
Blanqui, 13e, Paris) National organisation; regional
branches have local information.
**Groupement pour l'Insertion des Personnes
Handicapées Physiques** (☎ 01 43 95 66 36; www
.gihpnational.org in French; 10 rue Georges de Porto Riche,
14e, Paris; Ⓜ Porte d'Orléans) Provides vehicles outfitted
for people in wheelchairs; the national office will put you
in touch with local services.

VISAS
For up-to-date details on visa requirements,
see Foreign Affairs Ministry site www.diplo
matie.gouv.fr and click 'Going to France'.

EU nationals and citizens of Switzerland,
Iceland and Norway need only a passport
or national identity card in order to enter
France and stay in the country. However,
for nationals of the 10 new (in 2004) member countries, conditions for living and
working in France vary from those for nationals of the original countries.

Citizens of Australia, the USA, Canada,
New Zealand, Japan and Israel do not need
visas to visit France as tourists for up to
three months; the same goes for citizens of
EU candidate countries (except Turkey).

As a practical matter, if you don't need a
visa to visit France, no-one is likely to kick
you out after three months. The unspoken
policy seems to be that you can stay and
spend your money in France as long as you
don't try to work, apply for social services
or commit a crime. Being in a *situation ir-
régulière* is nonetheless illegal, and without
a *carte de séjour* you can face real problems

DIRECTORY

renting an apartment, opening a bank account and so on.

Carte de Séjour

Once issued with a long-stay visa, you can apply for a *carte de séjour* (residence permit), and are usually required to do so within eight days of arrival in France. Make sure you have all the necessary documents before you arrive. EU passport-holders and citizens of Switzerland, Iceland and Norway do not need a *carte de séjour* to reside or work in France. Other foreign nationals must contact the local *préfecture* (prefecture) or *commissariat* (police station) for their permits.

Students of all nationalities must apply for a *carte de séjour* at the **Centre des Étudiants Étrangers** (Map pp108-9; 13 rue Miollis, 15e, Paris; (M) Cambronne or Ségur) in Paris. For more information see the Paris Préfecture website (www.prefecture -police-paris.interieur.gouv.fr in French).

Long-Stay & Student Visas

This is the first step if you'd like to work or study in France, or stay for more than three months. Long-stay and student visas will allow you to enter France and apply for a *carte de séjour* (residency permit). Contact the French embassy or consulate nearest your residence, and begin your application well in advance as it can take months. Tourist visas cannot be changed into student visas after arrival. However, short-term visas are available for students sitting university-entrance exams in France.

Tourist (Schengen) Visa

Those not exempt need a Schengen Visa, named after the agreement that abolished passport controls between Austria, Belgium, Denmark, Finland, France, Germany, Greece, Iceland, Italy, Luxembourg, the Netherlands, Norway, Portugal, Spain and Sweden. It allows unlimited travel throughout the entire zone within a 90-day period.

Applications are made with the consulate of the country you are entering first, or that will be your main destination. Among other things, you will need medical insurance and proof of sufficient funds to support yourself. See www.eurovisa.com for information.

If you enter France overland, it is unlikely that your visa will be checked at the border, but major problems can arise if you don't have one later on.

Tourist visas *cannot* be extended except in emergencies (such as medical problems); you'll need to leave and reapply from outside France when your visa expires.

Working Holiday Visa

Citizens of Australia, Canada, Japan and New Zealand aged between 18 and 29 years (inclusive) are eligible for a one-year, multiple-entry Working Holiday Visa, allowing combined tourism and employment in France. You have to apply to the embassy or consulate in your home country, and must prove you have a return ticket, insurance and sufficient funding to get through the start of your stay. Make sure you get in early with the application, as quotas apply.

Once you have arrived in France and have found a job, you must apply for a Temporary Work Permit (*autorisation provisoire de travail*), which will only be valid for the duration of the employment offered. The permit can be renewed under the same conditions up to the limit of the authorised length of stay.

The idea is to supplement your funds with unskilled work. You can also study or do training programmes, but the visa cannot be extended, nor turned into a student visa. After one year you *must* go home.

Once in France, the Centre d'Information et Documentation Jeunesse (CIDJ; opposite) can help with information.

VOLUNTEERING

Websites like www.volunteerabroad.com and www.transitionsabroad.com throw up a colourful cross-section of volunteering opportunities in France: helping out on an organic farm in Provence, restoring century-old castle walls, landscaping public parks or digging ponds to attract amphibians are but some of the golden opportunities awaiting those keen to volunteer their skills and services.

Interesting volunteer organisations include the following:

Rempart (☎ 01 42 71 96 55; www.rempart.com; 1 rue des Guillemites, 4e, Paris) Brings together 170 organisations countrywide committed to preserving France's religious, civil, industrial and natural heritage.

Volunteer for Peace (☎ 802 259 2759; www.vfp.org; 1034 Tiffany Rd, Belmont, Vermont 05730 USA) Volunteer for one of 400-odd work camps a year; grass-roots projects cover social work, environment, education and the arts.

WWOOF (www.wwoof.org; PO Box 2675, Lewes BN7 1RB, UK) Work on a small farm or other organic venture (harvesting chestnuts, renovating an abandoned olive farm near Nice etc); volunteer opportunities in France are listed online by *département*.

WOMEN TRAVELLERS

For information about health issues while travelling, see p986.

Safety Precautions

Women tend to attract more unwanted attention than men, but need not walk around in fear; people are rarely assaulted on the street. Be aware of your surroundings and of situations that could be dangerous: empty streets, lonely beaches, dark corners of large train stations. Using metros late at night is generally OK, as stations are rarely deserted, but there are a few to avoid (see p125).

In some places women may have to deal with what might be called low-intensity sexual harassment: 'playful' comments and invitations that can become overbearing or aggressive, and which some women find threatening or offensive. Remain polite and keep your distance. Hearing a foreign accent may provoke further unwanted attention.

Be alert to vibes in cheap hotels, sometimes staffed by apparently unattached men who may pay far more attention to your comings and goings than you would like. Change hotels if you feel uncomfortable, or allude to the imminent arrival of your husband (whether you have one or not).

On overnight trains, you may prefer to ask (when reserving) if there's a women's compartment available. If your compartment companions are overly attentive, don't hesitate to ask the conductor for a change of compartment. Second-class sleeping cars offer greater security than a couchette.

You can reach France's national **rape crisis hotline** (☎ 0 800 059 595) toll-free from any telephone without using a phonecard. It's run by a Paris women's organisation, **Viols Femmes Informations** (Map pp98-9; www.cfcv.asso.fr in French; 9 villa d'Este, 13e, Paris; Ⓜ Porte d'Ivry).

The **police** (☎ 17) will take you to the hospital if you have been attacked or injured.

Organisations

Women-only **Association Maison des Femmes de Paris** (Map pp120-1; ☎ 01 43 43 41 13; http://maisondes femmes.free.fr in French; 163 rue de Charenton, 12e, Paris; Ⓜ Reuilly Diderot) is the main meeting place for women of all ages and nationalities.

WORK

EU nationals have an automatic right to work in France. Non-EU citizens will need to apply for a work permit, for which they first need a *carte de séjour* or a Working Holiday Visa (see opposite), as well as a written promise of employment. Permits can be refused on the grounds of high local unemployment.

Working 'in the black' (that is, without documents) is difficult and risky for non-EU travellers. The only instance in which the government turns a blind eye to workers without documents is during fruit harvests (mid-May to November) and the *vendange* (grape harvest; mid-September to mid- or late October).

Even with a permit, employers generally must pay 'foreigner fees' for non-EU employees, and must prove that the job cannot be done by an EU citizen (there are some exceptions for artists and computing and translation specialists). So getting qualified work is extremely difficult.

Summer and casual work is more flexible, and can be found in restaurants, bars and hotels (particularly in the Alps during the winter skiing season; for bar work www.moun taintradingco.com is a good place to start). Teaching English is another option, either for a company or through private lessons.

Au-pair work is also very popular and can be done legally even by non-EU citizens, but they must contact the placement agency from their home country at least three months in advance.

The administration for freelance workers (*travailleurs indépendants*) is **URSSAF** (☎ 01 49 20 10 10; www.urssaf.fr in French). Organising freelance work status is complicated; it is highly advisable to consult a local attorney experienced in immigration matters.

France's national employment service, the **Agence National pour l'Emploi** (ANPE; www .anpe.fr in French) has offices throughout France; the website has job listings.

In Paris the **Centre d'Information et de Documentation Jeunesse** (CIDJ; Map pp108-9; ☎ 01 44 49 12 00; www.cidj.com; 101 quai Branly, 15e; Ⓜ Champ de Mars) provides all sorts of information for young people, on jobs (including seasonal summer jobs), housing and education and more.

Paris-based mag *FUSAC* (p946) advertises jobs for English speakers, including au-pair work, babysitting and language teaching.

Transport

CONTENTS

GETTING THERE & AWAY

ENTERING THE COUNTRY

European integration means you'll usually cross fluidly between France and other EU countries without passing through customs or border checkpoints. If you're arriving from a non-EU country, you will have to show your passport (and your visa permit if you need one – see p965) or your identity card if you're an EU citizen, and clear customs.

AIR

Budget carriers account for an increasing share of the flights into France, particularly from other European destinations, resulting in competitive fares from many major airlines.

Airports

France has two major international airports in Paris: **Roissy Charles de Gaulle** (CDG; ☎ 01 48 62 12 12) and **Orly** (ORY; ☎ 01 49 75 15 15), both run by **Aéroports de Paris** (☎ 01 43 35 70 00; www.adp.fr in French). For details on these airports see p187.

A number of other airports have significant international services (mainly within Europe):

Bordeaux (BOD; ☎ 05 56 34 50 50; www.bordeaux .aeroport.fr)
Lille (LIL; ☎ 03 20 49 68 68; www.lille.aeroport.fr)
Lyon (LYS; ☎ 0 826 800 826; www.lyon.aeroport.fr)
Marseille (MRS; ☎ 04 42 14 14 14; www.mrsairport .com)
Nantes (NTE; ☎ 02 40 84 80 00; www.nantes .aeroport.fr)
Nice (NCE; ☎ 0 820 423 333; www.nice.aeroport.fr)
Strasbourg (SXB; ☎ 03 88 64 67 67; www.strasbourg .aeroport.fr)
Toulouse (TLS; ☎ 0 825 380 000; www.toulouse .aeroport.fr)

Some carriers use small provincial airports for flights to/from the UK, continental Europe and, sometimes, North Africa. Smaller airports with international flights include Biarritz, Brest, Caen, Carcassonne, Deauville, Dinard, La Rochelle, Metz–Nancy-Lorraine, Montpellier, Mulhouse–Basel (EuroAirport), Nîmes, Poitiers, Rennes, St-Étienne, and Tours. Relevant local airports are listed in destination chapters.

Airlines

Most of the world's major carriers serve Paris at the very least. (See p971 for budget airlines.)

Aer Lingus (☎ 01 70 20 00 72; www.aerlingus.com; airline code EI; hub Dublin)
Air Canada (☎ 0 825 880 881; www.aircanada.ca; airline code AC; hub Toronto)
Air France (☎ 0 820 820 820; www.airfrance.com; airline code AF; hub Paris)

THINGS CHANGE...

The information in this chapter is particularly vulnerable to change. Check directly with the transport provider or a travel agent to make sure you understand how a fare (and ticket you may buy) works, and be aware of the security requirements for international travel. Shop carefully. The details given in this chapter should be regarded as pointers and are not a substitute for your own careful, up-to-date research.

Alitalia (☎ 0 820 315 315; www.alitalia.com; airline code AZ; hub Rome)

American Airlines (☎ 0 810 872 872; www.american airlines.com; airline code AA; hub Dallas)

Austrian Airlines (☎ 0 820 816 816; www.austrianair lines.com; airline code OS; hub Vienna)

BMI BritishMidland (☎ 01 41 91 87 04; www.flybmi .com; airline code BD; hub London)

British Airways (☎ 0 825 825 400; www.britishairways .com; airline code BA; hub London)

Cathay Pacific (☎ 01 41 43 75 75; www.cathaypacific .com; airline code CX; hub Hong Kong)

Continental Airlines (☎ 01 42 99 09 09; www.contin ental.com; airline code CO; hub Houston)

Iberia (☎ 0 820 075 075; www.iberia.com; airline code IB; hub Madrid)

KLM (☎ 0 890 710 710; www.klm.com; airline code KL; hub Amsterdam)

Lufthansa (☎ 0 820 020 030; www.lufthansa.com; airline code LH; hub Frankfurt)

Olympic Airlines (☎ 01 44 94 58 58; www.olympicair lines.com; airline code OA; hub Athens)

Qantas Airways (☎ 0 820 820 500; www.qantas.com; airline code QF; hub Sydney)

Singapore Airlines (☎ 01 53 65 79 01; www.singapore air.com; airline code SQ; hub Singapore)

South African Airways (☎ 01 55 61 94 55; www.flysaa .com; airline code SA; hub Johannesburg)

Thai Airways International (☎ 01 44 20 70 15; www.thaiair.com; airline code TG; hub Bangkok)

Tickets

Calling around, checking internet sites, comparing the airline and travel agent prices, and scouring major newspapers' travel sections can result in significant savings on your air ticket. Start early: some of the cheapest tickets have to be bought well in advance.

Prices quoted in this section (and most advertised fares) don't include taxes, which will add from around €25 for the shortest hauls to upwards of €120 for long-haul flights – check with the airlines or a travel agent.

Well-known travel agents are listed later in this chapter under individual country headings. Good online agencies for cheap tickets:

Cheap Tickets (www.cheaptickets.com)

Expedia (www.expedia.com) Partnered with French discount site, Anyway (www.anyway.com in French)

Last Minute (www.lastminute.com)

Priceline (www.priceline.com) Bid for a ticket online (USA departures only).

Travel Cuts (www.travelcuts.com)

Travelocity (UK www.travelocity.co.uk; US www.travelo city.com; Asia-Pacific www.zuji.com.au)

Budget carriers such as Ryanair and easyJet have mushroomed across Europe – see p971.

TRANSPORT

CLIMATE CHANGE & TRAVEL

Climate change is a serious threat to the ecosystems that humans rely upon, and air travel is the fastest-growing contributor to the problem. Lonely Planet regards travel, overall, as a global benefit, but believes we all have a responsibility to limit our personal impact on global warming.

Flying and Climate Change

Pretty much every form of motorised travel generates CO2 (the main cause of human-induced climate change) but planes are far and away the worst offenders, not just because of the sheer distances they allow us to travel, but because they release greenhouse gases high into the atmosphere. The statistics are frightening: two people taking a return flight between Europe and the US will contribute as much to climate change as an average household's gas and electricity consumption over a whole year.

Carbon Offset Schemes

Climatecare.org and other websites use 'carbon calculators' that allow travellers to offset the level of greenhouse gases they are responsible for with financial contributions to sustainable travel schemes that reduce global warming – including projects in India, Honduras, Kazakhstan and Uganda.

Lonely Planet, together with Rough Guides and other concerned partners in the travel industry, support the carbon offset scheme run by climatecare.org. Lonely Planet offsets all of its staff and author travel.

For more information check out our website: www.lonelyplanet.com.

Australia & New Zealand

Many major airlines fly to Europe from Melbourne or Sydney. Return tickets to Paris range from A$1950 to A$3000. Fares from Perth are about A$200 cheaper. A return flight from Auckland will cost from around NZ$2300. A round-the-world (RTW) ticket may work out cheaper than a return fare.

Major dealers in cheap fares, with many branches:

Flight Centre (Australia ☎ 13 11 31, New Zealand ☎ 0800 24 35 44; www.flightcentre.com)

STA Travel (Australia ☎ 1300 733 035; www.statravel.com.au; New Zealand ☎ 0508 782 872; www.statravel.co.nz)

Canada

From Toronto or Montreal, return flights on Air Canada to Paris are available from about C$750 in low season; prices are around C$200 to C$300 more from Vancouver. **Travel CUTS** (☎ 1 888 359 2887; www.travelcuts.com) has branches across Canada. **Transat** (www.transat.com) offers travel services and operates low-cost flights between Canada and Europe. **Zoom Airlines** (www.flyzoom.com) is a popular Canadian budget airline serving France.

Continental Europe

Most European airlines fly into Paris. Air France offers competitive fares on most of its routes, and often good discounts for young people, seniors and couples (married or legally cohabiting). Local travel agencies and online ticket sites follow.

DENMARK

Kilroy Travels (☎ 70 80 80 15; www.kilroytravels.com; Skindergade 28, Copenhagen)

STA Travel (☎ 33 14 15 01; www.statravel.dk; Fiolstraede 18, Copenhagen)

GERMANY

STA Travel (☎ 030-310 00 40; www.statravel.de; Hardenbergstrasse 9, Berlin)

ITALY

CTS Viaggi (☎ 06 462 043 116; www.cts.it; Via Genova, Rome)

THE NETHERLANDS

Kilroy Travels (☎ 020-524 51 00; www.kilroytravels.com; Singel 413, Amsterdam)

ISSTA (☎ 020-618 80 31; 226 Overtoom Straat, Amsterdam)

NORWAY

Kilroy Travels (☎ 81 55 96 33; www.kilroytravels.com; Nedre Slottsgate 23, Oslo)

STA Travel (☎ 81 55 99 05; www.statravel.no; Karl Johansgate 8, Oslo)

SWEDEN

Kilroy Travels (☎ 0771-545769; www.kilroytravels.com; Kungsgatan 4, Stockholm)

STA Travel (☎ 0771-611010; www.statravel.se; Kungsgatan 30, Stockholm)

SWITZERLAND

STA Travel (☎ 022-818 02 00; www.statravel.ch; rue de Rive 10, Geneva)

The UK & Ireland

Low-cost carriers offer astounding rates from the UK and Ireland to destinations throughout France, especially to destinations other than Paris – see opposite. Prices vary wildly from a ridiculously low UK£23 between London and Paris. Aer Lingus flies from Dublin or Shannon to Paris for as low as €28.

Air France and British Airways link cities throughout the UK and France, fares are also often very reasonable.

Look for special deals in the travel pages of the weekend broadsheet newspapers, as well as in *Time Out*, the *Evening Standard* and the free magazine *TNT*.

Recommended travel agencies and online ticket sites:

Cheap Flights (www.cheapflights.co.uk)

Cheapest Flights (www.cheapestflights.co.uk)

Online Travel (www.onlinetravel.com) Good deals on flights from more than a dozen British cities.

STA Travel (☎ 0870 1600 599; www.statravel.co.uk)

Usit Voyages (Republic of Ireland ☎ 01 602 1904, Northern Ireland ☎ 028 90 327 111; www.usitworld.com)

The USA

The flight options across the North Atlantic, the world's busiest long-haul air corridor, are bewildering. A return flight from New York to Paris costs around US$400/850 in low/high season, but lower promotional fares are often available. Tickets from the west coast are US$150 to US$250 higher.

In addition to major newspapers, independent periodicals such as the *San Francisco Guardian* and New York's *Village Voice* are good places to check for low fares.

DISCOUNT DESTINATIONS

Low-budget, no-frills carriers allow you to travel around Europe for often unbeatable rates. Tickets usually need to be bought using a credit card online or by phone. These companies and their flight routes change regularly, so check the websites to see who's going where. Budget carriers often have limited luggage allowances and charge steeply for excess baggage.

Some of the cut-price companies serving various destinations in France at the time of publication follow.

Atlas Blue (www.atlas-blue.com) Moroccan budget airline.
bmiBaby (www.bmibaby.com) Budget subsidiary of BMI; generally offers good ticket flexibility.
easyJet (www.easyjet.com) UK budget carrier; also has domestic flights within France.
Flybe (www.flybe.com) Regional UK budget carrier.
Flyglobespan (www.flyglobespan.com) Scottish budget carrier.
Hapag-Lloyd Express (www.hlx.com) German budget airline.
Ryanair (www.ryanair.com) Extensive destinations throughout France.
Transavia (www.transavia.com) Budget subsidiary of Dutch airline KLM.
Virgin Express (www.virgin-express.com) Brussels-based budget carrier.

There are a number of local travel agencies and online ticket sites:
Expedia (www.expedia.com)
Flight Centre (www.flightcentre.com)
STA Travel (www.statravel.com)
Travelocity (www.travelocity.com)

STAND-BY & COURIER FLIGHTS

Other rock-bottom options for discounted – and even free – air travel include charter, stand-by and courier flights.
Airhitch (www.airhitch.org)
Courier Travel (www.couriertravel.org)
International Association of Air Travel Couriers (www.courier.org)

LAND

If you are doing a lot of travel around Europe, look for discount bus and train passes, which can be conveniently combined with discount air fares.

Bus

Buses are slower and less comfortable than trains, but are cheaper, especially if you qualify for discount rates (people under 26, over 60, teachers and students) or get one of the reduced-price fares sometimes offered.

BUSABOUT

From May to October, the London-based **Busabout** (UK ☎ 0207 950 1661; www.busabout.com) links 36 European cities in 11 countries. Within France the buses stop at Bordeaux, Tours, Paris, Avignon and Nice. There are two types of pass available:

Flexipass Allows for a set number of stops within the entire six-month operating season; additional stops can be purchased onboard, but each sector can only be travelled once. A six-stop pass costs UK£225; additional stops cost UK£25.
Busabout Pass Allows for use of the bus system within a regional 'loop' throughout the whole six-month season. France is situated in the Western loop and the pass costs UK£275.

You can hop on or off the buses as you like (buses generally travel every other day within the season), and can pay extra for additional links to places like Croatia and Morocco. Onboard guides can take care of hostel reservations or you can book ahead online – in many places the pick-up/drop-off point is a central hostel. For information and bookings, check out Busabout's website.

EUROLINES

Eurolines (☎ 0 892 899 091; www.eurolines.com) groups together 32 European coach operators and links points all across Europe as well as Morocco and Russia. Eurolines' website provides links to each national company's site and gives detailed information about fares, routes, bookings and special promotional fares. You can usually make your booking online. Return tickets cost about 20% less than two one-way fares. In summer it's best to make reservations at least two working days in advance. The main French hub is Paris. Sample one-way fares:

TRANSPORT

Route	Full Fare (€)	Duration (hr)
Paris–Prague	68	16
Paris–Brussels	21	3¾
Bordeaux–Barcelona	57	10¼
Nice–Rome	55	10
Lyon–Berlin	88	20

The Eurolines Travel Pass is a flexible ticket that allows for unlimited travel within a set period between 40 European cities, including several in France – but you are not able to visit other cities en route. A 15-/30-day pass during high season (June to September) costs €329/439 for adults and €279/359 for youth (under 26) fares. Mid-season fares cost €229/319 for adults and €199/259 for youth fares, and low-season fares cost €199/299 for adults and €169/229 for youth fares.

INTERCARS

French coach company **Intercars** (☎ 08 92 89 80 80; www.intercars.fr in French) links France with cities throughout Europe, notably Eastern Europe and Russia. The office in **Paris** (☎ 01 49 03 40 63; paris@intercars.fr; 139bis rue de Vaugirard, 15e; Ⓜ Falguière) links with European destinations such as Prague (€56, 16 hours) and Warsaw (€90, 28 hours). From **Lyon** (☎ 04 78 37 20 80; lyon@intercars.fr; Perrache bus station) you can reach Naples, Porto, Minsk or Zagreb. From **Nice** (☎ 04 93 80 08 70; nice@intercars.fr; Nice bus station) you can reach San Sebastian, Casablanca and Venice.

You can reserve by emailing the agency closest to your place of departure.

Car & Motorcycle

Arriving in France by car is easy to do. At some border points you may be asked for passport or identity card (your driver's licence will not be sufficient ID). Police searches are not uncommon for vehicles entering France, particularly from Spain and Belgium (via which drugs from Morocco or the Netherlands can enter France). See p977 for details about driving in France.

EUROTUNNEL

The Channel Tunnel, inaugurated in 1994, is the first dry-land link between England and France since the Ice Age.

High-speed **Eurotunnel shuttle trains** (UK ☎ 0870 5353 535, France ☎ 03 21 00 61 00; www.euro tunnel.com) whisk cars, motorcycles and coaches from Folkestone through the Channel Tunnel to Coquelles, 5km southwest of Calais, in air-conditioned and sound-proofed comfort. Shuttles run 24 hours a day, every day of the year, with up to five departures an hour during peak periods (one an hour from 1am to 5am). LPG and CNG tanks are not permitted, which eliminates many campers and caravans.

Prices start from UK£49 one way for a car including all passengers, unlimited luggage and taxes; discounts for advance bookings are often available on the website. The fee for a bicycle, including its rider, is UK£32 return; advance reservations are mandatory.

Train

Rail services link France with every country in Europe; schedules are available from major train stations in France and abroad. Because of different track gauges and electrification systems, you sometimes have to change trains at the border (eg when travelling to Spain). Many national rail companies are linked to Paris:

Austria (☎ 01-93 00 00; www.oebb.at)
Belgium (☎ 02-528 28.28; www.b-rail.be)
Germany (☎ 0800 1 50 70 90; www.bahn.de)
Italy (☎ 89 20 21; www.trenitalia.it)
The Netherlands (☎ 06 92 96; www.ns.nl)
Spain (☎ 902 24 02 02; www.renfe.es)
Switzerland (☎ 0900 300 300; www.sbb.ch)

The **Thalys** (www.thalys.com) service links Paris' Gare du Nord to Brussels-Midi (from €74.50, 1½ hours, 20 per day), Amsterdam CS (from €97.50, 4¼ hours, five per day) and Cologne's Hauptbahnhof (€85.50, four hours, seven per day).

You can book tickets and get information from **Rail Europe** (www.raileurope.com) up to two months ahead. In France ticketing is handled by the national train network **SNCF** (☎ 0 892 353 535; www.sncf.com). Telephone and internet bookings are possible, but SNCF won't post tickets outside France. See p983 for information about discounts.

If you like to travel in style, **Elipsos Trenhotel** (www.elipsos.com) has 'train hotels' complete with an onboard chef-staffed restaurant and luxury facilities operating between many European cities, including a number in France (domestic trips aren't possible).

The fare from Paris to Barcelona costs from €120 for a 'super reclining seat' to €353 for a grand class cabin.

A helpful resource is the information-packed website **the Man in Seat 61** (www.seat61 .com), which lists train timetables and travel tips for France and beyond.

EUROPEAN TRAIN PASSES

These discount passes are worthwhile only if you plan to travel extensively around France and other European countries by train.

A variety of **Eurail Passes** (www.eurail.com) are available to non-European residents for travel in 17 countries. For people over/under 26, 15 days' consecutive, unlimited travel costs €588/414; and five days' travel over a two-month period costs €356/249.

InterRail (www.raileurope.co.uk/inter-rail) and **Eurodomino** (www.eurodomino.com) passes are available to European residents. All are valid on the French national train network and allow unlimited travel for varying periods of time.

See p983 for discounts and passes from the SNCF and for travel within France. Eurail and some other train passes must be validated at a train station ticket window before you begin your first journey, in order to begin the period of validity.

Websites that help you work out if a pass will be economical for the itinerary you have in mind include **Railkey** (www.railkey.com).

EUROSTAR

The highly civilised **Eurostar** (France ☎ 0 892 353 539; www.voyages-sncf.com; UK ☎ 0870 5186 186; www.eurostar.com) whisks you between London and Paris in just two hours and 35 minutes. There are direct daily services between London and Ashford (Kent) and Paris, Brussels, Lille, Parc Disneyland Paris and Calais-Fréthun. A direct seasonal service operates on Saturday from London and Ashford to Avignon (July to early September). Ski trains run on Friday night and Saturday between London and Ashford and the French Alps (December to April).

Eurostar fares vary enormously. A standard 2nd-class one-way ticket from London to Paris costs UK£149; from Paris, the standard fare to London is €223.50. You'll get the best deals if you book a return journey, stay over a Saturday night, book 14 or seven days ahead, if you're under 25 or if you're a student. Student travel agencies may have youth fares not available directly from Eurostar. Eurail pass–holders receive discounts.

SEA

Tickets for ferry travel to/from the UK, the Channel Islands and Ireland are available from most travel agencies in France and the countries served. Except where noted, the prices given below are for standard one-way tickets; in some cases, return fares cost less than two one-way tickets. Prices vary greatly according to the season and the demand. There are discounts for children.

If you're travelling with a vehicle, for safety reasons you are usually denied access to it during the voyage.

The Channel Islands

Passenger-only catamarans operated by **Hugo Express** (France ☎ 02 33 61 08 88) link the Channel Islands with two small ports on the western coast of Normandy: Granville and Carteret. Both usually operate between April and September, but services vary depending on the tides, so there may be daily ferries for five days, then a short break in service. The one-way pedestrian fare is around UK£40.

Services to/from St-Malo were undergoing changes at press time; contact the St-Malo Tourist Office (p309) for updates.

Ireland

Eurail pass–holders pay 50% of the adult pedestrian fare for crossings between Ireland and France on Irish Ferries (make sure you book ahead).

Irish Ferries (Ireland ☎ 0818 300 400, France ☎ 01 43 94 46 94; www.irishferries.ie) has overnight services from Rosslare to either Cherbourg (18½ hours) or Roscoff (16 hours) every other day (three times a week from mid-September to October, with a possible break in service from November to February). A foot passenger/car and driver costs from €56/99; bicycles can be taken onboard for free. The €15 booking fee is waived if you book online.

From April to October, **Brittany Ferries** (Ireland ☎ 021-427 7801, France ☎ 0 825 828 828; www .brittany-ferries.com) runs a car ferry every Saturday from Cork (Ringaskiddy) to Roscoff

TRANSPORT

(13 hours), and every Friday in the other direction. Foot passengers pay between €146 and €180 for a bunk in an inside, two-person cabin with shower and toilet.

Italy

From late April to mid-October, the **Société Nationale Maritime Corse-Méditerranée** (SNCM; France ☎ 0 825 888 088; www.sncm.fr) has five or six car ferries per week from Marseille or Toulon to Porto Torres on the Italian island of Sardinia (Sardaigne in French). The crossing takes about 11 hours. The one-way adult pedestrian fare is around €118, plus €22 for a bunk in a shared cabin with shower and toilet.

NORTH SEA

Legend	
Fast track sections	Normal SNCF track
	TGV Nord, Thalys & Eurostar – depart from Gare du Nord
	TGV Atlantique Sud-Ouest & TGV Atlantique Ouest – depart from Gare Montparnasse
	TGV Sud-Est & TGV Midi-Mediterranée – depart from Gare de Lyon
	TGV Est Européen – depart from Gare de l'Est (scheduled to open from mid 2007 onwards)

PARIS DEPARTURE STATIONS

Gare du Nord
Gare de l'Est
Gare de Lyon
Gare d'Austerlitz
Gare Montparnasse
Gare St-Lazare

Several ferry companies ply the waters between Corsica and Italy. For details, see p916.

North Africa
SNCM (see opposite) and **Compagnie Tunisienne de Navigation** (CTN; www.ctn.com.tn) link Marseille with the Tunisian capital, Tunis (about 24 hours, three or four a week). The standard adult fare is €276 one way for a seat, plus an additional €12 to €43 for a cabin. There are discounts for seniors and those under 25. In France, ticketing is handled by SNCM, which also links Marseille with Algiers (Alger in French; Algeria).

Two Moroccan companies, **Comanav** (www .comanav.co.ma in French) and **Comarit** (www.comarit .com in French) link Sète, 26km (20 minutes by train) southwest of Montpellier, with the Moroccan port of Tangier (Tanger; 36 hours, once or twice weekly). Fares start from €250 one way. Discounts are available if you're aged under 26 or in a group of four or more. In France ticketing is handled by **SNCM** (Sète ☎ 04 67 46 68 00).

Spain
If you're travelling between England and southwestern France, a couple of ferry services to/from nearby northern Spain are worth considering.

P&O Ferries (UK ☎ 0870 5980 555, France ☎ 0 825 013 013; www.poferries.com) links Portsmouth with Bilbao (Santurtzi port, 35 hours including two nights *to* Bilbao, 29 hours including one night *from* Bilbao), about 150km west of Biarritz, twice a week (once a week from late October to late March; no services from early January to early February). A one-way pedestrian ticket including a mandatory sleeping berth costs around €185.

From mid-March to mid-November, **Brittany Ferries** (UK ☎ 0870 3665 333, France ☎ 0 825 828 828; www.brittany-ferries.com) runs twice-weekly car-ferry services from Plymouth to Santander (24 hours), which is around 240km west of Biarritz. Foot passengers pay around €90 one way including a mandatory reclining seat.

The UK
Fares vary widely according to seasonal demand (July and August are especially busy) and the time of day (a Friday night ferry can cost much more than a Sunday morning journey); the most expensive tickets can cost almost three times as much as the cheapest ones. Three- or five-day excursion (return) fares generally cost about the same as regular one-way tickets; special promotional return fares, often requiring advance booking, are sometimes cheaper than a standard one-way fare.

Check out **Ferry Savers** (☎ 0870 9908 492; www .ferrysavers.com), which guarantees the lowest prices on Channel crossings. Ferry companies may try to make it hard for people who use super-cheap, same-day return tickets for one-way passage; a huge backpack is a dead giveaway.

Eurail passes are *not* valid for ferry travel between the UK and France. Transporting bicycles is often (but not always) free.

TO BRITTANY
From mid-March to mid-November, Plymouth is linked to Roscoff (six hours for day crossings, one to three per day) by **Brittany Ferries** (UK ☎ 0870 3665 333, France ☎ 0 825 828 828; www .brittany-ferries.com). The one-way fare for foot passengers ranges from UK£23 to UK£73.

Brittany Ferries also links Portsmouth with St-Malo (8¾ hours for a day crossing, one per day). Pedestrians pay from UK£48 one way; a reclining seat (UK£5) or cabin is mandatory for overnight sailings.

From April to September, **Condor Ferries** (UK ☎ 0870 243 5140, France ☎ 02 99 20 03 00; www .condorferries.com) has at least one daily ferry linking Weymouth with St-Malo (UK£41, seven to 10 hours).

TO FAR NORTHERN FRANCE
The Dover–Calais crossing is handled by **SeaFrance** (UK ☎ 0870 5711 711, France ☎ 0 804 044 045; www.seafrance.com; 70min-1½hr; 15 daily). Foot-passenger fares start at UK£6 to UK£12 return. Fares for a car and up to nine passengers cost from UK£24 to UK£45 one way. **P&O Ferries** (UK ☎ 0870 5980 555, France ☎ 0 825 013 013; www.poferries.com; 1-1½hr; 29 daily) also operates a Dover–Calais service starting from UK£25 including a small car.

Ferries run by **Norfolk Line** (UK ☎ 0870 8701 020, France ☎ 03 28 28 95 50; www.norfolkline.com) link Loon Plage, about 25km west of Dunkirk (Dunkerque), with Dover from UK£19 one way for a vehicle and up to nine passengers, while **Speed Ferries** (UK ☎ 0870 2200 570, France ☎ 03 21 10 50 00; www.speedferries.com) offers an ultramodern, ultrafast catamaran service

TRANSPORT

between Boulogne and Dover from UK£19 one way for a vehicle and up to five passengers (50 minutes, five daily).

TO NORMANDY
Transmanche Ferries (UK ☎ 0 800 917 1201, France ☎ 0800 650 100; www.transmancheferries.com) operate the Newhaven–Dieppe route. The crossing (up to three daily) takes four hours. A one-way foot-passenger fare starts at UK£12; the one-way fare for a car and two adults starts from UK£33.

There's a 4¼-hour crossing (two or three per day) from Poole to Cherbourg with **Brittany Ferries** (UK ☎ 0870 3665 333, France ☎ 0 825 828 828; www.brittany-ferries.com). Foot passengers pay from UK£48 one way.

On the Portsmouth–Cherbourg route, Brittany Ferries and Condor Ferries have two or three car ferries a day (five hours by day, eight hours overnight) and, from April to September, two faster catamarans a day. Foot passengers pay from UK£38 one way.

Brittany Ferries also has car-ferry services from Portsmouth to Caen (Ouistreham; six hours, three per day). Tickets cost the same as for Poole–Cherbourg.

LD Lines (UK ☎ 0870 428 4335, France ☎ 0 825 304 304; www.ldlines.co.uk) offers an afternoon service from Le Havre to Portsmouth (7½ hours, from UK£9.90), and an overnight crossing in the opposite direction.

The USA, Canada & Elsewhere
The days when you could earn your passage to Europe on a freighter are long gone, but it's still possible to travel as a passenger on a cargo ship from North America (and ports further afield) to France's Atlantic Coast. Expect to pay from around UK£70 per day. Such vessels typically carry five to 12 passengers (more than 12 would require a doctor on board). Good websites:
The Cruise People (www.cruisepeople.co.uk) In the UK.
Freighter World Cruises (www.freighterworld.com) In the USA.

GETTING AROUND

The state-owned Société Nationale des Chemins de Fer Français (SNCF) takes care of most land transport between *départements*, and short-haul bus companies are either run by the *département* or grouped

so each local company handles different destinations. In recent years domestic air travel has been partly deregulated, but local smaller carriers continue to struggle.

While the efficient train system can get you to major cities and towns, travel within rural regions on public bus services can be slow and infrequent – if not impossible. To visit rural areas and visit small towns off the major train routes, you really need your own wheels.

AIR
All of France's major cities – as well as many minor ones – have airports, which we mention in the destination chapters. National carrier **Air France** (☎ 0 820 820 820; www.airfrance .com) continues to control the lion's share of France's long-protected domestic airline industry. British budget carrier easyJet has flights linking Paris with Marseille, Nice and Toulouse. Other European budget carriers may soon try to muscle in on France's domestic market.

Until then, the stiffest competition in the transport price war comes from the *Train à Grande Vitesse* (TGV), which has made travel between some cities (eg Paris and Lyon or Marseille) faster and easier by train than by air.

Any French travel agency or Air France office can make bookings for domestic flights and supply details on the complicated fare options. Outside France, Air France representatives sell tickets for many domestic flights.

You can save up to 84% if you fly during the week and buy your ticket three weeks in advance. Significant discounts are available to children, young people, families, seniors, and couples who are married or have proof of cohabitation. Special last-minute offers are posted on the Air France website every Wednesday.

BICYCLE
In general, France is a great place to cycle, thanks in part to its extensive network of secondary and tertiary roads, many of which carry relatively light traffic. One pitfall: the roads rarely have proper shoulders (verges). Many French cities have a growing network of urban and suburban *pistes cyclables* (bicycle paths), and in some areas (eg around Bordeaux) such paths link one

town to the next. *Never* leave your bicycle locked up outside overnight if you want to see it or most of its parts again.

French law dictates that bicycles must have two functioning brakes, a bell, a red reflector on the back and yellow reflectors on the pedals. After sunset and when visibility is poor, cyclists must turn on a white light in front and a red one in the rear. When being overtaken by a car or lorry, cyclists are required to ride in single file.

Bicycles are not allowed on most local or intercity buses or on trams. On some regional trains you can take a bicycle free of charge. On train timetables, a bicycle symbol indicates that bicycles are allowed on particular trains. On some regional trains, bikes have to be covered and stored in the luggage van. The SNCF baggage service **Sernam** (☎ 0 825 845 845) will transport your bicycle door-to-door in France for €49, with bicycles delivered within 48 hours excluding Saturday, Sunday and public holidays.

European Bike Express (UK ☎ 01642-713 710; www .bike-express.co.uk) transports cyclists and their bikes from the UK to places all over France.

More information of interest to cyclists can be found on p949. A useful resource is the **Fédération Française de Cyclisme** (☎ 01 49 35 69 00; www.ffc.fr in French).

Hire & Purchase

Most towns have at least one shop that hires *vélos tout terrains* (mountain bikes), popularly known as VTTs (around €15 to €25 a day), or cheaper touring bikes. They generally require a deposit of around €150 to €300, which you forfeit if the bike is damaged or stolen. Some cities, such as Strasbourg (p385), have remarkably inexpensive rental agencies run by the municipality. For details about rental shops, see the city and town listings throughout this book.

A VTT can be purchased from around €250. Reselling your bike at the end of your trip (for around two-thirds of its purchase price) is possible at certain bike shops and pawnbrokers. The French-language website www.velo101.com has classified ads and advice.

BOAT

For information on ferry services linking towns along the coast of France see individual town and city sections. For informa-

tion on ferry services from other countries, see p973.

Canal Boating

One of the most tranquil trips through France is to rent a houseboat and cruise along canals and navigable rivers, stopping at whim along the way. Changes in altitude are taken care of by a system of *écluses* (locks).

Boats generally accommodate from four to 12 passengers and are fully outfitted with bedding and cooking facilities. Anyone over 18 can pilot a riverboat without a special licence, but first-time skippers are given a short instruction session. The speed limit is 6km/h on canals and 10km/h on rivers.

Prices start at around €1100 a week for a small boat. Weekends (usually 55% of the weekly price) and short four- or five-night cruises are sometimes possible. Reservations are essential during holiday periods. See the Limousin, the Dordogne & Quercy (p611) and Burgundy (p457) chapters. The **Syndicat National des Loueurs de Bateaux de Plaisance** (☎ 01 44 37 04 00; Port de Javel, 75015 Paris; Ⓜ Javel) publishes a booklet listing rental companies.

Online rental agencies:

Barging in France (www.barginginfrance.com)

Canal Boat Holidays (www.canalboatholidays.com)

Worldwide River Cruise (www.worldwide-river-cruise .com)

BUS

For travel between regions, a train is your best bet since inter-regional bus services are limited. Buses are used quite extensively for short-distance travel within *départements*, especially in rural areas with relatively few train lines (eg Brittany and Normandy) – but services are often slow and few and far between.

Over the years, certain uneconomical train lines have been replaced by SNCF buses, which – unlike regional buses – are free for people with train passes. City and town entries include bus connections with other destinations.

CAR & MOTORCYCLE

Having your own wheels gives you exceptional freedom and allows you to visit more remote parts of France. Unfortunately it can be expensive and in cities parking and

TRANSPORT

ROAD DISTANCES (KM)

	Bayonne	Bordeaux	Brest	Caen	Cahors	Calais	Chambéry	Cherbourg	Clermont-Ferrand	Dijon	Grenoble	Lille	Lyon	Marseille	Nantes	Nice	Paris	Perpignan	Strasbourg	Toulouse	Tours
Bayonne	---																				
Bordeaux	184	---																			
Brest	811	623	---																		
Caen	764	568	376	---																	
Cahors	307	218	788	661	---																
Calais	164	876	710	339	875	---															
Chambéry	860	651	120	800	523	834	---														
Cherbourg	835	647	399	124	743	461	923	---													
Clermont-Ferrand	564	358	805	566	269	717	295	689	---												
Dijon	807	619	867	548	378	572	273	671	279	---											
Grenoble	827	657	1126	806	501	863	56	929	300	302	---										
Lille	997	809	725	353	808	112	767	476	650	505	798	---									
Lyon	831	528	1018	698	439	755	103	820	171	194	110	687	---								
Marseille	700	651	1271	1010	521	1067	344	1132	477	506	273	999	314	---							
Nantes	513	326	298	292	491	593	780	317	462	656	787	609	618	975	---						
Nice	858	810	1429	1168	679	1225	410	1291	636	664	337	1157	473	190	1131	---					
Paris	771	583	596	232	582	289	565	355	424	313	571	222	462	775	384	932	---				
Perpignan	499	451	1070	998	320	1149	478	1094	441	640	445	1081	448	319	773	476	857	---			
Strasbourg	1254	1066	1079	730	847	621	496	853	584	335	551	522	488	803	867	804	490	935	---		
Toulouse	300	247	866	865	116	991	565	890	890	727	533	923	536	407	568	564	699	205	1022	---	
Tours	536	348	490	246	413	531	611	369	369	418	618	463	449	795	197	952	238	795	721	593	---

traffic are frequently a major headache. Motorcyclists will find France great for touring, with winding roads of good quality and lots of stunning scenery. Just make sure your wet-weather gear is up to scratch.

France (along with Belgium) has the densest highway network in Europe. There are four types of intercity roads, which have alphanumeric designations:

Autoroutes (eg A14) Multilane highways, usually with tolls (*péages*).

Routes Nationales (N, RN) National highways.

Routes Départementales (D) Local roads.

Routes Communales (C, V) Minor rural roads.

Information on tolls, rest areas, traffic and weather updates and more is available on www.autoroutes.fr. The websites www.via michelin.com and www.mappy.fr plot itineraries for your specified departure and arrival points.

By *autoroute*, the drive from Paris to Nice (about 950km; eight hours of driving) costs at least €150 in petrol and *autoroute* tolls. By comparison, a regular one-way, 2nd-class TGV ticket for the 5½-hour Paris–Nice run costs around €106 per person (and often much less – see p983).

Roads throughout France block up during holiday periods and long weekends.

As insurance is compulsory for all cars in France, the number of the appropriate roadside assistance company is written on the insurance papers that will be in the car or stuck to the inside of the windscreen. Rental drivers should call their rental company for assistance.

Make sure your car is fitted with winter or all-season tyres if there's a chance you'll be driving through snow.

Motorcycle and moped rental is popular in southern France, especially in the beach resorts, but accidents are all too common. Where relevant, details on rental options appear at the end of city and town listings. To rent a moped, scooter or motorcycle you usually have to leave a large *caution* (deposit), which you then forfeit – up to the value of the damage – if you cause an accident or if the bike is damaged or stolen.

Bring Your Own Vehicle

A right-hand drive vehicle brought to France from the UK or Ireland must have deflectors affixed to the headlights to avoid dazzling oncoming traffic. A motor vehicle entering a foreign country must display a sticker identifying its country of registration. In the UK information on driving in France is available from the **RAC** (☎ 0870 0106 382; www.rac.co.uk) and the **AA** (☎ 0870 6000 371; www.theaa.com).

Driving Licence & Documents

All drivers must carry at all times: a national ID card or passport; a valid driver's licence (*permis de conduire;* most foreign licences can be used in France for up to a year); car-ownership papers, known as a *carte grise* (grey card); and proof of third-party (liability) insurance. An International Driving Permit (IDP) is valid for a year and can be issued by your local automobile association before you leave home.

Fuel & Spare Parts

Essence (petrol or gasoline), also known as *carburant* (fuel), costs around €1.30/L for 95 unleaded. Filling up *(faire le plein)* is most expensive at the rest stops along the *autoroutes* and cheapest at supermarkets.

Many small petrol stations close on Sunday afternoons. If you're out in the country you may have to drive to a self-service supermarket petrol station and pay by credit card.

If your car is *en panne* (breaks down), you'll have to find a garage that handles your *marque* (make of car). Peugeot, Renault and Citroën garages are common, but if you have a non-French car you may have trouble finding someone to service it in more remote areas.

Hire

To hire a car in France you'll generally need to be over 21 years old and in possession of a valid driver's licence and an international credit card. Arranging your car rental or fly/drive package before you leave home is often considerably cheaper. Major rental companies include:

ADA (☎ 0 825 169 169; www.ada.fr in French)
Avis (☎ 0 820 050 505; www.avis.com)
Budget (☎ 0 825 003 564; www.budget.com)
Easycar (UK ☎ 0906 333 333 3; www.easycar.com)

Europcar (☎ 0 825 358 358; www.europcar.com)
Hertz (☎ 0 825 342 343; www.hertz.com)
OTU Voyages (☎ 01 40 29 12 12; www.otu.fr in French) For students.
Sixt (☎ 0 820 007 498; www.sixt.fr in French)

Deals can be found on the internet, with travel agencies and through companies like **Auto Europe** (US ☎ 1-888-223-5555; www.autoeurope .com) in the US, and **Holiday Autos** (UK ☎ 0870 5300 400; www.holidayautos.co.uk) in the UK. In this book, car-rental addresses are listed under large cities and towns.

Note that rental cars with automatic transmission are *very* rare in France. You will usually need to order one well in advance, with a much smaller (and invariably costlier) range of models to choose from.

For insurance reasons, you are usually not allowed to take rental cars on ferries such as to Corsica.

All rental cars registered in France have a distinctive number on the licence plate, making them easily identifiable (including to thieves – never leave anything of value in the car, even in the boot).

Insurance

Unlimited third-party liability insurance is mandatory for all automobiles entering France, whether the owner accompanies the vehicle or not. As proof of insurance, the owner must present an international motor insurance card showing that the vehicle is insured while in France. Normally cars registered in other European countries can circulate freely in France; check with your local insurance company before you leave to make sure you are covered. If necessary a temporary insurance policy, valid for eight to 30 days, is available from the vehicle insurance department of the **French Customs Office** (La Douane; www.douane.gouv.fr) at the point of entry (border-crossing or seaport).

Third-party liability insurance is provided by car-rental companies, but things such as collision-damage waivers (CDW, or *assurance tout risqué*) vary greatly from company to company. When comparing rates, the most important thing to check is the *franchise* (excess/deductible), which is usually around €350 for a small car. Your credit card may cover CDW if you use it to pay for the car rental.

TRANSPORT

Purchase-Repurchase Plans

If you'll need a car in Europe for 17 days to six months (one year if you're studying or teaching in France), by far your cheapest option is to 'purchase' a brand-new one from **Citroen** (www.citroen.com), **Peugeot** (www.peugeot-openeurope.com) or **Renault** (www.eurodrive.renault.com), then at the end of your trip, 'sell' it back to them. In reality, you pay only for the number of days you use the vehicle. Eligibility is restricted to people who are not residents of the EU (citizens of EU countries are eligible if they live outside the EU); contact the office in your home country.

Prices include unlimited kilometres, 24-hour towing and breakdown service, and comprehensive insurance with – incredibly – no excess (deductible), so returning a damaged car is totally hassle-free. Extending your contract is possible (using a credit card), but you'll end up paying about double the prepaid per-day rate.

Cars can be picked up in cities all over France and returned to any other purchase-repurchase centre, including other European capitals.

Road Rules

Enforcement of road safety rules has been stepped up in France over the last few years. French law requires that all passengers, including those in the back seat, wear seat belts. Children weighing less than 10kg must travel in backward-facing child seats; and children weighing up to 36kg must travel in child seats in the vehicle's rear seat. A passenger car is permitted to carry a maximum of five people. North American drivers should remember that turning right on a red light is illegal in France.

You will be fined for going 10km over the speed limit. Unless otherwise posted, a limit of 50km/h applies in *all* areas designated as built-up, no matter how rural they may appear. Speed limits outside built-up areas:

- 90km/h (80km/h if it's raining) on undivided N and D highways
- 110km/h (100km/h if it's raining) on dual carriageways (divided highways) or short sections of highway with a divider strip
- 130km/h (110km/h in the rain, 60km/h in icy conditions) on *autoroutes*

Under the *priorité à droite* rule, any car entering an intersection (including a T-junction) from a road on your right has the right-of-way, unless the intersection is marked 'vous n'avez pas la priorité' (you do not have right of way) or 'cédez le passage' (give way). *Priorité à droite* is also suspended on priority roads, which are marked by an upended yellow square with a black square in the middle.

It is illegal to drive with a blood-alcohol concentration over 0.05% (0.5g per litre of blood) – the equivalent of two glasses of wine for a 75kg adult. There are periodic random breathalyser tests. Mobile phones may only be used when accompanied by a hands-free kit or speakerphone.

Motoring in Europe, published in the UK by the RAC, gives an excellent summary of road regulations in each European country, including parking rules. British drivers committing driving offences in France can receive on-the-spot fines and get penalty points added to their driving licence.

Riders of any type of two-wheeled vehicle with a motor (except motor-assisted bicycles) must wear a helmet. No special licence is required to ride a motorbike whose engine is smaller than 50cc, which is why you often find places renting scooters rated at 49.9cc.

HITCHING

Hitching is never entirely safe in any country in the world, and we don't recommend it. Travellers who decide to hitch should understand that they are taking a small but potentially serious risk. Remember that it's safer to travel in pairs and be sure to inform someone of your intended destination. Hitching is not really part of French culture, and is not recommended for women in France, even in pairs.

Hitching from city centres is pretty much hopeless: take public transport to the outskirts. It is illegal to hitch on *autoroutes*, but you can stand near the entrance ramps as long as you don't block traffic. Remote rural areas are a better bet, but once you get off the *routes nationales* there are few vehicles. If your itinerary includes a ferry crossing, it's worth trying to score a ride before the ferry goes, since vehicle tickets sometimes include a number of passengers free of charge. At dusk, give up and think about finding somewhere to stay.

Ride-share Organisations

A number of organisations around France put people looking for rides in touch with drivers going to the same destination. Usually you pay a per-kilometre fee to the driver, as well as a flat administration fee. The best known is Paris-based **Allostop** (☎ 0 825 803 666; www.allostop.net in French).

LOCAL TRANSPORT

France's cities and larger towns generally have excellent public-transport systems. City centres are small and compact – most can be visited entirely on foot.

There are underground subway systems (metros) in Paris, Lyon, Marseille, Lille and Toulouse.

Ultramodern tramways exist in Paris, Grenoble, Nantes, Lille, Strasbourg, Lyon, Nancy and Bordeaux, and are being built in cities across the country. Bus systems tend to be less reliable.

Details on routes, fares, tourist passes etc, are available at tourist offices and from local bus companies. We list information in the individual destination sections.

See p949 and p976 for information on bicycles and bike hire.

Taxi

All large and medium-sized train stations – and many small ones – have a taxi stand out the front. For details on the tariffs and regulations applicable in major cities, see p204.

In small cities and towns, where taxi drivers are unlikely to find another fare anywhere near where they let you off, there are four kinds of per-kilometre tariffs, set locally by the *préfecture*. Rates are more expensive at night and on Sundays and holidays.

Travel under 20km/h (or thereabouts) is calculated by time (about €15 an hour) rather than distance. There may be a surcharge of €1 to get picked up at a train station or airport, and a small additional fee per bag or for a fourth passenger.

TOURS

Local tourist offices, museums, wineries, chateaux and private companies all over France offer a wide variety of guided tours that you arrange locally. Some tourist offices also offer tours to destinations out-

side of town. Details appear under Tours in city listings. Guided hikes, cycling tours and other organised outdoor activities appear under Activities. Some places are difficult to visit unless you have wheels, or are much more interesting with expert commentary.

The **Association of British Tour Operators to France** (www.holidayfrance.org.uk) has an extensive list of UK-based companies offering trips to France.

A multitude of companies run activities-based tours, usually including accommodation, meals and transport.

ATG Oxford (www.atg-oxford.co.uk) Cycling and rambling holidays for independent travellers.

Butterfield & Robinson (www.butterfield.com) Canada-based upmarket walking and biking holidays.

CBT Tours (www.biketrip.net) Cycling tours from the USA.

Classic Bike Provence (www.classicbikeprovence.com) Motorcycling tours in Provence and beyond astride classic 1950s-'80s bikes.

Cycling for Softies (www.cycling-for-softies.co.uk) Unescorted cycling trips through rural France.

French Travel Connection (www.frenchtravel.com.au) Australia-based themed tours including language study.

French Wine Explorers (www.wine-tours-france.com) Small-group wine tours of Beaujolais, Bordeaux, Burgundy and the Rhône Valley.

Olde Ipswich Tours (www.ipswichtours.com) Specialist wine tours (USA based).

Ramblers Holidays (www.ramblersholidays.co.uk) Tours based on outdoor activities such as walking, trekking and cross-country skiing.

TRAIN

France's superb rail network reaches almost every part of the country. Many towns and villages not on the SNCF train and bus network are served by bus lines linking *départements*.

France's most important train lines radiate from Paris like the spokes of a wheel, making train travel between provincial towns situated on spur lines infrequent and often slow. In some cases you have to transit through Paris. For details, see the map on p974.

Since its inauguration in the 1980s, the pride and joy of SNCF – and the French – is the world-renowned TGV (*Train à Grande Vitesse*, www.tgv.com). Pronounced 'teh-zheh-veh', it literally is a 'high-speed train', travelling at speeds of over 300km/h (186mph).

TRANSPORT

TRANSPORT

TGV Atlantique Sud-Ouest & TGV Atlantique Ouest
These link Paris' Gare Montparnasse with western and southwestern France, including Brittany (Rennes, Quimper, Brest), Nantes, Tours, Poitiers, La Rochelle, Bordeaux, Biarritz and Toulouse.

TGV Est Under construction at press time, this line will connect Paris with Strasbourg and continue to Germany, Austria and Eastern European destinations. The first sections are due to open in mid-2007.

TGV Nord, Thalys & Eurostar These link Paris' Gare du Nord with Arras, Lille, Calais, Brussels, Amsterdam, Cologne and, via the Channel Tunnel, Ashford and London Waterloo.

TGV Sud-Est & TGV Midi-Méditerranée These link Paris' Gare de Lyon with the southeast, including Dijon, Lyon, Geneva, the Alps, Avignon, Marseille, Nice and Montpellier.

TGV lines are interconnected, making it possible to go directly from, say, Lyon to Nantes or Bordeaux to Lille, without switching trains in Paris. Stops on the link-up, which runs east and south of Paris, include Roissy Charles de Gaulle airport, Massy and Disneyland Paris. For details on Thalys and the Eurostar, see p972.

A train that is not a TGV is often referred to as a *corail*, a *classique* or a TER *(train express régional)*.

Between major stations, passengers can rent a DVD player from €9.95.

Classes & Sleeping Cars
Most French trains have 1st- and 2nd-class sections. On overnight trains the 2nd-class couchette compartments have six berths, while those in 1st class have four. In addition to bed linen, you are issued a bottle of water and a little 'welcome kit'. Some couchette compartments are reserved for women travelling alone or with children.

Many overnight trains have *voitures-lits* (sleeping cars), which provide private facilities, a continental breakfast and greater security. Second class holds up to three people; 1st-class compartments are somewhat larger and accommodate one or two people.

Costs
Significant discounts are available (see opposite) on regular train fares. Full-price fares can be very expensive (eg TGV Paris–Lyon €76.30 one way). Full-fare return (round-trip) passage costs twice as much as one-way fares. Travel in 1st class is 50% more expensive than 2nd class. Train tickets (including the TGV) are more expensive during the peak periods (commuting hours, weekends, holiday periods).

Tickets & Reservations
You can buy a ticket with a credit card via the SNCF's website and either have it sent to you by post if you have an address in France or collect it from any SNCF ticket office. Nearly every SNCF station in the country has at least one *billeterie automatique* (automatic ticket machine) that accepts computer-chip credit cards. Large stations often have separate ticket windows for *international, grandes lignes* (long-haul) and *banlieue* (suburban) lines, and *achat à l'avance* (advance purchase) and *départ du jour* (same-day departure).

Before boarding the train you must validate your ticket by time-stamping it in a *composteur*, one of those yellow posts located at the start of the platform. If you forget, find a conductor on the train so they can punch it for you to avoid being fined.

Reserving in advance (€1.50) is optional unless: you're travelling by TGV, Eurostar

---

STOWING YOUR LUGGAGE

Security on French trains has heightened considerably in recent years. Security measures change regularly, but bags may not be allowed to be stored in racks between carriages, but instead kept with the passenger. Where such storage is permitted, clear labelling of items with name and address of the owner is required.

Left-luggage lockers located at train stations countrywide are no longer in operation, but in some larger cities like Paris, Lyon and Marseille staffed left-luggage facilities – where items are handed over in person and x-rayed before being stowed – are still available. See Left Luggage under Information in the destination sections for details of opening hours, rates etc. The SNCF baggage service **Sernam** (☎ 0 825 845 845) offers door-to-door luggage delivery of up to three items of 30kg, from €25 for the first piece, and €11 for each subsequent piece.

SNCF DISCOUNT FARES

Fantastic deals are available on the website www.sncf.com. Last-minute offers at up to 50% off are published on the site every Tuesday; 'Prem's' early-bird deals (eg Paris–Toulouse €25) are available for online bookings made three months to two weeks in advance. These tickets cannot be exchanged or refunded.

Discounted fares and passes are available at all SNCF stations. See earlier for discount European bus (p971) and train (p972) passes.

Children aged under four travel free of charge; those aged four to 11 travel for half-price. Discounted fares (25% reduction) apply, subject to the trains and conditions of reservation, to: travellers aged 12 to 25, seniors aged over 60, one to four adults travelling with a child aged four to 11, two people taking a return journey together or anyone taking a return journey of at least 200km and spending a Saturday night away.

Guaranteed reductions of 25% to 50% are available with a **Carte 12-25** (€49), aimed at travellers aged 12 to 25; the **Carte Enfant Plus** (€65) for one to four adults travelling with a child aged four to 11; and a **Carte Sénior** (€50), for those aged over 60. A **Carte Escapades** (€99), for those aged 26 to 59, guarantees savings of 25% on a return journey of at least 200km including a Saturday night away.

If you're spending three months to one year in France, ask about *Fréquence* travel cards offering savings of up to 50%.

The **France Railpass** entitles nonresidents of France to unlimited travel on SNCF trains for four days over a one-month period. In 2nd class it costs US$229; each additional day of travel costs US$30. The **France Youthpass** entitles holders to four days of travel over a one-month period. In 2nd class it costs US$169, plus US$23 for each extra day. These two passes can be purchased from travel agencies, or online through agencies such as www.raileurope.com.

or Thalys; you want a couchette (sleeping berth; €16) or a bed; or you'll be travelling during peak holiday periods when trains may be full. Reservations can be made by telephone or via the SNCF's website. Reservations can usually be changed before departure time by telephone.

Long-distance trains sometimes split at a station; that is, each half of the train leaves for a different destination. You should verify the destination as you board the car, or you could wind up very, very far from wherever it was you intended to go.

TRANSPORT

Health

CONTENTS

Travel health depends on your predeparture preparations, your daily health care while travelling and how you handle medical problems that do develop. France is a healthy place. Your main risks are likely to be sunburn, foot blisters, insect bites and mild stomach problems from eating and drinking too much.

BEFORE YOU GO

Prevention is the key to staying healthy. Planning before departure, particularly for pre-existing illnesses, will save trouble later. See your dentist before a long trip, carry a spare pair of contact lenses and glasses, and take your optical prescription. Bring medications in their original, clearly labelled, containers. A signed and dated letter from your physician describing your medical conditions and medications, including generic names, is also helpful. If carrying syringes or needles, be sure to have a physician's letter documenting their medical necessity.

INSURANCE

Citizens of the EU, Switzerland, Iceland, Norway or Liechtenstein receive free or reduced-cost state-provided health care cover with the European Health Insurance Card (EHIC) for medical treatment that becomes necessary while in France. The EHIC replaced the E111 in 2006. Each family member will need a separate card. In the UK, get application forms from post offices, or download them from the Department of Health website (www.dh.gov.uk), which has comprehensive information about the card's coverage.

Citizens from other countries will need to check if there is a reciprocal arrangement for free medical care between their country and France. If you need health insurance, strongly consider a policy covering the worst possible scenario, such as an accident requiring an emergency flight home. Find out in advance if your insurance plan will make payments directly to providers or reimburse you later for overseas health expenditures.

RECOMMENDED VACCINATIONS

No vaccinations are required to travel to France. However, the World Health Organization (WHO) recommends that all travellers should be covered for diphtheria, tetanus, measles, mumps, rubella and polio, regardless of their destination.

IN TRANSIT

DEEP VEIN THROMBOSIS (DVT)

Blood clots may form in the legs during plane flights, chiefly because of prolonged immobility. The main symptom of DVT is swelling or pain of the foot, ankle or calf, usually but not always on just one side. When a blood clot travels to the lungs it may cause chest pain and breathing difficulties. Travellers with any of these symptoms should immediately seek medical attention.

To prevent the development of DVT on long flights walk about the cabin, contract the leg muscles while sitting, drink plenty of fluids and avoid alcohol and tobacco.

JET LAG

To avoid jet lag (common when crossing more than five time zones) drink plenty of nonalcoholic fluids and eat light meals.

Upon arrival, get exposure to natural sunlight and readjust your schedule (for meals, sleep and so on) as soon as possible.

IN FRANCE

AVAILABILITY & COST OF HEALTH CARE

Excellent health care is readily available and for minor illnesses pharmacists can give valuable advice and sell medications. They can also advise on more specialised help and point you in the right direction. Dental care is usually good, however it is sensible to have a dental checkup before a long trip.

DIARRHOEA

If you develop diarrhoea, drink plenty of fluids, preferably an oral rehydration solution (eg Dioralyte). If diarrhoea is bloody, persists for more than 72 hours, or is accompanied by fever, shaking, chills or severe abdominal pain seek immediate medical attention.

ENVIRONMENTAL HAZARDS
Altitude Sickness

Lack of oxygen at high altitudes (over 2500m) affects most people to some extent. Symptoms of Acute Mountain Sickness (AMS) usually develop in the first 24 hours at altitude but may be delayed up to three weeks. Mild symptoms are headache, lethargy, dizziness, difficulty sleeping and loss of appetite. Severe symptoms are breathlessness, a dry, irritative cough (followed by the production of pink, frothy sputum), severe headache, lack of coordination and balance, confusion, vomiting, irrational behaviour, drowsiness and unconsciousness. There's no rule as to what is too high: AMS can be fatal at 3000m, but 3500m to 4500m is the usual range.

Treat mild symptoms by resting at the same altitude until recovered, usually a day or two. Paracetamol or aspirin can be taken for headaches. If symptoms persist or grow worse, however, *immediate descent is necessary;* even 500m can help. Drug treatments should never be used to avoid descent or to enable further ascent. Diamox (acetazolamide) reduces the headache of AMS and helps the body acclimatise to the lack of oxygen. It is only available on prescription.

To prevent AMS:

- Ascend slowly – have frequent rest days, spending two to three nights at each rise of 1000m. Acclimatisation takes place gradually.
- Sleep at a lower altitude than the greatest height reached during the day if possible. Also, once above 3000m, care should be taken not to increase the sleeping altitude by more than 300m per day.
- Drink extra fluids. Monitor hydration by ensuring that urine is clear and plentiful.
- Eat light, high-carbohydrate meals for more energy.
- Avoid alcohol, sedatives and tobacco.

Heat Exhaustion

Heat exhaustion follows excessive fluid loss with inadequate replacement of fluids and salt. Symptoms include headache, dizziness and tiredness. Dehydration is already happening by the time you feel thirsty – aim to drink enough water to produce pale, diluted urine. To treat heat exhaustion, replace lost fluids by drinking water and/or fruit juice, and cool the body with cold water and fans.

Hypothermia

Even on a hot day in the mountains weather can change rapidly; carry waterproof garments and warm layers, and inform others of your route. Acute hypothermia follows a sudden drop of temperature over a short time. Chronic hypothermia is caused by a gradual loss of temperature over hours. Hypothermia starts with shivering, loss of judgment and clumsiness. Unless rewarming occurs, the sufferer deteriorates into apathy, confusion and coma. Prevent further heat loss by seeking shelter, warm dry clothing, hot sweet drinks and shared bodily warmth.

SEXUAL HEALTH

Emergency contraception is available with a doctor's prescription in France. Condoms are readily available; when buying, look for a European CE mark, which means they've been rigorously tested. Keep them in a cool dry place or they may crack and perish.

TRAVELLING WITH CHILDREN

All travellers with children should know how to treat minor ailments and when to seek medical advice. Be sure children are

HEALTH

up to date with routine vaccinations, and discuss possible travel vaccines well before departure, as some vaccines are not suitable for children under a year.

If your child has vomiting or diarrhoea, lost fluids and salts must be replaced. It may be helpful to take rehydration powders for reconstituting with boiled water.

WOMEN'S HEALTH

Emotional stress, exhaustion and travelling across time zones can all contribute to an upset in the menstrual pattern. Some antibi-otics, diarrhoea and vomiting can interfere with the effectiveness of oral contraceptives and lead to the risk of pregnancy – remember to take condoms just in case. Time zones, gastrointestinal upsets and antibiotics do not affect injectable contraception.

Travelling during pregnancy is usually possible but you should always consult your doctor before planning your trip. The most risky times for travel are during the first 12 weeks of pregnancy and after 30 weeks.

Language

CONTENTS

Modern French developed from the *langue d'oïl*, a group of dialects spoken north of the Loire River that grew out of the vernacular Latin used during the late Gallo-Roman period. The *langue d'oïl* – particularly the Francien dialect spoken in the Île de France – eventually displaced the *langue d'oc*, the dialects spoken in the south of the country and from which the Mediterranean region of Languedoc got its name.

Standard French is taught and spoken in France, but its various accents and dialects are an important source of identity in certain regions. In addition, some of the peoples subjected to French rule many centuries ago have preserved their traditional languages. These include Flemish in the far north; Alsatian in Alsace; Breton (a Celtic tongue similar to Cornish and Welsh) in Brittany; Basque (a language unrelated to any other) in the Basque Country; Catalan in Roussillon (Catalan is the official language of nearby Andorra and the first language of many in the Spanish province of Catalonia); Provençal in Provence; and Corsican on the island of Corsica.

For more information on food and dining in France, see p87. If you'd like a more comprehensive guide to the French language

Lonely Planet's compact *French Phrasebook* will cover most of your travel needs.

PRONUNCIATION

The pronunciation guides included with each French phrase should help you in getting your message across. Here are a few of the letters that may cause confusion:

j	**zh** in the pronunciation guides; as the 's' in 'leisure', eg *jour*, zhoor (day)
c	before **e** and **i**, as the 's' in 'sit'; before **a**, **o** and **u** it's pronounced as English 'k'. When underscored with a 'cedilla' (**ç**) it's always pronounced as the 's' in 'sit'.
r	pronounced from the back of the throat while constricting the muscles to restrict the flow of air
n, m	where a syllable ends in a single **n** or **m**, these letters are not pronounced, but the preceding vowel is given a nasal pronunciation

BE POLITE!

While the French rightly or wrongly have a reputation for assuming that all humans should speak French – until WWI it was the international language of culture and diplomacy – you'll find any attempt to communicate in French will be much appreciated.

What is often perceived as arrogance is often just a subtle objection to the assumption by many travellers that they should be able to speak English anywhere, in any situation, and be understood. You can easily avoid the problem by approaching people and addressing them in French. Even if the only sentence you can muster is *Pardon, madame/monsieur, parlez-vous anglais?* (Excuse me, madam/sir, do you speak English?), you're sure to be more warmly received than if you stick to English.

An important distinction is made in French between *tu* and *vous*, which both mean 'you'; *tu* is only used when addressing people you know well, children or animals. If you're addressing an adult who isn't a personal friend, *vous* should be used unless the person invites you to use *tu*. In general,

LANGUAGE

younger people insist less on this distinction between polite and informal, and you will find that in many cases they use *tu* from the beginning of an acquaintance.

GENDER

All nouns in French are either masculine or feminine and adjectives reflect the gender of the noun they modify. The feminine form of many nouns and adjectives is indicated by a silent **e** added to the masculine form, as in *ami* and *amie* (the masculine and feminine for 'friend').

In the following phrases both masculine and feminine forms have been indicated where necessary. The masculine form comes first and is separated from the feminine by a slash. The gender of a noun is often indicated by a preceding article: 'the/a/some', *le/un/du* (m), *la/une/de la* (f) ; or one of the possessive adjectives, 'my/your/his/her', *mon/ton/son* (m), *ma/ta/sa* (f) . In French, unlike English, the possessive adjective agrees in number and gender with the thing in question: 'his/her mother', *sa mère*.

ACCOMMODATION

I'm looking for *Je cherche ...* zher shersh ...
a ...

camp site	*un camping*	un kom·peeng
guesthouse	*une pension*	ewn pon·syon
	(de famille)	(der fa·mee·ler)
hotel	*un hôtel*	un o·tel
youth hostel	*une auberge*	ewn o·berzh
	de jeunesse	der zher·nes

Where can I find a cheap hotel?
Où est-ce qu'on peut trouver un hôtel pas cher?
oo es·kon per troo·vay un o·tel pa shair
What is the address?
Quelle est l'adresse?
kel e la·dres
Could you write the address, please?
Est-ce que vous pourriez écrire l'adresse, s'il vous plaît?
e·sker voo poo·ryay ay·kreer la·dres seel voo play
Do you have any rooms available?
Est-ce que vous avez des chambres libres?
e·sker voo·za·vay day shom·brer lee·brer

I'd like (a) ... *Je voudrais ...* zher voo·dray ...
single room	*une chambre à*	ewn shom·brer
	un lit	a un lee
double-bed	*une chambre*	ewn shom·brer
room	*avec un grand*	a·vek un gron
	lit	lee

MAKING A RESERVATION
(for phone or written requests)

To ...	*À l'attention de ...*
From ...	*De la part de ...*
Date	*Date*
I'd like to book ...	*Je voudrais réserver ...*
in the name of ...	*au nom de ...*
from ... (date) **to ...**	*du ... au ...*
credit card	*carte de crédit*
number	*numéro*
expiry date	*date d'expiration*
Please confirm	*Veuillez confirmer la*
availability and	*disponibilité et le prix.*
price.	

twin room	*une chambre*	ewn shom·brer
with two beds	*avec des lits*	a·vek day lee
	jumeaux	zhew·mo
room with	*une chambre*	ewn shom·brer
a bathroom	*avec une salle*	a·vek ewn sal
	de bains	der bun
to share a dorm	*coucher dans*	koo·sher don
	un dortoir	zun dor·twa

How much is it ...? *Quel est le prix ...?* kel e ler pree ...
per night	*par nuit*	par nwee
per person	*par personne*	par per·son

May I see it?
Est-ce que je peux voir es·ker zher per vwa la
la chambre? shom·brer
Where is the bathroom?
Où est la salle de bains? oo e la sal der bun
Where is the toilet?
Où sont les toilettes? oo·son lay twa·let
I'm leaving today.
Je pars aujourd'hui. zher par o·zhoor·dwee
We're leaving today.
Nous partons noo par·ton o·zhoor·dwee
aujourd'hui.

CONVERSATION & ESSENTIALS
Hello.	*Bonjour.*	bon·zhoor
Goodbye.	*Au revoir.*	o·rer·vwa
Yes.	*Oui.*	wee
No.	*Non.*	no
Please.	*S'il vous plaît.*	seel voo play
Thank you.	*Merci.*	mair·see

You're welcome.
Je vous en prie. zher voo·zon pree
De rien. (inf) der ree·en

Excuse me.
Excusez-moi. ek·skew·zay·mwa
Sorry. (forgive me)
Pardon. par·don

What's your name?
Comment vous ko·mon voo·za·pay·lay voo
appelez-vous? (pol)
Comment tu ko·mon tew ta·pel
t'appelles? (inf)
My name is ...
Je m'appelle ... zher ma·pel ...
Where are you from?
De quel pays êtes-vous? der kel pay·ee et·voo
De quel pays es-tu? (inf) der kel pay·ee e·tew

I'm from ... *Je viens de ...* zher vyen der ...
I like ... *J'aime ...* zhem ...
I don't like ... *Je n'aime pas ...* zher nem pa ...
Just a minute. *Une minute.* ewn mee·newt

SIGNS

Entrée	Entrance
Sortie	Exit
Renseignements	Information
Ouvert	Open
Fermé	Closed
Interdit	Prohibited
Chambres Libres	Rooms Available
Complet	Full/No Vacancies
(Commissariat de)	Police Station
Police	
Toilettes/WC	Toilets
Hommes	Men
Femmes	Women

DIRECTIONS
Where is ...?
Où est ...? oo e ...
Go straight ahead.
Continuez tout droit. kon·teen·way too drwa
Turn left.
Tournez à gauche. toor·nay a gosh
Turn right.
Tournez à droite. toor·nay a drwat
at the corner/at traffic lights
au coin/aux feux o kwun/o fer

behind	*derrière*	dair·ryair
in front of	*devant*	der·von
far (from)	*loin (de)*	lwun (der)
near (to)	*près (de)*	pray (der)
opposite	*en face de*	on fas der

EMERGENCIES

Help!
Au secours! o skoor
There's been an accident!
Il y a eu un accident! eel ya ew un ak·see·don
I'm lost.
Je me suis égaré/e. (m/f) zhe me swee·zay·ga·ray
Leave me alone!
Fichez-moi la paix! fee·shay·mwa la pay

Call ...! *Appelez ...!* a·play ...
a doctor *un médecin* un mayd·sun
the police *la police* la po·lees

---

beach	*la plage*	la plazh
bridge	*le pont*	ler pon
castle	*le château*	ler sha·to
cathedral	*la cathédrale*	la ka·tay·dral
church	*l'église*	lay·gleez
island	*l'île*	leel
lake	*le lac*	ler lak
main square	*la place centrale*	la plas son·tral
museum	*le musée*	ler mew·zay
old city (town)	*la vieille ville*	la vyay veel
palace	*le palais*	ler pa·lay
quay	*le quai*	ler kay
river bank	*la rive*	la reev
ruins	*les ruines*	lay rween
sea	*la mer*	la mair
square	*la place*	la plas
tourist office	*l'office de*	lo·fees der
	tourisme	too·rees·mer
tower	*la tour*	la toor

HEALTH
I'm ill.	*Je suis malade.*	zher swee ma·lad
It hurts here.	*J'ai une douleur*	zhay ewn doo·ler
	ici.	ee·see

I'm ...	*Je suis ...*	zher swee ...
asthmatic	*asthmatique*	(z)as·ma·teek
diabetic	*diabétique*	dee·a·bay·teek
epileptic	*épileptique*	(z)ay·pee·lep·teek

I'm allergic	*Je suis*	zher swee
to ...	*allergique ...*	za·lair·zheek ...
antibiotics	*aux antibio-*	o zon·tee·byo·teek
	tiques	
bees	*aux abeilles*	o za·bay·yer
walnuts	*aux noix*	o nwa
peanuts	*aux cacahuètes*	o ka·ka·wet
penicillin	*à la pénicilline*	a la pay·nee·see·leen

antiseptic	*l'antiseptique*	lon·tee·sep·teek
aspirin	*l'aspirine*	las·pee·reen
condoms	*des préservatifs*	day pray·zair·va·teef
contraceptive	*le contraceptif*	ler kon·tra·sep·teef
diarrhoea	*la diarrhée*	la dya·ray
medicine	*le médicament*	ler may·dee·ka·mon
nausea	*la nausée*	la no·zay
sunblock cream	*la crème solaire*	la krem so·lair
tampons	*des tampons*	day tom·pon
	hygiéniques	ee·zhen·eek

LANGUAGE DIFFICULTIES

Do you speak English?
Parlez-vous anglais?   par·lay·voo ong·lay

Does anyone here speak English?
Y a·t·il quelqu'un qui   ya·teel kel·kung kee
parle anglais?   par long·glay

How do you say ... in French?
Comment est·ce qu'on   ko·mon es·kon
dit ... en français?   dee ... on fron·say

What does ... mean?
Que veut dire ...?   ker ver deer ...

I don't understand.
Je ne comprends pas.   zher ner kom·pron pa

Could you write it down, please?
Est·ce que vous pourriez   es·ker voo poo·ryay
l'écrire, s'il vous plaît?   lay·kreer seel voo play

Can you show me (on the map)?
Pouvez·vous m'indiquer   poo·vay·voo mun·dee·kay
(sur la carte)?   (sewr la kart)

NUMBERS

0	*zero*	zay·ro
1	*un*	un
2	*deux*	der
3	*trois*	trwa
4	*quatre*	ka·trer
5	*cinq*	sungk
6	*six*	sees
7	*sept*	set
8	*huit*	weet
9	*neuf*	nerf
10	*dix*	dees
11	*onze*	onz
12	*douze*	dooz
13	*treize*	trez
14	*quatorze*	ka·torz
15	*quinze*	kunz
16	*seize*	sez
17	*dix·sept*	dee·set
18	*dix·huit*	dee·zweet
19	*dix·neuf*	deez·nerf
20	*vingt*	vung
21	*vingt et un*	vung tay un

22	*vingt·deux*	vung·der
30	*trente*	tront
40	*quarante*	ka·ront
50	*cinquante*	sung·kont
60	*soixante*	swa·sont
70	*soixante·dix*	swa·son·dees
80	*quatre·vingts*	ka·trer·vung
90	*quatre·vingt·dix*	ka·trer·vung·dees
100	*cent*	son
1000	*mille*	meel

PAPERWORK

name	*nom*	nom
nationality	*nationalité*	na·syo·na·lee·tay
date/place	*date/place*	dat/plas
of birth	*de naissance*	der nay·sons
sex/gender	*sexe*	seks
passport	*passeport*	pas·por
visa	*visa*	vee·za

QUESTION WORDS

Who?	*Qui?*	kee
What?	*Quoi?*	kwa
What is it?	*Qu'est·ce que*	kes·ker
	c'est?	say
When?	*Quand?*	kon
Where?	*Où?*	oo
Which?	*Quel/Quelle?*	kel
Why?	*Pourquoi?*	poor·kwa
How?	*Comment?*	ko·mon

SHOPPING & SERVICES

I'd like to buy ...
Je voudrais acheter ...   zher voo·dray ash·tay ...

How much is it?
C'est combien?   say kom·byun

I don't like it.
Cela ne me plaît pas.   ser·la ner mer play pa

May I look at it?
Est·ce que je peux le voir? es·ker zher per ler vwar

I'm just looking.
Je regarde.   zher rer·gard

It's cheap.
Ce n'est pas cher.   ser nay pa shair

It's too expensive.
C'est trop cher.   say tro shair

I'll take it.
Je le prends.   zher ler pron

Can I pay by ...? *Est·ce que je peux* es·ker zher per
      payer avec ...? pay·yay a·vek ...

credit card	*ma carte de*	ma kart der
	crédit	kray·dee
travellers	*des chèques*	day shek
cheques	*de voyage*	der vwa·yazh

more	plus	plew
less	moins	mwa
smaller	plus petit	plew per·tee
bigger	plus grand	plew gron

I'm looking for ...	Je cherche ...	zhe shersh ...
a bank	une banque	ewn bonk
the ... embassy	l'ambassade de ...	lam·ba·sahd der ...
the hospital	l'hôpital	lo·pee·tal
an internet café	un cybercafé du coin	un see·bair·ka·fay dew kwun
the market	le marché	ler mar·shay
the police	la police	la po·lees
the post office	le bureau de poste	ler bew·ro der post
a public phone	une cabine téléphonique	ewn ka·been tay·lay·fo·neek
a public toilet	les toilettes	lay twa·let

TIME & DATES

What time is it?	Quelle heure est-il?	kel er e til
It's (8) o'clock.	Il est (huit) heures.	il e (weet) er
It's half past ...	Il est (...) heures et demie.	il e (...) er e day·mee

in the morning	du matin	dew ma·tun
in the afternoon	de l'après-midi	der la·pray·mee·dee
in the evening	du soir	dew swar
today	aujourd'hui	o·zhoor·dwee
tomorrow	demain	der·mun
yesterday	hier	yair

Monday	lundi	lun·dee
Tuesday	mardi	mar·dee
Wednesday	mercredi	mair·krer·dee
Thursday	jeudi	zher·dee
Friday	vendredi	von·drer·dee
Saturday	samedi	sam·dee
Sunday	dimanche	dee·monsh

January	janvier	zhon·vyay
February	février	fayv·ryay
March	mars	mars
April	avril	a·vreel
May	mai	may
June	juin	zhwun
July	juillet	zhwee·yay
August	août	oot
September	septembre	sep·tom·brer
October	octobre	ok·to·brer
November	novembre	no·vom·brer
December	décembre	day·som·brer

TRANSPORT
Public Transport

What time does ... leave/arrive?	À quelle heure part/arrive ...?	a kel er par/a·reev ...
boat	le bateau	ler ba·to
bus	le bus	ler bews
plane	l'avion	la·vyon
train	le train	ler trun

I'd like a ... ticket.	Je voudrais un billet ...	zher voo·dray un bee·yay ...
one-way	simple	sum·pler
return	aller et retour	a·lay ay rer·toor
1st class	de première classe	der prem·yair klas
2nd class	de deuxième classe	der der·zyem klas

I want to go to ...
Je voudrais aller à ...   zher voo·dray a·lay a ...
The train has been delayed.
Le train est en retard.   ler trun et on rer·tar
The train has been cancelled.
Le train a été annulé.   ler trun a ay·tay a·new·lay

the first	le premier (m)	ler prer·myay
	la première (f)	la prer·myair
the last	le dernier (m)	ler dair·nyay
	la dernière (f)	la dair·nyair
platform number	le numéro de quai	ler new·may·ro der kay
ticket office	le guichet	ler gee·shay
timetable	l'horaire	lo·rair
train station	la gare	la gar

Private Transport

I'd like to hire a/an...	Je voudrais louer ...	zher voo·dray loo·way ...
car	une voiture	ewn vwa·tewr
4WD	un quatre-quatre	un kat·kat
motorbike	une moto	ewn mo·to
bicycle	un vélo	un vay·lo

Is this the road to ...?
C'est la route pour ...?   say la root poor ...
Where's a service station?
Où est-ce qu'il y a   oo es·keel ya
une station-service?   ewn sta·syon·ser·vees
Please fill it up.
Le plein, s'il vous plaît.   ler plun seel voo play
I'd like ... litres.
Je voudrais ... litres.   zher voo·dray ... lee·trer

| petrol/gas | essence | ay·sons |
| diesel | diesel | dyay·zel |

LANGUAGE

ROAD SIGNS

Cédez la Priorité	Give Way
Danger	Danger
Défense de Stationner	No Parking
Entrée	Entrance
Interdiction de Doubler	No Overtaking
Péage	Toll
Ralentissez	Slow Down
Sens Interdit	No Entry
Sens Unique	One Way
Sortie	Exit

(How long) Can I park here?
(Combien de temps) Est-ce que je peux stationner ici?
(kom·byun der tom) es·ker zher per sta·syo·nay ee·see?

Where do I pay?
Où est-ce que je paie?
oo es·ker zher pay?

I need a mechanic.
J'ai besoin d'un mécanicien.
zhay ber·zwun dun may·ka·nee·syun

The car/motorbike has broken down (at ...)
La voiture/moto est tombée en panne (à ...)
la vwa·tewr/mo·to ay tom·bay on pan (a ...)

The car/motorbike won't start.
La voiture/moto ne veut pas démarrer.
la vwa·tewr/mo·to ner ver pa day·ma·ray

I have a flat tyre.
Mon pneu est à plat.
mom pner ay ta pla

I've run out of petrol.
Je suis en panne d'essence.
zher swee zon pan day·sons

I've had an accident.
J'ai eu un accident.
zhay ew un ak·see·don

TRAVEL WITH CHILDREN

Is there a/an ...?	*Y a-t-il ...?*	ya teel ...
I need a/an ...	*J'ai besoin ...*	zhay ber·zwun ...
baby change room	*d'un endroit pour changer le bébé*	dun on·drwa poor shon·zhay ler bay·bay
car baby seat	*d'un siège-enfant*	dun syezh·on·fon
children's menu	*d'un menu pour enfant*	dun mer·new poor on·fon
disposable nappies/diapers	*de couches-culottes*	der koosh·kew·lot
formula (milk)	*de lait maternisé*	de lay ma·ter·nee·zay
(English-speaking) babysitter	*d'une baby-sitter (qui parle anglais)*	dewn ba·bee·see·ter (kee parl ong·glay)
highchair	*d'une chaise haute*	dewn shay zot
potty	*d'un pot de bébé*	dun po der bay·bay

Do you mind if I breastfeed here?
Cela vous dérange si j'allaite mon bébé ici?
ser·la voo day·ron·zhe see zha·layt mon bay·bay ee·see

Are children allowed?
Les enfants sont permis? lay zon·fon son pair·mee

LANGUAGE

Glossary

For a glossary of food and drink terms, see the Food & Drink chapter (p73).

(m) indicates masculine gender, (f) feminine gender and (pl) plural

accueil (m) – reception
alignements (m pl) – a series of standing stones, or menhirs, in straight lines
alimentation (f) – grocery store
AOC – *appellation d'origine contrôlée*; system of French wine classification
arrondissement (m) – administrative division of large city; abbreviated on signs as 1er (1st arrondissement), 2e or 2ème (2nd) etc
atelier (m) – workshop or studio
auberge de jeunesse (f) – (youth) hostel

baie (f) – bay
bassin (m) – bay or basin
bastide (f) – medieval settlement in southwestern France, usually built on a grid plan and surrounding an arcaded square; also a country house in Provence
belle époque (f) – literally 'beautiful age'; era of elegance and gaiety characterising fashionable Parisian life in the period preceding WWI
billet (m) – ticket
billet jumelé (m) – combination ticket, good for more than one site, museum etc
billetterie (f) – ticket office or counter
boulangerie (f) – bakery or bread shop
boules (f pl) – a game not unlike lawn bowls played with heavy metal balls on a sandy pitch; also called *pétanque*
BP – *boîte postale*; post office box
brasserie (f) – restaurant usually serving food all day (original meaning: brewery)
bureau de change (m) – exchange bureau
bureau de poste (m) or **poste** (f) – post office

CAF – Club Alpin Français
carnet (m) – a book of five or 10 bus, tram or metro tickets sold at a reduced rate
carrefour (m) – crossroad
carte (f) – card; menu; map
caserne (f) – military barracks
cave (f) – wine cellar
chambre (f) – room
chambre d'hôte (f) – B&B
charcuterie (f) – pork butcher's shop and delicatessen; the prepared meats it sells

cimetière (m) – cemetery
col (m) – mountain pass
consigne or **consigne manuelle** (f) – left-luggage office
consigne automatique (f) – left-luggage locker
correspondance (f) – linking tunnel or walkway, eg in the metro; rail or bus connection
couchette (f) – sleeping berth on a train or ferry
cour (f) – courtyard
crémerie (f) – dairy or cheese shop
cyclisme (m) – cycling

dégustation (f) – tasting
demi (m) – 330mL glass of beer
demi-pension (f) – half-board (B&B with either lunch or dinner)
département (m) – administrative division of France
donjon (m) – castle keep
douane (f) – customs

église (f) – church
embarcadère (m) – pier or jetty
épicerie (f) – small grocery store
ESF – École de Ski Français; France's leading ski school

fauteuil (m) – seat on trains, ferries or at the theatre
fest-noz or **festoù-noz** (pl) – night festival
fête (f) – festival
FN – Front National; National Front
forêt (f) – forest
formule or **formule rapide** (f) – similar to a *menu* but allows choice of whichever two of three courses you want (eg starter and main course or main course and dessert)
fouilles (f pl) – excavations at an archaeological site
foyer (m) – workers or students hostel
fromagerie (f) – cheese shop
FUAJ – Fédération Unie des Auberges de Jeunesse; France's major hostel association
funiculaire (m) – funicular railway

galerie (f) – covered shopping centre or arcade
gare or **gare SNCF** (f) – railway station
gare maritime (f) – ferry terminal
gare routière (f) – bus station
gendarmerie (f) – police station; police force
gîte d'étape (m) – hikers accommodation, usually in a village
gîte rural (m) – country cottage
golfe (m) – gulf
GR – *grande randonnée;* long-distance hiking trail
grand cru (m) – wine of exceptional quality

halles (f pl) – covered market; central food market
halte routière (f) – bus stop
horaire (m) – timetable or schedule
hôte payant (m) – paying guest
hôtel de ville (m) – city or town hall
hôtel particulier (m) – private mansion

intra-muros – old city (literally 'within the walls')

jardin (m) – garden
jardin botanique (m) – botanic garden
jours fériés (m pl) – public holidays

laverie (f) or **lavomatique** (m) – laundrette

mairie (f) – city or town hall
maison de la presse (f) – newsagent
maison du parc (f) – a national park's headquarters and/or visitors centre
marché (m) – market
marché aux puces (m) – flea market
marché couvert (m) – covered market
mas (m) – farmhouse in southern France
menu (m) – fixed-price meal with two or more courses
mistral (m) – incessant north wind in southern France said to drive people crazy
musée (m) – museum

navette (f) – shuttle bus, train or boat

Occitan – a language also known as langue d'oc or sometimes Provençal, related to Catalan

palais de justice (m) – law courts
parapente – paragliding
pardon (m) – religious pilgrimage
parlement (m) – parliament
parvis (m) – square
pâtisserie (f) – cake and pastry shop
péage (m) – toll
pensions de famille (f pl) – similar to B&Bs
pétanque (f) – a game not unlike lawn bowls played with heavy metal balls on a sandy pitch; also called boules
piste cyclable (f) – bicycle path
place (f) – square or plaza
plage (f) – beach
plan (m) – city map
plan du quartier (m) – map of nearby streets (hung on the wall near metro exits)
plat du jour (m) – daily special in a restaurant
pont (m) – bridge
port (m) – harbour or port

port de plaisance (m) – marina or pleasure-boat harbour
porte (f) – gate in a city wall
poste (f) or **bureau de poste** (m) – post office
préfecture (f) – prefecture (capital of a département)
presqu'île (f) – peninsula
pression (f) – draught beer
puy (m) – volcanic cone or peak

quai (m) – quay or railway platform
quartier (m) – quarter or district

refuge (m) – mountain hut, basic shelter for hikers
région (f) – administrative division of France
rez-de-chausée (m) – ground floor
rive (f) – bank of a river
rond point (m) – roundabout
routier (m) – trucker or truckers restaurant

sentier (m) – trail
service des urgences (f) – casualty ward
ski de fond – cross-country skiing
SNCF – Société Nationale des Chemins de Fer; state-owned railway company
SNCM – Société Nationale Maritime Corse-Méditerranée; state-owned ferry company linking Corsica and mainland France
sortie (f) – exit
spectacle (m) – performance, play or theatrical show
square (m) – public garden
supplément (m) – supplement or additional cost
syndicat d'initiative (m) – tourist office

tabac (m) – tobacconist (also selling bus tickets, phonecards etc)
table d'orientation (f) – viewpoint indicator
taxe de séjour (f) – municipal tourist tax
télécarte (f) – phonecard
téléphérique (m) – cableway or cable car
télésiège (m) – chairlift
téléski (m) – ski lift or tow
TGV – Train à Grande Vitesse; high-speed train or bullet train
tour (f) – tower
tour d'horloge (f) – clock tower

vallée (f) – valley
v.f. (f) – version française; a film dubbed in French
vieille ville (f) – old town or old city
ville neuve (f) – new town or new city
v.o. (f) – version originale; a nondubbed film with French subtitles
voie (f) – train platform
VTT – vélo tout terrain; mountain bike

Behind the Scenes

THIS BOOK

For this 7th edition of *France*, Nicola Williams coordinated a skilled team of authors composed of Oliver Berry, Steve Fallon, Catherine Le Nevez, Daniel Robinson and Miles Roddis. Nicola, Oliver, Steve, Daniel and Miles also made major contributions to previous editions, as did Teresa Fisher, Jeremy Gray, Annabel Hart, Paul Hellander, Jonathan Knight, Leanne Logan, Oda O'Carroll, Jeanne Oliver and Andrew Stone. Dr Caroline Evans reviewed and contributed to the Health chapter.

This guidebook was commissioned in Lonely Planet's London office, and produced by the following:

Commissioning Editor Judith Bamber
Coordinating Editor Laura Gibb
Coordinating Cartographer Csanad Csutoros
Coordinating Layout Designer Margie Jung
Managing Editor Suzannah Shwer
Managing Cartographer Mark Griffiths
Assisting Editors David Andrew, Carolyn Bain, Barbara Delissen, Kate Evans, Charlotte Harrison, Margedd Heliosz, Helen Koehne, Anne Mulvaney, Joanne Newell, Dianne Schallmeiner, Louise Stirling
Assisting Cartographers David Connolly, Hunor Csutoros, Diana Duggan, Jimi Ellis, Tony Fankhauser, Joshua Geoghegan, Corey Hutchison, Valentina Kremenchutskaya, Sophie Reed, Amanda Sierp, Herman So, Simon Tillema
Assisting Layout Designers Laura Jane, Wibowo Rusli
Cover Designer Rebecca Dandens
Colour Designer Indra Kilfoyle
Project Manager Fabrice Rocher
Language Content Coordinator Quentin Frayne

Thanks to David Burnett, Helen Christinis, Sally Darmody, Mark Germanchis, Rachel Imeson, Katie Lynch, Trent Paton, Fiona Siseman, Tashi Wheeler, Celia Wood, Meg Worby

THANKS
NICOLA WILLIAMS

The enormous graciousness, professionalism and good humour of the contributing authors of this book cannot be emphasised enough: thank you.

On the snowy Jurassien road, a *grand merci* to Cristelle and Pascal at Au Douillet Gourmet for the advance extreme-weather warning and fabulous farmstay *à la fondue*; and to Muriel and David Blanchard at Escargot Comtois for the fascinating insight into snail farming and snail cuisine. In Lyon, dozens of friends and acquaintances have uncovered places to eat, drink and enjoy over the years, Lise Pederson, Sally Urwin and Chiara B included.

At home on the lake front, love and kisses to Matthias, Niko and Mischa for tolerating the long hours and absences with a smile; to my sister Michelle Ovenden, and Ella and Scott for entertaining while I was gone; and to Christa and Karl-Otto Lüfkens for helping out way above and beyond the call of in-law duty.

OLLY BERRY

As always, far too many names and far too little space for thank yous. Firstly to Jenks for all those late nights on The Ark, and for keeping the boat afloat in my absence; to Susie Berry for doing the same back at the ranch; and to Abi and Jas and Si and Helen and Tails and Daisy for birthday messages while I was out on the road. Over on the

THE LONELY PLANET STORY

The story begins with a classic travel adventure: Tony and Maureen Wheeler's 1972 journey across Europe and Asia to Australia. There was no useful information about the overland trail then, so Tony and Maureen published the first Lonely Planet guidebook to meet a growing need.

From a kitchen table, Lonely Planet has grown to become the largest independent travel publisher in the world, with offices in Melbourne (Australia), Oakland (USA) and London (UK). Today Lonely Planet guidebooks cover the globe. There is an ever-growing list of books and information in a variety of media. Some things haven't changed. The main aim is still to make it possible for adventurous travellers to get out there – to explore and better understand the world.

At Lonely Planet we believe travellers can make a positive contribution to the countries they visit – if they respect their host communities and spend their money wisely. Every year 5% of company profit is donated to charities around the world.

other side of the Channel, thanks to Jean-Claude Lamartine, Melanie Duchamp, Claude Fourcade, Robert Martin, Sophie Lambert and all the other people I met along the way; to John Huston and Stephen Ambrose; to all the boys of Bayeux and Colleville-sur-Mer; and to the staff at Normandy's war cemeteries. Over at the Planet, to Nicola for steering the ship even when everyone else seemed to have abandoned the helm; to Meg Worby, Tashi Wheeler and all the people in the map-room for making sense of my scrawl. Lastly, thanks to the Hobo, as always, for being there when all other lights went out.

STEVE FALLON
A number of people helped in the updating of my portion of *France*, in particular resident Brenda Turnnidge, who provided invaluable support and insider's information with her usual efficiency and enthusiasm. Thanks too to Zahia Hafs, Caroline Guilleminot and Olivier Cirendini for assistance, ideas, hospitality and/or a few laughs along the way. As always, I'd like to dedicate my share of Paris to my Partner (now with a capital – and legal) Michael Rothschild.

Finally, to all the wonderful *and* infuriating Parisians I met along the way this time round – elegant and stylish, cultured and entertaining, bitchy and attitudinous *à l'extrême* – *merci encore une fois*. You're just what the world needs more of.

CATHERINE LE NEVEZ
Many thanks to all who helped on my journey, including all of the unfortunately-too-numerous-to-mention-individually tourism professionals throughout the Côte d'Azur, Provence, Atlantic Coast, Brittany and Corsica. Thanks especially to Suzanne in Marseille, Michel in Toulon, Florence in Nice, Josian in Bastia, and Katia in Nantes. A major *merci* to my brother Adam for being an awesome and very patient travel guide throughout Brittany, for the trip to the old family mill, and for teaching me to (finally!) drive a manual car. Thanks too to Matthias in Bordeaux, Isabelle in Concarneau, and Frank in Oz. Cheers to Meg Worby for giving me the gig, Nicola Williams and the *France* team, Tashi Wheeler, and everyone at LP. Above all, heartfelt thanks to my family for their unfailing support.

DANIEL ROBINSON
In the Far North, warm thanks to Hélène Giguet and Valérie Meteier in Lille and to Hélène Muller and Guillaume Norbert in Dunkirk. In Épernay, my research was nourished by Patrick Michelon and Oz-bound Florine Lambert. 'Twas, as always,

a pleasure to see Thierry di Constanzo and his family and Raquel and Elie Margen in Troyes. In Alsace, many thanks to Della Meyers of The Bookworm and Aurélien, Patricia and Jean-Michel Kempf. Many and excellent were the suggestions about living well in Burgundy from Laurent de Courtivon and Caroline Boutefou. My best post-graduation wishes to Snezhana Zlatinova and Max Otto. And a special *merci* to Myrna and Albert Huberfel for their warmth and hospitality in Dijon.

Finally, I would like to thank Emily Silverman and Max for their *Gastfreundschaft* and my brother Micah Robinson for his nimble and determined scanning – all three saved my maps from catastrophe; and Kristy Zofrea of DriveAway Holidays for the purchase-repurchase Peugeot 206 that served me for 6900 problem-free kilometres.

MILES RODDIS
Huge thanks, as always, to Ingrid, chauffeur, proofer, stalwart supporter and first lady. Thanks too to so many cheerful and informed tourist office staff: Sylvie (Ax-les-Thermes), Catherine Goxe and Corinne Cayrey (Condom), Maïte and Mireille (Albi), Mélissa Buttelli and Sandra (Toulouse), Laetitia (Pau), Anne Laloi (Bayonne), Cécilia (Biarritz), Fabienne (St-Jean de Luz), Myriam (Bedous), Myriam (Lescun), Marie-Pierre (Cauterets), Stéphanie, (Gavarnie), Isabelle (Lourdes), Natalie (Luchon), Muriel Bastié (Carcassonne), Isabelle (Collioure), Marilyn Mouche (Perpignan), Sylvie and Julie (Castres), Annie (Millau), Cyrielle (Florac), Anthony (Ste-Énimie), Marie and Muriel (Murat), Philippe (Clermont-Ferrand), Anne-Marie (St-Nectaire), Florie (Riom), Françoise Gioux (Vichy), Matthieu Aubignat-Fournet (Thiers), Christelle (Ambert), Patricia (Vichy), Patricia (Le Puy), Jérome (Alès), Linda (Nîmes), Irena Milosevic (Sète), Lucie (Narbonne) and Alicia (Montpellier).

OUR READERS
Many thanks to the travellers who used the last edition and wrote to us with helpful hints, useful advice and interesting anecdotes:

A Gill Abbott, Sarah Abrams, Lynda and Percy Acton-Adams, Katie Affleck, James Angresano, Jan Aniskowicz, Caroline Ashley-Cooper, Dina Avila **B** Melda Beanette, Michelle Bishop, Anne Brasier, Cheryl Buckeridge, Christian Byhahn **C** Francis Cagney, Michelle Cahalone, Don Carter, Romelle Castle, Pauline Charleston, Yvan Chaxel, Phil Chubb, Krista Coleman, Matt Cooper, Carlos Coupland, Barbara Cribb, Chris Crowther, Alys and Jo Cummings **D** Emma and Rebecca Davis, Régis de la Haye, Heather Delanghe, Dianne Deveaux, Kelly Duke-Bryant **E** Graeme and Nicola Edwards **F** Lynette Filips, Yuet Yee Foo, Steven Forbes, William Frugal **G** Channa Galhenage, Tapan

Ganguli, Grimaldi Ghjuvan-Andria, Catrina and Bill Gilliam, Estelle Green, Ruth Gregory, Michael Griffith **H** Paul Hagman, Trevor Hamersley, Linda Harper, Jennifer and Steve Hart, David Hilton, Adam Hobill, Tony Holden, Andrew Hood, Cecile Hubert, John and Joan Hunter **I** Dale Ivens **J** Paul Jackson, Kylie Jane, Steve and Carol Jones, Rashaad Jorden **K** Russell Karlson, Jo Kent, Andrew Killoran, Eva Kisgyorgy, Michaela Kviat **L** Leo Lacey, Colin Lamont, Ame Latine, Anthony Lee, Tony Lees, Mauro Leoni, David Lowry, Andrew Lyons **M** Dawn MacDonald, Michael Marcus, Jennifer Marks, Johan Marynissen, Carlo Massini, Diana McCall, Charley McGlinchey, Andrew McLoughlin, Seema Mehtq, Fergus Mitchell, Tina Mizgalski, Heather Monell **N** Annelie Norde **O** Paul O'Dwyer, Stefan Oeberg, Bill Orkin, Paul Ostroff **P** Stephanos Papadopoulos, Patin Pascal, Pablo Pena, Eliel Pimentel, Catherine Plant, Thea Platt, Ruth and Moss Potter, Sandra Pozzobon **R** Denise Reich, Frank and Carol Rhodes, Christiane Rochon, Andrew Roper, Katrina Roper, Katherine Roussos, James Royal, Sue Royal **S** Michel Schmid, Pierre Seltz, Jonathan Shepherd, Kristie Sheppard, Natashya Sherbot, John Simmonds, Krys Smith, Ian Southwell, John Stein, Kenneth Stein, Michael Stuart, Karin Sturzenegger, Niles Szwed **T** Andrew Talbot, Alex Talsma, Irene Taylor, Lynette Taylor, Francis Tebbe, Martina Tomassini, Helen Townsend, Cameron Trost **V** John van Bavel, J van der Laar, Jos van Oord, Helen Varley **W** Alexandria Waldron, Michael Waldron, Tory Waterman, Patrick Wehrlin, Jeremy White, Neil Whitehead, Ian Williams **Y** Ronit Yadin, Tammy Yee, Barbara Yoshida **Z** Julia Zhogina

Index

000 Map pages
000 Photograph pages

INDEX

000 Map pages
000 Photograph pages

INDEX

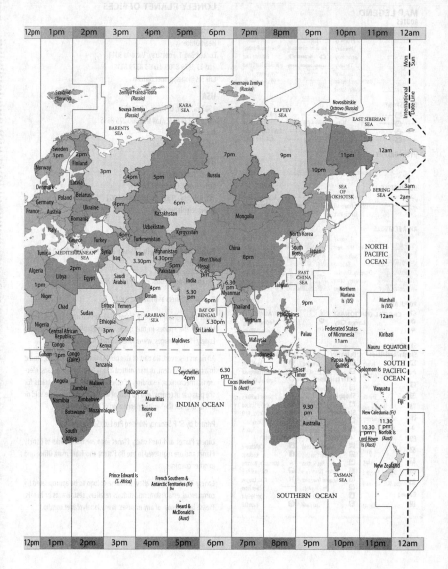

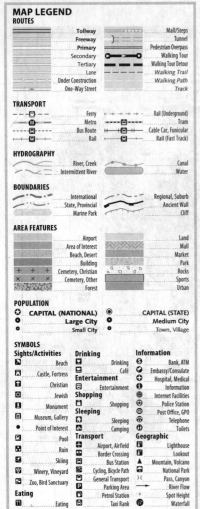

MAP LEGEND

ROUTES

Tollway	Mall/Steps
Freeway	Tunnel
Primary	Pedestrian Overpass
Secondary	Walking Tour
Tertiary	Walking Tour Detour
Lane	Walking Trail
Under Construction	Walking Path
One-Way Street	Track

TRANSPORT

Ferry	Rail (Underground)
Metro	Tram
Bus Route	Cable Car, Funicular
Rail	Rail (Fast Track)

HYDROGRAPHY

River, Creek	Canal
Intermittent River	Water

BOUNDARIES

International	Regional, Suburb
State, Provincial	Ancient Wall
Marine Park	Cliff

AREA FEATURES

Airport	Land
Area of Interest	Mall
Beach, Desert	Market
Building	Park
Cemetery, Christian	Rocks
Cemetery, Other	Sports
Forest	Urban

POPULATION

○ CAPITAL (NATIONAL)	◉ CAPITAL (STATE)
● Large City	● Medium City
○ Small City	○ Town, Village

SYMBOLS

Sights/Activities
- Beach
- Castle, Fortress
- Christian
- Jewish
- Monument
- Museum, Gallery
- Point of Interest
- Pool
- Ruin
- Skiing
- Winery, Vineyard
- Zoo, Bird Sanctuary

Eating
- Eating

Drinking
- Drinking
- Café

Entertainment
- Entertainment

Shopping
- Shopping

Sleeping
- Sleeping
- Camping

Transport
- Airport, Airfield
- Border Crossing
- Bus Station
- Cycling, Bicycle Path
- General Transport
- Parking Area
- Petrol Station
- Taxi Rank

Information
- Bank, ATM
- Embassy/Consulate
- Hospital, Medical
- Information
- Internet Facilities
- Police Station
- Post Office, GPO
- Telephone
- Toilets

Geographic
- Lighthouse
- Lookout
- Mountain, Volcano
- National Park
- Pass, Canyon
- River Flow
- Spot Height
- Waterfall

LONELY PLANET OFFICES

Australia
Head Office
Locked Bag 1, Footscray, Victoria 3011
☎ 03 8379 8000, fax 03 8379 8111
talk2us@lonelyplanet.com.au

USA
150 Linden St, Oakland, CA 94607
☎ 510 893 8555, toll free 800 275 8555
fax 510 893 8572
info@lonelyplanet.com

UK
72–82 Rosebery Ave,
Clerkenwell, London EC1R 4RW
☎ 020 7841 9000, fax 020 7841 9001
go@lonelyplanet.co.uk

Published by Lonely Planet Publications Pty Ltd
ABN 36 005 607 983

© Lonely Planet Publications Pty Ltd 2007

© photographers as indicated 2007

Cover photograph by Getty Images: Av des Champs Élysées, Paris.
Many of the images in this guide are available for licensing from
Lonely Planet Images: www.lonelyplanetimages.com.